*The Complete*
# BIBLICAL LIBRARY

## THE NEW TESTAMENT

## STUDY BIBLE

### Volume 2

## Acts–Revelation

**Executive Editor:** Ralph W. Harris, M.A.

**Editor:** Stanley M. Horton, Th.D.

**Managing Editor:** Gayle Garrity Seaver, J.D.

**EMPOWERED**LIFE
A C A D E M I C

**Tulsa, Oklahoma 74145**

formerly published by:

**World Library Press, Inc.**

**Springfield, Missouri, U.S.A.**

The Complete Biblical Library, a two volume study series on the New Testament. Volume 2: Study Bible, Acts-Revelation.

20 19 18 17 16          5 4 3 2 1

Complete Biblical Library Volume 2

ISBN: 978-168031-123-5

Published by:

**E MPOWERED**LIFE

Empowered Life, an imprint of Harrison House Publishers

www.empoweredlifebooks.com

Tulsa, OK 74145

Printed in Canada.

# THE NEW TESTAMENT

## Study Bible, Volume 2 Acts–Revelation

## INTERNATIONAL EDITOR

## Thoralf Gilbrant

**Executive Editor:** Ralph W. Harris, M.A.

**Computer Systems:** Tor Inge Gilbrant

## National Editors

**U.S.A.**
Stanley M. Horton, Th. D.

**NORWAY**
Erling Utnem, Bishop

Arthur Berg, B.D.

**DENMARK**
Jorgen Glenthoj, Th.M.

**SWEDEN**
Hugo Odeberg, Ph.D., D.D.
Bertil E. Gartner, D.D.
Thorsten Kjall, M.A.
Stig Wikstrom D. Th.M.

**FINLAND**
Aapelii Saarisalo, Ph.D.
Valter Luoto, Pastor
Matti Liljequist, B.D.

**HOLLAND**
Herman ter Welle, Pastor
Henk Courtz, Drs.

**Project Coordinator:** William G. Eastlake

## International and Interdenominational Bible Study System

# Table of Contents

# FOREWORD

The original *Complete Biblical Library* consisted of Old and New Testament commentaries, Greek and Hebrew dictionaries, and interlinear Greek and Hebrew texts. It covered all aspects of Bible study, providing a truly unique study experience appealing to the international and interdenominational Christian church at large. The original set of 39 hardcover volumes, has become an indispensable addition to the libraries of many scholars and lay people alike fortunate enough to acquire one of these treasured sets. For the last thirty years, the *Complete Biblical Library* has remained an essential resource to any serious Bible student.

Because the original *Complete Biblical Library* has been out of print since 2001, printed volumes are now rare, only available used from second-hand markets. And since they continue to increase in value and popularity, it is quite common to find the individual volumes sold at five to ten times their original price. Obtaining a full set is nearly impossible.

Most recently, this treasured work has been available in a limited digital format. Using the digital version has its advantages, and it is a great way to study, but computers and software platforms are ever changing. In recent times we have seen companies and platforms disappear, leaving valuable content and investment in jeopardy. It is comforting to look on your library shelf and see a wonderful printed book that cannot crash or be erased, and even though the printing press that printed it may be long gone, the book remains your own. To avoid the risk of losing such a wonderful asset, a printed version can remain a permanent, treasured reference work.

We are committed to bringing this great work to another generation of Christian scholars hungry to know God's Word and discern it correctly. And so it is our pleasure to take this first step in reintroducing the *Complete Biblical Library*. Our two-volume New Testament commentary includes the various versions, original contributors, outlines, endnotes, and individual bibliographies. We have also included the *Harmony of the Gospels* at the end of Volume I. We did not, however, include the Interlinear Greek text, saving enough space to condense the original nine volumes into two.

A special thanks to Tor Inge Gilbrant and Tarjei Gilbrant—son and grandson of Thoralf Gilbrant, the original founder and visionary of the *Complete Biblical Library*—for their confidence in us to republish and redistribute this great work. Without their permission, this offering would not be possible.

Finally, we offer this commentary with a prayer that it will prove to be a great blessing to those who use it, especially those who are "filled with the Spirit" and seeking God's will for their lives. May that same Spirit use this study of God's word to empower readers to do "signs and wonders" today, just as Jesus and the apostles did in their times.

The Empowered Life Staff

# CONTRIBUTORS

## Acts

**Verse-by-Verse Commentary**
Stanley M. Horton, Th.D.

**Various Versions**
Gerard J. Flokstra, Jr., D.Min.

**Board of Review**
Zenas Bicket, Ph.D.
Jesse Moon, D.Min.
Charles Harris, Ed.D.
Opal Reddin, D.Min.

**Editor of Greek-English Dictionary**
Denis W. Vinyard, M.Div.

**Associate Editor of Greek-English Dictionary**
Donald F. Williams, M.Div.

**Production Coordinator**
Cynthia Riemenschneider

**Senior Editors**
Gary Leggett, M.A.; Dorothy B. Morris

**Editorial Team**
Faye Faucett; Charlotte Gribben; Connie Leggett

**Art Director**
Terry Van Someren, B.F.A.

**Layout Artist**
Jim Misloski, B.A.

**Word Processing and Secretarial**
Sonja Jensen; Rochelle Holman; Rachel Wisehart Harvey, B.A.

## Galatians–Philemon

**Executive Editor**
Ralph W. Harris, M.A.

**Editor**
Stanley M. Horton, Th.D.

**Managing Editor**
Gayle Garrity Seaver, J.D.

**Verse-by-Verse Commentary**
Erich H. Kiehl, Th.D., Galatians
Bernard Rossier, Ph.D., Ephesians, Philippians, Colossians, Philemon
Gary Leggett, M.A., 1, 2 Timothy, Titus
Stanley M. Horton, Th.D., 1, 2 Thessalonians

**Various Versions**
Gerard J. Flokstra, Jr., D.Min.

**Board of Review**
Zenas Bicket, Ph.D.
Jesse Moon, D.Min.
Charles Harris, Ed.D.
Opal Reddin, D.Min.

Staff
**Production Coordinator**
Cynthia Riemenschneider

**Research Editor**
Denis Vinyard, M.Div.

**Senior Editors:**
Gary Leggett, M.A.; Dorothy B. Morris

**Editorial Team:**
Lloyd Anderson; Ken Barney; Betty Bates; Norma Gott; Charlotte Gribben; Faith Horton, B.A.; Mary Jane Jaynes; Connie Leggett; Brenda Lochner; Marietta Vinyard

**Art Director:**
Terry Van Someren, B.F.A.

**Word Processing and Secretarial**
Faye Faucett; Sonja Jensen; Don Williams, M.Div.; Rachel Wisehart, B.A.
Material written by Bernard Rossier adapted by him from his book Praise from Prison: Ephesians, Philippians, Colossians and Philemon, published by House of Bon Giovanni ©1968.

## Hebrews–Jude

**Executive Editor**
Ralph W. Harris, M.A.

**Editor**
Stanley M. Horton, Th.D.

**Managing Editor**
Gayle Garrity Seaver, J.D.

**Verse-by-Verse Commentary**
Paul O. Wright, Th.D., Hebrews
Hardy W. Steinberg, B.A., James
Robert C. Cunningham, M.A., 1, 2 Peter
John D. Bechtle, D.Min., 1, 2, 3 John, Jude

**Various Versions**
Gerard J. Flokstra, Jr., D.Min.

**Board of Review**
Zenas Bicket, Ph.D.
Jesse Moon, D.Min.
Charles Harris, Ed.D.
Opal Reddin, D.Min.

**Editor of Greek-English Dictionary**
Denis Vinyard, M.Div.

**Editor of the Old Testament**
Don Williams, M.Div.

**Production Coordinator**
Cynthia Riemenschneider

**Senior Editors:**
Gary Leggett, M.A.; Dorothy B. Morris

# Contributors

## Contributing Editors of the Complete Biblical Library

The names which follow represent those who have assisted in producing the original entire set. Although their contributions have been made in the Study Bible and the Bible Dictionary, it seems fitting to pay tribute to them in each volume of the entire Library. They are listed alphabetically by countries.

### United States
Abshier, Carolyn, B.A.
Aker, Benny C., Ph.D.
Albrecht, Daniel E., M.A.
Alexander, Donald L., Ph.D.
Alexander, Patrick, M.A.
Anderson, Carl, B.D.
Anderson, Gordon, M.A.
Arrington, French L., Ph.D.
Autry, Arden C., Ph.D.
Bailey, Gary D., M.A.
Bailey, Mark, Th.M.
Baker, Carmen, B.A.
Baldwin, Donald, Ph.D.
Ballantyne, Jeff K., B.A.
Barlow, John, M.Div.
Barton, Freeman, Ph.D.
Beacham, A. D, Jr., D.Min.
Beaty, James M., Ph.D.
Bechtle, John D, D.Min.
Bibb, Charles W., B.A.
Bicket, Zenas, Th.D.
Bishop, Richard W., D.Min.
Black, Daniel L., Th.D.
Black, David Alan, D.Theo.
Boonstra, Gerald D., B.A.
Broadus, Steve, B.A.
Brock, Raymond T., Ed.D.
Brookman, William R., Ph.D.
Brown, William K., Ph.D.
Brubaker, Malcolm, M.Div.
Bundrick, David R., M.Div.
Buswell, Robert C, D.Min.
Cargal, Eric Michael, B.A.
Carlson, G. Raymond, D.D.
Carlson, John, B.A.
Castleberry, Joseph L., B.A.
Chamberlain, Ernest H., B.D.
Clyde, Terese, B.A.
Cohen, Gary G., Th.D.
Cole, Greg, B.A.
Collins, Oral, Ph.D.
Cornet, R. Dale, M.Div.
Cotton, Roger D., Th.D.
Crabtree, Dan, B.A.

Darnell, Lonnie L., II, M.A.
Dayton, Wilber T., Th.D.
Dean, David A., Th.D.
Deisher, John, M.Div.
Dippold, David, M.A.
Doerksen, Vernon D., Th.D.
Drury, Rodney A., B.A.
Dusing, Michael, M.Div.
Dyce, Shelley L., M.A.
Elliott, William E., Th.D.
Esposito, David, B.A.
Estridge, Charles A., D.Min.
Eustler, Steve, B.A.
Faber, Charles H., M.Div.
Fettke, Steven M., Th.M.
Fiensy, David, Ph.D.
Fisher, Robert E., Ph.D.
Flokstra, Gerard, Jr., M.T.S.
Flower, Joseph, B.A.
Flower, John, M.A.
Ford, Joseph Michael, M.A.
Foreman, Kenneth K., Th.D.
Franklin, Karen, M.Div.
Franklyn, Paul, Ph.D.
Fransisco, John C, M.Div.
Freeman, Ernest R., Ph.D.
Friskney, Thomas E., B.D.
Gause, R. Hollis, Ph.D.
Gerlicher, John, Th.M.
Gilley, Bobby Lee, M.Ed.
Gilman, Tom, M.A.
Glandon, Arvin W., D.Min.
Good, Sanford, M.Th.
Grabill, Paul, Th.M.
Graves, Robert W., M.A.
Hackett, Gregory A., B.A.
Haight, Larry L., M.A.
Haltom, Michael F., D.Min.
Hammock, Hoyt, Jr., B.A.
Hampton, Ralph C., Jr., M.Div.
Hancock, Trey, B.A.
Hands, Greg, Th.M.
Hansen, Wesley, B.A.
Hardman, Samuel G., B.S.
Harris, Ralph W., M.A.
Hartman, Dawn, B.A.
Hatchner, Walter, B.A.
Heady, Jerry, M.A.
Henes, Kenneth E., M.Div.
Hernando, James D, M.Div.
Heuser, Roger, Ph.D.
Hewett, James Allen, Ph.D.
Hillis, David P., B.A.
Holman, Charles L., Ph.D.
Home, Edward S., B.A.
Horner, Jerry W., Th.D.

Horton, Stanley, Th.D.
Indest, Michael, M.A.
Israel, Richard D, M.Div.
Jackson, Bill, M.Div.
Jenkins, James D., Ph.D.
Jenney, Timothy P., M.A.
Johns, Donald A., Ph.D.
Johnson, Dave, B.A.
Johnson, Fred R., Ph.D.
Jones, Randall Wayne, B.A.
Kath, Gerald, M.Div.
Kerkeslager, Allen, B.A.
Kiehl, Erich H., Th.D.
Kime, Harold A., M.Th.
Klaus, Byron D, M.R.E.
Koffarnus, Richard A., M.Div.
Krause, Mark, M.Div.
Kyser, Winston, M.A.
LaBelle, Lisa, B.A.
Linderman, Albert, M.A.T.S.
Lohr, Philip K., B.A.
Lowen, A. Wayne, M.Div.
Lucas, Howard, M.Div.
Macy, David C., Th.M.
Maempa, John, M.A.
Mainse, Ronald, B.A.
Manley, Grady W., Sr., M.A.
Mansfield, M. Robert, Ph.D.
Markham, Thomas E., M.Div.
Martin, Phil, B.A.
Mattingly, Gerald L., Ph.D.
McCaslin, Keith, M.Div.
McMahan, Oliver, D.Min.
McNaughton, Daniel, B.A.
McReynolds, Paul, Ph.D.
Melton, Terri L. C., B.A.
Menken, Debbie L., M.Div.
Menzies, Robert P., B.A.
Menzies, William W., Ph.D.
Meyer, Don, M.A.
Millard, Amos D., D.Min.
Miller, Johnny V., Th.D.
Miller, Kevin, M.A.
Miller, Steven E., M.Div.
Molina, John, M.Div.
Moyer, Dale, B.A.
Nash, Fred D., M.A.
Neal, Jeff, B.B.A.
Nelson, G. Edward, M.Div.
Neumann, Matthew L., B.A.
Newman, John, B.A.
Nicholaides, Stasie T., M.Div.
Nichols, Larry, B.A.
O'Grady, Brian, B.A.
Olsen, Wesley A., D.Ed.
Paris, Andrew, M.A.

Paschal, R. Wade, Ph.D.
Perrin, Jac, B.A.
Penchansky, David, M.A.
Peterson, Eugene H., M.Th.
Pettis, Bob, B.A.
Phillipps, John P., D.D.
Picirilli, Robert E., Ph.D.
Pledge, Joel K., M.Div.
Plummer, Hubert Lee, B.A.
Powell, Timothy, Ph.D.
Pratt, Thomas D, S.T.M.
Price, James D., Ph.D.
Quinn, Christopher L., B.A.
Railey, James H., Jr., Th.M.
Ray, Randall, B.A.
Reid, Garnett H., M.A.
Reinhard, David L., B.A.
Reynolds, Steven R., M.A.
Richardson, James E., M.Div.
Rossier, Bernard, Ed.S.
Rymer, David D., Minister.
Saglimbeni, Dan, M.Div.
Sanderson, Dave, B.A.
Schatzmann, Siegfried, Ph.D.
Shaner, Danny L., M.Div.
Shelton, James B., Ph.D.
Sherrer, Stormy, B.A.
Shuert, Norman, M.Div.
Simkins, Ron, M.A.T.S.
Smith, David E., M.A.
Sonia, John, B.A.
Starner, Roger, M.A.
Steward, Stan, Th.M.
Stockton, Greg, B.A.
Stout, Maury, Th.M.
Stronstad, Roger, M.C.S.
Stroud, Robert, M.Th.
Stuart, Streeter S., Jr., Ph.D.
Suthers, Edwin B., B.A.
Swanson, Mary, B.A.
Tharp, Stan, M.A.
Tedeschi, Edmund L., M.A.
Terrell, Terry L., B.A.
Thee, Francis, C. R., Ph.D.
Thomas, John Christopher, Th.M.
Thomas, Mark S., B.A.
Tourville, Robert E., M.A.
Tracy, Brian, B.A.
Tunstall, Frank G., B.A.
Van Doren, Michael, D.Min.
Walker, Paul, Ph.D.
Warren, Virgil, Ph.D.
Williams, Don, B.A.
Williams, Larry, M.A.
Williams, Marjorie.
Williams, William C, Ph.D.
Williamsen, Kelleen, B.A.
Wilser, Joseph, Th.D.

Wilson, Doug, M.A.
Wilson, Ralph F., D.Min.
Wimer, Barney, Ph.D.
Wisehart, Russell, M.Div.
Wittstock, Peter A., B.A.
Wretlind, Dennis O., Th.M.
Wright, Paul O., Th.D.
Yantz, Buddy, B.A.
Young, Richard A., Ph.D.
York, Gary, M.Div.

## Norway
Almaas, Ragnhild, B.D.
Andersen, Hakon E., Dean.
Andersen, Oivind, B.D.
Aske, Sigurd, D.D.
Berg, Arthur, B.D.
Berg, Marie, B.D.
Bjerkrheim, Trygve, B.D.
Breen, Hakon Fred, B.D.
Danbolt, Erling, D.D.
Dordal, Ole, B.D.
Fjeld, Bjorn Oyvind, B.D.
Gilbrant, Tor Inge, Computer specialist.
Hauge, Dagfinn, Bishop.
Hove, Odd Sverre, B.D.
Jensen, Sonja Lie, Secretary.
Kjelle, Edvard, Editor.
Kvalbein, Hans, D.D.
Kvarme, Ole Chr. M., B.D.
Lunde, Age, B.D.
Maeland, Jens Olav, B.D.
Nilsen, Oddvar, Editor.
Reigstad, Leif, B.D.
Ruud, Erling, Pastor.
Rudd, Kjell, B.D.
Solli, Einar, Professor.
Strand, Egil, Editor.
Saugstad, Anne Margrete, B.D.
Utnem, Erling, Bishop.
Senstad, Magne Valen, B.D.
Saeveras, Olav, D.D.
Vik, Jofrid, B.D.
Wisloff, Carl Fr., D.D.
Wisloff, Fredrik, B.D.
With, Thor, Bishop.
Yri, Norvald, B.D.

## Sweden
Abrahamsson, Stig, General Superintendent.
Bernspang, Erik, Pastor.
Corell, Alf, D.D.
Djurfeldt, Olof, LL.D.
Giertz, Bo, D.D.
Gartner, Bertil E., D.D.
Heinerborg, Karl Erik, Pastor.
Johansson, Carlo, Pastor.
Josephsson, Torsten, B.D.
Kjall, Thorsten, B.D.

Lindholm, Hans, B.D.
Mangs, Frank, National evangelist.
Norlander, Agne, D.D.
Olingdahl, Gote, B.D.
Paulson, Berthil, National evangelist.
Svensson, Samuel, B.D.
Termen, David, B.D.
Wigholm, Anders, Salvation Army officer.
Wikstrom, Stig, B.D.

## Denmark
Bech, Robert, Dr. Jur.
Behrens, Carl Peter, B.D.
Berno, Aage, B.D.
Christiansen, Henrik, Bishop.
Frokjaer-Jensen, Flemming, Pastor.
Geil, Georg S., B.D.
Glenthoj, Jorgen, B.D.
Hansen, K. Robert, B.D.
Haystrup, Helge, B.D.
Hoffman, Poul, J.D.
Kjaer-Hansen, Kai, B.D.
Langagergaard, Poul, B.D.
Legarth, Peter V., B.D.
Lorenzen, Alfred, Superintendent.
Nissen, Hans Erik, B.D.
Paaske, Oluf E., B.D.
Prenter, Regin, D.D.
Rasmussen, Leif, B.D.
Ruager, Soren, B.D.
Svendsen, Flemming Kofoed, B.D.
Wagner, Hartvig, B.D.

## Finland
Koilo, Toivo, M.Div.
Liljeqvist, Matti, B.D.
Luoto, Walter, Pastor.
Saarisalo, Aapeli, Ph.D.

## Holland
Van den Brink, Gys, Ph.D.
Courtz, Henk, Ph.D.

## Canada
Du Pont, Dennis E., M.Div.
Hayward, David R., M.A.T.S.
Przybylski, Benno, Ph.D.
Pugerude, Dan, M.Phil.
Ruthven, Jon, Ph.D.

## France
Bachke, Gerard A., M.A.
Stotts, George R., Ph.D.

## New Zealand
Williams, S.J., Gen. Supt.

## West Germany
Herron, Robert W. Jr., M.A

# INTRODUCTION

**Editor's Note:** The introduction that follows on the next four pages makes several references to the original resources that were available when the *Complete Biblical Library* was first in print. As this work is brought back into print the first two-volumes that will be available contain the New Testament verse by verse commentary and the Various Versions translations. Although it is our intentions to bring back in print the entire work it will be a process which will take a few years. We chose to leave most of the introduction as it was originally so that our readers can understand how they can benefit when the rest of the work is available.

## Features of the Study Bible

The Study Bible is a unique combination of study materials which will help both the scholar and the layman achieve a better understanding of the New Testament and the language in which it was written. All of these helps are available in various forms but bringing them together in combination will save many hours of research. Most scholars do not have in their personal libraries all the volumes necessary to provide the information so readily available here.

The editors of The Complete Biblical Library are attempting an unusual task: to help scholars in their research but also to make available to laymen the tools by which to acquire knowledge which up to this time has been available only to scholars.

## The major divisions of the Study Bible:

## Overview

Each volume contains an encyclopedic survey of the New Testament book. It provides a general outline, discusses matters about which there may be a difference of opinion, and provides background information regarding the history, culture, literature, and philosophy of the era covered by the book.

study between the Study Bible and the Greek-English Dictionary the ultimate in simplicity. Each Greek word has been assigned a number. Alpha is the first word in alphabetic order as well as the first letter of the Greek alphabet, so the number 1 has been assigned to it. The rest of the

almost 5,000 words follow in numerical and alphabetic sequence.

The Greek-English Dictionary follows the same plan with each word listed in alphabetic sequence. If a student desires further study on a certain word, he can find its number above it and locate it in the dictionary. In moments he has access to all the valuable information he needs for a basic understanding of that word.

## Verse-by-Verse Commentary

Many Bible-loving scholars have combined their knowledge, study, and skills to provide this. It is not an exhaustive treatment (many other commentaries are available for that), but again it provides a basic understanding of every verse in the New Testament. It does not usually deal with textual criticism (that can be dealt with in another arena), but it opens up the nuances of the Greek New Testament as written by the inspired writers.

## Various Versions

This offers a greatly amplified New Testament. Each verse is broken down into its phrases; the King James Version is shown in boldface type; then from more than 60 other versions we show various ways the Greek of that phrase may be translated. The Greek of the First Century was such a rich language that to obtain the full meaning of words, several synonyms may be needed.

## Translation of Greek Words

No word-for-word translation can be fully "literal" in the sense of expressing all the nuances of the original language. Rather, our purpose is to help the student find the English word which most correctly expresses the original Greek word in that particular context. The Greek language is so rich in meaning that the same word may have a slightly different meaning in another context.

In any language idioms offer a special translation problem. According to the dictionary, this is an expression which has "a meaning which cannot be derived from the conjoined meanings of its elements." The Greek language abounds in such phrases which cannot be translated literally.

We have come to what we consider a splendid solution to the problem, whether the translation should be strictly literal or abound in a plethora of idiomatic expressions. From more than 60 translations, the Various Versions column presents the various ways phrases have been translated. Here the student will find the translations of the idioms. This enables us to make our English line in the Interlinear strictly literal. The student will have available both types of translation—and will have a fresh appreciation for the struggles through which translators go.

## How the New Testament Came to Us

Volume 1 of The Complete Biblical Library, the Harmony of the Gospels, contains information on how the four Gospels came into being. The preponderance of proof points to the fact that the rest of the New Testament was written before A.D. 100. Like the Gospels, it was written in Greek, the universal language of that era. It was qualified in a special way for this purpose. Probably no other language is so expressive and able to provide such fine nuances of meaning.

Yet the New Testament Greek is not the perfectly structured form of the language from the old classical period. It is the more simple Koine Greek from the later Hellenistic age. This had become the lingua franca of the Hellenistic and Roman world. The Egyptian papyri have shown that the language which the New Testament writers used was the common language of the people. It seems as though God accomodated himself to a form of communication which would make His Word most readily accepted and easily understood.

At the same time we should recognize that the language of the Greek New Testament also is a religious language, with a tradition going back a couple of centuries to the Septuagint, the Greek translation of the Old Testament.

## The Manuscripts

None of the original manuscripts (handwritten documents) still exist. Even in the First Century they must have often been copied so as to share their treasured truths with numerous congregations of believers. The original documents then soon became worn out through use. Evidently, only copies of the New Testament still exist.

Over 5,000 manuscripts of the New Testament have been discovered up to the present time. Most of them are small fragments of verses or chapters, a few books of the New Testament, some copies of the Gospels. Very few contain all or nearly all of the New Testament.

The manuscripts have come to us in various forms: (1) Egyptian papyri, (2) majuscules, (3) minuscules, (4) writings of the Early Church fathers, (5) lectionaries, and (6) early versions.

## The Egyptian Papyri

These are the oldest copies of parts of the Greek New Testament. The earliest are dated about A.D. 200, a few even earlier, and the youngest are from the Seventh Century. Most of them date back to the Third, Fourth and Fifth Centuries of the Christian Era.

They were found in the late 1800s in Egypt. The dry climatic conditions of that country enabled them to be preserved. The largest fragments contain only a few dozen pages, while the smallest are the size of a postage stamp.

The papyri are listed in the back of this volume under the heading "Manuscripts."

## The Majuscules

These are the second oldest kind of copies of New Testament manuscripts. They received this description because they were written in majuscules; that is, large letters (the uncials are a form of majuscules). Three major majuscules are the following:

1. Codex Aleph, also called Codex Sinaiticus, because it was discovered in the mid-1840s by the great scholar Tischendorf at St. Catharine's Monastery, located at the foot of Mount Sinai. Numbered 01, it contains all the New Testament and is dated in the Fourth Century.

2. Codex A, numbered 02, is named Alexandrinus, because it came from Alexandria in Egypt. In the Gospels, this manuscript is the foremost witness to the Byzantine text type.

3. Codex B, 03, is called Codex Vaticanus, because it is in the Vatican library. Along with the Sinaiticus, it is the main witness for the Egyptian text type. However, it is important to realize there are more than 3,000 differences between these 2 manuscripts in the Gospels alone (Hoskier).

See the list of majuscules in the back of this volume, under "Manuscripts."

## The Minuscules

This is a kind of manuscript written in small letters. They are only a few hundred years old, beginning with the Ninth Century. Most come from the 12th to the 14th Century A.D. They form, by far, the greatest group of the New Testament manuscripts, numbering almost 2,800.

The minuscules represent the unbroken text tradition in the Greek Orthodox Church, and about 90 percent of them belong to the Byzantine text group. They are numbered 1, 2, 3, etc.

## Lectionaries and Church Fathers

Lectionaries include manuscripts which were not Scripture themselves but contain Scripture quotations, used for the scheduled worship services of the annual church calendar. These are numbered consecutively and are identified by lect.

Practically all the New Testament could be retrieved from the writings of early Christian leaders, called church fathers. These lists are located in the back of this volume.

## Early Versions

Translations of the New Testament from Greek are also of value. They are listed under "Manuscripts" in the back of this volume. The best known is the Latin Vulgate by Jerome.

## Major Greek Texts

From the manuscripts which have just been described, various types of Greek texts have been formed:

The Western text can possibly be traced back to the Second Century. It was used mostly in Western Europe and North Africa. It tends to add to the text and makes long paraphrases of it. Today some scholars do not recognize it as a special text type.

The Caesarean text may have originated in Egypt and was brought, it is believed, to the city of Caesarea in Palestine. Later, it was carried to Jerusalem, then by Armenian missionaries into a province in the kingdom of Georgia, now a republic of the U.S.S.R. Some scholars consider it a mixture of other text types.

The two most prominent text types, however, are the Egyptian (also called the Alexandrian) and the Byzantine. These are the major ones considered in our Interlinear and Textual Apparatus. Except for the papyrus texts which are highly varied, these are the only text families which have any degree of support. References to numerous text groups which were so common a few decades ago must now probably be considered out of date. At any rate, out of practical considerations, we have kept the Byzantine and Egyptian (Alexandrian) as fixed text groups in our Textual Apparatus. Following is historical information about them.

## The Byzantine Text

Many titles have been applied to this text type. It has been called the K (Koine), Syrian, Antiochian, and Traditional. It is generally believed to have been produced at Antioch in Syria, then taken to Byzantium, later known as Constantinople. For about 1,000 years, while the Byzantine Empire ruled the Middle East, this was the text used by the Greek Orthodox Church. It also influenced Europe.

Because of this background it became the basis for the first printed text editions, among others the famous Textus Receptus, called "the acknowledged text."

The Byzantine text form is also called the Majority text, since 80 to 90 percent of all existing manuscripts are represented in this text, though most of them are quite recent and evidently copies of earlier manuscripts. Like the Egyptian text, the Byzantine text can be traced back to the Fourth Century. It also contains some readings which seem to be the same as some papyri which can be traced back to a much earlier time. Among the oldest majuscules the Byzantine is, among others, represented by Codex Alexandrinus (02, A), 07, 08, 09, 010, 011, 012, 013, 015, and others.

## The Egyptian Text

This text type originated in Egypt and is the one which gained the highest recognition and acceptance there in the Fourth Century. It was produced mainly by copyists in Alexandria, from which it received the name Alexandrian. This text form is represented mostly by two codices: Sinaiticus (01, Aleph) and Vaticanus (03, B) from the Fourth Century, also from Codex Ephraemi (04, C) from the Fifth Century. The use of this text type ceased about the year 450 but lived on in the Latin translation, the Vulgate version.

## Printed Greek Texts

The invention of printing about 1450 opened the door for wider distribution of the Scriptures. In 1516 Erasmus, a Dutch scholar, produced the first printed Greek New Testament. It was based on the Byzantine text type, with most of the New Testament coming from manuscripts dated at about the 12th Century. He did his work very hurriedly, finishing his task in just a few months. His second edition, produced in 1519 with some of the mistakes corrected, became the basis for translations into German by Luther and into English by Tyndale.

A printed Greek New Testament was produced by a French printer, Stephanus, in 1550. His edition and those produced by Theodore Beza, of Geneva, between 1565 and 1604, based on the Byzantine text, have been entitled the Textus Receptus. That description, however, originated with the text produced by Elzevir. He described his second edition of 1633 by the Latin phrase Textus Receptus, or the "Received Text"; that is, the one accepted generally as the correct one.

## Contribution of Westcott and Hort

Two British scholars, Westcott and Hort, have played a prominent role in deciding which text type should be used. They (especially Hort) called the Byzantine text "corrupt," because of the young age of its supporting manuscripts and proceeded to develop their own text (1881-86). It was really a restoration of the Egyptian text from the Fourth Century. It depended mainly on two codices, Sinaiticus and Vaticanus, but was also supported by numerous majuscules such as 02, 04, 019, 020, 025, 032, 033, 037, and 044.

Westcott and Hort opposed the Textus Receptus because it was based on the Byzantine text form. Most scholars agreed with their contention, and the Textus Receptus fell into disrepute. However, Westcott and Hort made their assumptions before the Greek papyri were discovered, and in recent years some scholars have come to the defense of the Byzantine text and the Textus Receptus. They have learned that some of the readings in the Byzantine text are the same as those found in the earliest papyri, dated about A.D. 200 and even earlier (p45, p46, p64 and p66, for example). This seems to take the Byzantine text back at least as far as the Egyptian.

Two important statements must be made: (1) We should always remember there are good men and scholars on both sides of the controversy, and their major concern is to obtain as pure a text as possible, to reassure Bible students that the New Testament we now possess conforms to that written in the First Century. (2) Since it was the original writings which were inspired by the Holy Spirit, it is important for us to ascertain as closely as possible how well our present-day text agrees with the original writings. It should alleviate the fears some may have as to whether we have the true gospel enunciated in the First Century to know that most of the differences in the Greek text (about 1 percent of the total) are minor in nature and do not affect the great Christian doctrines we hold dear. Significant differences may be found in only a very few cases.

We have consciously avoided polemics in the area of textual criticism. There is legitimacy for such discussion, but The Complete Biblical Library is not the arena for such a conflict. (1) Often the opposing views are conjectural. (2) There is insufficient space to treat subjects adequately and to raise questions without answering them fully leads to confusion.

## Literary and Biblical Standards

Several hundred people, highly qualified scholars and specialists in particular fields have participated in producing The Complete Biblical Library. Great care has been taken to maintain high standards of scholarship and ethics. By involving scholars in Boards of Review for the Study Bible and the Greek-English Dictionary, we added an extra step to the editorial process. We have been particularly concerned about giving proper credit for citations from other works and have instructed our writers to show care in this regard. Any deviation from this principle has been inadvertent and not intentional.

Obviously, with writers coming from widely differing backgrounds, there are differences of opinion as to how to interpret certain passages.

We have tried to be just. When there are strong differences on the meaning of a particular passage, we have felt it best to present the contrasting viewpoints.

## Study Helps

As you come to the Scripture section of this volume, you will find correlated pages for your study. The facing pages are designed to complement each other, so you will have a better understanding of the Word of God than ever before. Each two-page spread will deal with a group of verses.

The Verse-by-Verse Commentary refers to each verse, except when occasionally it deals with some closely related verses. The Various Versions provides an expanded understanding of the various ways Greek words or phrases can be translated. The phrase from the King James Version appears first in boldface print, then other meaningful ways the Greek language has been translated. This feature will bring to you the riches of the language in which the New Testament first appeared.

## General Abbreviations

In a work of this nature it is necessary to use some abbreviations in order to conserve space. In deference to the Scriptures it is our custom not to abbreviate the titles of the books of the Bible, but abbreviations are used elsewhere. Becoming familiar with them will enable you to pursue in-depth study more effectively.

The following are general abbreviations which you will find used throughout the book:

| cf. | compared to or see |
|---|---|
| ibid. | in the same place |
| id. | the same |
| idem | the same |
| i.e. | that is |
| e.g. | for example |
| f. ff. | and following page or pages |
| sic | intended as written |
| MS(S) | manuscript(s) |
| ET | editor's translation |

## Old and New Testament Books and Apocrypha

As a service to you, we have listed the books of the Bible in their order. The Apocrypha is a series of books which were included in the Vulgate version (the Latin translation of the Bible endorsed by the Roman Catholic Church). Though not considered part of the canon by either the Jews or Protestants, they give interesting insights, on occasion, concerning the times with which they deal. They are not on the same level as the 66 books of our canon. These lists are located in the back of the book.

## Bibliographic Citations

The Complete Biblical Library has adopted a system of coordinated citations in the text and bibliography material which accommodates every type of reader. For the sake of simplicity and space, information given in the text to document a source is minimal, often including only the last name of the writer, or a shortened title and a page number.

Those who would like to research the subject more deeply can easily do so by looking in the Bibliography in the back of the book under the last name or shortened title. The Bibliography lists complete information necessary to locate the source in a library, supplemented by the page number given in the citation in the text.

# ACTS

## Overview

The Book of Acts forms a natural transition between the Gospels and the Epistles of the New Testament. The Gospels record what "Jesus began both to do and teach" (Acts 1:1); Acts picks up the story of Christ's continued work by His Holy Spirit through the apostles.

Actually Acts is the second part of a two-part work, the first part being the third Gospel. The opening words of Acts show this clearly, for they refer to the "first book" written by the author and dedicated to Theophilus. Although this concerns two distinct pieces of literature, there is a connection between them. The last document picks up the theme where the first ends. It is rather obvious from a comparison of Acts and Paul's letters that it is the physician Luke who has authored both of these writings. The ancient church, likewise, supports this tradition (cf. the opening of Luke's Gospel).

For many years Luke was Paul's coworker. Together they are responsible for over one-half of the New Testament, each writing about one-fourth. This alone indicates what a vital place Luke has among the New Testament writers.

## Sources and Background

One quite natural question arises when examining the Books of Acts: Where did Luke get his material? Concerning his "first book," the Gospel of Luke, Luke directly states that he has utilized sources: "Forasmuch as many have taken in hand to set forth in order a declaration of those things which are most surely believed among us, even as they delivered them unto us, which from the beginning were eyewitnesses, and ministers of the word; it seemed good to me also, having had perfect understanding of all things from the very first, to write unto thee in order" (Luke 1:1-3). He mentions "which from the beginning (were) eyewitnesses and ministers of the word" as among his sources of information (verse 2). Thus we may say that Luke does not record an account solely based upon his own experience; rather, he relies upon oral and written sources.

With regard to the second portion of his two-part work, the Book of Acts, Luke says nothing about using particular sources; nevertheless, it is apparent that he maintains the same thoroughness and accuracy in telling the story. Luke displays very remarkable reliability as a historian. W.M.

Ramsay calls him a historian of first quality who should be considered among the greatest.

Throughout the last half of Acts, Luke to a large extent did not depend upon outside sources. He did not have to. As the coworker of Paul he could chiefly draw from his own experiences, as the so-called we-sections indicate. Neither was Luke necessarily dependent upon written sources for the first half, which principally takes place in and around Jerusalem and Israel. Internal evidence of Acts, as well as the letters of Paul, demonstrate that Luke enjoyed personal contact with and knowledge of those who lived in the midst of the events he describes. For example, Mark and Luke were in Rome simultaneously (Colossians 4:10-14); Mark had firsthand knowledge of the Jerusalem church (Acts 21:17, 18). Luke contacted Philip the evangelist, one of Stephen's coworkers (Acts 21:28). In addition to this he associated with Paul and his companions. All of this made firsthand information readily accessible. The Book of Acts contains no less than 65 historical facts about Paul, which are referred to in 11 of his letters.

## Time and Location of Composition

Since we know that Luke accompanied Paul during his imprisonment in Rome (Acts chapters 27 and 28; cf. Colossians 4:14), it is reasonable to suppose that Acts was written in Rome during this time. This might explain the rather abrupt ending of Acts. Luke records the history up until the time he is writing and thus closes the book. However, it is not universally accepted that the ending is actually as abrupt as it appears.

Since it states that Paul worked unimpeded for 2 whole years, we can probably conclude that the period in which the opponents had to accuse Paul before the emperor's court had expired. If the legal precepts were enforced, then Paul would have been released at this time.

Additional evidence may further support the view that Acts was written during Paul's imprisonment in Rome: the book gives one the impression of being a defense of Paul and Christianity. Paul's legal battles are covered from the initial confrontation with the Jewish High Court until he reaches the supreme court of the land—the court of the Roman Emperor.

Therefore, much indicates that the Book of Acts was written in Rome, no later than A.D. 64-65 and perhaps earlier. The first volume, the Gospel of Luke, precedes this, probably around A.D. 60.

The hypothesis that Acts intends to justify/ defend Paul in his case before the emperor's court is intriguing. Although it may be merely secondary, a slight apologetic intent does seem to appear throughout the document. The matter itself, however, is of primary interest: what is the relationship between Christianity and Roman government?

As long as Christianity was regarded as a sect of Judaism believers could take advantage of the special privileges afforded the Jews by Rome. As an accepted religion, Judaism was tolerated; its adherents were exempt from worshiping the emperor. The Jewish leaders attempted to deprive Christians of that same freedom. If the Roman government believed the Jews, Christianity would be considered a new cult. The effect of that would mean serious consequences to the churches. Early Christians had to emphasize that they were neither revolutionary nor anti-social; Christianity was not a "kingdom of this world." Jesus was not an insurrectionist and neither were His disciples. One theme permeating Acts is that the Roman officials were much kinder to the Christian heralds than were the countrymen of these witnesses.

This leads us to another theme of the book. Evidently Acts intends to demonstrate that it is the Jews' own fault that the promises of the gospel went from the Jews to the Gentiles. In every case the message was preached "to the Jew first"; their status as God's "chosen people" was honored. The first chapters of Acts reveal that many Jews did in fact receive the gospel and did believe in Jesus as Messiah. However, overall, as a nation they rejected the Messiah. Consequently, a tremendous shift occurs with respect to God's design—salvation moves from being exclusively Jewish to being universal.

Although the external impetus for the mission to the Gentiles might be the Jewish rejection of the gospel, the deeper cause lies in God's own design. He fully intended from the outset that through His people Israel "all people should be blessed" (cf. the promise to Abraham, Genesis 12:3). Now the fulfillment of that promise occurs in the gospel. In accordance with its universal character, the offering of the gospel to the Gentiles is a major theme of Acts.

The chief purpose of Acts is to record salvation history. The main point of Acts is not that the writing initiates the history of the Church; rather it forms the climax of salvation's revelation in Jesus Christ. Many have discussed the appropriateness of "Acts" as descriptive of the book's contents. It should be considered in this regard that one of the book's primary goals is to validate the apostle's ministry. Without the authentication of the apostles that one finds in Acts, the New Testament epistles would lack a great deal of their authority.

Just as Jesus began both "to do and teach" (Acts 1:1), the apostles of Christ continue to "do" as well as to "teach" by the power of the Holy Spirit. Just as Jesus' mighty miracles confirmed His being Messiah, the works of the apostles confirm their endorsement and authorization by God (e.g., 2 Corinthians 12:12).

Those offering instruction in the faith in the epistles of the New Testament are authorized as men taught by God. This further explains why Paul's activity receives such a large amount of attention. References to Paul are first and foremost because he is the apostle to all peoples, not because he was such an effective missionary.

At this point the intent of Acts is reflected in the opening words of the third Gospel: "That thou mightest know the certainty of those things, wherein thou hast been instructed." Luke desires to affirm the reliability of the Christian faith. Every other recognized motif must be subordinate to this dominant theme.

And this is a matter which must take place within full public view. The book was possibly made available to the public by the chief recipient of the work, Theophilus. Similar to the Gospel of Luke, the Acts of the Apostles is especially directed to the cultured Greco-Roman world. Simultaneously it presents history and proclamation.

## Content and Character

Without any hesitation one can call Acts the first church-and-mission history of its kind. But the work does not provide a complete description of the history and growth of the early Christian faith. For example, Luke tells us nothing of the gospel's spread into the countries east and south of Israel. What Luke shows is the path of the gospel's spread from Jerusalem, the religious center of Judaism, to the center of the world at that time, Rome. Chronologically the book covers approximately 30 years, from around A.D. 30 to A.D. 60.

Acts 1:8 affords a programmatic outline for the whole book: "Ye shall be witnesses unto me both in Jerusalem, and in all Judea, and in Samaria, and unto the uttermost part of the earth." When the Holy Spirit descended upon the disciples they filled Jerusalem with their teaching (Acts 5:28). The second phase, the evangelization of Judea and Samaria, began seriously when persecution broke out and scattered the believers (Acts 8:1). The third phase was initiated with Peter's preaching to the house of Cornelius (Acts 10:34f.). It became fully realized in the missionary journeys of Paul. Their groundbreaking work will continue and extend "unto the uttermost part of the earth" (Acts 1:8) through the body of Christ, His Church. This will be the objective of the Church "unto the end of the world (the time)" (Matthew 28:20).

Acts naturally divides itself into two sections. In chapters 1-12, which especially deal with the early missionary efforts among the Jews, Peter is the principal character. The second part centers on Paul. Here the primary theme is the missionary thrust to the Gentiles. The following outline reflects the structure of Acts:

## Section 1: The Focus on Peter (chapters 1-12)

I. Jerusalem (chapters 1-7)

1. The ascension of Jesus and the selection of Judas' replacement (chapter 1)

2. The Day of Pentecost:

   a. The outpouring of the Spirit (2:1-13)

   b. Peter's sermon (2:14-40)

   c. The Early Church (2:41-47)

3. The healing of the lame man and Peter's sermon on the porch of Solomon (3:1-26)

4. First appearance before the Sanhedrin (4:1-22)

5. The life in the ancient church (4:23-37)

6. Ananias and Sapphira (5:1f.)

7. Stephen

   a. Ministry (6:8-15)

   b. Sermon (7:1-53)

   c. Martyrdom (7:54-60)

II. Judea and Samaria (chapters 8-9)

1. Philip in Samaria (8:1-25)

2. The Ethiopian eunuch (8:26-40)

3. The conversion and first preaching of Paul (9:1-30)

4. The missionary activity of Peter (9:31-43)

III. The Gentile Mission (chapters 10-12)

1. Peter in the house of Cornelius (chapter 10)

2. The church in Jerusalem approves the Gentile mission (11:1-18)

3. The first Gentile Christian church in Antioch (11:19-30)

4. The persecution of Herod; Peter's deliverance (chapter 12)

## Section 2: The Focus on Paul (chapters 13-28)

I. First Missionary Journey (chapters 13-15)

1. Cyprus (chapters 13:4-12)

2. Asia Minor (13:13-14:28)

3. Jerusalem Council (chapter 15)

II. Second Missionary Journey (chapters 16-18)

1. Journey through Asia Minor (15:40-16:8)

2. Missionary activity in Europe (16:9-18:22)

III. Third Missionary Journey (chapters 19, 20)

1. Ministry in Ephesus (chapter 19)

2. New visit to Europe (20:1-4)

3. Troas and Miletus; farewell to Ephesian elders (20:5-38)

IV. The Journey to Jerusalem (chapters 21-26)

1. Tyre and Caesarea (21:1-16)

2. In Jerusalem (21:17-23:22)

3. Two years in Caesarea (23:23-26:32)

V. The Voyage to Rome (chapters 27, 28)

1. Voyage and shipwreck (chapter 27)

2. Stay on Malta (28:1-10)

3. From Malta to Rome (28:11-16)

4. Two years in Rome (28:17-31)

## The Acts of the Apostles: The Title

"The Acts of the Apostles," *praxeis tōn apostolōn* in the Greek or *acta apostolorum* in Latin—hence the name "Acts" in common parlance—is the ancient title of the book. By and large the ancient church knows of no other title. The only variation is that three manuscripts omit the article *tōn*, so the title reads "Acts of Apostles" or "apostles' acts." The question remains: Is this the original designation of the book?

The data against this being the author's choice include that the subject matter to a certain extent cloes not agree with that title. It is true that all the apostles are mentioned by name (1:13), but the focus does not fall upon each one's activity. As mentioned above, the first twelve chapters are devoted to Peter's activities primarily; John plays only a secondary role, and the only mention of James his brother is that he died.

From chapter 13 on the only "acts" recorded are those of Paul, who for good reason is not one of the apostles in the list of 1:13. Witnesses other than the apostles do receive a lot of attention; for example, Stephen (chapters 6, 7) and Philip the Evangelist (chapter 8) are given a lot of space. Above all, it is clear that Luke is not merely writing "biographies" of the apostles. In fact, the source of the "acts" is resurrected, ascended, and glorified Jesus Christ. He, through His Spirit, performs His mighty works through His apostles, who are merely His instruments.

However, strong evidence indicates that the heading is the title selected by the author himself. The book originally was titled. A writing dedicated to a person of such high standing and caliber as Theophilus, as well as probably being "published" by him, almost certainly had the name of the book and the name of the author. "The Acts of Apostles" conveys a somewhat broader meaning than we first imagine. It actually relates the ministry of Jesus Christ through His apostles and His church. The earliest apostles had witnessed the resurrection of our Lord. It is to this group that Paul belongs for he received a special revelation of the Risen Lord and a unique call. Also included among others who continued the ministry of Jesus are the coworkers of the apostles who built upon the "foundation of the apostles and prophets" (Ephesians 2:20). The apostolic witnesses proclaimed the gospel from Jerusalem—the focal point and beginning of the salvation message—to Rome, the heart of the Gentile world.

## The Most Ancient Witnesses to Acts

Polycarp, bishop of Smyrna, writes a letter to the church in Philippi around the year A.D. 107. In it he quotes so freely from Acts of the Apostles that it is obvious the document was generally known to the church at large. Perhaps this insight confirms a close relationship between the author of Acts and the church at Philippi (see below).

## The Author

The author is not mentioned in connection with the title of the work or within the document itself. But at least two facts are clear and are useful for identifying the author's background, his environment, and his purpose.

First, the opening words of the Book of Acts (1:1, 2) together with verse 3 form not so much an introduction as they do a "summary" of what preceded. The first-person "I" of the opening verses of Acts is undoubtedly the same "I" in the opening words of the third Gospel. While the third Gospel has a true "introduction," the opening words of Acts are a summary and continuation—a reference to Luke 1:1-4—of Jesus' words and work. This theme is merely resumed.

Since this indeed is the intent of the author of Acts, we can be certain that this is the same individual responsible for the third Gospel. Acts is the second volume of two by the same author. Further supporting this is the fact that the language and style of both works are the same.

Second, we observe from the introduction to the third Gospel that the Book of Acts is written to the same individual—"most excellent Theophilus." The name literally means, "he who loves God." Some interpreters suggest that Theophilus is actually a personification of the (any) person seeking God, a Gentile seeking the truth—all of fallen humanity yearning for their God and Creator, who may be "unknown" but not forgotten (cf. Acts 17:23). Now God has revealed himself to all mankind through the gospel of Jesus Christ.

Others speculate that Theophilus is a pseudonym of an individual whose name must remain anonymous. "Theophilus" characterizes him nonetheless. Both of these opinions could in one sense

pick up the intent and purpose of the writing very adequately. Nonetheless, both suppositions are unacceptable. First, the kind of dedication such as the one made to Theophilus—lacking any pseudonymic qualities or personification—were common in Hellenistic literature of that period. Second, the use of the name in the Gospel diminishes the chances of its being merely a literary convention. Whether or not the title "most excellent" refers to the high office of its bearer or whether it is simply a respectful address, we can be sure that Theophilus was a man of high social status and wealth.

Moreover, the dedication of literary work to an individual of significant social status corresponds with the custom of the time. In so doing the work came under the auspices of the person to whom it was dedicated; his name thus became a sort of "recommendation" for the book. The need for such an endorsement of a book is entirely in keeping with the custom of the time, when no commercial marketing of a book was possible. Thus, the use of the adjective *kratistos* to describe Theophilus helped fill a need. *Kratistos* itself means "the most excellent," "the highly esteemed" (formally a superlative form). "Your Excellency" (Today's English Version) thus describes a real person.

Luke's introduction to his Gospel affords no insight into the identity of Theophilus or his whereabouts. Historical records offer no help in that regard, since Theophilus was a relatively common name in both Hellenism and Judaism, being attested by literature and inscription.

Even the title *kratistos* provides little information about the recipient of the work. It corresponds to the Latin *vir egregius*, a title applied to the Roman governors of the emperor or the Roman procurators, such as Felix in Judea (Acts 23:26; 24:3) or Festus (Acts 26:25). Thus it may be describing Theophilus as a man having a high political position; however, it may also simply be a title of respect without any reference to social standing. It often occurs in dedications to a wealthy benefactor who placed money and influence at the disposal of his scribes (slaves), who were responsible for publishing a work.

If one then couples this with the unanimous tradition that Luke the physician (see below) authored Acts, and keeping in mind that physicians were often, though not always, released slaves, the picture emerges that as a physician and a freed slave, Luke was favored by a prosperous man, perhaps in a high political office. Theophilus then would be the "patron" or "benefactor" of the work as well as the recipient.

But the introduction of the third Gospel and its transitional "bridge" in the opening paragraphs of the Book of Acts can teach us much more about the relationship between Luke and Theophilus.

This somewhat formal dedication, typical of its historical climate, tells us that the recipient was a cultured Hellenist. A rather late tradition of the Early Church notes that he lived in Antioch in Syria. But this may have been influenced by another tradition that the author was from Antioch (see discussion below).

Of more importance is the last sentence of the Gospel's introduction that informs us that Theophilus had received instructions concerning the Christian faith: "those things, wherein thou hast been instructed" (Luke 1:4). The verb here, *katēcheo* (actively, "to give lessons"; passively, "to be taught"), implies "to inform," such as a teacher "informs" a student (cf. Acts 22:3). In the language of the Church this stood for the "teaching" of the way of Christianity (cf. Acts 18:25). About the middle of the Second Century *katēcheo* became a technical term for catechetical instruction (see e.g., 2 Clement 17:1). A recipient of such instruction was a catechumen. As early as the New Testament this trend is beginning. We read of the "elementary teachings about Christ" (Hebrews 6:1) and "elementary truths of God's word" (Hebrews 5:12). Possibly a form of baptismal catechesis (instruction) was instituted quite early. There may be a trace of it, for example, in 1 John 2:20-27 and Ephesians 4:20.

Naturally, it cannot be determined for certain whether Theophilus was baptized already or he was a catechumen, i.e., a candidate for baptism. If he were a catechumen, it can probably be assumed that the Gospel that was dedicated to him, along with the Book of Acts, are related to his instruction and that of his fellow disciples. Thus, if this is true, Luke would be his *kathēchōn*, "teacher" (cf. Galatians 6:6). A similar teacher in the Church is called a *didaskalos* on another occasion. There were many of them in Antioch (Acts 13:1).

We are uncertain of the spiritual heritage of the "most excellent Theophilus," or why he became a catechumen in the Church. Possibly he was one of the many "devout" men (*sebomenos*) touched by the gospel (e.g., Acts 13:50; 17:4, 17), or perhaps a "God-fearer" (*phobumenos*) like Cornelius (10:2). He might have regularly attended synagogue or he might have been a Jewish proselyte (convert), "fruit" of the Jewish mission among the Gentiles (cf. 13:43, a reference to one in Antioch). He could also have been an enlightened Gentile, tired of the emptiness of paganism, such as Sergius Paulus, the proconsul of Cyprus who "desired to hear the word of God" (Acts 13:7). He subsequently became a believer who listened, "being astonished at the doctrine of the Lord" (Acts 13:12).

One purpose of the book, clearly discernible from the final words in the dedication (Luke 1:4), is that both the Gospel and Acts were written in order to give Theophilus spiritual guidance. There is an "in order that" *hina* clause which implies more than simply providing information. This involved Christian proclamation. We encounter the teaching of historical data: the human origins of Jesus; His words and deeds; His death and resurrection. Since God has wrought a saving work in Christ, the message about Jesus Christ is "words by which we become saved." Through personal witness in the first and second parts of this work the author assists the reader in personally experiencing that "faithful saying . . . worthy of all acceptation: that Christ Jesus came into the world to save sinners" (1 Timothy 1:15).

Saving faith involves a knowledge of the events surrounding Christ's salvation. We have all assurance that the message of salvation has been handed down faithfully and unchanged; it is reliable and eternal.

Theophilus is not the only reader. The dedication implies that—in accordance with the custom of the day—the book is for all those in the same situation as Theophilus. The document is particularly relevant to Gentiles inquiring into the Christian faith as well as those Gentile Christians in need of confirmation of the reality of the Christian message. Everyone willing to be led *ad fontes* "to the sources," discovers the dependable, solid, tradition of the Christian church—the apostolic witness.

The writer does not repeat or elaborate upon the first dedication. The most natural explanation is that the two volumes are so closely tied together in terms of time and content that the shortened opening is adequate since there had been a complete statement in the first volume.

## A Historian

With regards to discovering the character of the author of Acts we can extract much more insight from the introduction of the Gospel of Luke and its relationship to the opening words of Acts.

The author is a historian and works historically and methodically. He presents himself to the reader in this way in Luke 1:3: "It seemed good to me also, having had perfect understanding of all things from the very first, to write unto thee in order." The Acts of the Apostles corroborates this purpose in its careful and exact presentation at every turn. The author possesses firsthand knowledge of the world and time in which he recounts the course of the spread of the gospel. He fully grasps the historical situation, realizing from personal experience the impact of the gospel. For example: He makes accurate geographical statements. He knows from experience that Perga lies in Pamphylia (13:13); Antioch in Pisidia (13:14); Lystra and Derbe in Lycaonia (14:6); while Myra can be located in Lycia

(27:5). He has a thorough knowledge of the territorial divisions of Macedonia (16:12). He knows that Philippi is a Roman settlement. He is aware of Fair Havens near the city of Lasea. He knows Phoenix, the harbor, faces both the southwest and northwest (27:12). The divine Author, the Holy Spirit was able to use Luke's knowledge and abilities as He inspired him to write this part of the Scriptures.

Luke records many details. It should also be pointed out he knows the names of the apostles and their coworkers, he also knows their addresses. Paul is living in the "street which is called Straight" in Damascus (9:11). Peter lodged with Simon, a tanner, "whose house is by the sea side" (10:6). Lydia, whose house became the base for the first European missionary outreach, was a "seller of purple" from Thyatira (16:14). In Thessalonica Jason and his household suffered because he opened it to "these" (17:5f.). Paul was hosted in Corinth by Titius Justus, "whose house joined hard to the synagogue" (18:7).

The author is able to provide information about the Roman governmental structure without difficulty. He is thoroughly familiar with the historical data. He knows that in the senate of the provinces the proconsul presides (13:7f.; 18:12; 19:38). He is familiar with the "Asiatics" in Ephesus (19:31), and he is aware of the "strategists" in Philippi (16:36f.) and the "politicians" in Thessalonica (17:6f.). Modern historians specializing in the Roman judicial system discover that Luke is accurate in regard to Roman judicial proceedings in his description of Paul's trial before Gallio (18:12f.), Felix (chapter 24), as well as Festus (25:26). He, furthermore, fully understood the implications of what it means to be a Roman citizen (16:37f; 21:39; 22:25f.; 23:27). Indeed, Luke so presents the geographical, political, and judicial circumstances of the First Century A.D. in the regions around the Mediterranean Sea—even in minute details—that we are forced to regard him as a reliable historian. His writing must be considered as a primary source of the first order for the investigation of such matters.

## A Theologian

Nonetheless, the author of Acts is more than a mere historian. He is first and foremost a theologian, a careful and historical theologian; a theologian who believes his message—his heart burns for the gospel of Jesus Christ (cf. Luke 24:32).

This becomes apparent in the introduction to his first volume in the opening sentences of the second: "The former treatise have I made, O Theophilus, of all that Jesus began both to do and teach, until the day in which he was taken up." Not expressed, but implied in this is: "In this second volume I will continue to relate the deeds and words of Jesus from the time He was taken up until today."

The entire two volume work—Luke-Acts—its goal, its unity, as well as its appearing in two volumes, is of a theological nature. The Gospel of Luke and the Acts of the Apostles do not involve two different subjects or themes. Both are concerned with what Jesus "did and taught." In one word the theme of both is the "gospel," the joyous message of God's saving, redeeming work for all of creation and for fallen humanity by Jesus Christ. The first volume presents this gospel, the history of its origins. The second volume recalls the history of the spread of that message. Or, to put it another way: the Gospel tells of the work fulfilled in Jerusalem for the salvation of all the world; the second part, the Book of Acts, involves the preaching of the salvation "unto the uttermost part of the earth!" (Acts 1:8).

The relationship between these two books as a unified whole as well as their uniqueness as two separate works can also be expressed in these terms: The first volume concerns the Son of God, Jesus Christ, who became man, and who, through His life, death, and resurrection, demonstrates in word and deed God's saving power. In the second volume Jesus continues to carry out His mission, but now He does it as the one who has been "taken up," i.e., the "ascended Lord." Now He accomplishes His work through His new body, the Church, by His word and by the Holy Spirit. Thus we see two phases, two epochs of salvation history. But prior to telling the history of the second epoch there are five basic affirmations to be noted:

(1) The "taking up" the Ascension (Acts 1:9-11) brought to a close the first volume and it opens the second. It therefore unites the two epochs. Just as the Son of God "descended" to earth becoming a man among men, He "ascended" when He fulfilled His work; that is, He left the human realm of time and space and moved into the realm of the eternal, into the almighty and divine realm of the omnipresent God. A "cloud," the Shekinah of God—the symbol of His glory and presence—overshadowed Christ, and now He "sits at the right hand of God." Just as the mystery of the Incarnation, Christ's becoming a man, opened the first epoch, the mystery of the Ascension underlies the second epoch.

(2) The Ascension itself is the background for the events of the Book of Acts. Because Jesus ascended the Spirit comes (Acts 2:1-13). Through the Spirit the Risen Lord is present in the world. Now the Third Person of the Trinity continues the ministry of the Ascended Lord.

(3) The Spirit as the one carrying on the work of Jesus is not a vague influence. Rather, He works in and through the Church, the ekklēsia, the people of God on earth. This explains why chapter 2 not

only relates the arrival of the Spirit, but necessarily the "birth" of the Church that had been "conceived" (created) when Jesus called His disciples. Therefore, the Church is the new body of Jesus Christ, the sign of His presence and the instrument and dwelling place of His Spirit.

(4) Just as a person needs skills to perform a certain task, or just as a worker needs tools to be efficient, the Church needs a "tool" for carrying out the ministry of the Spirit. That "tool" is the Word of God. Peter in his sermon on the Day of Pentecost emphasizes its role and authority. Later we see the power of the Word revealed in the preaching, in missionary outreaches, in baptism or in the Lord's Supper, and in fellowship and worship, throughout the entire work.

(5) That a new epoch is in effect is confirmed by the reestablishment of the apostles (Acts 1:12-26). The ministry of the true Church is apostolic. The Church and the apostles cannot exist independently of one another.

This is chiefly because the Church is built upon the foundation of the apostles and the prophets, Jesus Christ himself being the chief cornerstone (Ephesians 2:20). This takes place because the apostles are the authentic, original, and principal witnesses of Jesus and they are responsible—according to God's own choice and will (Acts 1:2)—to continue Jesus' words and deeds. They witnessed the Resurrection and Jesus' triumphant victory over death—the announcement of salvation. Thus Acts opens with the fact that the Risen One "showed himself to these men and gave many convincing proofs" (NIV). For 40 days He instructed them about their testimony (cf. Moses on Sinai, Exodus 24:18). He did not appear in "visions"; He was truly seen. He revealed himself to them and confirmed their apostolic calling.

Furthermore, the 12 apostles represent the sum of the people of God, the "12 tribes." Israel awaited the promise of restoration, when the 12 patriarchs, the sons of Jacob, along with the 12 tribes they ruled over, would be reunited. Now the fulfillment of the promises becomes fully realized. The people of God is made up of all peoples, tribes and tongues, to the glory of God. The 12 apostles of Jesus Christ are the firstfruits, the promise of a larger harvest. From them people of God would grow and become great. This would take place in Jerusalem (Luke 24:47).

## An Eyewitness

An important feature of Luke's writing is that in certain sections of the documents there are "we passages." According to the reliable Western text representative, Codex Bezae (D), considered by some to be a "rough draft" or a "first edition," there is a first-person plural ("we") reading as early

as 11:28: "when we had gathered together." Generally Codex D is regarded as being relatively accurate historically and it contains many fascinating details not otherwise attested.

Elsewhere, the "we passages" include 16:10-27; 20:5-21:18; 27:1-28:16. By writing "we," the writer indicates he personally participated in the events and missionary work he describes. The personal nature of these recollections serves to underscore the reliability of what is being told. Here we have the testimony of an eyewitness.

The "we" of the sections mentioned naturally refers back to the "I" in the opening sentences of the work. This, in turn, points back to the "I" in the introduction to the third Gospel. In every instance we meet the careful, accurate hand of a historian and theologian of literary and personal integrity inspired by the Holy Spirit.

Neither can linguistic or stylistic differences be appealed to as indicating a difference in the "we passages" from the remainder of the book. From start to finish Luke-Acts represents a homogeneous authorship. Even a scholar of such critical views as Adolf von Harnack strongly endorses the unity and homogeneity of the various elements of the two books, including the "we sections" of the Book of Acts (Harnack, p. xlii).

In addition to von Harnack others strongly advocate a common authorship and a date for Acts around the end of Paul's first Roman imprisonment. According to the tradition, and as yet most probable chronology, this means about the year A.D. 60. One of the weightiest arguments is that Acts almost certainly was not composed after the Pauline epistles. They all existed, except for the Letters to Titus and 1 and 2 Timothy, when Paul was released (ca. A.D. 60). These should also be regarded as "epistles," in other words, preaching and admonition intended for the churches. At that time the letters undoubtedly were circulating among the churches; nonetheless, the author of Acts would not have had access to any "collection" of these letters, since it was still too early for that.

The chronological relationship between the Pauline epistles and Acts, and their respective recording of Paul's whereabouts, is not always clear. This in fact supports the trustworthiness of Acts. Acts is an independent recollection of selected events, many of which come from the hand of an eyewitness. If the date of composition were later one can be sure that the writer would have made his material conform to Paul's own letters. This would be easily discernible, since it would have included "quotes" or allusions to Paul's letters.

## The Lucan Tradition

A unanimous tradition of the ancient church ascribes the authorship of the third Gospel as well as Acts to Luke. The first occurrence of this tradition is the prologue to the Gospel of Luke in the anti-Marcionite canon, around A.D. 150. It is also attested in the Muratorian Canon, named after its discoverer, L.A. Muratori (d. 1750). This fragment is supposedly an official ecclesiastical document issued from Rome around A.D. 170. The Muratorian Canon was written by an ecclesiastical authority, and it deals with which documents the Church accepts and permits to be read in the worship service as a part of its liturgy—Gospels, Epistles and lection (according to a church calendar). The purpose is obvious: The list combats heretics and their false writing. As a result of that struggle the Church is forced to determine standards of faith and practice. *Kanōn*, thus means "rule," "guide."

An Early Church father wrote that the third Gospel was written by Luke, that he wrote about what he had learned from others, because he himself had not seen Jesus in the flesh. He collected all the available information and began his account with the birth of John. The writer also stated that the acts of the apostles were recorded in one book. Luke presented to Theophilus a report of the events he had "firsthand" information of. He was selective in his presentation. For example, he omitted the martyrdom of Peter and Paul's journey from Rome to Spain.

The records of the ancient church mention no name other than Luke in speaking of the authorship of the third Gospel and Acts. In actuality, neither is it rejected by later critics, at least not to the extent that it has gained wide acceptance. Furthermore, it is totally incredible to think that someone in the Second Century could have affixed a name of a First-Century disciple or apostle to a document later accepted into the New Testament canon, especially in a period in which such a practice was so commonly denounced (cf. the apocryphal "acts" of the various apostles written from the second through the fifth centuries).

## Luke in the New Testament

Who, then, is this "Luke"? The name *Loukas* (Greek) is actually a variation of the Roman *Lucanus* (the name of a Roman poet at the time of Nero), just as Silas is the abbreviated form of the Roman name *Silvanus*. Some have speculated that these may be the same person, since Silvanus comes from the Latin *silva*, "wood," and Luke might be connected with *Lucus*, which means a "grove" (of trees?) that is dedicated to the gods. But this is merely fanciful speculation and it does not correspond to Acts, which refers to the apostle/disciple Silas in the third person.

## A Gentile Christian

We learn from Colossians 4 that Luke was apparently a Gentile Christian. Although it is not stated

explicitly it is plain from the context. At the close of his letter to the church in Colossae Paul mentions his coprisoners Aristarchus and Mark—Barnabas' nephew—together with Jesus Justus, as the only coworkers of the circumcised group who comforted him. In addition to the founder of the church, Epaphras, Paul mentions Luke and Demas (cf. Colossians 4:10, 11, 12-14). Thus these three were not members of the circumcised group, being non-Jewish Gentiles. Therefore, Luke is probably the only New Testament author not of Jewish descent.

## A Greek Physician

From the same text we learn that Luke was a trained physician (Colossians 4:14). With respect to the training and skills of doctors at this time we know that in the Fourth Century B.C. the science of medicine, after the time of Hippocrates (d. ca. 380 B.C.), was studied first in Alexandria, Egypt, and from there it reached Rome.

Physicians in the capital of the empire were initially Greeks, ordinarily released slaves. During Luke's time the famous writing of Celsus, *De Medicina,* was in circulation. Also at that time there was a "board of health" under the control of the Government. This group, in part, examined and authorized men to practice medicine in the empire. New doctors were closely supervised by their older colleagues; mistakes were severely punished. For example, their right to practice, *just practicandi,* might be suspended.

Thus Luke, as a physician, possessed no small amount of technical and practical experience, and because he came into contact with so many individuals he also had a wealth of knowledge about human nature. As a Greek by birth and as a physician by training and occupation, Luke was understandably more cultured and precise in his use of the Greek language than the other New Testament writers. The Holy Spirit used all these qualites and background as He inspired the writer.

During earlier times of research, importance was often attached to unique medical expressions in both Luke's writings. For instance, in Acts 9:18—the description of Paul regaining his sight—appeal was made in support of the tradition that Luke was the author. However, not as much significance is attached to "medical terminology" in current studies. Although Luke does use medical terminology, at times we find the same expressions used in authors who are not physicians. Thus the words and phrases must be in common use.

## From Antioch?

Much indicates that we are on historical grounds when we investigate the tradition of the ancient church that Luke was from Antioch, or at least that he lived in Antioch in Syria. Antioch was the capital of Syria and the third largest city in the Roman

Empire with a half million inhabitants. Eusebius (d. 340) maintains that Luke was from Antioch. (Eusebius, *Historia Ecclesiastica,* Books 3, 4:7, 8). He had studied there. Jerome (d. 420) also supports the tradition and he, too, grew up in Antioch as a child.—Jerome, *De viris illustribus,* chap. 7)

The New Testament can lend support to this hypothesis. The thoroughness and personal concern reflected in the accounts of Acts about particular locations or events in and around Antioch indicate such a relationship may indeed be possible. He knows and tells about the establishment of the church in Antioch. He realizes that some of those who lived in Antioch were among Jesus' disciples who had to flee from Jerusalem because of the persecution following Stephen's martyrdom. These Jews from Cyprus and Cyrene, he recounts, in contrast to others, testified to Greeks that Jesus from Nazareth was Lord *kurios* and Christ. With obvious joy he relates the outcome of their preaching: a great number believed (Acts 11:20ff.). Furthermore, he knows that Barnabas, as the first emissary from the Jerusalem church, was responsible for this Gentile outreach. He states that Barnabas himself went to Tarsus, sought out Paul, and asked him to join him in the work of the church in Antioch. They worked together there for an entire year. Luke also remembers that it was in Antioch that believers were first called "Christians" because they confessed Jesus the Christ as Lord (Acts 11:22- 26).

Luke was also aware of the close relationship between the mother church in Jerusalem and the young gathering in Antioch; he knew the liaison between them. He remembers the occasion that Agabus (from Jerusalem) prophesied by the Spirit of a coming famine. As a result the church sent some to minister to those in Judea (Acts 11:27f.).

Luke was moreover familiar with the names of the prophets and teachers in the Antiochean church (Acts 13:1). Why did he mention them specifically by name—besides Barnabas and Paul, Simeon, who was called Niger, Lucius from Cyrene, as well as Manaen, who was brought up with Herod—unless he knew them personally? He perhaps regarded their teaching and preaching very highly.

We find a brief but vivid account of the church service in which the church in Antioch, with the laying on of hands, sends out Barnabas and Paul as missionaries called by the Lord (Acts 13:2). For the most part Antioch is considered by Luke to be the home church of the missionaries. They return there in between missionary journeys and report to all the church what the Lord is doing in the mission fields (Acts 14:26-28; 15:35; 18:22).

Additionally, Luke's familiarity with the local and theological issues in Antioch is impressive. He gives detailed accounts of the choosing and sending of representatives to the Jerusalem Council, a decisive point in the early history of the Church. He recalls the delegates' stop along the way in the churches of Phoenicia and Samaria. In precise detail he describes the proceedings of the Jerusalem Council as well as recalling the recollections of the delegates upon their return. Indeed, he knows the meeting's resolution (Acts 15:1-34).

He must also intimately know the life of the church in Antioch and without hesitation—an indication of the integrity of Luke—he recalls the disputes in the church, even the unfortunate, bitter dispute between Paul and Barnabas that resulted in their breakup. Barnabas and John Mark travel one direction and Paul and Silas another, but both pairs are carrying on the work of the gospel (Acts 15:35-41).

In light of all of this it is not unreasonable to conclude that Luke the physician was an active member of the Gentile church in Antioch.

The enthusiasm with which he remembers the revival that swept over the city may indicate that he himself was one of its "fruits." Barnabas comes to the forefront as the leader of this revival and other missionary pushes (11:22ff.). Even after Paul arrives, Barnabas continues to be mentioned first (e.g., 11:30; 12:25; 13:1, 2, 7; 14:14). As the older servant of the Lord, Barnabas would have naturally assumed a position of leadership. But the emphasis placed upon Barnabas could indicate that Barnabas played an important role in the conversion of the Greek physician Luke. If that is the case, Luke's calling Barnabas "a good man and full of the Holy Spirit and of faith" takes on a quality of personal thankfulness and respect.

## The Coworker of Paul

According to the New Testament it was Paul with whom Luke was so closely associated, both as a fellow-worker in the gospel and as a personal friend to the end. During his first imprisonment in Rome, Paul writes of "Luke, the beloved *agapētos* physician" (Colossians 4:14). This could, of course, simply mean "our dear doctor Luke." It might also indicate that he was a believer and a member of the Church, a man who together with Paul knows that he is obligated to show the love *agapē* of God in Jesus Christ. Nevertheless, the words may also connote a special bond of friendship and confidence between Paul and Luke.

Perhaps the phrase "beloved physician, Luke" can be understood to mean all these things, for in Philemon (verse 24) Luke is explicitly called Paul's coworker. In Paul's supposedly last epistle, the farewell letter to Timothy, Luke is portrayed as being special to Paul, "Only Luke is with me" (2 Timothy 4:11). Paul is writing this at a time in which almost everyone else has deserted him. It is immediately prior to his death, apparently: "I am now ready to be offered, and the time of my departure is at hand" (2 Timothy 4:6f.).

What bond united these two men of God? If we can assume that Luke was connected with the church in Antioch (see above), then their original meeting took place during the early 40s. The joining of forces began around the year 50, however, when Paul's missionary focus rested upon Europe.

Paul and Silas set out on foot through Syria and Asia Minor at this time on their second missionary journey. The disciples "increased in number daily" (Acts 16:5). Thus it was necessary to expand the missionary workers. Timothy from Lystra joined their ranks and together these three worked their way through Phrygia, Galatia, and Mysia. In Troas Paul and his coworkers met another great and unexpected challenge: the call to go to Macedonia (16:9) and to preach the gospel in Europe. They could not refuse this call and responded "immediately" (Acts 16:10).

Precisely at this intersection we encounter the "we passage" phenomenon mentioned before. We might conclude that at this juncture, impressed by the tremendous challenge before them, Paul sent to the base church in Antioch for "reinforcements." Here Paul mentions Luke as useful in that capacity. Luke, as quickly as possible—either by ship or over land through Asia Minor—joined the group. The time was around A.D. 50.

Why did Paul choose Luke, or more precisely, why did the Spirit set him apart (cf. 13:2)? As we have noted, there were other possibilities, such as Simeon Niger, Lucius, and Manaen. One answer bringing the gospel to the heart of Greek civilization. What better choice than the Greek-educated Luke?

Some would claim Paul needed Luke's help as a physician. However, Paul's frequent recollections of his gospel-related suffering give no indication that he was sick (1 Corinthians 4:9-13; 2 Corinthians 4:8, 9; 6:4-10; 11:23-29). For the same reason 2 Corinthians 12:7, "a thorn in the flesh" cannot be adduced as proof that Paul was so chronically ill as to need the services of a physician on a regular basis.

From the "we passages" and the aforementioned places in the Pauline epistles we may conclude that Luke remained with Paul and his group except on those occasions where the ministry of the gospel demanded he be elsewhere.

## The Sources of Luke

Every author, even the most "original" draws from certain or unconsciously from sources. This is especially true of an historical author.

Of course, this applies to Luke too. He himself describes this in his introduction to his first volume, the Gospel of Luke (Luke 1:1-4). He used many sources, for "many have taken in hand." They wrote "to set forth in order a declaration." These originated from eyewitnesses of the ministry of Jesus and they rest upon a conscientious, reliable, accurate, oral tradition of the Church "delivered unto us," and "which are most surely believed among us."

In Acts the author included himself in the circle of the eyewitnesses and his own testimony. The origin of the "we passages" is interpreted differently. Are they abstracts of a diary kept by Luke? Keeping a journal would not be strange for a physician or unparalleled. Or it might include written testimony at the "lawcourt of the emperor" during Paul's trial in Rome. Perhaps similar notes were kept by the author during the shipwreck at Malta and the events that took place there.

These eyewitness accounts cover the period of Paul's second missionary journey in the years 49-51. According to the "snorter text" this includes the journey from Troas. According to the longer reading of Codex D, it includes the journey from inland Mysia up to and including Philippi. Apparently Luke remained in Philippi to protect the gains made by the gospel into that area. Next the "we" sections span the years 52-55, the third missionary journey from Philippi to Jerusalem, including Paul's arrest and imprisonment. The "we" sections probably include Paul's imprisonment in Caesarea (A.D. 55-57). At least they cover Paul's dramatic voyage to Italy in the winter of A.D. 57-58 and his first two-year imprisonment in Rome (A.D. 58-60). This last point is substantiated by Paul's mentioning Luke in two letters written during this period.

What sources has Luke drawn upon for the rest of his story? Undoubtedly he had access to the same kind of sources he employed in his first volume. This would especially hold true in the accounts immediately after the Resurrection, the Ascension, and the outpouring of the Spirit on the Day of Pentecost, as well as in the earliest history of the church in Jerusalem. Included here too should be the account of the gospel's first being preached to the Gentiles—Peter's visit to Cornelius' house.

In telling of the establishment of the different churches Luke could depend upon traditions and personal conversations he had with those who were present. Luke learned of the traditions on his journeys and he includes them in his second volume. When he tells of the establishment of the church in Antioch, he is certainly relying upon his own recollection.

Involved in the writing of Acts is the personal knowledge and recollection of the author, together with his investigation of the "eyewitnesses and ministers of the word." A glance at Acts with this "source" in mind reveals that the prime sources of information of that day and time were none other than such men as Peter, John, and James the brother of our Lord (cf. 21:17f.)—the early apostles, as well as the evangelists and apostolic coworkers like Barnabas, John Mark, and Silas. Just think what Paul and Luke must have discussed as they traveled on foot across the miles and lived together for 2 years in Rome while Paul was under house arrest.

But to underscore the unity of the document again: Acts is a unified whole in both language and content. It possesses a literary and technical consistency unmatched. It is a unity which at the deepest level comes from the Spirit who inspired its writing.

That is not just a pious remark by a believer oblivious to the critical questions. Of course there are "sources." But the ultimate source is the gospel, the Word and the Spirit, the Church and the apostolate that the author serves.

## The Time of Writing of the Document

Nothing in the first or second volume (Luke-Acts) indicates the year of the composition. In order to estimate the time of composition we must deduce it from the arguments themselves in light of history. Opinions are wide-ranging in this regard. Some have thought that Acts was written around the Second Century with the intention to "harmonize" divergent views between Pauline and Petrine Christianity. Others assert that the book originates in the anti-Marcionite struggle. Still others regard Acts as a defense of Paul designed to declare his apostolic authority as genuine.

In contrast to these opinions is the theory that the document is genuine history drawn from the apostolic period. The earliest time of composition is apparently A.D. 60, the date of the last events it records. There is strong evidence against a late date of composition:

(1) The relationship to the third Gospel, whose themes clearly continue into Acts; the well-attested Lucan tradition.

(2) The similarities between Luke and Acts, on the one hand, compared with the "unique" style and format of later "acts" written during the post-apostolic period, on the other.

(3) The convincing arguments of von Harnack: a late date would be evident in harmonizing tendency between Acts and the Pauline letters. This "harmonizing" is not present.

(4) The accuracy of historical, geographical, and cultural statements about the First Century and the unmistakable sense that it is an eyewitness telling the story.

All of the above demonstrate that the document was written during the First Century. But can we narrow the date of composition any further? The evidence suggests the answer is "yes."

(1) Acts must have been written prior to A.D. 70. The temple in Jerusalem is still standing according to Acts (cf. 2:46; 21:26). If Acts were written after the Jewish War and after the destruction of the temple (A.D. 70), then the writing would have naturally reflected that.

(2) Some interpreters suggest A.D. 64 as the date of composition. This was the year Paul was martyred, during Nero the emperor's persecution of Christians, because of the Rome fire he charged they set.

We learn from 2 Timothy 4:9-11 that Paul, immediately prior to his death, sends for Timothy and asks him to bring along Mark. He requests also that he bring "the books, especially the parchment books." Luke is at this time the only coworker of Paul remaining. Some have interpreted this data as indication of Paul's last literary work. Probably with the help of Luke and Mark—both effective writers—Paul wished to complete this task.

However, nothing can be proven, although it may have a certain degree of possibility. If there had been such a cooperation, what would it have involved? A continuation of Acts would be fitting; that document ends abruptly and it seems as if something was supposed to follow. It is true that Luke-Acts does achieve the goal it sets for itself (cf. Acts 1:8): the spread of the gospel from Jerusalem to Rome, the "end of the earth" symbolically and the capital of the known world. Even if Luke meant the "end of the earth" in a literal sense he would have meant the pillars of Hercules in Spain, because the then-known world ended there. Indeed, Luke could have continued.

Almost without doubt Paul was acquitted in his trial before the emperor in A.D. 60. From that time he began a new ministry. The New Testament may offer credible support of this. Paul was in the province of Asia once more and he returned to Macedonia and Achaia (1 Timothy 1:3). He visited Crete and Nicopolis (Titus 1:5; 3:12). The tradition of the Early Church holds that Paul succeeded in fulfilling his objective of reaching Spain with the gospel before he died (Romans 15:28). The First Epistle of Clement (before A.D. 100) testifies to this.

This letter, up until the Second Century, was placed on the same level as other writings which later became canonical. According to Irenaeus, Clement knew Peter and Paul. Clement says in chapter 5: "Let us set before our eyes the good apostles: Peter, . . . (and) Paul . . . seven times he was in bonds, he was exiled, he was stoned, he was a herald both in the East and in the West, . . . and when he had reached the limits of the

West he gave his testimony before the rulers, and thus passed from the world. . . ." (1 Clement 5:3-7, Loeb Classical Library).

An author like Clement, who himself lived in Rome, could not have meant Rome by "limits of the West." He must have thought of Spain. It would have been difficult to invent a story about Paul traveling to Spain from Rome only 30 years after his death. And from Clement's description of Paul's suffering as a missionary it is apparent that he does not have Paul's letters or Acts in front of him. He relates some generally known information.

All this suggests the unlikelihood that Acts was written during this time. An additional volume to Acts is conceivable, but not the writing of the New Testament Book of Acts.

Given the political and ecclesiastical turmoil of the years around A.D. 64, the positive, irenic messages of Luke and Acts do not belong. That was a time of dangerous conflict. Acts' thoroughly positive portrayal of the empire and Roman government are inconsistent with such an atmosphere as A.D. 64. The Emperor Nero's persecution of the Christian church culminated in mass trials and executions of such proportions that they remained etched on the mind of the world for a long time. Ecclesiastical documents remember it again and again.

(3) On the other hand the picture of Acts corresponds nicely with the political and ecclesiastical climate of the year A.D. 60. That is not to say that there was peace and tranquility. The insanity of the young emperor, who appeared so promising on other respects, was beginning to show, but nothing to the extent it did later! The judicial system was still intact. Paul's trial ends in acquittal, in accordance with due process of law in Jerusalem, Caesarea, and Rome (Philippians 1:7).

Acts closes on a somewhat positive note: Although Paul is a prisoner, he is free to come and go as he pleases (Acts 28:16) and he lives in his own lodgings (Acts 28:30). He has visitors (28:23) and in fact has companions with him. And most importantly, from dawn to late at night he preaches and teaches Jesus Christ is Lord *kurios* without restrictions and in all honesty and boldness (Acts 28:23-31).

Not only this, there are some indications that Paul's preaching of Jesus as Lord became a topic of conversation not only among his own countrymen but among Gentiles, too, even those in high official capacities. "The entire Praetorium" ("whole palace guard," NIV) listened to and contemplated Paul's message. Members of the "household of the emperor" were won to Christ and followed Him in baptism, becoming members of the church (Philippians 1:13; 4:22).

This is where Acts fits. As it was mentioned, some parts of Acts may have evolved from the written records of Paul's trial. Indeed, the whole work, Luke-Acts might have formed part of Paul's defense. Of course it is speculation to think that Theophilus could have been Paul's "attorney" in his trial before the emperor and Luke-Acts evidence for Paul's defense; nevertheless, such a bold hypothesis does explain the ending of Acts. If the objection is raised that there is too much irrelevant material in the volumes for this to have been the case, it might be supposed that it was only later expanded for Theophilus' personal use.

Whatever the case, the notion that Luke-Acts is essentially an apologetical (a "defense") work is correct. This is especially true of their political stance. It is hardly an accident that the Roman authorities are consistently spoken of in positive terms.

For example, Pilate does not find Jesus guilty and he wants to release Him (Luke 23). The governor of Cyprus becomes a believer (Acts 13:7-12). The magistrates of Philippi discreetly come to the aid of Paul and Silas after they see they were unjustly treated (Acts 16:37f.). Likewise, Gallio, the governor of Achaia (18:12f.), comes to Paul's defense against the attacks of the Jews. The local "Asians" in Ephesus are accepted by the Roman officials, thus as their friends, Paul and his companions receive fair treatment by the city clerk who comes to their aid (19:31). Felix and Festus, Roman proconsuls, treat Paul in keeping with Roman law (Acts 24:1-26:32). And finally, Paul's Roman citizenship is respected everywhere (16:37; 25:10 and elsewhere).

## Later Traditions

An author of the personality and status (apostolic coworker) of Luke naturally evokes the interest of later times. Just out of gratitude for his preservation of the early history of the Church, we have made him the topic of much study. We even desire to know more about his life than the historical sources provide.

Origen of Alexandria, an Early Church father (d. ca. A.D. 251) thought that Luke was one of the 70 disciples sent out by Jesus during His earthly ministry (Luke 10). This, however, can be dismissed, since it fails to correspond with Luke's own description of himself in the preface to the Gospel.

He clearly states he was not among the "eyewitnesses and ministers of the word."

In the same way we must disregard Theophylact's (an Eastern exegete, ca. A.D. 1000) comments upon Luke 24:13f. He concludes on the basis of silence that the unnamed disciple on the Emmaus road was actually Luke the evangelist, who was too modest to mention his own name, choosing only to name his fellow-disciple Cleopas. Since Luke was not an eyewitness of Jesus' earthly ministry, he cannot be among the Greeks wanting to see Jesus during Passover Week (John 12:20).

Nothing absolute is known about Luke's death, but there appears to be a rather firm tradition that he died in Greece. Supposedly he worked there for a number of years following Paul's death. Ancient tradition says he died a martyr's death there. We cannot be certain of his martyrdom, but his two-volume masterpiece of Luke-Acts is one of the tremendous witnesses to the life, death, and resurrection of our Saviour, and of the ancient church.

## Religious Groups

Five different religious groups existed in the First Century which are relevant to the time in which Christianity developed. Before outlining each of these groups, a rough distinction can be made: Jews and Jewish Christians are of Jewish birth; Proselytes, Godfearers, and Gentiles are all Gentile-born.

Proselytes are Gentiles who became Jews. Godfearers had a close affinity for Judaism, but they never fully adopted the Jewish religion (circumcision was often the distinguishing step they did not take). The New Testament indicates that individuals from both of these groups later became Christians. Jewish Christians are those Jews who acknowledge that Jesus is Messiah. They did not see themselves as forsaking Judaism; rather, Jesus was the fulfillment of Jewish expectation. Others did not view them as "ex-Jews" either. Gentile Christians have faith in God through Jesus Christ, but this does not make them Jews.

## Jews

The label *Jew* was used by Jew and non-Jew alike for those people who confessed faith in the God of Abraham, Isaac, and Jacob. It denotes a national and religious affiliation—actually inseparable concepts in Israel's religion. Some writers of that day do use the term in a derogatory manner, but since it is also employed by Jewish authors, *Jew* can be understood in a neutral manner. In the Book of Acts *Jew* at times stands in parallel to the term "Israelite." Jews often made use of this latter term in reference to their position as "the people of God." *Israelite* is only rarely used by Gentile writers to denote the Jewish people.

*Jew* and *Israelite* appear to be used synonymously in Acts. For example, in Acts 2:14 we read the exhortation, "Ye men of Judea!"; but in Acts 2:22; 3:12; 5:35; 13:16 and in similar contexts we hear, "Ye men of Israel!" It is difficult to discern any difference in usage.

Elsewhere in Acts we observe that the term *Jew* often functions neutrally or objectively in reference to the Jewish people or their religion. Paul thus testifies to the Jews that Jesus is the Christ (Acts 18:5). The inhabitants of a city are depicted in two groups: Jews and Greeks (Acts 18:4; 19:10, 17). The false prophet Bar-Jesus was Jewish, but there is nothing negative in that fact. Furthermore, Luke presents Christian Jews as Jews, for example, Aquila and Apollos (cf. below, Jewish Christians). Indeed, even following Paul's experience on the Damascus road Paul can introduce himself as "a man which am a Jew of Tarsus" (Acts 21:39).

Jesus ministered in the "land of the Jews" (Acts 10:39). Luke takes it for granted that Jesus from Nazareth is himself a Jew with whom the God of Abraham, Isaac, and Jacob has dealt in a unique way (Acts 3:13).

Although some interpreters attempt to show that the author of Acts intentionally distanced himself from the Jewish people through his use of the term *Jews,* this theory does not hold water. His use of that terminology can be compared with how the Jewish historian Josephus describes his own people when he writes to non-Jewish people. Moreover, all of the speeches in Acts, all the material about Jesus, indeed, all of Acts, has Jewish coloring. It is the God of Israel, the God of the Jews, who sent Jesus, the Messiah and Lord of all who believe.

Clearly Luke shares Paul's opinion that those who are truly "Jews" are those who believe in Jesus. Anyone who rejects Jesus Christ—whatever nationality he or she may be—has only a doubtful claim to that name. But Luke does use the term often when speaking of the Jewish rejection of the gospel. Nonetheless, just as both Jews and Greeks believe (14:1), so too, both Gentiles (Greeks) and Jews want to harm or kill the apostles (14:5).

For example, in Acts 9:23 we read that the Jews plotted to kill Paul. Of course this refers to those Jews living in Damascus and not to the entire Jewish people (cf. 9:22). In Acts 13:48, 50 we are told that the two groups in the synagogue in Iconium split. The "Gentiles" probably are the "Godfearers." When it is said in 17:5 that the Jews were jealous of Paul, this refers to those Jews in Thessalonica. Thus *Jews* refers to a local constituency of Jews, say from a synagogue. It does not refer to Jews in general. Luke clearly distinguishes between those Jews who believe and those who oppose the gospel (cf. the reputation of the Jews in Berea: "These were more noble than those in Thessalonica" [17:11]).

Some texts reading "Jews" might be interpreted as a reference to Jews in general. In the account of the murder of James, the brother of John, it is said: "And because he saw it pleased the Jews, he proceeded further to take Peter also" (Acts 12:3). A similar understanding may occur in the expression "the Jewish people," a symbol of all of Judaism (Acts 12:11). Such an expression, however, must not be exaggerated or interpreted apart from the larger portrait of Jews in Acts. There was no monolithic response to Christianity by the Jewish people.

With respect to the responsibility for Jesus' death, the Jews are not viewed as solely responsible. Herod and Pilate are both mentioned in that connection; the Gentiles as well as the people of Israel participated: "For of a truth against thy holy child Jesus, whom thou hast anointed, both Herod, and Pontius Pilate, with the Gentiles, and the people of Israel, were gathered together" (Acts 4:27). The same attitude recurs in Acts 2:23, where the mystery of the divine plan is explained: "Him, being delivered by the determinate counsel and foreknowledge of God, ye have taken, and by wicked hands have crucified and slain."

Finally it should be noted that the use of "Jew" in the Book of Acts carries no anti-Semitic overtones. Luke plainly states that the God of the Christians is the God of Jews. Jesus was a Jew; the first Christians were themselves Jews who preached to Jews and Gentiles alike. Some Israelites accepted the gospel message; others rejected it. Those who acknowledged its truth did not cease being Jewish. This is the best evidence that the term *Jew* does not carry negative implications in Acts. But there are differences among the Jews, just as there are differences among the Gentiles (cf. Romans 2:28f.: true Jews are those who believe in Jesus as Messiah and Lord).

## Proselytes

Proselytes and Godfearers are those not of Jewish ethnic descent. Both groups appear in Acts, and in contrast to other Gentiles and Greeks, proselytes and Godfearers were attracted to the Jewish religion, to the one true God, and to the ethical life-style of Judaism. Thus they share a positive relationship to Judaism. Nevertheless, one must distinguish between these two groups. Proselytes became Jews in the fullest sense of the word; Godfearers remained Gentiles.

From the Jewish perspective a proselyte is a Gentile who converts to Jewish religion, who believes in the God of Israel, and who attempts to follow the Mosaic law. For Gentile men proselytes, becoming a proselyte involved three steps: circumcision, a ritual bath (baptism), and offering a sacrifice. For women only the last two were applicable. Following the destruction of the temple (A.D. 70) even sacrificing was no longer allowed.

As a proselyte one was obligated to keep all the commandments of the Mosaic law. Since a proselyte was technically a Jew, it meant both responsibilities and privileges. Rabbinic sources disclose that discussions often concerned the rights of proselytes. For example, it was debated by some that proselytes in private prayer should say: "the God of *the* fathers of Israel," and in their synagogue prayers: "the God of *their* fathers"—instead of the normal "God of *our* fathers."

Furthermore, proselytes were forbidden from holding certain public positions. The female proselyte could not marry a priest. Nevertheless, technically they were Jews and had both the obligations and duties of any other Jew.

The rabbis, however, tried to further distinguish between the righteous and true proselyte, who genuinely desired to follow the God of Israel, and the proselyte, who became such for improper reasons. For example, a man or woman wishing to marry a Jew would become a proselyte in order to be able to do so; however his or her intentions might be unrelated to any desire to serve the God of Israel. Rabbis declared such pretenders "false proselytes." Another reason for becoming a proselyte might be a desire to advance socially and economically. This too was condemned.

Accounts of forcing someone to become a proselyte are rare. One exception is John Hyrcannus, who toward the close of the Second Century B.C. forced the Idumeans to be circumcised. The various schools of rabbinic thought differed in their opinions about whether or not it was even desirable that Gentiles be converted to Judaism. Particular examples of this are the schools of Shammai and Hillel. Shammai tried to make the path to Judaism as difficult as possible for potential proselytes. Hillel, on the other hand, wanted to make the step relatively easy. There is a familiar story about Hillel's teaching of a Gentile: "What you do not like that anyone do to you, you shall neither do your neighbor. This is the law. The rest is explanation. Go and learn this."

The term "proselyte" occurs only four times in the New Testament. Jesus disparages the eagerness of the scribes and Pharisees to make converts/proselytes (Matthew 23:15). Some have questioned the historicity of His statement. Although present discussion continues about the extent of Jewish missionary efforts, available Jewish sources clearly state that some Jewish groups encouraged Gentiles to adopt the Jewish religion. And most agree that the number of proselytes within Judaism at the time of Jesus was great. This held especially true in the region of the Diaspora, where the faith and practice of Jews often sharply contrasted the corrupt Gentile pattern of life. Nevertheless, many rabbis were skeptical about inviting Gentiles to become Jews. One reason for their hesitancy might be because during periods of intense persecution the proselytes often returned to their former way of life.

The three remaining instances of "proselyte" occur in the Book of Acts. Jews and proselytes are present on the Day of Pentecost (2:5). In the list of those appointed to minister to the needs of the widows, Nicolas, the last one mentioned, is described as a "proselyte" from Antioch (6:5). The other six should probably be considered fully Jewish.

A puzzling usage occurs in Acts 13:43, where the issue concerns "Jews and religious proselytes." The conjunction of the words "religious" and "proselytes" is unique. Some think that "proselyte" is an early "gloss" (explanatory comment) that entered the text at a very early stage. However, there is no textual support for such a view. Thus, it is best to not try and separate the two; it is a unique expression for proselytes. It might be compared with the expression in Acts 2:5, "Jews, devout men."

## God-Fearers

Using different Greek terms Luke describes one group of Gentiles in Acts as "Godfearers." Although this terminology elsewhere does not function this way, the similar idea occurs in his descriptions of the centurion of Luke 7:1-10 as a Godfearing Gentile. He had even given money to build a synagogue. Cornelius is a God-fearer according to Acts 10:2, 22, and we observe that in the synagogue in Antioch in Pisidia Paul addresses two groups of listeners:

"Men of Israel, and ye that fear God, give audience" (Acts 13:16). This phenomenon is repeated in Thessalonica and Athens (Acts 17:4, 17). Lydia, the seller of purple, is described as a worshiper of God (16:14). Later in 18:7 we read that Paul stayed in Corinth in the house of "one that worshipped God," Titus Justus.

This group of individuals are those who did not take the final step of conversion to Judaism. They did not become proselytes; however, Judaism appeals to them. They participate in the synagogue services and abide at least by the Noahic covenantal commands. Regardless of how closely a God-fearer followed Jewish guidelines and laws, this still did not make him or her a Jew. To the Jews, "Godfearers" were called "righteous Gentiles." They were thought to have a share in the Age to Come. Although rabbis differed in their estimate of these Godfearers, most regarded them with much skepticism.

Paul's preaching especially appealed to this group, which continued to be closely associated with other Gentiles (cf. Acts 13:48). When Paul preached in the synagogues these Godfearers were often present. A large crowd of Godfearing Greeks join Paul in Thessalonica (Acts 17:4; cf. 14:1; 17:12; 18:4). In contrast to synagogue custom Paul preached that circumcision was unnecessary for those believing the gospel message and putting their faith in Jesus.

## Jewish Christians

The common denominator between Jewish Christians and Gentile Christians is their faith that Jesus is the Messiah and the Lord. They are united by faith and in baptism without being totally alike. Gentiles did not have to become Jewish before becoming Christian. Christian Jews regarded themselves as fully Jewish.

The Early Christian Church began as a Jewish Christian congregation in Jerusalem. The earliest Jewish Christians did not "change Gods" when they accepted Jesus as Messiah. Neither did they consider themselves "ex-Jews." Rather, they understood their faith as the true religion of the Old Testament. They thought themselves the true people of God in contrast to their countrymen who rejected Jesus.

Just as Jesus was Jewish, with a Jewish mother and reared in Jewish environment, with the Old Testament Scriptures as His Bible, likewise, the first apostles were Jewish. Paul was Jewish and regarded himself to still be one even after his "conversion." He would have protested if someone had maintained that by believing in Jesus he ceased being Jewish. This holds true despite the fact that later Jewish factions disassociated themselves from Paul because of his missionary efforts among the Gentiles and his contention that Gentile Christians were free from the obligations of the Law.

The mother church in Jerusalem primarily consisted of Jewish Christians. During its early stages, the missionary activity of the Early Church was directed toward Jew and Gentile alike by Jewish Christians. Gentiles considered these Jewish Christians as Jews. One part of the charge against Silas and Paul in Philippi shows this plainly: "These men, being Jews, do exceedingly trouble our city" (Acts 16:20). (Cf. also the comments of Gallio, the Roman proconsul, 18:15.)

A brief examination of the principal characters in Acts reveals the same tendency. Most of the main personages are Jewish Christians. The apostles are Jewish (Acts 1): six of the seven chosen to minister to the needs of the widows are Jewish (Nicolas was a proselyte); and James, the brother of our Lord and one of the leading figures in the Jerusalem church, was also Jewish. Likewise Paul, Barnabas, Silas, and John Mark came from Jewish stock. Timothy's mother was Jewish, although his father was a Greek (Acts 16:1). Paul had him circumcised. Aquila and Priscilla and Apollos were of Jewish lineage (cf. Acts 18:2, 24). Although one of Luke's chief objectives is to explain how the Christian message reached from Jerusalem to Rome and how it is welcomed by Gentiles but largely rejected by the Jews, he strongly emphasizes now it is Jewish Christians who carry the gospel message into the world. Neither does he tone down the Jewish character of the message; instead, it is more the opposite.

The Jewish character of the Jerusalem church surfaces in a number of ways. There is no indication that Sabbath-Day observances were dropped, other than its being reinterpreted in terms of what Jesus did on the Sabbath. In addition to continuing the practice of going to the temple to worship, the Early Church members also met in homes or other special spots where they could pray, study the Old Testament Scriptures, sing together, and share the Lord's Supper. Like Jesus, they probably continued to attend the synagogue service as well.

Evidence abounds in support of this: "And they, continuing daily with one accord in the temple" (Acts 2:46); "Peter and John went up together into the temple at the hour of prayer, being the ninth hour" (Acts 3:1); "They were all with one accord in Solomon's porch" (Acts 5:12); and "Go, stand and speak in the temple to the people all the words of this life" (Acts 5:20).

The above examples depict the situation in the first year of the new movement as Luke sees it. A short time later the situation remains largely the same, despite the inclusion of Gentiles. Some interesting material is given about the situation following Paul's third missionary journey (Acts 21:17f.). The above examples do not tell us whether the Jewish Christians continued to participate in the temple sacrifices. However, we cannot ignore the fact that Acts 21:17f. indicates that this is indeed the case. The Jewish Christian believers in Jerusalem tell Paul: "Thou seest, brother, how many thousands of Jews there are which believe; and they are all zealous of the law" (verse 20).

It is of particular interest that Paul, following the advice of James, joins four men of Jerusalem who had taken a vow, and he even pays their expenses. Thus in doing this Paul puts to rest rumors which speculated that he had forsaken the Law. Paul's actions suggest that when he finished his third missionary journey he might have participated in the sacrifice at the temple. At the least he paid for and consented to other believers doing so. The sacrifices offered by these four men (which Paul paid for) were probably eight lambs, four rams, and oil and flour (cf. Numbers 6:13-21).

It would be a likely mistake to assume that Paul was compelled to join them. Jews are Jewish just as Greeks are Greek (1 Corinthians 9:20). Paul clearly taught that circumcision has no spiritual value, but he also taught that not to be circumcised had no spiritual value either (Galatians 6:15). If these four men had hoped to be justified by these sacrifices Paul would never have sponsored them. The issue

was the fulfillment of a Nazarite vow. The old covenant was weak and ineffective (Hebrews 7:18), but it was only injurious to someone if he considered such action as means of securing salvation.

Christ abolished the old covenant. The new covenant is in effect, but the old must pass off the scene. The author of the Letter to the Hebrews states that the old "is ready to vanish away" (Hebrews 8:13). When he wrote these words the sacrificial service still existed and it would continue as long as the "first tabernacle was yet standing" (Hebrews 9:8, 9). The worship service of the temple continued up until the time the temple was destroyed (A.D. 70). At that time the vestiges of an antiquated sacrificial system were lost.

Since Paul submitted to the ritual purification in the temple, and since he paid the expenses of the sacrifices (burnt, sin, thanksgiving), we can deduce that Paul did not require Jewish Christians to relinquish their unique Jewish heritage, not even when this involved the Jewish system of sacrifice. Apparently one could continue to live like a Jew if one were born a Jew.

The judgment and decision of the Apostolic Council, in light of the preceding evidence, do not disagree with this understanding. The issue of the Apostolic Council involved the life-style and moral conduct of Gentile Christians (Acts 15). After "much discussion" (15:7) everyone agreed that the Gentiles did not have to become Jews or live as Jews in order to be a part of the people of God. This decision rested on the opposite premise that Jews were not required to live as Gentiles in order to be saved.

Paul, as well as the church in Jerusalem, apparently abided by this decision. Nevertheless, not all the issues were resolved. Some from the Pharisaic party who had become believers raised some questions. For one, must Gentiles be circumcised in order to be saved? (cf. 15:1-5). A similar problem occurs in Galatia. Concerning the assertion that Gentiles must be circumcised Paul says just one thing: "If ye be circumcised, Christ shall profit you nothing" (Galatians 5:2).

The Christian freedom of the Jewish Christians thus has its limits, as Galatians 2:11-16 makes clear. Peter ate with Gentile Christians, but when Jewish Christians from James arrived, Peter withdrew from table fellowship with them. Paul sharply rebukes such action. The superior principle of love supersedes any Jewish Christian custom. We cannot investigate this difficult problem any further, but Acts transparently depicts the first Jewish Christians as thoroughly Jewish and as living essentially in keeping with Jewish customs. Not even Paul criticizes them for this.

Several items warrant discussion in order to explain the Jewish element in the faith of the earliest believers.

(1) Early Christian proclamation and missionary preaching is thoroughly saturated with material from the Old Testament. The God of Israel, the God of the covenant, is the Father of those who believe in Messiah (see, e.g., Acts 2:5 and elsewhere in Acts).

(2) A few of the sermons in Acts contain some formulaic, stock phrases, such as the phrase "our fathers." This phrase appears in Stephen's defense about 10 times. Whereas Stephen identifies himself with the transgression of the patriarchs, at the close of his sermon he says "your fathers" instead of "our fathers." He says: "Ye stiffnecked and uncircumcised in heart and ears, ye do always resist the Holy Ghost: as your fathers did, so do ye" (Acts 7:51). The "fathers" here, however, are not Abraham, Isaac, Jacob, Moses, David, etc. These men were revered by Jewish Christians too. The continuity between the Old Testament and its story of salvation history is highlighted. Jewish Christians are the true children of the true fathers.

(3) Another minor stock phrase is "brothers" ("brethren"). This may mean "Christian brethren" (e.g., 1:16), but it is also used of fellow Jews who do not believe in Jesus (e.g., 2:29; 7:2; 28:17). By calling non-believing Jews "brothers," the Jewish Christians reveal that they consider themselves Jews. They do not feel they have broken away from the Jewish people. Jews unreceptive of Jesus are merely Jews who reject the God of their fathers.

(4) A couple of terms descriptive of Jewish Christians prove interesting as well. They may be termed "Jews who believe" or even "Pharisees who believe" (Acts 15:5). Those confronting Peter in Jerusalem, called the "circumcised believers," were Jewish Christians. And, as pointed out earlier, most of the central characters in Acts are Jewish (e.g., Acts 18:1f.).

These observations demonstrate that Jewish Christians continued to regard themselves as Jews. It was also shown that Paul and the Jerusalem church ultimately agreed upon the relationship between Jewish Christians and Gentile believers. Some interpreters have sought to resolve the differences in the Early Church by suggesting that the issues were never resolved and that an ongoing struggle existed between Paul and the Jerusalem church. Acts, however, points to another solution: agreement between the two was most likely.

This is not to say that Paul had no opposition. Some Jewish Christians resisted Paul's missionary efforts among the Gentiles from the outset. It is entirely possible that their allegiance to Judaism proved stronger than their newfound faith in Jesus the Messiah. Despite the lack of the necessary historical data for answering these questions fully, we do know from Second-Century sources that Jewish Christianity existed in many different forms. Such branches—like those which occurred when not all accepted the decision of the Apostolic Council (Acts 15), or like those who disagreed with Paul's outreach to the Gentiles—probably originated very early. Some advocate an early date for such "splits," although evidence only confirms that the separation occurred later. The reason for the Apostolic Council and the attitude of some Jewish Christians there favor an early fragmentation of the new movement.

It would be impossible to isolate each group that formed from the Jewish Christians "stock" of early believers. However, it is beyond question that some of these gradually became more Jewish in their orientation, while others drifted into the currents of Gnosticism. Below we will examine the two basic forms of Jewish Christianity, which were at least present during the Second Century. Their origin, however, is not certain.

(1) One group within Jewish Christianity was essentially the same as the Gentile church; that is, the Gentile church which continued in the apostolic tradition. (Even among Gentile Christianity there were peripheral groups.) Both groups respected the decisions of the Apostolic Council. For the most part Jewish Christians continued to live as Jews, but they did not insist that the Gentiles must follow Jewish customs and practices. With respect to Jesus' identity, these Jewish Christians held the virgin birth of Jesus to be an essential element of their Christology.

(2) Another group within Jewish Christianity insisted that Gentiles must live in accordance with Jewish custom if they were to be truly Christians. Thus they opposed the Gentile church. They refused to accept Paul's apostolic claim, perhaps because before his "conversion" Paul had persecuted the Church. And more importantly, in their eyes Paul continued to destroy the Church because he advocated the inclusion of Gentiles into the new covenant and reinterpreted the old covenant and law in terms unacceptable to many. This group, furthermore, denied the deity of Christ and rejected His virgin birth.

Gentile Christianity, which was theologically oriented around the message of the New Testament and the apostolic tradition, could not, of course, accept the latter group. At the same time, it is regrettable that the former group was not always received with understanding and appreciation for its unique place in salvation history. In Justin's *Dialogue with Trypho* (Trypho was Jewish), written around the middle of the Second Century, we find an example of Justin's conviction that Jewish Christians will be saved if they do not demand that Gentile Christians live as Jews. But in the same breath Justin concedes that there are Gentile Christians who do not agree with him.

That last point of view came to be the dominant one in Christianity. Gradually the Jewish element of the Christian faith diminished; Jewish Christians lost out. After numerous struggles, in which Gentile Christianity should have shown more understanding for the Jewish Christian's search for identity, Jewish Christianity disappeared around the Fourth Century.

Finally to emphasize our findings: The first Jewish Christians did not meet a new God through faith in Jesus Christ; rather, they met God in a new way. Faith in Christ did not mean they relinquished their Jewish identity; instead, they became the people of God that God desired for all peoples.

## Gentile Christians

The preceding pages have indirectly discussed the group of Christianity made up principally of Gentiles. Consequently, summary comments will be sufficient. One of Luke's chief objectives is to demonstrate the spread of the Christian faith among the Gentiles. Faith in Jesus extends to cities in Asia Minor, Macedonia, Greece, and Rome, the capital of the world at that time. Philip the evangelist preaches to the Samaritans, who were not Jewish or Gentile; later he baptizes an Ethiopian eunuch on the road to Gaza (Acts 8). Peter baptizes Cornelius (Acts 10). Those Jewish Christians scattered in connection with the persecution following the stoning of Stephen initially preach to Jews. Later, though, they proclaim the gospel to Greeks in Antioch and Syria (Acts 11:19f.). Antioch became one of the main centers for Christianity outside of Jerusalem. Believers in Christ first received the name "Christians" in Antioch (Acts 11:26).

Elsewhere we can point to Paul's missionary efforts. Normally he enters the synagogues, where he preaches to Jews as well as Godfearing Gentiles. The gospel is most welcomed among the latter. Through faith in Jesus and by following Him in baptism they could become full members of the Christian faith. Jews and Gentiles alike heard the message of "repent, believe, and be baptized." Paul sharply rejected any notion that Gentiles had to become Jewish in order to be Christians. All peoples were to travel the same road to salvation; nonetheless, it is tragic that many in the Church soon forgot that the God of Christianity was the God of Israel who had revealed himself in Jesus Christ. Moreover, Paul's caution in Romans 11:16f. not to be arrogant or unconcerned about the unique problems of Jewish Christianity, was soon forgotten. The relationship between Jewish Christianity, the Jewish people as a whole, and the Gentile element of Christianity is admittedly a dark chapter in the history of the Church. However, it must not be forgotten but confessed.

## The Damascus Event

On more than one occasion in his letters Paul refers to what happened to him on the road to Damascus. He mentions it at least 20 times, 5 times explicitly and 15 whose meaning would be hard to pin down apart from the background of his experience on the road to Damascus. This does not imply that Paul's understanding revolves solely around his "conversion." Even given the impact that the experience had upon Paul's life, that alone does not entitle it to the place of prominence it receives. But, as we will see, Paul's experience involves a final link in the actualization of God's plan. On the road to Damascus Paul was confronted by the Risen Lord; on this basis the founding of the Church begins.

The centrality of the event is also reflected in the fact that Luke includes it three times in his Book of Acts (chapters 9, 22, 26). The principal elements are as follows:

(1) *The first account (chapter 9).* The account in chapter 9 picks up on the aside-like comments of 7:58 and 8:1-3. There we learn that Saul (Paul) hated the disciples of Jesus. This is particularly "fleshed out" in his probable official role in the stoning of Stephen. He continued to persecute the church in Jerusalem, entering house by house and dragging out men and women alike and casting them into prison. Jerusalem, however, is not enough! He takes it upon himself to expand his persecution of the "people of the Way." He requests that Caiaphas, the high priest (from A.D. 18-36) and leader of the Sanhedrin, give him permission and authority to track down and capture disciples of Jesus in the Syrian city of Damascus. He was to bring them back to Jerusalem for trial.

Evidently a large Jewish population existed in Damascus; there were several synagogues. These synagogues came under the jurisdiction of the authorities in Jerusalem, the spiritual "capital" of all of Judaism. However, Saul's actions were not solely based upon religious motives. The Roman government gave authority to the Sanhedrin to carry out police action among the Jews outside Palestine. Those disciples of Jesus who fled Jerusalem because of the persecution following Stephen's death were Jewish. Consequently they could be tracked down to Jewish synagogues elsewhere.

Saul, together with his traveling companions— probably "policemen" and other persecutors— is traveling towards Damascus when something happens: Suddenly a bright light from above, from heaven (the dwelling place of God), shines forth. The "glory" (Greek *doxa*; Hebrew *kabod*) of flashing light, the eternal and almighty majesty of God which no man can stand to see, surrounds Saul (cf. Exodus 24:16f.; 33:18-23; Ezekiel 1:4f.; Isaiah 6:1f.; 1 Timothy 6:16). Like Ezekiel (Ezekiel 1:28), Saul is forced to the ground. He looks for a human being in the midst of the glorious light (Acts 9:7, 17, 27), but he does not know who it is. Is it an angel? But out of the glorious light a voice calls out his Jewish name, "Saul, Saul, why do you persecute me?" (Acts 9:4).

Not understanding, Saul asks, "Who are you, Lord?" "I am Jesus, whom you are persecuting," answered the Voice. Now Saul realizes that the divine light is coming from none other than Jesus of Nazareth, who is risen from the dead and is alive and ascended into heaven. There Jesus shares in the glory *doxa* of God. It is none other than the gloried Christ, the Lord *Kurios*, the very one of whom the disciples of Jesus were proclaiming. By persecuting these disciples Saul was persecuting the living and glorified Christ. As Augustine puts it, "The head of the church in heaven has cried out on behalf of his earthly members."

From this moment Saul relinquishes control of his life and person. He is under the command of the Lord: "Arise, and go into the city, and it shall be told thee what thou must do." No discussion or arguing is possible; Saul is subdued and drafted into the service of his Lord (cf. Ezekiel 2:1f.).

Paul's traveling companions also experienced something on that day. Thus it is clear that this was no "subjective" experience of Paul; rather, it. was an external, verifiable event. Those with him stand speechless with fear. They hear the Voice, but they do not see anyone.

Saul rises, but the blinding effects of the light are not just temporary. Blind and helpless he is led by the hand into the city. Once there he lodges with a countryman named Judas, who lives on "the street which is called Straight." Saul's blindness continues for 3 days. This blindness is a sign that the glorified Jesus Christ wants to tell him something. Blinded, Saul is totally dependent and subdued. Neither eating nor drinking Saul fasts, makes atonement, repents, and prays. He thus prepares himself to receive his call, the command of the Lord Jesus. During his fasting and praying Saul receives a vision of a man named Ananias (Hebrew, *Hananya*, the "Lord is compassionate"). Ananias becomes the instrument of the Lord's compassion as he leads Saul into a new life in Christ.

Ananias is himself called to this task, and he answers the call in a prophetic manner (cf. 1 Samuel 3:1f.; Isaiah 6:8; Exodus 3:4). He is an ordinary disciple of Jesus, but he exemplifies the promise of the Day of Pentecost, the fulfillment of Joel's prophecy: "On my servants and on my handmaidens I will pour out in those days of my Spirit, and they shall prophesy" (Acts 2:18). He is instructed by the Lord to visit Paul, but he initially refuses—in typical prophetic character (e.g., Exodus 3:11; Jeremiah 1:6). Ananias has no personal knowledge of Saul, but he has heard rumors about him from many quarters. He heard of his hatred of disciples of Jesus and he knew of his intention in Damascus. But we can probably say that Ananias was not among those disciples scattered from Jerusalem. He was perhaps persuaded by their testimony. The Lord changes Ananias' mind, but it is interesting to note that the Lord does not demand "blind obedience" from His servant; instead, He explains that He chose Saul to be His instrument in the proclamation of His name, the Lord *Kurios* (Philippians 2:11). Saul is thus called to be a witness to the Resurrection to the Gentiles and the Jewish people alike. Part of this call includes the inevitable sufferings preaching Jesus will incur.

Ananias obeys the Lord; he finds Saul and greets him with these words: "Saul, brother!" Next he lays his hands upon him and becomes the Lord's instrument for restoring Paul's sight. Paul is baptized into Christ and is welcomed by the Christians in Damascus. He vividly illustrates that which he writes to the church in Corinth many years later: "If any man be in Christ, he is a new creature: old things are passed away; behold, all things are become new" (2 Corinthians 5:17).

Paul immediately breaks his fast and begins to preach what he is convinced to believe: Jesus from Nazareth is the Messiah, the Son of God. Preaching this throughout the synagogues in Damascus not only creates natural interest among the people, they are amazed that the former persecutor of the Church is now a chief spokesperson. Paul's former association with the Jerusalem church was well known in this Syrian city and so was his previous purpose for going to Damascus.

Those Jews not believing in Jesus responded with their familiar arguments, but Paul was strengthened in spiritual power and wisdom (cf. Stephen, Acts 6:8-10) to prove to them from the Scriptures that the crucified Jesus was indeed the Messiah. The Greek word used to describe Paul's efforts is the term *sumbibazō*, "to demonstrate, prove, instruct." Paul demonstrates that Jesus is Messiah by "uniting" (another meaning of *sumbibazō*) Jesus of Nazareth with the messianic prophecies of Scripture. As a teacher he wins disciples (Acts 9:25).

As time went by the enmity against Paul increased (Acts 9:23). The "Jews" conspire to kill Paul, but the disciples in Damascus thwart their plans and save Paul by letting him down over the wall in a basket. Later editions, such as the United Bible Societies' 3d edition *Greek New Testament* and *Nestle-Aland's 26th edition Novum Testamentum,* read "his disciples" .in verse 25. However, the editorial committee's comments upon that verse indicate that it is totally unreasonable to assume the Jewish converts to Christianity would be termed "Paul's disciples." They conclude that in all likelihood the original reading was *auton* instead of *autou*. The transcriptional error, therefore, took place at a very early stage. Later manuscripts, particularly from the Byzantine text type and the so-called Textus Receptus text, read *auton* in an effort to rectify the difficulties. The actual sense in any case is that the disciples took him and let him down over the wall. "The disciples" occurs seven other times absolutely in this chapter (see Metzger, *A Textual Commentary on the Greek New Testament,* 366).

After Paul arrived in Jerusalem, he naturally tried to contact the followers of Jesus there; however, his attempts were understandably met with great suspicion. Barnabas then "took him under his wing" and introduced him to the circle of apostles. At that point he was received into the church. For a period he preached in Jerusalem, especially among the Hellenistic Jews living there. But hatred and plots against his life prompted the church to intervene and to advise Paul to "go underground" in his native city of Tarsus.

*(2) The second account (Acts 22:2-21).* In this version Paul himself recalls what happened to him that caused him to believe that Jesus was Messiah and to be called an apostle. He begins by stating that he is a Jew, not a Gentile who had unlawfully entered the temple. Actually he was born in Tarsus in Cilicia, but he "grew up" in Jerusalem. The verb here, *anatrephō,* can either mean "brought up" (as a child) or "taught" (as a student). This recalls Paul's "sitting at the feet of Gamaliel," the famous rabbi through whom Paul received his instruction in the Law. Under Gamaliel Paul learned the strictness of the Law and he calls himself "zealous" for God.

This "zeal" for God and the Law manifests itself in Paul's persecution of those who declared and followed the only way of salvation, the way of Jesus Christ. A similar account of this occurs also in chapter 9.

Paul's experience on the road to Damascus is described in essentially the same terms as before (chapter 9); here, though, it is noted that the brilliant light flashed around Paul and his companions "about noon," that is, in the middle of the day. Paul describes his companions' experience as seeing the light but not hearing the voice. Furthermore, the Lord's command is more explicit here than in chapter 9. He is instructed to rise and go into Damascus, and "there it shall be told thee of all things which are appointed for thee to do." This involves the divine will for Paul's life, and the use of the verb *tetaktai* (*tassō,* often used in classical

Greek for the installing of someone in an office) suggests Paul's impending apostleship.

Ananias' Christian faith is not mentioned in this account, and neither does Paul tell of his dual vision (Acts 9:10, 12). Actually Ananias is portrayed as a devout Jew, who was highly respected by his fellow countrymen. His devotion to the Law is also noted. Apparently Paul intends to portray Ananias as first and foremost a reliable witness.

The plan for Paul's life following his "conversion," which according to Acts 9:15 is told to Ananias during his vision, and which presumably Paul learned about at the house of Judas, is relayed to Paul in Acts 22:14. Ananias says, "The God of our fathers hath chosen (cf. Paul's terminology in Galatians 1:15f.) thee (Paul), that thou shouldest know his will (i.e., the counsel of God concerning the salvation of mankind through Jesus Christ; Ephesians 1:9) and see that Just One (i.e., to see Jesus, who is authenticated as God's Messiah by the Resurrection; John 16:10) and shouldest hear the voice of his mouth."

Ananias goes on to say that Paul's experience on the road to Damascus established Paul as a witness to the resurrected Jesus Christ. Thus, what Paul "saw and heard" will be the basis of his testimony to "all men." In other words, Ananias declares by the Spirit that Paul is called to be an apostle. This means an apostolic calling on par with that of the early apostles. He witnessed the Resurrection just as they did, and in the same way he has "seen and heard" Jesus. In every aspect Paul's apostolic calling is identical to those first apostles. Just like them he is called to preach the message "both in Jerusalem, and in all Judea, and in Samaria, and unto the uttermost part of the earth" (cf. 1:8; 4:20). There in the house of Judas, in the street called "Straight," Paul stood on the same foundation and in the same position as the 12 apostles whom Jesus selected from His followers during His earthly ministry (Luke 6:13). One morning, following a night of prayer (Mark 3:13f.; Luke 6:12f.), Jesus chose 12 to be His apostles; now that "morning" came for Paul following 3 days of "darkness" like night.

Since the Risen, exalted Lord summoned Paul, there was no excuse for delay. Ananias makes this plain with his question: "And now why tarriest thou (Paul)? arise, and be baptized, and wash away thy sins, calling on the name of the Lord" (Acts 22:16). The baptismal confession of the most ancient of churches is brief but totally effective: Jesus is Lord *Kurios* (1 Corinthians 12:3; Romans 10:9; 1 John 2:22f.; 4:14f.).

This account offers no other information about what happened in Damascus. Paul's stay with the disciples there, his sermon and teaching in the synagogues, the persecution against him, and his escape are all omitted. Paul begins relating immediately his experience in Jerusalem: in the temple, where in a trance he sees the Risen Lord and hears Him say, "Make haste, and get thee quickly out of Jerusalem; for they will not receive thy testimony concerning me" (Acts 22:18).

At first Paul disagrees with this advice, thinking that he, better than anyone else, had the qualifications to minister in Jerusalem. The Lord interrupts his stalling saying, "Depart: for I will send thee far hence unto the Gentiles" (cf. Ephesians 2:13, 17). We should note that Paul's well-intended and logical plans were contradicted by the Lord on other occasions (see, e.g., Acts 16:6f.).

(3) *The third account (Acts 26:1-20).* In the third account of Paul's experience on the Damascus Road we are, for the second time, given Paul's own version. But this second recollection is given in an entirely different context.

Once again Paul recalls his former life. He always lived as a Jew; as a youth he lived in the heart of Judaism, Jerusalem. Everyone should know this. They should also be aware that he was a member of that party in Judaism which emphasized strict obedience to the law of God—the Pharisees. He puts his hope in God's promise to Israel that the Messiah would come and bring salvation, the same hope that many of the "12 tribes" sought to obtain through fulfilling the demands of the Law and through continual temple attendance.

Paul explains that his zeal for this hope and for the temple service caused him to feel obligated to contest the offensive name of Jesus of Nazareth and to battle that power causing divisions in Israel. Paul's descriptions of his actions in this regard do not differ from the earlier accounts.

He explicitly states that he acted under official authority when he arrested, tried, and sentenced to death disciples of Jesus. This does not necessarily mean that Paul was a member of the Sanhedrin. It might suggest that as some kind of "prosecuting attorney" he sentenced those he captured in accordance with the law. Furthermore, he admits that he tortured people in the synagogues. He scourged followers of Jesus with "forty strokes minus one," just as Jesus had predicted (Mark 13:9). He attempted to force believers to blaspheme the name of Jesus, perhaps as some were doing in the Corinthians church later (1 Corinthians 12:3: "Jesus is accursed!"). Paul states that his intense hatred for Christians prompted him to expand his persecution efforts to cities abroad as well as to Damascus.

The heavenly light that surrounded Paul en route to Damascus is said to be brighter than the sun (Acts 26:13). Just like Acts 22:9 it is emphasized that the traveling companions also were illumined by this light. It is also stated that all of them—Paul as well as his fellow travelers—fell to the ground when the light hit them. In contrast only Paul heard the voice of the Risen One. In addition we are told that the voice spoke to him in Hebrew (perhaps Aramaic) and told him, "It is hard for thee to kick against the pricks."

One aspect of this account that stands out is that Ananias' role is omitted. Both chapters 9 and 22, the other accounts, tell that Paul is told to go into Damascus for further instructions. Next they describe how the Lord uses Ananias as his instrument and spokesman. But in chapter 26 Paul, then and there, receives a revelation about his calling from the Lord with these words: "Rise, and stand upon thy feet!" Chapters 9 and 22 indicate more clearly that this involves a prophetic call similar to the call of the Old Testament prophets (see e.g., Ezekiel 2:1; Daniel 10:11).

At this point the Lord chooses Paul to be His servant and witness. He is to testify of what he has seen here—his experience on the road to Damascus. Later he will bear witness to other things that will be revealed to him (cf. the vision in the sanctuary, 22:17-21). Paul's apostolic calling is for the people of Israel as well as the Gentiles (26:17). The prediction that the Lord will deliver him from the hands of "the people" (Israel) and from the Gentiles (cf. Jeremiah 1:8) indicates the opposition and hardship that will be part and parcel of his apostolic call. Ananias was also shown what lay in store for Paul (9:16). Serving the Lord and suffering are inseparably bound together. Suffering is the sign of service (Ephesians 3:13). Just as the prophets of old were persecuted, so too, were the apostles (Luke 11:49f.).

Another indication that the Damascus experience resembles the prophetic vision of call to ministry is that the call of Paul to the Gentiles comes from Isaiah 42:1-7, the first of the servant songs of the Lord. This text indicates that the Servant of the Lord will be a "covenant for the people," i.e., Israel. But it also says he will be a "light unto the Gentiles." Both groups, Israel and non-Israelites alike, will be made holy and saved by the same grace of God—through faith in the Risen Lord Jesus Christ (cf. Ephesians 2:11-22).

Paul concludes this account of his call by stating to Agrippa the king that he was not disobedient to his divine vision of the glorified Jesus. Such action would have been to resist stubbornly the living God himself. When Paul reflects upon his life he realizes—just like Jeremiah—that he was persuaded and compelled into the Lord's service by God himself (cf. Jeremiah 20:7-12). From the moment of his call to that point, Paul was not his own master; he had a master superior to him—the Lord. As a result of this relationship he was compelled to journey throughout the world preaching the message of the Resurrected Lord—first to Israel, in Damascus as well as Jerusalem and Judea—and then to the "nations."

## Unity and Diversity

As we have seen, there are differences among the three accounts at various points. Some interpreters emphasize these differences so much that one must distinguish between "genuine" and "artificial" elements. As a result the "discrepancies" become "ammunition" in the battle to prove that Acts is a composite of conflicting sources. It is argued that the author did not even know these "discrepancies" existed, but he took them as he received them and joined them carelessly and in haphazard fashion. Finally, some have undertaken to judge the accounts' quality; thus, the account in chapter 26 is considered "the oldest and most valuable." Chapters 9 and 22, on the other hand, are regarded as embellished versions based upon chapter 26 (e.g., Ananias would be considered as "embellishment").

To this assertion it must be immediately responded that none of the differences are of such a magnitude as to pose any serious problem to the integrity of the accounts. All three accounts are essentially the same. Only the manner in which the recollections are given is different. That even eyewitness testimonies of one and the same account seldom, if ever, coincide exactly is widely recognized. One person witnessing an event might perceive something one way, while another might have an entirely different impression. Even one's own recollection of personal experiences may unconsciously differ in terms of vocabulary, length, details, or focus, according to one's audience and the reason for the retelling.

The multiple context and occasion for the giving of the three accounts explain the variation within the telling of Paul's experience on the road to Damascus:

(1) *The context of chapter 9.* In this section Luke recalls the experience as he personally heard it from Paul or as he had received it from a grateful Christian church in Damascus. This has to do with the tradition of the church in Damascus that was carefully received and passed on in accordance with the well-established pattern of tradition. Quite understandably we see the Damascus tradition version contains the information about Ananias (himself from Damascus).

(2) *The context of chapter 22.* This passage centers around Paul's opening defense of himself (he was interrupted before he could continue). From the steps of the Roman army barracks Paul asks permission to speak to the furious shouting crowd that surrounded him. Except for the presence of the Roman officer Paul would have been lynched.

Luke emphasizes twice that the speech was given in Aramaic. Paul stresses his unquestioned Jewish ancestry, his upbringing in Jerusalem, and his studies under Gamaliel, the famous rabbi. This is the context of the speech. The account of Ananias also functions to highlight his close connection with Judaism. Ananias is characterized as a devout man, highly respected among his people.

More importantly for the purpose and audience of this speech, Paul does not mention his stay in Damascus, choosing instead to explain immediately what happened to him upon his return to Jerusalem.

Because of his setting he emphasizes that it was during a worship service in the temple, while he was praying in the sanctuary, that he received his call to undertake a mission to the Gentiles to tell them of the saving grace of Jesus the Messiah. At this time he was also forewarned of the negative reaction his Jerusalem countrymen would have to him and his message. His explicit description of his actions as a persecutor of Christians prior to the Risen One's breaking into his life additionally fits well the context of Jerusalem.

(3) *The context of chapter 26.* An entirely different situation elicits Paul's telling of his Damascus Road experience in chapter 26. On this occasion the setting is the audience room in the palace of Herod in Caesarea, the residence of Festus the Roman governor; and the language Paul speaks is Greek. The speech has a twofold purpose. In part, Paul appears because Fetus, who has inherited Paul from his predecessor, needs some information in order to carry out his investigation of the matter. But at the same time Paul wants to testify before Herod Agrippa II, the king, who, along with his sister, was welcoming the new governor. The Roman governor perhaps wished to entertain the Jewish King Herod with something he supposes will be of interest to him, since he supervises the temple of the Jews.

Formally the speech is directed to the king. During his opening Paul compliments Agrippa for his intimate knowledge of Jewish affairs, customs, and controversies. Here we note one particular aim of the speech: Paul intends to emphasize his attitude toward the Law. He belongs to the party of the Pharisees and he believes in the messianic promises. In fact, Paul sees his being accused because he takes God's promises seriously. Jesus from Nazareth, the son of a carpenter, was sentenced to death and executed on a Roman cross. That He is the fulfillment of the messianic promises was not just offensive to the Jew; Paul used every means possible to overcome its message in the beginning and he thought he was doing his duty.

Up until the moment the Risen Lord stood alive and glorified before him, Paul kept this attitude.

The Lord "stopped him in his tracks" and called him to be His servant and witness. After falling to the ground and believing that Jesus is indeed the Messiah of God, Paul is sent by God throughout the world telling people about Jesus. In time Festus, thinking Paul is insane because of his excitement and ardor, interrupts. It seems natural that Paul's passionate telling of his "conversion" left little room for details about his stay with Ananias. Paul's call is the fulfillment of the expectations of Moses and the prophets: life is proclaimed to the dying: light to those dwelling in darkness; all this is possible only through Jesus Christ, the crucified and Risen Lord.

As we said, the different ways of saying and the different circumstances in which they were told, clearly explain the differences in the accounts. And in regard to this also, one must not overlook the relationship between Paul and Luke. Throughout the years, off and on, Luke worked closely with Paul. This should caution us against perceiving "discrepancies" in the various versions. In the Letter to the Galatians, which was probably not written any later than A.D. 55 at the latest (5 years before Luke wrote Acts), Paul guarantees his truthfulness in telling history (Galatians 1:20). This may suggest the presence of other versions of his experience during his time. But a friend and companion as loyal, dependable, and close to the apostle Paul as Luke would by no means risk inaccuracy. Even less likely is the possibility that he would lie or distort the truth.

None of the variations of the accounts that are called into question by some offer compelling reason for detecting essential disagreement among the accounts.

Often great emphasis is placed upon the fact that in Acts 9:7 Luke writes that companions of Paul "stood" speechless during the experience, while in Acts 26:14 Paul says that "we were all fallen to the earth." Actually everyone was driven to the ground by the awesomeness of the event. Soon, however, Paul's fellow travelers rose to their feet, where they stood confused and ignorant to what took place. Saul, though, continued to lie on the ground, stunned not only by the divine light but by the heavenly Voice that spoke to him as well.

Another point of controversy is that in 9:7 it is recalled that the fellow travelers heard a voice but did not see anyone. Acts 22:9, however, states that they "saw indeed the light, and were afraid; but they heard not the voice of him that spake to me." Both stories tell only that part of the event that the others might have experienced; but the ultimate meaning of the event was only understood by Paul.

From a linguistic standpoint it can be noted that the Greek verb *akouō* ("I hear") can indicate that perception takes place through hearing; thus hearing equals understanding and from that one obeys what is understood. Moreover, the Greek word *phōnē* ("sound") can describe sound in general or an articulate sound, i.e., a voice, speech that is understood. These two meanings may be determined from the context on a grammatical basis. *Phōnē* stands alone 9:7; the fellow travelers heard the *phōnē*, the "sound," but they did not see anyone. They saw no one in the glorious light, although they did hear something, is perhaps the correct understanding.

The other instances of *phōnē* in the account of the Damascus Road are accompanied by an explanatory modifier. Sometimes it is followed by the present participle of *legō* ("I say, I speak"). Thus in 9:4 it is said that Saul "heard a *phōnē* speaking to him"; and in 22:7, "I heard a voice saying unto me" and in 26:14, "I heard a *phōnē* speaking to me in Hebrew." *Phōnē* is often followed by a noun in the genitive case denoting the source of the voice. For example in 22:9: "The companions heard not the *phōnē* of him that spake to me."

A third point of dispute, which we already discussed somewhat, is the three different accounts of Paul's call to be the apostle to the Gentiles. We are told in chapter 9 that Ananias receives a revelation of the Lord's purpose for detaining and manifesting himself to Paul. Chapter 22 concerns Ananias' revelation in Damascus (verses 12-15) as well as Paul's vision in the temple in Jerusalem (verses 17-21). Then in chapter 26 we read that Paul received his call as apostle to the Gentiles on the road to Damascus and that he received it from the Lord himself.

All three accounts unanimously agree that it is the Risen Lord who called Paul into the apostolic outreach to the Gentiles. They also concur that this took place in connection with the experience of Paul on the Damascus Road. The call, however, was confirmed to Paul in various ways. Chapter 9 highlights that Ananias' objections and suspicions about Paul are laid to rest when God declared to Ananias that Saul from Tarsus was a chosen instrument of God to preach the gospel. Chapter 22 reiterates that Ananias confirmed what God had already told Saul about his future work. In that same context we read that Paul, too, received a confirmatory vision of his call in the temple. Chapter 26 informs us that on the road to Damascus Paul was initially called to be an apostle.

As we have seen before, the explanations for this are closely tied to the context in which the events are recounted. That the divine call was put into effect by a human agent like Ananias may have proved of decisive interest for certain Christian readers. Furthermore, that part emerged out of the tradition of the Damascus church, so it fits naturally in this context of chapter 9. This was also important for believers in Jerusalem who may have known Ananias, who was himself Jewish. Naturally Paul would mention this in his speech from the steps of the Roman barracks in Jerusalem (as we read in chapter 22). But to King Agrippa and the governor Festus such information would not be of any interest. Such details would only appear irrelevant and unrelated at the trial in Caesarea.

Some skeptical interpreters reject all three versions. They point to the fact that the historical basis for Paul's call to a mission to the Gentiles is quite obviously Barnabas, who searched him out in order to enlist Paul in the preaching of the gospel to Gentiles in Antioch (11:19-26). They place the three accounts in the category of "anecdotes." Against this reasoning stands Paul's express statement that his call to be the apostle to the Gentiles came through his encounter on the Damascus Road with the Resurrected Lord Jesus Christ.

Nevertheless the call came to Paul in a variety of ways; one might say in stages. This kind of experience is typical of the call of a missionary or a preacher. Many of the Lord's servants can testify that ever since they were children they have known their calling in life. This does not negate the possibility that they can receive additional, personal revelations at a later date. Neither does this prevent their inner call from God from being confirmed by the external call of the church of God. The fact that Ananias told Paul of his call and life's work in no way abolished the call that Paul personally received from the Lord on the Damascus Road—a revelation to which Ananias himself refers (9:17). Neither did Barnabas' invitation to join him in mission work (11:26) or the sending by the church in Antioch (13:2) eliminate the validity of Paul's testimony in Galatians: "I certify you, brethren, that the gospel which was preached of me is not after man. For I neither received it of man, neither was I taught it, but by the revelation of Jesus Christ" (Galatians 1:11f.).

Even though Paul stresses the divine source of his apostolic call as well as his gospel message (he did not consult with "flesh and blood"; Galatians 1:16), this can in no way be interpreted to mean that Paul never incorporated the insights of others' call and "conversion." Just as Peter was sent to Cornelius, Ananias was sent to Saul. Entrance into the fellowship of the Church through baptism always requires a human instrument. Moreover, the fact that Paul received a divine revelation from the Lord did not exclude the possibility that God still spoke to him through the Holy Scriptures, where the Word of the Lord was put into effect by "the holy men of God" (2 Peter 1:20, 21). Neither does

it remove the possibility that God spoke to Paul through members of His living church.

The Lord indeed sent Ananias to Paul with His message. And more importantly, we know from Paul's own words that the gospel—which Paul strongly perceives as being directly from God—is the holy tradition of the Church. He "passed this on" in his own preaching. Paul summarizes this holy tradition in 1 Corinthians 15:1-11: Christ died for our sins according to the Scriptures; He was buried; He arose; He was seen alive by witnesses. Paul adds to this: "And last of all he was seen of me also"; he assures his readers that his preaching is identical to that of the other apostles: "Therefore whether it were I or they, so we preach and so ye believed."

Paul's use of the terms *receive* and *deliver* is recognized as a use of Jewish technical terminology for sacred tradition. It denotes transmission by word of mouth, which acquired so much significance that the tradition was repeated word for word and in the same form when it was passed on. Furthermore the term *tradition* became equivalent to Christian tradition, such as the gospel tradition, the ritual tradition, the confessional tradition, or the admonition tradition. This applies to ancient Christian tradition since the time of the apostles. Paul did not position himself outside of that tradition. As an apostle and witness to the Resurrected Lord, Paul transmitted the gospel tradition; but the gospel message is first and foremost "from the Lord."

Paul declares emphatically in his letter to the Galatians that his gospel has divine origins. He stresses the "objectivity" of the revelation and apostolic call he received on the road to Damascus. Only the Sovereign Lord is responsible for his call. That did not originate with some internal, psychological, moral, mental, or religious decision on his part. Neither did he acquire his through instruction by others, not even the original apostles. All three versions distinctly testify to this objectivity.

*Psychological Explanations.* The experience on the Damascus Road is interpreted in various ways. Those unwilling to acknowledge any supernatural element in the account often attempt to present a psychological explanation. Paul's encounter with God on the Damascus Road, therefore, is explained as the result or climax of a lengthy process.

With various modifications the account is presented thus:

A young Jewish theologian from Tarsus, during his training in Jerusalem, decides to follow the teachings of the Pharisees. Paul is convinced that righteousness before God can be obtained by fulfilling the Mosaic law and the prescriptions of oral tradition. Such thinking is not merely abstract theory; he takes it seriously, applying it to his religious as well as ordinary existence.

But being honest and having integrity, he has to admit his inability to fulfill this system's obligations. Especially in his struggle to keep the Law's commandments, he recognizes the power of sin. His pangs of conscience increase steadily. The spiritual turmoil intensifies; he recognizes that it is unavoidably true that "cursed is every one that continueth not in all things which are written in the book of the law to do them!" (Galatians 3:10; cf. Deuteronomy 27:26). He feels himself under this curse. The despair implicit in the words of Romans 7:14 and 24: "I am carnal, sold under sin—O wretched man that I am! Who shall deliver me from the body of this death?" echo his own condition that gradually emerged as he tried to adhere to the Pharisaic legalism.

But parallel to this is another thought: From his earliest childhood Paul lived in Jerusalem; indeed, he is "brought up in this city" (Acts 22:3). More precisely we learn from 2 Corinthians 5:16 that Paul actually saw and heard Jesus of Nazareth "after the flesh." This might suggest that Paul knew Jesus from the perspective of his (Paul's) fallen nature. He judged Jesus a blasphemer. Or it might be interpreted to mean according to Jesus' human appearance as a carpenter from Galilee. In either case the person and words of Jesus left an indelible mark on Paul's conscience that he was unable to remove.

In any case, Paul took great offense at the thought that the Man from Galilee might be the Messiah. A poor, homeless Galilean, surrounded by unlearned followers and persons of questionable character such as tax-collectors, prostitutes, and sinners; the One sentenced to death and crucified; the One who died under the curse of the Law; could this man possibly be the promised king for whom Israel had waited throughout its history? To Saul such a thought was utterly absurd and not worth taking seriously.

Moreover, the sect of the Nazarenes, followers of Jesus increased steadily. They believed in Jesus as Messiah, the Son of God, the Lord. They asserted that He had risen from the dead and that He continued to live and act in history. They must have indirectly influenced Paul's thinking.

Soon Saul began to debate with these followers of Jesus the Nazarene. With zeal and because of his formal training, he combats that which he can only interpret as blasphemy. Saul does not come out of the battle unscathed; their application of Scripture and their burning hearts have to make their impression. Stephen's wisdom and spirit could not be resisted. While Saul struggles to stick to his training, the doubt continues to grow. Could those followers of Jesus be correct? Their joy and their openness contrast his own burdensome obligation to the demands of the Law.

Next the doubt drives him from debate to persecution. But as he contests with the Nazarenes it increasingly becomes a wrestling with his own doubt; he does not want to be conquered by their faith. He intensifies his efforts. With the authority of the high priest Paul is present at scourgings, imprisonments, trials, inquiries, and even at the stoning of Stephen, the "blasphemer." In a last effort to conquer his anxiety Paul volunteers to lead an expedition to Damascus, a prominent city containing a large Jewish population, where the members of the Way were gaining more and more adherents. There he hopes to arrest many and bring them to trial. With the authority of the high priest he hurries with other "vigilantes" to carry out the task. Motivated by guilt, doubt, and indecision, Paul tries to get rid of his doubt by planning the tracking, capture, arrest, and trial in Jerusalem of the Nazarenes.

But then, just outside of Damascus, the pressure of his doubts becomes unbearable and a "psychological explosion" devastates him. The disciples of Jesus are correct; Jesus is the Messiah, Kurios! Saul must give in!

Subsequently Paul's thoughts reverse totally. Everything that previously seemed scandalous and offensive to his Pharisaic and scribal character now becomes understandable. It now becomes the foundation to Pauline theology: The Son of God in the form of a servant died on the cross and in so doing He provided salvation which the Law could not afford; He brought righteousness through the forgiveness of sins.

Thus is the "psychological interpretation" of Paul's transformation (with some degree of variation). However, this theory of the spiritual transformation of the apostle Paul, the former Pharisee, has one essential flaw: There is serious lack of any concrete evidence that this is indeed what happened. It is a psychological analysis of a nonexistent personage who is more at home in poetry than in Biblical narrative. Such a theory fails to correspond with Luke's portrait of Paul in Acts and with Paul's own story in his letters. In fact, the primary sources give an entirely different portrait!

None of the primary material offers any basis for supposing that such a personality shift took place. Moreover the conjecture that an internal crisis culminated in the Damascus Road experience is a psychological absurdity.

Of course it cannot be ignored that Paul, as a person with deep and sincere feelings, probably did experience internal turmoil in the time prior to his "conversion." Paul knows the Law as "our schoolmaster to bring us unto Christ" (Galatians 3:24), but a passage like Romans 7:7-25 has a depth of understanding that would be foreign to someone not born anew; consequently these are not merely autobiographical confessions of the pre-Christian life. The words reflect that experience, but Paul is evaluating that existence in light of the Spirit's transforming power. It is almost certainly not a picture of normative Christian living, but neither is it strictly the frustration of an unregenerate person living under the Law rather than being born of the Spirit.

It is true that recognition of one's sin comes through the Law (Romans 3:20). But it is also correct that the distorted view of Pharisaic Judaism was not its failure to admit sin; rather, it was their distortion of the Law as a means of attaining righteousness (cf. Luke 18:9). Paul was a Pharisee of the Pharisees. He lived his life in a "clear conscience" not only after becoming a Christian, but during his former life as a Pharisee (Acts 23:1; cf.2 Timothy 1:3). He persecuted the church of God "ignorantly" (1 Timothy 1:13), and he was deeply persuaded in his soul that according to his Jewish obligations he was right and actually doing what God wanted!

According to the standards of Judaism, if anyone could put trust in their "flesh" it was Paul, who considered himself "touching the righteousness which is in the law, blameless" (Philippians 3:4-6). His eagerness and zeal for the tenets and customs of Judaism surpassed many of his peers' (Galatians 1:14). Furthermore, he was pleased with himself. In light of all of this hard evidence it is difficult to endorse the construction of a psychological profile of his conversion. Such an approach lacks any degree of probability. The conversion and apostolic call of Paul was not an internal psychological process. It is a consequence of a divine encounter on the road to Damascus.

*A Visionary Experience?* Another attempt to explain the Damascus Road encounter in psychological terms involves interpreting it as a visionary experience. At this point the question emerges, what precisely constitutes a vision? To some interpreters a "vision" could be a natural experience, explainable as a psychological phenomenon. In this type of experience one hears or sees things in a kind of dream-like state that are not based in reality. This resembles a kind of variation of mental "enlightenment," a change based upon sensation.

Many interpreters quickly adopt such a view of Paul's mental condition. They consider Paul's experience on the Damascus Road a "vision," in the sense that internal factors—not external, or only slightly external—led to the event. This view sees the experience as a fabrication of Paul's conscience; it has no basis in reality. The three accounts recorded by Luke as well as the other Pauline references to his experience on the Damascus Road are likewise catalogued in such terms. Although Paul sees his divine encounter on that day as a starting point of his faith and call, according to this theory Paul should be reckoned among those whom Paul himself condemns: those "intruding into those things which he hath not seen" (Colossians 2:18), those who "make you vain" and speak "a vision of their own heart" (Jeremiah 23:16).

But there is another point of view as to what constitutes a "vision." This might resemble what the prophets term "visions from God" (Ezekiel 1:1), such as the "vision" which foresaw the coming events on the Day of Pentecost (Joel 2:28). This understanding does not deny the supernatural nature. The basis for such genuine, spiritual visions is not the "internal condition of conscience," but the revelation of God.

However, what is perplexing in this case is that this understanding of "vision" does not describe what transpired on the road to Damascus. It is true that Paul was open to the reality of visions. Although he sees nothing inherently advantageous in having visions, he does speak of "visions and revelations of the Lord" (2 Corinthians 12:1). These are particularly associated with a previous experience of being caught up into heaven, where he heard "unspeakable words, which it is not lawful for a man to utter" (2 Corinthians 12:4).

With less hesitation he recalls visions relating to God's guiding him in his ministry. Following his return to Jerusalem after a stay in Damascus, Paul was worshiping in the temple when he saw Jesus in a trance and heard Him speak. Through this vision Paul receives his confirmation as the Apostle to the Gentiles (Acts 22:17-21). He also comes to realize that Gentiles will receive a full share of the inheritance (Ephesians 3:2-7).

A revelation also preceded Paul's visiting the apostles in Jerusalem one final time (Galatians 2:2). Luke also is aware of the "vision in the night"—and who else could have told him of this except the apostle himself?—which summons Paul to Europe (Acts 16:9, 10). Later, when Paul almost seems to give up the idea of missionary work in Corinth because of the severe opposition, it was once again a "vision in the night" which the Lord used to tell him to continue without fear, and which prompted him to extend his stay there for 1 1/2 years (18:9-11). And at the height of crisis on the voyage to Rome, when everyone had abandoned hope of being saved, Paul encourages them not to be afraid, because that night "the angel of God, whose I am, and whom I serve," stood before him in a vision saying, "fear not" (Acts 27:22-24).

Thus we note that Paul was personally familiar with visions and revelations. Likewise, "vision" forms a part of his experience on the Damascus Road. This type of vision was both visual and audible, i.e., Paul saw somebody as well as he heard the One he saw (Acts 9:4-7, 17; 22:14; 26:16). Nonetheless, our primary sources—Luke's Acts and Paul's letters—draw a clear distinction between visionary revelations and the unique encounter Paul had on the way to Damascus. All three accounts make it plain that the "vision" stressed the prophetic nature of the event, as we mentioned before (cf. Exodus 24:16f.; 33:18-23; Isaiah 6:1f.; 42:1-7; Ezekiel 1:4f.; 2:1f.; Jeremiah 1:8; 20:7-12; Daniel 10:11).

A frequently found phrase among many interpreters is "the Damascus experience." Instead, the "Damascus event" might be more appropriate. This distinction would help separate the visionary experiences of Paul from this dramatic event. This would also place his event on the road on a par with the other apostolic witnesses who saw the risen, living Lord Jesus Christ. The entire life of Paul and his attitude before the Damascus event are "separated by a chasm over which no other bridge crosses other than the visible revelation of Christ" (cf. O. Moe).

Therefore, there is no difference between the revelation of the Risen Saviour to Paul on the road to Damascus and those appearances of Jesus to His disciples in between the Resurrection and the Ascension. Luke introduces his second volume by referring to these appearances as the indication that the beginning of the end has begun. He speaks of chosen apostles to whom Jesus presented himself alive following His death, proving himself alive with many undisputable proofs, being seen by them for 40 days while He spoke to them about the kingdom of God (Acts 1:1-3). By virtue of witnessing these appearances the apostles became "apostles," that is, being a witness to the Resurrection is a requirement for the status of apostle (verse 22). This is precisely what Paul experienced on the road to Damascus.

"Last of all he was seen of me also," says Paul in 1 Corinthians 15:8. By saying this Paul puts himself on a par with Cephas, the Twelve, more than 500 brethren, James, and all the apostles. The reality of the empty tomb, the certainty of the Resurrection confront us here, not just some subjective, internal experience. Here we have assurance that Jesus lives in spite of His death and burial.

As mentioned previously, in 1 Corinthians 15 Paul recalls some of the fundamentals of gospel proclamation. The Word of God has the power to save (verse 2; cf. Acts 11:14: "words, whereby thou and all thy house shall be saved"). The saving Word is the message of the person and work of Christ, His death and resurrection. This announcement of salvation was passed on through the apostolic tradition, by witnesses of the Resurrected Lord. Consequently, any visionary dimension to the Da-

mascus event must be subordinated to the historical reality of Christ's resurrection. Whenever the New Testament speaks of the apostolic tradition that was passed on, it never refers to subjective, internal experience; rather, it always suggests actual historically verifiable facts. The events that took place on the Damascus Road firmly belong to such a historical category.

*The Apostolic Call.* That Paul's apostolic calling is intricately bound to the Damascus event is evident not only from 1 Corinthians 15:1-11, but also from several passages in his letters.

In the salutation of the Epistle to the Romans Paul introduces himself as "called to be an apostle." This call to apostleship is expressly connected with Him, who according to His spiritual origin is "declared to be the Son of God with power, according to the spirit of holiness, by the resurrection from the dead" (Romans 1:4). Through Jesus Christ Paul received grace and his apostleship in order to lead the Gentiles to an obedience of faith (verse 5).

We encounter the same understanding in the first letter to the Corinthian church. With the Damascus event in the background Paul poses the question: "Am I not an apostle? am I not free? have I not seen Jesus Christ our Lord?" (1 Corinthians 9:1).

The resurrection of Christ once again confirms Paul's apostolic calling in Paul's opening words to the Galatians (Galatians 1:1). This theme is picked up again in verse 12, a reference to Paul's reception of the gospel through "the revelation of Jesus Christ." From this basis Paul maintains his equality with Peter as an apostle of Jesus Christ (cf. Galatians 2:8).

Actually, it is only recognizing the background of the Damascus event as the basis for Paul's emphatic conviction of his apostolic call that keeps Paul from sounding arrogant in asserting his authority. Apart from this context Paul's strident assertion of apostleship and its implicit authority would be pointless; or worse yet, a by-product of his own psyche.

## The Missionary Journeys of Paul

*First Missionary Journey (ca. A.D. 45-47) (Acts 13:4-14:26).* Paul and Barnabas, along with Mark as their helper, crossed Seleucia and sailed from there to Cyprus, where they preached in the cities of Salamis and Paphos. From there they traveled to the south of Asia Minor. Arriving in Perga in Pamphylia, John Mark departed and returned to Jerusalem. Paul and Barnabas continued to Pisidian Antioch and from there on into Iconium, Lystra, and Derbe. At each stop they began in the Jewish synagogues, but when the Jews rejected their message they also announced the good news to the Gentiles. Paul's missionary strategy was: "to the Jew first and also to the Greek" (Romans 1:16). Their preaching was confirmed by signs and wonders, and in spite of persecution churches were founded.

In many ways the times were "ripe" for the gospel. Already the beginnings of a trend toward monotheism were stirring. This was a direct response to the religious decay of the time. Elsewhere, philosophies—also in response to this decline—developed in the direction of a more religious nature. They stressed high moral ideals in an effort to counter the moral degradation that was sweeping through society at that time (cf. Romans 1). Many saw life as worthless and even despised.

Diaspora Judaism persisted in promoting the Jewish religion during these times, thus it laid much of the groundwork for the early Christian missionary efforts. The well-structured Roman governmental system afforded public peace and security. This, together with a sophisticated public transportation system (some Roman roads are still extant) and a common commercial language throughout the empire, contributed to the "perfect timing" of the early Christian mission. The cities visited by Paul were ordinarily prominent and large, making it possible for Paul to contact a large number of people from a variety of cultures.

*Second Missionary Journey (ca. A.D. 49-52) (Acts 15:36-18:22).* This journey began with a sharp conflict between Paul and Barnabas. Barnabas wanted to invite John Mark, while Paul obviously felt hesitant, since John Mark had left them during their first missionary outing (Acts 13:13). Paul opposed having John Mark along and the result was a split in the team. Barnabas and Mark left for Cyprus, while Paul chose Silas (Silvanus) to accompany him. They visited the churches in Syria and Asia Minor. In Lystra Timothy joined them.

Guided by the Holy Spirit, Paul and his coworkers arrived in Troas via Phrygia and Galatia. At this point Luke joins them (cf. the "we" in 16:10f.; perhaps he joined them even earlier). While staying in Troas Paul has a vision in the night instructing him to take his group over to Macedonia. Here they met Philip the evangelist and traveled to Thessalonica and Berea, where they established two new churches in spite of the opposition. Leaving Timothy and Silas behind in Berea, Paul traveled to Athens. There he gave his famous speech on Areopagus (Acts 17:22-31). Although he was interrupted as soon as he mentioned the resurrection of Jesus, some believed in the gospel (verse 34).

Paul spent his longest time in Corinth. Once again he was reunited with his coworkers. At that time Corinth stood as the largest city in Greece as well as being the political capital for that region. Paul's hosts in Corinth were Priscilla and Aquila, who later had a great impact upon the missionary efforts in Ephesus and Rome (Acts 18:24-26; Romans 16:3, 4) as "advance men" for Paul. From Corinth Paul wrote his two letters to the church in Thessalonica. First Thessalonians is considered the oldest New Testament document; it is dated with relative certainty around the end of the year A.D. 50 or the first part of A.D. 51. (Some statisticians date the writing of James' Epistle as A.D. 47, 48.) These letters express the apostle's deep love for this church (1 Thessalonians 3:6-10; 2 Thessalonians 1:11). Apologizing for having to leave them so quickly (cf. Acts 17:10), Paul now instructs and admonishes them on the basis of Timothy's report (1 Thessalonians 3:6). Next Paul travels to Caesarea via Ephesus; after a visit to Jerusalem he returns to Antioch.

*Third Missionary Journey (ca. A.D. 52-56) (Acts 18:23-21:17).* Once again Asia Minor was the primary target of the mission, especially Ephesus, the capital of the province of Asia. It served as a center for Paul's activity for almost 3 years. Prior to his arrival Priscilla and Aquila worked there. In addition to other activity they had guided Apollos, the educated Alexandrian Jew, in the rudiments of the faith. During his efforts in the synagogues Paul came in contact with some disciples of John the Baptist who were perhaps associated with Apollos in some way.

When the opposition forced Paul to vacate the synagogue, he relocated in the school of Tyrannus. In fact, it was so effective that the silversmith of Ephesus, who made shrines for the goddess Diana and sold them, threatened to cause a public riot when they saw their income dwindling as a result of the gospel. The church in Ephesus probably emerged during this period.

Residing in Ephesus Paul composes the Letter to the Galatians. In it he contests the Judaistic tendencies of some. He also writes the first letter to Corinth, where he is faced with both opposition and misconduct by the church. On his journey through Macedonia he sends the second letter to that church, and in it he must defend himself against the false accusations of his opponents. Later, spending the winter in Corinth, he writes the more "theological" Epistle to the Romans. Although he does not know them personally yet, he hopes to meet them at a later time (Romans 15:23, 24). From Corinth Paul returns to Jerusalem via the same route as before. He is taking to Jerusalem a "gift" to the mother church (2 Corinthians 8-9).

## The Purpose of Acts

Supposedly the close of Acts provides relatively reliable evidence of when and where the book was written: In Rome during the interval of Paul's waiting for trial before the court of the emperor.

It may also be a clue as to the primary intent of the overall writing: to provide a written defense for Paul in his appearance before the Roman high court.

Nevertheless, when a document has the distinction of being a sacred writing and inspired by the Holy Spirit, one must exert caution before jumping to such conclusions. According to God's larger purposes the double volume of Luke-Acts was written in order that the church of God might read it until the end of time. In that case we clearly have something more than a draft of a written legal defense.

On the other side of things, there is not necessarily a contradiction between these tacitly different purposes. Paul sees God's divine purpose at work in his imprisonment and impending trial: that the gospel might be known and that he might defend the gospel (Philippians 1:12f.).

Luke was closely associated with Paul and accompanied him on a number of his journeys, at least on those paths depicted in the so-called "we-passages." If he intended to compose a biography of Paul much more could have been written. From Paul's epistles we learn of other dramatic events not recorded in Acts. Items that a contemporary story might dwell upon are passed over silently.

The question might be raised, what principle of selection did Luke follow when he wrote Acts? A very striking tendency appears to be present here. Throughout his Gospel account Luke emphasizes the Jewish authorities' and the crowd's role in sending Jesus to the cross. But the Roman authorities as well as King Herod do not get blamed. With respect to Acts it is not difficult to see that the book's structure is built around a series of accusations, trials, and vindications by the Roman authorities. This can be detected in the arrest of the apostles in chapters 4 and 5, and had Stephen been tried in accordance with Roman law he would not have been sentenced.

Luke's account of the spread of Christianity from Jerusalem to Judea and Samaria and on into the Greco-Roman world contains much data that would substantiate Paul's case before the Roman court, and that would put the accusations of the Jews in another perspective. The trouble that arose because of Paul's efforts was primarily caused by the Jews themselves. It is the Jews who incited the people against Paul in Antioch in Pisidia (Acts 13), just as it is in Iconium and Lystra (chapter 14). But in Philippi (chapter 16) and Ephesus (chapter 19) the Gentiles assault him. The picture of Jewish enmity reappears in chapter 21: the Jews stir up the crowd against Paul, but the Roman authorities protect him and give him an opportunity to defend himself in a legal court setting. The court does not find Paul guilty, in spite of the accusation of the Jews. Ultimately the court of the Roman emperor will make the final decision in the case.

Acts 17, the account of Paul's appearance on the Areopagus, also contains material that might have proved crucial in his appearance before the emperor's court. Although no judicial proceedings took place on Areopagus, there may have been an official board that monitored the education of youths in Athens.

All of Paul's defenses (speeches) under the different trial circumstances were actually Christian proclamation. The speeches are legal briefs in the form of theology; "testimonies" in the legal as well as the religious sense of that word. Thus Acts focuses much of its attention on these speeches. The larger divine purpose, therefore, is to afford Christians in the generations to come valid testimonies of the origin and message of the Christian faith.

We can regard these speeches as sworn depositions of the authenticity and historicity of Christianity. As a legal document and as Holy Scripture, Acts has one and the same purpose. The reliability of the Christian tradition is presented.

Acts apparently ends very abruptly; however, it may not be as abrupt as it seems. If the book originally served as a draft of Paul's defense before the emperor, then its ending is not as abrupt as it seems. As was mentioned earlier, according to an official edict of the emperor, cases to be heard by the emperor were delayed 1 1/2 years (Eger, 1919, made this conclusion in a study of the Roman legal system). If the accusers failed to appear within the 1 1/2 years, the indictment was dropped. Luke's recalling that Paul preached from his rented quarters for 2 years, and yet not mentioning any appearance before the royal court, suggests that the case was dropped against Paul.

# The Acts of the Apostles

## and Various Versions

## Commentary

### Chapter 1

1. **The former treatise have I made, O Theophilus:** . . . O God-lover, *—KLGS* . . . In my earlier work I dealt with everything, *—JB* . . . first account, *—CNDT* . . . first historical narrative, *—WUST* . . . I wrote my first volume, *—WLMS* . . . composed the first discourse, *—DRBY* . . . In the former book, *—CNFT* . . . I made a continuous report, *—AMPB.*

**of all that Jesus began both to do and teach:** . . . from the very first, *—TCNT.*

**1:1.** Originally this book had no title. Since the middle of the Second Century A.D., however, it has been known as *The Acts of the Apostles,* probably because the apostles are named in 1:13. Yet the Holy Spirit is more prominent than the apostles. A better title would be "The Acts of the Risen Lord by the Holy Spirit in and Through the Church," since the "former treatise" (Luke's Gospel) recorded what Jesus "began" to do and teach, and Acts records what the risen, ascended Lord continued "to do and teach."

Theophilus ("lover of God; dear to God") was the first recipient of this book, as he was of Luke's Gospel. Most likely he was a personal friend. Luke could count on him to read the book and to have copies made and circulated.

The fact that Luke's Gospel was what Jesus "began to do and teach" shows two things. First, the Church had its beginning in the gospel. Luke's Gospel ends with a convinced group of believers. The Cross put the new covenant into effect (Hebrews 9:15). Jesus "opened . . . their understanding, that they might understand the Scriptures" (Luke 24:45). They were no longer an easily scattered group of disciples, but a commissioned, New Testament Body, united, worshiping, waiting to be endued with power from on high (Luke 24:46-53). They were already the Church.

Second, the work of Jesus did not end when He ascended. As has already been noted, the Holy Spirit continued the work of Jesus in and through the Church. During His life and ministry on earth Jesus practiced what He was teaching the apostles. The truth of His doctrines was confirmed by the miracles He performed and by the purity of His life-style.

2. **Until the day in which he was taken up:** . . . until the day of His ascension, *—BRKL* . . . Before he ascended, *—PHLP.*

**after that he through the Holy Ghost had given commandments:** . . . through the intermediate agency, *—WUST* . . . when through the Holy Spirit He gave . . . their orders, *—WLMS* . . . their instructions, *—NORL* . . . charged the apostles, *—DRBY* . . . having equipped, *—FNTN.*

**unto the apostles whom he had chosen:** . . . those legates, *—MRDK.*

3. **To whom also he showed himself alive:** . . . gave ample proof, *—NEB* . . . presented himself living, *—DRBY.*

**after his passion:** . . . His death, *—ET.*

**by many infallible proofs:** . . . in many convincing manifestations, *—MNTG* . . . sure tokens, *—RTHM* . . . clear and certain signs, *—BB* . . . convincing demonstrations, *—AMPB.*

**being seen of them forty days:** . . . at successive intervals, *—WUST* . . . He appeared to them from time to time, *—TCNT* . . . over a period of forty days, *—ADAM* . . . appearing to them at intervals, *—PNT* . . . appeared to them repeatedly, *—PHLP.*

**and speaking of the things pertaining to the kingdom of God:** . . . discussing the interests, *—BRKL* . . . regarding the welfare, *—FNTN* . . . God's empire, *—ADAM.*

**1:2, 3.** Jesus did not ascend until after He gave instructions through the Holy Spirit to the apostles whom He had chosen to carry out His work. "Taken up" reminds us of Elijah's translation (2 Kings 2:9-11). It was the occasion of the beginning of Elisha's ministry, just as Christ's ascension was the beginning of the Church's ministry.

Acts here includes those to whom Jesus presented himself in definite ways at definite times after His suffering, giving many positive proofs (or sure signs) and unmistakable, convincing evidence that He is alive.

In these appearances He made it clear He was not a spirit or a ghost. They touched Him. He showed them His hands and feet, saying, "It is I myself" (Luke 24:28-43). During 40 days He came to them again and again. These were not visions. They were objective, real, personal appearances. They knew Him, and He taught them truth concerning the Kingdom (or rule, royal power, and authority of God). Now they understood how the Cross and the Resurrection are both necessary for salvation. Both are revelations of God's mighty power and love.

During Moses' 40 days on Mount Sinai God gave him the Law. But during these 40 days Jesus gave His disciples a better "law." (The Hebrew word for law, *torah*, means "instruction.") He was preparing them to carry on after His departure.

**4. And, being assembled together with them:** . . . While he was staying with them, —NOLI . . . and once when, —MNTG . . . On one occasion, while he was eating with them, —NIV.

**commanded them that they should not depart from Jerusalem:** . . . charged them, —ASV . . . ordered them, —BECK . . . he emphasized, —PHLP . . . Do not leave Jerusalem, —NOLI . . . told them not to leave, —NAB.

**but wait for the promise of the Father:** . . . You must wait, —NEB . . . for the fulfillment of the promise made, —NORL . . . but to wait for the Father's promised gift, —WEYM . . . of my Father's promise, —NAB.

**which, saith he, ye have heard of me:** . . . You have heard me speak of it, —WLMS.

**1:4.** Luke's Gospel condenses his account of the 40 days after the Resurrection and jumps to the final exhortation for the 120 to wait in Jerusalem until they had received the Promise of the Father (Luke 24:49). In Acts Luke goes again to the time immediately preceding the Ascension. Jesus repeated the command not to leave Jerusalem.

"The promise of the Father" relates the gift of the Spirit to Old Testament prophecies. The idea of promise is one of the bonds that unites the Old and New Testaments. The promise to Abraham spoke of personal blessings, and blessings to the nation, as well as to all the families of the earth (Genesis 12:3).

The story of God's dealings with His people is a step-by-step revelation. First was the promised defeat of that old serpent, the devil, through the seed of the woman (Genesis 3:15). Next, the promise was given to Abraham, to Isaac, and to Jacob. The chosen line was then narrowed down to Judah, then to David. This led to Jesus, David's greater Son. Now through Jesus would come the Promise of the Father, the gift of the Spirit.

**5. For John truly baptized with water:** . . . For John indeed immersed with water, —RTHM . . . baptized people in water, —WLMS . . . was with water, —BB.

**but ye shall be baptized with the Holy Ghost:** . . . immersed, —HBIE.

**not many days hence:** . . . within a few days, —CMPB . . . after a little time, —BB.

**1:5.** Jesus had already promised this mighty outpouring of the Spirit to His followers (John 7:38, 39 and chapters 14-16). So had John the Baptist. Jesus, as John promised, would baptize them in the Holy Spirit (Mark 1:8). Now Jesus further promised that it would be after "not many days."

**6. When they therefore were come together:** . . . On one occasion, when the Apostles had met together, —TCNT . . . Those who were present then, —NORL . . . While they were with him, —NAB.

**they asked of him, saying:** . . . They . . . began to question him, —RTHM . . . they asked Jesus this question, —TCNT.

**Lord, wilt thou at this time restore again the kingdom to Israel?:** . . . are you now going to make Israel an independent kingdom again, —BECK . . . dost thou duly establish the kingdom, —RTHM . . . set up the kingdom again, —WLMS . . . the sovereignty of Israel? —NEB . . . will you now bring back the kingdom to Israel? —KLGS . . . to restore the rule to Israel now? —NAB.

**1:6.** Acts and the Epistles contain a great deal more about the Holy Spirit and the Church than about the kingdom of God. But the Kingdom was important in Jesus' teaching. Jesus told the disciples it was the Father's good pleasure to give them the Kingdom. *Kingdom* in the New Testament deals primarily with the King's power and rule. Righteousness, peace, and joy in the Holy Spirit show God is ruling in the lives of believers and they are in His kingdom (Romans 14:17).

The future rule of Christ was what the disciples had in mind here. They knew the prophecy of Ezekiel 36:24-27. They knew God's promise to Abraham included not only the seed, but the land. All through the Old Testament God's promise to Israel was connected with the promise of the land.

**7. And he said unto them:** . . . He answered, —NOLI.

**It is not for you to know the times or the seasons:** . . . your business to learn times and dates, —WLMS . . . your affair, —BRKL . . . to decide dates and times, —EVRD . . . and occasions, —MNTG . . . or periods, —FNTN . . . the chronological events, —WUST . . . moments, —DOUY.

**which the Father hath put in his own power:** . . . under His personal authority, —BRKL . . . has appointed by his own authority, —SAWR . . . has reserved at His own absolute disposal, —FNTN . . . has decided, —JB . . . set within his own control, —NEB . . . is the only One who has the authority, —EVRD . . . has a right to fix, —WLMS . . . has kept within his own providence, —NOLI.

**1:7.** Jesus did not deny that it was still God's plan to restore the kingdom (the rule) of God (the theocracy) to Israel. But on earth they would never know the specific times and proper occasions of that restoration before Jesus returned.

In Old Testament times God did not reveal the timespan between the first and second comings of Christ. Sometimes the prophets jump from one to the other in almost the same breath. At Nazareth, Jesus stopped His reading from Isaiah 61 in the middle of verse 2 because the rest of the verse refers to the Second Coming. Again and again Jesus warned the disciples that no man knows the day or the hour of His return (Mark 13:32-35, for example). Jesus also warned that the kingdom of God would not immediately appear (Luke 19:11, 12). The Father has placed the times and seasons under His own authority. He alone has the knowledge and wisdom to take all things into account. In His wisdom He has made the times and seasons His business; it is not the concern of the Church.

**8. But ye shall receive power:** . . . Instead, —ADAM . . . you shall be obtaining power, —CNDT . . . receive energy, —MRDK . . . you shall lay hold of power, —KLGS.

**after that the Holy Ghost is come upon you:** . . . from the Holy Spirit coming upon, —FNTN . . . descends upon, —NOLI.

**and ye shall be witnesses unto me:** . . . will testify of Me, —BECK . . . my witnesses, —DRBY.

**both in Jerusalem, and in all Judaea, and in Samaria, and unto the uttermost part of the earth:** . . . even to the remotest parts, —CMPB . . . the farthest ends, —NORL . . . to the utmost limit, —WORL . . . farthest parts, —BECK . . . the very last part of, —KLGS . . . the very ends of, —TCNT . . . in every part of the world, —EVRD.

**1:8.** What is the believers' business? Verse 8 gives the answer. The disciples would receive power after the Holy Spirit came upon them. Through the Spirit's power their business would be to serve as Christ's witnesses (1 John 1:1) telling what they had seen, heard, and experienced. Beginning at Jerusalem they would carry their witness through Judea (probably including Galilee) and Samaria, and then to the uttermost parts of the earth. This method of procedure for witnessing gives a virtual table of contents for the Book of Acts.

Christians do not need to fail. The coming of the Spirit is an empowering experience. "Ye shall receive power" (Greek, *dunamis*, "mighty power, ability"). Jesus (Matthew 24) emphasized that His followers could not wait for ideal conditions before spreading the gospel to the nations. He told them this age, and especially the end times, would be characterized by wars, rumors of wars, famines, and earthquakes. Followers of Jesus must spread the gospel to all nations despite all these natural calamities and political upheavals. How would this be possible? Jesus promised they would receive power as a result of being filled with the Spirit. This would be the secret of success in the Church Age until its final consummation when Jesus returns.

**9. And when he had spoken these things, while they beheld, he was taken up:** . . . Jesus had no sooner said this than he was caught up before their very eyes, —TCNT . . . With these words, while they

were looking, —NOLI . . . as they were looking on, he was lifted up, —RSV . . . as they were watching, —EVRD.

**and a cloud received him out of their sight:** . . . a cloud swept under Him and carried Him out, —WLMS . . . caught him away from their eyes, —RTHM . . . hid him, —EVRD . . . a cloud took Him up from, —ADAM.

**1:9.** Luke's Gospel is climaxed by Christ's ascension. Luke 24:50 indicates Jesus led His followers out to the Mount of Olives opposite Bethany. As He blessed them He was taken up into heaven (that is, taken gradually, not snatched away). Acts 1:10 adds that this happened "while they looked." They were not dreaming. They actually saw Him go. Then "a cloud," not an ordinary cloud but undoubtedly a glory cloud like the Old Testament Shekinah, took Him up. This could well mean the cloud swept under Him and He rode it up out of their sight. But not only did He leave the surface of the earth, He ascended to the right hand of the Father, and He is still bodily present in heaven. Stephen saw Him there (7:55).

**10. And while they looked stedfastly toward heaven as he went up:** . . . They were still looking intently up to heaven, watching His departure, —NORL . . . . while they were in rapt attention toward heaven, —SWAN . . . gazing intently, —WORL . . . gazing up into the heavens, —NAB . . . at His departure, —FNTN . . . they were looking earnestly up, —WMCK . . . while He was departing, —BECK . . . after him into the sky, —GDSP . . . As he was going, —EVRD, —HNSN . . . going away from them, —MLNT.

**behold, two men stood by them in white apparel:** . . . at that moment, —KLST . . . All at once two men dressed in white, —NLTG . . . suddenly there were two men in white garments standing by them, —WEYM . . . two angels, —SEB . . . in white robes suddenly appeared, —NOLI . . . two men in white, —NAB . . . in white clothes were standing right beside them, —BECK.

**1:10.** After Jesus disappeared, the disciples stood there in amazement with their gaze fixed on the heavens where He had gone. Suddenly, two men in white clothing stood beside them. The white speaks of purity. Though the Bible does not call them angels, it is generally assumed they were. Hebrews 1:14 states that angels are ministering *spirits;* however, on this occasion God enabled the disciples to see them. The white clothing is a reminder of the angels who appeared at the tomb the morning of the Resurrection. Luke calls them "men" (Luke 24:4), John says "angels" (John 20:12).

**11. Which also said:** . . . Who also said, —ASV.
**Ye men of Galilee, why stand ye gazing up into heaven?:** . . . Men! Galileans! —KJII . . . of the country of, —NLTG . . . fixed on the sky? —TCNT . . . looking up to

heaven, —MOFT . . . into the sky? —EVRD . . . up at the skies? —NAB.

**this same Jesus, which is taken up from you into heaven:** . . . This very Jesus, —PHLP . . . This Jesus who has been taken from you, —NAB . . . was caught away, —AMPB . . . who ascended into, —NOLI . . . who had been caught up from you, —GDSP.

**shall so come in like manner as ye have seen him go into heaven:** . . . He will come back in the same way, —EVRD . . . will come in just the way that you have seen him go up, —GDSP . . . in the same manner in which, —MLNT . . . will return in the same way as you have seen him going there, —TNT.

**1:11.** The angels asked why these disciples, men of Galilee (only Judas was of Judea), stood gazing into heaven. This implies they were straining their eyes as if they hoped to see into heaven where Jesus had gone. But Christ's first coming was fulfilled. His work of redemption was complete. It would be a long time before His return, but He would be with them as truly as He had been before (Matthew 28:20). Furthermore, He had left them a great commission, a work to do. He had given them instructions to wait in Jerusalem for the Promise of the Father and for power to be His witnesses. They must obey with the assurance He would come again.

The promise of His return is as emphatic as it could possibly be. Many have tried to interpret this return in some symbolic or spiritual way. Some say it was fulfilled by the outpouring of the Holy Spirit at Pentecost. But Paul makes it clear, long after Pentecost, that "the Lord *himself* shall descend from heaven with a shout, with the voice of the archangel (Michael), and with the trump of God: and the dead in Christ shall rise first," then living believers who remain will "be caught up (snatched up, raptured up) together with them in the clouds," for a meeting with the Lord in the air (1 Thessalonians 4:16, 17).

Others have said the Second Coming is fulfilled when Christ comes for believers at death, but the passage just quoted shows the dead will rise to meet Him. Still others say some other person from some other place will arise or come into prominence and be the Christ, the Messiah. Any such claim reminds us of Jesus' warnings against false christs (Matthew 24:5, 11). In fact, if anyone has time to say, "Here is Christ, or there" (Matthew 24:23), Christians will know he is false. When Jesus comes back, believers will be caught away and changed in the twinkling of an eye. No one will have to tell them Christ has come (1 Corinthians 15:23, 51, 52).

The Greek makes it perfectly clear. "*This same* Jesus . . . shall *so* come in like manner (in the *same* way) as ye have seen him go." He had already told

them He would return in the clouds (Mark 13:26). At His trial He identified himself with the "Son of man," whom Daniel speaks of as coming with clouds (Daniel 7:13, 14). No wonder the fact of His return continues to be one of the most important motivations for Christian living. (See 1 John 3:2, 3.)

**12. Then returned they unto Jerusalem from the mount called Olivet:** . . . After that, —NAB . . . The followers went back to, —NLTG . . . Then they went back to, —EVRD, —MLNT . . . the Olive-yard, —PNT . . . the hill called 'The Olive-Orchard,' —GDSP, —MOFT.

**which is from Jerusalem a sabbath day's journey:** . . . which is near Jerusalem, —RSV . . . This was near Jerusalem, a **little** over a half mile away, —NORL . . . only half a mile away, —WLMS . . . a mere sabbath's journey away, —NAB.

**1:12.** The Gospel of Luke describes the return of Jesus' followers to Jerusalem as being "with great joy" (Luke 24:52). It was only a Sabbath day's journey (about 1,000 yards) from the Mount of Olives back to the city. (Compare Exodus 16:29 and Numbers 35:5.)

**13. And when they were come in:** . . . When they got there, —TCNT . . . When they reached the city, —WLMS . . . and when they had entered, —RSV . . . On entering the city, —WMCK

**they went into an upper room:** . . . they ascended into the upper chamber, —CNDT . . . to the second-floor room, —BECK . . . upper-story, —RTHM . . . to the upstairs room, —EVRD.

**where abode:** . . . which was now, —PNT . . . their fixed place for meeting, —WEYM . . . where they usually met, —BRKL . . . where they were making their abode, —NOYS . . . where they were accustomed to meet, —MNTG . . . where they were in the habit of meeting, —KLGS . . . where they were indefinitely staying, —AMPB . . . Among those present were, —NOLI.

**both Peter, and James, and John, and Andrew: Philip, and Thomas, Bartholomew, and Matthew, James the son of Alphaeus, and Simon Zelotes:** . . . Simon the Zealot, —ASV . . . known as the Revolutionary, —SEB . . . the Zealot party member, —NAB.

**and Judas the brother of James:** . . . Judas the son of James, —ASV.

**1:13.** The 11 apostles were staying in a large upper room. Judas the son of James is called Thaddeus in Matthew 10:3. Zealots were Jewish nationalists (cf. the Aramaic Kan'ana, "Canaanite" in Mark 3:18). The Upper Room may be the place of the Last Supper and the Resurrection appearances. Some believe it was at the home of Mary the mother of John Mark (12:12).

**14. These all continued with one accord in prayer and supplication:** . . . Together they devoted themselves to constant prayer, —NAB . . . all unanimously persevered, —CMPB . . . They were all united, —NOLI ... were persevering, —CNDT ... continued stedfastly in prayer, —ASV ... engaged constantly, —BRKL ... All of these with one mind continued earnest in prayer, —WEYM ... All these engaged constantly and with one mind in prayer, —BRKL ... These all gave themselves to prayer together, —WMCK ... persevering in prayer together, —ADAM ... joined in continuous prayer, —JB ... all kept praying together, —BECK.

**with the women:** ... together with some women, —WEYM ... along with their wives, —KLGS ... There were some women in their company, —NAB.

**and Mary the mother of Jesus, and with his brethren:** ... his brothers, —NAB.

**1:14.** Five things are seen here: (1) The Eleven were in one accord, in contrast to the jealousy exhibited before the Cross where each wanted to be the greatest (Matthew 20:24). Jesus had dealt with them all after the Resurrection. Now all were restored and recommissioned. There was no more conflict, no more jealousy. All were with one mind, with one accord. "One accord" (Greek, *homothumadon*) is an important repeated word in Acts. Being in one accord is an important key to getting God's work done.

(2) They all continued steadfastly in prayer. This included faithfulness to the morning and evening hours of prayer at the temple as well as prayer in the Upper Room. Prayer and praise were the chief occupation during those days (Luke 24:49).

(3) The women joined them in prayer with the same steadfastness. Actually, the women were present all along. In those days, if one man was present, the masculine pronoun was used for the mixed group. Even when Peter calls them brethren (verse 16), the women were included. The Jews all understood this. But Luke wanted the Gentiles to know the women were present and praying, so he mentioned them specifically. They included Mary Magdalene, Salome, Joanna, Mary and Martha of Bethany, John Mark's mother, and others.

(4) Mary the mother of Jesus is given special mention. She was present because the apostle John was fulfilling Jesus' request to take care of her. She was not there as a leader but simply joined the others in prayer and in waiting for the Promise of the Father, the baptism in the Holy Spirit. This also indicates she had accepted Jesus as her Saviour from sin and as her Lord and Master. She was obeying His command to stay in Jerusalem. She, along with the others, felt her need of the power of the Spirit. Thus, it is certain she received the Spirit even though this is the last time she is mentioned in the Book of Acts. Some traditions say she died in Jerusalem and point to a tomb near St. Stephen's gate. Other writers of the Early Church said she went with the apostle John to Ephesus and died there.

(5) The brothers of Jesus were present, though before the Cross they did not believe on Him (John 7:5). Some say these were cousins of Jesus or children of Joseph by a previous marriage. However, Matthew 1:25 makes it clear that Joseph entered into a physical marriage relation with Mary after Jesus was born. Thus, there is every reason to believe these brothers were actual children of Mary and Joseph. Their names were James (a form of Jacob), Joses (a form of Joseph), Judah, and Simon (Mark 6:3).

After His resurrection, Jesus made a special appearance to His eldest brother James (1 Corinthians 15:7). James later became the leader and chief elder, or bishop, of the Jerusalem church. Jude also became a leader in the church (Acts 12:17; 15:13; 21:18; Galatians 2:9; James 1:1; Jude 1). Now these brothers were in one accord with the apostles and the rest of the 120 as they all waited for the promised Holy Spirit.

15. **And in those days Peter stood up in the midst of the disciples, and said:** ... During this time there was a meeting of the believers, —EVRD, —NCV ... At one point ... Peter stood up in the center, —NAB ... About this time, at a gathering of the Brethren, Peter rose to speak, —TCNT ... stood up at a meeting of the brethren, —WMCK ... in the midst of the brethren, —ASV ... among the brotherhood, —BRKL ... in the congregation, —JB ... and addressed them, —KLST.

**(the number of names together were about an hundred and twenty,):** ... they were a large group numbering, —TNT ... the number of names assembled, —HNSN ... the company of persons was in all, —RSV ... there were about a hundred and twenty persons present, —GDSP.

**1:15.** Apparently not all the 500 or more who saw Jesus in Galilee (1 Corinthians 15:6) followed Him back to Jerusalem. But about 120 men and women returned after Christ's ascension and were united in this atmosphere of prayer and praise. But they did more than pray. They also gave attention to the Scriptures. What Peter saw in the Scriptures caused him to stand up and address the 120, who are here called disciples (students, learners, eager to learn more about the gospel and about God's will and plan).

Some ancient manuscripts, which form the critical text used by the NIV and NASB, read "brothers" (*adelphōn*) in place of "disciples" (*mathētōn*). If "brothers" is the original, the word still includes the women who were present (cf. verse 14). Luke, to a greater extent than all other New Testament writers, relates the important role women had in the ministry of Christ and in the Early Church (for example, the virgin Mary, Elisabeth, Anna, Martha and Mary, the women in the parables of the Lost Coin and the Unjust Judge, and others [in the Gospels]; Tabitha, Lydia, Priscilla, and the four daughters of Philip the Evangelist [in Acts]).

**16. Men and brethren:** ...Brethren, *—ASV* ...Brothers, *—TCNT.*

**this scripture must needs have been fulfilled:** ... it was necessary that the Scripture should be fulfilled, *—WEYM* ... that the passage of Scripture, *—KLST* ... the prediction of the Scriptures, *—GDSP* ... what he wrote had to come true, *—BECK* ...was destined to be fulfilled, *—NAB* ...according to the prediction of, Noli.

**which the Holy Ghost by the mouth of David spake before concerning Judas:** ...predicted, *—CNDT* ... long ago, *—BECK* ... foretold through the lips of David, *—BRKL* ... uttered by the mouth of David, *—WLMS* ... dictated through the mouth of David, *—FNTN* ... the fate of Judas,

**which was guide to them that took Jesus:** ... who acted as guide to those who arrested Jesus, *—WEYM* ... who became leader, *—SWAN* ... who was the leader, *—DOUY* ... of those apprehending Jesus, *—CNDT* ...that Judas would lead men to arrest Jesus, *—EVRD* ...to the men that arrested Jesus, *—TCNT.*

**1:16.** Peter drew attention to the fulfillment of David's prophecy, spoken by the Spirit, through David's mouth. Peter saw that Psalms 41:9 and 109:8 applied to Judas who acted as a guide to those who arrested Jesus in the Garden of Gethsemane. Peter recognized that the Holy Spirit is the real author of God's written Word, and that what David said about God's enemies in his day applied to the enemies of Jesus (since David is seen by some as a type pointing to Jesus, and God's covenant with David finds its complete and final fulfillment in Jesus).

The phrase "men and brethren" apparently was a style of formal address in the First Century. The phrase does not occur in the extant literature of the day (except Maccabees 8:19), but it is common in Acts, always in a context where there was a gathering of Jews. Peter (2:29; 15:7), Stephen (7:2), James (15:13), and Paul (13:26, 38; 22:1; 23:1, 6; 28:17) all use this same phrase.

The verb *edei* is related to *dei*, "it is necessary," a term Luke frequently used to indicate divine necessity. It speaks of the providence of God governing the events of history, especially in relation to His plan of redemption. As in this passage and in verse 21, the word is occasionally used specifically in connection with the fulfillment of Scripture (see Luke 22:37; 24:7, 26, 44, 46; Acts 17:3).

**17. For he was numbered with us:** ... one of our number, *—WLMS* ... Judas was one of us twelve, *—BECK* ... he was enumerated with us, *—FNTN.*

**and had obtained part of this ministry:** ...and received his portion in, *—ASV* ...and having had his part allotted him in this work of ours, *—TCNT* ...obtained

the inheritance of this service, *—SAWR* ...was alloted his share, *—ADAM* ...actually sharing, *—JB* ...his allotted share, *—MNTG.*

**1:17.** The tragedy was that Judas was numbered among the apostles as one of the Twelve, and yet he failed. Jesus included him when He called together a large group of disciples and out of them chose 12 to be with Him (Luke 6:12, 13). Jesus did this knowing the character of Judas (John 6:70). Yet He also knew the Scripture must be fulfilled (John 13:18). Even though Jesus knew what Judas would do, He gave him an assigned portion in the ministry which He gave to all of the Twelve. Judas was sent out with the same commission and the same authority as the others.

Judas was present also when Jesus declared He was appointing a kingdom (a kingly rule and authority) for His 12 apostles like the one His Father had appointed for Him. They would have a special place in His kingdom. They would sit on 12 thrones judging (and therefore ruling) the 12 tribes of Israel (Luke 22:29, 30).

Even at the Last Supper Jesus washed the feet of Judas along with the others. When Jesus took the sop (a broken piece of bread), dipped it, and offered it to Judas, it was a final offer of His love. But Judas turned his heart from Jesus. Then Satan entered Judas, and he went out to betray the Lord.

**18. Now this man purchased a field with the reward of iniquity:** ...acquired a field, *—HBIE* ...bought a farm, *—FNTN* ...had bought a piece of land with the payment for his treachery, *—TCNT* ... the wages of crime, *—BRKL* ...the price of his villainy, *—NEB* ...the wages of injustice, *—CNDT* ...wages of sin, *—MRDK* ...reward of unrighteousness, *—YNG* ...which he took for his treachery, *—WLMS* ... the money he got for his crime, *—BECK* ...his dishonest money, *—SEB.*

**and falling headlong:** ...and falling from a height, *—TCNT* ...having fallen down head first, *—NORL* ...fell there face downward, *—WLMS* ...having fallen prone (on his face), *—PNT.*

**he burst asunder in the midst:** ...his intestines, *—ADAM* ...his body burst open, *—TCNT* ...he was ruptured in the middle, *—NORL* ...brake asunder in-the-midst, *—RTHM* ...his body broke in two, *—WLMS.*

**and all his bowels gushed out:** ...his intestines gushed out, *—BRKL* ... all his entrails were poured out, *—MRDK* ...his intestines poured out, *—BECK* ...all his entrails poured out, *—JB* ... he became disembowelled, *—PNT.*

**1:18.** At this point Acts adds a parenthetic note about the death of Judas which adds some new details to the account in Matthew 27:3-5. Matthew says Judas, when he knew the Jewish leaders had condemned Jesus, changed his mind, brought the money back, and confessed he had sinned. When these leaders rejected him, he threw down the money, went out, and hanged himself. Acts says Judas purchased a field with the reward money, and falling headlong, he burst open, and all his internal organs gushed out.

Since Luke had searched out all that was written about Jesus, he knew the priests took the money, bought the potter's field where Judas hanged himself, and used it as a cemetery to bury foreigners in (Matthew 27:6, 7). He also knew Judas hanged himself and added this further information about the event.

This incident can be understood better by recognizing that hanging by a rope was not common in ancient times. The two common methods of hanging were crucifixion and impalement through the middle of the body over a sharp stake. Judas, of course, could not nail himself to a cross. But he could set up a sharp stake and fall headlong over it with the result described here. There is evidence also that the Greek includes the idea that when he fell over the stake, his body first swelled up and thus burst open.

It is also true that since the priests took the money which they considered still belonging to Judas, they bought the potter's field in the name of Judas. They called the field *Aceldama* (verse 19, Aramaic for "the field of blood") because the 30 pieces of silver were the price of blood, that is, of Christ's death.

**19. And it was known unto all the dwellers at Jerusalem:** ... And it became known, —ASV ... Everybody living in Jerusalem heard about it, —BECK.
**insomuch as that field is called in their proper tongue:** ... and so the field got its name, in their language, —TCNT.
**Aceldama, that is to say, The field of blood:** ... a bloody piece of ground, —WUST ... Blood-Farm, —FNTN ... the Bloody Acre, —JB.

**1:19.** Judas' suicide soon became known to all the residents of Jerusalem. They also called the field Aceldama, but they had in mind the violent death of Judas which took place there.

**20. For it is written in the book of Psalms, Let his habitation be desolate:** ... Let his homestead, —ADAM ... camp, —JB ... dwelling, —TCNT ... should not go near his property, —SEB ... Let his habitacion be voyde, —GNVA ... Let his house be a ruin, —WMCK ... May his place be empty, —EVRD.
**and let no man dwell therein:** ... And let no one live in it, —TCNT ... let no resident be in it, —MRDK ... let there be no one living there, —NORL ... No one should live there! —SEB.
**and his bishoprick let another take:** ... and His office, —RSV ... his office of oversight, —ADAM ... Let another man replace him as leader, —EVRD ... let another person of a different character take, —WUST ... His work, —WEYM ... His supervision, —CNDT ... let

another take his service, —MRDK ... Let someone else take his position, —GDSP ... let a different one take, —RTHM ... his overseership, —DRBY.

**1:20.** Peter's emphasis, however, was on the fulfillment of Psalms 69:25 and 109:8, with special attention to the latter: "His bishopric (overseership, rulership) let another take." The Twelve were chosen by Jesus himself as primary witnesses to His teaching. They had heard His words and sayings again and again as they followed Him from place to place and listened to Him teach. They had the promise also that the Holy Spirit would bring to their remembrance all Jesus said (John 14:26). They would have positions of authority, ruling the 12 tribes of Israel in the coming kingdom (Luke 22:29, 30; Matthew 19:28).

It is important to notice also that it was only because Judas became a lost soul for all eternity that it was necessary to replace him. When the apostle James, the brother of the apostle John, was martyred by King Herod Agrippa I, no one was chosen to replace him (12:2). James would rise again at the second coming of Christ and would reign on 1 of the 12 thrones along with the rest of the Twelve in the coming kingdom.

**21. Wherefore of these men which have companied with us:** ... It is necessary, therefore, that of the men who have been with us, —WEYM ... This person must be one ... who has been associated with our company, —NOLI ... who have been associated, —WLMS ... who have been in our society, —WMCK.
**all the time that the Lord Jesus went in and out among us:** ... the whole time ... Jesus was traveling, —JB ... moved about among us, —TCNT ... who were part of our group, —EVRD.
**22. Beginning from the baptism of John:** ... during all the time the Lord Jesus was with us, —EVRD ... from his baptism by John, —TCNT.
**unto that same day that he was taken up from us:** ... down to the day on which he was taken away from us, —TCNT ... to the day of his Ascension, —NOLI ... unto His ascension, —ET.
**must one be ordained to be a witness with us of his resurrection:** ... must one become a witness, —ASV ... someone must be found to join us as a witness, —TCNT ... must be an eyewitness, —PHLP ... as a witness to, —NOLI.

**1:21, 22.** Peter then proceeded to lay down the qualifications for the one who would replace Judas. Jesus had chosen the Twelve out of a large group of disciples. Many of these other disciples continued to follow Jesus. Among the 120 in the Upper Room there were some men who had accompanied the Twelve while Jesus went in and out among the people, traveling from place to place, from village to village.

This implies the one chosen would need to be a firsthand witness to the sayings and teachings of Jesus. Jesus did not give brand-new teachings in every one of the many villages He visited on His teaching tours in Galilee, Judea, the Decapolis, and Peraea. He undoubtedly introduced such teachings as are found in the Sermon on the Mount at the place indicated in Matthew's Gospel (chapters 5-7). But there is indication that He also taught these same truths in other places.

It is also evident in many cases that the Gospels condense or give key points of the teaching of Jesus. Often Jesus spent hours teaching, even all day. In line with Old Testament methodology, He undoubtedly used a great deal of repetition to bring emphasis. This methodology also would bring out the same truths by using different words. The audience of Jesus sometimes included Gentiles, especially in the Decapolis and Peraea. People often asked questions. Thus Jesus must have given much explanation. He did to His own disciples. This may help to explain why the wording of the Gospels sometimes differs a little from each other. The Holy Spirit inspired each of the Gospel writers to select out of the actual words of Jesus the terminology that would bring home the truth to the audience to which the particular Gospel was addressed.

It is worth noting also that the apostle Paul had to defend his apostleship, since he was not among this group who heard the sayings of Jesus and since he was not commissioned before the Ascension as a witness to the resurrection of Jesus.

He defended his apostleship in three ways. First, in Galatians 1:11, 12, 16 he declared he did not receive his gospel from man but by revelation of Jesus Christ. Some believe this took place during Paul's 3 years in Arabia. Paul thus claimed to be a *firsthand* witness to the teachings and sayings of Jesus. In fact, he gave one saying of Jesus not recorded in the four Gospels (Acts 20:35). Second, Paul defended his apostleship by declaring he was a *firsthand* witness to the resurrection of Jesus, even though the appearance of Jesus to him was after the Ascension (1 Corinthians 15:8). He was personally commissioned by Jesus to be an apostle. Third, God wrought apostolic miracles through him (2 Corinthians 12:11, 12).

It is probable also that the qualifications set down by Peter fitted best those who were among the 70 Jesus sent out (Luke 10:1-20). They were directly commissioned by Jesus to heal the sick and proclaim the Kingdom.

23. **And they appointed two:** . . . . At that, —NAB . . . And they put forward two, —RSV . . . Then they nominated two men, —WLMS . . . they proposed two,

—GDSP, —NOLI, —NOYS . . . Having nominated two candidates, —JB . . . brought two men in front of them, —NLTG . . . They put the names of two men before the group, —NCV.

**Joseph called Barsabas:** . . . also called Barsabbas Justus, —NLTG.

**who was surnamed Justus:** . . . was known as, —ET.

**and Matthias:** . . . The other was, —NCV.

**1:23.** Peter laid down the conditions, but the people made the choice. Two men met the conditions best. One was Joseph named Barsabas ("son of the Sabbath," born on the Sabbath) who, like so many Jews, had a Roman name, Justus. The other was Matthias. Eusebius, the third-century church historian, says he was indeed one of the Seventy sent out in Luke 10:1.

24. **And they prayed, and said:** . . . Then the followers prayed, —NLTG . . . and they offered this prayer, —TCNT.

**Thou, Lord, which knowest the hearts of all men:** . . . knower of all hearts, —BRKL . . . Heart-knower, —ADAM . . . you know the minds of everyone, —EVRD . . . you read the hearts of men, —NAB.

**shew whether of these two thou hast chosen:** . . . show of these two the one whom thou hast chosen, —ASV . . . Make known to us which of these two you choose, —NAB . . . make clear which one of these two, —BRKL . . . thou didst select, —HNSN . . . manifest, —MRDK.

**1:24.** To make the choice between Joseph Barsabas and Matthias, the apostles first prayed. They knew they needed divine guidance. They did not attempt to make the decision on the basis of their own reasoning or wisdom. In their prayer they addressed Jesus as Lord. This indicated their recognition of Jesus as the divine Lord, truly God as well as truly man. They recognized too that they could not make the decision on the basis of the outward appearance or apparent qualifications of these men. They needed the help of the One who knows the hearts of everyone. Some note that this verse lays down an important principle in understanding election: God's sovereign election takes into consideration the heart of the individual whom He chooses.

They wanted Jesus to make the choice also because He had chosen them. When Jesus told the Twelve, "Ye have not chosen me, but I have chosen you" (John 15:16), He was not talking of their salvation, but of their ministry as apostles. Actually, no Christian has the right to follow his own desires, inclinations, dreams, or fantasies in order to decide what kind of ministry he would like to pursue. Just as the Holy Spirit distributes gifts as He wills (1 Corinthians 12:11), so Jesus alone knows enough about each believer's heart, nature, and the future, to know where he can fit best into His purpose and plan.

**25. That he may take part of this ministry and apostleship:** . . . to take the place in this ministry, *—RSV*. . . this apostolic ministry, *—KLST, —NAB*. . . to take a share in this service as an apostle, *—WLMS* . . . to serve in this office of apostle, *—BECK*. . . to succeed to this apostolic service, *—TNT*. . . to take the place of this dispensation, *—CNDT*. . . as servant and apostle, *—WMCK*. . . and be a missionary, *—NLTG*.

**from which Judas by transgression fell:** . . . replacing Judas, who deserted the cause, *—NAB*. . . from which Judas broke away, *—MRDK*. . . Judas went aside, *—RTHM* . . . Judas went astray, *—FNTN* . . . Judas abandoned, *—JB, —TNT* . . . Judas forfeited, *—PHLP* . . . Judas fell from, *—WMCK* . . . Judas turned away from it, *—EVRD* . . . Judas has fallen away, *—NOLI* . . . Judas left, *—GDSP*. . . Judas lost his place . . . because of sin, *—NLTG*.

**that he might go to his own place:** . . . left to go where he belonged, *—BECK*. . . to go to his own place, *—ADAM*. . . and gone to his own doom, *—NOLI*.

**1:25.** So Jesus alone could know which of the two was His choice for this ministry, or service, and this apostleship (the office of apostle from which Judas fell).

They also recognized that Judas fell away by his own choice and by his deliberate, rebellious sinning. He went to his own place, that is, the place he had chosen, the place of punishment.

**26. And they gave forth their lots:** . . . Then they drew lots between them, *—TCNT* . . . Subsequently, they cast lots, *—NOLI*.

**and the lot fell upon Matthias:** . . . and so Matthias was chosen, *—BECK*.

**and he was numbered with the eleven apostles:** . . . he was added to the number of, *—TCNT*. . . elected to work, *—FNTN* . . . as one of the twelve apostles, *—JB* . . . the Eleven Missionaries, *—KLGS* . . . was considered equally an apostle, *—PHLP* . . . So he took his place, *—NOLI*.

**1:26.** They used the Old Testament method of casting lots, probably following the precedent of Proverbs 16:33. They believed God would overrule the laws of chance and show His choice by this means. The Book of Acts never mentions the use of this method again, however. After Pentecost they relied on the Holy Spirit for guidance.

Some modern writers question whether Peter and the others were right in doing this and say Paul should have been chosen. But he was the apostle to the Gentiles. Though He was equal in calling and authority to the others, he never included himself with the Twelve (1 Corinthians 15:7, 8).

Actually, the Bible states without adverse comment that Matthias was numbered with the 11 apostles. In 6:2 he is still included with the Twelve.

Though he is not mentioned again by name, neither are most of the other apostles.

Because Judas became a lost soul, his replacement was necessary. He had been commissioned. He had the opportunity. But through his own choice he became "the son of perdition," a Hebraistic way of saying he was headed for eternal loss.

# Chapter 2

**1. And when the day of Pentecost was fully come:** . . . . During the celebration, *—FNTN* . . . In the course of the Harvest Thanksgiving-day, *—TCNT* . . . when the actual day, *—PHLP* . . . When the fyftith daye, *—TNDL*. . . When Pentecost day came round, *—JB* . . . being fulfilled, *—YNG* . . . had arrived, *—ADAM* . . . was now accomplishing, *—DRBY* . . . were drawing to a close, *—CNFT*.

**they were all with one accord in one place:**. . . they were all together in one place, *—RSV*. . . the disciples had all met together, *—TCNT*. . . unitedly, *—BRKL*. . . assembled together, *—MRDK* . . . harmoniously assembled, *—FNTN* . . . at the same place, *—YNG* . . . for the same object, *—RTHM*. . . and of one mind, *—NORL*.

**2:1.** On the 50th day after the waving of the sheaf of firstfruits (Leviticus 23:15), the Jews waved two loaves for firstfruits (Leviticus 23:17). Thus this feast of harvest was called *Weeks* (because of the "week" of weeks between) or *Pentecost* ("fiftieth"). Pentecost was now being completed or fulfilled, a word indicating that the period of waiting was coming to an end, and Old Testament prophecies were about to be fulfilled. The Sadducees who controlled the temple took the "sabbath" of Leviticus 23:15 to be the weekly Sabbath after Passover. This made Pentecost occur on a Sunday.

The 120 were still in one accord in one place. The Bible does not name the place, but most believe it was the Upper Room. Others, in view of Peter's statement that it was the third hour of the day (9 a.m.), believe they were in the temple, probably in the Court of the Women. Believers were habitually in the temple at the hours of prayer. One of the roofed colonnades on the edge of the court would have provided a good place for them to gather. (The temple is called a "house" in 7:47.) This would help explain the crowd that gathered after the Spirit was outpoured. (Others believe the Upper Room was open to the street, or that the 120 left the Upper Room.)

**2. And suddenly there came a sound from heaven:**. . . there came suddenly out of the heaven, *—YNG*. . . from the sky, *—FNTN*. . . came from the heavens a noise, *—TCNT*. . . a roaring, *—BRKL*.

**as of a rushing mighty wind:**. . . like that of a strong wind coming nearer and nearer, *—TCNT*. . . as of a rushing violent wind, *—CMPB*. . . as a violent carrying blast, *—CNDT* . . . like a terrific blast of wind,

—WLMS ... violent tempest-blast, —FNTN ... like a roar, —NORL ... a violent impetuous blowing, —DRBY.

**and it filled all the house where they were sitting:** ... entire house, —JB ... was full of it, —BB.

**3. And there appeared unto them cloven tongues like as of fire:** ... tongues parting asunder, —ASV ... like split tongues, —ADAM ... tongues of what appeared to be flame, separating, —TCNT ... fiery tongues, —FNTN.

**and it sat upon each of them:** ... on the head of each person a tongue alighted, —WEYM ... separating and resting on their heads, —WLMS ... distributing themselves over the assembly, —PNT.

**2:2, 3.** Suddenly a sound came from heaven like that of a violent rushing wind or tornado. But it was the sound that filled the house and overwhelmed them, not an actual wind.

The sound of wind would remind them of Old Testament divine manifestations (Exodus 14:21; Job 38:1; 40:6). Thus, the sound of the wind indicated God was about to manifest himself by His Spirit in a special way.

Just as suddenly, cloven tongues looking like flames of fire appeared. "Cloven" means "distributed." What looked like a mass of flames appeared and then broke up, and a single tongue of flame settled on the head of each person. Fire and light are common symbols of the divine presence (as in Exodus 3:2; 19:18).

The fire here signified God's acceptance of the Church body as the temple of the Holy Spirit (1 Corinthians 3:16; Ephesians 2:21, 22). It also indicated the acceptance of individual believers as being temples of the Spirit.

Notice also that these signs *preceded* the filling with the Holy Spirit. They were not part of it, nor were they repeated on other occasions when the Spirit was outpoured.

**4. And they were all filled with the Holy Ghost:** ... all were controlled by the Holy Spirit, —WUST.

**and began to speak with other tongues:** ... different languages, —CNDT ... diverse languages, —MRDK ... strange tongues, —TCNT ... foreign languages, —FNTN.

**as the Spirit gave them utterance:** ... granted them expression, —BRKL ... was giving them to declare, —YNG ... was giving them to be sounding out, —RTHM ... granted them to utter divine things, —WLMS ... endowed them with clear expression, —FNTN ... gave them the gift of speech, —JB ... enabled them, —NIV ... gave them words to utter, —PNT ... prompted them to speak, —CNFT ... gave them power to proclaim his message, —PHLP.

**2:4.** Now that God had acknowledged the Church as the new temple, the next thing was to pour out the Holy Spirit on the members of the Body.

In 1:5 Jesus said, "Ye shall be *baptized* with the Holy Ghost." Here, Luke wrote that the 120 were "filled with the Holy Ghost," in fulfillment of Jesus' promise. In 11:16 Peter connected the outpouring of the Spirit in Caesarea to Jesus' promise that He would baptize in the Spirit. Actually, the Bible uses a variety of terms. It was also a pouring out of the Spirit as Joel prophesied, a receiving and an active taking of the Spirit as a gift (2:38), a falling upon (8:16; 10:44; 11:15), a pouring out of the gift (10:45), and a coming upon (19:6).

As soon as they were filled, the 120 began to speak with other tongues (languages). This speaking came as the Spirit proceeded to give them utterance (to speak out). They spoke, but the words did not come from their mind or thinking. Through the Spirit they spoke out boldly. This is the one sign of the baptism in the Spirit that was repeated (10:44-47; 19:1-7).

**5. And there were dwelling at Jerusalem Jews:** ... residing in, —PNT ... sojourning Jews, —RTHM.

**devout men:** ... God-fearing, —NIV ... religious men, —KLGS ... of deep faith, —PHLP.

**out of every nation under heaven:** ... from every part of the world, —WEYM ... from many and distant lands, —MNTG.

**2:5.** "Dwelling" usually implies permanent residence. Many Jews from the dispersion had settled in Jerusalem. But on the Feast of Pentecost many Jews from all over the known world would be there. Actually, more would be present than at Passover, since travel on the Mediterranean was safer at this season.

**6. Now when this was noised abroad:** ... this sound took place, —ALFD ... this speaking was heard, —NORL ... this report having been circulated, —WLSN.

**the multitude came together:** ... throng, —RTHM ... they came crowding together, —WEYM ... the crowd rushed together, —WLMS ... they all assembled, —JB ... a crowd quickly collected, —PHLP.

**and were confounded:** ... confused. —CNDT ... thrown into confusion, —RTHM ... amazed, —WEYM ... they were bewildered, —RSV ... agitated, —MRDK ... dumbfounded, —BECK ... in great excitement, —WLMS.

**because that every man heard them speak in his own language:** ... because each of them heard the disciples speaking, —TCNT ... they were hearing words in their own language, —NLTG ... his own vernacular, —CNDT ... proper dialect, —YNG ... peculiar dialect, —FNTN ... native language, —MLNT.

**2:6.** As the sound of the 120 speaking in tongues became heard, a crowd came from all directions. All were confounded for each kept hearing them speak in his own language. "Own" is emphatic, meaning his own language he used as a child. *Tongue* means a distinct language. They were not speaking merely in a variety of Galilean or Aramaic dialects but in a variety of different languages.

**7. And they were all amazed and marvelled:** . . . They were beside themselves with wonder, *−WEYM* . . . The whole occurrence astonished them . . . in utter amazement, *−NAB* . . . They were surprised and wondered about it, *−NLTG* . . . utterly amazed, *−TCNT* . . . were delighted, *−FNTN* . . . were perfectly amazed and . . . in their astonishment, *−GDSP.*

**saying to one another:** . . . and kept saying in their astonishment, *−TCNT* . . . They asked, *−NAB.*

**Behold, are not all these which speak Galileans?:** . . . Look! *−ADAM* . . . all these men who are speaking, *−GDSP.*

**2:7.** The result was total amazement. The listeners were astonished. They were filled with awe-struck wonder, for they recognized, perhaps by their clothing, that the 120 were Galileans. They could not understand how this was happening.

**8. And how hear we every man in our own tongue, wherein we were born?:** . . . How does it happen, *−JB* . . . how can it be possible . . . our own private dialect, *−WUST* . . . how is it that each of us hears his own native tongue? *−GDSP* . . . we each hear them in our . . . speech in which we were born? *−MLNT* . . . our own language, *−ASV.*

**2:8.** Some suppose the 120 were all really speaking the same language and by a miracle of hearing the multitude were made to hear it in their mother tongue. But verses 6 and 7 are too specific for that. Each man heard them *speak* in his own dialect without any Galilean accent. There would have been no surprise if the 120 had spoken in Aramaic or Greek.

Others suppose the 120 really spoke in tongues but no one understood them. They propose that the Spirit interpreted unknown tongues in the ears of the hearers into their own language. But verses 6 and 7 rule that out too. The 120 spoke in real languages which were actually understood by a variety of people from a variety of places. This gave witness to the universality of the Gift and to the universality and unity of the Church.

**9. Parthians, and Medes, and Elamites:** . . . We are, *−NAB, −NLTG* . . . Some of us are Parthians, some Medes, some Elamites, *−TCNT.*

**and the dwellers in Mesopotamia, and in Judaea, and Cappadocia, in Pontus, and Asia:** . . . and some of us live in Mesopotamia, *−TCNT* . . . and from the countries of, *−NLTG* . . . residents of, *−GDSP* . . . inhabitants of Mesopotamia, *−WEYM* . . . the province of Asia, *−NAB.*

**2:9.** The places named were in all directions, but they also follow a general order (with exceptions), beginning in the northeast. Parthia was east of the Roman Empire, between the Caspian Sea and the Persian Gulf, in the southern part of Persia. Mesopotamia was the ancient Babylonia, mostly outside the Roman Empire. Babylon had a large Jewish population in New Testament times and later became a center for orthodox Judaism (1 Peter 5:13). There is evidence that the listeners included members of all 12 tribes. (Some of the northern 10 tribes settled in Media and later joined the synagogues. Compare James 1:1; see also Acts 26:7.)

Judea is mentioned because Jews there still spoke Hebrew and would have been amazed at the lack of a Galilean accent. It is also possible that Luke included all of Syria with Judea, in fact, all the territory of David and Solomon from the Euphrates river to the River of Egypt (Genesis 15:18). Cappadocia was a large Roman province in northern Asia Minor on the Black Sea. Asia was the Roman province comprising the western third of Asia Minor.

**10. Phrygia, and Pamphylia, in Egypt, and in parts of Libya about Cyrene:** . . . Egypt and the parts of Libya belonging to Cyrene, *−RSV* . . . and the district of Africa, *−GDSP* . . . the regions of Libya, *−NAB* . . . near Cyrene, *−NLTG.*

**and strangers of Rome:** . . . some of us are visitors from Rome, *−TCNT* . . . transient dwellers from Rome, *−WLMS.*

**Jews and proselytes:** . . . either Jews by birth or converts, *−TCNT* . . . Jews and those who have accepted the Jewish religion, *−BECK.*

**2:10.** Phrygia was an ethnic district, part of which was in the province of Asia and part in Galatia. Pamphylia was a Roman province on the south coast of Asia Minor. Egypt to the south had a large Jewish population. The Jewish philosopher Philo said in A.D. 38 that about a million Jews lived there, many in Alexandria. Cyrene was a district west of Egypt on the Mediterranean coast.

Others present in Jerusalem were strangers (sojourners, temporary residents) in Jerusalem, citizens of Rome, including Jews and proselytes (Gentile converts to Judaism). Full proselytes took circumcision, a self-baptism, and offered a sacrifice to declare their purpose to keep the Jewish law and live as Jews.

**11. Cretes and Arabians, we do hear them speak in our tongues the wonderful works of God:** . . . about the majesty, *−WEYM* . . . the excellencies, *−BRKL* . . . the great things, *−CNDT* . . . the wonders, *−MRDK* . . . magnificent things, *−RTHM* . . . the great acts, *−ADAM* . . . the marvels, *−JB* . . . mighty wonders, *−NORL* . . . the greatness, *−KLGS* . . . of the triumphs, *−MOFT.*

**2:11.** Still others were from the island of Crete and from Arabia, the district east and southeast of Palestine.

All these kept hearing in their own languages the wonderful works (the mighty, magnificent, sublime deeds) of God. This may have been in the form of ejaculations of praise to God. No discourse or preaching is implied. There is no record here or elsewhere, however, of the gift of tongues being used as a means of preaching the gospel.

**12. And they were all amazed, and were in doubt:** ... Nay, all were ... quite at a loss, –RTHM ... and upset, –ADAM ... bewildered, –CNDT ... utterly amazed and bewildered, –TCNT ... astounded and bewildered, –WEYM ... amazed and puzzled, –BECK ... in ... perplexity, –CMPB ... wholly at a loss what to think, –WUST ... they were all excited and did not know what to think, –KLGS.

**saying one to another, What meaneth this?:** ... How will this turn out, –BRKL ... From whom is this thing? –MRDK ... What can it all possibly mean? –NORL.

**2:12.** Instead, the hearers were amazed (astounded) and in doubt (perplexed). "What meaneth this?" is literally, "What will this be?" It expresses their total confusion as well as their extreme amazement. They understood the meaning of the words, but not the purpose.

**13. Others mocking said:** ... But others said with a sneer, –TCNT ... taunting, –CNDT ... But others, scornfully jeering, –WEYM ... laughed it off, –JB ... said contemptuously, –NEB ... in mockery, –NORL ... made fun of them, –NIV.

**These men are full of new wine:** ... They are brimfull of sweet wine, –WEYM ... They are running over with new wine, –WLMS ... They are simply drunk with new wine, –NORL ... are intoxicated, –MRDK.

**2:13.** Others apparently did not understand any of the languages, and because they could not understand the meaning they jumped to the conclusion that it had no meaning. Therefore, they proceeded to mock, saying the people were "full of new wine" (sweet wine). "New wine" here is the Greek *gleukous* from which we get our word *glucose*, a name for grape sugar. It is not the ordinary word for new wine and probably represents an intoxicating wine made from a very sweet grape which would have a higher alcoholic content. It would be some time before the grape harvest began in August and real new wine or grape juice would again be available.

Some drinkers do become noisy and this may be what the mockers were thinking of, but one must not suppose there was any sign of the kind of frenzy that marked heathen drunken debauchery. The chief emotion of the 120 was still joy. They had been thanking and praising God in their own language (Luke 24:53), and now the Holy Spirit had given them new languages to praise God.

Their hearts were still going out to God in praise, even though they did not understand what they were saying.

**14. But Peter, standing up with the eleven:** ... Then arose Peter, representing the eleven, –BRKL.

**lifted up his voice, and said unto them:** ... spoke forth unto them, –ASV ... addressed them in a loud voice, –WEYM ... raised his voice, –WUST ... and declared to them, –YNG ... and addressed them, –PHLP.

**Ye men of Judaea, and all ye that dwell at Jerusalem:** ... all you inhabitants of Jerusalem, –WEYM ... Jewish men and Jerusalem residents, –BRKL ... all men residing in Jerusalem, –FNTN.

**be this known to you:** ... let me tell you what this means, –TCNT ... understand this, –BECK.

**and hearken to my words:** ... pay attention, –NOLI ... and give ear unto my words, –RSV ... and mark my words, –TCNT ... and attend to what I say, –WEYM ... and give close attention to my words, –WLMS ... give ear to my declarations, –CNDT ... mark my assertions, –FNTN ... I will explain this to you, –ADAM ... take note of this, –NORL ... I will tell you something you need to know, –SEB.

**2:14.** When Peter and the 11 other apostles (including Matthias) stood, the whole crowd gave their attention to Peter (the 120 probably stopped speaking in other tongues). Still anointed by the Spirit, he raised his voice and proceeded to "utter forth" (*apephthenxato*) or speak out to them. The word used for this speaking is from the same verb used of the utterance in tongues in 2:4. It suggests that Peter spoke in his own language (Aramaic) as the Spirit gave utterance. In other words, what follows is not a sermon in the ordinary sense of the word. Certainly, Peter did not sit down and figure out three points. It seems likely this was a spontaneous manifestation of the gift of prophecy (1 Corinthians 12:10; 14:3).

Peter's address was directed to the Jewish men and the inhabitants of Jerusalem. This was a polite way to begin and followed their custom, but it does not rule out the women.

**15. For these are not drunken, as ye suppose:** ... You are wrong in thinking that these men are drunk, –TCNT ... as you imagine, –ADAM.

**seeing it is but the third hour of the day:** ... indeed it is only nine in the morning! –TCNT ... for it is still the middle of the forenoon, –KLGS.

**2:15.** Apparently, as the 120 were speaking in tongues, the mocking increased until most were mocking. Even some of those who understood the languages may have joined them. Peter drew no attention to the fact that some did understand. He answered only those who mocked.

The 120 were not drunk as the crowd supposed. Actually, even the sweet wine was not very strong.

In those days they had no way of distilling alcohol or fortifying drinks. Their strongest drinks were wine and beer, and they made it a practice to dilute wine with several parts of water. It would have taken a great deal to make them drunk that early in the morning. Also, they would not be drinking in a public place at that hour. Thus, the mockers were shown to be absurd.

16. **But this is that which was spoken by the prophet Joel:** ... On the contrary, —ADAM, —NOLI ... declared through, —CNDT ... spoken through, —BRKL ... this is something that the Prophet Joel foretold, —NORL ... Joel predicted, —MNTG.

**2:16.** Peter declared that what they had seen and heard was a fulfillment of Joel 2:28-32. The context in Joel goes on to deal with the coming judgment at the end of the age. But Joel, like the other Old Testament prophets, did not see the timespan between the first and second comings of Christ. Even Peter himself did not understand how long it would be. He did see, however, that the Messianic Age was coming and that the present fulfillment of Joel's prophecy would continue until then.

17. **And it shall come to pass:** ... And it shall be in the last days, —ASV ... It will occur in the last days, —WLMS ... In the days to come, —JB ... it shall come about, —KLGS.

**in the last days, saith God:** ... This is what God says, —NORL ... God declares, —NOLI.

**I will pour out of my Spirit upon all flesh:** ...abundantly bestow my Spirit, —WUST ... upon everyone a portion, —NEB ... all mankind, —NOLI, —TCNT ... all people, —BECK.

**and your sons and your daughters shall prophesy:** ... Then will, —NORL ... shall become Prophets, —TCNT ... will speak God's Word, —BECK ... shall speak forth by divine inspiration, —WUST ... preach, —FNTN.

**and your young men shall see visions:** ... your youths, —CNDT.

**and your old men shall dream dreams:** ... your elders, —CNDT ... will have special dreams, —NCV.

**2:17.** Peter made one apparent change in the prophecy. Under the inspiration of the Spirit he specified what the word "afterward" in Joel's prophecy means: *the outpouring* is "in the last days." Thus he recognized that the last days began with the ascension of Jesus (3:19-21). This evidences that the Holy Spirit recognizes the entire Church Age as the "last days."

The first part of the quotation from Joel had an obvious application to the 120. The many languages highlight God's purpose to pour out His Spirit on all flesh. In the Hebrew "all flesh" usually means "all mankind," as in Genesis 6:12.

The emphasis (verses 17, 18) is on the pouring out of the Spirit so those filled would prophesy.

In the Bible, to prophesy means to speak for God as His spokesman or "mouth." (Compare Exodus 4:15, 16; 7:2.) It does not necessarily mean to foretell the future.

"All flesh" is then broken down to sons and daughters. Concerning this outpouring of the Spirit there would be no distinction with regard to sex. This is another indication that all 120 were baptized in the Spirit, including the women.

Young men would see visions and old men dream dreams. No division with respect to age would exist. Nor does there seem to be any real distinction here between dreams and visions. The Bible often uses the words interchangeably. Here, at least, they are parallel. (See 10:17; 16:9, 10; and 18:9 for examples of visions.)

18. **And on my servants and on my handmaidens:** ... And even upon my men-servants and upon my maid-servants, —RTHM ... At that time I will give my Spirit even to, —EVRD ... Even on the servantsfor they are mineboth men and women, —TCNT ... Even on your servants, men and women alike, —NORL ... bondmen and ... bondwomen, —DRBY ... on my very slaves, —MOFT ... and my slave-girls, —WMCK

**I will pour out in those days of my Spirit:** ... At that time I will pour out My Spirit, —WEYM ... pour out a portion of, —NAB.

**and they shall prophesy:** ... And they will become prophets, —WLMS ... and they will prophesy also, —NOLI.

**2:18.** Even upon male and female slaves God would pour out His Spirit. Thus, the Spirit would pay no attention to social distinctions. Though there were probably no slaves among the 120, the Roman Empire had many areas where slaves comprised as high as 80 percent of the population. Fulfillment would come. The gospel has often reached the lower levels of society first.

19. **And I will shew wonders in heaven above:** ... I will display marvels in the sky above, —WEYM ... will work wonders, —NAB ... I will show miracles, —EVRD ... I will give you startling wonders in the sky above, —BECK ... strange things, —KLGS ... I will show amazing things, NCV, —SEB ... I will show portents, —NOLI.

**and signs in the earth beneath:** ... marvelous signs, —BECK ... prodigies, —MRDK ... and tokens in the erth benethe, —TNDL ... and miracles, —NOLI ... on the earth below, —TCNT.

**blood, and fire, and vapour of smoke:** ... mist of smoke, —TCNT ... cloud of smoke, —WEYM ... and thick smoke, —EVRD.

**2:19.** Many interpret verses 18 and 19 symbolically. Others suppose they were somehow fulfilled during the 3 hours of darkness while Jesus hung on the cross. It seems rather that the mention of the signs indicates the outpouring and the prophesying would continue until these signs come at the end of the age. Peter also meant that these signs can just as confidently be expected.

The gift of the Spirit can also be seen as the firstfruits of the age to come (Romans 8:23). The unregenerate human heart and mind has no conception of what God has prepared for those who love Him, but God "hath revealed them unto us by his Spirit" (1 Corinthians 2:9, 10). The believers' future inheritance is no mystery, for they have already experienced it, at least in a measure. As Hebrews 6:4, 5 points out, all who have tasted (really experienced) the heavenly gift and are made partakers of the Holy Spirit have already experienced the good word (promise) of God and the mighty powers (miracles) of the age to come.

Some also see in the fire and smoke a reference to the signs of God's presence at Mount Sinai (Exodus 19:16-18; 20:18), and view Pentecost as the giving of a new law or the renewing of the new covenant. However, as Hebrews 9:15-18, 26, 28 indicates, the death of Christ inaugurated the new covenant, and there was no need for anything further.

**20. The sun shall be turned into darkness:** ...shall be changed into darkness, —MOFT...be transformed to, —FNTN ... converted into darkness, —CNDT...turned dark, —BECK.

**and the moon into blood:** ...blood-red, —TCNT.

**before that great and notable day of the Lord come:** ... Before the day of the Lord come, That great and notable day, —ASV...the great and manifest day, —KLST, —RTHM ... To usher in the day of the LordThat great and illustrious day, —WEYM ... the great advent day, —CNDT ... Before that great and conspicuous Day of the Lord arrives, —BRKL ...splendid day, —BECK ...great and glorious, —NIV...obvious day, —AMPB.

**2:20.** The signs here also include blood and refer to the increasing bloodshed, wars, and smoke from wars that will cover the sun and make the moon appear red. These things will happen before "that great and notable (manifest) day of the Lord" comes. They are part of the present age.

The Day of the Lord in the Old Testament, in some contexts, spoke of God's judgment on Israel and Judah and of their being sent into exile to rid them of their idolatry. It also spoke of the judgment on nations God brought in due time, such as Assyria and Babylon. In other contexts the Day of the Lord spoke of end-time judgments on the nations of the world which the Book of Revelation places in the tribulation period. It also includes the restoration of Israel to the Promised Land and a spiritual restoration, as well as the establishment of the messianic kingdom.

**21. And it shall come to pass:** ...And it shall be, —RSV.

**that whosoever shall call on the name of the Lord:** ...every one who invokes, —TCNT...trusts in the name of the Lord, —SEB.

**shall be saved:** ...shall live, —MRDK.

**2:21.** This verse gives the purpose of the outpouring of the Holy Spirit. Through its empowering, the convicting work of the Spirit will be done in the world, not just in the end of the age but throughout the entire age right down to the great Day of the Lord. All during this period, whoever calls (for help for his need, that is, for salvation) on the name of the Lord will be saved. The Greek is strong, "all whoever." No matter what happens in the world or what forces oppose the Church, the door of salvation will remain open. Based upon this, believers can expect many to respond and be saved. There was a tremendous response in the First Century as the gospel was spread to all parts of the known world of that day. There have been periods of great revival from time to time since then. Now, as the end of the age approaches, even greater revival is evident in all parts of the world.

**22. Ye men of Israel:** ...Men of Israel, —TCNT.

**hear these words:** ...listen to this, —TCNT...listen to what I say, —WLMS.

**Jesus of Nazareth:**

**a man approved of God among you:** ...a Man pointed out of God unto you, —RTHM...a man whose mission from God was proved, —TCNT...a man accredited to you from God, —WEYM...a man attested to you by God, —RSV...a Man divinely accredited, —BRKL ... demonstrated to be from God, —CNDT...made known to you, —NORL...God showed you who the Man is, —BECK...a man chosen of God, —KLGS...celebrated among you, —WLSN...a very special man, —SEB ... God clearly showed this to you, —EVRD...whom God has revealed to you, —NOLI.

**by miracles and wonders and signs, which God did by him in the midst of you:** ...through him, —RTHM...was proved by miracles, —TCNT...by means of, —NORL...by powers, marvels, and evidences, —FNTN...right here among you, —WLMS...which God did among you through Him, —PNT.

**as ye yourselves also know:** ... as you personally know, —BRKL ...you yourselves know positively, —WUST.

**2:22.** The main body of Peter's message centers around Jesus, not the Holy Spirit. The outpouring on the Day of Pentecost was intended to bear powerful witness to Jesus (Acts 1:8; John 15:26; 16:14).

Peter first drew attention to the fact that the inhabitants of Jerusalem knew the "man" of Nazareth, Jesus. (*Nazareth* in Hebrew is derived from the word *branch*, Hebrew *nētser*, used in Isaiah

11:1 of the greater Son of David, the Messiah. *Nazarene,* Hebrew *nētseri,* can mean either "the man of Nazareth" or "the man of the branch," and thus identifies Jesus as the Messiah. Jeremiah 23:5; 33:15; Zechariah 3:8; 6:12 and other passages use related words to describe the Messiah as the righteous Branch, the new shoot that will arise from the stump of what was left of David's line and bring in the coming Kingdom.)

Peter's audience knew how God had approved Jesus for their benefit by miracles (mighty works, mighty manifestations of power), wonders, and signs. These are the three words used in the Bible for supernatural works. They refer to the variety of miracles Jesus did, and Peter had in mind especially the miracles Jesus did in the temple at the feast times when many in this crowd had undoubtedly been present (John 2:23; 4:45; 11:47).

**23. Him, being delivered by the determinate counsel and foreknowledge of God:** . . . in accordance with, *—WLMS* . . . by the settled purpose, *—NOYS* . . . by the settled counsel, *—HBIE* . . . resolute decision, *—FNTN* . . . in accordance with God's definite plan and with his previous knowledge, *—TCNT* . . . deliberate intention, *—JB* . . . God definitely planned and intended to have Him betrayed, *—BECK* . . . it was part of His plan, *—SEB* . . . by the predetermined plan, *—PHLP* . . . in the predestined course of God's deliberate purpose, *—MOFT.*

**ye have taken, and by wicked hands:** . . . Ye by the hand of lawless men, *—ASV* . . . with the help of heathen men, *—TCNT* . . . with lawless hands, *—CNDT* . . . and you used for your purpose men without the Law! *—PHLP.*

**have crucified and slain:** . . . . assassinate, *—CNDT* . . . nailed him to a cross and put him to death, *—TCNT.*

**2:23.** Peter next declared that the Jews in Jerusalem, by wicked hands (the hands of lawless men, men outside the Jewish law, that is, the Roman soldiers), crucified and slew (nailed up and slew) this Jesus. The Jerusalem Jews were responsible. But Peter also made it clear that Jesus was delivered up (given over) to them by the determinate counsel (the designated will) and foreknowledge of God. (Compare Luke 24:26, 27, 46.) If they had understood the prophets they would have known Messiah had to suffer. Peter did not intend, however, to lessen their guilt by saying this. Note that the Bible never puts this kind of responsibility on the Jews in general.

**24. Whom God hath raised up:** . . . But God has raised Him to life, *—WEYM* . . . resurrected Him, *—ADAM.*

**having loosed the pains of death:** . . . released him from the pangs, *—TCNT* . . . by unfastening the cords, *—BRKL* . . . having liberated from the grip, *—FNTN* . . . cords of the grave, *—MRDK* . . . putting an end to the agony, *—BECK.*

**because it was not possible that he should be holden of it:** . . . it being impossible for death to retain its hold upon Him, *—TCNT* . . . for him to be held fast by death, *—WEYM* . . . to be mastered by it, *—WUST* . . . to continue held fast under it, *—RTHM* . . . death could not possibly hold Him in its power, *—NORL.*

**2:24.** Peter quickly added that this Jesus is the One whom God raised up. The Resurrection took away the stigma of the cross, which was the Roman method of hanging criminals whom they considered enemies of society. It is hard for us to realize today how much shame there was in being crucified. As Hebrews 12:2 brings out, Jesus, as the Author (leader) and Finisher (perfecter) of our faith, for "the joy that was set before him, endured the cross," caring nothing for the shame, and He is now seated "at the right hand of the throne of God."

By the Resurrection also, God released Jesus from the pains (pangs) of death because it was not possible for Him to be held by it. *Pangs,* "pains," here usually means "birth pangs," so that the "death" here is perceived as labor. Just as labor pains are relieved by the birth of a child, so the Resurrection brought an end to the pangs of death.

Why was it not possible for Jesus to be held by death? Since the wages of sin is death (Romans 6:23), some say the reason death could not hold Him was because He had no sin of His own for death to claim Him. Hebrews 9:14 points out that Jesus, through His own eternal Spirit, offered himself without spot to God. He was in all points tempted (and tested) just as believers are, yet without sin (Hebrews 4:15). As the Lamb of God He was undefiled, without blemish and without spot (1 Peter 1:19; 2:22-24). Because He was righteous He was able to bear away our sins without being defiled himself (Romans 5:18; Hebrews 7:26). In 2 Corinthians 5:21, the Bible says God made Jesus to be sin for us, who knew no sin. But this does not mean He was made sinful or made a sinner. In fact, the Old Testament word for sin means both *sin* or a *sin offering,* depending on the context. The context in 2 Corinthians 5 is of reconciliation accomplished because He died for all and thus became a sin offering, literally, "instead of us." But He remained always the spotless Lamb of God.

**25. For David speaketh concerning him:** . . . in reference to Him, *—PNT*

**I foresaw the Lord always before my face:** . . . I beheld, *—ASV* . . . I have ever fixed my eyes upon the Lord, *—WEYM* . . . I always kept my eyes upon the Lord, *—WLMS.*

**for he is on my right hand, that I should not be moved:** ... may not be shaken, –*RTHM* ... not be disquieted, –*TCNT* ... need not be disturbed, –*NORL.*

**2:25.** Peter's reason for the fact that death could not hold Jesus, however, is that His resurrection was necessary in order to fulfill the prophetic Word of God. Under the inspiration of the Spirit Peter said David was speaking of Jesus in Psalm 16:8-11. Jewish tradition of the time also applied this to the Messiah. David foresaw the Lord before his face (present with him) and at his right hand to help, so that he would not be moved (so he would be established).

**26. Therefore did my heart rejoice:** ... my heart was glad, –*RSV* ... my heart was cheered, –*TCNT.*
**and my tongue was glad** rejoiced, –*ASV* ... exulted, –*RTHM* ... my tongue exults, –*CNDT* ... told its delight, –*TCNT* ... greatly rejoiced, *ABUV* ... is jubilant, –*BRKL* ... rejoiced exceedingly, –*WUST.*
**moreover also my flesh shall rest in my hope:** ... Yea further even my flesh shall encamp on hope, –*RTHM* ... And my body still lives in hope, –*WLMS* ... repose in hope, –*WLSN* ... shall dwell, –*ASV.*

**2:26.** God's presence caused David's heart to rejoice and his tongue to express gladness. His flesh also made God-given hope his rest, his tabernacle, his place of encampment.

**27. Because thou wilt not leave my soul in hell:** ... For thou wilt not abandon my soul to the Place of Death, –*TCNT* ... to the underworld, –*HBIE* ... to the nether world, *NAB* ... unto hades, *ASV.*
**neither wilt thou suffer thine Holy One to see corruption:** ... Nor give up Thy Holy One to undergo decay, –*WEYM* ... Your Loved One experience decay, –*BECK* ... your faithful servant to suffer death, –*NOLI* ... to undergo, *NAB* ... to see utter-corruption, –*RTHM* ... experience decay, –*WLMS.*

**2:27.** The central point of David's prophecy is the promise that God would not leave (abandon) His soul in hell (Greek, *hadēs*, the place of the afterlife, a translation of the Hebrew word *she'ôl*), and that He would not permit His Holy One to see corruption (putrefaction).

Some contend that the Old Testament does not reflect a belief in a resurrection of the dead. This passage from Psalm 16 seems to indicate otherwise as do the following: Daniel 12:2—"And many of them that sleep in the dust of the earth shall awake, some to everlasting life, and some to shame and everlasting contempt"; Job 19:25-27—"I know that my Redeemer lives ... Even after my skin is destroyed, Yet from my flesh I shall see God" (NASB); Psalm 17:15—"As for me, I will behold thy face in righteousness: I shall be satisfied, when I awake, with thy likeness." (See also Deuteronomy

32:39; 1 Samuel 2:6; Psalms 49:15; 73:24; and Isaiah 26:19 for passages that may point to an Old Testament teaching on resurrection.)

Everywhere else in the New Testament *Hades* refers to the place of punishment during the intermediate state between death and the final (Great White Throne) judgment. It, along with death, will be cast into the lake of fire (Revelation 20:14). That is, it will be fused with the lake of fire so that the lake of fire will then be the only place of death and punishment.

According to some scholars, the view that Hades was a place of punishment developed during the period between the Testaments. Until then the term *Hades* simply referred to the grave or to the underworld abode of the dead. This understanding, they say, is reflected in the Septuagint where *hades* is used to translate the Hebrew term *she'ôl*. If this is the case, Sheol is the place everyone went after they died. However, others hold that in the Old Testament *she'ôl* referred to the place where the wicked were punished after death. In this verse, the quotation taken from Psalm 16 does not seem to convey either theological conclusion; it simply says Death could not hold the Messiah.

**28. Thou hast made known to me the ways of life:** ... Thou hast shown me the path of life, –*TCNT.*
**thou shalt make me full of joy with thy countenance:** ... Thou wilt fill me with happiness in thy presence, –*TCNT* ... You will fill Me with joy by being with Me, –*BECK* ... fill me with gladness, –*WEYM* ... with delight, –*MOFT* ... with good cheer, –*BRKL* ... in your presence, –*NAB.*

**2:28.** "The ways of life" is best understood in terms of Proverbs 15:24 where the Hebrew reads: "The way of life is to the place above for the wise (the godly), that he may avoid Sheol beneath." For Christ they would speak of His resurrection and ascension to the right hand of the Father. There, the Father's countenance would be turned toward Him and make Him full of joy. (Compare Hebrews 12:2.)

**29. Men and brethren:** ... Brethren, –*ASV* ... Brothers, –*NAB.*
**let me freely speak unto you of the patriarch David:** ... I can speak to you confidently about, –*TCNT* ... I can tell you with confidence, –*ADAM* ... say to you with boldness, –*CNDT* ... I can tell you frankly, –*BECK* ... As to the patriarch David, I need hardly remind you, –*WEYM* ... our progenitor David, –*WUST.*
**that he is both dead and buried:** ... That he both died and was buried, –*ASV* ... that he is deceased also, –*CNDT* ... not only that he died, –*NORL.*
**and his sepulchre is with us unto this day:** ... his monument, –*DRBY* ... His tomb is known to us, –*NOLI* ... we still have his tomb among us, –*WEYM* ... His grave is still here with us today,

—*EVRD*...is in our midst to this day, —*NAB*...until the present time, —*FNTN*.

**2:29.** Peter declared it was proper for him to say boldly (freely and openly) of the patriarch (chief father, ancestral ruler) David that the psalm could not possibly apply to him. He not only died and was buried, his tomb was still there in Jerusalem. Obviously David's flesh did see corruption. But Jesus' did not. This clearly implies Jesus' tomb was empty.

There have been several suggestions concerning the precise location of David's tomb. Some place it in the town of Bethlehem, the place of David's birth. Others believe it was somewhere in the vicinity of Gethsemane. More likely the tomb was actually near Siloam. This conclusion is based upon a statement made in Nehemiah 3:16 concerning the work which was done in repairing the walls of Jerusalem: "After him Nehemiah the son of Azbuk . . . made repairs as far as a point opposite the tombs of David, and as far as the artificial pool and the house of the mighty men" (NASB). The artificial pool referred to in this verse is apparently the pool of Siloam which served as a major source of water for the city of Jerusalem. The Jewish historian Josephus reports that during the siege of Jerusalem (ca. 135 B.C.). John Hyrcanus, the high priest during the period of the Maccabees, robbed the tomb of David. About 100 years later King Herod made a similar attempt but was thwarted, supposedly through God's intervention (see *Wars of the Jews* 1.2.5; *Antiquities* 8.8.4; 16.7.1; cf. Bruce, *New International Commentary, Acts,* p. 66).

**30. Therefore being a prophet:** ...Speaking, then, as a Prophet, —*TCNT*...He was one who spoke for God, —*NLTG*...but he was a prophet, —*WMCK*

**and knowing that God had sworn with an oath to him:** ...had solemnly sworn to him, —*TCNT*, —*TNT*...sworn to him with an oath, —*NORL*.

**that of the fruit of his loins, according to the flesh:** ...that of the fruit of his loins, —*ASV*...of his body, —*WMCK*...From his family, —*NLTG*...to set one of his descendants, —*TCNT*.

**he would raise up Christ to sit on his throne:** ...Christ would come and take His place as King, —*NLTG*...he would set one upon his throne, —*ASV*...place one of his descendants, —*ADAM*...set (one) upon his throne, —*PNT*.

**2:30.** Because David was a prophet (a speaker for God), and because he knew God had sworn an oath that of the fruit of his loins One would sit on his throne, he foresaw and spoke of the resurrection of Christ (the Messiah, God's Anointed One). The reference here is to the Davidic covenant. In it God promised David there would always be a man from his seed for the throne. This was first given with respect to Solomon (2 Samuel 7:11-16). But it recognized that if David's descendants sinned they would have to be punished. God, however, would never turn His back on David's line and substitute another as He had done in the case of King Saul (Psalms 89:3, 4; 132:11, 12).

Because the kings of David's line did not follow the Lord, God finally had to bring an end to their kingdom and send the people to Babylon. His purpose was to rid Israel of idolatry. But the promise to David still stood. There would yet be One to sit on David's throne and make it eternal.

**31. He seeing this before:** ...he foreseeing this, —*ASV*...David looked into the future, —*TCNT*...with prophetic foresight he spoke of, —*WEYM*...David saw what was ahead, —*BECK*...knew this before it happened, —*EVRD*, —*NCV*...thus proclaiming beforehand, —*NAB*...with a prevision, —*MOFT*.

**spake of the resurrection of Christ:** ...and was referring to, —*TCNT*...the resurrection of the Messiah, —*NAB*...and said the promised Saviour would rise again, —*BECK*.

**that his soul was not left in hell:** ...that he had not been abandoned to the Place of Death, —*TCNT*...abandoned in the unseen, —*CNDT*...to the underworld, —*NOYS*...to the effect that He was not left forsaken in the grave, —*WEYM*...He was not deserted when He was dead, —*BECK*...abandoned to the realm of the dead, —*BRKL*...neither was He left...in the unseen world reserved for the human dead, —*WUST*...was not deserted in death, —*PHLP*...was not abandoned to the nether world, —*NAB*.

**neither his flesh did see corruption:** ...nor did His body undergo decay, —*WEYM*...did not experience decay, —*BECK*...nor was His flesh acquainted with decay, —*CNDT*...his body was never destroyed, —*PHLP*...did not rot, —*EVRD*...his flesh was not allowed to suffer death, —*NOLI*.

**2:31.** Peter did not give any details of Christ's descent into Hades. The notion that Jesus spent the 3 days following His crucifixion leading the righteous dead out of paradise and snatching the keys of Hades and Death from Satan is not supported by the Scriptures. Speculation about this goes beyond what the Scripture teaches. Instead, Peter declared that what David foresaw in the psalm was the resurrection of Christ (literally, the Christ, that is, the Messiah, God's Anointed Prophet, Priest, and King). In other words, Peter declared Jesus to be the messianic King. Because God raised Him up, He was not left in Hades, nor did His flesh see corruption.

**32. This Jesus hath God raised up:** ...It was this Jesus, whom God raised to life, –TCNT...Jesus is this one, –NLTG.

**whereof we all are witnesses:** ...and of that fact we are ourselves all witnesses, –TCNT ... a fact to which all of us testify, –WEYM...and we have all seen Him, –NLTG.

**2:32.** Again Peter emphasized that God is the One who raised up Jesus from the dead. He and all of the 120 who were gathered in the Upper Room were witnesses to His resurrection. First Corinthians 15:6 states that having appeared to Peter and then to the Twelve, Jesus also was seen by more than 500 men and women. It is reasonable to surmise that some or all of those now gathered for prayer were among the 500 who had seen the resurrected Christ.

This was important. The elders of the Sanhedrin knew the tomb of Jesus was empty, and the soldiers who were set to watch it told them of the angel who rolled back the stone. But they spread the story that the disciples came by night and stole the body while the guard slept. Peter made no reference to this story, but the crowd had undoubtedly heard it. Actually, it was ridiculous to believe that a Roman guard or even temple guards would sleep on duty and that the Roman seal could have been broken by disciples who had fled when Jesus was arrested. Now the people were faced, not by a few fearful disciples, but by 120 who were firsthand witnesses to the fact of Christ's resurrection, and who were filled with power through the baptism in the Holy Spirit.

**33. Therefore being by the right hand of God exalted:** ...So then, now that he has been exalted to the right hand of God, –TCNT ...when He was exalted, –ADAM...Being therefore lifted high by the right hand of God, –WEYM ... Since he is by the mighty hand of God exalted, –MNTG ... Lifted up to God's right side, –BECK.

**and having received of the Father:** ...and, as promised, –NORL.

**the promise of the Holy Ghost:** ...the promised gift of the Holy Spirit, –TCNT...that Spirit, –EVRD.

**he hath shed forth this:** ...He hath poured forth this, –ASV...He was pouring forth this, –WORL...flows from him, –NEB ... So now Jesus has poured out, –EVRD ... this Spirit, –CNFT...which he poured out as you see, –NOLI.

**which ye now see and hear:** ...This is what you, –EVRD...you are observing, –CNDT...as you now see and hear for yourselves, –TCNT.

**2:33.** Christ's resurrection, however, was only part of a process whereby God, by His right hand of power, raised Jesus to an exalted position of power and authority at His right hand. (Both *by* and *at* His right hand are indicated in the Greek.) This is also the place of triumph and victory. By paying the full price, Jesus won the battle against sin and death. He remains at God's right hand. (See Mark 16:9; Romans 8:34; Ephesians 1:20, 21; Colossians 3:1; Hebrews 1:3; 8:1; 10:12; 12:2; 1 Peter 3:22.)

In Christ, believers also are seated "in heavenly places" (Ephesians 2:6). Because this is their position in Christ, they do not need their own works of righteousness to claim His promise. There can be no higher position than they already have in Christ.

Next Peter used Christ's exalted position to explain what had just occurred. Now at the Father's right hand, He had received from the Father the Promise of the Spirit and poured out the Spirit, as the crowd had seen and heard as the 120 spoke in other tongues. The outpouring of the Spirit was *evidence* that Jesus was actually exalted at the Father's right hand.

Before His death Jesus told the Twelve that it was necessary for Him to go away in order for the Comforter to come (John 16:7). Though the baptism in the Spirit is the Promise of the Father, Jesus is the One who pours it forth. God is the Giver; Jesus, the Baptizer. There is clear distinction between the Persons of the Trinity here.

**34. For David is not ascended into the heavens:** ...For it was not David who went up into Heaven, –TCNT...did not go up into heaven, –WMCK.

**but he saith himself:** ...Indeed he says himself, –TCNT.

**The LORD said unto my Lord:** ...The Lord said to my master, –TCNT.

**Sit thou on my right hand:** ...Sit at my right hand. –WEYM.

**35. Until I make thy foes thy footstool:** ...Till I put thy enemies as a footstool under thy feet, –TCNT...for those who hate You will be a place to rest Your feet, –NLTG...put your enemies under your control, –EVRD, –NCV ... the footstool of your feet, –WLMS...underneath thy feet, –WLSN.

**2:34, 35.** That none of this could apply to David is further evidenced by another quotation from Scripture. David did not ascend into the heavens as Jesus did, but he prophesied that exaltation of Jesus in Psalm 110:1. Again, David could not be speaking of himself for he said, "The Lord said unto my Lord, Sit thou at my right hand, until I make thine enemies thy footstool." Making enemies a footstool signified complete and final defeat, a total triumph over them. (See Joshua 10:24 where Joshua had his generals put their feet on the necks of the conquered kings.) Jesus also referred to Psalm 110:1 in Luke 20:41-44 where He recognized that David called his greater Son "Lord." (See also Matthew 22:42-45; Mark 12:36, 37.)

The resurrection and ascension of Jesus are inseparably linked. Though they were separated by 40 days, they are both important elements of the redemption act. (Hebrews 9:12, 24 also emphasizes that Christ's entrance into heaven was necessary for the completion of the believer's redemption.) Jesus was not simply raised from the dead, He was raised to the right hand of the Father where He is now exalted. In John 17:5 Jesus prayed that the Father would glorify Him with His own self, with the glory which He had before the world was brought into being. This was accomplished when Jesus rose and ascended to the place of authority in heaven which is His by right of His eternal sonship.

36. **Therefore let all the house of Israel know assuredly:** . . . the whole nation . . . must understand, —GDSP . . . So let all Israel know beyond all doubt, —TCNT . . . Without a shadow of doubt, then, let the whole house of Israel acknowledge, —BRKL . . . The whole Jewish nation must know for sure, —NLTG . . . certainly know, —WLSN . . . should know this truly, —EVRD, —NCV . . . safely know, —SWAN.

**that God hath made that same Jesus, whom ye have crucified both Lord and Christ:** . . . that God has declared, —GDSP . . . that God has made him both Master and Christ this very Jesus whom you crucified, —TCNT . . . and Messiah, —NAB . . . He is the man you nailed to the cross! —EVRD.

**2:36.** The conclusion Peter drew is that all the house of Israel needed to know assuredly that God has made this Jesus, whom they (the Jerusalem residents) crucified, both Lord and Christ (Messiah, God's anointed Prophet, Priest, and King).

In fulfillment of Joel's prophecy, Jesus is the Lord on whom all must call for salvation. Paul also recognized that God has highly exalted Him and given Him a name that is above every other name (Philippians 2:9). *The Name* in the Old Testament Hebrew always means the name of God. (The Hebrew has other ways of referring to the name of a human being without using the word *the*, so whenever the Hebrew uses *the* with the word *name* it refers to the name of God.) *The Name* stands for the authority, person, and especially the character of God in His righteousness, holiness, faithfulness, goodness, love, and power. *Lord* was used in the New Testament for the name of God. Mercy, grace, and love are part of the holiness, the holy Name by which Jesus is recognized as "Lord," the full revelation of God to man.

37. **Now when they heard this, they were pricked in their heart:** . . . As they were listening, —MLNT . . . heard this statement, they were deeply moved, —NOLI . . . it went straight to their hearts, —MOFT . . . stabbed to the heart, —WLMS . . . moved to the depths of their hearts, —BRKL . . . cut to the heart, —RSV, —TNT . . . they felt crushed, —BECK . . . their heart was pricked with compunction, —CNDT . . . they were deeply shaken, —NAB . . . stung to the heart, —GDSP, —WUST . . . their consciences pricked them, —TCNT . . . their hearts were troubled, —NLTG, —NORL . . . pierced to the heart, —CNFT, —HNSN . . . felt a sharp, cutting pain in their conscience, —SEB . . . they were sick at heart, —EVRD.

**and said unto Peter and to the rest of the apostles:** . . . They asked Peter and the other apostles, —BECK . . . and to the other missionaries, —NLTG.

**Men and brethren, what shall we do?:** . . . What are we to do, Brothers, —TCNT . . . Fellow Jews, what should we do, —BECK.

**2:37.** The response to this manifestation of the gift of prophecy was immediate. The listeners were pierced to the heart. No longer were they saying, "What does this mean?" Peter's words from the Holy Spirit stung their consciences. They cried out to him and to the other apostles (who were evidently still standing with him), "Brothers, what shall we do?"

They did not feel completely cut off, however. Peter had called them brothers, and they responded by calling the apostles brothers. Their sin in rejecting and crucifying Christ was great, but their very cry shows they believed there was hope.

38. **Then Peter said unto them, Repent:** . . . Each one of you must turn from sin, return to God, —TALR . . . change your minds, —FNTN . . . Get a new mind, —KLGS . . . Amend your lives, —GNVA.

**and be baptized every one of you in the name of Jesus Christ:** . . . and, as an expression of it, let every one, —WLMS . . . and be immersed, ABUV . . . for the pardon of your sins, —CNDT . . . on the basis of the name of Jesus Christ, —ADAM . . . in reliance on the name, —HBIE.

**for the remission of sins:** . . . that you may have your sins forgiven, —WLMS . . . for a release, —FNTN . . . for the forgiveness of your sins, —TCNT.

**and ye shall receive the gift of the Holy Ghost:** . . . you will be given the Holy Spirit, —BECK . . . the gratuity of, —CNDT . . . the free-gift of the Holy Spirit, —RTHM.

**2:38.** Peter answered by calling them to repent, that is, to change their minds and fundamental attitudes by accepting the change required. This would produce a renewing of their minds as well as a change in attitude toward sin and self.

The repentant ones could show that change of mind and heart by being baptized in the name of Jesus. A survey of New Testament passages discussing water baptism for believers reveals it is described in various ways. In verse 38 the phrase *"in* the name of Jesus Christ" employs the preposition *epi* with the dative case. Matthew 28:19 reads *"in* the name of the Father, and of the Son, and of the Holy Ghost" and uses the preposition *eis* ("in, into") along with the Trinitarian confession. Acts 8:16 and 19:5 use the phrase "in (*eis*) the name of the Lord Jesus" while 10:48 shows "in (*en*) the name of the Lord" (KJV) or "in the name of Jesus Christ" (NIV), depending on the Greek manuscripts being followed. (Modern versions translate the Greek differently either in an attempt to clarify what is meant or because the manuscripts which serve as a basis for the translation show numerous variants at these passages.) The various Greek prepositions which are used do not greatly change the meaning of the phrase "in the name of Jesus." It may be understood to mean upon the authority of Jesus. (For similar uses of this phrase in Luke's writings see Luke 9:49; 10:17; Acts 3:6, 16; 4:7; 9:27.)

This baptism would also be for (*eis*) the forgiveness of sins. *Eis* here means "because of" or "with a view toward" just as it does in Matthew 3:11 where John baptized "because of" repentance. John baptized no one to produce repentance. Rather, he demanded works demonstrating true repentance.

**39. For the promise is unto you, and to your children:** ... For the promise is for you, *–TCNT* ... this great promise, *–PHLP* ... For to you belongs the promise, *–WEYM* ... What is promised belongs to you, *–BECK* ... the promise is meant for you, *–MOFT.*

**and to all that are afar off:** ... all who are far away, *–BECK.*

**even as many as the Lord our God shall call:** ... as many as the Lord our God invites and bids come to Himself, *–AMPB* ... shall call unto him, *–ASV* ... every one whom the Lord our God calls to him, *–RSV* ... with a divine summons call to himself, *–WUST* ... our God may call unto him, *–RTHM* ... shall call to himself! *–PHLP* ... those who may be marked out, *–BB.*

**2:39.** Peter identified the gift with the Promise (1:4). This promise, or "gift of the Holy Ghost," was not limited to the 120. It would continue to be available, not only to the 3,000 who responded, but to their children (including all their descendants), and to all who were far away, even to as many as the Lord should call to himself. In verse 38 Peter said that in order to receive the Promise of the Father a person must "repent, and be baptized . . . in the name of Jesus Christ."

The "calling" here may refer to Joel 2:32, but it cannot be limited to the Jews. In Isaiah 57:19 God speaks peace to the one far off. Ephesians 2:17 applies this to the Gentiles. Acts 1:8 speaks of the uttermost part of the earth. It is clear that the promise of the Spirit is for the Gentiles also.

**40. And with many other words did he testify and exhort, saying:** ... In many other ways Peter bore his testimony, and urged the people, *–TCNT* ... And with many different words bare he full witness, and went on exhorting them saying, *–RTHM* ... more appeals he solemnly warned and entreated them, saying, *–WEYM* ... With many more words he continued to testify and to plead with them, *–WLMS* ... using many arguments, *–JB* ... with emphasis on the plea, *–NORL.*

**Save yourselves from this untoward generation:** ... Be saved from this perverse age, *–TCNT* ... this crooked generation, *–ASV* ... this pointless generation, *–KLGS* ... the punishment coming on this wicked people! *–TEV.*

**2:40.** Luke did not record the rest of Peter's witness and exhortation. But in this exhortation Peter was evidently exercising another of the gifts of the Spirit. (Romans 12:8 lists exhortation as a distinct gift of the Holy Spirit, though 1 Corinthians 14:3 includes it as part of the gift of prophecy. The Bible does not draw hard and fast lines between gifts.) Thus, Peter became the instrument or agent through whom the Holy Spirit carried out the work foretold by Jesus in John 16:8, for there was indeed conviction with respect to sin, righteousness, and judgment to come.

The essence of Peter's exhortation was that they should save themselves (the Greek is better translated "be saved") from this "untoward" (perverse, crooked) generation. That is, they should turn away from the perversity and corruptness of those around them who were rejecting the truth about Jesus. (Compare Luke 9:41; 11:29; 17:25. In these passages Jesus is disturbed by the unbelief, perversity, and evil of that generation, and He knew He must endure many things from them and be rejected by them.)

**41. Then they that gladly received his word were baptized:** ... Those therefore, who joyfully welcomed his word, *–WEYM* ... Then those, who welcomed his message, *–BRKL* ... They were convinced ... and they accepted, *–JB* ... readily received his discourse, *–MRDK.*

**and the same day there were added unto them about three thousand souls:** ... and about three thousand joined the disciples on that day alone, *–TCNT.*

**2:41.** Those who received (welcomed) Peter's message then testified to their faith by being baptized in water. The Bible shows baptism was an important element in the conversion experiences of the Early Church.

Though Luke did not mention it, it seems certain all the 3,000 who were added to the Church received the Promise of the Father, as Peter had said they would.

**42. And they continued stedfastly:** ... And they went on to give constant attention, –RTHM ... They were regularly present, –TCNT ... and they were constant in attendance, –WEYM ... They were loyal, –BECK ... firmly adhering to, –RTHM ... they persevered, –ADAM ... constantly attending, –HBIE ... kept their attention fixed, –BB.

**in the apostles' doctrine and fellowship:** ... to the instruction, –MOFT ... at the teaching of the Apostles and at the sharing of the offerings, –TCNT ... to the teaching of the apostles and to fellowship with one another, –WLMS ... the teaching and companionship of the apostles, –SAWR.

**and in breaking of bread, and in prayers:** ... eating the supper of the Lord, –SEB ... were associated together in prayer, –MRDK.

**2:42.** By the Spirit they also were baptized into the body of Christ (1 Corinthians 12:13). God never saves a person and then lets him wander off by himself. Thus, the 3,000 did not scatter but remained together, continuing steadfastly in the apostles' doctrine (teaching) and fellowship, and in the breaking of bread and prayers.

A further evidence of their faith was this persistent desire for teaching. Their acceptance of Christ and the gift of the Spirit opened up to them a whole new understanding of God's plan and purpose. With joy, they became hungry to learn more. This shows also that the apostles were obeying Jesus and teaching (making disciples) as He had commanded them (Matthew 28:19). It also shows that discipleship includes this kind of eager desire to learn more of Jesus and God's Word.

Fellowship was experienced in the teaching. It was more than just getting together. It was partnership in the ministry of the Church, sharing the message and the work. As in 1 John 1:3, the Word, as witnessed by the teaching of the apostles, brought this fellowship, one that was also with the Father and with the Son.

Some take the breaking of bread to be the Lord's Supper, but it also included table fellowship. They could not observe the Lord's Supper in the temple, so this was done in homes, at first in connection with a meal (since Jesus instituted it at the close of the Passover meal).

Their prayers also included daily gathering in the temple at the hours of prayer, which they still continued, plus prayer meetings in the homes.

**43. And fear came upon every soul:** ... A deep impression was made upon every one, –TCNT ... Awe came upon everyone, –WEYM ... A sense of reverence seized everyone, –WLMS ... a reverential fear, –WUST ... a sense of awe came over everybody, –ADAM.

**and many wonders and signs were done by the apostles:** ... and many wonders and signs through means of the apostles were coming to pass,
–RTHM ... and many marvels ... were wrought by the Apostles, –WEYM.

**2:43.** The continuing witness of the apostles to the resurrection of Jesus brought a reverential fear on every soul (every person) who heard. Their "fear" included a sense of awe in the presence of the supernatural. The word "soul" is used here in the Old Testament sense where it often means "person" (Genesis 46:26).

This reverential fear was further enhanced by the many wonders and signs done by the apostles, that is, done by God through the apostles. (The Greek *dia* here is used of secondary agency; hence, God really did the work.) The apostles were God's instruments, His agents. As Paul indicated in 1 Corinthians 3:6, Paul planted, and Apollos watered, but all the while Paul was planting and Apollos was watering, God was giving the increase.

Later God gave miracles through many others, including ordinary disciples who had no office. But here God was using the apostles to train all the believers so they could all do a work of ministry or service. (See Ephesians 4:8, 11-16 where those taken captive by Christ were given to the Church to train the saints to do the work of ministry.)

The apostles were the primary witnesses to the teaching of Jesus, which they had received from Him personally. They had the background of His commission and His encouragement to their faith. These miracles were not for, display, but rather were to confirm the Word, the teaching, as Jesus promised (Mark 16:20). The miracles also helped to establish the faith of the new believers.

**44. And all that believed were together:** ... All who had become believers in Christ, –TCNT ... And all the believers kept together, –WEYM ... The believers all met together, –BRKL ... All the believers lived together, –NORL.

**and had all things common:** ... had everything jointly, –BRKL ... agreed in having everything in common, –TCNT ... formed an organized community, –FNTN ... and held all they had as common goods to be shared by one another, –WLMS ... had a common treasury, –KLGS.

**45. And sold their possessions and goods, and parted them to all men, as every man had need:** ... And so they continued to sell their property and goods and to distribute the money to all, –WLMS ... sold their possessions and belongings, –KLGS ... shared them with all, –ADAM ... to anyone as he needed it, –BECK ... as anyone might have need, –DRBY.

**2:44, 45.** The believers remained together and had things common; that is, they shared with one another what they had. From time to time many sold pieces of land they owned and personal property as well. The money was distributed (by the apostles) to those who had need. The words "as every man had need" is a key statement. They did not sell property until there was a need.

This was not communism in the modern sense. Neither was it communal living. It was just Christian sharing. They all realized the importance of becoming established in the apostles' teaching (which today is the written New Testament). Some of those from outside Jerusalem soon ran out of money, so those who were able simply sold what they could to make it possible for these Christians to remain nearby. Later Peter made it clear that no one was under any compulsion to sell anything or give anything (5:4). But the fellowship, joy, love, and the example and teachings of Jesus made it easy for the believers to share what they had.

**46. And they, continuing daily with one accord in the temple:** . . . Every day, too, they met regularly in the Temple Courts, –TCNT . . . Daily they regularly frequented the temple with a united purpose, –BRKL . . . All were one at heart as they went to the temple regularly every day, –BECK . . . regularly attended, –WLMS . . . in harmony, –FNTN . . . in unity of spirit, –ADAM.

**and breaking bread from house to house:** . . . they practiced breaking their bread together in their homes, –WLMS . . . They had their meals in their homes, –BECK.

**did eat their meat with gladness and singleness of heart:** . . . they were partaking of food with exultation, –RTHM . . . combined with humility, –FNTN . . . partaking of their food in simple-hearted gladness, –TCNT . . . they took their meals with great happiness and single-heartedness, –WEYM . . . with joy and simplicity of heart, –CMPB . . . partook of nourishment with exultation and simplicity, –CNDT . . . shared their food gladly and generously, –JB . . . with happy and unruffled hearts, –BRKL . . . with joyful and generous hearts, –KLGS.

**2:46.** The picture then is of a loving body of believers meeting daily in the temple with one accord, one mind, one purpose, and sharing table fellowship in their homes. ("From house to house" means by households.) Each home became a center of Christian fellowship and worship. Mark's mother's home was one such center. Probably the home of Mary and Martha in Bethany was another. Jerusalem was not able to hold such a multitude, and many certainly stayed in surrounding villages.

The table fellowship was very important. They took their food with rejoicing (delight and great joy) and with simplicity of heart. There was no jealousy, no criticism.

**47. Praising God, and having favour with all the people:** . . . They praised God, and all the people liked them, –EVRD . . . continually praising God, and

winning respect from all the people, –TCNT . . . and enjoying the good will of all the people, –BRKL . . . stood in favor, –NORL . . . They praised God continually, –PHLP . . . praised God constantly . . . won the favor of, –NOLI . . . and approved by all the people, –WMCK

**And the Lord added to the church daily such as should be saved:** . . . to them day by day those that were saved, –ASV . . . Also day by day the Lord added to their number those whom He was saving, –WEYM . . . And every day the Lord continued to add to them the people who were being saved, –WLMS . . . while daily the group who were being saved, –BRKL . . . added daily to the assembly, –MRDK . . . multiplied every day, –NOLI . . . to the congregation, –WLSN . . . those who were in the path of Salvation, –TCNT . . . who were getting saved, –ADAM . . . those who were saved, –WSLY.

**2:47.** The joy in the hearts of believers kept them praising God. Their praise found expression also in psalms (the word includes musical accompaniment especially on stringed instruments), hymns, and spiritual songs coming from their hearts (Colossians 3:16).

The result was that they found favor with the whole of the people of Jerusalem. At this point there was no opposition, no persecution. The common people who had not yet accepted Christ saw the believers' worship, their good works, and their joy, and were attracted by what they saw. Thus the Lord kept adding (together, to the Church) day by day those who were being saved. Certainly, the Church accepted the new believers joyfully into their fellowship and brought them under the teaching of the apostles.

The phrase "were being saved" does not suggest that salvation is a progressive experience. Rather, the Greek is a simple statement that every day some were being saved and the saved ones were added to the Church. Notice too that no high pressure methods were used to persuade others to come and join. The people saw the joy and the power, and they opened their hearts to the truth about Jesus.

## Chapter 3

**1. Now Peter and John went up together into the temple:** . . . One day Peter and John went to, –EVRD.

**at the hour of prayer, being the ninth hour:** . . . during the time of the three o'clock Prayers, –TCNT . . . at three in the afternoon, –BECK . . . in the middle of the afternoon, –KLGS.

**3:1.** Luke often made a general statement and then gave a specific example. Acts 2:43 states that many wonders and signs were done through the apostles. Luke then proceeded to give one example to illustrate this.

On this occasion Peter and John were going up the temple hill into the temple to join the others for the hour of evening prayer, "the ninth hour" (about 3 p.m.). Sacrifice and incense were being offered by the priests at the same time.

Peter, James, and John constituted the inner circle of Jesus' disciples during much of His ministry. Yet James and John had asked Jesus for the chief places in His coming kingdom, and this had excited the jealousy of others, including Peter. But all that was in the past. In many ways Peter and John were opposites. But now they were going into the temple together. This was part of the new unity brought about by Christ's commission and by the Holy Spirit. Together, in one accord, they were going up to worship God and exalt the name of Jesus.

Between the Court of the Gentiles and the Court of the Women was a Corinthian-style, bronze gate with beautifully carved gold and silver inlays. It was worth more than if it had been made of solid gold. (The Court of the Gentiles was as far as Gentiles were allowed to go. The Court of the Women was as far as the women were allowed to go. Pharisees had long used the Court of the Women to gather both men and women for their teaching sessions. So it was the best place for the Church to gather also.)

2. **And a certain man lame from his mother's womb was carried:** ... and, just then, some men were carrying there one who had been lame from his birth, *–WEYM* ... whose lameness was due to prenatal causes, *–WUST* ... who had been crippled all his life, *–EVRD* ... been a cripple from his birth, *–BECK* ... had had no power in his legs, *–BB.*

**whom they laid daily at the gate of the temple which is called Beautiful:** ... those accustomed to bring, *–MRDK* ... The man used to be set down every day ... of the Temple called the Beautiful Gate, *–TCNT* ... placed daily at the entrance, *–NOLI* ... at the door, *–ASV.*

**to ask alms of them that entered into the temple:** ... to beg from the people as they went in, *–WEYM* ... so he could beg the people for gifts as they went, *–BECK* ... to ask a kindness, *–YNG* ... to beg for money, *–WMCK* ... from those who entered the sanctuary, *–NOLI* ... from the people on their way in, *–GDSP.*

**3:2.** At this Beautiful Gate, Peter and John were confronted by a man, lame from birth, who daily was carried and laid outside it to ask alms (gifts of charity). The man was over 40 years old (4:22). Jesus had passed this way many times, but apparently the man had never asked Him for healing. Possibly Jesus, in divine providence and timing, left this man so he could become a greater witness when he was healed later.

3. **Who seeing Peter and John about to go into the temple asked an alms:** ... on their way into, *–NOLI* ... on the point of going, *–GDSP* ... was requesting to receive an alms, *–RTHM* ... asked them for money, *–EVRD* ... he kept asking them for alms, *–MNTG.*

**3:3.** When this man who was born lame saw Peter and John about to enter the temple, he asked them for a gift of charity. Giving to the poor and disabled was encouraged by the Law and was considered by the Jews an important way to please God. This man did not seem to recognize Peter and John. After spending his days at the temple gate begging, he was then carried by friends or relatives back to some lonely room. If he had heard about what was going on in Jerusalem or of the miracles done through the apostles, he did not seem to have any idea that this could affect him.

4. **And Peter, fastening his eyes upon him with John:** ... But Peter directed his gaze at him, *–RSV* ... But Peter looking steadfastly at him, *–RTHM* ... Peter fixing his eyes on him, as did John also, *–WEYM* ... looked straight at him, *–EVRD* ... Peter looked him straight in the eye, and so did John, *–WLMS* ... with a piercing gaze, *–WUST* ... Peter, as well as John, looked intently at him, *–NORL.*

**said, Look on us:** ... Look at us, *–WMCK*, *–GDSP.*

**3:4.** When this man asked to receive a gift of money, Peter, together with John, fastened his eyes on him. What a tremendous contrast to the jealousy that once characterized the disciples (Matthew 20:24). Now they worked in complete unity of faith and purpose. As the spokesman Peter said, "Look on us."

It may seem strange that Peter and John called attention to themselves. But this man, like so many beggars, must have been lying there listlessly with a rather pitiable, hopeless expression on his face. Daily as the crowds passed by, he probably paid no attention to who they were or what they said to him. His only concern was the few coins that were dropped into his hand. Peter and John needed to get his attention. They needed to raise his expectation. Expectation is at least a step toward faith.

5. **And he gave heed unto them:** ... The man gave them his attention, *–TCNT* ... He looked at them attentively, *–NOLI* ... So he looked and waited, *–WEYM* ... So he watched them closely, *–BRKL* ... attended to them, *–CNDT.*

**expecting to receive something of them:** ... supposing that they were going to give him something, *–GDSP* ... he thought they were going to give him some money, *–EVRD.*

**3:5.** Peter's words did catch the man's attention, and he did in fact rivet his full attention on them.

They also aroused an expectation that he would receive something. Probably he expected money. But money is not always the thing people really need. In fact, this man did not know what he really needed. Since he was born lame, he had never known what it was to walk. If his parents had taken him to physicians, both they and he had long ago given up any hope that he would ever walk.

**6. Then Peter said, Silver and gold have I none:** ... I do not possess, −CNDT ... I possess none, −FNTN ... I don't have any, −EVRD.
**but such as I have give I thee:** ... I'll give you what I have, −BECK.
**In the name of Jesus Christ of Nazareth rise up and walk:** ... By the power of Jesus Christ, −EVRD ... walk, −CNDT ... start walking and keep on walking, −WUST ... be walking about, −RTHM.

**3:6.** Peter, however, did not do the expected. What money he possessed had probably already been given to needy believers. But he did have something better to give. His statement, "Silver and gold have I none; but such as I have give I thee," took faith on Peter's part. Then Peter gave the positive command, "In the name (and by the authority) of Jesus Christ of Nazareth rise up and walk."

**7. And he took him by the right hand, and lifted him up:** ... And gripping him, −MLNT ... And laying hold of him by the right hand he raised him up, −RTHM ... having seized him by the right hand, −YNG ... Grasping the lame man ... Peter lifted him up, −TCNT ... and pulled him up, −NAB.
**and immediately his feet and ankle bones received strength:** ... and instantly were his feet and ankles strengthened, −RTHM ... his feet and the bones in his legs became strong, −NLTG ... Instantly his feet and ankles grew firm, −BRKL, −MLNT ... insteps and ankles were given stability, −CNDT ... and ankles became strong, −EVRD ... and he positively jumped, −PHLP ... immediately became strong, −GDSP ... instantly grew strong, −WLMS.

**3:7.** As Peter spoke these words, he put his own faith into action by taking hold of the man's right hand and, with a firm grip, lifted him up. This must have encouraged the man to exercise faith as well. An atmosphere of faith does help encourage faith in others, and it is certain these apostles exuded an atmosphere of positive faith wherever they went. They had seen Jesus. They had experienced God's power. They knew what Jesus could do.

At the very moment Peter took hold of the man's hand, strength went into the man's feet and ankle bones, and the wobbly ankles were made firm. It is quite possible also that the man's faith was stirred by the mention of the Messiah, Jesus of Nazareth. It may be that some of the 3,000 saved at Pentecost

had witnessed to him. He had heard perhaps of others healed by Jesus, and he may have wondered why Jesus passed him by. But now, even though up to this point he had felt hopeless, the positive faith and the positive action of Peter brought the healing power of God into his body.

**8. And he leaping up stood, and walked:** ... he stood erect, −KLST ... and leaping forward he stood, −RTHM ... he staggered, −FNTN ... jumped up on his feet, −NLTG ... and jumping up, he began to walk about, −TCNT ... He jumped up, stood on his feet, and began to walk, −EVRD ... springing, −YNG ... at once he leaped to his feet, −WLMS ... stood for a moment, then began to walk around, −NAB ... And he sprange, stode and also walked, −TNDL.
**and entered with them into the temple:** ... and then went with them into the Temple Courts, −TCNT ... went into the house of God with them, −NLTG.
**walking, and leaping, and praising God:** ... walking, jumping, and praising God, −TCNT ... jumping about, −NAB ... and laude God, −TNDL ... He gave thanks to God as he walked, −NLTG.

**3:8.** As strength flowed into his feet and ankles, Peter no longer had to lift the man. He jumped to his feet, stood for a moment, and then began to walk for the first time in his entire life.

Now that the man was healed he could go into the temple. Since he had been laid outside the gate every day for all those years, it is probable that he had never been through the gate before. Now he went into the temple walking normally, not limping, not stumbling, but joyfully erect. Every few steps he would leap for pure joy and excitement. All the while he was shouting the praises of God.

As verse 11 indicates, the man still held on to Peter's hand and had taken a firm hold on John's hand as well. This was not to help hold himself up. It was rather in a joyful sense of fellowship with them. In his new, God-given strength he was taking the lead. What a scene this must have been as the man came walking and jumping in the temple court where crowds of the Jews were gathered for prayer.

**9. And all the people saw him walking and praising God:** ... walking about, −TCNT ... walking around, −MLNT ... moving and giving praise, −NAB ... and giving thanks to God, −NLTG ... recognized him, −EVRD.

**3:9.** As they were praying in the temple, the Jews may have been sitting, standing, kneeling, or prostrate. Many may have been crying out to God for help. But now they saw this man as he kept walking through the temple court, shouting God's praises.

**10. And they know that it was he which sat for alms at the Beautiful gate of the temple:** . . . And they began to recognize him, that the same was he who for the alms used to sit at the . . . Gate, −RIEU . . . All the people recognized him, −NCV . . . this was the very man, −MOFT.

**and they were filled with wonder and amazement at that which had happened unto him:** . . . They were surprised he was walking, −NLTG . . . they were filled with awe and amazement, −WEYM . . . filled with amazement and transport, −RTHM . . . mingled with ecstasy, −FNTN . . . They were struck with astonishment utterly stupefied at what had happened to him, −NAB . . . they were completely astounded and bewildered, −WLMS . . . filled with wonder and admiration at what had occurred, −MRDK . . . unable to explain, −JB . . . very much surprised, −BECK . . . they were at a loss to know what had happened, −KLGS . . . they were all overcome with wonder and sheer astonishment, −PHLP . . . filled with excitement and wonder, −WMCK . . . at the miracle which healed him, −NOLI.

**3:10.** The people could hardly believe their eyes. They all recognized that this was the man born lame who had always been sitting at the Beautiful Gate begging for alms. He was a very familiar sight to all of them, and there was no question about his identity.

His healing therefore filled them with wonder and amazement when they saw what had happened to him. The word "wonder" is not the ordinary word so translated, but another word related to awe. The people were overwhelmed with a sense that something great, something totally supernatural had taken place.

The word "amazement" also implies bewilderment, the kind of bewilderment that comes when a person is in a state of shock. Their minds were in a whirl trying to figure out how this could have happened. Yet it was obvious something had happened. Like most ancient beggars, this man's shriveled ankles and misshapen feet were undoubtedly displayed when he was placed at the Beautiful Gate. Attention was usually drawn to such things by beggars in order to excite pity and stir people to give. If the man had any shoes (and he probably did not), they would have been sandals. So as the man walked and jumped it was easy for them all to see the well-formed feet and strong, firm ankles that he now had. They were completely astonished.

**11. And as the lame man which was healed held Peter and John:** . . . While he was still clinging to, −WLMS . . . As he clung, −ADAM . . . while the man kept his hands on, −WMCK

**all the people ran together unto them:** . . . all the people quickly gathered round them, −TCNT . . . the entire crowd, −WUST . . . all the people crowded awestruck around them, −MNTG.

**in the porch that is called Solomon's:** . . . in the portico called Solomon's, −RSV . . . in the Colonnade called after Solomon, −TCNT . . . in what was known as Solomon's Portico, −WEYM.

**greatly wondering:** . . . greatly amazed, −RTHM . . . in the greatest astonishment, −TCNT . . . awe-struck, −WEYM . . . in utter amazement, −WLMS . . . overawed, −CNDT . . . completely flabbergasted, −WUST . . . stunned, −SEB . . . full of astonishment, −WMCK

**3:11.** The temple area was quite large. King Herod was a megalomaniac and wanted to make everything bigger than it had been before. When he rebuilt the temple he could not make it bigger because the dimensions were given in the Scriptures, so he made the courts twice as big as they had been in Solomon's time and in Zerubbabel's rebuilding. The so-called Wailing or Western Wall is just a retaining wall which was necessary to enlarge the top of the temple mount so he could make the courts larger. Thus, it took a few minutes for the man to walk across the court. By the time he reached Solomon's Porch, still holding the hands of Peter and John, the crowd began to gather.

God has often used miraculous healings to get people's attention. There was very little of the miraculous during the Intertestamental Period before Jesus came. His miracles and the miracles done by the 12 and the 70 helped to draw the crowds. But this crowd did not yet know the power of Christ's resurrection. They probably thought the day of miracles was past. They needed a visible manifestation of the supernatural to let them know God was still visiting His people. Miraculous healings in many parts of the world today are again bringing crowds.

**12. And when Peter saw it, he answered unto the people:** . . . On seeing this, Peter spoke to the people, −TCNT.

**Ye men of Israel, why marvel ye at this?:** . . . why are you surprised at this? −NORL.

**or why look ye so earnestly on us:** . . . or why fasten ye your eyes on us, −ASV . . . Or upon us why are ye intently looking, −RTHM . . . and why do you stare so at us, −TCNT . . . Or why gaze at us, −WEYM.

**as though by our own power or holiness we had made this man to walk?:** . . . Do you think this happened because we are good? −EVRD . . . power or godliness, −RTHM . . . or devoutness, −CNDT . . . our own individual power, or active piety, −FNTN . . . as though we, by any power or piety of our own, had enabled this man to walk, −TCNT.

**3:12.** This was Peter's opportunity, and he was quick to answer the unspoken questions on the perplexed and astonished faces. His message follows the same general pattern given by the Spirit through the gift of prophecy on the Day of Pentecost, but adapted to this new situation.

Peter addressed them as Israelite men. (This was the custom even though there were women in the crowd, and the message was for them too.) By referring to them as "Israel," instead of as Jews, he was using the more honorific title, the name given to Jacob as God's fighter and God's prince. It would remind them too of God's promises and of His good purpose for His people.

Peter asked the people why they marveled at this happening and why they fastened their eyes on him and John as if the man's ability to walk had its source in their own power or holiness. The word "power" here is mighty, supernatural power. No man has this on his own. It is God's power ministered through the gifts of the Holy Spirit. No one ever receives a reservoir of this power. Believers can only become channels through whom the Holy Spirit can work. If the connection is broken, if individuals lose touch with the divine Source, they have nothing.

The word "holiness" here is not the ordinary word used but one often translated "godliness." It implies a Godfearing attitude that gives respect and obedience to God because it is His right, His due. But this is only what God deserves. It does not give any person any special merit or make him the source of power, so he cannot take any credit to himself. God is always the believer's Source. True godly people do not call attention to themselves. Rather, they direct attention to the Lord.

**13. The God of Abraham, and Isaac, and of Jacob:**
the God of our fathers: ... The God of our ancestors, –TCNT ... the God of our forefathers, –WEYM.
hath glorified his Son Jesus: ... hath done honour, –TCNT ... has done it, –NORL ... glorified his servant, –NOLI.
whom ye delivered up: ... though you indeed surrendered him, –TCNT ... whom you yourselves betrayed, –WLMS ... handed over and then disowned, –JB.
and denied him in the presence of Pilate: ... and disowned him even before Pilate, –TCNT ... denied him to Pilate's face, –RTHM ... renounced him, –WSLY ... turning your backs on him, –BB.
when he was determined to let him go: ... when he had decided to release him, –RSV ... after he had made up his mind to set Him free, –NORL ... that one's verdict to release Him, –WUST ... resolved to release him, –WLSN.

**3:13.** Peter continually bore witness to Jesus. Here he identified Jesus as the One glorified by the God the Bible describes as the God of Abraham, Isaac, and Jacob, the God of their fathers (Exodus 3:6, 15). This God had exalted His Son Jesus on high.

The word "Son" here is not the ordinary word but one that may mean "child" or "servant." Another word is used when the Bible talks about the divine sonship of Jesus. Here Peter probably had in mind the identification of Jesus with the Suffering Servant of Isaiah 52:13. The servant of the Lord is the one who does the Lord's work. This healing was thus the result of the fulfillment of Isaiah's prophecy that spoke of the sufferings of Jesus on the sinner's behalf when He bore his griefs (literally, his "sicknesses") and carried away his sorrows (literally, his "pains") as in Isaiah 53:4.

Again Peter reminded the people that they were the ones who were responsible for arresting Jesus and denying Him before Pilate, even when Pilate had decided to release Him.

**14. But ye denied the Holy One and the Just:** ... Righteous One, –ASV ... You disavowed the ... man, –NOLI ... Yes, you disowned the holy and righteous One, –WEYM.
and desired a murderer to be granted unto you: ... and asked for yourselves the release of a murderer! –TCNT ... to be surrendered, –CNDT ... and asked as a favour, –WEYM ... demanded the reprieve, –JB ... and asked a murderer to be pardoned as a favor to you, –WLMS ... the man you requested, –KLGS.

**3:14.** The One they denied was the Holy and Just (righteous) One. Again, this was a reference to the Suffering Servant in Isaiah 53:11. (Compare Zechariah 9:9.) These two terms would have been recognized by those who listened as prevalent messianic titles. This is reinforced further in Acts 7:52 which says, "Which one of the prophets did your fathers not persecute? And they killed those who had previously announced the coming of the Righteous One, whose betrayers and murderers you have now become" (NASB). (See also 1 John 2:1.) As in his Gospel, Luke placed full responsibility for the death of the Messiah on the Jews, not on Pilate who sought to have Jesus released (Luke 23:4, 14-16, 20-25). But the people had turned from Jesus so completely that they asked for a murderer to be released to them instead.

The murderer was, of course, Barabbas, whom the Bible also describes as one who caused a certain sedition (political upheaval and riot) in Jerusalem (Luke 23:19, 25). Jesus not only died in his place, but also in the place of every individual.

**15. And killed the Prince of life:** ... The very Guide to Life you put to death, –TCNT ... You killed the Lord and Giver of, Bed: ...... . Inaugurates of, –CNDT ... Author of the life, –WUST ... originator of, –DRBY.
whom God hath raised from the dead: ... Whom God raised from among the dead, –RTHM.

**whereof we are witnesses:** ... and of that fact we are ourselves witnesses, *—TCNT* ... We saw this with our own eyes, *—SEB.*

**3:15.** Because of the determination of the Jerusalem Jews to have Jesus crucified, they became guilty of killing the "Prince of life." What a contrast! They gave death to the One who gave them life. "Prince" (Greek, *archēgon*) is a word that usually means originator, author, or founder. In Hebrews 2:10 it is translated "captain." In Hebrews 12:2 it is translated "author." It speaks of the part Jesus had in creation. As John 1:3 says of Jesus, the living, active Word, "All things were made through Him, and apart from Him was not anything made that was made" (literal translation). In other words, the preincarnate Jesus was the living Word who spoke the worlds into existence, and through Him God breathed life into the first man, Adam (Genesis 2:7). They had killed this Jesus, the very source of both physical and spiritual life, but God had raised Him from the dead. Peter and John were witnesses to this.

**16. And his name through faith in his name:** ... And it is by faith in the name of Jesus, *—TCNT* ... In virtue of faith in, *—WEYM* ... It is His name, that is, on condition of faith in, *—WLMS.*
**hath made this man strong, whom ye see and know:** ... has strengthened this man whom you behold and know, *—WEYM* ... that has made strong again this man whom you see and recognize, *—WLMS* ... gives stability to him whom you are beholding, *—CNDT* ... has entirely restored this man, *—PNT.*
**yea, the faith which is by him:** ... Yes, it is the faith inspired by Jesus, *—TCNT* ... and the faith which He has bestowed, *—WEYM.*
**hath given him this perfect soundness in the presence of you all:** ... unimpaired soundness, *—CNDT* ... that has made this complete cure of the man, before the eyes of you all, *—TCNT* ... has given this man the perfect health you all see, *—WLMS* ... has completely restored this man, *—NORL.*

**3:16.** Notice the repetition of the Name in this verse. "And his name, through faith (on the grounds of faith, on the basis of faith) in his name, hath made this man strong, whom ye see and know." And the faith that is by (through) Him (Jesus) had given him this freedom from bodily defect "in the presence of you all."

The Name, of course, refers to the character and nature of Jesus as the Healer, the great Physician. The healing came on the ground of faith in Jesus for who He is. But it was not their faith as such that brought the healing. It was the Name, that is, the fact that Jesus is true to His name, His nature, His character. He is the Healer. Faith had a great part, of course, but it was the faith that came

through Jesus. The faith Jesus himself had imparted (not only to Peter and John, but also to the man) gave complete freedom from defect to this lame man before their very eyes. ("Perfect soundness" reflects the terminology used in the Law for the freedom from defect necessary for animals used in Jewish sacrifices.) Jesus had healed the lame when He was on earth. He was still healing them through His disciples.

**17. And now, brethren, I wot that through ignorance ye did it, as did also your rulers:** ... fellow Jews, *—BECK* ... you did not realize what you were doing, *—WLMS* ... you had no idea what you were doing, *—PHLP* ... with your rulers also, *—PNT.*

**3:17.** Peter added that he knew it was because of ignorance they and their rulers killed Jesus. (Paul later confessed that he persecuted the Church because of ignorance and unbelief [1 Timothy 1:13].) Peter's words imply they did not really know Jesus to be Messiah, nor did they know He is God's own Son. This ignorance did not lessen their guilt, yet even in the Old Testament there was always forgiveness for sins done in ignorance. On the cross Jesus cried out, "Father, forgive them; for they know not what they do" (Luke 23:34). Thankfully, the Bible says, "God hath not cast away his people which he foreknew" (Romans 11:2).

**18. But those things, which God before had shewed:** ... But the things which God foreshowed, *—ASV* ... But in this way God has fulfilled the declarations He made, *—WEYM* ... God accomplished what He had foretold, *—NORL* ... in this way God did what He predicted, *—BECK* ... he made it come true in this way, *—TEV.*
**by the mouth of all his prophets, that Christ should suffer, he hath so fulfilled:** ... by the lips of all the Prophets, *—TCNT* ... that His Christ would suffer, *—WEYM* ... suffer many hard things, *—NLTG* ... He fulfilled in this way, *—ADAM* ... he thus fulfilled, *—ASV.*

**3:18.** The sufferings and death of Jesus were also the fulfillment of prophecies God had revealed by the mouth of all His prophets, that is, by the body of prophets as a whole. Their message, taken as a whole, had for a focal point the death of the Messiah, the Christ. Even so, this did not lessen the guilt of the people of Jerusalem. God has never accepted ignorance as an excuse for sin. Sin always brings guilt.

**19. Repent ye therefore, and be converted:** ... Change your minds, *—SAWR* ... and turn again, *—RSV* ... you must be sorry for, *—NLTG* ... You must, therefore, repent and turn, *—WEYM* ... and turn around, *—ADAM* ... you must turn to God, *—NORL.*
**that your sins may be blotted out:** ... for your sins to be wiped away, *—TCNT* ... cancelled, *—WEYM* ... for the erasure of your sins, *—CNDT* ... that

your sins may be obliterated, —WUST . . . maye be done awaye, —TNDL.

**when the times of refreshing shall come from the presence of the Lord:** . . . so there may come seasons of refreshing, —ASV . . . and then better and brighter days will come direct from the Lord himself, —TCNT . . . that times of revival may come, —WLMS . . . a time of recovery, —NEB . . . when the Lord refreshes you, —BECK . . . your soul will receive new strength, —NLTG.

**3:19.** As on the Day of Pentecost, Peter then called on the people to repent, to change their minds and attitudes about Jesus. Let them be converted (turn to God) he said, so that their sins (including the sin of rejecting and killing Jesus) might be blotted out (wiped away, obliterated) when (literally, in order that) times (seasons, occasions) of refreshing from the presence (face) of the Lord might come.

This can be taken as a general principle. Whenever a person changes his mind and attitude and turns to God, his sins will be obliterated, and he can have seasons of refreshing from the throne of God.

Too many put all their emphasis on the warnings of perilous times to come and on the statement that there will be a falling away (2 Timothy 3:1; 2 Thessalonians 2:3). These things will come. The falling away, of course, may mean spiritual falling away, though the Greek word ordinarily means revolt or revolution and war. Though the warnings are necessary, the Christian does not need to make them the focus of his attention. Repentance (a real change of mind and attitude) and a turning to God will still bring seasons of refreshing from the presence of the Lord.

**20. And he shall send Jesus Christ, which before was preached unto you:** . . . And he may send forth him who had been fore-appointed for you Christ Jesus, —RTHM . . . the pre-appointed Messiah, —FNTN . . . and he will send you, in Jesus, your long-appointed Christ, —TCNT . . . your long-heralded Christ, —PHLP.

**3:20.** To those who repent, God will send the appointed-for-you Messiah Jesus. Christians must keep their eyes on Jesus as the One who is to come. But it does not mean they have to wait until Jesus comes back before they can enjoy God-sent times of refreshing. It is clear in the Greek that they can have them now and continue to do so until the time Jesus comes again.

**21. Whom the heaven must receive:** . . . But Heaven must be his home, —TCNT . . . Yet heaven must retain him, —WLMS.

**until the times of restitution of all things:** . . . of universal restoration, —TCNT . . . of the reconstitution

of all things, —WEYM . . . until the final recovery of all things from sin, —LIVB . . . times of spiritual rest, —SEB.

**which God hath spoken by the mouth of all his holy prophets since the world began:** . . . of which God has spoken from the earliest ages through the lips of His holy Prophets, —WEYM . . . from a remote age, —RTHM.

**3:21.** These times of refreshing can come even though Jesus is not personally present. The heavens must receive Him until the times of restoration (reestablishment) of all things which were spoken by God through the mouth of His holy prophets from the beginning of the age (or from of old). "Since the world began" is a paraphrase which could mean "from eternity" or "from the beginning of time." The sense is "all the prophets ever since there ever were prophets."

The times of reestablishment refer to the coming age. Then God will restore and renew the Kingdom, and Jesus will reign personally on the earth. The restoration includes a further outpouring of the Spirit. But care must be taken as to the interpretation of this. Only those things which God has spoken by the prophets will be restored.

The prophets also show the Kingdom must be brought in through judgment. Daniel 2:35, 44, 45 shows the Babylon image (representing the entire world system) must be destroyed. Even the good in the present system must be ground to powder and blown away in order to make room for the better things of the Kingdom.

No one knows when that will be. But the important thing is that believers do not have to wait for the Kingdom to come before they experience God's blessings and power. The Holy Spirit even now brings believers an earnest, a first installment of things to come.

**22. For Moses truly said unto the fathers:** . . . Moses indeed said, —ASV, —KJII . . . In fact Moses said, —MLNT.

**A prophet shall the Lord your God raise up unto you of your brethren, like unto me:** . . . The Lord your God will raise up from among your brothers a Prophet, as he did me, —TCNT . . . will give you a prophet like me . . . He will come from, —NCV . . . One Who speaks for God, —NLTG . . . as he raised me, —GDSP, —WEYM . . . He will be one of your own people, —EVRD . . . from among your own kinsmen, —NAB . . . One like me, —KJII.

**him shall ye hear in all things whatsoever he shall say unto you:** . . . You must attentively listen to everything that he tells you, —BECK . . . You must obey everything he tells you, —EVRD . . . listen to whatever He tells you, —ADAM . . . listen to all the things that he shall say to you, —WMCK . . . To him you must hearken, —KLST . . . to everything He says, —NLTG.

**3:22.** Peter next referred to Moses and quoted from Deuteronomy 18:18, 19 where God promised to raise up a prophet like Moses. The people must listen to (and therefore obey) this Prophet. In fact, they must give heed to everything He says, whatever it might be. Moses did not know what this coming Prophet would say, but he was sure He would speak for God, and the people could have full confidence in Him and His words. (See also Leviticus 26:12; Deuteronomy 18:15; Acts 7:37.)

This was the promise the people had in mind also when they asked John the Baptist if he were "that prophet" (John 1:21, 25). Now Peter was speaking of a specific Prophet foretold by Moses. Peter said Jesus was the complete and final fulfillment of God's promise of the Prophet like Moses.

In what sense was Jesus like Moses? God used Moses to bring in the old covenant; Jesus brought in the new covenant. Moses led the nation of Israel out of Egypt and brought them to Sinai where God brought them to himself, that is, into a covenant relation with himself. (See Exodus 19:4, 5.)

Moses also gave Israel the command to sacrifice the Passover lamb; Jesus is the Lamb of God, our Passover. Moses was used by God to perform great miracles and signs; Jesus performed many miracles and signs, but most were signs of love rather than of judgment. Moses instituted the Day of Atonement where the blood was sprinkled on the mercy seat (the solid gold cover of the ark of the covenant); Jesus is the believer's "propitiation," literally, his "mercy seat" (Romans 3:25). By His blood He entered into heaven's Holy Place once for all, and by His blood He obtained eternal redemption for believers (Hebrews 9:12).

**23. And it shall come to pass, that every soul, which will not hear that prophet:** . . . And it shall be true, *–KJII* . . . And every one who refuses to listen to the Prophet, *–WEYM* . . . Everyone among the people who will not listen, *–NLTG* . . . Anyone that will not listen, *–GDSP* . . . that every life that shall not hear, *–HNSN* . . . that refuses to obey, *–WMCK* . . . to hearken to, *–KLST.*

**shall be destroyed from among the people:** . . . shall be utterly destroyed, *–ASV* . . . utterly exterminated, *–CNDT* . . . will be cut off entirely, *–ADAM* . . . will be put to death, *–NLTG* . . . shall be ruthlessly cut off from, *–NAB* . . . will be annihilated from among, *–GDSP* . . . then he will die, *–NCV* . . . separated from God's people, *–EVRD.*

**3:23.** Moses warned the people they would be cut off if they did not receive and obey this Prophet. Thus, though God is good, there is a penalty for those who do not repent. Peter emphasized the meaning of Moses' warning. They would be destroyed from among the people. That is, God would not destroy His people Israel as a whole, but individuals could lose out.

**24. Yea, and all the prophets from Samuel and those that follow after, as many as have spoken:** . . . All the early preachers who have spoken from Samuel until now, *–NLTG* . . . all the prophets that have spoken successively, *–MLNT* . . . and all the other prophets who spoke for God after Samuel, *–NCV* . . . Yes . . . Samuel onwards, and all of their successors who taught the people, *–TCNT.*

**have likewise foretold of these days:** . . . have also predicted these days, *–WEYM* . . . these times of ours, *–MLNT* . . . proclaimed, *–TNT* . . . announced the events of, *NAB.*

**3:24.** Samuel was the next great prophet after Moses (1 Samuel 3:20). From that time on, all the prophets foretold of "these days," that is, the days of God's work through Christ. Since those who were listening to Peter's sermon were mainly Jews, his argument in these verses (22-26) appealed to those with whom the Jews would be most familiar and accept. In verses 22 and 23 the appeal is to Moses. Longenecker states that the implied emphasis of Peter's argument was twofold: "(1) True belief in Moses will lead to a belief in Jesus, and (2) belief in Jesus places one in true continuity with Moses" (*Expositor's Bible Commentary, Acts,* p. 298). In verse 24 the continuity with their Jewish heritage is described in terms of the prophet Samuel who anointed David, the man chosen by God to establish an everlasting kingdom, as the ruler over His people (1 Samuel 13:14; 16:13). Through Jesus, the son of David, all prophecy either has been or will yet be fulfilled. Some may not have given specific prophecies, but all gave prophecies which led up to or prepared for "these days."

**25. Ye are the children of the prophets:** . . . You are yourselves the heirs of the Prophets, *–TCNT* . . . the descendants of, *–GDSP* . . . You are of the family of the early preachers, *–NLTG* . . . You have received what the prophets talked about, *–EVRD.*

**and of the covenant which God made with our fathers:** . . . and the heirs of the covenant, *–NOLI* . . . God covenanted, *–RTHM* . . . which God instituted for your fathers, *–SWAN* . . . and of the promise that God made with our early fathers, *–NLTG* . . . You have received the agreement God made with your ancestors, *–EVRD* . . . that God established with, *–MLNT* . . . and of the bond which God made, *–WMCK* . . . and the heirs of the sacred compact, *–WLMS.*

**saying unto Abraham:** . . . when he said unto Abraham, *–GDSP* – *TCNT.*

**And in thy seed shall all the kindreds of the earth be blessed:** . . . In your descendants will all the nations, *–TCNT* . . . And in your Descendant all the people, *–BECK* . . . In thy children's children, *–WMCK* . . . through one of your children, *–NCV* . . . all the races of the earth, *–NORL* . . . all the families, *–MNTG* . . . will receive God's favor through, *–NLTG* . . . are to be blessed through your posterity, *–WLMS* . . . in your offspring, *–NAB.*

**3:25.** Peter next reminded these residents of Jerusalem and Judea that they were the literal descendants of the prophets, heirs also of the Abrahamic covenant with its promise that in Abraham's seed all the families of the earth would be blessed (Genesis 22:18). This promise is actually repeated five times in Genesis. Some modern versions of the Bible translate Genesis 22:18 (et al.) as follows: "In your seed shall all the nations of the earth *bless themselves*." However, the Greek rendering of this same passage in verse 25 is ". . . all the kindreds of the earth (will) *be blessed*." The verb for "be blessed" is a future tense, passive voice form, *eneulogēthēsontai*; if the verb was to have been translated "bless themselves," the future middle form could have been selected, *eneulogēsontai*. Although the original Hebrew could be rendered either way, the Septuagint version and Luke (inspired of God) used the passive form which maintains the prophetic nature of the Genesis passage.

Galatians 3:14, 16 also shows that believers become heirs of this promise through faith in Jesus, for Jesus is the one "Seed" through whom the promise comes. Thus, by faith all can become children of Abraham, heirs of the same promise.

**26.** **Unto you first God:** . . . It was for you first that God, *—TCNT* . . . he sent him to you first, *—NAB* . . . It is to you first that God, *—WEYM* . . . for you primarily, *—BRKL.*

**having raised up his Son Jesus:** . . . after raising His Servant from the grave, *—WEYM* . . . His special servant, *—SEB* . . . after he had raised him from the dead, *—GDSP.*

**sent him to bless you:** . . . Hath sent him forth, ready to bless you, *—RTHM* . . . and sent him with blessings for you, *—TCNT.*

**in turning away every one of you from his iniquities:** . . . by turning each of you from his wicked ways, *—TCNT* . . . by causing every one of you to turn from his wickedness, *—WEYM* . . . as each of you turns from his evil ways, *—BRKL.*

**3:26.** The blessing promised to all the families of the earth came first to the people of Israel. What a privilege! Yet this was not favoritism on God's part. It was their opportunity to receive the blessing by repenting and by turning from their "iniquities" (their sins, their evil or malicious acts).

Actually, someone had to be the first to carry the message of the gospel. (Compare Romans 1:16; 2:9, 10; 3:1, 2 which emphasize that the gospel came to the Jew first, and the responsibility to do God's work and to spread the gospel was put on them first.) Paul always went to the Jew first because they had the Scriptures and the background and knew about the Promise. But they could not carry the message and the blessing to others without first repenting and experiencing the blessing for themselves. God had prepared the Jews for this. The first evangelists (spreaders of the good news) were all Jews.

# Chapter 4

**1.** **And as they spake unto the people:** . . . While Peter and John were still speaking to, *—TCNT.*

**the priests:** . . . the Chief Priests, *—TCNT.*

**and the captain of the temple, and the Sadducees:** . . . the Commander of the Temple Guard, *—WEYM* . . . the military commander of the temple, *—WLMS.*

**came upon them:** . . . came up to them, *—TCNT* . . . surprised them, *—BRKL* . . . stepped up to them, *—BECK* . . . burst suddenly upon them, *—WUST.*

**4:1.** Peter and John continued to speak to the crowd for a considerable time. As verse 3 indicates, it was now evening. Since the miracle took place about 3 p.m., Peter and John had continued to talk to the crowd about 3 hours. Suddenly, the priests (chief priests), the captain of the temple (the priest next in rank to the high priest who commanded the temple guard of chosen Levites), and a group of their Sadducean supporters came upon them.

The high priest was a Sadducee, as were many of the priests in Jerusalem. They did not accept the traditions of the Pharisees, denied the existence of angels and spirits, and said there was no resurrection (Acts 23:8; Matthew 22:23).

**2.** **Being grieved that they taught the people:** . . . being indignant, *—NOYS* . . . chagrined, *—BRKL* . . . much annoyed, *—TCNT* . . . exasperated, *—CNDT* . . . being tired out because, *—RTHM* . . . extremely annoyed, *—JB* . . . angered, *—NORL* . . . being sore troubled, *—ASV* . . . highly incensed at their teaching, *—WEYM.*

**and preached through Jesus the resurrection from the dead:** . . . and announcing in Jesus, *—RTHM* . . . preaching Jesus as an example, *—BB* . . . and preaching that in Jesus the dead rise, *—BECK.*

**4:2.** At first the high priest and these Sadducees were disturbed because of the great crowd around Peter and John, and they may have feared a possible riot. But when they understood what Peter and John were saying, they became "grieved" (deeply annoyed) because the apostles proclaimed through or in Jesus the resurrection from the dead. They thought Jesus would stay dead. That would be the end of His teaching and would cause His followers to scatter. But now here were two of the once frightened disciples speaking out boldly, with everyone in the temple court listening to them, just as had been the case when Jesus performed His miracles there.

The high priest and even the Pharisees who were members of the Sanhedrin never denied the reality of the miracles of Jesus. In fact, after

Lazarus was raised from the dead the priests and the Pharisees, who were usually on opposite sides of the fence, consulted together and said, "What do we? for this man doeth many miracles. If we let him thus alone, all men will believe on him; and the Romans shall come and take away both our place and nation" (John 11:47, 48). In other words, they were more concerned over their own status, position, and power than they were over the truth of God.

They knew Peter was preaching a resurrected Jesus. They understood he was presenting this as evidence for the truth of the resurrection of all believers. The Sadducees felt they could not tolerate this teaching.

3. **And they laid hands on them:** . . . They arrested the Apostles, —TCNT.

**and put them in hold unto the next day:** . . . in ward unto the morrow, ASV . . . in custody for the morrow, —RTHM . . . in prison till, —TCNT.

**for it was now eventide:** . . . for it was already evening, —RSV . . . already dusk, —CNDT.

**4:3.** These temple officials therefore arrested Peter and John and put them in jail overnight. It was evening, too late to call the Sanhedrin together.

4. **Howbeit many of them which heard the word believed:** . . . Many, however, of those who had heard their Message believed it, —TCNT . . . of those who had heard the sermon, —NORL.

**and the number of the men was about five thousand:** . . . and it raised the number of the people, —KLGS . . . increased, —NORL . . . The group of followers was now about, —NLTG . . . came to be about, —ASV . . . and the number of the men alone mounted up to some five thousand, —TCNT . . . grew to about five thousand, —BECK . . . There were now about 5,000 men, —NCV . . . in the group of believers, —EVRD.

**4:4.** It was too late also to stop the gospel from having its effect. Many who heard the Word believed; they were truly born again, saved by grace through faith. No doubt they were soon baptized in water, perhaps the next day in one of the several pools in and around Jerusalem. (Compare 2:41, 42.)

The number is given as about 5,000 men. The Greek may mean "became about 5,000 men," so some writers today understand this to mean the total number of believers was now up to 5,000. But the way it is stated here indicates the number was so large they counted only the men. There must have been a great number of women who believed also.

5. **And it came to pass on the morrow:** . . . The next day, —TCNT . . . it chaunsed on the morowe,

—TNDL . . . And it occurred on, —HNSN . . . On the following day, —NOLI.

**that their rulers, and elders, and scribes:** . . . the Jewish leaders, the older Jewish leaders, and the teachers of the law, —EVRD . . . the leading men, Councillors, and Rabbis, —TCNT . . . the leaders of the court and the leaders of the people, —NLTG.

**4:5.** Luke presented a rather detailed description of the prestigious group that had assembled in Jerusalem. Among the 71 members of this Council were the *archontas* which consisted of the high priest and other senior priests. These men conducted worship and were in charge of the daily functioning of the temple. Others, such as temple wardens, treasurers, and perhaps former high priests, also made up this first group. The second were the *presbuterous*, composed primarily of the Sadducees. Lastly, the *grammateis* (scribes, experts in the Law, Pharisees) were also present (see Haenchen, p. 215).

6. **And Annas the high priest, and Caiaphas, and John, and Alexander:** . . . the head religious leader, —NLTG.

**And as many as were of the kindred of the high priest:** . . . in fact, all the members of the high priestly family were there, —NORL . . . of high-priestly descent, —RTHM . . . and all the High Priest's relations, —TCNT . . . all who were of, —TNT . . . and the other members of the High Priest's family, —WEYM . . . and all who were in the family of the head religious leader, —NLTG . . . and whoever belonged to the high priest's clan, —BRKL.

**were gathered together at Jerusalem:** . . . assembled, —CNDT . . . came together, —SWAN.

**4:6.** Among the Sanhedrin who came were Annas, Caiaphas, John, Alexander, and all the rest of the relatives of the high priest who happened to be in the city.

Annas is called the high priest. He was officially high priest from A.D. 6-15. Then his son Jonathan was appointed for about 3 years. Next Caiaphas, the son-in-law of Annas, was made high priest and remained in office until A.D. 36. But Annas remained the power behind the throne. The people did not accept his deposition by the Romans and still considered him to be the true high priest. In the Old Testament Aaron was made high priest for life. The Law made no provision for the secular governors or kings to change this. Consequently, Jesus was taken to Annas' house first (John 18:13), then to Caiaphas (who probably occupied a portion of the same building around the same courtyard). Annas and Caiaphas, along with some of the rest of the relatives of Annas, actually formed a closed corporation that ran the temple.

John may have been Jonathan the son of Annas. (Codex Bezae, manuscript D of the New

Testament, has Jonathan here.) Alexander was probably one of the leading Sadducees.

**7. And when they had set them in the midst:** ... They had Peter and John brought before them, −TCNT ... Then they made the men stand before them, −MNTG ... and placing them in the center, −BRKL ... put the missionaries in front of them, −NLTG.

**they asked:** ... and repeatedly inquired of them, −WLMS ... inquired to ascertain, −CNDT ... they interrogated them, −MRDK ... demanded to know, −NORL ... repeatedly demanded, −AMPB.

**By what power, or by what name, have ye done this?:** ... In what power, or in what name, −ASV ... By what sort of power and authority, −WLMS ... What power do you have or whose name did you use? −TEV ... have you done this healing? −NOLI.

**4:7.** They made Peter and John stand in the midst of the assembled court. This was the Sanhedrin, called the *Gerousia* (Council or Senate) as in 5:21, and the *Presbuterion* (Body of Elders) as in 22:5. According to Josephus, they met just west of the temple area. According to the Mishnah (a collection of oral laws and traditional Jewish doctrines compiled before A.D. 200), the Sanhedrin sat in a semicircle, apparently around the accused.

The inquiry began with two important questions. First, the Council wanted to know what sort of power effected this healing. They apparently suspected idolatry or black magic was involved. Second, the Council asked "by what name" had they healed this man. Magical formulas discovered on papyri reveal that the ancients believed there was a potential power resident in the names of certain gods and demons. This power, it was thought, could be released or controlled by invoking the name (Bietenhard, "*onoma*," *Kittel*, 5:250f.). While the Council may not have believed such myths, the evidence which stood before them needed an explanation. The question raised by the Sanhedrin, therefore, was an attempt to discover the source of the power as well as the authority behind the men who performed the miraculous healing. The question they posed could be restated as "How were you able to do this?" or "Who gave you the ability to heal this man?"

**8. Then Peter, filled with the Holy Ghost:** ... because he was filled, −WLMS ... being controlled, −WUST.
**said unto them:** ... spoke as follows, −TCNT.
**Ye rulers of the people, and elders of Israel:** ... Princes of the people, −FNTN ... Leaders of the people, and Councillors, −TCNT ... Rulers and Elders of the people, −WEYM.

**4:8.** Peter had once cringed before a girl in the courtyard of the high priest. Now there was a difference. As he began to speak, Peter was filled

with the Holy Spirit. The form of the Greek verb indicates a new, fresh filling. This does not mean he had lost any of the power and presence of the Spirit he received on the Day of Pentecost. In view of the pressures of this critical situation, the Lord simply enlarged his capacity and gave him this fresh filling to meet this new need for power to witness.

There was also a practical application of Jesus' instructions given in Matthew 10:19, 20 and Luke 21:12-15. They were to take no advance thought of what they should speak, for the Spirit of their Heavenly Father would speak in (and by) them. Thus, instead of trying to defend themselves, the Spirit would make their words a witness. Knowing this Peter and John probably slept well during the night in jail and awakened refreshed.

Filled anew with the Spirit, Peter did not let the Jewish leaders frighten him. Truly, God has not given believers a spirit of cowardly fear, but of power, of love, and of a sound mind; that is, a mind that shows self-discipline (2 Timothy 1:7). Politely, Peter addressed the Council as rulers and elders.

**9. If we this day be examined of the good deed done to the impotent man:** ... are you questioning us about a good thing that was done, −EVRD ... if we are being cross-examined today, −KLGS ... we are under investigation today concerning a benefit done to, −NOLI ... are to be examined for doing good to a sick man, −RTHM ... since we are on trial to-day for a kind act done to a helpless man, −TCNT ... benevolent service to a cripple, −BRKL ... benefit to a feeble man, −FNTN ... a benefit conferred upon a cripple, −MNTG ... that we are today being tried, −WLMS ... on a man helplessly lame, −PNT.

**by what means he is made whole:** ... In whom this man hath been made well, −RTHM ... as to how this man has been cured, −WEYM ... by what means this man has been healed, −RSV ... Maybe you are questioning us as to how he was healed, −NORL ... to learn how he was cured, −WLMS ... restored, −NOYS.

**4:9.** Then, in a dignified way, he told them that if they were making a judicial examination concerning the good deed done for a weak human being, if they wanted to know by what means the man had been and still was restored (saved, healed), then he had the answer.

**10. Be it known unto you all, and to all the people of Israel:** ... So let me tell you all, −TCNT ... then you and all ... should know, −BRKL.
**that by the name of Jesus Christ of Nazareth:** ... that it is by the authority of, −TCNT ... that through the name of, −WEYM.
**whom ye crucified, whom God raised from the dead:** ... whom God raised from among the dead, −RTHM.

**even by him doth this man stand here before you whole:** ... in him does this man stand before you strong and well, —MNTG ... it is, I say, by his authority that this man stands here before you cured, —TCNT ... in prime condition, —BRKL ... stands healthy, —BECK ... doth this (man) stand here before you recovered, —MRDK ... is standing restored before you, —NOLI.

**4:10.** What a contrast there is in this verse between what Jewish leaders did to Jesus and what God did to Him!

Peter proclaimed that in (by) the name of Jesus, whom they ("you" is plural) crucified, whom God raised from the dead, by Him (in Him—Jesus) this man stood before them whole (restored to sound health). Again Peter recognized that the lame man was both saved and healed and was now "in Christ"; that is, he was in right relationship to Christ as a member of the body of Christ.

**11. This is the stone which was set at nought of you builders:** ... He is the stone, —ASV ... the Scriptural stone, —NOLI ... scorned by you, the builders, —TCNT ... treated with contempt, —WEYM ... cast aside, —MNTG ... thrown away, —WLMS ... the stone despised by you, —BRKL ... by you builders, —KLGS.

**which is become the head of the corner:** ... which was made, —ASV ... but it has been made the Cornerstone, —WEYM ... the keystone, —JB ... the capstone, —NIV.

**4:11.** Peter quoted a passage these same chief priests and elders had heard from Jesus himself. On one occasion they had challenged Jesus' authority to teach. He gave them parables and then quoted Psalm 118:22. (See Matthew 21:23, 42, 45; 1 Peter 2:7.) Peter, however, made it personal. *This* One (emphatic) "is the stone which was set at nought (ignored, despised) of you (plural) builders," but this stone (Jesus) had "become the head of the corner." (That is, because He is now exalted to the Father's right hand.)

**12. Neither is there salvation in any other:** ... And Salvation comes through no one else, —TCNT ... No one else can save us, —BECK ... by anyone else, —WLMS ... by nobody else, —ADAM.

**for there is none other name under heaven given among men:** ... for there is no other Name in the whole world, given to men, —TCNT ... His name is the only means under heaven, —NOLI ... for no one else in all the wide world has been appointed among men, —WLMS ... this is the only one, —JB ... no second name, —PNT.

**whereby we must be saved:** ... to which we must look for our Salvation, —TCNT ... as our only medium by which to be saved, —WLMS ... we must needs be saved, —RTHM.

**4:12.** Next Peter explained what this means. There is no salvation in any other. The promised salvation which the Jews hoped would be brought by the Messiah is not in any other than Jesus. "For there is none other name under heaven given among men (human beings)" by which "we must be saved." (Some ancient Greek manuscripts have "you must be saved.") "Must" is an emphatic word. If a person does not find salvation through the name of Jesus, he will never find it. (Here, the "name" means the person of Jesus.)

The healing of the lame man thus witnessed to Jesus as the only Saviour. The Jewish leaders could see no value in Jesus, yet God had made Him of unique and supreme worth. In Him, as Isaiah chapter 53 also shows, is (the promised) salvation. There is only one salvation, only one way to God (Hebrews 10:12-22).

Many have claimed to be messiahs or saviors. Many have presented other ways of salvation. But they are all put in opposition to our Lord Jesus Christ. There is only one choice when an individual faces the claims of Christ: he can accept or reject. Other ways which may seem right lead to destruction (Proverbs 14:12; Matthew 7:13).

It is not popular to be so exclusive. Many unbelievers who are not atheists want to think there are many ways to find God. Some of the so-called world religions would be quite happy to include Jesus in their list of gods, or in their list of prophets or saviors. Some cults even try to combine what they suppose is the good in a variety of religions. But all this is in vain; God has rejected all other ways. Even in the Old Testament the prophets condemned idolatry, but they condemned the worship of the Lord *plus other gods* even more strongly. Such mixed worship has never been acceptable to God.

**13. Now when they saw the boldness of Peter and John:** ... beholding the openness, —YNG ... Seeing how boldly Peter and John spoke, —TCNT ... As they looked on ... so fearlessly outspoken, —WEYM ... the glad fearlessness of Peter and John, —MNTG ... when they saw the intrepidity of, —NOLI ... the courage, —WLMS ... the freedom of speech, —BRKL.

**and perceived that they were unlearned and ignorant men:** ... they took note, —NIV ... and having discovered that they were unlettered and obscure men, —RTHM ... ordinary men, —CNDT ... illiterate persons, untrained in the schools, —WEYM ... men without schooling or skill, —BRKL ... in private stations in life, —CMPB ... uneducated laymen, —ADAM ... had no education or training, —BECK ... uninstructed, —DRBY ... unordained and unschooled, —KLGS ... ungifted, —WLSN.

**they marvelled:** ... they were surprised to note, —NORL ... they were staggered, —PHLP.

**and they took knowledge of them that they had been with Jesus:** ... realized that they had been companions of Jesus, —TCNT ... now they recognized them as having been, —WEYM.

**4:13.** The priests and elders marveled (wondered) when they saw the boldness (freedom in speech) of Peter and John, especially since they perceived they were unlearned (uneducated in the sense of not having attended a rabbinic school or having sat under a great rabbi like Gamaliel) and ignorant men (unprofessional men, laymen). This does not mean they were totally unschooled. They had gone to the synagogue schools in their hometowns, but they were not professional teachers or trained speakers like the rabbis, scribes, and lawyers. Ordinary laymen did not speak with such authority.

It must have been hard for Peter and John to face such snobbishness. But the key to their boldness and freedom in speaking was, of course, the new fresh filling with the Spirit. He gave them the words to say.

Then something else struck these Jewish leaders. The phrase "took knowledge of them" does not mean they inquired further of them. Rather, the Greek simply means the Jewish leaders gradually began to recognize that the disciples (apostles) had been with Jesus. Perhaps the words of Peter jogged their memory of what Jesus had said. As these men thought about their confrontation with Jesus, they remembered Peter and John were His disciples.

Jesus had spoken with authority. The leaders had believed they would be rid of Jesus by crucifying Him. But now the disciples, trained by Him, were speaking with the same authority. Jesus had done miracles as signs. Now the apostles were also working miracles.

**14. And beholding the man which was healed standing with them:** . . . But since they saw, —MNTG . . . even the (man) who had been cured, —RTHM.

**they could say nothing against it:** . . . they had nothing wherewith to contradict, —RTHM . . . they had nothing controversial to say, —BRKL . . . they could say nothing to confront them, —MRDK . . . nothing to say in opposition, —ADAM . . . they had nothing to answer, —MNTG . . . no effective reply, —PHLP.

**4:14.** The elders were confronted with something else. The man who was healed was standing there with Peter and John. (The man himself was not on trial.) Suddenly, the priests and elders had nothing else to say. What could they say against such an obvious miracle?

**15. But when they had commanded them to go aside out of the council:** . . . So they ordered them out of court, —TCNT . . . So they ordered them to withdraw from the Sanhedrin, —WEYM.

**they conferred among themselves:** . . . and then began consulting together, —TCNT . . . they parleyed with one another, —CNDT . . . held a consultation, —NORL . . . talked the matter over among themselves, —BECK.

**4:15.** The leaders then commanded Peter and John to go outside the council, that is, out of the room where the Sanhedrin was meeting. The Sanhedrin then engaged in a discussion.

**16. Saying, What shall we do to these men?:** **for that indeed a notable miracle hath been done by them is manifest to all them that dwell in Jerusalem:** . . . a notorious sign, —RTHM . . . a remarkable sign, —TCNT . . . an unmistakable wonderwork, —WLMS . . . a signal miracle, —CMPB.

**and we cannot deny it:** . . . We cannot say it is not true, —EVRD, —NCV.

**4:16.** They did not know what to do with Peter and John. They could not deny that a notable miracle (a known supernatural sign) had been done through them, visible to all the inhabitants of Jerusalem.

This could imply they were aware of the resurrection of Jesus. What bothered them was the fact that the apostles were using it to teach a future resurrection for all believers. In order to avoid this problem earlier, they had bribed the soldiers to say the body of Jesus had been stolen (Matthew 28:12, 13). Some even today contend the women and the disciples looked into the wrong tomb. But the women paid special attention to where Jesus was laid (Luke 23:55). Actually, these Jewish leaders were neither stupid nor unsophisticated. They knew how difficult it is to get rid of a body. If they had thought the body of Jesus was in some other tomb they would have made an intensive search for it. They did not, because they *knew* He had risen from the dead. But this knowledge did not help them. It takes more than a head belief or a mental acceptance of the truth of Christ's resurrection to be saved. (See Romans 10:9, 10.)

**17. But that it spread no further among the people:** . . . But, that it may go no further with, —WMCK . . . this report must not be spread any further, —NOLI . . . But we must warn them not to talk to people anymore, —EVRD . . . lest it may disseminate more, —CNDT . . . to keep the news of it from spreading farther, —NORL.

**let us straitly threaten them:** . . . let us warn them, —TCNT . . . let us stop them by threats, —WEYM . . . severely threaten, —WLMS . . . we must give them a stern warning, —NAB . . . let us terrify them with threats, —FNTN . . . forbid them, —WMCK

**that they speak henceforth to no man in this name:** . . . not to plead the Cause, —TCNT . . . to say anything to anyone, —WMCK . . . never to mention that man's name to anyone again, NAB . . . to preach no more to anyone, —NOLI.

**4:17.** Since the priests and elders had no logical reply to Peter and John, they decided the best course was to try to suppress their teaching about Jesus and the Resurrection. They would threaten the disciples to speak no longer in (on the ground of, on the authority of, or concerning) this Name.

Like so many in the later history of the Church, they had committed themselves to a religious structure, a religious hierarchy, and a religious system that was largely of human devising and human interpretation. They knew what was in the Scriptures, but they ignored or twisted those parts that did not fit their system. They were not open to searching the Scriptures to see whether these things were so.

Since Peter and John were outside the room, some wonder where Luke got his information. Some suggest that Saul, who became the apostle Paul, was in this session of the Sanhedrin and later told Luke what was said in that meeting.

18. **And they called them:** . . . So they recalled the Apostles, *—WEYM* . . . called them back, NAB.

**and commanded them not to speak at all nor teach in the name of Jesus:** . . . and charged them, *—ASV* . . . and ordered them altogether to give up speaking or teaching, *—WEYM* . . . commanded them not to utter even a sound nor to teach, *—SWAN* . . . made it clear that under no circumstances were they to speak the name, *—NAB* . . . imperatively forbade them, *—FNTN* . . . ordered them bluntly . . . a single further word, *—PHLP* . . . under no condition, *—TEV* . . . to speak or teach a single sentence about the Name of Jesus, *—MOFT.*

**4:18.** When the elders called Peter and John back into the room, they commanded them not to speak (open their mouth, utter a word) at all or teach in the name of Jesus. They, of course, were the Supreme Court of the Jews. Except for the death penalty, the Roman government gave them full authority in matters pertaining to the temple and to the conduct of their religious rites and duties. They were used to giving imperious, dictatorial commands, and they were used to having them obeyed. In this case they must have sensed that men who were this bold, this free to speak, would need an extra authoritative command. So they spoke as emphatically as possible.

19. **But Peter and John answered and said unto them:** . . . replied to them, *—BRKL.*

**Whether it be right in the sight of God to hearken unto you more than unto God, judge ye:** . . . What do you think is right? What would God want? Should we obey you or God? *—EVRD* . . . to listen to you rather than to himyou must decide, *—TCNT* . . . Does God consider it right to listen to you, *—BECK* . . . you must judge, *—WMCK* . . . Judge for yourselves, *—NOLI.*

**4:19.** These threats did not intimidate the two apostles. Courteously, but very firmly, they put the responsibility back on the Jewish leaders to judge or decide whether it was right before God to listen to them rather than to Him.

Clearly, the apostles were not afraid of the threats of the Sanhedrin. They had already done their worst to Jesus. They could not do any more than that to the apostles, and because of the hope of the resurrection of the dead they were not afraid of death. Moreover, they had committed themselves to Jesus, not as to a human leader, but as to the divine Son of God.

From that day to this, followers of Jesus have faced the same question. The commands of human leaders, even religious leaders, have all too often been contrary to the commands of God and Christ. Paul warned Timothy the time would come when some church members would not put up with sound, healthy, Biblical teaching. Instead, following their own desires, they would heap to themselves teachers who would tell them what they wanted to hear. They would turn away their ears and refuse to listen to the truth. They would instead turn to (and believe) fables (idle tales, fanciful stories coming from the imaginations of these false teachers). (See 2 Timothy 4:3, 4.)

20. **For we cannot but speak:** . . . as for us, we cannot help speaking of, *—TCNT* . . . keep from telling, *—WLMS* . . . refrain from telling, *—BRKL* . . . We can't stop telling, *—BECK* . . . We cannot keep quiet, *—EVRD.*

**the things which we have seen and heard:**

**4:20.** The apostles then boldly declared they were not able to stop telling what they had seen and heard. They had in mind, of course, the Great Commission. All four Gospels and the Book of Acts tell of this command of Jesus given not only to the apostles but to all His followers. Some have said the believer's chief purpose is to glorify God and enjoy Him forever. There is truth in this, but God is also glorified when believers serve Him, praise Him, and worship Him in Spirit and in truth. They glorify God also as they fulfill His purposes as expressed in the Great Commission.

21. **So when they had further threatened them:** . . . But after further threats, *—NOLI* . . . After they had spoken more sharp words to them, *—NLTG.*

**they let them go:** . . . the Council set them at liberty, *—TCNT* . . . they turned them loose, *—WLMS* . . . and then freed them, *—BRKL* . . . they released them, *—NOLI.*

**finding nothing how they might punish them:** . . . not seeing any safe way of punishing them, *—TCNT* . . . nothing to accuse them of, *—KLGS* . . . could not find a way to punish, *—EVRD.*

**because of the people:** ... on account of the people, —RTHM ... because all the people, —EVRD ... before the people, —KLGS.

**for all men glorified God for that which was done:** ... continued to praise God for what had taken place, —WLMS ... everybody was praising God for what had happened, —ADAM ... everybody was glorifying God, —MNTG ... This miracle was a proof from God, —EVRD.

**4:21.** After the high priest and elders added further threats to their warnings, they released Peter and John from custody. Though they searched their minds to try to find some way to punish the apostles, they could not think of any way to do it. At least they could not think of how to do it without antagonizing the people. The people were glorifying God because of what had taken place. The man who was healed had come into the temple glorifying and praising God. Peter and John had given God all the praise. For the Sanhedrin to punish the apostles at this point could have made the people think they were against God.

Actually, the very fact that the leaders let the apostles go must have made the crowd believe God was putting His approval on the gospel the apostles were proclaiming. It also let the people know God could deliver from the Sanhedrin. The crowd understood from this also that the Sanhedrin had no case against the apostles, nor did they have any way to refute their message.

22. **For the man was above forty years old:** ... was more than forty years old, —TCNT.
**on whom this miracle of healing was shewed:** ... the more so as the man who was the subject of this miraculous cure, —TCNT ... this sign of healing, —RTHM ... this act of power, —BB.

**4:22.** This miracle of healing was especially outstanding because the man was over 40 years old. If normal muscles are not used even for a few weeks or months, one does not stand up and begin to walk and jump the way this man did. For a person whose muscles were shriveled and his ankles without strength suddenly to do so was beyond any human expectation.

The Greek word translated "miracle" here literally means a "sign," an outward, visible manifestation of the truth of the gospel the apostles were preaching. John's Gospel uses the same Greek word for the miracles of Jesus that were signs pointing to His authority and deity as the Son of God.

23. **And being let go:** ... After they had been set at liberty, —TCNT ... After their release, —WEYM ... were free again, —BECK ... On their release, —NIV ... after

their dismissal, —CNFT ... When the Apostles were released, —NOLI.

**they went to their own company:** ... they came unto their own friends, —RTHM ... the apostles went to their companions, —WLMS ... their associates, —WUST.

**and reported all that the chief priests and elders had said unto them:**

**4:23.** As soon as they were released, Peter and John went back to their own company, their own people. The Greek expression used here could mean to the people of their own nation or tribe, or it could mean to their own family. In this case it meant the body of believers who had become the true family of God. It corresponds to what Ephesians 2:19 calls the household of God, the family that belongs to God.

From what Luke records on other occasions, it seems certain these believers were gathered together to pray for Peter and John, and that they rejoiced and gave God praise for their release. Then the apostles reported all the high priest and elders had said to them, holding nothing back.

24. **And when they heard that they lifted up their voice to God with one accord:** ... When they heard their report, —NOLI ... moved by a common impulse, they raised their voice to God in prayer, —TCNT ... one and all lifted up their voices to God, —WEYM ... they prayed to God with one purpose, —EVRD ... with one consent, —SAWR.
**and said, Lord, thou art God:** ... O Sovereign! —RTHM ... O Sovereign Lord, —TCNT ... O Master, —WMCK ... absolute in power, —WUST.
**which hast made heaven, and earth, and the sea, and all that in them is:** ... you are the Maker of, —WLMS ... thou that didst make, —ASV ... it is thou who hast made the sky ... and everything that is in them, —TCNT.

**4:24.** The warnings and threats of the Jewish leaders did not frighten the believers. Neither did they ignore them. They took them to God. The word "voice" is in the singular here, which means they all joined together and prayed in unison. They prayed also in one accord, that is, with one purpose. Probably, however, the prayer which the Bible records here was given by one of them who became the spokesman for them all.

Much can be learned from this prayer. First, as in the case of most of the prayers in the Bible, they recognized who God is. They addressed Him as Lord (a different word from that used elsewhere in the Bible, this one meaning Master, Owner, Sovereign) and thus presented themselves before Him as His servants, even as His slaves. They were not making demands on Him. They were throwing themselves on His mercy, looking for His grace, His unmerited favor.

Then they recognized that He alone is God, the God of all power, for He is the Creator of the universe and all that is in every part of it. He is Sovereign over the universe, the true King of the universe, by right of creation.

**25. Who by the mouth of thy servant David hast said:** ... and who by the lips of our ancestor, thy servant David, speaking under the influence of the holy Spirit, hast said, –TCNT ... and didst say through the Holy Spirit by the lips of our forefather David, Thy servant, –WEYM ... who was inspired by the Holy Spirit, –NOLI.
**Why did the heathen rage:** ... Gentiles, –ASV ... Unto what end did nations rage, –RTHM ... Why are the nations so angry? –EVRD ... heathen roar, –WMCK ... rage haughtily, –DRBY.
**and the people imagine vain things?:** ... And peoples busy themselves with empty things, –RTHM ... And the nations form vain designs, –TCNT ... and the peoples form futile plans, –MNTG ... the peoples plan in vain? –WMCK ... Why are the people making useless plans? –EVRD ... and the nations plot in vain? –NOLI ... empty stratagems? –ADAM ... study emptiness? –KLGS.

**4:25.** Second, they based their petition on the inspired Word of God, spoken by the Holy Spirit through the mouth of King David. Again, most of the prayers of the Bible are based on the Word of God already given. Psalm 2:1, 2 was a word from the Lord that fitted their situation and made them feel God knew in advance what their situation was and how to deal with it.

Psalm 2 speaks of an opposition like that of the Jewish leaders. It asks why the heathen (the nations, the Gentiles) were raging (with a general hostility against God). It emphasizes the question by repeating it in a little different way and asking why the peoples (plural) imagined (planned, were devising) a vain (empty, foolish, ineffective) thing.

This psalm was, of course, speaking first of all of the Gentiles, the nations who were enemies of God and His people. It tells believers that all the plans men try to devise, hoping to hinder or stop the plan of God, are doomed to failure. God is still in control, but He is also patient.

**26. The kings of the earth stood up:** ... set themselves in array, –ASV ... took their stand, –WLMS ... took a belligerent stand, –ADAM ... prepare to fight, –EVRD.
**and the rulers were gathered together against the Lord:** ... assembled together, –HBIE ... conspired together against, –NOLI ... mustered themselves against, –MLNT ... were united against the Lord, –NORL.
**and against his Christ:** ... his Anointed, –ASV.

**4:26.** David further identified this raging, foolish planning as the kings of the earth standing by each other, trying to support each other against

God. This idea is repeated for emphasis by saying that the rulers "were gathered together against the Lord (that is, against the divine Lord, 'Lord' standing for the personal name of God, the Hebrew *YHWH*), and against his Christ," that is, against His Messiah, His Anointed One, God's anointed Prophet, Priest, and King.

This prayer, inspired by the Spirit, recognized that the Jewish leaders were in the same class as the outside nations who were always conspiring against God and His Anointed, in this case, against Jesus. There is precedent for this in that the Old Testament prophets sometimes used the word *gôyim* (usually translated "Gentiles") for Israel because Israel had turned from God.

**27. For of a truth against thy holy child Jesus:** ... conspired against Jesus, your holy servant, –NOLI.
**whom thou hast anointed:** ... whom thou hast consecrated the Christ, –TCNT ... whom thou didst appoint, –WMCK
**both Herod, and Pontius Pilate, with the Gentiles, and the people of Israel:** ... not Herod and Pontius Pilate only, but the nations and the people of Israel besides, –TCNT.
**were gathered together:** ... They did ... assemble, –WEYM ... they have actually gathered in this city, –MLNT.

**4:27.** This prayer then specifically identifies Psalm 2 with those who were gathered together (with hostile purpose) against God's holy child Jesus. Herod here is Herod Antipas, the tetrarch of Galilee and Peraea, the same ruler who put John the Baptist to death. In his Gospel, Luke records how Herod and his soldiers mocked Jesus, threw a brightly colored robe around Him, and sent Him back to Pilate (Luke 23:11). The same day Herod and Pilate were made friends. Their treatment of Jesus caused them to be among those who were gathered together against God and His Son, Jesus.

These enemies of God and Christ also included the Gentiles, in this case the Roman soldiers and the peoples of Israel. *People* is a word ordinarily used of Israel as God's chosen people. The Greek is in the plural here, possibly because the 12 tribes were all represented in Israel, but more probably because the Israelites were divided into various sects, such as the Pharisees and Sadducees. It may also be a recognition that they were in the same category as the Gentiles (literally, *nations,* also in the plural).

As before, Luke used the word "child" (Greek, *paida*) in the sense of "servant." "Holy child" thus means the dedicated, consecrated Servant of the Lord, the same Suffering Servant prophesied in Isaiah 52:13-53:12.

**28. For to do whatsoever thy hand and thy counsel determined before to be done:** ... but only to do all that thy providence and thy will had already determined should be done, –TCNT ... to carry out what your hand and will had destined should happen, –GDSP ... made your plan happen, –NCV ... your plan had beforehand decreed to be done, –KLST ... to do all that thy power and thy will had predetermined should be done, –MNTG ... to do what thy hand and thy purpose had determined, –WMCK ... marked out beforehand, –RTHM ... and Thy purpose preordained to take place, –MLNT.

**4:28.** Yet they could do only what God's hand (that is, God's power) and God's will had determined before (decided beforehand) to be done. They were, however, responsible for their deeds, for they chose freely to do them.

The believers based their petition on what God did through Jesus. God's hand was in control when He permitted the death of Jesus; Jesus was indeed God's Servant who accomplished God's will in their behalf. They could come to God on the basis of what was fully accomplished through the death and resurrection of Jesus (1 Corinthians 1:23, 24; 3:11; 2 Corinthians 1:20).

**29. And now, Lord, behold their threatenings:** ... look upon their threats, –RSV ... give heed to their threats, –TCNT ... give attention to their threats, –WLMS ... listen to their threats, –PNT ... listen to what they are saying, –EVRD ... consider, –KLST ... notice, –MLNT.

**and grant unto thy servants:** ... and enable thy servants, –TCNT ... Thou endowing Thy slaves, –CNDT ... endow Thy servants with fearlessness to speak Thy word, –BRKL ... Your bond servants, –AMPB.

**that with all boldness they may speak thy word:** ... with all freedom of utterance to speaking, –RTHM ... with all fearlessness, to tell thy Message, –TCNT ... to proclaim Thy word with fearless courage, –WEYM ... with perfect courage to continue to speak your message, –WLMS ... fearlessly, –PHLP.

**4:29.** Their petition was that the Lord would now look on the threatenings of the Sanhedrin and give His servants (slaves) opportunities to keep on speaking the Word with all boldness (and freedom of speech). Perhaps they felt less confident after they left the courtroom than while they were in it. Even after a spiritual victory Satan may suggest that believers have acted foolishly, so they must pray for continued boldness. Abraham also became afraid after boldly testifying before the king of Sodom, but God reassured him (Genesis 15:1).

**30. By stretching forth thine hand to heal:** ... while thou stretchest, –ASV ... stretchest forth thy hand to heal, –MNTG.

**and that signs and wonders may be done:** ... and to give signs and marvels, –WEYM.

**by the name of thy holy child Jesus:** ... through the name of thy holy servant Jesus, –RSV ... Through the power of thy holy Servant Jesus, –TCNT ... by the authority of your holy Servant Jesus, –WLMS.

**4:30.** What would provide new opportunities for the apostles to speak boldly and freely for their Lord? They knew how the Lord had used the healing of the lame man to spread the gospel and add new believers to the Church. But the healing of the lame man was just a beginning. There would be more such opportunities provided by God's stretching out His hand (extending through them His power) for healing and for signs and wonders to be done through the name of His holy child (Servant) Jesus. Here the word "holy" means separated to God and His service and emphasizes the consecration and dedication of Jesus to the work His Heavenly Father gave Him to do. Jesus made it clear He was sanctified (made holy, set apart, consecrated, dedicated) by the Father and sent by the Father into the world (John 10:36). He finished the work His Father gave Him to do (John 17:4).

The entire company of believers joined in with this prayer for boldness to keep on doing the same thing that had brought the arrest of Peter and John and the threats of the Sanhedrin. They did not want miracles for miracles' sake, however. Rather, they were opportunities to preach the gospel and signs to help the people recognize that Jesus was indeed risen from the dead and is truly the Christ, the Son of God.

**31. And when they had prayed:** ... And when they had made supplication, –RTHM ... at their beseeching, –CNDT.

**the place was shaken where they were assembled together:** ... their meeting-place shook, –BRKL ... the place where they were was violently moved, –BB.

**and they were all filled with the Holy Ghost:** ... and one and all were filled, –RTHM.

**and they spake the word of God with boldness:** ... and began speaking ... with freedom of utterance, –RTHM ... and continued to tell God's Message fearlessly, –TCNT ... and continued courageously to speak God's Message, –WLMS ... fearlessly they gave utterance to God's message, –BRKL ... spoke out the message of God with freedom, –FNTN ... with confidence, –DOUY ... without fear, –BB.

**4:31.** After they prayed, the place where they were gathered was shaken, not by an earthquake but by the Spirit, indicating a mighty move of God. It is probably true that the people were shaken as well. As they felt this shaking, the whole company of believers were all filled with the Holy Spirit; and in His power they all continued speaking the Word of God with boldness (and freedom of speech). This was as great a work of the Spirit as the miracles.

The Greek indicates again a new, fresh filling of the Spirit. Some writers contend that only the new people (the 5,000 mentioned in 4:4) were filled at this time. But the Greek does not uphold this. All the believers, including the apostles, received the fresh filling to meet the continued need and to withstand the pressures upon them. New, fresh fillings of the Holy Spirit are part of God's wonderful provision for all believers.

**32. And the multitude of them that believed were of one heart and of one soul:** . . . of the throng, *—RTHM* . . . The whole body of those who had become believers in Christ were animated by one spirit, *—TCNT* . . . Now the multitude of the believers, *—MNTG* . . . in the vast number of those who had become believers, *—WLMS* . . . The host of believers were one in heart and soul, *—BRKL* . . . united in spirit, *—SEB*.
**neither said any of them that ought of the things which he possessed was his own:** . . . Not one of them claimed any of his goods as his own, *—TCNT* . . . no one claimed his belongings just for himself, *—BRKL* . . . And nobody called anything he had his own, *—BECK*.
**but they had all things common:** . . . but everything was held for the common use, *—TCNT* . . . but everything they had was common property, *—WEYM* . . . but they shared everything that they had, *—WLMS* . . . was for the use of all, *—FNTN*.

**4:32.** The increasing number of believers continued in one heart and one soul. They formed a community of believers who were in one accord, with a unity of mind, purpose, and desire. None of them said, "What I have is mine and I am afraid I might need it all myself." Instead, they felt a love and responsibility for each other. They recognized they were all partners in the work of God, so all things were shared. God was supplying their needs, and they believed He would continue to provide. The same attitude that sprang up after they were first filled on the Day of Pentecost still prevailed (2:4, 5). Again, there was no compulsion. Their sharing was simply an expression of their love and their unity of mind and heart.

This does not mean they turned away from unbelievers who were in need. The Bible urges Christians to be considerate of the poor and to do good to all men, "especially unto them who are of the household of faith," that is, the believers who are in the family of God (Galatians 6:10). Christians have a special responsibility to help fellow believers who are in need.

**33. And with great power gave the apostles witness of the resurrection of the Lord Jesus:** . . . The Apostles continued with great power to bear their testimony to the resurrection of Jesus,

their Master, *—TCNT* . . . propagated the evidence, *—FNTN* . . . rendered testimony, *—CNDT* . . . told the truth, *—BECK* . . . with great effect, *—WEYM*.
**and great grace was upon them all:** . . . great favour, *—RTHM* . . . and divine help was given to them all abundantly, *—TCNT* . . . and much good will rested, *—BECK* . . . grace rested liberally on all of them, *—BRKL* . . . all held in high esteem, *—NEB* . . . God's favour rested richly on them all, *—WLMS* . . . a wonderful spirit of generosity, *—PHLP* . . . goodwill, *—FNTN*.

**4:33.** In answer to their prayer, the apostles were able to keep on giving witness to the resurrection of the Lord Jesus with great power, that is, with mighty deeds of supernatural power. At this point the apostles were still the chief channels of the miraculous power of God, just as they were the primary witnesses to the resurrection of Jesus. Apparently, this continued to be so for some time. Much later, the apostle Paul declared that through him the signs of an apostle were truly done among the Corinthians in all patient endurance with all kinds of miraculous signs, wonders, and deeds of supernatural power (2 Corinthians 12:12).

This implies also that the thousands of believers were still looking to the apostles, not only to give them teaching but to be the primary ones who were doing the work of God. Later, God did begin to use others. Even at this point, however, the work of the Spirit was not limited to the apostles, for the Word says "great grace was upon them all" (the believers). That is, free grace, the wonderful unmerited favor of God, was mightily upon them all. Grace is also manifested through the gracious gifts of the Spirit, the *charismata*, and these Spirit-filled believers were open to the distribution of His gifts by the Holy Spirit as He willed. (Compare 1 Corinthians 12:11.)

**34. Neither was there any among them that lacked:** . . . There was not a needy person among them, *—RSV* . . . Indeed, there was no poverty among them, *—TCNT* . . . And, in fact, there was not a needy man among them, *—WEYM* . . . Not one among them suffered need, *—BRKL* . . . Neither was there one indigent person, *—CMPB* . . . no one among them was needy, *—SAWR* . . . was ever in want, *—JB*.
**for as many as were possessors of lands or houses sold them:** . . . for all who were owners of, *—TCNT* . . . proceeded to sell them, one by one, *—WLMS*.
**and brought the prices of the things that were sold:** . . . and continued to bring the money received for the things sold, *—WLMS* . . . and bring the proceeds of the sales, *—BECK*.

**4:34.** This verse shows a special way in which the grace and graciousness of God were expressed through the believers. There was a gracious gift of giving of help. No one lacked, that is, no one was in need or a needy person, for as many as were owners of fields or houses were selling them and kept bringing the price of the things that were sold.

The Greek here does not mean that everyone sold his property at once. Rather, from time to time someone would sell a piece of property, then later another would sell another piece as the Lord brought the need to their attention.

**35. And laid them down at the apostles' feet:** . . . and gave it to the Apostles, –WEYM . . . They used to lay them, –NAB . . . They put the proceeds at the disposal of, –NOLI . . . They gave it to the missionaries, –NLTG.

**and distribution was made unto every man according as he had need:** . . . then they were shared with everyone, –GDSP . . . and then everyone received a share in proportion to his needs, –TCNT . . . it was then divided up according to every man's need, –WMCK . . . then distribution was continuously made to everyone in proportion to his need, –WLMS . . . It was divided to each one, –NLTG . . . Then each person was given what he needed, –NCV . . . as anyone might have necessity, –WLSN.

**4:35.** Those who sold the property brought the money and laid it at the apostles' feet. They gave it over to the apostles and gave the apostles full authority to use it as they saw fit. The apostles were faithful to this responsibility, and they distributed the money here and there to each needy person in proportion to the need.

This was an added responsibility put upon the apostles. At first they undoubtedly shared what they had, as did all the rest. But now with the additional 5,000, plus others who were being added to their number daily, the number of needy ones seems to have increased. Thus the distribution to meet their needs was a growing task. But the indication is that the apostles, as leaders and fellow believers, accepted the additional work without complaint.

The distribution of the money was a continuing ministry. As long as there was a need, and as new needs arose, the apostles were made aware of the need and help was given in proportion to the need. They did not help a person once and then forget him or her. On the other hand, there is evidence from later passages that as time went on fewer people needed this monetary help. The Bible always encourages those who are able to work to find employment, so they can be able to give to others and to the work of God. (Compare Ephesians 4:28.)

**36. And Joses, who by the apostles was surnamed Barnabas:** . . . And Joseph, –ASV . . . for example, –BECK . . . who had received from the Apostles the additional name of Barnabas, –TCNT . . . was called Barnabas by the apostles, –MLNT.

**(which is, being interpreted, The son of consolation,):** . . . when translated, –RTHM . . . Son of exhortation, –ASV . . . which means The Preacher, –TCNT . . . signifying Son of Encouragement, –WEYM . . . One who encourages, –TNT.

**a Levite, and of the country of Cyprus:** . . . a native of Cyprus, –WEYM . . . a Cyprian Levite, –BRKL . . . a Cyprian by birth, –SWAN . . . a Cypriot by race, –TNT.

**4:36.** After making the general statement that those who had land sold it, Luke gave a specific example. This particular example is important because it provides a background for the events of the next chapter.

"Joses" is from a Greek form of *Joseph,* a very common name among the Jews. The apostles gave him special recognition by giving him a very distinctive surname or additional name of "Barnabas."

It is not clear whether the apostles gave him this name at this time or whether they had already done so because of his previous actions. From what is recorded about Barnabas later, he had a character which fitted the meaning of the name *Barnabas,* "son of consolation," which also means "son of exhortation or encouragement." *Son of* was often used in Hebrew and Aramaic to indicate a person's character or nature.

**37. Having land, sold it:** . . . having a field, –ASV . . . sold a farm that belonged to him, –TCNT . . . sold land which he owned, –WMCK

**and brought the money, and laid it at the apostles' feet:** . . . and brought the proceeds which he deposited, –BRKL . . . brought the payment, –SWAN . . . put it at the disposal of the apostles, –WLMS . . . and made a donation of the money, –NAB.

**4:37.** When Barnabas saw the need, his spirit was stirred. He sold a field, brought the money, and laid it at the feet of the apostles. The Greek indicates it was agricultural land, and it was probably of good quality and brought a good price. But the amount of money is not important. From what the Bible says about Barnabas, it seems certain it was the spirit in which he gave that impressed the apostles. He was a good example of those who were concerned about the needy believers.

## Chapter 5

**1. But a certain man named Ananias:** . . . There was, however, a man named Ananias, –TCNT . . . Another man named, –NAB.

**with Sapphira his wife:** . . . in partnership with his wife Sapphira, –WLMS.

**sold a possession:** . . . sold some property, –TCNT . . . sells an acquisition, –CNDT . . . sold some real estate, –BRKL . . . an estate, –FNTN.

**5:1.** With the example of Barnabas before them, two individuals who had joined the believing community conspired to get the same kind of attention given to him without experiencing the pain of sacrifice. So they, as Barnabas did, sold a field, a piece of farm property. But in every other way what they did was in strong contrast to Barnabas' actions.

Although they listened to the teaching of the disciples and saw the miracles, whether Ananias and Sapphira were really Christians like Barnabas is not specifically stated. But verse 13 says that the divine judgment upon the couple had the following effect: "Of the rest durst no man join himself to them." This could be an indication that Ananias and Sapphira were just such "joiners."

"Ananias" is used in the Greek Septuagint version for both the Hebrew *Hananiah* ("the Lord is gracious") and *Ananiah* ("the Lord protects"). "Sapphira" may mean a sapphire stone, which was considered very precious, or it may be an Aramaic word meaning "fair" or "beautiful." Someone has suggested that their names were not appropriate.

**2. And kept back part of the price:** ... retained, —BRKL ... deducted part of the price, —FNTN ... some of the proceeds, —TCNT ... but ... dishonestly kept back part of the price received for it, —WEYM ... embezzles from the price, —CNDT ... and carried away (part) of the price and concealed it, —MRDK ... kept back for themselves a part of the money, —WLMS ... appropriated a part, —WLSN ... reserved part of the price for himself, —PHLP ... by fraud, —DOUY.

**his wife also being privy to it:** ... his wife also being aware of it, —HBIE ... with her connivance, —TCNT ... with her full knowledge and consent, —WEYM ... with her knowledge and agreement, —KLGS.

**and brought a certain part:** ... though he brought the rest, —WEYM.

**and laid it at the apostles' feet:** ... and gave it to the Apostles, —WEYM.

**5:2.** Unfortunately, sometimes those who claim to be believers become liars and deceivers. Ananias made up his mind to keep back part of the price. "Kept back" (*enosphisato*) is from the same verb translated "purloining" (Titus 2:10) in the sense of stealing or embezzling. The Septuagint version of Joshua 7:1 uses it of Achan's sin when he took from Jericho things that were to be dedicated to God. The idea is that Ananias appropriated part of the money for his own benefit and set it aside. Sapphira shared the knowledge of this and was equally guilty since she was in full accord with her husband's actions. Ananias brought a certain part of the money and laid it at the apostles' feet, giving the impression that, like Barnabas, he had done a noble deed.

**3. But Peter said, Ananias, why hath Satan filled thine heart to lie to the Holy Ghost:** ... how is it that Satan has so taken possession of your heart, that you have defrauded the holy Spirit, —TCNT ... the Adversary, —YNG ... so possessed your mind, —NEB ... to falsify, —CNDT ... so that you would cheat, —BRKL ... that you should try to deceive the Holy Spirit, —WEYM ... thou shouldest be false, —RTHM.

**and to keep back part of the price of the land?:** ... and dishonestly keep back part of the price paid you for this land, —WEYM ... and covertly withdraw some of the field's price, —BRKL ... keep a part of the receipts from the sale, —ADAM.

**5:3.** Peter, acting as representative and spokesman for the 12 apostles, knew immediately what was done. He did not have spies out to report to him, but he had the Holy Spirit. Perhaps this was revealed to him through one of the Holy Spirit's gifts of revelation.

Peter then asked Ananias why Satan (the Satan, the Adversary—compare Revelation 12:9, 10) had filled his heart to lie to the Holy Spirit and keep back for himself part of the price of the field. The question "why?" draws attention to the fact that their action was voluntary. There was no excuse for what they did.

**4. Whiles it remained, was it not thine own?:** ... While it was unsold, was it not your own? —TCNT ... you could have kept it, couldn't you? —ADAM.

**and after it was sold, was it not in thine own power?:** ... was not the money at your own disposal, —TCNT ... you could have used the money any way you wanted, —EVRD, —SEB ... the money was under your control, —NOLI.

**why hast thou conceived this thing in thine heart?:** ... How is it that you have cherished this design in your heart, —WEYM ... How could you have the heart to do such a thing, —WLMS ... How could you think of committing such a sin? —NOLI ... Why did you think of doing this? —EVRD ... How have you let this thing find a place in your heart? —WMCK

**thou hast not lied unto men, but unto God:** ... You have not defrauded men, but God, —TCNT ... You did not cheat men but God, —BRKL.

**5:4.** Peter made it very clear that no one had asked them to sell their field; they were under no compulsion to sell it. Before they sold it, it remained theirs and could still have remained theirs. After they sold it, the money was still in their power, that is, they had the authority over what they should do with it. There was nothing compelling them to give it all. What they had conceived in their hearts was a lie, not to men but to God.

Satan was behind what Ananias and Sapphira did. They were guilty of jealousy, unbelief, and love of money. This grieved the Spirit of the Lord. These things had not happened overnight. By the time they conspired together, Satan had filled their hearts (their whole inner beings), and they followed a pathway of deceit.

They could have resisted Satan (James 4:7). But they let pride, self, and the love of money possess them. The love of money is the root of all (kinds of) evil (1 Timothy 6:10). Once the love of money takes possession of a person, there is no evil that he cannot or will not do. With the love of money in control, a person will do things he never would do otherwise, including murder and every other sin. It is clear also that if a person is filled with the love of money he cannot love God (Matthew 6:24).

In lying to the Holy Spirit who was guiding the Church, the believers, and the apostles, Ananias and Sapphira were also lying to God. This comparison in verses 3 and 4 makes it clear that the Holy Spirit is a divine Person.

**5. And Ananias hearing these words fell down, and gave up the ghost:** ... And as Ananias heard these words he fell and expired, —RTHM ... fell down dead, —WEYM ... breathed his last, —ALFD ... he collapsed and died, —PHLP.

**and great fear came on all them that heard these things:** ... This made a profound impression, —JB ... and all who heard the words were awestruck, —WEYM ... a strange awe seized everybody who heard it, —WLMS ... And all who heard of it were terrified, —BECK ... Those who witnessed the event were appalled, —NOLI.

**5:5.** Judgment was immediate. While Ananias was still listening to Peter, he fell down and breathed out his last breath. This sudden death may seem severe punishment. It was indeed. But God brought this judgment near the beginning of the Church's history to let them know what He thinks of unbelief, greed, and self-seeking hypocrisy that lies to the Holy Spirit, lying not just to men but to God. As Peter later reminded believers in 1 Peter 4:17, "The time is come that judgment must begin at the house of God: and if it first begin at us, what shall the end be of them that obey not the gospel of God?"

It should be emphasized also that Ananias' lie was premeditated. When he died "great fear (including terror and awe) came on all" who heard about it. They knew now that the Holy Spirit is a mighty power. He is indeed holy, and it does not pay to lie to Him.

**6. And the young men arose:** ... But the younger men got up, —TCNT ... came forward, —NAB.

**wound him up:** ... and after winding the body in a sheet, —TCNT ... covered his body, —NLTG ... enshroud him, —CNDT ... wrapped up the body, —NAB.

**and carried him out, and buried him:**

**5:6.** They did not wait long to bury people in those days. Peter and the apostles called in some younger men. Some consider these a class of younger men who assisted the elders of the church. More probably, they were just some of the younger believers who were present. These young men quickly wrapped Ananias in a linen winding sheet, took him out of the city, and buried him. Because of the seriousness of his sin, there was no funeral service or procession, and none of the weeping and mourning that was usually expected among the Jews.

**7. And it was about the space of three hours after:** ... And it came to pass, after about three hours interval, —RTHM ... About three hours later, —EVRD.

**when his wife, not knowing what was done, came in:** ... still not knowing, —KLGS ... not knowing what had happened, —RSV ... ignorant of what had occurred, —BRKL.

**5:7.** About 3 hours later Sapphira came in, not knowing what had happened to her husband. She obviously was looking for commendation and praise because of what she hoped had been accepted as a generous gift.

**8. And Peter answered unto her:** ... Peter at once questioned her, —WEYM ... Peter said to her, —WMCK ... asked her, —MLNT, —NOLI.

**Tell me whether ye sold the land for so much?:** ... Tell me! was it for so much ye gave up the field, —RTHM ... Is it true ... that you sold the land for such and such a sum, —TCNT ... Tell me how much money you got for your field. Was it this much? —EVRD, —NCV ... was this the price for which you sold the field? —TNT ... did you sell that piece of property, —NAB ... such a price? —NOLI ... for this amount of money? —NLTG.

**And she said, Yea, for so much:** ... Yes, she said, that is right, —TNT ... Yes, that was the price, —NCV ... Yes, for so much, —MLNT ... Yes, that was the sum, —NAB ... the full amount, —TEV.

**5:8.** She did not see her husband, nor did she sense any of what she expected. Peter answered her inquiring look by asking her if she and her husband had sold the land for the amount he brought in. Peter thus gave her an opportunity to confess the truth. But she too lied.

Like her husband, Sapphira was not sensitive to the Holy Spirit. She too had allowed Satan to fill her heart. There's a lesson here for believers. If they remain sensitive to the Spirit, He is faithful to check, convict, and help them. They do not need to allow Satan to take control. The Bible says, "Submit yourselves therefore to God. Resist the devil, and he will flee from you" (James 4:7). Satan is not yet bound, He still goes about like a roaring lion seeking whom he may devour. Believers need to be vigilant, but they also need to keep calm and claim the victory over him (1 Peter 5:8, 9).

**9. Then Peter said unto her:** ... Peter then came back at her, —BRKL ... then asked her, —MLNT.

**How is it that ye have agreed together:** ... conspired together, —CMPB ... How could you two scheme, —NAB ... How could you two have talked together, —NLTG.

**to tempt the Spirit of the Lord?:** ... to try, —ASV ... to put to the proof, —RTHM ... to provoke, —TCNT ... about lying to, —NLTG ... to put the Spirit of the Lord to the test, —WEYM ... to defy the Holy Spirit? —NOLI.

**behold, the feet of them which have buried thy husband are at the door, and shall carry thee out:** ... Listen! The footsteps of those who, —TCNT ... are standing at the door, —NLTG ... can be heard at the door. They stand ready to carry you out too, —NAB.

**5:9.** Peter was just as severe with Sapphira as he had been with Ananias. His question clearly indicated he knew she and her husband had agreed together to tempt (test) the Holy Spirit. They were deliberately trying to see how far they could go in their disobedience without provoking God's wrath. They were also testing the Holy Spirit's knowledge, for they conspired secretly and acted as if they thought even the Holy Spirit would not know what they were doing. This was, in a sense, a denial of His deity.

Like the Israelites who complained to Moses, they acted as if they were just dealing with a man, but they were really putting God to the test (Exodus 17:2). They were acting presumptuously, what the Hebrew calls "with a high hand," and that was casting reproach on the Lord. Under the Law it deserved death (Numbers 15:30). Jesus recognized that it is the devil who tries to get believers to put God to the test in this way, and He reminded Satan of God's warning against this (Luke 4:12; Deuteronomy 6:16).

After his question, Peter directed Sapphira's attention to the young men at the door who had now returned from burying her husband. They would carry her out too. As in the case of his words to Ananias, Peter was not saying this as a result of his own thinking or his own reasoning. He was moved by the Holy Spirit to give this judgment.

**10. Then fell she down straightway at his feet, and yielded up the ghost:** ... At that, —NAB ... And she fell down immediately at his feet, —ASV ... Instantly she fell down dead at his feet, —WEYM ... And she fell instantly at his feet, and expired, —RTHM ... At once she collapsed at his feet and died, —TNT ... At that moment Sapphira fell down by his feet, —NCV.

**and the young men came in, and found her dead:** ... When the young men entered, —NOLI.

**and, carrying her forth, buried her by her husband:** ... They took her out, —NLTG ... carried her out, —GDSP ... entomb her, —CNDT ... by her husband's side, —TCNT.

**5:10.** Thus, by the same kind of miracle of divine judgment, Sapphira fell down immediately at Peter's feet and breathed out her last breath. The same young men then came in, found her dead, proceeded to carry her out, and then buried her beside Ananias.

Some people wrestle with the severity of God's judgment of Ananias and Sapphira. However, this was the advent of a new era. The Holy Spirit had just recently been poured out and the Church was in its infancy. In light of this, such harsh judgment created a reverent fear of the Lord which protected the Early Church. Believers learned that though God is a God of mercy, He also will send judgment on sin.

In addition, the property this couple gave was no longer theirs—it was devoted to God. Others in the Old Testament were judged in exactly the same way when they did not show proper respect for the holy things of the Lord, e.g., Nadab and Abihu (Leviticus 10:2), Achan (Joshua 7:25), Uzzah (2 Samuel 6:7).

**11. And great fear came upon all the church, and upon as many as heard these things:** ... And there came ... upon the whole of the assembly, —RTHM ... and all who heard of these events were appalled, —TCNT ... great awe fell upon the whole church, —MLNT ... was awestruck, and so were all who heard of this incident, —WEYM ... All the members of the church ... were terrified, —NOLI ... were struck with awe, —WMCK

**5:11.** Once more the Bible emphasizes that great fear came upon the whole Church or Assembly. The Greek word *ekklesia* was used for the "congregation" of Israel. It was also used in everyday Greek for any assembly of free citizens. Here the word is used of the whole body of believers in Jerusalem and the surrounding area. It shows that the believers already considered themselves a distinct Body, though they still thought of themselves as Jews.

This great fear also came upon all those outside the Church who heard of these things. But the fear was a holy fear that stirred a reverence for God and a respect for His holiness. It did not split up the Church, nor did it hinder the work of God. But it made them all very careful to walk softly before the Lord.

**12. And by the hands of the apostles were many signs and wonders wrought among the people:** ... The missionaries did many powerful works,

—*NLTG* ... numerous startling evidences, —*FNTN* ... performed many wonders, —*NOLI* ... continued to occur ... through the instrumentality of the Apostles, —*TCNT.*

**(and they were all with one accord in Solomon's porch:** ... They gathered on, —*NLTG* ... they all met unitedly, —*MLNT* ... and by common consent they all met in Solomon's portico, —*WEYM* ... met together in Solomon's colonnade, —*NOLI.*

**5:12.** Luke now gave another summary statement. The apostles continued to be full of the Holy Spirit and power, that is, they were full of power because they were full of the Holy Spirit. They kept right on doing many miraculous signs and supernatural wonders that were impossible to do apart from the mighty power of God.

The Church also remained in one accord, meeting daily at the hours of prayer in Solomon's portico (and probably overflowing into the Court of the Women beside it). This, of course, was the very place where Peter and John had addressed the crowd after the healing of the lame man, where they had been arrested and thrown in jail overnight.

**13. And of the rest durst no man join himself to them:** ... No one from outside their own group came in with them, —*NLTG* ... but none of the rest ventured to stand by them, —*TCNT* ... None of the outsiders, —*MLNT* ... But none of the others dared to attach themselves, —*WEYM* ... None of the leaders dared to associate with them, —*NOLI* ... no one of the rest dared join them, —*KLST.*

**but the people magnified them:** ... On the other hand, the people were full of their praise, —*TCNT* ... But those outside the church had respect for the followers, —*NLTG* ... And although the common people made much of them, —*KLST* ... Yet the people held them in high honour, —*WEYM* ... continued to hold them in high regard, —*WLMS* ... spoke highly of them, —*ADAM* ... thought very highly of them, —*BECK.*

**5:13.** The fear that resulted from the death of Ananias and Sapphira also affected the unbelievers so that none of them dared to join in with the crowd of believers in the temple.

Some have suggested that the believers also did not dare to join with or come into the company of the apostles lest they be judged as Ananias and Sapphira were. But the evidence is that all the believers continued in just as great a fellowship with the apostles as before, so this interpretation is unlikely.

It is clear that no unbeliever dared to mix in with the crowd of believers. Perhaps out of curiosity some had been pretending to be Christians; or perhaps they hoped to receive part of the overflow of the blessing of the Lord, so evidently upon the believers.

This did not mean, however, that the Church's growth was slowed down. When the people saw how God dealt with sin among the believers, they realized that the Church as a whole was pleasing God and held high standards of honesty and righteousness. Therefore they "magnified them," that is, they held the believers in high esteem.

**14. And believers were the more added to the Lord, multitudes both of men and women.)** and, more than ever, —*WMCK* ... and the more were being added when they believed in the Lord, throngs, —*RTHM* ... while large numbers, both men and women, kept joining them more readily than ever as they became believers in the Master, —*TCNT* ... However, throngs of men and women who believed in the Lord were increasingly added, —*BRKL* ... in increasing numbers believed in the Lord, —*NOLI.*

**5:14.** The actual result was that more and more believers were "added to the Lord," that is, to the Lord Jesus, not just to the Church as an external body. This amounted to "multitudes (crowds) both of men and of women." It has been suggested the number of believers was over 10,000 by this time.

**15. Insomuch that they brought forth the sick into the streets:** ... In consequence people, —*MNTG* ... They went so far as to bring out their sick, —*MLNT* ... They actually brought the sick, —*ADAM* ... even into the broadways, —*RTHM.*

**and laid them on beds and couches:** ... mattresses and mats, —*TCNT* ... beds and pallets, —*HBIE* ... to lay them on rugs and mats, —*MLNT* ... light couches or mats, —*WEYM.*

**that at the least the shadow of Peter passing by might overshadow some of them:** ... in the hope that, as Peter came, at least his shadow, —*TCNT* ... even the shadow, —*CMPB.*

**5:15.** Because the believers had such confidence in the Lord to meet all their needs, they brought the sick (including the lame, the crippled, the diseased, and the infirm) out "into the streets," that is, into wide streets or into public squares, and "laid them on beds and couches," litters and mattresses or mats, so that when Peter passed by, even his shadow might overshadow them. They believed the Lord would honor Peter's faith and theirs even if Peter was not able to stop and lay hands on each one of them. This undoubtedly also stimulated the faith of those who were sick. It is not always easy for those who are sick to express faith.

Although some claim the Bible never says people actually were healed as the shadow of Peter went over them, the clear implication of the context is that people were healed. God used similar methods to restore health to individuals through supernatural means. For example, the woman with an issue of blood was made whole when she touched the hem of Jesus' garment (Matthew 9:20 and parallels). Also, Acts 19:11, 12 says God performed "extraordinary miracles" (NIV) through the apostle Paul. When handkerchiefs and aprons touched by Paul were taken to the sick, diseases were cured and evil spirits departed those who had been demonized.

**16. There came also a multitude out of the cities round about unto Jerusalem:** . . . Even from towns outside Jerusalem the crowd came streaming in, —BRKL, —MLNT . . . the inhabitants of the neighbouring towns flocked, —TNT . . . Crowds flocked together to, —NOLI.
**bringing sick folks:** . . . They took with them their sick people, —NLTG.
**and them which were vexed with unclean spirits:** . . . those molested, —CNDT . . . and such as were harassed by impure spirits, —RTHM . . . those afflicted by, —NOLI . . . and those who were bothered by evil spirits, —EVRD . . . troubled with demons, —NLTG.
**and they were healed every one:** . . . all alike cured, —TCNT . . . all of whom were, —NORL.

**5:16.** The word of what God was doing soon spread into the surrounding cities (including towns and villages) of Judea. Soon, because of their newfound faith, crowds of believers began to come and kept on coming, bringing the sick (again, including the diseased, the weak, the lame, and the crippled) and those who were vexed (tormented, troubled) by unclean spirits, that is, by demons.

As in the Gospels, the Bible makes a clear distinction between the sick and the people who were tormented or possessed by demons. There is nothing in the Bible to teach that all who are sick are demon possessed. The Bible indicates that sickness is in the world because of the activity of Satan and because of man's sin. But the Bible again and again makes it clear that in individual cases the sickness may not be caused by either sin or Satan. (Compare John 9:1-3.)

All of the sick and those tormented by unclean spirits were healed. This undoubtedly includes the sick mentioned in verse 15 as well. This was a critical point in the history of the Early Church, and God was doing special things.

**17. Then the high priest rose up, and all they that were with him:** . . . On this the High Priest and all his supporters . . . were aroused, —TCNT . . . Now the high priest took a stand, and all his friends, —WLMS . . . and all his party, —WEYM.
**(which is the sect of the Sadducees,):** . . . the Sadducee party, —BRKL . . . the party of the liberals, —KLGS . . . who believe no one will be raised from the dead, —NLTG.
**and were filled with indignation:** . . . they were insufferably jealous, —BRKL . . . in a fit of jealousy,

—TCNT . . . made them furious, —NORL . . . became very jealous, —EVRD, —NLTG.

**5:17.** Once again the local Sadducees in Jerusalem, including the high priest with his family and his close friends, were upset. In fact, they were very upset. This time they were "filled with indignation." The Greek word *zēloō* can mean zeal, enthusiasm, or eagerness in a good sense, or it can mean the worst kind of jealousy, the sense of the word as it is used here. It also implies a party spirit and a zeal for their Saducean teachings against the resurrection of the dead.

**18. And laid their hands on the apostles:** . . . arrested, the Apostles, —TCNT . . . So they seized, —BRKL . . . took hold, —NLTG . . . they apprehended the apostles, —MNTG . . . grabbed the apostles, —SEB.
**and put them in the common prison:** . . . and had them placed in custody, —TCNT . . . official custody, —NEB . . . the public prison, —HBIE . . . public ward, —ASV . . . the public jail, —NOLI.

**5:18.** Jealous indignation, then, caused these Sadducees to rise up, go into action, arrest the apostles, and throw them into the common prison. The Greek also indicates they did this publicly. "Common" here is actually an adverb which means "publicly." They made the arrest with the whole crowd looking on. Apparently the priests and Sadducees had become desperate. Many times they had been afraid to arrest Jesus publicly because they were afraid of the reaction of the crowds. When they finally did arrest Him, it was at night when the crowds were not around. But now they were more afraid that if they did not show their authority, the crowds would lose their respect for and fear of the Sanhedrin altogether.

**19. But the angel of the Lord by night:** . . . during the night, —WEYM . . . a messenger of the Lord, —CMPB.
**opened the prison doors, and brought them forth, and said:** . . . threw open the jail doors, —WLMS . . . conducted them out, —BRKL . . . and leading them out said, —RTHM . . . led the apostles outside, —EVRD.

**5:19.** During the night an angel of the Lord came to the prison. (The Greek does not have the article "the," but simply means one of the host of angels who are available as ministering spirits to be sent out to minister to or serve those who are and shall be heirs of salvation; see Hebrews 1:14.) "Angel" means "messenger," and this angel was a messenger sent from the Lord with the power to open the doors of the prison, which he proceeded to do. The prison had guards, but the account does not say what happened to them.

From what the Bible says in other places, it is probable that the Lord caused a deep sleep to come upon these guards so they were totally unaware of the opening of the gates and the departure of the Twelve.

**20. Go, stand and speak in the temple to the people all the words of this life:** ... Go ... and take your stand in the Temple Courts, and tell the people all you have to say about the new Life, –TCNT ... stand where you have been standing, –NLTG ... keep on telling the people, –BECK ... the full message, –NIV ... and continue proclaiming, –WEYM ... proclaim all the doctrines of the Gospel, –NOLI ... the declarations of this life, –CNDT ... all about this life, –WMCK ... everything about this new life, –EVRD.

**5:20.** After bringing the apostles out, the angel commanded them to go and take their stand and keep on speaking "in the temple to the people all the words of this life," that is, the words that were giving life to those who believed. Similar phraseology was used by Peter and the Twelve when they recognized that Jesus had the words of eternal life (John 6:68). Later Peter identified this as the Word of the Lord which endures forever, the Word which by the gospel is preached (1 Peter 1:25). In all these instances a form of the Greek *rhēma* is used. *Rhēma* is often a spoken word or utterance, the concrete expression of the Word (*logos*) of God.

**21. And when they heard that, they entered into the temple early in the morning, and taught:** ... Following this instruction, –NORL ... they went into the house of God, –NLTG ... just before daybreak, and began to teach, –WEYM ... Then they did as they were told, –WMCK

**But the high priest came, and they that were with him:** ... Meanwhile the chief priest and his party came, –KLST ... When the head religious leader, –NLTG ... and his supporters arrived, –NAB.

**and called the council together:** ... they summoned the Sanhedrin, –MNTG ... They called a meeting of, –NCV ... they gathered the men of the court, –NLTG ... they convoked the Sanhedrin, –NAB ... the Supreme Council, –TNT.

**and all the senate of the children of Israel:** ... even the whole Senate of the sons of Israel, –BRKL ... the full council of the elders of Israel, –NAB ... and the leaders of the Jews together, –NLTG.

**and sent to the prison to have them brought:** ... They sent word to the jail that the prisoners were to be brought in, –NAB ... the prison house, –ASV.

**5:21.** Because of the angel's command, the 12 apostles rose up very early in the morning and went into the temple. By dawn they were already proceeding to teach publicly. This must have astonished the people who had seen them arrested and thrown into the prison the night before.

It must also have encouraged the believers and helped all the people to see that God was still with the apostles. It was also further confirmation that their message was true and God was standing behind both them and His Word which they were proclaiming with such boldness.

Sometime later that morning, the high priest and his associates called the Council (the Sanhedrin) together. This Council is further identified as the whole Senate of the people of Israel. (And in Greek sometimes means "even." This is the meaning here. The Council and the Senate were the same body.) This seems to mean that all 71 members were present. In the Greek the words "and all the senate of the children (sons) of Israel" are nearly a word-for-word quote of Exodus 12:21 taken from the Septuagint. The Old Testament passage is a reference to the elders whom Moses called prior to the Exodus.

It also implies that on the previous occasion when Peter and John were arrested (as well as on some other occasions such as the trial of Jesus) only those who were Sadducees under the domination of the high priest were called. The Sadducees did make up the major portion of the Sanhedrin and constituted a quorum, so the high priest was able to carry on business this way if he wished. But this time, because they knew they were going against the feeling and desires of most of the people in Jerusalem and Judea, they brought in the full body, expecting them to concur in their decision and uphold the punishment of the apostles. Then they sent to the prison to have the apostles brought in.

**22. But when the officers came, and found them not in the prison:** ... But when the attendants came, –SWAN ... But when the temple guard got to the jail, –NAB ... when the officers arrived, –WMCK ... they couldn't find them in the jail, –ADAM ... they failed to find them, –MLNT.

**they returned, and told:** ... and hurried back with the report, –NAB ... and reported, –RSV ... told the court, –NLTG.

**5:22.** The officers who were sent to bring the apostles were not high officers. The word indicates they were servants or attendants of the high priest or of the temple. Imagine their surprise when they came to the prison and found the apostles were not there. This was something unprecedented. When Jesus was arrested, He submitted and made no attempt to escape, though He could have had 12 legions of angels to help Him. When Peter and John were arrested after the healing of the lame man, they were still in the jail the next morning, and when they were sent for there was nothing to hinder their being brought before the Council.

But God does not always work in the same way. He has His surprises.

**23. Saying, The prison truly found we shut with all safety:** . . . The jail was closed and locked, —EVRD . . . we found closed in all safety, —SWAN . . . we found locked with all security, —CNDT . . . very securely locked, —BRKL . . . carefully closed, —MRDK . . . quite securely shut, —TCNT.
**and the keepers standing without before the doors:** . . . with the guards stationed at the doors, —MNTG . . . and the guards on duty at the doors, —WMCK . . . the sentries standing at the doors, —NOLI . . . the guards at their posts outside the gates, NAB . . . and the soldiers watching the doors, —NLTG . . . standing outside in front of the doors, —KJII.
**but when we had opened, we found no man within:** . . . when we went in, —NOLI . . . no one inside, —SWAN . . . the jail was empty! —NCV.

**5:23.** Apparently these temple servants or attendants did not waste any time. There were no hidden corners for the apostles to hide in. So all these attendants could do was go back quickly to the Sanhedrin and tell them what they found. They explained that the prison doors were still "shut with all safety," that is, with full security, which means the doors were all locked. The keepers (the guards) were still standing outside in front of the doors. The Sanhedrin had been careful to be sure that no one could come in and try to rescue the apostles. There was no evidence that anyone had been careless. But when they opened the doors, they found there was no one inside the prison.

**24. Now when the high priest and the captain of the temple and the chief priests heard these things:** . . . both the magistrate of the temple, —HNSN . . . When the religious leaders and the leader of the house of God heard this, —NLTG . . . and the leading priests, —NCV . . . heard this report, —NOLI.
**they doubted of them whereunto this would grow:** . . . were confused, —EVRD . . . utterly at a loss concerning them, —RTHM . . . were perplexed about the apostles, wondering what could have happened, —TNT . . . they were utterly at a loss to know how this might turn out, —WLMS . . . wondering what would happen next, —WEYM . . . they were completely at a loss how to account for it, —BRKL . . . they wondered what had become of them, —NOLI . . . wondered anxiously what it could mean, —WMCK . . . they were much perplexed about it as to how this thing could have happened, —KLST . . . they were much troubled as to what might happen, —NLTG . . . what might result from this, —SWAN.

**5:24.** This report of the attendants caused the high priest and his associates, including the captain of the temple guard, to be in doubt (troubled and at a loss concerning the apostles, wondering what would come of this). "Grow" here translates a form of the Greek word for *become* or *happen*.

This also implies they wondered and were very worried about what would happen next.

What a contrast there was between these religious leaders and the common people of Israel. The people were giving respect to the apostles and the believers. They were rejoicing and giving God the praise for the miracles. But these leaders cared nothing for the common people or their needs. They did not want to see revival. They did not want to see God move. All they wanted was to preserve the status quo and to keep their own power structure which they had set up. They did not really want to serve the people or the temple. They wanted the people and the temple to serve them. The question that really filled their minds was how they were going to stop this and keep anything else from happening that would disturb them.

**25. Then came one and told them, saying:** . . . but a man came up and reported, —WMCK . . . Then someone, coming, announced to them, —SWAN.
**Behold, the men whom ye put in prison are standing in the temple, and teaching the people:** . . . At this very moment, —JB . . . are actually in the temple, —TNT . . . are standing right here in the temple square, —WLMS . . . preaching to the people, —NOLI.

**5:25.** While the Sanhedrin members were still sitting there wondering and upset, someone arrived and reported that the men who were supposed to be in the prison were in the temple, standing there openly and publicly teaching the people. They were doing again the very thing that had brought their arrest the day before.

These Jewish leaders should have learned from this that though they could throw the preachers or proclaimers of the gospel into prison, there is no way God would let them stop the gospel from being preached.

**26. Then went the captain with the officers:** . . . military commander, —WLMS . . . The leader of the house of God took his men, —NLTG.
**and brought them without violence:** . . . and got them. They did not hurt the missionaries, —NLTG . . . but without using violence, —WEYM . . . not, however, by force, —MNTG . . . the soldiers did not use force, —EVRD, —NCV.
**for they feared the people, lest they should have been stoned:** . . . afraid of being pelted with stones, —WLMS . . . would kill them with stones, —EVRD . . . afraid the people would throw stones at them, —NLTG.

**5:26.** The captain (commander of the temple guard) then went with the officers (servants, attendants of the temple) and brought the apostles without violence, that is, without the use of force.

This probably means they came up to them in the temple very quietly, gathered around them, and talked to them very politely. These temple officers were very careful because they were afraid the people would turn on them and stone them. They had dealt with mobs before. They knew what a mob spirit and mob violence could do when it was stirred up.

Actually, of course, they did not need to use force. The apostles went willingly even though they also knew they had but to say the word and the mob would have stoned these officers as blasphemers of God's servants and enemies of God. Stoning in Old Testament times had been the punishment of willful, high-handed sin and rebellion.

The apostles did not resist, however, because they had the words of Jesus that they would appear before councils and kings, and the Holy Spirit would give them the words to say (Matthew 10:17-20). They undoubtedly hoped this arrest would become another opportunity to witness for their Messiah and Saviour.

**27. And when they had brought them, they set them before the council:** . . . and made them stand before, –NCV . . . the Sanhedrin, –WEYM . . . stand in front of the court, –NLTG.

**and the high priest asked them:** . . . The High Priest demanded an explanation from them, –TCNT . . . examined them, –BRKL . . . questioned them carefully, –KLGS.

**5:27.** When they brought the apostles into the room where the Sanhedrin was meeting, they made them stand before the Council, that is, before its 71 members. It should be noted that when the high priest began speaking, he avoided asking the apostles how they got out of the prison. It was obviously something supernatural, and it may very well be that he did not want to hear about angels he did not believe in. He probably did not want to hear praise to God for this deliverance either.

**28. Saying, Did not we straitly command you that ye should not teach in this name?:** . . . Did we not give you strict orders . . . to not teach in this name, –NORL . . . Did we not positively forbid you, –WLMS . . . We absolutely prohibited you, –FNTN . . . We gave you a formal warning, –JB . . . We strictly enjoined you, –DRBY . . . We told you and told you, –KLGS . . . We gave you very clear orders, –BB . . . We gave you strict orders not to go on teaching, –EVRD.

**and, behold, ye have filled Jerusalem with your doctrine:** . . . you have actually flooded Jerusalem, –TCNT . . . You are spreading this teaching over, –NLTG . . . with your teaching, –RSV.

**and intend to bring this man's blood upon us:** . . . and are wishing to make us responsible for the death of this man, –TCNT . . . accuse us as responsible for this man's death, –NOLI . . . and now want to bring on us the people's vengeance for this man's death, –WLMS . . . And you want to get us punished for killing this Man, –BECK . . . you wish to bring upon us the blood of this man, –KLGS . . . Now you are making it look as if we are guilty of killing this Man, –NLTG . . . You are determined to make us responsible for, –KLST.

**5:28.** The high priest began by asking the apostles if the Sanhedrin had not given them strict orders not to teach in this name. Other versions (NIV, RSV) translate these words as a statement rather than a question. Since the Greek term *parangellia* has the meaning of "injunction," in essence the Sanhedrin was saying, "We gave you an injunction not to teach in this name!" The word "this" was used by him in a belittling sense and was intended to be a derogatory reference to the name of Jesus.

The high priest accused the apostles of filling Jerusalem with their doctrine (teaching), desiring to bring on the Jewish leaders "this man's blood"; that is, they accused the disciples of wanting the people to believe they were guilty of murder in the death of Jesus, hoping the crowd would avenge His death. He evidently forgot the declaration of the crowd recorded in Matthew 27:25, "His blood be on us, and on our children."

The statement that they had filled Jerusalem with their teaching was a great admission of the effectiveness of the apostles' witness. Yet the high priest totally misunderstood their purpose, probably because, in spite of himself, he felt guilty for what had been done to Jesus. The statement that the apostles wanted to bring vengeance on them for the death of Jesus was nothing but pure slander and was completely false.

**29. Then Peter and the other apostles answered and said:** . . . and the missionaries said, –NLTG.

**We ought to obey God rather than men:** . . . We must obey, –RSV . . . Better for us, –NAB . . . the orders of God, –PHLP.

**5:29.** Peter and the apostles did not apologize. Without hesitation they answered (with Peter as the spokesman), "It is necessary to obey God rather than human beings" (author's translation). "Obey" is a word used of obedience to one in authority as in Titus 3:1. With a consciousness of Christ's authority, the apostles said the equivalent of "We must obey." Before, in 4:19, they said, "You judge." But the Sanhedrin did not judge that the apostles were under divinely appointed necessity to spread the gospel. Therefore, the apostles had to declare themselves very strongly here.

**30. The God of our fathers raised up Jesus:** . . . of our early fathers, −NLTG . . . ancestors has raised Jesus from the grave, −TCNT . . . raised Jesus to life, −WEYM.

**whom ye slew and hanged on a tree:** . . . whom you crucified and put to death, −WEYM . . . whom you yourselves put to death, by hanging him on a cross, −TCNT . . . whom you murdered by crucifying him, −NOLI . . . you killed and nailed to a cross, −NLTG.

**5:30.** The high priest had not mentioned God or His will. Neither did he mention the name of Jesus. But Peter did not hesitate to point them to the God of their fathers, who had raised up Jesus. Then, once again, he contrasted the way God treated Jesus in raising and exalting Him with the way the Jewish leaders treated Him, hanging Him on a tree. (Both the Hebrew and Greek words for *tree* also mean wood or anything made of wood, and so "tree" here includes the cross. The cross was made of rough-hewn wood.)

**31. Him hath God exalted with his right hand to be a Prince and a Saviour:** . . . It is this Jesus, whom God has exalted to his right hand, to be a Guide, −TCNT . . . to his right side, −TEV . . . with his right hand to be captain and saviour, −WMCK . . . as a Ruler, −ADAM . . . our Pioneer, −KLGS . . . our Leader, −EVRD.

**for to give repentance to Israel, and forgiveness of sins:** . . . so that the people of Israel would have opportunity for repentance, −LIVB . . . Who saves from the penalty of sin, −NLTG . . . so that all Jews could change their hearts and lives and have their sins forgiven, −EVRD.

**5:31.** Contrary to their fears, it was not the apostles' desire, nor was it God's purpose, to punish the Jewish leaders for crucifying Jesus. Rather, God had exalted Jesus, the very One they crucified, with (and also "to") His right hand, to be a Prince (author, founder) and a Saviour, in order to give repentance to Israel and the forgiveness of sins. God's purpose was to offer the opportunity for repentance and forgiveness of sins to Israel.

Peter, of course, did not mean to restrict this offer of repentance and forgiveness to the people of Israel. God's purpose has always been to bring blessing to all the families of the earth by offering forgiveness and salvation to all sinners. Their guilt will be canceled if they repent, whoever they are. By exalting Jesus, God put Him in a position where it should be easy for sinners to repent.

**32. And we are his witnesses of these things:** . . . We saw all these things happen, −EVRD . . . We have seen these things and are telling about them, −NLTG.

**and so is also the Holy Ghost:** . . . The Holy Spirit makes these things known also, −NLTG.

**whom God hath given to them that obey him:** . . . who submit to his government, −CMPB . . . who obey his commands, −PHLP.

**5:32.** As before, the apostles emphasized they were Christ's witnesses to "these things," that is, to these words (*rhematōn*, used of the "*words* of this life" in 5:20 and therefore of the gospel message the apostles were teaching and preaching). Peter added that the Holy Spirit whom God has given is also a witness. Peter made it clear that God gave, and still gives, the Holy Spirit to those who obey Him. This corresponds to Galatians 3:2 where Paul reminded the Galatians that they received the Spirit by the hearing of faith, and both the hearing and the faith imply obedience. This also points back to Luke 11:13 which says God as a good Father gives the Holy Spirit to them that ask Him, assuming they have right motives (see James 4:3). So asking is normally a part of obedience. He is the Giver (John 15:26). It is also quite clear that the giving of the Spirit was not to be limited to the apostles or to their time.

**33. When they heard that, They were cut to the heart:** . . . The members of the Council grew furious on hearing this, −TCNT . . . And hearing it, they were convulsed with rage, −HBIE . . . Infuriated at getting this answer, −WEYM . . . they were enraged, −CMPB . . . burned with indignation, −MRDK . . . they were stung to madness, −WMCK

**and took counsel to slay them:** . . . and determined to destroy them, −BRKL . . . and made up their minds, −WMCK . . . and planned to kill them, −NORL . . . consulted to put them to death, −CMPB . . . they talked of killing them, −KLGS.

**5:33.** Apparently the majority of the Sanhedrin took Peter's words to mean the apostles not only considered them guilty of Christ's death but also guilty of a refusal to accept God's authority and obey Him. The apostles had linked their witness to the Spirit's witness. But instead of accepting the offer of repentance, the members of the Sanhedrin were cut to the heart (sawn through, cut through, cut to the quick with anger, indignation, and jealousy). Immediately they started proceedings to kill the apostles. The same word for *kill* is used of killing (murdering) Jesus in 2:23.

**34. Then stood there up one in the council:** . . . But there stood up one in the Sanhedrin, −HBIE . . . a man of the religious leaders' court, −NLTG.

**a Pharisee, named Gamaliel, a doctor of the law:** . . . a Teacher of the Law, −TCNT . . . a professor of law, −BRKL . . . He was a proud religious law-keeper, −NLTG.

**had in reputation among all the people:** . . . honoured by all the people, −RTHM . . . held in universal respect, −TCNT . . . who was highly respected by, −NOLI.

**and commanded to put the apostles forth a little space:** ... ordered the apostles to leave the meeting for a little while, —EVRD ... gave orders to put the men outside for a little time, —RTHM ... the men to be removed for a short time, —WMCK ... said that the missionaries should be sent outside, —NLTG.

**5:34.** This time the entire Sanhedrin was meeting together, and it included some prominent Pharisees. *Pharisees* probably means "separated ones," possibly referring to their emphasis on washings and ceremonial purity. The Sadducees dominated the temple and the priesthood at this time, but the Pharisees had the most influence in the synagogues and among the majority of the Jews. Pharisees were generally careful not to exceed the demands of justice in the administration of the Mosaic law.

Among the Pharisees was Gamaliel, a doctor (authoritative teacher) of the Law, a person valued highly by all the people. In the Jewish Talmud Gamaliel is said to be the grandson of the famous rabbi Hillel. Hillel was the most influential teacher of the Pharisees, a man who continued to be held in high esteem by all later orthodox Jews. The apostle Paul was trained by Gamaliel and became one of his most prominent students. Possibly, Paul, then known as Saul of Tarsus, was already a member of the Sanhedrin at this time.

At this point Gamaliel stood up, took charge of the situation, and ordered the apostles to be taken outside for a little while. Again, it is probable that Paul later told Luke what Gamaliel said and what went on while the apostles were outside.

**35.** **And said unto mem, Ye men of Israel:** ... Then Gamaliel said ... Jewish men, —NLTG.

**take heed to yourselves what ye intend to do as touching these men:** ... consider carefully, —NIV ... be careful what you are about to do in dealing with these men, —WEYM ... beware what you are going to do, —TNT ... think well before you take any action against these men, —NOLI ... be careful how you intend to treat these men, —BRKL.

**5:35.** Gamaliel gave a stern warning to the Sanhedrin. That the Sanhedrin received such advice from him is a strong indication of the great respect afforded to this rabbi. F.F. Bruce quotes the following statement recorded in the Mishnah: "When the Rabban Gamaliel died ... the glory of the Torah ceased, and purity and 'separateness' died" (*New International Commentary on the New Testament, Acts*, p. 115). Bruce goes on to explain that "Rabban" (Aramaic for "our teacher") was a title of great honor bestowed only upon the most distinguished teachers. This title set them apart from others who were called "rabbi," which means "my teacher" (ibid.).

Gamaliel warned the Council that they must be cautious about (and give careful attention to) what they were intending to do (or, were about to do) to these men. Obviously Gamaliel sensed the anger and indignation rising up in the hearts of the members of the Sanhedrin. This kind of anger can become irrational. It can turn thinking men into an unthinking mob, just as it did at the trial of Jesus when the priest-dominated crowd cried out, "Crucify Him!" (Just a few days earlier the crowd had cried out, "Hosanna! Blessed is he who comes in the name of the Lord.")

Again it must be remembered that the high priest gathered only part of the Sanhedrin at night for the trial of Jesus. It is evident that men like Gamaliel were not present on that night. Neither was the crowd that had cried "hosanna" present. Most of them were staying outside the city in the villages around about. Jesus was already being led out by the Roman soldiers to be crucified when the crowds began coming into Jerusalem the following morning. But in the providence of God, the high priest and the Sadducees were not alone this time. Gamaliel and others were present. Perhaps also Gamaliel did not feel the same anger and indignation; he was a highly respected, rational, and well-educated man.

**36.** **For before these days rose up Theudas:** ... Years ago, —MNTG ... Remember that some time ago, —NOLI ... For it is not long ago that Theudas appeared, —TCNT ... who became notorious, —JB ... made himself conspicuous, —PHLP.

**boasting himself to be somebody:** ... affirming himself to be, —RTHM ... claiming to be, —TCNT ... professing to be a person of importance, —WEYM ... He said that he was a great man, —EVRD ... claimed to be a divine messenger, —NOLI.

**to whom a number of men, about four hundred, joined themselves:** ... espoused his cause, —WLMS ... adhered to him, —BRKL.

**who was slain:** ... He himself was killed, —TCNT ... who was assassinated, —CNDT.

**and all, as many as obeyed him, were scattered:** ... all his supporters, —BRKL ... all his followers were dispersed, —WEYM ... were divided, —NLTG.

**And brought to nought:** ... and came to nothing, —RSV ... and as a party annihilated, —WLMS ... They were able to do nothing, —EVRD, —NCV ... and that was the end of them, —TNT ... and their movement was suppressed, —NOLI ... and nothing came of his teaching, —NLTG.

**5:36.** By two examples Gamaliel reminded the Sanhedrin that individuals in the past had gathered a following, but came to nothing.

The first example was Theudas, who said of himself that he was something, that is, something great. He was probably a man of the same order as Simon the sorcerer who deceived the Samaritans by his trickery and pretended to be the great power of God.

*Theudas* was a common name, and he was probably one of the rebels who arose after Herod the Great died in 4 B.C. Some have confused this Theudas with a later Theudas of whom Josephus, the Jewish historian, speaks. Josephus referred to this latter individual as a "magician" who persuaded a great many people to gather all their possessions and follow him to the Jordan River. This self-proclaimed prophet boasted that he would command the Jordan to part, as did Elijah and Elisha (*Antiquities* 20.5.1). His grandiose plans were short-lived: Fadus, the procurator who succeeded Agrippa I in A.D. 44, beheaded him (Carter and Earle, *Acts*, p. 83). To this Theudas about 400 men attached themselves. He was murdered, and all who obeyed him (and believed in him) were dispersed and came to nothing.

**37. After this man rose up Judas of Galilee:** . . . came into prominence, *—ADAM.*

**in the days of the taxing:** . . . at the time of the census, *—TCNT* . . . of the enrollment for the Roman tax, *—WLMS* . . . at the time of the registration, *—EVRD.*

**and drew away much people after him:** . . . and drew a people into a revolt after him, *—RTHM* . . . and got people to follow him, *—TCNT* . . . and was the leader in a revolt, *—WEYM.*

**he also perished:** . . . but he too was destroyed, *—WMCK*

**and all, even as many as obeyed him, were dispersed:** . . . were scattered abroad, *—ASV* . . . to the winds, *—NORL.*

**5:37.** After Theudas, Judas the Galilean rose up in the days of the taxing, that is, of the census which was taken for the purpose of taxing.

The Romans ordered the first census of the people and their property in 10-9 B.C. It reached Palestine about 6 B.C., at the time Jesus was born in Bethlehem (Luke 2:2). There was another similar census every 14 years after that. The second census reached Palestine, however, in A.D. 6 when this Judas arose and, according to Josephus, taught the people not to pay tribute to Caesar.

This Judas of Galilee succeeded in drawing away a considerable number of the Jewish people after him. But he also perished, and all who obeyed him (and believed in him) were scattered.

**38. And now I say unto you:** . . . And in this present case, my advice to you is, *—TCNT* . . . What I suggest, therefore, *—JB* . . . And so not I tell you, *—EVRD.*

**Refrain from these men, and let them alone:** . . . Stand aloof from these men, *—RTHM* . . . leave them alone, *—NORL* . . . keep away from these men, *—BECK* . . . keep your hands off these men, let them alone, *—WMCK* . . . Stay away from these men, *—EVRD* . . . let them go, *—NIV.*

**for if this counsel or this work be of men:** . . . If this teaching and work is from, *—NLTG* . . . for if this scheme or work, *—WEYM* . . . if their movement is of, *—NOLI* . . . are only of human origin, *—TCNT* . . . For, if this program or movement has its origin in man, *—WLMS* . . . For if what they are planning or doing is man's work, *—WMCK*

**it will come to nought:** . . . come to nothing, *—WEYM* . . . go to pieces, *—WLMS* . . . fail, *—RSV* . . . break down, *—BECK* . . . it will collapse, *—MOFT* . . . it will be wrecked inevitably, *—NOLI.*

**5:38.** Gamaliel's conclusion was that they should refrain from "these men" (the apostles), that is, withdraw from them and leave them alone. In other words, they should let them go, for if "this counsel or this work" was from (out from) men (it had a mere human source from human ideas, human thinking, or human plotting) it would come to nought, it would be overthrown or destroyed.

**39. But if it be of God, ye cannot overthrow it:** . . . you will be powerless to put them down, *—WEYM* . . . If it is of divine origin, you cannot put it down, *—NOLI* . . . it is not in your power to frustrate it, *—MRDK* . . . you won't be able to stop them, *—ADAM.*

**lest haply ye be found even to fight against God:** . . . lest perhaps you find yourselves to be actually fighting against God, *—WEYM* . . . find yourselves to be God resisters, *—BRKL* . . . opposing God, *—NORL.*

**5:39.** On the other hand, Gamaliel continued, if it was from God they would not be able to overthrow it (or them, that is, the apostles and the movement they were leading). They must therefore let these men go, lest perhaps they also would be found to be "ones fighting against God" (one word in the Greek).

It is important to keep in mind here that this was the Pharisee Gamaliel speaking. The Bible here gives us the inspired record which makes it clear that Gamaliel really did say this. But no one must jump to the conclusion that what Gamaliel himself said was inspired. His recorded words were the conclusions of his own thinking, his own human reasoning.

There is a measure of truth in what Gamaliel said. Gamaliel did know the Old Testament Scriptures, and they make it very clear that what is from God cannot be overthrown. It is true also that it is foolish to try to use physical means to overthrow spiritual forces. But it is not true that everything from men will always be quickly overthrown; not every movement or political system of mere human origin has been short-lived.

**40. and to him they agreed:** . . . And they were persuaded by him, *—RTHM* . . . And to him they assented, *—HBIE* . . . His advice carried conviction, *—WEYM* . . . Gamaliel's advice prevailed, *—NORL* . . . They gave in to him, —MNTG... They were convinced by him, —WLMS... They listened to his advice, —KLGS.

**and when they had called the apostles and beaten them:**... had them flogged, —TCNT... lashing them, —CNDT... they beat them, —DRBY.

**they commanded that they should not speak in the name of Jesus, and let them go:**... they charged them to stop speaking on the authority of Jesus, and then turned them loose, —WLMS... released them, —NORL.

**5:40.** The whole body of the Sanhedrin was persuaded by the words of Gamaliel. Therefore, they called the 12 apostles back into their council chamber and had them severely flogged with whips. The Greek word for "beaten" actually means "skinned," and is the same word used of flaying, that is, skinning the animals who were sacrificed under the Law. Thus the Sanhedrin still took out their spite and indignation on the apostles. Undoubtedly they followed the law of Deuteronomy 25:2, 3 which indicated the persons to be beaten had to lie face down and that the limit was 40 stripes.

Jesus had anticipated this and had warned His disciples they would be beaten (Mark 13:9). Jesus never promised that His followers would always be prosperous in a material sense or that they would always be free from persecution. He told them they would have tribulation (persecution, affliction, distress, pressure), but He promised, "Be of good cheer (take courage); I have overcome (conquered, and am still conqueror over) the world" (John 16:33).

After beating the apostles, the Sanhedrin again commanded (ordered) them not to speak in the name of Jesus (that is, with a view to promoting the authority of Jesus). Then the Council let them go (set them free).

**41. And they departed from the presence of the council:**... But the Apostles left the Council, —TCNT... They, therefore, left the Sanhedrin, —WEYM.

**rejoicing that they were counted worthy to suffer shame for his name:**... they were fit to suffer, —KLGS... the honor of suffering dishonor, —SEB... to suffer disgrace on behalf of the Name, —WEYM... deemed worthy to be dishonored, —CNDT... suffer abuse, —MRDK... of suffering humiliation, —JB... suffer indignity, —NEB... to suffer shame for Jesus, —BECK.

**5:41.** The apostles went away from the presence of the Sanhedrin rejoicing and continuing to rejoice because they were counted worthy to suffer shame (suffer disgrace, be treated disgracefully, dishonored, insulted, and despised) for the sake of the Name. They rejoiced to be disgraced (beaten with the punishment the Law commanded for evil men and criminals) for the sake of all that

the name of Jesus includes. They understood the Name to include His character and nature, especially His messiahship, deity, saviourhood, and lordship.

**42. And daily in the temple, and in every house:**... or in private houses, —TCNT.

**they ceased not to teach and preach Jesus Christ:**... they did not for a single day cease, —CNFT... to teach unceasingly, —PHLP... the Gospel of Jesus, the Messiah, —MNTG... Jesus is the promised Saviour, —BECK... announcing the glad tidings, —DRBY... they kept right on teaching, NASB... evangelizing, —ALFD.

**5:42.** It seems that this beating satisfied the anger of the Jewish priests and leaders for the time being, and their opposition subsided for a considerable period. But the apostles still knew they must obey God rather than men, so they refused to obey the command of the Sanhedrin, and they kept right on preaching and teaching the gospel and honoring the name of Jesus.

Every day in the temple and also going from house to house they never ceased teaching and preaching the good news (the gospel) of Jesus the Christ (the Messiah Jesus). They boldly defied the orders of the Sanhedrin and paid no attention to their threats. They did not even wait for their backs to heal. Instead they engaged in a regular program of teaching and evangelism.

## Chapter 6

**1. And in those days:**... About this time, —TCNT.

**when the number of the disciples was multiplied:**... was constantly increasing, —TCNT... kept growing, —BRKL... the number of the students was increased, —KLGS.

**there arose a murmuring of the Grecians against the Hebrews:**... protests were made, —BB... the Greeks in the group began to complain, —NORL... low, undertone murmuring... secretly complaining against, —WUST... complaints were made by the Greek-speaking Jews against the native Jews, —TCNT... a complaint was brought against those who spoke Aramaic by those who spoke Greek, —BECK.

**because their widows were neglected in the daily ministration:**... were being overlooked in the daily distribution, —TCNT... were habitually overlooked in the distribution of alms, —MNTG... daily provision of food, —WUST... daily serving of food, —ADAM... daily rationing, —KLGS... distribution of relief, —FNTN... when the food was handed out, —BECK.

**6:1.** As a result of this regular program of teaching and evangelizing, the number of disciples (learners, believers desiring to learn more about Jesus and the gospel) kept multiplying.

All these newcomers crowding in caused problems. In this case the growing Church was a cross section of society as it was in Jerusalem and Judea.

Some of the believers were born there and spoke Hebrew in their homes. (Jerusalem Jews kept alive the Biblical Hebrew.) They knew Greek as a second language, for Greek was the language of trade, commerce, and government since the time of Alexander the Great. But the Jews born outside of Palestine did not know Hebrew well and normally spoke Greek.

In the previous chapters Luke recorded that believers contributed to a common fund for the needy. As time went on, most believers found work and no longer needed this help. Widows, however, could not go out and get a job, and soon they were the only ones left who still needed help from this fund. As the Early Church developed, concern for these widows became more evident. The Epistle of James, for example, considers caring for widows (and orphans) one aspect of the kind of a pure and faultless religion God accepts (James 1:27). Later, Paul specified how congregations were to provide for their widows (1 Timothy 5:3-10).

It seems that the Greek-speaking widows who did not understand Hebrew held back, so they were easily overlooked. The result was that tension built up between the Greek-speaking and Hebrew-speaking believers. Finally a murmuring (a grumbling half under their breath) arose among the Greek-speaking believers against the Hebrew-speaking believers because their widows were being neglected (overlooked) in the daily ministration (service).

**2. Then the twelve called the multitude of the disciples unto them, and said:** ... The Twelve, therefore, summoned the general body of the disciples and said to them, —TCNT ... then convened, —FNTN ... the main body, —MOFT ... addressed them, —RIEU.

**It is not reason that we should leave the word of God:** ... It will not do for us to neglect God's message, —TCNT ... it would be a grave mistake, —NEB ... neglect the teaching of God's word, —BRKL ... forsaking, —RTHM ... drop preaching, —MOFT.

**and serve tables:** ... to attend, —TCNT ... to wait on, —WLMS ... to attend to mere money matters, —FNTN ... to look after the accounts, —PHLP ... to hand out food, —NLTG.

**6:2.** When the 12 apostles (including Matthias) realized how serious this division was becoming, they called the multitude (the whole mass) of the disciples together. They told them it was not reasonable (pleasing, satisfactory, or acceptable) for them to leave or abandon the teaching and preaching of God's Word to serve tables (in this case, to take care of money tables). They would have to quit preaching and teaching and give all

their time to this ministry if they were to personally see that no widow was neglected.

**3. Wherefore, brethren, look ye out among you:** ... choose, —NLTG ... pick out from among yourselves, —WEYM ... from your number, —NOLI.

**seven men of honest report:** ... who can be well-attested, —RTHM ... of an attested character, —CMPB ... reputable, —CNDT ... good testimony, —MRDK ... of good standing, —NOLI ... who are respected, —NLTG.

**full of the Holy Ghost and wisdom:** ... full of the Spirit, and of good practical sense, —WLMS ... who are both practical and spiritually-minded, —PHLP.

**whom we may appoint over this business:** ... and we will appoint them to undertake this duty, —WEYM ... We will turn this responsibility over to them, —NIV ... We will have them take care of this work, —NLTG ... We will put them in charge of this service, —NOLI.

**6:3.** The apostles told the believers to choose from among themselves seven men full of the Holy Spirit and practical wisdom. These the apostles would appoint (set) "over this business" (need). In other words, the apostles laid down the qualifications and the people looked over the congregation to see who had these qualifications to a high degree. Then the people chose the seven through some kind of election. The apostles did not arbitrarily put seven men in charge. The congregation did the choosing, not the apostles.

The seven are not called deacons here, though the verb is related to *diakoneō*, from which *deacon* is derived. Most probably, this election gave a precedent for the office of deacon mentioned later. (See 1 Timothy 3:8-12; Romans 16:1, where Phoebe is called a *diakonon*, the word which is elsewhere translated "deacon, servant," or "minister.")

Some see a special significance in the number seven here as a number of completeness. More likely the only reason for having seven deacons was that seven were needed to keep the accounts and give out the money from the money tables (as the Greek word indicates) to the widows. Notice too that there were no deacons until deacons were needed.

**4. But we will give ourselves continually to prayer:** ... But, as for us, we will devote ourselves to prayer, —WEYM.

**and to the ministry of the word:** ... and to the delivery of the Message, —TCNT ... and to preaching, —NOLI.

**6:4.** Choosing the 7 would enable the 12 apostles to give themselves to prayer and the ministry (*ministration;* Greek *diakonia*, the same word used in verse 1 for the daily ministration to the widows) of the Word. The apostles would serve the Word, while the seven served tables.

**5. And the saying pleased the whole multitude:** . . . the whole group was pleased with the apostles' proposal, *—TEV* . . . was pleasing in the sight of all the throng, *—RTHM* . . . This proposal was unanimously agreed to, *—TCNT* . . . This recommendation met with the approval of, *—NOLI* . . . The suggestion met with general approval, *—WEYM* . . . The whole group liked the idea, *—BECK* . . . This plan commended itself to the whole body, *—MNTG.*

**and they chose Stephen:** . . . and they selected Stephen, *—RTHM* . . . they elected Stephen, *—SAWR.*

**a man full of faith and of the Holy Ghost, and Philip, and Prochorus, and Nicanor, and Timon, and Parmenas:**

**and Nicolas a proselyte of Antioch:** . . . and Nicholas of Antioch, a former convert to Judaism, *—TCNT.*

**6:5.** There was no dissent to this direction given by the apostles, for the saying (*word,* Greek, *logos*) pleased the whole crowd of the believers (implying also, that they were all willing to do their part even if it meant serving in this capacity).

They then proceeded to choose Stephen (Greek for *victor's crown* or *wreath*), a man full of faith and the Holy Spirit; Philip (Greek for *lover of horses*), Prochorus, Nicanor, Timon, Parmenas, and Nicolas, a proselyte (a Gentile convert to Judaism) from Antioch of Syria. (Later traditions tried to connect this Nicolas with the Nicolaitans of Revelation 2:6, 15, but there is no real evidence of this.)

All of the seven who were chosen had Greek names and were undoubtedly from the Greek-speaking believers. Surely this shows the grace of God and the work of the Holy Spirit in the hearts of the Hebrew-speaking believers. They were in the majority, but they chose all the "deacons" out of the minority group. These seven would have charge of the administration of the fund for the needy of both groups. Thus, no possible complaint could now be lodged by the Greek-speaking believers. This was wisdom and it shows how the Holy Spirit broke down this first barrier that rose up in the Church. Language is still a barrier in the world. But the Holy Spirit can help people of different languages to love and serve one another.

**6. Whom they set before the apostles:** . . . These men were taken to the missionaries, *—NLTG.*

**and when they had prayed they laid their hands on them:** . . . who then prayed and placed their hands on them, *—TCNT* . . . and, after prayer, they, *—WEYM* . . . After praying, the missionaries laid their hands on them, *—NLTG.*

**6:6.** The people brought the seven before the apostles, who laid their hands on them. This laying on of hands was probably like the public recognition of Joshua in Numbers 27:18, 19. Stephen and the others were all full of the Spirit before this. The laying on of hands symbolized prayer for God's blessing on them. The apostles probably prayed also that the Spirit would give these men whatever gift and graces would be necessary for this ministry.

**7. And the word of God increased:** . . . So God's Message spread, *—TCNT* . . . Meanwhile God's word continued to spread, *—WEYM* . . . In the meantime, the message of God continued to spread, *—NOLI* . . . message of God extended, *—FNTN* . . . God's Word kept on spreading, *—BECK* . . . word of God went on growing, *—PNT* . . . spread further, *—NLTG.*

**and the number of the disciples multiplied in Jerusalem greatly:** . . . exceedingly, *—ASV* . . . rapidly, *—TCNT* . . . multiplied tremendously, *—CNDT* . . . continued to grow, *—WLMS* . . . greatly increased, *—FNTN* . . . became much larger, *—NLTG.*

**and a great company of the priests were obedient to the faith:** . . . a vast throng, *—CNDT* . . . and a large body of the priests accepted the Faith, *—TCNT* . . . and a great multitude . . . were obeying the faith, *—HBIE* . . . a large number even of priests continued to surrender to the faith, *—WLMS* . . . subdued to the faith, *—FNTN* . . . Many of the religious leaders believed in the faith of the Christians, *—NLTG.*

**6:7.** Luke concluded this incident with another summary statement: "The Word of God increased" (kept on growing). This implies that not only the apostles were involved in spreading the Word. All the believers were involved in proclaiming the Word. As a result the number of disciples kept on multiplying (increasing) in Jerusalem. Among these new disciples were a large crowd of priests, and they too became obedient to the Faith, the body of truth proclaimed and taught by the apostles. Josephus said there were 20,000 priests at this time. That a large number of them accepted the gospel probably means that many of them were Sadducees. Since they did not believe in the Resurrection, this was a major breakthrough. (Some writers say the priests who were converted were humble priests, like the father of John the Baptist, who were obviously not Sadducees. But most of the priests were Sadducees, so this large number would include at least some of that party.)

**8. And Stephen, full of faith and power:** . . . full of grace and power, *—ASV* . . . full of God's gifts and power, *—BECK* . . . active benevolence, *—FNTN.*

**did great wonders and miracles among the people:** . . . wrought great wonders and signs, *—ASV* . . . wrought notable wonders, *—BRKL.*

**6:8.** The fact that the seven (deacons) were chosen to carry out a rather routine service with the wisdom and grace of the Spirit did not limit their ministry in other areas. Stephen was full of faith (or *grace,* as many Greek manuscripts read). He was both the recipient and the channel of God's grace, God's unmerited favor. He was also full of mighty power, and he began to do (and kept on doing) wonders and great signs among the people. The people were not merely spectators. They also experienced the mighty miracles as God's gifts (or gifts of the Holy Spirit) to meet their needs.

This is the first time the Book of Acts indicates miracles were done by those who were not apostles. The important thing, however, is that the Holy Spirit was working through Stephen.

**9. Then there arose certain of the synagogue, which is called the synagogue of the Libertines, and Cyrenians, and Alexandrians, and of them of Cilicia and of Asia:** . . . the Freedmen, —NOYS . . . But some members from the Synagogue known as that of the Freed Slaves and . . . as well as visitors from Cilicia and Roman Asia, —TCNT.

**disputing with Stephen:** . . . They all came and argued with, —EVRD.

**6:9.** Soon opposition arose. This time it came from Greek-speaking Jews who, like Stephen, had returned from the Dispersion to live in Jerusalem. They had their own synagogue or synagogues. ("Synagogue," literally, "gathering together place," was a combination community center, school, a place for reading and commenting on the Scriptures on the Sabbath. The word here is singular, but many take it as a distributive word and apply it to each group, for Jewish tradition says there were a great many synagogues in Jerusalem at this time.)

The opposition included Jews who were Libertines, former slaves who had been set free by their Roman masters. When the Romans conquered a city they usually took the doctors, lawyers, teachers, and skilled workers and gave them as gifts to their friends. But the Romans also considered it a religious thing to set slaves free, so there was a large class of these freedmen in Rome. Also included in the opposition were Cyrenians from Cyrene, west of Egypt on the Mediterranean coast, and Alexandrians from Alexandria in Egypt where there was a very large Jewish quarter. Others were from Cilicia (Paul's home province in southeastern Asia Minor) and from the province of Asia (in western Asia Minor) where Ephesus was the chief city.

Most of these Jews in the Dispersion had to face many threats to their teaching, living as they did, surrounded by Gentiles. As a result they were quicker to defend themselves against anything different from what their rabbis taught them. So they engaged Stephen in debate and kept trying to dispute the truth of his teachings about Jesus.

**10. And they were not able to resist the wisdom and the spirit by which he spake:** . . . But the Spirit was helping him to speak with wisdom, —EVRD . . . they could not match, —NORL . . . to withstand the wisdom, —ASV . . . and inspiration, —TCNT . . . but they could not cope with his good practical sense and the spiritual power, —WLMS . . . to be unable to stand up against his wisdom, —WUST . . . They were not able to say anything against what he said, —NLTG . . . the intelligence, —FNTN . . . either his practical wisdom or the spiritual force, —PHLP.

**6:10.** Stephen had a distinct advantage. He was not depending on his own wisdom to proclaim the truth, but on the anointing and gifts of the Holy Spirit. So all their arguments fell flat. They did not have the strength or power to stand against the wisdom and the Spirit by which Stephen was speaking.

**11. Then they suborned men, which said:** . . . In desperation, —PHLP . . . So they paid some men to say, —EVRD . . . they secretly instigated men, who said, —RSV . . . they induced some men to say, —TCNT . . . they bribed men to say, —WMCK . . . Then they privately put forward men who declared, —WEYM . . . men who alleged, —NEB.

**We have heard him speak blasphemous words against Moses, and against God:** . . . We heard him slander Moses and God, —BECK.

**6:11.** Though they did not have the Scriptures or reason on their side, these Greek-speaking Jews still refused to believe and only became more and more determined to get rid of Stephen. They suborned men (obtained them in some unfair way) who said they had heard Stephen speaking blasphemous (abusive, scurrilous) words against Moses and against God.

**12. And they stirred up the people:** . . . In this way they excited the people, —WEYM . . . Thus they got the people wrought up, —BRKL . . . And they roused the people, —DRBY.

**and the elders, and the scribes:** . . . and the presbyters, —HNSN . . . as well as the Councillors and Rabbis, —TCNT . . . and the men of the Law, —BECK.

**and came upon him, and caught him:** . . . coming suddenly, —WLSN . . . and arrested, —TCNT . . . seized him with violence, —WEYM . . . they attacked and grabbed him, —BRKL . . . took him by force, —KLGS . . . set upon him, arrested him, —NOLI.

**and brought him to the council:** . . . Sanhedrin, —HBIE . . . before the court, —BECK.

**6:12.** In order to carry out their plan to stop Stephen, these Greek-speaking Jews stirred up the (Jewish) people (violently) and also the elders (who were members of the Sanhedrin) and the scribes (who not only copied the law of Moses, but who claimed to be experts in its interpretation).

With all these groups supporting them, they came upon Stephen suddenly and unexpectedly, caught him (took hold of him violently and kept a firm grip on him), and brought him to the Council.

**13. And set up false witnesses, which said:** ... Then they produced, *—WMCK* ... Here they brought forward false witnesses who declared, *—WEYM* ... There they had witnesses stand up and lie, *—BECK* ... The people were told to lie and say, *—NLTG* ... They brought in some men to tell lies about Stephen, *—EVRD.*

**This man ceaseth not to speak blasphemous words against this holy place, and the law:** ... this man never quits uttering statements against, *—BRKL* ... constantly saying things against, *—GDSP* ... speaks incessantly against, *—SAWR* ... is constantly uttering, *—NOLI* ... contrary to the law, *—MRDK* ... incessantly saying things, *—TCNT* ... never ceases speaking words against, *—KLST.*

**6:13.** Then those who were trying to stop Stephen set up false witnesses, witnesses who misrepresented the words of Stephen in a false and misleading way, putting him in as bad a light as possible. They took the stand and said this man continued to speak words against this holy place (the temple) and against the Law (of Moses).

It is probable that all Stephen had done was tell how Jesus had overthrown the tables of the money changers in the temple and said they had made the temple a den of thieves (Matthew 21:13). He must have also told of the many times Jesus corrected the misinterpretations of the law of Moses, misinterpretations that the scribes and Pharisees promoted, who, for example, criticized Jesus for doing good on the Sabbath Day (John 5:16; Luke 13:11-17).

**14. For we have heard him say** indeed, we have heard him declare, *—TCNT.*

**that this Jesus of Nazareth shall destroy this place:** ... that Jesus, the Nazarene, *—WEYM* ... will demolish this place, *—BRKL* ... will tear this sanctuary down, *—NOLI* ... pull down this place, *—NLTG.*

**and shall change the customs which Moses delivered us:** ... change the rites, *—MRDK* ... change the constitutions which has been transmitted, *—FNTN* ... will change the things that Moses told us to do, *—EVRD* ... handed down to us, *—WMCK* ... change what Moses taught us, *—NLTG.*

**6:14.** These false witnesses also claimed they had heard Stephen say that this Jesus the Nazarene would destroy this place (the temple) and change the customs (including the ceremonies, rites, and institutions) which Moses had delivered (handed down) to them.

On two occasions Jesus did speak of destroying the temple. The first time Jesus chased the money changers (John 2:15), the Jews asked Him, "What sign showest thou unto us, seeing that thou doest these things?" and Jesus answered, "Destroy this temple, and in three days I will raise it up." As so often in the Gospel of John, the Jews misunderstood Jesus, took His words literally, and gave a mocking reply, "Forty-six years was this temple in building and wilt thou rear it up in three days?" But, as the Bible goes on to state, Jesus was speaking of the temple of His body (John 2:18-21).

Jesus also told His disciples that not one stone of the temple would be left upon another (Matthew 24:2). This was something that normally did not happen. All over Palestine and the Middle East are ruins where conquerors destroyed cities, palaces, temples, but left the lower course or at least the foundation stones intact. But the words of Jesus were fulfilled when the armies of the Roman Titus destroyed Jerusalem in A.D. 70.

Actually, there is a sequence of worship in the Bible. First, were the altars of the patriarchs before Moses; second, the tabernacle in the wilderness; third, the temple built by Solomon, rebuilt by Zerubbabel, and rebuilt again by Herod the Great; fourth, the Church as the temple (Greek, *naos*, the inner sanctuary where the presence of God is manifest). (See 1 Corinthians 3:16 where the word "you" is plural and refers to the local assembly as a body.)

**15. And all that sat in the council, looked stedfastly on him:** ... At once the eyes of all who were sitting in the Sanhedrin were fastened on him, *—WEYM* ... And giving undivided attention to him, *—SWAN* ... The men sitting in the religious leader's court, *—NLTG* ... As all those seated in the Sanhedrin gazed at him, *—BRKL* ... The men seated in the council were all staring at Stephen, *—NORL* ... The eyes of all the members of the council were riveted upon Stephen, *—TCNT* ... were watching Stephen closely, *—EVRD* ... looked intently at him, *—TNT.*

**saw his face as it had been the face of an angel:** ... and they saw his face looking like, *—TCNT.*

**6:15.** At this point all those who were seated in the Sanhedrin fixed their eyes on Stephen and saw his face as if it were the face of an angel. This probably means there was a glow or a brightness that was more than human and came from heaven. Possibly this was similar to the glory on the face of Moses when he came down from the presence of God on Mount Sinai (Exodus 34:29-35).

## Chapter 7

**1. Then said the high priest, Are these things so?:** ... Then the High Priest asked him, Are these statements true, *—WEYM* ... The head religious leader asked, —NLTG . . . are these statements correct? —BRKL . . . These charges are true, are they not? —NORL . . . Is this true? —WMCK . . . Is this accusation true? —NOLI . . . this statement true? —GDSP . . . Is this so? —TNT.

**7:1.** The high priest (probably Caiaphas) gave Stephen an opportunity to respond to the charges by asking him if these things were so. At least the high priest was going through the proper form of a trial, though he probably did not expect Stephen to take such full advantage of it as he proceeded to do. Stephen did not attempt to refute the charges made against him—he was not primarily interested in clearing himself. Instead, he reiterated the truths which were creating such an uproar among the Jewish leaders (Harrison, p. 111).

**2. And he said, Men, brethren, and fathers, hearken:** . . . To this Stephen replied, —NAB . . . And he said, Brethren and fathers, hearken, —ASV . . . Brothers and Fathers, listen, —TCNT . . . Fellow Jews, —BECK . . . listen to me, —NLTG.

**The God of glory appeared unto our father Abraham:** . . . The Glorious God appeared to our ancestor, —TCNT . . . Our glorious God, —EVRD . . . The great God showed Himself to our early father, —NLTG . . . our forefather, —WEYM.

**when he was in Mesopotamia:** . . . while, —RTHM . . . he was living in, —WEYM . . . in the country of, —NLTG.

**before he dwelt in Charran:** . . . This was before he moved to, —NLTG . . . before he settled in Haran, —NAB, —TCNT . . . previous to his settling, —BRKL . . . before he ever made him home in Haran, —WLMS . . . before he resided in Haran, —WLSN.

**7:2.** Stephen politely addressed the Sanhedrin as "Men, brethren, and fathers." By calling them men who were brothers, he wanted them to know he still considered himself an Israelite, a descendant of Abraham, a member of the chosen nation. He had done nothing to cut himself off from his heritage. By calling them fathers, he wanted them to know he still respected the institutions of Israel and was willing to subject himself to any decision they might make that would be in line with God's purpose for Israel which promised blessing to all the families of the earth (Genesis 12:3).

**3. And said unto him:** . . . and told him, —BRKL.

**Get thee out of thy country, and from thy kindred:** . . . Leave your country and your kindred, —TCNT . . . Get away from, —MLNT . . . Go forth from, —KLST . . . Depart from, —FNTN . . . your relationship, —CNDT . . . and your relatives, —EVRD, —NOLI . . . your kinsfolk, —NAB . . . leave your family and this land where you were born, —NLTG.

**and come unto the land which I shall shew thee:** . . . and go into whatever land I point out to you, —WEYM.

**7:3.** Then Stephen began a review of the history of Israel, a history they all knew well. His purpose was to defend the gospel against false charges and to show a parallel between the way Old Testament Israelites had treated their prophets and the way the Jewish leaders had treated Jesus.

First, Stephen reminded them how the God of glory (the God who reveals himself in glory and who is glorious in all that He is and does) appeared to Abraham while he was in Mesopotamia, that is, in Ur of the Chaldees. (Some archaeologists, such as Cyrus Gordon, believe this was a northern Ur rather than the Ur on the Euphrates east of Babylon [p. 132]. There is some evidence that the Chaldeans came from the north and that they did not come into Babylonia until long after Abraham's time.)

The Book of Genesis does not mention this revelation to Abraham in Ur, but it must have been recorded in other ancient records. Nehemiah 9:7 refers to it and shows that it was God who brought Abram out of Ur and later gave him the name Abraham.

**4. Then came he out of the land of the Chaldaeans:** . . . Thereupon he left Chaldaea, —WEYM . . . So he left the country, —NOLI . . . He went from the land of, —NLTG.

**and dwelt in Charran and from thence, when his father was dead:** . . . and from there, after his father's death, —TCNT.

**he removed him into this land, wherein ye now dwell:** . . . God removed him into this land, —ASV . . . to migrate, —NEB . . . he was led to this land, —NORL . . . moved him from there, —ADAM.

**7:4.** After Abraham left Ur of the Chaldees, he settled in Haran and lived there until Terah, his father, died. The Greek indicates a rather permanent establishment of a home there. The Book of Genesis confirms that Haran remained the permanent residence of Abraham's relatives even in the days of Jacob (Genesis 29:4, 5). Ancient Jewish tradition says Terah was a maker of idols, especially idols of the moon god, and that he settled in Haran because it was the center of worship for the moon god in western Mesopotamia.

It is not clear from the Hebrew of Genesis 12:1 whether God again spoke to Abraham at the time of his father's death, or whether he simply remembered what God had said in Ur of the Chaldees and now he was free to obey by leaving not only his land but also his relatives.

**5. And he gave him none inheritance in it:** . . . God did not give him any property in it, —TCNT . . . no possession in it, —WEYM . . . no allotment to enjoy in it, —CNDT . . . He gave him no heritable property in it, —BRKL . . . Yet God did not give him any ownership in the land, —NORL...But He gave him no estate in it, —FNTN...He gave him nothing to call his own, —BECK.

**no, not so much as to set his foot on:** ...not even a foot...not even for the sole of his foot, —KLGS.

**yet he promised that he would give it to him for a possession:** ...And yet He promised to bestow the land as a permanent possession on him, —WEYM...promised to give it to him, —WUST...the land should be his, —NORL...that it should eventually belong, —PHLP...as a tenure, —CNDT.

**and to his seed after him:** ...and for his descendants after him, —TCNT...on him, —MNTG...and his posterity, —WEYM...it should belong to his children and children's children after him, —NORL.

**when as yet he had no child:** ...and promised this at a time when Abraham was childless, —WEYM...though up to that time he had no children, —TCNT...even before he had children, —KLGS.

**7:5.** Though Abraham came into the land because of the obedience of faith, God gave him no inheritance in it, not even the space which could be covered by a footstep. Genesis 12:6 shows that Abraham traveled through the land when he first came and found everywhere that "the Canaanite was then in the land." The land was already occupied.

Yet God, while Abraham still had no child, had promised to give the land to him and to his descendants for a (permanent) possession. After Abraham allowed Lot to choose the garden land of the Jordan Valley before Sodom and Gomorrah were destroyed, Abraham was left with the dry hillsides and the unoccupied land between the cities of Palestine where no one else wanted to live. But God saw Abraham's faith and told him to look in every direction, including the direction Lot had taken, and He promised to give it all to him and to his descendants forever. Then God told him to stand up and start walking through the length and breadth of the land, for God was going to give it all to him. Actually it was Abraham's to enjoy, even though he personally did not receive it as an inheritance.

Archaeological discoveries show there were further reasons why it really took faith for Abraham to claim the land. Abraham was not only a shepherd; he was also a merchant prince who dealt in gold, silver, and spices. The Canaanites had laws which allowed such merchant princes to travel in their territory but which made it illegal for them to acquire any land.

**6. And God spake on this wise:** ...What God said was this, —TCNT...conversed with him, —MRDK.

**That his seed should sojourn in a strange land:** ...Abraham's descendants will live in a foreign country, —TCNT...will be aliens in a foreign land,
—ADAM...should lodge, —FNTN...in an alien land, —CNDT...foreign land, —RTHM.

**and that they should bring them into bondage:** ...where they will be enslaved, —TCNT...into servitude, —RTHM.

**and entreat them evil four hundred years:** ...and treat them ill, four hundred years, —ASV...illtreated, —TCNT...ill-use, —RTHM...mistreat them, —BECK...they will do cruel things to them, —EVRD...and be cruelly treated, —WMCK...and oppressed, —NAB.

**7:6.** God also spoke of Abraham's descendants living temporarily as resident aliens in a land belonging to others who would make them slaves and treat them badly 400 years. "Four hundred" is a round number both here and in Genesis 15:13. In Exodus 12:40, 41 the exact number of 430 years is given. Paul, however, seemed to understand (Galatians 3:17) that the 430 years included all the time from Abraham to Moses.

The reference in Genesis 15:13 is part of a passage where God confirmed His promise of the land to Abraham and his descendants by making a covenant (Genesis 15:18-21). This was after Abraham met Melchizedek and refused to take anything for himself from the king of Sodom. That night God's word came to Abraham in a vision telling him to stop being afraid, for God was his Shield and would protect him. God was also his exceeding great reward; that is, God himself would be Abraham's portion. This was God's way also of telling Abraham, "Be concerned with Me!" Then God renewed the promise of a son by taking him out and showing him the stars and saying his descendants would be just as numerous. Because Abraham believed God, his faith was accounted for righteousness.

God gave Abraham further assurance He would fulfill His promise of the land. Abraham was asked to lay out a sacrifice before the Lord. God moved through the midst of the sacrifice from one end to the other in the symbol of a warming oven with a flame coming out of it. By this action God was indicating that He would begin the work of fulfilling His promise and He would finish it.

**7. And the nation to whom they shall be in bondage will I judge, said God:** ...But I will myself judge the nation, to which they shall be enslaved, —TCNT...I will pass sentence, —WLMS...But I will punish the nation where they are slaves, —EVRD...the nation that has enslaved them, —NOLI...that nation which they serve, —NAB.

**and after that shall they come forth:** ...and after that they will leave the country, —TCNT...they will be freed, —NORL...Then they will be liberated, —NOLI.

**and serve me in this place:** ...and render divine service unto me, —RTHM...and worship me in this very place, —TCNT.

**7:7.** God also promised to judge the nation that would make Israel slaves (Genesis 15:14). This, of course, was fulfilled by the 10 plagues which climaxed in the death of the firstborn of Egypt, and in the destruction of Pharaoh's cavalry and chariots in the Red Sea.

Then God promised Abraham that after that his descendants would come out of Egypt and serve God "in this place," the Promised Land. "Serve" here is not the word for serving as a slave or even as a servant. It is especially used of the service of worship rendered to God. God wanted a people who would worship Him and Him alone.

**8. And he gave him the covenant of circumcision:** ... And with Abraham He made the sacred compact of, −WLMS ... the sign for this . . . was, −NCV . . . .made a covenant, −NAB . . . agreement, −EVRD, −PHLP . . . gave him the bond of circumcision, −WMCK ... circumcision being its seal and sign, −WUST.
**and so Abraham begat Isaac, and circumcised him the eighth day:** ... and it was under these circumstances that Abraham became the father of Isaac, −TCNT ... and under this covenant he became the father of, −WEYM.
**and Isaac begat Jacob; and Jacob begat the twelve patriarchs:** ... and Isaac became the father of Jacob, −TCNT ... Isaac circumcised his son Jacob, −TEV ... and Jacob did the same for his sons, −NCV.

**7:8.** God also gave Abraham the covenant of circumcision, so that Isaac was circumcised the eighth day after his birth. Actually, God gave the covenant of circumcision before Isaac was born and assured Abraham by it that Sarah his wife would bear a son and he should call his name Isaac. Then God would establish His covenant with Isaac.

Abraham, then at the age of 99, circumcised himself as a sign of the covenant. He also circumcised Ishmael who was then 13. But the pattern would be to circumcise 8 days after birth (Genesis 17:12). Thus it was Isaac, who was born and circumcised a year later, who set the pattern and began the line of descent that then continued through Jacob and the 12 patriarchs (tribal heads or tribal rulers). This emphasizes that they were all born under the covenant of circumcision. This was a change from the situation before Abraham.

For Abraham and his descendants, circumcision was both the outward sign that one had entered into a covenant relationship with God and also the seal. Paul showed that God imputed righteousness to Abraham solely on the basis of faith (Romans 4), and the sign of circumcision was added later "as a seal of the righteousness of faith which he had yet being uncircumcised" (Romans 4:11). Stephen did not address the legalism that developed around the subject (cf. Acts 15:1).

**9. And the patriarchs, moved with envy:** ... famous ancestors, −TEV ... Now our forefathers were jealous of Joseph, −WMCK ... moved with jealousy, −ASV ... out of jealousy, −TCNT ... burning up with envy of Joseph, −WUST... envious of Joseph, −NOLI.
**sold Joseph into Egypt:** ... sold Joseph into slavery in Egypt, −TCNT ... and sold him as a slave into Egypt, −WLMS... They sold him to be a slave in Egypt, −EVRD... as a slave to the Egyptians, −NOLI.
**but God was with him:** ... But God helped him, −NOLI.

**7:9.** The patriarchs, actually the 10 sons of Jacob by Leah and his concubines, were moved and filled with envy and jealousy, so they sold Joseph into Egypt. But God was with him.

Stephen was preparing to make a strong contrast between the way Joseph's brothers treated him and the way God treated him. The envy and jealousy arose partly because Joseph was a younger son but was given the tunic of a priest or king, indicating Jacob had chosen him to receive the birthright, and partly because of his dreams where he had seen his brothers and even his father and Leah bowing down to him. That a father and mother would bow down to a son (Leah was now the mother of the family since Rachel had died), or even that older sons would bow down to a younger son, was something unheard of in their culture.

Stephen recognized also that God was with Joseph all along. Joseph reported to his father the misdeeds of his half brothers, the sons of Bilhah and Zilpah (possibly idolatry; Genesis 37:2). The dreams of Joseph showed God was with him. God was with him even when he was sold into Egypt. He could have been sold to a farmer somewhere up the Nile. But he was sold to an officer of the king and put in a position where he could learn to become a business manager and then where he could learn how to handle men.

**10. And delivered him out of all his afflictions:** . . . Joseph had many troubles there, −EVRD...God rescued him from them all, −SEB...from all his trials, −KLST... extricates him out of all his afflictions, −CNDT ... and took him out of all his tribulations, −RTHM ... rescued him from all his afflictions, −NOLI ... his troubles, −TCNT.
**and gave him favour and wisdom in the sight of Pharaoh, king of Egypt:** ... and gave him grace, −WMCK ... caused Pharaoh ... to approve him for his wisdom, −TNT ... and enabled him to win favour and a reputation for wisdom with Pharaoh, −TCNT ... respected him, −SEB.
**and he made him governor over Egypt and all his house:** ... who appointed him Governor of Egypt and of his whole household, −TCNT ... and all the royal household, −WEYM ... appointed him prime minister, −FNTN ... chief, −MRDK ... in charge of all the people in his palace, −EVRD.

**7:10.** God delivered Joseph out of all his afflictions and distressing circumstances. He became the best business manager Potiphar ever had. When he was falsely accused and thrown in prison, he was put, not in an ordinary prison, but one where the king's prisoners were kept, which showed Potiphar still had a high regard for him. This high regard was further shown when he was asked to take care of special prisoners, the king's butler and baker. This led to the opportunity to interpret Pharaoh's dream, which gave him favor before Pharaoh and made Pharaoh and his advisers realize the Spirit of God was in Joseph.

Pharaoh recognized his wisdom and made him governor (leader, leading man) over Egypt and over all Pharaoh's household, including all his business affairs. Actually, Joseph was both the business manager for Pharaoh and the prime minister over the whole land. Though his brothers mistreated Joseph, God used it all to bring him to a place of high position, power, and great honor. Truly God was taking care of Joseph.

**11. Now there came a dearth over all the land of Egypt and Canaan:** ...a famine over all Egypt and Canaan, –ASV ...Then a famine spread over the whole of Egypt and Canaan, –TCNT ...became so dry that nothing would grow there, –EVRD.

**and great affliction:** ... causing great distress, –TCNT ...a lot of hardship, –ADAM ...and no little suffering, –KLST.

**and our fathers found no sustenance:** ...since our fathers, –KLST ...and our ancestors could find no food, –TCNT ...and our forefathers could not find the simplest food, –WLMS ...so that our fathers failed to find nourishment, –BRKL ...were not finding sustenance, –YNG ...not finding pasture, –RTHM ...found no Provisions, –HNSN, –WLSN ...lacked food, –MRDK.

**7:11.** When the famine came over the land of Egypt, it also spread to Canaan. The patriarchs, now identified as "our fathers," found no food.

Stephen here skipped over the 7 good years in Egypt and the provision Joseph made for the 7 years of famine that followed. Some have wondered why Joseph did not contact his brothers after he was elevated to this high position in Egypt. But Joseph had no desire to tell his brothers, "I told you so." He knew too that if they were jealous of his tunic they might be even more jealous and vindictive if they saw the robes he now wore. More important, he recognized God was with him and he believed God was working it all out for good, so he was leaving it all in God's hand. But while Joseph was still prospering, his brothers were getting into a desperate situation through lack of food. They were used to having plenty, now the famine put them into a state of distress.

**12. But when Jacob heard that there was corn in Egypt:** ... when Jacob learned, –MLNT ...there was food, –NLTG ...grain, ASV ...wheat, –BRKL.

**he sent out our fathers first:** ...sent our early fathers, –NLTG ...he sent forth our fathers the first time, –ASV ...our forefathers on their first visit there, –GDSP ...Jacob sent our ancestors on their first visit to that country, –MOFT ...This was their first trip to Egypt, –EVRD, –NCV ...sent ...there on a first trip, –MLNT ...there on a first mission, –NAB.

**7:12.** When Jacob heard there was wheat (or bread) in Egypt, he sent the 10 "fathers" of Israel's tribes to Egypt. (The word "corn" in the King James Version is Old English for grain. The Hebrew word means both wheat and the bread made from wheat.)

Joseph immediately knew his brothers. They were mature men when he left them and they had not changed much. But they bowed down to Joseph without knowing who he was. To them he was Zaphnath-paaneah, the Prime Minister of Egypt. His Egyptian name was given as a way of conferring Egyptian citizenship so he could hold his high office. He was dressed like an Egyptian and at 39 looked much different from the 17-year-old boy the brothers had sold into Egypt.

Joseph made sure they would return to Egypt by making his brother Simeon a prisoner and by demanding that they not come back without bringing Benjamin with them. He wanted to be sure they had changed and that they had not shown the same kind of envy to Benjamin they had shown to him. He wanted to help them, but he knew he could not help them very much if they still had the same old attitudes.

**13. And at the second time Joseph was made known to his brethren:** ...On their second visit, –GDSP ...Then they went there a second time. This time, Joseph told his brothers, –NCV ...The second time they went to the country, –NLTG ...In the course of their second visit, –TCNT ...told ...who he was, –BECK.

**and Joseph's kindred was made known unto Pharaoh:** ...and Pharaoh learnt the parentage of Joseph, –TCNT ...Joseph's kin, –KJII ...and his family ties became known, –NAB ...Joseph's origin became known, –TNT ...and thus Joseph's race was revealed to Pharaoh, –WLMS ...Pharaoh came to hear of Joseph's parentage, –WMCK ...learned about Joseph's family, NCV.

**7:13.** As the famine continued, Jacob sent the brothers down to Egypt the second time to buy more grain. He hesitated for a time because he did not want to send Benjamin. But again the lack of food caused such distress that he finally was willing to let him go. This time Joseph had a dinner prepared where the seating arrangement for the

11 brothers was according to their age, and where Benjamin's portion was five times as large as any of the others. This would make it perfectly obvious that the arrangement was not accidental and that somehow Benjamin was the favored one. If they were still full of the old jealousy, this would have spoiled the dinner for the 10 brothers. After one further testing (cf. Genesis 44), Joseph could hold back no longer and revealed himself to his brothers. At first they were afraid of revenge, but Joseph told them not to fear. He saw that God had made all they had done turn out for good.

**14. Then sent Joseph, and called his father Jacob to him:**... Then Joseph sent an invitation to his father, –*TCNT*...Joseph sent some men, *NCV*...asked his father, –*NLTG*...sent for, –*NAB*...to invite Jacob, his father, to come to Egypt, –*EVRD*.

**and all his kindred, threescore and fifteen souls:**... He also invited all his relatives, –*NCV*...all his relations, seventy-five persons in all, –*TCNT*...all his kinsfolk, –*NAB*...the whole family, –*MLNT*...and all his family, numbering seventy-five persons, –*WEYM*...There were seventy-five people in the family, –*NLTG*...lives, –*HNSN*...souls, –*SWAN*.

**7:14.** Then Joseph sent for Jacob and all his relatives who were in Canaan, 75 souls. (The word "souls" here means persons, a very common meaning of the Hebrew word.) Stephen used the number found in the Greek Septuagint version of Genesis 46:27; Exodus 1:5; and in some copies of Deuteronomy 10:22. The Masoretic Hebrew text has the round number 70.

**15. So Jacob went down into Egypt:**... And Jacob moved down to Egypt, –*NORL* ... came down, –*GDSP*. –*MLNT*.

**and died, he, and our fathers:**...where he and our fathers finished their course, –*BRKL*...There he died and our ancestors too, –*TCNT*...There he died, and so did our forefathers, –*WEYM*.

**7:15.** Jacob at first refused to believe Joseph was still alive. He had believed Joseph was killed by a wild animal and may have inferred that perhaps he and Joseph were both under God's judgment. But when he saw the wagons Joseph sent to bring them, he believed. For the first time since he thought Joseph was killed, he was comforted and received encouragement from God to go to Egypt, where he was satisfied to die now that he had seen Joseph. Later, all the brothers died there, that is, "our fathers" from whom the 12 tribes of Israel received their names.

**16. And were carried over into Sychem:**...Later their bodies were moved, –*NCV*...and their bodies were removed to Shechem, –*TCNT*...their bodies were brought back, –*JB*.

**and laid in the sepulchre that Abraham bought for a sum of money of the sons of Emmor the father of Sychem:**...and laid in the tomb, –*ASV*...and put in a grave there, –*EVRD*...which Abraham had bought for silver, –*WMCK*...for its value in silver, –*SWAN*.

**7:16.** After their deaths, the fathers (Jacob's sons) were transferred to Shechem and placed in the tomb bought for a price of silver from the sons of Emmor (the Greek form of *Hamor*), the father of Shechem (Genesis 33:19).

The reference here is to the burial of the 12 patriarchs. Jacob was buried in the cave of Machpelah near Hebron where Abraham and Sarah were buried (Genesis 23:17, 19; 50:13). Joseph also was buried in Shechem (Joshua 24:32). Genesis 33:19 and Joshua 24:32 indicate Jacob did the actual buying of the plot in Shechem. However, Abraham was still alive, and it was undoubtedly done in the name of Abraham as the head of the clan.

In all this there is a subtle emphasis on the way Joseph was sold by his jealous brothers, yet was used by God to save their lives. There is also an emphasis on the faith of Abraham who believed God's promise even when he saw absolutely no evidence that it would be fulfilled.

These members of the Sanhedrin were refusing to believe God even though He had provided evidence of the fulfillment of His promise through the resurrection of Jesus. The treatment of Joseph by his brothers and the contrast to the way God treated him was a parallel to the way the Jewish leaders had treated Jesus.

**17. But when the time of the promise drew nigh:**... Now just as the time of the promise was drawing near, –*TCNT*...But as the time drew near for the fulfilment, –*WEYM* ... that God set in His promise, –*BECK*...The promise...was soon to come true, –*EVRD*...But as the promised time approached, –*BRKL* ... for realizing the promise, –*WLMS* ... The time approached for the fulfillment of the promise, –*NOLI*...drew near, –*KLST*...was about to happen, –*NLTG*.

**which God had sworn to Abraham:**.... that God made to Abraham, –*EVRD*...which God vouchsafed, –*ASV*...had made, –*NOLI*, –*TCNT*...promised, *HBIV*...ratified, –*ALFD*...The promise...was soon to come true, –*NCV*.

**the people grew and multiplied in Egypt:**... the people increased largely in numbers in Egypt, –*TCNT*...the people grew greatly in numbers, –*TNT*...The number of people in Egypt grew large, –*EVRD*...increased and grew in number, –*WMCK*...the people became many times more numerous, –*WEYM*.

**7:17.** Stephen next recounted the way the Israelites grew and multiplied in Egypt as the time came for the fulfillment of the promise God had sworn to Abraham, the promise that Abraham's descendants would possess the land of Canaan.

Joseph had secured for them the land of Goshen in the well-watered eastern part of the Nile delta. There they would be separated from the people of Egypt and yet be close to Joseph. They would also be able to retain their own customs and language. Through Joseph's provision they prospered and kept increasing in number until the land (Goshen) was filled with them (Exodus 1:7). Later, Moses was able to say that their fathers had gone down into Egypt 70 persons, but by Moses' time the Lord their God had made them "as the stars of heaven for multitude" (Deuteronomy 1:10; 10:22). Truly God had been fulfilling the promise given to Abraham in Genesis 15:5!

**18. Till another king arose, which knew not Joseph:** ... till a new king, who knew nothing of Joseph, came to the throne, —*TCNT* ... a different king, —*BECK* ... a foreign king, —*PNT* ... became ruler of Egypt, —*NOLI* Egypt, —*EVRD* ... who had not been acquainted with Joseph, —*CNDT.*

**7:18.** This increase of prosperity and numbers continued until a king arose who did not know Joseph. Joseph lived to see his greatgrandchildren and died at the age of 110. He was obviously still in favor and was able to help his brothers and their children, grandchildren, and greatgrandchildren during this time.

It is not known exactly how long this prosperity continued, for the exact time of the rise of the Pharaoh who knew not Joseph is unknown. First Kings 6:1 indicates that Solomon began to build the temple in the fourth year of his full reign (that is, the fourth year after David died). This would put the Exodus from Egypt at 1440 B.C., and the birth of Moses 80 years before that. Some believe Hatshepsut, Egypt's well-known individualistic queen, was the Pharaoh's daughter who rescued Moses. Arguments for a later date are all very weak and can be easily refuted.

This king was undoubtedly of a different dynasty or ruling family from the one under whom Joseph served. He would thus have no regard for the previous kings of Egypt, to say nothing of their prime ministers.

**19. The same dealt subtilly with our kindred:** ... This king acted deceitfully towards our race, —*TCNT* ... By taking a cunning advantage of our race, —*WLMS* ... He defrauded our race, —*BRKL* ... He exploited our race, —*NORL* ... He took advantage of our race, —*ADAM* ... This man's policy was to exterminate our race, —*FNTN* ... shrewd in scheming, —*BECK* ... adopted a crafty policy, —*PNT* ... He worked some tricks, —*KLGS* ... outwitted our race, —*WLSN* ... victimized our race, —*PHLP* ... He oppressed our people, —*NOLI.*

**And evil entreated our fathers:** ... ill-treated, —*ASV* ... oppressed our forefathers, —*WEYM* ... abused, —*BRKL* ... mistreated, —*ADAM* , ... He outraged, —*FNTN* ... afflicted, —*CNFT.*

**so that they cast our their young children:** ... compelled them to expose their infants, —*NOLI* ... so as to cause their babies to be exposed, —*RTHM* ... making them abandon their own infants, —*TCNT* ... with the object that our race might not be reproduced, —*FNTN.*

**7:19.** This king of Egypt victimized Israel by trickery and underhanded methods. The reference here is probably first of all to the way he set slave drivers over them and made them work harder and harder. Second, it probably refers to the way the king gave a command, possibly secret, to the midwives to kill the boy babies and let only the girls live.

When the midwives managed to avoid doing what the king commanded, the king told all the Egyptians to throw every son born to the Israelites into the river. Stephen says they cast out their infants so they would not live. "Cast out" is a term used for exposing babies in some place where the elements or wild animals would cause them to die. The later Romans used it of putting unwanted babies out where wild animals would come at night and take them. Here it refers to exposing them in the river to be eaten by crocodiles.

**20. In which time Moses was born:** ... At which season, —*ASV* ... At this juncture, —*AMPB* ... At this period, —*NOLI.*

**and was exceeding fair:** ... beautiful in God's sight, —*BRKL* ... lovely to God, —*MRDK* ... delightful, —*ADAM* ... a divinely beautiful child, —*MNTG* ... he was no ordinary child, —*NIV* ... child of remarkable beauty, —*PHLP.*

**and nourished up in his father's house three months:** ... reared, —*TCNT* ... cared for, —*WEYM* ... nurtured in his parental home, —*BRKL.*

**7:20.** During this time Moses was born and was *asteios* (Hebrew *tôv*, "goodly, fair, beautiful," cf. Exodus 2:2), literally, *fair* (lovely, fine) *to God.* This may mean he was made so by God or considered so by God.

The Bible shows God is always with those He plans to give opportunities for unusual service and God prepares them even from birth. God told Jeremiah, "Before I formed you in (your mother's) body, I knew you, and before you came out of (her) womb I sanctified you (set you apart for my service) and ordained you as a prophet to the nations" (Jeremiah 1:5, author's translation). John the Baptist was filled with the Holy Spirit even from his mother's womb (Luke 1:15).

The parents of Moses were sensitive to God's will and carefully nourished him, keeping him hidden for 3 months.

**21. And when he was cast out:** ... At length he was cast out, —WEYM ... but when he was exposed, —RTHM ... and, when he was abandoned, —TCNT.

**Pharaoh's daughter took him up:** ... rescued him, —RTHM ... adopted him, —WEYM ... lifts him up, —CNDT.

**and nourished him for her own son:** ... for herself as a son, —RTHM ... and reared him as her own son, —TCNT ... and brought him up as her own son, —WEYM ... raised him, —BECK.

**7:21.** God's care was shown when Moses was exposed by the water's edge. Of course, his mother's faith and confidence in God made her take an active part in expressing that faith. She made an ark (a vessel for floating, the same word that is used of Noah's ark) in the form of a waterproofed woven basket and put it among the bulrushes growing near a place where Pharaoh's daughter came to bathe. She also had Miriam, Moses' sister, keep a lookout.

Stephen was drawing attention to God's care through Pharaoh's daughter who took the baby up out of the water and reared him as her own son.

**22. And Moses was learned in all the wisdom of the Egyptians:** ... instructed, —ASV ... trained, —RTHM ... educated in, —WLMS ... the science, —BRKL ... the philosophy, —FNTN.

**and was mighty in words and deeds:** ... and showed ability in both speech and action, —TCNT ... in discourse and in deeds, —BRKL.

**7:22.** As a prince then, Moses was trained or educated in all the wisdom of Egypt and was mighty (powerful) in his words and deeds. This is significant, for the Egyptians had already made great advances in science, engineering, mathematics, astronomy, and medicine.

**23. And when he was full forty years old:** ... in his fortieth year, —TCNT ... As he was rounding out his fortieth year, —WLMS.

**it came into his heart to visit his brethren the children of Israel:** ... the thought came into his mind that he would visit his brother Israelites, —TCNT ... it occurred to him to visit his brethren the descendants of Israel, —WEYM ... visit his own people, —BECK ... for the purpose of acquainting himself with their needs, —WUST.

**7:23.** The first 40 years of Moses' life were spent as an Egyptian prince. Jewish tradition says he took part in some of Egypt's military campaigns, going up the Nile into Cush (the ancient Ethiopia,

now called the Sudan). The same traditions indicate that Moses married a Cushite woman (of the Caucasoid race, not Negroid), who was left behind when he fled Egypt and did not rejoin him until after he had successfully brought Israel out of Egypt.

But Moses never forgot he was an Israelite. In the providence of God, the princess hired his mother to nurse him, and she had him long enough to instill in his heart the promises God gave to Abraham, Isaac, and Jacob, for it is clear that at the burning bush Moses knew what kind of God they served.

At the age of 40, the desire came into Moses' heart to visit his Israelite brothers. "Visit" here is a word that means to look after, take care of, relieve, or protect. It means Moses left his duties at Egypt's capital and went into Goshen with a deep desire to do something to help his people.

**24. And seeing one of them suffer wrong:** ... and seeing one being wronged, —RTHM ... and seeing an Israelite ill-treated, —TCNT ... being imposed upon, —WEYM ... being mistreated, —WLMS ... treated unfairly, —BRKL ... suffer injustice, —YNG.

**he defended him:** ... he took his part, —WEYM ... defended the oppressed man, —NORL ... he wrought redress, —MNTG ... took the part of the wronged man, —KLGS.

**and avenged him that was oppressed:** ... and secured justice for the ill-treated man, —WEYM ... avenges the one being harried, —CNDT.

**and smote the Egyptian:** ... by striking down, —TCNT ... by slaying, —BRKL.

**7:24.** When Moses saw one of the Israelites being injured unjustly, he defended him, avenged the ill-treated one, and struck down the Egyptian. "Avenged" here does not speak of revenge. Rather, it means that Moses was concerned to bring justice, and as a prince of Egypt he felt he had the right to bring that justice.

**25. For he supposed his brethren would have understood:** ... he concluded, —FNTN ... He supposed his brethren to be aware, —WEYM ... he inferred that his brethren understood, —CNDT.

**how that God by his hand would deliver them:** ... that God through his hand would give them deliverance, —RTHM ... that God through his instrumentality, —WLMS ... that he was foreordained by God to liberate them, —NOLI ... was using him to save them, —EVRD ... that God would give them freedom by his help, —NORL ... he was the one by whom God was freeing them, —BECK.

**but they understood not:** ... but they failed to understand, —BRKL ... his brethren failed to understand his mission, —NOLI.

**7:25.** Stephen explained why Moses was seeking to help the Israelites and why he tried to bring justice to this mistreated Israelite. Actually, also, this is the point Stephen was leading up to. Moses did this because he supposed his Israelite brothers (his fellow Israelites) would understand that God, by his hand, would give them deliverance. "Deliverance" here is the Greek *sotērian*, a word usually translated "salvation," though it is also used of deliverance, health, and well-being.

Moses not only must have had faith in God's promise to Abraham, Isaac, and Jacob, but he was sensitive to those promises, and probably remembered the way God had prepared Joseph to bring a great deliverance from the famine. He saw that God's hand had been guiding and preparing him to deliver his people. But though Moses understood this and thought his people would see it too, they did not.

Stephen's emphasis here shows he was making a clear parallel to the way the Jewish leaders failed to understand what God had done through Jesus to provide salvation. Their rejection of Jesus was no reason to despise Jesus, for their fathers for a time rejected Moses.

This should have brought back to the memory of these Jewish leaders the way Jesus pronounced woes on the scribes and Pharisees who were building the tombs of the prophets as great memorials to them and were decorating the sepulchers of the righteous men of God who had been martyred in earlier times. By this they were saying that if they had lived in the days of their fathers they would not have been partakers with them in the murder of those prophets. But Jesus recognized that all this was for show. Their attitudes were no different from their ancestors, and they would do as they had done.

**26. And the next day he shewed himself unto them as they strove:** . . . the ensuing day, —*CNDT* . . . he came and found two of them fighting, —*WEYM* . . . he came across two of them quarreling, —*NOLI.*

**and would have set them at one again:** . . . and would have reconciled them in peace, —*RTHM* . . . and tried to make peace between them, —*TCNT.*

**saying, Sirs, ye are brethren:** . . . Men! ye are brothers! —*RTHM.*

**why do ye wrong one to another?:** . . . how is it that you are ill treating one another, —*TCNT* . . . why should you harm each other, —*WLMS* . . . why abuse each other, —*BRKL* . . . Why do you injure one another? —*NOLI.*

**7:26.** Continuing the history, Stephen reminded the Sanhedrin how Moses went out the next day and found two Israelites fighting with each other. This shocked him. He was troubled when he saw how the Egyptians were mistreating the Israelites. He was even more disturbed when he saw his own people mistreating each other. In the midst of all

this mistreatment from the Egyptians, they should have been upholding and encouraging one another. So Moses' first thought was to try to reconcile them and have them at peace. So he said, "Men, you are brothers, why do you harm each other?" that is, "Why do you injure each other unfairly?"

**27. But he that did his neighbour wrong thrust him away, saying:** . . . was wronging his neighbour, —*RTHM* . . . But the aggressor thrust him aside, —*NOLI* . . . The man who was ill treating his fellow workman pushed Moses aside with the words, —*TCNT* . . . But the man who was doing the wrong resented his interference, —*WEYM* . . . the aggressor of his neighbour retorted, —*FNTN.*

**Who made thee a ruler and a judge over us?:** . . . Who hath appointed, —*RTHM* . . . a chief and a justice, —*CNDT.*

**7:27.** But the one harming his neighbor repelled Moses, saying, "Who made you a ruler and a judge over us?" In other words, these Israelites were resisting and rejecting God's purpose. Exodus 2:19 indicates that when Moses came to Midian he was still dressed as an Egyptian and was thought by the Midianites to be an Egyptian. So these Israelites, even if they knew Moses was born of Israelite parents, did not think of him as one of themselves. Nevertheless, Stephen's point was that they did not see God's purpose and for that reason resisted Moses.

**28. Wilt thou kill me, as thou didst the Egyptian yesterday?:** . . . Dost thou seek to kill me, —*MRDK* . . . like you killed that enemy Egyptian? —*KLGS* . . . Do you mean to murder me,

**7:28.** The Israelite who was in the wrong then said, "Do you want to kill me the way you killed the Egyptian yesterday?" He was looking at Moses as if he were self-righteous in what he was doing and was not really wanting to help the Israelites. Part of the reason for what he said was undoubtedly a sense of guilt on his part. He knew he was in the wrong, but was trying to put the condemnation and the guilt on Moses instead of admitting his own wrongdoing.

**29. Then fled Moses at this saying:** . . . Alarmed at this question, Moses fled from the country, —*WEYM* . . . On hearing this, —*NAB* . . . At that, —*WMCK* . . . At these words Moses fled, —*NOLI* . . . took to flight, —*FNTN.*

**and was a stranger in the land of Madian:** . . . lived as, —*WMCK* . . . took up his residence as an alien, —*NAB* . . . and became an exile, —*TCNT* . . . and lived . . . in exile, —*NOLI* . . . became a temporary resident, —*WUST* . . . and became a sojourner in the land of Midian, —*ASV,* —*HNSN.*

**where he begat two sons:** . . . There he became the father of two sons, —*WEYM.*

**7:29.** Fearing for his life, Moses fled to the land of Midian where he lived as a resident alien and where two sons were born.

Hebrews 11:24-28 skips over this part of Moses' life. It records only that by faith Moses, when he grew up, repudiated his position where he was called the son of Pharaoh's daughter. He chose rather to be ill-treated along with (to take his share of suffering along with) the people of God, rather than to enjoy the pleasures of sin for a season. He esteemed the reproach of the Messiah (God's anointed) "greater riches than the treasures of Egypt," for he turned his attention to the reward. By faith Moses left Egypt, not fearing the wrath of the king. But at this point Hebrews 11 is talking about how Moses led Israel out of Egypt in connection with the 10th plague and the keeping of the Passover.

Stephen skipped over the second 40 years of Moses' life, telling nothing of his marriage to Zipporah (*little bird*), the daughter of the priest of Midian, telling only of the fact that he had two sons. These 40 years were important in Moses' preparation, however.

**30. And when forty years were expired:** ... were fulfilled, —*ASV* ... At the end of forty years, —*TCNT* ... When forty years had passed, —*WLMS* ... Forty years later, —*NAB*, —*NOLI*.

**there appeared to him in the wilderness of mount Sina an angel of the Lord:** ... in the uninhabited region, —*WUST* ... in the wilds of, —*WLMS C.K* ... An the Desert of Mount Sinai, —*TCNT*.

**in a flame of fire in a bush:** ... in the flame of a burning thornbush, —*BRKL*, —*NAB* ... in a flame of fire of brambles, —*KLGS*.

**7:30.** When 40 years had passed, an angel of the Lord appeared to Moses in the desert of Mount Sinai in the flame of fire in a thorn bush. Exodus 3:1 calls this the "back side of the desert" and calls the mountain Horeb, the mountain of God.

The angel here was no ordinary angel, but the Angel of the Lord, a manifestation of God himself, or rather of the preincarnate Son. In this passage He is distinguished as a separate person, and yet is identified with God. Jesus is, and has always been, the one Mediator between God the Father and man. He was in Creation (John 1:3). He was and is in redemption (1 Timothy 2:5, 6; Hebrews 8:6; 9:15; 12:24). He will be in the coming judgments (John 5:22, 27). Thus, it is evident He was the one Mediator in Old Testament times as well.

**31. When Moses saw it, He wondered at the sight:** ... marvelled, —*RTHM* ... was astonished, —*TCNT* ... marvels at the vision, —*CNDT* ... at the sight, —*MNTG* ... wondered at the spectacle, —*NOLI*.

**and as he drew near to behold it:** ... and as he was going near to observe, —*RTHM* ... but, on his going nearer to look at it more closely, —*TCNT* ... and as he drew near to consider it, —*HBIE* ... and as he approached to investigate, —*BRKL* ... He went near to look closer at it, —*EVRD* ... to examine it, —*NOLI*.

**the voice of the Lord came unto him:** ... there came a voice of the Lord, —*ASV* ... the Lord said to him audibly, —*MRDK*.

**7:31.** As Moses continued to look, he saw the bush did not burn up, and he was filled with wonder and amazement at this surprising phenomenon. Curiosity caused him to go near to get a closer look. This was something that deserved careful observation.

As he did so, the voice of the Lord (God) came to him. After 40 years in the desert, it took something unusual to get Moses' attention before he would be sensitive to the voice of God. This voice was the same as that of the Angel mentioned in the preceding verse. "The sight" (Greek, *to horama*) is often translated "the vision," but it is used of objective visions, real appearances that can be seen by the eyes. In other words, this was not a figment of Moses' imagination. He really heard the voice of God.

**32. Saying, I am the God of thy fathers:** ... I am the God of your ancestors, —*TCNT* ... I am the same God your fathers had, —*NCV* ... forefathers, —*WEYM*.

**the God of Abraham, and the God of Isaac, and the God of Jacob. Then Moses trembled, and durst not behold:** ... Moses trembled all over, and did not dare to look, —*TCNT* ... began to tremble and dared look no more, —*NAB* ... Moses began to shake with fear and was afraid to look, —*EVRD* ... Quaking with fear Moses did not dare to gaze, —*WEYM* ... Moses shook! He was so afraid he did not look at the bush, —*NLTG* ... Moses felt so shaken, he did not dare to investigate, —*BRKL* ... becoming terrified, —*RTHM* ... was so frightened, —*MLNT* ... was so terrified, —*WLMS* ... dared not look, —*HNSN* ... and turned away his face, —*NOLI* ... dared not examine it, —*HBIE*.

**7:32.** God then declared himself to be the God of his fathers, the God of Abraham, Isaac, and Jacob. When the Sadducees confronted Jesus with their refusal to believe in the Resurrection and the future life, Jesus referred to this passage and pointed out that God made it clear here that He *is* (not He *was*) the God of Abraham, Isaac, and Jacob. Thus, they have continued existence after death, for God is not the God of the dead, but of the living (Matthew 22:32; Mark 12:26, 27; Luke 20:37).

When Moses heard God thus identify himself, he trembled and did not dare to look. Exodus 3:6

says he hid his face for he did not dare to look on God.

This indicates that Moses knew the kind of God which Abraham, Isaac, and Jacob served. It is not likely there were any written records of the history of these patriarchs. (Some archaeologists would dispute this, for people did keep extensive business records and detailed accounts of government relationships long before Abraham's time, as the Ebla records show.) Nevertheless, Moses' mother trained him and must have passed on to him the stories of these patriarchs.

**33. Then said the Lord to him, Put off thy shoes from thy feet:** . . . Loose the shoes from thy feet, –ASV . . . Loose the sandals of thy feet, –RTHM, –SWAN . . . Untie the sandals from your feet, –BRKL . . . Remove the sandals from, –NAB . . . Take off your shoes, –NOLI . . . off your feet! –NLTG.

**for the place where thou standest is holy ground:** . . . for the spot, –WEYM.

**7:33.** God commanded Moses to take off his sandal, a leather sole fastened to the foot by leather straps. (The singular is used here in a collective or distributive sense, so in English it is best translated "sandals.") The ground all around the burning bush was holy ground because of the presence of God manifested there. Joshua had a similar experience when he was out looking over the situation with regard to the conquest of Jericho. There the Captain (prince, head, king) of the Lord's host appeared to him, and Joshua worshiped Him. This shows this also was a preincarnate manifestation of Christ, not an ordinary angel. An ordinary angel would have forbidden Joshua's prostration before him. The command for Joshua to remove his sandals also confirms the divine nature of the Captain or Prince. The Law also describes the clothing of Aaron and his sons, but says nothing about sandals or shoes, so it is evident the priests were barefoot as they served at the altar. It should be noted also that the presence of the Lord made it holy ground even though it was far from the Promised Land. It was always important that men be reverent and tread softly in the presence of the Lord.

**34. I have seen, I have seen the affliction of my people which is in Egypt:** . . . I have surely seen, –ASV . . . I have certainly observed, –MLNT . . . I have attentively seen, –MRDK . . . I have witnessed, –NAB . . . I have indeed seen the ill-treatment, –RTHM . . . the evil treatment of, –HNSN . . . the evil condition, –WMCK . . . I have indeed seen the oppression of my people, who are in Egypt, –TCNT . . . seen the evil against my people, –SWAN . . . seen the troubles my people have

suffered, –EVRD . . . seen My people suffer in the country of, –NLTG.

**and I have heard their groaning:** . . . their groans, –TCNT . . . heard My people moaning, –SEB . . . have heard their cries, –WMCK, –NLTG.

**and am come down to deliver them:** . . . and I have come down, –RSV . . . to rescue them, –NAB, –RTHM . . . to let them go free, –NLTG . . . to save them, –GDSP.

**And now come, I will send thee into Egypt:** . . . So get ready! I am going to send you, –NOLI . . . So come! I will make you, –GDSP . . . I should dispatch you, –CNDT . . . I will send you back to Egypt as my messenger, –WLMS . . . I will give you a mission to Egypt, –KLST.

**7:34.** The repetition of "I have seen" is a Hebrew way of giving strong emphasis to the fact that God had definitely seen the ill treatment of His people in Egypt and had heard their groaning. The repetition also draws attention to the faithfulness of God. Though God has His timing, believers can depend on Him to show himself to be the kind of God He is. He will always be true to His own nature. He will always keep His promises.

In response to Israel's need, God had "come down," that is, He had come down into the earthly scene to go into action, for His purpose was to deliver Israel, to take them out for himself. He wanted them for His people. He wanted to bring them into a new relationship to himself. To bring about this deliverance God called Moses saying, "Come!" (This is the same word used by Jesus when He called His disciples to come after Him and follow Him.) But then God added the request (Greek, subjunctive, not a command), "Let me send you into Egypt."

**35. This Moses whom they refused, saying:** . . . This same Moses, whom they had disowned with the words, –TCNT . . . This Moses was the same man, –NCV . . . The people had put Moses aside, –NLTG . . . the Jews said they did not want, –EVRD . . . whom they denied, –HBIE, –SWAN . . . whom they rejected, –WEYM . . . whom they renounced, –WLSN . . . whom they disavowed, –HNSN . . . when they said, –MNTG . . . with the words, –NAB.

**Who made thee a ruler and a judge?:** . . . Who has appointed you, –NAB . . . referee? –WLMS . . . a ruler and adjudicator? –RTHM . . . Who made you a leader over us? Who said you are the one to say what is right or wrong? –NLTG.

**The same did God send to be a ruler and a deliverer:** . . . a saviour, –BB . . . this one has God commissioned to be a chief as well as a redeemer, –CNDT . . . God sent both to rule and to deliver them, –GDSP . . . But God made this man a leader . . . who brought them out of the country, –NLTG . . . a liberator, –NORL.

**by the hand of the angel which appeared to him in the bush:** . . . with the help of the angel, –NCV, –TCNT . . . with the assistance of the angel, –ADAM.

**7:35.** Stephen now emphasized his main point in this part of the history. This Moses, whom they had refused (denied, rejected), God sent with the hand (that is, the power) of the Angel who appeared to him in the thorn bush, to be a ruler and a deliverer (a ransomer, a liberator). "Deliverer" here is a word originally used of those who paid a ransom to liberate slaves or set prisoners free.

Thus, the answer to those who first said to Moses, "Who made thee a ruler and a judge?" is "God made him that and more." Once again Stephen had in mind the saying that the stone the builders refused was made the head of the corner (Psalm 118:22). The same God who gave honor and power to Moses gave honor and power to Jesus.

It was because of this that Stephen dared to stand and talk in this manner to the Sanhedrin. Jesus had said, "The disciple (the student) is not above his master (his teacher), nor the servant (the slave) above his lord (his master)." He had also warned them that they would be brought before governors and kings "for my sake, for a testimony against them and the Gentiles" (Matthew 10:18, 24). Although Stephen was an unknown, he had the courage to face the Council.

Stephen was in no way demeaning Moses; instead, his speech held him in the highest esteem possible. His high regard for the person and the work of Moses further developed the analogy Stephen was drawing between their actions toward Christ and the actions of their "fathers" toward the prophets who foretold His coming.

36. **He brought them out:** . . . This man led them forth, –ASV . . . He it was who led them out, –TCNT. **after that he had shewed wonders and signs in the land of Egypt:** . . . having wrought wonders, –ASV . . . He did powerful works, –NLTG . . . after performing marvels and signs, –WEYM . . . by performing wonders and signs, –WLMS . . . having produced terrors and evidences, –FNTN. **and in the Red sea, and in the wilderness forty years:** . . . and at the Red Sea, –WEYM . . . he led them in the place where no people live, –NLTG . . . in the desert, –RTHM.

**7:36.** Moses, this very person whom the Israelites had earlier rejected, brought them out of Egypt. They had been ready to deliver him up to Pharaoh and to his death. But Moses forgot all this and became their deliverer. Not only so, God used him to do mighty wonders and supernatural signs in Egypt, and then in bringing them through the Red Sea, and caring for them in the wilderness for 40 years.

In all those miraculous events God was revealing himself. For example, Moses let Pharaoh have the advantage by allowing him to set the time for the removal of the plague of the frogs so he might know "that there is none like unto the Lord our God" (Exodus 8:9, 10). With the plague of flies, there were no flies in Goshen that Pharaoh might know that God is the Lord "in the midst of the earth" (Exodus 8:22); in other words, God is immanent, not a far-off God. The deliverance at the Red Sea (sea of reeds or weeds) caused Moses and Israel to sing to the Lord and give Him glory. The manna for food and water from the rock provided for their needs. In all of this Moses was God's agent, even though he had once been refused and rejected.

37. **This is that Moses, which said unto the children of Israel:** . . . unto the sons of Israel, –RTHM . . . to the people of Israel, –TCNT . . . to the descendants of Israel, –WEYM . . . to the Israelites, –NAB. **A prophet shall the Lord your God raise up:** . . . God will raise up for you, from among your brothers, a Prophet, as he raised me up, –TCNT . . . one who speaks for Him like me, –NLTG . . . just as he appointed me, –NORL. **unto you of your brethren, like unto me; him shall ye hear:** . . . He will be one of your own people, –EVRD . . . He will come from among, –NCV.

**7:37.** As a climax to this section of his defense, Stephen reminded the Sanhedrin that this was the same Moses (the Moses whom they had rejected and God used to save them out of Egypt) who told the Israelites God would raise up a prophet for them like himself. Him they should hear (listen to and obey).

The Jewish leaders knew how the apostles applied this passage about the prophet like unto Moses. In fact, all the believing Jews applied it to Jesus. They knew Stephen was saying that by not listening to Jesus they were disobeying God and treating not only Jesus, but Moses, with contempt. Jesus himself had told them He would not accuse them to the Father (in heaven), Moses, the very one they put their trust in, was the one accusing them. "For had ye believed Moses, ye would have believed me: for he wrote of me. But if ye believe not his writings, how shall ye believe my words?" (John 5:45-47). Instead of Jesus dishonoring Moses, it was the Jewish leaders who were doing so.

In some ways, Stephen was also building a case for the superiority of Jesus, similar to the writer of Hebrews who said, "This man (Jesus) was counted worthy of more glory than Moses, inasmuch as he who hath builded the house hath more honor than the house" (Hebrews 3:3).

38. **This is he, that was in the church in the wilderness with the angel that spake to him in the mount Sina, and with our fathers:** . . . He was the ambassador, –FNTN . . . was the go-between between

the angel, —NORL . . . he that was in the assembly in the wilds, —WMCK . . . who appeared at the assembly in the Desert, —TCNT . . . who took part in the assembly of our forefathers, —NOLI . . . with the gathering of the Jews in the desert, —EVRD . . . church in the waste, —BB.

**who received the lively oracles to give unto us:** . . . living oracles, —ASV . . . ever-living utterances to hand on to us, —WEYM . . . who was entrusted with words of life, —JB . . . living Word of God, —NORL . . . living truths, —BECK . . . living words to give them, —WMCK . . . [the] living sayings, —HNSN . . . received life-giving oracles to pass on to you, —KLST . . . He received commands from God that give life, —EVRD . . . to be handed down to you, utterances that still live, —WLMS . . . received living messages to give to us, —TNT . . . the eternal commandments and delivered them to us, —NOLI.

**7:38.** In this section (verses 38-43) Stephen referred to an even worse rejection, a rejection of God himself. Again Stephen spoke of Moses. Moses was in the church in the wilderness. "Church" (Greek, *ekklēsia*, assembly) here refers to the congregation of the people of Israel in the wilderness. (The word *church* in the Bible always refers to an assembly of people, never to a building or an organization or hierarchy.) This Moses was with the angel that spoke to him on Mount Sinai. He was also with all the fathers; that is, with the fathers of Israel (in this case, the 12 tribes of Israel in the wilderness). Keep in mind this mention of the fathers. It prepared for the conclusion Stephen gave in verse 51.

Moses received the living oracles to give to Israel. "Received" also means "welcomed." Moses was happy to receive these words, the Ten Commandments, from God. "Oracles" means "sayings" and is generally used of revelations of God, sayings of Jesus, and of the Scriptures in general. Here the Ten Commandments are called "living" because they provide guidance for the conduct of life, and because they had their source and authorship in the living God.

**39. To whom our fathers would not obey:** . . . our fathers would not become obedient, —HNSN . . . were not willing to become obedient, —HBIE . . . Our forefathers, however, would not submit to him, —WEYM . . . our fathers refused to obey him, —BECK . . . did not want to obey Moses, —EVRD . . . would not listen to him, —NLTG.

**but thrust him from them:** . . . thrust him aside, —NAB . . . thrust him off, —GDSP . . . more than that, they rejected him, —TCNT . . . but spurned his authority, —WEYM . . . on the contrary, they revolted, —FNTN . . . they ignored him, —NORL . . . disregarded him, —PHLP . . . they repudiated him, —NOLI.

**and in their hearts turned back again into Egypt:** . . . while their hearts longed for Egypt, —NORL . . . in their hearts they hankered after Egypt, —WLMS . . . turned back to Egypt in their hearts,

—KLGS . . . They wanted to go back to Egypt again, —EVRD.

**7:39.** The fathers, that is, the entire body of the 12 tribes of Israel, had no such longing after the words of God. So instead of waiting patiently for Moses to come down from Mount Sinai, they refused to become obedient to him, rejected him, and in their hearts turned back to Egypt. This, actually, was an attitude that became habitual among the Israelites. Again and again they remembered the spicy food, the leeks, the garlic, and also the fish they had back in Egypt. But they forgot the whip of the slave drivers. They forgot the bondage, the misery, the oppression that caused their boy babies to be thrown to the crocodiles in the Nile River. It is so easy for people even today to remember the so-called pleasures of the world and to forget the hangovers, the spiritual darkness, the satanic oppression.

**40. Saying unto Aaron, Make us gods to go before us:** . . . Make gods for us, to march in front of us, —WEYM . . . Make gods for us, who will lead us, —BECK . . . who shall go before us, —DRBY.

**for as for this Moses, which brought us out of the land of Egypt:** . . . who led us forth, —ASV.

**we wot not what is become of him:** . . . we do not know what has, —TCNT . . . what had happened to him, —EVRD.

**7:40.** In addition to their rejection of Moses, the Fathers showed the desires of their hearts by asking Aaron to make gods to go before them. "Gods" here is in the plural, but used this way because the fathers' hearts were not toward Moses and therefore were not in right relation to the one true God. Actually, the fathers had only one God in mind. Joshua at this time called them to a feast to the Lord (YHWH, the divine name of the one true God in Exodus 32:5).

They also showed the attitude of their hearts by despising Moses, for they said in a derogatory way, "As for *this* Moses who brought us out of Egypt, we do not know what has become of him." (See Exodus 32:1.)

**41. And they made a calf in those days:** . . . Moreover they made a calf at that time, —WEYM.

**and offered sacrifice unto the idol:** . . . and brought sacrifice to the image, —BRKL.

**and rejoiced in the works of their own hands:** . . . and held festivities in honour of their own handiwork, —TCNT . . . held a celebration, —WLMS . . . and kept rejoicing in the gods which their own hands had made, —WEYM . . . applauded the work of their hands! —ADAM . . . and they celebrated a holiday in honor of their own handiwork, —NOLI . . . were proud of what they had made with their own hands! —EVRD . . . they rejoiced over their own handiwork, —FNTN . . . in great glee, —NORL . . . delighted, —BECK . . . over what their own hands had manufactured, —MOFT.

**7:41.** Then they made an image of a calf and sacrificed to this image and rejoiced (made merry, reveled) in the works of their own hands.

Many believe this image of a calf was of a small golden bull but was called a calf because of its small size. Aaron made it from the earrings of the people. Since slaves in ancient times did not wear earrings, these were part of the gifts the Egyptians gave them before they left. God gave them favor so they were able to leave, not as slaves fleeing for their lives, but as a triumphant army carrying the spoils of victory, as free people, signified by the earrings in their ears. But now they were going into a different kind of slavery, a slavery to false concepts of religion and of God.

Actually, it was not just Moses they despised. By rejecting their God-given leader they had taken God off the throne of their hearts and put self in His place.

Exodus 32:6 says the people sat down to eat and drink and then rose up to play. "Play" is a word used of joking and amusing themselves. The dancing that Moses saw (Exodus 32:19) was not part of spiritual worship. They were delighting in the work of their hands, so self and the flesh were dominant.

Whether this golden calf was supposed to be a representation of the Lord or simply an idol (cf. Exodus 32:1-6), their attitude toward it was the same as the attitude of the heathen. Thus, even before Moses came down from Mount Sinai with the Decalogue, the people had violated the second commandment, "Thou shalt not make unto thee any graven image" (Exodus 20:4).

**42.** **Then God turned:** . . . So God turned away, —TCNT . . . So God turned from them, —WEYM . . . God abandoned them, —NORL . . . So God turned his back on them, —NOLI.
**and gave them up to worship the host of heaven:** . . . He did not try to stop them from worshiping, —EVRD . . . and abandoned them, —BRKL . . . to serve, —ASV . . . the Starry Host, —TCNT . . . the army of the sky, —FNTN . . . the sun, the moon, and the stars, —BECK . . . the demons of the sky, —NOLI.
**as it is written in the book of the prophets:** . . . This is written in the book of the early preachers, —NLTG.
**O ye house of Israel, have ye offered to me slain beasts and sacrifices by the space of forty years in the wilderness?:** . . . Nation of Jews, was it to Me you gave gifts of sheep and cattle on the altar, —NLTG . . . all those forty years in the Desert, —TCNT . . . offered me victims and sacrifices, —DRBY.

**7:42.** Because Israel's worship of the golden calf was a rejection, not merely of Moses but of God,

"God turned." This may mean God turned away from the Israelites as no longer giving them the fullness of His blessing while they were in the wilderness. Or it may mean God turned the Israelites toward the worship of the heavenly bodies. Stephen said God gave them up; that is, handed them over to worship and serve the host of heaven. Thus they received the consequences they deserved because of their action.

Stephen saw this confirmed in the Book of the Prophets, the 12 Minor Prophets which were written on one scroll in his day and called the Book of the Twelve, or the Book of the Prophets. The quotation is from Amos 5:25-27. Stephen quoted the question of Amos in a way that called for a negative answer. It might be paraphrased, "You didn't offer sacrifices and offerings to Me 40 years in the desert, did you?" They had not offered sacrifices to God alone, nor did they offer them with the love and faith they should have.

It is also true that they had neglected the covenant they had accepted, for none of the males who were born in the wilderness were circumcised, and thus they were not brought under the covenant until after they entered the Promised Land at Gilgal (Joshua 5:5). It seems also they may have neglected to keep the Passover during this 40-year period (at least, after the second year). They apparently did go through the forms, but the idolatry that began with the golden calf continued to tempt Israel and did so until they went into exile in Babylonia.

**43.** **Yea, ye took up the tabernacle of Moloch:** . . . Nay, you lifted up Moloch's tent, —WEYM . . . No, you offered me the tent of Moloch, —WLMS . . . You took with you the tabernacle of Moloch, —TCNT . . . No, it was Moloch's tent that you took along, —TNT . . . the false god Molech, —EVRD.
**and the star of your god Remphan:** . . . And the star of the god Rephan, —TCNT . . . the constellation of your god Raiphan, —CNDT . . . and of your god, the star Remphan, —FNTN . . . star symbol of the god Rampha, —MNTG.
**figures which ye made to worship them:** . . . The forms which ye made to bow down unto them, —RTHM . . . The images which you had made to worship, —TCNT . . . to bow down to them, —TNT.
**and I will carry you away beyond Babylon:** . . . So I will exile you, —TCNT . . . and I will remove you, —RSV . . . Therefore I will deport you, —NOLI . . . I will relocate you beyond Babylon! —BRKL.

**7:43.** Even in the wilderness after seeing God's glory, the fathers took up the tabernacle (tent) of Moloch (a Venus god worshiped by the Ammonites and several other Semitic peoples). What a contrast this was to the "tabernacle of witness" set up by Moses according to the pattern given in Mount Sinai and decorated by men who were filled with the Spirit of God (Exodus 35:30-35).

They also worshiped the star of the god Remphan (probably the Assyrian name for the planet Saturn, called *Chiun* in Amos 5:26). Both were figures (images) they made for themselves to worship, thus breaking the First Commandment. (These images were probably small images or figurines carried secretly by these Israelites.) As a result, God told Israel He would transport them beyond Babylon. (Stephen was quoting from the Septuagint, and the KJV and other English versions are primarily based on the Masoretic Text [written in Hebrew]. This, in part, accounts for the different wording one finds.)

Stephen was saying it was their fathers who had rejected Moses and the Law, thereby rebelling against the God who gave the Law. Though Stephen did not say so, his audience knew Jesus was not like that.

**44. Our fathers had the tabernacle of witness in the wilderness:** ... The tent of witness was with our fathers in the desert, −*RTHM* ... The Holy Tent where God spoke to our fathers, −*EVRD* ... the tabernacle of the testimony, −*ASV* ... the tabernacle of Revelation, −*TCNT* ... the tent in which God spake to His people, −*BECK* ... Covenant Tent, −*TEV.*

**as he had appointed, speaking unto Moses:** ... according as he who was speaking ... gave instructions, −*RTHM* ... even as he directed, −*HBIE* ... as He prescribes, −*CNDT* ... as he had arranged, −*KLGS.*

**that he should make it according to the fashion that he had seen:** ... according to the figure, −*ASV* ... according to the model, −*RTHM* ... in imitation of the model, −*WEYM* ... pattern, −*WUST* ... like the model Moses had seen, −*WLMS.*

**7:44.** Stephen continued by answering their accusation concerning what Jesus said about the temple. He did not try to explain what Jesus really meant by "destroy this temple." Instead, he reminded them that the fathers had the tent of the testimony which contained the tablets of stone which were a witness to the covenant between God and His people.

**45. Which also our fathers that came after:** ... This Tabernacle, which was handed on to them, −*TCNT* ... which also our fathers in turn received, −*HBIE* ... That Tent was bequeathed to the next generation of our forefathers, −*WEYM* ... received it by succession, −*WLSN.*

**brought in with Jesus:** ... with Joshua, −*RSV.*

**into the possession of the Gentiles:** ... When the Gentiles had been dispossessed by God, −*NOLI* ... actually brought into the land, −*MRDK* ... entered on the possession of the nations, −*ASV* ... at the conquest of the nations, −*TCNT* ... when they were taking possession of the land of the Gentile nations, −*WEYM* ... into the land of the Pagans, −*KLGS.*

**whom God drove out before the face of our fathers:** ... that God thrust out, −*ASV* ... that God drove out, −*KLGS.*

**unto the days of David:** ... and remained here down to the time of David, −*TCNT* ... So it continued till David's time, −*WEYM.*

**7:45.** The next generation of the fathers received the tabernacle (the tent) in their turn. They brought it in with Joshua (Greek, *Iēsou,* English *Jesus,* which is derived from the Greek form of Joshua, as in Hebrews 4:8), into what was previously the possession of the Gentiles (the nations) whom God drove out before the fathers until the days of David. This indicates the driving out was not completed until the days of David. Actually, the Book of Joshua indicates the land was subdued in his day, but there was much land yet to be possessed (Joshua 13:1). The Book of Judges shows also that in the days after Joshua the people did not drive out the Canaanites, but instead fell into Canaanite idolatry. They did so again and again, even though God was faithful to raise up judges to deliver them. Not until David's time was Israel fully united and in control of its territory.

Stephen's attention, however, was focused on the tabernacle, and he showed it lasted until the time of David. After the capture of the ark of the covenant by the Philistines the tabernacle was pitched at Nob, a short distance north of Jerusalem, possibly on Mount Scopus. Later, it was at the high place at Gibeon (1 Samuel 21:1; 1 Chronicles 16:39). Finally, Solomon brought to the temple what was left of the nearly 500-year-old tent (1 Kings 8:4; 2 Chronicles 5:5).

**46. Who found favour before God:** ... David won favour with God, −*TCNT* ... who found grace before God, −*BRKL.*

**and desired to find tabernacle for the God of Jacob:** ... and asked to find a habitation, −*ASV* ... and asked permission to find a dwelling, −*TCNT* ... he might find a residence, −*MRDK* ... begged to design a dwelling, −*WLMS.*

**7:46.** David found favor before God. This was shown, of course, by his victories and by the fact that God used him to establish the kingdom of Israel, something King Saul had failed to do.

After David brought back the ark to Jerusalem, he placed it in a temporary tent shelter. But he personally desired to find a tabernacle for the God of Jacob. (Several ancient manuscripts have "for the house of Jacob.") "Tabernacle" here is used as a general word for a dwelling, even more permanent dwellings, and Stephen was thinking of David's desire to build a temple as a dwelling place for God. David expressed this in Psalm 132:4, 5 by saying "I will not give sleep to mine eyes or slumber to mine eyelids, until I find out a place for the Lord, a habitation for the mighty God of Jacob."

**47. But Solomon built him an house:** ... But it was Solomon who built a House for God, *—TCNT* ... who actually built it, *—SEB.*

**7:47.** God did not allow David to build the temple. David served his generation as a warrior, which was necessary for the nation to be established. But God wanted a man of peace to build the temple, so that was designated as Solomon's prime task. (His name means "Peaceful," in Hebrew, *Shelōmôh,* from *shālôm,* "peace.") Nevertheless, it was David's vision for building a temple that was passed down to his son. It was also David who made preparations and gathered the materials for its construction (see 1 Chronicles 22).

**48. Howbeit the most High dwelleth not in temples made with hands:** ... the Highest One, *—SEB* ... does not live in houses, *—EVRD* ... does not dwell in anything handmade, *—BRKL* ... Yet it is not in buildings made by hands that the Most High dwells, *—TCNT* ... dwells not in hand-made structures, *—FNTN* ... made by human hands, *—BECK.*

**7:48.** Solomon's Temple, however, was not God's permanent dwelling place, and Stephen declared that the Most High (God) does not dwell (or settle down to stay permanently) in what is made by hands.

Solomon himself recognized this. At the dedication of the temple in his prayer before God, he said, "But will God indeed dwell on the earth? behold the heaven and heaven of heavens cannot contain thee; how much less this house that I have builded?" (1 Kings 8:27).

**49. Heaven is my throne:** ... The sky is a throne for me, *—TCNT* ... the place where I sit, *—NLTG.*

**and earth is my footstool:** ... a rest for my feet, *—FNTN* ... where I rest my feet, *—NLTG.*

**what house will ye build me? saith the Lord:** ... What manner of house, *—ASV* ... What kind of a house, *—HBIE.*

**or what is the place of my rest?:** ... Or what place is there where I may rest, *—TCNT* ... Or what resting-place shall I have, *—WEYM* ... no place where I need to rest! *—EVRD, —SEB* ... On what spot could I settle? *—MOFT.*

**7:49.** To prove that God did not dwell permanently in the temple, Stephen quoted Isaiah 66:1 and part of verse 2. There, God told Isaiah that heaven is His throne and the earth His footstool (the place where He will show that He is Conqueror). In view of that, what house could they build for Him, or what was the place of His rest? In other words, in what place could God settle down and make His permanent abode (on earth)?

Rest also suggests the ceasing of activity. Where would God do this? As Isaiah 40:28 tells us, God is never weary. He never gets tired. He never ceases His divine activity.

**50. Hath not my hand made all these things?:** ... Was it not my hand that made, *—TCNT* ... Did not my hand make this universe, *—MNTG* ... Remember, I made all these things! *—EVRD.*

**7:50.** The unreasonableness of limiting God's presence to a temple built by human hands is further seen by the fact that God made the heavens and the earth and everything in them. How could anything made by man match what He has made?

Stephen was not denying that God had manifested His presence in the temple. God did manifest His glory there in the Holy of Holies from the time of Solomon to the time of the destruction of the temple by the Babylonians. Isaiah 57:15 also recognizes that God is the high and lofty One who inhabits the eternity of time and space (who fills the universe) and whose name (and character) is Holy. He dwells in the high and holy place, that is, He has His chief manifestation of His glory in heaven, but He dwells also with the one who has a contrite and humble spirit.

**51. Ye stiffnecked and uncircumcised in heart and ears:** ... You obstinate race, heathen in heart and ears, *—TCNT* ... uncircumcised heathen, *—FNTN* .... pagan at heart and deaf to the truth, *—BECK* ... stubborn in will, heathenish in hearts and ears, *—WLMS* ... Stubborn people with pagan hearts and ears! *—NOLI* ... You have hard hearts and ears that will not listen to me! *—NLTG.*

**ye do always resist the Holy Ghost:** ... you are continually at strife with the Holy Spirit, *—WEYM* ... you are forever resisting the Holy Spirit, *—TCNT* ... ever clashing with, *—CNDT* ... set yourselves against, *—MRDK* ... you are always in opposition, *—FNTN* ... continually fighting, *—KLGS* ... working against, *—NLTG.*

**as your fathers did, so do ye:** ... Your early fathers did. You do too, *—NLTG* ... your ancestors did it, and you are doing it still, *—TCNT* ... just as your forefathers did, *—GDSP, —NOLI.*

**7:51.** Stephen apparently saw that his message was not being accepted. Possibly there was angry whispering among his hearers. He therefore rebuked them sharply. They were stiffnecked, they were stubborn and uncircumcised in heart and ears. Their attitude and their refusal to listen to the gospel put them in the same class as the Gentiles who were outside God's covenant and were rejecting Him. They were hearing, thinking, and planning in the way unbelieving Gentiles did. Their fathers were actually warned against this.

Deuteronomy 10:16 and 30:6 calls for a circumcision of the heart lest they become rebellious and be cut off from God's promises. (See also Jeremiah 6:10; 9:26; Ezekiel 44:7.) In fact, these Jewish leaders were actively resisting the Holy Spirit just as their fathers had.

**52. Which of the prophets have not your fathers persecuted?:** ... Was there ever a prophet your fathers didn't persecute, *—BECK* ... every prophet who ever lived, *—SEB* ... Can you name a single prophet whom your fathers did not persecute? *—PHLP.*
**and they have slain them which shewed before of the coming of the Just One:** ... they killed the men who foretold, *—WEYM* ... they murdered those who foretold the coming, *—FNTN.*
**of whom ye have been now the betrayers and murderers:** ... whose betrayers and murderers you have now become, *—WEYM* ... now you yourselves have become His betrayers and murderers, *—NORL* ... you have now handed over, *—KLGS* ... and now you betrayed and murdered him, *—BECK.*

**7:52.** None of the prophets escaped persecution by the fathers. (See Matthew 5:11, 12; 23:30, 31). They killed those who announced beforehand the coming of the Just One (the Righteous One). It was He these Jewish leaders had now betrayed and murdered.

Stephen threw the guilt of Judas back on the ones who commanded that information be given them in order that they might arrest Jesus (which they did some time before Judas came to them; John 11:57).

**53. Who have received the law by the disposition of angels:** ... Angels were ordered, *—BECK* ... ordination of angels, *—MRDK* ... by arrangement of messengers, *—YNG* ... injunction, *—ALFD* ... as ordained by the ministry of angels, *—DRBY* ... that angels transmitted, *—MOFT.*
**and have not kept it:** ... and have not guarded it, *—SWAN* ... but you did not obey them, *—NOLI.*

**7:53.** These Jewish leaders would have acknowledged the guilt of those who killed the prophets was great. But their guilt was even greater. They had received the Law which was given by the disposition (the ordaining, the ordinance) of angels, but they did not keep or observe it.

The mention of angels here comes from Jewish traditions and also from the Septuagint translation which interpreted Deuteronomy 33:2, 3 to mean that angels were active in the giving or expounding of the Law. This was part of Moses' blessing given shortly before his death. There he spoke of the Lord's coming from Sinai and His glory shining forth from Seir and Paran (that is, from the direction of Edom). He came with "ten thousands of saints" (holy ones), and at the same time "from his right hand went a fiery law." The saints or holy ones were taken to be angels.

Since the Jewish leaders did not keep the Law, they were the guilty ones. That is, they, not Jesus, nor His followers, had disregarded the Law in killing Jesus, the very One the Law as well as the prophets had prophesied would come.

**54. When they heard these things:** ... As they continued to listen to this address, *—WLMS.*
**they were cut to the heart:** ... grew frantic with rage, *—TCNT* ... they were becoming infuriated, *—WLMS* ... enraged, *—WLSN.*
**and they gnashed on him with their teeth:** ... grind their teeth at him, *—WLMS* ... clinched their teeth, *—ET.*

**7:54.** This severe rebuke cut (sawed through) to the heart of these Sanhedrin members who heard Stephen and brought a vicious reaction. These dignified "senators" of the Jewish people gnashed (crunched) their teeth over Stephen. By this expression of rage and exasperation they only proved they really were resisting the Holy Spirit as Stephen said they were.

**55. But he, being full of the Holy Ghost:** ... but possessing fulness of Holy Spirit, *—FNTN* ... But since he was full, *—WLMS* ... filled through all his being with the Holy Spirit, *—PHLP.*
**looked up stedfastly into heaven, and saw the glory of God:** ... looking intently into heaven, *—CNDT* ... he looked right into heaven and saw the glory of God, *—WLMS* ... he saw a Divine Majesty, *—FNTN.*
**and Jesus standing on the right hand of God:** ... at his right hand, *—NOLI.*

**7:55.** In contrast to them, Stephen, being still full of the Holy Spirit, fixed his gaze into heaven and saw the glory of God and Jesus standing at the right hand of God (that is, in the place of honor, power, and authority). Other passages speak of Jesus seated at the right hand of God where He is now interceding for believers (Mark 14:62; Luke 22:69). This seems to indicate that Jesus rose to welcome the first martyr who gave a witness for Him at the cost of His life. (The word *martyr* comes from the Greek *martus* which has a genitive form *marturos* and means "a witness." During the later persecutions of the Early Church so many bore witness to Jesus as they were being killed for their faith that the word came to have its present meaning of martyr as one who dies for his faith.)

**56. And said, Behold, I see the heavens opened:** . . . Look, −NOLI . . . I see an opening in the sky, −NAB.

**and the Son of man standing on the right hand of God:** . . . the Messiah, −NOLI . . . at God's right side, −NCV.

**7:56.** Stephen immediately told what he saw. But this time he did not use the name of Jesus. Instead, he called Him "the Son of man." This was a term the Jewish leaders in the Sanhedrin had often heard Jesus use of himself. During His ministry He used it because of His identification with mankind whom He came to redeem. The term *son of* was also used to indicate nature or character. So Jesus was declaring himself to be truly human as well as truly divine. But it was not a term His enemies could use against Him. Jesus did not want to be arrested and killed before He had opportunity to teach and train His disciples. However, at His trial, Jesus declared He was the Son of Man prophesied by Daniel 7:13, the Son of Man who would come in clouds to receive the kingdom promised to Israel.

**57. Then they cried out with a loud voice:** . . . At this, they shouted with all their might, −NORL . . . they uttered a great shout, −GDSP . . . The onlookers were shouting aloud, −NAB . . . yelled at the top of their voices, −BECK . . . With a loud outcry, −MNTG . . . With a loud shriek, −MOFT.

**and stopped their ears:** . . . holding their hands over their ears as they did so, −NAB . . . holding their hands to, −MLNT.

**and ran upon him with one accord:** . . . did rush, −YNG . . . and they all pushed on him, −NLTG . . . with one thought in mind, −ADAM . . . and rushed with one accord upon him, −SWAN . . . rushed . . . in a body, −MLNT . . . as one man, −NAB.

**7:57.** The words of Stephen caused the Sanhedrin to start crying out, yelling and shrieking with a loud voice. At the same time they put their hands over their ears to shut out anything further that Stephen might say. Then "with one accord" (that is, with one spontaneous impulse and purpose) they rushed upon him. (The same word is used of the swine rushing down into the sea when the legion of demons took possession of them, Matthew 8:32; Mark 5:13; Luke 8:33. It was also used of the mob rushing into the theater when they were upset because the sale of images was falling off; Acts 19:29.)

**58. And cast him out of the city, and stoned him:** . . . dragged him outside the city, −MNTG . . . drove him, −TNT . . . threw him, −MLNT . . . Then they took him . . . and threw stones at him, −NLTG . . . they pelted him, −CNDT.

**and the witnesses laid down their clothes at a young man's feet, whose name was Saul:** . . . Meanwhile, the witnesses, −NIV . . . The men who told lies against Stephen, −EVRD . . . The men who were throwing the stones laid their coats down in front of a young man, −NLTG . . . deposited their clothes, −FNTN . . . throwing down their clothes, −GDSP . . . meanwhile were piling their cloaks, −NAB.

**7:58.** Then they dragged Stephen out of the city and stoned him. This time they were still following the letter of the law of Moses where a willful, high-handed unrepentant sinner was to be stoned "outside the camp" (Numbers 15:35).

By stoning him, however, they were defying Roman law which did not allow the Jews to carry out the death penalty (John 18:31). They had bowed to Roman law in seeking to get the death penalty for Jesus, and this led to His being crucified instead of being stoned. It should be noted, however, that this took place probably near the close of Pilate's governorship when he had fallen into disfavor with the Roman government, and these Jews were taking advantage of his weakness.

The Sanhedrin also followed the externals of Jewish legal procedure with the witnesses casting the first stone (Deuteronomy 17:7). They, in fact, took off their outer garments in order to be more free to throw the stones and laid the garments at the feet of a young man named Saul. ("Young man" here means a man in his prime, up to the age of 40. Saul [Paul] was old enough to be a member of the Sanhedrin. Acts 26:10 indicates he cast his vote, and he had to be a member to do that.) Saul was an eyewitness to Stephen's death and probably to his preaching in the synagogue. This is the first mention of Saul, a preparation for what comes later.

**59. And they stoned Stephen, calling upon God, and saying:** . . . While they threw stones at Stephen, he prayed, −NLTG . . . While they were throwing rocks, −NCV . . . while he is invoking and saying, −CNDT . . . as he called upon the Lord, −MLNT . . . called out again and again, −WMCK

**Lord Jesus, receive my spirit:** . . . take my spirit, −KLGS.

**7:59.** While they were stoning Stephen he was calling on God saying, "Lord Jesus, receive (welcome) my spirit." He knew that to be absent from the body is to be present with the Lord (2 Corinthians 5:8). Although there is a great similarity between Stephen's confession and Jesus' (see verse 60), there is one striking contrast: Jesus "commended" His spirit to the Father but Stephen, to the Lord Jesus. This is one of the earliest and clearest testimonies to Jesus' deity by His followers.

**60. And he kneeled down, and cried with a loud voice:** ... He fell on his knees, —EVRD ... Falling on his knees, he called out loudly, —MLNT.

**Lord, lay not this sin to their charge:** ... mayest thou not lay to them this sin, —YNG ... do not hold this sin against them! —EVRD ... do not count this sin against them, —NOLI ... weigh not, —FNTN ... to their account, —WMCK

**And when he had said this, he fell asleep:** ... and with these words, —BRKL ... he fell into the sleep of death, —PHLP ... slept the sleep of death, —MOFT ... he died, —TNT ... fell asleep in death, —MLNT.

**7:60.** Then Stephen knelt down and cried out with a loud voice "Lord, do not let this sin stand against them." ("Lay not this sin to their charge" is a paraphrase which gives the meaning.) How like Jesus this was! It reminds us of His cry, "Father, forgive them; for they know not what they do" (Luke 23:34).

Having said this, Stephen fell asleep. There was something peaceful about his death in spite of its violent nature. Stephen went to be with Jesus and became the first martyr of the Early Church, the first of a long line of believers who gave their lives for Jesus and the gospel.

## Chapter 8

**1. And Saul was consenting unto his death:** ... Saul agreed that the killing of Stephen was a good thing, —EVRD ... Saul, for his part, concurred in the act of killing, —NAB ... was taking pleasure with them in his death, —RTHM ... fully approved of his murder, —WEYM ... entirely approved, —GDSP ... was altogether agreed to his murder, —BRKL ... endorsing his assassination, —CNDT ... heartily approved, —WLMS ... and participating, —MRDK ... was well pleased with his slaughter, —CMPB, —SWAN ... applauding it, —WUST ... in hearty agreement with, —NASB.

**And at that time there was a great persecution against the church which was at Jerusalem:** ... And there arose on that day, —ASV ... On that very day a great storm of persecution burst upon the Church in Jerusalem, —PHLP ... That day a great persecution ... began, —WMCK ... Just then a violent persecution broke out, —FNTN ... That very day ... began to suffer cruel persecution, —TEV ... started that day against the church, —KLGS ... a fierce attack on the congregation, —SEB.

**and they were all scattered abroad throughout the regions of Judaea and Samaria, except the apostles:** ... All Church Members, —PHLP ... were all dispersed, —MRDK ... among the districts, —CNDT.

**8:1.** The first sentence of this verse really belongs with the end of chapter 7. The Greek is a strong statement. Saul was not only consenting to Stephen's death, he wholly and completely approved of Stephen's murder and continued to act accordingly. He did not share the feelings of his former teacher, Gamaliel, as they were expressed in 5:38. Instead, he considered Stephen's ideas

dangerous and felt they should be rooted out. (It seems possible that due to Stephen's strong defense, even Gamaliel may have changed his mind and joined in with the stoning of Stephen.) But they were all going to learn that neither Saul nor the rest of the Sanhedrin could root out the work of the Holy Spirit.

Saul was undoubtedly one of the chief instigators of the great persecution that arose against the Church in Jerusalem at that time (on the very day Stephen was murdered). So intense was this persecution that the believers were scattered in various directions throughout Judea and Samaria.

Some commentators believe the persecution was primarily, or even entirely, against the Hellenistic or Greek-speaking Jewish believers and that only these fled. But the Bible specifically says they all fled except the apostles. Some modern writers also suppose that the Jerusalem church contained no Hellenist believers after this. But the presence of Barnabas, a Hellenist, in 11:22, and his being sent as a representative of the Jerusalem Church, refutes this idea.

The 12 apostles remained undoubtedly because they were constrained to believe that God would still have a church in Jerusalem and that the city still needed to be a center for the further spread of the gospel.

**2. And devout men carried Stephen to his burial:** ... And God fearing men, —BB ... While reverent men, —PHLP ... religious men, —EVRD ... buried Stephen, —ASV ... took charge of Stephen's funeral, —BRKL.

**and made great lamentation over him:** ... making a great weeping, —BB ... sorrowed much, —NORL ... cried very loudly for him, —EVRD.

**8:2.** This verse indicates that many of the Jerusalem Jews were sympathetic to the believers. Devout men carried Stephen out, buried him, and made a great lamentation, weeping and beating their breasts over him. This was unusual, for Jewish tradition was against showing this kind of respect or sorrow for an executed person.

"Devout men" refers to men like those of 2:5 where the same title is used. They were sincere, godly Jews who had not yet accepted Christ as their Messiah and Saviour, but who respected Stephen and rejected the decision of the Sanhedrin as wrong and unjust. Through them the Church in Jerusalem would grow again.

**3. As for Saul, he made havoc of the church:** ... But Saul laid waste the church, —ASV ... But Saul began ravaging the church, NASB ... Now Saul devastated the Ecclesia, —CNDT ... On that day the Jews began trying to hurt the church in Jerusalem, —EVRD ... continued, —WLMS ... to harass, —TCNT ... shamefully treated, —LIVB . . . worked for the total destruction, —JB.

**entering into every house:** . . . entering house after house, —TCNT . . . forcing himself into homes, —BRKL.

**and haling men and women committed them to prison:** . . . and dragging off, —WEYM . . . both men and women by their feet along the street, —WUST.

**8:3.** In contrast to the devout men who lamented over Stephen, Saul became more and more furious, more energetic in his persecution. "He made havoc" of the Church. Literally, he ravaged and devastated it. (The Septuagint version uses the same word of a wild boar tearing up vineyards.) Entering into house after house, he dragged out men and women and handed them over to be put into prison.

**4.   Therefore   they   that   were   scattered abroad:** . . . Nevertheless, —CMPB . . . As a result, —ADAM . . . Now those who were scattered in different directions, —TCNT . . . were dispersed, ABUV . . . had taken flight, —BB . . . All the believers . . . went to different places, —EVRD.

**went every where preaching the word:** . . . went from place to place, with the good News of the Message, —TCNT . . . spreading the gospel of God's Word, —WEYM . . . proclaiming good newsthe word, —YNG.

**8:4.** If Saul thought persecution would stop the spread of the gospel he was wrong. In fact, it had exactly the opposite effect. Prior to this persecution the believers were receiving teaching and training from the apostles. Now they were ready to move out. It took the persecution to make them do it but move out they did.

Those who were scattered did not go into hiding. Neither did they settle down. Instead, they kept traveling from place to place, spreading the good news, the gospel.

**5.   Then Philip went down to the city of Samaria, and preached Christ unto them:** . . . and proclaimed unto them the Christ, —ASV . . . and there began proclaiming the Messiah, —RIEU.

**8:5.** Many preached or proclaimed the gospel publicly, however. After the general statement in verse 4, Luke gave an example of what must have happened all over. Philip the deacon was chosen as this example, not because what happened in Samaria was greater than what happened elsewhere but because of the lessons learned there and because Samaria was next in line in the commission given in 1:8.

Jews avoided going through Samaria if at all possible, so it took courage for Philip to go there. But, like the others, he was led by the Spirit. (The city was rebuilt by Herod the Great and renamed Sebaste, which is Greek for Augustus and thus honored the Emperor, Caesar Augustus, but the Jews still called it Samaria. It was about 10 miles north of where Jesus talked to the woman at the well.) As soon as he arrived, Philip began to preach Christ, proclaiming the truth about Him as the Messiah and Saviour. The ministry of Jesus in Samaria (John 4) was not forgotten. These things were not done in a corner.

**6.   And the people with one accord gave heed unto those things which Philip spake:** . . . Crowds of people with one accord gave attention, —WEYM . . . The crowds unanimously attended to the teachings of Philip, —BRKL . . . listened very carefully, —SEB . . . one and all, listened attentively, —TCNT . . . acquiesced, —MRDK . . . unitedly paid attention, —ADAM.

**hearing and seeing the miracles which he did:** . . . when they heard of, and saw, the signs, —TCNT . . . especially when they saw, —BECK . . . they watched him do powerful works, —NLTG.

**8:6.** The crowds (including all classes of people) with one accord paid attention to Philip's message, listening to him, both hearing and seeing the miracles (signs) he kept doing. The Lord's promise to confirm the Word with signs following was not limited to the apostles (Mark 16:20).

**7.   For unclean spirits, crying with loud voice:** . . . For there were many cases of people with wicked spirits, —TCNT . . . came shrieking out of many, —JB . . . For many of those under the power of foul spirits, —WLMS . . . screaming with a loud voice, —MLNT.

**came out of many that were possessed with them:** . . . where the spirits, with loud screams, came out of them, —TCNT . . . those who were plagued, —BECK.

**and many taken with palsies, and that were lame, were healed:** . . . and many who were paralyzed and lame were cured, —TCNT . . . and many paralytics and lame persons were restored to health, —WEYM . . . Many weak and crippled people were also, —NCV . . . people could not move their bodies or arms and legs, —NLTG.

**8:7.** The people heard those having unclean spirits shouting with a loud voice as they came out. They saw those who were paralyzed and who were lame healed. (Palsy here means paralysis.) Here the Bible clearly distinguishes between afflictions that were due to the direct activity of demons and those which were simply "diseases." In both cases, the miraculous healings and deliverances functioned as "signs" which confirmed the message Philip was preaching.

**8.   And there was great joy in that city:** . . . much joy, —ASV . . . so that there was great rejoicing throughout that city, —TCNT . . . much rejoicing in that city, —BRKL . . . The rejoicing in that town rose to fever pitch, —NAB . . . So the people in that city were very happy, —EVRD.

**8:8.** In contrast to the rejection and persecution going on in Jerusalem, the people of Samaria were open to the gospel. There was no opposition, no criticism. Instead, there was great joy and rejoicing. This was the joy of health and salvation.

**9. But there was a certain man, called Simon:** . . . Simon by name, —ASV.

**which beforetime in the same city used sorcery:** . . . had been using, —KJII . . . magical arts, —RTHM . . . who had been practising magic there, —TCNT . . . practicing witchcraft, —BECK . . . did magic tricks, —SEB . . . and who made great pretensions, —GDSP.

**and bewitched the people of Samaria:** . . . and amazing the nation of Samaria, —HBIE . . . amazed all the people, —EVRD . . . and astonishing the Samaritans, —WEYM . . . who had kept the Samaritan people thrilled, —WLMS . . . and holding the Samaritans spellbound, —NAB . . . he fooled them with his witchcraft, —NLTG.

**giving out that himself was some great one:** . . . He boasted, —NIV . . . pretending that he was more than human, —WEYM . . . bragged and called himself a great man, —EVRD . . . some extraordinary person, —CMPB . . . a man of note, —NORL . . . that he was a remarkable person, —MLNT . . . someone momentous, —JB.

**8:9.** The success of the gospel in Samaria was an even greater miracle than it first appeared, for these people previously had been filled with astonishment and amazement by a man named Simon. He practiced sorcery (Greek, *mageuōn*, a plural, meaning magic arts or magic tricks). "Bewitched" in the King James Version is the same Greek word which is rendered "wondered" in verse 13. It does not imply any supernatural power on the part of Simon. He depended on trickery, though he may also have dabbled in the occult. He did not claim to be in touch with evil spirits or demon powers as so many heathen magicians did. Instead, he claimed he was someone great (or some great being).

Apparently, he did not say he was a divine being or a messiah, but he talked enough about his greatness and about his powers that he was obviously trying to give the impression that he was more than human.

Simon, also referred to as Simon Magus, is the subject behind a great deal of legend popularized in the Early Church. Irenaeus, for example, reports that Simon was the father of gnosticism. Furthermore, in an apocryphal work by Hippolytus entitled *The Acts of Peter,* Simon is said to have boasted against Peter and claimed that he would rise on the third day if buried alive. He did not

(Bruce, *New International Commentary on the New Testament, Acts,* pp. 178f.). At this point it is not possible to verify for certain if the Simon of these legends and traditions is in fact the Simon of Acts chapter 8. Nevertheless, the people of the area revered him.

**10. To whom they all gave heed, from the least to the greatest, saying:** . . . Every one, high and low, listened attentively to him, —TCNT . . . all sorts and conditions of people attached themselves, —MOFT . . . inclined towards him, —MRDK . . . To him people of all classes paid attention, —WEYM . . . Everybody, high and low, kept running after him, —WLMS . . . all paid regard, —CMPB . . . was fascinated by him, —PHLP.

**This man is the great power of God:** . . . He must be what they call, —WMCK . . . This man, they used to say, must be that Power of God which men call The Great Power, —TCNT . . . the Power of God, known as the Great Power, —WEYM.

**8:10.** To Simon, all (from the least to the greatest in Samaria) gave attention, giving heed to him, even considering themselves to be his followers, for they said, "This man is the power of God which is called great." (Or, as many ancient manuscripts have it, "This man is the great power of God.")

The people were thus deceived by one who drew attention to himself. Like most who dealt with the occult, he encouraged the people to follow their own pride and fleshly inclinations.

Actually, such magicians were quite common in the Roman Empire in New Testament times. The emperor Tiberius, especially in the latter part of his reign, kept a large number of magicians as advisers in his court. The apostle Paul later came in contact with another of them, Elymas, on the island of Cyprus (13:8).

**11. And to him they had regard:** . . . And they gave heed to him, —ASV . . . They paid attention to him because, —TNT . . . the people became his followers, —EVRD.

**because that of long time he had bewitched them with sorceries:** . . . he had for long astonished them, —WMCK . . . thrilled them with his magical performances, —WLMS . . . he had astounded them, —ADAM . . . deeds of magic, —YNG . . . his enchantments, —CMPB . . . his skill in magic, —NORL.

**8:11.** The people of Samaria had given heed, paid attention, and considered themselves followers of Simon for some time, because he amazed them with his magic tricks. The Greek word *mageiais,* "magic tricks," is sometimes translated "sorcery." Actually, sorcery, divination, astrology, witchcraft, fortune-telling, demon worship, and various kinds of magic were all part of the heathen religions of ancient times and are all condemned in the Bible.

This was all the devil's territory, and anything that seemed supernatural had to have come from Satan's power or from magic tricks. Archaeologists have found speaking tubes, trap doors, and other such things in ancient temples and shrines. These were used to fool the people and make them think something supernatural was happening. Hypnotism and drugs were also used by ancient magicians to produce special effects. How much of this Simon used is not known, but he probably used a combination of the occult and trickery to amaze the people. The Greek indicates this had a continuing effect on them. They were astounded, astonished, and almost afraid of him.

**12. But when they believed Philip preaching the things concerning the kingdom of God, and the name of Jesus Christ:** . . . But now they believed, —LIVB . . . Philip's good news, —WMCK . . . message of the good news of the kingdom, —WEYM . . . and the authority of Jesus, —SEB.

**they were baptized, both men and women:** . . . were constantly baptized. —WLMS.

**8:12.** When Philip came, the people saw something far more wonderful in his miracles. The tricks and false miracles of Simon faded into insignificance in the presence of the genuine power of God. Furthermore, Philip did not draw attention to himself or exalt himself. He brought the good news of the kingdom of God, that is, of God's divine power, rule, and authority that was and is the assurance that God is carrying out His great plan of redemption. He also brought good news of the Name, that is, the authority, nature, and character of Jesus. Philip told the people the facts of the gospel that are found not only in the preaching in the Book of Acts but also in the Gospels. He showed them from the Old Testament Scriptures that the rule and power of God is and will be manifest through Christ in His character and nature.

The people believed, not just Philip but also the truth he proclaimed. They accepted what Philip told them about Christ's work as the crucified and risen Saviour and Lord and were all baptized, both men and women.

**13. Then Simon himself believed also:** . . . Indeed Simon himself believed, —TCNT . . . became a believer, —WMCK.

**and when he was baptized:** . . . after his baptism, —KLST . . . baptized like the rest, —NAB.

**he continued with Philip:** . . . devoted himself to Philip, —GDSP . . . and attached himself closely to Philip, —TNT . . . kept close to, —MLNT, —WMCK . . . and became a devoted follower of, —NAB . . . He went along with Philip everywhere, —NLTG.

**and wondered, beholding the miracles and signs which were done:** . . . and was full of amazement at seeing such signs and such great miracles performed, —WEYM . . . he was always thrilled, —WLMS . . . As he saw the signs and remarkable demonstrations of power which took place, he lived in a state of constant wonder, —PHLP . . . was amazed at the sight of the signs and exceedingly great miracles being effected, —KLST . . . was astonished, —WMCK . . . he was continually performing, —NORL.

**8:13.** Finally, even Simon himself believed and was baptized. Then he attached himself persistently and constantly to Philip, following him around, not letting him out of his sight. Simon was accustomed to deceiving people by his magic tricks and knew astonishing things can be done by trickery. He had watched Philip with the professional eye of a magician and had come to the conclusion that the miracles done by Philip were real. Clearly, these signs and great deeds of power were supernatural. So he too "wondered," that is, he was filled with wonder and amazement. He had to admit these miracles were quite unlike the magic tricks and occult practices by which he had gained attention.

Some have questioned whether Simon truly believed. This verse indicates he did. It uses the same form of the verb as is used of the others in Samaria and does not qualify the statement in any way. Moreover, it is likely that Philip, a man led by the Holy Spirit, would not have baptized Simon if he had not given evidence of being a true believer. (Even John the Baptist had enough spiritual discernment not to baptize the Pharisees and Sadducees who came to him but had not genuinely repented. See Matthew 3:7.)

**14. Now when the apostles which were at Jerusalem heard that Samaria had received the word of God:** . . . The apostles were still in Jerusalem, —NCV . . . heard that the Samaritans had welcomed God's Message, —TCNT . . . welcomed the message of God, —MLNT . . . accepted God's message, —WLMS.

**they sent unto them Peter and John:** . . . sent on a mission to them, —WUST . . . they despatched, —MOFT.

**8:14.** The news that Samaria had "received (welcomed and was continuing to welcome) the Word of God" soon reached the apostles in Jerusalem. They sent Peter and John to Samaria. As a body the apostles commissioned Peter and John as their representatives and sent them with a message and a purpose to encourage the new believers. There is no indication, however, that they wanted to take control of what was going on. Neither is there any indication that they thought Philip's ministry was in any way deficient, inferior, or lacking in any way. They just wanted to help him and encourage and strengthen the new believers. Neither is there any thought that Peter and John were the chief apostles or that Peter was some sort of a pope.

**15. Who, when they were come down, prayed for them, that they might receive the Holy Ghost:** ... On their arrival, they prayed that the Samaritans might receive the Holy Spirit, —TCNT ... prayed for the believers to receive the Holy Spirit, —BRKL ... in order that, —WUST ... prayed that the new followers, —NLTG.

**16. (For as yet he was fallen upon none of them:** ... so far, —ADAM ... For He had not as yet fallen upon any of them, —WEYM ... alighted upon, —FNTN ... thus far, —BRKL ... had not yet come down on any of them, —SEB.

**only they were baptized in the name of the Lord Jesus.):** ... they had simply been baptized, —MNTG ... they had received nothing so far except, —KNOX ... into the Faith of Jesus, —TCNT ... having been baptized, they belonged to the name of the Lord Jesus, —CNDT.

**8:15, 16.** When Peter and John arrived, the first thing they did was to pray for the Samaritan believers to receive the Holy Spirit. Elsewhere in Acts, the Holy Spirit was received both at the time of being baptized in the name of Jesus (cf. 2:38, 41) and even before water baptism (10:44-48). Several explanations have been given to explain the present situation. Some believe the Spirit was given only when an apostle (or some official delegate of God) laid his hands on an individual. Others say the faith of the Samaritans was somehow defective, that is, they were not truly converted through the preaching (and baptism) of Philip. Another view states that God withheld the Holy Spirit until delegates from the Jerusalem (Jewish Christians) church arrived. He did this in order to emphasize that Samaritans were not to be excluded fellowship in the body of Christ. This "Samaritan Pentecost" was to serve as evidence that God accepts the Gentile as well as the Jew.

One final explanation is that although the Samaritans had become Christians, they had not received the "promise of the Father" which Jesus told His disciples to tarry for (1:4, 5). It is presumed, from what follows in verse 19, that the supernatural signs recorded in 2:4-8 also accompanied this outpouring of the Holy Spirit. This text, then, serves as evidence for a second work of grace following conversion and is referred to as the baptism of (in) the Holy Spirit, using the wording of 1:5 (see also 2:4ff.).

**17. Then laid they their hands on them:** ... Then they put their hands on them, —BB ... Then, when the two apostles began laying their hands on the people, —EVRD ... placed their hands on them,

—BRKL ... The pair upon arriving imposed hands on them, —NAB ... one after another, —WUST.

**and they received the Holy Ghost:** ... so that the Holy Spirit was given them, —KNOX.

**8:17.** Not until after they prayed for the Samaritan believers did the apostles lay hands on them. Then God confirmed the faith of the believers, and they received the Holy Spirit, and they kept receiving the Spirit publicly as the apostles laid hands on them.

**18. And when Simon saw that through laying on of the apostles' hands the Holy Ghost was given:** ... perceiving that, —CNDT ... was conferred, —WLMS ... was imparted through, —GDSP, —KLST ... by the imposition of a hand, —MRDK ... was given to people, —EVRD ... was granted through the imposition of the apostles' hands, —KNOX.

**he offered them money:** ... he brought them a sum of money, —TCNT.

**8:18.** Whether or not the apostles laid hands on Simon is not explicitly stated in the text. What is stated, however, is that Simon was very interested in possessing the power he observed in Peter and John. He was prepared to pay for the power of imparting the Holy Spirit through the laying on of hands. (Note that the word "simony" refers to buying or selling a position in the church.)

Verse 13 indicates that Simon, after believing and being baptized, observed the miracles which followed Philip's ministry. Nevertheless, he was more impressed by the signs which accompanied the receiving of the Spirit. Many insist that these believers spoke in tongues just as on the Day of Pentecost. This may have been the power Simon sought to purchase: power to impart the gift of speaking in tongues.

**19. Saying, Give me also this power:** ... Give this power to me too, —EVRD ... Let me too ... have such powers, —KNOX ... this authority, —RTHM ... this prerogative, —MRDK.

**that on whomsoever I lay hands, he may receive the Holy Ghost:** ... to communicate the holy Spirit, —GDSP ... Then I can give the Holy Spirit to anyone, —NLTG ... when I lay my hands on a person, —EVRD.

**8:19.** Simon's offering was conditional. He would give them the money if they would give him the power (the authority) to lay his hands on people and have them receive the Holy Spirit.

In saying this he jumped to the wrong conclusion. The Bible does not indicate that the apostles could lay hands on whomever they wanted to and have them receive the Spirit. As we have seen, they prayed first. Then they laid hands on the believers. Simon was wrong too in thinking that the laying on of hands was necessary for receiving the

Spirit. There was no laying on of hands on the Day of Pentecost or at the house of Cornelius. Nor was the laying on of hands limited to the apostles or to those delegated by them. Ananias, a layman of Damascus, laid his hands on Saul (who became Paul) for both healing and the receiving of the Holy Spirit. The laying on of hands here was a means of welcoming them as fellow believers and of encouraging their faith to receive (actively) the gift of the Spirit.

**20. But Peter said unto him, Thy money perish with thee:** ... Thy silver with thee go to destruction! —RTHM ... May your money go to, —MLNT ... Take thy wealth with thee, —KNOX . . . Take your money to perdition with you! —TCNT . . . May you and your money rot, —NAB . . . Death to you and your money, —MOFT ... To hell with you and your money! —PHLP ... A curse on you and your money, —WMCK ... should both be destroyed! —EVRD, —SEB.

**because thou hast thought that the gift of God may be purchased with money:** ... because you have imagined that you can obtain God's free gift with money, —WEYM ... because you have supposed, —MNTG ... to acquire, —HBIE ... How dare you think you could buy the gift of God? —PHLP . . . the gratuity of God, —CNDT ... by a worldly substance, —MRDK.

**8:20.** Peter rebuked Simon severely. Literally, he said, "Let your money (silver) together with you go into destruction (probably the destruction of the lake of fire) because you thought the gift of God (that is, God's gift of the Holy Spirit, as in 2:38; 10:45) could be purchased with money (earthly riches)."

**21. Thou hast neither part nor lot:** ... You have no share or part, —TCNT.

**in this matter:** ... in our Message, —TCNT ... in the proclamation of this message, —ADAM.

**for thy heart is not right in the sight of God:** . . . not sincere, —WLMS . . . not straight, —BRKL ... not honest, —PHLP.

**8:21.** Peter further stated that Simon had neither part (share) nor lot (portion) in this matter. "Part" and "lot" are synonyms here. The repetition is for emphasis. The very fact that he tried to buy this power ruled out the possibility of his having any part in it whatsoever.

This further suggests that Simon could have had part or lot in this matter if he had come in faith and received the gift of the Spirit himself instead of offering money.

Peter also, by the insight given him by the Spirit, saw into the heart of Simon. Behind the money he offered, apparently as a generous gift, was a heart which was not right, that is, not upright or straight before God.

**22. Repent therefore of this thy wickedness:** ... Let your heart be changed, —BB ... So, repent of this crookedness of yours, —BRKL ... Change your heart! —SEB ... of this evil plan of yours, —TEV ... Turn your mind, —SAWR.

**and pray God:** ... pray the Lord, —ASV ... beseech the Lord, —MNTG ... plead with the Lord, —BRKL.

**if perhaps the thought of thine heart may be forgiven thee:** ... to forgive you for what you had in mind, —BRKL.

**8:22.** Peter then showed that Simon's case was not entirely hopeless by exhorting him to repent from his wickedness and pray to God (request of the Lord) if perhaps the thought (including the purpose) of his heart might be forgiven. There is no question here about God's willingness to forgive. God always freely forgives those who come to Him confessing their sin (1 John 1:9). Peter added the "if perhaps" because of Simon's heart condition. Simon must turn from the pride and greed that caused him to sin in this way.

**23. For I perceive that thou art in the gall of bitterness:** . . . for I see that you have fallen into bitter jealousy, —TCNT . . . you are a bitter weed, —WLMS . . . For I can see inside you, and I see a man bitter with jealousy, —PHLP . . . I see you're turning to bitter poison, —BECK . . . poisoned with envy, —NORL ... you are trapped, —TEV.

**and in the bond of iniquity:** ... and the fetters of sin, —TCNT ... and a pack of evil, —MOFT ... and a bundle of crookedness, —WLMS ... and being chained by wickedness, —BECK . . . fetter of injustice, —CNDT ... slave of wrong-doing, —NORL ... the bond of unrighteousness, —HBIE ... a prisoner of sin, —TEV ... the chains of sin, —JB ... captive to sin, —NIV.

**8:23.** Peter further perceived and recognized that Simon had an embittered, resentful spirit, because the people ceased to give him prominence. (Compare how the "gall of bitterness" is used in the Old Testament, as in Deuteronomy 29:18.) This may even imply some jealousy because of the attention now given to the gospel and to those who proclaimed it. Such a spirit of bitterness often rejects reconciliation and certainly grieves the Holy Spirit (Ephesians 4:30, 31). It is an evil root that can defile everyone around the person who has it (Hebrews 12:15).

Simon was also in the "bond (that is, in the grip) of iniquity" (including injustice and unrighteousness). He was unjust in wanting to receive this power or authority for himself. Also, his wrong attitude had such a grip on him that it would be difficult for him to break loose from its grasp.

However, the Greek could mean Simon was in danger of being in the "gall of bitterness" and the "bond of iniquity." This would mean he was not yet bound by bitterness and unrighteousness, and therefore there was still hope for him if he would repent immediately.

**24. Then answered Simon, and said, Pray ye to the Lord for me:** ... Simon responded, I need the prayers of all of you, —NAB ...You plead, —BRKL ...Both of you pray for me, —NCV ...Plead with the Lord for me yourselves, —MLNT.

**that none of these things which ye have spoken come upon me:** ...that none of this harm you have spoken of may fall upon me, —KNOX ...so that what you have just said may never happen to me, —NAB ...that nothing you have said will come to me, —NLTG ...may happen to me, —MNTG.

**8:24.** Simon responded by begging Peter and John to pray for him so none of these things Peter had spoken would come upon him. This is emphatic. Some believe this implies Simon was praying.

There is considerable controversy about what happened to Simon. Some suggest he only wanted prayer because he was afraid of judgment. But the fact that he wanted the apostles to pray for him possibly shows a change of attitude, a change of heart, and therefore may indicate Simon did repent. The Bible says no more about him.

Later writers use the term *simony* for the buying or selling of church office or for the attempt to use a position in a church organization to increase personal gain. By the middle of the Second Century A.D., legends about Simon began to be circulated. Some say he introduced a gnostic sect or that he defended one gnostic sect against another and denied the deity of Christ, making Him just one of the Jewish prophets. Other traditions try to connect him with an Italian deity and say he went to Rome and made himself a god there. In these stories they have Simon constantly opposing Peter, saying that he also died in Rome. But these traditions have no Biblical basis.

**25. And they, when they had testified and preached the word of the Lord:** ... having fully borne witness and spoken, —RTHM ...So the Apostles, after giving a solemn charge and delivering the Lord's Word, —WEYM ... Then after they had thoroughly testified and talked over the Lord's teachings, —BRKL ... after having given earnest personal testimony, —NORL ...after telling what they had seen and heard, —NLTG.

**returned to Jerusalem:** ... began their return, —RTHM ... began their journey back, —KNOX ... made their way back to Jerusalem, —TCNT.

**and preached the gospel in many villages of the Samaritans:** ... carrying the gospel into, —KNOX ... telling the Good News, as they went, in many Samaritan villages, —TCNT ... evangelizing many Samaritan villages as they went, —MNTG ... to many Samaritan communities, —MLNT.

**8:25.** Peter and John continued in Samaria for a time, giving strong witness (strong Biblical evidence) and speaking the Word of the Lord. Probably they included more of the life, ministry, and teachings of Jesus. They would certainly be concerned that these believers should receive the same body of teaching that they taught in Jerusalem, the body of teaching recorded in the Gospels.

They preached the same good news in many Samaritan villages on their way back to Jerusalem.

**26. And the angel of the Lord spake unto Philip, saying:** ... Meanwhile an angel, —TCNT ... then addressed himself to, —NAB ... was commanded by an angel of the Lord, —KNOX.

**Arise, and go toward the south unto the way that goeth down from Jerusalem unto Gaza:** ... Rise and proceed south to the road that runs down from Jerusalem to Gaza, —WEYM ... about midday go down the road, —MLNT ... Get ready and go south, —NCV ... Get up and go south, along the road from, —MOFT ... Rise up and go south. Take the road, —NORL ... go south to meet the road which leads from, —KNOX.

**which is desert:** ... (The town is now deserted), —GDSP ... (It is now deserted.), —TCNT ... crossing the desert, —WEYM ... this is the desert road, —WLMS ... a lonely road, —BRKL, —MLNT ... the desert route, —NAB ... It goes through the place where no people live, —NLTG ... out in the desert, —KNOX.

**8:26.** At this point the angel (Greek, an angel) of the Lord spoke to Philip telling him to rise and go toward the south to the road going down from Jerusalem to Gaza, which is desert. "Desert" also means deserted, abandoned, desolate. Here the emphasis is that the area was largely uninhabited. Gaza was the most southern of the five cities of the Philistines in Old Testament times. It was about 60 miles southwest of Jerusalem, and this road was the old road which was seldom used anymore.

The New Testament tells of angels appearing to people comparatively seldom. For example, they appeared to Elisabeth, Zechariah, and Mary (Luke 1:11-38); Joseph (Matthew 1:20-23); Jesus (Mark 1:13; Luke 22:43); and Peter (Acts 12:7); cf. Matthew 28:3; Acts 1:10. Yet they are often present and function as "ministering spirits, sent forth to minister for them who shall be heirs of salvation" (Hebrews 1:14).

Jesus himself referred to their number and activity. When they came to arrest Jesus He said He could have had more than 12 legions of angels to defend Him if He were to ask His Father for them (Matthew 26:53). Hebrews 12:22 speaks of an innumerable company of angels. Revelation 5:11 also speaks of great numbers of them. But they must be sent forth by God.

There may have been a special reason for sending an angel to Philip. He was in the midst of a great revival in Samaria. It probably took something unusual to get him to leave the crowds and go down to a deserted back road. Some take "which is desert" to refer to Old Testament Gaza which was destroyed in 93 B.C. In 57 B.C. a new city was built nearer the Mediterranean Sea. The road to old Gaza might be called the road to desert (deserted) Gaza.

**27. And he arose and went:**...So he got busy and departed, —*KLST*...he rose up, —*KNOX*...So he set out on his journey, —*TCNT*...So Philip got ready and went, —*EVRD*, —*NCV*.

**and, behold, a man of Ethiopia, a eunuch of great authority under Candace queen of the Ethiopians:**...On the road he saw a man...an important officer, —*EVRD*...and found there...a courtier, —*KNOX*...an Ethiopian official, —*WLMS*...He had been made so he could not have children, —*NLTG*...and on his way he came upon an official of high rank, in the service of Candace, Queen of the Abyssinians, —*TCNT*...a high officer, —*NOYS*...had come from Cush, —*MRDK*.

**who had the charge of all her treasure:**...He was her Treasurer, —*TCNT*...He was responsible for taking care of all her money, —*NCV*...as her treasurer, —*WEYM*...of all her finances, —*MLNT*...in charge of the entire treasury, —*NAB*...her chief treasurer, —*GDSP*...He cared for all the riches that belonged to Candace, —*NLTG*.

**and had come to Jerusalem for to worship:**...had gone to, —*EVRD*, —*NCV*.

**28. Was returning, and sitting in his chariot read Esaias the prophet:**...was now on his way home, sitting in his carriage and reading, —*TCNT*...As he was going back home, he was sitting in his wagon, —*NLTG*...reading aloud, —*LIVB*.

**8:27, 28.** When the angel spoke, Philip did not hesitate or demur. He arose and went in obedience and with faith and expectation.

At the very time he reached the Gaza road, the chariot of an Ethiopian eunuch was approaching. "Behold" indicates something unexpected or surprising. Philip was surprised, but God's timing was exactly right.

Most officers in palaces were eunuchs in ancient times. This man was a highly placed officer (a potentate), a member of the court of the Ethiopian queen Candace, in charge of all her treasures, with full responsibility for the care and disbursement of funds.

Candace was the hereditary title of the queens of Ethiopia, whose seat of government was on the island of Meroe in the Nile River. Ethiopia here corresponds to what is today called the Sudan, though it probably included part of modern Ethiopia.

This eunuch had come a long distance to worship in Jerusalem. Though he was probably a proselyte to Judaism, because of his being a eunuch, he could only go as far as the Court of the Gentiles. (Some believe he could not have been a full proselyte either, and this would cause him to be classed as a Godfearing Gentile, which would also limit him to the court of the Gentiles.)

Even so, he had purchased scrolls of the Old Testament to take back with him. These were hand-copied and extremely expensive in those days. Usually a whole community of the Jews would join together to buy a set for their synagogue and would keep it locked up for use in worship and teaching.

Now the eunuch was returning home, sitting in his chariot reading the Book (roll, scroll) of Isaiah.

**29. Then the Spirit said unto Philip, Go near, and join thyself to this chariot:**...Go up and keep close to the carriage, —*TCNT*...walk by the side of, —*TNT*...contact that chariot, —*BRKL*...Go over to that wagon and get on it, —*NLTG*...and stay near it, —*EVRD*, —*NCV*...and stay by that car, —*GDSP*.

**8:29.** Then the Holy Spirit spoke to Philip. It took an angel to get Philip to leave Samaria, but now that he was aroused to do God's will, he did not need another angel to prompt him. All he needed was the inner voice of the Spirit. Guidance by the Spirit is a prominent theme in the Book of Acts and is worthy of special study. All the early believers learned to be sensitive to the moving and checks of the Spirit. Philip was undoubtedly looking to the Lord, praying as he went along, expecting the Lord to show him what to do.

The Holy Spirit's command was clear and simple. Philip was to go and join himself closely to this chariot. He was to cling to it. He must not let this opportunity pass him by.

**30. And Philip ran thither to him:**...And running near to him, —*KJII*...ran toward the chariot, —*EVRD*.

**and heard him read the prophet Esaias, and said:**...and overheard the Etheopian reading, —*KLST*...reading aloud, —*LIVB*...from the writings of the early preacher Isaiah, —*NLTG*...He inquired, —*KLST*.

**Understandest thou what thou readest?:**...Do you really understand what you are reading, —*TCNT*, —*TNT*...Do you really grasp, —*NAB*.

**8:30.** Philip did not need any further exhortation. In obedience he ran to the chariot and began to run alongside it. As he did so he heard the eunuch reading aloud from the prophet Isaiah. (Reading was almost always done aloud in those days.) Philip probably listened for a few moments and then interrupted the eunuch and asked if he understood what he was reading; did he really know and comprehend what Isaiah was writing about?

**31. And he said, how can I, except some man should guide me?:** ... How in the world could I ... teaches me, *—WLMS* ... unless someone will explain it to me, *—TCNT* ... should no one be guiding me? *—CNDT* ... someone interprets it, *—KLST* ... I need someone to explain it to me! *—EVRD* ... unless some one instruct me? *—MRDK* ... show me the way? *—MNTG* ... unless someone teaches me? *—NLTG.*

**And he desired Philip that he would come up and sit with him:** ... And he earnestly invited Philip to come up, *—WEYM* ... to get in, *—KLST* ... begged him to get up and sit with him, *—WLMS* ... to climb in and to be seated with him, *—BRKL.*

**8:31.** The eunuch's question shows he did not feel capable of understanding what he was reading. The message of the Book was a mystery to him. The quotation which follows shows he was reading from the Septuagint version, translated in Alexandria, Egypt, beginning about 250 years before Christ. The educated Ethiopians would know Greek, and a person in government service would need to know it very well, for most government business was carried on in Greek in those days. Thus, it was not the language that was causing him difficulty.

Perhaps his difficulty came from his heathen background. The Ethiopians, like the Egyptians, were still pagans at this time, worshiping idols. There were Jewish communities among them, and it may be that the eunuch first heard the Old Testament Scriptures read as he sat with other Gentiles in the back seat of some synagogue. This must have stirred him to go to Jerusalem and learn more. Now he was returning, still with a desire to learn. But he could not grasp what he was reading. He needed someone to guide him, someone to show him the way into an understanding of God's truth. So he welcomed Philip's question and gave Philip a sincere and urgent invitation to come up into the chariot and sit with him.

**32. The place of the scripture which he read was this:** ... the portion of Scripture, *—MNTG* ... the contents of the Writing, *—YNG* ... This was the passage of Scripture, *—GDSP* ... the verse of Scripture, *—EVRD.*

**He was led as a sheep to the slaughter:** ... when it is taken, *—NCV* ... being led to be killed, *—EVRD* ... taken away to be killed, *—SEB* ... to be put to death, *—NLTG.*

**and like a lamb dumb before his shearer:** ... And as a lamb is mute in the hands of its shearer, *—TCNT* ... He was quiet, as a sheep is quiet, *—EVRD* ... is not bleating, *—CNDT* ... is silent, *—MRDK* ... voiceless, *—BRKL, —MLNT* ... a lamb that makes no sound when someone cuts off its wool, *—NCV* ... does not make a

sound while its wool is cut, *—NLTG* ... before the man who cut off her wool, *—BECK.*

**so opened he not his mouth:** ... So he refrains from opening his lips, *—TCNT* ... So he made no sound, *—BB, —NLTG* ... He says nothing, *—NCV* ... in his humility, *—MRDK.*

**8:32.** In the providence of God the eunuch was reading Isaiah 53:7, 8. Chapter 53 of Isaiah has been called the Mount Everest of messianic prophecy. There is no other chapter in the Old Testament that more clearly or more specifically tells of the redemptive work of Christ. There is little or no evidence to suppose that the eunuch, or the Jews, would have understood Isaiah 53 as a reference to the Messiah. Jesus was the first to interpret these passages describing the Suffering Servant in messianic terms. For example, Jesus said that He came to give His life as a "ransom for many" (Mark 10:45). While elsewhere in the chapters surrounding Isaiah 53, the "servant" of the Lord may refer to the nation of Israel, the vicarious and propitiatory nature of Isaiah 53:4-6 cannot be applied to anyone but the Lord Jesus Christ.

The discussion of Christ's redemptive work actually begins with Isaiah 52:13 where God refers to the coming Messiah as "my servant." As the Lord's Suffering Servant, the Messiah would be the One to carry out God's work. He would be the Lamb of God who would take away the sin of the world. Like a sheep led to be slaughtered for sacrifice, so He would give His life for sinners. Like a lamb, He would come patiently, and without any word against His captors He would give himself. Surely it must have been exciting to Philip as he saw how wonderful and how exact God's timing was.

**33. In his humiliation his judgement was taken away:** ... In his lowly condition justice was denied him, *—TCNT* ... In his humiliation he was deprived of his trial, *—BRKL* ... He was humiliated and deprived of justice, *—TNT* ... He was shamed; and all his rights were taken away, *—NCV* ... was refused him, *—NOYS* ... deprived of the justice due Him, *—NORL* ... No one listened to Him because of His shame, *—NLTG.*

**and who shall declare his generation?:** ... Who will tell the story of his age, *—TCNT* ... who shall describe, *—CMPB* ... his offspring? *—BRKL* ... Who will make known His posterity, *—WEYM* ... Who can tell, *—WLMS* ... Who will tell the story to His generation, *—NORL* ... There will be no story about his descendants, *—SEB* ... without children to continue, *—EVRD* ... Who will describe his descendants? *—TNT* ... his family, *—KLGS.*

**for his life is taken from the earth:** ... For He is destroyed from among men, *—WEYM* ... His life is removed, *—WLMS* ... For His life on this earth is taken away, *—NORL* ... he is deprived of his life on earth? *—NAB* ... his life on earth has ended, *—EVRD, —NCV.*

**8:33.** The Hebrew text used by the later Masoretes (Jewish scholars of tradition) reads "from oppression and from judgment he was taken." One scholar, C.R. North, has translated the Hebrew text from which this quote is derived as follows: "After arrest and sentence he was taken off, And on his fate who reflected? For he was cut off from the land of the living" (see Bruce, *New International Commentary on the the New Testament, Acts,* note 49, p. 188). Certainly this passage would have been quite an enigma to anyone not familiar with the life of Jesus and His death on the cross.

The Greek text of this verse reads, "In the humiliation his judgment (that is, his punishment) was taken away." He humbled himself to take the place of a servant. Then He humbled himself even further to die the most humiliating kind of death known at that time. But death could not hold Him, and through the Resurrection the punishment He received on our behalf was taken away. (Compare Philippians 2:7-11.) "Who shall declare his generation?" may mean "Who can describe his origin?" (Compare 1 Corinthians 2:8, "Had they known it, they would not have crucified the Lord of glory.") The Masoretic text also reads "for he is cut off from the land of the living." The Greek for "taken" implies killing, thus there is no essential difference between the readings.

**34.** **And the eunuch answered Philip, and said, I pray thee, of whom speaketh the prophet this?:** ... I beg of you, —*KJII* ... Will you tell me whom the Prophet is speaking about, —*TCNT.*
**of himself, or of some other man?:** ... himself, or someone else, —*TCNT.*

**8:34.** The eunuch then requested Philip to tell him about whom the prophet Isaiah was speaking—of himself or of some other person. Isaiah 53 speaks of the One who was to suffer wholly for the sins of others and not for any of His own. The eunuch knew no one who could do that, and he was puzzled.

Some writers speculate that the eunuch could not have been in Jerusalem any length of time without hearing at least something about Jesus, His miracles, His sufferings, death, and resurrection. But it is not known how long he was there. He may have simply come to worship among the thousands who thronged the temple and then gone on his way without coming into contact with any of the believers. If he had heard of Jesus he did not make any connection between Him and Isaiah 53.

**35.** **Then Philip opened his mouth:** ... Then Philip began, —*TCNT* ... began to speak, —*EVRD.*
**and began at the same scripture:** ... and taking this passage as his text, —*TCNT* ... launched out with this Scripture passage as his starting point, —*NAB* ... and starting from this passage, —*GDSP* ... started with this same Scripture, —*EVRD* ... started with this part of the Holy Writings, —*NLTG.*
**and preached unto him Jesus:** ... told him the Good News about Jesus, —*TCNT* ... proclaimed good news to himJesus, —*YNG* ... he preached to him the gospel of Jesus, —*KJII* ... he announced to him, —*WMCK* ... gave him the good news, —*BB.*

**8:35.** This was Philip's great opportunity. Beginning at that very Scripture passage, he preached Jesus; he told the eunuch the good news, the gospel about Jesus. Jesus had never sinned and had never done anything to deserve suffering or death. No passage in the Prophets more clearly pictures the vicarious suffering, death, resurrection, and triumph of Jesus.

Philip undoubtedly pointed out the many ways in which Isaiah 53 speaks of Jesus. But that was only the beginning. He went on to explain the gospel further with its commands, promises, call to repentance, its assurance of salvation, and other aspects of the kingdom of God.

**36.** **And as they went on their way:** ... Presently, as they were going along the road, —*TCNT* ... As they continued down the road, —*WLMS* ... As they journeyed along, —*KLST* ... Proceeding on the road, —*MLNT* ... While they were traveling down the road, —*EVRD, —NCV* ... as they were going along the way, —*KJII* ... As they moved along the road, —*NAB* ... going on their way, —*BB* ... Now as they went on their journey, —*WMCK*
**they came unto a certain water:** ... came to some water, —*EVRD, —KLST, —TNT* ... a brook, —*FNTN.*
**and the eunuch said, See, here is water; what doth hinder me to be baptized?:** ... The officer said ... What is stopping me from, —*EVRD* ... what is to prevent my being baptized, —*TCNT* ... why may I not have baptism? —*BB* ... What is there to keep me from being baptized, —*WLMS* ... what forbids my being immersed, —*HBIE* ... is there any reason why I should not be baptized now? —*PHLP.*

**8:36.** As Philip and the eunuch continued on down the road they came to some water ("certain water"). "Certain water" here can refer to a spring, a pool, or a stream. The eunuch immediately called attention to it. "See" is the same word translated "behold" in verse 27 and indicates something unexpected, even surprising. Most of southern Palestine is rather dry. Not only was this pool or stream unexpected, it might be a long time before they would come to another one. The eunuch did not want to pass it by without being baptized.

The eunuch put his request in the form of a question, "What hinders me from being baptized?" or, "What is there to prevent me from being baptized?" Probably, he was afraid his being a Gentile and a eunuch might bar him from this ordinance of the Church, just as it barred him from most of the Jewish worship.

**37. And Philip said, If thou believest with all thine heart, thou mayest:** ... Philip answered, —EVRD ... If you heartily believe, —BRKL ... from the whole heart, it is lawful, —KJII ... it is allowable, —MRDK ... it can be done, —TNT ... it is permitted, —MLNT.
**And he answered and said, I believe that Jesus Christ is the Son of God:**

**8:37.** Philip then asked for a confession of faith coming from the heart of the eunuch. To believe with the whole heart would mean that he really understood now and that he was willing to commit his whole being to Christ to follow and obey Him.

The eunuch's response shows that he accepted Jesus as the Messiah, God's anointed Prophet, Priest, and King, and that he understood who Jesus is, the Son of God, and therefore the believer's Saviour and Lord.

This verse is omitted by some ancient manuscripts and by many modern scholars, but it fits the context and reflects the practice of the Early Church. Several of the ideas represented here are clearly stated elsewhere in the Bible (e.g., Romans 10:8-10, 13). It is also quoted by Early Church fathers such as Cyprian and Irenaeus. The Early Church did not hesitate to baptize new believers immediately if they had sufficient background in the Scriptures.

**38. And he commanded the chariot to stand still:** ... Then the officer, —EVRD ... So he ordered the carriage to stop, —TCNT.
**and they went down both into the water, both Philip and the eunuch and he baptized him:** ... the two descended into, —WUST ... and the official, —KLST ... and he immersed him, ABUV ... Philip gave him baptism, —BB.

**8:38.** With the assurance that his faith was accepted, the eunuch commanded the driver of the chariot to stop. Then both the eunuch and Philip left the chariot and went down into the water. In fact, Luke drew attention to the fact that both went down (*katabainō*), not merely to the edge of the water, but into the water. Then Philip baptized him and they came up out of the water.

In this context the word "baptized" appears to have its usual meaning of "immerse, submerge, dip under." Archaeologists have also discovered

baptistries in the ruins of second-century church buildings, showing that baptism by immersion was practiced quite early in the Church. Nevertheless, many scholars are not willing to be too dogmatic on the issue of whether baptism must only be by immersion.

The important thing, however, is that the eunuch wanted to obey the command of Jesus and become His disciple and follower. His baptism was the testimony of a good conscience that had been cleansed by his faith in Jesus and His shed blood.

**39. And when they were come up out of the water:** ... But no sooner had they come up, —WEYM ... from the water, —MLNT.
**the Spirit of the Lord caught away Philip:** ... snatched Philip away, —MNTG, —NAB ... suddenly took Philip away, —WLMS ... hurriedly transported Philip, —BRKL ... was carried off by the spirit, —KNOX ... hurried Philip away, —GDSP ... seized Philip, —WMCK
**that the eunuch saw him no more:** ... the eunuch lost sight of him, —MOFT ... the officer never saw him again, —NCV ... saw nothing more of him, —GDSP.
**and he went on his way rejoicing:** ... but continued, —MNTG ... With a glad heart he resumed his journey, —WEYM ... so he went joyfully on his way, —BRKL ... full of joy, —BB.

**8:39.** Again Luke had said two men both went down into the water. Now they came up out of the water. Then the Spirit of the Lord suddenly snatched Philip away, and the eunuch never saw him again. A few ancient manuscripts and versions add that the Holy Spirit fell on the eunuch before Philip was snatched away.

**40. but Philip was found at Azotus: and passing through he preached in all the cities, till he came to Caesarea:** ... As for Philip, he was next heard of ... and from there, —KNOX ... appeared in a city called, NCV ... found himself at Ashdod and passing through the country he announced the good news to all the towns, —WMCK ... he preached the gospel to all the cities, —ASV ... and went on telling the good news, —GDSP.

**8:40.** Apparently, the Spirit of the Lord gave Philip a miracle ride over to the coast of the Mediterranean Sea at Azotus (near the site of the ancient Ashdod, about 20 miles north of Gaza).

From there Philip proceeded northward along the coast, preaching the gospel (evangelizing, telling the good news, the same good news he told the eunuch) in all the cities along the way until he came to Caesarea. This Caesarea, built by Herod the Great, was the capital of the Roman province of Judea. Philip was still there years later. Evidently he made it his headquarters from this time on.

But he still traveled around telling the good news and became known as Philip the evangelist (21:8).

## Chapter 9

**1. And Saul, yet breathing out threatenings and slaughter against the disciples of the Lord:** ... In the meantime, —TEV ... still uttering murderous threats against, —TCNT ... still breathing threats of death, —KLST ... was still trying to frighten the followers ... by saying he would kill them, —EVRD ... and murder against, —KJII ... was still talking much about how he would like to kill the followers of the Lord, —NLTG.

**went unto the high priest:** ... called on, —BRKL.

**9:1.** Now the Book of Acts returns to Saul. Some of the Sanhedrin and others who joined in the persecution of 8:1 may have lost their zeal against the Christians, but not Saul. He was still "breathing out threatenings" (the Greek is singular, not plural) and "slaughter" (murder) against those who were disciples (learners, students, and followers) of the Lord Jesus. Later, when he was speaking before King Agrippa, he told how he put many of the saints (the dedicated believers) in prison and how he voted for their death.

"Breathing out" here is literally "breathing in." It is a Greek participle (*empneōn*) indicating this had become characteristic and continuous. Saul created an atmosphere around him of threat and murder so that he was constantly breathing it in. As oxygen enables an athlete to keep going, so this atmosphere kept Saul going.

As a result of this persistent persecution, most of the believers left Jerusalem. What happened in Samaria did not concern Saul. But Philip was only one of those who were scattered in all directions. Saul must have heard rumors that these believers were having success in preaching the gospel. So he determined to do something about it and went to the high priest for permission to do so. This led to an event so important that the Book of Acts records it three times.

**2. And desired of him letters to Damascus to the synagogues:** ... asked him to write letters to, —NCV ... and requested of him letters to, —MLNT ... addressed to the Jewish congregations at, —TCNT ... wanted the high priest to give him the authority, —NCV ... to the Jewish places of worship, —NLTG ... to the synagogues, —EVRD ... to the meeting-houses at, —WMCK

**that if he found any of this way, whether they were men or women:** ... which would empower him to arrest ... living according to the new way, —NAB ... to find people, —NCV ... If he found any there ... people in Damascus who were followers of Christ's Way, —EVRD ... giving him authority, —TNT ... that were of the Way, —ASV ... any men or

women there who belonged, —GDSP ... belonging to The Way, —WLMS ... to this religion, —WMCK

**he might bring them bound unto Jerusalem:** ... bring them in chains, and taken to, —TCNT ... convey them shackled to, —BRKL ... he would arrest them and bring them back to Jerusalem, —EVRD ... he might bring them in bonds to, —KLST ... as prisoners, to Jerusalem, —BB, —MLNT.

**9:2.** Some of those who were scattered went north and on to Damascus. Damascus was the oldest and most important city in Syria. At this time it was probably outside the Roman Empire and under King Aretas who made it part of Arabia. Aretas was anti-Roman as were the Jews. It seems Aretas allowed Jews freedom and gave the Jerusalem leaders authority over the Jews in Damascus. Saul went to the high priest and asked for official letters giving him authority to arrest any of "this way." He would then bring them bound to Jerusalem (26:11, 12). This would mean a trial before the Sanhedrin and probably the death sentence.

Since there was more than one synagogue in Damascus it indicates the city must have had a large Jewish population. Quite a number of them must have responded to the gospel. *The Way* is an interesting title for the believers, one they could accept. Christ is the way of salvation, the way of life. (See 19:9, 23; 22:4; 24:14, 22.) But it was a way of life Saul was determined to destroy.

**3. And as he journeyed, he came near Damascus:** ... On his trip, —ADAM ... was drawing near, —TNT ... it came to pass that he drew nigh unto, —ASV ... He was on his way there, —WMCK ... as he was getting near, —TCNT ... As he traveled on he finally approached, —WLMS ... as he came near the city, —EVRD ... During his journey, it happened, —KLST.

**and suddenly there shined round about him a light from heaven:** ... suddenly a light from the sky flashed all round him, —TCNT ... a light out of heaven flashes about him, —CNDT ... suddenly beamed all around him, —BRKL.

**9:3.** Damascus was about 140 miles northeast of Jerusalem, probably nearly 200 miles by road at that time. Near the end of the journey, a light from heaven suddenly shined (like lightning) around Saul.

*Light* in the Bible is often associated with manifestations of the presence of the Lord. In John 17:5, Jesus prayed to His Father, saying, "Glorify thou me with thine own self with the glory I had with thee before the world was." When Jesus rose from the dead, His resurrection body was transformed—it was immortal and incorruptible, no longer subject to aging or decay. Now He appeared to Saul as the risen and glorified Christ. Later on, in 1 Corinthians 15:8, Saul (Paul) referred to this: "Last of all (after the other resurrection appearances of Jesus) he was seen of me also, as of one born out of due time (as a miscarriage, an untimely birth)."

**4. And he fell to the earth:** . . . He fell to the ground, *—NAB, —TCNT* . . . and falling to the ground, *—KLST.*

**and heard a voice saying unto him, Saul, Saul, why persecutest thou me?:** . . . why are you persecuting me, *—TCNT* . . . why are you working so hard against Me? *—NLTG* . . . Why are you doing things against me? *—EVRD.*

**9:4.** As this brilliant light shone around him, Saul fell to the ground overwhelmed. Then he heard a voice, "Saul, Saul, why do you keep persecuting me?" "Persecuting" also includes pursuing and driving out, the very thing Saul was intent on doing to the believers in Damascus, just as he had done to them in Jerusalem.

In referring to Saul, Luke always used the Greek form of his name (*Saulos*, as in 9:1). But here Luke quoted Jesus using the Hebrew form of his name (*Saoul*), which the Book of Acts is careful to preserve here. Saul later confirmed that Jesus was speaking in the Hebrew language (26:14). *Saul*, in Hebrew, means "asked for," that is, asked of God. Now the Lord was asking for him. He wanted this zealous persecutor for himself.

**5. And he said, Who art thou, Lord? And the Lord said, I am Jesus whom thou persecutest:** . . . Saul said . . . The voice answered . . . I am the One you are trying to hurt, *—EVRD* . . . he asked. Jesus replied, *—KLST* . . . Who are you, sir? *—GDSP* . . . I am Jehoshua, *—WUST* . . . I am Jesus, whom you are persecuting, *—RSV* . . . whom you have been, *—MLNT* . . . Whom you are working against, *—NLTG* . . . and you are persecuting me, *—WMCK* . . . whom you are attacking, *—BB* . . . was the response, *—FNTN.*

**it is hard for thee to kick against the pricks:** . . . This is a thankless task of thine, kicking against, *—KNOX* . . . the goads, *—MLNT, —MRDK* . . . to resist and rebel, *—NORL.*

**9:5.** This appearance of Jesus was something special, something extraordinary, something beyond the normal. Saul did not know who it was at first, but he knew his Hebrew Bible very well and recognized that this light from heaven had to be a divine manifestation. But the question confused him. Who was he persecuting other than the Christians? So he asked, "Who are you, Lord?" Some take this to mean, "Who are you, sir?" using the word *lord* merely as a term of polite address. But in response to this obviously supernatural manifestation, the word can only mean divine Lord.

The answer came at once, "I (emphatic) am Jesus whom you (emphatic) keep persecuting." In persecuting the Church, Saul was persecuting, driving out, pursuing the body of Christ whose individual members are in Christ. (See Matthew 25:40, 45; Ephesians 1:23; 2:6.) Then Jesus added, "It is hard (rough, dangerous) for you to kick against the pricks (against the ox goads)."

By this Jesus recognized that much of Saul's persecution of the Christians was because he knew he had no answer for their arguments. It was a reaction by which he was trying to resist the conviction of the Holy Spirit.

This does not mean Saul was conscious that these were goads, or that he even realized he had no good arguments against the believers. He was so full of fury that he could think of nothing but how he could punish the believers and stop the spread of the gospel. He was zealous for the Jewish religion.

**6. And he trembling and astonished said, Lord, what wilt thou have me to do:** . . . dazed and trembling, *—KNOX* . . . thou wish me to do? *—YNG* . . . what do you want me to do? *—KJII* . . . was shaken and surprised, *—NLTG.*

**And the Lord said unto him, Arise, and go into the city:** . . . Get up now, *—EVRD* . . . and go into the town, *—WMCK*

**and it shall be told thee what thou must do:** . . . Someone there will tell you, *—NCV* . . . you will be told what you ought to do, *—GDSP* . . . it will be made clear to you what you have to do, *—BB* . . . what thy work is, *—KNOX.*

**9:6.** Now that Saul was faced with Jesus, not just a man, but the divine Lord, his whole attitude changed and he answered simply, "What shall I do, Lord?" (This response of Saul was omitted here, probably by an early copyist's mistake, and it is not found in any of the Greek manuscripts now extant. It is found in 22:10, however, and in the Latin Vulgate version it is found in 9:6.)

In response to this evidence of genuine repentance, Jesus told Saul to rise and go into the city of Damascus. There he would be told what would be necessary for him to do. Jesus actually told Saul more at this time, but Luke left the rest for Saul (as the apostle Paul) to tell in his defense before King Agrippa (26:16-18). In Galatians 1:1, 11, 12, and 16, Saul also made it clear that he was commissioned directly by Jesus himself, not by any man. In other words, Saul was a genuine apostle or "sent one," sent out and commissioned by Jesus himself.

**7. And the men which journeyed with him stood speechless:** . . . Meanwhile his traveling companions remained speechless, *—KLST* . . . His companions stood in bewilderment, —KNOX...standing dumb with amazement, —WEYM ... His fellow-travellers stood, —MOFT...the men who were with him stood speechless, —WMCK ... stood there but they said nothing, —EVRD, —NCV...were not able to say anything, —BB, —NLTG...The men accompanying him, however, were stunned, —FNTN.

**hearing a voice but seeing no man:**... hearing the sound of the voice, —TCNT ... they heard the voice well enough, —BRKL, —MLNT... hearing indeed the voice, —NOYS ... no one was visible to them, —MRDK... but saw no one, Kliest... but seeing no one, —BB, —FNTN, —WMCK

**9:7.** Meanwhile, the men who were traveling with Saul stood speechless (from fright), hearing the voice (the sound, not the words) but seeing no one. When Paul later repeated this incident, the details he emphasized are slightly different. For example, 22:9 says those who were with Saul saw the light but did not hear the voice of the One speaking (cf. 26:13f.). Apparently, the men saw a light but not Christ himself; they heard the sound of a voice but not the words. Only Saul was able to hear both the voice and the words Jesus spoke. As 26:14 says, they all fell to the ground but the men with Saul were able to get up before he did.

**8. And Saul arose from the earth:**... Saul got up from the ground, —MOFT.

**and when his eyes were opened, he saw no man:**... he saw nothing, —ASV... though his eyes were open, he could see nothing, —MLNT... his eyes were wide open, —WLMS ... He opened his eyes, —EVRD... but on opening his eyes, —FNTN... he could not see, —TNT... unable to see, —NAB...saw no one, —KLST.

**but they led him by the hand, and brought him into Damascus:**... They had to take him by the hand, —GDSP, —NAB... They accordingly, leading him, entered into, —FNTN... So the men with Saul took his hand and led him, —EVRD...and he was guided by the hand, —BB...took him by, —WMCK

**9:8.** Saul, it seems, shut his eyes because of the continuing brightness of the glory, but not until after he saw Jesus. He made it very clear in all his testimony that he was as much an eyewitness to the resurrection of Christ as the other apostles. (See especially 1 Corinthians 9:1; 15:8.)

When Saul got up off the ground, he was blind. His traveling companions led him into Damascus. What a contrast this was with the way he had begun the journey. Once leading, now he was being led. Intending to arrest the believers, he had been arrested by Christ. Having the authority of the high priest, he had come under the authority of the great High Priest. Expecting to put chains on helpless believers, now he was the helpless one.

**9. And he was three days without sight:**... For three whole days, —KLST...and for three days he was unable to see, —TCNT ... and for three days he remained blind, —BRKL...Saul could not see, —EVRD...he continued blind, —NAB...Here...he remained without sight, —KNOX.

**and neither did eat nor drink:**...and he took no food, —BB...and neither ate nor drank, —RSV, —WMCK

**9:9.** Saul remained 3 days in the house where he was taken. Unable to see, he neither ate nor drank anything. The Jewish way of counting made the first day the day he entered Damascus, and the third day the day Ananias came. This gave Saul a day to think things over and to pray. Probably, he was so absorbed in prayer and meditation that he had no desire to eat or drink. It also gave the Holy Spirit opportunity to reveal Christ to his heart, mind, and soul.

Now that Saul knew he was wrong about Jesus and the believers, he could not help but realize he had been wrong about his interpretation of the Old Testament and its prophecies.

He had been depending on who he was and what he could do (see Philippians 3:5, 6). His zeal was a jealous eagerness to uphold what he thought was God's honor, but that zeal was not according to knowledge (Romans 10:2). It was misdirected. Paul now realized that what he had said and done against Christ and the Church was blasphemy. Surely Saul began to realize all this during these important 3 days. He was in darkness, but the light and love of Christ was being shed abroad in his heart.

**10. And there was a certain disciple at Damascus, named Ananias:**... a follower of Jesus, —NCV...a student, —KLGS.

**and to him said the Lord in a vision, Ananias:**... The Lord spake to this man in a dream, —PHLP...to whom the Lord said in, —KLST...to him the Lord called in a vision, —KNOX...showed him in a dream what He wanted him to see, —NLTG.

**And he said, Behold, I am here, Lord:**...Yes, Master, —TCNT...Yes, Lord, —GDSP...I am here, Lord, —PHLP...Behold me, Lord, —YNG...Here I am, Lord, —KLST ... came the answer, —NAB ... was his reply, —FNTN.

**9:10.** On the third day the Lord appeared in a vision to a disciple named Ananias. This was supernatural, not a dream, not a figment of the imagination. Ananias was not asleep, but fully awake and able to respond. He knew it was the Lord, and by saying, "Here I am, Lord," he expressed his availability and willingness to obey the Lord and to do whatever the Lord wanted him to do. Later (22:12) Paul pointed out that Ananias was a devout Jew (converted to the Lord) who still had a good reputation among all the Jews in Damascus.

**11. And the Lord said unto him, Arise, and go into the street which is called Straight:** ...Get up! —EVRD, —NLTG...and go to Straight Street, —WEYM...Go at once, —NAB...go to the road, —KNOX.

**and enquire in the house of Judas for one called Saul, of Tarsus: for, behold, he prayeth:** ...Ask for a man named, —NCV...ask for a certain Saul, —NAB...Find the house of, —EVRD...and make search at the house of Judas for one...for he is at prayer, —BB...inquire at the house of Judah for...a Tarsian, —FNTN...enquire...for a man of TarsusEven now he is at his prayers, —KNOX...for he is even now praying, —WEYM.

**9:11.** Jesus told Ananias to arise (that is, get ready) and go to the street (the narrow street) called Straight. In ancient times this street went straight from one end of the city to the other, and it is still an important street in Damascus today. There he was to inquire (that is, seek, search) in the house of Judas for Saul of Tarsus. The directions are detailed. Ananias was well-known in the Jewish community of Damascus and he would know which Judas lived on Straight Street. Saul was a common name also, so he is identified as being from Tarsus. Tarsus was a city of about a half million people, in Cilicia about 10 miles from the Mediterranean coast.

The reason Ananias was to go was that Saul was praying. The word "behold" (Greek, *idou*) is used to draw attention to something surprising and unexpected. It also gives strong contrast to the atmosphere of threatening and murder Saul had previously created around himself. Notice too that he was not just saying prayers, as he might have done as a Pharisee, but he was really praying. He was humbly waiting before God.

**12. And hath seen in a vision a man named Ananias coming in:** ...and he has seen a man named, —WMCK...he has had a vision of a man called, —KNOX...in a dream, —NLTG...comes to him, —EVRD...enter, —KLST.

**and putting his hand on him, that he might receive his sight:** ...entering and laying hands, —MLNT...laying his hands on him in order that he may recover his sight, —TNT...to bring back his sight, —MOFT...so that he might see, —KJII...Then he sees again, —NCV...to restore his sight, —GDSP...that he may get his sight back, —WMCK...so that he may be able to see, —BB...to cure him of blindness, —KNOX.

**9:12.** Another reason Ananias was told to go to Saul was that Saul, while he was praying, had already seen a vision (a supernatural, God-given vision) of a man named Ananias coming in and laying his hands on him in order that he might regain his sight. God was preparing Saul even before he began to deal with Ananias to prepare him to go to Saul. This vision given to Saul was in answer to his prayer. It was also intended to raise his faith

and help him anticipate further answers to prayer when Ananias came.

Notice too that God did not send for Peter and John, nor was it necessary for any apostle to lay hands on Saul. Ananias was a godly man, but not an apostle. The Book of Acts shows God can and does use ordinary believers to do His will and bring His healing. It also shows Paul did not get his commission through another apostle. He was commissioned directly by Jesus himself and then given further help and direction by another humble believer.

**13. Then Ananias answered, Lord, I have heard by many of this man:** ...Ananias, however, objected...! I have heard from many a person, —KLST...At this, Ananias answered, —KNOX...heard from many sources about this man, —NAB...many people have told me, —EVRD...I have had accounts of this man from a number of people, —BB.

**how much evil he hath done to thy saints at Jerusalem:** ...about all the harm, —KLGS...all the hurt, —KNOX...especially the great suffering he has brought on your people, —WLMS...and the terrible things he did to your saints, —NCV...he hath perpetrated towards, —MRDK...how much wrong, —BECK...how much injury he has done to Your holy ones at, —FNTN...how many hardships, —NORL...He is the reason many of Your followers...had to suffer much, —NLTG...your holy people in Jerusalem, —PHLP.

**9:13.** Though Ananias had at first expressed his willingness to obey the Lord, he began to object to the Lord's command as soon as he heard what it was. He knew about this Saul of Tarsus. Many people had told him about the many terrible things Saul had done to the Lord's saints at Jerusalem.

Ananias thus distinguished himself from the believers in Jerusalem. He was either born in Damascus or had lived there a long time. Obviously many of the believers who fled from the persecution after Stephen's death had come there and brought news of Saul's fury.

By the Lord's saints, Ananias meant all the believers. They were saints (holy, dedicated people who were separated and consecrated to the Lord and to His service) because they had turned their backs on the world and sin to follow Jesus. The word *saint* does not imply perfection. Rather, it simply means they were headed in the right direction. In the preaching and writings of the apostle Paul believers are called saints about 40 times.

**14. And here he hath authority from the chief priests to bind all that call on thy name:** ...to put in chains all those who invoke your name, —TCNT...and here he is authorized by the High Priests, —WEYM...with authorization from, NAB...He came here with the right and the power from the head religious leaders, *—NLTG* ... given him the power to arrest everyone who believes in you, *—NCV* ... to put in chains, *—TNT* ... to arrest all who invoke your name, *—KLST* ... to chain all who call on Your name, *—KJII* ... who worships you, *—EVRD*.

**9:14.** The news had already come that Saul had authority from the chief priests to bind (with chains and thus make prisoners of) all who called on the name of Jesus. This can mean all who made a practice of calling on the name of Jesus, appealing to Him in prayer. Or, it could mean all who called themselves by the name of Jesus, admitting that they belonged to Him.

It seems probable from this that the Church in Damascus not only knew Saul was coming, but they were getting ready to face the same sort of scattering that had occurred because of the persecution in Jerusalem. All that Ananias had heard made him want to avoid Saul. It seemed it would not be safe for a believer to go near him. Yet Jesus was asking Ananias to go to him. Ananias' first thought must have been that the Lord wanted him to become another martyr like Stephen, and he was not anxious to suffer that way.

**15. But the lord said unto him, Go thy way:** ... Go, *—WEYM* ... Still, you must go, *—TCNT* ... You must go! *—NAB* ... the Lord commanded him, *—KLST*.
**for he is a chosen vessel unto me:** ... my chosen instrument, *—TCNT* ... My choice instrument, *—BRKL* ... an elect vessel, *—DRBY* ... a chosen tool, *—KLGS* ... I have chosen Saul for an important work, *—NCV* ... This man is the means I have chosen, *—GDSP*.
**to bear my name before the Gentiles, and kings, and the children of Israel:** ... to bring my name, *—WMCK* ... He must tell about me to non-Jews ... and to the people of Israel, *—EVRD* ... to carry my name among nations, *—KLST* ... before the heathen and their kings, *—TCNT* ... among the people who are not Jews, *—NLTG* ... as well as before the sons of Israel, *—MOFT*.

**9:15.** The Lord was patient with Ananias. He did not rebuke him for this expressed unwillingness to go. He understood how Ananias felt. So He again commanded Ananias to go and reassured him that he did not need to worry about any trouble or persecution from Saul. Not only was he praying, Saul was Christ's own chosen vessel to carry His name (including His character, nature, and authority) before the Gentiles (that is, before all the nations outside of Israel) and also before kings and the children (sons, descendants, people) of Israel.

"Vessel" is a general word used of anything or any equipment that is useful. "Chosen" also has the idea of choice, excellent, outstanding, well-adapted. Thus, Jesus was saying He considered Saul a choice instrument who would be eminently

suited and useful to carry out His purpose in spreading the gospel to the Gentiles. His background, his education, his knowledge of the Old Testament Scriptures, his knowledge of the Greek writers, and his energy and zeal, were all things the Holy Spirit could use once he was brought into right relationship with Jesus, and once he was taught the facts of the gospel. (He was taught many of these facts and even some of the sayings of Jesus by Jesus himself. See Galatians 1:11, 12, 16.) Thus, the apostle Paul did become the outstanding apostle to the Gentiles.

**16. For I will shew him how great things he must suffer for my name's sake:** ... Indeed, I myself will show him, *—PHLP* ... I shall make clear to him, *—NORL* ... I myself shall indicate to him, *—NAB* ... I will show him how much suffering he must bear, *—WMCK* ... how great are the sufferings, *—WLMS* ... he will have to endure for my sake, *—GDSP* ... on behalf of, *—MLNT*.

**9:16.** Moreover, Ananias did not need to fear Saul, for it was Saul who would have to suffer. In fact, Jesus himself would show Saul (warn him, point out to him) how much it would be necessary for him to suffer for the sake of His name.

The necessity of Saul's suffering is emphatic here. But he would not suffer as punishment for his persecution of the Church. He would not suffer because of any failures or lack of faith on his part.

**17. And Ananias went his way, and entered into the house:** ... And Ananias departed, *—ASV* ... With that Ananias left, *—NAB* ... left and went into, *—TNT* ... set out and went to, *—GDSP* ... entered the house, *—KLST* ... went out and came to, *—WMCK*
**and putting his hands on him said:** ... and laying, *—ASV* ... He laid his hands on Saul, *—NCV*.
**Brother Saul, the Lord, even Jesus, that appeared unto thee in the way as thou camest, hath sent me:** ... who appeared to you on your journey, *—GDSP* ... on the road you traveled, *—MLNT* ... has commissioned me, *—CNDT* ... He is the one you saw on the road on your way here, *—EVRD*.
**that thou mightest receive thy sight:** ... He sent me so that you can see again, NCV ... to help you recover, *—NAB* ... so that you may recover your sight, *—TCNT* ... regain your sight, *—MOFT*.
**and be filled with the Holy Ghost:**

**9:17.** Ananias did not hesitate any longer. He obeyed the Lord's command, went to the house of Judas, entered it, and immediately laid his hands on the sightless Saul, calling him "Brother Saul." By this he recognized that Saul was now a believer, and that by faith Saul had been accepted into the family of God with Christ as his elder Brother. Calling each other brother and sister was not just a form in the Early Church. It was something very precious, a wonderful expression of their new relationship to each other in Jesus Christ.

Then Ananias explained that the Lord had sent him, and he identified the Lord as Jesus who had appeared to Saul on the road. This explanation probably seemed necessary to Ananias, for the Jews normally used the term *Lord* to mean Jehovah or Yahweh (the proper pronunciation of this divine Name of the one true God is not known for certain). But it really was not necessary, for Saul had already recognized Jesus as the divine Lord and therefore the divine Son of God.

Ananias added that the Lord had sent him for two reasons. First, that Saul might recover his sight; second, that he might be filled with the Holy Spirit (that is, empowered for the ministry to which the Lord was calling him).

Notice that though Ananias was a "layman," God did not limit this ministry of healing and encouraging believers to the apostles or to officers of the Church. Also, since Ananias was a native of Damascus and the apostles had not left Jerusalem, no apostle had laid hands on him to receive the Spirit, yet he had obviously been filled. Now he was laying hands on Saul because he was acting in simple faith and obedience to the command of Jesus.

**18. And immediately there fell from his eyes as it had been scales:** ... Instantly something like scales fell from Saul's eyes, —*TCNT* ... something that looked like, —*NCV* ... And all at once, —*WLMS* ... what seemed to be scales, —*WEYM* ... something like a scab, —*MRDK* ... the appearance of incrustations, —*WUST* ... as if a scaly substance fell from, —*TNT* ... like fish scales, —*EVRD.*

**and he received sight forthwith:** ... and his sight was restored, —*GDSP,* —*TCNT* ... and he could see once more, —*WEYM* ... he regained his sight, —*MOFT* ... he instantly saw again, —*KJII* ... He was able to see again! —*EVRD,* —*NCV.*

**and arose, and was baptized:** ... Then he got up, —*TCNT* ... and was immersed, *ABUV* ... Upon this he rose and received baptism, —*WEYM.*

**9:18.** Immediately, without any long prayers or any great effort on the part of Ananias, the Lord accomplished His purpose in sending Ananias. Something like scales (fish scales) fell from Saul's eyes and he could see again. A similar incident is recorded in Tobit, an apocryphal work written in the Second Century B.C. (cf. 3:17; 11:13). Then he rose up (probably from his knees) and was baptized in water, thus bearing witness publicly to his newfound faith.

This verse does not tell how Saul received the Spirit; however, Jesus sent Ananias to lay hands on Saul for the recovery of his sight *and* for the filling with the Holy Spirit. It is possible that both

happened at the same time. Verse 12 does not say Jesus commanded Ananias to lay hands on Saul so that he might be filled with the Spirit. The testimony he shared with Saul shows that verse 12 does not report everything Jesus said to him in the vision. (Titus 3:5-7 confirms that the Holy Spirit was poured out on Paul abundantly though it does not specify when this occurred.)

**19. And when he had received meat, he was strengthened:** ... he took food, —*ASV* ... After eating some food, his strength returned, —*EVRD,* —*NCV* ... felt his strength return, —*TCNT* ... his strength returned to him after he had taken food, —*NAB* ... and regained his strength, —*WEYM* ... was invigorated, —*MRDK.*

**Then was Saul certain days with the disciples which were at Damascus:** ... Then he remained some little time, —*WEYM* ... For several days, —*MOFT* ... For some time Saul remained with, —*MLNT* ... stayed with the followers of Jesus, —*EVRD.*

**9:19.** Then Saul ended his fast, took food, and became strong. After that he stayed some days with the disciples in Damascus. Nothing more is said about Ananias. He undoubtedly continued to serve the Lord in humble obedience.

**20. And straightway he preached Christ in the synagogues:** ... he began right away, —*ADAM* ... And immediately he preached Jesus, —*NOYS* ... and began at once to declare, —*GDSP* ... he proclaimed Jesus, —*ASV* ... in the Jewish places of worship, —*NLTG.*

**that he is the Son of God:**

**9:20.** Saul immediately became part of the body of disciples in Damascus. No doubt Ananias brought him to the meetings of the local assembly and explained to them what the Lord had done and how He had commissioned Saul to preach the gospel.

Because Saul accepted the Lord's commission, he did not wait to start preaching Christ. Immediately he went to the very synagogues where he had intended to search out the believers and send them bound to Jerusalem. Boldly he preached Christ (that is, that Jesus is the promised Messiah and Saviour) and declared that He is the Son of God. (This is the first time in Acts that the title "Son of God" is used of Jesus.) From what is seen later, it is clear that Saul's preaching included proofs from the Old Testament Scriptures that Jesus died "according to the Scriptures," and that He rose again, "according to the Scriptures," and that He is God's promised Anointed One, God's anointed Prophet, Priest, and King. His proofs that Jesus is the Son of God were also taken from the Scriptures as well as from the fact that God raised Jesus from the dead (Romans 1:4).

21. **But all that heard him were amazed, and said:** ... All his hearers were staggered and kept saying, –PHLP ... Any who heard it were greatly taken aback, –NAB ... was excited, –KLGS.

**Is not this he that destroyed them which called on this name in Jerusalem:** ... He was trying to destroy those who trust in this name! –NCV ... who went about ravaging those, –MLNT ... made havoc of them, –ASV ... harassed, –WLMS ... ravages those who are invoking this Name? –CNDT ... who beat and killed, –NLTG ... spread desolation among them, –CMPB.

**and came hither for that intent:** ... with the sole object of, –PHLP ... Did he not come here purposely to apprehend such people, –NAB ... and who came here especially for the purpose, –GDSP.

**that he might bring them bound unto the chief priests?:** ... put in chains, –TCNT ... for the purpose of taking them, –TNT ... of arresting such persons and taking them before the high priests? –GDSP ... all such people as prisoners, –PHLP ... to take them as prisoners shackled, –MLNT.

**9:21.** Saul's proclamation of the gospel brought amazement to the people in the synagogues who heard him. They were totally astonished, almost knocked out of their senses. They could hardly believe this was really the same person who had brought destruction on those in Jerusalem who called on the name of Jesus (those who called themselves by the name of Jesus, the followers of Jesus). The Jews in Damascus had all heard about Saul's zeal in persecuting the believers. They had also heard the news that Saul's purpose in coming to Damascus was to bring the believers bound to the chief priests in Jerusalem for trial before the Sanhedrin (bad news traveled fast even in those days). Now he was worshiping the One he had hated.

22. **But Saul increased the more in strength:** ... Saul's power ... kept steadily increasing, –TCNT ... gained power more and more, –WEYM ... went on from strength to strength, –PHLP ... grew steadily more powerful, –NAB ... were so strong, –NCV ... being endued with power, –WUST ... gained more and more influence, –MNTG.

**and confounded the Jews which dwelt at Damascus:** ... was confounding, –RTHM ... continued to put to utter confusion, –WLMS ... reduced the Jewish community of Damascus to silence, –NAB ... put to confusion the Jews, –TNT ... couldn't withstand his proofs, –LIVB ... could not argue with him, –NCV.

**proving that this is very Christ:** ... proving that Jesus was the Christ, –RSV ... he demonstrated that this, –MRDK ... shewing, by comparison, –RTHM ... with his proofs, –WEYM ... His proofs that Jesus is the Christ, –NCV ... proving beyond doubt, –PHLP ... His proofs ... were so strong, –EVRD ... by which he made it clear that Jesus was, –BB ... is the promised Savior, –BECK ... to be the Messiah, –TNT.

**9:22.** Saul, however, was more and more filled with mighty, supernatural power. He confounded the Jews living in Damascus, proving (deducing from the Scriptures) that this One (Jesus) is the Christ, the promised Messiah, God's Anointed One. He used Old Testament prophecies and showed how they were fulfilled in Jesus.

The fact that he "confounded the Jews" means he not only amazed and surprised them, he also agitated them and threw them into confusion and consternation. Many were upset by what he said, even distraught. The word also implies that some of them looked on him as one stirring up trouble. They knew Saul was not the only one involved in the death of Stephen and in the persecution that followed. If the chief priests had given permission for Saul to come and bind believers, there might soon be others who would come with the same purpose. Saul was ready to suffer for the sake of Christ's name now, but many of these Jews were not. Apparently, Saul's proofs from the Scriptures only angered them and roused further opposition just as Stephen's arguments had done earlier in Jerusalem. But now Saul was on the other side, and their opposition only caused him to look to the Lord and the Holy Spirit for even more of His mighty power.

The objections of some were overcome and at least some did accept Jesus as their Messiah and Saviour. The believers also must have been encouraged and strengthened by Saul's conversion and the tremendous change they saw in him. What a proof this is of the power of the gospel!

23. **And after that many days were fulfilled:** ... After some time had gone by, –TCNT ... after a number of days had elapsed, –MOFT ... After considerable time, –BRKL ... had elapsed, –FNTN.

**the Jews took counsel to kill him:** ... the Jews laid a plot to kill Saul, –TCNT ... the Jews consulted together, ABUV ... but they were seeking to kill him, –ASV ... But they kept trying to murder him, –WLMS ... made an agreement together, –BB ... conspired to destroy him, –MLNT.

**9:23.** After a considerable time, the unbelieving Jews who were rejecting the gospel and who were separating themselves from the Jews who had become followers of Christ counseled with one another and came up with a plot to kill Saul.

Acts does not record how long the "many days" were. But Paul told the Galatians that he received the gospel he preached by revelation directly from Jesus himself, not from the other apostles, not from any man (Galatians 1:11, 12, 16). Even some of the sayings of Jesus may have been given him by Jesus himself. In 20:35 Paul quoted a saying of Jesus that is not recorded in the Gospels: "It is more blessed to give than to receive." In 1 Corinthians 11:23 he said he received the account of the Lord's Supper from Jesus himself. In other places he said he had a word from the Lord, by which he meant he had a saying of Jesus to back up what he was writing in his epistles. He had a commission from Christ himself.

Paul also told the Galatians that he left Damascus for a time during this period and went into Arabia and returned again to Damascus before going to Jerusalem.

Galatians 1:18 also says that it was not until after 3 years that the "many days" were fulfilled. Jesus may have given Saul some of His revelation of the gospel during the time he was blind, but probably most of it was given during the time he was in Arabia.

**24. But their laying wait was known of Saul:** ... but their plot became known, –RSV ... but information of their intention was given to him, –WEYM ... but Saul got wind of their plot, –BRKL ... but Saul discovered their plot, –ADAM ... But their plan became known, –KJII ... but Saul learned about their plan, –NCV ... their plot came to his attention, –NAB.

**And they watched the gates day and night to kill him:** ... and they were even narrowly watching the gates, both day and night, that they might kill him, –RTHM ... They went so far as to keep close watch on the city gates, –NAB ... Day and night they kept guarding the city gates, to murder him, –WLMS ... plan to assassinate him, –CNDT.

**9:24.** The plot of the Jews to kill Saul became known to him. Undoubtedly there were some who secretly admired Saul and let the details slip to one of the believers.

The Jews kept watching the gates of Damascus very carefully day and night. Second Corinthians 11:32 indicates that the governor (literally, the ethnarch) under King Aretas IV of Arabia (who reigned from 9 B.C. to A.D. 40) cooperated in this plot, or perhaps was paid by the Jews to give them help in seizing Saul. Saul's life was in danger, but this was only the first of many times when he would risk his life for the sake of the gospel.

**25. Then the disciples took him by night:** ... some of his converts, –LIVB ... managed one night, –MOFT ... conveying him by night, –FNTN ... contrived, –KNOX.

**and let him down by the wall in a basket:** ... lowering him in a basket, –RTHM ... let him down over the wall, –RSV ... by lowering him in a hamper-basket, –WLMS ... conveying him, –FNTN ... through an opening in the city wall, –EVRD.

**9:25.** The disciples (those converts who had become true students of the gospel and followers of Christ) foiled the plot of the Jews. They let Saul

down "by the wall" in a large, flexible basket made of rushes, or something similar, woven together. Second Corinthians 11:33 adds that he was let down through a window. It was common in those days to build houses directly against the city wall. Then some would add an upper story with a section built over the top of the wall. The exact date of this escape is not certain, but it probably took place in A.D. 38. It was certainly a daring escape.

**26. And when Saul was come to Jerusalem:** ... On his arrival at Jerusalem, –TCNT ... On reaching Jerusalem, –MLNT.

**he assayed to join himself to the disciples:** ... and made several attempts to associate with the disciples, –WEYM ... and tried to join the disciples, –MOFT ... made efforts to associate, –BRKL, –MLNT ... endeavoured, –LIVB ... the group of followers, –EVRD.

**but they were all afraid of him, and believed not that he was a disciple:** ... not believing that he was, –ASV ... They even refused to believe, –NAB ... unable to believe that he was really, –MOFT ... that he was really a disciple, –WLMS ... finding it impossible to believe, –PHLP ... thought he was faking! –LIVB ... and all avoided his company, –KNOX ... that he was really a follower, –EVRD.

**9:26.** After escaping from Damascus, Saul went south to Jerusalem. The road was familiar, but he was an entirely different person from the one who had traveled that road over 3 years before on the way to Damascus. Arriving in Jerusalem he kept trying to join with the disciples (in the worship and service of the Church), but they were all afraid of him and continued to fear him.

They had not forgotten what Saul had done to the believers, persecuting them, having them put in prison or killed. Perhaps their first thought was that this was surely some sort of trick or deception to find out who they were in order to destroy them.

The news of what had happened in Damascus apparently had not reached them. They had seen the persecution and heard the threats of Saul. After Saul left Jerusalem everything had quieted down. The apostles continued their witness, so many more Jews were converted to Christ, and the Church was reestablished and continued to grow.

No doubt, the believers felt it was wise to be cautious. They knew God does not expect us to believe everyone who comes along. It was hard to believe that the one who was most furious was now a true follower of Christ. But they were soon to learn that the gospel has power to save and deliver even the worst enemies of Christ.

**27. But Barnabas took him, and brought him to the apostles:** ... Barnabas, however, introduced him to the apostles, −TCNT... took him up and presented him, −WLMS... accepted Saul, −EVRD.

**and declared unto them how he had seen the Lord in the way, and that he had spoken to him: and how he had preached boldly at Damascus in the name of Jesus:**... he had spoken out fearlessly, −TCNT... he had fearlessly taught, −WEYM... and how courageously he had spoken, −WLMS... he had discoursed openly, −MRDK... with the utmost boldness, −PHLP.

**9:27.** Barnabas, however, was sympathetic, living up to the meaning of his name as the "son of encouragement." Some writers suggest that as a Hellenistic (Greek-speaking) Jew he had come from Cyprus to Jerusalem about the same time as Saul (also a Hellenistic Jew) came from Tarsus to study under Gamaliel, and that they might have known each other in earlier days.

Now Barnabas took an interest in Saul and apparently did some investigation. Then he "brought him to the apostles," that is, to some of the apostles. Galatians 1:18-24 shows that Saul (Paul) met only Peter and James the brother of Jesus at this time, and that he only stayed in Jerusalem 15 days on this visit. Though not one of the Twelve, James was considered an apostle because of Jesus' special appearance to him after the Resurrection (1 Corinthians 15:7). Barnabas explained how Saul had seen the Lord and how he continued to speak boldly, freely, and openly in the name of Jesus in Damascus.

28. **And he was with them coming in and going out at Jerusalem:** ... After that, Saul remained at Jerusalem, on familiar terms with the Apostles, −TCNT... he associated with them freely in, −GDSP... Henceforth Saul was one of them, −WEYM... So Saul moved freely among them in Jerusalem, −KLST... And he went about in the company, −FNTN.

**9:28.** For a time Saul was associated with the believers, for they now accepted him. But he did not spend all of his time with them. He went in and out among them, which means he visited other synagogues and probably visited synagogues in the surrounding towns and villages.

29. **And he spake boldly in the name of the Lord Jesus:** ... speaking courageously, −KLST... preaching boldly, −ASV, −WMCK... spoke eloquently, −FNTN... conversed boldly, −BRKL.

**and disputed against the Grecians:** ... also spoke and argued, −KLST... and especially talked and argued with, −MLNT... talking and arguing with the Greek-speaking Jews, −TCNT... And he often talked with the Hellenists and had discussions with them, −WEYM... he also held conversations and debates with the Hellenists, −MOFT... And

he... reasoned with, −KJII... Jews who understood Greek, −MRDK... Grecian Jews, −MNTG.

**but they went about to slay him:** ... were endeavoring, −NOYS... these set themselves to kill him, −WMCK... They for their part responded by trying to kill him, −NAB... but they conspired, −FNTN... But they kept trying to murder him, −WLMS... but they undertook to murder him, −MLNT... but they were working for his death, −BB.

**9:29.** During this time Saul continued to speak boldly and freely in the name (and with the authority) of the Lord Jesus. But, because of his own heritage, he was especially attracted to the "Grecians," that is, the Hellenistic or Greek-speaking Jews. He spent much of his time talking to them and disputing (discussing, debating) with them. Thus, he went to the Hellenistic synagogues, including the same ones that had debated with Stephen. He did not visit the churches of Judea (outside Jerusalem) however, for he said later that he was "unknown by face" to them at this time (Galatians 1:22).

The Hellenistic Jews were undoubtedly offended because Saul had once been one of them. His message of the gospel and his proofs from the Scriptures roused their anger. It is strange how many people become angry when they realize they do not have a good case for their own beliefs.

Because of their anger they kept trying to kill Saul. Probably they considered him a traitor who did not need a trial. It is clear however that these attempts failed. God surely protected him.

30. **Which when the brethren knew:** ... But when the Brethren found this out, −TCNT... When the brothers learned about this, −EVRD... heard of this attempt, −KLST... had knowledge of it, −BB... became aware of it, −FNTN.

**they brought him down to Caesarea, and sent him forth to Tarsus:** ... took him down... and sent him off, −FNTN... and then sent him by sea to Tarsus, −WEYM... sent him on his way to, −WMCK

**9:30.** As soon as the Jerusalem believers found out about these attempts on Saul's life they decided they did not need another martyr and another siege of persecution. So they took Saul and brought him down to Caesarea and sent him away to Tarsus. Jesus also appeared to him and told him to leave Jerusalem (22:17-21).

The believers did not send him away simply to save him from being a martyr, however. The Greek *exapesteilan* means they sent him out as a representative and with a commission. They recognized he was a person qualified to take the gospel to Tarsus, his birthplace. Tarsus, about 300 miles to the north, was the most important city of Cilicia. It was a free city and a well-known university city (which means there were a number of outstanding teachers located there). Its educational opportunities were exceeded only by Athens and Alexandria. Saul was needed there. It was a place where he could freely work and develop his ministry.

**31. Then had the churches rest throughout all Judaea and Galilee and Samaria, and were edified:** ... the assemblies, *—NOYS* ... So the church ... had peace, *—ASV* ... The church everywhere ... had a time of peace, *—EVRD* ... being built up, *ABUV* ... and became well-established, *—TCNT* ... continued to be built up spiritually, *—WLMS* ... The church was made strong, *—NLTG* ... it was consolidated, *—MOFT* ... to make progress, and it went on increasing, *—TNT* ... accordingly had rest, *—FNTN.*

**and walking in the fear of the Lord:** ... lived in reverence for, *—GDSP* ... ordering its life by reverence for the Lord, *—TCNT* ... It showed that it feared the Lord by the way it lived, *—NCV* ... and, progressing in the reverence of, *—FNTN* ... showed that they respected the Lord by the way they lived, *—EVRD.*

**and    in    the    comfort    of    the    Holy Ghost:** ... and help, *—TCNT* ... and it was given comfort by, *—NLTG* ... the encouragement of the Holy Spirit, *—WEYM* ... in the strengthening presence of the Holy Spirit, *—PHLP* ... and, stimulated by the holy Spirit, *—GDSP* ... the consolation, *—CNDT* ... the encouragement that the Holy Spirit gave, *—WLMS* ... by the advocacy of the Holy Spirit, *—RTHM.*

**were multiplied:** ... Because of this, the group of believers grew, *—EVRD* ... they were being increased through, *—FNTN* ... increased greatly, *—BB* ... More people were added to the church, *—NLTG.*

**9:31.** With Saul gone, everything quieted down again. This verse is another brief summary, showing that the Church throughout the whole of Judea, Galilee, and Samaria had rest (peace and blessing), was edified (built up both spiritually and in numbers), walked (lived, conducted themselves) in the fear (reverential awe) of the Lord and in the encouragement of the Holy Spirit, and was multiplied.

Up to this point there is not much in Acts to indicate churches were being established in Galilee. But it is clear from this verse that both Galilee and Samaria had been well-evangelized by this time. Notice that the word *church* is in the singular. The various assemblies in these regions were in fellowship with each other and constituted one body (Church) under the headship of Christ (Ephesians 1:22, 23).

**32. And it came to pass, as Peter passed throughout all quarters:** ... While travelling about in all directions, Peter, *—TCNT* ... Now Peter, as he went to town after town, *—WEYM* ... It now occurred

that Peter, journeying, *—FNTN* ... was traveling through all the area, *—EVRD.*

**he came down also to the saints which dwelt at Lydda:** ... went down to visit the People of Christ living at, *—TCNT* ... the holy people living in Lydda, *—BECK* ... God's people, *—EVRD.*

**9:32.** Acts says no more about Saul until 11:30. After the summary statement of verse 31, Luke began a sequence which led to Peter's bringing the gospel to the Gentiles in Caesarea. This was a key turning point in the spread of the gospel. Without this experience of Peter it would have been much more difficult for the Church to approve Saul's ministry as it did at the Jerusalem Council (see chapter 15).

Since the conditions in Jerusalem were now peaceful, Peter was able to leave the city. His purpose was to visit the various congregations which had sprung up as the result of the scattering after the death of Stephen and to build the believers up in the Faith. Like Jesus, he went about doing good, strengthening and edifying the believers, and bringing blessing and healing wherever he went.

As he journeyed about he eventually came to visit the believers at Lydda, called saints because they were dedicated believers who had separated themselves from the ways of the world and to the worship and service of the Lord Jesus.

Lydda was an ancient city on the road to Joppa about 23 miles northwest of Jerusalem and 10 miles southeast of Joppa. It was rebuilt after the Jews returned from Babylon, then taken over by the governor of Samaria. In 145 B.C. it was made part of Judea.

**33. And there he found a certain man named Aeneas:**

**which had kept his bed for eight years, and was sick of the palsy:** ... who had been bed-ridden for eight years with paralysis, *—TCNT* ... lain on a pallet, *—HBIE* ... being completely paralyzed, *—WUST* ... could not move his body, *—NLTG* ... without power of moving, *—BB.*

**9:33.** At Lydda Peter found a certain man named Aeneas (Greek, *Aineas*, a Greek name popularized because it was the name of a Trojan hero. It seems to be derived from the Greek word for *praise*.)

Paralyzed, this man had been confined to his bed for 8 years. ("Palsy" here is not the shaking palsy with its uncontrollable tremors. Rather, it is an old word meaning "paralysis.") Since Aeneas had been in this helpless condition for 8 years, his family and friends had long ago given up any hope he would ever get better.

Jesus did not avoid such cases when He was on earth. Peter and John had already experienced what Jesus could do with hopeless cases when they received a gift of healing for the lame man at the Gate Beautiful (chapter 3). They knew that nothing is impossible with the Lord. They had seen Jesus heal people who were paralyzed on more than one occasion. (See Matthew 4:24; 8:6; 9:2-6.)

**34. And Peter said unto him, Aeneas, Jesus Christ maketh thee whole:** . . . Jesus Christ healeth thee, *—ASV* . . . Peter, addressing him, said . . . the Messiah, *—FNTN* . . . cures you, *—GDSP, —TCNT*

**arise, and make thy bed:** . . . Get up, and make your bed, *—TCNT* . . . smooth thy bed for thyself, *—RTHM* . . . Stand up, *—EVRD* . . . make yourself a meal, *—TNT.*

**And he arose immediately:** . . . Aeneas got up instantly, *—TCNT* . . . He at once rose to his feet, *—WEYM* . . . At once he rose to his feet, *—MNTG* . . . stood up immediately, *—EVRD.*

**9:34.** Peter spoke to this man with the assurance that surely came from the Holy Spirit: "Aeneas, Jesus Christ is healing you. Rise and make your bed." This was a command calling for immediate action. Aeneas must get up off his mattress immediately, and make his own bed, which probably meant he should roll it up and put it away. ("Make your own bed" is a phrase that in Greek can be used of either making a bed or preparing a meal. In Mark 14:15 and Luke 22:12 it is used of preparing the Passover meal in the Upper Room. Thus, another possible meaning here is that Aeneas should immediately prepare himself some food to be strengthened.)

His healing was instantaneous. The fact that he arose immediately showed that Peter was speaking with the authority of Jesus when he used the present tense and said, "Jesus Christ is (now, at this moment) healing you." Notice too that Peter made it very clear that Jesus was the One who was doing the healing. He is the Great Physician, and all the credit, all the glory belongs to Him.

**35. And all that dwelt at Lydda and Saron saw him:** . . . All the inhabitants of Lydda . . . were converted to the Lord, *—NAB* . . . all who inhabited, *—DRBY* . . . who were living, *—WMCK*

**and turned to the Lord:** . . . came over to the Lord's side, *—TCNT* . . . and were converted to, *—KLST* . . . and so they turned to the Lord, *—WLMS.*

**9:35.** The result of this healing was a great spread of the gospel. All the inhabitants of Lydda and Sharon "saw him, and turned to the Lord." This implies Aeneas was well-known in that area. "Sharon" here means the whole Sharon coastal plain west and northwest of Lydda, stretching toward Mount Carmel and extending east to the hills of Samaria. It was a fertile region, famous for its flowers, especially lilies and anemones. The fact

that the people in this region saw him indicates that Aeneas, now that he was healed, was restored to such vigor and such excellent health that he walked all through that region giving his testimony and telling of the wonderful works of the Lord.

**36. Now there was at Joppa a certain disciple named Tabitha:** . . . a certain female disciple, *—RTHM* . . . Among the disciples at Joppa was a woman called Tabitha, *—WEYM* . . . a follower, *—EVRD.*

**which by interpretation is called Dorcas:** . . . or, as the name may be translated, Dorcas, *—WEYM* . . . that is, Gazelle, *—WLMS* . . . means "a deer," *—EVRD.*

**this woman was full of good works and almsdeeds which she did:** . . . Her life was full of the good and charitable actions which she was constantly doing, *—WEYM* . . . Her life was marked by constant good deeds, *—NAB* . . . a woman bubbling over with helpful activities and practice of charities, *—BRKL* . . . She was always busy doing good and helping the poor, *—NORL* . . . she was conspicuous, *—FNTN* . . . full of good and kindly actions, *—PHLP* . . . loving acts which she was always doing, *—KLGS* . . . charitable practices, *—MOFT* . . . good deeds and acts of charity, *—AMPB* . . . and of kind-hearted acts, *—KJII* . . . and acts of mercy, *—WMCK*

**9:36.** Joppa (called Japho in Joshua 19:46) was the only seaport between Haifa and the borders of Egypt. It was important in ancient times, though today it has been reduced to a suburb of Tel Aviv which is on its northern border. From it Jonah fled as he tried to avoid the Lord's command to go to Nineveh.

At Joppa lived Tabitha (her Aramaic name). She was also known by her corresponding Greek name, *Dorcas*, which means "gazelle." The gazelle was a small antelope, a swift runner, and so graceful that it became a symbol for gracefulness. The fact that Dorcas was so well-known by her Greek name shows she was one of the Hellenistic Jews and was probably wealthy and well-educated. But her real riches were her good deeds. She was full of them and constantly enriched the lives of others through them. She was especially active in "almsdeeds," that is, in kind deeds and charitable giving to the poor.

**37. And it came to pass in those days, that she was sick, and died:** . . . It happened that at that time she fell ill, *—WMCK* . . . that she fell sick, *—ASV* . . . became sick, *—EVRD.*

**whom when they had washed, they laid her in an upper chamber:** . . . and when they had washed her, they, *—ASV* . . . After washing her body they laid it out in a room upstairs, *—WEYM* . . . in a room on the second floor, *—NLTG* . . . in a room which was high up, *—BB.*

**9:37.** While Peter was at Lydda, Dorcas became sick and died. The Bible does not state the cause of her illness, and there is no indication that she was lacking in faith. Her godly life and good works did not prevent either her sickness or her death. It seems she rapidly became worse and her death was an unexpected shock to her friends and to the entire Christian community. Her friends washed her body as was the custom, but instead of wrapping it in linen with spices for burial, they took her body and placed it in an upstairs room. (This was a large upstairs room in her own house, another indication that she was a fairly wealthy woman. Most of the poor in those days lived in one-room homes and would not have an upper room large enough for people to gather.)

**38. And forasmuch as Lydda was nigh to Joppa:** . . . Lydda, however, being near Jaffa, *—WEYM* . . . Then because, *—WMCK*

**and the disciples had heard that Peter was there:** . . . The followers in Joppa, *—EVRD* . . . the disciples, learning that, *—BRKL* . . . having knowledge, *—BB.*

**they sent unto him two men, desiring him that he would not delay to come to them:** . . . with the urgent request, NAB . . . Please come to us without delay, *—RSV* . . . and begged him, hurry, please come to us! *—NCV* . . . to ask him to come at once, *—NLTG* . . . begging him to be good enough to come to them, *—WMCK*

**9:38.** Lydda was near Joppa (only about 10 miles away). Most probably, the news about the healing of Aeneas had reached the believers in Joppa. Now the believers in Joppa learned that Peter was in Lydda. The believers, here called "disciples" (learners, students and followers of Christ), were not only concerned about Dorcas, but as believers must have spent time asking guidance of their Master Teacher, so they sent two men from their number to Peter. Some writers have wondered why they sent for Peter since there is no previous record in the Book of Acts of the apostles raising the dead. But Jesus raised the dead, and when He first sent out the Twelve He gave them authority to raise the dead (Matthew 10:8). The news that Peter had brought Christ's healing to a man paralyzed for 8 years must also have raised their faith.

The two men were sent with an urgent message, literally, "Do not delay to come to us." The custom in those days was to bury people the same day they died. Their request to Peter "to come" was very emphatic.

**39. Then Peter arose and went with them:** . . . Peter started with them at once, *—TCNT* . . . Peter set out with them, *—NAB* . . . So Peter at once got up, *—WLMS* . . . got ready and went, *—EVRD.*

**When he was come, they brought him into the upper chamber:** . . . On his arrival they took him upstairs, *—WEYM* . . . they conducted him to the upper room, *—BRKL.*

**and all the widows stood by him weeping:** . . . All the women whose husbands had died, *—NLTG* . . . came round him in tears, *—TCNT* . . . stood by his side, *—TNT* . . . weeping audibly, *—WUST* . . . crying, *—EVRD* . . . and with tears, *—KLST.*

**and shewing the coats and garments which Dorcas made, while she was with them:** . . . and showing him all the clothing and cloaks that Dorcas used to make, *—WEYM* . . . the undergarments and coats, *—BRKL* . . . all the shirts, *—WMCK* . . . the tunics . . . which Dorcas used to make, *—KLST* . . . the various garments, *—NAB* . . . the dresses and cloaks, *—PHLP* . . . inner and outer garments, *—BECK* . . . when she was still alive, *—NCV.*

**9:39.** Peter immediately got up and went with the two men from Joppa. As soon as he arrived at the house of Dorcas, they took him upstairs and brought him into the room where she was lying. The room was full of weeping widows who immediately presented themselves to Peter. They were self-appointed mourners and were undoubtedly following the custom of weeping, wailing, and beating their breasts. But they were not like the professional mourners so often hired in those days. Their sorrow was genuine. They could not understand why Dorcas had been cut off in the midst of such a godly and useful life. They were also weeping because they loved and appreciated her for all she had done for them.

While they still wept, they kept showing Peter the tunics (long garments like T-shirts worn next to the skin) and the outer garments (cloaks, robes) that Dorcas was in the habit of making "while she was with them." The Greek indicates the women were wearing the garments they were showing Peter and they were commending her, not only for her charity, but for her constant hard work in their behalf and on behalf of others who were needy.

In some ways Dorcas reminds us of the ideal wife of Proverbs 31 who was industrious and stretched out her hands constantly to help the poor and needy (Proverbs 31:19, 20). But she was either not married or her husband was already dead. (The latter is most probable.)

**40. But Peter put them all forth:** . . . But Peter sent everybody out of the room, *—TCNT* . . . first made everyone go outside, *—NAB* . . . Peter made them all leave the room, *—NLTG, —NORL* . . . made them all go, *—BB* . . . ejecting them all, *—CNDT* . . . put them out of the room, *—WMCK* . . . sending them all out, *—KLST.*

**and kneeled, and prayed:** . . . went down on his knees in prayer, *—BB* . . . then he knelt down and prayed, *—MOFT* . . . and having knelt, he prayed, *—FNTN* . . . went on his knees to pray, *—KNOX.*

**and turning him to the body said, Tabitha, arise:** . . . and turning to the body, *—ASV* . . . Tabitha, stand up, *—EVRD, —NAB* . . . get up, *—BB, —WMCK* . . . rise up! *—FNTN.*

**And she opened her eyes: and when she saw Peter, she sat up:** . . . seeing Peter, —KLST . . . she fell backwards, —FNTN . . . and got up, —BB . . . sat up on the bed, —KNOX.

**9:40.** The widows' words about Dorcas shows they thought of her as dead and her work ended. They obviously had no expectation that Peter would be able to do more than give them sympathy and comfort.

Peter made them all leave. An atmosphere of eastern mourning with its hubbub and commotion was not conducive to prayer or faith. The Greek implies that Peter had to force them to leave. Peter knew he had to get alone with God. So after they were gone, he went to his knees in humble prayer. He knew also that the power to raise the dead was inherent in Jesus. In himself he was nothing, so he put himself at the disposal of the risen Christ.

After prayer, Peter turned to the body and said in faith, "Tabitha, arise!" Many see here a parallel to what Jesus did when He raised the daughter of Jairus (Mark 5:41) where He said, "Talitha cumi," because the Aramaic for what Peter said is "Tabitha cumi."

At these words Dorcas opened her eyes. Life had returned and it was as if she had been wakened out of a sleep. Her health had returned as well, so when she saw Peter, she sat up.

**41. And he gave her his hand, and lifted her up:** . . . But giving her a hand, he assisted her up, —FNTN . . . took her hand, lifting her up, —BB . . . Peter raised her up, —TCNT . . . he raised her to her feet, —WEYM . . . helped her to her feet, NAB, —PHLP . . . helped her up, —EVRD . . . helped her rise, —KLST.

**and when he had called the saints and widows, presented her alive:** . . . Then he called the members of the congregation, —TNT . . . calling the holy ones, —FNTN . . . into the room, —EVRD . . . and, sending for the saints and widows, he gave her to them, living, —BB . . . he gave her back to them alive, —GDSP, —WEYM . . . he showed her alive, —KJII . . . a living person, —NLTG.

**9:41.** Peter gave her his hand and helped her to her feet. Then, calling the saints and the widows, he "presented her alive."

The saints surely included all the believers in the Christian community. Dorcas apparently did not limit her acts of love to believers but reached out to all who were in need. Her name Tabitha, the Aramaic name for the gazelle, also has a meaning that includes beauty, splendor, and honor. Her faith, hope, and love expressed in a godly life gave her a charm and a loveliness that made the people love her and rejoice as Peter presented her to them alive again.

What an evidence it was to these saints and widows that the living Christ was in their midst! Peter took no credit for this. Christ alone had done the work. He alone deserved all the credit, all the glory. Peter's faith-filled and faithful ministry was needed. But God did not give this ministry or this miracle because Peter or Dorcas deserved it. All His healings, all His gifts, flow out of the exceeding riches of His mercy and grace. Believers dare not look to man or put their trust in man's abilities.

**42. And it was known throughout all Joppa:** . . . And it became known, ASV . . . news of it went all through, —BB . . . all over Joppa, —MOFT . . . through the whole of, —FNTN . . . learned about this, —EVRD.

**and many believed in the Lord:** . . . and a number of people had faith in the Lord, —BB . . . many became believers, —WMCK . . . put their trust in, —NLTG . . . believed on, —FNTN.

**9:42.** Unlike Aeneas, Dorcas did not travel around after her restoration to life. God does not ask everyone to witness in the same way. Apparently, Dorcas just went back to her work among the widows and among the poor where her gracious smile and deeds of love and compassion continued to spread comfort and cheer as they had before. But that was enough. The news spread quickly throughout all the city of Joppa, and many believed on Jesus as Lord.

It is worth noting that the city of Lydda was burned by the Roman Cestius during the time of Nero, and Joppa was destroyed a few years later in A.D. 68. Many souls must be in heaven because of Peter's miracle ministry and the faithfulness of Aeneas and Dorcas.

**43. And it came to pass, that he tarried many days in Joppa with one Simon a tanner:** . . . Meanwhile Peter stayed some days in Jaffa, —TCNT . . . It happened that he continued to stay for some time, —KLST . . . He afterwards remained in, —FNTN . . . he was living . . . for some time with, —BB . . . stayed many days in, —WMCK . . . remained for a considerable time, —WEYM . . . who was a leatherworker, —NCV.

**9:43.** Because of the open door for ministry, Peter stayed in Joppa for a considerable time with a certain Simon, a tanner. This shows the Holy Spirit was still working to break down the barriers which separate people from each other. The occupation of a tanner was considered unclean. Because of the bad odor, the craft was usually carried on outside a town or city. Usually, the workers would remove the hairs from a hide by lime and then treat it with an infusion of bark (usually oak) to make it firm and pliable. The fact that Peter stayed with a tanner shows he had overcome some of the Jewish scruples, for he recognized God's grace in Simon.

## Chapter 10

**1. There was a certain man in Caesarea called Cornelius:** ... There was then in Caesarea a man named Cornelius, –TCNT.

**A centurion of the band called the Italian band:** ... a Captain in the regiment known as the Italian Regiment, –TCNT ... a centurion of a cohort, ABUV ... a captain in an Italian company of the Roman army, –NORL ... a centurion, of the squadron, –CNDT ... a colonel, –WLMS ... of the detachment, –FNTN ... of an Italian group of the army, –NLTG.

**10:1.** Acts now begins a sequence leading to an important turning point for the gospel. Though Jesus commissioned the apostles to make disciples of all nations (Matthew 28:19), those who were scattered by the persecution after Stephen's death at first preached the gospel to Jews only (11:19). But God was already working in the hearts of Gentiles at Caesarea.

Caesarea, about 30 miles north of Joppa, was built by Herod the Great from 25 to 13 B.C. It became the capital of Judea. Stationed there was a special band, or cohort, of soldiers known as the Italian cohort. (Usually a cohort had 600 foot soldiers under a tribune, but there is evidence that this was an auxiliary cohort of 1,000 men.) One of them, Cornelius, was a centurion commanding 100 infantry.

**2. A devout man, and one that feared God with all his house:** ... a religious man and one who reverenced God, as also did all his household, –TCNT ... who venerated, –AMPB ... He was religious and God-fearing, and so was every member of his household, –WEYM.

**which gave much alms to the people:** ... He was liberal in his charities to the people, –TCNT ... He practiced liberal benevolences among, –BRKL ... He was generous in giving alms to the people of Israel, –RIEU ... He gave much money to the people, –NLTG ... gave liberally, –ADAM.

**and prayed to God always:** ... constantly, –TCNT ... and was a real man of prayer, –PHLP.

**10:2.** Like all the centurions mentioned in the New Testament, Cornelius was a good man, and like the one Jesus commended in Matthew 8:10, 11, he was also a man of faith.

Some Gentiles in those days were tired of the foolishness and immorality of the religions of Rome and Greece. Many, including Cornelius, found something better in the teaching of the synagogues and accepted the truth of the one true God who is holy, righteous, and good.

Luke called Cornelius "devout." In other words, he was right in his attitudes toward both God and

man and by grace was living a godly life. He also feared (that is, reverenced and worshiped) God, as did his entire household (including both his family and his servants). But they had not become full proselytes or converts to Judaism.

Cornelius, however, was generous in charitable giving and prayed to God always (literally, "through all", that is, daily, and in every circumstance of his life and work). In other words, he really trusted the Lord to guide him in all things. From 10:37 it is also quite evident that Cornelius knew the gospel. He had not only heard about Jesus, he knew about His resurrection and the promise of the Holy Spirit.

**3. He saw in a vision evidently about the ninth hour of the day:** ... He saw in a vision openly, –ASV ... One afternoon, about three o'clock, he distinctly saw in a vision, –TCNT ... in a vision manifestly, –YNG ... saw in a vision plainly, –NOYS ... clearly and distinctly, –WUST ... he saw in a dream what God wanted him to see, –NLTG.

**an angel of God coming in to him, and saying unto him, Cornelius:** ... an angel of God enter his house, –KLST ... coming into his room, and calling him by name, –TCNT.

**10:3.** Without a doubt God saw the desire of Cornelius' heart. About 3 o'clock in the afternoon, the Jewish hour of evening prayer, he was fasting and praying. In the temple at Jerusalem, the evening sacrifice was being offered by the priest at about this same time each day. Therefore, praying at this very hour was quite significant; it was almost a way of participating in the priest's offering. (Cf. Psalm 141:2, "Let my prayer be set forth before thee as incense; and the lifting up of my hands as the evening sacrifice.") (See 10:30.) Suddenly an angel appeared to him in a vision ("something seen"), that is, in an actual appearance or revelation, openly in full daylight.

**4. And when he looked on him, he was afraid:** ... Looking steadily at him, and being much alarmed, –WEYM ... Gazing at the angel in awe he said, –KLST ... when he looked intently at him, –KJII ... overcome with awe, –TNT ... Gazing at him earnestly, and becoming terrified, –FNTN ... looking on him in fear, –BB ... He stared at the sight, –NAB ... He fixed his eyes on him in fear, –WMCK ... stared at him in terror, –GDSP ... being seized with fear, –DOUY.

**and said, What is it, Lord? And he said unto him, Thy prayers and thine alms are come up for a memorial before God:** ... and said in fear ... and your generosity have risen in God's sight, –NAB ... What do you want, Lord? –EVRD ... Sir, –FNTN ... replied the angel, –KLST ... and your gifts of money, –NLTG ... and your offerings have come up ... and he has kept them in mind, –BB ... He has seen what you give to the poor, –EVRD ... as a sacrifice to be remembered, –MOFT ... and your gifts to the poor, *—WMCK*... have ascended as worthy to be remembered, *—BRKL*... your charitable acts, *—TNT*... come to the notice, *—KLGS*.

**10:4.** As Cornelius directed his gaze on the angel, he became afraid (full of awe, fear, or even something akin to terror). This was a natural reaction to the supernatural by a man who had never before experienced anything supernatural. But in spite of his fear, he asked, "What is it, Lord?" thus taking the angel to be a divine manifestation. The angel, however, directed his attention to God. Cornelius' prayers and charitable giving had gone up (ascended) as a memorial (reminder, or better, a remembrance offering, which is the meaning in the Old Testament) to God.

**5. And now send men to Joppa, and call for one Simon, whose surname is Peter:** ... invite over a man named Simon, *—WLMS* ... and summon, *—NAB*... and get one Simon, *—BB*... and fetch, *—KLST*... and bring back a man named, *—EVRD*... who is called, *—WMCK*

**10:5.** The angel did not give any further explanation to Cornelius. He did not tell him what God had in store for him. Neither did he give him any additional teaching to help him. God has not given angels the responsibility to spread the gospel or teach and train the believers. He has given that responsibility to the members of His Body, the Church. Actually, the Church needed to learn some lessons here, and so did the apostles. What Peter was about to learn would help him as much as it would help Cornelius.

The angel directed Cornelius to send men (of his own choosing) to Joppa to summon Simon who was given the (additional) name of Peter. *Simon* (the Hebrew Simeon or Symeon) means "hearing" in the sense of being obedient, and he was obedient to the call to follow Jesus. But Jesus gave him the additional name of Cephas (Aramaic, *Kephâ*, "a stone, a piece of rock"), which corresponds to the Greek *petros*, also meaning a stone or a piece of rock (John 1:35-42). Peter had not been much like a rock in his earlier days, but by the grace of God he had been changed into the strong leader he had now become. Peter would be the one to help Cornelius.

**6. He lodgeth with one Simon a tanner:** ... Who is living with Simon, *—BB* ... the same is a guest, *—RTHM* ... He is being entertained at the house of, *—GDSP*... is staying with a man, also named Simon, *—EVRD*... the man who works with leather, *—NLTG*...a leather-worker, *—WMCK*

**whose house is by the sea side:** ... who has a house close to the sea, *—WEYM* ... whose house stands by the sea, *—MOFT*... is by the seaside, *—KLST*.

**he shall tell thee what thou oughtest to do:** ... thou wilt learn from him what thou hast to do, *—KNOX*.

**10:6.** The angel then gave further directions. The messengers of Cornelius would find Peter being entertained as a guest by a certain Simon who was a tanner and whose house was by the shore of the (Mediterranean) Sea, that is, outside of the city of Joppa itself. This is now modern Jaffa.

The statement "This one will tell you what it is necessary to do," is found in the margin of one of the late manuscripts of the Greek New Testament (cursive or minuscule #69) and in the A.D. 1592 edition of the Latin Vulgate of the Roman Catholic Church, but it is not found in any other ancient manuscripts of any importance. However, it does fit the context and explains why Cornelius should send for Peter.

**7. And when the angel which spake unto Cornelius was departed:** ... who spoke to him had left, *—MOFT*... had disappeared, *—NAB*... had gone away, *—WLMS*.

**he called two of his household servants:** ... calling two of the domestics, *—RTHM* ... his houseboys, *—KLGS*.

**and a devout soldier of them that waited on him continually:** ... and a religious soldier who was one of his constant attendants, *—TCNT* ... and a God-fearing soldier, *—WEYM*... and a godly soldier, *—WMCK* ... who belonged to his personal retinue, *—MOFT*... one of his orderlies, *—TNT*... in continual attendance, *—WUST*.

**10:7.** As soon as the angel left, Cornelius called two of his household slaves to himself. As verse 2 indicates, these were Godfearers who had accepted the truth about the one true God and were worshiping Him. Cornelius also summoned a devout, loyal soldier.

*Devout* means godly, Godfearing, and reverent. So this soldier must have listened to God's Word in the synagogue and joined in the prayers. He too must have heard about Jesus, His teachings, His ministry, His miracles, His death, and His resurrection. This soldier was also closely attached to Cornelius and must have talked and prayed with him, so Cornelius knew him very well and felt he could trust him to go along with this mission to summon Peter and bring him to Caesarea.

These men were in the military service of Rome as a career. They were part of the Empire's attempt to maintain what was called the "Roman peace," a peace that enabled the gospel to spread more rapidly than it otherwise could have in those days. But the believers were seeking a better peace than Rome could give.

**8. And when he had declared all these things unto them:** ... and having rehearsed, *—ASV* ... after telling them the whole story, *—TCNT* ... told them everything, *—WMCK*

**he sent them to Joppa:** ... dispatches them, *—CNDT.*

**10:8.** Cornelius did more than give a command to his servants and this soldier. He, in fact, did not treat them as servants, but as friends, and explained in detail what the angel had said. Cornelius had received an assurance from God that He had heard his prayers, and he wanted all God had for him. He was also sure that what God had for him was good, so these servants and his soldier would want what God had to offer as well. Then Cornelius sent the three men to Joppa.

**9. On the morrow, as they went on their journey:** ... as those men were journeying, *—RTHM* ... The next day, while they were still on their journey, *—WEYM.*

**and drew nigh unto the city:** ... and just as they were getting near the town, *—TCNT* ... not far from the town, *—WLMS* ... approaching the town, *—BRKL.*

**Peter went up upon the house top to pray about the sixth hour:** ... ascended the balcony, *—FNTN* ... about mid-day, *—TCNT* ... about noon, *—WEYM.*

**10:9.** The next day about the sixth hour (about noon) the three men sent by Cornelius were nearing Joppa. But at this point the Bible's attention shifts to Peter. God is always faithful to work on "both ends of the line," and it was time now to prepare Peter to go with these men to Caesarea to the house of Cornelius.

At that very time Peter went up to the flat roof of Simon's house by an outside stairway with the purpose of spending some time alone in prayer.

Most Jews considered noon one of the hours of prayer. As the psalmist David said, "Evening, and morning, and at noon, will I pray, and cry aloud: and he shall hear my voice" (Psalm 55:17).

**10. And he became very hungry, and would have eaten:** ... and desired to eat, *—ASV* ... and wished to eat, *—RTHM* ... wanted something to eat, *—TCNT* ... wished for some food, *—WEYM* ... he became ravenous, *—CNDT* ... would have taken a little refreshment, *—CMPB* ... craved something to eat, *—NORL* ... longed for something, *—PHLP* ... And he was in need of food, *—BB* ... longed to taste something, *—FNTN.*

**but while they made ready:** ... and while they were making ready, *—RTHM* ... but, while they were preparing it, *—WEYM* ... But as they were getting the meal ready, *—MOFT* ... While they were fixing a meal, *—KLGS* ... But while the food was being prepared, *—EVRD, —NCV.*

**he fell into a trance:** ... he fell into an ecstatic reverie, *—FNTN* ... there came upon him a trance, *—RTHM* ... he fell into a deep sleep, *—WMCK* ... he saw in a dream things God wanted him to see, *—NLTG* ... he fell into an ecstasy, *—KLST* ... he had a vision, *—EVRD* ... a deep sleep came on him, *—BB.*

**10:10.** Apparently Peter prayed for a time, then he became very hungry and wanted to eat. His heart was open to the Lord, and undoubtedly it was the Lord who put this unusual hunger upon him to prepare him for the revelation God was about to give him.

While Peter remained on the roof enjoying the cool breezes off the Mediterranean and waiting for them to prepare the food, he "fell into a trance." This does not mean a trance in the modern sense of the word, however, nor does it imply a hypnotic or unconscious state. The Greek says an *ekstasis* came over him. This simply means his mind was distracted from whatever he was thinking about as he sensed something important was about to happen. It was a consciousness of the presence of the supernatural, a feeling akin to astonishment or amazement. God was about to do something special.

**11. And saw heaven opened:** ... opening, *—KNOX* ... and saw that the sky was open, *—TCNT* ... He saw a rift in the sky, *—NEB.*

**and a certain vessel descending unto him, as it had been a great sheet:** ... and a bundle, *—KNOX* ... something like a great sail was descending, *—TCNT* ... what seemed to be an enormous sheet was, *—WEYM* ... and an object come down that looked like a big canvas, *—NAB* ... resembling a large sheet, *—FNTN* ... and a receptacle descending like, *—KLST* ... a container coming down like a wide sheet, *—BRKL* ... a great linen sheet, *—DOUY* ... an enormous sail, *—MNTG* ... a big piece of canvas, *—KLGS* ... like a great sail, *—TNT* ... like a giant sheet, *—KJII* ... like a large linen cloth, *—NLTG* ... a great cloth, *—BB.*

**knit at the four corners, and let down to the earth:** ... let down by four corners, ASV ... let down by its four corners towards the earth, *—TCNT* ... supported at the four corners, *—FNTN* ... by ropes at the four corners and lowered to the ground, *—WEYM.*

**10:11.** Then Peter saw a sight that must have really filled him with amazement. He saw heaven opening, and a kind of vessel, or container like an enormous sheet or sailcloth tied at the corners, was descending to him as it was let down to the earth.

Seeing the heavens opened is a reminder of Jacob's dream at Bethel where he saw the heavens opened, and the Lord appeared to him (Genesis 28:12-16). It meant God was accessible and He had a message for Jacob. God had a message for Peter, but He gave it in a way quite different from when He sent the angel to Cornelius. The angel was an objective, real appearance. But this experience of

Peter was a vision dealing with symbolic things, a dream-type vision, though Peter was fully awake and saw it with his eyes.

**12. Wherein were all manner of four footed beasts of the earth, and wild beasts, and creeping things, and fowls of the air:** ... In which were all sorts of, —BB ... In it were all kinds of quadrupeds, reptiles, and birds, —TCNT ... animals, —EVRD ... and snakes of the earth, —NLTG ... things that creep on the earth, —KNOX ... and wild birds, —WMCK ... and birds of the sky, —FNTN.

**10:12.** The sheet, or sailcloth, was filled with all kinds of quadrupeds, wild animals, reptiles of the earth, and birds of the air. The implication is that they did not include the domesticated animals that were considered clean by the law of Moses and therefore suitable for sacrifice and for eating. Furthermore, all these animals and birds were mixed together. They did not have any of the separation required by the Law.

Many of the prohibitions of the Mosaic law were included by God so that there might be a distinction between and even a separation of the Jews from the heathen around them. As one reads Leviticus 11 and Deuteronomy 14, several if not most of the dietary restrictions seem to be included for just this reason; there seems to be nothing intrinsically harmful about consuming the various foods that were prohibited. In fact, Genesis 9:3 states that God gave Noah "every moving thing that liveth" for food. However, he commanded Noah not to eat meat with the blood still in it (verse 4). This vision was telling Peter that the distinction between Jew and Gentile was abolished at the Cross.

**13. And there came a voice to him, Rise, Peter; kill, and eat:** ... Sacrifice! —CNDT ... Up, Peter, —WMCK ... Slaughter, then eat, —NAB.

**10:13.** While Peter was observing the contents of the sheet, a voice came to him and commanded him to rise up, kill (these animals and birds), and eat them.

**14. But Peter said, Not so, Lord:** ... On no account, lord, he replied, —WEYM ... By no means, Lord, —BRKL ... No, Sir, I cannot, —TCNT ... Far be it, —MRDK ... Sir, it is unthinkable, —NAB.

**for I have never eaten any thing that is common or unclean:** ... for I have never eaten anything defiled and impure, —TCNT ... unhallowed and unclean, —WEYM ... undedicated and unclean, —BRKL ... prohibited or unclean, —NORL ... polluted, —MRDK ... vile, —FNTN.

**10:14.** Peter's response shows he was spiritually sensitive enough to know this was the voice of the Lord. But his life-style of strict obedience to the Law overcame his normal desire to obey the Lord. So he replied very emphatically, "Not so (not at all, certainly not, never), Lord." He had never eaten anything common (unsanctified, dirty) or unclean (nonkosher). Peter had made some progress. He had accepted the Lord's work in saving the Samaritans. But they were circumcised and kept the forms of the Law about as well as many of the Jews did.

Peter had not faced the biggest barrier, however. Many laws and customs separated the Jews from the Gentiles, especially the dietary laws. They realized these laws were for their good. Actually, Jesus had already prepared His disciples for the abolishing of these food laws by His discussion of what really defiles a man. He made it clear that the true source of spiritual defilement is from within. External washings cannot get rid of the unclean thoughts, greed, malice, pride, and spiritual ignorance that can fill the heart and become the root of all sorts of evil (Mark 7:15-23).

**15. And the voice spake unto him again the second time:** ... Once more the voice came to him, —BRKL.

**What God hath cleansed, that call not thou common:** ... What God has pronounced pure ... you must not call defiled, —TCNT ... you must not regard as unhallowed, —WEYM ... stop declaring unhallowed, —WUST ... never treat as defiled! —FNTN.

**10:15.** Peter's reply was a contradiction. He called Jesus "Lord," yet refused to do what Jesus asked him to do. It was a human reaction, the same kind that still keeps many people from making a forward move with God. Therefore the voice (of the Lord Jesus) gave an even more emphatic reply, "What God has cleansed, don't you regard as common (unclean)." The negative used here by Jesus is indeed very emphatic.

It is best to be generally conservative, for not every proposed change is of God. On the other hand, a hidebound conservatism can be harmful, if it hinders bringing a wider dissemination of the gospel.

**16. This was done thrice:** ... This happened, in all, three times, —TCNT ... This took place three times, —WEYM.

**and the vessel was received up again into heaven:** ... and then suddenly it was all taken up into the sky, —TCNT ... then the thing was at once taken up into heaven, —WMCK ... and immediately the sheet was drawn up out of sight, —WEYM.

**10:16.** For further emphasis, the command to kill and eat was given three times. A lifetime of careful obedience to the Law is not easy to set aside. But the Lord made the command so emphatic that Peter had to give attention to it.

**17. Now while Peter doubted in himself what this vision which he had seen should mean:** . . . was still worrying over the meaning, *–JB* . . . was much perplexed in himself, *–ASV* . . . While Peter was still puzzling over the meaning of the vision he had seen, *–TCNT* . . . wondering as to the meaning, *–WEYM* . . . quite at a loss to know the meaning, *–MOFT* . . . was mulling over in his mind, *–BRKL* . . . was bewildered in himself, *–CNDT* . . . was still at a loss to know, *–WLMS* . . . was reflecting on the vision, *–CMPB.*

**behold, the men which were sent from Cornelius had made enquiry for Simon's house:** . . . having just asked the way to Simon's house, *–TCNT* . . . having made search for simon's house, *–BB* . . . just then, *–KLST* . . . having asked for the house of, *–KJII* . . . and on the next day, *–MOFT* . . . having made diligent inquiry regarding, *–WUST* . . . having found out the house of Simon, *–FNTN.*

**and stood before the gate:** . . . came up to the entrance, *–TNT* . . . came to the door, *–BB, –WEYM* . . . They were in fact standing at the very doorway, *–PHLP.*

**10:17.** Peter had enough discernment to understand this vision was symbolic. The fact that he "doubted" means that it was difficult to understand what the vision meant.

Peter's reaction was not unusual. Visions are sometimes open to more than one interpretation. Peter wanted to be sure he discovered the right one. But he did not find the meaning of this vision by weighing the possibilities in his mind. Rather, he was going to be asked to take a step of faith and obedience in response to the guidance of the Holy Spirit.

God did not let Peter speculate for long. The men sent by Cornelius had already asked the way to Simon's house and were standing at the gate. Once again, it is clear how exact God's timing is in all of His dealings. This was a very critical time in the history of the Church, but God was in control.

**18. And called, and asked whether Simon, which was surnamed Peter, were lodged there:** . . . inquiring for Simon's house, *–KLST* . . . calling out to ascertain whether Simon . . . was a guest there, *–BRKL* . . . Is Simon Peter staying here? *–NCV* . . . was living there, *–BB* . . . lodged there, *–FNTN.*

**10:18.** The three men at Simon's gate were inquiring if Simon who was also called Peter was staying as a guest there. The people in the house were busy preparing the meal, and Peter was lost in his thoughts about what the vision might mean. Fortunately, the men were persistent and did not give up or go away.

**19. While Peter thought on the vision:** . . . as Peter was pondering, *–RTHM* . . . was earnestly considering the vision, *–ABUV* . . . was meditating on the vision, *–WLMS* . . . was reflecting about, *–FNTN* . . . was turning over the vision in his mind, *–BB* . . . thinking deeply about the vision, *–PHLP* . . . was musing, *–LIVB* . . . is engrossed, *–CNDT.*

**the Spirit said unto him, Behold, three men seek thee:** . . . See, *–BB* . . . three men are looking for you, *–RSV* . . . looking for you at this moment, *–TCNT* . . . are now inquiring for you, *–FNTN.*

**10:19.** Peter was still thinking about the vision, pondering over it, weighing this and that possible interpretation in his mind. He was still trying to understand it by his own reasonings, probably not willing to admit to himself that the unclean animals and birds might represent people who needed the gospel.

So the Holy Spirit interrupted his thoughts and told him to pay attention, for three men were looking for him. Thus, in spite of his background in Judaism, Peter was sensitive enough to the Holy Spirit to recognize His voice (His inner voice) and be open to His leading.

**20. Arise therefore, and get thee down:** . . . So get up and go down, *–TCNT* . . . but rise up, descend, and accompany them, *–FNTN.*

**and go with them, doubting nothing:** . . . and do not hesitate to go with them, *–TCNT* . . . and go with them without any misgivings, *–WEYM* . . . and depart with them, *–KLST* . . . set out with them unhesitatingly, *–NAB* . . . Don't treat them as different people, *–BECK* . . . let not thy mind hesitate, *–MRDK* . . . without hesitation, *–TNT* . . . without scruple, *–NOYS.*

**for I have sent them:** . . . for I have sent them myself, *–TCNT.*

**10:20.** The Holy Spirit then commanded Peter to get up, go down (the outside stairway) from the flat roof, and go with these men. (Outside stairways made of stone may be seen in the ruins of Biblical cities excavated by archaeologists in Palestine.)

The Holy Spirit further commanded that Peter must go with the three men doubting nothing, that is, without any hesitation. (*Doubt* in this verse translates a different Greek word *diakrinomenos* from the one used in verse 17 *diēporei.* The word used in verse 20 implies being at odds with oneself, wavering, and therefore hesitating to obey, in fact, hesitating to do anything at all. The verb in verse 17 emphasizes perplexity about meaning. In verse 20 the perplexity is about whether to take action.) It was important for Peter to meet these men and go with them. Peter must act and act immediately.

It was also important for Peter to meet them and to realize the Holy Spirit had sent them. When the angel gave directions to Cornelius, the Holy Spirit also moved Cornelius to summon and send these three men. The Holy Spirit moved also on their hearts to encourage them to obey with all diligence. Thus, the Holy Spirit was the One who really sent them.

**21. Then Peter went down to the men:** ... So Peter went down and said to the men, *—WEYM*...accordingly, *—FNTN.*

**which were sent unto him from Cornelius; and said:** ... So Peter went down and said to the men, *—WEYM.*

**Behold, I am he whom you seek:** ... I am the man you are looking for, *—TCNT*... I am the man you want, *—FNTN.*

**what is the cause wherefore ye are come?:** ... What is your object in coming, *—TCNT*...What is the purpose, *—WLMS*...What brings you here, *—BECK*...Why have you come? *—NLTG.*

**10:21.** This was enough for Peter. Casting all doubts, perplexities, and indecision aside, he rose up in obedience to the voice of the Holy Spirit and went down to the men who were sent to him from Cornelius. He told them he was the person they were looking for, and he politely asked the reason for their coming. Courtesy is an important aspect of the love of Christ.

Even though Peter already had the Spirit's command to go with these men, he did not thrust himself upon them, nor did he immediately reveal to them what the Holy Spirit had told him. Instead, he gave them opportunity to explain their mission. It would be good for their spiritual experience for them to give their testimony of what God had done.

**22. And they said, Cornelius the centurion:** ... Cornelius, a colonel in the army, *—WLMS*...an army officer, *—NCV*...a captain, *—FNTN.*

**a just man, and one that feareth God:** ...a pious officer who reverences God, *—TCNT*...an upright and God-fearing man, *—WEYM*...righteous, *—FNTN*...and he honors God, *—NLTG.*

**and of good report among all the nation of the Jews:** ... and is well spoken of by the whole Jewish nation, *—TCNT*...who enjoys a good reputation, *—KLST*...of good reputation among all, *—MLNT*...and a man of high reputation with, *—WLMS* ... whose character can be vouched for by, *—PHLP*...is attested by the whole of, *—FNTN*...All the Jewish people respect him, *—NCV.*

**was warned from God by an holy angel to send for thee into his house:** ... had word from God, *—BB*...has been divinely instructed, *—WEYM*...divinely warned, *—YNG*...to summon you to his house, *—NAB*...to bring you into, *—FNTN.*

**and to hear words of thee:** ...and listen to what you have to say, *—TCNT*...He wants to hear what you have to say, *—NLTG*...and to listen to your message, *—MNTG*...to hear your suggestions, *—BRKL*...to listen to instructions from you, *—FNTN*...to give hearing to your words, *—BB*...so that he can hear what you have to say, *—EVRD.*

**10:22.** The men then explained, first by drawing attention to the character of Cornelius, the centurion who had sent them. Their first emphasis was on the fact that he was a just man. That is, he was upright, righteous, law-abiding, not only conforming to the laws of the land, but also recognizing the sovereignty of God and keeping a right relationship to Him by trying to live a life that would be pleasing to Him. It also implies honesty, goodness, and even mercy. Cornelius must have been a wonderful person to work for and a wonderful officer to serve under.

His uprightness was the result of his being a fearer of (the one true) God. He had turned his back on all the whole pantheon of Roman gods, goddesses, and semi-divine heroes of their mythology. All those things which were part of his religious background and upbringing in heathenism were now behind him. He no longer believed any of that mythology or followed any of the forms and ceremonies of Roman worship. He had committed himself to worship the true God who had revealed himself in the sacred writings of the Law, the Prophets, and the Psalms, inspired by the Spirit. As a God-fearer, he continually showed reverence and respect for God, and faithfully worshiped Him.

As a result of this, he had a good testimony borne to him by the whole of "the nation of the Jews." He was not only a man of good reputation among them, he was a man whose merit was well-attested and well-known so they approved of and spoke well of him. This implies he had been a member of Rome's occupation force in Palestine for a long time, probably for many years. Though he was now stationed in Caesarea, he may have been assigned previously to other places in Judea and Galilee as well. It is evident also that he had given generously to the needs of the poor among the Jews wherever he went. He had become well-known among the Jewish people.

The men then explained how Cornelius had been given a divine revelation through a holy angel to summon Peter to his house. The "angel of God" of verse 3 is here called a "holy angel," which shows he must have radiated some of the glory of God, just as the seraphim did in Isaiah chapter 6. This made Cornelius conscious that this angel was indeed a messenger from heaven. The angel further directed that they should hear words (Greek, *rhēmata*) from Peter, implying that they should also listen and obey these words of Christian teaching.

**23. Then called he them in, and lodged them:** ... Upon this Peter invited them in and entertained them, *—TCNT*...So he took them in for the night, —BB . . . and housed them, —KJII . . . He accordingly invited them in, —FNTN . . . asked the men to come in and spend the night, —EVRD, —NCV . . . and treated them as guests, —NAB . . . and asked them to stay with him, —WMCK.

**And on the morrow Peter went away with them:** . . . The next day he set out with them, —WEYM . . . But next day he got up and traveled with them, —BRKL . . . the day after, —BB . . . on the following morning, arising, he went with them, —FNTN . . . got ready and went, —EVRD . . . he set off with them, —TNT . . . he went off with them, —NAB . . . started off with them, —GDSP.

**and certain brethren from Joppa accompanied him:** . . . taking some of the brothers, —BB . . . and some of the brothers in Joppa went along with him, —WLMS . . . by some of the disciples from, —FNTN . . . joined him, —EVRD.

**10:23.** Though it was only a little after noon, they did not insist on starting back at once. Peter invited the three men into Simon the tanner's house, and Simon, at Peter's request, probably provided them hospitality for the night. Whatever reservations Peter initially had concerning the distinctions between clean and unclean foods were set aside. His encounter with the Lord had an immediate impact on his behavior, and likely, his attitudes and beliefs. As a Jew who had spent a lifetime trying to fulfill the requirements of the Law and the traditions of Judaism, Peter could have understandably been uncomfortable eating with and boarding these three Gentiles. Even though eating with Gentiles would have been strictly forbidden to him according to the customs of current Judaism, the text gives no indication that he was reluctant to receive these visitors. Apparently he quickly grasped the deeper truth portrayed in the vision.

The next day Peter went along with them. But he was careful to take six good, believing Jewish brothers from Joppa with him. (See 11:12.) He knew he would be called into question by other believers for entering a Gentile house, so he wanted witnesses he could depend on. Just to be sure, he took double the two or three required by the Law (Deuteronomy 19:15; compare Matthew 18:16).

**24. And the morrow after they entered into Caesarea:** . . . and the following day, —TCNT . . . and on the next day, —MOFT . . . The day after, —ADAM . . . day after that, —BB . . . they came to, —EVRD . . . he reached, —KLST . . . they arrived at, —FNTN.

**And Cornelius waited for them:** . . . was expecting them, —RTHM . . . was awaiting their arrival, —WEYM . . . was looking for them, —NLTG.

**and had called together his kinsmen and near friends:** . . . his kinsfolk and intimate friends, —RTHM . . . relatives, —EVRD . . . had collected his . . . more intimate friends, —FNTN . . . and close

friends, —RSV . . . gathered all his family, —NLTG . . . having got together his relations and his near friends, —BB . . . all the kindred, —MRDK . . . whom he had invited, —KLST.

**10:24.** The next day this company of 10 men arrived in Caesarea. They found Cornelius waiting for them with a house full of people. He not only believed the Lord was looking with favor on him, as the angel had said, he also believed this meant God wanted to bless him, for he had learned to know God as a good God. He had shared his material wealth with others. So he could not think of keeping to himself all of the blessing he expected God would bring him through Peter. He felt this too should be shared.

He was sure Peter would come. God would see to that as well. Therefore, he estimated the time of Peter's arrival and took it upon himself to call together all his relatives and close friends. He must have explained to them also about the angel's visit. He undoubtedly had already led them to a belief in the one true God and told them what he already knew about Jesus and the gospel. So they were all waiting with great expectation.

**25. And as Peter was coming in, Cornelius met him:** . . . So when Peter entered the city, —TCNT . . . When Peter entered the house, —WEYM . . . came in,

**and fell down at his feet, and worshipped him:** . . . and throwing himself at Peter's feet, bowed to the ground, —TCNT . . . did homage, —RTHM . . . and did reverence to him, —BRKL . . . showed him respect by bowing at his feet, —FNTN.

**10:25.** As Peter was coming into the house, Cornelius was very conscious that God had sent him. Therefore, as soon as he met Peter, he fell down at Peter's feet and worshiped. That is, he went down on his hands and knees before Peter, prostrating himself, and possibly even kissing his feet. This was the way the Persians bowed before their kings (whom they considered gods). The Greeks and Romans also did it before their gods. It was considered the way to show the highest reverence to them.

Some scholars believe Cornelius only meant to do this as a means of giving Peter a respectful welcome. But it is probably more likely that the excitement of actually seeing this man, whom the angel told him to summon, brought an emotional feeling in his heart and mind that caused him to react the way he was taught to react in his childhood and youth in Rome.

**26. But Peter took him up, saying:** ... raised him up, *—ASV* ... made him stand up, *—BECK* ... lifted him up, *—WMCK*

**Stand up; I myself also am a man:** ... I am only a man like you, *—TCNT* ... Rise, I am a human being, too, *—BRKL* ... Stand up! I'm not a god! *—TALR*.

**10:26.** Peter was probably shocked to see Cornelius bowing before him. He knew the commandment that the Jews were not to bow down or worship any other god (Exodus 20:5). He knew that by the time of the Book of Esther, the Jews had learned the further lesson that they were not to bow down to any man either (see Esther 3:2-4).

Therefore, Peter took hold of Cornelius quickly and raised him up, telling him to stand up, and saying to him very emphatically, "I myself also am a man." The Greek here is *anthrōpos*, not a man in the sense of being a male, but man or mankind in the sense of being a human being. Thus he reproved Cornelius very gently, yet firmly. At the same time he did not belittle Cornelius. Peter did not want any exaltation for being used of God. Neither did he want anyone to give any human personality preeminence in the Church.

**27. And as he talked with him, he went in:** ... And conversing with him, *—RTHM* ... Talking with him as he went, *—TCNT*.

**and found many that were come together:** ... where he found a large gathering of people, *—TCNT* ... a large company assembled, *—WEYM* ... a great crowd had gathered, *—WLMS* ... a large number gathered together, *—WMCK* ... a great many gathered, *—NORL* ... a considerable assemblage, *—FNTN*.

**10:27.** Peter then began to converse with Cornelius, and while doing so came into the room where all the relatives and close friends of Cornelius were gathered. The text implies Peter was surprised to see so many people.

**28. And he said unto them, Ye know how that it is an unlawful thing for a man that is a Jew to keep company, or come unto one of another nation:** ... it is a violation of established order, *—WUST* ... You are aware ... that it is forbidden for a Jew to be on intimate, or even visiting, terms with a foreigner, *—TCNT* ... a Jew is strictly forbidden to associate with a Gentile of visit him, *—WEYM* ... how wrong it is, *—BECK* ... how abominable it is, *—DOUY* ... to be uniting with, *—RTHM* ... an alien, *—MRDK* ... a person of any other nationality, *—KLGS*.

**but God hath shewed me that I should not call any man common or unclean:** ... unhallowed, *—BRKL*.

**10:28.** Peter reminded the assembled crowd that it was unlawful for a Jew to keep company with or come to a foreigner (for fellowship or association). By saying it was unlawful, he was not referring primarily to the law of Moses. "Unlawful" here could be used of any act that showed a lawless spirit or an undisciplined desire or purpose to break the rules accepted by a particular group or society. A better way to put it might be that to a Jew it was not merely illegal but something abominable to join in closely with a foreigner. (The same word is used of Paul's attempting to join in with the disciples and become part of their fellowship at Jerusalem in 9:26.) Coming to these Gentiles also implies more than simply entering the house. It indicates an agreeing with them, acceding to or even giving consent to their heathen ways and desires.

But Peter was there, not because he was turning his back on Jewish ways and customs, but because God had showed him not to call any man (any human being) common (ordinary, profane, ceremonially impure) or unclean (defiled or defiling, and therefore cut off from coming into the presence of God).

**29. Therefore came I unto you without gainsaying:** ... I came readily, *—MRDK* ... So I came immediately, *—KLGS* ... without raising any objection, *—TCNT* ... without any demur, *—MOFT* ... I didn't object to coming here, *—BECK* ... came without debate, *—CMPB* ... without any hesita-

**as soon as I was sent for: I ask therefore for what intent ye have sent for me?:** ... when you sent for me, *—WMCK* ... when I was summoned, *—KLST* ... when I was asked to come here, *—EVRD* ... I may now be allowed to ask for what reason you have brought me, *—FNTN* ... I therefore ask why you sent for me, *—WEYM* ... Now I want to know what made you send for me, *—PHLP* ... I should, of course, like to know why you summoned me, *—NAB*.

**10:29.** Peter did not explain about his vision or how the Lord brought him to the conclusion that he must not call any person common or unclean. It was enough to remind them of the tremendous barrier of prejudice that the Jews had placed between themselves and the Gentiles. From this Cornelius and his friends would have to understand that it would have to be a revelation from God himself if that barrier was to be broken down. The fact that it was indeed broken down in Peter's experience was shown by his making no objections to their request, and by his coming to them immediately. He wanted their attention to be on what God was doing, not on himself.

Then Peter politely inquired about their reason for sending for him. He had heard this from the two slaves and the soldier Cornelius had sent. But he wanted to hear it from Cornelius himself. Thus he gave Cornelius an opportunity to express what God had told him and in this way to express his faith.

**30.** **And Cornelius said, Four days ago I was fasting until this hour:** ... Just three days ago this very hour, –TCNT ... about this time, –WMCK ... at this very hour, –KLST.

**and at the ninth hour I prayed in my house:** ... I was keeping the ninth hour of prayer, –ASV ... observing the time of the three o'clock prayer, –TCNT ... I was home for my three o'clock worship, –BRKL ... in my house saying the afternoon prayers, –WMCK ... It was at this same time, –EVRD.

**and, behold, a man stood before me in bright clothing:** ... All at once, I saw, –NLTG ... when suddenly, –WMCK ... in bright apparel, –ASV ... in dazzling clothing, –GDSP, –TCNT ... in shining raiment, –WEYM ... dazzling robes, –NAB ... shining garments, –KLST ... wearing shining clothes, –EVRD.

**10:30.** In answer, Cornelius recounted how 4 days before (2 days before yesterday in their method of counting days) he was fasting and praying in his house until about 3 o'clock in the afternoon, and suddenly he looked and a man in bright (shining) clothes stood before him.

Though the Bible called this one an angel (verse 3), Cornelius is giving his first impressions here. It is uncertain if the angel appeared to him in the form of a man, or if God opened his eyes in order that he might perceive a being which was spiritual, not physical by nature. (Cf. 2 Kings 6:16f., where Elisha asked God to open his servant's eyes so that he could see the spiritual forces which surrounded them.)

**31.** **And said, Cornelius, thy prayer is heard:** ... and your acts of charity have been remembered by God, –WEYM ... your charitable gifts, –PHLP ... God has heard your prayer, –BECK, –EVRD.

**and thine alms are had in remembrance in the sight of God:** ... He has seen what you give to the poor, and he remembers you, –NCV ... your generosity remembered, –NAB ... are remembered before, –LIVB ... have been recalled to mind by God, –GDSP ... has remembered your gifts of love, –NLTG.

**10:31.** *Angel* means "messenger," and this young "man" in shining clothes bright with the glory of God had a message. Cornelius now recounted how his prayer had been heard (had been really and truly heard). His charitable giving had also been called to remembrance by God.

This does not mean God had ever forgotten or failed to take notice of either the prayers or the generosity of Cornelius. When the Bible talks about God remembering something or someone, it means God had that person or thing in mind all along, but now the time had come for God to do something specific about it.

God had been taking note of Cornelius and his godliness and his giving to the poor of God's people. In response God was about to bring the proper answer to his prayer.

The prayer here is speaking of one particular prayer, a prayer which must have been on the heart of Cornelius in the midst of all his praying. It undoubtedly involved a desire to have closer fellowship with God and with His people.

**32.** **Send therefore to Joppa, and call hither Simon, whose surname is Peter:** ... and invite Simon. –WEYM ... and summon Simon, –KLST, –MOFT ... and ask Simon Peter to come, –EVRD.

**he is lodged in the house of one Simon a tanner by the sea side: who, when he cometh, shall speak unto thee:** ... is staying in the house, –EVRD ... the man who works with leather, –NLTG.

**10:32.** Cornelius next repeated the command to send for Simon Peter, drawing attention again to the specific details given by the angel of where to find him at the house of Simon the tanner (outside of Joppa) by the seaside.

At this point the majority of the Greek manuscripts have the phrase "who, coming (when he comes), will speak to you." Some of the oldest manuscripts leave it out, but it does fit the context, and it seems obvious that the reason for summoning Peter was to give him opportunity to tell them God's message.

The fact that the Book of Acts takes valuable space to repeat the details of the visit of the angel and the directions to send for Peter shows that God wanted to emphasize the fact that the gospel preached by Peter and the other apostles was and is from God.

This also shows that God prepares hearts to receive the gospel. From time to time there have been unusual revivals in the history of the Church that cannot be explained apart from a sovereign move of God. God has not changed His purpose that He revealed to Abraham so long ago. He still wants all the nations of the world to be blessed.

**33.** **Immediately therefore I sent to thee:** ... So, I sent to you at once, –RSV ... Accordingly at once I sent for, –KLST.

**and thou hast well done that thou art come:** ... and I thank you heartily for having come, –WEYM ... it was very good of you to come, –EVRD ... and you have been kind enough to come, –NAB ... you were good enough to come, –WMCK ... and you acted nobly, –BRKL ... and you have been most kind in coming, –PHLP.

**Now therefore are we all here present before God:** ... That is why all of us are now assembled here in God's presence, –WEYM ... at this moment, –NAB.

**to hear all things that are commanded thee of God:** ... to listen to what the Lord has commanded you to say, –WEYM ... to hear everything the Lord has commanded you to tell us, –NCV ... to hear whatever directives, NAB ... in which the Lord has instructed

154

you, —MLNT...whatever the Lord has told you to say, —NLTG.

**10:33.** Cornelius then let Peter know he had not hesitated to obey the angel's command. Immediately (within the same hour), he sent for Peter. Now Peter had "done well" to come. However, Cornelius did not mean here that Peter had done a good thing by coming. The language used by Cornelius is idiomatic and really means they were pleased that Peter had come. Now all of them were gathered there in the presence of God, to hear from Peter everything God had instructed him to tell them. The Greek implies Peter would tell them truths established by God, and therefore fixed, unchangeable, dependable.

**34. Then Peter opened his mouth, and said:**...Then Peter began to speak, —EVRD, —WEYM...began to address them, —KLST.

**Of a truth I perceive that God is no respecter of persons:**...I discover, —MRDK...to show partiality, —TCNT...I conclude, —RTHM...Now I truly see that God cares nothing for outward appearances, —WMCK...God makes no distinction between one man and another, —WEYM...God has no favourites, —MOFT, —TNT...I really understand now that to God every person is the same, —EVRD, —NCV...thoroughly understand the truth, —MLNT...I now thoroughly grasp the truth that God is not partial, —BRKL...doesn't prefer one person to another. —BECK.

**10:34.** The phrase "opened his mouth," was used in New Testament times to introduce an important discourse. In fact, this sermon at the house of Cornelius was a landmark in the history of the Early Church for more than one reason. A number of scholars have drawn attention to the fact that there are important similarities between Peter's preaching here and the Gospel of Mark. Irenaeus, the pastor of the church at Lyons in Gaul wrote in the Second Century A.D. (as did Papias and others before him) that Mark was Peter's disciple and reported Peter's preaching about Christ in his Gospel. In other words, the Gospel of Mark embodies the essence of the teaching that Peter gave wherever he went, with Peter commissioned by Christ and Mark inspired by the Holy Spirit to write.

This sermon is important also because from the start Peter showed that he understood fully the meaning of his vision that was repeated three times on the rooftop. He saw that God truly is no respecter of persons; He does not show favoritism or partiality.

Actually, this was not a new truth. The Old Testament recognized this truth (2 Samuel 14:14, for

example). But up to this time Peter had been able to apply it only to the Jews, not to Gentiles.

**35. But in every nation he that feareth him, and worketh righteousness:**...God accepts anyone who worships him and does what is right...It is not important what country a person comes from, —NCV...he who reverences him, —TCNT...and practices doing right, —WLMS.

**is accepted with him:**...God makes no distinction between one man and another, —WEYM...He is pleased with any man, —NLTG...God has no favourites, —MOFT...I now thoroughly grasp the truth that God is not partial, —BRKL...welcomes the man, —GDSP...is welcomed by him, —WMCK

**10:35.** Now Peter understood that the barrier that had kept people away from the Lord was broken down by Christ. So Peter emphasized that the way to God is open to all. Anyone who fears (worships and gives reverence to) God and works righteousness (proving he has received divine grace by faith) is acceptable to Him.

God's impartiality was also taught in such passages as Deuteronomy 10:17 and 2 Chronicles 19:7. (See also Amos 9:7.) The New Testament emphasizes it even more in such passages as Romans 2:11, and 1 Peter 1:17. This does not mean God cannot make a choice, but rather that He does not base His choice on, or limit it to national, racial, social, or any other type of external differences. Therefore, these Gentiles, if they fulfilled the qualifications of worship, faith, and faithfulness, were just as acceptable to God as any Jew who worshiped God in spirit and in truth.

Peter now realized this in a new way. So did this houseful of Gentiles. Jewish exclusivism had kept them away from full fellowship. They had undoubtedly heard the Gentiles called dogs. But they probably had never heard any emphasis on the promise that in Abraham and his seed all the families (of all the nations) of the earth would be blessed, a promise that is repeated five times in the Book of Genesis (12:3; 18:18; 22:18; 26:4; 28:14).

**36. The word which God sent unto the children of Israel:**...This is the message he has sent to the sons, —NAB...God has sent his Message to the Israelite people, —TCNT...to the sons of Israel, ABUV.

**preaching peace by Jesus Christ: (he is Lord of all:):**...announcing the glad tidings of peace through, —RTHM...spreading, —WMCK...by telling them the good news of peace through, —WLMS...He is Lord of all, —CNDT...of everything, —ADAM...of all people! —NCV.

**10:36.** Peter next reminded Cornelius and his friends of the word (the message, Greek, *logon*) God sent to Israel preaching (literally, telling) the good news (the gospel) of peace by (through)

Jesus Christ. The content of the gospel, the central truth of the good news, is that God has made full provision for the believer's peace through Jesus Christ. That peace includes not only peace with God through the cleansing and forgiveness that comes through Christ's death on the cross, but also all of God's provisions and promises for the believer's entire well-being. Christ has put the "yes" and the "amen" ("truly") on them all (2 Corinthians 1:20).

**37. That word, I say, ye know, which was published throughout all Judaea:** . . . you yourselves know what happened throughout, —WMCK . . . you know how the message spread, —MNTG . . . I take it you know what has been reported, —NAB . . . You know the things that occurred up and down Judaea, —BRKL . . . been published, —DOUY . . . which came throughout, —KJII.
**and began from Galilee, after the baptism which John preached:** . . . beginning in Galilee, —WEYM.

**10:37.** Peter continued, reminding them of the "word" (the message [Greek, *rhēma*], used here as a synonym interchangeable with *logos*) they already knew. In fact, "you know" is emphatic in the Greek here. This means they already knew the facts about Jesus, about His life, death, and resurrection. Someone had given them the message.

It is one thing, however, to hear the facts of the gospel. It is quite another thing to receive the message as it is given by a Spirit-filled messenger of God. Peter repeated the well-known gospel story so the Spirit could apply it to the hearts and minds of the hearers. Peter made Christ the central part of his message and trusted the Holy Spirit to do the work.

**38. How God anointed Jesus of Nazareth with the Holy Ghost and with power:** . . . how God consecrated him his Christ by enduing him with the Holy Spirit and with power, —TCNT . . . how God appointed, —WMCK . . . when God had endowed Him, —FNTN . . . with the power of the Holy Spirit, —PHLP.
**who went about doing good:** . . . went everywhere, —EVRD . . . who traversed the land doing good, —BRKL.
**and healing all that were oppressed of the devil:** . . . and making well, —BB . . . and curing all who were under the power of, —TCNT . . . and curing all who were harassed by, —MOFT . . . and curing all who were overpowered by, —FNTN, —WLMS . . . all those who are tyrannized over by the Slanderer, —CNDT . . . that were suffering from evil, —MRDK . . . all who were troubled by, —NLTG . . . all who suffered from the devil's power, —PHLP . . . all that were pressed down by, —KJII . . . those who were ruled by, —EVRD, —NCV . . . all who were in the grip of, —NAB.
**for God was with him:** . . . with God at his side, —KNOX . . . because God was, —RTHM . . . since, —WMCK . . . was with Jesus, —EVRD.

**10:38.** Actually, the message is always Jesus himself. It is Jesus from Nazareth whom God anointed with the Holy Spirit and mighty supernatural power. This anointing was in fulfillment of the prophecies of Isaiah 11:2 which speak of the sevenfold Spirit of the Lord resting upon Him: (1) the Spirit of the Lord, (2) of wisdom, (3) of understanding, (4) of counsel, (5) of might, (6) of knowledge, and (7) of the fear of the Lord. It also fulfilled Isaiah 61:1, 2, "The Spirit of the Lord God is upon me," which Jesus declared was spoken of Him (Luke 4:18, 19).

This Jesus, said Peter, went about doing good (kind) deeds and healing all who were oppressed (overpowered or treated harshly) by the devil ("the slanderer," the chief slanderer of all), for God was with Him. God not only sent Jesus, He continued to be with Him in all His ministry so His miracles showed the goodness and kindness of God as well as God's power in every realm, thus giving proof that Jesus was and is indeed God's "Anointed One."

**39. And we are witnesses of all things which he did both in the land of the Jews, and in Jerusalem, whom they slew and hanged on a tree:** . . . We have seen and heard everything He did, —NLTG . . . all that he did in the country of, —KLST . . . both in the villages of, —FNTN . . . whom they put to death, —BB . . . they hung him up on a tree and killed him, —WMCK . . . hanging him on, —KLST . . . and they murdered Him, —MLNT . . . They killed him, finally, —NAB . . . by nailing him to a cross, —EVRD.

**10:39.** Next, Peter added, "We (meaning the apostles rather than the six believers from Joppa) are witnesses of all things which He did in the land of the Jews (Judea), and in Jerusalem." This emphasis on the apostolic witness is important. Jesus chose the Twelve to be the primary witnesses to the facts of the gospel.

Peter continued his message by pointing out this One who did nothing but good, the One who brought such blessing, healing and deliverance, the Jews killed and hung on a tree.

*Hung* here means crucified. It seems Peter used this word here rather than the ordinary word for "crucify" in order to emphasize the shamefulness of Christ's death. "Tree" basically means "wood," and the word was used to mean any object made of wood. It is translated "wood" in 1 Corinthians 3:12 and Revelation 18:12. It also translates the Hebrew word *'ets*, as, for example, when Galatians 3:13 refers to Deuteronomy 21:23. But *'ets* is a general word and is translated "wood" over 100 times in the Old Testament. Thus the "tree" here means the cross. The Romans sometimes crucified on an X-shaped cross, but the fact that the inscription was placed over Jesus' head shows that the usual form of the cross was used.

**40. Him God raised up the third day:** ... This Jesus God raised from the grave, −TCNT ... only to have God raise him up, −NAB ... raised Jesus to life, −EVRD ... God gave him back to life, −BB.

**and shewed him openly:** ... permitted him to appear, −WEYM...allowedhimtobeseen, −BB, −MOFT...and caused him to be, −EVRD, −KLST ... let him be seen clearly, −KLGS ... with naked eyes, −MRDK ... and caused Him to be seen, −KJII ... and grant that he be seen, −NAB ... to be plainly seen, −GDSP, −WLMS ... and granted Him to become visible, −FNTN ... granted the clear sight of him, −KNOX.

**10:40.** In contrast to what men did to Jesus, God raised (resurrected) Him on the third day. (Some see in this statement a reference to Hosea 6:2 since the apostle Paul spoke of Christ rising on the third day "according to the Scriptures." See 1 Corinthians 15:4, 20, 23.)

Then God permitted the risen Jesus to be manifest, to be visible, to be revealed. What God did was not something hidden, something mystical, or something merely spiritual.

The Gentiles who were listening to Peter had heard of Christ's resurrection, but they may also have heard the stories circulated by the Jewish leaders who said the disciples stole away the body of Jesus (Matthew 28:13). So Peter emphasized the reality of the bodily resurrection of Jesus and the reality of His appearances.

**41. Not to all the people:** ... But he was not seen by all the people, −EVRD ... not to the general public, −TALR ... not of all the people, −DRBY.

**but unto witnesses chosen before of God, even to us:** ... but to us witnesses previously selected of God, −BRKL ... Only the witnesses that God had already chosen saw him, and we are those witnesses, −EVRD ... whom God had designated beforehand, −GDSP.

**who did eat and drink with him:** ... and we ate and drank with Him, −NORL.

**after he rose from the dead:** ... after his resurrection from the dead, −TCNT ... after he was raised from death, −EVRD.

**10:41.** Peter added that these appearances were not made to all the people, but to witnesses chosen by God beforehand, namely to Peter and the others who ate and drank with Jesus (and thus enjoyed fellowship with Him around the table) after He arose from (out from among) the dead. This was concrete proof of the reality of Christ's resurrection body. He was not a spirit, not a ghost, not a figment of their imagination, but a very real Person who could give them genuine fellowship in this way.

It is also evident that Jesus did not intend to stay on the earth and teach the general public anymore. He gave His time after the Resurrection to opening the minds of His chosen witnesses to the Scriptures so they would be able to understand and proclaim the gospel after He ascended to His place at the Father's throne. (See Luke 24:25-27, 32, 44-49, noting that He caused the truth to burn in their hearts.)

Actually, 1 Corinthians 15:5-8 reports there was a sufficient number of witnesses. The resurrected Christ was seen by more than 500 believers at once (probably in Galilee), and most of them were still alive at the time Paul wrote to the Corinthians. He was seen also by His half-brother, James, and by all who were apostles, including Paul.

**42. And he commanded us to preach unto the people:** ... And he charged us, −ASV ... And to us He gave orders, −MLNT ... to proclaim, −RTHM ... to herald, −BRKL ... to announce to the people, −GDSP.

**and to testify:** ... and solemnly declare, −WEYM, −TNT ... to testify fully, −NORL ... and to tell them, −EVRD.

**that it is he which was ordained of God to be the Judge of quick and dead:** ... that He is the One, −NORL ... appointed by God, −TCNT ... the Judge of the living and the dead, ASV ... God-ordained Judge, −AMPB.

**10:42.** Peter then drew attention to the need for forgiveness in view of the coming judgment day.

Because of Christ's command, these chosen witnesses were proclaiming the good news to the people. (The Great Commission is found in all four Gospels as well as in Acts 1:8.) But Peter did not stop with speaking of the good news. He continued by showing the importance of accepting the good news. As witnesses to Christ's resurrection, the apostles were also under obligation to testify solemnly that Jesus was ordained (designated, appointed) as Judge of the living and the dead.

Peter did not mean the spiritually living and the spiritually dead. Rather, Jesus is and will be the Judge of all who have lived or whoever will live on earth. This bears out what Jesus said in John 5:22, "The Father judges no one, but has given (and continues and will continue to give) all judgment to the Son" (RSV).

**43. To him give all the prophets witness:** ... To Him all the prophets bear witness, −WEYM ... All the early preachers spoke of this, −NLTG ... All the prophets say this is true, −EVRD.

**that through his name whosoever believeth in him shall receive remission of sins:** ... forgiveness of sins, −TCNT ... that remission of sins is to be received through his name by every one that believeth on him, −RTHM ... remission of the penalty of sins, —WUST ... God will forgive his sins through Jesus, —EVRD.

**10:43.** The coming judgment need not frighten them, however. For Peter emphasized again the fact that the way is open to all, so no one need be excluded from the benefits of Christ's death and resurrection. But this time Peter drew attention, not to his own vision, but to the command of the Lord and the witness of the prophets to the written Word.

**44. While Peter yet spake these words:** ... Before Peter had finished saying these words, —TCNT ... Even while Peter was preaching this sermon, —NORL ... Peter had not finished these words when, NAB ... was still saying this, —EVRD.
**the Holy Ghost fell on all them which heard the word:** ... came down on all those who were listening, —EVRD ... listening to his message, —NORL ... overshadowed all them, —MRDK ... who hearkened to the message, —FNTN.

**10:44.** While Peter was still speaking these words (Greek, *rhēmata*, the plural of *rhēma*), there came a sudden unexpected interruption from heaven. The Holy Spirit fell on all those who were listening to the Word (Greek, *logon*). Notice here that what Peter spoke was referred to as *rhēma*, but what they heard, *logos*. Again it is clear that the two Greek words are used interchangeably.

The Holy Spirit is spoken of here as falling on them, using the same word found in 8:16 which says the Holy Spirit had not yet fallen upon those in Samaria who were saved under the preaching of Philip and were baptized in water by him. Thus, in the present context, "falling upon" speaks of receiving the Holy Spirit in a "baptism" for power (cf. 1:5, 8).

**45. And they of the circumcision which believed were astonished, as many as came with Peter:** ... And all the Jewish believers who had come with Peter were astonished, —WEYM ... The Jewish faithful, Peter's companions, —KLST ... And the circumcised believers, —BRKL ... were surprised, —BECK ... were absolutely amazed, —PHLP.
**because that on the Gentiles also was poured out the gift of the Holy Ghost:** ... the holy Spirit had actually been poured out on the Gentiles, —MOFT ... bestowed even upon the heathen, —TCNT ... the free-gift, —RTHM ... the grace of the Holy Ghost, —DOUY ... that the gift of the Holy Spirit had been given even to the non-Jewish people, —EVRD ... had been showered upon the heathen too, —WLMS ... had also been poured forth on, —KLST ... on the Pagans, —KLGS.

**10:45.** This outpouring of the Holy Spirit totally amazed the six Jewish believers who had come with Peter. In fact, they could hardly believe they

were observing the Holy Spirit poured out on these Gentile Romans.

Luke referred to these six men as "they of the circumcision." Peter, of course, was circumcised, but his mind had been opened. But the Bible draws attention to the fact that these six men, even though believers in Christ, were still very conscious of who they were as heirs of the promise given to Abraham, a promise confirmed by a covenant whose outward sign was circumcision. They did not feel the importance of the part of the promise that spoke of blessing to all the nations of the earth, nor did they see themselves as opening the way for that promise to come to non-Jews. Even Peter's experience had not convinced them their prejudices were wrong, and the truth that God is no respecter of persons had not become as clear in their minds as it had in the mind of Peter. Thus, they did not really expect God to save these Gentiles and fill them with the Holy Spirit in the same way He had done for the Jewish believers.

"Poured out" is used to mean the same thing as "fell upon," and it shows that Peter and the six Jewish believers saw in this experience the same thing that happened on the Day of Pentecost (2:17, 33).

**46. For they heard them speak with tongues, and magnify God:** ... These Jewish believers, —EVRD ... for they could hear them speaking with tongues and extolling God, —TCNT ... and declaring, —GDSP ... speaking in other languages and praising God, —BECK ... exalting God, NASB ... with diverse tongues, —MRDK ... in various languages, —ADAM.
**Then answered Peter:** ... At this Peter asked, —TCNT ... Peter said, —EVRD ... Then Peter made the decision, —KLST.

**10:46.** The fact that this whole crowd of Romans spoke with tongues (languages they had never learned) and magnified God also relates this outpouring to the outpouring on the Day of Pentecost (2:4). They magnified God as they kept on speaking in other tongues. (The Greek indicates continuous action for both the speaking in tongues and the magnifying or praising, extolling, exalting, and glorifying God.) Since there were not the people of various languages present as there were on the Day of Pentecost, this seems to mean their praise was addressed to God.

Peter apparently observed this for a time, and then he gave a response that was surely inspired by the Holy Spirit.

**47. Can any man forbid water, that these should not be baptized:** ... Can any one refuse the water for the baptism of these people, —TCNT ... Can anyone keep these people from being baptized with water? —EVRD...Can anyone refuse the baptism of water to these people, —KLST.

**which have received the Holy Ghost as well as we?:**...since they have received the Holy Spirit, —WLMS...who the Holy Spirit did receive, —YNG...have been given, —BB...as well as ourselves? —FNTN...as we ourselves did, —MLNT...even as we also did? —KJII...just like ourselves? —WMCK...as we did, —KLST...just as we have, —LAMS.

**10:47.** Peter saw that this kind of evidence was sufficient for the Church to accept these believers, so no one could forbid baptism in water. Peter recognized that these Gentiles were not only accepted by God but were also a part of the Church. The Holy Spirit was poured out on believers who were already identified as the Church and as the temple of the Holy Spirit in chapter 2. Thus, their experience was the same as that of the Jewish believers at Pentecost.

**48. And he commanded them to be baptized in the name of the Lord:**...And he ordered, —MOFT...So he directed, —MLNT, —TCNT...And he gave instructions, —TNT...So he commanded his companions, —NOLI...gave orders for them to be baptized in the name of Jesus Christ, —PHLP, —WMCK...to have baptism, —BB...of our Lord, —LAMS.
**Then prayed they him to tarry certain days:**...after this, they asked him to stay on some days, —KNOX...Afterwards they asked him to stay with them for some days, —PHLP...after which they asked him to stay there a few days longer, —TCNT...Then they begged him to remain with them for a time, —WEYM...they besought him to stay on there, —KLST...Then they kept him with them, —BB...for some days, —WMCK...to stay certain days, —KJII...they urged him to remain, —LAMS...to remain for some days with them, —NOLI.

**10:48.** Peter did not hesitate any longer. He saw that these Gentile Romans had believed the Word while he was preaching, and were saved, born again from above. Then, while he was still preaching, the Holy Spirit had been poured out upon them. Later, in 15:8, Peter said, "God, which knoweth the hearts, bare them witness, giving them the Holy Ghost, even as he did unto us."
So Peter gave instructions, and they were all baptized in the name (that is, by the authority) of the Lord (Jesus Christ, as is stated in many ancient manuscripts). The authority of Jesus, of course, points back to the command in Matthew 28:19.
This baptism was a public declaration of their faith, a witness to the faith they already had, a witness to the faith that had already brought cleansing to their hearts (15:9).
After being baptized in water, the people asked Peter to remain with them a few days. Undoubtedly, they wanted more instruction in the truths of the gospel and desired to share spiritual fellowship with him, just as the 3,000 who were saved, baptized in water, and filled with the Spirit on the Day of Pentecost wanted to continue in the teaching and fellowship of the apostles (2:42).

## Chapter 11

**1. And the apostles and brethren that were in Judaea heard that the Gentiles had also received the Word of God:**...brothers who lived in, —MLNT...who were resident in Judea, —FNTN...that even the heathen had welcomed God's Message, —TCNT...The non-Jewish people, too, have accepted God's Word, —BECK...and brothers all over, —KLST...had news that, —BB...heard that the heathen had also accepted, —GDSP...also had received the Gospel, —NOLI...were told how the word of God had been given to the Gentiles, —KNOX.

**11:1.** Peter was right in believing he would need witnesses with him when he returned to Jerusalem. He also found it necessary to explain everything that happened in Caesarea. The fact that Luke records this, repeating much of what was said in chapter 10, shows how important these events were. From them the Church learned that God would accept the Gentiles without circumcision and without their keeping the forms of the Law, that is, without their becoming Jews. Christianity was not something added to or tacked on to Judaism. Gentiles could come to God directly under the new covenant without coming first under the old covenant.
It was striking news that the Gentiles at the house of Cornelius had received (welcomed) the Word of God willingly, acknowledged its truth, and accepted its full message of repentance, forgiveness, and salvation. But to some of the Jewish believers in Jerusalem this was not good news. Such news, especially when it is considered bad news, travels fast. It reached the apostles and the rest of the believers in Jerusalem before Peter returned.

**2. And when Peter was come up to Jerusalem:**...went up, —TCNT...returned to, —GDSP, —WEYM...came up, —KNOX, —TNT...had come up to, —LAMS...So when Peter next visited Jerusalem, —PHLP.
**they that were of the circumcision:**...those converts who held to circumcision, —TCNT...the party of circumcision, —WEYM...those insisting on circumcision, —BRKL...those who still held to the need of circumcision, —NORL...in favor of circumcising Gentiles, —TEV.
**contended with him:**...began to find fault with him, —RTHM...began attacking him, —TCNT...disputed with him, —MNTG...began to bring charges against him, —WLMS...criticized him, —RSV...were full of criticism, —PHLP.

**11:2.** When Peter arrived, "they of the circumcision" (which included all the believers in Jerusalem, for they were all Jews or proselytes) were ready for him. Immediately they "contended with him," criticizing him severely.

3. **Saying, Thou wentest in to men uncircumcised, and didst eat with them:** ... You went into the houses ... and you ate with them, —WEYM.

**11:3.** The believers in Jerusalem were quick to take issue with Peter for entering the house of uncircumcised men (which they considered defiling). Even worse, Peter had gone so far as to eat nonkosher food with them.

These believers were so greatly upset that they did not use the usual word for "uncircumcised." Instead, they used a slang word for *foreskin* that was a scornful expression and very derogatory toward the Gentiles.

It is quite probable also that another reason they were upset was because they were afraid Peter's action in bringing Gentiles into the Church might turn the unconverted Jews against them. This would bring an end to the period of peace and quiet they had been enjoying since Saul had ceased his persecution.

4. **But Peter rehearsed the matter from the beginning, and expounded it by order unto them, saying:** ... But Peter expounded the matter by order unto them from the beginning, saying, —ALFD ... So Peter began, and explained the facts to them as they had occurred, —TCNT ... and gave them an orderly account, ABUV ... Peter, however, explained the whole matter to them from the beginning, —WEYM ... gave them the details, —JB ... in consecutive order, —NORL ... to them point by point, —BECK ... to explain how the situation had actually arisen, —PHLP ... precisely as it had happened, —NIV.

**11:4.** Peter understood how they felt, for he had felt the same way. So he did not rebuke them or pass judgment on them the way they were passing judgment on him. Neither did he take a superior attitude. Even as an apostle, he was a member of the Body, subject to submitting himself to their judgment if that judgment came from the guidance of the Spirit and the Word.

5. **I was in the city of Joppa praying:** ... as I was praying, —JB ... I was praying in the town of Joppa, —GDSP ... in prayer, —WLMS.
**and in a trance I saw a vision:** ... and while in a trance, —TCNT ... and while completely unconscious of my surroundings, —PHLP.
**A certain vessel descend, as it had been a great sheet, let down from heaven by four corners:** ... something like a big sheet being let down, —JB ... something coming down ... from heaven, —TEV.

**and it came even to me:** ... a sort of vessel, —NOYS ... and it came right down to me, —TCNT ... and it came close to me, —WEYM.

**11:5.** Beginning then with Joppa, Peter told the believers how he was praying. Then he had seen, not in a trance in the modern sense of the word but in astonishment, a vision of a certain object coming down out of heaven. It was like a very large sheet. Chapter 10 states the sheet was let down to the earth. Peter here said it came "to where I was." Thus Peter recognized the vision was specifically for him, and since it came down from heaven, God had a lesson in it for him. Even though the vision was symbolic, there was something very personal in the way it was presented to Peter. The Jerusalem Jews were concerned over Peter because they thought what he had done was wrong. Peter wanted them to see that God was concerned over him for a different reason.

In all of this Peter was asking the believers to identify with him, to try to understand why he had done this thing that had caused them to censure him. Believers would not be so critical if they could see things as others see them, especially when God has been dealing with them.

6. **Upon the which when I had fastened mine eyes:** ... into which steadfastly looking, —RTHM ... Looking closely at it, —TCNT ... On which looking intently, ABUV ... I examined it carefully, —MNTG.
**I considered, and saw:** ... I began to observe, and saw, —RTHM ... I examined it closely, and saw, —WEYM ... and when I looked at it closely, —PHLP ... considered it attentively, —WUST ... Looking in, I fixed my eyes, —KJII ... I saw there were in it, —LAMS.
**fourfooted beasts of the earth, and wild beasts, and creeping things, and fowls of the air:** ... all sorts of, —BB ... quadrupeds, wild beasts, reptiles, and birds, —TCNT ... animals and beasts of prey, —RSV ... and the wild birds, —MOFT ... of the sky, —KJII.

**11:6.** Peter added that the sheet not only came down to him, but came so close he was able to fasten his eyes on it, looking closely and inspecting the contents without any possibility of being mistaken. What he had observed so carefully and contemplated were quadrupeds of the earth, wild animals, reptiles (specially snakes), and birds of the air. As before, the implication is that none of these were domestic animals or clean animals the Law allowed to be used for food or sacrifice. Some of them, it is also implied, were dangerous animals. It was not something any of these believers or any ordinary Jew would like to confront.

**7. And I heard a voice saying unto me:** ... And I heard also a voice, —ASV.

**Arise, Peter; slay and eat:** ... Simon, arise, —LAMS ... Get up, Peter! Kill something and eat it! —GDSP ... sacrifice and eat! —FNTN ... take them for food, —BB.

**11:7.** Peter then told how he heard a voice telling him to get up (implying going into action), kill, and eat. This was not a mere suggestion. The words were imperative commands, commands given with his name attached. There was no way he could avoid them or shift the responsibility to someone else. The commands left him no alternative.

**8. But I said, Not so, Lord:** ... On no account, Lord, I replied, —WEYM ... It cannot be, Lord, —KNOX ... By no means, Sir, —FNTN ... Never, Sir! —GDSP ... No, Lord, —KJII.

**for nothing common or unclean hath at any time entered into my mouth:** ... because that which is unhallowed or unclean, never yet did it enter my mouth, —WUST ... I have never eaten anything that is unholy, —EVRD ... for never has anything defiled, —LAMS ... nothing that was not ceremonially cleansed, —GDSP ... has ever passed my lips, —PHLP.

**11:8.** Then Peter told of his refusal to obey, using in his reply a strong word meaning "certainly not!" or, as modern language might put it, he gave the Lord a flat "No!" Never would he do such a thing, for nothing common (profane, unsanctified, dirty) or unclean (ceremonially unclean, nonkosher) had ever entered his mouth. Peter wanted these Jerusalem saints to know he had reacted as strongly as any of them would have.

**9. But the voice answered me again from heaven, What God hath cleansed, that call not thou common:** ... And a second utterance came from, —KNOX ... spoke a second time, —PHLP ... the voice from heaven answered again, —EVRD ... hath purified, —LIVB ... has made clean do not you make, —WMCK ... you do not make common, —KJII ... do not call unclean, —LAMS.

**11:9.** The same voice came to Peter again and gave him the answer that what God had cleansed he was not to call common or unclean.

Most of the commands in the Old Testament that have reference to cleansing are commands for the people to cleanse various things or to cleanse themselves. But David in Psalm 19:12 cried to God to cleanse him from secret faults (things hidden from him, things David was not conscious of). God also prophesied in Joel 3:20, 21 concerning Judah and Jerusalem that He would cleanse their blood that He had not (previously) cleansed. But none of this applied to Gentiles. The idea that God would cleanse Gentiles without making them Jews had not occurred to these Jewish believers.

They did know that Gentiles could be saved and enjoy the blessings of God. All through the Old Testament the door was always open. Moses invited his brother-in-law, a Gentile (a Midianite) to come with Israel, indicating he could share the good things God had promised for Israel if he would become one of them (Numbers 10:29). Rahab the Canaanitess, and Ruth the Moabitess, also put their faith in God, and each found an important place in Israel and even became ancestresses of David and of Christ. But all these Gentiles became Jews in their faith.

**10. And this was done three times:** ... This happened, in all, three times, —TCNT ... This occurred, —FNTN.

**and all were drawn up again into heaven:** ... when everything was drawn up again into the sky, —TCNT ... Then the whole thing was taken back, —EVRD ... then everything was lifted up into heaven, —LAMS ... it was all drawn back again into the sky, —GDSP.

**11:10.** Peter told his listeners the vision was repeated three times so they would know he had not been carried away by a vision or interpretation that could have been his own imagination. The threefold repetition shows that the vision was not to be ignored. Peter had not arbitrarily changed his mind about the Gentiles. God had changed it for him. God had also made it clear that He was able to cleanse Gentiles. These wild animals and birds still looked outwardly like the same animals and birds they were. But God had cleansed them. So these Gentiles still dressed as Romans and ate the same nonkosher food they were in the habit of eating. But God was not only able to cleanse them, He had done so.

**11. And, behold, immediately there were three men already come unto the house where I was, sent from Caesarea unto me:** ... The extraordinary thing is ... sent to me personally, —PHLP ... And at that minute, —BB ... just at that moment, —GDSP ... And in that very hour ... sent to me by Cornelius from Caesarea, —LAMS ... And at that very moment, —WMCK ... three men stood before the house in which we were, having been sent, —ASV ... three men, who had been sent from Caesarea to find me, —GDSP ... appeared at the door, —KNOX ... approached the house where we were, —FNTN ... stood at the house ... having been sent, —KJII.

**11:11.** Peter next told how God had not left him in doubt about the interpretation of the vision. To his surprise, immediately three men were standing by the house where Peter was (or, approaching the house), men sent from Caesarea to Peter (sent with a message, sent with a purpose or a commission). The choice of the verb for "sent" is significant here. It is the same verb used of God's sending Jesus and of Jesus' sending out the apostles. They did not just happen to be there. They were there because of God's divine purpose and because of God's perfect timing.

**12. And the spirit bade me go with them:** ... The Spirit told me to go with them, —*TCNT* ... then instructed me, —*FNTN* ... gave me orders to go, —*BB* ... said for me to go, —*KJII* ... to accompany them, —*KLST.*

**nothing doubting:** ... making no distinction, —*RSV* ... without hesitation, —*TCNT, —WMCK* ... without the least hesitation, —*FNTN* ... without any misgivings, —*WEYM* ... without any scruple, —*CMPB* ... doubting nothing, —*LAMS.*

**Moreover these six brethren accompanied me:** ... these six brethren who are now present, —*WEYM* ... These ... brothers here, —*GDSP* ... six of these brothers went with me, —*KJII.*

**and we entered into the man's house:** ... and together we entered, —*KNOX* ... the house of the man, —*KJII.*

**11:12.** The Holy Spirit then told Peter to go along with these men, that is, they were to go together. Peter was not to go alone, he was not to follow them at a distance, but he was to accompany them, giving them his fellowship as they traveled along. Again, he was to go with them without doubting, without wavering, without hesitation, without being at odds with himself. The Greek may also indicate he was not to take issue or dispute with them, neither was he to pass judgment on them, or separate himself from them as if he were superior in any way. He was to go along simply as a humble servant of the Lord, identifying with them.

Peter was also careful to refer to the six brethren (that is, believers) whom he took along as witnesses and who went in with him when he came to the house of this (uncircumcised) man.

Peter did not tell anything about who Cornelius was or his high position as an officer in the Roman army. He said nothing about all of Cornelius' good works and charitable deeds. He drew no attention to his good reputation or the way he was highly regarded all through the land by the Jews. In fact, he did not even mention the name of Cornelius. Peter knew that none of this would outweigh the fact that Cornelius was uncircumcised, a Gentile, an alien excluded from the commonwealth (citizenship) of Israel. He was a foreigner separated from the covenants of promise, and in their eyes outside of Christ, without hope unless he became a Jew, and therefore without God in the world. (See Ephesians 2:12.)

**13. And he shewed us how he had seen an angel in his house, which stood and said unto him:** ... and he related to us, —*LAMS, —RTHM* ... Then he described to us, —*WEYM* ... he gave us an account of how, —*BB* ... he saw the angel standing in his house, —*KJII.*

**Send men to Joppa, and call for Simon, whose surname is Peter:** ... Send to the city of Joppa and bring, —*LAMS* ... and bring, —*MLNT* ... and bid Simon, —*KNOX* ... and fetch, —*FNTN* ... whose last name is, —*KJII.*

**11:13.** As a further proof of God's leading, Peter told how Cornelius reported to Peter and the six witnesses that he had seen an angel in his house who appeared and took his stand firmly so that there could be no question about the objective reality of his presence there. The call to send for Peter thus came from an angelic messenger from heaven, a messenger from God, who gave specific directions. Cornelius did not get the idea to send for Peter from his own reasoning or imagination.

**14. Who shall tell thee words, whereby thou and all thy house shall be saved:** ... He will teach you truths by which you and all your household will be saved, —*WEYM* ... will speak words to you, —*KJII* ... he shall speak to you words by which you and all of your household, —*LAMS* ... He will tell you how you can be saved; yes, you and your whole household, —*NORL* ... who will explain to you the means by which you, as well as all your family may be saved! —*FNTN* ... The things he will say will save you, —*EVRD.*

**11:14.** The angel further stated that Peter would speak words (Greek, *rhēmata*) to Cornelius by which Cornelius and all his house would be saved. "House" here means household and normally included the family plus the extended family and the servants or slaves. Peter gave further details which show the angel encouraged Cornelius to bring in his family and friends to hear Peter, for his words were to be the means by which the entire household would be saved.

The expression "words whereby thou and all thy house shall be saved" shows the gospel, the good news about Jesus Christ and His atoning work, is the only message whereby men must be saved (cf. 4:12). This message must never be changed or corrupted (cf. Galatians 1:6-9). It is now the written Word of God.

**15. And as I began to speak:** ... I had just begun to speak, —*TCNT* ... No sooner had I begun to speak than, —*WEYM* ... But in the beginning of my speech, —*BRKL* ... at the beginning of my message, —*MLNT* ... when I had set about speaking to them, —*KNOX* ... When I began my speech, —*EVRD* ... While I was beginning to tell them, —*PHLP.*

**the Holy Ghost fell on them, as on us at the beginning:** ... descended upon them, —*KLST* ... just as He fell upon us at the first, *—WEYM*...in the same way as upon us, *—FNTN*...fell on them, exactly as it did on us, *—TCNT*...even as on us, *—KJII*...as He originally came on us, *—BECK*...on them as also on us, *—SAWR*...just as upon us also originally, *—RTHM*.

**11:15.** Peter knew he could have gone on for hours explaining the gospel and telling more about Jesus. So he told the Jerusalem believers that it was at the beginning of his speaking that the Holy Spirit fell on Cornelius and his household.

Actually, these believers in Jerusalem did not need to hear a summary of Peter's sermon, for they knew the facts of the gospel very well. Nor did Peter want to draw attention to what he preached or how well he preached. The thing that counted, the thing that was important, was what the Holy Spirit did. The fact that the Holy Spirit fell on Cornelius and the other Gentiles gathered in his home was enough to let the Jerusalem believers know that these Gentiles had heard and believed the gospel and that their faith was in Jesus.

By the words "the beginning" Peter meant the Day of Pentecost when the Holy Spirit was first given. Now the Spirit had been poured out upon the Gentile believers just as He was on Jewish believers. This was important not only as a personal experience for Cornelius and his friends, but it also served as a manifestation and divine testimony that the whole New Testament Church, Gentiles as well as Jews, were baptized by one Spirit into one Body. (Cf. 1 Corinthians 12:12f.)

**16. Then remembered I the word of the Lord, how that he said:**...Then I remembered the Lord's words, *—WEYM*...Then I was reminded of what, *—KNOX*...the declaration of, *—FNTN*...the saying of the Lord, *—GDSP, —MOFT*...came into my mind, *—BB*...so I was mindful of the Lord's message, *—MLNT*...the words of our Lord, *—PHLP*.

**John indeed baptized with water; but ye shall be baptized with the Holy Ghost:**...John's baptism was with water, *—KNOX*.

**11:16.** Peter next added something that had gone on in his own mind. He remembered the word of the Lord (Jesus) given in 1:5, that John baptized in water but they would be baptized in the Holy Spirit. ("In water" and "in the Holy Spirit" are the proper translations here.)

Peter recognized that the gift of the Spirit had been given. The new dispensation, the age of the Spirit prophesied in the Old Testament and promised by Christ, was for all people regardless of race or national origin. Peter had seen it happen to the Jews on the Day of Pentecost (chapter 2), to the Samaritans (chapter 8), and now to the Gentiles in the house of Cornelius (chapter 11).

**17. Forasmuch then as God gave them the like gift as he did unto us:**...If then, *—RSV*...God had given them the very same gift, *—TCNT*...exactly the same gift, *—MOFT*...gives them the equal gratuity, *—CNDT*...the identical thing, *—JB*...equally to them, *—SAWR*.

**who believed on the Lord Jesus Christ:**...after believing, *—NOYS*.

**what was I, that I could withstand God?:**...who was I that I should be able to thwart God, *—TCNT*...could I stop God? *—BECK*...to obstruct God? *—CMPB*...I could hinder God? *—HBIE*...to stand in God's way? *—JB*...be able to interfere, *—CNFT*.

**11:17.** Peter then went on to say that God had given these Gentiles the like gift as He had given to the Jewish believers. *Like* in the Greek means "equal" or "identical." (The masculine form of the same word is *isos*, and is found in the word *isosceles,* a triangle where two sides are equal, that is, identical.)

The barriers which had been established in the Law were now, and for all time, being broken down. In the plan of God, these "barriers" had served their purpose. Initially they were designed in order to set apart God's people from the idolatrous nations surrounding them. They were to protect Israel from the corrupting elements of heathen religions practiced by their neighbors. But now, God was doing a new thing. His Spirit was being poured out upon the Gentiles. Not even the Jewish converts who still held to a great many of their fathers' traditions (traditions that went beyond the Law and created a barrier God had never intended) doubted that God was at work here.

For Peter to refuse to accept these Gentiles to whom God had given this gift of the Spirit would have been to withstand God, and who was he—who is any man—to do that!

**18. When they heard these things:**...On hearing this statement, *—TCNT*...On hearing this, *—WEYM*.

**they held their peace:**...they ceased to object, *—TCNT*...they were silenced, *—RSV*...they quieted down, *—BRKL*...they were satisfied, *—NORL*...they stopped arguing, *—SEB*...This account satisfied them, *—JB*...they had no further objections, *—NIV*.

**and glorified God, saying:**...and broke out into praise of God, *—TCNT*...and they extolled the goodness of God, *—WEYM*...but gave God the glory, *—WLMS*.

**Then hath God also to the Gentiles granted repentance unto life:**...So even to the heathen...the repentance which leads to Life! *—TCNT*...also to the non-Jewish people so that they will live, *—BECK*...the opportunity to repent and live! *—TEV*...resulting in life, *—WUST*...God gives life...through repentance! *—NORL*...conversion into life, *—FNTN*...has actually allowed the Gentiles to repent and live! *—MOFT*.

**11:18.** The same thing that convinced Peter convinced the believers in Jerusalem. They could not withstand God either. The facts of the the case silenced all their previous objections. They were responsive enough to the Holy Spirit and to the Word of God to glorify God and to recognize that God had given the Gentiles repentance unto life. God had accepted their repentance and given them spiritual life.

**19. Now they which were scattered abroad upon the persecution that arose about Stephen:** . . . the fugitives, *—WLMS* . . . by reason of the tribulation that took place on account of Stephen, *—RTHM* . . . dispersed by the distress, *—FNTN.*

**travelled as far as Phenice, and Cyprus, and Antioch:** . . . made their way to Phoenicia, *—WEYM* . . . went all the way to, *—GDSP* . . . even to the land of, *—LAMS* . . . traversed as far as, *—FNTN.*

**preaching the word to none but unto the Jews only:** . . . telling the Messagebut only to Jews, *—TCNT* . . . they told the message to none but, *—GDSP* . . . giving the message as they went, *—PHLP* . . . speaking the message to nobody but, *—KLST* . . . to none except, *—MLNT* . . . except to Jews only, *—KJII.*

**11:19.** Though the Jerusalem apostles and believers accepted the fact that Gentiles in Caesarea were saved and had become part of the Church, it did not excite them very much. There was no rush to go out and win more Gentiles to the Lord. Even Peter continued to consider his ministry as primarily to the "circumcision" (to the Jews) and kept ministering on most occasions to Jews only (Galatians 2:7-9). Thus, Luke turned his attention at this point to a new center for the spread of the gospel, Antioch of Syria, located on the Orontes River, over 300 miles north of Jerusalem. It was a great trade center, the largest city in Asia Minor, and the capital of the Roman province of Syria.

This verse makes a connection with 8:1, 4. (See also 9:31.) Up to this point the examples of what happened in the spread of the gospel were taken from Judea and Samaria. But the wave of itinerant evangelism did not stop there. Luke did not try to cover everything that was happening everywhere. Instead, following the inspiration of the Holy Spirit, he selected one direction this evangelism took and presented it as an example of what was going on in many different localities. There was a special reason for choosing the direction toward Antioch, however, because it formed a link with the apostle Paul and was a preparation for the account of his journeys.

Even outside of Palestine, however, those who spread the gospel preached the Word only to Jews. This may not have been entirely due to prejudice. The Jews had the Old Testament Scriptures and knew the prophecies, which was a great advantage in dealing with them (Romans 3:1, 2). These traveling evangelists based their message on the fact that God, through Jesus as the Messiah, had fulfilled prophecy. Most Gentiles had no background to understand this. But these evangelists were overlooking the fact that many Gentiles had lost their confidence in their idols and were looking for something better.

The Book of Acts mentions certain evangelizers who traveled up the coast of Asia Minor as far as Phenice (Phoenicia) where churches were established in Tyre and Sidon (as 21:3-4 and 27:3 show). From there some went to the island of Cyprus and then to Antioch of Syria.

**20. And some of them were men of Cyprus and Cyrene:** . . . But there were some of them, *—FNTN* . . . However, among their number were natives of, *—PHLP* . . . certain ones of them were men of, *—KJII* . . . there were some men among them, *—LAMS.*

**which, when they were come to Antioch:** . . . and these men, on their arrival at, *—PHLP* . . . who, on coming to Antioch, *—WEYM* . . . who on reaching Antioch, *—MOFT* . . . who arrived at, *—MLNT* . . . these men entered into, *—LAMS.*

**spake unto the Grecians:** . . . proclaimed their message to, *—PHLP* . . . began to speak to the Greeks too, *—WLMS* . . . spoke to heathen men as well, *—WMCK* . . . to the Gentiles also, *—TNT* . . . to the Greek-speaking Jews, *—KJII.*

**preaching the Lord Jesus:** . . . announcing the glad-tidings as to the Lord Jesus, *—RTHM* . . . publishing the good news of the Lord, Jesus, *ABUV* . . . and preached concerning our, *—LAMS* . . . the gospel of, *—KJII* . . . good news about, *—MLNT.*

**11:20.** Some of those who went on to Antioch were men of Cyprus, an island off the coast of Asia Minor over 200 miles northwest of Jerusalem. With them were men of Cyrene, a beautiful city founded by Greek colonists in North Africa nearly 800 miles west of Jerusalem.

These men may have been among the 3,000 who were saved and filled with the Spirit on the Day of Pentecost. Now, at Antioch, they began to speak to Greek-speaking Gentiles, telling them the good news (the gospel) of the Lord Jesus.

**21. And the hand of the Lord was with them:** . . . The Lord's power was with them, *—TCNT, —TNT* . . . The Lord's hand, *—GDSP* . . . went with them, *—KNOX* . . . The Lord blessed their efforts, *—KLST.*

**and a great number believed, and turned unto the Lord:** . . . and there were a vast number who believed, *—WEYM* . . . and a great number had faith, *—BB* . . . and there were a great many, *—GDSP* . . . and very many turned to the Lord, believing, *—KJII* . . . became believers, *—TNT.*

**11:21.** When these men of Cyprus and Cyrene took the first step to tell Gentiles about Jesus, the hand of the Lord was with them. This expression, "the hand of the Lord," was used frequently in the Old Testament of the mighty manifestations of the power of God in behalf of His people. Now God was showing the same mighty hand to bring Gentiles out of the bondage of sin.

The same expression was also used in parallel to the Spirit of the Lord (as in Ezekiel 1:3; 3:14, 22, 24; 8:1; 11:1). It is likely therefore that the miracle-working power of the Lord was manifest, confirming the Word just as was the case with Philip in Samaria (8:5-8). As a result a great number believed and turned to the Lord. They turned away from their heathen customs and worldly ways to follow Jesus and joined the company of those whom the Bible calls saints. As Peter declared, God is not a respecter of persons, He does not show partiality but makes His good gifts available to all.

**22. Then tidings of these things came unto the ears of the church which was in Jerusalem:**... And the report concerning them, −ASV...The news about them reached, −TCNT...When word of it came to the attention of, −BRKL.

**and they sent forth Barnabas, that he should go as far as Antioch:**... and they despatched Barnabas to Antioch, −MOFT... And they commissioned Barnabas, −FNTN.

**11:22.** When news of the conversion of these Gentiles in Antioch reached the Jerusalem church, they recognized that this great spread of the gospel among Gentiles was an important new development. Antioch itself was significant, since it was the third most important city in the entire Roman Empire, exceeded only by Rome and Alexandria. So they sent Barnabas to go as far as Antioch (probably ministering along the way).

The choice of Barnabas is important. It shows that the Jerusalem church (not just the apostles) was concerned about this new assembly in Antioch and sent out their best encourager to help the believers.

Some writers have assumed that sending Barnabas meant the Church in Jerusalem wanted to maintain control over this new development. However, there is no evidence of this. It was brotherly love and concern, the same loving spirit that sent Peter and John to Samaria to help the people there moved the Jerusalem believers also. Barnabas did not have to report back to Jerusalem, nor did he have to seek their advice about further steps in ministry that might be necessary. (See verse 25.)

**23. Who, when he came, and had seen the grace of God, was glad:**...On arriving he was delighted to see the grace of God, −WEYM...the favor God had shown them, he was delighted, −GDSP...how gracious God had been to them, he rejoiced, −NORL...and saw the effects of God's grace, −KLST...he was delighted to see what God's love had done, −BECK.

**and exhorted them all, that with purpose of heart they would cleave unto the Lord:**...and encouraged them all to make up their minds to be faithful to the Master, −TCNT...and he encouraged them all to remain, with fixed resolve, faithful to the Lord, −WEYM...to continue to be devoted to the Lord, −WLMS...and he made clear to them the need of keeping near the Lord with all the strength of their hearts, −BB...with a firm purpose, −KLGS...He urged them all to be resolute, −PHLP.

**11:23.** At Antioch the sight of the manifest grace (unmerited favor) of God made Barnabas rejoice. He accepted these Gentiles just as Peter had accepted the believers at the house of Cornelius. He then lived up to his name by exhorting (and encouraging) them all to purpose openly from their hearts to abide in (or continue with) the Lord. Barnabas knew that difficulties, persecutions, and temptations lay ahead. Persistence in a close walk with the Lord would be needed.

**24. For he was a good man, and full of the Holy Ghost and of faith:**... for he was a genial man, −FNTN...a splendid man, −BRKL.

**and much people was added unto the Lord:**... and the number of believers in the Lord greatly increased, −WEYM... Considerable numbers of people were brought in for the Lord, −MOFT...So a large number of people were united to the Lord, −WLMS... A great multitude was won over to the Lord, −KLST.

**11:24.** Because Barnabas was a good man and full of the Holy Spirit and faith, a considerable crowd of people were added to the Lord, that is, to the body of Christ, the Church, by entering into a personal relationship and walk with the Lord. His life, not simply his preaching and teaching, proved to be a most effective witness. No doubt his "goodness" meant he was entirely free from Pharisaic judgment. (See Luke 18:11.)

**25. Then departed Barnabas to Tarsus, for to seek Saul:**...Afterwards Barnabas left for Tarsus to look for Saul, −TCNT...He then proceeded to Tarsus, to search for, −FNTN.

**11:25.** The growth in numbers made Barnabas realize he needed help. He did not, however, seek assistance from those in Jerusalem; he did not ask them to send someone. Instead he went to Tarsus to search for Saul. Since he was the one who took the time and effort to find out about Saul and introduce him to the apostles in Jerusalem earlier (9:27), he obviously knew what God had said about sending Saul to the Gentiles. (See 22:21.) Now it was God's time for Saul to begin this ministry. (Some suggest that Saul had been disinherited by friends and family because of his faith in Christ [cf. Philippians 3:8], and that he had already begun his work of evangelizing Gentiles in his native province of Cilicia.)

**26. And when he had found him, he brought him unto Antioch:** . . . and when he had come across him, —BB.

**And it came to pass, that a whole year they assembled themselves with the church:** . . . it came about that they were working together in that assembly, —FNTN . . . they were gathered together with the church, —ASV . . . For a whole year after this they were made welcome, —KNOX . . . where for an entire year they conducted church meetings, —BRKL . . . they took part in the meetings of the congregation, —KLST.

**and taught much people:** . . . and taught a large number of people, —TCNT . . . and teach a considerable throng, —CNDT . . . a great multitude, —KLST.

**And the disciples were called Christians first in Antioch:** . . . the disciples, too, at Antioch first called themselves, —FNTN . . . and it was in Antioch that the disciples first got the name of 'Christians,' —TCNT . . . the followers were called . . . for the first time, —EVRD . . . are styled, —CNDT . . . also were divinely called first, —YNG . . . called themselves, —FNTN.

**11:26.** The search for Saul probably took some time. When Barnabas found him, he brought him back to Antioch. The two of them then became the chief teachers of the Church, gathering the believers together and teaching a considerable crowd.

Obviously, these Gentile believers could not be given a Jewish name, nor could they any longer be considered a sect of the Jews. They needed a new name. Soldiers under particular generals in the Roman army often took the name of their general and added "ian" (Latin, *iani*; Greek, *ianos*) to indicate they were soldiers and followers of that general. For example, Caesar's soldiers were called *Caesariani*, and Pompey's soldiers were called *Pompeiani*. Political parties were also designated by the same sort of suffix.

So the people of Antioch began to call the believers *Christiani* or *Christians*, soldiers, followers, partisans of Christ. Some believe the name was first given in derision, but there is no great evidence of this. The believers did not reject the name. They were indeed in the Lord's army, clothed with the full armor of God. (See Ephesians 6:11-18.)

**27. And in those days came prophets from Jerusalem unto Antioch:** . . . some preachers came down, —FNTN.

**11:27.** The various assemblies of believers in different places continued to keep in touch with each other. After Barnabas, others came from Jerusalem to help and encourage the believers in Antioch. About the time Saul's first year in Antioch was up, several prophets from Jerusalem came. These men were regularly used by the Holy Spirit in the ministry of the gift of prophecy for edification (to build up spiritually and confirm faith), exhortation (to awaken, encourage, and challenge every believer to move ahead in faithfulness and love), and comfort (to cheer, revive, and encourage faith and expectation), as in 1 Corinthians 14:3. Thus they met the spiritual needs of the believers.

**28. And there stood up one of them named Agabus:** . . . came forward, —TCNT . . . rising, —CNDT . . . having stood up, —YNG . . . said publicly, —BB.

**and signified by the Spirit that there should be great dearth throughout all the world:** . . . explained by the Spirit, —KLGS . . . and spoke with the help of . . . A very hard time is coming, —EVRD . . . announced, through the influence . . . that a severe famine would come over all the empire, —FNTN . . . and revealed through the Spirit, —KLST . . . and, under the influence of the Spirit foretold, —TCNT . . . publicly predicted by the Spirit the speedy coming of a great famine, —WEYM . . . under inspiration of the Spirit, —NORL . . . being instructed, —MNTG . . . there would be serious need of food all over the earth, —BB . . . over all the inhabited earth, —HBIE.

**which came to pass in the days of Claudius Caesar:** . . . This actually happened, —PHLP . . . which, indeed, did occur under, —FNTN . . . This happened in the time of, —TNT . . . a famine which actually occurred in the reign of Claudius, —TCNT . . . as it did in the reign of, —KNOX.

**11:28.** Sometimes the Holy Spirit used these New Testament prophets to reinforce their exhortations with a foretelling of the future. This was the exception rather than the rule, however. Prophecy in the Bible is always primarily "forthtelling" (speaking for God whatever His message may be) rather than foretelling the future. God has always been more interested in helping people to walk with Him in the now than He ever is in giving all the details some would like to know about the future (though He has revealed in His Word that He has a glorious future waiting for believers).

On this occasion Agabus, one of the prophets, stood up and indicated by a word from the Spirit that a great famine was about to come over the whole world (Greek, *oikoumenēn*, "inhabited earth"). To them this meant the Roman Empire, for they used the Greek word in those days to mean the Roman world. The Romans did not think anything outside their empire was worth noticing. The famine did take place in the days of Claudius Caesar who reigned from A.D. 41-54. Two Roman historians, Tacitus and Suetonius, have recorded that during this period there were several localized famines or "dearths." This serves as further evidence that Luke was quite a careful historian himself. Even the small details of his accounts are accurate and verifiable through secular sources. This helps to support the reliability of the Bible. (The date of the arrival of Barnabas in Antioch was about A.D. 41, so Claudius was already on the throne.)

**29. Then the disciples, every man according to his ability:** ... So the disciples, without exception ... in proportion to their means, —TCNT ... The disciples resolved, each according to his means, —TNT ... put aside money, every one in proportion to his means, —WEYM ... to their individual ability, —FNTN ... as each of them was able to afford it, —MOFT ... as much as he could, —EVRD ... what each man could afford, —WMCK

**determined to send relief unto the brethren which dwelt in Judaea:** ... planned to send them, —EVRD ... to send something to help the Brethren living in Judaea, —TCNT ... made a decision to send help to, —BB ... for the relief of the brethren living in Judaea, —WEYM.

**11:29.** It is wonderful to see the quick response of God's people to a need presented by the moving of the Spirit. Their faith was not dead. (See James 2:14-17.) Furthermore, the disciples in Antioch felt genuine gratitude for the blessings and teaching brought them from Judea.

Church history shows that Gentiles pronounced *Christiani* the same as *Chrestiani*, "followers of Chrestos," which means good, kind, lovingly benevolent, useful, and generous. But it was more than this that made the Gentiles view believers like these as good followers of the Good. They showed their love in practical ways.

They were not illogical in their giving, however. They did not give beyond their means. Each one gave what he could, based on the financial ability the Lord had given him. The believers in Antioch were going to suffer from the famine too. But they knew the Jerusalem believers had already sacrificed their property and possessions for the benefit of the poor and the widows.

**30. Which also they did, and sent it to the elders by the hands of Barnabas and Saul:** ... sent it to the Officers of the Church, —TCNT ... sending the money officially to the elders by the hand of, —WMCK ... forwarding their contribution, —WEYM ... the rulers of the church, —BB ... and in sending it to

the presbyters they entrusted it to the hands of, —KNOX ... personally through Barnabas, —PHLP.

**11:30.** When the believers in Antioch had gathered their offering together, they sent it to Jerusalem by Barnabas and Saul. The two men were sent to insure proper accounting of the funds, and the funds were turned over to the elders, the administrative officers of the Jerusalem assembly.

## Chapter 12

**1. Now about that time Herod the king:** ... It was at that time, —TCNT ... surnamed Agrippa, —LAMS.

**stretched forth his hands to vex certain of the church:** ... exerted his authority to persecute some of those who belonged to the Church, —KNOX ... put forth his hands to afflict, —ASV ... laid his hands upon certain, —ALFD ... to do them violence, —WEYM ... arrested some, —WLMS ... made cruel attacks on, —BB ... laid violent hands on some members of, —WMCK ... those connected with the assembly, —FNTN.

**12:1.** From A.D. 6 to 41 Judea was governed by procurators sent by the Roman emperor. These men were never popular. In A.D. 41 the emperor added Judea to the realm of King Herod Agrippa I, who is the King Herod of this chapter. He was a grandson of Herod the Great. Because Herod Agrippa I was a friend of the Roman emperors, Gaius made him king of part of Syria in A.D. 37. Then, in A.D. 39, he added Galilee and Peraea after exiling Herod Antipas, the Herod who killed John the Baptist.

When Herod Agrippa I became king over Judea and Jerusalem, he did everything he could to gain and hold the favor of the Jews. Unlike most of the other Herods, he practiced the forms of the Jewish religion faithfully. Apparently, he also saw and heard enough from the Jewish leaders to know of their fears and frustration with respect to the apostles and with respect to the continued spread of the Church. He undoubtedly heard also how the Sanhedrin had threatened the apostles and how the apostles continued to preach Jesus.

Somewhere in the early part of his reign over Jerusalem he took steps to show his authority. He seized some from the Church with the intention of treating them badly.

**2. And he killed James the brother of John with the sword:** ... he beheaded, —WEYM ... murdered with a sword, —WLMS.

**12:2.** Among those arrested was the apostle James, the son of Zebedee. The apostle James, his brother John, and Peter constituted the inner circle of Jesus' disciples while He ministered on earth. Luke did not give any details, but there does not seem to have been a trial. James was given no opportunity even to witness to his faith. Herod simply had him killed (murdered) with a sword (that is, decapitated).

**3. And because he saw it pleased the Jews:** ...And when he saw, −ASV...Finding that this gratified the Jews, −WEYM...was agreeable to the Jews, −WLMS ...was a pleasing thing to the Jews, −WUST.

**he proceeded further to take Peter also:** ...he went further and arrested Peter as well, −TCNT...he took a next step, −NORL...to apprehend Peter also, −NOYS...he also set about the apprehension of Peter, −FNTN.

**(Then were the days of unleavened bread.):** ...And those were the days of, −ASV...That was during the Passover days, −BRKL...the time of unfermented bread, −FNTN.

**12:3.** The murder of James pleased (was very acceptable to) the Jewish leaders and their friends. They had never forgotten how the apostles defied them. Moreover, since most of these leaders were Sadducees, they did not like the teachings of the Christians.

When Herod saw how pleased they were, he proceeded to arrest Peter, who was the most outspoken of the apostles. But this arrest took place during the 7 days of the Feast of Unleavened Bread, which was combined with Passover at this time, so that all 8 days beginning with the 14th of Nisan (March-April) were usually called Passover.

**4. And when he had apprehended him:** ...And when he had taken him, −ASV...After seizing Peter, −TCNT...He had him arrested, −WEYM.

**he put him in prison:** . . . and put in jail, −GDSP...was kept in jail, −SEB.

**and delivered him to four quaternions of soldiers to keep him:** ... and entrusted him to the keeping of four Guards of four soldiers each, −TCNT ... handing him over to the care of sixteen soldiers, −WEYM ...four detachments, with four in each detachment, −NORL...four files of soldiers to be kept, −DOUY...to guard him constantly, −WUST.

**intending after Easter to bring him forth to the people:** ...to put him on trial in public, −TEV.

**12:4.** For some reason Herod decided to wait until after Passover before bringing Peter out before the people so they would be able to witness his execution.

*Passover* here means the whole Passover season. The King James Version translates *Passover* (Aramaic, *Pascha*) as "Easter." (The Romance languages still use derivatives of *Pascha* as a name for Easter.) But Passover is clearly meant here.

Herod probably wanted to show how strict he was in keeping the Passover season. He may also have wanted to wait until he could get the whole

attention of the people for the display he intended to put on. Whatever the reason, Herod put Peter in prison with a heavy guard of four squads of four soldiers each. Herod had heard how apostles had escaped from prison before.

**5. Peter therefore was kept in prison:** ...So Peter was closely guarded in prison, −MOFT...confined in prison, −FNTN...and well guarded, −NORL.

**but prayer was made without ceasing of the church unto God for him:** ...were being earnestly offered to God on his behalf, −TCNT...fervent prayer was offered, −WEYM...was persistently made by the church, −WLMS ...the congregation was constantly praying, −SEB...for him unremittingly, −JB...all the time, −KLGS.

**12:5.** The prison where Peter was kept was probably in the Tower of Antonia at the northwest corner of the temple area. The soldiers probably guarded him in 6-hour shifts. He would be chained to two of them, and the other two would guard the door.

In the meantime, prayer was being made to God continuously and very earnestly on Peter's behalf. The believers must have been overwhelmed by the suddenness and vigor of this new persecution. There was no way they could free Peter, and in the natural the situation seemed hopeless. But they did not give up. They went to God in prayer. The Greek indicates they threw themselves into the work of intercession. This was no silent, sleepy prayer meeting. They loved Peter, and they did not spare themselves. At any hour of the day or night for the next 7 days many were crying out to God earnestly, fervently, strenuously, and continuously. They knew they were in a spiritual battle against the powers of the enemy. Unseen forces of the world, the flesh, and the devil were moving King Herod to try to put a stop to the Church. Herod, of course, was deceived. He could not alter the fact that Jesus had risen from the dead by putting a few church leaders to death.

**6. And when Herod would have brought him forth, the same night Peter was sleeping between two soldiers:** ... The very night before, −MOFT...on the very night...he was to be delivered up, −LAMS...before Herod was going to bring him up for trial, −KLST...Herod was-on-the-point, −RTHM...was about ready, −KLGS...was to try him, −JB...was about to produce him to the people, −FNTN...bring him into court, −TNT.

**bound with two chains:** ...chained with double chains, −PHLP...securely bound by two chains, −WUST.

**and the keepers before the door kept the prison:** ...and sentries, −RSV...guarding the prison, −TCNT...others were guarding the door, −LAMS...and there were warders at the door, −KNOX...and guards were on duty outside the door, −WEYM...in front of, −KJII...while guards maintained a strict watch on the doorway of the prison, −PHLP.

**12:6.** When the Passover season was finally over, Herod was ready to bring Peter out. He was sure the execution of Peter would please the strict Jews, for Peter was the one who had taken the gospel to the Gentiles at Caesarea and who was known to fraternize with them. It is implied that Herod had also given out the word that the Jews were not to rush away from Jerusalem after the Passover season. He wanted them to remain for the grand spectacle he intended to put on for them.

The night before Herod intended to bring Peter out for trial, sentencing, and execution, Peter was sleeping soundly. The Greek here is like that used in 25:26 of the apostle Paul being brought before King Agrippa. Thus it seems clear that Herod did intend to conduct a trial this time, and Peter knew it. Nevertheless, Peter did not let that trouble him. He must have been able to sleep soundly because he had committed his case to the Lord, even though he expected to face execution the next day. He was at peace. He had Christ with him and the Holy Spirit dwelling within. Death could not separate him from Christ. In fact, if he died it would only mean more of Christ. Like Paul, for him to live was Christ and to die would be gain in Christ, more of Christ (Philippians 1:21). The early believers were so full of Christ they did not fear death. Like Peter, they could face it without any signs of worry and dismay.

7. **And, behold, the angel of the Lord came upon him:** ... stood by him, −ASV... stood over, −TNT... All at once an angel, −TCNT... Suddenly an angel, −WEYM... stood by, −KJII.

**and a light shined in the prison:** ... shined in the cell, −ASV... a light shone in his cell, −WLMS... a light illumined the building, −NORL... shone in all the prison, −LAMS.

**and he smote Peter on the side, and raised him up:** ... hitting Peter ... he awakened him, −KJII... and by striking Peter on the side the angel woke him, −WLMS... then touching Peter in the side, he roused him, −BRKL... He tapped Peter on the side and woke him up, −PHLP... he pricked his side, −MRDK... slapped Peter on the side, −NORL... He poked Peter's side, −ADAM... so that he came out of his sleep, −BB.

**saying, Arise up quickly:** ... and said to him, −LAMS... saying as he did so: ... Get up quickly, −TCNT... Get up! Quick! −BECK... Rise quickly! −CNDT... Arise, instantly, −MRDK... Rise in haste, −YNG... Hurry and get up! −NORL... Get up in a hurry, −KLGS.

**And his chains fell off from his hands:** ... The chains dropped from his wrists, −TCNT... The fetters dropped, −MOFT... fell away from, −PHLP.

**12:7.** Seven days had gone by without any answer or any sign of deliverance. Yet, though God often delays His answers in order to test and develop our faith and patience, He does not delay more than is necessary. Someone has said, "The trains of divine promises arrive in the depot of history always on time."

Peter's faith, however, was in God, not merely in the idea of deliverance. He had committed his way to God (Psalm 37:5). In humility he felt he was no better than Stephen, James, and others who had died for the Lord's sake. Furthermore, he knew from the lips of Jesus himself that he would die a martyr's death (John 21:18, 19).

Thus, the sudden appearance of an angel in the middle of the night was unexpected. At the same time as the angel appeared standing by Peter, a bright light shined in the prison, possibly from the angel, or possibly as a separate manifestation so Peter could see what to do. The angel then struck him sharply on the side, aroused him, and told him to get up quickly. (The Greek verb does not necessarily mean that the angel raised him or lifted him up, but simply that he woke him up.) At the same time, the chains fell off his hands without waking up the soldiers who were guarding him.

Though Peter was willing to die for his Lord, it was not God's time, and Peter's work was not yet done. After this, Peter went to Babylon to the large Jewish community there and, some think, to Rome. The Church would not have his two epistles were it not for this deliverance, and perhaps not even the Gospel of Mark, for Mark, according to early tradition, recorded the preaching of Peter in his Gospel.

8. **And the angel said unto him:** ... Then the angel said, −BB.

**Gird thyself, and bind on thy sandals:** ... Put on your belt and your sandals, −TCNT... Tighten your belt and put on your shoes, −WLMS... Hurry! Get up ... get dressed, −EVRD... Dress yourself and put on your sandals, −RSV... Put on your clothes, −NIV.

**And so he did, And he saith unto him:** ... When Peter had done so, the angel added, −TCNT.

**Cast thy garment about thee, and follow me:** ... Throw your cloak round you, −TCNT... Wrap your mantle around you and follow me, −RSV.

**12:8.** After the chains fell off from Peter's hands (or from his wrists, which were considered part of the hands), the angel continued to give Peter directions. It was as if Peter was still half asleep and was slow to respond. So the angel told him to gird himself, that is, tighten his belt around his tunic. Then the angel told him to put on his sandals, throw his long outer garment around him, and follow him.

All this was done very quickly, once the angel finally got Peter to respond. The angel knew what he was doing even if Peter did not. Yet the angel must have kept anyone else in the prison from hearing what was going on. Neither did anyone see the bright light that shone in the prison. Truly God was in control!

**9. And he went out, and followed him:** ... Peter went out and followed the angel, —TCNT ... And he followed him out, —MOFT.

**and wist not that it was true which was done by the angel:** ... without knowing that what was happening under the angel's guidance was real, —TCNT ... yet could not believe that what the angel was doing was real, —WEYM ... having no idea that the angel's activity was real, —BRKL ... not realizing the angel was actually doing this, —BECK ... but he was not conscious that what was being done by the angel was real, —WLMS.

**but thought he saw a vision:** ... but supposed that, —WEYM ... but imagining that, —MOFT ... he thought he was dreaming it, —WLMS ... he thought it was just a vision, —NEB ... thought it was a dream, —KLGS ... he felt he must be taking part in a vision, —PHLP.

**12:9.** Peter obeyed the angel and followed him out of the prison cell. But all the time he did not know what was happening to him was real. He thought he was seeing a dream-type vision. He knew the angel was real, but he did not think what was happening was true. He was probably expecting all this to vanish away and find himself back in his cell still chained to the two soldiers.

This was not due to any lack of faith on Peter's part. By faith he had committed himself into the hands of the Lord for whatever God might allow.

Neither did Peter fear death. He knew that to be absent from the body was to be present with the Lord (2 Corinthians 5:8). Like Paul, he knew that to be with Christ is far better than anything believers can experience here on this earth. He had heard Jesus tell how the angels came and carried the poor beggar Lazarus into Abraham's bosom, and this gave Peter assurance that the angels would carry the humblest believer into the presence of Jesus in paradise. He was once afraid of death, but Jesus had long ago set him free from slavery to that fear. (Compare Hebrews 2:14, 15.)

**10. When they were past the first and the second ward:** ... After passing the first Guard, and then a second, —TCNT ... the first and second watchmen, —BB ... guard-points, —PHLP.

**they came unto the iron gate that leadeth unto the city:** ... and at last came to the iron gate which led into the city, —WLMS ... that separated them from the city,

**which opened to them of his own accord:** ... of itself, —TCNT ... and it automatically opened for them, —BRKL ... opened to them automatically, —WUST.

**and they went out, and passed on through one street:** ... and they passed out and proceeded one block, —WLMS ... and they went outside and up the street, —BECK.

**and forthwith the angel departed from him:** ... and immediately, —RSV ... and straightway, —ASV ... all at once the angel left him, —TCNT ... and then suddenly the angel left him, —WEYM.

**12:10.** Still following the angel, Peter passed one gate with its guards, then another gate with its guards. This shows that Herod had taken the further precaution of putting Peter in the innermost prison. (Some believe Peter was held prisoner in Herod's palace. Most, however, say the prison was in the fortress of Antonia which was built by Herod the Great in honor of Mark Antony.) Then they came to the great iron gate that opened into the street outside the prison. That gate opened of its own accord (Greek, *automatē*, automatically). Early western manuscripts (represented by Codex Bezae [D]) add that they went down seven steps to the street. This fact was probably added in the margin of the manuscript by an early copyist who was familiar with Jerusalem and who knew about the steps leading down to the street.

The angel led Peter down the narrow street, possibly to the end of the street, or possibly to the first cross street. Then the angel suddenly left him and disappeared.

The angel stayed with Peter as long as Peter needed him. But now Peter was out of danger. The great gate of the prison had undoubtedly closed behind him, also of its own accord. The guards were still completely unaware of what had happened, so Peter would have time to get away before morning. Peter could see where he was, and now it was up to him to act. God's miracles do not relieve believers of responsibility for action. God had done His part, now it was up to Peter to take the next step. He did not need another miracle at this point.

**11. And when Peter was come to himself, he said:** ... Peter coming to himself said, —WEYM ... Then Peter came to his senses and said, —MOFT ... said Peter to himself, —NORL ... finally realized what had happened! —LIVB.

**Now I know of a surety:** ... Now I know of a truth, —ASV ... Now I know for certain, —TCNT ... I really know, —WLMS ... I am sure, —RSV.

**that the Lord hath sent his angel:** ... hath sent forth his angel, —ASV ... sent forth his messenger, —RTHM.

**and hath delivered me out of the hand of Herod:** ... rescued me from Herod's hands, —TCNT.

**and from all the expectation of the people of the Jews:** ... the Jewish people were anticipating, —WEYM ... were expecting to do to me, —WLMS ... what the Jews were devising against me, —MRDK ... and from all the things the Jewish people thought would happen, —EVRD ... expected to see, —NORL.

**12:11.** Not until the angel disappeared and Peter found himself alone out in the street of the city did he come to himself and realize that the Lord had actually sent His angel to rescue him from Herod's power and from the expectation of the Jewish people, that is, from the expectation that Herod would do to Peter what he had done to the apostle James.

Peter's first thought was to recognize that God had done this, and thus he gave God the glory. The angel was God's messenger. The hand of Herod was powerful, a heavy hand of persecution and oppression. But the hand of God, that is, the power of God was greater. The victory was God's victory, and undoubtedly Peter's heart was overflowing with praise to Him. Peter did not have any questions anymore. He really knew it was God.

**12.** **And when he had considered the thing:** ... And when he was aware of it, —ALFD ... As soon as he understood what had happened, —TCNT ... So, on reflection, —WEYM ... As the truth broke upon him, —PHLP ... having taken in his situation clearly, —WUST ... Then, after thinking it over, —NORL ... Aware of his situation, —TEV ... after he had thought things over, —MNTG ... When this had dawned on him, —NIV ... When he realized his situation, —CNFT ... And when he became clear
**he came to the house of Mary the mother of John:** ... he went, —TCNT.
**whose surname was Mark:** ... whose other name was Mark, —RSV ... the one called Mark, —BECK.
**where many were gathered together praying:** ... a considerable number, —RTHM ... a large number, —WEYM ... many thronged together, —YNG ... in prayer, —PHLP.

**12:12.** When Peter "considered" this (realized this), he did not waste any time. Though it was the middle of the night, he knew he could count on Christians being in prayer. So he went to the house of Mary, John Mark's mother. (*Mark*, or *Marcus*, was an added Latin name.)

Many believe this was the house of the Upper Room and that Mark's father was now dead. The house was on the higher southwestern hill (wrongly called Zion by the Crusaders, who, as someone has well said, were long on zeal but short on knowledge). Many of the finest homes in Jerusalem were located there.

As Peter expected, a considerable number of believers were gathered together in a prayer meeting. After several days, people were still praying day and night for Peter. Faithful prayer marked the Early Church.

**13.** **And as Peter knocked at the door of the gate:** ... the door of the porch, —RTHM ... When he knocked, —GDSP ... the door of the gateway, —RSV ... the entrance gate, —BECK ... at the vestibule door, —NOYS.
**a damsel came to hearken, named Rhoda:** ... a maid came to answer, —ASV ... a servant-girl, —WLMS ... a young maid called Rhoda came to answer it, —PHLP ... by the name of Rose, —BECK.

**12:13.** Mark's mother's house was a large one. The gate here was more than an ordinary gate. It was actually an entrance passageway which led through the front part of the house to the inner courtyard around which the main rooms of the house were built. The believers were probably assembled in this inner court.

The fact that a slave girl, Rhoda (Greek, *Rodē*, "rose bush"), answered the door shows it was a wealthy home as well. It was obviously the meeting place for a large group of believers. Peter knew he would find people there. He felt a special kinship with the group because Mark was his convert and one to whom he had given special training. (See 1 Peter 5:13 where Peter refers to Mark as "my son" in the sense of "my student.")

Mark (Latin for "a large hammer") was also the cousin of Barnabas (Colossians 4:10 where the Greek *anepsios* means "cousin"). He later accompanied Paul and Barnabas on Paul's first missionary journey, but left them in the lurch just when he was needed. Many speculate that he decided he could not take the hardships of missionary life and deserted them to go back to the comfort of his mother's beautiful home in Jerusalem where he would have servants to wait on him. Barnabas, however, gave Mark another chance, and he matured under Barnabas' leadership and probably with further training from Peter. Thus, Paul later considered Mark profitable for the ministry (2 Timothy 4:11).

Rhoda is called a *paidiskē* in Greek, meaning she was a slave girl employed as a household servant. But she had accepted Jesus as her true Lord and Master. Many slaves in those days became Christians.

**14.** **And when she knew Peter's voice:** ... and recognizing the voice of Peter, —RTHM.
**she opened not the gate for gladness, but ran in:** ... but in her joy, left the gate unopened, and ran in, —TCNT ... so overjoyed, —LIVB ... failed to open the door from sheer joy. Instead she ran inside, —PHLP ... for very joy she did not open the door, but ran in, —WEYM ... did not open the entry, —DRBY ... instead of opening the door, —MOFT.

**and told how Peter stood before the gate:** . . . and told them that Peter was standing there, —WEYM . . . and reported that Peter was standing on the doorstep, —PHLP . . . and announced, Peter is standing at the gate, —BECK.

**12:14.** The sound of Peter's familiar voice so filled Rhoda with joy that in her excitement she did not open the door to the gateway (the passageway to the inner court). Instead, she ran back into the courtyard and announced Peter's presence to the assembled believers. The logical thing would have been to open the door as soon as she recognized Peter's voice. Her joy and delight should have made her want to welcome him. But when something unexpected takes place, a person does not always do the most logical thing. In her simplicity, the first thing that occurred to her was that she must tell the others that Peter was standing outside the door and their prayers had been answered.

15. **And they said unto her, Thou art mad:** . . . Thou art raving, —RTHM . . . Thou art delirious, —MRDK . . . You are distracted, —CMPB . . . You are crazy! —NORL . . . You're out of your mind, —NIV . . . You must be mad! —PHLP.

**But she constantly affirmed that it was even so:** . . . But she stoutly maintained that it was true, —WEYM . . . But she insisted up and down that it was so, —BRKL . . . confidently affirmed, —CMPB . . . asserted strongly, —SAWR.

**Then said they, It is his angel:** . . . It is his guardian angel, —WEYM.

**12:15.** The believers told Rhoda she was raving mad, absolutely crazy, out of her mind completely. But she kept asserting emphatically that it was so; Peter was really there. Then they began to say that it was his angel. Some of the Jews had a tradition that a guardian angel could take a person's form. There is absolutely no Biblical ground for such a teaching, but Luke records what they said here to show they thought Peter was already dead, that somehow he had died in prison.

It had been several years since the apostles were delivered from prison, but it was not the passage of time alone that made them lose hope for Peter's deliverance. The shock of James' death made them wonder if perhaps the Lord might allow Peter to be killed too.

Actually, the Bible makes no explanation of why God let James be killed at this time and rescued Peter. But in His divine wisdom He knew James' work was done, and Peter was still needed on earth. God does all things well!

16. **But Peter continued knocking:** . . . Meanwhile Peter went on knocking, —TCNT . . . persisted in knocking, —CNDT . . . to stand there knocking on the door, —PHLP.

**and when they had opened the door:** . . . until at last they opened the door, —WEYM . . . when they opened up, —KJII.

**and saw him, they were astonished:** . . . and saw that it was really he, and were filled with amazement, —WEYM . . . and recognized him they were simply amazed, —PHLP . . . they saw to their astonishment that it was he, —MLNT.

**12:16.** While all this discussion was going on in the prayer group, Peter was still standing out in the street knocking on the door. (The front wall of the houses in old Jerusalem was at the edge of the street.) But finally they opened the door and the sight of Peter astonished them. These believers knew there was no natural explanation for Peter's presence.

17. **But he, beckoning unto them with the hand to hold their peace:** . . . Peter made signs to them to be quiet, —TCNT . . . But he motioned with his hand for silence, —WEYM . . . He waved his hand to quiet them down, —BECK . . . made a gesture to them to stop talking, —PHLP . . . waving to them, —KJII . . . motioned to them to be quiet, —GDSP . . . to hush, —CNDT . . . to be silent, —YNG.

**declared unto them how the Lord had brought him out of the prison:** . . . and then related to them, —GDSP . . . while he explained to them, —PHLP . . . and then described to them, —WEYM . . . and explained how the Lord had conducted him out of the prison, —BRKL.

**And he said, Go shew these unto James, and to the brethren:** . . . Tell these things, —ASV . . . Go report these things, —ALFD . . . Give the news, —BB . . . Let James and the brothers know all this, —MLNT . . . what has happened, —PHLP.

**And he departed, and went into another place:** . . . And going out he went his way unto some other place, —RTHM . . . Then he left the house, —TCNT . . . After this he left them, —PHLP.

**12:17.** Apparently the assembled believers started to cry out excitedly. But Peter waved his hand to silence them and told them how the Lord brought him out of the prison. Then he asked them to take the report of this to James the brother of Jesus and other leaders.

Knowing that by dawn Herod's men would be searching for him, Peter left and went to another place (other than Jerusalem). He did not tell anyone where he was going so they could say honestly that they did not know where he was. Some writers speculate that Peter went to Rome at this time, but there is no evidence for this. In fact, there is no real evidence that Peter ever visited Rome before his martyrdom. Peter was back in Jerusalem for the Jerusalem Conference of chapter 15. He also visited Babylon later, for it was the greatest center of orthodox Judaism outside Palestine.

(See 1 Peter 5:13, which must mean actual Babylon, since there was no reason to disguise Rome by calling it Babylon at that time.)

From what Peter says here, it is clear the increasing place of leadership given to James. This may be partly due to the fact that he was Jesus' brother. But Jesus had other brothers, and there is no evidence that any of them drew attention to their relationship to Jesus or that they tried to capitalize on it in any way. Both James and Jude in their epistles simply refer to themselves as servants (slaves) of the Lord Jesus. James continued to be a leading elder in the church at Jerusalem until he was stoned to death in A.D. 61 just after Festus died.

It does seem that after Jesus appeared to James (1 Corinthians 15:7), James won his other brothers to the Lord, and then they all received teaching from the apostles. From that point they gave themselves to prayer and to the service of others. James especially seems to have quickly grown spiritually. A later tradition says he had calluses like those of a camel on his knees from praying. All agree that the anointing of the Spirit made him a spiritual leader.

**18. Now as soon as it was day:** . . . And when it became day, —RTHM . . . In the morning, —TCNT . . . At daybreak, —NORL . . . when morning came, —GDSP . . . With the break of day, —PHLP.

**there was no small stir among the soldiers:** . . . no small commotion, —RTHM . . . no little consternation, —BRKL . . . no little commotion, —WLMS.

**what was become of Peter:** . . . as to what could possibly have become of Peter, —TCNT . . . as to what could have happened to Peter, —PHLP.

**12:18.** At dawn there was more than a little disturbance among the soldiers as they tried to find out what had become of Peter.

**19. And when Herod had sought for him:** . . . had search made for Peter, —TCNT.

**and found him not:** . . . and had failed to find him, —TCNT . . . and could not find him, —WEYM.

**he examined the keepers:** . . . he cross-questioned the Guard, —TCNT . . . arraigned, —MRDK . . . he cross-examined, —NIV.

**and commanded that they should be put to death:** . . . ordered them to be led away to death, —RTHM . . . and ordered them away to execution, —TCNT . . . he gave orders to have them put to death, —NORL.

**And he went down from Judaea to Caesarea, and there abode:** . . . stayed there, —RTHM . . . and remained there, —WEYM.

**12:19.** Though Herod had a thorough search made for Peter, he was not found. Then Herod brought the guards in for a preliminary examination, but did not give them a formal trial. Although

the Greek simply says the guards were led away, it is nearly certain that they were led away to be executed. According to Roman law (*Code of Justinian*), which Agrippa may not have been bound to in this case, a guard who permitted someone to escape was subject to the same punishment the prisoner would have suffered. In light of James' execution (verse 2), it can be assumed that Peter, and now the guards, faced certain death (Bruce, *New International Commentary of the New Testament, Acts,* p. 253). After that, Herod left Judea and went to the provincial capital on the seacoast (Caesarea) and stayed there. He perhaps felt disgraced by Peter's escape, so he never returned.

**20. And Herod was highly displeased with them of Tyre and Sidon:** . . . Now he was bitterly hostile to, —RTHM . . . had incurred Herod's violent displeasure, —WEYM . . . Now Herod cherished a bitter grudge against, —WLMS . . . bitter animosity, —AMPB.

**but they came with one accord to him:** . . . So they sent a large deputation to wait on him, —WEYM.

**and, having made Blastus the king's chamberlain their friend:** . . . and having won over Blastus, —TCNT . . . and having secured the good will of Blastus, his treasurer, —WEYM . . . the king's household steward, —NORL . . . the king's chief valet, —WUST.

**desired peace:** . . . they were suing for peace, —RTHM . . . they begged Herod for a peaceful arrangement, —TCNT.

**because their country was nourished by the king's country:** . . . because their country was dependent on the King's for its food supply, —TCNT . . . their country depended for its food-supply upon the king's country, —WLMS.

**12:20.** At this time, and probably for some time previously, Herod was furiously angry with Tyre and Sidon. He was practically at the point of waging war with them, though war would not have been allowed between two Roman provinces or dependencies. To try to quiet him, the leaders of Tyre and Sidon got together in one accord (with a unity of purpose) and came to Herod. But first they made friends of Blastus, the king's chamberlain, who was one of Herod's confidential advisers. Using his influence, they asked for peace for themselves. They had good reason. Tyre and Sidon are on a narrow strip of land between the Lebanon Mountains and the Mediterranean Sea. That strip varied from a few yards to about 5 miles. Thus they had very little land suitable for agriculture and they were dependent on Palestine for their food supply. (See 1 Kings 5:10, 11 where Solomon exchanged food for cedar and fir trees from Lebanon; see also Ezra 3:7; Ezekiel 27:17.)

It is indicated that Barnabas and Saul were in Jerusalem at this time bringing an offering for famine relief. This famine would have affected Tyre and Sidon too, so they must have been desperate for a share of the food Palestine produced. Peace for them was a real necessity.

**21. And upon a set day:** ... And on an appointed day, —*RTHM.*

**Herod, arrayed in royal apparel:** ... putting on royal apparel, —*RTHM* ... put on his state-robes, —*TCNT* ... having arrayed himself in royal robes, —*WEYM.*

**sat upon his throne:** ... took his seat on the tribunal, —*WEYM* ... sat in the judgment seat, —*DOUY.*

**and made an oration unto them:** ... and addressed the assembly, —*LAMS* ... began to make them a speech, —*TCNT* ... a public address, —*NIV.*

**12:21.** Herod responded favorably, and the leaders of Tyre and Sidon, and undoubtedly many of the people of Lebanon gathered in Caesarea on an appointed day. The crowd probably gathered in the Greek-style stadium or amphitheater beside the Mediterranean Sea, built by Herod the Great. It is still there and its structure is in better condition than most ancient ruins.

With a great deal of pomp and ceremony, King Herod appeared in his royal robes. According to the Jewish historian Josephus, the outer robe was of silver (either adorned with silver or actually woven of silver threads), and the sun's rays were reflected brilliantly from Herod's silver robe.

After taking his seat on an elevated throne especially prepared for him, Herod began a speech using proper oratory in the best Greek or Roman style.

**22. And the people gave a shout, saying:** ... and the assembled people raised the shout, —*WEYM* ... The mob shouted, —*BRKL* ... started to applaud, —*NORL* ... were crying out, —*KJII.*

**It is the voice of a god, and not of a man:** ... This sounds like the voice of, —*LAMS* ... There is a god speaking, —*PHLP.*

**12:22.** The people of Tyre and Sidon had not only adopted the Greek language, they had adopted the full spectrum of Greek culture including Greek idolatry. It is quite evident that Herod did not say anything about the strict Judaism he practiced to please the Jews. His speech obviously was intended to please the people of Tyre and Sidon, which it did. In fact, it pleased them so much that they began to shout out, "A god's voice, not a man's!" The inference is that when they did so Herod did not rebuke them or try to stop them in any way. Instead, he let them keep on shouting, repeating the same phrase. Thus he accepted their flattery.

Apparently Herod's pride, so deflated by Peter's escape, was greatly puffed up again by the flattering cries of these people who called him a god.

Instead of humbling himself, he became quite willing for others to treat him as a little god.

**23. And immediately the angel of the Lord smote him:** ... Instantly an angel of the Lord struck him, —*WEYM* ... in that very hour, —*LAMS* ... But the angel of the Lord struck him down immediately, —*GDSP* ... struck him down with a deadly disease, —*NORL* ... afflicted him with a disease, —*WUST.*

**because he gave not God the glory:** ... because he had usurped the honour due to God, —*NEB.*

**and he was eaten of worms:** ... and being eaten up by worms, —*WEYM* ... and his flesh was wasted away by worms, —*BB* ... and he was eaten by disease, —*LAMS.*

**and gave up the ghost:** ... and died, —*RSV.*

**12:23.** The Bible emphasizes that Herod did not make any objection to the cries of the people of Tyre and Sidon, and he did not give the true God any glory whatsoever. This called for the righteous judgment of God. Immediately an angel of the Lord struck him down. He was eaten by worms and died (expired). He had brought his own doom on himself. Josephus adds that Herod lingered 5 days with agonizing pains in his belly. This agrees with the Bible text which only says he was struck down immediately, not that he died on the spot. Luke the physician said more than Josephus, however, for Luke gave the cause of Herod's death.

This took place in A.D. 44. After that the Roman emperors again appointed procurators over Judea.

**24. But the word of God grew and multiplied:** ... Meanwhile the Lord's Message kept extending, and spreading far and wide, —*TCNT* ... But the word of the Lord continued to gain ground and increase its influence, —*PHLP* ... made progress, —*MRDK* ... extended and increased, —*FNTN* ... continued to increase and spread, —*NIV* ... went on spreading and increasing, —*TNT* ... continued to be preached and to reach many, —*LAMS.*

**12:24.** None of these events hindered the continued growth of the Church or the spread of the gospel in Palestine. In spite of James' death, Peter's arrest, Herod's attitude, and Herod's death, "The word of God grew and multiplied."

This is a beautiful way of expressing the secret of the growth of the Church. The growth was not due to the leadership of any man. It was not due to better methods or clever new ways men thought up for propagating the gospel. It was due to the power of the Word of God to bring life and growth.

**25. And Barnabas and Saul returned from Jerusalem, when they had fulfilled their ministry;** ... after visiting Jerusalem in the discharge of their commission, —*TCNT* ... When Barnabas and Saul had finished their helpful service, —*WLMS* ... having performed their service, —NOYS...when they had finished their ministry there, —MLNT...their relief work, —NORL...having fulfilled their service, —LIVB...after carrying out, —TNT...had performed their mission to Jerusalem, they went back, —GDSP...from Jerusalem to Antioch, —LAMS.

**and took with them John, whose surname was Mark:**...also bringing with them, —KJII...taking John...with them, —GDSP...and brought along, —MLNT...and took along with them John who was called Mark, —WLMS.

**12:25.** It seems possible that Barnabas and Paul were in Jerusalem, at least during the Passover season, when these events took place. Because Josephus indicates the famine took place in A.D. 46, 2 years after Herod's death, others suggest the visit of Paul and Barnabas did not take place until then.

Though the date is not certain, it is clear that Saul and Barnabas fulfilled their ministry and delivered the famine relief to the Jerusalem elders. (It is possible that because the famine was prophesied in advance by Agabus, Saul and Barnabas brought the money well in advance so it would be available as soon as it was needed.)

The choice of Mark shows they saw in him a desire for ministry and calling they wanted to nurture and develop. There were no schools for the training of Christian workers and Christian ministers. But Jesus had set a precedent by selecting the Twelve to be with Him and to be trained by Him. Now that the Church was beginning to spread out in so many different directions, more workers would be needed to help teach and train the believers.

## Chapter 13

**1. Now there were in the church . that was at Antioch:** ... among the members of the Church there, —TCNT...In the congregation at, —SEB...In the local church, —TNT.

**certain prophets and teachers:**...both prophets and, —PHLP...some Prophets and Teachers, —TCNT...doctors, —DOUY.

**as Barnabas, and Simeon that was called Niger:**...namely, —SWAN...Simeon who went by the name of Black, —TCNT...called Black, —BECK.

**and Lucius of Cyrene:**...from the city of, —SEB.

**and Manaen, which had been brought up with Herod the tetrarch, and Saul:**...Manael, who was the son of the man who brought up, —LAMS...foster-brother of Prince Herod, —TCNT...who was an intimate friend of the governor, —WLMS...a childhood companion of Herod, —BRKL...the foster-brother, —NOYS...a member of the court of Herod, —AMPB, —NOLI...who had grown up with, —EVRD.

**13:1.** In time, as the church at Antioch grew, God raised up others besides Barnabas and Saul to aid in ministering to the believers. They are called prophets and teachers here. This may mean they

were all prophets and teachers, or it may mean the first three named were prophets and the last two were teachers (as the Greek could be interpreted). As prophets they were used by the Spirit to bring edification, exhortation, and comfort or encouragement. As teachers they received gifts from the Holy Spirit which would enable them to teach the Word of God effectively.

These included Simeon (Simon) called Niger. *Simeon* (Simon) was a common Hebrew name; *Niger* means "black." Some writers believe he was the child of a Jew who had married a Negro. Others speculate he may have been Simon the Cyrenian who carried Christ's cross (Mark 15:21; Luke 23:26).

The next prophet or teacher, Lucius, is definitely said to be from Cyrene in North Africa (west of Egypt). Possibly he was one of those who first brought the gospel to Antioch (11:20).

Manaen (a Greek form of *Menahem,* "comforter"), the other prophet or teacher, was brought up with Herod the Tetrarch (Herod Antipas, who killed John the Baptist). He was literally called a foster brother and was about the same age as Herod. He grew up in the palace, and some believe he also became a courtier or officer of this Herod. John the Baptist must have influenced him. Later Manaen was saved. It is also possible that he was among those present on the Day of Pentecost when the Holy Spirit was first outpoured.

**2. As they ministered to the Lord, and fasted:** ... While they were worshipping the Lord, —TCNT ... While the Christians were worshipping, —BECK...making supplication, —MRDK...all serving, —SEB...as they were serving the Lord, —KJII.

**the Holy Ghost said:**...said to them, —LAMS.

**Separate me Barnabas and Saul for the work whereunto I have called them:** ... Set apart for me, ABUV ... Appoint for me, —LAMS ... Separate me forthwith, —ALFD ... have allotted them, —FNTN...Give...to me to do a special work, —EVRD...a special job, —LIVB...for a task to which, —PHLP...I have chosen them to do a special work, —SEB.

**13:2.** These, along with the congregation, were ministering to the Lord in a public service (as the Greek indicates here). They were also fasting.

During the service, the Holy Spirit spoke and commanded them (the whole church) to separate "to me" (set apart for me) Barnabas and Saul for the work to which He had (already) called them. The Greek is imperative here and includes a particle expressing a strong command.

How the Holy Spirit gave this message is not indicated. Likely it was a message in prophecy given by one of the other prophets and teachers named in verse 1. This does not give grounds for so-called "directive prophecy," however. It was not meant to give direction for Barnabas and Saul. The Greek perfect tense used here means an action in the past with present results. This shows that the Holy Spirit had already dealt with both Barnabas and Saul personally. But they had responsibilities in ministry to the local church, and the church must be willing to let them go. So the Spirit's message was directed to the whole assembly.

**3. And when they had fasted and prayed:**...At this, —PHLP...So, the congregation, —SEB...after further fasting and prayer, —PHLP...they gave up eating and prayed, —EVRD.

**and laid their hands on them:**...put their hands on, —SEB...and the laying on of hands, —WEYM.

**they sent them away:**...and sent them on their way, —TCNT...and set them free for this work, —PHLP...let them go, —BECK...dismissed them, —CMPB....and sent them off, —NOLI...sent them out, —EVRD, —SEB.

**13:3.** The whole assembly then fasted and prayed further. Later, Paul wrote to the Corinthians (1 Corinthians 14:29) that prophecies should be judged by other members of the Body. It is always wise to hold steady until it is certain prophetic messages are from the Lord.

The assembly also must have prayed for God's blessing on this new ministry. Then they sent Barnabas and Saul away (literally, set them free, released them, from their obligations at Antioch and permitted them to depart).

This was another important step in the progress of the gospel. Up to this point the gospel was carried to new places by those who were scattered abroad by persecution. But there were none who gave themselves specifically to the work of going to new places to start and organize new churches.

**4. So they, being sent forth by the Holy Ghost:**...sent on this mission, —TCNT...So these two, sent at the Holy Spirit's command, —PHLP...Being sent out in this way, —GDSP...Thus, designated by the, —NOLI...Indeed, it was really the Holy Spirit who had sent them out, —NORL...Under the guidance, —FNTN.

**departed unto Seleucia:**...went down to Seleucia, —ASV.

**and from thence they sailed to Cyprus:**...they sailed away, —ALFD...to the Island of, —SEB.

**13:4.** The Bible next emphasizes that Barnabas and Saul were sent out by the Holy Spirit. The believers gave them their blessing and let them go. Both the Holy Spirit and the church were involved.

Their first missionary journey took them to the island of Cyprus, over 100 miles to the southwest, then to the mainland cities in the southern part of the Roman province of Galatia, and finally back to

Antioch where they reported to the home church (14:26, 27).

Seleucia was a city on the Syrian coast of the Mediterranean Sea, 5 miles north of the mouth of the Orontes River and about 16 miles from Antioch.

At Seleucia, Antioch's harbor, they took a sailing ship to Cyprus. There was wisdom in the Holy Spirit's taking them first to the island where Barnabas was born and grew up (4:36).

**5. And when they were at Salamis:**...And arriving at Salamis, ABUV...On reaching Salamis, —TCNT...when they had entered the city of, —LAMS...When they came to, —EVRD.

**they preached the word of God in the synagogues of the Jews:**...they proclaimed, —ASV...they declared, —RTHM...they began to tell God's message in the Jewish Synagogues, —TCNT...they began to announce, —WEYM...they announced, —DRBY...they preached the divine Gospel, —NOLI...they were preaching God's message in, —SEB.

**and they had also John to their minister:**...as their attendant, —ASV...as their assistant, —WEYM...as their helper, —NORL.

**13:5.** At Salamis on the eastern end of the island of Cyprus, they took advantage of the opportunities given by the synagogues for visiting rabbis to preach and teach. It was always Saul's practice to go to the Jews first, for they had the Scriptures and the background to understand the gospel. (See Romans 1:16; 3:2; 9:4, 5.)

The Bible draws attention to the fact that they took John Mark along as their minister, their attendant. Some believe that like Elisha who waited on Elijah, Mark helped them as a personal servant while he trained for the ministry. Luke 1:2 uses the same word for "ministers of the Word," however. Others believe they took Mark because he was an eyewitness of the arrest, death, and resurrection of Jesus, probably being the young man mentioned in Mark 14:51, 52.

**6. And when they had gone through the isle unto Paphos:**...the whole island, —RSV...They covered the whole island as far as Paphos, —MOFT...Traversing the entire island, —BRKL.

**they found a certain sorcerer, a false prophet, a Jew:**...they there met with a Jewish magician and false prophet, —WEYM...a Jewish false prophet, —NOYS...wizard, —AMPB.

**whose surname was Bar-jesus:**...whose real name was Bar-joshua, —TCNT...Bar-Jesus by name, —WEYM.

**13:6.** After proclaiming the gospel at Salamis, they traveled throughout the island. The Greek indicates they covered it rather thoroughly stopping at all or most of the towns and cities until they came to Paphos on the western end of Cyprus.

Saul (Paul) changed this method after they left Cyprus. After this, instead of trying to cover the whole territory of a region or province, they went to key cities to establish churches. These local assemblies then became centers where the local body could spread the gospel into the surrounding area.

Paphos here is probably New Paphos. Old Paphos was a city founded by the ancient Phoenicians. New Paphos was a harbor city which became important after the Romans annexed the island in 58 B.C.

At Paphos they came in contact with a Jew named Bar-Jesus ("son of Joshua" or "son of Jesus"). He may have claimed to be a new Joshua sent to lead people into a new promised land of spiritual power. Or he may have claimed to be a follower of Jesus, but only to try to get a following for himself by his trickery.

The Bible identifies him as a sorcerer who falsely claimed to be a prophet. Like Simon the sorcerer in Samaria, he practiced magic to fool the people and gain power over them.

7. **Which was with the deputy of the country:** . . . He was at the court of the Governor, −*TCNT* . . . who was a friend of the Proconsul, −*WEYM* . . . an intimate friend, −*WLMS* . . . an attendant, −*NIV.*

**Sergius Paulus, a prudent man:** . . . a man of understanding, ASV . . . an intelligent man, −*RTHM* . . . a man of considerable intelligence, −*TCNT.*

**who called for Barnabas and Saul:** . . . who sent for, −*TCNT* . . . He summoned, −*MNTG* . . . who urgently invited, −*BRKL.*

**and desired to hear the word of God:** . . . and sought to hear, −*RSV* . . . and asked to be told God's Message, −*TCNT.*

**13:7.** Saul and Barnabas found this sorcerer with the deputy (literally, the *proconsul*, the governor appointed by the Roman Senate; Luke used the correct title). This man, Sergius Paulus, was prudent; he was sensible, intelligent, and well-educated. As governor, he apparently was careful to keep himself informed about what was going on in the island and heard good reports of the ministry of Saul and Barnabas and its effects. So he called in Barnabas and Saul, earnestly seeking to hear the Word of God.

8. **But Elymas the sorcerer:** . . . the magician, −*ALFD* . . . the fortune teller, −*KLGS.*

**(for so is his name by interpretation):** . . . for so, when translated, is his name, −*RTHM* . . . for that is the meaning of the name, −*TCNT* . . . for that is the sense of his name, −*BB* . . . for this was his nickname, −*KLGS.*

**withstood them:** . . . opposed them, −*TCNT* . . . put himself against them, −*BB.*

**seeking to turn away the deputy from the faith:** . . . seeking to turn away the proconsul from the faith, −*ASV* . . . and tried to prevent the Proconsul from accepting the faith, −*WEYM* . . . to divert, −*MRDK* . . . to dissuade the proconsul from accepting the faith, −*PHLP.*

**13:8.** Then the sorcerer, now called by an interpretation of his name, Elymas, took a stand against Saul and Barnabas, actively seeking to turn away (pervert, twist away) the proconsul from the Faith.

This implies Saul and Barnabas presented "the faith," the complete content of the gospel with its full message of the life, death, and resurrection of Jesus, the outpouring of the Holy Spirit, and the hope of His future return. It also means the proconsul was not only listening to the message, he was accepting it.

9. **Then Saul, (who also is called Paul,):** . . . however, Saul (who is the same as Paul), −*TCNT* . . . Saul-hereafter called Paul, −*NORL.*

**filled with the Holy Ghost:** . . . because he was full of the Holy Spirit, −*WLMS.*

**set his eyes on him:** . . . fastened his eyes on him, −*ASV* . . . fixed his eyes on him, −*ALFD* . . . looked steadily at him, −*MOFT* . . . looked him straight in the eye, −*WLMS.*

**13:9.** This was a crisis time for the spread of the gospel in Cyprus. But the Holy Spirit knew how to deal with the situation. He gave Saul the power and authority to confront Elymas. The Greek expression here is like that used when Peter received a new special rilling of the Holy Spirit when he faced the Sanhedrin (4:8).

Acts notes at this point also that Saul had another name, a Roman name, Paul (from the Latin, *Paulus*, "little"). This is significant because in the rest of the Book of Acts he is always called Paul. In his epistles also he always calls himself Paul.

Also by this filling of the Spirit, the Lord gave Paul the leadership in the missionary journey. Looking ahead to verse 13, instead of Barnabas and Saul, it is "Paul and his company." This is in line also with the prophecy given to Ananias in Damascus after Paul was converted. (See 9:15.)

What Paul did next was not his own idea. It was a prompting given directly by the Holy Spirit who had just filled him anew. This new filling gave him a holy boldness that caused him to fix his eyes on Elymas, looking at him intently, straight in the eye.

10. **And said, O full of all subtilty and all mischief:** . . . O full of all guile and all villany, −*ASV* . . . You incarnation of deceit and fraud! −*TCNT* . . . You who are full of every kind of craftiness and unscrupulous cunning, −*WEYM* . . . You expert in every form

of deception and sleight-of-hand, –*WLMS* . . . O you, who are full of false tricks and evil ways, –*BB* . . . all knavery, –*CNDT* . . . full of every deceit and villainy, –*BRKL* . . . You professional deceiver, –*NORL* . . . you monster of trickery and evil, –*PHLP* . . . You master in every form of deception, –*AMPB*.

**thou child of the devil:** . . . thou son of the devil, –*ASV.*

**thou enemy of all righteousness:** . . . and foe to all that is right, –*WEYM* . . . hating all righteousness, –*BB*.

**wilt thou not cease to pervert the right ways of the Lord?:** . . . Will you never cease diverting the straight paths of the Lord, –*TCNT* . . . plotting against the saving purposes of God, –*BRKL* . . . Won't you stop twisting the Lord's right ways? –*BECK* . . . always keep trying to turn the Lord's truths into lies! –*TEV.*

**13:10.** The Holy Spirit gave Paul a message that exposed Elymas for what he was. (Some believe this is one way the gift of the discerning of spirits may be manifested; see 1 Corinthians 12:10.)

Paul addressed Elymas as a person full of all kinds of subtlety (deceit, guile, treachery) and mischief (wickedness, unscrupulousness, reckless facility for doing evil, fraud), a son of the devil, an enemy of all righteousness. *Son of* can mean "having the character of," or a disciple of. (See Genesis 3:15, the seed of the serpent, and John 8:44, "your father the devil." The "devil" means the slanderer, and thus, the "false accuser," as the plural form is translated in 2 Timothy 3:3.)

Then Paul asked a rhetorical question which was really an affirmation that Elymas was determined not to cease perverting (twisting, distorting) the right (upright, straight) ways of the Lord (including the way of salvation and God's purposes for the believer).

**11. And now, behold, the hand of the Lord is upon thee:** . . . Listen! The hand . . . is upon you even now, –*TCNT* . . . Right now the hand, –*WLMS* . . . Now listen, the Lord Himself will touch you, –*PHLP.*

**and thou shalt be blind, not seeing the sun for a season:** . . . and you shall be blind for a time and unable to see the sun, –*TCNT* . . . for a time, –*NOYS.*

**And immediately there fell on him a mist and a darkness:** . . . and instantly, –*RTHM* . . . a mist and then an utter blackness came over his eyes, –*PHLP.*

**and he went about seeking some to lead him by the hand:** . . . and he went feeling about for someone to guide him, –*TCNT* . . . and he groped about for someone to take him, –*MOFT* . . . going about, he sought someone to lead him, –*SWAN* . . . walked around lost, trying to find someone to lead him, –*SEB* . . . seeking people to lead him, –*NOLI* . . . begging people to lead him by the hand, –*WLMS.*

**13:11.** Because Elymas was so determined to oppose and pervert the ways of the Lord, Paul declared God's judgment upon him. The hand (power) of the Lord would be (at last) upon him

to bring the judgment he deserved. Elymas would be totally blind until a fitting season when God would enable him to see again. Probably, this meant God would be merciful and give even Elymas an opportunity to repent.

Mist and darkness immediately fell on Elymas, and he went around searching for someone to lead him by the hand. Apparently the people all withdrew from him, and he had a hard time finding anyone to lead him.

This was God's righteous judgment. Paul did not do this sort of thing very often. Very few can exercise such supernatural discipline. The words must come from the Holy Spirit and not from the mind or the emotions. Those who attempt to act in such a way in the power of the flesh could be like the mockers mentioned in Jude 14, 15, 18, and 19, people characterized as "not having the Spirit."

**12. Then the deputy, when he saw what was done, believed:** . . . When the Governor saw what had happened, he became a believer in Christ, –*TCNT* . . . the Proconsul, –*SWAN* . . . he believed, –*SEB* . . . saw what had come to pass, –*NOYS* . . . for he had witnessed what had happened, –*NORL.*

**being astonished at the doctrine of the Lord:** . . . being greatly struck with the teaching about the Master, –*TCNT* . . . was thunderstruck, –*WLMS* . . . for he was shaken to the core at the Lord's teaching, –*PHLP* . . . being gladly amazed at, –*KJII* . . . was overcome with awe at the Gospel, –*NOLI* . . . the teaching about the Lord, –*MLNT.*

**13:12.** As soon as the proconsul saw what happened, he believed. But too much emphasis should not be put on the effect of the miracle here. The proconsul was not astonished (astounded, thunderstruck) so much by the judgment on Elymas as by the doctrine (teaching) of the Lord. This event drove home the truth about Jesus, the Cross, the Resurrection, and the rest of the gospel that had been presented to him. The Holy Spirit used the truth to bring him to the place of faith and salvation. (See Romans 10:9, 10; Ephesians 2:8; Hebrews 11:6.)

The Bible does not tell anything further about the experience of Sergius Paulus. Archaeologists have found evidence that this proconsul's daughter and her son were baptized believers. This should be taken as further evidence that the proconsul was a true believer. The gospel was reaching into every stratum of society.

**13. Now when Paul and his company loosed from Paphos:** . . . his companions, –*PHLP* . . . and those with him sailed away from, –*NCV* . . . set sail, –*ASV* . . . put to sea, –ALFD ... put out to sea, –WEYM ... leaving Paphos, –SWAN.

**they came to Perga in Pamphylia:** ... Paul's company came to, –WORL ... They continued their trip from, NCV.

**and John departing from them returned to Jerusalem:** ... Here John quit them, –WLMS ... withdrawing from them, –RTHM, –WORL ... left them, –TCNT ... separated himself from them, –BRKL ... deserted them, –LIVB ... he went back home to, –SEB.

**13:13.** From Paphos, Paul and his company set sail for Perga in Pamphylia (a district on the south coast of Asia Minor). Barnabas was still with Paul, of course.

At Perga, John Mark left (deserted) them and returned to Jerusalem. Later (15:38) it is implied that Mark did so when they really needed him. Possibly, the work became more difficult as they encountered unfamiliar territory on the mainland. Since Mark was from a wealthy home where there were servants, perhaps he decided to go home where life would be easier. Paul may have been suffering from some sort of physical sickness. In any case, Paul looked at this as an almost inexcusable failure on the part of Mark. Nor did Mark have any grounds for resenting Paul. Even though Paul had been promised a position of missionary leadership about 15 years before this, Paul had taken the place of humble service through long years of training and preparation, and he had done it willingly. (Notice that Paul was mentioned last in verse 1.) In God's time, the Spirit put Paul in the place God had for him. Paul knew God would do the same for Mark in due time if he would be faithful. Later, Mark was reinstated in Paul's favor (2 Timothy 4:11).

**14. But when they departed from Perga:** ... They continued their trip from, –SEB ... But they themselves, passing through, –WEYM.

**they came to Antioch in Pisidia:** ... a city near, –NCV.

**and went into the synagogue on the sabbath day:** ... On Saturday they went into the synagog, –BECK.

**and sat down:** ... and took their seats, –PHLP, –TCNT.

**13:14.** From Perga they went to Antioch in (of) Pisidia; so called to distinguish it from other cities named Antioch and because it was near the border of Pisidia (not actually in Pisidia but in Phrygia) in the southern part of Galatia.

**15. And after the reading of the law and the prophets:** ... After the lessons, –JB ... After the lesson from, –NOLI ... After the rulers had read from, –NORL.

**the rulers of the synagogue sent unto them, saying:** ... the synagogue-rulers sent unto them, –RTHM ... officers of, –TNT ... the leaders of the

synagogue worship, –WLMS ... the Presidents of the Synagogue sent them this message, –TCNT ... sent a message to, –NCV.

**Ye men and brethren:** ... Brethren, –RSV ... Fellow Jews, –BECK.

**if ye have any word of exhortation for the people, say on:** ... if you have any helpful words to address to the people, now is your opportunity, –TCNT ... any message of encouragement for ... you may speak, –WLMS ... any comforting message, –FNTN ... if you have any message that will encourage the people, please speak! –NCV ... if there is among you any word of exhortation for the people, –WORL ... any word of counsel, –MOFT ... by all means speak, –PHLP ... proceed, –NOLI.

**13:15.** In the synagogue on the Sabbath Day, they listened as usual to someone reading the selections from the Law (the Pentateuch) and from (one of) the Prophets (which in the Hebrew Bible consist of Joshua, Judges, Samuel, Kings, Isaiah, Jeremiah, Ezekiel, and the Book of the Twelve, the Minor Prophets).

Then the rulers (the leaders, the elders) of the synagogue sent to them (for Paul and Barnabas were sitting in the back of the synagogue) and courteously asked them to give a word of exhortation, a word of encouragement or challenge.

**16. Then Paul stood up, and beckoning with his hand said:** ... So Paul rose, and motioning ... for silence, –WEYM ... standing up, and beckoning with his hand, –WORL ... and suggesting silence by a wave, –BRKL ... He raised his hand and said, –NCV.

**Men of Israel:** ... Israelites, –WEYM.

**and ye that fear God:** ... and such as revere God! –RTHM ... and all here who reverence God, –TCNT ... and you Godfearing people, –NORL ... and God-fearing brothers, –NOLI.

**give audience:** ... hearken, –ASV, –WORL ... listen to me, –TCNT ... pay attention to me, –WEYM ... hear my words, –LAMS.

**13:16.** Paul then stood, waved his hand for silence, and asked the Israelites and the Godfearers to listen. This implies there were interested Gentiles in the synagogue audience, Gentiles who recognized the Lord as the one true God.

As mentioned previously, many Gentiles were tired of the immorality and idolatry of heathen religion. They were hungry for something better and were attracted to the synagogues and to the worship of the holy, righteous, loving God revealed in the Old Testament, the God so unlike their heathen gods. Yet many of them did not become full proselytes or converts to Judaism because they hesitated to accept circumcision, self-baptism, and the other Jewish rites and ceremonies. Some rabbis did not give them much encouragement to do so, for they would not promise them salvation if they did become Jews. They would only say their children would be counted as Jews and be under the covenant blessings. But these Gentiles still came every Sabbath to hear the Word of God and to learn more about the Holy One of Israel.

Paul's sermon here at Pisidian Antioch is given in considerable detail. Luke recorded it as an example of the kind of preaching Paul did in the Jewish synagogues. It is probable Paul used essentially the same approach the first time he spoke in a synagogue in a new town. The Book of Acts does not go into such detail in the record of later sermons.

As Paul began, he courteously addressed both the Jews and Gentiles in the audience and recognized both groups as "brethren," keeping both in mind throughout the sermon.

17. **The God of this people of Israel:** ... of this people Israel, *–RSV* ... of the people of Israel, *–NIV* ... The God of our nation,

**chose our fathers:** ... selected our fathers, *–BRKL* ... chose out, *–KJII* ... chose our ancestors,

**and exalted the people when they dwelt as strangers in the land of Egypt:** ... and made the people great during their stay in Egypt, *–WEYM* ... during the time they lived in Egypt, *–NCV* ... exalted and multiplied them, *–LAMS* ... lifted up the people in their stay, *–KJII* ... he uplifted by the sojourn in Egypt's land, *–RTHM* ... prospered the people even while they were exiles, *–PHLP* ... when they were living as strangers in, *–TNT* ... during their residence, *–NOLI.*

**and with an high arm brought he them out of it:** ... until with wondrous power He brought, *–WEYM* ... with an uplifted arm, *–SWAN* ... With mighty power, *–NIV* ... He led them forth out of it, *–WORL.*

**13:17.** The first part of Paul's sermon (verses 17-25) reviewed the history of Israel, beginning with God's choice of Israel and their deliverance from Egypt, and leading up to God's choice of David. All this was very familiar to the Jews in the audience and showed them Paul knew the Scriptures.

Unlike Stephen, Paul did not emphasize Israel's failures. Rather, he spoke of God's choosing (for His own purpose and service) and God's exalting of the Israelites during their sojourn as foreigners (resident aliens) in Egypt. The Israelites who were made subject to oppression and slavery in Egypt saw God set them apart as His special people even during the plagues. When the terrible plague of flies covered Egypt there was not a fly in Goshen. When the plague of darkness affected Egypt, the sun was shining brightly in Goshen.

Then God confirmed His choice of Israel by leading them out of Egypt with a high arm (corresponding to a lifted-up arm in the Hebrew, that is, by mighty manifestations of His supernatural power; see Exodus 6:1-6; 19:4; Psalm 136:11, 12).

18. **And about the time of forty years:** ... For about forty years, *–TCNT.*

**suffered he their manners in the wilderness:** ... he bore with them in the Desert, *–TCNT* ... He fed them like a nurse in the desert, *–WEYM* ... he put up with their ways, *–BB* ... He endured their behavior, *–BRKL* ... he was patient with them, *–NCV* ... after he had taken care of them, *–GDSP* ... he nourished them, *–NOYS* ... tenderly cared for them, *–WUST.*

**13:18.** Next Paul mentioned how God endured the manners (ways) of the people during the wilderness journey. (Several ancient Greek manuscripts read a word with only one letter different, a word which means God "carried them" as a nurse would a child. Deuteronomy 1:31 in the Septuagint version has the same variant.)

Paul was reminding his listeners of the patience of God with the Israelites during all those times of murmuring, criticizing, and complaining throughout the 40 years. The Book of Numbers shows how God had to deal with human nature in the raw. In Numbers 11, their problem was appetite; Numbers 12, jealousy; Numbers 13, unbelief; Numbers 14, presumption; Numbers 15, rebellion; Numbers 16, mutiny.

19. **And when he had destroyed seven nations in the land of Chanaan:** ... Then, after overthrowing ... Canaan, *–WEYM.*

**he divided their land to them by lot:** ... he gave them their land for an inheritance, *–ASV* ... he allotted their land to the people, *–TCNT* ... He divided that country among them as their inheritance, *–WEYM* ... gave their land to Israel to possess, *–TNT* ... giving their land to His people, *–SEB* ... gave the land to his people, *–NCV* ... distributed the land, *–KLGS* ... distributed by lot, *–WORL.*

**13:19.** Next, Paul quickly summarized Joshua's conquest. The seven nations were the tribes of the Canaanites and others that were in Palestine. (See Deuteronomy 7:1 which names them.)

Then Paul reminded his listeners that God divided or parceled out the land among the tribes of Israel by lot. This refers to Joshua 14:1 which says Joshua distributed the land "for inheritance to them."

20. **And after that he gave unto them judges about the space of four hundred and fifty years, until Samuel the prophet:** ... Later on he gave them Judges, of whom the Prophet Samuel was the last, *–TCNT* ... all of which took about, *–MLNT* ... All this happened in

**13:20.** Paul summarized the period of the judges. The 450 years (a round number) refers not merely to the period covered by the Book of Judges, but to the whole time after they entered the land up to the beginning of David's reign (with

Samuel the prophet being the last judge). (Some manuscripts apply the 450 years to the 400 years in Egypt, plus the time of the conquest up to the time of the dividing of the land in chapter 14 of Joshua; that is, they say that after the 450 years, God gave them judges up to the time of Samuel.)

It should be noted that the periods during which the judges ruled overlapped in many cases. For example, the 40 years of Philistine oppression mentioned in Judges 13:1 began with Judges 10:7 and ended with 1 Samuel 7:10. A careful comparison of the Bible passages concerned shows that the Ammonites oppressed Israel from the east while Philistines oppressed them from the west.

Again, Paul did not emphasize the negative side of the period of the judges. He reminded his listeners only that it was God who gave them the judges, and he named Samuel, the judge who was more than a judge, the only judge who was able to unite all 12 tribes and through his ministry bring a spiritual revival (1 Samuel 7:3-9).

**21.** **And afterward they desired a king:** ... And when, after a while, they demanded a king, *—TCNT* . . . Next they asked for a king, *—WEYM* . . . Then when they begged for, *—PHLP.*
**and God gave unto them Saul the son of Cis:** ... the son of Kish, *—ASV.*
**a man of the tribe of Benjamin:** ... a Benjamite, *—WEYM* . . . from the family group of, *—NCV.*
**by the space of forty years:** ... He was king for, *—SEB* . . . who reigned for forty years, *—TCNT.*

**13:21.** Next Paul reminded them of how the people asked for a king and God gave them Saul (which means "asked for"). The fact that the people asked for a king reminded Paul's listeners of the whole story of how the people wanted a king to be like the other nations. But what Paul was emphasizing is that God was guiding the history of Israel, and He was the One who gave Saul to the people. Saul was also identified as "of the tribe of Benjamin," the same tribe to which the apostle Paul belonged.

The 40 years of King Saul's reign are confirmed by the Jewish historian, Josephus, but they are not given in the Old Testament. (Actually, Josephus seems to mean that Saul reigned 20 years and Samuel judged 20 years, together making the 40.)

First Samuel 13:1 reads literally, "Saul was a son of year in his reigning (when he began to reign), and he reigned two years over Israel." This follows the usual formula for giving the length of a king's reign, like that found in 2 Kings 14:2; 16:2; 18:2. Many believe this means that early in the process of copying the Books of Samuel, the scribe accidentally left out the age of Saul and the length of his reign. Many Bible scholars conjecture that

Saul was 40 years old when he began to reign and that he reigned 32 years. This would mean Paul was including in Saul's reign the 7 1/2 years when David reigned in Hebron and Saul's son continued Saul's reign and kingdom. Jews in those days usually rounded off the last half year or part year of a reign and added it as a year to the total, thus giving 40 years here. Other writers conjecture that King Saul reigned 42 years and that Paul rounded it off here to 40 years.

**22.** **And when he had removed him:** . . . After removing him, *—TCNT* . . . And taking him away, *—KJII* . . . After deposing him, *—MOFT* . . . But God took the throne away from him again, *—BECK* . . . And when in time God took Saul away, *—LAMS* . . . deposing him, *—BRKL.*
**he raised up unto them David to be their king:** . . . he raised David to the throne, *—TCNT* . . . He raised up David for their king, *—BRKL.*
**to whom also he gave testimony, and said:** . . . and he bore also this testimony to him, *—TCNT* . . . a man of whom God Himself bore witness in the words, *—PHLP* . . . This is what God said about him, NCV.
**I have found David the son of Jesse:**
**a man after mine own heart:** . . . a man I love, *—WEYM* . . . a man dear to my heart, *—BB* . . . a man agreeable to my mind, *—BRKL* . . . is the man I like, *—SEB* . . . the kind of man I want, *—NCV.*
**which shall fulfil all my will:** . . . who will carry out all my purposes, *—TCNT* . . . obey all My commands, *—WEYM* . . . do all that my will requires, *—WLMS* . . . carry out My whole program, *—BRKL* . . . who does all my will, *—KLGS* . . . He will do all the things I want him to do, *—SEB.*

**13:22.** The climax of this historical part of Paul's sermon came when he pointed out that God removed Saul from his throne and gave them (raised up for them) David as their king. One thing was really important about David. God bore witness to him that he was a man after God's own heart, one who would do all God's will. Saul became a self-willed king. In contrast to him, David, deep in his heart, really wanted to do all of God's will. This is what made him a man after God's own heart. God wanted a person who would do all His will whether he felt like it or not.

Outwardly, David was not an obvious choice, a young boy who was relegated to keeping the sheep. But the radiance of his personality and the brightness of his eyes (1 Samuel 16:12) showed that his inner life was clean and pure. He was a young man who looked out over the hills and into the sky, not to dream, but to see the glory of God (Psalm 19:1).

**23.** **Of this man's seed hath God:** . . . It was from this man's descendants that God, *—TCNT* . . . Of this man's posterity, *—RSV* . . . this man's offspring,

—*LAMS* . . . God has brought one of David's descendants, —*SEB*.

**according to his promise:** . . . in fulfillment of His promise, *Wey*-

**raised unto Israel a Saviour, Jesus:** . . . brought Israel a Saviour, —*TCNT* . . . given Israel a Saviour, —*NORL* . . . to be their Savior, —*SEB*.

**13:23.** The people in Paul's audience knew of God's promise to David. After David brought back the ark to Jerusalem, he wanted to build a temple. It was not God's time nor God's will for David. But God did not let David go away in disappointment. Because David submitted to God's will, God gave him a new promise, a promise beyond David's expectations. This promise, known as the Davidic Covenant, is one of the great covenants of the Bible. It included the promise that David's son would succeed him on the throne and build a temple as a place where God's name could be mentioned in prayer with assurance that God keeps His promises. The covenant also revealed God's purpose to make David's throne eternal (2 Samuel 7:11-16; Psalm 89:29-34). Individual kings of David's line would still be punished for sin, but God would not let David's line be replaced as Saul's had been.

Paul's audience also knew the prophecies that God would raise up a greater seed to David (Isaiah 9:6, 7; 11:1-5), as well as the prophecy that He would give David's throne to the One whose right it is (Ezekiel 21:27). Paul declared that God had fulfilled His promise, and from the seed (descendants) of David raised up a Saviour, Jesus (Matthew 1:21).

24. **When John had first preached before his coming:** . . . John had proclaimed, before Jesus came among them, —*TCNT* . . . John's pre-proclamation, —*CNDT* . . . Before whose coming, —*LAMS*.

**the baptism of repentance to all the people of Israel:** . . . baptism as an expression of repentance, —*WLMS* . . . the baptism which goes with a change of heart, —*BB* . . . of changed hearts and lives, —*NCV* . . . to change their hearts and to be immersed, —*SEB*.

**13:24.** Paul further identified Jesus as the One John the Baptist recognized as the One who was to come. John the Baptist's ministry was well known everywhere. He had awakened the nation of Israel to their need of repentance as preparation for the coming of the Messiah. Many were sincerely waiting for the consolation (or the Consoler) of Israel and for redemption to come (Luke 2:25, 38). John's baptism was a baptism because of repentance, a baptism that symbolized a repentance which had already taken place.

25. **And as John fulfilled his course:** . . . As John was drawing towards the end of his career,

—*TCNT* . . . was finishing his course, —*RSV* . . . he was finishing his race, —*MNTG* . . . was completing his work, —*BB* . . . finishing the course of his office, —*WUST* . . . was about finished with his work, —*NORL* . . . completing his mission, —*FNTN* . . . reached the end of his time, —*PHLP* . . . was nearing the end of his life-work, —*TNT*.

**he said:** . . . he used to say, —*TCNT* . . . repeatedly asked the people, —*MNTG*.

**Whom think ye that I am? I am not he:** . . . What do you think I am? I am not the Christ, —*TCNT*.

**But, behold, there cometh one after me:** . . . No, but after me one is coming, —*RSV* . . . no, he is coming after me, —*MOFT* . . . He is coming later, —*NCV*.

**whose shoes of his feet I am not worthy to loose:** . . . He is so superior to me that I am not worthy, —*NOLI* . . . whose shoe, even, I am not worthy to untie, —*TCNT* . . . whose sandal . . . to unfasten, —*WEYM* . . . to untie his shoestrings, —*MRDK*.

**13:25.** John the Baptist's denial that he was the One to come was also well-known. John's testimony to Jesus was therefore important. John was not trying to start a new sect or religion. He did not seek to build an organization around himself. He was preparing men to meet the Mighty One who held their eternal destiny in His hands. John gained many disciples who became very loyal to him. Yet he kept pointing them ahead to the coming One, the One who would take a position ahead of John in importance and dignity.

John therefore was willing to take the humble place. He confessed he was not worthy to loose (unloose, take off) the shoes (the sandals) of that One. He felt he was not worthy to do the most menial task, a task usually done by a slave.

26. **Men and brethren, children of the stock of Abraham:** . . . Brethren! sons of the race of Abraham, —*RTHM* . . . descendants of the family of Abraham, —*WEYM*.

**and whosoever among you feareth God:** . . . all among you who fear God, —*PHLP* . . . and you non-Jews who worship God, —*NCV*.

**to you is the word of this salvation sent:** . . . it was to us that the Message of this Salvation was sent, —*TCNT*.

**13:26.** The second part of this sermon in Antioch (verses 26-37) deals with the death and resurrection of Jesus and with the witness of the apostles as well as the witness of the Old Testament Scriptures.

Paul addressed the Jews in his audience as men, brothers, descendants of the family of Abraham. By this he drew attention to their common heritage of the promises and blessings given to Abraham, a heritage that was intended to bring blessing to all the families (nations) of the earth (Genesis 12:3). He also addressed the Gentiles as those who were "fearers of," that is, those who continually reverenced (the one, true) God. "To you (both Jew and Gentile) is the word (*logos*, message) of this salvation sent." The message of salvation through faith in Christ was sent to them personally through those commissioned by the Lord Jesus.

**27. For they that dwell at Jerusalem, and their rulers:** ... for the inhabitants of, *—TNT.*

**because they knew him not:** ... not recognizing him, *—RTHM* ... failing to recognize Jesus, *—TCNT* ... refused to recognize him, *—PHLP* ... because they were ignorant of Him, *—WEYM* ... did not realize it, *—SEB.*

**nor yet the voices of the prophets which are read every sabbath day:** ... did not understand the predictions of, *—NOLI* ... and not understanding the utterances of, *—TCNT* ... and to understand the voice of the prophets, *—PHLP.*

**they have fulfilled them in condemning him:** ... Yet they made the prophets' words come true by condemning Jesus, *—TEV* ... have actually fulfilled the predictions, *—WEYM* ... the utterances of, *—TNT.*

**13:27.** Paul next showed that the death of Jesus was the fulfillment of God's prophetic Word and that it was carried out by the Jews living in Jerusalem and their rulers.

It is important to notice here that Paul did not blame the death of Jesus on all the Jews or even on the Jews in general. He put the blame only on those Jews and their rulers in Jerusalem who were actually involved. He also recognized that they did it because they were ignorant of Jesus and of the voices of the prophets whose books were read every Sabbath in their synagogues. The Greek word used here sometimes implies willful ignorance or a deliberate ignoring of the truth. Since they did know these prophecies and had often heard them read, willful ignorance is indeed meant here.

The result was that these Jerusalem Jews and their rulers (which might include the Romans) fulfilled those prophecies by condemning Jesus and handing Him over for sentencing.

**28. And though they found no cause of death in him:** ... They found no ground at all for condemning him to death, *—TCNT* ... Without having found Him guilty of any capital offence, *—WEYM* ... For though they found no cause, *—PHLP* ... couldn't find any real reason why he should die, *—SEB* ... they did not find any reason for the death sentence, *—TNT* ... found nothing to justify his death, *—JB.*

**yet desired they Pilate that he should be slain:** ... and yet demanded his execution from Pilate, *—TCNT* ... they urged Pilate to have Him put to death, *—WEYM* ... begged Pilate to have him executed, *—PHLP* ... asked Pilate to kill him, *—SEB.*

**13:28.** Paul also said the Jerusalem Jews found no cause, no real grounds for a death sentence, yet they asked Pilate to have Him killed (done away

with, destroyed, put to death in a violent manner). The Jerusalem leaders did seek to find some grounds for condemning Jesus to death but they were never successful.

**29. And when they had fulfilled all that was written of him:** ... After carrying out everything written about him, *—TCNT* ... And when they had completed, *—PHLP* ... had accomplished all that, *—TNT* ... when they finished all things, *—KJII.*

**they took him down from the tree:** ... they took Jesus down from the cross, *—TCNT.*

**and laid him in a sepulchre:** ... and laid him in a tomb, *—RSV.*

**13:29.** The Jerusalem dwellers fulfilled all the prophecies concerning the death of the Messiah, the Christ. In their preliminary scourging they fulfilled Isaiah 50:6 and 53:5. In their mockery as they bowed the knee, they portrayed the fact that Jesus is the King of kings and Lord of lords and before Him every knee shall someday bow (Revelation 19:16; cf. Isaiah 45:23; Philippians 2:10, 11). The further mocking and beating of their helpless victim and His silent acceptance of it brought a further fulfillment of Isaiah 53:7. Taking Jesus to a place outside the city walls fulfilled the typology of the sin offering on the Day of Atonement (Leviticus 16:27; Hebrew 13:11). Even in casting lots over His clothes, the calloused executioners unconsciously were fulfilling the great prophecy of Psalm 22:16-18.

These prophecies having been fulfilled, Jesus was taken down from the "tree" (the rough wooden cross; compare Deuteronomy 21:23 and Galatians 3:13) and laid in a tomb. "Tree" is a general term here for anything made of wood. Paul did not name Nicodemus and Joseph of Arimathea as the ones who actually took Jesus down from the cross and put Him in Joseph's new tomb (John 19:38, 39). Probably they were unknown to the people in the synagogue at Antioch.

**30. But God raised him from the dead:** ... from among the dead, *—RTHM* ... out from among the dead, *—WUST* ... raised him up from death! *—SEB.*

**13:30.** In contrast to what man did to Jesus, God raised Him from the dead (out from among those who had died). This was in contrast also to the expectations of those who had Him crucified. God did what to men seemed impossible. The tomb could not hold Him.

**31. And he was seen many days of them which came up with him from Galilee to Jerusalem:** ... Who appeared during many days unto them who, *—RTHM* ... After this, for many days, Jesus was seen by the people who had gone with him,

—*SEB*...those who had gone with Jesus...saw him, —*NCV.*

**who are his witnesses unto the people:**...They are now telling the people the truth about Him, —*BECK* ... these men are his witnesses before, —*NOLI* ... These are the ones who tell the people about him, —*NLTG.*

**13:31.** After His resurrection Jesus was seen over a period of many days by those who came up with Him to Jerusalem from Galilee. These were not only the 11 apostles who were all from Galilee, but also included the 120 who were present on the Day of Pentecost, and probably others as well. Paul said these were (now, at that time) witnesses to the people. ("The people" here could mean the people of Israel or it could be used in a universal sense meaning "all the people.")

**32. And we declare unto you glad tidings:**...We, too, have the good News to tell you, —*TCNT*...So we are bringing you the joyful tidings, —*BRKL*...We also proclaim to you, —*NOLI*...preach to you, —*LAMS*...We are telling you the Good news, —*SEB.*

**how that the promise which was made unto the fathers:** ... What God promised our fathers, —*NIV*...about the promise made to our ancestors, —*TCNT*...God has fulfilled for us the promises which he made to, —*NOLI* ... about the promise made to our forefathers, —*WEYM*...to our early fathers, —*NLTG.*

**13:32.** Paul then said this was the glad tidings, the good news, the gospel that he and his company were proclaiming (preaching) to them. This good news concerned the promise given to the fathers (the Old Testament fathers, especially the patriarchs, Abraham, Isaac, and Jacob).

Paul was not speaking of the nearly 100 prophecies which were fulfilled in connection with the death and resurrection of Jesus. Rather, he was speaking of one particular promise, the promise given to Abraham and confirmed to Abraham, Isaac, and Jacob. This promise had its beginning in Genesis 3:15 that a future Seed of the woman would crush the head of the same old serpent who tempted Eve. It was a promise of blessing through the greater Seed of Abraham who is also the greater David, and who, as the Suffering Servant of Isaiah 53 would accomplish our redemption. It was good news too that this promise was not only for the Jews, but for all people of every language and of every nation, family, or group.

**33. God hath fulfilled the same unto us their children:**...We are their children, —*NCV*...that our children have had the promise fulfilled to them by God to the very letter, —*TCNT*...God has amply fulfilled it to our children, —*WEYM* ... has fulfilled the promise made to the fathers, —*TNT*...God has made

this promise come true for us, —*SEB*...God has finished this for us who are their children, —*NLTG.*

**in that he hath raised up Jesus again:**...by his raising Jesus from the grave, —*TCNT*...from death, —*SEB.*

**as it is also written in the second psalm:**...This is endorsed, —*PHLP*...This is just what is said in the second Psalm, —*TCNT*...We also read about this in Psalm 2, —*SEB.*

**Thou art my Son, this day have I begotten thee:**...My son art thou:...I this day have begotten thee, —*RTHM* ... Today I am Your Father, —*BECK*...I have given you life today, —*NLTG.*

**13:33.** The promise made to their fathers was now fulfilled (completely fulfilled) to their children by God's raising Jesus from the dead.

Paul confirmed this by quoting from Psalm 2:7 where God declares the Messianic King to be His Son, and says, "This day have I begotten thee." "Begotten thee" means "I have become your Father (and still am)." It translates a Hebrew phrase that means literally, "I have brought you out." It could be used of a woman who brings a child out into the world at birth. But when this phrase was used by a king, it was a technical formula declared by a king to one who was already his son and was now brought out to the people and declared to be king to share the throne with his father as his associate and as his equal. This was the kind of thing David did when he had Solomon brought out and declared to be king when Adonijah was trying to take over the throne. (See 1 Kings 1:33, 34, 48.)

Psalm 2 refers to Jesus being declared by God publicly to be His Son. God did this first when Jesus began His ministry and God sent His Spirit upon Him (Luke 3:22). He did it even more unmistakably when He raised Jesus from the dead. As Romans 1:3, 4 says, Jesus, who was "made of the seed of David according to the flesh" was "declared to be the Son of God with power, according to the Spirit of holiness (or, by means of the Holy Spirit), by the resurrection from the dead." Since Luke was condensing a sermon that took a considerable time to preach, it is probable that Paul explained these things more fully to his audience.

**34. And as concerning that he raised him up from the dead:** ... And in that he raised him from among the dead, —*RTHM* ... And as a proof that he has raised, —*MOFT*...he confirmed his Resurrection and his immortality, —*NOLI*...God proved that Jesus was His Son by raising Him, —*NLTG.*

**now no more to return to corruption:**...never again to be in the position of one soon to return to decay, —*WEYM*...never to turn to dust, —*BRKL*...never again to return to decay, —*NORL*...to death's decay, —*TNT*...He will never die again, —*NLTG.*

**he said on this wise:** ... He speaks thus, —*WEYM*...He expressed this way, —*BRKL.*

**I will give you the sure mercies of David:** . . . I will give you the sacred promises made to, *—TCNT* . . . the holy and trustworthy promises made to, *—WEYM* . . . the sure grace, *—MRDK* . . . will finish the promises made, *—NLTG* . . . sacred blessings, *—BRKL.*

**13:34.** Since God raised Jesus from the dead He will never again be on the point of returning to corruption (decay); He will never again return to the grave or the place of the dead. Paul meant that Christ's resurrection body is not subject to death or decay.

Paul continued by mentioning Isaiah 55:3 which refers to the sure mercies of David in a passage that speaks of pardon and salvation. By "mercies" he meant the divine decrees which are sure, trustworthy, dependable. The point is that the promises to David were not for David himself, nor for the people of his day, but for "you," that is, for a generation still future to Isaiah. The implication is that this refers to those who will be living after the sacrificial death of the Suffering Servant of Isaiah 53.

**35. Wherefore he saith also in another psalm:** . . . in another Psalm, it is said, *—TCNT.*
**Thou shalt not suffer thine Holy One to see corruption:** . . . Thou wilt not give up . . . to undergo corruption, *—TCNT* . . . You will not let your Loved One experience decay, *—BECK* . . . go back to dust! *—NLTG.*

**13:35.** Paul then pointed out that those mercies, those promises given to David, include Psalm 16:10 which says God will not permit (give) His Holy One to see corruption (decay or destruction or dissolution of the body). "Holy One" (Greek, *hosion*) is the singular of the same word used of the "mercies" or divine decrees pertaining to David (Greek, *hosia*). When it is used of a person it means consecrated, devout, pleasing to God, and therefore, holy. This fits with the words of Jesus' Heavenly Father who said, "You are my Son, whom I love; with you I am well pleased" (Luke 3:22, NIV). (The ordinary Greek word for holy is *hagios. Hosios* is used here to draw attention to the fact that the sure decrees relating to David point to the Messiah, David's greater Son or descendant.)

**36. For David, after he had served his own generation by the will of God:** . . . David, of course, after obediently doing God's will in his own time, *—TCNT* . . . after serving his divine missions, *—NOLI.*
**fell on sleep:** . . . fell asleep, *—RSV.*
**and was laid unto his fathers:** . . . was gathered to his forefathers, *—WEYM* . . . and was buried with his fathers, *—BRKL* . . . was put into a grave close to his Father's grave, *—NLTG.*

**and saw corruption:** . . . his body rotted, *—TEV* . . . He did in fart see corruption, *—PHLP* . . . He did suffer decay, *—TNT.*

**13:36.** Psalm 16:10 cannot apply to David for two reasons. First, David did not serve the future generation to whom Isaiah promised the sure decrees pertaining to David. He served his own generation, not the "you" of Isaiah 55:3. David served his own generation in the will of God, but the promise does not apply to him.

Second, after he had finished the work God gave him to do, David fell asleep (in the sleep of death) and was gathered to his forefathers, and his body did see corruption. Thus, the words of Psalm 16:10 cannot possibly apply to David.

**37. But he, whom God raised again, saw no corruption:** . . . this man, *—PHLP* . . . did not suffer decay, *—MOFT.*

**13:37.** In contrast to what happened to David, the One God raised up from the dead (Jesus) did not see corruption.

Though Paul presented this truth in a little different way than Peter did in 2:29, it is still the same truth. Clearly, the apostle Paul preached the same gospel the other apostles did. This is important, for some unbelievers have tried to put Paul in opposition to the other apostles. But as Galatians 1:8, 9; 2:2-8 show, Paul declared there is only one gospel, the one he preached. He presented that gospel to the apostles and elders in Jerusalem. They did not feel they had to add anything to it, but gave Paul full approval, not only to his gospel but to his ministry among the Gentiles.

**38. Be it known unto you therefore:** . . . I would, therefore, have you know, *—TCNT* . . . Understand therefore, *—WEYM* . . . And so, let it be clear to you, *—BB* . . . It should be clear then to you, *—BRKL* . . . It is therefore imperative, *—PHLP.*
**men and brethren, that through this man is preached unto you the forgiveness of sins:** . . . that our announcement is, that there is forgiveness of sins for you through Jesus, *—TCNT* . . . the putting away of sins, *—KLGS.*

**13:38.** Now comes the final part of Paul's sermon in Pisidian Antioch (verses 38-41). Its purpose is exhortation.

Again addressing his audience as brothers, Paul said that therefore (because of Christ's death and resurrection) "through this man is preached (proclaimed, announced) unto you forgiveness of sins." This is the good news, not only that Jesus died and rose again, but that He did so on the sinner's behalf so that through Him there can be pardon that includes forgiveness of sins and the cancellation of guilt, so those sins will never be remembered or brought up against any believer in the coming judgment.

**39. And by him all that believe are justified from all things:** ... and that, in union with him, all who believe in him are cleared from every charge, —TCNT ... and in Him every believer is absolved from all offences, —WEYM ... through union with Him ... is given right standing with God and freed from every charge, —WLMS ... righteous and free, —BECK ... acquitted, —CNFT.

**from which ye could not be justified by the law of Moses:** ... cleared under the Law of Moses, —TCNT ... from which you could not be absolved under, —WEYM ... from which you could not be freed by, —WLMS ... even those from which the law of Moses cannot set you free, —NORL ... not able to be acquitted, —FNTN ... could never set him free, —PHLP.

**13:39.** By this One (Jesus) also, all believers are justified; they are made righteous in God's eyes, acquitted, and treated as if they had never sinned. This further emphasizes that all who are believing and trusting Jesus are therefore forever freed from the guilt and punishment of their sins. Believers are forgiven of all those things for which the law of Moses was not able to provide justification.

The Greek word order here is, "even from all which you were not able to be justified by the law of Moses, in this One every one believing is justified." Some take this to mean the Law provided justification for some things, and the gospel provides justification for the rest. But the meaning is rather that the Law could not really provide justification at all: only through faith in Jesus Christ is a person justified.

**40. Beware therefore, lest that come upon you, which is spoken of in the prophets:** ... Take care, —TCNT ... So be careful the prophetic utterance does not become your experience, —BRKL ... Now be careful, or what the prophets said will happen to you, —BECK.

**13:40.** Paul concluded his sermon with a warning. Let his audience, Jews and Gentiles, beware lest the things spoken by the prophets come upon them. They knew the prophets not only spoke of good news, not only prophesied future blessings through the Messiah, but they also gave many warnings, severe warnings. In fact, the major portion of the prophetical books is full of warnings.

**41. Behold, ye despisers, and wonder, and perish:** ... Listen, —NORL ... See, ye despisers, and marvel and disappear, —RTHM ... you scorners, —KLGS ... and hide your heads, —TCNT ... Look, you scoffers! Then wonder and vanish away, —WLMS.

**for I work a work in your days:** ... For I am about to do a great work myself, —TCNT ... Because I am carrying on a work in your time, —WEYM.

**a work which ye shall in no wise believe:** ... A work which you will never believe, —TCNT ... in your times a deed, —NOLI ... utterly refuse to believe, —WEYM.

**though a man declare it unto you:** ... Though one relate it in full unto you, —RTHM ... even if it is made clear to you, —BB ... though one may tell you in detail, —WLMS ... even if someone were to explain it to you! —SEB ... someone tells you about it, —NLTG.

**13:41.** The warning Paul emphasized uses language taken from Habakkuk 1:5 in the Septuagint (LXX) version. (Notice the slightly different wording: the Septuagint reads, "Behold, ye *despisers*," while the Hebrew [Masoretic text] reads, "Behold ye *among the heathen* [or *nations*]"; cf. Isaiah 28:22.) In Romans 2:4 Paul warned the Jews against despising the riches of God's kindness. Here he warned his audience lest they become despisers of the message of Christ and of the forgiveness of sins Christ offers. Those who do so will be surprised and filled with fear when they face the coming judgment, for they will perish or be removed to destruction. Paul wanted his audience to be on their guard lest an even greater judgment would come on them than that which came on the rebels to whom Habakkuk spoke.

The work of God Habakkuk was talking about was the judgment He was bringing through the Chaldeans (Babylonians) who took the Jews captive and destroyed Jerusalem and Solomon's temple. They did not believe judgment would come, but it did. Many today do not believe the end of this age and the judgments are coming, but they will. The only hope for any person is the salvation and forgiveness of sins that Christ offers. Apart from Him all shall perish. (See John 3:16 where the word "perish" speaks of destruction, ruin, and eternal loss.) The word used to translate *Habakkuk* means to disappear into destruction or ruin. Those who reject Christ will not be present to enjoy the blessings salvation through Christ provides.

**42. And when the Jews were gone out of the synagogue:** ... And as they were going out, —PHLP, —RTHM ... out of the Jewish place of worship, —NLTG.

**the Gentiles besought that these words might be preached to them the next sabbath:** ... they kept on beseeching, —RTHM ... they were implored by the people, —NOLI ... the people begged for a repetition of this teaching, —TCNT ... the Gentiles asked that these words, —KJII ... this repeated to them, —MOFT ... on the same subjects the next Sabbath, —TNT ... the people asked them to talk about these things on the next Day of Rest, —NLTG.

**13:42.** As the people were leaving the synagogue, they asked that these words (this message) would continue to be spoken to them the next Sabbath. A large number of ancient manuscripts leave out the words "Jews" and "Gentiles" in this verse. It does seem likely that at this point both Jews and Gentiles wanted Paul to continue giving them these words (Greek, *rhēmata*) from God's Word, a fact which is confirmed by the following verse.

**43. Now when the congregation was broken up:** . . . Now when the meeting was ended, *—BB* . . . and when the synagogue was dismissed, *—BRKL* . . . had dispersed, *—TNT* . . . went from the place of worship, *—NLTG*.

**many of the Jews and religious proselytes:** . . . devout converts from heathenism, *—WEYM* . . . God-fearing Gentiles who had become Jews, *—BB*.

**followed Paul and Barnabas:** . . . allied themselves with, *—WLMS*.

**who, speaking to them:** . . . in conversation with them, *—TCNT* . . . who spoke personally to them, *—PHLP* . . . They preached to them again, *—NOLI*.

**persuaded them to continue in the grace of God:** . . . urged them to continue to rely on the mercy of God, *—TCNT* . . . on the unmerited favor, *—WLMS*.

**13:43.** When the meeting of the synagogue ended, many of the Jews and the worshiping (God-fearing) proselytes (converts to Judaism) followed Paul and Barnabas. Normally, they would have gone home to enjoy the Sabbath feast. (Compare Mark 1:29-31 where "she ministered" means she served a meal.) But these who followed Paul and Barnabas were concerned about spiritual food. The apostles had stirred a deeper hunger in their hearts.

Paul and Barnabas did not turn them away, but spent some time with them, speaking to them and effectually persuading them to remain in the grace of God.

This means they took time to explain the gospel more in detail and to show that salvation is indeed by grace through faith apart from the Law. They accepted that grace by believing the message. What joy must have filled the hearts of Paul and Barnabas as they encouraged those who believed to remain or continue in this grace. The same phraseology is used in 11:23 where Barnabas exhorted the new Gentile converts in Syrian Antioch to remain true to the Lord. These serious exhortations are repeated throughout the New Testament.

**44. And the next sabbath day came almost the whole city together to hear the word of God:** . . . on the coming Sabbath, *—KJII* . . . almost the whole population of the city, *—WEYM* . . . almost all the city, *—YNG* . . . almost the whole town, *—BECK* . . . almost the entire city, *—WUST* . . . almost all the inhabitants of the city had assembled, *—NOLI* . . . all the people of the

town came to hear, *—NLTG* . . . gathered to hear God's message, *—TCNT*.

**13:44.** The message, the exhortation, and the further teaching given by Barnabas and Paul must have stirred the new believers to a high pitch of enthusiasm. The Godfearing Gentiles must have been especially excited by this assurance of forgiveness and salvation through Christ. They spread the word about this good news so effectively that the next Sabbath nearly the whole city assembled to hear the words concerning the Lord Jesus. Pisidian Antioch was a center of Greek culture and a prosperous commercial center. It also had a large number of Roman colonists among its chief citizens. Jewish colonists had also settled there for over 200 years, primarily for business and commercial reasons. Since the synagogue had been there so long, the people of the city apparently knew at least something of their teachings, and quite a number of Gentiles had become proselytes or converts to Judaism.

**45. But when the Jews saw the multitudes:** . . . the crowds of people, *—TCNT* . . . immense crowd, *—NORL* . . . when they saw so many people, *—NLTG*.

**they were filled with envy:** . . . were filled with jealousy, *—RTHM* . . . they became exceedingly jealous, *—TCNT* . . . with angry jealousy, *—WEYM* . . . completely overcome by their jealousy, *—WLMS* . . . terribly jealous, *—BRKL*.

**and spake against those things which were spoken by Paul:** . . . and contradicted the things, *—ASV* . . . they interrupted Paul's address, *—NORL* . . . they bitterly opposed the words, *—LAMS* . . . and denied the things spoken by Paul, *—KJII* . . . They used abusive language, *—TNT* . . . argued against what Paul said, *—EVRD*.

**contradicting and blaspheming:** . . . in abusive language, *—TCNT* . . . and abused him, *—WEYM* . . . covering him with abuse, *—PHLP* . . . even to abuse him, *—WLMS* . . . talked abusively, *—BRKL* . . . saying slanderous and evil things, *—WUST* . . . said insulting things, *—EVRD* . . . by saying he was wrong, *—NLTG*.

**13:45.** The sight of the crowds thronging to hear Paul filled the Jews with jealousy. Like the Pharisees and Sadducees who became jealous of Jesus, they could not bear to think they were losing their influence and their religious leadership. They undoubtedly interpreted their jealousy, however, as a zeal for God and for the law of Moses. As Paul later said, the Christ-rejecting Jews did have a zeal for God, but not according to knowledge. Actually, the Greek word *zēlos* has the good meaning of zeal and the bad meaning of jealousy or envy. Romans 10:2 indicates that the zeal of the unconverted Jews was a jealous eagerness to uphold what they thought was God's honor.

Because of this jealousy and misplaced zeal, the unconverted Jews in Pisidian Antioch began to speak against what Paul was teaching. They even blasphemed the gospel.

This is a further indication they were afraid of losing their influence over these Gentiles who had been looking to them for teaching. It probably implies also that they had a zeal for a Judaism that had no room for blessings on Gentiles who did not first become Jews.

**46. Then Paul and Barnabas waxed bold, and said:**...speaking boldly said, –RTHM...spoke out fearlessly, –TCNT...courageously spoke out, –WLMS...did not mince their words but said, –PHLP...said to the people in plain words, –NLTG.

**It was necessary that the word of God should first have been spoken to you:**...We were bound to proclaim, –WEYM...We felt it our duty to speak the message, –PHLP...bound to preach the Gospel to you first, –NOLI...to you Jews first, –WLMS.

**but seeing ye put it from you:**... but since you reject it, –TCNT ... But since you spurn it, –PHLP, –WEYM...you refuse to listen, –EVRD.

**and judge yourselves unworthy of everlasting life:**... and declare yourselves unworthy of, –NOLI...to be unworthy, –WEYM.

**lo, we turn to the Gentiles:**...why, we turn to the heathen! –TCNT...we are now turning to the non-Jews, –BECK...So we will now go to the people of other nations! –EVRD.

**13:46.** The opposition of these unconverted Jews did not frighten Paul and Barnabas. Instead, they grew bold and responded with a great deal of fearless freedom of speech. Very openly they told these Jews it was necessary for them to go to the Jew first in order to fulfill God's plan. (Compare Romans 1:16.) Romans 3:2 indicates that the chief reason was because "unto them were committed the oracles (Greek, *logia*, 'sayings, utterances,' including the promises) of God." Romans 9:4, 5 adds that they had the adoption (the place of sons; see Exodus 4:22; Isaiah 1:2), the glory, the covenants, the giving of the Law, the service or worship of God, and the promises. It was God's plan that the gospel be announced to them first, but with the intention of using them to spread the gospel to all the nations of the world (as God promised Abraham, Genesis 12:3).

But since the Jews had scornfully thrust away and rejected the gospel, they thus judged themselves by their conduct to be unworthy of eternal life. (As John 5:26 and 15:1-6 show, eternal life is Christ's life in the believer, flowing as from the vine to the branches.)

Then the apostles declared that as a result of the Jews' rejecting the gospel, they were turning (at that moment) to the Gentiles. ("Behold" indicates

this turning to the Gentiles was something unexpected and surprising to the Jews.)

**47. For so hath the Lord commanded us, saying:**...For this is the Lord's order to us, –TCNT...The Lord gave us a commission. It is this, –NORL...This is what the Lord told us to do, –EVRD.

**I have set thee to be a light of the Gentiles:**...I have destined thee for a light to the heathen, –TCNT...I have appointed you to enlighten, –NOLI...for the non-Jewish nations, –EVRD.

**that thou shouldest be for salvation unto the ends of the earth:**...To be the means of salvation to, –TCNT...to bring salvation to, –MOFT...to save people all over the earth, –BECK.

**13:47.** Turning to the Gentiles was not really the apostles' own idea. Rather, it was obedience to the prophetic Word given in Isaiah 49:6 concerning the Messiah, God's Servant. In this context God is saying it was not enough for the tribes of Israel to be regathered and restored. His purpose was to make the Messiah light and salvation for all the nations of the world (which shows how the blessing promised through the Seed of Abraham would be fulfilled). Isaiah 42:6 also speaks of the Messiah as a light to the nations (the Gentiles). When Jesus was brought to the temple as a baby, the godly, Spirit-led Simeon also recognized Him as "a light to lighten the Gentiles, and the glory of thy people Israel" (Luke 2:32). Paul recognized they had the responsibility of bringing the light of Christ to the Gentiles.

**48. And when the Gentiles heard this, they were glad:**...On hearing this, the heathen were delighted, –TCNT...The Gentiles listened with delight, –WEYM ... The Gentiles were overjoyed when they heard this, –NORL.

**and glorified the word of the Lord:**...and extolled God's message, –TCNT...and praised God's message, –GDSP...and thanked God for His Message, –PHLP.

**and as many as were ordained to eternal life believed:**...and all who were predestined to eternal Life, –WEYM...and those marked out by God for, –BB...as many as are disposed, –ALFD...many...believed the message, –EVRD.

**13:48.** Hearing this, the Gentiles rejoiced and glorified the Word of the Lord. That is, they kept glorifying, giving honor to, and magnifying the Truth, the gospel preached by Paul and Barnabas. While the Jews were trying to contradict the Word concerning Jesus, the Gentiles were telling everyone how wonderful it was and giving God thanks for it.

There is some controversy over the word translated "ordained," (*tassō*). Elsewhere in the New Testament, the word means "to determine" (cf. 22:10, Jesus told Paul that certain things were "appointed," i.e., determined, assigned, for him to do). It can also mean to appoint (cf. 15:2, where Paul, Barnabas, and others were appointed by the church in Antioch to go to Jerusalem). (See also Matthew 28:16; Luke 7:8; Romans 13:1; 1 Corinthians 16:15.) While there is a strong indication of predestination, the text may simply be trying to distinguish between those who were converts (*hosoi*) and those who were not.

**49. And the word of the Lord was published throughout all the region:** ... was spread abroad, *–ASV* . . . was disseminated all over that region, *–NOLI* . . . the message of the Lord was spreading through the whole country, *–EVRD*.

**13:49.** The result of the enthusiastic witness by the Gentile believers was that the Word of the Lord (the Word; Greek, *logos*) concerning the Lord Jesus was carried or spread continually by them throughout the whole region.

**50. But the Jews stirred up the devout and honourable women:** . . . the Jews instigated, *–NOYS* . . . worked upon the feelings of religions and respectable, *–PHLP* . . . influenced the gentlewomen of rank who worshipped with them, *–WEYM* . . . the devout women of wealth, *–BRKL* . . . the most religious and respected women, *–NORL* . . . incited the women worshippers of high standing, *–TNT* . . . the pious ladies, *–NOLI*.

**and the chief men of the city;** ... and the leading men of the town, *–TCNT* . . . and the leading citizens, *–MNTG* . . . the outstanding men, *–BRKL* . . . the foremost men of, *–TNT*.

**and raised persecution against Paul and Barnabas:** . . . and so started a persecution, *–WLMS* . . . and instigated persecution, *–BRKL*.

**and expelled them out of their coasts:** . . . and drove them out of their neighbourhood, *–TCNT* . . . out of the district, *–WEYM* . . . *they* ejected them from their boundaries, *–CNDT* . . . out of their boundaries, *–WUST* . . . expelled them, *–PHLP* . . . from their region, *–NIV*.

**13:50.** The unbelieving Jews then got the attention of devout, worshiping, Godfearing women of honorable positions in society, convinced them that Paul and Barnabas were wrong, and urged them to do something. With their help the unbelieving Jews also persuaded the chief men of the city government to try to stop Paul and his company. By this means the unconverted Jews aroused persecution to the point that Paul and Barnabas were forced out of the district. "Their coasts" means the region or district under the control of these city officials. Paul made it clear in 1 Thessalonians 2:15, 16 that it was their speaking to the Gentiles that aroused the Jews to this kind of persecution.

**51. But they shook off the dust of their feet against them:** . . . They, however, shook the dust off, *–TCNT* . . . as a protest against them, *–WLMS*.

**and came unto Iconium:** . . . and went to Iconium, *–RSV*.

**13:51.** Paul and Barnabas did not try to confront the city officials. They knew there were faithful believers who would carry on the work of the Lord. So they simply shook the dust off their feet as a testimony against those who had forced them out of the city. This was something Jesus commanded His disciples to do (Matthew 10:14; Mark 6:11; Luke 9:5; 10:11). It was a sharp rebuke. By rejecting Paul and Barnabas, the Jews were rejecting Christ. By shaking the dust off their feet Paul and Barnabas were indicating the deadly effects of their rejection. It meant these people had broken every bond with God and His true people.

Paul and Barnabas went on to Iconium, a Phrygian city in the southern part of the Roman province of Galatia. It was about 60 miles east and a little south of Pisidian Antioch on a plateau of 3,370 feet elevation. It was a key city on the border between Phrygia near Lycaonia. It was also a center from which five Roman roads radiated. The Book of Acts makes it clear the Holy Spirit was directing Paul and Barnabas and thus it was God's purpose to make this important city the next new gospel center.

**52. And the disciples were filled with joy:** . . . leaving the disciples full of joy, *–TCNT* . . . and as for the disciples, they were more and more filled with joy, *–WEYM* . . . continued to be full, *–PHLP*.

**and with the Holy Ghost:** . . . controlled by the Holy Spirit, *–WUST*.

**13:52.** The persecutors did not destroy the Church in Pisidian Antioch. The believers continued to be true disciples and followers of Jesus as their Lord and Saviour and were filled with joy and with the Holy Spirit. The Greek tense here indicates they continued to be filled. They obeyed the injunction of Ephesians 5:18 to be "being filled," to keep on being filled with the Holy Spirit. (Though the Epistle to the Ephesians was not yet written, it was surely already part of Paul's teaching.) Notice too how often being filled with joy and being filled with the Spirit go together in the Scriptures!

# Chapter 14

**1. And it came to pass in Iconium:** . . . Their Iconium experience was similar, *–BRKL* . . . Much the same thing happened, *–PHLP*.

**that they went both together into the synagogue of the Jews:** . . . that they entered together, *–ASV* . . . went as usual to the Jewish synagogue,

—EVRD . . . went into the Jewish place of worship, —NLTG.

**and so spake:** . . . and preached, —WEYM . . . and spoke with such conviction, —PHLP . . . and spoke with such effect, —TNT . . . spoke . . . in such a way, —SEB.

**that a great multitude both of the Jews and also of the Greeks believed:** . . . that a large number of both Jews . . . believed them, —TCNT . . . joined the company of believers, —NOLI . . . believed what they said, —SEB.

**14:1.** The preaching at Pisidian Antioch, the great response of the Gentiles, and the persecution that followed set a pattern. Much or all of this was repeated in practically all of the cities Paul visited on his missionary journeys. Iconium was no exception. Arriving there, Paul and Barnabas went first to the synagogue, identified as "the synagogue of the Jews" as a reminder that even though they had turned to the Gentiles in Pisidian Antioch, they still felt it was God's will to go to the Jew first.

As usual, they were given opportunity to speak. Luke did not record the sermon. He simply indicated that they spoke in their usual manner. Paul preached essentially the same message concerning Christ and the forgiveness of sins as he had in Pisidian Antioch and gave the same warning and exhortation as well.

The results were similar. A very large number of both Jews and Greeks (Greek-speaking Gentiles) believed. This would mean they too would then be baptized. They too would be filled with joy and would become excited about spreading the good news to their friends in the city and in the surrounding area.

**2. But the unbelieving Jews:** . . . But the Jews who refused to believe, —TCNT . . . the unpersuaded Jews, —RTHM.

**stirred up the Gentiles, and made their minds evil affected against the brethren:** . . . stirred up the heathen, and poisoned their minds, —TCNT . . . rendered them antagonistic, —WUST . . . and embittered the minds, —ALFD . . . against the disciples, —NORL . . . making them evil-hearted against the brothers, —KJII . . . to oppress the brethren, —LAMS . . . made them persecute the brothers, —SEB.

**14:2.** Then, as before in Pisidian Antioch, unbelieving Jews rose up opposing them. "Unbelieving" here includes the idea of disobedience and rebellion. In fact, the King James Version translates the verb as "disobedient" in Romans 10:21 and 1 Peter 2:7, 8; 3:20. Belief brings obedience, unbelief brings rebellion.

These Jews in their mistaken zeal and jealousy aroused the Gentiles and turned them "against the

brethren," not only against Paul and his company but also against the new believers.

The Jews in this case, however, were not able initially to get as much support from the Gentiles and city officials as the Jews in Pisidian Antioch had, so Paul and Barnabas were not immediately forced out of the city. Therefore, they dared to stay in Iconium a considerable length of time.

**3. Long time therefore abode they:** . . . they tarried there, —ASV . . . remained there, —WEYM.

**speaking boldly in the Lord:** . . . speaking out fearlessly in dependence on the Lord, —TCNT . . . and continued to speak with courage from the Lord, —WLMS.

**which gave testimony unto the word of bis grace:** . . . who bare witness, ASV . . . who supported the Message of his mercy, —TCNT . . . confirmed the message of his grace, —TNT . . . who confirmed their gracious message, —NOLI . . . proved what they said was true, —SEB.

**and granted signs and wonders to be done by their hands:** . . . He helped them do miracles, —SEB . . . by permitting . . . to take place at their hands, —TCNT . . . by allowing, —MOFT . . . allowing them to perform, —PHLP . . . to be effected, —FNTN.

**14:3.** With boldness and freedom of speech they spoke for (or, in) the Lord Jesus (relying on Him and centering all their preaching and teaching in Him). As they did so, the Lord bore witness to the Word (Greek, *logo*, the message) of His grace (His unmerited favor in sending Jesus to save sinners) by giving signs (miraculous signs, supernatural signs) and wonders to be done by their hands.

By these miracles also, the apostles were recognized as Christ's agents doing His work by His authority. (Compare Galatians 3:5 where Paul later showed these Galatians that the miracles which were still being done in their midst were an evidence of God's grace and did not come as a result of the works of the Law.) Luke did not give any details of these miracles, but they surely included a variety as before.

**4. But the multitude of the city was divided:** . . . But the townspeople were divided, —TCNT . . . the great mass of the people of the city were divided in their opinions, —PHLP . . . the city split into parties, —WEYM . . . The inhabitants of the city, —NOLI . . . became divided, —TNT.

**and part held with the Jews, and part with the apostles:** . . . some siding with the Jews, some with the Apostles, —TCNT . . . agreed with, —SEB.

**14:4.** In time the city crowd, that is, the whole population of the city Iconium became sharply divided. Some were with the (unbelieving) Jews. Some held with the apostles.

Notice here that both Paul and Barnabas are called apostles. Barnabas was evidently a witness of the resurrection of Jesus and of His teachings. Possibly he was part of the 70 sent out (Luke 10:1), or possibly he was part of the 120 in the Upper Room. Paul, in defending his apostleship in 1 Corinthians 9:1-6, also included Barnabas with him, as he did in Galatians 2:9, 10.

**5. And when there was an assault made:** ...There was a plot afoot, *—NIV.*

**both of the Gentiles, and also of the Jews:** ...on the part of both heathen and Jews, *—TCNT.*

**with their rulers:** ... with their leading men, *—TCNT* ... with the sanction of their magistrates, *—WEYM* ...in collaboration with the authorities, *—PHLP.*

**to use them despitefully, and to stone them:** ... to treat them shamefully, *—ASV* ...to illtreat and stone them, *—TCNT* ...to insult, *—MOFT* ...in order to abuse, *—KJII* ... wanted to stone them to death, *—SEB.*

**14:5.** Both unbelieving Gentiles and unbelieving Jews joined together with hostile intent. They purposed to treat the apostles outrageously and to stone them to death. The Greek, however, does not mean there was any actual assault, but only the intent and instigation of one. This time, though, they had the support of their rulers including the city officials. Stoning, of course, shows that the Jews were justifying their action by the law of Moses against blasphemy. But they, by despising the gospel message, were blaspheming Christ and God.

**6. They were ware of it:** ... they were warned, *—KJII* ...they became aware of it, *—ASV* ...the Apostles heard of it, *—TCNT* ...the apostles got wind of it, *—MNTG* ... When they became aware of this danger, *—NORL* ...they found out about it, *—BECK* ...aware of the situation, *—AMPB.*

**and fled unto Lystra and Derbe, cities of Lycaonia:** ...made their escape into the Lycaonian towns of, *—WEYM* ...they left that town, *—SEB.*

**and unto the region that lieth round about:** ...and the neighbouring country, *—WEYM.*

**14:6.** The apostles became aware of the plot, however, and fled. Paul showed he was always willing to risk his life for the sake of spreading the gospel. But he did not seek to be a martyr. He fled because there were other places that needed the ministry of the gospel. So he and Barnabas went on eastward to Lystra and Derbe, cities of Lycaonia in the southern part of the Roman province of Galatia. Lystra was about 18 miles south-southwest of Iconium. Like Iconium, it was a Roman military colony.

Derbe was farther east. Recent discoveries have shown it was about 65 miles south-southeast of Lystra and was over the border of the Roman province of Galatia in the realm of King Antiochus of Commagene.

**7. And there they preached the gospel:** ...where they continued to tell the Good News, *—TCNT.*

**14:7.** In this whole region round about Lystra and Derbe, the apostles proceeded to preach the gospel and kept on doing so for some time.

Since they were well on the road back to their home base, and since there were no Jewish synagogues in the area, it would have been easy for Barnabas and Paul to remember how they had shaken the dust off their feet against the cities that had rejected them and decide to keep on going back to a place where they knew they would be appreciated. But they felt the pressure of their call and commission to which the Holy Spirit had separated them. So they stayed.

**8. And there sat a certain man at Lystra:** ...There used to sit in the streets of Lystra a man, *—TCNT.*

**impotent in his feet:** ...who had no power in his feet, *—TCNT* ...lame in his feet, *—MNTG* ...who had not strength in his feet, *—WLMS* ...who could not use his feet, *—RSV* ...whose feet were paralyzed, *—SEB.*

**being a cripple from his mother's womb:** ...he had been lame from his birth, *—TCNT* ... a cripple from birth, *—MNTG* ... who had never walked in his life, *—JB* ... had been born crippled, *—SEB.*

**who never had walked:** ...and had never walked at all, *—TCNT* ...in his life, NEB ...had never been able to walk, *—GDSP, —PHLP.*

**14:8.** What follows at Lystra gives an example of how Paul preached to Gentiles who had not come in contact with Jews and who had no knowledge of the Old Testament Scriptures.

At Lystra Paul did not go to a synagogue as was his usual custom, because there was none. Instead, it seems he went to the marketplace or to an open square just inside the city gates (as 14:13 indicates). There he began to preach. Among those nearby was a cripple. To draw attention to the utter hopelessness of his case, the Bible uses a threefold repetition. He was powerless in his feet, he was crippled from his mother's womb, and he had never walked.

**9. The same heard Paul speak:** ... He listened to Paul speaking, *—RSV* ...was hearing Paul, *—WORL* ...This man was listening to Paul speaking, *—TCNT* ... This man was sitting there and listening to Paul speak, *—SEB* ... listened as Paul spoke, *—NLTG* ... to Paul's sermon, *—NOLI* ...to Paul's preaching, *—KNOX.*

**who stedfastly beholding him:** ...who, fastening his eyes upon him, ASV ...looking him straight in the eye, *—PHLP* ... looked intently at him, *—TNT* ...looking earnestly upon him, *—SWAN* ...Paul watched him, *—NLTG* ... gazing at him, *—KLST* ... looking closely at him, *—KNOX* ...looked straight at him, *—EVRD.*

**and perceiving that he had faith to be healed:** ... and seeing that he had faith to be made whole, —ASV ... saw that the man believed that God could heal him, —SEB ... saw that he had faith in his salvation, —NOLI ... seeing that there was saving faith in him, —KNOX ... believed he could be healed, —NLTG ... to be cured, —KLST, —WEYM ... that there was faith in him, —LAMS ... to be made well, —BB, —TNT.

**14:9.** This cripple kept listening intently to Paul. Undoubtedly, Paul had to start at the beginning and give teaching about the one true God, His promises, and His plan of salvation. He must have told about the coming of Jesus, His death, resurrection, and the promise of the Spirit. This began to stir faith in the heart and mind of this cripple.

Paul noticed how the man kept listening, fixed his eyes on him, and that he had faith to be healed. ("Healed," Greek *sothenai*, is from the verb *sozo* which is ordinarily translated "saved," but which also means to rescue from danger or from severe situations and thus be restored, healed, or made whole.) From this incident it is clear Paul did not leave anything out of the gospel he preached.

10. **Said with a loud voice:** ... Calling to him, —NLTG ... said loudly, —TCNT ... So, Paul shouted, —SEB ... he shouted aloud to him, —WLMS ... So he cried out, —NCV.

**Stand upright on thy feet:** ... Stand up on your feet, —EVRD, —NCV, —TCNT ... Stand erect on your feet, —MOFT ... Get on your feet and stand erect! —WLMS ... Stand up straight on your feet, —BRKL.

**And he leaped and walked:** ... And he sprang up and began to walk about, —RTHM ... The man jumped up, and began walking about, —TCNT ... walking around, —SEB ... sprang up, stood, —MRDK ... he leaped up with a single bound, —WUST.

**14:10.** With his eyes still fixed on the cripple, Paul encouraged the man's faith to action by commanding him in a very loud voice to stand up straight (erect) on his feet. Without hesitation the man immediately leaped up. He not only stood up straight, he found he could walk and proceeded to do so.

He showed even greater faith than the cripple at the Gate Beautiful, for there Peter had to encourage the beggar's faith by taking him by the hand. Here the cripple stood up in response to the Word of God and the command given by the Holy Spirit through Paul.

11. **And when the people saw what Paul had done:** ... And the multitudes, —WORL ... The crowds of people, seeing what, —TCNT ... When the people saw Paul's miracle, —NOLI ... beholding what Paul had done, —SWAN.

**they lifted up their voices, saying in the speech of Lycaonia:** ... called out in the Lycaonian language, —TCNT ... in the language of the country, —MRDK.

**The gods are come down to us in the likeness of men:** ... The gods, made like unto men, have come, —RTHM ... The Gods have made themselves like men and come down to us, —TCNT ... in the form of men, —WEYM ... in human form, —MOFT ... disguised as men, —JB.

**14:11.** Undoubtedly Paul was preaching to a crowd that kept gathering as he preached. Some of them may have been idly curious. Some may have just been passing by and stopped for a moment to listen. Few, if any, were giving the kind of attention to the message the cripple did. But the loud command of Paul caught the attention of the whole crowd. When they saw the man jump up and start walking around, they began shouting excitedly. However, though they knew the Greek Paul was using in his preaching, in their excitement they reverted to their native Lycaonian language, which Paul and Barnabas did not understand. This sort of thing is a common occurrence. Usually, when a person is educated to use a second language, he will still fall back into his native language, the language of his childhood, when he is excited or under stress. Even Jesus did that on the cross when he quoted Psalm 22:1 in the Aramaic He grew up with, instead of in the Hebrew in which it was written (Mark 15:34).

The miracle made the people (who were pagan Gentiles) believe the Greek gods had come down, being made like human beings or taking the form of human beings. This would not have been a new idea to them, for their Greek mythology included many stories of gods coming to earth in human form, and the images of their Greek gods were in human form. Because they had never seen such a miracle, they jumped to the conclusion that the apostles were manifestations of their gods.

12. **And they called Barnabas, Jupiter:** ... They called Barnabas 'Zeus,' —WEYM ... And they began to call Barnabas "Zeus," —MNTG ... Lord of the Gods, —MRDK.

**and Paul, Mercurius, because he was the chief speaker:** ... and Paul, Mercury, —ASV ... and Paul Hermes, since he was the chief spokesman, —MOFT ... because he led the conversation, —BRKL ... because he was the principal speaker, —WLMS ... the main speaker, —BECK.

**14:12.** The people then began to call Barnabas *Dia* (in verse 13, *Dios*), a form of the Greek sky god Zeus, who was identified by the Romans with their chief god Jupiter and by this people with their chief Lycaonian god. Barnabas was identified with the chief god probably because he was older and a larger man than Paul.

Since Paul was the chief speaker (literally, "the leader [or, the guide] of the Word [the *logos*]"), they called him *Hermēn* (Hermes), the messenger and herald of the gods, especially of *Dios* (Zeus, Jupiter). Hermes was identified by the Romans with their god Mercurius (Mercury) who presided over eloquence and cunning as well as commerce and theft. (The King James Version uses Jupiter and Mercurius due to the influence of the Roman Catholic Latin version.) This also indicates Paul had been doing most of the preaching.

**13. Then the priest of Jupiter, which was before their city:** . . . And the priest of Zeus, whose temple was in front of the city, *–RSV* . . . The priest of Jupiter-beyond-the-Walls, *–TCNT* . . . And the priest of Zeusthe temple of Zeus being just outside the city, *–WEYM* . . . In fact, the city-priest for Zeus, *–BRKL* . . . What is more, the High Priest of Jupiter whose temple was at the gateway of the city, *–PHLP.*
**brought oxen and garlands unto the gates:** . . . brought bullocks and garlands to the gates, *–TCNT* . . . unto the doors of the house, *–ALFD.*
**and would gave done sacrifice with the people:** . . . was disposed, *–MRDK* . . . with the multitudes, *–ASV* . . . with the intention of offering sacrifices, *–TCNT* . . . and in company with the crowd was intending to offer sacrifices to them, *–WEYM.*

**14:13.** In view of this identification of the apostles with their gods, the people of Lystra took what they thought was appropriate action. They contacted the priest of the god *Dios* whose temple was in front of the city. He brought oxen (actually, bulls, the most costly victims they could offer in sacrifice). These were decorated with garlands (wreaths) as part of the sacrifice and brought to the gates of the city where the crowds 'were gathered, wanting to sacrifice.

Notice that Barnabas is again named first in verses 12 and 14. As *Dios* (Zeus, Jupiter) he was considered the chief god and the leading one for whom the sacrifices were to be made.

**14. Which when the apostles, Barnabas and Paul, heard of:** . . . understood what the people were doing, *–SEB* . . . of their intention, *–PHLP.*
**they rent their clothes:** . . . they tore their clothes, *–TCNT* . . . they ripped their own clothes, *–SEB.*
**and ran in among the people:** . . . and rushed out among the multitude, *–RSV* . . . and rushed out into the crowd, *–TCNT* . . . dashed forward among the crowds, *–BRKL.*
**crying out:** . . . exclaiming, *–WEYM* . . . shouting, *–MOFT* . . . crying at the top of their voices, *–PHLP.*

**14:14.** All of this was done with a great deal of excitement and shouting in the Lycaonian language, which Paul and Barnabas did not understand. Perhaps they made inquiries about what was going on. Finally, someone must have explained to

them in Greek what was happening. When the apostles heard and understood that the people were about to sacrifice these animals to them and offer the wreaths as well, they tore their clothes as a sign of grief and dismay. (This was usually done by taking two hands at the neck and ripping the clothes open part of the way down the front.) After they did this, they immediately rushed out (sprang out) into the midst of the crowd crying out loudly (shouting, almost screaming).

It is not strange that Paul was upset. He would not court or tolerate the praise and attention of man. He knew that loving God completely left no room for taking any part in heathen worship. He knew the foolishness and emptiness of idolatry, so it shocked both him and Barnabas that these people of Lystra would be looking at them as if they were gods and wanting to worship them. So immediately they began to shout out their protests.

What happened here also drives home the importance of the Jewish synagogues to the spread of the gospel in this initial thrust of the Apostolic Church during the First Century. Wherever they were scattered through the Roman Empire and beyond, they prepared the way. They taught one true God and high moral standards. The Gentiles who attended knew the Word; they had heard the prophecies. They knew God worked through men "of like passions," for they heard the stories of Moses and Elijah. The synagogues had enough influence on the community around them so no one would ever have interpreted miracles the way these people at Lystra did. The people at Lystra had no such background. All they could do was interpret the miracle in terms of their own pagan ideas.

**15. And saying, Sirs, why do ye these things?:** . . . Friends, why are you doing this, *–TCNT* . . . Why are you doing these things? *–CNDT* . . . why are you making all this fuss? *–NOLI.*
**We also are men of like passions with you:** . . . We are only men like you, *–TCNT* . . . We also are but human beings with natures like yours, *–WEYM* . . . We too are mortal, *–KLST* . . . are ordinary human beings, *–LAMS* . . . We are men with the same feelings as you, *–BB* . . . We are human, with emotions as yourselves, *–BRKL* . . . frail mortals, *–MRDK* . . . with experiences like yours, *–BECK* . . . men who possess the same kind of feelings, *–WUST.*
**and preach unto you:** . . . and bring you good tidings, *–ASV* . . . and we have come with the Good News, *–TCNT.*
**that ye should turn from these vanities:** . . . these follies, *–TCNT* . . . these empty things, *–MNTG* . . . these foolish things, *–WLMS* . . . these meaningless things, *–PHLP* . . . such superstitions, *–NORL* . . . these useless things, *–MRDK* . . . these worthless things, *–SEB* . . . from these vain gods, *–KLST* . . . turn from such futile ways, *–MOFT* . . . from these futile things, *–TNT.*

**unto the living God, which made heaven, and earth, and the sea:** ... who made the sky, the earth, the sea, –*TCNT* ... the Creator of earth and sky and sea, –*WEYM.*

**and all things that are therein:** ... and everything that is in them, –*TCNT.*

**14:15.** Paul and Barnabas tried to stop the sacrifices by declaring they were men, human beings with feelings like theirs (implying a nature like theirs). They had come to preach the gospel (the good news) to turn them from these vain (unreal, useless, unfruitful) things to the living God.

Paul took them back to the time of the Creation. He told them of the living God who made all things. Many modern missionaries have found they had to start where Paul did when dealing with people who have no knowledge of the Bible. There is indeed a revelation of God in nature and history for those who will see it.

**16. Who in times past suffered all nations to walk in their own ways:** ... In the generations that are passed he let all the nations follow their own ways, –*KLST* ... to go on in their own ways. –*PHLP.*

**14:16.** In times past (literally, generations gone by) God let all nations (all the Gentiles) go their own way (in contrast to going God's way). They all followed various roads, various ways of life of their own choosing, and God let them do it. But He did not give up His plan of redemption or his purpose to bring blessing to all the nations of the earth.

It is clear in Genesis chapters 1 through 11 that God dealt with the world as a whole and gave them a new start through the Flood. But with chapter 12 God ceased to deal with the world as a whole. He dealt with one man, Abraham, and his descendants through whom would come a blood line that would lead to Christ, the greater Seed of Abraham, the One who makes all God's promises good.

Noah worshiped the true God with a simple faith that pleased the Lord, but by the time of Abraham the whole world was full of idolatry. Abraham's relatives worshiped idols in Haran. (See Joshua 24:15 where the Hebrew means "the gods your fathers served [worshiped] on the other side of the [Euphrates] river.") According to Jewish tradition, Abraham's father Terah was actually an idol maker.

**17. Nevertheless he left not himself without witness, in that he did good:** ... Yet he has not omitted to give you, in his kindly acts, evidence about himself, –*TCNT* ... and yet by His beneficence He has not left His existence unattested, –*WEYM* ... without

testimony, –*LAMS* ... without some proof of what he is, –*NOLI* ... bestowing blessings, –*KLST.*

**and gave us rain from heaven, and fruitful seasons:** ... sending you, as he does, rain from Heaven and harvest, –*TCNT* ... he helped us with his bounties, –*NOLI* ... in that He sends you, –*WEYM* ... in that he bestowed good on them, –*LAMS.*

**filling our hearts with food and gladness:** ... and satisfying your desires with food and good cheer, –*TCNT* ... filling you with food, and making you happy, –*BECK* ... to your hearts' content, –*PHLP* ... filling your stomachs with food and your hearts with gladness, –*ADAM* ... satisfied their hearts, –*LAMS.*

**14:17.** In spite of all this human self-will and rebellion with its false worship, the one true God did not leave himself without witness. He did good deeds, giving rain from heaven and fruitbearing seasons, filling people with food and gladness.

By saying this, Paul pointed out that God is the real Source of all the good things the earth provides and that mankind as a whole enjoys. As Jesus declared, He is "our Father" (the Father of those who believe, who are born again), but He sets an example of how to treat unbelievers who oppose believers by making His sun to shine on the evil and on the good and by sending rain on the just and on the unjust (Matthew 5:44-48).

Also, after the Flood God gave the rainbow as a sign of His covenant that there would never be a universal flood again to destroy the earth (Genesis 9:8-17), and that as long as the earth remains, "seedtime and harvest, and cold and heat, and summer and winter, and day and night shall not cease" (Genesis 8:22).

As James 1:17 says, "Every good (useful, beneficial) gift ... is from above." Beginning with creation, God prepared good gifts for man. He put man into an environment where everything was "very good," perfectly suited to man's needs, provided with every opportunity for man's growth and development. Even after man fell, God continued to provide good things to enjoy.

**18. And with these sayings scarce restrained they the people, that they had not done sacrifice unto them:** ... Even with this appeal they could hardly prevent the people from offering, –*TCNT* ... Even with words like these they had difficulty in preventing the thronging crowd from, –*WEYM* ... they hardly restrained the crowds, –*KLST* ... with difficulty restrained the crowds, –*WUST* ... difficulty in stopping the crowds, –*TNT* ... the multitudes from doing sacrifice, –*ASV.*

**14:18.** Even with saying these things, Paul and Barnabas had a hard time stopping the crowds from their intent to offer sacrifices to them. At first, some in the crowds may have thought Paul and Barnabas were trying to test the sincerity of their intent to offer these sacrifices. Others may have been intent on carrying it out so they could enjoy the feast and carousing that usually accompanied such sacrifices. Still others may have already worked themselves up into some kind of heathen frenzy that often marked their celebrations. Or it may be that all the noise and excited talking in their native Lycaonian language may have made it hard for some to pick up what Paul and Barnabas were saying in Greek.

**19. And there came thither certain Jews from Antioch and Iconium:** . . . Presently, however, there came some Jews, *–TCNT* . . . But now a party of Jews came, *–WEYM*.

**who persuaded the people:** . . . who, after they had won over the people, *–TCNT* . . . and, having won over the crowd, *–WEYM* . . . who influenced the populace, *–BRKL* . . . and after turning the minds of the people against Paul, *–PHLP* . . . to their side, *–NOLI*.

**and, having stoned Paul, drew him out of the city:** . . . they stoned Paul, and dragged him, *–ASV* . . . dragged him by his feet outside of the city, *–WUST*.

**supposing he had been dead:** . . . supposing that he was dead, *–RSV* . . . thinking him to be dead, *–TCNT* . . . where they left him for dead, *–NOLI* . . . under impression he was dead, *–BRKL* . . . thinking that he had died, *–WUST*.

**14:19.** Obviously, at least some in the crowds gathered at the city gate did listen to Paul and Barnabas. In fact, there must have been such a great response with so many saved and discipled by the apostles, that the news reached Pisidian Antioch where the Jews had had Paul and Barnabas thrown out of the city. It also reached Iconium where the Jews had wanted to stone Paul to death. Jews from both cities traveled to Lystra and persuaded the heathen crowds to help them, or at least permit them, to carry out their plot. Stoning was the Jewish method of executing blasphemers. It may be that some of the unbelieving people of Lystra felt they were disgraced when Paul and Barnabas did not let them sacrifice to them. They may also have felt the preaching of Paul was blasphemy against their heathen gods, since Paul left no room for their existence. It probably was not too hard to persuade them to allow the stoning of Paul.

This time these unbelieving Jews did stone Paul and dragged his body out of the city, thinking he was dead. It is clear that he was not actually dead, though he was unconscious and must have been severely bruised all over his body. Undoubtedly he had broken bones as well.

In 2 Corinthians 11:25 Paul included this stoning between beatings and shipwrecks as calamaties he endured. There is no hint there or in this passage that he died. But the beatings and this stoning left scars. In Galatians 6:17 he calls these scars the marks of the Lord Jesus.

Paul was never surprised when he and other believers suffered for Christ's sake. He knew Jesus expected His disciples to suffer with courage and with rejoicing (Matthew 5:10-12; 10:24, 25, 28; John 15:18, 20). Never did he blame the Lord for the rough treatment he received for his faithful service. Always he spoke of his sufferings as but a "light affliction" working "a far more exceeding and eternal weight of glory" (2 Corinthians 4:17).

**20. Howbeit, as the disciples stood round about him:** . . . But when the disciples had gathered round him, *–TCNT* . . . But the disciples formed a circle about him, *–WLMS* . . . gathered in a circle round him, *–PHLP* . . . assembled around him, *–MRDK* . . . had surrounded him, *–TNT*.

**he rose up, and came into the city:** . . . he got up and went back into the town, *–TCNT* . . . to own, *–WLMS* . . . he arose suddenly, *–WUST* . . . and entered the city, *–BRKL*.

**and the next day he departed with Barnabas to Derbe:** . . . Next day he went off, *–MOFT*.

**14:20.** As soon as the crowd left, the believing disciples surrounded Paul's prostrate form. Undoubtedly they were looking to God, and God did not disappoint them. Suddenly, in what must have seemed like a resurrection, Paul rose up, obviously completely healed, and went back into the city with them. But knowing the mood of the crowds and how easily they might turn into a mob and bring violence on the new believers, he and Barnabas left the next day for Derbe. Jesus himself said that if people do not receive the message in one city, believers should go to another (Luke 10:10-12). Paul often went back and preached in spite of opposition. But he also was sensitive to the leading of the Holy Spirit.

**21. And when they had preached the gospel to that city:** . . . After telling the Good News throughout that town, *–TCNT* . . . After proclaiming the gospel to the people there, *–WEYM*.

**and had taught many:** . . . and making a number of converts, *–TCNT* . . . and winning many converts, *–MNTG* . . . and having discipled many, *–YNG*.

**they returned again to Lystra, and to Iconium, and Antioch:** . . . they retraced their steps to, *–WEYM* . . . they went back to, *–MNTG*.

**14:21.** At Derbe also, there was apparently no synagogue. Thus Paul and Barnabas must have preached the gospel much as they did at Lystra, but without the Jewish opposition, since Paul's enemies thought he was dead.

After they had made a considerable number of disciples, and thus established a growing church, they courageously returned to Lystra, Iconium, and Pisidian Antioch.

**22. Confirming the souls of the disciples:** . . . reassuring the minds, *–TCNT* . . . Everywhere they strengthened the disciples, *–WEYM* . . . They gave new courage to, *–TNT* . . . strengthening the hearts of the disciples, *–WLMS* . . . Strengthening the souls of the converts, *–LAMS* . . . They fortified the souls of, *–NOLI* . . . reassuring the disciples spiritually, *–BRKL* . . . had ordained to them priests, *–DOUY*.

**and exhorting them to continue in the faith:** . . . beseeching them to abide in the faith, *–RTHM* . . . urging them to remain true to the Faith, *–TCNT* . . . by encouraging them to hold fast, *–WEYM* . . . urging them to stand firm, *–PHLP* . . . persevere, *–MRDK*.

**and that we must through much tribulation enter into the kingdom of God:** . . . and showing that it is only through many troubles, *–TCNT* . . . and warned them saying, It is through many afflictions that we must make our way, *–WEYM* . . . We must suffer many things to enter God's kingdom, *–EVRD* . . . that only through much tribulation can we enter, *–LAMS*.

**14:22.** This time, however, they did not stir up the Jews. Apparently, they did no evangelistic work, leaving that to the local believers. Instead, they ministered to the Church. In each place, they confirmed (strengthened and established) the souls of the disciples. They also challenged and encouraged them to continue in the Faith. The Greek is very strong here. They told the people they must maintain the Faith (the whole gospel), standing by it, and living by its principles.

They also challenged the believers to share the suffering of the apostles and to accept the fact that through much tribulation (persecution, affliction, distress) it is necessary to enter the kingdom of God.

**23. And when they had ordained them elders in every church:** . . . They chose elders for each church, *–EVRD* . . . after electing elders for them, *–KJII* . . . had appointed elders, *–RSV* . . . they selected Elders by show of hands, *–WEYM* . . . helped them select elders, *–WLMS* . . . having elected for them elders, *–FNTN* . . . chose leaders, *–NLTG*.

**and had prayed with fasting:** . . . and, after prayer and fasting, *–TCNT* . . . by praying and giving up eating, *–EVRD* . . . They went without food during that time so they could pray better, *–NLTG*.

**they commended them to the Lord:** . . . entrusted them, *–MOFT* . . . these were dedicated, *–NORL* . . . they gave them to the Lord, *–KJII* . . . giving them over to, *–NLTG* . . . put them in the Lord's care, *–EVRD* . . . commended to the favor of God, *–SAWR*.

**on whom they believed:** . . . men who had trusted the Lord, *–EVRD* . . . on whom their faith rested, *–WEYM*.

**14:23.** Because the body of believers needed organization to be able to work together and carry out the work of the Lord, the apostles then "ordained" elders (overseers, superintendents of each congregation or assembly) in each place. This, however, was not an ordination in the modern sense. The Greek word for "ordained" here is *cheiratonēsantes*, where *cheir* means hand, and the whole word means they conducted an election by the show of hands.

At the beginning, these elders were Spirit-filled men chosen from among the members of the local congregation. Not until many years later did the churches begin to feel they needed to bring in pastor-teachers from outside the local assembly who could also be the administrative head of the assembly and who could combine the office of elder (also called bishop and presbyter) with the God-called, Spirit-empowered, and gifted ministry of pastor-teacher. (*Pastor* in the New Testament refers to a spiritual ministry, not an office.)

Before Paul and Barnabas went on to the next city, they always spent time in prayer and fasting with the believers. Then they entrusted them (as precious and valuable) to the care and keeping of the Lord (Jesus) in whom they had believed (and continued to believe).

**24. And after they had passed throughout Pisidia, they came to Pamphylia:** . . . Paul and Barnabas then went through, *–TCNT* . . . After traveling through, *–BRKL* . . . Then they crossed Pisidia, *–PHLP*.

**14:24.** Pisidian Antioch was situated on a plain at 3,600 feet elevation. The apostles took the road south which wound down through Pisidia and Pamphylia to Perga on the Cestrus River near the Mediterranean coast. Though the Bible does not specifically say they evangelized along the way, the Greek verb *dielthontes* is used in other passages of going from place to place preaching the gospel.

**25. And when they had preached the word in Perga, they went down into Attalia:** . . . They preached the message, *–EVRD* . . . having spoken the word in, *–SWAN* . . . they came down to, *–WEYM*.

**14:25.** Arriving on the rich coastal plain of Pamphylia, they went to Perga and preached the word there apparently without opposition or mistreatment. Some speculate that because Paul became ill there, they pushed on to the higher ground at Pisidian Antioch.

They stayed long enough at Perga to establish a church there. They undoubtedly organized it by having the believers elect elders. With proper organization people learn to work together for the glory of God.

From Perga they went down to Attalia, Perga's seaport, a city of increasing importance. This was the last stop on Paul's first missionary journey.

**26. And thence sailed to Antioch:** . . . and from there they sailed back to Antioch, . . . and from there set sail for Antioch. —NEB.

**from where they had been recommended to the grace of God for the work which they fulfilled:** . . . where they had originally been, —JB . . . had first received the divine grace for the mission, —NOLI . . . This is where the believers had put them into God's care, —NCV . . . commended to the help of God, —TCNT . . . from where they had been delivered up to the grace of God, —KJII . . . had first been commended to the grace . . . for the task which they had now completed, —PHLP.

**14:26.** From Attalia they sailed away to Syrian Antioch. Now they were back in the place where they had started on this missionary journey. At Antioch they had been given over to the grace of God to do the work which they had now completed. At this time, Paul and Barnabas felt they had fulfilled the ministry for which the Spirit sent them out (13:2-4).

**27. And when they were come:** . . . And when they had arrived, —RTHM . . . Upon their arrival, —WEYM.

**and had gathered the church together:** . . . they called the Church together, —WEYM . . . they called a church meeting, —BRKL.

**they rehearsed all that God had done with them:** . . . and gave an account of . . . with and through them, —TCNT . . . and proceeded to report in detail all that God, working with them, had done, —WEYM . . . and reported all that God had used them to do, —TNT . . . of all the work that God had achieved through them, —NOLI.

**and how he had opened the door of faith unto the Gentiles:** . . . especially how he had opened to the heathen a door, —TCNT . . . and how he had thrown open the gates of faith to the Gentiles, —NEB . . . so that the non-Jews could believe! —NCV.

**14:27.** Since Paul and Barnabas considered Antioch their home base, and since the people had fasted and prayed with them before sending them out, the apostles wanted to report to the believers all that God had done. Therefore, they "gathered the church together" and told what great things God did as they worked as fellow laborers with Him. To the Gentiles, also, God had opened a door of faith. (The Greek has "a door," not "the door" here.) This door was through the preaching of the Word.

It is noticeable that in this report Paul and Barnabas put the emphasis on the positive. During most of the journey they faced persecutions, trouble, and difficult circumstances as their daily lot. Yet none of these experiences had robbed them of

their zeal and enthusiasm. They finished this journey just as excited about preaching the gospel as they had been when the Lord sent them out.

**28. And there they abode long time with the disciples:** . . . they stayed . . . a long time, —TCNT.

**14:28.** After giving their report, the two apostles remained "not a little time" with the disciples at Antioch. They resumed a ministry of teaching and help in the assembly of believers for several months, possibly as much as a year.

## Chapter 15

**1. And certain men which came down from Judaea:** . . . In the meantime, —CMPB . . . some of those coming down, —FNTN.

**taught:** . . . tried to convince, —WEYM . . . and attempted to teach, —MNTG.

**the brethren, and said:** . . . and these were their words, —WUST.

**Except ye be circumcised:** . . . Unless you are circumcised, —RSV . . . that without circumcision, —BB.

**after the manner of Moses:** . . . the custom, —ASV . . . enjoined by Moses, —TCNT . . . with the rite of the law, —MRDK . . . in accordance with the Mosaic doctrine, —NOLI.

**ye cannot be saved:** . . . there is no salvation, —BB.

**15:1.** The Jerusalem Conference dealt with in this chapter is another important turning point in the history of the Early Church. According to Galatians 2:1-10, Paul visited Jerusalem and presented the gospel he preached among the Gentiles. The Church leaders gave their approval to his message and did not require Titus to be circumcised.

A little later (Galatians 2:11-16) Peter came to Antioch, enjoyed table fellowship and ate non-kosher food with the Gentiles. But when some Jewish believers "came from James" (not sent officially, but simply sent to help and encourage the believers), Peter withdrew from that fellowship. When he saw their critical looks, he forgot the lesson he had learned at the house of Cornelius.

Peter's example affected the other Jewish believers in Antioch. Even Barnabas was carried away with this hypocrisy. Paul therefore took a strong stand against Peter and faced him with a rebuke for the hypocrisy of what he was doing (Galatians 2:14).

Later, either these same Jews from James, or another group of what were probably converted Pharisees, went a step further and took things into their own hands. They began teaching the Gentile believers that unless they were circumcised according to the custom of Moses, they could not be saved.

For these "visitors" from Judea, the question was not whether Gentiles could be saved; the

Cornelius incident settled this matter (as did the Old Testament which prophesied that Gentiles would also trust in the Jewish Messiah [Isaiah 11:10; cf. Psalms 18:49; 117:1; Romans 15:8-12]). Rather, these Jews believed that Gentile conversion represented a transfer into a "Christianized" Judaism. Thus in addition to a demand for circumcision and obedience to the Law, intimate social contact with uncircumcised Gentiles (e.g., at fellowship meals or the Lord's Supper) was strictly forbidden. Apparently, Pharisees who became believers in Jesus supported these views (see verse 5). Although the Scriptures teach that a restored Israel would serve to proselytize the nations (Isaiah 2:3; 60:2f.; Zechariah 8:22f.), they held too closely to their own traditions and did not fully understand that a new age, a new "dispensation" of grace, had arrived. These men were later referred to as "Judaizers" (cf. Galatians 2:11-19).

Some false teachers still say a person will lose his salvation if he does not accept their particular doctrine. Others say a person is not fully saved unless he goes through certain prescribed rites or ceremonies. All these false teachers fail to recognize that salvation is by grace through faith alone, as is clearly taught in Romans 10:9, 10 and Ephesians 2:8, 9.

**2. When therefore Paul and Barnabas had no small dissension and disputation with them:** ... Between these newcomers and Paul and Barnabas there was no little disagreement and controversy, —WEYM ... This gave rise to a serious dispute, and much discussion between Paul and Barnabas and these men, —TCNT ... Naturally this caused a serious upset among them, —PHLP ... sharp dispute, —NIV ... in the discussion and disagreement that arose, —NORL ... got into a fierce argument, —TEV ... were very much opposed to this teaching, —SEB.

**they determined that Paul and Barnabas:** ...the brethren appointed, —ASV ... it was arranged that, —RTHM ... it was therefore settled that, —TCNT ... to have Paul, —MLNT.

**and certain other of them:** ...and others of their number, —TCNT ... and some other brethren, —WEYM.

**should go up to Jerusalem unto the apostles and elders about this question:** ... to consult ... the Church about the matter under discussion, —TCNT ... and presbyters, —MOFT ... about this dispute, —BRKL ... about the whole question, —PHLP ... about this controversy, —ADAM.

**15:2.** This Judaizing teaching brought quite an upheaval with much dissension, disturbance, discord, and disputation (or questioning) between them (that is, between the brethren) and Paul and Barnabas. They (the brethren) then assigned Paul, Barnabas, and some others to go to Jerusalem to

confer with the apostles and elders "about this question."

**3. And being brought on their way by the church:** ... So they set out, being accompanied for a short distance by the Church, —WEYM ... So they were endorsed and sent on by the church, —WLMS ... So then, fitted out for their trip by the church, —BRKL ... It was, in fact, the congregation that was sending them, —NORL ... Having therefore been dispatched, —ADAM.

**they passed through Phenice and Samaria:** ... and they made their way through, —TCNT.

**declaring the conversion of the Gentiles:** ... reporting the conversion, —RSV ... telling the story, —TCNT ... where they narrated in detail, —BRKL ... fully narrating, —RTHM ... they told the whole story how the non-Jews were turning to God, —BECK ... telling the details, —ADAM.

**and they caused great joy unto all the brethren:** ... to the great joy of all the Brethren, —TCNT ... and brought great rejoicing to all the brothers, —WLMS ... and thus made all the brothers very happy, —BRKL ... And all the brothers were overjoyed to hear about it, —PHLP ... unbounded delight, —FNTN.

**15:3.** The whole assembly of believers at Antioch turned out to escort Paul, Barnabas, and the others for a short distance on the way. By this the members of the assembly showed they still loved, respected, and had confidence in them in spite of the questions raised by these Judaizing teachers. In all the upheaval, discussion, and questioning, they had not lost their love for the leaders God had given them. But they felt that for the sake of the Church as a whole, the questions needed to be resolved.

Paul took the road south through Phoenicia and the province of Samaria, stopping to visit churches all along the way. Phoenicia at this time extended south to Mount Carmel on the Mediterranean coast, so it was not necessary to go through Galilee. From Mount Carmel they took the inland route through Samaria to Jerusalem. In each place Paul gave a complete account of how the Gentiles were turning to the Lord. By giving a full report, Paul undoubtedly included an account of the persecution as well as the miracles.

Now these churches in Phoenicia were made up of Jewish believers. Those in Samaria were Samaritans. Yet they all rejoiced with great joy when they heard the report of the success of the Word of God among the Gentiles. Apparently the Judaizers had not visited these churches. Since Paul and Barnabas had not founded them, the Judaizers probably thought they would reject the Gentiles unless they became Jews. But because they were open to the Word and the Spirit, they accepted what God had done without question.

**4. And when they were come to Jerusalem:** ...On their arrival at Jerusalem, –TCNT...When they reached Jerusalem, –GDSP.

**they were received of the church:** ...they were welcomed by the Assembly, –RTHM...they were cordially received, –WEYM...were welcomed gladly by, –KJII...they had a meeting with, –BB...the congregation, –CMPB...the church leaders were glad to see them, –NLTG.

**and of the apostles and elders, and they declared:** ...and they rehearsed, –ASV...and they recounted, –RTHM...they revealed all, –KJII.

**all things that God had done with them:** ...as many things as God wrought with them, –WORL...had helped them to do, –TCNT...working with them, –WEYM...how great things God has wrought with them, –HBIE.

**15:4.** Arriving in Jerusalem, the apostles and those with them were received (favorably) by the believers. The apostles and elders also welcomed them. Apparently the Judaizers had been so anxious to move on to spread their doctrines in the churches Paul and Barnabas had founded in South Galatia that they had not sent word back to the church in Jerusalem. So there was no opposition at first.

The apostles probably included the Twelve, with the exception of James, who had been martyred. At this point they were still in Jerusalem building up the church and teaching and training the believers in the surrounding area. The elders were probably the elected leaders of the local groups meeting in the various homes in Jerusalem and the surrounding communities.

They all listened to the report of what God had done with (along with) Paul and Barnabas. Paul and Barnabas were just fellow laborers with the Lord. They gave God all the glory. Not only had He been with them, He was the One who really had done the work.

Paul was always careful to recognize that Christian workers, no matter how wonderfully used of God, are but ministers or servants of God and the Church. Each believer has his part.

**5. But there rose up certain of the sect of the Pharisees which believed, saying:** ...Some of the Pharisees' party, who had become believers in Christ, came forward, –TCNT...there had been proud religious law-keepers, –NLTG...who had been converted from the sect of, –LAMS.

**That it was needful to circumcise them:** ...It is necessary to circumcise them, –RSV...it was absolutely essential, –PHLP...Gentiles must be circumcised, –MOFT...said that such converts ought to be, –GDSP.

**and to command them to keep the law of Moses:** ...and to charge them, –RSV, –WORL...and to direct them to observe, –TCNT...ordered to observe, –BRKL.

**15:5.** This welcome and pleasant atmosphere did not last. It was not long before some converted Pharisees rose up out of the assembly in Jerusalem. They forcefully expressed the view that it was (and continued to be) necessary both to circumcise the Gentiles and to command them to keep (observe) the law of Moses.

These Pharisees were still making Moses and the Law central in their religion. They made the covenant of the Law more important than the promise given to Abraham and actually, more important than Christ's crucifixion and resurrection. But the Cross was no afterthought in God's plan. Jesus was and is the Lamb of God "slain from the foundation of the world" (Revelation 13:8). The first promise looking ahead to Christ is in Genesis 3:15, long before the giving of the Law. The Pharisees thought Christianity should be added to the Law. But the reverse is true. As Galatians 3:19 indicates, the Law was added to the promise, not the other way around.

**6. And the apostles and elders came together:** ...were gathered together, –ASV...held a meeting, –NOLI, –TCNT...were assembled, –KJII, –WORL.

**for to consider of this matter:** ...to investigate this question, –MOFT...to see about this matter, –KJII...to study this problem, –SEB.

**15:6.** The apostles and elders then assembled to consider the matter. This was what the assembly in Antioch wanted, and this was the purpose for which Paul and Barnabas had come.

The apostles and elders did not ask for a closed meeting, however. Verse 12 indicates a multitude (a crowd) was present. This matter was very important to the believers in Jerusalem, for they all still followed the customs of their fathers with respect to the kosher food laws and other Jewish forms and ceremonies.

**7. And when there had been much disputing:** ...much debate, –RSV...much questioning, –ASV...After much discussion, –TCNT...After an exhaustive inquiry, –PHLP...after there had been much talk, –KJII...After a long time of much talking, –NLTG.

**Peter rose up, and said unto them:** ...Peter stood up and addressed them, –PHLP.

**Men and brethren:** ...Brethren, –RSV...Fellow Christians, –BECK.

**ye know how that a good while ago:** ...you are aware that, –TNT...that long ago, –TCNT...You will keep in mind that a good while back, –BRKL...you know what happened in the early days, –NCV.

**God made choice among us:** ...God singled me out, –TCNT...it was God's pleasure, –BB.

**that the Gentiles by my mouth:** ...that through my mouth the nations, –RTHM...that through my lips, –TCNT...the non-Jews, –BECK.

**should hear the word of the gospel:** ... the glad tidings, —RTHM ... the Message of the Good News, —TCNT.

**and believe:** ... and become believers in Christ, —TCNT.

**15:7.** At first there was much disputing, not in the sense of arguing, but rather there was a great deal of questioning and discussing as the apostles and elders and others tried to probe into the subject. Some may have favored Paul's view. Others may have favored the converted Pharisees who wanted all the Gentiles circumcised. But the Greek implies both sides were sincerely investigating the question, expecting to find a solution. Wisely, the leaders allowed the people to present various points of view. Apparently, this went on for some time, so no one could say he had not had an opportunity to be heard. Thus, the whole question with all its ramifications was brought into the open.

Finally, after this long period of discussion, Peter stood and reminded them that by God's choice he had taken the gospel to the Gentiles at Caesarea and they believed.

Everyone knew about this. Peter had explained the whole story in detail to the Jerusalem leaders and believers after he came back from Caesarea.

But apparently, during all this discussion no one had referred to what happened at Caesarea. This shows how little that important event had influenced most of the Jerusalem believers. They had accepted the fact that God had saved those Gentiles. They had accepted Peter back into their fellowship. But most of them seem to have treated this as an exception rather than something to be expected or sought after. Some may have thought it was all right for Peter to respond the way he did, but it was not for them. But Peter emphasized it was in their presence that God chose him out. In other words, what God had done for Peter was for the benefit of them all.

**8. And God, which knoweth the hearts:** ... who knows men's inmost thoughts, —PHLP ... who reads all hearts, —TCNT ... the searcher of hearts, —BB ... and the heart-observing God, —RTHM ... who can read men's minds, —NEB ... the heart-knowing God, —DRBY.

**bare them witness:** ... gave His testimony in their favor, —WEYM ... declared his acceptance of the Gentiles, —TCNT ... attested this, —MOFT ... gave this testimony in their behalf, —MNTG ... God bore witness, —WORL ... showed them they were to have His loving favor, —NLTG.

**giving them the Holy Ghost:** ... by bestowing, —WEYM.

**even as he did unto us:** ... exactly as he did to us, —PHLP ... just as he did upon us, —MNTG ... even as to us, —WORL.

**15:8.** Peter further reminded the Jerusalem believers it was not his choice to accept the Gentiles at the house of Cornelius into the Church. It was God's choice, for He knows what is in the hearts (and minds) of all. God saw the faith in their hearts. Then God bore witness to the fact that these Gentiles were believers by giving them the Holy Spirit, just as He had to all the Jewish believers. God saw their hearts, then the outpouring of the Holy Spirit became an outward evidence so Peter and the others could see that God had accepted them. It was a seal of His acceptance.

**9. And put no difference between us and them:** ... and he made no distinction, RSV ... Making no division, —BB ... does not discriminate, —CNDT ... not the slightest distinction, —MOFT.

**purifying their hearts by faith:** ... because he cleansed, —WLMS ... when He cleansed their hearts, —ADAM ... by their faith, —TCNT.

**15:9.** From this experience Peter learned that God does not distinguish between or make a separation between Gentile believers and Jewish believers in any way. Just as in the case of Jewish believers, God purified (cleansed) their hearts by faith, saving them by grace through faith alone (Ephesians 2:8). That is, God had already purified (cleansed) their hearts by faith before He showed there was no distinction by giving to them the Holy Spirit.

From this experience it is very clear that circumcision was not necessary for God to bear witness to the salvation of these Gentiles. Neither was the keeping of the law of Moses necessary for God to bear witness to that faith by pouring out His Holy Spirit.

**10. Now therefore why tempt ye God:** ... why make ye trial of God, —ASV ... why are you proving God, —RTHM ... Why, then, do you now provoke God, —TCNT ... Now then, why be a trial to God, —BRKL ... now strain the patience of God, —PHLP ... why do you try God, —FNTN ... we cannot call into question this act of God, —NOLI.

**to put a yoke upon the neck of the disciples:** ... by trying to put on the shoulders of these disciples a burden, —PHLP ... you are putting a heavy load around the necks of, —NCV ... by putting too heavy a load on the back of, —NLTG.

**which neither our fathers nor we were able to bear?:** ... our ancestors, —TCNT ... have the strength to bear? —CNDT ... strong enough to bear? —FNTN, —WORL.

**15:10.** Peter then asked why they would tempt God (put God to the test) by disregarding what He had done and made plain at Caesarea.

Tempting God, putting God to the test, is a very serious kind of unbelief. God had clearly made

His will known, pouring out the Holy Spirit upon the Gentiles. To doubt Him and make trial of Him to see whether He really meant what He did at Caesarea was to say that God is not consistent.

Furthermore, the yoke of the Law was something that neither these Jewish believers in Jerusalem nor their ancestors had been able to bear (had strength to carry). In their human weakness they had found it too burdensome. Even in the Old Testament, God repeatedly showed mercy and grace to those who were failing or falling short under the burden of the Law. (Compare Romans 4:6-8.)

> 11. **But we believe that through the grace of the Lord Jesus Christ:** . . . On the contrary, —FNTN . . . Instead, we believe that we are saved, —BRKL . . . No, we believe that both we and these people, —SEB . . . only on the mercy, —TCNT.
> **we shall be saved:** . . . are relying for Salvation, —TCNT . . . we are to be saved, —FNTN.
> **even as they:** . . . just as they are, —WLMS.

**15:11.** Peter concluded by declaring what "we" (the Christians who were gathered in Jerusalem) "believe": that through the grace of the Lord Jesus Christ Jewish disciples are saved in exactly the same way as Gentiles. (The Greek term for "believe" [*pisteuomen*] is in the present tense and represents continuous action.)

It is clear then that by grace, apart from the heavy yoke of the Law and apart from the legalistic bondage encouraged by the Pharisees, both Jewish and Gentile believers were to continue in their relationship with Christ. The Pharisees were very strict at this time. Jesus spoke of how "they bind heavy burdens and grievous to be borne, and lay them on men's shoulders; but they themselves will not move them with one of their fingers" (Matthew 23:4). Not only did the Pharisees make the legalistic burden heavy, they refused to help anyone carry it. God's grace has, through Christ, removed those burdens.

> 12. **Then all the multitude kept silence:** . . . Then the whole assembly remained silent, —WEYM . . . entire assembly kept quiet, —BRKL . . . the whole meeting quieted down, —CNFT . . . the whole group became quiet, —NCV . . . All those who were gathered together said nothing, —NLTG . . . assembly kept silence, —FNTN.
> **and gave audience to Barnabas and Paul:** . . . and began to hearken unto, —RTHM . . . as they listened to, —TCNT.
> **declaring what miracles and wonders:** . . . rehearsing what signs and wonders, —ASV . . . relating how many, —RTHM . . . through . . . evidences and deep impressions, —FNTN.
> **God had wrought among the Gentiles by them:** . . . God had performed, —MOFT . . . what God had produced . . . among the nations, —FNTN.

**15:12.** Peter's words quieted the crowd and they listened in silence, giving their full attention as Barnabas and Paul related (and explained) how many signs and wonders God had done through them among the Gentiles. (Barnabas is mentioned first again, for he was known and respected by the Jerusalem leaders and believers. Thus, this time he was the spokesman.)

The emphasis is on what God did and implies that the miracles showed God's concern for winning these Gentiles to Christ and establishing them in the faith. The miracles were witness to the fact that God had accepted the Gentiles. It is obvious He would not keep doing miracles among them if He had not accepted their faith and their response to the simple gospel of salvation by grace through faith.

> 13. **And after they had held their peace:** . . . After they had finished speaking, —TCNT . . . And when they had come to an end, —BB . . . After a time of silence, —SEB.
> **James answered, saying:** . . . James addressed the Council, —TCNT . . . James replied, —RSV.
> **Men and brethren, hearken unto me:** . . . hear what I have to say, —TCNT . . . listen to me, —BB.

**15:13.** After Barnabas and Paul finished speaking, the crowd waited until James broke the silence by asking them to listen. But in this request James spoke as a humble brother, not as one who had superior authority. Though he was the brother of Jesus, he was a servant of the Lord who was simply responding to the Holy Spirit.

> 14. **Simeon hath declared:** . . . hath fully told, —RTHM . . . has related, —RSV.
> **how God at the first did visit the Gentiles:** . . . the manner in which God first visited, —TCNT . . . how God first came to the non-Jews, —BECK.
> **to take out of them a people for his name:** . . . in order to take from among them a people to bear his Name, —TCNT . . . to gain, —BRKL . . . a people for Himself, —BECK.

**15:14.** First, James drew attention to what Peter had said, calling Peter by his Hebrew name, *Sumeôn* (another spelling of Simon; both Simon and Simeon are Greek forms of the Hebrew *shimeôn*, "hearing"). Then he summarized what Peter had said by saying that God, at the house of Cornelius (before other Gentiles were saved), first visited the Gentiles (the nations) to take out of the Gentiles a people for His name.

God's visiting the Gentiles meant a gracious divine intervention to bring salvation and blessings. It also expressed God's desire to win a people from among the Gentiles. He wanted a people for His name, a people who would honor His name and be His people.

**15. And to this agree:** ... This is in full agreement with, –PHLP ... This agrees with, –NLTG ... this is in harmony, –MNTG.

**the words of the prophets:** ... what the prophets wrote, –PHLP ... what the early preachers said, –NLTG ... the language of the Prophets, –WEYM.

**as it is written:** ... as Scripture has it, –NEB.

**15:15.** James then gave grounds for God's concern over the Gentiles by quoting from the Prophets. It was important for the Jewish believers to see that this truth was not based on the experience at the house of Cornelius alone but also was founded on the written Word of God that had already been given. Spiritual truths are learned through experience, but experience must always be checked by the Word of God and not the other way around.

**16. After this I will return:** ... Afterward, –GDSP ... After these things, –PHLP ... There will come a time when I shall return, –NORL ... I will return later, –SEB.

**and will build again the tabernacle of David:** ... re-erect it, –CNDT ... the dwelling of David, –RSV ... the tent of David, –RTHM ... the House of David, –TCNT

**which is fallen down:** ... that hath fallen, –RTHM.

**and I will build again the ruins thereof:** ... Its very ruins I will rebuild, –TCNT ... relay its foundations, –FNTN ... its broken parts, –BB.

**and I will set it up:** ... and restore it, –BRKL.

**15:16.** The passage James quoted is Amos 9:11, 12 from the Septuagint version. The prophet spoke of a time when God would return to associate himself with His people. His purpose would be to build up again the fallen tabernacle (tent) of David. He would build up its ruins and restore it. All this repetition was to emphasize that God will indeed fulfill His promises to David. Apparently also, James (under the inspiration of the Holy Spirit) took the setting up of the fallen tent of David to be parallel to the prophecy that the Messiah would come as a new shoot, or branch, out of the stump of Jesse and the root of David. Isaiah 11:1 speaks of this and applies it to the Messiah, adding that the Spirit of the Lord would rest upon Him.

By picturing the kingdom of David as a stump, Isaiah indicated that David's glory and David's kingdom would be like a fallen tree, leaving nothing but a stump behind. Yet, though David's glory was gone, the prophet said God would raise up the Messiah from David's descendants and restore the hope of Israel and also the Gentiles. Isaiah 11:10 goes on to say, "And in that day there shall be a root of Jesse, which shall stand for an ensign of the people (peoples; the Hebrew is plural); to it (to Him) shall the Gentiles seek: and his rest shall be glorious (glory)."

**17. That the residue of men:** ... that so the rest of mankind, –TCNT.

**might seek after the Lord:** ... may seek out, –RTHM ... may earnestly seek, –TCNT.

**and all the Gentiles:** ... Even all the nations, –WEYM ... all the heathen, –FNTN.

**upon whom my name is called:** ... which are called by My name, –WEYM ... upon whom my name has been bestowed, –TCNT ... over whom my name has been invoked, –BRKL ... may take my name upon them, –FNTN ... They can be My people, too, –SEB.

**saith the Lord:** ... The Lord says this, –BRKL.

**who doeth all these things:** ... whose work it is, –NEB.

**15:17.** Amos also spoke of the rest of mankind seeking the Lord. This differs from the ordinary Massoretic Hebrew text in that it substitutes "men" (mankind) for the "Edom" of that text. Actually, the Hebrew could also be read "mankind" (Hebrew, 'ādhām) instead of "Edom." The difference involves only a slight change in the vowels, which the ancient Hebrew did not write anyway. Note also that "Edom" in Amos is parallel to the heathen (the nations, the Gentiles). At least, Edom is representative of the Gentiles. But some Bible scholars believe the vowels for "Edom" were added by later Jews to change the meaning because they knew the Book of Acts used this verse to uphold the acceptance of uncircumcised Gentiles.

Actually, in the same chapter Amos showed that God was just as much concerned over the Gentiles as He was over the Jews. In Amos 9:7, God said, "Are ye not as the children (people) of the Ethiopians unto me, O children of Israel? saith the Lord. Have not I brought up Israel out of the land of Egypt? and the Philistines from Caphtor (probably, Crete), and the Syrians from Kir?" In other words, God was concerned about the Gentiles even though they did not know it.

**18. Known unto God are all his works from the beginning of the world:** ... From eternity all His doings are known, –BRKL.

**15:18.** This was, as the prophets said, the work of the Lord who has known all these things from the beginning of the world (or age), that is, from the beginning of time.

**19. Wherefore my sentence is:** ... In my judgement, therefore, –TCNT ... Therefore it is my opinion, –AMPB ... For this reason my decision is, –BB.

**that we trouble not:** ... we should not add to the difficulties of, –TCNT ... be not harassed, –BRKL ... we should not harass, –FNTN ... are not to be disquieted, –DOUY.

**them, which from among the Gentiles are turned to God:** ... those Gentiles who are turning to God, –TCNT.

**15:19.** "My sentence is" is better translated, "I think it good." James was not acting as a judge here, nor as a leading elder of the church. (See verse 28.) In this situation James was simply a Christian brother, a member of the Body, who gave a word of wisdom as the Spirit willed. (See 1 Corinthians 12:8, 11.)

The Spirit's word of wisdom was that they should not trouble the Gentile believers further. They should not add any further requirements to the faith and practice of the Gentile believers.

**20. But that we write unto them:** ... command them, —ALFD ... Yet, let us send them written instructions, —WEYM.

**that they abstain from pollutions of idols:** ... keep aloof from the defilement of, —MRDK ... Do not be guilty of, —NCV ... food that has been polluted by being sacrificed to idols, —TCNT ... things polluted by connexion with idolatry, —WEYM ... anything that has been contaminated by idols, —CNFT.

**and from fornication:** ... keep away from sex sins, —NLTG ... from impurity, —TCNT ... from sexual vice, —MOFT ... and from unchastity, —BRKL ... avoid unlawful sexual intercourse, —NORL ... prostitution, —CNDT ... sexual immorality, —WLMS ... sexual sin, —NCV.

**and from things strangled:** ... and from what is strangled, —ASV ... the flesh of strangled animals, —TCNT ... Do not taste blood, —NCV ... animals that have been killed in ways against the law, —NLTG ... from meat with the blood in it, —FNTN.

**and from blood:** ... and from blood-meat, —NOLI.

**15:20.** James suggested that a letter be written directing the Gentile believers to abstain (keep away) from the pollutions of idols (everything connected with idol worship), from fornication (the various types of heterosexual and homosexual immoralities habitually practiced by so many Gentile heathen), from things strangled (meat from animals killed without draining out the blood), and from blood.

The first two requests to keep away from idolatry and all forms of sexual immorality were to uphold the witness to the one true God and the high moral standards He requires. Gentiles should not keep anything from their former idol worship, even though they now knew these were meaningless and harmless, lest others misinterpret them, and lest Jewish visitors be offended.

The Gentile believers also had to be reminded of the high moral standards God requires. They had come from a background where immorality was accepted and even encouraged in the name of religion. Paul had to deal sternly with these things. (See Romans 6:12, 13, 19-23; 1 Corinthians 5:1, 9-12; 6:13, 15-20; 10:8; Ephesians 5:3, 5; Colossians 3:5, 6; 1 Timothy 1:9, 10.) In the Book of Acts the word "fornication" is used in the general sense that includes all forms of sexual immorality both before and after marriage.

The second two requests were for the sake of promoting fellowship between Jewish and Gentile believers. If there was anything that would turn a Jewish believer's stomach, it was to eat meat from which the blood had not been drained, or to eat blood itself. If the Jewish believers were going to give up a great deal by eating nonkosher food in Gentile believers' homes, then the Gentile believers could at least avoid serving and eating those things which no Jew, no matter how long he had been a Christian, could stomach.

There was a precedent for these last two requests because long before Moses' time, God had told Noah not to eat blood, for it represented the life.

**21. For Moses of old time hath in every city them that preach him:** ... from the earliest times, —FNTN ... has from ancient generations, —SWAN ... These prescriptions of the law, —NOLI ... has had his preachers in every town, —GDSP ... that proclaim him, —RTHM ... in every city from the early days, —NLTG ... for generations long past, —SEB ... from preceding generations, —FNTN.

**being read in the synagogues every sabbath day:** ... for he is read every sabbath, —RSV ... read as he is in the Synagogue, —TCNT ... read in the meeting-houses, —FNTN.

**15:21.** James was concerned about the testimony of the synagogues in every city (in city after city) where the Jews had been for generations, going back to ancient times.

**22. Then pleased it the apostles and elders:** ... Then it seemed good, —ASV ... It was then decided by the, —TCNT ... passed a resolution, —WLMS ... agreed, —PHLP.

**with the whole church:** ... with the assent of the whole Church, —TCNT ... with the approval of, —WEYM ... The group, —SEB ... the whole assembly, —FNTN.

**to send chosen men of their own company to Antioch with Paul and Barnabas:** ... to choose men out of their company, ASV ... to choose representatives, —PHLP ... resolved to select representatives and send them, —GDSP ... to select some of their men, —MLNT ... to choose some of their own men, —SEB ... men should be chosen from among themselves, —FNTN.

**namely, Judas surnamed Barsabas, and Silas:** ... Those chosen were, —TCNT ... Judah, called, —FNTN.

**chief men among the brethren:** ... who were leading men among the Brethren, —TCNT ... prominent members of the brotherhood, —MOFT ... leaders among the Christians, —BRKL ... These men were respected, —SEB.

**15:22.** The apostles, elders, and "the whole church" accepted the word of wisdom from James. But as they considered the situation, they agreed it would be best to send men chosen from themselves to go with Barnabas and Paul to Antioch to present the decision and the letter. They would be able to confirm the truth of what would be contained in the letter as well as the fact that the whole assembly was unanimous in standing behind it. Those chosen were Judas Barsabas (probably meaning "son of the Sabbath," that is, born on the Sabbath) and Silas (short for Silvanus; 2 Corinthians 1:19). These two were recognized as leading men among the believers in Jerusalem.

Some suppose that Judas Barsabas was the brother of Joseph Barsabas, the one who, along with Matthias, was proposed as a possible substitute for Judas (1:23). This, however, is only conjecture, and nothing more is said about him after this chapter.

Silas is better known. He was a Roman citizen (16:37-39), and since Paul always referred to him as Silvanus in his epistles, it may be that Silvanus was his Roman *cognomen* or surname, while Silas (a Greek form of the Aramaic *sheila* or Saul) was chosen because of its similar sound and was preferred by his Jerusalem friends, as well as by Luke. Beginning with Paul's second missionary journey, Silas became an important and highly esteemed fellow worker with Paul in the spread of the gospel. Later he worked with Peter and carried Peter's first epistle to the churches of Asia Minor.

**23. And they wrote letters by them after this manner:** ... with the following letter, −RSV ... They were bearers of the following letter, −TCNT ... They conveyed, −MOFT.

**The apostles and elders and brethren send greeting unto the brethren which are of the Gentiles in Antioch and Syria and Cilicia:** ... to the brothers from among the heathen, −WLMS ... to their non-Jewish fellow Christians, −BECK ... the Brethren of heathen birth, −TCNT ... to the Gentile Brotherhood, −MNTG.

**15:23.** The Jerusalem assembly also used Silas and Judas Barsabas as scribes to write the letter that was to be sent by them. This indicates they were well-educated and knew Greek very well. The letter would undoubtedly be written in Greek, since the Gentiles in Antioch, Syria, and Cilicia were Greek-speaking. The people in the other churches of South Galatia founded on the first missionary journey would also speak Greek, at least as a second language.

The letter began with a polite greeting from the apostles, elders and brothers (in the Jerusalem church) to the Gentiles in the churches in Asia Minor. The word for "greetings" actually means "to be glad" or "to rejoice," but it became a common form of greeting among the Greeks.

The letter was addressed specifically to "brothers, the ones out of the nations." That is, they recognized these Gentiles as brothers who were fellow members of the family of God. They had come out from among the nations. Their origin was Gentile, but they were no longer strangers and foreigners to the promises of God, they were brothers. Paul enlarged on this thought in Ephesians 2:11-22. These Gentiles were once outside of Christ, aliens separated from the commonwealth of Israel, strangers cut off from the covenants of promise, having no hope, and without God in the world. But now, through the blood of Christ, they were no longer foreigners but fellow citizens with the saints.

**24. Forasmuch as we have heard:** ... As we have been informed, −WEYM ... Having learned, −MOFT.

**that certain which went out from us:** ... that some of our number, −TCNT ... quite unauthorized by us, −MOFT.

**have troubled you with words:** ... they continue to upset you, −BECK ... had upset you by their orations, −TCNT ... have disturbed you by their teaching, −WEYM ... have caused you trouble by their claims, −NORL ... perplexed and disturbed you, −WUST.

**subverting your souls:** ... dismantling your souls, −RTHM ... and unsettled your minds, −TCNT ... continuing to unsettle your minds, −WLMS ... and they continue to upset you, −BECK.

**saying, Ye must be circumcised, and keep the law:**

**to whom we gave no such commandment:** ... although we gave them no instructions, −RSV ... without instructions from us, −TCNT.

**15:24.** The letter first drew attention to the fact that they had heard the report that some who went out from the Jerusalem assembly had troubled (disturbed, unsettled, agitated, thrown into confusion) these Gentile believers in Antioch and other places "with words," that is, with their message, implying a multitude of arguments. The result was a tearing down, an upsetting, an unsettling of their souls. This implies their words did not come from the Holy Spirit, no matter what these men from Jerusalem might have said.

**25. It seemed good unto us, being assembled with one accord:** ... we met and decided, −TCNT ... being unanimously assembled, −RTHM ... we have unanimously decided, −WEYM ... we have passed a unanimous resolution, −WLMS ... being of one opinion, −WSLY.

**to send chosen men unto you:** ... resolved to select, −NOLI ... to send you outstanding men, −BRKL ... and send them to you, −WMCK

**with our beloved Barnabas and Paul:** ... along with, –WMCK ... with our dear brothers, –TCNT ... in company with our beloved friends, –WEYM.

**15:25.** In order to make their decision known, it seemed best to the Jerusalem believers and their leaders to send chosen (choice) men to the Gentile believers to accompany Barnabas and Paul. This implies the leaders thought their decision and this letter were extremely important, so they sent choice men, excellent men, chosen because they were the best fitted to explain the decision and encourage the Gentile believers by it.

They were also sending back Barnabas and Paul with the same message. All four would confirm the fact that the decision was made with the assembled believers and their leaders in one accord, with one mind and one purpose, unanimously.

Their words "our beloved Barnabas and Paul" emphasized that the Jerusalem apostles, elders, and all the believers counted Barnabas and Paul as dear friends, worthy of love.

This was important because Paul's epistles indicate the Judaizers were not satisfied to upset the Gentiles by spreading their legalistic doctrines, they also attacked Paul personally.

26. **Men that have hazarded their lives:** ... endangered, –WEYM ... risked, –MOFT ... who personally have jeopardized their lives, –BRKL ... who have sacrificed themselves, –TCNT ... lives have been in danger for, –NLTG.
**for the name of our Lord Jesus Christ:** ... in behalf of the name of, –RTHM ... for the sake of, –WEYM, –WMCK

**15:26.** The letter further recommended Barnabas and Paul as men who had hazarded their lives for the name of our Lord Jesus Christ. The Greek is literally, "handed over their souls for the sake of the name." This must mean they had risked their lives for His name. They recognized that when individuals believe on the name of Jesus, they enter by faith into all He is to the believers. Thus believers are saved by His name—saved by what He is (4:12). Followers of Jesus have life through His name—through what He is to them and in them (John 20:31).

27. **We have sent therefore Judas and Silas:** ... So we are dispatching, –BRKL ... We therefore send, –WMCK
**who shall also tell you the same things by mouth:** ... who also themselves by word of mouth can tell you the same things, –RTHM ... who will personally announce these things, –BRKL ... what we are now writing, –TCNT ... by word of mouth, –GDSP ... who will confirm our message, –NOLI.

**15:27.** Judas and Silas would personally confirm the contents of the letter to the churches to whom it was addressed. They would also confirm by word of mouth the love and respect the apostles, elders, and the whole Jerusalem church had for Paul and Barnabas. Thus, Paul and Barnabas would not have to defend themselves or the letter.

28. **For it seemed good to the Holy Ghost, and to us:** ... We have, therefore, decided, under the guidance of the Holy Spirit, –TCNT ... The Holy Spirit and we have decided, –WMCK
**to lay upon you no greater burden than these necessary things:** ... thinks you should have no more burdens, –SEB ... these necessary conditions, –TCNT ... no burden heavier than these necessary requirements, –WEYM ... that you should not have a heavy load to carry, –NCV ... not to burden you more than is necessary, –BECK ... any additional burden, –MRDK ... except these essentials, –BRKL ... to put no further load on you than these necessary things, –WMCK ... only the following indispensable burdens, –NOLI.

**15:28.** Only the necessary things which seemed good to the Holy Spirit and to the Jerusalem believers would be asked of them. This shows that the whole assembly in Jerusalem accepted the words of James as a word of wisdom from the Holy Spirit.

All through the Book of Acts the Holy Spirit is shown breaking down barriers—language barriers, cultural barriers, national barriers. Unfortunately, there are always some people who want to build the barriers back up again, even in the name of religion, using Bible passages and twisting them to suit their prejudices. But the Holy Spirit will cause the love of Christ to constrain believers from prejudice and make them channels of His love.

29. **That ye abstain from meats offered to idols:** ... You are to avoid, –NORL ... Keep away from, –BECK ... from idol-sacrifices, –WORL.
**and from blood:** ... the eating of blood, –NORL.
**and from things strangled:** ... the meat of animals that have been strangled, –WLMS.
**and from fornication:** ... sex impurity, –NORL ... sexual sin, –BECK.
**from which if ye keep yourselves:** ... If you guard yourselves against such things, –TCNT.
**ye shall do well:** ... you shall prosper, –RTHM ... you will make good progress, –PHLP ... you will do right, –WMCK
**Fare ye well:** ... May you be happy, –BB ... be strong, –YNG ... Farewell, –WMCK

**15:29.** The letter repeated the four things felt to be necessary for fellowship between Jewish and Gentile believers. Since it was dealing largely with table fellowship, abstinence from the polluted things of idolatry meant abstaining from meats offered to idols. When animals were sacrificed in heathen temples, part of the meat would be taken to the town market and sold. Paul later recognized that the idols were nothing, so meat offered to them was the same as any other meat. However, he said love would not let him eat such meat if it would offend a weaker brother. In this case, even though the Jewish believers were not weaker, it would still offend them, so love would not allow Gentile believers to serve such meat to them.

"Fare ye well," literally, "Make yourselves strong," had become a common phrase used at the end of a letter to mean farewell or good-bye.

**30. So when they were dismissed:** ... So when they were sent off, —RSV ... So the bearers of this letter were sent on their way, —TCNT ... were dispatched, —MOFT.

**they came to Antioch:** ... arrived in Antioch, —BRKL.

**and when they had gathered the multitude together:** ... There they called a meeting of all the Brethren, —TCNT ... where they called together the whole assembly, —WEYM.

**they delivered the epistle:** ... they handed them the letter, —MOFT.

**15:30.** The Jerusalem believers then dismissed (set free, released and sent away) Paul and his company accompanied by much prayer and expressions of their love.

When Paul and Barnabas arrived in Antioch, they gathered the whole crowd of the believers together. Then Paul handed over the letter.

**31. Which when they had read, they rejoiced for the consolation:** ... The reading of which caused great rejoicing, —TCNT ... were delighted with the comfort it brought them, —WEYM ... When the letter was read it gave them both comfort and joy, —NORL.

**15:31.** The Bible does not say who read the letter to the assembled crowd, but it was probably given to one of their own elected elders.

When the letter was read, the believers rejoiced over the consolation, or comfort, it gave them. They were also glad because of the exhortation and requests contained in the letter. Now they could forget about all the arguments of the Judaizers. Now it was clear they did not need to follow the externals of the law of Moses. They were free from all that legalistic bondage. In return for this freedom, they were only too glad to accept the provisions for fellowship and the exhortations to high moral standards.

**32. And Judas and Silas, being prophets also themselves:** ... they also were prophets, —MRDK.

**exhorted the brethren with many words, and confirmed them:** ... with much discourse consoled and confirmed the brethren, —RTHM ... further encouraged the Brethren by many an address, —TCNT ... a long and encouraging talk, —WEYM.

**15:32.** Judas and Silas did more than confirm the facts of the letter. By the Holy Spirit they exhorted the brethren. They confirmed (upheld and supported) them. They gave them solid encouragement to forget the arguments of the Judaizers and to maintain their faith in Christ and in the gospel they had received of salvation by grace through faith alone (apart from the works of the Law).

Prophets are also revival men. Because the church at Antioch was upset and thrown into confusion by the Judaizers, the fires of their zeal and the fires of their worship were burning low. Judas and Silas, as prophets, restored, revived, and brought them back into the place where they could serve the Lord with gladness (Psalm 100:2, 5).

**33. And after they had tarried there a space:** ... And having remained a while, —HBIE ... And when they had been there for some time, —BB.

**they were let go in peace from the brethren unto the apostles:** ... before the brethren let them go home, —KNOX ... they were dismissed in peace, —ASV ... with kind farewells, —TCNT ... they were sent back by the brethren with (the greeting) Peace, —AMPB ... sent them back in peace to those who had commissioned them, —PHLP ... to those that had sent them, —WMCK

**15:33.** After a time the brethren (the believers at Antioch) released Judas and Silas with a farewell blessing of peace and well being to go back, not just to the apostles, but as the Greek shows, to the entire group of believers in Jerusalem.

**34. Notwithstanding it pleased Silas to abide there still:** ... to remain, —ET ... though Silas decided to stay there, —MLNT ... But Silas thought he should stay there, —NLTG.

**15:34.** Judas Barsabas decided to return, but Silas chose to remain. (Many modern versions omit verse 34 and suppose Silas went back to Jerusalem and returned to Antioch later.)

**35. Paul also and Barnabas continued in Antioch:** ... remained, —RSV ... tarried in, —WORL ... kept on, —BB ... stayed on in, —WMCK

**teaching and preaching the word of the Lord:** ... telling the joyful tidings, —RTHM ... told the Good News of the Lord's Message, —TCNT.

with many others also: . . . and joined with many others, −TNT . . . with the help of many others, −NLTG, −TCNT . . . with a number of others, −BB.

**15:35.** Paul and Barnabas also remained in Antioch to teach and preach the gospel. The church in Antioch was still growing, and God raised up many others (in addition to the prophets and teachers of 13:1) to teach and spread the good news of the word (Greek *logos*) of the Lord. The first teachers and preachers in Antioch were believers who came from outside. Most of these new teachers and evangelists were probably from the local assembly. They too were entering into the work of ministry for the edifying or building up of the body of Christ. God's plan is that the Body should be edified most of all spiritually (Ephesians 4:12, 15, 16). This is the reason Christ gave apostles, prophets, evangelists, and pastor-teachers to the Church. It was not for them to do the work of ministry, but for them to train believers and bring them to maturity in the work of ministry. The results were that the gospel spread and many came to the Lord.

**36. And some days after:** . . . Some time after this, −TCNT . . . On a later occasion, −JB . . . A few days later, −SEB . . . After some time, −WMCK
**Paul said unto Barnabas, Let us go again:** . . . Let us return now, −ASV . . . Let us go back, −TCNT . . . retracing our steps, −WUST . . . We should go back, −EVRD . . . Let us now pay a return, −FNTN.
**and visit our brethren:** . . . and look in on the brothers, −BRKL . . . and see how the brethren fare in, −SWAN.
**in every city where we have preached the word of the Lord:** . . . to all those towns, −EVRD . . . in which we proclaimed the message, −TNT . . . have told the Lord's Message, −TCNT . . . we proclaimed the word of the Lord, −WMCK . . . where we have given the word of God, −BB.
**and see how they do:** . . . and see how they are prospering, −TCNT . . . see how they are proceeding, −FNTN . . . to see how they are getting along, −MLNT.

**15:36.** After certain days (probably a considerable time, even up to a year), Paul suggested to Barnabas that they visit the brethren in the churches established during the first missionary journey in Cyprus and South Galatia to see how they were and what their situation was. All these churches were founded in the midst of all kinds of opposition and persecution. Paul had been stoned at Lystra. He had suffered persecution in every place where he preached the gospel. Now Paul felt it was time to go back and see how these churches were doing.

Throughout his ministry, Paul maintained a love and concern that kept him praying for the churches and believers to whom he had

ministered. He visited many of them again and again to give them further teaching and encouragement. He knew how important it is to follow up and disciple new believers. When he could not go to them, he wrote them letters. Even in the midst of his own persecution and perils, he did not forget them. Upon him daily was the care and concern for all the churches (2 Corinthians 11:28, 29). So now he wanted to visit every city where they had founded churches.

The word "visit" is the same word used of God's gracious visitations where He brought salvation and blessing to His people. It is also often used of visiting the sick to pray for them and to help them. *Visit* has the connotation of caring and looking after. Paul had the heart of a good undershepherd who felt the responsibility of caring for the Lord's flock.

**37. And Barnabas determined to take with them John:** . . . was bent on taking, −WEYM . . . But Barnabas persisted in wanting to take along John, −WLMS . . . had a desire to take with them, −BB.
**whose surname was Mark:** . . . who was called Mark, −ASV . . . whose other name was Mark, −TCNT . . . named, −BB.

**15:37.** Barnabas felt the same desire to visit and help these churches. But he saw someone else he wanted to help. His cousin John, the one called Mark, wanted to go along, and Barnabas decided to (willed to, purposed to) take him along with him and Paul. Barnabas, as we have seen, was an encourager. Even though Mark had failed them before, Barnabas encouraged him to come.

**38. But Paul thought not good to take him with them:** . . . did not think it wise, −NIV . . . didn't think it was such a good idea, −SEB . . . counted him unworthy, −CNDT . . . not fit to take along with them, −WLMS . . . was of the opinion that it was not right, −BB . . . thought it unwise, −MNTG . . . it was not right to admit such a man to their company, −KNOX.
**who departed from them from Pamphylia:** . . . who withdrew, −ASV . . . who had deserted, −TCNT . . . the one who had quit them, −BRKL . . . one who had gone away from them, −BB.
**and went not with them to the work:** . . . instead of accompanying them on active service, −MOFT . . . He had not helped them in the work, −NLTG . . . had not gone on with, −BB . . . and had not continued with them, −NORL.

**15:38.** Paul, however, did not agree. In fact, he kept insisting that they not take him along. He did not think Mark was worthy, fit, or suitable for this ministry. Mark had left them in the lurch at an important point where they needed him for the task of spreading the gospel in new and more difficult areas.

**39. And the contention was so sharp between them:** ... And there arose an angry feeling, —RTHM ... So there arose a sharp altercation, —WEYM ... so intense, —ET ... The disagreement was so sharp, —WLMS ... In consequence of this strife, —MRDK ... After a violent quarrel, —JB ... so stirred, —GNVA ... had a serious argument, —NCV ... there was a sharp argument, —BB.

**that they departed asunder one from the other:** ... which resulted in their parting from one another, —WEYM ... that they went their separate ways, —PHLP ... They separated and went different ways, —SEB ... so that they were parted from one another, —BB.

**and so Barnabas took Mark, and sailed unto Cyprus:** ... and went by ship to, —BB.

**15:39.** Barnabas, however, was determined to give his cousin another chance, so he refused to give in to Paul's demands that they leave Mark behind.

Both Paul and Barnabas felt so strongly about this that they felt temporary irritation, perhaps indignation. The Greek indicates sharp feelings between them. But they did not let this hinder the work of the Lord and they came up with a peaceful settlement. They decided it was best to separate and divide up the responsibility of visiting and encouraging the believers. Barnabas, therefore, took his cousin Mark and went to Cyprus to visit the churches founded on the first missionary journey. This was wise because Cyprus was familiar territory to Mark. He had been faithful there. It was better to take him back to the area where he had been a success rather than to the place where he had failed.

That Barnabas was right in wanting to give Mark a second chance is shown by the fact that Paul later asked Timothy to bring Mark with him because he was useful for ministry (2 Timothy 4:11). Mark was also with Peter on his visit to Babylon (1 Peter 5:13). Some writers take "Babylon" here to mean Rome. But Babylon had one of the largest Jewish communities outside Palestine. It should not be considered strange that Peter, the apostle to the circumcision, would go there.

**40. And Paul chose Silas and departed:** ... chose Silas and went forth, —SWAN ... set out, —WEYM.

**being recommended by the brethren unto the grace of God:** ... committed unto the favour of the Lord by the brethren, —RTHM ... to the gracious care of the Lord, —TCNT ... his fellow Christians entrusting him to the Lord's love, —BECK ... having been entrusted by the brethren to the blessing of the Lord, —FNTN ... into the Lord's care, —EVRD ... asked for the Lord's favor to be on, —NLTG ... commended ... to the grace of God, —WMCK ... with the blessing of the brothers, —BB.

**15:40.** Paul then chose Silas who was a mature believer, a prophet already used by the Spirit to challenge and encourage the churches. Silas would be an excellent helper to Paul in his efforts to encourage the churches in South Galatia which were in a most difficult environment.

Since Silas was also an outstanding member of the Jerusalem church, he would also be helpful in showing the Galatian churches the unity between Paul and the Jerusalem leaders. This would further put to rest the arguments of the Judaizers and would confirm the statements of Paul in Galatians 2:1-10 (where he said those leaders accepted his gospel as the same one they were teaching and gave him the right hand of fellowship). It was important also that Silas was an apostle in the sense that he not only heard Jesus teach and saw Him after His resurrection, but was directly commissioned by Him.

The brethren at Antioch then released Paul and Silas and committed them anew to the grace of God.

**41. And he went through Syria and Cilicia:** ... passed, —WMCK ... He accordingly travelled through, —FNTN.

**confirming the churches:** ... giving strength to, —NCV ... strengthening the Churches in the Faith, —TCNT ... where he established congregations, —NORL ... where he strengthened the congregations, —KLST ... helping the congregations grow stronger, —SEB ... making the churches stronger in the faith, —BB.

**15:41.** So Paul and Silas went on their way through Syria and Cilicia, confirming (strengthening) the churches, including the assembly in Paul's home city of Tarsus.

## Chapter 16

**1. Then came he to Derbe and Lystra and, behold, a certain disciple was there:** ... At the latter place they found a disciple, —TCNT ... he descended to, —FNTN.

**named Timotheus the son of a certain woman, which was a Jewess, and believed:** ... whose mother was a Jewess who had become a believer in Christ, —TCNT ... son of a woman, a believing Jewess, —FNTN.

**but his father was a Greek:** ... but of a Greek father, —SWAN ... of a Grecian, —WORL.

**16:1.** From Cilicia Paul and Silas went through the Taurus mountains by way of a famous pass called the Cilician Gates. Coming from this direction they would first arrive at Derbe, and then go to Lystra.

At Lystra Paul came across a young disciple named Timothy (short for *Timotheus,* "venerating, worshiping, honoring God"). His mother was a believing Jewess named Eunice. His grandmother Lois was also a godly believer. (See 2 Timothy 1:5; 3:14, 15.) His father, however, was a Greek, probably a member of a prominent and wealthy family but apparently still unconverted.

Fortunately, the faith and training given Timothy by his mother and grandmother had more effect upon him than the unbelief of his father; they had trained him in the Scriptures from earliest childhood.

**2. Which was well reported of by the brethren that were at Lystra and Iconium:**...who was well attested, –RTHM...was well spoken of, –RSV...was well recommended, –BRKL...They said good things about him, –SEB.

**16:2.** When Timothy accepted Christ, he made great progress in the Christian life. The believing brethren at Lystra and in the next town, Iconium, bore witness to him. This clearly means God had given Timothy a spiritual ministry in both cities, and his life and ministry was a blessing to the assemblies there.

It is probable that he was converted under Paul's ministry during one of Paul's previous visits to Lystra. However, when Paul later called him "my son," he was probably using the term *son* to mean "student," as well as younger fellow worker (1 Timothy 1:2, 18; 2 Timothy 1:2). Prophetic utterances confirmed Timothy's mission, and the Holy Spirit gave him gifts as Paul and the elders gathered around and laid hands on him. (See 1 Timothy 1:18; 4:14; 2 Timothy 1:6.)

**3. Him would Paul have to go forth with him:**...Wishing to take this man with him on his journey, –TCNT...wanted Timothy to travel with him, –EVRD...resolved to take him as a companion on his journey, –KNOX...being anxious that he should accompany him, –FNTN...for travel
**and took and circumcised him because of the Jews which were in those quarters:**...Paul caused him to be circumcised on account of the Jews in that neighbourhood, –TCNT...But he was careful to circumcise him, –KNOX...out of consideration for the Jews, –NEB...In deference to the Jews of the area, –TALR...due to the local Jews, –BRKL...out of respect to the Jews resident in these places, –FNTN...to please the Jews, –EVRD...on account of the Jews in those places, –WMCK
**for they knew all that his father was a Greek:**...for they one and all knew, –RTHM...for they all had knowledge, –BB.

**16:3.** In view of this, Paul wanted to take Timothy with him for further training as well as to help in the spread of the gospel. But when Paul decided to do this, he did something very unusual. He circumcised Timothy. Paul made quite a point in

Galatians 2:3-5 that the Jerusalem leaders did not require Titus to be circumcised. But Titus was a Gentile. To circumcise him would have meant yielding to the Judaizers who said Gentiles must become Jews to keep their salvation. Timothy, however, had been brought up in the Jewish traditions by a Jewish mother. Jews even today accept a person as a Jew if his mother is Jewish, even if his father is a Gentile. They rightly understand that the mother has the greatest influence on the values and religious attitudes of a young child.

Paul still went to the Jew first in every new city he visited. For him to take an uncircumcised Jew into a synagogue would be like taking a traitor into an army camp. It would be intolerable to the Jews. None of them would listen to him. Thus, for the sake of giving Timothy opportunity to witness to his fellow Jews, Paul took Timothy and circumcised him. From this it is clear Paul did not ask Jews to give up their Jewish customs, but he recognized that circumcision and uncircumcision in themselves mean nothing. (See Galatians 5:6; 6:15; 1 Corinthians 7:19.)

Perhaps 1 Corinthians 9:20-23 gives further insight into Paul's reasoning. He did not go against the cultural norms of the people to whom he ministered unless they were immoral or idolatrous. Thus he brought everything into line with the promotion of the gospel and the salvation of sinners. Everyone knew Timothy's father was a Greek, so Paul had to confirm Timothy's Jewish heritage before they could go on. The elders of the local assembly accepted this, prayed, and sent Timothy with their blessing (1 Timothy 4:14).

**4. And as they went through the cities:**...As they passed from, –WMCK...As they travelled from town to town, –TCNT...on their way through the towns, –BB.
**they delivered them the decrees for to keep:**...unto them for observance the decrees, –RTHM...they handed over into their keeping the decisions made by, –WMCK...they gave them the rules...so that they might keep them, –BB...they delivered into their custody the decrees, –FNTN...they recommended to their observance the decree laid down by, –KNOX...they gave the Brethren the decisions...for them to observe, –TCNT...those injunctions, –MRDK...gave the believers the rules and decisions from, –SEB.
**that were ordained of the apostles and elders which were at Jerusalem:**...which had been decided upon by, –RTHM...which had been reached by, –TCNT...which had been agreed upon by, –FNTN...which had been made by, –SWAN...and the rulers of the church, –BB...had written for the Christians to do, –NLTG.

**16:4.** As Paul, Silas, and Timothy went on their way through the rest of the cities of South Galatia, they handed over copies of the decrees, or regulations, from the letter recorded in chapter 15, decrees which the Gentile believers were to keep. These regulations were recognized as "ordained." They were decided by the apostles and elders in Jerusalem who then gave their approval to them and sent out the letter. But Paul and Silas no doubt drew attention to 15:28, "It seemed good to the Holy Ghost and to us."

The result was that the upsetting teachings of the Judaizers were counteracted. What had been a critical issue was no longer a threat or a cause of division. Everyone accepted the decision of the Jerusalem Council. Undoubtedly, the Epistle to the Galatians had helped to prepare the way for this. In it Paul dealt with the problem of the Law and circumcision as critical issues and gave strong arguments against the Judaizers.

**5. And so were the churches established in the faith:** . . . were being confirmed, –*RTHM* . . . through faith continued to grow in strength, –*WLMS* . . . were given stability, –*CNDT* . . . firmly established in the faith, –*KNOX* . . . accordingly strengthened in the faith, –*FNTN* . . . were made strong. BB.

**and increased in number daily:** . . . and grew in number from day to day, –*WEYM* . . . the number daily increased, –*FNTN* . . . and daily increased in membership, –*NORL* . . . increased in numbers every day, –*WMCK* . . . More people were added each day, –*NLTG* . . . were abounding in number, –*YNG* . . . grew larger every day, –*EVRD*.

**16:5.** The assemblies in the various cities were all strengthened not only in faith, but in "the faith." That is, they grew in their understanding of the truth of the gospel and in their obedience to its teachings and precepts. "The faith" was the whole body of truth that was preached and believed.

As a result of this encouragement and teaching the local assemblies continued to grow, increasing in number daily. This growth implies that the believers put their faith into action. They all became personal witnesses, spreading the truth about Jesus, telling of His death and resurrection, offering His grace and salvation to all of their friends and neighbors.

**6. Now when they had gone throughout Phrygia and the region of Galatia:** . . . And they passed through, –*RTHM* . . . And after they had gone through the land of, –*BB* . . . went through the provinces of, –*NCV* . . . Thus they crossed, –*WMCK*

**and were forbidden of the Holy Ghost to preach the word in Asia:** . . . kept them from preaching, –*NLTG* . . . they were prevented by, –*WMCK* . . . did not let them take the word into, –*BB* . . . but were restrained by, –*TCNT*.

**16:6.** After Paul and his company went through the region of Phrygia and Galatia, it would have been logical to go next into the Roman province of Asia. Its great city of Ephesus and many other outstanding cities could have provided great opportunities for the gospel. Though God later gave Paul a great ministry there, it was not yet God's time. The Holy Spirit had already forbidden them to speak the Word in that province. (The Greek means "having been forbidden.")

They did have to go through the province of Asia, however. For days, perhaps weeks, they had to travel without spreading the Word, saying nothing in behalf of their Lord. This must have been very difficult for Paul. He felt constrained, moved by the mighty compulsion of Christ's love. (See 2 Corinthians 5:11, 13, 14, 18, 20.) He felt necessity laid on him: "Woe is unto me, if I preach not the gospel!" (1 Corinthians 9:16).

**7. After they were come to Mysia:** . . . When they reached the borders of Mysia, –*TCNT* . . . when they got as far as Mysia, –*MOFT* . . . having come to, –*BB* . . . reached the frontier, –*WEYM*.

**they assayed to go into Bithynia:** . . . they were attempting to journey into, –*RTHM* . . . they were about to enter Bithynia, –*WEYM* . . . they tried to enter, –*KLST* . . . they made an attempt to go into, –*BB* . . . they attempted to proceed to, –*FNTN*.

**but the Spirit suffered them not:** . . . but the Spirit of Jesus did not permit them, –*TCNT* . . . would not allow them to, –*NIV* . . . did not let them, –*BB*, –*NCV* . . . permitted them not, –*MRDK* . . . would not let them go, –*NLTG* . . . forbad it, –*WMCK*

**16:7.** Since they were forbidden to preach in Asia, they moved north along the eastern border of Mysia and made an attempt to enter Bithynia to the northeast. Bithynia was another important Roman province which lay along the Black Sea.

Paul was never one to sit around and do nothing when he did not know where God wanted him to go or to do next. He was always conscious of the missionary burden upon him. So when he was checked by the Spirit from going in one direction, he would take a step in another, trusting the Holy Spirit to confirm or check that direction also. Thus he tried to go into Bithynia, but the Spirit would not let them go in that direction either. (However, 1 Peter 1:1 shows that Bithynia was later evangelized by others.)

**8. And they passing by Mysia came down to Troas:** . . . Passing through Mysia, they went down to Troas, –*TCNT* . . . passing along the frontier of, –*KLST* . . . going past . . . they came down to, –*BB* . . . having passed by . . . they went down to, –*FNTN*.

**16:8.** Since they were not allowed to go east, there was only one direction left, so they turned west and went to Troas. To do this they had to go through Mysia, another Roman province. The Greek says literally that they bypassed Mysia. This can only mean they were not given permission to preach the gospel in Mysia either. This must have been hard for Paul, but because he was obedient to the Spirit, God brought him to Troas when He wanted him there.

**9. And a vision appeared to Paul in the night:** ... and there one night Paul saw a vision, –TCNT ... That night Paul had a dream, –NLTG.

**There stood a man of Macedonia, and prayed him, saying:** ... A Macedonian was standing and appealing to him, –TCNT ... stood by him in entreaty, –KNOX ... and beseeching him, –RTHM, –WORL ... entreating him, –CMPB ... requesting him, –BB ... appealing to him in the words, –KLST ... stood there begging him, –SEB ... who stood imploring him, saying, –FNTN.

**Come over into Macedonia, and help us:** ... Pass over, –DOUY ... and bring us succour! –RTHM.

**16:9.** Troas was a harbor city of Mysia. It was some distance south of Homer's Troy, which gave the name to the district. It lay on the Aegean Sea across from Macedonia.

Another important turning point in Paul's ministry and missionary travels came at Troas. Had Paul gone into Bithynia, he might have continued eastward and never gone to Greece or Rome. But God had new centers He wanted to establish in Europe. There were opportunities there which would not only allow the establishing of churches, but would call forth several of Paul's epistles. Not only so, it is clear that it was God's purpose in Paul's ministry to establish new centers for the spread of the gospel. It was appropriate, therefore, that he should eventually end up in Rome. The capital of the Roman Empire became a new center from which the gospel could spread toward the uttermost parts of the earth.

Thus it was left for other apostles and believers to go eastward. There is strong tradition that the apostle Thomas went to South India, had a great ministry, and was martyred there near Madras.

The call westward was made clear in a night vision given to Paul. In the vision Paul saw a Macedonian pagan standing and begging him to come over to Macedonia to help them.

**10. And after he had seen the vision immediately we endeavoured to go into Macedonia:** ... As soon as he had the vision, we forthwith made efforts to set out for, –KLST ... That vision once seen, we were eager to sail for, –KNOX ... Accordingly, having seen this vision, we at once attempted to proceed to, –FNTN ... we were eager to start at once, –TCNT ... we immediately prepared to leave

for, –EVRD, –NCV ... we immediately sought to go into, –SWAN.

**assuredly gathering that the Lord had called us:** ... since we concluded, –BECK ... concluding that God had called us, –RSV ... We understood that God had called, –EVRD, –SEB ... convinced that God had called us, –PHLP ... concluding that God had summoned us, –RTHM ... inferring, –CMPB ... being sure, –CNFT ... being assured, –DOUY ... we agreed that God told us to go to, –NLTG ... had called us forward, –FNTN.

**for to preach the gospel unto them:** ... to evangelize there, –BRKL ... to bring the Good News to its people, –KLST ... evangelize them, –FNTN.

**16:10.** Paul and his company did not hesitate once this positive guidance was given. Immediately they sought to go to Macedonia, concluding that God had called them to preach the gospel there.

Up to this time the Book of Acts, in referring to Paul and his company, uses the word *they.* Here, for the first time, Luke used the word "we." This is the first of the "we" passages which indicate Luke, the beloved physician, was part of Paul's company on certain occasions. The other "we" passages are in 20:5-21:18 and 27:1-28:16. So Luke joined Paul at Troas and continued on the second missionary journey as far as Philippi. Then, on the third missionary journey, Luke rejoined Paul at Philippi and went with him to Jerusalem. Then, it seems, he stayed in Palestine and sailed with Paul from Caesarea to Rome. Luke was a Gentile (Paul distinguished him from his Jewish companions in Colossians 4:11, 14). Many early traditions of the church say Luke was a native of Antioch in Syria, and this is quite probable. If so, Luke was a first-hand witness to many of the events he recorded in the Book of Acts even before he became a fellow laborer with Paul.

**11. Therefore loosing from Troas we came with a straight course to Samothracia:** ... Setting sail therefore from ... we steered straight to, –FNTN ... and ran before the wind, –TCNT ... and struck a bee line for, –WLMS ... and sailed to the island of, –SEB.

**and the next day to Neapolis:** ... and the day following, –ASV ... and on the morrow unto New City, –RTHM ... The next day we arrived in Neapolis, –MNTG.

**16:11.** A ship took Paul and his company about 125 miles from Troas to Neapolis, the harbor town of Philippi, by way of the mountainous island of Samothrace. The wind must have been favorable, for it took only 2 days. Later, the journey in the other direction took 5 days (20:6).

Samothrace (off the coast of Thrace) is a small island of about 30 square miles. It has a 5,000-foot mountain which, in clear weather, guided them on a straight course to it. They were then able to circle north of the island and swing west to Neapolis, keeping fairly close to the coast. (Most ships in ancient times did not venture too far away from land.)

**12. And from thence to Philippi:** ... From there we made our way to Philippi, *—TCNT* ... Then we went by land to, *—EVRD.*

**which is the chief city of that part of Macedonia, and a colony:** ... a Roman colony, *—ASV* ... the first Macedonian city of the district, *—ALFD* ... the leading town in that part of, *—WLMS* ... This was an important city in the country of, *—NLTG* ... which is the most important town of, *—BB* ... which is the principal town of its district, *—WMCK* ... which is a capital, *—FNTN* ... It is a city for Romans, *—SEB.*

**and we were in that city abiding certain days:** ... we spent several days, *—TCNT* ... There we stayed for some time, *—MNTG* ... in this city abiding for some days, *—SWAN* ... we remained for some days, conferring together, *—KNOX* ... stayed there for a few days, *—SEB* ... And we rested for some days in the town itself, *—FNTN* ... in this town we stayed for some days, *—WMCK*

**16:12.** They did not stay in Neapolis, but went on about 10 miles to Philippi. Paul did not stop in every little town along the way; led by the Spirit, he went to the most important city in that part of Macedonia. His method was to go to the chief cities and establish churches as gospel centers. His converts would then have the privilege of taking the gospel to the surrounding cities and towns.

Philippi, named after Philip, the father of Alexander the Great, was a great city of what was called the first division of the Roman province of Macedonia, north of Greece. The city was also a Roman "colony." That is, in Philippi the Romans had settled a garrison of Roman soldiers who were citizens of Rome and who followed Roman laws and customs. The constitution of the city was modeled on that of Rome. Other cities were given honorary status as colonies, but the Bible only draws attention to the colonial status of Philippi. Apparently, when Augustus made Philippi a military colony, many Romans made it their home.

Philippi was an important city also because it was located at the eastern end of the famous Roman road, the Egnatian Way. Roman soldiers patrolled the road—another reason for the colonial status. The emperor also had given the citizens of Philippi the "Italic right," which meant they had the same rights as cities on Italian soil.

**13. And on the sabbath we went out of the city by a river side:** ... And on the day of rest we went

forth outside the gate, *—RTHM* ... On Saturday we, *—BECK* ... went outside the town, by the river, *—BB.*

**where prayer was wont to be made:** ... where we had an idea that there would be, *—BB* ... There we thought we would find a special place for prayer, *—NCV* ... where we were informed prayer was to be, *—FNTN* ... a place of worship, *—BRKL.*

**and we sat down, and spake unto the women which resorted thither:** ... and having sat down, we spoke to the women who were assembled, *—FNTN* ... and sitting down we went on to speak unto the women who had come together, *—RTHM* ... talked to the women who had gathered, *—WMCK*

**16:13.** There was no Jewish synagogue at Philippi, which probably means the city lacked the 10 adult Jewish men necessary to have a synagogue. It could also mean there was no organized Jewish community, no school for the Jewish children, and no public witness or systematic reading of the Old Testament Scriptures. Yet Paul did not go directly to the Gentiles as he had at Lystra and Derbe where there were no Jews at all. Paul continued to go to the Jew first (Romans 1:16). They at least had some background in the Scriptures.

Probably by making inquiries, Paul heard there was a place of prayer about a mile outside the city gate on the bank of the Gangues River. When the Sabbath Day came, Paul and his fellow workers went down to the riverside, sat down, and proceeded to talk to a group of women who met there. From what follows it is clear that some of the women were Jewish, and some were interested Gentiles; some were single, while others may have been widows or perhaps married to Gentiles.

**14. And a certain woman named Lydia:** ... Among them was a woman, named Lydia, *—TCNT.*

**a seller of purple:** ... Her job was selling, *—EVRD* ... purple fabrics, *—WUST* ... purple dyes, *—TCNT* ... a dealer, *—FNTN* ... purple goods, *—ADAM* ... a trader in purple cloth, *—BB.*

**of the city of Thyatira which worshipped God:** ... of the town ... and a God-fearing woman, *—BB* ... devout towards God, *—RTHM* ... reverenced God, *—MOFT.*

**heard us:** ... was listening, *—WORL* ... listened to us, *—MNTG* ... gave ear to us, *—BB.*

**whose heart the Lord opened:** ... The Lord touched this woman's heart, *—TCNT* ... The Lord opened her mind to pay attention to, *—NCV.*

**that she attended unto the things which were spoken of Paul:** ... that she accepted the message spoken by Paul, *—WLMS* ... to give attention to the things which Paul was saying, *—BB.*

**16:14.** As Paul talked about the Lord and began to explain the gospel, the Lord began to work, and the Spirit began to drive home the truth to the hearts of those who heard.

Strangely enough, the first convert was a Gentile, Lydia. She was a wealthy businesswoman, a seller (that is, an independent dealer) of purple-dyed woolen cloth. In ancient times the word *purple* included various shades of crimson and red. The "royal" purple of those days was actually a deep shade of crimson red, later called Turkey red. It was the product of the shellfish murex and was very expensive.

Lydia was from Thyatira, a city in Lydia north of Sardis (the capital of the Lydian region of the Roman province of Asia). Some believe she was named for her native land, though the name *Lydia* was common. Thyatira was famous for another purple dye made of madder root. Some believe it was the real source of Turkey red. Thyatira contained a Jewish colony. Lydia possibly became interested in the things of God by attending the synagogue there. At Philippi she continued to pray and seek God. Because she did, the Lord was able to open her heart to understand the truth of the gospel as she gave her full attention to the things Paul was preaching and teaching.

15. **And when she was baptized, and her household:** . . . And when she was immersed, *—RTHM* . . . when she and her family had had baptism, *—BB*.

**she besought us, saying:** . . . she urged us to become her guests, *—TCNT* . . . she made a request to us, *—BB*.

**If ye have judged me to be faithful to the Lord:** . . . If ye are really persuaded, *—MRDK* . . . in your judgement, *—WEYM* . . . If you think I am truly a believer, *—NCV* . . . If it seems to you that I am true to, *—BB* . . . to be a believer in the Lord, *—RTHM*.

**come into my house, and abide there:** . . . come into my house and be my guests, *—BB*.

**And she constrained us:** . . . And she insisted on our going so, *—TCNT* . . . she persuaded us to stay with her, *—NCV* . . . she would take no refusal, *—JB* . . . And she compelled us, *—SWAN*.

**16:15.** The result was that Lydia believed the gospel and was baptized in water with her entire household, that is, with her staff and servants. Through her influence they also believed, and together they became the first body of believers in Europe. (Compare Luke 24:32, 45; 1 Corinthians 2:13, 14.)

This took place over a period of time. By winning her household to the Lord, Lydia demonstrated her own faithfulness to the Lord. On this basis she besought Paul and his entire company to make her large home their home and headquarters. She wanted her household to be established in the Lord. No doubt also, she had many friends and business acquaintances who might not go down to the riverside but who would come to her house. Thus, it was in her house a church would be established.

Lydia kept urging Paul and his fellow workers to come until they finally did so. The assembly soon began to grow. At the end of chapter 16 there were not only women but "brethren" who were now part of the congregation. (See verse 40.) Thus, even though there were small beginnings, God was faithful.

16. **And it came to pass, as we went to prayer:** . . . One day, as we were on our way to the Place of Prayer, *—TCNT* . . . But it happened, as we were going to the prayer service, *—BRKL*.

**a certain damsel possessed with a spirit of divination met us:** . . . having a spirit of Python, *—RTHM* . . . we were met by a girl possessed by a divining spirit, *—TCNT* . . . a slave girl met us, possessed by a spirit of, *—MOFT* . . . by a fortune-telling demon, *—NORL* . . . a spirit of clairvoyance, *—PHLP* . . . the gift of magical fortune-telling, *—WLMS* . . . She had an evil spirit, *—SEB*.

**which brought her masters much gain:** . . . who made large profits for her masters, *—TCNT* . . . who afforded a vast income, *—CNDT* . . . she earned a lot of money for her owners, *—NCV* . . . Her owner made much money from her power, *—NLTG*.

**by soothsaying:** . . . by her power of fortune-telling, *—MOFT* . . . by telling the unknown, *—BECK* . . . by her prediction, *—SWAN* . . . which gave knowledge of the future, *—BB*.

**16:16.** One day as Paul, Silas, Timothy, and Luke were going down to the place of prayer, a demon-possessed slave girl met them. Her "spirit of divination" in the Greek means a spirit of ventriloquism. A demon spirit used her, in spite of herself, to speak and to practice soothsaying or fortune telling. The Greek also calls her a "pythoness." The python was a monstrous constricting snake that Greek mythology said was killed by the god Apollo. Thus the python became a symbol of the Greek god, Apollo. The masters of this slave girl claimed that her fortune telling was the voice of Apollo. This kind of fortune telling was popular and brought much gain (money) to her masters. It seems to be implied also that they used her to attract people to their other businesses.

Various types of fortune telling, astrology, and spiritism or spiritualism were common in all the ancient heathen religions of the Middle East and Europe. Isaiah 47:12-14 shows how all this was part of the heathenism of ancient Babylon and was of no spiritual profit to them. Isaiah 2:6 shows that one of the reasons God had turned away from His people and would have to judge them was because they were soothsayers like the Philistines. Many places in the Bible show that all these things are defiling. They are really part of the devil's territory. The believer who trusts God will have nothing to do with them. The believer's guidance comes through the Spirit and the Word, not through human, magical, or demonic means. God may use fellow believers to encourage Christians, and He may even use circumstances to check them, but He will never use any form of the occult.

**17. The same followed Paul and us:** . . . She used to follow after, *–MNTG* . . . followed Paul and us everywhere, *–SEB.*

**and cried, saying:** . . . crying out again and again, *–MNTG* . . . shrieking, *–MOFT.*

**These men are the servants:** . . . bondmen, *–DRBY* . . . are workmen who are owned by, *–NLTG.*

**of the most high God:** . . . of the Supreme God, *–NEB* . . . of the Highest God, *–NORL.*

**which shew unto us:** . . . who proclaim unto you, *–ASV* . . . who indeed are declaring unto you, *–RTHM* . . . and they are bringing you news of, *–TCNT.*

**the way of salvation:** . . . how you can be saved! *–NCV.*

**16:17.** This demon-possessed slave girl followed after Paul and his company, repeatedly shouting out in a shrieking, high-pitched voice, "These men are servants (slaves) of the most high God who are announcing to you a way of salvation." (Many Greek manuscripts have "to us" instead of "to you.")

The girl was right in saying Paul and his companions were committed servants, "slaves," fully subject to the Most High God. Her witness, however, was incomplete. It is a question what "the most high God" might mean to the Greeks and the Romans. They might have supposed she was talking about one of their gods, such as Zeus or Jupiter. The word has no definite article. It reads "a way," rather than "the way." Many even today are willing to call the gospel "a way" of salvation, but they are not at all willing to concede that the gospel is "the way," that is, the *only* way.

When missionaries went to India proclaiming Jesus as Saviour, some of the Hindus said, "Fine, we are glad to accept Him as a savior. We have many saviors; we can always use one more." Some would still be willing to treat Jesus as an avatar or incarnation of one of their heathen gods. But their universal being, the Brahman or Atman, is not a personal god. Their philosophers admit they cannot say whether this "great soul" exists or not.

**18. And this did she many days:** . . . And this she continued to do, *–RTHM* . . . This she persisted in for a considerable time, *–WEYM* . . . She kept this up, *–NCV* . . . on a number of days, *–BB.*

**But Paul, being grieved, turned and said to the Spirit:** . . . But Paul was annoyed, *–RSV* . . . worn out and turning unto, *–RTHM* . . . in a burst of irritation, turned round, *–PHLP* . . . This bothered Paul, *–SEB* . . . being much displeased, *–NOYS* . . . was

indignant, *–MRDK* . . . being exasperated, *–CNDT* . . . until Paul in vexation, *–WEYM* . . . being sore troubled, *–ASV.*

**I command thee in the name of Jesus Christ to come out of her:** . . . I order you out of her! *–MOFT* . . . to get out of her! *–BRKL* . . . By the authority of, *–SEB* . . . By the power, *–FNTN, –NCV* . . . I charge thee, *–SWAN.*

**And he came out the same hour:** . . . That very moment the spirit left her, *–TCNT* . . . Immediately, *–NCV.*

**16:18.** The slave girl kept following Paul and his companions for (during) many days. That is, she did not do it continuously, but during part of every day she would follow close after them, shouting out the same thing.

The slave girl's shrieks and cries must have attracted a great deal of attention. But it was not the kind of witness that brings real glory to God, because it did not proclaim the whole truth. Paul was greatly troubled, disturbed, and annoyed by her unpleasant shrieking. It was not the kind of witness Paul needed.

Finally, Paul felt this shrieking had to be stopped. So he claimed the name and the authority of Jesus. Turning to the woman, he spoke, not to her, but to the evil spirit in her, commanding it in the name (by the authority) of Jesus Christ to come out of her. In this he was following the example of Jesus who also spoke directly to the demons who possessed people. It came out of her "in that hour," which really means immediately. (Codex Bezae [D], along with other ancient "western" manuscripts, adds the word *immediately.*) Truly there is power in the name of Jesus.

**19. And when her masters saw that the hope of their gains were gone:** . . . seeing that the hope of their gain was gone, *–SWAN* . . . no hope of further profit from her, *–TCNT* . . . their way of making money for the future was gone, *–ADAM* . . . all their hopes of profit had vanished, *–KNOX* . . . knew that now they could not use her to make money, *–NCV* . . . could not longer use her, *–SEB.*

**they caught Paul and Silas:** . . . they took, *–BB* . . . they seized, *–TCNT* . . . they grabbed, *–BRKL* . . . arresting, *–FNTN.*

**and drew them into the marketplace unto the rulers:** . . . and dragged them . . . before the rulers, *–ASV* . . . pulling them . . . before the rulers, *–BB* . . . dragged them into the public square to the authorities, *–TCNT* . . . dragged them by their heels, *–WUST* . . . to the law courts, *–JB.*

**16:19.** Up to this point in Paul's missionary travels, most of the persecution and opposition to the gospel was stirred up by Jews. It came from jealousy over the success of the apostles and from a desire to retain their own position of religious leadership. But in Philippi there was no synagogue, and for the first time persecution came directly from Gentiles.

Actually, the Gentiles paid no attention to Paul at first. The owners of the slave girl did not object to her following Paul, for that only drew attention to the demon spirit in her, which in turn brought more people to her for fortune telling when her masters had their hours of business. But when Paul cast out the evil spirit, their attitude suddenly changed. To them the evil spirit was their hope of gains (profit). The deliverance of the poor demon-possessed girl meant nothing to them. All they saw was that their hope of profit was gone (literally, "cast out"). Greed for material gain all too often makes men take advantage of others. Money was the real god of these men. They cared nothing for Paul or his message. All they cared about was using this slave girl to make a profit.

Because the girl's masters were very upset at their loss, they seized Paul and Silas and dragged them into the marketplace (Greek, *agora*), the center of public life in Greek cities. There they rather violently brought them before the rulers, the two praetors or chief Roman magistrates of the city.

**20. And brought them:** . . . and took them, —TCNT . . . And when they had taken them, —BB.

**to the magistrates, saying:** . . . in front of the leaders, —NLTG . . . before the highest Roman officials, —BECK . . . before the authorities, —BB.

**These men, being Jews, do exceedingly trouble our city:** . . . mightily disturb, —CMPB . . . are perturbing, —CNDT . . . are making trouble in, —SEB . . . are greatly troubling our town, —BB.

**16:20.** As soon as they brought Paul and Silas before the Roman magistrates they presented their accusation. But they did not mention the real reason they were upset. Instead, they called Paul and Silas big Jewish troublemakers. The Greek word is emphatic. They claimed the apostles were troubling their city greatly (exceedingly).

**21. And teach customs:** . . . and are declaring customs, —RTHM . . . and announcing customs, —SWAN . . . they're teaching religious ways, —BECK . . . Teaching rules of living, —BB.

**which are not lawful for us to receive, neither to observe, being Romans:** . . . which it is not allowable for us either to accept or observe, —RTHM . . . teaching a religion that we Romans are not allowed to follow, —NLTG . . . which it is not right for us to have or to keep, —BB . . . aren't allowed, —BECK . . . to welcome, —BRKL.

**16:21.** They went on to say that Paul and Silas were proclaiming customs that were not lawful for Romans to welcome or practice.

Though Judaism was a legal religion in the Roman Empire, it was only tolerated by the majority of the people and was not looked on with any real favor by the government. The fourth Roman emperor, Claudius, had no love for the Jews and expelled them from Rome.

In most of the Greek-speaking cities of Asia Minor where there were synagogues, the Jews influenced quite a number of Gentiles. Also many Gentiles responded to the gospel and accepted Christ as Lord and Saviour. But since there was no synagogue in Philippi, and since they took pride in being Romans, the owners of this slave girl tried to stir up the city officials to take action against Paul and Silas.

**22. And the multitude rose up together against them:** . . . On this the mob rose as one man against them, —TCNT . . . The crowd, too, joined in the outcry against them, —WEYM . . . also joined in against them, —SWAN.

**and the magistrates rent off their clothes:** . . . stripped them of their clothing, —TCNT . . . ordered them to be stripped, —WEYM . . . tore off their garments, —HBIE . . . having torn their garments from them, —YNG . . . took their clothing off them, —BB.

**and commanded to beat them:** . . . and ordered them to be beaten with rods, —TCNT . . . to scourge them, —MRDK . . . were giving orders to beat with rods, —WORL . . . gave orders for them to be whipped, —BB.

**16:22.** The people were ready to believe that Jews could be troublemakers. It is always easy for people to blame their troubles on a minority group among them. The agora was always crowded with people. It was the civic center as well as the marketplace. People gravitated there when they had nothing else to do. The sight of these men dragging Paul and Silas before the magistrates could not help but get their attention. They listened to the accusation which stirred up the crowd and joined together in an outbreak of mob violence.

To satisfy the mob, the chief magistrates tore off the clothes from Paul and Silas and ordered them to be severely beaten (flogged) with a rod—a common Roman punishment. Paul (2 Corinthians 11:25) said he was beaten with rods on three different occasions. But on this occasion he had the additional indignity of having his clothes ripped off of him in public. This kind of punishment was illegal for Roman citizens who had not undergone a legal trial. But in all the confusion, no one paid any attention to anything but that these men were Jews.

**23. And when they had laid many stripes upon them:** . . . After beating them severely, —TCNT . . . and, after severely flogging them, —WEYM . . . when they had inflicted many lashes on them, *–KNOX* . . . after lashing them severely, *–FNTN* . . . After they had hit them many times, *–NLTG* . . . given them a great number of blows, *–BB.*

**they cast them into prison:** . . . the Magistrates put them in prison, *–TCNT.*

**charging the jailor to keep them safely:** . . . bade the gaoler keep them in safe custody, *–KNOX* . . . giving orders to the keeper of the prison, *–BB* . . . to guard them securely, *–BRKL* . . . guard them carefully, *–KLST* . . . be sure to keep them from getting away, *–NLTG.*

**16:23.** After Paul and Silas had been beaten with many blows (strokes of the rod), the magistrates had them thrown into prison. All this indicates the mob was still jumping around, shouting, and encouraging the officers, and that they followed while Paul and Silas were violently dragged away and thrown into the prison. Then the magistrates ordered the jailer to guard them securely.

**24. Who, having received such a charge:** . . . On receiving so strict an order, the jailor, *–TCNT* . . . heard this special order, *–SEB* . . . having such orders, *–BB.*

**thrust them into the inner prison:** . . . in the inner dungeon, *–NORL.*

**and made their feet fast in the stocks:** . . . and secured their feet in the stocks, *–TCNT* . . . with chains on their feet, *–BB.*

**16:24.** To make sure Paul and Silas could not escape, the jailer threw them into the inner prison and fastened their feet in wooden stocks. These stocks had holes for the feet and were constructed so the feet could be forced wide apart, causing much pain and making it impossible for the apostles to move their legs.

The inner prison was probably damp, cold, and insect-infested. After all their rough treatment, Paul and Silas must have found these circumstances to be almost unbearable.

**25. And at midnight Paul and Silas prayed:** . . . But about midnight Paul and Silas were praying, *–RSV* . . . But about the middle of the night . . . were making prayers, *–BB* . . . were worshipping, *–BRKL.*

**and sang praises unto God:** . . . and singing hymns, *–ASV.*

**and the prisoners heard them:** . . . in the hearing of the prisoners, *–BB* . . . were listening to them, *–WORL.*

**16:25.** But Paul and Silas made no complaint. Instead at midnight they prayed. The Greek means they were praying and probably that they had been praying for some time.

Some folk in the same circumstances might have decided at this point the Macedonian call was a mistake and the vision in Troas a bad dream. But Paul and Silas did not give up hope. In spite of

the torture, they could still look up to God. They might not have felt like praying at first; they certainly must not have felt like singing. But the times believers do not feel like praying are the times it is most important to pray. Evidently Paul and Silas must have prayed through to victory, for as they prayed joy flooded their souls and they broke out singing hymns of praise to the Lord. They saw that in spite of their discouraging and painful circumstances, God was still worthy to be praised. They had confidence that whatever happened they were still the Lord's. He would see them through!

Apparently, as Paul and Silas continued to pray and sing God's praises, the Holy Spirit lifted their spirits and they began to sing louder and louder, until the prisoners in the main part of the prison woke up and began to listen to them. Somehow, the songs of praise to God must have awed them, for they did not complain or shout out insults at Paul and Silas. At midnight they were still listening.

**26. And suddenly there was a great earthquake:** . . . an earthquake of such violence, *–TCNT* . . . a violent earthquake, *–FNTN.*

**so that the foundations of the prison were shaken:** . . . the jail was shaken to its foundations, *–TCNT* . . . so that the base of the prison was moved, *–BB* . . . of the prison rocked, *–KNOX.*

**and immediately all the doors were opened:** . . . all the doors flew open, *–TCNT* . . . At one stroke all the doors sprang open, *–BRKL* . . . all the doors of the jail broke open, *–EVRD* . . . came open, *–BB.*

**and every one's bands were loosed:** . . . and all the prisoners' chains were loosened, *–TCNT* . . . while every one was freed from his bonds, *–FNTN* . . . and the chains fell off every prisoner, *–WEYM* . . . all the chains fell apart, *–ADAM* . . . and every man's chains were undone, *–KNOX* . . . every man's chains unfastened, *–WMCK* . . . and the bands of all were removed, *–WSLY* . . . and the fetters, *–WLSN.*

**16:26.** Suddenly a great earthquake shook the very foundations of the prison. As the walls shook back and forth, the doors flew open and all the prisoners' chains, which were probably fastened into the wall, were broken loose.

One of the earth's great earthquake zones runs through the Mediterranean region. In both ancient and modern times, violent earthquakes have been fairly common there. Many have been violent enough to destroy entire cities. This one was not strong enough to knock down the prison, but it was enough to loosen the prisoners' chains and break the bars on the doors. It came at just the right time—when Paul and Silas had prayed through and gained the attention of the prisoners.

Earthquakes are caused by the build-up of forces along fault lines in the rocks. But God has often used natural phenomena in connection with His miracles to show His control and His timing. He does all things well. Clearly, this earthquake was no accident. God caused it. He saw Paul and Silas and let them suffer a short time to prepare for an even more important event.

**27. And the keeper of the prison awaking out of his sleep:** . . . When the jailer woke up, —WMCK . . . The warder being accordingly roused from his sleep, —FNTN . . . startled out of his sleep, —AMPB.
**and seeing the prison doors open:** . . . wide open, —WEYM.
**he drew out his sword, and would have killed himself:** . . . and was about to kill himself, —RSV . . . intending to kill himself, —TCNT . . . and was on the point of killing himself, —WEYM . . . intent on committing suicide, —NORL . . . was about to put himself to death, —BB.
**supposing that the prisoners had been fled:** . . . because he thought, —MNTG . . . under the impression, —TCNT . . . feeling sure, —BRKL . . . for he imagined that all the prisoners, —PHLP . . . inferring that the prisoners have escaped, —CNDT . . . fearing that the prisoners had got away, —BB.

**16:27.** The earthquake awakened the jailer. It seems he immediately rushed to the prison, saw the doors were open, and jumped to the conclusion that all the prisoners had escaped. He knew the penalty he would suffer. Under Roman law, the jailer was personally responsible for the lives of the prisoners and was subject to the death penalty if they escaped. The Book of Acts recorded what Herod Agrippa I did to the guards when the angel brought Peter out of prison (12:19). Rather than face the trial, the shame, and the disgraceful death that was sure to come, the jailer drew his sword, intending to commit suicide.

Suicide was not common among the Jews. Only a very few instances are known. One was the case of Ahithophel. He was one of David's trusted counselors. But when Absalom won over the hearts of many of the Israelites and prepared to declare himself king, he sent for Ahithophel and won him over too. But when Absalom did not follow Ahithophel's advice, Ahithophel knew Absalom's cause would lose. He could not bear to face David who had trusted him and whom he had betrayed. So he went home, put his household affairs in order, and hanged himself.

Suicide was more common among the heathen, however. It is still fairly common among many non-Christian religions where human life does not have the value the Bible places upon it.

**28. But Paul cried out with a loud voice, saying:** . . . But Paul at once shouted out to him,

—WLMS . . . shouted loudly to him, —WEYM . . . at the top of his voice, —PHLP.
**Do thyself no harm, for we are all here:** . . . Don't hurt yourself, —PHLP . . . Do not begin to do yourself one bit of harm, —WUST . . . Do yourself no damage, —BB . . . we are still here, —NAB.

**16:28.** From the deep darkness of the prison, Paul could see what the jailer was doing even though the jailer could not see into the darkness of the prison. Immediately Paul shouted out, telling the jailer not to harm himself, for all the prisoners were still there. This must have come as a shock to the jailer. After the way he had treated Paul, and after the beating Paul had received, the jailer would certainly have expected no mercy from Paul or from any other prisoner. Most prisoners in those days, if they had not yet escaped, would have waited in silence until the jailer killed himself and then made their escape. But Paul was always more concerned about others than he was about himself.

**29. Then he called for a light, and sprang in:** . . . Calling for a light, the jailer rushed in, —TCNT . . . Then he ran inside, —NCV . . . told someone to bring a light, —SEB . . . Demanding then a light, —FNTN . . . called for a lamp, —WMCK . . . sent for lights, —BB.
**and came trembling, and fell down before Paul and Silas:** . . . becoming agitated, —RTHM . . . trembling for fear, —ASV, —HNSN . . . and fell terror-stricken, —BRKL . . . and seized with a tremor, —FNTN . . . being in fear, —WORL . . . and flung himself trembling at the feet, —TCNT . . . shaking with fear, —BB . . . and got down in front of Paul . . . He was shaking with fear, —NLTG.

**16:29.** After asking for lights to be brought, the jailer rushed into the prison. Trembling with fear, he fell down beside Paul and Silas. That is, he was completely overcome by fear and awe because of what had happened and because Paul had saved him from suicide.

**30. And brought them out, and said:** . . . After a brief interval he led them out, —NAB . . . conducting them out, —FNTN . . . and leading them forth outside, —RTHM . . . as he led them out, —KNOX.
**Sirs, what must I do to be saved?:** . . . Masters, —SWAN . . . Men, what is it necessary for me to do that I may be saved, —AMPB . . . what am I to do, to save myself? —KNOX . . . what have I to do to get salvation? —BB.

**16:30.** Then, recovering his composure, he brought them out of the prison. The context indicates he brought them into his own house, which was undoubtedly next door. Codex Bezae (D) adds that he first secured the other prisoners. This was undoubtedly true. Apparently because they were so in awe of the prayers, the songs, and the earthquake, none of them had made any attempt to escape.

The jailer then asked Paul and Silas what he must do to be saved. This might seem a strange question from a pagan Roman, but he knew the accusation against Paul and Silas. He must have remembered the words of the ventriloquist spirit that possessed the slave girl—these men could tell him the way of salvation.

**31. And they said, Believe on the Lord Jesus Christ:** . . . Have faith in the Lord Jesus, —*BB*, —*BRKL* . . . Commit yourself, —*SEB* . . . Put your trust in, —*NLTG*.

**and thou shalt be saved, and thy house:** . . . and you shall be saved, you and your household too, —*TCNT* . . . and you and your family will have salvation, —*BB* . . . and all the people in your house, —*EVRD*.

**16:31.** Paul's answer let him know he must "believe" rather than "do" in order to be saved. When the people asked Jesus, "What shall we do, that we might work the works of God?" Jesus replied, "This is the work of God, that ye believe on him whom he hath sent" (John 6:28, 29). The jailer also needed to know who Jesus is and what it means to believe in Him.

The words "and thy house" must be connected with the believing. Paul did not mean the jailer's household would be saved simply because the jailer was. Neither did he mean the jailer's salvation would guarantee theirs. Paul wanted the jailer to know the offer of salvation was not limited to him. Some cults, popular among the Romans, were composed of all males; some catered to certain classes. But the salvation Christ brings is for all. If the rest of the jailer's household would believe, they too would be saved. Paul wanted to see them all saved, not just one.

**32. And they spake unto him the word of the Lord and to all that were in his house:** . . . they delivered the message of the Lord to him, with all those in his family, —*FNTN* . . . told the story of the Lord Jesus, —*SEB* . . . as well as to all who were in his house, —*WEYM* . . . to him and his family, —*NLTG*.

**16:32.** The jailer then gathered his entire household (including the servants) for a midnight evangelistic service and teaching session. Paul proclaimed the Word of God to them, explaining the truth and giving them a solid Biblical foundation for believing in Jesus and for following the Christian way of life.

**33. And he took them the same hour of the night:** . . . At that very hour, —*TCNT* . . . took personal charge of them, —*KLST* . . . he took them then and there in the middle of the night, —*WMCK* . . . It was late

at night, —*NLTG* . . . at that hour, —*LAMS* . . . at dead of night, —*KNOX*.

**and washed their stripes:** . . . and when he had given attention to, —*BB* . . . and washed their wounds, —*LAMS*, —*TCNT*.

**and was baptized, he and all his, straightway:** . . . and he and all the members of his household at once were baptized, —*WLMS* . . . on-the-spot, —*RTHM* . . . was baptized at once, himself and all his family, —*WMCK* . . . got baptized instantly, —*MOFT* . . . were immersed right away, —*SEB* . . . had baptism straight away, —*BB* . . . in that very hour, —*LAMS* . . . without delay, —*SWAN*.

**16:33.** The jailer first showed he truly believed in Jesus by recognizing Paul and Silas as God's messengers. He believed they did not deserve the stripes (the wounds from the beating with rods given by the Roman officers or lictors), so he washed off the dried blood and dirt to indicate this.

Immediately after that, he and all the members of his household (who had also heard the Word and believed) were baptized in water. This was probably done in a pool in the courtyard of the house. Such pools were not uncommon in the larger Roman-style homes of those days (as archaeology shows).

**34. And when he had brought them into his house he set meat before them:** . . . set food, —*ASV* . . . offered them food, —*PHLP*.

**and rejoiced, believing in God with all his house:** . . . and exulted, —*RTHM* . . . rejoicing that he, with all his household, had come to believe in God, —*TCNT* . . . and was filled with gladness, —*WEYM* . . . transported with joy, —*CMPB* . . . was extremely happy, —*BRKL* . . . was full of joy, having faith in God with all his family, —*BB* . . . were very happy because they now believed in God, —*EVRD* . . . filled with great joy, —*WMCK* . . . they now trusted in God, —*SEB*.

**16:34.** After being baptized, the jailer took the apostles back inside the house and set before them a table loaded with food. After the jailer and his household came to believe, they began to rejoice. Joy does not always come the moment a person believes on Jesus, but it will come. When it does, it is a joy the world knows nothing about.

This passage (see also 11:14; 16:15; 18:8) describes an entire household that was converted. Modern missionaries report a similar phenomenon (referred to as "people movements") in tribes dominated by one (perhaps a few) male leader. A decision by the designated and respected "household" affects each family member. This was not uncommon, for example, in the case of Greeks who converted to Judaism.

**35. And when it was day:** ... In the morning, —*TCNT* ... When day broke, —*MOFT*.

**the magistrates sent the serjeants, saying:** ... the chiefs of the police court sent policemen with the message, —*WLMS* ... the officials sent attendants, —*BECK* ... the praetors sent their lictors with the instructions, —*KLST* ... sent the police, —*BB* ... sent a soldier to say, —*NLTG* ... to tell the prison warden, —*LAMS*.

**Let those men go:** ... Release those men, —*WEYM* ... Dismiss those men, —*CMPB* ... Liberate these men, —*FNTN* ... Let these men go free! —*EVRD* ... Those men are to be discharged, —*KNOX*.

**16:35.** The rejoicing probably continued the rest of the night. It would be hard to sleep after such an experience. In the morning the chief magistrates sent officers, called lictors, who were orderlies or attendants (not sergeants in the modern sense), to tell the jailer to let Paul and Silas go. (These lictors were also "rod bearers" and may have been the very ones who had beaten Paul and Silas.)

The Bible does not say why these Roman magistrates changed their minds after commanding the jailer to be sure to guard the prisoners securely. It may be that after thinking over the charges against Paul and Silas, they realized no evidence had been presented against them; nor had there been any mention of any specific way Paul and Silas had agitated the people or thrown them into confusion. In fact, the confusion had come only after the slave owners had dragged Paul and Silas into the agora (the marketplace and civic center). It may be that the earthquake had seemed to be some sort of sign or omen that they had done wrong.

It is also possible that in some way word had come to them of how Paul stopped the jailer from committing suicide. This would have given them a different view of Paul and Silas and might have caused them to feel they should be rewarded by being released.

**36. And the keeper of the prison told this saying to Paul, The Magistrates have sent to let you go:** ... The jailer said to Paul, The officials, —*NCV* ... The Magistrates have sent an order for your discharge, —*TCNT* ... sent these soldiers to set you free, —*SEB* ... orders for you to be released, —*WEYM*.

**now therefore depart, and go in peace:** ... so you had better leave the place at once and go quietly away, —*TCNT* ... and go without any trouble, —*NLTG*.

**16:36.** The jailer obediently passed on the word from the chief magistrates that it was their decision to let the apostles go. Then he urged them to accept this, leave the prison area, and to proceed on their way in peace. He was undoubtedly very happy about this decision. His words may reflect a little of the Hebrew salutation of peace and blessing.

**37. But Paul said unto them:** ... But Paul's answer to them was, —*TCNT*.

**They have beaten us openly uncondemned:** ... They have flogged us in public without trial, —*TCNT* ... a public flogging without trial, —*NORL* ... Your leaders did not prove that we did anything wrong, —*SEB* ... cruelly beating us in public, —*WEYM* ... yet they whipped us in public, —*TEV* ... a public whipping, —*BB* ... unoffending men, —*MRDK*.

**being Romans:** ... despite the fact, —*PHLP* ... though we are Roman citizens, —*TCNT*.

**and have cast us into prison:** ... have thrown us, —*RSV* ... and sent us to prison, —*KNOX*.

**and now do they thrust us out privily?:** ... they are for sending us out secretly! —*TCNT* ... and are they now going to send us away privately, —*WEYM* ... to get rid of us in this underhand way, —*PHLP* ... Secretly now they are going to get rid of us, —*KLST* ... are ejecting us surreptitiously! —*CNDT* ... they want to make us go away quietly, —*EVRD* ... do they think they can send us away without anyone knowing? —*NLTG*.

**nay verily; but let them come themselves and fetch us out:** ... Certainly not, —*FNTN* ... No, indeed! Let them come and take us out themselves, —*TCNT* ... come in person and fetch us out, —*WEYM* ... I should say not! These should come themselves, —*BECK* ... and bring us out! —*NCV*.

**16:37.** Paul now did something he did not do very often—he took advantage of his Roman citizenship. In some situations he did this to forestall unnecessary persecution. This time he did it because he knew the crowds gathered around them in the Philippian agora still had a wrong idea, not only about them, but about both Jews and Christians. Paul therefore refused to sneak away like a beaten criminal. The chief magistrate had caused them to be beaten publicly, without any semblance of a trial, even though Paul and Silas were both Roman citizens. Then they had thrown them publicly into prison with the whole crowd looking on. Were they now going to throw them out of prison secretly? Let them come themselves and lead the apostles out publicly. In this way the city of Philippi would know the charges were false.

Paul probably had in mind the welfare and growth of the new assembly of believers. If the crowd was allowed to think Paul and Silas were the big troublemakers they were accused of being, persecution for the new believers would have resulted and would have hindered others in the city from accepting their witness. Paul could not let this happen.

**38. And the Serjeants told these words unto the magistrates:** ... the attendants announced these words to, —*SWAN* ... The officers then went and reported this demand to the magistrates, —*NORL*.

**and they feared, when they heard that they were Romans:** ... and they were struck with fear when, —*RTHM* ... who, on hearing that Paul and Silas were Roman citizens, were alarmed, —*TCNT* ... who were horrified to hear, —*JB*...they were alarmed by this talk of Roman citizenship, —*KNOX*...became terrified, —*FNTN*.

**16:38.** When the lictors reported the Roman citizenship of Paul and Silas to the chief magistrates of the city, they knew they were in the wrong. They should not have yielded to the mob without questioning Paul and Silas. They were afraid because Roman citizens had rights to trial before punishment, rights that could not be ignored with impunity. They knew also what could happen to them if the apostles were to lodge a complaint with the government in Rome.

Imperial Rome was a symbol of power. (Nebuchadnezzar's dream of Daniel 2 describes it as "iron.") But it did provide for the rights of its own citizens, so Paul's appeal to his Roman citizenship had the effect he hoped for.

One ancient manuscript, Codex Bezae (D), inserts an interesting addition at the end of verse 38 that reads as follows: "And when they were come with many of their friends to the prison, they besought them to go out saying: We were ignorant of your circumstances, that you were righteous men. And leading them out, they besought them saying, Depart from this city, lest they again make an insurrection against you, and clamour against you." More likely, the magistrates were ignorant not of Paul and Silas' righteousness, but of their Roman citizenship. Not even at this stage did they attempt to discover the true reasons behind the mob's actions.

**39. And they came and besought them:**...and went to the prison, and did their best to conciliate them, —*TCNT*...Accordingly they came and apologized to them, —*WEYM*...and came and plead with them, —*WLMS*...and came to appeal to them, —*KLST*...came to appease them, —*NIV*...apologizing to them, —*BRKL*...came and made prayers to them, —*BB*...came and begged their pardon, —*WMCK*...told Paul and Silas they were sorry, —*EVRD*.

**and brought them out, and desired them to depart out of the city:**...Then they took them out and begged them to leave the city, —*TCNT*...Then they escorted them out, —*NEB*...urging them, as they brought them out, to leave the city, —*KNOX*...and conducting them out, requested them to leave the town, —*FNTN*...kept asking them to leave, —*SEB*.

**16:39.** The chief officials of Philippi then came very humbly and besought Paul and Silas; they begged them not to bring charges against them. This was done in the prison, for Paul and Silas had voluntarily left the jailer's house and gone back into the prison so there would be no reason to question the jailer (who had been commanded to keep them locked up securely). The chief

magistrates led the apostles out of the prison compound publicly, as Paul had asked.

The magistrates then asked them to leave the city. This was not because they wanted in any way to stop the preaching of the gospel in Philippi. But they were most probably afraid Paul and Silas might change their minds and bring charges against them. They were probably afraid also that the sympathies of the people would now swing to Paul and Silas and against them, because of the unjust beating. So they asked the apostles to leave for the sake of peace in the city.

**40. And they went out of the prison:**...So they left the prison, —*MOFT*...Being thus liberated from custody, —*FNTN*.

**and entered into the house of Lydia:**...and visited Lydia, —*RSV*.

**and when they had seen the brethren:**...where they saw the brothers, —*BRKL*...They met with the Christians, —*NLTG*...having seen, —*FNTN*.

**they comforted them, and departed:**...they exhorted them, —*ALFD*...they consoled them, —*FNTN*...and encouraged them, they left the place, —*TCNT*...Then they left, —*EVRD*...then they set out on their journey, —*KNOX*...they left the place, —*WMCK*

**16:40.** Before leaving the city, Paul and Silas went to Lydia's house. There a large courtyard or upper room was full of believers who were gathered together, undoubtedly praying for Paul and Silas. After seeing and exhorting the brethren, the apostles left town.

Notice here that the believers were no longer limited to a few women converted out of the prayer group by the riverside. The brethren now took the leadership, though in Hebrew usage, the word *brethren* included the women (just as the phrase "children of Israel" in Hebrew is literally the "sons of Israel" but included both men and women).

It is evident at this point that Luke did not leave with Paul and Silas. The next chapter (17:14) shows that Timothy did leave with them, but Luke no longer used the word "we." It seems obvious Paul and Silas left Luke in Philippi to give further encouragement and teaching to the assembly there. (Luke was still in Philippi in 20:6.) His teaching and guidance is undoubtedly another reason why there were so few problems in this assembly.

## Chapter 17

**1. And when they had passed through Amphipolis and Apollonia:** ... And travelling through, —*RTHM*...Then they passed by the cities of, —*LAMS*...Travelling then through, —*FNTN*.

**they came to Thessalonica, where was a synagogue of the Jews:** ...Here the Jews had a

Synagogue, −TCNT . . . had a place of worship there, −NLTG . . . where there was a Jewish meeting-house, −WMCK

**17:1.** After Paul, Silas, and Timothy left Philippi, they proceeded westward on the Egnatian Road. The next two towns of any size (each about a day's journey apart) apparently had no Jewish synagogue and were probably left for the Philippians to evangelize. So the apostles pushed on 100 miles from Philippi to Thessalonica, the most important city of ancient Macedonia, and still important today. It was founded in 315 B.C., and named by Cassander (its founder) for his wife, who was a stepsister of Alexander the Great.

Again Luke's account draws attention to Paul's custom of going to the Jews first. Paul always took advantage of the Jews' background and of the opportunities given in the synagogue to teach.

**2. And Paul, as his manner was, went in unto them:** . . . as his custom was, −ASV . . . as he always did, −NCV, −NLTG . . . paid them a visit there, −KNOX.
**and three sabbath days reasoned with them out of the scriptures:** . . . addressed them, drawing his arguments from the Scriptures, −TCNT . . . he discoursed to them from, −SWAN . . . he argued with them, −WMCK . . . on three Saturdays had Bible discussions, −BECK . . . from the holy Writings, −BB.

**17:2.** Paul followed his usual custom (manner, habit, settled policy), and over the space of three sabbaths (or weeks) he ministered in the synagogue. It is possible this means he ministered daily during the entire time, addressing the people, and preaching to them. Discussion with questions and answers may also be implied.

The Book of Acts does not give any details here. But it does draw attention to one very important feature of Paul's preaching. It was Biblical. Paul did not spend time talking about human theories of ethics, economics, or politics. He did not lecture to them out of philosophy or out of the teachings of his former professor, Gamaliel. He knew God's Word is the Holy Spirit's sword to win victories, His tool to do the work of salvation and to make the power and wisdom of Christ effective. It is probable that in his first sermon Paul followed the same pattern as he had in his first sermon in the synagogue at Pisidian Antioch (13:16-41).

**3. Opening and alleging:** . . . He laid before them and explained, −TCNT . . . illustrating and proving, −FNTN . . . expounding these and bringing proofs, −KNOX . . . explaining and quoting passages to prove, −MOFT . . . and setting forth, −WORL . . . and clearly showed that, −SEB . . . and showing, −WMCK
**that Christ must needs have suffered, and risen again from the dead:** . . . that it was necessary for the Christ, −RSV . . . to suffer and rise again from the dead, −NLTG . . . had to be put to death and come

back to life again, −BB . . . rising from the dead were foreordained, −KNOX.
**and that this Jesus, whom I preach unto you, is Christ:** . . . and (saying) This is the ChristJesus whom I am declaring unto you, −RTHM . . . This Jesus, whom I announce to you, is the Messiah! −SEB.

**17:3.** The Jews and the believing Gentiles who attended the synagogue believed in a Messiah, but their ideas about the Messiah were rather vague. To most of them the whole subject seemed controversial and speculative. It was necessary for Paul to show them what the Bible teaches about the Messiah before they could believe that Jesus is the Messiah, or Christ.

Paul would open up the meaning of an Old Testament passage and discuss it with them, explaining it fully. Then he would refer to other passages that supported and proved his interpretation. After he was able to get them to see from the Scriptures that the Messiah or Christ would not only reign, but would suffer, die, and rise again, he could point to Jesus. Jesus fulfilled the prophecies. Jesus is the only One who could possibly be the Christ.

Behind Paul's anointed preaching was much prayer and Spirit-directed study of the Scripture. This careful study made it possible for Paul to become a good agent of the Spirit in driving home the truth to human hearts. It is clear also that Paul presented the proofs from the Word in a logical, connected, and reasonable way. (Compare 1 Peter 3:15.)

**4. And some of them believed:** . . . Some of the Jews were convinced, −NCV . . . were persuaded, −RSV . . . became believers, −NORL . . . were won over, −KLST . . . put their trust in Christ, −NLTG . . . had faith, −BB.
**and consorted with Paul and Silas:** . . . and cast in their lot with, −RTHM . . . and threw in their lot with, −KNOX . . . and attached themselves to, −WEYM . . . and joined themselves to, −HBIE . . . and associated themselves with, −FNTN.
**and of the devout Greeks a great multitude:** . . . as did also a large body of Greeks, −TCNT . . . including great number of God-fearing Greeks, −WEYM.
**and of the chief women not a few:** . . . and a great number of women belonging to the leading families, −TCNT . . . and by a considerable number of influential women, −PHLP.

**17:4.** This verse condenses what took place over a considerable period of time. Some indications point to at least 6 months.

Some of the Jews were persuaded; they believed in Jesus, obeyed the gospel, and threw in their lot with Paul. Weymouth's translation reads, "They attached themselves to Paul and Silas." The same was true of an even larger number of Gentiles. In fact, many Godfearing Greeks, including many wives of the chief men of the city, supported Paul.

First Thessalonians 2:1-13 gives a further description of the ministry of Paul and Silas at this time. Their preaching and ministry was very effective. The outrageous treatment they had received at Philippi did not cause them to be timid or fearful. At Thessalonica they preached in a bold, free, open, fearless manner, with pure motives as servants of Jesus Christ. They were gentle to the new converts, giving them all kinds of tender loving care. Yet they were firm in their stand for righteousness and encouraged each one of the believers to live in a manner worthy of the God who had called them to His own kingdom and glory.

**5. But the Jews which believed not, moved with envy:** ...in a fury of jealousy, —PHLP...the Jews became jealous, —EVRD.

**took unto them certain lewd fellows of the baser sort:** ...wicked fellows of the rabble, —RSV...found confederates among the riff-raff, —KNOX...enlisted the aid of some base loafers, —KLST...engaged some worthless fellows from the streets, —TCNT...and taking to them, of the idlers in the market-place, some vieious men, —HBIE...got some wicked rowdies to join them, —NORL...got some evil men from the marketplace, —EVRD...They hired some evil men from the city, —SEB.

**and gathered a company, and set all the city on an uproar:** ...formed a great mob...they alarmed the city, —MRDK...and gathered a mob, —ALFD...and started a riot, —EVRD.

**and assaulted the house of Jason:** ...and besieging, —RTHM...They attacked Jason's house, —TCNT.

**and sought to bring them out to the people:** ...with the intention of bringing Paul and Silas before the Popular Assembly, —TCNT...and searched for Paul and Silas, to bring them out before the assembly of the people, —WEYM.

**17:5.** Though some of the Jews rejected Paul's message it did not bother him. Even the most powerful, anointed proofs will not convince some people of the truth. The Bible shows believers can expect people to be saved, but they must not be disappointed if all do not believe. (See 2 Corinthians 2:14-16.) When God works it is not unusual for the devil to stir up opposition.

These Jews who rejected Paul's message soon became frustrated by the increasing numbers of Gentiles who were accepting the gospel. As a result, they rebelled against what God was doing. They even went so far as to forbid (hinder, prevent) Paul and his company from speaking (or even talking) to Gentiles with a view to their salvation (1 Thessalonians 2:14-16).

The Gentiles, however, continued to respond to the gospel and paid no attention to these Jewish

rebels. Since the Jews had no arguments (that is, no real or effective arguments against the gospel), they resorted to mob violence and proceeded to stir up a riot. First, they took to themselves a group of marketplace loungers who were ruffians always ready for mischief, always ready to join any agitators for the sake of a little excitement. With their help, these unbelieving Jews gathered a crowd and set up a disturbance that threw the whole city into a panic. The mob acted the way mobs always do. A mob does not think; it blindly follows its leaders or promoters and shouts what they shout. The same mob spirit moved those who shouted "Crucify Him!" when Jesus stood before Pilate's judgment seat.

Then the mob, led by the Jewish unbelievers, went to the house of Jason, taking Jason by surprise, seeking to bring out Paul and Silas to the rabble. But evidently Paul and Silas were able to get out another way, and they escaped to another part of the city.

**6. And when they found them not:** ...and, not finding them there, —TCNT...And when they were not able to get them, —BB.

**they drew Jason and certain brethren:** ...they proceeded to drag Jason and some of the Brethren, —TCNT.

**unto the rulers of the city:** ...before the rulers, —ASV...the City Magistrates, —TCNT...the politarches, —MOFT...the city fathers, —BRKL.

**crying:** ...loudly accusing them, —WEYM...were yelling, —EVRD...shouting out, —WMCK

**These that have turned the world upside down:** ...They who have thrown the inhabited world into confusion, —RTHM...These upsetters of the whole world, —MOFT...These fellows, who have turned the world topsyturvy, —WLMS...These world revolutionists, —BRKL...who are setting the world in an uproar, —KLST...who have been making trouble over all the world, —NLTG...turning the state, —KNOX.

**are come hither also:** ...have now come here, —TCNT...are here now, —BECK.

**17:6.** Because Paul and Silas were not there, the mob dragged Jason and some of his fellow believers before the rulers. The Greek calls these rulers *politarchs,* and archaeologists have found inscriptions in Thessalonica referring to them by this title. The word *Politarch* was a special title used by Macedonians for chief magistrates here and in a few other cities. Thessalonica had five or six of them.

As usual, the accusation made before the magistrates was not the real reason for wanting to get rid of Paul and Silas. The unbelieving Jews and their coconspirators accused the apostles of being agitators who were working against the Roman Empire.

The accusation that Paul and Silas had turned the inhabited world upside down has been a thrill and a challenge to true believers ever since. The world turned upside down is at last right side up. (The Romans used "the world" [the inhabited world] to mean the Roman Empire.)

**7. Whom Jason hath received:** . . . unto whom Jason has given welcome, −*RTHM* . . . and have been harboured by Jason! −*TCNT* . . . Jason is keeping them in his house, −*NCV,* −*SEB* . . . has taken into his house, −*BB.*

**and these all do contrary to the decrees of Caesar:** . . . They are all defying the decrees of the Emperor, −*TCNT* . . . All these folk defy the edicts of, −*KNOX* . . . working against Caesar's orders, −*WMCK*

**saying that there is another king, one Jesus:** . . . They say that some one else is kinga man called Jesus, −*TCNT* . . . claiming that there is another kingJesus, −*BRKL.*

**17:7.** The accusation then turned against Jason. The Jews accused Jason of joining with Paul and Silas to practice things contrary to the decrees of Caesar, speaking of another king (meaning a rival emperor), Jesus.

This was an accusation of open treason. Paul did declare that Jesus is alive at the right hand of the throne of God, and that He is and will be the true King. These Jews were out of character when they pretended to be concerned over the well-being of the Roman Empire and the honor and authority of Caesar. The Jews were notorious for their turbulence, and everyone knew they had no love for the Roman Empire. All Paul had done was to preach the gospel peacefully.

**8. And they troubled the people and the rulers of the city, when they heard these things:** . . . On hearing this, the people . . . were much concerned, −*TCNT* . . . Great was the excitement among the crowd . . . when they heard these charges, −*WEYM.*

**17:8.** The crowd and the politarchs were disturbed by these things. Part of their problem may have been that they had not observed any evidence of political activity. It is probable also that the believers who were wives of the chief men included the wife of one or more of the politarchs before whom these charges were being made.

There may have been some good in this. When Paul and his company first came into the city, it may be that few gave them more than a passing glance. The Gentiles who attended the synagogue and their friends were soon influenced. But now everyone in town knew that something was happening.

**9. And when they had taken security of Jason, and of the other:** . . . they took bail from Jason and the others, −*TCNT* . . . Jason and the rest gave a bond to keep the peace, −*WMCK*

**they let them go:** . . . they released them, −*HBIE* . . . and turned them loose, −*WLMS* . . . and were then dismissed, −*WMCK*

**17:9.** Apparently the politarchs did not take the charges seriously. To satisfy the crowd they took security (surety) from Jason and the others who had been brought before them. This probably means Jason and his friends provided bail as a guarantee that Paul and Silas would leave the city and not come back lest there be further disturbance.

**10. And the brethren immediately sent away Paul and Silas by night unto Berea:** . . . That very night the Brethren sent, −*TCNT.*

**who coming thither went into the synagogue of the Jews:** . . . who, as soon as they arrived, went, −*ALFD* . . . they made their way to the Jewish meeting-house, −*WMCK*

**17:10.** The Christian brethren saw how bitter and determined the unbelieving Jews were, so they took no chances. By night they sent Paul and Silas to Beroea, about 50 miles to the southwest on the road to Greece. The believers probably thought they would be safe there. It was a safer place than Thessalonica.

Paul did not let his experiences with the unbelieving Jews in Thessalonica discourage or intimidate him. At Beroea he went at once to the synagogue, still feeling the mandate that he must go to the Jew first, even though Jesus had sent him to the Gentiles.

**11. These were more noble than those in Thessalonica:** . . . These Jews of Berea were better disposed, −*TCNT* . . . were better people than the ones in, −*SEB* . . . were of a better breed than, −*KNOX* . . . of a nobler disposition than, −*WEYM* . . . were more broad-minded, −*WMCK*

**in that they received the word with all readiness of mind:** . . . for they welcomed the Message with great readiness, −*TCNT* . . . accepted the message most eagerly, −*PHLP* . . . for they gave serious attention to the word, −*BB* . . . were very happy to listen to the things, −*SEB* . . . welcomed the word with all eagerness, −*KNOX* . . . were eager to hear, −*NORL* . . . very eager to get the Word, −*BECK* . . . with eagerness, −*WMCK*

**and searched the scriptures daily:** . . . examining, −*RSV* . . . and made a daily study of the scriptures, −*MOFT.*

**whether those things were so:** . . . to see if what was said was true, −*TCNT* . . . to see whether it was as Paul stated, −*WEYM* . . . to find out if these things were true, −*NCV.*

**17:11.** At this synagogue Paul's faithfulness was rewarded. Instead of the usual opposition, he found an eager enthusiasm for the Word of God. Instead of opposing Paul's message, they welcomed the Word with eagerness. Even more important, they examined the Scriptures daily, to see whether these things were so. Because of their attitude and their searching of the Scriptures, the Bible says they were more noble than the Jews in Thessalonica.

The word "noble" does not have its usual sense of "aristocratic birth" here. Luke used it of God's men and women who showed their nobility by their high-minded, open, generous spirit. They did not let prejudice close their minds to the truth. They gave attention to the preaching of the Word. How this must have encouraged Paul! An expectant audience that loves God's Word draws out the preacher.

Those who honestly want to know the truth God has for all will subject what they hear and read to the test of the Scriptures. Any pet idea deserves to be thrown out if it will not stand examination in the light of the whole Bible. Believers will be blessed by truths the Holy Spirit drives home as they keep searching the Scriptures. The net result will be a strengthening of their faith.

**12. Therefore many of them believed:** ...As a consequence many of them became believers in Christ, *−TCNT*...So, many of them believed, *−NCV*...became Christians, *−NLTG.*
**also of honourable women which were Greeks, and of men, not a few:** ...a number of Greek women of good position, *−WMCK*...including outstanding Greek women and a goodly number of men, *−BRKL*...also many noble Greeks, women as well as men, *−BECK*...important Greek men and women also believed, *−NCV.*

**17:12.** In Thessalonica some of the Jews had believed. Others had let their old prejudices guide them, and they reacted against the gospel. In Beroea, however, many of the Jews believed, possibly the majority of them. There was no opposition stirred up among them. This indicates they not only accepted the truth of the gospel, but they opened their hearts and let the Holy Spirit apply it for both salvation and Christian living. The response of faith is always obedience.

Many Gentiles also believed, women who had an honorable position in society, and men as well. Notice also that these noble-minded Jews were not upset or jealous when these Gentiles were saved. In their searching of the Scriptures it seems they were reminded of God's promise that *all* the families of the earth would be blessed.

**13. But when the Jews of Thessalonica:** ...As soon, however, as the Jews, *−WEYM.*
**had knowledge:** ...came to know, *−RTHM*...found out, *−TCNT* ... heard that, *−WMCK* ... had news, *−BB*...became aware, *−BECK.*
**that the word of God was preached of Paul at Berea:** ...had been declared by Paul, *−RTHM*...was proclaimed, *−ASV.*
**they came thither also:** ...they came there too, *−RSV.*
**and stirred up the people:** ...exciting and disturbing the minds of the people, *−TCNT*...to cause trouble and spread alarm among the people, *−PHLP*...and incited the mob to a riot, *−WEYM*...to stir up and excite the crowds, *−KLST*...They upset the people and made trouble, *−EVRD* ... worked against the missionaries by talking to the people, *−NLTG*...to upset and disturb the minds of the multitude, *−KNOX*...troubling the people and working them up, *−BB* ... disturbing the common people, *−WMCK*

**17:13.** While the Beroean Jews were studying the Old Testament systematically, closely, carefully, and candidly, and as they considered Paul's teachings, in the light of the Scripture, somehow the news of Paul's effective proclamation of the gospel was carried back to Thessalonica. The synagogue at Beroea had caused no trouble. But Satan was determined to find some way to oppose the work of God. When he cannot find troublemakers nearby, he will bring them in from the outside. When the unbelieving Jews at Thessalonica heard the news, they came to Beroea and did the same sort of thing they had done at home. They aroused the crowds, trying to incite them to mob violence against Paul.

**14. And then immediately the brethren sent away Paul to go as it were to the sea:** ...promptly sent Paul down to the seacoast, *−WEYM* ... quickly sent Paul away to the coast, *−NCV*...sent away Paul to journey as far as to the sea, *−WORL*...to continue his journey up to the coast, *−KNOX* ... away to the sea, *−SEB*...Sent Paul away at once, *−WMCK*
**but Silas and Timotheus abode there still:** ... stayed behind there, *−RTHM* ... remained where they were, *−MOFT.*

**17:14.** Before these unbelieving Jews from Thessalonica could do any damage, the Beroean Christian brethren hurried Paul off in the direction of the Aegean Sea, probably intending to send him away by ship. Silas and Timothy stayed behind, since only Paul was the object of the Thessalonian Jews' wrath and bitterness.

Because the Beroean Christians knew this, they believed that with Paul gone, the Thessalonian Jews would go home, and the opposition they had stirred up would subside. Although they were well on their way toward being established in the faith (because of their searching the Scriptures for the basis of the truths of the gospel), Silas and Timothy stayed behind in order that they might further instruct, train, and encourage the whole assembly of believers. Evangelism must be followed by training in discipleship (cf. Matthew 28:19, 20).

**15. And they that conducted Paul:** . . . The men who accompanied Paul, *—PHLP* . . . The friends who escorted Paul, *—TCNT* . . . The men who acted as Paul's bodyguard, *—WLMS*.
**brought him unto Athens:** . . . took him to the city of, *—SEB* . . . took him as far as, *—KLST* . . . all the way to, *—WMCK*
**and receiving a commandment unto Silas and Timotheus for to come to him with all speed, they departed:** . . . then went back with his orders, *—WMCK* . . . and returned with instructions from him . . . to rejoin him as soon as possible, *—KLST* . . . and after receiving a message for Silas and Timothy to join him as quickly as possible, *—TCNT* . . . they carried a message from Paul back to, *—EVRD* . . . Come to me as soon as you can, *—NCV* . . . to come to him quickly, *—BB*.

**17:15.** Those who were conducting Paul toward the sea suddenly changed directions. Possibly they heard that the Thessalonian Jews had not gone home and were plotting something else. It may be they were sending some of their number on ahead to try to ambush Paul. Whatever the reason, the Beroean Christian brethren, or a part of their group, took Paul to Athens. There Paul saw he needed help and he sent the Beroeans back with the command for Silas and Timothy to come to him there as quickly as possible.

First Thessalonians 3:1, 2 indicates they did come, but Paul's concern over the Thessalonian assembly of believers caused him to send Timothy back to them to further establish and encourage them with respect to their faith. He knew the Jews who were disappointed in not catching him in Beroea could very well go back and cause further persecution and trouble for the believers in their own city. While he was with them, Paul had told them they would continue to suffer the affliction of trouble and persecution and he wanted to be sure the tempter had not successfully tempted them.

Timothy did come back to Paul later with a good report of the Thessalonian believers' faith and love and their desire to see Paul again. Paul also assured them he was praying most exceedingly, night and day, that he might see them and bring their faith into proper condition (1 Thessalonians 3:10).

In the meantime, with Timothy gone back to Thessalonica and Silas sent to minister elsewhere, Paul determined to wait in Athens. His stay there is important for it gives us an example of how Paul witnessed to those who had no background in Scripture study.

**16. Now while Paul waited for them at Athens:** . . . was waiting for, *—EVRD*.
**his spirit was stirred in him:** . . . his soul was deeply vexed, *—BRKL* . . . his spirit was stirred to its depths, *—WLMS* . . . was exasperated, *—KLST* . . . his heart was moved within him, *—KNOX* . . . felt deeply troubled, *—SEB* . . . it hurt him deeply, *—WMCK* . . . was grieved in his spirit, *—FNTN*.
**when he saw the city wholly given to idolatry:** . . . at seeing the whole city full of idols, *—TCNT* . . . seeing how the city was given to idols, *—RTHM* . . . to see the city completely steeped in idolatry, *—WLMS* . . . to see the city full of idols, *—WMCK* . . . to see the city devoted to idols, *—FNTN*.

**17:16.** Athens was famous for its Acropolis and all its temples. Some 600 years before Paul's time it was a world leader in art and philosophy. By this time, however, it had lost its former glory. It was no longer politically important. Its old leadership in culture and education had been taken over by Alexandria in Egypt. Other new centers such as Ephesus, Antioch, and Tarsus far surpassed it as educational centers. It had lost its drive and creativity. It was filled with curiosity seekers and with philosophical speculation that was without depth. Yet it still nurtured the memory of its past. Its temples were still beautiful examples of the best in Greek architecture. But everywhere Paul looked the city was full of images. Alongside the intellectual snobbery of Athens was the most degrading and immoral idolatry.

Paul did not look at the idols as glorious examples of Greek art. He was disturbed by them. His spirit was provoked (almost "angered") within him. All this idol worship made him realize all the more that "the world by wisdom knew not God" (1 Corinthians 1:21).

**17. Therefore disputed he in the synagogue with the Jews:** . . . So he reasoned, *—ASV* . . . argued, *—TCNT* . . . had discussions, *—WEYM* . . . in the meetinghouse with, *—WMCK*
**and with the devout persons:** . . . and with those who joined in their worship, *—TCNT* . . . and the devout proselytes, *—MOFT* . . . and the devout adherents, *—BRKL* . . . the God-fearing persons, *—WMCK*
**and in the market daily:** . . . and he even argued daily in the open market-place, *—PHLP* . . . in the business district of the city, *—SEB* . . . in the public square day by day, *—WMCK*
**with them that met with him:** . . . with them who happened to be at hand, *—RTHM* . . . with the passersby, *—PHLP* . . . with all he met, *—KNOX* . . . with those whom he chanced to meet, *—WMCK*

**17:17.** As always, Paul first went to the synagogue on the Sabbath Day and preached to the Jews and the godly Gentiles. But he was concerned about the rest of the Gentiles too. Their idolatry aroused him to give himself to the proclamation of the gospel as never before. He took every opportunity to speak to groups and to individuals about Jesus and the Resurrection. Throughout every day he carried on discussions with every person he met, especially in the marketplace (the agora, the civic center).

**18. Then certain philosophers of the Epicureans, and of the Stoicks:** ... Some members of the ... schools of wisdom, —WMCK
**encountered him:** ... also encountered him again and again, —MNTG ... joined issue with him, —TCNT ... were disputing with him, —HBIE ... began to debate with him, —WLMS ... argued with him, —EVRD ... also opposed him, —WMCK
**And some said:** ... Some would ask, —TCNT.
**What will this babbler say?:** ... What has this beggarly babbler to say, —WEYM ... Whatever does the fellow mean with his scraps of learning, —MOFT ... this amateur talker, —BRKL ... this cock sparrow, —PHLP ... This man doesn't know what he is talking about, —EVRD ... This man has lots of little things to talk about, —NLTG ... What can his drift be, this dabbler? —KNOX.
**other some:** ... and others, —ALFD ... while others would say, —TCNT.
**He seemeth to be a setter forth of strange gods:** ... announceth foreign deities, —MRDK ... a Preacher of foreign Deities, —TCNT ... Of foreign demons he seemeth to be a declarer, —RTHM ... He seems to be a herald of, —KLST.
**because he preached unto them Jesus, and the resurrection:**

**17:18.** Among those who met him in the marketplace were some Epicurean and Stoic philosophers, and they engaged him in a discussion.

Epicureans were followers of Epicurus (342-270 B.C.). Epicurus taught that nature is the supreme teacher and provides sensations, feelings, and anticipations for the testing of truth. By feelings he meant pleasure and pain. These he said could be used to distinguish between good and evil. He also taught that the gods were incapable of wrath, indifferent to human weakness, and did not intervene or participate in human affairs. Thus, he denied the possibility of miracles, prophecy, and divine providence. In the beginning Epicurus meant "real happiness" by *pleasure*. At first, his followers merely sought a quiet life free from fear, pain, and anger. Later, some made sensual pleasures the goal of life.

Stoics were followers of Zeno of Citium (335-263 B.C.). Zeno believed in a creative power and made duty, reason (or accordance with divine reason), and self-sufficiency the goal of life. He encouraged his followers to accept the laws of nature and conscience and to be indifferent to pleasure, pain, joy, and grief.

Some of these philosophers were quite contemptuous of Paul's gospel and called him a "babbler," literally, "a seed-picker." This term was also used as slang for parasites and ignorant plagiarists who would gather information from a variety of sources and try to market it as their own system of knowledge. Then, because Paul preached the good news of Jesus and the Resurrection, they said he seemed to be proclaiming not merely strange gods, but foreign demons. They sneered at the gospel as a foreign religion contrary to all they believed.

**19. And they took him:** ... So they laid hold of him, —TCNT ... they took him by the sleeve, —KNOX.
**and brought him unto Areopagus, saying:** ... and took him to the city auditorium and said, —WLMS ... and led him up, —KNOX ... to the Court of Areopagus, —TCNT ... to Mars' Hill, —NLTG ... to a meeting of the Areopagus Council, —SEB.
**May we know what this new doctrine, whereof thou speakest, is?:** ... May we hear what new teaching this is which you are giving, —TCNT ... May we know what is this novel teaching of yours, —MOFT ... Will you make clear to us what is this new teaching of yours, —BB ... Please explain to us this new idea that you have been teaching, —EVRD ... desire to know the purpose of these things, —SWAN ... We want to know what these things mean, —NLTG.

**17:19.** Undoubtedly, there were "seed-pickers" who prowled around the marketplace, picking up scraps of information and bits of philosophical ideas and retailing them secondhand. But as these Stoics and Epicurean philosophers listened to Paul, they apparently decided Paul's teaching was dangerous to their ideas and philosophies. Many of the Athenians may have believed in an afterlife and a vague sort of immortality of the soul. But the teaching concerning Jesus and a literal bodily resurrection was startling and bewildering. It could undermine their teachings and their influence. So they seized Paul and brought him before the Council of the Areopagus, the supreme court of Athens. This court formerly met on the Hill of Ares (Mars' Hill), a rocky outcrop or ridge facing the Acropolis. There is some evidence that it no longer met on Mars' Hill in New Testament times, but instead met in a colonnade or roofed portico in the public marketplace (the agora). In any case, it retained the same name wherever it met. It had jurisdiction, not only over criminal cases, but over all public lectures. Paul was taken before it for a sort of preliminary inquiry to give him opportunity to explain his teachings.

The request of the Council of the Areopagus was polite. They asked literally, "Are we able to ascertain something of that new teaching, the one (continually) spoken by you?" This was not an unusual request.

**20. For thou bringest certain strange things to our ears:** . . . scatterest in our ears, *—MRDK* . . . For the things you are saying sound strange to us, *—WEYM* . . . Thou dost introduce terms which are strange to our ears, *—KNOX* . . . are so new to us, *—SEB*. **we would know therefore what these things mean:** . . . we should like to know what they mean, *—TCNT* . . . we have a desire to get the sense of them. *—BB*.

**17:20.** The Council further defined these new things as "strange," not merely foreign or different, but startling and bewildering. It was their will, therefore, for Paul to explain what these things meant. They felt they had a right to know.

Notice that the Council did not give Paul time to prepare a sermon or a defense. But this did not upset Paul. He had the Holy Spirit with him and dwelling in him, so he had the Helper he needed. Not only so, he had been explaining the gospel to everyone he met, so his mind and heart were filled with the truth.

Furthermore, he knew what Jesus taught in Matthew 10:18-20. Jesus told His disciples they would be brought before councils, governors, and kings for His sake, for a testimony to them and to the Gentiles. But when they were arrested or brought before those who would put them on trial or examine them, they must not be anxious or worried about how or what they would speak. What they should speak would be given them at the very time they needed it.

**21. (For all the Athenians and strangers which were there:** . . . (Now everybody in Athens, *—BECK* . . . and the foreign residents, *—FNTN* . . . sojourning foreigners, *—RTHM*. **spent their time in nothing else:** . . . found no time for anything else, *—TCNT* . . . spent the whole of their leisure, *—FNTN*. **but either to tell, or to hear some new thing.):** . . . but telling, or listening to, the last new thing.), *—TCNT* . . . to talk about any new idea, *—SEB*.

**17:21.** This verse is a parenthesis explaining why the Council of the Areopagus wanted to know, ascertain, and determine the meaning of Paul's new and bewildering teaching. They were Athenians, and the Athenians as a whole, as well as the resident aliens who had accepted the Athenian culture and way of life, spent their (leisure) time telling and hearing something new. They were not great leaders and thinkers as their ancient forebears had been. Rather, they were curiosity

seekers and philosophical hangers-on whose only interest was what was new.

**22. Then Paul stood in the midst of Mars' hill, and said:** . . . taking his stand, *—RTHM* . . . in the centre of the High Court, *—FNTN*. **Ye men of Athens, I perceive that in all things ye are too superstitious:** . . . excessive in the worship of demons, *—MRDK* . . . on every hand I see signs of your being very devout, *—TCNT* . . . I observe at every turn that you are a most religious people, *—MOFT* . . . my own eyes tell me that you are in all respects an extremely religious people, *—PHLP* . . . very much given to the worship of divinities, *—HBIE* . . . you stand in greatest awe of the deities, *—SWAN*.

**17:22.** Standing in the midst, not of the hill, but of the Council of the Areopagus, Paul wisely began in a positive way. As at Lystra, he took the people where they were and tried to lead them into spiritual truth.

The translation (KJV) that says they were "too superstitious" sounds as if he was intending to insult them. Though the Greek words can bear that meaning, it is better to translate them here with the meaning of "very religious," in the sense of being very respectful to their gods. This was not a statement they would react against. They might have even considered it a compliment.

**23. For as I passed by:** . . . For as I was going about, *—TCNT* . . . going here and there, *—WLMS* . . . made my way here, *—PHLP*. **and beheld your devotions:** . . . and studying, *—FNTN* . . . I observed the objects of your worship, *—RSV* . . . looking at your sacred shrines, *—TCNT*. **I found an altar:** . . . I came upon an altar, *—TCNT* . . . I actually came upon, *—MOFT* . . . I particularly noticed an altar, *—PHLP*. **with this inscription:** . . . on which were inscribed the words, *—PHLP* . . . with this writing on it, *—BB*. **TO THE UNKNOWN GOD:** . . . THE HIDDEN GOD, *—MRDK* . . . TO GOD THE UNKNOWN, *—PHLP*. **Whom therefore ye ignorantly worship:** . . . What therefore you in your ignorance revere, *—RTHM* . . . what you don't know and yet worship, *—BECK* . . . What, therefore, you unknowingly worship, *—FNTN*. **him declare I unto you:** . . . that I am now proclaiming to you, *—TCNT* . . . announce to you, *—BRKL* . . . he is the One I will tell you about, *—NLTG* . . . that I am revealing to you, *—KNOX*.

**17:23.** Then Paul used an inscription on an altar in Athens to give him an opportunity to speak about the one true God in contrast to their many gods. During his walks around Athens he had come across this inscription, "To the Unknown God." In their desire to be sure they did not slight or overlook some god, the Athenians had erected this altar. This was evidence that Paul was not preaching something contrary to the laws of

Athens. He could tell them about the God who was unknown to them.

Paul did not mean by this that their worship was acceptable to God. God seeks those who will worship Him in spirit (and in the Spirit) and in truth, not in ignorance and empty forms. Actually, the Greeks did not feel close to any god. Like those who go to the heathen temples today, they would go from god to god, from altar to altar, hoping that somehow one of them might help them. Thus, in spite of their education and highly developed culture, these Greeks were badly in need of the gospel.

Paul used words here that carry another connotation. The word *worship* can mean serving or worshiping one who has a right to your service and worship. The word *ignorantly* often implies willful ignorance that is, therefore, guilty before God. Romans 1:18-32 shows that the Gentiles are guilty because they once knew God, but they turned from Him, refused to give Him glory and thanks, and became full of empty and unreal imaginings so that their foolish hearts were darkened through moral defect. The implication in Paul's letter to the Romans is that they took God off the throne, put self on the throne, and soon were worshiping gods of their own making, gods they thought they could manipulate to do their will.

**24. God that made the world and all things therein:** . . . the universe and everything in it, —WEYM . . . the world and all that it contains, —WLMS.
**seeing that he is Lord of heaven and earth:** . . . he, Lord as he is of Heaven and earth, —TCNT . . . the Lord of the land and the sky, —EVRD.
**dwelleth not in temples made with hands:** . . . is not housed in buuildings made with hands, —BB . . . does not dwell in sanctuaries built by man, —WEYM . . . He doesn't live in temples, —SEB.

**17:24.** Among the Jews who claimed the Old Testament as their authority, Paul always went right to the prophecies and promises of Scripture. But Paul never started with these when he was dealing with Gentiles who did not know or believe the Bible. In Athens he was led by the Holy Spirit to declare first some facts about the God who made the promises. It was necessary for the Athenians to understand that He is different from the gods they believed in.

Paul first emphasized that God is the Creator of all things, the world (the *kosmos*, the universe, the sum total of the created order) and everything in it. This was a new idea to the Greeks. In their myths they claimed that various gods created various things, always out of preexisting materials. In fact, they looked on the gods themselves as part of what we might call the created universe. They needed to know the true God is above and beyond the universe and that He created it all. This is basic. All through the Old Testament the Bible draws attention to the fact that God is both Creator and Redeemer. The Athenians had to understand first that He is the Creator before they could understand how He could be the Redeemer.

Then Paul emphasized the truth that God is Lord of heaven and earth. That is, by right of creation, He is Lord, Owner, Master. There is no room for other gods. He alone is worthy of our worship.

Furthermore, since He is the Creator and is above all, He is too great to dwell in sanctuaries made by human hands; that is, He cannot be limited to them. This was a truth well understood by Solomon when he said, "Behold, the heaven and heaven of heavens cannot contain thee; how much less this house that I have builded?" (1 Kings 8:27). The prophets also understood it. In Isaiah 66:1 God says, "The heaven is my throne, and the earth is my footstool: where is the house that ye build unto me? and where is the place of my rest?" What a contrast with the little gods of Athens!

**25. Neither is worshipped with men's hands:** . . . is waited upon, —RTHM . . . nor yet do human hands minister to his wants, —TCNT . . . And is not dependent on the work of men's hands, —BB . . . He doesn't need any help from men, —SEB.
**as though he needed any thing:** . . . as though in want of anything, —RTHM . . . as though he needed anything, —TCNT . . . as if he had need of anything, —BB . . . He does not need any help from them, —NCV . . . as if he stood in need of anything, —KNOX.
**seeing he giveth:** . . . for it is he who giveth, —MOFT.
**to all life, and breath, and all things:**

**17:25.** The true God does not need to be worshiped with what human hands can do. He does not need to be cared for as a physician would tend a patient, for He does not need anything. After all, how could He need anything and how could He need any care? He is the true Source of and Giver of all life, breath, and all things.

**26. And hath made of one blood all nations of men:** . . . And made all nations of men, (created) of one blood, —ALFD . . . He made all races of men from one stock, —TCNT . . . He caused to spring from one forefather people of every race, —WEYM . . . From one man he has created the whole human race, —KLST . . . From him came all the different people, —EVRD . . . of one single stock, —KNOX.
**for to dwell on all the face of the earth:** . . . and caused them to settle on all parts of the earth's surface, —TCNT . . . for them to live on the whole surface of the earth, —WEYM . . . to dwell all over the earth, —MOFT.

**and hath determined the times before appointed:** . . . marking out fitting opportunities, *—RTHM* . . . definitely appointing the pre-established periods, *—BRKL* . . . fixing a time for their rise and fall, *—TCNT* . . . He decided exactly when, *—NCV* . . . the cycles it was to pass through, *—KNOX.*

**and the bounds of their habitation:** . . . limits of their settlements, *—TCNT* . . . boundaries of their abodes, *—MOFT* . . . boundaries they live in, *—BECK* . . . and where they must live, *—NCV* . . . having provided proper methods and guides, *—FNTN.*

**17:26.** Paul further emphasized that God is the Creator of all by saying God has made out of one blood (that is, from one blood line, in other words, from Adam) every nation of mankind to dwell on the whole face of the earth.

Some ancient manuscripts omit the word "blood" in this verse. The meaning is still the same, however, for it would mean that out of one (person), Adam, God has made all the nations of the earth. This too is important. Some ancient peoples taught they were created by a separate creation from other nations. But in God's eyes, as well as in the facts of history, all are part of Adam's race. Most scientists today say the facts point to a single origin for the human race.

God has also fixed the limit of mankind's appointed seasons (times, occasions, and opportunities) as well as the boundaries of mankind's dwelling. Since this points back to what God has done in creation, it must refer to Genesis 1:9, 10 where God separated the dry land from the waters.

Other Old Testament passages show that God as the Creator is also the Guide of the family of nations. God regulates the rise and fall of nations (Daniel 4:34, 35; 5:18-21). He also is concerned over them and exercises authority over their location and limits their expansion (Amos 9:7; Deuteronomy 32:8).

**27. That they should seek the Lord:** . . . search for God, *—TCNT* . . . for their research in seeking God, *—FNTN.*

**if haply they might feel after him, and find him:** . . . if by any means they might feel their way to him, *—TCNT* . . . if perhaps they could grope for Him, *—WEYM* . . . somehow grope their way towards him? *—KNOX* . . . on the chance of finding him in their groping for him, *—MOFT.*

**though he be not far from every one of us:** . . . although in truth he is already not far, *—RTHM* . . . Though indeed he is close to each one of us, *—MOFT.*

**17:27.** By saying God has fixed the boundaries of mankind's dwelling, Paul did not mean mankind could not or should not move from one place to another. All people have done that throughout history to a greater or lesser extent. Rather, Paul meant God brought mankind to the places and

times where they would have opportunities to seek God, "if perhaps they might touch Him and find Him," though He is actually not far away, not distant from each one. So it should not be hard to find Him. (Romans 1:20, 21 points out that "the invisible things of him are clearly seen, being understood by the things that are made, even his eternal power and Godhead; so that they are without excuse." Just looking at the greatness, the complexity, and the beauty of creation should have let the Athenians understand that it was not some little god in a corner who brought all this into being.)

**28. For in him we live, and move, and have our being:** . . . For in him we have life and motion and existence, *—BB* . . . and keep on living, *—NLTG* . . . and exist, *—FNTN* . . . and are, *—WORL.*

**as certain also of your own poets have said:** . . . To use the words of some of your own poets, *—TCNT* . . . Some . . . have endorsed this in the words, *—PHLP.*

**For we also are his offspring:** . . . From him is our descent, *—MRDK* . . . You see, we are His children, *—BECK* . . . originate from Him, *—FNTN.*

**17:28.** To emphasize that God should not be hard to find, Paul added, "For in Him we live, and move, and are (exist, have our being)." This statement is a quotation from one of the ancient poets, possibly Minos or Epimenedes of Crete. Then Paul quoted another of their own (Gentile, Greek-speaking) poets (Aratus of Cilicia) who said, "For we are His offspring." Paul used these quotations, not because they were inspired, but because they are true. God is indeed the Source of our existence and is near us.

Paul's words emphasize that God as Creator is not only above and beyond us as created beings, He is also everywhere present in His creation and wants to be a Friend to all, even to fallen men and women who have lost their way. The Gentile poets did not, of course, understand the full implication of what they said. But the Holy Spirit brought them to Paul's memory to catch the attention of these Athenians and turn their thoughts toward God. Paul, however, made it clear later (verses 30, 31) that having their source in God did not make them ready to meet God. They still needed to repent because a final judgment is coming.

**29. Forasmuch then as we are the offspring of God:** . . . Now then, since we have our being from God, *—BECK* . . . possessing an origin from God, *—FNTN.*

**we ought not to think:** . . . to be supposing, *—RTHM* . . . we must not think, *—TCNT* . . . we ought not to imagine, *—FNTN, —WEYM* . . . it is not right for us to have the idea, *—BB.*

**that the Godhead is like unto gold, or silver, or stone:** . . . the Divine Nature to be like, *—FNTN* . . . that the Deity has any resemblance to anything made of, —*TCNT*...that His nature resembles, —*WEYM*.

**graven by art and man's device:**...a work of human art and imagination, —*TCNT*...sculptured by the art and inventive faculty of man, —*WEYM*...or anything humanly manufactured or invented, —*BRKL*.

**17:29.** Since human beings are the "offspring" of God (in the sense of being created in the image and after the likeness of God), mankind would be totally unreasonable to think of the Godhead (the divine Trinity) as gold, or silver, or stone, an engraved work of the art and meditations or thoughts of a human being.

This is one of the strong points of Old Testament teaching. In Deuteronomy 4:15-19 Moses reminded Israel that they saw a genuine manifestation of God's presence at Sinai. But they saw no physical form of any kind. What they saw was glory. (See also Exodus 33:18, 22.) Moses gave this as a reason for not making or worshiping idols. The infinite God does not have the kind of form of which you can make an image. Therefore, when men try to make or fashion images, they are getting further away from what God is really like. When they worship these man-made images they are thus worshiping something other than God.

Psalm 115:4-8 points out the foolishness of idols made with human hands. Idols that cannot see, speak, or hear call attention to the stupidity of those who make them (see also Psalm 135:15-18). Isaiah 40:18-22 also uses irony to contrast the goldplated gods that need silver chains to keep them from falling over with the true God who founded the earth and who sits above the sphere of the earth (see also Isaiah 41:24; 44:9-17).

The words "ought not" also imply guilt. The heathen are wrong to make idols. Their false worship is sin. It is rebellion against the God who made them. Paul said they should have known better.

**30. And the times of this ignorance God winked at:**...God overlooked, —*ASV*...True, God looked with indulgence on the days of man's ignorance, —*TCNT*...However, while God paid no attention to those seasons of ignorance, —*BRKL*...Now while it is true that God has overlooked the days of ignorance, —*PHLP*.

**but now commandeth all men everywhere to repent:**...but now he is announcing to every one everywhere the need for repentance, —*TCNT*.

**17:30.** All of this idolatry showed their ignorance of what God is really like. The times (time periods) of this ignorance God, in His mercy and longsuffering, overlooked. But now He (through the gospel) was announcing to all human beings everywhere that they should repent. They should

change their minds and attitudes toward God by turning to Him through Christ and the gospel.

This does not mean those idolaters of past ages were saved. The Old Testament indicates idolatry came into existence after the Flood, probably by the time of the Tower of Babel (Babylon). At least it seems the Tower of Babel became the model for the temple towers or ziggurats of Babylonia. But, though their idolatry was sin and deserved to be judged, God did not bring the judgment day in the time periods between the Flood and Christ.

**31. Because he hath appointed a day:**...fixed a day, —*RSV*...set a day, —*WLMS*.

**in the which he will judge the world in righteousness:**...on which he intends to judge the world with justice, —*TCNT*.

**by that man whom he hath ordained:**...by a man whom he hath pointed out, —*RTHM*...in the person of a man whom he has destined for this work, —*WEYM*...He will use a man to do this, —*EVRD*.

**whereof he hath given assurance unto all men:**...has given proof of this to all, —*MOFT*...He has made this credible to all, —*WLMS*...of which he has given a sign to all men, —*BRKL*...He has given everyone a good reason to believe, —*BECK*...having given the strongest evidence, —*FNTN*.

**in that he hath raised him from the dead:**...by raising him from among the dead, —*RTHM*...by giving him back, —*BB*.

**17:31.** Paul said the Gentiles must no longer look to their images as gods, for a judgment day is coming. Repentance is therefore imperative. God has indeed appointed a day in which He will judge the earth in righteousness by a Man whom He has revealed and designated as Judge. (Compare Daniel 7:13; John 5:22, 27.)

That the day is actually coming and that there will be no escape from it, God guaranteed to all by the fact that He raised that Man (Jesus) out from among the dead. The fact that God raised Jesus from the dead shows He is deity and His teachings are true. He will be the Judge and will judge in righteousness (Isaiah 9:7; 11:4).

**32. And when they heard of the resurrection of the dead:**...On hearing of a, —*TCNT*...When they heard Paul speak of a resurrection of dead men, —*WEYM*...The mention of, Fenton.

**some mocked:**...began to mock, —*TCNT*...began jeering, —*WEYM*...some of them laughed, —*EVRD*...laughed outright, —*PHLP*...some treated it as a joke, —*WMCK*

**and others said, We will hear thee again of this matter:**...that they should hear what he had to say about that another time, —*TCNT*...Let us go more fully into this another time, —*BB*...We want to listen to you again about this, —*NLTG*.

**17:32.** As always, there are only two attitudes toward God: faith-obedience and unbelief-rebellion.

So here, some rejected Paul's message in unbelief. In fact, the mention of the resurrection from the dead brought immediate mockery from some. Others said, "We shall hear you concerning this matter again." This may mean they were at least willing to give Paul's message another hearing.

**33. So Paul departed from among them:**...And so Paul left the Court, —TCNT...went forth out of their midst, —WORL...the auditorium, —WLMS...left the Council, —WMCK...went away from among them, —BB...left them, —LAMS.

**17:33.** The statement that they would hear Paul again was also a way of bringing the discussion to a close and thus dismissing Paul. He was now free to leave the council chamber and go his way.

**34. Howbeit certain men clave unto him:**...But certain persons joining themselves unto him, —RTHM...associated with him, —BRKL...gave him their support, —BB...and followed him, —FNTN.
**and believed:**...and became believers in Christ, —TCNT...and were converted, —LAMS.
**among the which was:**...including, —MOFT.
**Dionysius the Areopagite:**...the Mars-hill judge, —RTHM...a member of the Court of Areopagus, —TCNT...a member of the Court of Areopagus, —TCNT...the Judge of the High Court, —FNTN...one of the judges of, —LAMS.
**and a woman named Damaris, and others with them:**...and several others, —TCNT...There were some others, too, —SEB.

**17:34.** The sessions of the Council of the Areopagus were open to the public. Some responded and became Paul's followers. Among them was Dionysius, a member of the Council, and a prominent woman named Damaris.

Some writers say that what Paul said to the Corinthians, "I determined not to know any thing among you, save Jesus Christ, and him crucified" (1 Corinthians 2:2), means that Paul was disappointed in the results at Athens and was rejecting the approach he had used there. But Paul's words to the Corinthians do not mean he said nothing about other truths. And those who joined with Paul were a sufficient nucleus for a church.

## Chapter 18

**1. After these things Paul departed from Athens, and came to Corinth:**...Before long Paul left Athens and went on to Corinth, —PHLP...On leaving Athens, Paul next went to Corinth, —TCNT...taking his departure from, —FNTN.

**18:1.** When Paul left Athens the Holy Spirit led him to Corinth, the capital of the Roman province of Achaia. It was a very prosperous city and a Roman colony. It was also a center of idolatry and licentiousness. No city in the Roman Empire

was more corrupt. It was filled with Greek adventurers, Roman merchants, lustful Phoenicians, sharp-eyed Jews, ex-soldiers, near-philosophers, sailors, freedmen, slaves, tradesmen, and agents of every kind of vice.

**2. And found a certain Jew named Aquila:**...There he met a Jew, —TCNT...came across, —MOFT.
**born in Pontus:**...from the region of, —LAMS...a man of Pontus by birth, —BB...a native of, —WMCK
**lately come from Italy, with his wife Priscilla:**...He and his wife Priscilla had recently come from Italy, —WEYM...had but recently migrated from Italy, —BRKL...had recently moved to, —NCV.
**(because that Claudius had commanded:**...in consequence of the order which had been issued by, —TCNT...when Claudius decreed, —KNOX.
**all Jews to depart from Rome:):**...expelling all the Jews from Rome, —WEYM...to get out of Rome, —SEB...to leave, —WMCK
**and came unto them:**...Paul paid them a visit, —TCNT...called on them, —BRKL...went to see them, —WMCK

**18:2.** Paul's first task in this great and corrupt city was to find a place to stay and some way to pay expenses. He was alone and without friends or acquaintances in the city. Yet he was not alone. God was with him, and God was already working.

A short time before this the fourth Roman Emperor, Tiberius Claudius Caesar Augustus Germanicus, who ruled A.D. 41-54, had commanded all the Jews to leave Rome. The date was probably sometime in A.D. 49 or 50. Paul probably arrived in Corinth in A.D. 50.

Among the Jews who were expelled were a husband and wife who were to become Paul's most faithful friends and fellow laborers in the gospel. The husband, Aquila, was a Jew from a family of the Roman province of Pontus. Aquila's wife's name, Priscilla, a diminutive or familiar form of Prisca (2 Timothy 4:19), indicates she was a Roman lady of one of the upper classes of society. It is at least possible she was the daughter of Aquila's former master. He may have helped her to believe in the one true God, the God of Israel. Then, when he was set free, he married her.

When Paul found them he went to them, that is, to their home. He was undoubtedly being directed by the Holy Spirit, and he never regretted having found them. It is evident that though the Emperor Claudius had expelled them and they had had to leave their home in Rome, they had no bitterness in their hearts. They were godly people who had committed their lives to Him.

**3. And because he was of the same craft:**...of the same trade, —RSV...they were brothers of the same craft, —KNOX . . . of the same occupation, —BRKL . . . of the same profession, —FNTN.

**he abode with them:** . . . lodged with them, —WEYM . . . stayed with them, —MOFT.

**and wrought:** . . . and worked, —ALFD . . . and they all worked together, —MOFT . . . employing himself, —FNTN.

**for by their occupation they were tentmakers:** . . . their trade was tent-making, —TCNT . . . (They were workers in leather by trade.), —MOFT . . . they were landscape painters, —FNTN.

**18:3.** Priscilla and Aquila had set up their tent-making business in their home, and when Paul came to them, these two lonely hearts were quick to welcome him and open their home to him. This gave him a congenial place to carry on his tent-making business also.

Some writers believe they were also leather workers and makers of felted cloth for tents. Paul's native province of Cilicia was, however, famous for its goats' hair cloth, most of which was used for tentmaking, and tentmaking would be an obvious trade for him as a future rabbi. (Jewish rabbis were expected to learn a trade. Most did not take money for their teaching, and many also believed hard work would help keep them from sin.) There is nothing to indicate whether or not Priscilla and Aquila were Christians before Paul met them. It is possible they knew at least something about the gospel. If they were not believers already, Paul soon won them to the Lord. They became faithful followers of Christ.

**4. And he reasoned in the synagogue every sabbath:** . . . began reasoning, —RTHM . . . Sabbath after Sabbath, he preached, —WEYM . . . gave addresses, —TCNT . . . had discussions, —BB . . . argued, —MOFT . . . he held a disputation, —KNOX . . . debated with the Jews, —SEB.

**and persuaded:** . . . and tried to persuade, —MNTG . . . trying to convince, —TCNT . . . and tried to win over, —WEYM . . . was engaged in earnest discussion, —FNTN.

**the Jews and the Greeks:** . . . both Jews and Greeks, —RTHM.

**18:4.** As was his custom, Paul went to the synagogue and preached and taught on the Sabbath. This he continued to do every Sabbath for some time, seeking to persuade both Jews and Greeks. Aquila and Priscilla no doubt accompanied him and were further established in the truth of the gospel. Again, it is probable that Paul began the first Sabbath as he had in Pisidian Antioch. Then, as he continued to persuade his listeners from Sabbath to Sabbath, there must have been many who responded to the truth. It is clear that as in most synagogues there were quite a number of Godfearing Greeks who had turned their backs on idolatry and wanted to know more of God.

**5. And when Silas and Timotheus were come from Macedonia:** . . . Now at the time when Silas and Timothy arrived, —WEYM.

**Paul was pressed in the spirit:** . . . After this, Paul used all his time, —SEB . . . completely possessed by the message, —BRKL . . . was earnestly occupied in discoursing, —ALFD . . . was hard pressed with teaching the word, —NORL . . . was preaching fervently, —WEYM . . . After this, Paul used all his time telling people the Good news, —EVRD . . . devoted himself entirely to delivering the Message, —TCNT . . . was engaged in earnest discussion, —FNTN.

**and testified to the Jews:** . . . bearing full witness unto the Jews, —RTHM . . . earnestly maintaining before the Jews, —TCNT . . . solemnly affirming to, —WEYM . . . strongly urging upon, —BRKL . . . showing the Jews as clearly as he could, —PHLP . . . demonstrating to the Jews, —FNTN.

**that Jesus was Christ:** . . . that the Christ was Jesus, —RSV . . . Jesus is the promised Saviour, —BECK . . . was the Messiah, —FNTN.

**18:5.** When Silas and Timothy finally joined Paul at Corinth they found him wholly absorbed, not in tentmaking but in teaching the Word of God. The Greek indicates he felt a greater pressure than the pressure of making a living, a greater pressure than the desire for this world's pleasures and luxuries. He still did a good job in his tentmaking, but the need to teach the Word of God became the impelling, compelling pressure that bore in upon him from all sides. Like Jeremiah, he felt the Word of God as a fire within his bones, and he could not stop giving it out (Jeremiah 20:9).

Paul wrote First Thessalonians shortly after Silas and Timothy came to him, for they brought good news. In 1 Thessalonians 3:6-10 Paul spoke of this. Timothy reported concerning the faith and love of the Thessalonian believers. The enemies of the gospel had not been able to turn them away from the Lord or from Paul. This wonderful report of their faith and continuance in the gospel cheered him and relieved the pressure of his passionate concern for them, giving him courage to go on.

But he still felt the pressure of the Word and from the Word to spread the gospel in Corinth. Thus, he gave witness with greater and greater intensity and zeal. Everywhere he declared the fact that Jesus is the Messiah, God's anointed Prophet, Priest, and King.

**6. And when they opposed themselves:** . . . But as they began opposing, —RTHM . . . However, as they set themselves against him, —TCNT . . . However, when they turned against him, —PHLP.

**and blasphemed:** . . . and abused him, —MOFT.

**he shook his raiment:** . . . Paul shook his clothes in protest, —TCNT . . . shook out his robe, —FNTN.

**and said unto them, Your blood be upon your own heads:** . . . it will be your own fault! —SEB.

**I am clean:** ... Pure am I, –RTHM ... My conscience is clear, –TCNT ... I am not responsible, –WEYM ... I am innocent, –BRKL ... guiltless, –FNTN.

**from henceforth I will go:** ... From this time forward, –TCNT ... From now on, –MNTG.

**unto the Gentiles:** ... to the non-Jews, –BECK ... to the heathen, –FNTN.

**18:6.** In the Jewish synagogue this increased intensity on Paul's part caused most of the unbelieving Jews to cease their indifference and line up against the gospel. They even blasphemed. They used abusive, vile, and scurrilous language against Paul, calling him all sorts of bad names to gain support and organize the opposition. This seems to mean they persuaded others to speak evil against Paul and against the gospel.

This was too much for Paul. Jesus had told His disciples earlier that when they encountered this kind of opposition they were to leave. As they left they were to shake the dust off their feet as a witness against them (Matthew 10:14, 15; Mark 6:11). There are too many people who are hungry for the truth to waste time on those who prove themselves incorrigible rebels.

So Paul shook off his outer garments (robes) against them in a gesture that was like shaking worthless scraps off a work apron. It was a sign he was rejecting their blasphemy. Then he called down their blood on their own heads. That is, he declared they would be responsible for the judgment God would send on them.

The Jews would understand, of course, that he was referring to the responsibility God put on Ezekiel to warn the people (Ezekiel 3:16-21; 33:8, 9). Had Paul not been faithful in giving them warning, their blood would have been upon his hands. But he had been faithful. He had done all he could. Now there was nothing for him to do but to turn to others who had not enjoyed so many opportunities to hear the gospel. From this point on Paul would go to the Gentiles.

**7. And he departed thence:** ... So he left, –TCNT ... He accordingly took his departure, –FNTN.

**and entered into a certain man's house, named Justus, one that worshipped God:** ... went to the house of a God-fearing man, –FNTN.

**whose house joined hard to the synagogue:** ... was next door to, –RSV, –SEB ... which adjoined, –KLST ... who lived next door to the synagogue, –KNOX ... to the meeting-house, –WMCK

**18:7.** Again, God was already working. Just as God saw to it that Aquila and Priscilla were in Corinth in time to provide Paul a home and a place to work, so God had a Godfearing Gentile living right next door to the synagogue who was ready to open his house as a new evangelistic center. His name was Titus (or Titius) Justus. His Roman name indicates he was a Roman citizen. Sir William Ramsay and others have suggested his full name was Gaius Titius Justus and that he was the Gaius mentioned in Romans 16:23 and 1 Corinthians 1:14.

**8. And Crispus, the chief ruler of the synagogue:** ... the President, –TCNT ... warden, –MNTG ... a leading man, –WMCK

**believed on the Lord with all his house:** ... came to believe in the Lord, and so did all his household, –TCNT ... trusted in the Lord, –SEB ... became a believer ... and so did all his family, –WLMS.

**and many of the Corinthians:** ... by now many of, –KNOX.

**hearing believed, and were baptized:** ... as they listened to Paul, became believers in Christ, –TCNT ... hearing the word, had faith and were given baptism, –BB ... listened and found faith, –KNOX ... and were immersed, –SEB.

**18:8.** Paul, Silas, and Timothy were not the only ones to leave the synagogue. The ruler, that is, the chief elder of the synagogue, Crispus, had come to believe on the Lord. First Corinthians 1:14 shows that Paul baptized him and his household. This loss of their leader must have been quite a shock to the unbelieving Jews and must have set them back in their plans to bring further opposition against Paul. In fact, the conversion of Crispus must have broken up the organized opposition to Paul for a time.

Then many of the Corinthians, that is, the Greeks who were residents of the city, kept listening (to the gospel), and as they heard, they believed and were baptized.

The Jews did not succeed in stopping the spread of the gospel. The move to the house of the Gentile Justus gave an open door to many Gentiles who would never have been willing to set foot in a Jewish synagogue. Thus, there was a constant stream of people hearing the truth, believing, and being baptized.

**9. Then spake the Lord to Paul:** ... the Lord said to Paul, –FNTN.

**in the night by a vision:** ... by night through means of a vision, –RTHM ... in a vision by night, –WEYM ... in a night vision, –BRKL.

**Be not afraid:** ... Have no fear, –TCNT ... Dismiss your fears, –WEYM ... Stop being afraid, –WLMS.

**but speak, and hold not thy peace:** ... but continue to speak, and refuse to be silenced, –TCNT ... go on speaking, –WMCK ... Continue talking to people and don't be quiet! –NCV ... Do not be silent, –KLST ... Do not close your mouth, –NLTG.

**18:9.** The Lord soon confirmed to Paul that he had done the right thing. In a night vision He (Jesus himself) told Paul not to be afraid. The form of the Greek used here really means he must stop being afraid. This indicates Paul was beginning to be afraid he would have to leave Corinth as he had so many other cities when persecution began. But Jesus told him he should keep on spreading the Word in Corinth and not be silent (not even begin to be silent).

Paul needed this assurance. He was human like others. The very success of the mission must have reminded him of what had happened in other cities. Perhaps, too, it may have occurred to him that it might be a good idea to leave while things were still going well. More than that, Paul had caught a vision of the need of the world. He was always ready to push on to new fields as the Spirit led. But how tender Jesus was as He dealt with him. He knows how to give new boldness to His witnesses.

**10. For I am with thee:**
**and no man shall set on thee to hurt thee:** ...and no one shall attack you to injure you, —WEYM ... shall make an attack upon you, —SWAN . . . shall assault you to your hurt, —BECK ... shall lift a finger to harm you, —PHLP ...no one shall succeed in harming you, —WLMS.
**for I have much people in this city:** ... There are many in this city who belong to me, —PHLP ... many of my people, —EVRD ... in this town, —WMCK

**18:10.** Jesus also assured Paul that He was with him and would not allow anyone to lay hands on him (arrest him and bring him to trial) or harm him. The promise that they would not hurt (harm) him is very emphatic. (They did attack him, but they did not hurt him.)

The reason for this promise of protection was the fact the Lord had "much people" in Corinth. Many would yet come to Jesus and become part of the true people of God.

**11. And he continued there a year and six months:** ... So he settled there for a year and a half, —TCNT ... For he had already been in Corinth a year and six months, —LAMS ... And he dwelt there, —WORL ...he remained settled there, —WLMS C. K. ...for eighteen months, —PHLP.
**teaching the word of God among them:** ...teaching among them, —WMCK

**18:11.** With this encouragement, Paul remained in Corinth 18 months, teaching the Word of God among them. During all this time there was no violence and no one harmed Paul, just as the Lord had promised. Truly the Lord was with him.

**12. And when Gallio was the deputy of Achaia:** ... governor of Greece, —TCNT, —WMCK ... became proconsul, —WEYM ... was leader of the country of, —NLTG.
**the Jews made insurrection with one accord against Paul:** ... the Jews made a combined attack on Paul, —TCNT ... made a concerted attack, —KLST ... without exception, —MOFT ... unanimously, —WLMS ... worked against Paul, —NLTG ... with only one thing in mind to stop Paul, —SEB.
**and brought him to the judgment seat:** ...in front of, —NLTG ...They took him to court, —SEB . . . dragged him, —WMCK . . . took him to the judge's seat, —BB ... before the court, —WEYM ... the tribunal, —MOFT ...the Governor's Bench, —TCNT.

**18:12.** Paul's continued success was a source of constant irritation to the unbelieving Jews. In the spring of A.D. 52, a new proconsul named Gallio was appointed by the Roman Senate to govern the province of Achaia (Greece). He was the brother of the famous Stoic philosopher Seneca and a man of great personal charm, known for his great graciousness. He remained in office until the spring of A.D. 53. Later, the Emperor Nero had him put to death.

The unbelieving Jews apparently thought they could take advantage of the new governor's lack of knowledge of the situation. So they rose up against Paul with one accord and brought him before the governor's judgment seat.

Archaeologists have discovered this judgment seat (Greek, *bēma*) at Corinth. It was built of blue and white marble and must have been very impressive.

Now the opposition Paul anticipated had come. But the Lord was still with Paul. It seems Paul was conscious of this and did not offer any resistance as the Jews led him to the *bēma*. He was still trusting God that they would not be able to hurt or harm him.

**13. Saying, This fellow persuadeth men:** ... charging him with persuading people, —TCNT ... This man, they said, is inducing people, —WEYM ... declaring, This fellow advises the people, —BRKL ....This man is perverting men's minds, —PHLP.
**to worship God contrary to the law:** ...to give worship to God, —BB ...in a way forbidden by the Lew, —TCNT ...in an unlawful manner, —WEYM ... in ways that violate our laws, —WLMS ...a way that is against our law! —NCV...against the Jewish Law, —NLTG ...in a manner the law forbids, —KNOX.

**18:13.** To Gallio the Jews accused Paul of urging men (human beings) by evil persuasion to worship God in a way "contrary to the law." Since they were before a Roman court or tribunal, this would be taken by Gallio to mean contrary to Roman law. Roman law at that time distinguished between legal and illegal religions. Judaism under that law was considered a legal religion. Thus, the Jews were really accusing Paul of teaching men to worship God in a way contrary to their own views or interpretations of what the Old Testament taught. They knew, of course, that Paul used the Old Testament Scriptures to preach Christ.

Also, by saying that Christianity was illegal, they were declaring that in their view Christianity was not a sect of Judaism, but was a totally different religion. They were also referring to Paul in a derogatory way by calling him "this one" (this fellow).

Actually, Paul still considered himself a Jew, but a believing Jew. He never looked at Christianity as a brand-new religion. It was the continuation and fulfillment of God's plan and promises revealed in the Old Testament. What God is doing through the Church is not something different from what He revealed in the Old Testament; it is all part of His eternal purpose.

**14. And when Paul was now about to open his mouth:** . . . Just as Paul was on the point of speaking, −TCNT . . . was about to begin his defense, −WEYM . . . as Paul was desirous to open his mouth and speak, −LAMS . . . just beginning to speak, −WLMS . . . was about to say something, −BB.

**Gallio said unto the Jews, If it were a matter of wrong or wicked lewdness, O ye Jews:** . . . Jews, if this were a case of misdemeanor or some serious crime, −TCNT . . . If it had been some wrongful act or piece of cunning knavery, −WEYM . . . some injustice or villainy, −HBIE . . . of wrongdoing or vicious crime, −RSV . . . or a serious fraud, NAB . . . or reckless evil, −SWAN . . . some malicious contrivance, −KNOX.

**reason would that I should bear with you:** . . . there would be some reason for my listening patiently to you, −TCNT . . . I might reasonably have listened to you, −WEYM . . . It would be only fair that I listen to you, −BECK . . . to listen to you Jews with patience, −KNOX . . . I would give you . . . a patient and reasonable hearing, −NAB.

**18:14.** Paul did not have to defend himself. He was about to speak when Gallio answered the Jews. He was not the inexperienced man the unbelieving Jews took him to be. He was born in Cordova, Spain, and grew up in the midst of philosophers, poets, and orators in Rome. A man of intelligence and wit, he had sense enough to realize that no crime against the Roman state or against the Roman law was involved, neither was there any evidence of any wicked (evil, malicious) act against morality. Had there been any legal or moral crime indicated, he would have felt it reasonable to listen patiently.

Actually, Paul was a good citizen. He encouraged people to obey the laws of the land and submit to their rulers. He encouraged believers to pray and give thanks "for all that are in authority; that we may lead a quiet and peaceable life in all godliness and honesty" (1 Timothy 2:1, 2; see also Titus 3:1).

There was never anything malicious, evil, or immoral about Paul's life or ministry. Part of the proof of his apostleship was that he considered the gospel as a trust to which he must be true. He always endeavored to please God rather than men and never modified the truth to flatter others or gain something for himself.

A further proof of his apostleship was that he was never hard, harsh, high-handed or dictatorial in dealing with people. Rather, he was gentle, like a nurse or a loving father. He poured out his very life in service to the believers, and he lived the kind of devout, upright, blameless life he implored them to live (1 Thessalonians 2:4-12).

**15. But if it be a question of:** . . . But if they are questions about, −ASV . . . but, since it is a dispute about, −TCNT.

**words and names:** . . . words and persons, −MOFT . . . about terminology and titles, −NAB.

**and of your law:** . . . arguments about your own law, −NCV . . . and your own law, −RSV . . . and your kind of Law, −HBIE.

**look ye to it:** . . . you will have to see to it yourselves, −WLMS . . . So you must solve this problem yourselves, −NCV . . . you must see to it yourselves, −NAB . . . take care of it yourselves, −NLTG.

**for I will be no judge of such matters:** . . . I refuse to be a judge, −WEYM . . . I decline to adjudicate upon matters like that, −MOFT . . . I am not willing, −MNTG . . . I am not disposed to be a judge, −WORL.

**18:15.** It seemed to Gallio that the case against Paul involved nothing but questions (rather, a contemptible parcel of questions) about words and names and their own Jewish law. Therefore, he told them they could see to that for themselves. He refused to be a judge of such matters.

**16. And he drave them from the judgment seat:** . . . And he had them ejected from the court, −PHLP . . . made them leave the courtroom, −SEB.

**18:16.** Thus, Gallio dismissed the case and ordered the lictors to drive them from the court or tribunal, which was probably set up in an open public square.

The historian and archaeologist Sir William Ramsay considered this decision of Gallio the "charter of Christian freedom." It set a precedent in Corinth that would keep the Jews from ever trying to use the Roman government or Roman power against the Christians again.

**17. Then all the Greeks took Sosthenes:** . . . laying hold of, −RTHM . . . set upon, −TCNT . . . they all grabbed, NCV . . . they all pounced on, −NAB.

**the chief ruler of the synagogue, and beat him:** . . . began to strike him, −RTHM . . . and kept beating him, −WLMS.

**before the judgment seat:** . . . in front of the courthouse, −PHLP . . . right before the governor, −NORL . . . in full view of the bench, −NAB.

**And Gallio cared for none of those things:** . . . did not trouble himself about any of these things, −TCNT . . . did not concern himself in the least about this, −WEYM . . . did not let this trouble him, −NLTG . . . this did not bother Gallio, −NCV, −SEB . . . paid no attention to it, −NAB . . . took no notice, −MOFT, −WMCK

**18:17.** This pleased the crowd, for the Jews were not popular with them. They then took advantage of Gallio's attitude and seized Sosthenes, the new ruler of the synagogue, striking him down before he could leave the tribunal. Some ancient manuscripts leave out "the Greeks" in this verse. On this basis some commentaries suppose it was Jews who beat the president of their congregation, Sosthenes, because of his failure to gain the success of their cause against Paul. But this is not likely. Good manuscripts uphold the reading "the Greeks." The marketplace crowd would be largely Gentile, and they used this opportunity to express their feelings against these troublemakers and show their approval of the verdict of Gallic Gallio, as the people expected, paid no attention. He considered the whole matter outside his jurisdiction. The Jews who hoped to turn the governor against Paul found the tables turned. It had looked at first as if the promise Jesus gave Paul that he would not be harmed in Corinth could not be fulfilled. But Paul's enemies, not Paul, were the ones who were harmed.

This must have had a deep effect on Sosthenes. It seems Sosthenes finally yielded to the truth of the gospel. In 1 Corinthians 1:1 Sosthenes joined Paul in greeting the Corinthians. Apparently this is the same Sosthenes. It is unlikely that there would be another prominent Sosthenes who was well-known to the Corinthian church. Truly the grace of God is marvelous! The leader of the opposition became a brother in the Lord. With this victory before Gallio, and the conversion of Sosthenes, there must have been more freedom than ever for the Christians to witness for Christ in Corinth.

**18. And Paul after this tarried there yet a good while:** . . . Paul remained there some time after this, −TCNT . . . quite a while longer, −NORL . . . stayed a long time more, −WMCK

**and then took his leave of the brethren:** . . . but eventually he took leave, −NAB . . . said goodbye to the brothers, −MOFT.

**and sailed thence into Syria:** . . . and went by ship to Syria, −BB.

**and with him Priscilla and Aquila:** . . . accompanied by Priscilla and Aquilla, −MOFT.

**having shorn his head in Cenchrea:** . . . but not before his head had been shaved at Cenchreae, −TCNT . . . He had cut off his hair at Cenchreae, −WEYM . . . At the port of, −NAB.

**for he had a vow:** . . . because he was under a vow, −TCNT . . . bound by a vow, −WEYM . . . for he had taken an oath, −BB . . . made a promise to God, −EVRD.

**18:18.** After some time, probably after several months, Paul sailed for Syria in the final part of his second missionary journey. He took Priscilla and Aquila with him. As is usually the case, Priscilla is named first. She seems to have been gifted by the Spirit for ministry, but Aquila was always working with her. They must have been a wonderful team. (Note how Paul commended them in Romans 16:3, 4.)

At Cenchrea, the port of Corinth (9 miles east on the Saronic Gulf), Paul had his hair cut, for he had taken a vow, probably a modified Nazirite vow, to express total dedication to God and His will. (A few think Aquila took the vow, not Paul.)

**19. And he came to Ephesus:** . . . When they landed at, −NAB . . . arrived at, −WMCK

**and left them there:** . . . and there Paul left his companions behind, −WEYM.

**but he himself entered into the synagogue:** . . . while he went personally in the synagogue, −BRKL.

**and reasoned with the Jews:** . . . and debated with the Jews, −PHLP . . . to hold discussions with, −NAB.

**18:19.** When they came to the great city of Ephesus, Paul left Priscilla and Aquila behind to minister there while he went on to Jerusalem. They stayed several years in Ephesus, the capital of the Roman province of Asia. Its population was over 300,000, and it was a very prosperous center of trade and commerce. Thus, there was a great opportunity for witness.

Paul did stay at Ephesus over the following Sabbath, however. This time the Holy Spirit did not check him from preaching in Asia. So he went to the synagogue and found Jews willing to listen to his reasoned presentation of the gospel (and to discuss it with him). There was an openness among the Jews of Ephesus at this time that was more like the reception Paul had received at Beroea.

Their response to Paul was not because he rose to heights of oratory, however. Neither did he use the high-sounding vocabulary and technical language of the Greek philosophers and Jewish theologians. The apostle had a message from God, and he said it simply and directly under the anointing of the Holy Spirit. He trusted the Holy Spirit to drive home the truth to human hearts.

Not human wisdom, but the wisdom and power of God were the secret of Paul's success.

**20. When they desired him:** ... requested him, −RTHM ... wanted him, −NORL ... asked him, −WMCK
**to tarry longer time with them:** ... to prolong his stay, −TCNT ... to remain a longer time with them, −HBIE ... to stay on longer, −NAB ... a little longer, −FNTN.
**he consented not:** ... he declined, NAB, −RSV ... he said, No, −BB ... he refused, −PHLP.

**18:20.** The Jews in the Ephesian synagogue were not only impressed by Paul's teaching, they wanted to hear more. So they requested that he stay with them for a longer period of time, but he did not consent.

**21. But bade them farewell, saying:** ... but taking his leave of them, −ASV ... As Paul was leaving them, −SEB ... As he said goodbye he gave them his promise, −NAB ... took leave of them, saying, −WMCK
**I must by all means keep this feast that cometh in Jerusalem: but I will return again unto you:** ... I will come back to you again, −NAB.
**if God will:** ... please God, −TCNT ... if it is the will of God, −MOFT ... if God wants me to, −NLTG.
**And he sailed from Ephesus:** ... He put to sea from, −KLST ... took ship from Ephesus, −BB ... He then left Ephesus, −WMCK

**18:21.** As Paul took his leave, he explained why he could not stay longer. He felt it was necessary for him to get to Jerusalem in time for the coming feast. He did not explain which feast he was desiring to keep. Usually, when the feast was not specified it was the Passover, for it was the great feast of the Jews.

In his farewell Paul also promised to return to Ephesus again, "God willing." The word "if" is not in the Greek, though we might consider it to be implied. James 4:15 does use the word "if" and warns that believers ought to say, "If the Lord will (that is, if it is His will), we shall live, and do this, or that." This should always be the Christian's attitude, for no one knows what tomorrow will bring.

**22. And when he had landed at Caesarea:** ... On reaching Caesarea, −TCNT.
**and gone up, and saluted the church:** ... he went up to Jerusalem and exchanged greetings with the Church, −TCNT ... he went up to the town, −WMCK ... to pay his respects to the congregation, −KLST ... to say hello to, −NLTG ... visited, −FNTN ... saluting the assembly, −WORL.
**he went down to Antioch:** ... Then he descended to, −FNTN.

**18:22.** The sailing vessel Paul took at Ephesus brought him without incident to Caesarea, which was Jerusalem's seaport. Apparently he did not stay there but immediately made the 65-mile journey southeast to Jerusalem. When the phrase *to go up* is used by itself in the New Testament, it often means to go up to Jerusalem for a feast. (Compare John 7:8, 10; 12:20.) Though the feast is not mentioned either, it can be inferred that Paul did reach Jerusalem in time for the feast.

Apparently there were no incidents at the feast. Luke only reported that Paul visited the assembly (the Jerusalem church) and "saluted" (greeted, paid his respects to) them. He probably let them know he had been faithful to carry out the instructions of the Jerusalem Council of chapter 15.

From Jerusalem Paul went down to Antioch of Syria. (Note that he went up to Jerusalem and down to Antioch. Antioch was at a lower elevation, but Luke may have been thinking of the exalted position of the city of Jerusalem.)

Thus, Paul completed the circuit and brought his second missionary journey to a close. As before, he felt a responsibility to go back to the church where the Holy Spirit had given assurance that he was to go out into missionary travels to take the gospel to the Gentiles.

**23. And after he had spent some time there, he departed:** ... Paul stayed there for some time, −NLTG ... set out again, −NAB ... Paul set out on a tour, −WEYM ... he proceeded on his way, −FNTN.
**and went over all the country of Galatia and Phyrgia in order:** ... traveling systematically through the Galatian country, −NAB ... and went through, −ASV ... and made his way successively through, −BRKL ... and by a definite schedule travelled all over, −WLMS ... he set out on a tour through, −TCNT ... visiting in a regular manner the districts of, −FNTN ... he passed through all the country of, −WMCK
**strengthening all the disciples:** ... establishing, −ASV ... imparting new strength to, −WLMS ... in order to strengthen, −NORL ... strengthening the faith of all the disciples as he went, −TCNT ... making all the disciples strong in the faith, −BB ... encouraging all, −FNTN ... confirming, −ALFD.

**18:23.** Paul spent some time in Antioch, probably until the fall of A.D. 53, continuing his ministry of encouraging and teaching the believers. The church at Antioch continued to be an outstanding evangelistic center. It was important in the history of the Church in the early centuries. (The ruins of about 20 church buildings dated from the Fourth Century A.D. have been discovered by archaeologists.)

This was Paul's last visit to Antioch. Finally, he felt the pressure of the Holy Spirit directing him to begin his third missionary journey. From Antioch he went north by land on a 1,500 mile journey into the regions of Galatia and Phrygia. One after another he visited the churches established during his first and second journeys.

Paul never founded churches and then forgot them. He always sought to go back to give further teaching and to establish and strengthen the disciples. He was always as much or more concerned with following up the new believers as he was in getting them saved in the first place. This was also the reason for his epistles.

**24. And a certain Jew named Apollos, born at Alexandrea:** ...a native of Alexandria, —WEYM ...an Alexandrian by birth, —BB.

**an eloquent man:** ...a learned man, —RTHM ...a gifted speaker, —PHLP ...and a man of learning, —BB.

**and mighty in the scriptures:** ...well versed in, —RSV ...and mighty in the Bible, —BECK ...he had a great knowledge of the holy Writings, —BB ...an authority on Scripture, —NAB.

**came to Ephesus:** ...had arrived at, —WMCK ...arrived by ship at, —NAB.

**18:24.** While Paul was ministering in South Galatia and Phrygia, an eloquent Jew named Apollos (short for Apollonius, "pertaining to [the Greek god] Apollo") came from Alexandria to Ephesus.

Alexandria, located on the north coast of Egypt west of the mouth of the Nile River, was the second largest city of the Roman Empire. It was an important seaport and the empire's greatest cultural and educational center. Its library was world famous.

Not only was Apollos eloquent and a great orator, he was very well educated, a real scholar, and powerful in his use of the Old Testament Scriptures.

**25. This man was instructed in:** ...had been orally taught, —RTHM ...had been trained in, —BB ...He had had some teaching in, —WMCK

**the way of the Lord:** ...the Cause of the Lord, —TCNT.

**and being fervent in the spirit:** ...and with burning zeal, —TCNT ...and with spiritual fervor, —WLMS ...and burning in spirit, —BB ...and being an enthusiastic soul, —NORL ...his heart was warmed by, —WMCK

**he spake and taught:** ...he used to speak and teach, —WEYM ...he preached and taught, —MOFT.

**diligently the things of the Lord:** ...accurately, —RSV ...The things he taught about Jesus were correct, —SEB ...carefully the facts about Jesus, —TCNT.

**knowing only the baptism of John:** ...though he knew of no baptism but John's, —TCNT.

**18:25.** Apollos had already been instructed orally in the way of the Lord Jesus, probably in his home city of Alexandria. So enthusiastic was he about Jesus that his spirit (his own spirit) was literally boiling over as he spoke.

His teaching was accurate also. He had all the facts straight about the life and ministry of Jesus, as well as about His death and resurrection. But the only baptism he knew was the baptism of John, a baptism which expressed and declared a person's own repentance.

This suggests he must have heard the facts about Jesus from one of the witnesses of Christ's resurrection who, like many of the over 500 (1 Corinthians 15:6), did not come to Jerusalem and were not present at the outpouring of the Holy Spirit on the Day of Pentecost.

**26. And he began to speak boldly in the synagogue:** ...This man began to speak out fearlessly, —TCNT ...He began to speak freely, —BRKL ...speak out with confidence, —FNTN ...preaching ...without fear, —BB ...in the meeting-house, —WMCK

**whom when Aquila and Priscilla had heard, they took him unto them:** ...took him home, —TCNT ...took him aside, —PHLP ...made friends with him, —KNOX.

**and expounded unto him the way of God more perfectly:** ...and explained more accurately to him what the Way of God really meant, —MOFT ...and gave him fuller teaching about, —BB ...more correctly, —SWAN ...more particularly, —KNOX.

**18:26.** Apollos was excited about what he did know about Jesus, however. So he began to speak boldly and freely in the synagogue, pouring out his heart as he endeavored to show from the Scriptures that Jesus is the Messiah, the Christ.

Priscilla and Aquila were present in the synagogue service and heard him. They did not say anything to him in the synagogue to embarrass him. But they could not let him go on spreading a message that did not tell the fullness of what the gospel provides. So they took him aside to give him further instruction. The Greek also implies that they welcomed him and probably took him home with them to share the fellowship of the Sabbath feast around their table. Then they explained God's way to him more precisely. Just what they said the Bible does not say here, but the next chapter deals with 12 disciples who were in the same position, with the same need for instruction, and details are given there.

It is interesting to note that John Chrysostom ("John of the golden mouth," so nicknamed because of his oratory), the chief pastor of the church in Constantinople about A.D. 400, recognized that Priscilla took the lead in giving this instruction to Apollos. Apollos was a man of culture and education. Priscilla also must have been well educated and a very gracious woman. Paul's epistles also indicate she was, along with her husband, a fellow-worker and missionary.

**27. And when he was disposed to pass into Achaia:** ... When he wanted to cross to Greece, *—TCNT* ... Then, as he had made up his mind to, *—WEYM* ... of Southern Greece, *—EVRD.*

**the brethren wrote, exhorting the disciples to receive him:** ... urgently wrote unto the disciples to welcome him, *—RTHM* ... to the disciples in Corinth, begging them to give him a kindly welcome, *—WEYM* ... the Brethren furthered his plans, and wrote to the disciples there to welcome him, *—TCNT.*

**who, when he was come, helped them much which had believed through grace:** ... On his arrival he proved of great assistance to those who had, through the loving-kindness of God, become believers in Christ, *—TCNT* ... On his arrival he proved a source of great strength to those who had believed through grace, *—PHLP* ... was a welcome reinforcement to the believers, *—KNOX.*

**18:27.** That Apollos responded to the instruction he received is shown by the letters of recommendation the Christian brethren in Ephesus wrote for him when he wanted to go over to Achaia (Greece).

This statement shows that a church had been established in Ephesus by this time. Paul had preached in the synagogue only one Sabbath. Priscilla and Aquila must have been effective witnesses and must have been the ones God used to establish and train the church. Apollos probably stayed for a while also and by his powerful presentation of the Scriptures convinced quite a number more to take their stand for Christ.

In Greece the Holy Spirit made the ministry of Apollos effective. He became a channel of grace to help the believers. The words "through grace" may apply either to Apollos or to the Corinthian believers. That is, it may mean he was of great assistance through or because of the grace of God that was manifest in his life and preaching. Or it may mean that he was a great help to those who had already believed through grace. The use of the Greek perfect tense here indicates they had already believed before Apollos came. Actually, nothing in the context prevents the application of the phrase "through grace" to both Apollos and the Grecian believers.

**28. For he mightily convinced the Jews, and that publickly:** ... vigorously confuted, *—TCNT* ... successfully refuted the Jews in public, *—WLMS* ... He was a powerful debater and openly refuted, *—NORL* ... clearly proved, *—EVRD* ... He argued very convincingly in public, *—SEB* ... powerfully and in public overcame the Jews in argument, *—WEYM* ... for with great force he came out ahead in his public discussions with the Jews, *—BRKL* ... Publicly and vigorously he proved the Jews were wrong, *—BECK.*

**shewing by the scriptures:** ... proving by, *—TCNT* ... quoting from the scriptures to prove, *—PHLP* ... as he showed from the Bible, *—BECK.*

**that Jesus was Christ:** ... that Jesus is the promised Saviour, *—BECK* ... is the Messiah, *—SEB.*

**18:28.** One of the chief ways Apollos helped the believers was by vigorously and powerfully refuting the arguments of the unbelieving Jews, showing by the Scriptures that Jesus is the Messiah, the Christ, God's promised Prophet, Priest, and King. This strengthened the faith of the ones who had already believed.

In most of the churches in Greece it is probable that the believers gave God the glory for this help, recognizing it was indeed God who was giving the increase. But in Corinth some of the believers became enamored with Apollos and began to consider themselves his followers. Others reacted by expressing their loyalty to Paul. Still others declared themselves followers of Cephas (Peter). A fourth group may have decided to follow no man and thought themselves more spiritual, naming themselves the Christ party.

# Chapter 19

**1. And it came to pass, that, while Apollos was at Corinth:** ... During the stay of apollos in Corinth, *—WEYM* ... And it came about that while, *—BB.*

**Paul having passed through the upper coasts came to Ephesus:** ... Paul travelled over the hills to get to Ephesus, *—BECK* ... was visiting some places on the way, *—NCV* ... passed through the interior of, *—NAB* ... finished his journey through the inland country, *—KNOX* ... along the northern route to, *—SEB* ... passed through the highland district, *—FNTN.*

**and finding certain disciples:** ... There he found some disciples, *—TCNT* ... found a few followers, *—NLTG* ... where he found a few disciples, *—WEYM.*

**19:1.** After Paul visited the churches of South Galatia founded on his first missionary journey, he passed through the upper or higher-lying regions on his way to Ephesus instead of taking the main road through the fever-ridden valleys.

At Ephesus he found a group of 12 disciples. There can be no doubt that these disciples were truly godly and pious people, but there is much discussion whether they should be regarded as believers in the New Testament meaning (Christians), or if they still lived in an Old Testament relationship with God. Some writers believe they were disciples of John the Baptist, but one objection to this is that everywhere else in Acts, "disciples" means followers of Jesus. Others think these 12 men were won to Christ by Apollos, before Priscilla and Aquila instructed him (18:25), but then one may wonder why they were not more informed about the Holy Spirit at a later time.

**2. He said unto them:** . . . He asked them, —WEYM . . . to whom he put the question, —NAB.

**Have ye received the Holy Ghost:** . . . Did you get the Holy Spirit, —BB.

**since ye believed?:** . . . when you first believed, —WEYM . . . on your becoming believers, —BRKL . . . when you learned to believe? —KNOX . . . when you put your trust in Christ? —NLTG . . . when you had faith? —BB.

**And they said unto him, We have not so much as heard whether there be any Holy Ghost:** . . . These followers answered him, —SEB . . . On the contrary, —FNTN . . . Nay! not even whether there is Holy Spirit did we hear, —RTHM . . . No, they said, we never even heard of its existence, —MOFT . . . nobody even mentioned to us the existence of, —KNOX . . . we have had no knowledge of, —BB.

**19:2.** The narrative implies Paul discerned something was missing in their spiritual life. His question, "Have ye received the Holy Ghost since ye believed?" indicates they were missing the New Testament gift of the Holy Spirit. Because the final phrase translates an aorist participle, *pisteusantes*, one possible interpretation is "having believed" or "after you believed did you receive the Holy Spirit?" The tense of the participle normally shows its relation to the main verb. Frequently, the aorist participle indicates action that occurs prior to the action of the main verb. In this case, the implication is that belief (i.e., conversion) came prior to receiving the Holy Spirit. However, there are examples of an aorist participle whose action occurs at the same time as the main verb. The sentence would then read, "Did you receive the Holy Spirit *when* you believed?" The answer to Paul's question was quite surprising: "We have not so much as heard whether there be any Holy Ghost." If these men were followers of John, it is difficult to understand why they would not have heard about the Holy Spirit (cf. Matthew 3:11; Mark 1:8; Luke 3:16; John 1:33; Acts 1:5). It might be they probably knew about this element of John's message, but word had not yet reached them that the Holy Spirit had come as Jesus promised He would (Luke 24:49; Acts 1:8; see also John 7:39).

**3. And he said unto them, Unto what then were ye baptized?:** . . . What then was your baptism? Paul asked, —TCNT . . . What kind of baptism, —KLST . . . How were you baptized? —NLTG . . . Into what, then, were ye immersed? —WORL . . . What kind of immersion, —SEB . . . What sort of baptism, —BB . . . did you have? —EVRD.

**And they said, Unto John's baptism:** . . . The way John baptized, —NLTG . . . that John taught, —NCV.

**19:3.** Paul's second question is interesting. It shows he assumed these disciples had been baptized. But as they told that they had no knowledge about the Holy Spirit, Paul naturally must have wondered what kind of baptism they had received. Since Christian baptism is in the name of the Father and the Son and the Holy Ghost (Matthew 28:19), they would have known of the Holy Spirit if this was the way they were baptized. So Paul asked, "Unto what then were ye baptized?" It hardly came as a surprise to him when they said they were baptized with the baptism of John.

**4. Then said Paul, John verily baptized with the baptism of repentance:** . . . John . . . administered a baptism of repentance, —WEYM . . . John's baptism was a baptism upon repentance, —TCNT . . . a baptism that was an expression of repentance, —WLMS . . . was a baptism of changed hearts and lives, —EVRD . . . John baptized those who were sorry for their sins, —BECK . . . for conversion, —FNTN . . . which goes with a change of heart, —BB.

**saying unto the people:** . . . telling the people, —MOFT . . . bidding the people, —WEYM . . . but he always told the people, —PHLP.

**that they should believe:** . . . they were to have faith, —BB . . . they must believe, —PHLP . . . to put their trust, —NEB.

**on him which should come after him, that is, on Christ Jesus:** . . . Who followed him, —FNTN . . . on One who was to come after him; namely, on Jesus, —WEYM.

**19:4.** Paul explained that John's baptism was only preparatory, a baptism of repentance, that is, a baptism that testified to their repentance (cf. Luke 7:30). John refused to baptize those who did not repent (Matthew 3:7, 8). John himself told the people they should believe in the Coming One, Jesus. Apparently, this is what these 12 men did; Paul said they "believed" (verse 2). Paul seems to have no doubt they were genuine disciples. Still he did not accept their baptism as the Christian baptism which Jesus ordained after His death and resurrection.

**5. When they heard this:** . . . On hearing this, —RSV.

**they were baptized:** . . . immersed, —RTHM.

**in the name of the Lord Jesus:** . . . by the authority of, —SEB . . . into the Faith of the Lord Jesus, —TCNT.

**19:5.** Then, having heard, "they were baptized in the name of the Lord Jesus." They not only listened, they understood and obeyed. This is the only occasion in the New Testament where it is recorded that people received two baptisms. Paul must have further explained the meaning of Christian baptism, including identification with Jesus in His death and resurrection. (See Romans 6:3, 4.)

The phrase "in the name of the Lord Jesus" means they were baptized into the worship and service of Jesus, making Him Lord of their lives. This short designation is used several times for

Christian baptism. Because Jesus is the revealer of the Father (John 17:6) and the one who baptizes in the Holy Spirit (Matthew 3:11), the baptism "in Jesus name" should not be understood or interpreted as being opposed to baptism in the name of the Trinity. This expression in no way cancels the baptismal formula given by the Lord himself in Matthew 28:19. To do so would be like asserting that Romans 10:13 is in opposition to Acts 16:31 since the first says those who *call upon* the name of the Lord will be saved, and the latter states salvation is based on *belief in* Christ.

**6. And when Paul had laid his hands upon them:** . . . and, after Paul had placed his hands on them, *—TCNT.*
**the Holy Ghost came on them:** . . . the Holy Ghost came on them, *—TCNT* . . . came down, *—NAB.*
**and they spake with tongues, and prophesied:** . . . began speaking with tongues and prophesying, *—RTHM* . . . began to speak with tongues, *—TCNT* . . . in different languages, *—EVRD* . . . they had the power of talking . . . and acting like prophets, *—BB* . . . and they started to talk in other languages and to speak God's Word, *—BECK* . . . started to talk in special sounds, *—NLTG* . . . spoke languages and preached, *—FNTN* . . . and to utter prophecies, *—NAB.*

**19:6.** After Paul laid his hands on them, the Holy Spirit came upon them. What happened relates to earlier narratives in Acts which tell of an outpouring of the Spirit, variously referred to as a "baptism in the Spirit" (1:5), a "filling with" the Spirit (2:4), the Spirit "falling upon" believers (8:16; 10:44).

As in Samaria (8:17, 18) the Spirit was given through laying on of the apostle's hands. In the house of Cornelius the coming of the Spirit was spontaneous (chapter 10). This shows that laying on of hands was not in itself the cause of the giving of the Spirit. However, one cannot diminish the importance of laying on hands as a means or medium of imparting spiritual power, authority, or gifts (see Numbers 27:15-18; Mark 6:5; 16:18; Acts 8:18; 13:3; 28:8; 1 Timothy 4:14; 2 Timothy 1:6).

**7. And all the men were about twelve:** . . . There were about twelve of them in all, *—RSV* . . . These men numbered about, *—KLST* . . . In this group there were about, *—SEB.*

**19:7.** The number of these disciples was not large. It came to the sum total of about 12 men. There could have been 11 or 13. The exact number is not important, but their experience of the baptism in the Holy Spirit with the evidence of speaking in tongues is. Women are not mentioned, and since Luke usually mentioned them when they were present, it may be assumed that all were men.

**8. And he went into the synagogue:** . . . Paul went to the synagogue there, *—TCNT* . . . Then Paul made his way, *—PHLP.*
**and spake boldly for the space of three months:** . . . and for three months spoke out fearlessly, *—TCNT* . . . continued to preach fearlessly, *—WEYM* . . . courageously spoke, *—WLMS* . . . spoke with utmost confidence, *—PHLP* . . . debated, *—NAB.*
**disputing and persuading:** . . . giving addresses and trying to convince, *—TCNT* . . . persuasivley discussing, *—BRKL* . . . arguing and pleading about, *—RSV* . . . using both argument and persuasion, *—PHLP* . . . with persuasive arguments, *—NAB.*
**the things concerning the kingdom of God:**

**19:8.** On the following Sabbath Paul went to the synagogue. He was following his usual practice of going to the Jew first. But in this case he was also fulfilling his promise that he would return to the Ephesus synagogue and speak to them further (18:21).

For 3 months he was able to speak to them boldly, freely, fearlessly, and openly. No one stopped him as he "disputed" (preached and conducted discussions), seeking to persuade of the things concerning the kingdom of God. He brought reasonable proofs from the Old Testament Scriptures to show that the kingdom (rule, authority) of God is revealed in Jesus, who was now ascended to the right hand of the Father, seated at the Father's throne (2:30-33). Looking ahead to 20:24, 25, it is clear that the kingdom or royal rule and royal authority and reign of God is parallel to the gospel or the good news of the grace of God. Romans 14:17 shows that Paul must have dealt with righteousness (including righteous deeds, and the uprightness or righteousness based on faith and bestowed by God; the righteousness of Christ in which we stand), peace (harmony, order, and the well-being that comes with the salvation brought by Christ), and joy in the Holy Spirit (the joy that believers have as the result of the work of the Spirit in their lives).

**9. But when divers were hardened, and believed not:** . . . But when some, *—ASV* . . . were hardening themselves and refusing to be persuaded, *—RTHM* . . . When some in their obstinacy would not believe, *—NAB* . . . grew obstinate in unbelief, *—WEYM* . . . some obstinately resisted and disbelieved, *—FNTN* . . . grew harder and harder, *—WLMS.*
**but spake evil of that way before the multitude:** . . . denouncing the Cause before the people, *—TCNT* . . . what is more, spoke offensively about the way in public, *—PHLP* . . . actually criticizing, *—WLMS* . . . and slandered the Christian religion before the crowd, *—BECK* . . . and cursed the way of God, *—LAMS* . . . in the presence of the assembly, *—NAB.*
**he departed from them:** . . . he turned from them, *—BRKL* . . . Paul simply left them, *—NAB.*

**and separated the disciples:** ...and withdrew his disciples, —TCNT...and, taking with him those who were disciples, —WEYM.

**disputing daily in the school of one Tyrannus:** ...and gave daily addresses in the lecture-hall of Tyrannus, —TCNT...and went on holding daily discussions, —BRKL.

**19:9.** It took a little longer than usual in Ephesus, but eventually some (a number, but not the majority) of the unconverted Jews became hardened (obstinate, unyielding) and disobedient (rebellious). They showed their rebellious spirit by publicly speaking evil of the Way, that is, of the Christian faith and way of life, before the crowds who gathered to hear the gospel and packed out the synagogue. (It may be implied also that they spread their insults and vile comments through the whole community at Ephesus.)

"The Way" is significant in that it includes the whole of Christian teaching and comprehends all that Christianity and the gospel means. It is truly the better way, the one and only way of salvation.

The opposition of the unbelievers did not discourage Paul. He had learned to expect it. So he simply withdrew from them, separating the disciples (the ones who had set themselves apart to follow Jesus and learn more of Him) and taking them away (from the unbelieving Jews in the synagogue).

Then Paul found a separate place for the disciples to meet, in the schoolroom or lecture hall of Tyrannus. There, instead of meeting only on the Sabbath, Paul preached and taught the gospel daily, conducting discussions with all who would come.

**10.** **And this continued by the space of two years:** ... for two years, —RTHM ... This went on, —TCNT ... kept up, —BRKL.

**so that all they which dwelt in Asia heard the word of the Lord Jesus, both Jews and Greeks:** ... Thus all the inhabitants ... were acquainted with, —NOLI ... so that the whole population of the province, —MLNT ... so that everyone who lived in, —GDSP.

**19:10.** Paul continued these daily discussions and teaching sessions for a period of 2 years. It was his practice also to take the evenings (after 4 p.m.) as a time to go to various homes to teach and establish the believers and to help win their friends and neighbors to the Lord. (See 20:20.)

The result was that the whole of the Roman province of Asia was evangelized. Both Jews and Gentiles from all directions came in to the schoolroom and heard the Word.

Many other churches were established. Since Ephesus was a great center, people came from all over the province for business, trade, tourism, and various other reasons. Many of them were converted, filled with the Holy Spirit, and taught by Paul. Then they went back to their home cities and towns where the Spirit filled them with zeal and made them powerful witnesses for Christ, each one a nucleus for a new church which soon grew up in their homes.

**11.** **And God wrought special miracles:** ...God also continued to do such wonderworks, —WLMS...God gave most unusual demonstrations of power, —PHLP...special works of power, —BB...miracles of an unusual kind, —NEB...extraordinary miracles, —NOLI ... worked more than the usual miracles, —KLST...God kept performing special miracles, —WORL...did mighty, and unusual deeds, —SWAN.

**by the hands of Paul:** ...through Paul, —WEYM...by means of Paul, —MOFT...used Paul to do, —NCV.

**19:11.** An important factor in this spread of the gospel in the Roman province of Asia was that God did special (extraordinary) miracles (powers, manifestations of divine power, deeds which showed God's power) by the hands of Paul. The Greek implies mighty miracles were an everyday occurrence in Paul's ministry here.

Notice that the Bible gives first emphasis to Paul's preaching and teaching of the Word. Paul was always wholly absorbed in the Word. Because he was, God confirmed the Word with these unusual miracles. The city of Ephesus was full of heathen priests and magicians, but these miracles so surpassed heathen trickery, overcoming the power of demons and evil spirits, that all were able to see that it was God who was with Paul.

**12.** **So that from his body were brought unto the sick handkerchiefs or aprons:** ...so that people would carry home to the sick handkerchiefs or aprons that had touched his body, —TCNT...Kerchiefs or aprons, for instance, which Paul had handled, would be carried to the sick, —WEYM...or clothing which had been in contact with his body, —PHLP...or his garments, —NOLI ... People even carried away towels or aprons he had used, —MOFT...he had handled, —MLNT...which had touched his skin, —TNT.

**and the diseases departed from them:** ... to heal the sick of their diseases, —NOLI ... and they would recover from their ailments, —WEYM.

**and the evil spirits went out of them:** ...and the wicked spirits were goint out, —RTHM ... were made to go, —BRKL ... also went out, —SWAN ... left them, —NCV.

**19:12.** So powerfully was the Lord working through Paul that people did not want to wait for him to minister to them in the lecture hall of Tyrannus. They would come to his workroom where he was busy at his tentmaking and would carry off handkerchiefs (actually, the sweat cloths he used to wipe away perspiration while he was working) and work aprons that had been used and thus had been in contact with his body (Greek, his skin). These they laid upon the sick who were then freed from their diseases. Even evil spirits (demons) came out of those who were possessed, and they too were released, set free.

It seems to be implied that the people took these sweat cloths and work aprons without asking Paul. He did not send them out. Yet he did not seem to mind when the people took them. He knew there was nothing magic about these items. He knew he was not causing the miracles anyway—God was. Paul was only a channel God was using, so he was happy for whatever means God used to bring His healing to others.

Actually, a sick person may not find it easy to express faith. If a person is helped to touch God by any means, it should be a cause for rejoicing. Such rejoicing brings glory to God.

**13. Then certain of the vagabond Jews, exorcists:** ... some itinerant Jews, who were exorcists, –TCNT ... Some Jews who made it their business to go around and drive out evil spirits, –BECK ... Some traveling Jewish exorcists, –NOLI ... Some also of the itinerant Jewish exorcists, –TNT ... some also of the wandering Jews, –WORL ... who went from place to place, –GDSP.

**took upon them to call over them which had evil spirits the name of the Lord Jesus:** ... took it upon themselves to invoke the name of, –KNOX ... to use the Name of the Lord Jesus over those who had wicked spirits in them, –TCNT ... who attempted to invoke the name of the Lord Jesus when dealing with those who had, –PHLP ... were also trying to make evil spirits go out of people, –SEB ... tried to use the name ... in the cases of people who had evil spirits in them, –GDSP ... force the evil spirits out, –EVRD.

**saying, We adjure you by Jesus whom Paul preacheth:** ... I command you by that Jesus, –WEYM ... I conjure you, –KNOX ... I solemnly charge you, –TNT ... I charge you on oath, –SWAN ... I speak to you, –NLTG ... By the same Jesus that Paul talks about, –EVRD ... I order you to come out, –SEB ... whom Paul proclaimeth! –RTHM.

**19:13.** The success of Paul's ministry and the many complete cures and deliverances God gave caught the attention of a group of seven traveling (wandering, itinerant) Jewish exorcists who, for a fee, went about claiming to be able to cast out evil spirits or demons by magical formulas. Possibly following the example of other Jewish exorcists, they took it upon themselves to pronounce the name of the Lord Jesus over those who were demon possessed in an attempt to bring deliverance.

The Bible does not imply they had been successful in their previous attempts to cast out demons

by their magical formulas. What it does show is that they tried to make a magical formula out of the name of Jesus.

It seems that when they saw Paul cast out demons and heal the sick in the name of the Lord Jesus, they jumped to the conclusion that he was using a magical formula in the same way the heathen did. They thought they would add the name of Jesus to their list. What they did not realize was that Paul, in using the name of Jesus was recognizing Jesus for who He is. Moreover, Paul was filled with the Holy Spirit and in touch with Jesus, doing the work Jesus had called him to do. He did not minister gifts of healing just for the sake of building a reputation for himself. He was preaching the gospel, the true Word of God, and the Lord was confirming the Word with signs following (Mark 16:20). Thus the Word, not the signs, had the important place.

**14. And there were seven sons of one Sceva, a Jew, and chief of the priests:** ... The seven sons of Sceva, a Jewish chief Priest, –TCNT ... A Jewish leader of the people by the name of, –NLTG ... an important Jewish priest, –SEB ... was a leading Jewish priest, –NCV.

**which did so:** ... who did this, –ASV ... who were doing this, –WEYM ... practiced this, –BRKL, –MLNT ... pronounced this formula over a sick man, –NOLI ... were engaged in this practice, –PHLP.

**19:14.** These seven were sons of Sceva (possibly a form of *shāva'*, "oath") who was designated as a Jewish high priest. The title was used of those belonging to one of the high priestly families, especially if they belonged to the Sanhedrin. It was also used of the treasurer of the temple and the captain of the temple police. It could also be used of the head of one of the 24 orders or courses of priests who took turns ministering in the temple. Some writers suggest, however, that Sceva was the head of a company who made exorcism their business and that he took the title of Jewish high priest in order to impress the heathen who would buy their services.

**15. And the evil spirit answered and said:** ... But the evil spirit retorted, –MOFT ... But on one occasion the evil spirit answered, –WLMS ... The demon said, –NLTG ... replied, –SWAN ... said to these Jews, –SEB.

**Jesus I know:** ... Jesus I acknowledge, –TCNT ... Jesus I recognize, –KNOX ... I have heard about Jesus, –SEB.

**and Paul I know:** ... I understand, –HBIE, –SWAN, –WORL ... and I am acquainted with Paul, –PHLP ... I know about Paul, –NLTG ... Paul I know well enough, –KNOX.

**but who are ye?:** ... but who on earth are you, –PHLP ... but I do not know you, –NOLI.

**19:15.** The attempt to use the name of Jesus as a magic formula failed. The evil spirit answered, "Jesus I know (recognize, know about), and Paul I know (I know of, I understand who he is), but as for you, who are you?" (Two different words for "know" are used here.) Thus, the demon recognized that these sons of Sceva only knew Jesus as the name of someone whom Paul was preaching. They did not know Jesus for themselves. They had never come to a place of faith in Jesus as their own Lord and Saviour. The devil knows when there is faith. He is not deceived by ritual or formulas or mere words. It takes the power of Jesus made manifest by the Holy Spirit for evil spirits to tremble and flee.

Notice here also there is a clear distinction between the man in whom the evil spirit was and the evil spirit itself. The man was no longer in control of his senses. The evil spirit or demon who possessed him had taken charge and was able to use the man's speech organs to answer these sons of Sceva.

**16. And the man in whom the evil spirit was:** ... spirit dwelt, —MLNT ... in whom the evil spirit resided, —KJII ... in whom the evil spirit was living, —PHLP ... who had the evil spirit in him, —NCV.

**leaped on them:** ... sprang on them, —TCNT ... flew at them, —NEB ... jumped on these Jews, —NCV.

**and overcame them:** ... overpowered them all, —MOFT ... overcoming them both, —WORL ... He was much stronger than all of them, —NCV ... He gained the upper hand, —TNT ... gained the mastery over them all, —SWAN.

**and prevailed against them:** ... and so completely overpowered them, —TCNT ... and treated them with such violence, —WEYM ... and compelled them to rush out of, —NOLI ... and overcame them all, —TNT ... He beat them, NCV.

**so that they fled out of that house naked and wounded:** ... and tore their clothes off, —NCV ... stripped of their clothes, and wounded, —TCNT ... wounded, with their clothes torn off their backs, —PHLP ... tattered and bruised, —GDSP.

**19:16.** Then the demon-possessed man leaped upon the sons of Sceva and overpowered them all. Some ancient Greek manuscripts say he leaped on (*amphoterōn*, which in earlier Greek usage, before New Testament times, meant "both"). In view of this, some writers suppose that only two of the seven sons of Sceva were involved in this attempt to cast out the evil spirit. However, in New Testament times *amphoterōn* was used in everyday speech to mean "all." Many ancient Greek papyrus manuscripts from secular literature confirm this. So it is most probable that all seven sons were involved.

The demon-possessed man used his strength so effectively against the seven brothers that they all

fled out of the house naked (stripped of their outer garments) and wounded. (The Greek indicates the wounds were severe enough to affect them for a while.)

It is important to notice that this evil spirit had such power over this man that it was able to use the man's strength in a superhuman way. Casting out demons is not something to be undertaken lightly or casually. When Jesus came down from the Mount of Transfiguration, He found His disciples unable to cast an evil spirit out of a boy. After bringing the boy's father to a place of faith, Jesus commanded the demon to come out of the boy. But the demon did not come out without a struggle. It used the boy's speech organs to give a last rebellious scream or shriek, tore him with severe convulsions, then came out leaving the boy to all appearances dead. Jesus then reached down His hand, lifted the boy, and completed the healing. (See Mark 9:25-27.) Quite clearly, evil spirits are not to be faced unless believers are sure they have the power of Christ.

**17. And this was known to all the Jews and Greeks also dwelling at Ephesus:** ... This incident came to the knowledge of all the Jews and Greeks living at Ephesus, —TCNT ... When this incident became known, —NOLI ... All the people ... learned about this, —NCV.

**and fear fell on them all:** ... they were all awe-struck, —TCNT ... They were all frightened, —BECK ... filled with fear, —NCV.

**and the name of the Lord Jesus was magnified:** ... and great honor was given to the name of, —NCV ... and the Name of the Lord Jesus was held in the highest honour, —TCNT ... and they began to hold the name of the Lord Jesus in high honor, —WEYM ... while the name of the Lord Jesus became highly respected, —PHLP ... was highly praised, —BRKL ... was extolled, —RSV.

**19:17.** The sight of the seven sons of Sceva running out into the street naked and wounded surely must have caught the attention of bystanders. They must have inquired, learned the facts, and soon the news of what had happened spread throughout Ephesus. The result was that a fear (an awe inspired by the supernatural) fell upon Jews and Greeks (Gentiles) alike. This caused the name of the Lord Jesus to be magnified (glorified, praised, held in high esteem). The "name" means the person and authority of Jesus.

It may seem strange that the people felt this way when the attempt to use the Name failed. But it let the people know that such charlatans as these sons of Sceva could not make the name of Jesus a part of their bag of tricks. They saw a great contrast between the sons of Sceva and the apostle Paul. When Paul prayed in the name of the Lord

Jesus things happened. People were set free from sickness, disease, and demons, as the case might be. So they saw that the power of the name of Jesus was a revelation of His holy nature as well as of His divine love and grace. His power was nothing to be trifled with. Moreover, His holy name demanded a holy people.

Believers do need to "try the spirits" putting them to the test of God's Word (1 John 4:1). But genuine outpourings of God's Spirit always bring glory to Jesus no matter how the devil tries to hinder. The Holy Spirit will always make people know that the name of Jesus is a name above every name.

**18. And many that believed came:** ... Many of those who had professed their faith, —PHLP ... were coming, —WORL.

**and confessed, and shewed their deeds:** ... made public statement of their sins and all their acts, —BB ... began openly to admit their former practices, —PHLP ... with a full confession of their practices, —TCNT ... began to confess openly and tell the evil deeds they had done, —NCV ... giving a full account of them, —KNOX.

**19:18.** All this had an important effect on the believers also. Many of them came confessing and publicly reporting their deeds. The Greek indicates they now came out and out for the Lord (with a total commitment). They realized their need for holiness and righteousness as well as for salvation.

**19. Many of them also which used curious arts:** ... that practiced magical arts, —ASV ... while a number of people, who had practiced magic, —TCNT ... Numbers also of the professors of magic rites, —FNTN.

**brought their books together:** ... collected their books, —TCNT.

**and burned them before all men:** ... and burnt them publicly, —TCNT.

**and they counted the price of them:** ... The total value was reckoned, —WEYM ... They added up the cost of these books, —BECK ... Those books were worth about, —NCV.

**and found it fifty thousand pieces of silver:** ... came to about twenty-five thousand dollars, —NORL ... 50,000 silver coins, —NCV.

**19:19.** Another result was the fact that they now realized the true power over evil was only in Jesus. Ephesus was a center for the practice of magical arts, especially the putting of spells on people or things. A considerable number of the new believers had practiced magic, including attempts at foretelling or influencing the future. Most of them still had the books they used hidden away. (Archaeologists have discovered books of this kind.)

Now the believers saw that these books with their formulas, spells, and astrological forecasts, were of no value whatsoever. In fact, they were purely heathen, even demonic, in their origin. So they brought together all their books and burned them publicly. Books were very expensive in those days, and when they reckoned up the total price of the books it came to 50,000 pieces of silver (no specific coin is mentioned, though some believe it was the drachma). This was as much as 200 day laborers or soldiers would earn in a year.

**20. So mightily grew the word of God and prevailed:** ... So irresistibly did the Lord's message spread and prevail, —TCNT ... Thus mightily did the Lord's word spread and triumph, —WEYM ... In a way of just such power as this the Lord's message kept on spreading and increasing, —WLMS ... So in a powerful way the word of the Lord kept spreading and growing, —NCV.

**19:20.** Luke's account of this incident concludes the story of the success of the gospel in Ephesus. But it was the Word of the Lord (the Word concerning Jesus) that grew mightily (with divine might and power) and prevailed (in a healthy, vigorous way). The fact that later (20:17) there was a large number of elders in the church at Ephesus shows there were many house churches and that the whole church there continued to grow in a healthy way.

**21. After these things were ended:** ... Sometime after these events, —TCNT ... When matters had reached this point, —WEYM ... With these aims accomplished, —BRKL.

**Paul purposed in the spirit:** ... resolved in his spirit, —MNTG ... the thought in Paul's heart was to go to, —KNOX ... set his heart on going, —PHLP.

**when he had passed through Macedonia:** ... to go through Macedonia and Greece, —TCNT.

**to go to Jerusalem:** ... and then make his way to Jerusalem, —TCNT ... en route to Jerusalem, —KLST.

**saying, After I have been there, I must also see Rome:** ... I have a desire to, —BB ... After these journeys, I must visit, —NOLI ... I must see Rome as well, —PHLP.

**19:21.** Paul himself felt these things brought not just an end but a fulfillment to his ministry in Ephesus. "Ended" is literally "fulfilled" and indicates he had carried out the ministry he came to accomplish. The tremendous growth of the church during the previous more than 2 years and the training of the people and their leaders meant he could leave them now with confidence and go on to another place of ministry.

Paul's epistles show there had been problems. He says he fought with the "beasts" at Ephesus (1 Corinthians 15:32). This probably means he risked his life opposing men who acted like beasts. He also says he suffered such affliction in Asia (that is, in Ephesus) that he despaired of life but was delivered by God (2 Corinthians 1:8-10).

Now that everything was going well, Paul purposed in the spirit (or, in the Holy Spirit) to visit Rome (see Romans 1:11, 14, 15; 15:22-25). But he would first revisit the churches of Macedonia and Greece and take their offering to the Jerusalem church (Acts 24:17; Romans 15:26; 1 Corinthians 16:1-4). That purpose was finally realized but not quite the way Paul expected.

"In the spirit" usually means in the Holy Spirit. (In New Testament times the Greek did not distinguish between capital and lower case letters.) It is likely that Paul's own spirit was in harmony with the Holy Spirit and submissive to Him. His purpose was thus a God-planned purpose. This is further confirmed by the statement "I must see Rome." The Greek indicates a divine necessity laid upon Paul. He did not know yet how God was going to get him to Rome. But from this point Rome was the objective in view.

**22. So he sent into Macedonia:** . . . So he dispatched, –MOFT . . . ahead to, –NCV.

**two of them that ministered unto him:** . . . two of his assistants, –SWAN, –WEYM . . . two of his helpers, –NCV.

**Timotheus and Erastus; but he himself stayed in Asia for a season:** . . . remained for a while in Roman Asia, –WEYM . . . remained for some time longer in Asia, –MLNT.

**19:22.** That Paul's purpose to go to Rome was indeed pleasing to the Lord was confirmed later by Jesus himself (23:11) and by an angel (27:23, 24).

To prepare the churches in Macedonia for his visit, Paul sent Timothy and Erastus (Greek, "beloved") on ahead. Erastus was a convert who had probably been a high official in Corinth, possibly the city treasurer. He later joined Paul in sending greetings to the Roman converts (Romans 16:23; see 2 Timothy 4:20).

Paul himself stayed for a time in Ephesus. As he told the Corinthians, a great door and an effectual one was still open to him, but there were many adversaries (1 Corinthians 16:8, 9). Perhaps he had in mind some of the "beasts" he had been fighting.

**23. And the same time:** . . . And about that time, –ASV . . . But in process of time, –BRKL . . . During that time, –BECK . . . Just at that time, –GDSP.

**there arose no small stir:** . . . no small disturbance, –RTHM . . . there was some serious trouble, –NCV . . . no small commotion, –WEYM . . . no small tumult, –HBIE . . . a great riot, –NORL . . . the cause of a notable disturbance, –KNOX.

**about that way:** . . . concerning the Christians, –TALR . . . about the Road, –KLGS . . . the Way of Jesus, –NCV.

**19:23.** Just how many adversaries there were in Ephesus soon became apparent. Luke spoke of what happened next as no small stir (disturbance, tumult). Actually, it was an uprising that might easily have resulted in Paul's death.

**24. For a certain man named Demetrius, a silversmith:** . . . A silversmith named Demetrius, –TCNT . . . a silver-beater, –DRBY . . . who worked with silver, –NCV.

**which made silver shrines for Diana:** . . . who made models of the shrine of Artemis, –TCNT . . . silver boxes for the images of Diana, –BB . . . by manufacturing silver shrines of Artemis, –WLMS . . . made miniature silver shrines, –WEYM . . . silver models of, –KNOX . . . that looked like the temple of the goddess, –NCV.

**brought no small gain unto the craftsmen:** . . . men who did this work made much money, –NCV . . . a business which brought great profits to the craftsmen in his employ, –WEYM . . . was making large profits for his workmen, –GDSP . . . and provided the artisans with no small income, –BRKL . . . provided the artisans with a large income, –MLNT . . . no little gain to, –SWAN.

**19:24.** The disturbance started through the efforts of a silversmith named Demetrius. His chief product, like that of most silversmiths in Ephesus, was a small silver shrine of Artemis containing a miniature image of this many-breasted fertility goddess of Ephesus. These were used as amulets and charms. Many of them had tiny silver lions in attendance on the goddess. Others may have been models of the temple of Artemis with its 127 columns, many of which were beautifully carved. There is some evidence also that Demetrius and his fellow silversmiths were part of a guild connected with the temple and its priesthood. Most heathen temples in those days carried on large business enterprises. The temple at Ephesus was one of the seven wonders of the ancient world.

This Ephesian goddess actually had no relation to the other Artemis, the Artemis of Greece known as the maiden huntress and identified by the Romans with their goddess Diana (the daughter of Jupiter and Latona; the twin sister of Apollo; she was the Roman goddess of the moon and of hunting).

**25. Whom he called together:** . . . called a general meeting of his own men, –JB.

**with the workmen of like occupation:** . . . as well as the workmen engaged in similar occupations, –TCNT . . . and others who did similar work, –BECK.

**and said Sirs:** . . . Men, –RSV.

**ye know:** . . . you understand, –BRKL.

**that by this craft we have our wealth:** . . . this trade is the source of our prosperity, —*TCNT* . . . that by this business we make our money, —*MNTG* . . . we're getting a fine income from this business, —*BECK*.

**19:25.** Because sales of the shrines were falling off, Demetrius gathered all his fellow craftsmen together and made a speech. He began by appealing to their self-interest, "Men, you understand that by this business (trade) we get our prosperity." The Greek also implies they knew this was the way to earn a good living.

The way Demetrius began by stirring up self-interest shows their chief concern was not the worship or the honor of the goddess, but their own prosperity. Their attachment to the goddess was simply to make it a means of gain for themselves.

The apostle Paul warned Timothy that even Christians can fall into this same attitude. He warned against those who suppose "gain is godliness," that is, who suppose that the profession of Christianity is a means of making money or getting prestige. He was speaking of false teachers who make a show of their religion in order to collect large sums of money for themselves (1 Timothy 6:5). Then he called on believers to turn away from such teachers to real godliness, that is, to a godly faith that shows itself in devotion and duty, in service to the Lord and other believers in practical ways. This kind of godliness brings a contentment that comes from an inner sufficiency through the full appropriation of God's provisions for the inner man and which is therefore independent of outward circumstances. This benefits in every way. (See 1 Timothy 4:8.)

**26. Moreover ye see and hear:** . . . If you use your eyes and ears you also know, —*PHLP*.

**that not alone at Ephesus, but almost throughout all Asia:** . . . that not only at Ephesus, but in almost the whole of Roman Asia, —*TCNT* . . . the whole province of Asia, —*WEYM* . . . practically throughout Asia, —*PHLP* . . . the mass of all Asia, —*MRDK*.

**this Paul hath persuaded and turned away much people:** . . . has convinced and won over great numbers of people, —*TCNT* . . . this fellow Paul has led away a vast number of people, —*WEYM* . . . has succeeded in changing the minds of a great number of people, —*PHLP* . . . and enticed away, —*MRDK*.

**saying that they be no gods, which are made with hands:** . . . He declares that handmade gods are not gods at all, —*MOFT* . . . by persuading them that manufactured gods are not real gods, —*BRKL*.

**19:26.** The next words of Demetrius are a testimony to the power and effectiveness of the gospel. Paul's message had a great effect not only in the city of Ephesus, it had permeated practically the entire Roman province of Asia.

Getting the people to listen to the Old Testament prophets would be sufficient to persuade many of them that the gods, that is the idols were nothings. Isaiah 40:18-20 shows the true God is not to be compared with idols. With tremendous irony Isaiah pictured a rich man hiring a workman to cast and shape an image and then hiring a goldsmith to overlay it with gold. Then he has silver chains made to hold it up. After all, a rich man would not want his goldplated god to fall over! The poor man, of course, could not afford a goldplated god, so he goes out and cuts down a tree that would not rot and has a wooden god made with a broad base so it would not fall over. It would be a shame if his wooden god fell over and rotted!

**27. So that not only this our craft is in danger to be set at nought:** . . . So that not only is this business of ours likely to fall into discredit, —*TCNT* . . . will lose its reputation, —*WLMS* . . . will get a bad name, —*TEV*.

**but also that the temple of the great goddess Diana should be despised:** . . . but there is further danger that the Temple of the great goddess Artemis will be thought nothing of, —*TCNT* . . . her magnificence destroyed, —*NOYS* . . . will fall into utter disrepute, —*WEYM* . . . might come to be lightly regarded, —*PHLP*.

**and her magnificence should be destroyed:** . . . will soon be dethroned from her majestic glory! —*WLMS* . . . and so she . . . will have all her grandeur destroyed, —*NORL* . . . and then she . . . will be robbed of her glory, —*BECK* . . . her actual majesty might be degraded, —*PHLP* . . . It could end up by taking away all the prestige of a goddess venerated, —*JB* . . . will be shorn of her majestic rank, —*KLST* . . . will even be deposed from her greatness, —*TNT*.

**whom all Asia and the world worshippeth:** . . . she who is now worshipped by the whole province of Asia; nay, by the whole world, —*WEYM* . . . and all the world reveres, —*KNOX* . . . the world worship will be a thing of the past! —*GDSP*.

**19:27.** Because of Paul's message, the sales of the shrines were diminishing, and the trade of idol making was in danger of falling into disrepute, as more and more people were rejecting the idols and refuting their value.

Verse 37 indicates Paul may not have openly criticized either the silversmiths, their shrines, or their goddess. He preached Christ and taught the people of the greatness and power of the one true God who is our Creator and Redeemer. Nevertheless, 14:15 shows that he was bold in preaching against idols (cf. 17:22-31).

Then secondarily, Demetrius said something about their goddess. Again his purpose was still to stir up their self-interest. Thus he claimed that the temple of the goddess Artemis (called "Diana of the Ephesians" in KJV, verse 28) was in danger of being accounted as nothing. The goddess itself was also in danger of having its divine majesty (magnificence) diminished (or, destroyed).

Then Demetrius made the exaggerated claim that not only the whole province of Asia, but all the (inhabited) world worshiped it. It may be that many visitors did come from other parts of the Roman Empire, and while in Ephesus visited the magnificent temple and joined in the worship of the goddess. But there is little evidence that she was worshiped or revered elsewhere.

The heathen gods and goddesses were always considered to be limited in their power and in their sphere of activity. Most were considered to have more power in the area dominated by the temples or in the countries where they were especially worshiped. None were believed to be omnipotent, and certainly not everywhere present.

**28. And when they heard these sayings:** . . . After listening to this harangue, *−WEYM* . . . As they listened, *−BRKL* . . . When the workers heard this speech, *−NOLI.*

**they were full of wrath:** . . . the men were greatly enraged, *−TCNT* . . . they all became furiously angry, *−WEYM* . . . all overcome with rage, *−KNOX.*

**and cried out, saying:** . . . and began shouting, *−TCNT* . . . and cried out again and again, *−MNTG.*

**Great is Diana of the Ephesians:** . . . Great is Artemis of Ephesus! *−NCV.*

**19:28.** This speech, as Demetrius hoped, brought an outburst of passionate wrath among the silversmiths. They began crying out (and kept crying out again and again) with great emotion, "Great is Artemis (Diana, KJV) of the Ephesians."

The great wealth and prominence of the city of Ephesus was largely due to its great temple. The image was originally of wood (possibly ebony). Later images were of stone or metal. The image had a headdress representing a fortified city wall. From the headdress hung drapery on each side of her face to her shoulders. Rows of breasts completely covered the upper part of the body designating her as the mother goddess, the source of all life in their tradition.

The temple was also a museum where the finest statuary and the most beautiful paintings were preserved. It also employed a large number of people, including these silversmiths. Their livelihood, and the livelihood of many others, depended on making people believe Artemis of the Ephesians was great.

**29. And the whole city was filled with confusion:** . . . Then the city was agitated from end to

end, *−BRKL* . . . Soon the whole city was in an uproar, *−PHLP* . . . became confused, *−NCV.*

**and having caught Gaius and Aristarchus:** . . . and having seized, *−ASV* . . . The people grabbed, *−NCV* . . . carrying off with them, *−RTHM* . . . dragging with them, *−TCNT.*

**men of Macedonia, Paul's companions in travel:** . . . two Macedonians who were Paul's travelling companions, *−TCNT* . . . These two men . . . were traveling with Paul, *−NCV.*

**they rushed with one accord into the theatre:** . . . and the people rushed together into the amphitheatre, *−TCNT* . . . they jointly stormed, *−BRKL* . . . ran to, *−NCV* . . . and by a common impulse, *−GDSP.*

**19:29.** The Greek indicates the silversmiths kept up their shouting until their chant filled the whole city with confusion and disturbance. The result was that they all rushed into the theater which was a Greek-style amphitheater, stadium, or arena, open to the sky with room to seat 25,000 people.

First, however, they seized Gaius and Aristarchus, Macedonians who were among Paul's traveling companions. Their presence shows Paul's company was considerably larger on this missionary journey than on his earlier travels. These two were seized and dragged into the amphitheater because the crowd's anger was stirred against Paul, and they recognized these men as Paul's associates.

**30. And when Paul would have entered in unto the people:** . . . Paul wished to go into the amphitheatre and face the people, *−TCNT* . . . wanted to speak to the people himself, *−NOLI* . . . and address the people, *−WEYM.*

**the disciples suffered him not:** . . . would not hear of it, *−NORL* . . . restrained him, *−MRDK* . . . would not allow him to do so, *−NOLI* . . . tried to prevent it, *−KNOX.*

**19:30.** When Paul wanted to go in among the tumultuous crowd, the disciples would not let him. Paul probably wanted to make a defense before the crowd. But the disciples (the Christians) were concerned about his safety.

**31. And certain of the chief of Asia:** . . . the principal officers of Asia, *−WSLY* . . . Some of the Asiarchs, *−KLST* . . . some of the delegates of Asia, *−KNOX* . . . Some of the religious authorities also, *−GDSP* . . . some leaders of Asia, *−NCV.*

**which were his friends:** . . . being his friends, *−ASV* . . . friends of his, *−GDSP.*

**sent unto him, desiring him that he would not adventure himself into the theatre:** . . . also sent to beg him, *−MOFT* . . . sent him warning, *−BRKL* . . . not to venture, *−MNTG* . . . imploring him not to risk his life in the theatre, *−KNOX.*

**19:31.** Even some of the non-Christians were concerned for Paul's safety. Some of the Asiarchs (officials connected with Roman worship in the Province of Asia) who were friends sent him a message urging him not to offer himself in the amphitheater. No doubt they thought the crowd might tear him to pieces.

These Asiarchs were chosen from the wealthiest and most prominent citizens for an annual term, to which they might be reelected. They were delegates to the provincial council of cities, and presided over the athletic games and religious rites in the amphitheater. They were held in high honor by the people.

**32. Some therefore cried one thing, and some another:** ... Meanwhile some were shouting, *—TCNT.*
**for the assembly was confused:** ... for there was no order in the meeting, *—BB* ... for the mass meeting was just a tumult, *—BRKL* ... meeting was in confusion, *—GDSP* ... completely confused, *—NCV.*
**and the more part knew not wherefore they were come together:** ... and the majority, *—MNTG* ... and most of them, *—GDSP* ... not even knowing why they had met, *—TCNT* ... part had no idea why they had come together, *—WEYM.*

**19:32.** In the amphitheater, the crowd was still in confusion. Some were crying out one thing, some another. The major part of the assembly did not have any idea why they had come together.

The "assembly" here is the Greek *ekklēsia.* The derivation of *ekklēsia* from *ek* ("out of") and *kaleō* ("to call") shows it once had the meaning of a "called-out assembly," called out to transact official business, a sort of "town meeting." But by New Testament times, *ekklēsia* had lost the idea of being "called out." It was used in everyday Greek to mean any assembly of citizens, whether officially called, or whether it was an unruly, confused mob come together such as this one in the amphitheater.

In the New Testament, *ekklēsia* is translated "assembly" three times, all in this chapter (verses 32, 39, 41). In all other places (about 112 times) it is translated "church." But its proper meaning is still an assembly, not of citizens of Rome, but of citizens of heaven. What a contrast this is with the confused mob that made up this assembly in the amphitheater in Ephesus.

**33. And they drew Alexander out of the multitude:** ... A man called Alexander ... was pushed into the forefront of the crowd, *—PHLP* ... some brought out of the crowd Alexander, *—KLST* ... called up, *—GDSP.*
**the Jews putting him forward:** ... the Jews thrusting him forward, *—RTHM* ... whom the Jews pushed to the front, *—TCNT* ... Some of them had told him what to do, *—NCV.*
**And Alexander beckoned with the hand:** ... motioning with his hand to get silence, *—WEYM.*

**and would have made his defence unto the people:** ... wanted to defend himself before the people, *—MOFT* ... to show that he wanted to speak in their defence to the people, *—TCNT* ... tried to give an account of himself, *—KNOX* ... because he wanted to explain things to the people, *—NCV.*

**19:33.** At this point the Jews put forward Alexander out of the crowd with the intention of instructing them. They wanted Alexander to explain that the Jews were not responsible for what the Christians were doing.

Alexander was a very common Greek name and shows he was a Hellenistic Jew, well acquainted with Greek thought and Greek oratory. The Jews recognized that the wrath of the silversmiths was directed against the apostle Paul. But they also knew a riot like this could result in mob violence, and an unthinking mob could turn on them, since Paul was a Jew. The Jews were very anxious to let the mob know the Jews were completely innocent and had done nothing to stir up this riot.

Perhaps the Jews thought the name Alexander, with its reference to Alexander the Great, would command some respect from these Greek-speaking Ephesians. At least, his oratory would impress them. Some believe this Alexander was the same as Alexander the coppersmith named by Paul in 2 Timothy 4:14, 15. The Greek indicates he was a worker in copper, bronze, iron, and other metals. Secular Greek literature shows these metalsmiths also made idols, though Alexander as a Jew would not have done so. However, if this Alexander was indeed a coppersmith, it may be another reason why the Jews put him forward. As a fellow metal worker, he would be known by the silversmiths who had started this riot and hopefully might be able to influence them.

**34. But when they knew that he was a Jew:** ... But when they perceived that he was a Jew, *—ASV* ... But recognizing, *—RTHM* ... No sooner, however, did they see that he was a Jew, *—WEYM.*
**all with one voice about the space of two hours cried out:** ... one cry broke from them all, and they continued shouting for two hours, *—TCNT* ... then there arose from them all one roar of shouting, lasting about two hours, *—WEYM* ... they shouted as one man for about two hours, *—PHLP.*
**Great is Diana of the Ephesians:** ... Glory to Artemis, *—NOLI* ... Great Artemis of Ephesus! *—WLMS.*

**19:34.** Alexander did not get an opportunity to use his talents. They immediately recognized he was a Jew. Then the whole crowd went wild. With one voice they kept crying for about 2 hours, "Great is Diana (Artemis) of the Ephesians." This image and temple which was such a great source of civic pride to the Ephesians was being threatened, and they became more and more vociferous in proclaiming its greatness.

Actually, in spite of all their shouting, the greatness of Diana (Artemis) of the Ephesians had already begun its decline through Paul's preaching, and nothing would be able to stop it. In time, the pilgrims to the Temple of Artemis came in ever fewer numbers, while the church in Ephesus continued to flourish. Christian tradition tells us the apostle John spent many years in Ephesus in the latter part of his life and wrote his Gospel and Epistles there.

In A.D. 262 the Temple of Diana (Artemis) was again burned, and this time it was never rebuilt. Its influence was gone. Later, Ephesus was such a prominent Christian city that in A.D. 341 a great Council of the Church was held there.

**35. And when the townclerk:** . . . the chancellor, —CMPB . . . The Mayor, —TCNT . . . the main city official, —SEB . . . the chief secretary, —BB.

**had appeased the people, he said:** . . . having calmed the multitude, —RTHM . . . brought some order in the crowd, —BRKL . . . restored quiet among the crowd, —KNOX . . . succeeded in quieting, —NOLI.

**Ye men of Ephesus:** . . . Ephesians, —RTHM . . . Gentlemen of Ephesus, —PHLP.

**what man is there that knoweth not:** . . . who is there of mankind that doth not acknowledge, —RTHM . . . who in the world could be ignorant of the fact, —PHLP.

**how that the city of the Ephesians is a worshipper of the great goddess Diana:** . . . that this city of Ephesus is the Warden of the temple of the great Artemis, —TCNT . . . is guardian, —ALFD . . . a devotee, —YNG . . . is the custodian of, —ADAM.

**and of the image which fell down from Jupiter?:** . . . we also keep her holy stone, —NCV . . . statue which fell down from Zeus, —TCNT . . . that descended from heaven? —MRDK . . . which is Jupiter's offspring! —KNOX.

**19:35.** After 2 hours of shouting, the frenzy of the mob began to wane. Finally the town clerk (the secretary of the city) quieted (subdued) the crowd. The town clerk was a citizen of Ephesus. He was the official contact or liaison with the Roman government officials in Ephesus. Thus, he probably had a responsibility to the Romans to help keep order.

When the crowd was quiet he addressed them as men of Ephesus and asked, "Who is there of mankind who does not know the city of Ephesus is the temple keeper (literally, the temple sweeper) of the great Artemis, even the one fallen from the sky (or, from the sky gods)?"

It is probable that a large stone meteor was used as the pedestal for the image of the goddess, since the image itself was originally of wood. However, some of the earlier Greek writers speak of the

images of their gods as fallen from heaven, so this may have been fairly common for heathen to use meteorites as pedestals or as a part of the statue or image of their gods.

**36. Seeing then that these things cannot be spoken against:** . . . be contradicted, —RSV . . . are undeniable facts, —TCNT . . . is beyond question, —MOFT . . . being incontrovertible, —WORL . . . No one can say that this is not true, —NCV.

**ye ought to be quiet:** . . . you ought to keep calm, —TCNT . . . to maintain your self-control, —WEYM . . . compose yourselves, —BRKL . . . to be tranquil, —MRDK . . . you must preserve order, —NOLI.

**and do nothing rashly:** . . . and not act recklessly, —WEYM . . . and do nothing unwise, —BB . . . You must stop and think before you do anything, —NCV.

**19:36.** The town clerk then argued there was no reason to be so upset and excited since the greatness and reputation of the image, in his opinion, were undeniable. Therefore, it was their duty to quiet down. It would be wrong to do anything rash (impulsive, reckless, or in thoughtless haste).

**37. For ye have brought hither these men, which are neither robbers of churches:** . . . have not stolen anything from her temple, —NCV . . . who are neither sacrilegious, —RSV . . . temple destroyers, —BRKL.

**nor yet blasphemers of your goddess:** . . . nor insulters of, —BRKL . . . have not said anything evil against, NCV.

**19:37.** The town clerk also pointed out that the men they had brought into the amphitheater were neither temple robbers (or sacrilegious), nor were they blasphemers of their goddess. Although Paul had been nearly 3 years in Ephesus, there was no evidence that either he or the Christians ever said anything bad or scurrilous against the temple or the goddess. They simply kept preaching the good news of Jesus Christ. However, Paul certainly confronted the idolatry and heathen practices he observed on his missionary journeys (see 14:15 and 17:22-31, for example). He was not afraid to preach against sin and false religions.

The KJV translation "robbers of churches" is one word in the Greek, *hierosulos*. It was used literally of those taking the gold vessels, the funds, or the sacred books from a temple (Greek, *hieron*). It was also used for sacrilege in general. Here the town clerk obviously means sacrilege in general. He thus declared that Paul and his associates had not committed any offense against their religion or their goddess.

Temple robbery and sacrilege against a temple were considered very serious offenses by the Greeks and Romans. They put them in the same class as treason and murder. Paul in Romans 2:22 includes it in a list with robbery and adultery.

For the Christian this is significant, for our bodies are temples of the Holy Spirit. Fornication (including adultery and all other types of sexual immorality) is a sin against the temple of the Holy Spirit. (See 1 Corinthians 6:13-20.) When believers meet together they are together the temple of the Holy Spirit. Anyone who brings division or a party spirit into the Body is also committing sacrilege (1 Corinthians 3:3, 16, 17).

**38. Wherefore if Demetrius, and the craftsmen which are with him:** ... the artisans, —TCNT ... and his fellow tradesmen, —MOFT.

**have a matter against any man:** ... have a charge to make against anyone, —TCNT ... have a ground of complaint, —FNTN.

**the law is open:** ... They can press charges, —NIV ... the courts are in session, —ADAM.

**and there are deputies:** ... appointed judges, —ALFD ... Magistrates, —TCNT.

**let them implead one another:** ... let both parties take legal proceedings, —TCNT ... let them go to law, —WLMS.

**19:38.** The town clerk then proceeded to call for law and order. The court days were kept regularly in the marketplace. He implied also that the courts were in session at that very time. The proconsuls were available. (The plural is general and does not mean there was more than one at a time.) The proconsul was the governor appointed by the Roman Senate for provinces under their jurisdiction (rather than under the jurisdiction of the emperor). Thus the governor would be there to give judgment. If Demetrius and his fellow craftsmen had a case against anyone, let them bring their charges or accusations against "one another" (in a lawful way).

**39. But if ye enquire any thing concerning other matters:** ... But if you want some other matter cleared up, —NORL.

**it shall be determined in a lawful assembly:** ... it shall be settled in the regular assembly, —ASV ... settled in a lawful assembly, —ADAM ... It can be decided at the regular town meeting of the people, —NCV.

**19:39.** If anyone wanted to seek anything (of public concern) beyond that, or there was anything further they wanted to know or discuss, it should be explained in the legal (duly constituted) assembly (Greek, *ekklēsia*, the word usually translated "church"), that is, not in a riotous gathering (*ekklēsia*) like this. In other words, a disorganized, tumultuous assembly was no proper place for deciding anything that affected the public welfare or the city's well-being.

**40. For we are in danger to be called in question for this day's uproar:** ... For in connection with today's proceedings there is danger of our being charged with attempted insurrection, —WEYM ... of being accused of revolt, —RTHM ... we run the risk of being accused of rioting, —NOLI ... as seditious, —MRDK ... to be questioned for sedition concerning this day, —WSLY ... of starting a rebellion, —KLGS.

**there being no cause whereby we may give an account of this concourse:** ... we shall be at a loss to give any reason for this disorderly gathering, —TCNT ... there having been no real reason for this riot; nor shall we be able to justify the behaviour of this disorderly mob, —WEYM ... particularly as we have no real excuse to offer for this commotion, —PHLP ... we cannot give any justifiable reason, —NORL ... been tumultuous without a cause, —MRDK ... this disorderly riot, —WUST ... no culprit whom we can hold liable, —CNFT.

**19:40.** The clerk was actually upset about this riot for it put the city in danger of having a charge of sedition, rebellion, or revolution brought against it. This kind of uprising would run the very real risk of having the Roman government discipline them. In the Roman ruler's eyes, there would be no reason or excuse for the events of the day. They could give no account for this wild assemblage, which the Romans could take as a seditious meeting or conspiracy.

The Romans at this point in their history were very proud of what they called the *pax romana* or Roman peace. They did not tolerate any kind of uprising, or rebellion, or rioting, whatever the cause. In fact, since most rebellion and mob action was directed against the Roman government, they treated everything of that nature as political and as a breach of the Roman peace. They would not understand that this riot was over a purely religious matter.

**41. And when he had thus spoken:** ... With these words, —TCNT.

**he dismissed the assembly:** ... he told the people to go home, —NCV.

**19:41.** After having said these things, the town clerk dismissed the assembly (Greek, *ekklēsia*). Thus, they had to release Paul's companions, Gaius and Aristarchus. Just as Paul's Roman citizenship was useful in giving him further opportunities to spread the gospel, so Roman concern for law and order and for keeping the peace proved helpful to the church.

# Chapter 20

**1. And after the uproar was ceased:** ... When the tumult had been quieted down, —BRKL ... After this disturbance died down, —PHLP...When the riot, —KLST...had subsided, —ADAM...was allayed, —SAWR.

**Paul called unto him the disciples:**...Paul invited the disciples to see him, —BRKL.

**and embraced them:**...and, with encouraging words, bade them goodbye, —TCNT...and having exhorted and embraced them, —HBIE...he spoke many heartening words, —PHLP.

**and departed for to go into Macedonia:**...and started on his journey to Macedonia, —TCNT...and left for. —BRKL.

**20:1.** Part of the pressure on Paul in Ephesus was his care or deep concern for all the churches. His letters to the Corinthians show he was especially concerned about those in Macedonia and Greece. (See 2 Corinthians 11:28; 12:20.) He had already sent Timothy and Erastus to Macedonia. Now it was time for Paul himself to go there.

After the riot stirred up by the makers of the silver shrines was over, and all the noise had ceased, Paul sent for the disciples (the Ephesian believers) and exhorted or encouraged them. He wanted them to live holy lives and be faithful to the Lord (as the practical sections of all his epistles show). Then, after saying his farewells, he left and went to Macedonia. This was probably the last time he would see this body of believers. When he passed by Ephesus on the way back to Jerusalem later, he only stopped at the seaport and sent for the elders of the assembly.

**2. And when he had gone over those parts:** . . . After going through those districts, —TCNT...As he made his journey through those districts, —PHLP...He traveled through all that region, —NOLI...As he went through those parts of the country, —NLTG.

**and had given them much exhortation:**...and exhorting them with much discourse, —RTHM...and speaking many encouraging words to the disciples, —TCNT...and encouraging the brethren with many suggestions, —BRKL...with his sermons, —NOLI...he spoke words of comfort and help, —NLTG...He said many things to strengthen the followers, —NCV...in a long speech, —MLNT.

**he came into Greece:** . . . Then he went on to, —NLTG...then he entered, —KNOX.

**20:2.** It is probable that Paul went to Macedonia by way of Troas where the Lord opened a door for him to minister the Word and where he hoped to find Titus (2 Corinthians 2:13). Titus, however, was not there, and Paul went on to Philippi. He did not have an easy time there. He was hard-pressed (afflicted), distressed on every side with fightings (strife, disputes) on the outside and fears within. But then Titus did come with good news of the concern and prayers of the Corinthians for him (2 Corinthians 7:6, 7).

During the summer and fall Paul went through the various churches in Macedonia, giving them much exhortation (and encouragement), or, as the Greek says, he exhorted (encouraged) them with much discourse. Probably he also visited the cities west of those visited on the previous journey, since in Romans 15:19 he wrote he "fully preached the gospel" as far as Illyricum (Dalmatia) on the northwest side of Macedonia. The Acts account gives no details, but it is possible he made a journey into the mountainous region of Illyricum or to its coastal cities that were related to or even technically parts of Macedonia. Then, after a rather thorough tour of Macedonia, he went down to Greece.

**3. And there abode three months:**...where he stayed three months, —TCNT.

**And when the Jews laid wait for him:**...and a plot was laid against him by the Jews, —ASV...The Jews having planned to waylay him, —WEYM...were planning something against him, —NCV...had made a plan to take him, —NLTG.

**as he was about to sail into Syria:**...Just as he was going to sail for Syria, —GDSP...on the point of taking ship for Syria, —WEYM...As he was about to get on a ship for the country of, —NLTG...he was meaning to take ship for, —KNOX...of setting sail for, —PHLP.

**he purposed to return through Macedonia:**...he changed his mind, —WLMS...changed his plans and went back through, —NLTG...so he decided to return by way of Macedonia, —TCNT...So he resolved to return, —KLST...to make his way back through, —PHLP.

**20:3.** Paul spent the 3 winter months of A.D. 56-57 in Greece. Most of this time was probably spent in Corinth. Titus had told him of their "fervent mind" toward him, that is, their ardor on Paul's behalf (2 Corinthians 7:7). Paul's letters to the Corinthians show how concerned he was about them and their problems.

Paul was also concerned about the offering which was to be taken to the poor saints (believers) in Jerusalem. While in Macedonia he had used the generosity of the Corinthians to encourage the churches there to give. But when the Corinthians fell behind in their giving, Paul wrote to them, reminding them of God's law of sowing and reaping (2 Corinthians 9:5, 6).

Just as he was about to go to Syria, the unbelieving Jews formed a plot against him. So Paul changed his plans. Instead of taking a ship from Greece, he was counseled to return through Macedonia.

**4. And there accompanied him into Asia Sopater of Berea:** . . . He was accompanied by,

−TCNT . . . Some men were going along with him, −NLTG.

**and of the Thessalonians, Aristarchus and Secundus:** . . . of the city of, −NLTG.

**and Gaius of Derbe, and Timotheus:**

**and of Asia, Tychicus and Trophimus:** . . . of the countries of, −NLTG.

**20:4.** Seven men who were accompanying Paul into the Roman province of Asia apparently took the ship as originally planned. These seven included Sopater (also called Sosipater), the son of Pyrrhus of Beroea and therefore one of those who "searched the Scriptures"; Aristarchus, the Macedonian from Thessalonica who had been with Paul at Ephesus; Secundus, also from Thessalonica; Gaius of Derbe; Timothy, Paul's assistant from Lystra; Tychicus, from the province of Asia; and Trophimus, a Gentile Christian from Ephesus.

Many writers believe at least some of these men took the journey to represent the churches who gave money as an offering for the poor among the Jerusalem Christians (1 Corinthians 16:3; see also Acts 19:29; 27:2; Colossians 4:10; Ephesians 6:21, 22; 2 Timothy 4:20). They were to see what was done with the money and report to their home churches.

The Early Church was very careful to keep good financial accounts and just as careful to make them known to the members of the congregation. There is no place where honesty, integrity, and openness are more important than in the distribution of funds given by God's people for the service of the Lord and His people.

**5. These going before tarried for us at Troas:** . . . having gone before us, −PNT . . . These companions went on ahead, −NAB . . . These men went to Troas and waited for us there, −TCNT . . . The latter proceeded to, −NOLI . . . These went on in advance, −TNT . . . went first, ahead of Paul, −EVRD . . . waiting for us in the city of, −SEB . . . This party proceeded to Troas to await us there, −PHLP.

**20:5.** These seven men went ahead of Paul by ship from Greece to Troas where they waited for Paul. Since Luke used the word "us" in this verse, it seems clear that he remained with Paul and journeyed back into Macedonia with him.

**6. And we sailed from Philippi after the days of unleavened bread:** . . . after the Passover, −TCNT . . . after the Feast, −EVRD . . . after the Jewish Festival, −SEB . . . After the supper of bread without yeast we got on a ship in the city of, −NLTG . . . and we sailed away from, −WORL.

**and came unto them to Troas in five days:** . . . and joined them five days later, −TCNT . . . We met these men . . . It took five days to get there, −NLTG.

**where we abode seven days:** . . . where we spent a week, −PHLP . . . where we stayed for a week, −TCNT . . . where we tarried, −WORL.

**20:6.** Paul and Luke arrived in Philippi in time for the Feast of Unleavened Bread in April of A.D. 57. Paul had found it necessary to leave Philippi rather abruptly after the conversion of the Philippian jailer. He probably visited it during the previous summer and fall of A.D. 56. Now he was able to spend some time again with the Philippian believers during this feast. (The Jews called the whole period of Passover and Unleavened Bread *Passover.* Perhaps Luke used the old name because Christ is the believer's Passover.)

Later, toward the end of Paul's first Roman imprisonment, Paul wrote his Epistle to the Philippians. This letter was partly in response to a gift sent by the Philippian church and brought by Epaphroditus (Philippians 4:10).

Paul made it clear that his real trust was in the Lord. He had learned to be content whatever his situation. He knew how to be humbled and have everything swept away without feeling the Lord had deserted him. He knew how to abound with material blessings and not feel he deserved them. Christ was his strength, his real source of supply. Yet this did not mean he appreciated the gifts of the Philippians any less. They did right to share with him in his affliction. But he appreciated their sympathetic interest even more. He saw that as a fruit of the Spirit.

After the 7 days of the feast, which the Jewish Christians undoubtedly still celebrated, Paul sailed from Philippi with Luke accompanying him. At Troas they met the others and remained there for 7 days.

**7. And upon the first day of the week:** . . . On Sunday, −BECK . . . on the first day of the sabbaths, −WORL.

**when the disciples came together to break bread:** . . . when we had met for the Breaking of Bread, −TCNT . . . we all met together, −EVRD, −NCV . . . were assembled to break bread, −NOLI . . . come together for the holy meal, −BB . . . to eat the Lord's supper, −NLTG.

**Paul preached unto them:** . . . Paul addressed them, −GDSP . . . Paul was discoursing to them, −TNT . . . talked, −NLTG . . . spoke to the group, −NCV.

**ready to depart on the morrow:** . . . He thought he would leave, −NLTG . . . as he was going away the next morning, −GDSP . . . Because he was planning to leave, NCV . . . intending to depart, −ASV . . . since he expected to leave the next day, −NORL . . . He was ready to leave, −SEB . . . he intended to leave on the following day, −PHLP.

**and continued his speech until midnight:** . . . and prolonged his speech until midnight, −ASV . . . and he went on talking till after the middle of the night, −BB.

**20:7.** At Troas Paul probably went to the synagogue on the Sabbath Day as was his custom. Then on the day following, that is, on Sunday evening (Luke used the Greek method of reckoning days, not the Jewish), the believers gathered with Paul and his company to break bread. This means they all brought food, shared a fellowship meal, and concluded with an observance of the Lord's Supper.

Paul took the opportunity to preach, that is, to conduct a discussion and converse with the people. Since he was going to leave the next day, he prolonged his discourse until midnight. What a wonderful time of fellowship and learning this must have been! Surely it was a joy to listen to Paul talk about the things of God and Christ. He probably dealt with their problems and answered their questions. It was his great desire for them to walk and live in the Spirit and bring glory to Jesus.

**8. And there were many lights in the upper chamber:** . . . a good many lamps in the upstairs room, –TCNT.

**where they were gathered together:** . . . where we had met, –TCNT . . . were assembled, –HBIE . . . We were all together, –NCV.

**20:8.** Paul could continue, for there were plenty of olive oil lamps in the upper room where they were meeting. Such a room would be reached by an outside stairway and would probably hold 200 or 300 people.

**9. And there sat in a window a certain young man named Eutychus:** . . . And a youth by the name Eutychus, –WEYM . . . on the window sill, –PHLP.

**being fallen into a deep sleep:** . . . was gradually overcome with great drowsiness, –TCNT.

**and as Paul was long preaching:** . . . while Paul preached at unusual length, –WEYM . . . and as Paul's address went on and on, –MOFT . . . As Paul continued talking, –NCV.

**he sunk down with sleep:** . . . so as he sagged down in, –BRKL . . . a profound sleep, –CMPB . . . he went sound asleep, –KLGS.

**and fell down from the third loft:** . . . and fell to the ground from the third floor, –NCV . . . from the third story, –ASV.

**and was taken up dead:** . . . When they picked him up, NCV . . . a corpse, –MOFT . . . lifeless, –BRKL.

**20:9.** A young man, Eutychus ("fortunate"), was sitting on a window sill listening. About midnight he was "borne down" with sleep. That is, he gradually dropped off and was finally overcome by deep, sound sleep. Everyone's attention was on Paul, so no one noticed. As Paul kept on preaching, Eutychus finally fell from the third story window and was taken up dead. This means he was

really dead. Luke, as a physician, would be able to determine this.

This must have been quite a shock to the believers gathered there. Their first thought may have been that this young man whose name meant "fortunate" was not so fortunate after all. It is easy for people to feel a sense of tragedy when they see a young man or a young woman killed. The Bible just tells the story factually. It does not indicate why the young man was sitting in the window sill instead of joining in with the believers who were gathered around Paul.

Some suppose the smoke from the many lamps helped to put Eutychus to sleep. But this would hardly be the case by any open window. Others say the devil caused it in an attempt to disrupt the meeting. Still others say the Bible records it as a warning to all who do not give attention to the Word of God when it is being preached or taught. But there is no indication of any blame being put on Satan here; neither is there any reproach put on the young man for having fallen asleep.

The Bible shows he was not merely injured or dying. He was dead. Some writers suggest he was taken up for dead, or taken up as dead. But where that was the case, as in Matthew 28:4, Mark 9:26, and Revelation 1:17, the Greek clearly indicates this. Here the Greek is the same as is used elsewhere when people were actually dead. He was a lifeless corpse. In the natural there was no hope for him.

**10. And Paul went down:** . . . Paul hastened down, –NORL.

**and fell on him:** . . . threw himself upon him, –TCNT . . . lay on him, –BECK . . . knelt, –NCV.

**and embracing him said:** . . . took him in his arms and said, –BB . . . put his arms around him, –NCV . . . and holding him gently in his arms, –PHLP.

**Trouble not yourselves:** . . . Stop being alarmed, –WLMS . . . Have no anxiety, –BRKL . . . Cease your wailing, –WEYM . . . Do not make an uproar, –HBIE . . . Make no lamentations, –NOYS . . . Be not troubled, –WSLY . . . Do not weep, –KLGS . . . Make no tumult! –WORL . . . Do not worry, –NOLI.

**for his life is in him:** . . . he is still alive, –TCNT . . . He's alive, –BECK.

**20:10.** Immediately Paul went down the outside stairway and threw himself upon the young man, throwing his arms around him in a tight embrace, surely praying as he did so.

Paul had the example of Elijah in this. In 1 Kings 17:17-21 when the widow's son died, Elijah came and stretched himself over the child three times and prayed. The Hebrew indicates Elijah did not put any of his weight on the child. Rather, he bent over the child as an expression of faith in prayer. The emphasis is clearly on prayer.

In answer to prayer, the boy was brought back to life. Elisha had a similar experience when the son of the wealthy Shunammite woman died (2 Kings 4:34, 35).

After Paul embraced the young man Eutychus, he said, "Don't panic, for his life is in him." That is, his life had returned to him. ("life" here is the Greek *psuchē* which also means "soul" or "person," but in this case it means physical life.) Apparently, the people had already started noisy lamentations. Paul therefore told them to stop all this noise which was so traditional, especially among the Jews. God had given a miraculous restoration.

**11. When he therefore was come up again:** ... Then he went upstairs, –*TCNT*.

**and had broken bread, and eaten:** ... and, after breaking and partaking of the Bread, –*TCNT* ... broke the bread, and took some food, –*WEYM*.

**and talked a long while, even till break of day:** ... he talked with them at great length till daybreak, –*TCNT* ... and after much conversation that lasted till the sun rose, –*BECK* ... he conversed long with them, –*WSLY* ... even till daylight, –*WLMS* ... until it was early morning, –*NCV*.

**so he departed:** ... and then left, –*TCNT* ... at last he parted from them, –*WEYM* ... and so finally departed, –*PHLP*.

**20:11.** It was now after midnight on Monday morning. But Paul went back up to the upper room and broke bread, that is, had a meal which he ate ("tasted") with enjoyment. Then he kept on talking (conversing) a long time, and the believers stayed right with him until daylight. Again the Bible does not say what Paul talked about. But this surely would have been a wonderful opportunity to tell about how Jesus healed the sick and raised the dead and to say more about Christ's own death and resurrection which is the guarantee of every believer's. Then, at daybreak Paul left.

**12. And they brought the young man alive:** ... Meanwhile they had taken the lad away alive, –*TCNT* ... taken the lad home alive, –*WEYM* ... took the young man home alive, –*NCV*.

**and were not little comforted:** ... comforted beyond measure, –*RTHM* ... immeasurably consoled, –*CNDT* ... much to their relief, –*MOFT* ... were enormously encouraged, –*ADAM* ... relieved, –*PHLP* ... greatly comforted, –*NCV*.

**20:12.** The young man was also brought before the people alive (and fully recovered), and they were very greatly encouraged. Eutychus is called a boy (*paida*) here, which probably means he was still in his teens. (In verse 9 Eutychus is called a *neanias*, a youth.) However, *paida* is also used of a trusted servant or slave. Many slaves did become

Christians in those days. This could be another reason he fell asleep. He may have been working hard all day.

The encouragement of these believers was not merely a feeling of relief because Eutychus was alive. It was also undoubtedly an encouragement to their faith in Christ and to their belief in the truth of the resurrection that will take place when Jesus comes again (1 Thessalonians 4:13-18). Paul used the same verb there when he wrote "comfort (encourage) one another with these words."

**13. And we went before to ship:** ... We started first, went on board ship, –*TCNT* ... Meanwhile we had gone aboard the ship, –*PHLP* ... Embarking, –*FNTN*.

**and sailed unto Assos:** ... and sailed for Assos, –*TCNT* ... and sailed on ahead for Assos, –*PHLP*.

**there intending to take in Paul:** ... intending to take Paul on board there, –*TCNT* ... where we were to take Paul on board, –*WLMS* ... intending to pick up Paul there, –*PHLP*.

**for so had he appointed:** ... arranged, –*RTHM* ... He had planned it that way, –*NORL* ... for such was his arrangement, –*BRKL*.

**minding himself to go afoot:** ... intending himself to go by land, –*ASV* ... since he himself had planned to go overland, –*PHLP*.

**20:13.** Luke and the rest of Paul's company did not stay until daybreak. They went on ahead to the ship and set sail for Assos in Mysia south of Troas where they expected to take Paul on board. He had directed them to do this. The ship would go a longer route around a long peninsula (Cape Lectum). The sea journey was nearly twice as far as by land. Paul thus took the land route and walked to Assos. This was his choice.

Luke did not say why Paul did this. But for some reason he wanted to be alone. A little later he told the Ephesian elders that in every city the Holy Spirit bore witness to him that bonds (chains) and affliction (persecution, distress) awaited him in Jerusalem. Probably Paul felt he needed this time alone in order to settle it with the Lord whether it was truly His will for him to go on to Jerusalem. Paul had written to the Romans to pray to God for him that he might be delivered from the unbelievers in Judea so he might minister to the saints in Jerusalem (Romans 15:30, 31). But he needed time now to pray and talk to God.

**14. And when he met with us at Assos:** ... When he met us on our arrival at Assos, –*PHLP*.

**we took him in:** ... we took him on board, –*RTHM* ... aboard, –*NCV* ... taking him up, –*WORL*.

**and came to Mitylene:** ... and went on to Mitylene, –*TCNT* ... and sailed on to Mitylene, –*WLMS*.

**20:14.** By the time Paul reached Assos it seems he had no more doubts about it being God's will for him to go on to Jerusalem. So he met the ship and they took him on board and proceeded to sail along the coast of Asia Minor until they came to Mitylene, the capital of the island of Lesbos. There they stopped for a brief time. It was an important state at the crossroads of Europe and Asia. The Romans made it a favorite vacation spot. Its fine harbor faced toward the coast of Asia Minor and thus it was a convenient place for the ship to stop. It is probable that it picked up or dropped off cargo and passengers there.

Paul's journey by foot cannot be observed without developing a great deal of respect for the apostle. It was a difficult journey; so difficult, in fact, that Homer said traveling on foot to Assos was enough to kill a person. The trip attests not only to Paul's zeal for the gospel but also to his physical stamina.

**15. And we sailed thence, and came the next day over against Chios:** . . . The day after we had sailed from there, we arrived off Chios, —*TCNT* . . . and arrived off the coast of Chios the next day, —*PHLP* . . . From there we sailed and arrived off, —*NOLI* . . . and came to a place near, —*NCV* . . . And sailing away from there, —*KJII* . . . we reached a point opposite Chios, —*KNOX* . . . to a point facing, —*MLNT*.

**and the next day we arrived at Samos:** . . . put in at Samos, —*ALFD* . . . we sailed to, —*NCV* . . . we touched at, —*WORL* . . . docked at Samos, —*BRKL*.

**and tarried at Trogyllium; and the next day we came to Miletus:** . . . we came on the third day to Miletus, —*BB* . . . and, on the following day, —*WORL* . . . A day later, we reached, —*NCV*.

**20:15.** From Mitylene they sailed the next day across from Chios, a large island opposite Smyrna. Chios was a free city-state. The ship anchored in the lee of the island for a night. The next day they came near Samos, another large island southwest of Ephesus which had been made a free state by the Roman Emperor Augustus. The ship sailed between Samos and the mainland. This brought them to a narrow strait between the island of Samos and the promontory of Trogyllium. They remained there until morning since it would have been very difficult to make their way through the strait in the darkness. (Some ancient manuscripts leave out any mention of this waiting at Trogyllium, but the majority of Greek manuscripts recognize there was danger here, and this delay most surely did take place.) This promontory was actually between Ephesus and Miletus. So the next day they came to Miletus.

Miletus was on the seacoast of the Roman province of Asia about 36 miles south of Ephesus. It was located on the south shore of the Bay of Latmus near the mouth of the Maeander River (now called the Menderes). The city was founded by the Ionian Greeks. It was a very prosperous commercial city until it was destroyed by the Persians in 494 B.C. It never regained its past glories. The Maeander River brought down a great deal of silt, and in modern times what is left of its harbor is now a lake, leaving the site of the city of Miletus about 6 miles from the present seacoast.

**16. For Paul had determined to sail by Ephesus:** . . , Paul's plan was to sail past Ephesus, —*WEYM* . . . had already decided not to stop at, —*NCV*.

**because he would not spend the time in Asia:** . . . so that he might not be kept in Asia, —*BB* . . . with the idea of spending as little time as possible in Asia, —*PHLP* . . . as he did not want to be delayed in the province of, —*NOLI* . . . in order that he might not have to spend time in, —*TNT* . . . he did not want to stay too long in, —*NCV* . . . lest he spend much time in, —*KLST* . . . for fear of having to waste time in, —*KNOX*.

**for he hasted:** . . . since he was very desirous, —*WEYM* . . . he was eager, —*WLMS* . . . He wanted to hurry on, —*NORL* . . . For he was hastening to be in, —*NOLI*.

**if it were possible for him:** . . . if possible, —*TCNT* . . . if he possibly could, —*KLST* . . . if he found it possible, —*KNOX*.

**to be at Jerusalem the day of Pentecost:** . . . to arrive in Jerusalem, —*RTHM* . . . reach Jerusalem, —*KLST* . . . by the Festival at the close of the Harvest, —*TCNT*.

**20:16.** This trip had taken longer than usual with the ship sailing among the islands off the coast of Asia Minor and apparently sailing only by daylight. Paul had decided to bypass Ephesus. He knew if he went there the large number of local assemblies or house churches would all want him to come and visit them and it would take too much time. He had indeed settled it with God that he should go to Jerusalem. Now he was in a hurry to get there by the Day of Pentecost (in May) if possible. This would be a time when the Jewish believers in Palestine would be together, and the offering sent by the Greek and Macedonian churches would be most helpful.

**17. And from Miletus he sent to Ephesus:** . . . Notwithstanding, —*RTHM* . . . he sent messengers to, —*MLNT*.

**and called the elders of the church:** . . . and summoned, —*ALFD* . . . and invited the Officers of the church to meet him, —*TCNT* . . . of the assembly, —*RTHM*.

**20:17.** Paul did not bypass Ephesus because of any lack of concern for the church there. To show his care for them he sent to Ephesus and called the elders of the church, asking them to come and meet with him at Miletus. This would probably be the last time he would ever see them.

God gave Paul the heart of a true shepherd. His words reveal another side of his ministry. Chapter 13 has a summary of the kind of sermons Paul preached to Jews when he first went to the synagogue in a new town. Chapter 17 has a summary of Paul's preaching to purely Gentile audiences when he first met with them. But this chapter contains the only example in Acts of a sermon Paul preached specifically to Christians. It was a deeply moving farewell address. Now Paul gave his final challenge to the elders or administrative officers who were responsible for the teaching and direction of the believers in the great city of Ephesus.

**18. And when they were come to him:** ... When they came to him, —MOFT.

**he said unto them:** ... he spoke to them as follows, —TCNT ... he told them, —BRKL ... he addressed them in these words, —PHLP.

**Ye know:** ... You are well acquainted, —BRKL ... I am sure you know, —PHLP ... with my behavior, —MLNT.

**from the first day that I came into Asia:** ... ever since I set foot in Asia, —MOFT.

**after what manner I have been with you at all seasons:** ... the life that I always led among you, —TCNT ... the kind of life I lived among you the whole time, —WEYM ... what my whole life has been like, —BB.

**20:18.** Paul began by reminding them of the kind of person he had been from the first day he set foot in the province of Asia and how he had conducted himself the whole time he was there.

Paul did not intend to glorify himself. He always wanted all the glory to go to Jesus. But in many cases the work of Judaizers and other enemies of the gospel had degenerated into attempts to destroy Paul's message and divide the churches he founded by making personal attacks on him. Paul now reminded the Ephesians that they knew him.

**19. Serving the Lord:** ... and how I continued to serve the Lord, —WLMS ... Doing the Lord's work, —BB.

**with all humility of mind:** ... with all lowliness of mind, —ASV ... without pride, —BB ... with all modestie, —GNVA.

**and with many tears, and temptations:** ... with many a tear and many a trial, —MOFT ... and in trials, —BECK ... and what tears I have shed over the trials, —PHLP.

**which befell me:** ... which I encountered, —MOFT ... I endured, —BECK ... and this troubled me very much, —NCV.

**by the lying in wait of the Jews:** ... because of the evil designs of the Jews, —BB ... The Jews plotted against me, —NCV.

**20:19.** Paul also reminded the Ephesian elders that all the time he was with them he had served the Lord in all humility. He was a true servant-leader. He was humble-minded, modest, and unassuming. The people knew this was a strong contrast to the boastfulness of the false teachers who were trying to draw a following after themselves.

Paul also served with tears, weeping as he sought to bring sinners to Christ, weeping also over the needs of the believers. When he preached judgment, it was out of a broken heart full of love for the people with whom he was dealing. His tears flowed from the love and compassion of Jesus that flooded his own soul.

Paul also continued to serve the Lord with the same humility and tears in the midst of all the testing brought by the plots of unbelieving Jews.

In the midst of all these tests, Paul forgot his own dignity and desires for the sake of fulfilling his God-given task. He was not trying to build up a reputation or a fortune for himself. He was willing to do the jobs no one else wanted to do. He was willing to do anything, however unpleasant or dangerous, if it meant building up the body of Christ.

**20. And how I kept back nothing that was profitable unto you, but have shewed you:** ... I never shrank from telling you anything that could be helpful to you, —TCNT ... anything that was beneficial to you, —ADAM ... how I never refrained from telling you, —TNT.

**and have taught you publickly, and from house to house:** ... and teaching you publicly and in your homes, —RTHM ... or from teaching you both in public and in private, —TCNT ... in meetings and in homes, —BECK.

**20:20.** At the same time, Paul did not let danger or the plots of his enemies cause him to shrink from telling the Ephesians anything that was beneficial (helpful, profitable, useful, advantageous, for their good).

Paul had the heart of a true shepherd. The chief task of the eastern shepherd in Palestine is to find food and water for the sheep, and to protect them from enemies. So Paul was careful to give thorough teaching from the Word of God, both publicly and in every home that was open to him. Much of Paul's teaching and preaching was more like conversation or discussion. He did not try to impress the people with beautiful oratory.

**21. Testifying both to the Jews, and also to the Greeks:** ... bearing full witness both to Jews and to Greeks, —RTHM ... and how I earnestly warned,

−BECK . . . earnestly urged Greeks as well as Jews, −GDSP.

**repentance toward God:** . . . to change their lives and turn to God, −NCV . . . to turn from sin to God, −BECK.

**and faith toward our Lord Jesus Christ:** . . . and as to belief on our Lord Jesus, −RTHM . . . and trust in our Lord Jesus, −NEB . . . I told them all to believe in our Lord, NCV.

**20:21.** To both Jews and Greeks, then, Paul bore witness to their need of repentance (a fundamental change of mind and attitudes) toward God and faith in the Lord Jesus. This would include the promises of God and a faith, trust, and acceptance of all Jesus had provided. (See, for example, 1:4, 5; 2:4.)

**22. And now, behold, I go bound in the spirit unto Jerusalem:** . . . And now, under spiritual constraint, −TCNT . . . I am impelled by the Spirit, −WLMS . . . under the binding force of, −MOFF . . . a prisoner already, −JB . . . under spiritual compulsion, −KLST . . . a prisoner in spirit, −KNOX . . . now I must obey the Holy Spirit and go, −NCV . . . on my way to . . . for the Spirit compels me to go there, −GDSP.

**not knowing the things that shall befall me there:** . . . and I have no idea of, −NORL . . . what will happen to me, −TCNT.

**20:22.** Paul next indicated to the Ephesian elders why he believed it was the last time he would have the opportunity to see and encourage them. He told them he was going to Jerusalem, not only because of his own desire but because he was already bound by the Holy Spirit to go. That is, the Spirit had made it clear to him that divine necessity was still upon him to go to Jerusalem, though he did not know what he would encounter there.

Some believe that "bound in the spirit" means Paul was bound in his own spirit, for the King James Version does not capitalize the word "spirit" here. However, the most ancient copies of the New Testament were written completely in capital letters, so the small letter in our English translation tells us nothing. The original Greek uses the definite article here, however, and this would normally indicate the Holy Spirit. The whole context shows Paul was indeed bound or strongly constrained by the Holy Spirit to go on to Jerusalem, no matter what awaited him there.

**23. Save that the Holy Ghost witnesseth in every city:** . . . in town after town the Holy Spirit plainly declares to me, −TCNT . . . makes clear to me, −BB . . . emphatically assures me, −WLMS . . . the Holy Spirit assures me, −KNOX . . . fully testifies, −KJII . . . tells me, −NCV . . . testifieth to me, −WORL . . . in every town I visit, the holy Spirit warns me, −GDSP.

**saying that bonds and afflictions abide me:** . . . imprisonment and suffering are awaiting me, −WEYM . . . that imprisonment and persecution, , −KLST . . . prison and pains, −BB . . . and tribulations, −WORL . . . bondage and affliction await me, −KNOX . . . that troubles and even jail wait for me, −NCV.

**20:23.** The one thing Paul knew was that the Holy Spirit in city after city gave solemn witness (probably through the gift of prophecy) that bonds (chains) and afflictions (persecution, distress) awaited him in Jerusalem. (See also Romans 15:31.)

Clearly, these prophecies were not meant to give personal direction to Paul, nor were they intended to stop him from going to Jerusalem. The Bible indicates that prophecy, like most of the gifts of the Spirit, is intended to edify the church (the local assembly or congregations), not to guide individuals. The churches needed to know what was coming so when these things happened to Paul they would not be taken by surprise or have their faith shaken. Satan might have used Paul's imprisonment to discourage some if they had not been forewarned. Or some might have imagined that some sin brought on Paul's imprisonment.

**24. But none of these things move me:** . . . However, I am not concerned about anything, −BRKL . . . I make no account (of these things), −PNT . . . But I do not attach any importance to, −NOLI . . . I care nothing for all that, −KNOX.

**neither count I my life dear unto myself:** . . . frankly I do not consider my own life valuable to me, −PHLP . . . as of no value unto myself, −ALFD . . . But even the sacrifice of my life I count as nothing, −WEYM . . . worth nothing, −MOFF . . . I set no value, −MOFF . . . But I don't care about my own life, −NCV . . . count my life precious compared with my work, −KNOX.

**so that I might finish my course with joy:** . . . if only I may complete the course marked out for me, −TCNT . . . The most important thing is, −NCV . . . I want only to complete the race I am running, −NOLI . . . unless I can finish my race, −KLGS . . . if only I accomplish my course, −KLST . . . in order to complete my course and the mission, −TNT.

**and the ministry:** . . . and be faithful to the duty, −WEYM . . . the dispensation, −CNDT . . . I want to finish the work, −NCV . . . accomplish the ministry, −MNTG . . . to fulfill the mission, −NOLI . . . the commission, −FNTN . . . and complete the ministry, −PHLP . . . the task of preaching, −KNOX.

**which I have received of the Lord Jesus:** . . . was allotted, −TCNT . . . which I accepted from, −MLNT . . . which the Lord Jesus has entrusted to me, −WEYM . . . which the Lord Jesus has given me, −KNOX.

**to testify the gospel of the grace of God:** . . . to bear full witness, −RTHM . . . of faithfully telling, −WLMS . . . to proclaim the Gospel of the divine grace, −NOLI . . . to tell people the Good News about God's grace, NCV . . . so as to full testify, −KJII.

**20:24.** Paul was not only bound by the Holy Spirit to go to Jerusalem, he was willing to go. On no account did he make his life valuable (precious) to himself. He greatly desired to finish his run (as in a race) with joy, accomplishing the ministry (the service) which he had received from the Lord, giving serious witness to the good news of the grace of God.

In other words, the threat of danger could not turn Paul back from what he knew was God's will because he had already given up everything and put his life on the altar for the Lord (Philippians 3:8). He was not afraid of persecution or even death.

He had a secret. He had seen "the light of the knowledge of the glory of God in the face of Jesus Christ" (2 Corinthians 4:6). He felt in his body "the excellency of the power . . . of God" (2 Corinthians 4:7). He had received the "earnest" or first installment of what the Spirit will make fully real for every believer when Jesus comes again (2 Corinthians 1:22; 5:5; Ephesians 1:14). Therefore, he was willing "to be absent from the body, and to be present with the Lord" (2 Corinthians 5:8). Above all, the resurrection of Jesus from the dead gave him the assurance of his own resurrection, and made it such a real hope that all fear of death was gone (1 Corinthians 15:20, 51, 54; 2 Corinthians 4:14-16; Hebrews 2:14, 15). Death is not a defeat for the Christian for each believer shall rise in glorious victory. The Christian does not need to fear the consequences of anything the Holy Spirit directs him to do. He cannot lose.

25. **And now, behold, I know that ye all:** . . . I tell you, I know that none of you, –*TCNT* . . . I am perfectly sure that, –*NOLI.*
**among whom I have gone preaching the kingdom of God:** . . . All the time I was with you, –*NCV.*
**shall see my face no more:** . . . will ever seen my face again, –*TCNT.*

**20:25.** Paul next let the elders know this was a final farewell. They would never see him again.

But he did not simply draw attention to the finality of this visit. The thing that concerned him was that he had gone about among them preaching the kingdom of God. This would be the last time he would be able to reinforce that teaching and remind them of the grace of God. That grace had saved him from the life of a willful, murderous Pharisee and had called him to a worldwide, earth-shaking ministry where he proclaimed the kingdom or rule of God, made manifest in and through Jesus by God's grace.

In the same way, Paul showed that the gospel of the grace of God is the same as the preaching of the kingdom of God, and therefore is the same

as the gospel of the Kingdom. It is by God's grace that believers are brought under the rule and authority of God through the Lord Jesus, by His death and resurrection. Believers show they are under His rule by righteousness, peace, and joy in the Holy Spirit (Romans 14:17). There is only one gospel, and it includes the present rule of God as well as the future rule when Jesus will establish His kingdom on earth.

26. **Wherefore I take you to record this day:** . . . I take you to witness this day, –*ALFD* . . . Therefore I declare to you this day, –*TCNT* . . . So today I can tell you one thing that I am sure of, –*NCV* . . . solemnly affirm, –*WEYM.*
**that I am pure from the blood of all men:** . . . that I am clear from, –*MNTG* . . . that I am guiltless, –*BRKL* . . . that, should any of you perish, the responsibility is not mine, –*WEYM* . . . I am not responsible for the fate of any one of you, –*TNT* . . . that my conscience is clear as far as any of you is concerned, –*PHLP.*

**20:26.** In this final farewell Paul bore witness that he was pure (clean) from the blood of all. Paul undoubtedly had in mind here the reference to Ezekiel who was appointed a watchman and a warner to the people of Israel who were in exile in Babylon (see Ezekiel 3:16-21). God considered Ezekiel as a lookout or sentry watching for sin. A sentry who neglects his duty and lets the enemy through without sounding a warning is, in wartime, court-martialed and executed. God made it clear that if Ezekiel failed, the blood of those he failed would be on his hands; he would be guilty.

27. **For I have not shunned to declare unto you:** . . . For I have not fallen short at all of preaching to you, –*BRKL* . . . I have never hesitated to announce to you, –*TNT.*
**all the counsel of God:** . . . the whole counsel of God, –*RSV* . . . the whole purpose of God concerning you, –*TCNT* . . . the complete will of God, –*PHLP* . . . God's whole plan, –*WEYM.*

**20:27.** Paul was free from guilt. No one could say he had failed in giving warning. Even more important, he never shrank from proclaiming the whole counsel (all the wise counsel, all the wise plan and purpose) of God. He gave himself in full devotion to the Word and will of God. He also told the people what to expect, both with respect to persecutions and difficulties in the present and the glories to come.

Ephesians 1:3-14 also shows what Paul meant by the wise counsel or purpose of God. There Paul showed it is God's will or choice for Christians to be holy in a positive way through dedication and service to God. It is God's will or choice for believers also to be blameless. He pours out heaven's blessings on them, not so they can waste them on the desires of their own flesh and mind, but so they can be like Jesus.

**28. Take heed therefore unto yourselves:** ... Be watchful over yourselves, —TCNT ... Give attention to, —BB ... Be on guard for yourselves, —BRKL.

**and to all the flock:** ... and over the whole flock, —TCNT ... and for every flock, —PHLP.

**over the which the Holy Ghost hath made you overseers:** ... has appointed you as, —TNT ... has constituted, —CMPB ... you bishops, —ASV ... shepherds, —NORL ... has placed you in charge, —TCNT ... has given into your care, —BB ... has made you guardians, —PHLP ... sent you to watch, —KLGS ... The Holy Spirit chose you to guard this flock, —SEB.

**to feed the church of God:** ... to be shepherding the assembly of God, —RTHM ... to feed the congregation, —CMPB ... to rule the church of God, —DOUY.

**which he hath purchased with his own blood:** ... which he has bought, —WEYM ... at the cost of his own life, —TCNT ... which he acquired, —RTHM ... which he won for himself, —TNT ... with the blood of His own Son, —FNTN.

**20:28.** Paul had warned them before. Now he continued to challenge them with a warning which showed his concern over both the present and future welfare of the church.

First, he warned the elders themselves. Let them attend (give attention) to themselves for the sake of the flock. They must realize the greatness of their responsibility, taking care of their own spiritual well-being. They were also to take the same care and give the same attention to all the flock among whom the Holy Spirit had made them bishops (overseers, superintendents, ruling elders, presidents of the local congregations or house churches), to feed or shepherd the assembly (Greek, *ekklēsia*, as in 19:41) of God.

The "assembly of God" includes all whom He (Jesus) made His own through His own blood, that is, through the shedding of His blood when He died in agony on Calvary (Ephesians 1:7; Titus 2:14; Hebrews 9:12, 14; 13:12, 13).

It is clear here also that the elder and the bishop were interchangeable terms for the same elected office. They were Spirit-filled people who were led by the Spirit. Thus the Holy Spirit really gave the office. They were also dependent on the Holy Spirit for the gifts of administration (governments) and ruling necessary for the carrying out of their office (Romans 12:8; 1 Corinthians 12:28). In addition they needed Spirit-anointed, Christ-given ministries to be pastors (shepherds) and teachers of the assembly.

**29. For I know this, that after my departing:** ... when I am gone, —WEYM ... I know that after I leave, —NCV.

**shall grievous wolves enter in among you:** ... some men will come like wild wolves, —NCV ... merciless wolves will get in, —TCNT ... violent wolves will break in, —WLMS ... cruel, —WEYM ... ferocious wolves will enter, —NOLI.

**not sparing the flock:** ... and try to destroy the flock, —NCV ... that have no mercy on, —BRKL.

**20:29.** Another part of the work of the shepherd was to protect the sheep from enemies. The shepherd's staff guided the sheep. The shepherd's rod protected them from the wolves who came to destroy the sheep. Paul therefore warned these elders that after his departure, grievous (heavy, difficult to handle) wolves would come in among them, not sparing the little flock, but injuring them severely. (See Luke 12:32 where the flock means Jesus' disciples.)

**30. Also of your own selves shall men arise:** ... And even some of you men will start, —BECK ... men among your own number, —KNOX ... from your own group, —NCV.

**speaking perverse things:** ... speaking distorted things, —RTHM ... and will teach perversions of truth, —TCNT ... who will give wrong teaching, —BB ... and teach false doctrines, —NORL ... will speak contrary things, —KLGS ... who will pervert the truth, —TNT ... and twist the truth, —NCV ... with a false message, —KNOX.

**to draw away disciples after them:** ... in order to, —TNT ... make them followers of themselves, —PHLP ... The will lead away followers after them, —NCV.

**20:30.** These savage wolves would be false teachers who would bring terrible trouble (Matthew 7:15; 2 Timothy 3:5-8; Jude 4, 10, 12, 13; Revelation 2:2).

Not all of these wolves would come into the church from outside. Sad to say, some would rise up from among the believers, even from among these Spirit-filled, Spirit-anointed elders themselves. By perverting the truth or by twisting the Scriptures, they would seek to draw away a following for themselves from the disciples, even splitting up the local assemblies to do it.

Paul's warning indicated the real purpose of these false teachers would be to build up themselves rather than the assembly. They would attempt to draw away disciples who were already believers. They would have little interest in winning the lost for Christ, nor would they desire to build up the churches (assemblies) that were already established.

That this was a very serious and prevalent problem is shown by the many warnings in Paul's epistles. (See Romans 16:17, 18; Colossians 2:8; 1 Timothy 4:1-3; Titus 1:10, 11.)

**31. Therefore watch:** . . . be on your guard, —*TCNT* . . . be on the alert, —*WEYM* . . . Keep, therefore, on the lookout, —*BRKL* . . . be-on-the-watch, —*RTHM*.
**and remember, that by the space of three years:** . . . for three years, —*ET*.
**I ceased not to warn every one night and day with tears:** . . . I never failed . . . to warn every one of you, even with tears in my eyes, —*PHLP* . . . I did not cease counselling each one of you, —*TNT*.

**20:31.** The elders needed to be on their guard, not only against such wolves as these, but against becoming one themselves. (Compare 1 Timothy 1:19, 20; 4:1-10; 2 Timothy 1:15; 2:17, 18; 3:1-9; Revelation 2:2-4.)

Paul set them an example in this too. For the nearly 3 years he had been with them in Ephesus, he had never ceased warning each one of them with tears night and day. He was instant in season and out of season; he was always moved by tender love for them. Nor did he limit himself to office hours. He was always available to meet any need. Again, from Paul's epistles it is clear that during those years he was opposed by many "wolves" and false brethren.

**32. And now, brethren, I commend you to God:** . . . Now I am giving you to God, —*SEB* . . . I give you into the care of God, —*BB* . . . I give you to the Lord for protection, —*KLGS* . . . For the present I commend, —*KLST*.
**and to the word of his grace:** . . . and to the Message of his love, —*TCNT* . . . and to his gracious Son, —*NOLI*.
**which is able to build you up:** . . . a Message which has the power to build up your character, —*TCNT* . . . to make you strong, —*BB* . . . is able to give you strength, —*NCV*.
**and to give you an inheritance:** . . . your proper possession, —*WLMS* . . . your salvation, —*BECK* . . . give you your place, —*PHLP* . . . it will give you the blesings that God has, —*NCV*.
**among all them which are sanctified:** . . . among the saints, —*WEYM* . . . among all God's consecrated people, —*WLMS* . . . all those made holy, —*MLNT* . . . among all those who are consecrated to God, —*PHLP* . . . for all his holy people, —*NCV*.

**20:32.** Paul always did more than warn the believers. He also commended (entrusted) them to God and to His gracious Word which was able to edify them (build them up spiritually) and give them the inheritance among all those who are sanctified, that is, among those who are holy, set apart to follow Jesus.

The inheritance Paul was talking about is the very definite, well-known, promised inheritance. Jesus had sent Paul among the Gentiles "that they may receive forgiveness of sins, and inheritance among them which are sanctified by faith that is in me (in Jesus)" (26:18). It includes the blessing of Abraham and the promise of the Spirit through faith (Romans 4:13-16; Galatians 3:9, 14, 18, 26, 29).

There is a fullness of this inheritance coming to believers in the future as a reward from the Lord. This hope should cause believers to do whatever they do heartily ("out of soul," that is, with the whole being, putting everything they have into it), remembering that they are servants (loveslaves) of the Lord (Colossians 3:23, 24). God will not forget any labor of love or the way Christians serve their fellow believers.

**33. I have coveted no man's silver, or gold, or apparel:** . . . I desired no one's, —*HBIE* . . . never wanted anyone's money or fine clothes, —*NCV*.

**20:33.** It was in view of this inheritance that Paul could serve the Lord and the Church without coveting, even when other Christians had much more in the way of material things than he did. In all that he did, he set them an example of selfless service. He did not desire anyone's silver, gold, or clothing.

**34. Yea, ye yourselves know:** . . . yourselves acknowledge, —*RTHM*.
**that these hands have ministered unto my necessities:** . . . that these hands of mine provided not only for my own wants, —*TCNT* . . . that these hands supplied my needs, —*BRKL* . . . these hands worked for what I needed, —*BECK* . . . I always worked to take care of my own needs, —*NCV*.
**and to them that were with me:** . . . but for my companions also, —*TCNT* . . . and for the people with me, —*WEYM*.

**20:34.** The Ephesian elders well knew that Paul set an example, in that by his own hands he served (ministered to) his own needs and the needs of those who were with him. As Paul told the Thessalonians, he worked night and day that he might not be a burden to any of them (1 Thessalonians 2:9).

Paul did tell Timothy that elders who rule well should be given a double pay or honor, for the laborer is worthy of his hire (1 Timothy 5:17, 18). But Timothy would be dealing with well-established, growing churches, well-taught assemblies. When Paul came to a new area he was careful to show that he was not preaching the gospel in order to gain material benefits.

**35. I have shewed you all things:** ... In every way I have shown you, —WEYM ... I have in every way pointed out to you, —BRKL.

**how that so labouring:** ... that, labouring as I laboured, —TCNT ... how, by working as I do, —WEYM.

**ye ought to support the weak:** ... succor the needy, —MOFT ... the needy must be assisted, —MLNT ... and help, —NCV.

**and to remember the words of the Lord Jesus, how he said, It is more blessed to give than to receive:** ... There is more spiritual prosperity, —WUST ... There is a greater blessing in giving than in getting, —BB ... It is giving rather than receiving that brings happiness, —TNT.

**20:35.** Paul worked with his hands also, to set an example for all. The object of every believer should be to give, not just to receive. Christians should become mature and strong and work hard so they can give to help the weak (including the physically sick or weak, as well as those who are spiritually weak).

In Ephesians 4:17-32 Paul implored the Gentile believers to turn away from the empty, meaningless thinking and from the moral debauchery and greed of other Gentiles. The Greek calls for a decisive act of "putting off" their former way of life and "putting on" the new man, which is a new creation, created in the likeness of God and in righteousness (toward others) and true holiness (the kind of dedication to God the Bible calls for). Above all, they must guard against the sins of the disposition, for those sins give a place for the devil to take hold. Included among these exhortations is a command that those who stole steal no more, but work with their hands in order to be able to give to (share with) those in need. By this kind of hard work and gracious giving to the weak, they would be remembering the words of Jesus, "It is more blessed to give than to receive."

This saying of Jesus is not recorded in any of the four Gospels. However, as indicated by Galatians 1:11, 12 Paul received the central truths of the gospel by direct revelation from Jesus himself. In his epistles as well as here, Paul used sayings of Jesus to confirm the Word.

**36. And when he had thus spoken:** ... With these words, —MOFT ... When he had finished his talk, —NORL.

**he kneeled down, and prayed with them all:** ... he fell on his knees with them all and prayed, —WLMS.

**20:36.** When Paul had finished speaking, he and the elders of Ephesus went to their knees and prayed together. Praying on the knees was common in the Early Church (9:40; 21:5). But they also prayed standing and sitting.

Paul in his prayer expressed, no doubt, his desire for their spiritual welfare and committed them to God. The many prayers in Paul's epistles show he was moved by the Spirit as he prayed and poured out his heart in supplication and intercession for the people. On this occasion the time of prayer was no short, formal prayer. The Early Church knew how to seek God fervently and pour out their hearts to Him in prayer and supplication with thanksgiving.

**37. And they all wept sore:** ... There was much weeping among them all, —TNT ... much, —RTHM ... freely, —BRKL ... All were in tears, —TCNT ... with loud lamentation, —WEYM ... they cried bitterly, —KLGS.

**and fell on Paul's neck, and kissed him:** ... they embraced Paul, —TNT ... and throwing their arms round Paul's neck, they kissed him again and again, —TCNT ... ardently kissed, —DRBY ... kissed him fondly, —CNDT ... they kept on kissing him, —WUST ... they kissed him lovingly, —KJII ... affectionately, —PHLP.

**20:37.** After this time of prayer, there was a considerable amount of weeping from them all as they fell on (pressed on) Paul's neck and kissed him (probably on both cheeks). The kiss was a common greeting and farewell in all of Bible times. It was a sign of affection and love and also a sign of homage. Here it shows their friendship and affection. In fact, the Bible uses a stronger form of the word here to show how strong their love and concern for Paul was.

**38. Sorrowing most of all for the words which he spake:** ... They were pained most of all at the statement, —TNT ... grieving most of all over what he had said, —TCNT ... What saddened ... was his saying, —PHLP ... They were grieved especially over the remark, —MLNT ... being distressed especially on account of the word which he had spoken, —WORL ... they had the most anguish, —MRDK ... What made them sad most of all was because, —NLTG.

**that they should see his face no more:** ... that they would never see his face again, —TCNT ... never see him again, —NCV.

**And they accompanied him unto the ship:** ... Then they escorted him to the ship, —TNT ... And they went with him down to, —PHLP ... they were escorting him to, —WORL.

**20:38.** This was not the ordinary pain of parting. These elders were filled with acute pain and sorrow, most of all because Paul said they would see his face no more. Paul's self-sacrificing ministry in their behalf had indeed kindled a great love in their hearts for him. Such mutual love drew them together, as love always does. The real cause of divisions in an assembly is that love has gone, and self seeking lust (especially lust for power) has taken its place (James 4:1-4).

Then, after all the weeping and kissing were over, as a further mark of respect, the Ephesian elders escorted Paul to the ship. No doubt they waited on the shore to see the ship depart and to have a last glimpse of their beloved apostle.

## Chapter 21

1. **And it came to pass, that after we were gotten from them:** ... And when at last we had parted, Alford ... having torn ourselves, —RTHM ... And when we were torn away, —WSLY ... having been torn away, —WORL ... After we left them, NCV, —NLTG ... having departed from them, —SWAN ... When the parting was over, —GDSP ... After we all said good-bye to the elders, —SEB.

**and had launched:** ... launched forth, —PNT ... we sailed away, —SEB ... we put out to sea, —NAB.

**we came with a straight course unto Coos:** ... we ran before the wind to Cos, —TCNT ... we struck a beeline for Cos, —WLMS ... straight for Cos Island, —SEB ... and sailed straight to, —NAB.

**and the day following unto Rhodes:** ... the next day, —RSV ... we came to Rhodes, —TCNT.

**and from thence unto Patara:**

**21:1.** The farewell at Miletus must have been very hard for Paul and for Luke and Paul's other companions as well. This verse indicates they literally had to tear themselves away from the crowd of Ephesian elders who pressed around them to the last. Nor would things get any easier. There would be more sad farewells all along the way to Jerusalem.

When they finally put out to sea, the first day's travel took them by a straight course to Coos (Cos), a very mountainous island about 21 miles long and 6 miles wide. Dorian Greeks first colonized it. The Romans made it a free state though it was still part of the province of Asia.

The next day they sailed to Rhodes ("rose"). The city was the capital of a large island also called Rhodes. The island is about 45 miles long and 20 miles wide. The city was a commercial center, for it was at a point where great commercial sea routes crossed. The city was a splendid one, and the Colossus, a great lighthouse at its harbor, is said to have been about 105 feet high, one of the seven wonders of the ancient world.

From Rhodes, they sailed to Patara, a seaport on the southwest coast of Lycia, a small district on the south coast of Asia Minor. The Western text (Codex Bezae, D) adds "and Myra." But it is not likely Paul went on to Myra. Because of the prevailing winds, Patara was the best starting point for the next part of the trip which would take them to Phoenicia.

2. **And finding a ship sailing over unto Phenicia:** ... we found a ship which was going to, —SEB ... a ship bound for, —GDSP ... crossing over to, —WORL.

**we went aboard, and set forth:** ... and put to sea, —WEYM ... we embarked and set sail, —BRKL ... We got on it and went along, —NLTG ... we boarded it and sailed off, —NAB.

**21:2.** At Patara Paul, Luke, and the rest of Paul's company found a ship scheduled to sail directly across to Phoenicia, so they took passage on it. This would be a nonstop journey of about 600 miles.

3. **Now when we had discovered Cyprus:** ... And sighting Cyprus, —RTHM ... We sailed near the island of, —SEB ... We caught sight of, —NAB.

**we left it on the left hand:** ... and leaving it behind to the left, —RTHM ... leaving it on our left, —WLMS ... passed it on our left, —NORL ... We could see it on the north side, but we did not stop, —SEB.

**and sailed into Syria:** ... we went on to Syria, —BB ... as we continued on toward, —NAB ... to the country of, —SEB.

**and landed at Tyre:** ... and docked at Tyre, —BRKL ... We stopped at the city of, —SEB ... we put in at Tyre, —NAB.

**for there the ship was to unlade her burden:** ... since that was where, —PHLP ... was to discharge her cargo, —RTHM ... was to unload her cargo, —GDSP, —HBIE ... its freight, —CMPB.

**21:3.** About halfway to Phoenicia, they sighted the west end of the large island of Cyprus. They kept Cyprus on the left hand and continued sailing southeast to the Roman province of Syria (which included Phoenicia). The ship landed at Tyre and waited there while its cargo was unloaded. Tyre originally had two harbors, one on the coast and one on an island. But when Alexander the Great conquered the island city, he had to build a causeway, or mole, out to it in order to do so. Thus, the city was turned into a peninsula. Long before Paul's time it had recovered much of its importance and was still a major city and seaport.

4. **And finding disciples:** ... Having searched for the disciples and found them, —WEYM ... we found some followers of Jesus, —SEB ... We looked for the Christians, —NLTG.

**we tarried there seven days:** ... we stayed with them, —SEB ... and remained there seven days, —RTHM ... and stayed a week with them, —TCNT.

**who said to Paul:** ... They advised Paul, —BRKL ... they warned Paul, —TCNT ... Some of them advised, —FNTN ... they tried to tell Paul, —NAB.

**through the Spirit:** ... Speaking under the influence of the Spirit, —TCNT ... felt led by the Spirit again and again, —PHLP ... because of impressions made by the Spirit, —WLMS ... Instructed by the Spirit, —GDSP ... taught by the Spirit, —WEYM ... Under the Spirit's prompting, —NAB.

**that he should not go up to Jerusalem:** ... he should not set foot, —MNTG ... not to proceed to Jerusalem, —WEYM.

**21:4.** Paul had never visited Tyre before, but he knew there were believers there. The city was probably evangelized by some of those who were scattered by the persecution which followed the death of Stephen. Paul did not know where the Christians were, but he sought them out and spent 7 days visiting with them.

While Paul and his company were enjoying fellowship with the believers in Tyre, the Spirit, as in many places before, warned of what was going to happen to Paul in Jerusalem. The Bible does not say how the Spirit did this, but from what happened a little later in Caesarea, the warning no doubt came through a prophecy.

The believers "through the Spirit" said (kept saying) to Paul not to go up to Jerusalem. This did not mean God had changed His mind. God is not fickle. He does not change His mind in that way. Moreover, Paul was sensitive to the Holy Spirit. When he was forbidden by the Holy Spirit to preach in the Roman province of Asia, in obedience he bypassed it immediately.

Actually, the Greek does not mean the Spirit did not want Paul to go to Jerusalem. The word "through" (Greek, *dia*) is not the word used in previous passages for the direct agency of the Holy Spirit. (See 13:4 where the Greek is *hupo*, a word used for direct or primary agency.) Here the Greek is better translated "in consequence of the Spirit," that is, because of what the Spirit said. The Spirit himself definitely did not forbid Paul to go on to Jerusalem. The Spirit was, in fact, constraining Paul to go (20:22). Paul knew the Holy Spirit does not contradict himself. It was not the Spirit but the believers' love for Paul that made them say he should not go. In other words, because of the prophecy of bonds and imprisonment the people voiced their own feeling that he should not go. But Paul refused to let them force their feelings on him. So he still obeyed what the Holy Spirit directed him personally to do, that is, to go on to Jerusalem.

**5. And when he had accomplished those days:** ... When, however, our time was up, —WEYM ... When we finished our visit, —EVRD ... When our time was up, —NLTG ... when the days had passed, —SWAN.

**we departed and went our way:** ... we left and continued our trip, —EVRD, —SEB ... went out, —SWAN ... we started out on our journey again, —WMCK ... we were resuming our journey, —WORL.

**and they all brought us on our way, with wives and children:** ... escorting us, —TCNT ... All of themwives and children included, —NAB ... escorted by all the believers with their wives and children, —MLNT ... They all came out to see us off ... accompanying us, —PHLP ... being conducted by all, —SWAN.

**till we were out of the city:** ... as far as outside the city, —RTHM ... went with us out of town, —NLTG.

**and we kneeled down on the shore, and prayed:** ... kneeling on the beach, —CNDT.

**21:5.** Paul no doubt ministered in Tyre as he had elsewhere, with a deep love for the Lord and for the people. Since this was already a well-established assembly, they knew the facts of the gospel, and they were filled with the Holy Spirit. Thus, Paul was able to give them further instruction and encouragement.

It is clear that during the 7 days all the believers came to know and love Paul. For when the week was up, all of them, along with their wives and children, escorted Paul out of the city to the level, sandy beach outside Tyre. There beside the beautiful blue Mediterranean Sea they knelt and prayed. What a volume of prayer must have gone up before the Lord as they joined in unison, praying for Paul and his company. It is likely that Paul also led out in prayer for them.

**6. And when we had taken our leave one of another:** ... and then said goodbye to one another, —TCNT ... and said farewell, —SWAN ... then we bade one another goodbye, —GDSP ... then embraced one another, —MLNT.

**we took ship:** ... we went on board the ship, —RSV ... and embarked in the ship, —ALFD ... we boarded the ship, —NAB ... our ship, —WMCK.

**and they returned home again:** ... they went home, —GDSP ... went back to their homes, —MLNT.

**21:6.** After prayer they gave parting greetings to each other. These were very warm greetings and were probably accompanied by a kiss and probably some tears. Then Paul and his company entered the ship, and the believers and their families returned to their homes. This was apparently the one and only time Paul visited the city of Tyre. On his journey as a prisoner to Rome the ship touched at Sidon but not Tyre (27:2f.).

The assembly at Tyre seems to have shown a unity and maturity that must have blessed Paul. The warning of what awaited Paul in Jerusalem also shows that the gifts and ministries of the Spirit were present in the assembly. The Bible shows God uses many types of ministries to train believers and to bring them to a maturity where they can all do a work of ministry and service. Notice, however, that God used Paul in a special way. God does not use merely ministries, but ministers.

**7. And when we had finished our course from Tyre, we came to Ptolemais:** ... We continued our sailing, going from Tyre to Ptolemais, —BECK ... We continued our trip from, —*EVRD* . . . The same ship took us from, —*NLTG* . . . when we finished the voyage from, —*SWAN*.

**and saluted the brethren:** . . . and exchanged greetings, —*TCNT* . . . There we greeted our fellow Christians, —*BECK* . . . Here we inquired after the welfare of, —*WEYM* . . . greeted the believers, —*EVRD*.

**and abode with them one day:** . . . spent a day with them, —*TCNT* . . . stayed, —*WMCK*

**21:7.** After they left Tyre, the ship sailed smoothly to Ptolemais where it stopped for 1 day.

Ptolemais was the Old Testament Accho mentioned in Judges 1:31 and is now called Acre or Akka. The city is on a small promontory about 8 miles north of the headland of Mount Carmel, and about 25 miles south of Tyre. In the division of the land after Joshua's conquest, the city was assigned to the tribe of Asher, but they never took possession of it. It remained under the dominion of Tyre and Sidon until the Assyrians took it in about 70 B.C. About 200 B.C. its name was changed to Ptolemais, probably in honor of Ptolemy Philadelphus (285-246 B.C.). In New Testament times it was an important seaport for trade with Galilee, the Decapolis, and Arabia. Many Jews lived there, and in the Roman period the Emperor Claudius settled a group of ex-soldiers from the Roman army in Ptolemais. By the time of Paul's visit there was a well-established church. Paul and his company greeted the believers and stayed with them for the day.

**8. And the next day we that were of Paul's company departed:** . . . And on the morrow we, —*ASV* . . . The next day we left, —*TCNT* . . . The following day we departed, —*MLNT*.

**and came unto Caesarea:** . . . and arrived at, —*MLNT* . . . and reached Caesarea, —*TCNT*.

**and we entered into the house of Philip the evangelist:** . . . where we went to the house of Philip, the Missionary, —*TCNT* . . . were guests in the house of Philip, the preacher, —*BB* . . . where we called at the home of, —*MLNT* . . . He was a preacher who goes from town to town, —*NLTG*.

**which was one of the seven:** . . . who was one of the Seven, —*TCNT* . . . seven servants, —*SEB* . . . was one of the seven church leaders, —*NLTG* . . . of the seven helpers, —*NCV*.

**and abode with him:** . . . and stayed with him, —*WMCK* . . . by whom we were entertained, —*MLNT*.

**21:8.** The next day the ship brought them to Caesarea. There they left the ship for the land journey to Jerusalem. But first they went to the house of Philip the evangelist.

God must have blessed Philip materially, for his home was large enough to entertain Paul and his company. It is probable that his home was the chief Christian center in Caesarea and that an assembly of believers gathered there.

This may mean also that Paul had visited there on previous occasions when he had passed through Caesarea and that he was well-known to Philip. Philip obviously welcomed him and persuaded him and his company to stay with him for a time. Hospitality for fellow believers and for traveling teachers and preachers is very strongly advocated in the New Testament.

**9. And the same man had four daughters, virgins:** . . . unmarried daughters, —*BECK* . . . four maiden daughters, —*FNTN*.

**which did prophesy:** . . . who had the gift of prophecy, —*TCNT* . . . who were prophetesses, —*WEYM* . . . all of whom spoke by the Spirit of God, —*PHLP* . . . They spoke the Word of God, —*NLTG*.

**21:9.** The Bible now draws attention to Philip's four virgin daughters who prophesied. This is significant for several reasons. First, it indicates Joel's prophecy that both sons and daughters would prophesy was being fulfilled in the Early Church (Joel 2:28; Acts 2:17). The Greek here does not call them prophetesses, but uses an attributive participle in order to emphasize this fulfillment of Joel's prophecy. They were four prophesying virgin daughters.

The use of the participle also indicates they were regularly used by the Holy Spirit in this ministry of prophesying. That they were virgins further indicates they had given themselves to this ministry. It was unusual in those days for a woman not to be married. These daughters had separated themselves for the service of the Lord.

This shows something about Philip also. Ordinarily the father had the responsibility to make arrangements for his daughters to be married. The fact that Philip did not do so shows he was more concerned that his daughters follow the Lord than that they follow the social customs of the day.

The church historian Eusebius (A.D. 260-340) quotes Papias as saying these daughters moved to Asia, lived long lives, and continued to minister and witness to the Early Church. Thus they were used "as the Spirit wills." (In 1 Corinthians 12:11 "every man" is literally "each one," including both men and women.)

**10. And as we tarried there many days:** . . . During our visit, which lasted several days, —*TCNT* . . . Now during our somewhat lengthy stay, —*WEYM* . . . After we had stayed there for many days, —*SEB* . . . After we had been there for some time, —*EVRD* . . . as we remained, —*FNTN* . . . During our few days' stay, —*NAB* . . . When we had stayed there, —*WMCK* . . . During our stay there, —*PHLP* . . . We had stopped there for several days, —*MLNT* . . . While we were there a few days, —NLTG...We spent a number of days there, and in the course of them, —GDSP.

**there came down from Judaea a certain prophet, named Agabus:**...a man who speaks for God, —NLTG...by the name of, —PHLP...arrived from, —NAB...a preacher of the name of, —FNTN.

**21:10.** At Miletus Paul was anxious to hurry on his way. But here the blessing of the Lord was so rich that he stayed a considerable number of days. It seems obvious that the ministry of Philip's four daughters as they prophesied must have brought encouragement and blessing to Paul and his company. According to 1 Corinthians 14:3, when a person prophesies, he or she speaks for God by the Spirit in a language everyone understands. The speaking is to men (human beings, including both men and women). The words of the prophesying bring edification (that builds up spiritually and develops or confirms faith), exhortation (that encourages and awakens, challenging all to move ahead in faithfulness and love), and comfort (that cheers, revives, and encourages hope and expectation). By prophesying, these daughters were blessing, edifying, and building up spiritually all the believers who heard.

Possibly Philip gave Luke much information concerning the early days of the church at Jerusalem, facts which the Holy Spirit was able to direct Luke to use in writing the Book of Acts.

After a number of days the prophet Agabus, the same one who prophesied in 11:28, came down from Judea. He had probably heard the news that Paul was in Caesarea, though it is also possible the Holy Spirit simply directed him to go.

**11. And when he was come unto us, he took Paul's girdle:**...and called on us, —MLNT...He came up to us, and taking Paul's belt, —NAB...When he came to see us, —PHLP...borrowed Paul's belt, —EVRD.
**and bound his own hands and feet, and said:**...and, tying his feet and hands, —BRKL...and used it to tie, —NLTG...and fastened his own hands, —WMCK.
**Thus saith the Holy Ghost:**...This is what the Holy Spirit says, —TCNT...Thus speaks, —MLNT...These are the words of the Holy Spirit, —WMCK...tells me, —SEB.
**So shall the Jews at Jerusalem bind the man that owneth this girdle:**...This is how the Jews, —EVRD...In like manner shall, —FNTN...will tie the man this belt belongs to, —BECK...The man whose belt this is will be fastened like this, —WMCK...will be bound like this, —PHLP.
**and shall deliver him into the hands of the Gentiles:**...and will hand him over to, —WEYM...to the heathen! —GDSP...to heathen hands, —FNTN.

**21:11.** Agabus took Paul's belt (probably a wide belt made of linen cloth, long enough to be wrapped several times around the waist) and

bound his own feet and hands as an object lesson. Then he gave a prophecy from the Holy Spirit that the Jews would bind (or be the cause of binding) Paul and give him over into the custody of the Gentiles (the Romans). In general, Paul knew of the things he would suffer because of the gospel (see 9:16), but in particular, he was fully aware of the problems that faced him in Jerusalem (20:23; 21:4). The Spirit, speaking through Agabus, did not forbid the journey to Jerusalem. The trip was too important to cancel just when the goal was in sight.

**12. And when we heard these things:**...As soon as we heard these words, —WEYM...On hearing this, —BRKL, —MLNT...heard him say this, —PHLP.
**both we, and they of that place:**...the residents, —MRDK...the people there, —EVRD.
**besought him not to go up to Jerusalem:**...began to entreat Paul, —TCNT...begged Paul not to go, —EVRD.

**21:12.** Because of the prophecy of Agabus, those who were meeting in Philip's house along with Paul's companions all begged him not to go up to Jerusalem. This was undoubtedly like what happened at Tyre. The people, when they heard the Spirit's message, expressed their own feelings and their own concern for Paul's welfare. The Greek indicates they kept on doing so.

**13. Then Paul answered:**...His reply was, —WEYM.
**What mean ye to weep and to break mine heart?:**...What do you achieve by weeping and discouraging me, —BRKL...unnerving me with all your tears, —PHLP...and crushing my heart? —RTHM...making me weak in my purpose, —BECK...disheartening me? —MOFT...weaken my resolution, —JB...Why are you making me so sad? —SEB...with your grief? —MNTG.
**for I am ready not to be bound only:**...not only to be a prisoner, —BB...I am prepared not merely to be bound, —BRKL...I am ready to be tied up, —EVRD...to be put in chains, —NLTG.
**but also to die at Jerusalem:**...but even to suffer death, —TCNT.
**for the name of the Lord Jesus:**...in behalf of the name of, —RTHM...for the sake of the Lord Jesus! —WEYM.

**21:13.** Not only did they keep begging Paul not to go, they became quite emotionally distraught and began to weep. They could not bear to think of anything happening to Paul, they loved and respected him so.

Paul, however, said, "What are you doing, weeping and making me feel crushed to pieces?" Breaking (crushing to pieces) the heart was a phrase used to mean breaking the will, weakening the purpose, or causing a person to "go to pieces" so that he could accomplish nothing. To get them to stop their weeping and begging, Paul declared he was ready not only to be bound, but to die in Jerusalem for the sake of the name of the Lord Jesus. Actually, he had long ago made this kind of commitment. He had often risked his life for the sake of the gospel and for the sake of winning the lost to Christ. He knew too that death might strip him of this present body, but he would be immediately in the presence of the Lord (2 Corinthians 5:6-8). Later he said he was hard pressed to decide between life and death. He had a desire to go and be with Christ, but for the sake of those who needed him, he was willing to stay and be a help (Philippians 1:20-25).

Thus, Paul in this case did not let his friends hinder him. Through the constraint of the Holy Spirit in his own soul, he had a clearer vision of the will of God than they did. For this reason, the threat of persecution did not bring despair to his heart. He had the assurance that whatever happened, even death, it would bring glory to Jesus' name. Though he now had no hope of escaping chains and imprisonment, he voiced his determination to do God's will.

**14. And when he would not be persuaded:** ... So when he was not to be dissuaded, *—WEYM* ... Paul would not listen to us, *—NLTG* ... So as he would not yield, *—GDSP.*

**we ceased, saying:** ... we said no more to him, *—TCNT* ... we ceased remonstrating with him, *—WEYM* ... we stopped begging him, *—WLMS* ... we kept quiet, *—ADAM* ... we acquiesced, *—CNFT* ... So, we stopped trying, *—SEB* ... we were silent, *—SWAN.*

**The will of the Lord be done:** ... Let the purpose of God be done, *—BB* ... We pray that what the Lord wants will be done, *—EVRD.*

**21:14.** Finally Paul's friends gave up. They had to recognize that they, not Paul, had been unwilling to submit to the will of God. (Compare Luke 22:42.) It was indeed God's will for Paul to go to Jerusalem.

The events which followed show that Paul was right. If he had not gone to Jerusalem, he would have missed a new vision of Jesus (23:11), plus many miracles and opportunities to witness. He would also have missed God's way of getting him to Rome. God's way is sometimes a hard way, but it is always the best way!

It was important also for the Church to have these warnings from the Spirit. Had Paul gone up to Jerusalem without them, there were Judaizers around who would have been quick to take Paul's arrest as a judgment of God. They would have said, "See, did we not tell you? Paul's preaching is all wrong. You Gentiles must become Jews and be circumcised or you will lose your salvation."

This would have brought great confusion into the churches. But through these prophecies the Holy Spirit bore witness to Paul and the gospel he preached. At the same time, the Church itself was protected from forces which could have caused division.

**15. And after those days:** ... At the end of our visit, *—TCNT* ... A few days afterwards, *—WEYM.*

**we took up our carriages:** ... we packed our baggage, *—ASV* ... we got ready, *—EVRD, —WLMS* ... we packed up, *—TCNT* ... we made our preparations, *—GDSP.*

**and went up to Jerusalem:** ... and continued our journey, *—WEYM* ... and started for, *—MOFT* ... we ascended to, *—FNTN.*

**21:15.** After those days in the house of Philip, Paul and his company made preparations to go up to Jerusalem. This probably means they hired horses and saddled them up. Some writers, however, believe it means simply that they packed their bags (their luggage).

**16. There went with us also certain of the disciples of Caesarea:** ... Some of the disciples from Caesarea, *—TCNT* ... also joined our party, *—WEYM* ... also accompanied us, *—FNTN.*

**and brought with them one Mnason of Cyprus:** ... by whom we were introduced to, *—FNTN.*

**an old disciple:** ... a disciple of long standing, *—TCNT* ... an aged disciple, *—WORL* ... He was one of the first followers, *—NLTG* ... a disciple from the first, Fenton.

**with whom we should lodge:** ... we were to stay, *—TCNT.*

**21:16.** Some of the disciples from Caesarea went with Paul and his company. These believers from Caesarea knew a believer from Cyprus, Mnason (the M is not pronounced). Mnason, like Barnabas, was one of the "old" (original) disciples, that is, one of the 120. (He was not necessarily "old" in age.) He was known as one who delighted to entertain strangers (foreigners).

Some translations indicate that Mnason was visiting in Caesarea at the time Paul was there and came up with them to Jerusalem. But the Greek text does not need to be interpreted this way. It is more likely that the Caesarean believers simply brought Paul and his company to Mnason's house in Jerusalem. The Western text (Codex Bezae, D), however, takes it to mean that Mnason's house was in a village on the way to Jerusalem. Actually, the journey to Jerusalem was too long for 1 day, so it is possible the Western text is correct here in that Mnason's house was west of Jerusalem and became a convenient headquarters for the Jerusalem visit.

**17. And when we were come to Jerusalem:** ... On our arrival at Jerusalem, —TCNT ... when we arrived at, —FNTN.

**the brethren received us gladly:** ... gladly welcomed us, —RTHM ... gave us a hearty welcome, —GDSP, —TCNT ... a very warm welcome, —PHLP ... were pleased to see us, —BB ... glad to see us, —NLTG.

**21:17.** At Jerusalem the brethren (including Mnason) welcomed them joyfully and entertained them hospitably. They were really glad to see Paul and his company, including the Gentile believers.

**18. And the day following:** ... And on the next day, —RTHM ... on the following morning, —FNTN.

**Paul went in with us unto James:** ... Paul went with us to have an interview with, —TCNT ... accompanied us to James, —FNTN ... to visit James, —PHLP.

**and all the elders were present:** ... and all the Officers of the Church, —TCNT ... where all the elders assembled, —FNTN ... presbyters, —MOFT.

**21:18.** The next day Paul took Luke and the rest of his company to see James, the brother of Jesus, who was now the chief elder of the church in Jerusalem. The other elders were also present. These were undoubtedly the elders (administrative officers, much like the pastors of today) who were responsible for taking care of the house churches or local assemblies in Jerusalem and its environs. What follows shows there were a large number of them.

At this point it is worth noting also that none of the apostles are mentioned. Seven years before, at the Council of Jerusalem (A.D. 49), they were all present. Now it seems, as much of early church tradition says, they were already scattered, spreading the gospel in many different directions. John, for example, went to Ephesus. Some say Andrew was martyred in Scythia, others say in Greece. Tradition is strong that Thomas was martyred in India.

**19. And when he had saluted them:** ... After greeting them, —FNTN, —TCNT ... After exchanging greetings, —WEYM.

**he declared particularly:** ... he went on to narrate one by one, —RTHM ... Paul related in detail, —TCNT ... described in detail, —MOFT ... he recounted to them step by step, —BRKL ... he carefully explained, —KLGS ... Then he told them exactly how, —SEB ... gave a detailed account of, —GDSP ... and told them everything, —NCV.

**what things God had wrought among the Gentiles by his ministry:** ... each of the things, —RTHM ... that God had done among the Gentiles through his efforts, —TCNT ... through his service, —WLMS.

**21:19.** Paul greeted the Jerusalem elders warmly, undoubtedly with a holy kiss, as was the custom (Romans 16:16; 1 Corinthians 16:20; 2 Corinthians 13:12; 1 Thessalonians 5:26). He probably pronounced blessings on them in the name of the Lord Jesus.

After greeting them, Paul gave a detailed account of what God had done among the Gentiles through his ministry. This must have been a step-by-step rehearsal of his second and third missionary journeys. Specifically, he told them everything that had happened since the last time he was with them at the Council referred to in chapter 15. He must have emphasized the vision that gave him the Macedonian call, the conversion of the Philippian jailer, the success at Beroea, the victories at Corinth, the 2 years he taught in the schoolroom of Tyrannus in Ephesus, the special miracles, the burning of the books of magic, and the establishment of the churches in the various cities of the Roman province of Asia.

The brief account of these journeys in the Book of Acts fills believers' hearts with praise to God and admiration for the men God used. But the Book of Acts does not record all that happened. Think what the whole story must have been! Think too that Paul accomplished all this without a printed Bible, and without the help of newspapers, magazines, radio, or television. He had no monthly check, no guaranteed support. In addition, Jews, heathen, and false brethren opposed him on every hand. Again and again he risked his life for the gospel, but the Lord saw him through it all in triumph. As he was leaving for Jerusalem, he wrote the Romans and was able to say, "I will not dare to speak of any of those things which Christ hath not wrought by me, to make the Gentiles obedient, by word and deed, through mighty signs and wonders, by the power of the Spirit of God; so that from Jerusalem, and round about unto Illyricum (on the coast of the Adriatic Sea opposite Italy), I have fully preached the gospel" (Romans 15:18, 19).

**20. And when they heard it:** ... and they, on hearing this account, —PHLP.

**they glorified the Lord:** ... they began praising God, —TCNT ... gave glory to God, —WEYM ... thanked God, —FNTN.

**and said unto him:** ... They told him, —BECK ... remarked, —FNTN.

**Thou seest, brother:** ... You see, —NLTG.

**how many thousands of Jews there are which believe:** ... how many myriads there are, —RTHM ... that the Jews who have become believers in Christ may be numbered by tens of thousands, —TCNT ... of Christians there are among, —NLTG.

**and they are all zealous of the law:** ... naturally earnest in upholding the Jewish Law, —TCNT ... zealots for the law, —HBIE ... and every one of them is a staunch upholder of the law, —PHLP ... all zealous supporters of the law, —NORL ... they all think it is very important to obey, —SEB ... ardent upholders, —MOFT.

**21:20.** James and all the Jerusalem elders glorified God because of what He was doing among the Gentiles. But they had a problem. Another matter of deep concern was affecting the Jerusalem church. Though the elders were rejoicing and were willing to congratulate Paul, he would have to do something more if his good report was to influence the thousands of Jewish believers in Palestine.

"Thousands" here is literally tens of thousands. The Jerusalem church was still growing by leaps and bounds. All of these converts from Judaism had accepted Jesus as their Messiah, Lord, and Saviour. Yet they were still zealous of the Law, eagerly devoted to the law of Moses, ardent observers of the Law. Undoubtedly their newfound faith in Christ stirred them up to serve God with new zeal, so they applied this to obeying the Law as they had been taught all their lives.

**21. And they are informed of thee:** ... Now they have heard it rumoured concerning thee, —RTHM ... again and again, —MNTG ... Now what they have been told about you is, —WEYM ... were informed by report concerning you, —WORL.
**that thou teachest all the Jews which are among the Gentiles to forsake Moses:** ... to discard Moses, —TCNT ... to turn their backs on Moses, —WLMS ... to give up the law of Moses, —BB ... to disregard the Law of Moses, —PHLP ... apostasy from Moses, —PNT ... to abandon the law, —SEB ... to break away from, —NLTG ... to leave the law, —NCV.
**saying that they ought not to circumcise their children:** ... advising them not to, —FNTN ... you continue to tell them to stop circumcising, —WLMS ... telling them to not do the religious act of becoming a Jew, —NLTG.
**neither to walk after the customs:** ... or even to observe Jewish customs, —TCNT ... old-established customs, —WEYM ... the cherished customs, —WLMS ... and not to keep the old rules, —BB.

**21:21.** False teachers had come among the Jewish believers. These were probably Judaizers who were still teaching that Gentiles must become Jews in faith before they could be genuine Christians and be truly saved. Or they may have been unconverted Jews from Asia Minor, Macedonia, or Greece, who were enemies of Paul. They had followed Paul from place to place before and stirred up trouble. They looked on Paul as a sort of religious anarchist or revolutionary who launched malicious attacks on the law of Moses and who was urging Jews everywhere to forsake the Law.

These false teachers told the Jerusalem believers again and again that Paul was teaching all the Jews who lived among the Gentiles (the nations outside of Palestine) not to circumcise their children. They also said Paul taught these Jewish believers to stop walking (conducting their lives) according to their (Jewish) customs.

This was nothing but slander. Paul never taught the Jews they had to become Gentiles or give up their Jewish manners and customs in order to follow Christ. Paul had even circumcised Timothy. He had also taken a vow recently himself.

**22. What is it therefore?:** ... What shall we do about it, —BECK ... Now, how about it, —BRKL ... What then ought you to do, —WEYM ... What is your duty, then, —WLMS.
**the multitude must needs come together:** ... Undoubtedly, —CNDT ... A crowd of them will surely gather about you, —NORL.
**for they will hear that thou art come:** ... as they are certain to hear of your arrival, —TCNT ... for they will learn, —BRKL ... for they are simply bound to hear, —PHLP.

**21:22.** These accusations against Paul were false, but everyone in Jerusalem had heard them again and again, and thousands of Christians in Palestine who were faithful to the Law misunderstood Paul's ministry and motivation.

Now since everyone in Jerusalem would surely hear that Paul had come, the crowd would come together; so before they did, something had to be done to prevent trouble or even a riot. What should be done?

**23. Do therefore this that we say to thee:** ... Do what we are going to suggest, —TCNT ... why not follow this suggestion of ours, —PHLP.
**We have four men which have a vow on them:** ... who of their own accord put themselves under a vow, —TCNT.

**21:23.** James and the elders had a suggestion. They saw a way to stop the rumors and show that the bad report about Paul was false. Four of the Jewish believers had taken a vow upon themselves, obviously a temporary Nazarite vow.

The Nazarite vow was instituted after God set apart the Levites to serve the tabernacle and the family of Aaron as priests. God did not want the people to think the priests and Levites were closer to Him or more dedicated to Him than He wanted the people to be. So God gave the Nazarite vow as an opportunity whereby men or women could declare their total dedication to God and His will.

Usually the vow was taken for a limited period of time. During the time they were observing the vow, they were not to cut or trim any of the hair on the head. By this they declared God's will was more important to them than any human custom. They were not to drink wine or grape juice, nor eat grapes or raisins. The grapevine had become a symbol of human pleasures, so they put everything connected with it aside in order to declare that God was their chief joy. They were not to touch any dead human body. Preparing a body for burial was considered the last act of love. By refraining from this, they were declaring their love for God was greater than any human love. It was a complete consecration.

At the close of the period they had chosen for the vow, they would offer rather expensive sacrifices, including a male and female lamb, a ram, and other offerings. They would then shave their heads as a sign the vow was completed (Numbers 6:14-20).

**24. Them take:** ... Make friends, —TCNT ... Associate with these men, —WEYM ... Take them along with you, —WLMS.

**and purify thyself with them:** ... Join in their abstinence, —TCNT.

**and be at charges with them:** ... and bear their expenses, —TCNT ... and pay their expenses, —WEYM ... and incur expense for them, —WORL ... and bear the costs for them, —HBIE ... Pay their bills, —KLGS.

**that they may shave their heads:** ... so that they may have their hair cut short, —PHLP ... shall shave, —MRDK.

**and all may know:** ... and then all will see, —TCNT ... Then everyone will realize, —BRKL.

**that those things, whereof they were informed concerning thee, are nothing:** ... that the things which they have heard rumoured, —RTHM ... there is nothing in these stories, —MOFT ... that there is no truth in the things they have been told about you, —TCNT ... that there is no basis for the reports, —BRKL.

**but that thou thyself also walkest orderly, and keepest the law:** ... on-the-contrary, —RTHM ... you yourself rule your life in obedience to the Jewish Law, —TCNT ... living as a constant observer, —WLMS ... but that you personally order your life in observance, —BRKL ... but you live strictly according, —BECK ... guarding the law, —RTHM ... respect the law of Moses in your own life, —SEB.

**21:24.** Paul did not have to take the vow himself. But he was asked by the Jerusalem leaders to go through the ceremonies of purifying himself along with the four who were taking the vow and pay their expenses, especially pay for the sacrifices so they could complete their vow and shave their heads.

Numbers 6:9-12 shows that if someone died suddenly beside a person who was observing a Nazarite vow, this would defile him, that is, make him ceremonially unclean. Then he would have to go through 7 days of ceremonial purification.

It is possible the Jewish Christians considered Paul ceremonially unclean because of his contact with the Gentiles, for he had lived in Gentile homes and eaten nonkosher food with the Gentiles. Thus, Paul would please them by going through the ceremonies of purification himself. This, along with his paying the expenses of the four Jewish believers, would show the whole assembly of believers and everyone else in Jerusalem that Paul did not teach Jewish believers to go against the customs of their fathers. It would also answer all the false things said about Paul and would demonstrate that Paul himself was still willing to observe the Law.

**25. As touching the Gentiles which believe:** ... As to the Gentiles who have become believers in Christ, —TCNT ... as for non-Jewish believers, —SEB ... As for the people who are not Jews, —NLTG.

**we have written and concluded:** ... we have sent our decision, —TCNT ... we have sent them our resolution, —WLMS.

**that they observe no such thing:** ... they should keep themselves from things, —ASV.

**save only that they keep themselves from things offered to idols, and from blood, and from strangled, and from fornication:** ... that has been given to gods ... must keep away from sex sins, —NLTG ... from whoredom, —MRDK ... any kind of sexual sin, —SEB.

**21:25.** James and the elders then confirmed the decision of the Council (see chapter 15), a decision Paul had already carried to the Gentile believers. Though they wanted Paul, as a Jewish believer, to show he did not ask Jews to live like Gentiles, they were willing to accept Gentile believers without asking them to become Jews.

The Jewish Christian leaders reminded Paul of the previous decision (15:13-21). The Gentile believers did not need to be circumcised or keep the Law. These things had been written in the letter sent out, and as far as the Jerusalem church leaders were concerned, they still stood. They had not changed their minds.

**26. Then Paul took the men:** ... On this Paul joined the men, —TCNT ... So Paul associated with the men, —WEYM ... Then Paul took the men along with him, —WLMS.

**and the next day purifying himself with them:** ... shared in the washing ceremony, —SEB ... went through the religious worship of washing with them, —NLTG.

**entered into the temple:** ... the house of God, —NLTG.

**to signify the accomplishment of the days of purification:** ... announcing the completion of the days of the purification, —HBIE ... when the days of the cleansing ceremony would be ended, —SEB.

**until that an offering should be offered for every one of them:** ... and there he remained until the sacrifice for each one of them was offered, —WEYM ... Then the gift for each one of them would be given as an act of worship, —NLTG.

**21:26.** The next day Paul took the four men and did as he was asked to do, spreading the news of the completing of the days of purification until the sacrifice was brought for each of them.

This was not a compromise on Paul's part. Paul knew these Jewish ceremonies had no value as far as salvation is concerned. But he did recognize that God had instituted them and that they had a value as symbols to teach, illustrate, and implant truth in the hearts and minds of Jewish believers. Thus, the Jewish believers could still carry out these ceremonies, not to gain salvation, not to get in right relation with God, but to express a dedication to God that was already settled in their hearts through Christ and through their acceptance of His work on the cross and the justification that comes through His resurrection.

It was also Paul's practice to meet people half-way as long as no fundamental principle of the gospel was compromised. He said, "Unto the Jews I became as a Jew, that I might gain the Jews; to them that are under the law, as under the law, that I might gain them that are under the law; to them that are without law (outside the Jewish law), as without law, (being not without law to God, but under the law to Christ,) that I might gain them that are without law. To the weak became I as weak, that I might gain the weak: I am made all things to all men, that I might by all means save some. And this I do for the gospel's sake, that I might be partaker thereof with you" (1 Corinthians 9:20-23).

Paul taught that Christ fulfilled all the sacrifices of the Law at the Cross. He taught also that it was not circumcision or uncircumcision that counted but being a new creature (creation) in Christ (2 Corinthians 5:17; Galatians 6:15). He also warned the Gentiles that it was foolish to begin in the Spirit and then seek growth and development through legality and outward fleshly ceremonies (Galatians 3:1-5). But neither Gentile liberty nor any of these principles were at stake, so Paul graciously yielded to the request of the Jerusalem elders. Thus he set an example for all believers when they are faced with questions that are a matter of doing or not doing some nonessential thing. If this means giving up or putting aside personal ideas, wishes, preferences, or intentions, the Christian thing to do is to yield.

**27. And when the seven days were almost ended:** ... But, just as the seven days were drawing to a close, —TCNT ... were-on-the-point of being concluded, —RTHM ... were almost finished, —NLTG ... almost completed, —SWAN ... at an end, —WMCK

**the Jews which were of Asia:** ... the Jews from the province of Asia, —WEYM ... some of the Asiatic Judeans, —FNTN ... from Roman Asia, —WMCK

**when they saw him in the temple:** ... caught sight of him, —GDSP ... caught a glimpse of him in the temple, —WLMS ... observing him, —FNTN ... saw Paul in the house of God, —NLTG.

**stirred up all the people:** ... and began to stir up all the crowd, —MNTG ... They excited the whole crowd into an uproar, —NORL ... They caused all the people to be upset, —EVRD ... They made the people turn against him, —NLTG ... incited the whole of the rabble, —FNTN ... threw the whole crowd into disorder, —WMCK

**and laid hands on him:** ... by seizing Paul, —TCNT ... and seized him, —WLMS ... and grabbed hold of him, —BRKL ... they threw their hands upon, —FNTN.

**21:27.** Paul's charitable action of paying for the sacrifices of these four men worked well as far as the Jewish believers were concerned. But as far as the majority of the people who came to the feast in Jerusalem was concerned, it failed. Instead of satisfying the non-Christian Jews, the opposite happened. When the 7 days of purification were almost ended, Jews from the Roman province of Asia were in Jerusalem for the Feast of Pentecost (a harvest festival to the Jews). These may have been some who had persecuted and beaten Paul in their home synagogues. They saw him in the temple. Immediately they went to work stirring up a riot and laid violent hands on Paul.

This was not the first time they had thrown a crowd into confusion. They looked at Paul as a false prophet and considered the miracles he performed as signs meant to test their loyalty to God and to the law of Moses. Back in their hometowns Paul had escaped them. Now was their opportunity. Now they had him.

**28. Crying out:** ... as they kept shouting, —WLMS ... yelling, —BECK.

**Men of Israel, help:** ... Men! Israelites! —FNTN ... help! help! —WLMS ... come to our help, —BB ... to our aid! —BRKL.

**This is the man:** ... here is the fellow, —WMCK

**that teacheth all men every where against the people:** ... who by his teaching sets everyone everywhere against our people, —WMCK ... who goes everywhere preaching to everybody against the Jewish people, —WEYM.

**and the law, and this place:** ... our law, and this sanctuary, —NEB ... and the temple, —WMCK

**and further brought Greeks also into the temple:** ... and besides, —GDSP ... and now he has even brought, —WMCK ... and, what is more, he has actually brought Greeks into the Temple, —TCNT ... non-Jews, —BECK.

**and hath polluted this holy place:** . . . defiled, —RSV . . . desecrated, —WEYM . . . and made this holy place unclean, —BB . . . contaminated, —CNDT . . . has profaned this holy place, —WUST . . . made this holy place common! —ADAM . . . this holy place dirty, —NLTG.

**21:28.** As these Asian Jews grabbed Paul they began shouting accusations against him. They addressed the rest of the Jews in the temple court as "Men of Israel," drawing attention to them not just as Jews but as God's covenant people crying out for their help.

They kept shouting that Paul taught everyone everywhere against the people, that is, against the Jews and against the law of Moses. Then they added that he had now defiled the temple by bringing in Greeks, that is, Greek-speaking Gentiles.

This was a serious charge. The temple in New Testament times was surrounded by three courts. The innermost court was the Court of Israel. Here the men could come as Israelites and offer sacrifices required by the Law. But that was as far as the men could go. Only the consecrated priests could enter the temple building itself, and only the high priest could enter the inner sanctuary.

The second court was the Court of the Women, so called because it was as far as the women could go. Actually, the whole family could gather in this court for prayer and worship. Rabbis, including Jesus, taught in this court. Christians gathered in it daily at the hours of prayer. But only Jews were allowed to enter it.

The outer court was called the Court of the Gentiles because it was as far as Gentiles could go. Archaeologists have found two of the inscriptions once placed at the entrances to the Court of the Women. They read (in Greek), "No foreigner may enter within this barricade which surrounds the temple and enclosure (its two inner courts). Anyone caught doing so will have himself to blame for his ensuing death."

29. **(For they had seen before with him in the city Trophimus an Ephesian, whom they supposed that Paul had brought into the temple.):** . . . and were under the impression, —TCNT . . . and surmised that Paul had brought him into the temple, —BRKL.

**21:29.** These false charges of unpatriotic conduct, blasphemy, and sacrilege were reinforced by the mention of a Gentile because these Asian Jews had seen Paul in the city earlier with Trophimus, a Gentile believer from Ephesus. So they jumped to the false conclusion that Paul had brought him into the temple.

Trophimus was well-known as a companion of Paul's. He traveled with Paul during the latter part of his third missionary journey and was with him from Greece all the way through Macedonia, Asia, and the final journey to Jerusalem. Trophimus was thus the innocent cause of the accusation of these Jews from Asia. The very thought that a Gentile who was not a proselyte or convert to Judaism would enter the temple court and defile it filled them with fury. This fury was directed against Paul because they thought he was the one who had brought Trophimus in, deliberately in defiance of the Law. Tertullus later repeated this charge against Paul.

Second Timothy 4:20 indicates that Trophimus remained loyal to the Lord and to Paul. He traveled with Paul again after Paul was released from his first imprisonment in Rome. Many believe also that Trophimus was the unnamed brother mentioned in 2 Corinthians 8:16-24. Paul speaks very highly of him there.

30. **And all the city was moved:** . . . And the whole city, —RTHM . . . was stirred, —TCNT . . . was thrown into turmoil, —MOFT . . . was thrown into uproar, —MNTG . . . The excitement spread through the whole city, —WEYM.

**and the people ran together:** . . . quickly collected, —TCNT . . . and a mob collected, —PHLP . . . surged together, —MNTG.

**and they took Paul:** . . . and they laid hold on Paul, —ASV . . . seized Paul, —TCNT.

**and drew him out of the temple: and forthwith the doors were shut:** . . . the doors were immediately shut, —TCNT . . . and the Temple gates were immediately closed, —WEYM . . . and the doors were slammed behind him, —PHLP . . . instantly, —MRDK.

**21:30.** The cries of these Jews from Asia stirred up the whole city of Jerusalem, for many people were already in the temple courts by this time. The Jews ran together from all directions, seized Paul, and dragged him out of the temple (that is, out of the Court of the Women), beating him as they did so. Immediately the great doors of the temple Court of the Women were shut so that the mob would not desecrate the temple. No one seemed to notice that Paul had no Gentiles with him, however.

The gate they closed was probably the gate of Nicanor, that is, the Beautiful Gate. It was the principal gate and was the gift of a wealthy Alexandrian Jew named Nicanor. It was solid Corinthian bronze, 50 cubits (75 feet) high and 40 cubits (60 feet) wide. It was beautifully carved and glittered like gold. From it steps led down into the Court of the Gentiles.

**31. And as they went about to kill him:** ... They were bent on, *−TCNT* ... But while they were trying, *−WEYM* ... were endeavoring to kill him, *−NOYS.*

**tidings came unto the chief captain of the band:** ... when it was reported to the officer commanding the garrison, *−TCNT* ... the allegation ... captain of the squadron, *−CNDT* ... reached the commandant, *−BRKL.*

**that all Jerusalem was in an uproar:** ... was in confusion, *−ASV* ... was in a ferment, *−WEYM* ... was out of control, *−BB* ... that the people were rioting all over Jerusalem, *−NORL* ... learned that there was trouble in the whole city, *−EVRD.*

**21:31.** It is clear the mob actually was intending to kill Paul. But the uproar caught the attention of someone who took the news up the steps to the Roman tribune. He was the officer over a cohort of 600 to 1,000 soldiers stationed in the Tower (castle, fortress) of Antonia on the northwest side of the temple where the guards could overlook the temple area. The messenger told the tribune that all Jerusalem was in an uproar or state of confusion.

**32. Who immediately took soldiers and centurions:** ... He instantly got together some officers and men, *−TCNT* ... So he at once got together some soldiers and captains, *−WLMS* ... and sergeants, *−WMCK*

**and ran down unto them:** ... and charged down upon the crowd, *−TCNT* ... he ran to the place where the crowd was gathered, *−EVRD* ... he marched down at once upon them, *−WMCK*

**and when they saw the chief captain and the soldiers:** ... At the sight of, *−WEYM* ... But as soon as they saw, *−WLMS* ... when they saw the colonel, *−GDSP* ... saw the commander, *−SEB.*

**they left beating of Paul:** ... they stopped hitting Paul, *−BECK.*

**21:32.** Immediately the tribune took at least two centurions with the soldiers under their command. Since the centurions were officers over 100 men, this made quite a show of force as they ran down the steps from the Tower of Antonia into the Court of the Gentiles.

The Romans stationed these soldiers at the Tower of Antonia for the specific purpose of keeping order in the temple, especially during the Jewish feast days. The law of Moses made three pilgrimage feasts compulsory. These were Passover, Pentecost, and Tabernacles. During these periods a great crowd of Jews gathered in the temple at the hours of prayer. But, like all dictators and oppressors of subject peoples, the Romans were fearful of what might happen when large crowds came together without having a loyalty to Rome. Furthermore, Jewish mobs had been troublesome before.

The sight of the tribune, the centurions, and all the soldiers made the mob stop beating Paul,

thus saving his life. The people, of course, knew the soldiers meant business. They had not forgotten the Galileans whose blood Pilate had mingled with their sacrifices (Luke 13:1). These Galileans were probably Jews who refused to pay tribute to Rome. Pilate's men waylaid them and probably slaughtered them and the animals they were about to sacrifice.

**33. Then the chief captain came near:** ... came up, *−WMCK* ... went up to Paul, *−TCNT* ... making his way to him, *−WEYM.*

**and took him:** ... arrested him, *−TCNT* ... and seized him, *−MOFT* ... took charge of him, *−BRKL.*

**and commanded him to be bound with two chains:** ... told his soldiers to tie up Paul, *−NCV* ... to be doubly chained, *−TCNT* ... gave orders that he should be fastened up with two chains, *−WMCK*

**and demanded who he was, and what he had done:** ... and began to inquire who he might be, *−RTHM* ... What has he done wrong? *−NCV.*

**21:33.** Though the tribune (or as we might say, the colonel) rescued Paul from the violence of the mob, he did not set Paul free. Instead, he jumped to the conclusion that Paul, as the cause of all this confusion, must be some vicious criminal. So he immediately placed him under arrest and chained him with hand chains to two soldiers, one on each side. Chaining a prisoner to a soldier was a common practice among the Romans. Chaining Paul to two soldiers was an extra precaution. This was similar to the custom today of handcuffing a prisoner.

The tribune then asked the Jews who Paul was and what he had done. He was anxious to know what had caused the uproar.

**34. And some cried one thing, some another, among the multitude:** ... Some of the crowd shouted one accusation against Paul and some another, *−WEYM.*

**and when he could not know the certainty for the tumult:** ... and, as he could get no definite reply on account of the uproar, *−TCNT* ... so, unable to get at the facts, *−BRKL* ... was not able to find out what had happened, *−NLTG* ... could not learn the truth about what had happened, *−SEB* ... since he could hear nothing for certain, *−WMCK* ... not being able to ascertain the truth, *−WLSN* ... because of the shouting that was going on, *−PHLP* ... Because of all this confusion, *−NCV* ... on account of the noise, *−ET.*

**he commanded him to be carried into the castle:** ... he ordered Paul to be taken into the barracks, *−TCNT* ... gave orders that he should be taken into the fort, *−WMCK* ... the citadel, *−CNDT* ... to be conveyed to the fortress, *−FNTN* ... to the army building, *−EVRD* ... led away to headquarters, *−NAB.*

**21:34.** In response, the crowd broke out into a confusion of contradictory statements. Everyone was shouting different things, all at the same time.

Actually, most of the people in the crowd did not know Paul, but had run together and joined in when they heard the noise of the riot. Rumors of the wildest kind arise quickly in such a situation. Once a mob spirit takes over, people are swept along and take part in the violence without thinking. It was God's merciful providence that this Roman officer was there to protect Paul.

Paul in his letters had already recognized that God is the One who authorized civil authority. Without it the world would have nothing but anarchy. The Bible teaches respect for officers of the law because of what they stand for and for the sake of the protection they give. The Bible says further that those who are not lawbreakers really have nothing to fear from them.

Because there was no way the tribune could be sure of what was being said in the midst of all the hubbub, he then ordered the soldiers to take Paul into the castle, that is, into the barracks of the fortress, the Tower of Antonia.

**35. And when he came upon the stairs:** ... When Paul reached the steps, *—TCNT* ... got to the steps, *—PHLP.*

**so it was, that he was borne of the soldiers:** ...he had to be carried by, *—WEYM* ... had to carry him on their shoulders, *—KLGS.*

**for the violence of the people:** ... because the people were so wild, *—SEB* ... cried out so loud and pushed so hard, *—NLTG* ... of the crowd, *—WMCK* ... of the mob, *—PHLP.*

**21:35.** The crowd was so violent the soldiers were having a hard time protecting Paul. As they moved toward the stairs which led from the temple court up to the Tower of Antonia, the crowd surged around them. When they reached the stairs, the pressure was so great the soldiers had to lift Paul up and carry him.

The Jews kept up this pressure because they still thought the temple had been desecrated. They were very proud of the temple building with its courts, porticoes, and great stones. But many of them had become like those in Jeremiah's day who trusted more in the temple than they did in God (Jeremiah 7:4, 14). It is always easier to give attention to a religious symbol than it is to seek the Lord and do His will.

The mob was also taking something into their own hands that belonged to the Lord. The Law provided for a just and fair trial. These Jews were moved by a false patriotism, and they were going contrary to the Word of God.

**36. For the multitude of the people followed after, crying:** ... for the people were following in a mass, shouting out, *—TCNT* ... for a tremendous crowd, *—WLMS* ... The mob was right behind them,

yelling, *—BECK* ... The whole mob was following them, *—NCV* ... pushing and calling out, *—NLTG.*

**Away with him:** ... Kill him! *—NLTG, —TCNT* ... Down with him, *—WMCK*

**21:36.** Even on the stairs the crowd kept following the soldiers, trying to pull Paul away from them. They also kept crying out, shrieking again and again, "Away with him!" By this they meant they wanted Paul killed. Possibly some in the crowd had cried out in the same way against Jesus (Luke 23:18; John 19:15). But it seemed the crowd was even more angry here. In fact, they would have torn Paul apart if the soldiers had not protected him.

**37. And as Paul was to be led into the castle:** ... When Paul was on the point of being taken into the fort, *—WMCK* ... barracks, *—PNT* ... fortress, *—FNTN* ... citadel, *—CNDT.*

**he said unto the chief captain:** ... asked the colonel, *—PHLP* ... to the commander, *—WMCK*

**May I speak unto thee?:** ... Do I have the right to say something to you? *—SEB* ... May I say something, *—WMCK*

**Who said, Canst thou speak Greek?:** ... the commander exclaimed, *—NAB* ... You know Greek! *—MOFT* ... Can you speak the Greek language? *—NLTG* ... So you know Greek, do you? *—PHLP.*

**21:37.** The crowd dropped behind as the soldiers came to the top of the steps and were about to enter the safety of the Fortress of Antonia. At this point Paul, using the Greek language, politely asked the tribune's permission to speak to him. The fact that Paul spoke Greek surprised the tribune, and he showed his surprise by asking a question that had an obvious answer. It showed he could not believe Paul was really speaking Greek.

This should not have been so surprising. Educated people and business people spoke Greek in those days, for it was the language of trade, commerce, education, and government communication all over the Roman Empire. Even the fishermen of Galilee had to know Greek in order to sell their fish in the Greek-speaking cities and towns of Phoenicia and the Decapolis. The Bible makes a point that the Syrophoenician woman was Greek-speaking, so Jesus must have conversed with her in Greek (Mark 7:26). Peter undoubtedly spoke in Greek to Cornelius and those gathered at his home. Greek was a second language for many of the Jews at that time.

**38. Art not thou that Egyptian:** ... Are you by chance, *—BB* ... Then you are not the man I thought you were, *—SEB.*

**which before these days madest an uproar:** ... who some time ago raised an insurrection, *—TCNT* ... who some years ago excited the riot,

—WEYM...who not long ago raised a riot, —PHLP...who caused the riot some time ago, —NAB ... recently stirred up the rebellion, —BRKL ... headed a rising, —WMCK

**and leddest out into the wilderness four thousand men that were murderers?:** ... led a band of, —NAB ... and led the four thousand Bandits out into the desert, —TCNT ... of the 4000 cutthroats and led them out into the Desert, —WEYM ... the four thousand men of the assassins? —DRBY ... and led those four thousand assassins into the desert, —PHLP...and led out the four thousand armed rebels into the wilds? —WMCK...hoodlums, —KLGS.

**21:38.** The real reason the tribune was so surprised was that he had jumped to a conclusion about Paul's identity. He thought Paul was a certain dangerous, dagger-carrying Egyptian assassin who had turned things upside down as a political revolutionist.

About A.D. 54 this Egyptian came to Jerusalem claiming to be a prophet. He led a great crowd of about 4,000 fanatical Jews to the Mount of Olives and promised that the walls of Jerusalem would fall down at his word. The Roman governor Felix sent soldiers who killed about 400 and captured another 200, but the Egyptian, with some of his fanatical followers, escaped into the desert.

His followers were murderers, literally dagger-men (*sikariōn*). These fanatical Jews were known even before this time to mingle with the crowds in Jerusalem during the festival times and would use their daggers to stab to death pro-Roman Jews.

Josephus also mentions this Egyptian but says he gathered 30,000 Jews under his influence and that they all marched toward the Mount of Olives to see the walls of Jerusalem fall.

**39. But Paul said, I am a man which am a Jew of Tarsus, a city in Cilicia:** ... No, said Paul, I am, —TCNT ... a citizen of, —NAB ... a native of Tarsus, —MNTG.

**a citizen of no mean city:** ... of that not insignificant city, —PHLP ... no obscure city, —RTHM ... no unimportant city, —WEYM ... a city of some note, —TCNT...of a notable town, —WMCK

**and, I beseech thee, suffer me to speak:** ... and I beg you to give me permission to speak, —TCNT...I ask you to let me speak, —PHLP...Please give me leave to speak, —WMCK...Please let me speak, —WLMS...let me address, —NAB.

**unto the people:**

**21:39.** Paul answered the tribune by identifying himself as a Jew and a citizen of Tarsus, a city that was neither unimportant nor obscure. In fact, it was the chief city of Cilicia in the eastern part of Asia Minor. It was famous also as a university city, and its schools were in the same class as those of Alexandria and Athens. Anyone born and educated there would certainly be fluent in the Greek

language and would certainly not be ashamed of his birthplace.

Then Paul asked permission to speak to the people. What a courageous thing this was for Paul to do. All the confusion, the beatings, and the threats would have shattered some people's nerve. Some might have vowed never again to preach to such unappreciative people. Others might have called down Roman judgment on the people and demanded that the soldiers treat the crowd the way they had treated the crowd that followed the Egyptian. But Paul had no desire for revenge, nor did he think of his own feelings or the chains that still bound him to the two soldiers. Love and compassion gave him courage to want to plead and reason with his people about the gospel.

**40. And when he had given him license:** ...The Commanding Officer gave his permission, —TCNT...He granted the request, —WLMS ... On being given permission, —PHLP.

**Paul stood on the stairs:** ... Paul, from the steps, —BB.

**and beckoned with the hand unto the people:** ... and motioned to the people to be quiet, —WEYM ... made a gesture with his hand to the people, —PHLP...to silence, —NAB.

**And when there was made a great silence:** ...great hush came over them, —MOFT...comparative silence, —TCNT...when they were quite quiet, —WMCK ... great silence ensuing, —FNTN ... deep hush, —PHLP ... become fairly quiet, —KLST ... all of them were quiet, —MLNT.

**he spake unto them:** ... he addressed them, —RTHM ... as he began to speak to them, —PHLP.

**in the Hebrew tongue, saying:** ... Hebrew dialect, —CMPB ... vernacular, —CNDT...Jewish language, —BECK ... Aramaic, —SEB ... as follows, —FNTN ... in these words, —MLNT.

**21:40.** When the tribune gave his permission, Paul was allowed to stand on the stairs. Signaling his desire to speak, he gained the attention of the crowd, and there was sudden quiet. Paul then began to speak in the Hebrew language.

This is generally taken to be Aramaic, the language the Jews brought back from Babylonia after their exile there in the Sixth Century B.C. Aramaic is closely related to Hebrew and belongs to the same branch of the Semitic family of languages. Abraham's relatives in Haran spoke Aramaic (Genesis 31:47 shows Laban gave the "heap of witness" its Aramaic name). Aramaic was also the language of trade and commerce in the fertile crescent from Babylonia to Egypt from before the time of Abraham until Alexander the Great replaced it with Greek.

However, there is some evidence that Jerusalem Jews took pride in being able to use the old (Biblical) Hebrew. Every week in all the synagogues they read the Scriptures. They were first read in Hebrew and then paraphrased into Aramaic. As a result they would all be familiar with the Old Testament Hebrew. Yet, since they would understand both, it is not clear which is meant here. In some other New Testament passages the word "Hebrew" is used to designate Aramaic. Aramaic was used in the homes of Galilee and probably in most of the homes of Judea.

## Chapter 22

1. **Men, brethren, and fathers, hear ye my defence which I make now unto you:** . . . listen to the defence which I am about to make, —TCNT . . . my vindication, —HNSN.

**22:1.** Paul's defense given on the stairs was the first of five he was permitted to make. In it he emphasized his heritage as a Jew and his encounter with Christ. The verses which follow record Paul's answers to the major charge the Jews were leveling against him: that he was an apostate. Although he never specifically answered the accusation that he had defiled the temple by taking a Gentile, Trophimus, into the inner courts, his defense made it clear he was living in a manner consistent with his orthodox heritage. In truth, Paul had taken great care not to offend the Jews upon his arrival in Jerusalem. In fact, he had joined with four Christian Jews who were completing their Nazarite vows (cf. 21:24-26).

Paul politely addressed the crowd as gentlemen who were his brothers and fathers, using the word father as a respectful title for the older men among them. Then he asked them to listen to his defense.

2. **(And when they heard that he spake in the Hebrew tongue to them:** . . . And on hearing him address them in Hebrew, —WEYM.

**they kept the more silence:** . . . they quieted down still more, —BECK . . . they were still quieter, —BRKL . . . they kept more quiet, —WORL.

**and he saith,):** . . . and Paul went on, —TCNT . . . and he continued, —WLMS.

**22:2.** Though the Roman tribune had been speaking to the crowd in Greek and Paul had spoken to him in Greek, Paul was wise to switch to Hebrew in speaking to the crowd. For when the crowd recognized he was speaking in Hebrew, they became even more quiet and gave him full attention. This was not because Hebrew was a sacred language, but because it made them realize he was a Jew, not a Gentile, for Gentiles carried on all their business with the Jews in the Greek language.

3. **I am verily a man which am a Jew:** . . . I am, without question, a Jew, —NORL.

**born in Tarsus, a city in Cilicia:** . . . a native of Tarsus, —TCNT.

**yet brought up in this city:** . . . but nurtured in this city, —RTHM . . . but I had my education in this city, —BB.

**at the feet of Gamaliel:** . . . under the teaching of Gamaliel, —WEYM.

**and taught according to the perfect manner of the law of the fathers:** . . . trained after the strictness of our ancestral law, —RTHM . . . trained according to the exactness of the ancestral law, —WORL . . . accurately instructed, —HNSN . . . educated according to, —TCNT . . . strictness of the law, —SWAN . . . strictest observance of our fathers' law, —PHLP.

**and was zealous toward God:** . . . I was as zealous in God's service, —TCNT . . . I worked hard for God, —NLTG . . . as jealous for the honour of the law, —KNOX . . . very serious about serving God, —EVRD, —SEB . . . given up to the cause of God with all my heart, —BB.

**as ye all are this day:** . . . just as are all of you here today, —EVRD.

**22:3.** Paul then identified himself as a Jew born in Tarsus but brought up in Jerusalem at the feet of Gamaliel. This probably means Paul came to Jerusalem in his early youth, possibly in his early teens.

Gamaliel, a member of the Sanhedrin, was one of the best known rabbis of the day. All the people in the crowd would know who he was. According to the Jewish Talmud, Gamaliel was the grandson of the famous rabbi Hillel, still considered by many as the most outstanding rabbi in the history of the Pharisees. They would have to agree with Paul that as a student of Gamaliel he would have been educated strictly and accurately according to the law of the fathers. That is, Gamaliel trained him with strict attention to every detail, not only of the law of Moses, but the additional laws contained in the traditions of the Scribes and Pharisees.

Paul also declared he was, as a result of his training, a zealot for God, eagerly devoted to God, just as all in his audience were. Clearly, Paul was not blaming or criticizing the people for beating him and trying to kill him. He let them know he understood how they felt, for he in his former zeal would have done the same thing. In fact, he recognized their zeal as a zeal for God. Paul sometimes had to warn believers in the assemblies he founded that false teachers would come among them who claimed to be Christians but who had wrong motives. Paul always gave credit to the Jewish persecutors that they had a zeal for God, even though it lacked knowledge (Romans 10:2). This attitude was one of the things that helped Paul to win so many Jews to Christ in all of his journeys.

(Compare Romans 10:1 and 11:1 for more about Paul's attitude.)

**4. And I persecuted this way unto the death:** . . . In my persecution of this Cause I did not stop even at the taking of life, *—TCNT* . . . persecuted this religion, *—LAMS* . . . I hurt the people who followed . . . Some of them were even killed, *—EVRD.*

**binding and delivering into prisons both men and women:** . . . I put in chains, and, *—TCNT* . . . I arrested . . . and put them in jail, *—EVRD* . . . throwing them into prison, Weymouth.

**22:4.** Paul then admitted he had in fact persecuted the Christians, referring to the Church as "this way," that is, the way of life that follows the teachings of Jesus and the gospel. He admitted that he actually pursued the believers up to the point of causing their death, binding both men and women and having them put in prison. As chapters 8 and 9 have already shown, he hounded them, creating around himself an atmosphere of violence and murder.

**5. As also the high priest doth bear me witness, and all the estate of the elders:** . . . the council of the elders, *—ALFD* . . . The head religious leader, *—NLTG* . . . and all the Eldership, *—RTHM* . . . and to that the High Priest himself and all the council can testify, *—TCNT* . . . are witnesses, *—MNTG* . . . and all the presbytery, *—HNSN* . . . can tell you that this is true, *—EVRD, —SEB.*

**from whom also I received letters unto the brethren:** . . . For I had letters of introduction from them, *—TCNT* . . . These leaders gave me letters to, *—EVRD.*

**and went to Damascus:** . . . and I was on my way to, *—TCNT.*

**to bring them which were there bound unto Jerusalem, for to be punished:** . . . So I was going there to arrest these people, *—EVRD* . . . where they would be beaten, *—NLTG.*

**22:5.** The high priest was a witness to Paul's zeal, as were all the elders of the Sanhedrin. Though Paul did not mention it, he had been with them when they listened to Stephen's defense and took him out to stone him. Paul never forgot how he had persecuted the Church in those days, and he was humbled by that memory, even though he knew he had done it in ignorance. From the high priest and the elders of the Sanhedrin he received letters to the Jews of Damascus, probably to the leaders or rulers of their synagogues. Then he went there with the determined purpose of bringing the believers bound to Jerusalem to be punished.

The Roman government had given the high priest and the Sanhedrin (Jewish Senate and High Court) considerable authority in matters relating to their religion. Though Damascus at this time was outside the limits of the Roman Empire and was ruled by Nabatean Arabs, apparently the Arab king allowed them the same authority in his territory. The Arabs at that time were idolaters, as were all the nations round about Israel. The Jews were still a little island of monotheism in the midst of a whole world that did not worship the one true God. But their persecution of the Christians only helped to spread the gospel.

**6. And it came to pass, that, as I made my journey:** . . . But something happened to me, *—NCV* . . . While I was still on my way, *—TCNT.*

**and was come nigh unto Damascus:** . . . just as I was getting close to Damascus, *—TCNT* . . . just before I reached Damascus, *—WLMS* . . . on my way to, *—NCV* . . . and was drawing nigh to, *—WORL* . . . when I came close to the city, *—SEB.*

**about noon:** . . . suddenly about midday, *—TNT.*

**suddenly there shone from heaven a great light round about me:** . . . a bright light from heaven flashed all around me, *—EVRD* . . . suddenly out of heaven there flashed a great light all around me, *—RTHM* . . . a sudden blaze of light, *—WEYM* . . . suddenly a dazzling light blazed around me, *—NOLI* . . . an intense light . . . beamed, *—BRKL* . . . a great light shone on me, *—KJII* . . . shined all around me, *—SEB.*

**22:6.** The question in the mind of Paul's hearers at this point was undoubtedly, "What changed Saul the persecutor into Paul the apostle?" So Paul told the crowd the story of the journey to Damascus and how, as they approached the city, suddenly a very bright light shone from heaven and surrounded him. Later Paul described it as brighter than the noonday sun (26:13). The angels who announced the birth of Jesus to the shepherds had the glory of the Lord shining around them (Luke 2:9). But this was an even greater manifestation of the glory of God, the glory which Jesus himself had prayed the Father would restore to Him (John 17:5).

**7. And I fell unto the ground:** . . . I fall flat, *—CNDT* . . . And when I went down on the earth, *—BB* . . . fell upon the ground, *—GDSP.*

**and heard a voice saying unto me:** . . . a voice asking me, *—BECK.*

**Saul, Saul, why persecutest thou me?:** . . . why do you persecute me, *—RSV* . . . why do you work so hard against Me? *—NLTG* . . . why are you attacking me so cruelly? *—BB* . . . why are you doing things against me? *—EVRD.*

**22:7.** Overwhelmed by the brightness of the heavenly light, Paul fell to the ground. He heard a voice asking, "Why do you keep persecuting me?" The One who spoke addressed him with the Hebrew form of his name, Saoul. This too drew attention to the fact Jesus was addressing him as a Jew. Even though Saul was the name of a king who failed, the name was a good name and meant "asked for," that is, asked of God. Yet on the Damascus Road Paul was acting in a very self-willed manner, just as King Saul had.

**8. And I answered, Who art thou, Lord?:** ... Sir? —WLMS.

**And he said unto me:** ... The voice answered, —SEB ... he answered me, —MNTG ... So he told me, —BRKL.

**I am Jesus of Nazareth, whom thou persecutest:** ... I am Jehoshua, —WUST ... the Nazarene, —TNT ... Jesus from Nazareth ... the One you are trying to hurt, —EVRD ... whom you are attacking, —BB.

**22:8.** Paul then inquired who it was that was speaking to him, addressing Him as "Lord." In doing this, Paul was not just being polite. That light made him realize this incident was something more than could be explained by natural causes. It had to be a divine manifestation, a manifestation of God. So he meant "divine Lord" when he said "Lord."

The reply was instant and plain. The One speaking to him was Jesus of Nazareth, the One Paul kept persecuting. Jesus made this very emphatic, meaning literally, "You, yourself are continuing to persecute me." Most of the other Jews had quit persecuting the Christians in Jerusalem. Paul had been the one to keep it up.

Jesus emphasized the fact that Paul was persecuting Him. He is the Head of the Church, and the Church is His body. So, in a very real sense Paul was persecuting Christ when he persecuted Christians. To put it another way, the Christians were Christ's witnesses, His representatives, His ambassadors. An insult to an ambassador is an insult to the country or the king he represents.

This vision of Jesus was behind the prayer of Paul "that the God of our Lord Jesus Christ, the Father of glory, may give unto you the spirit of wisdom and revelation in the knowledge of him: the eyes of your understanding being enlightened; that ye may know what is the hope of his calling, and what the riches of the glory of his inheritance in the saints, and what is the exceeding greatness of his power to usward who believe, according to the working of his mighty power, which he wrought in Christ, when he raised him from the dead, and set him at his own right hand in the heavenly places, ... and gave him to be the head over all things to the church" (Ephesians 1:17-20, 22).

**9. And they that were with me saw indeed the light:** ... The men with me saw the light, —TCNT ... (My companions), —MOFT ... My traveling companons saw, —NOLI ... The men who were with me ... saw

the light, —SEB ... certainly saw, —BRKL ... naturally saw, —PHLP.

**and were afraid:** ... but they did not understand, —WORL.

**but they heard not the voice of him that spake to me:** ... but the voice of him who spoke to me they did not understand, —HBIE ... did not distinctly hear, —CMPB ... but they understood not the voice, —WLSN ... but could not catch the voice of him who spoke to me, —KNOX ... came not to their ears, —BB.

**22:9.** Paul's companions also saw the light, but its intensity was not focused on them as it was on Paul. They also did not hear the voice of Jesus. But this does not mean they did not hear the sound of His voice. The sense is that they did not hear with understanding.

The brightness of the light was enough to make them afraid, however. In fact, it both startled and terrified them.

**10. And I said:** ... And I asked, —WEYM.

**What shall I do, Lord? And the Lord said unto me:** ... answered, —WLMS.

**Arise, and go into Damascus:** ... Get up, —TCNT ... and proceed to Damascus, —NOLI.

**and there it shall be told thee:** ... and it will be made clear to you, —BB.

**of all things which are appointed for thee to do:** ... about all you are destined to do, —MOFT ... that has been laid out for you to do, —BRKL ... everything you are ordered to do, —BECK ... all that you have been assigned to do, —NIV ... everything that has been arranged for you, —ADAM ... all things which have been arranged, —WORL ... the work you are foreordained to accomplish, —NOLI ... that is destined for thee, —KNOX ... which have been appointed to you to do, —KJII.

**22:10.** Then Paul told how he asked the Lord what he should do. Then he added, "And the Lord said." This is important. Paul had just told the crowd the voice speaking out of the midst of the light from heaven was Jesus of Nazareth. Now he called Jesus "Lord" with full knowledge of who He is. This makes it clear Paul had immediately accepted Jesus as the divine Lord and as the Lord of his life. He showed it further by putting himself at his Lord's disposal and asking for His direction concerning what to do. It must be remembered also that Lord was the title the Jews used to refer to God the Father in their reading of the Scriptures and in their worship in the synagogues. This does not mean Paul was identifying Jesus as the same Person as God the Father. He was recognizing Jesus as deity.

Jesus then told Paul to get up and go into Damascus. There he would be told of all the things which were appointed for him to do. The use of the Greek perfect tense here means the things Paul would be told had already been appointed for him in advance and were still being commanded or ordered for him. God had a great plan for Paul's life. Now that he had accepted Jesus as Lord of his life, God was ready to put that plan into effect. All Paul needed to do was follow in faith and obedience. But the first step was to go to Damascus where he had intended to arrest the believers. They needed to see that God could turn around the one who persecuted "the Way" and make him a loyal follower of Jesus in the way God had ordained.

**11. And when I could not see for the glory of that light:** ... In consequence, —TCNT ... But as I could not see clearly owing to, —RTHM ... As I did not see on account of the glory of that light, —SWAN ... Due to the brilliancy of that intense light, —BRKL ... As I was blinded by the dazzling light, —NOLI.

**being led by the hand of them that were with me:** ... guided by the hands of my companions, —BRKL.

**I came into Damascus:** ... and in this way I reached Damascus, —WLMS.

**22:11.** Because of the glory of the light from heaven, Paul could not see. His companions had to take him by the hand and lead him into the city. Paul's mention of the glory of the light again drew attention to the fact that it was more than an ordinary light. The glory identified it clearly with the Shekinah, the divine manifestation of glory and light in the Old Testament. Paul was declaring to the crowd that he was now convinced that Jesus is the supernatural Lord, the Son of God, just as the Christians were saying.

**12. And one Ananias:** ... a certain, —KJII.

**a devout man according to the law:** ... a man devout in strict observance of the law, —WLMS ... a pious man who obeyed the Law, —WEYM ... a God-fearing man who kept the law, —BB ... devout by the standards of the law, —ADAM ... for his pious observance of the Law, —NOLI ... a man devoted according to the Law, —KJII.

**having a good report of all the Jews which dwelt there:** ... well spoken of by, —RSV ... by all the resident Jews, —WORL ... respected him, —NCV ... all the Jews in that place had a high opinion, —BB.

**22:12.** Paul also drew attention to the fact that Ananias of Damascus was a devout (godly, God-fearing) man according to the Law, that is, in the way he was careful to keep the Law. He followed Jewish customs and did not despise his Jewish heritage.

The Bible recognizes here that it was important what non-Christians said about Ananias. A believer's reputation in the community may not seem important, but it is important for his witness. God expects Christians to walk in wisdom toward those who are outside the Church (Colossians

4:5). This is a practical wisdom that shows up in right conduct of life. Also, Christians must walk honestly toward non-Christians (1 Thessalonians 4:12). More literally, this means believers must conduct themselves in a life-style that shows decency, dignity, and good order. A Christian's deportment should be above reproach in all things. This includes good social behavior and little details of courtesy in the home and everywhere.

**13. Came unto me:** ... called on me, —BRKL.

**and stood, and said unto me:** ... stood by me, —EVRD.

**Brother Saul, receive thy sight:** ... Saul, my Brother, recover your sight, —TCNT ... you may see again! —PHLP ... see again! —BECK, ... look up and see, —KNOX ... let your eyes be open, —BB.

**And the same hour:** ... And then and there, —TCNT ... And at that instant, —KNOX ... At that very moment, —NOLI ... Immediately, —EVRD.

**I looked up upon him:** ... I recovered my sight and looked up at him, —TCNT ... At that moment, —SEB ... I regained my sight, —NOLI ... I looked up into his face, —KNOX ... I was able to see him, —BB, —EVRD.

**22:13.** Ananias came to Paul and stood by him. Here Paul just summarized what happened. Chapter 9 provides more details and tells how Ananias laid his hands on Paul and records more of what Ananias said. It was Jesus who appeared to Ananias and told him to go to Paul and pray for him to receive his sight. In his defense Paul merely drew attention to the fact that Ananias called him "brother," and he recovered his sight and was able to see the man the Lord had sent to him.

It seems from this that the terms brother and sister were already becoming meaningful to the Christians. They recognized that whether they were Jews or Gentiles they were in the family of God. Paul had had a great education. He had the right to be called "Rabbi." But it was his own studies that gave him that right. Only the Lord could make him a brother.

**14. And he said, The God of our fathers hath chosen thee:** ... Ananias told me, —EVRD ... You have been marked out by the God of our fathers, —BB ... chose you a long time ago, —SEB.

**that thou shouldest know his will:** ... to recognize his will, —BRKL ... to learn what he wants, —BECK ... to understand His intention, —FNTN ... to have knowledge of his purpose, —BB ... to know his plan, —EVRD.

**and see that Just One:** ... the Righteous One, —ASV.

**and shouldest hear the voice of his mouth:** ... and hear Him speak, —WEYM ... to hear words from him, —EVRD.

**22:14.** Ananias then told Paul that the God of their fathers (the God of Abraham, Isaac, and

Jacob) had chosen him, that is, appointed him (selected him, a word used always of appointment to an important duty). God's purpose was that Paul would come to know His will (to realize what His will is), that he would see the Just One (the Righteous One, the Righteous Servant of God, that is, the Messiah), and that he would hear His voice, not from a distance but face-to-face.

By referring to Jesus as the Just or Righteous One, Ananias connected Jesus with Old Testament prophecies of the Messiah. (See Isaiah 9:7; 11:4, 5; 53:11; Jeremiah 23:5, 6.) The fact that Paul heard the voice of Jesus from His mouth also makes it clear that this was not a dream-type vision or a ghostly manifestation. Jesus was present in bodily form. Jesus came to Paul in a way just as real and literal as the way in which He had come to the other apostles after His resurrection. This made Paul a witness to His resurrection on the same level as those who saw Him alive before His ascension.

15. **For thou shalt be his witness unto all men:** . . . to all the world, —TCNT . . . to all mankind, —CNDT.

**of what thou hast seen and heard:** . . . You will tell them about the things, —EVRD.

**22:15.** Ananias specifically told Paul he was to be Christ's witness to all men concerning what he had seen and heard. This means Paul was to be a firsthand witness, just as the other apostles were. His commission was the same as the Great Commission. It was to all mankind (including both men and women). Behind it was the promise to Abraham that in his Seed all the families of the earth would be blessed. Behind it also was the love of God for the whole world, the same love that caused Him to send His Son (John 3:16).

16. **And now why tarriest thou?:** . . . why wait any longer, —TCNT . . . why lingerest thou? —DRBY . . . Now, don't wait any longer, —SEB . . . why are you waiting? —BB . . . why art thou wasting time? —KNOX.

**arise, and be baptized:** . . . Get up, —EVRD . . . Be baptized at once, —TCNT . . . and be immersed, —HNSN.

**and wash away thy sins:** . . . be cleansed of your sins, —BRKL . . . and wash your sins away, —WLMS.

**calling on the name of the Lord:** . . . and invoke his name, —TCNT . . . by calling on His name, —WLMS . . . as you call on his name, —PHLP . . . having previously called, —WUST . . . by praying to him, —TEV . . . at the invocation of his name, —KNOX . . . Do this, trusting in him to save you, —EVRD.

**22:16.** Then Ananias said, "Now what do you intend? Rise, be baptized, and wash away your sins, calling on the name of the Lord" (editor's translation). This was a call to express faith. Paul's sins would be washed away, however, through calling

on the Lord's name, not by the water of baptism. The only other place where this word for "wash" is used is in 1 Corinthians 6:11. There it is the Spirit of God that does the washing.

As Peter pointed out, the waters of baptism in and of themselves do not have the power to wash away sins (1 Peter 3:20, 21). However, one must not underestimate the value God places on the act of baptism. Jesus himself said, "He that believeth and is baptized shall be saved" (Mark 16:16; cf. Matthew 28:18ff.). Paul also pointed to its importance when he assumed the disciples in Ephesus had been baptized (19:3). Elsewhere he taught that baptism relates the believer to Christ's redemptive work (Romans 6:3-6). Baptism, then, is intimately connected to calling upon Jesus by faith for forgiveness, that is, for the "washing away" of sin.

17. **And it came to pass, that:** . . . Then it came about that, —NORL . . . Later, —EVRD.

**when I was come again to Jerusalem:** . . . when I had returned, —ASV.

**even while I prayed in the temple:** . . . I was praying, —EVRD.

**I was in a trance:** . . . in an ecstasy, —CNDT . . . I had a dream, —NLTG . . . I saw a vision, —EVRD, —NCV.

**22:17.** Paul skipped over the experiences he had in Damascus and told how he returned to Jerusalem. There, while praying in this very temple, he was in a trance. This was not a trance in the modern or heathen sense, but a state in which he felt an overwhelming astonishment; after all, he was in the very presence of Christ. This also shows Paul was not the polluter or defiler of the temple the Asian Jews were saying he was. He was treating it as God's house of prayer.

18. **And saw him saying unto me:** . . . I saw Him and He said to me, —WEYM . . . saw the Lord saying, —EVRD.

**Make haste:** . . . Hurry, —BRKL.

**and get thee quickly out of Jerusalem:** . . . and leave Jerusalem at once, —NOLI, —TCNT . . . leave Jerusalem quickly, —WEYM . . . leave Jerusalem with all speed, —KNOX . . . Leave . . . now! —EVRD, —NCV.

**for they will not receive thy testimony concerning me:** . . . The people here will not accept the truth about me, —EVRD . . . not accept thy witness, —RTHM . . . not accept the truth you tell about me, —BECK . . . your evidence about me, —MOFT.

**22:18.** While Paul was in this state and as he continued to pray, he saw Jesus speaking to him and telling him to hurry out of Jerusalem, for the people of Jerusalem would not receive his witness to them.

This gives us some additional details beyond those already mentioned in chapter 9 which records how Paul spoke boldly to the Hellenistic

Jews, probably in the same synagogues where Stephen had witnessed for Christ. The result was that they were making plans to kill him. So the Christians took him down to Caesarea and put him on a ship to Tarsus.

Now it is clear Paul did not go just because his fellow Christians in Jerusalem were afraid he might become another martyr like Stephen. Paul went with them because he had the command of Jesus. This warning from Jesus himself also drew attention to the fact that He is alive and knows what is going on here on earth.

**19. And I said, Lord, they know:** . . . I replied, *—WEYM* . . . it is within their own knowledge, *—KNOX.*
**that I imprisoned and beat in every synagogue them that believed on thee:** . . . how active I was in imprisoning, and flogging, *—WEYM* . . . I put the believers in jail and beat them, *—EVRD* . . . and manhandled, *—BRKL* . . . and scourging, *—CMPB* . . . I had them beaten, *—NLTG* . . . and scourge them, *—KNOX.*

**22:19.** Paul tried to argue that these Hellenistic Jews knew how he imprisoned and beat believers in every synagogue. That is, he systematically went through synagogue after synagogue, arresting, beating, and imprisoning the believers.

The Jewish believers all went to the synagogues on the Sabbath as their custom had been from childhood. Living in a community, they were part of its synagogue. The synagogue was the center of Jewish community life.

**20. And when the blood of thy martyr Stephen was shed:** . . . They also know that I was there when . . . your witness, was killed, *—EVRD* . . . that when Stephen your witness was put to death, *—BB* . . . was poured out, *—SWAN.*
**I also was standing by, and consenting unto his death:** . . . even I myself, *—RTHM* . . . and well pleased, *—HBIE* . . . I was there, giving approval, *—BB* . . . I stood there and agreed, *—EVRD* . . . endorsing it, *—CNDT* . . . I myself was then Chief Justice, and gave the Decision, *—FNTN* . . . agreed that they should kill him, *—NCV.*
**and kept the raiment of them that slew him:** . . . and watched over the garments of, *—KNOX* . . . and took charge of the clothes of those who were murdering him, *—TCNT* . . . I even held the coats of the men who were killing him! *—EVRD* . . . was in charge of the garments of them who stoned him, *—LAMS* . . . the clothes of those who killed him, *—KJII.*

**22:20.** Paul argued further that they knew he was present at the violent death of Stephen. Though Stephen was stoned, Paul spoke of the shedding of his blood in order to emphasize the violence of his death. He also spoke of Stephen as Christ's martyr. Marturos is translated "witness" about 29 times in the King James Version. "Witness" is the basic meaning, but in time, because so

many died because of their Christian witness the word gained its technical sense of a martyr. But in New Testament times those who witnessed for Christ were risking their lives whether they were actually killed or not.

By telling this also, Paul wanted the audience in the temple court below to see that Jesus was patient with him, yet was still in control and knew what the situation really was.

**21. And he said unto me, Depart:** . . . Go, *—TCNT* . . . Leave, *—BRKL* . . . But the Lord said to me, *—EVRD.*
**for I will send thee far hence unto the Gentiles:** . . . because I am to send you out and far away among the heathen, *—WLMS* . . . to a people who are not Jews, *—BECK* . . . I mean to send thee on a distant errand, *—KNOX* . . . I will send you as my Apostle to the Gentiles all over the world, *—NOLI.*

**22:21.** Jesus knew Paul's reasoning was wrong. So He said again to him, "Depart." Paul was to leave Jerusalem at once.

Jesus made it clear to Paul, however, that He was not through with him just because he was stirring up so much opposition, or because his ministry was not successful in winning the thousands to the Lord as the rest of the apostles had been doing in that area. God had not changed His plan. Jesus would send Paul (as an apostle) far away to the Gentiles (the nations outside of Israel).

The emphasis here is not on Paul's leaving Jerusalem, but on the fact that Jesus was sending him out with a commission to reach the Gentiles with the gospel. Because Jesus was now his Lord, he could not disobey. Furthermore, the fact that Jesus sent him out with His commission made Paul an apostle. He was not one of the special group of 12 apostles Jesus first chose, and he never claimed to be. But he was personally sent out by Jesus and was therefore entitled to be called an apostle.

**22. And they gave him audience unto this word:** . . . Until they heard this, *—WEYM* . . . Till he said that, *—MOFT* . . . Up to this point the people had been listening to Paul, *—TCNT.*
**and then lifted up their voices, and said:** . . . but now with a roar of disapproval they cried out, *—WEYM* . . . But at that they shouted, *—MOFT.*
**Away with such a fellow from the earth:** . . . Kill him! *—TCNT* . . . Down with him! *—NEB* . . . Rid the world, *—BECK.*
**for it is not fit that he should live:** . . . A fellow like this ought not to have been allowed to live, *—TCNT* . . . A scoundrel like that is better dead! *—NEB* . . . it is a disgrace that he should live, *—KNOX.*

**22:22.** The Jews listened to Paul until he spoke of the command to go to the Gentiles. That God cares about the Gentiles is clear in the Old Testament.

God's purpose in calling Abraham was to bring blessing to all the families of the earth (Genesis 12:3). Every time the promise was repeated to Abraham, Isaac, and Jacob, the same truth was reemphasized (Genesis 18:18; 22:18; 26:4; 28:14). Though two different forms of the verb are used in these passages, the context and the continued revelation of the promise confirm that God was promising blessing through the Seed of Abraham for all the peoples and nations of the earth.

However, Roman oppression had blinded the minds of these Jews who were listening to Paul. In their minds Gentiles were dogs, scavengers, as well as enemies of God. Thus, in their prejudice they went into an emotional tantrum and began crying out again for Paul's death. Referring to him scornfully as "such a fellow," they expressed their feeling that he was not worthy to live.

23. **And as they cried out:** ... They were howling, *−NOLI* ... And when they continued their furious shouts, *−WEYM* ... They kept on yelling, *−NORL*.

**and cast off their clothes:** ... tearing off their clothes, *−TCNT* ... . and tearing their mantles, *−RTHM* ... and ripping their clothes, *−PHLP* ... throwing their clothes into the air, *−WEYM*.

**and threw dust into the air:** ... and hurling dust into the air, *−PHLP*.

**22:23.** While the Jews were shouting out their demands for Paul's death, they were also throwing their outer garments around as an expression of their uncontrollable anger. The throwing off of their garments may also have expressed their desire to stone Paul for what they considered blasphemy, just as the elders threw off their garments when they stoned Stephen. At the same time, they threw dust in the air as a symbol of their rejection of Paul and his message. No doubt they would have thrown mud if it had been available. Prejudice continued to dominate them and kept them from searching the Scriptures to see if Paul's message was so, as the more noble Beroeans had done (17:11).

24. **The chief captain commanded him to be brought into the castle:** ... ordered Paul to be taken into the Fort, *−TCNT* ... into the army building, *−BB*.

**and bade that he should be examined by scourging:** ... and directed that he should be examined under the lash, *−TCNT* ... by flogging, *−WLMS* ... to get information from Paul by whipping him, *−BECK* ... wanted to force Paul, *−SEB* ... saying that he would put him to the test by whipping, *−BB*.

**that he might know:** ... to tell him, *−SEB* ... that he might find out, *−RTHM* ... in order to ascertain, *−WEYM* ... to learn, *−MNTG*.

**wherefore they cried so against him:** ... the reason for their outcry against him, *−TCNT* ... the reason

for such an uproar, *−PHLP* ... exactly why they were shouting, *−ADAM* ... they were thus clamoring him, *−WORL* ... why the people were shouting against him like this, *−SEB*.

**22:24.** Because the Roman tribune was responsible to stop riots, he quickly brought Paul inside the fortress and undoubtedly barred the door against the mob. Because Paul was speaking in Hebrew and the shouts of the mob were in the same language, the tribune did not understand anything that was being said. Therefore he jumped to the conclusion that Paul must have said something terrible to stir up the mob to such violence again. He did not expect Paul to confess the truth about what he was saying, so he told the soldiers to examine him by scourging. That is, they were to question him while torturing him with a whip made of leather thongs with pieces of bone and metal sewn in them. This was a common type of Roman punishment, one to which Pilate had subjected Jesus (John 19:1).

25. **And as they bound him with thongs:** ... But when they had stretched him out with the straps, *−RTHM* ... with the thongs, *−HNSN* ... But just as they had tied him up to be scourged, *−TCNT* ... with the straps (for the lash'), *−WEYM*.

**Paul said unto the centurion that stood by:** ... standing near, *−TCNT* ... who was present, *−BB*.

**Is it lawful for you to scourge a man that is a Roman:** ... Is it legal for you to scourge a Roman citizen, *−TCNT* ... Have you the right to scourge a man, when he is, *−KNOX*.

**and uncondemned?:** ... and one who is uncondemned at that, *−WLMS* ... unconvicted, *−TCNT* ... and that without a trial? *−CNFT* ... not been proven guilty? *−SEB* ... when no one has said he is guilty? *−NLTG* ... and has not been judged? *−BB*.

**22:25.** Paul was no stranger to torture. He had already been whipped by Jews five times and beaten with rods by the Romans three times (2 Corinthians 11:24, 25). But the punishment by a Roman scourge was far worse and often crippled or killed its victim. In Paul's condition, after having just been dragged by the Jews and nearly beaten by them, a scourging would have meant his death.

To prepare Paul for the scourging, the soldiers made him bend over and stretch forward. They bound him in that position with thongs, that is, with leather straps, to receive the flogging. (This was the more common way of preparing a victim for scourging. However, some writers believe what was done here was even more severe. They interpret this to mean Paul was hung up by the thongs so that his feet dangled a few inches above the floor of the fortress.)

At this point Paul stopped the proceedings. He had been rushed into the fortress, grabbed by the soldiers, and rushed off to wherever they were going to torture him. In the confusion, no one paid attention to anything he was trying to say. But now he was able to get the attention of the centurion who was standing there supervising the soldiers. Paul asked him if it was legal to scourge (whip, flog) a man who was a Roman citizen and uncondemned, that is, his case not even brought to trial.

Paul, of course, knew what they were doing was illegal. He had used his Roman citizenship to help him before. He was willing to suffer for the gospel's sake, but he never sought suffering when it could be avoided.

**26. When the centurion heard that:** . . . On hearing this question, —WEYM . . . And hearing this, —KJII . . . as soon as he heard this, —KNOX . . . When the officer heard, —SEB.

**he went and told the chief captain, saying:** . . . went to the commander, —EVRD . . . reported it, saying, —WORL . . . went to the colonel, —GDSP . . . reported this statement to the tribune, —NOLI . . . and told him about it, —NCV . . . and gave him an account of it, —BB.

**Take heed what thou doest:** . . . What are you intending to do? —WEYM . . . Be careful what you do, —LAMS . . . Do you know what you are doing? NCV, —TCNT . . . Do you realize what you were about to do? —PHLP . . . Listen! What are you doing? —NLTG . . . What art thou about? —KNOX . . . What are you about to do? —BB . . . What do you propose to do? —GDSP.

**for this man is a Roman:** . . . This man is a Roman citizen, —TCNT.

**22:26.** As soon as the centurion heard Paul was a Roman citizen, he reported it to the tribune, warning him to be careful about what he was doing. The centurion could not rescind the order of the tribune on his own, for the tribune was his superior officer. But he could remind the tribune what was being done was by his orders and, therefore, he (the tribune) would be responsible.

The tribune (chief captain) in Greek, chiliarchos, means literally "the chief of 1,000 (soldiers)." But the title was used more broadly of the chief officer or commandant of a garrison or fortress, whether there were exactly 1,000 soldiers under him or not. In the same way, the centurion (hekatontarchēs) means "chief of 100 (soldiers)," but was used whether there were exactly 100 or not. Here the centurion stood by the soldiers who were preparing Paul for the scourging, even though it was probably a squad of four men who were doing the work.

Both the centurion and the tribune knew very well the rights of Roman citizens, as well as the penalties that would fall on them if they disregarded those rights. Valerian and Porcian laws

provided that no judge or officer had the right to bind, scourge, or kill a Roman citizen without proper trial. At first this was by the decision of the general assembly of the citizens of Rome. Later the power was transferred to the emperor, to whom appeal could be made. All a person had to do to claim his rights was to say the words *I am a Roman citizen*. When Paul claimed his rights as a citizen, it was enough to stop the proceedings.

**27. Then the chief captain came, and said unto him:** . . . Then the tribune came, —NOLI . . . commander came, —TNT . . . going forward, —WORL . . . came to Paul and asked him, —WEYM.

**Tell me, art thou a Roman?:** . . . Give me an answer, —BB . . . are you really, —EVRD . . . a Roman citizen? —TNT.

**He said, Yea:** . . . Yes, replied Paul, —TCNT . . . He answered, Yes, —EVRD.

**22:27.** The tribune immediately went to Paul to ask if he was indeed a Roman citizen. He wanted to hear this for himself before he rescinded the order to scourge Paul. Without hesitation, Paul answered, "Yes!"

**28. And the chief captain answered:** . . . Whereupon the colonel replied, —PHLP . . . The commander said, —EVRD.

**With a great sum obtained I this freedom:** . . . I had to pay a heavy price for my position as citizen, —TCNT . . . I paid a large sum for this citizenship, —WEYM . . . I, for a great sum, acquired this citizenship, —WORL . . . I paid a lot of money to become a Roman, —EVRD . . . I got Roman rights for myself at a great price, —BB . . . I purchased this citizenship with, —HNSN . . . I bought this citizenship at a great price, —SWAN . . . it cost me a heavy sum to win this privilege, —KNOX . . . I bought this citizenship with a great sum, —KJII . . . a great sum of money to obtain this citizenship, —TNT.

**And Paul said, But I was free born:** . . . I am one by birth, rejoined Paul, —TCNT . . . But I was born a citizen, —HBIE . . . Ah, said Paul, but I am a citizen by birth, —KNOX.

**22:28.** The tribune then remarked that he bought his Roman citizenship with a great sum of money. But Paul replied he was born a Roman citizen.

Originally the privileges of Roman citizenship were limited to the free people living in the city of Rome itself. Later, citizenship was extended to a number of Italian tribes and cities, then to most of Italy. Emperors kept adding to the places outside Italy that could have Roman citizenship. Often individuals who had rendered some outstanding service to the empire would also receive citizenship for themselves and their families. Paul's father, or grandfather, most probably was in this category because of some unusual service.

It was also possible to purchase Roman citizenship for money, even in towns and cities that had no special privileges otherwise. This selling of Roman citizenship was especially encouraged in the reign of the Emperor Claudius. His wife and other court favorites were allowed to do this, apparently as a means of lining their own pockets. This explains how the tribune gained his Roman citizenship. He probably bought his citizenship as a means of gaining a higher commission in the Roman army.

(Some older commentaries say the entire city of Tarsus was given Roman citizenship and that was how Paul's family became citizens, but the historical evidence is against this. Paul's father or grandfather must have gained citizenship as individuals.)

**29. Then straightway they departed from him which should have examined him:** ... The men who were to have examined Paul immediately drew back, —*TCNT* ... So the men who had been on the point of judicially examining him immediately left him, —*WEYM* ... Then those who were about to scourge him, —*MNTG* ... moved away from him, —*WEYM* ... kept their hands off, —*BRKL* ... intending to scourge him, fled from him, —*MRDK* ... going to torture him left him, —*CNFT* ... The men who were preparing to torture Paul, —*SEB* ... immediately departed from him, —*HNSN.*

**and the chief captain also was afraid:** ... was struck with fear, —*RTHM* ... felt worried, —*BRKL* ... the captain himself was alarmed, to find out, —*KNOX* ... was frightened, —*NCV.*

**after he knew that he was a Roman:** ... when he found out, —*RTHM* ... finding that Paul was a Roman citizen, —*TCNT* ... on discovering that, —*BRKL.*

**and because he had bound him:** ... especially since he had him bound, —*NORL* ... had stretched him (for scourging), —*MRDK* ... strapped him for the lash, —*ET* ... because he had already tied Paul up, NCV.

**22:29.** The soldiers who were about to question and torture Paul quickly left. The tribune also was afraid. He knew that Paul, as a Roman citizen, had a right to bring charges against him for even putting him in chains.

Paul seemed to take all this as part of the providence of God. He considered civil government to be ordained by God. He therefore accepted the responsibilities the government put upon him and claimed the rights and privileges that went with them. In this Paul set an example for all, and especially believers, with respect to both civic rights and civic duties.

Paul brought this out further in Romans 13:1-7. There he showed that every person is to subject himself of his own free will to the powers or authorities of the government he lives under. This is not a matter of expediency or of fear of the consequences of disobedience. Rather, it is because God has ordained that there be civil government, and therefore to resist government in a stubborn, obstinate way is to resist the ordinance of God. God is still on the throne of the universe, and He is the One who is in ultimate control, as Nebuchadnezzar found out when he had to live like an animal for seven seasons (Daniel 4:25, 32, 34-37; 5:18-22). Even where the government is not the best, it must be recognized that civil government is of God. Without it there would be nothing but anarchy, society would disintegrate, and in the confusion life would become more and more miserable for all.

Paul's admonition was given despite the fact that the Roman government could be oppressive and that the emperor at this very time was the infamous Nero.

**30. On the morrow:** ... On the next day, —*TCNT.*

**because he would have known the certainty:** ... wishing to find out the real reason, —*TCNT* ... wishing to know exactly, —*WEYM.*

**wherefore he was accused of the Jews:** ... as to why he was being accused by the Jews, —*RTHM* ... why Paul was denounced by the Jews, —*TCNT.*

**he loosed him from his bands:** ... released him, —*RTHM* ... had his chains taken off, —*TCNT.*

**and commanded the chief priests and all their council to appear:** ... to come together, ASV ... to assemble, —*ALFD,* —*HNSN* ... to gather for their court, —*NLTG.*

**and brought Paul down:** ... and took, —*TCNT* ... he brought Paul out, —*EVRD.*

**and set him before them:** ... and brought him before them, —*TCNT* ... to face them, —*BRKL* ... and stood him before their meeting, —*EVRD,* —*NCV* ... and set him among them, —*KJII.*

**22:30.** The tribune kept Paul in custody, however, though probably without all the chains. He could not release Paul simply because Paul was a Roman citizen. As the representative of the Roman government, the tribune had the responsibility to try to keep peace in Jerusalem. He therefore had to give the Jews an opportunity to present their case.

Thus, the next day, because he wanted to know for sure why the Jews were accusing Paul, he brought him out, ordered the chief priests and the Sanhedrin to assemble, and made Paul stand up before them.

Actually, it was the Roman custom at this time to let the Jews settle religious matters among themselves. Authority in these matters was delegated to the Sanhedrin. If it had not been for the riot, the tribune would have turned Paul over to them and let them settle the matter. But because of his responsibility to keep the peace, he made them assemble in his presence.

The Sanhedrin (*sunedrion*) had a long history behind it. Persians granted the Jews authority over their own affairs. When the Persian Empire fell, a governing body arose which was called the *gerousia* (senate). The Romans around 57 B.C. divided Judea into five districts, each governed by a *sunedrion* (assembly). But in A.D. 47 the emperor gave the *sunedrion* (or as the Jews pronounced it, the Sanhedrin) of Jerusalem authority over all Judea. After A.D. 6, under Roman procurators, the Sanhedrin's powers were increased and extended even beyond Judea. Seventy of its members were elders whose Jewish descent was pure and unquestionable.

Verse 30 actually begins the sequence that continues in chapter 23 and thus really belongs with that chapter.

## Chapter 23

**1. And Paul, earnestly beholding the council, said:** . . . Then Paul, fixing a steady gaze on the Sanhedrin, said, —WEYM . . . looking steadfastly, —ASV . . . looking intently, —HBIE . . . Paul looked straight at the council members and said, —NORL . . . With a stedfast gaze, —MNTG.

**Men and brethren:** . . . My brothers, —BB . . . Fellow Jews, —BECK.

**I have lived in all good conscience before God until this day:** . . . I in all good conscience have used my citizenship for God, —RTHM . . . for my part, I have always ordered my life before God, with a clear conscience, up to this very day, —TCNT . . . I have lived my life in a good way before God up to this day, —EVRD . . . in the presence of God with an altogether clear conscience, —BRKL . . . my life has been upright before God, —BB . . . with a heart that has said I am not guilty to this day, —NLTG.

**23:1.** Paul must have understood what he was facing. Some believe he had once been a member of the Sanhedrin and had cast his vote to stone Stephen. Now he stood before them as an accused prisoner.

Paul, however, showed no fear or hesitation. He knew he was in the will of the Lord, and he had learned to depend on the Holy Spirit to guide him and give him the words to say. Fixing his eyes on the council, he began to speak with deep earnestness and yet with friendliness, addressing them as brethren. He still felt a kinship with his brethren or kinsmen in the flesh.

Now Paul declared he had lived his life (and fulfilled his duties) before God with all good conscience up to that day. (See 1 Corinthians 4:4; Philippians 3:6, 9.)

**2. And the high priest Ananias commanded them that stood by him:** . . . At this . . . ordered the men standing near, —TCNT . . . On hearing this ordered those who were standing near Paul, —WEYM . . . ordered the attendants, —BRKL.

**to smite him on the mouth:** . . . to strike him, —RSV . . . to give him a blow, —BB.

**23:2.** Paul's declaration that he was not guilty of any of the charges brought against him infuriated the high priest Ananias. He ordered his attendants who were standing beside him to strike Paul on the mouth, probably as a rebuke for blasphemy.

Some believe Ananias thought Paul arrogant for calling the Sanhedrin his brothers. Others believe Ananias thought Paul was lying. Most probably, it was his own guilty conscience that made Ananias act as he did. This Ananias was well-known as an unscrupulous, grasping politician. He had been appointed about 9 years earlier through political influence. He ruled like a tyrant and, according to the Jewish Talmud, was also a terrible glutton. Such a man as he could not believe anyone could live with a clear conscience before God.

**3. Then said Paul unto him:** . . . to Ananias, —EVRD.

**God shall smite thee:** . . . God will strike you, —TCNT . . . God is about to slap you, —KLGS.

**thou whited wall:** . . . You whited sepulcher, —MNTG . . . you whitewashed wall! —TCNT . . . you painted pigpen, —LIVB.

**for sittest thou to judge me after the law:** . . . How dare you, —PHLP . . . Are you sitting there to try me in accordance with law, —TCNT . . . Yet in defiance of the Law, —NOLI . . . Do you sit as a judge to try me. —WLMS.

**and commandest me to be smitten contrary to the law?:** . . . and yet, in defiance of law, order them to strike me, —TCNT . . . and you yourself break the Law by ordering me to be struck! —WEYM . . . and give orders for me to be struck, which is clean contrary to the Law, —PHLP . . . to be beaten illegally! —CNDT . . . yet you are telling them to hit me, —SEB . . . and that is against the law, —EVRD.

**23:3.** Paul reacted to this immediately because his sense of justice was aroused. This unwarranted and illegal blow on the mouth caused him to say to the high priest, "God will strike you, you whitewashed wall" (TCNT). Whitewash was used to cover over dirt and filth, so this was a strong rebuke.

The elders who were members of the Sanhedrin were sitting there to judge him according to the Law. The Law treated a man as innocent until he was proven guilty. Nevertheless, some today believe Paul's indignation here was a failure in self-control. Others see it as justified anger without sin (Ephesians 4:26).

**4. And they that stood by said:** ... The bystanders objected, —NORL ... The men standing near Paul said to him, —EVRD.

**Revilest thou God's high priest?:** ... Do rail at, —WEYM ... Do you revile, —WORL ... Do you dare to insult, —PHLP ... Is that the way to talk to, —LIVB ... Do you slander, —KLGS, —KJII ... Do you know that you are insulting God's High Priest, —TCNT ... Are you reproaching, —SWAN ... You must not talk like that to, —SEB.

**23:4.** Those who had struck Paul immediately rebuked him for reviling (abusing, insulting) God's high priest. They felt his office deserved respect since God had instituted the high priesthood.

**5. Then said Paul:** ... Paul answered, —WLMS.

**I wist not, brethren, that he was the high priest:** ... I knew not, —ASV ... I was not aware, —RTHM ... I had no idea that, —BB.

**for it is written:** ... after all, —ADAM ... for Scripture says, —TCNT ... The Bible does say, —BECK.

**Thou shalt not speak evil of the ruler of thy people:** ... You must not defame a ruler of the people, —BRKL.

**23:5.** Paul was quick to take the humble place and apologize, for he too recognized the man's position was given honor by the Scriptures regardless of whether the man himself deserved it or not (Exodus 22:28; Deuteronomy 17:8-13).

It is not clear why Paul did not recognize Ananias as the high priest. Some believe on the basis of Galatians 6:11 that Paul had weak eyesight, but there he was emphasizing his own handwriting so the Galatians could recognize it as genuine and not a forgery.

Actually, Paul had no occasion to see this high priest before this time. Ananias was made high priest in A.D. 47 by Herod of Chalcis. Paul had been in Jerusalem since then only a few times and for short periods, so it is not strange he had never before seen this high priest. It is probable also that since the tribune had assembled the Sanhedrin on this occasion, the high priest was sitting among the other members of the court instead of presiding.

Actually, Paul's prediction was carried out. Ananias was deposed a little over a year later. Then in A.D. 66 Jewish zealots assassinated him as pro-Roman.

**6. But when Paul perceived:** ... But when Paul saw, —BB ... was well aware, —JB ... As Paul knew, —KLGS.

**that the one part was Sadducees, and the other Pharisees:** ... that some of those present were Sadducees and other Pharisees, —TCNT ... that the Sanhedrin consisted partly of Sadducees and partly of Pharisees, —WEYM ... were Liberals and part Orthodox, —KLGS.

**he cried out in the council:** ... shouted, right in the Sanhedrin, —BRKL ... raised his voice and said to them, —PHLP.

**Men and brethren, I am a Pharisee, the son of a Pharisee:** ... and my father was a Pharisee! —EVRD.

**of the hope and resurrection of the dead:** ... concerning the hope and, —ALFD ... It is because of my hope of a resurrection of the dead, —WEYM.

**I am called in question:** ... that I am on my trial, —TCNT ... I am here to be questioned, —BB ... I am accused, —BRKL.

**23:6.** At this point Paul realized there was an issue he could declare. As he already knew, but now noticed again, part of the Sanhedrin were Sadducees, part Pharisees. The Sadducees were a party made up mostly of powerful priestly families who were aristocrats and who had been influenced by Greek culture and philosophy. They put emphasis on the written laws of the Pentateuch, ignored the rest of the Old Testament, and rejected the traditions of the Pharisees. They denied the resurrection, the afterlife, and any future rewards or punishments.

The Pharisees were a minority party which arose during the time of the Hasmonaeans (Maccabees) in the Second Century B.C. They believed temple worship was not enough and said the individual must fulfill the Law. By their traditions they often modified the Law to meet conditions not expressly mentioned. They claimed to make religion ethical rather than theological, and they believed God overruled in all acts, even in those which seemed to come from man's free will. They also taught the immortality of the soul and believed the hope of the resurrection was fundamental to the hope of Israel.

Paul therefore took advantage of the situation with courage. It was an opportunity to witness to the truth of the resurrection and to the fact of the resurrection of Jesus. He was not out of order.

Some believe Paul can be criticized for seizing on the controversy between the Pharisees and Sadducees to divert attention from himself. They say it was a mere stratagem, ducking the blow, avoiding the issue. However, Paul saw that the truth, not his own personal safety, was the real issue at stake.

Even before his conversion, as a Pharisee Paul realized how deep and important the doctrine of the future resurrection is. Crying out that he was a Pharisee, the son of Pharisees, he declared it was with respect to the hope and resurrection of the dead that he was being called into question.

**7. And when he had so said:** ... As soon as he said this, −TCNT ... At these words, −PHLP.

**there arose a dissension:** ... a dispute arose, −TCNT ... there was an argument, −BB ... a quarrel broke out, −MOFF ... a split occurred, −FNTN.

**between the Pharisees and the Sadducees:**

**and the multitude was divided:** ... the court, −WLMS ... and there was a sharp division of opinion among those present, −TCNT ... and the assembly took different sides, −WEYM.

**23:7.** Paul's declaration split the Sanhedrin into two camps. As they talked to one another, the discord grew. Ordinarily they avoided this issue when they met together.

**8. For the Sadducees say:** ... claim, −PHLP.

**that there is no resurrection:** ... no such thing as a resurrection, −TCNT ... no coming back from the dead, −BB.

**neither angel, nor spirit:** ... and that there is neither angel, nor spirit, −TCNT ... and no such thing as an angel or spirit, −WLMS.

**but the Pharisees confess both:** ... while the Pharisees believe in them, −TCNT ... acknowledge them all, −WEYM ... confess the one as well as the other, −BRKL.

**23:8.** Actually, the chief thing the Sadducees denied was personal immortality. Like some of the Greek philosophers, they considered body, soul, and spirit to be a unity, so that one could not exist without the other.

In dealing with the Sadducees, Jesus emphasized that God declares himself the God of Abraham, Isaac, and Jacob, that He is not the God of the dead but of the living, so that Abraham, Isaac, and Jacob are indeed still alive to Him (Matthew 22:23-33; Mark 12:18-27; Luke 20:27-40). Jesus recognized the chief argument of the Sadducees was that souls do not exist apart from their bodies, and it was on this basis they denied the resurrection. By showing that Abraham, Isaac, and Jacob are still alive though their bodies were in their graves, Jesus counteracted the chief argument of the Sadducees and removed their grounds for denying the resurrection.

Actually, the Old Testament gives clear teaching of a future resurrection. Job's testimony is outstanding (see Job 19:23-27). Psalm 16:10 shows the Messiah would be raised from the dead (Acts 2:24-32; 13:34-37). Psalm 17:15 shows a hope, not only of going to be with the Lord, but of a change when believers are raised at Christ's coming (1 Corinthians 15:51, 52; 1 John 3:2). Psalm 73:23-26 shows faith in personal immortality to be ever with the Lord and implies the hope of the resurrection. Isaiah 53:8-12 also shows the resurrection of the suffering Messiah, and Daniel 12:2 specifically prophesies two resurrections (John 5:29; Revelation 20:4, 5, 12, 13).

**9. And there arose a great cry:** ... So a great uproar ensued, −TCNT ... The meeting became very noisy, −NORL.

**and the scribes that were of the Pharisees' part:** ... and some of the teachers of the Law belonging to the Pharisees' party, −TCNT ... and some of the scribes on the side of the Pharisees, −BB.

**arose, and strove, saying:** ... stood up and hotly protested, −TCNT ... sprang to their feet and fiercely contended, −WEYM ... got up and argued vehemently, −BRKL ... jumped to their feet and protested violently, −PHLP.

**We find no evil in this man:** ... Nothing bad find we in this man, −RTHM ... We find nothing whatever wrong in this man, −TCNT ... We cannot find any fault in this man, −KNOX.

**but if a spirit or an angel hath spoken to him:** ... Suppose a spirit did speak to him, or an angel, −TCNT ... maybe an angel or a spirit did speak to him, −NCV ... what if he has had a revelation from, −BB.

**let us not fight against God:**

**23:9.** The discussion soon became a great outcry as Pharisees and Sadducees clamored against each other. Some of the scribes (experts in the interpretation of the Mosaic law) who were on the side of the Pharisees stood up and greatly strove in Paul's behalf. They found no evil (nothing bad) in him. They even suggested an angel or spirit may have spoken to him and warned that in condemning Paul they might be fighting against God.

**10. And when there arose a great dissension:** ... But when the dissension became violent, −MNTG ... The dispute was becoming so violent, −TCNT ... And as a great fight began, −KJII ... They argued all the more, −NLTG ... Since the dispute kept getting hotter and hotter, −WLMS ... But the discord grew so bitter, −BRKL ... As the debate became very heated, −NORL ... The argument was beginning to turn into, −NCV.

**the chief captain, fearing lest Paul should have been pulled in pieces of them:** ... would be pulled in two by them, −BB ... fearing that they would tear him to pieces, −NOLI ... was afraid that the Jews would tear Paul to pieces, −EVRD.

**commanded the soldiers to go down:** ... ordered the military to, −RTHM ... a detachment to march down, −BRKL.

**and to take him by force from among them:** ... and rescue him from them, −NOLI, −TCNT ... and take him out of their hands, −WLMS ... and snatch him from their midst, −BRKL ... and take Paul away, −EVRD.

**and to bring him into the castle:** ... and take him into the Fort, −TCNT ... and lead him into, −WORL ... and bring him safe to the soldiers' quarters, −KNOX ... and put him in the army building, −EVRD.

**23:10.** The mention of angel and spirit must have stirred up the Sadducees. Even though Jesus had once silenced them, they refused to give up their interpretations. Paul had been right in taking his stand with the Pharisees on the matter of the resurrection here, and at this point they were inclined to listen to him. Actually, it was easier for a Pharisee to become a Christian than it was for a Sadducee. In fact, many Pharisees had already become Christians (15:5; 21:20). But a Sadducee would have to cease being a Sadducee altogether and give up all his basic presuppositions in order to accept the resurrected Christ as his Messiah and Saviour. (Acts 6:7 tells of the great number of the priests who were obedient to the Faith, however, and at least some of them must have been Sadducees.)

Here the Sadducees created so much upheaval, and the discord became so great the tribune became afraid Paul might be torn apart by the Sanhedrin members. So he ordered the soldiers to go down and snatch him out of their midst and bring him back into the Fortress of Antonia. Once again when Paul's life was in jeopardy, God's providence saw to it that the Romans rescued him.

**11. And the night following the Lord stood by him, and said:** . . . That night the Lord came, —TCNT . . . But that same night, —WLMS.

**Be of good cheer, Paul:** . . . Be of good courage! —RTHM . . . Paul, be brave, —NORL . . . Take heart! —BRKL . . . Be strong, —LAMS, —SEB.

**for as thou hast testified of me in Jerusalem:** . . . You have borne witness for me in Jerusalem, —TCNT . . . as you fully testified as to the things concerning Me, —WORL . . . as you have been witnessing for me, —BB . . . testified concerning me at, —LAMS . . . You have told people in Jerusalem about me, —EVRD . . . For just as you have given a full account of me in Jerusalem, —NORL.

**so must thou bear witness also at Rome:** . . . testify also at Rome, —HBIE . . . just so it is necessary for you to testify at Rome, —BRKL . . . and now thou must carry the same witness to, —KNOX . . . You must also go to Rome to do the same thing there! —SEB . . . You must do the same in Rome also, —EVRD.

**23:11.** It had been a hard day for Paul. But during the night following, the Lord Jesus suddenly stood beside him and said, "Be of good cheer" (be of good courage, cheer up and do not be afraid). As Paul had testified (given a clear witness) for Christ in Jerusalem, so must he also witness (testify) in Rome. Paul's desire to go to Rome had seemed impossible when he was arrested. But Jesus now said it was still God's will for him. This encouragement upheld Paul in the sufferings and difficulties that were still to come.

One of the marvelous things in the New Testament is the way the Lord Jesus gave encouragement to His servants, sometimes by angels, sometimes by a vision or dream, and sometimes by a personal appearance of the Lord himself.

Paul was human. He really needed this encouragement. After being beaten by the mob he attempted to witness to them, but his witness brought only more riot and rejection. His witness before the Sanhedrin seemed a better opportunity, but the result was the same. In neither case was anyone converted. In fact, it was obvious Paul's enemies were more determined than ever to destroy him.

That night after the excitement was over, Paul must have felt a sense of his own weakness and must have wondered where it would all end. The very words of Jesus imply Paul was beginning to feel a little discouraged and afraid. But how wonderful it must have been when suddenly in the darkness he saw Jesus standing beside him telling him to stop being afraid (as the Greek most probably means).

There was no condemnation in the words of Jesus, only comfort, cheer, and approval. Even though no one was converted, Paul had pleased the Lord with his witness in Jerusalem. Jesus accepted his sincerity and the earnestness and truth of his witness.

**12. And when it was day:** . . . In the morning, —TCNT . . . At daybreak, —BRKL.

**certain of the Jews banded together:** . . . combined together, —TCNT . . . the Jews conspired, —HNSN . . . came together, —BB . . . held a conclave, —KNOX . . . made a plot, —KJII.

**and bound themselves under a curse:** . . . and took an oath, —TCNT . . . and solemnly swore, —WEYM . . . and pledged themselves under an oath, —BRKL . . . They promised each other, —NLTG . . . They made a vow, —NCV . . . made a plan, —EVRD.

**saying that they would neither eat nor drink till they had killed Paul:** . . . that they would not take food or drink till they had put Paul to death, —BB.

**23:12.** Paul slept with new peace and confidence, but as soon as it was day some of the Jews met to plot Paul's death. It seems they saw the Romans were determined to protect Paul and give him a fair trial, and they began to despair of ever putting an end to him by legal means. So these plotters determined they would find some way to murder Paul.

This conspiracy was carried on in the same spirit of violence that had characterized the mob that attacked Paul in the temple court. They went so far as to invoke a curse on themselves, saying they would neither eat nor drink until they had killed Paul.

Binding themselves under a curse means they anathematized themselves or invoked a curse on themselves. That is, they said something like: "May God himself punish us by making us the objects of His wrath to destroy us if we eat or drink until we have killed Paul."

By invoking such a curse upon themselves, they were trying to put God in a position where He would have to do their will. But they were heathenish in their thinking when they felt they could bargain with God or put Him in a corner and force Him to do their will. No one can hold a club over God or demand that He do something contrary to His will or contrary to His nature.

Those who are following the Lord in faith and obedience do not need to bargain with God. Out of pure grace He will pour out His blessings upon those who belong to Him. Even under the Law the people were told that if they obeyed God and did His will, they would not need to run after the blessings. The blessings would literally pursue them and overtake them (Deuteronomy 28:1, 2). It does no good to bargain with God, because those who try to do so forget that God is God.

**13. And they were more than forty which had made this conspiracy:** . . . There were more than forty in the plot, –TCNT . . . who swore to carry out this plot, –BECK . . . established this compact by oath, –MRDK . . . those that formed this conspiracy were more than, –HNSN . . . were involved in this plot, –NOLI . . . who had made this plot, –KJII . . . made this plan, –EVRD.

**23:13.** Over 40 Jews joined in this conspiracy. They could not believe God would destroy them or make them anathema for the sake of one little despised man like Paul. Possibly they believed that by Paul's becoming a preacher of Christ to the Gentiles, he had become a false prophet. They believed he was enticing people to turn away from the way in which the Lord their God had commanded them to walk, as Deuteronomy 13:5 warns when it commands the death penalty for all who do this. Actually, Deuteronomy is dealing with false prophets who turn the people to the worship of false gods, but the conspirators included it to mean turning from Jewish traditions.

**14. And they came to the chief priests and elders, and said:** . . . approached, –PHLP . . . They went and talked to the leading priests and the older Jewish leaders, –EVRD . . . to the most important priests, –SEB.

**We have bound ourselves under a great curse:** . . . taken a solemn oath, –TCNT . . . sworn ourselves to liability of a curse, –BRKL . . . solemn anathema, –CMPB.

**that we will eat nothing until we have shun Paul:** . . . to taste nothing until we have killed Paul, –ASV . . . to let nothing pass our lips, –PHLP.

**23:14.** These 40 conspirators then went to the chief priests and elders and explained their plan, telling them how they had bound themselves under a great curse, or anathema, that they would not eat, not even taste anything until they had killed Paul.

These plotters were not really depending on God. They probably would not have invoked such a serious curse on themselves if they had not been so sure of their own cleverness. They thought they could put Paul in a position where he could not escape them. They were sure the high priest and his company, along with the Sadducee portion of the Sanhedrin, would go along with them.

**15. Now therefore ye with the council:** . . . So we want you now, with the consent of the Council, –TCNT . . . Now then, you, in cooperation with the Sanhedrin, –BRKL . . . We therefore ask you, together with the council, –NORL.

**signify to the chief captain:** . . . ask, –MNTG . . . must now notify, –WLMS . . . send word to, –BRKL . . . must make it plain to, –PHLP . . . make it appear to the officer, –SWAN.

**that he bring him down unto you to morrow:** . . . that you want him to bring Paul down to you, –PHLP.

**as though ye would enquire something more perfectly concerning him:** . . . determine his matter more regularly, –ALFD . . . as if you meant to get more exact information about him, –BECK . . . as though you intended to go more fully into his case, –TCNT . . . It will look as if you want to ask him some things, –NLTG . . . as if you intended to inquire more minutely about him, –WEYM . . . as if you meant to examine his cause more precisely, –KNOX . . . pretending you want more correct information about him, –NCV.

**and we, or ever he come near:** . . . before he comes near, –ASV . . . Then we, if he comes anywhere near, –BRKL.

**are ready to kill him:** . . . are prepared to assassinate him, –WEYM . . . will be waiting to put him to death, –BB.

**23:15.** They asked these leaders to get the Sanhedrin to make an official request to the tribune to bring Paul down, as if they intended to determine more precisely the facts concerning him. Before he got near, they would be waiting, prepared to kill him. That is, they would ambush him on the way, so the Sanhedrin would not be held responsible for his death. Thus the unsuspecting Romans would become tools in their hands.

It is probable also that they did not tell the Pharisees in the Sanhedrin that they intended to ambush Paul. Some of them, at least, were still fearful they might be fighting against God by condemning Paul. But they would be willing to ask for further questioning, since that seemed reasonable.

Unfortunately for the conspirators, they did not know Jesus had already promised to send Paul to

Rome, and their plot was therefore doomed to failure. Yet if they had known, it would probably have made no difference to them. They had already rejected Paul's testimony about the appearance of Jesus on the Damascus Road.

It is not known who these plotters were except that they were not members of the Sanhedrin. Since they went to the priests it is probable they were already under the influence of the priests. It is a fact that any society governed by a corrupt priesthood or clergy spawns wicked men who are quite willing to resort to violence and murder in the name of religion.

Thank God, there was no way Paul's enemies could have thwarted God's plan to get Paul to Rome. With the Lord as their Helper, believers need not fear what man can do to them (Hebrews 13:6). David learned this in the midst of difficult circumstances, and he was able to proclaim that the Lord was his light and his salvation, the strength of his life, so he did not need to be afraid of any enemies that might arise (Psalm 27:1-3). The Levitical singers, the sons of Korah, sang out, "God is our refuge and strength, a very present help in trouble" (Psalm 46:1). (See also Psalms 56:4; 91:1-6; 118:6.)

Actually, there was only one person who could have thwarted God's plan for Paul, and that was Paul himself. He could have done it through unbelief (Hebrews 3:19; 4:1, 11).

**16. And when Paul's sister's son:** ... But Paul's nephew, —SEB, —WEYM . . . Paul's sister had a son, —KNOX.

**heard of their lying in wait:** ... hearing of the plot, —TCNT . . . heard of the intended attack upon him, —WEYM . . . got wind of the ambush, —BRKL . . . who heard of this ambush being laid, —KNOX.

**he went and entered into the castle, and told Paul:** ... He went to the fortress, —SEB . . . went to the army building, —NCV . . . went to the Fort, and on being admitted, told Paul about it, —TCNT . . . and he came and got into the barracks, —GDSP . . . he went and gained entrance to, —TNT . . . came and found his way into, —PHLP . . . so he came along and entered the barracks to inform Paul, —BRKL . . . went to the soldiers' quarters, —KNOX . . . entering the fortress, he reported to Paul, —KJII . . . and gave news of it to Paul, —BB . . . reported it to, —WORL.

**23:16.** While the conspirators were discussing their plot with the chief priests and elders, Paul's sister's son happened to come on the scene in time to hear them. Some writers believe he had come to Jerusalem from Tarsus to be educated, just as Paul had years before. The Bible does not say how he happened to be there, but God saw to it that he was. Though Paul himself was not aware of the danger, God knew it and provided for it. One of

the thrills of eternity will be to learn of the dangers believers did not see, but which God saw and kept them from.

Paul's nephew did not hesitate. He went immediately and told Paul about the plot against him.

From this it is evident Paul's nephew was intelligent. He kept his eyes and ears open, and when he found out about this plot, he understood the danger for Paul. It is clear that he loved his uncle. Whether he was a Christian or not, Luke did not say. Possibly he was not, since Luke in Acts usually identified those who were Christians by calling them disciples. But in this sudden peril, the nephew did not let any religious differences that might have existed keep him from trying to help his uncle. He also was prompt. He did not let excuses or any of his own plans or desires keep him from immediate action. He could have been like so many who know their duty but fail to do it. Paul's nephew could have decided he did not want to get involved. He could have told himself he was just a young man without influence and there was nothing he could do. But, thank God, he resisted any of these excuses or temptations that might have come to his mind. He was willing to do what he could and leave the rest in the hands of God.

**17. Then Paul called one of the centurions unto him, and said:** ... called one of the officers and said, NCV.

**Bring this young man unto the chief captain:** ... to take the lad to, —TCNT . . . Take this young man to, —WEYM . . . Conduct this young man to, —BRKL . . . to the officer, —SWAN . . . to the commander, —EVRD.

**for he hath a certain thing to tell him:** ... for he has information to give him, —WEYM . . . he has something to tell him, —NLTG . . . he has news to give him, —KNOX . . . He has a message for him, —EVRD, —NCV . . . has something to report to him, —PHLP.

**23:17.** Paul then called a centurion and asked him to take the young man to the tribune. It took courage for the young man to go to see Paul. If his visit to Paul became known, it could have caused Paul's enemies to direct their wrath against him. It took even more courage for him to be willing to share what he knew with the Roman authorities. He had no way of knowing how they would react. He might have been afraid the tribune would not believe him and would turn him over to the Jews, for he surely knew the Romans allowed the Sanhedrin authority over Jewish affairs. But he was willing to take the risk in order to save Paul.

**18. So he took him, and brought him to the chief captain, and said:** ... So the officer took him to the commander, saying, —MOFT . . . brought Paul's nephew to the commander, −EVRD . . . brought him into the colonel's presence, −PHLP.

**Paul the prisoner called me unto him:** . . . made a request to me, −BB . . . had me summoned, −KNOX . . . asked me, −EVRD.

**and prayed me to bring this young man unto thee:** . . . and asked me, −ASV . . . made a request to me, −BB . . . and begged me to bring this youth to you, −WEYM . . . bring this young man to you, −LAMS . . . and asked me to take this young man into thy presence, −KNOX.

**who hath something to say unto thee:** . . . as having somewhat to tell thee, −RTHM . . . as he has something to say, −GDSP . . . He wants to tell you something, −EVRD.

**23:18.** The centurion took the young man to the tribune. He explained how Paul had said the young man had something to say to him. Paul wisely had not told the centurion about the plot. Only the tribune would be able to do anything about it, and it was better that not too many people know about it.

Paul is called a prisoner here. Actually, he was under protective custody. It may be also that (as was later the case in Rome) his right hand was chained to the left hand of a soldier. But this did not trouble Paul. Later he made it clear that he considered himself a prisoner, not of Rome, but of the Lord (Ephesians 3:1; 2 Timothy 1:8; Philemon 1, 9). He had been brought into the glorious freedom and liberty of the children of God (Romans 8:21). Christ had set him free and the Spirit of the Lord gave continued liberty. Nothing could change that.

**19. Then the chief captain took him by the hand:** . . . taking him by the arm, −WEYM . . . led the young man, −EVRD.

**and went with him aside privately, and asked him:** . . . began privately to ask, −RTHM . . . stepped to one side with him privately and inquired, −BRKL . . . and drew him aside (where they could not be overheard), −PHLP . . . withdrew to a private place, −SWAN . . . to a place where they could be alone, −SEB . . . drew him off to one side, asking, −KJII.

**What is that thou hast to tell me?:** . . . What have you to tell me, −WEYM . . . What is it which thou hast to report unto me, −RTHM.

**23:19.** The tribune received the young man courteously, took him by the hand, and retired into a place where they could talk privately. Then he asked him what he had to tell him.

There must have been something about the bearing of Paul's nephew that impressed the tribune with the seriousness of what the young man had to say. He was probably impressed too by the fact that the young man had not tried to come directly to him, but had gone first to Paul, and then through the centurion. This young man was

quite different from the violent, riotous Jews the tribune had been dealing with in the temple court and even in the Sanhedrin. He showed an attitude of trust toward the tribune.

Actually, though Rome's conquests were often barbaric, Rome ruled its conquered territories with a statesmanship that was humane and very tolerant. Beginning with the Emperor Augustus it became Rome's policy to preserve peace throughout the whole empire. They wanted to spread civilization and what they considered to be just laws. They encouraged the spread of Greek culture. But they were tolerant of Judaism and made it one of the licensed religions of the empire. At times the Roman government even protected the Jews from the enmity that was sometimes stirred up against them by their heathen neighbors.

**20. And he said:** . . . He answered, −WLMS . . . And he replied, −PHLP.

**The Jews have agreed to desire thee:** . . . have decided to ask, −EVRD . . . to ask thee, −ASV . . . to request thee, −RTHM.

**that thou wouldest bring down Paul to morrow into the council:** . . . to ask you to bring Paul to the courtroom tomorrow, −NLTG . . . to their council meeting, −EVRD.

**as though they would enquire somewhat of him more perfectly:** . . . on the plea of your making further inquiry into his case, −TCNT . . . as though you were going to examine his case more carefully, −WLMS . . . on the pretext of obtaining more precise information about him, −NEB . . . as if they would inquire somewhat more exactly concerning him, −WORL . . . They want you to think that they plan to ask Paul more questions, −SEB . . . They want you to think that they want more information about him, −NCV.

**23:20.** The young man told the tribune how the Jews had agreed together to make a request of the tribune that he would bring Paul down to the Sanhedrin the next day in order to determine or decide his case by a more thorough and exact investigation. This was something that under ordinary circumstances the tribune would certainly consider a reasonable request.

Paul's nephew meant the Jewish leaders had done so, that is, the Jews with whom the tribune had been dealing in the previous trial. The New Testament often uses the term "the Jews" when it means the Jewish leaders who were the representatives of the Jews before the Roman government. It does not mean that every Jew or even every Jew in Jerusalem was involved in the plots and opposition against the Christians or against Christian leaders like Paul.

It does seem strange that these Jews who were the highest religious leaders of the Jewish people would consent to a plot that was pure deception.

But this was not the first or last time that high religious leaders had promoted deception and trickery under the guise of religion. But it is a sad thing when lies and deception are used by those claiming to represent the one true God. However, the Jewish leaders were not the only ones guilty of such things. The history of the church is not blameless either.

**21. But do not thou yield unto them:** ... but do not you give in to them, —*BRKL* ... Do not grant them this request, —*NOLI* ... But do not let them persuade you, —*TCNT* ... I beg you not to comply, —*WEYM* ... Do not pay attention to them, —*KLGS* ... Do not let them talk you into it, —*NLTG.*

**for there lie in wait for him of them more than forty men:** ... have ganged up, —*KLGS* ... are waiting in secret, —*NLTG* ... who are hiding and waiting to kill, —*SEB.*

**which have bound themselves with an oath, that they will neither eat nor drink:** ... have taken a solemn oath, —*NOLI.*

**till they have killed him:** ... assassinated him, —*WEYM* ... destroyed him, —*BRKL.*

**and now are they ready:** ... and they are at this very moment in readiness, —*TCNT* ... and they are all set, —*NORL* ... even now they are in readiness, —*KNOX* ... Now these conspirators are lying in ambush for him, —*NOLI.*

**looking for a promise from thee:** ... only waiting for thy consent, Knox ... awaiting your consent, —*MOFT* ... all they want now is for you to give the order, —*PHLP* ... will receive a favourable reply from you, —*FNTN* ... They are all waiting for you to say the word, —*NLTG* ... now they are waiting for you to say yes, —*NCV* ... are waiting for a favorable answer from you, —*NOLI.*

**23:21.** Paul's nephew went to warn the tribune not to be persuaded by the Jews who would come in a very convincing manner. The young man was very bold and emphatic here as he put the responsibility on the tribune not to be convinced, not to follow the Jews' advice or yield to their request.

Then he informed the tribune of the reason. Even now the men were prepared to carry out their plot. They were just waiting until they received a promise from the tribune. Then they would take their place in the ambush in order to carry out their terrible plot.

The way the young man presented himself to the tribune shows he was sincere, earnest, and had the facts. He showed no fear of the tribune. He did not waste time with undue politeness, but was straightforward and went right to the point. This also must have appealed to the tribune as a Roman. The Gospel of Mark, which was directed to the Romans, shows the same straightforward manner and direct approach. The Holy Spirit must have given this young man wisdom as well as courage.

Jesus had promised that when His disciples came to trial before governors and kings, the Holy Spirit would give them what to say (Matthew 10:18-20). Now it is evident that the Spirit guides others who are raised up to help His people.

**22. So the chief captain then let the young man depart:** ... therefore dismissed the young man, —*RTHM* ... So the Tribune sent the youth home, —*WEYM* ... sent the young man away, NCV.

**and charged him:** ... cautioning him, —*TCNT* ... with strict directions, —*WLMS* ... with the strict advice, —*NORL* ... with the injunction, —*MNTG* ... with the following command, —*NOLI.*

**See thou tell no man:** ... Tell nobody, —*MOFT* ... Do not let anyone know, —*WEYM* ... Don't let a soul know, —*PHLP* ... not to mention to anyone, —*TCNT* ... not to divulge to anyone, —*CNFT* ... warning him not to let anyone know, —*KNOX.*

**that thou hast shewed these things to me:** ... that he had given him that information, —*TCNT* ... that you have informed me of this, —*MOFT* ... that he had notified him of this plot, —*WLMS* ... that he had revealed this secret to him, —*KNOX.*

**23:22.** The tribune then dismissed the young man (let him go, sent him away) with a command forbidding him to tell anyone what he had revealed (reported) to him.

The tribune gave this order in such an emphatic manner to impress on the young man the need of secrecy and discretion to insure the safety of Paul. It is certain Paul's nephew obeyed the tribune's order. The young man's manner impressed the tribune and caused the tribune to believe him. But the tribune also recognized the youth of his informant. He knew that youth is not always characterized by discretion. So this was another reason he made the command so emphatic.

God was working in all of this. Jesus had appeared to Paul and given him assurance that He would see him through to Rome. But Paul still did not see how this could or would be done. But God was working things out step by step. The very fact that Paul's nephew came must have given Paul's faith further encouragement. The Bible does not say so, but it is very probable that the young man stopped by to see Paul on the way out of the fortress and told him of the favorable way the tribune had received him. Thus, the Lord was encouraging Paul's faith at every step of the way.

It must not be supposed Paul did not need this repeated encouragement. James 5:17 is a reminder that Elijah was a man with a nature like everyone else. In spite of the great faith he showed and the miracles he saw, he too could become discouraged. But God dealt with him and brought him to renewed faith and courage. He encourages believers today as well.

**23. And he called unto him two centurions, saying:** . . . He summoned two of the officers, —MOFT . . . and ordered them, —TCNT.

**Make ready two hundred soldiers to go to Caesarea:** . . . to have two hundred men ready to go to Caesarea, —TCNT.

**and horsemen threescore and ten:** . . . and seventy horsemen, —RTHM . . . as well as seventy troopers, —TCNT.

**and spearmen two hundred:** . . . and two hundred lancers, —TCNT . . . men with spears, —EVRD.

**at the third hour of the night:** . . . and have them ready to start, —BECK . . . starting . . . tonight! —WEYM . . . Be ready to leave at nine o'clock tonight, —EVRD.

**23:23.** The tribune knew he would be held accountable for Paul, as a Roman citizen in his custody, if Paul were assassinated. That is, the tribune himself would be punished. Therefore, he did not waste any time. Immediately he had 2 centurions get 200 foot soldiers ready to go to Caesarea, along with 70 cavalry and 200 soldiers of another class. Apparently, these were the usual constituents of a Roman army corps. By 9 o'clock that night they were to be on their way to the Roman capital of Palestine, about 55 miles northwest of Jerusalem.

Caesarea was built by Herod the Great on the coast about 30 miles north of Joppa. Herod also constructed a 200-foot-wide causeway of huge stones in water 60 feet deep in order to enclose an artificial harbor that was unusually large for that day. The Roman procurators or governors made this city their chief residence. Archaeologists have found the name of Pilate inscribed on one of the stones.

**24. And provide them beasts, mat they may set Paul on:** . . . and to have horses ready for Paul to ride, —TCNT . . . get some horses for Paul to ride, —EVRD.

**and bring him safe unto Felix the governor:** . . . and convey him safely, —HNSN . . . and conduct him safely to governor Felix, —BRKL . . . He must be taken to Governor Felix safely, —EVRD.

**23:24.** Horses were also to be provided for Paul to ride so he might be brought safely to Felix, the Roman governor of the province.

Marcus Antonius Felix was procurator of Judea from A.D. 52 to 59. He was a freedman (former slave) of the Emperor Claudius or of the emperor's mother. A violent man, he slaughtered many Jews as well as others. Tacitus, the Roman historian, wrote that Claudius reveled in cruelty and lust, and wielded the power of a king with the mind of a slave.

But though Felix was a fierce and violent man, Paul was not afraid to be sent to him, for Jesus had promised to be with him.

In the meantime, the more than 40 Jews who had planned to wait in ambush were left without their victim. Perhaps they just went home feeling thwarted in their plans to do away with Paul.

**25. And he wrote a letter after this manner:** . . . somewhat as follows, —TCNT . . . He also wrote a letter of which these were the contents, —WEYM . . . after this fashion, —RTHM . . . to whom he sent the following letter, —WLMS . . . after this model, —CNDT.

**23:25.** The tribune, of course, could not send Paul to the governor without some explanation, so he wrote a letter to Felix.

Acts says it was "after this manner" (type, pattern, copy). A possible meaning is that what follows is an actual copy of the letter. There has been conjecture that Paul saw the letter, made a copy, and gave it to Luke. How the Holy Spirit worked in this case is not explained.

**26. Claudius Lysias unto the most excellent governor Felix sendeth greeting:** . . . to His Excellency, —NOLI.

**23:26.** In the letter the tribune stated his name, Claudius Lysias. Claudius was a Roman name taken by the tribune, probably at the time he bought his Roman citizenship. Lysias was a Greek name common in Syria, indicating his background in Greek culture.

Next he sent greetings to Felix, addressing him as the most noble or most excellent (imperial) governor (a title used of the procurators).

**27. This man was taken of the Jews:** . . . This man, having been apprehended, —RTHM . . . When this man was set upon, —BRKL . . . had been seized by the Jews, —TCNT . . . The Jews had taken this man, —EVRD.

**and should have been killed of them:** . . . and was on the point of being killed by them, —TCNT . . . and was within an inch of being murdered by them, —BRKL . . . almost assassinated by them, —FNTN . . . They were ready to murder him, —NOLI . . . who intended to kill him, —LAMS.

**then came I with an army:** . . . but I intervened with Roman soldiers, —LAMS . . . came upon them with the force under my command, —TCNT . . . came upon them suddenly, with the troops, —HNSN . . . with my regiment, —NORL . . . when I arrived with my troops, —PHLP.

**and rescued him:** . . . and took him out of danger, —BRKL.

**having understood that he was a Roman:** . . . as I learnt that he was a Roman citizen, —TCNT . . . as I had ascertained that, —MOFT . . . since I had discovered, —PHLP.

**23:27.** The tribune explained how Paul was seized by the Jews and was about to be killed violently by them. Then, because he had learned Paul was a Roman citizen, he came and rescued Paul.

It was not true that Lysias learned Paul was a Roman before he went to rescue him. He did not learn of this until after he gave orders for his soldiers to scourge Paul. But Lysias does not mention this mistake on his part. Perhaps he felt that to admit this would get the violent Felix sidetracked on another issue. Also he wanted to put himself in the best light possible.

It is in the tribune's favor, however, that from the start he wanted to give the impression that Paul had been unjustly seized and attacked by the Jews. He seemed really concerned to protect Paul and put Paul in the best light possible. The special emphasis on the fact that Paul was a Roman citizen was also intended to get Felix to receive him favorably.

**28. And when I would have known:** ... And wishing to know, –HBIE ... Wishing to ascertain exactly, –TCNT ... And desiring to get at, –BB ... In the hope of discovering, –BRKL.

**the cause wherefore they accused him:** ... the ground of the charges they made against him, –TCNT ... the offence of which they were accusing him, –WEYM ... the crime for which they were accusing him, –HBIE ... the reason for their attack, –BB ... the exact charge, –WLMS ... what complaint it was they had, –KNOX.

**I brought him forth into their council:** ... I took him down into their High-council, –RTHM ... Sanhedrin, –WEYM.

**23:28.** Lysias further explained he had not jumped to conclusions about Paul. He wanted to learn and ascertain exactly and thoroughly the charge or ground for complaint by which the Jews accused or brought charges against Paul. Therefore he brought Paul down to their Sanhedrin.

This, of course, was true. Even though the tribune had made a mistake in commanding Paul to be scourged, he did want to get at the root cause of all the disturbance that had centered around Paul. The tribune did not give the details of this encounter in his letter, but he was still wanting to put Paul in a good light.

Most of the Roman officers described in the New Testament were well-disposed toward the Jews and later on to the Christians. The centurions especially are shown in a good light. Two centurions are mentioned by name: Cornelius of Caesarea and Julius (chapter 27), who conducted Paul to Rome and treated him with consideration and kindness. Other centurions believed and put their faith in Jesus.

**29. Whom I perceived to be accused of questions of their law:** ... where I found he was accused of matters relating to, –MOFT ... when I found that their charges were connected with questions of their own Law, –TCNT.

**but to have nothing laid to his charge worthy of death or of bonds:** ... and that there was nothing alleged involving either death or imprisonment, –TCNT ... and that nothing was said against him which might be a reason for prison or death, –BB ... but there was none for which he deserved to die or be in chains, –BECK.

**23:29.** The tribune further explained that when Paul was before the Sanhedrin, he (the tribune) found the accusations all pertained to controversial questions related to their (Jewish) law. He further explained he found nothing in their charges or accusations worthy of putting Paul to death or even of putting him in chains or imprisonment.

This letter, as an official Roman report to the governor, declared Paul was innocent of any crime worthy of punishment. It not only showed Paul in a good light, it gave him an advantage should the Jews bring further accusations against him in the future. Obviously, the tribune wanted to make sure Paul would get justice.

**30. And when it was told me:** ... But when I was informed, –RTHM ... on its being divulged to me, –CNDT.

**how that the Jews laid wait for the man:** ... that there would be a plot against the man, –ASV ... that a plot was being concocted against this man, –BRKL ... that a conspiracy was preparing against the man, –ALFD.

**I sent straightway to thee:** ... I am sending him to you at once, –TCNT ... without delay, –PHLP.

**and gave commandment to his accusers also:** ... and I have directed, –TCNT ... I also told those Jews, –EVRD ... giving orders to these who are against him, –BB ... At the same time I have notified his accusers, –PHLP.

**to say before thee what they had against him:** ... to prosecute him before you, –TCNT ... to state before you the case they have against him, –WEYM ... that they must plead their cause before thee, –KNOX ... to tell you what they have against him, –NCV ... to go and contend with him before you, –LAMS ... to state ... whatever accusations they have against him, –NOLI.

**Farewell:**

**23:30.** The tribune explained how he was told of the Jews' plot to ambush Paul and how he immediately sent Paul to Felix. Then he added something not mentioned before. He gave commandment to Paul's accusers to bring their charges or accusations to Felix also. In view of the fact that he sent Paul away immediately, the tribune probably meant he was about to send this order to the Sanhedrin.

It is clear also that the tribune wanted both Felix and the Sanhedrin to know Paul was now out of his jurisdiction. Whatever happened to Paul now would be their affair, not his. He seemed anxious to make sure that if anything did happen to Paul the Roman government would know he had done his part well, and no accusation could be brought against him. This is not to say he was more concerned about himself than he was about Paul. But he probably breathed a sigh of relief when he saw the 400 foot soldiers and 60 horsemen leaving the city of Jerusalem, taking Paul and the letter to Felix.

Such a troop movement, even at night, must have attracted attention. Though it may not have been known Paul was in the midst of them then, it was surely known by the next morning. If the traditions of the Jewish Mishnah were held at this time there was provision for a sacrifice or offering to atone for the failure to keep a vow. Thus, there may have been over 40 extra sacrifices brought to the temple that day.

**31. Then the soldiers, as it was commanded them, took Paul:** . . . The soldiers, in accordance with their orders, took charge of Paul, *—TCNT* . . . did the things they were told, *—SEB* . . . acting on their orders, *—PHLP* . . . obeying their orders, *—KNOX* . . . did what they were told, *—EVRD.*

**and brought him by night to Antipatris:** . . . and, riding through the night, brought him down to Antipatris, *—PHLP* . . . conducted him, travelling all night, *—KNOX* . . . brought him to the city . . . that night, *—EVRD.*

**23:31.** That night the soldiers brought Paul as far as Antipatris, about 30 miles northwest of Jerusalem (possibly about 38 miles by the old Roman road, and about 24 miles from Caesarea). It was located on a fertile plain near the foothills between Judea and Samaria. Herod the Great built the city and named it after his father, Antipater. The Romans had located a Roman colony there, so it was a convenient and safe place for the Roman soldiers to stop and spend the rest of the night.

**32. On the morrow they left the horsemen to go with him, and returned to the castle:** . . . On the next day, leaving the troopers to go on with him, they returned to the Fort, *—TCNT* . . . dismissed the footmen, *—LAMS* . . . The next day the infantry returned to the barracks, leaving the cavalry to proceed with him, *—WEYM* . . . the horsemen went with Paul to Caesarea, *—EVRD.*

**23:32.** The next day the 400 foot soldiers returned to their barracks in the Fortress of Antonia in Jerusalem. They probably kept watch along the way to be sure none of the Jews were trying to follow Paul.

Then the 60 cavalry conducted Paul the rest of the way to Caesarea. It was felt that the 60 horsemen would be enough to protect Paul for the remainder of the journey. This undoubtedly gave Paul further opportunity to spread his witness for Christ.

**33. Who, when they came to Caesarea:** . . . They went into Caesarea, *—PHLP.*

**and delivered the epistle to the governor:** . . . and delivered the letter, *—RSV* . . . gave the letter to, *—EVRD.*

**presented Paul also before him:** . . . and brought Paul before him, *—TCNT* . . . and turned Paul over to him, too, *—WLMS* . . . Then they gave Paul to him, *—SEB.*

**23:33.** When the horsemen arrived in Caesarea it must have been an unusual sight to see such a company escorting a prisoner. Those who saw them probably thought Paul was some hero or notable person being escorted to the governor's palace by an honor guard. God has ways of overruling the intentions of the enemies of His people.

The cavalry first delivered the letter to the Roman governor, or procurator, Felix. Then, after giving the governor the letter (and an opportunity to read it), they presented Paul to him also. (It is probable that a centurion accompanied the cavalry. The centurion may have been the one who actually delivered the letter and presented Paul to Felix.)

**34. And when the governor had read the letter:** . . . As soon as Felix had read the letter, *—TCNT* . . . Felix, after reading the letter, *—WEYM.*

**he asked of what province he was:** . . . he inquired, *—TCNT* . . . What part of the country do you come from? *—BB* . . . What area are you from? *—EVRD.*

**And when he understood that he was of Cilicia:** . . . When he learned, *—RSV* . . . that he came from Cilicia, *—TCNT.*

**23:34.** When Felix read the letter he also understood the reasons for sending Paul to him, as well as the reasons for the extra precautions for the protection of Paul on the journey to Caesarea.

After reading the letter, Felix asked Paul what province he was from. Probably Felix asked the question because he had to know if Paul came from a Roman province. Only if he came from a Roman province could Felix, as a Roman governor, take charge of Paul on his own authority (that is, without getting the emperor's permission).

Cilicia was an important district or province in southeast Asia Minor between the Taurus mountains and the Mediterranean Sea. It was separated from Syria on the east by Mount Amanus and was bound on the west by Pamphylia. The western part of the province is mountainous. The eastern part is a fertile, alluvial plain with Tarsus, the birthplace of Paul, as its chief city. The Romans took control of Cilicia beginning with Pompey's conquest about 66 B.C. Cicero, the famous Roman orator, was its governor for a short time in 51-50 B.C.

The fact that Paul was a Roman citizen from this important province meant Felix could not ignore him. Neither could he ignore the complaints of the Jewish leaders of Jerusalem. As governor or procurator he was the chief one responsible to keep peace and promote Roman justice in Judea.

**35. I will hear thee, said he:** . . . hear your case, —MNTG . . . will give you a full hearing, —NORL . . . I will listen to all of this, —NLTG.

**when thine accusers are also come:** . . . as soon as your accusers have arrived, —TCNT . . . when thy accusers, too, are present, —KNOX . . . as soon as your accusers make their appearance, —NOLI . . . when those who are against you come here too, —EVRD.

**And he commanded him to be kept:** . . . In the meantime, —NOLI . . . and gave orders that . . . he should be kept under guard, —RTHM . . . that he should be kept safe in, —KNOX.

**in Herod's judgment hall:** . . . in the praetorium of Herod, —HBIE, —LAMS . . . in the palace, —EVRD.

**23:35.** Upon hearing that Paul was from Cilicia, Felix told him he would give him a hearing whenever his accusers arrived to present their case against him. Then Felix commanded that Paul be guarded in Herod's Praetorium. This was the lavish palace built by Herod the Great. It served as the capitol building as well as the official residence of the Roman procurators. Thus, Paul was in a better situation than in Jerusalem, where he had been kept in the soldiers' barracks.

## Chapter 24

**1. And after five days:** . . . Five days later, —MOFT.

**Ananias the high priest descended with the elders:** . . . They went to Caesarea, —SEB . . . came down to Caesarea with a number of Elders, —WEYM . . . with certain presbyters, —HNSN.

**and with a certain orator named Tertullus:** . . . a barrister named Tertullus, —TCNT . . . a prosecuting attorney, —WLMS . . . and a certain attorney named, —NOLI . . . by an advocate named, —KNOX.

**who informed the governor against Paul:** . . . who made a complaint against Paul before Felix, —NORL . . . to present their evidence, —BRKL . . . to make charges against Paul before the governor, —SEB.

**24:1.** Only once did the Jews bring formal charges against the apostle Paul. It happened after Paul had been in Caesarea 5 days. Then Ananias the high priest came down from Jerusalem with some of the members of the Sanhedrin. Undoubtedly, these elders were mostly Sadducees who were friends of the high priests.

They had hired an orator, a professional public speaker, to act as an advocate, that is, as the counsel for the prosecution.

Tertullus ("little third"), a common Roman name, was probably a Jew who was a Roman citizen trained in Roman oratory and legal methods. The high priest must have given him a large sum of money to get him to go to Caesarea to try to counteract the effect of Paul's Roman citizenship as well as to impress Felix.

**2. And when he was called forth:** . . . So Paul was sent for, —WEYM . . . was summoned, —MOFT . . . Paul was called into the meeting, —NCV.

**Tertullus began to accuse him, saying:** . . . began to impeach him as follows, —WEYM . . . began his charge by saying, —NORL . . . began his speech for the prosecution, —TCNT . . . began the prosecution in these words, —PHLP.

**Seeing that by thee we enjoy great quietness:** . . . we are enjoying profound peace, —TCNT . . . we dwell in much tranquility, —MRDK . . . We owe it to you personally . . . that we enjoy lasting peace, —PHLP.

**and that very worthy deeds are done unto this nation by thy providence:** . . . it is due to your foresight that the nation enjoys improved conditions of living, —PHLP . . . by your prudent administration, —CMPB . . . your wise care, —MOFT.

**24:2.** Paul was then called, and Tertullus was given opportunity to present his accusation against him.

Tertullus did not immediately prefer charges. Instead, he began by flattering the governor with flowery traditional oratory that sugarcoated the truth. He said that through him the Jews were enjoying great peace. This, Felix must have known, was mere flattery, for he well knew it was contrary to the facts. The facts are that Felix had incited robbers to assassinate the high priest, Jonathan, who had displeased him. Then he had many of the same robbers captured and crucified. When false prophets led crowds into the wilderness, Felix attacked them and had great numbers of them killed. When an Egyptian came and led a mob to the Mount of Olives, Felix sent an army, killed about 400 of them, and took about 200 more prisoners.

Tertullus then said reforms had come to the Jewish nation through the forethought (foresight and care) of Felix.

Some ancient manuscripts have "success" (prosperity, good order) instead of "reforms" (Greek *katorthōmatōn*, instead of *diorthōmatōn*). But Felix had brought neither reforms nor great prosperity and success to the Jews. Instead, there was constant turmoil throughout his governorship. His ineffective rule was an important factor leading to the revolt "of the Jews which brought the destruction of Jerusalem in A.D. 70.

**3. We accept it always, and in all places, most noble Felix, with all thankfulness:** ... In all things and in all places we are conscious of our great debt to you, —BB ... with profound gratitude, —WLMS ... At all times, and indeed everywhere, we acknowledge these things with the deepest gratitude, —PHLP.

**24:3.** Tertullus went on to say these things (peace and reforms or great prosperity) the Jews accepted in all ways and in all places with thankfulness. This also was pure flattery. Actually, the Jews were always complaining about Felix. Even after he was replaced and returned to Rome they sent more complaints.

By calling him "most noble," Tertullus was merely using the traditional tide of honor given to officials, a title better translated "most excellent," as in 23:26.

**4. Notwithstanding, that I be not further tedious unto thee:** ... However, not to take more of your precious time, —BRKL ... Not to keep you too long, —BECK ... intrude on thy time, —DRBY ... for I must not detain you too long, —PHLP.

**I pray thee:** ... I entreat thee, —ASV ... I beseech thee, —RTHM ... I beg you, —TCNT ... I make a request to you, —BB ... I simply want to ask you, —NORL.

**that thou wouldest hear us of thy clemency a few words:** ... with your accustomed fairness, to listen to a brief statement of our case, —TCNT ... to grant us in your courtesy a brief hearing, —MOFT ... to listen to a few words from us, —MNTG ... with your usual candor, —CMPB.

**24:4.** As a further gesture of politeness or deference to Felix, Tertullus suggested he did not want to hinder the governor more. The Syriac Peshitta and the Armenian versions (translations) took this to mean "in order not to weary you any further." But he may have meant "in order not to delay or detain you any further." Tertullus promised to be brief and to the point, and declared that he expected Felix to be fair (even though secular history shows Felix was a violent, unfair man).

**5. For we have found this man a pestilent fellow:** ... a public pest, —TCNT ... The fact is, we have found this man is a perfect pest, —MOFT ... a source of mischief, —WEYM ... to be a veritable plague, —BRKL.

**and a mover of sedition among all the Jews throughout the world:** ... he stirs up sedition among the Jews all over the world, —MOFT ... an inciter of insurrection among all the Jews of the empire, —MNTG ... raiser of insurrections, —PNT ... a promoter of seditions, —CNFT ... a pestilential disturber of the peace ... all over the world, —PHLP.

**and a ringleader of the sect of the Nazarenes:** ... and the chief mover in the society of the Nazarenes, —BB ... of the party of, —WMCK ... the

Nazarene heretics, —TCNT ... heresy of the Nazarenes, —MNTG ... of the Nazareth sect, —PHLP.

**24:5.** By a mixture of lies and cleverly twisted half-truths, Tertullus began to accuse Paul falsely on four points.

First, he said Paul was a pestilent fellow; that is, like a disease he was spreading an epidemic that would destroy the people. There was hardly anything worse they could have said about Paul.

Second, Tertullus said Paul was constantly stirring up sedition (discord, revolution, and riot) among all the Jews who were in all the inhabited world.

By the inhabited world, Tertullus meant the Roman Empire (as the phrase was commonly understood in those days). It is as if he was accusing Paul of being the causer or arouser of all the uprisings, riots, and strife among the Jews in those times.

Third, Tertullus implicated all the Christians by calling Paul a ringleader of the sect of the Nazarenes, the party or group of people who followed the teachings of the Man of Nazareth.

By calling the Christians a sect, he did not necessarily mean a heretical sect. The same term was used of the various schools of philosophy among the Greeks, and it was applied to the Pharisees and Sadducees by the Jews. This indicates also that Tertullus was looking on the Jewish believers as a Jewish sect.

**6. Who also hath gone about to profane the temple:** ... who also attempted to desecrate even the temple, —RTHM ... He actually tried to desecrate, —MOFT ... who, in addition, was attempting to make the Temple unclean, —BB ... he was on the point of desecrating, —PHLP ... even tried to bring unclean things into the temple, —WMCK

**whom we took:** ... whom we also seized, —RTHM ... but we caught him, —TCNT ... when we overcame him, —PHLP.

**and would have judged according to our law:** ... and would have sentenced him by our Law, —BRKL.

**24:6.** Fourth, after these general accusations, Tertullus gave the specific charge. Paul, he said, had tried to profane the temple, that is, he had attempted to desecrate it. But they laid hold on him and arrested him before he could desecrate it.

This, of course, was false. Actually, they seized Paul and tried to lynch him without a trial. But Tertullus did not tell of their violence and how they were in the process of beating Paul to death as an act of mob violence.

**7. But the chief captain Lysias came upon us, and with great violence took him away out of our hands:**

**24:7.** As most ancient New Testament manuscripts indicate, Tertullus claimed Paul was being judged properly by their law when the tribune Lysias intervened and took Paul out of their hands.

Tertullus made a serious mistake when he tried to put the Roman tribune in a bad light. His claim that the Jews had arrested Paul and were about to give him a fair trial made it seem wrong for Lysias to intervene violently, using the force of Roman soldiers wrongfully.

Felix, however, knew that Roman officers had a responsibility to keep order in Jerusalem. He knew they would not have interfered unless there were near-riot conditions. Besides, Felix had the letter from Lysias which put an entirely different light on the subject. Lysias had said Paul was seized by the Jews and was about to be killed by them. Lysias had only done his duty in rescuing Paul from the mob.

**8. Commanding his accusers to come unto thee: by examining of whom thyself:** ... Examine him for yourself, —MOFT ... on all these points, —TCNT ... If you will personally cross-question him, —BRKL.

**mayest take knowledge of all these things, whereof we accuse him:** ... to ascertain the things of which we are accusing him, —RTHM ... to learn the truth as to all this we allege against him, —WEYM ... you will be able to find out from him all the facts of the case that we bring against him, —WMCK ... will soon discover from the man himself all the facts about which we are accusing him, —PHLP.

**24:8.** Tertullus further implied Lysias was wrong in sending Paul to Felix. Tertullus said nothing about the plot to assassinate Paul and the willingness of the Jewish Sanhedrin to be a part of the plot by asking that Paul be sent to them for further investigation. But again the letter the tribune sent to Felix told how they were plotting to ambush and kill Paul, so Felix knew the dealings of the Jews were not as honest and legal as Tertullus was trying to say they were.

Tertullus confidently declared that by examining Paul himself the governor would be able to find out these things (these accusations against Paul) were true.

**9. And the Jews also assented:** ... joined in the charge, —ASV ... joined in the attack, —RTHM ... agreed, —HBIE ... While Tertullus was speaking the Jews kept joining in, —PHLP ... also corroborated the charges, —FNTN.

**saying that these things were so:** ... asserting, —PHLP ... maintaining that these were the facts, —WEYM ... and declared that all he said was exactly so, —BRKL ... confirming the accuracy of, —TCNT ... declaring that these accusations were true, —NORL ... insisting that this is the way it was, —KLGS ... affirming their accuracy, —FNTN.

**24:9.** The Jews who had come down to Caesarea with the high priest then joined in, pressing charges against Paul, saying again and again that these things were so.

**10. Then Paul, after that the governor had beckoned unto him to speak, answered:** ... And Paul answered, when the governor had motioned him to be speaking, —RTHM ... On a sign from the Governor, Paul made his reply, —TCNT ... at a nod from the governor, —PHLP ... made signs to Paul to speak, and he made his reply, —WMCK

**Forasmuch as I know that thou hast been of many years a judge unto this nation:** ... I am well aware, —PHLP ... Knowing, as I do, for how many years you have acted as Judge to this nation, —TCNT ... have administered justice to this nation, —WEYM.

**I do the more cheerfully answer for myself:** ... it is with confidence that I undertake my own defence, —TCNT ... I find it easier to defend myself on these charges, —BRKL ... I can therefore make my defense with every confidence, —PHLP ... I answer all the more confidently for myself, —FNTN.

**24:10.** When the governor indicated to Paul that he might speak, Paul addressed the governor courteously, but without the insincere flattery Tertullus had used. Since Felix had been for many years a judge of the Jews, and therefore understood Jewish customs and laws, Paul felt he could make his defense with good courage.

Paul could say this truthfully, and he did not add empty flattery. Of course, Felix knew how the Jews detested him, and he probably appreciated the sincerity of Paul more than the wordy insincerity of Tertullus.

**11. Because that thou mayest understand:** ... For you can easily ascertain, —TCNT ... find out, —NORL ... for you can verify the fact, —WLMS.

**that there are yet but twelve days:** ... it is not more than twelve days ago, —PHLP ... have elapsed, —FNTN.

**since I went up to Jerusalem for to worship:**

**24:11.** Paul then made his defense in a way that showed he was more than a match for the padded rhetoric and ineffective conclusion of Tertullus.

Some commentators believe Paul should have ignored the false charges against him instead of defending himself. No doubt, there are times when a Christian should ignore false accusations. But Paul had good reasons not to ignore them, for they had to do with his attitude toward God and the truth.

Paul, in fact, gave a very skilled and wise defense. His presentation would have done justice to the best lawyer in the Roman Empire. Of course, he did have the best Lawyer there is, a better Lawyer than any human lawyer or advocate—one of the meanings of the title Comforter, which is given to the Holy Spirit, is Advocate.

Paul began with the accusation that he stirred up riots and discord. He knew this would be of major concern to the Roman government. This accusation really made him the causer of sedition, rebellion, and revolution. In fact, the Jews put this in because they knew it was the only charge a Roman court was likely to convict him on.

Paul did not have difficulty in showing how foolish this charge was. At this time it was still only 12 days since Paul had come to Jerusalem, and this was already the fifth day he had spent in Caesarea (according to the usual Jewish method of counting days). What time did that leave for him to stir up riots or start a revolution? In addition, it was too short a time for the Jews to have investigated him and found him such a dangerous character as they said he was. Furthermore, Paul came to worship, not to cause strife or defile the temple.

**12. And they neither found me:** . . . and it is not true, *—JB* . . . I was never found, *—PHLP.*

**in the temple disputing with any man:** . . . disputing with any opponent, *—WEYM* . . . holding discussions with any one, *—TCNT* . . . found either arguing with anyone, *—PHLP.*

**neither raising up the people:** . . . the multitude, *—ALFD* . . . or causing a crowd to collect, *—TCNT* . . . or causing a riot, *—MOFT* . . . gathering a crowd, *—PHLP* . . . nor collecting any company, *—MRDK* . . . nor making any insurrection among the multitude, *—WSLY.*

**neither in the synagogues, nor in the city:** . . . or throughout the city, *—RTHM* . . . either in the Temple, *—TCNT* . . . or in the open air, *—PHLP.*

**24:12.** In every instance when the Jews met him in the temple, Paul was quietly doing what he came to do, worshiping the Lord. In no case did they find him disputing. He had not even become involved in an argument, to say nothing of being a pest. Nor had he stirred up a crowd in the temple, in the synagogues, or in the city.

Paul was not intending to deny there had been riots and disturbances in other places. Actually, in those cases Paul had simply preached the good news, the gospel. Those who had rejected the gospel were the ones who stirred up the people and caused the riots, not Paul. Furthermore, Paul was not on trial for what had happened in other places, but for what had happened in Jerusalem. He was right in saying he had done absolutely nothing to stir up trouble there.

**13. Neither can they prove the things whereof they now accuse me:** . . . These men are quite unable to prove the charges, *—PHLP* . . . they cannot furnish you with any proof of their present charges against me, *—MOFT* . . . to substantiate, *—WUST.* . . . and they are not able to give facts in support of the things they say against me now, *—BB* . . . Neither can they produce any evidence to substantiate these present charges, *—BRKL.*

**24:13.** Paul further challenged his accusers by saying that in no way could they prove any of their accusations. They had no evidence, and Paul knew they could prove nothing. He also implied that Tertullus made the accusations in terms of generalities because he had no proof of any of them. Paul's point was well-taken.

**14. But this I confess unto thee:** . . . This, however, I do acknowledge to you, *—TCNT* . . . I certainly admit to you, *—MOFT* . . . I will freely admit to you, however, *—PHLP.*

**that after the way which they call heresy:** . . . that it is as a believer of the Cause which they call heretical, *—TCNT* . . . according to the way which they call a heresy, *—PHLP.*

**so worship I the God of my fathers:** . . . that I worship the God of my ancestors, *—TCNT* . . . I continue to worship the God of my forefathers, *—WLMS.*

**believing all things which are written in the law and in the prophets:** . . . At the same time, I believe everything that is in accordance with, *—TCNT* . . . taught in the Law or written, *—WEYM* . . . in the scriptural authority of both the Law and the Prophets, *—PHLP.*

**24:14.** Paul was not satisfied merely to deny the charges made against him by the Jews. He seized the opportunity to make a public declaration or confession of his Christian faith and hope. At the same time he made Felix see that the real charge against him was not political, not civil, but religious. The chief thing the Jews had against him was that he worshiped God in a different way from them. Paul was willing to confess this and give clear testimony to it. But he denied he was preaching a new or false religion.

To confirm this, Paul declared that according to the Way called a sect (which they implied was a self-chosen opinion), he continued to serve the God of his fathers. That is, he worshiped the same God the rest of the Jews did, the God of their ancestors. He was no less loyal to the one true God than they were.

Paul also declared that by the way he worshiped God he showed he was still a believer in everything that was according to the Law and everything written in the Prophets. By "the law and . . . the prophets" Paul probably meant the whole of the Jewish sacred books, the entire Old Testament.

The word *believe* also implies he continued to trust and obey God and His Word. Belief, in both the Old and New Testaments, always implies personal confidence and faithfulness. It shows itself always in action, not just in a mental attitude.

**15. And have hope toward God:** ... and I have a hope that rests in God, —*TCNT* ... and trust God, —*BECK*.

**which they themselves also allow:** ... a hope which they also cherish, —*TCNT* ... for the same thing they're looking for, —*BECK*.

**that there shall be a resurrection of the dead, both of the just and unjust:** ... that a resurrection there shall certainly be both of righteous and unrighteous, —*RTHM* ... that there will one day be a resurrection of good and bad alike, —*TCNT* ... of both good men and bad, —*PHLP*.

**24:15.** By the Law and the Prophets Paul also had a confident hope in God, a hope that these Jews shared or, at least, the majority of Jews shared. This hope involved a confidence in the plan of God, a plan that would culminate in the resurrection of the dead, both of the just and the unjust. It would demonstrate the justice of God.

Paul, of course, did not give all the details in this brief statement. Daniel 12:2 gave the Jews a specific prophecy that many who sleep in the dust of the earth (actually including all of the dead) will awake (be resurrected in a bodily resurrection), some to everlasting life, and some to shame and everlasting contempt.

Jesus made it clear this includes two distinct resurrections, one a resurrection to life (eternal), and the other a resurrection to damnation or judgment (John 5:29). However, He did not draw attention to the time between the two resurrections. God did not reveal to the Old Testament prophets the time between the first and second comings of Christ. Zechariah 9:9, for example, tells of Christ's triumphal entry into Jerusalem, which took place in connection with His first coming. Zechariah 9:10, the next verse, prophesies that His dominion or rule will be from sea to sea and from the river (the Euphrates) even to the ends of the earth. This applies to His second coming and shows that His kingdom will not be limited to the territory promised to Abraham and his descendants, which was only from the River Euphrates to the River of Egypt (Genesis 15:18). Rather, it will cover the entire earth. In the same way Jesus did not reveal the times and the seasons, but left them under the Father's authority.

**16. And herein do I exercise myself:** ... In this I myself also take pains, —*HBIE* ... And in this I do my best, —*BB* ... I therefore exert myself, —*BRKL* ... With this hope before me I do my utmost to live my whole life, —*PHLP*.

**to have always a conscience void of offence toward God, and toward men:** ... to keep my conscience clear before both God and man, —*TCNT* ... to have in all respects a clear conscience in my relations with God and with men, —*BRKL* ... to live my whole life with a clear conscience, —*PHLP*.

**24:16.** Because of his confident hope in the resurrection, Paul exercised himself continually to have a conscience free from causing offense to God and men.

This did not mean he tried to conciliate the different parties or sects in Judaism. Actually, they differed too much in both faith and practice. (Judaism today is just as full of diverse elements, from the Orthodox who are much like the Pharisees to the liberal Reformed Jews who accept all the theories of the antisupernatural, destructive critics of the Bible.) What Paul directed attention to was the spiritual religion actually taught in the Old Testament, the genuine spirituality promoted in the Law, the Prophets, and the Psalms. This was true Old Testament religion and found its completion, fulfillment, and highest expression in and through Christ.

**17. Now after many years:** ... Now after several years' absence, —*WEYM*.

**I came to bring alms to my nation, and offerings:** ... I had come to bring charitable gifts ... and to make offerings, —*TCNT* ... to bring a sum of money to my countrymen, and offer sacrifices, —*WEYM* ... I came to give help and offerings to my nation, —*BB* ... to offer sacrifice and fulfill vows, —*CNFT*.

**24:17.** After this discourse on the resurrection, Paul returned to recounting the facts of his case. Now, after many years, he had returned to Jerusalem to bring alms to his people and an offering to God. He had been accused of being an enemy of his people. But bringing charitable gifts and offerings was not enmity.

**18. Whereupon:** ... while engaged in this, —*TCNT* ... While I was busy about these things, —*WEYM* ... While I was performing these duties, —*WLMS* ... It was in the middle of these duties, —*PHLP*.

**certain Jews from Asia found me purified in the temple:** ... that they found me in the Temple, after completing a period of purification, —*TCNT* ... they found me just as I had completed my rites of purification, —*WLMS* ... a man purified, —*PHLP*.

**neither with multitude, nor with tumult:** ... or disorder, —*TCNT* ... with no crowd about me and no uproar, —*WEYM* ... I was not mixed up in any mob or riot, —*MOFT*.

**24:18.** Paul further showed reasons why his conscience was clear. While presenting these offerings, the Jews found Paul in the temple purified. He had entered the temple as a worshiper and was actively fulfilling the requirements of the Law. He was quietly submitting to what was asked of him and was demonstrating that he did not ask the Jews to cease being Jews when they became Christians. He was honoring the Law and the temple. How could they say he was about to defile the temple?

Furthermore, they found him with no crowd, creating no disturbance. Nothing was going on around him. He was giving his whole attention to the worship of God and was doing nothing to draw the attention of the people to himself. But there were certain Jews from the Roman province of Asia who falsely accused him. (They had jumped to a wrong conclusion because they had seen Paul in the city with a Gentile and they supposed Paul had brought him into the temple. Tertullus had not mentioned this because he wanted to give the impression that the Jews had arrested Paul to keep him from defiling the temple.)

19. **Who ought to have been here before thee:** ... who should in my opinion have come before you, —PHLP ... who ought to have appeared, —WMCK
**and object:** ... and to accuse me, —ALFD ... and to have made any charge, —TCNT ... and to have been my prosecutors, —WEYM ... to prosecute me, —FNTN ... and made their accusation, —PHLP ... and charged me, —WMCK
**if they had ought against me:** ... if they knew anything tangible against me, —BRKL.

**24:19.** Paul then declared that these Jews from the province of Asia were the real accusers. It was really their duty to be the ones to come before Felix and make their accusation if they really had anything against Paul.

Paul was taking advantage of the Law's demand for witnesses to make the accusation. The Law, in fact, demanded at least two or three witnesses in the case of any accusation of wrong for the matter to be established (Deuteronomy 17:6, 7; 19:15). Jewish writings after Old Testament times also stressed the importance of the witnesses being cross-examined to be sure they were not false witnesses. This is also indicated in Deuteronomy 19:18. None of this was being done in this trial or any of the previous times Paul had to face the Jews.

20. **Or else let these same here say:** ... let my opponents, —TCNT ... let these now present declare, —FNTN ... let these men themselves speak out now and say, —PHLP ... Let those who are here declare, —NAB.
**if they have found any evil doing in me:** ... what misdemeanor they found me guilty of, —WEYM ... what crime, —HBIE ... what fault they found

in me, —FNTN ... what they found to complain of in me, —WMCK ... they found me guilty of, NAB.
**while I stood before the council:** ... when brought up before the senate, —FNTN ... the Sanhedrin, —WEYM.

**24:20.** Paul made it clear that none of the priests and elders present were witnesses of anything they were claiming against Paul or of anything that went on in the temple. This again meant they were paying no attention to their own law, for they brought no witnesses with them. The passages in Deuteronomy 17:6 and 19:15 indicate there was to be no trial without witnesses. (The New Testament also upholds this; see 2 Corinthians 13:1.) Roman law also recognized the need for witnesses. But all that Paul's accusers brought with them was a clever lawyer.

21. **Except it be for this one voice:** ... except as to the one sentence, —TCNT ... Unless it was that one expression of which I made use, —WEYM ... Yes, there was one thing they resented, —NORL ... unless it be this one exclamation, —FNTN ... unless it was that one sentence, —PHLP.
**that I cried standing among them:** ... it was what I called out as I stood in their presence, —NAB ... that I shouted out as I stood among them, —TCNT ... standing in their midst, —FNTN ... All I said was this, —PHLP.
**Touching the resurrection of the dead:** ... It is about, —PHLP ... Concerning the raising of the dead, —RTHM.
**I am called in question by you this day:** ... am I to be judged this day by you, —RTHM ... that I am on my trial before you today, —TCNT ... that I am accused this day before you, Fenton.

**24:21.** There was really only one thing this priest and the elders were witnesses of with respect to Paul. They were present when Paul stood before the Sanhedrin in Jerusalem and cried out that it was with respect to the resurrection of the dead that he was called into question. He would willingly let them accuse him of saying that.

Because Paul was first of all a witness for Christ, he could not rest his case without once more bringing to the attention of both the Jews and Felix that the central and basic issue in the promises of God is the hope of the resurrection.

The high priest and elders failed to say anything in reply at this point. They knew very well the Sanhedrin would have acquitted Paul if the Pharisees had been in the majority. The Sadducees also knew that to bring it up again would expose their own sectarian attitude to Felix and would hurt their case.

**22. And when Felix heard these things:** ... At this point Felix, —WEYM.

**having more perfect knowledge of that way:** ... who was fairly well informed about the new faith, —WEYM ... who had a fairly clear conception of the principles involved in the Way, —WLMS ... who was better acquainted with the Way than most people, —PHLP ... who knew the Christian religion rather well, —BECK.

**he deferred them, and said:** ... adjourned the case ... with the promise, —TCNT ... adjourned the trial, saying to the Jews, —WEYM ... postponed the case, saying, —NORL.

**When Lysias the chief captain shall come down:** ... As soon as, —RTHM ... Colonel Lysias arrives, —PHLP.

**I will know the uttermost of your matter:** ... I will decide your case, —RSV ... adjudge your matter, —ALFD ... give my decision in your case, —TCNT ... go carefully into the matter, —MNTG ... finish the examination of your case, —NORL.

**24:22.** In view of the lack of evidence, Felix should have set Paul free. But Felix gave in to the same temptation that controlled Pontius Pilate. When Pilate found no fault or crime in Jesus, he did not set Jesus free for fear of the Jews. Felix had already angered the Jews on several occasions, and he shrank from offending them further lest they get a hearing for their complaints against him before the emperor in Rome.

Felix had been governor over Judea long enough to have an accurate knowledge of the teachings and way of life of the thousands of Jewish Christians who lived under his rule. He also knew enough about the Jews to realize that if he turned Paul over to these Jewish leaders he would be condemning an innocent man.

Yet, instead of setting Paul free, he compromised and put the Jews off, saying that when the tribune Lysias came down he would learn the details of the things that concerned them. There is no evidence, however, that he ever sent for Lysias.

Felix probably hoped that time and chance would make things easier for him. So, after giving this empty promise to make further investigation, Felix kept Paul in custody.

**23. And he commanded a centurion to keep Paul:** ... So he gave orders to the Captain in charge of Paul to keep him in custody, —TCNT.

**and to let him have liberty:** ... a measure of liberty, —RTHM ... but to relax the regulations, —TCNT ... but to allow him some freedom, —MOFT ... but to grant him reasonable liberty, —PHLP ... treated with indulgence, —MNTG ... to allow him out on parole, —FNTN.

**and that he should forbid none of his acquaintance to minister or come unto him:** ... and not to prevent any of his personal friends from attending to his wants, —TCNT ... and allow any of his personal friends to look after his needs, —PHLP ... from showing him kindness, —WEYM.

**24:23.** To salve his conscience, Felix turned Paul over to a centurion, ordering him to give Paul a considerable amount of freedom. More than that, he must not forbid any of Paul's own people from ministering to him. Paul's many friends among the Christians would be allowed to visit him, bring him food, and give him whatever else he needed. In a sense, Paul was in what might be called "house arrest." His friends were free to minister to him in any way at any time.

These friends would include Luke, the physician, who later stood by him so faithfully on the journey to Rome and in both Paul's Roman imprisonments (2 Timothy 4:11, "only Luke is with me"). Many believe Luke wrote his Gospel while Paul was in custody in Caesarea for the following 2 years. Luke would be free also to travel to Jerusalem and talk to Mary and the apostles to confirm the facts. Luke must also have gathered much material for the Book of Acts at the same time. Philip and many other eyewitnesses lived in Caesarea. Still others were nearby.

The many Christians in Caesarea could be counted on to help make Paul's imprisonment there as comfortable as possible. Also, many of Paul's friends from the churches he had established would enter Palestine on their way to Jerusalem for the Feasts by way of Caesarea.

**24. And after certain days:** ... Some days later, —TCNT ... Not long after this, —WEYM.

**when Felix came with his wife Drusilla, which was a Jewess:** ... Felix brought along his wife Drusilla, a Jewess, —BRKL ... Felix came again. His wife Drusilla, who was a Jew, was with him, —BECK.

**he sent for Paul, and heard him concerning the faith in Christ:** ... and sending for Paul, listened to what he had to say about faith in Christ Jesus, —TCNT ... and heard what he had to say about, —PHLP ... faith toward Christ, —YNG ... about this Christ Jesus faith, —KLGS.

**24:24.** At first it may have been hard for Paul to see how his continued imprisonment in Caesarea fitted in with God's purpose for him. But part of Paul's mission was to testify before rulers (9:15). After some days he had an opportunity to carry this out. Felix, with his wife Drusilla, summoned Paul and listened to him tell of his faith in Christ Jesus; literally, he told of the "in Christ Jesus" faith, that is, the gospel.

Drusilla was the young daughter of Herod Agrippa I, the Herod who had arrested James the brother of John and killed him with the sword (12:1, 2). She was the sister of Herod Agrippa II and Bernice. Felix had seduced her from her former husband, King Aziz of Emesa in the western part of Syria. She was actually the third wife of

Felix. His first wife was a granddaughter of Marc Antony, the Roman orator and general, and Cleopatra, the queen of Egypt. His second wife was a princess. Divorce and remarriage were very common among both Romans and Jews in those days. Felix and Drusilla also had a son who died in the eruption of Mount Vesuvius that buried Pompeii in A.D. 79.

Herod Agrippa I was educated in Rome, but when he became king, he was tactful in his treatment of the Jews and tried to curry their favor. Like all the Herods, he was nominally a Jew through his mother who was descended from the Hasmonean (Maccabean) priests who had temporarily reigned over Jerusalem. Through Drusilla, Felix would have learned a great deal about the history and customs, as well as the religion of the Jews.

**25. And as he reasoned of righteousness:**...But while Paul was speaking at length about righteousness, *—TCNT*...about justice, *—WEYM*...was talking about goodness, *—PHLP*...But when he discussed purity of life, *—BRKL*.

**temperance:**...self control, *—ASV*...the mastery of passions, *—BRKL*...self-mastery, *—MOFT*.

**and judgment to come:**...and the coming judgment, *—TCNT*...and the future judgment, *—WEYM*...the coming Day of Judgment, *—TEV*.

**Felix trembled, and answered:**...Felix was terrified, *—RTHM*...was afraid, *—ALFD*...became alarmed, *—NOYS, —PHLP*...became terrified, and broke in with, *—TCNT*...being filled with fear, *—DRBY*...grew uneasy, *—MOFT*.

**Go thy way for this time:**...For the present, *—RTHM*...leave me, *—WEYM*.

**when I have a convenient season:**...and when I find an opportunity, *—RTHM*...When I can spare the time, *—BRKL*...and when the right time comes, *—BB*...when it will be convenient for me, *—NORL*...When I get a chance, *—BECK*...some future opportunity, *—CMPB*...a convenient moment, *—PHLP*.

**I will call for thee:**...I will send for thee, *—RTHM*...I will summon you, *—RSV*.

**24:25.** To Felix and Drusilla, Paul not only presented the facts and the theology but, as he did in all his epistles, he went on to discuss practical matters of righteousness, self-control, and the coming judgment.

There is no doubt Paul told Felix all about the life and teachings of Jesus, as well as about His death, resurrection, and second coming. Paul had recently written the Epistle to the Romans in which he declared he was not ashamed of the gospel (Romans 1:16). He had gone on to tell how all, both Gentiles and Jews, have sinned and need the gospel. Then Paul had told the Romans the gospel means justification by faith, assurance,

freedom from sin, and the ultimate glorification of believers.

But when Paul began to deal with God's requirements with respect to righteousness, self-control, and the coming judgment, Felix became terrified. Now their positions were reversed. This time Felix was on trial. The conviction of the Holy Spirit made him tremble.

Jesus said the Holy Spirit would guide into all truth and convince the world with respect to sin, showing that their real sin was unbelief; with respect to righteousness, not their own righteousness or lack of it, but of what righteousness really is as it is seen in Jesus; and with respect to judgment, for they will share in Satan's judgment (John 16:8-11).

Felix, however, resisted the Spirit's conviction and told Paul to go for now. In his "spare time" he would see him again.

**26. He hoped also that money should have been given him of Paul:**...At the same time he nursed a secret hope that Paul would pay him money, *—PHLP*...He was hoping, too, for a bribe from Paul, *—TCNT*.

**that he might loose him: wherefore he sent for him the oftener:**...and so he used to send for him frequently, *—TCNT*...and so he kept sending for him, *—WLMS*...which is why Paul was frequently summoned to come, *—PHLP*.

**and communed with him:**...he used to converse with him, *—RTHM*...and talk with him, *—TCNT*...and talked things over with him, *—BRKL*.

**24:26.** Felix was also motivated by greed. The real reason he promised to see Paul again was he hoped Paul would give him a great deal of money (riches) in order to gain his freedom. It is quite possible that when he saw how loyal Paul's friends were, Felix hoped that many of them would get together and present to him a bribe for Paul's release.

In any case, Felix was still motivated by the hope for a big bribe when he sent for Paul more often and conversed with him. It seems certain that whatever Felix brought up in these sessions Paul would use as an opportunity to talk about Jesus and the gospel. All of these sessions must have continued to deal with righteousness, self-control, and the coming judgment.

**27. But after two years:**...But at the close of two years, *—WLMS*...when two full years had passed, *—PHLP*.

**Porcius Festus came into Felix' room:**...Felix was succeeded by Porcius Festus, *—RSV*...Porcius Festus took the place of Felix, *—BB*...succeeded, *—BECK*.

**and Felix, willing to shew the Jews a pleasure:**...and desiring to gain favor with the Jews,

Felix, *–ASV*... to gain popularity, *–TCNT*... and being desirous of gratifying the Jews, Felix, *–WEYM*... and because he wished to curry favor with, *–MNTG*... willing to ingratiate, *–CMPB*... as he wanted to remain in favor with, *–PHLP.*

**left Paul bound:** ... he left Paul a prisoner, *–TCNT*... in custody, *–MOFT*... kept Paul in chains, *–BB.*

**24:27.** These conversations with Paul continued over a 2-year period. Then Felix was replaced by Porcius Festus, who arrived in A.D. 59 and remained in office until his death in A.D. 61. The date of Paul's arrest was thus A.D. 57.

Because Felix still wanted to seek favor with the Jews, he left Paul bound (imprisoned), that is, he left him behind as a prisoner. Truly, Felix not only let his desire for money cause him to resist the Holy Spirit, he now allowed his own self-interest to cause him to turn his back on justice in this last act of his regime. But this did not help him. After he returned to Rome the Jews sent complaints to the emperor Nero. Nero would have punished him if it had not been for the influence of his brother Pallas, who interceded on his behalf. (Pallas at the time was a favorite of the emperor.)

Possibly Felix was removed because of the trouble that was going on in Judea. The assassins who believed in using force to kill and overthrow Romans, as well as to kill Jews who seemed to be favored by the Romans, were active again, murdering and robbing or plundering the countryside. A little later another false messiah led a great crowd of adherents into the wilderness in rebellion against Rome, and Festus was forced to go out after them and slaughter them. Thus, while it was fairly quiet in Caesarea there was trouble elsewhere in Judea.

## Chapter 25

**1. Now when Festus was come into the province:** ... Festus, having entered on his duties as governor of the province, *–WEYM*... having entered into the government of the province, *–FNTN*... after entering upon his provincial office, *–BRKL*... had taken over his province, *–PHLP*... after he had taken charge of the province, *–WMCK*

**after three days he ascended from Caesarea to Jerusalem:** ... three days later went up from Caesarea to Jerusalem, *–WEYM*... Festus went up from Caesarea to Jerusalem, *–BRKL.*

**25:1.** The Jews in Jerusalem had not given up. They still considered Paul their archenemy and wanted his death. So they were waiting to take advantage of the new governor Festus, with the intent of seeking an opportunity for carrying out their plots.

Festus knew Felix had done much to antagonize the Jews, so he was anxious to conciliate them. After Festus took office in Caesarea, he rested a day and then the next day (according to the Jewish method of counting), he went up to Jerusalem. Though Caesarea was the capital of the province over which he was now governor, Jerusalem was still the center as far as the Jews were concerned, and they carried on their religious government through the high priest and the Sanhedrin in Jerusalem.

**2. Then the high priest and the chief men of the Jews:** ... leading men among the Jews, *–TCNT*... Jewish leaders, *–MOFT*... Jewish elders, *–WLMS*... most prominent Jews, *–BRKL.*

**informed him against Paul:** ... made manifest to him, *–YNG*... laid information before him against Paul, *–RTHM*... informed him of the case against Paul, *–PHLP*... complained about Paul, *–KLGS*... appeared before him against Paul, *–FNTN.*

**and besought him:** ... urged and begged, *–BECK*... and appealed to him, *–FNTN.*

**25:2.** As soon as Festus arrived, the chief priests and chief men of the Jews informed him of their charges against Paul. These chief Jews were members of the Sanhedrin, probably the Sadducees in it who were friends and allies of the high priest.

Clearly, the act of Felix in leaving Paul imprisoned was not enough to satisfy the Jewish leaders. The Greek indicates they began to besiege Festus with repeated accusations against Paul. Undoubtedly the fact that Paul had escaped the hands of the more than 40 Jews who had plotted to ambush and kill him was still a sore point with them. Then they began to beg Festus.

**3. And desired favour against him:** ... and asked a favour of him, to Paul's injury, *–TCNT*... asking it as a favour, to Paul's prejudice, *–WEYM*... as a special favour, *–WMCK*

**that he would send for him to Jerusalem:** ... to have Paul brought, *–TCNT*... send him back to, *–FNTN*... send for him to come to, *–WMCK*

**laying wait in the way to kill him:** ... intending to, *–WMCK*... making an ambush to kill him on the way, *–RTHM*... They meant to lay in wait for him and kill him on the way, *–MNTG*... themselves plotting to murder him on the road, *–FNTN.*

**25:3.** They were begging Festus, not for justice, but for a favor. They were definitely trying to get him to help them do something against Paul. They urgently requested him to send for Paul and have him brought to Jerusalem. Again there was a plot to ambush him and kill him along the road.

**4. But Festus answered:** ... to which Festus replied, —BRKL ... told them in reply, —FNTN.

**that Paul should be kept at Caesarea:** ... would be kept in Caesarea, —BECK ... that Paul was under guard, —BRKL ... be detained at, —FNTN.

**and that he himself would depart shortly thither:** ... meant to leave for Caesarea before long, —MOFT ... he himself was soon to leave, —WMCK ... he was himself about to return there at an early date, —FNTN ... intended to go there shortly, —RSV.

**25:4.** Festus must have been informed of their previous plot, so he replied that Paul was kept (guarded) in Caesarea where he would soon be going.

From this we see that Festus, though he wanted to please the Jews, did have a sense of justice which would not allow him to yield entirely. Thus, God used Festus to protect Paul from the renewed plots.

It seems strange these Jewish leaders could be so emotionally disturbed about Paul that they would be willing to subvert justice and resort to murder. They knew the law of Moses taught justice and included even establishing of the rights of the weak, the poor, and the foreigners, as well as seeing to it that they were given their rights. In fact, the entire Old Testament teaches the justice of God. He is the true King, and He is concerned about establishing and maintaining what is right and righteous according to His holy and righteous nature.

Obviously, these Jewish leaders were supposing the end justifies the means. But they were letting their own ideas guide them rather than the Word of the Lord.

**5. Let them therefore, said he, which among you are able:** ... They therefore among you (saith he) who are in power, —RTHM ... He also added, Let those therefore who are in authority among you, —FNTN ... So let the influential men among you, —TCNT ... Let those then, he said, who are in authority among you, —MNTG ... let the proper officials, —WMCK

**go down with me:** ... come down, —WMCK

**and accuse this man, if there be any wickedness in him:** ... charge him formally with it, —TCNT ... and charge the man with whatever crime he has committed, —MOFT ... they can indict him, —FNTN ... present their charges against the man, if he has done anything wrong, —WMCK

**25:5.** Festus then suggested that those among them of power or authority go down with him to Caesarea. If there was anything wrong (out of place, or improper) in Paul, let them accuse him there.

Festus yielded to the Jews to a degree. Though he had politely refused to bring Paul up to Jerusalem, he did rule for a new official trial. This does not mean Festus had prejudged the case or accepted their accusations against Paul. He simply said they would be permitted to present their accusations if they believed there was anything improper or out of place in Paul. Nevertheless, by the very language he used, Festus showed he considered their accusations up to that point to be rather trivial from the point of view of Roman law. He did not yet see that Paul had committed any serious crime. Perhaps if the Jews could send their most prominent men who had real ability and influence, they might be able to come up with something.

**6. And when he had tarried among them more than ten days:** ... After spending among them not more than eight or ten days, —RTHM.

**he went down unto Caesarea:** ... and then went, —PHLP.

**and the next day:** ... On the day after his arrival, —PHLP.

**sitting on the judgment seat:** ... after taking his seat on the judge's bench, —WLMS ... he took his place in court, —WMCK

**commanded Paul to be brought:** ... ordered, —RSV ... and sent for Paul, —BB ... gave orders that Paul should be brought in, —WMCK ... to be brought before him, —TCNT.

**25:6.** Festus spent some time in Jerusalem ("more than ten days"), probably just getting acquainted with the city. He may have visited the Fortress of Antonia and acquainted himself with the Roman officers and soldiers stationed there. He probably stayed in the palace built by Herod the Great. This magnificent palace stood on the west side of Jerusalem south of the modern Jaffa gate. It had been the official residence of Pilate whenever he visited Jerusalem.

The next day after returning to Caesarea Festus sat on the judgment seat, that is, on his official judge's throne or tribunal. This meant he was calling for a new official trial. Then he had Paul brought in. The Jews who had come down from Jerusalem were also present.

Festus could do this because Felix had never officially handed down a decision. He had only indicated he would carry out further investigation, which he did not do. So, Festus felt justified in calling this new official trial.

The judgment seat or judicial bench was usually on a raised platform in order to give the judge the prominent place and to give an appearance of power and authority. In this case it was in the palace built by Herod the Great, where Paul was also kept.

The same word used here was used by the rabbis of the judgment seat of God and by the New

Testament of the judgment seat of Christ. Actually, although neither Festus nor the Jewish leaders seemed to realize it, they were all standing before the judgment seat of God in a real sense. That is, God knew what was going on. God saw the hearts of the Jews. He knew their plots. He knew their concern for themselves and their position and reputations. He saw that Festus was torn between a desire for justice and a desire to please and conciliate the Jews.

But God also saw the heart of Paul. He knew how Paul was committed to Christ and to the preaching of the truth of the gospel. Moreover, God was working out His plan, and it was about to come to an important turning point, though neither Paul, the Jews, nor Festus knew it.

**7. And when he was come:** . . . As soon as he arrived, −PHLP. . . . When he came in, −WMCK . . . But when he was produced, −FNTN.

**the Jews which came down from Jerusalem stood round about:** . . . collected round him, −BRKL . . . stood up on all sides of him, −PHLP.

**and laid many and grievous complaints against Paul:** . . . and presented their chargesnumerous and weighty, −BRKL . . . and made all sorts of serious statements against him, −BB . . . charging him with many and serious offenses, −NORL . . . bringing many heavy accusations, −CMPB . . . bringing forward many serious accusations, −PHLP . . . bringing forward numerous as well as serious charges, −FNTN.

**which they could not prove:** . . . which they failed to establish, −TCNT . . . were unable to substantiate, −WEYM . . . which they were not able to prove, −RTHM . . . which were not supported by the facts, −BB.

**25:7.** The Jerusalem Jews stood around Festus, making many weighty charges or accusations against Paul. They made it clear they considered these charges very important, but they could prove none of them. The charges against Paul were undoubtedly similar to those Tertullus had brought before Felix.

What follows implies they did add one new accusation, however. Paul had rights and privileges as a Roman citizen. These Jews hoped to counteract those rights by adding the charge that Paul had committed offenses against Caesar, that is, against the current Roman emperor, Nero. But again they had no proof.

**8. While he answered for himself:** . . . While Paul said in his defense, −ASV . . . Paul, in his defense, maintained, −PHLP . . . In reply, Paul said, −WEYM . . . Paul's defence was, −WMCK

**Neither against the law of the Jews, neither against the temple, nor yet against Caesar, have I offended any thing at all:** . . . have not committed any offense against the, −TCNT . . . have committed no crime against, −MNTG . . . I have done nothing wrong, −WMCK . . . have I offended in any way, −FNTN . . . I have committed no offense in any way against, −PHLP.

**25:8.** It is clear Paul had no trouble defending himself. Luke merely summarized Paul's defense. Paul contended he had not sinned in any way against the Jewish law, the temple, nor against Caesar (including the whole Roman government).

It must have been hard for Paul to listen to the same old accusations again and again. He must have felt like crying out, "Enough is enough!" But he had learned long before that God's grace is sufficient under even the most trying circumstances (2 Corinthians 12:9). He was in a position of weakness now as a prisoner, but God's strength was there to help him answer with a graciousness, wisdom, and maturity that was in strong contrast to the way the Jews were acting in their accusations.

Later, Festus showed that Paul bore witness to Christ's death and resurrection as well. As before, Paul never let an opportunity for witness to go by. (See 25:19.) He was always looking for some way to bring in the good news about Jesus and His salvation. Defending the gospel and presenting Christ was always more important to him than defending himself. Yet he did not do it in an offensive way. He always tried to show the meekness and love of Christ in his own attitude as he proclaimed the truth about Jesus, and the Holy Spirit inspired and helped him as he did so.

**9. But Festus, willing to do the Jews a pleasure:** . . . Festus, as he wished to gain popularity with the Jews, −TCNT . . . Then Festus, in hope of winning the favor of the Jews, −NORL . . . to conciliate the favor, −MRDK . . . wishing to gratify, −WLSN . . . wishing to do the Jews a favour, −WMCK . . . wishing to gain the goodwill of the Jews, −PHLP . . . anxious to ingratiate himself with the Jews, −FNTN.

**answered Paul, and said:** . . . interrupted Paul with the question, −TCNT . . . spoke direct to Paul, −PHLP.

**Wilt thou go up to Jerusalem:** . . . Art thou willing, −RTHM . . . Are you prepared to, −PHLP . . . Do you want to, −BECK . . . Do you desire to go, −FNTN.

**and there be judged of these things before me?:** . . . and be tried on these charges before there, −TCNT . . . and stand your trial over these matters in my presence there? −PHLP . . . to be tried in respect of these matters before me? −FNTN . . . and take your trial there on these charges before me? −WMCK

**25:9.** Festus, then, desired to do the Jews a favor that would give them pleasure. He wanted to gain favor with them. So he responded to Paul by asking him if he would be willing to go up to Jerusalem for another trial before him. That is, he would do as the tribune Lysias had done. He would bring in the whole Sanhedrin and let them bring their accusations against Paul before him.

Like Lysias and Felix, Porcius Festus was trying to avoid giving a decision. He saw that the Jewish leaders were loud, persistent, and determined. He must have also realized that since they were so persistent in bringing false charges against Paul, they would probably be just as persistent and determined in bringing false charges against him if he did not satisfy them. It was easy for Festus to yield to the crowd against his better judgment, the judgment he had expressed when he had earlier refused to have Paul brought up to Jerusalem.

Once again, it is evident that those who seem to be in the majority at the moment are not always right. Paul was all alone in the courtroom. He had no lawyer to defend him. Obviously, none of his faithful friends were allowed. But the Holy Spirit was with him.

**10. Then said Paul, I stand at Caesar's judgment seat:** ... But Paul said, I am standing before, —RSV ... Paul replied, I am standing in Caesar's court, —PHLP ... the seat of Caesar's authority, —BB ... at Caesar's tribunal, —BRKL ... in the Emperor's court, —WMCK ... before the tribunal of the Emperor, —FNTN.

**where I ought to be judged:** ... where alone I ought to be tried, —WEYM ... and that is where I should be judged, —PHLP.

**to the Jews have I done no wrong:** ... I have not wronged the Jews, —TCNT ... I have done the Jews no injury of any sort, —WEYM ... no harm, —PHLP ... I have never injured Judeans, —FNTN.

**as thou very well knowest:** ... as you yourself are well aware, —TCNT ... you know that perfectly well, —MOFT ... as also you have clearly ascertained, —FNTN.

**25:10.** Paul, of course, knew what it would mean if he were to go up to Jerusalem. Friends probably had informed him of the new plot to ambush and kill him on the way. Luke, at least, knew about it, and others must have.

Paul, however, knew he had one recourse to keep out of the clutches of the Jewish leaders. Paul recognized that the authority behind the judgment seat or tribunal where Festus sat was Caesar's (that is, it was the current Roman emperor's). As a Roman citizen he had a right to appeal to Caesar. To the Jews he had done no harm or injury, as Festus well knew. Paul's emphasis was that it was necessary, proper, and fitting for him as a Roman to be judged at Caesar's tribunal.

**11. For if I be an offender:** ... If, however, I am breaking the law, —TCNT.

**or have committed any thing worthy of death:** ... any offense deserving death, —TCNT ... for which I ought to die, —MNTG ... some crime which deserves the death penalty, —PHLP.

**I refuse not to die:** ... I am ready for death, —BB ... I do not ask to escape it, —TCNT ... I am not begging to keep from dying, —WLMS.

**but if there be none of these things:** ... But if there is no truth, —WEYM ... But as in fact there is no truth, —PHLP.

**whereof these accuse me:** ... in the accusations of these people, —TCNT ... in what these men allege against me, —WEYM ... in any of their charges against me, —MOFT.

**no man may deliver me unto them:** ... no man hath power to give me unto them as a favour, —RTHM ... I will let no man turn me over to them, —NORL ... no one may sacrifice me to their pleasure, —MRDK ... to surrender me to them, —JB ... to dispose of me to gratify them, —FNTN.

**I appeal unto Caesar:** ... Let my cause come before Caesar, —BB.

**25:11.** Paul then stated his case for his appeal to Caesar. If he had done anything worthy of death, he would not object to the death penalty.

Paul had faced death often before. In the great resurrection chapter, 1 Corinthians 15, he told how he stood in jeopardy (danger, peril) every hour and he died daily, that is, he faced death every day. To the unbeliever, life is a dead-end street. If he makes a billion dollars he will still die and lose it all. The believer, on the other hand, makes God's work his work. The believer looks forward to his resurrection and knows God will finish His work.

But since there was nothing true about the acts of which Paul was accused, no one had the power and authority to turn him over to the Jews as a favor to them. Therefore, Paul appealed to Caesar.

Up to this point Nero, the emperor at this time, had good advisers, and Paul had reason to believe he would get a fair trial in Rome. But that was not the only reason he wanted to go to Rome. Jesus had assured him he would witness for Him in Rome (23:11).

**12. Then Festus, when he had conferred with the council:** ... having consulted with his council, —HBIE ... after a conference with his advisors, —PHLP.

**answered:** ... replied to Paul, —PHLP.

**Hast thou appealed unto Caesar? unto Caesar shalt thou go:** ... You have said, Let my case come before Caesar; to Caesar you will go, —BB.

**25:12.** Festus may not have been pleased with Paul's demand to be sent to Caesar. Festus knew it would not please the Jews. But he conferred with his advisers on the provincial council. They must have made it clear that Paul was within his rights. There was nothing Festus could do but send him to Caesar.

Citizens of Rome were given the right of appeal as early as 509 B.C. At that time they could appeal to the assembly when a judge pronounced sentence on any serious crime. Later on, in 449 and 299 B.C., further enactments reinforced this right of appeal. Then when Rome became an empire the governors or procurators of the provinces had the duty to grant the privilege of a trial at Rome when any Roman citizen demanded it. At first, the trial might be either before the Roman senate or before the emperor, but at this time it was before the emperor.

13. **And after certain days:** ... Some days later, —TCNT ... A short time after this, —WEYM.

**king Agrippa and Bernice came unto Caesarea:** ... King Herod Agrippa II, —SEB ... arrived at Caesarea, —ASV.

**to salute Festus:** ... and paid a visit of congratulation to Festus, —TCNT ... to pay a complimentary visit to, —WEYM ... to pay official respects, —WLMS ... to bid Festus welcome, —BRKL ... to congratulate Festus, Fenton.

**25:13.** Some days later, King Agrippa, with his widowed sister Bernice, came to Caesarea to bring official greetings and pay his respects to the new governor of Judea.

Herod Agrippa II, also known as M. Julius Agrippa II, was the son of Herod Agrippa I, the Herod of 12:1-23. The emperor Claudius made him king of Chalcis between the Lebanon and Anti-Lebanon mountains in A.D. 50. Later (A.D. 53) the emperor made him king of the tetrarchy of Philip, east of the Sea of Galilee, and of Lysanius, west and northwest of Damascus. Then in A.D. 56, Nero added cities around the Sea of Galilee, including parts of the Decapolis and Peraea. Agrippa II died in Rome in A.D. 100, still greatly honored as a "praetor" or high officer of Rome.

Bernice ("Victorious") was married first to her uncle, Herod of Chalcis. After his death she married Polemon, king of Cilicia, but deserted him and came to live with her brother, Herod Agrippa II. She lived a very immoral life. Later she became the mistress of the emperor Vespasian and then of the emperor Titus.

14. **And when they had been there many days:** ... And as they were spending more days there, —RTHM ... and, during their rather lengthy stay, —WEYM ... They prolonged their stay for some days, —PHLP ... Since they were staying there some time, —WMCK

**Festus declared Paul's cause unto the king:** ... Festus acquainted the king with Paul's situation, —BRKL ... put Paul's case before the king, —WMCK ... submitted the case of Paul to, —FNTN.

**saying, There is a certain man:** ... remarking, —FNTN ... I have a man here, he said, —PHLP ... There is a man here, —WMCK

**left in bonds by Felix:** ... left a prisoner by Felix, —ASV ... who was left in prison by Felix, —WMCK

**25:14.** Though Agrippa II was educated in Rome, he was a Jew, and the emperor Claudius had given him (in A.D. 50) the government of the temple in Jerusalem. This caused Festus to look on Agrippa II as an authority in the Jewish religion.

Since they were there many days, Festus decided to lay Paul's case before Agrippa, desiring to consult with him about it. Festus would need to write an opinion to send with Paul when he went as a prisoner to Rome. He felt Agrippa could help him.

King Agrippa's general attitude and friendliness must have encouraged Festus to do this. King Agrippa never showed the sort of cold disdain that some of the other Herods often did with regard to their subjects. He helped the Jews whenever he could. For example, he persuaded the emperor to restore the custody of the high priestly robes to the Jews. The Romans had allowed them to be used only on certain occasions.

15. **About whom, when I was at Jerusalem, the chief priests and the elders of the Jews informed me:** ... respecting whom, on my arrival in Jerusalem ... Judean senators, —FNTN ... made allegations against him, —PHLP ... laid information against him, —WMCK

**desiring to have judgment against him:** ... demanding judgement against him, —TCNT ... and continued to ask, —WLMS ... and demanded his condemnation, —MOFT ... and asked me to condemn him, —BECK ... asked for sentence to be pronounced against him, —FNTN ... pass judgment upon him in their favor, —MRDK.

**25:15.** After telling how Felix had left Paul imprisoned, Festus related how the chief priests and elders of the Jews in Jerusalem informed him (that is, brought charges or accusations against Paul and asked for a sentence of condemnation).

What Festus indicated is that the Jewish leaders in Jerusalem did not really want another trial for Paul. What they wanted was for Festus to accept their accusations at face value and pronounce the death sentence for Paul without any further trial or investigation.

The Jewish leaders were trying the same tactics they used when they brought Jesus before Pilate. When Pilate asked them what formal charge they were bringing against Jesus, they said if He were not an evildoer or criminal they would not have brought Jesus to him.

Now this was a new generation of Jewish leaders and a new high priest. But they had not learned anything from the way the previous generation treated Jesus. They still thought the Romans ought to accept their decision without investigation. It seems they thought the death penalty would get rid of both Paul and the gospel he preached, just as the previous generation had thought that crucifying Jesus would get rid of Him and His teachings.

16. **To whom I answered:** . . . I replied to them, —WMCK

**It is not the manner of the Romans:** . . . the practice of Romans, —TCNT . . . that with Romans it is not customary, —BRKL . . . the custom, —WMCK

**to deliver any man to die:** . . . to give up any man to the accusers, —TCNT . . . for punishment, —WEYM . . . to hand a man over gratuitously, —BRKL.

**before that he which is accused have the accusers face to face:** . . . until he has been face to face with those who are attacking him, —BB . . . until he has met those that charge him face to face, —WMCK

**and have license to answer for himself:** . . . and have had opportunity to make his defence, —ASV . . . and an opportunity afforded him of, —FNTN . . . been given the opportunity of defending himself, —PHLP.

**concerning the crime laid against him:** . . . on the charges made against him, —PHLP.

**25:16.** Festus answered the Jewish leaders by saying it was not the manner or custom of the Romans to hand over any human being (to the death penalty) before the accused person was brought face to face with his accusers and given opportunity to defend himself with respect to the accusation made against him.

Because of his education in the imperial palace in Rome, King Agrippa would be very familiar with Roman law and custom. Actually, it had developed over several hundred years and had often been modified to meet changing needs of the republic and then of the empire. It was eventually codified, and the Roman law codes have influenced the laws of western Europe and America. But at this time much was in the hands of the governor or the king of the particular part of the Roman Empire.

It was also part of the Roman custom to bring in experts who would help the judge, governor, or king make his decisions. So it was not out of order for Festus to ask Agrippa for his opinion.

Actually, what Festus said about Roman law and custom was part of the Jewish law and custom as well. When the chief priests and Pharisees wanted to arrest Jesus, the officers sent to arrest Him were so impressed by His teaching that they did not do so. This upset the Pharisees and they remarked that the crowds who were following Jesus did not know the Law and were accursed. But Nicodemus responded by asking whether their Law judged anyone before giving a hearing and finding out what he was doing (John 7:44-51). The Pharisees were implying that because they knew the Law they had more sense than to believe in Jesus. But they were wanting to kill Jesus without a trial, something which was contrary to the Law.

17. **Therefore, when they were come hither:** . . . So they met here, —TCNT . . . When, therefore, a number of them came here, —WEYM . . . Since these Jews came back here with me, —PHLP.

**without any delay on the morrow I sat on the judgment seat:** . . . I lost no time to occupy the judgment seat, —BRKL . . . I didn't delay matters, —ADAM . . . I did not postpone the case, —WMCK . . . I wasted no time but on the very next day I took my seat on the bench, —PHLP.

**and commanded the man to be brought forth:** . . . gave orders for, —WMCK . . . and ordered the man to be brought before me, —TCNT.

**25:17.** Festus then related how, after refusing to give the Jews the favor they desired, and after telling them that Paul, as a Roman, deserved to face his accusers, the Jewish leaders came to Caesarea.

Festus had not delayed or postponed the matter. The next day he had taken his seat at the tribunal and given the command or order that Paul be brought out. Festus thus made it clear to Agrippa there had been no laxity on his part. He had done his duty as a Roman governor as he put Paul on trial.

18. **Against whom when the accusers stood up:** . . . and standing up around him, —HBIE . . . But when his accusers got up to speak, —PHLP.

**they brought none accusation of such things:** . . . they did not charge him with misdemeanours, —WEYM . . . charged him with none of the crimes, —WMCK . . . not able to substantiate, —MRDK.

**as I supposed:** . . . such as I had expected, —TCNT . . . as I had in mind, —BB . . . as I had anticipated, —PHLP.

**25:18.** Then when the accusers stood up (took their stand), Festus, as a Roman, was surprised they did not charge Paul with any of the evil things he supposed they would.

The Roman courts considered criminal cases to include extortion, embezzlement, treason, corrupt practices, murder, fraud, and assault. Since the Jewish leaders were obviously wanting Paul killed, Festus supposed Paul must be guilty of something that would be in the same class as these criminal practices. But Paul was not guilty of anything like any of these, and the Jewish leaders did not try to accuse him of any such matters.

19. **But had certain questions against him of their own superstition:** . . . in dispute between them, —TCNT . . . But they quarrelled with him, —WEYM . . . in regard to their system of religion, —NORL . . . they only had certain differences of

309

opinion, —WMCK...Their differences with him were about their own religion, —PHLP.

**and of one Jesus, which was dead:**...and concerning one Jesus, who had died, —RTHM ... and about some dead man called Jesus, —TCNT... one Jesus deceased, —DOUY.

**whom Paul affirmed to be alive:**...whom Paul declared to be alive, —TCNT, —WMCK... but, so Paul maintained, is now alive, —WEYM... but whom Paul affirmed over and over was alive, —MNTG... whom Paul affirmed to be alive, —DOUY... asserted to be alive, —FNTN.

**25:19.** Instead, the Jewish leaders had questions against Paul concerning what Festus, as a Roman pagan, considered to be controversial questions or issues concerning "their superstition." Superstition was a word which could be used in a good sense, for it originally meant simply fear of or reverence for a divine being. But the word came to have a bad sense also. The context must determine which meaning is intended. In this case, since King Agrippa was a Jew, it is not likely that Festus would be using the word in an unfavorable sense. It may be better to translate his words "they had some points of dispute about their religion."

Festus added that the dispute also was concerning a certain Jesus who had died (who was put to death), but whom Paul alleged to live (claimed or asserted to be alive).

The truth of the resurrection of Jesus was, of course, the central point at issue, though Festus seemed almost to hesitate to tell King Agrippa about it and added it as if it were something of an afterthought. To Festus, as to the Greek philosophers in Athens, the idea of the Resurrection was something foreign to their thinking. Festus, however, did not mock or make fun of the idea, although he obviously neither understood nor believed Paul's claim.

**20. And because I doubted of such manner of questions:**...I was at a loss how to investigate such questions, —WEYM... As I felt uncertain about the proper investigation of such issues, —BRKL...I was puzzled, —BECK...I was perplexed, —MNTG...And being myself at a loss how to deal with such questions, —FNTN...was myself uncertain how to enquire into such matters, —WMCK

**I asked him whether he would go to Jerusalem:**...I asked Paul if he were willing to go, —TCNT...I made the suggestion to him to go, —BB.

**and there be judged of these matters:**...and there stand his trial on these matters, —WEYM...and be tried there on these charges, —MOFT.

**25:20.** Festus, however, did not admit to King Agrippa it was because he wanted to seek favor with the Jews that he had asked Paul to go to Jerusalem for another trial before the Jewish priests and elders of the Sanhedrin. Instead, he told

Agrippa he was at a loss as to how to investigate these matters. There was truth in this statement. Probably, this was the first time Festus had ever come up against religious questions in a criminal case. Since the Romans had decreed Judaism to be a legal religion in the Roman Empire and had turned over decisions on Jewish religious matters to the Sanhedrin and the high priest, it is not likely Festus ever thought he would have to face a case like Paul's.

**21. But when Paul had appealed:**...Paul, however, appealed, —TCNT.

**to be reserved unto the hearing of Augustus:**...that his case be retained for examination by Augustus, —BRKL...to have his case reviewed for the decision of the Emperor, —MNTG...for his case to be deferred for the decision of, —FNTN...appealed to be kept under guard, —WMCK...the emperor's decision, —NORL...for his Majesty's decision, —WLMS.

**I commanded him to be kept:**...I ordered him, —RTHM...to be detained in custody, —TCNT...to be held, —BRKL.

**till I might send him to Caesar:**...until I could send him up to, —WMCK

**25:21.** Next Festus reported how Paul had refused to go to Jerusalem and had appealed to be kept for the decision of the Augustus, the emperor.

*Caesar* was the family name of the famous Gaius Julius Caesar who was assassinated in Rome in 44 B.C. His grandnephew Octavius became the first Roman emperor and took the name *Augustus Caesar.* "Augustus" then became a title applied to his successors who were also Caesars. *Augustus* means "worthy to be reverenced." It implied respect and veneration that was usually given to their gods and to sacred things. But the title soon became used to encourage the worship of the emperor.

Because of Paul's appeal, Festus ordered Paul to be kept under guard until he could send him to Caesar, that is, to Nero.

The original name of Nero was Lucius Domitius Ahenobarbus. His mother Agrippina was the sister of the emperor Caligula and niece of the emperor Claudius. His father died when Nero was 3 years old, and by intrigue Agrippina married Claudius and had Nero adopted as his son. Claudius was poisoned, and Nero became emperor in A.D. 54. During the first 5 years of his reign, good advisers helped him initiate many reforms, though Nero himself began to indulge in all kinds of excesses.

**22. Then Agrippa said unto Festus:**...Agrippa remarked to Festus, —BRKL.

**I would also hear the man myself:**...I have a desire to give the man a hearing myself, —BB.

**To morrow, said he, thou shalt hear him:** ... you may give him a hearing, —BB.

**25:22.** Agrippa apparently had heard of Paul and of Jesus and had been wishing for an opportunity to hear Paul. This desire pleased Festus, and he promised to arrange a special hearing.

Agrippa spent his early life in Rome and then reigned to the north and northeast of Palestine. As a Jew he must have made pilgrimages to Jerusalem. The Law required all male Jews to go there for the Feasts of Passover, Pentecost, and Tabernacles.

The multitudes of Jewish believers in Jerusalem and Judea could not have escaped his notice. There were also assemblies of believers in Galilee, Peraea, Samaria, and the Decapolis. No doubt, the believers who were scattered after the death of Stephen had established assemblies in his kingdom as well. Agrippa surely had to know something about Jesus. Since there was a great deal of travel and communication between churches, the news about Paul's travels and the churches he established must have been spread in all directions too. So it is not strange that Agrippa wanted to hear Paul.

**23. And on the morrow:** ... So the next day, —TCNT ... Accordingly, the following day, —BRKL ... When the next day came, —PHLP.

**when Agrippa was come, and Bernice:** ... proceeded, —WMCK ... arrived, —MLNT.

**with great pomp:** ... in full state, —TCNT ... with great pomp and ceremony, —PHLP ... with great display, —MLNT, —RTHM ... in great state, —WMCK ... with stately pomp, —FNTN.

**and was entered into the place of hearing:** ... and they had entered the audience-chamber, —RTHM ... to the hall of audience, —WMCK ... the audience hall, —MLNT.

**with the chief captains, and principal men of the city:** ... in the company of military officers, NAB ... superior officers and the principal people, —TCNT ... together with the officers of high rank and the chief men of the town, —WMCK ... with an escort of military officers and prominent townsmen, —PHLP ... with the Generals and the principal men of the city, —FNTN ... accompanied by the chief military men and the prominent citizens of the city, —MLNT.

**at Festus' commandment Paul was brought forth:** ... by the order of Festus Paul was brought before them, —TCNT ... was also brought in, —FNTN.

**25:23.** The next day King Agrippa and his sister Bernice came with great pomp and display. They took it as an opportunity to let the city of Caesarea and all the Jews and Gentiles there see the glory of a Jewish king. So they made a great parade from wherever they were staying to the palace of Herod where Paul was being kept and where the governor Festus had a large audience hall. They paraded in with all their royal robes and with all their attendants in a great show of magnificent pageantry.

Joining in with them were the tribunes of the Roman army stationed in Caesarea and all the prominent men of the city as well. It must have been an impressive sight.

The population of the city included Jews, Jewish and Gentile believers in Christ, Romans, and a great many Syrians. The city had a theater, an amphitheater, and a Roman temple, all built by Herod the Great. It was a cosmopolitan city with a very mixed population. The Gentiles among them had caused trouble already for the Jews under Felix. One reason for all this display of pomp and ceremony may have been to encourage the Jews and show the Gentiles that a neighboring Jewish king had power. If so, it did not have any permanent effect, for it was only a few years later that the Syrians vented their jealousy in a wholesale massacre of Jews in the city. (This was another thing that helped to bring about the revolt of the Jews that ended with the destruction of Jerusalem in A.D. 70.)

**24. And Festus said, King Agrippa, and all men which are here present with us:** ... and then he spoke, —PHLP ... The governor began to speak, —NAB ... and all other men now present with us, —FNTN.

**ye see this man:** ... you are looking at the person, —BRKL ... look at this man! —NAB ... you see before you, —WMCK

**about whom all the multitude of the Jews have dealt with me:** ... about whom the whole mass of the Judeans ... have distracted me, —FNTN ... on whose account the whole constituency of the Jews have made complaint to me, —BRKL, —MLNT ... the whole Jewish nation ... have made complaint to me, —WMCK ... the whole Jewish people ... have petitioned me, —PHLP.

**both at Jerusalem, and also here:** ... and in this city, —PHLP.

**crying that he ought not to live any longer:** ... They loudly insist he ought not to live any longer, —MOFT ... clamoring that he should live no more, —NAB ... shouting that he ought not to live, —MLNT ... They din it into my ears, —PHLP.

**25:24.** After Paul was brought in, Festus addressed King Agrippa and all the others who were present, calling on them to look at this man about whom the whole multitude of the Jerusalem Jews petitioned, both in Jerusalem and at Caesarea, crying out that he must not live any longer.

Festus was quite dramatic in this and exaggerated the truth for the sake of the effect. Actually, the multitude of the Jews in Jerusalem, and the population of Jerusalem as a whole, had not cried out that Paul must be killed. The mob in the temple had when the Jews from the Roman province of

Asia stirred them up. But there were many other Jews, including the thousands of Jewish believers who had no part in this. After that, the Jews who demanded the death penalty were primarily the chief priests and the Sadducean members of the Sanhedrin.

Possibly Festus also called on them to look at Paul because he was not an impressive figure as far as his outward appearance went. On the other hand, Paul bore himself with the dignity of a Roman gentleman as he faced these rulers and prominent people.

Actually, it is not certain what Paul really looked like. The fictional apocryphal book, The Acts of Paul and Thecla pictures him as "a man of small stature, with a bald head and crooked legs, in a good state of body, with eyebrows meeting and a nose somewhat hooked, full of friendliness" (Barnstone, p. 447). Some believe this description was based on ancient tradition that had some basis in fact, but it seems Festus wanted the people to wonder how such a man as this could cause so great a disturbance.

**25. But when I found:**... But I for my part discovered, —*PHLP*... I did not find, —*NAB*.

**that he had committed nothing worthy of death:**... that he had not done anything deserving death, —*TCNT*... nothing he has done that deserves death, —*MLNT*... which deserves the death penalty, —*PHLP*.

**and that he himself hath appealed to Augustus:**... and as he himself has made a request to be judged by Caesar, —*BB*... Since, however, he himself made the appeal, —*KLST*... his Imperial Majesty, —*TCNT*... His Majesty the Emperor, —*NAB*.

**I have determined to send him:**... I decided to send him, —*RSV*... to Rome, —*WEYM*... send him on, —*NAB*.

**25:25.** Then very emphatically Festus again stated that Paul had not committed any crime worthy of death (or anything at all worthy of death). His words might be translated, "As for me, I have found (and fully understand) that he has done (and still has done) nothing worthy of death."

Festus, like many rulers of the day, was primarily concerned with pleasing those who could affect his political career. Although it is quite probable he knew Paul was innocent right from the beginning, Festus would have gladly submitted him to the Jews in order to win their support. However, when Paul appealed to "Caesar," Festus knew it would be unwise or even dangerous to circumvent the appeals system established by Roman law as a means of protecting Roman citizens. Now, before Agrippa, he tried to present himself in the best possible light.

Unfortunately, though Festus had come to an understanding of the fact that Paul was not guilty of anything worthy of death, he had not come to an understanding of what Paul's message was all about. Martin Luther once said, "The object of his (Paul's) mission is to open their eyes—that is, to open and awaken the mind to the truth, and this in order to their conversion. The change is denoted by a twofold contrast—by that between darkness and light, and by that between the ruling power of Satan and the liberating fellowship of God. Finally, the ultimate design of God in their conversion consisted in the forgiveness of sins, and the bestowal of an inheritance, that is, a share in the glory." Festus was still blinded to these truths.

**26. Of whom I have no certain thing to write unto my lord:**... The trouble is, I have nothing definite to write about him to our sovereign, —*NAB*... But I have nothing definite to write about him to my Imperial Master, —*TCNT*... Frankly, I have nothing specific to write to the emperor about him, —*PHLP*... anything reliable to write, —*BECK*... nothing substantial to write, —*MLNT*... our Sovereign, —*WLMS*.

**Wherefore I have brought him forth before you:**... and for that reason, —*TCNT*... That is why I have brought him before all of you, —*NAB*... and I have therefore brought him forward before you, —*PHLP*.

**and specially before thee, O king Agrippa:**... and particularly before you, —*BRKL*.

**that, after examination had:**... as the result of your cross-examination, —*MOFT*... that from this investigation, NAB... so that after due examination, —*MLNT*... after an examination of him has been made, —*KLST*.

**I might have somewhat to write:**... I may find something which I can put into writing, —*WEYM*... there may emerge some charge which I may put in writing, —*PHLP*.

**25:26.** Festus had a problem when it came to making arrangements to send Paul to Rome. He had nothing reliable, nothing definite, nothing trustworthy to write to his lord, that is, to the emperor Nero.

Paul was not on trial here; he was simply being questioned at what may be called an informal hearing. Because the entire matter had become a lightly or dismiss it all together. However, the "evidence" presented both by Paul and the Jews was theological and may not have been understandable to these Roman rulers.

"My lord" in the Greek is simply "the lord." The Greek *kurios*, "lord," was often used in a way that was to imply showing respect to anyone and would be translated, "Sir!" Among the Romans, however, it was more often used to mean "master" of servants or slaves. It was also used of high officials, and by this time among the Romans it was used of their gods.

Festus then expressed his hope that after this examination before King Agrippa he would have something to write. He hoped Agrippa would be able to ask the right questions and give him something more definite.

**27. For it seemeth to me unreasonable:** ... For it seems to me absurd, —*TCNT* ... ridiculous, —*PHLP* ... odd, —*BRKL* ... to me pointless, —*JB*.

**to send a prisoner:** ... to send a prisoner up for trial, —*NORL*.

**and not withal to signify the crimes laid against him:** ... without at the same time stating the charges made against him, —*TCNT* ... without specifying, —*WLMS* ... without reporting what he's accused of, —*BECK* ... without indicating the charges against him, —*PHLP* ... the crimes alleged against him, —*CMPB* ... not to designate his offence, —*MRDK*.

**25:27.** Festus further emphasized that it seemed unreasonable to him to send a prisoner to the emperor without pointing out in a letter the charge against him. It apparently was customary to send such a letter, just as Lysias had sent a letter to Felix concerning Paul (23:25).

Obviously, Paul had successfully defended himself against all the flimsy charges the chief priests and elders of the Jews had brought against him. There was certainly nothing in the various categories of Roman civil or criminal law that would cover Paul's case. Festus undoubtedly knew better than to write the confused charges and generalities the Jewish leaders had included in their accusations.

Such a letter, of course, would not determine the emperor's decision. Paul's accusers would have to send representatives to bring charges against him as well. But a favorable letter from Festus would help a great deal.

## Chapter 26

**1. Then Agrippa said unto Paul:** ... Turning to Paul, Agrippa said, —*TCNT*.

**Thou art permitted to speak for thyself:** ... You are at liberty to speak for yourself, —*TCNT* ... You have permission, —*PHLP* ... You may put your case before us, —*BB*.

**Then Paul stretched forth the hand:** ... So Paul, extending his hand, —*NORL* ... with that characteristic gesture of the hand, —*PHLP*.

**and answered for himself:** ... went on to make his defence, —*RTHM* ... began his defense, —*PHLP*.

**26:1.** This final hearing before Agrippa was not an official trial, since its purpose was to gain additional information for the benefit of Festus. Here the Book of Acts records for the third time, the account of Paul's conversion, giving some details not previously recorded in chapters 9 and 22.

Consider the setting. King Agrippa sat there in all the finery of his royal robes. Beside him sat his beautiful 32-year-old sister Bernice, "blazing in all her jewels." All around were the town notables dressed in their best. Then there were the tribunes in their uniforms with glittering swords at their sides.

King Agrippa turned to Paul and told him he was permitted to speak for himself. Paul did not hesitate. Filled once again with the power of the Holy Spirit, he began his defense.

**2. I think myself happy, king Agrippa:** ... I have been congratulating myself, King Agrippa, —*TCNT* ... I think myself fortunate, —*WEYM* ... I must say how fortunate I consider myself to be, —*PHLP*.

**because I shall answer for myself this day before thee:** ... in being able to defend myself today before you, —*MOFT* ... in making my defense before thee personally today, —*PHLP*.

**touching all the things whereof I am accused of the Jews:** ... with regard to the charges brought against me by, —*TCNT* ... against all the charges which the Jews have preferred against me, —*WLMS* ... in answering all the charges that the Jews have made against me. —*PHLP*.

**26:2.** Paul made no criticism of the king's empty display, nor did he refer to the jewelry of Bernice or her unsavory reputation. He was intent not on defending himself but his Master. The cause of Christ was always more important to him than his own cause. Thus, with all courtesy and deep earnestness he began his defense.

He first let King Agrippa know he counted himself happy to make a defense before him and to give an answer with respect to all things of which the Jews were accusing him.

**3. Especially because I know thee to be expert:** ... Especially as thou art well versed, —*RTHM* ... especially as you are well acquainted with, —*KLST* ... for you are so thoroughly acquainted, —*BRKL* ... because you are expert, —*BB* ... you are thoroughly familiar, —*PHLP*.

**in all customs and questions which are among the Jews:** ... in all the Jewish customs and questions, —*RTHM* ... that prevail among the Jews, —*WEYM* ... and controversial questions, —*NORL* ... the controversies, —*MRDK* ... and disputes that exist among, —*PHLP*.

**wherefore I beseech thee to hear me patiently:** ... Pray listen to me then with patience, —*MOFT* ... with indulgence, —*MRDK*.

**26:3.** Paul felt happy or fortunate that it was Agrippa who was to hear his case because Agrippa was an expert in all the things concerning Jewish customs and questions.

Agrippa's father was zealous for the Jewish law up to almost the end of his life. He was concerned about Jewish customs and the temple. Because Agrippa himself was now the Roman official in charge of the temple, he must have learned a great deal from his own experiences as well as from his father's. He would know too how controversial many of the questions were that arose among the Jews and how the customs varied among the different sects such as the Pharisees, Sadducees, and Essenes.

Therefore, because of this expert knowledge, Paul begged Agrippa to listen patiently to what he was about to say. Paul was implying in this that his words would be helpful to Agrippa also, for Agrippa was a Jew and needed to know the facts, not only of Paul's life, but of Paul's message, the gospel.

**4. My manner of life from my youth:** ... The kind of life I have lived from, –WEYM ... The fact that I lived from my youth upwards, –PHLP.

**which was at the first among mine own nation at Jerusalem:** ... as exemplified in my early days among, –WEYM ... the early part of which was spent among, –KLST ... among my own people, –PHLP.

**know all the Jews:** ... is known to all the Jews, –WEYM ... all the Jews know, –KLST.

**26:4.** Paul pointed out first that all the Jews knew his manner of life from the beginning (in Tarsus) and during his youth among his own people in Jerusalem.

Paul did not draw attention to his birth in Tarsus, the chief city of Cilicia. Nor did he mention the wealth and influence of his family in that city or even his Roman citizenship. He emphasized that from his early youth he had lived among the Jews in Jerusalem, and they all knew the kind of life he lived. He was open and aboveboard in all that he did. He took part in the affairs of the Jews in Jerusalem, so that they all came to know him well.

He was sent early to Jerusalem to be educated and taught a trade. His teacher, Gamaliel, was one of the most distinguished rabbis of that time and was a grandson of the famous Hillel who is still revered by orthodox Jews. At his feet the young Paul (then called by his Hebrew name, Saul) learned the Old Testament and all the rabbinical traditions and interpretations.

**5. Which knew me from the beginning:** ... They are fully aware, –BRKL ... They have known all the time, –PHLP ... In fact they have long been acquainted with me, –KLST.

**if they would testify:** ... if only they are willing to give evidence, –KLST ... if they choose to give evidence, –TCNT ... if they would but testify to the fact,

–WEYM ... if they want to tell the truth, –BECK ... and could witness to the fact if they wished, –PHLP.

**that after the most straitest sect of our religion:** ... according to, –DRBY ... the strictest sect, –NORL ... the most rigid Sect, –WLSN ... the strictest party of our religion, –BECK.

**I lived a Pharisee:** ... I lived a true Pharisee, –TCNT ... I spent my life as. –KLST.

**26:5.** If those who knew Paul from the beginning (of his stay in Jerusalem) would testify (bear witness), they would have to say Paul lived as a Pharisee, following the teachings of the strictest of the Jewish sects.

The Pharisees were separatists. They not only separated themselves from Greek culture and idolatry, they took a stand against the Maccabean (Hasmonean) priests about 100 years before Christ. They did not like the fact that they took the title of king even though they were not of the line of David. Alexander Jannaeus, a Hasmonean king, showed his hostility toward the Pharisees by crucifying about 800 of them. But force did not stop them, and they maintained their strict religious convictions.

Clearly, Paul was not some stranger or foreigner coming in trying to start a new religion. He was a Jew, a Pharisee, and he lived up to their customs to the best of his ability.

**6. And now I stand and am judged:** ... Even now ... I stand here on my trial, –TCNT.

**for the hope of the promise made of God unto our fathers:** ... because of my hope in the promise given by God to our ancestors, –TCNT ... because I trust the promise God made, –BECK ... which came from God a promise to, –FNTN ... because of a hope that I hold in a promise that God made, –PHLP.

**26:6.** Now Paul was being judged, not because he had done anything wrong, not because he had turned against his true heritage, but because of the hope of the promise God made to the patriarchs (Abraham, Isaac, Jacob, and the other ancestors of the Jews who received His promises). These would include the promises of blessing, not only for Israel, but for all the families of the earth (Genesis 12:3).

**7. Unto which promise our twelve tribes:** ... a promise which our Twelve Tribes, –TCNT.

**instantly serving God day and night, hope to come:** ... hope to attain, –ASV ... by earnest service night and day, hope to see it fulfilled, –TCNT ... as they worship earnestly night and day, hope to gain, –WMCK ... serve God zealously day and night, hoping to see it fulfilled, –PHLP ... in confident expectation to secure, –FNTN.

**For which hope's sake, king Agrippa:** ... It is for this hope, your Majesty, –TCNT ... And I am actually impeached by Jews, –MOFT.

**I am accused of the Jews:** . . . that I am accused and by Jews themselves! —TCNT . . . And I am actually impeached by Jews, —MOFT . . . I am charged, —WMCK . . . I am accused as a criminal by the Judeans! —FNTN.

**26:7.** This promise, Paul said, "our twelve tribes" in earnestness served (worshiped) God day and night hoping to attain it (reach it as their God-given destination).

Paul, of course, recognized that the Jews of his day included all 12 tribes, although Judah comprised the largest group who originally returned from Babylon. He was of the tribe of Benjamin. The Jews at that time knew the tribe to which they belonged. The 10 northern tribes were obviously never lost. (Actually, some had intermarried and became Samaritans. Others purified themselves and joined in the worship of the temple after Cyrus sent the Jews back.)

The Jews' accusations against Paul, then, did not refer to any crime. They really concerned this hope of their fathers.

**8. Why should it be thought a thing incredible with you:** . . . Why is it deemed with all of you a thing past belief, —WEYM . . . do you find it impossible to believe, —WMCK

**that God should raise the dead?:** . . . if God doth raise the dead, —ASV.

**26:8.** Paul then gave his full attention to Agrippa and asked a pointed question, "Why does it seem incredible (unbelievable) to you that God should raise the dead?"

Agrippa would know that as a Pharisee Paul always believed in the future resurrection of the body and future judgments. Agrippa must also have known the Christians believed God had raised Jesus from the dead and made His resurrection the guarantee of theirs. Actually, since God is God, and since the Old Testament teaches that nothing is too hard, too wonderful, or too impossible for God, it should not have been hard for Agrippa to believe, especially now that God had raised Jesus from the dead.

**9. I verily thought with my self:** . . . Fact is that I was possessed of the idea, —BRKL.

**that I ought to do many things contrary to the name of Jesus of Nazareth:** . . . my duty to oppose in every way the Name of, —TCNT . . . a duty to be active in hostility to the name of Jesus, the Nazarene, —WEYM . . . to do everything to oppose the name of, —WMCK . . . to oppose with the utmost vigor the name of, —PHLP . . . to take extreme measures in hostility to the name, —WLMS.

**26:9.** Paul did not want to imply that Agrippa was foolish or stupid for thinking it hard to believe in the Resurrection. Paul himself had not had an easy time believing in the resurrection of Jesus either. In fact, he had thought it necessary to do many things against the name of Jesus of Nazareth, that is, against what the Name represented: the character, nature, and authority of the Son of God.

Paul did not elsewhere call Jesus "Jesus of Nazareth." Perhaps he did so here because he was thinking of the words of Jesus on the Damascus Road where He identified himself as "Jesus of Nazareth, whom you keep persecuting." But this was the name by which Jesus was known to the Jews, and Agrippa would have no question about which person this was.

**10. Which thing I also did in Jerusalem:**

**and many of the saints did I shut up in prison:** . . . I myself threw many of the People of Christ into prison, —TCNT . . . I locked up many of the holy people in prison, —BECK . . . where I shut up in prison many of the holy, —FNTN.

**having received authority from the chief priests:** . . . Acting on the authority of the Chief Priests, —TCNT . . . armed with authority received from, —WEYM.

**and when they were put to death:** . . . executed, —BRKL . . . condemned to death, —MNTG . . . on trial for their lives, —PHLP . . . and when it was proposed to put them to death, —TCNT.

**I gave my voice against them:** . . . I voted against, —MOFT . . . I gave my decision against them, —BB.

**26:10.** Paul had shown his antagonism to Jesus by putting many of the saints in prison, not on his own authority but on the authority he received from the chief priests.

After his conversion Paul called the Christians saints "holy, dedicated, consecrated ones," that is, dedicated or set apart for God and for the worship and service of God. The same adjective is applied to God, Christ, and the angels. Israel was called to be a holy people, that is to be saints. Christians have the same calling (Romans 1:7). In the New Testament a saint is one who has turned his back on the world to follow Jesus.

Paul did more than hold the clothes of the witnesses who stoned the martyr Stephen. He cast his vote against him and many other Christians, a vote that called for the death penalty.

On the basis of Paul's casting his vote against them some have surmised Paul was a member of the Sanhedrin. However, such a young man would not normally be chosen to become a member. Nevertheless, his zeal for the Law, his great intelligence, and the progress he made in his studies under Gamaliel gave him a reputation that caused him to be sought after.

**11. And I punished them oft in every synagogue:** ... there was not a synagogue where I did not often punish them, —MOFT ... I tortured them, —MRDK ... I frequently forced them, by torturing, —FNTN.

**and compelled them to blaspheme:** ... and forced them to blaspheme, —WEYM ... to make them renounce their faith, —NEB.

**and being exceedingly mad against them:** ... So frantic was I against them, —TCNT ... and in my wild fury, —WEYM ... frantic fury, —MOFT ... mad fury, —MNTG ... furious rage, —NORL ... furiously mad against them, —FNTN.

**I persecuted them even unto strange cities:** ... as far as foreign cities, —BRKL ... that I pursued them even to towns beyond our borders, —TCNT ... and I hounded them to distant cities, —PHLP ... into foreign cities, —NORL.

**26:11.** Paul's zeal against Jesus and against those who believed in Him also caused him to go from synagogue to synagogue. He sought out the believers and punished them. Even worse, he tried to compel them to blaspheme the name of Jesus. However, the Greek may indicate he was not able to make them do it; the imperfect tense implies he repeatedly "compelled" them to blaspheme.

So exceedingly and madly enraged had Paul been against the Christians that he pursued them even to foreign cities. Later, in 1 Timothy 1:13, Paul pointed out that he acted in ignorance of the truth. But he never forgot what he had done. He reminded the Galatians that they had heard of his manner of life when he was engaged in the Jews' religion. He said, "Beyond measure I persecuted the church (assembly) of God, and wasted it (tried to destroy it): and profited (advanced, made progress) in the Jews' religion above many of my equals (those of my own age) in mine own nation, being more exceedingly zealous of the traditions of my fathers" (Galatians 1:13, 14). He showed this zeal by the way he never let up in his persecution of believers. His aim was to destroy the Church by getting all the Christians to renounce Christ.

**12. Whereupon as I went to Damascus:** ... While thus engaged, I was travelling one day to Damascus, —WEYM.

**with authority and commission from the chief priests:** ... entrusted with full powers, —TCNT ... with discretionary authority, —ADAM ... and approval of, —BRKL ... authorized and appointed by, —BECK ... based on a commission, —WLMS.

**26:12.** After painting such a word picture of his violence against the Christians, Paul recounted for Agrippa the story of his conversion on the Damascus Road. Again Paul made it clear that he had not hounded the Christians on his own authority. He went to Damascus with authority and the full power of a commission from the chief

priests. Likely, his anger and the anticipation of arresting the Jewish believers in Damascus caused him to lead the group as he pressed on toward the city. All this provides a contrast for what followed.

**13. At midday, O king, I saw in the way:** ... On this journey, —NAB ... on the journey, at noon, O King, I saw, —WEYM ... upon the road, —FNTN ... when in the middle of the day, your Majesty, —WMCK

**a light from heaven, above the brightness of the sun:** ... a light brighter than the glare of the sun, —TCNT ... a light from heaven, more dazzling than the sun, —MOFT ... more brilliant than the sun, —BRKL, —MLNT ... eclipsing the splendour of the sun, —FNTN ... far brighter than, —PHLP ... a light from the sky, brighter than sunshine, —KLST ... shining in the sky, —NAB.

**shining round about me and them which journeyed with me:** ... It surrounded me, —NAB ... flash round me and my fellow-travellers, —MOFT ... blazing about me and my fellow travelers, —PHLP ... and those travelling with me, —FNTN ... and the men who were traveling, —EVRD.

**26:13.** Paul again addressed the king and told him how in the middle of the day while he was going along the road he saw a great light coming out of heaven and shining around him. Although the story of Paul's conversion is recorded three times in the Book of Acts, this is the only place where the time of day is recorded. The brilliance of the light was greater than the brightness of the noonday sun, and it enveloped not only Paul but the whole company of men who were traveling with him.

Paul here was drawing attention to the supernatural character of this light. Paul was out on the open road. This was no illusion, no mirage. No trick could produce a light brighter than the sun at midday. Nor was it a mere lightning flash. The light shone around them for quite some time. The New Testament uses the word only here and in Luke 2:9 where the glory of the Lord shone around the shepherds when the angel appeared to announce the birth of Jesus.

To King Agrippa, who knew the Old Testament, this would speak of a divine manifestation like the glory Moses saw, or like the glory of God that was manifest in the Holy of Holies above the mercy seat from the time the glory first appeared as recorded in Exodus chapter 40 until it departed (see Ezekiel chapters 8-11). This had to be a manifestation sent by God.

**14. And when we were all fallen to the earth:** ... We all fell to the ground, —TCNT.

**I heard a voice speaking unto me:** ... and then I heard a voice, —TCNT ... saying to me, —NAB.

and saying in the Hebrew tongue: ... asking me in the Jewish language, *—BECK* ... in the Hebrew dialect, *—FNTN* ... the Hebrew language, *—MLNT.*

**Saul, Saul, why persecutest thou me?:** ... Saul! Saul! Why do you continue to persecute me, *—WLMS* ... why are you attacking me so cruelly, *—BB* ... why are you doing things against me? *—EVRD.*

**it is hard for thee to kick against the pricks:** ... By kicking against the goads you are punishing yourself, *—TCNT* ... It is hurting you to keep on kicking, *—WLMS* ... It hurts you to kick against the goad, *—WMCK* ... It is not easy for you to kick against your own conscience, *—PHLP* ... You cannot kick against, *—GDSP* ... to rebel and to resist, *—NORL* ... You are only hurting yourself by fighting me, *—EVRD.*

**26:14.** The light was so bright that none of them could stand it. Probably in trying to shield themselves they all fell to the ground. It is likely this brilliant light terrified both Paul and his companions. (The word used of its brightness is also used of a joyousness such as the believer feels when God is pouring out spiritual blessing on those who worship Him.) The sense of the supernatural prepared Paul for the voice that spoke to him by name in the Hebrew language, asking him why he kept persecuting Him, and adding that it was hard for him to kick against the goad. The picture is that of an ox who kicks against the goad of a driver and gets a more severe wound. The present active infinitive of the Greek verb also shows Paul was continually kicking against the goad and had been doing so undoubtedly ever since he heard the defense of Stephen.

The goad was a pointed stick used in place of a whip to spur animals on. The same word is used of a sting, and normally the goad would simply prick the hide of the ox and sting a little without really injuring him unless he kicked against it. Its use here meant that it was hard for Paul to keep resisting God. Though he did it in ignorance, all this human effort and fleshly anger he was expending against the Christians was hurting him more than he knew.

**15. And I said, Who art thou, Lord?:** ... But I said, *—MLNT* ... I said, at that, *—NAB* ... Who are you, Sir? *—FNTN* ... I inquired, *—KLST* ... said I, *—GDSP.*

**And he said, I am Jesus whom thou persecutest:** ... The Lord said ... I am the One you are trying to hurt, *—EVRD* ... I am that Jesus, NAB ... the Lord replied, *—KLST* ... and you are persecuting me, *—WMCK*

**26:15.** Paul's response showed he recognized not only the light but the Person who spoke to him was from heaven. When he called Him Lord and asked Him to identify himself, it is evident he knew the Person had the right to be addressed as Lord.

What the Lord said must have been as surprising to King Agrippa as it was to Saul (Paul) on the Damascus Road: "I am Jesus whom you keep persecuting." All Paul had done in persecuting the believers both in Jerusalem and in other cities, he had really done to Jesus, for He is the Head of the Church and the believers constitute the Body.

**16. But rise, and stand upon thy feet:** ... get up and stand upright, *—TCNT* ... Stand up! *—EVRD.*

**for I have appeared unto thee for this purpose:** ... for I have shown myself to you for a reason, *—PHLP* ... I have chosen you, *—EVRD.*

**to make thee a minister and a witness:** ... to ordain you a minister, *—CMPB* ... to appoint thee, *—ASV* ... to designate you as, *—NAB* ... you are chosen to be my, *—PHLP* ... a servant, *—TCNT.*

**both of these things which thou hast seen:** ... you will tell people, *—EVRD* ... of those revelations of me which you have already had, *—TCNT* ... of what you have seen of me today, *—PHLP.*

**and of those things in the which I will appear unto thee:** ... and also of what I will reveal to you, *—NORL* ... This is why I have come to you today, *—EVRD* ... what you will see of me, *—NAB* ... and of those in which I will still show Myself to you, *—MLNT* ... and to the visions you shall have of me, *—KLST* ... and of other visions of myself which I will give you, *—PHLP* ... and to what I will make you see of me, *—WMCK*

**26:16.** Next Paul described the way Christ commissioned him and what was included in his call in greater detail than he had done in his previous trials. Jesus commanded him to get up off the ground and stand on his feet. Jesus wanted his full attention. He told Paul that He had appeared to him to appoint him for the important task of being a minister (a servant) and a witness both of the things he had seen and of future revelations from Christ.

Paul was first of all to be a minister. The Greek words translated "minister" all mean servant. The word used here means a "helpful assistant." The word was often used of a physician's assistant as well as other types of practical service. Paul was thus called to be a faithful workman for the Lord.

Paul was also called to be a witness, not only of what he had seen, but of what Christ would continue to reveal to him. This visit of Jesus made him a firsthand witness to Christ's resurrection. Later Jesus revealed to him many other details and made him a firsthand witness of the gospel message as well (Galatians 1:12, 16).

**17. Delivering thee from the people, and from the Gentiles:** ... Rescuing thee from, *—RTHM* ... I will keep you safe, *—BB* ... I will not let your own people hurt you, *—EVRD* ... delivered you from this people,

*—NAB* . . . both from your own people, *—PHLP* . . . and from the heathen, *—WMCK*

**unto whom now I send thee:** . . . to whom I am going to send you, *—WLMS.*

**26:17.** It is possible the verb used here means to select or choose out for oneself; thus Paul would be saying Jesus chose him out for himself from the people and the nations. But in this context the other meaning of the verb, "save, deliver, rescue," seems to fit better. That is, Jesus promised to save him from the people and from the nations to whom He was sending him.

Agrippa would understand that "the people" meant the Jews, while the nations meant the Gentiles, that is, all the other nations. This was the common way the Jews looked at the rest of the world.

The mention of the Gentiles did not evoke the kind of reaction it had in Jerusalem (22:21, 22). Agrippa had associated with Gentiles in Rome and in the kingdom he ruled. So he was accustomed to treating them more graciously than the Jerusalem Jews were.

**18. To open their eyes:** . . . I sent you to open their eyes, *—PHLP* . . . that their eyes may be opened, *—MOFT* . . . for the opening of their eyes, *—MLNT.*

**and to turn them from darkness to light:** . . . that they may turn, *—MOFT* . . . and their turning from, *—MLNT.*

**and from the power of Satan unto God:** . . . authority of, *—RTHM* . . . dominion of, *—HBIE* . . . the devil's control, *—BECK* . . . of the Adversary, *—YNG* . . . to God himself, *—PHLP.*

**that they may receive forgiveness of sins:** . . . so that they may know, *—PHLP* . . . remission of sins, *—ASV* . . . pardon for their sins, *—TCNT* . . . release from sins, *—FNTN.*

**and inheritance among them which are sanctified by faith that is in me:** . . . and have a possession among, *—WLMS* . . . and take their place with all those who are made holy, *—PHLP* . . . and get a share of what the people enjoy who are made holy, *—BECK* . . . by faith in me, *—DRBY.*

**26:18.** Jesus had then made it clear to Paul what he was to do when He sent him to the Gentiles. The light of Christ and the truth of the gospel would open their eyes. The power of Christ and the Holy Spirit would turn them from darkness to light and from the power of Satan to God, that they might receive the forgiveness of sins.

With their forgiveness they would receive an inheritance among those who are sanctified (treated as holy, set apart to God as His people to do His will) by faith in Christ.

King Agrippa and the other Jews present would recognize that much of the language Jesus used in giving this commission to Paul was drawn from the Old Testament. The phraseology comes especially from Isaiah 42:6, 7 and 61:1, 2. These are prophecies of God's ministry through His Suffering Servant, the Messiah, and point specifically to Jesus.

Paul, in his epistles, recognized the reason unbelievers need to have their eyes opened is because "the god of this world (Satan) hath blinded the minds of them which believe not, lest the light of the glorious gospel of Christ, who is the image of God, should shine unto them" (2 Corinthians 4:4).

**19. Whereupon, O king Agrippa:** . . . After that, King Agrippa, *—TCNT.*

**I was not disobedient unto the heavenly vision:** . . . I could not disobey, *—WLMS* . . . I did not go against the vision from heaven, *—BB* . . . not apathetic, *—FNTN.*

**26:19.** Paul again addressed Agrippa. He declared he was not disobedient to the heavenly vision. The word "vision" here does not mean a dream-type vision but an actual appearance where Jesus spoke to him. This was as real as the appearances of Jesus to the apostles and disciples before His ascension. It made the apostle Paul a firsthand witness to the resurrection of Jesus, and the commission of Jesus made him an apostle, one personally sent out by Jesus himself with the same power and authority He had given to the other apostles.

**20. But shewed first unto them of Damascus:** . . . but I proceeded to preach first to the people in Damascus, *—WEYM* . . . but first I told, *—BECK.*

**and at Jerusalem, and throughout all the coasts of Judaea:** . . . and Jerusalem, and then through the whole of Judaea, *—TCNT.*

**and then to the Gentiles:** . . . and to the Gentiles as well, *—TCNT* . . . and I preached even to the Gentiles, *—NORL.*

**that they should repent and turn to God:** . . . to turn from sin to God, *—BECK.*

**and do works meet for repentance:** . . . and a life befitting that repentance, *—TCNT* . . . and live lives consistent with such repentance, *—WEYM* . . . and live lives to prove their change of heart, *—PHLP* . . . live lives consistent, *—NORL* . . . to do things to show that they really had changed, *—EVRD.*

**26:20.** Paul did not use this declaration of obedience to honor himself. Rather, he used it as a further opportunity to clarify the meaning of the gospel and to show what it means to accept Christ as Lord and Saviour.

He declared that his obedience was shown in the way he proclaimed the gospel to the Jews at Damascus, Jerusalem, and all Judea, and also to the Gentiles, that they should repent, turn to God, and then do works worthy of repentance.

"To repent" means to change the mind, not in a superficial way but a deep change that affects one's fundamental attitudes. Christians once loved darkness, now they love the light of the gospel, the light of Christ (John 3:19). They once loved the world and the things in the world, now their love is given to the Lord and to His people as they reach out in love to the lost (1 John 2:15). They were careless about sin before, but now they realize that all sin is against God and they seek first His kingdom (rule) and His righteousness (Matthew 6:33).

Christians must also turn to God. If they truly repent, they will commit their lives to God and cultivate a trusting relationship with Him. Their repentance, if it is genuine, will be shown by works or deeds worthy of repentance. The Greek verb here also indicates this must be ongoing. Believers must keep on doing works or deeds worthy of the changed minds and attitudes they profess.

**21. for these causes the Jews caught me in the temple:** . . . That is why, —TCNT . . . It was on this account that, —WEYM . . . For these very things the Jews arrested me, —WLMS . . . On account of these facts the Jews grabbed me, —BRKL . . . the Jews seized me in the Temple, —PHLP.
**and went about to kill me:** . . . and kept on trying, —WLMS . . . and made attempts upon my life, —TCNT.

**26:21.** Paul then declared it was because of this message, which included blessings for the Gentiles, that the Jews seized him in the temple and attempted to kill him.

Paul's words emphasized this was a violent arrest and that the Jews in the temple were really trying to murder him. He wanted Agrippa to know the Jewish leaders were not orderly, nor were the Jews giving him a fair trial as they claimed they were.

**22. Having therefore obtained help of God:** . . . To this day I have received help from God himself, —PHLP . . . And so, by God's help, —BB . . . But God helped me, —EVRD.
**I continue unto this day:** . . . to this very day and so stand here, —TCNT . . . I have stood firm until now, —WEYM . . . and is still helping me today, —EVRD.
**witnessing both to small and great:** . . . and have solemnly exhorted, —WEYM . . . and bear my testimony to high and low alike, —TCNT . . . telling all people what I have seen, —EVRD.
**saying none other things than those which the prophets and Moses did say should come:** . . . saying nothing beyond, —WMCK . . . claiming nothing else than, —NORL . . . without adding a word to what the Prophets, as well as Moses, declared should happen, —TCNT . . . But I am saying nothing new . . . what Moses and the prophets said would happen, —EVRD . . . adding nothing to what the prophets and Moses foretold

should take place, —PHLP . . . never uttering a single syllable beyond, —MOFT.

**26:22.** God's help was indeed with Paul in all that followed. At every step along the way, Paul was able to witness (give testimony to Christ) to both small and great, that is, to those of little importance in the eyes of the world as well as to those who had great position and power. In this way he had continued (stood firm) to that very day. His witnessing was now being directed to the great ones present at this hearing, especially to King Agrippa.

Paul's witness was not limited to his own experience, however. Again he emphasized that everything he said was only what the prophets and Moses had already said would come. His total message was based on the Old Testament Scriptures. He consistently proclaimed the gospel out of the Old Testament. He was faithful to the same Scriptures the Jews who tried to kill him professed to believe.

Paul encouraged others to be faithful to the same Word of God. He had the Old Testament Scriptures in mind when he told Timothy to "Study (be eager, be zealous, make every effort, do your utmost) to show thyself approved unto God, a workman that needeth not to be ashamed, rightly dividing (cutting a straight path for and refusing to be turned aside from) the word of truth" (2 Timothy 2:15).

**23. That Christ should suffer:** . . . how that the Christ was to be a suffering Christ, —WEYM . . . the Suffering Messiah, —FNTN . . . would be a sufferer, —WLSN . . . would die, —EVRD.
**and that he should be the first that should rise from the dead:** . . . and being the first to rise from the dead, —WEYM . . . from death, —EVRD.
**and should shew light unto the people, and to the Gentiles:** . . . he would declare the word of light, —WMCK . . . he was destined to be the first to bring news of light, —TCNT . . . he was to proclaim a message of light both to the Jewish people and to the Gentiles, —WEYM . . . would communicate light, —WLSN . . . would bring light to the Jewish and non-Jewish people, —EVRD . . . and so proclaim the message of light both to our people, —PHLP.

**26:23.** Paul showed how the Scriptures declared Christ (the Messiah, God's anointed Prophet, Priest, and King) must suffer. They also showed how He, as the first to be resurrected from the dead, would proclaim light to the people (the Jews) and to the Gentiles (the nations).

With this Paul came back to the heart of the gospel: the resurrection of Jesus is the guarantee that God will raise believers from the dead.

In 1 Corinthians 15:20 Paul called Jesus the firstfruits. That is, he pictured the resurrection of the just, which Jesus called the resurrection to life (John 5:29) and John called the first resurrection (Revelation 20:5), as a harvest. The believers' resurrection, which comes at the time when the dead in Christ will rise first (1 Thessalonians 4:16, 17), is part of the same harvest, that is, it is part of the same resurrection. This only recognizes the scriptural order: "Christ the firstfruits; afterward they that are Christ's at his coming." Revelation 20:4 adds the further truth that the tribulation martyrs are also part of the same resurrection. They could be thought of as gleanings after the main part of the harvest, and therefore the final part of that harvest. The rest of the dead do not live again (are not resurrected) until after the Millennium (Revelation 20:5, 11, 15). This message is part of the light of Christ for Jews and Gentiles alike.

**24. And as he thus spake for himself;** As he was defending himself in this way, −BECK...And when he made his answer in these words, −BB...At this point in Paul's defence, −WMCK

**Festus said with a loud voice:** . . . Festus exclaimed in a loud voice, −WEYM...Festus burst out, −PHLP.

**Paul, thou art beside thyself:** . . . Paul, you are raving mad, −MNTG...Paul, you are out of your mind, −BB . . . Paul, you are insane! −NORL . . . You're crazy, Paul! −BECK...You are going crazy, Paul! −WLMS...you are distracted, −CMPB.

**much learning doth make thee mad:** . . . Much scripture, −CNDT...That great learning, −WLMS...Your great study, −KLGS...is turning your brain, −WEYM...has made you unbalanced, −BB . . . All this learning is driving you mad, −WMCK...your excessive study has turned you to frenzy, −BRKL.

**26:24.** This was powerful preaching. Festus felt its conviction and reacted against it by interrupting Paul. Shouting out loudly, he said, "You are raving mad, Paul. Your much learning is turning you into a raving madman." By "much learning" he meant "many writings." He was referring to the Old Testament Scriptures about which Paul had been speaking. He meant it was Paul's (and the Jews') Bible that was turning Paul into a raving maniac right before his eyes.

For the first time Festus was experiencing what the energizing and anointing of the Holy Spirit can do, and he did not understand it. It astonished him. It also made him uncomfortable.

Many of the Romans and Greeks followed philosophies which taught them to have a contempt for the body. This made the very idea of the resurrection of the body abhorrent to them. None of their mythologies or philosophies had any place for bodily resurrection.

**25. But he said, I am not mad, most noble Festus:**...No, your Excellency, −WMCK...I am not out of my mind, −BRKL.

**but speak forth the words of truth and soberness:**...on the contrary, the statements that I am making are true and sober, −TCNT...I am speaking words of sober truth, −WEYM...the straight truth, −WLMS...of truth and rectitude, −MRDK...speaking the truth in all soberness, −WMCK

**26:25.** Paul replied in a very courteous manner: "I do not speak as a madman, most excellent Festus, but I utter forth (anointed by the Holy Spirit) words (Greek, *rhēmata*, the plural of *rhēma*) of truth and sound good sense" (literal). "Speak (utter) forth" is a form of the same Greek word used in 2:4 where the 120 spoke in other tongues as the Spirit gave "utterance", and which is used also in 2:14 where Peter proclaimed (uttered forth) a message that was the expression of a prophetic gift given by the Holy Spirit. The word used here shows that Paul, in expressing these ideas, was speaking directly under the inspiration of the Holy Spirit. The prophetic anointing which was on the words of Paul demanded a response of faith, rather than the reaction given by Festus.

**26. For the king knoweth of these things:**...Why, the king is well aware of this! −MOFT...The King understands these things, −WMCK

**before whom also I speak freely:** . . . To the king I can speak without the slightest hesitation, −MOFT...speak boldly, −ALFD.

**for I am persuaded:**...I am sure, −TCNT...I do not believe, −WEYM.

**that none of these things are hidden from him:**...that any detail of them has escaped his notice, −WEYM . . . none of these things escaped him, −CNFT...that he has failed to notice any of them, −WMCK

**for this thing was not done in a corner:**...some obscure corner, −NORL.

**26:26.** The fact that Paul's words were sound good sense, not mad ravings, was something others could verify. King Agrippa knew of these things. He could verify them if he wished to do so.

With this Paul turned his attention again to the king. Paul could speak boldly (and freely) to him, for he was persuaded that none of these things were hidden to him (or had escaped his notice), for this (the facts of Christ's death and resurrection, the events of the gospel) had not been done in a corner. They were done publicly and were well known.

The origin of many cults and heathen religions is shrouded in the mists of fancy and legend, but not the origin of Christianity. Eyewitnesses accurately recorded its beginnings.

Even the Pharisees recognized the tremendous effect of the teaching, ministry, and miracles of Jesus for they said, "Behold (look!), the world is gone after him" (John 12:19). The preaching of the gospel also had a tremendous effect, so much so that the unbelieving Jews and their conspirators accused Paul and Silas of turning the inhabited world upside down (17:6). Truly, these things were "not done in a corner." King Agrippa could not help but know of them.

**27. King Agrippa, believest thou the prophets?:** ... do you believe the Prophets, —WEYM ... Hast thou faith, —RTHM.

**I know that thou believest:** ... I know you do, —TCNT ... I am sure you believe, —WMCK ... know you believe that, —FNTN.

**26:27.** Then Paul addressed Agrippa in a very pointed manner, asking him if he believed the prophets. Without waiting for an answer, he added that he knew the king believed.

As a Jew, under other circumstances King Agrippa would not have hesitated to say he believed the prophets. That is, he recognized the prophetic books of the Old Testament as part of the Jewish sacred books. But he might have hesitated at this time. To admit that he believed the prophets would mean, in this context, he approved Paul's message and believed the gospel. Paul did not give him a chance to hesitate.

**28. Then Agrippa said unto Paul:** ... answered, —WEYM ... But Agrippa turned to Paul, —BRKL ... returned Agrippa, —PHLP.

**Almost thou persuadest me to be a Christian:** ... You are with a little effort convincing enough to make me a Christian, —BRKL ... Much more of this ... and you will be making me a Christian, —PHLP ... In brief, you are confident that you can make me a Christian, —WEYM ... you are trying to persuade me and make a Christian of me! —WLMS ... In short, you are doing your best to persuade me to become a Christian, —MNTG ... you are persuading me, —KLGS ... Much more of this, Paul ... and you will be making me a Christian! —PHLP ... You are not taking long to persuade me to become a Christian, —WMCK ... almost persuade me to be made, —FNTN.

**26:28.** Suddenly, and with surprise, Agrippa realized Paul was trying to convert him. It overwhelmed him that Paul would be trying to get him to make a commitment to the truth of Christ and to all Paul was saying about Jesus and the resurrection.

Agrippa's reply has been translated and interpreted in a number of ways by Bible-believing scholars. Some ancient manuscripts read literally, "In (by) a little, you seek to persuade me to be a Christian." Some take this to be an admission

that King Agrippa was almost persuaded to be a Christian.

Other ancient Greek manuscripts read, "In (by) a little, you seek to persuade me to act a Christian," that is, act the part of a Christian. Many Bible scholars take this as a rejection, that he did not want Paul to use him to corroborate the gospel.

"In (by) a little" could also mean "in brief" or "in a few words." Or it may mean "in a very short time." Thus some Bible scholars say Agrippa meant "in brief, you are seeking to persuade me to become a Christian," and they interpret this simply as an expression of surprise. Others interpret the reply as irony: "In so short a time do you really think you can persuade me to become a Christian (act, live like a Christian)?" Still others take Agrippa's words to be a sharp rejection: "In brief, you are trying to persuade me to act (play the part of) a Christian." Whatever the translation, it is clear Agrippa was rejecting Paul's efforts to convert him and was closing his heart and mind to the conviction of the Holy Spirit.

**29. And Paul said, I would to God, that not only thou:** ... Paul replied, —FNTN ... I could pray God, —HBIE ... Long or not, I wish to God, —WMCK ... whether in brief or at length, —WEYM ... whether it means 'much more' or 'only a little,' —PHLP.

**but also all that hear me this day, were both almost, and altogether:** .... all who listen to me ... might become in every respect, —FNTN.

**such as I am, except these bonds:** ... just what I am myself except for these chains, —TCNT ... might stand where I stand but without these chains, —PHLP ... in my condition not including these shackles, —BRKL ... except for these handcuffs, —WMCK

**26:29.** Paul, however, refused to be discouraged. He replied, "I pray to God that both in brief or at length (or in a great degree), not only you, but all who are listening to me today might become such as I am (that is, a Christian like me), except for these chains" (literal). It is possible that at this point Paul held up his hands to show the chains on his wrists.

**30. And when he had thus spoken, the king rose up, and the governor, and Bernice:** ... Then the king rose to his feet and so did, —PHLP ... as well as the governor, —FNTN.

**and they that sat with them:** ... all that were seated, —WMCK ... with their retinue, —KLST ... and the rest of the company, —NAB.

**26:30.** Paul's courtesy and dignity in his reply still did not convince Agrippa. But he realized that when Paul said that whether in brief or in great measure (or, in a short or a long time, easily or with difficulty), Paul was putting Agrippa on trial, and Agrippa did not like that. He had heard enough. So he stood up, thus indicating the hearing was over.

**31. And when they were gone aside:**...and stepping to one side, —BRKL, —MLNT...retired from the assembly, —PHLP...and withdrawing, —FNTN...After they had left the chamber, —NAB...when they had left the hall, —WMCK...and left the room, —EVRD.

**they talked between themselves, saying:**...discussed the case among themselves, —TCNT...they discussed the matter among themselves and agreed, —PHLP...they said to one another, —WMCK...They were talking to each other, —EVRD...they kept talking the matter over, saying, —KLST...they talked matters over among themselves and admitted, NAB...they talked it over together and concluded, —MLNT.

**This man doeth nothing worthy of death or of bonds:**...There is nothing...deserving death or imprisonment in this man's conduct, —TCNT...There is no reason why this man should die or be put in jail, —EVRD...is engaged in no activity that deserves, —KLST...punishable by death or even imprisonment, —NORL...or prison, —MLNT.

**26:31.** Then they all went out and discussed the hearing. All agreed Paul had done nothing worthy of death or imprisonment. Nothing in Roman law could hold him guilty.

It is probable too they were all feeling uncomfortable because of the conviction of the Holy Spirit. Though Paul addressed Agrippa directly, Festus was affected, and probably the others also. Paul's testimony had the ring of truth to it. They could not deny that the appearance of Christ in His resurrection glory had made a tremendous change in the apostle Paul. They did not try to deny either that the Old Testament Scriptures prophesied the death and resurrection of Jesus and upheld the truth of the gospel. These truths were in their minds, but they did not discuss them.

**32. Then said Agrippa unto Festus:** ... Agrippa remarked to Festus, —PHLP ... further remarked, —NAB.

**This man might have been set at liberty:**...He might easily have been discharged, —PHLP ... We could let this man go free, —EVRD ... This man could have been released, —TNT ... set free, —MNTG.

**if he had not appealed unto Caesar:**...but he has asked Caesar to hear his case, —EVRD ... to the Emperor, —FNTN.

**26:32.** Agrippa told Festus that Paul might have been set free if he had not appealed to Caesar. In fact, Agrippa was really saying Paul could and should have been set free. In other words, Festus was wrong in not setting Paul free at once after the hearing.

Agrippa implied also that the emperor would recognize Paul's innocence too and would have to set him free. Though Nero was the emperor

in A.D. 59, he had not yet embarked on any campaign against the Christians. Under Roman law at this time it was not a crime to be a Christian. Not until Paul's second imprisonment did it become dangerous under the Romans to be a Christian.

It seems from this also that the appeal to Caesar had already been signed and sealed, or at least officially registered, so it was necessary to go through with it. Some Bible students have wondered if Paul had second thoughts now that he knew his appeal to Caesar was the only thing that kept him from being set free. But Paul must have been convinced it was God's will for him to make that appeal. He always obeyed the voice of the Spirit, so he was confident the Spirit was guiding him and was not disturbed. As he told the Philippians, he had learned in whatever state he was to be content, that is, to be content in the sense of being able to keep on an even keel and being able to maintain his purpose to serve God. He never gave up. He never gave way to discouragement (Philippians 4:11). Christ was his strength in every situation. Christ was his sufficient source of supply.

## Chapter 27

**1. And when it was determined that we should sail into Italy:**...As it was decided that, —TCNT...As soon as it was decided that we should sail away to, —PHLP...should sail for, —KLST.

**they delivered Paul and certain other prisoners unto one named Julius:** ... Paul and some other prisoners were put in charge of, —TCNT...they committed ... some other prisoners, —MLNT...they handed over Paul and a few other prisoners into the custody of Julius, an officer of the Augustan battalion, —WEYM.

**a centurion of Augustus' band:**...from the cohort known as, —NAB...a captain of the Augustan Cohort, —MLNT...who served in the Emperor's army, —EVRD...an imperial regiment, —NORL.

**27:1.** It was not long before arrangements were made for Paul's journey to Rome to present his appeal to Caesar. This account of Paul's journey to Rome gives one of the most interesting and factual accounts of a sea voyage and a shipwreck to be found anywhere in ancient literature. Luke uses "we" throughout the passage, so it is clear he accompanied Paul and was an eyewitness to it all.

For the trip from Caesarea to Italy, Paul and other prisoners were turned over to a centurion named Julius who belonged to the cohort of Augustus, a cohort directly responsible to the emperor. "Cohort I Augustus" had its headquarters in Bananaea in northeastern Palestine, east of the southern end of the Sea of Galilee, in the territory of King Agrippa II. From the kindness Julius showed Paul some have speculated he might have been present at Paul's trial before King Agrippa. Others speculate he may have known the Roman centurion Cornelius who was converted and filled with the Spirit when Peter came to Caesarea years before. Or it may be that, like other centurions mentioned in the New Testament, he had visited Jewish synagogues and was impressed by the worship of the one true God. (See Mark 15:39; Luke 7:2-10.) He had soldiers under him who were sent along to guard the prisoners (verse 42).

**2. And entering into a ship of Adramyttium:** ...And going on board, *—RTHM*...We boarded a ship from, NAB...We embarked on a ship sailing from Adramyttium, *—PHLP.*

**we launched, meaning to sail by the coasts of Asia:** ...that would make the ports along the coast, *—MLNT*...bound for ports in the province of, NAB...about to sail along the coasts of Asia, we put to sea, *—HBIE*...that was going to sail to the ports on the coast of the province of Asia, and we started out, *—BECK.*

**one Aristarchus, a Macedonian of Thessalonica, being with us:** ...went with us, *—TCNT.*

**27:2.** Paul sailed on three different ships on this journey to Rome. They first took passage on a ship belonging to Adramyttium. It was headed up the coast of Asia Minor.

Luke took passage on this ship to be with Paul. So did Aristarchus, a Macedonian believer from Thessalonica. They went along to help Paul and to serve him in every way possible. It must have been a comfort for Paul to have Christian companions with him on this rather long sea voyage.

**3. And the next day we touched at Sidon:** ...And on the next day we put into Zidon, *—RTHM*...landed at, *—HBIE*...docked at, *—BRKL*...made a stop at, *—NORL*...we put in at, *—NAB.*

**And Julius courteously entreated Paul:** ...in a friendly manner, *—TCNT*...with thoughtful kindness, *—WEYM*...treating Paul kindly, *—MLNT*...humanely, *—HBIE.*

**and gave him liberty to go unto his friends:** ...and allowed him to go to see his friends, *—TCNT*...to visit his friends, *—WEYM*...and permitted him, *—HBIE.*

**to refresh himself:** ...and receive their hospitality, *—TCNT*...and enjoy their care, *—WEYM*...who cared for his needs, *—NAB.*

**27:3.** The next day the ship docked at the port of Sidon, 67 miles north of the starting point (Caesarea). There, Julius, treating Paul with humanitarian kindness, permitted him to go to his Christian friends to obtain care. He was allowed to stay with them until the ship was ready to sail again. To Paul this must have seemed further evidence of the providence of God. God was with him; God

was guiding. It was not by chance that he was on his way to Rome.

This is the only mention of Paul's stopping at Sidon. It seems quite clear Paul had not founded the church there. But it is certain there was a well-established church in the city. The church in Sidon is just another evidence that what happened when Philip visited Samaria (chapter 8) was happening in all directions as others spread the good news after the death of Stephen. The believers in Sidon knew of Paul, and it may be that some of Paul's converts now lived there.

**4. And when we had launched from thence:** ...After setting sail from there, *—WLMS*...Putting to sea from there, *—MLNT*...putting out from, *—NAB.*

**we sailed under Cyprus, because the winds were contrary:** ...we had to sail under the lee of Cyprus, as the wind was against us, *—MOFT*...we sailed along the south coast of Cyprus, *—BRKL*...and sailed close to the island of, *—EVRD.*

**27:4.** The Bible does not tell us how long the ship stayed at Sidon. It may have taken several days to unload or load cargo and take care of the shipowner's business.

Then from Sidon they put out to sea and sailed under the lee of the island of Cyprus, battling contrary westerly winds. Normally they would have sailed directly northwest from Sidon to Myra, the next port of call for this ship. But the westerly winds forced them to take the longer route east and then north of the island. Since Cyprus is about 141 miles long, this took them a considerable distance out of their way.

**5. And when we had sailed over the sea of Cilicia and Pamphylia:** ...and, after crossing the sea of, *—TCNT*...and, sailing the whole length of the sea that lies off, *—WEYM*...the deep sea, *—PNT*...steering across the open sea, *—FNTN*...went across the sea, *—EVRD.*

**we came to Myra, a city of Lycia:** ...we reached Myra in Lycia, *—TCNT*...we landed at, *—BRKL.*

**27:5.** The north side of Cyprus brought them opposite the coast of Cilicia, Paul's native province. After sailing along the coast of Cilicia and the coast of the next province, Pamphylia, they came to the port of Myra in the next province, Lycia. This was almost directly across the Mediterranean from Alexandria in Egypt. Myra was built on a cliff about 2 miles from the seacoast. Its seaport was an important stopping place for ships from Egypt and Cyprus. Its ruins are better preserved than most of those of the ancient cities of that region. They indicate it was a very prosperous city. From it a gorge leads into the rugged interior. In some parts of the province high mountains come down almost to the sea. It had been a Roman province since A.D. 53. Myra, for a time, was its capital and one of its chief trading centers.

**6. And there the centurion found a ship of Alexandria sailing into Italy:** . . . There the sergeant found a ship, –WMCK . . . on her way to Italy, –TCNT . . . bound for Italy, –WEYM.

**and he put us therein:** . . . and put us on board of her, –TCNT . . . transferred us to that, –BRKL.

**27:6.** At Myra, the centurion transferred Paul and the other prisoners (as well as Luke and Aristarchus) to a ship from Alexandria that was sailing to Italy with a cargo of wheat. (See verse 38.)

Egypt was the chief source of wheat for the city of Rome, and the ships that carried wheat were considered very important. Most of the wheat grown in Egypt was a bearded wheat with multiple heads on the same stalk, rather than the ordinary wheat with a single head, which was the variety commonly grown in Palestine.

Alexandria (founded in the year 332 B.C.) had an excellent harbor. Normally the grain ships would sail directly from its port to Puteoli on the north shore of the Bay of Naples in Italy. But the same contrary westerly winds that caused the first ship to take the lee side of Cyprus had most probably forced this ship off its course so that it stopped at Myra. Otherwise the centurion might have had to wait some time for a ship going to Italy.

Since ancient peoples ate very little meat, bread was the most important article of their diet. The poor in Palestine would eat the cheaper barley bread. But even the poor in Rome wanted wheat bread. With its increased population as the capital of the empire, Egyptian wheat became very important.

**7. And when we had sailed slowly many days:** . . . For several days our progress was slow, –TCNT . . . For several days we beat slowly to windward, –PHLP.

**and scarce were come over against Cnidus:** . . . and it was only with difficulty that we arrived off Cnidus, –TCNT . . . and only just succeeded, –PHLP . . . we had a hard time reaching, –EVRD.

**the wind not suffering us:** . . . As the wind was still unfavorable, –TCNT . . . Then, since the wind was still blowing against us, –PHLP . . . checked our progress, –MOFT.

**we sailed under Crete, over against Salmone:** . . . we ran under the lee of Crete off Salmone, –WEYM . . . we sailed south of Crete off Salmone, –BRKL . . . So we sailed by the south side of the island of, –EVRD.

**27:7.** The winds continued to be contrary, so they sailed very slowly westward along the south coast of Asia Minor trying to reach the port of

Cnidus on the coast of Caria at the southwest point of Asia Minor. The captain probably hoped to reach it, but contrary winds from the northwest forced them southward until they came under the lee of the island of Crete off the promontory of Salmone at the eastern tip of the island.

**8. And, hardly passing it:** . . . And with difficulty, by keeping close in shore, –TCNT . . . And though hardly making any headway, –NORL . . . We sailed along the coast, but the sailing was hard,

**came unto a place which is called The fair havens:** . . . we reached a place called, –TCNT . . . Fair Harbours, –WMCK . . . Safe Harbors, –EVRD.

**nigh whereunto was the city of Lasea:** . . . near the town of Lasea, –WEYM . . . with the town of Lasea near it, –WMCK

**27:8.** Crete is a 160-mile-long island southeast of Greece. A mountain chain runs through it from east to west, which may have given some protection from the force of the winds. They sailed about half the length of the island to reach Fair Havens, near the island's most southerly point. Its harbor was a small bay easily entered from the east but with two small islands blocking it on the southwest. Lasea was 5 miles to the east and would be the only source of food and supplies. Some authorities call Fair Havens just a "roadstead," a place where ships could ride at anchor, rather than a real harbor.

**9. Now when much time was spent:** . . . And when a considerable time had passed, –RTHM . . . After considerable delay there, –FNTN . . . we had lost much time, –EVRD . . . It was now far on in the season, –WMCK

**and when sailing was now dangerous:** . . . and the navigation being now unsafe, –WEYM . . . and the journey was now full of danger, –BB . . . and the voyage had become dangerous, –WMCK . . . was now hazardous, –CMPB.

**because the fast was now already past:** . . . it was late in the year, –BB . . . day of fasting had already gone by, –BECK . . . Day of Atonement, –TEV . . . autumn fast was already over, –WMCK . . . it was already after the Day of Cleansing, –EVRD.

**Paul admonished them:** . . . Paul began to advise, –RTHM . . . and so Paul gave this warning, –TCNT.

**27:9.** Because considerable time had passed due to the strong winds that forced them off their course, "the fast" had gone by. By "the fast" Luke meant the Day of Atonement on the 10th day of the 7th month of the Jewish year. This was the only fast commanded by the law of Moses and it lasted just the 1 day. During the Babylonian exile some of the poor Jews left in Palestine had added other fast days to commemorate the destruction of the temple by Nebuchadnezzar and the assassination of the Jewish governor, Gedaliah. But Zechariah prophesied that it was God's purpose to turn their fasts into joyful feasts (Zechariah 8:19). Thus, in New Testament times, the Day of Atonement remained the only fast.

In A.D. 59 the Day of Atonement was on October 5, and Paul recognized that since this had gone by it would be dangerous to continue their voyage. He was an experienced traveler and had been in three shipwrecks already (2 Corinthians 11:25). He knew how dangerous winter storms could be. In fact, he had spent a night and a day adrift on the open sea after one of those shipwrecks.

Sailing was actually considered dangerous on the Mediterranean Sea after September 14. Storms were more frequent, and the sky was so often overcast they could not see the stars and navigation was difficult. Most ships therefore spent the winter in a safe harbor.

**10. And said unto them, Sirs, I perceive:** . . . My friends, I see, —TCNT.

**that this voyage will be with hurt and much damage:** . . . with danger and heavy loss, —WEYM . . . there will be a lot of trouble on this trip, —EVRD . . . will involve hardship and considerable damage, —BRKL . . . end in disaster and great loss, —NORL.

**not only of the lading and ship:** . . . not only of the cargo and of the ship, —RTHM . . . The ship and the things in the ship will be lost, —EVRD.

**but also of our lives:** . . . but to our lives, —WMCK . . . Even our lives may be lost! —EVRD.

**27:10.** Paul went to those in charge of the ship and advised them of the certainty of injury and great loss to the ship and its cargo, as well as danger to their lives, if they continued on. Paul's perception here undoubtedly came not only from his experience, but also from the leading of the Spirit. He was always sensitive to the Holy Spirit, and here he felt a strong sense of disaster ahead. Thus he dared to go and volunteer his advice.

**11. Nevertheless the centurion believed:** . . . paid more attention to, —RSV . . . was more persuaded by, —RTHM . . . put his faith in, —NORL . . . was convinced by, —TEV . . . But the sergeant had more confidence in. —WMCK

**the master and the owner of the ship:** . . . the captain and the owner, —TCNT . . . the navigator, —CNDT . . . the skipper, —WUST.

**more than those things which were spoken by Paul:** . . . rather than by Paul's arguments, —WEYM . . . rather than in Paul's suggestions, —BRKL.

**27:11.** The centurion seems to be the one really in charge. This gives confirmation to the suggestion that this ship was part of the imperial grain fleet that had as its chief business the carrying of wheat from Alexandria to Italy. Most of these ships were quite large for that day: as much as 180

feet long by 45 feet wide with a capacity of over 1,200 tons.

The ship had a "master" who was the shipmaster in the sense of directing or steering the ship. Today he would be considered the pilot. It also had a captain. The Greek term could mean the captain was the owner of the ship. But since the ship was in the state service of *the* empire, the same term was applied to the captain even though he was not the actual owner. Instead of listening to Paul, the centurion Julius was persuaded by the pilot and the captain to keep going.

**12. And because the haven was not commodious to winter in:** . . . was not fit, —WLMS . . . And that harbor was not a good place for the ship to stay for the winter, —EVRD . . . Moreover, since the harbor is unsuitable for a ship to winter in, —PHLP . . . was not well situated, —HBIE . . . was ill-adapted for, —PNT . . . was badly placed, —MOFT.

**the more part advised to depart thence also:** . . . the majority were in favour of continuing the voyage, —TCNT . . . So most of the men decided that the ship should leave, —EVRD.

**if by any means they might attain to Phenice:** . . . The men hoped we could go to Phoenix, —EVRD . . . in the hope of being able to reach Phoenix, —TCNT . . . on the chance, —RSV.

**and there to winter:** . . . for the winter, —BB.

**which is an haven of Crete:** . . . a harbour of Crete, —TCNT.

**and lieth toward the south west and north west:** . . . facing, —WEYM . . . open to the northeast and southeast, —TCNT.

**27:12.** The chief argument against staying in Fair Havens was simply that the harbor was poor, unfavorably situated, and therefore unsuitable to winter in. Apparently, others joined in the discussion and the majority gave counsel to try to reach Phoenix, a harbor which was better located whether the winds came from the northwest or from the southwest.

Phoenix (Phenice, Phinika, Greek, Phoinix, "palm tree"; also the name of the fabled bird of Egypt) was on the south coast of Crete, west of Lasea, over 50 miles west of Fair Havens.

There has been some question about the identification of Phoenix. However, there was only one safe harbor in that part of Crete which was large enough for the imperial grain ships to winter in, and that is at or beside the village of Loutro, directly north of the small island of Cauda. All of the ancient writers who mention Phoenix agree it was in the area of Loutro. Archaeologists have found an inscription from the reign of the emperor Trajan that shows grain ships from Egypt often wintered there.

The harbor at Loutro is open toward the northeast and toward the southeast. This presents a difficulty because the Greek in this verse normally means "open to the southwest and open to the northwest." However, Luke may have been thinking of how it would look to the sailors coming into the harbor.

Some writers have suggested another reason Paul might have desired to stay in Fair Havens was the fact that the city of Gortyna, not much more than a dozen miles away, had a large Jewish population where he could have done some missionary work. Jews in Gortyna had been protected by the Romans since 141 B.C. It may be also that the officers of the ship wanted to go to Phoenix where other ships would be. But the chief concern seems to have been the finding of a safer harbor.

**13. And when the south wind blew softly:** ... So when a light wind sprang up from the south, —TCNT ... When a light breeze from the south began to blow, —WLMS.

**supposing that they had obtained their purpose:** ... so that they supposed they were now sure of their purpose, —WEYM ... thinking their purpose was about to be realized, —WLMS ... found their opportunity, —TCNT ... thinking they had obtained just what they wanted, —PHLP ... they felt they could easily make it, —BECK ... This is the wind we wanted, —SEB.

**loosing thence:** . . . they weighed anchor, —RSV ... they let the ship go, —BB.

**they sailed close by Crete:** ... and kept along the coast of Crete, close in shore, —TCNT ... and coasted along, hugging the shores of Crete, —PHLP . . . very close to the island, —EVRD.

**27:13.** The ship remained in the bay of Fair Havens as long as the northwest winds continued to blow. After a time the direction of the winds changed and a gentle wind came from the southwest. This persuaded the centurion and the other officers they could fulfill their purpose and make it to Phoenix. So they sailed west, keeping close to the south coast of Crete. Paul was not convinced. He undoubtedly had that spiritual sensitivity that let him know there was danger ahead. But the centurion only looked at the immediate present and thought he could take advantage of the pleasant weather.

**14. But not long after:** ... But shortly afterwards, —TCNT ... But before long, —PHLP.

**there arose against it a tempestuous wind, called Euroclydon:** ... a hurricane came down on us off the land, —TCNT ... a furious northeast wind, coming down from the mountains, burst upon us, —WEYM ... a terrific gale, —NORL ... a typhoon, —RTHM ... a very strong wind named the "Northeaster" came from the island, —EVRD.

**27:14.** It was not long before Paul's prediction came true. A vehement, turbulent wind

called Euroclydon rushed against them from the east-northeast.

"Euroclydon" seems to mean "the southeast wind that stirs up waves." Another spelling is *eurukludōn*, "the wind that stirs up broad waves." *Eurakulōn* was a word developed by the sailors of these ships from the Greek *euros* and the Latin *aquilo* as a name for a violent northeast wind.

**15. And when the ship was caught:** ... The ship was snatched along by it, —WLMS ... This wind took the ship and carried it away, —EVRD.

**and could not bear up into the wind:** ... and since she could not be brought up into, —PHLP ... so, unable to head against, —BRKL ... couldn't face, —BECK ... could not sail against it, —EVRD.

**we let her drive:** ... so we had to give way and let her drive before it, —TCNT ... so we gave up and let her drift, —BRKL ... we let her go and were borne along, —RTHM . . . we surrendered, —WLSN . . . we stopped trying and let the wind blow us, —EVRD.

**27:15.** This violent northeast wind caught the ship in its grip and drove it away from the shores of Crete. The sailors tried to make the ship face into the land, but the wind was too strong.

The Greek indicates the wind caught the ship and literally tore it away from its projected course toward Phoenix. The same word is used of the demoniac who was seized by a violent unclean spirit (Luke 8:29). The ship was completely under the control of this wind, and the sailors were totally unable to do anything about it. They could only give themselves up to the wind and let themselves be driven wildly. Some have compared them to a kite in a windstorm. The ship must have been tossed like a cork on the waves.

The apostle Paul did not say "I told you so!" right away. It was quite obvious now that he was right and that the centurion, pilot, and captain had been wrong. No doubt, by the time the sailors gave up and let the ship be driven by the wind, they were all exhausted and this was no time to say anything.

Paul, however, even with all the danger must have had a deep peace in his heart and mind. He still had the assurance given by Jesus himself that he would bear witness in Rome. No storm, no wind or waves could rob him of that promise from His Lord. He knew Christ was with him, and the Holy Spirit gave him peace in the midst of the storm.

**16. And running under a certain island which is called Clauda:** ... As we passed under the shelter of, —NORL ... We went below a small island named, —EVRD.

**we had much work to come by the boat:** ... we were able, though it was hard work, to make the ship's boat safe, —*BB* . . . Then we were able to bring in the lifeboat, but it was very hard to do, —*EVRD*.

**27:16.** The wind kept driving the ship toward the southwest. After several hours it brought them close along the south side of the small island of Clauda. It was also called Cauda, or Kauda, and in later times was known as Gaudos, Gavdhos, Gozzo, and more recently as Gaudho.

Clauda was about 23 miles from where the storm first hit them. In the lee of the island they found a little temporary relief from the full force of the storm. Even then it was with difficulty that they regained control over the small boat that was being towed behind the ship.

17. **Which when they had taken up:** . . . and after hoisting it on a board, —*TCNT*.

**they used helps, undergirding the ship:** . . . they put cords under and round the ship, —*BB* . . . to reinforce it, —*BECK* . . . tied ropes around the ship to hold it together. —*EVRD*.

**and, fearing lest they should fall into the quicksands:** . . . But, afraid of being driven on to the Syrtis Sands, —*TCNT* . . . Fearing they would run on the great sandbank near Africa, —*BECK*.

**strake sail:** . . . lowered the sail, —*WLMS*.

**and so were driven:** . . . and went running before the wind, —*BB* . . . drifted under bare poles, —*TCNT*.

**27:17.** After the sailors hoisted the small boat onto the deck of the ship, they used "helps" to undergird the ship. They fastened strong ropes or cables vertically around the ship to try to keep the timbers from straining too much or giving way because of the violence of the wind and waves.

The slight protection of the lee of the island of Clauda was soon behind them. Then, because there was no sign of the storm letting up, they became afraid they would be driven off their course into Syrtis, a quicksand off the coast of North Africa west of the ancient city of Cyrene. So they slackened their tackle (which may mean they took down the topsail) and were carried along by the continuing force of the northeast wind.

*Quick* is Old English for "living." Thus, the quicksand here refers to sandbanks that seem alive in that they move. The ones mentioned here were a terror to the sailors of ancient times.

18. **And we being exceedingly tossed with a tempest:** . . . terribly battered, —*MOFT* . . . because we were so violently beaten, —*WLMS* . . . And still fighting the storm with all our strength, —*BB*.

**the next day they lightened the ship:** . . . began to throw the cargo overboard, —*RTHM* . . . they jettisoned, —*CNDT* . . . the freight overboard, —*MNTG*.

**27:18.** The next day, because they were still in the grip of the storm, the crew began throwing things overboard to lighten the ship so it would

ride higher and not be swamped by the worsening waves. Usually they would begin by throwing part of the cargo overboard. But this ship's cargo of wheat was so important to Rome it was the last thing they would get rid of. They probably began with personal baggage and the cabin furniture.

19. **And the third day:** . . . while two days later, —*MOFT*.

**we cast out with our own hands the tackling of the ship:** . . . flung out, —*PNT* . . . the sailing apparatus go over the side, —*BB* . . . the ship's equipment, —*BECK* . . . *the* ship's gear, —*MOFT*.

**27:19.** The third day (according to their way of counting, the day after they began throwing things overboard), with their own hands, they tossed overboard the ship's tackle (probably including the main yard that supported the mainsail).

20. **And when neither sun nor stars in many days appeared:** . . . As neither sun nor stars were visible for several days, —*TCNT* . . . And as we had not seen the sun or stars for a long time, —*BB*.

**and no small tempest lay on us:** . . . and, as the gale still continued severe, —*TCNT* . . . and the terrific gale still harassed us, —*WEYM* . . . and a great tempest still beat upon us, —*MNTG* . . . and we were still in the grip of the gale, —*PHLP*.

**all hope that we should be saved was then taken away:** . . . all hope of our being saved was at last reluctantly abandoned, —*TCNT* . . . and at last we had to give up all hope of being saved, —*MOFT* . . . the last ray of hope was now vanishing, —*WEYM* . . . wholly cut off, —*MRDK* . . . being stripped away from us, —*WUST*.

**27:20.** The storm continued many days. By comparing verse 27, which mentions the 14th night, it is probable the storm had continued 11 days at this point. Without any sighting of the sun, moon, or stars, they had no way of knowing where they were, for they had no other means of navigation.

Finally, as this great storm continued to buffet them and press upon them, all hope of rescue was stripped away. Up to this time those on the ship had maintained some hope or expectation or anticipation that something good would happen. They kept before them the prospect that the storm would come to an end, or at least that the winds would lessen and there would be a break in the clouds. But now, after furling the sails and after the grueling work of throwing overboard everything possible, they were cold, wet, and thoroughly exhausted. It is no wonder the men lost all hope and now thought all would be lost, not only the ship but their own lives as well.

21. **But after long abstinence:** . . . It was then, when they had gone a long time without food, —*TCNT* . . . . Since hardly anybody wanted to eat,

—BECK ... been long fasting, —YNG ... upon the verge of starvation, —FNTN.

**Paul stood forth in the midst of them, and said:** ... that Paul came forward, and said, —TCNT ... stood up before them, —EVRD ... among them, —NAB.

**Sirs, ye should have hearkened unto me:** ... My friends, you should have listened to me, —TCNT ... you should have taken my advice, —EVRD.

**and not have loosed from Crete:** ... I told you not to leave, —EVRD ... and not set sail from, —NAB.

**and to have gained this harm and loss:** ... and so incurred this injury and damage, —TCNT ... You would then have escaped this suffering and loss, —WEYM ... you would not have all this trouble, —EVRD ... this disastrous loss, —NAB.

**27:21.** For a long time the 276 people on the ship (see verse 37) had abstained from food. The Greek word could mean they lacked food, and some have speculated the sea water had ruined most of their food. But verses 34 to 36 indicate they still had food in good condition on board. The Greek word can also mean abstinence from food because of loss of appetite or from seasickness. Because of the storm, many must have been seasick. Even if a person is not seasick himself, the sight and odor of seasickness in others is enough to cause a well person to lose his appetite.

At this point the apostle Paul stood up in the midst of the people and reminded them of the warnings he had given them before they left Fair Havens in Crete. He was not simply saying, "I told you so." He remembered they had refused to listen to him then. He had something very important to say to them now. He wanted them to be sure to listen this time. So he caught their attention by getting them to admit (in their minds) that he was right.

Paul's manner indicated also that he did not share the despair of the rest. Paul later told Timothy God has not given believers a spirit of cowardly fear, but of power, of love, and of a sound mind, that is, of self-control (2 Timothy 1:7).

**22. And now I exhort you to be of good cheer:** ... But now I tell you, —EVRD ... And even now I advise you to cheer up, —BRKL ... Yet, even as things are, I urge you not to lose courage, —TCNT ... But now take courage, —WEYM ... keep up your courage, —NAB.

**for there shall be no loss of any man's life among you:** ... for there will not be a single life lost among you, —TCNT ... None of you will die! —EVRD ... None among you will be lost, NAB.

**but of the ship:** ... only the ship, —NAB, —TCNT ... the ship will be lost, —EVRD.

**27:22.** If Paul had not reminded the people that his previous words had proved true, they might have turned away in the bitterness of their despair and refused to listen. Now, in the midst of this

most hopeless situation, Paul began with words of renewed hope and expectation. He called them to be of good courage. Paul explained why they must keep up their courage because not one among them would lose his life. Only the ship would be lost.

**23. For there stood by me this night the angel of God:** ... For this very night, —RSV ... Last night ... God's angel said, —EVRD ... a messenger of, NAB.

**whose I am, and whom I serve:** ... This is the God I worship, and I am his, —EVRD ... whose man I am, —NAB ... to whom I belong and whom I worship, —RSV.

**27:23.** There was good reason for his encouraging words. That very night an angel of God had appeared to Paul and stood beside him. The Greek has the article here, so Paul is not referring to just any god, but to the one true God, the God to whom Paul belonged, the God Paul served.

The word "serve" here is also rendered "worship" in the King James Version. In the temple Anna worshiped God with fastings and prayers night and day (Luke 2:37). Paul worshiped and served God with his own spirit as he spread the gospel (Romans 1:9).

**24. Saying, Fear not, Paul:** ... Have no fear, Paul, —TCNT ... Dismiss all fear, Paul, —WEYM ... Stop being afraid, Paul, —WLMS ... do not be afraid! —EVRD.

**thou must be brought before Caesar:** ... You must stand before, —EVRD ... You are destined to appear before, NAB ... you must appear before the Emperor, —TCNT.

**and, lo:** ... and note this, —WEYM ... and listen! —WLMS ... and be assured, —BRKL ... Therefore, as a favor to you, —NAB ... And God has given you this promise, —EVRD.

**God hath given thee all them that sail with thee:** ... made a gift to thee, —MRDK ... God has granted safety to all who are sailing with you, NAB ... He will save the lives of all those men sailing with you, —EVRD.

**27:24.** After giving God the glory, Paul continued with the message of the angel who had told Paul to stop being afraid. It was necessary for him to come before Caesar. This, of course, was a necessity not because of Paul's appeal to Caesar, or because of the charges brought against him by the Jews. Rather, it was necessary because of the divine plan.

Up to that time all hope was lost. Paul had cooperated with those who were trying to save the ship. With his own hands he threw many things overboard. But when all seemed hopeless, Paul did not give up and do nothing. He must have found some corner where he could be alone and seek the Lord. Then he learned the truth again that angels are ministering spirits, "sent forth to minister for them who shall be heirs of salvation" (Hebrews 1:14).

Furthermore, the centurion, the pilot, and the captain had all given up hope along with the rest of the ship's crew. No one seemed to have the wisdom, knowledge, or power to bring the passengers and crew to safety. The ship would have been doomed if there had not been a man on board who still had a God-given work to do.

Then, by the grace of God, that is, by His unmerited favor, the angel gave assurance that for Paul's sake, all those on board, helpless and unworthy though they were, would be saved.

**25. Wherefore, sirs, be of good cheer:** ... Therefore, courage, my friends! *—TCNT* . . . be cheerful! *—EVRD.*

**for I believe God:** ... for I have confidence in my God, *—WLMS* . . . I trust in God, NAB.

**that it shall be even as it was told me:** ... it will all work out, NAB ... that everything will happen exactly as I have been told, *—TCNT.*

**27:25.** Paul concluded in the same way he had begun. He challenged them to keep up their spirits, to be courageous. The situation had not changed. The storm was still raging. But now they had grounds for courage, hope, and expectation—Paul's faith in God. He did not condemn them for their fears. He had shared them. But now God had spoken. They must get their eyes off the storm, off the discouraging circumstances, and fix their eyes on God.

**26. Howbeit we must be cast upon a certain island:** ... But we are to be stranded on a certain island, *—WEYM* . . . But we will crash on an island, *—EVRD* ... though we still have to face shipwreck on some island, NAB.

**27:26.** Paul then added a further revelation given by the angel. They must drift with the storm until the ship would run aground on a certain island. This word also gave further assurance that God knew the future and that Paul was not just guessing. The crew and passengers did not know where they were, but God knew where they were and where they were going. However, God did not reveal which island it was.

**27. But when the fourteenth night was come:** . . . arrived, *—MOFT* . . . It was now the fourteenth night of the storm, *—TCNT.*

**as we were driven up and down in Adria:** ... we were still being driven across the Ionian Sea, NAB ... we were floating around in the Adriatic Sea, *—EVRD.*

**about midnight the shipmen deemed:** ... when toward midnight, *—NAB*...the mariners, *—CMPB*...the

sailors suspected, *—RTHM*...sensed, *—PHLP*...began to suspect, *—NORL*...thought, *—EVRD.*

**that they drew near to some country:** ...That they were drawing near land, *—TCNT*...that we were nearing land, *—PHLP*...we were close to land, *—EVRD.*

**27:27.** On the 14th night they were still being driven by the wind in whatever direction it blew. As they later found out, they were drifting across the Sea of Adria, which is the part of the Mediterranean Sea southeast of Italy (not the Adriatic Sea).

As far as they knew, this was open sea. But about midnight the sailors supposed (had a suspicion) that they were approaching land. Some ancient manuscripts of the New Testament read that the land was resounding. In other words, the sailors thought they could hear waves breaking on the beach in the distance.

**28. And sounded:**...let down the lead, *—BB*...They took a sounding, *—NAB*...threw a rope into the water with a weight on the end, *—EVRD.*

**and found it twenty fathoms:** ... and found a depth of, NAB...and found the water 120 feet deep, *—BECK.*

**and when they had gone a little further:**...and a little further on, *—MOFT*...after sailing on a short distance, *—NAB.*

**they sounded again:**...threw the rope in again, *—EVRD.*

**and found it fifteen fathoms:**...and it was ninety feet, *—BB.*

**27:28.** The crew threw out a weighted rope to sound the depth and found it to be 20 fathoms, that is, about 120 feet or 36 meters. The fathom was originally the distance measured by the arms stretched out horizontally and it came to be standardized as 6 feet. It was used as a nautical measure of depth.

After they went a little farther, they threw out the weighted rope to sound the depth again and found it to be 15 fathoms (90 feet; about 28 meters). From this it was obvious they were indeed coming close to land of some sort.

**29. Then fearing lest we should have fallen upon rocks:**...being driven upon some rocky coast, *—TCNT*...So, for fear that we might be hurled on the rocks, *—PHLP*...lest on rough places, *—YNG*...afraid that we would hit the rocks, *—EVRD*...we should be dashed against some rock coast, *—NAB.*

**they cast four anchors out of the stern:**...they let down four hooks from the back of the ship, *—BB*...threw four anchors into the water, *—EVRD.*

**and wished for the day:**...and kept wishing for daylight to come, *—WLMS*...and longed for daylight, *—TCNT*...for break of day, *—BRKL*...and began praying, *—RTHM*...for morning to come, *—BECK*...prayed for daylight to come, *—EVRD*...and earnestly wished, *—PNT.*

**27:29.** No doubt by now the sailors could indeed hear the waves breaking on the shore. They became afraid the ship would run aground on the rocks and break up before they could escape. So they tossed out four sea anchors from the rear of the ship. These anchors were probably of iron or lead and each had two flukes shaped to catch on the sea bottom.

Since it was not long after midnight, it was still pitch dark, and there was nothing else they could do but hope the anchors would keep them from drifting nearer the rocks. Probably in the excitement no one could sleep so they all "wished for the day."

The Greek word could mean "wish." But it more commonly means they kept praying for the day to come. The King James Version translated it "pray" in 2 Corinthians 13:7 and in James 5:16. In the latter case believers are told to pray one for another. In this situation they were no doubt praying that the ship would hold together until there would be enough light to see where they were and what it might be possible for them to do. Even Paul knew he would have to put his faith into action.

**30. And as the shipmen were about to flee out of the ship:** . . . as the sailors, —ASV . . . Some of the sailors wanted to leave the ship, —EVRD . . . tried to abandon, —BRKL . . . the ship, —NORL.

**when they had let down the boat into the sea:** . . . and they got as far as letting a boat down, —PHLP . . . they let the ship's boat down, —NAB . . . lowered the lifeboat, —EVRD . . . the skiff, —CNDT.

**under colour as though they would have cast anchors out of the foreship:** . . . by pretext as though, —RTHM . . . on pretence of running out anchors from the bows, —TCNT . . . These sailors wanted the other men to think that they were throwing more anchors from the front of the ship, —EVRD.

**27:30.** The crew did more than wish and pray, however. They decided it would be dangerous to wait the several hours until the daylight, so they made an attempt to flee from the ship.

When they were discovered, they had lowered the small boat under the pretense of putting out anchors from the prow, that is, from the bow or the front end of the ship. They intended to make it to the shore and at least save themselves. Obviously, they did not share the faith of Paul, nor did they accept his assurance that everyone on board would be saved.

It seems also the captain did not interfere and the centurion did not know what to do. It is obvious too that these sailors and their officers were still fearful, so full of fear, in fact, that they thought only of themselves. They were quite willing to leave the more than 200 other people on the ship to die.

These sailors were wrong too to use deception to gain their ends. Moreover, they had no command to put out anchors from the prow. Thus they were also guilty of disobedience.

**31. Paul said to the centurion and to the soldiers:** . . . But Paul, addressing Julius and the soldiers, said, —WEYM . . . told the officer and the other soldiers, —EVRD . . . alerted the centurion and the soldiers to this, NAB.

**Except these abide in the ship:** . . . Unless the sailors remain on board, —TCNT . . . Unless these men remain on the ship, —MNTG . . . If these men do not stay with the ship, —NAB.

**ye cannot be saved:** . . . you will not be safe, —BB . . . Your lives will be sacrificed, —WEYM . . . you can't be rescued, —BECK . . . you have no chance to survive, —NAB.

**27:31.** Again Paul took command of the situation. With a sense of authority given him by the Holy Spirit, he told the centurion that unless these sailors stayed with the ship none of the crew or passengers could be saved.

As it turned out, these sailors were needed to try to get the ship to go aground in the best place. Though Paul had the promise of God that all those on board would be saved, God was not going to send angels to carry them to safety. Nor could they simply let the boat drift in the storm any longer. They were going to have their part to do. God is sovereign; yet He sometimes uses even the ungodly to help accomplish His will. He used the ungodly Assyrians to bring His judgment on Israel, even though they did not know He was using them (Isaiah 10:5-7). He used the idol-worshiping Cyrus to send the Jews back to rebuild the temple (Isaiah 45:1-4). He used heathen sailors to throw Jonah overboard, and a big fish to get Jonah headed back in the direction He wanted him to go. There is no limit to what God can use to accomplish His purposes. It is obvious Paul was not using his own imagination to decide how he wanted God to act or what miracle he would like performed. Rather, he was sensitive to the Holy Spirit and was acting on the wisdom given him by the Spirit.

**32. Then the soldiers cut off the ropes of the boat:** . . . the ropes which held the boat, —TCNT.

**and let her fall off:** . . . and let her drift away, —TCNT . . . go adrift, —MRDK . . . and let the lifeboat fall into the water, —EVRD . . . fall away, —WMCK

**27:32.** The soldiers under the centurion not only accepted Paul's authority, they had common sense enough to know he was right. They did not want to take any further chances that some, under the cover of darkness, might try the same thing again. So they cut the ropes holding the small boat and let it fall into the sea. Now they were all going to have to trust Paul's advice.

**33. And while the day was coming on:** ... And as day was dawning, *—WEYM* ... And when dawn was near, *—BB* ... Just before dawn, *—EVRD*.

**Paul besought them all to take meat, saying:** ... Paul urged all on board, *—NAB* ... Paul gave them all orders to take food, saying, *—BB* ... began persuading all the people to eat something, *—EVRD* ... kept begging them ... to eat, *—WLMS*.

**This day is the fourteenth day that ye have tarried:** ... For fourteen days now, *—WMCK* ... For the past 14 days you have been waiting and watching, *—EVRD* ... that you have been on the strain, *—WEYM* ... you have uninterruptedly been on the alert, *—BRKL* ... you have been constantly waiting, *—WLMS* ... your being on watch, *—NORL* ... you have been in constant suspense, *—NAB*.

**and continued fasting, having taken nothing:** ... and have fasted, eating little or nothing, *—WEYM* ... you have gone without food, *—TCNT* ... you have gone hungryeaten nothing, *—NAB* ... not even taking a bit, *—WLMS* ... that you have not had time to eat, *—NORL* ... without a proper meal, *—MOFT* ... without regular rations, *—FNTN*.

**27:33.** As they were nearing daybreak, Paul, still in command of the situation, again took charge and encouraged everyone to take food for their own bodily health and welfare. This was the 14th day they were tarrying or waiting. The Greek implies they were expecting the worst. They really thought the storm was going to destroy the ship and that all would be lost. Thus, during all this time they were continually without food.

In recounting his sufferings, Paul had already told the Corinthians of his three previous shipwrecks and also the many perils he faced. Then he added he was "in weariness (labor, toil) and painfulness (hardship), in watchings (wakefulness, sleepless nights) often, in hunger and thirst, in fastings (because lack of food made fasting necessary) often, in cold and nakedness (not stark naked, but poorly dressed because of the lack of clothing)." (See 2 Corinthians 11:27-29.)

**34. Wherefore I pray you to take some meat:** ... So I urge you to take something to eat, *—TCNT* ... I therefore strongly advise, *—WEYM* ... Now I beg you, *—EVRD* ... So I implore you to eat something, *—BRKL*.

**for this is for your health:** ... it is necessary for your safety, *—MLNT* ... your safety depends on it, *—TCNT* ... it will sustain your health, *—BRKL* ... this is conducive, *—CMPB* ... in order to survive, *—TEV* ... You need it to stay alive, *—EVRD, —SEB* ... the beginning of your deliverance, *—WORL*.

**for there shall not an hair fall from the head of any of you:** ... for not one of you will lose even a hair of his head, *—TCNT* ... not a hair of your head will perish, *—MLNT* ... will be lost, *—WMCK*

**27:34.** Again Paul urged them to take nourishment for their "health" (since it was going to be for their deliverance, preservation, salvation). They were going to need some energy to be able to get to the shore.

Then Paul gave them further positive assurance that not a hair would be lost from anyone's head. Not only would they be saved from what had seemed to be certain death, there would not be the slightest injury to anyone. Paul was encouraging them, not only to take food, but to believe and trust in the promise God had given through the angel who had appeared to him.

God gave this promise, of course, to meet this particular situation. He does not promise believers will always be protected from any injury. But He is always with them.

**35. And when he had thus spoken, he took bread:** ... With these words he took some bread, *—TCNT*.

**and gave thanks to God in presence of them all:** ... he gave thanks unto God before all, *—RTHM* ... he gave praise to God, *—BB* ... before them all, *—WMCK*

**and when he had broken it, he began to eat:** ... He broke off a piece and began eating, *—EVRD*.

**27:35.** Paul did more than urge the people on the ship to take nourishment. He set the example by taking a loaf of bread. But he did not begin to eat at once. Before the whole crowd he gave thanks to God. This was no mere formal prayer. It came from the depths of Paul's heart. It was an anointed prayer. All the people on the ship must have felt the impact of the Holy Spirit as he prayed. Then Paul broke the bread and began to eat.

**36. Then were they all of good cheer:** ... Then they all cheered up, *—MOFT* ... This raised the spirits of all, *—WEYM* ... And they all took heart, *—WMCK* ... All the men felt better, *—EVRD* ... This gave them new courage, *—NAB* ... Then they all were encouraged, *—MLNT*.

**and they also took some meat:** ... and had something to eat themselves, *—TCNT* ... and began themselves to eat, *—WMCK* ... and started eating too, *—EVRD* ... and they too had something to eat, *—NAB* ... and partook of nourishment, *—MLNT*.

**27:36.** Paul's example had the effect he wanted it to have. When they saw Paul's joy in the Lord, they were all encouraged. With cheerfulness and in good spirits they also began to take nourishment for themselves.

Paul's faith and example had inspired them with new hope, real hope for the first time since the storm began. It is likely they sensed Paul's love as well. The combination of faith, hope, and love is unbeatable under all circumstances. Paul wrote to the Corinthians, "For whether we be beside ourselves (that is, if we are out of our senses), it is to God: or whether we be sober (that is, in our right mind), it is for your cause (that is, for you). For the love of Christ constraineth us (that is, impels us, urges us on, at the same time embracing us, controlling us, and keeping us within the boundaries set by God's Word); because we thus judge, that if one died for all, then were all dead; and that he died for all, that they which live should not henceforth live unto themselves, but unto him which died for them, and rose again" (2 Corinthians 5:13-15).

**37. And we were in all in the ship two hundred threescore and sixteen souls:** . . . There were two hundred and seventy-six of us, crew and passengers on board, –WEYM . . . all told there were 276 of us on board, –BRKL . . . in all in the ship, –WMCK

**27:37.** The Bible now draws attention to the fact there were 276 souls on board the ship. "Souls" here means living persons, living human beings. This was not the largest audience the apostle Paul had stood before and influenced, but it was an unusually large number to be on any one ship in those days. It was also probably the first time an entire crowd had followed his advice.

**38. And when they had eaten enough:** . . . After satisfying their hunger, –TCNT . . . After eating a hearty meal, –WEYM . . . When they had had enough, –NAB, –WMCK . . . We ate all we wanted, –EVRD.

**they lightened the ship:** . . . they further lightened the ship, –TCNT.

**and cast out the wheat into the sea:** . . . by throwing the grain, –TCNT . . . by dumping the wheat into the sea, –BRKL.

**27:38.** After they had all eaten their fill and were satisfied with food, everyone went to work throwing the cargo of wheat overboard. Up to this time they had thrown overboard everything else they could move. But somehow, even after they had given up all real hope that they would be saved, they still had a vague hope that something would happen to make it possible for them to get the cargo of wheat to Rome so they could collect their money. But now they not only believed Paul's promise that they would be saved, they remembered that he said the ship would be lost. Thus, there was no longer any point in making any attempt to save the cargo of wheat. Furthermore, by throwing the wheat overboard they would lighten the ship so it would ride higher. This would help them get closer to the shore and give them a better chance of reaching land safely.

**39. And when it was day:** . . . And when day came, –RTHM . . . In the morning, –BECK . . . When day arrived, –MLNT.

**they knew not the land:** . . . they could not recognize the coast, –WEYM . . . they could not make out what land it was, –TCNT.

**but they discovered:** . . . But they noticed, –WEYM . . . but gradually could see, –BECK.

**a certain creek with a shore:** . . . a certain creek in which there was a beach, –TCNT . . . an inlet with a sandy beach, –WEYM.

**into the which they were minded:** . . . they consulted, –TCNT . . . and they began conferring, –MNTG . . . on which they determined, –HBIE . . . into which they decided, –MLNT.

**if it were possible, to thrust in the ship:** . . . to run the ship aground, –ALFD . . . as to whether they could run this ship safely into it, –TCNT . . . to beach the ship if they could, –PHLP.

**27:39.** When daylight came they did not recognize the land. Because they had seen neither sun nor stars, they had no idea of their course. It seems the island of Malta was not a regular stopping place for the grain ships going from Egypt to Rome. Undoubtedly, no one on board had ever been there before. But they noticed a bay and decided that if they were able they would run the ship aground on the beach. This would make it easy for them all to go ashore.

St. Paul's Bay, as it is called today, fits exactly the account recorded in this chapter. There are places near the west side of the bay where the depth is actually 20 fathoms and then a little farther in, 15 fathoms. The bay is about 2 miles northwest of Valetta.

**40. And when they had taken up the anchors:** . . . And when they had cut away the anchors, –ALFD . . . clearing away the anchors, –RTHM . . . After severing the anchors, –BRKL . . . After casting off the anchors, –MLNT.

**they committed themselves unto the sea:** . . . and dropping them in the sea, –MLNT . . . and abandoned them to the sea, NAB.

**and loosed the rudder bands:** . . . cut the ropes which held the steering oars, –PHLP . . . unlashed the gear of the steering oars, –TCNT . . . and meanwhile loosening the ropes that held the rudders, –MLNT.

**and hoisted up the mainsail to the wind:** . . . spread out the foresail to catch the wind, –BECK . . . hoisted the foresail to the wind, –MLNT.

**and made toward shore:** . . . and steered the ship to the shore, –BECK . . . and made for the beach, –MLNT.

**27:40.** The sailors, now that they could see the bay and the opportunity to reach the beach, went to work. They knew what to do, and they no longer hesitated. First, they released the anchors and left them in the sea, because this also would lighten the ship. At the same time they unfastened the rudder (or steering paddle), so they could head the ship in the right direction. Then they raised the foresail (which was set on the bow of the ship) to catch the wind, and headed for the beach.

The storm had not yet ended. It was still raining and the wind was still blowing. The sailors needed to use all the skills they had in order to get the ship as close to the shore as possible. God's promise was good. But He still allowed adverse conditions to test their faith and obedience. Sometimes believers would like Him to bring them to the desired shore on a magic carpet. But instead He makes sure the right people are there with the right skills to help those who need help. In this case it was sailors who knew how to steer the ship and how to set the sail. But whatever the situation, believers too can count on the Lord's care and concern for them. At the same time, believers should not be afraid to use the means which He has made available. Paul and his companions must have been asking God to help the sailors.

These were tense moments. The sailors were doing their best. Many of the others on board may have been feeling a bit apprehensive again, but the believers were trusting in the Lord.

**41. And foiling into a place where two seas met:** ... but the ship hit a sandbar, —NAB ... hit a sandbank, —EVRD.

**they ran the ship aground:** ... they drove the ship aground, —MOFT ... They struck a bank in the water, —BECK.

**and the forepart stuck fast:** ... the stem having bilged, —FNTN ... and her prow sticking fast, —HBIE ... The front of the ship stuck there, —EVRD ... The bow stuck fast, —NAB ... was fixed in the sand, —BB.

**and remained unmoveable:** ... and could not be moved, —TCNT ... and remained fixed, —MNTG ... and could not be budged, —NAB.

**but the hinder part was broken:** ... but the stern, —ASV ... while the stern was shattered, NAB ... began to go to pieces, —WEYM ... break the back of the ship to pieces, —EVRD.

**with the violence of the waves:** ... Then the big waves began to, —EVRD ... under the violent pounding of the waves, —NORL ... by the pounding of the sea, —NAB ... under the strain, —TCNT ... under the heavy hammering of the sea, —WEYM.

**27:41.** But even using the best of their skills, the winds were such that the sailors could not control the ship. Instead of reaching the beach, they accidentally came to a place between two seas. This was a narrow channel, too shallow for the ship to make it through. Actually, there is a little island called Salmoneta near the entrance to the bay. The rush of breakers on both sides of the island give the appearance of two seas meeting.

The bow of the ship ran aground in mud and clay and stuck fast. Then the stern of the ship began breaking up because of the force (violence) of the waves. It was immediately obvious that everyone would have to leave the ship at once. The ship had already been battered by the storm for a long time and there was no possibility of it holding together.

**42. And the soldiers' counsel was:** ... Now the soldiers recommended, —WEYM ... And the design, —SAWR ... had in mind, —NORL ... And it was the plan of the soldiers, —HBIE ... decided to, —EVRD ... thought at first, —NAB.

**to kill the prisoners:** ... that they should kill, —HBIE.

**lest any of them should swim out, and escape:** ... for fear that any of them should swim away and make their escape, —TCNT.

**27:42.** The soldiers then conferred with one another and their counsel was to kill the prisoners lest they swim away and escape. Their concern was over what would happen to them if they were not able to produce the prisoners when they finally arrived in Rome. They knew the government would hold them responsible and their own lives would be in jeopardy. The Book of Acts has already provided an example of this after the angel brought Peter out of prison just before King Herod Agrippa I was going to have him killed. Herod conducted a legal examination of the guards who had custody of Peter while he was in the prison and had them put to death because of their failure (12:19). To save themselves the soldiers thought it best to kill the prisoners.

**43. But the centurion, willing to save Paul:** ... desiring to save, ASV ... anxious to save, —TCNT ... wanted to let Paul live, —EVRD.

**kept them from their purpose:** ... prevented their carrying out their intention, —TCNT ... put a stop to their plan, —CNFT ... he opposed their plan, —NAB ... He did not allow the soldiers, —EVRD.

**and commanded that they which could swim:** ... and ordered that those who could swim, —TCNT.

**should cast themselves first into the sea:** ... should be the first to jump into the sea, —TCNT ... to leap off first, —BRKL ... to jump into the water, —EVRD.

**and get to land:** ... and try to reach shore, —TCNT ... and make for shore, —BRKL ... and swim to land, —EVRD.

**27:43.** The centurion, however, now exercised his authority as the one in command. He wanted to save Paul, so he stepped in and prevented the soldiers from carrying out their purpose.

The word "save" here is an emphatic one. It seems to imply the soldiers were already intent on carrying out their purpose. They may have already gathered the prisoners together. The centurion actually had to rescue Paul and the other prisoners from them. The same word was used when Lysias provided a guard of 460 men to bring Paul safely to the governor, Felix, in Caesarea, thus preventing the Jews from carrying out their purpose to kill Paul at that time (23:23, 24).

This was another time this centurion showed favor to Paul. All the way along the kindness of this Roman army officer has been evident. He knew, of course, that Paul was a Roman citizen, but that does not seem to have been the issue here. Rather, the centurion had a personal desire to see Paul safely through to Rome. He was probably grateful for the way Paul had brought new hope and courage, and even for Paul's encouragement for them to eat and gain strength so they would all be able to make it to shore.

The centurion commanded all who could swim to jump overboard first and get to the land. This shows that even though the ship did not make it to the beach, it was still close enough for good swimmers to get to shore without any difficulty.

**44. And the rest:**
**some on boards:** . . . used wooden boards, −EVRD.
**and some on broken pieces of the ship:** . . . or on other debris from the ship, −NAB.
**And so it came to pass:** . . . In these various ways, −TCNT . . . In this way it turned out, −MOFT . . . And this is how, −EVRD.
**that they escaped all safe to land:** . . . everyone managed to get safely ashore, −TCNT . . . they all got safely to land, −WEYM . . . all the people made it safely, −EVRD.

**27:44.** After the swimmers jumped in, the rest followed them, some on planks or whatever boards of the ship they could grab, and others on whatever else they could find that would float. So they were all brought safely through the waves to the land. Paul's words of assurance given him by the angel of the one true God were thus proved true. But as Paul also warned, the ship was a total loss.

All of them must surely have been thankful to be alive. But undoubtedly there was praise and thanksgiving in the hearts of Paul and his friends to God and to the Lord Jesus who loved them, died for them, and was now risen, ascended to the right hand of the Father's throne where He was interceding for them through all this. Truly God had kept His promise, not only for Paul, but also for the 275 others who were on board.

## Chapter 28

**1. And when they were escaped:** . . . And when we were safely through, −RTHM . . . When we were

all safe, −TCNT . . . After our escape, −CNFT . . . Once on shore, −NAB.
**then they knew that the island was called Melita:** . . . discovered, −WEYM . . . ascertained, −MNTG . . . we learned, −NAB . . . we found that the island was called Malta, −TCNT.

**28:1.** After arriving safely on land they learned the island was called Melita (Phoenician or Canaanite for "refuge"), now called Malta.

Malta is about 174 miles from Italy and about 56 miles from the southern tip of Sicily. The African coast lies about 187 miles to the south. (The African coast then curves north, so it can be reached from Malta by going about the same distance to the west.) The island itself is a little over 17 miles long and a little over 9 miles wide, giving it an area of about 95 square miles. Its capital in modern times is Valetta. Because of its central position in the Mediterranean Sea, the Romans made it an important naval station.

**2. And the barbarous people shewed us:** . . . the barbarians, −MRDK . . . And the natives shewed us, −ALFD.
**no little kindness:** . . . remarkable friendliness, −BRKL . . . unusually kind, −NORL . . . extraordinary kindness, −NAB . . . remarkable kindness, −WLMS.
**for they kindled a fire:** . . . for they lit a fire, −TCNT.
**and received us every one:** . . . and took us all under shelter, −TCNT . . . and made us all welcome, −WEYM . . . and took us in, −BB . . . and gathering us all around it, −NAB.
**because of the present rain:** . . . because it was raining, −BB . . . the pelting rain, −WEYM . . . driving rain, −PHLP . . . there was a cold, drenching rain, −NORL . . . it had begun to rain, −NAB.
**and because of the cold:** . . . and the cold, −WEYM.

**28:2.** The local people had seen what was happening to the ship and how this crowd of 276 people were coming to shore. They spread the word and gathered to try to help the shipwrecked people.

Throughout this passage, Luke called the local inhabitants of Malta barbarians. But he did not mean they were degraded or uncivilized. To the Greeks any foreigner who could not speak Greek was a barbarian. Later they gave the Romans a little leeway by including among the barbarians those who could not speak Greek or Latin.

Actually the people of Malta were descended from Phoenician colonists who probably spoke a dialect closely related to Hebrew. It had for a time been under the domination of Sicilian Greeks, then of Carthage. But the Romans took it from the Carthaginians in 218 B.C. So it had long been under Roman rule.

It is easy to see that the citizens of Malta were good people even if they could not speak Greek.

Their kindness went beyond the ordinary. They lit a fire and welcomed all 276 of these strangers who had escaped from the wrecked ship. Because of the rain and the cold, the fire was an act of great kindness and must have been a welcome sight to all who came from the ship. Later the islanders showed further kindness and continued to prove they were a hospitable people. So it was definitely in the providence of God that Paul and his companions were shipwrecked on this particular island.

**3. And when Paul had gathered a bundle of sticks:** . . . an armful of dry branches, *—BECK* . . . Paul had collected a bundle of faggots, *—KNOX* . . . having gathered a certain lot of fuel, *—WORL* . . . had gathered some wood, *—NLTG* . . . had got some sticks together, *—BB* . . . picked up a pile of sticks, *—SEB*.

**and laid them on the fire:** . . . and had thrown them, *—WEYM* . . . was about to put it on, *—PHLP*.

**there came a viper out of the heat:** . . . a poisonous snake, *—SEB* . . . a snake came out, *—BB* . . . crawled out of the heat, *—NORL* . . . coming out to escape the heat, *—KNOX* . . . because of the heat, *—NLTG* . . . driven by the heat, *—LAMS*.

**and fastened on his hand:** . . . It held fast to Paul's hand, *—NLTG* . . . and gave him a bite on the hand, *—BB*.

**28:3.** A little later, knowing the fire would need more fuel, Paul took the place of a servant and went out to gather brushwood. Paul, great spiritual leader that he was, never asked others to do what he was not willing to do himself. He had worked hard all during his ministry at his tentmaking to support not only himself but the labors of his entire evangelistic party. He was always ready to serve others, and he was never afraid to soil his hands in doing so. What an example he set!

Soon he returned with a large bundle of the brushwood and put it on the fire. The heat brought out a viper that had been picked up with the wood. Before Paul could pull away the viper fastened its fangs on his hand.

The viper is a poisonous snake, and many writers take notice of the fact that there are no vipers on Malta today. Some even try to imply that the Bible must be wrong here. However, Malta is a small island and the people eventually got rid of the vipers after Paul's day. The historical facts in the Bible have been vindicated and confirmed so many times that it has been proven the mistakes are in the critics, not in the Bible. Even when there seems to be no answer to the allegations of the critics, the best thing is to hold steady. Time is the best judge.

**4. And when the barbarians saw the venomous beast hang on his hand:** . . . the reptile hanging on his hand, *—MNTG* . . . coiled round his hand, *—KNOX* . . . saw the reptile hanging from, *—NOLI*.

**they said among themselves:** . . . one to another, *—ASV*.

**No doubt this man is a murderer:** . . . Evidently, *—TCNT* . . . Assuredly this man is, *—WORL* . . . It may be that, *—LAMS* . . . Beyond doubt, *—WEYM* . . . This man must be a murderer! *—MOFT* . . . This man is a killer, *—NLTG* . . . This man is certainly a criminal, *—NOLI* . . . has put someone to death, *—BB*.

**whom, though he hath escaped the sea:** . . . for, though he has been saved from the sea, *—TCNT* . . . he has been rescued from, *—LAMS* . . . He didn't die in the ocean, *—SEB* . . . did not die in the sea, *—NCV* . . . whom, though safely escaping from, *—WORL*.

**yet vengeance suffereth not to live:** . . . Justice has not allowed him to live, *—TCNT* . . . will not permit him, *—SEB* . . . yet it is not right for him to live, *—NLTG* . . . divine justice will not let him live, *—NOLI* . . . God will not let him go on living, *—BB* . . . does not want him to live, *—NCV* . . . justice permitted not to live, *—WORL*.

**28:4.** When the people of Malta saw the wild creature dart out of the brush and bite Paul (vipers can dart several feet in a single quick motion), they jumped to the conclusion that Paul must be a murderer who, though he escaped safely from the sea, vengeance (literally, "the Justice") had not let him live. Paul, as a prisoner, must have had either a chain still attached to one of his wrists, or else the marks of the chains. (It would hardly seem logical that he would be able to make it to shore if they had not taken the chains off at least for the time.) In any case, the obvious fact that he was a prisoner must have helped the islanders to think he was surely a murderer.

By "the Justice" they may have meant their heathen goddess of justice. Or the reference may be simply to a vague sense of retributive justice which was common even among the heathen.

They were like the friends of Job who thought any trouble or misery was always judgment. But the Bible does not treat accidents as punishment. What Paul said about temptations in 1 Corinthians 10:13 can be applied to accidents as well, for they can become a temptation to unbelief and rebellion, or they can become an opportunity to trust God and learn what He can do. As Paul says, these things are common to mankind.

**5. And he shook off the beast into the fire:** . . . But he simply shook the reptile, *—WLMS* . . . shook off the creature, *—SWAN*.

**and felt no harm:** . . . without suffering any ill effect, *—PHLP* . . . and was none the worse, *—KNOX* . . . He was not hurt, *—SEB* . . . he got no damage, *—BB*.

**28:5.** Paul did not get excited or worried. He did not even cry out, though he must have felt the pain. Neither did he question God, even though he had picked up the snake while he was working hard because of his faithful concern for others.

Note too that he had not picked up the snake deliberately, nor did he do it as an attempt to show his faith. Unfortunately, some have misinterpreted Mark 16:18 to make it a command. However, the Greek word used there is often used of taking away or removing. Matthew 24:39 uses it of the flood sweeping everyone away. Luke 23:18 uses it of the crowd crying out "Away with him!" Other ancient Greek writings outside the New Testament also use the verb in the sense of removing, taking away, and blotting out. It should be kept in mind also that the serpent was symbolic of evil, and the whole context of Mark 16 indicates victory over the works of the devil. The same is true of Luke 10:19 where Jesus said, "Behold, I give (have given and still give) unto you power (authority) to tread on serpents and scorpions, and over all the power (mighty power) of the enemy; and nothing shall by any means hurt you."

Early Christians certainly did not go around picking up snakes. In fact, in Mark's context, the picking up of snakes is presented as something very unlikely. Thus, when Paul accidentally picked up this viper, he simply shook the wild creature off his hand into the fire and suffered no harm.

**6. Howbeit they looked when he should have swollen:** . . . were expecting inflamation to set in, –TCNT . . . they had the idea that they would see him becoming ill, –BB . . . The natives kept on looking for him to swell up, –WLMS . . . they thought he soon would become inflamed, –KJII.

**or fallen down dead suddenly:** . . . or suddenly drop dead, –WLMS.

**but after they had looked a great while:** . . . but after waiting for a long time, –TCNT . . . in suspense, –FNTN . . . having waited a considerable time, –SWAN.

**and saw no harm come to him:** . . . observed nothing unusual happening to him, –RTHM . . . found that there was nothing amiss with him, –KNOX . . . but nothing bad happened, –SEB . . . and saw nothing extraordinary occur, –HNSN . . . seeing that no damage came, –BB.

**they changed their minds:** . . . their opinion, –BB.

**and said that he was a god:** . . . and said over and over, –MNTG.

**28:6.** The local people who had no doubt seen others bitten by the same kind of viper expected Paul to swell up or drop dead. For a long time they kept waiting and watching, but nothing unusual happened to him. So they changed their minds and said he was a god. Based on these outward circumstances their opinion thus shifted from one extreme to the other.

This must have bothered Paul. He had seen how the people of Lystra had thought he and Barnabas were gods and were preparing to sacrifice to

them, then very shortly went to the other extreme and were persuaded to stone Paul (14:13, 19). He knew how fickle the opinion of the crowd could be.

**7. In the same quarters were possessions of the chief man of the island, whose name was Publius:** . . . In that neighborhood there was an estate belonging to the Governor of the island, –TCNT . . . In the same part of the island there were lands, –WEYM . . . the property of the chief man of the island, –BB . . . There were some fields around that same area, –SEB . . . in the vicinity of that place were, –HNSN . . . owned by the island chief, –KJII.

**who received us:** . . . who welcomed us to his house, –WEYM . . . took us into his house as his guests, –BB.

**and lodged us three days courteously:** . . . hospitably entertained us, –RTHM . . . We stayed in his house for, –SEB . . . and gave us everything we needed, –NLTG.

**28:7.** Nearby were the fields (lands, properties) belonging to the chief man (the governor) of the island, whose name was Publius (meaning "popular"). There is evidence that he held his office under the governor of Sicily, and as the chief Roman official on the island he would be responsible for any Roman soldiers and their prisoners who might come there.

Publius did far beyond what was necessary, for he welcomed them with kindness, and for 3 days entertained them with friendly thoughtfulness. As his name indicates, he was a Roman citizen and no doubt felt special concern for these Romans. Yet it seems that even this does not account for his unusual kindness. In the providence of God, Paul came in contact here with a good man who would help him.

**8. And it came to pass:** . . . And it so happened, –RTHM . . . But, –LAMS.

**that the father of Publius lay sick:** . . . was lying prostrate, –RTHM . . . was lying ill, –WEYM . . . happened to be sick, –BECK . . . lay in distress, Swarm . . . lay overcome with, –KJII.

**of a fever and of a bloody flux:** . . . and dysentery, –ASV . . . with a stomach sickness, –NLTG . . . with a disease of the stomach, –BB.

**to whom Paul entered in:** . . . So Paul went to see him, –TCNT . . . went to him, –NCV . . . went in to where he was lying, –LAMS.

**and prayed, and laid his hands on him, and healed him:**

**28:8.** There was another reason God in His providence brought Paul to Malta at this time. There was a great need here that would become an opportunity for the ministry of the Holy Spirit and for the spread of the gospel of Christ.

It happened that at this time the father of Publius lay sick, suffering from fevers and dysentery. The Greek indicates these were recurring fevers. He had suffered from them all too often before. Luke, the physician, was careful to make note of this. Yet Luke did not go to work to try to apply the knowledge and skill he had as a physician. He, like Paul, was led of the Holy Spirit. He could have used his skill if the Holy Spirit had directed him to do so. But with even the best of ancient medical practice, the care and recovery of the father of Publius would have been a long drawn-out process. Something more was needed, especially to bring a witness to the power of the gospel. God often uses a miracle as an entering wedge to open a new door for the proclamation of the good news about Jesus.

When Paul heard about this sickness of the father of Publius he went in, prayed for him, laid hands on him, "and healed him." Paul, of course, acted as a fellow laborer with the Lord. God did the actual healing.

9. **So when this was done:** ... And when this happened, —RTHM ... After this, —TCNT ... After this miracle, —NOLI ... occurred, —SEB.

**others also, which had diseases in the island, came, and were healed:** ... the rest of the sick folk in the island also came and got cured, —MOFT ... a steady procession, —WUST ... suffering from infirmities, —KNOX ... sick in the island, —LAMS ... kept coming to him, —WLMS.

**28:9.** The news of this miraculous healing soon spread over the whole of this rather small island. It was like a small town. There were no secrets and news spread quickly. So it was not long before the other people of the island who had illnesses began coming to Paul and were all healed.

Though Luke did not mention it here, Paul surely did more than pray for the sick. Throughout the four Gospels and the Book of Acts the healing ministry was closely tied with the ministry of teaching and the message of the forgiveness of sins.

Luke may not have had a part other than prayer in this ministry, for it is possible he did not know the language and the people did not know Greek. It is probable that people spoke a dialect of Phoenician or Canaanite Hebrew, so Paul may well have been able to communicate with them. At least, it should not have been hard for them to find someone who knew both languages and could interpret for them.

10. **Who also honoured us with many honours:** ... Consequently, —PHLP ... They also loaded us with honours, —WEYM ... There also showed us honor in many ways, —NORL ... every kind of respect,

—BRKL ... They had great respect, —NLTG ... They also presented us with many gifts, —TCNT ... made us rich presents, —MOFT, —NOLI ... they bestowed on us many rewards, —SAWR.

**and when we departed:** ... and when at last we sailed, —WEYM ... when we embarked, —KNOX ... when we put to sea, —SWAN ... When we were ready to leave, —NCV.

**they laded us with such things as were necessary:** ... they supplied all our needs, —BRKL ... what should minister to our wants, —DRBY ... loaded us with all the supplies we needed, —KNOX ... they heaped on us, —KJII ... whatever we needed, —BECK ... whatever things we were in need of, —BB ... gave us the things we needed, —NCV.

**28:10.** Paul no doubt kept ministering to the people of Malta during the 3 winter months that followed. Many of the people must have come to a knowledge of Jesus Christ as Lord and Saviour. It is clear also that the healings of all these illnesses prepared the way for an effective ministry of evangelism. In spontaneous appreciation the people honored Paul and his friends with many honors. The honors probably included gifts of food, clothing, and money to help them stay alive during those winter months. The people surely must have opened their homes and shared fellowship with them as well.

When Paul and the others set sail in the spring, the people placed on board the things they needed for the journey. Apparently, the islanders provided not only for Paul, but for all the other 275 people who had been shipwrecked as well.

11. **And after three months:** ... Three months later, —GDSP ... Three months having elapsed, —FNTN ... We stayed there three months, —SEB.

**we departed in a ship of Alexandria:** ... we put to sea in, —BRKL ... we left, sailing in, —LAMS.

**which had wintered in the isle:** ... that had stayed there during the winter, —NLTG.

**whose sign was Castor and Pollux:** ... and which bore the sign of, —LAMS ... whose ensign was The Twin Brothers, —RTHM ... was the sign for the twin gods, —SEB.

**28:11.** The rest of the journey to Italy took place on another ship of Alexandria that had wintered in Malta, probably at the good harbor of Valetta. Its figurehead was the Dioscuri. This was their name for the "sons of (the Greek chief god) Zeus," that is, Castor and Pollux. In some of the Greek mythology these were said to be the sons of Zeus and Leda and were considered patrons of sailors and their protectors when in distress. The constellation Gemini ("the Twins") is named after them, and its two brightest stars are called Castor and Pollux.

12. **And landing at Syracuse:** . . . We docked at, —BRKL . . . We put in at, —TCNT . . . going into the harbour at, —BB.

**we tarried there three days:** . . . we remained there, —LAMS . . . and stayed there, —TCNT.

**28:12.** The ship took a course that went north-northeast and then north in order to go between Sicily and the toe of Italy's boot. When they came to Syracuse on the east coast of Sicily, they stopped 3 days. Syracuse was a famous and beautiful city about 80 miles north of Malta founded and colonized by the Greeks. The Romans made it the capital of the province.

13. **And from thence we fetched a compass:** . . . whence removing, —HNSN . . . we made a circuit, —AMPB . . . From there we circled around, —LAMS . . . from there we coasted around, —SWAN . . . going in a circuitous course, —DRBY . . . we sailed around, —BECK . . . Then tacking round, —MOFT . . . from there, going about in a curve, —BB . . . after going around, —KJII . . . we went around to, —KLGS.

**and came to Rhegium:** . . . and arrived at, —LAMS.
**and after one day:** . . . next day, —MOFT.
**the south wind blew:** . . . began to blow, —WLMS . . . blew in our favor, —LAMS.
**and we came the next day to Puteoli:** . . . and in two days, —LAMS.

**28:13.** When the ship left Syracuse the wind was not favorable, so they had to "make a circuit," that is, they had to tack against the wind all the way to Rhegium (the modern Reggio) in the toe of Italy's boot opposite Messina in Sicily.

After another day the wind changed, and it took them only one more day to sail the approximately 180 miles between Rhegium and Puteoli (the modern Pozzuoli), the chief port on the bay of Naples. It stood on the north shore of an indentation in the bay and was protected by a massive breakwater.

Because the coast nearer Rome had no good harbors until an artificial one was made by the emperor Claudius, and because Puteoli was a very safe harbor, the Romans made it their chief seaport. Thus, it became the center of commercial activity and was very prosperous. The grain ships that brought wheat from Egypt made it their home port. Other ships brought goods and spices from the Orient by way of the countries bordering on the eastern Mediterranean. At this time its population was about 100,000.

14. **Where we found brethren:** . . . found some Christians there, —NLTG.
**and were desired to tarry with them seven days:** . . . and were entreated, —ASV . . . and were urged to stay, —KJII, —TCNT . . . and they begged us, —WLMS . . . and were invited to remain with them, —HNSN . . . who invited us to stay, —LAMS.

**and so we went toward Rome:** . . . and thus towards Rome we came, —RTHM . . . Finally, we

**28:14.** After Paul and his companions went ashore at Puteoli, they found Christian brethren who successfully urged them to stay with them 7 days. Probably they did so because they wanted and felt they needed the teaching and fellowship of the apostle. This week of rest and fellowship must have meant much to Paul and his companions.

15. **And from thence, when the brethren heard of us:** . . . When the Christians heard of our coming, —NLTG . . . had heard about our affairs, —SWAN . . . heard of our arrival, —ALFD, —LAMS . . . who heard our story, —KNOX.

**they came to meet us as far as Appii forum, and The three taverns:** . . . to have a meeting with us, —BB . . . as far as the street which is called Appiiforum, —LAMS . . . Appius' Market, —WLMS . . . the Market of Appius, —FNTN . . . the Three Shops, —BECK . . . and Three Tabernacles, —BRKL . . . and Three Inns, —TEV . . . the Three Stores, —NLTG.

**whom when Paul saw:** . . . And as soon as Paul caught sight of them, —WLMS.

**he thanked God, and took courage:** . . . and took renewed courage, —NORL . . . and felt encouraged, —BECK . . . and was much cheered, —TCNT . . . greatly encouraged, —LAMS, —NOLI.

**28:15.** From Puteoli, Paul and his companions proceeded on foot toward Rome, taking the famous Roman road, the Appian Way. Paul knew, of course, the Lord wanted him in Rome (23:11), but he did not know what awaited him or how his trial would turn out. As he trudged along, he may have looked back over the 3 years that had passed since he had written to the Romans, expressing his desire to visit them (Romans 1:10, 11, 15). What a weary 3 years they had been! There had been persecutions and false accusations. The imprisonment at Caesarea had dragged on and on until he had appealed to Caesar. What further severe ordeal awaited him now?

But God had a pleasant surprise for Paul. When he reached the Appii Forum ("the marketplace of Appius"), about 40 miles south of Rome, a delegation of people met him. They were Christians who had come out in order to give him a royal welcome. It was not honor that brought Paul joy, however. The sight of Christian brothers who would walk and talk with him caused him to thank God and take courage. Even mature, spiritual believers need the inspiration and strength which can be derived from Christian fellowship with other believers.

Again, at the village of Three Taverns (rather, Three Shops), about 30 miles from Rome, another delegation of believers met Paul. This was the regular expression for the official welcome of an official or dignitary. The same phrase is used of the Church going for the meeting with Christ in the air (1 Thessalonians 4:17).

**16. And when we came to Rome:** ... When at last we reached, *—NOLI* ... When we finally entered Rome, *—MNTG* ... On our reaching Rome, *—TCNT* ... Once we were in Rome, *—KNOX.*

**the centurion delivered the prisoners to the captain of the guard:** ... commander of the prison camp, *—NORL.*

**but Paul was suffered to dwell by himself with a soldier that kept him:** ... Paul was allowed to live by himself except for the soldier who was in charge of him, *—TCNT* ... Paul received permission to live by himself, guarded by a soldier, *—WEYM* ... to live alone with the soldier who was guarding him, *—PHLP* ... was allowed to have his own residence, *—KNOX* ... gave permission to Paul to live wherever he pleased with a soldier to guard him, *—LAMS* ... reside where he pleased, *—MRDK* ... outside the garrison, *—FNTN* ... allowed to live where he wanted to ... a soldier was always by his side to watch him, *—NLTG* ... with the soldier who guarded him, *—SWAN* ... the armed man who kept watch over him, *—BB.*

**28:16.** At Rome Paul and the other prisoners were handed over to the commander of Nero's praetorian guard (that is, to the general in charge of the Roman legion stationed at the Roman praetorium to guard the emperor Nero and the palace). The other prisoners were probably thrown into a prison. But Paul was permitted to live by himself, lightly chained by the wrist to a soldier who guarded him. As verse 30 indicates, he was able to rent an apartment in a private house and keep it for the 2 years he was in Rome. Luke and Aristarchus also remained in Rome to help him during this period. Paul mentions them in some of the prison Epistles written during this period. (See Colossians 4:10, 14; Philemon 24.) The apartment was large enough for quite a few people to gather, as verses 23-25 indicate.

The guard who was chained to Paul's wrist was probably a member of the emperor's praetorian guard, since Paul was appealing to Caesar. They probably served in shifts, with different ones from time to time. Thus the whole praetorian guard came to hear the gospel. (See Philippians 1:13, where "the palace" is literally the praetorian guard.)

Paul was also permitted to have his friends come and go so he could enjoy their fellowship and hospitality. As a Roman citizen he was given better treatment than the other prisoners. Also the centurion Julius may have put in a good word for him with the commander of the guard.

**17. And it came to pass, that after three days:** ... Three days after our arrival, *—TCNT* ... And it occurred after, *—HNSN* ... Three days later, *—NOLI.*

**Paul called the chief of the Jews together:** ... Paul invited the leading Jews to meet him, *—TCNT* ... he called a meeting of the leading men among the Jews, *—KNOX* ... those that were the principal of the Jews, *—HNSN* ... for some of the most important Jewish leaders, *—SEB.*

**and when they were come together:** ... when they had convened, *—SAWR* ... when they were assembled, *—HNSN.*

**he said unto them:**

**Men and brethren:** ... Fellow Jews, *—BECK.*

**though I have committed nothing against the people:** ... nothing hostile to the interests of our nation, *—TCNT.*

**or customs of our fathers:** ... or the way our early fathers lived, *—NLTG* ... or contrary to the customs of our forefathers, *—WEYM* ... of our ancestors, *—SEB.*

**yet was I delivered prisoner from Jerusalem into the hands of the Romans:** ... handed over to the Romans, *—TCNT* ... yet I was made a prisoner at Jerusalem, *—NORL* ... yet I was arrested in, *—SEB.*

**28:17.** After 3 days Paul called together (that is, sent out an invitation to) the Jewish leaders in Rome, asking them to come to his apartment. Ancient Roman inscriptions show there were several Jewish synagogues in Rome at this time. In fact, the Roman government at the time did more than tolerate the Jews. They favored them by allowing them the privilege of governing themselves and making laws and ordinances for their own community. They even let them send an annual contribution to the temple in Jerusalem.

During his missionary journeys Paul normally went first to the synagogue on his first visit to any city in order to give the Jews the first opportunity to accept the gospel. When he wrote to the Roman Christians, he reminded them the gospel was given to the Jew first (Romans 1:16). He also declared to them his own deep love and concern for his unsaved Jewish brothers (Romans 9:1-5; 10:1). But now, since he was a prisoner, he could not visit the synagogues, so he did the next best thing and invited their leaders to visit him.

When they came he showed a courteous and conciliatory spirit as he humbly explained how he came to be in Rome as a prisoner. He made it clear that his chain did not mark him as a renegade Israelite. He had, in fact, done nothing at all against the people of Israel or against the customs of their fathers to cause him to be handed over out of Jerusalem as a prisoner to the Romans. This was true. He was actually in the process of showing his willingness to follow those customs when he was attacked and arrested.

18. **Who, when they had examined me:** . . . After examining me, —*WLMS* . . . The Romans asked me many questions, —*SEB* . . . sharply questioned me, —*WEYM* . . . when they had put questions to me, —*BB*.

**would have let me go:** . . . were minded to, —*RTHM* . . . were willing to, —*WEYM* . . . were prepared to, —*PHLP* . . . desired to release me, —*HNSN* . . . they wished to let me go, —*KJII* . . . were ready to let me go, —*BB* . . . go free, —*SEB*.

**because there was no cause of death in me:** . . . nothing in my conduct deserving death, —*TCNT*.

**28:18.** Paul then explained his innocence by telling how the Romans had examined him (in an official court hearing) and had wanted to set him free, for they found no legal grounds at all for putting him to death. In other words, the Roman authorities were ready to give him a full pardon.

It seems Paul felt it necessary to begin this way in case the Jews in Rome had already had a report from the Jerusalem Jews, or perhaps in anticipation that such a report would soon come. He had no way of knowing how much they knew about him.

19. **But when the Jews spake against it:** . . . made protest against it, —*BB* . . . But owing to the opposition of the Jews, —*WEYM* . . . But the Jews objected, —*BECK* . . . objected, so, —*WLMS*.

**I was constrained to appeal unto Caesar:** . . . and forced me to appeal, —*BECK* . . . I was compelled, —*ALFD* . . . I had to put my cause into Caesar's hands, —*BB* . . . forced to ask to have my trial before, —*SEB*.

**not that I had ought to accuse my nation of:** . . . not that I'm accusing my people of anything, —*BECK* . . . I have no charge to bring against my people, —*NCV*.

**28:19.** After emphasizing his innocence, Paul explained why he appealed to Caesar, being careful not to put any blame on the Jewish nation (the Jewish people) as a whole.

The Jews in Jerusalem, however, had continued to speak against him, opposing him, refusing to accept the decision of the Roman authorities. Therefore, Paul had felt obliged to appeal to Caesar. But his purpose in doing so was not to make any accusation against his nation (his people, the Jews). Rather, he simply wanted the opportunity to defend himself. Thus, he was in Rome as a prisoner, not because he had done anything wrong, but because circumstances had made it a necessity.

The fact that Paul did not want to bring any charge against his own people shows how loving and forgiving he was toward them. No matter what they did to him, he could not hold a grudge or keep anything in his heart against them.

He told the Romans, "I have great heaviness (pain, grief of mind and spirit) and continual sorrow in my heart (my heart is continually grieved). For I could wish that myself were (would be) accursed (*anathema*, accursed and therefore separated) from Christ for my brethren, my kinsmen according to the flesh: who are Israelites" (Romans 9:2-4). That is, Paul would have been willing to give up his own salvation if that could have guaranteed the salvation of the Jews. He knew that was not possible, but that is how much he loved them!

Paul went on in the Book of Romans to show that the Jews who were rejecting Christ were trying to set the conditions on which God would give His mercy and salvation. They trusted in their own works instead of taking the God-appointed way of faith. They trusted in who they were instead of who Christ is. They stumbled at Christ, took offense at Him, when He was really the Chief Cornerstone. So it was not God's fault the Jews rejected Him.

In all this Paul expressed a tremendous concern over the Jews and a heartfelt desire for their salvation, at the same time recognizing their zeal for God, a zeal that was without right knowledge, just as his had been.

20. **For this cause therefore:** . . . This, then, is my reason, —*TCNT* . . . This is the reason why, —*MNTG* . . . on account of, —*NOLI* . . . But it is because of this accusation of the Jews, —*PHLP*.

**have I called for you, to see you, and to speak with you:** . . . for urging you to come to see me, —*TCNT* . . . I have invited you here, —*WEYM* . . . I have asked for the opportunity of seeing you, —*KNOX*.

**because that for the hope of Israel:** . . . for on account of, —*RTHM* . . . because I believe in the hope of Israel, NCV . . . the Messianic hope of Israel, —*NOLI*.

**I am bound with this chain:** . . . that I wear this chain, —*KNOX* . . . I am branded with, —*FNTN*.

**28:20.** Paul's purpose in calling together the Jewish leaders was, however, more than just to explain why he was in Rome as a prisoner. He wanted to testify to the truth that it was for the hope of Israel he was bound by a chain.

In his prison epistles, Paul never drew attention to the fact that he was a prisoner of Rome. Rather, he called himself a prisoner of his Lord (Ephesians 3:1; 4:1).

In his epistles, Paul also called himself a servant, literally, a slave of Jesus Christ (Romans 1:1). In those days the most common way of becoming a slave was to be taken captive by some conqueror. Paul considered he had been taken captive by the risen Christ who then gave him, still as His slave, as an apostle to the Church (Ephesians 4:11). In other words, when Paul accepted Jesus as Lord on the Damascus Road, he gave himself up to Christ completely as his Lord and Master. From that time on he was Christ's captive and slave to do His will. Thus, his whole life was under his Lord's direction. He was in Rome, then, because of the Hope of Israel, Christ.

**21. And they said unto him:** ... At this they said to him, −KNOX.
**We neither received letters out of Judaea concerning thee:**
**neither any of the brethren that came:** ... and not one of our Jewish brother has come, −WLMS.
**shewed or spake any harm of thee:** ... and reported or said anything bad about you, −TCNT ... or told us anything bad about you, −NCV ... anything to your disadvantage, −WEYM ... with a bad report or gossip about you, −BRKL ... with any ill report or hard words about thee, −KNOX ... or say any evil about you, −BB ... officially or unofficially, −PHLP.

**28:21.** The Jewish leaders replied that no letters had come from Judea, nor had anyone brought a report of Paul's trial or spoken anything bad concerning him. There is evidence that Roman law punished unsuccessful prosecutors of Roman citizens. So it is possible the Jewish leaders in Jerusalem simply decided it was the better part of wisdom not to oppose Paul in Rome.

**22. But we desire to hear of thee what thou thinkest:** ... But we shall be glad to hear from you what your views are, −TCNT ... We think it only right to let you tell your own story, −MOFT ... But we deem it fitting to hear from you what you think, −SWAN ... But we are eager to hear from you what it is you believe, −MNTG ... We want to hear your ideas, −NCV ... we have a desire to give hearing to your opinion, −BB ... We ask nothing better than to hear, −KNOX ... So we want to hear you state your views, −NOLI ... what thine opinions are, −RTHM.
**for as concerning this sect:** ... for with regard to this sect, −TCNT ... As for this new religion, −NLTG ... concerning this teaching, −LAMS ... regarding this belief, −KJII.
**we know:** ... we are well aware, −TCNT ... all we know is, −WEYM.
**that every where it is spoken against:** ... that it is spoken against on all sides, −TCNT ... objections to it, −MOFT ... it is condemned everywhere, −NORL ... is not received by any one, −MRDK ... it is not acceptable to any one, −LAMS ... it is everywhere denounced, −WLMS ... it is everywhere decried, −KNOX ... that in all places it is attacked, −BB ... everyone is talking against it, −NLTG.

**28:22.** These leaders of the Roman Jews expressed a desire to hear Paul tell what he had in his mind. They were not complimentary to the Christians, however, for they called Christianity a sect that everywhere was opposed. Up to this time most of these leaders may have been indifferent to

Christianity, knowing only that it was unpopular. Now, at least, their curiosity was aroused.

Paul's epistle to the Romans shows that the church in Rome was already well-established by A.D. 57 and probably long before that. It probably spread as a sect or party under the umbrella of Judaism as a protected religion. The word "sect" here does not necessarily mean a heretical sect. The same word is used of the Pharisees and Sadducees. However, the fact that the Jewish leaders referred to it as everywhere opposed, shows that the Jews in Rome were beginning to consider it somewhat heretical. Yet their leaders obviously had never bothered to investigate for themselves.

**23. And when they had appointed him a day:** ... having arranged with him, −RTHM ... So they set a date with Paul, −TEV ... So they made an appointment with him, −KNOX ... set a day for a meeting, −SEB.
**there came many to him into his lodging:** ... came in large numbers, −WLMS ... in even larger numbers, −NOLI ... many gathered together and came to him where he was staying, −LAMS.
**to whom he expounded and testified the kingdom of God:** ... earnestly telling, −BECK ... bearing full witness, −RTHM ... he solemnly explained, −WEYM ... earnestly testifying the reign of God, −HNSN ... preached to them about the holy nation of God, −NLTG.
**persuading them concerning Jesus:** ... tried to convince, −TCNT ... tried to persuade them, −NOLI.
**both out of the law of Moses, and out of the prophets:** ... by arguments drawn from, −TCNT ... by appealing to, −NEB ... Using the law of Moses, −SEB ... by quoting passages from, −NOLI.
**from morning till evening:** ... spoke to them all day long, −SEB.

**28:23.** The Jews set a date among themselves and came in considerable numbers to Paul's apartment to receive his hospitality. To these he gave explanation of what was in his mind by bearing solemn witness to the kingdom (rule, power, authority) of God. This would include God's rule manifest through Jesus and through the Holy Spirit. It would also speak of the coming Kingdom when Jesus will return to this earth, take the throne of David, and make it eternal.

Then, as he always did in all the synagogues he visited, Paul used the books of Moses and the prophets, books accepted as God's Word by these Jews, seeking to persuade them that Jesus is truly the Messiah, God's anointed Prophet, Priest, and King.

Paul kept their attention as he continued this teaching from early morning until evening. This means he must have given them the same kind of teaching he gave the Jews in the synagogue at Pisidian Antioch. (See 13:16-41.) He also had time to explain the body of teaching found in the four Gospels. No doubt, there were many questions which he answered from the Scriptures. Paul would not treat this opportunity as an academic exercise. He must have spent much time in prayer preparing for this special day. Nor would he be casual in presenting the truth. His earnestness must have brought tears to his eyes as he sought to explain the truth and exhort these fellow countrymen to accept the gospel, the wonderful good news about Jesus and about the grace of God that brings salvation.

**24. And some believed the things which were spoken:** ... Some of them were convinced by what he said, –*NOLI* ... were in agreement, –*BB* ... indeed persuaded, –*KJII* ... were convinced by his reasonings, –*BRKL.*

**and some believed not:** ... others refused to believe, –*WEYM* ... others, however, rejected it, –*TCNT* ... yet some disbelieved, –*CNDT* ... were skeptical, –*JB* ... Others did not share his views at all, –*NOLI.*

**28:24.** Some of the Jews who listened to Paul were persuaded. They believed and obeyed Paul's message and exhortation. A faith in Jesus as their Messiah, Lord, and Saviour sprang up in their hearts. They accepted the truth and believed in their hearts that God had raised Jesus from the dead and therefore that Christ's death was effective for the redemption of soul and body (Romans 8:18-23). They also accepted the truth that Christ's resurrection is the believers' guarantee, and that His coming is an encouragement to holy living now as well as an encouragement to have hope for the future. So they became born-again believers, members of the body of Christ, sharers in the blessed hope and the heavenly inheritance that Paul proclaimed (Romans 10:9, 10). Paul no doubt urged them to join in the worship of Christ as part of one of the local assemblies in Rome.

Others of the Jews disbelieved. In spite of Paul's testimony, in spite of all the proofs he brought from the Old Testament Scriptures, they refused to put their faith in Jesus. Paul did not consider this a failure on his part, however. He always gave thanks to God, "which always causeth us to triumph in Christ, and maketh manifest the savor (fragrance) of his knowledge (the knowledge of God) by us in every place" (2 Corinthians 2:14).

**25. And when they agreed not** among **themselves:** ... Unable to agree, –*WEYM* ... still at variance among themselves, –*KNOX* ... they did not agree with each other, –*NLTG.*

**they departed:** ... began to disperse, –*TCNT* ... and they took their leave, –*KNOX.*

**after that Paul had spoken one word:** ... but not before Paul had spoken a parting word, –*WEYM* ... one last word, –*KNOX* ... added this last remark, –*NOLI.*

**Well spake the Holy Ghost:** ... The Holy spirit spoke the truth, –*BECK* ... It was a true utterance the Holy Spirit made, –*KNOX* ... an apt word, –*MOFT* ... beautifully expressed it, –*WLMS.*

**by Esaias the prophet unto our fathers:** ... to your ancestors, –*TCNT.*

**28:25.** The fact that some believed and were saved while others rejected the truth brought disagreement and a line of separation, just as the truth always does. Jesus himself warned His disciples that when the truth about Him was proclaimed it would bring division (Luke 12:51).

Paul did not let them leave without one final exhortation, however. He quoted for them what the Holy Spirit in Isaiah 6:9, 10 said to their ancestors in the year King Uzziah died because of his presumptuous sin. (The quotation here follows the Greek Septuagint version of the Old Testament, a version much used by the Early Church.)

**26. Saying, Go unto this people, and say:** ... and tell them, –*KNOX.*

**Hearing ye shall hear:** ... You will hear with your ears, –*TCNT* ... You will listen and listen, –*KNOX.*

**and shall not understand:** ... without ever understanding, –*TCNT* ... but not catch the meaning, –*BRKL.*

**and seeing ye shall see:** ... And will look and look, –*WEYM* ... and never see, –*NLTG.*

**and not perceive:** ... and yet will in nowise, –*RTHM* ... understand, –*ET.*

**28:26.** Paul quoted from Isaiah because he wanted those Jews who were rejecting the gospel to realize they were not merely turning away from him and his message. They were closing their hearts and minds to God and His plan, and in doing so they were coming under judgment just as the Israelites did who rejected Isaiah's message when it was first given over 700 years before.

God sent Isaiah to a people who would hear but not understand, who would see but not perceive. That is, they would not consider that there was any truth in the prophet's message. They would have no expectation that God would bring any fulfillment of the prophet's warnings. Later they mocked Isaiah and, though he did see a period of revival after Sennacherib left Jerusalem, they eventually killed him.

**27. for the heart of this people is waxed gross:** ... hath become dense, –*RTHM* ... For the mind of this nation, –*TCNT* ... has grown callous, –*WEYM* ... For this people's soul, –*WLMS* ... For this people's heart is stupefied, *—HNSN* . . . this people's mind is dull, *—NOLI* . . . is grown obtuse, *—MNTG.*

**and their ears are dull of hearing:** . . . scarcely hear, *—WLMS* . . . hardly hear, *—NORL* . . . their ears are slow to listen, *—KNOX* . . . they hear with difficulty, *—SWAN.*

**and their eyes have they closed:** . . . they keep their eyes shut, *—KNOX* . . . They have shut their eyes, *—SEB* . . . shut tight, *—WLMS* . . . their eyes are blind, *—NOLI.*

**lest they should see with their eyes:** . . . So they will never see with, *—NOLI* . . . for fear they might, *—NORL* . . . so that their eyes don't see, *—BECK* . . . Otherwise, they would see, *—SEB.*

**and hear with their ears:** . . . will never hear with, *—NOLI.*

**and understand with their heart:** . . . never understand, *—NOLI* . . . with their minds, *—WEYM* . . . with that heart, *—KNOX* . . . their minds do not understand, *—NLTG.*

**and should be converted:** . . . will never turn back to me, *—NOLI* . . . and turn to me, *—WLMS.*

**and I should heal them:** . . . let Me heal them, *—NORL* . . . and I cure them, *—SWAN.*

**28:27.** The reason for Israel's rejection of Isaiah's message was the fact that their hearts had grown fat (that is, such a thick layer of unbelief had grown around their hearts and minds that the truth had a hard time penetrating). Their ears had become dull, and they had closed their eyes. In other words, they were deliberately unreceptive with an arrogance that willfully disregarded God and His Word. Moreover, this willfullness was keeping them from repenting (turning back to God) so God could heal (and deliver) them. God wanted to give them healing from their sins and deliverance from their enemies, but their unbelief was shutting them off from Him and from the good things He wanted to do for them.

Isaiah's prophecy did not in any way imply God's plan would fail, however. Isaiah saw a godly remnant among the Jews, as did Amos and many of the other Old Testament prophets.

Paul also recognized there was a godly remnant among the Jews in his day who were accepting the Lord Jesus Christ as their Messiah and Saviour (Romans 9:6; 11:5). The problem was that the unbelieving Jews were trying to dictate to God what the way of salvation should be. They forgot how Israel had lost out back in the days of Isaiah and Hosea, so God said they had become Lo-ammi, "not my people" (Hosea 1:9). Only God's grace and mercy preserved a remnant of the people in that day and kept the nation from complete destruction. The remnant were the ones who realized God made faith a condition on which His mercy and blessing is given. His promises are never a wholesale gift presented to everyone whether

they want it or not. They are only for those who accept God's conditions of faith and obedience.

**28. Be it known therefore unto you:** . . . Understand, then, *—TCNT* . . . Let it be plainly understood then, *—PHLP* . . . You should know, *—BECK* . . . let it be a matter of knowledge to you, *—SWAN* . . . Take notice, then, Knox.

**that the salvation of God is sent unto the Gentiles:** . . . that this salvation, *—ALFD* . . . God has sent His salvation to non-Jewish people, *—SEB* . . . this Gospel of divine salvation will be preached to, *—NOLI* . . . how to be saved from the penalty of sin has been sent to the people who are not Jews, *—NLTG.*

**and that they will hear it:** . . . and they will listen, *—TCNT* . . . they, at least, will listen to it, *—KNOX* . . . they . . . will give heed, *—WEYM* . . . they also will hear, *—HNSN.*

**28:28.** Paul then added that God's salvation was also sent to the Gentiles (a reference to his own call). They (emphatic) would also hear (and obey).

Paul thus declared the door was wide open to the Gentiles. As he told the Romans, they could be grateful for the goodness and severity of God which has resulted in the spread of the gospel to all nations and has made possible the salvation of all who hear.

The believers' attitude toward the Jews, however, should be one of compassion, not pride or superiority. Though they have rejected Christ and have been cut out of what Paul calls the "olive tree" (of God's continuing plan and blessing), God is able to graft them in again; and the Bible implies He will (Romans 11:17-24).

**29. And when he had said these words, the Jews departed:**

**and had great reasoning among themselves:** . . . with much dissension among themselves, *—KNOX* . . . arguing at great length with one another, *—NOLI.*

**28:29.** After Paul concluded these exhortations, the Jews left his apartment, but they were still carrying on a great discussion or debate among themselves. No doubt those who believed and obeyed were trying to persuade their friends to accept the truth of the gospel Paul had proclaimed and demonstrated to them from the Scriptures.

**30. And Paul dwelt two whole years in his own hired house:** . . . paid money to live in a house by himself, *—NLTG* . . . two entire years, *—SAWR* . . . which he rented for himself, *—TCNT* . . . in his rented lodging, *—SWAN* . . . at his own expense, *—NOLI.*

**and received all that came in unto him:** . . . He welcomed, *—NOLI* . . . and was wont to welcome, *—WORL* . . . welcoming all, *—TCNT* . . . He was happy for all who came to see him, *—NLTG* . . . to visit him, *—MOFT.*

**28:30.** This day of presenting the gospel to the Jews was not Paul's last opportunity. For 2 whole years he was able to live in his own rented apartment in a house where all who wished to visit him could come and go freely. Paul was happy to welcome them all.

Some believe Paul was released after those 2 years when he was called before the emperor, and the Jerusalem Jews had sent no accusation and no lawyer to represent them.

Others believe there was no trial and the case was automatically dismissed at the end of the 2 years because no charges were presented. Roman law gave the prosecution a limited time to present its case, depending on the distance they had to come. Philemon 22 shows Paul did expect to be released.

**31. Preaching the kingdom of God:** ... He continued to preach, *—MNTG* ... publishing the reign of God, *—HNSN.*

**and teaching those things which concern the Lord Jesus Christ:** ... teaching openly about, *—LAMS* ... and boldly taught the truth about, *—BECK.*

**with all confidence, no man forbidding him:** ... with perfect fearlessness, unmolested, *—TCNT* ... He was very bold, *—SEB* ... with utmost freedom and without hindrance from anyone, *—PHLP* ... fearlessly and unhindered, *—NORL* ... with entire freedom, none forbidding him, *—HNSN* ... with full freedom and without any hindrance, *—NOLI* ... without any restraint, *—CMPB* ... unforbidden, *—CNDT* ... and nobody stopped him, *—BECK* ... with unlimited freedom,

*—FNTN* ... freedom of speech, *—WSLY* ... with all freedom of speech, *—WORL* ... openly, *—KLGS* ... and unhindered, *—SWAN* ... without being hindered, *—KJII* ... and no one tried to stop him from speaking, *—NCV.*

**28:31.** During the 2 years Paul was able to preach and teach boldly and freely, proclaiming the kingdom or rule of God and teaching the things concerning Jesus Christ openly, boldly, and with freedom of speech. This was an answer to his requests for prayer sent to some of the churches he had founded (Ephesians 6:19, 20; Colossians 4:3, 4). Even some from Caesar's household were converted (Philippians 4:22). This probably came about through the witness the soldiers made to the whole praetorian guard or palace (Philippians 1:13).

First Timothy shows Paul was indeed released and went to the Roman province of Asia. Ancient tradition says he went to Spain also. This was followed by Paul's second imprisonment and death. Second Timothy 4:13 indicates he left his cloak at Troas, possibly because of a sudden arrest. By the time Paul wrote his last epistle, Second Timothy, it had then become a crime to be a Christian.

The Book of Acts breaks off suddenly. It has no formal conclusion. Some believe Luke intended to write another volume. Others believe Luke suffered martyrdom along with Paul. But the important point is that the Book of Acts had no formal ending. It is still going on today.

# ROMANS

## Overview

The New Testament can be divided into two basic parts. First there is a historical part, the Gospels and Acts; these contain apostolic testimony about Jesus and the Early Church. The second is a didactic (teaching) part consisting of the various letters (epistles) which give the apostolic interpretation of the events surrounding salvation. Just as the literary genre "gospel" was unique and unparalleled in antiquity, so too, the content of the letters is uniquely Christian. That also is due to Christianity's being grounded in history as well as a religion founded upon divine revelation. The oral proclamation of the apostles ceased with time, but through their letters they continue to speak to the Church until the end of time. *Apostle* means "one sent"; *epistle* denotes a "sent letter."

There are 2 groups of New Testament letters: the 13 letters of Paul and the Epistle to the Hebrews as well as the 7 so-called General Epistles. Paul's letters may be broken into four groups: (1) Eschatological Epistles (1 and 2 Thessalonians); (2) The Chief Epistles (sometimes referred to as "soteriological," concerning the doctrine of salvation— Romans, 1 and 2 Corinthians, Galatians); (3) The Prison Epistles (sometimes called ecclesiastical, that is, "church epistles"), written during Paul's imprisonment in Rome (Ephesians, Philippians, Colossians, and Philemon); (4) The Pastoral Epistles (1 and 2 Timothy, Titus).

Paul's letter to the church in Rome is the longest and most structured of the Pauline correspondence. It is regularly ascribed the most importance. There is general consensus that Paul, inspired by the Holy Spirit, authored it; arguments in favor of that include the self-testimony of the letter (1:15), its style, its content, and the tradition of the Early Church.

Apparently the letter was composed during the years A.D. 56-57, and probably from Corinth near the close of Paul's third missionary journey. At this point Paul was nearing the close of an epoch. He could reflect upon 20 years of Christian ministry. On every strategic front of the Roman Empire Christianity had made advances and had planted churches. The great apostle to the Gentiles now set his sights on the West; he intended to go all the way to Spain. On the way he wanted to fulfill his earnest desire to visit Rome, where a church was already thriving.

Just as Antioch was the base camp for the missionary outreach to the Gentiles in the East, now Rome would be the headquarters for the evangelization of the western Roman Empire. Paul wrote to advise them of his upcoming visit; thus Romans is in a sense a letter of introduction to the church. However, it was not a personal introduction but a presentation of the gospel that Paul preached. He outlined the message he hoped they would join him in spreading.

From such a background it becomes understandable why Paul summarized the gospel in such a highly didactic (teaching) way. Luther called Romans "the correct main piece of the New Testament and the 'most evident gospel.'" Chapter 1, verses 16 and 17, capsulize the major theme of the letter: "The gospel . . . is the power of God unto salvation to every one that believeth; to the Jew first, and also to the Greek. For therein is the righteousness of God revealed from faith to faith."

Romans can be divided into a section on teaching (chapters 1 to 8); a section on the history of salvation that deals with God's plans for Israel and the rest of mankind (chapters 9 to 11); and a section of admonition (chapters 12 to 16). Although dogmatic, Romans is not polemical, as is, for example, Galatians. Several passages address practical problems (chapter 14). In these Paul instructed the church about how to handle its current struggles. By and large, though, basic questions are discussed. The logic of the letter flows smoothly and serenely, despite Paul's natural inclination to preach. (See below for a fuller discussion of the character of the letter as a whole.)

The absence of verses 1-24 in chapter 16 of some manuscripts has caused some consternation. The most likely explanation is that the letter was closed temporarily in 15:33 but it was not sent until Phoebe could take it to Rome (16:1f.). Thus Paul added further greetings to those he knew in Rome—among others Priscilla and Aquila who apparently returned after the edict against Jews was lifted (ca. A.D. 54; cf. Acts 18:2)—then he closed the letter. Origen indicates a knowledge of this section in the oldest manuscripts. Because the passage is of such a personal nature it may have been omitted in those manuscripts that circulated for the Church at large. If the letter was read aloud it might be omitted for the same reason. No person in the Ancient Church denied the authenticity of chapter 16 except for the heretic Marcion, who excised the passage, including chapter 15, for his own dogmatic reasons.

The letter to the Romans is considered by many to be the most significant theological document in the New Testament. Throughout the history of the Church it has maintained its major position. During the Reformation it became the pivotal book for the doctrine of justification by faith alone. The following structure can be presented:

I. OPENING (1:1-17)

A. Authorship and Greetings (1:1-15)

B. Major Themes (1:16, 17)

1. The Gospel Is the Power of God Unto Salvation

2. Through the Gospel God's Righteousness Is Revealed

3. The Source of the Gospel's Power Is Faith

4. The Message of the Gospel Is Universal

II. TEACHING SECTION (1:18-8:39)

A. Concerning Sin (1:18-3:20)

1. The Guilt of the Gentiles (1:18-32)

a. Ungodliness, spiritual ignorance, and idolatry (1:18-23)

b. Unrighteousness and moral decay (1:24-32)

2. The Guilt of the Jews (2:1-3:20)

a. The principle of judgment (2:1-16)

1. God's judgment rests on the principle of truth (2:1-5)

2. God's judgment considers one's works (2:6-10)

3. God does not show partiality in His judgment (2:11-15)

4. God judges according to the gospel (2:16)

b. False and true Judaism (2:17-29)

1. The claim of the Jews (2:17-20)

2. The failure of the Jews (2:21-27)

3. The true Jewish religion (2:28, 29)

c. The Jewish advantage (3:1-8)

d. The world's guilt (3:9-20)

1. The accusation (3:9)

2. The proof of Scripture (3:10-18)

3. The conclusion (3:19, 20)

B. Concerning Justification (3:21-5:21)

1. The Basis of Justification (3:21-31)

a. The new revelation of God's righteousness (3:21, 22)

1. The righteousness of God revealed in the Law.

2. Witnessed by the Law and the Prophets.

3. The righteousness of God is by faith.

b. The three metaphors (3:23-26)

1. The legal metaphor (3:23)

2. The slave market metaphor (3:24)

3. The temple metaphor (3:25, 26)

c. The two addenda (3:27-31)

1. Boasting is excluded (3:27, 28)

2. Salvation is for everyone (3:29, 30)

2. Illustration of Abraham's Faith (4:1-5:11)

a. Not by works (4:1-8)

b. Not by circumcision (4:9-12)

c. Not by the Law (4:13-16)

d. The father of believers (4:17-25)

e. The blessings of justification (5:1-11)

1. Faith (5:1, 2)

2. Hope (5:2-4)

3. Charity (love, 5:5-11)

3. Adam and Christ (5:12-21)

C. Concerning Sanctification (6:1-8:39)

1. Freedom from Sin (6:1-23)

a. Baptized into His death (6:1-14)

b. Analogy of the slave (6:15-23)

2. Freedom from the Law (7:1-25)

a. Analogy from marriage (7:1-6)

b. The Law activates sin (7:7-13)

c. The "man" in Romans 7 (7:14-25)

1. A pre-Christian experience

2. A normal Christian life

3. A compromise solution

3. Freedom in Christ (8:1-39)

a. Justification and freedom (8:1-4)

b. The Spirit of liberty (8:5-14)

c. Our adoption (8:15-39)

III. HISTORY OF SALVATION SECTION (9:1-11:36)

A. The Doctrine of Election

B. Paul's Grief Because of the Unbelief in Israel (9:1-5)

C. God's Relationship With Israel (9:6-29)

1. Israel's Rejection and God's Promises (9:6-13)

2. Israel's Rejection and God's Righteousness (9:14-29)

D. Israel's Rejection and the Responsibility of the People (9:30-10:21)

1. Israel Rejects Christ (9:30-33)

2. Israel Rejects God's Righteousness (10:1-11)

3. Israel Rejects the Gospel (10:12-21)

## I. Opening (1:1-17)

The letter to the Romans is termed the first great theological work in Christian literature; such a title is fully deserved. But since this major Christian document is in the form of a letter, it has an opening.

## A. Authorship and Greetings (1:1-15)

Paul first identified himself as the sender, just as custom dictated. But he did this in a manner totally different from, say, the letter to his friend Philemon. Paul wrote to the church in Rome not so much for personal reasons but as the servant and apostle of Jesus Christ. The letter to Rome outlines the gospel Paul preached. He appealed both to his apostolic authority and to the authority of Scripture as the basis for the veracity of his message. The opening shows by what authority the apostle was writing. Paul did not himself found the church in Rome; however, at the same time he was no "outsider." He was writing as the apostle to the Gentiles and as an instructor in faith and truth (Romans 11:13; cf. 1 Timothy 2:7).

Paul's gospel is the gospel of God, and it is about the Son of God. Jesus Christ is the main character of the gospel story; in fact, He is the story itself. "According to the flesh," according to His human origin, He came from the line of David in keeping with messianic promises. "According to the Spirit of holiness," according to His spiritual heritage, He is the almighty Son of God. He proved this by being raised from the dead. The Pauline portrait of Christ does not simply point to the human and divine natures of Jesus; rather, it directs our attention to the two different positions He assumed in His manifestation: humiliation and exaltation.

## B. Major Themes (1:16, 17)

With a classic understatement Paul declared that he was not ashamed of the gospel. Actually the cross of Christ was his only glory (Galatians 6:14). At the same time Paul knowingly placed himself at odds with the world's attitude toward the gospel, because the preaching of the Cross is foolishness to those who are perishing (1 Corinthians 1:18). Nothing causes as much offense to the sinful man as the message of the Cross.

## 1. The Gospel Is the Power of God Unto Salvation

Thus Paul could declare he was not ashamed of it. It is superior to any human claim of personal merit in that it accomplishes something. It is the *dunamis* ("power") in contrast to the "powerlessness" of man to do anything to save himself. The gospel is God's solution to the problem of sin; it makes the dead alive and makes one a new creation in Christ. Salvation is mankind's greatest need, and only God can fulfill it. He alone can save us (Isaiah 35:4). He accomplishes this through Jesus Christ. The gospel then is the vibrant, powerful message of that salvation that has been procured for all mankind.

## 2. Through the Gospel God's Righteousness Is Revealed

The gospel becomes God's power for our salvation because in it God reveals His righteousness "by faith from first to last," as the apostle says. The phrase "the righteousness of God" appears for the first time in this passage. There is particular significance to that expression here. It does not simply refer to an attribute of God but to an action on God's part (Dodd, *The Moffatt New Testament Commentary,* p. 10). God's righteousness is expressed in His action in that He saves mankind: "The Lord hath made known his salvation: his righteousness hath he openly showed in the sight of the heathen" (Psalm 98:2).

The gospel offers the solution to the question of how can God be just in justifying the ungodly (3:26; 4:5). In the Law, God's righteousness is revealed in judgment, but in the gospel it is manifest for salvation. Thus the "righteousness of God" is not only an attribute of God but that which He freely gives to man. This great truth became apparent to Martin Luther and became a leading force behind the Reformation. Luther realized that what was previously thought to be an expression of God's strict expectations was in fact a declaration that God justifies. His righteousness does not condemn or judge the sinner; it invites him by grace to share in God's life (cf. 8:33).

### 3. The Source of the Gospel's Power Is Faith

It is for the one who believes "the power of God unto salvation." The righteousness of God that is revealed in the gospel is "first and last of faith," that is, no one can obtain salvation or righteousness through keeping the Law. It can only be received by faith. Faith in this context concerns the gospel itself. This includes the fact that the sinner places his trust in the gospel message; he depends upon it to guide his/her life and puts his trust in its message.

This faith is moreover based upon certain salvation events accomplished by God in Christ: When Jesus rose from the dead He justified those believing in Him (4:25). Faith is the condition upon which the gospel depends. The believer receives God's righteousness "by faith." At the same time the gospel demands that Christians act upon their faith. "Faith cometh by hearing" (10:17). Believers are saved by hearing and not by doing (Acts 11:14). The righteous will live by faith!

### 4. The Message of the Gospel Is Universal

Although it is "for the Jew first," it is not like the Mosaic covenant whose blessings were restricted to Jews and proselytes of the Jewish religion. The gospel is "to the Jew first, and also to the Greek." When Paul spoke from the Greek perspective the pagans were excluded (1:14). But from a Jewish point of view the Greek was a typical Gentile, i.e., he was excluded and outside of the covenant (Moody, *Broadman Bible Commentary,* 10:168). Paul proclaimed a gospel in which "there is neither Jew nor Greek!" (Galatians 3:28). Before the apostle began to condemn the world before God, his opening words acknowledged that salvation in Christ is just as universally affective as the guilt of mankind.

## II. Teaching Section (1:18-8:39)

### A. Concerning Sin (1:18-3:20)

The counterpart to God's grace is His wrath. Just as the righteousness of God is revealed in the gospel (1:17), so too, God's wrath is revealed from heaven against sin (1:18). God's kindness is offset by His sternness (11:22). Paul demonstrated how justified God is in His wrath and how necessary the gospel is if we are to escape this wrath. Justification can only be appreciated against the backdrop of God's wrath because of sin. The one not knowing guilt has no comprehension of innocence either. The most serious consequence of

sin is not that it leads to Satan's snares; rather, it puts one under the judgment of God (Luke 12:5). Paul shows in 1:18-3:20 that both Gentiles and Jews stand before God without excuse; each has incurred the wrath of God.

### 1. The Guilt of the Gentiles (1:18-32)

God directs His wrath toward two things: ungodliness and unrighteousness (1:18). Ungodliness refers to sin of a religious nature; unrighteousness involves sin in the moral sense of that word.

*a. Ungodliness, spiritual ignorance, and idolatry (1:18-23).* The ungodly one does not perceive God worthy of knowing (1:28), and he desires no fellowship with God. Ungodliness involves sinning against those commandments on the first table. It also concerns the spurning of the greatest commandment, to "love the Lord thy God with all thy heart, and with all thy soul, and with all thy mind" (Matthew 22:37).

Ungodliness leads to spiritual ignorance (1:18-23), which results from a hardened heart (Ephesians 4:17, 18). Because God has afforded men the opportunity to know Him through natural revelation, such as the Creation (1:19, 20), as well as through his (man's) conscience (2:14, 15), mankind is without excuse before God. He is ignorant of God not because of an intellectual deficiency; rather, it is due to his moral deficiency. It is the evil delusion about which the Bible has so much to say; it is the very essence of sin (Ecclesiastes 7:25). Sin corrupts the cognitive life of man and darkens his heart (1:21). In the end, the mind ruled by sin is utterly worthless (1:28).

Furthermore, spiritual ignorance results in idolatry (1:23-25). The void in the soul of man must be filled by something, and where God is excluded something else moves in and takes His place. At the heart of every denial of God—in one form or another—is a worship of the creation rather than the Creator (1:25). Eventually demonic forces are worshiped (1 Corinthians 10:20); the devil becomes one's god (2 Corinthians 4:4). The most serious aspect of idolatry is not its threat to life; instead it is its essentially sinful character. It offends God and subjects men to God's wrath.

*b. Unrighteousness and moral decay (1:24-32).* Unrighteousness as well as every other sin is a violation of God's law and a conscious rejection of His will (1 John 3:4). In actuality unrighteousness is rooted in ungodliness—a religious sin results in a wrong moral action. Eventually one discovers that unrighteousness lies at the root of many other sins (Murray, *New International Commentary on the New Testament,* 1:43). Paul's sin lists are paralleled elsewhere in earlier Jewish literature (e.g., Wisdom of Solomon 12-14). His own "catalogue of vices" are not that far removed from common social standards found elsewhere in Gentile writings. Paul divided the sins into two groups.

First he spoke of sexual impurity (1:24-28). Idolatry is a source of most immorality, and paganism is characterized by much sexual perversion. Paul indicted the worst kind of immorality—unnatural sexual relations. In an effort to relay the extent of pagan immorality and the degree to which it can control men, Paul first showed he was appalled that "even their women exchanged natural relations for unnatural ones" (1:26).

Three times Paul stressed that because men are held captive to their desires there is implicit judgment; God has handed them over to their own lusts (1:24, 26, 28). Ultimately, God allows men to choose their own route. Nevertheless, there is an element of God's judgment—active judgment—in this. God punishes sin with sin; the one who loves sin is handed over to his own lusts. This is not to say that God tempts men to sin (James 1:13), but He does permit man free choice. Man receives the due penalty of his sins—in part because of the corrosive, destructive character of sin, and in part because it is a judgment from God.

Second, in 1:29-32 Paul focused upon those sins that defile the spirit of man. These include social sins, sins against the second table of the Law, and sins against the great commandment: love your neighbor. He also mentioned hatred against God.

The list culminates in 1:32, which states that those who live in such sins know very well the judgment of God as well as His sentence for such sins—death. However, these reprobates do not simply live in sins themselves, they also encourage others who participate in like sins. Thus there is a "fellowship" in sin, an evil unity in which sinners support one another in their rebellion against God. This mystery of lawlessness is fundamental to the superstructure of Satan's realm.

## 2. The Guilt of the Jews (2:1-3:20)

Paul knew that voices from many sources would agree with his condemnation of the sins of the Gentiles. A contemporary of Paul, Seneca, a Stoic philosopher, wrote a number of pieces on virtue and sin that are entirely compatible with what the apostle to the Gentiles wrote. Paul would have received an even more thoroughgoing endorsement from the Jewish community for his indictment of Gentiles. But when Paul moved into a well-planned dialogue/ argument (which never actually occurred) called a diatribe (in which he took the Jewish religiosity to task, they became his opponents rather than advocates. Some—by their own positions—were compelled to agree with this indisputable logic. Using rhetorical questions, Paul virtually "tied up" his opponents. Thus Paul moved the Jew to the center of his readers' field of vision

and kept him there, not just in the central portion of this section, but in 2:1-16 and 3:9-20 as well.

*a. The principle of judgment (2:1-16).* The Jews must not fall into the error of thinking that if they judged others they themselves would not be judged. In sharp contrast to human judging stands God's judgment. Paul then proceeded to outline the principles used by God.

(1) *God's judgment rests upon the principle of truth (2:1-5).* "According to truth" (verse 2), the Lord is "the righteous judge" (2 Timothy 4:8). Apparently Paul was referring to the common Jewish misconception that God would use different standards for judging Jews and Gentiles (cf. the Wisdom of Solomon, chapters 11 to 13 especially). Paul denounced such an attitude (2:9, 11, 27). "Wherein thou judgest another, thou condemnest thyself; for thou that judgest doest the same things" (2:1).

(2) *God's judgment considers one's works (2:6-10).* Far from getting off easy, the Jews will be judged first, just as they will be rewarded first (2:9, 10). At the Judgment words will not replace deeds. Being judged according to deeds does not contradict the doctrine of justification by faith, because judgment based upon works is not the same as judgment by works (Moody, *Broadman Bible Commentary,* 10:174). Being judged according to works is a consistent principle of Scripture (e.g., Psalm 62:3; Proverbs 24:12; Jeremiah 17:10; 2 Corinthians 5:10; 2 Timothy 4:14; 1 Peter 1:17; Revelation 2:23; 20:12). Individuals may be denied not only because of unbelief, but also because of evil deeds. Good works, furthermore, are evidence of faith and salvation. Salvation is solely by faith (Romans 3:28), but faith never stands alone (James 2:14-20). It produces works.

(3) *God does not show partiality in His judgment (2:11-15).* Precisely because of this each man will be judged according to his own merits. Jews having the Law will be thus judged according to the Law (2:12). But Gentiles also have a law, the law of conscience that teaches them right from wrong. They have the work of law written in their hearts, according to Paul. This thought verbally resembles Jeremiah 31:31, but it has a different meaning.

"There is no nation so lost to everything human that it does not keep within the limits of some laws. Since then all nations, of themselves and without monitor, are disposed to make laws for themselves, it is beyond all question evident that they have some notions of justice" (Calvin, *Calvin's Commentaries: Romans,* p. 96).

(4) *God judges according to the gospel (2:16).* The teaching of a final judgment does not contradict the message of the gospel; in fact, it is integral to the announcement of grace. This was not fully realized until the proclamation of the gospel, thus

Paul only infrequently pointed to the gospel as the basis for judgment. Paul suggested that a new principle of judgment is in force: "That they all might be damned who believed not the truth" (2 Thessalonians 2:12; cf. John 16:9 and its context).

b. False and true Judaism (2:17-29). The next section opens with the words: "Behold, thou art called a Jew . . ." (2:17). At this juncture Paul began a most curious argumentation. In response to the boast of those Jews who pointed to their Jewish heritage Paul questioned their adherence to Judaism: You are called a Jew, but are you really? Thus Paul was redefining "Jewish" not in terms of natural descent, but in terms of a spiritual position.

(1) The claim of the Jews (2:17-20). In short statements Paul summarized some of the privileges the Jews appealed to as an indication of their "superiority" over the Gentiles. His stipulations are not without irony; nevertheless, he did not deny that being Jewish has certain actual advantages. Still, he undermined their basis for such claims to superiority.

(2) The failure of the Jews (2:21-27). Paul posed five questions to the Jewish legal expert or teacher of the Law: First, "Thou therefore which teachest another, teachest thou not thyself?" Paul asserted, just as Jesus had, that the ultimate sin of Judaism was its hypocrisy (cf. Matthew 23:1f.). The adherents knew the Law; they taught others the Law, but they did not themselves do what the Law demanded. Thus Paul could regard their "religion" as useless.

Circumcision meant Jews must keep the Law (cf. Galatians 5:3)—all of it! Perhaps, Paul argued, circumcision was of some small value ("profiteth") if one indeed kept the whole Law. But any violation of the Law, even in its smallest point, was a violation of the whole Law. The violator, thus, must be regarded in the same manner as an uncircumcised Gentile (2:25). This reasoning would not have set well in Jewish ears, for to them circumcision had a value all its own. Some rabbis taught that the sign of circumcision prevented any Jew from going to Gehenna (Moody, Broadman Bible Commentary, 10:177). Paul regarded these speculations as empty self-delusion.

(3) The true Jewish religion (2:28, 29). Jews regarded themselves superior to Gentiles on the basis of ethnic heritage (nationality) and religion (especially monotheism). They saw themselves certainly on a par with Christians and more typically above. They considered Christians, especially Jewish Christians, as deceivers. However, at a very early stage of development Christianity responded to this charge.

Peter redirected this charge of deceit upon the Jews themselves in his public accusation that they betrayed the Messiah by delivering Him to the Romans (Acts 3:13; cf. 4:27). Even Paul's deep love for his kinsmen did not prevent him from using scathing language against them (1 Thessalonians 2:15).

With words charged with indignation Paul attacked the Judaizers and called them "dogs, those men who do evil, those mutilators of the flesh" (Philippians 3:2, NIV). The kind of Judaism that had crucified the Messiah and had persecuted His disciples ceased being "true Judaism" to Paul. Paul reserved the title Jew for those who believe in Christ. Over against those "putting confidence in the flesh" are those of the (true) circumcision, those who "worship God in the spirit" (Philippians 3:3). "For he is not a Jew, which is one outwardly; . . . but he is a Jew, which is one inwardly; and circumcision is that of the heart, in the spirit, and not in the letter; whose praise is not of men, but of God" (Romans 2:28, 29).

There is some dispute over the final words. Jews are named in keeping with their ancestor Judah. Some contend that Judah means "the praised one," and is from the Hebrew word yadah, "praise." Leah, who worshiped God because of her son, named him Judah in keeping with her praise of God (Genesis 29:35). His father Jacob blessed him from his death bed with the words: "Thou art he whom thy brethren shall praise" (Genesis 49:8).

c. The Jewish advantage (3:1-8). In this next section Paul gave his imaginary opponent one opportunity to defend himself. It consists of two of the standard arguments against Christianity which Paul undoubtedly met in the synagogues. The first relates to the perception mentioned above: Judaism and circumcision. The second relates to the Jewish objection that God would be unjust if "our unrighteousness brings out God's righteousness more clearly."

(1) Is Judaism actually practiced in vain? Paul's challenger raised an objection which might mistakenly be concluded from Paul's earlier arguments. If what Paul said about the value of "inwardly" belonging to God's people is true, and if only the "circumcision of the heart" by the Spirit has significance, "What advantage then hath the Jew? or what profit is there of circumcision?" (3:1). "What advantage is there in being Jewish and in being circumcised as a sign of the covenant?" asks his imaginary opponent.

Paul, however, did not concede to such reasoning. On the contrary, he responded that the advantage of being Jewish is "much every way" (3:2). The privileges of the Jewish people are actual, although they have been abused and neglected in the past.

One of the main advantages of the Jewish people is that they were entrusted with God's Word in the Holy Scriptures. The Scriptures speak on behalf of God in the same way the prophets did. Circumcision was a sign of God's covenant with Abraham, the patriarch of the nation (Genesis 17). God remains faithful to this covenant in spite of the unfaithfulness of the Jewish people.

(2) The second Jewish objection, that it is "unjust" that "our unrighteousness brings out God's righteousness more clearly" (3:5, NIV)—and hence an invitation to sin that grace may abound, was soundly refuted by Paul. Mankind's sin is no less reprehensible because it does not affect God, thus Paul ignored such reasoning. God is the judge of the world and the moral standard of the universe; this is revealed truth. "The reply to objections is proclamation" (Murray, *New International Commentary on the New Testament,* p. 99).

Still, Paul had more to say than this. The imaginary opponent rephrased the objection, and this time Paul—in obvious disbelief—admitted that some had erroneously insinuated that this is what he taught. Heralds of the gospel, and especially Paul, were continually suspected of encouraging "lawlessness" (antinomianism). The New Testament is plagued with traces of the struggle against those who pervert the freedom of the gospel into license for immorality (Galatians 5:13-21; Titus 1:16; 2 Peter 2:1f.; 2:18f.; Jude 4).

This distortion of the Christian message afforded the legal experts in Judaism as well as the philosophers of the Gentile world the opportunity to infiltrate the gospel ranks. They asserted that lawlessness was a natural by-product of gospel proclamation. Paul's letters indicate they claimed much of their authority (unjustly) from Paul's own teachings. Paul readdressed himself to this issue in 6:1f., and he took it as a point of departure for his teaching on sanctification. In 3:8 though, he only rejected scornfully such agitators with the words "whose damnation is just."

*d. The world's guilt (3:9-20).* In this section Paul moved toward concluding his argument. He posed the question: "Are we Jews any better than the Gentiles?" Although Jews may have advantage "much in every way," they are "in no wise" better than Gentiles in God's eyes (cf. Bruce, *Tyndale New Testament Commentaries,* 6:92).

(1) *The accusation (3:9).* Paul summarized and restated the accusation he made earlier: Jew and Greek alike are under the condemnation of sin. To be under sin means that sin controls and dominates one's existence. But it also signifies one's guilt before God. One already stands under God's judgment. In the next two sections Paul discussed these two dimensions of sin.

(2) *The proof of Scripture (3:10-18).* Having summarized the charge in the preceding verse, Paul now began his argument with the evidence of Scripture. He employed a method of interpretation commonly used by the rabbis of his day.

It derived its name, *charaz,* from the process of threading beads on a string, such as a string of pearls. The practice of *charaz* involved using, for example, a Pentateuchal text as a basic text; then one would "string" other texts to this on the basis of corresponding words or phrases. These other texts came from the Prophets, Psalms, and other portions of Scripture (Edersheim).

In this instance Paul created a chain of six citations from the Old Testament which demonstrate man's sinful nature and conduct. Five times it is noted that none are righteous and none seek God (verses 10-12).

In highly metaphorical language Paul noted those physical parts of the body capable of serving unrighteousness (verses 13-15). Fallen man is characterized by his "worthlessness" (verse 12; cf. 1:28). No one does anything good or makes any effort to seek God.

(3) *The conclusion (3:19, 20).* The final verses pronounce the sentence: All the world is guilty before God. It is guilty because of sin—actual concrete sin, not some subjective feeling of guilt. This guilt and sin separate man from an offended and holy God. Sin itself devastates man, creating inner conflicts as well as binding him to wrongdoing.

The actual problem of guilt before God places man under His judgment and wrath. Mankind is enabled to recognize this problem only through the convicting power of the Holy Spirit through preaching and the Word of God. Through the power of the Holy Spirit man comes to realize that he needs something more than deliverance from a bad conscience; what he really needs is to be justified—made righteous—before God, so he will not perish eternally.

In no uncertain terms Paul asserted that "by the deeds of the law there shall no flesh be justified in his sight" (3:20). Because the Law permits man to recognize sin he can confess it. However, the Law is not able to release man from the guilt of that sin, nor can it set him free from sin's power. Only the gospel of the "good news" of Jesus Christ has that ability.

## B. Concerning Justification (3:21-5:21)

Someone once said that this is the most important section of the most important book in the Bible. Although this is an overstatement, there is something to be said for its element of truth. There is perhaps no other portion of Scripture which condenses so much of the essence of the gospel.

## 1. The Basis of Justification (3:21-31)

In this section Paul began to proclaim the gospel in the same manner as he had in the opening (see above), having laid the groundwork in between. The thunder of the Law closes every mouth; sin is stilled in silence. It is in this setting that the still voice of the gospel can be heard.

The gospel cannot meet an unrecognized need, but where men are awakened from their worldly slumber and their religious self-righteousness the gospel can penetrate and accomplish mighty things. Jesus himself declared that He had not come for the righteous but for the unrighteous; it is the sinner who needs to be justified.

a. The new revelation of God's righteousness (3:21, 22). Section 3:21-26 is actually made up of a hymn of three verses, each containing four lines and arranged in balance.

1). verses 21, 22a

2). verses 22b-25a

3). verses 25b, 26

The following breakdown, however, is according to content.

The main focus of this section of the letter to Rome is the issue of righteousness—the dispute between the unrighteous man and the righteous God. Prior to this point Paul had stressed that God's righteousness is revealed in His judgment. Here Paul shifted gears and began to describe an entirely different manifestation of the righteousness of God.

(1) The righteousness of God revealed in the Law. The words of the Law announce the arrival of a totally new age and order—what some have called "God's eschatological now." In sharp contrast to the role of the Law in manifesting God's righteousness Paul had previously outlined, now he spoke of a new righteousness that is revealed apart from the Law. This does not concern righteousness in the subjective sense, such as an attribute of God; rather, it involves an objective righteousness that God imputes to those who believe. This is the righteousness that Paul introduced as early as 1:17: "The righteousness of God revealed from faith to faith"—that is, a righteousness by faith in contrast to a righteousness through the Law.

God could not satisfy His demand for righteousness apart from destroying the moral universe. Only the righteous can stand before God (Psalm 15). However, man cannot attain this righteousness through his own efforts; therefore, God gives to man the righteousness he needs by offering him salvation. Even if the path of the Law had been an avenue to righteousness, it was a path no one could follow. Indeed, Paul argued that the Law was never a means of attaining righteousness.

Since man is unable to win righteousness by doing the works of the Law, God gives it to him as a free gift. By His own sovereignty God declares sinners righteous if they accept His provision for their redemption. This enigmatic event is termed "justification" in the Scripture. All those believing in the One who justifies the ungodly may experience it (4:5).

This is a righteousness apart from the Law; that is, it is not something that man earns by keeping the Law. This righteousness is given on a totally different basis—Jesus Christ.

(2) Witnessed by the Law and the Prophets. Whenever Paul spoke of a righteousness apart from the Law it must not be assumed that the gospel contradicts the old covenant and the Holy Scriptures. At its heart even the old covenant was founded upon promise rather than Law (Galatians 3:17). True Judaism is not a legalistic religion but a religion of promise. Thus Paul declared that the righteousness of God that is apart from the Law is nevertheless precisely the righteousness to which the Law and the prophets bore witness. Later Paul offered a series of texts in support of this claim. The very point at which the faith of the Bible differs so radically from every other human religion in the world is that God's righteousness is something He gives, and it cannot be earned.

(3) The righteousness of God is by faith. Over against one's "own righteousness, which is by the law" (Philippians 3:9), the true righteousness, now revealed, is called "the righteousness of God which is by faith of Jesus Christ" (Romans 3:22). Unlike legalistic religions or human religions that depend upon man's own efforts, the righteousness of God depends upon the work of Christ. Man does not deserve it, and yet for Christ's sake it is imputed to those who believe. It rests upon an individual's being forgiven and having repented of his sins. God demands righteousness, but He provides the believer with the very righteousness He wants.

Whereas the "righteousness of the law" was thought to be won through keeping the Law, God's righteousness comes through faith. The centrality of faith is highlighted by the deliberate redundancy of verse 22: "righteousness of God which is by faith of Jesus Christ unto all and upon all them that believe!" Faith here is not some nebulous "faith" without substance; neither is it simply believing that God exists. The faith which justifies is faith in Jesus Christ, the Son of God (1:3, 4), who "was delivered over to death for our sins and was raised to life for our justification" (4:25, NIV). The one justified by faith is the one believing in Jesus' person and Christ's work on his behalf.

b. The three metaphors (3:23-26). Justification by faith is the great theological theme in Romans. It stands in sharp contrast to the rabbis' doctrine of justification by works. Paul did not present the arguments for his teaching by mere logic, although what he said is indeed logical. Instead, he used a series of pictures or parables, the language of the prophet and the poet.

The apostle used three metaphors. One comes from the courtroom: The accused is acquitted; although guilty, he is justified by God's own decision. The second metaphor is from the slave market: The one in bondage is released through the price of redemption paid by Jesus Christ. The third metaphor is taken from the temple offerings: The blood of Jesus Christ is the real basis of justification. Through the repentant sinner's faith, the blood of Jesus becomes a propitiation that satisfies God's wrath against sin.

(1) *The legal metaphor (3:23).* The repentant sinner is justified on the basis of what Paul called "the righteousness of God."

Justification is not synonymous with forgiveness, although it is clearly granted only on the basis of forgiveness of sins. The way the word *justification* is used, it indicates it is not identical with forgiveness. If an individual actually kept the Law he was no sinner and therefore did not need to be forgiven. No one could actually be justified through fulfilling the commands of the Law, but if he could, it could not accurately be described as forgiveness.

Romans 3:4 speaks of God's being justified. The same Greek word for justification is used in Luke 7:29 where it is said the people justified God, i.e., acknowledged God to be in the right. Justifying God means acknowledging His completely righteous character. Thus, justification is something other than forgiveness of sins.

Justification is the opposite of condemnation: "By thy words thou shalt be justified, and by thy words thou shalt be condemned" (Matthew 12:37). See also Romans 5:16; 8:33, 34. A court does not make a man a criminal. It simply arrives at a decision about what he already is.

If he is acquitted, this is a public declaration that no guilt can be placed upon him. The term *justification* has the same meaning in the Bible. It means to be acquitted of what one is accused of, to be declared righteous by God (G.H. Clark).

In his teaching about justification, Paul described what takes place in God's courtroom. Here the guilty one is acquitted; the sinner is justified. His sins are canceled, and the righteousness of Christ is imputed to him. If God rendered such a decision only on the basis of what the sinner is himself, it would be unjust. Of course, this would be contrary to the character of God. Proverbs 17:15 says, "He that justifieth the wicked, and he that condemneth the just, even they both are abomination to the Lord."

The main question in the Book of Romans is: how then can a just God acquit and justify the ungodly one? It was of special importance to Paul to defend God's character and actions in the matter, to show that He can be just and still justify the sinner. No doubt Paul encountered objections to this teaching in his discussions with the Jews. They could not understand that the gospel did not contradict the righteousness of God. The apostle's reply to the Jews' opposition was this: God can be just and still justify the person who believes in Jesus because the believer stands before God clothed in Jesus' own righteousness. He has a new relationship with God secured for him by what Paul called "the redemption that is in Christ Jesus" (3:24).

(2) *The slave market metaphor (3:24).* The Greek word used here for "redemption" is *apolutrōseōs*. The term was used in connection with redeeming a slave or prisoner of war. In the Septuagint *lutroō* is used of God's redemption of His people from Egypt and from Babylon (Deuteronomy 7:8; Isaiah 51:11). In the New Testament the word has the double meaning of being redeemed and being bought by a price, a ransom, *lutron*. This last term is used in Matthew 20:28 and Mark 10:45. In both passages it is said that Jesus would give His life "a ransom for many." This substitutionary atonement is the basis of redemption. Jesus gave His own life as the price paid for that redemption.

God taught His people under the old covenant that He had the right to redeem His people (Rosenius). If an Israelite had been sold into slavery because of a debt, he could be redeemed by a brother. In the Old Testament the subject of redemption already had a distinct spiritual context. It is written in Psalm 49:7, 8: "None of them can by any means redeem his brother, nor give to God a ransom for him: (for the redemption of their soul is precious, and it ceaseth for ever)." This passage concerns the relationship between man and God. It requires a ransom, but no man can save his brother from death by paying a price. The ransom is now paid in full by Jesus Christ, and God himself is the One who has actually paid the price so that He and man can have a restored relationship.

(3) *The temple metaphor (3:25, 26).* Paul took his third picture from the temple and the ritual of the old covenant. He used the word *hilastērion*. The only other place the term is used in the New Testament is Hebrews 9:5. There it means the mercy seat, the golden cover of the ark of the covenant where the blood was sprinkled on the great Day of Atonement. The word is also used in such a manner 22 times in the Septuagint. Most scholars agree that in 3:25 Paul wanted to include the symbolism of the mercy seat. Origen and all the Greek fathers of the Church understood the verse this way. In fact, it has always enjoyed widespread support among Bible scholars.

Such a reference to the mercy seat of the old covenant does not limit the meaning of the Greek word since it is used in other ways. Although Paul alluded to the mercy seat by using the word *hilas-*

*tērion*, there is no reason to believe he confined the meaning of the word only to the mercy seat. The term belongs to a group of words used in connection with atonement and reconciliation.

Besides *hilastērion*, which is used this way twice, three related Greek words are used in the New Testament—each of them twice.

The verb *hilaskomai* stands in Greek usage for soothing an offended person or securing his favor through a gift or an atoning sacrifice. It is the offended party, not the offender, who becomes softened in his attitude. In the New Testament this word is used in Hebrews 2:17, where it refers to Christ who as a high priest made reconciliation for sin. It is also used in Luke 18:13 where the publican prayed that God would be merciful to him. The publican was praying in the temple—the place where atonement must be made. Thus his prayer was consistent with the thought of atonement.

The adjective *hileōs* is used in Matthew 16:22 where Peter rebuked Jesus with the words "Be it far from thee," or more literally, "Have mercy on you." The word is also used in Hebrews 8:12 where the word of the prophet is quoted: "I will be merciful to their unrighteousness."

The noun *hilasmos* is used in 1 John 2:2; 4:10 concerning Christ as the propitiation for our sins.

Thus the usage of these words in the New Testament is consistent with their usual meaning in Greek usage. This is also true in Romans 3:25. Paul could have employed a word used in the New Testament concerning Christ as an atonement, i.e., *hilasmos*, but he did not. Instead, he chose to use the well-known word for mercy seat, *hilastērion*, a word used for the place of the atonement, not the offering made there. It is difficult to believe the Holy Spirit inspired writer did not do this intentionally. It seems clear that he wanted to bring the mercy seat into the picture, thus connecting Christ's sacrifice with the Day of Atonement. The Jews understood the mercy seat to be God's throne on earth. Thus the usage of the mercy seat as a picture of Christ in His sacrifice fits in with the temple metaphor very well.

Paul was also dealing with another basic theological problem: When God justifies sinners, how can it be just when He bore with sins throughout the Old Testament period? Under the old covenant the various sacrifices—and especially those on the Day of Atonement—were to remind the people that God would one day make atonement for sin by one perfect sacrifice (Hebrews 10:3). However, the Jews did not understand this symbolism of the Day of Atonement, for only the high priest saw the blood-sprinkled mercy seat.

Now something new and unheard of had taken place: the mercy seat was displayed openly. It was no more hidden behind the veil of the temple. It was presented publicly, thus demonstrating God's righteousness to the whole universe, to heaven and earth (Manson, *Peake's Commentary on the Bible*). The mercy seat God had now set forth was not an imperfect copy of the one in the tabernacle and temple. The day of types and shadows was past, for reality had now come (Hebrews 9:11). God is gracious and He has shown the reason for it. Paul declared it is Jesus Christ himself "whom God hath set forth to be a propitiation through faith in his blood."

The mystery is not that God punishes sin, but how can He *not* do so? Only the gospel can give the correct answer. Jewish teachers of the Law accused the gospel of contradicting the righteousness of God. Paul, however, showed that the Jews themselves could not really explain how God can be righteous when He has borne with the sins of past generations. In the shedding of His blood, Jesus displayed the answer to God's forbearance in the past and His justifying grace in the present. God has placed His Son not only before His own eyes, but has exhibited Him to all the world.

*c. The two addenda (3:27-31).* Now Paul returned to the format of the dialogue. However, it is evident that the apostle himself was asking the rhetorical questions as the antagonist. Several facts need to be noted:

(1) *Boasting is excluded (3:27, 28).* In Paul's writings the matter of "boasting" was taken very seriously. First Corinthians 1:29 says God has chosen that which is low in the world so no flesh could boast before Him. In 3:27 Paul resumed the line of thought from the final verse in the preceding chapter. Earlier he had declared men have nothing to boast about. Their violation of the Law has deprived them of all right to boast. Such an attitude is inconsistent with the law of faith. No one can boast about his works, because works are not the basis of salvation. The basis is faith, thus excluding everything about which a believer might boast.

Christians are justified by faith and faith alone. Luther did not add anything to the actual construction of the text when he added his famous "alone" because this is exactly what the verse emphasizes. Unfortunately, the Council of Trent went against the plain meaning of the text by finally deciding to omit "without works of the law" in quoting Paul. The apostle was emphasizing here that believers are justified by faith alone apart from the works of the Law.

(2) *Salvation is for everyone (3:29, 30).* All have sinned, including both Jews and Gentiles and confirmed by Paul in the preceding chapter, but all may be saved. As an argument for this, Paul pointed to the Shema, Israel's great confession of faith: God is one (Deuteronomy 6:4). The one true God is not only the God of the Jews. He is also the God

of the whole earth. In other statements Paul emphasized the fact that God chose Abraham and his family in order that He might bless all people, not just the Jews. Now the apostle stressed the truth that this was through faith, not by the Law, proving that salvation has been provided for (*all*) who believe. Those who have had the Law (the Jews) must come to God the same way as those without the Law (the Gentiles). God justifies by faith the circumcised as well as the uncircumcised.

## 2. Illustration of Abraham's Faith (4:1-5:11)

Chapters 4 and 5 can be considered as comments on the basic proclamation of justification by faith in the latter part of chapter 3. There are a number of questions and objections which must be answered so that conclusions can be made. Paul treated this material in two sections. Here the apostle made another of his surprising points. He presented his argument around two prominent Old Testament persons, Abraham as the type of the one justified by faith (chapter 4) and Adam as the type of Christ (5:12-21). By doing this Paul made his presentation lively and clear and gave a series of proofs from the Scripture for justification by faith. He had already done this in 3:21, where he said the Law and the prophets bear testimony to this truth.

In 3:21 Paul explained the real foundation of justification, based on the redemptive work of Christ. In chapter 5 he explained faith more thoroughly as the subjective means by which the righteousness of God is imputed to man. Paul pointed to Abraham the ancestor of Israel, showing from his life that justification is by faith, not by works (4:1-7), not by circumcision (4:9-12), not by the Law (4:13-16). Then Abraham was presented as the father of believers (4:17-25). Following this is a passage which concerns the blessing resulting from justification (5:1-11).

*a. Not by works (4:1-8).* Abraham was a justified man. Paul here opposed the rabbis' teaching that Abraham fulfilled the Law and therefore was justified by works. The apostle quoted the Scripture, "Abraham believed God, and it was counted unto him for righteousness." Of all the just men in the Old Testament, none surpasses Abraham. Moses was called the servant of God, but Abraham was called the friend of God. From the Lord himself he received testimony that he had kept all His commandments and laws (Genesis 26:5). But even the most righteous and perfect man must be justified by his faith, not by his works. The rabbis listed Abraham's faith among his good works, but Paul placed faith in opposition to works. By faith and by faith only was Abraham justified.

*b. Not by circumcision (4:9-12).* Some may raise the question, "When Abraham's faith was counted

to him for righteousness, did this not take place because he had entered the covenant of circumcision with God?" Paul rejected such a thought by reminding his readers that righteousness by faith was ascribed to Abraham at least 14 years before he was circumcised. Justification is by faith, not by religious rites.

*c. Not by the Law (4:13-16).* Since the covenant of circumcision was not the basis of Abraham's justification, neither can the Law given at Sinai. In Galatians 3:15-22 Paul pointed out that the Law was given 430 years later. In Romans he presented these principal arguments: law and promise are two entirely different categories. God's promise did concern blessing (Genesis 12:2, 3; Galatians 3:8, 9), but the Law works wrath (Romans 4:15). If Law makes men heirs of God's promise, then faith is made void.

Therefore, Paul declared that Abraham and his family did not receive the promise of being heirs of the world by the Law, but by the righteousness of faith. Abraham received the promise by faith because it was by God's grace. If he had received it from works it would be like a salary which he earned by his labors. But the promise was by grace, not earnings. Works would render grace meaningless. Where does faith enter the picture? It is the means by which an individual accepts and receives the grace of God which is given apart from works.

*d. The father of believers (4:17-25).* When Paul spoke of Abraham as the father of believers, the subject becomes one of spiritual relationship. To a certain extent chapter 4 presents a contrast to chapter 5 where Adam is presented as the ancestor of the human race (according to the flesh). This argument had great relevance to the Jews. They were descendants of Abraham, and they must be saved in the same way as their great ancestor. When Paul insisted that natural descent was not enough to save them, it was language the Jews understood. They must also have a spiritual relationship with Abraham, which meant they must have the same kind of faith he had. Paul was echoing the preaching of John the Baptist (Matthew 3:7-9) and of Jesus himself (John 8:33-58).

Abraham's faith was characterized by his belief that God makes the dead alive and that He is the Creator who by His word brings into existence what did not previously exist. Thus his faith in God concerned His being both Redeemer and Creator. When God promised Abraham posterity as innumerable as dust and stars, he was still childless, but he believed God (4:18-22). When Abraham went to the mountain to sacrifice Isaac, he believed God could raise from the dead the son through whom the promise was to be carried out (compare Hebrews 11:19).

By this faith Abraham was justified, but this is not recorded in Scripture just to honor Abraham's memory. It is written because of all those who have the same faith in God. The faith of Abraham was displayed first because he believed God had power to raise up Isaac the son of promise. The Christian faith leads believers to accept the fact that God gave His Son to die for the sinner and raised Him from the dead for the believer's justification.

e. *The blessings of justification (5:1-11).* In 4:13 the promise to Abraham is interpreted as meaning he would become heir to the world. In 8:17 Paul spoke of believers as "heirs of God, and joint-heirs with Christ." They share with the only begotten Son His undivided inheritance (John 1:14; Revelation 21:7). This inheritance is "all things."

Paul mentioned the believer's inheritance briefly in 4:13, and then proceeded with his series of arguments. In all of this he was focusing on the important subject of salvation. Paul returned to this subject after completing his interpretation of Abraham's justification. In 5:1-11 the apostle dealt with the other blessings resulting from justification. This passage forms a transition to the next section of the epistle which concerns sanctification. Chapter 5 deals with what believers *have* in Christ, while chapter 6 speaks of what they *are* in Christ.

Next Paul summed up the blessings shared by Christ and the believer, and he did it under the headings of three well-known words—faith, hope, and charity (1 Corinthians 13:13).

(1) *Faith (5:1, 2).* The apostle mentioned three things produced by faith. First, as discussed previously, is justification. The first evidence of justification is peace with God. This peace must be understood theologically, not psychologically. The subject is not peace in one's heart and mind, but peace with God. The peace a believer *feels* is simply the result of the peace he has *received* from God. Unsaved man lives in rebellion against his Creator, which is the reason for his restlessness and internal discord. When he is justified by faith, this warfare ceases. The repentant sinner is reconciled to God, so he no longer lives under His wrath. Enmity and revolt are gone. Therefore, peace with God is something much more than a feeling. A total change in man's relationship with God has taken place.

Furthermore, "we have access by faith into this grace wherein we stand." One commentator says this statement could refer to being introduced to a royal person—a striking and beautiful illustration. The real meaning, however, is that since believers are now in favor with God they have been given great privileges.

(2) *Hope (5:2-4).* Faith and justification do not only provide rich treasures of peace and grace

now, they give hope of enjoying the glory of God in the future. What the believer now possesses is evidence that the future has already begun and is a foretaste and pledge of that which is to come. Even the believer's present tribulations only strengthen and increase this hope.

(3) *Charity (love, 5:5-11).* A believer is secure in the knowledge that he will not be ashamed in his hope—a security resting in the love of God. This love has been poured out into his heart by the Holy Spirit, who is himself the guarantee of the believer's inheritance until the day of redemption when he actually enters into it. The overwhelming love of God in the believer's heart is the great force which guides his life.

The amazing thing is that this love was shown "when we were still powerless, Christ died for the ungodly" (NIV). Sinners did not win (earn) God's love. His love won and keeps them. Christ died for the ungodly at a time God had already fixed. Much more then, being justified by Christ's blood, believers will be saved from wrath through Him. The believer does not boast of himself or his own works as the basis of his salvation and hope. He boasts of God by the Lord Jesus Christ. This means that in Christ he trusts God as Guarantor that his hope will be realized.

This discussion of love is actually a hymn about love, as 3:21-26 is a hymn about righteousness. In both passages there is a poetic section of three verses, each containing four lines and two parallels. Verse 1 of the hymn says Christ died "when we were . . . without strength" in verse 2 while men were sinners, in verse 3 while they were enemies (Moody, *Broadman Bible Commentary,* 10:193). The hymn in 3:21 exalts the death of Christ as the perfect revelation of God's righteousness, while the hymn in 5:6-11 exalts the Cross as the ultimate proof of God's love.

### 3. Adam and Christ (5:12-21)

Paul explained the connection between justification and faith in chapter 4. In 5:12-21 he ended that explanation and presented the connection between justification and the Fall. In chapter 4, justification is illustrated by the faith of Abraham. In chapter 5 it is seen in connection with the fall of Adam. Paul built on the truth that the record of the Fall tells of realities, that sin actually entered the world through a man. From this fact Paul declared that Adam is a type and Christ a countertype (5:14). As sin entered the world by one man, God has sent one Man to take away sin.

The focus of Paul's teaching in this section was to answer the question: How can the One take the place of the many? He knew this was an objection some had to the gospel, so he replied to it. This passage does not take form as dialogue, although some of it may be dialogue in a limited sense. Actually it is a rather complicated discourse.

Verse 12 is unfinished, as if the apostle had been suddenly interrupted. He inserted two great parentheses (13, 14 and 15-17) and replied to two important questions. First, in verse 18 he resumed the line of thought begun in verse 12 and carried through the explanation which was started there. In verses 20, 21 he ended his discussion about justification by establishing that grace is greater than sin and rules in those who are justified. This forms the transition to the next section of the epistle concerning sanctification, i.e., that the believer must not let sin rule him (6:12).

In 5:12-21, justification was still discussed, but the apostle's main intent was to justify God, to show that God is righteous. In chapter 3 this question was addressed: How can God be just when He justifies the ungodly? In chapter 5 the reply is given to another question: How can God be righteous when He allows one Man to bear the punishment for the sins of all humanity?

The apostle gave the answer immediately: "As by one man sin entered into the world, and death by sin; and so death passed upon all men, for that all have sinned." Paul ended the statement without making any conclusion. For the time being he did not clarify it further but inserted his parenthetical remarks.

In the first parenthesis Paul defended his teaching that all sinned when one sinned (verse 12). Adam's influence on the human family was not just his bad example or his creation of a moral climate which made it easy for his descendants to sin. Paul was not emphasizing the fallen nature Adam passed on to his descendants but the sentence God passed on them—an imputed guilt which Adam as the head of the human race brought on every member of the race. God placed the entire family of Adam under sin because of the fall of Adam.

Now Paul moved to prove that the sentence resulting from Adam's sin rests on the human race. He presented the argument that even those who did not bear personal guilt because of breaking God's commandments were under the dominion of death anyway. Such was the case from Adam to Moses, i.e., the period before the Law was given.

This is not mere theory. Paul was discussing a guilt which is demonstrated daily. Each innocent child that dies is a testimony to the sentence of death which rests on mankind.

This imputed guilt can be abolished only when men are granted righteousness by God, i.e., justified. Fundamentally this can happen in two ways, but practically and in reality in only one. Fundamentally man can be justified by the Law, which Paul maintained distinctly (Romans 10:5; Galatians 3:12). This means that the descendant of Adam who fulfills the law of God will not be condemned on the Day of Judgment because of Adam's sin even though in this life he is under judgment because of that sin. Here man stands at the tension point between two declarations of God, i.e., that God visits on children the sin of their fathers (Exodus 20:5) and that a son shall not die because of his father's sin if he is converted (Ezekiel 18:20). However, the Law is a "way of salvation" only in theory. Just as distinctly as Paul said that he who fulfills the Law is justified by it, he also said that nobody is justified by works of the Law. The reason is that no such man ever lived. No one has ever fulfilled the Law. "All have sinned, and come short of the glory of God" (Romans 3:23; cf. 3:20; Galatians 2:16; 3:10, 11, 21).

In addition to judgment because of Adam's sin, there rests over each man the judgment for his personal sins. Therefore, the justification Christ provides is not only to restore what Adam forfeited, but is a "free gift of many offenses unto justification" (5:16). Two interpretations of Paul's arguments are presented. Verses 15-17 consist of two contrasts expressed by the antithesis—not by the Fall but much more (compare verses 9, 10). Verses 19, 20 consist of two similarities, expressed by the comparison: as—so (compare verse 12).

To counteract the results of Adam's fall and the "many falls" which have followed this first fall, the work of Christ had to be powerful. Adam is a type of Christ as the head of a creation—Adam, head of the first; Christ, head of the second creation. However, Adam is also a contrast to Christ as shown by their different characters and the totally opposite effects of their works. Anyone can tear down and destroy—this was the work of Adam. But to build up and restore is more difficult, and this is Christ's work. His work is more powerful because it has cancelled the disastrous results of Adam's fall. That fall had terrible repercussions lasting to this present moment, but it did not hinder God from fulfilling His plan. The work of Christ is a work of God; Adam's work was the rebellion of a human against his Creator. In a sense Christ's work is also the work of "the first man" since He as "the second man" and the "last Adam" restored what the first man destroyed (1 Corinthians 15:45).

God's placing the whole human race under sin because of Adam's fall was an act of grace because it enabled Him to have mercy on all (cf. Romans 11:32; Galatians 3:22). If one man, as head and representative of the race, could bring such disaster on all mankind, it is an astounding miracle that Jesus Christ as the new head and representative of the race can bring salvation and blessing to all. If Adam's sinful action had such results, how much greater are the results of Christ's righteous work and obedience. Righteousness is not weaker than evil. Satan's seduction of Adam and Eve brought distress and anguish on mankind, but nothing could prevent God from redeeming those who were seduced!

The sin and guilt of man were real. The offense was great. "But where sin abounded, grace did much more abound" (5:20).

## C. Concerning Sanctification (6:1-8:39)

In chapter 6 Paul began a new section of the Epistle to the Romans. Sin needs a "double cure." The sinner needs forgiveness and justification—the theme in chapters 3 to 5. But he also needs deliverance from the power and control of sin. This is the subject Paul discussed in this section of Romans. The theme now is sanctification. While justification is a single decisive act on God's part, sanctification is continuous in the believer's life. The one who is holy must remain holy (cf. Revelation 22:11).

In an epistle as rich and comprehensive as Romans, there will be passages which follow one theme and then there is a break as the apostle began another subject. The following chapters deal with various themes as shown below (chapter 5 has already dealt with freedom from wrath; that is, reconciliation):

Chapter 6: Freedom from sin—or, positively, sanctification.

Chapter 7: Freedom from the Law—or, positively, emancipation.

Chapter 8: Freedom from death—or, positively, the believer's inheritance. (See Nygren, pp. 230, 265, 304.)

Such an outline may help in developing a survey of these chapters. However, the material cannot be squeezed into tight compartments.

We must not lose sight of the fact that Paul, guided by the Spirit, developed a consecutive line of thought from 6:1-8:16. The main focus is on emancipation from sin. In 6:1-11 Paul pointed to Christ's death as the basis of emancipation. In 6:14, 15 he equated emancipation from sin with liberty from the Law. Since believers are not under the Law, they are not under the dominion of sin.

Then Paul used metaphors to illustrate these truths. To show our freedom from sin, he used the slave or servant analogy (6:16). To show our freedom from the Law, he used the illustration of marriage (7:1-4).

A new section follows in which the apostle explained why it is so important to be free from the Law and why the Law cannot make anyone free (7:5). In this section of the epistle Paul emphasized that emancipation is the work of the Spirit, which is based on the work of Christ (8:1-16).

Finally, the apostle presented the Christian hope. The believer's spiritual emancipation is just the beginning of his complete and eternal emancipation, "the glorious liberty of the children of God" (8:21).

## 1. Freedom From Sin (6:1-23)

Paul opened the new section of the epistle by mentioning again the question from 3:8, expressing it this way: "Shall we continue in sin, that grace may abound?" There is but one answer: "God forbid!" The question is rhetorical but not just hypothetical. Paul dealt with the objection of Jewish legalists to Christianity. But it was even more unthinkable that Christians could consider adopting such a lawless principle. It amounted to receiving the grace of God in vain (2 Corinthians 6:1) and turning that grace into lasciviousness (Jude 4). Paul warned against such a delusion (1 Corinthians 6:9, 10; Galatians 5:21).

As a reaction against lawless tendencies, some demanded that new converts keep the Mosaic law. This may have been understandable, but it was not a legitimate conclusion. Paul rejected it emphatically. He could never employ legalism as a cure for looseness in conduct (Bruce, *Tyndale New Testament Commentaries*, 6:128). On the contrary, Paul pointed to the Law as the basis for sin's dominion (6:14), a subject on which he enlarged in chapter 7. For Paul the basis for victorious living was not the Law but abiding in Christ.

*a. Baptized into His death (6:1-14).* As a starting point Paul referred to Christian baptism, which illustrates a spiritual reality in the believer's experience. He has been crucified with Christ, was buried, and has risen with Him.

The death of Christ happened but once and cannot be repeated. Paul was not speaking of a repetition of our Lord's crucifixion when he referred to our being "planted together in the likeness of his death." He was emphasizing the righteousness of Christ that is imputed to the believer as a result of his union with Christ and identification with His death. Christ not only died but He arose and His life is the believer's sanctifying power. Christ for us and we in Him—our righteousness. Christ in us—our sanctification.

Baptism symbolizes a subjective experience in the believer's life—a reality springing from his union with Christ.

He who believes in Christ is "justified from sin" (6:7). This means he is liberated from serving sin as a way of life. Therefore the apostle can command: Let not sin reign! It is a contradictory thought that he who is dead to sin should continue to live in sin. As Christ died *for* sin, the believer dies *to* its dominion and attraction.

*b. Analogy of the slave (6:15-23).* The second part of the chapter begins in the same manner as the first part. There are four parallel expressions in verses 1-3 and 15, 16. Each contains the same opening challenge: "What then?" and the same rhetorical question, "Shall we continue in sin?" Each has the same reply of rejection: "God forbid!" There is also the same appeal: "Know ye not . . ."

In this chapter "slaves" is a better translation of the word *doulos* than "servants." A slave had no rights. Paul was here describing two kinds of service and two kinds of slaves. Man has a right to decide which he will choose. He can become the slave of sin or the slave of Christ.

There are also two kinds of freedom. The person who is the slave of sin is "free from righteousness," because he is not bound by any kind of moral code. He makes his own rules for living, he sets his own standards, and determines his own conduct. But he who is the slave of Christ is free from the slavery of sin. The believer has changed masters. He has discovered genuine freedom.

This section concludes with verse 23. There Paul declared that while Christ's servants receive eternal life as a gift of grace, the servants of sin receive the wages they deserve—death. Usually it is God who punishes sin, but here is one of the few places in the Bible where sin brings along its own punishment. Compare James 1:15 that teaches us when sin is finished, it brings forth death.

## 2. Freedom From the Law (7:1-25)

Paul wrote of emancipation from sin in chapter 6. Here in chapter 7 he discussed emancipation from the Law. It is not difficult to understand that we need emancipation from sin, but why is the apostle so concerned that believers must be set free from the Law? The answer is already indicated in 6:14. Being delivered from sin means being delivered from the Law which causes sin's dominion.

This teaching may have been puzzling to some and needed further explanation, so Paul treated the matter thoroughly in chapter 7. As an introduction he wrote that he was addressing those who knew the Law. The entire context shows he was referring to the Law given at Sinai. Those who "know the law" are not just Jews but even believers whose Bible was the Old Testament. Paul wanted all believers to know Christ had emancipated them from the Law. In the Early Church this became a subject of great controversy and disturbed many Gentiles who had turned to Christ. Paul had already shown how powerless the Law is to justify a man. Now he explained it is just as powerless in sanctifying believers.

*a. Analogy from marriage (7:1-6).* Paul presented a new allegory. He compared man's connection with the Law and the believer's union with Christ to marriage. A woman cannot at the same time be married to two men, and no man can at the same time be under the authority of the Law and the authority of Christ. The believer has no higher authority than Christ, and neither is there any authority equal to Christ. The terms for a person's union with Christ require that he also be emancipated from the Law.

This is a legal matter. As long as a woman's husband is alive, she is bound to him by law. But if the husband dies, the wife is free to marry another man. Paul said that in the same manner he who dies to sin is free from the Law. This was a well-known teaching of the rabbis. It was commonly maintained that such obligations ceased at death.

Paul concluded that as the believer is to be considered as dead with Christ (6:2-11), he is also dead to the Law. By His death Christ has delivered us from the Law so we may belong to Him (cf. Galatians 2:19-21; 2 Corinthians 5:15; Colossians 3:3). For the believer the old, unhappy marriage, with sin as "offspring," has ceased. A new marriage producing the fruits of righteousness has been contracted.

Thus it is through Christ's death that the believer is freed from the Law. What a tremendous price Christ paid! Therefore, to return to the Law is spiritual unfaithfulness to Christ just as idolatry in the Old Testament was considered spiritual adultery. From Galatians 4:3-11 we note that returning to the Law is equivalent to returning to idolatry and worshiping idols "which by nature are no gods." We are set free from the Law by Christ's death and he who returns to the Law crucifies God's Son afresh (Hebrews 6:6), i.e., considers Him as dead and the union with Him dissolved (cf. Galatians 5:2-4).

From verse 7 to the end of the chapter the content falls naturally into two parts: (1) The power of the Law to stir sinful desires and make sin active in the life (verses 7-13); and (2) the conflict between the two "laws" in man (verses 14-25).

*b. The Law activates sin (7:7-13).* Paul already had shown that the Law's purpose was to reveal and identify sin so that it "abounded" (5:20). Now he went a step further, showing that the Law even stirs up sin, awakening it to life and activity. Thus the Law has an influence on man which is quite contrary to what one might be inclined to think. The Law brings death, not life. It does not produce holiness but sin—deceiving man into believing otherwise. The Law is not the reason for sin, but it shows what sin is, and man's sinful nature automatically rises up against the teaching and leads him to disobedience and sin. Sin is so vicious that it uses what is actually good in order to destroy its victim.

Paul related this conflict in an autobiographical section which is one of the great confessions of Scripture. The apostle's testimony is very personal, but it is also the history of each man who ever lived. It is the history of mankind itself. The apostle made distinct references to the Fall, showing that the enemy, Satan, uses exactly the same tactics today. He takes the holy commandments of God to deceive man and make him fall. "I was alive without the Law once," Paul wrote. This is a picture of the relative innocence of childhood, illustrating the original innocence of man before the Fall.

The first autobiographical verses are rather simple to interpret. Paul spoke in the past tense and what he said seems to belong to his life before he became a believer. The rest of the chapter is totally different and is one of the most controversial passages in Romans.

c. The "man" in Romans 7 (7:14-25). Who is this "wretched man" who is sounding his call of distress? This is the question upon which the correct interpretation of this passage rests.

The interpretation of chapter 7 has a long and interesting history all the way back to the church fathers. Three main views have emerged through the centuries: (1) that Paul is describing his spiritual experience prior to his becoming a Christian; (2) that this is the testimony of a normal Christian experience; (3) that the interpretation is to be found in both of the first two views—a compromise interpretation.

(1) A pre-Christian experience. During the first three centuries the church fathers agreed largely that Paul was describing his experiences under the Law before his conversion. Augustine also had this view at first, but changed his mind later. At the time of the Reformation the Greek fathers in the western church embraced this interpretation. Chief among these were Erasmus, Socinus, and others of similar caliber and level of leadership. Arminius and his followers, including Grotius, held to this view. Later it was maintained by men like Francke, Spencer, and Bengel in Germany, and by John Wesley and Adam Clarke in England. Among recent scholars this view seems to be the one most favored. However, many stand on the other side.

There are a series of arguments supporting the view that this passage relates to Paul's pre-Christian experience. Dodd says it would make all of Paul's teaching ridiculous if he admitted that at the time he was writing his epistles he was "a miserable wretch, a prisoner to sin's law" (The Moffatt New Testament Commentary, p. 108). M. Black finds Dodd's arguments convincing (New Century Bible, pp. 101-108). Clarke asks what benefit Paul received by his conversion if he was still a prisoner under the law of sin and death: "He had found no salvation under an inefficient Law; and he was left

in thraldom under an equally inefficient Gospel" (Clarke's Commentary, 6:92). L. Allen says that in this chapter, Paul dramatically relives his life as a Pharisee.

Those who share this interpretation find it inconceivable that Paul could say concerning himself in his present standing as a Christian that he is "carnal, sold under sin" (verse 14) and that he is a "wretched man," torn by internal conflicts, unable to do the good he wants to do, and forced to commit the evil he does not want to do.

(2) A normal Christian life. Other interpreters find that all the struggles Paul mentioned belong to a normal Christian experience. Augustine was the first church father to maintain forcefully that Paul was describing an aspect of his life as a Christian. Later this became the usual interpretation in the western church and was maintained, for instance, by Thomas Aquinas. The reformers Luther, Melanchthon, Calvin, and Beza agreed with this view of Augustine. Calvinists usually maintain this opinion, which is contrary to the belief of the Arminians. Lutherans are more divided on the question. A number of more recent scholars share this second interpretation (i.e., Hodge, p. 246; Nygren, p. 301; Barth, pp. 266-268; Murray, New International Commentary on the New Testament, 1:267-269; G.H. Clark, and others).

These scholars, of course, have a number of arguments to substantiate their view. Some believe it would be contrary to the whole format of the Epistle to the Romans if a prominent passage about the unconverted man suddenly appeared in an explanation of sanctification. They state that it is logical to expect to find the problem about the believer's two natures discussed here. Conflict with sin and fleshly impulses is part of the normal experience of the believer. Chapter 8 speaks just as distinctly about this as chapter 7. A Christian cannot overlook the fact that within himself is a nature to which he cannot yield without losing his spiritual life (8:13). This includes an apostle as well as all other believers. The more holy a Christian becomes, the more painfully he will feel this internal conflict. Paul also spoke of these two conflicting tendencies in other passages (Galatians 5:17). Such an intense contrast between an inner desire to obey God's law and will and the carnal nature's opposition to God's law could not be experienced by an unconverted person. Paul used strong expressions to describe this conflict, but did he really say more than we all have felt when we cried but to God in our private closet of prayer? Haven't we felt the strong spiritual longings of the apostle as well as his weakness? Haven't we experienced the paradox of the cry of distress from the "wretched man" and the joyful praises over being set free: "I thank God through Jesus Christ our Lord!"

(3) *A compromise solution.* A controversial passage like this naturally leads us to seek a compromise interpretation. Both views have their strong arguments as well as their great difficulties. If Paul was describing a sinner, how could he have such a deep desire to do God's will? Paul said that they who are after the flesh do mind the things of the flesh. He declared the carnal mind is in a state of enmity against God (8:5-7). On the other hand, how can a Christian say he does evil that he does not want to do, committing acts he hates? (7:15, 19). Is this not describing slavery to sin? One might say that the "man" in chapter 7 is too spiritual to be a sinner and too bound by sin to be living a true Christian life.

This puzzling section of Romans is closely related to the preceding passage that describes the experience of an awakened conscience under the Law. Is it possible this is an extension and further development of the same theme? Is it not possible that this concerns the experiences of man under the Law but also those experiences with which a Christian grapples? Ramifications of this view vary somewhat with different scholars, but basically the conclusions are the same. A number of commentators, both recent and past, share this view. (See Moody, *Broadman Bible Commentary*, 10:211-213.)

Gerlach claims that the struggle Paul describes is a struggle under the Law. He does not believe it is the struggle of a believer who possesses the spiritual weapons provided by the gospel. He sees it as a powerless attempt to avoid evil and do good with the help of the Law, never the gospel. However, the struggle which is depicted is not just something that happened in the past. It is one which is easily encountered in the present. The Galatians fell back under the Law and were in danger of straying from the gospel. This can happen to anyone who forsakes the liberty of the gospel.

Oivind Andersen maintains that chapters 6 and 7 together create the foundation for chapter 8. Chapter 6 speaks of Christ's death and our death with Him as the basis of sanctification. While the first part of the autobiographical section (7:7-13) is in the past tense, verse 14 speaks in the present. This is not accidental. This section describes an individual's feelings when his conscience has been aroused but he is not yet converted. However, a Christian can also have these experiences because sin and the old nature in us must still be contended with.

The apostle wrote of a Christian's relation to the Law in his struggle to live a holy life. It is not just the construction of the passage in the present tense which makes it clear that Paul spoke as a Christian. It is the content of his statements. The basic attitude toward sin and the law of God described in this section is possible only for the Christian. It is not the believer's normal struggle against sin which is described here. The apostle is showing what a Christian experiences struggling against sin if he uses the Law as his source of power to conquer sin and live a holy life. A Christian cannot conquer sin and the old nature by the Law, but by Jesus Christ.

Since the Church has debated this passage through the centuries, we cannot hope to draw conclusions which all will accept. In fact, we can only present the different views and the arguments for them. It is puzzling that capable, spiritual men can present such important and logical points of view that are so contradictory to each other. This would seem to indicate that the third may be the best. It softens the other two interpretations. Sometimes a compromise solution like this comes the closest to the correct one.

## 3. Freedom in Christ (8:1-39)

Chapter 8 distinctly marks a new section of Romans. We can tell this even by the first verses, which introduce us to a life of spiritual emancipation, governed by the law of the Spirit of life (8:1-4). In this new section the Spirit stands in contrast to the flesh, not the Law (8:5-13). Adoption stands in contrast to bondage (8:14-17).

*a. Justification and freedom (8:1-4).* It is remarkable that Paul makes a connection here with the main theme of the epistle, justification: "There is therefore now no condemnation to them which are in Christ Jesus." In contrast, verse 3 says that God "condemned sin in the flesh." God condemned that which condemned us. The sinner is acquitted and justified in Christ because sin has been condemned in the flesh of Christ.

That which was impossible under the Law, God did. This is explained in three short statements in 8:3.

First, He sent His own Son in the likeness of sinful flesh. Paul used an expression here which closely guards the sinlessness of Christ. When he wrote in 1 Timothy 3:16 that Christ put on human flesh he said, "God was manifest in the flesh." Thus he differentiates between Christ's being manifest in the flesh and manifest in the *likeness* of the flesh. To have said that Christ was manifest in the likeness of flesh would have been error, casting doubt about the reality of Christ's humanity. But here in 8:3 another expression is necessary because the topic is sinful flesh. The apostle cannot say that Christ, who knew no sin (2 Corinthians 5:21), came in sinful flesh. Therefore, he added here the word "likeness," *homoiomati*. The subject is also expressed like this: Christ was revealed in flesh, but He came in the likeness of sinful flesh. He came in real flesh, but it was not sinful flesh.

Paul spoke from a Hebrew background in using the term "flesh." To the Hebrews, the Greek dualism between *sarx* (flesh) and *psuchē* (soul) was strange. The Hebrew *basar* and its Greek equivalent *sarx* expressed to a Jew the being and personality of man. Flesh is not something a man has, but something he is (cf. Genesis 6:3). The word often expresses man's being a weak, feeble, earthly person in contrast to the power of the eternal God. Thus in the Incarnation Christ put on flesh, experiencing deep humiliation compared with His place in the Godhead. His putting on flesh was real, not symbolical.

More is implied in Jesus' coming in the likeness of sinful flesh than His coming in flesh. This fact emphasizes that He became united with the fallen, sinful human race. The human nature He put on was not the glorious and perfect nature which Adam possessed before the Fall. It was our human nature, reduced and debased by sin. Yet sin itself was not in Him (Hodge, pp. 252f.).

When God sent His Son to partake of our nature (but without sin), it was to deal with the sin in our nature. The expression "for sin" is one used in the Septuagint for "sin offering." The expression is used often in the Old Testament—more than 50 times in Leviticus alone. Paul used this second expression in connection with Christ's offering: "Who gave himself for our sins" (Galatians 1:4). Apparently the expression has the same meaning in 8:3 where the thought of sacrifice is dominant. Through Christ's sacrificial death, God did what the Law could not.

God condemned sin in the flesh. This third statement connects naturally with the two preceding ones. It can have but one meaning—sin has received its judgment and punishment. The Greek term *katakrinō* means "to condemn." God condemned sin in the flesh. He made His Son to be sin in order to justify us (2 Corinthians 5:21). God made Him to become a curse for us in order to be able to bless us (Galatians 3:13, 14). It pleased the Lord to bruise Him when He presented the sin offering (Isaiah 53:10).

Jesus suffered in our nature as one of the human race and as the race's representative. He had to partake of flesh and blood and be like His brethren in all things to be able to act as high priest in atoning for sin (Hebrews 2:14-18). He came in the likeness of sinful flesh and in this flesh was condemned. Therefore, there is no condemnation for those who are in Christ Jesus. Having been justified, the believer can now be set free from the power and control of sin.

This passage teaches that emancipation from sin's power objectively is connected with the death of Christ and related subjectively to justification. This is a truth we meet many places in the Epistle to the Romans and elsewhere in the New Testament. However, 7:21-25 especially sheds light on this matter. Here we note that Paul spoke of the power of sin as a law. The law of sin and death rules over men. This is no casual designation, for it is a law in the clearest and deepest meaning. It is a declaration of God which emphasizes that sin rules over the sinner.

The law that declares a sinner the slave of sin is based on the righteousness of God. The one who chooses sin has to take sin with all its consequences. Three times in chapter 1 Paul declared that God gives men up to their sin (1:24, 26, 28). Man is in double bondage—to the devil and to his own flesh (Ephesians 2:2, 3). God has promised to deliver the sinner from this bondage only when he accepts Christ.

The Spirit of God is the only power which can set men free from sin. But the Spirit of God sets them free only when they have been forgiven. Only the one who has been acquitted of the guilt of sin can be set free from the power of sin. Only in Christ Jesus will the law of the Spirit of life set one free from the law of sin and death.

*b. The Spirit of liberty (8:5-14).* In verse 3 Paul repeated what he said positively in chapter 6 and negatively in chapter 7: "For what the law could not do" (cf. 7:1-25), "God sending His own Son . . ." (cf. 6:1-12). Only the Spirit of God can accomplish the possibilities shown in chapter 6 and conquer the "impossibilities" spoken of in chapter 7. The new life cannot produce itself—this can only come by the Spirit of God.

Paul called this new principle of life the law of the Spirit of life. Jesus had said the Spirit would come as rivers of living water (John 7:37-39). Christianity broke forth as a spiritual river, something new in the history of mankind, different from all other religions and all forms of religion. This is the age of Pentecost which the prophets foretold.

Liberty is the distinct mark of the new age (Galatians 5:1)—liberty from bondage to sin and the Law. "Where the Spirit of the Lord is, there is liberty" (2 Corinthians 3:17). The new servitude is by the Spirit, not the letter (Romans 7:6). The law is written in the heart, not on tables of stone. In chapter 7 the Law stands in contrast to the flesh, but in chapter 8 it is the Spirit who stands in contrast to the flesh. This makes all the difference.

The flesh is still the same. It is not any better in chapter 8 than it was in chapter 7. The flesh is still at war with God and cannot be subject to His law (verse 7). But now the works of the flesh are conquered by the Spirit: "As many as are led by the Spirit of God, they are the sons of God" (verse 14).

*c. Our adoption (8:15-39).* Believers move from bondage to adoption. Instead of the spirit of bondage which creates fear, they have received the

Spirit of adoption which cries Abba, Father. The Spirit himself makes intercession for them and testifies with their spirit that they are the sons of God. Even during the present time of tribulation believers can rejoice because they know these sufferings are not worthy to be compared with the glory which shall be revealed in them.

"And if children, then heirs." Those who have received the Spirit as the firstfruits and pledge sigh for the total possession of that which includes their adoption. This will be achieved fully at the redemption of the body from mortality and death.

"For we are saved by hope." It is not a hope which one can see, but it is firm and secure. "I am persuaded!" the apostle said. Nothing shall be able to separate us from the love of God in Christ Jesus our Lord.

## III. History of Salvation Section (9:1-11:36)

Chapter 9 begins a new section of the Epistle to the Romans. These 3 chapters belong to what has been termed the teaching part of the epistle, but they differ clearly from the preceding chapters.

It is correct in general to say that chapter 9 relates to Israel's past, chapter 10 relates to Israel's current situation, and chapter 11 deals with Israel's future. The two major subjects discussed in these chapters are God's relationship with Israel and the doctrine of election.

This section must not be considered as an appendage to the epistle. On the contrary, it is related to the major theme of the Epistle to the Romans (1:16, 17), that the gospel is the power of God for salvation—explained in the first section of the epistle (chapters 1 to 8). However, what is *not* discussed there is Paul's declaration that the gospel is provided to "the Jew first, and also to the Greek" (1:16).

## A. The Doctrine of Election

It has been said that chapter 9 is the most difficult passage in Scripture to interpret. In fact, the difficulties are so great that few will claim to understand the passage thoroughly. This is because the subjects of election and predestination are among the most difficult aspects of the Christian faith. Paul often mentioned the elect, and in his epistles he discussed the matter more thoroughly in three places: Ephesians 1:1-11; Romans 8:28-30; 9 to 11; and especially 9:6-29. This last section is usually considered to be the main passage that deals with the subject of the so-called double predestination doctrine. This teaching maintains that God from eternity has irrevocably chosen a group of people for salvation and another group for perdition. In Bruce's interpretation he regrets that some theological schools formed their election doctrine too quickly from the preliminary stage

of Paul's presentation in chapter 9, without paying sufficient attention to his conclusion in 11:25-32. Bruce is undoubtedly correct and in more recent exegetical work, greater care seems to have been taken than was often the case earlier (*Tyndale New Testament Commentaries,* 6:180).

It is not surprising that such conflicting opinions prevail within Protestant Christianity about the doctrine of election. Great denominations and great leaders within them have held opposing views. Rather than being discouraged over this, we should be humbled over it because it reveals how human all of us are even in our attempts to discover God's truth and His will.

Of course it is virtually impossible to draw dogmatic conclusions about this matter. The most we can achieve is probably to find a view that satisfies us in our own mind (14:5)—and many of us must probably settle for less! The matter of election is connected with the eternal counsels of God. We have to accept the fact that God acts "so that no man can find out the work that God maketh from the beginning to the end" (Ecclesiastes 3:11). Then we have to rest satisfied with the knowledge which is now partial but will one day become clear (1 Corinthians 13:9).

Election and predestination are among the most difficult areas of Christian doctrine because they touch on the great mystery: Why has God created man who will finally be lost forever? No doctrine of election gives any satisfactory reply to this question whether it maintains the complete sovereignty of God or gives room for man to influence his own final destiny. In any case it is evident that God knew the end from the beginning. He knew the eternal destiny of the creation of His own hand. The Scripture says God's election took place "before the foundation of the world" (Ephesians 1:4). This implies election in creation itself. God's sovereignty is unquestioned in His work of creation whatever we might think about His sovereignty concerning the destiny of men.

We do not actually avoid the problems of predestination by speaking of "free will." The difficulties are still there, but when we consider man's free will in our search for the correct interpretation, it brings the different opinions close together.

As already mentioned, more recent efforts at exegesis agree that chapters 9 to 11 are a discussion of salvation history rather than a dogmatic statement about predestination and election. Certain portions of Scripture have too often been taken out of their context and used as arguments in religious quarrels. It is evident that the contents of these chapters do not possess the dogmatism sometimes attributed to them.

This section of Scripture containing the most detailed discussion of the subject of election that is found anywhere else in the Bible. This is not coincidental, but appears to be part of Paul's intent in writing the Epistle to the Romans. In the first part of the epistle he discussed such basic truths of the Christian faith as justification and sanctification. It is logical that he then would proceed in the second part of the epistle to explain God's election. We should not overlook the fact that the presentation in chapter 9 connects naturally with the last part of chapter 8 that mentions election. Thus the subject becomes a principal one in the teaching part of the epistle. The theme of election is so central in the Christian faith that it can claim such a prominent place in this epistle.

But the matter is taken up in the context of salvation history. This is logical in more than one way. Israel is the elected nation and it would be inconceivable to overlook it in such a discussion. The history of Israel is a demonstration of God's election. We must have this view of salvation history if we are to understand at least part of what is implied in being elected. We must avoid forcing our interpretation into some kind of dogmatic system. On the contrary, the dogmatic questions should be considered against the background of salvation history.

## B. Paul's Grief Because of the Unbelief in Israel (9:1-5)

The beginning of this section (verses 1-5) opens with Paul's expression of sorrow over Israel's unbelief and ends with a doxology of praise for God's plan of salvation.

During Paul's discussion of God's plan of salvation in the first part of the epistle, a central theme is the connection between Law and the gospel. Many times the apostle obviously had the Jews in mind. In the opening words of the epistle Paul said the gospel he preached was something God had promised in the holy Scriptures which were committed to the charge of the Jews (1:2; 3:2). Before he began the "admonishing" part of the letter, he addressed this problem: How can it be explained that the Jews—the people who were especially prepared for God's promise—did not know their Messiah when He came, while so many Gentiles who did not have the messianic promises and prophecies received Him?

This matter was of deep personal interest to Paul. He was a Jew himself, "an Hebrew of the Hebrews," and he had strong ties to his people. He began the discussion with a solemn assurance of the heaviness and continual sorrow he felt because his "kinsmen according to the flesh" rejected the gospel. If it would make a difference for them, Paul was willing to be "accursed from Christ" (9:2, 3).

When Paul took up the question about Israel's place in God's plan of salvation, he hinted at

a question of current interest to Christians in the Church. Almost everywhere there were Jewish minorities in those local congregations. This was true in Rome where the church from the beginning consisted of "strangers of Rome" who were present on the Day of Pentecost in Jerusalem (Acts 2:10). The Gentiles were in the majority generally where there were Christian congregations. It was important to them as well as to Jewish Christians to have insight into God's plan for His covenant people, the descendants of Abraham. There might be a tendency for the Gentile Christians to hold the Jew in contempt—something to which Paul objected (11:18). On the other hand, Jewish Christians could be in danger of letting loyalty and love for their own people overshadow the glory of belonging to God's *new* covenant people. These problems were later taken up and discussed in the Epistle to the Hebrews. Their existence when Paul wrote to the Romans is surely one of the reasons he focused on this theme here.

However, the main question concerned the situation of Israel at that time. Understanding this was of vital importance in understanding the gospel which Paul had explained in the first main section of the epistle. One of Paul's key arguments was that this gospel had been preached previously in the prophecies of the Old Testament (1:2; 16:26). When the Jews rejected the gospel it meant they rejected the evidences from the Scriptures to which Paul referred. Thus they doubted the trustworthiness of the gospel. How could one expect then that the Gentiles should receive a Jewish Messiah whom the Jews themselves had rejected? The Jews' rejection of the gospel caused problems which required an answer. In the Epistle to the Romans Paul gave a systematic statement of the gospel he preached and its connection with the old covenant, but he could not overlook the problems arising because the people who had received the messianic promises had rejected the Messiah.

In his Epistle to the Romans Paul proclaimed the entire message of the gospel. In the first part he discussed the main truths: sin and grace, the person and work of Christ, justification and sanctification. He also gave a basic presentation of ecclesiology and eschatology. The position of the Church as it related to Israel must also be explained. The connection between the people of the old and new covenants must be discussed. In the first part of the epistle the gospel is shown as applying chiefly to the questions about personal salvation. In the second section the theme is the kingdom of God and its completion. Here in three short chapters the apostle Paul set forth the greatest eschatological perspectives in the entire New Testament.

The section comprised of chapters 9 to 11 is thus not to be considered as an irrelevant parenthesis inserted between the two main parts of the epistle. This section forms an important main section of this most systematic epistle in the New Testament.

Chapters 1 to 5 concern the grace of God in justification; chapters 6 to 8 concern His grace in sanctification; chapters 9 to 11 discuss His grace in election. The place of election is treated nowhere else in the New Testament in such detail as it is here.

The parallelism between chapters 3 and 9 shows how close the connection is between the first and second main parts of the Epistle to the Romans. The objections against the gospel which are discussed in chapter 3 are discussed once more in chapter 9, and here they get their final reply. This involves three particular questions:

(1) The first objection is that the gospel would abolish the privileges which had been given the Jews. "What advantage then hath the Jew? or what profit is there of circumcision?" (3:1). Paul replied in 3:2: "Much every way: chiefly, because that unto them were committed the oracles of God." In 9:4, 5 Paul once more discussed the question and showed what privileges are given to the Jewish people.

(2) The second objection in chapter 3 concerns the validity of God's promises to Israel: "For what if some did not believe? shall their unbelief make the faith of God without effect?" (3:3). Paul rejected such a thought immediately in verse 4: "God forbid: yea, let God be true, but every man a liar." But he took up the objection once more in 9:6 and assured: "Not as though the word of God hath taken none effect."

(3) The third objection made in chapter 3 is the question about the righteousness of God: "But if our unrighteousness commend the righteousness of God, what shall we say? Is God unrighteous who taketh vengeance?" (3:5). Again Paul replied immediately: "God forbid: for then how shall God judge the world?" (verse 6). In 9:14 Paul discussed the same question once more: "What shall we say then? Is there unrighteousness with God? God forbid." The three objections to the gospel which are set forth in chapter 3 are thus fully answered in chapter 9.

We note then that the content of chapters 9 to 11 is related to the theme of Romans (1:16, 17) and answers questions arising from the subjects discussed in the first part of the epistle. But actually this section breaks the pattern. Here light is thrown on problems which concern the entire revelation of the Bible, God's sovereignty, and election. In these chapters Paul constantly referred to the Old Testament because the matters on which he threw light have their background and origin in the Old Testament. Now they can be interpreted in the light of fulfillment. But because these themes are among the most difficult that man has struggled with, their interpretation is far from simple.

## C. God's Relationship with Israel (9:6-29)

The apostle took up the theme of Israel's rejection very carefully. He knew this was a matter that could seem harsh and hurtful to his Jewish brethren. Therefore, he opened the section with a solemn assurance of his love for his countrymen and relatives. He was the apostle to the Gentiles, and he magnified his office (11:13). But his first desire was to go to his own people with the gospel and he was willing to go to the Gentiles only when the Lord himself warned him the Jews would reject his testimony about Jesus (Acts 22:17-21). Later the Jews had persecuted him from city to city and he knew now they were continually adding to their sins (1 Thessalonians 2:16). It was because of this bitter opposition from his own people that it was very important for Paul to emphasize he did not have any personal grudges against them. It was of no satisfaction to Paul that the Jewish people were not the sole recipients of God's special favor and that God was choosing a people from among both Jews and Gentiles. On the contrary, Paul would have willingly made the greatest sacrifices if it could have brought his countrymen to Christ.

Paul said he could wish himself "accursed from Christ" if this could be of any profit to his brethren. The form of the statement implies that this would be impossible. It is hypothetical, but the words express a love patterned after the example of Jesus, who was made a curse for our sake (Galatians 3:13). Whatever this desire might mean, it does not indicate that Paul was willing to become an enemy of Christ or live in sin. It is wrong to imagine that good can come from doing evil (3:8), and it is also wrong to suppose that one could serve a good cause by becoming evil. The deep concern of Paul's heart was the suffering and loss the Jews were experiencing by turning away from Christ. If it would save his brethren, he was willing to give up the glory and blessedness he enjoyed through Christ and which Israel forfeited by rejecting Him (cf. Colossians 1:24).

Paul accepted fully the privileges granted the Jews and he set them forth in seven expressions:

(1) *The adoption:* The Lord calls this people His son (Exodus 4:22; Hosea 11:1). They are His property more than any other people on earth (Exodus 19:5).

(2) *The glory:* The glory of God was given to Israel by the Lord's personal presence with His people (Exodus 24:16, 17; 40:34, 35; Leviticus 16:2; 1 Kings 8:10, 11).

(3) *The covenants:* These are the covenants of promise which God made with Abraham (Genesis

12 and 15), the covenant of Law on Sinai (Exodus 19:5), and the covenant with King David (2 Samuel 7; 1 Chronicles 17).

(4) *The giving of the Law:* Israel received the Law through divine revelation. On Sinai God explained what was good and holy and what was evil and sinful. Only Israel has received such a revelation and through this revelation the will of God has been known among the nations.

(5) *The divine service:* This includes holy actions—the sacrifice and purification rituals; holy places—the tabernacle and temple; the priesthood—the Levites and the prophets; holy times—the Sabbath and the calendar of feasts. The divine service of the Old Testament illustrated and prepared for the salvation provided in the New Testament.

(6) *The promises:* The promises of God and not the Mosaic law were the basis of salvation for Israel. It was when the Israelites believed the promises God had given that they were saved in ancient times (cf. Hebrews 11).

(7) *The fathers:* This refers to the first ancestors of the Jewish people—Abraham, Isaac, and Jacob—and also the holy men of God who kept and proclaimed the covenant through the centuries.

Finally Paul mentioned the great climax of Israel's privileges: From this nation Christ came—He who is the fulfillment and realization of the messianic promises. Of course He came from Israel in only one sense—according to the flesh, that is, according to His human nature. Spiritually He is "over all, God blessed for ever" (9:5). That verse is one of the great Christological statements of the New Testament and shows the true humanity of Christ as well as His deity.

This passage has been thus understood from the early days of the Church. Among the church fathers agreement was almost absolute. For three centuries it was unanimous. Then in the Fourth Century another view arose among interpreters under the influence of Arianism, which attempted to explain away Christ's deity. However, the interpretation was completely rejected. Calvin wrote, "They who break off this clause from the previous context, that they may take away from Christ so clear a testimony to his divinity, most presumptuously attempt to introduce darkness in the midst of the clearest light; for the words most evidently mean this, *Christ who is from the Jews according to the flesh, is God blessed forever*" (italics original, *Calvin's Commentaries: Romans,* p. 342).

Linguistically there is no doubt that the entire passage proclaims Christ's deity. Among those who tried to make it mean something else were those with wrong motives. Some maintained that Paul could not have meant to say Christ is God. By inserting a period after "the flesh" (*sarx* in the Greek

text) one interpreter tried to separate the last part of the verse and change its construction so it had no connection with the preceding part. All of this is farfetched and a completely unnatural exegesis. Westcott said such a change of the subject seems unlikely. Nigel Turner declared it is grammatically unnatural that a participle which goes together with Christ "first be divorced from it and then be given the force of a wish, receiving a different person as its subject" (p. 15). Adam Clarke said with considerable indignation in his comment: "I pass by the groundless and endless conjectures about reversing some of the particles and placing points in different positions, as they have been all invented to get rid of the doctrine of Christ's divinity, which is so obviously acknowledged by the simple text" (6:110).

Linguistically it seems completely unreasonable to conclude that the last sentence in this verse is meant as a disconnected exclamation of praise. No such doxology can be found anyplace in the Bible. The basic text lacks a relative sentence or the relative pronoun which Paul always adds to such praise elsewhere in his writings (Andersen). Also, the succession of words here is different from that used in doxologies. Such passages of praise read like this: "Blessed is he," not—as here—"God blessed." In the Septuagint as well as the New Testament all doxologies are formed this way (Matthew 21:9; 23:39; Mark 11:9, 10; Luke 1:42, 68; 13:35; 19:38; John 12:13; 2 Corinthians 1:3; Ephesians 1:3; 1 Peter 1:3). In Romans 9:5 the succession of the words is the way it occurs in declarations, not forms of praise, i.e., Romans 1:25; 2 Corinthians 11:31: "He who is blessed for ever" (cf. Hodge, p. 300; Barrett, *Harper's New Testament Commentaries,* pp 177f.; Murray, *New International Commentary on the New Testament,* 2:5ff.). Paul is declaring in this verse the deity of Jesus Christ.

For objective reasons and not just because of linguistic and grammatical considerations, "God blessed for ever" must refer to Christ. The context requires it. In this section the apostle wrote of his deep grief because his people were under judgment and curse and it would be absurd for him to conclude with a praise to God. It is also unimaginable that Paul would reduce his testimony concerning Jesus to merely mentioning that He is "according to the flesh." The expression in itself indicates that Jesus in His person possesses something which is higher than flesh (Calvin, *Calvin's Commentaries: Romans,* p. 342). We have an antithesis here and something is required to balance the expression "according to the flesh" (Bruce, *Tyndale New Testament Commentaries,* 6:176). The word here is a parallel to 1:3, 4 where it is said that Christ "was made of the seed of David according to the flesh, and declared to be the Son of God with power, according to the Spirit of holiness, by the resurrection from the dead." It is typical of Paul that when he spoke of what Christ is according to the flesh, His human side, he also spoke of what Christ is according to the divine side (Andersen). In 1:4 He is called "the Son of God with power." In 9:5 He is called "God blessed for ever."

All of this fits the context. Christ came as the fulfillment of God's revelation and the salvation history of the Old Testament which Paul has outlined briefly. Jesus is that "child" who is born, the "son" who is given, the one the prophet called "mighty God" (Isaiah 9:6). This is the Jewish people's greatest glory and greatest tragedy: "He came unto his own, and his own received him not" (John 1:11). This was the cause of Paul's deep distress for his people—they had rejected their Messiah, their God.

## 1. Israel's Rejection and God's Promises (9:6-13)

Since God has put aside His people of the old covenant and given His kingdom to a people who bring forth its fruits (Matthew 21:43), has He then broken His covenant promises to the fathers? Paul replied immediately to this question: "Not as though the word of God hath taken none effect" (9:6). This expansion of God's call to all mankind corresponds with the promise itself which was given to Abraham when God called him: "In thee shall all families of the earth be blessed" (Genesis 12:3). But when the great part of the people of Israel are now excluded and receive no share of the promised blessing, it is plainly because they do not belong to "the children of the promise" (9:8). "For they are not all Israel, which are of Israel" (9:6).

The Israel for whom the promises of God shall be fulfilled is not "the children of the flesh." Not all the posterity of Abraham are considered to belong to the family which owns the promise. To prove this, Paul set forth an argument he knew all Jews would accept. He referred to the relationship between Ishmael and Isaac and between Esau and Jacob. Both Ishmael and Esau were descendants of Abraham, but no Jew would claim that their posterity belonged to the nation of promise. Paul transferred this truth to the Jewish people. Already in 2:28, 29 he had said that he was not a Jew which was one outwardly but he was a Jew which was one inwardly. In 4:12 Paul also followed this thought. Abraham is "the father of circumcision to them who are not of the circumcision only, but who also walk in the steps of that faith of our father Abraham."

This is in fact a truth taken from the Old Testament. The true Israelites are those with a clean heart (Psalm 73:1), those who seek God's face (Psalm 24:6). John the Baptist maintained the

same view. When the Jews pleaded that they were the children of Abraham, John replied that God could give Abraham children of "these stones." Jesus had a sharp conflict with the unbelieving Jews for His teaching along this same line. He told them He knew they were of Abraham's lineage but He did not accept them as Abraham's children (John 8:37-39). Thus it is no new thought Paul put forth when he maintained that an election takes place among the chosen ones. This is what has taken place throughout the history of the people. Only the believing Israelites inherited the promise, and they were almost always in the minority among their people. What has taken place before is now being repeated. If the great part of the Jewish people reject their Messiah, this does not mean that God's promise has been discarded or that His word has failed.

## 2. Israel's Rejection and God's Righteousness (9:14-29)

The next objection to Paul's preaching is that God would be unfair to turn away from His people of the old covenant. This was a deeply rooted delusion in Israel—that they had a claim on God which He could not escape. Now Paul showed that everything God gives is of grace, and God is completely sovereign as to whom He will show grace. When Jacob and Esau were still unborn and neither had done good nor bad, God made His choice between them. When Jacob was chosen, this was grace. When Esau was rejected, no wrong was done to him. It is not of him that wills, nor of him that runs, Paul said. Abraham wanted Ishmael to inherit the promise. Isaac wanted Esau to inherit the promise. But God chose otherwise. Esau went hunting to get venison for his father and receive the blessing, but this did not help him. The will of God according to election stood firmly.

Even God's enemies must serve His intentions. Pharaoh was raised up for God to show His power in Him. God handed him over to his reprobate mind and hardened his heart while He had mercy on Israel. "He hath mercy on whom he will have mercy, and whom he will he hardeneth" (9:18). Just as the clay cannot complain to the potter, man cannot say to God, "Why hast thou made me thus?" (verse 20). God maintains His unrestricted right over His creation to act as He wishes concerning what belongs to Him.

Paul applied this to Israel as the prophets did (Isaiah 45:9). However, when he used this Old Testament picture of God's sovereign power, it was not because he was pleading for any despotic action on God's part. The will of God is for the good of people and those Old Testament passages to which Paul referred speak of the care God has for His people: "But now, O Lord, thou art our father;

we are the clay, and thou our potter; and we all are the work of thy hand. Be not wroth very sore, O Lord, neither remember iniquity for ever: behold, see, . . . we are all thy people" (Isaiah 64:8, 9).

The picture of the clay in the potter's hand should not cause the Jews to have a fatalistic attitude. They were acquainted with Jeremiah 18:1-10 where it is said that a vessel which was marred was taken up once more and formed into another vessel. "O house of Israel, cannot I do with you as this potter? saith the Lord. Behold, as the clay is in the potter's hand, so are ye in mine hand, O house of Israel. At what instant I shall speak concerning a nation, and concerning a kingdom, to pluck up, and to pull down, and to destroy it; if that nation, against whom I have pronounced, turn from their evil, I will repent of the evil that I thought to do unto them." Just this way Paul described the situation of his people. God has shown His power by rejecting the nation because they rejected His Messiah, but God is also able to graft them in again if they do not continue in their unbelief (11:23).

To sum up, chapters 9 to 11 fall into three sections. In chapter 9 Paul justified God's actions concerning Israel by referring to His sovereignty. He is God and is within His rights to act as He wishes without accounting to any man. Israel's history shows that God dealt with His people this way in the past. Chapter 10 shows that God's rejection of the covenant nation is no casual action. Israel had placed herself outside God's blessing because of her unbelief. But even though Israel as a nation was put aside, there was also a remnant who believed. Paul himself and his brethren who believed in Christ represented this true Israel. Chapter 11 speaks of Israel's future. Israel will eventually be saved, that is, the Jews as a nation will be restored as the people of God.

Paul then summed up the matter in 11:32: "God hath concluded them all in unbelief, that he might have mercy upon all." This corresponds with 5:12-20, which says that God has placed the entire human race under judgment because of Adam's fall. He was the first man, but through the second Man, Jesus Christ, God can justify those who believe and give life to all men who receive His Son. This is the intent and goal of the eternal counsels of God. Here the choice of grace in Christ has its place.

In the Scripture God has pulled aside the veil over the mystery of election just enough to show us that here are some secrets we cannot completely comprehend. But we must keep in focus that the question of election is placed in the context of salvation history where the salvation of both Israel and the Gentiles is concerned. Thus we must view predestination and election in light of God's will and saving love. Everything must finally serve the salvation plan of God. Therefore, Paul concluded by praising God for His wisdom. Paul admits that God's judgments are unsearchable and His ways past finding out. However, those judgments and ways—which are so much higher than ours—lead to the great goal which God has fixed: His eternal kingdom.

## IV. Admonition Section (12:1-13:14)

Paul followed his general practice when he added a section of admonition to his doctrinal presentation. This practical application of Christian doctrine can be found in most of his epistles. The preaching of sound doctrine, declaring the gospel and the person and work of Christ, is basic and must come first. Here in the Epistle to the Romans Paul laid the foundation of the believer's new lifestyle in chapters 6 to 8. There he taught about the new life the believer has received in Christ. This new life is the source of the new conduct expressed in his daily walk. Christian practice has Christian truth as its origin and the two are inseparably connected. With Paul's "therefore" in 12:1 this final section connects with the first doctrinal section of the epistle. This reference to the gospel (in the first section) is a necessary background to admonition. These admonitions are given in light of "the mercies of God" (12:1). They are also set forth by the authority of Christ and the Holy Spirit (15:30).

The admonition section of the epistle falls into one general part (chapters 12, 13) where the teaching concerns basically all age groups, and a special part (14:1-15:13) which contains admonitions relating primarily to conditions in the church at Rome but also to matters among all believers.

The general part contains a series of admonitions which cover the greatest area of the Christian life and gives some examples which illuminate different situations. This concerns the believer's body (12:1) and mind (12:2). This is vital to his relationship with God (12:1, 2), fellow Christians (12:4), those outside the Church (12:17), and governing authorities (13:1). Paul taught obedience to the laws of the community (13:1) and the faithful fulfillment of God's law (13:10).

## A. Personal Life (12:1, 2)

The first basic admonition concerns each believer's relation to God and the worship of Him. The expression Paul used about consecration to God is taken from ritual language, but the contrast to the divine service of the Old Testament is striking. Here in Romans the subject is a living sacrifice; the believer should *live* for God. This divine service includes both body and mind (verses 1, 2). Paul emphasized that what makes the believer different from the world comes from within through the renewing of his mind.

## B. Church Life (12:3-8)

Then Paul wrote about the life of the Church. In verse 1 the subject is the physical body, while in verse 5 it is the spiritual body of Christ, the Church. Christian love should first of all be expressed to those "who are of the household of faith." Proper relationship to those outside the Church depends on brotherly love inside the Church (cf. 2 Peter 1:7).

## C. Social Life (12:9-21)

Our love must extend to all men, beginning with our fellow believers. Our love for the world is an extension of our love for those in the Church. A Christian must not be conformed to this world (verse 2), but neither should he be isolated. We have a relationship with all fellow humans. The Christian mind is to be expressed in actions among believers by unfeigned love. This means, among other things, to have willing fellowship with those who are not highly esteemed and even considered "low." In relation to the world the Christian mind will express itself by an attitude of peacemaking which leaves no room for vengeance but conquers evil with good. This section echoes Jesus' preaching distinctly. Some of it reminds us of the Sermon on the Mount. None of the four Gospels had been written at this time, but Paul had a knowledge of Jesus' teachings.

## D. Obedience to Authority (13:1-7)

When Paul discussed the social relationships of Christians, their relationship with governing authorities also came into view. Before this, the Roman authorities had been rather indifferent to Christian activity and had even shown considerable tolerance. They considered Christianity a Jewish "denomination" and to a large extent had granted Christians the same privilege and protection the Jews had enjoyed as a legal, registered religious group in the empire. In a few more years this would change, and persecution of Christians would begin. Paul knew from experience how critical the situation was already and how important it was that Christians not challenge their rulers unwisely. This was particularly true in Rome where the Church lived under the eye of the highest authorities. What happened there could produce repercussions for Christians all over the Roman Empire. There had already been some trouble in Rome. The historian Suetonius wrote that Emperor Claudius had exiled all Jews from Rome because they constantly caused turmoil (Acts 18:2). This shows there were controversies among the Jews because of Christianity. This was the background of the emperor's edict.

Paul did not here discuss this question: How shall a Christian behave toward an authority who abuses his power? But the apostle declared that all authorities are the servants of God—dreaded by evil and praised by the good. As long as the governing authority fills its God-given place, it can demand Christians' loyalty. Obedience to the authorities is an extension of the believer's obedience to the Lord. Therefore, it is not just because of the fear of punishment that the Christian should subject himself to the governing authorities. It is a matter of conscience.

## E. Fulfillment of the Law (13:8-10)

After speaking about obedience to human law, Paul wrote about fulfilling the law of God. We still hear echoes from Jesus' teaching, and the section concludes with the great declaration: "love is the fulfilling of the law."

## F. The Eschatological Section (13:11-14)

Paul, after writing of Christian love, expressed the theme of Christian hope. Everything in this passage emphasizes and reinforces what has been said previously: Romans 12:1 refers to the teaching in chapters 6 to 8 about holy living based on the preaching of the gospel; 13:10 refers to love as the new impelling power that enables us to fulfill the Law; 13:11 looks forward to the return of Christ as the motive for holiness (cf. 1 John 3:3). Salvation, the final salvation, is nearer than when we believed (1 Thessalonians 5:8, 9; 1 Peter 1:5; 2:2). The New Testament teaches that the day of redemption is near: Philippians 4:5; James 5:8. The first generation of believers expected the return of Christ in their day (John 21:23; 1 Thessalonians 1:10; 4:17). However, this expectation took into consideration that to the Lord "one day is . . . as a thousand years, and a thousand years as one day" (2 Peter 3:8). When Paul wrote "the night is far spent," he put the present evil age alongside the age to come. "The night" includes all the dark times until the Second Coming, which is "the day." The first coming of Christ took place at the end of the times (Hebrews 9:26; cf. Hebrews 1:1) and the present age belongs to the end of the world (1 Corinthians 10:11). Therefore the night is far spent and the day is at hand.

## V. The Strong and the Weak (14:1-15:13)

The entire Epistle to the Romans is of course addressed to the church in Rome and clearly shows this background. However, it has a message to all Christians. It seems correct to say that 14:1-15:13 treats in a special way questions which presented problems in Rome at that time. There were difficulties about those considered "strong" and others labeled "weak." Those who had a strong conscience and used their Christian liberty freely were in conflict with those who had weak consciences and were confused about questions of food and the observance of certain days. Paul took these matters up in other epistles also. The matters of the Jewish Sabbath and feast days are mentioned in Galatians 4:10 and Colossians 2:16, 17. Jewish eating customs are mentioned in Colossians 2:21. What is unusual is that Paul discussed the situation in Rome in a way that shows an entirely different reaction than when he wrote to Galatia and Colossae. The only conclusion we can draw is that there were different backgrounds in those churches. In the Epistle to the Galatians Paul opposed the Judaizers who taught that it was necessary to follow the Law in order to be justified and actually were preaching "another gospel." In the Epistle to the Colossians Paul struggled against a Gnostic error that taught extreme asceticism to discipline the desires of the body and encouraged worship of angels. None of these problems are mentioned in the Epistle to the Romans. There Paul addressed believers who because of a weak conscience had imposed unnecessary burdens on themselves. These "weak" ones in Rome remind us of the "weak" in Corinth who did not dare to eat meat, fearing it may have been offered to idols before being sold in the market (1 Corinthians 8 and 10).

Paul admonished the believers in Rome to be tolerant toward those with different viewpoints in this matter. He told those on both sides not to judge or scorn fellow believers with different opinions (14:1-12). He also cautioned the "strong" not to put a stumbling block or an occasion to fall in the path of the weak brother but rather to sacrifice the use of one's own liberty if necessary (14:13-23). As a motive for such an attitude Paul referred to the example of Christ, who did not live to please himself but honored God by His concern for the well-being of others (15:1-13).

## VI. Conclusion of the Epistle (15:14-16:27)

The long ending of the epistle falls into a number of sections. First, Paul discussed personal conditions and told of his own plans (15:14-33). He recommended to them Phoebe, who ministered to the church in Cenchrea (16:1, 2), then gave a series of personal greetings which show that Paul had a great circle of friends in the church (16:3-16). He implored them seriously to pay close attention to people trying to cause division and to disassociate themselves from them (16:17-20). The epistle concludes with a doxology in which Paul reiterates what he wrote in the opening verses.

# The Epistle to the Romans

## and Various Versions

## Commentary

### Chapter 1

**1. Paul, a servant of Jesus Christ:** ... My name is Paul, *—NORL* ... a slave, *—HNT* ... a bondservant, *—WEYM* ... a bondsman, *—CNBR.*

**called [to be] an apostle:** ... especially selected for, *—SEB* ... appointed a special apostle, *—FNTN* ... an ambassador by divine summons, *—WUST.*

**separated unto the gospel of God:** ... permanently separated to God's good news, *—WUST* ... put apart to preache, *—GNVA.*

**1:1.** Paul related himself to the Lord he served, to his apostolic office, and to the ministry God had given to him. He was the *doulos* ("slave") of Jesus Christ. His will was totally submitted to the will of his Lord.

Paul's vocation was a *klētos apostolos*, a chosen messenger. There are many servants, but not all are apostles.

Paul's entire life was "separated unto the gospel of God." The meaning is to "mark off by boundaries." The proclamation of the gospel was his only pursuit.

Four words describe Paul and his mission. Two relate to character and two relate to service. He called himself "a servant" and "an apostle." Two words picture his career of service, "called ... separated." Life to Paul was commitment (a servant), commission (an apostle), and consecration (called, separated).

**2. (Which he had promised afore:** ... in advance, *—BRKL.*

**by his prophets in the holy scriptures,):** ... holy Bible, *—BECK.*

**1:2.** *Ho proepēngeilato,* "which he had promised afore by his prophets in the holy Scriptures" indicates that Christ is the good news that fulfills God's promises.

*Hagion* ("in the *holy* Scriptures") is that which belongs to God. *Graphais hagiais* is the Old Testament, containing God's promises written by inspired men *dia ton prophētōn autou,* "through his prophets."

**3. Concerning his Son Jesus Christ our Lord: which was made of the seed of David according to the flesh:** ... as regards His human descent, belonged to the posterity of David, *—WEYM* ... born of David's offspring, *—HNT* ... as to His human nature, *—BRKL.*

**1:3.** The good news focuses on the Son of God who became the Son of Man. *Tou genomenou* means "came" or "born" (Galatians 4:4); *ek spermatos,* "of the seed of David." By His physical birth Jesus became a descendant of Israel's great king.

**4. And declared [to be] the Son of God with power:** ... was predestinate the sonne of God, *—RHEM* ... installed as Son of God, *—HNT* ... was marked out, *—CNBR* ... openly designated, *—BRKL* ... miraculously proved to be the Son of God, *—ADAM* ... powerfully defined a Son of God, *—FNTN* ... declared mightely to be, *—GNVA.*

**according to the spirit of holiness:** ... bi the spirit of halow-ynge, *—WCLF* ... the spirit of sanctification, *—RHEM* ... on the holy spiritual side, *—WLMS.*

**by the resurrection from the dead:** ... of the agenrisynge of deed men, *—WCLF* ... rose agayne from deeth, *—TNDL.*

**1:4.** Jesus was "declared" the Son of God. Here again the meaning is "marked off by boundaries" (*horisthentos*). The Resurrection declared Him to be what He is, the Son of God, which identifies Him as deity.

The birth and the resurrection of Christ are linked together. Divinely born, He was divinely raised. Here is the crowning proof of His deity, "according to the Spirit of holiness." This refers to the spiritual nature of the One who is human and divine.

**5. By whom we have received:** ... Through him God gave me the privilege, *—TEV.*

**grace and apostleship:** ... the undeserved gift, *—BRKL* ... and our apostolic mission, *—JB* ... a charge and commission to subdue all nations, *—FNTN* ... favour of my commission, *—MOFT* ... even the apostolic office, *—CMPB.*

**for obedience to the faith among all nations, for his name:** ... to urge upon all the heathen obedience, *—WLMS* ... to promote an obedience of faith, *—SCLT* ... to secure for his Cause submission to the Faith, *—TCNT* ... to bring all maner hethen people vnto obedience of the fayth, *—TNDL* ... in alle folkis, *—WCLF.*

**1:5.** Apostleship came to Paul through grace (unmerited favor). "Obedience to the faith" refers not to doctrine or belief, but belief itself. Grace comes before apostleship, salvation before service. Commitment to the truth comes before commitment to the task.

6. **Among whom are ye also the called of Jesus Christ:** . . . of whose nombre you be, —*CRNM* . . . you also are divinely summoned ones, —*WUST* . . . you are also the Invited ones, —*WLSN.*

**1:6.** The previous verse concludes with "among all nations" which indicates Paul's special calling to be the apostle to the Gentiles. Paul now wrote to the Roman believers, "Among whom are ye also." They too were "the called of Jesus Christ."

7. **To all that be in Rome, beloved of God, called [to be] saints:** . . . to all God's loved ones in Rome, —*BRKL* . . . who are God's loved ones, —*WLMS* . . . God's beloved ones, —*HNT* . . . the holy chosen friends, —*FNTN* . . . called to be His holy people, —*BECK* . . . called to become Christ's People, —*TCNT* . . . and Sainctes by callyng, —*GNVA* . . . Constituted Holy ones, —*WLSN.*
**Grace to you and peace from God our Father, and the Lord Jesus Christ:** . . . May gracious love, —*SEB* . . . spiritual blessing, —*WLMS.*

**1:7.** God knows the whereabouts of those He has called. This verse speaks of a specific group, not all Romans. The called are "beloved of God"; literally "God's loved ones."

Believers are "called to be saints," meaning "holy ones." The emphasis is on being set apart to God. Christians are not called by the Church to sainthood posthumously.

Paul greeted these saints with the words "grace . . . and peace." Grace, the unmerited favor of God, always precedes peace. When one has grace from heaven, he has peace wherever he may go. Grace and peace are forever proceeding from God the Father and the Lord Jesus Christ.

Grace comes from *chaireim,* the typical greeting among the Greeks. Then as now the greeting used among Hebrews is *Shalom,* "peace." Possibly Paul used both of these words for he was writing to churches composed of both Jews and Gentiles. The Old Testament form of greeting was "Peace be to you." But in the New Testament grace is God's provision. By grace we are converted, by grace we live, by grace we draw from His bountiful provision. All the blessings of the gospel emanate from God's grace and peace. Peace with God, peace in one's conscience, peace in daily living, living in peace with others; all this is because of and through grace.

The first seven verses of this epistle, while given to greetings, develop a fundamental groundwork of Christian doctrine. Note the theology: the deity and humanity of Jesus, the place of believers as "saints," and the relationship of God the Father and God the Son. No word is wasted. Even the opening words of greeting present doctrine.

8. **First, I thank my God:** . . . At the very outset, —*HNT* . . . I am constantly thanking, —*WUST.*
**through Jesus Christ for you all:**
**that your faith is spoken of throughout the whole world:** . . . the whole world is getting to know about your faith, —*NORL* . . . because the tidings of, —*CNBR* . . . your faith is proclaimed, —*RSV* . . . your faith is publisshed throughout all, —*GNVA* . . . your faith is renoumed in the whole world, —*RHEM* . . . is celebrated in, —*FNTN.*

**1:8.** Following the salutation (verses 1-7), the epistle proper opens with thanksgiving for the faith of the Roman Christians which was widely known. Paul's thanksgiving was "through Jesus Christ." All our activities are pleasing to God only through Jesus Christ. God is well-pleased with His Son. The believer is accepted in the Son (Ephesians 1:6). Our praise to God is accepted in Christ, and our prayers are addressed to God in the name of Jesus Christ (John 14:13, 14; 15:16; 16:23, 24, 26).

9. **For God is** my **witness:** . . . that what I say is true, —*TEV.*
**whom I serve with my spirit:** . . . I render holy service, —*MNTG* . . . my whole heart, —*NORL.*
**in the gospel of his Son:** . . . by telling the good news about, —*WLMS.*
**that without ceasing I make mention of you always in my prayers:** . . . without intermission I make a memorie of you, —*RHEM* . . . how incessantly, —*SCLT* . . . I regularly mention you, —*ADAM* . . . I make mynde of you euer in my preiers, —*WCLF.*

**1:9.** The phrase "with my *spirit*" is significant. Here Paul spoke of his spirit in worship (cf. John 4:24; 1 Corinthians 14:14). The terms "spirit" (*pneuma*) and "soul" (*psuchē*) are sometimes used interchangeably, but never in Paul's writings. The emphasis of Romans is spiritual life vs. natural life (cf. 1 Corinthians 2:14, 15). Just as by the will of God Paul gave the clearest presentation of the gospel, so he also gave the clearest treatment of man's constitution (as in 1 Thessalonians 5:23). A study of these terms in the Epistles will cause one to agree with F.F. Bruce that "'spirit' and 'soul' are not only distinguished in Paul, but set in contrast to each other" (*Tyndale New Testament Commentaries,* 6:47). First Thessalonians 5:17 urges us to "pray without ceasing." *Adialeiptōs,* "without ceasing," means "without letting up or leaving off." Paul practiced what he preached. Although he was not personally acquainted with many of the Roman Christians, he prayed for all of them.

**10. Making request:** . . . always entreating, —*WLMS* . . . supplicating, —*NOYS* . . . pleading, —*BRKL* . . . besechynge, —*CRNM* . . . continually inquiring, —*FNTN*.

**if by any means now at length:** . . . that sometime, somehow, —*NORL* . . . that by some meane . . . one tyme or other, —*CRNM* . . . if it be possible, —*NOYS*.

**I might have a prosperous journey by the will of God to come unto you:** . . . succeed in coming to you, —*BECK* . . . I may be sped upon my way, —*HNT* . . . myght fortune me, —*TNDL* . . . be favored with an opportunity of coming to you, —*NOYS*.

**1:10.** Paul's desire to visit the Roman Christians was so strong that he said "if by any means." God took him up on that offer, for he later went to Rome as a prisoner. He considered himself to be a prisoner of Christ and not of Nero (Philippians 1:12-14). How different his entrance to Rome was from the anticipated voluntary arrival. After a tempestuous voyage filled with peril, he arrived as a prisoner to plead for his life before the emperor.

The apostle earnestly prayed for the privilege of visiting this assembly located in the capital of the Roman Empire. While all men of that time aspired to see the fabled capital city of the world of that day, Paul did not measure his longing on the basis of the outward magnificence of the great city; he longed to meet with his fellow believers. Some were his kinsmen, some had been fellow workers, some were prisoners, but all were his Christian brothers and sisters. The ties of Christian fellowship are very special, and particularly so during times of opposition and persecution. Love for Christ prevents narrowness of spirit. The richer our vertical relationship is to Christ, the greater will be our horizontal relationship with others.

The reason for Paul's desired visit was the mutual edification of himself and the assembly. He prayed that he would "have a prosperous journey." The Greek word is *euodoō* which comes from *eu*, "well" or "good," and *hodos* meaning "way." He expected to find that way "by the will of God." To find the will of God is the greatest discovery. To know the will of God is the greatest knowledge. To do the will of God is the greatest achievement.

Scorching suns, raging seas, weary miles, and bitter persecutions were to be a part of that journey. All was endured not for friends, fame or fortune, but for fruit.

**11. For I long to see you:** . . . I do long to meet you, —*NORL* . . . I am yearning, —*BRKL*.

**that I may impart unto you some spiritual gift:** . . . may give you, —*ADAM* . . . myght bestowe,

amonge you, —*GNVA* . . . spiritual privilege, —*HNT* . . . spiritual help, —*WEYM* . . . spiritual grace, —*RHEM*, . . . *CNFT*.

**to the end ye may be established:** . . . for your confirmation, —*BRKL*, —*NOYS* . . . give you fresh strength, —*TCNT* . . . make you strong, —*TEV*, . . . for the establishment of your steadfastness, —*CNBR* . . . resulting in your being stabilized, —*WUST*.

**12. That is, that I may be comforted together with you by the mutual faith both of you and me:** . . . and I can obtain mutual comfort, —*NORL* . . . and I may find encouragement in, —*TCNT* . . . receaue exhortation together with you through the commen faith, —*GNVA* . . . that I might haue consolacion, —*CRNM*.

**1:11, 12.** Paul desired to "impart . . . some spiritual gift" (*ti charisma*). He would "impart"; they would be "established." Their mutual relationship would comfort preacher and people. The word "comforted" (*sumparakaleō*) can also be translated "encouraged or strengthened together." Paul expressed with delicate courtesy and gracious humility that he needed them. Both would be benefactors and both would be beneficiaries.

**13. Now I would not have you ignorant, brethren:** . . . wish you to ignore, —*FNTN*.

**that oftentimes I purposed to come unto you: (but was let hitherto,):** . . . But, until now, I was stopped, —*SEB* . . . so far I have always been hindered, —*NORL* . . . but thus far I have been prevented, —*BRKL*.

**that I might have some fruit among you also:** . . . that I might reap some harvest among you, —*BRKL* . . . enjoy some results of working among you, —*BECK*.

**even as among other Gentiles:** . . . even as also in the rest of the Gentiles, —*ALFD* . . . as in other folkis, —*WCLF*.

**1:13.** "I would not have you ignorant" is a favorite expression of Paul meaning, "I want you to know." "Oftentimes I purposed to come." He had often tried to get to Rome but was hindered. "Let" has changed its meaning completely since King James' day. It now means "allow."

Verse 13 concludes with an expression of the driving force in his desire to come to the imperial city—"that I might have some fruit among you also, even as among other Gentiles." That was the passion of the great apostle to the Gentiles. Fruit (*karpas*) denotes the result of labor. He was ready to labor to see that fruit.

**14. I am debtor:** . . . I owe a duty, —*MOFT* . . . under obligations, —*WEYM* . . . I have a debt to discharge, —*MNTG*.

**both to the Greeks, and to the Barbarians:** . . . alike to Greek-speaking races, —*WEYM* . . . and non-Greeks, —*BECK* . . . and to uncivilized nations, —*TCNT* . . . to the civilized and to the savage, —*TEV* . . . and to all the other nations, —*WLMS*.

**both to the wise, and to the unwise:** . . . to the educated, —*ADAM* . . . both to clever and to simple-minded people, —TCNT . . . philosophers, and illiterates, —FNTN . . . and the foolish, —BECK.

**1:14.** The word "debtor" (*opheiletēs*) means "one held by some obligation, bound to some duty." Paul felt this great obligation, and the only way he could repay was by loving service. The term "Barbarians" (*barbaros*) was applied to any foreigners who did not speak the Greek language. To the Greeks all non-Greeks were barbarians.

Paul had already given proof of his passion to share Christ with all men, whether a runaway slave like Onesimus or a proud king like Agrippa. The apostle's great desire was to preach to the wise and the unwise, the learned and the unlearned. His debt was to all men, whether divided by language or culture.

**15. So, as much as in me is:** . . . hence my deep-felt eagerness, —BRKL . . . so, as far as it depends upon me, —ADAM . . . to the extent of my ability, —WLMS.

**I am ready to preach the gospel:** . . . I am sincerely eager, —NORL.

**to you that are at Rome also:**

**1:15.** Wherever Paul went to preach he met opposition. Often the price was physical suffering even to the point of being left for dead. At Jerusalem, the religious center, he was mobbed. At Athens, the intellectual center, he was mocked. At Rome, the governmental center, he was martyred. But he was ready to preach at Rome. The only limit to that obligation was "as much as in me is."

**16. For I am not ashamed of:** . . . For I am proud of the Gospel, —MNTG.

**the gospel of Christ:** . . . the Glad-tidings, —CNBR.

**for it is the power of God unto salvation to every one that believeth:** . . . a Divine power, —FNTN . . . for saving anyone who believes it, —SEB . . . by which God brings Salvation, —TCNT . . . it is God's saving power for everyone who has faith, —MOFT . . . of everyone who trusts, —WLMS.

**to the Jew first, and also to the Greek:** . . . then non-Jews, —SEB.

**17. For therein is the righteousness of God revealed:** . . . God's plan to justify us, —NORL . . . the iustice of God, —RHEM . . . is uncovered, —WLMS.

**from faith to faith:** . . . It is by faith, first and last, —NORL . . . It begins and ends by faith, —SEB.

**as it is written:**

**The just shall live by faith:** . . . will find Life as the result of faith, —TCNT . . . by faith shall the upright live, —HNT.

**1:16, 17.** Now comes the next assertion, one of the greatest: "For I am not ashamed of the gospel of Christ." The other assertions were positive; this one is also, but stated with a negative, "I am not ashamed." The word "for" relates to the assertion

"I am ready." Paul felt it was a privilege to preach the gospel.

Verses 16 and 17 are the theme of the entire Book of Romans. When Paul boldly declared, "I am not ashamed," his statement was based on two premises: (1) the gospel is the power of God; (2) the gospel reveals the righteousness of God.

Verse 1 shows God as the source of the gospel. Verses 16 and 17 show further: (1) the dynamics of the gospel—"the power of God"; (2) the aim of the gospel—"salvation"; (3) the extent of the gospel—"to every one"; (4) the condition of the gospel—"that believeth"; and (5) the reason for the gospel—"the just shall live by faith."

Paul gloried in the gospel and felt it a great honor to proclaim it. The gospel is more than human might; we might call it today the *dynamics* (dynamo, dynamite, power, ability, strength); the inherent power of the Almighty employed for our salvation.

Salvation (*sōtēria* from *sōtēr*, "saviour") is the all-inclusive word in describing redemption. Righteousness is one of the key words. The *gospel* is God's *power* unto *salvation*, consisting of God's *righteousness*, which comes by *faith*. Salvation is from "faith to faith" meaning all of faith and not of works.

The gospel is God's righteousness revealed in a twofold manner: (1) how sinners can come to be "in the right" with God, and (2) how God vindicates His personal righteousness in the very act of declaring us righteous.

**18. For the wrath of God is revealed from heaven:** . . . God's indignation is revealed, —BRKL . . . Divine displeasure, —FNTN . . . God in heaven shows He is angry, —BECK.

**against all ungodliness and unrighteousness of men:** . . . upon every lack of reverence, —WLMS . . . against irreligion and wrong-doing in every form, —TCNT . . . vpon al impietie and iniustice, —RHEM.

**who hold the truth in unrighteousness:** . . . pervert the true into the false, —FNTN . . . that de-teine the veritie of God, —RHEM . . . their wicked ways suppress the truth, —NORL, —BRKL . . . who smother the truth, —MNTG . . . through iniquity suppress the truth, —WEYM . . . whose evil ways prevent the truth from being known, —TEV . . . who use sin to hide the truth, —SEB . . . who keep truth imprisoned in their wickedness, —JB . . . of those who hinder the Truth, —MOFT . . . who impede the truth, —HNT.

**1:18.** God's wrath (*orgē theou*) is revealed against all ungodliness (*asebia*) and unrighteousness (*adikia*). Asebeia means ungodlike. It connotes licentious living, but it also includes respected people who are ungodlike in heart and life. The basic idea is irreverence, disregard for God's law and disregard for God's person. *Adikia* refers to an absence of a right attitude inwardly and right conduct outwardly.

To "hold the truth in unrighteousness" implies to suppress, to hinder the truth. Although there may be verbal agreement given to doctrine, it is meaningless if there is unrighteous living.

God's wrath is the result of the clash of His righteousness with sin. He cannot love good unless He hates evil. God's wrath is revealed because of human ungodliness, human unrighteousness, and human unbelief. Attention is drawn to the righteousness of God in verse 17, the manifest wrath of God in verse 18, followed by the analysis of the sinful heart.

Sin established a process of degeneration, ending in judgment. The black background of gross sin and God's hatred of it is provided to bring into bright focus the blessing of God's provision for deliverance from sin's condemnation. We must see man "unrighteous and condemned" to get the full impact of man made "righteous and redeemed."

**19.** **Because that which may be known of God:** ... what can be known about God is apparent to them, *—ADAM.*

**is manifest in them:** ... is clear to them, *—BECK* ... is plain to their inmost consciousness, *—WEYM.*

**for God hath showed [it] unto them:** ... He himself gave it to them, *—TCNT.*

**20.** **For the invisible things of him:** ... His invisible qualities, *—BRKL* ... His unseen attributes, *—FNTN.*

**from the creation of the world:**

**are clearly seen, being understood by the things that are made:** ... brought within men's apprehension, *—TCNT* ... have been dearly perceptible, *—NORL* ... they have seen the unseen things of God, *—BECK* ... have been rendered intelligible, *—WEYM* ... being perceived, *—WORL* ... and clearly visible, *—WLMS.*

**[even] his eternal power and Godhead:** ... they can tell He has everlasting power, *—BECK* ... and divine character, *—TCNT* ... and divinity, *—CNFT* ... and deity, *—SAWR.*

**so that they are without excuse:** ... Men have no excuse at all, *—NORL* ... they are inexcusable, *—RHEM.*

**1:19, 20.** Now comes the proclamation of the tragic wickedness of man, leading from one stage of depravity to another.

The term "that which may be known of God" is not that which is knowable, but that knowledge of God as the Creator. Men see the attributes of God in His creation; they see His person only in His Son, the Lord Jesus Christ.

The witness of God is unmistakable (verse 19) and universal (verse 20). It is one of the most astounding facts of all Scripture that to *all* human beings of *all* time God has given a revelation of himself. As any person walks in the light he has, he will always be given more light from God. The

Psalmist understood this truth when he wrote that the heavens and the firmament "declare the glory of God; ... Day unto day ... and night unto night" they give knowledge of God; "There is no speech nor language, where their voice is not heard" (Psalm 19:1-4). All created beings are accountable to their Creator for what has been "clearly seen." This witness from nature brings knowledge of the truth of His eternal power and the truth of Godhood (*theiotēs*). "Eternal power" emphasizes the eternity of God himself as well as of His power. *Theiotēs* emphasizes His deity—His being separate from and above His creation. A.W. Tozer speaks of the divine transcendence: "Forever God stands apart, in light unapproachable. He is as high above an archangel as above a caterpillar ... they are alike created. They both belong in the category of that-which-is-not-God" (p. 76). The greatness and detail of God's creation shows man His omnipotence and omniscience. Natural revelation shows that God exists and can be clearly seen by all mankind. The expression "without excuse" (*anapologētus*) means that men are defenseless on judgment day.

**21. Because that, when they knew God:** ... though they knew God, *—ALFD.*

**they glorified [him] not as God, neither were thankful:** ... they did not joyfully honour Him, *—FNTN* ... nor gave him thanks, *—HNT.*

**but became vain in their imaginations:** ... but trifled in, *—FNTN* ... they busied themselves with silly speculations, *—NORL* ... they indulged in their useless speculations, *—BRKL* ... became vain in their reasonings, *—WSLY, —CNFT* ... their thoughts turned to worthless things, *—BECK* ... their thinking became nonsense, *—SEB* ... waxed ful of vanities in their imaginations, *—GNVA* ... are become vaine in their cogitations, *—RHEM.*

**and their foolish heart was darkened:** ... their insensible hearts have been shrouded, *—WLMS* ... and their senseless minds, *—MNTG* ... their inconsiderate heart, *—CMPB* ... their heart being without understanding, *—ALFD.*

**1:21.** The universal willful rejection of God's salvation is seen in man's history. God revealed, but man rejected; he willfully chose not to receive the revelation of God. The downward path is tragic. Irreverence, "glorified him not as God," gives birth to ingratitude, "neither were thankful." This in turn begets rationalism, "became vain in their imaginations" (reasonings), followed by spiritual blindness, "their foolish heart was darkened." Filled with intellectual pride, "professing themselves to be wise," they became idolaters.

All who are charged with unrighteousness are under God's wrath; neither their character nor conduct are acceptable. Unbelievers are guilty and inexcusable because they have seen God's eternal power and deity and yet have rejected it.

**22. Professing themselves to be wise, they became fools:** . . . Claiming to be smart, —BRKL . . . The more they called themselves philosophers, the more stupid they grew, —JB . . . but became moronic, —KLGS.

**1:22.** Claiming themselves to be wise, they became simpletons instead. The word for "wise" had the connotation among the Greeks of persons of culture and learning. The Greek word translated "fools" is *mōrainō*, the source of the English word *moron*. Moral denseness is implied.

Paul pointed out to the Athenians how foolish it was for them to claim to be the offspring of God and then call an idol of "gold, or silver, or stone" that God (Acts 17:28, 29). The Areopagites prided themselves on their intellectual superiority; how ridiculous to worship something at best "unknown" and logically inferior to living human beings.

**23. And changed the glory of the uncorruptible God:** . . . So they exchanged the glory, —NORL, —SEB . . . and have transformed the splendor of the immortal God, —WLMS . . . transformed the majesty of the imperishable God, —FNTN . . . of the undying God, —KLGS.
**into an image made like to corruptible man:** . . . into an Image-likeness of Corruptible Man, —WLSN . . . for idols graven in the likeness of, —CNBR . . . substituted images in the likeness, either of mortal man, —TCNT . . . into a similitude, —RHEM . . . for a worthless imitation, —JB . . . of man, who dies, —BECK.
**and to birds, and fourfooted beasts, and creeping things:** . . . reptiles, —WEYM, —SCLT . . . and of serpentes, —TNDL.

**1:23.** Four stages of idolatry are listed: worship of man, of birds, of beasts, and at the lowest level, snakes ("creeping things").

Man did not glorify God, but changed His glory by making images that looked like other men and even animals which were beneath him. By this process man sought to deify himself which resulted in degrading his concept of God. The vacuum of refusing the truth was filled with this exchange for idolatry. The glory of God was exchanged for humanism, the truth of God for a lie, and God-given relations of life for that which is unnatural.

Man is directly affected by the way he lives. His emotions, intellect, and body are affected by his rejection of God. By that rejection man has regressed to his own lusts, vile affections, and all unrighteousness.

The willful blindness of man became penal blindness. They would not see; therefore, they could not see. The next verses are not beautiful.

Three times the expression "for this cause God gave them up" occurs. He gave them up to uncleanness, to vileness, and to a reprobate mind. The Greek word *paradidōmi* is the same in each instance and means "to give or hand over, to deliver to judgment or prison." Man's deliberate rejection of God brings judicial punishment.

**24. Wherefore God also gave them up to uncleanness through the lusts of their own hearts:** . . . They became sexually unclean, —SEB . . . abandoned them in the lusts of their hearts to filthiness, —FNTN . . . gave them up to live immorally, —BECK . . . their own depraved cravings, —WEYM . . . in the evil trend of their heart's desires, —WLMS . . . in the passionate cravings, —WUST.
**to dishonour their own bodies between themselves:** . . . make a degrading use of their bodies, —TCNT . . . to bestial profligacy, —WUST . . . their bodies be dishonored among them, —PNIN . . . to disgrace their bodies, —SAWR . . . to sexual vice, —MOFT.

**1:24.** God gave them over to lusts (*epithumias*), which means desire. In this instance the desire is evil. The picture is one of retrogression, not progression; downward, not upward, from illumination to futility to folly. Moral degradation went to the depths. The passionate desire (*epithumia*) was for forbidden pleasure, a desire that defied all reason. Those who are taken up with such evil, cease to be aware of God and give themselves to shameless cravings.

**25. Who changed the truth of God into a lie:** . . . seeing they had bartered the truth, —CNBR . . . changed the veritie of God into lying, —RHEM . . . they traded the true God for a lie, —BECK . . . for a false religion, —WLSN.
**and worshipped and served the creature more than the Creator:** . . . rendered religious service to the creation, —WUST . . . reverenced and worshipped the things made instead of the Maker, —CNBR . . . for they had bartered the reality, —WEYM . . . neglecting the Creator, —GNVA.
**who is blessed for ever. Amen:** . . . who is to be eulogized forever, —WUST.

**1:25.** The word "changed" occurs in verses 23, 25, and 26. The word can also be translated "exchanged." Men exchanged the glory of the immortal God for images representing and resembling mortal man and birds, animals, and reptiles. They exchanged the truth of God for a lie, and God-ordained natural relations for unnatural functions.

God made man with the spirit dominant over the body. The order is inverted through sin. Sin begets sin. When men give themselves to sin, they become slaves to sin. When they abandon themselves, their free will eventually fades into oblivion. Man's only freedom is in total worship to God;

his only alternative is bondage to Satan through worship of "the creature."

God has given people a free will. They have the privilege of choice. Choice is essential for a proper relationship between God and man. Without choice there would be neither love nor goodness. God has done everything possible to bring righteousness to men, but if they reject, He cannot make the choice for them. Coerced love is not true love; coerced goodness is not true goodness.

**26. For this cause God gave them up unto vile affections:** . . . shameful lusts, *—BECK* . . . abandoned them to shameful passion, *—FNTN* . . . to dishonorable passions, *—RSV, —ADAM, —WUST, —KLGS* . . . to degrading passions, *—TCNT* . . . to immoral, unnatural drives, *—SEB* . . . passions of ignominie,.Rheims.

**for even their women did change the natural use into that which is against nature:** . . . exchanged their functions for practices contrary to nature, *—NORL* . . . perverted the natural use to one contrary to nature, *—FNTN* . . . indulged in unnatural lust, *—NOYS* . . . from natural intercourse, *—JB* . . . natural sexual drives, *—SEB*.

**1:26.** For the second time we read "God gave them up." This time it was to disgraceful passions. Sexual sins stand out first on the list. These include lesbianism and homosexuality. There are abuses of normal appetites, such as fornication and adultery, but this is a baser sin, for it is perversion. Paul mentions women first which accentuates the abomination of their sin.

The conjunction *te* may be translated "and" or "both" or "even." Here the meaning is best brought out, "for even their women. . . ." John Murray has written, "It is the delicacy which belongs to the woman that makes more apparent the degeneracy of homosexual indulgence in their case" (*New International Commentary on the New Testament*, 1:47). Women should be the bulwark of society. When they yield to sinful desires, the home and the nation are doomed. Lost men and women plunged deeper and deeper into the cesspool of shameful iniquity and did so unashamedly. The apostle here uses *thēleiai* for "women" rather than the usual *gunē* and *arsēn* for "men" rather than the usual *anēr*. A literal translation would be "females" and "males." This usage emphasizes the physical obsession with sex, de-emphasizing the emotional, intellectual, and spiritual aspects of a right relationship in marriage according to God's plan.

**27. And likewise also the men, leaving the natural use of the woman:** . . . disregarding that for which women were intended by nature, *—TCNT* . . . leaving the natural enjoyment of the female, *—SAWR* . . . forsook their natural relationships,

*—BRKL* . . . abandoning the, *—HNT* . . . neglecting that for which nature intends women, *—WEYM*.

**burned in their lust one toward another:** . . . were burnt up with their furious lust, *—WLSN* . . . consumed by flaming passion, *—WLMS*.

**men with men working that which is unseemly:** . . . men perpetrating shameless acts with their own sex, *—MOFT* . . . males with males, *—SEB* . . . working filthiness, *—WSLY* . . . men perpetrating unseemliness, *—HNT* . . . practicing shameful vice, *—WEYM, —WLMS* . . . doing the shameful act with men, *—BECK* . . . wrought filthines, *—GNVA*.

**and receiving in themselves that recompense of their error which was meet:** . . . getting an appropriate reward for their perversion, *—BECK* . . . on account of their wrong behavior, *—BRKL* . . . the inevitable punishment, *—TCNT* . . . the full penalty that their error deserves, *—ADAM* . . . the rewarde of their erroure, *—TNDL* . . . the consequences for this error, *—SEB* . . . because of their deviation, *—WUST* . . . for their own foul acts, *—KLGS* . . . of their perversity, *—MOFT*.

**1:27.** All sin is hideous, but the hideousness of sexual perversion brings an inevitable penalty. The threefold expression "God gave them up to uncleanness" describes a judicial abandonment.

The judgment of God on such sin was not arbitrary or capricious. Judgment came because of the refusal to recognize as God the One who revealed himself as deity through creation.

The *New English Bible* translates the latter part of verse 27, "and are paid in their own persons the fitting wages of such perversion." The penalty is to suffer "in their own bodies and personalities the inevitable consequences and penalty of their wrongdoing and going astray, which was (their) fitting retribution" (*The Amplified Bible*).

The transition from deification of man and turning loose of animal passions ends in frightening immorality. Licentious practices become entwined in religious practices. When men worship genius and passion and the lower creation, there is no end to the extremes of sin in which they mire themselves. Sin has a tendency to lead to unnatural practices. Sin breeds sin. Wickedness fosters greater wickedness. Unrestrained licentiousness proceeds to outrageous lengths. First, the homosexual leaves the *phusikēn chrēsin* ("natural use") of sex. God created the male and the female sex organs so that they provide for union in marriage (Genesis 2:21-25). Anatomy clearly reveals the "natural use." Oral or anal sex is not natural; it is considered criminal in many legal systems. Sodomy is just as abhorrent in God's eyes today as when He destroyed the cities by fire (Genesis 19).

We read that men "burned in their lust one toward another." *Ekkaiō* ("burn") is found nowhere else in Scripture. The literal meaning is "burned out." They were "set ablaze" and "consumed" with passion for one another.

**28. And even as they did not like to retain God in [their] knowledge:** ... refused to see it was rational to acknowledge God, *—BECK.*

**God gave them over to a reprobate mind:** ... to a disapproved mind, *—ADAM* ... vnto a lewde mynde, *—GNVA.*

**to do those things which are not convenient:** ... they do what is not fitting, *—CNFT* ... they lived immorally, *—BECK.*

**1:28.** Moral perversion also brings mental perversion. As men did not see fit to acknowledge God, He gave them up to a "reprobate mind." The word "reprobate" (*adokimion*) means "rejected after testing." Since men rejected God, He rejected them. William's translation reads, "And so, as they did not approve of fully recognizing God any longer, God gave them up to minds that He did not approve."

God does not compel or entice men to evil. Responsibility rests with men. They give themselves to uncleanness and God gives them up to the judgment of their sin. The retributive act of God is a penal infliction of justice and punishment consistent with the holiness of God.

**29. Being filled with all unrighteousness:** ... crammed with, *—FNTN* ... all kinds of wrong, *—SEB* ... they overflow with every sort of evil-doing, *—WLMS.*

**fornication:**
**wickedness:** ... maliciousness, *—WSLY.*
**covetousness:**
**maliciousness:** ... viciousness, *—MOFT.*
**full of envy:** ... crammed with, *—BRKL* ... filled to the brim with, *—MOFT* ... jealousy, *—TEV.*
**murder:**
**debate:** ... wrangling, *—WUST* ... quarreling, *—BECK.*
**deceit:** ... treachery, *—BECK.*
**malignity:** ... spite, *—TCNT.*
**whisperers:** ... They gossip, *—BECK.*

**30. Backbiters:** ... open slanderers, *—WLMS.*
**haters of God:** ... loathed by God, *—MOFT,* *—HNT.*
**despiteful:** ... outrageous, *—CNBR* ... insolent, *—WUST.*
**proud:** ... haughty, *—WEYM.*
**boasters:** ... braggarts, *—HNT* ... swaggerers, *—WUST.*
**inventors of evil things:** ... devisers of evil, *—HNT* ... new forms of sin, *—WEYM.*
**disobedient to parents:**

**31. Without understanding:** ... senseless, *—ADAM* ... bereft of wisdom, *—CNBR.*
**covenantbreakers:** ... They break their promises, *—BECK* ... untrue to their word, *—HNT.*
**without natural affection:** ... heartless, *—NORL.*
**implacable:** ... ruthless, *—NORL* ... callous, *—MOFT.*
**unmerciful:** ... heartless, *—SEB* ... without human pity, *—WEYM.*

**1:29-31.** Paul writes of men who had God-rejected minds, unable to distinguish between right and wrong. Conybeare and Howson translate the preceding verse: "And as they thought fit to cast out the acknowledgement of God, God gave them over to an outcast mind, to do the things that are unseemly" (p. 501).

These men were given over to think thoughts, do deeds, and live lives for which they were not created. Man was created in God's image and for God's glory. How he has fallen!

The last verses of this chapter list a catalog of sins which are the results of total depravity. The record presents a picture of the heathen world, but it is also a portrayal of the headlines of today's newspaper. God says man is filled with these sins—filled without limit—whether he belongs to a savage tribe or to high society.

Twenty-three frightful sins are listed. The first, "all unrighteousness," is a generic term. It is the genus that spawns all the other sins that follow. These are sins of thought, word, and deed. They are both against one's self and against one's neighbor. Some sins are inward, others are outward.

Some of the sins are wrong attitudes toward God, the beginning point of all evil. When men are destitute of a capacity for spiritual things, they become haters of God and constantly discover new evils. They are just plain wicked.

Sins of the spirit are also listed. They include greed, envy, pride, haughtiness, boastfulness. Evils in the area of human relationship are cataloged, including secret gossip and open slander. Deceitfulness, craftiness, faithlessness to one's word, sowing of discord, feelings of ill will, and holding of grudges are on the list. Abusiveness to others, lack of mercy, an unforgiving attitude, and a spirit of harming others are a part of the lurid picture.

Sins concerning the family include the absence of natural love and disobedience to parents. Character is defiled, conduct is defiled, conversation is defiled, companionship is defiled. The list of these sins is introduced by *peplērōnemous* from *plēroō* which means "fill to the full." All rules of conduct are broken, every kind of injustice is practiced, all kinds of new mischief are invented. Loyalty to parents, conscience, and fidelity to one's word are lacking. Natural affection and pity for others are totally absent.

**32. Who knowing the judgment of God:** ... though knowing the judicial decision of God, *—SCLT* ... knowing the righteous sentence, *—CLMT.*

**that they which commit such things are worthy of death:** ... deserve death, *—SAWR.*

**not only do the same, but have pleasure in them that do them:**...and what is worse, –JB...even give their approval to those, –BRKL...but they also that consent to them, –DOUY...but heartily approve of those who practice them, –ADAM...but also on terms of intimacy with those who indulge in them, –TCNT...but even encourage and applaud others, –WEYM...but are even well pleased, –SCLT...but also favour them, –GNVA...but delight in their fellowship with the sinners, –CNBR.

**1:32.** Here the climax is reached. This verse sums up all that has been written, beginning with verse 18. The most degraded persons are not destitute of the knowledge of God and of His righteous judgments. God's wrath has been revealed to man, and yet man ignores His judgment. Man goes all out in iniquity, revels in it, boasts about it, and has pleasure in others who do the same. This is the climax of sin. Man may deny the accusation and try to evade it, but man is guilty and without excuse. Degeneracy and disaster go hand in hand.

The rebellion of fallen men is epitomized in that they find pleasure in iniquity. Iniquity is most prevalent when it is not controlled by the disapproval of others, but rather it receives approbation and applause. One has only to observe the plots of popular entertainment to know that unregenerate men love sin as pigs love mud and dogs love their vomit.

Those who enjoy seeing others sin show that they hate their fellowman, because they know that such sin risks damnation. Rebellious human beings are not only bent on damning themselves but also stay busy seeing to it that others will also be damned. Thus, they judge themselves worthy of eternal death.

## Chapter 2

**1. Therefore thou art inexcusable, O man, whosoever thou art that judgest:**...So no matter who you are, –JB...you have no excuse for condemning others, –NORL...who set yourself up as a judge, –TCNT.
**for wherein thou judgest another, thou condemnest thyself:**...thou art passing sentence, –SCLT...thou judgest thy neighbour, –ALFD.
**for thou that judgest doest the same things:**...You, the judge, are habitually practising, –MNTG...the same things that you are condemning! –SEB...since you behave no differently, –JB...indulge in the very same practices, –TCNT.
**2. But we are sure that the judgment of God is according to truth against them which commit such things:**...We know that the doom of God, –HNT...God's judgement falls unerringly, –TCNT...God's judgment justly falls, –WLMS...will be factual and impartial, –NORL...against them who practise such things, –WSLY.
**3. And thinkest thou this, O man, that judgest them which do such things, and doest the

**same:**...But, mister, –SEB...who condemn those practicing, –BRKL.
**that thou shalt escape the judgment of God?:**...that you will elude, –MNTG...do you reckon upon escaping, –TCNT...schalt ascape the dome of god? –WCLF.

**2:1-3.** After charging the Gentiles with sin and guilt in chapter 1, Paul now speaks to the Jew. The Gentiles who rejected God's revelation of himself in nature were "without excuse," but the Jews who had God's revelation in the Law were also "inexcusable." While the Jews are not named earlier in the chapter, it is evident from verse 17 and on that the principles of divine judgment (2:1-16) are also applied to the Jew (2:17-24) and his covenant status (2:25-29).

The Jewish moralists were as guilty of *practicing* sin as were the Gentile heathen (1:18-32). The main differences were in the degree of knowledge possessed by each group and in the hypocrisy of the moralists. While the pagans openly approved of the sins of others, the moralists pronounced judgment and pretended to hate sins. Fallen man can no more stop sinning than he can stop breathing. All God asks is that he humbly accept the One who saves from sin. The common usage of "inexcusable" (*anapologētos*) came to mean "defenseless." The self-righteous man is defenseless. "Judgment" (*krina*) has the basic meaning of decision, and as used here indicates a judicial verdict with the sense of a sentence of condemnation.

The emphatic meaning of "thou" is "thou, of all men." This is an expansion of the revelation of the wrath of God to include another class of men, namely, "every man who passes judgment." The self-righteous moralist represented by the Jew is as guilty as the idolatrist Gentile. They practice or do (*prassō*) the same things that they condemn. The self-righteous moralist knows neither God's holiness nor man's sinfulness. The sin of judging and boasting is born of self-justification and indicates an unwillingness to recognize God's condemnation of all that we are as fallen men.

Man's judgment can only be partial, for he does not have all the facts. Paul describes in this chapter four simple principles upon which men are judged: "according to truth" (verse 2); "according to his deeds" (verse 6); "there is no respect of persons with God" (verse 11); "according to my gospel" (verse 16).

God's judgment is made "according to truth" (*kata alētheian*), according to the facts of the case, according to reality. It is made by God's standards. The hypocrite is indignant at other peoples' failure and indulgent of his own. The answer to the rhetorical question, "Do you think you will escape the judgment of God?" is an emphatic, "No."

**4. Or despisest thou the riches of his goodness and forbearance and longsuffering:** ... Or perhaps you despise his great kindness, tolerance, —TEV, —SEB ... Or do you play fast and loose, —KLGS ... mistake the wealth of His mercy and the gentleness of His forebearance, —FNTN ... do you underestimate His wealth of kindness, —BRKL ... Or do you think lightly of, —TCNT ... are you slighting all his forbearance, and patience? —MOFT.

**not knowing that the goodness of God leadeth thee to repentance?:** ... the kyndnes of God, —GNVA ... to get you to feel sorry for your sins? —BECK ... invites you to a reformation? —CMPB ... leads you to a change of mind? —SAWR ... to a change of heart, —SEB.

**2:4.** The word "or" introduces the alternative. Is your estimate of God's goodness such that you have license to sin? Three words stand out for those who are trifling with the mercy of God.

The Greek term here for "goodness" is *chrēston* ("loving kindness") rather than the usual *agathos* ("rebuke, discipline").

"Forbearance" (*anochē*) is the word for a cessation of hostility, but with a limit, giving an opportunity for repentance.

"Long-suffering," or patience, (*makrothumia*) expresses patience with people. God's kindness is always active in the pursuit of repentance.

**5. But after thy hardness and impenitent heart:** ... Your stubborn refusal to repent, —JB ... your perverse and unchanging heart, —FNTN ... But according to your obstinate, —WUST ... you stubbornly refuse to turn from sin, —BECK ... harde herte that cannot repent, —TNDL.

**treasurest up unto thyself wrath:** ... you are storing up, —RSV ... heapest vnto thy selfe, —CRNM ... heapest the togedder the treasure of wrath, —TNDL.

**against the day of wrath and revelation of the righteous judgment of God:** ... against a day of fury, —FNTN ... when God will reveal the justice of His judgments, —NORL ... the just doom of God is revealed, —MOFT ... of the just judgment, —CNFT.

**2:5.** Verses 4 and 5 set forth sharp contrasts: repentance and impenitence, despising riches of goodness and treasuring up wrath. God's goodness is manifested to lead (present tense in the Greek) to repentance; it is a continuing activity.

As men continue to despise God's goodness, they amass an accumulation of divine wrath. Day by day a new deposit of wickedness is stored up for judgment in a coming day.

The phrase "*impenitent* heart" (*ametanoētos*) occurs in no other New Testament passage. It means "unrepentant." This is the apex of sin.

"Treasurest" (*thēsaurus*) had the meaning of a place of safekeeping, a treasury or a storehouse. As the word developed it came to mean the treasure which was stored. But the word here is the verb *thēsaurizō*. It has the basic meaning of laying up, keeping in store, of storing. And what is stored up? God's wrath. His wrath is the abhorrence of wrong. His holiness and character require that unrepented and unforgiven sin must come under the judgment of His wrath.

**6. Who will render to every man according to his deeds:** ... God will pay back, —SEB ... since He will pay every person exactly what his deeds deserve, —ADAM ... He will make an award corresponding to his actions, —WEYM ... according to his works, —CNFT ... what his actions deserve, —TCNT.

**7. To them who by patient continuance in well doing seek for glory and honour and immortality, eternal life:** ... by patiently doing good, —MOFT ... by perseverance in doing good ... to attain, —NORL ... in good works, —PNT ... of persistent right-doing, —WEYM ... seek rectification, —FNTN ... enduring Life, —TCNT ... the imperishable eternal life, —HNT ... and life with no end, —SEB ... and incorruptibility, —WUST ... and incorruption, —ASV.

**2:6, 7.** The second principle of judgment is "according to his deeds." This refers to the justice of the judgment, not to the divine provision of eternal life. The passage does not teach that salvation is earned by good deeds. Eternal life is not attained by patient continuing in well-doing. That would be a violation of the whole tenor of Scripture. Salvation is by faith, judgment is according to works.

*Hupomonē* is translated "patience" 28 times in the King James Version. In 2 Corinthians 1:6 it reads "enduring." It means "patient waiting" in 2 Thessalonians 1:4, and in Romans 2:7 it is "patient continuance." Other translations render the word "steadfastness," "endurance," "perseverance," "patiently enduring," and "enduring patiently." See *Various Versions. Makrothumia* refers to the long-suffering and patience of God. *Hupomonē* speaks of the patience of the believer. The steadfastness of patience is never passive. It is not mere endurance; it is perseverance in good work that is active and positive.

*Aphtharsia*, translated "immortality" in the King James Version, comes from the verb *phtheirō* which means "destroy, corrupt, spoil." The basic meaning is "incorruption."

**8. But unto them that are contentious:** ... for the unsubmissive, —JB ... to those who are divisive, —ADAM ... to those who factiously disobey, —HNT ... vnto them that are rebelles, —CRNM ... Other people are selfish and reject, −TEV . . . to them who are obstinate, −PNT . . . that seek their own, −ALFD.

**and do not obey the truth, but obey unrighteousness:** . . . and refuse to listen to the truth, −BECK . . . but assent to iniquity, −CNFT.

**indignation and wrath:**

**2:8.** The word translated "contentious" may also be rendered "strife," "self-seeking," "factious," "governed by selfish ambition." "Do not obey the truth" can be rendered "disloyal to the truth," "always resisting the right." Such persons are responsive only to what is wrong and yield to the wrong.

The last three words of the verse, *thumos kai orgē*, express God's abhorrence of sin and His hot anger, His fury that flows out in judgment.

9. **Tribulation and anguish:** . . . Affliction and anxiety, −BRKL . . . Distress and calamity, −HNT . . . Affliction and Distress on every Soul, −WLSN . . . Affliction and anguish will come, −ADAM . . . crushing suffering and awful anguish, −WLMS.

**upon every soul of man that doeth evil:** . . . who deliberately does wrong, −WEYM . . . that perpetrates evil, −HNT . . . and yielding to the wrong, −WLMS.

**of the Jew first, and also of the Gentile:**

**2:9.** *Thlipsis*, from the verb *thlibō*, is usually translated "tribulation," but on occasion it is "affliction." The verb means to "press," such as pressing out grapes in a winepress. Thus tribulation denotes the heavy pressures that make one almost despair of life. The tribulation referred to here is that of those who "do not obey the truth." The *New English Bible* states, "There will be grinding misery." Goodspeed's translation is "crushing distress."

*Stenochōria*, translated "anguish," is from *stenos* ("narrow") and *chōra* ("space"). One commentator defines it as "torturing confinement." How true the Scripture, "The way of transgressors is hard" (Proverbs 13:15). The apostle speaks of treasuring up "wrath against the day of wrath" (Romans 2:5) and "he that soweth to his flesh shall of the flesh reap corruption" (Galatians 6:8).

10. **But glory, honour, and peace, to every man that worketh good:** . . . But distinction and honor, −BRKL . . . shall come prayse, −CRNM . . . shall be awarded, −CNFT.

**to the Jew first, and also to the Gentile:** . . . also a non-Jew, −SEB.

**2:10.** It may seem difficult to reconcile a judgment according to works with justification by faith. But as human society provides punishment for the evildoer and rewards for the one who does good, so it is in God's society. Grace through faith alone saves, but there is a reward in proportion to work. The fact is that no human being can "work

good" in the absolute sense. Jesus asked, "Why callest thou me *good?* none is good, save one, that is, God" (Luke 18:19). *One* bad act spoils all "good" acts (James 2:10). Man's good works can come only by the life of Christ within.

11. **For there is no respect of persons with God:** . . . For God is impartial and treats everyone alike, −NORL . . . God has no favorites, −JB . . . God doesn't prefer one to another, −BECK . . . God does not recognize human distinctions, −TCNT . . . God pays no attention to this world's distinctions, −WEYM . . . For ther is no parcialyte with god, −TNDL.: . . . For God judges everyone by the same standard, −TEV . . . there is no acceptance of faces, −YNG . . . there is no flattery with God, −FNTN.

**2:11.** This verse states the third principle of God's righteous judgment: "There is no respect of persons with God." *Prosōpolēpsia*, "respect of persons," comes from *prosōpon*, "face," and a form of the verb *lambanō*, "receive." Thus it means "receiving of face." It is variously rendered "no partiality," "no human preferences," "no favoritism," "no attention to this world's distinctions," "undue favor or unfairness."

In Mayor's commentary, *The Epistle of St. James*, the author states, "In its strict sense the Greek would mean to accept the outside surface for the inner reality, the mask for the person" (p. 78).

Whatever advantages certain races of mankind seem to have above others, all men stand on an equal footing at the bar of God's justice. Whether Jew or Gentile, none have a monopoly of divine favor with regard to salvation.

12. **For as many as have sinned without law shall also perish without law:** . . . For whosoever have sinned, −DOUY . . . will be lost without reference, −BRKL . . . will be destroyed, −SEB . . . without reference to the law, −NORL . . . are lost apart from the Law, −TEV.

**and as many as have sinned in the law shall be judged by the law:** . . . whilst living under the Law, −WEYM . . . in the sphere of law, −WUST.

13. **(For not the hearers of the law [are] just before God:** . . . For merely hearing the law read, −WLMS . . . are put right with God, −TEV.

**but the doers of the law shall be justified:** . . . but those who practice, −BRKL . . . it is his obedience to the law, −NORL . . . who will be acquitted, −MOFT . . . shall be accounted righteous, −PNT.

**2:12, 13.** *Anomōs* is rendered "without law." The word "law" would seem to refer to the law of Moses. The *New English Bible* translates it, "Those who have sinned outside the pale of the law of Moses will perish outside its pale."

The judgment of God will be in accordance with the light men have. Those who "have sinned without law shall . . . perish without law." Those who "have sinned in the law shall be judged by the law." In both cases man has a responsibility to God. All will be dealt with fairly.

Those who have the Law have much more light than those without it. But light is light no matter how dim or bright it may be. Judgment and doom await all who reject the light, but those who have more light have less excuse and a greater measure of guilt. Knowing what is right is not enough. We must act accordingly.

In verse 13 we have the first occurrence of the term "justified." The verb *dikaiaō* ("justify") comes from the noun *dikē* ("law"). It is a forensic term meaning "to pronounce not guilty of breaking any law." Logically the one who "does the law" is justified. Of course, no human being can "do the law" perfectly. See comment on verse 7.

**14. For when the Gentiles, which have not the law:** . . . not possessing the law, —*FNTN*.

**do by nature the things contained in the law:** . . . obey instinctively the Law's requirements, —*MOFT* . . . do habitually, —*WUST* . . . perform by natural disposition, —*SCLT* . . . what the Law prescribes, —*CNFT*.

**these, having not the law:** . . . may not actually "possess" the Law, —*JB*.

**are a law unto themselves:** . . . they are their own law, —*SEB*.

**15. Which show the work of the law written in their hearts:** . . . They can point to the substance of the Law engraved on their hearts, —*JB* . . . their conscience attesting, —*FNTN* . . . Their actions show, —*SEB* . . . they exhibit the effect of the Law, —*MOFT* . . . since they exhibit proof . . . is engraven on their hearts, —*WEYM*.

**their conscience also bearing witness:** . . . their conscience also testifies, —*ADAM* . . . testifying with it, —*WORL* . . . too, corroborate it, —*TCNT* . . . giuing testimonie to them, —*RHEM*.

**and [their] thoughts the mean while accusing or else excusing one another;):** . . . and their inner thoughts, —*WLMS* . . . arguing a case, either condemning or justifying it, —*NORL* . . . they argue either in self-accusation or, it may be, in self-defence, —*TCNT* . . . even when conflicting thoughts accuse or defend them,. —*CNFT*.

**2:14, 15.** The law of the Gentiles to whom Paul was writing was not in code but in conscience. They did not have a specific set of rules, but they did have the basic moral concepts which are contained in the Law. The judgment of such people will be based on God's revelation through nature and the standard of right and wrong as revealed through conscience.

Anthropologists know by research what God has revealed in His Word. There is *no* societal group that is devoid of law in the sense of a standard of right vs. wrong. Also, all men know that they break their own laws and they suffer guilt.

No one will be *saved* by the light he has; he will *be judged* by that light. Light will condemn. Christ alone can save.

"Conscience" is a word often used by Paul. Scripture has a great deal to say about conscience. It speaks of a good conscience (1 Timothy 1:5, 19), a convicting conscience (John 8:9), and a seared conscience (1 Timothy 4:2).

The conscience must be governed by the Word of God. Apart from the Word, conscience is an uncertain faculty. The Holy Spirit in His work of conviction takes hold of conscience and brings God's Word to bear upon it with great forcefulness.

Conscience can be said to be the mental faculty by which man judges his actions and passes judgment on those actions. The verdict of God on the Day of Judgment will be in line with what man has done at the heart of his existence with the measure of light and power that God's revelation has brought to his life. "Accusing or else excusing" suggests that as a rule the conscience condemns.

**16. In the day when God shall judge the secrets of men by Jesus Christ according to my gospel:**

**2:16.** How devastating will be the judgment of God. All unbelievers live under the judgment of God, whether they are unrighteous or self-righteous. What we do with the light of the gospel determines our sentence. There will be no secrets on that day.

This verse states the fourth principle of God's judgment: "according to my gospel." Verse 12 connects with verse 16. The matter begins with "the law" (verse 12) and ends with the "gospel" (verse 16). All men will be brought face-to-face with Christ. What we have done with Christ now determines what He will do for us in eternity. Men will not be judged for keeping "the law" but for accepting or rejecting life through Jesus Christ.

**17. Behold, thou art called a Jew:** . . . be entitled a Jew, —*FNTN* . . . since thou bearest the name of a Jew, —*CLMT*.

**and restest in the law:** . . . You depend on, —*SEB* . . . rest comfortably in your Law, —*BECK* . . . and trustest in the lawe, —*CRNM* . . . and have a blind and mechanical reliance, —*WUST* . . . and dost rely upon the Law, —*CNFT*.

**and makest thy boast of God:** . . . You brag about being in God, —*SEB* . . . and are proud of your God, —*JB* . . . exulting in God, —*HNT* . . . and reioysist in God, —*TNDL* . . . and gloriest in God, —*PNIN*.

**2:17.** *Ioudaios* is the Greek word for "Jew." Abraham was known as Hebrew. Most of those who returned from exile were from the tribe of Judah and became known as Jews.

This verse states the three reasons for which the Jews prided themselves. They were proud to be called Jews; they "rested," "felt secure" in the Law; and they "boasted," "bragged," "prided" themselves on a special favor or relationship with God.

**18. And knowest [his] will:** . . . and understand His will, —WORL.

**and approvest the things that are more excellent:** . . . you can appreciate the more excellent way, —NORL . . . appreciate moral excellence, —TCNT . . . and dost discern superior things, —WLSN . . . and vote for the best, —KLGS . . . and provest the things that differ, —PNT, CLMT . . . and approvest the more profitable things, —DOUY.

**being instructed out of the law:** . . . have an idea of the essentials, —BRKL . . . with a sense of what is vital in religion, —MOFT.

**2:18.** The Jew was certain that God looked upon him with special favor, because of his national descent from Abraham and the badge of circumcision in his body. In these verses Paul shatters that confidence and continues to emphasize the truth again and again.

*Katēchoumenos,* from which we get the word *catechumen,* is the word used for one who is being instructed. From this we get our word *catechism.* The Jew had the advantage of being born a Jew. From childhood he was taught in the synagogue. He was indoctrinated in the Law, he kept the Sabbath, he was aware of the need of sacrifices and kept himself separate.

**19. And art confident that thou thyself art a guide of the blind:** . . . if you have convinced yourself, —ADAM.

**a light of them which are in darkness:** . . . be a beacon to the unlearned, —JB.

**20. An instructor of the foolish:** . . . a trainer of the simple, —BRKL . . . a master over uneducated people, —SEB . . . a corrector of the stupid, —HNT . . . a schoolmaster for the dull and ignorant, —WEYM . . . of them which lacke discretion, —GNVA.

**a teacher of babes:** . . . a maister of yong children, —WCLF . . . of the immature, —BRKL . . . of the childish, —TCNT.

**which hast the form of knowledge and of the truth in the law:** . . . you have the framework of knowledge, —NORL . . . possessing in the Law the perfect pattern of knowledge, —CNBR . . . thou hast the embodiment of knowledge, —HNT.

**2:19, 20.** The Jew was confident that he was not only the possessor of truth, but that he was a teacher of others. He prided himself on his position to the extent that he looked with contemptuous scorn on those who did not have his good fortune.

Paul affirmed that it was a distinct privilege to be a Jew (3:1, 2). But he charged the Jew that he thought too highly of himself and too poorly of others. This made his peril all the more real.

To have access to truth, to be born into a family where God and His Word are a central part of daily living, brings great responsibility to a person. To have such privileges and then to become a spiritual bigot exposes one to searing condemnation. Paul dwelt on the fact that the Jews preached too little to themselves.

**21. Thou therefore which teachest another, teachest thou not thyself?:**

**thou that preachest a man should not steal, dost thou steal?:** . . . You who proclaim, —CMPB.

**22. Thou that sayest a man should not commit adultery, dost thou commit adultery?:** . . . Do you forbid adultery, and yet commit it? —TCNT . . . breakest diou wedlocke? —GNVA.

**thou that abhorrest idols, dost thou commit sacrilege?:** . . . You who detest idols, —BRKL . . . You are disgusted with idols, —BECK . . . You loathing idols, —FNTN . . . You who find idols an abomination, —ADAM . . . who shrink in horror from idols, —WLMS . . . and yet. rob their temples? —TCNT . . . and yet robbest God of his honoure, —CRNM.

**2:21, 22.** These verses deal with spiritual insensitivity. Paul charged that the Jew preached high standards of holiness but was not concerned with the fact that he was living a lie. No man can expect to have God's blessing simply because the light of divine revelation shines brightly around him.

The word "therefore" placed here introduces an inference from the preceding words. If the Jew had such privileges, was it not reasonable to expect that he would live up to them?

From God's viewpoint all men are on the same level. Men may classify people by race, civilization, culture, wealth, education, and other human standards. God declares that "all have sinned." Human rationalization and judgment are inexcusable. The man who renders judgment upon another whom he considers below him by any natural standard is like a person in an airplane trying to determine the size of human beings on the earth beneath him.

Moral responsibility increases in direct ratio to knowledge and light. To excuse oneself from known duty on the basis of God's favoritism brings greater condemnation. Knowing never cancels doing; rather it calls for it.

**23. Thou that makest thy boast of the law:** . . . You feel proud, —BECK.

**through breaking the law dishonourest thou God?:** . . . do you dishonor God by its violation? —BRKL . . . do you habitually dishonor, —MNTG . . . by trangressing its commandments? —ADAM . . . by your breaches of the Law? —MOFT.

**2:23.** The court scene continues. The self-righteous boaster is being stripped of his cloak of self-righteousness. The proud, self-sufficient Jew, the religious man of that day, with his claim to personal privilege, is shown for what he is—a hypocrite. Knowing the will of God only increases his condemnation. He claims privilege for both who he is and then for what he has done. Paul could well understand these claims, for no one had been more zealous as a Jew than he. The picture is that of being religious without being redeemed.

The Jew claimed profession, but God, in refuting his proud claim, demanded possession. He claimed precept; God demanded practice. He claimed religion; God demanded reality. Orthodoxy in religion does not make a person more acceptable with God. Neither are men impressed, for they too look for reality.

**24. For the name of God is blasphemed among the Gentiles through you:** ... You make the non-Jews slander God's name, —BECK ... The very name of God is reviled among, —TCNT ... God's name is maligned, —HNT ... is dishonored among the heathen, —NORL ... is defamed among the heathen, —FNTN.

**as it is written:**

**2:24.** The thought expressed in the words "the name of God is blasphemed" is "to speak injuriously, to malign." In 3:8 and 14:16 the Greek is rendered "be slanderously reported" and "be evil spoken of." Paul wrote that the Jews were to a great extent responsible for causing the Gentiles to blaspheme (speak evil of) God.

"As it is written" refers to Isaiah 52:5. This was not a new revelation to the Jews but they needed to be reminded of it. They obviously fell into the same sort of thought patterns over and over just as all men do in all ages. All men need the Word of God every day of their lives "for doctrine, for reproof, for correction, for instruction in righteousness" (2 Timothy 3:16).

With this statement, Paul reaches the apex of his indictment of the hypocritical Jews. He reminds them that what the Gentiles know of the God of Abraham is what they see in Abraham's descendants. The Gentiles reason that a people are like their God; if the Jews can perpetrate such crimes, then their God must be wicked, and they can therefore desecrate His name with impunity.

The Jews who claimed to be leaders for the true worship of God became the instruments to provoke the nations to blasphemy. This solemn and searching charge should startle all who profess the name of *Christian*. Those who profess to be possessors of the truth should not parade lip service without exemplifying standards of holy living.

**25. For circumcision verily profiteth, if thou keep the law:** ... is really worthwhile, —ADAM ... benefits only if you practice the Law, —BRKL.

**but if thou be a breaker of the law:** ... but if you are a Lawbreaker, —WEYM ... a trespassour, —WCLF ... a transgressor, —ASV, —CNFT.

**thy circumcision is made uncircumcision:** ... you have lost your circumcision, —BECK ... your circumcision becomes paganised, —FNTN ... has practically ceased to exist, —TCNT ... counts for nothing, —WEYM.

**2:25.** The Word now pursues the Jew into his last retreat of self-justification, his trust in circumcision. The apostle makes clear that circumcision itself is neutral. It *can* profit if it indeed is a sign of that which is of ultimate value; otherwise, it can be a liability. The word "circumcision" (*peritomē*) occurs 35 times in the New Testament, 15 times in Romans (6 times in this chapter) and 7 times in Galatians. Romans and Galatians give major attention to the means of salvation alike for both Jew and Gentile.

**26. Therefore if the uncircumcision keep:** ... the physically uncircumcised, —BRKL.

**the righteousness of the law:** ... meets the requirements of the law, —NORL ... the ordinance of the law, —HNT ... the precepts, —CNFT.

**shall not his uncircumcision be counted for circumcision?:** ... would not his paganism be considered equivalent, —FNTN ... be regarded by God as if he were? —TCNT ... be reckoned equivalent to, —MOFT.

**27. And shall not uncircumcision which is by nature, if it fulfil the law, judge thee:** ... those who are physically uncircumcised, —ADAM ... and yet scrupulously obeys the Law, —TCNT.

**who by the letter and circumcision dost transgress the law?:** ... for all your written code, —MOFT ... in spite of being circumcised, —JB ... art a preuaricatour of the Law? —RHEM ... who violate the Law in spite of instruction, —FNTN.

**2:26, 27.** *Akrobustia*, "uncircumcision," occurs 19 times in the New Testament, 10 times in Romans and 3 times in Galatians. These two words are almost exclusive to Paul's epistles.

Paul's argument is that a rite or ritual has no meaning unless it is an outward expression of an inward experience. For circumcision to be of any value, the Jew must keep the Law. To keep the Law was humanly impossible. So, to break the Law was to make the rite null and void. The apostle proved that the ordinance of circumcision, which is a seal, was useless without personal righteousness. True circumcision is that of the heart.

The advantage of circumcision lapses unless the moral conditions to which the rite is joined are fulfilled. Wuest renders verse 25: "For indeed, circumcision is profitable if you are a practitioner of the law, but if on the other hand you are a transgressor of the law, your circumcision has become uncircumcision" (*Word Studies from the Greek New Testament, Romans in the Greek New Testament,* 1:49).

Paul makes three points: (1) The rite without reality is unrighteousness (verse 25); (2) The reality without the rite is righteousness (verses 26, 27); (3) The reality is praised by God, the rite by men (verses 28, 29). The uncircumcised Gentiles who kept the Law were more pleasing to God than the circumcised Jews who did not keep the Law.

**28. For he is not a Jew, which is one outwardly:** ... is not a real Jew, –*TCNT* ... who is such in appearance, –*SCLT* ... who is so in an outward fashion, –*WUST* ... who just looks like one, –*KLGS* ... is not one manifestly, –*PNIN*.

**neither [is that] circumcision, which is outward in the flesh:** ... nor is outward bodily circumcision real circumcision, –*TCNT*.

**29. But he [is] a Jew, which is one inwardly:** ... who is a Jew in soul, –*TCNT* ... that is in secrete, –*RHEM* ... in the sphere of the inner man, –*WUST*.

**and circumcision [is that] of the heart:** ... of the herte is the true circumcisyon, –*CRNM*.

**in the spirit, [and] not in the letter:** ... not literal, –*WEYM* ... performed by the Spirit, not the written code, –*SEB*.

**whose praise [is] not of men, but of God:** ... This man's praise originates, –*WLMS* ... the commendation of which is not of men, –*SAWR* ... wins praise from God, –*TCNT*.

**2:28, 29.** *Phaneros*, "outwardly," carries the meaning of "apparent, manifest, evident, known." This speaks of that which can be observed on the outside. *Kruptos*, "inwardly," has the sense of "hidden, secret, concealed" and speaks of the soul-life of a man, his inner part.

The Jew who inwardly maintains his covenant relationship with God is truly a Jew in contrast to the one who is merely professional in his lifestyle. There must be concern to keep the heart right. It is not a matter of keeping "the letter of the law." The spiritual implications are far greater. Circumcision is reckoned as uncircumcision if not accompanied by heart devotion. Uncircumcision is reckoned as spiritual circumcision if obedience to God is practiced. Circumcision must be that of the heart. Circumcision relates to the organ that God ordained to transmit life. Without spiritual life there is no true spiritual circumcision.

"Whose praise is not of men, but of God." The Jews derived their name from their ancestor Judah whose name is associated with praise. His mother named him Judah at birth declaring, "Now will I praise the Lord." On his deathbed, his father stated, "Judah, thou art he whom thy brethren shall praise." But Paul states in verse 29 that the true

Jew receives his praise from God and not from men.

## Chapter 3

**1. What advantage then hath the Jew?:** ... What special privilege, then, –*WLMS* ... what is the Jew's superiority? –*MOFT*.

**or what profit [is there] of circumcision?:** ... what benefit does circumcision confer? –*WLMS* ... or what aduauntageth circumcisyon? –*CRNM*.

**2. Much every way:** ... Considerable in every respect, –*BRKL* ... from every point of view, –*WEYM*.

**chiefly, because that unto them were committed:** ... First indeed, –*DOUY* ... principally in that, –*PNT* ... The most important advantage, –*BECK* ... This at the outset ... were intrusted to them, –*HNT*.

**the oracles of God:** ... the vvordes of God, –*RHEM* ... God's revelatory words, –*ADAM* ... God's utterances, –*TCNT* ... God's truth, –*WEYM*.

**3. For what if some did not believe?:** ... showed a want of faith, –*TCNT*.

**shall their unbelief make the faith of God without effect?:** ... Will their unfaithfulness, –*BECK* ... lack of faith cancel God's loyalty? –*SEB* ... destroy God's trust? –*FNTN* ... make God break faith? –*TCNT* ... cancel God's fidelity? –*JB* ... make the promes of god with out effecte? –*TNDL* ... make null and void God's faithfulness? –*WLMS*.

**3:1-3.** Paul's preceding statements were disastrous blows to Jewish pride and ceremonies. His argument might at first reading appear to make invalid God's institutions for Israel in the Old Testament. His statement in 2:17, in particular, might be construed to imply that circumcision itself created a disadvantage. Therefore, two logical questions are posed in verse 1. The matter of Jewish superiority is dealt with briefly and then considered more fully in chapters 9, 10, and 11. Paul then shows that the Jew had an advantage, but it became his condemnation.

The answer to the first question is found in verse 2. It is "much." He says "chiefly" because, first of all, the Word of God was committed to the Jews. These oracles contain promises yet to be fulfilled. Note that Israel is set aside, not cast away.

*Logia* occurs four times in the New Testament and is translated "oracles." In every instance it means the words or utterances of God. At the time Paul was writing, these "oracles" comprised the Old Testament.

The second question is answered in 2:28, 29.

A third question, posed in verse 3, is answered in verse 4. Though the advantage of the Jew did not serve God's intended purpose, their unfaithfulness did not cancel God's faithfulness.

"For what" is *ti gar*, "for how." "Did not believe" is the verb *pisteuō* meaning they were without faith. Several translations carry the thought of unfaithfulness. Commentators are divided on the rendering, but most agree that the "faith of God" refers to His faithfulness.

"Make . . . without effect" (*katargeō*) carries the thought of rendering it inoperative. Some prefer the rendering "to make inefficient" rather than "to make without effect."

**4. God forbid:** . . . No, never! —*NORL* . . . That would be absurd, —*JB* . . . By no means, —*SCLT.*
**yea, let God be true, but every man a liar:** . . . God must prove true, —*TCNT* . . . though every man be a cheat, —*BRKL* . . . though all mankind prove false, —*MNTG.*
**as it is written:**
**That thou mightest be justified in thy sayings:** . . . be vindicated in, —*BRKL* . . . be declared righteous in thy words, —*CLMT.*
**and mightest overcome when thou art judged:** . . . and will win the case when You are brought to trial, —*ADAM* . . . mayest be victorious, —*CNFT* . . . And mightest prevail, —*ASV* . . . when you go into court, —*WLMS.*

**3:4.** The question raised in the third verse is here answered with a firm "God forbid." Phillips renders it "of course not!"

*Mē genoito* literally means "let it not be" or "may it not come to pass." The expression occurs 15 times in the King James Version of the New Testament, 14 times by Paul, 10 of them in Romans.

Israel's unbelief does not nullify the faithfulness of God. What if some are unfaithful? Will their unfaithfulness make God unfaithful? The answer to the question is very simple. The faithfulness of God holds true even if men would be able to contend with Him in court. A guilty verdict will be returned against men even if it becomes necessary to declare all men are liars. God is true. His truth is due to the fact that He is a perfect Being, even though all men are proved to be liars.

"Let God be true." *Ginomai* is the verb and it means "become." The apparent meaning is that it becomes an apparent condition, that it "proves to be," "is seen to be."

*Gegraptai*, "as it is written," occurs 66 times in the New Testament. Its clearest meaning is, "It has been written and still stands written."

**5. But if our unrighteousness commend the righteousness of God:** . . . if our wrongdoing brings out so strikingly, —*BRKL* . . . if our iniquitie, —*RHEM* . . . But if our wickedness, —*CNFT* . . . simply serves to magnify God's righteousness? —*NORL* . . . demonstrates God's righteousness so clearly, —*ADAM.*
**what shall we say?:**
**[Is] God unrighteous who taketh vengeance?:** . . . Is God wrong . . . when He's angry,

—*BECK* . . . be wrong to punish us, wouldn't He? —*SEB* . . . that the angerbearing God is unjust? —*FNTN* . . . wrong in inflicting punishment? —*TCNT* . . . when inflicteth vengeance? —*SCLT.*
**(I speak as a man):** . . . I am only speaking as men do, —*TCNT* . . . I speak after a purely human manner, —*CNFT.*

**3:5.** The righteousness of God as used here is not a reference to His righteousness that is given in justification to men who believe. It is an attribute of righteousness which includes His faithfulness and truth, what has been called the "inherent equity of God."

The Jews' "unrighteousness" consisted of national disobedience to the Law given at Sinai, neglect of the Law (aptly illustrated in Josiah's time), pride because they were possessors of the Law, and ignorance of the spiritual meaning of the Old Testament Scriptures. They even killed the Righteous One (Acts 13:27).

*Sunistēmi*, "commend," can be rendered "demonstrate, show, prove, establish." "Taketh vengeance" is also translated "inflict anger, wrath." The answer to the question in this verse is given by another question: "God who inflicts wrath is not unjust, is He?" God's justice cannot be questioned.

When Paul said "I speak as a man," he was not speaking in his character as an apostle but rather in the character of men in general. He was voicing those questions that arise in flawed human reasoning, for the purpose of dealing with them and to express his horror at the very thought of any possibility of God's being unjust.

**6. God forbid:** . . . That be far from us, —*CNBR.*
**for then how shall God judge the world?:**

**3:6.** The foregoing questions again bring Paul's resounding answer, "God forbid!" God is just and righteous. God's righteousness is not determined by sin in itself, but by sin as God deals with it, whether punished by His wrath or pardoned by His grace. The sinner is under divine judgment. He can claim no merit if God turns his sin to His glory. "Shall not the Judge of all the earth do right?" (Genesis 18:25).

**7. For if the truth of God hath more abounded through my lie unto his glory:** . . . a falsehood of mine has made God's truthfulness more conspicuous, —*WEYM* . . . if my lie results in His glory by making God's truthfulness all the more obvious, —*ADAM.*
**why yet am I also judged as a sinner?:** . . . why am I still sentenced, —*SCLT* . . . why am I still tried as a sinner? —*MNTG* . . . as a wrong-doer? —*FNTN.*

**3:7.** Commenting on the words "through (by) my lie," Vincent states, "The expression carries us back to verse 4, and is general for moral falsehood, unfaithfulness to the claims of conscience and of God, especially with reference to the proffer of salvation through Christ" (3:3-4). The two questions in verses 7 and 8 are as impertinent and out of place as those in verse 5. Paul knew that all men in general, and the Jews in particular, were always looking for a basis on which to rationalize away their accountability. By twisting what he was teaching, as in the first part of verse 5, they could "logically" progress to the total error of verse 8 (cf. 6:1).

**8. And not [rather], (as we be slanderously reported, and as some affirm that we say,) Let us do evil, that good may come?:** ... Perhaps we should say, —SEB ... insulted me by accusing me, —TEV ... as people abusively say of us, —WLMS ... Why not say ... as some slanderously claim, —ADAM ... Do evil as a means to good, —JB ... so that good may result! —BRKL ... that good may come out of it? —MOFT.

**whose damnation is just:** ... The question justly deserves condemnation, —NORL ... Deservedly are such talkers condemned, —BRKL ... Such arguments are rightly condemned, —MOFT ... The condemnation of those who would so argue is just, —WEYM ... Such conduct is justly condemned, —HNT ... They deserve to be condemned, —SEB ... Of such men the doom is just, —CNBR.

**3:8.** Some had said that Paul was saying, "Let us do evil, that good may come." But Paul was not teaching the doctrine that sin magnifies the grace of God. This, they said, was accomplished by the contrast between man's failure and God's perfection. The absurd conclusion that sin enhances the glory of God and therefore excludes judgment, is not only incompatible with future judgment, but also ruinous to all morality. *Krima*, rendered "damnation" in the King James Version, is generally translated "condemnation."

**9. What then? are we better [than they]?:** ... What defense then have we? —SAWR ... Are the Jews better off? —SEB ... we are the superior? —FNTN ... Do we come out ahead? —BRKL ... Do we excel them? —DOUY ... in any better condition, —TEV.

**No, in no wise:** ... No, not so, —DOUY ... Not at all, —WORL.

**for we have before proved both Jews and Gentiles, that they are all under sin:** ... we haue argued, —RHEM ... under sin's dominion, —JB ... being in thraldom to sin, —WEYM ... in subjection to sin, —TCNT ... under the sway of sin, —WLMS ... decided to serve sin, —FNTN.

**3:9.** The question of unrighteousness among Gentiles and Jews has been fully considered. Both are unrighteous. Now Paul charges that both are guilty. They are under the dominion of sin. The condemnation of God is upon them.

The Gentiles have been charged with sin and guilt in 1:18-32. The guilt of the Jews is declared in 2:8-3:8. The principles of divine judgment are outlined (2:1-16), with application being made to the Jews (2:17-24) and their covenant status (2:25-29). The answer to the counterclaims of the Jews is given in 3:1-8.

*Proaitiaomai* is a word not found elsewhere in the New Testament. While it is translated "proved" in the King James Version, most other translators render it "charged." Man is a sinner by nature, man is a sinner by deliberate choice, man is a sinner in God's sight. All men are under sin, and God will deal with them accordingly and without argument.

The idea "that they are all under sin" is also expressed in Galatians 3:22, "The Scripture hath concluded all under sin." This seems to indicate that they are not only sinners, but are under an empire of sin.

**10. As it is written:**
**There is none righteous, no, not one:** ... not one just man, —CNFT ... who stands right with God, —TCNT ... single human creature is upright, —WLMS.

**11. There is none that understandeth:**
**there is none that seeketh after God:** ... diligently seeketh, —NOYS.

**12. They are all gone out of the way:** ... All have swerved, —HNT ... Al haue declined, —RHEM ... All have left the ranks, —FNTN ... Everyone has side stepped, —KLGS.

**they are together become unprofitable:** ... they have become utterly useless, —BRKL ... one and all become worthless, —BECK ... one and all have become vile, —ADAM ... become depraved, —TCNT ... gone wrong, —MOFT ... have turned bad together, —HNT ... become corrupt, —WEYM.

**there is none that doeth good, no, not one:** ... Not a single one practices kindness, —NORL.

**3:10-12.** Verse 10 begins an extended quotation from the Old Testament which runs through verse 18. The quotes are from six psalms and from Isaiah 59:7, 8. God speaks as a judge (verses 10-12); as a physician (verses 13-15); and as a historian (verses 16-18).

The judge brings six sweeping charges of guilt: "There is none righteous ... there is none that understandeth, there is none that seeketh after God. They are all gone out of the way, they are together become unprofitable; there is none that doeth good."

These are the evidences for the indictment. Two major emphases stand out. Sin is universal. All are under its power and condemnation. Not one person is excluded. The second emphasis is upon the depravity and intensity of sin. Every aspect of a man's life is affected, his thoughts, words, and deeds.

"None righteous." No mortal soul has ever been righteous. Even Adam was not righteous; he was innocent, that is, not knowing good from evil (Psalms 14:1; 53:1; Ecclesiastes 7:20). "Understandeth." Man by nature can understand nothing of God (1 Corinthians 1:21). "Gone out of the way" implies turning aside, backsliding. Apostasy is first described in 1:21. "Together" (*hama*) means "one and all," everyone individually.

**13. Their throat [is] an open sepulchre:** . . . are yawning graves, *—JB*, *—FNTN* . . . an open tomb, *—PNT.*
**with their tongues they have used deceit:** . . . They use their tongues to trick people, *—SEB* . . . they are treacherous with their tongues, *—MOFT.*
**the poison of asps [is] under their lips:** . . . Their lips hide the poison of snakes, *—BECK* . . . cobras, *—ADAM* . . . the venym of snakis is vndir her lippis, *—WCLF.*

**14. Whose mouth [is] full of cursing and bitterness:** . . . full of imprecations, *—WUST.*

**3:13, 14.** God as physician diagnoses five deadly ailments: (1) Their throat is like an open sepulcher—death, decay, stench. (2) Their tongues use deceit—deceitful. (3) The venom of asps is under their lips—uncharitable. (4) Their mouth is full of cursing and bitterness—blasphemous. (5) Their feet are swift to shed blood—murderous. Four different bodily organs connected with speech and one connected with the feet are mentioned. This illustrates how man's sinfulness is exemplified in his words.

"Their throat is an open sepulchre," the grave has been opened and remains open. The stench is not due to the grave itself but to the rottenness within. Can you imagine a worse odor than that of a decaying carcass? That reeking smell depicts the corruption of so much of human speech. As the contents of the grave cause the stench, so the contents of the human heart and mind cause the unclean, unkind utterances.

The fangs of deadly serpents are to be feared. Their poisonous venom is easily fatal. Man is born with this venom under his tongue. Bitter, deceitful, poisonous words maim and kill. We will be held accountable for our words (Matthew 12:36). Words are like a bag of feathers in the wind. Once they are released they cannot be gathered again. Poisonous words do untold damage to God's work, to others, and to the speaker himself.

**15. Their feet [are] swift to shed blood:** . . . They move quickly to kill someone, *—SEB.*

**3:15.** The first recorded sin following the Fall was murder. The first sin separated man from God in Eden; the second sin separated man from man. In worship to God, Cain could not slay an animal, but in anger he could slay his brother.

**16. Destruction and misery [are] in their ways:** . . . Ruin and misery mark their path, *—WEYM* . . . wherever they go there is havoc, *—JB* . . . people are suffering and destroyed, *—SEB* . . . break down and misery are in their road, *—KLGS* . . . wretchednes, *—TNDL* . . . calamitie, *—GNVA* . . . dog their steps, *—TCNT.*

**17. And the way of peace have they not known:** . . . And the path to peace, *—TCNT.*

**3:16, 17.** Man's wicked ways bring nothing but "destruction and misery." This is true whether he is a Hitler, a well-known criminal, or an unknown sinner. Sin leaves a tragic trail.

"There is no peace, saith my God, to the wicked" (Isaiah 57:21). Isaiah 59 catalogs the way of sinners. They walk continually in paths of violence. Their crooked paths leave a trail of waste and destruction (Isaiah 59:8).

**18. There is no fear of God before their eyes:** . . . No reverence of God is, *—BRKL* . . . God does not terrify them, *—BECK.*

**19. Now we know that what things soever the law saith:** . . . whatever the Law enjoins, *—SCLT.*
**it saith to them who are under the law:** . . . it says to those under its control, *—BRKL* . . . who are under its authority, *—WLMS.*
**that every mouth may be stopped:** . . . in order to stop all human excuses, *—TEV.*
**and all the world may become guilty before God:** . . . may become liable to divine retribution, *—BRKL* . . . made answerable to God, *—MOFT* . . . may be brought under the judgment of God, *—ALFD*, *—CLMT* . . . that the whole world may be under the sentence, *—WORL.*

**3:18, 19.** All man's sin seems to be summed up in Psalm 36:1 referred to here: "The transgression of the wicked saith within my heart, that there is no fear of God before his eyes." The wicked completely ignore God; they act as though He is nonexistent.

*Hupodikos*, found only here in the New Testament, means "under sentence of condemnation." The whole world is brought to trial before God, is found guilty, and is under a sentence of condemnation.

**20. Therefore by the deeds of the law there shall no flesh be justified in his sight:** . . . as the result of actions done in obedience to Law, *—TCNT* . . . by the practice of a ritual, —FNTN . . . into right standing with God, —WLMS.

**for by the law [is] the knowledge of sin:** . . . that one becomes fully aware of his sin, —ADAM . . . there comes a clear conception of sin, —TCNT . . . a recognition of sin comes by means of, —FNTN . . . comes the consciousness of sin, —MNTG.

**3:20.** The words "deeds of the law" appear to go beyond the Mosaic law. "No flesh" can be "justified" in God's sight "by the law." The verb *dikaioō* indicates that only God can declare man righteous. Justification is the judicial act of God wherein He shows man free from guilt and acceptable to God (Ephesians 1:6).

At this point Calvinists and Arminians divide. It is imputation versus impartation. Calvinists state that in justification the righteousness of Christ is imputed to the sinner. The Arminians teach that God in one act of justification makes man righteous and then pronounces him righteous. Their reasoning is that God will not declare righteous what is not righteous.

The Law was given through Moses to give us the "knowledge of sin." God knew that the Law could never save us because of the weakness of our flesh. It could only give us the knowledge of sin's awful character.

Two expressions, "before God" (verse 19) and "in his sight" (verse 20), are significant. All the world is guilty "before God," and no flesh is justified "in his sight." The Law has done its work. It could not justify; it only condemned. The old covenant brought death, but the new covenant brings life.

The Law may be compared to a scale which tells us how much we weigh; it will not add to or subtract from our weight. The Law discovers the fact of sin, exposing its presence and revealing its nature in order that God might prescribe the remedy.

**21. But now the righteousness of God without the law is manifested:** . . . a Divine righteousness is exhibited, —FNTN . . . the iustice of God, —RHEM . . . has been revealed, —SEB . . . has been disclosed apart from law, —HNT.

**being witnessed by the law and the prophets:** . . . testified to by the law, —YNG . . . point toward this truth, —SEB.

**3:21.** For generations people had been sinning and learning that it was neither possible to put away or to conquer sin. "But now" God clearly and openly had revealed the way.

Since the Law cannot justify, man's only hope is for a "righteousness without the Law." It is not an unlawful righteousness or one that allows man to sin, but a change of position and condition

produced apart from the Law. This does not mean that justification without the Law was now for the first time revealed and that earlier men had reason to believe that they could be justified by works of the Law. To prevent any such misunderstanding, Paul expressly stated that this righteousness of God was witnessed by the Law and the Prophets, the usual phrase signifying the entire Old Testament.

There is supernatural continuity between the two Testaments. What is emphasized here is the *manifestation* of God's righteousness. It can be stated unequivocally that Christ Jesus *is* God's righteousness. He who was promised in the Old Testament had now been manifested in the flesh, having been "delivered for our offenses, and was raised again for our justification" (4:25).

**22. Even the righteousness of God:** . . . rightewesnes no dout which is good before God, —TNDL.

**[which is] by faith of Jesus Christ unto all and upon all them that believe:** . . . that is channeled through faith, —ADAM.

**for there is no difference:** . . . For there is no distinction, —BRKL . . . It makes no difference who you are, —SEB.

**3:22.** "The righteousness of God" is not a law-righteousness (verse 21) but a faith-righteousness (verse 22). It comes by faith in Jesus Christ and is imparted to all who believe.

"By faith of Jesus Christ" can be understood as faith of Him as well as faith *in* Him. It is impossible to have one without the other. In the Greek phraseology, we have the genitive form; this shows that it is faith possessed by Christ which He gives to those who are willing to receive. Of course, it operates as faith *in* Him. Faith as described in the Bible is God's gracious gift: "For by grace are ye saved through faith; *and that not of yourselves*" (Ephesians 2:8). To believe is to respond to God's gracious gift, exercising the faith He offers to all.

"No difference." The word *diastolē* is used in only two other places, Romans 10:12 and 1 Corinthians 4:7. Many translators render the word "distinction." There may be difference essentially between two things and yet no distinction is made, so "distinction" seems to be the better translation.

**23. For all have sinned:**

**and come short of the glory of God:** . . . and are destitute of, —GNVA . . . and forfeited God's glory, —JB . . . and are without God's glory, —BECK . . . all fall short of God's glorious ideal, —TCNT . . . and have need of the glory of God, —CNFT . . . and everybody continues to come short, —WLMS . . . and fall short of the majesty of, —HNT . . . and all consciously come short of, —WEYM . . . and fail of obtaining the glory which cometh from God, —NOYS . . . are in need of rectification from God, —FNTN . . . and lacke the prayse that is of valoure, —TNDL.

**3:23.** This is the most clear-cut statement about sin in all Scripture. All have fallen short. "There is none righteous, no, not one" (3:10). God has made no charges that He has not substantiated. The proof is clear and convincing. There is no appeal and no reversal of the verdict.

**24. Being justified freely by his grace:** . . . become righteous by a gift of His love, —BECK . . . they are justified for nothing, —MOFT . . . gaining acquittal from guilt, —WEYM . . . being justified gratuitously by, —WUST . . . being declared righteous freely, —YNG . . . Iustified gratis by his grace, —RHEM.
**through the redemption that is in Christ Jesus:** . . . through the ransom that Christ Jesus provided, —BRKL . . . which is paid in Christ Jesus, —CNBR . . . by His free unpurchased grace, —WEYM . . . paid to free them, —BECK.

**3:24.** *Apolutrōsis*, "redemption," is the theme of this epistle. Christ paid the ransom and we are redeemed. We are justified (acquitted) and declared righteous "freely by his grace."

**25. Whom God hath set forth [to be] a propitiation through faith in his blood:** . . . whom God hath proposed, —RHEM . . . God once publicly offered Him in His death, —WLMS . . . as a reconciling sacrifice, —BRKL . . . by his sacrifice of himself, —TCNT . . . as a Mercy-Seat, rendered efficacious through faith, —WEYM . . . to be the obtayner of mercy thorow fayth, —CRNM . . . to be a pacification, —GNVA . . . as an offering of atonement, —MNTG . . . as an expiatory satisfaction, —WUST.
**to declare his righteousness for the remission of sins that are past:** . . . for the manifestation of His righteousness, —WORL . . . for a demonstration of his own justice, —CMPB . . . that sins are taken away, —SEB . . . because of the passing by of the errors committed previously, —SAWR . . . of the bygone sins, —YNG.
**through the forbearance of God:** . . . in His tolerance, —ADAM.
**26. To declare, [I say], at this time his righteousness:** . . . for the showing, I say, —PNIN . . . in our present period, —BRKL.
**that he might be just, and the justifier of him which believeth in Jesus:** . . . stand right with himself, —TCNT . . . might justify the children of Faith, —CNBR . . . on the score of faith in Jesus, —MOFT.

**3:25, 26.** The word *justify* as employed in the New Testament means more than to forgive sin and remove condemnation; it means also to place the offenders in the position of righteousness. God blots out the past with all its sin and then considers the sinner as if he had never sinned. The sinner is pronounced "justified." Justification has been purchased through the propitiatory sacrifice of Christ.

Propitiation means bringing together, making favorable, thus enabling someone to act with mercy and forgiveness. A propitiation is a sacrifice or gift which averts the wrath of God and enables Him to be merciful and favorable to the sinner.

*Hon . . . hilastērion* is always used for the "lid of the ark" or the "mercy seat" (Hebrews 9:5), so called from the fact of its being sprinkled with the blood of the sacrifices on the Day of Atonement. Mercy seat means literally "to cover." The great privilege of access to God has been purchased at a great price, the blood of Christ.

*En tō autou haimati. En* is instrumental expressing means. *Haimati*, "blood," is the instrument. The reference is to the life blood of Jesus as the means of propitiation. Blood is regarded as the reservoir of life (Leviticus 17:11). Its application was the application of life, and the offering of the blood to God was an offering of life.

*Autou* ("his") emphasizes the identity of the sacrifices as that of the life of Jesus. The emphasis is on the voluntary offering of Jesus' life to God. His sacrificial death becomes in a twofold sense the means by which God does away with a person's sin. The sin is removed not only from the believer's life but also from the presence of God. The *hilastērion* which God provided in Christ not only removes the ungodliness and unrighteousness of men, but also averts the wrath and retribution which is its just due. Christ died in order to save us from God's wrath and to secure His favor for us.

The propitiation becomes effective *dia pisteōs*, "through faith" (Hebrews 10:19, 20, 22).

The effect of Christ's redemption was retroactive. Before Calvary God gave proof of His anger against sin by now and then inflicting punishment on sinners. But He did not inflict the full penalty, for if He had the race would have perished.

*Paresin* ("remission," literally "passed over") indicates a temporary passing by and not a permanent absolution of sin. Sins prior to Calvary were temporarily covered awaiting the perfect sacrifice: "for the remission of sins that are past, through the forbearance of God."

*En tō nun kairō*, "at the present time," is in contrast to the sins previously considered. Christ's blood was shed to cover and wash away sins that had been temporarily covered in the past and also to declare God's righteousness "at this time."

**27. Where [is] boasting then?:** . . . What then, becomes of our vain human pride? —NORL . . . Where is then the reioysyng? —GNVA . . . where is the exulting? —HNT.
**It is excluded:** . . . There is no room left for it, —TCNT . . . outlawed, —NORL . . . It is ruled out

absolutely, —MOFT... for ever shut out, —WEYM... banished, —FNTN... It was once for all excluded, —WUST.

**By what law? of works? Nay: but by the law of faith:**... On what principle? —WLMS... What sort of Law forbids it? A Law prescribing acts? No, a Law prescribing faith, —TCNT... through the principle of faith, —SEB... a law of deeds? —HNT... On the ground of merit? —WEYM.

**28. Therefore we conclude that a man is justified by faith without the deeds of the law:**... We are convinced, —BECK... for our reasoned conclusion, —WUST... altogether apart from the deeds, —MNTG... independently of the works of the Law, —CNFT.

**3:27, 28.** Man was not made righteous by the Law. Peter expressed the Jews' inability to keep the Law (Acts 15:10). The Law revealed he was not righteous. The law of *faith,* the gospel, completely excludes boasting. Righteousness is dependent upon merit. We receive it by accepting by faith the Christ who has merit.

**29. [Is he] the God of the Jews only? [is he] not also of the Gentiles?:**... of the heathen? —TCNT.

**Yes, of the Gentiles also:**... Assuredly, of Gentiles also, —HNT.

**30. Seeing [it is] one God, which shall justify the circumcision by faith, and uncircumcision through faith:** ... Agreeing there is but one God, —BRKL... assuming that there is one God... through the intermediary instrumentality of faith, —WUST... For it is God only whych iustyfyeth, —CRNM... who will pronounce the circumcised to be acquitted, —WEYM.

**31. Do we then make void the law through faith?:**... Do we then use faith to overthrow Law? —TCNT... Do we then render law invalid, —MNTG... cancel the Law? —BECK... do we nullify the law by this faith? —ADAM... destroy the Law? —CNFT... make the Lawe vnprofitable, —GNVA... make law useless through the faith? —CMPB.

**God forbid:**... Let not such a thing be considered, —WUST... on the contrary, —MNTG.

**yea, we establish the law:** ... we establish its authority, —TCNT... rather it strengthens the law, —NORL... giving the Law its true value, —JB... We uphold the Law, —BECK, —RSV, HNT... we give the Law a firmer footing, —WEYM... we corroborate law, —FNTN... we rather mayntayne the lawe, —TNDL... we make it stand, —MNTG.

**3:29-31.** God's plan of salvation casts all the provision on a God who cannot fail and brings all men to the same level of need and dependence on the grace of God. Pride is eliminated (3:27, 28). There is no place for boasting. Prejudice is eliminated (3:29, 30). There is no favored group and no special person. Presumption is eliminated. One dare not presume upon the grace of God.

If justification were possible by the Law, then God belonged only to the Jew, but since

justification is by faith, He is God of both Jew and Gentile. There can be no boasting if man examines his record. It is black (1:18-32). There can be no boasting if man considers the Law, for the Law is a rigid, impartial measuring rod (2:17-3:8). There can be no boasting if man remembers the Cross, for there man's helplessness and God's love and mercy are revealed.

Three statements are made: (1) If the way of salvation is by faith alone, there is no place for human effort. (2) If the way of salvation is by faith alone, there is no difference between Jew and Gentile. "The Lord our God is one God" (Deuteronomy 6:4) is the basis of the Jewish creed and the opening words of every synagogue service. There is not one God for the Gentiles and another for the Jews.

(3) Though the way of salvation is by faith alone, it does not mean an end of the Law. Paul says in verse 31, "We establish the law." The doctrine of grace does not render the moral law void. In reality it confirms and establishes its validity. The Law required the death penalty for violation. Paul preached that Christ died for our sins. He tasted "death for every man" (Hebrews 2:9). Israel, under the Law, was redeemed from the curse of the Law through Christ who was made a curse at Calvary.

When Paul asked, "Do we then make void the law through faith?" he anticipated the questions dealt with in detail in chapter 6. He was well aware of the dangers of the antinomian inferences some wanted to draw from the doctrine of grace. He dealt that heresy a death blow summarily, saying that faith actually establishes the Law. Only Christ *can* establish (fulfill) the Law (8:2, 3)!

Jew and Gentile alike are justified by faith. Righteousness comes by faith alone. No other claim will do. The law of faith does no violence to the law of Moses. That law is established through God's act in fulfilling it. All its benefits accrue to the believer through faith in the work of Christ. The believer, through Christ, attaches a new sacredness to the commands of the Law and finds a new power to fulfill its demands.

## Chapter 4

**1. What shall we say then that Abraham our father, as pertaining to the flesh, hath found?:**... our human ancestor, —BRKL... the ancestor of our nation? —TCNT... What did he gain from his human experience? —SEB... found with reference to the flesh? —WUST... according to the flesh, —CNFT.

**2. For if Abraham were justified by works:**... made righteous by rituals, —FNTN... by human effort, —SEB... as the result of his actions, —TCNT... on the score of what he did, —MOFT... on the ground of his actions, —WEYM.

**he hath [whereof] to glory; but not before God:** ... he has something to brag about, –BRKL ... he has something to exult about, –HNT ... he hath ground of boasting, –ALFD ... he has something to be proud of. But not to be proud of before God, –MOFT ... But he couldn't feel proud before God, –BECK.

**3. For what saith the scripture?:** ... for what doth the writing say? –YNG.

**Abraham believed God:** ... had faith in God, –NOYS.

**and it was counted unto him for righteousness:** ... and his faith was regarded by God, –TCNT ... so God declared him, –SEB ... placed to his credit, –WEYM ... and it was reputed him to iustice, –RHEM ... and it was paid to him in righteousness, –FNTN ... and it was credited to him as right standing with God, –WLMS.

**4:1-3.** Romans is a lawbook; its terms are law terms. The argument follows legal precedents and is in logical order. The indictment against sin and sinners has been argued and every plea known to legal practice has been exhausted. At Calvary "mercy and truth are met together; righteousness and peace have kissed each other" (Psalm 85:10). But the Jews could not understand that righteousness could come apart from the Law. Note how skillfully Paul builds support for the doctrine of justification. He cites the example of Abraham.

Abraham, of all men, is an example of righteousness. He had many qualities, but the only basis for his justification was that he believed God (John 8:56). It was not on the merit of his faith, but faith in God. This is the second time Paul quoted Genesis 15:6; he also referred to it while writing to the Galatians when they were threatened by the Judaizing heresy (Galatians 3:6). Some teachers seem to place more emphasis on faith than on the God whom we believe. Note that the Word does not say that Abraham believed *in* God; he "believed God." To believe God removes all doubt once God has clearly spoken to an individual.

A fairly common teaching is that faith is a "leap in the dark." It is actually the opposite of that. It is a step in the light as God reveals the light. By faith Abraham "went out, not knowing whither he went" (Hebrews 11:8), but knowing full well that he was walking with God, who is Light. Faith is not a work; faith caused Abraham to leave Ur, but the faith was genuine and complete before he left.

**4. Now to him that worketh is the reward not reckoned of grace, but of debt:** ... is not imputed according to grace, –RHEM ... as a favor, –SEB ... pay is not reckoned a favour but a debt, –WEYM ... the remuneration is not put down on his account ... but as a legally contracted debt, –WUST ... are not credited

as a favor but as an obligation, –BRKL ... a worker has his wage counted to him as a due, –MOFT.

**4:4.** "Worketh" is *ergazomai*, meaning "to do that from which something results." "Reward," *misthos*, means "dues paid for work, wages." "Reckoned," *logizomai*, means to "think, impute, count, account." "Grace," *charis*, speaks of "God's favor." "Debt," *opheilēma*, means "that which is justly or legally due, a debt."

Under works the sinner feels he can earn his salvation; under grace he understands he must rely totally on God. Under law God gives a fair trial; under grace He gives pardon. Work and wages are contrasted with faith and grace. Conybeare and Howson translate verse 4 as follows: "Now, if a man earn his pay by his work, it is not 'reckoned to him' as a favor, but it is paid him as a debt."

**5. But to him that worketh not, but believeth on him that justifieth the ungodly:** ... the impious, –RHEM ... who declares the guilty to be innocent, –TEV.

**his faith is counted for righteousness:** ... there is put to his account his faith, –WUST.

**4:5.** God's justification is given to a person as a sinner, not as a saint. Justification does not depend on growth in spiritual maturity. That is sanctification. The person who sees the futility of trying to obtain God's favor by works and casts himself wholly on God will be justified.

"Ungodly" is *asebēs*, meaning a person totally lacking in piety, destitute of reverential awe of God. But such are justified by faith. In the Old Testament the condemnation of the innocent and the acquittal of the sinner are alike censured as acts of unjust judges. God himself states, "I will not justify the wicked." How startling and paradoxical that under grace God justifies the sinner. But through the provision of Calvary God maintains His own character. Almost beyond human understanding, God solved this moral problem by His grace.

**6. Even as David also describeth the blessedness of the man:** ... Precisely as David mentions the blissfulness, –BRKL ... also pronounceth blessing upon the man, –PNIN ... describes the happiness, –WLMS ... that man to be "happy," –HNT ... speaks of the spiritual prosperity of the man, –WUST.

**unto whom God imputeth righteousness without works:** ... whom God ascribeth ryghtuousnes wythout dedes, –GNVA ... credits justice, –CNFT ... irrespective of good deeds, –JB ... apart from rituals, –FNTN ... without human effort, –SEB.

**7. [Saying], Blessed [are] they whose iniquities are forgiven:** ... Spiritually prosperous, –WUST ... Happy are they, –WSLY ... whose breaches of the Law, –MOFT ... whose lawless acts, –ADAM, –YNG ... whose crimes are forgiven, —JB . . . whose wrongdoings have been forgiven, —TCNT.

**and whose sins are covered:** . . . whose sins are obliterated, —FNTN . . . and over whose sins a veil has been drawn, —TCNT.

**8. Blessed [is] the man to whom the Lord will not impute sin:** . . . will not record any sin, —NORL . . . whom the Lord considers sinless, —JB . . . if the Lord doesn't count sins against you, —BECK . . . will in no wise reckon sin, —CLMT.

**4:6-8.** The use of *kathaper* ("even as") introduces the revelation God gave to David also, regarding imputation of righteousness without works. It is clear that David understood by the Spirit exactly what Abraham knew and demonstrated, thus becoming the father of those of faith. The principle of God's acceptance of Abraham, the friend of God, by faith is the same as that used to accept the vile sinner. David was a man of God, yet his violation of three of the Ten Commandments—coveting, adultery, and murder—precludes the idea that he was justified by works.

In the case of Abraham, Paul dealt with the positive side of justification and shows how God reckons righteousness to the believer. In David's case Paul touched the negative side and showed how God does not impute (reckon, count, credit) sin to those whom He justifies.

Paul used the convincing illustration of David (Psalm 32; compare Psalm 51 and Proverbs 28:13). There was nothing that David could do to restore chastity to Bathsheba or life to Uriah. Into that hopeless case God by sovereign grace came and canceled his sin, counting him righteous. David was undeserving of pardon; he did not merit forgiveness. Forgiveness was freely bestowed and his sin was "covered," forever canceled. David rejoiced not only that sin was not imputed but also in the positive imputation of righteousness, the pronouncement of acquittal.

**9. [Cometh] this blessedness then upon the circumcision [only], or upon the uncircumcision also?:** . . . Does this happiness, therefore, come, —WORL . . . does this ascription of bliss apply only, —BRKL.

**for we say that faith was reckoned to Abraham for righteousness:** . . . for we affirm, —WLSN . . . was placed to his credit, —WEYM.

**4:9.** Abraham's example was the bulwark of the whole Jewish system of theology. After Paul introduced David as a demonstration of the faith of Abraham, he returned to discussing Abraham. He was ready to clinch the thesis that works can never produce faith nor procure righteousness. To do this he showed the absolute impossibility of Abraham's circumcision having any justifying merit. If

that were the case with Abraham, then it applied also to Abraham's seed.

*Peritomē* ("circumcision") and *akrobustia* ("uncircumcision") occur six times each in verses 9 through 12. Paul is making the point that Abraham was justified by faith at least 14 years before he was circumcised. Circumcision is not essential to salvation. Man is always trying to claim credit for himself, but there is nothing he can do to earn salvation.

**10. How was it then reckoned?:** . . . Under what circumstances, —WLMS . . . How then was it put to his account, —WUST.

**when he was in circumcision, or in uncircumcision?:**

**Not in circumcision, but in uncircumcision:** . . . Not after, but before, —BRKL.

**11. And he received the sign of circumcision:** . . . As a matter of fact, —ADAM . . . he received the Symbol, —WLSN . . . it was a seal to prove that the faith he had, —SEB . . . he received the attesting sign of circumcision, —WUST.

**a seal of the righteousness of the faith which [he had yet] being uncircumcised:** . . . as a mark to confirm the righteousness he got by believing, —BECK . . . as a seal of the righteous character of the faith, —WUST . . . as a sign or seal of the righteousness, —MOFT . . . which belonged to the faith he had, —HNT . . . on condition of faith, —WLMS . . . while in uncircumcision, —WORL.

**that he might be the father of all them that believe:** . . . the father of all uncircumcised believers, —BRKL.

**though they be not circumcised:**

**that righteousness might be imputed unto them also:** . . . might be accredited, —BRKL . . . who are declared righteous, —SEB . . . they also may be regarded by him as righteous, —TCNT.

**4:10, 11.** The Jewish disputant is still in Paul's mind. Paul has proved that Abraham and David were not justified by works. But some will argue that this great provision is only for Jews—those who follow rites of religion. Justification in the Old Testament, as in the New Testament, is independent of ordinances.

This portion of Scripture gives emphasis to the fact that the sacraments and ceremonies of the Church do not save. As circumcision will not bring righteousness, baptism will not bring regeneration. As works are set aside as a basis for justification, so divine ordinances are also set aside.

Circumcision is spoken of as the "sign" and the "seal." Abraham had been justified before he was circumcised. Why, then, was circumcision ever practiced? The answer is twofold. First, circumcision was an outward sign given to Abraham as a seal of the righteousness he had received 14 years earlier. To seal means to validate. In other words, circumcision attested or bore witness to an existing righteousness. Circumcision was not the means of Abraham's justification. Of itself it did nothing for Abraham, other than giving the great assurance that the promise was certain.

Second, circumcision bore witness to the fact that Abraham "might be the father of all them that believe, though they be not circumcised." By this illustration God defines righteousness and establishes the basis on which a person is made righteous.

Abraham is not the father of those who have been circumcised; he is the father of all who exercise the same act of faith in God as he did. Every person in every age who takes the Word of God as Abraham did is a child of Abraham. The descendants of Abraham are those in every nation who belong to the family of God regardless of race, color, or national origin.

**12. And the father of circumcision to them who are not of the circumcision only:** ... do not rely on that fact alone, *—JB* ... who are not merely circumcised, *—ADAM.*
**but who also walk in the steps of that faith of our father Abraham, which [he had] being [yet] uncircumcised:** ... those also who tread in the footsteps of the faith, *—WLSN* ... to all arranging themselves in the path of the faith, *—FNTN* ... before the tyme of Circumcision, *—GNVA* ... while yet uncircumcised, *—CNFT.*

**4:12.** On the other hand, a man could be a Jew with no mixed blood line, and yet in a spiritual sense not be a descendant of Abraham. Abraham can only be his father as he acted in faith the way Abraham did. Circumcision provides neither God's saving grace nor immunity from punishment. The children of Abraham are those who have the faith of Abraham. The Jews failed to understand this essential truth, believing that the rite brought them rightness with God.

Was there no relation at all between Abraham's faith and circumcision? Was circumcision merely a secular rite to mark racial identity? Such is not the case. Circumcision in no way contributed to the exercise of his faith nor indeed to his justification; yet there was a relationship. Circumcision received its meaning from the fact that it was an act of faith; Abraham obeyed because he believed God. Thus it was both sign and seal.

The principle of faith is vital. We are saved and justified by faith alone. To illustrate, to believe in the doctrine of baptismal regeneration is a refutation of the doctrine of justification by faith. Baptism does not save us; it is in a sense a seal, outwardly indicating the inward work of grace. Water baptism, like circumcision, can be performed by

unbelievers. It receives its meaning only as an act of obedience motivated by saving faith.

The genuineness of New Testament Christian experience is that of circumcision of the heart—not a flesh mark, but a spirit mark. After faith has laid hold of the promise, then the ordinances are meaningful, and they bring blessing.

A great principle is established. The way to God is not through belonging to a given nation, nor through an ordinance which makes a mark on a person's body. Relationship to God is by faith, not through personal achievement.

**13. For the promise, that he should be the heir of the world, [was] not to Abraham, or to his seed, through the law:** ... that they should possess the earth, *—NORL* ... would inherit the world, *—SEB* ... that the world should be theirs, *—BECK* ... that he should own the world, *—WLMS* ... and to his posterity, *—CNFT* ... did not reach him through the Law, *—MOFT* ... conditioned by Law, *—WEYM.*
**but through the righteousness of faith:** ... produced by faith, *—BRKL.*

**4:13.** God promised that Abraham would become a great nation and that in him all the families on the earth would be blessed (Genesis 12:2, 3; 15:5; 22:17, 18). This promise was given 430 years before the Law was given to Moses. The promise was not contingent on Abraham's obedience to the Law; it was unconditional.

The word *promise* may be translated from either of two Greek words, *huposchesis* and *epangelia*. The first word is made with a condition, the second is made unconditionally. The latter is the word used here. God's promise was not based on merit but strictly on grace. The Law dealt with the conduct of people who were already in a covenant relationship with God.

"The promise" was that Abraham should be "heir of the world." In geographic terms the inheritance touched land at the east of the Mediterranean. But Abraham's inheritance cannot be limited to such frontiers. He "looked for a city which hath foundations, whose builder and maker is God" (Hebrews 11:10).

Abraham had two seeds. One was of "the law" and the other "of faith." There are three words translated "seed" in the New Testament. *Spora* and *sporos* come from *speirō* ("sow"). These two are used regarding seed that is sown. The third which occurs in verses 13, 16, and 18 is *sperma*. In 38 of the 44 times where it appears it refers to descendants. The true interpretation comes through in Galatians 3:16, "And to thy seed, which is Christ." This gives understanding to Genesis 17:7, 8. Heirship for the believer is through being in Christ (Ephesians 2:12, 13; 3:5, 6).

**14. For if they which are of the law [be] heirs:** ... For if it is adherents of the Law, *—MOFT* ... For if the subjects of the law, *—SAWR* ... are to possess the world, *—TCNT.*

**faith is made void, and the promise made of none effect:** ... then is faith but vayne, *—GNVA* ... then faith is pointless, *—JB* ... faith is worthless, *—ADAM* ... then faith is useless, *—WEYM* ... is robbed of its value, *—TCNT* ... faith is empty of all meaning, *—MOFT* ... faith would be nullified, and the promise abolished, *—FNTN* ... the promise is made void, *—CNFT* ... has been rendered inoperative, *—WUST* ... the promise abrogated, *—SAWR* ... God's promise is worthless, *—SEB* ... and the promise is empty, *—KLGS.*

**4:14.** "Is made void" carries the meaning "has been voided and as a present result is in a state of invalidation." *Katargeō* means "made of none effect," "to render inoperative." If fulfillment depends on law-keeping, the inability of men to keep the Law makes certain that the promise will never be fulfilled.

**15. Because the law worketh wrath:** ... the law abolished anger? *—FNTN* ... the law results in wrath alone, *—WLMS.*

**for where no law is, [there is] no transgression:** ... Where no law exists, there can be no sin, *—SEB* ... there is no breaking of the Law, *—BECK* ... no breach of it is possible, *—TCNT* ... there can be no violation of it, *—WLMS* ... there can be no law-breaking, *—CNBR.*

**4:15.** God's promise is by grace through faith. In contrast, the Law cannot fulfill the promise. The Law can diagnose the malady but cannot effect a cure. It condemns but cannot save.

The phrase "no law ... no transgression" brings out several principles. First, there must be law to have transgression of it. Second, there must be divine dispensations where the Law is not the principle of relationship with God. Third, man must be completely removed from under the principle of the Law if he is to come to a spiritual place where there will be no transgression. Fourth, the only place of freedom from the Law is the place of the inheritance.

**16. Therefore [it is] of faith, that [it might be] by grace:** ... For this cause, *—ALFD* ... that it may be according to grace, *—YNG* ... [it was] on the ground, *—PNT.*

**to the end the promise might be sure to all the seed:** ... that it might be secure for all the offspring, *—CNFT* ... should hold for all descendants, *—BECK* ... may rest on a solid basis for all his descendants, *—ADAM* ... should be guaranteed as God's free gift, *—TEV.*

**not to that only which is of the law:**
**but to that also which is of the faith of Abraham:** ... but also to the adherents of, *—BRKL.*

**who is the father of us all:**

**4:16.** *Ek pisteōs* ("of faith") indicates that it is "out of faith as a source." Salvation is by grace through faith and not of works. *Bebaian* ("sure") means "stable, valid, something realized." Abraham was given a promise which, in the natural, could not be fulfilled. But he believed God!

**17. (As it is written, I have made thee a father of many nations,) before him whom he believed:** ... for I haue sette thee fadir of many folkis, *—WCLF* ... I have constituted thee, *—PNT* ... I have appointed thee, *—CNFT* ... I have established you permanently, *—WUST.*

**[even] God:** ... bifor god, *—WCLF.*

**who quickeneth the dead:** ... could make dead people come back to life, *—SEB* ... who gives life to the dead, *—TCNT* ... whych restored the deed vnto lyfe, *—CRNM.*

**and calleth those things which be not as though they were:** ... calls into existence what has no being, *—BRKL* ... and names the non-existent as if existent, *—FNTN* ... things which do not exist as existing, *—SAWR* ... and calls the no being to being, *—KLGS.*

**18. Who against hope believed in hope:** ... Under hopeless circumstances, *—WEYM* ... Vvho contrarie to hope, *—RHEM* ... past hope, *—WORL* ... contrary to what he could expect, *—BECK* ... calls into being what does not exist, *—MOFT* ... in spite of hopeless circumstances, *—WLMS* ... Though things looked hopeless ... sustained by hope, put faith in God, *—TCNT.*

**that he might become the father of many nations, according to that which was spoken:** ... as many as the stars, *—JB* ... in agreement with the words, *—WEYM.*

**So shall thy seed be:** ... So numberless shall your descendants be, *—WLMS, —MNTG* ... So shall thy offspring be, *—CNFT.*

**4:17, 18.** In addition to their natural parents, believers have a threefold fatherhood relationship: (1) that of Abraham, the whole household of faith; (2) the person who was used of Christ to bring them to Christ ("I have begotten you through the gospel," 1 Corinthians 4:15); (3) God who begat us by the Holy Spirit through His Word. The first two fatherhoods are fatherhoods of relationship, but the last one is that and more; it is of life.

These verses and their context form a great and encouraging passage of Scripture. Faith is shown as bringing a person into right relations with God. The relationship will, in turn, encourage habits of submission and obedience to God. For Abraham to be the "father of many nations" was beyond human expectation and natural possibility. But Abraham exercised faith. His life became the great example of faith to us.

Abraham's faith was in God. It is most important to bear in mind that our faith is primarily not in a doctrine, not in a fact, even a fact such as Calvary, or a doctrine such as the Atonement. Faith must be in a Person who is what He is and does what He does by virtue of His death on the cross and all that is involved in the great doctrine of the Atonement.

Because Abraham believed in this Person, he could reckon "those things which be not as though they were." He believed in the God who calls the dead to life and who brings into being even things which were not in existence. Without faith there is no capacity for contact and communion with God. The things of God are spiritual and invisible—the natural eye cannot see them. Faith is the eye that sees. Faith is the taking hand of the soul. Without that hand man has no grasp of eternal things.

Abraham's faith was in the God "who quickeneth the dead" and in the God who actually creates new existences. "Against hope" Abraham "believed in hope." In hope he anticipated; by faith he appropriated. Humanly speaking, his case was hopeless.

Believing that God could bring the dead back to life, Abraham trusted in the omnipotence of God. When God told him, "Look now toward heaven, and tell (count) the stars . . . So shall thy seed be," Abraham immediately responded with faith. "And he believed in the Lord; and he counted it to him for righteousness" (Genesis 15:5, 6).

**19. And being not weak in faith:** . . . His faith never quailed, —MOFT . . . faith didn't weaken, —SEB . . . there was no weakening, —BRKL . . . yet his faith did not fail him, —TCNT, —MNTG . . . And without weakening in faith, —CNFT.

**he considered not his own body now dead, when he was about an hundred years old:** . . . when he thought about his almost dead body, —KLGS . . . even when he noted the utter impotence of, —MOFT . . . then utterly worn out, —TCNT . . . although he realized . . . he couldn't have children any more, —BECK.

**neither yet the deadness of Sarah's womb:** . . . nether yet that Sara was past chyldeberinge, —TNDL . . . or the impotence of, —MOFT . . . was far too old to bear children, —NORL.

**4:19.** The matter of a promised land had been considered. The matter of a promised seed is presented next. The promise of a son was given to Abraham when he was 75 years of age. His wife was 65. Obviously both were beyond the age of bearing children. But the patriarch believed. He believed in the One who made something out of nothing, as in creation (Hebrews 11:3), and in the One who could raise the dead as in the case of Isaac (Hebrews 11:19).

Note the expressions regarding the patriarch's faith: "not weak in faith . . . considered not his

own body . . . staggered not at the promise of God." The same power that brought forth Christ from the grave brought Isaac into the world. Isaac's birth is set forth as a resurrection from the dead in a sense (Hebrews 11:11, 12). "Against hope" Abraham "believed in hope." Against a promise that in the normal course of events was unlikely to be fulfilled, Abraham's faith did not grow weak for he was fully assured, not just wishfully hoping. God had spoken, and with God nothing is impossible.

*Katanoeō*, "considered," means "to consider attentively, fix one's eyes or mind upon." Many manuscripts and translations omit the word "not" in "considered not." This gives greater impact to the expression. Abraham considered his own body being dead as far as its procreative functions were concerned, but he refused to accept the natural implications of his age, concluding that the certainty of the divine promise outweighed every natural improbability.

**20. He staggered not at the promise of God through unbelief:** . . . There was no unbelief to make him doubt, —BECK . . . no unbelief made him waver about, —MOFT . . . Nor did he doubtingly criticise the promise of God, —FNTN . . . did not through unbelief question God's promise, —NORL . . . was not led by want of faith to doubt God's promise, —TCNT . . . He was not shaken by unbelief, —KLGS.

**but was strong in faith:** . . . but fortified by faith, —ADAM . . . his faith gave him strength, —TCNT.

**giving glory to God:** . . . gave honour, —TNDL . . . gaue God the prayse, —CRNM.

**4:20.** *Diakrinō*, "stagger," means "to be divided in one's mind, to hesitate, doubt." The word is translated "waver" twice in James 1:6. Abraham's confidence in God never wavered.

*Endunamoō*, "was strong," is "to make strong, endue with strength." A better translation seems to be "was made strong." *Tē pistei*, "in faith," translates "with respect to faith." There was no vacillation by Abraham between belief and unbelief.

Abraham gave "glory to God." Abraham weighed the human impossibility of becoming a father when both he and Sarah were far beyond childbearing age against the divine impossibility of God being able to break His word. If God be God, nothing is impossible. Look at the circumstances and one staggers; look to God and one is strong. Abraham did not stagger because he gave glory to God. Great men of faith bring glory to God.

**21. And being fully persuaded that:** . . . He was absolutely certain, —NORL . . . most

fully knowing, —RHEM . . . since he was thoroughly convinced, —ADAM . . . in the firm conviction, —TCNT.
**what he had promised, he was able also to perform:** . . . was able also to make it good, —CRNM.

**4:21.** This verse may be the best definition of faith to be found in the Word. Faith is described in Hebrew 11:1; here it is defined. Abraham received and believed God's promise. His secret was that he did not waver but gave glory to God.

In the study of righteousness, it is unnecessary to argue imputation versus impartation. The term *dikaiosunēn*, translated "righteousness" (verse 22), describes *what* God imparts. *Dikaiōsin*, translated "justification" (verse 25), names the *act* of God who does the imputing. Both are received when one receives Christ (1 Corinthians 1:30). Abraham was righteous; God declared him so, just as He did for Abel (Hebrews 11:4), Noah (Genesis 7:1), and other Old Testament saints.

22. **And therefore it was imputed to him for righteousness:** . . . That is why he was counted righteous, —BECK.

23. **Now it was not written for his sake alone, that it was imputed to him:** . . . that it was reckoned to him, —TNDL, —CRNM.

24. **But for us also, to whom it shall be imputed:** . . . to whom it shalbe counted for, —GNVA.
**if we believe on him that raised up Jesus our Lord from the dead:**

**4:22-24.** Paul has given a great analysis of faith to show how justification comes by faith. The principle of justification, which Abraham experienced, is "for us also . . . if we believe on him that raised up Jesus our Lord from the dead."

25. **Who was delivered for our offences:** . . . who was surrendered to death, —WEYM . . . who was put to death for our sins, —JB . . . who was handed over to die for our sins, —BECK . . . delivered up for our trespasses, —MOFT, —ASV . . . who was betrayed to death, —MNTG.

**and was raised again for our justification:** . . . because of the acquittal secured for us, —WEYM . . . and rose agayne for to iustifye vs, —CRNM . . . to make us right with God, —SEB.

**4:25.** Justification comes on the same principle, "(Christ) was delivered for our offenses, and was raised again for our justification." Abraham looked forward to the work of Christ (John 8:56); we look back to the finished work of Christ. The account of Abraham's faith and justification was written for the benefit of believers of all ages.

Notice how Paul turns to the personal touch in verses 24 and 25, "us also . . . we . . . our Lord . . . our offenses . . . our justification." We have been through the black scenes of the courtroom as all men were declared guilty. From there we came to the glorious light of God's provision of justification.

The Son of God "was delivered"—God spared not His own Son. Nothing less than the death of Jesus on the cursed tree would do. It was because of "our offenses." Calvary was essential because of a righteous God and His law. Nothing but the atoning death of Christ could meet the need of sinful man.

Our Lord was raised from the dead "for our justification." His resurrection was the validation of the sacrifice of His death and the proof of our acceptance. Our place of acceptance is in the risen Christ. The ungodly who believe on the Lord are declared righteous and are given a new standing in the risen Christ. All the promises center around the empty tomb. As Christ's resurrection was the proclamation of His acceptance as the propitiation, it is the demonstration of our acceptance in Him. By Him we are made righteous and acquitted of the Law's claims (1 Corinthians 15:17).

## Chapter 5

1. **Therefore being justified by faith:** . . . Standing then acquitted as the result of faith, —WEYM . . . Having been declared righteous, —YNG . . . Since we stand justified as the result of faith, —MNTG.
**we have peace with God through our Lord Jesus Christ:** . . . let us continue enjoying peace, —WLMS . . . let us have peace, —CLMT.

**5:1.** The chapter opens with the word "therefore," meaning in view of the foregoing exposition. The statement of the benefits which follow shows the result of having been declared righteous. "Therefore" relates directly to chapter 4. Justification is not by works (4:1-8), not by ordinances (4:9-12), not by obedience to the Law (4:13-25). It is by faith.

Most scholars prefer the translation "let us have peace with God" rather than "we have." More than mere tranquility of mind, this peace is cessation of hostility. God has ceased righteous hostility toward us because we who were hostile toward Him have been reconciled to Him in Jesus.

2. **By whom also we have access by faith into this grace wherein we stand:** . . . we have been introduced into this grace, —SAWR . . . by whom we have awaye in thorow fayth, —TNDL . . . by whom also it chaunsed vnto vs, —CRNM . . . we have obtained access to this grace in which we stand, —NORL . . . through whom we also have access, —CNFT . . . we have obtained our access, —HNT . . . we have obtained admission, —TCNT . . . we have had admission by faith, —SCLT . . . who gave us the way to come to God's love, —BECK . . . we have as a permanent possession,

—*WUST* . . . entrance to this grace, —*BRKL* . . . in which we safely stand, —*WLMS.*

**and rejoice in hope of the glory of God:** . . . And we feel proud as we hope for God's glory, —*BECK* . . . and glorie, —*RHEM* . . . and exult in the hope, —*CNFT* . . . and let us continue exulting in the hope, —*WLMS* . . . We feel good, because, —*SEB* . . . So let us triumph in our hope of attaining God's glorious ideal, —*TCNT.*

**5:2.** We have "access by faith." We are not shut out because of our sins but are given a "pass" through faith "into this grace." "Access" (literally, introduction) brings another benefit, "wherein we stand." The believer is introduced into a place that is one of standing, not falling. His stand before God is the standing of Christ himself (2 Corinthians 5:21). Exultation is in God, not in self.

**3. And not only [so], but we glory in tribulations also:** . . . we also boast about afflictions, —*ADAM* . . . but we triumph even in our troubles, —*MOFT* . . . we exult also in our distresses, —*HNT* . . . but we also rejoice, —*WORL* . . . we also are exulting in our tribulations, —*WUST.*

**knowing that tribulation worketh patience:** . . . that suffering produces fortitude, —*WEYM* . . . that trouble produces endurance, —*TCNT* . . . that suffering develops endurance, —*SEB* . . . results in patient endurance, —*HNT* . . . works fortitude, —*MNTG* . . . stedfastness, —*ASV.*

**5:3.** The implied meaning of this verse is that the justified person, enjoying his standing in God, is able to triumph not just in tribulation, but even because of it.

**4. And patience, experience:** . . . and patience approval, —*ADAM* . . . and patience, probation, —*RHEM* . . . brings perseverance, —*JB* . . . stability of character, —*TCNT* . . . is the proof of soundness, —*CNBR* . . . tested character, —*WLMS.*

**and experience, hope:**

**5. And hope maketh not ashamed:** . . . this hope is not deceptive, —*JB* . . . And we need not be ashamed of hope, —*ADAM* . . . In this hope we're not disappointed, —*BECK.*

**because the love of God is shed abroad in our hearts by the Holy Ghost which is given unto us:** . . . has been diffused in our hearts, —*WLSN* . . . is povvred forth in our hartes, —*RHEM* . . . flooded our hearts, —*WLMS* . . . has overflowed, —*MNTG.*

**5:4, 5.** Jesus came into the world to atone for our sinful actions as well as to deal with our proneness to sin. Both the first Adam and the last Adam (Christ) were sinless before they were tempted of the devil. The first Adam fell. The last Adam did not fall. As we have our standing in Christ, we have the confidence that tribulation cannot destroy our hope. The believer glories in hope and in suffering, knowing that tribulation works

patience (endurance); and endurance works experience; and experience, hope.

*Dokimi,* "experience," means "tested, accepted, approved." "Patience" can be rendered "endurance," "steadfastness." "Experience" relates to character, "strength of character," "ripeness of character," "tested character." Paul is saying that endurance produces character. "Experience" works hope. This hope will never make one ashamed (*kataischunō*), meaning it will never "dishonor, disgrace, or put to shame," or, as others translate it, will never "disappoint" or "prove illusory."

All these privileges assure us of this unashamed hope, for the "love of God is shed abroad in our hearts by the Holy Ghost." This is the first mention of the Holy Spirit in the Book of Romans. He, the Third Person of the Trinity, has brought us into all these blessings.

"Shed abroad" (*ekcheō*) is translated "pour out" 11 of 18 times in the King James Version and is so rendered in several other translations. The word *love* has probably been abused more than any other in the English language. Here it is "the love of God" that is being given to and through those who are justified. This love is defined in 1 Corinthians 13 and modeled perfectly in Jesus.

For a human being, even a redeemed one, to try to produce this love is an exercise in futility. When we are willing to receive, the Holy Spirit miraculously produces His fruit within us. With this kind of love, we never have to be ashamed before Him.

The very character of our present privilege, "peace," participates in our future perspective, "the glory of God." We rejoice in what is now ours and rejoice in what will then be fully ours. These two faith actions become fused as we appropriate in life the sanctification our justification provides.

**6. For when we were yet without strength:** . . . We were entirely helpless, —*NORL* . . . when we were still strengthless, —*BRKL* . . . being yet helpless, —*WLSN* . . . when we were yet weak, —*TNDL, CRNM* . . . in our being still ailing, —*YNG.*

**in due time Christ died for the ungodly:** . . . in a strategic season, —*WUST* . . . at exactly the right time, —*SEB* . . . precisely at that time when it was needed, —*ADAM* . . . Christ at the right moment, —*WEYM* . . . when Christ, in His appointed time, —*NORL* . . . died on behalf of the godless, —*TCNT* . . . die for the impious? —*RHEM.*

**5:6.** The descending scale of man before God is described in verses 6, 8, and 10 as "without strength (weak) . . . sinners . . . enemies." *Asthenēs* translated "without strength" in the King James Version is rendered in various translations as "weak . . . feeble . . . helpless and hopeless apart from God's grace." Too weak to live a righteous life, man is a sinner disobeying God's law, and is in reality an enemy of God.

**7. For scarcely for a righteous man will one die:** ... It is rare to find anyone willing, —NORL ... Why, it is scarcely conceivable, —WEYM ... one wouldn't ordinarily die, —ADAM.

**yet peradventure for a good man some would even dare to die:** ... though once in a while ... for a generous friend, —WLMS ... yet perhaps one might bring himself to die, —CNFT ... for perhaps for a good man, —RHEM ... a benevolent person, —BRKL ... someone really worthy, —JB ... for a kind person, —BECK ... though for a benefactor some might perhaps hazard death, —FNTN ... some one might actually have the courage to die, —TCNT ... for a good and lovable man, —WEYM ... some one might even venture, —WLSN.

**5:7.** "Righteous ... good." The meaning is simply "right or just" (*dikaios*), and *agathos* = "good," that is, "kind, generous, benevolent."

**8. But God commendeth his love toward us, in that, while we were yet sinners, Christ died for us:** ... But God reassures us of His love, —SEB ... god comendith his charite in us, —WCLF ... But God is constantly proving His own love, —WUST ... But God setteth out his loue toward vs, —CRNM ... established His love towards us, —FNTN ... But God recommends His own Love to us ... died on our behalf, —WLSN ... but God gives proof of His own love, —CNBR ... beyond doubt, —TCNT.

**5:8.** "Sinners" (*hamartōlōn*) includes everyone, for it means those who have "missed the mark" and that includes all. The proof of God's love is in the gift of His Son. Some might die for a friend or a kind and good person, but Christ died for sinners who were at enmity with Him. Such is the character of God's love that anchors our hope. Our Lord died instead of us, taking our penalty, and in our place. His death was in our interest.

**9. Much more then, being now justified by his blood:** ... Much rather therefore, —PNIN ... we have now been pronounced free from guilt, —WEYM.

**we shall be saved from wrath through him:** ... save us from God's anger, —BECK ... saved from God's punishment, —SEB ... from the madness of sin, —FNTN.

**10. For if, when we were enemies, we were reconciled to God by the death of his Son:** ... while we were His enemies we were made God's friends, —BECK ... we were led back to God, —FNTN.

**much more, being reconciled, we shall be saved by his life:** ... was used to make us God's friends, —SEB ... by sharing Christ's Life, —TCNT ... we shal be preservid by his lyfe, —TNDL.

**5:9, 10.** The expression "much more" occurs repeatedly in this chapter. Christ's work at

Calvary did much more than restore what was lost in Adam. Because of the Cross and as the sons of God, we enjoy a richer relationship with God than did Adam. We are "justified by his blood" which denotes the laying down of His life and is synonymous with "by the death of his Son" (verse 10).

"Saved from wrath" means saved from anger, indignation, and divine reaction toward evil. Paul writes concerning the future wrath of God. If the believer has already been justified, Paul reasons, he will surely be spared the future judgments of God. If as an enemy he was reconciled to God, surely as a reconciled person he will be spared punishment on judgment day.

The expression "much more" occurs again. As offending sinners we are reconciled by the vicarious death of our Saviour. He provided for our restoration to a place of harmonious relationship.

"Justified by his blood," "saved from wrath through him," "reconciled to God by the death of his Son"—all great provisions. But there is more— "we shall be saved by his life." God's love reached us before when we were sinners, but now "much more" as we are linked to Him. We "shall be saved from wrath" and shall be kept "saved by his life." Christ's death was a sacrificial ministry for us, and His life is now an intercessory ministry for us.

Great mercies came as a result of His love. We have been saved from the guilt and penalty of sin; we are being saved from the power of sin in daily life: we shall be saved from the presence of sin in eternity. That is our threefold salvation.

Reconciliation is the work of God, whereby He effects in the believing sinner a thorough change from enmity and aversion to love and trust. This work is also through the death of Christ.

Reconciliation, the result of justification, is something *we* have, not God. It is something *we* needed, not God. Propitiation is the Godward side whereby He restores His favor manward. Reconciliation is the manward aspect of the death of Christ; our enmity Godward is removed (2 Corinthians 5:18, 19). Our message is, "Be ye reconciled to God." Man must choose to lay down his arms and cease hostilities against God.

**11. And not only [so], but we also joy in God through our Lord Jesus Christ:** ... But that is not all, —NEB ... And this is not merely a future hope, —BRCL ... we are filled with joyful trust, —JB.

**by whom we have now received the atonement:** ... to whom we owe our reconciliation, —NORL ... through whom we have now received reconciliation, —CNFT ... who has now given us this friendship, —BECK ... we have been made friends with God, —BRCL ... by whom we haue now obtayned, —CRNM.

**5:11.** "Atonement" is literally "reconciliation" and is so translated in verse 10. In reconciliation, Christ is always the Reconciler and man is the object of reconciliation. When Adam and Eve sinned there came an aversion to God. They hid from His presence. Those who accept reconciliation find "joy in God."

**12. Wherefore, as by one man sin entered into the world:** ... This comparison, *−WEYM* ... For this cause, *−ALFD* ... It is therefore as follows, *−BRKL* ... as through one man, *−WORL* ... gained an entry, *−BRCL.*

**and death by sin:** ... and through sin came death, *−TCNT* ... death came into the world through sin, *−SEB* ... by the meanes of synne, *−GNVA.*

**and so death passed upon all men:** ... In this way death spread to all men, *−SEB* ... thus death pervaded the whole human race, *−NEB* ... to all mankind in turn, *−WEYM.*

**for that all have sinned:** ... inasmuch as all men sinned, *−MOFT* ... because everyone has sinned, *−JB* ... supposing indeed that all sin, *−FNTN* ... because all committed sin, *−CNBR.*

**5:12.** The section of verses 12-21 is an analogy of contrast between the disobedience of Adam resulting in universal death and the obedience of Christ Jesus making eternal life possible for all human beings. The main point of the passage is to show that just as the death of all rests on Adam, so the righteousness of all rests on Jesus Christ. "Death" in verse 12 refers specifically to physical death, as seen in verses 6-8, 10, 14, and 17. Spiritual death includes eternal damnation in hell. Jesus did not die spiritually, nor do infants (see commentary on verse 13).

The phrase *pantes hēmarton* ("all have sinned") is in the aorist tense, showing that a completed act was committed. In some way *all* sinned. Adam's fall introduced the virus of sin into the entire human race; every human being is born with the sinful nature. There are three basic theological positions.

Calvinism says that "all have sinned" means that every human being, including infants, is individually guilty of Adam's sin and that all men are "totally depraved," meaning that the human will cannot choose anything but evil. It is unscriptural: (1) some die who are not guilty of Adam's sin (verse 14); (2) God commands each human to choose; (3) infants who die would be irrevocably damned in hell.

Pelagianism teaches that Adam's sin affects others only as a bad example, and that each person starts life as free from effects of sin as Adam was prior to the Fall. (1) If this were true, man can "save" himself, and Jesus did not need to die for all (verse 18); (2) Ephesians 2:3 says we "were by nature the children of wrath."

Arminianism says that when Adam sinned, the race sinned. No human baby has been born with the original righteousness Adam had prior to the Fall but is born with a nature bent toward sin that results in actual sin when he reaches the age of accountability; each can and must then volitionally choose between God and Satan.

**13. (For until the law sin was in the world:** ... For prior to the Law, *−WEYM* ... earlier than the Law, *−BRKL* ... There was sin in the world, *−BECK* ... sin actually existed in the world, *−MNTG.*

**but sin is not imputed when there is no law:** ... as long as there is no law, *−GNVA* ... in the absence of law, sin is not charged, *−HNT* ... in the absence of law no reckoning is kept of sin, *−NEB* ... sin is not charged up, *−BRKL* ... sin is not debited to anyone's account, *−BRCL* ... the sin of "law-breaking," *−JB* ... sin is not put to account, *−PNIN* ... sin was not thought of as sin, *−SEB* ... cannot be charged, *−TCNT* ... no account is kept of sins, *−TEV* ... if a law did not exist, *−FNTN.*

**5:13.** "The law" referred to here is the Mosaic law, as verse 14 shows. There was law prior to Moses, else there could have been no sin (4:15). Cain was guilty of sin (Genesis 4:7-11). Abel was righteous by faith (Hebrews 11:4) which motivated his obedience.

We can say with certitude that "when there is no law" describes the condition of infants and children prior to the age of accountability. Jesus made clear that children are in the Kingdom (Matthew 18:3; 19:14). Paul said, "I was alive without the law once: but when the commandment came, sin revived, and I died" (7:9). This is true of every person who lives to the age of accountability. David knew he was born with a sinful nature (Psalm 51:5); he also knew that his infant son who died was with God (2 Samuel 12:23).

**14. Nevertheless death reigned from Adam to Moses:** ... But death held sway, *−NEB.*

**even over them that had not sinned after the similitude of Adam's transgression:** ... in which Adam broke the command, *−BRCL* ... in a way that was exactly like, *−ADAM* ... didn't break the law as Adam did, *−BECK* ... by disobeying a direct command, *−NEB.*

**who is the figure of him that was to come:** ... Adam foreshadowed One who was to come, *−NORL* ... who is a Type of that being about to come, *−WLSN* ... a type of the future, *−FNTN* ... Him whose coming was still future, *−WEYM* ... Adam was a picture of what was going to happen, *−SEB.*

**5:14.** For Adam's sin God pronounced the sentence of death on him and all his descendants. Adam is an antithetical type ("figure") of Christ who is "the last Adam" (1 Corinthians 15:45). The period from Adam to Moses served to illustrate that it was not the Mosaic law that determined the reign of death or the reality of sin.

As stated above (see verse 12), the death spoken of here is physical death. It is true that there is a relationship between the sin of Adam and spiritual death. We cannot scripturally say, however, that Adam's sin caused the spiritual death of all. If that were true, the section 1:18-3:19 would be completely unnecessary. That section has already proved that all (assuming the age of accountability) are guilty (3:19) because they have knowingly rejected God's revelation of himself (1:18-32); they have knowingly broken the law they had (2:1-16); and all like sheep have gone astray, knowingly transgressing God's law as they understood it (2:17-3:19).

The sinful nature will inevitably manifest itself in actual sins as the person reaches the age of accountability. It is God's prevenient grace in Christ that prevents the spiritual death of the child until he can knowingly choose. This is not a set age but is governed by the principles of 1:18-2:16. At that time, he can realize his sin and the necessity of the new birth from above (John 3:1-8), if he is to be a partaker of "the divine nature" (2 Peter 1:4).

This passage marks a transition from the question of *sins* to that of *sin*. The matter of justification has been the apostle's burden, now he begins to lead up to sanctification.

**15. But not as the offence, so also [is] the free gift:** ... but not as the fall, –*SAWR* ... not as the trespass, –*WORL* ... But there is no comparison between, –*BRCL* ... there is a great contrast between Adam's offence and God's gift of mercy, –*TCNT* ... thus also is the gratuitous favor, –*WUST* ... free gift immeasurably outweighs the transgression, –*WEYM* ... considerably outweighed the fall, –*JB* ... in proportion to Adam's transgression? –*NORL*.

**For if through the offence of one many be dead:** ... through the lapsing of one person, –*BRKL* ... if the wrongdoing of that one man brought death upon so many, –*NEB* ... the mass of mankind have died, –*WEYM* ... the whole race of men have died, –*WLMS*.

**much more the grace of God, and the gift by grace, [which is] by one man, Jesus Christ, hath abounded unto many:** ... to a much greater degree, –*WLMS* ... infinitely greater is the generosity ... have been bestowed on the mass of mankind, –*WEYM* ... his mercy which found expression ... were lavished upon the whole race, –*TCNT* ... has the freeness of God's bounty overflowed, –*CNBR* ... overflowed far more richly upon the rest of men, –*MOFT* ... have been richly poured out on all people, –*BECK* ... came to many in great surplus, –*KLGS*.

**5:15.** In bringing the justification section to an end, Paul clearly establishes the grounds of it all. The sinner is not only justified by faith and

reconciled to God by Christ, but his redemption is by grace alone. The words "gift" and "grace" are used repeatedly in this chapter.

"Through the offense of one many be dead," and "by one man's offense death reigned by one" (verse 17). If the person is not born again on reaching the age of accountability, he dies spiritually; spiritual death includes eternal death in hell. The fall of Adam caused untold evil, but the work of the last Adam "by grace" shall do "much more" good. He gave much more than was lost in the first Adam. The act of grace far outbalances Adam's act of sin.

The fact that sin and death are universal through the first Adam does not mean that salvation is universal through the last Adam. The former is a matter of sentence; the latter is a matter of choice. God planned for man to choose. He knows how we will choose, but He allows that to be a matter of choice (Joshua 24:14, 15). And He always honors our choices. Eternal life is the reward for choosing the gift of God's grace; eternal death is the penalty of unforgiven sin, of not accepting God's gift by grace.

Our sins are imputed to Christ; He became sin on our behalf. He bore the penalty of our guilt. Because His sacrifice was acceptable to the Father, His glorious righteousness is imputed to us so that we are pronounced righteous in God's sight (1 Peter 2:24).

**16. And not as [it was] by one that sinned, [so is] the gift:** ... Nor is the gift like the effect of the sin, –*ADAM* ... as it was in the case of one man's sin, –*CNFT* ... like the effect of the one man's sin, –*MOFT* ... exceeds the fruit of Adam's sin, –*CNBR*.

**for the judgment [was] by one to condemnation, but the free gift [is] of many offences unto justification:** ... that the judgment following the sin was a death sentence, –*NORL* ... ensuing on a single sin resulted in doom, the free gift ... issues in acquittal, –*MOFT* ... The sentence ... condemns us, but the gift, –*BECK* ... followed many sins and made people right with God, –*SEB* ... but divine grace led to, –*BRKL* ... the free gift had to be great enough to result in, –*ADAM* ... after a multitude of transgressions results in acquittal, –*WEYM* ... led to our standing right with him, –*TCNT* ... the undeserved gift of "Not guilty!" –*TEV* ... to a declaration of 'Righteous,' –*YNG* ... came rectification from many transgressions, –*FNTN* ... to a righteous ordinance, –*SAWR*.

**5:16.** Here we have a contrast of the catastrophic result of the one offense of one man, Adam, and the gift by grace which is by one man, Jesus Christ. The gift by grace is much more than the consequence of the offense. Adam's offense brought physical death, but it could not doom all men to eternal death. Men go to hell for their own sins, not Adam's. Jesus was able to bring to all who are in Him eternal life.

Man was involved in circumstances in which there was no hope. Sin and death had man in their power and there was no escape. Into this setting Christ came. He conquered sin and death. By His death and resurrection He broke the stranglehold of sin. Man can escape but only by an act of his will, his free choice. Our relationship with the first Adam is automatic; our relationship with the last Adam is voluntary.

This verse tells us that out of Adam's one trespass came judgment but that out of many trespasses that were laid upon Christ came not judgment but a righteous act (*dikaiōma*).

Three Greek words translated "gift" appear in verses 15 and 16: *charisma, dōrea*, and *dōrēma*. *Charisma* is translated in the American Standard and the King James versions as "free gift." This suggests that there is a distinction between *charisma* and the other two words and that *charisma* carries a special sense.

**17. For if by one man's offence death reigned by one:** ... if the reign of death was established...through the sin of him, alone, —CNBR...death is king, —BRKL...to seize the sovereignty, —WEYM.

**much more they which receive abundance of grace and of the gift of righteousness shall reign in life by one, Jesus Christ.):** ... it is far more certain that those who obtain in rich abundance God's mercy, —TCNT...much more will God's abundant mercy and His gift of sanctification reign, —NORL...who receives the free gift that he does not deserve, —JB.

**5:17.** God's grace abounds. "They which receive" is based on the principle of "the one for the many," but this does not include all men because some reject. The believer may receive the "abundance of grace." "Abound" and "abundance" are used many times to express the gracious kindness of the loving heart of God towards sinners. The believer may also receive the "gift of righteousness." This is apart from works, the Law, ordinances, and worthiness.

When speaking of God's grace, here as elsewhere, Paul seems compelled by the very nature of that grace to place extreme emphasis on its abundance. The point of this entire passage is to stress how "much more" effective God's grace is than any effects of sin. The Greek verb translated "to abound" carries with it the sense of being plentiful to the point of excess. The noun "abundance" may well be translated "superabundance."

Christ's atoning death, designed in the counsels of eternity and carried out on Golgotha's cross, is God's marvelous way of combining in one great and glorious act His holiness, righteousness, and justice together with His love, mercy, grace, and

forgiveness. He bridged the great gulf which no man could span. The eternal Son of God, the perfect Son of Man, became the one Person who could take on himself the guilt, the penalty, and the effects of sin for time and eternity, thereby making it possible for the believer to become righteous in God's sight.

**18. Therefore as by the offence of one [judgment came] upon all men to condemnation:**...It follows then, —MNTG...just as a single offence resulted, —TCNT...by one offence the sentence of death came upon, —WSLY...as by one sin all people were condemned, —BECK...is a condemnation which extends to the whole race, —WEYM...sentence passed upon all men, —SCLT.

**even so by the righteousness of one [the free gift came] upon all men unto justification of life:** ... so also one Person's righteous act, —ADAM...so, too, a single decree, —TCNT...to all men there resulted a righteous standing, —WUST ... so likewise the fruit of one acquittal shall reach to all, —CNBR . . . leads to acquittal and life for all men, —RSV...spryngeth good vpon all men, —CRNM.

**5:18.** A key word in 5:12-21 is "one," occurring 12 times. One man brings the curse of sin and death. Without choice, all men are "in Adam." His offense (Genesis 3:6, 17-19) brought the judgment of God in a universal way. It brought physical death on every one in Adam's race, and it caused a sinful nature to be imparted to every human being. This sinful nature leads to condemnation because it will manifest itself in actual sin in everyone when he attains accountability to God.

Likewise, Jesus, by His death and resurrection (4:25), made the justification of life available to every person in Adam's race. If we take the words of verse 18 literally without interpreting in the light of all Scripture, we could assume a teaching of universal salvation of all men. This is totally unscriptural, as any true Bible student knows. Christ's atonement is efficacious for all men *potentially,* for no man *unconditionally,* and for all believers *efficiently.* In 1 Corinthians 15:22, Paul wrote: "As in Adam all die, even so in Christ shall all be made alive." Only those who are in Christ, by faith which includes voluntary obedience, receive the free gift.

One Man, the last Adam, brings all men who believe into a supernatural generation. We died with Him, we rose with Him, and we sit in "heavenly places" with Him. Offsetting "sin" and "death" is His bestowment of "grace," "righteousness," and "eternal life," which are ours "by Jesus Christ our Lord" (verse 21). As the guilt of Adam was reckoned to our account for condemnation, so the righteousness of Jesus Christ has been reckoned to us for our justification. When Christ died, He paid the penalty of sin in our stead. He took our place. He was our Representative, our Substitute.

**19. For as by one man's disobedience:** ... For as bi inobedience of, —WCLF.

**many were made sinners:** ... many were constituted sinners, —HNT, —WUST.

**so by the obedience of one:** ... through one righteous act, —WORL.

**shall many be made righteous:** ... the whole race will be set right with God, —TCNT... be constituted upright, —HNT... will be constituted righteous, —WUST.

**5:19.** The apostle continues his series of contrasts. Disobedience is contrasted with obedience. Sinners are contrasted with the righteous. This verse contrasts the vast difference between condemnation and justification, with the background indicating the prospect of judgment for the unbeliever as opposed to the assurance of acquittal for the believer.

The just rewards for the deeds of the ungodly are shown over against the rewards of those who accept God's free gift of righteousness.

Death is contrasted with life. In Jesus Christ we have righteousness and life, not as gifts apart from Him, but as life in Him. This life "in Christ" will be unfolded in the next three chapters of the epistle. Compare Colossians 3:3, 4.

**20. Moreover the law entered, that the offence might abound:** ... Now law was brought in, —MNTG ... But a law intervened, —FNTN ... the result was that trespasses were on the increase, —NORL ... in to make the trespass more serious, —BRKL ... Law slipped in to aggravate the trespass, —MOFT ... came to multiply sin, —BECK ... that gilte schulde be plenteous, —WCLF ... that synne shuld encreace, —TNDL, —CRNM.

**But where sin abounded, grace did much more abound:** ... But where the sin was augmented, —WUST ... where the sin exceeded, the gift went far beyond it, —FNTN ... grace surpassed far more, —PNIN ... grace overflows the more, —BRKL ... but however great the number of sins committed, grace was even greater, —JB ... God's gift of love was so much greater, —BECK ... the wider was God's mercy, —TCNT ... there was more plenteousnes of grace, —TNDL ... grace was superabundant, —SAWR.

**21. That as sin hath reigned unto death:** ... Sin used death to rule, —SEB ... in its deadly way, —BECK.

**even so might grace reign through righteousness unto eternal life by Jesus Christ our Lord:** ... and result in enduring Life, —TCNT ... which issues in eternal life, —MNTG ... unto life everlasting, —DOUY.

**5:20, 21.** The final contrast is between the Law and grace. The Law entered (*pareiserchomai*). Other renderings are "came in beside," "intruded into this process," "slipped in." According to Galatians 3:19, the Law was given "to make wrongdoing a legal offense" (NEB).

The Law caused man to see the great wickedness of sin. By the Law the knowledge of sin increased. But as the guiltiness of sin became apparent, God manifested His grace, His unmerited favor, to guilty sinners. Grace did "much more" superabound.

To accept the affirmation of God's abundant grace is to free one once and for all from anxiety and concern about one's salvation. The message of divine grace can properly be received only with thanksgiving and joy. It is truth to be celebrated, truth that is more liberating, exhilarating, and gladdening than one could imagine.

## Chapter 6

**1. What shall we say then?:** ... What inference, —TCNT.

**Shall we continue in sin, that grace may abound?:** ... continue living in sin, —SEB ... shall we persist in sin that the gift of grace may be more abundant? —CNBR ... so as to give more room for grace? —NORL ... to let grace become more plentiful? —BRKL ... to let grace have greater scope? —JB ... that the grace extended to us may be the greater? —WEYM ... that favor may abound? —SCLT ... that grace may be multiplied? —ALFD.

**6:1.** The great theme of Romans, God's method of making sinners righteous, continues. Earlier the epistle showed how God changes a man's position, now we learn how God provides for a change in a man's condition. The former section dealt with the *sins* questions; now we consider the *sin* question. The former dealt with the pardon of sin's guilt; now we learn of deliverance from sin's power.

One of the last verses in chapter 5 states, "Where sin abounded, grace did much more abound." Some have wanted to use this and other verses to prove that justification encourages sin. They say if the guilty sinner is declared righteous, solely by faith and not by works, then, "Let us do evil, that good may come." If the more heinous the sins, the more abundant the grace to pardon, then may we not go on in sin that the grace of God may be the more magnified?

Such was the slanderous accusation that the Jews made of Paul's teaching (3:7, 8). He defended the doctrine of justification against the charge that it encourages increasing sin in order to display grace more abundantly. This defense is the doctrine of sanctification.

This truth is set forth perhaps more completely in Romans 6 than anywhere else in Scripture. There are two divisions in the chapter, and both are introduced by a question which Paul answers with the firm statement, "God forbid."

**2. God forbid:** ... Surely not! –NORL ... Certainly not, –TCNT ... No, indeed, –WEYM ... May such a thing never occur, –WUST ... It could not be! –WORL.

**How shall we, that are dead to sin, live any longer therein?:** ... how can we endure living in it? –NORL ... who have been separated once for all from the sinful nature, any longer to live in its grip? –WUST ... we have ended our relation to sin, –WLMS ... We died to it! –SEB.

**6:2.** To show how unreasonable the proposition of verse 1 is, Paul answers the question with another. "How shall we, that are dead to sin, live any longer therein?"

There are three kinds of death: (1) physical death, the separation of the personality from the physical body; (2) spiritual death, the separation of the person from the life of God; (3) death to sin, the separation of the believer from the power of the sinful nature.

**3. Know ye not, that so many of us as were baptized into Jesus Christ were baptized into his death?:** ... Do you not know, –CNFT ... Are you ignorant that, –RHEM ... all of us were immersed into Christ Jesus, –SEB ... in union with Christ Jesus, –BRKL ... made us share his burial, –MOFT.

**4. Therefore we are buried with him by baptism into death:** ... Consequently, –TCNT ... we are jointly interred, –BRKL ... and joined him in death, –JB ... We have therefore been entombed with him, –WLSN ... by means of Baptism, –CNFT.

**that like as Christ was raised up from the dead:**

**by the glory of the Father:** ... through the Father's glorious power, –BRKL ... by a display of the Father's power, –TCNT.

**even so we also should walk in newness of life:** ... so we too shall conduct ourselves in a new way of living, –BRKL ... ought to conduct ourselves in a renewed life, –FNTN.

**6:3, 4.** The believer's experience involves a transformation so great as to be described as a resurrection to life. Water baptism pictures the experience. The believer's immersion testifies to the fact that because of his union with the crucified Saviour he has died to sin. Being raised from the watery "grave" testifies to the fact of his union with the risen Saviour and that he now walks "in newness of life." Christ died *for* sin that we might die *to* sin.

There is also a deeper significance to the phrase "baptized into Jesus Christ." Water baptism can be a mere ritual, a "work," apart from faith. According to Galatians 3:27, to be "baptized into Christ" means to have "put on Christ." "For by one Spirit are we all baptized into one body" (1 Corinthians

12:13). Water baptism is the outward symbol of what the Holy Spirit has done inwardly. The believer is separated from the evil nature, no longer compelled to follow its dictates. He receives a new nature (2 Peter 1:4), causing him to hate sin and love righteousness.

**5. For if we have been planted together in the likeness of his death:** ... if we have become like-natured with him, –PNIN ... if we have been united with him, –CNFT ... by sharing His death, –NORL ... by an experience resembling his death, –TCNT.

**we shall be also [in the likeness] of [his] resurrection:** ... we shall much more be, –SAWR ... by a resurrection like his, –MOFT.

**6:5.** "Planted together" is literally "united together." We share the life of Christ just as a branch that is grafted into a tree shares the life of the tree (John 15:5). The believer becomes grafted into Christ.

Christ's death was our death, His burial was our burial, His resurrection was our resurrection. As a result of our union with Him, the power of sin is broken. God placed us in Christ when He died so we might share His death and receive the benefits of that identification with Him, specifically, to be separated from the evil nature as part of our salvation. We were also placed by the Holy Spirit in Christ in order to share a new environment, the sharing of newness of life through His resurrection power.

**6. Knowing this, that our old man is crucified with [him]:** ... our old sinful self, –NORL ... was nailed with Him, –BECK.

**that the body of sin might be destroyed:** ... so that the sin-controlled body might be devitalized, –BRKL ... might be made ineffective, –ADAM ... may cease to be under the tyranny of Sin, –TCNT ... might be deprived of its power, –WEYM ... that is liable to sin inactive, –WLMS ... might be rendered null, –PNT ... may be made useless, –YNG ... might be brought to nought, –WORL.

**that henceforth we should not serve sin:** ... and free us from any further slavery to sin, –MOFT ... that we should no more be in bondage to sin, –WORL ... that we should no longer be subservient to sin, –PNT ... rendering a slave's habitual obedience, –WUST.

**7. For he that is dead is freed from sin:** ... For a corpse is considered guiltless of sin, –BRKL ... he who has paid the penalty of death stands absolved from his sin, –WEYM ... is acquitted of sin, –CNFT ... is absolved from sin, –HNT.

**6:6, 7.** "Old man" refers to our former self, the unregenerate son of Adam. We were put to death with Christ. The emphasis is on the conclusion or results of an action. We have been buried, we have become united. The person we once were is now dead. While the "old man" is ourselves in union with the first Adam, the "new man" is ourselves in union with the last Adam. God says that my old life was destroyed, put to death, at Calvary. God's Word is the basis of fact. Our first step is "knowing."

The term "destroyed" does not mean annihilated but rendered "powerless." Sin is not destroyed, but is robbed of its power. The one who is born again is commanded to take his stand on this verse for "he that is dead is freed from sin." Death breaks all ties and cancels all obligations. By his union with Christ the Christian dies to the old self and is free from it, even as the Law has no jurisdiction over a dead man, regardless of his crime. The only power that can cause the believer to sin now is his own power of choice. He *can* sin, but he does not *have* to do so.

**8. Now if we be dead with Christ, we believe that we shall also live with him:**

**9. Knowing that Christ being raised from the dead dieth no more:** ... He will never die again, —NORL ... never dies after his resurrection, —MOFT.

**death hath no more dominion over him:** ...death holds lordship over Him no longer, —BRKL ... death no longer holds lordship, —ADAM ... Death over Him no longer exercises lordship, —WUST ... Death is no longer his boss, —KLGS ... can no more dominate Him, —FNTN ... no longer lords it over him, —WLSN.

**6:8, 9.** With great triumph Paul declares that the Resurrection forever ended the reign of death over the body of Christ. Jesus died "once for all." He arose from the grave immortal, never to be subject to death again. Death is an end. Once it is over for the Christian, it is forever ended. Life is a process. It will continue forever for the believer.

The significance of the Resurrection is that as we were identified with Christ in His death, we are also identified with Him in His resurrection. Since death has no more dominion over Christ, sin has no more dominion over us.

Because of the believer's union with the crucified and resurrected Christ, sin has been robbed of its power over the Christian, or, as someone stated, it has been put "out of commission." This truth is realized by faith in the fact of the Word and by the word we "know." Faith concludes about us what God has declared about us. When we believe what God says, something real and powerful happens.

**10. For in that he died, he died unto sin once:** ... The death He died was because of sin, —NORL ... and once only, unto sin, —CNBR ... He once for all ended His relation to sin, —WLMS.

**but in that he liveth, he liveth unto God:** ...He lives in unbroken relation to God, —WLMS.

**6:10.** Christ's death ended the earthly state in which He had contact with sin. His life is now one of unbroken communion with God. He is no longer on the cross or in the tomb. He is alive and holds the keys of hell and of death. Death has dominion over Him no more.

In the first 10 verses of this chapter, 2 main facts are laid before us. First, a Christian has a permanent relationship of freedom from his sinful nature. He need not submit to it or obey it. Second, by the miracle of the new birth he receives a new nature; he becomes a new creature. He is given the desire and the power to do God's will.

**11. Likewise reckon ye also yourselves to be dead indeed unto sin, but alive unto God:** ...Even so count yourselves, —MNTG ...Thus do you consider yourselves, —CNFT ... regard yourselves as dead to sin, —TCNT ... but you have been restored to life again, —NORL.

**through Jesus Christ our Lord:** ...in the Anointed Jesus, —WLSN.

**12. Let not sin therefore reign:** ... rule as king, —MNTG.

**in your mortal body:** ...over your dying bodies, —SEB ...in your dying bodies, —BECK.

**that ye should obey it in the lusts thereof:** ...compelling you to obey its lusts, —MNTG ...with a view to obeying it ... in its passionate cravings, —WUST...your obedience to bodily passions, —JB...to make you obey their passions, —RSV, —MOFT ... with the result that you, —ADAM...and compel you to obey its cravings, —TCNT ...causing you to be in subjection to their cravings, —WEYM ... obey in its licentious desires, —SCLT ... obey the concupiscences thereof, —RHEM ...to obey its whims, —KLGS...to obey it in its evil propensities, —PNT.

**6:11, 12.** Verses 6 and 9 brought us the facts. We "know" our position of death to self and new life in Christ. But we must act on knowledge. It is one thing to "know," it is something else to "reckon." Verses 11-13 set forth the means for living that life of victory. It is a matter of appropriation.

We have now come to man's responsibility. We are to "reckon" two things: (1) that the "old man" has died, and the sinful nature has been rendered powerless; (2) that we are "alive unto God," new life has been imparted to us.

The term "reckon" is a mathematical term. It means "to count, compute, to take into account." The believer is to take into account the fact that he is dead to sin, that he is set free from the old evil nature, that he has been brought into new life, and that being a new creation (2 Corinthians 5:17), he can live above the desire to sin. When a sinner believes in Christ, he receives a new heart and becomes a new creature. He is under new management.

When we reckon ourselves dead to sin, we are free from it. Death breaks sin's dominion. The presence of sin is not removed; that will take place when salvation is complete on Resurrection Day. But while sin is still present, it is powerless, except by a deliberate act of reuniting ourselves with the enemy.

But it is more than death; it is life (Galatians 2:20; Philippians 1:21). The divinely given self-control (verse 12) is as normal to a Christian as sin is to a sinner. But it must be appropriated and continually acted on. Faith concludes about ourselves what God has declared about us.

**13. Neither yield ye your members [as] instruments of unrighteousness unto sin:** . . . stop putting your members at the disposal of, –WUST . . . Do not give up any part of your body to Sin, to be used in doing wrong, –TCNT . . . But neither doe ye exhibite your members as instruments of iniquitie, –RHEM . . . as evil tools for sin, –SEB . . . no longer lend your faculties as unrighteous weapons for Sin to use, –WEYM . . . turn into an unholy weapon, –JB . . . for the service of vice, –MOFT . . . as implements for vice, –HNT . . . as instruments for wrongdoing, –WLMS.

**but yield yourselves unto God, as those that are alive from the dead:** . . . surrender your whole being to him, –TEV . . . as living persons who rose from, –BRKL . . . as people who have come back from the dead and live, –BECK.

**and your members [as] instruments of righteousness unto God:** . . . and give up to him the various parts of your bodies to be used in doing right, –TCNT.

**6:13.** Paul goes on to show how we can put this matter of reckoning into actual practice. It is doing something that is a work of faith. The positive is prefaced by the command: "neither yield . . . but yield." This involves the matter of making right choices. Constantly we must choose between right and wrong, good and evil. The will is the steering gear of the soul, and we choose the right or the wrong road.

Often one comes across a highway sign, "Road Closed." Break down the barrier or drive around it and you will have trouble. Break down God's "Road Closed" barriers and you will pay the price.

**14. For sin shall not have dominion over you:** . . . Sin must not be your lord and master, –ADAM . . . Let not sinne haue power ouer you, –GNVA . . . must not any longer exert its mastery, –WLMS . . . must not govern you, –FNTN.

**for ye are not under the law, but under grace:** . . . for you are not governed by Law, –BRKL . . . you are under God's gracious love! –SEB . . . You are living under the reign, not of Law, but of Mercy, –TCNT . . . but as subjects to God's favor, –WLMS . . . but under a gift, –FNTN.

**6:14.** Man is so made that he must be mastered. He was created a free moral agent, but he was not made to be his own sovereign; he was created to be mastered by God. When man fell, he came under the mastery of sin. Christ came to deliver us from sin. He provided grace to conquer sin. The work has been done for us, but we must yield ourselves to the divine will for it to be operative within us.

When the believer obeys the instructions of this passage relative to adjustment to the evil nature and the divine nature, this verse promises, "Sin need never again be your master, for now you are no longer tied to the law where sin enslaves you, but you are free under God's favor and mercy" (*Living Bible*).

**15. What then? shall we sin, because we are not under the law, but under grace?:** . . . What are we to conclude? –WLMS . . . Shall we sin occasionally, –WUST . . . Shall we commit an act of sin, –MNTG.

**God forbid:** . . . Away with the thought, –WUST . . . Be it not so, –PNIN . . . let it not be! –YNG.

**6:15.** It is totally false to believe that it is of no consequence whether or not Christians sin. Such doctrine is propounded by "no-Law people" otherwise known as antinomians. True, the Law was uncompromising, but grace while forgiving is never lenient. To be free from the Law does not mean one can sin with freedom from punishment. Being under grace must not be taken as liberty or license to sin. The grace of God is not in the heart of a man who looks upon grace as a loophole to sin. Those who continue in sin are the servants of sin (John 8:34).

**16. Know ye not, that to whom ye yield yourselves servants to obey:** . . . whomever ye choose to obey as a master, –NOYS.

**his servants ye are to whom ye obey:** . . . as obedient servants, –BRKL . . . as obedient slaves, –HNT . . . when you submit to someone as master, –NORL . . . that one whom you are in the habit of obeying, –WLMS . . . his bondmen ye are, –NOYS.

**whether of sin unto death, or of obedience unto righteousness?:** . . . with death as the result, –WEYM . . . obedience to His standard of teaching, –NORL.

**6:16.** "Servants" in this passage is literally "slaves." There were two kinds of slaves; namely, those captured in war and those born in slavery. Paul used the word referring to those born slaves. By nature we were born slaves—slaves to sin and Satan. The believer is a former slave of Satan, delivered by the power of God. Being identified with Christ he becomes bound to Him as his new Master.

Obedience is a key word along with yielding. We choose to whom we yield and whom we obey.

The choice is between "sin unto death" or "obedience unto righteousness."

Note that this is addressed to believers. They are warned that sin leads to death. This is not speaking of physical death, for all will die physically, saints included. It is eternal death of "everlasting destruction from the presence of the Lord" (2 Thessalonians 1:9).

The apostle is dealing with the great truth of sanctification, of holy living. Sanctification is not eradication (1 John 1:8). Sin is not dead, but the believer can be dead to sin. Neither is sanctification suppression. It is not boiling over inside with anger and suppressing our feelings so no one knows about it.

Sanctification is the operation of the law of life over the law of sin and death. It is not natural law, not legal law, but spiritual law. The believer is able to live above the selfish demands of self and live in triumph in a new life.

**17. But God be thanked, that ye were the servants of sin:**
**but ye have obeyed from the heart:** . . . now you heartily obey, —FNTN . . . you have rendered whole-hearted obedience, —MOFT.
**that form of doctrine which was delivered you:** . . . the rules of discipline under which you enlisted, —FNTN . . . the standard of teaching, —RSV . . . the pattern of teaching, —SEB . . . that model of doctrine into which ye have been moulded, —SCLT . . . in which you were instructed, —SAWR.

**6:17.** "Servant" (*doulos*) should be translated "slave." Men are slaves of sin until freed by Christ. Jesus said, "Every one who commits sin is the slave of sin" (John 8:34, NASB).

Literally the meaning of "that form of doctrine" is "that form of doctrine into which you were delivered." "Form" reminds one of a mold into which molten metal is poured to be fashioned into the desired shape. The believer is the molten material and the gospel is the mold. The gospel delivers from sin and fashions character.

**18. Being then made free from sin, ye became the servants of righteousness:** . . . from the tyranny of Sin, —WEYM . . . having been emancipated from sin, you became subservient to righteousness, —WLSN . . . ye became bondservants of righteousness, —CLMT.

**6:18.** The idea of slavery carries over into the balance of the chapter. Slavery was common in Paul's day. The Roman Christians no doubt clearly understood Paul's language. Possibly some of them had been in servitude.

"Being . . . made free" is *eleutheroō*, "to liberate, set free from bondage, to set at liberty." Believers are set free from the bondage of sin and Satan. But

they are freed to a new slavery, to become slaves of righteousness. In verses 18 and 20 the expression "became . . . servants" is a form of the verb *douloō*. As used in these verses it means to "become a slave to someone." Freed from the slavery of sin, the believer has a glorious freedom enjoying a higher slavery, a slave to God.

In essence Paul is saying that at one time you gave yourself to sin as its slave, and when you did that righteousness had no claim over you. Now that you have given yourself to God as a slave to righteousness, sin has no claim on you.

*Doulos* ("slave") carries the thought of one who serves another to the disregard of his own interests. The sinner disregards his own interests when he serves Satan and receives nothing but eternal death. The Christian must be a slave to Christ with disregard for his personal desires, but he is guaranteed eternal joy.

**19. I speak after the manner of men because of the infirmity of your flesh:** . . . I am using human illustrations, —ADAM . . . I am using an illustration drawn from human affairs, —WUST . . . I am speaking in familiar human terms because of the frailty of your nature, —WLMS . . . because you are naturally weak, —BECK . . . Because of your human weakness, —SEB . . . because of your natural limitations, —RSV.
**for as ye have yielded your members servants to unclean-ness and to iniquity unto iniquity:** . . . the various parts of your bodies to the service of impurity, —TCNT . . . to moral impurity, —SEB . . . to impurity and to wickedness in wickedness, —SAWR . . . always getting worse and worse, —NORL . . . to greater and greater iniquity, —RSV . . . and unrestrained lawlessness, —FNTN . . . from one iniquitye to another, —CRNM.
**even so now yield your members servants to righteousness unto holiness:** . . . now you must surrender your faculties, —MNTG . . . as slaves of justice unto sanctification, —CNFT . . . which leads on to holiness, —TCNT . . . that means consecration, —MOFT . . . that ye maye be sanctifyed, —CRNM . . . in order to become holy, —NOYS.

**20. For when ye were the servants of sin:**
**ye were free from righteousness:** . . . you are freemen, —FNTN . . . you weren't free to serve righteousness, —BECK.

**6:19, 20.** The apostle apologized for using the analogy of slavery. He says, "I am using this human illustration so your human minds can understand." The Roman believers did not yet have the spiritual insight to grasp the significance of their position as identified with Christ.

One way or another every person is a slave to someone. But every person must choose to whom he will be a slave. Either one is a slave to the tyranny of uncleanness and iniquity, or a slave to "righteousness unto holiness." If slaves to sin there is no righteousness.

Paul was reminding them that in their former state of slavery to sin they were in no way bound by righteousness. Righteousness had no mastery or authority over them. They could sin all they wanted to, with no respect to the demands of righteousness.

He was using this fact, which they all could understand, to show them that likewise they now were free from the mastery of sin. His thought could be paraphrased: "Consider how that you once were carefree where righteousness was concerned. No one could say to you, 'You must be holy,' for you made no claim to holiness. One slavery always brings freedom from the other. Slavery to sin is coexistent with freedom from righteousness; slavery to righteousness is coexistent with freedom from sin."

These verses show clearly that the believer still is faced with the decision of whether to yield his members to sin and uncleanness or to yield his members to righteousness unto holiness. Paul had already warned them of the possibility of losing their life in Christ if they chose to yield themselves to sin (verse 16).

**21. What fruit had ye then in those things whereof ye are now ashamed?:** . . . that now make you blush, —JB.

**for the end of those things [is] death:** . . . Death is their consequence, —BRKL . . . actions whose outcome is death, —HNT . . . for the reward of these things is death, —CMPB.

**6:21.** The apostle calls attention to the shameful fruit of the life of sin. The old life was characterized by uncleanness and lawlessness. Evil desires reigned and, as is always true, sin begat sin. Sin becomes less repulsive as it is repeated. When indulged in, it eventually becomes effortless to sin. The road to sin leads down more and more. It leaves one with shame, remorse, and regret.

Believers are ashamed of their past sins; this leads to a horror of any new occurrence of sin. "Death," which is the end of such sins, includes the second death (Revelation 20:14).

**22. But now being made free from sin, and become servants to God:**

**ye have your fruit unto holiness, and the end everlasting life:** . . . your fruite vnto sanctification, —RHEM . . . you have the fruit of your consecration, —FNTN . . . you are being made holy, —TCNT . . . You get something good for being holy, —SEB . . . you have your reward in being made holy . . . the Life of the ages as the final result, —WEYM . . . your fruit is growth in holiness, —CNBR . . . the final destiny is eternal life, —WLMS . . . and the end eonian life, —CLMT.

**6:22.** The new life is different. The birth and resultant end of sin is that "when it is finished, (it)

bringeth forth death" (James 1:14, 15). In sharp contrast slaves to God have "fruit unto holiness, and the end everlasting life." The believer, justified and sanctified, enjoys daily fruit, revealed in holiness and climaxing in eternal life.

Here Paul was showing the "double" aspect of holiness. We are sanctified by Christ (1 Corinthians 1:30). Then we are commanded to "cleanse ourselves from all filthiness of the flesh and spirit, perfecting holiness in the fear of God" (2 Corinthians 7:1).

Believe and behave! The first brings us into fellowship with God; the latter gives evidence that we have fellowship with God. When we believe, we enter the "strait gate"; when we behave, we walk in the "narrow way."

**23. For the wages of sin [is] death:** . . . Sin pays off with death, —BECK . . . For the stipends of sin, —RHEM . . . For the subsistence pay which the sinful nature, —WUST . . . The pay you get for sinning is death, —SEB . . . the poor wages, —MNTG . . . For death is the wages of sin, —WSLY.

**but the gift of God [is] eternal life through Jesus Christ our Lord:** . . . but the free gift, —MNTG . . . is the Life of the ages bestowed upon us, —WEYM . . . is aionian Life, by the Anointed Jesus, our Lord, —WLSN . . . through union with, —TCNT, —WLMS . . . our Lord and Master, —CNBR.

**6:23.** Thayer states that the definition of "wages" (*opsōnion*) is "whatever is bought to be eaten with bread, as fish, flesh, and the like. And as corn, meat, fruits, salt, were given to the soldiers instead of pay, *opsōnion* began to signify that part of a soldier's support given him in place of pay (i.e., rations) and the money in which he is paid" (Thayer, "*opsōnion*"). This was the pay which the soldier earned with the sweat of his brow and the risk of his body. It was due him and could not be taken from him.

On special occasions an emperor handed out a free gift of money to his soldiers. This was not earned and came through the emperor's kindness and grace. This was *charisma*.

Sin pays wages and the pay is death. In contrast to the horrible wages of sin, there is the gift of "eternal life through Jesus Christ our Lord." Men merit hell not eternal life. Christ alone procured that kind of life and gives it freely to all who believe.

## Chapter 7

**1. Know ye not, brethren, (for I speak to them that know the law,):** . . . Are you ignorant brethren, —RHEM . . . to those who have an experiential knowledge of law, −WUST . . . them that are skilful in the Lawe, −GNVA.

**how that the law hath dominion over a man as long as he liveth?:** . . . that the law rules a man's actions only during his lifetime? −NORL . . . the lawe hath lordship in man, −WCLF . . . That the Law controls a man, −WLSN . . . the law governs man, −FNTN.

**2. For the woman which hath an husband:** . . . for the married woman, −YNG.

**is bound by the law to [her] husband so long as he liveth:** . . . the woman which is in subiection to a man, −GNVA . . . is by law secured to the husband, −BRKL . . . binds a married woman, −BECK . . . has legal obligations, −JB . . . to the living Husband, −WLSN . . . during his lifetime, −MNTG.

**but if the husband be dead:** . . . should die, −SCLT.

**she is loosed from the law of [her] husband:** . . . she is released from the law of marriage, −SEB . . . she is discharged, −RSV, −SCLT, −PNIN.

**3. So then if, while [her] husband liveth, she be married to another man:** . . . during her husband's lifetime, −TCNT, −MNTG . . . she couple her selfe, −GNVA . . . she connect herself with another man, −NOYS . . . if she lives with another man, −KLGS.

**she shall be called an adulteress:** . . . she shall be styled "adulteress," −HNT . . . she will be stigmatized as an adulteress, −WEYM . . . shalbe counted a wedlocke breaker, −CRNM.

**but if her husband be dead, she is free from that law:** . . . she is legally free, −BRKL . . . no longer under the old prohibition, −WEYM . . . from that marriage bond, −WLMS . . . she is delivered from the law, −DOUY.

**so that she is no adulteress, though she be married to another man:** . . . she is legally a free woman, −TEV . . . even though she marries again, −WEYM . . . to a different man later, −SEB.

**7:1-3.** Denny's comment on this chapter, which is complicated and difficult, is helpful. "The subject of chapter 6 is continued. The apostle shows how by death the Christian is freed from the law, which, good as it is in itself and in the divine intention, nevertheless, owing to the corruption of man's nature, instead of helping to make him good, perpetually stimulates sin. Verses 1-6 describe the liberation from the law; verses 7-13, the actual working of the law; in verses 14-25 we are shown that this working of the law is not due to anything in itself, but to the power of sin in the flesh" (*The Expositor's Greek Testament*, 2:637).

Sanctification, introduced in chapter 6, is the theme of chapters 7 and 8. All three chapters deal with the believer's deliverance from the power of sin and his growth in holiness. In chapter 6 we see that victory over sin is achieved by the attitude and work of faith. Another ally, the Holy Spirit, is introduced in chapter 8. Chapter 7 describes a man who earnestly desires to be holy by his own efforts—by the Law—apart from grace. The

chapter presents the hopeless conflict of the better side of a man with his sinful nature.

Chapter 6 makes clear what was meant by "ye are . . . under grace" (6:14). Chapter 7 shows that the Law has no claim on the believer. Christ terminated the Law at Calvary for He met its demand of death when He died on the cross. The believer who dies with Him is also dead to the Law.

Verse 1 lays down the general principle that death frees a man from the dominion of the marriage vow. The wife is bound to her husband as long as he lives. Both husband and wife are free from the other when either one dies.

Paul then compares the Law to a husband and shows that we cannot be married to Christ and enjoy the blessings of grace until the Law is dead to us, or we to the Law. To do otherwise is to be "fallen from grace" (Galatians 5:4).

Believers are dead to the Law as the wife is dead in respect to the marriage vow when her husband dies. Paul makes the application: when the Christian died in Christ to sin, he became dead to the Law. The bondage imposed by the law of sin was completely severed.

Some will ask the question, who or what dies? Is it the Law? Christ? or we? True, Christ died, but more than that, we died with Him. The Law did not die, but we did, and when we died we were separated from the former husband of sin and united with Christ by faith. All the virtues of Christ's death, in meeting the claims of the Law, became ours, and we were set free from the power of sin to which the Law had committed us.

**4. Wherefore, my brethren, ye also are become dead to the law by the body of Christ:** . . . are put to death, −SCLT . . . The crucified body of Christ, −MOFT . . . the incarnation of Christ, −WEYM.

**that ye should be married to another, [even] to him who is raised from the dead:** . . . You can marry someone elsethe one who was raised from death, −SEB . . . that ye might be joined to another, −WORL . . . to marry AnotherHim who rose from the dead, −BECK.

**that we should bring forth fruit unto God:** . . . that we might yield God a harvest, −BRKL . . . that we should bear fruit, −SAWR.

**7:4.** The word "body" in the phrase "dead to the law by the body of Christ" means sacrifice, not the Church.

It is important to remember that freedom from the former union is not an end in itself. This severance is for a positive purpose—to be "married to another." And He is none other than the One "who is raised from the dead." By the spiritual union with Jesus, the representative of the sinner on the cross, we have had the payment of the death penalty imputed to us by faith. Death in

Christ leads to resurrection in Him. We are united with Him and come under His authority.

The purpose of this new union with Jesus is "that we should bring forth fruit unto God." In our natural condition we "walked according to the course of this world . . . children of disobedience . . . lusts of our flesh . . . children of wrath . . ." (Ephesians 2:2, 3). The issue from that union, the offspring of that relationship, made us ashamed. It worked "in our members to bring forth fruit unto death" (7:5). It worked actively in our faculties, both mental and physical, resulting in death.

In chapter 5 we read that we are brought to peace with God through our Lord Jesus Christ, having been justified in Him. In chapter 6 we see that we are serving a new master, Christ. In chapter 7 we are viewed as united to a new husband, Christ. The old marriage to the Law brought unbearable bondage (Acts 15:10) and continuous frustration because we could never fully please the old husband (James 2:10). That marriage has been ended not by divorce, but by death to the Law so that we might be married to Christ Jesus (cf. Ephesians 5:32; Revelation 19:7).

**5. For when we were in the flesh:** . . . Before our conversion, *−JB* . . . we were in our sensuality, *−FNTN* . . . whilst we were under the thraldom of our earthly natures, *−WEYM* . . . while we were unspiritual, *−MNTG* . . . with our lower nature, *−WLMS*.

**the motions of sins:** . . . sinful passions, *−NORL, −BRKL, −JB, −TCNT, −ASV, −CNFT* . . . the passions of sinnes, *−RHEM, −DOUY, −WORL* . . . the stirrings of sins, *−ALFD* . . . the sinful cravings, *−MOFT* . . . the lustes of synne, *−CRNM*.

**which were by the law:** . . . quite unsubdued by the Law, *−JB* . . . aroused by the Law, *−TCNT* . . . whych were stered vp by the lawe, *−CRNM* . . . excited by the Law, *−MOFT*.

**did work in our members to bring forth fruit unto death:** . . . wrought effectually in our members, *−CMPB* . . . were active in every part, *−TCNT* . . . to bring a harvest of death, *−NORL*.

**7:5.** "In the flesh" refers to the unrenewed and legal state, under the Law and not under Christ, under control of the evil nature. *Pathēmata*, rendered "motions" in the King James Version, is more often rendered "passions" in other translations. Very possibly the King James translators chose "motions" since in earlier English the word was sometimes used in the sense of "emotion." "Which were by the law" may also be rendered "occasioned or aroused by the law." "Did work in our members" implies working both physically and mentally. And it brought "forth fruit unto death." How the Law can arouse sinful passions is defined in verses 7-13. The "fruit unto death"

comprises those evil works whose end is death, according to verse 21.

**6. But now we are delivered from the law:** . . . now we have been loosed, *−ALFD* . . . set free, *−CNFT* . . . fully discharged, *−WORL*.

**that being dead wherein we were held:** . . . We died to what bound us, *−SEB* . . . held us captive, *−RSV* . . . kept us under restraint, *−TCNT* . . . wherin we were deteined, *−RHEM*.

**that we should serve in newness of spirit, and not [in] the oldness of the letter:** . . . under new and spiritual conditions, *−TCNT* . . . but in the new service of the spirit, *−CNBR* . . . not under the written code as of old, *−MOFT* . . . in the old age of a writing, *−SAWR* . . . not by following a strict code, *−SEB*.

**7:6.** "Now . . . delivered" could be translated "now released." The Jewish believer was put under the Law at Sinai. Now he is released from the Law. If so, the Gentile has also been released from the Law. "That being dead" is better translated "having died" (*apothanontes*); it is we who died to that which held us in bondage. The bondage was marriage to the Law. That was a union that could only produce death. The Law could not deliver from sin; that was not God's purpose in giving it. It was given to inform men that death is the inevitable result of sin. God had a better plan, provided through the death of His Son. "Wherein we were held" really means "in which we were constantly held down." We were dead in sins while under the Law and held helpless to free ourselves from its bondage and death.

Deliverance brings us freedom to "serve in newness of spirit, and not in the oldness of the letter." "Letter" is *gramma* which was used of a "bond, a document, a letter one writes." The word "oldness" used here is *palaiotēs* meaning that which is obsolete. Newness means that which is new as to quality in contrast to that which is worn out. Spirit refers to the Holy Spirit.

The believer is not bound to the minute particulars of legal observances according to the traditions of the fathers. His life does not consist in mere conformity to a list of rules and regulations. He serves in a new spiritual state in Christ and not in the old bondage of the Law. He is free from the slavish fear of the Law.

Note the word "serve." Even though married to a new husband, we must still serve. But this is a service of freedom in contrast to the drudgery of the old life. Service is not determined by the old externals but by new spiritual principles (2 Corinthians 5:14, 15).

7. **What shall we say then?:** ...do we conclude? —*BRKL.*

**[is] the law sin?:** ...That the Law is equivalent to sin? —*MOFT.*

**God forbid:** ...Far be it from our thoughts, —*BRKL.*

**Nay, I had not known sin, but by the law:** ...I should not have comprehended the sin, —*FNTN*...Yet, if it had not been for the law, —*WLMS*...it was the law that made clear my knowledge of sin, —*NORL*...I should have known nothing of sin as sin, —*WEYM*...an experiential knowledge of sin except through the instrumentality of law, —*WUST.*

**for I had not known lust, except the law had said, Thou shalt not covet:** ...I had not known even inordinate desire, —*CMPB*...strong desire, —*WLSN*...except the Law had repeatedly said, —*MNTG*...Don't lust, —*BECK.*

8. **But sin, taking occasion by the commandment, wrought in me all manner of concupiscence:** ...when sin had gained a vantage-ground, —*MNTG*...Sin found its rallying point, —*WLMS*...Taking the commandment as a challenge, sin worked in me every kind of wrong desire, —*BECK*...to make me want all kinds of things which didn't belong to me, —*SEB*...made that command a fulcrum that effected in me all sorts of covetousness, —*BRKL*...to arouse in me every form of covetousness; —*TCNT.*

**For without the law sin [was] dead:** ...In the absence of Law sin shows no sign of life, —*TCNT*...disconnected from law, sin is non-existent, —*FNTN*...for apart from law sin is dead, —*PNIN*...sin is lifeless, —*NORL, HNT, WLMS.*

**7:7, 8.** This section begins in the logical sequence by asking a question, which is a pattern in Romans. No doubt the question, like others which Paul raised, was being asked by the legalists who were constantly attempting to bring the Church back into bondage. They taught that the believer, even though justified by faith, was after justification put under Law as a rule of faith. Is the Law sinful? Is the Law the cause of sin? Is there something wrong with the Law?

Paul answers clearly. He does not reflect dishonorably on the Law. The Law is like the Lawgiver. It is holy, just, and good, commanding holiness and outlining those things which are right and just. But the Law is powerless to save and sanctify, not because it is not good, but because of the sinful bias in human nature.

There was a time when sin was dead; without the Law sin was dead. Before God gave Adam the law regarding the tree of the knowledge of good and evil, sin was dead in that man was separated from it. The Garden was all holy until man rebelled against God's law. Adam and Eve were free from sin in a way that none of their progeny can be. However, Paul knew by revelation and by experience that he was alive without the Law once, when as a child he was "without the law" in that he was not then personally accountable to God for

his sinful nature. The child has selfish desires but is not aware of lust or coveting per se.

9. **For I was alive without the law once: but when the commandment came:**

**sin revived, and I died:** ...sin sprang into life, —*WEYM*...synne lyued agen, —*WCLF*...sin lived again, —*WLSN*...sin came to life, —*ALFD.*

**7:9.** Paul was speaking both by revelation and by his experience (and the experience of all human beings who live to the age of accountability) when he wrote, "I was alive without the law once." He could be alive without the Law, because sin was dead (verse 8). Sin was dead because as a child he was not aware of what was sin. Then—by the revelation of God in (1) creation (1:18-20), (2) the written Word (as in verse 7), and (3) his conscience as pricked by the Holy Spirit (2:15)—sin came to life because he then knew what was sin against God. Being bent toward sin by his sinful nature he died spiritually; he was separated from God by his sin from then until he was born again.

10. **And the commandment, which [was ordained] to life:** ...that was aimed to give life, —*BRKL*...which was intended for life, —*WSLY*...whose design was life, —*NOYS*...which should have meant life, —*MNTG.*

**I found [to be] unto death:** ...actually proved to be a sentence of death to me, —*NORL*...brought death instead! —*SEB*...I found to result in Death! —*TCNT*...proved in my experience death, —*HNT*...this I found unto death, —*WSLY*...me tending to death, —*SCLT*...vnto me an occasion of deeth, —*TNDL*...I found to issue in death, —*NOYS.*

11. **For sin, taking occasion by the commandment, deceived me, and by it slew [me]:** ...Taking the commandment as a challenge, sin seduced me, —*BECK*...beguiled me and, —*WUST, PNIN*...to take hold of me, —*SEB*...gave sin a chance, and sin deceived me, —*NORL*...by taking its incentive from the command, cheated me, —*BRKL*...beguiled me through the commandment, —*HNT*...seized the advantage, —*WEYM*...to mislead me, —*JB*...and slew me by the sentence of the Law, —*CNBR.*

**7:10, 11.** The Law reveals the sinful nature of man and the vile nature of sin. Sin is shown in its seriousness (verses 10, 11) and its sinfulness (verses 12, 13). The Law revealed the fact (verse 7), the occasion (verse 8), the power (verse 9), the deceitfulness (verse 11), the effect (verses 10, 11), and the sinfulness of sin (verses 12, 13). The Law made Paul discover his sin. It served as a mirror to reveal his need of washing. The Law, reflecting the holy will of God, defined evil. Sin has no existence apart from the Law, for sin is the transgression of the Law.

The Law was a schoolmaster to bring us to Christ (Galatians 3:24, 25). The Roman schoolmaster was a pedagogue who did not teach but was the slave whose duty it was to take the child to school. Paul tells the Galatians that the person who is justified by faith is no longer under the schoolmaster.

"Ordained to life" has the meaning of "tending to life." The aim was to life, for it set forth nothing but that which was right and perfect; to keep it perfectly insured life eternal. "Found to be" means proved to be death to me because I could not keep it.

The word "deceived" is *exapataō* which literally means "completely make one lose one's way." Sin leads one to confusion and lostness, to completely lose the way. Sin, like the tempter before Eve, took the commandment for a starting point and deceived him.

**12. Wherefore the law [is] holy, and the commandment holy:** . . . The conclusion, then, is, —TCNT . . . and its specific commands are, —WLMS . . . holy, fair and good, —SEB.
**and just, and good:**
**13. Was then that which is good made death unto me? God forbid:**
**But sin, that it might appear sin, working death in me by that which is good:** . . . that it might be manifest as sin, —CNFT . . . clearly used this good thing to kill me, —BECK . . . producing death to me, —SAWR . . . that it might be shown to be sin, —WORL.
**that sin by the commandment might become exceeding sinful:** . . . that the unutterable malignity of sin, —MNTG . . . might be beyond doubt excessively sinful, —FNTN . . . how intensely sinful sin is, —TCNT . . . the unspeakable sinfulness of sin might be plainly shown, —WEYM . . . myght be out of measure synfull, —CRNM . . . sin might appear surpassingly sinful, —WLMS . . . might become immeasurably sinful, —CNFT.

**7:12, 13.** There is no defect in the Law, "the law is holy." It is holy because it was given by God and expresses part of His will. The Law being "holy," "just," and "good," heartily approves righteousness but without reservation condemns evil. Other than Jesus, the Law never saw a man righteous through obedience.

Paul again poses a question. If the Law is holy, just, and good, how then is it the cause of death? Again comes the firm response, "God forbid." Paul points out that it was not the Law that killed him but sin that would not let him obey the Law. This made sin appear for what it really is—a decision, a deadly enemy, a killer.

Earlier the question was posed, "Is the law sin?" (verse 7). The Law is good for it is "the commandment . . . ordained to life" (verse 10). It is "holy" as God's revelation of himself, "just" in its prerequisites, and "good" because of its end.

Sin is basically disobedience, and there must be a law to disobey before one is conscious of

sin. Dormant sinful nature springs into life, sin revived when the Law came. It was not the Law that brought the state of death. The Law was good, but the villain was sin. Sin seized the opportunity when the Law revealed what was right and what was wrong. The Law was powerless to help a person do the right and unable to avoid the wrong. Sin works in men, against their better judgment, causing them to do what the Law showed them to be wrong, thus bringing condemnation and death.

**14. For we know that the law is spiritual:**
**but I am carnal, sold under sin:** . . . It is I who am sensual, —NORL . . . but I am unspiritual, —JB, —WEYM . . . but I am earthly, —TCNT . . . I am made of flesh that is frail, —WLMS . . . and I am fleshly, —YNG . . . bought and sold under the dominion of sin, —MNTG.
**15. For that which I do I allow not:** . . . For what I work I know not, —PNIN . . . what I perform, —ALFD . . . what I accomplish, —WORL . . . I do not understand my own actions, —RSV . . . I do not practise what I would, —WSLY . . . what I work out, I do not approve, —WLSN . . . I don't always do what I really want to do, —SEB.
**for what I would, that do I not; but what I hate, that do I:** . . . What I want to do I don't practice, but instead what I hate is exactly what I do, —ADAM . . . I do not act according to my will, —HNT . . . I do what I detest, —MOFT . . . doing what I actually hate, —SEB . . . but what I am averse to is what I do, —WEYM . . . that I habitually do, —MNTG.
**16. If then I do that which I would not:** . . . In view of the fact then, —WUST.
**I consent unto the law that [it is] good:** . . . I agree that the Law is right, —BECK . . . I admit that the Law is good, —CNDT . . . that it is noble, —FNTN . . . I concur in the excellence of the law, —HNT.
**17. Now then it is no more I that do it:** . . . it is no longer I who perform the action, —NEB.
**but sin that dwelleth in me:** . . . sin which has its home within me, —WEYM . . . that lodges in me, —NEB.
**18. For I know that in me (that is, in my flesh,) dwelleth no good thing:** . . . I am well aware that, as far as my lower nature goes, —BRCL . . . that is, in my human nature, —TEV . . . in my unspiritual nature, —NEB . . . in my sensuality, —FNTN . . . does not live in me, —SEB.
**for to will is present with me; but [how] to perform that which is good I find not:** . . . I can will what is right, but I cannot do it, —RSV . . . for though the will to do good is there, the deed is not, —NEB . . . To will I find is attainable, —HNT . . . but I am not producing fine things, —ADAM . . . but not the power of doing what is right, —MOFT . . . the power to carry it out is not, —WEYM . . . but I fynde no meanes to performe that, —TNDL, —GNVA . . . but I do not find the strength to accomplish what is good, —CNFT . . . but to accomplish that which is good, —RHEM . . . to avail myself of its benefit? —FNTN . . . but to do it, I find difficult, —CMPB . . . but to work the good, —PNIN . . . the power to do it I do not possess, —BRCL . . . but to work out what is excellent I find not, —WLSN.

**7:14-18.** Three words are used by Paul to describe man. *Pneumatikos* is the spiritual man who "walks after the Spirit." *Psuchikos* is the unsaved or natural man. *Sarkikos* is the carnal Christian who does not have victory in his life. The spiritual man is delivered from the Law. The natural man is doomed by the Law. The carnal man is defeated by the Law.

Paul, who seems to be describing his own past experience, says that the Law which he desired so much to obey stirred sinful impulses within him. He was hindered from doing the good that he wanted to do and was driven to do the thing that he hated. This civil war raged between his mind and his flesh. The passage presents the picture of a man under law who has come to grips with the searching spirituality of the Law, but in his attempt to keep the Law finds himself stymied by indwelling sin.

When Paul wrote "I am carnal," he was not necessarily speaking of his life prior to conversion. In 1 Corinthians 3:1-3 Paul described as carnal those who were immature believers who should have developed beyond the stage of being "babes in Christ." They were carnal because they were choosing to give way to envy, strife, and divisions. They were regenerate; they were "brethren" and they were "in Christ," even if only "babes." They were behaving, however, like unregenerate men.

When the believer tries to be spiritual by keeping the Law, any law, he becomes very aware of his carnality. His sinful human nature is aroused by law because the Christian is to live from Christ's life within rather than by trying to do good works of law. The Law was spiritual, a written expression of the character of God and could only be kept by one who was perfect spiritually. Paul, and every man, was "sold under sin" by Adam who made it impossible for anyone except Jesus Christ to be perfect spiritually in himself.

This particular passage has been the battleground of theological difference. Able Bible students are divided in interpreting this experience as being that of the regenerate or unregenerate. (1) Some say it is the struggle of one who is endeavoring to overcome sin by his own strength. (2) Others say that this is the experience of all true Christians in their disappointing conflict with inward sin and no deliverance is to be expected until they reach heaven. (3) Others hold that it is the struggle that can only be won by a second definite work of grace in becoming "wholly sanctified." (4) Still others hold that these verses describe the struggle and defeat of devout Jews in their attempt to keep the Law which they reverenced so highly.

Very possibly there is a measure of truth in some if not all of the various interpretations; however, most evangelicals are inclined to agree with the first statement. It is certain that application can be made in every instance. The fact remains that this experience describes a man who struggles to be holy and good in his own strength but fails miserably because of sin's power.

The contrast between chapters 7 and 8 is most significant. In chapter 7 the pronoun "I" occurs 31 times (KJV) without one mention of the Holy Spirit, unless verse 6 refers to the newness *He* brings. Obviously "I" am struggling to do and completely failing for it is an attempt in my own strength. In chapter 8 the Holy Spirit is mentioned at least 20 times. In chapter 8 law is scarcely mentioned while there are 20 references to law in chapter 7.

The carnal Christian finds it impossible to behave the way God expects him to because he is in bondage to the flesh. The unbeliever has only one nature, the Adamic or human nature with which he was born. When he reaches the age of accountability he either immediately chooses to obey God by receiving Christ as Saviour, or he chooses to live according to that nature and becomes a literal sinner, a slave of Satan. If he rejects God's revelation to him he is then under the wrath of God (John 3:36). The only thing that keeps him out of hell at any moment is the mercy of God who is longsuffering, "not willing that any should perish" (2 Peter 3:9).

The believer has two natures. He has the nature with which he was born, the Adamic nature, which is unable to obey God's law. This nature is also called the "flesh" (verse 18), "carnal" (verse 14), the "I" that does what the new nature hates (verse 15), "the body of this death" (verse 24), the "old man" (6:6). This nature is to be reckoned dead; but it is not nonexistent, as any truthful believer can attest. In the Bible *death* never means annihilation, but always separation. When we died with Jesus (6:3-7), we were indeed separated from this nature, but it is a separation that depends on constant reckoning (6:11) and conscious yielding to the new nature (6:12-19). Just as in the case of the Law (verse 4), we died to the old nature, but the old nature itself did not die.

The believer has been made partaker of the "divine nature" (2 Peter 1:4), the "new man" (Colossians 3:10), the "I" that delights in the law of God (Romans 7:22) because of being crucified with Christ (Galatians 2:20).

Chapters 6 to 8 all deal with the believer's sanctification. Chapter 6 gives the machinery, chapter 7 describes the malfunction when the believer tries to "do it" himself, and chapter 8 shows the victory that comes by being led of the Spirit, trusting Him for actualization.

**19. For the good that I would I do not:** ...I desire, —ALFD...I intend to do, —MNTG...I fail to do, —NEB.

**but the evil which I would not, that I do:** ...I practice the bad I do not want to practice, —BRKL...that I habitually do, —TCNT...I do wrong against my wishes, —MOFT...is what I constantly do, —WEYM...that I am ever practising, —MNTG...that I perform, —CNFT.

**20. Now if I do that I would not:**

**it is no more I that do it:** ...it is no longer I who am responsible for the results, —TCNT.

**but sin that dwelleth in me:** ...but sin living in me, —BECK...that makes itself at home in me, —BRKL.

**7:19, 20.** Paul had just stated that he had a will to do right. The predicament that he was describing could be that of a Jewish legalist trying to become holy by doing works of self-righteousness. It can also be that of any Christian who is trying by his own willpower to be holy. The clue to the problem is in the emphasis on "I." The flesh thrives on what "I" can do and on what "I" do not do. No believer has to settle for fleshly efforts, bringing the wretched state of doing what he does not want to do. His deliverance is as near as Calvary.

If to know to do right was to do it, how easy life would be. Knowing what is right behavior does not necessarily make us perform correctly. Human resolution is inadequate. The human will, apart from the strength of the Holy Spirit, is destined to fail under pressure. In human nature there is a weakness in the will. And yet the will is an obstacle of God's own creation. He never violates that will; He never crosses the threshold of the door to man's will unless invited to do so.

The carnal believer finds himself at cross purposes, desiring two different patterns of life at the same time. He is trying to do the impossible—to serve two masters at the same time. He is allowing sin to dwell in him when he has actually been set free (6:16). It seems that he is unaware of the freedom that is his, just as some slaves lived on in slavery after the close of the Civil War because they did not know they were free.

**21. I find then a law:** ...Consequently, —WORL...this seems to be the rule, —JB...I discover this law, —CNFT.

**that, when I would do good, evil is present with me:** ...when I intend to, —MNTG...when I have a will, —DOUY...that every single time I want to, —JB...when I desire to do that which is good, —ALFD...it is easier for me to do wrong! —TCNT...but wrong is all I can manage, —MOFT...is lying in ambush for me, —WEYM...is always in my way, —WLMS...evil is

controlling me, —SEB...lies near me, —WLSN...close at hand, —PNT.

**7:21.** We must keep this portion of Scripture in context if we are to interpret it correctly. The Holy Spirit desired to portray the flesh in all its hideousness and viciousness. Paul by inspiration of the Spirit was describing the misery of one who has not yet yielded to the deliverance provided and described in verses following (7:25; 8:1-4). He was not delineating what should be the normal experience of the believer. Chapter 6 had already made that clear.

The military motif of verse 13 is continued in verse 23. Paul stated that if he tried to overcome the "law in my members" with "the law of my mind," he could not have victory. Rather, the law of sin brought him into captivity; he was pitting his own strength against the flesh. In 8:2, 3, he described the "law" that can give victory, "the law of the Spirit of life in Christ Jesus."

**22. For I delight in the law of God after the inward man:** ...In my inmost self I dearly love God's Law, —JB...for I consent gladly to the law of God, —CNBR...I gladly approve God's law, —HNT...all my sympathy is with the Law, —WEYM...in accordance with my better inner nature, —WLMS.

**23. But I see another law in my members:** ...but I perceive a foreign law, —FNTN...but I find a different law in my bodily faculties, —MNTG...and I behold another law, —YNG...but I see another power operating, —WLMS...I see a different law, —ASV, —PNIN.

**warring against the law of my mind:** ...battling against the principles which my reason dictates, —BRKL...rebelling against, —GNVA...fighting against, —DOUY...operated by, —WLMS.

**and bringing me into captivity:** ...and holding me captive, —ADAM...It is making me a prisoner to the sinful law, —SEB...making me a prisoner of war, —WUST...and captivating me, —SCLT, —WSLY.

**to the law of sin which is in my members:** ...and subduynge me vnto the law of synne, —CRNM...that controls my bodily organs, —BRKL...which is in my bodily faculties, —MNTG.

**7:22, 23.** The apostle goes on to speak of the various laws which bring conflicting purposes and principles to bear upon him. They are four in number.

There is the "law of God" in which his better nature, his inner nature delights or takes "sympathetic pleasure." This is the moral law, written or unwritten.

There is the "law of sin" which is also called the "law of sin and death" (8:2). The entire human race came under the dominion of this law through the Fall in Eden. This law operates in the moral realm as the law of gravity acts in the physical realm. Unless its power is revoked by the "law of the Spirit" (8:2), it can only bring one down on a relentless march to hell.

There is the "law of my mind." "Mind" is variously rendered "will," "reason," "conscience." This is the moral sense in man.

There is the "law in my members." It wars against the law of the mind and brings man's faculties into captivity as a prisoner of "the law of sin." By this means "the law of sin" asserts itself. Mentally there is the desire to do right. Intellectual assent is given to the law of God. But the law of the members (bodily faculties, lower nature, or self) asserts itself. The eyes look with lust, the untamed tongue builds fires of evil through gossip, boasting, and evil speech (James 3), and the ears listen to that which is unedifying.

24. **O wretched man that I am!:** ... What a miserable man I am! —NORL ... Man of toils and troubles that I am, —BRKL ... Vnhappie man that I am, —RHEM. **who shall deliver me from the body of this death?:** ... Who will rescue me, —MOFT, —SCLT, —WLSN ... from this slave of death? —MNTG ... help me escape, —SEB ... from this death-burdened body? —WEYM ... from this body which turns life into death, —BRCL ... from my own sinful body? —NORL ... from this deadly carcase? —FNTN ... this body doomed to death? —BRKL ... from this deadly lower nature? —WLMS ... which is dragging me down to Death? —TCNT.

**7:24.** The gulf between the demands of the Law and the ability of the flesh to fulfill them is like a vast chasm which seems impossible to bridge. It results in a wail of anguish and a cry for help. "Wretched" is translated from *talaipōros* which carries the thought of being "wretched through the exhaustion of hard labor."

The words "the body of this death" seem to be an allusion to an ancient custom from days of horrible tyranny. At times a convicted criminal was bound face-to-face, hand to hand, to the corpse of his victim and forced to carry it, until he died of contagion from the putrid, decaying body. That is the result of the conflict described in the previous verses. From that wretched condition comes the cry of despair: "Who can rescue me," "who can save me," "who can set me free?"

25. **I thank God through Jesus Christ our Lord:** ... He does it through, —BECK ... God alone, through Jesus Christ, —NEB. **So then with the mind I myself serve the law of God:** ... This, then, is my condition, —TEV ... I myself, subject to God's law as a rational being, —NEB ... with the spiritual part of my nature, —BRCL. **but with the flesh the law of sin:** ... but by my sensuality, —FNTN ... yet in my animal nature, —MNTG ... yet, in my unspiritual nature, a slave to the

law of sin, —NEB ... but my human nature is under sin's control, —BRKL.

**7:25.** Paul's answer is clear. Deliverance must come through Christ and, in turn, through yielding to the Holy Spirit, whose work is to produce the Christ life in those who receive Him. The chasm has been completely spanned. There is deliverance from the penalty of sin in the past as we believe and from the power of sin in the present as we walk by the law of the Spirit. Sin and Satan are conquered foes and the self-nature can also be brought into subjection.

The mind is willing, the flesh is weak, but the defeat described in chapter 7 yields to the victory of chapter 8, if we allow the law of the Spirit to reign.

## Chapter 8

1. **[There is] therefore now no condemnation to them which are in Christ Jesus:** ... Consequently, there is now, —WORL ... For this very reason, —BRKL ... there is no doom, —MOFT ... no death sentence hanging over those, —NORL ... not even one bit of, —WUST ... no damnation ... who are in union, —TCNT. **who walk not after the flesh, but after the Spirit:** ... and behave in no flesh-governed way, —BRKL ... whiche wandren not aftir the fleisch, —WCLF.

**8:1.** This chapter puts the capstone on the doctrinal portion of the book. Vividly setting forth the life of triumph, the chapter begins with "no condemnation," ends with "no separation," and in between there is "no defeat." The work of the Holy Spirit is introduced. The Holy Spirit is referred to 19 times in Romans 8. The dominant theme is the victorious message of deliverance from sin by the power of the Holy Spirit.

The word *katakrima* ("condemnation") is often misunderstood; many take it to mean no more conviction for sin for believers. F.F. Bruce has well defined it as "punishment following sentence—in other words, penal servitude. There is no reason for those who are in Christ Jesus to serve sin as if they had never been pardoned and never been liberated from the prison-house of sin" (*Tyndale New Testament Commentaries*, 6:159).

2. **For the law of the Spirit of life in Christ Jesus:** ... The rule, —BECK ... the life-giving Spirit, —TCNT. **hath made me free:** ... hath delyuerid me fro, —WCLF ... liberated me, —WLSN. **from the law of sin and death:** ... from the rule of sin that kills, —BECK ... that deals only with sin and death, —WEYM.

**8:2.** The deliverance from condemnation and the bondage of legalism is achieved through the operation of a new law, "the law of the Spirit of life in Christ Jesus," which is more powerful than the law of sin and death. Those who are "in Christ" have escaped the realm of the Law's condemnation and have a vantage point from which they can subdue the flesh.

The believer is positionally "in Christ Jesus" as a result of his union with Christ in death, burial, and resurrection (6:1-13). Notice three ways in which believers are "in Christ": (1) by birth as we were in Adam, we are born again in Christ (1 Corinthians 15:22; Romans 5:12-21); (2) vitally, as the branch is in the vine (John 15:1-7), or as all members are in the body (1 Corinthians 12:27; Ephesians 1:23); (3) by faith (Ephesians 3:17; Galatians 3:26, 27).

**3. For what the law could not do, in that it was weak through the flesh:** ... What the Law, weakened by the flesh, —BECK ... because of the inability of the Law, —FNTN ... For the law being powerless, —PNT ... that which is an impossibility for the law, —WUST ... because of our unspiritual nature, —JB ... as our earthly nature weakened its action, —TCNT ... because it was made helpless, —WLMS.

**God sending his own Son in the likeness of sinful flesh, and for sin:** ... For God effected, —HNT ... in the guise of sinful flesh, —MOFT ... with a nature like man's sinful human nature, —SEB ... in the similitude of, —RHEM ... in a body like that of sinful human nature, —WEYM ... to atone for sin, —TCNT ... as a sin-offering, —HNT ... who on account of sin, —NOYS ... and, respecting sin, —WORL.

**condemned sin in the flesh:** ... He pronounced sentence upon sin in human nature, —WEYM ... overcame sin, —CNBR.

**8:3.** Two words keep appearing again and again in this chapter: "flesh" (*sarx*) and "spirit" (*pneuma*). Paul often uses these words in his epistles. *Sarx* is used in three different ways. He speaks of literal flesh, such as physical circumcision, "in the flesh" (2:28). Then he speaks of *kata sarka*, or "according to the flesh," which means from the human point of view, such as the Jews were Jesus' *kata sarka*, or kinsmen (1:3). Such usage refers to human relationships (1:3; 9:3). The word is again used in a way peculiar to Paul, such as *en sark* (7:5; 8:4-6, 8, 9, 12). In these instances he is not referring to our bodies, flesh and blood, but rather to human nature, dominated by the desires of the sinful, lower side of man's nature (Galatians 5:19-21).

The words "what the law could not do" could be rendered "the impossible (thing) of the Law." The Law was "weak through the flesh" in that it could do nothing with flesh except stir it up (7:7-14). It could condemn the sinner (3:19), but it could not

stop his sinning. Christ Jesus could and did solve both problems.

He came "in flesh" (Romans 1:3; John 1:14), but not in *sinful* flesh. He "knew no sin" (2 Corinthians 5:21), even though He was fully human. He came in the *likeness* of sinful flesh; His flesh was not sinful flesh for there was no sin in Him (Hebrews 4:15).

Christ's mission was "for sin." He came and condemned sin through the Atonement. Jesus became the perfect sin offering when He took our nature, lived a sinless life that condemned sin in our lives, and then, nailed to the cross, took God's condemnation of sin. By this act, conceived in the counsels of eternity, sin's doom was pronounced, and God rejected its claim upon us.

**4. That the righteousness of the law:** ... that the requirement of the law, —WORL ... in order to secure the fulfilment, —MOFT ... as righteous as the Law demands, —BECK ... the Law's just demands, —JB ... that the righteous ordinance of the law, —SAWR.

**might be fulfilled in us:** ... be satisfied, —JB ... may be performed by us, —SAWR.

**who walk not after the flesh, but after the Spirit:** ... who do not live by the standard, —WLMS ... for our lives are regulated, —WEYM ... not in harmony with sensuality, —FNTN ... not in a fleshly but in a spiritual way, —BRKL ... not as dominated by the sinful nature, —WUST.

**8:4.** "Righteousness" (*diakaiōma*) is used here in its most usual meaning as "righteous requirement." It is fulfilled in us by the One who lives within: "Christ in you, the hope of glory" (Colossians 1:27). The Law could not become flesh and live within us. Jesus became flesh, fulfilled the Law, and now lives in us. As we walk after the Spirit, we are "dead indeed unto sin" (6:11) and to self (8:8-10), and alive to God through Christ Jesus (6:11).

**5. For they that are after the flesh do mind the things of the flesh:** ... meditate about the gratification of their sensuality, —FNTN ... give their attention to the things, —MNTG.

**but they that are after the Spirit the things of the Spirit:** ... have their interests in the Spirit, —MOFT ... usually thinking the things suggested by the Spirit, —WLMS ... are gostly mynded, —TNDL.

**8:5.** This verse sets forth two classes of men. Those who live to the flesh and those who live to the Spirit are set in contrast. The believer does not have to walk after the flesh, but he can still allow the flesh to dominate his life.

Note the significance of the mind. We can know to what extent the old nature is influencing us by what our minds like to dwell on.

**6. For to be carnally minded [is] death:** ... For the inclination of the flesh, –CNFT ... For the wisdom of the flesh, –DOUY ... The way human nature thinks, –SEB ... to have the mind dominated, –WUST ... to limit oneself to what is unspiritual, –JB.

**but to be spiritually minded [is] life and peace:** ... but the minding of the Spirit, –SAWR.

**8:6.** "Mind" (*phroneō*) occurs in verses 5 and 6. It means to have understanding, to feel or think, to direct the mind, to seek or strive for. The human mind is indeed difficult to define fully. Words are at times frail vehicles by which to convey the concepts of deep reality. The mind uses the brain, but it cannot be completely identified with the brain. The brain per se is not what is being discussed here; it is physical and is not necessarily changed by the new birth.

It could be said that the mind is the way the spirit of man uses the brain. Without the brain the mind cannot manifest itself. It is closely related to the basic attitude or stance in the heart (Romans 10:10; Proverbs 4:23; 23:7; Philippians 4:7; 1 Peter 3:4) or spirit of man (1 Corinthians 2:11; Hebrews 4:12).

"To be carnally minded" is literally the mind of the flesh. The noun *phronēma* is found only in Romans 8 (verses 6, 7, 27) and means the pattern of thought and motive, the interests and aims. The carnal mind is the mind dominated by the flesh.

"To be spiritually minded" is to have "the mind of Christ" (1 Corinthians 2:16). A renewed spirit will result in a renewed mind as we walk after the Spirit.

**7. Because the carnal mind [is] enmity against God:** ... the mind of the flesh, –PNIN ... which is interested only in carnal things, –NORL ... worldly-mindedness is hostile to God, –BRKL ... is an enemy against, –KLGS.

**for it is not subject to the law of God:** ... such a limitation never could and never does submit to God's law, –JB ... It refuses to obey God's Law, –BECK ... is not subordinate, –SCLT.

**neither indeed can be:** ... for neither is it able, –YNG.

**8. So then they that are in the flesh:** ... So, those controlled by the flesh, –BRKL ... they who are carnal, –CNFT ... they who are earthly minded, –MNTG ... they whose hearts are absorbed in, –WEYM ... on the plane of the lower nature, –WLMS ... controlled by human nature, –SEB ... who are in a Sensual state, –WLSN.

**cannot please God:** ... do not have the power, –KLGS ... are unable to please God, –BRKL.

**9. But ye are not in the flesh, but in the Spirit:** ... But you are not earthly, –MNTG ... are not devoted to earthly, –WEYM ... you are not Sensual, –WLSN.

**if so be that the Spirit of God dwell in you:** ... is at home in you, –BRKL ... has made his home in you, –JB ... is in residence in you, –WUST.

**Now if any man have not the Spirit of Christ:** ... But, assuming that a person does not have, –WUST ... No one who does not possess the Spirit, –BRCL ... if one doth not profess, –SCLT.

**he is none of his:** ... he does not belong to Him, –BRKL ... he does not belong to Christ, –TCNT, –SEB ... such a one does not belong to Him, –WEYM ... he is not of him, –WLSN.

**10. And if Christ [be] in you:** ... if Christ lives in you, –WLMS.

**the body [is] dead because of sin:** ... even though your body is dying (because of sin), –SEB ... though the body is a dead thing owing to Adam's sin, –MOFT ... even though your bodies are going to die, –TEV ... the physical part of you may be doomed to death because of, –BRCL ... your body must die because of sin, –NORL ... indeed, is dead, with respect to sin, –CMPB ... as a consequence of sin, –TCNT ... by reason of sin, –ALFD, –CNFT ... because you were sinful, –BECK.

**but the Spirit [is] life because of righteousness:** ... your spirits are now enjoying life because of right standing, –WLMS ... is destined for life because of the right relationship with God, –BRCL ... full of life because of righteousness, –MNTG.

**11. But if the Spirit of him that raised up Jesus from the dead dwell in you:** ... is in residence in you, –WUST.

**he that raised up Christ from the dead shall also quicken your mortal bodies:** ... will animate even, –SCLT ... will make your dead bodies live, –SEB ... will revive your deadened bodies by His indwelling Spirit, –FNTN ... shall give life also, –ASV ... shall endow with life also your dying bodies, –CNBR ... shall make alive also, –PNIN ... also your dying bodies, –YNG ... also make your dying bodily self live, –MNTG.

**by his Spirit that dwelleth in you:** ... by his Spirit that keeps house in you, –KLGS.

**8:7-11.** The carnal mind is an enemy to God and is in rebellion against the law of God. Therefore carnality will always bring God's displeasure and rob the believer of peace.

The law of sin and death is in operation in human nature, but that law is counteracted by the law of the Spirit of life. The presence of Christ within is a higher law than any other; it can permeate our motives and innermost desires.

The Law could not meet our need. In itself the Law was good, but man, being carnal, was without power to obey it. Someone has said that the anchor of the Law was strong in itself, but it could not hold firm in the soft earth of the heart. God did not change the principles of righteousness, but He made provision for changing human nature by sending forth a new spiritual power which was released through the atoning work of Jesus Christ. The Holy Spirit is able to produce a righteous life in us by Christ's work at Calvary.

We have died to the first Adam to be united to the last Adam. We have died to sin, the old master, to be raised with Christ, our new Master. We have died to the old husband, the Law, to "be married to another," our heavenly Bridegroom (7:4). "There is therefore now no condemnation."

Through union with the risen and glorified Saviour, a new power—the Holy Spirit—enters human nature to subdue sin. Through the Spirit the righteousness which the Law required is fulfilled in us (not *by* us), because we walk in yieldedness to the Spirit.

When our life is in Christ, He inspires new desires and new affections. A holy life gives evidence that our life is in Christ. Though a saved person can and at times may yield to the flesh, he is not "in the flesh," the domain of sin. He will not practice a walk in the flesh. The word "flesh" refers to the old, unrenewed sinful nature by which the unregenerate man lives. The life in the flesh can be lived by the cultured, educated, and refined, as well as the murderers, thieves, and harlots. Every Christian has the Spirit of Christ. At the moment of our new birth we were placed in Christ and He in us. This is the instant aspect of sanctification. This experience does not make it *impossible* for us to have fleshly attitudes or deeds, but it does make it possible for us *not* to have them.

The process by which we are being conformed to the image of Christ (verse 29) is the practical, continuing aspect of sanctification. The Holy Spirit is doing in us what He has done for us. We do not grow *into* sanctification, but we grow *in* sanctification.

All human activities that center around self are in the flesh. As the hub of our life changes from self to God we begin walking in the Spirit instead of in the flesh. The walk in the flesh brings death or separation from God. The carnal (fleshly) mind resents the will of God. It opposes God and loves to have self pampered and praised. No matter how good a person might be, no matter how benevolent one's work might be, if self has the center, such a person "cannot please God." But if the Spirit of God is in us, we are enabled to live above the desires of the flesh; if we do not have the Spirit of Christ we do not belong to God.

The Spirit of Christ is the Holy Spirit. Every believer has the Holy Spirit within, but not every believer is baptized in the Holy Spirit. The Holy Spirit baptizes the repentant sinner into the body of Christ (1 Corinthians 12:13); this is salvation. Jesus himself, and no one else, baptizes the believer in the Holy Spirit (Acts 1:5) as all four Gospels declare; this is the baptism in the Holy Spirit (Acts 2:4). Even if a believer has not been baptized in the Holy Spirit, he has the Spirit; this should make

it easy for him to allow Jesus to pour upon him the fullness of the Spirit (Acts 2:33).

When Christ is in us we have life—even though our bodies are doomed to death—because of the active principle of righteousness. The redemption of the body, which is still under the curse, is future. The implanted righteousness of the Spirit possesses the human spirit, but physical death prevails over the body.

Each human being dies physically because of Adam's sin. It seems God has allowed the body, even of the saint, to suffer, grow old and die, to constantly remind us of our need to draw our spiritual life from Him. Just as we do not have natural life within ourselves except as God gives it, so we have no spiritual life apart from Him. If the human being dies spiritually it is because of the person's own sin, not Adam's.

Verses 10 and 11, contrast the human body and the spirit. The body dies physically because of Adam's sin, but the spirit indwelt by the Holy Spirit becomes a living power. The indwelling Spirit is a guarantee of a future bodily resurrection. Not only are we delivered from the law of sin (verses 3-8), we shall be delivered from the law of death.

**12. Therefore, brethren, we are debtors, not to the flesh, to live after the flesh:** ... Accordingly, then, —WORL ... bound not to the Flesh, —CNBR ... we don't owe it, —BECK ... we are under no obligation to our earthly nature, that we should live in obedience to it, —TCNT ... bound to follow the standards set by our fleshly natures, —NORL.

**8:12.** With the gracious privilege of having Christ in our lives, there come certain obligations—"we are debtors." There is danger if we live according to the flesh after what God has done for us. It is to court disaster.

**13. For if ye live after the flesh:** ... if you go on living according to the flesh, —MNTG.

**ye shall die:** ... you are on the road to death, —MOFT ... death awaits you, —HNT ... you are doomed to die, —CNBR.

**but if ye through the Spirit do mortify the deeds of the body:** ... by the helpe of the sprite, —TNDL ... you deaden the practices of the body, —BRKL ... kill the evil deeds, —SEB ... you put an end to the misdeeds, —JB ... you kill the activities of, —BECK ... you destroy the practices of sensuality, —FNTN ... through being under the sway of the spirit, you are putting your old bodily habits to death, —WEYM.

**ye shall live:** ... you will attain to life, —CNBR.

**8:13.** To allow the things of the world to completely dominate one's life is spiritual suicide. This verse is perhaps the clearest, most concise statement of the way a person once in grace can lose his salvation. John Murray is basically Calvinistic in his theology, but in commenting on 8:13 he states: "Paul is speaking here to believers and to them he says, 'If ye live after the flesh, ye shall die.' The death referred to must be understood in its broadest scope and does not stop short of death in its ultimate manifestation, eternal separation from God" (*New International Commentary on the New Testament,* 1:293).

The believer finds his victory in Christ by the power of the Holy Spirit. Nothing is owed to the flesh. It is to have no more control. He is to mortify the deeds of the body. *Thanatoō* means to "put to death, destroy, render extinct."

**14. For as many as are led by the Spirit of God, they are the sons of God:** ... All who are moved by God's Spirit, —*BECK* ... All who are guided by, —*TCNT,* —*WLMS.*

**15. For ye have not received the spirit of bondage again to fear:** ... you do not have a sense of servitude to fill you with dread again, —*WLMS* ... that would re-enslave you to fear, —*BRKL* ... received no slavish spirit that would make you relapse into fear, —*MOFT* ... to fall back into fear, —*RSV* ... to fill you once more, —*TCNT* ... with terror, —*WEYM* ... leading back unto fear, —*ALFD.*

**but ye have received the Spirit of adoption:** ... Who adopts you, —*ADAM* ... who places you as adult sons, —*WUST.*

**whereby we cry, Abba, Father:** ... by which we shout, —*KLGS.*

**8:14, 15.** To be led of the Spirit is to live a normal Christian life. By following the Spirit's leading we realize and prove our sonship. It is God's purpose that all New Testament saints are to be the "sons of God." But some turn "again to the weak and beggarly elements, whereunto ... (they) desire again to be in bondage" (Galatians 4:9).

Servants obey because they are subject to rules; sons of God obey because they are led by the Spirit into a clear realization that the Father's will is the best possible way. Like their Elder Brother they delight to do God's will.

Jesus did not come to give us a system by which we could live; He came to be our life. The Holy Spirit bears unmistakable witness to our spirit that we are children of God. The new birth (John 3:3-6) gives spiritual life; the adoption as sons guarantees privileges of sonship.

If we are to live a victorious life, there must be a definite assurance of our standing in grace and of our relationship to God. Unbelievers may call on God in times of calamity, but only a son can truly pray, "Our Father."

**16. The Spirit itself beareth witness with our spirit:** ... the Spirit him self, giueth testimonie to our spirit, —*RHEM* ... This Spirit assures, —*BECK* ... The same

sprete certyfyeth, —*CRNM* ... bears witness jointly with our spirits, —*BRKL* ... is a co-witness, —*SAWR.*

**that we are the children of God:**

**8:16.** Not all men are children of God. The liberals' teaching of the brotherhood of man and the fatherhood of God is a doctrine that is foreign to Scripture (John 8:44; 1 John 3:10). On the contrary, how wonderful is sonship. By and through Christ is the only way to be brought into the family of God.

The knowledge of sonship comes through the witness of the Holy Spirit. It is not necessary for us to tell people they are saved; that is the Spirit's prerogative. The Spirit makes our position as sons (literally, "adult sons") real to us as believers.

The word *tekna* is used here, while *huioi* appears in verse 14. *Tekna* refers to children; *huioi* to sons. The words are used interchangeably.

The King James translation, "the Spirit itself," is better rendered "the Spirit himself," for He is a person.

**17. And if children, then heirs; heirs of God, and joint-heirs with Christ:** ... And if sonnes ... co-heires of Christ, —*RHEM* ... in fact, God's heirs, —*BRKL* ... who share Christ's inheritance with Him, —*BECK.*

**if so be that we suffer with [him], that we may be also glorified together:** ... we have a share in His sufferings, —*NORL* ... so that we may also enjoy glory jointly, —*BRKL.*

**8:17.** The apostle points out another great privilege. Because believers are children of God, they are "heirs of God, and joint-heirs with Christ." The saints are called "joint-heirs with Christ" because God "hath in these last days spoken unto us by his Son, whom he hath appointed heir of all things" (Hebrews 1:2). The words *inheritance, inherit, heir,* and *joint heir* are all from the same root in the Greek. The believers' joint-heirship with Christ begins at once and includes suffering with Him in this present time, as well as glory with Him at His return. If we are to enter into our "adoption," or rights and privileges, we must accept the whole inheritance, suffering as well as glory (John 15:19, 20). All that belongs to Christ as the Firstborn belongs to His brethren as well, and this includes both a dark and a bright side. It was necessary for Him to suffer to enter into His glory (Luke 24:26; Acts 17:3). We are joint heirs, "if so be that we suffer with him." To wear the crown, we must share the Cross.

**18. For I reckon that the sufferings of this present time:** ... I confirme, that the afflictions, —*GNVA* ... I have come to a reasoned conclusion, —*WUST* ... what we suffer now isn't important, —BECK . . . this temporal suffering is of no account, —BRKL.

**[are] not worthy [to be compared] with the glory which shall be revealed in us:** . . . is a mere nothing, —MOFT . . . are of no weight, —WUST . . . are of no account in comparison, —ALFD, —WORL . . . which will soon be unveiled to us, —MNTG.

**8:18.** The trials of those who are the sons of God are not inconsistent with the ultimate glory of those who are "in Christ Jesus," and that theme is dominant in the entire chapter. The trials are limited to the "present time." It is noteworthy that this passage which begins with glory and ends with glory, in between deals with suffering. The believer in his suffering is hemmed by glory. The suffering is so minor in comparison with the greatness of the glory, that there is no real comparison. Think of Hebrews 11:35-38 in that light.

**19. For the earnest expectation of the creature waiteth for the manifestation of the sons of God:** . . . For in eager anticipation, —HNT . . . For all nature is expectantly waiting for the unveiling, —WLMS . . . the feruent desire, —GNVA . . . the eager longing of creation, —CNFT . . . gazing eagerly as if with outstretched neck, —WEYM . . . is waiting for the revelation of, —WORL . . . is waiting on tiptoe to see the unveiling of God's family, —BECK . . . the making plain, —KLGS.

**20. For the creature was made subject to vanity:** . . . Nature must waste away, —BECK . . . had to submit to imperfection, —TCNT . . . was tied to worthlessness, —SEB . . . was subjected to failure, —NORL . . . under the bondage of transitoriness, —BRKL . . . to a perishable condition, —SAWR . . . to frailty, —WLSN.

**not willingly, but by reason of him who hath subjected [the same] in hope:** . . . It was not for any fault on the part of creation, —JB . . . not from choice, —BRKL . . . not voluntarily, —PNT.

**8:19, 20.** When God's sons are unveiled, the whole creation, now groaning under the bondage of sin, will be redeemed. Dominion over a renewed creation, lost in Adam, will be restored to the redeemed race.

The vegetable kingdom involved in the curse, since the temptation in Eden related to a tree, will be delivered. The animal kingdom involved, since the Fall was introduced by a serpent, will be set free. All of the earth came under the curse because man relinquished his God-given dominion to Satan. The creation was thus made subject to pain and futility "not willingly." Animals and vegetables did not sin, but God "subjected" them "in hope" that man will learn that all sin exacts too great a price. The entire human family awaits the lifting of the curse. When that comes all creation will be delivered. The whole creation is now on "tiptoe" awaiting the completion of redemption.

**21. Because the creature itself also:**
**shall be delivered from:** . . . shall be liberated from the enslavement, —BRKL . . . will be set free from, —ADAM . . . will be emancipated from, —WLSN.

**the bondage of corruption:** . . . from the seruitude, —RHEM . . . from its enslavement to corruption, —TCNT . . . from the slavery of decay, —SEB . . . from the bondage of a perishing state, —CMPB . . . from the thraldom of decay, —MNTG.

**into the glorious liberty of the children of God:**

**8:21.** "Delivered" and "liberty" are from the same root in the Greek. The whole creation will gain the glorious freedom of God's children when His children are glorified. Creation will be rescued from the tyranny of change and decay. James 1:18 expresses the thought: "Of his own will begat he us with the word of truth, that we should be a kind of firstfruits of his creatures." Creation will be delivered from corruption, decay, and ruin.

**22. For we know that the whole creation groaneth and travaileth in pain together until now:** . . . We are conscious, somehow, —NORL . . . euery creature, —RHEM . . . the entire creation sighs and throbs with pain, —MOFT . . . creation is to this day sighing and in throes in unison, —BRKL . . . and laboureth in pain, —SCLT . . . travailing together until this hour, —MNTG . . . up to this very hour, —TCNT . . . up to this moment, —WUST.

**8:22.** Two compound verbs are found only here in the New Testament: *sustenazō* means "groan together"; *sunōdinō* means "travail together." "Together" refers to all the elements of creation having a common longing, a common groaning. The following passages present the thought of nature's cry: Psalm 98:7; Isaiah 35:1; Hosea 2:21. The transformation that will take place at the time of that deliverance is revealed in Psalms 96:11-13; 98:7-9; Isaiah 11:6-9; 65:20. The whole world of nature sighs for release from the agony of the ages, convulsing in birth pangs and awaiting deliverance. As a woman in travail has the hope of bearing her child, creation groans in hope. The groaning is not that of death throes, but of birth. That gives meaning to the cry of travail which nature now endures.

**23. And not only [they], but ourselves also:**
**which have the firstfruits of the Spirit:** . . . the Spirit whom we have is our first taste of heaven, —BECK . . . who enjoy the Spirit as a foretaste of the future, —WLMS . . . pledge of the glorious future, —WEYM.
**even we ourselves groan within ourselves:** . . . also groan inwardly, —ADAM . . . groan with pain also, —SEB.
**waiting for the adoption, [to wit], the redemption of our body:** . . . as we await that right of son-ship that involves our bodily redemption, —BRKL . . . for our privileges as sons, —TCNT . . . waiting

to become true sons, —SEB...for open recognition as sons, —WEYM... for the delivraunce of oure bodyes, —TNDL...the redemption from our sensuality, —FNTN.

**8:23.** The pains of birth are not only the experience of "dumb" creation, but Christians groan awaiting the redemption of the body. The obstetric metaphor used by Paul in one other passage (Galatians 4:19) illustrates how God's children and all creation are in the hour of labor, but the anguish will all be forgotten in the day of glory (John 16:21).

Present distress will give way to future glory when the curse is lifted. God's people are His sons. They have the Spirit. Sonship and Spirit are inseparably entwined in this chapter (verses 9, 14). Sons of God have the Holy Spirit. That possession is a promise of the harvest yet to come as stated concerning those who await the resurrection: "Christ the firstfruits; afterward they that are Christ's at his coming" (1 Corinthians 15:23).

All creation groans with a common cry, awaiting deliverance from the tensions and yearnings. Christians long for release from the final traces of sin and death. They are heirs of God and joint heirs with Christ, but they still tabernacle in mortal bodies subject to pain and death, with the vestment of a fallen nature to overcome (2 Corinthians 5:2; Romans 7:24).

**24. For we are saved by hope: but hope that is seen is not hope:**...is attained, —CMPB.

**for what a man seeth, why doth he yet hope for?:**...for who hopeth for that which he beholdeth? —CLMT.

**25. But if we hope for that we see not:**

**[then] do we with patience wait for [it]:**...we eagerly anticipate it, —ADAM...we steadfastly endure the present, —CNBR...we wait for it with endurance, —KLGS.

**8:24, 25.** Full and final redemption, the culmination of our "adoption," will see the transformation of our bodies into a glorified state. That is our hope, a hope rooted in God himself.

Take note of the development of the theme: "the glory which shall be revealed in us" (verse 18); "the manifestation of the sons of God" (verse 19); "the glorious liberty of the children of God" (verse 21); "the adoption, to wit, the redemption of our body" (verse 23). We are brought to our anchor of hope. Our salvation is partial now; it will be complete with the redemption of our body.

"Saved by hope" is not in conflict with being saved by faith. The salvation spoken of here relates to the redemption of the body.

Complete deliverance through redemption will be accomplished only when "this corruptible shall have put on incorruption, and this mortal shall have put on immortality" (1 Corinthians 15:54). That is the "hope which is laid up" (Colossians 1:5) and "the hope set before us" (Hebrews 6:18). It is the "blessed hope" (Titus 2:13). Further, it is "Christ in you, the hope of glory" (Colossians 1:27). Hope inspires joy in the believing heart. Those saved by faith find themselves rejoicing in hope.

**26. Likewise:**...And in like manner, —PNT, —PNIN.

**the Spirit also helpeth our infirmities:**...also supports us, —TCNT...also takes hold with us in our weakness, —MNTG ... assists us in our weakness, —MOFT.

**for we know not what we should pray for as we ought:**...we do not know how to pray aright, —MOFT.

**but the Spirit itself maketh intercession for us with groanings which cannot be uttered:**...He personally talks to God for us with feelings which our language cannot express, —SEB...requesteth for vs, —RHEM...comes to our rescue, —WUST...strongly intercedeth for us, with unutterable groans, —SCLT...the like spirit axeth for us with sorwynge, —WCLF...pleads for us with unutterable groanings, —CNFT ... pleads for us with unspeakable yearnings, —WLMS...pleads for us with sighs that are beyond words, —MOFT ... that words cannot express, —TEV ... with yearnings that can't find any words, —BECK.

**27. And he that searcheth the hearts:**...Yet he who fathoms the depths of our hearts, —TCNT.

**knoweth what [is] the mind of the Spirit:**...knows what the Spirit thinks, —WLMS...what is the meanynge of the spryte, —CRNM...knovveth vvhat the Spirit desireth, —RHEM.

**because he maketh intercession for the saints according to [the will of] God:**...he pleads for the saints, —CNFT...talks to God in behalf of holy people, —SEB...for holi men, —WCLF...in agreement with God's will, —TCNT...according to the pleasure of god, —TNDL.

**8:26, 27.** Chapter 8, solving the defeat of chapter 7, brings into focus the provision of victory: (1) a new law, "the law of the Spirit of life in Christ Jesus" (8:2), and (2) a new power to replace the weakness of the flesh.

This new power, the Holy Spirit, fulfills the righteousness of the Law (verse 4), provides power to please God (verse 8), power to live (verse 13), and power in prayer (verse 26). Verse 37 tells us that God also empowers us in suffering.

The *Amplified New Testament* gives this rendering: "So too the (Holy) Spirit comes to our aid and bears us up in our weakness." He takes the burden on himself and in our place, to share the load and make our part easier.

The Holy Spirit "maketh intercession." The ministry of prayer is spiritual ministry, and that is why we need the help of the Holy Spirit. He is able to express what we cannot put into words. Also, He knows the mind of God, so whatever the Spirit prays through us will be in perfect harmony with the will of God. Intercessory prayer reaches its greatest impact when it passes beyond the realm of our words and finds expression in the words of the Spirit and "with groanings which cannot be uttered." One of the most valuable ministries of the Spirit is that of helping us in prayer. The Spirit possessing all knowledge joins in intercession. Since He knows the will of God, we have assurance that since the intercession is according to God's will, we have the guarantee it will be answered (1 John 5:14, 15).

We have two intercessors: (1) the Lord Jesus Christ at the right hand of God prays for us; (2) the Holy Spirit here on earth prays in and through us.

**28. And we know that all things work together for good to them that love God:** . . . worcke for the best, —GNVA . . . co-operate for good, —SCLT.

**to them who are the called according to [his] purpose:** . . . to those being invited, —WLSN . . . to those who are set apart, —FNTN.

**8:28.** Though we do not always know what we should pray for as we ought, we do know that God causes all things to continually work together for our good. This does not mean Paul is teaching fatalism, the resignation to the inevitable. The assurance is conditional. Subjectively, it is to all who "love God." Objectively, it is to those "who are the called according to his purpose."

Our interests are never absent from the heart of God; our destinies are never adrift from His loving and guiding hand.

**29. For whom he did foreknow:** . . . whom God knew about long ago, —SEB . . . those on whom He set His heart beforehand, —WLMS.

**he also did predestinate:** . . . He also appointed long ago, —BECK . . . he also marked out, —TCNT . . . he predetermined, —SCLT . . . he also ordeyned before, —GNVA.

**[to be] conformed to the image of his Son:** . . . to become just like His Son, —SEB . . . to be made like to the pattern, —CNBR . . . to share the likeness of His Son, —BRKL . . . that they shulde be lyke fassyoned vnto the shape, —CRNM.

**that he might be:**

**the firstborn among many brethren:** . . . so that he might be the eldest of a great brotherhood, —MNTG . . . be the fyrst begotten, —GNVA . . . in a vast family of, —WEYM.

**30. Moreover whom he did predestinate:** . . . those whom he before approved, —SCLT . . . whom he appoynted before, —CRNM.

**them he also called: and whom he called:**

**them he also justified:** . . . He has also declared free from guilt, —WEYM . . . he also accepted as righteous, —NOYS.

**and whom he justified:** . . . He declared righteous, —YNG.

**them he also glorified:** . . . he shared his glory, —JB . . . also crowned with glory, —WEYM . . . and distinguished them, —FNTN.

**8:29, 30.** A study of Scripture on the subject of foreknowledge and predestination shows us that the way is predestined, not the individual. If that were not so, we would be saved by decree, not by faith. In His omniscience God sees all things in advance. He predestined Christ as the way, and He predestined all who are "in Christ" to be conformed to the image of Christ. He predestined that we would not have to bring ourselves to glorification by practices of legalism and religious forms.

The Greek word here translated "foreknow" is used five times in the New Testament (Acts 26:5; Romans 8:29; 11:2; 1 Peter 1:20; 2 Peter 3:17). To "foreknow" does not imply prompting or the extraordinary working of God's selective will. He foreknows by the ordinary process of His prescience (knowledge of events before they take place). No future event or thing could hide itself from God. The knowledge of those who would accept Christ could not be eliminated from the omniscience (all-knowledge) and omnipresence (everywhere present) of God. To foreknow is a divine attribute of God. He sees the past and the future just as clearly as the present. Being infinite He is not in any way limited by time or space. That God knows what will take place does not mean He is responsible for all that happens. His foreknowledge declares that He is unmistakably certain about all that will take place, but He does not determine what takes place. He knows all wrongdoings of men as well as their good deeds.

The sequence which defines the purpose of God as given in verses 28-30 is as follows: The passage begins with a statement of certainty, "And we know," followed by a reason based on that certainty, "For." God's call is associated with His purpose.

The term *predestination* has often been misunderstood. John Calvin defined predestination by saying, "God has once for all determined, both whom he would admit to salvation, and whom he would condemn to destruction" (*Institutes of the Christian Religion*, 3:21:181). He went on to state that their perdition depends on the predestination of God (ibid.).

Scripturally, predestination is never related to any person outside Christ. It always refers to those whom God foreknew would be in Christ (Romans 8:29, 30; Ephesians 1:5, 11). And the predestination is not to heaven per se, but "to be conformed to the image of his Son." To those God gives their calling, justification, and glorification.

God's purpose will be complete in us when our glorification is complete. We shall be like Jesus, the firstborn of many. Already we are glorified spiritually—sanctification begun. We are being changed "from glory to glory" (2 Corinthians 3:18). At the first resurrection (verse 23) our bodies will be glorified—sanctification completed.

**31. What shall we then say to these things?:** ... our response to these facts? —ADAM.

**If God [be] for us, who [can be] against us?:** ... If God be on our syde, —GNVA ... In view of the fact that God is on our behalf, —WUST ... what does it matter who may be against us? —NORL.

**32. He that spared not his own Son, but delivered him up for us all:** ... who did not protect, —KLGS ... but parted with Him for us all, —FNTN ... to benefit us all, —JB.

**how shall he not with him also freely give us all things?:** ... Therefore, wouldn't God give us everything, —SEB ... how can he fail to grant us also all things with him? —CNFT ... what is to hinder His favoring us with everything along with Him? —BRKL ... also bestow on us all, —HNT.

**8:31, 32.** Here is the first of six questions. From this point on through the balance of the chapter we are given the grand climax, the mountaintop of Christian position and experience. The apostle's heart was filled with absolute confidence. God who gave the best (His Son) will in no wise withhold the rest. He lavished mercy and grace, and He has more than sufficient to bestow upon His redeemed children, providing all that is needed for their good.

It was the Father who handed His Son over to suffering and death. Since God did this, and since the Son is seated at His right hand in heaven, what will He not do for His children on earth? If He was not reluctant to make such a major provision, will He not respond to any smaller favor?

**33. Who shall lay any thing to the charge of God's elect?:** ... Who shall impeach those, —WEYM ... accuse against, —RHEM ... bring a charge against, —PNIN ... accuse God's elect? —MNTG ... make accusation against the elect, —CNFT ... bring an accusation against God's elect? —WORL ... bring an accusation against God's Chosen ones? —WLSN ... the approved people of God? —SCLT.

**[It is] God that justifieth:** ... Shall God that justifieth? —ALFD ... God acquits them, —MNTG.

**8:33.** In triumphant tone Paul declares that no one dare lay a charge against the elect of God since God himself has justified them. There is no ground for bringing charges. Neither men nor Satan can resurrect the believer's past. No forgiven sin can ever be held against the forgiven since God has justified them. Satan, the "accuser of the brethren," may try to harass, but that which God has forgiven He will never remember against us anymore.

God alone is the Judge. When He justifies, no claim of past wrong will be held against us. Unconfessed sin is a different matter.

The word "justified" appears often in this epistle. It is used for the last time in this verse. And who shall accuse the man whom God declares righteous? No accusation will stand when God, the righteous Judge, has justified a person.

**34. Who [is] he that condemneth?:** ... who is the condemner? —BRKL ... What judge can doom us? —CNBR.

**[It is] Christ that died:**

**yea rather, that is risen again:** ... more than that, He rose, —BECK.

**who is even at the right hand of God:** ... at God's right side, —SEB.

**who also maketh intercession for us:** ... is there to intercede for us ... He pleads in our behalf, —NORL ... who actually pleads for us! —MOFT.

**8:34.** The next stroke of the hammer drives the nail with greater finality. There is no ground for condemnation. The Christ who died for us is at the Father's right hand interceding for us. Four great truths are our assurance and protection: (1) Christ died for our sins. He is our propitiation. (2) He is risen again for our justification (4:25). We are "saved by his life" (5:10). (3) "At the right hand of God," He is our representative. (4) Making intercession, He is our Advocate pleading our case (1 John 2:1).

Our future in glory is assured by the perfect defeat of our adversary, and the perfect intercession of our Advocate. Christ died, He arose, He ascended, He intercedes—all for us!

**35. Who shall separate us from the love of Christ?:** ... What can drive us from the love of Christ? —FNTN ... from the charitie of Christ? —RHEM.

**[shall] tribulation, or distress:** ... Will sorrow, hardship, —BECK ... Will trouble, or difficulties, —TCNT ... Will trouble, pain, —SEB ... shall anguish, or calamity, —MNTG ... or oppression? —FNTN.

**or persecution, or famine, or nakedness, or peril, or sword?:** ... or even attacked, —JB ... persecution, having no food, —SEB ... or want of clothing, —TCNT ... or danger? —RHEM.

**36. As it is written:**

**For thy sake we are killed all the day long:** ... on account of you! —FNTN ... we are being put to death the livelong day, —WLMS ... we are being massacred daily, —JB ... we are in danger of death at all times, —TEV ... trying to kill us, —WEYM.

**we are accounted as sheep for the slaughter:** ... We are regarded, —FNTN ... as sheep destined for slaughter, —WEYM, —WUST...as shepe apoynted to be slayne, —TNDL.

**8:35, 36.** With another masterful stroke of the hammer Paul drives home the truth of "no separation." No one can drive a wedge and create distance between Christ's love and us. No one can cause Him to cease loving us. No power outside us can cause us to cease loving Him.

The apostle was convinced beyond the shadow of a doubt that no opposing force can bring about separation between Christ and the Christian. He lists several forces which work to separate us from His love.

"Distress" speaks of being surrounded by difficult circumstances until one is literally in a tight squeeze. "Persecution" is associated with tribulation and affliction. "Famine" is absence of food. Of this, we in this land know little, but millions in other countries suffer and die because of this. "Nakedness" does not refer to immodest, immoral dress, but to the fact of not having sufficient clothing and no means of securing any. Paul spoke of being "in fastings often, in cold and nakedness" (2 Corinthians 11:27). "Peril" refers to danger and risk. "Sword" refers to the threat of martyrdom. This threat was in Paul's mind. He knew what it was to be left for dead after being stoned. Hebrews 11 records other heroes of faith who were victorious over all types of external difficulties, including death.

The perils mentioned by Paul may not be common to us where we live, but we are faced with numberless spiritual perils which threaten our relationship. The one thing that can separate us is spiritual death, described in verse 13. The believer can choose to leave Christ out of his life; then he is separated from salvation by his own will.

**37. Nay, in all these things we are more than conquerors:** ... Yet amidst all these trials we are more than victorious, —TCNT ... Yet amid all these things, —WEYM ... helps us win an overwhelming victory, —BECK ... we overcome strongly, —TNDL ... we have complete victory, —TEV ... we keep on gloriously conquering, —WLMS ... we do more than overcome, —WLSN ... we more than come out ahead by him, —KLGS ... we overcome because of him, —CNFT.
**through him that loved us:**

**8:37.** *Hupernikōmen* is rendered "we are more than conquerors." The word comes from *huper* (Latin, "super") meaning "above," and *nikaō*, from *nikē*, meaning "victory." The literal meaning is "we are super victors." A whole phrase in English is needed to translate one strong, vivid Greek word.

Despite the seven enemies listed in verse 35, we are super victors. Through the centuries Christians have often been "accounted as sheep for the

slaughter," but they lived triumphantly through it all.

The ability to be a super victor is not based on human ability or self-determination. The victory comes "through him that loved us." The Christ who conquered every foe because of His love for us imparts His grace and strength to make us "more than conquerors." *Hupernikōmen* is a very expressive term. *Nike* was the god of victory; in Christ we can be "hyper" victorious, *super*conquerors.

**38. For I am persuaded:** ... For I am sure, —RHEM ... I have full assurance, —WLMS ... I am fully persuaded, —MNTG.
**that neither death, nor life:**
**nor angels, nor principalities, nor powers:** ... neither the lower ranks of evil angels, —WEYM ... among angels or spiritual powers, —NORL ... no angels or their rulers, —BECK ... nor any force, —TCNT ... nether vertues ... nether strengthe, —WCLF ... nor all the Principalities and Powers of Angels, —CNBR.
**nor things present, nor things to come:** ... nothing that exists, —JB ... neither present nor future affairs, —BRKL ... nor the forces of nature, —WEYM.

**39. Nor height, nor depth, nor any other creature:** ... nor evil forces above or beneath, —WLMS ... nothing above or below, —BECK ... nor anything else in all creation, —RSV ... nor any other created thing, —WEYM ... nor any power in the whole creation, —CNBR.
**shall be able to separate us from the love of God:** ... will be able to part us, —MOFT ... shalbe able to depart vs, —GNVA.
**which is in Christ Jesus our Lord:** ... which rests upon us, —WEYM ... displayed in Christ Jesus, —TCNT ... made visible in, —JB ... shewed in Christ, —TNDL.

**8:38, 39.** "I am persuaded" can be translated "absolutely convinced," "certain," "stand convinced." There was no uncertainty in Paul's mind. Nothing need "separate us from the love of Christ" (verse 35). The one thing required of us, made possible by grace, is that we be willing to let His victory be made real in us moment by moment. This means that all self-interest will be subordinated to His lordship.

In triumphant confidence Paul wrote of the enemies which must be contended with and defeated. For the most part they are in couplets.

"Death" and "life." There is nothing to fear from the aloneness of one and the trials of the other. Physical death cannot alter the believer's spiritual union with Christ Jesus (1 Corinthians 6:17). It can only enhance the reality of His presence (2 Corinthians 5:6; Philippians 1:21).

"Angels" and "principalities." Invisible, mysterious forces aligned against God's people are conquered foes through Christ. "Powers" refers to hostility in the spirit world. In context these angels would be only evil angels who fell with Satan. God's angels are busy ministering to those who "shall be heirs of salvation" (Hebrews 1:14). The principalities are high-ranking fallen angels. Gabriel needed help from Michael to overcome the "prince of the kingdom of Persia" (Daniel 10:13); evil spirits are no match for Jesus!

"Things present" and "things to come" sum up the unlimited dimensions of time, as "height" and "depth" sum up the endless proportions of space. *Hupsōma* was worshiped as the god of high places, and *Bathos* as the god of the deep. No "god" can be high enough to surpass the love of God; nor can any be deep enough to undermine His love.

The secret is to remain "in Christ." Eternal security is provided, but it is only available as long as we remain "in Christ." By the decision of our will we came into the relationship of being "in Christ." By a decision of our will we can choose to terminate that relationship. If we do that we have lost our security. In summary, there is nothing in all creation that can separate us from the love of Christ outside of ourselves. The only thing that can effect that separation is human will.

## Chapter 9

**1. I say the truth in Christ, I lie not:** . . . I am not falsifying, *—BRKL* . . . I speak the verity in Christ, *—RHEM* . . . I speak the truth in Christ, *—CNFT* . . . as a Christian man, *—WLMS* . . . as a Christian, *—TCNT* . . . and do not misrepresent, *—MRDK* . . . I do not speak falsely, *—CMPB* . . . now is no pretence, *—JB.*

**my conscience also bearing me witness in the Holy Ghost:** . . . because my conscience enlightened by the Holy Spirit, *—WLMS* . . . guided and enlightened by the Holy Ghost, *—LOCK* . . . and my own conscience, prompted by the Holy Spirit, *—WAY* . . . my conscience in union with the Holy Spirit assures me of it too, *—JB* . . . fortified by the Holy Spirit, *—BRKL* . . . ruled by the Holy Spirit, *—TEV* . . . bearing joint-testimony, *—WUST.*

**2. That I have great heaviness and continual sorrow in my heart:** . . . I suffer endless anguish of heart, *—MOFT* . . . my heart is never free from sorrow, *—TCNT* . . . intense grief and unceasing distress, *—BRKL* . . . I have a consuming grief, *—WUST* . . . I have great sadness, *—DOUY* . . . great grief and unceasing anguish, *—MKNT* . . . a pain that never leaves me, *—BECK* . . . and incessant anguish, *—SCLT* . . . and never-ending pain, *—KLGS.*

**9:1, 2.** The first eight chapters of the Book of Romans are doctrinal, setting forth great basic truths. Chapters 12 through 16 are practical exhortations. Chapters 9 to 11 have often been called parenthetical, and a casual reader might consider them unrelated to the rest of the book. Closer study, however, reveals they are an integral part of

Romans. Understanding how the principles apply to Israel makes it possible to move properly from the theological portion to the practical section.

Chapter 9 opens with Paul's great burden for his Jewish brethren. He stated that he had a joint witness of his conscience and of the Holy Spirit regarding the sincerity of his expression of the "great heaviness and continual sorrow" he carried in his heart for them.

His concern bore witness to the fact that his beloved kinsmen were eternally lost apart from the saving grace of Christ. What a Christlike spirit Paul exhibited in his intense love for those who beat him, cast him into prison, cursed him, and reviled him.

**3. For I could wish that myself were accursed from Christ:** . . . For I was on the point of praying to be accursed, *—MNTG* . . . would I be myself the accursed scapegoat, *—WAY* . . . that I myself might be sentenced to separation, *—NORL* . . . and banished from Christ, *—HNT* . . . to be anathema, *—RHEM* . . . cut off from Christ, *—RSV.*

**for my brethren, my kinsmen according to the flesh:** . . . if so I might deliver my brothers, *—WAY* . . . my own blood relatives, *—NORL* . . . my kindred, *—YNG.*

**9:3.** Paul outlined God's dealings with His chosen people in the past, in the present, and in the future. He had been writing concerning the Church; now he discussed a nation and its destiny. In this division of Romans the objections and questions regarding the promised special privileges of Israel are clarified. God will keep His word to Israel, for Israel is only temporarily set aside because of unbelief. Chapter 9 deals with Israel's election, chapter 10 with Israel's rejection, and chapter 11 with Israel's restoration.

This division begins with the expression of Paul's pain, his "heaviness" and "sorrow." The Berkeley Version expresses it as "intense grief and unceasing distress." Paul was so burdened for his kinsmen in the flesh that he could wish himself accursed from Christ, were that possible, if that would bring about the salvation of Israel.

The tense used in the Greek is the imperfect of the verb *euchomai* and is well expressed by "I could wish." Paul knew that one person cannot take the place of another in the matter of his will. Each one must decide for or against God for himself. The intensity of his love prompted his strong statement.

There is only one source of love such as Paul experienced. It comes from the heart of God. It is the same kind of love that caused God to send the Son and that caused Jesus to be made a curse for us (2 Corinthians 5:21; Galatians 3:13). The only way we can be recipients of this love is for the Holy Spirit to pour it into our hearts (5:5).

His comment reminds one of the similar expression of Moses (Exodus 32:32f.). Moses was prepared to perish for his people; Paul was also prepared to perish for them.

**4. Who are Israelites:**
**to whom [pertaineth] the adoption, and the glory, and the covenants:** ... the sonship, the glorious Presence, *—BRKL* ... theirs the Glory of the Visible Presence ... were His covenants made, *—WAY* ... They were made God's family, *—BECK* ... whom God adopted as sons, *—NOYS* ... the Shekinah glory, *—MNTG* ... and the testament, Douay.
**and the giving of the law, and the service [of God], and the promises:** ... the divine legislation, *—MOFT* ... To them was revealed the Temple-ritual, *—WAY* ... and a form of divine worship, *—LOCK.*
**5. Whose [are] the fathers:** ... They trace their descent, *—TCNT* ... from the famous Hebrew ancestors, *—TEV.*
**and of whom as concerning the flesh Christ [came]:** ... in so far as He is human, theirs is the Messiah, *—WAY* ... in human lineage sprang, *—BRKL* ... according to His body came Christ, *—BECK* ... as a human being, *—TEV.*
**who is over all, God blessed for ever. Amen:** ... is supreme over all things, *—TCNT* ... is exalted above all, *—WEYM* ... to whom be praises and benediction, *—MRDK* ... unto the ages, *—CLMT.*

**9:4, 5.** The earnestness of Paul's pain, and of his deep desire for the salvation of his kin, is explained in part in these verses. Paul wrote of the greatness of his people, their special privileges, the magnificence of their inheritance and hopes, all of which they forfeited by their unbelief.

Eight special privileges are listed: (1) adopted, sonship in God's earthly family; (2) glory, the Shekinah presence of God; (3) covenants, made to "the fathers"; (4) the Law given at Sinai; (5) the service of God, worship as detailed in Leviticus; (6) the promises of the Messiah and others through Him; (7) the Fathers—Abraham, Isaac, and Jacob—God's chosen leaders for a special people; (8) the promised Messiah, who came in the Person of One virgin born, the Son of God.

Paul ascribed full deity to Christ here. The most natural translation of the Greek is "Christ who is God over all, forever praised! Amen!" There is the same ascription of full Godhood to Jesus here as in John 1:1, Philippians 2:6, and Hebrews 1:8.

**6. Not as though the word of God hath taken none effect:** ... Not as implying that God's message fell short, *—BRKL* ... I am not implying that God's promise 'to Israel' has been stultified, *—WAY* ... I am far from suggesting, *—TCNT* ... it is not that God's word has failed, *—WLMS* ... not such as that the word of God has lapsed, *—CNFT* ... has come to naught,

*—HNSN* ... is frustrate, *—RHEM* ... had fallen to the ground, *—WSLY* ... has failed of being accomplished, *—SAWR* ... hath miscarried, *—DOUY.*
**For they [are] not all Israel, which are of Israel:** ... Not all who are descended from Israel are the real Israel, *—BECK* ... that comprise the true Israel, *—WAY.*
**7. Neither, because they are the seed of Abraham, [are they] all children:** ... who are the race, *—LOCK* ... are for that reason his real children, *—BECK* ... nether are they all chyldren strayght waye, *—CRNM* ... does not constitute them all his sons, *—WAY.*
**but, In Isaac shall thy seed be called:** ... your posterity be reckoned, *—WEYM* ... your descendants will be counted, *—WLMS.*

**9:6, 7.** God had given great honor to Israel. His Son was born into the human family by a Jewish mother. He was raised in a Jewish home, attended a Jewish synagogue, and received a Jewish education.

Paul never denied that the Jews were God's chosen people. Not all Jews rejected Christ; nearly all His early followers were Jews. God always had a righteous remnant who were true to Him. The apostle in summary stated that Israel is the chosen people, but to be a member of Israel means more than racial descent.

God had not failed to keep His promise. It was limited to the remnant. Physical descent from Abraham does not make one a child of God (John 8:37-44; Galatians 3:7). Ishmael was the seed of the flesh. Isaac was the child of promise. Mere birth into the nation did not make a person a real Israelite. God-accepted Israelites were those of spiritual character.

The Israel distinguished from the Israel of natural descent is the true Israel. Jesus made a parallel distinction when He spoke of Nathanael as "an Israelite indeed" (John 1:47). Paul referred to the true Israel as Israel "according to the Spirit" (Galatians 4:29, NASB). The same distinction was stated earlier as related to the term "Jew" and to circumcision (2:29). Both believing Jews and believing Gentiles are included in "the Israel of God" (Galatians 6:16).

**8. That is, They which are the children of the flesh:** ... Which means: ... Not his physical descendants make up the children of God, *—BRKL* ... children born in a natural way, *—BECK* ... by natural descent, *—WEYM.*
**these [are] not the children of God:**
**but the children of the promise are counted for the seed:** ... to whom the promise applied, *—WAY* ... will be spoken of as descendants, *—KLGS* ... reckoned as a posterity, *—CNFT.*
**9. For this [is] the word of promise:**
**At this time will I come, and Sarah shall have a son:** ... About this time next year, *—BRKL.*

**10. And not only [this]; but when Rebecca also had conceived by one, [even] by our father Isaac:** ... Even more to the point, –JB ... Nor is that all. There is also the case of Rebecca, –TCNT ... when she had cohabited with one [man], –MRDK ... She was soon to bear two children, –WEYM ... when Rebecca became pregnant, –MOFT ... who was impregnated by our forefather Isaac, –WLMS ... when she was to have twins, –NORL ... had conceived two sons by the same husband, –CNBR.

**9:8-10.** The "children of the promise" were those who, like Abraham, believed the promise of God and as a result were Abraham's spiritual offspring. Paul made it very plain that the Jews could not base their claims to "election" upon their fleshly relationship to Abraham. The fleshly children were not necessarily the children of God. This was contrary to the general viewpoint.

Israel "according to the flesh" was the avenue by which God chose to bring the Messiah, and as such Israel enjoyed certain privileges. God's promise to Abraham or his seed that he should be the heir of the world was not by the Law, but through righteousness by faith (4:13). That promise still continues even to this day. Abraham is the father in a spiritual sense of all those who believe, Jew or Gentile, who walk in the steps of that faith (4:12). Paul exploded the idea that being a physical descendant of Abraham automatically made one a child of God.

The emphasis here is on the premium God places on our standing on His promises. The "word of promise" of verse 9 is the same as "word of God" in verse 6. Children of God are the children of promise (verse 8).

God promised Abraham a son and kept His promise by performing a miracle. That son of promise was Isaac. In God's sovereign plan, Sarah's son, not Hagar's or Keturah's son, was the one selected.

The Jews understood the selection process among their forebears. Ishmael was the son of Abraham, born into the patriarchal family. But no Jew would acknowledge Ishmael's descendants, the Arabs, as being the chosen people. Esau was as much a son of Isaac as was Jacob, and yet no Jew would countenance Esau as their leader. Abraham pleaded with God on behalf of Ishmael (Genesis 17:18), and Isaac tried to give the patriarchal blessing to Esau (Genesis 27:1-4, 30-33). But the promise came through Isaac.

By that line of argument Paul presented the fact that the seed was not by human lineage but through the righteousness of faith.

**11. (For [the children] being not yet born, neither having done any good or evil:** ... nor having practiced, –WUST ... and had done nothing, –HNT.

**that the purpose of God according to election might stand:** ... to confirm the divine purpose in election, –MOFT ... dominated by an act of selecting out, –WUST ... in order that the purpose of God's choice might prevail, –BRKL ... so that God's purpose of choice might stay, –KLGS ... may carry out His purpose according to His choice, –BECK ... according to election might continue, –SAWR ... according to the predetermination of his own choice, –LOCK ... might not be frustrated, –WEYM ... God's purpose ... is unconditional, –WAY.

**not of works, but of him that calleth;):** ... not on human merit, –JB ... independent of deeds, entirely a matter of his calling, –HNT ... yet God had made an election, –NORL ... conditioned not on men's actions but on God's calling them, –WLMS.

**9:11.** Two expressions need explanation. First, "the purpose of God" was to have a family who, through the righteousness provided by His Son, would be like His Son (8:29). The second term needing explanation is "election." Election is not based on the "flesh" (verse 8), nor on "works" (verse 11). The basis is "him that calleth."

The Jew cannot say, "I am elected because I descended from Abraham." The self-righteous cannot say, "We are elected because of our good works." The legalist cannot say, "I am chosen because I have obeyed the Law." Election is not based on works, but on the call of God. Those who answer the call are the elected. The Jew, the self-righteous, the legalist, all could argue their case, but to no avail. God will save whom He will. And who is the saved one? The answer is, "Whosoever believeth in him should not perish, but have everlasting life" (John 3:16).

God has made possible a way, a predestined way, whereby all (Jew and Gentile) who believe are elected. The unrighteous Gentiles and the self-righteous Jews can be saved only through faith.

**12. It was said unto her:**
**The elder shall serve the younger:** ... The superior shall be subject to the inferior, –WLSN ... The elder shall be subject to the younger, –WAY ... The greater shall be slaving for the inferior, –CNDT ... will be bondservant, –WEYM ... will be a slave to the younger, –WLMS.

**13. As it is written:**
**Jacob have I loved, but Esau have I hated:** ... To Jacob I was drawn, but Esau I repudiated, –BRKL.

**9:12, 13.** Not all the descendants of Abraham, Isaac, and Jacob were within the design of God to carry out His plan. There was more than physical descent; there was specific selection. Paul noted that there was electing within the family of

Abraham's physical descendants, a point the Jews understood and accepted.

A further point is that the election was not on the basis of deed or merit; Jacob was chosen and Esau was rejected before they were born. The only preference would normally be priority of birth, and God disregarded that. No legal works, no Jewish birth, could give a person a claim that God must honor. He acts according to His sovereign will.

Esau never served Jacob; therefore, we know that God was speaking of something besides individual election. God was speaking of the time when Esau's descendants the Edomites would serve Israel (Malachi 1:1, 4). Therefore the election here is corporate.

Jacob was chosen to be in the line of Christ. All election pertaining to salvation is corporate in the Elect One, Christ Jesus (Ephesians 1:4).

"Loved" and "hated" are contrasted. It is not a literal hatred, but the same kind Jesus requires, as stated in Luke 14:26. A form of the Greek term *miseō* ("hate") is used here in verse 13 (*emisēsa*). It does not mean to detest or to reject. It means to place in much lower priority in one's concern.

It was not possible for both Esau and Jacob to receive the birthright and be in the line of Messiah. Therefore one must be chosen (elected) and the other not chosen (hated).

Our love for Jesus must be so much greater than our love for father, mother, and all else, that by comparison the lesser love could be called "hate." There will be times when we have to choose between Him and other loved ones. When choice is unavoidable, the "not chosen," whether Esau or our treasures, may be described as "hated."

The choice of Jacob rather than Esau had nothing to do with their eternal salvation. Esau still had the opportunity to serve God and put his faith in Him. The repentance he could not find was the recovery of the birthright he had forfeited; he did not seek to repent of his profane lifestyle and immorality (Hebrews 12:16, 17).

The destiny of Israel has been shaped by their experience with two persons—Moses and Jacob. The Jews were separated from other peoples to be God's witness to the nations and to be custodians of His law. Their choice was not based upon (1) numerical strength—Deuteronomy 7:7; (2) power and wealth—Deuteronomy 8:18; or (3) righteousness—Deuteronomy 9:6.

This passage lays the foundation for the truth of God's sovereignty over Israel. Israel, God's chosen nation, came into existence by the supernatural act of God. The bodies of Abraham and Sarah were as good as dead, but God performed a miracle to beget Abraham's seed. If God had not acted, there would have been no nation.

**14. What shall we say then? [Is there] unrighteousness with God?:** ... what do we infer? That with God there is injustice? —BRKL ... what shall we conclude? That God is unjust? —NORL ... Do you dare insinuate that partialityinjustice, in factis an attribute of God? —WAY ... Is there iniquitie with God? —RHEM.

**God forbid:** ... Perish the thought! —BRKL ... No indeed, —MNTG ... Away with the thought! God's decision is beyond challenge, —WAY.

**15. For he saith to Moses:**
**I will have mercy on whom I will have mercy:** ... I will do kindness, —YNG ... on whom I choose to have mercy, —MOFT.

**and I will have compassion on whom I will have compassion:** ... I will pity whom I want to pity, —BECK.

**16. So then [it is] not of him that willeth, nor of him that runneth:** ... it isn't a question of, —ADAM ... is not on account of man's will or his readiness, —NORL ... So it depends not upon man's will or exertion, —RSV ... nor of him who is racing, —CNDT ... it doesn't depend on anyone wanting it or trying hard, —BECK ... not on human wishes or human efforts, —TCNT.

**but of God that showeth mercy:** ... that exercises mercy, —SAWR ... but of the pitying God, —HNSN ... but on His own fiat, —WAY.

**17. For the scripture saith unto Pharaoh:**
**Even for this same purpose have I raised thee up, that I might show my power in thee:** ... For this very thing, —PNIN ... to high position ... to show My power in dealing with you, —NORL ... I set you up high, to present in you the evidence of My power, —BRKL ... that I may exhibit my power, —HNSN ... to demonstrate My power, —BECK.

**and that my name might be declared throughout all the earth:** ... so that My name may be famed, —BRKL ... my name may be scattered abroad, —KLGS ... might be published abroad, —HNT, —WORL ... might be renowned through, —LOCK ... the entire earth, —CNDT ... in all the land, —YNG.

**9:14-17.** In the pattern found so often in Romans, Paul opened this portion with a question, "Is there unrighteousness with God?" The answer is a resounding, "God forbid." Paul presented a discussion that contains one of the most profound mysteries of our world: Israel must leave God to His sovereignty. Like Jacob, Moses received the mercy of God and by obeying became the deliverer of Israel. Like Esau, Pharaoh rejected God's mercy and was hardened. Moses was the vessel of mercy; Pharaoh, the vessel of wrath.

God does not create human beings for the purpose of condemning them; nor is He responsible for the sinfulness of men. In Pharaoh's case God gave him chance after chance to repent. Pharaoh's heart was not hardened until after he had rejected the light which came from God. The Scripture recounts 10 times when it is said that Pharaoh hardened himself. Pharaoh did not want God; he hardened his heart first of his own volition; then God made him an example of His displeasure with sin and of those who spurn His love and grace.

God gave Pharaoh, as well as Moses, an outstanding revelation of His power and of His mercy. Moses was responsive, but Pharaoh was rebellious. The revelation melted and shaped Moses, while it hardened Pharaoh. The gospel does the same wherever it is preached; some will yield, and others will reject (2 Corinthians 2:15-17).

God has elected that "whosoever believeth" on His Son shall have eternal life. If the Jew objects that God ignores his rights by lineage, by law, and by nationality, God reminds him that He has elected that all who believe shall be saved.

Recognition of the will of God for the salvation of all men completely negates any deterministic system of theology. God "will have all men to be saved" (1 Timothy 2:4); He "is the Saviour of all men, specially of those that believe" (1 Timothy 4:10). Potentially He is the Saviour of every person born. Only those who believe and receive are actually saved, but His mercy extends to all (Romans 5:18; 2 Peter 3:9).

God's sovereignty never excludes His mercy. The fact that any person enjoys God's blessing is of His mercy freely given.

**18. Therefore hath he mercy on whom he will [have mercy], and whom he will he hardeneth:** . . . He hardens the heart, —WEYM, —RSV . . . and he makes anyone stubborn just as he pleases, —MOFT . . . He confirms in their stubbornness, —WAY . . . just as he chooses, —TCNT.

**19. Thou wilt say then unto me:** . . . you will retort, —MOFT.

**Why doth he yet find fault?:** . . . Why does He still complain, —BRKL . . . Why does He still blame people, —ADAM . . . He still persist in finding fault? —WUST.

**For who hath resisted his will?:** . . . For who withstandeth his purpose? —PNIN . . . for His counsel who hath resisted, —YNG . . . since no one can oppose his will? —JB . . . who can oppose his purpose? —HNT . . . who hath withstood His will? —CLMT.

**9:18, 19.** This is one of the strongest statements in the New Testament about the sovereignty of God's will. This must be balanced with the many invitations in the New Testament to believe and accept Christ.

God does not entice nor cause men to do evil (James 1:13, 14). When people do wrong, it comes from their depraved nature.

The rabbis of Paul's day looked upon God's covenant with Israel as such that no matter how sinful

Israel was, their place in God could never change. They held to the premise of absolute predestination; the Gentiles were to be destroyed, but nothing could dissolve God's covenant with the Jews.

Paul meets the objection offered by sincere Jewish believers. They could not understand how Israel, to whom belonged the honors listed in 9:4, 5, could be set aside for the Gentiles, who were brought from their alienated and lost status to the place of blessing. The apostle proves that the Word of God cannot fail. He makes a distinction between the natural offspring and the spiritual offspring. God-accepted Israelites are those of spiritual character.

Perhaps the following illustrates God's election. The door to the temple of salvation says "whosoever will may come," but inside is inscribed the message "chosen . . . in him before the foundation of the world" (Ephesians 1:4).

God has always had total omniscience, foreknowing all things potential and actual. Because He is God He can have total prescience and yet allow men to make genuine choices of their own wills. Man's will is not free in the absolute sense, as God's is, but man is totally free in the decision as to who will be his master—either God or Satan. This choice determines his eternal destiny.

**20. Nay but, O man, who art thou that repliest against God?:** . . . I might rather ask . . . frail mortal, who are arguing with God? —TCNT . . . who are you anyway, to talk back to God? —BRKL . . . mere human creature that you are, dare arraign God? —WAY . . . who art thou replying against God? —WLSN . . . whych disputest with God? —CRNM . . . to cross-examine God? —JB . . . to answer back to God? —RSV.

**Shall the thing formed say to him that formed [it]:** . . . Will anything shaped by a man say to him, —BECK . . . Doth the vvorke say to him that vvrought it, —RHEM . . . The moldable material shall not say, —WUST . . . say to him who moulded it, —WEYM.

**Why hast thou made me thus?:** . . . Why did you make me this shape? —JB . . . Why didst thou fashion me into this form? —WAY.

**9:20.** It is incongruous for the creature to judge the Creator. Men are not lost because God has hardened them. They are hardened because they are lost; they are lost because they are sinners. God is not responsible for man's sin, but He offers mercy to all.

**21. Hath not the potter power over the clay:** . . . dominion, —MRDK . . . in dealing with clay, a perfect right, —TCNT . . . authority over, —KLGS . . . rightful power, —WEYM . . . at his absolute disposal, —WAY.

**of the same lump to make one vessel unto honour, and another unto dishonour?:** . . . to fashion of the same paste, —WAY . . . out of the same mass, —SCLT . . . out of the same Mixture, —WLSN . . . the one for distinguished service, *—NORL* ... one utensil for noble use, *—BRKL* ... one thing for a noble purpose and another for a lowly purpose? *—BECK* ... one jar as a decorative item and another jar for everyday use? *—ADAM* ... another for degrading service? *—WLMS*.

**22.** **[What] if God, willing to show [his] wrath:** ... desiring to demonstrate His wrath, *—WUST* ... wishing to exhibit his displeasure, *—HNSN* ... wishing to exhibit his indignation, *—WLSN*.

**and to make his power known:** ... and to reveal all His irresponsible power, *—WAY*.

**endured with much longsuffering:** ... yet He endures long and patiently, *—NORL* ... has tolerated most patiently, *—MOFT* ... tolerated with much longsuffering, *—HNT* ... with great patience enduring the agents, *—BRKL* ... suffered wyth longe pacyence, *—CRNM* ... susteined in much patience, *—RHEM*.

**the vessels of wrath fitted to destruction:** ... the vases of wrath, *—ADAM* ... the objects of his anger, ripe and ready to be destroyed? *—MOFT* ... made ready to damnation, *—GNVA*.

**9:21, 22.** The apostle offers another illustration of God's sovereignty. As the potter has absolute sovereignty over the clay, so God has absolute sovereignty over men. God does not need to answer man because He is infinite and independent. Even though He is unanswerable for what He does, He can be trusted to act in consistency with His character. And though He is free to act according to His pleasure, He is patient and full of longsuffering. His sovereignty is exercised in mercy.

The potter may take a lump of clay. Twisting it in half, he places one part on the worktable and makes of it a beautiful, graceful, almost priceless piece of pottery. Out of the same lump of clay he will take the other half and make it into a common, ordinary vessel that could be bought for a few cents at some store. Both vessels are made from the same lump of clay, by the same master potter. First Corinthians 10:1-12 illustrates this point very well.

Isolate this passage from other Bible truths, and it seems to suggest partiality on God's part. Unfortunately, some, taking it out of context, have made it a basic doctrine. They have divorced teaching on election from teaching on divine foreknowledge, resulting in a religious fatalism giving license for sin.

**23.** **And that he might make known the riches of his glory on the vessels of mercy:** ... made his mercy flow forth, *—MRDK* ... to the recipients of mercy, *—BRKL* ... which he had previously prepared for majesty, *—HNT* ... which He flooded with His mercy, *—WAY*.

**which he had afore prepared unto glory:**

**9:23.** The omnipotent God may do with that which belongs to Him just as He wills. So even if a distorted teaching of election were correct, and

if God would assign certain men to go to hell and certain men to go to heaven, God would still be just because He would be disposing of His property as He wills. He is the omnipotent God.

God's sovereignty, however, is always in harmony with divine foreknowledge. Being omniscient, or all-knowing, knowing the end from the beginning, and knowing before the world was ever made what I would do concerning His Son, knowing what all my decisions would be, God predestinated me as a Christian to be conformed to the image of His Son and to be made an heir of the inheritance of life as it is in Christ Jesus. God in His mercy has based His every move and plan upon His divine foreknowledge of choices we would make.

God's patience is revealed again and again. The judgments of His wrath have always been preceded with much longsuffering. That was true of Cain, of Pharaoh, of Lot and Sodom. Warning after warning is given until the offender crosses an invisible line and there remains no more repentance but "a certain fearful looking for of judgment and fiery indignation" (Hebrews 10:27).

**24.** **Even us, whom he hath called:**

**not of the Jews only, but also of the Gentiles?:** ... not only from among the Jews, *—BRCL*.

**9:24.** Not only has God been longsuffering in judgment, but the bestowal of His mercy has always been impartial and all of grace. There is no difference between Jew or Gentile (Romans 10:12; cf. Lamentations 3:22, 23). The called were not found among the Jews only but also among the Gentiles. The promise of salvation was not based on nationality but is "of him that calleth" (verse 11).

**25.** **As he saith also in Osee:** ... That is exactly what God says in Hosea, *—JB* ... as was prophesied in Hosea, *—ET*.

**I will call them my people, which were not my people:** ... I will give the title of, *—BRCL* ... that was not mine, *—WAY* ... I will make them my people who were not my people, *—ET*.

**and her beloved, which was not beloved:** ... I will call My loved ones, *—BECK* ... I will love her which I did not love, *—ET* ... and an unbeloved, beloved, *—CNFT* ... I never loved, *—JB* ... and the unloved nation, *—NEB*.

**26.** **And it shall come to pass, [that] in the place where it was said unto them, Ye [are] not my people:** ... and it will happen that, *—ET* ... in the very place where they were told, "you are no people of mine," *—NEB*.

**there shall they be called the children of the living God:** ... of the ever-living God, *—WEYM* ... they shall be numbered with God's people, *—ET* ... sons of the living God, *—BRCL*.

**9:25, 26.** Hosea, through his own tragic domestic life, saw a picture of the relationship between God and Israel. When he took Gomer as his wife, and she later gave birth to a son, he acknowledged the child as his. But he was convinced that the second and third children were not his. The names he gave them expressed his disappointment—Lo-ruhamah (meaning one for whom no natural affection is felt) and Lo-ammi (meaning no kin of mine). Their names pictured God's attitude toward His people Israel. But God will not allow that broken relationship to remain forever. He looks forward to the day when those who at present are estranged from Him will again be His people, and when those who now have no claim on His kindly feelings will again be objects of His mercy.

There is a principle of divine action at work in God's extension of His mercy. He is always desirous of restoring those who have departed from His favor. The Gentile rejection of God is described in a general way in 1:18-32. Just as God promised to restore Israel to His love and favor, He promised grace and mercy to Gentiles.

The revelation that Jews and Gentiles stood on equal ground before God was astounding to Jews. As the "minister of Jesus Christ to the Gentiles" (15:16), Paul placed great importance on that revelation. He called it "the mystery, which was kept secret since the world began" (16:25). Ephesians 3:1-9 explains this mystery, defined as "that the Gentiles should be fellow heirs" to Christ.

It was always God's will that all men be saved. Ruth is one example of the Gentiles who came to God through Jewish witness. When God chose Abraham it was with the intent that all the world be blessed. The Jews had lost the sense of their reason for being. When they failed to take the Word to all, both they and Gentiles suffered inestimable loss.

God's dealings with Israel were based on His wisdom, His sovereignty, and His Word. The prophecy of Hosea foretold a revival by which the blessing of God would ultimately reach Gentiles also. No Gentiles had ever been called the people of God, but now both Jews and Gentiles are brought into the Church, the great New Testament body (Ephesians 2:12-19).

**27. Esaias also crieth concerning Israel:** ... Isaiah shouted out about Israel, –KLGS ... Besides, Isaiah crieth, –MKNT ... Isaiah also prophesied over Israel, –ET ... cries in anguish concerning Israel, –WUST ... exclaims concerning Israel, –TCNT ... how the cry of Isaiah peals over Israel, –WAY.

**Though the number of the children of Israel be as the sand of the sea:** ... schal be as grauel of the see, –WCLF ... are as numberless as the sands,

–WLMS ... are as uncountable as, –ET ... be countless as the sands, –NEB.

**a remnant shall be saved:** ... but it is only the remnant who will be saved, –BRCL ... the residue, –CNDT ... only a remnant, –RSV ... the leftovers shall be saved, –BRKL ... the remaines shal be saued, –RHEM ... there will always be some leftovers, –ET ... of them will live, –MRDK.

**28. For he will finish the work, and cut [it] short in righteousness:** ... for "a conclusive and concise accounting," –CNDT ... the Lord fulfills his word speedily in justice, –CNFT ... for he executes and performs his word, –SAWR ... abbridging it in equitie, –RHEM.

**because a short work will the Lord make upon the earth:** ... for thoroughly and with dispatch, –BRKL ... fully and without delay, –TCNT ... the Lord will carry out His orders, –NORL ... will completely and decisively execute His sentence, –BECK.

**29. And as Esaias said before:** ... as Isaiah has before announced, –HNSN ... Even as in an earlier passage, –MNTG.

**Except the Lord of Sabaoth had left us a seed:** ... Unless the Lord of hosts, –WSLY ... If the Lord of armies hadn't left us some survivors, –BECK ... had left us a posterity, –CNFT.

**we had been as Sodoma, and been made like unto Gomorrha:** ... our nation would have disappeared as utterly, –WAY ... and had bene lykened to, –CRNM ... and should have resembled Gomorrah, –WLSN ... and should have fared like, –MNTG.

**9:27-29.** The prophecies of Hosea and Isaiah are quoted to show that the call of the Gentiles had been foretold. The backslidings and waywardness of Israel would result in the acceptance of but a remnant of a people as numerous "as the sand of the sea."

Hosea had said that God would make His people a people who were not His people (Hosea 2:23), and that those people would be called the sons of God (Hosea 1:10). He also showed how Isaiah had been made aware that Israel would have been wiped out had not a remnant been left (Isaiah 10:22, 23; 37:32). The apostle is saying that Israel would have known her fate if she had listened to and understood the Word of the Lord to her.

The context of Isaiah's prophecy was the impending Assyrian invasion of Israel. Only a minority survived the captivity and exile (Isaiah 10:21). Isaiah's elder son was named Shear-jashub ("remnant will return") as a sign to Judah. Only a remnant were true to God.

Israel did not fail of righteousness because of nonelection. Their failure was their own fault. They stumbled over Christ. He is either a steppingstone or "a stumblingstone and rock of offense" (9:33).

Israel's "stumblingstone" was the necessity of faith in Christ as the Messiah. They had prayed for, hoped for, and looked for the promised Messiah. But when He came as the crucified Christ they would not accept Him. The Cross was an "offense" to the Jew. Calvary did away with works, with legalism.

**30. What shall we say then?:** ... what is our inference? *—BRKL.*
**That the Gentiles:**
**which followed not after righteousness:** ... who never ran in the race for righteousness, *—WAY* ... who did not pursue righteousness, *—MKNT.*
**have attained to righteousness:** ... haue ouertaken rightuousnes? *—GNVA* ... haue apprehended, *—RHEM.*
**even the righteousness which is of faith:** ... a right standing conditioned on faith, *—WLMS.*

**9:30.** This verse shows the Gentiles have attained that for which they had no desire, and the Jews have failed in securing that to which they had devoted their lives. The condition of the Gentile world, apart from Christ, is pictured in Ephesians 2:12. We "followed not after righteousness." Romans 3:11 tells us there is "none that understandeth, ... none that seeketh after God."

But now we, who were outside and had no aspirations spiritually or Godward, have through the infinite mercy and grace of God attained to that righteousness which the Jews desired, but were never able to attain.

**31. But Israel, which followed after the law of righteousness:** ... Contrary wise, *—CRNM* ... was in search of a Law, *—TCNT* ... for the securing of, *—BRKL.*
**hath not attained to the law of righteousness:** ... did not arrive at that law, *—CLMT.*

**9:31.** Why could not Israel attain to the righteousness they desired? The key is in the preceding verse. The Gentiles had attained righteousness by faith. In a sense there are two kinds of righteousness. There is the righteousness which Paul describes, the righteousness which the Gentiles attained. Then there is the righteousness which the Jews sought after, what the Bible calls their own righteousness, which is "as filthy rags" (Isaiah 64:6).

All that we receive from God comes through faith. We are saved by faith (Ephesians 2:8, 9). We are justified by faith, not by the works of the Law (Romans 5:1; Galatians 2:16). We have access to God's throne by faith (5:2). All that we have comes by faith and is entirely divorced from works and self-effort: "Not of works, lest any man should boast" (Ephesians 2:9). It is all based on faith.

Paul makes the point clearly. The Jews had no claim to salvation as a national right. The way was plain, but they refused to accept it. On the other hand, the Gentiles who were not seeking righteousness, gladly accepted salvation by faith when they heard the good news of the gospel. By the hundreds and thousands, they "turned to God from idols to serve the living and true God; and to wait for his Son from heaven" (1 Thessalonians 1:9, 10).

Except for a believing remnant, the Jews turned in hatred on the Christians, driving them from their homes and scattering them abroad.

All Jews believed that possession of the law of Moses was all that was required, providing they lived by it. That goal was unattainable. When Messiah came, they rejected Him. They wanted a militant Lion; God sent a Lamb. They wanted a throne; God gave the Cross.

**32. Wherefore?:** ... For what reason? *—SAWR* ... And why? *—CNFT.*
**Because [they sought it] not by faith:** ... their principle was not faith, *—BRKL* ... they did not pursue it, *—RSV* ... has relied not on faith, *—MOFT* ... they did not try through faith, *—WLMS* ... they shaped their course not by faith, *—WAY.*
**but as it were by the works of the law:** ... but thought to gain it by works, *—MNTG* ... they relied on good deeds, *—JB* ... on what they could do, *—MOFT* ... from what they regarded as merit, *—WEYM* ... but in reliance on meritorious deeds, *—WAY.*
**For they stumbled at that stumblingstone:** ... they tripped over the, *—ADAM.*

**9:32.** The puzzling, haunting question is: How could Israel have missed out on righteousness when it was ostensibly their number one concern? It was because they did not seek righteousness in the only way it can come—by faith. Their "works of the law" nullified faith and blinded them to God's righteousness (seen in Christ when He came). If God had intended that man could become righteous by his works, He would never have given His Son to die. The Jews, like Cain, decided to bring what they wanted to bring rather than what God had commanded to be brought (Jude 11).

**33. As it is written:**
**Behold, I lay in Sion a stumblingstone and rock of offence:** ... people will trip over and a rock that will make them fall, *—ADAM* ... even a rock to trip them up, *—MOFT* ... and a rock of hindrance, *—HNT* ... and a stoon of sclaundre, *—WCLF* ... that men shallbe offended at, *—CRNM* ... a rocke which shal make men fall, *—GNVA* ... and a rocke of scandal, *—RHEM* ... a rock from which they shall recoil, *—WAY.*
**and whosoever believeth on him shall not be ashamed:** ... yet, he who rests his faith thereon, *—WAY* ... yet no one relying on it shall be disappointed, *—WLSN* ... schal not be confoundid, *—WCLF.*

**9:33.** The major reason for the Jews' failure to attain righteousness is that they stumbled over Christ Jesus. There is implicit imagery in verses 30 and 31 of a race, or an obstacle course, in the pursuit of righteousness. When Christ came across their path as the goal which they sought, the Jews instead stumbled and fell, missing the goal entirely.

God had forewarned Israel of the possibility of falling as a result of stumbling over the coming One. Isaiah prophesied that the "Lord of hosts" would be a stone of stumbling and a rock of offense (Isaiah 8:14) over which many would stumble and fall. Isaiah 28:16 foretold of "a tried stone, a precious corner stone, a sure foundation," promising that "he that believeth shall not make haste."

The Psalmist foresaw the Jews' rejection of Jesus as he wrote, "The stone which the builders refused is become the head stone of the corner" (Psalm 118:22). Jesus applied this prophecy to himself and warned His hearers that "whosoever shall fall on this stone shall be broken: but on whomsoever it shall fall, it will grind him to powder" (Matthew 21:42-44).

When Jesus asked the Jewish leaders to explain Psalm 118:22, they had no answer (Luke 20:17). When He applied it to himself, they understood His claim and tried to take Him for trial, but His time had not yet come (Mark 12:10-12).

The joyous aspect of the stumbling stone is that "whosoever believeth on him shall not be ashamed." Isaiah 28:16 stated that the believer would "not make haste." The two ideas are complementary.

The believer rests on the solid rock Christ Jesus; he does not have to rush about in anxiety but can move in deliberation and peace. Jesus will never allow him to be put to shame. In a world of mutability and uncertainty, Jesus never changes (Hebrews 13:8).

## Chapter 10

1. **Brethren, my heart's desire and prayer to God for Israel is:** ... the kindly intent, —BRKL ... the will of my heart, —DOUY ... the pleasure indeed of my heart, —YNG ... indeed and my supplication, —CLMT ... and my intercession, —MRDK ... the longing of my heart ... for my countrymen, —MNTG ... my entreaty to God, —WAY.

**that they might be saved:**

**10:1.** God has offered righteousness to Israel three times: (1) under the prophets (9:30-33); (2) under the Law (10:1-13); (3) under the gospel (10:14-21).

Paul did not discuss Israel's rejection with coldness and anger. He felt deeply about the matter (cf. 9:1-3). Paul's life was often endangered by the Jews; many a beating and stoning left marks upon his body. But despite this he was deeply grieved over their ways; he desired above all else that they might be saved. The burden of souls left no room in his heart for the condemnation of souls.

2. **For I bear them record that they have a zeal of God:** ... I can vouch for, —MOFT ... I bear witness that they possess an enthusiasm for God, —WEYM ... to their jealousy for God's honour, —WAY ... that they haue a feruent mynde to Godwarde, —GNVA.

**but not according to knowledge:** ... their zeal is misguided, —JB ... their zeal is not guided by true knowledge, —LOCK ... but they lack certain knowledge, —NORL ... but it is an unenlightened enthusiasm, —WEYM ... but they are not intelligently so, —WLMS ... but not according to a full and accurate knowledge, —WUST.

3. **For they being ignorant of God's righteousness:** ... They are densely ignorant, —NORL ... They steadily ignore, —WAY ... they have not submitted, —BRKL ... which is alowed before God, —TNDL.

**and going about to establish their own righteousness:** ... and seeking to establish, —PNIN, —HNSN ... while they try to earn, —NORL ... they try to set up a private standard of righteousness, —WAY ... to make stidfast her owne, —WCLF ... and were trying to set up one of their own, —WLMS.

**have not submitted themselves unto:** ... haue not bene obedient vnto, —GNVA ... they haue not been subiect to, —RHEM ... they were not submissive, —WLSN, —HNSN.

**the righteousness of God:**

4. **For Christ [is] the end of the law for righteousness to every one that believeth:** ... For Messiah is the aim of the law, —MRDK ... is the fulfyllynge of the lawe, —CRNM ... For the termination of the law, —WUST ... is the consummation of the Law, —CNFT.

**10:2-4.** The Jews failed to submit to the righteousness of God. They had great zeal, they knew the Law, they gave themselves to the Law, and they endeavored to convert Gentiles to the Law. But since their zeal was "not according to knowledge," it was not acceptable. It was misguided to a wrong cause.

The Jews had not properly interpreted the purpose of the Law. Ignoring the sinfulness of their hearts, they had come to trust in the keeping of the letter of the Law. When Jesus came, offering free pardon for sin, they felt they had no need of Him. "They answered him, We be Abraham's seed, and were never in bondage to any man: how sayest thou, Ye shall be made free?" (John 8:33). On more than one occasion they asked, "What shall we do?" Notice John 6:28, 29 where we read they asked, "What shall we do, that we might work the works of God?" Jesus answered, "This is the work of God, that ye believe."

The human desire to merit God's favor by works is present among all men; it is not limited to the Jew with his alms, prayers, and traditions. The African brings offerings to his fetish; the Hindu bathes in the Ganges; those of the Roman Church do penance, count beads, and journey to shrines.

Christ came both to fulfill the Law and to remove the need for the Law. Myer Pearlman (pp. 232, 233) likened the Law to a train. In the days of train travel, we used a train as a means to an end. We had no intention of making the train our home. When we reached our destination, we left the train. But the self-satisfied Jews refused to move from the seats of the old-covenant train even though they were at the end of the line. Christ is the "end of the law" in that He fulfilled it (Matthew 5:17). He did not destroy it nor make it void; He is our righteousness and He fulfills the Law in us (Romans 3:21, 31; 1 Corinthians 1:30). The Law can find no fault in Him.

**5. For Moses describeth:** ... For Moses wryteth of, —CRNM.

**the righteousness which is of the law:**
**That the man which doeth those things shall live by them:** ... The man who fulfils its requirements (which no man ever did) shall find life in it, —WAY.

**6. But the righteousness which is of faith:** ... based on faith, —RSV.

**speaketh on this wise:**
**Say not in thine heart, Who shall ascend into heaven?:** ... Do not say to yourself, —ET.
**(that is, to bring Christ down [from above]:):** ... This, in its implications, —WUST ... euen to fetche Christ downe from aboue, —GNVA ... to drag the Messiah down from heaven, —ET.

**10:5, 6.** Moses described "righteousness which is of the law" (cf. Leviticus 18:5). Paul reiterated that same principle in 2:7: God could not deny eternal life to the person who totally always kept His law.

Scripture is very clear, however, that no human being except our Lord Jesus ever met that qualification. Adam could have, but since the Fall there has been no human who could keep even the first commandment in totality (Romans 3:20, 23; Acts 15:10; Galatians 3:10; James 2:10). Blood sacrifice was always necessary for atonement (Hebrews 9:22).

The Law declares that if a person wants to be right with God, then he must do right. Salvation by grace declares that if a person wants to do right, he must be right with God. Imputed righteousness consists of a Person rather than an effort. Through Christ we have a righteousness which is not dependent upon us or what we have done but upon Christ himself.

The Law was given to Israel as a temporary thing, a "ministration of death" (2 Corinthians 3:7) to reveal sin and the necessity of Calvary. The day of the Law is over, since Christ, having paid the penalty for sin, disannulled it (Hebrews 7:18).

**7. Or, Who shall descend into the deep?:** ... who schal go doun in to helle? —WCLF ... who is able to descend into the grave, —ET ... down to the underworld? —JB ... into the depths? —BECK ... into the abyss? —HNT ... to the abyss of the grave, —MRDK.
**(that is, to bring up Christ again from the dead.):** ... that is, to bring again Christ, —MKNT ... back from the dead, —NORL ... to be leading Christ up, —CNDT ... restore Christ from among the dead, —ET.
**8. But what saith it?:** ... But what does it say? —MNTG ... what do the scriptures say? —ET.
**The word is nigh thee, [even] in thy mouth, and in thy heart:** ... The matter is nigh thee, —MKNT ... it is the inspired word on your very tongue, —ET ... near you, on your lips, —RSV ... and in your mind, —SAWR.
**that is, the word of faith, which we preach:** ... That is the very word of faith, —MNTG ... the word of the faith, —PNIN ... that is, the saying of the faith, —YNG ... or the doctrine of the Gospel, —LOCK ... which we publish, —HNSN ... which we are heralding, —CNDT ... We proclaim the Word that brings faith, —ET.

**10:7, 8.** Imputed righteousness provides an ever-present spiritual standard for believers. In other words, it is a righteousness that is centered in the Word of God. In writing of this, Paul asks questions that may have appeared foolish. In essence, he asks those who are searching for righteousness if they must go up to heaven and bring Christ down in order to have someone to keep them righteous. Or must they go down to the grave to bring Him up from the dead to have someone to keep them righteous.

Paul's use of Deuteronomy showed that he was not preaching a new concept; the only new part was the work Jesus had accomplished. Hebrews discusses the relationship of Jesus to the Levitical system, showing the "better" way of Jesus' finished work (John 19:30; Hebrews 10:9-14).

Verses 6-8 are taken from Moses' inspired teaching in Deuteronomy 30:12-14. When Jews were inclined to say that it was impossible to please God, Moses reminded them that "it is not hidden from thee, neither is it far off" (Deuteronomy 30:11). God through Moses was saying to Israel that He had made faith and life accessible to them. For every sin and transgression He had made a plan for forgiveness. Their faith was demonstrated by their obedience.

The Jews of Paul's day were liable to make the same error as those of Moses' day. To question how they could "ascend into heaven" in order to find a way of perfection was a denial of the incarnation of Christ. To question the need for bringing someone from "the deep" was a denial of Jesus' resurrection.

Paul's answer was that the Word was near them, seated at the right hand of the throne of God, and He (Jesus) is identified and inseparably connected with the written Word, which is "even in thy mouth." The righteousness by faith can be maintained by adhering to and abiding in the Word of God.

The message of salvation by faith conveys the good news that Christ, the Son of God, came down from heaven to become the Son of Man and to die for us, and that He has ascended again from the dead. The two greatest miracles of the Christian faith are the Incarnation which tells us that Christ came down from heaven, and the Resurrection which tells us He came up from the regions of the dead. These truths must be believed in the heart. The Scriptures, "the word of faith," are the means of relaying this to us.

**9. That if thou shalt confess with thy mouth the Lord Jesus:** ...that Iesus is the lorde, —*TNDL* ...For yf thou knowledge wyth thy mouth, —*CRNM* ...if you will openly confess, —*CMPB* ...if thou wilt openly confess, —*WLSN* ...openly own Jesus the Lord, —*LOCK* ...that Jesus is the Lord, —*CNFT.*

**and shalt believe in thine heart:** ...and have faith or trust in your inward being, —*ET.*

**that God hath raised him from the dead:** ...that God actually raised him, —*MNTG* ...that God did really raise Him, —*WAY.*

**thou shalt be saved:** ...thou shalt live, —*MRDK* ...you shall find salvation, —*WAY.*

**10. For with the heart man believeth unto righteousness:** ...For with the inmost heart, —*WAY* ...faith is exercised, —*WUST* ...in order to be justified, —*ADAM.*

**and with the mouth confession is made unto salvation:** ...and to knowledge with the mouth maketh a man safe, —*TNDL* ...profession of faith is made, —*CNFT* ...they make open acknowledgement and so find Salvation, —*TCNT* ...they make confession and obtain salvation, —*WEYM* ...is restored to life, —*MRDK.*

**10:9, 10.** God's great plan of righteousness is so wonderful and so complete that man's efforts are excluded. Salvation can only be received by faith. Faith does not earn a Saviour, faith accepts a Saviour. All that is required is the act of believing; proof is the act of confessing Him. Salvation is as close as the air we breathe. We only need to receive Him and confess Him. Salvation is for "whosoever shall call upon the name of the Lord" (verse 13).

Most translations render "confess ... the Lord Jesus" as "confess ... Jesus as Lord." The emphasis is on the lordship of Christ.

At the very heart of the gospel is the Resurrection. Salvation is to confess with the mouth the lordship of Christ and to believe in the heart His resurrection. Believing comes before confession. Lack of confession indicates lack of faith. Confession is first of all Godward in the heart, then outward and manward. Heart trust and true confession cannot be separated.

Believing with the heart is in contrast with intellectual belief. Faith, as used in Scripture, is not a natural attribute of fallen man. Faith is "not of yourselves; it is the gift of God" (Ephesians 2:8). Calvinists are scriptural when they say that man cannot believe apart from God's gracious help. They are unscriptural when they say He offers it only to a predetermined few. The Holy Spirit offers faith to all mankind (verse 11), but man must will to exercise that faith by receiving Christ, committing himself to Jesus as his Lord.

Confession of mouth and belief of heart are the prime requisites of salvation, representing the believers' outward and inward responses. Inward conviction must find outward expression. Salvation comes by faith which inevitably will cause the believer to confess Christ both in word and deed.

**11. For the scripture saith:** ...for the Writing saith, —*YNG.*

**Whosoever believeth on him shall not be ashamed:** ...Whoever depends on Him, —*ADAM* ...shall not be put to shame, —*BRKL* ...shall not be confounded, —*CRNM* ...shall not be disgraced, —*CNDT.*

**10:11.** This verse is a quotation from Isaiah 28:16. "He" in Isaiah is changed to "whosoever." Several translations render "ashamed" as "disappointed." There is nothing mentioned about law; it is all by faith. None of these renderings—ashamed, put to shame, disappointed—mean to be ashamed of the Lord. Rather, whosoever anchors his faith in Christ can be certain that the gospel works; it has power to save and deliver.

**12. For there is no difference between the Jew and the Greek:** ...are on precisely the same footing, —*WEYM* ...it discriminateth neither, —*MRDK* ...there is no distinccioun, —*WCLF.*

**for the same Lord over all is rich unto all that call upon him:** ...the same Person is Lord, —*ADAM* ...His riches are for everyone who calls, —*KLGS* ...full of blessing for all who at any time call upon Him, —*WAY* ...and He gives richly to all, —*CNBR* ...and he is bountiful to all who invoke his aid, —*TCNT* ...is infinitely kind to all, —*WEYM* ...constantly rich toward all, —*WUST* ...for all who invoke him, —*MOFT.*

**10:12.** "Difference" is rendered "distinction" in several translations. There is no distinction between Jew and Greek (Gentile) in their sinfulness (3:22, 23), and no distinction in the plan to deliver them from sin. God's mercy is rich unto all. The lordship of Christ is equally relevant to all in the matter of salvation.

13. **For whosoever shall call upon the name of the Lord shall be saved:** ...Everyone who invokes the name, —MOFT... For everyone, without exception, —WEYM.

**10:13.** Nothing can be simpler: "Whosoever"— one and all, anyone; "call"—call on the name of the only One who can help; "shall be saved"—it is just that simple. Jew or Gentile, rich or poor, bond or free, black or white, educated or uneducated, refined or crude—anyone can simply call. No longer is there a special people. It is all who call. Those who call are the elect, the chosen. They are the Israel of God.

The thrust of these verses is an appeal to the Jews to forsake the road of legalism and walk the way of grace. Paul appeals to them to see that their zeal is wrongly placed. Generations before the prophets had declared that faith is the way to God and that the door is open to all who believe.

14. **How then shall they call on him in whom they have not believed?:**
**and how shall they believe in him:** ...Moreover, how is it possible, —WUST... can men believe in a Lord, —WAY.
**of whom they have not heard?:** ...in one whose words they have not heard? —TCNT... of whom they did not hear? —CLMT.
**and how shall they hear without a preacher?:** ... how shall they listen, —BRKL... if no one preaches? —CNFT... unless some one proclaims him? —TCNT... apart from one heralding? —CNDT.

15. **And how shall they preach, except they be sent?:** ... unless they are sent as his messengers? —TCNT... if ever they should not be commissioned? —CNDT.
**as it is written:**
**How beautiful are the feet of them that preach the gospel of peace, and bring glad tidings of good things!:** ... How pleasant is the coming of men, —MOFT... hou faire ben the feet of hem, —WCLF... those who bring a glad gospel, —MNTG... that euangelize peace, of them that euangelize good things, —RHEM... that proclaim glad-tidings of blessings! —WAY... are the heralds of peace, —MRDK... who bring the good tidings of peace, —WSLY.

**10:14, 15.** At this point Paul turned emphatically to the responsibility of the Church to get the Word to everyone. He had already said that the Word is near (verse 8). He had already shown in chapters 1 and 2 that even pagan Gentiles who had not heard the written Word did have the unwritten

revelation of God in creation (1:18-20) and in their conscience (2:6-16).

The only way, however, that the pagan can ever find salvation is to hear the Word in some way. Scripture indicates that the person who does not have the Bible but walks in all the light he has will be given more light. Examples are Abraham, Ruth, Rahab, the Ethiopian eunuch, and Cornelius. If we could see God's agenda in heaven, we would see that He has someone in mind to take the good news to every unreached person.

In the Great Commission, recorded five times (Matthew 28:19, 20; Mark 16:15; Luke 24:47-49; John 20:21-23; Acts 1:8), Jesus made clear that the responsibility for taking the good news of salvation rests on His followers. The responsibility of each human being to God (1:18-3:20) in no way lessens the responsibility of every Christian to do his part in taking the gospel to every creature.

Nowhere in Romans is this set forth more plainly than in this Jewish section of the book. But faith or belief in this gospel depends on hearing it; and this requires preaching; and preaching requires pastors, evangelists, and missionaries carrying the good news to all parts of the world.

The oft-repeated "how" in these verses represents vital, searching, and challenging questions. These questions must be carefully considered today. Paul was talking about evangelizing the world, about getting the good news to all men. The Great Commission calls for living preachers to be living messengers of a living Saviour to a dying world.

The preacher must be sent. He must be God-called. God calls, but men do not hear. Jesus charged the Church to pray that God would send forth laborers (Matthew 9:37, 38). How will people hear without a preacher? Preaching is God's plan (1 Corinthians 1:21). There are other means of declaring the message, but they must never replace preaching. Righteousness is proclaimed by preaching.

The feet of the preacher are beautiful to the one who is in the prison of sin, just as Isaiah described the beauty of the feet of the messenger coming with good news of deliverance for the Jews in Babylonian captivity (Isaiah 52:7).

16. **But they have not all obeyed the gospel:** ... they have not all accepted the glad news, —NORL ... But not all lent an obedient ear, —WUST... they did not all hearken to the glad tidings, —ASV, —CLMT... they have not all heeded, —RSV... they all have not listened to the good news, —HNSN... it is not to be expected that all should receive and obey it, —LOCK.
**For Esaias saith:**

**Lord, who hath believed our report?:** ... what they heard from us? —MOFT ... who hath beleued oure sayinges? —CRNM ... who has put faith in what we told? —WLMS ... Lord, who did give credence to, —YNG ... our message? —KLGS ... our proclamation? —MRDK ... that which he heard from me? —WAY.

**10:16.** Evangelization is purposeless to those who believe that salvation comes by election with no decision being made by the elected. But the Word clearly teaches that man has a free will and must choose. Free will and faith are involved in receiving God's saving grace. Man's will must respond to God's will. Those who believe are the chosen, but God never crosses the threshold of human will unless He is invited. As a result some "have not ... obeyed the gospel." If salvation comes to all who call on the Lord, then it is imperative that all hear so they can know on whom to call.

**17. So then faith [cometh] by hearing:** ... Consequently, —WORL ... So belief, —ASV ... faith comes from the message, —HNT ... must depend upon having heard the Message, —WAY ... comes from a Report, —WLSN.

**and hearing by the word of God:** ... is through the message of Christ, —BRKL ... comes by the preaching of Christ, —RSV.

**10:17.** While emphasis is placed on preaching, let it never be forgotten that the preaching of the gospel is not the exclusive responsibility of the clergy (Acts 8:4).

With regard to the question of hearing (Romans 10:14), salvation is not imparted apart from the Word of God (John 5:24; Acts 10:44; Ephesians 1:3). And with regard to believing, lost men cannot call without believing. Here is where faith enters in.

Why do the heathen bow to idols of wood and stone? It may be because no one ever told them of the living God and the loving Saviour. Or, why do honest people sincerely believe in the perpetual sacrifice of Christ? It may be because no one has ever taught them that Jesus died once for all on the cross, and the price was fully paid. All one needs to do is repent and believe, and sin will be cleansed away, never to be remembered against the sinner again. Or, why do Jewish friends seek the answers through following the legalism of the Law? Could it be because they have not understood that Isaiah 53 pictures their Messiah?

To receive this message of salvation requires faith. Much is being said and written about faith today. The simple truth is that faith comes from hearing the Word of God. The Word is the source of all true faith. The faith which the Word produces brings an awareness of God to the soul. By faith

the believer hears God's voice. Faith enables the believer to walk through deep waters and suffer in the furnace of afflictions, for he sees God's hand in all things. Faith which the Word produces enables the believer to exercise confidence in God and to believe Him for impossible things.

The energizing power of the Word assures us that if we will attune our ears to hear, our faith will be quickened and God will work wondrous things on our behalf.

The responsibility of man comes clearly into focus. The Word must be preached. That requires a human channel. The Word must be heard. That requires the listener who really hears. The Word must be believed. That requires the listener to act in faith on the facts of the Word as presented.

**18. But I say, Have they not heard?:**
**Yes verily:** ... No doubt, —GNVA.
**their sound went into all the earth:** ... Fly Abroad, Thou Mighty Gospel, —MNTG ... All over the earth their voices have gone, —WLMS ... into the extremities of the inhabited earth, —WUST.
**and their words unto the ends of the world:** ... to the very ends of the habitable world, —NORL ... the ends of the inhabited earth, —CLMT.
**19. But I say:** ... But I demaunde, —TNDL, —CRNM.
**Did not Israel know?:** ... not understand? —RSV.
**First Moses saith:**
**I will provoke you to jealousy by [them that are] no people:** ... I will fire you with jealousy, —WEYM ... make you jealous, —NORL ... will move you to jealousy, —SCLT ... I will prouoke you to enuy, —CRNM ... to rivalry, —WORL ... with a nobody people, —KLGS.
**[and] by a foolish nation I will anger you:** ... against a Gentile nation without understanding will I make you wroth, —CNBR ... with an irreligious people, —JB ... With a nation void of understanding, —PNIN ... I will infuriate you, —BRKL ... make you angry over a senseless nation, —ADAM ... I vvill driue you into anger, —RHEM ... I will excite you to indignation, —NOYS ... By an unenlightened nation, —HNSN ... as yet untutored, —WAY.

**10:18, 19.** In these verses Paul shifted the emphasis from the responsibility of the messenger to that of the hearer. Verse 18 deals with mankind in general; verse 19 focuses on Israel in particular. Paul indicated that Israel had no excuse. Even their prophets had declared salvation by faith.

When Paul referred to Psalm 19:4 in verse 18, he was showing that all human beings have heard the "sound" and the "words" of God. This is the same concept developed in 1:18-32. Some can say they never heard the gospel per se, but no one can say he never heard God speak.

In verse 19, quoting Deuteronomy 32:21, Paul reminded unbelieving Jews that their mental assent (they *knew* the truth) was not enough. There are two kinds of hearing, physical and spiritual. Hearing with a receptive heart produces faith; otherwise it hardens (Hebrews 4:2).

**20. But Esaias is very bold, and saith:** ... Nay, Isaiah throws off all reserve, –WAY ... said more clearly, –JB ... dares to say, –CNFT ... quite boldly says, –ADAM ... with strange boldness, exclaims, –WEYM.

**I was found of them that sought me not:** ... who don't look for Me find Me, –BECK ... who were not seeking me, –MNTG.

**I was made manifest unto them that asked not after me:** ... I have shown myself, –RSV ... I have been made plain, –KLGS ... I appeared openly to those who made no inquiry of me, –CNFT ... who did not consult me, –JB ... who were not consciously enquiring for me, –WAY.

**21. But to Israel he saith:** ... But in regard of Israel he saith, –ALFD ... But in respect to Israel, –WORL.

**All day long I have stretched forth my hands: unto a disobedient and gainsaying people:** ... contradicting people, –BRKL ... a people who disobey Me and oppose Me, –BECK ... that is disobedient and obstinate, –WLMS ... antagonistic people, –ADAM ... contrary people, –MOFT, –RSV ... but speaketh agaynst me, –TNDL, –CRNM ... cantankerous people, –WUST ... complaining people, –KLGS.

**10:20, 21.** Throughout this section Paul had been driving home to the Jews their responsibility. They should have known better, they had every chance to know better, but they rejected God's appeal. Of all people, they should have understood. Even though Moses and Isaiah had foretold the salvation of the Gentiles, with Isaiah even foretelling Israel's opposition to that action, the Jews persisted in their rejection of salvation provided by faith through Christ.

The emphasis in these two verses is that the Gentiles who had much lesser revelation responded with greater faith. This contrast, described in Romans 9:30, 31, was foretold by Isaiah (Isaiah 65:1, 2).

God's outstretched arms are an indication of His great love and mercy. The fact that they were coldly rejected indicates how hard and cantankerous were the hearts of God's people. The Jews had been chosen to be God's primary messengers (3:2; 9:4). When as a nation they rejected their Messiah, they lost that place. The teaching that God sovereignly decreed that some men reject Him is shown to be utterly false. If He had predetermined that Israel reject Him, He surely would not have pleaded with them to return to Him. He would have let them go without the poignant pleading we read in the writings of prophets such as Hosea, Jeremiah, and Isaiah.

Paul maintained his profound feeling for perishing Israel. To coldhearted Christians the passionate love of Paul in 9:3 may seem like a mystery.

God grant that our hearts may so feel for lost men today that with heartfelt prayer (10:1) and willing feet (10:15) we may with great faith and perseverance propagate the faith-inspiring Word of God (10:17) to men everywhere.

## Chapter 11

**1. I say then, Hath God cast away his people?:** ... must we think that, –CNBR ... God repudiated his People, –TCNT, –MOFT ... Does not God thrust away, –CNDT ... has God rejected his people? –RSV ... push His people aside? –ADAM.

**God forbid:** ... By no means, –CMPB ... It never was, –KLGS.

**For I also am an Israelite, of the seed of Abraham, [of] the tribe of Benjamin:** ... a member of the tribe of Benjamin, –WLMS ... of the posterity, –WEYM ... of the race, –SAWR.

**2. God hath not cast away his people:** ... has not disowned His people, –NORL, –WLMS ... hath not rejected, –RHEM.

**which he foreknew:** ... his predestined People! –MOFT ... he chose specially long ago, –JB ... of whom he took note from the first, –TCNT ... whom formerly he acknowledged, –CMPB ... whom He marked out for His own so long ago, –WAY.

**Wot ye not what the scripture saith of Elias?:** ... know you not? –ET.

**how he maketh intercession to God against Israel, saying:** ... hovv he requesteth God, –RHEM ... how he pleadeth with, –PNIN ... how he complains to God, –WLSN.

**11:1, 2.** In enunciating the theme of Romans, Paul said, "To the Jew first" (1:16). Now he asks if God has forgotten His promise? Has "God cast away his people?" he says. Notice Paul's clear answer: "God forbid." God is concerned for His people. He will see to it that the glorious promises in which the prophets delighted will come to complete fulfillment. The chosen people are only temporarily set aside. When the gathering of all believers takes place at the end of this age of grace, God will turn again to Israel and make good His covenant promises.

The solemn promises made to Abraham and his seed regarding the Hebrew racial family, and those God gave to David and his seed regarding the Hebrew royal family, have not been canceled—only postponed. In this Church age, the Jewish nation is blinded, yet individual Jews are being saved.

The first answer to the important question, "Hath God cast away his people?" is the great apostle himself. The salvation of Paul proves there is still a remnant. His conversion is a striking preview to Israel's future conversion. The learned Pharisee in his campaign against the Church illustrated Israel's zeal for God was without knowledge. Even the manner of Paul's miraculous meeting with Jesus on the Damascus Road prefigures

Christ's glorious appearing to the Jews as their Messiah.

Though under chastisement and temporarily set aside, the Jews are still God's people, and they will be restored. Israel's future gave the prophets one of their most glorious themes. And Israel's future is still glorious. Even though God deals with Israel in a disapproving way at the present time, He is doing so with the prospect of Israel's restoration in mind.

There are many evidences that God is turning His attention toward the Jewish people and their land. The fulfillment of prophecy indicates that we are nearing the "fulness of the Gentiles" (11:25).

**3. Lord, they have killed thy prophets:** . . . they haue slaine thy Prophets, —*RHEM* . . . they have massacred thy prophets, —*WAY.*

**and digged down thine altars:** . . . they tore down, —*ADAM* . . . they have demolished thine altars, —*MOFT* . . . they have razed thy altars, —*CNFT* . . . they have dug up the very foundations, —*WAY.*

**and I am left alone:** . . . I alone am left over, —*BRKL* . . . I am the sole survivor, —*WAY.*

**and they seek my life:** . . . They are thirsting for my blood, —*WEYM* . . . and they are trying to kill me, —*WLMS* . . . and they hunt for my life, —*KLGS.*

**4. But what saith the answer of God unto him?:** . . . But what says the divine oracle to him? —*WLSN*, —*HNSN* . . . what is God's reply, —*RSV* . . . what doth the divine answer say, —*SCLT.*

**I have reserved to myself seven thousand men, who have not bowed the knee to [the image of] Baal:** . . . I have yet left to myself a remnant, —*CNBR* . . . kept for myself, —*RSV* . . . so loyal that they have never bowed a knee, —*WAY.*

**5. Even so then at this present time also:**

**there is a remnant according to the election of grace:** . . . a remnant God has chosen by His love, —*BECK* . . . in agreement with His gracious choice, —*BRKL* . . . a remnant according to a choice of grace, —*WUST* . . . chosen by gift of grace, —*CNBR* . . . selected by grace, —*MOFT* . . . to a gratuitous election, —*SCLT* . . . in accordance with God's unmerited favor, —*WLMS* . . . to an Election of Favor, —*WLSN* . . . chosen by favor, —*KLGS* . . . by the election of grace, —*MRDK.*

**6. And if by grace, then [is it] no more of works:** . . . else the grace is coming to be no longer grace, —*CNDT* . . . His choice is not conditioned by works of theirs, the era for which is past, —*WAY* . . . it can no more be deemed the wage of works, —*CNBR.*

**otherwise grace is no more grace:** . . . would cease to be mercy, —*TCNT* . . . is no longer a favour, —*SCLT* . . . would be a mere misnomer, —*WAY.*

**But if [it be] of works, then is it no more grace: otherwise work is no more work:** . . . for work claims wages, and not gifts, —*CNBR* . . . otherwise it wouldn't be His unearned love anymore, —*BECK.*

**11:3-6.** God has always had a faithful group. Elijah felt he was all alone, but God revealed 7,000 had not bowed their knees to Baal. As it was in the time of Elijah, so now the elect are a remnant. Although the Jewish leaders called for the death of Christ and asked that His blood be upon them—a much worse condition than Ahab's Baal worship in Elijah's day—there was a remnant that received Jesus and were put into His body, the Church. Every converted Jew abandoned his Jewish hopes and became a "partaker of the heavenly calling" (Hebrews 3:1). The Book of Acts gives us the record of thousands of Jews who became the early Christians, from the Day of Pentecost and on. All these came in by grace only and not by works. Not by the keeping of the Law but by the grace of God alone has there been a faithful remnant among the chosen people. Those who thus partake are no longer Jew or Gentile; they are called saints (Romans 1:6, 7; 1 Corinthians 1:2; Ephesians 1:1). The Church is not Jewish, nor national, nor earthly; the Church is a "new body," a heavenly Body.

In this passage Paul presents the Jews in two classes—a minority who believed and accepted salvation by grace and a majority who rejected with blinded eyes and hardened hearts.

There has never been nor will there ever be a time when God does not have a corps of loyal followers. Before the Flood there was Noah and his family. The Scriptures are replete with the accounts of the lives of those who were true to God—an Abraham, a Moses, an Ezra, a Nehemiah, and many others.

On the other hand there never was a time that a whole nation was true to God. Again and again God had to send His prophets and leaders to call Israel to repentance. But always there was a faithful remnant. The prophets became aware of this loyal remnant. Micah envisioned the gathering of the remnant as did Zephaniah and Jeremiah (Micah 2:12; 5:3; Zephaniah 3:12, 13; Jeremiah 23:3). Isaiah even named his son Shear-jashub which means "The Salvation of the Remnant." Over and over Isaiah writes of the faithful remnant who will be saved (Isaiah 7:3; 8:2, 18; 9:12; 6:9-13). Amos presents the picture of God sifting people as corn in a sieve and saving only the good (Amos 9:9). He indicates the word from God as a promise that the house of Jacob will not be utterly destroyed. When writing of the remnant, Ezekiel clearly states that people are not saved because of either national or inherited righteousness (Ezekiel 14:14, 18, 20, 22).

Relationship with God must be on an individual basis. And that comes only by grace. The believing remnant were those "according to the election of grace." The term *eklogēn* can be translated either "election" or "choosing, choice." It is the same term used in the Gospels to tell of Jesus' choosing of the Twelve. That an individual's election is not unconditionally secure is seen in Judas' fall. Jesus used the same term as applied to Judas as to the other 11 (John 6:70; 15:16). It was not by God's predestination (though He foreknew), but by his own choice that Judas fell, losing his election (Acts 1:17, 25).

Anyone chosen of God, at any time, Jew or Gentile, is the elect of God. All men are called to become God's elect or chosen ones. Grace elects to save all who will believe.

**7. What then?:**
**Israel hath not obtained that which he seeketh for:** ... It was not Israel as a whole, *—JB* ... failed to obtain what it sought, *—RSV* ... enthusiastically sought, *—ADAM* ... he has not attained, *—WAY.*

**but the election hath obtained it:** ... Only the chosen remnant got it, *—NORL* ... yet the chosen encountered it, *—CNDT.*

**and the rest were blinded:** ... the rest grew callous, *—TCNT* ... the rest have been hardened, *—HNT* ... The remnaunt are blynded, *—TNDL* ... The rest have become insensible to it, *—WLMS* ... the rest have been callously indifferent, *—WAY.*

**8. (According as it is written, God hath given them the spirit of slumber:** ... hath cast them into a trance of stupor, *—WAY* ... them a sluggish spirit, *—JB* ... has given them a deadness of mind, *—TCNT* ... a spirit of stupidity, *—SCLT* ... the sprete of vnquyetnes, *—TNDL* *—CRNM* ... given them over to an attitude of insensibility, *—WLMS* ... a spirit of deep sleep, *—CMPB* *—YNG* ... a spirit of sleepiness, *—KLGS.*

**eyes that they should not see, and ears that they should not hear;) unto this day:** ... eyes to see nothing, *—WEYM* ... unseeing eyes and inattentive ears, *—JB* ... a condition that continues, *—ADAM* ... ears for the purpose of not hearing, *—WUST* ... down to this very day, *—RSV.*

**11:7, 8.** Election is of grace, not of works, so while the remnant obtained grace, the rest were "blinded." "Election" may be given a very simple, yet scripturally sound, explanation by thinking of political process based on majority rule. For every individual God votes "yes," Satan votes "no," and therefore the deciding vote is left to the individual. The moment he votes "yes" he and God have settled his sure election. As long as he continues to say "yes" to God his election is secure.

The majority of individuals in Israel lost their election by saying "no" to God. God's judgment has its ground in antecedent sin. Those Jews who loved God—such as Zacharias, Elizabeth, Mary, Joseph, Anna, Simeon, and many others—were not blinded, but recognized Jesus as Saviour. The reason the others did not is that they had willfully closed their eyes and ears to God's revelation so long that they became spiritually blind and deaf.

This was foretold (Deuteronomy 29:4; Isaiah 6:9; 29:10; Jeremiah 5:21; Ezekiel 12:2).

In outlining this history, God said the Jews were to be scattered to all corners of the world because they were blinded and had forsaken God. Their apostasy and decline were clearly delineated.

The Greeks of Paul's day were consumed with a passion for knowledge. The Romans lusted for power, but the Jews searched for righteousness. They did not find the righteousness they desired because they rejected the only One who could make them righteous. This rebellion against God resulted in blindness. The word "blinded" bears the meaning of "hardened" or "calloused." The verb is *pōroō* and the noun is *pōrōsis*, a medical word meaning a callous. Calluses become hardened and more or less insensitive to feeling.

As a callous forms on the hand, a spiritual callous can grow on the heart. For a person to insist on going his own way despite the warning flags will eventuate in his becoming insensitive to the voice of God. That is what happened to Israel. Their hearts were insensitive and thus insensible to the gospel. Their eyes were sightless, and their ears were deaf. Paul had previously related God's dealings with Pharaoh as an example of judicial hardening. The more God demanded that Pharaoh let Israel go, the more stubborn and rebellious he became.

**9. And David saith:**
**Let their table be made a snare, and a trap:** ... in stede of a snare, and a net, *—GNVA.*

**and a stumblingblock, and a recompense unto them:** ... a scandal and repayment, *—KLGS* ... an occasion to faule, and a rewarde vnto them, *—TNDL* ... a pitfall, a retribution, *—WAY.*

**11:9.** The reference to the "table" is a quotation from Psalm 69:22, 23. There was a table in the tabernacle of Israel which was not reserved for the priests alone. The people could bring their peace offerings to this table (Leviticus 6:16; 7:18, 20). This high and holy privilege became a trap to the people, for they became more absorbed in the outward ceremonial than in the spiritual reality.

The word "table" also suggests feasting. The thought may well be that while they were lounging at the feast in presumptuous security, they were suddenly caught and destroyed.

**10. Let their eyes be darkened that they may not see:** ... may their eyes be struck incurably blind, *—JB* ... Let their eyes be shrouded in gloom, *—WAY.*

**and bow down their back alway:** ... make thou their back stoop beneath this burden for ever! *—WAY.*

**11:10.** The word for "bow down" is the compound *sunkamptō*, meaning "bend completely" or "bend together." The bowed back is a striking picture of servitude. The curse of anti-Semitism has driven the Jew from land to land. The torture and suffering has been almost unbelievable. The price has been bitter and will continue, for ahead lie the horrors of the Great Tribulation. But the final agony will end as they "shall look upon (Him) whom they have pierced" (Zechariah 12:10-12). Until that day the blinded majority of Israel will continue with unseeing eyes and bowed backs as the prophets warned.

11. **I say then:**
**Have they stumbled that they should fall?:** ... have the Jews fallen for ever, —JB ... to be lost altogether? —BECK ... did they trip in order to fall? —ADAM ... that they shuld vtterly fall, —CRNM ... to fall in utter ruin, —WLMS.

**God forbid:**

**but [rather] through their fall salvation [is come] unto the Gentiles:** ... But through the instrumentality of their fall, —WUST ... But by their offense, —DOUY, —CNFT ... that by their lapse, —MOFT ... through their misbehavior, —BRKL ... By their error, —BECK ... through their false step, —TCNT ... it is by their slip, —HNT ... But by their trespass, —WORL ... has left the field clear for the salvation of the Gentiles, —WAY.

**for to provoke them to jealousy:** ... to excite them to emulation, —HNSN ... to make the Jews jealous, —BECK ... that they may emulate them, —RHEM ... to provoke them to rivalry, —WORL.

**11:11.** The many promises made to Israel in the Old Testament have not been canceled. They relate to matters of national position and blessing.

This chapter shows that Israel's failure is neither complete (verses 1-11) nor permanent (verses 11-32). Israel's fall is not complete because the remnant, made up of Jews like Paul, have accepted Christ. Neither is Israel's fall permanent, because God will fulfill the national promises made to His people. True, Israel has stumbled—"we preach Christ crucified, unto the Jews a stumblingblock" (1 Corinthians 1:23)—but their failure is not permanent. God will not allow their fall to be the dismal climax to a marvelous history. God has a glorious future in store for them.

Rather, God has overruled and "through their fall salvation is come unto the Gentiles." The sons of Jacob persecuted their brother Joseph and finally sold him into slavery, but God overruled their wicked actions for the good of the Gentiles. The Jews were provoked to jealousy by observing the blessings being outpoured upon the "unworthy" Gentiles (Deuteronomy 32:21; Acts 13:45).

12. **Now if the fall of them [be] the riches of the world:** ... the world's enrichment, —BRKL ... is the Wealth of the World, —WLSN.
**and the diminishing of them the riches of the Gentiles:** ... and their failure, —HNSN ... if their defection, —MOFT ... if even their shortcoming gave such riches to, —WAY.
**how much more their fulness?:** ... their perfectnesse? —CRNM ... when the full quota of Jews comes in, —WLMS ... will their full inclusion mean! —RSV ... when their whole nation shall be restored? —LOCK ... shall their full reinstatement bring! —WAY.

**11:12.** When the Jews rejected Christ, they were set aside as God's witnesses on a sidetrack. A new chosen people (the Church) was placed on the main line. But the setting aside is not permanent, and it has been used to bring salvation to the Gentiles. If their fall and diminishing brought riches to the Gentiles, how much more will their restoration to full privilege.

13. **For I speak to you Gentiles:** ... I turn now to you, the Gentiles, —WAY.
**inasmuch as I am the apostle of the Gentiles, I magnify mine office:** ... I attach great importance, —NORL ... I insist upon the grandeur of my function, —WAY ... I magnify my ministry, —RSV ... I take pride in my service to them, —ADAM ... I lay great stress on my office, —MOFT ... I vvil honour my ministerie, —RHEM.

14. **If by any means I may provoke to emulation [them which are] my flesh:** ... awaken my own people to interest, —NORL ... make my own people envious of you, —JB ... I shall arouse to jealousy, —YNG.
**and might save some of them:**

**11:13, 14.** Paul stated he was the apostle to the Gentiles. He magnified his office, that is, his ministry (*diakonia*) to the Gentiles, before the Jews. The Jews did not want the gospel, but they did not want the Gentiles to have it either. Paul was showing, before his kinsmen in the flesh, the blessing of his ministry to the Gentiles, for God was saving them and filling them with His Spirit.

In effect he was saying that he was interested in the Jews for the sake of the Gentiles. According to the prophets, the restoration of Israel will be the starting point for the coming of God's kingdom on earth. Knowing the blessing to the world that will be brought by their restoration, Paul wanted to do all he could to further that goal. He wanted to provoke the Jews to emulation, "jealousy," that they might accept the Messiah and be saved.

15. **For if the casting away of them [be] the reconciling of the world:** ... For if the losse of them, —RHEM ... For if their rejection, —HNSN ... if their exclusion means, —MOFT.
**what [shall] the receiving [of them be], but life from the dead?:** ... what will their restoration

be, —MNTG . . . so what will their final acceptance mean, —NORL.

**11:15.** Up to this point Paul had spoken mainly of Israel's disobedience and futile attempts at self-righteousness. Here he began to reveal God's acts of judgment. Jesus had warned the Jews of this (Matthew 21:43). Scripture clearly indicates that after Christ came unto His own and His own rejected Him, He was preached to the Gentiles. The failure of Israel brought salvation to the Gentiles. Their fall was the wealth of the world; their loss the wealth of the Gentiles, and their casting away the reconciliation of the world. How much greater will be the blessing to the world when Israel is received (in restoration) back again. It will be "life from the dead." (See Isaiah 11:9; 40:1-5.) The nation will be saved by the sovereign grace of God out from a spiritually dead state and from those who remain spiritually dead.

Paul thrilled with thoughts of the future. If the tragedy of rejection has had such wonderful results, what will the glorious ending be, when the tragedy of rejection has changed to the glory of reception. It will be like life from the dead.

**16.** For if the firstfruit [be] holy, the lump [is] also [holy]: . . . If the first part of the dough, —NORL . . . if the first portion of the dough is holy, —NOYS . . . of the dough are holy, —WEYM . . . If the first handful of dough is consecrated, —WLMS . . . for if a litil part of that that is taastid be holi, —WCLF . . . the whole produce of the year, —LOCK . . . the mass is also, —HNSN . . . the whole mass of dough . . . shares in the consecration, —WAY . . . so is the loaf, —KLGS . . . is given to God, —TEV.

and if the root [be] holy, so [are] the branches: . . . the boughs are also, —CNDT.

**11:16.** Paul used two pictures to show that the Jews can never be finally rejected. The Law provided (Numbers 15:19, 20) that all food before it was eaten was to be offered to God. When the dough was being prepared, the first part was to be offered to God. That firstfruit of the bread, the first cake, was set aside for the priests. When that was done, the entire lump of dough became sacred. The offering of the first part sanctified the whole. When a sapling was planted, it was dedicated to God and from then on every branch that came from it was sacred to God.

A key word is "holy." The meaning is that the call and destiny of Israel sets them apart unto God. The "firstfruit" can refer to the first Jews blessed in the gospel and the "lump" to the whole nation that will be blessed and become holy in the end. Or, in connection with Israel, the "firstfruit" would be Abraham, Isaac, and Jacob. The "lump" would be the whole line of descent from the patriarchs. The

"root" would be Abraham and the "branches" the descendants of Israel.

**17.** And if some of the branches be broken off: . . . have been pruned away, —BRKL.

and thou, being a wild olive tree, wert grafted in among them: . . . a wild olive shoot, —BRKL, —RSV . . . art grafted in their place, —CNFT.

and with them partakest of the root and fatness of the olive tree: . . . to share the rich growth of the olive-stem, —MOFT . . . and there partakest of the blessings promised, —LOCK . . . and a fellow-partaker of the root, —YNG . . . in the fertility of the olive, —WAY . . . and art become a joint partaker, —MKNT . . . the strong spiritual life of the Jews, —TEV . . . nourishes you too, —BECK.

**18.** Boast not against the branches: . . . beware of assuming airs of superiority over those branches, —WAY . . . glorie not, —RHEM . . . do not boast over the branches, —RSV . . . glory not over the branches, —CLMT . . . don't brag of being more than the other branches, —BECK . . . you must not exult over the other branches, —TCNT.

But if thou boast, thou bearest not the root, but the root thee: . . . If you must brag remember, —ADAM . . . If you are inclined to look down on them, let this reflection sober you, —WAY . . . thou sustainest not the root, —MRDK . . . it is not thou that supportest the stem, —CNFT . . . you are not sustaining the root, —WUST . . . instead, the root supports you, —BRKL . . . the root upholds you, —WEYM.

**19.** Thou wilt say then:
The branches were broken off, that I might be grafted in: . . . branches have been snapped off, —WAY . . . have been lopped off, —WEYM.

**11:17-19.** The natural branches are the Jews and the ingrafted branches are the Gentiles. The Gentile does not become a Jew nor does he become "of Israel." He comes directly into the promise of blessing given by God to the Gentiles through Abraham (Genesis 12:3).

There are three figures of botanical speech relating to Israel. The "fig tree" speaks of Israel's national privilege (Matthew 24:32-34). The "vine" symbolizes Israel's spiritual privilege (Isaiah 5:1-7; Matthew 21:33, 34). The "olive tree" symbolizes Israel's religious privilege (Romans 11:16, 17; Judges 9:9; Zechariah 4:3).

As a result of unbelief the Jews were broken off. Not all were broken off; it was an individual matter. The ones who were broken off were formerly in vital connection with the root. In other words, they were at one time in the election of grace. By their own rejection of God they lost their elect position and perished.

We see the same principle in John 15:1-6. Jesus, speaking to believers, told them that He was the Vine. They were in vital union with Him. He warned them of the necessity of their abiding in Him, showing that the branches do not have an unconditional union with the vine. The branches must abide of their own volition, or they will be cut off, rejected, and cast into the fire. It is not God's predestination but man's volitional attitude toward God that determines his destiny.

The Gentiles in turn were grafted in as wild olive branches. They were given the privilege of sharing the root and riches of the olive. They share the benefits of the covenant made to Abraham.

Just as not all Jewish branches were broken off, so not all Gentiles are grafted in. Only some branches of the wild olive tree were grafted in and made to draw life from the root. Gentiles must always remember that they owe much to the faithful Jews; they have been grafted in among them and live by the same root.

**20. Well; because of unbelief they were broken off:** . . . True, −MNTG . . . right! −YNG . . . for infidelity, −SCLT . . . because of incredulitie, −RHEM.

**and thou standest by faith:** . . . yet you stand in faith, −CNDT . . . you owe your position to your faith, −MOFT . . . but you stand by believing, −BECK.

**Be not highminded, but fear:** . . . So you must not be proud; you ought rather to be fearful, −NORL . . . Stop having a superiority complex, −WUST . . . Do not be puffed up, −MNTG . . . be not to highly wise, −RHEM . . . There is no ground for arrogance here, but rather for dread, −WAY . . . Be not haughty, but feel awe, −BRKL . . . Do not cherish lofty thoughts, −WORL . . . Stop your haughty thinking; instead be concerned, −ADAM . . . do not become proud, but stand in awe, −RSV . . . You should feel awed instead of being uplifted, −MOFT . . . Be not exalted, −MRDK . . . . but take warning, −TCNT . . . tremble rather, −WEYM . . . continue to be reverent, −WLMS.

**21. For if God spared not the natural branches:** . . . own natural branches, −NORL.

**[take heed] lest he also spare not thee:** . . . perhaps, neither will he spare you, −CMPB.

**11:20, 21.** Unbelief is what brought about the breaking off of the Jews. But the Gentiles "stand by faith." It is not superiority in which the Gentiles stand; it is only by faith.

The Gentiles must not allow a spirit of contempt to possess them. The Jews of that day were hated, and it would have been easy for Gentile Christians to have wrong attitudes toward the Christ-rejecting Jews. We must remember that there never would have been such a thing as Christianity unless there had been Judaism first. Christians must never forget the roots from which they sprang.

Israel chosen, blessed, favored above all others, was not spared. The Gentiles are the wild branches grafted into their place. The Gentiles are enjoying the privileges and blessings of the olive tree. The olive tree is named as king of the trees. The only evergreen in the Parable of the Trees (Judges 9:8-15), the olive tree speaks of Israel's covenant blessings and privileges. Its enduring green illustrates the enduring covenant which God made with Abraham. The tree is characterized by fatness (privileges). Surely no other nation has ever been so blessed of the Lord. And yet, with all of their privileges, some of the branches were cut off.

Israel's greatest privilege was the gift of God's Word and God's Son. Think of it—Gentiles believing on God's Son as Saviour and preaching God's Word—blessings through Israel.

If God did not spare unbelieving Israel, He will not spare faithless Gentiles. The Jews had been more securely rooted in the Kingdom as natural branches. How much more then must the wild branch (the Gentiles) be careful to maintain the relationship which is by faith alone.

**22. Behold therefore the goodness and severity of God:** . . . Consider carefully, −NORL . . . Fix your gaze, −MNTG . . . Now see how kind and how severe God can be, −BECK . . . and rigorousnes of God, −GNVA.

**on them which fell, severity; but toward thee, goodness, if thou continue in [his] goodness:** . . . them surely that are fallen, −RHEM . . . if you cling to His kindness, −BECK . . . if thou abidest in his goodness, −CNFT . . . on the one hand, strictness toward those, −ADAM.

**otherwise thou also shalt be cut off:** . . . will be pruned away, −WLMS . . . else, you also shall be hewn away, −WAY.

**11:22.** Israel fell in unbelief. That brought God's severity. Rejecting the righteousness which God provided in Christ, they followed self-righteousness and pride. They did not submit to God's provision but went about to establish their own righteousness (10:3).

While God's severity fell on Israel, His goodness and kindness came to the Gentiles. They were given the place of privilege even though they had not merited the place of blessing. This came about entirely by grace; it was by the "goodness" of God. Goodness as used here is "kindness," "benignity."

*Epimenō* rendered "continue" bears the thought of "to remain, to abide." The message is clear. If one is to avoid the severity of God—avoid being cut off—be he Jew or Gentile, he must remain and abide in God's grace. *Epimenō* speaks of relationship to and position in. The word is used to express friendship and companionship and often expressed the idea of abiding in a home as a guest.

The phrase "if thou continue" has a parallel in Colossians 1:23. These verses make clear that our security in Christ is based on our being willing to continue to abide. Christ is always willing to abide if we will welcome and acknowledge Him as Lord. (Compare John 15:1-6.)

Some theologians say that Israel the nation lost her election but that no individual can lose his place in Christ—"once saved, always saved." That is as fallacious as to say that all sins are sins of society rather than of individuals. The fact is that only an individual can sin, and only an individual can be saved. The only way a nation can fall is by the fall of individuals. Paul made this clear in 11:1 where he showed that he, an individual Christian, proved that not all Israel had been cast away.

Neither the position of security nor the position of being cut off is unconditional. Both are conditional on the attitude and will of the individual; God has sovereignly made it so.

**23. And they also:**
**if they abide not still in unbelief:** . . . if they give up their unbelief, *—JB.*
**shall be grafted in:**
**for God is able to graft them in again:** . . . is able to graft them back, *—CNFT* . . . is amply able to graft them in, *—WLMS.*

**11:23.** If Israel will not persist in their unbelief, God is able to graft them in. Israel's blindness will be taken away (2 Corinthians 3:13-16). The Jews do not have to abide in unbelief just as they did not have to abide in faith. A broken, dried branch cannot in the natural be grafted back in, but God brings life from the dead (verse 15).

**24. For if thou wert cut out of the olive tree which is wild by nature:** . . . from your natural stock, *—TCNT.*
**and wert grafted contrary to nature into a good olive tree:** . . . in violation of Nature, *—WLSN* . . . by a process which is the very opposite of the natural one, *—WAY* . . . a cultivated olive tree, *—ADAM* . . . into a garden olive, *—HNT.*
**how much more:** . . . is it not much more reasonable, *—WAY.*
**shall these, which be the natural [branches]:**
**be grafted into their own olive tree?:** . . . be regrafted into, *—MNTG* . . . on to their parent-tree? *—WAY* . . . into the fruitful stock, *—CNBR* . . . into their parent olive tree, *—NORL* . . . on their own original tree! *—BRKL.*

**11:24.** Paul speaks of being grafted contrary to nature. Normally the good branch or graft is grafted into a poor stock. The good shoot receives the needed sap for growth from the inferior tree or stock. The graft retains the characteristics and qualities of its own heritage though it receives the sap of the inferior stock and is thus enabled to produce good fruit.

If God grafted the wild olive (Gentiles) into good stock (Israel), He is able to graft the natural branches, which were broken off, back into the good stock. God will bring all of this about. He will bring Israel to a place of repentance and faith and lead them to the Messiah.

Even then, each individual will have to choose, just as now in the time of the Gentiles each has to choose. Not every Jew will be saved, just as in the "fulness of the Gentiles" not every Gentile will be saved. God foreknows all things, but His prescience is not necessarily causative.

Prior to Calvary, Gentile salvation was accompanied by becoming a part of Jewish religious life, a type of the coming grafting described here. The restoration of Israel is very important and should be understood. What will it be when the natural branches come back into their own!

**25. For I would not, brethren, that ye should be ignorant of:** . . . be hyd from you, *—GNVA.*
**this mystery:** . . . There is a hidden reason for all this, *—JB* . . . I want you to know this secret truth, *—BECK* . . . you should learn this Secret of the Initiated, *—WAY.*
**lest ye should be wise in your own conceits:** . . . keep you from thinking too well of yourselves, *—BECK* . . . lest you may be passing for prudent among yourselves, *—CNDT* . . . that you might not be self-opinionated, *—BRKL* . . . To save you from self-conceit, *—TCNT* . . . for fear you should attribute superior wisdom to yourselves, *—WEYM.*
**that blindness in part is happened to Israel:** . . . Hardness in some Measure, *—WLSN* . . . a hardening in part hath befallen Israel, *—PNIN* . . . only temporary insensibility, *—WLMS* . . . that the partial obduracy, *—WAY* . . . partial obtuseness, *—BRKL* . . . that callousness, *—TCNT.*
**until the fulness of the Gentiles be come in:** . . . will last only until the full ingathering of the Gentiles has been secured, *—WAY* . . . until the full number of the Gentiles should enter, *—CNFT* . . . until all the rest of the world, *—TCNT* . . . until the great mass, *—WEYM* . . . until the full quota of the heathen peoples, *—WLMS* . . . until the completion of the pagans comes, *—KLGS* . . . until the complement of the nations, *—CNDT.*

**11:25.** In his characteristic way, Paul drew attention to this important truth as he used the words "ignorant," "mystery," "blindness," and "fulness."

On six occasions Paul declared, "I would not have you ignorant" (Romans 1:13; 11:25; 1 Corinthians 10:1; 12:1; 2 Corinthians 1:8; 1 Thessalonians 4:13). In this verse Paul refers to ignorance concerning a mystery.

The word "mystery" refers to a truth, once hidden, now revealed, the understanding of which requires spiritual perception. What is that mystery? That Israel's blindness and rejection will continue "until the fulness of the Gentiles be come in." This connects with the statement of James at the Council in Jerusalem (Acts 15:14).

The blindness of Israel refers specifically to their refusal to see God's plan in Jesus (verse 7). In a general sense it describes the spiritual condition of any individual who rejects light. Because he refuses to acknowledge God's truth, God gives eyes that cannot see and ears that cannot hear (verse 8).

In this age God is dealing particularly with the Gentiles, and He who knows all things and controls the times and seasons will one day bring this period of time to an end and begin dealing with the Jews in a special way.

The "fulness of the Gentiles" should be distinguished from the "times of the Gentiles." The latter was ushered in with the destruction of Jerusalem by Nebuchadnezzar and will continue through the Great Tribulation to the return of Christ to establish His kingdom on earth. The "fulness of the Gentiles" began with the calling out of the Church (on the Day of Pentecost) and will continue until the rapture of the Church.

**26. And so all Israel shall be saved:** . . . And when this has happened, —TCNT . . . And, in this way, all Israel will be saved, —ADAM . . . shall be converted, —LOCK.
**as it is written:**
**There shall come out of Sion the Deliverer:** . . . shall be the Rescuer, —CNDT.
**and shall turn away ungodliness from Jacob:** . . . rid Jacob of his ungodliness, —NORL . . . He shall banish impieties, —HNT.

**11:26.** Paul is nearing the end of his argument. As a Jew he has faced a heartbreaking situation. He has shown, however, that God has turned Israel's failure into salvation for the Gentiles. Now he looks ahead to a glorious prospect—"all Israel shall be saved." He was not saying that all individuals will be saved, but was speaking of national destiny. Putting it simply, Israel as a nation will be delivered from her enemies, both spiritually and earthly, and be restored to her ancient privileges as God's witness.

**27. For this [is] my covenant unto them:** . . . And this will be my agreement with them, —KLGS . . . is the promise, —SAWR.
**when I shall take away their sins:** . . . I should be eliminating their sins, —CNDT.

**11:27.** Jesus is the Deliverer who will rescue the Jews from their enemies (Zechariah 12:10). Best of all, He "shall turn away ungodliness" for this is His covenant. The reference to "taking away their sins" goes back to Isaiah 27:9. Their acceptance of the new covenant of grace, in contrast to the conditional covenant at Sinai, will find fulfillment (Jeremiah 31:31-34).

Israel's restoration is seen in the restored branches and the renewed fatness of the olive tree in that day when "all Israel shall be saved." God's Word also predicts a restoration of the fig tree which will put forth leaves and bear fruit again (Matthew 24:32, 33; Luke 21:29-31). This is happening today. The fig tree is budding; there are great signs of life in the Holy Land. Read Psalm 80:14-19.

There will be a spiritual revival among the Jews. It will be the fulfillment of Ezekiel's vision of the valley of dry bones. At present the bones seem to have come together; there is again a nation of Israel. But there is no spiritual life. That will come at the time of the Millennium.

**28. As concerning the gospel:** . . . As touching, —ALFD . . . As regards, —RSV . . . In view of, —CNFT . . . In relation to the good news, —HNSN.
**[they are] enemies for your sakes:** . . . enemies on your account, —YNG.
**but as touching the election, [they are] beloved for the fathers' sakes:** . . . in view of the divine choice, —CNFT . . . from the point of view of God's irrevocable choice, —WAY . . . for Abraham, Isaac, and Jacob's sake, —LOCK.

**11:28.** The Jews are the enemies of the gospel, but beloved for the Father's sake. Note two things. The Jews in their relation to the gospel are regarded by God as enemies for the sake of the Gentiles. But in respect to election the Jews, having been God's choice (Deuteronomy 7:6), are beloved for the fathers' sake (Abraham, Isaac, and Jacob).

**29. For the gifts and calling of God [are] without repentance:** . . . God never takes back his gifts or revokes his choice, —JB . . . for no change of purpose can annul God's gifts and call, —CNBR . . . never changes His mind when He gives anything or calls anyone, —BECK . . . are with respect to a change of mind irrevocable, —WUST . . . and the vocation of God, —RHEM . . . God never regrets, —TCNT . . . For unregretted are the graces, —CNDT . . . are unchangeable, —NORL . . . are not recalled, —ADAM.

**11:29.** Paul was discussing the earthly destiny of Israel, not the heavenly destiny of the individual.

The gifts and calling are subject to no recall; they are irrevocable. God will not change His mind regarding His chosen people and their mission and destiny. His promises concerning them are unconditional.

**30. For as ye in times past have not believed God:** . . . as you once disobeyed, —HNSN.
**yet have now obtained mercy through their unbelief:** . . . through stepping into the place they vacated, —WAY.
**31. Even so have these also now not believed:** . . . they are temporarily disobedient, —WAY.
**that through your mercy they also may obtain mercy:** . . . that through the occasion of the mercy which is yours, —WUST.

**32. For God hath concluded them all in unbelief:** ... has shut up all in unbelief, —CNFT ... has locked up all in the prison of disobedience, —MNTG ... has consigned all men to disobedience, —RSV, —MOFT ... For God had wrapped all nacyons in vnbeleue, —CRNM.

**that he might have mercy upon all:** ... in order to be merciful to all, —BECK.

**11:30-32.** Paul points to God's mercy four times in these verses. First, there is God's mercy to the Gentiles (verse 30). God's dealings with Israel have been the means of extending His grace and mercy to the Gentiles. Verse 31 relates God's mercy to the Jews. The Gentiles had been the unbelievers but found mercy because of the disobedience of the Jews. Now by the mercy of the Gentiles the unbelieving Jews may find mercy. Finally God's mercy reaches to all the world (verse 32).

The word *sunekleisen*, translated "concluded," is more often rendered "imprisoned." It is used only here, in Galatians 3:22, 23 and in Luke 5:6 where the thought is of the fish enclosed in the net.

The Law was God's net in which to enclose all men. This would include the pagan who is a law to himself (2:14). No human being can say that he has without fail kept his own law. All men thus are caught in the awareness of their sinfulness and their helplessness to escape, apart from Christ Jesus.

**33. O the depth of the riches both of the wisdom and knowledge of God!:** ... What an inexhaustible mine, —TCNT ... O fathomless abyss of God's rich bounty, —WAY ... how incomprehensible, —RHEM ... of the aboundaunt wysdome, —TNDL.

**how unsearchable [are] his judgments, and his ways past finding out!:** ... how inscrutable, —SAWR ... How incomprehensible, —DOUY ... how impossible to penetrate his motives, —JB .... how untraceable His footsteps, —BRKL ... how impossible it is to find out His decisions, —BECK ... How mysterious his methods! —MOFT, —WLMS ... How impossible it is to search into His decrees, —WEYM ... his ways past tracing out! —SCLT ... past reaching the end his ways, —KLGS.

**34. For who hath known the mind of the Lord? or who hath been his counsellor?:** ... Who can explore His decisions, —WAY ... Who has ever comprehended, —TCNT ... Or who has begun to tell him what to do? —KLGS.

**35. Or who hath first given to him: and it shall be recompensed unto him again?:** ... that He is indebted to return to him? —ADAM ... so as to receive payment in return, —MNTG ... and it shall be repaid him? —SAWR.

**36. For of him, and through him, and to him, [are] all things:** ... For the universe owes its origin to Him, —WEYM ... For from Him is the beginning, and by Him the life, and in Him the end of all things, —CNBR.

**to whom [be] glory for ever. Amen:** ... through the eternities! —WAY.

**11:33-36.** Just as the doctrinal portion of Romans (chapters 1 to 8) climaxes in a glorious and grand expression of worship to God (8:31-39), the dispensational portion (chapters 9 to 11) is brought to a sublime conclusion in these verses.

This section is praise, pure praise, and is not given to argument at all; yet it is the greatest argument of all. If we do not understand God's ways in His dealings with all men, Jew and Gentile, or even with the Church, it is because we are unable to comprehend the wisdom and knowledge and ways of God.

It has been said that the ways of God are beyond all human inferences (verses 33-35) and beyond all human interferences (verse 36). The mind of man constantly searches to know and to understand. God created him with this ability. But God's thoughts are not man's thoughts, nor are God's ways man's ways. God declares that His thoughts and ways are higher than those of men (Isaiah 55:8, 9).

Human interferences will never stop the fulfillment of God's will. All things and events are of Him, through Him, and for Him. He makes "known unto us the mystery of his will, according to his good pleasure, which he hath purposed in himself" (Ephesians 1:9; cf. 1 Corinthians 2:7). We are ignorant of the mind and purposes of God unless He chooses to reveal them to us (cf. Job 38:4, 36). When those ways are revealed to us, all we can do is bow and worship.

*Anexereunētos*, found only here in the New Testament, is rendered "unsearchable" in the King James Version. Several translations render it "unfathomable"; others use the word "inscrutable." Translations struggle to plumb the depths of the meaning of the Greek which is used to describe the profundity of the riches of the wisdom and knowledge of God. It is impossible for the human mind to grasp!

The apostle states God's ways are "past finding out." The translation comes from the adjective *anexichniastos*. The word comes from "to track out," so that literally it means "that cannot be traced out." Like the previous word it can be translated "inscrutable, incomprehensible, unfathomable." Expressed in simplest terms, Paul is saying that this reservoir of divine wisdom and knowledge cannot be searched to the depths, nor traced to the end.

Three prepositions, *ek*, *dia*, and *eis*, in verse 36 show God is the source, the agency, and ultimate end. He is the Creator, Sustainer, and Goal of all life. All events are of Him, through Him, and for Him. One can only join the apostle in the outburst of praise to our great God whose greatness and glory are unsearchable, unfathomable, and beyond comprehension.

## Chapter 12

**1. I beseech you therefore, brethren:**...I appeal to you, *−RSV*...I intreat you, *−HNSN*...I exhort you, *−CNFT.*

**by the mercies of God:**...because of God's compassion, *−NORL*...tender mercies, *−SCLT*...the pities of God, *−CNDT.*

**that ye present your bodies a living sacrifice:**...to make a decisive dedication of your bodies, *−WLMS*...bring your lives, and set them by the altar, *−WAY*...all your faculties, *−WEYM.*

**holy, acceptable unto God:**...dedicated to his service, *−TEV*...pleasing unto God, *−DOUY*...consecrated, *−MOFT.*

**[which is] your reasonable service:**...and so worship Him as thinking beings, *−BECK*...your spiritual worship, *−NOYS*...which is the reasonable way to serve Him in worship, *−ADAM*...your rational, sacred service, *−WUST.*

**12:1.** In chapters 1 to 8 the plan of salvation (doctrinal) is presented; the hope of Israel (dispensational) in chapters 9 to 11; and an exhortation to godliness (devotional) in chapters 12 to 16. Doctrine must be followed by duty, for privilege brings responsibility and precept must have practice.

**2. And be not conformed to this world:**...Do not live according to the fashions of the times, *−NORL*...Do not model yourselves on the behavior of the world, *−JB*...Do not conform to the externalities, *−WAY*...and not to be configured, *−CNDT*...stop assuming an outward expression, *−WUST*...do not follow the customs, *−WEYM*...Instead of being moulded to this world, *−MOFT*...do not be patterned, *−KLGS*...to the way of our modern age, *−ADAM*...to the present world scheme, *−BRKL.*

**but be ye transformed by the renewing of your mind:**...Be completely made over, *−KLGS*...by your new attitude of mind, *−TCNT*...by the renovation of your mind, *−WLSN.*

**that ye may prove what [is] that good, and acceptable, and perfect, will of God:**...be able to determine, *−ADAM*...that ye may search out, *−SCLT*...that ye may discern, *−ALFD*...that by an unerring test, *−CNBR*...that you may approve the will of God, *−CMPB*...how kind, how gladdening, how flawless it is, *−WAY*...and perfect pleasure of God, *Murdoch.*

**12:2.** From the pinnacle of glorious exultation over the greatness of God in the last verses of chapter 11, believers are brought to the valley of daily duty. The journey in the valley is not irksome, not tiring; it is realistic. The plane of service is made easy because of the glorious heights of Christian doctrine and experience.

The laws of Christian life are discussed in 12:1-13:7; the laws of Christian love are discussed in 13:8-16:24. Verses 1 and 2 of chapter 12 deal with the Christian attitude toward God. Verses 3-13 consider the Christian attitude toward fellowmen. Verses 14-21 discuss the Christian attitude toward enemies.

Service to God is vitally related to consecration and separation. Paul does not command, he entreats. The compassion of our Lord, not His stern command, is the basis of the appeal.

Believers consecrate themselves to God because of His "mercies." The glorious mercies listed in the previous chapters, including justification by faith, assurance, freedom from the penalty and power of sin, and the promise of ultimate glorification, are the bases for moving Christians toward God.

Believers' bodies are to be presented (offered) a "living sacrifice" in contrast to the dead sacrifices of the Levitical priesthood. Fallen creatures can be cleansed and become holy and acceptable. The body is physical, but the intent seems to include all members and faculties. That is reasonable (intelligent) service.

The call is for nonconformity to the world. This is not merely an outward act of self-renunciation. Anything that would displease God and dishonor His holy name is conformity to the world. The Christian is to have God's viewpoint in relation to the world. The word "world" refers to the Spirit which moves humans contrary to the will of God—the spirit of selfishness, the pleasing of self, and submission to the devil. J.B. Phillips renders it: "Don't let the world around you squeeze you into its own mold."

The Christian is called upon to be transformed (transfigured, or changed) by the renewing of his mind. *Metamorphoō*, translated "transformed" here, occurs four times in the New Testament—twice in the account of the Transfiguration and in 2 Corinthians 3:18 where it is rendered "changed."

From these instances believers gain insight as to how to live the transfigured life. When Jesus was transfigured before Peter, James, and John, God's glory shone through Him, not upon Him. Even so, the indwelling Christ is to control the believer's entire being so he will reflect His glory. This is that which is willed by God; it is good, acceptable, and therefore perfect.

The term used here for "mind" (*noos*) can include the intellect, the will, and the emotions. As Paul made clear in 8:5-7, the mind is the battlefield where most of Satan's attacks come. The outcome of the battle depends on whether we yield our minds to the flesh or to the Spirit. James warned that the double-minded man is unstable in all his ways (James 1:8). The goal God has for His children is to have "the mind of Christ" (1 Corinthians 2:16).

The "renewing" indicates present continuous action on the mind. In the new birth, the believer receives a renewed spirit (John 3:1-8); this is regeneration. The continuous renewing of the mind is a major part of the process of sanctification. When one's mind is being renewed by the Word, prayer, and right choices, it becomes easy to know and to live in God's perfect will.

**3. For I say, through the grace given unto** me, **to every man that is among you:**...I command every one, —MKNT...I warn every individual among you, —WEYM...who is self-important, —MOFT.

**not to think [of himself] more highly than he ought to think:**...let no one rate himself more than he ought, —CNFT...no man stonde hye in hys owne conceate, —CRNM...not to value himself higher, —BRKL...not to exaggerate his real importance, —JB...not to estimate himself above his real value, —WLMS.

**but to think soberly:**...Let your thoughts tend to sober views, —WAY...but to make a sober rating of himself, —WLMS...with a view to a sensible appraisal of himself, —WUST...think modestly, —CMPB...so as to think wisely, —YNG.

**according as God hath dealt to every man the measure of faith:**...each measuring himself by the faith which God has allotted to him, —TCNT...as God has apportioned to each one the measure of faith, —CNFT...distributed to each of you, —ADAM...God has assigned to each, —HNT...which God hath imparted to each, —NOYS...has allotted to each man, —WAY.

**4. For as we have many members in one body:**...we have a union of many parts, —TCNT...as we have many limbs, —CNBR...compose collectively one body, —WAY.

**and all members have not the same office:**...all the same function, —MOFT...are not appointed to the same work, —LOCK.

**12:3, 4.** Christians are to render service in humility (verse 3) and in unity (verse 4) to fellow members in the body of Christ. As in the human body there should be no rivalry between members, only mutual respect and harmony.

Verse 3 deals with the believer's self-esteem. He is not to esteem himself more highly than he should; this would cause one to think he is better than others. If he thinks "soberly," he will know that others are not better either. He will be neither conceited nor the victim of an inferiority complex.

The statement that God has given to each one "the measure of faith" applies only to those who are in the body of Christ. In Scripture faith is much more than mental assent or trust because of experience. It is a gift of grace from God (1 Corinthians 12:9; Galatians 5:22; Ephesians 2:8).

**5. So we, [being] many, are one body in Christ:**...as individual members are mutually dependent, —WAY.

**and every one members one of another:**...and are all fellow-members one of another, —LOCK.

**12:5.** Humility is a noteworthy characteristic of the new nature. Paul is saying believers should not overestimate their own importance. Whatever success may come their way is not due to their ability—rather, it is God who has blessed. The possession of spiritual talent should not make Christians feel superior to other members in the Body. Spiritual power is a gift of God (1 Corinthians 4:6, 7). To avoid pride and maintain humility involves the recognition of one's dependence upon fellow Christians, appreciating the place and ministry each one fills and fulfills in the assembly.

Christians, collectively, are linked to a Body. Each member in the Body fulfills his own office (function). Each member is needed. The members have different functions, and these functions are not interchangeable. The person who has given himself to God has a big reason for doing anything, be it ever so small, in a big way.

**6. Having then gifts differing according to the grace that is given to us:**...but possessed of varied talents, —BRKL...according to the respective favour that is bestowed upon us, —LOCK.

**whether prophecy, [let us prophesy] according to the proportion of faith:**...whose gift is inspired eloquence, —WAY...exercise it in accord with the analogy of the faith, —CNDT.

**7. Or ministry, [let us wait] on [our] ministering:**...if it is the gift of administration, —WEYM...then faithfulness in that ministry is required, —NORL.

**or he that teacheth, on teaching:**...take hede to his doctrine, —TNDL...led him be occupied in teaching, —GNVA.

**8. Or he that exhorteth, on exhortation:**...if he is a counselor, in counseling, —ADAM...the entreater, in entreaty, —CNDT.

**he that giveth, [let him do it] with simplicity:**...who has wealth to distribute, —WAY...imparts, —WORL...who contributes, —HNT...without display, —NORL...in singleness of mind, —CNBR.

**he that ruleth, with diligence:**...presideth over others, —NOYS...the office-holder must be faithful, —NORL...he who is leading, —YNG...do it with care, —MKNT.

**he that showeth mercy, with cheerfulness:**...he that pities, —HNSN...he that shows compassion, —PNT...with a joyous abandon, —WUST.

**12:6-8.** In the Church members have "gifts differing according to the grace that is given" them. Seven gifts are enumerated. The purpose of the variety is to enable the whole Body to function as a unit (1 Corinthians 12:12). The various gifts and ministries are as integral to the body of Christ as the parts of the natural body.

Three sections of Scripture in the New Testament describe Body ministry gifts: Romans 12:3-8; 1 Corinthians 12:4-31; and Ephesians 4:4-16. They have much in common, yet each has a different perspective. All are dealing with gifts of grace operative in the Body, and yet each has a distinctive. All are showing the unity of the Body comprised of the diversity of various members with various gifts.

Ephesians 4:11 lists the gifts of Christ to the Body. These are *persons* who have a lifelong calling to be apostles, prophets, evangelists, pastors, or teachers. First Corinthians 12:8-10 is a distinctive list of *manifestations,* rather than persons with a calling for life. They are never called gifts of Christ as in Ephesians 4:11; they are in a special sense gifts (or better, manifestations) of the Holy Spirit. The Holy Spirit is sovereign in bestowing these gifts; they are apportioned according to His will. They are resident in the Spirit and are available at any time as the need exists. They never really belong to the believer in the sense that he does not need to depend on Him in faith for every expression of them. Here in Romans 12 we have a composite list which covers a broad scope, naming gifts of grace which are not distinctive as to a specific Giver, or as to a calling for life, or a temporary manifestation.

The gifts mentioned here are only a partial list. They are: "Prophecy"—the gift of uttering God's will under the direct impulse of the Holy Spirit. The utterance will always be in accord with Scripture which is the criterion for creed and conduct. "Ministry"—this is one of the Greek words (*diakonia*) for a servant. This can include many kinds of service. "Teaching"—to instruct in the truths of Scripture. "Exhortation"—to encourage, to entreat, an appeal to the will in comparison to teaching which is an appeal to the mind. "Giveth"—sharing substance readily and liberally. "Ruleth"—referring to the office of elders and deacons. "Showeth mercy"—engaging in practical deeds of helpfulness and doing so cheerfully.

9. **[Let] love be without dissimulation:** . . . perfectly sincere, —BRKL . . . genuine, —RSV . . . without hypocrisy, —ADAM . . . without pretense, —CNFT . . . unfeigned, —HNSN.

**Abhor that which is evil:** . . . Regard with horror, —WEYM . . . Loathe all wickedness, —WAY . . . Detest the evil, —WLSN.

**cleave to that which is good:** . . . Stick fast, —WUST.

**12:9.** This verse begins a list of 20 commands regulating Christian brotherhood. Verse 9 must be interpreted in the light of those that follow.

There must be love without "dissimulation" (without hypocrisy, genuine, sincere). This is a warning against being two-faced, pretending an affection which is not meant. See 1 John 3:18. Believers are to be glued to that which is good (Psalm 97:10). Those who love righteousness intensely will hate sin. They must regard evil with horror.

10. **[Be] kindly affectioned one to another with brotherly love:** . . . Louing the charitie of the brotherhod one toward an other, —RHEM . . . in a brotherhood of mutual love, —BRKL.

**in honour preferring one another:** . . . in matters of worldly honour, —WEYM . . . put others before yourselves, —TCNT.

**12:10.** The Church is a spiritual family, and warm affection should characterize the members of a family. The idea expressed here is that of the affection between a mother and her children. One of the evidences of Christianity in the Apostolic Church (and today it should be the same) was the testimony in word and deed of brotherly love, an evidence of real discipleship.

11. **Not slothful in business:** . . . never let your zeal flag, —MOFT.

**fervent in spirit:** . . . Be boiling hot, —KLGS . . . be aglow with, —RSV . . . always on fire, —WLMS.

**serving the Lord:** . . . slaving for the Lord, —CNDT.

**12:11.** Christians are not to be lazy, slothful, or careless in zeal. They are to import God's love and grace, then export what they have received in praise to God and service for Him.

The word rendered "fervent" here occurs in only one other place (Acts 18:25) and carries the thought to "boil," to be ardent in boiling over with holy enthusiasm. To lack this is to result in what the Scripture calls a lukewarm or cold condition (Matthew 24:12; Revelation 2:4; 3:15).

12. **Rejoicing in hope:** . . . Let your hope be something exultant, —WAY.

**patient in tribulation:** . . . be steadfast in time of trouble, —NORL . . . in affliction, —MKNT . . . in distress, —HNT.

**continuing instant in prayer:** . . . earnest and persistent in prayer, —WEYM . . . persevering in prayer, —SCLT.

**12:12.** The hope of the Christian is the imminent return of Christ. Believers are not without hope (1 Thessalonians 4:13). The hope of future glory should make them patient. Paul has already written on the subject of patience (5:3, 4; 8:25) and says more in 15:4, 5.

*Hupomenontes* ("patient," KJV) is given a stronger rendering by many translators by the use of "enduring" or "steadfast." The general sense is to stand one's ground, to hold out, to endure. Paul urges believers to continue "instant in prayer." In 1611 the word *instant* had a different meaning. "Insistent" seems to be more correct.

**13. Distributing to the necessity of saints:**...Help the saints, —NORL...Be liberal to the needs of the saints, —CNBR...Contributing to the wants of the saints, —WLSN.

**given to hospitality:** . . . Eagerly welcome strangers as guests, —BECK...always practise hospitality, —WEYM...shewing hospitality to strangers, —SCLT...be readie to harboure, —CRNM.

**12:13.** The word *saint* means "belonging to God." The amazing results are that God will supply the believer's necessities as he ministers to the ones "belonging to Him." The literal meaning of "hospitality" is "love to strangers." See 1 Timothy 3:2; Titus 1:8; Hebrews 13:2; 1 Peter 4:9.

**14. Bless them which persecute you: bless, and curse not:**...Shower blessings on those who persecute you, —WAY.

**12:14.** In this verse Paul reiterates Jesus' teaching as found in Matthew 5:44 and Luke 6:27, 28.

**15. Rejoice with them that do rejoice, and weep with them that weep:**...Share the joy of those who are glad, —BRKL...Be mery with them that are mery, —TNDL...lamenting with those lamenting, —CNDT.

**12:15.** The believer should enter into both the joys and sorrows of other believers. The best example of this is our Lord who could enter into the joyfulness of the wedding in Cana of Galilee, yet weep at the tomb of Lazarus.

It is far easier to weep with the other person in his troubles, than to rejoice with the person whose successes are greater. To be able to rejoice with and for him is the test of true Christian character.

**16. [Be] of the same mind one toward another:**...Live in harmony together, —NORL.

**Mind not high things, but condescend to men of low estate:**...Do not pay special attention to important persons, —KLGS...Avoid being haughty; mingle with the lowly, —NORL...Don't be too ambitious, —BECK...do not aspire to eminence, but willingly adjust yourselves to humble situations, —BRKL...Do not cherish a spirit of pride, —TCNT...but make youre selues equall to them of the lower sorte, —CRNM.

**Be not wise in your own conceits:** . . . Do not over-estimate your own discernment, —WAY...Don't think you are wise, —BECK...Do not be self important, —KLGS...in youre awne opinions, —TNDL...in your own estimation, —HNSN.

**12:16.** The literal Greek is "thinking the same thing toward another." Without agreeing on all things, Christians can have a mutual trust which makes for unity. Snobbishness is not Christian. Believers are not to think too highly of themselves.

**17. Recompense to no man evil for evil:**...Never pay back injury with injury, —TCNT...Repay no one, —RSV.

**Provide things honest in the sight of all men:** . . . Be concerned with things that everybody considers noble, —BECK...Aim to do what is honorable, —MNTG...what all men will recognize as honourable, —TCNT.

**18. If it be possible, as much as lieth in you:**...without sacrificing your principles, —WAY.

**live peaceably with all men:** . . . live on good terms, —TCNT.

**12:17, 18.** The desire to get even has no place in the life of the believer. Christ gave the example; His followers are to forgive even as He forgave them (Colossians 3:13). There are those who will treat a Christian unkindly and often with purpose, and to retaliate is a natural response. But to turn the other cheek, to go the second mile, is Christlike.

The Christian will do his best to live at peace with all men and avoid giving offense to any. Rather than to avenge himself of unjust attacks, he is to return good for evil.

In all his social and business dealings the Christian must maintain a standard that is above reproach. His word must be his bond. There must be no policy other than honesty. The Christian's conduct must at all times commend the gospel witness. He declares by his actions the righteousness of God.

*Pronoeō*, translated "provide," means literally to take thought in advance, to foresee, to think beforehand. *Kala*, rendered "things honest," is one of several Greek words describing that which is good. *Kalos*, the root of the word used here, speaks of that which is fitting and useful. The Christian is to exercise care, to plan in advance so his way of life will properly represent his inward experience.

The believer who lives by Biblical principles will take thought for things honorable "not only in the sight of the Lord, but also in the sight of men" (2 Corinthians 8:21). Character is of supreme importance, but reputation is also of vital importance (Acts 6:3; 16:2).

Christians are to love peace and not be guilty in claiming their rights at the expense of others. The initiative in disturbing peaceful relations with those around them must never be theirs.

"If it be possible" indicates the time may come when courtesy needs to submit to principle. Easygoing tolerance is not always right. The Christian should not back off from a battle if principle is violated.

**19. Dearly beloved, avenge not yourselves:**
**but [rather] give place unto wrath:** ... let God handle it, *—NORL* ... leave room for divine retribution, *—BRKL* ... for God's judgement, *—TCNT* ... leave a place for God's anger, *—WLMS.*
**for it is written:**
**Vengeance [is] mine:** ... Judgment is mine, *—SAWR* ... To me belongs punishment, *—WUST* ... Vengeance belongs to me, *—CMPB* ... is my prerogative, *—WAY.*
**I will repay, saith the Lord:** ... I will pay them back, the Lord says, *—BRKL.*
**20. Therefore if thine enemy hunger, feed him:** ... And if thy adversary, *—MRDK.*
**if he thirst, give him drink:** ... in case he is thirsty, *—BRKL* ... quench his thirst, *—WEYM.*
**for in so doing thou shalt heap coals of fire on his head:** ... you will make him burn with shame, *—TEV.*

**12:19, 20.** Any thought of taking revenge must be banished from the mind. Opposition, persecution, and hatred are to be repaid positively with good.

Scripture makes it very clear that vengeance belongs to God, not to the Christian. God's way of avenging is infinitely better for all concerned and brings glory to Him.

Christians need to realize that they live in a moral universe that is under the authority of God. They must not play God by seeking revenge for personal affronts. God has His way of dealing with offenders either through governmental authority (13:4) or in the final judgment.

When the Christian avoids avenging himself and returns good for evil, he gives God an opportunity to work. Further, he transforms enemies into friends. Kindness shown to one who has caused injury will make him ashamed of his meanness. Vengeance may break an enemy's spirit, but kindness will break his heart. Kindness can bring shame like burning coals of fire on the offender's head.

Those who take vengeance into their own hands are apt to find that at the last it produces bitter fruit. When God avenges wrong it is not done with a retaliation which is so representative of human scheming. God avenges wrong with perfect equity and justice.

**21. Be not overcome of evil, but overcome evil with good:** ... Stop being conquered by evil, *—WLMS* ... Be not subdued by evil, *—WLSN* ... but master evil with good, *—BRKL* ... conquer evil by kindness, *—WAY.*

**12:21.** Those who stoop to vengeance are themselves conquered by evil. To think to overcome evil with evil, hatred with hatred, anger with anger, is to expect that two wrongs make a right,

and that is never so. To meet wrong with wrong is to only increase the wrong. There is power for overcoming evil in the simple might of goodness. If there is anything that will cause an enemy to change his mind, it will be the goodness he sees in the one he has wronged. The only real way to destroy an enemy is to make him a friend.

The risk Paul saw was that a Christian, by giving way to revengeful conduct, would be "overcome of evil," that the wrong in others would produce wrong in his own life. The believer must guard against this by taking the initiative of love and so "overcome evil with good."

## Chapter 13

**1. Let every soul be subject unto:** ... Let every person, *—RSV* ... submitte him selfe, *—GNVA* ... be in subjection, *—WORL* ... be submissive, *—HNSN.*
**the higher powers:** ... governing authorities, *—RSV* ... supreme authorities, *—SCLT* ... superior powers, *—SAWR* ... authorities that are over him, *—WORL.*
**For there is no power but of God:** ... there is no government, *—BECK* ... no one is a ruler except by God's permission, *—WEYM* ... for there exists no authority except from God, *—CNFT.*
**the powers that be are ordained of God:** ... the existing authorities are instituted by, *—HNT* ... stand permanently ordained, *—WUST* ... have been arranged under God, *—WLSN* ... those in charge are divinely constituted, *—BRKL* ... have had their rank and power assigned to them by, *—WEYM* ... are placed under God, *—MKNT* ... by God's sanction, *—WAY.*

**2. Whosoever therefore resisteth the power:** ... So that he which setteth himself against the authority, *—ALFD* ... he who sets himself in opposition to, *—CMPB.*
**resisteth the ordinance of God:** ... he really sets himself against a plan that God has ordained, *—NORL* ... stands against the command, *—KLGS* ... is opposing the divine order, *—MOFT* ... is rebelling against God's decision, *—JB* ... resists what God has appointed, *—RSV* ... is resisting God's will, *—WEYM* ... is a rebel against God's arrangement, *—WAY.*
**and they that resist:**
**shall receive to themselves damnation:** ... bring on themselves condemnation, *—CNFT* ... shall be sentenced, *—HNT* ... will incur judgment, *—RSV* ... shall procure punishment to themselves, *—MKNT.*

**3. For rulers are not a terror to good works, but to the evil:** ... Magistrates are no terror, *—MOFT* ... only criminals have anything to fear, *—JB* ... is not terrible to, *—CNBR* ... to good conduct, *—HNT* ... but by wrong-doers, *—WEYM* ... but to bad actions, *—WAY.*
**Wilt thou then not be afraid of the power?:** ... Would you like to be unafraid of, *—TEV* ... Dost thou desire not to be afraid, *—ALFD.*
**do that which is good, and thou shalt have praise of the same:** ... Act uprightly, *—WAY* ... Do what is right, *—BECK* ... and you will be commended for it, *—WLMS.*

**13:1-3.** In chapter 12 Paul exhorted the believer, as a member of the body of Christ, to perform duties related to his gifts and callings. Romans 13:1-7 deals with the Christian's responsibility as a citizen. His citizenship is in heaven (Philippians 3:20), but he lives in this present world and as a Christian citizen must walk circumspectly. The believer, united to Christ, must still obey the laws of the state. To violate these laws is to sin against God.

Both the Church and the state are institutions of God. Spiritual obligations concern the Christian's relationships to Christ and the Church. Other obligations which some choose to call divine obligations relate to institutions which came into existence before the Church.

Human government is a divine institution. The Christian is a member of a spiritual institution, the Church, and is under the law of God. He is also a member of a divine institution, the state, and is subject to the law of the state. The Church is a spiritual institution; the state is a secular institution. The saved and the unsaved are both under the laws of the state.

Believers must never reject governmental authority; they are never terrorists or anarchists. However, if government opposes God's laws then they must "obey God rather than men" (Acts 5:29). Unless governmental authority opposes God's commands, they are to submit to it, even though the men who administer the authority are ungodly and wicked.

Christians have the duty of civil obedience. Disobedience to governmental authority is disobedience to God and will be judged. Since governments are appointed by God, they must be obeyed. The rule of law militates against the right of the person to decide which laws are right and which are wrong, or to assume the responsibility to obey or disobey as he may please.

While not all rulers are chosen by God, all rule is divinely ordained. The only ones who should live in fear of the representatives of the law are those who break the law. The man who does right has nothing to fear from the authorities, for government, a terror to crime, has no terrors for good behavior.

**4.** **For he is the minister of God to thee for good:** ... It is God's servant to help you, *—BECK* ... The magistrate should be, in your eyes, God's steward, *—WAY* ... for he is God's servant, *—RSV* ... is God's minister appointed, *—MNTG* ... for thy wealth, *—GNVA.*

**But if thou do that which is evil:** ... doest amiss, *—LOCK.*

**be afraid:** ... then be alarmed, *—BRKL.*

**for he beareth not the sword in vain:** ... for not in vain does it wear the sword, *—HNT* ... He does not

carry the sword uselessly, *—KLGS* ... just for show, *—NORL* ... without a purpose, *—BECK* ... without cause, *—RHEM* ... is not without meaning! *—TCNT* ... his power to punish is real, *—TEV* ... is invested with the power of life and death, *—WAY.*

**for he is the minister of God, a revenger to [execute] wrath upon him that doeth evil:** ... the exponent of God's wrath, *—WAY* ... to bring deserved punishment on the evildoer, *—BRKL* ... a revenger to inflict wrath on him, *—CMPB* ... for the infliction of divine vengeance, *—MOFT* ... since he is God's avenging Servant, *—WLSN* ... they carry out God's revenge by punishing wrongdoers, *—JB* ... to him who practiseth evil, *—CLMT.*

**5.** **Wherefore [ye] must needs be subject:** ... there is a necessity for putting one's self in subjection, *—WUST* ... you are absolutely bound to loyal submission, *—WAY.*

**not only for wrath, but also for conscience sake:** ... not for feare of vengeance onely, *—GNVA* ... not only for the sake of escaping punishment, *—WLMS* ... for conscientious reasons, *—TCNT.*

**13:4, 5.** The scriptural point of view is that God commands respect for government, whether good or bad. Paul, with real significance, based his emphasis upon the God-appointed aspect of governmental authority. Five times in the first four verses of this chapter the phrase "of God" occurs. It indicates the origin of government; the origin is God's authority. All government goes back to God. In the covenant with Noah (Genesis 9), God gave the renewed earth into man's hand and instituted human government. God has never revoked that covenant. Therefore, it is the Christian's duty to be a good citizen. Not only is this the teaching of Paul in Romans, but Peter also gives the same counsel (1 Peter 2:12-17).

God has decreed governments but not what form they shall be. Among the nations, there has been every form of government from tribal rule to democracy, monarchy, and dictatorship.

The first clause of verse 4 gives the chief purpose of civil authority. The ruler is the minister "for good," so that "we may lead a quiet and peaceable life in all godliness and honesty" (1 Timothy 2:2). The second clause tells us that the evildoer should fear because the magistrate "beareth not the sword in vain." In most countries the current counterpart of the sword is a gun. The sword or gun is the sign of his authority to use the weapon when necessary.

The fact that an official carries an instrument of death makes clear the God-ordained right of the state to require the death penalty for some crimes. Genesis 9:6, given prior to the Law, has never been revoked. In the New Testament the sword is associated with death as the instrument of execution (Matthew 26:52; Luke 21:24; Acts 12:2; Hebrews

11:34, 37; Revelation 13:10). As John Murray has observed, "To exclude its use for this purpose in this instance would be so arbitrary as to bear upon its face prejudice contrary to the evidence" (*New International Commentary*, 2:153). A sword is not used to rap knuckles; "in vain" would be to a wrong purpose.

Paul was here writing to the Christians in Rome, the capital of the great Roman Empire. Its government was an absolute dictatorship. The emperor had the power of life and death over the empire, and there was no appeal. At the time Nero was emperor. He was a man so sinful and blood-thirsty that his very name remains to this day a synonym for lust, cruelty, and corruption. Yet Paul wrote to the Christians of the Roman Empire that they were to be "subject unto the higher powers" (verse 1).

Those in authority are placed in the position of rulership. They protect law-abiding citizens and they have power to restrain evil men from their wicked deeds. To disobey the law is to resist God's ordinance. Those who keep the law will have nothing to fear; if believers are good citizens those in authority will usually have a good word for them.

In these verses the ruler is twice called "the minister of God"—another testimony to the essentially divine character of civil authority. First Peter 3:13 states, "And who is he that will harm you, if ye be followers of that which is good?"

The Christian's submission should be motivated by more than that which is morally wrong. He obeys the law for a civil reason as well as a moral reason. He obeys in order to escape the wrath of rulers, but a higher law also motivates him. Paul was very concerned about keeping a good conscience before God and man (Acts 23:1; 24:16; 2 Corinthians 1:12; 4:2; 5:11; 1 Timothy 1:5; 3:9; 2 Timothy 1:3). We obey God's ministers because of our obligation to God himself.

The moral "conscience," however, limits obedience. If the civil power commands us to violate the law of God, we must obey God before man. Obtaining, by lawful means, the abrogation of unjust laws must be by legitimate protest and not disobedience.

God has ordained that government shall prescribe laws and then punish the offenders. Government is to protect the community and to punish the criminal.

**6. For for this cause pay ye tribute also:** . . . For the same reason, *—NORL, —RSV* . . . On the same principle, *—WAY* . . . therefore you are settling taxes, *—CNDT* . . . tribute money, *—MRDK.*

**for they are God's ministers:** . . . are God's official servants, *—WLMS* . . . they are God's public ministers, *—HNSN.*

**attending continually upon this very thing:** . . . to this very business, *—CMPB* . . . that constantly attend to this task, *—BRKL* . . . who must attend to this very matter, *—ADAM* . . . devoting themselves to this special work, *—TCNT* . . . serving unto this purpose, *—DOUY.*

**7. Render therefore to all their dues:** . . . Pay to all whatever you owe them, *—BECK* . . . Pay promptly to all men what is due to them, *—WEYM* . . . Deliver to all the debts due them, *—WUST.*

**tribute to whom tribute [is due]; custom to whom custom:** . . . tariff to whom tariff is due, *—NORL* . . . rates where rates are due, *—TCNT* . . . fees to the fees, *—KLGS* . . . revenue to whom revenue is due, *—RSV.*

**fear to whom fear; honour to whom honour:** . . . respect to those who should be respected, honor to those entitled to it, *—NORL* . . . reverence to whom reverence, *—HNSN* . . . homage to whom homage is due, *—MNTG, —WAY* . . . to whom drede: . . . drede, *—WCLF.*

**13:6, 7.** Because government is of God, we are to pay taxes. Even if taxes seem exorbitant, tax collectors "are God's ministers, attending continually upon this very thing." The office, and not necessarily the man, is a ministry ordained by God. Christians are to pay taxes, show proper respect to officers, and courteous deference to all. Just as we owe money in payment of taxes and dues, so we owe a debt of "fear" and "honor" to those whom God has appointed to care for us.

**8. Owe no man any thing, but to love one another:** . . . Avoid getting into debt, *—JB* . . . Stop owing even one person even one thing, *—WUST* . . . Be under obligation to no one, *—TEV* . . . except mutual love, *—WEYM* . . . save the debt of love alone, *—CNBR.*

**for he that loveth another:** . . . that loveth his neighbour, *—DOUY.*

**hath fulfilled the law:** . . . has perfectly satisfied, *—WLMS* . . . has fully performed the law, *—SAWR* . . . has already completed the law, *—KLGS.*

**13:8.** Christians must live with a view to Christ's return, and verses 8-14 tell us how. In addition to obligations to the state the Christian has obligations to members of the state.

The Christian is to "owe no man any thing, but . . . love." No conscientious Christian will assume more financial obligations than he can care for. To go beyond his means in contracting a debt may be plain carelessness; to make no effort to settle the debt is plain dishonesty. Believers should never dishonor the name of Christ by dishonest treatment of the creditor. Every man's word should be absolutely dependable. Nothing will ruin a Christian's testimony faster than chronic indebtedness. The Apostolic Church was given a first requisite for the candidates for the office of deacons—that they should be "men of honest report" (Acts 6:3).

Verse 8 brings a transition, broadening the scope from our relationship to the state to our relationship to all people. Not only are we to render to rulers their just dues, we also are to pay our debts to all. This is in the imperative mood; it is our Lord's command.

This does not necessarily mean that credit is always a sin. For example, a person buying a home with a plan for paying off a mortgage does not "owe a debt" as long as he makes payments on time. The collateral of the home itself covers the lender so that neither the buyer nor the creditor is at loss. This principle should be followed in all purchases involving any credit. A believer is wise to use credit very sparingly, if at all.

Financial obligations can be paid, but there is another obligation that can never be fully paid—the debt to love one another. If a Christian loves his neighbor as he loves himself, he will take as much care of his neighbor's interests, his property, his good name, as he would of his own. He will never do anything to harm him and will thus fulfill God's law and man's law.

To say that love fulfills the Law does not mean that love displaces law. Love is a higher motive than law, but it is law that love fulfills. Love, as defined by the Bible, will never cause a person to break any of God's laws nor to influence anyone else to do so. Jesus said that if we love Him we will keep His commandments (John 14:15).

The love described here is supernatural, given by the Holy Spirit (5:5). It is the love of God manifested in and through His children.

**9. For this:**...For, take the prohibitions, —WAY.
**Thou shalt not commit adultery:**
**Thou shalt not kill:**...Thou shall not murder, —ET.
**Thou shalt not steal, Thou shalt not bear false witness:**
**Thou shalt not covet:** ... don't be greedy, —BECK...thou shalt not lust, —CRNM...do not desire what belongs to someone else, —TEV.
**and if [there be] any other commandment:**...any other precept, —CNDT.
**it is briefly comprehended in this saying, namely:**...it all heads up in one word, —BRKL...are summed up in this one command, —WEYM ... are gathered up in this word, —HNT...it in short is comprehended in this, —LOCK...it is comprised in this word, —RHEM...in this one injunction, —WAY.
**Thou shalt love thy neighbour as thyself:**...thy fellow man as much as thou lovest thyself, —WEYM.

**10. Love worketh no ill to his neighbour:**...Love is the one thing that cannot hurt your neighbor,

—JB ... works no evil, —CMPB ... can perpetrate no wrong, —WAY ... permits us to do no harm to our neighbour, —LOCK.
**therefore love [is] the fulfilling of the law:**...so love meets all the Law's requirements, —BRKL...and is therefore complete obedience to Law, —WEYM...so love is the perfect satisfaction, —WLMS.

**13:9, 10.** When a person becomes a child of God he comes under the influence of the law of love, and that law inspires the love of law. If a person tries to pay the debt of love, he will instinctively keep the commandments.

God gave Moses two tables of commandments. One concerns man's relationship to God, the other man's duty and attitude toward his fellowman. Paul stated that the last five are summed up in this law, "Thou shalt love thy neighbor as thyself."

A person who truly loves will not commit adultery. If two people allow physical passions to entice them to sin, it is not because they love each other too much, but because they love each other too little. In true love there is respect and restraint. One who truly loves will never kill, for love never seeks to destroy; it is always kind, even to an enemy. One who truly loves will never steal, for love is more concerned with giving than getting. One who truly loves will not covet, for to covet is to desire that which is forbidden. God's love removes all such unholy desires.

Love works no ill. If a person's heart and life is controlled by love, he will need no other law.

**11. And that, knowing the time:**...What I have said is the more urgent, —TCNT...knowing the strategic season, —WUST...the critical period at which we are living, —WEYM...if you recognise the imminence of a great crisis, —WAY.
**that now [it is] high time to awake out of sleep:**...because the hour has struck for us to wake up, —BRKL...it is now the hour for us to rise, —DOUY.
**for now [is] our salvation nearer than when we believed:**...Our Great Deliverance, —WAY...we are now nearer being rescued, —BECK...than when you first entered into the profession of Christianity, —LOCK.

**13:11.** The imminence of the Lord's return was a message used by the apostles to urge people to live holy lives. Considering the nearness of eternity, Christians should fulfill every duty. Paul emphasized the need for believers to do everything in the light of the uncertainty of life and the certainty of eternity. He underscored the tendency to slumber and sleep. To "sleep" indicates unconcern. Being "awake" implies spiritual readiness. The reference is to salvation as the consummation of God's final redemptive act.

**12. The night is far spent:** ... The night is far gone, —NORL ... The night is passed, —RHEM, —DOUY.

**the day is at hand:** ... and dawn is at hand, —NORL ... the day is drawing near, —SCLT.

**let us therefore cast off the works of darkness:** ... cast away the dedes of darkenes, —GNVA.

**and let us put on the armour of light:** ... put on the weapons of light, —ADAM.

**13:12.** The last four verses of this chapter list eight commands for Christians: (1) cast off the works of darkness; (2) put on the armor of light; (3) live honorably; (4) stop rioting and drinking; (5) shun all immoral living; (6) refrain from quarrels, contentions, jealousies; (7) clothe one's self with the character of Jesus Christ; (8) make no provision for lust. These verses are a call to holiness.

The "night" symbolizes a time of great spiritual darkness, a time when planet Earth is beset with the darkness of sin, evil, war, hunger, and suffering. The "day" pictures the coming of Christ as the "Sun of righteousness (who shall) arise with healing in his wings" (Malachi 4:2).

It is time to "cast off the works of darkness" as one would shed an unclean garment. All wicked ways and acts are to be thrown off. The antithesis between light and darkness is found repeatedly in Paul's epistles (2 Corinthians 6:14; Ephesians 5:8; Colossians 1:12, 13; 1 Thessalonians 5:4, 5).

It is time to "put on the armor of light." "Armor" is *hopla*, meaning weapons. "Put on" is from *endunō* meaning to put on or clothe as with a garment. By prayer, self-discipline, reading and studying God's Word, we put on holy character, so that people can recognize us as belonging to Christ. The "armor of light" is listed in Ephesians 6:11-17.

**13. Let us walk honestly:** ... Let us live nobly, —BECK ... behave ourselves with propriety, —HNT ... walk decently, —WSLY ... walk becomingly, —SAWR, —CNFT ... walk seemly, —ALFD.

**as in the day:** ... that is appropriate to the daytime, —ADAM ... in broad daylight, —WEYM.

**not in rioting and drunkenness:** ... Let us not carry on in carousing, —NORL ... not indulging in revelry, —WEYM ... not in glotonie, —GNVA ... and drunken entertainments, —WSLY.

**not in chambering:** ... not in prostitution, —BRKL ... nor in lust, —WEYM ... not in sexual orgies, —ADAM ... with no lewd or any sensual acts, —HNT.

**and wantonness:** ... or living wild, —BECK ... debauchery, —WEYM ... a dissolute abandon, —WUST ... excesses, —SAWR ... licentiousness, —PNT.

**not in strife and envying:** ... in quarreling, —RSV ... in contention and emulation, —RHEM ... strife and jealousy, —ASV.

**13:13.** *Peripateō* which means "walk" or literally "walk around" is also rendered "behave," "live," "conduct ourselves."

*Euschēmonōs* means "becomingly" or "decorously" and is so rendered in several translations. *Kōmos*, meaning "revelry," was a riotous procession at night of half-drunken carousers who made themselves a nuisance; *methē*, "drunkenness," was particularly disgraceful to the Greeks. *Koitē*, rendered "chambering," was sexual immorality. *Aselgeia*, "wantonness," described more than immorality. It was unbridled and shameless. *Eris*, contention, "strife," results from placing self first. *Zēlos*, "envy," means a contentious and jealous rivalry.

**14. But put ye on the Lord Jesus Christ:** ... But clothe yourselves, —MNTG ... be enveloped with, —BRKL ... put on the character of the Lord Jesus, —MOFT.

**and make not provision for the flesh, to [fulfil] the lusts [thereof]:** ... and take no forethought, —ALFD ... don't make plans to satisfy, —ADAM ... never think how to gratify the cravings of the flesh, —MOFT ... to gratify the irregular desires of, —SCLT ... for the indulgence of appetites, —MRDK.

**13:14.** The believer is to "put on the Lord Jesus Christ." This is first done at regeneration and is to be a daily experience (Titus 3:5). This is a walk in the Spirit (8:2). There must be no provision for either gross appetites or refined carnal attitudes; all must be denied.

# Chapter 14

**1. Him that is weak in the faith receive ye:** ... who is feeble ... reach forth the hand, —MRDK ... receive into full Christian fellowship, —WLMS ... be giving a cordial welcome, —WUST.

**[but] not to doubtful disputations:** ... and not just to argue about different opinions, —BECK ... about his personal opinions, —TEV ... not for mutual judgings of opinions, —PNT ... without regard to differences of opinions, —CMPB ... yet not for decisions of scruples, —WORL.

**14:1.** This chapter comes to grips with the problems related to balancing two spiritual laws. The law of liberty permits a Christian to do certain things which may be perfectly lawful but may raise a question in the minds of others. The law of love motivates the Christian to readily sacrifice his liberty rather than to cause the other brother to stumble.

Christians are free from sin and bondage, but not from spiritual obligations. We have liberty, but not license, for none of us are free to live as we please without regard to others.

The Spirit was instructing the church not to discriminate against those who had conscientious scruples regarding things considered nonessentials by the more mature believers.

It is difficult to know the exact meaning of "doubtful disputations" (*diakriseis dialogismōn*, literally "judgment of thoughts"). It seems that God, who alone sees the heart, was telling the stronger not to subject the convictions of the weaker to censorious scrutiny.

**2. For one believeth that he may eat all things:** ...allows him to eat anything, *—WEYM* ...has confidence, *—WUST.*

**another, who is weak, eateth herbs:** ...yet the infirm one is eating greens, *—CNDT* ...lives upon vegetables, *—SCLT.*

**3. Let not him that eateth despise him that eateth not:** ...despise the vegetarian, *—NORL* ...should not feel contempt for the abstainer, *—BRKL* ...belittle the one who does not eat, *—KLGS.*

**and let not him which eateth not:**

**judge him that eateth:** ...must not criticize, *—MOFT* ...condemn him who eats, *—HNSN* ...censure the eater, *—BRKL.*

**for God hath received him:** ...has fully accepted, *—WLMS.*

**4. Who art thou that judgest another man's servant?:** ...condemnest another's household servant? *—MKNT.*

**to his own master he standeth or falleth:** ...own personal master, *—WUST* ...own lord, *—WORL.*

**Yea, he shall be holden up:** ...Yea, he shall be made to stand, *—PNIN.*

**for God is able to make him stand:** ...for the Master is able to make him stand, *—KLGS* ...is able to set him up, *—CNBR* ...He will succeed, *—ET* ...he will assuredly stand, *—MRDK.*

**14:2-4.** There are certain essentials upon which all followers of Christ must agree, such as the inspiration and infallibility of the Bible, the deity of Christ, the Virgin Birth, the necessity of the vicarious sacrifice, the new birth, and many others. There are, however, matters over which Christians may disagree but are not essential to salvation. These are not the great questions of doctrine, nor are they questions of spirituality or morality; they are the smaller details which arise from day to day. In chapter 13 Paul condemned those things which are immoral, but in chapter 14 he warned against the dangers of being too severe in questionable matters that are not contrary to scriptural principles.

Verse 4 shows the danger of judging a brother in the area of his conscience. This does not eliminate all judging. Speaking to Pharisees, Jesus said, "Judge not" (Matthew 7:1), but in the same sermon He said, "By their fruits ye shall know them" (Matthew 7:20).

Paul, no doubt, was writing on this matter because of a problem in the church at Rome. Some of the Christians, whom he called "weak" brethren, were in bondage to regulations concerning food and holy days. Some Gentile Christians, influenced by pagan customs, believed in abstaining from meats (1 Timothy 4:3). Another group influenced by Judaism, felt it was sinful to eat food forbidden by Mosaic law. One group, the vegetarians, felt the meat eaters were backslidden, while the other group even thought of excluding the vegetarians from fellowship.

Romans 14 and 1 Corinthians 8 are devoted to a burning question in the Apostolic Church. Large quantities of meat were brought to the heathen temples for idol worship. What the priest could not consume was sold to the public in the marketplace. Since it was almost impossible to know if the meat purchased at the market had come from an idol's temple, the weaker brethren found themselves unable to eat *any* meat for fear it might have been offered unto an idol (1 Corinthians 8:7). Therefore, to avoid defiling their conscience they confined their diet to vegetables.

Notice how Paul dealt with the problem. He did not put the strong in bondage, nor did he remove the scruples of the weak. Instead, he laid down principles which made it possible for both to live in peace with each other. These same principles are applicable today in matters between God's saints. As long as fundamental matters are not involved, Christians should live with harmonious consideration of each other. Paul warned believers neither to despise nor to judge another "for God hath received him," and he will stand or fall before the Lord whose servant he is.

**5. One man esteemeth one day above another:** ...decides for the superior sacredness, *—WAY* ...discriminateth between days, *—MRDK* ...as holier than others, *—JB* ...some make one day more sacred than another, *—ET* ...as better than another, *—RSV.*

**another esteemeth every day [alike]:** ...another man counteth all dayes, *—GNVA* ...rates all days alike, *—BRKL* ...subjects every day to a scrutiny, *—WUST* ...another makes every day holy, *—ET.*

**Let every man be fully persuaded in his own mind:** ...Let every one be convinced, *—MKNT* ...should firmly make up his own mind, *—TEV* ...know what he believes, *—ET* ...be fully assured, *—WUST.*

**14:5.** Another problem was that of the observance of days. The Christian's Sunday is not a Sabbath in the sense of the old covenant Sabbath. The first day of the week was set apart by the resurrection of our Lord Jesus. On that day He appeared to His disciples. The Christians broke bread on that day (Acts 20:7), and on that day they brought their offerings to the Lord (1 Corinthians 16:2). The first day of the week is the Lord's Day. We are not told exactly how to keep the day, but it is to be observed in worship as a special day.

Regarding things not specifically regulated, Paul stated, "Let every man be persuaded in his own mind."

This chapter is often entitled "Questionable Things." Another term that perhaps best describes food and days is *neutral*. A neutral thing is anything that in itself is neither good nor bad; it can be used for either good or for bad. Along with food and days we could mention many things, such as money and houses. The list could be very lengthy.

**6. He that regardeth the day:** ... who observes the day, *—HNSN* ... that observes the day, *—SAWR* ... he who reverences a day, *—ET* ... obserueth one day, more than another, *—GNVA.*

**regardeth [it] unto the Lord:** ... reverences it to the Lord, *—ET* ... does so in the Lord's service, *—WAY* ... should observe it in the Lord's honor, *—NORL* ... observes it with the Lord in view, *—BRKL* ... means to honor the Lord, *—BECK* ... to the Master's honour, *—TCNT.*

**and he that regardeth not the day, to the Lord he doth not regard [it]:** ... He that is not concerned about a day, *—ET.*

**He that eateth, eateth to the Lord:** ... So also the non-abstainer eats, *—WAY.*

**for he giveth God thanks:**

**and he that eateth not, to the Lord he eateth not:** ... refrains for the Lord's sake, *—BRKL* ... he who abstains, *—MNTG* ... abstains to the Lord, *—MOFT* ... is doing it as unto the Lord, *—ET* ... abstains for the Lord, *—CNFT.*

**and giveth God thanks:** ... since he, too, gives God thanks, *—MNTG.*

**14:6.** Frequently a great deal of unbrotherliness has been generated in the Christian community by assuming judgmental attitudes concerning those who differ with us on some of the implications of the Christian life. The end product is a feeling of hostility and a breach of fellowship which is sometimes far worse from a Christian standpoint than the conduct being condemned. There comes a point at which we must leave the judgment of someone else's behavior up to the Lord.

At times, when we are wearied with controversy, we wish it were possible for all persons to be in agreement. To think that is to assume an impossibility. There will always be the stimulus of conflicting opinions. But we must learn to disagree without being disagreeable. There must be no compromise on doctrine, no concessions concerning truth, but there will be some give-and-take in the area of opinions.

Church members of Jewish background among the Romans and Corinthians tended to cling to the seventh day of the week for worship purposes. This viewpoint was in conflict with the trend toward observing the first day of the week. Opponents of this viewpoint apparently said that those who really wanted to honor the Lord would honor Him every day. The same conflict existed regarding eating meat which may have been dedicated to an idol.

**7. For none of us liveth to himself:** ... No man's life concerns only himself, *—BRCL* ... none of us can live alone by himself, *—WLMS* ... as if he were his own man, *—LOCK* ... lives for himself alone, *—ET.*

**and no man dieth to himself:**

**8. For whether we live:** ... If we live, *—ET.*

**we live unto the Lord:** ... In life we live for the Lord, *—BRCL* ... we always live in relation to the Lord, *—WLMS* ... our life is appropriated to the Lord, *—LOCK.*

**and whether we die:** ... or if we die, *—ET.*

**we die unto the Lord:**

**whether we live therefore, or die, we are the Lord's:** ... In life and in death we belong to the Lord, *—BRCL* ... we belong to our Lord, *—MNTG.*

**14:7, 8.** In verse 5 Paul stated, "Let every man be fully persuaded in his own mind." Over against that we have this verse which indicates that there is not one whose life or death concerns himself alone. It is impossible to live in isolation. One cannot disentangle himself either from his fellowmen or from God. For this reason, among others, no one can make his own practice the universal standard. It is well to remember that believers have a right to have their own convictions, but they also have the duty to allow others to have theirs without regarding them as sinners.

Personal conviction is important. Christian lifestyle should not be governed by convention or by semisuperstitious taboos, but by a prayerfully and carefully thought-out conviction as to what is right and what is wrong.

There must be room for toleration and liberty of conscience. Extremes infect a man's thoughts and actions. Differences of opinions must not divide brethren. Each should treat the other in love, and avoid condemning another, for the Lord has received all believers into His divine favor.

Note that the questionable things under consideration are in themselves totally neutral. Jesus made clear that it is not food that defiles a man but rather those things that proceed out of his mouth, from his heart (Matthew 15:17-20). Food can, however, be used in a sinful way; this was true under the Law, and it is true now.

To eat something one knows to be harmful to the body is wrong (1 Corinthians 6:19; 10:31). Gluttony is condemned in the same way alcoholism is

(Proverbs 23:21; Galatians 5:21). Jesus was called by His enemies a glutton and winebibber because He ate with sinners, but that was a false charge like many others made against Him. He never did anything that was in any way sinful.

Any neutral thing can be used in a sinful way. The motive is what God judges (1 Corinthians 4:5). Money can be used for good (Luke 16:9) or for evil (1 Timothy 6:10). A musical instrument can also be used for God or for Satan. Lyrics of songs are not neutral; they communicate meaning which always says something either conducive to godly living or to sinful living. Many believe that the same is true of music itself; there can be no doubt that some music communicates an evil message.

**9. For to this end Christ both died, and rose, and revived:** ... For this purpose, —MNTG ... For this very reason, —NIV ... for because of this, —YNG ... The very reason why Christ died and came to life again, —BRCL ... and continues alive, —SCLT.

**that he might be Lord both of the dead and living:** ... to establish his lordship over dead and living, —NEB ... be lorde both of deed and quicke, —TNDL ... that He might exercise lordship, —WUST, —SAWR ... that he might rule over both, —MKNT.

**14:9.** The Lord's will and His glory are always to be in view, in life and in death. Jesus died to redeem us and rose from the grave to reign. As the dying Christ, He saved us; as the living Christ, He regulates our daily walk. Christians should live in the shadows of the Cross by the power of the Resurrection. Whether liberty is enjoyed or scruples are adhered to, the Christian lives with Calvary in view and his life conditioned by the living Christ.

**10. But why dost thou judge thy brother?:** ... Then why should you criticize, —WLMS ... Why do you pass judgment, —RSV ... as some of you have done, —JB.

**or why dost thou set at nought thy brother?:** ... Why do you put down, —ET ... why do you look down on your brother? —BRKL ... why do you look on your brother with contempt? —ADAM ... why do you regard your brother with contempt? —BRCL ... why do you look down upon, —WEYM ... why doest thou despyse thy brother? —TNDL.

**for we shall all stand before the judgment seat of Christ:** ... Surely, we shall all stand before God, —WLMS ... seat of God, —ALFD ... at the tribunal of God, —SAWR ... the tribunal of Christ, —SCLT, —WLSN ... that we shall all have to present ourselves, —WAY.

**14:10.** Paul declared that we must all stand before the Judgment Seat (*bēma*). God is the Judge, not we. Therefore we should leave the judging to Him.

In the New Testament the word *bēma* refers to the judgment of believers for their works, in contrast to the Great White Throne Judgment where sinners will be judged. One can see the word today carved on the wall where Gallio sat on the judgment seat at Corinth (Acts 18:12, 16, 17). It is used of Pilate's judgment seat (Matthew 27:19), and also that of Festus (Acts 25:6, 17). Here these governors passed judgment on offenders and exonerated the innocent. Paul lived his life with an awareness that he and all of us must stand before the great Judge of all. Little wonder that he sought always to have "a conscience void of offense toward God, and toward men" (Acts 24:16).

Only believers will be present; therefore the issue is not whether one is saved or not. It is rather that "every one may receive the things done in his body, . . . whether it be good or bad" (2 Corinthians 5:10).

God is very concerned about our stewardship with the gifts and opportunities He has given us. Jesus said He would come quickly to reward every believer according to his works. Works motivated by faith and love (Galatians 5:6) will prove to be gold, silver, and precious stones (1 Corinthians 3:12-15). Works done without *agapē* love as the motive will be burned, bringing loss of reward.

**11. For it is written:**
[As] **I live, saith the Lord, every knee shall bow to me:** ... everyone will kneel to Me, —BECK.
**and every tongue shall confess to God:** ... and every tongue shall make confession to God, —NORL ... shall render acknowledgment to God, —BRKL ... shall give praise to God, —HNSN ... shall be acclaiming God! —CNDT.
**12. So then every one of us shall give account of himself to God:** ... shal render account, —RHEM ... will give his own report to, —KLGS ... each of us concerning himself, —YNG ... is to be answerable for his own actions, —WAY.

**14:11, 12.** Every individual believer will answer; an individual inquiry will require individual responsibility. Let us not judge others, but rather let us keep our own house in order. Our personal liberty is to be enjoyed in the light of the presence of the Master of our lives and the certainty that each of us "shall give account of himself to God."

**13. Let us not therefore judge one another any more:** ... let us no longer pass judgment, —MNTG ... let us never again find fault, —KLGS ... stop criticizing one another, —NORL, —MOFT.
**but judge this rather:** ... but let us rather decide this, —BRKL ... let this be your resolution, —TCNT ... but rather determine this, —SCLT ... But rather let us make up our minds, —KLGS.
**that no man put a stumbling-block or an occasion to fall in [his] brother's way:** ... that it is wrong to set in your brother's path anything, —WAY ... decide not to lay any stumbling block or

trap, —BECK ... not to put any hindrance, —HNT ... a cause of offence, —PNT ... nor anything to trip him up, —WEYM ... or a scandal before a brother, —SCLT.

**14. I know, and am persuaded by the Lord Jesus:** ... As one who lives in union, —WEYM ... For I know with an absolute knowledge, —WUST ... My union with the Lord Jesus, —TEV ... I know and am confident, —CNFT ... and am full certified by, —CRNM ... and am fully assured, —LOCK.

**that [there is] nothing unclean of itself:** ... no food is impure, —WEYM ... not even one thing is unhallowed, —WUST ... nothing is common, —PNIN ... nothing is contaminating, —CNDT.

**but to him that esteemeth any thing to be unclean, to him [it is] unclean:** ... only to him that accounteth anything unclean, —ALFD ... to those who so regard it, —TCNT ... vnto him that iudgeth it to be vnclene, —GNVA ... to him it is defiled, —SAWR.

**14:13, 14.** It has been said that those who are weak in faith live by conscience, those who are strong in faith by knowledge, but the more mature by love. The apostle chided those with a weak conscience, but in the fellowship of the Church, he put the burden for maintaining right relationship on the strong. If concessions had to be made, they must make them in a spirit of love. The weaker brethren were their solemn responsibility, and they must do nothing to offend their conscience or jeopardize their standing.

Paul's conclusion is emphatic. Even though he was stronger in faith, even though eating meat offered to idols did not bother him, he refrained voluntarily for the sake of his weaker brother. His cardinal concern was his brother's welfare.

The right use of liberty is important. Under the gospel the Christian is perfectly free from the externals of the law of Moses and from the bondage that some might be in, having not realized their liberty in Christ. But the gospel that grants liberty may also require the believer to sacrifice that liberty to help the weak. One is not truly free until he recognizes this. Otherwise he is a slave to liberty.

Liberty gives way to a brother's weaker conscience. He will do nothing to bring his brother spiritual harm. Christians are warned against placing a stumbling block or hindrance in a brother's way. In other words, believers should not glory in their religious freedom in such a way as to cause a weaker, overscrupulous brother to stumble and fall. True love will put the interests of others first. Nothing is worth enjoying if it causes someone to lose his soul. The test by which we are to judge our life and action is not our own welfare but that of our brother.

**15. But if thy brother be grieved with [thy] meat:** ... is hurt by what you eat, —KLGS ... is continually pained because of your food, —MNTG ... for a matter of mere food, —HNT.

**now walkest thou not charitably:** ... you are not conducting yourself, —MNTG ... your life has ceased to be ruled by love, —TCNT ... you are not living by the standard of love, —WLMS.

**Destroy not him with thy meat, for whom Christ died:** ... you lead to ruin a man for whom, —WEYM ... Do not persist in ruining him, —WAY.

**14:15.** The strong may be called upon to exercise great self-denial and sacrifice their liberty. Otherwise they would be slaves to liberty. They do this for three reasons: (1) for the good of the weaker brother (verse 13); (2) for Jesus' sake (verse 15); (3) for the good of the Church (verse 20).

If Jesus gave His life for these, should not the strong be willing to give up a small item of personal liberty for Jesus' sake?

*Lupeō* is translated "grieved" in the King James. Other translations use stronger words such as "pained, hurt, being injured." Possibly the latter is the best rendering.

*Apollumi*, translated "destroy" here, literally means to "destroy utterly." It is used frequently in the New Testament of sinners perishing without salvation. This makes it clear that it is not a matter of a weak brother having his life wasted or his reputation ruined. Our selfish liberties may cause his soul to perish.

**16. Let not then your good be evil spoken of:** ... what is wholesome for you, —BRKL ... Your rights must not get a bad name, —MOFT ... become a subject of reproach, —NORL ... be not oure good thing blasfemed, —WCLF ... be spoken of in a reproachful and evil manner, —WUST ... be injuriously spoken of, —SAWR.

**14:16.** *Blasphēmeō*, translated "evil spoken of," is the Greek word from which comes our word *blaspheme*. It is not enough for the Christian to do what he feels is right. He must guard against doing anything that could cause his "good (to be) evil spoken of." He should be concerned about the impression he makes on others, as well as the relations of his own conscience to God.

**17. For the kingdom of God is not meat and drink:** ... For the Reign of God, —CMPB, —YNG ... since God's empire, —ADAM ... do not consist in the enjoyment of greater variety of meats and drinks, —LOCK.

**but righteousness, and peace, and joy in the Holy Ghost:** ... but justice, —KLGS ... but of right conduct, —WEYM ... in the sphere of the Holy Spirit, —WUST.

**14:17.** The discussion of whether or not to eat certain foods became the occasion for Paul to make this profound statement of truth. The kingdom of God is not a matter of externals. God's kingdom is concerned with far greater matters than the mere question of eating and drinking. The apostle sweeps away the debris of rituals and traditions of men. Those externals are all too often the center of controversy and only hinder the growth of the Church.

The spiritual life of the believer receives experiences of: (1) righteousness—the state of being right and doing right in the sight of God; (2) peace—peace that passes understanding is the portion of all who are right with God and with men; (3) joy in the Holy Spirit—rightness with God brings the indwelling of the Holy Spirit.

**18. For he that in these things serveth Christ [is] acceptable to God, and approved of men:** . . . is well-pleasing to God, and cannot be condemned by men, *—CNBR* . . . finds favor with God and is approved also by men, *—NORL* . . . and esteemed by men, *—MOFT* . . . and men highly commend him, *—WEYM.*

**14:18.** When a person follows these principles he becomes a slave of Christ. Living for these, one serves Christ and has the approval of God and man. Christians should remember that their rights are far less important than their obligations. While they have Christian liberty, it is never to be used to cause pain and grief to a brother. The Church suffers if the members do not in love consider one another. There are people who need to be set right, but there is a right way to do it (Galatians 6:1-3).

The weak brother, in turn, is to avoid a critical spirit of faultfinding. A censorious person is usually a weak person.

**19. Let us therefore follow after the things which make for peace:** . . . So then let us eagerly pursue, *—MNTG* . . . let us strive after peace, and mutual edification, *—CMPB* . . . that contributes to one another's peace, *—BRKL* . . . after the things productive of peace, *—WORL.*

**and things wherewith one may edify another:** . . . the upbuilding of each other, *—MNTG* . . . and mutual upbuilding of character, *—WEYM* . . . the upbuilding of the fabric of the church, *—WAY* . . . the things that tend to mutual edification, *—WORL.*

**14:19.** How often the bickerings of believers have brought discredit to the work of God. Christians should never tear down the work of God in the hearing of a weak believer or in the eyes of the unconverted for the sake of their own gratification. The believer's self-denial does not involve asceticism—painful inflictions, torturous pilgrimages, living as a hermit—rather, it is lofty purpose within his own desire for the sake of others.

*Diōkō,* translated "follow after," means to "pursue." We are to keep on pursuing the things of peace.

The word "edify" as used here has the meaning of "building up." The message is, let us then pursue what makes for peace and for mutual upbuilding.

**20. For meat destroy not the work of God:** . . . Don't ruin God's work, *—BECK* . . . Overthrow not for meat's sake, *—PNIN* . . . We must not undo God's work, *—ADAM* . . . must not break down God's work for the mere sake, *—MOFT* . . . for a meal of meat, *—CNBR* . . . Do not demolish, *—HNSN.*

**All things indeed [are] pure:** . . . . indeed are clean, *—DOUY.*

**but [it is] evil for that man who eateth with offence:** . . . when it makes another stumble, *—WLMS.*

**14:20.** The unwise example of the strong may lead to the spiritual ruin of the weak. We are counseled not to break down, undo, and destroy the work of God for the sake of food. Even though everything may be ceremonially clean, we do wrong to bring damage to the conscience of others or to make them fall by what they eat.

The "all things" that are pure include only those things that are genuinely neutral. A television set, for example, is "pure," but the program will be either pure or impure according to the message communicated.

**21. [It is] good neither to eat flesh, nor to drink wine, nor [any thing]:** . . . The right course is to go without meat, *—TCNT* . . . is to forego eating, *—WEYM* . . . It is an excellent plan to abstain from flesh, *—HNT* . . . It is better to forbear flesh, *—LOCK.*

**whereby thy brother stumbleth, or is offended, or is made weak:** . . . that affords an occasion for your brother to stumble, *—ADAM* . . . so as to be an occasion of sin, *—NOYS* . . . or is weakened, *—CMPB.*

**14:21.** Conscious limitation for the sake of others is the Christian way. The believer must look at his lifestyle not only as to how it affects him personally but also how it affects others.

In Romans 14:21 and 1 Corinthians 8:13 Christians have a God-given code of conduct that is not determined by conscience or knowledge, but by love operating through truth.

The way a person uses his power is a good test of his character. Authority can become overbearing. The strong can look down on the weak, the prosperous can despise those of limited means, the educated can belittle the unlettered.

**22. Hast thou faith? have [it] to thyself before God:** . . . Have it personally in the presence of God, *—BRKL* . . . keep your own conviction on the matter,

−MOFT . . . keep it for thine own comfort before God, −CNBR.

**Happy [is] he that condemneth not himself in that thing which he alloweth:** . . . that is not self-condemned in the thing that he practises, −LOCK . . . who has no qualms of conscience in what he allows himself to do, −BRKL . . . if you never have to condemn yourself, −BECK.

**23. And he that doubteth is damned if he eat:** . . . But the person who entertains doubts, −BRKL . . . But he who has scruples, −PNT . . . he who discerns a difference, −CMPB . . . he who feels any hesitation, −HNT . . . he who has misgivings, and yet eats meat, −MNTG . . . And he who doubts is condemned, −WORL.

**because [he eateth] not of faith:** . . . it was not an act of faith, −NORL . . . because he doesn't go by what he believes, −BECK . . . his action is not based on faith, −MNTG.

**for whatsoever [is] not of faith is sin:** . . . and every act which is not from Conviction, −WLSN . . . and any action that is not based on faith, −MOFT . . . for whatever is not from full persuasion is sin, −SCLT . . . whatever does not proceed from faith, −RSV . . . and every faithless deed is sin, −CNBR.

**14:22, 23.** These verses point out two perils of liberty. First, the strong brother is not to parade his liberties and injure the feelings of others. If one is positive of his position, he need never make a display of it. The proper action for the strong brother is to choose, not on the basis of liberty, but for the sake of God and others. Quietly he makes his decision, and in refraining, he finds happiness beyond compare. The highest and holiest ambitions will call for abstinence instead of indulgence; for a walk on the narrow way instead of a broad-minded way.

Second, the weak brother has a peril too. If he by the example of a stronger one becomes bold to eat despite his conscience, he will be condemned. The term *katakekritai* ("has been condemned") is from the same root as *katakrima* ("condemnation") in 8:1. It is also translated "damned." This shows two very important truths. (1) "Condemnation," as used by Paul, includes being damned, doomed to hell. As long as one is "in Christ," he of course cannot be damned (8:1). (2) The one who is in Christ can, by his own attitude and action, leave Christ; i.e., he can be damned (condemned at the judgment) after having been saved.

This is the main point of the warnings here. The stronger can cause the weaker to stumble and fall (verse 13), thus destroying his brother (verse 15), causing him to be lost in hell forever (verse 23).

It is good to hesitate if one is not sure about indulgence, amusements, and recreation. Let conscience become clear on the basis of decisive Biblical principles.

# Chapter 15

**1. We then that are strong ought to bear the infirmities of the weak:** . . . We then, who are able men, ought to bear the weaknesses of the unable, −MKNT . . . we of the robust faith have a duty to take up the burden of the tender scruples, −WAY . . . are indebted to carry, −KLGS . . . must susteine, −RHEM . . . with the failings, −RSV . . . with the scruples of, −NORL . . . with the qualms of the weak, −JB.

**and not to please ourselves:** . . . and not seek our own pleasure, −WEYM.

**2. Let every one of us please [his] neighbour for [his] good to edification:** . . . should please his neighbor . . . as conducive to edification, −MRDK . . . unto his upbuilding, −MNTG.

**15:1, 2.** With tenderness and patience Paul continues the matter of Christian example and liberty. Christians should help each other and consider the good of the weaker brother, while receiving one another in unity and fellowship to the glory of God before the Gentiles. The strong and enlightened must tolerate and bear with the weaker and less enlightened until they too become strong in faith and knowledge.

Spiritual unity in the Church is vital. To develop and maintain that unity requires that all parties, weak and strong, must be welcomed. The strong must relinquish certain things they are free to do, for the sake of those who are weaker.

When the stronger accepts the weaker he should not do so with the idea of arguing over scruples. He is not to criticize the weaker person's views. He should not even try to settle the doubtful points. Unfortunately, trouble usually begins when one side tries to argue the issue with the purpose of getting the other side to change. The essence of Christian fellowship does not require unanimity on doubtful points.

Churches sometimes divide because they attempt to require unanimity on debatable matters. That is a fruitless effort. It denies the nature of true Christian fellowship. Christian fellowship is built around the centrality of each person's relationship to Christ. Every believer is to be received warmly and openly, regardless of his views on nonessentials.

**3. For even Christ pleased not himself:** . . . never once consulted His own pleasure, −WAY . . . did not gratify himself, −SCLT . . . even the Messiah did not his own desires, −ET.

**but, as it is written:** . . . as the Scripture says, −ET.
**The reproaches of them that reproached thee fell on me:** . . . The insults of those who insulted you, −ADAM . . . The insults which are hurled at you, −TEV . . . The yackety yak of those who yaked at you, −KLGS . . . who denounced . . . fell upon me, −HNT.

**15:3.** The Lord Jesus is our example of self-sacrifice as the governing principle regarding our brother's conscience. His example teaches us to set aside personal prerogatives that may be all right in order to help those who are weak. He "pleased not himself."

In some decisions it is possible to please God, others, and oneself at the same time. Many times, however, one cannot please oneself and also please God. Even Jesus prayed "not my will, but thine, be done" (Luke 22:42).

The Scripture passage referred to here is Psalm 69:9 which speaks of the indescribable humiliation and suffering of Jesus in His passion. He could not please himself and also save the lost sinners He loved.

Paul was so much as saying that if Jesus could give His life to save a soul, it should be easy for a believer to sacrifice some meat—or any liberty—that might cause that soul to be lost forever.

Jesus occupied His whole life with ministry to others. The multitudes thronged Him, taking His time, His strength, His ministry of teaching, healing, and blessing. He "came not to be ministered unto, but to minister" (Matthew 20:28).

As believers are identified with Jesus, their first concern will be to please Him and, in turn, their neighbor whenever it will promote the neighbor's good and Christian growth. The Lord Jesus received us when we were sinners, and He is very patient with us from day to day. He received the weaker brother. Can the "strong" refuse to be of the "same mind"? He is not only our Example; as our Redeemer and Sustainer, He will provide sufficient grace to enable us to imitate Him. He will help us not only by example but also by His presence through the Holy Spirit as we use the resources of the Word (verse 4) and prayer (verse 5).

**4. For whatsoever things were written aforetime were written for our learning:** ... whatever was written in former days, *−RSV* ... written of old has been written for our instruction, *−MNTG* ... whatever the Prophets prophesied, *−ET.*

**that we through patience and comfort of the scriptures might have hope:** ... by means of the steadying and comforting power, *−BRKL* ... we might continuously cherish our hope, *−WLMS* ... through patient endurance and the encouragement to be gained from the Scriptures, *−TCNT* ... and consolation of, *−RHEM* ... and admonition, *−CMPB.*

**15:4.** The "for" at the beginning of this verse shows that Paul's appeal to Psalm 69:9 was an example of principles we learn from the Old Testament (1 Corinthians 10:6, 10; 2 Timothy 3:16, 17). The Christian fellowship should not only be stamped by consideration of its members one for

another; it should be known for its study of Scripture. The Bible is our great source of comfort and strength. By the Scriptures we learn that it is always better to be right with God and to suffer, than to be wrong to avoid trouble. The promises of God's Word comfort us in our sorrows and encourage us in our struggles.

**5. Now the God of patience and consolation:** ... May the God of Dependableness and Encouragement, *−KLGS* ... Now the God who provides, *−ET* ... the God of the endurance, *−YNG* ... who gives men patient endurance and encouragement, *−WLMS* ... of steadfastness and encouragement, *−NORL* ... and of comfort, *−CLMT.*

**grant you to be likeminded one toward another according to Christ Jesus:** ... help you all to be tolerant with each other, *−JB* ... grant you a Christ-like spirit of harmony, *−TCNT* ... give you that harmony, *−KLGS* ... may allow you to agree together, *−ET* ... be in full sympathy with one another, *−MNTG* ... enable you to have the same point of view, *−TEV* ... and of comfort giue you to be of one minde, *−RHEM* ... after the ensample of, *−GNVA.*

**15:5.** This verse is a prayer of the apostle, the first of several wherein he petitioned for seven divine graces to be poured into the hearts of the Roman believers. He desired that they would find harmony which the disputes recorded in chapter 14 disturbed. The qualities which make for harmony in the local fellowship of believers are to be found in God. If each Christian would get to really know and follow the God of patience and comfort there would be no strife over nonessentials. The spirit of Christ would rule.

**6. That ye may with one mind [and] one mouth glorify God, even the Father of our Lord Jesus Christ:** ... that unanimously as with one voice, *−BRKL* ... That with one accord, *−ALFD, −YNG, −CLMT* ... grant to you to attain mutual unanimity, *−WAY* ... That ye may unanimously with one mouth, *−SCLT* ... that you may unite in a chorus of praise, *−MOFT* ... that ye all agreynge [agreeing] together, *−TNDL* ... with one mouth prayse God, *−CRNM* ... with one heart and with one voice, *−MNTG* ... in magnifying the God, *−HNT* ... that you may be in perfect harmony, *−ET.*

**15:6.** Paul was asking a strange thing. He was suggesting that the strong and the weak, who disagreed concerning things, speak with "one mouth" and with "one mind" glorify God. He requested this after having made the point that there is room for differences of opinions concerning nonessential things and that every believer must be persuaded in his own mind. How can this be? Was he contradicting himself? What he was saying is that while believers may not be in total agreement concerning nonessentials, they can and should be in agreement that none should please himself but rather "his neighbor for his good to edification" (verse 2). With the "one mind" of self-denial, brethren can with "one mouth" glorify God.

**7. Wherefore receive ye one another:** ... Welcome one another, *—RSV* ... Habitually therefore give one another a friendly reception, *—WEYM* ... receive one another into the fellowship, *—CNBR.*

**as Christ also received us to the glory of God:** ... even as the Messiah has welcomed us, *—ET.*

**15:7.** The injunction to receive one another was possibly addressed to Jews and Gentiles. All through the epistle there are evidences of the possibility of differences between these two sections in the Church. Throughout his writing the apostle defended the Gentile against the self-satisfied national pride of the Jew, and the Jew against the probable contempt of the Gentile.

**8. Now I say that Jesus Christ was a minister of the circumcision:** ... I maintain that Christ became a minister, *—NORL.*

**for the truth of God:** ... in order to prove God's honesty, *—MOFT* ... to prove God's truthfulness, *—WLMS* ... in vindication of God's truth, *—MNTG.*

**to confirm the promises [made] unto the fathers:** ... by fulfilling, *—MOFT* ... in order to ratify the promise made to the patriarchs, *—SCLT* ... to confirm the patriarchal promises, *—CNDT* ... to complete the covenant made, *—ET.*

**15:8.** Note the change in the use of terms. Paul switched from the words "strong" and "weak" to terminology indicating two nationalities in the Church—Jews and Gentiles. Very possibly the "weak" were for the most part Jews and the "strong" were Gentiles.

As the "minister of the circumcision" Christ fulfilled the whole Mosaic requirement in His person and His work. He was the minister of the covenant that brought salvation to Israel and, in turn, to all people. He validated and carried out the promises made to Abraham, Isaac, and Jacob.

**9. And that the Gentiles might glorify God for [his] mercy:** ... prayse God, *—GNVA* ... to honour God, *—RHEM* ... for His uncovenanted mercy to them, *—WAY.*

**as it is written:**
**For this cause I will confess to thee among the Gentiles:** ... Therefore I will offer praise, *—MNTG* ... I will openly confess, *—WUST* ... will I render thanks, *—PNT* ... will I give praise unto Thee, *—CLMT.*

**and sing unto thy** name: ... And sing to honor Your name, *—BECK* ... shall I be playing music, *—CNDT.*

**15:9.** Christ came to the Jews because God had pledged himself by many promises to send the Redeemer to them. Jesus himself manifested concern for "the lost sheep of the house of Israel"

(Matthew 10:6; 15:24). Paul in the opening of Romans declared that "the gospel . . . is the power of God unto salvation . . . to the Jew first" (1:16).

But while Christ honored the Jews by coming first to them, they by no means had exclusive possession of Him and His mercy. He came "that the Gentiles might glorify God for his mercy."

The quotation in the verse is from Psalm 18:49. Linking verses 8 and 9 to the quotation from Psalm 18 shows us that Christ's coming to the Jew was in the way of God's truth and to the Gentile it was in the way of mercy. The Jew can praise God for His faithfulness and the Gentile for His grace.

The underlying appeal of the apostle is that the Gentiles should not be contemptuous of the scruples of the Jewish saints and the Jews should not be censorious of the Gentile's liberty in the grace of God.

**10. And again he saith:**
**Rejoice, ye Gentiles, with his people:** ... Be happy, *—NORL* ... you heathen peoples, with His people! *—WLMS.*

**11. And again, Praise the Lord, all ye Gentiles; and laud him, all ye people:** ... and once more, *—BRKL* ... and magnify him, *—DOUY* ... Be extolling, all you Gentiles, *—WUST* ... Rejoice, pagans, with his people, *—JB* ... Extol the Lord, *—HNT* ... And highly praise him, *—PNT* ... And let all the people extol him, *—MNTG* ... and exceedingly praise him, *—MKNT* ... And sing his praises, all you peoples, *—CNFT* ... Praise the Lord . . . and laud him, all ye nations, *—LOCK.*

**12. And again, Esaias saith, There shall be a root of Jesse:** ... The noted Son of Jesse, *—WLMS* ... shall be a sprout from, *—BRKL* ... A descendant of Jesse, *—TEV.*

**and he that shall rise to reign over the Gentiles:** ... to rule, *—RSV* ... he who rises to govern the pagans, *—KLGS* ... to rule the heathen, *—TCNT* ... to be Chief of the nations, *—CNDT.*

**in him shall the Gentiles trust:** ... and hethen men, *—WCLF* ... build their hopes, *—WEYM* ... shall the Gentiles place their hope, *—CMPB.*

**15:10-12.** Old Testament prophecy has much to say about the bringing of the Gentiles into the place of blessing. The apostle, in support of his argument, called attention to several passages. He quoted from Psalm 18:49 (verse 9), Deuteronomy 32:43 (verse 10), Psalm 117:1 (verse 11), and Isaiah 11:10 (verse 12).

In quoting Psalm 18:49, the Holy Spirit showed that David knew by revelation that God wanted His chosen people to proclaim Him to the Gentiles. He exhorted them to confess His name and sing praises to Him in their midst. When the Jews were in captivity in Babylon, Gentiles asked them to sing for them one of the songs of Zion (Psalm 137). What an opportunity to witness for God. They, however, were too engrossed in their sorrow to sing. They hung their harps on the willow trees and wept. Sometimes we become so self-centered and filled with self-pity because of temporal problems that we miss opportunities to win a soul for eternity.

Verse 10 uses a quotation from Deuteronomy 32:43. This is in the song of Moses shortly before his death. God was giving him prophetically a new understanding of God's judgments as well as His blessings. He was calling on Gentile nations to rejoice with Jews as they learned of God's power and glory.

Verse 12 draws the assurance from Isaiah 11:10 that Gentiles will surely respond to the good news. They will put their trust in the true and living God, as they hear of His mighty acts of grace.

The Old Testament lists many Gentiles who came to know God through the witness of Jews. Peoples of earth were divided into Jew/Gentile through the calling out of Abram from Gentile idolatry to become the ancestor of the Jewish race. One of the first Gentiles to come to know God was Hagar as she served in that home. The people of Nineveh were Gentiles won to God by a reluctant missionary, Jonah.

All three divisions of the Hebrew Bible—the Law, the Prophets, and the Psalms—were used to support the argument. The quote from Isaiah declares that the One who comes in the Davidic line will also rule over the Gentiles. Jew and Gentile alike will be united under Christ in a common hope. This is the hope which will be fulfilled in the Millennium. Israel will come into its own, and the Gentiles will be blessed in Christ.

**13. Now the God of hope:** . . . May the hope-inspiring God, *—WLMS* . . . the fountain of hope, *—BRKL* . . . the source of hope, *—TEV* . . . the God of expectation, *—CNDT.*

**fill you with all joy and peace in believing:** . . . so fill you with perfect joy and peace through your continuing faith, *—WLMS* . . . replenish you, *—RHEM* . . . fill you with perfect happiness, *—BECK* . . . with every sort of joy, *—ADAM* . . . grant you perfect happiness, *—TCNT* . . . fill you with continual joy, *—WEYM* . . . through the exercise of your faith, *—WAY.*

**that ye may abound in hope:** . . . may be ryche, *—GNVA* . . . you may be overflowing with hope, *—MNTG* . . . you may have abundant hope, *—WEYM* . . . may have a surplus of hope, *—KLGS* . . . this hope of yours may be an overflowing fountain, *—WAY* . . . you may bubble over, *—WLMS.*

**through the power of the Holy Ghost:** . . . and in the vertue, *—RHEM.*

**15:13.** Paul had a beautiful way of concluding an argument with benediction. Here it is "the God of hope." There is nothing hopeless about the Christian experience. "The God of hope" is both the

One who gives hope and the object of that hope. The joy is the joy of the Lord (John 15:11; Galatians 5:22; 1 John 1:4). The peace is not "as the world giveth" (John 14:27). It is Jesus' peace given by the Holy Spirit to those who hope in God (Galatians 5:22; Philippians 4:7). The Christian does not build on the experience of an hour or the happenings of a century; hope is in God, the One who sees the end from the beginning, planning and understanding it all. The result of joy and peace abounds "through the power of the Holy Spirit."

To summarize the argument, note these: (1) welcome the weaker brother (Romans 14:1, 2); (2) do not despise one another (Romans 14:3); (3) don't pass judgment on your brother (Romans 14:4); (4) don't cause your fellow believer to sin (1 Corinthians 8:7-13); (5) accommodate the weaker brother in a spirit of love (Romans 14:14-23); (6) show the spirit of Christ (Romans 15:1-8).

**14. And I myself also am persuaded of you, my brethren:** . . . also am confident regarding you, *—MNTG* . . . And I am assured, *—HNSN* . . . I have reached a settled conviction, *—WUST.*

**that ye also are full of goodness:** . . . that you are very good-hearted, *—NORL* . . . that you also are ful of loue, *—RHEM* . . . you yourselves also are bulging with goodness, *—CNDT* . . . you are filled with perfect spiritual illumination, *—WAY.*

**filled with all knowledge:** . . . replenished with, *—MRDK* . . . amply furnished with knowledge, *—BRKL* . . . perfectly well instructed, *—JB* . . . fully equipped with every kind of knowledge, *—TCNT.*

**able also to admonish one another:** . . . and competent to counsel one another, *—ADAM* . . . also competent to instruct one another, *—WEYM* . . . and are able to exhorte, *—GNVA.*

**15:14.** In the concluding verses of this great Epistle to the Romans, Paul, the great example of Christian grace, speaks of his apostleship. He was writing not with a low estimate of the spirituality of the Roman Christians, but with the purpose of putting them in mind of what they already knew.

The concluding section, like the introductory section, is filled with personal allusion and revelation. While Paul carried the theme of the power of the gospel and Christian responsibility regarding its power throughout the epistle, the closing portion reveals the warmth of fellowship of all saints.

Few passages reveal Paul's character better that this. He was coming to the end of his letter and wanted to lay the groundwork for his forthcoming visit, the first ever for him. Ever gracious and tactful, he is a great pattern for all to emulate.

The gracious man is gentle. Strong men often have a special gentleness born of compassion and love through Christ. Paul recognized the goodness of the Romans. Goodness must keep pace with knowledge if a person is to be truly successful.

It may be that Paul referred to goodness and knowledge because of their special relevance to the subject dealt with in 14:1-15:13. Goodness will cause the stronger to refrain from what would damage the weaker. Right knowledge will correct the weakness of faith. The strong are in particular need of goodness; the weak are in particular need of knowledge.

Paul was careful to guard against any merely personal boastfulness, yet with unaffected modesty he did not hesitate to glory in the triumph of the gospel. The only glory he claimed was that he was the servant of Christ.

15. **Nevertheless, brethren, I have written the more boldly unto you in some sort:** ... I write you with somewhat greater boldness, —HNT ... written to you in some things pretty freely, —LOCK ... with more freedom, —HNSN ... in some measure, —ASV ... quite unreservedly, —WAY.

**as putting you in mind:** ... as it were to refresh your memory, —CNFT.

**because of the grace that is given to me of God:** ... has given me this special position, —JB ... the foregoing principles, —WAY.

**15:15.** On the official basis of his God-appointed office Paul wrote them "the more boldly." Gentiles are accepted, apart from the Law, through Christ as preached by Paul. Paul was the apostle to the Gentiles. His ministry was astonishing, strong, and authoritative, for it was God-ordained. Therefore Paul wrote boldly.

His reason for writing was to "put them in mind" of what they already knew. He did not criticize to cause pain. He spoke with honesty and forthrightness, but always because he wished to enable people to be what they could be by the grace of God.

16. **That I should be the minister of Jesus Christ to the Gentiles:** ... the officiating priest of the Glad-tidings of God, —WAY.

**ministering the gospel of God:** ... exercising a sacred ministry, —WUST ... doing priestly service, —CLMT ... sanctifying the Gospel, —RHEM ... in the sacred service of the gospel, —HNT ... in which holy ministration I officiate, —LOCK ... as a priest presents the offering, —CNBR ... I serve like a priest in preaching, —TEV ... acting as priest in the good news of God, —YNG ... of my divine commission as a priest of Christ, —MOFT ... the glad tydinges of God, —GNVA.

**that the offering up of the Gentiles might be acceptable:** ... my charge being to make the sacrificial offering of the Gentiles, —WAY ... an acceptable offering, —MOFT ... that the oblation, —RHEM.

**being sanctified by the Holy Ghost:** ... hallowed by the working of, —CNBR ... consecrated by, —MOFT.

**15:16.** Paul made no apology, for he knew God had called him to minister to the Gentiles. God's chosen man is great in office; he is the "minister of Jesus Christ." The true preacher's office is the greatest in the world. He does priestly work, offering up the gospel as his sacrifice as he stands between time and eternity. Many offer up people as a sacrifice on the altar of mammon. But Paul was a minister of the gospel acting as a priest of God's good news in order that the Gentiles when offered might be an acceptable sacrifice.

This offering of the Gentiles was consecrated and made holy by the Holy Spirit. No doubt some maintained that the Gentiles were "unclean" because they were not circumcised. To such Paul's reply was that they were "clean" because they were sanctified by the Holy Spirit.

17. **I have therefore whereof I may glory through Jesus Christ in those things which pertain to God:** ... legitimate cause to exult in the presence of Jesus, —WAY ... reason to be proud of the work, —TCNT ... In union with ... in some affairs related to God, —BRKL ... My exultation then is in, —HNT ... the work for God in which I am engaged, —WEYM.

18. **For I will not dare to speak of any of those things which Christ hath not wrought by me:** ... For I will not presume, —WEYM ... For I will venture to speak, —WORL ... wrought by my means, —SCLT ... has not performed by me, —SAWR.

**to make the Gentiles obedient, by word and deed:** ... to win the allegiance of the pagans, —JB ... to make the nations obedient, —BECK ... both in profession and practice, —LOCK.

**15:17, 18.** Paul gloried in his labors because it was the preaching of the gospel message which had its basis in Christ. To the Galatians he wrote, "God forbid that I should glory, save in the cross of our Lord Jesus Christ" (Galatians 6:14).

The apostle was careful to give the credit to the One to whom it belongs. Note the expression "Christ ... wrought by me." This is a commentary upon the proper position of the Christian worker. Christ is the actual worker, and the servant is the instrument through whom Christ accomplishes His purposes. Such a relationship leaves no room for personal pride, and yet therein is the place for great confidence and glorying in the Christ who does the work.

Paul saw himself as an instrument in the hands of Christ. He did not talk of what he had done, but of what Christ had done with him. He never said, "I did this, I did that"; it was always, "Christ used me to do this or that."

History is precept teaching by example; history is recorded experience, and this is all the more so when history is the biography of a person. The insights into the character of Paul afford tremendous examples which believers would do well to adopt for their lives and ministries.

**19. Through mighty signs and wonders, by the power of the Spirit of God:** ... has armed me with arguments, *–WAY* ... by the force of miracles and marvels, *–MOFT* ... through the energy of signs, *–SCLT* ... in vertu of tokenes and greet wondris, *–WCLF.*

**so that from Jerusalem, and round about unto Illyricum:** ... complete circuit of all countries as far as Illyricum, *–WAY* ... and the outlying districts, *–WEYM* ... as far as the East of Europe, *–TCNT.*

**I have fully preached the gospel of Christ:** ... I haue replenisyhed, *–RHEM* ... fulfylled myne office of preaching, *–GNVA.*

**15:19.** As Paul worked to bring the Gentiles to obedience by word and work, God worked through him, confirming the Word with signs following. The God Paul proclaimed is the God who parted the waters, healed the sick, raised the dead, quieted the storm, delivered the faithful from prison, furnace, and lion's den. God confirmed His Word by working miracles. There are three Hebrew words which are translated by the English word *miracle* in the Old Testament: *mōpheth* ("sign," "wonder"); *'ōth* ("signs," "miracles," as pledges or attestations of divine presence and interposition); and *palá* ("wonder acts"), (see Brown, Driver, and Briggs). Two Greek words occur in the New Testament: *dunamis* ("power, might, strength, force") and *sēmeion* ("sign" or distinguishing mark by which something is known) (see *BAGD*).

Everywhere Paul went he saw results. The Holy Spirit clothed him with divine authority. Mighty demonstrations of miracle-work-ing power wrought great changes not only in the lives of people but in the cities in which they lived. God truly confirmed the Word that was preached. Despite terrible obstacles and fierce persecution, God's servant pressed on and saw churches established from "Jerusalem . . . unto Illyricum."

**20. Yea, so have I strived to preach the gospel, not where Christ was named:** ... also, that I was strongly desirous to declare, *–CMPB* ... thus making it my ambition, *–RSV* ... to announce the glad tidings, *–WUST* ... So have I endorsed my selfe to preache, *–TNDL* ... I have fully dispensed the Gospel, *–WORL* ... not where Christ has [already] been announced, *–PNT.*

**lest I should build upon another man's foundation:** ... so as studiously to avoid the carrying of it to those places, *–LOCK* ... leest I bilde [vpon] anotheris grounde, *–WCLF.*

**15:20.** Paul considered his work was to lay the foundation (1 Corinthians 3:10). Others were to follow and do the building. He proceeded upon the principle of preaching the gospel to those who had never heard the message. He was possessed of a holy ambition to preach in Christless regions. He went to those who needed the message the most.

**21. But as it is written:** ... but to act on the principle embodied in these words of Scripture, *–WAY* ... my chief concern has been to fulfill the text, *–JB.*

**To whom he was not spoken of, they shall see:** ... nothing was announced, *–WORL* ... who have never been told of him, *–RSV* ... it hath not been preached of him, *–RHEM* ... no tidings of Him came, *–CLMT.*

**and they that have not heard shall understand:**

**15:21.** This is the 19th and last Old Testament prophecy referred to in Romans. The quote from Isaiah 52:15 is translated in the *Amplified Bible,* "For that which has not been told them shall they see and that which they have not heard shall they consider and understand." Other translations are very similar. The reference is to the surprise of the nations and their leaders when they see the exaltation of the Suffering Servant, the One whom they had despised and rejected.

Paul was consumed with a burning ambition to fulfill this prophecy with respect to the spread of the gospel in heathen countries. Whenever God has work to do, He raises up men with a heart to do it.

**22. For which cause also I have been much hindered from coming to you:** ... I have been prevented, *–NORL* ... All this press of work has again and again hindered me, *–WAY.*

**15:22.** The apostle mentioned in the beginning of his letter his long-cherished desire to come to Rome (1:9-13). He here repeated it. The cause which had frustrated fulfillment of this desire was the principle given in verses 20 and 21. City after city had been his challenge. He did not pretend that Rome was the sole object of his journey. Nor did he, for the sake of self-serving, make more of the Roman believers than the truth warranted. Hypocritical courtesy is wrong. It is better to say nothing if courtesy is stated at the expense of truth.

Paul had purposed to visit Rome but was hindered until he had finished the task at hand. He had been too busy in reaching the unreached to fit Rome into his immediate plans. Rome had been on the itinerary, but again and again the Holy Spirit had directed otherwise. Believers must never become slaves to plans. Plans must never be "set in concrete." God may have some better thing in mind.

**23. But now having no more place in these parts:** ... I can find no fresh field of labour in this country, —WAY ... as there is no more unoccupied ground, —WEYM ... there are no further openings, —TCNT ... But now having no more opportunity in these regions, —NOYS.

**and having a great desire these many years to come unto you:** ... a longing to come unto you, —ALFD ... to pay you a visit, —WEYM.

**15:23.** Now his ministry had been accomplished "in these parts." Rome was to be the next stop. A review of the events surrounding Paul's trip to Rome as recorded in the Book of Acts is most interesting. The great pioneer arrived in Rome, not as a free church planter but as a prisoner. God, however, was glorified, for Paul's chains gave him access to Caesar's household.

**24. Whensoever I take my journey into Spain, I will come to you:** ... I hope to see you in passing, —RSV ... So now whenever I can go to Spain, —KLGS ... as ever I extend my travels into Spain, —WEYM.

**for I trust to see you in my journey:** ... I do hope to see you with my own eyes, —BRKL ... as I proceed, —PNT ... on my intended journey, —WAY.

**and to be brought on my way thitherward by you:** ... to have an escort from you on the way, —BRKL ... to be furnished with the necessities of travel, —WUST.

**if first I be somewhat filled with your [company]:** ... having enjoyed your fellowship for a while, —BRKL ... your society, —TCNT ... after being somewhat satisfied with your companionship, —HNT ... after that I haue som what enioyed your acquayntaunce, —CRNM ... I shall have enjoyed you, —DOUY ... to some extent enjoyed your society, —WAY.

**15:24.** Having been delayed by his church planting efforts, he was now at last setting his face toward Rome. And yet Rome was not his final goal. His eyes were looking at the vast harvest field in the regions beyond. His intention was to reach Spain. His journey to Spain would afford him an opportunity to realize his long-cherished desire to see Rome and to meet the Christians in the capital of the world of that day. Above all, he looked forward to being refreshed by their fellowship.

Paul's aim was always to preach the gospel and establish local assemblies. He purposed to preach the gospel where it had not been preached before. Having completed his work in the east he set his face toward the west. He proposed to evangelize Spain and to visit Rome en route.

**25. But now I go unto Jerusalem to minister unto the saints:** ... Right now I am going, —BECK ... Just now I am going to, —MNTG ... being employed in a ministration to the saints, —CNBR ... I am setting out for Jerusalem, —LOCK ... on an errand to the saints, —MOFT ... performing a service, —PNT ... on a service of relief, —NOYS.

**26. For it hath pleased them of Macedonia and Achaia:** ... For it has been the good pleasure, —MNTG ... For it delights, —CNDT ... have freely decided, —TEV ... have determined of their own accord, —TCNT.

**to make a certain contribution:** ... to send a generous contribution, —JB ... to make a certayne distribution vnto, —GNVA ... to make a contribution, —WLMS ... jointly contributed for the poor, —WUST.

**for the poor saints which are at Jerusalem:**

**27. It hath pleased them verily; and their debtors they are:** ... they certainly owe it to them, —BRKL ... and they really are under obligation to them, —WLMS.

**For if the Gentiles have been made partakers of their spiritual things:** ... For the converts from heathenism, —TCNT ... Since the Jews shared their spiritual blessings, —TEV ... spiritual possessions, —BRKL ... have been admitted into partnership with the Jews, —WEYM ... have participated in, —PNT ... spiritual riches, —MNTG.

**their duty is also to minister unto them in carnal things:** ... they owe it in return, —CNBR ... they ought certainly, —SCLT ... they are bound also ... in fleshly things, —HNSN ... a debt of aid in material blessings, —MOFT ... they are under moral obligation ... of things needed for the sustenance of the body, —WUST ... bodily thynges, —CRNM ... physical things, —CLMT.

**28. When therefore I have performed this:** ... So after discharging this duty, —WEYM ... I have despatched this business, —LOCK ... I have accomplished this, —ASV, —PNIN ... I have settled this, —MNTG ... when I have completed this, —CNFT ... having finished this affair, —CMPB.

**and have sealed to them this fruit:** ... and consigned to them this fruit, —DOUY ... the fruit of this collection, —MNTG ... and officially handed over, —JB ... have delivered to them the proceeds, —CNFT.

**I will come by you into Spain:** ... I will return through you, to Spain, —YNG ... passing through Rome on my way there, —WEYM.

**15:25-28.** Paul had an immediate and a future plan. His future plan was to go to Spain. At the time Spain was, in a sense, the far end of the civilized world, and that alone was enough to motivate the apostle, for he wished to take the gospel where it had not been heard before.

It is possible that Paul did go to Spain. He may have been set free after his first imprisonment in Rome (Acts 28:30). He expected to be set free (Philemon 22). Some scholars believe the visit to Asia of 1 Timothy 1:3 was between imprisonments and that it was then he left the cloak at Troas (2 Timothy 4:13). J.B. Lightfoot states that Clement of Rome recorded Paul's ministry in the western part of Spain between the imprisonments

(*The Apostolic Fathers,* 2:30). Of this we cannot be sure at this time.

But Paul had an immediate goal and that was to go to Jerusalem. He had been collecting the contributions of the Gentile saints to take to the poor in Jerusalem. This was a matter of great importance to him, a ministry very dear to his heart.

The desire to take this collection to the Jerusalem "saints" was born in the apostle's heart and met several obligations. No doubt it would bring about a better understanding between Gentiles and Jews (2 Corinthians 8 and 9). Cleavage between Jerusalem and the Gentile churches could only hinder the cause of Christ. This generous gesture of brotherly love could do nothing but forge the bonds of fellowship.

Not all the saints in Jerusalem were poor, but the poor saints (better translated "the poor of the saints") found themselves impoverished for several reasons. Possibly some were widows and family members whose husbands and fathers had been slain by Paul and his cohorts in the days of his persecution of the Church. Also much of the income of people in Jerusalem revolved around the religious activities in the temple and their worship. The Christians, of course, could have no further employment in these activities; they were despised by the Jews.

For Paul this was payment of a debt. When the Jerusalem brethren agreed that Barnabas and Paul should go to the Gentiles, they requested one thing—that they should remember the poor in Jerusalem—a matter Paul was only too ready to do (Galatians 2:9, 10). Duty now called Paul to take money to Jerusalem rather than the gospel to Rome.

This generous act was a beautiful gesture of practical action and demonstrated to one and all the essential unity of the Church—Jew and Gentile alike. The fellowship of the saints is not limited to one church but to the Church.

The Gentile Christians had become recipients of the blessings which had come to and through the Jews. Now they could fulfill a duty and minister to them with material things. The contribution was a voluntary gesture on the part of the Gentile section of the Church; yet it was the recognition of a moral debt. Paul left no stone unturned to do what he could to repay the debt.

The Gentile believers were debtors (*opheiletai*), just as Paul was a debtor (*opheiletēs*) to all, both Jews and Gentiles (1:14). They owed a debt, however, to Jewry, beyond the general sense in which Paul had earlier used the term.

They were, and are, in a sense indebted to Jews for their very hope of eternal life. They were

partakers of spiritual blessings which emanated from God's chosen people, Israel.

Isaiah, among others, spoke of Israel as the source of blessings for all the earth (Isaiah 2:3; 11:1; 25:6; 42:1; 60:3). Jesus told the Samaritan woman, "Salvation is of the Jews" (John 4:22). Paul had already spoken to the Romans of the same fact (3:2; 4:16, 17; 9:5; 11:17-24).

Paul mentioned the Christians in two provinces, Macedonia and Achaia, where he had been ministering for several months. But he had also organized a similar collection in the churches of Galatia (1 Corinthians 16:1-3). The party which would travel with Paul to Jerusalem was very representative—Sopater, Aristarchus, and Secundus from Macedonia; Gaius of Derbe and Timothy of Lystra, representatives of Galatia; and Tychicus and Trophimus of Asia Minor (Acts 20:4).

**29. And I am sure that, when I come unto you: I shall come in the fulness of the blessing of the gospel of Christ:** ... with abondance of, *—GNVA* ... with Christ's abundant blessing on me, *—WLMS.*

**15:29.** Paul was confident that when he came to Rome he would do so with a full measure of blessing from Christ. He did not know when he would come; he did not know that he would be in chains when he came; but he was certain of the condition of his soul. There is tremendous assurance when one knows he is in the will of God.

**30. Now I beseech you, brethren: for the Lord Jesus Christ's sake:** ... in behalf of our Lord Jesus Christ, *—ET.* **and for the love of the Spirit:** ... and by the charitie of the holy Ghost, *—RHEM* ... by the love that the Spirit inspires, *—WLMS.* **that ye strive together with me in [your] prayers to God for me:** ... to wrestle with me in prayers, *—WLMS* ... struggle together with me in prayers, *—CNDT* ... to help me in my struggle, *—MNTG* ... agonize together with me, *—KLGS* ... to help me through my dangers by praying, *—JB* ... rally round me by praying, *—MOFT* ... to join with me in straining every nerve in prayer, *—BRCL.*

**15:30.** The request of Paul for the prayers of the Christians in Rome is very touching and beautiful. The request reveals that this great warrior and pioneer who had undergone so much for the sake of the gospel (2 Corinthians 11:23-33) was very conscious of the perils which lay ahead. He was aware that people in Jerusalem were very suspicious of him, and he was evidently conscious that his coming could be an occasion for strife and persecution. He needed the assurance of the undergirding of prayer.

The apostle appealed to the believers at Rome to pray for him while they awaited his coming. Although he was absent from them, they were colaborers with him and could pray for him. The greatest gift we can give a fellow believer is that of prayer. "Pray one for another" (James 5:16). If you cannot help another to meet his need, whatever it may be, you can perform a beautiful ministry by praying with and for him.

31. **That I may be delivered from them that do not believe in Judaea:** ... that I may escape the clutches of, *−BRCL* ... that I may be rescued from the disobedient, *−HNT* ... that I may escape unhurt from, *−WEYM* ... kept safe from unbelieving Jews, *−ET* ... rescued from the stubborn, *−CNDT* ... fro[m] the vnfeithful men, *−WCLF* ... from the infidels, *−RHEM* ... who reject the Faith, *−TCNT* ... from them which are disobedient, *−GNVA.*

**and that my service which [I have] for Jerusalem may be accepted of the saints:** ... that my mission to Jerusalem may be favorably received, *−MNTG* ... that my errand to Jerusalem may find acceptance with God's people, *−NEB* ... and the oblation, *−RHEM* ... and that my ministration, *−ASV, −YNG* ... and that that gift-bearing of mine may be acceptable, *−WLSN* ... that the offerings will be well received, *−ET* ... may welcome the help I bring to them, *−BRCL.*

**15:31.** Paul appealed to the Roman saints for prayer for the sake of the Lord Jesus Christ and for the love of the Spirit. It is noteworthy that Paul never felt he was so full of the fullness of God that he did not need the prayers of fellow believers.

"For the love of the Spirit" is parallel to "for the Lord Jesus Christ's sake." While this can mean the love that is the fruit of the Spirit (Romans 5:5; Galatians 5:22), it is more likely that Paul was speaking of the love the Holy Spirit, who is God, bore for the saints in Rome and indeed has for all saints. He is a Person who loves.

Paul gave the Roman believers specific prayer requests. He was definite in his request that he might be rescued from those in Judea who rejected the Faith. Even within the church there were those who were not willing to welcome Gentiles into the Body. The *New English Bible* rendering is, "Be my allies in the fight; pray to God for me." He apparently anticipated the trouble he was to face in Judea (Acts 21:27-26:32).

In addition, the Romans were asked to pray that the contribution he was taking from the churches would be received. Since the gift was basically from Gentile churches to a Jewish church, he foresaw the possibility of a racial issue due to the pride of Jewish prejudice. He did not want problems that would bring division to the body of Christ.

32. **That I may come unto you with joy by the will of God:** ... that I may subsequently come to you, *−BRKL* ... in a happy frame of mind, *−NEB* ... I want to come joyfully to you, *−BRCL* ... with a happy heart, *−WLMS.*

**and may with you be refreshed:** ... be renewed, *−ET* ... and may with you find rest, *−ALFD* ... with a light heart, *−TCNT.*

**15:32.** Finally he asked that they would pray that he might come to them "with joy by the will of God" and together with them find rest. The great pioneer desired a respite from the rigors of personal dangers and the ecclesiastical struggles which he constantly faced. Even coming to them in chains, as he later did, could not destroy this joy. God's will is always best, even in circumstances such as Paul faced.

Paul reached Rome and yet how different was his arrival from what he had originally expected. What did it matter, if it was in the will of God? That was the qualifying petition that was answered.

33. **Now the God of peace [be] with you all. Amen:**

**15:33.** Paul closed the epistle proper with a benediction, breathing blessing on the church. Knowing danger and hatred lay ahead of him, he could face the journey to Jerusalem in peace because he knew "the God of peace." This was the benediction he gave to the saints at Rome.

## Chapter 16

1. **I commend unto you Phebe our sister:** ... I recommend to you, *−NORL, −MKNT* ... Now I introduce to you, *−WLMS* ... I commend to your care, *−TCNT.*

**which is a servant of the church which is at Cenchrea:** ... She is a worker, *−BECK* ... being a servant also of the ecclesia, *−CNDT* ... who is a ministering servant, *−CNBR* ... being a ministrant, *−YNG* ... a deaconess, *−SCLT* ... who ministers to the Community, *−HNT* ... a minister of the congregacion, *−TNDL* ... who is a minister of the church, *−SAWR* ... who is in the ministerie, *−RHEM* ... a Servant of the Congregation, *−WLSN* ... of the assembly, *−WUST.*

2. **That ye receive her in the Lord, as becometh saints:** ... Make her welcome in the Lord, *−NORL* ... as befits the saints, *−RSV* ... give her a Christian welcome, *−MNTG* ... as saints deserve, *−BRKL* ... in a manner becoming God's people, *−WLMS* ... in a way that is fitting for saints, *−ADAM* ... as a fellow Christian ... of God's people, *−WEYM* ... as holy ones should, *−KLGS* ... worthily of the saints, *−WORL.*

**and that ye assist her in whatsoever business she hath need of you:** ... give her any help she may require, *−MOFT.*

**for she hath been a succourer of many, and of myself also:** ... she, indeed, has been a benefactor, *−ADAM* ... For she herself has been made an overseer to many people, *−MNTG* ... for she also became a leader of many, *−YNG* ... she also has been a patroness of many and especially of me, *—HNSN*... she has looked after a great many people, *—JB*... she has been an assistant to many, including myself, *—BRKL*... she has indeed been a kind friend to many, *—WEYM*.

**16:1, 2.** Although Paul had never visited Rome at the time he wrote the epistle, he had many beloved friends there. Thirty-five names are listed, most of them mentioned in no other place. His mention of them illustrates this interest and love.

Phoebe was a *diakonos* in the assembly in Cenchreae, the seaport of Corinth. Her name indicates that she was a Gentile and she was probably a widow. According to Greek custom, she could not have traveled in the independent manner described if she had a husband or had never been married. She was given the honor of bearing to Rome the greatest theological document of the Christian Church.

Commentators have differed regarding her position in the church. In the Gospels, *diakonos* is sometimes used for "servant" as in John 2:9. In the Epistles, however, it is always used to indicate an official position of ministry in the church. *Diakonos* occurs 22 times in the Epistles. In the KJV it is translated "minister" 18 times, "deacon" 3 times (actually a transliteration), and "servant" only once—here in 16:1.

*Diakonos* is a title used of Paul, Timothy, Apollos, Tychicus, and Epaphras (1 Corinthians 3:5; 2 Corinthians 3:6; Ephesians 3:7; 6:21; Colossians 1:7; 4:7; 1 Thessalonians 3:2; 1 Timothy 4:6)— all of them recognized as full-fledged preachers, ministers. Phoebe's possible role of leadership is also shown by the term *prostatis* ("succorer") which, according to Liddell and Scott, means "one who is a leader or ruler; a front-rank person; one who exercises authority" (*LSJ*, "*prostateia*"). We have no parallel usage of this noun in the New Testament, but the verb form always calls for some aspect of leadership, ruling, commanding (Matthew 1:24; 8:4; 21:6; Luke 5:14; Acts 10:33, 48; Romans 12:8; 1 Thessalonians 5:12; 1 Timothy 3:4, 5, 12). Because of these facts, some scholars believe Phoebe may have had some official position in the Cenchreae church.

**3. Greet Priscilla and Aquila:** ...Remember me to, *—WLMS*...Give my good wishes, *—TCNT*.

**my helpers in Christ Jesus:** ... my co-laborers, *—SAWR*.

**4. Who have for my life laid down their own necks:** ...friends who have endangered their own lives for mine, *—WEYM*...who exposed their necks for my life, *—SAWR*...who risked death, *—JB*...exposed their own to danger, *—LOCK*...who have risked their lives for me, *—MOFT*...for the sake of my soul, jeopardize their own necks, *—CNDT*.

**unto whom not only I give thanks:** ...to whom not I alone owe my thanks, *—SCLT*...feel grateful, *—BRKL*...to owe them a debt of gratitude, *—JB*.

**but also all the churches of the Gentiles:** ...also all the churches of the nations, *—PNIN*...among the non-Jews, *—BECK*.

**16:3, 4.** Next on the list are Priscilla and Aquila. Here and in Acts 18:18 and 2 Timothy 4:19 the wife's name is first, indicating that she was the dominant one. Paul met this couple first at Corinth. They were tentmakers, the trade of Paul also (Acts 18:1-3). He made his home with them as he pioneered the Corinthian church. When Paul left Corinth they accompanied him to Ephesus and settled there. The brilliant scholar Apollos came to the city. He did not have a full grasp of the Christian faith, although he was mightily used of God. Aquila and Priscilla took him into their home, giving him fellowship and instruction (Acts 18:24-19:6). Their ministry, no doubt, did much to prepare the ground for the outpouring of the Holy Spirit when Paul returned to the city.

This fascinating couple risked their lives to save Paul's. We do not know how, nor when and where. It may have been during the riot in Corinth (Acts 18) or in Ephesus (Acts 19). This latter was so violent Paul compared it to fighting "with beasts" in the arena (1 Corinthians 15:32). It is quite certain that the reference is to beastly men and not to wild beasts.

**5. Likewise [greet] the church that is in their house:** ... Also, greet the assembly which meets, *—WUST* ... grete the congregacion that is in their house, *—CRNM* ... their domestical Church, *—RHEM*...that meets in their home, *—MNTG*.

**Salute my wellbeloved Epaenetus:** ...My greetings to, *—BRKL*...Greet my beloved, *—KLGS*.

**who is the firstfruits of Achaia unto Christ:** ...who was the earliest convert to Christ, *—WEYM*...the first man in Roman Asia to believe in Christ, *—MNTG*...to be reaped for Christ, *—MOFT*.

**16:5.** Priscilla and Aquila had been driven from Rome along with all other Jews. We find them in Corinth, then Ephesus, back in Rome, and finally in Ephesus. Wherever they lived they were used of God. Their home became the place where the local assembly met. Our homes are our castles. We welcome the privacy they afford. At the sacrifice of comfort and privacy, they opened the doors of their household, and the home of Priscilla and Aquila became known as the church in Rome.

The next friend mentioned is the well-beloved Epenetus. Only two things are said of him. Paul called him, first of all, "well-beloved" and then spoke of him as his "firstfruits" of Achaia. It is possible that he was of the house of Stephanas, which is also called the firstfruits of Achaia (1 Corinthians 16:15).

Two-thirds of all the names are Greek. In all probability these are names of persons whom Paul had actually known in his work in Asia. All of those listed have an interrelationship as saints based upon their common relationship to Christ. Scattered throughout the record are phrases which indicate this common bond: "In the Lord . . . in Christ Jesus . . . unto Christ."

All the situations of life and service rest upon their relationship to Christ. Phoebe was to be received "in the Lord." Priscilla and Aquila were fellow workers "in Christ Jesus." Epenetus was the firstfruits of Achaia "unto Christ." His kinsmen, Andronicus and Junia, were "in Christ." The bond of service and the ties of fellowship knit by the impulse of love came about through union with Christ. Christ was their life. His love controlled their beings. The work they did was the activity of their Lord through them.

All these beloved people who are spoken of in this chapter became what they were through the life, the ministry, and the example of the apostle. In turn, Paul found comfort and encouragement in them. They provided him with assistance in the ministry.

**6. Greet Mary, who bestowed much labour on us:** . . . who went through much trouble for you, —BRKL . . . who toiled terribly for you, —MNTG . . . who has laboured strenuously, —WEYM . . . who expended much labor for you, —ADAM . . . she laboured actively for you, —HNT . . . who toils much for you, —CNDT.

**16:6.** Mary was known for her strenuous labor on behalf of God's servants. This is the only reference to this Mary, one of six women bearing the name in the New Testament.

**7. Salute Andronicus and Junia:**
**my kinsmen, and my fellow-prisoners:** . . . my relatives, —HNSN . . . my cosins and fellow captiues, —RHEM . . . who once shared my imprisonment, —WEYM.
**who are of note among the apostles:** . . . who are distinguished, —CNFT . . . who are of excellent reputation, —WUST . . . who are well known by the apostles, —ADAM . . . who are noble, —RHEM . . . among the legates, —MRDK . . . They are well thought of among the missionaries, —KLGS.
**who also were in Christ before me:** . . . of longer standing than myself, —WEYM . . . who accepted the Messiah long before me, —ET . . . they were Christians before I was, —BRCL.

**16:7.** The Bible only mentions Andronicus and Junia here. There is uncertainty as to whether or not Junia is male or female. Some versions use the masculine *Junias*.

All the Early Church fathers and commentators up to the 13th Century recognized Junia as a woman. For example, Chrysostom wrote, "Oh how great is the devotion of this woman that she should be even counted worthy of the appellation of apostle!" In recent times some translators have used the masculine form, *Junias*. The name does not appear elsewhere.

Paul wrote of them as his kinsmen. This could mean they were blood relatives or else they were Jewish. They were early converts, having become Christians before Paul which must mean they had an early link with the Jerusalem church. It is evident that they were prominent for they were "of note among the apostles." Apparently they had been incarcerated with Paul during one of his imprisonments (2 Corinthians 11:23).

**8. Greet Amplias my beloved in the Lord:** . . . Give my good wishes to Ampliatus, my dear Christian friend, —BRCL . . . my dear friend in the fellowship, —NEB . . . my fellow toiler in Christ, —MNTG.

**16:8.** *Amplias* is an abbreviated form of *Ampliatus*. The name was found repeatedly among the members of the imperial family and in Roman inscriptions of that day. There is reason to believe that he was a slave but that he was of high standing in the church. During Paul's 20 years of labor in many lands he had won to Christ many who had afterward moved to the great city which was like the center of gravity of the world. He was not only commending them with sincere affection, he was preparing the church for his forthcoming visit. Paul was always thanking God for his friends and pouring love upon them.

**9. Salute Urbane, our helper in Christ, and Stachys my beloved:** . . . who shares with me in the work and in the fellowship of Christ, —BRCL . . . our co-laborer, —SAWR . . . my comrade in Christ, —NEB.

**16:9.** *Urbane* or *Urbanus* ("belonging to the city") was a name which by its very nature was quite common in Rome. On the other hand *Stachys* ("ear of grain") was not common. The name shows up once or twice in association with the imperial household. Urbane was Paul's "helper" and Stachys was his "beloved." While our information regarding these men is very limited, they were honored to be named in this great epistle by their friend and leader.

**10. Salute Apelles approved in Christ:** . . . who has been tried and found trustworthy, —CNBR . . . who has been tested and approved by, —ADAM . . . that sterling Christian, —BRCL . . . well proved in Christ's service, —NEB . . . attested in Christ, —CNDT . . . approved in Christ's service, —NORL . . . that tried Christian,

*—MOFT . . . that veteran believer, —WEYM . . . that most venerated Christian, —WLMS.*

**Salute them which are of Aristobulus' [household]:**

**11. Salute Herodion my kinsman:** . . . to my fellow-countryman, —BRCL . . . to my compatriot, —JB.

**Greet them that be of the [household] of Narcissus, which are in the Lord:** . . . the believing members, —MNTG . . . who have embraced the Gospel, —LOCK . . . who are in the Lord's fellowship, —NEB.

**12. Salute Tryphena and Tryphosa, who labour in the Lord:** . . . to those strenuous Christian workers, —BRKL . . . to those Christian workers, —WEYM . . . who are such strenuous workers in the Lord's service, —BRCL . . . who labour in our Lord, —RHEM . . . who are ever toiling, —MNTG.

**Salute the beloved Persis:** . . . to my dear Persis, —BRCL.

**which laboured much in the Lord:** . . . who has toiled in his service so long, —NEB . . . who has toiled terribly in the Lord's service, —MNTG . . . a consistant hard worker, —ET . . . who has worked hard, —RSV . . . unwearied worker, —BRKL.

**16:10-12.** There must have been many more names in the church at Rome, names possibly known to Paul in addition to those mentioned; but their names are not listed in this eternal scroll. It is very special to be among the blood washed, but how privileged to be listed as a worker with extra commendation. To leave behind a name which the world will not let fade into oblivion is significant; how much more to have a name that our Lord will mention with approval before the angels.

Such a person was Apelles. He was "approved," but most importantly, he was approved "in Christ." The word translated "approved" here is rendered "tried" in James 1:12. Origen says that Apelles was "approved by suffering and great tribulation."

Herodion may have belonged to the Herod family. The households of Aristobulus and Narcissus were very possibly slaves.

Tryphaena and Tryphosa which are slave names were near relatives, most likely sisters and possibly twins, to whom it was quite common to give names derived from the same root. Persis may have been older for she "labored" as compared to the other two who "labor."

**13. Salute Rufus chosen in the Lord:** . . . eminent in the Lord, —RSV . . . the choice one, —YNG . . . that choice Christian, —MOFT, —BRCL . . . to that eminent Christian, —TCNT . . . that choice character in Christ, —HNT . . . that outstanding worker, —TEV . . . an outstanding follower of the Lord, —NEB . . . the elect in our Lord, —RHEM . . . who is noted in the Lord, —KLGS . . . the special one, —ET . . . selected to be a disciple, —LOCK.

**and his mother and mine:** . . . who has also been a mother to me, —WEYM . . . who has always treated me like a son, —TEV . . . who is the mother both of him and of me, —MKNT . . . whom I call mother too, —NEB.

**16:13.** The name *Rufus* (meaning "red" or "red-haired") was so common among Italians that it would not be noted if it were not for two items. First, Rufus is mentioned in Mark 15:21 as one of the two sons of Simon of Cyrene, and second, the reference to the mother of Rufus as being a mother to Paul.

Mark addressed his Gospel to the Romans. Some 30 years after Simon bore Jesus' cross, Mark identified him to the Romans as the father of Alexander and Rufus. The fact that there was a well-known Rufus "chosen in the Lord" in Rome, may indicate that he was the one whose father was Simon of Cyrene. Simeon surnamed Niger ("the dark-skinned") was a colleague of Paul at Antioch (Acts 11:25, 26; 13:1). Simeon has been identified with Simon of Cyrene.

All of those greeted show a relationship to Christ. Special attention was called to Phoebe, Priscilla and Aquila, Epenetus, Andronicus and Junia. Note how Amplias was "beloved in the Lord." Urbane was a "helper in Christ." Apelles was "approved in Christ." The greeting to those in the household of Narcissus was to those "in the Lord." Tryphaena and Tryphosa labored "in the Lord" and Persis "labored much in the Lord." Rufus was "chosen in the Lord."

**14. Salute Asyncritus, Phlegon, Hermas, Patrobas, Hermes:**

**and the brethren which are with them:** . . . and all friends in their company, —NEB . . . and to all the members of their Christian community, —BRCL . . . and the brothers who are associated with them, —MNTG.

**15. Salute Philologus, and Julia, Nereus, and his sister, and Olympas:**

**and all the saints which are with them:** . . . and all God's people associated with them, —NEB . . . all the saints associated with them, —BRKL, —MNTG . . . the brethren associated with them, —WEYM.

**16:14, 15.** The 10 persons mentioned in these verses are named only here. At least seven women are named in this chapter: Phoebe (verse 1), Priscilla (verse 3), Mary (verse 6), Tryphaena, Tryphosa, and Persis (verse 12), Julia (verse 15). In addition, there is Junia (verse 7), although some scholars believe that the person was a man named Junius. Mention is also made to an unnamed sister of Nereus (verse 15). All of them were Christian workers, deaconesses, and prophetesses who "labored . . . in the Lord" (verse 12). This would seem to indicate that some of them labored in the ministry of the Word. The Gospels name several women who proclaimed the good news (Matthew 28:1-10; Luke 24:9-11; John 4:28-30; 20:16-18).

Bearing out the prophecy of Joel 2:28-31, Peter's sermon on the Day of Pentecost promised that this would be fulfilled in the last days (Acts 2:14-21). Philip the evangelist had four daughters who were prophetesses (Acts 21:9). See also Philippians 4:2, 3.

Paul has at times been interpreted as being opposed to women in places of leadership in ministry. Stanley Horton has shown that Paul encouraged the public ministry of women (p. 235). In spiritual gifts and ministries there are no racial, social, or sexual exclusions (Galatians 3:28). This does not impinge on the headship of the man in marriage and family structure (1 Corinthians 11:3). This basic distinction clarifies difficult Scripture passages.

**16. Salute one another with an holy kiss:** . . . Greet each other with the kiss of peace, *—BRCL* . . . with a Christian kiss, *—ET* . . . with a sacred kiss, *—TCNT* . . . with a consecrated kiss, *—WLMS.*
**The churches of Christ salute you:**

**16:16.** The custom of combining a greeting and a kiss is still the custom in many parts of the world. There can be no doubt that the kiss was practiced as a token of Christian love. Jesus marked its absence in reprimanding Simon the Pharisee (Luke 7:45). Paul enjoined the practice elsewhere (1 Corinthians 16:20; 2 Corinthians 13:12; 1 Thessalonians 5:26). Peter gave the same admonition calling it a kiss of love (1 Peter 5:14). "Holy" distinguishes the greeting from the ordinary greeting of natural affection. The holy kiss is seldom practiced in churches in the West. Some leaders have thought that problems related to immorality among church members may have been aggravated by the practice; this applies especially to the heinous vice of homosexuality. It may also be that *agape* love is less prevalent now than then.

**17. Now I beseech you, brethren:** . . . I implore you, *—JB* . . . And I call upon you, *—YNG* . . . Now I am entreating you, *—CNDT.*
**mark them which cause divisions and offences:** . . . watche diligently, *—GNVA* . . . to take note, *—RSV* . . . who cause splits and obstacles, *—BRKL* . . . who encourages trouble, *—JB* . . . create difficulties, *—TCNT* . . . who cause disagreements, *—BECK* . . . who are making factions and stumbling-blocks, *—HNSN* . . . put hindrances in your way, *—MOFT* . . . geve occasions of evyll, *—TNDL.*
**contrary to the doctrine which ye have learned:** . . . in opposition to, *—RSV* . . . quite out of harmony with the doctrine you have been taught, *—BRKL* . . . in defiance of the instruction which you have received, *—WEYM* . . . by disregarding the teaching that you have learned, *—ADAM.*

**and avoid them:** . . . to dissociate yourselves from them, *—TCNT* . . . turn away from them, *—PNIN* . . . always avoid, *—WLMS.*

**16:17.** "Mark them" and "avoid them" was Paul's solemn warning concerning those who caused "divisions" in the church. The consciousness of unity in Christ, evident in the greetings to the Roman believers, caused Paul to write this final and urgent caution. False teachers prowl stealthily to lead God's people into divisions and difficulties. Dissensions and discord cause the unwary to stumble and fall. Beware of those who come to divide and destroy.

**18. For they that are such serve not our Lord Jesus Christ:** . . . for the master whom they serve is not, *—CNBR.*
**but their own belly:** . . . but are slaves of their own appetites, *—ADAM* . . . slaves of their own base desires, *—MOFT.*
**and by good words and fair speeches deceive the hearts of the simple:** . . . By their honeyed words and flattery they deceive the hearts of the unsuspecting, *—NORL* . . . by smooth and complimentary speech, *—HNSN* . . . with their plausible and pious talk they beguile, *—MOFT* . . . by svveete speaches and benedictions seduce, *—RHEM* . . . with swete preachinges and flatteringe wordes . . . of the innocentes, *—TNDL* . . . of the harmless, *—YNG* . . . of ynnocent men, *—WCLF.*

**16:18.** There was the potential danger of the opponents of the gospel destroying the harmony and unity of the church. Throughout Paul's ministry opposition, especially by the Judaizers, came to disrupt. This was true almost everywhere he went, and he knew it would eventually get to Rome.

The believers were warned to avoid fellowship with these opponents of Christ. They are marked by deceitfulness, serving their own ends and purposes rather than the Lord's.

Some people apparently take pride in causing trouble and find satisfaction in sowing strife and dissension. Others mask their true motives behind a facade of piety. They lead people astray by subtle words and actions, avoiding a direct attack. They speak well but act with evil intent. False brethren cause divisions, occasion offenses, and pervert doctrines. Their motives are impure, their words deceptive, their victims the simple.

There is danger from without the Church, and there is danger from within. As the earth is assailed by two perils—storms from without and volcanic forces from within—the Church suffers from the same kind of dangers. The most dangerous is the volcanic force from within. Winds and waves may beat and cause exterior damage, but when internal fires and rumblings take place, the foundations quake, mighty rocks shiver and split, and the planet shakes.

The spirit of pride, discontent, jealousy, and all the other works of the flesh, along with false doctrine, are the greatest dangers as they attack the Church from within.

**19. For your obedience is come abroad unto all [men]:** ... Your fidelity to the truth, *—WEYM* ... For your submission to the faith, *—CNFT* ... The story of your Christian obedience is known to everyone, *—BRCL* ... The fame of your obedience has spread everywhere, *—NEB* ... is famous everywhere, *—JB* ... is published into euery place, *—RHEM.*

**I am glad therefore on your behalf:** ... so I am delighted about you, *—WLMS* ... You make me very happy, *—BRCL* ... I rejoice therefore over you, *—ALFD.*

**but yet I would have you wise unto that which is good:** ... be well versed when it comes to goodness, *—BRKL* ... but I want you to be experts in goodness and, *—BRCL* ... experts in good, *—MOFT* ... be wise with respect to, *—SCLT.*

**and simple concerning evil:** ... and guileless, *—CNFT* ... but simpletons in evil, *—NEB* ... and innocents in evil, *—MOFT* ... and pure with respect to evil, *—MKNT* ... and harmless as to the evil, *—YNG* ... and to be innocentes concerninge evyll, *—TNDL* ... but unskilled about the evil, *—KLGS.*

**16:19.** The "for" introduces a reason for the preceding admonition regarding erroneous doctrines. The church in Rome had been so well indoctrinated in truth that Paul could exhort them to judge any new teaching against what they had learned. He intensely desired that their doctrine be kept pure.

The reputation of the church at Rome for fidelity to the gospel was such that a brief warning against those who would sow discord was sufficient. Paul had confidence in them and yet he was constrained to warn them to "mark ... and avoid" those who caused division. They were to be wise regarding good and simple concerning evil. *Akeraious* ("simple") is better translated "innocent." Paul hoped that they would be immune to any evil. Prior to disobedience, Adam and Eve were innocent, "simple" regarding the dichotomy of good and evil. His entreaty was to be "in malice ... children" but "in understanding be men" (1 Corinthians 14:20).

**20. And the God of peace shall bruise Satan under your feet shortly:** ... our source of peace, *—TEV* ... shall treade Satan vnder youre fete, *—CRNM* ... so crushes Satan that you will trample on him, *—BRCL* ... will soon rid you of these ministers of Satan, *—LOCK* ... will soon bruise the adversary, *—HNSN* ... will soon crush Satan, *—ADAM* ... vndir youre feet swiftli, *—WCLF* ... will trample Satan under your feet, *—WUST* ... under your feet quickly, *—CLMT* ... under your feet speedily, *—DOUY.*

**The grace of our Lord Jesus Christ [be] with you. Amen:**

**16:20.** All of the deceptions which plague the Church and the members of the body of Christ are from Satan. The Father of Lies is behind it all. A massive struggle has gone on over the centuries between right and wrong, truth and error, God and Satan. But Satan shall soon be crushed to pieces and defeated. He will be finally defeated at the time of the Second Coming and chained for 1,000 years before being cast into the lake of fire.

The God of peace shall crush Satan under our feet. The saints are going to share with Christ in His final absolute triumph over Satan. Heretics may plague the Church, Satan may scheme to defile and destroy it, but the God of peace shall conquer.

The apostle closed this section with a reminder of the channel through which ultimate victory is made possible—"The grace of our Lord Jesus Christ be with you."

**21. Timotheus my workfellow, and Lucius, and Jason, and Sosipater, my kinsmen, salute you:** ... my compagnion, *—GNVA* ... my colleague, sends you his good wishes, *—BRCL.*

**16:21.** The apostle had sent greetings to many at Rome, and now those laboring with him sent greetings as well. Timothy, of course, is well known. A native of Lystra, Timothy was Paul's convert and was chosen by him as an assistant and colleague in his apostolic ministry (Acts 16:1-5). The relationship was "as a son with the father" (Philippians 2:19-22). Paul's constant companion, Timothy became a special representative of the apostle from time to time. A great student of Scripture (2 Timothy 1:5; 2:15; 3:15), he was ordained the first bishop of the church at Ephesus. Timothy not only knew the rigors of travel with Paul, but he also knew the persecution for he too suffered imprisonment (Hebrews 13:23).

Lucius, Jason, and Sosipater are also mentioned elsewhere (Acts 13:1; 17:5; 20:4). Some feel that Lucius could be Luke the physician-turned-evangelist and the inspired writer of Luke and Acts.

**22. I Tertius, who wrote [this] epistle, salute you in the Lord:** ... who recorded this letter, *—ADAM* ... the one who is putting this letter in writing, *—WUST.*

**16:22.** Tertius acted as Paul's secretary, writing the epistle at Paul's dictation. Paul's gracious courtesy should be noted. He allowed Tertius to make his greeting personal instead of being treated as a dictating machine—"I Tertius . . . salute you in the Lord." The expression "in the Lord" establishes the fact that his greeting was on the basis of being a fellow Christian.

**23. Gaius mine host, and of the whole church, saluteth you:** . . . who is entertaining me, *−JB* . . . who extends his hospitality to, *−TCNT* . . . and host of the whole assembly, *−WUST* . . . the hoste of all the congregacions, *−TNDL, −CRNM.*

**Erastus the chamberlain of the city saluteth you:** . . . tresorer of the citee, *−WCLF.*

**and Quartus a brother:**

**16:23.** Gaius was one of the first converts at Corinth (1 Corinthians 1:14) and Paul's host at Corinth. There is a likelihood that he is the believer in whose home Paul ministered in Corinth earlier (Acts 18:7). Sir William Ramsey has so identified him, stating that he was a Roman citizen and giving his full name, consisting of praenomen, nomen gentile, and cognomen, as Gaius Titius Justus (p. 205). This verse seems to indicate that he was also the host "of the whole church." This could mean that the Corinthian church met in his house or that he hosted all the visiting brothers and sisters who came to Corinth.

Erastus was the city treasurer, showing that people of prominence had accepted the gospel message.

In contrast there was Quartus. His name means "four." There is conjecture that he had been a slave, for many slaves had only numbers for a name. Whether he had been or was a slave, he had a beautiful tribute—he was "a brother." Since *Tertius* means "three," it may be that Tertius and Quartus were brothers, both freedmen.

**24. The grace of our Lord Jesus Christ [be] with you all. Amen:**

**16:24.** This is Paul's familiar benediction (cf. 1 Corinthians 16:23; 2 Corinthians 13:14; Philippians 4:23; 1 Thessalonians 5:28; 2 Thessalonians 3:18).

**25. Now to him that is of power to stablish you:** . . . Now I commend you to Him who is able to keep you stedfast, *−MNTG* . . . who has power, *−KLGS* . . . that is able to confirme you, *−RHEM* . . . to make you strong, *−WEYM* . . . to establish you, *−CNDT.*

**according to my gospel:** . . . in agreement with my Gospel, *−BRKL* . . . in an adherence, *−LOCK* . . . as promised in the Good News, *−TCNT.*

**and the preaching of Jesus Christ:** . . . and the proclamation, *−WORL.*

**according to the revelation of the mystery:** . . . whereby is unveiled the secret truth, *−MNTG* . . . according to the revelation of the secret, *−ADAM* . . . according to the mandate of the eternal

God, *−WUST* . . . which involves the revealing of the secret, *−BRKL* . . . by revealing the secret purpose, *−MOFT* . . . in vtteringe of the mistery, *−TNDL.*

**which was kept secret since the world began:** . . . that has been obscure for ages, *−NORL* . . . veiled in silence for long ages, *−BECK* . . . after the silence of many centuries, *−BRKL* . . . that was kept quiet for ages, *−ADAM* . . . which has been kept silent, *−HNT* . . . which in the periods of past ages remained unuttered, *−WEYM* . . . which for eternal ages was unrevealed, *−NOYS* . . . not revealed in ancient times, *−SAWR* . . . having been kept in silence, *−CLMT* . . . kept secret in times of the ages, *−KLGS* . . . which was kept secret through immemorial ages, *−MNTG* . . . from eternal ages, *−CNFT* . . . from eternal times kept secrete, *−RHEM* . . . through times eternal, *−ASV* . . . for long ages, *−RSV.*

**16:25.** Paul began the Epistle to the Romans with the prayer that he might "impart unto you some spiritual gift, to the end ye may be established" (1:11). He longed to visit them for that purpose, but although he had not been able to do so at the time of writing, he had through this letter been able to impart a rich treasure to them.

Paul concluded the epistle with an ascription of praise. All glory belongs to God—"to him." He alone has the power (is able) to keep the Christian in the right path and to keep him from falling (Ephesians 3:20; Jude 24). He is the One who will make the believer stable, strengthen and make him firm and able to stand (14:4). Saints are to be established in and by the gospel which Paul preached. Those doctrines which Paul preached and defended presented Christ as the answer. That communication long concealed had now been revealed.

When Paul said "my gospel," (cf. Romans 2:16; 1 Thessalonians 1:5; 2 Timothy 2:8), he was speaking of the gospel as it was revealed to him by Jesus. When Paul returned to Jerusalem (Acts 9), he had a clearer revelation of the gospel than any other apostle (Galatians 1:12-17).

**26. But now is made manifest:** . . . But now is opened, and published, *−GNVA* . . . But now disclosed, *−HNSN* . . . with the uncovering of the secret, *−WLMS* . . . but is now disclosed, *−RSV* . . . brought out into the open, *−TEV.*

**and by the scriptures of the prophets:** . . . and through the prophetic Scriptures, *−ADAM* . . . by means of prophetic scriptures, *−PNT* . . . on the basis of the prophetic scriptures, *−MOFT.*

**according to the commandment of the everlasting God, made known to all nations:** . . . according to the precept of the eternal God, *−CNFT* . . . to an appointment of the aeonian God, *−HNSN* . . . of god withouten bigynnynge [and] endynge, *−WCLF* . . . according to the precept of the eternal God, *−RHEM* . . . publisshed amonge all nacions, *−TNDL* . . . to the precept of the eternal God, *−DOUY.*

**for the obedience of faith:** ... to bring about obedience to the faith, —RSV ... to secure submission to the Faith, —TCNT.

**16:26.** The "mystery" of verse 25 was the divine secret that Gentiles would be fellow heirs with Jews in the body of Christ (Ephesians 3). The gospel brought Gentiles to glory, and so glory came to God. This mystery is now being made known to all nations.

Paul constantly used the Old Testament Scriptures in his preaching. It was "according to the Scriptures" (1 Corinthians 15:3, 4). His gospel, the mystery, was witnessed to by the Law and the Prophets but only became known as revealed by the one who had the key. Paul had that key, the knowledge of Christ which God had revealed to him. It was only in the light of the new revelation in Christ that Paul and the apostles were able to understand and expound the Scriptures (1 Peter 1:10-12).

This revelation was "according to the commandment of the everlasting God." He is the Eternal One and therefore unchanging. He had concealed this truth but He intended that it should be revealed. By His command the gospel has been known in and by His Son.

The expression "the obedience of faith" was also used in 1:5. The tendency of faith is to produce obedience. There is no true faith that does not produce obedience. This is a constant affirmation in the New Testament (Romans 15:18; 16:19; 2 Corinthians 7:15; James 2).

The original commission which Jesus gave His disciples was that the gospel was to be preached "among all nations" (Luke 24:27). It was the special commission which Paul received at his conversion (Acts 9:15). It is the privilege of all to receive and appropriate the message of the gospel; the duty of all who accept is to transmit the good news to others.

**27. To God only wise, [be] glory through Jesus Christ for ever. Amen:** ... into worldis of worldis, —WCLF ... to the ages! —SCLT ... for the eons of the eons, —CNDT.

**16:27.** Paul resumed the doxology with a great expression of praise to God. The attribute of wisdom is brought into view, for it has surely been particularly on display in God's plan to save men as revealed in this great epistle. God's wisdom is shown in devising the plan and in bringing it about.

All men have been found guilty; the whole world was declared guilty before God. Justification by faith in Christ crucified is the only remedy for sin. It is by faith alone.

The remedy of the gospel for indwelling sin is sanctification. By union with Christ in His death and resurrection the dominion of sin is broken. "The law of the Spirit of life in Christ Jesus" (8:1, 2) makes it possible for the believer to live victoriously with no condemnation and no separation.

God has turned His attention to the Gentiles, but the Jew is only temporarily set aside and will return to God.

Christian life and service calls for all believers to be considerate of others and to be motivated with an outflow of the love of Christ.

The long argument of the letter comes to a close with a great song of praise "to God only wise, be glory through Jesus Christ for ever. Amen."

# 1 CORINTHIANS

## Overview

The city of Corinth was located in southern Greece in the province of Achaia, on the narrow isthmus connecting the Greek mainland with Peloponnesus, that peninsula extending into the Mediterranean Sea. Even prior to the Corinth of the New Testament, a strategic city had existed on the site. "Old Corinth," however, was destroyed by the Romans in 146 B.C. Nevertheless, because of its being ideally suited for trade—with harbors on the Aegean Sea on the east and the Gulf of Corinth, which connected to the Ionian Sea on the west—it was eventually rebuilt. Almost all of the east-west trade had to travel through Corinth; the other option was to sail around the Peloponnesus, an option often dangerous and difficult. After the city lay dormant for 100 years, Julius Caesar ordered it rebuilt (46 B.C.). Originally the newer city was settled by army veterans from Italy. These Italian immigrants spoke Greek, so the entire province was Greek-speaking. Later, Greeks returned to populate it. Because of its being a trade center, the population was a composite of people from all over the Mediterranean region. From 27 B.C. on, Corinth was the capital city of Achaia.

Corinth had a bad reputation, even among Gentiles and pagans. To "live like a Corinthian" meant to live licentiously. The expression "Corinthian girls" became an idiom throughout the Roman Empire for "harlots." In the city's temple of Aphrodite there were countless numbers of temple prostitutes. Aphrodite was the Greek goddess of love, beauty, and life and was synonymous with the Roman goddess Venus or the Phoenician deity Astarte.

On his second missionary journey, Paul visited Corinth and conducted his work there for 18 months. During this period he established the Corinthian church composed of Jewish and Gentile Christians. Later, after he had moved to Ephesus for a 3-year period, he apparently made brief visits to the city while he was on his third missionary journey. A third visit to Corinth probably took place towards the end of that missionary journey, just as the Ephesian ministry was coming to a close.

Paul began his ministry in Corinth from the Jewish synagogue. Later, he moved to a house church perhaps adjacent to the synagogue (Acts 18:4-7). Crispus, the ruler of the synagogue, and his family were converted to Christ. Most of the others in the church had a Greek/Gentile background. A few may have belonged to the upper class, for we read of one "Erastus, who is the city's director of public works" (Romans 16:23, NIV). Most, though, were from the lower classes, such as slaves, freedmen, etc. (1:26ff.; 7:21).

Paul wrote several letters to the church at Corinth; we know of at least three, two of which we have. First Corinthians 5:9 indicates that Paul wrote one letter to the church prior to the one we call "First Corinthians." Paul also received a letter from the Corinthians (7:1). First Corinthians then, is partially a response to that letter, and at the same time, Paul's means of addressing other current issues. Whereas in the Epistle to the Romans we meet Paul the teacher, in 1 Corinthians we encounter Paul the spiritual leader. Just as the Epistle to the Romans contains much doctrinal instruction, 1 Corinthians holds much ethical teaching. Paul discussed the situation at Corinth in a very forthright manner; issues were evaluated and a response was given on the basis of Christian faith and teaching. Because the letter takes such a fundamental approach to resolving issues, it was of utmost importance to the Corinthian believers individually, but also to the Church throughout the ages.

First Corinthians was written from Ephesus, probably a little while before Pentecost, A.D. 55 (cf. 16:8; i.e., toward the end of Paul's 3-year stay in Ephesus). There is general agreement that this is indeed an authentic Pauline letter. Robertson and Plummer remark that those attempting to show Paul was not the author only succeed in proving their own ignorance (*The International Critical Commentary, Corinthians,* p.xvi). The genuineness of the epistle is attested by both external and internal evidence. Among the external witnesses are Clement of Rome, who around A.D. 95 refers to a letter which can only be 1 Corinthians. Irenaeus' writings contain more than 60 quotes or allusions to 1 Corinthians; Clement of Alexandria's around 130; and Tertullian's around 400. Moreover, the authenticity is attested by Ignatius, Polycarp, Hermas, Justin Martyr, Athenagorus, and by the *Didache* (The Teaching of the Twelve Apostles). In the Muratorian Fragment it is placed first among the writings of Paul. The internal witnesses—the style, vocabulary, and content—corroborate the external evidence and coincide with what is known both about Paul and the church to which he wrote.

First Corinthians was a reply to a letter Paul received from believers in Corinth. In that letter questions were raised concerning sexual relations, meat offered to idols, and perhaps the exercise of spiritual gifts in the congregation. The letter may have also inquired about proper procedure in worship (e.g., the Lord's Supper). Paul replied very directly to their questions.

However, before discussing their questions (7:1ff.), Paul devoted six chapters to what he evidently regarded as more crucial and urgent problems in the Corinthian church. Paul had learned from others about these other problems (1:11; 5:1). Divisions had arisen in the church body because some were identifying themselves according to Paul, Apollos, or Peter; some even claimed to be "of Christ" (1:12). The Corinthians seemed not to view these divisions as a serious matter, but Paul thought otherwise. Furthermore, he had received word of adultery in the church of such a morally degenerate nature that it was not even heard of among the Gentiles. It had even caused moral offense among the city's inhabitants, who were otherwise accustomed to moral laxity. Paul had another complaint: believers were taking one another to pagan courts to settle their petty differences.

Paul wrote to correct these problems as well as to answer the questions in the Corinthians' letter. In addition, he addressed certain doctrinal issues, particularly concerning the resurrection of believers, and he affirmed some of the basic tenets of Christian proclamation (cf. 2:2; 15:1ff.). Paul endeavored to prevent two things: the influence of the moral corruption that existed outside the church; and the infiltration of a teaching based upon Greek philosophical ideals which threatened to destroy the heart of the gospel.

Even though the scheme of 1 Corinthians does not follow the same kind of rigid structure as the Epistle to the Romans, the main sections are rather easy to identify:

## I. Christian Proclamation (1:1-4:21)

The first main section of 1 Corinthians concerns Christian proclamation, the most crucial distinctive of the Christian Church. Here that theme is especially discussed in relation to the problem of dissension among the Corinthians and their arguments over which preacher was "better" or "right." Paul's teaching, therefore, did not merely inform about the nature of Christian proclamation, it also reflected the place of heralds of the gospel and the attitude the Church is to exhibit towards them.

First, the apostle addressed the problem of interpersonal strife that had arisen in the church; he rejected it outright (1:10-16). Next he related how such dissension could occur: the Corinthians were indiscriminately accepting preaching modeled after Greek "wisdom" (i.e., rhetoric and persuasion), rather than the word of the Cross (1:17-2:5). Paul wrote that the Corinthians were too immature to handle actual spiritual "wisdom." He then explained that the conflict over preachers was pointless, since every witness sent by God is merely a servant performing those duties for which the Lord has equipped him (3:3-23). Paul lastly commented on the hazards of preaching (chapter 4).

The dispute in Corinth ran far deeper than simple preference for one leader/preacher over another. This attitude reflected a fundamentally defective understanding of the gospel—the message of the Cross. They had allowed interests other than the gospel to affect their judgment; this will always result in schism. Paul exposed the heart of the problem. They had allowed interests other than the word of the Cross to control them. Instead of sorting out the various factions into "correct" and "incorrect" categories, Paul directed their attention to the element necessary for unity in the body—the message of the Cross. At the same time he uncovered the actual reason for the divisions: The church had succumbed to strange teachings and had been deceived by Hellenistic "wisdom." The elevation of human wisdom and human beings resulted in factions and caused dissent in the church at Corinth.

A truth emerges here which applies to almost any conflict over doctrine: many of those involved in conflict do not really grasp the issue or its consequences. The believers in Corinth were not intentionally rejecting the gospel, they merely wanted to modify the message to make it more acceptable. What they failed to recognize, however, was that to dress the gospel in the garments of Greek philosophy would be to rob it of its distinctive character. A gospel preached in "words of human wisdom" is no gospel at all (1:17).

The gospel of the first Christian churches was in risk of being distorted from two sources: paganism and Judaism. The epistolary literature of the New Testament generally reflects such conflict, but 1 Corinthians and Galatians are the clearest responses to this danger.

The Epistle to the Galatians cautions against legalistic Judaism's influence upon the young church. It does not appear that these "Judaizers" were in any way connected with James, the leader of the Jewish-Christian congregation in Jerusalem (Acts 15:24). Further, it seems they did not go so far as to deny Jesus' messiahship and His status as Saviour. Nonetheless, Paul declared that they preached "another gospel" (Galatians 1:6-9). Their teaching is summarized in Acts 15:1: "Except ye be circumcised after the manner of Moses, ye cannot be saved." Verse 5 says that these Judaizers had a pharisaic background but they "believed." Thus, they did not deny that belief in Jesus is essential for salvation, but they asserted that believers must also "keep the law of Moses." This mixture of Law and gospel is a distortion of the gospel, said Paul (Galatians 1:7). He strongly condemned it: "But though we, or an angel from heaven, preach any other gospel unto you than that which we have preached unto you, let him be accursed" (verse 8).

Any "gospel" that neutralizes grace and relies upon works is not the gospel but its annulment!

While one main assault on the gospel originated from pharisaic Judaism, the other source of attack came from Gentile/pagan philosophy. Just as Judaism was a legalistic religion, Hellenistic philosophical speculation was the ultimate in pagan religion. "Pagan" here does not mean some simplistic, animistic philosophy; rather, it was one of the most sophisticated philosophies of all time. Hellenistic paganism had sunk into deep idolatry and moral decay, but for Paul it was the Greeks' worship of "wisdom" that typified paganism. Precisely at the point of "wisdom" paganism launches its sharpest attack on Christianity.

The idolatry and immorality surrounding the first Gentile churches had their effect upon the newly converted. Yet even more dangerous was the subtle infiltration of Gentile thoughts and ideas, such as the attack from so-called "wisdom." This is what Paul picked up on in the first section of his letter. Just as he showed in the Epistle to the Galatians that it is impossible to unite Christianity with Jewish legalism, in 1 Corinthians he demonstrated that the gospel and Hellenistic wisdom are altogether incompatible. Any plan of salvation that "unites" law and grace perverts the gospel and becomes "another gospel," and to join Greek philosophy with the gospel strips the gospel of its power. Faith and "wisdom" are as incompatible as faith and works of the Law in relation to receiving salvation. Any compromise between the gospel of God and human wisdom is impossible.

The New Testament renounces the kind of wisdom exposed and denounced here and elsewhere in its pages. The "wisdom cult" originated in the Gnostic mystery religions, which adopted myths from the Orient and mixed them with Hellenistic philosophy. "Christian" Gnosticism mixed the gospel of Jesus Christ with Hellenistic "wisdom," asceticism, and worship of angels. These were merely a "spiritualized" form of idolatry. Such a form of "Christian" Gnosticism may also have been threatening the church at Colossae.

The strange "wisdom" teaching that threatened the early Christian churches surfaced in a variety of forms. While the wisdom at Colossae was decidedly mythological in character, the type in Corinth was more rational and intellectual. But Paul condemned this worldly "wisdom" whatever its form. It is foreign to the gospel and an enemy to it. It was the root of the divisions that emerged in Corinth threatened to destroy the church.

## A. Greeting and Thanksgiving (1:1-9)

Paul began his letter with a greeting and an offering of thanks to God for the believers in Corinth. His generous acknowledgment of the good in the church—its richness of doctrine, knowledge, and spiritual gifts—was in no way sarcastic. Neither was it flattery designed to ingratiate the church to himself. That kind of reasoning was foreign to Paul. On the contrary, the apostle stated with great joy that not everything was going badly in Corinth. Much true piety and spiritual abundance existed in the church. Paul's letter addressed the errors and abuses in the Corinthian church but the believers needed to be reminded immediately that there was much that was positive about the church. This would keep them from losing courage and thinking that Paul was denouncing everyone.

Paul wrote with apostolic authority, as one with the authority to act on behalf of the Lord and to speak with the authority of Jesus. His letter was more than a friendly correspondence; it was a holy letter to be read in the church and received as the Word of God.

## B. Dispute Over Preachers (1:10-17)

To begin his discussion of the problem of divisiveness in Corinth, Paul opened with an appeal for unity. He explained that he learned of the conflict not from some vague rumor but from reliable witnesses whom he named: "those who are of the house of Chloe."

To say Paul was seriously concerned about divisions in the church would be an understatement. No less than 4 of the 16 chapters are devoted to that issue and its ramifications. Still it is noteworthy that he did not refer to the disputing factions as "sects" (*hairesis*), but as "schisms" (*schismata*, pl.). This denotes "splits," or "divisions."

Paul's choice of words may reflect the state of affairs in Corinth. Perhaps they were not the result of heretical groups; their error may not have gone that far . . . yet. Nevertheless, the seed of division sown among them resulted in a spiritual cleavage in the church. Members had selected their "favorite preacher" and were taking sides against one another—despite the fact that the preachers themselves did not want or encourage such division.

Paul mentioned four such groups, but he did not elaborate on what specifically distinguished each group. A great deal of literature has been devoted to trying to identify the various features of each group; however, such an attempt is ultimately doomed to failure. There is simply not enough hard evidence.

The general consensus argues that those claiming to be "of Paul" or "for Paul" attached a great deal of importance to Paul's teaching on Christian freedom. Those "of Apollos," an eloquent scholar from Alexandria, perhaps put a great deal of emphasis upon a polished, rhetorical style. The members of the Cephas group are regarded by many as representatives of a Jewish-Christian faction; these would naturally affiliate with Peter, the apostle to the circumcised. The above may be true, but it cannot be confirmed.

The greatest conflict of opinion concerns the nature of the fourth group, those "of Christ." Some interpreters regard this to be Paul's reply to the first three groups. Although possible, it is not probable. Paul continued with the indignant rhetorical question, "Is Christ divided?" This would seem to indicate that even the name of Christ was being used by a faction.

Opinions differ as to what characterized this the "Christ group." It may have asserted a special "spirituality" that regarded itself above human authority and the only true followers of Jesus. Their error lay in claiming Christ exclusively for themselves. The very name that should have united all the people had become a party name. Paul rejected it just as he had the others.

Naturally Paul rejected those claiming to be "of Paul." He would not tolerate any group of Pauline "disciples"; he was in the business of making disciples of Jesus Christ and Him alone. Peter and Apollos apparently felt the same as Paul. The question of who was the "greatest" interested Peter no more than Paul (cf. Galatians 2:6). Paul's confidence in Apollos becomes clear when he asked him to go to Corinth (1 Corinthians 16:12).

The conflict in Corinth probably did not concern any actual doctrinal issues, but the consequences of their divisions included their being "puffed up for one against another" (4:6). This kind of conflict was moreover totally unjustified, since the only kind of justifiable dispute would concern doctrine. To contend for the Faith is the obligation of every believer; personal conflict is usually unauthorized. In the eyes of the people the personalities of the preachers overshadowed their message, which was Biblical and in total agreement. As the personalities became the focus of attention the gospel receded into the background. If the gospel had been given its rightful place in the community, those who heard it would not have made the messenger more important than the message. The basis of Christian unity is the cross of Christ; only the preaching of the Cross can lead believers into that unity.

## C. The Foolishness of Preaching (1:18-2:5)

For Paul the cross became a religious symbol, a new and radical viewpoint in the ancient world. In fact, "the cross" has become the central symbol in Christian proclamation. Paul spoke of "the preaching of the cross," which equals the gospel itself, the power of God unto salvation (1:18; cf. Romans 1:16). The very gospel the Corinthians believed and by which they were saved is the same gospel received by Paul: Christ died for our sins according to the Scriptures, He was buried, and He rose from the dead (15:1ff.). The message of salvation is the announcement of the reality of what God has done in Christ. This makes the gospel "good news," and its truth cannot be compromised. "The preaching of the cross" was an offense to the Jews, a stumbling block that made them fall. Paul linked this to their demand for a "sign" before they would believe (1:22). They thought the Messiah would authenticate himself with signs from heaven, like Moses or Elijah. Even though they saw Him heal the sick and raise the dead, they continued to demand a sign from heaven. Jesus told them the only sign they would be given would be the sign of Jonah the prophet. As Jonah was in the belly of the great fish for 3 days, so too would the Son of Man be in the heart of the earth for 3 days. The ultimate sign given to them was the death and resurrection of Jesus, and this was the "sign" Paul preached. Nevertheless, the scandal of "the cross" made it virtually impossible for the Jews to accept its message. The Law stated that "He that is hanged, is accursed of God" (Deuteronomy 21:23; cf. Galatians 3:13). To reconcile the dilemma of a Messiah dying in such total weakness and defeat was virtually impossible. Furthermore, that any "Messiah" should die under the judgment and curse of God was absurd and a contradiction within itself.

The Jewish leaders who later had stoned Stephen and caused the death of so many other believers took care to see that Jesus died a Roman death; that was all the "proof" they needed that Jesus was not the promised Messiah. They could not accept a humiliated Messiah. Their unbelief stemmed directly from a failure to believe the Scriptures. They were blind to the Old Testament's anticipation of the Suffering Servant of God, spoken of in Isaiah 53. They had no use for any Messiah who would allow himself to bear the sin and its penalty of all peoples. However, this is precisely the kind of Messiah Paul preached: Christ crucified (2:2); Christ made sin for us (2 Corinthians 5:21); Christ made a curse for us (Galatians 3:13). There is no other way to salvation than this.

To the Greek "the preaching of the cross" was the ultimate folly. One could not expect its absurdity to be taken seriously. A crucified Jew the saviour of the whole world? Impossible. The Greeks regarded the message of the Cross as an insult to their intelligence. The danger facing the church at Corinth was that it would adopt the world's attitude toward the message of the Cross. Undoubtedly some were urging that the message be adapted to suit the cultural situation and to make it more acceptable to outsiders. Paul was responding to the efforts of some to cloak Christianity in the guise of the wisdom of the world, i.e., Hellenistic rhetorical methods and terminology.

Paul was not against adapting to one's environment; he had done it himself. He became a Jew to the Jews and a Greek to the Greeks (9:19-22). His sermon on Mars Hill in Athens, just before he went to Corinth reflected this (Acts 17:22ff.). But when it came to modifying the gospel according to the Hellenistic "wisdom" philosophy, he was immovable. His solid reluctance to alter the gospel's heart at this point resembles his similar ardor against the Judaizers in Galatians. He would not preach the gospel with "wise words"; his listeners' faith could not rest upon human wisdom but upon the power of God (1:17; 2:4). This explains why Greeks seeking wisdom did not find it in the preaching of the apostles. Instead of human wisdom they met the "foolishness" of preaching, the plain, unaltered truth of the gospel. The preaching of the Cross is carried out in the "demonstration of the Spirit's power" (2:4, NIV). The expression "demonstration" (*apodeixis*) here denotes "proof," a term often appearing in argumentation in which the premise is known to be true and reliable. At the same time, it denotes more than a logical truth, because an argument may be logically sound yet still unconvincing. The "proof" has real power to convince; it has a spiritual impact upon the inner person. This cannot be produced by human eloquence; it comes only from the convicting power of the Holy Spirit (cf. John 16:8). When Paul declared that his preaching was in the demonstration of the Spirit's power, he was probably referring to those supernatural manifestations that accompanied his ministry. He himself observed that signs and wonders were worked in Corinth (2 Corinthians 12:12). In this case, though, there was undoubtedly something more than external miracles; rather, it included the spiritual power that was the key to apostolic preaching.

As Paul's own ministry attests, the power of the Cross is not revealed in human power and ability, but in weakness and humiliation (2:3; cf. 2 Corinthians 10:10; 12:5-9). He therefore avoided any appearance of using "enticing words of man's wisdom" or the methods of philosophers, because human wisdom has already proved inadequate for leading man to God. Through its wisdom the world did not know Him (1:21). With a series of rhetorical questions Paul invites the "wise person" to step forward. Where is the wise? where is the scribe, (the expert in the law)? where is the disputer (debater) of this world (age)? The last expression is somewhat sarcastic. Together the three summarize the essence of what was regarded as "wise." But which of these three understood salvation on the basis of their "wisdom"? The world might expect them to be at the forefront, but their wisdom had not led them to faith or shown them the way to God.

On the contrary, not many considered "wise" in the world's eyes are called. Neither are many called whom the world regards as powerful or influential. And not many esteemed as "noble" receive the gospel. That which a person might boast about or exalt himself for is captured in these three expressions: intellectual superiority, political and economic power, and social status. Against these the apostle Paul juxtaposed the elect of God. God chooses the "foolish things" of this world, not the "wise." He calls the weak, not the strong; He invites the lowly and even despised, not the exalted. He summons those disowned by human society— "nonpersons" who are not even recognized by the rest of society. These are like slaves, the lowest dregs of society. To be "nothing" or nonexistent was abhorrent to the Greek mind. But for Paul it stood at the crux of God's new act in which He was creating a new creation from nothing. The words of the Old Testament ring out clearly: "Those who were not a people will become a people," the new people of God (Hosea 1:7ff.; cf. Romans 9:25, 26; 1 Peter 2:10).

A word of caution is in order here. Paul was not suggesting that the "lowly" are really the "lofty" and the "powerful" the "powerless." God chooses the things which are indeed lowly, not for the purpose of exalting them according to worldly standards, but precisely because they are lowly. None have reason for boasting in the presence of God (1:29). The sole criterion for salvation remains faith (Romans 3:27); no one can take credit for what God's grace accomplishes. Both the exalted and the debased stand in need before God. God's choosing the lowly and humble shows that it is by grace alone that salvation comes. It is altogether the work of God: "Of him are ye in Christ Jesus, who of God is made unto us wisdom, and righteousness, and sanctification, and redemption" (1:30).

Paul made it perfectly clear that the preaching of the Cross is foolishness to those who are perishing, but to those who believe it is the power and wisdom of God (1:18, 24). With this as his background, Paul proceeded to explain the nature of true spiritual wisdom.

## D. Preaching Wisdom (2:6-16)

Paul's argument revolved around two contrasts: the weakness of God is stronger than men, and the foolishness of God is wiser than men. These two concepts are interlaced with one another continually, but the first section (1:17-2:5) focuses upon how the "weakness" of God accomplishes what the "power" of humanity cannot. The foolishness of preaching is superior to every human philosophy or epistemology because it acts. The preaching of the Cross, which might appear "rough-cut" in the company of "gems" of human oratory, nevertheless has the power to set men and women free and transform their lives.

In 2:6-16 Paul began to discuss the second major contrast: the foolishness of God is wiser than men. Lacking any ability to grasp the foolishness of the preaching of the Cross, fallen man, ruled not by the Spirit of God but by his own corrupt nature, cannot receive the things of the Spirit. They are "folly" to him. To modify the Christian message in order to accommodate Gentiles, therefore, is useless. In fact, it is not the simple, plain presentation of the gospel that prevents men from receiving, but the reality that the gospel is foreign to the natural man. He is hostile to it. Therefore, the gospel must be proclaimed in simple, direct terms. Only then can the Spirit of God use it to convince men of their need to be saved.

This principle applies not only to the evangelistic efforts of proclaiming the gospel, but to the teaching ministry within the Church itself. Just as the kerygma—the essence of the proclamation of the gospel—owes nothing to the world, so too, the Christian teaching or *didachē* is not to be overly influenced by human teaching. Rather, teaching should be marked by the Spirit's instruction. The Spirit teaches spiritual things which can only be interpreted by spiritual words; spiritual matters must be compared with other spiritual matters (2:13).

The simple message Paul preached could help some to grasp its forthright message. But this does not mean the gospel is not sophisticated, lacks depth, or anything similar. That would be a total misrepresentation. The Christian message is one of the deepest mysteries of all time: God and the human condition, sin and redemption, time and eternity, and the beginning and the consummation. The wisdom given by God can grant insight into the mysteries of the earth never before accessible by merely human methods. Wisdom indeed characterizes the gospel: "But we speak the wisdom of God in a mystery, even the hidden wisdom, which God ordained before the world unto our glory" (2:7). Related to this, Paul raised two questions: What does the deeper wisdom of Christ consist of? Who participates in this secret wisdom?

When Paul explained the nature of Christian wisdom, he began—quite understandably given the problem of wisdom in Corinth—by setting out very clearly that the hidden wisdom of God is entirely different from the wisdom of the world. Worldly wisdom is an invention of mankind, thus it is colored by sin's influence (cf. Ephesians 4:17, 18). Consequently, it is empty and restricted to this present world. Christian wisdom, however, being of a divine origin, consists of the concepts which God "ordained before the world" (2:7), i.e., what God thought before He created. It therefore reflects the wisdom of God himself and His plan of salvation. "Christ . . . the wisdom of God" is the essence of this wisdom, and in Him are "hid all the treasures of wisdom and knowledge" (Colossians 2:2, 3). Spiritual wisdom does not lead one away from the Cross, as worldly wisdom does; rather it points toward it, since Christ is what spiritual wisdom is all about.

Because spiritual wisdom comes from God and is hidden in God, it is unobtainable for anyone not having the Spirit of God. Only the Spirit of God knows what dwells in God (2:10ff.). "The princes of this world" did not know this wisdom. If they had known it they would not have crucified the Lord of glory (2:8).

It is not strange that the world and its leaders did not grasp the deep wisdom of God. It is amazing that "the wisdom" is also unknown by carnal and immature believers. Preaching of this wisdom is "meat" in contrast to the "milk" of preaching basic gospel truths. Paul declared that the Corinthians were not able to bear preaching on wisdom (3:1, 2). It can be dangerous to immature believers because it can be misinterpreted (cf. 2 Peter 3:15, 16). The kind of insight referred to here is more than intellectual. It is closely related to a person's spiritual condition. This wisdom is for the "mature," the "spiritual" (2:6, 15). Spiritual maturity in this instance is necessary to comprehend the deep things of God. It also denotes the condition of an individual as "spiritual" rather than "carnal, fleshly" (3:3). These are not just "babes" in Christ, but "carnal Christians," whose lifestyle is inconsistent with their Christian testimony.

The New Testament writings encourage the Christian to grow in knowledge. This is not just mental, but includes the entire personality. Spiritual immaturity leads to all kinds of destructive influences (Ephesians 4:13, 14). To be deficient in Christian knowledge can lead to backsliding (Hebrews 6:1ff.). Against this background Paul desired all believers to obtain "all the riches of the full assurance of understanding" (Colossians 2:1f.). The apostle must not be misunderstood here as saying that wisdom is available only for the mature. By no means would he have endorsed some spiritual hierarchy within the body of Christ. All believers may achieve "the unity of the faith, and of the knowledge of the Son of God" (Ephesians 4:13). Knowledge here is not merely intellectual information, but spiritual growth, maturity (2 Peter 3:18). When Paul stated that the Corinthians were "babes in Christ," he meant that they needed more than teaching to obtain the hidden wisdom of God.

## E. The Role of Preachers (3:1-23)

Having explained the essence of Christian proclamation in 1:17-2:5 and the nature of Christian wisdom in 2:6-16, Paul returned (chapter 3) to a theme introduced in 1:10-16: divisions in the church over leaders. The apostle explained in this section the role of the preacher and his place in the Church. He showed how utterly pointless was their favoring one preacher over another. Their attitude showed they were still living a fleshly existence; they were still immature and therefore not ready to receive deeper spiritual instruction (3:1-3).

"Who, then is Paul, and who is Apollos, but ministers by whom ye believed?" Paul asked (3:5). They were servants of God, their special ministry was given to them by God alone. Paul used two illustrations. He compared the Church with a field and with the temple of God. In each case His servants have their different roles.

In God's field some plant and others water. How absurd it would be to say "I'm for the planter," or "I'm for the waterer." They are coworkers, not competitors. Together they work for God who alone can grant growth. Apart from Him neither the one who plants nor the one who waters is anything. But because they are working together toward the same objective, it is ridiculous for anyone to align with one and reject the other. It is disastrous when Christians become "puffed up for one against another" (4:6). If the leaders were esteemed for who they truly are—servants of the Lord—there would not be any conflict or division.

The second image Paul utilized is that of the temple, God's holy habitation of old. The Old Testament spoke of a new temple that would be erected in the last days (Isaiah 28:16). The early Christians saw the Church of the New Testament as the spiritual fulfillment of these prophecies. Paul declared that he had laid the foundation of this spiritual building in Corinth. This foundation was none other than that which God himself had laid—Jesus Christ (3:11). He is the cornerstone of the "foundation of the apostles and prophets." In Him the various churches or "buildings" are fitted together into a "holy temple . . . an habitation of God through the Spirit" (Ephesians 2:20-22). Jesus' work and His person are the foundation of the Church. When Jesus said He would build His Church, He associated this with Peter's confession at Caesarea Philippi: "You are the Christ, the Son of the living God" (Matthew 16:16ff.). No one else can lay another foundation, declared Paul. Any organization built on another foundation is not a church. Christ and His presence authenticate the Church.

The "building" rests upon this foundation. Its erection, first and foremost, comes through preaching. To continue the imagery, preaching the gospel, i.e., evangelization, brings new "stones" for the building. Teaching doctrine places and fits the stones properly into the larger structure. The object is that everyone should be presented "perfect" in Christ (Colossians 1:28) and be "thoroughly equipped" for service (Ephesians 4:12ff.). Later Pauline churches had to endure "preachers" who tried to build on another foundation. These were sharply rebuked (Galatians 1:6f.; Philippians 3:2, 18; Colossians 2:8). In 1 Corinthians Paul spoke of those who build upon the same foundation but with different materials. Those who build on Christ's foundation, provided their work stands, will be rewarded. But those who build with "cheap" or "worthless" material, will not be rewarded. Instead, their work will burn in the fiery judgment. Nevertheless, the one building upon the proper foundation will not lose his soul, even though he loses his reward. He will be saved, but only as through fire. A genuine believer never relies upon his own efforts to save him, but the work of Christ. Although the believer may fail and his work perish, the work of Christ stands firm. This is what saves him.

It is a different matter when divisions are caused in the Body of Christ. Paul uses two Greek words, *dichostasia* and *schismata*, which are translated "divisions." He also speaks of *hairesis* ("heresies") as dividing the church (see 11:19 and 2 Peter 2:1) and calls them a work of the flesh (Galatians 5:20).

Paul uses strong language: "If any man destroy the temple of God, him shall God destroy" (3:17), stating that believers are the temple of God. To destroy the Church is a heinous crime. It is like touching the "apple of his eye" (cf. Zechariah 2:8) and defiling the bride of Christ. The larger Church can never be destroyed (Matthew 16:18), but from Revelation (2:5; 3:16; etc.) it is apparent that some individual churches can be. Whether Paul's warning of God's judgment was directed at certain individuals cannot be determined for sure (cf. Galatians 5:10).

Paul concluded this subsection by warning the Corinthians not to "glory in men" (3:21). How could they choose sides or follow a particular teaching, when in actuality everything was theirs? Whether Paul, Apollos, or Cephas, they were all servants given to the Church by God (cf. 12:28; Ephesians 4:11). Indeed, whether the world, life, or death, whether present or future, everything belongs to the children of God and will work for their good (cf. Romans 8:28). Why limit to a part what God has given in totality? Why choose the world's empty wisdom when the eternal wisdom of God—the things "eye hath not seen not ear heard, neither have entered into the heart of man"—are available (cf. 2:7-10).

## F. The Hardships of Ministry (4:1-21)

Paul concluded this section on preachers and preaching with a discussion of their low status in the world and the hardships endured by servants of Christ. He opened the section and united it with what had preceded it by asking the Corinthians to regard their leaders not as leaders of factions, but as ministers and stewards of Christ.

The two terms he used express both the low position of the witnesses as well as their uniqueness. The term for servant here, *hepēretas*, originally denoted the rowers who sat on the lowest bench in the ship. From this it came to describe any "assistant" or "helper." The second term, *oikonomous*, signified a slave who was the overseer of his master's household and property. This "steward" was in charge of his fellow slaves, but depending upon the extent of his master's flexibility, he was nevertheless a slave like the rest.

The first obligation of a steward is to be faithful. Where faithfulness was at stake, the opinions of others did not matter to Paul. Indeed, he did not even judge himself; he left that to God. Although he had not knowingly been unfaithful in his service, he realized he could make mistakes. Thus he declared, "He who judges me is the Lord." Paul was not concerned that the Corinthians would look into his record. He knew his record would be evaluated by the One who will bring to light everything that has been hidden in the darkness and the inner motives of hearts. When the Lord returns hidden motives will be exposed—Paul's as well as those of everyone else's. Then all men will praise God. Apparently every believer will receive praise for something. Paul looked confidently, but with a holy respect, toward the time when he would stand before the judgment seat of Christ (2 Corinthians 5:10, 11).

Next comes the most biting portion of the entire letter. It contains the harshest rebuke and is marked by a painful irony. But Paul gave it in deep love, calling his listeners "brethren" and his "dear children" (4:6-14). First, he explained why he had referred to himself and Apollos (1:12; 3:4, 22). It was not because this was necessarily a Corinthian concern, but because he and Apollos were models of what he was talking about. Paul customarily supported his arguments with references to Scripture (cf. 1:19f., 31; 2:9, 16; 3:19f.). Apparently there were some teachers in the Corinthian church who thought their vision was superior in authority to Scripture. They incited division in the church. To supersede what was written was itself divisive. Consequently, the danger of elevating the teaching of men above Scripture by giving them authority and power is plain.

Typically, Paul set things in order with one of his penetrating rhetorical questions. "For who maketh thee to differ from another?" Paul questioned. The only answer could be, "I did it myself!" No one would admit to that, however. But Paul was relentless: "And what hast thou that thou didst not receive?" Only a fool boasts of something he obtained from others.

Within the Corinthian church were individuals who imagined they had already reached a perfection that cannot occur in this life. That perfection belongs to the time of the consummation. They not only judged before the time (verse 5), they also took credit (glory) in advance. They were already satisfied. They had become rich already! But Jesus declared, "Blessed are those who are hungering and thirsting after righteousness." Jesus also said, "Blessed are the poor in spirit."

The Corinthians were acting as if the kingdom of God had already come and they had been appointed rulers. "I truly wish it were so," commented Paul sarcastically. "If that were true," he reasoned, "we apostles could rule with you." The pretense of glory and the illusion of divine living experienced by the Corinthians was entirely foreign to the apostles. While the Corinthians listened to the wisdom of the world, the apostles were preaching the word of the Cross. They lived their lives under the Cross; they followed the rejected Messiah, the humiliated Son of Man.

The church in Corinth, or at least some of its members, was influenced by the deadly teaching of Laodicea. They imagined themselves wealthy to the exclusion of Christ (Revelation 3:17). To shock them into awareness of what was happening, Paul compared them with the apostles: "We are fools for Christ's sake, but ye are wise in Christ; . . . ye are honorable, but we are despised" (4:10). As heralds of the suffering Messiah, the Son of God, the apostles were the most lowly of all. Their fate was as much sealed as those waiting to die in the arena. They were a spectacle to all the world, both angels and mankind. They had not obtained the kingdom of God, and at the present time some were hungry, thirsty, naked, mistreated, homeless, and tired.

The Greeks despised manual labor and those who performed it. Only slaves worked with their hands. However, Paul declared that he and the other apostles had worked with their own hands. He continued, "Being reviled, we bless; being persecuted, we suffer it: being defamed we entreat" (4:12, 13). To the Greek such ideas sounded despicable. Aristotle declared that the highest priority was not to endure insult, that it was the characteristic of a big soul. But the apostle endured suffering as "the scum of the earth." Such were the conditions of the servants of Christ. This was the apostolic call to which Paul had been summoned and set apart from the beginning (Acts 9:16; cf. 2 Corinthians 4:11; 11:23f.; 12:10; 1 Thessalonians 2:6). How unfair it was for his own spiritual children to lay further burdens on the already encumbered apostle. How petty divisions and partiality are when the true servants are enduring affliction on behalf of the Church (Colossians 1:24).

The first main section of the letter concludes with a deeply personal appeal: "For though ye have ten thousand instructors in Christ, yet have ye not many fathers: for in Christ Jesus I have begotten you through the gospel" (4:15). Paul recognized others shared in the upbuilding of the Church through preaching and teaching. But he asked the Corinthians to listen to him as their spiritual father. "Be followers of me!" He did not say, "Do as I tell you!" but rather, "Do as I do." Instead of searching for the wisdom and honor of the world, they were to follow Paul as he followed Christ.

## II. Christian Morality and Ethics (5:1-7:40)

The introduction to the second major section may seem abrupt. Omitting any transitional statement, Paul immediately gave the serious charge: "It is reported commonly that there is fornication among you." Far from having any justification for their boasting, because of spirituality or knowledge, the Corinthians should instead have been mourning because of the moral decay of the church (5:2).

### A. Moral Laxity (5:1-6:20)

*1. Immorality and Congregational Disputes (5:1-13).* Paul charged that the Corinthians were tolerating a brand of immorality so decadent that it did not even occur among Gentiles. Apparently a man was living with his stepmother, his own father's wife. Perhaps she was divorced or widowed. We are not told whether they were married, but apparently their relationship was long-term. It is disturbing enough that such a thing would take place in the church at all, but what is truly alarming is that the church did not take any disciplinary action against it. The church, therefore, was also guilty. A church is responsible for what takes place within it and must face God's judgment for laxity. Moreover, its members are exposed to sin, which can spread like a disease: "Know ye not that a little leaven leaveneth the whole lump?" (5:6).

Realizing their irresponsibility, Paul demanded that they rid themselves of this sinner. This was not only for the sake of the church but for the sake of the individual as well. If the church did nothing, the man could only think his conduct was acceptable. This would make him blind to his own sin and make it difficult for him to repent. Consequently, the church must act and remove him from the congregation. They must "deliver such an one unto Satan for the destruction of the flesh, that the spirit may be saved in the day of the Lord Jesus" (5:5).

The expression "deliver unto Satan" also occurs in 1 Timothy 1:20. When a person is expelled from the spiritual refuge of the church, he must face the evil one in his own strength. That one is destined to fall under Satan's power. It is hard to make the "destruction of the flesh" mean anything except physical sickness and suffering brought on by the enemy (cf. Job 2:5-7; 2 Corinthians 12:7-9).

That the church in Corinth could ignore such a flagrant violation of God's commandments reflects the same kind of fleshly nature that caused its members to put value on worldly wisdom and to "glory in men" (3:21). They boasted of their "libertine views" and their "tolerance," which actually ignored a condition that should only be stamped as sin. But Paul cautioned them, "Your glorying is not good" (5:6).

Furthermore, Paul straightened out a misunderstanding in an earlier letter—they were riot to have any fellowship with adulterers. He was not referring to those outside the church, however. If Christians avoided contact with such people altogether, they would have to "leave the world." Instead, Paul was referring to "adulterers" who profess Christianity, yet continue in sin. A genuine Christian must not fellowship with such a person. On the other hand, it is not possible to avoid contact with the outside world. Elsewhere the apostle cautioned against having any kind of intimate relationship with the ungodly (2 Corinthians 6:14.).

In an effort to separate themselves from the world, some believers have avoided any contact with it. However, when the issue concerns those inside the church, it is the responsibility and obligation of the church to pass judgment (5:12, 13).

2. *Lawsuits Before Pagan Courts (6:1-11).* The right of the Church to judge its members and in the age to come the world (6:2), and even angels (6:3), was ignored by the Corinthians. Even worse, they were taking their disputes against one another before pagan courts! With biting sarcasm Paul asked, "Is it so, that there is not a wise man among you? no, not one that shall be able to judge between his brethren?" (6:5). While the Corinthians took pride in their "wisdom," in actuality they did not even view themselves as competent to render judgment in trivial matters!

No matter what, it is a tragedy for believers to have lawsuits against one another. Actually a Christian should be willing to be defrauded rather than fight for his "rights" in such a manner (this recalls the Sermon on the Mount, Matthew 5:39ff.). But even more seriously, such a lawsuit would determine one "right" and the other "wrong." Paul thus asked, "Know ye not that the unrighteous shall not inherit the kingdom of God?" (6:9). It is therefore preferable for a Christian to suffer unrighteousness. After all, the unrighteous person excludes himself from the kingdom of God (cf. Matthew 13:41-43).

In addition to this Paul offered a so-called vice list (6:9, 10). Sins against the general commandments are listed here, as well as violations of the sixth commandment. Paul placed the same demands upon homosexuals as he did upon unmarried heterosexuals; all married people are warned against adultery. Such sins invite the judgment of God; anyone who thinks differently is headed for destruction.

Some of these sins may lie in the past of some believers, but now they are "washed" (cf. Revelation 7:14; especially Acts 22:16, where the same Greek word is used in connection with washing). This recalls the symbolism of baptism which washes away not only the guilt and feelings of guilt, but the sins themselves (cf. Romans 6:1ff.).

3. *The Body as the Temple of God (6:12ff).* Following the parenthetical section about lawsuits, Paul resumed his primary theme: sexual conduct and holiness of believers. He again showed that adultery is a particularly deplorable sin, since it profanes the body of the believer.

Two circumstances made the situation in Corinth critical. First, the morally bankrupt condition of the pagan society around the church might easily have influenced believers' attitudes towards moral issues. Those "living like Corinthians" did not consider immorality a serious problem. An individual's moral conduct was not believed to have any effect upon one's spiritual life at all. Second, some had perverted Christian liberty into a license for immorality and lawlessness. Every ancient congregation had to battle this delusion (cf. Titus 1:16; 2 Peter 2:18; Jude 4; Revelation 2:20). Freedom was being exploited as an "occasion to the flesh" (Galatians 5:13).

When Paul said, "All things are lawful," he was not giving a blanket endorsement of all actions. He qualified it by saying not all things are expedient; that is, for the best. He repeated this statement in 10:23, where he applied it to eating meat sacrificed to idols, which he would not do, if it caused a brother to stumble. The great principle of action is found in 10:31: "Whether therefore ye eat, or drink, or whatsoever ye do, do all to the glory of God."

Freedom is to be used for good. It runs counter to the nature of freedom to use it to permit something else to rule. In the original language the passage has a play on words: "To have the authority to do something must not mean we become under the authority of something else."

Any notion that sexual relations are nothing besides a bodily function like eating and drinking was abhorrent to the apostle. He categorically rejected such an idea by affirming, "Meats for the belly, and the belly for meats: but God shall destroy both it and them" (6:13). However, the body is not for fornication (6:15). His reasoning is virtually identical to Jesus' words in Mark 7:18-23. There the Lord contrasted "that whatsoever thing from without entereth into the man" and does not defile the person, with the evil which comes out of the heart and defiles him. Among the evil things coming from within, Jesus explicitly mentioned lewdness.

When a man and woman live together the two become "one flesh," their bodies joint possessions. The physical union between a man and his wife is according to the will of God and does not prevent the body from belonging to the Lord. But in an adulterous situation, the "members of Christ" join with the members of a prostitute. This disrupts communion with the Lord. "The body is for the Lord"—it is thus a terrible insult to profane that which belongs to Him.

Sexual immorality profanes the very temple of God. When Paul talked about the body as the dwelling place of the human spirit, he called it a house (2 Corinthians 5:1; cf. 2 Peter 1:13, 14, tabernacle), but as the residence of the Holy Spirit, it is the temple of God (6:19). When Paul commented that the adulterer sins against one's own body, he apparently had a twofold point. One, it refers to the body of the individual, and two, it refers to the body of Christ, the Church, the true temple of God.

Paul concluded his comments by urging the Corinthians to honor God in their bodies. While those disrupting the community defended adultery and viewed the body as worthless and meaningless, Paul forbade adultery by demonstrating what a high position the body has as the temple of the Holy Spirit.

## B. Married and Unmarried States (7:1-40)

Beginning with 7:1 Paul addressed issues raised by the Corinthians in an earlier letter to him. Many divide the letter at this juncture.

Each time Paul discussed a Corinthian issue (from their former letter) he began with the Greek phrase *peri de*, "now concerning." The following topics fall under this category: marriage and divorce (7:1); marriage of young women 7:25; sacrifices to idols (8:1); spiritual gifts (12:1); collection for the saints in Judea (16:1); and, Apollos (16:12).

In chapter 7 Paul answered questions concerning the married and unmarried states. He defended both states as legitimate before God. He said something positive about both being married and unmarried, but he opposed extreme views in either direction.

He began by saying that it is good for a man "not to touch a woman." This phrase, of course, is not intended to be taken literally, and neither was he saying it is better to be unmarried than married.

Here, "not to touch a woman" is a euphemism for having sexual relations. Paul fully recognized the temporal and spiritual advantages of being unmarried; spiritual because the unmarried person can devote more time to the things of the Lord (7:32), and temporal because the unmarried person is spared some of the hardships of the married state (7:26-28). But what is best for each individual is a personal decision. It depends on the gift of grace received by each, and thus on God's will for each (7:7). What Paul intended to assert, however, was that avoiding illicit sexual relations (as a single or married person) is good. Being single is not morally inferior to being married. People of that time may have considered singleness and sexual purity as almost mutually exclusive in the morally depraved society in Corinth. Anyone living the single life was naturally assumed to be immoral. Paul rejected such a prejudice.

The other extreme rejected by Paul was that being married is sinful. However, sexual relations outside of matrimony are indeed sinful. To prevent rampant adultery Paul wrote that each was to have his or her own spouse. Marriage is not some "higher," "spiritual" union which rejects sexual relations. Marriage does not become more spiritual if the partners abstain from sex. Neither partner should defraud the other, unless both agree to devote themselves to prayer—and then only for a given period of time. Therefore, Paul distanced himself from any position espousing some artificial union between men and women that claims higher spirituality. Avoiding sex in marriage does not bring about a preferred spiritual condition either; on the contrary, it can lead to greater temptation by Satan and to adultery.

Paul remained consistent in this position when he addressed the issue of virgins and matrimony (7:25ff.). It is absurd to think that the apostle would first distance himself from any "spiritualizing" of matrimony and then turn around and favor what he had just argued against! These kinds or forms of "marriage" were unknown to the Ancient Church, although an ascetic position did at times emerge. The first examples of spiritual marriages come from the Second Century, almost 150 years after Paul wrote 1 Corinthians, and then it appeared only in isolated, fanatical circles. Those joined in such "engagements" or "marriages" mutually pledged to live celibate lives; any union would be "spiritual."

In 7:36-38 it seems that Paul was giving advice to one having custody of a young girl. Ordinarily this is taken to mean a father's normal authority over his unmarried daughter. Other commentators have thought it could refer to a man and his fiancee. At the close of the last century, however, some theologians suggested a new theory that

Paul was advising an individual living in the so-called spiritual marriage or engagement condition, who found celibacy increasingly difficult to maintain. According to this new interpretation Paul consented that the man could marry his "fiancee," but he (Paul) contended that he would do better if he sent his "fiancee" away and continued to live in celibacy. Thus according to this theory, Paul advocated some kind of divorce. The theory runs counter in many ways to what Paul wrote earlier in the chapter.

The theory of a spiritual engagement also lacks any contextual support. The original verb in 7:38 is *gamizō*, which means "to give in marriage." This is over against *gameō*, "to marry," which occurs a total of seven times in the chapter (verses 9, 10, 28, 30, 34, 36, 39). (See the commentary for 7:36-38.)

## III. Christian Freedom (8:1-10:33)

One of the dominant issues discussed in 1 Corinthians is the misuse and abuse of Christian freedom. The second major section of the epistle dealt with the moral side of that issue. Next Paul turned to other aspects of the same subject. He warned those who were thinking Christian freedom made adultery acceptable: *"Flee* fornication" (6:18). The third major section examined the Christian's freedom in relation to idolatry. Paul's teaching on that subject concluded with the same admonition: *"Flee* from idolatry" (10:14).

The members of the church in Corinth were not in disagreement about exactly what constituted idolatry. Like many other early assemblies, they had left idolatry when they decided to follow the living and true God (cf. 1 Thessalonians 1:9). What caused difficulties was more practical in nature. The Corinthians lived in a place where idolatry affected every aspect of social existence. Social gatherings often took place in idol temples. In addition, nearly all of the meat sold in the marketplace had at one time been offered to an idol. This raised two questions: One, should a Christian participate in a feast in an idol temple with his Gentile family and friends? And two, could a believer purchase and eat meat that was previously offered to an idol. Paul treated these questions at a very basic level, and offered some practical solutions.

First, Paul opposed the arrogant "knowledge" or "enlightment" concerning these things some in Corinth boasted they had. This kind of "knowledge" is the kind of prideful display Paul had just spent four chapters denouncing. Just as he disavowed false wisdom (3:18): "If any man among you seemeth to be wise..."—he now rejected false knowledge: "If any man think that he knoweth any thing" (8:2). Later he warned against a false, fleshly sense of security, "him that thinketh he standeth" (10:12; cf. Romans 11:25; Galatians

6:3). Those who boast of knowledge, he said, never really know anything as they should.

In contrast to a knowledge that is "puffed up," Paul preached a love that "builds up." The one who loves God possesses something greater than knowledge. He himself is known by God (8:3; cf. Galatians 4:9). But those who abuse Christian freedom because they lack love are a stumbling block to their "weaker" brethren. Causing offense means to make another fall, stumble. These are not simple barbs or insults. The offense was that some who professed knowledge and freedom were enticing others to exceed what their consciences allowed. Such a stance is destructive to the Christian life and faith of those enticed and can result in a fall (10:11). In order to avoid such a situation, Paul argued that it is better to relinquish one's freedom. Paul was himself an example. Throughout most of the chapter he showed how he gave up his rights as an apostle to become the servant of all in order to win souls.

Having thereby emphasized that regard for one's brother was reason enough to avoid anything associated with idolatry, he proceeded to demonstrate that this was also necessary for each individual. Actually, idols do not exist; they are fictions, for there is but one God. But behind the idolatrous image lies an evil power. What is offered in sacrifice to the idol is sacrificed to the evil spirit. Idols are thus indeed linked to evil. This applied to Christians who were partakers in idol feasts.

Paul drew a comparison with the Lord's Supper. He reminded the Corinthians that those eating the bread and drinking the cup were partakers of and shared communion with the body and blood of Christ. The same held true for a pagan sacrificial meal, a religious ceremony signifying commonality and fellowship. Paul conluded, "Ye cannot drink the cup of the Lord, and the cup of devils: ye cannot be partakers of the Lord's table, and of the table of devils" (10:16-21).

The one who may "think that he knoweth any thing" in fact knows nothing as it should be known. He only has a knowledge that leads him astray. Those claiming "knowledge" superior to the weak who do not have such knowledge have themselves been snared by the sin of idolatry—a real enough sin, although idols are nothing and meaningless. With a piercing earnestness, Paul recounted the history of Israel as a warning: "Now all these things happened unto them for ensamples" (10:11).

After giving explicit instructions that Christians were not to share in pagan sacrificial meals, Paul discussed another question raised by the Corinthians: Can a believer eat meat bought at the marketplace or served at another's home? It is quite possible that such meat—almost all meat—had been offered in sacrifice to an idol. In these circumstances the issue was not sharing in a pagan sacrifice, but eating the meat. It was made holy through the Word of God and prayer (cf. 1 Timothy 4:4, 5). What God has created is clean.

But, Paul said, if the meat was expressly identified as meat formerly sacrificed to an idol, for the sake of another's conscience, it should not be eaten. A Christian is to strive not to cause offense to any—Jews, Greeks, nor to the household of God (10:32).

## IV. Christian Worship (11:1-14:40)

The theme of the next major section of this letter is worship in the church. Paul complained about and corrected certain problems. Initially he praised the Corinthians for following his commands—the "traditions" which he passed on to them. He did not want to discourage them with one-sided criticism.

This major section falls into four smaller sections. First Paul commented on the conduct of women during the worship service (11:2-16). Next he reprimanded the church because it was abusing the love feast and Lord's Supper (11:17-34). Then he answered the church's question about spiritual matters, including the use of spiritual gifts (chapters 12 to 14). In the midst of the latter there is Paul's ode to love, one of the most marvelous passages in all of Scripture (chapter 13).

## A. The Conduct of Women (11:2-16)

Perhaps one of the most significant changes that took place in the ancient Christian assemblies was the revolutionary shift in the social position of women. While the Greeks commonly regarded women as having no soul, the apostle Peter called them "heirs together of the grace of life" (1 Peter 3:7). Paul's words, "There is neither male nor female" (Galatians 3:28), are perhaps some of the most socially and religiously radical words ever uttered.

In Christian worship services women played an active role, unlike those in the Jewish synagogues where they were entirely passive. Although women were permitted in the synagogue, they were not allowed to share in the service in any way. They were not even counted to obtain the required 10 necessary for a service. However, in the Christian churches women at least shared in both prayer and prophecy (11:5).

Some of the women in the church at Corinth brought the custom of praying without a head covering into the church, perhaps as a misunderstanding of their newfound Christian freedom. As was seen in the two earlier major sections, an "overrealization" of Christian teaching results in a distortion of the gospel. Paul opposed their new custom because it challenged some fundamental principles. He regarded it as more than a forsaking of cultural custom; it violated the order of God's creation. From the most ancient of times, women in the Middle East and Asia grew their hair long and covered their heads as a symbol of their dependence upon the man. Later, Christian churches adopted this custom (11:16).

The Greek word Paul used to denote the woman's head covering is *exousia*, "authority, power." However, underlying this Greek term is the Aramaic word *shaltōnyah*, which has the twofold idea of "covering" and "power" (Kittel, cited by Foerster, "*exousia*," *TDNT*, 2:574). Paul apparently intended this double meaning when he used *exousia*. It suited his purpose by showing the significance of women's headcoverings: It showed her dependency upon the man, while at the same time it represented authority. The woman was under the authority of her husband, but she maintained her dignity. The context suggests that "authority" here has a passive sense. The interpretation goes as far back as the church father Chrysostom, who also used the term in this manner.

Paul said that the man is the head of the woman. "Head" expresses will and authority. This is a puzzling thought since the common view of that day saw the "bowels, inward parts" as the seat of emotions and contemplation. Paul asserted that the woman is simultaneously subject to the man as well as equal to him. For this logic he appealed to creation (cf. Genesis 2:18) and to Christ's relationship with the Father. Christ is in no way demeaned or called inferior when Paul says God is His "head" (11:3). In the same way, a woman should not be viewed as inferior or less than a man even though God has ordered that man is the "head."

## B. Love Feasts and the Lord's Supper (11:17-34)

In this section Paul again referred to the splits within the church (11:18). The kind of division he was now confronting did not concern differences in leaders or doctrines but revolved around the social and cultural differences among the members. Remarkably, Paul considered this kind of division as serious as a doctrinal split. He employed the term *haireseis*, "sects, parties," here; this sin will exclude some from the kingdom of God (Galatians 5:20, 21). It reflects how seriously Paul viewed the problem of cliques in the church.

The divisions especially appeared in the love feasts and the Lord's Supper (11:20f.). Many had turned these occasions into opportunities to eat and drink; some were even getting drunk! Whatever the situation, this kind of conduct was sinful, but in the context of a sacred meal, the Lord's Supper, it was a profanation of something holy and sacred. The one participating in such an unfitting manner was eating and drinking condemnation upon himself (11:29). The injunction of verse 28 to "examine" oneself is a call to look closely at one's heart before partaking in the Lord's Supper. An outward appearance of reverence is inadequate. What is in question is one's attitude of heart towards Christ.

By recounting the apostolic tradition of the institution of the Lord's Supper (11:23), Paul demonstrated that the event the Corinthians had been profaning was in actuality a truly sacred moment in Christian worship. When Paul commented that he received the words of the Supper from the Lord, he did not use the preposition *para*, "by," which would have indicated a direct communication, but the preposition *apo*, "from," which assures the words originated from the Lord. Nevertheless, the formula did not prevent Paul from referring to a personal revelation (cf. Acts 18:9f.; 22:18; 23:11; 27:23; 2 Corinthians 12:7; Galatians 1:12; 2:2). Moreover, one case does not eliminate the possibility of the other. Paul's words are virtually technical language denoting the reception and transmission of holy tradition, which appears in the Gospel records. It is crucial to realize that only 25 years had passed since Jesus instituted the Supper—and it would be almost as many again before the first Gospel was written. Already there was a detailed record of the institution of the Supper and its centrality in early Christian communities.

## C. The Gifts of Grace (12:1-31 and 14:1-40)

One of the major questions the Corinthians asked Paul about in their earlier letter apparently concerned the *charismatōn*, which were experienced regularly in the worship and church services of ancient Christian churches. With respect to the church in Corinth, Paul commented that it lacked no gift (1:7). At the same time, he also said that he did not want them to be ignorant about the exercise and purpose of the gifts of the Spirit. He implied that they actually knew very little about the workings of the Spirit.

Chapter 12 gives a summary description of the gifts of the Spirit, and chapter 14 offers instruction on the proper use of the charismata. Placed between these two chapters are Paul's comments on love. He referred to love as greater than any of the gifts and the only legitimate motive for using the gifts.

First, Paul affirmed that spiritual manifestations in the Christian congregation are much more than the idol trances the Gentile believers had experienced before their conversion. Such pagan phenomena were of course fleshly demonstrations, whereas Christians experience the effects of the Holy Spirit's manifestation. Pagan demonstrations were in part the result of spiritual forces, to the extent that their source was other than what the believer experienced. Before their conversion the

Corinthians were drawn to the dumb idols (12:2), now they were driven by the Spirit of God (cf. 8:1-4). The Triune God was the One causing their spiritual utterances. The charismata, services, and manifestations of power were different, but one and the same Spirit was behind them all. The same Lord, and the same God "worketh" in all (12:4-6).

Different from other more "natural" gifts of the Spirit, the list of the Spirit's workings given in 1 Corinthians 12 are often described as "supernatural" gifts of the Spirit. The term *charismata* is often applied to these "gifts." Such a distinction between supernatural and nonsupernatural is undoubtedly legitimate, but this can easily result in elevating some as more "spiritual" than others. This can lead to some of the gifts being overlooked and underused. Moreover, it is not always easy to distinguish between what is natural and what is supernatural in a world that is led by an almighty and ever-present God. One thing is clear, though; spiritual gifts are in no way a guarantee of spirituality or holiness. The Corinthians were well equipped with the charismata, but they were still oriented towards this world and lacked spiritual maturity.

This in no way negates any argument that the gifts are not important. They are, in fact, God's response to the Church's need for spiritual power in carrying out its mission. The charismata are the basis of the special positions or "offices" that the Lord established for His church (12:28f.; cf. Ephesians 4:20).

The apostle Paul referred to these gifts as "the manifestation of the Spirit." Some have debated whether this is a comprehensive list of the Spirit's workings or a series of examples. Both sides have strong and weak arguments. On the one hand, certainly many different spiritual "effects" or "gifts" exist other than the categories Paul provided, but on the other hand, virtually every gift can be linked to one or more in the list he gave.

Some have attempted to categorize the gifts according to the three dominant properties of the human soul: understanding, will, emotion. Such a breakdown looks like this: (1) gifts of understanding (knowledge, wisdom, and discerning of spirits); (2) gifts of power (faith, healing, working of miracles); (3) gifts of inspired utterance (prophecy, tongues, interpretation of tongues). The gifts can also fall into four groups: (1) the word of wisdom, which gives God's counsel, and the word of knowledge, which affords special insight into the truths of God's Word; (2) faith, which here must refer to miracle-working faith (cf. 13:2; Matthew 17:20), the gifts of healing, and the power to work miracles; (3) the gift of prophecy, which is always to be associated with the ability to discern spirits; and (4) speaking in tongues, which can only be for the blessing of the church when it is interpreted.

According to many interpreters, the way the gifts are listed implies there is some disparity or heirarchy in their character. Thus, it is argued, the gift of tongues is the least worthy, while the word of wisdom and prophecy are among the greatest. But from Paul's point of view, it seems that he may have regarded tongues among the highest (14:1). He considered speaking in tongues plus the interpretation of tongues as equivalent to prophecy (14:5). Even though some might argue tongues is the "least" of the gifts, it cannot be too insignificant, for the apostle Peter received it (Acts 2:4) as did Paul. Paul even thanked God for his gift of speaking in tongues (14:8); it is clearly not to be ignored.

The Corinthian congregation was richly equipped with the charismata, but they lacked wisdom in using the gifts in a sound and fitting manner. Paul instructed them about the nature and number of the charismata. He concluded by saying, "Covet to prophesy, and forbid not to speak with tongues. Let all things be done decently and in order!" (14:39, 40).

## D. The Song of Love (13:1-13)

Surpassing in importance any of the gifts of the Spirit is the fruit of the Spirit, love ("charity," KJV; cf. Galatians 5:22). The charismata are equipment given to the believer for service. The fruit of the Spirit is the mind and nature of Christ being realized in the character and conduct of the life of the believer who is being conformed to the image of Christ (Galatians 4:19). One cannot be a Christian without producing some of the fruit of the Spirit. Thus Paul could not encourage seeking spiritual gifts without emphasizing that something is more important: i.e., to follow after love (12:31; 14:1). This is the "more excellent way."

This "Song of Love" is unparalleled in its beauty. Harnack referred to it as "the greatest, strongest, and deepest which Paul ever wrote." The lyrical style and rhythmical form of the passage remind one of a hymn. Its very penetrating message is typical of only the loftiest poetry. There is almost nothing elsewhere in the writings of Paul requiring so little explanation.

Some interpreters have conjectured that since this section differs so much from the style and message of its context that it must have been added from another source. True, Paul may have used these thoughts elsewhere, but the way in which it presently appears does not represent any great digression. With his opening words Paul compared love with the charismata; when the end comes love will remain while everything else—including the charismata—will fail.

Paul demonstrated that without love, even the greatest of gifts is meaningless. Speaking in tongues, prophesying, knowing all things, and having all faith—none of these can replace love, not even a great sacrifice. Self-denial without love is as useless as using the gifts of the Spirit without love.

Paul described two great qualities of love: it is patient and it is kind. He then stated in negative terms what love does not do. To the last he added the positive qualifier: Charity (love) "rejoiceth not in iniquity, but rejoiceth in the truth." The kind of love Paul was referring to here is not a kind of moral laxity which sacrifices truth and right for the sake of ease. Rather four short words summarize the extent of love: It *bears* all things, *believes* all things, *hopes* all things, and *endures* all things.

Finally, Paul asserted that love will always remain. He contrasted one group of three items against another group of three. Three will remain until the end, and three will pass away. Prophecy, tongues, and knowledge will end when that which is perfect is come, and believers can know fully. But faith, hope, and love will remain until the end of all things. And of these, "the greatest . . . is love" (13:13).

## V. Christian Hope for the Future (15:1-58)

In this final major section of 1 Corinthians, Paul discussed the question of the believer's hope for the future. His immediate reason for this can be detected in 15:12, where he wrote that some of the Corinthians were claiming there was no resurrection of the dead. Paul received word of this and found it necessary to speak to the matter. He demonstrated that the doctrine of the Resurrection is central to the entire Christian message and faith. The Christian's hope for the future does *not* rest in some shadowy, spiritual existence in which the soul is "freed" from the body's prison (to put it in Greek philosophical language). The gospel does not preach that believers are redeemed "from" their physical bodies, rather, it teaches the "redemption of the body" (Romans 8:23). Paul then argued that the power of the Resurrection was proven in Christ whom God raised from the dead (cf. Ephesians 1:18-20). Christ is the "firstfruits of them that slept" (15:20). Thus He is the "guarantee" of the future resurrection awaiting believers. The resurrection of Christ is inseparable from His work of redemption (15:14). Therefore, it follows that the resurrection of the believer is an inseparable element of the redemption in which he participates.

In addition to addressing the pressing problems in Corinth, Paul had already instructed the Corinthians in the fundamental doctrines of the Faith. Now, using the controversy over the Resurrection as a springboard, he offered the most comprehensive discussion of resurrection in the entire New Testament. First, he discussed the importance of

Christ's resurrection. Second, he outlined what the future holds for Christians and showed the place of the Resurrection in that hope. Third, he commented on how the dead will rise.

## A. The Resurrection of Christ (15:1-22)

*1. The Essence of the Gospel (15:1-5).* Paul opened his remarks by calling attention to the early portions of the letter, where he discussed the centrality of the "preaching of the cross" to the Christian proclamation of salvation. Now he again "validated" the authenticity of the gospel he had preached to them. That gospel is what had saved them when they believed (cf. Acts 11:14). This is a unique aspect of the Christian faith and differs from every manmade religion or philosophy. The message of the gospel, delivered by Paul to the Corinthians, is that which he himself received: "That Christ died for our sins according to the scriptures" (15:3).

Now Paul proceeded to show that it is not only the death of Jesus, but His resurrection that is an indispensable element of Christian proclamation. The opening verses of chapter 15 summarize the main content of gospel tradition. This involves the death of Christ, His burial, His resurrection, and His appearances as the risen Lord. At the same time, Paul offered the apostolic witness to the historicity of the gospel (verses 6-9), and the apostolic interpretation of the events of salvation, namely, that Christ died for our sins (verse 3).

*2. Witnesses of the Resurrection (15:6-11).* This section contains the Church's first written testimonies of the resurrection of Christ. It was composed many years prior to any of the Gospels. Jesus revealed himself many times in the time between His resurrection and His ascension; the Gospels record 9 or 10 such events. Paul mentioned only the ones which would have the greatest impact upon the Corinthians. He mentioned in particular Jesus' appearance to Simon Peter, a leader among the apostles, to James, the overseer in the Jerusalem church. He mentioned the large number of witnesses who were apparently still living: "above five hundred brethren at once; of whom the greater part remain unto this present." This was written just 20-25 years after the events, when the first generation of believers was still around to confirm the truth of what was being preached.

At least two of the events Paul referred to are not mentioned in the four Gospels. Both concern people who did not believe Jesus was Messiah until after they encountered the risen Lord. One was James, the brother of Jesus. During Jesus' earthly life, His brothers did not believe in Him (John 7:5), but after the Resurrection we find them together with the apostles in the upper room in Jerusalem (Acts 1:14). Shortly thereafter James became the undisputed leader of the Jerusalem church (Galatians 1:19).

The other appearance of Jesus not mentioned in the Gospel accounts was to Paul. Although this event took place several years after the Resurrection and Ascension, Paul nonetheless joined this appearance with those experienced by the other apostles. He considered this appearance not just a "vision" or "trance"; rather, it was a genuine occurrence. The risen Christ appeared to him just as He had to others following His resurrection. Therefore, Paul declared that he had not received the gospel from another man, but from the risen Lord (Galatians 1:12). Immediately he began to preach the message revealed to him (Acts 9:20-22; Galatians 1:16f.). But this does not imply Paul had no contact with or had adopted apostolic traditions about the life and death and resurrection of Jesus (Galatians 1:18ff.; 2:1ff.). His own encounter with the risen Lord did not cause him to deny the testimony of others. On the contrary, he said that he himself both received and passed on this holy tradition (15:3).

*3. The Importance of Christ's Resurrection (15:12-22).* Apparently those who denied the final Resurrection, did not deny the resurrection of Christ. Paul, however, pointed out the logical end of their reasoning. If there is no resurrection of the dead, then Christ could not have risen either. And if Christ had not risen, then the very foundation of the Christian faith had been removed. In a dramatic series of "if-then" statements, Paul rehearsed the logical consequences of thinking Christ had not risen from the dead.

*First,* if Christ had not risen, "then is our preaching vain" (verse 14). The apostolic proclamation would be "emptiness," that is, without any substance or basis. Christian proclamation would thereby be reduced to nothing more than the empty "wisdom" of the world. Christianity would be only one more religion in the world's philosophical and religious systems. Further, their "faith is also vain" (verse 14). Faith comes by hearing (Romans 10:17). Faith can be of no more value than the message it stands on. If preaching is empty, then faith in its message is no more than a miserable emptiness.

*Second,* if Christ is not risen, then the heralds of the gospel were "false witnesses of God" (verse 15). Their preaching was not just empty, it was a false and fraudulent testimony (the main character of apostolic preaching was that of a witness). The apostles had not defended some concept, philosophy, or human teaching; rather, as witnesses they announced the truth of what they had "seen and heard" (Acts 4:20) in the life and ministry of Jesus. If what they proclaimed was not true, then they were false witnesses, bearing false witness against God himself. Paul was fully aware of the responsibility resting upon those preaching the gospel. If its basis is in real events, then it indeed announces a mighty saving act of God in time and space, whose impact affects all mankind. But the validity of the entire message rests on whether or not it is true. As someone once said, "For Paul, any Christianity that is not based on reality does not benefit the life of the community, but becomes a tragic self-delusion."

If Christ is not risen, "your faith is vain" (verse 17). Thus Paul found it inconceivable that an empty or false faith could have any positive benefit for a believer. From his perspective, the advantage of faith depends completely on the fact that it receives and participates in the actual gifts of salvation: the forgiveness of sins and salvation from the judgment of sin. This depends altogether on the truth of the gospel message: Christ died to atone for our sins; He was raised for our justification (cf. Romans 4:25).

This enabled Paul to argue further that if Christ was not risen, "ye are yet in your sins" (verse 17). The forgiveness of sins was a reality to Paul. It involved much more than being released from the feeling of guilt. It involved actual forgiveness from the one God, who alone can forgive sin and nullify its consequences. The individual who believes moves from being under the judgment of God to being in His grace; it is the difference between being saved and being lost. If the gospel's offering of grace is not founded upon the facts of God's saving act in Christ, then those who believe the gospel remain in their sins. This applies not only to those believers who are living, but also to those who have died. If Christ is not risen, then they died in their sins, deluded into putting faith in a false hope.

False hope is worse than no hope: "If in this life only we have hope in Christ, we are of all men most miserable" (verse 19). Paul admitted, in fact, in verse 32 that a life without hope for eternal life is reflected in the pagan proverb recorded in Isaiah 22:13: "Let us eat and drink; for tomorrow we shall die." Of course, for Paul, the fear of God offered something for this life also (cf. 1 Timothy 4:8). He realized that the joy of the world is empty and temporary. Not much is lost in relinquishing what the world offers. Nevertheless, a Christianity that exists only for the present life and which has no hope for the future—because it involves a delusion—was unimaginable to Paul. He did not see any advantage in exchanging a worldly life "without hope" (Ephesians 2:12) for a "false religious hope" that is just as deceived. Hence, if Christ is not risen, then the Christian hope is just as false as the Christian faith.

Paul's argument in this section is designed to show how the entire Christian faith would crumble if some of the Corinthians' claim that the dead did not rise were true. If it were so, faith in Christ's resurrection must also be relinquished (verses 12, 13). Also, the veracity of the apostolic witness would be called into question (verses 14, 15), and finally salvation itself, and the Christian hope of eternal life would be regarded as false (verses 16-19). But such reasoning is based upon a faulty foundation, and Paul demolished such logic in verse 20 with the triumphant cry, "But now Christ is risen!" Thereby he confirmed the truth of the gospel. He secured the reality of salvation; and demonstrated that the resurrection of the dead is a fact because Christ has been raised, "the firstfruit" from the dead. He is the beginning of the resurrection awaiting all who belong to Christ. "But now" marks the shift from the hypothetical to the actual.

## B. Eschatological Perspectives (15:20-34)

*1. The Fact of Resurrection (15:20-22).* The fact that Christ rose from the dead guarantees the resurrection of believers. Just as those who believe in Christ have been in a spiritual sense "crucified with" and "risen with" their Lord (cf. Galatians 2:20; Colossians 3:1), they will also in the consummation share in bodily resurrection together with Christ. Paul thus drew a parallel between Adam and Christ: Adam, the ancestor and head of the human race, and Christ, the progenitor and head of a new race (cf. Romans 5:12-19). All coming from Adam—those "in Adam"—come under the power of death because of Adam's fall. In the same way, all those "in Christ" share in His victory over death. Just as Adam's sin affected the rest of the human race, so too, Christ's resurrection affects those for whom He died and rose. The resurrection for salvation or condemnation takes place at the directive of Christ (cf. John 5:28, 29). But to be "alive in Christ" involves more than merely the resurrection. It must also point to what is called "the resurrection of life." This includes the abundance of life that is in Christ which is shared by those who are in Him (cf. Romans 8:11).

*2. Stages in the Consummation (15:23-28).* Next Paul proceeded to show that being made fully alive in Christ takes place step by step and in various stages. These verses provide a rich glimpse into the future. The last days began with the first coming of Christ (Hebrews 1:1; 9:26) and cover a long period of time prior to the consummation. At various stages God manifests His kingdom. Not all are made alive simultaneously; each is raised according to his own "turn" (NIV). The term for "turn" here is *tagmati*, originally a military technical term, which later had a more general usage. Originally it meant a "division" of an army; later a "class" or "group" of any kind. The implication of *tagmati*'s use here is that the individual is being made alive together with the "division" to which he belongs.

Opinions differ among interpreters whether Paul was thinking of two or three stages in the resurrection. Those who maintain there are only two stages—Christ the firstfruit and the believers as the rest of the harvest—point to Paul's comments in verse 54 that "Death is swallowed up in victory," when the mortal puts on immortality. This may suggest that Paul regarded death, as the last enemy, as vanquished by the Parousia. But the picture in verses 23-28 suggest that there are three stages in the eschatological program. Paul outlined them in this manner: First, Christ rose as the firstfruit, the firstborn from the dead (Colossians 1:18). His resurrection initiated and guaranteed the resurrection of believers. Second, those who belong to Christ will be made alive at His coming, i.e., His parousia (verse 23). And third, as indicated by another "then" in verse 24, "Then cometh the end, when he shall have delivered up the kingdom to God, even the Father." It is difficult to interpret this "then" as anything but a third stage. Similarly "then" functions in verse 23 to show the distance of time between the Parousia and the "End" (cf. Revelation 20:1ff.). During the interim between the return and the final judgment, Christ will destroy all the spiritual powers that resist God (verse 25). Three expressions for these "spiritual powers" occur: *archēn*, "rulers"; *exousian*, "authorities"; and *dunamin*, "powers." All three designations occur in Ephesians 1:21; the first and last occur in Romans 8:38; and the first two occur in Ephesians 6:12; Colossians 1:16; 2:10. When all these forces are overcome, Christ will hand over the purified and cleansed Kingdom to His Father, and God shall be all in all.

This highly significant prophetic word concludes with the puzzling words in verse 28 that the Son himself will be subject to the Father. All theories of interpretation aside, this undoubtedly involves a relationship between the Persons of the Godhead; we cannot expect to grasp fully this divine mystery. But when such a theme recurs throughout Holy Scriptures, we should do our best to consider what this divine disclosure does tell us. Many of Christianity's greatest teachers have debated the issue; their comments are pertinent. Augustine, Beza, and Theodoret understood this text as reflecting Paul's understanding that when Christ presents the Church to the Father the saints will share fully in God's salvation. Because His work as mediator of salvation is complete, Christ lays aside His role as the revelation mediator between God and mankind.

Luther, Melanchthon, Bengel, and many others agree that the passage speaks of the end of Christ's mediatorial role—where there is no more sin there is no longer need of redemption or intercession. Interpreters like Meyer (*Meyer's Commentary on the New Testament,* 6:362f.) maintain that it alludes to the kingly dominion and the authority to judge which Christ has exercised over the enemy (also discussed in the preceding verses). Hofmann argues that when the Son subjects himself to the Father, it involves, from a human standpoint, the fact that He no longer assumes the role of mediator between God and the world.

None of these interpretations alter the trinitarian picture of God. However, a number of them imply that the passage about the Son's subjection to the Father does not merely reflect the mission of the Son, but the interrelationship between the Persons of the Godhead. Here some have attempted to differentiate between the divine and human natures of Christ, and have argued that the Son can be subject only at the human level. Others, though, do not regard the Son's being subject to the Father as inconsistent with the trinitarian understanding that the members of the Trinity are identical in nature and substance.

Godet reminds us that Paul previously in this letter stated that "Christ is God's" (3:23), that "the head of Christ is God" (11:3), and that both of these refer to Christ's status in glory, (pp. 795-804). He suggests, therefore, that the idea that the Son was subject to the Father was an inherent aspect of the writings of Paul, just as the preexistence of the Son was an established fact. Both concepts are conveyed by the term "Son," which simultaneously expresses equality in essence and yet the possibility of being in subjection. According to this view, subjection thus is in keeping with the relationship between the Father and Son during both His divine and human existence.

Others echo the same opinion. The other Person in the Trinity, in keeping with His nature, must accept the authority, will, and desires, of the First Person. Therefore, He declares himself the Son and the First Person His Father. Although identical to the Father in eternality, power, and honor, the Son finds His joy in doing the will of the Father; that is His desire. The obedience of the God-man on earth to the Father above did not reflect a new relationship effected by the Incarnation, but it continued the eternal fellowship that existed between the Son and Father in heaven. The submission of the Son to the will of the Father does not deprive Him of any of His divine honor and glory. As far as His personal humility in the Incarnation (cf. Philippians 2:5ff.) and His handing over of the Kingdom to the Father are concerned, they are totally of His own free will. These acts express His love for the

Father (cf. John 14:31). The kingdom of the Father is dear to Jesus. Because of this He does not seek a personal eternal kingdom; rather, He joins His Father on His throne and invites His followers to sit with Him (Revelation 3:21).

*3. Practical Concerns (15:29-34).* After presenting these tremendous prospects, and before he dealt with the question of how the dead rise, Paul included in the passage some practical arguments for the reality of the resurrection. Next he reviewed some of the ethical consequences of resurrection faith.

First, Paul reminded the Corinthians that baptism implies a belief in the resurrection. Within the rite of baptism is a drama of the Resurrection: we are "raised together with Christ" (Colossians 2:12; cf. Romans 6:3-5). When Paul introduced baptism here it is with the phrase "they which are baptized for the dead." This is either referring to some kind of substitutional baptism for the dead practiced by some of the Corinthians, or, more likely, it is a reference to those who were baptized in order to be reunited with their deceased Christian friends or family. In either case such a baptism was meaningless. Substitutional baptism is of no avail to the dead if the dead do not indeed rise; and there is no possibility of being reunited with fellow believers after death unless there is a resurrection. Chrysostom rejected substitutionary baptism for the dead as outside of orthodoxy. He interpreted it instead by noting that in the baptismal rite the one being baptized confesses, "I believe in the resurrection of the dead." He continued, "And on this faith we are baptized." By speaking of baptism Paul was confirming the basic and commonly accepted tenet of the Church that the dead will rise.

As far as he was concerned, Paul demonstrated in both word and practice that he believed in the resurrection. Why else would he have risked serious danger and trials for the sake of the gospel? Paul then continued to show how doctrine influences behavior. The resurrection is indeed a doctrine of the Church, and it has ethical consequences. If there is no resurrection then the rally cry of the hedonists of this age, "Eat drink, and be merry, for tomorrow we die!" is justified. It may be that some of those in Corinth who were denying the resurrection had already adopted such a moral stance. To deny the reality of the resurrection is in itself a sin and it leads to greater sin. "Be not deceived!" the apostle warned. As the Greek proverb says, "Evil communications corrupt good manners" (Menander, *Thais*). The Greek followers of "wisdom" denied the resurrection. A Christian risks much when he fellowships with any who reject a central tenet of the gospel. With the utmost sincerity the apostle warned, "For some have not the knowledge of God."

## C. How Do the Dead Rise? (15:35-58)

*1. The Resurrection of the Body (15:35).* Objections concerning the Christian proclamation of the resurrection of the body had arisen from two different sources: Greeks and Jews.

Greeks rejected any notion of resurrection as a consequence of a main assumption of Greek philosophy: a dualism which drew a sharp distinction between the "physical body" and the "spiritual soul." From their perspective the dualistic nature of man was his dilemma and downfall. Greeks considered the physical body as only part of this life and felt the soul to be immortal, once it was released from the "prison" of the physical body. Therefore, to conceive of the soul "putting on" again that which was regarded as evil was both reprehensible and impossible. The Greeks viewed eternal existence as only being possible when the body and soul were separated. Paul, however, did not even discuss the possibility of an eternal existence apart from a body. He did not deny that the soul exists after death—he called this as being "unclothed" and viewed it as temporary (2 Corinthians 5:4-8). For Paul, as for Jesus (Matthew 22:29-32), the resurrection of the body is necessary because of the eternal nature of the soul. But an eternal existence without a resurrection is worse than annihilation, because it would be in sin. As he had just shown, if there is no resurrection, then Christ did not rise, and if that is true, we are still in our sins!

Pharisaic Judaism, such as the apostle Paul followed at one time, maintained a resurrection, but only to a life of the same essence and nature as present existence. The body that was raised was to be identical to the body that died. The Syriac Apocalypse of Baruch (50:2) reads that when the earth will restore the dead, "it shall make no change in their form, but as it has received, so shall it restore them." The Sadducees of the Gospels directed their disdain at such views. Moreover, Paul abandoned such a viewpoint, for it is far removed from the Christian belief in a resurrection in glory and incorruptability.

Paul denounced both the Jewish misunderstanding of resurrection and the Greek denial of it. He asked rhetorically two aggressive questions: "But some will say, 'How are the dead raised?' and 'with what body do they come?'" The questions show how impossible resurrection was thought to be by some skeptics. The questions of how the body will be raised are difficult enough if an individual has just died; but what of the person's body who has long been dead, how is a resurrection possible then?

Paul began by answering the last question about the kind of body with which the dead will be raised. He clarified the issue with a series of analogies (verses 36-41), and a series of antitheses (verses

**495**

42-44). Next he answered the question about how it is possible for the dead to be raised by referring to Christ as the "life-giving spirit" (verses 45-49). Then he spoke of the transformation that those living at the time of Christ's return will experience (verses 50-54). He concluded the most detailed teaching on resurrection in the New Testament by offering a hymn of praise (verses 55-57).

*2. Analogies (15:36-41).* Responding to possible objections his opponents might raise, Paul gave a series of analogies from nature. An analogy can illuminate an issue, but it does not necessarily prove it. Paul had previously offered historical proof of the resurrection of Christ. His resurrection was attested to and proclaimed by men who had nothing to gain in this life. On the contrary, because of their testimony they hourly risked their lives; they died daily (15:30f.). When the world responded to the challenge of the gospel with empty arguments, the apostle was less than tolerant. "Thou fool," he exclaimed. He thereby showed how he felt about his opponents' arguments.

To the opponent who maintained he believed only in the laws and principles of nature, Paul challenged: "But doesn't nature itself testify to the reality of the resurrection. Don't you throw seed on the ground, which, because it dies, is made alive again in a new plant?" God gives a body according to His will; it is different and yet at the same time similar. Creation does not merely reveal the power of God to create something from nothing, it also shows His ability to re-create from death to life. What is sown is not precisely what is raised; it comes not in its old, corruptible form, but in a new and glorious appearance. So too is the resurrection.

Paul employed other analogies to remind the Corinthians of other forms of life created by God. First, there is a great difference between men and animals, birds and fish. Likewise, the sun differs from the moon and other stars in its brilliance. If there is such variation within nature, shouldn't God be able to create spiritual bodies rather than earthly bodies in the resurrection? Some see in Paul's expression "heavenly bodies" (verse 40) an allusion to the celestial bodies in verse 41. However, he could also have been alluding to the "spiritual bodies" he spoke of in verse 44.

*3. Four Antitheses (15:42-44).* In order to show the difference between the body that dies and the body that is raised, Paul offered four antitheses. The statements have a poetical, rhythmical form, and are reminiscent of the kind of poetic message of the prophets. They also bring to mind the kind of sayings Jesus used to teach His disciples.

The body that dies is perishable, corruptible. It belongs to that part of the creation which falls under the dominion of sin's effects; it shares in the groaning of all creation (Romans 8:20-23). Still, it is not redeemed. It is like a house that is torn down (2 Corinthians 5:1). But the resurrection body is imperishable, incorruptible. It is "eternal in the heavens." It should not be overlooked that the verse also suggests an analogy between physical and moral corruption (Morris, *Tyndale New Testament Commentaries,* 7:226). The strongest objections made by Greeks to the Christian message of resurrection were that the physical body, by nature, was corruptible, even evil. Their hope for the future was that the soul would be released from the confinement of the body, but Paul said that the resurrection body is incorruptible and imperishable.

The body that dies is subject to "dishonor." It lacks "glory" (Romans 3:23). Paul even called it "our lowly body" (Philippians 3:21, NIV), but there is no trace of the Greek contempt for the body as evil. Paul declared that it is precisely the lowly body that will be transformed into a glorious body like Christ's. That sown in dishonor will be raised in glory.

On the one hand, the body which dies is viewed as weak; it succumbs to sickness and death. It is only an inadequate instrument for the reborn spirit (cf. Mark 14:38). The resurrection body, on the other hand, will be characterized by power, might, and physical and mental vitality, empowered by the same power that raised Jesus from the dead (Romans 8:11; Ephesians 1:19f.).

The body that dies is a "natural" body. The expression points to the physical and mental qualities of the body. The same term, *psuchikos,* appears in 1 Corinthians 2:14 to describe the "natural" man. The emphasis is not that the body is *composed* of *psuchē,* "life, breath," but that the fleshly body is *controlled* by the *psuchē* (especially here the mental attitude). At the same time, the human soul (*psuchē*) is influenced and tempted by sinful impulses and desires (cf. 1 Peter 2:11). The world influences the *psuchē* through the "conduit" of the body. The "soul" is the rational principle of life; the body ruled by its "soul" is ruled by the "natural man," i.e., that part of the individual given to its natural inclinations.

In the eternal, spiritual realm all this will be different. The natural body—controlled by the *psuchē,* "soul"—dies and is transformed into a "spiritual body" in the resurrection. This is not to say that the body is "spirit" or some other "spiritual substance," but it will be governed by the spirit of man instead of the present, natural man. The spiritual body will be a perfect expression of the individual's personality and spiritual being. This being "clothed with our heavenly dwelling" (2 Corinthians 5:2, NIV) means that finally the believer will become what God intended him or her to be.

*4. The First and Last Adam (15:45-49).* Having responded to the question about what kind of body the dead rise with, Paul returned to the answer to the first question, "How do the dead rise?" "What is the power at work in the resurrection?" In his preceding explanation, Paul employed the image of the seed of grain which becomes a mature plant by saying the body is "sown a natural body." But he also guarded against the misinterpretation that the body somehow reproduces itself. He stated explicitly in verse 38 that God gives a new body. It is further clarified when he says Christ is the Last Adam, "a life-giving spirit" (15:45).

The concept that Messiah would be the Second Adam appears in the teachings of Rabbi Abraham, of Catelonia (Godet, p. 849; cf. Sadler, pp. 289-292). In Romans 5:12-21 Paul presented the concept of the Second Adam. Jesus Christ is the new representative of the people of God; He restores what the first Adam lost. Undoubtedly this was included in Paul's oral preaching, and the Corinthians were probably familiar with it. Now Paul inserted the concept in this context. He demonstrated that Adam, not only because of the Fall but because he is "of the earth," had only an earthly inheritance to pass on to his descendants. Paul alluded to the Creation account, which says that man became a living soul. The earthly man was *psuchikos*; and as Adam was, so are his offspring. But the Last Adam, Christ, the "man from heaven" is a life-giving spirit. Through the redemption provided by Christ, the entire person is transformed. Not only is there a spiritual rebirth, the believer will also share in a new form of bodily existence, the same kind of existence that Jesus Christ has in His body of glory.

*5. Resurrection and Transformation (15:50-58).* No one will be able to participate in eternal life with God apart from the transformation of the body into a spiritual body. The physical body has some innate restrictions: "Flesh and blood cannot inherit the kingdom of God" (verse 50). However, this raises the question, "What about those who are alive at Christ's return? How will they be able to share in the Kingdom and its glory?" The Corinthians' problem was exactly opposite that of the Thessalonians, who wondered, "What about those who are asleep when the Lord returns?" (1 Thessalonians 4:13f.).

Paul may have been referring to two groups (verse 50). If that is true, "flesh and blood" would equal those who are alive at the coming of the Lord, while "that which is perishable" concerns the former "flesh and blood" which is dead and already decomposing (Godet, p. 862). Some interpreters regard the two expressions as too synonymous to convey any strict division (Bruce, *New Century Bible,* 38:153f.), but the Semitic construction "flesh and blood" is used for persons alive, and this seems its usage in the New Testament. One thing is certain: no one, alive or dead, will share in the kingdom of God without experiencing a transformation. Having shown the possibility of such a transformation, Paul now showed its importance.

The Corinthians were invited to listen very carefully by Paul's use of the word "Behold." The term also emphasizes the significance of what is being said. Paul revealed something that was previously a "mystery," a "secret once hidden." Now, through a special revelation it has come to light. The mystery involves the great eschatological event for which the Church waits—the Parousia, the Second Coming of Christ and the consummation of all things. To some degree, all of God's plan of salvation might be termed a "mystery" (cf. Romans 16:25; Ephesians 3:3f.) that is known only through revelation by God. The apostle earlier spoke of the "hidden wisdom of God," the counsel of God which concerned what "God ordained before the world unto our glory" (2:7ff.). Paul reintroduced this thought toward the close of the letter. He explained that the glory destined for those who love the Lord also affects the redemption of the body at the return of Christ. Then the dead will rise imperishable; those alive at His coming will be "changed."

These are the two groups of believers. Resurrection awaits one group and transformation the other. In both instances the body is given a new form. Interestingly, as he did in a similar context in 1 Thessalonians 4:16ff., Paul utilized the "we-form" when he spoke of those alive at the coming of the Lord. Since he did not know precisely when the Lord would return, it is only natural that he would include himself among the living. As Jesus commanded, Paul lived in the expectation of Christ's imminent return (Luke 12:36). The apostle saw such expectation as normal for every believer (1 Thessalonians 1:10). Plainly Paul expected the return of Christ in his lifetime. If the first generation of Christians eagerly expected the Lord's return, how much more so should later generations look for their Lord's coming? There is no indication that Paul ever altered his position that the Lord's return could happen at any moment. Later, when he acknowledged his death was near (e.g., Acts 20:29; 2 Timothy 4:6ff.), he was not saying the Parousia was any less imminent.

The resurrection/transformation will occur "in a moment, in the twinkling of an eye, at the last trump." The Old Testament depicts the Day of the Lord as accompanied by a trumpet sound (Zephaniah 1:16), and trumpets are afforded a significant role in the apocalyptic portions of Scripture (e.g., Revelation). The coming of the Son of Man and the gathering of the elect will take place at the "sound of the trumpet." In the Book of Revelation a series of trumpet blasts are given. Paul explained in 1 Thessalonians 4:13-18 that the coming of the Lord, the resurrection of believers, and their transformation will be accompanied by the "trump of God."

Paul considered the resurrection/transformation as triumph over death. Those changed at the coming of Christ will never experience death; neither will those who died be conquered by death. Those who "sleep," as Paul put it, will be "awakened" from death. In principle, therefore, death has already been vanquished. It will be—and indeed has been—"swallowed up in victory" through Christ's death and resurrection. "O death where is thy sting? O grave, where is thy victory?" Like the scorpion without a sting, it has no poison. From Paul's perspective, all of this is in fulfillment of the promises of Scripture (cf. Isaiah 25:8; Hosea 13:14). Paul utilized both passages elsewhere.

Paul next offered praise to God who alone gives us the victory through Christ our Lord. In his second epistle to the Corinthians (2:14) he also offered thanksgiving to God for giving believers victory in all of life's circumstances. In this first epistle (15:57) he praised God for the final victory, salvation, and life in the eternal kingdom of God.

Moving abruptly from this climactic hymn of triumph, Paul suddenly warned: "Therefore, my beloved brethren, be ye stedfast, unmoveable, always abounding in the work of the Lord, forasmuch as ye know that your labour is not in vain in the Lord" (15:58). This shift is typical for Paul, and it often occurs in 1 Corinthians. Paul taught the deepest spiritual truths in conjunction with practical guidance. He joined the truths of the resurrection (chapter 15) with a discussion on assistance for the believers in Judea (chapter 16). The epistle concludes with greetings and a closing.

# The First Epistle of Paul to the Corinthians

## Commentary

### Chapter 1

**1. Paul, called [to be] an apostle of Jesus Christ through the will of God:** . . . by vocation an Apostle, *—GNVA* . . . a Constituted Apostle, *—WLSN* . . . chosen by divine will, *—FNTN* . . . and sent by Jesus Messiah, *—MRDK.*

**and Sosthenes [our] brother:**

**1:1.** This letter opens in the usual first-century way, listing the writer(s), those addressed, and a prayer. That this letter was written by the apostle Paul is beyond doubt. This is the Paul who once called himself a "Hebrew of the Hebrews" (Philippians 3:5), saw the Lord on the Damascus Road, wrote nearly half the books of the New Testament, and has been designated "the Apostle of the Gentiles." In this verse, while suggesting his position and authority ("apostle"), he also noted its divine origin ("called") and its divine order ("will of God"). In the beginning, Paul wanted his readers to know that what he was writing to them was from the Lord.

The cowriter of this letter is not so easily identified. Apparently he was a fellow minister of more local rank. It could be he was a Corinthian. Some have suggested this is the Sosthenes mentioned in Acts 18:17. It is possible, but the name was common and it is difficult to be certain.

**2. Unto the church of God which is at Corinth:** . . . Unto the congregacyon, *—CRNM* . . . to the ecclesia, *—CNDT* . . . to the Community of God, *—HNT* . . . to the assembly of God existing, *—FNTN.*

**to them that are sanctified in Christ Jesus:** . . . hallowed, *—CNDT, —CNBR* . . . to hem that ben halowid in crist, *—WCLF* . . . who are consecrated, *—MOFT.*

**called [to be] saints:** . . . the chosen saints, *—FNTN* . . . sainctes by callynge, *—TNDL.*

**with all that in every place call upon the name of Jesus Christ our Lord:** . . . along with all, *—HNT* . . . to all them, *—MRDK* . . . in conjunction with all, *—RTHM* . . . wherever they are, *—MNTG* . . . with al that inuocate the name, *—RHEM* . . . invoke the name, *—MOFT* . . . all appealing to the Power of our, *—FNTN.*

**both theirs and ours:** . . . which is their homeand our home also, *—CNBR.*

**1:2.** When we read further in this letter and see the problems plaguing the Corinthian Christians, we find it interesting that Paul called them saints.

Yet it is the work of Christ that makes someone a saint, not the work of a body of men. Sainthood is caused by the internal purification and reformation of the soul, as here suggested by the word "sanctified."

We might conclude that this letter was intended at least for more than just the Corinthians. The phrase "with all that in every place" would suggest that.

In verse 10 Paul began to discuss the problem of division at Corinth. But even in this verse Paul made a veiled reference to that when he spoke of Christ as Lord of all. True sanctification will produce genuine fellowship with other believers in Christ.

**3. Grace [be] unto you, and peace:** . . . favour unto you, *—RTHM* . . . be granted to you, *—WEYM.*

**from God our Father, and [from] the Lord Jesus Christ:**

**1:3.** The greeting of grace and peace from both God the Father and God the Son was to become the typical Christian greeting. Especially is that true of Paul's writings. (See, for example, Romans 1:7; 2 Corinthians 1:2; Galatians 1:3; Ephesians 1:2; Philippians 1:2; Colossians 1:2; 1 Thessalonians 1:1; 2 Thessalonians 1:2; 1 Timothy 1:2; 2 Timothy 1:2; Titus 1:4; Philemon 3.) The greeting spoke of God's gifts and blessings, and His attitude and desires toward those who love and serve Him.

**4. I thank my God always on your behalf:** . . . I always thank, *—HNT* . . . continually on your behalf, *—WEYM, —CNBR.*

**for the grace of God which is given you by Jesus Christ:** . . . granted to you, *—FNTN* . . . bestowed on you, *—MOFT.*

**1:4.** Paul said some difficult things before he concluded this letter. Yet despite the problems Paul encountered, he always found something for which to thank the Lord. This is the response of a man who spends more time dwelling on the goodness of the Lord than on his circumstances. Thanksgiving is essential to the Christian life, and Paul wanted the Corinthians to understand this. The grace of God has as its source Jesus Christ. He is its life-spring and the vessel through which it is imparted to the Church. Because of this, the grace of God is effective, even though the change may seem more apparent in some believers than others.

**5. That in every thing ye are enriched by him:** ... ye are made riche in hym, *–GNVA* ... so richly blessed in Him, *–WEYM* ... received a wealth of all blessing, *–MOFT.*

**in all utterance, and [in] all knowledge:** ... with readiness of speech and fulness of knowledge, *–WEYM* ... in all expression, *–CNDT* ... all the gifts of speech, *–CNBR* ... with full reason and full knowledge, *–FNTN* ... in all discourse, *–RTHM* ... and all extraordinary gifts, *–LOCK.*

**1:5.** This grace is clearly of God; thus, the work done is of God also. He had enriched the Corinthian Christians in a large way. Surprisingly, Paul noted their enrichment in two particular ways: in utterance or telling of truth, and in knowledge or the grasp of truth. Later, it appears that he rebuked the readers for these very things. A careful reading, however, will lead us to understand that what Paul rebuked was the pride or the attitude in these things. With a proper, tender attitude, knowledge and utterance can be a very powerful combination.

**6. Even as the testimony of Christ was confirmed in you:** ... by the which thynges the testimony of Iesus Christ, *–CRNM* ... which verifies the testimony, *–MOFT.*

**1:6.** This richness in Christ came as a result of clear and specific witness concerning Christ. We may conclude that there was certain testimony concerning Christ's death, burial, resurrection, ascension, and return, as well as specific teaching on the whole life of salvation and the work of the Holy Spirit.

This witness was confirmed in them. How was it confirmed? They heard the gospel, repented, believed on Christ, accepted the gospel, and the consequence was their fellowship and equality with other Christians.

**7. So that ye come behind in no gift:** ... you do not suffer want in any privilege, *–HNT* ... may not be deficient in any spiritual gift, *–FNTN* ... lack no spiritual endowment, *–MOFT* ... you lack no divine gift, *–MNTG* ... in any one gift-of-favour, *–RTHM.*

**waiting for the coming of our Lord Jesus Christ:** ... looking earnestly for the time, *–CNBR* ... awaiting the unveiling, *–CNDT* ... expecting the reuelation, *–RHEM* ... waiting for the revelation, *–MNTG* ... for the re-appearing, *–WEYM* ... and wayte for the apperynge of oure lorde Iesus Christ, *–TNDL* ... shall be revealed to sight, *–CNBR.*

**1:7.** Experientially, the Corinthians were not lacking in any "gift." This "gift" may refer to salvation, to good gifts in general, or to a special equipment of the Holy Spirit. Certainly it was intended to make them mature, effective Christians in life, deed, and thought. Whatever its precise reference,

these so blessed were thus pointed to the second coming of Jesus Christ, when their use of these gifts would be tested or examined and they would see the culmination of the work of the Spirit.

**8. Who shall also confirm you unto the end:** ... also support you until absolutely perfect, *–FNTN* ... keep you perfectly steadfast unto the end, *–MNTG* ... until the consummation, *–CNDT.*

**[that ye may be] blameless in the day of our Lord Jesus Christ:** ... there may be no charge against you, *–LOCK* ... to be irreproachable, *–HNT* ... you will be unreprovable in the Day, *–MNTG* ... he will guarantee that you are vindicated on the day, *–MOFT* ... unaccusable in the day, *–RTHM* ... unimpeachable, *–CNDT.*

**1:8.** Until that day Christ will continue what He has begun; i.e., the work of confirming, sanctifying, maturing, and making unreprovable or blameless. God's goal is to present us complete and accepted in Christ on that day when He shall return. As *The Expositor's Greek Testament* suggests, He will confirm character as they have confirmed their testimony (Nicoll, 2:761).

**9. God [is] faithful:** ... may be relied on, *–LOCK.*

**by whom ye were called unto the fellowship of his Son Jesus Christ our Lord:** ... were chosen into a fellowship, *–FNTN* ... into the societie of his sonne, *–RHEM.*

**1:9.** We must be assured that this confirmation will continue because God is faithful; our security rests in the character of God. What He commits himself to will always be finished. Phillips' translation reads: "God is utterly dependable...." It is this God who calls us to fellowship with His Son Jesus. This fellowship may be either subjective (with His Son) or objective (in His Son). The subjective sense would seem to be best because nowhere else is this noun used as the objective genitive of person, and the reference in context seems to be communion, of which Christ is the sum.

God will finish the beautiful work He has begun, if we remain in Christ. After all, Jesus Christ, under the direction of the Father, is the "author and finisher of our faith" (Hebrews 12:2).

**10. Now I beseech you, brethren:** ... Now I appeal to you, *–HNT* ... But I beg of you, *–FNTN.*

**by the name of our Lord Jesus Christ:**

**that ye all speak the same thing, and [that] there be no divisions among you:** ... that ye hold the same doctrines, *–LOCK* ... you would all reason alike, *–FNTN* ... to be all in unison, *–HNT* ... to shun disputes, *–CNBR* ... that there be no dissencion amonge you, *–TNDL* ... that there be no schismes among you, *–RHEM* ... must be no cliques, *–MOFT* ... to speak in accord, *–MNTG* ... to cultivate a spirit of harmony, *–WEYM.*

**but [that] ye be perfectly joined together:** ... but be ye knyt togither, —GNVA ... but be at harmony together, —HNT ... but you may be attuned, —CNDT ... may be trained in, —FNTN ... into one entire body, —LOCK ... perfect in one sense, —RHEM.

**in the same mind and in the same judgment:** ... to be knit together in the same mind, —CNBR ... to the same opinion, —CNDT ... in a common mind and temper, —MNTG ... and in one knowledge, —RHEM.

**1:10.** After his very positive opening remarks, however, it did not take Paul long to begin to correct the difficulties at Corinth that had come to his attention. "Now" contrasts what follows with what has preceded. He appealed to them with great solemnity, yet great gentleness, to be united together under Christ. Some might argue that it was very difficult to be so united because of differences in background, personality, and approach. But when Paul urged them to "speak the same thing" and to be in unity, he was referring to unity in love, doctrine, and purpose which is both essential and mandatory. In fact, "speak the same thing" is a classical expression used of political communities that were free from factions, or of different states that entertained friendly relations with each other. Besides, the Spirit of Christ draws us together around a common theme and into a common bond.

*Katērtismenoi* is also used in Mark 1:19 of "mending" fishing nets. In the same way that torn fishing nets could be restored and mended, the factionalized people at Corinth were to be knit together. The word is also used by the Greek historian Herodotus for restoring peace after civil unrest and discord. The church at Corinth was acting more like a group of political rivals than the church of God. The knitting together that Paul desired for the church was a matter of both mind and judgment, that is, by true and correct doctrine.

Paul wished his readers to be restored to a rightful condition of love in Christ, and if there could not be a unity of choice, there could be a unity of feeling and affection. It is possible to hold someone in regard and love and treat him as a brother, without agreeing with him on everything. Without unity, the Church cannot present an effective witness to the world around it.

**11. For it hath been declared unto me of you, my brethren:** ... For it was signified to me, —RTHM ... For I have been distinctly informed, —WEYM ... to me respecting you, —FNTN.

**by them [which are of the house] of Chloe:**

**that there are contentions among you:** ... to this effect, —HNT ... that ther is strife among you, —GNVA ... that you are quarrelling, —MOFT ... that party

feeling exists among you, —TCNT ... there are strifes, —CNFT ... disputes among you, —ADAM ... there are wranglings among you, —WLMS ... ye are fallen into parties, —LOCK ... each of you is a partisan, —WEYM.

**1:11.** Lest the Corinthians deny the difficulties, Paul recorded his source of information. The reports had come from "the house of Chloe." These were friends Paul respected and trusted. They had a deep and genuine concern for the church at Corinth. The reports were true beyond any reasonable doubt. Such problems need to be established as true before the minister of God proceeds with correction.

**12. Now this I say, that every one of you saith:** ... And I mention this, —MKNT ... I mean by this that one of you, —MNTG ... that you each declare, —FNTN ... each one belongs to a faction, —NORL.

**I am of Paul; and I of Apollos:** ... Paul certainly is my leader, —BRKL ... I follow Paul, —TCNT ... I holde of Paul, —TNDL, —CRNM ... I belong to Apollos, —SEB.

**and I of Cephas; and I of Christ:**

**1:12.** Paul told them precisely what they had been doing and saying. Unwilling to let the dishonor and sin continue, Paul confronted them directly and in love. It seems four major divisions had developed: One group followed Paul, with whom we are familiar already; one followed Apollos, who differed not in message but apparently in method, having a more rhetorical, eloquent style. His method of presentation was very popular with those of Greek background. One group followed Cephas or Peter, the "hero" of Pentecost and a true apostle (these were probably conservative Jewish-Christians). Another group said they followed Christ. These may have been ultraconservative followers, or individuals who were trying to satisfy their ego by convincing themselves that their religion was more pure and spiritual than anyone else's.

If he had been a lesser man, Paul might have been tempted to side with those who supported him. After all, he had begun this church and he had taught and trained them. Did that not make him right? But Paul did not yield to such temptation. This was Christ's church, not his, and such division had no place or value. They only make the Church weak, self-centered, and unprofitable.

**13. Is Christ divided?:** ... Can you gamble upon Christ? —FNTN ... Is Christ dismembered? —BRKL ... divided up into pieces? —SEB ... divided into parties, —MKNT ... You have torn the Christ to pieces! —TCNT ... Christ is parted! —CNDT ... Is the Christ in fragments? —WEYM.

**was Paul crucified for you?:** ... Paul was not nailed to the cross, —SEB ... on your behalf? —WEYM.

or were ye baptized in the name of Paul?: ... were ye immersed? —*RTHM* ... to be Paul's adherents? —*WEYM*.

**1:13.** Whatever the supports on which these groups rested, Paul quickly brought them to the real point with three short questions. These questions suggest the unity, work, and supremacy of Christ, and Paul intended a negative answer to each question. Christ is not divided; He died for all; He is Lord of all. Such division is the heart of folly. There is one Body and Paul made it clear, when he used those who followed him as examples, that it must remain one church under Jesus Christ.

14. **I thank God that I baptized none of you, but Crispus and Gaius:** ... that I christened none of you, —*TNDL* ... immersed on my authority, —*SEB*.

15. **Lest any should say that I had baptized in mine own name:** ... Then nobody can say, —*BECK* ... so that no one might say, —*TCNT* ... may claim baptism in my name, —*BRKL* ... to be my adherents, —*WEYM*.

**1:14, 15.** Paul noted his thanks that he had not baptized many at Corinth in water, and especially that he had not baptized in his own name. "Name" implied ownership, fellowship, and allegiance. Paul did nothing to develop such a relationship with those he led to Christ.

Verse 15 begins with a *hina* clause (*hina me tis*) which can be taken either as a purpose clause or a result clause. The KJV takes it as a purpose clause ("lest any should say . . .") whereas a result clause would be rendered, "For this reason, none of you can say. . . ." The important thing to stress here is that Paul avoided anything in his ministry which could lead to division or factionalism, even where the sacraments were concerned.

16. **And I baptized also the household of Stephanas:**
**besides, I know not whether I baptized any other:** ... beyond this I do not recollect, —*FNTN* ... I did not think, —*MNTG* ... for the rest, I do not remember, —*HNT* ... I am not aware, —*CNDT*.

17. **For Christ sent me not to baptize, but to preach the gospel:** ... does not commission me, —*CNDT* ... but to euangelize, —*RHEM* ... but to be declaring the joyful message, —*RTHM* ... but to publish the Glad-tidings, —*CNBR* ... but to proclaim the Good News, —*WEYM*.
**not with wisdom of words:** ... with no fine rhetoric, —*MOFT* ... not with philosophical argument, —*FNTN* ... not in mere learned language, —*WEYM*.
**lest the cross of Christ should be made of none effect:** ... might not be fruitless, —*FNTN* ... should be rendered void, —*HNT* ... be made an empty thing, —*MNTG* ... be deprived of its power, —*WEYM*.

**1:16, 17.** Paul's primary mission was to preach, not in his own wisdom or ability, but in the power of the Holy Spirit, the cross of Christ being the center of his message. To have ministered by his own eloquence or wit would have served only to detract from the message. It would have lifted up him instead of the Cross. Depending on the Holy Spirit instead of himself kept him where the Cross could be the center and source of Christian unity.

18. **For the preaching of the cross is to them that perish foolishness:** ... For the discourse, —*RTHM* ... the word of the cross to those in the way perdition is folly, —*CNBR* ... is stupidity, —*CNDT* ... folly to the reprobate, —*FNTN* ... those on their way to destruction, —*MNTG*.
**but unto us which are saved it is the power of God:**

**1:18.** Paul wished to turn the minds of his readers to the source of our union and unity—the Cross. He did so by displaying it as the greatest expression of wisdom and power the world has ever seen. To some it does not appear that way; it appears foolish. How could a cross be of any value? Paul spoke in irony. The "preaching of the cross" seems foolish merely because the message is simple and the listeners are blind, proud, and mocking. Those who are perishing (who are being brought to nothing, who are being destroyed) stubbornly take their own way and consider the Cross foolish. But it is this choice and consideration that is causing them to perish. They mock their only hope. And the fact of their perishing proves the fallacy of their thinking.

But there is another group. To those who are being saved (who are being saved, rescued, and preserved from harm), the Cross is the very expression of God's power. Notice that Paul includes himself ("us") in those who are heirs of salvation. It is not glory in himself, but in the cross of Christ. He had experienced its power for himself and he wanted to share it. The range of God's power covers not only the material realm of controlling the universe, and not only the mental realm of changing men's opinions, particularly at salvation, but also the realm of the moral and spiritual. By the Cross we see the wonder of God's redemption; by the Cross we are united with Christ; by the Cross we are cleansed and purified, and by the Cross we are "kept" unto salvation.

19. **For it is written, I will destroy the wisdom of the wise:** ... I will ruin, —*HNT* ... exhibit the nothingness, —*WEYM* ... the philosophy of the philosophers, —*FNTN* ... of the sages, —*MOFT*.
**and will bring to nothing the understanding of the prudent:** ... And the cleverness of the clever I will frustrate, —*HNT* ... confound the insight,

—MOFT . . . and upset the cleverness of the clever, —FNTN . . . the discernment of the discerning ones will I set aside, —RTHM . . . will I confound, —MNTG . . . shall I be repudiating, —CNDT . . . I vvil reiecte, —RHEM.

**1:19.** Paul made an important comparison. While the Cross is exalted and shown in its true light, we are told of God's view of man's wisdom. Isaiah 29:14 is quoted in spirit, with slight alterations. God rendered useless the imagined wisdom of Jerusalem, and as it happened then so it will happen again. When God spoke to Jerusalem, she refused to hear Him, considering herself too high to respond to God. Exalted by God, she discovered what it was to be brought low by God.

Paul tells us that men of this world professed themselves to be wise, and in pride lifted themselves up. That very act was the beginning of their downfall (Romans 1:22). James tells us that true wisdom cannot be manufactured on this earth. It must come from above (James 3:17). Repeatedly Proverbs reminds us that real understanding and applicable knowledge is found in a proper attitude toward and fellowship with God.

**20.** **Where [is] the wise? where [is] the scribe?:** . . . Sage, rabbi, skeptic of this present age, —MNTG . . . the professor of human arts and sciences? —LOCK . . . your man of letters? —WLMS . . . your expounder of the Law? —WEYM.

**where [is] the disputer of this world?:** . . . the reasoner, —CNBR . . . your logician of this age? —WLMS . . . the discusser of this eon, —CNDT . . . the debater of this age? —HNT . . . your investigator of the questions of this present age? —WEYM.

**hath not God made foolish the wisdom of this world?:** . . . to be utter foolishness? —WEYM . . . utter folly, —NORL . . . useless for the discovery of the truths of the Gospel? —LOCK.

**1:20.** Paul established his point with four questions. "Where is the wise?" establishes that where the Cross is preached human wisdom cannot stand. How can it? What religion is there on the face of the earth that has brought salvation and peace to the hearts of men? Only the gospel of Jesus Christ and the message of the Cross has been able to do that. Paul did not say that there are no worldly-wise men left, only that they fade to nothing beside the Cross.

Paul used the word *sophian* ("wisdom") extensively throughout 1 Corinthians in a variety of ways, both negatively and positively. Paul used the word in at least two negative ways: the first as a manner or style of preaching which emphasizes eloquence based on logic and rhetoric apart from Christ (as at 1:17); also negatively as the very essence of salvation, that it equaled salvation. Paul was thus attacking a Gnostic view of wisdom which equated knowledge with the way of salvation rather than seeing Jesus as the way to salvation (cf. John 14:6).

In question two, the scribe is mentioned because wisdom in the human sphere may use Holy Writ by referring to some truth in Scripture. But a knowledge of the Word without submission to it only creates helplessness and a chaotic state. "Where is the scribe?" By the message of the Cross, he is silenced.

Again, in question three, "Where is the disputer of this world?" there is an indication of one who understands his own "times," who perceives something of the motivations of men; but that is not enough.

Question four is not so much an addition as it is a summation and answer to the other three questions.

**21.** **For after that in the wisdom of God the world by wisdom knew not God:** . . . For since in accordance, —WLMS . . . by its philosophy, —MNTG . . . with all its wisdom failed to know God, —MOFT, —HNT.

**it pleased God by the foolishness of preaching to save them that believe:** . . . God took delight, —RTHM . . . God delights, through the stupidity of the heralding, —CNDT . . . by the apparent foolishness of the Message . . . to save those who accepted it, —WEYM . . . to quicken them who believe, —MRDK.

**1:21.** God deliberately chose a way that would confound man's wisdom and reason. Man in his wisdom could not discover what God is like. He has never discovered his duty to God without revelation, and that is part of God's wise providence. God deliberately chose the "foolishness of preaching." It is possible that Paul was referring to content, the foolishness of the thing preached (the Cross).

**22.** **For the Jews require a sign:** . . . Jews demand miracles, —MOFT . . . are always asking for proofs, —SEB . . . demand extraordinary signs, —LOCK . . . demanding spectacular signs, —WLMS . . . continue to ask for miracles, —MNTG.

**and the Greeks seek after wisdom:** . . . are ever wanting philosophy, —MNTG . . . demand wisdom, —MRDK . . . require wisdom, —HNT.

**23.** **But we preach Christ crucified:** . . . we are heralding Christ crucified, —CNDT . . . a crucified Messiah, —MNTG.

**unto the Jews a stumbling-block:** . . . a certain offence, —FNTN . . . a snare, —CNDT . . . a hindrance, —HNT . . . an occasion of fallinge, —TNDL . . . a doctrine offensive to the hopes, —LOCK.

**and unto the Greeks foolishness:** . . . and folly to the heathen, —FNTN . . . foolish to the acute men of learning, —LOCK.

**1:22, 23.** These verses point to actual demonstrations of man's foolishness. One example is the

Jews. They sought God in tradition, in the letter of the Law. They demanded evidence and visible positive affirmation and were interested in the practical. Yet they framed God in and offered Jesus only one pattern to fit. They stumbled over the fact of a crucified Messiah because it was not a "good sign." This ruined their selfish expectations.

The other example is the Greeks. They were absorbed in speculative philosophy, as Acts 17:21 points out. They were intellectual beings and proud of their reasoning which did not allow true faith; consequently, they considered the Cross ridiculous. To both Jew and Greek the Cross came simply and free, but that was too much for those who should have understood so much. They could not accept a God who was that gracious.

**24. But unto them which are called, both Jews and Greeks:** . . . to those who have received the Call, —WEYM.

**Christ the power of God, and the wisdom of God:** . . . a Divine power, and a Divine philosopy, —FNTN.

**1:24.** The preaching of the cross of Christ has great effect. It changes people, calls them to faith, and unites and crosses all manmade boundaries, for it is the direct revelation and plan of God. Man, with his highest achievements, cannot touch God; he cannot find Him; he cannot exhaust Him; he cannot understand Him. The gospel, which speaks so eloquently of Jesus Christ, reveals God and demonstrates His power to every generation. To those who accept, it is power and wisdom.

**25. Because the foolishness of God is wiser than men:** . . . the feble thing of god, —WCLF.

**and the weakness of God is stronger than men:** . . . that which is the infirme of God, —RHEM . . . the feebleness of God, —MRDK . . . is mightier than men's might, —WEYM . . . surpasses the power of men, —LOCK . . . than human strength, —FNTN.

**1:25.** The reason the Cross is so powerful to those who accept is because of the nature of God in comparison with man. It is difficult, even impossible, to believe God could do anything foolish or weak. That is not the point. The point is twofold. If God ever did anything foolish or weak, it would still far exceed man's capabilities. Yet even that falls somewhat short of Paul's point. Man often views something that God does as foolish or weak because he is too frail to understand God, too weak to see the power of His purposes. Thus, even though God appears foolish and weak in the eyes of men, it is because God's work is so much higher and better than men can grasp with their limited perception. So, in pride and weakness, they reject the program of God.

**26. For ye see your calling, brethren:** . . . For consider your own calling, —MNTG . . . behold your invitation, —WLSN . . . contemplate your vocation, —FNTN.

**how that not many wise men after the flesh:** . . . many eminent philosophers, —FNTN . . . are wise with merely human wisdom, —WEYM.

**not many mighty, not many noble, [are called]:** . . . how few are powerful, —CNBR . . . not many principal men, not many of high birth, —HNT . . . not many of hye degre, —TNDL, —CRNM . . . not many of position and influence, —WEYM . . . many high-born, —FNTN . . . many leading men, —MOFT.

**1:26.** Because the Cross was considered foolish by many, God's call was readily heard by the weak and foolish, by those who needed Him. This has always been true. The poor, the hungry, the hurt, the needy were the ones that heard Jesus most eagerly. Within the context, Paul reminded the Corinthians of their own calling and experience. Paul explained the term "wise men after the flesh" with what immediately follows. Not many "mighty" men or men of influence, men of rank and government, are chosen. Not many noble men, or men of high birth (Roman nobles?) were called. There were some, but not many.

An examination of Acts 18:18, Romans 16:23, and several passages in First Corinthians reveals that in the church at Corinth (among people who might be considered well-to-do) were Crispus, the former synagogue ruler; Erastus, the city chamberlain; and Gaius, the director of the city public works. Overwhelmingly, however, the church at Corinth consisted of the poor, uneducated, and slaves. There was thus no excuse for any vanity or pride on their part. Simple faith is difficult for men of such position. The gospel was addressed to those the world considered fools and weaklings.

**27. But God hath chosen the foolish things of the world to confound the wise:** . . . He might shame the philosophic, —FNTN . . . put its wise men to shame, —WEYM . . . to confound its philosophy, —MNTG . . . to confound its wisdom, —CNBR . . . to shame the wise, —MOFT.

**and God hath chosen the weak things of the world to confound the things which are mighty:** . . . the low-born things, —HNT . . . to confound its strength, —MNTG . . . to make strong people humble, —SEB . . . to put the strong to shame, —WLMS . . . shame the strong, —FNTN.

**28. And base things of the world, and things which are despised, hath God chosen:** . . . chosen the low-born, —FNTN . . . beneath regard, —TCNT . . . of low degree, —WLMS . . . the ignoble of the world, —CMPB . . . the ignoble ones, —MKNT . . . And byle thynges, —CRNM . . . and the contemptible, —RHEM . . . the worthless, the trash, —KLGS . . . which the world thinks are not important, —SEB . . . which it sets utterly at nought, —WEYM.

**[yea], and things which are not:** ... those that are nothing, *—CMPB* ... and thinges of no reputacion, *—TNDL.*

**to bring to nought things that are:** ... to put down things that are, *—MOFT* ... to annihilate what amounts to something, *—BRKL* ... them who are something, *—MRDK* ... things that do exist, *—WEYM.*

**1:27, 28.** But God does nothing because of capriciousness or because He can get nothing better. He had a purpose in His calling. God chose the weak and lowly. The world may laugh, but it is God himself who does the choosing. It must be added that not only does the world consider these weak and foolish; they really are. What a blow to pride! What a blow to those who have been seeking the world's approval, when they should be seeking only God's good pleasure. Yet Paul went further. He called them "despised," which Knox translated "contemptible." In "things" the neuter concentrates on the quality of foolishness possessed rather than on the individuals themselves (Morris, *Tyndale New Testament Commentaries,* 7:48).

**29. That no flesh should glory in his presence:** ... to prevent any mortal man, *—WEYM* ... that no person, *—MOFT* ... Natural human abilities, *—LOCK* ... to keep anybody from bragging, *—BECK* ... should exult before God, *—HNT* ... can boast, *—FNTN* ... can brag in front of God, *—SEB* ... should pride itself before him, *—CNFT.*

**1:29.** God chose these apparently insignificant ones to shame and confuse the strong; to reduce to insignificance the great of the world. In so doing, He expressed His love, in that He would willingly choose and lift the lowly and ugly.

The words "that no flesh should glory in his presence" reminded the Corinthians of Paul's precise reason for writing. Paul was not especially concerned about the world's glorying and false boasting, but he did write to counter the false pride in the church at Corinth. The thought expressed in 1:5 made clear to the Corinthians that they were rich in utterance and knowledge, not because of human rhetoric and wisdom, but "by him" (God). Because they had wrongly evaluated their gifts and believed wisdom to be from man, they gloried in men (3:21) instead of realizing that they were believers because they had been called according to the purposes of Christ, not according to human wisdom.

God has done this so "no flesh," including all of mankind, could boast before Him. God has refuted the so-called wisdom of this world, and the Church is nothing without the Lord. There is nothing that a man can take hold of in the program of redemption and say, "This is what I did to help God and the Church along. Therefore I deserve some praise for this." We have a part, but it is God's work, from beginning to end.

**30. But of him are ye in Christ Jesus:** ... And vnto him partayne ye, *—TNDL* ... you have your existence, *—BRKL.*

**who of God is made unto us wisdom:**
**and righteousness, and sanctification, and redemption:** ... our means of right standing, *—WLMS* ... being holy and free, *—SEB* ... justification, *—CMPB* ... holiness and deliverance, *—CNDT* ... our salvation, *—NORL* ... ransom from sin, *—BECK.*

**31. That, according as it is written:**
**He that glorieth, let him glory in the Lord:** ... Let the triumphant triumph with the Lord, *—FNTN* ... Let him who takes pride, *—CNFT* ... boast of the Lord, *—MOFT.*

**1:30, 31.** The opposite side of the argument is that we are nevertheless blessed and rich because of the work of Jesus Christ. The debased are now exalted. But now the exaltation is real and is based on the right foundation. We are blessed because we are "in Christ." It is to be noted that Paul presented the work of Christ as also the work of the Father. Christ is made to all believers "wisdom," which stands alone and may be explained by the last three words of verse 31, "in the Lord."

God turned the world's wisdom to foolishness for our salvation. Christ is our "righteousness," which refers specifically to the doctrine of justification by faith and speaks of a law court where the verdict is "Not guilty." He is our "sanctification," which refers to the continuous process of holiness and perfection as we remain in Christ. He is our "redemption," which refers to deliverance by ransom, as when slaves are liberated with a purchase price. Our life in God is grounded in Jesus Christ, and that life "in Christ" will produce union and fellowship with others who are "in Christ." When we discover the merits of Christ, we will glorify Him for this great revelation of wisdom and power. No other name can be placed alongside the name of Jesus. Paul transferred the idea of Jeremiah 9:23, 24 where the reference is to Jehovah, to Christ, placing Him above all other names (except God the Father) and personalities. Jesus Christ is Lord.

## Chapter 2

**1. And I, brethren, when I came to you:** ... And as for myself, *—WEYM.*

**came not with excellency of speech or of wisdom:** ... I did not endeavour to set it off with any ornaments of rhetoric, *—LOCK* ... not in the highness of word, *—WCLF* ... in magnificent speech, *—MRDK* ... with pretentious speech, *—SAWR* ... with grand reasoning or philosophies, *—FNTN* ... with any elaborate words or wisdom, —*MOFT* . . . with superiority of word, —*CNDT* . . . with no transcendent eloquence, —*WAY* . . . no distinction of eloquence, —*BRKL* . . . in gloriousnes of wordes or of wysdome, —*TNDL* . . . not in loftinesse of speache, —*RHEM* . . . not with surpassing power of eloquence, —*WEYM*.

**declaring unto you the testimony of God:** . . . come proclaiming the testimony, —*HNT* . . . that I came announcing, —*WEYM*.

2. **For I determined not to know any thing among you:** . . . I did not govern myself among you, as if I knew anything, —*MRDK* . . . decided not to know, —*HNT* . . . to be utterly ignorant, —*WEYM*.

**save Jesus Christ, and him crucified:** . . . and him a crucified Christ, —*MNTG*.

**2:1, 2.** "And I" begins to illustrate the truth of chapter 1. When Paul came to Corinth, from Athens with its idolatrous emphasis on philosophy, he came not as the usual itinerant professor of wisdom with which the Corinthians were so familiar. He was not witty, brilliant, or vain. Rather, his preaching was determined by the will of God and made effective by the power of God.

There is some debate as to whether Paul wrote that he came declaring the testimony (*marturion*) or mystery (*mustērion*) of God, but the evidence favors "testimony." One important reason is that "*testimony* is more suitable to the initial proclamation of the Gospel, whereas *mystery* suggests the wisdom Paul was able to speak among mature Christians" (Barrett, *Harper's New Testament Commentaries,* pp. 62, 63).

To enlarge and emphasize the thought, Paul reminded his readers of how he did not preach. Despite the comments of some modern expositors, it is entirely possible that Paul did have some oratorical ability. But if he did possess such, he made it a point not to depend on it at Corinth. Nor did he try to make the message sound humanly brilliant or intellectually intriguing. His presentation and the content of his message were rather plain and simple.

It is not necessary to distinguish the individual parts of his presentation. The dominant consideration that governed every part of his work among the Corinthians was to present nothing except the glory and power of Christ and the Cross. This is typical of Paul. In all the work he did and in each of the problems he discussed in his many letters, he always brings us back to the same point. How should this be considered in the light of the work of Christ? What does He teach us is the proper mode of action and response? Therefore, it is not surprising that Paul emphasized that here. The difficulties at Athens may have affected Paul's perspective, but they did not change, they only

reinforced, Paul's fundamental attitude. Christ must be preeminent.

3. **And I was with you in weakness:** . . . I in sikenesse, —*WCLF* . . . in bodily weakness, —*WAY* . . . in conscious feebleness, —*WEYM*.

**and in fear, and in much trembling:** . . . and great timidity, —*FNTN* . . . timid and greatly agitated, —*TCNT* . . . and drede, —*WCLF* . . . and in deep anxiety, —*WEYM*.

4. **And my speech and my preaching:** . . . And my thoughts and my language, —*FNTN* . . . my proclamation, —*RTHM*.

**[was] not with enticing words of man's wisdom:** . . . not adorned with persuasive words of earthly wisdom, —*WEYM* . . . not clothed in captivating philosophical phraseology, —*FNTN* . . . not rest on the plausible arguments of 'wisdom,' —*MOFT* . . . on the persuasive language of philosophy, —*MNTG*.

**but in demonstration of the Spirit and of power:** . . . but in shewinge of the sprete, —*TNDL* . . . but in playne euidence of spiritual power, —*GNVA* . . . on the proof supplied by the Spirit and its power, —*MOFT* . . . which the Spirit taught and mightily carried home, —*WEYM*.

**2:3, 4.** Paul came to the Corinthians in "weakness." This may refer to physical illness, but more probably it is a description of Paul's feeling of inadequacy in himself. Paul came in "fear," which is an inward emotion expressing fear of failure. Paul came with "trembling." This is used to describe the anxiety of one who distrusts his ability completely to meet all requirements, but does his utmost to fulfill his duty. (See Thayer, "*astheneia*," "*phobos*," and "*tromos*.") What preacher of the gospel is there anywhere who has not often known exactly what Paul is describing?

Yet the results were excellent. Paul preached with power, and God confirmed the Word with signs following. Paul understood his own deficiencies to present such a glorious gospel. He had to depend wholly on the Holy Spirit. The support was there in time of need. The premise on which he stood was true; the promises he declared were true; the power with which he spoke was true. Established on truth, presented in power, spoken in love, the results came. The only logical result was the persuasion of men concerning Christ and the enlargement of His kingdom.

In order to give fuller force to Paul's statement translated "in demonstration of the Spirit and of power," the dative preposition *en* is a dative of instrumentality and could thus be translated, "enforced by a demonstration of Spirit and power." The words "Spirit" and "power" are a hendiadys, that is, they are two words used to express the same thought. To preach in the Spirit is the same as preaching with power.

There is no substitute for God-ordained, Holy Spirit-anointed preaching of the Word of God. It may seem foolish to some, but it will produce results.

**5. That your faith should not stand in the wisdom of men:** . . . that your trust, —WEYM.
**but in the power of God:** . . . but in the vertu of god, —WCLF.

**2:5.** Paul's writing in this vein is clearly applied in this verse. If these believers stood on what someone said through his wisdom only, in time the foundation would crumble. This world's wisdom will fail, and so will those who rely upon it. But if these believers trusted in God they would not fall or fail. Faith in God's wisdom as displayed in Christ will produce maturity and also miracles.

**6. Howbeit we speak wisdom among them that are perfect:** . . . we can speak philosophy, —FNTN . . . among the full-grown, —RTHM . . . those who are mature, —MNTG.
**yet not the wisdom of this world, nor of the princes of this world:** . . . which belongs to this age, —HNT . . . nor of the useless leaders of this time, —FNTN . . . nether of the chiefest of this world, —GNVA.
**that come to nought:** . . . who are being discarded, —CNDT . . . who are to be set aside, —RTHM . . . who are soon to pass away, —WEYM.

**7. But we speak the wisdom of God in a mystery, [even] the hidden [wisdom]:** . . . the hidden mystery, —FNTN . . . which is in secrete and lieth hyd, —TNDL . . . which has been concealed, —CNDT.
**which God ordained before the world unto our glory:** . . . fore-appointed before the ages, —HNT . . . which God did predestinate, —RHEM . . . which God marked out beforehand, before the ages, —RTHM . . . decreed from all eternity, —MOFT . . . for our rectification, —FNTN . . . that it should result in glory to us, —WEYM.

**2:6, 7.** Paul continued to demolish step-by-step the foundation of natural wisdom on which the Corinthians were tempted to build. In thus comparing spiritual wisdom with natural wisdom, Paul noted that among "perfect" or "full-grown" believers the gospel is recognized as wisdom. These mature thinkers have freed themselves from the world and its values and so can acknowledge and pursue truth. God's wisdom is not dependent on the world, for it is permanent, and the world is on its way to a foolish, nonsensical end. True wisdom is not governed by leaders who set the patterns of this world in general. Yet while noting that this simple gospel is free from human additives, we must also recognize that in another sense it is the most brilliant "philosophy" to ever appear.

Because it does not come from men it appears as a mystery, a secret which man by himself could never unfold. But when Paul used it in his epistles

he used it in the sense of something long hidden, but now revealed. Indeed, when Christ came the mystery of the gospel was unfolded by God himself. Thus, Paul told the Corinthians that while they had been toying with the idea of abandoning this simple wisdom, in reality they were possessors of great benefits and the only true wisdom in all the world.

**8. Which none of the princes of this world knew:** . . . None of the leaders of this age, —HNT . . . not one of the chief men, —CNDT . . . none of the heades of this world, —GNVA . . . of the Powers, —MOFT . . . of this age recognised, —FNTN . . . world's leaders understands it, —WLMS . . . of this world comprehended, —NOYS.
**for had they known [it], they would not have crucified the Lord of glory:** . . . for if they had possessed it, —WEYM . . . for had they understood, —BRKL . . . would not have nailed the lord of glory to the cross, —SEB . . . the Lord of majesty, —HNT . . . our glorious master, —TCNT.

**2:8.** The "princes of this world" (including the Jews) did not fully comprehend God's plans or revelation. They did not really understand God's plan for salvation. Otherwise, they would have never crucified Christ. "Known" carries the idea of acknowledgment and so involves man's will. The implication is that God in His foreknowledge knew man would crucify Christ and worked it to man's hope or shame depending on personal choice. In any case, Christ, "the Lord of glory," of great position and title, would not have been crucified by wise men. In passing, our position is also noted by this term "Lord of glory," a position by association.

Some scholars prefer to take "princes of this world" as a reference to Satan because he is referred to as the *archōn tou kosmou* ("ruler of the world") in John 12:31; 14:30; and 16:11. There are, however, several reasons for not accepting this interpretation and for holding to the view that "princes of this world" refers to earthly princes. First of all, there is no evidence until the Second and Third Centuries that *archōn* was used in reference to devils, although in the singular it could sometimes be used of Satan. More importantly, however, is that *archōn* much more frequently explicitly refers to earthly rulers as it most certainly does in Romans 13:3. Finally, it was both Roman and Jewish leaders who caused Jesus' crucifixion.

**9. But as it is written, Eye hath not seen:** . . . according as it is written, —RTHM . . . What no one ever saw, —TEV.
**nor ear heard, neither have entered into the heart of man:** . . . never have occurred to human hearts, —WLMS . . . what no one ever thought could happen, —TEV . . . no human heart ever conceived,

507

—NORL ... No human being has ever imagined this, —SEB ... neither has it come up in the human heart, —BRKL.

**the things which God hath prepared for them that love him:** ... all that God has in readiness for, —WEYM.

**2:9.** That the plan of God would be a mystery was foretold by Scripture. Paul quoted from Isaiah 64:4 and 65:17. He referred to wonder beyond the senses, perception, or imagination of men. Here "heart" does not refer to the emotions, but to the understanding of natural man. "Mind" would be a better translation. Among the Greeks the seat of the emotions was the intestines. This revelation was beyond the ability of man to discover. We needed the help of the Holy Spirit. God had to tell us plainly of His wonderful plans for us.

**10. But God hath revealed [them] unto us by his Spirit:** ... God used the Spirit to show this secret to you, —SEB ... God made known his secret, —TEV ... hath opened them vnto vs, —TNDL ... has unveiled them, —MNTG ... which are not discoverable by man's natural faculties and powers, —LOCK ... has drawn aside the veil through the teaching of the Spirit, —WEYM ... through the Spirit, —HNT.

**for the Spirit searcheth all things:** ... Spirit fathoms everything, —MOFT, —MNTG, —TCNT ... finds out everything, —BECK ... examines everything, —BRKL ... exploreth all things, —MRDK ... can explore all things, —WAY ... investigates all, —FNTN.

**yea, the deep things of God:** ... ye the bottome of Goddes secretes, —TNDL ... even the high purposes, —FNTN ... the abysmal depths, —MNTG ... the profoundest secrets, —TCNT ... yea the profoundities of God, —RHEM ... including the depths of the divine nature, —WEYM.

**2:10.** It took a specific revelation by the Holy Spirit for us to understand the wisdom of God. The Holy Spirit has been a part of all God's work in this world; when the Church came into existence, His work took on a new feature. This verse does not refer to future glories still to be unfolded, but to wonders already shown to us. In other words, verse 9 has already begun to be fulfilled. Christ comes from God and so does the recognition of Him. The Holy Spirit must show those living in spiritual darkness that Christ is the wisdom of God.

This the Holy Spirit can do because He "searches" the things of God. This is basic. The word "searches" does not suggest incompleteness, but rather the opposite—fullness of knowledge, action, and penetration. The work He does can be done because He is God and understands all divine things. He searches the deep things of God. Salvation belongs here, but much more than just initial salvation is meant. Included is wisdom,

knowledge, and judgment—the work of the Holy Spirit himself.

**11. For what man knoweth the things of a man:** ... what comprehends the human faculties, —FNTN ... can understand his own inner thoughts, —WLMS ... the depths of man, —MNTG ... man is inscrutable to his fellow-man, —WAY.

**save the spirit of man which is in him?:** ... except the spirit of humanity, —CNDT ... except the man's own spirit, —WEYM.

**even so the things of God knoweth no man, but the Spirit of God:** ... In the same way, —SEB ... the thoughts of God no man knows, —CMPB ... no one comprehends the inner life of God, —TCNT ... is acquainted with God's inner thoughts, —WEYM ... knows the deeps profound of God, —MNTG ... knows all about God, —SEB.

**2:11.** Paul magnified his discussion with an illustration. From a human viewpoint, only the spirit of a man knows and understands the inner thoughts of a man. In other words, there are secrets kept from others. The comparison is made with the Spirit of God, but a point of clarification must be offered. "Spirit of man" refers to ego or self-consciousness. The "Spirit of God" could not be God's self-consciousness because this would take away the Spirit's personality and individuality. The point of comparison is that He can know that which no one except God could know. Only the Holy Spirit can recognize, understand, and reveal the heart and mind of God.

**12. Now we have received, not the spirit of the world:** ... Now we obtained, —CNDT.

**but the spirit which is of God:** ... but the Spirit proceeding from, —FNTN ... which comes forth from God, —WEYM.

**that we might know the things that are freely given to us of God:** ... that we may understand, —SEB ... we can distinguish the gifts, —FNTN ... we may realize the graces, —BRKL ... we may appreciate the gifts lavished on us, —WAY ... we may realize the blessings freely given us, —MNTG ... things which are gifted to us, —CMPB.

**2:12.** Now man may know the "things ... of God" because, and only because, he has received the Spirit of God. What is meant by "the spirit of the world"? It refers to the attitudes and motivation which controls a world that is not in subjection to God. It is a part of fallen human nature. In contrast, when we become "partakers of the divine nature" (2 Peter 1:4), the Spirit of God comes to indwell us. Believers must battle against the spirit of the world and yield to the Spirit of God. Almost every chapter of 1 Corinthians abounds with examples of the way the Corinthians were in bondage to the spirit of this world—the spirit of worldliness. In chapters 1 to 4 the spirit of this world created petty divisions within the church; in chapter 5 the spirit of the world led to sexual immorality; in chapter 6 it led to legal suits; in chapters 8 and 10 it led to idolatry. Finally in chapters 11 to 14 this same spirit of the world led to a failure of love even in a worship service. That we have not received the "spirit of the world" may also refer to something human, an attitude, a disposition. If so, it is a reference that may allude to Pentecost and the historic coming of the Holy Spirit. Paul tells us "we have received . . . the Spirit which is of God."

The Holy Spirit was sent that we might understand, discern, and possess the gifts of the Spirit. He was sent that the fruit of the Spirit might be growing and maturing in our lives in a practical fashion. He was sent that we might discern what is spiritual and what is fleshly or satanic. Grace, which sums up all the work of God in our lives, can only be understood through the eyes of the Spirit. The Spirit desires that we know more than just the powerful displays of God. Israel saw God's actions. The Spirit desires that we understand the motives and character of God. Moses was shown the ways of God. The Spirit urges these deeper matters upon us.

Once more, notice the emphasis on God's free decision to allow us to know these deeper things of God. To know true wisdom and the gifts of God, the presence of the Spirit is mandatory.

**13. Which things also we speak, not in the words which man's wisdom teacheth:** . . . We are not using human ideas, *—SEB* . . . not in the connynge wordes, *—TNDL* . . . not in the rhetoric of the schools, *—WAY* . . . not in the learned words, *—DOUY* . . . vvordes of humane vvisedom, *—RHEM.*
**but which the Holy Ghost teacheth:** . . . but in the doctryne of spirit, *—WCLF* . . . but in the Spirit's school, *—WAY* . . . but by spiritual teachings, *—FNTN.*
**comparing spiritual things with spiritual:** . . . We interpret what is spiritual in spiritual language, *—MOFT* . . . Interpreting spiritual things, *—HNT* . . . matching that which is spiritual, *—CNDT* . . . connecting what is spiritual, *—NOYS.*

**2:13.** Closely connected with knowledge is speaking. Spiritual things will come from the spiritual man. This verse points to what Christians endowed with the Spirit are always doing, for the verbs are in the present tense. These "spiritual" words have a definite color and lead in a definite direction. Thus, Christians do speak what the world does not often understand. There is a comparison of "spiritual things" (a neuter referring to thoughts, opinions, and precepts attributable to the Holy Spirit working in us) with spiritual. These matters are formed into a correlated system.

**14. But the natural man receiveth not the things of the Spirit of God:** . . . But the sensual man, *—RHEM* . . . the soulish man, *—CNDT* . . . brutish man does not entertain, *—FNTN* . . . perceaveth not, *—TNDL* . . . cannot grasp the revelations of the Spirit, *—WAY* . . . rejects the teachings, *—MNTG.*
**for they are foolishness unto him: neither can he know [them]:** . . . They are for him meaningless, *—WAY* . . . for it is foli to hym, *—WCLF* . . . they are 'sheer folly,' he cannot understand them, *—MOFT* . . . and he cannot ascertain [them], *—RTHM* . . . and cannot attain to the knowledge of them, *—WEYM.*
**because they are spiritually discerned:** . . . for they are estimated spiritually, *—HNT* . . . spiritually investigated, *—FNTN* . . . they are spretually examined, *—CRNM, —CNDT.*

**2:14.** Again, lest there be uncertainty in the minds of his readers, Paul compared the natural man and the spiritual man. The distinction is both absolute and general. It would seem that Paul suggests a total ignorance and rejection of *all* spiritual things. Unregenerate man calls the gospel nonsense because he has not received the Spirit to enlighten him, and he cannot by reasoning discover these things; they must be revealed. A deaf man cannot accurately "judge" music; a blind man cannot accurately "judge" the landscape; a natural man cannot receive or discern or "judge" spiritual things.

**15. But he that is spiritual judgeth all things:** . . . discerns everything, *—MNTG* . . . discusseth all thinges, *—TNDL.*
**yet he himself is judged of no man:** . . . be criticised by no one, *—FNTN.*

**2:15.** But the spiritual man is able to "judge" or compare and examine all things because his source of wisdom is completely accurate. The basis for this is found in verse 10. This is not to say, however, that the Christian believer could express knowledge and understanding on every subject. Since the believer is part of the world, however, his judgment involves secular as well as sacred matters. In judging the world's direction, philosophy, and attitude, some men are led to despair and even suicide. But as the Christian compares, examines, and in this specific sense "judges" but does not condemn, he is led to see the hope and victory for the man in Christ Jesus. At the same time, it is impossible for the natural man to make a similar judgment on the Christian, for he has no accurate source of knowledge. This is not pride, for the source of Christian confidence is not in oneself, but in the Holy Spirit.

**16. For who hath known the mind of the Lord, that he may instruct him?:** . . . who ever understood the thoughts, *—MOFT* . . . who has penetrated the mind, *—WEYM* . . . the sense of our Lord,

*—RHEM* . . . and who knewe the witte of the lord? *—WCLF* . . . have taught Him, *—FNTN.*

**But we have the mind of Christ:** . . . we possess, *—FNTN* . . . But we vnderstande the mynde of Christ, *—CRNM* . . . our thoughts are Christ's, *—MOFT.*

**2:16.** In this verse Paul gives proof for the previous verse. By his question (to which he expects a particular answer), he tells us no man has ever given the Lord instruction, counsel, or advice, and no natural man is able to ascend to God or find out anything about Him apart from divine revelation. The quotation is from Isaiah 40:13. Rather, a gift from God by His Spirit must come. That gift is the mind of Christ, to know and understand. It must be implanted and exercised by the presence of the Holy Spirit. What we have presented, then, is a mystical union, difficult to fully comprehend yet miraculously true, a marvelous work of controlling grace. This discussion leads to understanding a deeper dimension of the Spirit's control and work. God has come to be in us.

## Chapter 3

**1. And I, brethren, could not speak unto you as unto spiritual:** . . . As for me, brothers, *—MNTG.*

**but as unto carnal:** . . . address you as worldlings, *—MOFT* . . . as to animal, *—FNTN* . . . but as to fleischli men, *—WCLF* . . . to be as to worldlings, *—WEYM* . . . as creatures of flesh, *—HNT, —MNTG* . . . in whom the fleshly nature predominated, *—WAY.*

**[even] as unto babes in Christ:** . . . As it were to litle ones, *—RHEM* . . . as to minors, *—CNDT* . . . as to litil children in crist, *—WCLF* . . . mere infants in the New Life, *—WAY.*

**3:1.** Sad to say, these brethren at Corinth, with whom Paul had such a personal and loving relationship, were not mature, spiritual men. Up to this point in his discussion on wisdom Paul had been more general. Now he became specific and pointed. In chapter 2 Paul made clear that the wisdom of this world and the wisdom of this age are to be shunned, for they are contrary to the message of the Cross. There is, however, a proper way to view wisdom, and that is to see Jesus Christ as the wisdom of God (2:7). In chapter 3 Paul went on to say that although there is a spiritual wisdom, the Corinthians were not mature enough for it. When Paul first came to Corinth, these men had been converted and became spiritual "babes." They were young and weak. There is nothing wrong with that. Every Christian begins without experience, with little understanding; the need is for growth. But as we will shortly see, this entire section teaches the incapacity of the natural man for spiritual things. These believers were "carnal" Christians. They had not grown spiritually. They still showed traits of the old life.

**2. I have fed you with milk, and not with meat:** . . . not with solid food, *—MOFT.*

**for hitherto ye were not able [to bear it]:** . . . you were not yet strong enough, *—WEYM* . . . you could not have assimilated, *—WAY* . . . were not stronge, *—TNDL* . . . were not yet ready for it, *—CNFT.*

**neither yet now are ye able:**

**3:2.** Paul began his ministry by feeding them "milk." Paul was not saying he fed them on anything but the principles of Christ, but there is a realm in God that young Christians do not know and for which they are not yet ready. This soft diet was necessary because as spiritual babes they were not ready for the deeper truths of the gospel.

At this point Paul leveled a terrible charge. They had remained babes; they had not grown spiritually. They remained on the same plateau as when they first began and so proved themselves to be "carnal Christians." This was a strong rebuke to the Corinthians' pride and sense of accomplishment.

**3. For ye are yet carnal:** . . . you are still worldly, *—MOFT* . . . still in the flesh, *—MRDK.*

**for whereas [there is] among you envying, and strife, and divisions:** . . . where [there are] among you jealousy, *—RTHM* . . . is among you rivalry, *—NOYS* . . . is rage and strife, *—FNTN* . . . and quarrels, *—MOFT* . . . and factious parties, *—CNBR* . . . and sectes, *—CRNM.*

**are ye not carnal, and walk as men?:** . . . is it not evident that you are carnal, *—CNBR* . . . you are unspiritual, *—WEYM* . . . conducting yourselves like men? *—FNTN* . . . walking after the manner of men? *—HNT* . . . behaving like worldlings, *—MNTG* . . . like ordinary men? *—MOFT.*

**3:3.** This verse explains what is meant by the previous two verses. The meaning of the word "carnal" in verse 1 is different from the word "carnal" in this verse. The first word means "fleshy" or fleshly and one *cannot* help it. The second means "fleshly" and one *will* not help it. They should have been bearing the fruit of the Spirit; instead they were producing the works of the flesh. This was particularly true as it applied to divisions in the Corinthian church. The divisions were not only bad; they proved these believers were immature. Their wrong attitudes, words, and actions proved their inclination toward natural, worldly living.

**4. For while one saith, I am of Paul; and another, I [am] of Apollos:**

**are ye not carnal?:** . . . can you deny, *—CNBR* . . . are you not mere men, *—CNFT* . . . you not merely man-followers? *—FNTN* . . . is not this the way men of the world speak? *—WEYM.*

**3:4.** With strong words Paul attacked this specific arm of the problem. He denounced those in particular who followed him and Apollos. He might have done this to prove his own unworthiness; and he might have used Apollos because he was a close friend at Ephesus with him. Or these could have been the two strongest or the most quarrelsome parties. The question was intended to gain a positive answer.

5. **Who then is Paul, and who [is] Apollos: but ministers by whom ye believed:**...Servants are they, —*CNDT*...just God's servants, —*WEYM*...They are simply used by God to give you faith, —*MOFT*...We are simply God's servants, —*TEV*...Ministers through whom you believed, —*HNT*...through whose agency you came to accept, —*TCNT.*

**even as the Lord gave to every man?:**...The Lord gave each of us a job to do, —*SEB*...gave each his task, —*BRKL*...gave each of us his task, —*WLMS*...granted power to each, —*WEYM*...each endowed as the Lord decided, —*FNTN*...only as the Lord appointed, —*ADAM.*

**3:5.** The mature laborer for Christ does not involve himself in party dissension. The men whom God uses for work in His kingdom are really servants called to bring men to belief in Christ. God had given each minister a particular work, ability, and ministry which He used with the Word to bring the Corinthians to salvation. The emphasis is on God. As John wrote in his Gospel concerning John the Baptist: "There was a man sent from God, whose name was John" (John 1:6).

Paul here asked the question, "Who then is Paul, and who is Apollos . . . ?" Although a response of "nothing" might be expected because they were merely human instruments of God, Paul did not say that. Indeed, Paul and Apollos were *diakonoi* ("servants" or "ministers"). Paul said in 2 Corinthians 4:5 that they were "your servants for Jesus' sake." Paul also used the word "steward" (*oikonomous*) to describe his ministry (4:1).

Here in 1 Corinthians the word *diakonos* is used only in the general sense of servant (and probably not an exalted servant at that, since the word was also used of waiters!). By the time Paul had written the Pastoral Epistles, however, the word *diakonos* was a technical term denoting a specific function and office in the local church (cf. especially 1 Timothy 3:8-13).

Grammatically, the expression "and to each (*kai hekastō hōs*) as the Lord gave" could refer back to the verb "believed" (*episteusate*), meaning the Lord gave faith to each, but it is better to interpret the clause in terms of verse 7 suggesting that the Lord gave specific tasks to each servant to perform (such as planting, watering, etc.).

6. **I have planted, Apollos watered; but God gave the increase:**...apollo moistide, —*WCLF*...Apollos irrigates, —*CNDT*...watered the plant, —*TEV*...but

God prospered it, —*FNTN*...God caused to grow, —*RTHM*...made the growth, —*HNT*...produced the growth, —*MRDK*...made the seed grow, —*MOFT, —MNTG, —CNBR*...gave the crop, —*KLGS.*

**3:6.** Paul supported his point by way of illustration. He called attention to the illustration of a farmer or gardener. Paul had initiated the work; Apollos had strengthened and nurtured it. But these men had cooperated together under the direction of God, for it was God alone who gave the increase or harvest. The first two verbs of this verse are aorist and point to work already done. But God's activity is in the imperfect tense and indicates work continuing after a specific beginning.

7. **So then neither is he that planteth any thing:**...Consequently, the planter, —*FNTN*...nor the waterer counts for much, —*WLMS*...is of any importance, —*WEYM*...is not important, —*SEB.*

**neither he that watereth:**...the man who waters, —*TEV.*

**but God that giveth the increase:**...the only One who counts is God, —*ADAM.*

**3:7.** Divisions such as were occurring at Corinth should not be allowed because leaders and laborers are merely instruments. God accomplishes through them what He will. The Christian worker must maintain the humility, submission, and unity that come from understanding that all men work in the place to which God calls them, and all are important under God. God does not have "big" preachers or "small" preachers, just faithful preachers.

8. **Now he that planteth and he that watereth are one:**...so far from being rivals, —*WAY*...are for one thing, —*CNDT*...are one in aim, —*WLMS*...are nether better then the other, —*TNDL*...are equal, —*FNTN*...are on the same level, —*MOFT*...are on a par, —*MRDK*...are together, —*BECK*...work together, —*SEB.*

**and every man shall receive his own reward according to his own labour:**...and eche schal take his owne mede, —*WCLF*...each will receive his own special reward, —*WEYM*...his own pay, —*FNTN*...his own wage, —*MOFT*...his individual reward, —*HNT*...will be paid according to his work, —*KLGS*...his proper reward, according to his proper labor, —*CMPB*...according to his own service, —*MNTG.*

**3:8.** All ministers and laborers then are on an equal plane. The job does not make one person more important than another. All share a common goal. Therefore, the reward given to these co-workers will depend on their personal labor. The emphasis seems to be on the labor, not the success; on the faithfulness of the servant involved. If man does his part in the work of the gospel, God will certainly do His part.

**9. For we are labourers together with God:**...for we ben the helpers of god, −WCLF...joint laborers, −CMPB...fellow-laborers, −CNBR...are but labourers employed by God, −LOCK...in God's service, −MOFT.

**ye are God's husbandry, [ye are] God's building:**...You are God's farm, −FNTN...you are God's field, −WEYM...God's tillage, −HNSN...and God's edifice, −MRDK.

**3:9.** "We are laborers together with God"; that is, we are fellow workers who belong to God, and we are working with one another. The emphasis is on God. He is mentioned emphatically three times in this verse. We are, in keeping with the figures already suggested, God's "husbandry" and God's "building." "Husbandry" conveys the idea of cultivation, and "building" suggests the process of construction. God is cultivating and building the Church. God's possession then is in close view. If these Corinthians came to see God's proper place here then they would also come to see His minister's proper place. Without exception, the problems in the Church seem to be caused when we have a faulty view of God and His work. The problems would be resolved if we grasped His motive for doing something. To summarize, three things would be accomplished: The Corinthians (and we also) would come to a true view of human teachers, and would listen to them but not idolize them; we would not mistreat God's workers because they belong to God; and we would not mistreat ourselves because we belong to God.

**10. According to the grace of God which is given unto me, as a wise masterbuilder:**...In discharge of the task...God graciously entrusted to me, −WEYM...In virtue of my commission, −MOFT...By virtue of God's grace granted me, −HNT...having been imparted to me, −WLSN...as a wise maister carpenter, −WCLF...as a wise foreman, −CNDT...as a wyse bylder, −TNDL...as a skilful master builder, −GNVA...like a skilful architect, −FNTN.

**I have laid the foundation, and another buildeth thereon:**...and another bildith aboue, −WCLF...another is now carrying on the structure, −WAY.

**But let every man take heed how he buildeth thereupon:**...let him be careful how, −MOFT...take care how, −FNTN.

**3:10.** So then man as a colaborer with God builds for Him. Paul as a master builder, architect, and superintendent, had skillfully laid a foundation. Paul guards against usurping divine glory, for he indicates that his wise building was due to the grace of God and not his own abilities. In his comment on this verse Matthew Henry says, "It is no crime in a Christian, but much to his commendation, to take notice of the good that is in him, to the praise of divine grace" (6:3:10).

**11. For other foundation can no man lay than that is laid:**...The foundation is already laid, −MNTG. **which is Jesus Christ:**

**3:11.** But those who follow must be careful as to what they build on top of this wise foundation. In this chapter Paul introduced three classes of builders: (1) Those who are truly wise; (2) those who are unwise and introduce wrong material but do not leave the foundation; and (3) those who are fools and try to destroy God's temple. Paul acknowledged other builders besides himself, but he acknowledged no foundation other than Jesus Christ. Everything must be built on the person and doctrine of Christ. In an absolute sense, there can be no other foundation.

**12. Now if any man build upon this foundation:**...is erecting on that foundation, −WEYM. **gold, silver, precious stones, wood, hay, stubble:**...costly stones...straw, −FNTN...grass, −CNDT...reeds, −HNSN...tymber, −TNDL.

**3:12.** In building, men use different materials. Paul listed at least two categories of materials—good and bad. But he also set the stage for his next figure, fire, by listing three incombustible and three combustible types of material. These materials have been said to refer to one of three areas: (1) Different sorts of persons in the Church; (2) moral fruits; and (3) doctrines of the different teachers. It seems difficult and impractical to distinguish so finely among the three suggestions, since they have a relationship with one another. There is, however, some emphasis on speculative, curious doctrine versus solid doctrine. At this point one thing is certain, the emphasis is on *what* is done, not *how* it is done. In the process of building the work of Christ it is essential that the best materials be used because the work will be exposed and evaluated.

**13. Every man's work shall be made manifest:**...the true character of each individual's work, −WEYM...the nature of his work will come out, −MOFT...shall be disclosed, −HNT...become apparent, −CNDT.

**for the day shall declare it, because it shall be revealed by fire:**...the day of the Lord will declare it, −CNFT...will disclose it, −WEYM...will make it plain, −HNT...will make it evident, −CNDT.

**and the fire shall try every man's work of what sort it is:**...the fire itself will test, −RTHM...the fire will prove, −FNTN...will test each man's sort of work, −HNT...will assay the quality of everyone's work, −CNFT...what kind it is, −CNDT.

**3:13.** Whatever is built will be tested. God uses the process of accountability. This verse clearly teaches there will be a definite judgment of

Christians' works. This does not refer to salvation but to rewards. Paul is referring to the Bema judgment and the judging of believers for their service to God. This is a purging fire. The intent of the fire is to prove the value and good of the item tested. Sadly, some of the work will not stand the test of God's examination; it will be shown to be useless and without value and will be destroyed.

**14. If any man's work abide which he hath built thereupon:** . . . If one man's work stands, −*FNTN* . . . structure raised by any man survives, −*MOFT*, −*HNT* . . . stands the test, −*WEYM*.

**he shall receive a reward:**

**15. If any man's work shall be burned, he shall suffer loss:** . . . he shal suffer detriment, −*RHEM* . . . he will forfeit it, −*CNDT* . . . He shall be a loser, −*HNT*.

**but he himself shall be saved:** . . . yet he will himself be rescued, −*WEYM* . . . he will be snatched, −*MOFT*.

**yet so as by fire:** . . . but in this wayas through fire, −*RTHM* . . . by passing through the fire, −*WEYM* . . . from the very flames, −*MOFT*.

**3:14, 15.** On the basis of the test, the builder will receive his reward. If his service has stood the fire of judgment, he will receive his honest and just reward. But what is built must be of the strongest materials to withstand the fire. "By fire" is proverbial for a hairbreadth escape; a very close, perilous, narrow escape, not necessarily without injury. The figure is slightly different from that in verse 13.

Note that the reward is conditional. If a man builds with the wrong materials, he will lose his reward but still retain eternal life. Apparently some built with the wrong materials on the right foundation. The verb *zemiōthēsetai* is capable of several translations, but the best way to understand the word is that the servant who uses faulty materials "will miss the reward he might have had" (Barrett, *Harper's New Testament Commentaries*, p. 89). It must be said, however, that there appears to be a very fine line between the foolish builder of verse 15 and the one destroyed of verse 17. It is certainly a solemn warning to all who labor for the Lord, to be very careful not to be enticed by fads and doctrines that are only half true.

**16. Know ye not that ye are the temple of God:** . . . Are ye not ware that, −*TNDL* . . . Are you not aware, −*CNDT* . . . you are a Divine temple, −*FNTN* . . . you are God's Sanctuary, −*WEYM*.

**and [that] the Spirit of God dwelleth in you?:** . . . wherein God's Spirit dwells, −*CNBR* . . . lives in you, −*FNTN*, −*BECK* . . . has His home within you? −*WEYM* . . . has His permanent home in you? −*WLMS*.

**3:16.** The reason for the mason's care is that this "building" is God's temple, the habitation of God's Spirit. This carries a collective meaning. The

thought regarding the individual is better indicated in 6:19, 20. "Know ye not" suggests something the Corinthians should have remembered but had forgotten. The "temple" (the word used here suggests especially the structure containing the Holy Place and the Holy of Holies) was the noblest of buildings, for it was consecrated to the highest purposes—seeking and worshiping Almighty God.

**17. If any man defile the temple of God, him shall God destroy:** . . . If any one corrupts, −*FNTN*, −*KLGS* . . . If any man ruin, −*CNBR*, −*BRKL* . . . is marring, −*RTHM* . . . defaceth, −*NOYS* . . . if anyone destroys God's temple, −*TEV* . . . corrupt the sanctuary, −*PNT*, −*PNIN* . . . violate the temple, −*DOUY* . . . him will God mar, −*WEYM* . . . will bring him to ruin, −*NORL* . . . will waste him away, −*FNTN*.

**for the temple of God is holy, which [temple] ye are:** . . . for God's temple is hallowed, −*WAY* . . . for God's temple is sacred, −*MOFT*, −*WLMS* . . . and you yourselves are his temple, −*TEV*.

**3:17.** The man who would destroy this building, then, would reap the most terrible of punishments. Actions are joined together here. The reason this man would be destroyed is that he attempted to destroy "the temple of God." No man may touch the Church in this way without paying for it. God will not allow evil to taint His possession, for He is holy and His own must be holy. In spite of her failures and weaknesses, the Church is blessed with great glory. She is precious in the sight of her God and protector.

Some object to the translation of *phtheirei* as "destroy" since the word elsewhere can mean "corrupt" or "spoil." It is true, on the one hand, that even the gates of hell cannot overcome the Church (Matthew 16:18), yet Paul here is speaking of a local church which has been beset by bitter factions. Nothing can destroy a local church like divisiveness. It is precisely because the church at Corinth was in such danger that Paul wrote so emphatically. Furthermore, we read in Revelation that God himself will bring judgment to any church which does not repent or is lukewarm (Revelation 2:5; 3:16).

**18. Let no man deceive himself:** . . . Let no one fool himself, −*BRKL*, −*SEB* . . . Make no mistake about it, −*JB* . . . No one should fool himself, −*TEV* . . . be deluding himself, −*CNDT* . . . beguile himself, −*HNT*.

**If any man among you seemeth to be wise in this world:** . . . imagines he is wise, −*RTHM*, −*WEYM*, −*MOFT* . . . imagines that, in regard to the present, he ranks among you as a wise man, −*TCNT* . . . is presuming, −*CNDT* . . . to be wise in this age, −*KLGS* . . . in the ordinary sense of the word, −*JB* . . . wise by this world's standards, −*SEB*, −*TEV*.

**let him become a fool, that he may be wise:** ...in order to be truly wise, —NORL...in order to be really wise, —TEV...to become really wise, —BECK.

**3:18.** Since so much emphasis must be placed on God, then man must take his proper place. To believe oneself to be wise is really dangerous self-deception. The word "seemeth" is better translated "thinketh." This is an obvious reference to those who thought themselves wise, attaching themselves to a certain teacher. The source of such self-deceit is pride. The antidote to such pride is humility which fosters a dependence on a higher source. A man cannot be wise in both the "world" (verse 19) and the Church. The world thinks Christian thinking and wisdom is foolish, and there is much that the world considers acceptable which is not acceptable to the Church. At the heart of wisdom is the Cross. Either a man will despise it or cling to it. If he holds to it, he will gain much. If he despises it, he will lose everything.

As God looks at man's wisdom from the viewpoint of its inability to discover and obtain salvation, He considers it utter nonsense. It has no value. This world has a tendency to consider symptoms and build elaborate systems on them. God looks at root causes.

**19. For the wisdom of this world is foolishness with God:** ... For God ranks this world's wisdom, —MOFT...this world's wisdom to be foolish, —BECK...is folly compared to God, —FNTN...is mere nonsense to God, —WLMS...in God's estimation, —BRKL...in God's sight, —WEYM, —WAY.
**For it is written, He taketh the wise in their own craftiness:** ... He catcheth the wyse, —GNVA...He seizes, —MOFT...He catches the philosophers in their own craft, —FNTN...He snares the wise with their own cunning, —WEYM...in their subteltie, —RHEM.

**3:19.** God considers the wisdom of the world to be "foolishness." More than that, God proves it is foolish. He intervenes and brings it to nothing. How is this proved? Look at the Scriptures. Paul quoted first from Job 5:13. It is more of a summary than an exact quotation. The words were spoken by Eliphaz, who applied them inaccurately. The apostle did not refer to the application, but used the words themselves, which concerning God are true. God catches the crafty and exposes them. They are brought face-to-face with the fact that His wisdom totally surpasses theirs. He can so expose the faulty roots of a person's thinking that it is seen to be deceit and trickery.

**20. And again, The Lord knoweth the thoughts of the wise, that they are vain:** ... takes note of the speculations of the wise, —RTHM ... the reasonings, —CNDT, —MOFT ... the cogitations of the

wise, —RHEM ... the designs of the wise are futile, —HNT ... they are empty, —FNTN ... how useless they are, —WEYM.

**3:20.** Paul also quoted from Psalm 94:11 with minor changes. But the thought is clear. The idea is of total knowledge. No thought, not even the most secret, is hidden from God. This is part of the reason the Lord can intervene in the plans of men. He knows their thoughts from the very beginning.

**21. Therefore let no man glory in men:** ...about his human teachers, —WEYM.
**For all things are yours:** ... Everything belongs to you, —SEB.

**3:21.** "Let no man glory in" or boast of other men or himself. The creation must not be elevated above the Creator. In reality, Paul was not so much arguing against the lifting up of men as he was presenting the idea that these Corinthians were limiting themselves. Why should they listen to only one teacher, when all the teachers in their different aspects were given to benefit the Church?

**22. Whether Paul, or Apollos, or Cephas:** ...or a ritual, —FNTN.
**or the world, or life, or death, or things present, or things to come:** ...or that which is impending, —CNDT.
**all are yours:** ... everything belongs to you, —WEYM...all belongs to you, —MOFT.
**23. And ye are Christ's; and Christ [is] God's:**

**3:22, 23.** Paul did not stop here. He enlarged the circle to include things of special interest to this particular church. The first group consisted of Christian ministers and teachers. There was Paul with his logical, anointed, and singular ministry. There was Apollos with his brilliant rhetoric. There was Peter with his fond memories of personal acquaintance with Christ on earth. Why should the Corinthians not appreciate all that was given by God.

The second group consisted of the world, life, and death. "World" refers to the ordered universe, "life" to the spiritual life in Christ (Philippians 1:21), and "death" to that painful obstacle which has become a servant through Jesus Christ.

The last group, "things present" and "things to come," included not only present blessings, but an array of yet unknown blessings. At the end Paul placed the foundation. We are laid at the feet of Christ. We are the stewards of certain riches, and we are possessions of Jesus Christ. Paul returns the reader to the idea of Christ's mastery. Our subordination to Christ is given a supreme example in Christ's subordination to God. Paul was taking nothing away from the deity of Christ, but was speaking of His office and mission.

## Chapter 4

1. **Let a man so account of us, as of the ministers of Christ:** . . . Let a man regard us, —FNTN . . . let any one take this view of us —WEYM . . . esteeme vs, —RHEM . . . as deputies of, —CNDT . . . as officers of Christ, —RTHM.

**and stewards of the mysteries of God:** . . . and administrators, —FNTN . . . and the dispensers, —RHEM . . . and disposers of the secretes of God, —TNDL . . . of God's secret truths, —MOFT.

**4:1.** To us then, who are servants of Christ, comes the designation of stewardship. This is the practical outcome of unity, wisdom, and service. Paul was a "minister of Christ." While he might be too highly valued by some of the Corinthians, nevertheless, he was a minister and should not be considered too lightly. A balance is needed. Ministers are not lords, but their stewardship deserves respect.

2. **Moreover it is required in stewards, that a man be found faithful:** . . . in this matter of stewardship, —HNT . . . to prove each one's fidelity to his trust, —WAY . . . that a man be founden trewe, —WCLF . . . fidelity is what is required, —WEYM . . . they must be trustworthy, —MOFT.

**4:2.** It is required in the very nature of such a man that he be faithful to his work. As he had been doing, Paul reproved the pride and disunity of the Corinthians by indicating that ultimately the test of a steward is not his "ability" but his faithfulness. A steward is expected to act in the interest of his master, not in his own interest. Such is the requirement of all stewards, not just some, because sometime their faithfulness will be judged. A steward is not always closely supervised, but he is always expected to work diligently.

3. **But with me it is a very small thing that I should be judged of you, or of man's judgment:** . . . it is a light matter, —MRDK . . . of perfect indifference to me, —WAY . . . of very little importance, —WLSN . . . it is quite indifferent whether I am criticised by you, —FNTN . . . undergoing your scrutiny, —WEYM . . . I should be cross-questioned by you or by any human court, —HNT . . . or by a human tribunal, —NOYS.

**yea, I judge not mine own self:** . . . I do not even scrutinize myself, —WEYM . . . I do not even cross-question myself, —MOFT . . . do I criticise my own self, —FNTN.

**4:3.** Lest the Corinthians get the idea from 3:22 that they could judge these stewards, Paul added that neither they nor any other steward could judge another man's fidelity. In fact, not even Paul's own conscience was the final judge. Paul

was not rejecting the place of conscience. He was simply comparing inferior with superior. Nor was he rejecting the importance of other men's ideas and opinions. But men are often fickle and prejudiced in their examination, and a man may find it difficult to be objective and honest with himself.

4. **For I know nothing by myself:** . . . I am conscious to myself of no fault, —CMPB . . . though I am conscious of nothing against myself, —HNT.

**yet am I not hereby justified:** . . . not in this am I declared righteous, —RTHM . . . am I cleared of blame, —NOYS . . . I am not acquitted on account of that, —FNTN . . . that does not clear me, —HNT . . . not for that reason stand acquitted, —WEYM.

**but he that judgeth me is the Lord:** . . . He Who is examining me, —CNDT.

**4:4.** The Scriptures advise heart searching, but there is such a thing as too much self-examination. As far as Paul knew he had done his best and therefore knew no reason for condemnation. But he freely admitted his knowledge was limited. He that judges is the Master, the Lord himself. Paul was justified on the basis of Christ's righteousness. As Titus 3:5-8 indicates, this was the basis of his whole stand before God.

Good conscience is fine, but it cannot be relied on apart from the verdict of the Lord. The appraisal at the end will come from Him who justified at the beginning. Therefore, for the present, Paul left to Christ the testing of his actions, which Christ is doing for every believer in preparation for the judgment described in 3:11-15. At this point in time the criticism and the praise must rest with the Master Paul served.

5. **Therefore judge nothing before the time, until the Lord come:** . . . So make no hasty judgment, —MNTG . . . do not risk any premature judgment, —WAY . . . form no premature judgements, —WEYM . . . judge nothing hastily, until the coming of the Lord, —CNBR.

**who both will bring to light the hidden things of darkness:** . . . who will pour light upon, —MRDK . . . also illuminate the hidden, —CNDT . . . the secrets of darkness, —WLSN . . . the concealments of darkness, —FNTN.

**and will make manifest the counsels of the hearts:** . . . will openly disclose the motives, —WEYM . . . lay open the counsels of, —CMPB . . . bring to the light the plans people have in their hearts, —BECK . . . the purposes of men's hearts, —MNTG.

**and then shall every man have praise of God:** . . . then applause will be coming, —CNDT . . . then shall the due praise be awarded, —WAY . . . then the commendation will come, —FNTN . . . experience his due approval from God, —BRKL.

**4:5.** In 3:13 and 15 Paul made his readers aware that there would be a judging at the Bema, the judgment seat of Christ. Now in 4:5 Paul reinforced this by saying that all judging would be at the time (*kairou*) when the Lord comes. *Kairou* is one of two Greek words for time, and this word always has in mind that critical, crucial moment of time when one's personal destiny is decided (cf. Luke 12:56). When we arrive at this natural conclusion, we must understand that Paul was not forbidding examination, but was objecting to the proud judgment of teachers and the usurping of Christ's position. Only Christ can judge correctly because only He can see the unknown, the secret, the hidden things. The apostle Paul put all human judgments into proper perspective by telling the Corinthians that the only judgment that matters to believers is Christ's decisions at the Bema judgment. Frequently the Holy Spirit guided Paul to provide information concerning future judgment. In 6:3 he said that we would later judge the angels. Even the reference in 11:26 to drinking the cup of the Lord's Supper until He comes again is in the context of judgment, because the Corinthians were in danger of drinking damnation to themselves by not discerning the body of Christ (11:17-34, especially 11:29). The Lord will make manifest the counsels and purposes of the heart. "Counsels" is neuter, indicating good or evil. Each one shall then receive his due praise from God.

**6. And these things, brethren, I have in a figure transferred to myself and [to] Apollos for your sakes:** . . . In writing this much, *—WEYM* . . . I haue figuratiuely described, *—GNVA* . . . I have figuratively applied to myself, *—CMPB, —HNSN* . . . for an en-sample described in myne awne person, *—CRNM.*

**that ye might learn in us not to think [of men] above that which is written:** . . . so that from our case you might learn, *—HNT* . . . learn from our example, *—SEB* . . . might learn the lesson, *—WLMS* . . . learn not to assume a rivalry between us, *—WAY.*

**that no one of you be puffed up for one against another:** . . . Don't be more proud of one person, *—SEB* . . . be puffed up with rivalry, *—MOFT* . . . may not be arrogantly for one teacher against the other, *—BRKL* . . . brag about one man at the expense of another, *—BECK* . . . in favor of one teacher against another, *—WLMS* . . . exalt himself in comparison with his fellow, *—MRDK.*

**4:6.** Paul used a literary figure to apply what he had just said to Apollos and himself. The example was intended to help the Corinthians quell their pride and teach them not to exalt men unduly. "That which is written" refers to Scripture. Paul made this general reference to Scripture so that through this example the Corinthians would learn the subordination of man. The Bible exalts God. The Corinthians were exalting man.

What was even more damaging, not only were they exalting man instead of God, they were apparently also exalting their own traditions as equal to or better than the Scriptures. Literally, the Greek reads that "you may learn not above what is written," meaning that no human tradition or view can be placed above Scripture.

Paul dealt with this issue from many angles, going ever deeper until he had considered all aspects and came to the heart of the matter.

In this spirit of pride the Corinthians had made judgments on their teachers, and in adhering to one had really denounced and rejected the others. For that reason they were unbalanced; they were lacking part of the wisdom and counsel of God. Pride is a deadly sin. For that reason Paul attacked it from every side until he had fully exposed and dealt with the sin.

**7. For who maketh thee to differ [from another]?:** . . . For who distinguisheth thee? *—DOUY* . . . Who singles you out? *—MOFT, —HNT* . . . who is discriminating between, *—CNDT* . . . who gives you your superiority, *—WEYM.*

**and what hast thou that thou didst not receive?:** . . . been given you, *—MOFT.*

**now if thou didst receive [it]:** . . . But if you got it from someone, *—WLMS.*

**why dost thou glory, as if thou hadst not received [it]?:** . . . as if it hadn't been given to you? *—BECK.*

**4:7.** With three rhetorical questions Paul attacked the problem. The first question dealt with the fact that some of the Corinthians considered themselves superior in some way. Paul asserted that this personal conceit was presumptuous. The question demanded an answer that cut away at pride. The second question really answered the first. The Corinthians had received all they had from God. He was their sole supply. They had no right to boast and think they had obtained their position by their own hand. The third question went a step further. They could not boast as if they had not been given what they had; in so doing, they were glorifying themselves. It was a terrible response to a gracious God.

**8. Now ye are full, now ye are rich:** . . . you are wealthy, *—FNTN* . . . you are already enriched! *—WLSN* . . . have all your heart's desire, *—MOFT.*

**ye have reigned as kings without us:** . . . have reigned like princes, *—LOCK* . . . you have ascended your thrones! *—WEYM.*

**and I would to God ye did reign, that we also might reign with you:** . . . I too might share your royalty! *—WAY* . . . might have jointly become kings, *—RTHM.*

**4:8.** Paul painted a darker picture with each stroke of his brush. "Full" and "rich" denote the sense of satisfaction and attainment the

Corinthians felt. Thinking they had come to some ultimate plateau, to some superior spiritual level, they did not think they needed the apostles and believed them unnecessary. After all, their accomplishments had come from their own hands.

Luther commented: "Paul mocks them, for he means the opposite of what he says" (cited in Lenski, p. 179).

The truth is they had not attained. They were really spiritually weak when they thought themselves strong. They were foolish when they thought themselves very wise. Paul wished they had attained, that they were mature.

**9. For I think that God hath set forth us the apostles last:** . . . For I fancy God has exposed us, –FNTN . . . hath appoynted vs, –GNVA . . . God demonstrates with us, –CNDT . . . has exhibited us as apostles, –HNT, –RTHM . . . has exhibited us apostles last of all, –WEYM . . . for the lowest of all, –TNDL.

**as it were appointed to death:** . . . like the doomed gladiators in the arena! –MOFT . . . like criminals condemned to die, –CNBR . . . doomed to death, –HNT.

**for we are made a spectacle unto the world, and to angels, and to men:** . . . became a theater, –CNDT . . . we are a gasynge-stocke, –TNDL . . . we may become an exhibition, –FNTN . . . to all creation, –WEYM.

**4:9.** Paul established the position of the apostles and himself quickly, and it was far from what the Corinthians imagined it to be. It seemed as though the apostles were last in line and like men "appointed to death." In Paul's time criminals condemned to death were exhibited to amuse the crowds in the amphitheater. They were then brought to the arena to fight wild beasts; they did not leave the arena alive. More than one Christian faced unfair martyrdom in the arena, hearing the insults, the ridicule, the mockery, the slander. As men in the arena were exhibited to the crowds, so the apostles were exhibited to "the world," "to angels," which in comparison to men are not specifically noted as good or bad, and "to men" which might include good and bad.

Unlike what the Corinthians thought, Christian responsibility is not a "joyride." It is not attaining worldly success and involving oneself in the drive for the top and then sitting back and enjoying the world's applause and approval. The world does not like the Christian. The world does not like those who lead the vanguard toward spiritual heights. The apostles, as do all true spiritual leaders, suffered for their stand; they knew the pain of responsibility and the burden of continuing on when men did not speak well of them.

**10. We [are] fools for Christ's sake, but ye [are] wise in Christ:** . . . we are labelled as "foolish": . . . you . . . are men of shrewd intelligence, –WEYM . . . you in Christ are sensible, –MOFT . . . but you are quite philosophic in Christ, –MNTG . . . prudent in Christ, –RTHM.

**we [are] weak, but ye [are] strong:** . . . we are feeblebut you mighty, –FNTN.

**ye [are] honourable, but we [are] despised:** . . . You are glorious, –CNDT . . . you are illustrious, we unhonoured, –HNT . . . but we in contempt, –FNTN . . . we are in disrepute, –MOFT . . . we are outcasts, –WEYM.

**4:10.** Next Paul specifically compared the apostles and the Corinthians. The contrast of "we" and "ye" is important. The opinion of the world was that the apostles were fanatical and foolish. Meanwhile, the Corinthians were supposed to be wise. "In Christ" the Corinthians really were wise, but they were building on the wisdom of the world, which Paul had already refuted. "For Christ" and "in Christ" carry a shade of distinction and meaning which shows the depth of the apostles' work. The world may have given some honor to this church because it desired it and had gone after it, but the apostles preached only Christ and so received dishonor from the world.

**11. Even unto this present hour we both hunger, and thirst:**

**and are naked, and are buffeted, and have no certain dwellingplace:** . . . with scanty clothing, –WEYM . . . are ill-dad and knocked about, –MOFT . . . are stripped and flogged, and homeless, –FNTN . . . and are boffetted with fistes, –TNDL . . . we are victims of mob-violence, –WAY . . . and we ben vnstable, –WCLF . . . and are wanderers, –RTHM . . . and have no fixed abode, –CNFT.

**12. And labour, working with our own hands:** . . . work hard for our living, –MOFT . . . and toil, –RTHM . . . at our own expense, –FNTN.

**being reviled, we bless:**

**being persecuted, we suffer it:** . . . we bear it patiently, –WEYM.

**4:11, 12.** The list of difficulties continues. The apostles were enduring trials for the gospel even to the moment of writing. Paul may be reminded of what he was undergoing at Ephesus. They were enduring many privations.

There is here little of the philosophy that Christians will always receive the best of this world here and now. As far as this world was concerned, Paul had little or nothing, and he supported himself by work that was exhausting. Again, this was for Christ and His church. To the Greeks, manual labor was low and insulting and debasing to those who did it. To the Greeks, life was in philosophical speculation, not in the work that produced dirt under the fingernails. That was beneath them.

**13. Being defamed, we entreat:** . . . We are evyll spoken of, and we praye, —TNDL . . . we are blasphemed, —RHEM . . . we give consolation, —FNTN . . . we try to conciliate, —MOFT.

**we are made as the filth of the world, [and are] the offscouring of all things unto this day:** . . . we are made the refuse of, —RHEM . . . as the mere dirt and filth . . . even to this hour, —WEYM . . . refused by alleven until now! —FNTN . . . the scum of all things hitherto, —CNDT . . . as the scum of the earth, the very refuse, —MOFT.

**4:13.** But the picture is not quite finished. They were regarded as "filth" and "offscouring." "Filth" refers to the rubbish heap or litter gathered when one cleans. "Offscouring" is what is removed by scouring a filthy object. Beyond this Paul did not or could not go. Again the present and continuous is indicated by "unto this day" (even until now).

All of this is in opposition to the self-assertive spirit of the world and the self-sufficient, self-possessed spirit of the Corinthians. Paul and other men had sacrificed everything for Jesus, that the plan of salvation might be made known to all men. There can hardly be a more significant comparison than the one just made by Paul. What is most obvious is not the difference in work or position, but the difference in spirit. The Corinthians were motivated by a selfish, get-all spirit; the apostles and messengers of the gospel were motivated by a selfless, give-all spirit.

**14. I write not these things to shame you:** . . . Not to confound you, —RHEM . . . Not to be abashing you, —CNDT.

**but as my beloved sons I warn [you]:** . . . but I am offering you advice as my dearly-loved children, —WEYM . . . as my moost dereworthe sones, —WCLF . . . I wish to correct you, —FNTN . . . to instruct you, —MOFT . . . I admonish you, —RHEM.

**4:14.** It was not Paul's aim to shame or embarrass the Corinthians. Rather, he wished to bring them to reason, to give them counsel, to make them understand their true position in Christ and the world and how foolish their pride and bigotry were. That is a painful lesson. Paul showed his deep feelings for them by calling them his "beloved sons." Their wrong actions and attitudes touched Paul deeply.

**15. For though ye have ten thousand instructors in Christ:** . . . though perchance myriads of tutors, —RTHM . . . escorts in Christ, —CNDT.

**yet [have ye] not many fathers:**

**for in Christ Jesus I have begotten you through the gospel:** . . . I fathered you in Christ, —SEB . . . begotten you by preaching, —MRDK.

**4:15.** Paul had been strongly aroused by the Corinthians' behavior, yet the rebuke of verse 14

was mild. This verse helps explain why. The Corinthian believers had had many "instructors" or "tutors," that is, nurses or governors. "Ten thousand" may well be a hyperbole, but it emphasized Paul's point. Paul laid claim to the right to especially admonish and to be especially heeded because, unlike these other instructors, he was their spiritual father. Why did he claim this? He was the one who first brought the gospel to Corinth. It was through him by Christ that the Corinthian church was founded, and by his preaching many of the converts there first met Christ. Spiritual fatherhood carries with it a solemn obligation, and Paul was fulfilling that by correcting the Corinthians and by admonishing them to godly living.

**16. Wherefore I beseech you, be ye followers of me:** . . . Then imitate me, I beg of you, —MOFT . . . I plead with you, —NORL . . . I advise you, —FNTN . . . I urge you, —BECK . . . I entreat you therefore to become like me, —WEYM . . . make it your habit to follow my example, —WLMS . . . to copy my example, —TCNT . . . imitate my example, —MNTG.

**17. For this cause have I sent unto you Timotheus:** . . . For this reason, —WEYM.

**who is my beloved son, and faithful in the Lord:** . . . who is my deerest sonne, —RHEM . . . faithful child in the Lord, —NORL . . . in the Master's service, —TCNT.

**who shall bring you into remembrance of my ways which be in Christ:** . . . might bring to your recollection, —MRDK . . . remind you of my principles, —BRKL . . . remind you of my habits as a Christian, —WEYM . . . will call to your minds my methods in the work, —WLMS.

**as I teach every where in every church:** . . . in all Congregations, —GNVA . . . in every Community, —HNT . . . in every assembly, —FNTN.

**4:16, 17.** Paul continued the father-child figure by urging that as a child follows a father so they should follow him. It is a mark of Paul's deeply spiritual life that he could ask the Corinthians to imitate his example. We must set limitations, though, and say that Paul meant his example in Christ Jesus. This would not stir up divisions again. It was one thing to say "I am of Paul," and quite another to follow in Paul's steps as he pointed to the Master.

Because he had so much concern for the welfare of the Corinthians, Paul had sent Timothy to admonish and encourage them in the Lord. When Paul said that he had sent Timothy, the aorist verb (*epempsa*) is not used in its usual past sense but is an "epistolary aorist" meaning that by the time they receive the letter Timothy will have been sent (thus removing any apparent inconsistency with 16:10). Timothy was on his way, traveling by land before Paul wrote his first epistle to the Corinthians, but the letter, traveling by sea, would arrive first. We have a small profile on Timothy here. He was like a son, greatly loved by Paul. It may be Paul had a part in bringing Timothy to Christ. Certainly he influenced his spiritual maturation, and Timothy was a faithful Christian, true to his calling.

Timothy's purpose was to remind the Corinthians of Paul's actions and teachings in Christ. It is difficult to say exactly how this was to happen, but perhaps it would be by Timothy's teaching and life. In doing this, Paul was being very fair, for his life and doctrine remained constant—they began in Christ and ended there. He did not teach a different message according to the crowd, but everywhere proclaimed the same things.

Paul was consistently building the Church. He did it by consistent teaching; he did it by consistent living; he did it by preparing others such as Timothy, training and adding to their responsibility, and then sending them out to carry on the work to which he had given so much.

18. **Now some are puffed up, as though I would not come to you:** . . . Some, I hear, are elated, —TCNT . . . are acting proud, —SEB . . . have been filled with arrogance, —CNBR . . . have grown inflated with pride, —BRKL . . . may be elated at my failing to come to you, —FNTN . . . insinuating that I dare not come to you, —WAY . . . I would not [dare] come to you, —MRDK.

19. **But I will come to you shortly, if the Lord will:** . . . I shall come to you without delay, —WEYM . . . to you swiftly, —CNDT . . . to you before long, —MOFT . . . if the Lord wants me to, —BECK . . . will permit, —FNTN.
**and will know, not the speech of them which are puffed up, but the power:** . . . how great is their supernatural power, —WAY . . . I shall learn the power of those who are puffed up, —CNFT.

**4:18, 19.** Because Timothy had been sent and Paul had not come, some of the Corinthians had become proud and said Paul was afraid to face them. It may be they hoped he would not come, so they had convinced themselves that he would not. Paul set the record straight. He would come, provided the Lord so directed, which is all any servant can say. In coming, he would not be interested in their speeches but in their effectiveness, their power. Again we are reminded that the gospel is not mere theory, but practice, with power to make that practice effective. We are also reminded of the comparisons Paul made between words (1:17) and power (1:24), and between excellency of speech (2:1) and power (2:4).

20. **For the kingdom of God [is] not in word, but in power:** . . . the reign of God, —CMPB . . . For apostolic authority is not a thing of words, —WEYM . . . is not in talk, —FNTN . . . but in the miraculous operations of the Holy Ghost, —LOCK . . . For mighty deeds,

not empty words, are the tokens of God's kingdom, —CNBR.

**4:20.** This verse supplies the base for verse 19. The Corinthians must show God's power in their lives because the kingdom of God is not in word, but power and deed. Thus, Paul not only revealed the objective nature of the kingdom of God, but he also condemned pride. It is also interesting to note that in 2 Corinthians 13:1-10, Paul applied this same test to himself.

21. **What will ye? shall I come unto you with a rod:** . . . What are ye wishing? —RTHM . . . What do you want? —FNTN . . . What do you incline? —CMPB . . . Which shall it be? —WEYM . . . with a rod of discipline? —MOFT.
**or in love, and [in] the spirit of meekness?:** . . . with a loving and gentle spirit? —FNTN . . . in the sprete of softnesse? —CRNM . . . and the spirit of mildnes? —RHEM, —NOYS . . . and tender spirit? —WEYM . . . and gentleness, —MOFT.

**4:21.** The decision was left to the Corinthians. Paul had been stirred by what he had already written and by what he was about to write. But how he would come to them would be determined by their future actions. He could come with sharpness and discipline, albeit in love, or he could come in love and gentleness, with a special manifestation of his care and regard for them.

## Chapter 5

1. **It is reported commonly [that there is] fornication among you:** . . . There goeth a commen sayinge, —TNDL . . . it is absolutely notorious, —WAY . . . It is heard for a trueth, —GNVA . . . It is absolutely heard, —DOUY . . . It is actually reported that there is immorality among you, —MOFT . . . commonly reported there is depravity, —FNTN . . . that there is prostitution, —CNDT . . . is incest among you, —SAWR.
**and such fornication as is not so much as named among the Gentiles:** . . . such depravity, —FNTN . . . and of a kind unheard of, —WEYM . . . even among pagans, —MOFT.
**that one should have his father's wife:** . . . living in intercourse, —WAY.

**5:1.** Without preamble, Paul began the discussion of the next problem in the Corinthian church: indifference toward immorality. The case of incest was very serious, but Paul could not treat it until he had spoken to the problem of division (chapter 8). Church discipline could not be handled by a disunited church. Incest was an undoubted, talked-about fact. "Fornication" normally denotes participation with a harlot, but here Paul used it in the sense of general sexual misconduct. While incest was not entirely unknown among the Gentiles, Paul indicated that it was not common and definitely not condoned. Since it was so shameful, it was not even named or mentioned among them. Both Greek and Roman law stamped it with infamy, and Jewish law provided harsh penalties for this act.

The sin was between a man and his "father's wife." It has been suggested this refers to a stepmother, that the offender had seduced his stepmother, that she was divorced, or the father had died, leaving her a widow. Such specifics are not stated. We only know this disgraceful union had been established and, as "should have" tells us, it was a continued relationship. Its existence reflected a weak church needing restoration.

2. **And ye are puffed up:** ... you are self elated! —FNTN ... are filled with self-complacency, —WEYM.
**and have not rather mourned, that he that hath done this deed might be taken away from among you:** ... instead of being crushed with grief, —WAY ... rather be sorrowfully indignant, —FNTN ... sitten down in grief, —MRDK ... instead of mourning and removing from among you the man who has done this thing, —MNTG ... Expel the perpetrator of such a crime, —MOFT ... expelling from your membership, —NORL ... the man who has behaved in this way, —SEB ... that wrought this work! —RTHM ... should be removed, —SAWR ... from your midst, —CNDT.

**5:2.** The reaction of the church had been sadly amiss. The Corinthians' pride had reached such a point that they considered themselves above the standard of God. Perhaps they considered themselves broad-minded. They were not sorrowful over their indifference and reproach; they were blinded to what should have been their response. Paul indicated that they should expel the sinner. The honor of God and the holiness of the Corinthian church were at stake.

The attitude of the Corinthian believers concerning this gross sin shows they still had a long way to go to rise above the wicked environment in which they lived. The city had become so notorious for its wickedness that its very name had become a symbol for the worst kind of immorality. Some scholars have deduced from the grammatical structure of the sentence that it was stated in the form of a question, but the situation was so gross it probably demanded a strong imperative from the apostle.

3. **For I verily, as absent in body, but present in spirit:**
**have judged already, as though I were present:** ... have decided already, —FNTN ... already passed sentence, —MNTG ... judged the one effecting this, —CNDT ... judged him who has so acted, —WEYM.
**[concerning] him that hath so done this deed:** ... him who thus perpetrated this thing, —RTHM, —MRDK ... who has consummated this crime, —WAY.

4. **In the name of our Lord Jesus Christ:** ... And my sentence is this, —MKNT.
**when ye are gathered together:** ... meet in solemn congregation, —WAY ... that you convene an assembly, —CNBR ... when you are all assembled, —WEYM ... call a meeting in the name of our Lord Jesus Christ, —NORL.
**and my spirit, with the power of our Lord Jesus Christ:** ... and yours agreeing together, —FNTN ... in conjunction with the power, —RTHM.

**5:3, 4.** Paul thought of himself as present "in spirit" and having characterized the man by his deed, Paul disciplined with authority. The verb is in the perfect, which adds an air of finality. By this Paul had in mind both the welfare of the sinner and the purity of the local church. "In the name of our Lord Jesus" is the opening for a solemn judicial sentence and tells us under what authority all proper church gatherings and administrations must operate.

"When ye are gathered together" is probably associated with "with the power of our Lord Jesus" and indicated this was not to be a minority meeting but the gathering of the whole church to perform a solemn act. Paul would be there "in spirit" heading the proceedings. If the Corinthians had called Paul's spirit and teachings to remembrance and followed them, this discussion would have been unnecessary. "With" suggests not only Christ's power and presence would be there, but also His cooperation. It must be noted that Paul did not try to make his presence and Christ's co-equal. The proceedings must be in Christ's authority and for His glory. His presence was necessary with Paul's spirit and the congregation, to make the sentence valid.

5. **To deliver such an one unto Satan for the destruction of the flesh:** ... I have consigned that individual, —MOFT ... to the perischynge of fleisch, —WCLF ... for the extermination, —CNDT ... for the destruction of his fleshly lusts, —CNBR ... for the destruction of his body, —WEYM ... to be physically disciplined, —NORL ... that he may blast the sinner's body, —WAY.
**that the spirit may be saved in the day of the Lord Jesus:**

**5:5.** The purpose of this judgment is discussed here. "Deliver ... unto Satan" may mean excommunication, or it may mean some physical affliction and spiritual visitation on the guilty. Those who support the first sometimes suggest that Paul had in mind the idea of letting the flesh go as far as it could in Satan's realm, and then the sinner would remember God's goodness and return. Those who support the second view remind us that physical maladies and even death are sometimes ascribed to Satan in the New Testament (Luke 13:16; John

8:44; 2 Corinthians 12:7; Hebrews 2:14), and sickness is sometimes the result of being withdrawn from the secure realm of fellowship with God. Affliction is often made an instrument of spiritual benefit (1 Corinthians 11:30-32; 2 Corinthians 4:16-18; 12:7; 1 Peter 4). The apostles did on occasion pronounce penal sentences in the physical realm (Acts 5:1-10; 13:1-12).

But we do know the intent of the sentence: to bring the offender back to Christ, that on the "day of the Lord," when every man's position shall be finalized, he would stand with the company of the redeemed. One note should be added. In this account Satan was pictured as subject to God, and it is clear that God will gain final glory in every situation. Satan's power is limited and must serve the purpose of God which is redemptive. Paul was faithful to keep his priorities straight in this matter in loving the sinful and preserving the Church.

**6. Your glorying [is] not good:** ... It isn't good for you to feel proud, *—BECK* ... Your pride is not noble, *—FNTN* ... not right that you boast about this case, *—NORL* ... in a leader who drew you into this scandalous indulgence, *—LOCK* ... Your boasting is no credit to you, *—MOFT* ... is not praiseworthy, *—MRDK* ... is discreditable, *—HNT.*
**Know ye not that a little leaven leaveneth the whole lump?:** ... a morsel of dough, *—MOFT* ... a lytle leven sowreth the whole lompe of dowe, *—TNDL* ... a little ferment ferments the whole mass? *—FNTN* ... a little yeast corrupts the whole of the dough? *—WEYM* ... the whole kneading? *—CNDT.*

**5:6.** Having given this situation attention, Paul returned to the root of the problem—pride. He plainly stated that the resultant boasting of the Corinthians was wrong. Strictly speaking, "glorying" suggests content, not action. What Paul was really upset about was what they were bragging about. Paul used the illustration of yeast. It takes only a little to cause bread to rise. The application was that both the church as a whole and the individual, in allowing evil, would in time corrupt the whole Christian community, collectively and individually.

**7. Purge out therefore the old leaven:** ... Clean out, *—ADAM* ... Cleanse out every trace of this old leaven, *—WAY* ... Houseclean the old yeast, *—KLGS.*
**that ye may be a new lump, as ye are unleavened:** ... as ye are swete bread, *—GNVA* ... may be an untainted mass, *—CNBR* ... you are free from corruption, *—WEYM* ... may be a fresh lump, *—MOFT.*
**For even Christ our passover is sacrificed for us:** ... for our passover also was slain, *—RTHM* ... our paschal lamb, *—MOFT, —CNBR* ... oure estherlambe is offered vp, *—TNDL.*

**5:7.** The command was to clean out the evil, probably meaning the pride and boasting, but also

the sin they had allowed to be practiced among them. With that Paul reminded them of another figure. Certain ceremonies preceded the eating of the Passover. For 7 days Israel ate unleavened bread, having removed the leaven from their homes on the first day. This was to remind them of the Exodus and the liberation from the bondage of Egypt. What the Israelites used on their journey was different from that used in Egypt. The application? Too much of the heathen lifestyle remained with the Corinthians. They should have been new, fresh, and free in Christ, and in order for that to happen they must remove the leaven.

The figure was expanded. Israel ate the unleavened bread after the Passover. Christ as the Paschal Lamb enables His people to remain unleavened. Believers are free from sins objectively and, subjectively, are called to walk in holiness, confessing and forsaking all known sin. Christ has made believers free from corruption, and Christians should not allow old "yeast" to reenter the "new lump."

**8. Therefore let us keep the feast, not with old leaven:** ... celebrate the festival, *—NORL* ... keep the unending feast, *—MNTG.*
**neither with the leaven of malice and wickedness; but with the unleavened [bread] of sincerity and truth:** ... leaven of wickedness and bitterness, *—MRDK* ... but with unfermented batches of purity, *—BRKL* ... the bread of transparent, *—WEYM* ... of innocence and integrity, *—MOFT.*

**5:8.** Paul exhorted the Corinthians to "keep the feast," not literally, but symbolically; not with the "leaven of malice and wickedness; but with the unleavened bread of sincerity and truth." "Let us keep" is present continuous and indicates a continued operation. "Malice" refers to an evil habit of the mind, and "wickedness" refers to the results of that mindset. Contrasted with it is purity of motive and purity of action. Purity must be retained in the Church. Christ is our example in this.

**9. I wrote unto you in an epistle not to company with fornicators:** ... I enjoined you, *—CNBR* ... in my letter, *—FNTN* ... you were not to associate, *—WEYM, —MNTG, —MKNT* ... to have no association, *—HNSN* ... not to mingle, *—PNIN* ... not to get mixed up with those who are sexually immoral, *—ADAM* ... not to be mixing yourselves up with fornicators, *—RTHM* ... be not medlid with leccherous, *—WCLF* ... to be commingling with paramours, *—CNDT* ... with licentious men, *—WAY* ... with the immoral, *—MOFT.*

**5:9.** This subject had apparently come up before. We do not have the epistle referred to, but it seems fornication was a problem with which the Corinthian church had repeated difficulty. The command had been to forbid social intimacy with those who were guilty of this sin.

**10. Yet not altogether with the fornicators of this world:** ... you are to keep wholly aloof, —WEYM ... not altogether meaning, —CLMT ... I was not referring to the licentious of the heathen world, —WAY.

**or with the covetous, or extortioners, or with idolaters:** ... nor of the avaricious, —MRDK ... or with the debauched, —FNTN ... or people who worship false gods, —SEB.

**for then must ye needs go out of the world:** ... to leave the world altogether, —MOFT, —MNTG.

**5:10.** Now, Paul discovered, a problem had arisen in an opposite direction. A misunderstanding had developed over the force and purpose of Paul's command, and now the Corinthians claimed a separation in a way that was impossible. Paul did not mean they should avoid contact with sinners in a general way; such absence of contact was impossible. Yet, Paul contended that in many circumstances the Corinthian Christians should not participate in the activities of those who did not obey the Lord. He listed, along with fornicators, the "covetous," those who are possessed by greed, "extortioners," who take what is not theirs (robbers in any form), and "idolaters" who worship the wrong things. The relationship of the Church to the world must be carefully balanced.

**11. But now I have written unto you not to keep company:** ... But my meaning was, —CNBR ... let me explain that, —ADAM ... I have set it down plainly at this time, —WAY ... not to be associated, —HNSN ... not to be associating with, —FNTN.

**if any man that is called a brother be a fornicator:** ... who calls himself a Christian, —BECK.

**or covetous, or an idolater, or a railer, or a drunkard, or an extortioner:** ... or a wanton, —CNBR ... a slanderer, —ADAM ... avarice or idol-worship or abusive language, —WEYM ... or debauchee ... or a blackguard ... or rapacious, —FNTN ... or a curser, —WCLF.

**with such an one no not to eat:** ... do not even sit at table, —MNTG ... do not even eat with him! —MOFT.

**5:11.** Paul made clear his meaning of "separation." The Corinthians could choose those with whom they formed close friendships and whether or not evil pervaded their fellowship. "I have written" allows a stronger possibility for meaning the present letter, but this is unnecessary. The kingdom of God is not of this world and cannot be carried out by worldly associations. It is preserved by the power of God. If one who professes himself a Christian is really involved in evil living he cannot be an intimate friend of a true believer. And to the list in verse 10 Paul added the "railer" who

abuses others, and the "drunkard," which speaks for itself.

"Not to eat," according to many, refers to ordinary meals and not to the Lord's Supper, although that too would be forbidden. The difficulty is that Jesus ate with sinners, and Paul, in 10:27, allows one to accept invitations to eat in heathen homes. The answer may be in comparison of "not to keep company" and "not to eat." The former may denote regular fellowship and the latter not so. Without numerous hotels, private hospitality was important. The main theme remains: There is to be no close fellowship with one who claims to be a Christian, but whose life belies that claim.

**12. For what have I to do to judge them also that are without?:** ... For what business have I, —MRDK ... It is none of my business to judge, —SEB.

**do not ye judge them that are within?:** ... judge people on the inside, —SEB.

**13. But them that are without God judgeth:** ... who are outside? —WEYM.

**Therefore put away from among yourselves that wicked person:** ... In conclusion, —NORL ... Throw out the profligate, —FNTN ... that bad man, —NOYS ... Remove the wicked man from among you, —WEYM ... Banish the wicked one from your midst, —HNT ... Expel the wicked from your company, —MOFT, —BRKL ... from your membership, —WLMS.

**5:12, 13.** Paul claimed no authority to judge sinners or those outside the Christian community. But the Church must guard and watch those inside the Church. God will judge those outside the Church. "Within" and "without" denoted in synagogue usage members and nonmembers of the sacred community (Nicoll, *Expositor's Greek Testament*, 2:813). The Corinthians' indifference toward impurity must be resolved. Verse 12 points to their responsibility, and verse 13 limits that responsibility.

The injunction was to remove the unrepentant offender because he was within the fold; he must be left to God's judgment. The purpose of this was to warn sinners of judgment and point them to the grace of God. But the injunction rises to the greater principle that the Church must continually examine itself and keep itself from all unrighteousness for Christ's sake, for the Church belongs to Him.

In verse 13 Paul summed up the two most important aspects of this section. First was the command to exclude the "wicked person" (the fornicator) from the church. This thought is true not only of fornicators, but of any who would defile the Church, because it is the body of Christ. Second, because the Church is the body of Christ, Paul changed the Old Testament quote (Deuteronomy 17:7) from the singular to the plural to emphasize that the entire church community was involved in this action.

## Chapter 6

**1. Dare any of you, having a matter against another:** . . . has a grievance against an opponent, —WEYM . . . an action, —FNTN . . . against his neighbor, —MOFT.

**go to law before the unjust:** . . . their private differences into the courts of law, —CNBR . . . before irreligious men, —WEYM . . . a sinful pagan court, —MOFT.
**and not before the saints?:**

**6:1.** The problem discussed in chapter 5 and that of lawsuits (6:1-8) are related because both result from a spirit of greed and a lack of church discipline. Paul opposed the taking of difficulties between Christians before pagan courts. To do so was a bad example and showed immaturity. Generally, as Romans 13 indicates, Paul's opinion of pagan magistrates was favorable. But here we are carried back to the arguments on wisdom and reminded that the Corinthians could not settle disputes because they did not heed the revelation of God to them.

"Not before the saints" indicates that it was not forbidden to seek justice. Law and order and an honest court are blessings from God. But the Corinthians were seeking the wrong advice and disputing petty matters. Paul never used the courts to accuse his opponents but in defense of his work.

**2. Do ye not know that the saints shall judge the world?:** . . . are you not aware, —CNDT . . . the saints are to manage the world? —MOFT.
**and if the world shall be judged by you:** . . . the world is subjected to your judgment, —CNBR.
**are ye unworthy to judge the smallest matters?:** . . . are you unworthy of the least tribunals, —CNDT . . . are you unfit to deal with these petty matters? —WEYM . . . are you incapable of the smallest arbitrations? —FNTN . . . are you incompetent to adjudicate upon trifles, —MOFT . . . to iudge small trifles? —CRNM.

**6:2.** Paul thought the Corinthians should know already that the saints will participate with Christ in judging the world. They will applaud His actions and just decisions. Paul intended to emphasize a dignity, privilege, and association beyond the idea even of Christian magistrates. It is a picture of Christ and His saints in session, with the world brought in before them for judgment. With this position awaiting, are you unable, Paul asked, to handle petty matters among yourselves? Can you not form a "court" to settle your own disputes? The Corinthian church had forgotten its glory and the honor of God. This was an insult to God's ability to impart wisdom and ability in

Christ. "Matters" actually denotes the rules and means of judging and thus means the court itself.

**3. Know ye not that we shall judge angels?:** . . . judge messengers, —RTHM.
**how much more things that pertain to this life?:** . . . let alone mundane issues, —MOFT . . . how much more secular things? —RHEM . . . not to mention life's affairs? —CNDT . . . then why not business matters? —FNTN.

**6:3.** The Holy Spirit inspired Paul to add an interesting fact, that the Church will judge angels. This is discussed elsewhere in such passages as 2 Peter 2:4, Jude 6, and Revelation 20:10, but details are not included there either. Therefore, a discussion of the details would only be conjecture. Paul's purpose was to pick something lofty and beyond this world. The Church would judge these. Why could it not, then, handle smaller, less exalted matters?

**4. If then ye have judgments of things pertaining to this life:** . . . have iudgementes of worldely matters, —TNDL . . . which need to be decided, —WEYM.
**set them to judge who are least esteemed in the church:** . . . let the parties contending choose arbitrators, —LOCK . . . who are of no account, —HNSN . . . who have been denied authority in the assembly? —FNTN . . . the most despised, —DOUY . . . the meanest member of your own church is good enough, —WAY.

**6:4.** The crucial issue here is, who are the "least esteemed (or count for nothing) in the church." The NIV takes *kathizete* as an imperative ("appoint as judges") making people within the church those who are least esteemed. It is much better, however, to take *kathizete* as an indicative and a question ("do you appoint as judges . . . ?") which makes secular judges the object of "least esteemed in the church." Nobody within the church counts for nothing!

Church matters should not be decided by secular judges. That would be foolish. But that is exactly what the Corinthians were allowing. By placing their cases before pagan judges, these men, who were less than the least in the church from a spiritual standpoint, had become their judges. We want the most competent judge that we can find for ourselves. The Corinthians were using the least competent. How foolish indeed!

**5. I speak to your shame:**
**Is it so, that there is not a wise man among you?:** . . . there is not an intelligent man, —FNTN . . . not a single wise man, —MOFT.
**no, not one that shall be able to judge between bis brethren?:** . . . capable of deciding, —MNTG . . . to adjudicate amidst his, —CNDT . . . competent to settle a case in his brother's matter? —CNFT.

**6:5.** To the further shame of the church, they had not even considered the idea of finding a wise man in their own midst to settle judiciary disputes, one who could discern the will of God, who was instructed in the wisdom of God, who was sensitive to the moving of the Spirit of God. An arbiter was needed, one who knew how to settle disputes as God desired. There is a sting here because the Corinthians considered themselves wise, yet they had not considered doing the wise thing.

**6. But brother goeth to law with brother:**...contendeth in iudgement, *—RHEM*...but brother is suing, *—CNDT*...is suing for judgment, *—RTHM.*
**and that before the unbelievers:**...before infidels? *—RHEM.*

**6:6.** This verse answers the previous verse. Brothers fought; wisdom was lacking; evil ruled the day. It was absurd that brothers should dispute like this. Yet it was the natural result where pride was dominant, where self was lifted up, and where love was lacking. Faith was not being built. Paul pointed to a proper answer and attitude, for at the base of their problem was a motivating attitude that was wrong.

If the spirit of a Christian or a church is wrong, it will affect its witness before unbelievers. There will be a misrepresented, misunderstood, and ineffective witness before those the church is seeking to win to Christ.

**7. Now therefore there is utterly a fault among you, because ye go to law one with another:**...there is plainly a fault, *—DOUY*...there is indeed altogether a shortcoming, *—PNT*...it is total defeat for you, *—RTHM*...it is wholly a loss to you, *—WORL*...it is a deep degradation to you, *—FNTN*...altogether a defect, *—MNTG*...Even to have lawsuits with one another, *—MOFT.*
**Why do ye not rather take wrong?:**...Why not rather endure injustice? *—WEYM*...you not rather being injured? *—CNDT*...Why not rather endure to be wronged? *—FNTN.*
**why do ye not rather [suffer yourselves to] be defrauded?:**...not rather being cheated? *—CNDT*...why rather susteine ye not harme? *—GNVA*...Why not rather be swindled? *—FNTN.*

**6:7.** This litigation was soundly denounced. "Fault" is properly "defeat" or loss. While lawsuits were not branded as sinful, the nature and boasting behind them proved the Corinthians were defeated Christians. The defeat was proved by the lawsuits. Paul offered a solution and established the proper attitude for a Christian. Christians must serve their brethren (Matthew 20:25-28; John 13:13-20, 34, 35). Paul's aim was to show that seeking justice, particularly on external

things, is not the highest goal; the rule of love is. By this statement Paul revealed the Corinthians' lack of understanding and maturity in Christian principles.

**8. Nay, ye do wrong, and defraud, and that [your] brethren:**...But ye injure, *—MKNT, —SAWR*...ye youselves commit wrong, *—MRDK*...you impose injustice, *—BRKL*...and you cheat, and swindle even your brothers, *—FNTN*...yourselves inflict injustice and fraud, *—WEYM*...you inflict wrong and practise frauds, *—MOFT.*

**6:8.** Paul pointed out the hatred, self-righteousness, and jealousy in their midst. They were doing wrong to others. They were defrauding their own brothers in Christ. They were not ready to suffer wrong; they were committing wrong. The duty and the fact were leagues apart.

**9. Know ye not that the unrighteous shall not inherit the kingdom of God?:**...that wrongdoers, *—RTHM*...that dishonest people, *—BRKL*...the unjust will not possess the kingdom, *—CNFT*...*—DOUY.*
**Be not deceived: neither fornicators, nor idolaters:**...Cherish no delusion here, *—WEYM*...Don't be misled, *—ADAM*...neither profligates, *—BRKL.*
**nor adulterers, nor effeminate, nor abusers of themselves with mankind:**...nether wantons, *—GNVA*...nor voluptuaries, *—HNT*...nor sodomites, *—MOFT*...nor sensualists, *—WAY*...guilty of unnatural crime, *—WEYM*...nor male prostitutes, *—ADAM*...not liers with mankind, *—DOUY.*

**10. Nor thieves, nor covetous, nor drunkards, nor revilers:**...nor avaricious people...addicted to hard drinking, *—WEYM*...greedy person, *—ADAM*...nor misers, *—CMPB*...nether cursed speakers, *—TNDL*...nor the evil-tongued, *—CNFT*...nor foul-mouthed men, *—WAY, —MNTG.*
**nor extortioners, shall inherit the kingdom of God:**...nor plunderers, *—FNTN*...nor robbers, *—ADAM*...will possess, *—CNFT.*

**6:9, 10.** Lumped with the misconduct of the Corinthians were other evidences of unrighteousness, all of which will keep a man from the kingdom of God. The Corinthians had committed sins typical of the unrighteous, reflecting the condition of their hearts. Paul did not suggest they had committed all the sins listed, but he did suggest that by their sin they had joined this unrighteous company. They thought themselves kings (4:8), but they ran the risk of being outside God's kingdom because their spirits reflected the attitude of this world instead of that of Christ.

The list included "fornicators," which involved all trespassers of the seventh commandment; the "effeminate" and "abusers of themselves with mankind" designated passive and active homosexuals respectively; "idolaters" violated the first commandment; "adulterers," a more specific term than "fornicators," violated the seventh commandment also, and in particular the marriage bed. "Thieves" was a general description for robbers or thieves; the "covetous" included those who always lusted after someone else's possessions, although they might not steal.

To this point Paul was attentive to the commandments laid down in Exodus 20. Now he expanded the list somewhat. "Drunkards" consumed alcoholic beverages to excess; "revilers" were those who abused others; and "extortioners" suggested taking by force, violently. There was an air of undisciplined, "me-first" motivation.

Those who do these things have no part in the kingdom of God; the Spirit of Christ is not in them, and the Corinthians were in danger of missing the Kingdom. The list seems to fall into the rough categories of sins against self or against the temple of God and sins against others.

Such implications and associations should have moved the Corinthians to reexamine their actions in the light of God's desires. If they were sensitive at all to the conviction of the Holy Spirit, such potential association should have caused them to reject their desires and seek the Master's will.

11. **And such were some of you:** . . . And all this describes what some of you were, —WEYM.

**but ye are washed:** . . . had every stain washed, —WEYM . . . but you have washed away your stains, —CNBR.

**but ye are sanctified:** . . . been set apart, —WEYM . . . you have been consecrated, —MNTG . . . made holy, —NOYS.

**but ye are justified in the name of the Lord Jesus, and by the Spirit of our God:** . . . you were pardoned in the name, —TCNT . . . ye were declared righteous, —RTHM . . . you have been pronounced righteous, —WAY . . . pronounced free from guilt, —WEYM.

**6:11.** Before their conversion some of these Corinthians were members of this group. Their lives had been changed. "Washed" carries the force of "you go yourselves washed." This could not refer to water baptism, because water cannot cleanse from sin. Others suggest the washing of Revelation 1:5. The tense is past, the aorist referring to a decisive action. "Sanctified" is in the same tense. They were set apart. "Justified" is also an aorist and looked back to the time of their acceptance as righteous before God. "In" indicated both the sphere and ground of these actions. Note the full names of the Deity which suggest Christ in all His relationships. "The Spirit of our God" points to the source of the keeping power in these relationships. A great deliverance had occurred in their lives.

12. **All things are lawful unto me:** . . . I am allowed to do anything, —BECK . . . I may do anything I want to do, —SEB . . . is permissible for me, —WLMS . . . I maye do all thynges, —CRNM.

**but all things are not expedient:** . . . are not profitable, —GNVA . . . not all are good for me, —MOFT . . . not everything is good for me, —NORL . . . not everything is beneficial, —BRKL . . . everything does not benefit, —FNTN . . . But not everything is useful, —KLGS.

**all things are lawful for me:** . . . are allowable, —RTHM.

**but I will not be brought under the power of any:** . . . I will not let myself be enslaved by anything, —NORL . . . not be deluded by any, —FNTN . . . I will not be mastered by anything, —BRKL . . . not going to let anything master me, —MOFT.

**6:12.** Paul concluded his statement by reminding the Corinthians that the body belongs to Christ. "All things are lawful" must have been a common saying in this church. Certainly the Holy Spirit speaking through the apostle Paul did not intend to tell Christians that "anything goes." Rather the Holy Spirit countered that slogan with "but all things are not expedient." In this verse Paul gave a principle of Christian liberty. Although "all things are lawful," there are certain limitations. The truth of this statement is important because it deals with what is possible, but not necessarily best. "All things" cannot be taken in an absolute sense. Paul's intent was to lead the readers to admit the truth of this verse and then later to see their wrong. If the Christian is free to do all things, he is still not free to sin. Limitations to a Christian's liberty are set by consequences and what is right.

Also, the possibility of being brought under the wrong power would limit the sentiment expressed in this verse. The Corinthians thought they were free, but their actions had brought them under the power of sin. The Christian shares the authority of Christ, but that does not give freedom to do all things, even if the right to do them is there.

13. **Meats for the belly, and the belly for meats:** . . . Food exists for, —TCNT . . . Meates are ordeyned for, —GNVA . . . Foods for the bowels, —CNDT . . . the stomach craves food, —NORL . . . The stomach is supposed to receive food, —SEB.

**but God shall destroy both it and them:** . . . God will put an end to both, —TCNT . . . shall bring to an end, —ALFD . . . will bring to nought, —CLMT . . . will finally put a stop to both of them, —WLMS . . . God will eventually cause both of them to cease their work, —NORL.

**Now the body [is] not for fornication:** . . . Committing sexual sin is not the purpose, —SEB.

**but for the Lord; and the Lord for the body:** . . . for the service of the Lord, —WLMS.

**6:13.** God has an express purpose for the body. It may well be the Corinthians had placed fornication on a morally indifferent level, arguing that the presence of bodily appetites was enough reason to gratify them. Perhaps they considered body and soul separate, and since the body was to be done away with, it made little difference what it did. Paul quickly demolishes this viewpoint.

Paul admitted the fact there are certain natural appetites, but relegated them to a particular sphere because they are passing. In due time God will render them inoperative. But the body is not to be so done away with. Nor is fornication, etc., transient. It has a permanent effect. Likewise, the connection is not between body and fornication (as between meats and belly), but between the body and the Lord. "God did not design the body for fornication as He did the belly for food" (Morris, *Tyndale New Testament Commentaries,* 7:100). The body, the physical part of man, belongs to God who created it. The value of the body is increased because of the new birth. It is to be treated with honor; it is for the Lord and needs His help to function properly.

**14. And God hath both raised up the Lord:** ... raised the Master to life, *−WEYM.*
**and will also raise up us by his own power:** ... and will also restore us, *−FNTN* ... will He resurrect us, *−BRKL* ... by His mighty power, *−CNBR* ... by the exercise of his power, *−TCNT.*

**6:14.** The potential of the body must be seen. As the Father raised Christ, so shall He raise believers by His power. The emphasis is on the importance of the body. The destiny of the "belly" and "meats" is destruction. The destiny of the body is the resurrection and eternal life in Christ.

**15. Know ye not that your bodies are the members of Christ?:** ... Surely you realize, *−SEB.*
**shall I then take the members of Christ:**
**and make [them] the members of an harlot?:** ... join them to a prostitute, *−NORL* ... of a prostitute? *−WEYM.*
**God forbid:** ... It could not be, *−WORL* ... Never! *−MOFT, −RSV.*

**6:15.** Paul said the body is the Lord's and cannot function properly without Him, then he made the union more intimate by establishing union with Christ as prohibitive to impurity. Paul asked a question intended to receive a negative answer: Shall I take the members of Christ away and make them members of a prostitute or submit them to sin? Absolutely not! This would involve deliberate alienation and defilement. Moral and spiritual ruin would be caused by such actions.

Paul is emphasizing the intimate and binding relationship between Christ and believers. As the Church is the body of Christ, so the various persons in the Church are members of Christ (verse 20).

**16. What? know ye not that he which is joined to an harlot is one body?:** ... he who is connected, *−NOYS* ... he who is strongly attached, *−MKNT* ... when one is united with a prostitute, *−NORL* ... he which coupleth him selfe with an harlot, *−TNDL* ... who has sex with a whore is one body with her? *−SEB* ... is in union, *−WEYM* ... that union, *−FNTN* ... is one with her in body, *−MOFT.*
**for two, saith he, shall be one flesh:** ... The two shall be physically one, *−WLMS* ... They twain shall be one body, *−MRDK* ... shall be united into one flesh, *−LOCK.*

**6:16.** On the other hand, being joined to a prostitute is also a complex union, for it involves physical, mental, and spiritual aspects. One unit is formed. Paul reminded his readers of such passages as Genesis 2:24, Matthew 19:5, and Mark 10:8. The "harlot" is associated with evil, and by this illicit union the union with Christ is damaged or even broken.

**17. But he that is joined unto the Lord is one spirit:** ... who unites with, *−BRKL* ... is stongly attached, *−MKNT* ... he that is ioyned vnto the Lord, is one spirite, *−GNVA.*

**6:17.** However, a proper relationship with Christ forms a total relationship that affects every part of the individual. It is a proven fact that the mind affects the body and spirit and vice versa. This relationship is on a far higher plane than the first. A man "joined to a harlot" descends to her filthiness. A man "joined unto the Lord" becomes one "spirit" and ascends to heavenly places. The believer's thoughts, desires, and actions become one with His in a spiritual, wondrous union. "Joined" (as in verse 16) is used of close bonds of various kinds. Literally, it refers to the process of gluing. A very close tie is the result.

**18. Flee fornication:** ... Keep on running from, *−WLMS* ... Shrink away from, *−WAY* ... Avoid fornication, *−SAWR* ... Shun immorality! *−MOFT, −NORL* ... Shun unchastity, *−BRKL* ... Shun all such immorality, *−TCNT* ... Flee from sexual sin, *−BECK.*
**Every sin that a man doeth is without the body:** ... Any other sin, *−WEYM* ... Every crime, *−WLSN* ... The penalty of every sin, *−CNDT* ... The root of sin is not in the body, *−CNBR* ... is outside the body, *−FNTN* ... is external to the body, *−HNSN.*
**but he that committeth fornication sinneth against his own body:** ... when one indulges in sexual immorality, *−NORL* ... sins against his own constitution, *−FNTN* ... the sinner thereby blasts his own body, *−WAY.*

**6:18.** Paul's conclusion was based on what has preceded: "Flee fornication." Recall the story of Joseph in Potiphar's house. We have to stand up to and fight some sins, but the answer to this one is flight. The sexual drive is very strong, and we must guard against striking a spark in the passions that would lead to such sin. Other sins which may affect the body, do not wreak the devastation this one does, for this sin aims only at the satisfaction of lust. God's chosen possessions dare not be defiled by such sacrilege. This sin goes against the very nature and purpose of the body. It becomes a self-violation, as well as a sin against God. It demands the participation of the whole person, for it stems from the heart, the spring of being (Mark 7:18-23). Most of the pagan temples of this part of the world, including the temple of Aphrodite in Corinth, not only condoned it, they encouraged it because it brought profit to them. Though condoned there, it is not to be condoned in the temple of God.

**19. What? know ye not that your body is the temple of the Holy Ghost:** ... that your members, —DOUY ... are a sanctuary, —WEYM.

**[which is] in you, which ye have of God:** ... Holy Spirit is inside you, —SEB . . . you have as a gift, —WLMS ... you have received from God, —MOFT.

**and ye are not your own?:**

**6:19.** For the third time in this section, Paul turned to a fact the Corinthian readers should have known: "Know ye not. . . ." The Christian's body is the temple of the Holy Spirit. Filth has no right to be there. Paul referred to the whole Christian Church in 3:16, 17; here he was speaking to the individual member in the body of Christ. The Holy Spirit, sent from God, abides within the Christian and purifies the temple. But believers as priests have a part in it also. This temple was purchased by God through the blood of Jesus Christ and is now possessed by Him, with the result that this shrine is owned and possessed by the Holy Spirit. The temple does not draw dignity or purity from itself, but from the God who inhabits it.

**20. For ye are bought with a price:** ... For ye are dearly bought, —TNDL ... have been redeemed at infinite cost, —WEYM ... bought at a great price, —CNFT ... you cost something, —SEB ... and at what a price! —NORL.

**therefore glorify God in your body:** ... By all means, —CNDT.

**and in your spirit, which are God's:** ... since both are God's, —CNBR ... both of which belong to God, —NORL.

**6:20.** Here we have the basis for the previous verse. "Bought" is an aorist and points to a single decisive action in time past. This view of God as the One purchasing our salvation is the "ransom" theory of atonement. It reminds us of a custom in Paul's day. A slave could save the price of his freedom, pay it into the temple treasury, and be purchased by the god. He then served that god. It should be the Christian's constant goal to glorify God because he has been bought with a great "price." That principle of life applies directly to the body, and it requires immediate obedience.

## Chapter 7

**1. Now concerning the things whereof ye wrote unto me:** ... Now about the things you wrote, —BECK ... The chief business of the foregoing chapters, —LOCK ... I now deal with the subjects mentioned in your letter, —WEYM ... now to the subjects on which you wrote to me, —TCNT ... To come to the subjects of your correspondence, —BRKL . . . those questions about which you wrote, —ADAM . . . this is my answer, —CNBR.

**[It is] good for a man not to touch a woman:** ... the ideal state is abstention from marital intercourse, —WAY ... it is praiseworthy for a man not to approach, —MRDK ... an excellent thing for a man to have no intercourse, —MOFT ... have no intercourse with a woman, —MNTG ... not to be entangling himself, —RTHM ... not to marry, —SEB ... to have sex relations, —BECK ... to be encumbered with a wife, —FNTN ... to abstain altogether from marriage, —WEYM.

**7:1.** The matter introduced here has often been the subject of controversy, partly because some reject its teaching, and partly because some misunderstand what Paul said. An understanding of the context will clear up this misunderstanding. This section was written in response to questions from the Corinthians themselves. This seems to be suggested throughout the letter by the phrase "now concerning." It is important to observe the use of the word "good" here. It denotes a commendable rather than a commanded attitude and refers to sexual relationships within marriage, as we see from "touch a woman." The question was whether or not one should marry. Later in this chapter, Paul offered his major reason for celibacy (verse 32).

Paul wanted the virtues of marriage understood. He was aware of the low moral tide in Corinth and of the dangers of fornication, as chapter 6 discussed.

It must be admitted that some scholars hold to the view that Paul is referring to sexual activity outside of marriage. (See the word study on "*haptō*" in the *Greek-English Dictionary*.)

**2. Nevertheless, [to avoid] fornication:** ... to avoyde fornicacion, —TNDL ... to avoyde whordome, —CRNM ... but for fear of unchastity, —FNTN.

**let every man have his own wife, and let every woman have her own husband:**

**7:2.** Marriage is an antidote to perversion and lust. A particularly strong type of marriage is meant: "Every man" suggests a monogamous marriage, which is a commandment. This was applied first to the man, then to the woman. There is to be one mate (of the opposite sex). This restricts verse 1 which is only a restriction, not a universal rule. Paul was not downgrading marriage; he was replying within the context of a historical setting and problem. The emphasis was on the avoidance of sin.

It must be remembered that the primary heresy Paul was rebutting in Corinth, which appeared in various guises, was a form of gnosticism. Gnosticism taught that the spirit is good but that anything material or physical is evil. This in turn led to two opposite errors. The first error is that because the body is evil, the body can do anything it wants to, since it is totally unrelated to the spirit and to spiritual things. This error is manifest in chapter 5 where believers in Corinth seem unperturbed by the sexual immorality exhibited by the man sleeping with his father's wife, possibly his stepmother. The other error that arose from this heresy was the view that since the body is evil, the body must be thoroughly subdued and denied. As a result, even good and proper things that God had ordained for people, such as intercourse between married people, were rejected.

This latter error is in view here in chapter 7 where married men, in an effort to be "spiritual," were denying the right of intercourse to their wives. This heresy, and the word *heresy* is to be stressed, is thoroughly condemned by the apostle Paul.

**3. Let the husband render unto the wife due benevolence:** ... render his dette to the wife, *—RHEM* ... should do his duty to his wife, *—FNTN* ... the kindness, *—MRDK* ... must fulfill his obligation, *—ADAM* ... the conjugal obligation, *—WLSN* ... her conjugal dues, *—MOFT.*
**and likewise also the wife unto the husband:**

**7:3.** The marriage contract includes obligations. Both the husband and the wife have duties to each other. Each partner has certain rights that should be respected. This is a mark against the one-sidedness of the Jewish marriage, where the woman was considered so inferior. "Due" involves the idea of a debt or what is owed.

**4. The wife hath not power of her own body, but the husband:** ... The wife has not undisputed control, *—WAY* ... is not the sovereign, *—MRDK* ... is not mistress of her own person, *—MNTG* ... has not the command of her own person, *—CMPB* ... the jurisdiction of her own body, *—CNDT* ... cannot do as she pleases with her body, *—MOFT* ... controls not her

own Body, *—WLSN* ... has not absolute disposal of her own body, *—FNTN.*
**and likewise also the husband hath not power of his own body, but the wife:** ... does not control, *—HNSN* ... has not dominion over his own body, *—CNBR* ... is not master of his own person, *—MNTG* ... the wife has her rights, *—WAY* ... has certain rights, *—WEYM.*

**7:4.** It is a fair deduction that some members of the Corinthian church advocated sexual abstinence in marriage. This is wrong because it involves needless temptation and can lead to dangerous sins. The husband and wife have some authority over each other. A mutual surrender is involved. The husband, for example, cannot do what he pleases with his body. The wife has rights and privileges and vice versa. In view of the widespread exaltation of celibacy in Corinth, Paul's statements on the indispensability of the sex act in marriage are noteworthy.

**5. Defraud ye not one the other:** ... Withdrawe not youre selves one from another, *—TNDL* ... Withhold not yourselves from one another, *—SAWR* ... You should not separate from one another, *—FNTN*, *—CNBR* ... Do not refuse one another, *—WEYM*, *—CLMT* ... Deny not one another, *—HNSN* ... Do not deprive each other, *—WLSN*, *—CNFT* ... Do not withhold sexual intercourse from one another, *—MOFT.*
**except [it be] with consent for a time:** ... except by agreement, *—ADAM* ... by mutual consent for a season, *—CLMT.*
**that ye may give yourselves to fasting and prayer:** ... in order to devote yourselves, *—MOFT* ... you may have leisure for prayer, *—HNT* ... to leave yourselves free for prayer, *—JB.*
**and come together again:** ... resume conjugal relations, *—WAY* ... may then associate again, *—WEYM.*
**that Satan tempt you not for your incontinency:** ... lest the Adversary ... because of your deficiency in self-control, *—WEYM* ... should begin to take advantage of your want, *—TCNT* ... in case Satan should take advantage of your weakness to tempt you, *—JB* ... when you are weak, *—NORL* ... because you lack self-control, *—CNFT* ... through your fleshly passions, *—CNBR* ... through not having enough self-control, *—SEB* ... for your want-of-self-control, *—RTHM* ... may not tempt you through passion, *—FNTN* ... because of the concupiscence of your body, *—MRDK.*

**7:5.** What was stated positively in verse 3 is now stated negatively: Do not "defraud" your mate, for he/she has certain rights over your body. Paul approved separation from sexual intercourse only under certain conditions. It must involve mutual consent; therefore it is not really separation. It must be only for a limited time, a fixed, agreed-upon time. It must have a definite purpose: to give oneself to prayer. The Greek includes the article, indicating a specific prayer. Married life may place such demands on a person that such specific prayer cannot be maintained. This is not right. At such times, under the conditions noted above, abstinence would be more profitable (1 Corinthians 7:33-40; 1 Peter 3:7).

Paul added a more general admonition, which was the real reason for his writing. It involved Satan's temptation of the Christian. Satan seeks to trap every Christian. Man was created with a desire to express himself in a sexual manner. This expression is proper in marriage. But Satan tempts people by urging them to express themselves in an illicit manner, such as fornication or adultery. And the temptation to "incontinence" is stronger if such matters are not properly handled in the marriage.

**6. But I speak this by permission, [and] not of commandment:** . . . From my own knowledge, *−SEB* . . . I saye of fauoure, *−CRNM* . . . I am giving this advice, *−NORL* . . . I say this by indulgence, *−RHEM, −DOUY* . . . by way of advice, *−LOCK* . . . by suggestion, *−SAWR* . . . by way of concession, not by way of injunction, *−RTHM,* . . . not as an injunction, *−CNDT, −WLSN* . . . not command, *−MOFT* . . . not as a regulation, *−BRKL* . . . not of positive precept, *−MRDK* . . . not by a special command, *−FNTN.*

**7:6.** Paul speaks "by permission." Commandment is the opposite of concession. The crucial issue here has to do with what Paul meant by "this" when he said, "I speak this by permission." Some argue that it refers to 7:2-5, which would mean that Paul was conceding that it is permissible to marry. A second option is that by "this" Paul was referring to the latter portion of verse 5, which would then mean that Paul was conceding the necessity of resuming intercourse, although he was not commanding them to resume it. The first option is perhaps possible, but our discussion thus far has shown the second option to be untenable. Paul did not command Christians to marry. But on the other hand, neither did he reluctantly admit the right to marry. Every Christian has the right to marry, but exercising this right is not compulsory. The best option is to take "this" to refer to all of verse 5 which therefore means that intercourse is a necessity for marriage, and only as a concession to a season of prayer is abstinence allowable.

**7. For I would that all men were even as I myself:** . . . that all had my own powers of self-control, *−WAY* . . . had my own attitude, *−BRKL.*
**But every man hath his proper gift of God:** . . . has a personal gift, *−RTHM* . . . has his own, *−MNTG* . . . own special gift, *−WEYM, −WLMS* . . . is endowed with his gift, *−MRDK.*
**one after this manner, and another after that:** . . . one this wise, *−PNIN* . . . one of this sort,

*−ADAM* . . . one in one direction, *−WEYM, −BRKL* . . . and another with a gift for the opposite, *−JB.*

**7:7.** The exception is found in a man like Paul himself. The Corinthians knew what and who he was. It seems that Paul was unmarried at this time. Whether he was ever married is a more difficult question, which has not a conclusive answer. This ability, nonetheless, to remain unmarried and refrain from fornication, was due to a special ability and gift from God. It aided in the spread of the gospel (Matthew 19:9-12).

Paul did not exalt himself above any other Christian. God gives as He chooses, in His will and wisdom. This principle will appear again in 1 Corinthians 12. Paul's intention was that the gospel should be preached with great power and that nothing should interfere with it whether one was married or single. Purity and power with God were his goals. Paul may have preferred the celibate state, but he recognized that both marriage and celibacy are acceptable to God. Each person should recognize God's gifts and will for him.

**8. I say therefore to the unmarried and widows:** . . . to single people, *−SEB.*
**It is good for them if they abide even as I:** . . . that it is ideal, *−CNDT* . . . that it is advantageous, *−MRDK* . . . would be a fine thing, *−WLMS* . . . if they so continue, *−DOUY* . . . is an excellent thing if like me they remain as they are, *−MOFT.*

**7:8.** Having established basic principles regarding marriage, Paul now applied these principles to individual situations. He spoke first to the unmarried and widows. "Unmarried" probably refers to unmarried men, the article being masculine, and the widows are especially mentioned because of their dependence and vulnerability. The principle of verse 1 is seen. It is good for them to remain as they are—unmarried.

**9. But if they cannot contain, let them marry:** . . . But if they have not the gift of continency, *−LOCK* . . . are not excercising self-control, *−MNTG* . . . have not self-restraint, *−FNTN* . . . cannot control themselves, *−WLSN.*
**for it is better to marry than to burn:** . . . preferred to the flames of lust, *−LOCK* . . . than to be on fire, *−CNDT* . . . than to be incontinent, *−SAWR* . . . than to be feverish, *−FNTN* . . . than the fever of passion, *−WEYM* . . . than be aflame with passion, *−MOFT* . . . to be burning with sexual desire, *−SEB.*

**7:9.** The controlling rule depends on the gift of continence. Otherwise, "let them marry" appears as a command, not as permission. It is better to marry than to continually burn with sexual desire. Paul did not regard the suppression of sexual desire as meritorious in itself. There had to be a greater purpose. "To burn" is in the present, indicating a continuous urge, while the answer lies in the single definite act of marriage. The principle is that whatever is morally better, within God's call, should be the determining factor.

**10. And unto the married I command, [yet] not I, but the Lord:** . . . to them that be ioyned in matrimonie, *—RHEM* . . . I give charge, *—RTHM* . . . I give this authoritative instruction, *—WLSN* . . . but by the Lord's inspiration, *—WAY.*

**Let not the wife depart from [her] husband:** . . . not to separate, *—MOFT* . . . be separated from, *—CRNM.*

**7:10.** Paul turned his attention next to those who had Christian marriages. This time Paul gave his advice on the basis of a direct command of the Lord (Matthew 5:32; Mark 10:11, 12). He was emphasizing the correct attitudes believers should have toward marriage.

Paul mentioned the wife first. In the gospel passages referred to, Christ was speaking primarily to Jews. In that society it was the husband who put away his wife, not the wife her husband. In Corinth, women were more liberated. Paul wanted it understood that neither partner had the right to leave.

**11. But and if she depart, let her remain unmarried:** . . . or if she has already left him, *—WEYM* . . . remain without a husband, *—MRDK* . . . remain single, *—MOFT.*

**or be reconciled to [her] husband:** . . . or be conciliated, *—CNDT* . . . or let her return, *—FNTN* . . . or come back to, *—SEB.*

**and let not the husband put away [his] wife:**

**7:11.** If a woman did depart, however, one of two things should happen. Paul was not approving divorce here; instead he was saying if it happened in spite of everything done to prevent it, the wife must remain alone or be reconciled to her husband. He offered no other alternatives. Reconciliation would probably have to begin with the party who did the departing or divorcing. God made one husband for one wife, and anything contrary was, in this setting, breaking Christ's command.

Similarly the husband was not to separate from his wife. The verb is different but the result is the same.

**12. But to the rest speak I, not the Lord:** . . . To other people, *—MOFT* . . . To the remnant, *—GNVA* . . . on my own private judgment, *—WAY* . . . The rest is from me and not from the Lord, *—JB.*

**If any brother hath a wife that believeth not:** . . . haue an vnfeithful wiif, *—WCLF* . . . an infidel, *—RHEM.*

**and she be pleased to dwell with him, let him not put her away:** . . . if she agrees to, *—ADAM* . . . yf

she be content to dwell, *—TNDL* . . . consents to live, *—MOFT* . . . is well pleased, *—RTHM* . . . she approves of making a home, *—CNDT* . . . is willing to live with him, *—NORL* . . . and she agrees to live with him, *—FNTN* . . . let him not dismiss her, *—HNT* . . . he must not divorce her, *—WLMS* . . . he should not divorce her, *—TCNT* . . . he must not send her away, *—JB.*

**7:12.** Paul now began his application of the principles already cited to what he termed the "rest," which specifically involved various mixed marriage relationships, that is, where a believer and an unbeliever were married. He expressly dealt with a situation where the unbeliever was willing to continue the marriage relationship. It also apparently referred to one partner who became a believer after marriage. There is no legitimate basis for a Christian marrying a non-Christian in order to win him to the Lord.

Paul said, ". . . speak I, not the Lord." Verse 10 carries an express command of Christ. Here Paul did not have such words of Christ directly; but he was speaking by divine authority and under the inspiration of the Holy Spirit.

**13. And the woman which hath an husband that believeth not, and if he be pleased to dwell with her, let her not leave him:** . . . but he likes being married to her, *—SEB* . . . he agrees to live with her, *—BECK* . . . he consents to live with her, *—CNFT* . . . to dwell with her, *—HNT* . . . let her not forsake, *—MRDK* . . . let her not separate from him, *—WEYM* . . . put her husband away, *—MOFT.*

**7:13.** Some Corinthians thought it was necessary to divorce a mate when the latter remained pagan. There was concern that such pagan contact would defile the new Christian. But "if he be pleased" or content rendered this action unnecessary and even forbidden. The decision of the believer depended on the attitude of the pagan partner.

In a mixed marriage, the believing partner is not to take the initiative for a divorce. The reason for this is given in 7:14-16. Verse 14 speaks of the believing partner sanctifying the other spouse, and verse 16 speaks of the possibility of the other spouse being saved by the believing partner. This does not mean, of course, that a marriage partner is automatically converted by a believing spouse; rather, it means that the believing partner's Christian life will influence the other partner.

**14. For the unbelieving husband is sanctified by the wife:** . . . An unbelieving man married to such a woman serves a holy purpose, *—BECK* . . . is hallowed, *—CNDT* . . . is, so to speak, sanctified, *—NORL* . . . has become holy, *—RTHM* . . . has become consecrated, *—TCNT* . . . is made one with the saints through his wife, *—JB* . . . is purified, *—FNTN* . . . is consecrated,

—*MOFT* . . . consecrated through union, —*MNTG* . . . by union, —*WLMS.*

**and the unbelieving wife is sanctified by the husband:** . . . is halowid bi, —*WCLF* . . . is made acceptable to God by being united to her Christian husband, —*TEV.*

**else were your children unclean; but now are they holy:** . . . or else the children would be defiled; but now they are pure, —*FNTN*, —*MRDK* . . . are impure, —*RTHM* . . . in reality they have a place among God's people, —*WEYM* . . . they belong to God, —*TCNT.*

**7:14.** Paul offered an explanation for what he had said. He referred to a sanctifying influence, which pertained to a certain relationship to God, not moral uprightness. It did not mean the unbeliever was holy before God in Christ. He used the word in the same sense in 1 Timothy 4:5. The believer was set apart to God. His relation to God was not diminished because before believing he married an unbeliever. Rather, the believer exerts an influence on the unbelieving partner and the home. If they live together in love, the unbeliever showed externally that he belonged with believers. Being one flesh with the believer is very important for the unbeliever. Such scriptural blessings from a fellowship with God also extended to others, not just to the immediate recipients (Genesis 15:18; 17:7; 18:26; 1 Kings 15:4; Isaiah 37:4).

The children of such a union also served as examples. Through the sanctified life of the believer the children would be brought into contact with Christian influences. Until the age when a child was able to make a personal decision in the matter, his life was influenced and to an extent controlled by the faith of his parents. Indeed, the believing partner exerted a holy, sanctifying influence on the whole family. This did not mean that each member of the family automatically had a personal relationship or salvation experience with Jesus Christ. That remained in the domain of personal choice. But it did mean that a holy influence was brought to bear on the members of the family, and they enjoyed some of the blessings of a Christian presence.

**15. But if the unbelieving depart, let him depart:** . . . the unbelieving companion, —*SAWR* . . . be determined to leave, —*MNTG* . . . be determined to separate, —*MOFT* . . . seeks for separation, —*CNBR* . . . let the separation take place, —*WAY* . . . let him separate, —*ADAM.*

**A brother or a sister is not under bondage in such [cases]:** . . . is not subiect to seruitude in, —*RHEM* . . . is not enslaved, —*CNDT* . . . is not under servitude, —*DOUY* . . . is not tied to marriage, —*MOFT* . . . is not bound to remain under the yoke, —*CNBR* . . . is not enslaved in such a case, —*LOCK* . . . is fettered in such a case, —*WAY.*

**but God hath called us to peace:**

**7:15.** But the unbeliever could choose not to remain with the believing partner. The fact that the unbeliever is the subject places the full burden of separation on his shoulders. "Depart" is in the middle voice—"take himself off." If the unbeliever chose not to abide willingly and peacefully with the believer but to depart, he should be allowed to go. In such cases the believer was not under bondage. The question of remarriage did not technically appear here. On the basis of verse 11, it would seem that for the divorced to remain unmarried was the proper course. The divine Author of Scripture who inspired Paul would not contradict a command of Christ, who allowed divorce only on the grounds of unfaithfulness. Some believe, however, that if the unbeliever formed a new union then the exception of Matthew 5:32 would come into play and the divorced believer might remarry a believer.

The Christian spouse now forsaken was free from the former yoke. What should be the guiding attitude? A desire for peace. The work of Christ resulted in peace with God, as Romans 5:1 tells us. This causes internal peace to prevail in all aspects of life.

**16. For what knowest thou, O wife, whether thou shalt save [thy] husband?:** . . . For what assurance have you, —*WEYM* . . . What reasonable expectation have you, —*WAY* . . . you might convert, —*SEB* . . . whether thou wilt procure life, —*MRDK.*

**or how knowest thou, O man, whether thou shalt save [thy] wife?:**

**7:16.** Some would argue that the marriage should be preserved because the unbelieving partner might be saved. But Paul said this is uncertain, and marriage is more than a tool of evangelism. Conflict causes tension and frustration and the aim should be peace. The argument of this verse hinges on the "if" (*ei* in Greek), which should probably be interpreted or translated as "whether." Salvation requires a personal decision. Paul did not exclude the possibility of the unbeliever's salvation at any time here. The emphasis was on the believer and maintaining inner peace (verse 15). Marriage is an intimate, deep, lasting relationship that joins spirit as well as body. Ultimately, a relationship with God is individual and must take priority.

Paul was not advocating divorce or separation. He listed certain qualifications, and this was the last possible move after all steps had been taken to maintain the relationship under God, and after the conscience had been totally absolved of blame. The situation was specifically limited and again the unbeliever must initiate the action.

**17. But as God hath distributed to every man:** ... The Lord has given a role to each person, *—SEB* ... the Lord has imparted to each one, *—SAWR* ... has apportioned to each, *—WLSN* ... originally allotted to him, *—WAY* ... whatever be the condition in life, *—WEYM* ... whatever be the lot in life, *—MNTG* ... assigned him by the Lord, *—MOFT.*

**as the Lord hath called every one, so let him walk:** ... let each man walk in the same path which God alloted, *—CNBR* ... walk as the Lord has assigned him, *—ADAM* ... everyone must lead the lot, *—MOFT* ... continue to walk in the lot which the Lord appointed him, *—NOYS* ... when he heard God's call, *—WAY.*

**And so ordain I in all churches:** ... And thus am I prescribing, *—CNDT* ... I order the same, *—FNTN* ... This is what I command, *—WEYM* ... Such is the rule I lay down for all, *—MOFT* ... in all congregacyons, *—CRNM.*

**7:17.** In summary, Paul reminded the Corinthians of what he had been saying and allowed an enlargement of this basic principle to apply to all of life. One must remain in one's calling. In Corinth, there had been a disregard for the Christian's station in life. Paul called them back to contentment and service.

God both calls and maintains. He distributes blessings and gifts. "Hath distributed" implies God's governing influence. In the marriage relationship, freedom is not license. Opposed to liberty is the fact that the Christian has certain marital obligations, including the maintenance of one's present state as normal Christian practice. "Hath called" denotes that when God chooses, He expects one to live the pattern of life He sets before him, using the gifts He gives. This was a consistent message with Paul.

**18. Is any man called being circumcised?: let him not become uncircumcised:** ... Let it not be rejected, *—FNTN* ... let him not revert, *—MRDK* ... let him not adde vncircumcisyon, *—CRNM* ... be de-circumcised, *—CNDT* ... he is not to efface the marks of it, *—MOFT* ... Let him not have recourse to the surgeons, *—WEYM.*

**Is any called in uncircumci-sion? let him not be circumcised:**

**19. Circumcision is nothing, and uncircumcision is nothing:** ... counts for nothing, *—MOFT.*

**but the keeping of the commandments of God:** ... but observing Divine commands, *—FNTN* ... of the precepts of God, *—CNDT* ... obedience to God's commands is everything, *—MOFT.*

**7:18, 19.** Paul applied the principle stated above to the racial distinction of circumcision and uncircumcision. Paul said this is a matter of the outer man and of no importance. The Jews demanded circumcision, but the Gentiles often thought it a sign of liberty when, as sometimes happened, a Jewish youth underwent surgery to remove

the marks of circumcision, to better please the Greek culture within which he lived. It is difficult to say whether there were those in Corinth who were trying to conceal their Jewish origin. Perhaps they thought circumcision necessary to obey God more fully. Paul's point was this: Men find themselves in various circumstances when they are called by the Lord. This outward distinction is of no importance. The important thing is to keep the commandments of God. A person should not worry over his circumstances or seek to be what he is not. He is simply to walk according to his calling from God.

**20. Let every man abide in the same calling wherein he was called:** ... whatever be the condition in life in which a man was, *—WEYM* ... remain in the condition of life, *—MOFT* ... in the same state, *—GNVA* ... in the condition, *—FNTN.*

**7:20.** Paul here reiterates the principle he stated in verse 17. Believers in the First Century came from highly varied backgrounds. Most of them were from the middle or lower classes. As he stated earlier: "Ye see your calling, brethren, how that not many wise men after the flesh, not many mighty, not many noble, are called" (1:26). Often, even slaves found salvation through Christ.

This undoubtedly caused severe problems. What now was the relationship between the Christian master and his Christian slave? In Christ they were equals, but the customs of the day still had to be observed.

**21. Art thou called [being] a servant?:** ... called when in slavery, *—MNTG* ... a bondman? *—RHEM.*

**care not for it:** ... Never mind, *—MOFT* ... Let not that trouble you, *—MNTG* ... let it not trouble thee, *—MRDK* ... Let not that weigh on your mind, *—WEYM.*

**but if thou mayest be made free, use [it] rather:** ... then prefer it, *—FNTN* ... make use of the opportunity, *—MNTG* ... you had better avail yourself of. the opportunity, *—MOFT* ... yet prefer freedom to slavery, if thou canst obtain it, *—LOCK.*

**22. For he that is called in the Lord, [being] a servant, is the Lord's freeman:**

**likewise also he that is called, [being] free, is Christ's servant:** ... is Christ's bondman, *—PNIN.*

**7:21, 22.** Slaves may have thought natural freedom was their first concern, but Paul's advice was that believers accept the circumstances they were in when they first found Christ. He said to the slaves, "You were a slave when God called you to become His child. Accept your present social status." He used an interesting phrase, *mallon chrēsai.* Literally, it means "rather use (it)." This could mean a number of things, but most likely it has the import of "make use of your present position as a slave." Although the slave was serving his master from a state of bondage, he could serve as though it was for Christ (see Colossians 3:22, 23).

Paul was consistent in his treatment of the master/servant relationship. While he recognized that in Christ all were one, and there were no class distinctions (see Galatians 3:28; Colossians 3:11), he did not advocate change by society by radical methods. He even sent the converted Onesimus back to his master Philemon. Though Paul did not support slavery, he was not aiming for social revolution, but spiritual reformation. He pointed out that it is possible to be a Christian in any situation.

If the slave had an opportunity to be free, he should take advantage of it. But the slave was not to worry for he had been called by Christ. The world does not determine a man's position before God. In Christ all are equal.

**23. Ye are bought with a price:** . . . Christ paid a price for you, —SEB . . . you were dearly bought, —BRKL.
**be not ye the servants of men:** . . . you must not turn slaves to any man, —MOFT.

**7:23.** Paul returned to his thesis of 6:20. Believers have been bought with the blood of Jesus Christ. This is the reason for prompt obedience. One might be a slave, but he was free from sin and guilt. Another might be free, but he was bound to obedience and service in Christ. They dared not become captive to worldly distinctions or philosophies.

**24. Brethren, let every man, wherein he is called, therein abide with God:** . . . remain in the position, —TCNT . . . remain in the presence of God, —BRKL . . . let him stay, close to God, —MNTG.

**7:24.** Paul repeated the principle of this section: A man is to serve God where he is until God calls somewhere else. "Was called" is an aorist, pointing back to the time of God's call; "therein abide" is present continuous, indicating continuity. The ever-present God, who is also faithful, is the One with whom we are able to "abide." The will and pleasure of God must be consulted in every change and type of work: "Abide with God."

**25. Now concerning virgins I have no commandment of the Lord:** . . . I have no command, —TCNT . . . I have no orders from, —MOFT . . . I have no divine injunction, —BRKL . . . unmarried women, —WEYM . . . the young girls, —FNTN . . . the celibates . . . I have no injunction, —CNDT . . . I have no ordinance, —SAWR.
**yet I give my judgment, as one that hath obtained mercy of the Lord to be faithful:** . . . but counsel I giue, —RHEM . . . but I give counsel, —MRDK, —DOUY . . . I will give you the opinion, —MOFT . . . that I be trewe, —WCLF . . . to be

trustworthy, —HNSN . . . is deserving of your confidence, —WEYM, —MNTG.

**7:25.** "Now concerning" indicates yet another matter on which the Corinthians had apparently submitted questions. "Virgins" refers to women (and includes the question of daughters at home and the father's responsibility). As before where there are no specific commandments or words of Christ, the position is made clear. There is no distinction here between rule and advice. "Judgment" does not leave the case open to doubt or uncertainty. What was said was based on the risen Christ's mercy to Paul. It points out Paul's significance while giving the glory to God. When Paul gave this advice it was done in faithfulness to the Lord; it must, therefore, be pleasing to Him. It could, then, be trusted. God's grace had made Paul a trustworthy servant and apostle.

**26. I suppose therefore that this is good for the present distress:** . . . I judge a single life to be convenient, —LOCK . . . to encounter more easily the present distress, —FNTN . . . on account of, —MRDK . . . owing to the imminence of distressful times, —WAY . . . the imminent distress in these days, —MOFT . . . this is well in consequence of the present distress, —HNSN . . . is suitable on account of the necessity of the times, —MRDK . . . time of suffering now imminent, —MNTG . . . in view of the impending distress, —BRKL . . . of the existing distress, —RTHM.
**[I say], that [it is] good for a man so to be:** . . . to remain as he is, —NOYS.

**7:26.** Paul stressed two things: It is a good thing to be a virgin because of the present need, and it is a good thing in itself. The "present distress" was a general reference to the circumstances and pressures all Christians faced in that era of time. The context includes descriptions like "tribulation in the flesh" (verse 28, ASV), "time is short" (verse 29), and "fashion of this world passeth away" (verse 31). The Christian, whether married or unmarried, was caught in struggles and pressures, which are not closely defined, but the reference is to difficult circumstances. Paul's advice was to remain, then, as they were.

**27. Art thou bound unto a wife? seek not to be loosed:** . . . Art thou tied to a wife? —RHEM . . . in the bonds of wedlock? —LOCK . . . do not attempt to be free, —FNTN . . . Seek not release, —MRDK . . . Never try to untie the knot, —MOFT.
**Art thou loosed from a wife? seek not a wife:** . . . Are you unattached to a woman? —BRKL.

**7:27.** Paul enlarged on the thought. The moment he recommended remaining single under the "present distress," he had to answer questions concerning those already married. Should they separate? The answer was no. And such unity was a command of the Lord (verse 10). The application here is to men. "Art thou loosed" means simply unmarried.

**28. But and if thou marry, thou hast not sinned:** . . . if perchance thou even marry, *—RTHM.*
**and if a virgin marry, she hath not sinned:** . . . if your virgin daughters marry, *—CNBR* . . . if a maid marries, *—MOFT* . . . she has not done wrong, *—MNTG.*
**Nevertheless such shall have trouble in the flesh: but I spare you:** . . . Yet affliction in the flesh, *—CNDT, —CMPB* . . . will have outward trouble, *—WEYM* . . . will have tribulation, *—RTHM* . . . they will have bodily privations, *—FNTN* . . . will have added troubles, *—NORL* . . . will have trouble in worldly affairs, *—MNTG* . . . will have sorrows in the flesh, *—CNBR* . . . many troubles at this time, and I would like to protect you, *—SEB* . . . my wish is to spare you, *—TCNT* . . . and I am trying to spare you, *—ADAM.*

**7:28.** This verse makes it clear first to men, then to virgins, that marriage is not a sin. Perhaps some Corinthians had misinterpreted Paul's words and had this view of marriage. Paul made no absolute prohibitions concerning marriage. Marriage may produce distress, but it is a barrier to immorality. The Corinthians appeared to have a strong antipathy toward marriage. Paul must deal with this wrong attitude. Repeatedly the apostle Paul, directed by the Holy Spirit, made clear that marriage in and of itself is not a sin or sinful. Paul acknowledged that the marriage relationship entailed difficulties, but observation teaches us that it is not possible to escape difficulties or anxiety just by remaining single.

Some claim that the phrase "trouble in the flesh" refers to bodily difficulties of married women. But this appears too limited. "Such" is masculine, embracing more than married women. Some see a reference to complications with regard to the ministry, problems which are increased by a man's regard for his wife and children. Such blessings enrich a man's life, but mishaps to them are more difficult to handle. Sometimes a decision must be made between God and family. It was Paul's intention to spare them these difficulties, to aid and help rather than to add pressure.

**29. But this I say, brethren, the time [is] short:** . . . I warn you, brethren, *—WEYM* . . . the era is limited, *—CNDT* . . . the interval has been shortened, *—MOFT.*
**it remaineth, that both they that have wives be as though they had none:** . . . behave as if they had none, *—BRKL.*

**7:29.** By saying "brethren" Paul addressed the whole congregation with this important message. In "the time is short" some see a reference to the Second Coming, others to a crisis in Corinth.

Christians live between the descent of the Holy Spirit and the return of Jesus Christ. The Second Coming leads to the end of all things and hastens us toward that end. This does not necessarily mean Paul was certain of the coming of the Lord in his own lifetime, though his writings indicate it was his constant hope. He lived expectantly, while always planning for the future. "It remaineth" or "henceforth" (ASV) carries the idea that there remained only one thing necessary: the eye must be directed toward heaven.

From this point Paul listed five examples of the Christian's freedom from the transient world. Each item can be connected with the married state. "As though they had none" is not an exhortation to marital neglect, but an indication that marriage must be kept in proper perspective, with the advance of the gospel always having top priority.

**30. And they that weep, as though they wept not:** . . . People who are crying must act, *—SEB* . . . let mourners live, *—MOFT* . . . those lamenting, *—CNDT.*
**and they that rejoice, as though they rejoiced not:** . . . let the joyful live, *—MOFT.*
**and they that buy, as though they possessed not:** . . . as if they acquired not, *—MRDK* . . . had no hold on their goods, *—MOFT.*

**7:30.** Every Christian is going to weep, rejoice, and buy as he shares in the events of his world and time. But these are not to be the determinants in the character or actions of the Christian. In each situation the heart must be directed heavenward for guidance. The Christian is not acquiring lasting possessions here. The world has merely the passing fashion of the theater or stage. As J.H. Newman wrote: "Then what this world to thee, my heart? Its gifts nor feed thee nor can bless. Thou hast no owner's part in all its fleetingness" (Nicoll, *Expositor's Greek Testament,* 2:831).

**31. And they that use this world, as not abusing [it]:** . . . Those who do business with the world must act as though they don't care, *—SEB* . . . though using it sparingly, *—MNTG* . . . not going beyond the just using, *—MRDK* . . . must not be overly absorbed in them, *—NORL.*
**for the fashion of this world passeth away:** . . . for the arrangement, *—FNTN* . . . the present phase, *—MOFT* . . . as it now exists is passing away, *—WEYM.*

**7:31.** This addition and summary appears with an air of detachment. "Use this world" (to the full) indicates a man who uses the world in that manner and then has nothing left when the world passes. Rather it should be as the song tells us, "This world is not my home, I'm just passing through." For the world has a transitory nature and form, and it will pass away. This is inevitable. This world has been judged and stands condemned. A present action is involved in this "passing away." What a solemn warning this comment provides. Attachments in this world will pass away.

**32. But I would have you without carefulness:** ...I want you to be free from all preoccupation, —*WAY*...free from worldly anxiety, —*WEYM*, —*MNTG*...to be free from cares, —*ALFD* ... to be without worry, —*CNDT*...be without bidynesse, —*WCLF*...be without solicitude, —*DOUY*...be without anxiety, —*FNTN*.
**He that is unmarried careth for the things that belong to the Lord:**...The syngle man careth, —*GNVA*...He that is without a wife, —*RHEM*...is solicitous about, —*CNDT*, —*DOUY*...has time and liberty to mind things of religion, —*LOCK* ... is anxious about the Lord's affairs, —*MOFT*...is concerned about the Lord's things, —*SEB*...the Lord's business, —*MNTG*.
**how he may please the Lord:**

**7:32.** Instead of assigning value to this passing world, Paul desired unworried service for the Lord. Paul once again criticized the ascetic tendency found in Corinth; people were fooling themselves if they thought that singleness would release them from anxiety. The New Testament resounds with commands to be free from anxiety (e.g., Matthew 6:25; 1 Peter 5:7) because Christ by His death has delivered us, justified us, and given us peace with God (cf. Romans 5:1). Because of this, Paul made it clear (cf. Romans 8:15) that any *human* attempt to escape anxiety (i.e., celibacy) is insufficient.

Paul wanted his friends to be free from care and unnecessary pressure. This care would detract from perfect service toward God. The unmarried man does not have such "cares" or hindrances to serving the Lord as marriage sometimes brings; hence, Paul's preference for celibacy. His whole aim and guiding principle was what would provide the best service for the Lord whom he loved. He aimed to see how this service might best be accomplished. He desired undistracted service for the Lord.

**33. But he that is married careth for the things that are of the world:**...concerns himself with the business of the world, —*WEYM* ... is anxious about worldly affairs, —*MNTG*.
**how he may please [his] wife:**...how best to satisfy his wife so he is torn in two directions, —*MOFT*.

**7:33.** The cares of the married and the "freedom" of the single are further compared. Paul said that the married man cannot help but have some concern for "the things that are of the world." This does not denote "worldliness" or sin. It is rather a note that the married man must face the question of "how he may please his wife," which is a direct contrast with "how he may please the Lord." Such a man is divided in interest and purpose between God and wife. He cannot be as intense or "devoted" in his service for the Lord.

**34. There is difference [also] between a wife and a virgin:**...And there has been a distinction, —*CLMT*.
**The unmarried woman careth for the things of the Lord:** ... The single woman careth for the thinges, —*TNDL* ... should attend to the wishes, —*FNTN*...concerns herself with the Lord's business, —*WEYM*...can be absorbed in her duties to her Lord, —*WAY*...care for the Master's interests, —*TCNT*.
**that she may be holy both in body and in spirit:**...how to be consecrated, —*MOFT*...how she may be pure, —*MNTG*.
**but she that is married careth for the things of the world:**...about worldly affairs, —*MOFT*.
**how she may please [her] husband:**

**7:34.** The difference that exists between married and unmarried men is also found sometimes between married and unmarried women. Often the unmarried can more fully concentrate on the things of God (unless, as in some cases in today's world, they too have family responsibilities). The unmarried can have a singleness of purpose regarding consecration and the pursuit of holiness. This does not make the virgin any more righteous than the wife. But since the wife must take into account the needs of her husband, her consecration is "modified" by her dual purpose. For example, at some point she might want to do an act of charity. But her commitment is also to her husband, and if he is not agreeable, it may be difficult or impossible for her to perform that good act. She may wish to spend much time in prayer, but it may be difficult with family responsibilities calling to her. Thus Paul was stressing one obvious difference between the two states. The married individual has more responsibilities, usually, than the unmarried person, making it harder to find time for serving God.

Paul was speaking in a general sense. We must remember Paul's admonitions elsewhere about the sanctity of marriage (Ephesians 5 and 6) and the needs for which it provides.

The expression "that she may be holy both in body and in spirit" is applied directly to the unmarried woman. Elsewhere in Paul's letters when he speaks of holiness he makes it a requirement for all Christians, not just one group of Christians. It may be, therefore, that this expression was used by ascetics in Corinth to keep women from marriage, since intercourse in their view defiled the body.

Although Paul did not agree with this asceticism, he certainly agreed in general with the necessity of being holy in body and in spirit. Even a casual glance at his epistles indicates his overwhelming concern with purity. He urges Christians, "Present your bodies a living sacrifice, holy, acceptable unto God" (Romans 12:1). Paul says much the same elsewhere in Romans with his exhortation, "Let not sin therefore reign in your mortal body, that ye should obey it in the lusts thereof" (Romans 6:12).

The very first letters Paul wrote show that from the beginning of his ministry he was concerned about immorality. In 1 Thessalonians he wrote, "And the very God of peace sanctify you wholly; and I pray God your whole spirit and soul and body be preserved blameless unto the coming of our Lord Jesus Christ" (1 Thessalonians 5:23). Most of his statements concerning holiness, however, are found here in 1 Corinthians (6:13, 15, 19, 20; 15:44).

**35.** **And this I speak for your own profit:** ... your own application, —FNTN ... your own benefit, —CMPB ... your own advantage, —HNT ... in your own interests, —MOFT.

**not that I may cast a snare upon you:** ... I'm not trying to add an extra burden to you, —SEB ... not to make it harder for you, —NORL ... not to lay a trap for you, —WEYM ... not with any intention of putting a halter round your necks, —TCNT ... to bridle you by it, —ADAM ... to restrict your freedom, —MOFT ... be casting a noose over you, —CNDT ... restraint upon you, —WORL.

**but for that which is comely:** ... but with a view, —RTHM ... but for that which is honest, —TNDL ... but to promote propriety, —HNT ... to promote choice behavior, —BRKL ... to secure decorum and concentration, —MOFT ... rather to promote decency, —ADAM.

**and that ye may attend upon the Lord without distraction:** ... that ye may quyetly cleaue vnto the Lord without separation, —GNVA ... and enable you to wait, —WEYM ... without impediment, —RHEM, —DOUY ... in a suitable manner, while not minding worldly things, —MRDK ... undivided devotion to the Lord, —ADAM ... with a seemly and undivided service, —CNBR.

**7:35.** Paul's purpose was not to place undue restraints or absolutes on the Corinthians. Rather, his advice was for the purpose of gaining their best, undistracted service to the Lord. Paul was speaking of spiritual matters. For the third time they were advised that he was writing for their welfare. He was not insisting on celibacy; he was only reminding them of principles to consider in service for the Lord. "Snare" means the noose or lasso by which a wild creature is snared.

**36.** **But if any man think that he behaveth himself uncomely toward his virgin:** ... he acts improperly, —WLSN, —CMPB ... he is not behaving properly to the maid, —MOFT ... not treating his unmarried daughter properly, —HNT ... it is not suitable for his daughter, —FNTN ... toward his betrothed, —NORL.

**if she pass the flower of [her] age, and need so require:** ... if she passe the tyme of mariage, —TNDL ... if she is getting on in years, —NORL ... be beyond marriageable age, —ADAM ... be over her meridian, —CNDT ... beyond-the-bloom of youth, —RTHM ... and he hath not presented her to a husband, —MRDK ... and is under engagement to do thus, —FNTN ... if there are good reasons for the proposed match, —WAY ... so the matter is urgent, —MNTG.

**let him do what he will, he sinneth not: let them marry:** ... let him do what she desires ... she and her suitor should be allowed to marry, —WEYM ... let them be coupled in mariage, —GNVA.

**7:36.** It is admittedly difficult to discover the meaning of verses 36 through 38. Numerous explanations have been offered.

Some have interpreted the passage to mean that a man and a woman had agreed to a "spiritual marriage." They would go through the marriage ceremony but would remain celibates. However, the first examples of this sort of reasoning did not appear until the Second Century, almost 150 years after Paul wrote this letter.

Others have stated that the word *parthenos* ("virgin") may be translated "virgin state" or "celibacy" and be applied to either a man or woman. So, they say, the situation is that of a man or woman who gives up marriage in order to serve God more effectively. This may have influenced the system that developed that called for priests and nuns to remain unmarried.

Some believe that "any man" refers to one who was betrothed (in those days betrothals were contracts usually arranged by parents, often years before the marriage was to take place). This view pictures the man as undecided what to do. He feels he is not behaving honorably toward his fiancee by not marrying her, but will he be sinning if he goes against Paul's advice on celibacy?

The problem with this view is the meaning of the two Greek words whose translations are similar but importantly different. *Gameō* is the word used throughout this chapter, except in verse 38, where the word *gamizō* occurs. *Gameō* has the meaning of "marry," while *gamizō* means "give in marriage." Thus it is incorrect to refer to them as synonyms. Note that a husband-to-be could not give his fiancee in marriage.

The interpretation which has received most wide acceptance in the past is that "any man" refers to the father of a virgin daughter. In those times a daughter was under the absolute control of her father, who had the power to give her in marriage or to refuse to let her do so. The term might also apply in the case of a slave girl and her master, for he also had power to make the decision.

Related to the problem of who the "any man" and "virgin" are, is the problem of the word *huperakmos* which can mean either "past the prime of age," "of marriageable age," or more usually, "given to strong physical passions." If the first meaning is intended here, that is added weight for the view that "any man" refers to a father. However, this requires *parthenon* to mean daughter, which it does not usually do. If *huperakmos* has here its more usual meaning, then "any man" and "his virgin" probably refers to an engaged couple which would explain Paul's concern for their not sinning. It is verse 38, however, which provides the strongest case for the father/daughter option.

**37. Nevertheless he that standeth stedfast in his heart:** . . . if a father stands firm, —WEYM . . . he that hath determined, —RHEM . . . already firmly decided, —SEB.

**having no necessity, but hath power over his own will:** . . . he is not obliged, —FNTN . . . being under no constraint, —CNFT . . . is under no compulsion, —BRKL . . . finds himself under no necessity of marrying, —LOCK . . . complete control of his sexual will-power, —SEB . . . a sure control over his desires, —NORL . . . but is free to act as he will, —NOYS . . . as regards his own wish, —RTHM.

**and hath so decreed in his heart that he will keep his virgin, doeth well:** . . . has determined privately, —RTHM . . . to retain the girl at home, —FNTN . . . keep his unmarried daughter at home, —TCNT . . . to keep his betrothed untouched, —NORL . . . to preserve his virgin as a virgin, —BRKL . . . keep his maid a spiritual bride, —MOFT . . . he will keep his virginity, —LOCK . . . to maintain his Celibacy, —WLSN . . . he doeth commendably, —MRDK.

**7:37.** Paul indicates that the man must be fully convinced in his own mind. In making his earlier decision that the girl should remain a virgin, he may have failed to realize she might not want to remain single. He had "power over his own will." He was free to make the decision. If he insisted she remain single, or if he allowed her to marry, it was not sin.

**38. So then he that giveth [her] in marriage doeth well:** . . . If, then, he marries his girl, —BECK . . . So the man who marries does well, —TEV . . . the one who consents to his daughter's marriage, —TCNT . . . gives his unmarried daughter in marriage, —HNT . . . marries his bride-to-be, —SEB . . . his virgyn in matrymonye, —WCLF . . . will be doing the right thing, —MOFT . . . does right, —NIV.

**but he that giveth [her] not in marriage doeth better:** . . . the one who opts against her marriage, —ADAM . . . will do better, —WEYM . . . does even better, —NIV.

**7:38.** Verse 38 gives the strongest evidence for the view that verse 36 is addressing a father and his daughter. The reason for this is that Paul here

used a different word for marriage (*ekgamizōn*) than he did in verses 28 and 36 (*gameitōsan* and *gēmē*). In Mark 12:25 *gamizō* means "given in marriage" and this is its use in classical Greek. It is also true, however, that the classical distinction between *-eō* and *-izō* verbs (e.g., *gameō* and *gamizō*) was no longer consistently held to in Koine Greek.

To recapitulate this complex section, in verse 25 Paul addressed himself to an issue the Corinthians had brought to Paul's attention (either in the letter they sent to him, cf. 7:1, or else by the representatives from Chloe's household, cf. 1:11), namely, *parthenon* (virgins). Although there are several particular kinds of situations that Paul has addressed, the bottom line to all of Paul's comments, given as they were by the Holy Spirit, is that there is nothing inherently good or evil regarding singleness or marriage. Each is an option; each can be positive; each can be negative.

The only concern that Paul has is that when people make their choice (and it must be a choice) for singleness or marriage they are obedient to God and do not take undue concern for this world which is passing away.

Paul returns to his original theme, that because of circumstances which he calls "the present distress" (probably the persecutions through which the church was going) that the unmarried state would be better. So he says that marriage is acceptable, but the single state is better.

Notice that Paul was not encouraging celibacy on moral grounds, that it is morally better to remain celibate. It is better only because it would make possible greater service for Christ.

**39. The wife is bound by the law as long as her husband liveth:** . . . bound by the law of wedlock, —CNBR . . . during the whole period that he lives, —WEYM.

**but if her husband be dead, she is at liberty to be married to whom she will:** . . . but if her husband sleepe, —RHEM . . . if he be fallen asleep, —HNT . . . should be reposing, —CNDT . . . anyone she pleases, —MOFT.

**only in the Lord:** . . . only in a Christian way, —BRKL . . . provided he is not an unbeliever, —TCNT . . . provided that he is a Christian, —WEYM . . . provided he be a believer, —WAY . . . it must be a Christian, —MOFT, —WLMS.

**7:39.** In conclusion, Paul advised regarding widows and remarriage. The last group to fall under the heading of "virgins" in chapter 7 is widows. Paul has asserted all along that marriage and singleness are both legitimate options; that is the case here as well. In one of Paul's final letters, he once again took up the issue of widows (1 Timothy 5:9-15) and took the same stance that he took here.

A wife is obligated as long as her husband lives. If her husband should die, the woman is free to marry according to her choice and will, with one exception. Her new spouse must be a believer, one "in the Lord." This would also require seeking the Lord's will in the matter.

**40. But she is happier if she so abide, after my judgment:** . . . But more blessed shall she be, –DOUY . . . But she'll be happier, –BECK . . . her state is a more enviable one if she remains as she is, –WEYM . . . if she continue as she is, –CMPB . . . if she stays as she is, –NIV . . . if she stayed a widow, –SEB . . . according to my opinion, –HNSN . . . that is my opinion, –MOFT . . . in my opinion, –MRDK.

**and I think also that I have the Spirit of God:** . . . I, too, lay claim, –NORL . . . I also know God's intention, –FNTN.

**7:40.** But Paul was of the opinion that she would be happier if she remained a widow. She would be, in particular, happier in her undisturbed devotion to the Lord. And Paul concluded that in these matters he had not merely been bending to personal bias, but had been advised by the Spirit of God, in his position as a called apostle. He voiced not merely private opinion, but that which had come from divine enablement.

## Chapter 8

**1. Now as touching things offered unto idols:** . . . And concerning, –RHEM . . . Relative to food that has been offered to idols, –BRKL . . . With regard to food, –MOFT . . . about idol-offerings, –FNTN . . . sacrificed vnto, –GNVA.

**we know that we all have knowledge:** . . . we are aware, –RTHM, –HNT.

**Knowledge puffeth up, but charity edifieth:** . . . Understanding makes you vain, –FNTN . . . tends to make people conceited, –WEYM . . . maketh a man swell, –CRNM . . . Knowledge breeds conceit, while love builds up character, –TCNT . . . love edifieth, –MRDK . . . love builds up, –MOFT.

**8:1.** The Scriptures approve some things as always right for the Christian; others are always wrong. In between are questions of conscience, considered wrong by some, right by others. The problem at Corinth was the eating of meat that had been sacrificed to idols. The Corinthian Christians were continually confronted with it. Such meat could appear on nearly any table.

In dealing with this problem, and others, Paul set forth certain principles which are valid and useful to this day (1 Corinthians 6:12; Romans 14:1-15:13). The phrases "now concerning" or "now as touching" remind us that this was a question which came from the Corinthians themselves. In pursuit of the answer they had begun with a wrong premise. Paul had to correct them.

Knowledge was of great value to the Corinthians, and Paul agreed with the importance and exercise of knowledge, but the Corinthians tried to solve their problems with knowledge alone. Paul made it clear that knowledge must be tempered with love.

Paul contrasted knowledge and love. He reminded the Corinthians that "knowledge puffeth up"; it can create pride, intellectual snobbery, and a "party spirit." Love, on the other hand, "edifieth" or builds up. The great Corinthian flaw was their poverty of love. The verb "edifieth" really refers to the putting up of buildings. Paul used it figuratively to mean the building of Christian character and the church. Knowledge alone could destroy the church; love and knowledge together could build it. Edification is the natural outgrowth of love (Ephesians 4:15f.; Matthew 22:37-40; 1 John 4:16-21).

**2. And if any man think that he knoweth any thing:** . . . Someone may seem to know a lot, –SEB . . . is confident, –CMPB . . . is presuming to know, –CNDT . . . fancies he knows anything, –TCNT . . . thinks that he knows a lot, –NORL.

**he knoweth nothing yet as he ought to know:** . . . he still has a lot to learn, –NORL . . . he still has something to learn, –BECK . . . as it ought to be comprehended, –FNTN.

**8:2.** Knowledge by itself has limitations. No matter how much a man thinks he knows, he still does not know fully. Paul used the perfect tense of the verb, implying full and complete knowledge.

**3. But if any man love God, the same is known of him:**

**8:3.** What really matters is not our knowledge but God's (2 Timothy 2:19; Galatians 4:9). For to be known (*egnōstai*) by God means to share in His grace, having first been recognized by Him. "Is known" implies a knowledge that is complete and full. Proper knowledge, in the hand of love, gives a right foundation for our actions.

**4. As concerning therefore the eating of those things that are offered in sacrifice unto idols:** . . . In regard to eating food, –HNT . . . offered to false gods, –SEB.

**we know that an idol [is] nothing in the world:** . . . we are fully aware, –WEYM . . . that they really don't exist, –SEB . . . that the fictitious gods, –LOCK . . . has no true being, –CNBR . . . has no real existence, –RSV . . . existence in the world, –NORL . . . existence in the universe, –MNTG, –TCNT.

**and that [there is] none other God but one:**

**8:4.** Paul then returned to the immediate question. "We know" (*oidamen*) continues the thought from verse 1. This is typical of Paul's style of writing.

When Paul wrote that "an idol is nothing," he was really saying it had no real place in the world; it had no power over the elements of nature. Rather, there is one God who controls earth and sky. Belief in the truth that the world is controlled by Him will deliver any Christian from superstition and fear. An idol is the product of man and thus has no real influence in the realm in which God Jehovah operates.

**5. For though there be that are called gods:** ...For if so-called gods do exist, *—WEYM* ...there be many imaginary nominal gods, *—LOCK* . . . there are so-called gods, *—ADAM* ...there are nominal gods, *—CMPB* . . . those being termed gods, *—CNDT.*
**whether in heaven or in earth:** ...either in the sky or on the earth, *—TCNT* ...either celestial or terrestrial, *—CNBR.*
**(as there be gods many, and lords many,):** . . . there are plenty of them, *—MOFT* . . . indeed, a vast number, *—WLMS* ...and many demi-gods, *—FNTN* ...but they are not real, *—SEB.*

**8:5.** It is true there are claims to the godship (deity) and lordship (dominion) of idols. In point of fact, there are literally multitudes of these claims. The devil makes lying claims and performs lying wonders. But this very multitude proves inadequacy on their part. "Many" (*polloi*) shows the desire to compensate for truth and authority by numbers. But the fact remains that there is only one true God whether or not He is acknowledged in heathen societies.

**6. But to us [there is but] one God, the Father, of whom [are] all things, and we in him:** ...He is the Source of everything, *—SEB* ...who is the source of all things and the goal of our living, *—WLMS* ...for whose service we exist, *—WEYM* . . . and we live for him, *—BECK.*
**and one Lord Jesus Christ:**
**by whom [are] all things, and we by him:** ...He made everything, *—BECK* . . . through whom everything was made, *—WLMS* ...through Whom all things exist, including us who ourselves exist through Him, *—ADAM* . . . and for whom we exist, *—MOFT* . . . and we exist through him, *—HNT.*

**8:6.** On this hinge of the concept of one true God Paul hangs an important argument. Christians contrast sharply with idolaters. "Father" (*patēr*) denotes a special relationship to God as Creator and spiritual Father. All things exist by Him. Believers are reserved for His purposes and glory. He will reap in "us" His glory, as a father would through his children.

This relationship is possible through the "Lord Jesus Christ" who is seen in His functions of Master, Mediator, and Friend. Such faith leaves no

place for false deities. The sacrificial rites were hollow and ineffective.

The central conviction governing Paul's remarks here about food offered to so-called gods is the fact that God is one. This statement is based on Deuteronomy 6:4, 5, the Shema, which all faithful Jews recite twice a day. So important are the words of this passage, "Hear, O Israel: The Lord our God is one Lord: and thou shalt love the Lord thy God with all thine heart, and with all thy soul, and with all thy might," that Jesus himself called this the first and greatest commandment in Mark 12:29-31. One scholar has appropriately labeled the Shema "the most important word" for Christian life and doctrine (Miller, p. 17).

The oneness of God is the most important word for Christians because it encompasses and explains how every facet of life belongs to God. Because God is one, our loyalty must be exclusive to Him alone. This is why the first commandment says, "Thou shalt have none other gods before me" (Deuteronomy 5:7) because there are no other gods—period. Thus, for Israel, "the absence of faith was not seen as a possibility. The only options for human existence are faith in the living God or idolatry" (Miller, p. 25).

The Shema, then, has a twofold significance. The theological implication is that "there is only one ultimate or absolute—the power that undergirds all reality is one" (Miller, p. 28). The anthropological implication means "God is that which keeps our lives from being chaotic and divided beyond the limits of human management . . . (and therefore) is that one and absolute object of our allegiance and loyalty" (Miller, p. 29).

**7. Howbeit [there is] not in every man that knowledge:** . . . But everybody doesn't know this, *—ADAM* . . . all believers do not recognize these facts, *—WEYM* . . . this knowledge of God is not shared by everyone, *—NORL* . . . by [their] familiarity, until even now, *—RTHM.*
**for some with conscience of the idol unto this hour:** . . . Some, having been accustomed to idol worship, *—NORL* ...because of their past habits with idols, *—WLMS* ...still idol-conscious, *—CNFT* ...think in terms of idols, *—BRKL* . . . their quite recent familiarity with idols, *—TCNT* . . . by familiarity with the idol, *—WORL* ...accustomed until now, *—MNTG* ...still have the habit of treating idols, *—SEB.*
**eat [it] as a thing offered unto an idol:**
**and their conscience being weak is defiled:** ...their moral sense, being still weak, receives a shock, *—TCNT* ...is polluted, *—RHEM* ...are polluted, *—WEYM* . . . is contaminated, *—MOFT* ...is being guilt-stained, *—WAY.*

**8:7.** But there is another consideration. Not everyone in Corinth understood this. What knowledge these had did not rid them of the consciousness that what they ate was sacrificial idol meat and that they had somehow become connected with the idol. In verse 1 Paul said knowledge was not confined to a certain group in Corinth. But that did not mean all Christians possessed it. If a person lived with a haunting sense that what he ate belonged to idols, he was associated with idols; he had sinned (Romans 14:23). This one with the weak conscience, unable to discern whether the act was right or wrong, lived with guilt.

**8. But meat commendeth us not to God:** ... But food will not bring us before God, *−ADAM* ... Now our food cannot change our place in God's sight, *−CNBR* ... will not give us a standing, *−CNDT* ... does not recommend us, *−CMPB, −BRKL* ... doth not bring us near to God, *−MRDK* ... does not bring us nearness to God, *−MNTG.*

**for neither, if we eat, are we the better; neither, if we eat not, are we the worse:** ... We are not any better off, *−SEB* ... if we abstain we do not lose anything, *−MOFT* ... we are neither inferior to others if we abstain from it, nor superior to them if we eat it, *−WEYM* ... are we the richer ... are we the poorer, *−GNVA* ... are we lacking, *−WORL* ... are we deficient, *−MKNT* ... shal vve abound ... shal vve lacke, *−RHEM* ... do we come short, *−RTHM* ... shall we have the less, *−DOUY* ... we do not fall short by abstaining, *−NORL* ... are we worse Christians, *−LOCK.*

**8:8.** Paul made the point that neither partaking nor abstaining would affect the relationship of the Corinthians to God. Food is too small a matter and God is too great to allow it to determine a believer's relationship to Him. Abstinence will not bring him closer to God, nor drive him away, as the weak might have been led to believe. In like manner indulgence would not make him better as the proud might have wished. This was not the heart of the problem. What Paul was leading up to was having the right motive toward God and others.

**9. But take heed lest by any means this liberty of yours become a stumblingblock to them that are weak:** ... Now beware, *−CNDT, −SAWR* ... lest this same strength of yours, *−FNTN* ... lest this your authority, *−MRDK* ... that this mastery of yours, *−BRKL* ... that the exercise of your right, *−MOFT* ... your freedom in this matter, *−TCNT* ... cause not the weake to faule, *−TNDL* ... be an offense to, *−RHEM* ... be an occasyone of falling, *−CRNM.*

**8:9.** Paul issued a solemn warning about asserting one's personal rights. This can affect one's standing with God. Jesus made it abundantly clear that love toward God shows itself in the way we treat the stranger, our enemies, and our brother. Love is essential in our relationship with God;

therefore it is vital in our relationship with our Christian brothers.

The issue is not that we are strong or have a good knowledge of the things of Christ. Nor is the issue that of our wonderful freedom in Christ. The point is that we must consider the frailties of the weak. The stronger we are, the more that attitude is demanded of us.

Meat in itself is a neutral item and may be refrained from for the good of another. "Stumblingblock" (*proskomma*) is something that lies in the path, over which an unwary, unsuspecting foot might trip or stumble. Naturally, this could cause the person to fall. From a spiritual viewpoint a "stumblingblock" is anything that can cause another to sin, to act outside of faith, and so injure his soul or Christian life.

**10. For if any man see thee which hast knowledge sit at meat in the idol's temple:** ... the possessor of comprehension, *−FNTN* ... sit feasting in an idol-temple, *−LOCK* ... an idol's shrine, *−CNDT.*

**shall not the conscience of him which is weak be emboldened to eat those things which are offered to idols:** ... his conscience, uncertain as it is, *−BRKL* ... won't you be encouraging him, *−BECK* ... embolden him to violate his scruples of conscience, *−MOFT* ... be encouraged to eat, *−FNTN.*

**8:10.** To reinforce his point, Paul presented an illustration for the Corinthians. He pictured the example of a knowledgeable, strong Christian at a temple feast. He might be there from obligation or for an official ceremony, for such an event in a pagan city would not occur apart from a meal in the temple. Or it might be the result of the general conduct of a Corinthian who considered idol meat as merely ordinary.

Paul censured this because of its effect on others. In 10:18-22 he opposed it on its own account. A "weak" brother, as was possible in open feasts, might observe the actions of the "stronger" brother. By use of a question, Paul pointed out that the weak brother, seeing the example of the stronger brother, might eat thinking it was permissible for him also.

Paul said the weaker brother might be "emboldened" (*oikodomēthēsetai*) or strengthened; that is, encouraged, to partake of the idol meat. This same word is translated as "edifieth" in verse 1. The phrase is full of irony. Perhaps the stronger brother thought of "building" up by his poor example. But faith was not built, and the result was destruction.

The "stronger" Corinthians in their pride no doubt assumed that by their example they could show the weaker brothers "a better way." The problem with this is that Paul said that "whatsoever is not of faith is sin" (Romans 14:23). It is important to note that Romans 14:1-15:5 (which was written while Paul was in Corinth) also deals with the issue of the strong and the weak. Both in Romans and 1 Corinthians Paul personally favors the stronger position, but he would not prescribe this for any who might be offended. As with the issue of singleness and marriage, Paul did not make absolute assertions; Paul's task as an apostle of Jesus Christ and a willing tool of the Holy Spirit was to teach that any and all actions must come from faith, not from the well-meaning (or not so well-meaning) advice of other Christians. God is not glorified by actions performed under duress; rather God looks at the inner motivation of a person and judges on that basis (Romans 15:5, 6).

**11. And through thy knowledge shall the weak brother perish:** ... In consequence, —BRKL ... you may bring spiritual destruction upon this weaker man, —NORL ... ruining the weak fellow Christian, —BECK ... he who is feeble, —MRDK ... the weak man is ruined, —TCNT ... is ruined by your enlightenment, —BRKL ... by your so-called knowledge, —WLMS ... will perish because of your "knowledge"! —TEV ... is utterly lost, —FNTN.
**for whom Christ died?:**

**8:11.** The result of such an action was that the weak brother perished or "is perishing"; he sinned. What compounded this picture was that this was one for whom Christ died. If Christ would die for the "weak," what should the "stronger" brother be willing to do.

**12. But when ye sin so against the brethren:** ... against your fellow Christians, —BECK.
**and wound their weak conscience:** ... and striking their vveake conscience, —RHEM ... injuring their moral sense, —TCNT ... and smiting their conscience, —RTHM, —WORL.
**ye sin against Christ:** ... in reality, sinning, —WEYM ... you are actually sinning against Christ, —WLMS.

**8:12.** The sin of wounding a weak conscience is against the brethren, the Church as a whole. A wound is inflicted, because the conscience of the weaker believer is influenced to make a decision which it would not have done on its own and which it should not make. Sin then occurs.

Worst of all, it is a sin against Christ. He is robbed of the soul for which He died. Christ's work on the cross is not appreciated properly.

**13. Wherefore, if meat make my brother to offend:** ... if food is any hindrance to my brother's welfare, —MOFT ... if meat causes my brother to sin, —SEB ... if food makes my brother sin, —TEV ... is the cause of my brother's downfall, —NORL ... a cause of my brother's falling, —RSV ... I shall never eat meat

again, —ADAM ... so that I may not cause my brother to stumble, —FNTN ... to fall, —WEYM.
**I will eat no flesh while the world standeth:** ... under no circumstances, —CNDT ... I eat flesh to the latest age, —RTHM ... will I touch any kind of animal food, —WEYM.
**lest I make my brother to offend:** ... for fear I should cause my brother to fall, —WEYM ... I should be snaring my, —CNDT.

**8:13.** In conclusion, Paul's admonition was clear. Abstinence, under such circumstances, was best. But a warning must be offered. Not just any situation demands such forbearance, for some go to an opposite extreme. Nonetheless, Paul would under no circumstances bear the awful burden of causing someone to stumble and sin; that must be prevented at all costs.

Actually, Paul's statement was more comprehensive than some would think; the word "meat" (*brōma*) is a general term relating to food, not just to idol meat. The issue was vital to Paul; he used "brother" four times in these last three verses. It should be important to all Christians to care for the weaker brother. Paul said he would abstain, if need be, "while the world standeth." Paul was willing to do this, and the Corinthians needed to follow his example in Christ. There is a certain freedom of knowledge in Christ, but it must be tempered by love. Paul intended to have a clear conscience in liberty and love.

As a summary to chapter 8, let us recall the Gnostic problem at Corinth. The Gnostics, here associated with the strong position, believed that the "spiritual" and the "physical" realms were completely unrelated. Consequently any act involving the body could not detract from their spirituality. This gave them a kind of superiority over other Christians because their freedom was unhindered.

The strong position can be identified particularly in three slogans: "We all have knowledge" (8:1); "there is no ... idol in the world" (8:4, NASB) and "all things are lawful" (10:23, also in the context of meat offered to idols). Although these statements may appear to be true in and of themselves, the Holy Spirit cannot condone the attitude of pride that lurks behind them. This is why Paul begins the following chapter with the statement that even though he has freedom as an apostle, he is actually subject to God and to his brothers.

## Chapter 9

**1. Am I not an apostle?:**
**am I not free?:** ... a freeman? —CMPB.
**have I not seen Jesus Christ our Lord?:** ... with my own eyes? —NORL.

**are not ye my work in the Lord?:** ... I have accomplished in, —MOFT ... You are the result of my efforts, —SEB ... that you are the fruits of my labor, —CNBR ... products of my work in the Lord? —NORL.

**9:1.** Having suggested his own example, Paul set out to show that his example could be trusted and followed. With "am I not free?" to which Paul expected a positive reply, he asserted that, like other Christians, he had certain Christian rights and privileges. Paul was not bound by Mosaic restrictions. He knew liberty in Christ. The positive response expected to "Am I not an apostle?" also indicated his privileges in the special position of God's called apostle. He had seen "Jesus Christ our Lord." The use of "Jesus" alone (cf. variant *c)* is rare with Paul. He may have been thinking of his Damascus Road experience or maybe of Christ's humanity.

Paul's work had borne fruit. While the emphasis was still clearly on God, the Corinthians were visible proof of the effectiveness of Paul's labors. They should be the last to doubt Paul's apostleship because he was their spiritual father. They were living proof of the effectiveness of his work.

Paul built his argument to a telling conclusion. Step by step, in thorough and convincing fashion, he involved the Corinthians in the process and presented such a strong base for his conclusions that when he finished, the Corinthian Christians understood what was right in the Lord.

**2. If I be not an apostle unto others, yet doubtless I am to you:** ... yet I am certainly so to you, —FNTN ... certainly at least to you I am, —RTHM ... I certainly am one to you, —BECK ... At least to you, —SEB.
**for the seal of mine apostle-ship are ye in the Lord:** ... for your very existence as a Christian church, —WEYM ... for you are the seal set, —MOFT ... for you are the stamp of my apostleship, —FNTN ... the seal which stamps the reality of my apostleship, —CNBR ... are the proof of ... by virtue of your union with the Lord, —WLMS ... the actual seal set on my mission-work, —WAY.

**9:2.** The Corinthians were the "seal" of Paul's apostleship. The seal (*sphragis*) was important in a day when many could not read. The mark stamped on clay or wax was first a mark of ownership and then a means of authentication (Morris, *Tyndale New Testament Commentaries,* 7:132). This was not only a defense to Paul's critics, it also bore directly on the question of rights.

**3. Mine answer to them that do examine me is this:** ... My defence to, —RTHM ... My defence to my accusers is this, —FNTN ... And [my] apology to my judgers, —MRDK ... My defense against those who question me, —CNFT ... my reply to my inquisitors, —MOFT ... how I vindicate myself, —WEYM ... who

question my authority, —NOYS ... who are investigating my claims is this, —ADAM ... who set up an inquisition upon me, —LOCK.

**9:3.** "This" relates to the two previous verses. It appears that what was really under attack was Paul's apostleship, not the rights of apostleship. Paul defended this to make his argument accepted. Even if Paul's use of his rights had been criticized, it would have been much easier to accept if he were regarded as a true apostle. Both "answer" and "examine" are legal words, as though defending against a charge. If Paul had established his apostleship, the rights should be granted as well.

The point that Paul was coming to was that all must be an example of love in liberty as he had been.

**4. Have we not power to eat and to drink?:** ... Have we not liberty, —CMPB ... my right to be maintained, —CNBR.

**9:4.** Paul had the right or freedom to "eat and to drink." Probably he was speaking of the right to maintenance at the church's expense, or support in other ways. Or he may still have been discussing the matter of food.

**5. Have we not power to lead about a sister, a wife:** ... May we not take along with us on our journeys, —NORL.
**as well as other apostles, and [as] the brethren of the Lord, and Cephas?:** ... like the rest of the apostles, —ADAM.

**9:5.** Paul did expect, if he so chose, to be able to "lead about ... a wife." But this particular question was not limited to marriage only. That would not have been argued. The question with its positive response expected led not only to support for the apostle but to the implication that the wife too should be supported by the church. To support his argument Paul pointed to the actions of other Christian leaders. The reference to "other apostles" would suggest that a number of them were married. The examples used were those who had a special place in the eyes of the Corinthians. This strengthened the general argument.

**6. Or I only and Barnabas, have not we power to forbear working?:** ... not liberty to, —CMPB ... are denied the right of abstaining from work, —MOFT ... right to forbear working? —RTHM ... to abstain from labor? —WLSN ... have no right to be maintained, except by the labor of our own hands? —CNBR ... excluded from the privilege of being maintained without working? —LOCK.

**9:6.** The questions continued, each anticipating a positive answer. Paul had the right, along with Barnabas, to refrain from working to support himself while preaching the gospel. His point was that he should be able to desist from manual labor, in order to spend full time spreading the gospel. This would mean that the church would find it necessary to support him.

Certainly, this church could not argue that these two alone were not to be offered such support, or did not have this right, when the many others did.

7. **Who goeth a warfare any time at his own charges?:** . . . Vvho euer plaieth the souldiar, —RHEM . . . Who campaigns, —FNTN . . . Who serveth as a soldier, —DOUY . . . Who serveth in the wars, —MKNT . . . goes on a military expedition at his own expense? —SAWR . . . at his owne cost? —GNVA . . . provide his own supplies? —MOFT . . . serves at his own cost? —WEYM . . . serves at his private cost? —CNBR.

**who planteth a vineyard, and eateth not of the fruit thereof?:** . . . debarred from eating of the produce of it? —WAY . . . without eating its fruit? —NOYS . . . does not eat any of its grapes? —NORL.

**or who feedeth a flock, and eateth not of the milk of the flock?:** . . . Does a shepherd get no drink, —MOFT . . . who shepherds a flock, —ADAM . . . Who takes care of sheep, —NORL . . . look after a herd and not get his living from the milk? —TCNT . . . and does not drink any of the milk the flock produces? —WLMS.

**9:7.** Having defended his rights and privileges by the acts of other Christian teachers, Paul now turned to the custom of society. Paul pointed to the examples of the soldier, the vinedresser, and the shepherd. Like Christ before him, Paul found great power in these simple illustrations (Matthew 20:1; 21:28; Luke 11:21, 22; 12:32; 14:31; John 10:1-16; 21:15; 1 Corinthians 3:6; 14:8; Ephesians 4:11; 6:10; 1 Thessalonians 5:8). Each one mentioned had a different place in life; one was an employee, one an owner, the shepherd was perhaps a slave. But each was fed from his occupation, each shared in the harvest of his work.

To this point through the first six verses of the chapter Paul, by three questions and answers, has asserted that he has the right to have his daily needs met, to have a wife to minister with him, and not to have to do manual labor. Paul then supported these claims with several analogies. In verse 7 the analogies are human. If every soldier goes to war with his needs met, why cannot Paul have his met? If it is to be expected that a vinedresser can nourish himself from his own produce, why cannot Paul expect to have his produce, his church, support him? If a shepherd drinks milk while tending the sheep, why should not Paul be fed for tending to his flock?

8. **Say I these things as a man?:** . . . Speake I these things according to man? —RHEM . . . Am I making use of merely worldly illustrations? —WEYM . . . Am I stating only a human rule? —BECK . . . Am I speaking from a human viewpoint, —ADAM . . . Human arguments, —MOFT . . . by way of human illustrations, —WLMS . . . from human examples, —SEB . . . purely from a human standpoint, —BRKL . . . am I guided only by human customs? —TCNT.

**or saith not the law the same also?:** . . . Does not the Law speak in the same tone? —WEYM . . . or does not the Law mention these matters? —BRKL . . . too lay down the same principle? —WAY.

**9:8.** Paul wanted to make it clear that he was not speaking from the standpoint of human wisdom alone. Some might have accused him of this on the basis of his previous "natural" illustrations. So Paul proceeded a step further, to a link with divine truth and legal justice. The conjunction *ē* ("or") both combines and contrasts the two major clauses of this sentence which are "I speak" (*lalō*) and "the law says" (*ho nomos . . . legei*). The conjunction *ē* lends emphasis to the second clause which makes clear that Paul speaks not on his own but by authority of the Scriptures.

Paul expected a negative answer to the first question in this verse and a positive answer to the second question. "The law" was regarded as authoritative. This did not mean the Christian was under the power of the Law, but it did acknowledge the truth of principles in the Law and that it had God's blessing. It was a source of truth and right, and Paul used it for Christian guidance.

9. **For it is written in the law of Moses:**
**Thou shalt not muzzle the mouth of the ox that treadeth out the corn:** . . . thou schalt not bynde the mouth, —WCLF . . . that is treading out your grain, —WLMS . . . the threshing bullock, —FNTN.
**Doth God take care for oxen?:** . . . Is it the bullocks that God is thinking of? —TCNT . . . thinking in terms of oxen, —BRKL.

**9:9.** The reference is to Deuteronomy 25:4. The "law of Moses" properly refers to the first five books of the Old Testament. Whether it was intended to be so limited or so specific here is difficult to say, but the reference is clear. It is to the ox who, while tramping the corn, shook the grain loose from its husk. After that the mixture was tossed in the air. The wind carried the lighter chaff away. The heavier grain fell back to the floor, and the animal was allowed to eat some of the grain which lay on the floor.

On the basis of this Paul asked, "Doth God take care for oxen?" This question raises an interesting problem. The Greek text contains a *mē* plus an indicative verb, and this normally requires a negative response. But Paul is surely not saying that God does not care for oxen. All through the Scriptures God's care is shown for all the creatures He created, as well as for man. And in itself the

Old Testament reference Paul quotes shows God's care for oxen. It appears, then, that here the apostle was making an important point: If God made provision for even an animal, would He not be concerned about those who were ministering for Him?

**10. Or saith he [it] altogether for our sakes?:** . . . Isn't He really speaking about us? —*ADAM* . . . doth he command this chiefly for our sakes, —*MKNT* . . . Is it not especially for our sakes? —*NORL* . . . or does he care particularly for us? —*KLGS* . . . Surely He has us in mind, —*BECK* . . . is it really in our interest, —*WEYM* . . . in our behalf? —*WLMS.*

**For our sakes, no doubt, [this] is written:** . . . certainly, it was written, —*CMPB* . . . to teach us something, —*SEB.*

**that he that ploweth should plow in hope:**

**and that he that thresheth in hope should be partaker of his hope:** . . . it should be in the hope of sharing, —*WEYM* . . . should have some hope of a share in the harvest, —*NORL* . . . in hope of partaking of the fruits, —*CNFT* . . . to share in the produce of his toil, —*CNBR* . . . we should expect to get a share of the crop, —*BECK* . . . to receive fruit, —*DOUY.*

**9:10.** The quote and application were made first and foremost to preachers of the gospel, to laborers in the ministry. God provides for the needs of the Christian laborer from the fruits of his labor; thus, "plowing" (sowing and caring for the seed) and "threshing" (the harvest process) should be done in hope and expectation.

Notice again that Paul was building the argument carefully so that the resulting application was the more forceful and binding.

**11. If we have sown unto you spiritual things:** . . . been busy planting spiritual seed in you, —*NORL* . . . Since we planted spiritual things among you, —*SEB* . . . sown spiritually for you, —*FNTN.*

**[is it] a great thing if we shall reap your carnal things?:** . . . is it a great matter, —*RHEM* . . . is it unreasonable that we should expect, —*LOCK* . . . if we reap the necessaries of life, —*FNTN* . . . reap your worldly goods, —*MOFT* . . . that we should reap a temporal harvest, —*WEYM* . . . we reape youre bodely thynges? —*CRNM* . . . to reap a material support from you? —*WLMS* . . . reap material benefits from you? —*ADAM.*

**9:11.** Paul also argued from the standpoint of natural justice. The opening conditional clause of this verse implies that the condition had been fulfilled. The man who labors to produce the harvest is entitled to share in the proceeds. Paul had labored in the things of the Spirit; he had shown himself a profitable servant. But one cannot eat "spiritual" things. Therefore, Paul was entitled to material and bodily, not sinful, benefits. Considering the vast gulf between "spiritual" and

"carnal," it is no wonder that Paul could ask "Is it a great thing?" and expect a negative answer.

Material things are not intended to be the final or suitable reward for spiritual labors. But supply for basic needs is a natural part of the process, and those who have benefited from the spiritual labor of the ministry may be expected to provide the basic elements of life to one who has been called of God to share "spiritual" life on a free and generous basis.

**12. If others be partakers of [this] power over you, [are] not we rather?:** . . . if others have this prerogative, —*MRDK* . . . do not we still more? —*NOYS* . . . have we not a stronger claim? —*WLMS* . . . Shouldn't we have it, too? —*SEB.*

**Nevertheless we have not used this power; but suffer all things:** . . . have not used this right, —*FNTN* . . . but forego every claim, —*CNBR* . . . We endure all of these things, —*SEB.*

**lest we should hinder the gospel of Christ:** . . . lest we should giue any offence, —*RHEM* . . . that we might in nothing impede the announcement of, —*MRDK* . . . rather than place any obstacle in the way of the good news, —*ADAM* . . . to keep from hindering the progress, —*WLMS* . . . that we may cause no impediment to the good news of the Christ, —*HNSN.*

**9:12.** "Others" had exercised this right of maintenance and Paul did not begrudge them this, for it was right and proper. Yet they had a lesser claim on the Corinthians than Paul; he was their spiritual father.

But Paul and others had not exercised these rights. Rather they had "suffered" (*stegomen*) for the gospel. They had endured patiently and put up with wrong and poor treatment without complaining. It had not been easy to support themselves and continue the heavy load of spreading the gospel. But Paul and his coworkers had done it.

Some thought Paul had not claimed maintenance because his calling and ministry were somehow "inferior." But his motive had been unselfish; he did not want to "hinder the gospel of Christ." "Hinder" (*enkopēn*) means literally "a cutting into" and was used of breaking up a road to prevent an enemy's advance (Morris, *Tyndale New Testament Commentaries*, 7:135, 136). Some would claim Paul was preaching only to make a living, and that would hinder the gospel. So Paul renounced his right.

**13. Do ye not know that they which minister about holy things:** . . . the priests who perform the temple-services, —*WAY* . . . they which vvorke in the holy place, *–RHEM* . . . those who work with the sacred things, *–ADAM* . . . perform temple-rites, *–MOFT.*

**live [of the things] of the temple?:** . . . eat food from the temple, *–ADAM* . . . lyue of the sacrifice? *–CRNM* . . . live upon the revenues of the temple, *–CNBR.*

**and they which wait at the altar are partakers with the altar?:** . . . they that serue the altar, participat, *–RHEM* . . . are partakers of the temple, *–CRNM* . . . with the altar share, *–RTHM* . . . have their portion with the altar, *–CNDT* . . . get their share of the sacrifices, *–MOFT* . . . all alike share with the altar? *–WEYM* . . . share in what is sacrificed on the altar? *–ADAM* . . . are maintained from the altar? Fenton.

**9:13.** Paul added to the point. He referred to the example of the "ministers" of the temple. It is doubtful that he was referring to heathen practices because Paul would give no merit to what God had renounced and from which the Christian had turned away. "Do ye not know . . . ?" suggests familiar knowledge, and it was well known that those who worked in sacred things also received their livelihood. Those who regularly served in the temple received a portion of the altar sacrifice. Part was burned on the altar, part was given to the priests.

**14. Even so hath the Lord ordained:** . . . so the Lord's instructions, *–MOFT* . . . So also the Lord commanded, *–CNBR* . . . has appointed to those, *–SAWR* . . . also prescribes, *–CNDT* . . . directed that those, *–CNFT.*

**that they which preach the gospel should live of the gospel:** . . . those who announce the good news, *–ADAM* . . . to maintain themselves, *–WEYM* . . . get their living by the gospel? *–MOFT* . . . to be maintained thereby, *–CNBR.*

**9:14.** Lastly, Paul considered an argument from the Lord's command. This was the strongest and highest consideration. God himself had established this arrangement. Jesus had said workers deserve adequate pay (Luke 10:7).

All of these arguments united to make a point about "rights." Paul had renounced his own rights to advance the spread of the gospel. He stresses this theme through the rest of the chapter. He records the principles which motivated him as a preacher of the gospel.

Thus far in his argument, Paul had made an appeal to reason and common sense, to Old Testament Scripture, to Jewish temple practices, and finally to the words of Jesus himself to support the claim that apostles are absolutely entitled to support and remuneration. There is a strange irony to this chapter because Paul has argued strongly and vigorously on behalf of his fellow apostles (such as Barnabas) that they should be supported; yet in the rest of the chapter Paul proceeded to deny any of that support for himself.

In the church of today, the issue of support for ministers has to do largely with salary and benefits. Sadly, few Christians heed both aspects of Paul's arguments in chapter 9. Many clamor loudly for money and large salaries because they deserve it, and yet they ignore the example set by Paul himself who eschewed a salary. There are also others, however, who begrudge ministers their due and require them to be "servants" in a way not intended by Paul. These people need to realize that ministers are highly called of God and deserve their due. All Christians today need to hear *all* of what Paul said in chapter 9.

**15. But I have used none of these things:** . . . I have availed myself of none, *–FNTN* . . . I have used none of these privileges, *–CMPB* . . . my full rights, *–WEYM.*

**neither have I written these things, that it should be so done unto me:** . . . any such provision for myself, *–MOFT* . . . so done in my case, *–CLMT.*

**for [it were] better for me to die:** . . . for I prefer to die, *–HNSN.*

**than that any man should make my glorying void:** . . . shuld take this reioysinge from me, *–TNDL* . . . make this boast of mine an empty one, *–WEYM* . . . deprive me of this, my source of pride, *–MOFT* . . . deprive me of this reason for boasting, *–ADAM.*

**9:15.** Paul had not exercised his rights or liberty, and his refusal to do so had become a rule of life for him. Nor was he writing to establish these rights for himself in the future. Fiercely, strongly, and with much emotion he announced that "it were better for me to die"—in the Greek original, Paul left this incompleted. He would hold to his claim; he would never be so dependent.

Paul did not boast in the wrong sense. He was not speaking from a sense of pride or selfish egotism. His motives were pure. He was speaking in the context of the progress of the gospel, of its furtherance and its success. He was not referring to his own accomplishments.

**16. For though I preach the gospel, I have nothing to glory of:** . . . it is no credit to me, *–FNTN.*

**for necessity is laid upon me:** . . . for I cannot help doing it, *–WLMS* . . . Necessity compels me to do that, *–NORL* . . . is imposed upon me, *–WEYM* . . . I am constrained to do, *–MOFT.*

**yea, woe is unto me, if I preach not the gospel!:** . . . because it is a punishment for me, *–FNTN* . . . woe awaits me if I declare not the gospel, *–CMPB* . . . I am accursed if I do not preach, *–WLMS* . . . if I euangelize not, *–RHEM.*

**9:16.** Even in the preaching of the gospel, Paul did not "glory." He could claim no real credit.

Rather "necessity" was laid heavily on him. The Greeks considered it ruin to fight against "necessity." Paul thought of the message of the gospel of Christ as laying so heavily upon him that some undefined disaster would come upon him if he did not preach what had been so gloriously given to him. This did not, however, violate the part Paul's free will played in the process.

Paul was a man of duty, motivated by mercy and grace. He had once been an enemy, opposed to the message of the Cross. But that was changed by the call of Christ. He was now an ambassador for the Lord. This speaks of the deep impact and responsibility the call of God brings to a minister's life.

**17. For if I do this thing willingly, I have a reward:** . . . if I am engaging in this voluntarily, —CNDT . . . if I do This voluntarily, —WLSN . . . of my own accord, —MOFT . . . And if I preach willingly, —WEYM.

**but if against my will:** . . . but if, not by choice, —RTHM . . . but if unwillingly, —NOYS.

**a dispensation [of the gospel] is committed unto me:** . . . I have been entrusted with an office, —FNTN . . . a steward to discharge his trust, —MOFT . . . entrusted with a Stewardship reluctantly, —WLSN . . . I still am entrusted with trusteeship, —WLMS . . . a stewardship has nevertheless been entrusted to me, —WEYM.

**9:17.** In this verse Paul may have been saying that the man who preaches willingly merits a reward; whereas, if he does it unwillingly, he is nevertheless not excused. But perhaps the idea in this verse is carefully built on the previous one. If Paul preached from choice he would merit a reward. As it was, it was not his own choice; he had been chosen to preach. The following verse would then begin, "What reward is possible under these circumstances?"

The picture is one of a servant whose work is determined for him and his merit is in his faithfulness. The picture is of a sovereign Lord and an obedient slave. The Lord had given Paul an assignment. Some find a hint of predestination in such a view, but if so, it is in the matter of apostleship, not in the matter of salvation. It is God's choice that is involved. He chooses special vessels for special service.

**18. What is my reward then? [Verily] that, when I preach the gospel:**

**I may make the gospel of Christ without charge:** . . . I may deliver the gospel, —DOUY . . . will cost my hearers nothing, —WEYM . . . without cost, —RHEM, . . . without expense, —CNDT, —SAWR . . . without expense to anybody, —WLMS . . . free of charge, —MOFT . . . free to all, —NORL . . . without compensation, —ADAM.

**that I abuse not my power in the gospel:** . . . so as not to use to the full my authority, —PNIN . . . that I misuse not myne auctoritie, —GNVA . . . and use not the prerogative given me, —MRDK . . . from insisting on all my rights, —MOFT . . . forego my right as an Evangelist, —CNBR.

**9:18.** Paul's real reward was that while he had to preach, he did not have to preach without pay. He did not have to give up this right and privilege. But from his Master's example, Paul too had learned to be gracious and giving, though in a lesser sense. If Christ could give up His life, Paul could certainly surrender his right to support.

Thus Paul rejected reward in the mercenary sense, to claim it in the wider ethical sense. Again, the purpose was not to "abuse" or make full use of his power or right in the gospel, but to provide a way in which the gospel might be more powerfully and successfully spread. Liberty bowed to love.

These comments reveal a continuous life of love and sacrifice. Paul had caught the gracious spirit of his Lord and Master Jesus Christ. The Master's motivation was the salvation of men. To this end, everything was committed. His disciples saw the motives behind His actions and caught the same dedicated, committed spirit. They were moved to yield everything to the same great cause, the salvation of men. Now Paul was calling the Church to the same spirit and purpose.

**19. For though I be free from all [men]:** . . . I was not the slave of any one, —TCNT . . . free from any human power, —WLMS . . . from all human control, —WEYM . . . I submit to restrictions, —WAY . . . no one has any claim on me, —NORL.

**yet have I made myself servant unto all:** . . . I have made myself a veritable bondman, —WAY . . . I enslave myself to all, —CNDT.

**that I might gain the more:** . . . and yet, to win more converts, —TCNT . . . win over as many, —MOFT . . . in order to win a larger number, —BRKL . . . that I might benefit the greatest possible number, —FNTN . . . winning as many converts as possible, —WEYM . . . that I might gain the most, —CNBR.

**9:19.** Paul's real aim now comes into view. He had established his right to have liberty, so he could choose self-abnegation. He had not become unnecessarily encumbered by the demands of men. Rather, he freed himself from everyone so that he might truly be everyone's servant. Paul had been accused of "gainseeking"; but the gain he sought was winning many to Christ.

**20. And unto the Jews I became as a Jew:** . . . I met the Jews on the footing of a fellow-Jew, —WAY . . . I became more Jewish, —SEB.

**that I might gain the Jews:** . . . that I might benefit the Jews, —FNTN . . . for the winning of Jews, —WLMS . . . that I might win Jews for Christ, —NORL.

**to them that are under the law, as under the law:** ... To those who are subject to Law, —*TCNT* ... I became like a man under the Law, —*BECK.*

**that I might gain them that are under the law:** ... so as to gain the devotees of the Law, —*WAY.*

**9:20.** Paul "became" to the Jews as a Jew. He had been rejected by many of them, but he would not unnecessarily antagonize them. The fact that Paul used the article here with "Jews" (*tois Ioudaiois*) is highly unusual in Paul and is thought therefore to be referring to a particular incident, such as the circumcision of Timothy in Acts 16:3. Blass and Debrunner suggest that it might even be translated "those with whom I had to deal on each occasion" (section 262). Another example of where Paul adapted himself to Judaism was over the issue of purification in Acts 21:23-26. Paul did not believe the law of Moses could save a man, nor could the Jewish ceremonies and traditions. He was under grace, not "law." But he respected Jewish scruples and conformed to practices that would enable him to approach the Jew more acceptably.

This was not a case of "watering down" his belief. Rather, it was a subjection of accommodation not of principle. He was not bound to obey the Law, but he did so voluntarily. Because he ministered to those "under the law," Paul was accused of still preaching circumcision. But Paul's goal was to "gain them" for Christ.

This highlights something quite important regarding what it meant for Paul to be a Jew. For Paul, Judaism was tied in with the Law and the Pharisees' hedge around the Law which had perverted God's original intention for the Law. Paul therefore repudiated legalism but did not dispense with the Law because Jesus Christ fulfilled the Law (Matthew 5:17-20). Paul wrote in Romans 10:4, "Christ is the end of the law for righteousness to every one that believeth." Paul, then, was not a "Jew" as such in his theology, but he could use the Law and the beliefs of Judaism *insofar* as it won Jews to Christ. Note that in this paragraph (9:19-23) Paul used *hina* ("in order that") seven times to show that his personal manner was subservient to winning people to Christ.

**21.** **To them that are without law, as without law:** ... To those who have no Law, —*TCNT* ... those outside the Law, —*MOFT.*

**(being not without law to God, but under the law to Christ,):** ... although not lawless toward God but committed to Christ's Law, —*BRKL* ... but closer bound in Messiah's law, —*WAY* ... but specially under Christ's law, —*WLMS.*

**that I might gain them that are without law:** ... so that I might gain those not possessing a

law, —*FNTN* ... who have no written law, —*WLMS* ... without any moral law, —*NORL.*

**9:21.** Paul next mentioned the Gentiles, or those "without law," the Jewish designation for all outside the cover of the Mosaic covenant. Paul did not practice the law of Moses or make it the basis for his preaching among the Gentiles. But in a true Christian sense, Paul was not "without law." He had advanced to the "law of Christ" which is certain of fulfillment because it is by the Spirit and is governed by "an implanted life," not by an external yoke.

**22.** **To the weak became I as weak:** ... I am made sike to sike men, —*WCLF.*

**that I might gain the weak:**

**I am made all things to all [men]:** ... I fasshyoned my selfe to all men, —*CRNM* ... To all these I adapted myself, —*FNTN* ... I became all things, —*DOUY* ... I have become all sorts of things to all sorts of people, —*ADAM.*

**that I might by all means save some:** ... by all and every means, —*MOFT* ... to saue at the least some, —*GNVA.*

**9:22.** Paul refers to the weak, reminding the Corinthians of the matters dealt with in chapter 8. He left his position of strength and felt their weakness in order to gain them.

Note the thrice-repeated "all." In all these actions there was no compromise or compliance with unchristian principles, but rather love and self-denial. Paul did not bend before opposition. But where no principle was at stake, he would go to extreme lengths to meet people and win them to Christ. "Some" indicated that not all would accept Paul's message, but that did not deter him from attempting to reach as many as possible.

**23.** **And this I do for the gospel's sake:**

**that I might be partaker thereof with [you]:** ... that I myght haue my parte therof, —*CRNM* ... so that I may become a partner with others in it, —*ADAM.*

**9:23.** In "all things" Paul's governing aim was "for the gospel's sake." His one purpose was to fulfill his stewardship of the gospel. Determined and versatile in his approach to his assignment, Paul's goal and personal ambition was that he might be a joint partaker in winning people to salvation and leading them to Christ and then to spiritual maturity.

This prepared the stage for the remarks following on discipline and spoke to the Corinthians of the rewards that were available to them if they followed the right way.

**24. Know ye not that they which run in a race run all:** ... racing in a stadium, –*CNDT.* **but one receiveth the prize?:** ... but a single one, –*FNTN* ... gains the prize? –*MOFT.*

**So run, that ye may obtain:** ... so as to win, –*MOFT* ... so that you may win it, –*FNTN* ... in order to win with certainty, –*WEYM* ... in such a way that you will get it! –*ADAM* ... that you may win, –*CNBR.*

**9:24.** That which had been suggested was now openly expressed. Self-discipline was necessary for both Paul's mission and his salvation. He drew an illustration from the Isthmian games which got their name from the isthmus on which Corinth stood.

Every second or third year, huge crowds gathered to watch the athletic contests. Only free men could participate in the games, and they had to provide proof that for 10 months before the contest they had participated in the necessary preliminary training, as well as spending the last 30 days in exercises in the gymnasium. The winner and his family were honored, and when he returned to his native city, a breach was made in the city walls to allow him to enter, indicating that with such a man they had no need of walls for defense. He also received a prominent seat at all future contests.

In the Greek games only one won the prize. In the Christian race the prize is open to all. The emphasis is on the disciplined, purposeful, hard-running winner. The Christian should run as the winner runs.

**25. And every man that striveth for the mastery is temperate in all things:** ... And every competitor restrains himself, –*FNTN* ... contending in the games ... uses self control, –*RTHM* ... practices self-restraint all round, –*MOFT* ... who competes in a contest exercises self-control, –*ADAM* ... who strives in the matches trains himself by all manner of self-restraint, –*CNBR* ... refraineth himself from all things, –*DOUY* ... abstaineth from all thinges, –*TNDL* ... readily submit themselves to severe rules of exercise and abstinence, –*LOCK.*

**Now they [do it] to obtain a corruptible crown:** ... for the sake of securing a perishable wreath, –*WEYM* ... to win a fading wreath, –*MOFT.*

**but we an incorruptible:** ... to obtayne an euerlasting crowne, –*CRNM* ... an unfading, –*MOFT.*

**9:25.** The point made was not mere abstinence, but strong control of appetite and passion. The crown won at the games was the most coveted honor in the Greek world. If these athletes would strive and discipline themselves for something so unenduring as a leafy wreath, how much harder should Christians be willing to strive for a prize that is "incorruptible" or lasts forever. To achieve this prize, the participant must discipline himself in "all things."

**26. I therefore so run, not as uncertainly:** ... thus am I racing, not as dubious, –*CNDT* ... I am not just running in one spot, –*SEB* ... run without swerving, –*MOFT* ... not like a trifler, –*FNTN* ... but not aimlessly, –*NORL* ... with a clear goal ahead of me, –*BECK.*

**so fight I, not as one that beateth the air:** ... not as the pugilist who strikes out against the air, –*CNBR* ... I'm not shadow-boxing, –*SEB* ... thus am boxing, as not thrashing air, –*RTHM* ... does not inflict blows on the air, –*WEYM* ... not punching the air, –*BRKL.*

**9:26.** This concept leads to thoughts of the runner and the boxer. In similar fashion, Paul did not act without purpose or aim. He knew where the finish line was. Nor was he shadowboxing; his opponent was real and he fought "not as one that beateth the air." Only by such effort would Paul win.

**27. But I keep under my body, and bring [it] into subjection:** ... I tame my body, –*TNDL* ... I beat my body, –*GNVA* ... I subdue my body, –*MRDK* ... I exercise my own body and make it serve me, –*NORL* ... bringing it under complete control, –*SEB* ... I chastise my body, –*RHEM, –DOUY* ... I severely discipline ... make it subservient, –*WLSN* ... master my body, –*MOFT* ... and lead it captive, –*MKNT.*

**lest that by any means, when I have preached to others:** ... lest perhaps, –*MKNT* ... after having trained others, –*FNTN* ... while heralding to others, –*BRKL.*

**I myself should be a castaway:** ... I should myself be a reprobate, –*SAWR* ... I my selfe sholde be reproued, –*GNVA* ... I am disqualified myself, –*MOFT* ... be rejected as unworthy, –*NOYS* ... become disqualified, –*CNDT* ... become unfit to run, –*WLMS* ... and be thrown out myself, –*KLGS.*

**9:27.** Paul disciplined his body to gain a permanent victory, to meet the test, and qualify for his reward. It appears that Paul accepted his severe bodily suffering as needful for his own sanctification. He dared not lose his crown through failure to satisfy his Lord, or through carelessness and lack of discipline.

The verb *hupōpiazō* literally means "to strike under the eye" and therefore carried the connotation of giving someone "a black eye," certainly a vivid metaphor of what Paul was willing to endure in order to accomplish his ultimate objective of gaining the prize—not only for himself but for the Corinthians as well.

This should not be taken at all as if Paul regarded the physical body as evil; that was Gnostic thought. Rather, Paul's meaning here is similar to Romans 6:13, 19 where the body is spoken of as a servant who must serve one of two masters:

righteousness or unrighteousness. As with many other things in life (e.g., money, cf. Luke 16:13) what matters most is how we use what we have at our disposal and that it is used for God.

## Chapter 10

**1. Moreover, brethren, I would not that ye should be ignorant:**
**how that all our fathers were under the cloud:** ... sheltered by the cloud, *—WEYM.*
**and all passed through the sea:** ... got safely through, *—WEYM* ... crossed through, *—MOFT.*

**10:1.** Indulgence is dangerous to others and one's effectiveness in service. It is also dangerous to one's own soul. To illustrate, Paul turned to Old Testament history. He stressed the importance of what he was saying and its vital nature to the Corinthians with the warning, "I would not ... should be ignorant" (*agnoein*) or unaware. "All our fathers," without exception, received of the blessings of God. "All" is repeated five times in the first four verses.

The events referred to seem most directly related to the time of the Exodus. The fate of the fathers should warn the children. They knew about the cloud of divine guidance (Exodus 13:20-22; 14:19) and the sea of deliverance (Exodus 14). These were glorious signs of God's presence, blessing, and salvation.

**2. And were all baptized unto Moses:** ... and all as companions of Moses, *—BRKL.*
**in the cloud and in the sea:**

**10:2.** Together these experiences constituted the inauguration of Israel's national covenant life. Israel was born into its divine estate. They were "baptized (*ebaptisanto*) unto Moses" since in these acts they committed themselves to the leadership of Moses, and "through" him entered acknowledged fellowship with God.

The Corinthians had also been symbolically "baptized into Christ" (Galatians 3:27). The Israelites were united to Moses, but this relationship was in no way as close as the union between Christ and the believer.

**3. And did all eat the same spiritual meat:** ... ate the same spiritual food, *—MOFT* ... the same supernatural food, *—RSV.*
**4. And did all drink the same spiritual drink:** ... all drank of the same spiritual stream, *—CNBR, —MNTG* ... the same supernatural water, *—TCNT.*
**for they drank of that spiritual Rock that followed them:** ... that flowed from the spiritual rock, *—WEYM* ... a supernatural rock, *—TCNT* ... from the attending spiritual rock, *—BRKL* ... that went with them, *—BECK* ... that attended them, *—MRDK* ... which accompanied them, *—MOFT, —WLMS.*

**and that Rock was Christ:** ... which rock typified Christ, *—LOCK* ... was the Messiah, *—FNTN.*

**10:3, 4.** The Israelites were sustained by manna from heaven (Exodus 16:11-15) and water from the rocks at Rephidim and Kadesh (Exodus 17:1-7; Numbers 20:1-11). These carried a spiritual meaning for the believing partakers. Paul called the water "spiritual." He did not say the rock from which it issued was spiritual and not material, but that there was a "spiritual Rock" following them; their spirits drank while their bodies drank. "That (other) Rock was Christ." Paul was calling attention to the food's supernatural origin.

This verse indicates that Christ existed in Old Testament times and was spiritually present with Old Testament Israel. It is necessary that the divine Head be so identified to relate the Old Testament example to the New Testament Church.

Christ existed amid this ancient people and yet they perished. How can Christians believe themselves totally secure from such a fate? In passing, the apostle suggested that the Lord's Supper is spiritual food and drink by the first analogy to baptism in 10:2-4 and by the reference to the same observance in 10:16-22. Nowhere else in the New Testament are the two so closely related.

By calling attention to Israel's equivalent of baptism in verses 1 and 2, and Israel's equivalent of the Lord's Supper in verse 3, Paul offered a warning against a false emphasis on the sacraments. As important as baptism and the Eucharist are, they are not of themselves guarantors of salvation. Paul elsewhere evidenced a noncommittal attitude toward baptism at 1:14-16 and 15:29. It must be remembered, however, that Paul was writing here to a congregation who overemphasized the sacraments. For a more complete view of Paul's perspective on baptism it is also necessary to consult passages such as Romans 6:3, 4.

**5. But with many of them God was not well pleased:** ... Yet, in spite of these privileges, *—WAY* ... But with most of them, *—WEYM, —ADAM* ... with the greater part of them, *—PNIN, —CMPB* ... Yet most of them disappointed God, *—NORL* ... with a multitude of them, *—MRDK* ... not with the majority of them, *—RTHM* ... in the more part of them, *—RHEM* ... Yet most of them lost God's favor, *—CNBR* ... had God no delyte, *—CRNM* ... was not at all satisfied, *—WLMS* ... God took no pleasure, *—WORL.*
**for they were overthrown in the wilderness:** ... for they were strewed, *—RTHM* ... laid low in the desert, *—MOFT, —MNTG* ... they were laid prostrate, *—WLSN* ... were struck down in the desert, *—TCNT* ... and were destroyed in the wilderness, *—LOCK* ... Their dead bodies were scattered all over the desert, *—SEB.*

**10:5.** Instead of recognizing Christ's presence and blessings, Israel murmured and disobeyed. The contrasted "but" is strong. Therefore, God was displeased and Israel was judged in the wilderness. The greater part died in the wilderness; only Caleb and Joshua reached the Promised Land (Numbers 14:30).

"Many" of the "all" of verse 4, so highly favored and blessed, received only God's dire judgment. Why? Because of wrong attitudes which resulted in disobedience. The point should have been clear to the Corinthians.

**6. Now these things were our examples:** ...they became a warning to us, –WEYM . . . these became types for us, –FNTN . . . took place as a warning for us, –MOFT.
**to the intent we should not lust after evil things, as they also lusted:** ...that we might not be Cravers, –WLSN . . . to keep us from hankering after what is evil, –WLMS . . . that we should not covet, –DOUY...we might not covet evil things, –WORL...we should not hanker after, –MRDK...in pursuit of what is evil, –WEYM . . . as they craved, –MOFT . . . as they longed, –MNTG.

**10:6.** These were to serve as examples and warnings to the Corinthians and to us to avoid similar disobedience. At the very heart of these disobedient actions were disobedient attitudes, which Paul proceeded to enumerate.

The first refers to attitude and desire: "We should not lust." It recalls Numbers 11:4 and the Israelites' desire for the old diet of Egypt and at the same time refers to the attraction of the idol feasts in Corinth. These incidents were repeated. Evil passions desire evil things.

**7. Neither be ye idolaters, as [were] some of them:** ...Neither should we serve idols, –MRDK...So do not worship false gods, –NORL . . . be ye worshippers of Images, –TNDL...Don't worship idols, –BECK.
**as it is written, The people sat down to eat and drink:**
**and rose up to play:** . . . rose up to sport, –NOYS...rose up thence for idol-dances, –WAY...rose up for idol dances, –MNTG . . . got up to dance, –WLMS...got up to play around, –SEB...stood up to revel, –ADAM...to be making sport, –RTHM...to make sport, –MOFT...to act like children, –KLGS.

**10:7.** From the general admonition, Paul enlarged his discussion to cover certain specific matters. He admonished against idolatry. This urgent warning was repeated in verse 14. Paul was referring to Exodus 32:18-20, and he quoted Exodus 32:6. Remember that the Israelites did this at a time when they were waiting to receive the divine law from God by Moses. Idolatry was a real and continuous problem for the Israelites.

It was a real danger for the Corinthians also. They had been delivered from the superstitions of heathen religion, but they were still drawn by its festivities. They should have stopped their association with such completely, because enjoying this wild, careless merriment could lead rather easily to idolatry again.

When Israel should have been turning to spiritual matters and concentrating on the Lord, they were tempted to treat their salvation carelessly. The same could happen to the Corinthians.

One of the most consistent messages of the entire Bible is that idolatry and sexual immorality are always linked together. The one always results in the other. This is the case here where Paul spoke not only of eating food offered to idols but also of "play." Both the Hebrew *qahas* and the Greek *paizein* have the meaning of sexual play (cf. Genesis 26:8).

**8. Neither let us commit fornication:** ... Nor must we act licentiously, –MNTG . . . let vs be defyled with fornicacion, –CRNM . . . Let us stop practicing immorality, –WLMS . . . commit lewdness, –BRKL.
**as some of them committed:**
**and fell in one day three and twenty thousand:** ...fell dead in one day, –TCNT.

**10:8.** The progression moves from lust and desire to idolatry to fornication. Paul's primary reference appears to be Numbers chapter 25. This verse records that 23,000 died, while Numbers 25:9 records that 24,000 died. However, since Deuteronomy 4:3 indicates that all those connected with Baal-peor were under God's judgment, it seems probable that 23,000 actually died in the plague and Moses included those executed by the judges in Numbers 25:5 to make the total of 24,000 killed. Other writers (such as Hodge) believe both Moses and Paul were using round numbers. The important thing is the very serious danger that Paul was warning his readers about.

**9. Neither let us tempt Christ:** . . . Neither let us try the long-suffering of Christ, –CNBR . . . let us grievously tempt Christ, –CMPB...must we presume upon the Lord, –MOFT...not go too far in testing the Lord's patience, –BECK . . . must we presume upon the patience of our Lord, –MNTG . . . Nor should we try the patience, –TCNT...stop trying the Lord's patience, –WLMS.
**as some of them also tempted:**
**and were destroyed of serpents:** ...and perished by, –RHEM...They were killed by snakes, –SEB.

**10:9.** The natural progression in such a path is simply and clearly stated by Paul. The next step is tempting Christ. First comes sensuality, then unbelief. The path remains the same in every generation. The Corinthians would commit this same sin of presuming on divine forbearance if they continued to trifle with idolatry and these related sins.

It is extremely foolish to try God to see how far He will let a person go in sin before He brings judgment to bear. Israel tempted God; the result was judgment from God in the form of fiery serpents. At Corinth it was not so much the participation in pagan feasts as it was dissatisfaction with the discipline of their new faith that caused the problem.

In a sense, because of their disregard for the principles of faith and love, the Corinthians were close to rebelling in the same way that produced such disastrous results for Israel.

**10. Neither murmur ye:** ... do you complain as, —SAWR ... nether grucche ye, —WCLF.
**as some of them also murmured:**
**and were destroyed of the destroyer:** ... perished by the exterminator, —CNDT ... by the Destroying angel, —MOFT.

**10:10.** A fifth item was listed: murmuring (*gonguzete*) or grumbling. This amounts to disbelief in God's goodness. It is the complete opposite of faith in God. Paul may have been referring to the rebellion of Korah recorded in Numbers 16:40. Such murmuring was visited by the destroyer or "death angel" (2 Samuel 24:16; Isaiah 37:36; Exodus 12:23; Hebrews 11:28). Murmuring is a sin of dissatisfaction and rebellion that will not stop until it ends in disaster. It is defiance that God will not tolerate.

**11. Now all these things happened unto them for ensamples:** ... these came upon them typically, —FNTN ... by way of warning for others, —MOFT.
**and they are written for our admonition:** ... and were recorded, —NOYS ... for our correction, —CNFT, —DOUY.
**upon whom the ends of the world are come:** ... to whom the consummations of the eons have attained, —CNDT ... who stand at the meeting of the ages, —MNTG ... upon whom the final age of the world has come, —CNFT ... the perfection of the ages has come, —FNTN ... in the closing hours of the world, —MOFT.

**10:11.** Having looked at the Old Testament, Paul proceeded to apply the lessons taught by these incidents. "Now" indicates summary and application. These admonitions are for those "upon whom the ends of the world are come." Jewish and pagan history converge at the point of Christianity. All history finds its apex in the Christian Era. For the lessons of history to go unheeded by this generation would be disastrous.

**12. Wherefore let him that thinketh he standeth:** ... who is supposing, —CNDT ... whoever imagines he stands, —FNTN ... let him that thinks himself safe, —LOCK ... is standing so securely, —MNTG.
**take heed lest he fall:** ... lest he fall into sin, —LOCK.

**10:12.** Paul wanted his readers to be spiritually alert to the dangers of sin. "Standeth" refers to the believer's position in Christ. The problem is one of pride. The Corinthians had the same proud attitudes as did the ancient Israelites; and unless they were corrected, the results would be similar. They would "fall" morally, that is, sin. "Take heed" that you do stand.

**13. There hath no temptation taken you:** ... Trial has not overtaken you, —FNTN ... No Trial has assailed You, —WLSN ... Only human temptation hath overtaken you, —PNIN ... has waylaid you, —MOFT ... apprehend you, —RHEM.
**but such as is common to man:** ... as foloweth the nature of man, —TNDL ... except what is human, —CNDT ... but such as appartayneth to man, —GNVA.
**but God [is] faithful:**
**who will not suffer you to be tempted above that ye are able:** ... Who will not permit you, —FNTN ... above youre strenght, —TNDL ... above your ability, —HNSN ... beyond what you can stand, —MOFT ... beyond your strength, —CNFT.
**but will with the temptation also make a way to escape:** ... but shal in the middes, —GNVA ... provide the escape by, —FNTN ... provide the way out of it, —MOFT ... furnish also the way, —NOYS.
**that ye may be able to bear [it]:** ... that you may be able to susteine, —RHEM ... be enabled to hold out, —RTHM ... you to undergo it, —CNDT ... you will be able to come out of it, —FNTN ... that you may be able to withstand, —MNTG.

**10:13.** This verse may be one of the most frequently quoted passages in all of Paul's letters, and indeed, it is one that offers hope in time of trial. Following verse 12 as it does, these words offer encouragement and assurance that it is not necessary, after all, to fall as did the Israelites. If the Corinthians were willing to heed the Old Testament examples, God would be with them to help them stand.

There is more than just hope to this verse however. The "wherefore" (*Dioper*) which begins verse 14 is a warning that if the Corinthians continued to test God (hence Paul's warning in verse 9 not to tempt [test] Christ) and did not flee from idolatry, then God would not help them stand and instead would destroy them.

It is important to note that *peirasmos* ("temptation") is capable of three different meanings. First of all, it may mean temptation to sin. This can only come from Satan; never from God. Secondly, people may test God, as Israel did in the wilderness and as the Corinthians were doing. Finally, there is a testing from God that is not enticement to sin but purposes refinement and purification (Deuteronomy 8:2).

The example that alarms the proud may give hope to the burdened and discouraged; this temptation is bearable. Paul offered consolation first in the fact that this temptation is common to man; it is such as can be borne; it is measured by the strength of the tempted. It is not so strong it cannot be resisted.

Further consolation is found in the fact that God does not originate the temptation, but He does control it. God is faithful to help. God not only limits temptation, He supplies the means of escape. The purpose of seeing the escape is that the tempted may be able to bear the trial and hold up under it. The Corinthians faced the temptation of idolatry and, if resisted, the possibility of persecution. But the door of help stood open in Christ.

**14. Wherefore, my dearly beloved, flee from idolatry:** ... ye moost dereworthe to me, —WCLF ... continually flee, —MNTG ... fly from, —CRNM ... Shun idolatry, —MOFT ... flee from the worship of idols, —CNFT ... flee from the seruing of Idols, —RHEM ... avoid idolatry, —FNTN.

**10:14.** This verse fits so well with what precedes and with what follows that it serves as a hinge on which the whole chapter hangs and turns.

"My dearly beloved" showed Paul's deep concern for his readers and the problems discussed. As he had counseled regarding fornication in 6:18, he did now regarding idolatry. "Flee" (*pheugete*) or "run from" was the admonition. The Corinthians were not to view this matter casually and linger nearby; they were to fly from its presence. They were not to see how far they could go with sin, but have nothing to do with it. Paul had promised them God would sustain them in time of temptation, but this was not a license to play with sin; rather it was an admonition to run fast away, flee.

**15. I speak as to wise men:** ... as to prudent [men], —RTHM ... I speak as to men of understanding, —CNBR ... I am speaking to men of sense, —MNTG ... to intelligent [persons], —PNT ... to reflective men, —FNTN ... which haue discrecyon, —CRNM.

**judge ye what I say:** ... use your own judgment upon my words, —CNBR ... weigh my words for yourselves, —MOFT.

**10:15.** The Corinthians prided themselves on their wisdom. Whether Paul mixed sarcasm into this statement or not, he wrote in such a way as to appeal to their attitude and thereby achieve his point. If his readers were really sensible, if they

were wise, they would judge and see the wisdom of what Paul wrote.

**16. The cup of blessing which we bless:** ... The chalice of benediction, —RHEM, —DOUY ... The cup of thanksgiving, —MRDK.

**is it not the communion of the blood of Christ?:** ... is not a fellowship, —RTHM ... partakinge of the bloude, —CRNM ... not participating in the blood, —MOFT.

**The bread which we break, is it not the communion of the body of Christ?:** ... a common participation, —MNTG ... the participation of the body, —RHEM ... partetakynge of the body of Christ? —TNDL.

**10:16.** Fellowship and communion are important words in this discussion: communion with Christ and communion with demons, which are incompatible. Two elements are involved in such fellowship: one has to do with the sacred object or person honored; the other has to do with the common association among the celebrants.

"Cup of blessing" was the name given to the third cup of the Passover meal and may have been the cup with which our Lord instituted the ordinance of Holy Communion. It seems natural to refer to it at this point. The blessing said over this cup by Jews was, "Blessed are thou, O Lord our God who givest us the fruit of the vine."

But Paul had a wider view than just "blessing" the cup and "breaking" the bread. He had in view the whole sacred means by which we have communion with Christ. The emphasis is on the breaking by which "one" was given to "many" and by which they in turn become one. These elements are a "communion" of the blood and body of Christ and represent a covenant.

**17. For we [being] many are one bread, [and] one body:** ... are a single body, —FNTN.

**for we are all partakers of that one bread:** ... since we all have a share of the one loaf, —ADAM ... are we not all partakers, —CNBR ... all of the one loaf partake, —RTHM ... for we all do share in the one loaf, —MNTG.

**10:17.** Unity is emphasized. A single loaf was used at Communion, which symbolized unity. The ordinance stems from unity and creates unity for those who partake. They are one in spirit, one in faith, and one in worship. "Bread" suggests also the idea of a common nourishment, sustaining and strengthening an identical life.

It is instructive to note Paul's use of "body" in relation to the Eucharist and to the Corinthian congregation. In the Synoptic Gospels Jesus identifies His actual physical body with the bread of the Last Supper. In 10:17 and 11:17-34 Paul makes a shift from viewing the body of Christ as the physical body which died on the cross to the Church, the Body, i.e., believers, for which He died. This is especially important for chapter 11 where the Corinthians, while partaking of the Eucharist in a wrong manner, were not discerning the body of the Lord (11:29). This means that the Corinthians were not only despising the actual physical body of Christ which was broken for them, but were also despising the body of Christ (believers) for which He died.

The Lord's Supper, therefore, has both a Christological meaning (the sacrificial aspect of Christ's death) as well as an ecclesiastical dimension (the way in which it affects relations among fellow believers). This ecclesiastical concern is present both in chapters 10 and 11 where Paul stressed the need for unity in the body of Christ.

18. **Behold Israel after the flesh:** . . . Observe Israel, *−CNDT* . . . Look at the Israelites in their practices, *−WLMS* . . . See how the Jews do it! *−NORL, −BECK* . . . the corporate Israel! *−FNTN* . . . Look at the rites of Israel, *−MOFT* . . . which walketh carnally, *−TNDL* . . . by natural descent, *−NOYS* . . . according to the flesh, *−RHEM.*
**are not they which eat of the sacrifices partakers of the altar?:** . . . they who eat the victims, *−MRDK* . . . joint partakers of the altar? *−CMPB* . . . are in partnership with the altar? *−CNBR* . . . participate in the altar, *−MOFT.*

**10:18.** To enlarge his discussion, Paul turned to the observances of "Israel after the flesh" for illustration. This expression distinguishes the nation of Israel from the Church, the "true Israel." Paul pointed to the fact that those who "eat of the sacrifices" are "partakers" or have communion with the altar.

Going further, participation in the sacrificial feast means fellowship in the sacrifice. Paul's mind is on the total Israelite communion (Leviticus 7:15, 16). In these celebrations, there was a recognition of fellowship and service. It was no small thing to eat of the sacrifices offered on the burnt altar in the Jewish temple.

19. **What say I then?:** . . . What, then, do I affirm? *−CMPB* . . . Now, what do I mean? *−NORL* . . . Then what do I mean? *−WLMS.*
**that the idol is any thing:** . . . that an idol-god really exists, *−NORL* . . . itself means anything, *−MOFT.*
**or that which is offered in sacrifice to idols is any thing?:** . . . is really changed thereby? *−CNBR.*
20. **But I [say], that the things which the Gentiles sacrifice:** . . . what the heathen sacrifice, *−FNTN.*
**they sacrifice to devils, and not to God:** . . . is sacrificed to daemons, *−MOFT.*
**and I would not that ye should have fellowship with devils:** . . . I do not want you to have, *−MNTG* . . . and be in league with devils, *−LOCK* . . . to participate in daemons, *−MOFT* . . . to become communicants with demons, *−FNTN* . . . that ye should be associates of demons, *−MRDK* . . . would not have you

become partners with the demons, *−CNBR* . . . to become joint partakers, *−CMPB.*

**10:19, 20.** Paul was building to his point. He had noted the meaning of the Lord's Supper and the "communion" involved to show the danger of attending idol feasts. Certain of those with "knowledge" at Corinth would argue that idolatry was merely illusion; that there was no genuine ground of reality, especially for the Christian. They would argue further that these idol feasts had no religious meaning and, therefore, did not touch the conscience; so, friendship or social obligation should allow them to go.

Paul had admitted the truth of the nonreality of the idol in itself as early as 8:4. But he realized the terrible presences behind the idol. Demons were worshiped and communicated with at these idol feasts. The riot and perversion attending the festivals showed evil spirits presided over the events. Therefore, the sacrifice was really being offered to evil spirits (Deuteronomy 32:17), and fellowship was established by the sharing of food.

21. **Ye cannot drink the cup of the Lord, and the cup of devils:** . . . and the chalice of deuils, *−RHEM.*
**ye cannot be partakers of the Lord's table, and of the table of devils:** . . . You cannot be a guest at both, *−NORL* . . . are not able to share the Lord's table, *−FNTN* . . . You can't share the Lord's table, *−BECK.*
22. **Do we provoke the Lord to jealousy?:** . . . do we intend to rouse the Lord's jealousy? *−MOFT* . . . are we trying to incite the Lord, *−WLMS.*
**are we stronger than he?:** . . . Are we mightier, *−RTHM.*

**10:21, 22.** The position of the Corinthian Christians who ate the Lord's Supper and still chose to participate in idol feasts was contradictory and unacceptable. Paul was speaking of the moral and spiritual impossibility of real participation in both the Lord's Communion and the devil's communion.

There cannot be two masters in one life; there cannot be two communions. The distinct reference to "cup" and "table" emphasizes the strength of this admonition. "Cup of the Lord" and other such phrases point to both possession and leadership. The Lord distributes "the cup," and it denotes true fellowship with Him.

In like manner, participation in the idol feasts was wrong because of the fellowship with demons which it allowed. To do this was to break fellowship with the Lord and provoke Him to jealousy. Israel did this often, as we see from Deuteronomy 32:21. To oppose God in this manner and provoke Him to jealousy suggests that we are stronger than He is. Such an idea is foolish and completely wrong.

To participate in both feasts would only cause confusion and spiritual apathy initially. As the matter progressed, it would cause spiritual rebellion and rejection of Christ because allegiances and desires were divided between the Lord Jesus Christ and Satan.

**23. All things are lawful for me:** ... Everything is permitted, —*FNTN* ... All sorts of things, —*ADAM* ... Every thing is in my power, —*MRDK*.
**but all things are not expedient:** ... everything does not benefit, —*FNTN* ... all things are not beneficial, —*WLSN* ... but not all are good for us, —*MOFT* ... but not all things are advantageous, —*ADAM* ... but not everything is constructive, —*NORL*.
**all things are lawful for me:**
**but all things edify not:** ... but not everything builds up their personality, —*WLMS*.

**10:23.** There must be expedient and edifying profit in our actions. "All things are lawful" states the great, general principle of liberty. It was repeated twice just in this verse. Paul also repeated part of the statement in 6:12.

But not everything that is "lawful" is in our best interest, or another's. "Expedient" (*sumpherei*) refers to what is wise, beneficial, and most proper at the moment. "Edify" (*oikodomei*) refers to building up, especially in the Christian faith.

The point is not whether it is allowable or not, but whether it is profitable in a genuine Christian sense. The pervading theme in Paul's conclusion on the eating of sacrificial meats, the questions of conscience, was the supremacy of love in church life, which is expressed by edification of others.

Note that when Paul spoke of edifying, he had more than just the weak in mind. The whole Church, the entire Christian community, must be safeguarded by love, and thus edified.

**24. Let no man seek his own:** ... his own advantage, —*ADAM* ... his own private, particular interest alone, —*LOCK* ... be looking after his own welfare, —*WLMS*.
**but every man another's [wealth]:** ... but the benefit of others, —*FNTN* ... but each his neighbor's good, —*CLMT* ... but also that of his neighbor, —*WLMS*.

**10:24.** Paul narrowed the principle even more. The Christian is to seek the good of others and promote their interests.

**25. Whatsoever is sold in the shambles, [that] eat:** ... in the market, —*MOFT* ... in the flesh-market, —*MRDK*.
**asking no question for conscience sake:** ... never inquiring about it, —*FNTN* ... without any inquiry, or scruple, —*LOCK*.

**10:25.** On the basis of these principles, Paul explained that idol meat offered in the market for sale should not be argued over or worried over, but accepted as from God.

**26. For the earth [is] the Lord's:** ... belongs to the Lord, —*SEB*.
**and the fulness thereof:** ... and all its contents, —*MOFT* ... and every last thing in it, —*ADAM* ... everything in it, —*SEB* ... and all its store, —*WAY*.

**10:26.** Idol meat was often difficult to avoid because the butcher generally burnt at least a few hairs of an animal as a sacrifice, and the priest would often sell extra meat in the market. Paul wrote that the Corinthians were to ask no question, but rather to accept the fact that their food was a blessing from the Lord, "for the earth is the Lord's." This comes from Psalm 24:1. It would have been difficult to discover the nature of the meat in such a shop without causing a disturbance. In such a situation, the Corinthian Christians were to recognize the divine origin of meat and the goodness of the Lord, and to rest in that. Such things may be used within the framework of the law of Christ.

**27. If any of them that believe not bid you [to a feast], and ye be disposed to go:** ... some unbelieving heathen, —*WLMS* ... invite you, —*FNTN* ... invites some of you to his house, —*TCNT* ... invites you to his house, —*MNTG* ... to an entertainment, —*LOCK* ... and if ye be disposed to go, —*GNVA* ... you want to go, —*CNDT* ... ye are wishing to go, —*RTHM*.
**whatsoever is set before you, eat:** ... eat everything which is presented to you, —*WLSN*.
**asking    no    question    for    conscience sake:** ... never examining it, —*FNTN* ... without an inquiry, —*MRDK* ... without raising any question, —*WLMS*, —*RSV* ... instead of letting scruples of conscience induce you to ask any questions about it, —*MOFT*.

**10:27.** A second specific situation was presented. This involved being invited to a dinner by an unsaved host. If the invitation was accepted, the believer was to eat whatever was set before him without questioning the origin of the food. (This involved a private meal, not a meal in an idol temple.)

Before an unbelieving host or family, the Christian would be closely watched. One of the great dangers of such a situation was offense or unprofitable action. Under such circumstances, the Corinthian Christian was not to ask foolish questions because of scruples that have no merit. He should eat what was set on the table. There was no more need to raise the question of conscience in the one case than in the other.

**28. But if any man say unto you, This is offered in sacrifice unto idols:** ... But if somebody tells you, —BECK ... if someone informs you, —BRKL ... This is dedicate vnto idols, —GNVA ... is an idol offering, —FNTN.

**eat not for his sake that showed it, and for conscience sake:** ... Don't eat it, —SEB ... make it your rule not to eat it, —WLMS ... because of that one who divulges, —CNDT ... for the sake of him who pointed it out, —CNBR ... for hurtynge of conscience, —TNDL ... of the person who brought up the issue, —ADAM ... considering your informant, —NORL.

**for the earth [is] the Lord's, and the fulness thereof:**

**10:28.** But at some time at such a dinner or in a marketplace, someone might approach the Christian and explain that the meat had been sacrificed first to an idol. The Corinthians were told specifically how this should be handled. The situation was changed, and the strong Christian should refrain from eating. The meat was not now simply a gift of God, having passed through unknown sources. Rather, it was known as the end product of idolatry and some believed that to then eat it would mean idolatry. The Christian must not eat "for conscience' sake."

Paul did not mean the conscience of the eater, but the conscience of the speaker. The speaker, or another, could not see or grasp this. In deference to this weaker conscience, the strong Christian should not eat such meat.

In summation, whether the speaker was a weak Christian or a pagan, and whether the intent was to warn or embarrass, at such a point the Christian was to announce his faith and for the sake of another, abstain from eating "sacrifice meat."

**29. Conscience, I say, not thine own, but of the other:** ... I mean not yours, but his! —SEB ... his conscience, not your own, —MNTG ... but his who told you, —MRDK.

**for why is my liberty judged of another [man's] conscience?:** ... why is my freedom limited, —SAWR ... why should my freedom be determined by another man's conscience? —NORL ... why should one's own freedom be called into question, —MOFT ... "But," you may object, "why should my freedom be decided upon another's scruples of con-science?" —MNTG.

**10:29.** Two interconnected questions arise out of this discussion. One of them relates to why anyone else should be able to guide and limit my actions? Can freedom be restricted even when motives are pure? The motive for Paul's using this question in the text is to point out that the exercise of liberty must not be made the means of offense to another. Actions done in the right spirit must have a profitable result.

Several alternatives have been posed to explain the question raised by verse 29. Some have suggested that this was an actual complaint of the strong, namely, "Why should I allow my liberty to be infringed on?" This is unlikely: (1) because Paul did not answer this question in the following verse, and (2) this clause begins with *gar* ("for") instead of "but" which would be more likely if Paul were dealing with an interjection by the "strong."

A better suggestion is that Paul, by use of a rhetorical question, elaborated further on why a person might limit his own liberty. Paul, then, was simply reinforcing the meaning of verses 28 and 29 by saying that if a Christian voluntarily restricts his freedom for the sake of another person's conscience, that Christian has not lost his freedom. He has merely put it "on hold" temporarily.

**30. For if I by grace be a partaker:** ... If I participate with thankes, —RHEM ... If I partake with thankfulness, —FNTN, —NOYS, —ASV ... If I partake with thanksgiving, —CNFT ... with gratitude, —RTHM.

**why am I evil spoken of for that for which I give thanks?:** ... why am I blamed, —SAWR ... why should I be slandered about that, —FNTN ... why am I called a sinner for that which I eat with thanksgiving? —CNBR ... why am I reproached for that, —MRDK ... why am I denounced, —MNTG.

**10:30.** A second question is added. As long as I eat with a heart of thankfulness to God, why should I be discredited for doing so? The answer is that the believer is responsible not only for a thankful heart but also for the effect his actions may have on a weaker brother. Definite harm could result. A person with a sensitive conscience could regard the act as sacrilegious and hypocritical, and the cause of Christ could be damaged. While there is a limit to which another's conscience should be regarded, nevertheless, consideration for others must be added to our free personal conscience and our true thanksgiving to God.

**31. Whether therefore ye eat, or drink, or whatsoever ye do:**

**do all to the glory of God:** ... do everything for God's glory, —ADAM ... do all to the prayse of God, —TNDL.

**32. Give none offence, neither to the Jews:** ... You should be inoffensive, —FNTN ... Put no stumblingblock in the way, —MOFT ... Give no cause of stumbling, —CNBR ... Be without offence to the Jews, —DOUY.

**nor to the Gentiles, nor to the church of God:** ... nether to the congregacion, —CRNM.

**10:31, 32.** Paul gave two major reasons for acting as he had presented. The first is that all believers' actions should redound to the glory of God. Anything and everything, "all" without exclusion, must be subordinate to the supreme maxim of Christian duty: bringing glory to God.

The second reason is that there be no occasion to stumble for anyone, in or outside the Church. "Jews" and "Gentiles" include everyone. Causing another to stumble would result in that one sinning. That would affect his salvation and bring dishonor to the Lord.

**33. Even as I please all [men] in all [things]:** ... Such is my own rule, —*MOFT* ... as I also strive, —*NOYS* ... just as I also make everything pleasant to every one, —*FNTN*.

**not seeking mine own profit, but the [profit] of many:** ... I do not strive for personal profit, —*NORL* ... my own expedience, —*CNDT* ... my own advantage, —*ADAM*, —*CMPB* ... the advantage of the greater number, —*MOFT*.

**that they may be saved:** ... that I may be instrumental to the salvation of as many as is possible, —*LOCK* ... that they may live, —*MRDK*.

**10:33.** Paul concluded by using himself as an example. The apostle attempted to teach not only from knowledge, but from personal life and example. No personal advantage was sought; he always sought the profit of others, and he urged Christians to imitate him. His aim was the highest; his goal the best. This is the proper balance of liberty and love.

## Chapter 11

**1. Be ye followers of me, even as I also [am] of Christ:** ... Copy me, as I copy Christ, —*MOFT* ... Pattern after me, as I pattern after Christ, —*BRKL* ... Imitate me, as I myself imitate Christ, —*TCNT*.

**11:1.** Paul next turned to matters related to public worship. His teaching is closely related to what has just preceded. The main concern should always be to "do all to the glory of God" (10:31).

**2. Now I praise you, brethren, that ye remember me in all things:** ... I commende you, —*CRNM* ... Now I am applauding you, —*CNDT* ... for remembering me in everything, —*MNTG* ... for remembering all my orders, —*LOCK* ... ye are mindful of me, —*MRDK*, —*TCNT*.

**and keep the ordinances, as I delivered [them] to you:** ... and that you retain the traditions, —*SAWR* ... and hold fast my precepts, —*CNFT* ... You are loyal to the teaching that I passed on to you, —*SEB* ... for maintaining the traditions I passed on, —*MOFT* ... in what I instructed you, you observe my instructions, —*FNTN* ... you are always mindful of my teaching, —*CNBR* ... you the instructions, —*RTHM* ... you keepe my precepts, —*RHEM* ... the suggestions I transmitted to you, —*BRKL*.

**11:2.** Paul begins with praise for the Corinthian believers. They had faithfully obeyed the rules for behavior he had laid down for them. These were new converts. They needed detailed instructions, and Paul had carefully outlined how they should conduct themselves.

**3. But I would have you know, that the head of every man is Christ; and the head of the woman [is] the man; and the head of Christ [is] God:** ... and of a wife her husband is head, —*MNTG* ... the head of every woman is her husband, —*NORL* ... Christ is over every male, —*SEB* ... God is the Head of Christ, —*WLMS*.

**11:3.** Some have denounced Paul as a woman hater, but we must remember it was Paul who insisted that in Christ all distinctions were to be removed between Jew and Greek, bond and free, and male and female (Galatians 3:28). Those are some of the most radical words ever uttered concerning social and religious matters.

The context shows that in the Corinthian church women took an active part in the worship services, unlike those in the Jewish synagogue who were not allowed such freedom. Some of these women may have misunderstood their newfound Christian freedom and refrained from wearing the head covering, which custom dictated they should wear when prophesying or praying in public. This is the problem which Paul now addresses.

The apostle stated the "chain of command" for that First Century church. God is the head of Christ, Christ is the head of man, and man is the head of woman. If this principle is examined closely, it reveals an important fact: subordination does not mean inferiority. The sexes are equal mentally, morally, and spiritually.

"Head" refers to a governing, controlling, ruling organ. It indicates a relationship of authority. "The head of every man is Christ" began the discussion. Every man has one head, Christ.

"The head of the woman is the man" establishes the order of authority God has ordained. Man holds headship directly from his Creator and is brought by his manhood into direct responsibility to Christ. The very law of marriage and the social order are grounded in Christ.

On the side of submission, the Lord set the pattern with His perfect loyalty and obedience to the Father. This should make it easier to submit, when we see that Christ is subject to God the Father and man to the Head, Christ. In nature there is equality; in office and work there is submission.

**4. Every man praying or prophesying:** ... when publicly praying or preaching, —*TCNT*.

**having [his] head covered:** ... havynge eny thynge on his heed, —*TNDL*.

**dishonoureth his head:** . . . disgraces his own head, —*FNTN* . . . shameth his head, —*GNVA* . . . puts to shame his head, —*PNT*.

**11:4.** This principle applied directly to the covering of women. Paul first wrote of the uncovered man. This was a strictly Christian matter, for the Jewish male covered his head.

Man's only head is Christ, and while both sexes worship Him in common, woman also has man as her head. The man who wore a covering dishonored his own place and this reflected on Christ, for he shamed Christ whose lordship he represented.

**5. But every woman that prayeth or prophesieth:** . . . or speaks God's Word, —*BECK*.
**with [her] head uncovered dishonoureth her head:** . . . bareheaded, —*WLMS* . . . without a veil, —*MOFT* . . . she brings shame upon her head, —*CNBR*.
**for that is even all one as if she were shaven:** . . . for she is like the abandoned shorn woman, —*FNTN* . . . for she is on a level with her whose head is shaven, —*MRDK* . . . for it is exactly the same as if she had her hair cut short, —*WEYM* . . . she is no better than a shaven woman, —*MOFT* . . . She might as well have her head shaven, —*NORL*.

**11:5.** The identical situation was repeated for the woman. It seems likely the reference ("prayeth or prophesieth") is to women who participated in public worship. It is important to recognize that verse 5 makes it quite apparent that women were in fact praying and prophesying in church. The problem Paul dealt with was not the fact of women praying and prophesying, but the way they did it. If Paul disapproved of women praying and prophesying in church, he could have explicitly said so. Instead Paul corrected the disorderly manner of their praying and prophesying by telling them that when they did pray and prophesy, they must do so with their heads covered. This is the background by which to better understand 14:33-36. It was necessary for the woman to have her head covered as a sign of submission to the man. If she did not do so she dishonored her "head." The dishonor done to the man fell on her and the shame came home to her. Again, it also reflected on Christ's lordship. For her to submit detracted nothing from her equality with man.

The head-cover, in verse 10 called "power," may seem to have a paradoxical meaning of standing under authority and being endowed with authority.

**6. For if the woman be not covered, let her also be shorn:** . . . let her also cut off her hair, —*WEYM* . . . let her shave her head at once, —*CNBR* . . . she should

cut off all her hair! —*SEB* . . . let her hair be cut off too, —*ADAM*.
**but if it be a shame for a woman to be shorn or shaven:** . . . it is disgraceful, —*MOFT* . . . it be a foule thing for a woman to be polled or made balde, —*RHEM*.
**let her be covered:** . . . let her wear a veil, —*WEYM*.

**11:6.** It was agreed that it was shameful for a woman to be shaved or shorn. According to Deuteronomy 21:12, for instance, women captured in war were to have their heads shaved as a sign of shame. It was unwomanly, rather manly. The woman who began to act like a man by unveiling should be consistent and be shorn also. But having the head shorn or shaved was a shame. Therefore, being unveiled was also a shame. Thus the veil was to be used.

**7. For a man indeed ought not to cover [his] head:**
**forasmuch as he is the image and glory of God:** . . . since he exists in the image, —*ADAM* . . . for he represents the likeness and supremacy of God, —*MOFT* . . . being inherently the image, —*CNDT* . . . and the manifestation of God's glory, —*CNBR* . . . and reflected glory, —*WLMS* . . . he is the image and representative of God, —*LOCK*.
**but the woman is the glory of the man:** . . . the female is the glory of the male, —*SEB* . . . is man's honour, —*FNTN*.

**11:7.** Paul drew support for his position from the story of creation (Genesis 1:26, 27). Man was made in the direct image of God. Woman appeared, in creation, as derived and auxiliary. It was as wrong for the man to cover his head as it was for the woman not to. For man to cover himself would be to hide the "image and glory of God." Man is the pinnacle of creation and should reveal God's glory. Therefore, there should be no outward sign of subordination when a man worships.

Woman, in her right, stands in a position, singular in nature, to the man and therefore is "the glory of the man." This affords her a high position and at the same time protects man's place. Faith, purity, and beauty show most excellently and proportionately in her. The man who degrades a woman degrades his manhood.

**8. For the man is not of the woman; but the woman of the man:** . . . As a matter of fact, —*ADAM* . . . For it was not man who was taken from woman, —*TCNT* . . . man did not originate from woman, —*WLMS* . . . does not take his origin from man, —*WEYM* . . . woman was made from man, —*MOFT*.
**9. Neither was the man created for the woman:**
**but the woman for the man:** . . . but the woman for the man's sake, —*MRDK*.

**11:8, 9.** Two more "fors" are added to a chain beginning with verse 6. Paul was speaking of origin and purpose in creation (see Genesis 2:21-24). In origin woman came from Adam's rib, and in purpose she was to be his helper and companion. Originally, in creation, man did not come from woman, nor was he created for her. To ignore or discredit this arrangement of God is to invite problems.

**10. For this cause ought the woman to have power on [her] head:**...Consequently, *—FNTN*...For this reason...to have on her head a sign of man's authority, *—NORL* . . . to have permission upon, *—RTHM*...a token of authority, *—BRKL*...to have on her head a symbol of subjection, *—WEYM*...a symbol of man's authority, *—WLMS*...ought to show some sign on her head that she is respecting authority, *—SEB*...wear on her head a sign of man's authority, *—TCNT*...must wear a symbol of subjection on her head, *—MOFT.*
**because of the angels:**...especially out of respect to the angels, *—WLMS*...out of respect for the angels, *—BECK*...because of her [guardian] angels, *—MNTG.*

**11:10.** The phrases "power on her head" and "because of the angels" must be explained. An important factor is the context. Paul had been speaking of the principle of subordination, and particularly of the design and purpose of woman in creation. The first phrase would seem to refer to that to which she submits, the covering being its symbol. This might be said, for example, about the soldier who wears his ruler's colors, proudly identifying with him.

It is interesting, however, that the only time the word "power" ("authority," *exousian*) is used in this passage, it is something which belongs to women. Although the context speaks of subordination, it is the woman here who has the sign of authority. The New International Version tries to solve this problem by translating *exousian echein epi* in a passive sense (to "have authority *over*" [her head]); but if so, this is the only time out of 103 New Testament appearances that it is passive.

Others see "authority" in terms of the newfound liberty/authority that the women experienced in Christ, but this interpretation is not readily apparent in the context. Whatever "authority" means, it must be consistent with the following statement regarding "angels."

"Because of the angels" has been looked at in various ways, some of them impossible. Paul could not have meant evil angels subject to sensual temptation. Some have seen in these angels: pious men, prophets, church officers, and matchmakers.

But the better explanation seems to be as follows. In 4:9 Paul mentioned the angels as interested observers of Christian conduct. In 6:3 he spoke of the judgment of certain angels by the saints. Scripture is filled with the fact that angels are associated with God's earthly kingdom and the maintenance of creational laws and limits. It is consistent that angels are present at divine worship and are disturbed by irreverence at such worship. No unseemliness should come before them.

**11. Nevertheless neither is the man without the woman:** . . . neither is man independent of woman, *—CNFT*...and a man needs a woman, *—BECK.*
**neither the woman without the man, in the Lord:** . . . is not separate, *—FNTN* . . . she is not independent, *—SEB* . . . is not independent of man, *—WEYM, —WLMS.*

**11:11.** Paul, at the same time, wanted to insure the position of both man and woman, their need for each other, and their equality under God. There is a basic responsibility of both to each other and to God. The woman is subordinate but not inferior. In the higher things, "in the Lord" and in faith, man and woman exist in partnership and equality.

**12. For as the woman [is] of the man:** . . . as woman originates from man, *—WEYM* . . . as woman was made from man, *—CNBR.*
**even so [is] the man also by the woman:** . . . so also is the man, *—MNTG*...so a man is born of a woman, *—BECK* . . . man comes by means of the woman, *—TCNT.*
**but all things of God:** . . . but alle thingis ben of god, *—WCLF* . . . but everything proceeds from God, *—FNTN* . . . . and everything, including humankind, *—NORL* . . . and they all have their origin from God, *—BRKL*...Everything comes from God, *—SEB*...and all things spring from God, *—CNBR.*

**11:12.** There is a balance between equality and subordination. Man is the initial cause; woman the instrumental cause. But the original Source and Ruler, to whom reverence is due, is God.

**13. Judge in yourselves:** . . . Consider about these yourselves, *—FNTN* . . . Judge of this matter by your own feeling, *—CNBR.*
**is it comely that a woman pray unto God uncovered?:** . . . is it proper, *—MOFT, —ADAM, —PNT* . . . is it decent, *—CMPB.*

**11:13.** Paul asked his readers to look at this carefully and judge; the inference was that they would come up with the same conclusion. "Yourselves" is emphatic. They could discover the truth for themselves. There is an appeal both to the fitness and suitability of things to nature or character and common sense.

The matter hinges on general propriety and the Christian influence involved with it, and Paul was sure when the Corinthians rightly considered this custom they would not find it improper.

**14. Doth not even nature itself teach you, that, if a man have long hair, it is a shame unto him?:**...if a man should have long tresses, *–FNTN*...it is an ignominie for him, *–RHEM*...while it is unmanly for a man to wear long hair, *–WAY*...is disgraceful, *–MOFT*...it is a dishonour to him, *–WEYM*...to wear his hair long is degrading, *–CNFT*.

**15. But if a woman have long hair, it is a glory to her:**...if her hair is abundant, *–MRDK*...And a prayse to a woman, *–GNVA*...but glorious for a woman? *–BRKL*.

**for [her] hair is given her for a covering:**...Her hair is God's gift to her, a natural veil, *–WAY*...instead of a Veil, *–WLSN*.

**11:14, 15.** Paul appealed to the instincts and teaching of nature to support a related item—that of a man's moral constitution. This reference to the moral nature of the world, is true of other times Paul used *phusis* ("nature") such as Romans 1:26 where Paul condemns homosexuality because it is against nature; i.e., against God's moral ordering of the world.

The preference for a man to wear short hair has prevailed in modern times as it did in ancient eras. It is true, there have been exceptions. Homer's warriors wore long hair and the fashion was retained at Sparta. But the Athenian cropped his head when 18 and, except for the aristocratic knights, it was a mark of effeminacy to let the hair grow long. The Nazarite of the Old Testament times was another exception.

On the other hand, a woman's long hair is her glory. It is the crown of her beauty. Her hair served as a natural covering, in addition to the physical covering to be worn in public meetings. Paul's reasoning was that it is necessary that there be a clear distinction of the sexes in appearance as well as every other natural and scriptural way. And there remains this principle of subordination: the man to Christ and the woman to the man.

**16. But if any man seem to be contentious:**...assumes to be censorious, *–FNTN*...is seyn to be ful of striif, *–WCLF*...If any man luste to stryue, *–CRNM*...presumes to raise objections on this point, *–MOFT*...is inclined to be disputatious regarding such a custom, *–MNTG*...seems to be quarrelsome, *–HNSN*...thinks to be contentious in defence of such a custom, *–CNBR*.

**we have no such custom:**...we have no such usage, *–CNDT*.

**neither the churches of God:**

**11:16.** Abruptly Paul cut off the discussion with his reference to custom (*sunētheian*) and contention (*philoneikos*). "Contentious" refers to a quarrelsome person, one who disputes for the sake of disputation. It seems this attitude among the Corinthians touched everything, a woman's veil or the position of an apostle.

Many arguments have come over Paul's use of the word "custom" here. Paul seems to be saying, "We have no such custom as women praying or prophesying with head uncovered." Paul appealed to universal custom and to the fact that this was the habit in the Christian churches. To adopt another view would suggest that Paul was doing away with what he had just spent 15 verses asserting.

Paul was not supporting a custom per se but a principle with which the custom was linked. There must be a clear distinction of the sexes, the clear recognition of roles, and the proper order of authority that God established.

**17. Now in this that I declare [unto you] I praise [you] not:**...And this I commaund, *–RHEM*...I must announce this, *–BRKL*...But while giving you these instructions, *–WEYM*...in giving these authoritative instructions, *–ADAM*...But in giving this charge, I do not commend you, *–CNFT*...I consider this not to be estimable, *–FNTN*...I cannot commend you, *–MOFT*.

**that ye come together not for the better, but for the worse:**...your solemn assemblies do more harm than good, *–MNTG*...not with proffit, but with hurt, *–GNVA*...with bad rather than good results, *–WEYM*...are for evil rather than for good, *–CNBR*...not to your improvement, but to your deterioration, *–WAY*...but for discomfiture, *–CNDT*...ye have not made progress, but have deteriorated, *–MRDK*.

**11:17.** The problem Paul now turned to was a glaring fault that had to be corrected. He did so with authority. The Corinthians came together "for the worse" instead of the better. Their meetings and the Lord's Supper were a desecration.

**18. For first of all, when ye come together in the church:**...in the first place, *–PNT*...when you meet as a church, *–ADAM*...as you meet in church session, *–BRKL*.

**I hear that there be divisions among you:**...I hear there are differences, *–FNTN*...there are schismes among you, *–RHEM*...ther is dissencion amonge you, *–TNDL*...that cliques prevail, *–MOFT*.

**and I partly believe it:**

**11:18.** Paul specified the causes of this disgraceful gathering. "When ye come together" indicated repeated occurrence. The trouble was chronic. A contentious spirit was consistently present.

Paul had heard various reports on the Corinthians' actions. He did not believe everything he heard, but he did accept as truth what he listed here. The proper Christian attitude is to believe and hope for the best possible (13:7).

**19. For there must be also heresies among you:** ... you should have parties, —FNTN ... be differences of opinion among you, —WEYM ... but also adverse sects, —CNBR.

**that they which are approved may be made manifest among you:** ... who are the men of sterling worth, —WEYM ... the tried and true may be recognized among you, —BRKL ... who are qualified, —CNDT.

**11:19.** There were factions in the Corinthian church. Paul was not advocating factions, but in this sinful world they do happen. Men get things out of balance sometimes. Such factions do serve the purpose of sifting the loyal from the disloyal, the good from the bad. The factions leave the genuine believers standing out ("approved") by their loyalty, strength, and constancy. Those approved by God become manifest to other men.

**20. When ye come together therefore into one place:** ... you hold your gatherings, —MOFT.

**[this] is not to eat the Lord's supper:** ... there is no true eating of the Lord's Supper, —MNTG ... there is no eating of the Lord's Supper, —ALFD.

**11:20.** The "therefore" in this verse anticipates a conclusion on what has already been said and, at the same time, lays a foundation for further remarks.

These divisions had produced a visible rift at this common meal, detracting from the real meaning of the Lord's Supper. It is impossible to relate what was done among the Corinthians with the true sacrament of the Lord's Supper.

**21. For in eating every one taketh before [other] his own supper:** ... prepares his own individual meal to eat alone, —FNTN ... is getting his own dinner, —CNDT ... personally to eat it, —BRKL ... Each one hastens to eat the supper that he has prepared for himself, —NORL.

**and one is hungry, and another is drunken:** ... so that one man goes away hungry, —NORL ... and one eats like a hungry man, —WEYM ... one has too little to eat, and another has too much to drink! —TCNT ... and another is satisfied, —WLSN ... and another drinks overmuch, —CNFT ... and that one imbibes too freely, —BRKL ... again, gorged, —FNTN.

**11:21.** Paul's description reveals scandalous behavior. The problem was one of gluttonous, self-centered disregard for anyone else. The "Lord's supper" here noted was a united supper with which the meeting of the church commenced, apparently taking place as often as once a week. This church supper, later called the Agape (Love Feast) was akin to the dinners held by the guilds. It began as a kind of enlarged family meal. It accorded so well with the social custom that it was a universal Christian custom in the First Century.

Later the Communion was separated from the meal for greater decorum, and the Agape faded into extinction.

Each guest brought contributions to supply the table; the poor brought whatever meager amount they had, the rich brought out of their abundance. Greedily, the Corinthians consumed their own supply as soon as they arrived. The poor man with insufficient supply might arrive late, because his time was not his own, and find the table empty, the fellowship gone, and he remained hungry.

Further, hunger and drunkenness sat together. To call such the Lord's Supper would have been a travesty.

**22. What? have ye not houses to eat and to drink in?:**

**or despise ye the church of God, and shame them that have not?:** ... Or have ye a contempt for the church, —LOCK ... or do ye think amiss of the church, —MKNT ... show disrespect to, —MOFT ... or do you look with contempt upon, —FNTN ... and to shame the poor? —CNBR ... and to humiliate the poor? —TCNT ... do you wish to show your contempt ... and make those who have no homes feel ashamed? —WEYM ... mortifying those, —CNDT ... and put to shame the needy? —CNFT ... Do you want to make poor people ashamed? —SEB ... and wish to humiliate those who have nothing? —ADAM ... those who don't have anything? —BECK.

**What shall I say to you? shall I praise you in this? I praise [you] not:** ... Shall I approve of you? —FNTN ... Commend you? —MOFT ... In this I certainly do not praise you, —MNTG ... No, I cannot approve, —NORL.

**11:22.** Paul spoke pointedly. His first question proved that home is the place to satisfy such hunger and thirst. His irony attacked their greed and pride. Paul here condemned the rich for their attitude toward the poor ("them that have not"). If those who had plenty of food wished to indulge themselves, then according to Paul they should at least have the consideration to do so at home and not shame those less fortunate.

Apparently this arrogant attitude of rich believers toward the poor was not limited to Corinth. The apostle James had to reprimand the church to which he wrote for showing partiality toward the rich and ignoring the poor (James 2:1-7).

Such inhospitality toward the poor was not only wrong in general, but it was especially shocking since this activity was taking place at a meal honoring the death of Christ. In Paul's second letter to the Corinthians he told them that the significance of the death of Christ is that it made reconciliation between God and man, and between man and man. The Corinthians obviously needed to be told about reconciliation, since their own actions fell deplorably below the expectations of a believer who claimed to partake of the new nature of Christ (cf. 2 Corinthians 5:17-19). The whole letter of First Corinthians, in fact, reveals that every facet of the Corinthians' lives exhibited a lack of reconciliation with other believers.

His second question exposed the fact that if this action was deliberate, then they were scorning and despising "the church of God" and they were shaming and insulting the poorer brethren.

The last two questions and the declaration showed remarkable restraint. Clearly, their actions needed reprimand, not praise.

**23. For I have received of the Lord that which also I delivered unto you:** . . . I accepted from, *—CNDT* . . . I received this account from the Lord, *—NORL* . . . what I taught you, *—BECK* . . . what I passed on to you, *—SEB* . . . that which I imparted to you, *—MRDK.*
**That the Lord Jesus the [same] night in which he was betrayed took bread:** . . . took a loaf, *—MOFT, —CMPB.*

**11:23.** Because Paul wished to correct such behavior, he held up before them, as a mirror, the institution, design, and meaning of the Supper as begun by the Lord himself.

What Paul passed on came "of the Lord." What Paul received he gave out. He delivered truth correctly, openly, and positively and fulfilled his trust.

The phrase "same night . . . betrayed . . ." displays more than a necessary time element in a historical sense. It speaks of the character of Jesus who determined to make this new covenant with His people and fulfill the entire will of God even in the dark shadow of betrayal and death.

Note the detail in Paul's teaching. Jesus "took bread," the unleavened cakes of Passover. But the Corinthians were not following Christ's example and Paul's teaching.

**24. And when he had given thanks, he brake [it], and said:** . . . and broke off some of it, *—SEB* . . . broke it in pieces, saying, as he did so, *—TCNT.*
**Take, eat: this is my body, which is broken for you:** . . . which shall be delivered for you, *—DOUY* . . . which is about to be broken, *—WEYM* . . . broken for your sakes, *—CNDT, —MRDK* . . . which is for you, *—SAWR* . . . which is given for you, *—WLMS* . . . my body given on your behalf, *—TCNT* . . . broken on your behalf, *—BRKL.*
**this do in remembrance of me:** . . . thus do ye, *—MRDK* . . . do for a recollection of Me, *—CNDT* . . . for the commemoration of me, *—RHEM, —DOUY* . . . in memory, *—MOFT* . . . in memory of me, *—WLMS.*

**11:24.** Christ pronounced a blessing of thanks which inaugurated this ordinance and then turned to the sacraments. Paul's account is similar to that of Luke. There occurred first the breaking

of the bread, being symbolic of the body of Jesus. What happened to Christ's body was for us.

The words "this is my body" has initiated a long dispute between those who favor the idea of a "real" or literal body in the elements and those who favor a "representative" presence of the Lord by the elements.

Without attempting to be exhaustive, consider these supports for the "representative" or symbolic Communion. Since "this" refers to the bread and "for you" is joined to "body," the word "is" cannot imply a complete identity but rather a close connection. The presence of the article before "body" does not justify the conclusion that the head is identified with the body. The article is necessary for purely grammatical reasons. There is a correspondence of relation rather than of substance.

The following verse points out that "cup" is connected with "testament." What the blood effects, the cup sets forth and seals. There is an equal analogy between "bread" and "body." The Communion leads to Christ. Faith appropriates the blessing of the ordinance.

"Which is . . . for you" states the purpose of Christ's work. It was done for us, for the whole world. It was done to draw God and man together. "This do" is present continuous. The design of the institution was that it be continually reenacted until Christ returns.

**25. After the same manner also [he took] the cup, when he had supped, saying:** . . . Similarly, *—CNDT, —BRKL* . . . In the same way, *—MOFT* . . . In like manner also the cup, *—SAWR* . . . the same way also the cup, *—RSV* . . . the chalice, *—RHEM* . . . the chalice, after he had supped, *—DOUY* . . . after the supper, *—HNSN.*
**This cup is the new testament in my blood:** . . . the new agreement with God, *—SEB* . . . the new covenant ratified by my blood, *—MOFT* . . . is the new institution, *—CMPB* . . . of which my blood is the pledge, *—WEYM* . . . is the New Settlement, *—FNTN* . . . is the new Agreement, *—KLGS* . . . ratified by my blood, *—WLMS* . . . [sealed] with my blood, *—SAWR* . . . for the remission of sins, *—NORL.*
**this do ye, as oft as ye drink [it], in remembrance of me:** . . . do this, whenever you drink it, *—MNTG* . . . as often as ye do it, *—LOCK* . . . for my Remembrance, *—WLSN.*

**11:25.** Paul referred next to the place and purpose of "the cup." "When he had supped" emphasizes the distinction and special importance of the meal. The impression is that the bread was partaken of during the meal and the cup at the end, although both were necessary to the Communion. This forged a new "testament" or covenant, initiated by God (Jeremiah 31:31-34). The shedding of Christ's blood established the new covenant and all it guarantees. The Communion celebration should be often and reverently observed.

**26. For as often as ye eat this bread, and drink this cup:** ... Every time you eat, —SEB ... For every time, —WLMS ... So that the eating of this bread, and the drinking of this cup of the Lord's supper, —LOCK.

**ye do show the Lord's death till he come:** ... you are announcing, —CNDT ... you proclaim, —MOFT, —ADAM ... you openly publish, —CMPB, Mac-knight ... you openly show forth, —CNBR ... you declare the death, —WLSN ... until He returns, —FNTN.

**11:26.** Christ commanded His disciples to perpetually commemorate Him by Communion. But in the Corinthian church familiarity had made the service seem common. Paul reminded the Corinthians that they showed forth the Lord's death and all it means every time they partook of the sacrament.

The celebration of Communion is to show "the Lord's death till he come." It looks not only back to Calvary, but also ahead to Christ's return and the Marriage Supper of the Lamb. We know not the time nor the date of Christ's return, but we may be assured of its factual nature and certainty.

Each time we participate in the Lord's Supper we are reminded that all the activities and ordinances in the Church are to center around the person of Jesus Christ. The ordinances of water baptism and Communion point us consistently to either the finished work of Christ on the cross or the anticipated work in which "all things" shall be summed up in Christ. In trouble, debate, or doctrine, all is to point directly to Christ, and all our actions are to be consistent with the fact that He is our Lord.

**27. Wherefore whosoever shall eat this bread: and drink [this] cup of the Lord, unworthily:** ... in an unworthy manner, —WEYM ... carelessly, —MOFT.

**shall be guilty of the body and blood of the Lord:** ... will be liable, —CNDT ... shall be responsible for, —RTHM ... will be responsible for, —FNTN ... will be held guilty of an offense against the body, —ADAM ... will be an offender against, —WLSN ... must answer for, —MNTG ... shall be guilty of profaning the body, —CNBR ... will have to answer for a sin against the body and the blood of the Lord, —MOFT.

**11:27.** "Wherefore" leads to certain conclusions. A judgment of sorts was necessary on those who were violating the table of the Lord. Throughout this passage the verbs speak of continued practice and habit. "Whosoever" excludes no one. Everyone, rich or poor, high or low, must approach Communion in a reverent, humble manner. By

doing violence to the sacraments, the Corinthians were actually desecrating the sacrifice and person of the Lord himself. The magnitude of such a sin is measured by the magnitude of the gift. The penalty is decided by the same measure.

**28. But let a man examine himself:** ... Let each man scrutinize himself, —MNTG ... proue him self, —RHEM ... let a man prove himself, —SAWR, —DOUY, —CNFT ... let a man test himself, —FNTN, —MOFT ... be putting himself to-the-test, —RTHM.

**and so let him eat of [that] bread, and drink of [that] cup:**

**11:28.** Great care in behavior should be taken toward the Communion. It was important that the Corinthian Christians honestly and carefully examine themselves before they partook of the elements of the Lord's Supper.

Any truly honest and serious attempt at self-probing would make the scene of verses 20-22 impossible. Such greed and selfishness could not hide under the self-examination that allowed the Holy Spirit to do the probing. Examination would properly involve confession, repentance over anything that weakened the importance of the Lord's Supper and its full significance, and an analysis of one's true faith in Christ.

This is something that must be done regularly by all believers. The implication is that such examination will prove fruitful and favorable. Paul reminds us yet again of the importance of this ordinance invoked by the Lord, of the tremendous reverence that must accompany our approach to His table, and of how terrible is unworthy participation.

**29. For he that eateth and drinketh unworthily:** ... without a proper sense of the Body, —MOFT ... not discriminating the body, —HNSN.

**eateth and drinketh damnation to himself:** ... eateth and drinketh iudgement to him self, —RHEM ... and drinks judgement, —WEYM ... drinks to his own judgment, —ADAM.

**not discerning the Lord's body:** ... not distinguishing the body, —CMPB ... without distinguishing the body, —CNFT ... setting apart the body, —RTHM ... not discriminating the body, —WLSN ... when not distinguishing the body, —FNTN ... if he fails to estimate the body aright, —WEYM.

**11:29.** Paul emphasized the need of worthy conduct at the Lord's Supper by stressing the judgment that rested on those who had not properly discerned the "Lord's body." "Discerning" (*diakrinōn*) involves the idea of judging clearly and rightly. In this case it refers to the Lord's Supper, rather than any other eating and drinking.

Because the Corinthians did not judge or act rightly regarding the elements, a sentence of judgment rested on them. "Damnation" (*krima*) does not refer to the final judgment, but to a judicial sentence of any kind.

**30. For this cause many [are] weak and sickly among you:** ... Consequently, *—FNTN* ... are infirm and ailing, *—CNDT* ... and feble, *—RHEM* ... and out of health, *—WEYM.*

**and many sleep:** ... and a number even dead, *—MOFT* ... a considerable number, *—CNDT, —CMPB.*

**11:30.** A literal physical affliction had settled on some in the church because they had desecrated the Lord's table. However, "sleep" would indicate death "in Christ," which would appear to justify the view that this visitation had affected more than just the desecrators of the Communion; the church community was suffering for their widespread offense. Paul had in mind, not "natural" effects of excesses, but a special chastening of the Lord. This is further proof of their disturbing behavior at the Lord's table.

**31. For if we would judge ourselves:** ... if we wolde trye our selues, *—GNVA* ... if we tested ourselves, *—FNTN* ... If, however, we estimated ourselves aright, *—WEYM* ... we were judging ourselves aright, *—MNTG.*

**we should not be judged:** ... we would not come under the Lord's judgment, *—MOFT.*

**32. But when we are judged:**
**we are chastened of the Lord:** ... we are trained, *—MNTG* ... we are being corrected, *—FNTN* ... are we being disciplined, *—RTHM.*

**that we should not be condemned with the world:**

**11:31, 32.** Paul provided the antidote in a two-step sequence. First, believers should judge themselves. That would solve problems immediately. But if they do not, the Lord will judge and chasten so they will repent and avoid final condemnation with the "world" of unbelievers. Even in the middle of such sinful activity, Paul had positive advice. The Lord has no desire to see His children fall, so He disciplines in order to turn them back to Him.

Once again we are reminded that the ultimate goal of judgment is redemptive and not destructive. In chapter 5 Paul wrote that the man who had committed fornication with his stepmother should be delivered to Satan "that the spirit may be saved in the day of the Lord Jesus" (5:5). The word *paideuometha* ("being chastened") is also used by Paul in 2 Corinthians 6:9 and 1 Timothy 1:20. This is consistent with Hebrews 12:6 which says that "whom the Lord loveth he chasteneth" (cf. Hebrews 12:5-11).

Paul, in his loving manner, with his great pastor's heart, uses "we" to associate himself with his readers. A tremendous amount of hope and faith

is present. Christ is overshadowing His church and is concerned about each member. He will accomplish His will and pleasure in the believer.

**33. Wherefore, my brethren, when ye come together to eat:**
**tarry one for another:** ... wait for one another, *—MOFT* ... entertain one another, *—FNTN* ... cordially receive each other, *—WLSN.*

**34. And if any man hunger, let him eat at home:**
**that ye come not together unto condemnation:** ... so as not to assemble in an improper manner, *—FNTN* ... so that your meetings do not bring condemnation upon you, *—MNTG* ... your coming together may not lead to judgement, *—WEYM* ... only to incur condemnation, *—MOFT.*

**And the rest will I set in order when I come:** ... The other matters I will deal with, *—WEYM* ... The other things I will arrange, *—SAWR* ... other matters I will adjust when I come, *—MNTG* ... instructions upon the other matters, *—MOFT* ... and I schal dispose other thingis, *—WCLF* ... I will arrange the rest when I come, *—FNTN.*

**11:33, 34.** "Wherefore" shows us the second step in Paul's antidote. It is a practical admonition that includes a note of warmth and closeness ("my brethren") after his severe rebuke. The actions of the feast and the Lord's Supper were to be governed by a loving and reverent spirit.

Self-examination will result in care for others. Therefore, Paul admonished the Corinthians to wait for each other. Those who arrived early should wait for those arriving later. Each individual must be considered of equal importance in the church. Waiting for the others would presume wanting to eat with them.

Someone might raise the objection that he was hungry when he arrived and could not wait. Paul quieted the objection by directing that he first eat something at home. The church supper was more for fellowship than for eating. Otherwise, it would exclude Christian thought and charity. The spirit of love must prevail.

Paul added a footnote, "and the rest ... when I come." Paul was probably referring to other features of the administration of the ordinance which were not so pressing and could await his visit with them.

## Chapter 12

**1. Now concerning spiritual [gifts], brethren:** ... Concerning those who exercise Spiritual Gifts, *—CNBR* ... the spiritual endowments, *—CNDT.*

**I would not have you ignorant:** ... I do not wish you to be, *—WORL.*

**2. Ye know that ye were Gentiles:** ... whanne ye weren hethen men, *—WCLF* ... when you were pagans, *—MOFT.*

**carried away unto these dumb idols:**...dragged to speechless idols, −FNTN... the voiceless idols, −CNDT.

**even as ye were led:** ... even as ye happened to be led, −MKNT ... you were blindly led astray, −CNBR... being seduced, −RTHM.

**12:1, 2.** With the words "now concerning," Paul turned to a new area of discussion, one of much interest to him. The expression *peri de* ("now concerning") appears six times in First Corinthians and each time addresses a concern raised by the Corinthians themselves. He wished his readers to be knowledgeable and understanding in the matters that followed (*pneumatikon*, literally "spirituals").

Paul reminded the Corinthian believers of what they used to be: "Gentiles," heathens, pagans, men following dumb idols. They were helpless, for they had been "carried away" by their worship of these dead and useless idols.

**3. Wherefore I give you to understand:** ... I inform you, −FNTN... I make known to you, −WORL.

**that no man speaking by the Spirit of God calleth Jesus accursed:** ... no one can affirm, −RTHM ... Anathema is Jesus, −CNDT ... under the influence, −WEYM ... calleth Iesus execrable, −GNVA... defieth Iesus, −TNDL, −CRNM.

**and [that] no man can say that Jesus is the Lord, but by the Holy Ghost:** ... whoever is brought to own Jesus to be the Messiah, −LOCK ... can declare Jesus Lord, −MKNT... unless he be inspired by, −CNBR.

**12:3.** A comparison of their former heathen condition and their present Christian state shows a change had taken place. A Christian at all times acknowledges the lordship of Jesus Christ.

It is possible, in the public worship, that someone under ecstatic influence may have cried, "Jesus is accursed," and because of the excitement under which the statement was made, some were tempted to believe this came from God. Another view is that the statement might be made by a false teacher.

Such a statement denied the lordship of Jesus Christ. An utterance under the influence of the Holy Spirit is different; it asserts the lordship of Jesus Christ. If this particular utterance involved glossolalia, it would also have involved interpretation (or be a prophecy), for the statement to be understood publicly.

**4. Now there are diversities of gifts:** ... But distributions, −RTHM ... different talents, −FNTN ... diuisions of graces, −RHEM ... various kinds, −WEYM ... varieties of talents, −MOFT... apportionments of graces, −CNDT.

**but the same Spirit:** ... yet the selfe same Spirit, −GNVA.

**12:4.** Having laid down the cornerstone of lordship, Paul turned his thoughts to the matter of "spirituals" (*pneumatikon*) or "spiritual matters."

The manifestations of the Holy Spirit have both unity and variety. They have not the same purpose or magnitude, but each is given by one and the same Holy Spirit. These manifestations of the Spirit are called "gifts," but the idea of gift lies in their quality and ground and must be carefully used. These, like salvation, are a work of grace, but they still reside in the Holy Spirit.

In other words, their presence in someone does not necessarily signify great holiness, sanctification, or maturity. The word "diversities" (*diaireseis*) or "varieties" gives the idea of distribution and (as is made clear throughout the discussion) this is done by the choice of the Spirit.

**5. And there are differences of administrations:**... apportionments of service, −CNDT... there are diversities of ministries, −WORL... various forms of official service, −WEYM... of ministrations, −RHEM.

**but the same Lord:**

**12:5.** "Administrations" (*diakoniōn*) or "ministries" also differ according to God's decisions. These refer to the functions and services of those having the "gifts." The word also indicates the purpose of spiritual manifestations; these are for the help and strength of the Church. It is a useful service. Notice, it is always "the same Lord" who is served.

**6. And there are diversities of operations:**...and the working whereby they are wrought is various, −CNBR... varieties of workings, −CNFT... varieties of effects, −MOFT... diversities of energies, −MRDK.

**but it is the same God which worketh all in all:** ... which worketh all thinges that are wrought, in all creatures, −TNDL ... Who is operating all in all, −CNDT ... energizing everything in them all, −FNTN... that inwardly works all things in all, −RTHM ... who effects everything in everyone, −MOFT ... that works all these extraordinary gifts, −LOCK.

**12:6.** "Operations" (*energēmatōn*) are also diversified, these workings revealing both the availability and the effect of divine power. They result from gifts and ministrations and are workings in virtue of the power operative therein.

But again "it is the same God," as the context shows, that "worketh all (things) in all" (people). Notice the strong Trinitarian bent in "Spirit," "Lord" (which is generally Christ in Paul's epistles), and "God."

**7. But the manifestation of the Spirit is given to every man to profit withal:** ... The declaration, −GNVA... to proffit the congregacion, −TNDL ... with a view to expedience, –CNDT . . . but for the good and advantage of the church, –LOCK . . . for the common good, –MOFT . . . that it may aid him, –MRDK.

**12:7.** These gifts are given for the purpose of spiritual "profit." "Manifestation" (*phanerōsis*) is a vital word; it clarifies the meaning of "gift" and helps to define this entire section. On the basis of context, it appears as a subjective genitive and means to make evident to the understanding by proof. It is a shining forth, as light makes manifest.

The exercise of the gifts makes the Spirit's presence evident. This is a "manifestation of the Spirit" and not a manifestation of a gift. He is the Source, and in Him these "charismi" reside. The result is worship, not admiration of the gift. The final purpose is that all the Church may profit. On this basis, the gifts are as needed now as they were then.

**8. For to one is given by the Spirit the word of wisdom:** . . . On one is bestowed through the channel of the Spirit philosophic eloquence, –WAY . . . the vtterance of, –GNVA.

**to another the word of knowledge by the same Spirit:** . . . the utterance of spiritual illumination, –WAY . . . comprehension of thought, –FNTN.

**12:8.** "Wisdom" (*sophias*) by itself includes practical skill in the affairs of life, and in particular in the things of Christ. It is the supernatural ability to see how to handle a particular situation as the Spirit directs. "Word" denotes not only expression, but time and place, beginning and end. The gift operates in a particular setting and time. See the *Greek-English Dictionary* for added helps.

"Word of knowledge" (*gnōseōs*) involves a supernatural utterance of facts, including fundamental principles of the Word. It would include understanding of the great facts of life as they are known by God. See the *Greek-English Dictionary* for further information.

**9. To another faith by the same Spirit:** . . . special faith, –WEYM.

**to another the gifts of healing by the same Spirit:** . . . the grace of doing cures in one Spirit, –RHEM.

**12:9.** "Faith" (*pistis*) is infinite trust and belief in God and often appears in times of great crisis or opportunity. It is divine certainty (Matthew 17:20; 1 Kings 18:30-46; Acts 3:1-10).

"Gifts of healing(s)" suggests different healings for different diseases. It is used of God in ministering health to the sick, appears as a sign gift, and is involved in the work of evangelism.

**10. To another the working of miracles:** . . . inward workings of deeds of power, –RTHM . . . operations of powerful deeds, –CNDT . . . the exercise of miraculous powers, –WEYM . . . workings of mighty deeds, –WORL.

**to another prophecy:** . . . while to another eloquence, –FNTN . . . inspired oratory, –WAY.

**to another discerning of spirits:** . . . iudgement of spretes, –TNDL . . . the power of discriminating between prophetic utterances, –WEYM . . . discernment of character, –FNTN . . . iudgement to discerne, –CRNM . . . the gift of distinguishing spirits, –MOFT . . . the faculty of detecting the truth or falsity of any inspiration, –WAY.

**to another [divers] kinds of tongues:** . . . species of languages, –CNDT.

**to another the interpretation of tongues:** . . . the ability to interpret languages, –ADAM . . . to another expownynge of wordis, –WCLF . . . translating languages, –FNTN.

**12:10.** The word "miracles" involves an orderly intervention in the regular operations of nature. These "works of power" may be negative and destructive as well as positive.

There are those who doubt the validity of miracles today, but if the experience of the Early Church and Scripture itself have any meaning for Christians, then we must believe in the continuing miracle-working power of God. Jesus, as well as Peter, Paul, and other apostles, lived their lives with the continual expectation of the miraculous. This century has witnessed many validated miracles.

Matthew 8:17, which quotes Isaiah 53:4, shows that one sign of the coming of the kingdom of God was to be miraculous healing. It is also true that some references to "healing" in the Gospels are metaphors for salvation and that Christ's death on the cross, although it brought physical healing, did not bring about healing in precisely the same way in which it brought about salvation. Nevertheless, Jesus' ministry, the apostolic ministry recorded in Acts, and prophecies regarding God's future activity for His people all reveal that miracles (especially, but not exclusively, healing) can be expected by all the people of God in every era of New Testament times.

"Prophecy" (*prophēteia*) means literally "to speak for another" (in this case, to speak for God). With the Day of Pentecost Joel's prophecy of the outpouring of the Holy Spirit was fulfilled (Joel 2:28-30), and it could now be expected that all believers would exercise the gift of prophecy. This gift, which includes forthtelling as well as foretelling, is a supernaturally inspired utterance by the Holy Spirit in one's own language. Its purpose (14:3) is to upbuild, instruct, and comfort.

"Discerning of spirits" is the policeman of the group and is to distinguish among three possible sources of operation: the Spirit, Satan, or the human spirit (1 John 4:1-6; Matthew 7:15-23).

"Kinds of tongues" is defined as the power to speak by the Holy Spirit in a language the speaker has not learned. "Interpretation of tongues" is to render glossolalia understandable to the audience in their language, producing profit. It must be judged by the Word of God for spiritual quality and scriptural correctness.

**11. But all these worketh that one and the selfsame Spirit:**...effectively work, —*CMPB*...that is the energising source, —*WAY*.

**dividing to every man severally as he will:**...distributing peculiarly to each one, according as it is disposed, —*RTHM*...who bestows His gifts upon each of us in accordance with His own will, —*WEYM*...distributing to each his proper gifts as he pleaseth, —*MKNT*...apportioning them severally to each individual as he pleases, —*MOFT*...according as He is intending, —*CNDT*...distributing to each person as He considers best, —*FNTN*...as he thinks fit, —*LOCK*...as He determines, —*ADAM*.

**12:11.** Once more Paul emphasizes this theme: these are gifts of the one Holy Spirit. He distributes to each individual as He wills and chooses. The choice is His, and the glory is God's.

**12. For as the body is one, and hath many members:**...yet it has many limbs, —*FNTN*...it has many organs, —*WAY*.

**and all the members of that one body, being many, are one body:**...many as they are, form one body, —*CNFT*...comprise but the one body, —*WAY*...together make up one body, —*ADAM*.

**so also [is] Christ:**...so it is with the church of Christ, —*WEYM*.

**12:12.** As Paul considers the operation of these manifestations of the Spirit within the Church, he is moved to think of the operation of the Church itself. The analogy used is that of the body; one body with many functions. He is moved to consider the Church as the body of Christ.

He notes in comparison that the body is single, but has many parts. These various parts cannot be separated from the one body. The same is true of Christ's body. "Christ" here means the body of Christ, for the person of Christ is not divided.

**13. For by one Spirit are we all baptized into one body:**...For in the communion of one Spirit, —*CNBR*...we were all immersed into One Body, —*WLSN*, —*HNSN*...we have through baptism been made members, —*NORL*...into one church, —*LOCK*.

**whether [we be] Jews or Gentiles, whether [we be] bond or free:**...slaves or freemen, —*FNTN*, —*MOFT*.

**and have been all made to drink into one Spirit:**...and we were all nourished by that one Spirit, —*WEYM*...were all made to drink of [the] one spirit, —*HNSN*...we have all been imbued with one Spirit, —*MOFT*.

**12:13.** Believers are initiated into Christ's body (meaning the Church) "by one Spirit" or "in one Spirit" (ASV). This cannot be water baptism, because clearly the baptizer is the Holy Spirit, and the element is the body of Christ. Therefore it is regeneration as in Galatians 3:27.

Some say that the Spirit is not the agent. But He cannot be the element of baptism here because the body of Christ is. Thus it has to mean "in virtue of His operation." This would make the phrase "by one Spirit" a dative of instrumentality rather than a dative of location.

This work is accomplished regardless of station or place in life. "Jews or Gentiles" (Greeks) probably refers to nationality and birth. Such hereditary matters do not influence or affect the work of God in our lives. He is available to "whosoever" will come.

"Bond or free" refers to rank or position. God is no respecter of persons. He does not look on the social attainment, the economic status, or the hereditary influence. He looks on the heart.

Representatives of all these were made to "drink into (or of) one Spirit." While some see a reference to Communion here, it is more than possible that this is a reference to the baptism in the Holy Spirit. Certainly, God has poured out His Spirit on all flesh, according to His promise (Acts chapters 2 and 10).

It is the one Spirit who does all this, working, organizing, administrating, bringing about the effective work of Christ in believers' lives.

The work of the one Spirit brings a common bond to each life. There is a sense of unity with Him and each other, a sense of close contact and fellowship, deep, lasting, eternal. When it is the Spirit doing the work, it produces certain specific results and fruit all the time.

**14. For the body is not one member, but many:**...Since, therefore, —*MKNT*...So, too, the body, —*PNT*...For a body also, —*MRDK*...does not have only one part, —*SEB*...is not one sole member, —*LOCK*...does not consist of one part, —*WEYM*, —*WLMS*...is not a single organ, —*FNTN*...does not have only one member, —*ADAM*...the body is not one organ, —*WAY*.

**12:14.** This one Body (of Christ), which has been so established, has many members, from many backgrounds, and each one is necessary and important.

**15. If the foot shall say, Because I am not the hand:**...Since I am not a hand, —*WLMS*.

**I am not of the body:**...not a part of the body, —*ADAM*, —*MNTG*...I am no part of the body, —*WLSN*...I do not belong to the body, —*RSV*.

**is it therefore not of the body?:** ... would it not indeed be a part of the body? *—MNTG* ... would that constitute it no part of the body? *—WAY* ... is it for this not of the body? *—WLSN* ... is it for this reason, *—NOYS* ... is it, on that account, *—MRDK* ... does it therefore not belong to the body? *—FNTN* ... would not make it any the less a part of the body, *—WEYM* ... that does not make it no part of the body, *—MOFT*.

**12:15.** This diversity in unity is illustrated in several ways. Paul used the illustration of the foot and the hand. The foot might feel inadequate in comparison with the dexterity of the hand. But the foot has a function that is vital.

16. **And if the ear shall say, Because I am not the eye, I am not of the body:** ... And if the ear may say, *—CLMT* ... As I am not an eye, *—PNT* ... I am not a part of the body, *—WLMS*.
**is it therefore not of the body?:** ... does it thereby sever itself, *—CNBR* ... would it be any less a part of the body? *—MNTG*.

**12:16.** Paul added comparison of the ear and the eye. Again, the sense of inadequacy and inferiority might arise. The eye carries a great deal of responsibility and is an obvious part of the body. Should that make the ear feel uninvolved or unimportant because its function is less obvious? Or can it say that because it is not another member of the body that it is not a part of the body? The obvious answer is "No," it cannot say that.

17. **If the whole body [were] an eye, where [were] the hearing?:** ... where would be the hearing? *—DOUY, —NOYS, —PNT* ... sense of hearing? *—FNTN*.
**If the whole [were] hearing:** ... If all were hearing, *—MNTG* ... were all ear, *—MOFT*.
**where [were] the smelling?:** ... where would the nostrils be? *—WEYM* ... where were the scent? *—CNDT*.

**12:17.** In carrying the analogy to its proper conclusion, Paul offered some insights on unity. First, he noted that in the human body each member is important because if some part is missing, some important function of the body is missing, and the body is incapable of performing as a healthy body should and would.

Any time a member of the body of Christ ceases to function, the cause of Christ is hurt because something vital is absent. The Church was formed very carefully to do the whole work of God in this world.

18. **But now hath God set the members every one of them in the body:** ... But as it is, *—NOYS* ... the fact is that God set each one, *—ADAM* ... has arranged the parts in the body, *—WEYM* ... has placed the members, each One of them, *—WLMS*.
**as it hath pleased him:** ... with the best adaptation, *—FNTN* ... as He has seen fit, *—WEYM* ... as he willed, *—CNFT, —PNIN, —CLMT* ... as He wished, *—ADAM* ... just

as He wanted them to be, *—WLMS* ... according to his pleasure, *—MRDK* ... according as he thought fit, *—PNT* ... as He chose to do, *—SEB*.

**12:18.** Secondly, Paul noted that the individual members of the human body do not choose their function or place. They do not reach into some grab bag and pull out a function to please themselves.

The human body was designed very carefully by God. He had a specific plan in mind when He did the work. Nothing was left to chance or accident. The plan was followed very carefully.

The plan was the one God desired. It was according to His delight and was grounded in wisdom, practicality, and love. It therefore pleases His heart to see the body working well and in unity.

That plan and design was intended to profit the rest of the body. He placed each member in order that together they would make the body function properly. And what is true of the physical body is true also of the Church, the body of Christ,

19. **And if they were all one member:** ... And if the whole were One Member, *—WLSN*.
**where [were] the body?:** ... what would become of the body? *—MOFT* ... where would the body be? *—MNTG* ... there would be no body! *—SEB*.

**12:19.** Thirdly, Paul argued that if the whole body were one member such as an eye or an ear, then the body would not really be a body. Without certain members and functions, there is no complete body. It has lost its purpose and identity. Again, Paul's question anticipated a set response.

20. **But now [are they] many members:** ... now indeed they are many members, *—CLMT* ... now there are many members indeed, *—DOUY* ... though we are many members, *—WLMS*.
**yet but one body:** ... but a single body, *—FNTN*.

**12:20.** By repetition, Paul drove his point home. Division has no part in a united body of members.

21. **And the eye cannot say unto the hand, I have no need of thee:** ... It is also impossible, *—WEYM* ... The eye is not able to say to the hand, *—WLSN* ... So the eye cannot say to the hand, *—PNT* ... You are not necessarie for me, *—RHEM* ... Thou art not needful to me, *—MRDK* ... I do not need thy help, *—CNFT* ... I do not need you, *—WLMS*.
**nor again the head to the feet, I have no need of you:**

**12:21.** The individual members must respect one another, because each has a necessary function in a healthy body.

Once more the illustration of eye and hand appears in Paul's discussion. The eye is a powerful, long-range, controlling member. It is valuable to the total body. Being blind is a deficiency, no matter how the other members may try to compensate.

Sometimes members in such positions in the body of Christ think they can do everything themselves. But the eye, despite its visionary work cannot get along without the menial working of the hand. Someone must bring the eye's vision into reality. "Hand" is singular and generally refers to the right or main hand. The body needs both the long-range and the close-at-work member to accomplish its purposes.

**22. Nay, much more those members of the body:** ... Quite the contrary, —*MOFT.*
**which seem to be more feeble, are necessary:** ... those very organs which might seem to have least influence are really indispensable, —*WAY* ... are considered rather delicate, —*MOFT.*

**12:22.** No member of the body is sufficient in itself. It is impossible in the physical body; it is impossible in the spiritual Body.

In fact, in contrast to what is often thought, the weaker members are essential to the proper functioning of the body. These may only seem to be weaker; they may actually be weaker. But the point is that they are a part of the body and they are there for a specific purpose, without which the body simply cannot function properly. They are necessary. They are vital. They are a part of the body.

**23. And those [members] of the body, which we think to be less honourable:** ... the least estimable, —*FNTN* ... to be the baser members, —*RHEM.*
**upon these we bestow more abundant honour:** ... clothe with, —*WEYM* ... surround with, —*CNFT* ... accord greater honor, —*ADAM* ... invest with special honour, —*MOFT.*
**and our uncomely [parts] have more abundant comeliness:** ... And oure vngodly parties have most beauty on, —*TNDL* ... and so our ungraceful parts, —*WEYM* ... the less beautiful parts, —*CNBR* ... and we exert greater effort to make the ugly members attractive, —*ADAM* ... our plainest organ, —*FNTN* ... our indecent members have more exceeding respectability, —*CNDT* ... on them we put the more decoration, —*MRDK.*
**24. For our comely [parts] have no need:** ... than we do for the more beautiful ones that do not need it, —*ADAM* ... have no deficiency, —*FNTN.*
**but God hath tempered the body together:** ... it was God who built up the body, —*WEYM.*
**having given more abundant honour to that [part] which lacked:** ... giving supreme honour, —*FNTN* ... with a special dignity for the inferior parts, —*MOFT* ... and given to the lowlier parts the higher honor, —*CNBR* ... which is deficient, —*CNDT.*

**12:23, 24.** There must be a mutual respect and honoring of lesser members. Delicate but vital organs must be cared for. In verses 23 and 24 Paul used two sets of puns to further his point. Those bodily parts which are less honorable (*atimotera*) must be given more honor (*timēn*), and those parts which are unpresentable (*ta aschēmona*) must be made presentable (*euschēmona*). "Less honorable" members must be given more honor. How do we do this? Simply, we give them special attention; they are provided with special care and we take the time to clothe them.

"Uncomely parts," within the framework of the analogy, may refer to organs of procreation and excretion. The reference to sexual organs is indicated by the word *peritithemen* ("we put about" = clothe) which recalls Genesis 3:7, 21 where God clothed Adam and Eve to cover their nakedness and shame. If this is true, we understand their vital nature, and yet they are weaker, and we must give them special attention to make them honorable in their function.

Whether Paul's point is intended to go this far or not, the point is clear that some parts are more and less attractive, probably because of function. But that does not make them not part of the body. Rather, each has a place and honor in the body.

The more attractive parts we make sure are noticed. They receive honor and attention from others. We do not hide them nor forget them. We provide them with honor and care.

But each member must receive equal honor and care, for God ordained the bodily operations as they are, and He has equalized the gaining and receiving of honor.

If this is the way God has planned for the human body, and He intends that each member function correctly and be a part of the whole, is it not more than reasonable to believe that He has done the same excellent thing in His spiritual body, the Church?

Paul's message could not have been made any clearer. He was writing to a church wracked by internal division, squabbling, and bitterness over such false notions as stronger or weaker, greater or lesser Christians. Just as every member of the physical body has an important function, so every believer (even if he is weak!) has a vital role to fulfill.

**25. That there should be no schism in the body:** ... that debate be not, —*WCLF* ... might be no disunion, —*MRDK* ... may be no division, —*ADAM.*
**but [that] the members should have the same care one for another:** ... same anxious care for one another's welfare, —*WEYM* ... might mutually attend to each other, —*FNTN* ... have a common concern,

−MOFT . . . are sympathizing, −CNDT . . . should care equally for one another, −ADAM.

**26. And whether one member suffer, all the members suffer with it:** . . . if one organ be in pain, all the organs sympathise, −WAY . . . share its suffering, −MOFT.

**or one member be honoured:** . . . is being esteemed, −CNDT.

**all the members rejoice with it:** . . . share its honour, −MOFT . . . share its pleasure, −WAY.

**12:25, 26.** God equalized the gaining and receiving of honor to prevent division and argument in the Body and to promote concern among the members for each other. This way, suffering and loss are shared, as well as joy and honor. The Body becomes a tightly-knit unity, affected by everything its individual members do and feel.

**27. Now ye are the body of Christ:**
**and members in particular:** . . . and individually you are members of it, −WEYM . . . and participating members, −FNTN . . . and severally members of it, −MOFT.

**28. And God hath set some in the church:** . . . by God's appointment there are, −WEYM . . . set in the assembly, −RTHM.

**first apostles:**

**secondarily prophets:** . . . after them, −MRDK . . . inspired preachers, −WAY.

**thirdly teachers:** . . . doctors, −RHEM . . . expounders, −WAY.

**after that miracles:** . . . then men of power, −FNTN . . . thereupon powers, −CNDT . . . next, powers, −CMPB.

**then gifts of healings:** . . . then the graces of doing cures, −RHEM . . . then talent for healing, −FNTN . . . then ability to cure diseases, −WEYM.

**helps:** . . . or render loving service, −WEYM . . . Serviceable Ministrations, −CNBR . . . services of help, −CNFT.

**governments:** . . . governors, −LOCK . . . guidings, −RTHM . . . and leaders, −MRDK . . . power of administration, −CNFT.

**diversities of tongues:** . . . the ability to speak different kinds of languages, −ADAM.

**12:27, 28.** Paul used the human body as an example to illustrate his point; now he directly applied what he had said to the Corinthians. As elsewhere, there is individuality in unity. All of these workers are called and ordained by God.

It must be remembered that the context for Paul's statements that all members of the Body are to rejoice and suffer together is spiritual gifts. This means that if a church member does not have a prominent gift, he should not be looked down on, but accepted as a member of the Body. Similarly, no one is to think that being used for a special manifestation makes him better in the church than another person.

What about the order, then, that Paul offered. Does listing them as he does tear down what he has been saying about equality? Paul was not talking about the essential nature of the items listed in verses 27-31, but about their relative importance in some of the work of the Church. It should also be noted that the list begins with persons and proceeds to gifts or items, so it is difficult to carry a list of importance too far.

"Apostles" were chief ministers entrusted with the powers necessary to found the Church and make an entire revelation of God's will known to the body of Christ. They were certainly authoritative witnesses to the fact of the gospel and especially to the Resurrection. "Apostles" were and are designated by God for a set task.

The word "prophets" (*prophētas*) seems to have in mind a settled office rather than an occasional manifestation. Their ministry was Holy Spirit inspired speech. They were enabled to speak in their own language by a supernatural anointing. (See 14:1-5.)

"Teachers" (*didaskalous*) labor in word and doctrine with or without a pastoral charge. The word itself lends us some help. In the Ancient Church they played an important role due to the extremely high cost of hand-copied books. In some cases this ministry was local (Acts 13:1; Ephesians 4:11).

"Then" transfers the discussion from people to gifts. Miracles, healings, and tongues have been discussed earlier. "Helps" is a ministry not found elsewhere. It appears to be those who have compassion and ministry to the sick, weak, or helpless in some fashion. Special persons without set offices may render special assistance in needy cases. There are those who parallel "he that giveth" (Romans 12:8) with "helps" and "he that ruleth" (idem) with "governments."

"Governments" (*kubernēseis*) or administrations, while not fully defined, apparently has to do with some type of higher department of leadership. First Timothy 5:17 indicates it may refer to elders who not only labor in teaching and doctrine, but also are charged with some form of leadership.

**29. [Are] all apostles?:** . . . Not all are apostles, −CNDT . . . Are they all legates? −MRDK.
**[are] all prophets?:**
**[are] all teachers? [are] all workers of miracles?:** . . . can all be marvel-workers? −WAY.

**12:29.** These questions expect a negative answer. They point to what Paul has said earlier. God has put diversity in the body of Christ; He has set in order a variety of functions and gifts for the good of the Church.

**30. Have all the gifts of healing?:** ... Are all endowed, —MOFT.

**do all speak with tongues?:**

**do all interpret?:** ... Are all able to interpret? —MOFT ... all do not translate, —FNTN.

**12:30.** Again the questions beg a "No" answer. Not everyone manifests these particular gifts. Paul was stressing diversity, not exclusiveness. It must be remembered that it is the Spirit who distributes as He wishes and manifests as He chooses.

**31. But covet earnestly the best gifts:** ... But pursue the better giftes, —RHEM ... But always seek to excel in the greater gifts, —WEYM ... Yet strive after the greater gifts, —CNFT ... if ye are emulous of the superior gifts, —MRDK ... I would have you delight in the best gifts, —CNBR ... But be envying the greater gifts, —RTHM ... Yet be zealous for the greater graces, —CNDT ... Set your hearts on the higher talents, —MOFT.

**and yet show I unto you a more excellent way:** ... But now, I am going to show you a far better way, —ADAM ... now I will point out to you a way of life which transcends all others, —WEYM ... I will show you a path wherein to walk, —CNBR.

**12:31.** Paul concludes with an exhortation to "covet ... the best gifts." How is this determined, and does it mean one gift is worth more than others? The criterion of worth is use; purpose determines value. Those most serviceable to others are the most valuable and thus the greater or best gifts.

This naturally leads to that "more excellent way." Paul did not abolish gifts; he just showed the environment in which they are to exist and the force by which they are to be guided. That environment and force is love.

## Chapter 13

**1. Though I speak with the tongues of men and of angels:** ... If I can speak all the languages of men, —WEYM ... If I could speak in every tongue of men, —MRDK.

**and have not charity:** ... but have not friendship, —FNTN ... but am destitute of Love, —WEYM.

**I am become [as] sounding brass, or a tinkling cymbal:** ... I should become an echoing trumpet, or a resounding drum, —FNTN ... a noisy gong or a clanging cymbal, —MOFT ... aloud-sounding trumpet, —WEYM ... resounding copper, —CNDT.

**13:1.** Henry Drummond called love the "summum bonum," the supreme good (p. 11). It comes from and is, at best, a part of God. "Love is more than a characteristic of God, it is His character." (See 1 John 4:7, 8.)

Love is discussed in many parts of the Word of God. It was a vital part of Jesus' ministry and thought. Yet it never reaches a fuller, stronger, deeper presentation than in this chapter. Inspired by the Holy Spirit, with Christ in full view, Paul wrote this stirring description of love.

The supremacy of love is quickly established. It is supreme over "tongues" and speech. No language in heaven or earth can be compared with the practice of love. The art of oratory, so highly valued at Corinth, could not surpass love.

"Brass" (chalkos) denotes first metal, copper, and then any object made from it. Here it probably refers to a gong. "Sounding" (ēchōn) might be rendered "resounding."

"Tinkling" (alalazon) is rather clashing like the sound of heavy cymbals. The sound may be attractive and entertaining; it may be alluring and persuasive. But if action is not motivated by love, it is only noise, "sound without soul."

**2. And though I have [the gift of] prophecy: and understand all mysteries, and all knowledge:** ... and see, in the law and the prophets, all the mysteries contained in them, —LOCK ... perceiving all secrets, —CNDT ... and am versed in all mysteries, —WEYM ... fathom all mysteries and secret lore, —MOFT ... and every science, —MRDK.

**and though I have all faith:** ... and have such absolute faith, —WEYM ... if I possessed perfect faith, —FNTN ... faith to the highest degree, —LOCK.

**so that I could remove mountains:** ... so as to transport mountains, —CNDT ... so that I meue hillis fro her place, —WCLF.

**and have not charity:**

**I am nothing:** ... I am of no value, —LOCK.

**13:2.** To understand the contrast Paul put forth between love and tongues, prophecy, understanding, knowledge, and faith in verses 1 and 2, it is necessary to take into consideration why chapter 13 is sandwiched between chapters 11 to 14. The larger context of chapters 11 to 14 is that of public worship. In chapter 11 Paul was concerned to draw limits for the proper role of women in church worship and how Christians should conduct themselves at the Lord's Supper. Chapters 12 and 14 have to do with the proper exercise of the gifts of the Spirit in church worship.

The apostle Paul was forced to deal with these issues specifically because various Corinthian Christians were exalting their "Christian liberty" and "knowledge" to such a degree that they made a mockery of orderly Christian worship. Paul insisted in chapter 13 that the model of Christian worship is love, not knowledge or any other special gift in which the Corinthians thought they excelled.

First Corinthians 13, therefore, is not a general treatise on the nature of love; it is a very specific instruction explaining how people are to relate to one another in public worship. Paul did not condemn the gifts of tongues or prophecy; rather, he insisted that they cannot be used indiscriminately or boastfully but must be subordinated to love.

Love is superior to great knowledge and understanding. This involves inspiration and prophecy: the work of the seer. Mysteries are known, truths that men could never learn and penetrate for themselves, but only because it pleased God to reveal them. "All" explains the extent of the knowledge. It is "nothing" without love.

Love is superior to great faith, the kind of faith that moves mountain after mountain. Without love as the motive, even such miracle-working faith as this, exciting and successful though it may be, is of no value.

**3. And though I bestow all my goods to feed [the poor]:**...if I should distribute, *—RHEM*...I morsel out, *—RTHM*...if I bestow all I have in relief of the poor, *—LOCK*...if I should feed out to the destitute all I possess, *—MRDK*.

**and though I give my body to be burned:**...deliver my body, *—FNTN*.

**and have not charity:**

**it profiteth me nothing:**...nothing do I benefit, *—CNDT*...I gain nothing, *—FNTN*.

**13:3.** Love surpasses great generosity of goods and self. There may be generosity to the point of becoming a pauper and yet be without love. Men of the First Century, as today, saw great merit in deeds of charity and suffering. But these without love have no merit. To be of value love must be the motive.

If one gave one's self as a martyr, which is as far as this point could be carried, without love as the motive, there would be no gain of any kind.

**4. Charity suffereth long, [and] is kind:**...patient, is gracious, *—RTHM*...Friendship forbears, *—FNTN*...is courteous, *—GNVA*...is gentle and benign, *—LOCK*.

**charity envieth not:**...nor jealousy, *—WEYM*...without emulation, *—LOCK*.

**charity vaunteth not itself:**...is not forward and self-assertive, *—WEYM*...is not vainglorious, *—FNTN, —PNT*...not bragging, *—CNDT*...love is not boisterous, *—MRDK*.

**is not puffed up:**...gives itself no airs, *—MOFT*...swelleth not, *—GNVA*...is not pompous, Fenton.

**13:4.** Love is supreme in its position and practical in its display. It has great patience toward evil and is kind when doing good. Love is

longsuffering (Ephesians 4:1-3; 2 Peter 3:9). It has an infinite capacity for endurance and patience.

Love is "kind" (Luke 6:27-35; James 3:17). It shows goodness toward those who ill-treat it. It gives itself in the service of others.

It "envieth not" (James 3:14-16); it is not jealous. It has no petty feelings toward those, for instance, who are doing the same work, only better. Love is not displeased at the success of others. Love "vaunteth not" itself. The root of this word points to a "windbag." It is "not puffed up." Humility is an ingredient of love.

**5. Doth not behave itself unseemly:**...is not ambitious, *—RHEM*...is never rude, *—MOFT*...is not indecent, *—CNDT*...dealeth not dishonestly, *—CRNM*...does not behave unbecomingly, *—WEYM*.

**seeketh not her own:**...never selfish, *—MOFT.*

**is not easily provoked, thinketh no evil:**...nor blaze out in passionate anger, *—WEYM*...not exasperated, *—RTHM*...not incensed, *—CNDT*...never irritated, never resentful, *—MOFT*...nor brooding over injury, *—FNTN*.

**13:5.** Love is concerned with giving itself rather than asserting itself. It does not "behave itself unseemly." This phrase carries the idea of anything disgraceful, dishonorable, or indiscreet.

Further, it is "not easily provoked." It "thinketh no evil." It imputes no evil to anyone nor does it hold anything against anyone. "Thinketh" (*logizetai*) is a word Paul used frequently for the reckoning or imputing of righteousness to believers. Here it is connected with the keeping of accounts, recording them, and reckoning them to someone.

**6. Rejoiceth not in iniquity:**...love is never glad when others go wrong, *—MOFT*...finds no pleasure in injustice done to others, *—WEYM*.

**but rejoiceth in the truth:**...joyfully sides with, *—WEYM*...rejoices with the right, *—FNTN*.

**7. Beareth all things, believeth all things:**...slow to expose...eager to believe the best, *—MOFT*...knows how to be silent...full of trust, *—WEYM*.

**hopeth all things:**

**endureth all things:**...waits for all, *—FNTN*.

**13:6, 7.** Love "rejoiceth in the truth" (John 14:6; Romans 14:17; Ephesians 4:21). Even love cannot rejoice when the truth is denied. Love rejoices in the gospel.

Love "beareth all things" (Ephesians 4:2; Colossians 3:13). It endures, without disclosing to the world its stress or complaint. There is no bragging.

It "believeth all things." With a good conscience it puts good to another's credit. In trust and faith it believes the very best it honestly can at all times.

Love "endureth all things." It is steadfast even in difficult circumstances. There is a patient, loving spirit.

8. **Charity never faileth:** . . . Love never disappears, —MOFT.

**but whether [there be] prophecies, they shall fail:** . . . as for eloquence it will cease, —FNTN . . . shalbe abolished, —GNVA . . . be made voide, —RHEM . . . will be discarded, —CNDT.

**whether [there be] tongues, they shall cease:** . . . they will be silent, —FNTN.

**whether [there be] knowledge, it shall vanish away:** . . . will be brought to an end, —WEYM.

9. **For we know in part:** . . . For out of an installment are we knowing, —CNDT . . . we only know bit by bit, —MOFT.

**and we prophesy in part:** . . . we teach with imperfection, —FNTN.

**13:8, 9.** This love shall endure forever. It is compared with prophecy, tongues, and knowledge, all items of value in this life, but in a sense "temporary."

The painfully acquired knowledge of earthly things will "vanish away" in light of the overwhelming knowledge of God. Its incompleteness will be evident to everyone. The knowledge of the Lord shall be full.

To "prophesy in part" probably means that the prophet has only a partial glimpse of truth; his prophecy is accurate but incomplete. God does not reveal everything. This is the pattern in the Old Testament, as we discover from Hebrews 1:1-3. What the prophets of old spoke was accurate and true, but there was a fuller revelation to come, a final revelation in the Son of God, God's Word to man. We are learning about and from that Word; we seek truth and wisdom; we grow in knowledge. But when He restores all things and human limitations are removed, the veil will be lifted to show understanding beyond our reach now, understanding rich, full, and final.

10. **But when that which is perfect is come:** . . . when the perfect state of things, —WEYM.

**then that which is in part shall be done away:** . . . all that is imperfect will be brought to an end, —WEYM . . . will be superseded, —MOFT . . . will become useless, —FNTN.

**13:10.** That is exactly Paul's point as this verse indicates. When He who is perfect is fully revealed in His glory, then anything and everything partial will be swallowed up in that fullness.

A day of completeness and perfection is coming. Everything partial, temporary, or inadequate shall vanish in the light of Christ's brilliant power and glory.

11. **When I was a child, I spake as a child:** . . . a litle one, —RHEM . . . a minor, —CNDT . . . in the imperfect state of childhood, —LOCK.

**I understood as a child, I thought as a child:** . . . I reflected like, —FNTN . . . I had the feelings of, —NOYS . . . reasoned like, —WEYM . . . I argued like, —MOFT.

**but when I became a man, I put away childish things:** . . . came to the state and perfection of manhood, —LOCK . . . I have laid aside, —RTHM . . . I have discarded childish manners, —HNSN . . . outworn for me are the things of the child, —WAY.

**13:11.** To explain more fully, Paul gave us the illustration of a child becoming a man. "Put away" is an indication of the determination on Paul's part not to be ruled by childish attitudes. The tense is perfect, which shows that Paul put away childish things with decision and finality. This is a normal process for normal growth. The child strives to be a man and works at becoming one with clear deliberation. The spiritual process is also like that. Out of a spiritual nature comes the desire for maturity, fullness, and "manhood."

12. **For now we see through a glass, darkly:** . . . For at present, —CNDT . . . we see as yet the Vision glassed in a mirror it is a dark riddle, —WAY . . . we only see the baffling reflections in a mirror, —MOFT . . . a mirror obscurely, —RTHM, —CLMT . . . the dim, and, as it were, enigmatical representation of things, —LOCK . . . in a dark manner, —DOUY . . . and are puzzled, —WEYM . . . and are baffled, —MNTG.

**but then face to face:** . . . as a man sees another, —LOCK . . . shall we gaze, —WAY.

**now I know in part; but then shall I know even as also I am known:** . . . Now I knowe vnparfectly, —TNDL . . . now I know partially, —FNTN, —MRDK . . . now I know in fragments, but then shall I understand even as I also have been understood, —MNTG . . . Now my knowledge comes from seeing but a part, —WAY . . . then I shall recognize, —CNDT . . . then shall I know fully, —CLMT, —PNIN . . . even as I am fully known, —WEYM.

**13:12.** To express it by yet another figure, Paul included the illustration of the mirror reflection. Mirrors were a specialty of Corinth, but they were made of polished brass so the image was dim at best. Silvering glass was not discovered until the 13th Century. This makes the point of Paul's illustration more obvious.

Here on earth our sight of eternal things is at best indistinct. Human limitations make the fullness of our spiritual destiny hazy. But that will change. Sometime, in eternity, we shall know as we are now known, and we will understand redemption and our Redeemer fully.

Paul's use of "mirror" as a metaphor or analogy for "seeing" has been the subject of much debate. Most frequently it has been taken in a negative sense implying that our knowledge of God is skewed and warped. The Hellenistic Jew Philo, for example, used the mirror in this way. C.K. Barrett, however, suggests that the metaphor "must take its sense from the context; always the glass is an instrument of revelation . . ." (*Harper's New Testament Commentaries*, p. 307). The fact that "mirror," by itself, was not a negative image is suggested by the following *en ainigmati* (literally, "in a riddle").

The most likely background for *ainigmati* (which occurs only here in the New Testament) is the Septuagint of Numbers 12:8 where God spoke "mouth to mouth" with Moses (i.e., directly), not *en ainigmati*, in "dark speeches" or riddles as He did to the prophets. The point is not so much the inadequacy of God's revelation to the prophets as it is the indirectness of it. Thus, the understanding here in verse 12 should focus on the indirectness of the knowledge of God's revelation more than on our utter inability to understand His revelation. By stressing its indirectness, and the fact that we will understand in full only later, Paul was counteracting the Gnostic view that God can be fully known in the present.

**13. And now abideth faith, hope, charity, these three:** . . . And now exist, *—FNTN* . . . endure, *—MNTG* . . . these abide unperishing . . . These three Gifts alone, *—WAY* . . . now are remaining faith, expectation, *—CNDT*.

**but the greatest of these [is] charity:** . . . but the chiefest of these, *—GNVA* . . . the greatest of them is friendship, *—FNTN*.

**13:13.** Love stands above faith and hope, both of which are essential in the plan and work of salvation. The reason is that love will not fail or "fall" in the sense of cessation. Love surpasses its companions, since it is the character of God. Love is the fruition of faith's efforts and hope's anticipations.

Fittingly, love is the last word of the chapter. The heart needs love, and the Christian must allow every thought, action, and attitude to be ruled by love, which is the greatest in all of life.

## Chapter 14

**1. Follow after charity:** . . . Labour for loue, *—CRNM* . . . Be eager in your pursuit, *—WEYM* . . . Make love your aim, *—MOFT*.

**and desire spiritual [gifts]:** . . . nevertheless, be envious, *—RTHM* . . . be zealous for spiritual endowments, *—CNDT* . . . earnestly pursue spiritual things, *—RHEM* . . . and then set your heart on, *—MOFT* . . . mental powers, *—FNTN*.

**but rather that ye may prophesy:** . . . but most chefly, *—CRNM* . . . especially those enabling you to instruct, *—FNTN* . . . but let it be chiefly so in order that you may prophesy, *—WEYM*.

**14:1.** Now begins an analysis of the utterance gifts: tongues, interpretation, and prophecy. The emphasis on prophecy is due to the pride of the Corinthians over tongues and their neglect of the other gifts of the Spirit. Paul was not speaking against tongues (14:5, 18) but emphasizing the need for edification in utterance.

He encouraged believers to "follow after charity (love)." Love is not to be pursued to the neglect of everything else but in the interest of all else. The constant need is that everything be done out of love.

"Desire" (*zēloute*) is the same word which is translated "covet earnestly" in 12:31. It is proper and good to desire these spiritual gifts (12:8-10). They should be earnestly sought within the framework of love. Every believer is to be Spirit-filled; therefore, any Spirit-filled believer may manifest these spiritual gifts.

Paul emphasized prophecy because of the principle of edification. The Corinthians overemphasized tongues. Paul was showing the need for balance and edification.

**2. For he that speaketh in an [unknown] tongue speaketh not unto men:**
**but unto God: for no man understandeth [him]:** . . . addresses God not men, *—MOFT* . . . for no man heareth, *—RHEM* . . . for no one is listening, *—RTHM*.

**howbeit in the spirit he speaketh mysteries:** . . . he speaketh secret things, *—GNVA* . . . he is speaking secrets, *—CNDT*.

**14:2.** Paul first explained the action and communion of tongues. There is adequate sound in "tongues," but there is not understanding. "Tongues" do not edify anyone else because no one can understand what is being said unless there is interpretation or, as occasionally happens, the "tongues" are in a foreign language understood by someone present. Only God understands.

"Not unto men" shows that, whatever the intention, the person speaking in tongues still speaks only to God. If there is no interpretation, and no one present understood the language, then only God understands. "In the spirit," on the basis of context and verses 14 and 15, may refer to the believer's spirit which is quickened and sanctified by the Holy Spirit. It is possible to speak "in the spirit" without the aid of the understanding. The public assembly is not the place for such "private" communion, unless the gift of interpretation is operating to produce edification.

**3. But he that prophesieth:** . . . On the other hand, *—MOFT* . . . but the preacher, *—FNTN*.
**speaketh unto men [to] edification:**
**and exhortation, and comfort:** . . . encouragement, *—WEYM* . . . and consolation and comfort, *—CNDT* . . . encourage, and console them, *—MOFT*.

**4. He that speaketh in an [unknown] tongue edifieth himself:** . . . The linguist instructs himself,

—*FNTN* . . . speaketh strange lan-gage, —*GNVA* . . . is building up, —*RTHM* . . . does good to himself, —*WEYM*.

**but he that prophesieth edifieth the church:** . . . the congregacion, —*TNDL* . . . instructs the assembly, —*FNTN* . . . does good to the church, —*WEYM*.

**14:3, 4.** Prophecy will result in edification. Its results are noted. "Comfort" touches sorrow and fear and is found only here in the New Testament. "Exhortation" refers to duty, and "edification" to knowledge, character, and progress of the Church.

"Tongues" in prayer and praise bring personal edification and therefore have value for the individual, but prophecy edifies to a greater extent because it edifies the whole church.

Speaking in a tongue is edifying to the speaker himself, because it is an exercise of his spirit with the Holy Spirit, Godward. It adds a new dimension to one's devotional life. Prophecy has a larger effect, because it reaches a larger audience.

**5. I would that ye all spake with tongues:** . . . I want you all, —*CNDT*.

**but rather that ye prophesied:** . . . but I would prefer you, —*MOFT*.

**for greater [is] he that prophesieth than he that speaketh with tongues:** . . . the preacher is greater than the linguist, —*FNTN* . . . the man who prophesies is superior, —*WEYM*.

**except he interpret, that the church may receive edifying:** . . . vnlesse perhaps he interpret, —*RHEM*, —*DOUY* . . . except he expound it also, —*GNVA* . . . unless, indeed, the latter adds a running interpretation, —*WAY* . . . in order that the church may get a blessing, —*WEYM* . . . that the assembly may receive edification, —*SAWR* . . . may receive instruction, —*FNTN* . . . may benefit by being built up, —*ADAM* . . . he edifieth the church, —*MRDK*.

**14:5.** In this verse Paul summarized what he had said by establishing the good of tongues but the greater good of prophecy. Prophecy, or the combination of tongues and interpretation, edifies the Church because it is an understandable message.

In doing this, Paul adds another reason for the excellence of prophecy. The one who prophesies, giving a message that can be understood, is of greater value to the Church than the speaker in tongues, unless there is an interpretation. Tongues plus interpretation accomplishes in two steps what prophecy accomplishes in one. In that case, they are on equal footing, for the same end is accomplished: edification for the body of gathered believers.

A general principle is clear: The gifts of the Spirit are intended for the edification of the members of the body of Christ.

**6. Now, brethren, if I come unto you speaking with tongues:** . . . if I should come among you, —*MRDK* . . . should I apply myself to you in a tongue

you knew not, —*LOCK* . . . speaking foreign languages, —*FNTN*.

**what shall I profit you, except I shall speak to you either by revelation:** . . . what shall I be benefiting you, —*CNDT* . . . if the utterance is neither, —*WEYM* . . . what good could I do you, —*MOFT* . . . unless I can communicate to you, —*ADAM*.

**or by knowledge, or by prophesying, or by doctrine?:** . . . ether in techinge, —*WCLF* . . . or science, or in a sermon, —*FNTN* . . . no inspired address, no exposition? —*WAY*.

**14:6.** Paul used a series of illustrations to show the profit provided to the Church by understandable words and messages. He referred to those gifts that carry clear messages. Paul was not depreciating the value of "tongues," but placing it in proper perspective.

The term "brethren" indicates his close relationship and feelings for the Corinthian believers.

Paul used himself as an illustration. If he came to them ministering by "speaking with tongues" it would be impossible for the congregation to understand the message (except by interpretation); therefore, it would be profitless to the church body. What help would he be if he brought a sound that could not be understood?

Paul was speaking about four ways a minister could convey truth: revelation, knowledge, prophesying, and doctrine. These had been demonstrated in his own ministry. Paul's use of *revelation* (*apokalupsei*) varied considerably depending on the context. Frequently it refers to the end times and Christ's coming (Romans 2:5; 8:19; 1 Corinthians 1:7; 2 Thessalonians 1:7), but it can also refer to the gospel of preaching Christ (Romans 16:25), or to visions (2 Corinthians 12:1, 7). Whichever of these possibilities might be in mind here, the coupling of revelation with teaching suggests that this revelation must be taught and understood. In 2:10-12 he had referred to the revelation and knowledge he had received from the Lord. He had also ministered prophetically and in doctrine. However, all these had come to the Corinthians in intelligible speech, so all could profit. Again Paul was emphasizing that tongues that are not understood are unprofitable to those who hear.

**7. And even things without life giving sound, whether pipe or harp:** . . . if lifeless instruments, —*MNTG* . . . So of irrational objects making a sound, —*SAWR* . . . Inanimate instruments . . . the flute, —*MOFT* . . . soulless things, —*CNDT* . . . when yielding a sound, —*WEYM*.

**except they give a distinction in the sounds:** . . . if they make no distinction between one sound and another, —*MRDK* . . . a distinction in the notes, —*RTHM* . . . a distinction to the utterances, —*CNDT*.

**how shall it be known what is piped or harped?:** . . . how shall it be ascertained, —RTHM . . . whereby the tune and composure are understood, —LOCK.

**14:7.** Paul used another illustration, this time from the inanimate world of music. "Pipe" (*aulos*) is a flute and represents the wind instruments. "Harp" (*kithara*), from which we get *guitar,* represents the stringed instruments (Morris, *Tyndale New Testament Commentaries,* 7:192). Music rightly presented will speak to the very heart of man. But for this to happen, there must be a variety and balance of harmony, expression, and chord.

Without purpose, balance, and clear expression, there is mere noise—aimless, profitless jangle. Sound and speech must communicate meaning and message in an understandable, receivable way.

**8. For if the trumpet give an uncertain sound:** . . . should be giving a dubious sound, —CNDT . . . sounds indistinct, —MOFT.

**who shall prepare himself to the battle?:** . . . what soldier will be prepared for battle? —MNTG . . . to the warre? —CRNM . . . who shal prepare him selfe to fyght? —GNVA.

**14:8.** From the inanimate world Paul also drew the illustration of the battle trumpet. One melody was for reveille, another for taps, another for advance in battle, another for retreat.

If there was no clear distinction in sound, the troops would not understand nor react in the proper manner. Then who would prepare for the battle? The answer is no one.

**9. So likewise ye, except ye utter by the tongue words easy to be understood:** . . . unless you produce an intelligible speech, —FNTN . . . if you should not be giving an intelligible expression, —CNDT . . . except ye speake wordes that haue signification, —GNVA . . . ye give intelligible discourse, —RTHM . . . you fail to utter intelligible words, —WEYM . . . if ye utter a discourse, —MRDK . . . that is readily understood, —MOFT.

**how shall it be known what is spoken?:** . . . how can people make out what you say? —MOFT.

**for ye shall speak into the air:** . . . for ye schuln be spekynge in veyn, —WCLF . . . You will be talking to the winds, —WEYM.

**14:9.** From the living world, Paul used yet another illustration and applied it directly to the situation at Corinth. "Likewise ye" means "take a lesson here"; understand and apply it. "By the tongue" appears to refer to the physical tongue, setting this verse in marked contrast to the inanimate realm of verses 7 and 8. What is true of the inanimate is true to a larger degree of the human tongue: it articulates as it is directed.

This was the problem at Corinth. The "words" had no meaning; they were not "intelligible" (RSV). They were like one speaking "into the air." This proverbial expression noted ineffectiveness and profitlessness.

**10. There are, it may be, so many kinds of voices in the world:** . . . let us say, —MNTG . . . we will suppose, a great number of languages, —WEYM . . . so many species of sounds in the world, —CNDT . . . many kinds of language in the world, —MOFT.

**and none of them [is] without signification:** . . . and no creature is without a language, —WEYM . . . and none meaningless, —FNTN . . . and not one unspoken, —RTHM . . . without distinct pronunciation, —PNT.

**14:10.** In his last illustration, Paul summarized all he had been saying. He drew from the widest possible source: "in the world." There are many hundreds of languages and many dialects within general language groups. There are a multitude of sounds in the world. None of them is without "signification." Paul asserted that each voice carries the real nature of a voice. In other words, the sounds mean something to somebody.

**11. Therefore if I know not the meaning of the voice:** . . . the meaning of the particular language, —WEYM . . . I do not know the force of the expression, —MNTG . . . if I do not know the import of the sound, —MRDK.

**I shall be unto him that speaketh a barbarian:** . . . to be talking gibberish, —MOFT.

**and he that speaketh [shall be] a barbarian unto me:** . . . a foreigner to me, —FNTN, —ADAM . . . is all gibberish to me, —LOCK . . . will seem a mere jargon to me, —WAY.

**14:11.** There must be an existing understanding between speaker and listener, or each will view the other as a "barbarian." "Meaning" (*dunamin*) has the idea of "force" or "power."

Speech is a persuasive and communicative force. But speech that is not understood is powerless, futile, and useless. The listener may hear, but try as he may he cannot understand. The speaker may repeat his message, but he cannot make his listener understand.

It is as Paul wrote in 14:2, "He speaketh mysteries." The result is that each considers the other a "barbarian." The Greeks divided the world into Greeks and barbarians. While Paul had in mind primarily unintelligent speech and the lack of communication, the fuller sense of the term "barbarian" (*barbaros*), one beyond the limits of civilization, was implied. In such a case, nothing profitable or edifying could be accomplished. What a tragic ending to something filled with promise and value.

The one clear conclusion is that something un-intelligible should not be part of public worship. What is done, whether prophecy or tongues and interpretation, must be of more than personal val-ue; it must profit the whole body of Christ.

**12. Even so ye, forasmuch as ye are zealous of spiritual [gifts]:** . . . ye are envious of spirits, —*RTHM* . . . you are ambitious for spiritual gifts, —*WEYM.*
**seek that ye may excel to the edifying of the church:** . . . try to proceed so as to promote, —*FNTN* . . . that you may be supera-bounding to, —*CNDT* . . . be zealous to abound in what builds up the church, —*ADAM* . . . make the edification of the church your aim, —*MOFT* . . . so as to benefit the church, —*WEYM* . . . of the congregacion, —*TNDL.*

**14:12.** The application was made to the Cor-inthians. "Even so ye" indicated the need to un-derstand and apply these instructions to their situation. The Corinthians coveted spiritual gifts; they were zealous and desirous of such, which was good as long as their aim was the profit of others. From his heart, Paul exhorted the Corinthians, who sometimes acted out of selfish motives, to excel in the gifts of the Spirit for the edification of believers.

Verse 12 is a reminder that chapter 13 presents not so much an abstract treatise on love, but the way in which individual Christians are to exer-cise their gifts. Paul encouraged the Corinthians to seek spiritual gifts, but only insofar as they were used in love to edify the body, rather than as a means of exulting in their own private, self-serving gifts.

**13. Wherefore let him that speaketh in an [unknown] tongue pray that he may inter-pret:** . . . pray for the power of interpreting them, —*WEYM* . . . ask God to enable him to give a concurrent interpretation, —*WAY.*

**14:13.** Paul next dealt with the use of tongues. If the church body was to be edified by an "un-known" tongue, they must understand what was said. Therefore, the admonition was for the person who spoke in tongues to pray for the interpretation.

These spiritual gifts are not static. A man who is used in the gift of tongues may also be used in another gift, such as interpretation. To this end he should pray.

**14. For if I pray in an [unknown] tongue:**
**my spirit prayeth:** . . . my spirit is praying, —*CNDT* . . . my spirit, it is true, accompanies my words, —*LOCK.*
**but my understanding is unfruitful:** . . . yet my mind is unfruitful, —*CNDT* . . . my meaning is unintel-ligible, —*FNTN* . . . but my mind is no use to anyone,

—*MOFT* . . . is barren, —*WEYM,* —*MNTG* . . . is without fruit, —*DOUY.*

**14:14.** This verse explains further why one should pray to interpret what he has said in a tongue. At the same time, Paul established the need for understanding and the place of tongues and prophecy.

"Spirit" (*pneuma*) refers to a man's spirit. It is contrasted with "understanding." Normally man works through his understanding. But with the gift of tongues this is not so. And this is where the problem arises. One's "spirit" does not com-municate the clear messages with another's spir-it that one's "understanding" does with another's understanding. Now he that prays and speaks in a tongue does well, but because the interpretation is not given it is comprehensible to no one else. Paul was not presenting man's spirit and under-standing as opposed to each other. God works with men by either avenue. The point is that it is necessary to recognize the proper place of each.

**15. What is it then?:** . . . How then does the matter stand? —*WEYM* . . . What is the answer to the prob-lem? —*ADAM.*
**I will pray with the spirit, and I will pray with the understanding also:** . . . I may pray, —*FNTN* . . . with my mind, —*MOFT.*
**I will sing with the spirit, and I will sing with the understanding also:** . . . I will sing in the Spirit's rapture, —*WAY* . . . sing praise with my mind, —*MOFT* . . . will I be playing music, —*CNDT.*

**14:15.** How does the matter stand? Paul an-swered the question by calling attention to two activities: praying and singing. The singing is of praise to God, perhaps even using some of the psalms. Paul indicated he would pray and sing "with the spirit" and "with the understanding." Paul recognized both the gift of tongues and the value of understandable speech. His motive was to edify the body of Christ. In this context, that meant he would interpret his "tongue" in a public gathering.

**16. Else when thou shalt bless with the spir-it:** . . . Otherwise . . . in spirit only, —*WEYM* . . . If you bless God in spirit only, —*TCNT* . . . if you pronounce a blessing in the Spirit, —*NORL* . . . by the impulse of the Spirit, —*LOCK.*
**how shall he that occupieth the room of the unlearned say Amen at thy giving of thanks:** . . . how can one of an uneducated condition express his assent, —*FNTN* . . . how is the outsider to say, —*MOFT* . . . how is he who occupies the position of the uninspired to add his 'Amen!' —*WAY* . . . how shall he that holdeth the place of the unlearned say, Amen, to thy blessing? —*DOUY* . . . who is filling up the place of a plain person, —*CNDT* . . . who is in the position of being ungifted, —*ADAM* . . . how can

those in the congregation who are without your gift say, –TCNT.

**seeing he understandeth not what thou sayest?:** . . . he is not aware, –CNDT . . . since he knows not what you say? –SAWR.

**14:16.** "Unlearned" (*idiōtou*) denotes a private individual, a layman, not necessarily a non-Christian, but one who is unskilled or ignorant in these matters. This word was used in some pagan associations to denote nonmembers who were allowed to participate in the sacrifices. Clearly, whether a non-Christian or an unlearned believer, this one was unlearned and unable to participate in the same way as mature believers.

Those who maintain that the *idiōtēs* of this verse is the same as the *idiōtēs* of verse 23, and therefore an unbeliever, argue that Paul had in view a proselyte or a catechumen (cf. *BAGD*, "*idiōtēs*"). It is true in the following centuries the Church had a special place for nonbaptized converts, but this kind of specialized meaning is highly unlikely for the situation of the Church in A.D. 54.

Another drawback to understanding *idiōtēs* in this instance is that the context is concerned with the edification of the church body. Since Paul was concerned that the *idiōtēs* be edified, the *idiōtēs* must be part of the Body.

The expression *ho anaplērōn ton topon*, "he that occupieth the room of," should be understood as "the one who fills the role" or "the one who takes the place of." Paul, therefore, was suggesting to those involved in the gift of tongues that they put themselves in the place of someone unlearned in the operations of the Spirit in worship. By doing so, they would realize that by not being interpreted their utterances would be unintelligible, and therefore unedifying, to outsiders.

By not understanding the utterance of tongues, an *idiōtēs* would be unable to respond with "Amen," the customary response to a prayer in both Jewish synagogue services and Christian worship services. Deuteronomy 27:14-26 contains an example of a communal "amen" said after individual prayers of blessing and curse. In the New Testament "amen" occurs frequently in places of praise and doxology (e.g., Romans 11:36).

He could not say "Amen" to the blessing of the Spirit because he could not understand it. By such an "Amen," the worshiper made another's prayer his own; assent is given. Others would have the same problem, but special concern was expressed for "the unlearned."

**17. For thou verily givest thanks well:** . . . Thou blessest, indeed, very well, –MRDK . . . Your thanksgiving may be excellent, –TCNT . . . It is well enough for

you to give thanks that way, –NORL . . . appropriately enough, –ADAM.

**but the other is not edified:** . . . but it is of no value to the man who cannot understand you, –NORL . . . and yet your neighbour is not benefited, –WEYM . . . but others are not helped by it, –TCNT.

**14:17.** There was nothing wrong with the prayer in relationship to God. Praising God or praying in other tongues provides a special liberty of expression. "Thou . . . givest thanks well." The problem was that there was no edification. The person listening did not profit because there was no understanding on his part.

**18. I thank my God:** . . . Thank God, –TCNT . . . I am thankful to God, –NORL.

**I speak with tongues more than ye all:** . . . I am a better linguist, –FNTN . . . I use the gift of 'tongues,' –TCNT . . . that I speak in more languages than all of you, –ADAM . . . with all your tongues, –DOUY . . . in an [unknown] tongue, –NOYS.

**19. Yet in the church I had rather speak five words with my understanding:** . . . Still, in public worship, –NORL . . . I would rather speak five words intelligently, –TCNT.

**that [by my voice] I might teach others also:** . . . so as to instruct others, –WEYM . . . to the teaching of other, –GNVA . . . to the informacion of other, –CRNM . . . for the instruction of other people, –MOFT.

**than ten thousand words in an [unknown] tongue:** . . . than myriads of words, –RTHM.

**14:18, 19.** Paul restressed the place of tongues and prophecy and their relationship. He used the first person singular. Speaking in tongues was widespread at Corinth. Yet Paul acknowledged that he exercised it to an even greater extent. Far from decrying it, he thanked God for it because it comes by the Holy Spirit for the aid and strength of the individual. He probably was referring to his private devotional times.

But Paul added a specific note regarding their use in the church assembly. Again, edification was to be the aim. Some of the Corinthians gloried in their ability to speak in a "tongue." Paul could have done the same. But he stressed what served the most. His thought was how best to benefit his brethren in the Lord. That meant speaking in an understandable language.

**20. Brethren, be not children in understanding:** . . . do not become childish, –FNTN . . . in your thoughts, –MRDK.

**howbeit in malice be ye children:** . . . But in evil be minors, –CNDT . . . but in baseness become babes, –RTHM . . . as concerning maliciousnes, –GNVA . . . to evil things be ye infants, –MRDK . . . in evil be mere infants, –MOFT . . . be utter babes, –WEYM.

**but in understanding be men:** ... but be mature, —*MOFT* ... prove yourselves to be men of ripe years, —*WEYM* ... be of a ripe age, —*GNVA*.

**14:20.** Another major reason for the excellence of prophecy in the public assembly has to do with spiritual persuasion, or the conviction to even the more skeptical that God is truly present. This should be the aim of everything done and said in the assembly: to see men convicted of their sin or immaturity and persuaded of the power of God in Christ to transform and mature them.

"In understanding" reflects reasoning. It refers to the midriff or diaphragm, for this is where the Greeks located thought. Proper understanding of spiritual matters is one sign of Christian maturity.

In malice or wrong believers should be children. Innocence, simplicity, and distaste for evil should be clear always. But in "understanding" they should be mature.

**21. In the law it is written:**

**With [men of] other tongues and other lips will I speak unto this people:** ... By men of alien tongues, —*MOFT* ... with strange lips, —*FNTN* ... With a foreign speech, —*MRDK*.

**and yet for all that will they not hear me, saith the Lord:** ... neither thus will they be hearkening, —*CNDT* ... even so also they will not hearken to me, —*MRDK* ... and then they will never understand Me, —*FNTN* ... even then they will not listen to Me, —*WEYM*, —*MNTG*.

**14:21.** Paul turned to the Old Testament to teach a truth. "The law" (*nomos*) in Jewish usage extended to Scripture in general—for them, the Old Testament. He referred to the prophecy in Isaiah 28:11, 12. Isaiah said that God would speak to His people "with stammering lips and another tongue," perhaps alluding to the judgment coming in the Assyrian invasion. But he added, "They would not hear."

There seems to be a further meaning, referring to the coming of the Holy Spirit upon the Early Church. Even though it was accompanied by a miracle of language and some believed, some would not respond. The moving of the Spirit has always had a dual result, turning to God in repentance or rejection of His message.

**22. Wherefore tongues are for a sign, not to them that believe:** ... is intended as a sign, —*WEYM* ... are for a warning, —*FNTN* ... not to the faithful, but to infidels, —*RHEM* ... to those that have faith, —*RTHM*.

**but to them that believe not:** ... but to those who disbelieve, —*CLMT*.

**but prophesying [serveth] not for them that believe not:** ... contrariwyse, —*GNVA*.

**but for them which believe:** ... is meant for believers, —*MOFT*.

**14:22.** "Wherefore" indicates a conclusion and application of what has just been said. Tongues are for a sign to the unbeliever: it would seem that surely he would be touched, and he would respond to this phenomenon of "tongues." It does not seem, however, that even this will affect some people enough to turn them to God.

Paul points out that the purpose of prophecy is to minister to believers especially. In verse 3 he had said it produces edification, exhortation, and comfort. Notice, however, that the results of tongues for the unbeliever or of prophecy for the believer depends upon the hearer. The manifestation comes from God, but the hearer must respond in a proper way.

**23. If therefore the whole church be come together into one place:** ... the whole church to be holding a united meeting, —*WAY* ... if the whole congregation is assembled, —*NORL*.

**and all speak with tongues, and there come in [those that are] unlearned, or unbelievers:** ... if all present use the gift of 'tongues,' —*TCNT* ... and everybody is speaking, —*MNTG* ... in private persons, —*RTHM* ... unlearned persons or infidels, —*DOUY* ... or such as believe not, —*MRDK*.

**will they not say that ye are mad?:** ... would they not imagine you were mad? —*FNTN* ... won't they say that you are crazy? —*ADAM* ... would they not say that you are demented? —*NORL* ... ye are out of youre wites? —*CRNM* ... you are insane, —*MOFT* ... you are raving? —*WAY*.

**14:23.** Paul added detail to what he had just written. He visualized the whole congregation gathering and all speaking in tongues. If an unbeliever or one "unlearned" walked in, and did not understand or see the spiritual sense in the scene, he would feel justified in declaring these Christians "mad" or raving (*mainesthe*).

A note aside, the text says "into one place." This is a support for the regular Lord's Day services and regular attendance at them.

The fact that Paul spoke of the whole assembly gathering together into "one place" has led many to wonder what kind of service is in mind here. It may be that this single gathering is the same as at 11:17 where the Corinthians gathered together for the love meal. It is not impossible that their worship service took place outside (since it is unlikely that all the believers met together in one house) and at the same time as the love feast. This would explain how unbelievers and others could happen to come to a service and hear people speaking in tongues.

If, as the Corinthians thought, tongues is the highest gift of the Spirit, then nothing could be better than to have the whole church speaking "with tongues." But the result was not what they had expected. There was a marked lack of edification for the "unlearned" or unbelieving who came in, and as a result they claimed madness and irrationality on the part of the Christians. This drove them away from the church, rather than drawing them into its fellowship.

**24. But if all prophesy:** . . . if all could preach, —FNTN . . . every one is prophesying, —WEYM . . . if all those present use the 'prophetic' gift, —TCNT.
**and there come in one that believeth not, or [one] unlearned:** . . . and one unlearned or an unbeliever should come among you, —MRDK . . . or a man without the gift, —TCNT.
**he is convinced of all, he is judged of all:** . . . one by one they probe his thoughts, —WAY . . . he is convicted . . . and closely examined by all, —WEYM . . . he is being exposed by all, he is being examined by all, —CNDT, —MOFT . . . he becomes conscious of his sin and is called to account, —TCNT . . . he is rebuked of all men, —TNDL . . . and all will put questions to him, —NORL.

**14:24.** The aim of prophecy stood in clear contrast to this. The direct, understandable message from God would have powerful results. The "outsider" would be "convinced of all." This means the unbeliever would be convicted; the prophetic word would show him his condition and state.

The phrase "judged of all" means to put on trial, to sift judicially, to examine by question after penetrating question. The Word of the Lord throws a searchlight into hidden recesses of the heart. The unbeliever would then realize, through the work of the Holy Spirit, that he was guilty of sin and was under the judgment of God.

**25. And thus are the secrets of his heart made manifest:** . . . so are the secretes . . . opened, —GNVA . . . the hidden evils . . . are brought to light, —MOFT . . . and the secrets . . . are laid open [to him], —MRDK . . . will be revealed, —NORL . . . will be disclosed, —ADAM.
**and so falling down on [his] face he will worship God:** . . . throwing himself, —TCNT . . . pay homage to God, —FNTN, —WAY . . . he will adore God, —DOUY.
**and report that God is in you of a truth:** . . . announcing, —FNTN . . . declaring, —SAWR . . . affirming that God is among you indeed, —DOUY . . . God is really among you, —MOFT.

**14:25.** The secrets of his heart would be "made manifest." That which he thought safely hidden in his own being would be brought to light. "Made manifest" may carry a double meaning. Perhaps some particular sin would be mentioned, or the unlearned or unbelieving would see an image of himself in a general prophecy on sin. In these cases, the sin might be manifested to the congregation or simply to the individual. In any case, profit and edification was the intention.

Generally, there appears first the inward work, then the outward product. First comes the penetration of the Law, the measuring stick of righteousness and morality. Then comes the gospel with its presentation of mercy, faith, and grace. The results are worship and witness.

The last part of this verse is reminiscent of Isaiah 45:14. So powerful would be the effect of the divine message and presence that the unbeliever would prostrate himself before God. There would be humility, confession, and surrender, as the man worshiped God. The once unbelieving person would leave the congregation announcing "God is in you." Such a church is successful.

**26. How is it then, brethren?:** . . . What follows, then, brothers? —MNTG . . . What then is [to be done] brothers? —SAWR . . . what is the upshot of all of this? —ADAM.
**when ye come together, every one of you hath:** . . . each contributes something, —MOFT.
**a psalm:** . . . has a hymn, —FNTN.
**hath a doctrine:** . . . has a lesson, —FNTN . . . another piece of exposition, —WAY.
**hath a tongue, hath a revelation:**
**hath an interpretation:** . . . has an explanation, —FNTN.
**Let all things be done unto edifying:** . . . with a view to the building up of faith and character, —WEYM . . . with a view to the spiritual advancement of the church, —WAY.

**14:26.** Paul next turned from the subject of edification to the difficult matter of order in the church assembly. Accordingly, any member of the church might be expected to take part in the service.

Generally, the Corinthians were energetic in their involvement. But this exuberance also created a problem in that everyone tried to speak at the same time. The result was disorder. One had a psalm, which could mean one of the 150 in the Psalms, but it could also denote a song with instrumental accompaniment. One had a "doctrine," which involved lessons in Christian truth. One had a "tongue," a "revelation" which might involve prophecy, an "interpretation." This was fine as long as the rules were remembered. The manifestation must be of a kind that edified, and it must be brought in an edifying manner.

**27. If any man speak in an [unknown] tongue: [let it be] by two, or at the most [by] three, and [that] by course:** . . . at one meeting, and that in turn, —MOFT . . . and that separately, one after another, —LOCK . . . not simultaneously, but in turn, —WAY . . . and they should do so in turn, —ADAM . . . and by turns, —SAWR . . . and let them speak one by one, —MRDK.
**and let one interpret:** . . . let someone interpret, —MOFT, —MNTG . . . and let those who have the

gift of discernment of inspiration then exercise it, —WAY...let one be translating, —RTHM.

**14:27.** Having set the standard for an orderly service, Paul showed the specific procedure regarding the exercise of "a tongue." He indicated a situation in the assembly where a man could speak aloud in an unknown tongue. The order was to be "by two, or at the most by three." This has generally been considered the number of times this particular manifestation should be exercised during one service. It appears that some had tried to speak at the same time as another. The result was disorder. Paul strongly opposed such action.

If one or more spoke "in an unknown tongue" there must be an interpretation, for the congregation must be edified. The presentation was to be clear, orderly, and spiritual. There seems no reason to stress this to mean only one person should interpret for the two or three speakers in tongues. What Paul was indicating was prompt interpretation. As one speaks in a tongue, one should then interpret.

28. **But if there be no interpreter:** ... if there is nobody who can fully interpret, —ADAM ... not a translator, —FNTN.

**let him keep silence in the church:** ... let him hold his peace, —RHEM...let him hush in the ecclesia, —CNDT...let not any one use his gift of tongues in the congregation, —LOCK.

**and let him speak to himself, and to God:**...let him, silently, within himself, —LOCK.

**14:28.** If there was no interpreter present in the assembly, Paul gave specific instruction to the speaker in a tongue: He must refrain from public utterance and be content to speak in tongues in solitude unto God. Or, according to verse 13, he should pray that God will give him the interpretation.

The reason for this prohibition was that such public unintelligible utterance would not edify the congregation. It also showed that God does not operate through robots, but through a person's will and personality.

29. **Let the prophets speak two or three:**
**and let the other judge:** ... let the others discriminate, —CNDT...the others should reflect, —FNTN...exercise their judgment upon what is said, —MOFT...let the others examine and discuss it, —LOCK.

**14:29.** This order is universal. Prophecy should be subjected to the same standard as tongues. Everything must edify the congregation. Again we see the order of two or three in a service.

"The other" is plural. The utterance was not to be accorded uncritical acceptance. It was to be "judged" or discerned.

30. **If [any thing] be revealed to another that sitteth by:**...if something is suggested, —FNTN.

**let the first hold his peace:** ... let the first be silent, —WEYM ... the first speaker must be quiet, —MOFT...let the first hush, —CNDT...let the first stop speaking, —MRDK.

**14:30.** A spirit of love and gracious consideration should be manifested in relation to the utterance manifestations. Paul suggests a situation where one person has been speaking, and the Holy Spirit impresses another person to say something that has been revealed to him. The first speaker should be willing to give way to the other person. It has been said that the Holy Spirit is a gentleman and will not bring disorder and disruption. The edifying of the congregation is the objective all should seek.

31. **For ye may all prophesy one by one:**...eche bi hym silf, —WCLF.
**that all may learn:**
**and all may be comforted:** ... all be consoled, —CNDT...all be encouraged, —MOFT.

**14:31.** Paul was establishing an orderly, loving, edifying exercise of prophecy. As each person was moved on by the Spirit, in wisdom he would have the opportunity to exercise the gift. He would not be slighted, but would minister within the framework of order and "preferring one another."

Anyone filled with the Spirit has the potential and opportunity of being used in any of these gifts of the Spirit. With due order and self-discipline each would have an opportunity to minister and profit the assembly.

The purpose is that "all may learn, and all may be comforted." If there is equal opportunity for utterance, then all the hearers will benefit. The result will be blessing, benefit, and learning.

32. **And the spirits of the prophets:** ... the spiritual endowments of prophets, —CNDT.

**are subject to the prophets:** ... are regulated by, —FNTN...yield submission to prophets, —WEYM ... are in the power of the Prophets, —GNVA ... are masters of their own actions, —LOCK...can control their own prophetic spirits, —MOFT.

**14:32.** Paul explained how the order of verses 29-31 is possible. The speaker is in control of himself. The "spirits of the prophets are subject to the prophets." This adds a subjective reason for regulation to the objective reason of verse 31. The speaker's will is important. The gift must be exercised in wisdom and love to accomplish the best possible ends. A false prophet will not so speak or act.

**33. For God is not [the author] of confusion, but of peace:** . . . is not disturbance, *—FNTN* . . . is not for turbulence, *—CNDT* . . . is not causer of stryfe, *—CRNM* . . . of disorder, *—WEYM* . . . of tumult, *—MRDK* . . . but of harmony, *—MOFT.*

**as in all churches of the saints:** . . . This custom prevails, *—MNTG.*

**14:33.** The submissiveness Paul urged is founded on the virtue and desire of God himself. He is a God of peace. In the character of God, there is a guarantee against disorderliness. He wanted to pass this on to the Church.

The laws of nature show a marked lack of confusion. It is foolish to suppose God's spiritual laws and works would be different. Paul infers order by indicating God's underlying motive: peace.

**34. Let your women keep silence in the churches:** . . . Let youre wyves, *—TNDL* . . . Let married women, *—WEYM* . . . must keep quiet at gatherings, *—MOFT* . . . hold their peace, *—RHEM* . . . in the assemblies, *—SAWR.*

**for it is not permitted unto them to speak:** . . . since they are not allowed to speak, *—ADAM* . . . to discourse there, *—LOCK.*

**but [they are commanded] to be under obedience, as also saith the law:** . . . let them be in submission, *—RTHM* . . . must take a subordinate place, *—MOFT* . . . but to be subject, *—DOUY* . . . but to be in subjection, *—MRDK* . . . be content with a subordinate place, *—WEYM* . . . as stated in the law, *—FNTN.*

**14:34.** Understanding the customs of the times helps to understand the reason for Paul's instruction for the women to "keep silence in the churches." He was not forbidding participation by women, for he had already mentioned praying and prophesying by women (11:5). He was speaking to married women, for he mentions their husbands in the next verse. In that era men and women sat apart. Sometimes the women had legitimate questions about what was being said. In such cases, Paul suggested they not disturb the meeting.

Paul's reference to the "law" is uncertain. Usually when he quoted from the Law he identified the citation but did not do so here. Usually Genesis 3:16 is taken as the source for Paul's statement.

**35. And if they will learn any thing:** . . . wish to ask questions, *—WEYM* . . . wish to be informed on any subject, *—MRDK.*

**let them ask their husbands at home:** . . . let them be inquiring, *—CNDT.*

**for it is a shame for women to speak in the church:** . . . For it is a foule thing, *—RHEM* . . . it is scandalous, *—FNTN* . . . it is improper, *—ADAM* . . . it is unbecoming, *—MRDK* . . . it is disgraceful for a married woman to speak at a church assembly, *—WEYM, —MOFT* . . . to be addressing a public meeting, *—WAY* . . . to discourse and debate with men publicly, *—LOCK.*

**14:35.** Paul advised the proper procedure. If the woman's motive was a true desire to learn, she should not interrupt the service by asking her husband. Rather than cause a disturbance she should wait and ask her husband at home. This was the rule to be followed. To do otherwise would be disruptive, against custom, and would not be edifying.

**36. What? came the word of God out from you?:** . . . Consider this, *—ADAM* . . . was it from you that the word of God came forth? *—MRDK.*

**or came it unto you only?:** . . . are you the only ones that it ever got to? *—ADAM* . . . as if the Gospel began at Corinth, *—LOCK* . . . Or did it reach only to you? *—MRDK.*

**14:36.** Paul reproved the situation with the use of irony and questions to which he expected a negative answer. He reminded the Corinthians that they had not originated the Word, nor were they the only ones to receive it. Therefore they must conform to the Biblical pattern and Christian custom.

Selfishness and pride were rebuked. Paul suggested that the haughty Corinthians were desiring to take the place of God and were thinking they knew better than God by trying to make His Word mean what they thought it should. This could not be allowed.

**37. If any man think himself to be a prophet, or spiritual:** . . . If any one deems himself . . . or a man with spiritual gifts, *—WEYM* . . . imagine himself to be an orator, or inspired, *—FNTN* . . . or gifted, *—MOFT.*

**let him acknowledge that the things that I write unto you:** . . . let him be recognizing that, *—CNDT* . . . that these rules, *—LOCK.*

**are the commandments of the Lord:** . . . it is an order, *—FNTN* . . . is a precept of the Lord, *—CNDT.*

**14:37.** What remained now was for Paul to establish his authority for what he had written. While in the context this summation belongs particularly to the words of chapter 14, in a wider sense it belongs to the whole of Paul's discussion on public worship.

Paul asserted his apostolic position and authority and the source of the truths he presented and then once again reaffirmed the directives concerning orderly manifestations and the overall theme of edification.

Paul stated that what he had written were the "commandments of the Lord." This provides insight into how the New Testament writers viewed their inspiration; no greater claim could be made.

If a man thinks himself to be spiritual he will acknowledge the inspired truth of what is said here. Paul made no personal judgments. He left the answer as to possession of gifts, etc., to the individual. Whatever the case, he was to obey these commands from the Lord. And his reception of Paul's words would decide the nature and quality of his prophecy or spirituality.

Paul was following Jesus' viewpoint as expressed in John 8:47. Some have thought that "spiritual" must refer to "tongues" because Paul first mentioned "prophet" and because of the context. But the word is more general than that. Anyone who possessed a spiritual gift or was genuinely spiritual would acknowledge the validity of Paul's statements.

38. **But if any man be ignorant:** ... if any man know not, —DOUY ... But if anybody disregards this, —ADAM.

**let him be ignorant:** ... disregard him, —ADAM ... he shall not be known, —DOUY.

**14:38.** This verse has been variously interpreted. But whether it is viewed as a response by Paul, the Corinthian church, or some future indictment, the fact is presented that to refuse Paul's directives carried disastrous consequences. Paul's relationship with the Corinthian Christians seemed always to be tenuous. In 4:21 Paul told them that if they did not heed his words he would come to them with the rod. Apparently this became necessary since he later paid them a painful visit (cf. 2 Corinthians 2:1-4). Paul, as an apostle and representative of Jesus Christ, had no choice but to seek His commands regardless of the opposition he might receive.

The words of verse 38 that "if any man be ignorant, let him be ignorant" represent the unequivocal stance of a man of God who proclaims God's Word even if it is rejected. This may be compared with the prophetic commission of Isaiah 6:9, 10. Rejection of truth leads to spiritual ignorance, and that can be tragic.

39. **Wherefore, brethren, covet to prophesy:** ... The conclusion, my brethren, —WEYM ... be envious of, —RTHM ... desire earnestly to prophesy, —SAWR ... desire the talent for oratory, —FNTN ... be emulous of prophesying, —MRDK ... be ambitious for the gift, —MNTG ... let prophecy have the preference, —LOCK.

**and forbid not to speak with tongues:** ... and do not prohibit, —FNTN ... and do not check speaking with tongues, —WEYM ... prohibit not, —MRDK ... to speak in other languages, —ADAM.

**14:39.** In conclusion, Paul wanted believers to desire and treasure spiritual manifestations. Notice that despite the problems associated with tongues he concludes by endorsing them.

40. **Let all things be done decently and in order:** ... let all occur respectably, —CNDT ... in a becoming and orderly manner, —WEYM ... with comeliness and arrangement, —RTHM ... decorously, —MOFT ... and according to order among you, —RHEM ... let everything be conducted with due regard to decorum and discipline, —WAY ... and regularity, —MRDK.

**14:40.** At the same time Paul reminded the Corinthians these manifestations of the Spirit are to remain within the framework of edification and order. Good taste and proper procedure are to be the standards always.

## Chapter 15

1. **Moreover, brethren, I declare unto you the gospel which I preached unto you:** ... the joyful message which I myself announced to you, —RTHM ... I imparted to you, —FNTN.

**which also ye have received:** ... which you accepted also, —CNDT.

**and wherein ye stand:** ... you have your footing, —MOFT ... and in the which ye continue, —TNDL.

**15:1.** The resurrection of Jesus Christ is the indisputable rock on which Christianity and the gospel stand. This chapter sets forth this great truth and the problems of denying it as well as the promise in affirming it.

Paul began with a gentle rebuke. Rather than reminding the Corinthians of the gospel he had preached, he declared it to them again. Some did not seem to realize the importance of the gospel Paul had preached to them even though they had received it.

2. **By which also ye are saved:** ... you are being saved, —SEB.

**if ye keep in memory what I preached unto you:** ... if you grasp it, —FNTN ... if you bear in mind the words in which I proclaimed, —WEYM ... if you retain those joyful tidings which I delivered to you, —CMPB.

**unless ye have believed in vain:** ... your faith was all haphazard, —MOFT ... unless your faith was empty, —ADAM ... has been unreal from the very first, —WEYM ... to no purpose, —CNFT, —CMPB ... you believed inconsiderately, —WLSN.

**15:2.** The gospel is the means used to bring salvation. "Ye are saved" is present continuous, indicating continuing activity: "You are being saved." From God's standpoint there is both a permanent, once-for-all sense and a progressive sense. Salvation is a growing, deepening, inexhaustible experience. However, believers have the obligation to maintain their walk with God.

If the Corinthians held to it, this gospel would save them unless they had "believed in vain." This phrase could refer to belief on an inadequate basis. If men are not really trusting Christ, their belief is empty. "Vain" (*eikē*) includes the idea of at random, or without serious apprehension. Paul may also have been making an early reference to what he would refute in verses 12-19.

**3. For I delivered unto you first of all that which I also received:** . . . the first thing I taught you, *—CNBR.*

**how that Christ died for our sins according to the scriptures:** . . . died on account of our sins, *—MRDK* . . . as the scripture had said, *—MOFT* . . . agreing to the Scriptures, *—GNVA.*

**4. And that he was buried:** . . . He was entombed, *—CNDT.*

**and that he rose again the third day according to the scriptures:** . . . in agreement with, *—ADAM* . . . in accordance with, *—FNTN.*

**15:3, 4.** Paul was a faithful steward, and he had delivered to the Corinthians the very essence and substance of the gospel. This he did "first of all." Preaching the gospel had first place on Paul's list of priorities. Necessity lay heavily upon him.

Paul delivered what he had "received." Galatians 1:12 says he received it by direct revelation. The three basic truths he preached were: (1) Christ's death for our sins, (2) Christ's burial, and (3) Christ's resurrection.

The second of these truths links the others together, for it certified the completeness of Christ's death and the reality of His resurrection. His death and burial are presented in the aorist tense as historical events; the Resurrection is emphatically placed in the perfect tense, as an abiding power. The perfect tense appears in this manner six more times in this chapter.

The Resurrection occurred on the third day, fulfilling the prophecies of Holy Writ as well as indicating restoration of life when, under normal circumstances, decay would have begun.

**5. And that he was seen of Cephas:** . . . he appeared to, *—RTHM.*

**then of the twelve:** . . . afterwards by the twelve, *—FNTN* . . . thereupon by the twelve, *—CNDT* . . . and after that to the Eleven, *—CNFT.*

**15:5.** There were many witnesses to this great event. Jesus appeared to Peter (Luke 24:34). It was not a vision; He was seen by human eyes. Peter was one of the leading apostles, and his witness would have a profound effect on the Church and the world.

Jesus appeared to "the twelve." This was a designation for this group without regard to number. Judas was gone.

**6. After that, he was seen of above five hundred brethren at once:** . . . Afterwards He was seen by more, *—WEYM* . . . appeared openly, *—FNTN* . . . more

then fiue hundred brethren together, *—RHEM* . . . over five hundred, *—ADAM.*

**of whom the greater part remain unto this present:** . . . most of whom are still alive, *—WEYM* . . . most of whom still remain alive, *—ADAM* . . . the majority of whom survive to this day, *—MOFT* . . . of whiche many lyuen yit but summe ben deede, *—WCLF* . . . the greater number remain, *—FNTN* . . . many of whom are with us still, *—CNFT.*

**but some are fallen asleep:** . . . some were put to repose also, *—CNDT.*

**15:6.** After that He was seen of "above five hundred brethren." The word used for "at once" (*ephapax*) is not so translated elsewhere and is perhaps better translated "once for all," indicating that this was the culminating manifestation of the risen Christ, made at the general gathering of His brethren (Nicoll, *Expositor's Greek Testament*, 2:920).

The majority of the group of over 500 remained alive when this epistle was written. There was a continuing witness to the Resurrection. Only a few had "fallen asleep." This was indeed one of the effects of the Resurrection: death was transformed into sleep in Christ.

**7. After that, he was seen of James:** . . . Next He was seen by, *—CNBR.*

**then of all the apostles:**

**15:7.** Jesus appeared to James. The most fitting conclusion is that this was James, the brother of the Lord. This appearance, only mentioned here, explains the presence of "his brethren" (Acts 1:14) among the 120 at Jerusalem and James' subsequent leadership of the Jerusalem church. When Paul wrote this epistle, James held a high position and would have been an impressive witness.

Then Jesus appeared to "all the apostles." Interpretation depends on whether the stricter or looser sense of "apostles" is used. Paul, presumably aware of the absence of Thomas on the occasion of verse 5 and his consequent skepticism, may have written of this appearance to show that all the apostles saw Christ, and the resultant witness was complete and unqualified. Most likely he was speaking of the original apostles.

"Apostles" also could have a general meaning. Paul indicates in 9:1, 2 that the seal of his apostleship, a sign that he was an apostle, was his founding of the church at Corinth ("for the seal of mine apostleship are ye in the Lord" [9:2]). A second factor in determining the meaning of *apostle* is that the 12 disciples of Christ were regarded as a special and distinct group known as "the Twelve" who were separate from the other apostles. Another indication that "apostle" could be a loose term is that words like *deacon* and *presbyter* designated general functions and not particular offices or hierarchical designations (especially since the Church was only 20 years old).

**8. And last of all he was seen of me also:** . . . and finally he, *—MOFT.*

**as of one born out of due time:** . . . even as if a premature birth, *—CNDT* . . . as to one of untimely birth, *—WEYM* . . . unto the untimely birth, *—RTHM* . . . as if to a laggard, *—FNTN* . . . as if by the one prematurely born, *—WLSN* . . . the one whose birth was an abnormality, *—ADAM.*

**15:8.** Lastly, Jesus appeared to Paul. Paul described himself as an untimely child in this reference to Christ's appearance to him. "Of me also" lends emphasis to the matter. Even to Paul, the Lord appeared in resurrection power.

Some find in this an indication of the suddenness and violence of Paul's birth into Christ. Some see here the unripe birth of one changed in a moment from persecutor to apostle instead of maturing normally for his work. It may have been one of the insults the Judaists threw at Paul. Perhaps his opponents took note of his personal appearance and his doctrine of free grace and called him an abortion. Paul adopted the title and gave it a deeper meaning.

**9. For I am the least of the apostles:** . . . I am the most insignificant of, *—FNTN* . . . Yes, I am the meanest of His apostles, *—WAY.*

**that am not meet to be called an apostle:** . . . one who doesn't deserve to be called, *—ADAM* . . . am not fit, *—WEYM* . . . and am not worthy, *—CNBR* . . . who am not competent to be called, *—CNDT* . . . unfit to bear the name, *—MOFT.*

**because I persecuted the church of God:**

**15:9.** The emphatic personal pronoun "I" shows the great grace and condescension of Christ. Paul held staunchly to two points: One was the high dignity of his position as an apostle; the other was his profound sense of unworthiness in the matter. He felt himself unworthy because he had "persecuted the church of God." He had been active in the greatest of injustices; he had willfully persecuted the "church of God."

**10. But by the grace of God I am what I am:** **and his grace which [was bestowed] upon me was not in vain:** . . . his grace in me hath not been void, *—RHEM* . . . His grace, which stooped to me, has not proved ineffectual, *—WAY* . . . he showed me did not go for nothing, *—MOFT* . . . did not come to be for naught, *—CNDT* . . . did not prove ineffectual, *—WEYM* . . . has not been useless, *—FNTN* . . . was not fruitless, *—CNBR, WLSN* . . . was not found void, *—PNIN* . . . His grace to me wasn't wasted, *—ADAM.*

**but I laboured more abundantly than they all:** . . . On the contrary, *—ADAM* . . . but I toiled more abundantly, *—PNIN* . . . in fact I have labored more than

any of them, *—CNFT* . . . more strenuously than all the rest, *—WEYM.*

**yet not I, but the grace of God which was with me:** . . . yet I do not ascribe to any thing of myself, but to the favour of God, which accompanied me, *—LOCK* . . . but the gift of God, *—FNTN* . . . God's unmerited favor, *—WLMS* . . . God's love that was with me, *—BECK* . . . that is joined with me, *—BRKL.*

**15:10.** But the grace of God worked a marvelous transformation in Paul's life. He was a sinner saved by grace; an apostle and servant of Jesus Christ by grace.

If at the outset Paul appeared last and least, his ministry gave him the premier position. By his efforts he extended the kingdom of Christ over a larger area than any other person. Yet "not I," he asserted. Grace did the work; Paul was the instrument.

**11. Therefore whether [it were] I or they:** . . . At any rate, *—MOFT* . . . whether I did it or they, *—BECK* . . . or the other apostles, *—LOCK.*

**so we preach, and so ye believed:** . . . this is what we preach, and this is what you believed, *—BECK.*

**15:11.** Concluding his comparison of himself and the other apostles, Paul noted that whether it was he or another, "we preach" and "ye believed." On the crucial matters of verses 1-4 and on the matter of the Resurrection there was not the slightest variation. The authoritative witness of Paul or Peter, Jerusalem or Corinth, was unified and in one accord.

**12. Now if Christ be preached that he rose from the dead:** . . . if what we proclaim about Christ, *—TCNT* . . . is being heralded, *—CNDT.*

**how say some among you that there is no resurrection of the dead?:** . . . individuals among you assert, *—MOFT* . . . There is no reviviscence of the dead? *—MRDK.*

**15:12.** Paul had asserted the fact of Christ's resurrection with barely a clue as to his purpose in so beginning. Now he made it clear. If the resurrection of Christ is true, how could anyone say the resurrection of the dead was not also a fact?

Some at Corinth had doubted the resurrection of the dead. Such skepticism wrecked the faith of the church, just as party divisions had damaged its love. But these people did not, apparently, doubt the personal resurrection of Jesus Christ. They just would not admit the recovery of the body.

This argument had its parallels with the doctrine of the Sadducees (Acts 23:8) and countless illustrations from the superstitions of the Greeks. Some Greek philosophies theorized that the soul continued to exist, but the body died forever. Their idea belonged to the "wisdom of this age."

Paul's opposing argument followed two basic lines: If the Resurrection is untrue, then the Christian faith and its witnesses are false; and if the Resurrection is not real, then neither are the effects derived from it.

**13. But if there be no resurrection of the dead: then is Christ not risen:** . . . the Messiah also hath not risen, —*MRDK.*

**15:13.** The resurrection of Jesus Christ was logically impossible if there was a denial of bodily resurrection. Christ's resurrection was not even an exception; it was a pattern for many who would follow. If there was no resurrection of the dead, neither had Christ been raised. However, we know that though He was dead, that God raised Him to life. A universal negative cannot be accepted if one fact to the contrary exists.

**14. And if Christ be not risen, then [is] our preaching vain:** . . . false certainly is our preaching, —*MKNT* . . . both our preaching is worthless, —*FNTN* . . . our proclamation is groundless, —*TCNT* . . . what we preach is a delusion, —*WEYM* . . . our preaching is idle talk, —*LOCK* . . . the message which we preach has nothing in it, —*WLMS* . . . then our preaching amounts to nothing, —*BRKL* . . . our preaching is wasted, —*KLGS.*

**and your faith [is] also vain:** . . . and our faith is equally so! —*TCNT* . . . there is nothing in our faith either, —*WLMS* . . . your faith is an idle dream, you are still sunk in your sins, —*WAY* . . . and your believing it is to no purpose, —*LOCK* . . . and your faith is futile, —*BRKL* . . . You have believed in something which is false! —*SEB* . . . is groundless, —*NORL.*

**15:14.** If the fact is untrue, the testimony is untrue. If the message is hollow, building on an untrue fact, then the faith is also hollow, building on an untrue message and fact. Such reasoning robbed the gospel of its vitality. The Corinthians must agree with Paul, for they knew of their own faith; they had believed and accepted the apostles' preaching.

**15. Yea, and we are found false witnesses of God:** . . . we are detected bearing false witness, —*MOFT* . . . we are found guilty of false witness against God, —*CNBR* . . . guilty of lying about God, —*WLMS* . . . we, who pretend to be witnesses for God and his truth, shall be found liars, —*LOCK* . . . found false witnesses concerning God, —*FNTN.*

**because we have testified of God that he raised up Christ:** . . . we gave evidence respecting, —*FNTN* . . . by affirming of him, —*MOFT* . . . concerning God, —*MRDK* . . . that He resurrected Christ, —*BRKL.*

**whom he raised not up, if so be that the dead rise not:** . . . whom He did not raise in case no dead are actually raised, —*BRKL.*

**15:15.** Additionally, Paul argued, if the dead are not raised, Paul and his fellow witnesses would be giving lying testimony of the worst kind about God. They would be literally testifying against Him. Either Christ arose from the dead or the apostles had lied in affirming it. There was no other solution. The second possibility never entered Paul's mind.

**16. For if the dead rise not:** . . . For if the dead are never raised, —*WLMS.*
**then is not Christ raised:**

**15:16.** This verse serves as a hinge for the section. What had already been said was repeated with minor adjustment. Paul then turned to a discussion of the unreality of effect if there is no raising of the dead.

**17. And if Christ be not raised, your faith [is] vain:** . . . your faith is futile, —*MOFT* . . . your faith is delusive, —*HNSN* . . . your faith is deceptive, —*WLSN* . . . your faith is inane, —*MRDK* . . . is a mere delusion, —*WLMS* . . . is to no purpose, —*LOCK,* —*ALFD* . . . is mere folly, —*TCNT.*

**ye are yet in your sins:** . . . your sins are not forgiven, but you are still liable to the punishment due to them, —*LOCK* . . . you are still under the penalty of your sins, —*WLMS.*

**15:17.** The effects of denying the resurrection of Jesus Christ included the fact that faith would be ineffective because it is built on a false foundation; therefore, our sin has not been removed, and we are still sinners. A faith is useless which does not save from sin. But without Christ's resurrection, both our justification and sanctification are meaningless.

But this was contrary to experience; the Corinthians had experienced salvation; therefore Christ had been raised from the dead.

**18. Then they also which are fallen asleep in Christ are perished:** . . . It follows also that, —*WEYM* . . . More than that, —*MNTG* . . . they also, who died in the belief of the Gospel, are perished and lost, —*LOCK* . . . those who went to their rest trusting in Christ perished! —*TCNT* . . . those who died trusting in Christ, —*NORL.*

**15:18.** Paul moved through this morbid maze to other necessary conclusions if Christ had not been raised from the dead. He spoke of those who had "fallen asleep in Christ." The sense of Christ's presence and His promises had turned death into sleep. But if the Resurrection was denied, then they had really perished "in sins," in ruin and damnation. Lying down to "rest" untroubled, they would find the promises they had believed were a lie.

In such a case, there would be no hope beyond the grave. This would make Christianity no better than the worst paganism. Death would be the final victor.

**19. If in this life only we have hope in Christ:**...If in this present life, —WEYM...If the advantages we expect from Christ are confined to this life, —LOCK.
**we are of all men most miserable:**...most to be pitied, —RTHM...to be pitied most, —MOFT...the most wretched of all men, —FNTN.

**15:19.** The bitterness of the last step in this argument now showed itself. Misery would be the conclusion of such negative reasoning. It is possible for the adverb "only" to modify either the phrase "in this life" or the verb "hope." It appears it modifies the phrase, since "hope" usually appears in the New Testament as a positive term for the certain future joy of Christians, and the second alternative gives "hope" a tentative, negative connotation. These words do not mean that there is no significance to this life but that if Christ is not risen neither this life nor the future life has any meaning. If hope in Christ exists in this world and life only, there is no present deliverance from sin and no future inheritance in heaven, and believers are of all men most to be pitied. If there is no resurrection Christians have made great sacrifices for an empty, fruitless hope without foundation. If such were the case, it is no wonder the Christian would be the object of great pity.

**20. But now is Christ risen from the dead:**...But the fact is that, —ADAM...But, in reality, Christ has risen from the dead, —WEYM...in truth, Christ is actually risen, —LOCK.
**[and] become the firstfruits of them that slept:**...a Fore-runner of the sleepers, —FNTN.

**15:20.** "But now" Paul broke into song and unconditionally asserted the resurrection of Christ. The ugly consequences of verses 12-19 are untrue because there *is* a resurrection of the dead; Christ *has* been raised. Paul used the perfect tense of the verb *to rise*. Not only did Christ rise, He is alive forever.

Christ's resurrection makes the resurrection of the members of His church inevitable. He is the "firstfruits" of many who shall follow. There is an allusion to the first harvest sheaf of the Passover which was presented in the sanctuary on the 16th Nisan (possibly the day of Christ's resurrection). The first ripe sheaf was an earnest of the harvest and was consecrated to God and given to Him in thankfulness and anticipation of what was to come.

Christ was not the first to rise from the dead. But the others died again. His resurrection was to a life that knows no death. His is the life and truth that conquered death.

**21. For since by man [came] death, by man [came] also the resurrection of the dead:**
**22. For as in Adam all die:**...as the death that all men suffer is owing to Adam, —LOCK...as it was by Adam, —MRDK...through Adam, —WEYM.
**even so in Christ shall all be made alive:**...alle men schulen (shall) be quykened, —WCLF...all will be revived, —FNTN...so also by the Messiah they all live, —MRDK...is procured them by Christ, —LOCK.

**15:21, 22.** Christ is identified with those sleeping in death because He is the antitype of Adam. He is the One through whom life comes as Adam was the one through whom death came. When Adam sinned he passed into a new state, one controlled and symbolized by death. But Christ brought life. Christ then is the principle and root of resurrection life.

There is also the suggestion here that death is not a law or necessity of fate. Man brought it on himself by an event in history, and it is removable, in degree, by another event in history: the Resurrection.

Adam is pictured as the natural, earthly founder of humanity of which Christ is the spiritual, heavenly counterpart and the giver of new life. However, Paul was not here linking all the dead, even the sinful dead, with Christ. He was linking the risen Christ with the Christian dead, as yet unresurrected. As death in every case is established in Adam, so life in all cases is established in Christ.

**23. But every man in his own order:**...But each in his own turn, —CNFT...in his proper rank, —RTHM...each in his own class, —CNDT...every one in his order, —MRDK...in the right order, —WEYM...in his own vision, —MOFT...in his proper band, —MKNT.
**Christ the firstfruits:**...the first to rise, —WEYM...to be reaped, —MOFT.
**afterward they that are Christ's at his coming:**...then those who belong to Christ at his appearing, —MNTG...next after him shall rise those, who are his people, his church, —LOCK...that beleeued in his comming, —RHEM...who have believed, at his coming, —CNFT...Christ's people rising at His return, —WEYM...in His presence thereafter the consummation, —CNDT...at his arrival, —MOFT.

**15:23.** But while there is a unity in nature and principle, there is a difference in agreement and a distinction in order. Christ was raised as the firstfruit, then at His coming those who are His shall be raised. The thought is of a military division. There is the Captain, above all in His solitary glory; and there is His army, now sleeping, which shall rise at His trumpet's sound (1 Thessalonians 4:16).

**24. Then [cometh] the end:** ... Then the end shall be, —MKNT ... will be the perfection, —FNTN ... And then will be the end, Murdoch

**when he shall have delivered up the kingdom to God, even the Father:** ... when he shall resign the kingdom, —CMPB ... when he hands over his royal power, —MOFT ... when He delivers the empire, —ADAM ... surrender the Kingship to God, —WEYM.

**when he shall have put down all rule and all authority and power:** ... he shall have abrogated All Government, —WLSN ... when he shall have abolished all government, —CMPB ... whensoever He may abolish all rule, —CLMT ... when he will destroy every principality, —SAWR ... whenever He should be nullifying all sovereignty, —CNDT ... when every prince, and every sovereign, and all powers shall have come to naught, —MRDK ... overthrown all other government, —WEYM ... all his foes are put under, —MOFT ... having destroyed all other dominion, —CNBR.

**15:24.** Christ's second advent, of which the Rapture is a part, concludes the present history of the world. "Then cometh (is) the end," which indicates the end of the drama of sin and redemption. "Then" indicates taking place at an unspecified time afterward.

The end will be culminated by Christ's delivering the Kingdom to God the Father before which He shall have abolished all opposition, "all rule, and all authority and power." The two verbs (*parado* and *katargese*) indicate distinct but related actions. When every opposing force has been destroyed, then Christ shall lay His kingdom at the Father's feet.

"To God, even the Father" explains the reason for Christ's act of submission. The thought is not one of loss, but of giving to another what was designed for Him. This does not indicate a demotion of Christ; it is not the cessation of Christ's dominion, but the inauguration of Christ's eternal kingdom; it is not the termination of Christ's rule but of the reign of sin and death. "All" is complete.

**25. For he must reign:** ... must continue King, —WEYM.

**till he hath put all enemies under his feet:**

**15:25.** There is a compelling necessity about the word "must." God decides finally on the matter and no uncertainty is involved. There is a reference to Psalm 110:1 which indicates the Messiah's obligation and power. This general eschatology indicates Christ's kingship and points to the task He fulfills today. His work is a prelude to and notice of the end.

**26. The last enemy [that] shall be destroyed [is] death:** ... Death is to be done away with, —RTHM ... being abolished, —CNDT ... is to be overthrown is Death, —WEYM ... will be rendered powerless, —WLSN.

**15:26.** Paul had spoken of the event occurring at the "end" of earthly history and of the event preceding that, which is the subjection of all rule and power to that of Christ. Death is the last enemy to be totally destroyed. This stands in opposition to the position held by "some" in verse 12. These said there is no resurrection; Paul countered that there is to be no death. Death shall be robbed of all its control and power. It shall be abolished.

This was the climax of Paul's argument. In fact, in experience and in principle, Paul had shown the victory of the Resurrection over death.

**27. For he hath put all things under his feet:** ... For He subjects, —CNDT ... he made subject under, —RTHM ... he hath subjected all under, —MRDK.

**But when he saith all things are put under [him:** ... All things are in subjection, —WEYM ... are subdued to him, —RHEM.

**it is] manifest that he is excepted, which did put all things under him:** ... it is evident, —HNSN, —MNTG ... that God is excepted, —CNBR ... it is dear that this doesn't include the One Who subjected everything to Him, —ADAM.

**15:27.** Acting as a supplement to Paul's main thought in verses 20-26, this verse reaffirms the unlimited dominion of Christ and the fact that only through His absolute victory can the kingdom of God be consummated.

There is a reference to Psalm 8, which promised man complete rule over his domain. As man, Christ is the Deliverer and Conqueror for man; He has conquered death. "When all things shall be subdued unto him (the Son)," His commission will be ended and the travail of His soul will be satisfied (Isaiah 53:11).

"But" adds a self-evident assertion concerning God the Father. Behind the messianic reign is the absolute supremacy of God.

**28. And when all things shall be subdued unto him:** ... whenever all may be subjected to Him, —CNDT ... when He has subjugated all to Him, —FNTN ... the whole universe has been made subject to Him, —WEYM.

**then shall the Son also himself be subject unto him that put all things under him:**

**that God may be all in all:** ... may be everything to everyone, —MOFT.

**15:28.** The first part of the next verse reaffirms objectively what was issued subjectively as the verdict by Christ himself on His own finished work. When this subjection of "all things" to Christ has been completed, then Christ shall be subjected to God the Father. This simply involves the subjection of sonship. There is no inferiority of nature or removal of power, but the free submission of love.

This was the spirit that motivated Christ in His earthly ministry. His intention was always to glorify the Father, who in turn glorified the Son. And the purpose of all this is fixed in conclusion: "that God may be all in all"; that God's will may be everywhere observed and His being everywhere immanent.

**29. Else what shall they do which are baptized for the dead:** ... what do they obtain, —*FNTN* ... on behalf of their dead? —*MOFT.*

**if the dead rise not at all? why are they then baptized for the dead?:** ... if the dead are not absolutely raised? —*FNTN.*

**15:29.** "Baptized for the dead" has been much debated for many centuries. To what was he referring? William Barclay, in his commentary on 1 Corinthians, has a plausible explanation of this verse. He says, ". . . this phrase can refer to only one custom, which has quite correctly passed out of Church practice altogether. In the Early Church there was vicarious baptism. If a person died who had intended to become a member of the Church and was actually under instruction, sometimes someone else underwent baptism for him. The custom sprang from a superstitious view of baptism that, without it, a person was necessarily excluded from the bliss of heaven. It was to safeguard against this exclusion that sometimes people volunteered to be baptized literally on behalf of those who had died. Here Paul neither approves or disapproves that practice. He merely asks if there can be any point in it if there is no resurrection and the dead never rise again" (*The Daily Study Bible*, p. 171).

The fact that Paul only parenthetically referred to this practice suggests that it held no importance for him at all. He was merely using it as an example to show that the Corinthians were being inconsistent in their view of the afterlife: if there is no future resurrection, what was the point of baptizing for the dead?

**30. And why stand we in jeopardy every hour?:** ... why should we run a risk every hour? —*FNTN* . . . are we in danger euery houre? —*RHEM,* —*MOFT* ... running into peril, —*RTHM* ... are we also in danger every hour? —*CNDT* . . . expose ourselves to danger every hour, —*WEYM.*

**15:30.** The New Testament refers often to the peril of the apostles and other Christian workers. They daily faced hazards with the hope of future joy and security because of the resurrection of the dead. If the resurrection of the dead is not a fact,

this constant exposure to danger was foolhardy, even madness.

**31. I protest by your rejoicing which I have in Christ Jesus our Lord:**
**I die daily:** ... but I am at death's door! —*MOFT.*

**15:31.** Lest the Corinthians think Paul was exaggerating his situation, he offered his exclamation. *Kath' hēmeran apothnēskō* (literally, "daily I die") comes first in the Greek for emphasis. His danger was real and constant. As well as daily facing danger, he in himself daily abandoned his life.

In the process Paul boasted of the results of his apostolic work, which was the very reason for which he died daily. It was this glorying in the work of the Lord and his commitment to it that caused Paul to die daily.

**32. If after the manner of men I have fought with beasts at Ephesus:** ... from merely human motives, —*WEYM.*
**what advantageth it me, if the dead rise not?:** ... If dead men do not rise, —*MOFT* ... what doth it profit me, —*RHEM* ... what is my gain, —*FNTN.*
**let us eat and drink; for to morrow we die:**

**15:32.** Paul experienced poverty and pain; if there is no "day of Christ," he had been a fool. It is believed by some that Paul actually fought in the Ephesian arena. However, since Paul was a Roman citizen, he could not ordinarily be compelled to fight in the arena. No such experience is listed in 2 Corinthians 11. It appears from Acts 19:31-40 that Paul had friends among the ranking officials at Ephesus who probably would have prevented such a thing. Paul probably had in mind those men in Ephesus who had fiercely opposed him. Thus "I have fought with beasts at Ephesus" is probably used somewhat figuratively.

Morbid unbelief will produce a certain desperation and sensuality. Paul quoted from Isaiah 22:13 which reveals the recklessness bred by the absence of a hope of life after death. This citation might have provided an axiom for the popular Epicureanism. It is also an excellent example of ancient popular morals and attitudes. This was the best that could be had, they thought. But it was not so if there is a resurrection from the dead.

**33. Be not deceived:** . . . Be not seduced, —*RHEM* ... Be not misled, —*FNTN* ... Make no mistake about this, —*MOFT.*
**evil communications corrupt good manners:** ... Evil companionships corrupt good morals, —*WEYM* ... vile teachings, —*FNTN* ... evil conversations, —*CNDT.*

**15:33.** Paul charged the Corinthian believers, "Be not deceived." They were attempting to be too broad in allowing tenets that produced skepticism and were demoralizing in their effect. The line the apostle quoted, "evil . . . manners," has been attributed to Menander's *Thais* (ca. 322 B.C.). But it was probably used even before that time.

**34. Awake to righteousness, and sin not:** . . . to perfect sobriety, *—FNTN.*
**for some have not the knowledge of God:** . . . some of you are insensible, *—MOFT.*
**I speak [this] to your shame:** . . . I speak this to your rebuke, *—GNVA* . . . I speak reproving you, *—FNTN* . . . in order to move you to shame, *—WEYM.*

**15:34.** Paul exhorted the Christians in Corinth to "awake . . . and sin not." *Awake* originally had the sense of becoming sober after drunkenness. Paul urged the believers to sober righteousness.

"Some" of the Corinthians had no "knowledge of God." This statement indicated a characteristic, persistent condition which these "some" shared with the heathen. Paul spoke this to move the Corinthian believers to shame. The error that had arisen among them was caused by a lack of real knowledge of God.

**35. But some [man] will say, How are the dead raised up?:**
**and with what body do they come?:** . . . with what sort of body, *—ADAM* . . . in what form will they come? *—TCNT* . . . do they come back, *—WEYM.*

**15:35.** Having established the fact of the resurrection, Paul turned to questions regarding the nature and experiential side of the resurrection of the body. The recorded questions in this verse refer to the possibility and conceivability of the resurrection of the body. They imply that the resurrection of the body is absurd. But Paul answered each one.

**36. [Thou] fool, that which thou sowest is not quickened, except it die:** . . . Imprudent one! *—CNDT* . . . Simpleton! what you sow is not made alive, *—CMPB* . . . Foolish man! . . . unless it dies, *—MNTG* . . . Senseless man, *—DOUY* . . . Senseless! . . . unless it arises from its bed, *—FNTN* . . . does not daily experience teach thee, *—LOCK* . . . is not brought to life, *—NOYS* . . . is not made alive, *—PNIN* . . . does not burst into life, *—TCNT* . . . till it hath partaken of death, *—CNBR.*

**15:36.** "Thou fool" showed Paul's estimate of the skepticism involved in the questions. Paul may have been reflecting the Old Testament definition of a fool as a man who has no regard for God (cf. Psalm 14:1, "The fool hath said in his heart, There is no God"). The Biblical fool is not simply unintelligent, he is morally reprehensible. He involved the objector personally in the discussion. If this foolish man would only look at the fields, at his

own work, he would realize that nature carries an analogy. The farmer plants a seed in the ground. But it cannot produce a plant or crop or enhance itself unless it first dies. Thus life comes out of death. The seed does not give itself life; God gives it life.

Jesus himself used the analogy of wheat being planted, dying, and sprouting to speak of His own death (John 12:24). Although Jesus was there speaking primarily of the necessity of His death, the passage strongly maintains that in death a transformation takes place and that the final product is more glorious than the initial one.

Paul did not explain the modus operandi, but what he did show is that the mystery creates no doubt or prejudice against the reality, for the same mystery is present in the vegetating seed. With this example from nature so evident, why should anyone think the transformation of a dead body impossible?

**37. And that which thou sowest, thou sowest not that body that shall be:**
**but bare grain, it may chance of wheat, or of some other [grain]:** . . . but a mere kernel, *—HNSN* . . . but a naked grain, *—FNTN* . . . but a naked kernel, *—CNDT, —RTHM* . . . or some other seed, *—MOFT.*

**15:37.** The purpose of the sower is to receive a different (new) form or product from his seed. Yet the sower knows it is the same body or seed. The truth of this lower "resurrection" supports the conceivability of the higher resurrection. "It may chance . . . grain" refers to the fact that the grain of wheat gives no more promise of a future body than any other seed or grain. But the raised "body" will be more wonderful than the "body" (seed) that was buried.

**38. But God giveth it a body as it hath pleased him:** . . . an appropriate body, *—RTHM* . . . at his pleasure, *—GNVA* . . . such as He intended, *—FNTN* . . . such as God has thought fit to give it, *—LOCK.*
**and to every seed his own body:** . . . and to each of the seeds, *—MKNT* . . . its proper body, *—CMPB, —DOUY* . . . its natural body, *—MRDK* . . . a plant, of a particular shape and size, *—LOCK* . . . he gives the form peculiar to itself, *—TCNT.*

**15:38.** That which arises from the dead seed is a God-given body, as is the resurrection one. God gives the body as He wills. This is the connection between seed and plant.

Additionally, as God finds a fit body for each of the numberless planted seeds, so He will provide a fit body for man's redeemed, glorified nature. The man sows; the seed dies; the plant is raised by the power of God. It is an ordained rising; so shall it be with the resurrection of the body. God gives continually the proper body to each seed.

**39. All flesh [is] not the same flesh:** ... even now, all flesh is not identical in composition, —WAY ... And every body is not alike, —MRDK ... there are different kinds of flesh, —LOCK ... differ the one from the other, —CNBR.
**but [there is] one [kind of] flesh of men:** ... but there is one kind for human beings, —ADAM ... for the body of a man is one thing, —MRDK.
**another flesh of beasts:** ... and that of a beast is another, —MRDK ... another is animal, —BRKL ... another flesh for cattle, —FNTN ... Flesh of Cattle, —WLSN.
**another of fishes, [and] another of birds:** ... and another of fowls, —CMPB ... is essentially different, —WAY ... is of a peculiar sort, different from them all, —LOCK.

**15:39.** Paul spoke of the varied forms in nature and the appropriateness of each for the life it clothes. For example, in the zoological realm there is countless differentiation rather than uniformity. The corporeity of each division listed has been established by God according to individual constitution and needs. If God can find the precise body necessary for these lower forms, and even for mortal man, can He not also provide the proper body for the resurrected man?

**40. [There are] also celestial bodies, and bodies terrestrial:** ... To look yet farther into the difference of bodies, —LOCK ... heavenly bodies ... earthly bodies, —MOFT ... bodies peculiar to the heavens, —TCNT.
**but the glory of the celestial [is] one:** ... the splendour of, —MOFT ... differs, —FNTN.
**and the [glory] of the terrestrial [is] another:**

**15:40.** Paul added to his illustrations by comparing celestial and terrestrial bodies. Again, countless differentiation is noted. While the heavenly and earthly bodies are alike in the sense that they are both bodies, there is a vast difference in "glory" between the two. Each is taken care of and provided for by God.

Although it is only implied in English, the Greek noun *doxa* ("glory") governs not only the phrase "celestial (heavenly) bodies" but also bodies "terrestrial (earthly)." It is true that Paul was drawing a distinction between the glory of the heavenly bodies in their brilliance (i.e., the sun, moon, and stars all reveal brightness) and that of earthly bodies, but it must still be recognized that Paul spoke of the earthly bodies (*sōmata*) as having glory.

It must be noted that the word for "bodies" here (*sōmata*) refers to the physical flesh and blood of a body in contrast to *sarx* which also means "body" but was used by Paul metaphorically to speak of human sinful nature (as, e.g., in Romans 7:5). The

difference between *sōmata* and *sarx* must be considered when speaking of the "body."

**41. [There is] one glory of the sun, and another glory of the moon:** ... One kind of splendor belongs to, —WLMS ... the glory of the sun is one thing, —MRDK.
**and another glory of the stars:**
**for [one] star differeth from [another] star in glory:** ... for star is excelling star in glory, —CNDT ... moreover, star excelleth star in glory, —MKNT ... star excels star in glory, —CMPB ... and one star exceedeth another star in glory, —MRDK ... does one star differ, —BRKL ... in brilliancy, —FNTN.

**15:41.** Paul specifically mentioned the sun, moon, and stars as examples of the point of differentiation in body and "glory." Each has a glory distinctly its own, ordained by God. Each has its unique function and place. All are glorious, but there are degrees of glory.

**42. So also [is] the resurrection of the dead:** ... It is the same with, —WEYM ... So likewise is, —CNBR.
**It is sown in corruption:** ... what is sown is mortal, —MOFT ... in a state of decay, —WEYM ... sown in decay, —WLMS ... in destruction, —SAWR ... is a poor, weak, contemptible, corruptible thing, —LOCK ... sown in decomposition, —BRKL.
**it is raised in incorruption:** ... When it is raised again, it shall be powerful, glorious, —LOCK ... they arise without corruption, —MRDK ... raised free from decay, —WEYM ... it is raised in indestructableness, —SAWR.

**15:42.** "So also ... of the dead" serves as both a summary and transitional sentence. Paul made a direct application to his theme, the resurrection body. From there, he began to describe its change more directly and specifically.

Paul first noted the states of both natural and resurrection bodies and the changes involved. There will be a change from corruption to incorruption. The figure of sowing suggests our mortal bodies which shall conclude with death and out of which a different body will emerge.

"Corruption" (*phthora*) refers most correctly to the perishableness of man's actual body. The word refers primarily to the physical body's gradual decaying tendency.

The "incorruption" (*aphtharsia*) of the resurrection state is well placed here. The major objection of the Greeks to this thought was that the body is basically corruptible. They thought only of the body of flesh and blood. Paul agreed that corruption is a property of the earthly body. But the resurrection body will be a transformed body of which incorruption is a characteristic.

**43. It is sown in dishonour; it is raised in glory:** ... that which is sown is disfigured, that which rises is beautiful, —TCNT . . . sown in contempt, —FNTN . . . sown inglorious, —MOFT . . . sown in a state of dishonor, —ADAM . . . sown in humiliation, it is raised in splendor, —WLMS.

**it is sown in weakness; it is raised in power:** . . . in a state of helplessness, —ADAM . . . it is raised in strength, —WLMS.

**15:43.** Paul spoke of a second change, that from dishonor to glory. There is nothing honorable about the body that is put into the grave without rights and left to decay. Its decomposition would in a short time cause us to shrink back in horror. But the Greeks' rising doubts on the dishonorable nature of the present body were unjustified; it shall be changed into a glorious body. As the beautiful plant far surpasses the seed from which it sprang, so shall the resurrection body far surpass this present one in glory.

**44. It is sown a natural body:** . . . it is sowen a beestli bodi, —WCLF . . . sown an animate body, —MOFT . . . an animal body, —WEYM, —MRDK.

**it is raised a spiritual body:**

**There is a natural body, and there is a spiritual body:** . . . For there is a body of the animal life, —MRDK.

**15:44.** There are distinctions in nature between the natural and the spiritual body. Paul added another "it is sown." "Natural" has to do with the present life in all its aspects, especially as it stands in opposition to the supernatural life. The human body is suited to this life, not the heavenly.

"Spiritual" refers to the type of body needed for the world to come. A change will take place.

**45. And so it is written, The first man Adam was made a living soul:** . . . was a living nature, —FNTN . . . became a living animal, —WEYM . . . became an animate being, —MOFT . . . became a living being, —MNTG . . . became a living creature, —WLMS.

**the last Adam [was made] a quickening spirit:** . . . the second Adam [became], —MRDK . . . a life-giving, —MOFT, —SAWR, —PNT, —MNTG . . . is a Life-producing Spirit, —FNTN . . . made of a spiritual constitution, with a power to give life to others, —LOCK.

**15:45.** The different natures are contrasted in the reference to Adam and Christ. The basic characteristic of man from the beginning has been the "soul." The first Adam passed on his nature to all who followed. As the father of the human race his nature was stamped on it.

Christ, in comparison, "was made a quickening spirit." He is the progenitor of the spiritual race. As such, He stamps His nature on those who are "in Him." But not only is this "last Adam" the pattern for all those in Him, He is also the source of that life which will result in the resurrection body.

The "last Adam" indicates Christ's humanity and our bodily relationship to Him.

The best view on "life-giving spirit" (NASB) seems to be that it is a reference to the resurrection of Christ. Not only did He then enter a "spiritual" form, He will pass that spiritual form (body) on to His followers in the resurrection (John 11:25; Romans 8:10f.).

**46. Howbeit that [was] not first which is spiritual:** . . . the spiritual was not first, —SAWR.

**but that which is natural:** . . . but the animal, —LOCK.

**and afterward that which is spiritual:** . . . and only then, —MOFT.

**15:46.** However, there is a logical and necessary order: first natural, then spiritual. This does not mean that Paul was equating the two; he was simply establishing the order. The spiritual outweighs the natural even in the context of the body.

**47. The first man [is] of the. earth, earthy:** . . . was from the Ground, —WLSN . . . of the ground, —RTHM . . . was made of earthly clay, —CNBR . . . made of dust, —PNT, —NORL . . . dust, or earthy particles, —LOCK . . . was made of the dust of the earth, —WLMS . . . material, —MOFT.

**the second man [is] the Lord from heaven:**

**15:47.** Paul then spoke of the origin of the two natures. The first man had an earthly origin. While Paul had in mind specifically the idea of bodily origin, the words "of the earth, earthy" denote the whole quality of this life. This first man refers to Adam (Genesis 2:7). "Earthy" (*choikos*) is different from "earth" and means "made of dust." The first man was bound to this earth.

The "second man" refers to Jesus Christ. The first use of the word "man" is contrasted with the second "man." "First" and "second" suggest that both Adam and Christ had great significance for others. But while Christ appeared on this earth (Philippians 2:7) and lived, died, and rose again, His origin was not of this earth, but of heaven. Most specifically, within a historical relationship, Paul was presenting Christ as following and displacing Adam in the course of human history. He came from heaven to do it. Since there is no verb in either clause of this verse, some scholars have inserted a form of "come" to suggest that the first Adam came from the ground and the second from heaven (although earth and heaven may be taken adverbially suggesting an earthly or heavenly nature).

**48. As [is] the earthy, such [are] they also that are earthy:** . . . As he was of the dust, so also those who are of the dust, —MRDK...have barely an animal life and constitution, —LOCK.

**and as [is] the heavenly, such [are] they also that are heavenly:** ...and as was he who was from heaven, so also are the heavenly, —MRDK.

**15:48.** All of Adam's descendants are in Adam's image just as all of Christ's followers are in His image. It seems that more than just a physical distinction between pre- and post-resurrection states is involved. There is some moral connotation (Romans 6:4; Philippians 3:17-21; Colossians 3:1-4).

All men are patterned after the first Adam in that they have "earthy" bodies. But Christians enjoy another relationship also. Their relationship with Christ indicates that they are also "heavenly." This involves both the present implication and the future certainty. In the words of 1 John 3:2, "We shall be like him

**49. And as we have borne the image of the earthy:** . . . as we resembled the earthly, —FNTN...even as we have borne the likeness of the earthy, —CNFT...as we have worn the likeness of him from the dust, —MRDK...a resemblance to the earthly, —WEYM...the likeness of material man, —MOFT...as in the animal, corruptible, mortal state, we were born in, —LOCK.
**we shall also bear the image of the heavenly:** . . . so shall we wear the likeness of him from heaven, —MRDK...of the heavenly one, —PNT.

**15:49.** "We have borne" (*ephoresamen*) involves the idea of what is continual and habitual. "Image" (*eikona*) is used of man being made in God's image. "Image" may denote simply representation, or it may be used more precisely to indicate the original.

Paul assured us that we shall be given a spiritual or resurrection body. The image we have borne is evidence of the one we will bear.

**50. Now this I say, brethren:** . . . And this I affirm, brethren, —CMPB.
**that flesh and blood cannot inherit the kingdom of God:** . . . our mortal bodies, —WEYM . . . can not possess, —RHEM . . . can obtain no part in the kingdom, —CNFT . . . cannot possess God's reign, —HNSN . . . is not able to enjoy an allotment in the kingdom, —CNDT...a Divine Kingdom, —FNTN.
**neither doth corruption inherit incorruption:** . . . perishable inherit what is imperishable, —WEYM . . . the perishing inherit the imperishable, —MOFT...nor shall destruction inherit indestructibleness, —SAWR.

**15:50.** Paul also quieted the minds of the living and exhorted the Corinthians to worthy accomplishment in Christ because of the fact and hope of the resurrection.

In the process, Paul made two important assertions. The first was that "flesh and blood cannot

inherit the kingdom of God." "Flesh and blood" denote first substance (flesh), then the life-giving principle (blood) of the physical body.

The natural body is unsuited for the kingdom of God. It must be changed. "Inherit" (*klēronomēsai*) points to the rights and possessions of believers, as yet unrealized.

The second assertion, built on the first, was that corruption (perishableness) cannot inherit incorruption (imperishableness). There must be a necessary change.

**51. Behold, I show you a mystery:** . . . Listen! I tell you a secret, —FNTN...Here is a secret truth for you, —MOFT...a Secret I disclose to you, —WLSN...To which let me add, what has not been hitherto discovered, —LOCK.
**We shall not all sleep, but we shall all be changed:**...we shall not, indeed, all die, —CMPB...Vve shal al in deede rise againe, —RHEM . . . We are not all going to die, —NORL...but we shall all undergo a change, —TCNT.

**15:51.** Paul applied this to those who might have wondered if they had to die before they could be changed. "Behold" calls for emphatic attention to the declaration that would follow. "Mystery" speaks of a secret that is impossible for man to penetrate. Man can only know it as God has chosen to make it known. Man could never have discovered what will happen at the resurrection, but God has revealed it.

"We" is used generally. Paul lived as though Christ might come at any time, even though he did not know when He was coming, nor did he claim to. Some believers will not die, but whether among that group or not, dead or alive, "we shall all be changed."

**52. In a moment, in the twinkling of an eye, at the last trump: for the trumpet shall sound:**...It will come about suddenly, quickly, —NORL...for the trumpet shal blowe, —GNVA . . . in an eye's glance, —FNTN...in the flash of an eye, —WAY, —ADAM.
**and the dead shall be raised incorruptible:**...incapable of decay, —WEYM.
**and we shall be changed:** . . . we, also, shall undergo a change, —TCNT.

**15:52.** Paul used three vivid phrases to describe this change that will take place. "In a moment" is "that which cannot be cut or divided," the smallest possible. We get our word *atom* from it. It describes the instantaneousness of the event. "Twinkling" (*rhipē*) suggests the idea of throwing. It refers to the time it takes to cast a glance or flutter an eyelid.

"At the last trump" represents the solemn finality of this transformation. In the Scriptures and contemporary Judaism, the trumpet was often associated with both festivals and the events of the end time (Morris, *Tyndale New Testament Commentaries,* 7:233). The Christian dead shall be raised incorruptible.

**53.** **For this corruptible must put on incorruption:** . . . For so it must be: . . . this perishable nature must clothe itself, *—WEYM* . . . this corruptible frame and constitution of ours, *—LOCK* . . . perishing body must be invested with, *—MOFT* . . . this destructible must put on indestructibleness, *—SAWR* . . . must be endowed, *—FNTN* . . . must needs clothe itself, *—RTHM* . . . must be clothed with, *—MNTG.*

**and this mortal [must] put on immortality:** . . . and that which dieth, *—MRDK* . . . this deedly thing to putte aweye vndeedly-nesse, *—WCLF.*

**15:53.** The necessity of change was reaffirmed as being due to our nature and condition. The human body, of which Paul was painfully conscious, must put on incorruption and immortality. It is bound to do so. But the power to make this happen comes from God. "To put on" (*endusasthai*) is the usual word for putting on clothing. This change is represented as an investiture with incorruption and immortality.

**54.** **So when this corruptible shall have put on incorruption, and this mortal shall have put on immortality:** . . . when this corruptible body shall, *—MKNT* . . . and this that dieth, immortality, *—MRDK.*

**then shall be brought to pass the saying that is written:** . . . then will take place the word that is written, *—MRDK* . . . the written declaration, *—FNTN* . . . then the saying that was written will come true, *—ADAM* . . . then indeed will the words of Scripture come true, *—TCNT* . . . then shall be fulfilled what was foretold, *—LOCK* . . . then shall the word be accomplished that is written, *—SAWR* . . . will be realized, *—MOFT* . . . shall be accomplished, *—CMPB.*

**Death is swallowed up in victory:** . . . is consumed in to victory, *—TNDL* . . . is swallowed up forever, *—CMPB, —MKNT* . . . is absorbed in victory, *—MRDK.*

**15:54.** It is characteristic of Paul to see fulfillment of Scripture in all of this. "When" indicates time. When these things shall have taken place, then certain Old Testament prophecies will be fulfilled. "Corruption" putting on "incorruption" and "mortal" putting on "immortality" are what must come to pass to fulfill the Old Testament. The quotation is from Isaiah 25:8 and there is a parallel with 1 Corinthians 15:24, 27.

The destruction of this last enemy, this "king of terrors," indicates absolute victory for Christ and His followers. "Swallowed" (*katepothē*) presents a dramatic figure and expresses complete destruction. Not only will death be destroyed so that it can do no more harm, all of its apparent victories in days and years past will be undone, reversed,

destroyed. Those who are in Christ shall live in absolute victory!

**55.** **O death, where [is] thy sting?:**
**O grave, where [is] thy victory?:** . . . Hell where is thy victory? *—CRNM* . . . Hades! where is thy victory? *—CMPB.*

**15:55.** Paul could contain himself no longer. He broke forth into a song of triumph over death. It is in the strain of Hosea's anticipation of Israel's resurrection from national death (see Hosea 13:14). The words of Hosea are freely adapted. "Sting" (*kentron*) gives us the picture of death as a creature with a deadly sting. The great harmfulness of death is pictured. But there is more than a question here. "Where" denotes an exclamation of victory, a challenge, that must be answered by "Nowhere!" Death holds no permanent victory. Believers are victors over death and its sting.

**56.** **The sting of death [is] sin:** . . . but the pricke of deeth: . . . is synne, *—WCLF*
**and the strength of sin [is] the law:** . . . and sin derives its power from, *—WEYM* . . . the power of sin is the law, *—CNDT, —CNFT* . . . and sin's power is, *—BRKL* . . . and the law gives sin its power, *—WLMS* . . . and the power of sinne, *—RHEM.*

**15:56.** Sin gives death its power; it is its sting. It gives death its penal character, its humiliating form, and its bondage of corruption. To those who fall "asleep" in Jesus Christ, however, the sting of death has been removed because Christ has taken their sense of guilt and fear of judgment.

Sin in turn receives its power from the Law. In a few words Paul gave a condensation of his teaching concerning the relation between sin and the Law. The Law imposed on sinful man necessary but impossible requirements, promising salvation on fulfillment of impossible terms and death on nonfulfillment. This in effect extended sin and involved the sinner in hopeless guilt. When death is "the wages of sin" it has a deadly sting. When death, because of pardoned sin, ushers the believer into the immediate presence of the Lord it is gain, not loss. The believer can sing with the hymn writer, "O the joy of sins forgiven" because they have been washed away by the death and resurrection of Christ.

**57.** **But thanks [be] to God, which giveth us the victory through our Lord Jesus Christ:** . . . The victory is ours, *—MOFT.*

**15:57.** Paul ended his song of triumph by asserting the Source of our victory. The apostle finally linked his doctrine of the bodily resurrection and transformation of the believer to his basic teaching on justification and forgiveness of sins.

The use of the present participle may carry the idea that it is God's characteristic to give victory. This is daily victory. "Victory" is just one word, but it sums up all Paul had written in this chapter. It denotes enemies and a battle, but not ours. This great victory is being given to believers by God because of the Victor, "our Lord Jesus Christ," who is the One through whom their victory comes.

**58. Therefore, my beloved brethren, be ye stedfast, un-moveable:** . . . Consequently, –BRKL . . . be firm, –FNTN, –WEYM . . . hold your ground, –MOFT . . . be stable, –CMPB . . . stand firm and unshaken, –TCNT . . . and be not vacillating, –MRDK . . . incapable of being moved, –WLMS.

**always abounding in the work of the Lord:** . . . but be ye at all times abundant in the work of the Lord, –MRDK . . . busily occupied at all times in the Lord's work, –WEYM . . . aboundingly active in the Lord's service, –BRKL . . . always letting the cup run over in the work of the Lord, –WLMS . . . always diligent in the Lord's work, –TCNT . . . always abounding in your obedience to the precepts of Christ, and in those duties which are required of us, –LOCK . . . alwayes ryche in the workes, –GNVA . . . superabounding in the work, –RTHM.

**forasmuch as ye know that your labour is not in vain in the Lord:** . . . your labour will not be lost, –LOCK . . . is not futile, –FNTN . . . is not worthless, –ADAM . . . your toil is not fruitless, –WEYM . . . that what you do in the service of the Lord is labor not thrown away! –NORL.

**15:58.** The word "therefore" brings the matter to the point of conclusion and application. "My beloved brethren" not only showed Paul's concern for them, it also called on them to prove themselves brothers. They were urged negatively not to be flighty, movable, or unstable in their Christian beliefs and actions, but steadfast and unmovable. Positively, they were urged to be "abounding" or overflowing in the work of the Lord.

Believers should always be "abounding" in the Lord's work because their labor is not in vain. Labor "in the Lord" is not illusion, not profitless, but profitable, rewarding, promised success, which should spur those who are Christ's to greater work.

## Chapter 16

**1. Now concerning the collection for the saints:** . . . With regard to, –MOFT . . . of the gaderingis of money, –WCLF . . . the tax collected, –FNTN . . . for the converts to Christianity, –LOCK.

**as I have given order to the churches of Galatia, even so do ye:** . . . you must carry out the same arrangements, –MOFT . . . as I have enjoined, –CNBR . . . as I arranged with, –FNTN . . . even as I prescribe, –CNDT . . . as I directed, –RTHM . . . as I haue ordeined, –RHEM . . . do you also, –CNFT.

**16:1.** Paul has almost completed his letter. Items of large importance have been discussed. But there were a few general items that were still on his heart; thus in shorter but necessary comments he added these needful reminders.

"Now concerning" introduced a new topic. The phrase is used in this letter to mark topics mentioned by the Corinthians in their letter to Paul.

The matter in question touched on the offering which was to be taken to Jerusalem to help those who had been totally devastated by severe economic conditions. Paul had not only made a promise concerning them (Galatians 2:10), he saw this as an opportunity to unite the Jewish and Gentile elements of the Church.

Paul urged this giving to come from the highest motives. It was a part of the work of the Lord in which Christians should abound because of their victory through the Lord Jesus Christ. The fact that this collection was being made for the saints should recommend it to saints everywhere.

**2. Upon the first [day] of the week:** . . . some sondaye, –TNDL.

**let every one of you lay by him in store:** . . . put aside a sum, –MOFT . . . each of you set apart a certain portion of his profits, –WAY . . . let each of you set apart whatever his gains may enable him to spare, –CNBR.

**as [God] hath prospered him:** . . . according as he thrives, –LOCK . . . depositing as he may be prospered, –WLSN . . . accumulating as he may prosper, –CLMT . . . putting it into the treasury, –CMPB . . . whatever gain has been granted to him, –WEYM.

**that there be no gatherings when I come:** . . . that there may be no need of, –LOCK . . . there may be no collections, –CNBR.

**16:2.** Paul gave instructions concerning this collection. It was to be generous and systematically arranged "upon the first day of the week." This was a support for the regular observance of that day (Sunday) as the time for the Church as a whole to gather. Also, the giving was to be regular, not just emotional.

Further, everyone should make a contribution, however large or small, and the giving was to be proportionate as "God hath prospered him." The blessing would determine the amount.

**3. And when I come, whomsoever ye shall approve by [your] letters:** . . . On my arrival, –MNTG . . . whomsoever you should be attesting through letters, –CNDT . . . you shall authorize, –HNSN . . . whoever you may choose, –FNTN . . . whomsoever you shall judge to be fitted for the trust I will furnish with letters, –CNBR . . . you accredit by letter, –WEYM . . . will furnish credentials for, –MOFT.

**them will I send to bring your liberality unto Jerusalem:** . . . to carry your gift,

—FNTN, —CMPB . . . convey your bounty, —MOFT . . . to carry your benevolence, —CNBR . . . your kind gift, —WEYM, —CLMT.

**16:3.** Another New Testament principle of giving was that financial gifts must be carefully administered. Reputable, honest, trusted individuals were to be picked by the Corinthians to carry these funds to the Jerusalem church.

This was an area of church administration that needed great care, and any hint of mismanagement must be guarded against. This arrangement would protect Paul from the accusation of an unhealthy interest in the offering. Moreover, those who did the giving should be able to have a voice in who would take their gift. This trip would bring the Corinthians into personal contact with the Jerusalem believers and strengthen the unity of the Church.

In the Greek there is nothing corresponding to the first "your" of the verse. Therefore the comma might come after "approve." The meaning then would be that after the Corinthians had picked men for the responsibility, Paul would write letters of commendation to be sent with them.

**4. And if it be meet that I go also:** . . . Which if it deserves, —LOCK . . . or if there shall seem sufficient reason, —CNBR . . . if it be vvorthie, —RHEM . . . if it is important enough for me also to go, —CNFT . . . is worth while for me also to make the journey, —WEYM . . . if it be suitable, —PNT . . . Or, if it be proper, —CMPB.
**they shall go with me:**

**16:4.** A thought was added on the possibility of Paul's going to Jerusalem with those who would be chosen to carry this gift. Paul inserted "if" because he was uncertain as to whether or not he would go.

The giving of Christians should be such as to indicate the blessings of God and their own proper stewardship of the things of this earth. They are to be generously given and shared. Paul was not certain of the liberality of the Corinthians, thus he was guarding his position as an apostle and their respect for him.

**5. Now I will come unto you, when I shall pass through Macedonia: for I do pass through Macedonia:** . . . when I traverse, —FNTN . . . for my plan will be to pass, —WEYM . . . for I intend to take that, —LOCK . . . after my tour, —MOFT.

**16:5.** Paul indicated that he would come to visit the Corinthians, although at the time of this writing the time was uncertain. In 4:18, 19, Paul had remarked on those who did not think he would actually come to them. Now he stated the fact with certainty.

The time was set as "when I shall pass through Macedonia." "When" is indefinite again. In Acts "pass through" regularly denotes an evangelistic tour. The last part of this verse appears to give new information to the Corinthians, as though they had not known before of Paul's trip.

**6. And it may be that I will abide:** . . . perhaps I shall make some stay, —LOCK . . . perhaps I shall remain with you, —CNBR.
**yea, and winter with you:** . . . or els tary all wynter, —CRNM . . . or even spend the winter, —PNT . . . possibly spending the winter, —MNTG . . . perhaps remain or even winter, —CNFT.
**that ye may bring me on my journey whithersoever I go:** . . . I may sojourn, —RTHM . . . you may speed me, —MOFT . . . that ye may accompany me, —MRDK.

**16:6.** But Paul did not wish to visit Corinth just in passing. Rather, he desired to abide with them for awhile. Both "it may be" and "whithersoever I go" indicate clear uncertainty as to the apostle's future plans.

Winter was the time when travel was normally suspended. This extended visit during the winter would allow the Corinthians opportunity to "bring (Paul) on (his) journey." In other words, it would give them a chance to provide what he had need of for the journey. "You" is emphatic.

It is interesting that this is what Paul finally did. Acts 20:1-3 records that he traveled from Ephesus to Macedonia, and after "much exhortation" he went to Greece where he stayed for 3 months.

Paul's writings show that balance between what he desired and thought he might do, and the certain will of God.

**7. For I will not see you now by the way:** . . . to pay you a brief visit now, —FNTN . . . on this occasion merely in passing, —WEYM . . . to call in upon you, as I pass by, —LOCK . . . now for a passing visit, —CNBR.
**but I trust to tarry a while with you:** . . . since I hope to stay, —CNBR . . . for I hope to continue some time with you, —SAWR.
**if the Lord permit:** . . . yf God shal suffre me, —GNVA.

**16:7.** Paul indicated he would not do this immediately. He did not wish to make a quick visit. The Corinthians had requested his speedy arrival and this could have been arranged. But such a visit could only have been "by the way" in passing and would have been of little help.

There remained a greater leading than the apostle's own wish and will. That was the Lord's will; "if the Lord permit." Paul was above all a servant, and he went where his Master, the Lord, directed.

**8.** **But I will tarry at Ephesus until Pentecost:** ... For **I** shall continue at, —MRDK ... the time of the Harvest Festival, —WEYM ... i.e. Whitsuntide, —LOCK.

**9.** **For a great door and effectual is opened unto me:** ... I have wide opportunities here for active service, —MOFT ... a wide door stands open before me which demands great efforts, —WEYM ... a great wide open door, —FNTN ... promising opportunity given me, —LOCK ... and operative, —CNDT.

**and [there are] many adversaries:** ... yet there are many op-posers, —CMPB ... there are many to thwart me, —MOFT ... and many are they who are trying to shut it in my face, —WAY.

**16:8, 9.** In connection with this, Paul explained when he would leave Ephesus and gave a brief testimony concerning his work there. He would remain until Pentecost, the 50th day from the 16th Nisan in the Passover Feast. Some scholars have made capital out of the apparent contradiction between Paul's words in verse 8 that he would "tarry" and his words in 4:19, "I will come to you shortly." The solution (as if there were even a problem!) is to be discerned from the context of each chapter. In chapter 4, Paul was filled with anger at the Corinthian divisiveness and was admonishing them that if they didn't improve their behavior he would come to deal severely with them. Paul's admonition has been paraphrased by C.K. Barrett: "Anyone would think I was never going to set foot in Corinth again; but look out! I'll be there sooner than you think" (*Harper's New Testament Commentaries*, p. 390).

In chapter 16, however, Paul had an entirely different purpose in mind. Although Paul was listing his itinerary to the Corinthians, his personal itinerary was always subject to the will of God.

"Door" is a figurative expression. "Effectual" (*energēs*) is unusual here, especially in regard to its modification of door. It means "active" or "effective," and speaks of the influence gained by entering. "Great" (*megalē*) speaks of the door's width and the region into which it opened. "Is opened" (*aneōgen*) indicates present and continuous opportunity.

But Paul also called the Corinthians' attention to the fact of great opposition. Wherever the work of the Lord goes forth, it increases and flourishes despite opposition and adversity.

**10.** **Now if Timotheus come, see that he may be with you without fear:** ... make him feel quite at home, —MOFT ... pray take care that he be easy, —LOCK ... be careful to give him no cause of fear, —CNBR ... he is free from fear in his relations

with you, —WEYM ... that he is not troubled by you, —FNTN ... without trepidation, —MNTG.

**for he worketh the work of the Lord, as I also [do]:** ... he is engaged in the Master's work, —WEYM ... he promotes, —LOCK.

**11.** **Let no man therefore despise him:** ... let no one slight him, —WEYM ... let no one disparage him, —MNTG ... should be scorning him, —CNDT ... Don't let anyone make light of him, —ADAM.

**but conduct him forth in peace, that he may come unto me:** ... but send him forward, —CMPB ... But set him forward on his journey, —PNIN ... but speed him on his way, —CNFT.

**for I look for him with the brethren:** ... for I expect him, —CMPB ... with his companions, —FNTN.

**16:10, 11.** Paul might not come immediately, but others would, such as Timothy. Paul therefore put in a good word for his young associate. His direction to make Timothy feel at ease pointed to the disposition both of Timothy and the Corinthian church. It shows Timothy's youth, sensitivity, and possibly his timidity. It may have indicated wrong attitudes on the part of the church at Corinth.

Paul was concerned about Timothy in the midst of such a situation. Therefore, he reminded his readers that he and Timothy were engaged in the same work, "the work of the Lord." They had the same purpose, the same calling, and the same Lord. If Timothy attempted the task of 4:17, there was the possibility of trouble.

Rather, Timothy was to be sent forward on his journey in peace. "Conduct him forth" uses the same verb as that in verse 6, of Paul being sent on his journey. The Corinthians were to arrange and obtain that which was necessary for Timothy's journey. It appears Paul expected Timothy's return before he departed from Ephesus.

The Church is to treat its messengers with equal care and concern. Such treatment is not to be based on personality or expertise, but on the messenger's calling and the value of the message he has been called to present.

**12.** **As touching [our] brother Apollos, I greatly desired him to come unto you with the brethren:** ... Now concerning ... I besought him much, —PNT ... I have often requested, —FNTN ... I have repeatedly urged, —WEYM.

**but his will was not at all to come at this time:** ... he is quite resolved not to do so at present, —WEYM ... he was quite unwilling to come at present, —CNFT.

**but he will come when he shall have convenient time:** ... when there is a good opportunity, —FNTN ... he will come when he shall have opportunity, —HNSN.

**16:12.** Paul added a word concerning Apollos. His use of the phrase "as touching ... Apollos" suggests that his coming had been mentioned in the Corinthian letter to Paul. Considering the factions in Corinth and the fact that Apollos was viewed as Paul's rival there, it is valuable to note that Paul urged him to go to Corinth. It gives an insight into Paul's character and his concerns.

13. **Watch ye, stand fast in the faith:** ... Stand firm, *—CNDT* ... Be vigilant, *—PNT* ... Be on the alert, *—WEYM.*

**quit you like men, be strong:** ... Be manly! Be staunch! *—CNDT* ... doe manfully, and be strengthened, *—RHEM* . . . be manly; be self-restrained, *—FNTN* ... play the man, *—MOFT.*

14. **Let all your things be done with charity:** ... Let all your actions occur in love! *—CNDT* ... be done in love, *—PNT* ... from motives of love, *—WEYM.*

**16:13, 14.** In these two verses Paul wrote a series of short, powerful phrases that ring like military commands and are filled with clear direction. "Watch" is a present imperative. Paul was speaking of a continuing state. All the imperatives, in fact, in these two verses are present imperatives. More is meant than the mere absence of sleep. There is the idea of determined wakefulness and alertness. In Scripture there is both the warning to watchfulness against temptation and sin and also for the second coming of the Lord. Speaking against the Corinthians' lack of stability, Paul directed them to a particular steadfastness: "Stand fast in the faith"; in the person and power of Jesus Christ and His love (13:2, 13; 15:14-17).

Further, they were urged to be mature and courageous. There was a challenge to "play the man" (Moffatt) in all the activities of the Christian life. It was a charge against the childishness of the Corinthians. They had not been able to succeed because of their entanglement with heathen society and influence. The fight over sin and opposition of every sort is not one for children; it is for men.

Paul instructed the Corinthians to be strong. Christians may feel weak, but then is the time to go to the Strong One for strength. They must be "mighty" in Christian activity, by the power of the Lord. This contrasted with the Corinthian tendency to moral weakness and unsteadiness.

They were also charged to love. The Greek states it better: "in love." It refers to agape love, the highest, complete love. It stands as more than an equal or companion to Christian action. It is the realm and atmosphere within which the Christian thinks, moves, and lives. It is the fountain out of which all proper action flows (1 Peter 4:8).

15. **I beseech you, brethren, (ye know the house of Stephanas:** ... Now I am entreating you,

brethrenyou are acquainted, *—CNDT* ... I ask this favour of you, *—MOFT* ... But I advise you, *—FNTN.*

**that it is the firstfruits of Achaia:** ... they were the pioneers of Achaia, *—FNTN* ... were the earliest Greek converts to Christ, *—WEYM.*

**and [that] they have addicted themselves to the ministry of the saints,):** ... they have appointed themselves, *—PNT* ... for service to the saints, *—FNTN.*

**16:15.** Paul set before the Corinthians men to pattern themselves after and to respect, such as the household of Stephanas. "Ministry" is a general term for service. It does not indicate clergy.

16. **That ye submit yourselves unto such:** ... to such as these do you also be subject, *—CNFT* ... you to put yourselves under people like that, *—MOFT* ... to show deference to such, *—MNTG.*

**and to every one that helpeth with [us], and laboureth:**

**16:16.** Paul noted the manner in which the Corinthians were to treat such as the house of Stephanas. Again the indication is not that the men mentioned were church officials.

Paul was asking for willing submission to the direction of those willing and able to lead in profitable and excellent work. Such extensive work and sacrifice deserves respect in the Church as a whole. Paul included in this sweeping statement not only the house of Stephanas, but also all who helped and labored in the church.

17. **I am glad of the coining of Stephanas and Fortunatus and Achaicus:** ... I reioyce in the presence of, *—RHEM, —DOUY* ... I was very happy, *—SEB* ... at the arrival of, *—FNTN.*

**for that which was lacking on your part they have supplied:** ... for they have made up for your absence, *—MOFT, —BECK* ... they have supplied what was deficient on your side, *—LOCK* ... they have accomplished your instructions, *—FNTN.*

18. **For they have refreshed my spirit and yours:** ... they gave rest, *—RTHM* ... they soothe my spirit, *—CNDT* ... they have lightened my spirit, *—CNBR* ... they have quieted my mind, *—LOCK.*

**therefore acknowledge ye them that are such:** ... therefore honour such men, *—FNTN* ... So cultivate the acquaintance of such men, *—MNTG* ... You should appreciate men like that, *—BECK* ... You should give special recognition, *—SEB* ... Cultivate friendships with such men as these, *—TCNT* ... To such render due acknowledgment, *—CNBR* ... have a regard to such men, *—LOCK.*

**16:17, 18.** Paul admonished the Corinthians about their manner toward Stephanas, Fortunatus, and Achaicus when they returned home. But at present, he expressed his joy over their being with him.

*Fortunatus* was a common Latin name. *Achaicus* was a rare Greek name. Because of their names, some have supposed one or both were slaves, although there is little to support this. These three men probably carried the church letter to Paul. And since Paul commended them at the close of this letter, it is probable they would carry his letter back to Corinth.

Paul said that these three had made up to him for the absence of the Corinthians. In other words, they had representatively supplied him with the desired fellowship of the Corinthians. This would fit Paul's nature and satisfies the word "coming." It expressed the tenderness and depth of his feeling for the Corinthians even though they had not always treated him in a fitting or proper manner.

The coming of these men had been enjoyable not only because they had supplied a need but also because they had refreshed Paul's spirit and, therefore, that of the Corinthians. It would please and cheer them to know this visit had such desirable effects.

**19.** **The churches of Asia salute you:** ... The assemblies, *—HNSN* ... The congregations, *—CMPB* ... send greetings, *—KLGS* ... send regards to you all, *—FNTN* ... greet you heartily in the Lord, *—CNFT.* **Aquila and Priscilla salute you much in the Lord:** ... send you a hearty Christian greeting, *—TCNT* ... Salute you most heartily, *—BRKL* ... in hearty Christian love, *—WEYM* ... with much Christian affection, *—LOCK* ... greetings in the Lord, *—BECK.*

**with the church that is in their house:** ... the congregacion, *—CRNM* ... the church at their home, *—BECK* ... which assembles at their house, *—CNBR.*

**16:19.** Paul delighted in binding the churches together with real expressions of love. This was the purpose of the following greetings.

Paul specifically noted Aquila and Priscilla and the believers who met in their home. "Asia" referred to what was then the Roman province of Asia and what is now western Asia Minor. These two were well-known to the Corinthians (Acts 18:1-3).

Originally from Rome, Aquila and Priscilla had been a large part of Paul's life. Priscilla and Aquila had been forced to leave Rome in A.D. 49 when the Roman Emperor Claudius banished all Jews from the city of Rome. This edict was lifted in A.D. 50, allowing the Jews to return. When Paul wrote his letter to the Romans in A.D. 54 Priscilla and Aquila were once again residing in Rome (cf. Romans 16:3). When Paul first came to Corinth, he worked and lodged with them. They had been generous to him. Because they, like Paul, were tentmakers by trade, they worked together in this craft to support themselves.

At the time of Paul's writing this epistle Priscilla (or Prisca as she was also known) and Aquila were living in Ephesus where they had their own house-church.

Further, they had at some time risked their lives for him. They had instructed and encouraged Apollos in the Faith. They are mentioned six times in the New Testament.

"Salute you much" is a deep, warm, affectionate Christian greeting. "With the church ... in their house" can hardly mean the whole Ephesian church. Perhaps it meant a neighboring section of it.

**20.** **All the brethren greet you:** ... All the brotherhood salutes you, *—MOFT* ... All the Christians greet you, *—BECK* ... send you good wishes, *—TCNT.* **Greet ye one another with an holy kiss:** ... Give one another, *—BB* ... with a sacred kiss, *—TCNT, —GDSP* ... with the kiss of peace, *—BRCL* ... I should like you to shake hands all round as a sign of Christian love, *—PHLP.*

**16:20.** Paul added a comprehensive salute and then indicated the proper response. "All the brethren" is not specific, but appears to be all-inclusive.

The admonition from Paul on a "holy kiss" has caused much discussion. The custom was common in Paul's day, and in some countries a kiss on both cheeks is common in our day. Such a greeting would be a rebuke to any division or haughtiness; it would note that they were in accord.

**21.** **The salutation of [me] Paul with mine own hand:** ... That which followeth is, *—LOCK* ... The good wishes, *—FNTN* ... The final greeting of me, *—WEYM* ... I, Paul, add this farewell in my own handwriting, *—TCNT* ... Here is the greeting that I, Paul, write with my own hand, *—BECK* ... send you these words of love in my writing, *—BB* ... The salutation, with my hand, of Paul, *—RTHM* ... Here is my own greeting, written by me, *—PHLP.*

**16:21.** It was Paul's custom to dictate his letters to an amanuensis. But to mark the letter's genuineness he would, at the end, sign and close it himself. This was what he did now. This was his letter and personal greeting.

**22.** **If any man love not the Lord Jesus Christ, let him be Anathema, Maranatha:** ... If any one is destitute of love, *—WEYM* ... If any one is not a friend to the Lord, *—SAWR* ... If any one be an enemy to ... let him be accursed, or devoted to destruction, *—LOCK* ... If any one is not loving the Lord, *—RTHM* ... has not love for the Lord, *—BB* ... A curse upon anyone who has no love for the Lord. Lord come quickly! *—GDSP* ... excommunicate to death, *—GNVA* ... let him be delivered to the Lord coming in Judgment, *—FNTN* ... a curse on him! Our Lord, come! *—BECK* ... he should be condemned! *—SEB* ... let him be accursed, when the Lord cometh! *—WORL* ... Our

Lord is coming, —WEYM, —ADAM ... may the Lord soon come! —PHLP.

**16:22.** With great feeling, Paul closed the epistle. If a man falsely pretended to love the Lord, let him be "Anathema" (*anathema*), Paul wrote. Such a one is accursed. "Love not" (*ou philei*) is a strong note of accusation. It declares the individual to be heartless, lacking even human affection for Jesus. Such men, as the apostle John pointed out, neither love nor know God.

The second clause is "Maranatha" (*Maran atha*). This is an Aramaic word translated into Greek. Dividing the word, it breaks down roughly like this: *Mar* means "Lord"; *an* or *ana* denotes "our," and the latter part is from the verb *atha*, which means "to come" (Morris, *Tyndale New Testament Commentaries,* 7:247, 248). This seems best translated, "Our Lord cometh." This accords with Philippians 4:5; 1 Thessalonians 4:14; James 5:7; Revelation 1:7; 3:11; 22:20. It fits the immediate context; it is in harmony with 1 Corinthians 15, and it agrees with the New Testament attitude towards Christ's return.

23. **The grace of our Lord Jesus Christ [be] with you:** ... The favour of, —LOCK, —KLGS, —RTHM ... the blessing of, —TCNT, —GDSP ... May the Lord Jesus love you! —BECK.

24. **My love [be] with you all in Christ Jesus. Amen:** ... My Christian love to all of you, —TCNT ... My love to you all, —BRCL ... My love is with you all in Christ Jesus, —FNTN ... through Christ Jesus, —GDSP ... So be it, —BB.

**16:23, 24.** Paul desired that the Corinthians should be constantly attended by the marvelous grace of "our Lord Jesus Christ," that it should be the constant source of ministry and blessing to them. It was a common farewell from Paul and was expanded in 2 Corinthians 13:14.

Paul also added a note of affection peculiar to this letter, but it was fitting in light of some of the harsh directives he had to give the Corinthians. He noted his love for them all, and he desired it in an abiding sense ("with you").

He noted the foundation and bond for love among them all: the bond of Jesus Christ. Division, bigotry, and non-Christian behavior were all products of the Corinthians' living. It should be otherwise.

It is fitting that the last words should show the great heart of the apostle and, even more importantly, the bond of all things, the person of Jesus Christ. Paul's last word was "Jesus."

Of Paul's writers, the first three mentioned were from the church at Corinth. Paul had baptized Stephanus' family (1:16). Timothy, of course, was Paul's son in the Faith.

# 2 CORINTHIANS

## Overview

The entire Second Epistle to the Corinthians deals with the need for Paul to reestablish his apostolic authority in the church at Corinth. The epistle can be outlined as follows:

## I. Paul's Apostolic Ministry (1:1-7:16)

Initially, Paul does not engage in an open confrontation with the false apostles who have entered the church. He does that in the last division of the epistle. In the first division he states his apostolic authority positively, explaining to the Corinthians the ministry with which God has entrusted him. One might get a glimpse of Paul's opponents in the background all the time, but he only hints at their presence in the church and in a few passages defends himself openly against the suspicion and accusations of these people. This approach creates a rather different tone in the first and last divisions of the epistle. While the last division is strongly polemic, the first division is richly edifying. The same concern for the church characterizes the entire epistle. It is probably the most personal of all Paul's letters, and both the first and last divisions show the same warm concern.

It is not easy to subdivide the first division of the epistle. The whole presentation is connected like links in a chain, and it is not always easy to see where a new section starts. Of course, many subdivisions are possible.

Some characteristic features can help us get an overview of the material. As mentioned, this first division is concerned with Paul's apostolic ministry, and it is possible to identify four sections which directly relate to various aspects of his work. We note that two sections refer to the comfort Paul received during his tribulations. These two sections form the beginning and end of the first division of the epistle. Finally, there is a section where Paul explains changes in his traveling plans which forced him to postpone the visit he had intended to make to Corinth. From this point the first division of the epistle falls into seven subsections. First there is a short opening greeting where Paul introduces himself as Christ's apostle, a truth which confirms his authority from the very beginning.

## A. Comfort in Christ (1:3-11)

Paul wrote of the need of comfort. He penned this epistle just after one of the most severe periods of trial in his life, and the crisis was not totally past. His continuing anxiety is evident from remarks throughout the epistle. In addition to outward opposition and persecution, great problems had arisen in many of the new churches Paul had founded. The Galatians had been influenced by agitators from Judaism and were on the verge of backsliding from the true Christian faith. In Corinth false apostles had entered the picture. They had undermined Paul's authority and were destroying the great work of God which had been accomplished there. Yet with all of this pressure on him, the apostle exclaimed, "Blessed be God, the God of all comfort!" (1:3).

*1. Comfort in Tribulation (1:3-7).* The apostle had a share in Christ's suffering (Romans 8:17; Philippians 3:10; 1 Peter 4:13). Therefore he could say, "So our consolation also aboundeth by Christ" (1:5). As always, Paul related his experiences to the great spiritual principles, the spiritual laws of life. Here was a man who had gone through the most severe tribulations and now was giving his views on the mystery of suffering. The reason God had allowed these heavy trials was that he could comfort others who were distressed. He could do this because of the comfort he had received from the Lord. His trials had not been just for his own experience but in order to enable him to give the comfort of Christ to others. In his own deep distress Paul felt the assurance that the Corinthians also would be delivered from their difficulties. "As ye are partakers of the sufferings, so shall ye be also of the consolation" (1:7).

*2. Comfort in Tribulation Recently Endured (1:8-11).* Paul did not write about old experiences. His severe period of tribulation was one he had just passed through, and he wanted the Corinthians to know this. They had added to his burden which was heavy enough before. Now that he was telling them, he hoped they would be "helping together by prayer" (1:11). The Corinthians probably had a knowledge of Paul's tribulations in Asia Minor, but they did not know how serious they had been. Now he wrote that he and his coworkers had even doubted at times whether they would continue to stay alive. Yes, they had the sentence of death in themselves so they would know that only God's intervention could save them. They had trusted the God who raises the dead and Paul could testify: "Who delivered us from so great a death, and doth deliver" (1:10).

## B. Changed Traveling Plans (1:12-2:17)

*1. Accused of Instability (1:12-22).* After this opening, Paul found it necessary to discuss immediately a matter about which his opponents in Corinth seemed to have made the most. He related that in the beginning he had planned twice to come to Corinth—first on his way to Macedonia and later on his way back from Macedonia (1:15, 16). He had informed the church in Corinth of these plans. However, he had changed his original intention and had gone to Macedonia directly without visiting Corinth. Now there were some who cited this as evidence of Paul's being inconsistent and fickle, that he said yes when he meant no. They seem to have implied that the apostle was not led by God in his traveling plans but made his own plans "according to the flesh" (1:17).

Paul spoke out strongly against these accusations that he was a person one could not rely on. He declared that he had lived a holy and consistent life among them (1:12). The Son of God, Christ Jesus, whom Paul preached to them "was not yea and nay" and neither was Paul. In Christ all the promises of God have their yea and amen (1:20). Paul also had kept his promises. He was faithful as his Lord is faithful.

*2. Cause of the Change (1:23-2:2).* There was an actual reason for Paul's changing his route (Jesus himself had once changed His travel plans: John 7:8). Paul had received information from Corinth which gave him two reasons for waiting before making his visit. First, it would spare the church the punishment he would have to inflict against people who had sinned (1:23). "I determined this with myself, that I would not come again to you in heaviness" (2:1). It seems Paul had made a previous short visit to Corinth, and it had not been a joyful one. He would rather avoid such an experience again. He did not want to be made sorry by those who ought to make him glad or to make sorry those whom he wanted to make glad (2:2, 3). Therefore, Paul postponed the visit so the church would have time to correct the bad situation before he arrived.

*3. "The Epistle of Tears" (2:3-11).* Instead of coming personally to Corinth, Paul had chosen to write an epistle. Now he tells the people he had written under great emotion: "Out of much affliction and anguish of heart I wrote unto you with many tears" (2:4). The traditional interpretation is that the epistle Paul spoke of here is the First Epistle to the Corinthians. However, during the last century opinions about this have differed. Some believe that in the period between the first two epistles Paul had paid a visit to Corinth as well as writing an epistle which has been lost. One of the arguments for this view is that the first epistle is not sharp enough to have made the church as sorry as Paul speaks of here and would not have caused him so much grief in writing it. In the first epistle he did not mention another visit to Corinth which should have caused grief, so the visit probably took place after the epistle was written, i.e., shortly before Paul wrote the second epistle.

On the other hand, some object to this more recent theory on the grounds that there would not be time for such a visit by Paul in the period between the two epistles. The change in travel plans which Paul explained in the second epistle had already taken place when he wrote the first epistle. In that message he said the same thing as he now says in the second, i.e., that he would not come to Corinth before he had been in Macedonia (1 Corinthians 16:5).

Although some object that Paul could not have felt such great distress when he wrote the first epistle, it must be admitted it is difficult for anyone to know how deeply concerned and sad Paul was when he wrote certain parts of this epistle (Odeberg). H.L. Goudge says it was probably easier for Paul to shed tears than it is for his modern interpreters (cf. Philippians 3:18) (*Westminster Commentaries, Second Corinthians,* p. 13). If we look at the sections in question it seems it is indeed "an epistle of tears" for the one who wrote it as well as for those who received it (1 Corinthians 1:10-13; 3:1-3; 5:1-6; 6:8-10; 8:10-12; cf. 15:12, 33, 34). From these sections it appears that there were divisions in the church (1 Corinthians 1:10). The Corinthians were carnal (1 Corinthians 3:3). Fornication was reported among them and they did not mourn over this sin (1 Corinthians 5:1, 2). They mistreated other believers, and Paul declared that those who did this would not inherit the kingdom of God (1 Corinthians 6:8, 9). Some of the Corinthians were eating meat in the temple where idols were worshiped (1 Corinthians 8:10). Some denied the resurrection (1 Corinthians 15:12) and Paul had to write to them: "Awake to righteousness, and sin not; for some have not the knowledge of God: I speak this to your shame" (1 Corinthians 15:34).

Thus Paul wrote in 2 Corinthians 2:4 that he penned his last letter with anguish and tears. He continued by saying that since the man who had fallen into sin had repented he should be restored to fellowship instead of being expelled (2:6, 7). It is generally believed that this was the same individual Paul wrote about in 1 Corinthians 5:1. However, if the theory about a lost "epistle of tears" is accepted, he must have been referring to another person who had fallen into sin. Some have thought this referred to a sin against Paul personally or he would not have reacted so strongly. If this is true, then the man in 1 Corinthians 5:1 had committed an ethical sin, while the one referred to in 2 Corinthians 2:5 was simply a "trouble maker." Different arguments have been presented for this point of view, but no proof has been found.

*4. Paul in Troas and Macedonia (2:12-17).* We meet here a peculiarity in the composition of the first division of the epistle. Paul wrote of his traveling plan and his journey from Ephesus to Macedonia in three different sections: 1:15, 16; 2:12, 13; and 7:5. In the middle section he also referred back to the first section concerning a plan which was changed to the one mentioned in 1 Corinthians 16:5. Paul continued speaking of the unrest he felt in his spirit over the Corinthian church when he came to Troas and did not meet Titus there in accordance with their previous plans. Then Paul traveled to Macedonia in order to meet Titus. But he ended the story abruptly and said nothing about this meeting or the news he received about Corinth. Instead, he took up again the train of thought he began in 7:4. After the brief interruption to tell of his visit with Titus, he added what was the main content of the first division of the epistle, i.e., the statement of his ministry as an apostle.

Paul wrote that when he came to Troas there was an open door for preaching the gospel. However, his knowledge of conditions in Corinth burdened him heavily. In addition to his personal feelings and his love for the church there, Paul had considered Corinth strategic to his missionary activity. Corinth was an important junction, a link between the eastern and western worlds. He had planned to travel farther west to Rome and all the way to Spain, but this would be very difficult if conditions in Corinth did not improve. If believers there were influenced by Judaizers, Gnostics, and teachers of so-called wisdom, it would mean that this strategic church had become a stronghold of the enemy. No matter what could be accomplished in Troas, it would not compensate for what was lost in Corinth (J.B. Meyer). Filled with deep unrest, Paul therefore left Troas and went to Macedonia to meet

Titus as soon as possible. He wanted information about developments in Corinth.

Paul interrupted the description of his travels to thank God who always causes believers to triumph in Christ. He did not surrender to defeat. Even if preaching the gospel has sharply contrasting results, (life and death, salvation and judgment), the work of God still moves on to victory. In the section composed of 2:14-17 Paul referred back to what he had already written. At the same time this passage is a transition that opens the great section about the glory of the apostles' ministry (chapters 3 to 6).

## C. Ministers of a New Covenant (3:1-18)

*1. The Epistle of Christ (3:1-3).* Paul had just finished telling of those who corrupt the Word of God for their own benefit (2:17). Now the apostle continued by hinting at "some others" who needed "commendation." They were infiltrating the church. They were false apostles, and for the first time he referred to them directly. These individuals had recommendations from certain people, and they made the most of the fact that Paul did not appear to have any. They used this to sow doubt about his relationship with the original apostles in Jerusalem (cf. Part III.A.3). Paul replied that he did not need any commendation from men (cf. Galatians 1:15-17). He was called to be an apostle by the Lord himself (1:1), and the Lord had written Paul's letter of recommendation. The Corinthians themselves were part of his recommendation. They were the work of God, brought into the kingdom of God through Paul's ministry. His letter of recommendation was not written on stone tablets but on "tables of flesh," i.e., the hearts of believers. Paul's recommendation had not been written with ink but by the Spirit of the living God.

*2. The Letter and the Spirit (3:4-6).* Verse 3 refers to God's covenant between himself and Israel in the Old Testament. This covenant had as its basis the Law which Moses received, written on stone tablets (Exodus 34:1). The prophecies of Jeremiah 31:33 and Ezekiel 11:19 and 36:26 foretold a day when God would make a new covenant where He would write His law in the minds and hearts of men. The covenant into which Paul's ministry had brought the Corinthians was this new covenant, not the old covenant associated with tablets of stone.

Paul hinted here at some who had letters of recommendation but falsified the Word of God. It seems clear that Paul was engaging in a thinly veiled attack on these heretics in his continuing discussion. The Judaizers clung to the old covenant that emphasized the letter of the Law. Paul was a minister of the new covenant based not on the letter of the Law but the spirit it was intended to convey (3:6). It was the Spirit of God who breathed life into the new covenant.

In making a transition to the new theme, Paul changed his use of the illustration he had been employing. First he contrasted ink with the Holy Spirit, then stone tablets and tablets of flesh. Ink and stone tablets do not, of course, belong together (Kvalbein), but it served Paul's intention to use this double picture of contrast.

The two different covenants are referred to by "Spirit" and "letter." This was Paul's way of showing the contrast between Law and grace. This does not mean the old covenant was worthless, for it served God's purpose for its time. Its weakness was that it only showed what God expected of men but gave them no power to keep His commandments. Under the new covenant we do not merely read the "letter" of the Word and try our best in our own strength to keep it. Through grace we have received power by the indwelling Spirit to obey the law God has written in our innermost being.

We must not misunderstand Paul's teaching by imagining he was saying that Scripture is the letter that brings death and that under the new covenant we are "free" from the Scriptures. The apostle's point is that the Judaizers were sticking to the letter of the Scripture but rejecting the Christ through whom we receive the Spirit who has inspired the Scripture. The Spirit inspired the Old Testament as well as the New, and the Old Testament testified of Christ (John 5:39, 40). In their apparent loyalty to the "letter," the Judaizers were ignoring what the Spirit had taught through the Scriptures. Thus they were destroying themselves by the Scripture they professed to believe. The testimony of Jesus is the spirit of the prophetic word (Revelation 19:10). The one who rejects the Spirit by rejecting Jesus has nothing left but the dead letter. This is the condition of the one who, in this age of grace, continues to "serve in the oldness of the letter" (Romans 7:6).

*3. The Veil and the Glory (3:7-18).* The apostles were ministers of a new covenant and the differences between the new and old were great. The old covenant did in fact have its glory, but it was a glory which disappeared just as the glory on Moses' face disappeared. Paul presented a series of contrasts. The difference between the old and new covenants is the difference between letter and Spirit (3:6), death and life (3:6), and condemnation and righteousness (3:9).

As an illustration, Paul mentioned the veil Moses put over his face when he had finished speaking to the people (Exodus 34:29, 30). That veil hid from the people the glory of the Lord which was reflected in Moses' face. The glory was hidden so the people would not see it fade away. Paul said a veil also covers the old covenant, the Old Testament (3:14). This veil of unbelief kept the Jews from seeing that the old covenant was fulfilled in Christ and that its glory had passed away. This is totally different from the experience of those who follow Christ: "We all, with open face beholding as in a glass the glory of the Lord, are changed into the same image from glory to glory, even as by the Spirit of the Lord" (3:18).

## D. Honesty in the Ministry: (4:1-5:15)

As one who had received such a ministry, Paul spoke openly and frankly and did not lose courage. He was constantly impelled by strong motives. First, he had received his ministry through grace. He owed it to God's mercy (4:1), and his faith in that mercy kept him fearless. Second, Paul had the hope of eternal life and eternal glory (5:1). Third, the love of Christ constrained him (5:14).

*1. The Motive of Faith (4:1-15).* "We faint not!" Paul declared. He expressed the honesty of his faith. He had received his ministry by grace, for he had not been deserving of it nor suited for it. Faith gave Paul the ability to speak honestly, and he was influenced by the indwelling Spirit who constantly quickened his faith (4:13). Paul wrote he had "renounced the hidden things of dishonesty, not walking in craftiness" (4:2). Those words imply a defense against the baseless accusations leveled at Paul. He assured the Corinthians that he acted openly in everything. He who stands before the Lord with an unveiled face (3:18) does not have to hide his face from men. Satan blinds the minds of unbelievers (4:3, 4), but some will be won to Christ anyway, and the gospel will be preached to more and more people (4:15). Paul had his spiritual treasure in a human container, and his tribulations and temptations kept him reminded of this. It is as though he was constantly delivered to death, yet the life of Christ continued to be active through him (4:10-12).

*2. The Motive of Hope (4:16-5:10).* The other reason Paul did not lose his courage was that he possessed a hope. That hope assured him that if our physical house (the human body) falls into ruins, yet the true man—the inward man—is being continually renewed. If the earthly tent we live in is finally taken down, "we have a building of God, a house not made with hands, eternal in the heavens" (5:1). Paul longed to move into that house. "Therefore we are always confident," he said, that when we are absent from the body we will be present with the Lord (5:6, 8). This hope impelled him in his work: "Wherefore we labor, that, whether present or absent, we may be accepted of him" (5:9). In this great hope there was also a holy fear: "We must all appear before the judgment seat of Christ" (5:10). "Knowing therefore the terror of the Lord, we persuade men" (5:11). This hope makes the believer invincible. It transforms all his suffering and humiliation into glory and exaltation.

*3. The Motive of Love (5:14, 15).* The third motive Paul referred to was: "The love of Christ constraineth us." In this verse, Paul was probably referring to love in its fullest extent, i.e., Christ's love for all men as well as His love poured out into believers' hearts by the Spirit of God (Romans 5:5). Paul was thinking here of Christ's love for us and our love for Him. He loved us first. It was that love which led Him to die as our sacrifice. His love for us is the foundation of all Christian love. Christ revealed His love for all by dying for all. Because He died for all, those who live must not live any longer for themselves alone but for Him who died for them and rose again.

## E. The Ministry of Reconciliation (5:16-21)

The ministry Paul had received was a ministry of reconciliation. It was based on the truth that God in Christ reconciled the world to himself. Paul became a participant in that reconciliation and prayed in Christ's stead, "Be ye reconciled to God" (5:20).

Paul's ministry was not based on knowing Christ "after the flesh" (5:16). Again we get a glimpse of Paul's opponents who appealed to a natural, human knowledge of Jesus. If we once knew Christ in such a way, Paul says, we do not know Him that way now. Paul's knowledge of Christ was a new spiritual knowledge obtained from the Spirit of God. That is why Paul did not know anyone "after the flesh" (5:16). He looked at his fellowmen in an entirely different way, i.e., as men for whom Christ died. And he who is in Christ is a new creature; the old is passed away, all things are become new.

Paul wrote that God had committed to him and his fellow apostles the "word of reconciliation" (5:19). That word of reconciliation is based on this truth: "He hath made him to be sin for us, who knew no sin; that we might be made the righteousness of God in him" (5:21). The message of the redemption provided in Christ was the central theme of Paul's preaching. Shortly after he wrote this epistle he came to Corinth, where he wrote the Epistle to the Romans, that mighty document of evangelical truth. We note here and in 2 Corinthians 5:15-21 how the message of the Cross penetrated and dominated all of Paul's preaching.

## F. The Ministry of Admonition (6:1-7:3)

*1. Exhortations by Paul (6:1, 2).* Paul's apostolic ministry was also a ministry of admonition (6:1). We meet this in all his writings. His epistles are often divided distinctly into sections of teaching and sections of admonition. The admonition is directed basically toward believers and is a vital part of the gospel. The intent of admonition is to "present every man perfect in Christ Jesus" (Colossians

1:28). All admonition is "by the Lord Jesus Christ" (1 Thessalonians 4:1, 2; 2 Thessalonians 3:12), "by the name of our Lord Jesus Christ" (1 Corinthians 1:10), "for the Lord Jesus Christ's sake, and for the love of the Spirit" (Romans 15:30), "by the meekness and gentleness of Christ" (2 Corinthians 10:1), "by the mercies of God" (Romans 12:1). "Receive not the grace of God in vain" is a challenge to bring forth fruit which demonstrates that our conversion is genuine.

2. *Without Offense (6:3-10)*. Paul was determined that his ministry should not be blamed. For this reason he strove diligently to avoid giving offense in any way (6:3). Through the false accusations of his enemies he might have had a bad reputation with some and might have been considered by them as being in disgrace rather than honor. But he always determined to live a blameless life so these accusations would be seen as false.

3. *Fellowship and Separation (6:11-7:1)*. This section concludes with a double admonition. First there is a plea to the Corinthians to enlarge their hearts and give Paul the room in their affections which he ought to have. He wanted their confidence and love, reminding them that he had never treated anyone unfairly nor wronged any of them. Then Paul gave a strong warning for believers not to be unequally yoked together with unbelievers.

## G. Comforted by the Corinthians (7:4-16)

Here Paul resumed the train of thought from 2:13. In that verse he wrote of leaving Troas to go to Macedonia. Yet in 7:5 he said that when he came to Macedonia, "our flesh had no rest." In Troas Paul had a peaceful time, but in Macedonia he faced difficulties and different kinds of opposition: "We were troubled on every side; without were fightings, within were fears."

Then he recounted the comfort he received when he finally met Titus, who came from Corinth with good news. Much in the church had already been made right. Paul's epistle to them had had its effect. Most of the Corinthians had come to their senses and turned away from the false apostles. Now they had renewed their interest in Paul and his coworkers and loved him (7:12). Titus had received so much encouragement from the church that his joy was shared by Paul (7:13). The first division of the epistle concludes with Paul's strong expression of his confidence in the church.

## II. Help for Jerusalem (8:1-9:15)

The second division of this epistle concerns money. Since Paul had been informed by Titus that the situation had improved in the church at Corinth, he could discuss again the matter about which he wrote them the previous year (1 Corinthians 16:1-4).

This concerned the assistance many churches had begun for the Christians suffering in Judea. No doubt Paul himself had taken the initiative. When Paul and the original apostles met in Jerusalem, one thing on which they agreed was to remember the poor (Galatians 2:6-10). At that time Paul and Barnabas had already brought a gift from the Gentile church in Antioch (Acts 11:27-30).

The part of the Second Epistle to the Corinthians which concerns financial help for the Jerusalem believers covers two chapters and can be divided into three sections: (1) Motive of the gift: 8:1-15. (2) The task of Titus: 8:16-9:15. (3) The blessing of the gift: 9:6-15.

## A. The Motive of the Gift (8:1-15)

1. *The Example of the Macedonians (8:1-5)*. As an encouragement to the Corinthians to give, Paul referred first to the example of the Macedonians. The apostle knew that it is often easier for people to make a sacrifice when they know others have already done so. The churches in Macedonia were very poor, yet they wanted a part in the financial ministry to their fellow believers in Jerusalem. Paul said their attitude came from God himself, that it was the "grace of God bestowed on the churches of Macedonia" (8:1).

2. *The Spiritual Abundance of the Corinthians (8:6-8)*. It is interesting to note how often Paul spoke of spiritual abundance in the church at Corinth, especially when he rebuked them at the same time because so much was wrong. Paul was not blind to their good side! He challenged them by saying that since they were rich in so many spiritual ways, they must also become rich in this performance of financial help. They must give in a way that was proportionate to the spiritual abundance with which they had been blessed. A church's spiritual background often determines the people's financial sacrifices more than their economic situation.

3. *The Example of Christ (8:9)*. The example of Christ himself is the third motive Paul presented for their giving. This verse says in essence that Christ became poor in order to make us rich. Thus the Corinthians' financial giving would express the mind of Christ. It would follow His great example.

4. *Similarity Between Believers (8:10-15)*. The Bible teaches a reasonable distribution of material benefits. Paul referred to the manna God gave the Israelites, pointing out that he who gathered much had none left over, while the one who gathered less had no shortage. To avoid allowing a small number of people to possess most of the property, God instituted the year of sabbath and the year of jubilee in Israel. At that time, property was returned to the original owner or his family. The New Testament makes frequent references to the

care of those who need assistance. In fact, Christianity is not compatible with indifference to those in need (1 John 3:17)). Paul only expected the Corinthians to give according to their ability (8:11), although he praised the Macedonians for giving beyond their means (8:3). There must be the balance of justice in the matter. Nobody can expect to live off the gifts of others when the givers are poor themselves. However, the poverty in the church in Jerusalem was well known. At the beginning the members of that church who had property sold it and contributed to the common treasury (Acts 4:32). But now they were in financial straits. Possibly persecution had something to do with this.

## B. The Task of Titus (8:16-9:5)

1. *Supervision of the Distribution (8:16-24).* It is evident from 12:16 that suspicion had been thrown on Paul. Apparently some were saying he had used some of the contributions for personal gain. Of course it was wicked of them to try to hurt Paul's reputation this way, but it is interesting how he responded to the accusation. He ordered the churches to choose their own representatives to collect the money and take it to Jerusalem, where they were to deliver it to the church. Paul would not receive the money himself and he was not willing that his close friend and co-worker Titus should bear all the responsibility. "Avoiding this, that no man should blame us in this abundance which is administered by us: providing for honest things, not only in the sight of the Lord, but also in the sight of men" (8:20, 21).

2. *The Collection Resumed (9:1-5).* When Paul sent Titus and others to Corinth, it was to resume the work of collecting financial aid for Jerusalem. When the false apostles were in power, there was probably little to give others! But now their influence had been reduced and circumstances were becoming more normal, so the interrupted work of love could be continued. Paul reminded the Corinthians of their promise. He told them he had commended them to the church in Macedonia when they agreed the year before to make the collection. If this was just an empty promise, both Paul and the Corinthians would be embarrassed by having this known among other churches. This must not happen!

## C. The Blessing of the Gift (9:6-15)

1. *Reaping Blessing (9:6-11).* Paul knew this church that was filled with newly converted people needed teaching about the blessing of giving. He used the illustration of sowing seed corn. The sower does not consider the seed lost; neither is a gift lost if it is made in love. It is seed which gives hope for a harvest because God makes it grow. But the stingy person who sows little cannot expect a bountiful harvest. To the one who gives, blessing shall be given. God himself gives willingly and richly, and He loves the one who gives with the same attitude (cf. Isaiah 55:10; Hosea 10:12; James 1:5, 17).

2. *Causing Thanksgiving to God (9:12, 13).* Paul considered it the highest joy and reward for others to thank God for the testimony of a believer's life (Ephesians 1:16; Philippians 1:3; Colossians 1:3; 1 Thessalonians 1:2; Philemon 4). The Corinthians' gift would cause many to thank God for them. They would be praised not only for their financial contribution but for their obedience to the gospel of Christ.

3. *Creating Spiritual Fellowship (9:13-15).* Those who received the gift would thank God for the fellowship they had with Gentile believers (9:13). This was one of Paul's chief motives for being so eager to arrange the gift. It would have great meaning for the unity of the Church. It would demonstrate that "the middle wall of partition" had been torn down (Ephesians 2:14). It would prompt the Jewish believers to pray for their Gentile brethren with a new sense of love for them (9:14). The whole matter opens up an eternal perspective. Many times Christians do not meet their benefactors personally on earth, but one day they will meet. Paul ended his "collection sermon" with praise: "Thanks be unto God for his unspeakable gift!"

## III. Paul's Apostolic Authority (10:1-13:14)

As we have seen, the Second Epistle to the Corinthians carries strong emphasis by Paul concerning his calling to be an apostle. In the first part of the epistle he referred to the glory of the new covenant of which he had become a minister. He built his defense by positive statements without paying any particular attention to his accusers and their accusations. Yet we do get glimpses of these opponents in the background. In 2:17 Paul said bluntly that these people falsify the Word of God. In 3:1 he referred to them as "some others" who need letters of recommendation.

In the third division of the epistle Paul attacked his opponents openly. First he unveiled them as heretics and false apostles and rebuked the Corinthians for being attracted toward such people. Then in forced self-praise, Paul compared himself with the pseudo-apostles.

## A. False Apostles (10:1-11:21)

1. *Who They Are.* Just who were these opponents of Paul and what was their doctrine? This was no mystery to the Corinthians who received this epistle. They knew very well who Paul meant by "certain others" (3:1; 10:12). He did not have to give details about the doctrine and activity of these opponents.

However, Paul did give information about them. They were not from Corinth, but came from the outside (11:4). They were Jews (11:22), and they had a letter of recommendation from some source (3:1). From 10:10 and 11:6 it is evident that they considered themselves superior to Paul in speaking ability (1 Corinthians 2:1). These false teachers had not founded any churches. Instead, they had invaded territory where others had done the work and exploited their labors for their own benefit (10:15). They also used the church for their financial benefit (11:12, 20). Their behavior was very arrogant, even offending members of the church (11:20).

Paul characterized these opponents as "false apostles, deceitful workers, transforming themselves into the apostles of Christ" (11:13), while in reality they were Satan's servants transformed into supposedly ministers of righteousness (11:15). They preached "another Jesus" and "another gospel." They had "another spirit" completely opposed to the Spirit of Christ (11:4).

We do not need to know more than this about these who were causing such division by their heresy. However, it is possible to some extent to find a more detailed picture of what their teaching consisted. The doctrine of these false apostles was probably not unique to Corinth. It is unlikely that they were merely an isolated group. The error had not arisen in Corinth but was imported from without. Therefore, there must have been traces of similar error in other early churches.

From the writings of the New Testament and especially from the epistles it is clear that the early churches fought on two fronts. The false doctrine that threatened to penetrate the congregations was partly Gentile philosophy and partly Jewish legalism based on the Law. In the Epistle to the Galatians Paul opposed the infiltration of Judaism. He spoke against the Greek "wisdom" also, especially in the First Epistle to the Corinthians. From Paul's writing it is evident that the "wisdom" in Colosse did not have the same intellectual form as the wisdom and philosophy being proclaimed in Corinth. The Gnosticism in Colossae had a more esoteric character, being a "wisdom" reserved for the initiated ones and consisting of a mixture of Greek philosophy and Oriental myths.

However, of greater interest to us is that in Colosse the Greek wisdom had evidently become mixed with Judaism. False teachers there were following Jewish food laws, observing the Sabbath and the feasts (Colossians 2:16). What is then more natural than the development of similar error in Corinth? The "wisdom" in Corinth was just as susceptible to Judaistic influence as the "wisdom" in Colosse. The different tendencies and teachings did not exist in isolation but had influenced each other mutually. As in other Gentile churches there were groups of Jews in Corinth along with Jew-

ish proselytes. Because of their synagogue background they were particularly vulnerable to Judaistic preaching. These may have formed the "Cephas party" (1 Corinthians 1:12).

It is worth noting that among the dispersed Jews a Jewish/Hellenistic religion had developed at this time. It was propagated by wandering Jewish preachers and originated with Philo of Alexandria, the Jewish philosopher. His central theme was that the Old Testament contained the highest philosophy which he would interpret for the "enlightened" and well-bred world in the vocabulary of Greek philosophy. In certain circles the division between Jewish theology and Greek philosophy was thus about to be torn down. It is just as reasonable that such a Greek-Jewish popular philosophy would appeal to certain groups in the new Gentile churches. It is also obvious that such a syncretism represented a deadly danger to the purity of the Christian message.

This period of early Christianity was a time of unusual doctrinal conflict. Within paganism as well as the Jewish religion there were many ideologies that contended with each other and influenced each other. The Judaism which penetrated the Christian churches was probably no united movement. In fact, the Jewish agitators sometimes acted differently from others in different areas, just as other false teachers did.

This may explain why Paul in the Second Epistle to the Corinthians did not attack the doctrine of the false apostles point by point. He could write to the Colossians: "Let no man therefore judge you in meat, or in drink, or in respect of a holyday, or of the new moon, or of the sabbath days" (Colossians 2:16). In Colosse a Jewish-Gnostic party had begun to agitate for celebrating the Sabbath and observing Jewish food laws. He could write to the Galatians: "Behold, I Paul say unto you, that if ye be circumcised, Christ shall profit you nothing" (Galatians 5:2), because in Galatia the Judaizers preached circumcision. But nothing seems to indicate that the false teachers in Corinth demanded such things of their audience—at least not yet. Up to this time they were being very cunning (cf. 11:3) as heretics always are. Their teaching was still in the early stages and was not as clearly exposed as error was in other places. If Paul referred to what the Judaizers were doing elsewhere, the false apostles in Corinth could claim no connection with them.

Another point to consider is that doctrinal questions in themselves had been secondary with the false apostles in Corinth. Their first goal was to seize power in the church and enrich themselves financially at the believers' expense.

The motive of false teachers was to make the gospel as widely acceptable as possible. To Paul the real message of Christianity was "the word of the cross," the deity of Christ, His atoning death, and His resurrection. To the false apostles, however, these teachings were obstacles. Their "gospel" was an ethical view of life. Their "Jesus" was no more than the promoter of this view. Their doctrine was a kind of popularized and "christened" Pharisaism. In Judaistic circles there had evidently been a tendency to adapt Christianity so it could be accepted as a part of the Jewish religion.

But at least in Corinth the Jewish teachers of error were concerned first of all with a practical goal: to make a financial profit for themselves. Thus there was probably no unified theme among them and they did not appear to be advocating any particular philosophy. They wanted to distort the gospel so it could pass for a "reasonable" view of life and not seem too different from other doctrinal systems of that time. When they tried to penetrate the church in Corinth they presented their teaching so carefully that it would provoke as little resistance as possible (Odeberg). Thus their error became an even greater threat to this church which consisted mostly of the recently converted.

Undoubtedly there were distinct proofs of heresy in Corinth or Paul could not have attacked his opponents so strongly. But it seems in fact that at first the false apostles were most concerned with undermining his influence. They attacked him personally. The conflict was over Paul's apostolic authority.

Therefore, Paul had to meet his opponents at their point of attack even though this must have been unpleasant to him personally. Unlike the epistles to the Galatians and Colossians, the Second Epistle to the Corinthians is not a confrontation with specific errors but a message about true and false apostles.

The false apostles rejected Paul's position as a preacher and apostle, "a teacher of the Gentiles in faith and verity" (1 Timothy 2:7). Thus they did raise the issue of doctrinal contrasts. Their teaching was a contrast to Paul's gospel (Romans 1:16; 16:25; 2 Corinthians 4:3; 2 Timothy 2:8), whose central theme was salvation by grace, not works, salvation by faith, not "wisdom." Therefore, the message of the false apostles was "another gospel" (11:4). They added to the gospel, subtracted from it, changed it, so their teaching ceased to be a real gospel.

*2. The Tolerance of Heresy.* The situation in Corinth was made all the more critical by the church's tolerance of the heretics. Paul had led these people to Christ and would have expected them to come to his defense when the false teachers began to slander him. Yet they listened readily to these individuals and did not object to the preaching of "another gospel" among them.

Afflicted in his spirit and in deep earnest, Paul wrote to them: "If he that cometh preacheth another Jesus, whom we have not preached, or if ye receive another spirit, which ye have not received, or another gospel, which ye have not accepted, ye might well bear with him" (11:4).

Paul's subject here is the actual situation in Corinth. He was not dealing with possibilities or suppositions. He wrote about things which had already taken place. The Corinthians were tolerating the behavior of the intruders as well as their false doctrine. Thus they were partners in others' sins (1 Timothy 5:22) and accomplices in the evil works of the heretics (cf. 2 John 11). That is why Paul's warnings were so sharp—the souls of the Corinthian believers were in danger.

Paul's strong reaction sprang from his deep concern for these, his converts. He was appalled at the thought of their being unfaithful to Christ. He used John the Baptist's illustration, picturing himself as "the friend of the bridegroom" who has won a bride for Christ: "I have espoused you to one husband, that I may present you as a chaste virgin to Christ. But I fear, lest by any means, as the serpent beguiled Eve through his subtilty, so your minds should be corrupted from the simplicity that is in Christ" (11:2, 3). The Christians at Corinth did not belong to Paul and were not baptized in his name (1 Corinthians 1:13). He had brought them into fellowship with Christ. Paul's picture was a well-known Old Testament illustration of God's people being called His wife. The Jews interpreted the Song of Solomon as an allegory about the Lord and the elect nation. Paul employed the same figure concerning Christ and the Church (cf. Ephesians 5:31, 32), but with the variation that the Church is compared to a betrothed young lady who must maintain her purity until the wedding day. The wedding will take place at Jesus' coming back to earth (cf. Revelation 19:7). This admonition keeps recurring in Paul's epistles, i.e., that believers must be diligent about keeping their purity until the day of Christ's return (Ephesians 5:25; Philippians 1:10; 1 Thessalonians 5:23). The believers in Corinth and all others Paul had won for God would be his praise when Christ comes back (1:14—cf. Philippians 2:16).

But now Paul was full of fear for the church in Corinth. He was afraid believers there would be deceived and seduced even as Satan through the serpent beguiled Eve through his subtilty. The loyalty of the people to Christ was in danger because the false apostles were destroying the simplicity of the gospel. The Jesus they preached was "another Jesus," not the Jesus Paul had preached. Their spirit was "another spirit," not the Spirit of God the Corinthians had received. The intruders' gospel was another gospel.

Paul used two different words for "another." When he said these individuals preach another Jesus he used the Greek word *allon*, which can refer to the same person but in a distorted sense. The false apostles preached about Jesus of Nazareth, not another Jesus from a different place, but they gave a completely false picture of Him. When Paul continued by saying the heretics had another spirit, he used the word *heteron*, which means another individual, one who is a different kind. False preaching about Christ was connected with a totally strange spirit. The Holy Spirit glorifies the true Christ and only the true Christ (John 16:14). When one confesses Jesus Christ as Lord it is a testimony to the activity of the Spirit of God (1 Corinthians 12:3). The spirit that confesses Jesus is the Christ who has come in the flesh is of God, but the spirit of antichrist proclaims a false christ (1 John 4:2, 3).

Also, when Paul said the false apostles preached another gospel he used the term *heteron*, signifying that the "gospel" they proclaimed was something quite different from the true gospel. In Galatians 1:6, 7 Paul used the difference of meaning in the two words and said the Galatians had turned away to a different gospel which was not another gospel of the same kind as the true gospel. In reality there is no other gospel than the one preached about the One who died for our sins and rose for our justification (Romans 4:25).

The heretics preached a false gospel, and it was alarming that the Corinthians were tolerating such a distortion of the truth. They were also enduring the bragging and self-exaltation of these men. With considerable irony Paul said the Corinthians were so wise that they endured fools. In other words, they showed their high intelligence by enjoying all the foolish bragging. Even more humiliating was the fact that the Corinthians tolerated the arrogant behavior of the "apostles." In one verse (11:20) Paul characterized this behavior in five indignant expressions, trying to bring the Corinthians to their senses so they could see how outrageous it was for them to be treated this way.

(1) They were being brought into bondage: The tyrannical heretics would enjoy having the Corinthians as their personal slaves. But even worse was the spiritual bondage into which they had brought their victims. The word Paul used for making slaves, *katadouloi*, is used in just one other New Testament verse. It is Galatians 2:4 where Paul writes about the Judaizers who had brought the Galatians under the bondage of the Law.

(2) They were being devoured: These men were using the Corinthians for their own financial gain and they were doing it shamelessly, just like the Pharisees who devoured widows' houses (Luke 20:47).

(3) They were being preyed upon: The false apostles were treating them like a bird caught in a snare or a fish in a net. They did not only take their money and property, they were taking the people themselves and making them slaves of men (cf. 1 Corinthians 7:23).

(4) They were being treated with contempt: The intruders were lording it over the believers and they were enduring it.

(5) They were being slapped in the face: The false apostles showed total disrespect for the church. It was similar to the treatment Micaiah the prophet received from the false prophet (1 Kings 22:24). Jesus endured similar humiliation from His enemies, although it was much more severe (Luke 22:64). Paul received the same kind of treatment (Acts 23:2; cf. Matthew 5:39), but this was not the situation at Corinth. It is clear that Paul considered the Corinthians' submission to the slaps in the face as a sign of their weakness. Their cowardice showed how completely they had been intimidated by these intruders. Paul had tried to appeal to the Corinthians' sense of spiritual responsibility in telling them to resist the false apostles. Now he appealed to their sense of honor and self-respect—the lack of which was evident by their meek submission to their mistreatment. Paul also reminded them that neither he nor his coworkers ever treated them in such a way. With friendly irony he wrote something like this: "I have to admit with shame that we have been weak compared with these domineering 'apostles' you now serve!" Some scholars think it is to be interpreted literally that the false apostles often struck their most obedient followers in the face. Such action expresses the most humiliating treatment.

By appealing to both their spiritual responsibility and their self-respect, Paul sought to urge the Corinthians to rid themselves of the authority of error under which they had allowed themselves to fall. Their weakness toward the intruders was inexcusable and could lead to the actual destruction of the church.

*3. The Accusations of Paul's Opponents.* Paul said bluntly that the false apostles were Satan's servants who were performing his work. They had been taught their sly methods of seduction by the great deceiver himself who transforms himself into an angel of light (11:14, 15). They showed themselves to be false apostles by preaching another gospel. They also showed it by their attempts to divide and destroy the church. The fact that they opposed true servants of God emphasized their true character further. (Cf. Galatians 4:29 where it is said, "As then he that was born after the flesh persecuted him that was born after the Spirit, even so it is now.") Significantly Paul's discussion of the false apostle's attack on his apostolic authority developed into some of the strongest language in the entire epistle (11:5-15). Paul knew he belonged to Christ (10:7) and that he was called by God to his apostolic ministry (1:1). Thus he knew also that these individuals who were trying to undermine his position and hinder his work were carrying out Satan's strategy.

The accusations of Paul's opponents can be traced throughout the epistle. They become a long list if we try to sum them up: (1) Accusation of inconsistency and unreliability for changing his travel plans and postponing his visit to Corinth (1:15-24). This is discussed under point 2 in the division of the epistle. (2) Suggestions that he did not have good relations with the original apostles because he had no letter of recommendation from them (3:1). This is discussed under point 3 in the first division. (3) Suspicion thrown on Paul in connection with his part in gathering money for the church in Jerusalem (8:18-21; 12:16-18). This is discussed under point 2 in the second division. (4) Criticism of Paul's lack of eloquence (10:10; 11:6). (5) Criticism for his strong and frank epistles when he was absent (10:10). (6) Criticism for his weak and insignificant physical appearance when he was personally present (10:10, 11; cf. 12:12). (7) Devaluating his ministry because he did not receive money from the church as salary for his work (11:7-13). The last four accusations will be discussed below.

Regarding Paul's lack of eloquence, he would not agree that he was inferior to his opponents except in one point. He admitted he was not a good speaker. He was not a professional orator as some of them claimed to be. Compared to Paul, his opponents did not really have much to boast about, so they had to make a great fuss over what they had. It seemed important to them that Paul lacked technical and professional education as a speaker. Paul himself, however, dismissed the entire matter as being unworthy of much attention. In the first epistle he discussed the situation and said he had arrived at a firm decision to conduct himself just as he did (1 Corinthians 2:1-5). As one who knew his call had come from God he had purposely desisted from the "wisdom of words" in his preaching of the gospel (1:17).

When Paul said he was "rude in speech" (11:6) he used a Greek term meaning "unlearned." Originally the word referred to one who was not interested in politics and public service. Such a person had little respect among the Greeks so the word gradually developed bad connotations. When the New Testament was written, the word was sometimes used in connection with being unskilled in a matter. Paul employed the term this way in 1 Corinthians 14:23, 24. It could apply to one who lacked instruction in a trade and therefore only dabbled in it. In Acts 4:13 the word is used of Peter and John because they were lay people who were not educated in the rabbinical schools.

The opening speech of the orator Tertullus before Felix (Acts 24:1) is a good example of the type of rhetoric which Paul had not been taught and which he refused to use. One of the distinctive features of this speech was shameless flattery. Paul refused to use flattering words when he preached the gospel (1 Thessalonians 2:5), for he had renounced the hidden things of dishonesty (2 Corinthians 4:2). But it was characteristic of false teachers trying to gain access to the churches that "their mouth speaketh great swelling words, having men's persons in admiration because of advantage" (Jude 16).

What gave strength to Paul's preaching was his unfailing love of the truth. His speech was characterized by unaffected sincerity and marked by an appeal to his listeners' consciences (4:2). The progress of the gospel was not dependent on bombastic rhetoric. Paul's opponents might say "his speech is contemptible" (10:10), but none believed his preaching was powerless or insignificant. His activity as portrayed throughout the New Testament shows he was anything but powerless. In the churches he preached the deep spiritual truths "which the Holy Ghost teacheth" (1 Corinthians 2:13). Paul was actually one of the most effective missionaries in the Church's history. Throughout his journeys he established strong churches that grew and flourished spiritually. When we study Paul's speeches in the Book of Acts we see they are masterpieces. He may not have had the eloquence of Apollos nor the ability to be a popular speaker like Peter, but he could adapt to different situations as no one else could. He spoke in Jewish synagogues (Acts 19:8), in Christian assemblies (19:9, 10), in Gentile marketplaces (17:22). He spoke to a gathering of excited Jews (22:1) and to a crowd of Gentiles (14:12ff.). He could speak before the high court of the Jews (23:1) and before kings and rulers (26:1). He spoke of the judgment to come in such a way that his examining judge was terrified (24:25). His testimony to the Christian faith caused King Agrippa to exclaim, "Almost thou persuadest me to be a Christian" (26:28). What argument could the so-called "apostles" in Corinth advance to counteract these facts, even with all their oratorical skill?

Regarding the strong nature of his epistles, Paul's opponents criticized him because they felt his epistles were too authoritative and bold. They accused him of being one who shoots best from a distance! They said the Paul who wrote letters was different from the one who visited Corinth. There was probably no more effective way to undermine his personal reputation and influence (10:10).

Even these opponents had to admit that Paul's letters were effective. The influence his epistles had on the church was demonstrated before their very eyes. Through one of his letters he had caused a sinning member of the church to "sorrow to repentance" (7:9). These apostolic epistles were considered as the Word of God by the churches and were read along with "the other epistles" with which they were compared (2 Peter 3:15, 16). It is interesting that Scripture has preserved this testimony of opponents from the apostolic era in which the epistles were written.

Admission by Paul's opponents that his epistles were authoritative and courageous does not imply their recognition of Paul as a genuine apostle. They denied his apostolic authority in spite of the nature of his epistles. In their opinion his epistles were simply a collection of empty words. They said the authority present in Paul's writings was totally absent in his personal appearance. Paul rejected these accusations: "Such as we are in word by letters when we are absent, such will we be also in deed when we are present" (10:11). The Lord himself had given Paul his authority and the power of the Lord was effective through him. This power, however, was used to build up the church, not tear it down as the false apostles were doing (10:8). Paul had used his apostolic authority for the church's edification. Believers at Corinth had been saved through his preaching. Why then should they be frightened by his authoritative epistle? Certainly Paul never intended that they should be (10:9).

Regarding his unimpressive physical appearance, Paul's opponents insisted he was so weak and unsure of himself that he dared to be brave only in writing from a distance. He did not show such authority and strength when he was personally present—as one would expect a real apostle to do! (10:10).

The false apostles and their followers had taken Paul's modesty and humility as a sign of weakness. Since they were strangers to the mind of Christ they could not understand or appreciate the spirit of a true Christian. This was Paul's natural behavior toward others. His tone and style in speaking were the same as in writing. This spirit is evident even now when Paul must openly confront the deceivers and their followers. Some modern commentators think Paul was unnecessarily severe in the third division of the epistle, but it should be noted that he soon pointed to the meekness and gentleness of Christ as his example (10:1).

Probably one reason for Paul's seeming severity was that he knew his opponents were receiving some support from members of the church concerning his being more outspoken in his epistles than when personally present. Paul often wrote his epistles because of some circumstance in a church which needed to be corrected. In this case he would have to admonish the offenders, who naturally thought he was too strict. It was different when he visited a church and lived among the people for a longer period. At those times situations could be prevented by dealing with a matter before it grew to larger proportions. Odeberg writes: "Thus it came to pass that his personal presence in a church left the memory of a modest, friendly, and humble man, but that his epistles did more show the strict corrector and warner," English translation.

But one thing emerges clearly: Paul was anything but a weak, passive man. The thought is absurd when we remember the kind of life he lived and the tribulations he endured. When we follow Paul's career in Acts and in his epistles we see an individual with a powerful personality. Depending on the kind of situation he was confronting, he could show tender care and compassion or the most determined inflexibility. The man who was put into stocks in the Philippian prison and filled the place with praise in the middle of the night was no weakling. His strength was probably shown even more by his refusal to leave the prison until high officials came to release him (Acts 16:37).

He pronounced a curse on Elymas the sorcerer (Acts 13:8-11). He called the high priest "thou whited wall" when that man behaved unjustly in court, and he was big enough to apologize for his words (Acts 23:2-5). Not for one moment did Paul retreat in cowardice from false brethren who would bring believers into bondage (Galatians 2:4, 5). When his fellow apostle Peter "walked not uprightly according to the truth of the gospel," Paul rebuked him to his face (Galatians 2:11-14). He would also dare to speak just as bluntly to the false apostles in Corinth when he arrived there!

Such is the picture the Scriptures draw of Paul, the apostle to the Gentiles. It is not the picture of a weak or fearful man. It is the picture of a prince of God.

Finally, one of the strongest complaints against Paul seems to have been that he did not receive financial compensation from the church in Corinth for his work (11:7-12). This "accusation" has been linked to the one that he got money from congregations by underhanded means. So here are two accusations that are actually opposite to each other. The intention of the false apostles was to pile up as many accusations against Paul as possible.

We would not think it was a serious charge against a preacher of the gospel that he did his work without receiving pay (cf. Matthew 10:8). However, Paul's behavior in this matter caused great problems for his opponents. Their main motive in pretending to be religious workers was to receive a good living from it. Thus they felt uncomfortable over Paul's demonstrating openly that his motives were quite different. To the false apostles, preaching was simply a "job" and the church was the place where they worked. As a modern illustration, we can imagine the irritation of workers in a factory against a man who worked there without pay and thus reflected badly on them.

To Paul it was a usual practice to preach without pay. He practiced this in many places (Acts 20:33-35; 1 Corinthians 4:12; 9:7-12; 1 Thessalonians 2:9; 2 Thessalonians 3:6-10). He did this for several reasons. No doubt it was a necessity in many of the new territories where he preached to earn his living by manual labor. He also did this to show by example that a Christian should never shun work or shirk his duties. Sometimes it was to make things easier for his listeners to receive the gospel. Wandering Greek philosophers received money from those who listened to them and Paul did not want to be considered one of them. His work as an unpaid preacher underscored the message that the salvation offered through Christ was by God's free grace and not something that could be earned.

In Corinth there was a special reason to follow this practice. It made it less convenient for the false apostles to receive pay from the church. Even apart from their erroneous theology and ideology, Paul considered these men traveling agitators who used the gospel only as a way of livelihood (1 Timothy 6:5; Titus 1:11; cf. 1 Peter 5:2; 2 Peter 2:3). They probably had heard how believers in the first church at Jerusalem gave their property to the apostles for the welfare of the whole congregation (Acts 4:34, 35). This may have prompted them to pass themselves off as apostles—thinking they also could obtain the property of believers by underhanded means. They saw the great power which Christianity had over the people and wanted to utilize the new religion for their own profit. To achieve their aim, they had to break the believers' trust in the apostles so they could take apostolic authority themselves. Of course, this was not easy in Jerusalem where the original apostles lived. They considered Paul's apostleship easier to attack, so it was natural that they concentrated their activity in the new Gentile churches he had founded.

However, the false apostles met obstacles in their attempts to gain an economic advantage in the church where Paul had carefully refrained from doing so. Their selfishness and love of money soon began to be seen. Partly in self-defense and partly to undermine Paul, they began their attacks on his authority by pointing to his practice of not receiving pay. They insinuated this actually showed that Paul himself realized he was not a real apostle and therefore could not claim the support to

which an apostle was entitled. Paul had worked as a tentmaker with Aquila and Priscilla when he was in Corinth (Acts 18:1-3). Was this consistent with the calling and authority of an apostle? This would arouse suspicion especially among the Greeks, who looked down on manual laborers.

If Paul answered the charge by saying he had received financial help from other churches to support his work in Corinth (11:8, 9), this could also be used against him. His opponents could say this was because Paul did not really care for the church in Corinth, so he did not want to feel any debt of gratitude toward them. Paul had to assure the Corinthians solemnly and call on God as his witness that he had no ulterior motives for not receiving pay from their church (11:11). False rumors and unjust accusations surrounded Paul. Behind them all stood the false apostles who were systematically trying to throw suspicion on him and destroy his influence.

In 1 Corinthians 9:4-18 Paul had already discussed the matter thoroughly. It should not be necessary for anyone to require further explanation. Paul declared the Lord had ordained that those who preach the gospel should live by the gospel. He emphasized that he had this privilege but did not always use it. There were times when he voluntarily chose to labor without pay from the church. The purity of Paul's motives shines through these words: "It were better for me to die, than that any man should make my glorying void" (1 Corinthians 9:15). We might wonder what made Paul use such strong language. In 2 Corinthians 11:10 he repeated the same thing in the form of an oath: "As the truth of Christ is in me, no man shall stop me of this boasting in the regions of Achaia." Here he continued giving the reasons for maintaining this practice: "But what I do, that I will do, that I may cut off occasion from them which desire occasion; that wherein they glory, they may be found even as we. For such are false apostles, deceitful workers, transforming themselves into the apostles of Christ" (11:12, 13).

Paul thus declared emphatically that he would not receive any salary from the church for his work and this made it impossible for the false apostles to use him as an example when they used the church for their financial benefit. Of course, the matter of money was not Paul's sole reason for discussing this matter. The economic side of the controversy was secondary to the real issue, which was the religious activity of the false apostles. Paul focused on the subject of money because it was what enabled these men to continue destroying the church spiritually. The church was paying them for destroying the church! Paul would not consent to any arrangement which could contribute to a continuation of these conditions. He would not touch the Corinthians' money with one finger if it gave the heretics more advantage in squeezing money from the church for their evil purposes.

Two things are evident concerning these accusations and Paul's reaction to them.

First: The real character of the false apostles was revealed by their list of false accusations against an apostle and servant of the Lord. These men had not merely strayed from the truth; they were vicious and evil.

Second: The temper and spiritual quality of Paul's life never appeared more clearly than when he answered these accusations. One must possess much grace to react correctly to injustice, and Paul was able to do so. He did not assume an injured air nor refuse to give any reply or explanation—as a guilty person often does when he is called to account. On the contrary, Paul wrote a long letter—a small book in fact—in order to deal with the matter and assert his right to the Corinthians' respect for his apostolic ministry and authority. It must have been extremely painful to be forsaken by his friends as he was, but courageously and without sentimental complaints, Paul responded to the problem. He argued forcefully and with unquestioned honesty. He explained everything patiently and diligently. In fact, he used every kind of approach: He spoke sharply, he used sarcasm, he employed friendly persuasion. What else could he do? Just one thing remained and he would make use of that too. Now he proceeded to meet his opponents on their own ground.

## B. Forced Self-Praise (11:22-12:19)

The false apostles in Corinth not only brought another gospel, they brought another spirit (11:4). Those who followed them were infected with the same spirit and became very confused. One of the most certain signs of this infection of spirit was their refusal to be persuaded by any kind of argument. Paul had addressed them intelligently and with careful instruction. But how can you speak sense to one who is overcome by folly? The Corinthians had debased themselves by following these intruders. They had been carried away by foolishness. This reflected on their own level of spirituality and intelligence.

Paul replied soberly and intelligently to the outrageous behavior of the false apostles. He followed the advice, "Answer not a fool according to his folly, lest thou also be like unto him." But this passage also says, "Answer a fool according to his folly, lest he be wise in his own conceit" (Proverbs 26:4, 5). Both aspects of this counsel have their time and place. In the very difficult situation prevailing at Corinth, Paul tried both approaches. He had previously tried to convince the Corinthians with sensible talk; now he would try with folly!

The false apostles had deceived the Corinthians by their folly and boasting. Paul would not be a fool who enjoys boasting, which is the greatest folly of all (11:16). Paul's nature rebelled against such a spirit. Seven times in these two chapters he declared how foolish boasting is. It is not "after the Lord" nor according to the mind, example, and will of Christ (11:17). In fact, boasting is totally incompatible with the One who was of a gentle spirit and humble heart and who humbled himself in order to provide salvation to the lost. Paul was willing to try any approach to rescue the Corinthians from those who had taken them captive. If false apostles had been able to gain entrance to the Corinthian church by false boasting, why should Paul not be able to win them back by truthful boasting?

Of course it should have been totally unnecessary for Paul to praise himself to the Corinthians because they knew him so well. On the contrary, they ought to be praising him! Yet none of his old friends in the church seemed to be willing to say a kind word for him to counteract the criticism and gossip, so they had forced him to commend himself (12:11). Paul did this very thoroughly, and the Holy Spirit inspired the inclusion of this teaching in the Scriptures. This is because it applied not only to the Corinthians at that time but to believers at all times when they are in danger of being seduced by boasting teachers of error.

The forced self-praise of Paul falls into four sections with their subsections. He boasted of his Jewish background, his sufferings as a servant of Christ, his revelations of truth, and finally of his weakness—his *real* self-praise.

*1. Jewish background (11:22).* Paul's opponents had capitalized on their Jewish ancestry. It might seem strange that this had such great appeal in a Gentile church like Corinth where Jewish members were in the minority. However, a traveling preacher's Jewish background gave him some advantages. Jesus was a Jew according to the flesh and the gospel had come from the Jews. The first disciples of Jesus were Jews. The Church's Bible at that time was the Old Testament, a Jewish book, and the great events of salvation history had taken place in the land of the Jews.

Paul used three expressions for the intruders' claim to authority because of their Jewish descent:

(1) "Are they Hebrews?" he asked and replied immediately, "So am I." Usually the word *Hebrew* is used to distinguish Jews from Gentiles. In this sense Paul was "an Hebrew of the Hebrews" (Philippians 3:5). He was born in Tarsus but had been brought up in Jerusalem and was educated at the feet of Gamaliel (Acts 22:3), so he could not be called a Jew of the diaspora in the real sense of the word. In race and religion Paul was a Hebrew. If someone could "have confidence in the flesh," he

could have even more confidence (Philippians 3:4-6). In Acts 6:1 the term *Hebrew* is used to identify the Jews of Palestine who spoke Aramaic in contrast to the Greek-speaking Jews of the diaspora. It is evident from Acts 22:2 that Paul understood and spoke Aramaic. Hugo Odeberg maintains that the word *Hebrew* in 11:22 refers to being able to understand and speak the Hebrew language rather than the popular Aramaic. To master the basic language of the Old Testament was a mark of education and theological skill. Paul could study the Hebrew Old Testament and he could also preach a sermon in the Aramaic language which was spoken in Jerusalem. In no way was he inferior to the false apostles in Corinth, even though they acted as Jewish scribes.

(2) "Are they Israelites?" This is a term for the people of the covenant, "to whom pertaineth the adoption, and the glory, and the covenants, and the giving of the law, and the service of God, and the promises; whose are the fathers, and of whom as concerning the flesh Christ came" (Romans 9:4, 5). Paul belonged to God's covenant people and not merely in the outward meaning of the expression. He was an Israelite in the true sense of the word. He did not lose his rights as an Israelite by becoming a Christian. On the contrary, "They are not all Israel, which are of Israel" (Romans 9:6).

(3) "Are they the seed of Abraham?" This identifies Israel as the people of the promise who participate in the blessing which God gave to Abraham and his descendants. In reply to the intruders' claims that they were Abraham's children, Paul replied, "So am I." However, he had just called these false apostles the servants of Satan (11:14, 15). This passage is somewhat of a parallel to Jesus' discussion with the Pharisees in John 8:33. The Pharisees insisted they were Abraham's children, but Jesus said their father was the devil. The assertion of these false apostles that they were the children of Abraham was in fact a fraud. Abraham's children are those who have his faith (Romans 4:12; Galatians 3:7). Paul was not inferior to his opponents in any manner. He was of Abraham's race, not just after the flesh but one of Abraham's spiritual children, an heir of the promises given to him (Galatians 3:9, 29).

*2. Paul's Suffering (11:23-33).* The false apostles called themselves Christ's servants, but Paul had just called them the servants of Satan (11:13-15). He gave reasons why he was much more entitled than they to be called a servant of Christ. He had not only labored more than these men, he had endured more suffering and persecutions, and this more than anything else marks a true servant of Christ: "The servant is not greater than his lord. If they have persecuted me, they will also persecute you" (John 15:20). Actually Paul was completely

wiping out the claims of these deceivers to apostleship. In short, concise sentences without sentimentality or extra elaboration, Paul showed that God had a plan for his life from the very beginning: "I will show him how great things he must suffer for my name's sake" (Acts 9:16).

*a. Christian activity (11:23).* When Paul said he had worked more, this must be understood in the proper context. He was not comparing his labors to the insignificant efforts of his opponents, which Paul easily surpassed. The very nature of his work was great and worthy of comparison with the efforts of anyone else. He had worked more than any of the original apostles, but he quickly added that it was the grace of God, not his natural ability, which accomplished so much. He had written about this to the Corinthians earlier (1 Corinthians 15:10).

*b. Persecution (11:23-25).* Paul then listed his sufferings. He had alluded earlier in this epistle to what he had undergone (4:8-10; 6:4-10), but now he gave details.

(1) Many times he had been imprisoned. From Acts 16 we have knowledge of one imprisonment before this epistle was written. This was in Philippi, but there were more imprisonments, including one at Ephesus, where there are ruins of a tower which from ancient times has been called "the prison of Paul." Later on there were times of imprisonment in Caesarea and Rome. Clement of Rome wrote that Paul was in prison seven times.

(2) Paul suffered corporal punishment from Jewish and Roman authorities several times. Five times he was punished by the Jewish lash, "forty stripes save one." That means in the most severe form possible. The Law stipulated that 40 stripes were the most which could be given (Deuteronomy 25:1-3). To be certain they did not exceed the limit of the Law, the Jews stopped with the 39th stripe. Paul was beaten three times by Roman authorities. He says concerning his punishment that it was *huperballontōs*, i.e., "immensely" or "beyond every reasonable limit."

(3) Once he had been stoned. According to Acts 14:19, 20 this took place in Lystra during Paul's first missionary journey. The people who stoned Paul thought he was dead and dragged him outside the city, but while the disciples crowded around him, he stood up.

(4) He was often in deadly danger. In 1 Corinthians 15:30 Paul said he stood in jeopardy each day; in fact, he "died daily." In Romans 8:36, 37 he quoted the Psalmist's words: "For thy sake we are killed all the day long; we are accounted as sheep for the slaughter." But he testified, "In all these things we are more than conquerors through him that loved us."

c. *Perils and danger (11:25, 26).* Paul said he suffered shipwreck three times. Later he experienced the same thing on his voyage to Rome. During one of the shipwrecks it seems he floated around on the wreckage for 24 hours. When he remembered what he had experienced on his journeys it was too much to be described in detail, so he wrote: "In perils of waters, in perils of robbers, in perils by mine own countrymen, in perils by the heathen, in perils in the city, in perils in the wilderness, in perils in the sea, in perils among false brethren. . . ."

d. *False brethren (11:26).* Besides all these difficulties and conflict with enemies outside the Church, Paul also had perils from false brethren. The first church had its traitors, counterfeit believers who spied on the others and could thus become their accusers (cf. Matthew 24:10). The Judaizing heretics followed Paul's steps like a shadow, and they bore a deadly hatred toward him. False brethren had now found their way to Corinth. From what Paul wrote, it seems he considered them a danger to himself personally. However, he had decided to visit the church at Corinth anyway. He was the great missionary to the Gentiles who founded new churches everywhere. It seems strange to read that so much of his time had to be diverted from soul-winning work to fighting against these false brethren who spied on the churches and constantly looked for reasons to attack Paul.

e. *A life filled with trouble (11:27).* "In weariness and painfulness." This is how Paul characterized his life. He was not one who took his heavenly rest in advance! Wakeful nights often followed busy days. He knew hunger and thirst, cold and nakedness. Besides spiritual duties, he often had to work for his living, not only for personal necessities but also to have something to give those in need (Acts 20:34).

f. *Church work (11:28, 29).* In addition to everything else, Paul had the daily supervision of members of the church and the care of the other churches. Concerning his stay in Ephesus he said, "Remember, that by the space of three years I ceased not to warn every one night and day with tears" (Acts 20:31). "Who is weak, and I am not weak? who is offended and I burn not?" (11:29). From his coworkers Paul received constant reports from the churches and kept in touch with them through his epistles. These epistles, as we know, form a large part of the New Testament. They were written originally to meet some urgent need in the Church or to answer spiritual questions, yet for nearly 2,000 years they have been the source of blessing to all Christians.

The man who wrote these epistles stood head and shoulders above his critics. Daily he carried the load of responsibility for the churches. Must he be considered suspect because of his opponents' accusations? Surely such questions must have arisen among the Corinthians when they read his words of forced self-praise.

g. *Damascus (11:32, 33).* At first it seems Paul has ended his list of sufferings with the solemn assurance that he spoke the truth (11:31). But in 11:32, 33 he continued by telling how in Damascus during the early days of his ministry, he avoided the guards of King Aretas who, with the Jews, kept watch at the city gate in order to seize him. Aretas was an Arab who ruled the area between the Red Sea and Euphrates River. Perhaps Paul had incurred Aretas' wrath after his stay in Arabia (cf. Galatians 1:17). When we compare Paul's statement in that verse with Acts 9:23-25, it seems that both the Jews and the people of King Aretas had combined their efforts in order to capture Paul. He avoided them because one night he was lowered in a basket outside the city wall. We can be certain that Paul could never forget that experience, which was the beginning of a long series of persecutions he met later. Now he added this at the end of his list, even though it should have been at the front. He mentioned all these situations to remind his friends in Corinth that throughout his entire life as a Christian, he had endured persecution for preaching Jesus Christ.

3. *Revelations (12:1-6).* "I will come to visions and revelations," Paul wrote as he continued his forced self-praise. One should be careful about telling others of experiences the Lord has given him for his personal spiritual benefit. Paul's visions and revelations were not given in order to glorify him. On the contrary, they marked the beginning of humiliation that lasted the rest of his life in the form of a painful "thorn in the flesh." He said this happened so he would not boast of what he had experienced. Paul now laid bare what was the most personal aspect of his life, his most intimate feelings, as he discussed experiences which brought him both pain and blessing.

Why did Paul reveal these spiritual secrets? Why did he allow the accusations of his enemies to force from him what he had carried inside himself for so long? It was because of the concern he had for his spiritual children in Corinth. They would naturally expect an apostle to tell of his visions and revelations. They could not understand why he did not answer his antagonists by revealing these special experiences. No doubt the false apostles had claimed special religious experiences of their own and thus were of the number who were "intruding into those things which he hath not seen" (cf. Colossians 2:18), thus building up their own reputation and deceiving unsuspecting believers. It was in "competition" with these pseudo-prophets that Paul now told how the Lord had spoken directly to him in special revelations.

Of course it was known that Paul had visions, although he was slow to tell of them. His opponents had possibly said the "vision" on which he based his call to apostleship was only a delusion. Paul had many visions, some of which are referred to in Acts: The vision of Ananias in Damascus (9:12), the vision in the temple (22:17-21), the vision in Troas (16:9), the vision in Corinth (18:9), the vision during his last visit in Jerusalem (23:11), the vision during the voyage to Rome (27:23). In most of these visions the Lord himself appeared to Paul. There were two revelations which Paul placed in a particular class. One was "the heavenly vision" (26:19) on the way to Damascus. Paul did not consider this an experience of ecstasy like his vision in the temple (22:17), but an actual experience of Christ like His revelations to the disciples after the Resurrection (1 Corinthians 15:7). This vision of the risen Christ on the Damascus Road was the basis of Paul's apostleship.

The other revelation which Paul placed in a particular class is the one he now recounts to the Corinthians. This was not an experience of ecstasy like the vision in the temple. On this occasion he was "caught up," *harpagenta*. The same word is used in Acts 8:39 concerning Philip when he was caught away and found in Azotus. It is used also in 1 Thessalonians 4:17 concerning those who are caught up at the return of the Lord, and in Revelation 12:5 to describe the male child's being caught up to the throne of God. What Paul experienced seems similar to the vision on the Damascus Road, except that on that occasion the Lord descended and revealed himself to Paul, while in this experience Paul was caught up into the heavenly world where he heard words he could not repeat. To Paul it was easy to believe he was caught away bodily but he was not certain: "Whether in the body, I cannot tell; or whether out of the body, I cannot tell" (12:2).

Paul said he was caught up into the third heaven. The Jews had formed concepts of many "heavens," and this idea carried over to the New Testament (cf. Ephesians 4:10). From 1 Kings 8:27 some have concluded there are three heavens. Later Jewish and apocalyptic writings speak of seven heavens. We cannot be sure whether Paul thought the third heaven was the highest one. Scholars differ in their opinions (cf. Tasker, *Tyndale New Testament Commentaries,* 8:169-172; and Bruce, *New Century Bible,* 38:245-247). One might judge Paul's experience from rare ones which seem to resemble his. In this case, being caught up may indicate passing through several spheres (Odeberg).

Paul also spoke of being caught up into paradise, so it seems he used this word synonymously with the third heaven. *Paradise* is originally a Persian word which means "park," and the word was taken into both Hebrew and Greek. In the Septuagint—the Greek translation of the Old Testament—"paradise" is used for the Garden of Eden. In the New Testament the word is used to describe the dwelling place of believers after death (Luke 23:43) and for the new Garden of Eden (Revelation 2:7). The Jews believed that after the Fall, paradise was removed from earth to be protected in heaven by God. This belief may form the background of the final visions in the Book of Revelation where the New Jerusalem comes down from heaven, from God, and conditions of paradise are established (Revelation 21). What Paul experienced was thus a real foretaste of life in eternity.

Paul said nothing of what he saw in paradise, but he did hear "unspeakable words." They were unspeakable because they could not be expressed in human words. They were too holy for a human to try to repeat them. In the Greek word *exon*, translated "not lawful," both meanings are implied. In Daniel 12:4-10 and Revelation 10:2-4 we have other instances where a prophet was not permitted to make known what he had seen. The knowledge Paul received through this revelation was meant only for him.

He did not mention this experience until 14 years later and he did it then with hesitation and restraint. He did not rush to make it known the same day it happened! He was called to preach the gospel of Christ, not his visions. This vision, however, must have meant a great deal to Paul personally. If Second Corinthians was written in A.D. 56, Paul had this great experience during the quiet years in Tarsus, perhaps not long before Barnabas visited him. Before Paul began his first missionary journey and his ministry as the apostle to the Gentiles, he may have seen the throne of God like Isaiah and other special messengers of God.

"Of such an one will I glory!" Paul said. He had not deserved such revelations; they were only manifestations of God's grace to him. It is apparently for this reason that he used the third person and called himself "a man in Christ," as though to distance this "man" from himself. Not all Christians receive such visions and revelations, but each "man in Christ" shall one day participate by undeserved grace in the heavenly glory of which Paul received a foretaste.

*4. The Thorn in the Flesh (12:7-10).* Probably Paul could have related many visions and revelations, but he stopped with just one. "Now I forbear," he wrote (12:6). He did not want the Corinthians to think too highly of him because of these unusual experiences. And he had received something which kept *him* humble—a thorn in the flesh. Whatever it was, Paul called it Satan's messenger who kept striking him so he did not become too exalted because of his revelations. A great deal of speculation has centered around the identity of this thorn, but no real answer has been found.

The Greek words Paul used are not easy to interpret. *Skolops* (translated "thorn") in classical Greek meant a pole or stake. It is close to *stauros*, translated "cross" in 1 Corinthians 1:18 and many other passages. In time, *skolops* came to mean frequently a thorn like the term used mainly in the Septuagint (Numbers 33:55; Ezekiel 28:24; Hosea 2:6).

*Sarx* is the Greek word translated "flesh" in this verse. If "in the flesh" is the correct translation, this seems to refer to the physical body and this has influenced the interpretation that the thorn was some kind of bodily weakness. If it should be translated "for the flesh," it would be more natural to understand "flesh" as the fallen human nature—an expression Paul used often in his writing. If this is the correct interpretation, the thorn could be anything that hinders the tendency of the human nature to exalt itself. These different views of the correct translation have divided the interpreters into two main groups and both have had their spokesmen from ancient times to the present.

Tertullian is the first who supported the view of the thorn's being a sickness. Some scholars have thought he was building on tradition. In more recent theology this view has probably become predominant. Several kinds of "diagnosis" have been made: (1) Tertullian and Hieronymus: headache and earache. (2) J.T. Brown (1858): inflammation of the eyes. (3) M. Krengel and J. Klausner: epilepsy. (4) M. Dibelius: convulsive attacks. (5) W.M. Ramsay and E.B. Allo: malaria. (6) H. Clavier: depression. Some have also thought the verse meant Paul was physically disfigured.

From these views, one would think Satan had been allowed to strike Paul with some kind of painful sickness or bodily weakness as he did Job. Some quote Galatians 4:12-15 to support this view, pointing out that Paul reminds the readers it was because of a sickness that he first came to Galatia. Adherents to this interpretation understand "infirmity of the flesh" as synonymous with "a thorn in the flesh."

The second main division of interpretations is just as varied. Church fathers like Augustine, Chrysostom, and others thought the thorn referred to persecutions by Jews who stirred up opposition to Paul everywhere he went. Roman Catholic scholars of early times thought Paul was struggling with the sexual temptations that attacked monks and hermits. The reformers would not accept such an opinion. Calvin thought the thorn included all kinds of temptation to which the fallen nature is prone (*Calvin's Commentaries, Corinthians,* p. 273). Luther limited the temptations to the internal spiritual kind, i.e., doubts and blasphemous thoughts inspired by Satan, but he also thought outward persecutions had to be included (*Luther's Works,* 26:420f.).

Among modern commentators, Tasker belongs to the group who find it most reasonable that the thorn refers to attacks from opponents (*Tyndale New Testament Commentaries,* 8:177) (cf. Numbers 33:55 where the Scripture says the Canaanites would be troublesome to Israel like "thorns in your sides"). Beasley-Murray believes the thorn stands for Satan's accusations against Paul because of his earlier persecution of the Church. As support, he uses 1 Corinthians 15:9, 10 and 2 Corinthians 12:7-9—two passages which contrast Paul's guilt to the grace of God. This thought can perhaps be developed further. If the thorn or stake in Paul's flesh was inner guilt over his persecution of the Church, this may throw light on the Lord's words to him on the Damascus Road: "Saul, Saul, why persecutest thou me? it is hard for thee to kick against the pricks" (Acts 26:14). Nothing indicates that Paul kicked against any "pricks" before his conversion. Neither is there any indication that the Lord used a "prick" to force him to be saved. When Jesus revealed himself to Paul and spoke to him, he asked immediately, "What shall I do, Lord?" (Acts 22:10). But it is evident from 1 Timothy 1:12-16 that the memory of that persecution period had been tormenting Paul throughout his later life. With this in mind he even went so far as to say (like his opponents) that he was not worthy to be called an apostle. It is only the grace of God which had made him what he is.

In Gethsemane Jesus prayed three times that the cup of agony should pass from Him. Three times Paul prayed to be delivered from his thorn. Disciples learn obedience through suffering just as their Master did. They learn to pray the greatest of all prayers: "Thy will be done!" As Jesus through His suffering and death in weakness (1 Corinthians 1:25) revealed the power of God for salvation, His apostle found that in his weakness the power of God was revealed. The climax of this passage is in the Lord's word of comfort for His servant: "My grace is sufficient for thee; for my strength is made perfect in weakness" (12:9). Then Paul declared his satisfaction was not in his own ability or strength, but his incapability (3:5) and weakness. "Most gladly therefore will I rather glory in my infirmities, that the power of Christ may rest upon me" (12:9).

*5. The Signs of an Apostle (12:11, 12).* As Paul reached the climax of his praise, he boasted of his infirmities. He was at least greater in weakness than the false apostles! And because of this weakness the power of Christ worked through him.

The Corinthians had forced Paul to this folly of comparing himself to his opponents. Now he continued by asserting that he was not behind "the very chiefest apostles" in anything.

Just one point remains. Some would probably say it is the most important one, but Paul finished it with only a few lines. It concerns the question of a real apostle's characteristics. "The signs of an apostle" include the entire supernatural equipment which God gives an apostle. This includes what Paul mentioned in his summary: signs and wonders and powerful works. These signs had followed Paul during his entire service as an apostle (Acts 13:8-12; 14:3; 15:12; 19:11, 12; Romans 15:18, 19). But Paul did not list here all the signs which had followed his ministry. He referred to what should be the plainest evidence of all—the supernatural works the Corinthians themselves have seen. However, they must not think more highly of Paul than they ought to just because of these mighty works (12:6). False apostles and imposters might use signs and wonders as advertisements, but not a true servant of the Lord.

Signs, wonders, and miracles or powerful works are not meant as three different manifestations of supernatural power. Paul was simply discussing miraculous works from three different points of view. The same expression is used of Jesus (Acts 2:22) and of God's confirmation of the salvation message (Hebrews 2:3, 4). However, it is not God's will that believers should follow every wonder-worker. In the last days the Antichrist will use signs and wonders to deceive people (2 Thessalonians 2:9). Jesus said that on the Day of Judgment many will point to mighty works they have performed in His name, yet they will be rejected (Matthew 7:22, 23). It appears that the false apostles in Corinth belonged to this group.

Signs and wonders are an indication of God's stamp of approval on a ministry only when they appear in the right context. They must be part of a total picture where sound doctrine and the fear of God are also given their rightful place. This had always been Paul's position. During trials and opposition of all kinds he had performed these works of power patiently and persistently. Those wonders did indeed belong to "the signs of an apostle."

## C. Final Admonition (12:15-13:14)

Paul had explained to his readers what his apostolic service consisted of and he had defended his apostolic authority. The controversy with opponents is ended. The epistle is almost finished. Paul concludes with some final and personal admonitions which should bless the church.

*1. Paul's Readiness (12:13-19).* In a way, Paul was back at the starting point. In the beginning of the epistle he had to defend himself against those who accused him of unreliability because of postponing his visit to Corinth. Some had probably indicated

he did not dare come at all. Now he assured the church, "The third time I am ready to come to you" (12:14).

Thinking of the visit which now was drawing near, Paul mentioned once more that he did not receive financial support from the church. With friendly irony he said this was the only injustice he had committed against the Corinthians and asked them to forgive the "injustice." However, he did not promise any change of methods. He would not receive their gifts this time either because he wanted much more than money, i.e., themselves. He was their spiritual father and it was a parent's duty to gather for his children, the apostle says. He willingly offered all to them even though the result might be that the more he loved them, the less they loved him (12:15). Here we notice some of Paul's inner pain at their attitude, and it reminds us of his words to the Galatians: "Am I therefore become your enemy, because I tell you the truth?" (Galatians 4:16).

*2. Paul's Fear (12:20-13:5).* In deep earnest Paul then turned toward the church and uttered his fear that something was wrong with many of them. He mentioned especially two kinds of sin. First he wrote in 12:20 of a series of sins against the commandment to love, which was destroying the unity and solidarity of the church. In 12:21 he spoke of sins against the commandments of purity.

Paul said that to him it would be a great humiliation if it should turn out that the Corinthians did not stand the test. He had called this church his "praise" (1:14), his epistle of commendation (3:1), "the seal" of his apostleship (1 Corinthians 9:2). And what then if all his work should be a failure!

Hitherto Paul had been mild and restrained among them, but this time he would not show leniency toward the unrepentant. So he asked them all to examine their own hearts to see if they were in the faith.

*3. Paul's Trust (13:6-10).* In spite of his fears, Paul hoped for better things. He trusted the Corinthians were aware that he would not be restrained this time. He may have implied that the judging and punishing of sin was one way that apostolic authority can be demonstrated. However, he was not limiting the purpose of his visit to such judgment and punishment. Actually, he considered this a humiliating defeat because it meant passing sentence on his own work (Meyer). What he hoped was that the church itself would examine itself carefully and be ready to pass the test when he saw them. Paul, too, would pass the test when his work stands (13:6, 7). Therefore he wrote so they could have the opportunity to correct what was wrong. Then during his visit he could use the power the Lord had given him to build up, not break down. This was the real purpose for which he had received the power.

4. *Greeting and Blessing (13:11-14).* The conclusion of the epistle is very short, but the words are warm and filled with love. There are no personal greetings to or from certain persons. Perhaps he did not want to name them in an epistle to a church that had such serious problems. Yet in spite of all his stern words, Paul greeted the readers as Christian brethren.

The final words have been called the apostolic blessing, different from Aaron's blessing (Numbers 6:24-26). The apostolic blessing is trinitarian. The epistles to the Corinthians are among the earliest in the New Testament. So we have here one of the earliest testimonies in the New Testament to the faith of the Early Church in a triune God: "The grace of the Lord Jesus Christ, and the love of God, and the communion of the Holy Ghost, be with you all" (13:14).

# The Second Epistle of Paul to the Corinthians

## Commentary

### Chapter 1

**1. Paul, an apostle of Jesus Christ by the will of God:** ... This letter comes to you from Paul, *—PHLP* ... Paul a legate, *—MRDK* ... appointed by God, *—JB* ... chosen by God, *—NLTG* ... a special messenger, *R—PNT* ... missionary, *—KLGS* ... of Yeshua Mashiach, *MJV* ... an ambassador belonging to Christ Jesus through the desire of God, *—WUST* ... by the purpose, *—BB* ... by the good pleasure of God, *—MRDK* ... because God willed it so, *—BRCL.*

**and Timothy [our] brother:** ... our colleague, *—JB, BRCL* ... our fellow worker, *—BECK.*

**unto the church of God which is at Corinth:** ... to God's congregation, *—BRCL* ... to the community of God, *—HNT* ... assembly of God, *—YNG.*

**with all the saints which are in all Achaia:** ... together with all who are dedicated to him, *—JB* ... in conjunction with, *—RTHM* ... with all God's people, *—WEYM* ... to all the faithful, *—GRBR* ... to all Christ's people throughout Greece, *—TCNT* ... the holy people everywhere in Greece, *—BECK* ... who are throughout Achaia, *NASB.*

**1:1.** In the salutation of all his epistles except 1 and 2 Thessalonians, Paul referred to himself as either an apostle, a servant, or a prisoner of Jesus Christ. His favorite word to describe himself, however, was "apostle" or "sent one." The phrase "of Jesus Christ by the will of God" qualified his office as a "sent one." He had been called and sent out by the Lord Jesus himself. Paul's calling was not of his own choosing. It was by God's will (Acts 9:15).

Paul's emphasis on being an apostle by the will of God here focuses on the privilege that was his in being sent on a mission as an ambassador by the King of heaven. In other places he qualified the reference to his apostleship by declaring he had the office "by the commandment" of God (1 Timothy 1:1). In this case he thought more of the responsibility the Lord laid on him than of the opportunity God afforded him in sending him out. In either case, though, Paul made it clear he did not initiate his entrance into the ministry. No man in the natural would have chosen for himself the kind of life Paul lived. He stated emphatically that God put him into the ministry (1 Timothy 1:12). Paul did not choose the ministry; God chose him for the ministry.

In these opening words Paul identified himself with Timothy "our brother." The word *brother*

was also used in pagan societies, but the Christian gospel gave it new meaning. Here it means "our fellow Christian." Not only was Timothy Paul's brother in the Lord, he was also his son in the Christian faith (1 Corinthians 4:17; 1 Timothy 1:2; 2 Timothy 1:2). The closest of bonds united Paul and Timothy in the ministry of the gospel.

**2. Grace [be] to you and peace from God our Father, and [from] the Lord Jesus Christ:** ... May unconditional love be yours, *R—PNT* ... spiritual blessing and peace to you, *—WLMS* ... the Lord Jesus Christ bless you and give you peace, *—TCNT* ... favour to you, *—RTHM* ... and every blessing from God, *—BRCL.*

**1:2.** This verse has been called a Christian version of a Jewish blessing. Here, and in the first part of verse 3, Paul gives a Christian sense to Jewish liturgy. God is more than just the God of the Old Testament patriarchs and of Israel. God is the Father of Jesus Christ, the Son whom God sent to redeem the world. Implied very plainly in these verses is the deity of Christ.

**3. Blessed [be] God, even the Father of our Lord Jesus Christ:** ... Give praise to God, *—SEB* ... Let us praise, *—BECK* ... a gentle Father, *—JB.*

**the Father of mercies:** ... of all consolation, *—FNTN, —WORL* ... of tender mercies, *—HNT, —MNTG* ... compassionate mercies, *—WUST* ... the compassionate Father, *—TCNT.*

**and the God of all comfort:** ... of all encouragement, *—KLGS* ... of every comfort, *—NORL.*

**1:3.** Also implied is the fact that God is not only the Father of the Lord Jesus Christ, He is *our* Father, the Father of *our* Lord Jesus. Believers are united to the Father and the Son through faith (1 John 1:3) and are given power to become sons of God (John 1:12). As God's sons Christians are recipients of His mercies and His comfort. God is the divine source of the believer's help. He is the channel through whom all blessings are communicated to men.

**4. Who comforteth us in all our tribulation:** ... He encourages us, *—SEB* ... who consoles us, *—RTHM* ... comfort in all our trials, *—PHLP* ... in all our distress, *—HNT* ... in all our afflictions, *—CNFT, —WSLY, —RSV* ... in all my troubles, *—MNTG.*

**that we may be able to comfort them which are in any trouble:** ... to make us capable, *—ADAM* ... give the same sort of strong sympathy to others, *—PHLP* ... in all distress, *—DOUY* ... in any kind of distress, *—BRKL* ... having all kinds of trouble, *—SEB* ... in any distress, *—CNFT.*

**by the comfort wherewith we ourselves are comforted of God:** ... the same comfort, —NORL ...with the very comfort which we ourselves receive from him, —TCNT ... God is ever comforting me, —MNTG ... we are divinely sustained, —BRKL.

**1:4.** Some form of the word *comfort* occurs 10 times in verses 3-7. All are derived from the Greek *parakaleō* from which we get *comforter.* Paul declared here that God comforts His children in times of tribulations. How? We are not told; possibly through the ministry of Christian friends, certainly through the Scriptures. Christ promised He would not leave His followers orphans but that He would send the Holy Spirit to be their Comforter (John 14:16-18; 15:26). The emphasis here is on the constancy of that comfort. It is not to be temporary or spasmodic. This verse could just as well read: "who *always* comforts us. ..."

Several times this epistle expresses a paradox, i.e., affliction and comfort appear to go together, but not without a purpose. The very comfort that is received in times of suffering brings with it an understanding of why the comfort is sent in the first place. It is not only for the one who is comforted, it will also through that one benefit others.

**5. For as the sufferings of Christ abound in us, so our consolation also aboundeth by Christ:** ... the more we share Christ's suffering, —PHLP ... we have more than our share of comfort, —WEYM ... my sufferings for Christ are running over the cup, —WLMS ... overflowed to us, —FNTN ... are overflowing towards us, —RTHM ... come into our lives plentifully, —NORL ... through Christ, —WSLY ... through the Christ, —PNIN.

**1:5.** It is a reassuring thought that the constant comfort of God attends the overflowing sufferings that may come the believer's way. The Greek adverbs *kathōs* ("for as") and *houtōs* ("so also") express a comparison in which the second element matches the first. "For as" the sufferings of Christ may be present in abundance (*perisseuei*), "so ... also" is the encouragement and comfort present in abundance (*perisseuei*) for enduring the trial. This word means "to provide in superabundance." It is used in Matthew 14:20 to describe the fragments taken up "over and above" what had been eaten. It is also used by Jesus in the Parable of the Prodigal Son to describe the "bread enough and to spare" in the father's house (Luke 15:17).

Paul was saying here that although the sufferings of Christ seem to be present in abundance, even to overflowing, the comfort and encouragement for enduring the trial is just as abundant if only the Corinthians were spiritually sensitive enough to recognize it.

Paul was not necessarily referring only to what he suffered in his own body. These "sufferings" are those common to all who are united with Christ (Romans 8:17; 2 Corinthians 1:7; 1 Peter 4:13). "For as" union with Christ may be the cause of affliction, "so also" is its source of consolation. Apart from Christ, suffering often leads to despair rather than comfort.

**6. And whether we be afflicted:** ... if we have trials to endure, —NORL ... we be in tribulation, —YNG, —DOUY ... we are grieved, —FNTN ... we are in tribulation, —RTHM.
**[it is] for your consolation and salvation:** ... for your instruction, —CNFT ... deliverance, and preservation, —WUST ... and be saved, —SEB.
**which is effectual in the enduring of the same sufferings which we also suffer:** ... enabling you to bear patiently, —NOYS ... endure patiently, —PHLP ... through your patient fortitude, —WEYM ... your energetic endurance, —FNTN ... we ourselves are enduring, —MRDK.
**or whether we be comforted, [it is] for your consolation and salvation:**

**1:6.** The conditional "if" found in some versions does not imply any doubt regarding the sufferings. It is a simple way of stating the case. The verse has been translated "whenever we suffer" or "every time we suffer." The affliction that came to Paul and his companions enabled them to share this comfort with the saints at Corinth in such a way that it resulted in the strengthening of their faith, patience, and endurance as they went through similar trials. One of the wider results of suffering is the ability to comfort others.

Paul began here to distinguish between himself and his companions and his readers. He endured distress, trouble, and afflictions for the consolation and salvation of the Corinthians. In this sense their salvation became effective as they endured the same kinds of sufferings Paul and his party were going through.

"Salvation" here means more than conversion. The term *salvation* (Greek, *sōtēria*) also implies the following: (1) deliverance (material, temporal, spiritual, and eternal); (2) present experience of God's power to deliver from the bondage of sin; (3) future deliverance of believers at the return of Christ; (4) inclusively, to sum up all the blessings given by God to men through Christ by the Holy Spirit.

Thus the comfort ministered abundantly by God to His children in times of suffering extends beyond this present life into eternity. Our Heavenly Father plans all on our behalf with eternity in view while we tend to think in terms of time. Seeing things with temporal eyes we conclude God's chief aim for us is constant health, wealth, and happiness in this world. Instead, His major concern is our spiritual growth. Paul told the Romans that tribulation—suffering—works patience or perseverance, and patience produces experience or character (Romans 5:3, 4). Character motivated by godly love as described in 1 Corinthians 13 is the one thing we will take with us into eternity (1 Corinthians 13:13).

**7. And our hope of you [is] stedfast:** . . . Our hopes for you do not waver, *—TCNT* . . . concerning you, *—WSLY* . . . respecting you is firm, *—PNT* . . . is unshaken, *—BRKL, —RSV* . . . constant, *—WUST* . . . is firmly grounded, *NASB.*
**knowing, that as ye are partakers of the sufferings:** . . . you are comrades, *—MNTG* . . . that as you are sharing our sufferings, *—TCNT.*
**so [shall ye be] also of the consolation:** . . . as you are participators, *—FNTN* . . . ye are joint-partakers, *—RTHM* . . . so you share also, *—HNT.*

**1:7.** Comfort does not mean suffering will be taken away. But it can be understood as suffering for Christ with the result being *hupomonē* (verse 6), i.e., patient endurance in suffering. Paul's knowledge of this caused him to regard the believers with an unshakable hope despite their deficiencies in love and loyalty.

He calls them fellow participants (*koinōnoi*) of the sufferings. This term means "to share with someone in something." For Paul, the law of fellowship with Christ meant that as they participated in the sufferings of Christ, so also would they share the divine comfort.

**8. For we would not, brethren, have you ignorant of our trouble which came to us in Asia:** . . . we do not want you to be, *—RSV* . . . you to be uninformed, *—WLMS* . . . of our affliction, *—HNSN* . . . which happened to us, *—ALFD* . . . which befell us, *—WSLY, —CLMT.*
**that we were pressed out of measure, above strength:** . . . We were crushed, *—CNFT* . . . we were completely overwhelmed, *—PHLP* . . . I was burdened altogether beyond my strength, *—MNTG* . . . The burdens were heavier than we could carry, *—SEB* . . . burdened far beyond human ability, *—ADAM* . . . that our strength could not hold out, *—NORL* . . . afflicted exceedingly, *—MRDK* . . . exceedingly burdened, *—YNG* . . . were excessively loaded, *—FNTN* . . . exceedingly weighed down, *—WEYM* . . . exceedingly oppressed, *—PNT* . . . beyond our power, *—WUST, —SAWR* . . . past our strength, *—HNT* . . . exceedingly, beyond power, were we weighed down, *—RTHM.*
**insomuch that we despaired even of life:** . . . we actually despaired of life, *—TCNT* . . . we lost hope of life, *—KLGS* . . . we told ourselves that this was the end, *—PHLP.*

**1:8.** Verses 8-10 indicate the reality of the sufferings of which Paul had been speaking. Although it is not certain the trouble which Paul and his companions faced in Asia, some conjectures are

shipwreck, rebellion and division in the Corinthian church, severe illness, some unrecorded problem from which there seemed to be no escape, and the riot at Ephesus (Acts 19). It does not appear that Paul was writing to tell the Corinthians *what* the trouble was, but to tell *how* they had been affected. In the last part of this verse Paul used graphic language to describe the utter hopelessness of their situation. They were prostrated beyond all power of endurance. They were like an overloaded ship that was gradually sinking. They were utterly at a loss, absolutely without a way of escape.

**9. But we had the sentence of death in ourselves:** . . . Yes, we felt sentenced to death, *—BECK* . . . feel like men condemned to death, *—NAB* . . . We thought we would die, *—NLTG* . . . we decided the end must be death, *—HNT* . . . the answer of death, *—HNSN, —DOUY.*
**that we should not trust in ourselves, but in God which raiseth the dead:** . . . that we might learn to trust, *—PHLP* . . . that I might not rely on myself, *—MNTG* . . . might not rely on ourselves, *—TCNT* . . . might not have confidence, *—CLMT* . . . might not repose confidence, *—RTHM.*

**1:9.** Paul even went so far as to say he and his companions had the *apokrima* of death passed on them. This Greek word is found only here in the New Testament. They were like men condemned to death who, having made a petition for mercy, had instead received the sentence that they must die.

Now we have the paradox. The weakening of Paul's self-confidence and the self-despair to which it led resulted in the growth of a radical confidence in God. In the depths of his despair suddenly Paul seemed to grasp the divine purpose and was inspired with a new trust in God. The word "trust" is from the Greek *peithō* from which we also get the words *faith, believe,* and *confidence.* It has a solid equivalence in the Hebrew, namely, *batach.* The concept of hope and trust in God in both Old and New Testaments carries with it the idea not only of God's help in present distress but also the thought of eschatological help that puts an end to all distress.

Here again the importance of looking beyond the confines of this life becomes apparent. The faith the Lord looks for seems always to be of the resurrection variety. Abraham believed Jehovah would raise Isaac from the dead when he sacrificed him (Hebrews 11:17-19). Only a faith that declares God indeed raised Jesus from the dead brings deliverance from sin (Romans 10:9).

**10. Who delivered us from so great a death, and doth deliver:** . . . Who rescued us, *—FNTN* . . . rescued us from imminent death, *–MRDK* . . . He saved us from imminent death, *–NORL* . . . from so imminent a death, *–WEYM* . . . from such great perils, *–CNFT* . . . from a death so horrible, *–WLMS* . . . and is rescuing, *–WLSN* . . . He will rescue us in the future, *–SEB.*

**in whom we trust that he will yet deliver [us]:** . . . He is our hope, *–BECK* . . . we have set our hope, *–SAWR* . . . we have fixed our hope, *–RTHM.*

**1:10.** Paul was inspired with a strong confidence in God who could not only *keep* from death but was also able to *raise* from the dead. In fact, the deliverance that God brought to them was so great it was tantamount to a resurrection from the dead. Here, deliverance appears to rise above all else. God has delivered us; He is still delivering us. He will continue to deliver us. What a hope!

11. **Ye also helping together by prayer for us:** . . . striving together for us, *–SAWR* . . . working together . . . by your supplication, *–YNG, –ALFD* . . . co-operating by prayer, *–WLSN* . . . co-operating on our behalf by your supplication, *–HNSN* . . . cooperate on our behalf by prayer, *–HNT* . . . at the intercession of many, *–WEYM.*

**that for the gift [bestowed] upon us by the means of many persons:** . . . for the mercy bestowed, *–WORL* . . . obtained for us, *–DOUY* . . . the blessings vouchsafed to me through the intercession of many, *–MNTG.*

**thanks may be given by many on our behalf:** . . . on our account, *–MRDK.*

**1:11.** Paul's deliverance was conditioned by two things: his own trust and the continual intercession of the Church. That intercession seemed of the essence. God may not have acted on Paul's behalf if they had not prayed. The Psalmist noted how critical Moses' petition for Israel was. He wrote, "Therefore he said that he would destroy them, had not Moses his chosen stood before him in the breach, to turn away his wrath, lest he should destroy them" (Psalm 106:23).

Here we have the manward and Godward aspect of deliverance. Paul's trust, born in the depths of despair, along with the Corinthian believers' help (*sunupourgountōn*—help and cooperation in prayer), resulted in *to eis hēmas charisma.* Most commentators take the *charisma* here to refer to "the gracious gift of rescue from mortal danger."

The word "persons" is from the Greek *prosōpon* in most places translated "face" or "presence." This meaning could be retained here, e.g., "thanks from many upturned faces" or "from many persons." Since many had interceded, many would be thankful.

12. **For our rejoicing is this, the testimony of our conscience:** . . . For this is our proud claim, *NTPE* . . . The reason for our exultation,

*–BRKL* . . . our chief satisfaction is this, *–TCNT* . . . our glorying, *–YNG* . . . For our pride is the exact evidence of our conscience, *–FNTN* . . . our conscience backs us up, *–NORL.*

**that in simplicity and godly sincerity:** . . . we have been absolutely aboveboard and sincere, *–PHLP* . . . was one of holy living, *–NORL* . . . acted from pure motives, *–WLMS* . . . marked by a purity of motive, *–TCNT* . . . frankness and honesty, *–FNTN* . . . holiness and with pure motives, *–WEYM* . . . holiness, purity, and unsullied character of God, *–WUST.*

**not with fleshly wisdom, but by the grace of God:** . . . without human cleverness, *–BECK* . . . not with fleshly cunning, *–HNT* . . . the gracious help of God, *–WEYM.*

**we have had our conversation in the world:** . . . we behaved ourselves, *–ASV, –HNSN* . . . we had our behaviour, *–RTHM* . . . I have conducted myself, *–MNTG* . . . we did conduct, *–YNG* . . . we have conducted ourselves, *–CNFT.*

**and more abundantly to you-ward:** . . . especially with you, *–BECK* . . . more especially toward you, *–PNT.*

**1:12.** With verse 11 Paul ended the introduction of this letter. He then turned immediately to the main concern of the correspondence. In the body of the epistle the apostle felt compelled to defend his ministry against a series of false charges. That requirement made this the most painful to write of all his letters.

Verses 12-14 imply there either was or had been a different atmosphere at Corinth, at least on the part of some, with regard to Paul's ministry. They said he was insincere and fickle.

Paul dealt with these charges by offering a two-fold defense. First, he affirmed his absolute and complete sincerity. The two Greek words *haplotēti* and *eilikrineia* have been called a hendiadys, i.e., the expression of one idea by the use of two independent words connected by the word *and* (*kai*). These two words together refer to the moral purity and godly sincerity of Paul's inner motives and outward conduct.

The apostle recognized the conscience as a creature of God intended to serve commendable moral purposes. In his several letters he spoke of a conscience that is weak (1 Corinthians 8:7-12); good (1 Timothy 1:5, 19); pure (1 Timothy 3:9); and seared (1 Timothy 4:2). Paul valued the approval of his conscience, though he placed the ministry of the Holy Spirit above it (Romans 9:1).

Paul's conscience bore witness to the fact that he had never deceived anyone. The sincerity and integrity of his behavior became the very grounds for his rejoicing (*kauchēsis* = "boasting"). However, here the term picks up the good sense of praise of God found in the Hebrew *halal* (see Psalms 34:2; 44:8).

Paul had no confidence in the flesh or the wisdom of this world (1 Corinthians 2:1-5). He was careful to give all credit to the grace of God. His cry was, "By the grace of God I am what I am" (1 Corinthians 15:10). The exceptional effects produced by God's grace in the life of Paul had never been more clearly manifested than in his dealings with the Corinthian church.

**13. For we write none other things unto you, than what ye read or acknowledge:** . . . and very well recognize, —MNTG.

**and I trust ye shall acknowledge even to the end:** . . . get a complete understanding, —SEB . . . that you will understand it perfectly, —WLMS . . . you will admit this even to the end, —NORL.

**1:13.** Paul's second defense had to do with his letters. He had been accused of writing one thing, saying another, and doing something else. But Paul indicated that he had always been perfectly honest. He meant exactly what he wrote.

The play on words is not discernible in English, but Paul indicated that there was no difference in what they read (*anaginōskete*) in his letters and what they acknowledged (*epiginōskete*) or observed firsthand in his conduct. His actions and his words were in complete harmony.

**14. As also ye have acknowledged us in part:** . . . you have understood, —CNFT.

**that we are your rejoicing:** . . . we are your theme of boasting, —RTHM . . . as your reason for boasting, —WEYM.

**even as ye also [are] ours in the day of the Lord Jesus:** . . . when Christ reveals all secrets, —PHLP.

**1:14.** Paul had spent 18 months at Corinth preaching and teaching the Word of God. The thought here is that the Corinthian saints had once been proud of Paul and Timothy. However, their confidence had been shaken by a minority of rebellious church members and ad hominem remarks by false teachers regarding Paul's ministry.

Paul told the Corinthians they could still be proud. Neither he nor Timothy had changed. Their ministry had always been in the light of "that day" and when that day comes the Corinthians will know more fully the veracity of Paul's ministry to them. As they understood him more fully they would appreciate what God's grace was doing through him.

The Corinthians may have only partially understood Paul and his companions during the time the church was being established. The time would come when both Paul and the Corinthians would rejoice together. He would be their rejoicing as the one who had introduced them to Christ. They would be his rejoicing as converts.

**15. And in this confidence I was minded to come unto you before:** . . . With this assurance, —CNFT, —BRKL . . . with this conviction, —TCNT . . . after mature consideration, —WUST . . . I was purposing, —YNG, —WLSN . . . I purposed, —PNT . . . I had planned at first, —ADAM . . . was I disposed, —RTHM.

**that ye might have a second benefit:** . . . ye might receive the grace doubly, —MRDK . . . would be helped two times, —NLTG . . . so that you would enjoy two visits, —NORL . . . you would be helped twice, —SEB . . . be having a second bestowment, —WUST . . . a second pleasure, —FNTN . . . a second gift, —CMPB . . . a double delight, —WLMS . . . a pleasure twice over, —MNTG . . . a double blessing, —BRKL.

**16. And to pass by you into Macedonia, and to come again out of Macedonia unto you:**

**and of you to be brought on my way toward Judaea:** . . . to be sent forward, —YNG . . . helped forward by you, —WEYM . . . and be sped by you, —HNT . . . be escorted from you, —BRKL . . . sent with full provisions by you to Judea, —ADAM . . . on my journey, —CLMT.

**1:15, 16.** Paul's original itinerary included sea travel from Ephesus to Corinth, a journey by land north into Macedonia, then a second visit to Corinth on the return trip. Regarding the apostle's explanation here Carver wrote, "He desired that they should have 'the benefit of a double visit' (15, NEB; lit., 'have a second grace'). The expression is peculiar. Wendland notes that 'a tremendous awareness of power comes to light in these words: The apostle is the bearer of divine grace, and his presence in the church signifies a time when grace is at work (see Romans 1:11; 15:29).' Paul wanted to be a blessing to them both going and coming" (*Beacon Bible Commentary*, 8:509).

However, the apostle had no unwholesome view of himself as the sole source of blessing. After declaring a similar desire to impart grace to the Romans by visiting them, he said, "That is, that I may be comforted together with you by the mutual faith both of you and me" (Romans 1:12). Likewise, the blessing was to flow in two directions during his trip to Corinth. Brethren of the congregation there would have opportunity to assist Paul in his missionary ministry. They would bring him on his way toward Judea by seeing he had needed funds and supplies. As he wrote Titus, "Bring Zenas the lawyer and Apollos on their journey diligently, that nothing be wanting unto them" (Titus 3:13, 14).

When Paul altered his plans to revisit the church at Corinth his opponents used his perfectly legitimate change from two short visits to one long visit as an excuse to charge him with insincerity and unreliability. Paul insisted that the modification of his original travel plan had been in good faith. In reality it was loving consideration that had caused this revision. A previous visit (12:14; 13:1) may have been unpleasant. For their sake Paul did not want to come in the same manner again.

**17. When I therefore was thus minded:** ... Because we had to change this plan, —PHLP ... Yes, I changed my mind, —NLTG ... I therefore intended thus, —PNIN ... In purposing this did I display, —MNTG ... being my intention, —WLSN ... in this my intention, —CNFT.

**did I use lightness?:** ... did I act thoughtlessly, —GRBR ... Was I vacillating when I wanted to do this? —RSV ... I was not vacillating, NASB ... am I, therefore, to be condemned of fickleness? —LOCK ... did I show fickleness? —CNFT, —HNSN ... as one inconsiderate? —MRDK ... because it was not carried out? —WAY.

**or the things that I purpose, do I purpose according to the flesh:** ... thought to be an uncertain man, —LOCK ... do I form them on worldly principles, —WEYM ... determined by self-interest, —NAB ... in planning that? —WLMS.

**that with me there should be yea yea, and nay nay?:** ... saying "yes" and meaning "no"? —PHLP ... Yes, yes, and No, no? —YNG ... It is and It is not, —DOUY ... "Yes, yes!" equals "No, no"? —BRKL ... to have my "Yes" mean "No," if I want it so? —WLMS ... and changing to "no, no," according to circumstance? —NORL.

**1:17.** Paul took this opportunity to point out that he had not changed his plans without a reason. In his question "did I use lightness" (i.e., "Was I vacillating and fickle?"), the use of the interrogative particle *mē* strengthens the expected negative answer. The change hadn't been a whim of his carnal nature, but a deliberate purpose—possibly to spare them a rebuke (cf. 1:23; 2:4).

Paul was not the kind to say "yes" and "no" in the same breath. In fact, his deep love and concern for the Corinthians was one of the reasons for his delay in coming to them. They should have known him well enough from previous experience to have realized this. When Paul's evangelistic party had preached Christ to the Corinthians, they had not proclaimed one thing out of one corner of their mouths and something contradictory out of the other side.

These two parallel rhetorical questions imply that Paul's ministry had not been carried out *kata sarka* ("according to flesh"), i.e., he had not been controlled by worldly or selfish considerations. Paul's ministry was always "according to the Spirit." This was in keeping with what he professed and what he lived.

In determining where he went in his ministry Paul followed a rule based on his missionary call to take the gospel to the Gentiles (Acts 9:15; 22:21; 26:17). He always selected sites where Christ had not yet been preached (Romans 15:20, 21). His burden for souls took him to the area of his hometown in his first missionary journey. A pastoral concern caused him to return there to begin his second trip (Acts 15:36). Yet he was always open to specific direction of the Holy Spirit as to where he should go (Acts 16:6-10). He never carelessly chose his own way.

**18. But [as] God [is] true, our word toward you was not yea and nay:** ... God is faithful, —YNG, —HNSN ... as God can be trusted, NTPE ... is dependable, —ADAM, —SEB ... my message to you, —MNTG ... our language to you, —WEYM ... our object towards you, —FNTN.

**1:18.** Paul found it difficult to believe that anyone could have thought changed plans indicated changed character. The charge of the Corinthians against Paul reflected back, not only on his message, but also on God himself. They were actually the fickle ones.

Paul then made a transition from his trustworthiness as a person to his consistency as a preacher. He pointed out that God is true (*pistos*, meaning "trustworthy, faithful, dependable"). In verse 12 Paul mentioned his conscience as a witness. Here he indicated that God also bore witness to Paul's integrity. Just as God could be fully trusted, so also could the Word of God preached by Paul and his companions be considered trustworthy. Paul took a solemn vow, appealing to the unchanging nature of God as he affirmed that their message was not inconsistent or contradictory.

**19. For the Son of God, Jesus Christ, who was preached among you by us:** ... who was proclaimed to you, —WLSN.

**[even] by me and Silvanus and Timotheus, was not yea and nay:** ... was not wavering between, —MNTG ... was not inconsistent! —SEB ... showed no wavering between 'Yes' and 'No,' —TCNT ... did not show himself a waverer between "Yes" and "No," —WEYM.

**but in him was yea:** ... in Christ is the confirming 'Yes,' —TCNT ... it has always been yes in Him, —ADAM ... it was ever one consistent affirmative, —WAY ... he is the divine "Yes," —PHLP.

**1:19.** Paul reminded the Corinthian believers that the Jesus Christ they knew was the same Jesus Christ that he and Silvanus (Silas) and Timothy had preached to them during the 18 months of their ministry in Corinth. In essence Paul wrote, "We were the instruments God used when we preached the gospel and you believed." Their message and their character went together. A positive Christ could scarcely have been preached by negative preachers.

**20. For all the promises of God in him [are] yea:** ... He is the yes that makes them come true, −BECK . . . But with Him it is always "Yes," −WLMS . . . finds it affirmative in him, −PHLP.

**and in him Amen, unto the glory of God by us:** . . . to the honor of God, −HNT.

**1:20.** The apostles preached a positive gospel. Their preaching was confirmed by positive proofs (Mark 16:20). They emphatically declared that God was working according to the Scriptures. Jesus Christ has added "yea" and "Amen" to every promise of God. He is God's guarantee that all of God's promises are true. God shows His faithfulness in keeping His promises to the letter. Jesus Christ is the grand affirmation to all of God's promises.

**21. Now he which stablisheth us with you in Christ:** . . . For he that established, −WSLY . . . He Who supports us, −FNTN . . . has securely united us together, R−PNT . . . he who confirms us, −RTHM, −PNT . . . who is confirming you, −YNG . . . into union with Christ, −TCNT.

**and hath anointed us, [is] God:** . . . God has chosen us, −SEB . . . and has commissioned us, −RSV.

**1:21.** To recapitulate then, Paul wrote to his converts: here is God—absolutely trustworthy; here is Christ—always "yes"; here is our message—as unchanging and dependable as God himself; here are Paul and his companions, God's instruments along with the Corinthians, all "stablished" or firmly united in Christ and made faithful disciples. Not only have they been established, but they have also been anointed for divine service just as Christ (the Anointed One) was.

**22. Who hath also sealed us:** . . . He attested us, −FNTN . . . He who consecrated us and set his mark on us, −TCNT . . . stamped us with his seal, −CNFT.

**and given the earnest of the Spirit in our hearts:** . . . as down payment, −ADAM . . . security deposit, −BRKL . . . as a pledge, −CNFT . . . a first installment, −WLMS . . . the first-fruits, −KJII . . . the token payment guaranteeing, −WUST . . . the living guarantee of the Spirit, −PHLP . . . the pledge and installment of the Spirit, −HNT . . . foretaste of future blessing, −WEYM.

**1:22.** In these verses (21, 22) four statements are made about what God has done to and for the apostles and the Corinthian believers. Note the Trinitarian implications: God *established* them in Christ. He *anointed* or commissioned them for service. They were *sealed* and *given the Holy Spirit*.

The Greek aorist middle participle *sphragisamenos*, translated "sealed," conveys a twofold idea; namely, to *mark* (with a seal) as a means of identification. This mark not only denoted ownership but also carried with it the protection of the owner. From this definition we can better understand the symbolic use of the term describing

those who became Christians as being sealed with or by the Holy Spirit (Ephesians 1:13; 4:30).

However, many feel that it means more here than to just provide with a mark of identification. It also includes an endowment with power from heaven as denoted by God's giving the *arrhabōna* of the Spirit. In modern Greek *arrhabōna* is an engagement ring. Here it refers to a pledge or partial payment that is only a small fraction of the future endowment. What is given in the partial payment is the same in kind as can be expected in the future endowment. It is not the promising of one thing and the giving of another.

**23. Moreover I call God for a record upon my soul:** . . . But I invoke God as a witness, −RTHM, −WLSN . . . I for a witness, −YNG . . . a witness upon my life, −HNSN . . . putting my soul on trial, −ADAM . . . to give evidence to my life, −FNTN . . . against my spirit, −KLGS.

**that to spare you I came not as yet unto Corinth:** . . . in order not to hurt you, −BECK . . . to spare you pain, −WEYM.

**1:23.** In this verse Paul returned to his explanation of why he changed his original plans. He used the language of the law court to give weight to his truthfulness. Some translate the first part of this verse "I stake my life on it." The Greek phrase "upon my soul" could mean "as one who knows my inmost thoughts." Paul's motives for not coming were love and concern. Deep down he had not wished to come to them "with a rod" (1 Corinthians 4:21) even though he had been ready to do so if necessary.

**24. Not for that we have dominion over your faith:** . . . Not that we excercise lordship, −HNT . . . Not that we exercise dominion, −ALFD . . . we do not dictate your faith, −KLGS . . . that we domineer over your faith, −HNSN.

**but are helpers of your joy:** . . . we are joint promoters, −CMPB . . . to promote your joy, −WLMS . . . we are fellow-workers, −CNFT . . . associates of your joy, −WLSN . . . we are partners in your pleasure, Fen-ton.

**for by faith ye stand:** . . . ye have stood, −WSLY . . . you have already gained a firm footing, −GRBR . . . you are standing firm, NASB, −WEYM, −TCNT.

**1:24.** Paul knew that faith could not be demanded. Nor could holiness be legislated. This is determined by God, not man. Paul did not wish to be a tyrant who made men tremble. His desire was to be a helper to strengthen faith.

## Chapter 2

**1. But I determined this with myself:** . . . In thinking it through, −NORL . . . I decided this, −YNG . . . I have definitely decided, *–WLMS*...So far as I am concerned, I have resolved, *–WEYM*.

**that I would not come again to you in heaviness:** . . . that my next visit, *–NOYS* . . . make you another distressing visit, *–BRKL* . . . make you sorrowful, *–DOUY* . . . again in grief, *–WSLY* . . . again in displeasure, *–NORL* . . . pay you another painful visit, *–ADAM, –TCNT, –WLMS* . . . with sorrow, *–ASV* . . . with distress, *–FNTN*.

**2. For if I make you sorry, who is he then that maketh me glad:** . . . For what point is there in my depressing the very people, *–PHLP* . . . I cause you grief, *–WUST*...that cheereth me, *–WSLY*.

**but the same which is made sorry by me?:**...but he that is grieved by me? *–WSLY* . . . except the very ones whom I have offended? *–NORL* . . . save him on whom I have inflicted sorrow, *–KLST* . . . that is grieved, *–CNFT*.

**2:1, 2.** Verse 2 provides a basis for verse 1. The Corinthian converts were the source of Paul's joy. How then could he have caused pain to those who were the very source of his happiness! The sorrow in view here is that which Paul would have experienced if there had been no repentance on the part of the Corinthians.

Pondering these facts, Zahniser declared, "Paul gives here what is heralded as a new doctrine in missionary service, a helpful rather than a directive role" (*The Wesleyan Bible Commentary,* 5:271). He observed further, "Administrative power is never exercised properly in displaying itself, but is only an aid to the spiritual progress of the Church" (ibid., 5:270, 271). He concluded, "Paul was a man who worked with concern (Acts 20:19, 31), administered his churches with a sense of burden (11:28), and rent his soul almost in twain as his fatherly spirit yearned over his erring children" (ibid., 5:271).

The apostle displayed here the same attitude toward leadership that Peter did. He wrote instructions to church elders of his day saying simply, "The elders which are among you I exhort, who am also an elder" (1 Peter 5:1). He claimed no higher office than that of a fellow elder. His charge to other leaders was that they take the oversight of the congregation not "as being lords over God's heritage, but being ensamples to the flock" (1 Peter 5:3).

Paul also demonstrated the spirit of Jesus here in showing a concern over the joy of his converts. To His students the Master said, "These things have I spoken unto you, that my joy might remain in you, and that your joy might be full" (John 15:11). He made provision for it through prayer. He declared, "Hitherto have ye asked nothing in my name: ask, and ye shall receive, that your joy may be full" (John 16:24). He gave the Spirit, in part, for the same reason. Thus Luke recorded on

various occasions that "the disciples were filled with joy, and with the Holy Ghost" (Acts 13:52).

Though doing all he possibly could on their behalf, the apostle realized in the end relationship with God is a highly personal matter. When the final word was said the Corinthians would stand or fall before the Lord on the basis of individual faith. He would not dominate as to their position in the presence of Jesus.

**3. And I wrote this same unto you:**...about this very matter, *–NOYS*.

**lest, when I came, I should have sorrow from them of whom I ought to rejoice:**

**having confidence in you all, that my joy is [the joy] of you all:**...being persuaded concerning you all, *–WSLY*.

**2:3.** Many scholars feel verse 1 refers to a painful visit Paul had made to the church at an earlier date (see 12:14; 13:1). The implications are that this visit had been under circumstances painful to both Paul and the church. In addition to a "painful visit" there is also the feeling that verse 3 refers to what some scholars have called the "Severe Letter" Paul had written instead of visiting the church at Corinth (see also 2:9; 7:8, 12).

Paul had asked the church to discipline an offender (1 Corinthians 5:13). It seems that at first the church had refused to do this. However, after the severe letter they did so, and the man humbly confessed and quit his sinning. Paul had written to the church for that very reason. He had hoped his letter would result in proper discipline in Christian love, repentance on the part of the offender, and changed attitudes on the part of some in the church. In terms of both sadness and happiness Paul stressed how closely he and his readers were joined in Christian love and fellowship.

**4. For out of much affliction and anguish of heart:** . . . I was much troubled, *–NORL* . . . in deep suffering and depression of spirit, *–WEYM*...in deep distress, *–BRKL*...agony of heart, *–FNTN*...distress of heart, *–WLSN*...a most unhappy heart, *–PHLP*...and pressure of heart, *–YNG*.

**I wrote unto you with many tears:**

**not that ye should be grieved:** . . . not to pain you, *–MNTG*...should be distressed, *–FNTN*.

**but that ye might know the love which I have more abundantly unto you:** . . . No, I wanted to show you the great love, *–SEB* . . . but to convince you of my love, *–MNTG*...come to know experientially, *–WUST*...how very much I love you, *–BECK*...the great love, *–CNFT*...I so richly bear you, *–BRKL*...I have for you especially, *–HNT*...I have especially for you, *NASB*.

**2:4.** Paul had written this previous letter out of *pollēs* ("great, strong, deep") *thlipseōs* ("trouble and anguish of heart"). The words Paul used reveal some of his deep inner feelings. He had come to the Corinthians once *en lupē* or in deep grief, sorrow, and pain of mind and spirit (2:1), and he did not want to go through such an experience again. Thus, he had written to them "with many tears." The word "with" denotes attending circumstances, i.e., "I was (actually) crying when I wrote the previous letter to you."

Paul had not written in order to cause the Corinthians the same hurt (*lupē*) they had caused him. He did not mean to inflict grief for its own sake. He *did* desire that a heaviness might be produced that would lead to repentance rather than simply remorse. Paul had not written to hurt but to heal. The very grief caused by his severe letter was a manifestation of his love for them.

This *agapē* love is described by the comparative adverb *perissoterōs*, which is taken to mean "especially" here. Paul's special love for the Corinthians was a deep and abiding kind. It was a love of understanding and purpose. It was also a love that might at times cause pain in order to bless and benefit.

5. **But if any have caused grief:**
**he hath not grieved me, but in part:** . . . he has not made me sorry, *—CNDT* . . . but to some extent at least, *—BRKL.*
**that I may not overcharge you all:** . . . I don't want to be too unkind, *—SEB* . . . not to be too severe, *—PNT, —CNFT* . . . may not burden you, *—YNG* . . . may not lay a load on you all, *—CMPB* . . . not to overstate the case, *—NORL, —MNTG.*

**2:5.** Here the apostle began a defense against the second charge directed at him in Corinth, that of harshness in the case of discipline. Apparently some member of the congregation opposed him, perhaps hinting he sought personal vengeance in the matter. He showed a delicacy of feeling by not naming the offender. The negation (*ouk . . . alla*), i.e., "not . . . but," is used in the absolute sense, not to render void the first conception but to direct undivided attention to the second. Someone had indeed grieved Paul, but it was primarily the congregation at Corinth that had been grieved.

6. **Sufficient to such a man [is] this punishment:** . . . has been sufficient, *—PHLP* . . . punishment enough, *—NORL.*
**which [was inflicted] of many:** . . . The majority of you have censured him for his misdeeds, *—NORL* . . . inflicted by the majority, *—WUST, —HNSN* . . . imposed by the majority, *—MNTG* . . . the majority of you, *—WEYM.*

**2:6.** Evidently the majority of the church had decided to discipline the offender. The "of many" implies the decision was not unanimous. Some felt the punishment was not severe enough. Paul

says that this *epitimia* was sufficient. This Greek term is used only here in the New Testament. It is a technical term relating to congregational discipline for censure by the church.

7. **So that contrariwise ye [ought] rather to forgive [him], and comfort [him]:** . . . On the other hand, *—WLSN, —CMPB* . . . Now you should turn around, *—BECK* . . . so, instead of further rebuke, *—BRKL* . . . is better to forgive and encourage, *—KLGS* . . . show him that you still love him, *—NORL.*
**lest perhaps such a one should be swallowed up with overmuch sorrow:** . . . lest by any means, *—ASV* . . . may overpower him, *—NORL* . . . be overwhelmed by too much sorrow, *—CNFT* . . . overwhelmed by despair, *—BRKL* . . . be driven to despair, *—WEYM* . . . be completely overwhelmed by remorse, *—PHLP* . . . with his excessive grief, *—HNSN* . . . by excessive sorrow, *—HNT* . . . by more excessive sorrow, *—CNDT* . . . abundant sorrow, *—YNG* . . . that excessive reproof may drown him, *—FNTN.*

**2:7.** Whatever the censure was, the offender had deserved it. But discipline should not go beyond what is fair. It must also leave room for repentance. Forgiveness and reconciliation should then follow with the result being comfort and renewed fellowship (cf. Luke 17:3). Undue severity is to be avoided as much as undue leniency.

In a case of laziness deserving discipline at Thessalonica the apostle gave similar instructions. He considered refusing to work in support of oneself the height of selfishness. As such it cuts across the core of unselfishness in Christianity. Christ came not to have others serve Him but to serve others (Mark 10:45). The offender's laziness was so serious that Paul instructed, "Have no company with him, that he may be ashamed" (2 Thessalonians 3:14f.). Then he quickly added, "Yet count him not as an enemy, but admonish him as a brother."

8. **Wherefore I beseech you that ye would confirm [your] love toward him:** . . . I entreat you publicly, *—WLSN* . . . I beseech you fully to restore him to your love, *—CNBR* . . . to reaffirm, *NASB* . . . to ratify your love, *—HNT* . . . fully reinstate him in your love, *—WEYM, —MNTG* . . . in your affection, *—BRKL.*

**2:8.** Paul appealed to the Corinthian church members to confirm (*kurōsai*) their love to the offender. This Greek word is a legal term meaning "to enforce" or "to validate." Combining the two somewhat opposite concepts of *agapē* ("love") and *kuroun* (the legal term of developing church law) was not accidental. The church had made the decision to discipline one of its members. Paul now begged them earnestly to reverse the disciplinary process by confirming or deciding in favor of love for the repentant offender. This practical assurance of their love was to be shown in forgiveness and restoration.

**9. For to this end also did I write:**

**that I might know the proof of you:** ... was something of a test, —PHLP.

**whether ye be obedient in all things:** ... whether respecting all things, —RTHM ... you meet the specifications laid down, —WUST ... you would follow my orders implicitly, —PHLP ... you are prepared to be obedient in every respect, —WEYM ... in carrying out my orders, —NORL.

**2:9.** In a former letter Paul had set forth a course of action to be taken in dealing with an erring member. The reaction of the Corinthians would serve as a *dokimēn* ("proof") of their willingness to obey his authority as an apostle of Jesus Christ. The Greek word meaning proof that is the result of testing is unique in that it expresses both the fact that a test was made and that it was successfully passed.

**10. To whom ye forgive any thing, I [forgive] also:** ... you grant pardon, —FNTN.

**for if I forgave any thing, to whom I forgave [it]:**

**for your sakes [forgave I it] in the person of Christ:** ... in the presence of Christ, —WEYM, —PNT.

**2:10.** If the church was ready to reinstate the offender, Paul was satisfied with their decision. The perfect tense found here in *kecharismai* ("forgive," see also verse 9) indicates a present condition resulting from a past action. If any forgiveness was necessary on Paul's part it could be considered already given. If the Corinthians had forgiven the offender they could include Paul's forgiveness as having been given along with theirs. Paul felt deeply his responsibility as an apostle. Thus the action he had taken had for its main object the total welfare of the Corinthian church. Paul strengthened his position by appealing to Christ as a witness to the sincerity of his forgiveness "in (the) *prosōpō* (literally 'face') of Christ," i.e., as though Christ were looking on. His action had been performed as though he were in the presence of Christ.

**11. Lest Satan should get an advantage of us:** ... Then Satan won't fool us, —SEB ... to keep the devil from getting the best of us, —BECK ... that we may not be circumvented, —SAWR ... that we may not be overmastered, —FNTN ... that we may not be defeated by Satan, —CNFT ... that we may not be overreached by Satan, —RTHM ... the Adversary, —YNG.

**for we are not ignorant of his devices:** ... We know what he has in mind, —BECK ... not ignorant of his purposes, —WUST ... of his designs, —ADAM, —RSV ... of his schemes, NASB ... of his schemings, —BRKL ... of his tricks, —KLGS ... well we know his methods! —PHLP.

**2:11.** Unwillingness on the part of the Corinthians to forgive and comfort the offender and to confirm their love toward him could cause him to be *katapothē* (swallowed up with total extinction as a possible result) with excessive sorrow (see 2:7). If this happened there would be the danger that the church would be outwitted by Satan and robbed of a member of its fellowship. This should never happen because both Paul and the Corinthian believers were well aware of Satan's *noēmata*. This term (in the plural here) carries a sinister connotation meaning "evil schemings."

For the Corinthians to display ignorance of the strength of their enemy made them poor soldiers. These devices, designs, and plots the devil uses against Christians all stem from his basic character. His major name which Paul used here, *Satana*, reveals him as the chief "adversary" of the work of God. Paul showed his opposition is most real and not just imagined, as some suggest. In his first letter Peter said his plans include devouring every believer he possibly can (1 Peter 5:8). In an effort to do that he accuses them both to their face and before God constantly (Revelation 12:9, 10). Another of his names, devil (*diabolos*), speaks of this diabolic work of "slandering" people.

**12. Furthermore, when I came to Troas to [preach] Christ's gospel:** ... for the joyful message, —RTHM.

**and a door was opened unto me of the Lord:**

**2:12.** Paul now returned to his report regarding his change of travel plans. His purpose in coming to Troas had been to preach the gospel. While there "a door was opened." The metaphor of the open door means to "make possible" or "feasible."

**13. I had no rest in my spirit:** ... I was on edge the whole time, —PHLP ... I have had no relaxation, —WUST ... I had no ease, —FNTN ... I was still very worried, —SEB ... no peace of mind, —NORL, —MNTG ... no relief for my spirit, —WEYM ... but my mind could not rest, —RSV.

**because I found not Titus my brother:** ... I did not meet, —BRKL ... I failed to find Titus, —TCNT.

**but taking my leave of them, I went from thence into Macedonia:** ... I bade them farewell, —WEYM ... bidding them farewell, —CNFT ... so that I parted from them, —CNBR ... I proceeded into Macedonia, —FNTN.

**2:13.** An unusual opportunity for Christian service had opened up for Paul. However, Paul's anxiety regarding the affairs at Corinth seems to have kept him from taking advantage of the open door at Troas. The distress he experienced is pictured in a very forceful way by the use of the perfect tense for the verb here, namely, "I *had* no rest (relaxation, relief) in my spirit." Even as he wrote, Paul still had a vivid realization of the agony of spirit he had felt at Troas when Titus failed to arrive with news from Corinth. Again, the perfect tense also shows the continuation of Paul's tension until it grew so strong that he said good-bye to his friends and converts and hurried on to Macedonia.

**14. Now thanks [be] unto God, which always causeth us to triumph in Christ:** . . . who at all times leads us, *–RTHM,* . . . always leads us, *–HNSN* . . . exhibiteth us, *–NOYS* . . . leads us in one continual triumph, *–TCNT* . . . leads us on triumphantly, *–BECK* . . . heads our triumphal procession, *–WEYM* . . . to victory, *–NORL* . . . to celebrate his victory over the enemies of Christ, *–CNBR* . . . who ever makes our life a pageant of triumph, *–HNT.*

**and maketh manifest the savour of his knowledge by us in every place:** . . . he shows forth, *–KLGS* . . . the sweet aroma, *NASB* . . . an odor of incense everywhere, *–MNTG* . . . penetrate every place, *–NORL.*

**2:14.** Scholars differ in their opinions as to whether these verses (2:14-7:4) are an actual digression or not. It appears very possible that Paul at last met with Titus, possibly at Philippi, and received a very favorable report. Paul did not report this meeting but implied it by breaking into a doxology (2:14).

In verse 13 we see Paul's anxiety. In verses 14 and following we see his gratitude to God for divine deliverance and continual triumph "in Christ" as the gospel was being spread abroad in every place. The Greek term *thriambeuonti* ("cause to triumph") is given various meanings. Whether Paul was envisioning himself and his coworkers as soldiers of the Lord or prisoners of Christ, a basic thought here is that of display in a triumphal procession. Every place Paul ministered God gave him the victory regardless of the circumstances. The knowledge (*gnōseōs*) spoken of here is specifically Christian knowledge and understanding of the Scriptures given by God. It is opposed to Gnosticism and the mystery religions of the First Century.

**15. For we are unto God a sweet savour of Christ, in them that are saved, and in them that perish:** . . . a sweet perfume, *–FNTN* . . . a fragrant odor, *–CLMT* . . . the pleasant smell of Christ, *–SEB* . . . the unmistakable "scent" of Christ, *–PHLP* . . . fragrance of Christ to God, *–CNDT* . . . among the destroyed, *–CMPB.*

**2:15.** This was not a special knowledge communicated *by* a favored few *to* a favored few. The

fragrance (*osmē*) of the knowledge of God (2:14) was spread throughout the New Testament world by the preaching and works of the apostles. In spreading the fragrance of Christ the apostles themselves became a sweet perfume (*euōdia,* i.e., from *eu* meaning "well," and *ozō,* meaning "to smell"). This word is used of the fragrance from a sacrifice pleasing to God. A tradition states that when Polycarp was burned at the stake a similar fragrance was noted.

**16. To the one [we are] the savour of death unto death; and to the other the savour of life unto life:** . . . we are the deadly scent of death, *–ADAM* . . . To the latter, it is the smell of doom and death, *–NORL* . . . to these a fatal odor, *–BRKL* . . . odour of deadily death . . . an odour of living life, *–FNTN* . . . odour of death predicitive of death, *–WEYM* . . . of death that kills, *–BECK* . . . to the former the odor of life, *–NOYS.*

**And who [is] sufficient for these things?:** . . . who is equal to this? *–FNTN* . . . who is competent? *–WEYM, –CNDT* . . . who is qualified for this? *–HNT, –BRKL.*

**2:16.** Here the primary thought is not so much sacrifice as it is the dual effect produced through the ministry of the gospel. A graphic example of this is in Mark 16:16, namely, "He that believeth . . . shall be saved; but he that believeth not shall be damned" (see also John 3:18; Luke 2:34). In a sense Paul saw ministers of the gospel as messengers of both life and death, of salvation and judgment. Little wonder he asked, "And who is sufficient for these things?"

**17. For we are not as many, which corrupt the word of God:** . . . For we are not as the majority, *–CNDT* . . . profiting by corrupting, *–KJII* . . . secondhand dealers in God's word, *–KLST* . . . bartering the word, *–PNIN* . . . making merchandise of the word, *–WORL* . . . peddling the word, *NASB* . . . trafficking in the word, *–MNTG, –WLSN* . . . making profit by teaching God's Word falsely, *–NORL.*

**but as of sincerity, but as of God, in the sight of God speak we in Christ:** . . . but I speak from a single heart, *–CNBR* . . . but from the purest motives, *–BRKL* . . . but as of full strength, *–PNT* . . . but with transparent motives, as commissioned by God, *–WEYM* . . . in the very presence of God, *–MNTG.*

**2:17.** Two words stand out in relation to Paul's solemn view of his position as a gospel preacher. First, there is *kapēleuontes* ("corrupt"). The word occurs only here in the New Testament. It comes from the world of merchandising, suggesting trickery and avarice. The *kapelos* was often suspected of things like putting the best fruit on top of the basket or adulterating pure wine with water.

Paul was no peddler of spiritual goods for material gain. He refused to make merchandise of the gospel. Nor would he ever cheapen it by diluting it with foreign elements.

The second word to note here is *eilikrineias* ("sincerity"). It is derived from *eile* which refers to the "warmth or the light of the sun" and *krinō*. Thus the full sense is often given as "tested by the light of the sun," "completely pure." This word always denotes moral purity. Thus Paul contrasted the deceitfulness of the religious "hucksters" of his day with his pure motives and honorable methods in preaching the gospel. He received his message from God, ministered before Him, and was answerable to Him.

## Chapter 3

1. **Do we begin again to commend ourselves?:**...Is this going to be more self-advertisement, *—PHLP* . . . Am I falling into self-recommendation again? *—GDSP* . . . Are we beginning to flourish our credentials all over again? *—BRCL* . . . attempting to put ourselves in the right? *—BB* . . . like a new attempt to commend ourselves to *you? —JB* . . . as if we were again boasting about ourselves? *—TEV* . . . to pat ourselves on the back, *—SEB.*

**or need we, as some [others], epistles of commendation to you:** . . . Unlike other people, we need no letters, *—JB* . . . that we, like some people, need letters of introduction, *—BRCL* . . . letters of approval, *—BB.*

**or [letters] of commendation from you?:** . . . commentary letters, *—CNDT.*

**3:1.** One of the charges brought against Paul by his enemies had been self-assertion and pride. Some feel these charges may have been made in connection with Paul's words in 1 Corinthians 4:16; 11:1, namely, "Follow me." However, lest his words in 2 Corinthians 2:17 be misinterpreted as self-praise he quickly assured the Corinthians that he needed no letters of recommendation either to them or from them. In the Greek the form of this question indicates that a negative answer is expected. Paul was not against letters of recommendation. Later on these letters became quite necessary because of large numbers of charlatans.

Indeed the apostle himself wrote such letters of recommendation on behalf of others. In fact, before he closed this very epistle he included several lines to commend Titus and other fellow workers to the Corinthians (8:16-19, 22, 23). This Early Church practice provided a pattern for the licensing of ministers in the Church of today.

2. **Ye are our epistle written in our hearts, known and read of all men:** . . . Our letter of recommendation is yourselves, *—WEYM* . . . Credentials! you, you are my credentials, *—WAY* . . . you are all the letter we need, *—NEB* . . . my commendatory epistle, *—LOCK* . . . inscribed in our hearts, *—RTHM, —PNT* . . . open to everyone to know and to read, *—BRCL.*

**3:2.** Paul used the pronoun "Ye" (*humeis*) with the verb *este* ("ye are"). When this is done it expresses a certain emphasis because the subject is already in the verb. This construction is used to express a special relationship between the subject "Ye" and the predicate noun "epistle." Paul's recommendation was not *letters,* but *lives* that were known and read by everybody. The implication is that the authenticity of the letters produced by other so-called apostles was suspect and would not stand close scrutiny.

3. **[Forasmuch as ye are] manifestly declared to be the epistle of Christ:** . . . It is clear that Christ himself wrote this letter, *—TEV* . . . it is plain that you are a letter that has come from Christ, *—NEB.*

**ministered by us:** . . . drawn up by us, *—JB* . . . produced by my service, *—WLMS* . . . transcribed by me, *—MNTG* . . . transmitted by us, *—FNTN* . . . delivered by us, *—SAWR, —WLSN, —BRCL* . . . committed to my charge, *—CNBR* . . . entrusted to our care, *—TCNT* . . . executed by our ministry, *—HNT* . . . the result of our ministry, *—NIV.*

**written not with ink, but with the Spirit of the living God:** . . . recorded not with ink, *—BB.*

**not in tables of stone, but in fleshly tables of the heart:** . . . not on slabs, *—ADAM* . . . not in the tablets, *—YNG* . . . not on stone plates, *—BECK* . . . but on the pages of the human heart, *—NEB.*

**3:3.** The words "manifestly declared" (*phaneroumenoi*) mean "to make known or be shown." The connotation is that of public display. Some think Paul may have had in mind a letter engraved on a monument displayed to public gaze where all who passed by could read it.

In a sense believers themselves are *epistolē* or authoritative letters of Christ "known and read of all men." Paul's work was not his own but that of Christ. He was simply a *diakonos*, or one of the King's "servants."

A second metaphor grows out of the first. So close to the hearts of Paul and his companions were the interests of the Corinthians that Paul wrote, "You are a letter of Christ inscribed upon our hearts." Their being a "letter" was the work of the Spirit of God in their hearts. Paul used two comparisons to show this. First, he compared the miracle-working power of God with human letters of recommendation written with ink. Paul's "letters" of recommendation were vastly superior to the scrolls of his rivals. The contrast between "ink" and "Spirit" takes on added meaning when it is remembered that the ink used in Paul's day washed off easily.

The second comparison deals with how the messages were written. The Ten Commandments were written on "tables of stone" (Exodus 24:12). The message of the gospel Paul preached was written by the Spirit of God in their hearts.

**4. And such trust have we through Christ to God-ward:** . . . This is the sort of confidence, −SEB . . . Such is the confidence, −WEYM . . . Such is the assurance I have, −CNFT . . . we have this great confidence, −FNTN . . . such confidence have we through the Christ, −HNSN.

**5. Not that we are sufficient of ourselves to think any thing as of ourselves:** . . . not because we possess self-sufficiency, −BRKL . . . not that we are personally qualified, −HNT . . . not that we are competent, −CNDT . . . that we could accomplish anything by ourselves, −ADAM . . . by our own reasonings, −WEYM.
**but our sufficiency [is] of God:** . . . but our competency, −CMPB . . . our capacity is, −FNTN . . . but God gives us our ability, −BECK . . . Our ability is of God, −KLGS . . . but our qualification is from God, −HNSN, −HNT . . . has its source in God, −WUST.

**3:4, 5.** Paul could say what he did because of the confidence given him through Christ. His was not self-confidence or arrogance. He claimed nothing for himself—all was God. His confidence would endure in the sight of God. His trust was not in his own ability to think out something: "as (if) of ourselves." It was God who made Paul and his companions adequate for any task. One of the great Old Testament titles for God was *El Shaddai*, sometimes interpreted to mean "The All-Sufficient One." It was the All-Sufficient One who made Paul more than adequate for his work as a minister of the gospel. With these words the apostle answers his question of 2:16, "And who is sufficient for these things?"

Paul's theology here is the same as that expressed by Peter in his exhortation to those who serve in the church. He wrote, "If any man minister, let him do it as of the ability which God giveth" (1 Peter 4:11). He recognized one could serve with human talents in such a way as to draw attention to self. Thus the reason he gave for his instruction was "that God in all things may be glorified through Jesus Christ: to whom be praise and dominion for ever and ever."

**6. Who also hath made us able ministers of the new testament:** . . . Who also qualified us, −WORL . . . makes us competent administrators, −PHLP . . . competent to serve, −WEYM . . . sufficient to be ministrants, −YNG . . . sufficient as ministers, −ALFD . . . efficient ministers, −PNT . . . dispensers of a new covenant, −CNDT . . . of a new institution, −CMPB . . . of a New Settlement, −FNTN . . . of a New Way of Worship, −NLTG.
**not of the letter, but of the spirit:** . . . but a spiritual principle, −TCNT.
**for the letter killeth, but the spirit giveth life:** . . . for the letter slays, −RTHM . . . for the

writing kills, −SAWR . . . the written law puts to death, −HNT . . . for the letter destroys, but the Spirit restores to life, −FNTN . . . the spirit makes the dead to live, −CNBR . . . doth make alive, −YNG.

**3:6.** The verb "hath made . . . able" is from the same word as "sufficient" in verse 5. Paul and his companions had been made able ministers of the new covenant. This new covenant is spoken of as early as Jeremiah 31:31. God's *diathēkēs* ("decree" or "covenant") which He directed toward Christians is described as *kainēs* ("new," Ezekiel 11:19; 36:26). Some feel the prophecy in Ezekiel 36:26 was fulfilled in the outpouring of the Holy Spirit on the Day of Pentecost and in the apostolic proclamation of the gospel which followed.

The letter of the Law which causes men to die (Romans 7:9-11) is contrasted with the life-giving Spirit (John 6:63). Note in this passage (3:3-6) it is not stone *but* flesh, not letter *but* Spirit, not external *but* internal, not Law *but* grace.

**7. But if the ministration of death:** . . . Now, if the dispensation of death, −WLSN, −CNDT . . . served to bring death penalties, −NORL.
**written [and] engraven in stones, was glorious:** . . . was brought into existence in glory, −RTHM . . . came with glory, −WEYM, −WORL . . . was inaugurated with glory, −PNT . . . accompanied with such splendour, −HNT . . . came with a blaze of glory, NTPE.
**so that the children of Israel could not stedfastly behold the face of Moses for the glory of his countenance:** . . . the sons of Israel could not continue looking at, −SEB . . . could not gaze steadily on, −MNTG . . . could not stare at, −KLGS . . . to look unflinchingly at, −PHLP . . . on account of the brightness, −SAWR . . . because of the brightness of his face a vanishing brightness, −WEYM . . . the transient glory that shone upon it, −CNFT . . . due to his facial brilliance, −BRKL.
**which [glory] was to be done away:** . . . a glory even then fading, −MNTG . . . a splendour that was waning, −HNT . . . which was being nullified, −CNDT . . . its brightness, fading as this was, −RSV . . . even though transitory, −PHLP . . . was soon to fade, −CNBR.

**3:7.** These verses continue the contrast made between the letter and the Spirit. Paul was careful not to leave the impression that the Law was bad (Romans 7:7) or against the promises of God (Galatians 3:21). It was not designed to kill, but to bring believers to Christ (Galatians 3:24). The greatness of the glory of the old covenant is described in such a way that the glory of the new covenant appears more striking in contrast.

Beginning with these lines the apostle addressed still another charge against him. His critics apparently claimed he despised or at least neglected the Law in his preaching. But how could he? The messages of both the Law and grace came from God; therefore both are good. The brilliance in the teachings of Moses dims in the presence of the truths of the gospel, as the light of the moon dims when the sun rises. One does not despise the moon when there is no sun. Nor does he despise the light of the lowly lamp he burns to illuminate his room when he has neither sun nor moon.

The Greek *kainēs* in verse 6 is used to describe the "new" covenant everywhere in the New Testament except Hebrews 12:24. In Hebrews 12:24 the word is *neos*. This latter word refers to "what is new and distinctive." *Kainos* suggests a difference in nature and it is this difference Paul sought to emphasize.

In the New Testament the Law is represented in Moses (cf. Jesus' words in Luke 16:29, "They have Moses . . .," also Luke 24:27, "and beginning at Moses . . ."). Moses was called the minister of an external covenant that produced death because of the condemnation under which offenders were placed. Paul referred back to the giving of the Law on Sinai. The accompanying circumstances then were so glorious that when Moses came down from the mount his face reflected the very glory of God. The Israelites could not "look intently" (NASB) at Moses' face.

**8. How shall not the ministration of the spirit be rather glorious?:** . . . But how much more glorious will be the ministry of the Spirit? —SEB . . . be more luminous? R–PNT . . . be still more glorious, —MRDK.

**3:8.** We are not told how long Moses' face shone. The implications are that it was outward and transient in contrast with the "ministration of the spirit" which is internal and lasting. This contrast is strengthened by the grammatical form of the negative. Rather than simply *ou* ("not"), it is *ouchi mallon*, "not to a greater degree."

More understanding comes regarding Paul's comparison between the blessings of the Law and grace by considering his statements of like nature in addressing the Romans. He used *mallon* repeatedly there to contrast the death that came to man through the first Adam and the life he may have through the second Adam, Jesus. As real as the death is that comes to all through Adam, the apostle declared the life Jesus provides is "much more" (*pollō mallon*) available to all who believe (verse 9). Thus the "rather more glorious" here becomes the "much more" of Romans.

**9. For if the ministration of condemnation [be] glory:** . . . that announces doom, —BRKL . . . which pronounces doom had glory, —WEYM.

**much more doth the ministration of righteousness exceed in glory:** . . . how much greater and more glorious, —NORL . . . far more is the religion that sets men right with God rich in splendor, —TCNT . . . the dispensation of righteousness, —CNDT . . . radiant in glory, —MNTG . . . exceed in splendour, —FNTN.

**3:9.** Notice again the antitheses. The Law ministers death, but to a greater degree the Spirit ministers life. The Law ministers condemnation, but to a *much* greater degree (*pollō mallon*) the Spirit ministers righteousness. The old order faded away. The Holy Spirit is working in the new order to bring about what the old order could not do because of the weakness of the flesh (Romans 8:3). In this area the righteousness (*dikaiosunēs*) bestowed by God closely approximates salvation. Keeping the Law could never produce *dikaiosunēs*.

**10. For even that which was made glorious had no glory in this respect:** . . . once resplendent in glory, —WEYM.

**by reason of the glory that excelleth:** . . . on account of the surpassing glory, —RTHM . . . the glory which surpasses it, —WEYM . . . because of the superior glory, —YNG.

**3:10.** Mount Sinai was a scene of awesome glory. However, it was nothing in comparison to the glory of Mount Calvary. When Moses came down from Sinai after receiving the Ten Commandments, his face shone with God's glory. But this glory faded and later Moses died. The glory ministered by the Spirit will never fade. Christ is alive and Christians are "changed into the same image from glory to glory" (3:18).

**11. For if that which is done away [was] glorious:** . . . If what passed away, —BRKL . . . which was fading away, —MNTG.

**much more that which remaineth [is] glorious:** . . . that which is permanent, —BECK . . . the present permanent plan, —PHLP . . . which abides, —CNFT, —BRKL . . . will exist in much greater magnificence, —FNTN.

**3:11.** Verses 7-11 assert three conclusions which use the comparative degree. The comparative is sometimes strengthened by the use of *mallon*, meaning here "very far better." This is *bad* English, but *good* Greek. Verses 7 and 8 conclude that if the dispensation of the Law which ministered death was attended by glory, then now to a *greater degree* is life ministered by the Spirit.

The second conclusion is similar. The Corinthians knew how glorious the ministry of Moses was. But if the ministry of Moses that brought condemnation was glorious, it is exceeded in glory to a *much greater degree* by the righteousness God provided.

The third conclusion is almost identical with that in verse 9. For if the old covenant existed with a genuine glory even though it was transitory, then now to a *much greater degree* there is the glory of the new covenant which is permanent.

**12. Seeing then that we have such hope:** ... Having, then, such an expectation, —CNDT.

**we use great plainness of speech:** ... I speak and act without disguise, —CNBR ... we use much freedom, —YNG ... great openness of speech, —RTHM ... we speak quite unreservedly, —BRKL ... we can be very bold, —ADAM.

**3:12.** Paul expressed his confidence in the abiding permanence of the gospel message. On this the Christian's hope is based, and in this hope there is no element of uncertainty. Several commentators connect this hope (*elpida*) with the gift of the Holy Spirit and all that results from it.

Paul's confidence was grounded in the abiding glory of the new covenant. Because of this he used *parrhēsia* ("boldness"). This Greek word was used in the political sphere, and some of the shades of meaning persist in later Christian usage. Some of these are the right to say anything and the truth of what is said. There is also the interesting idea that such freedom of speech may be opposed by those to whom it may apply. However, in the face of such opposition *parrhēsia* is the candor that opposes any who would hamper or limit the unveiling of the truth.

**13. And not as Moses, [which] put a veil over his face:** ... we do not imitate Moses, —WEYM.

**that the children of Israel could not stedfastly look to the end of that which is abolished:** ... to prevent the Israelites gazing at the disappearance of what was passing away, —TCNT ... were not to look intently, —CNDT ... could not stare at, —KLGS ... might not observe the glory of his countenance, —CNFT ... until the final fading of the glory, —ADAM ... the last rays of the fading glory, —BECK ... until the brightness faded away, —SEB.

**3:13.** The use of *parrhēsia* implied a face that was uncovered before men. The contrast here is between the openness brought in by the new covenant and the transitory character of the Mosaic dispensation. The glory on the face of Moses was real, so bright Moses had to cover his face (Exodus 34:29-35). But it was also a glory that would fade away.

**14. But their minds were blinded:** ... But their conceptions, —RTHM ... their senses, —DOUY ... their apprehensions were calloused, —CNDT ... their minds had become dense, —TCNT ... were hardened, —YNG, NASB ... were dulled, —BRKL ... were made dull, —WEYM, MNTG ... it dimmed their thoughts, —FNTN.

**for until this day remaineth the same veil:** ... the same veil remaineth unremoved, —WSLY ... the same covering remains, —WUST ... remains unmoved, —FNTN.

**untaken away in the reading of the old testament:** ... when they read in their synagogues the ancient covenant, —CNBR ... when the old contract is read, —KLGS ... during the reading of the book of the ancient Covenant, the same veil remains unlifted, —WEYM.

**which [veil] is done away in Christ:** ... because it is removed in Christ, NASB ... it is only removed by Christ, —FNTN.

**3:14.** The vacillating conduct of the Israelites in the Old Testament revealed that they did not understand the ministry of Moses. Their minds became dull and callous. They were unable, perhaps even unwilling, to understand. The situation had not changed in Paul's day. The Jews still failed to recognize the transitory character of the Law: that it was only a schoolmaster to bring them to Christ (Galatians 3:24). It is only through Christ that the veil is removed. Only through Him could the Jews and all others really understand the true meaning of the Law and the gospel.

**15. But even unto this day, when Moses is read: the veil is upon their heart:** ... a covering is lying on their heart, —CNDT ... a veil over their minds, —PHLP.

**3:15.** Those of Paul's day still could not see the glory of God in His Word. The Judaizers at Corinth pointed people back to the Law, taking care to always read publicly "Moses." The name of the writer stood not only for his writings but also included all the Old Testament. Abraham said to the rich man, "They have Moses and the prophets; let them hear them" (Luke 16:29). The most complete title for the Old Testament was "Moses, ... the prophets, and ... the psalms" (Luke 24:44).

As Moses descended the mount, of necessity he covered his face. Israel could not stand to look upon the glory of the Lord reflected on his countenance (3:7). Even in Paul's day the veil of unbelief concealed the truth from their minds. The fault did not lie with the Law (Romans 7:7), but with its readers.

**16. Nevertheless when it shall turn to the Lord, the veil shall be taken away:** ... Yet if they "turned to the Lord," —PHLP ... when they shall be converted, —DOUY ... the veil is rent away, —CNBR ... is stripped away, —MNTG ... is removed, —WLMS ... will be withdrawn, —WEYM.

**3:16.** Instead of returning to the Law, Israel needed to turn back to the Lord. Then He would take away (remove) the veil just as Moses did when he returned to the mountain to commune with Jehovah (Exodus 34:34). With the covering removed, they could see Christ as the theme of the Word.

The teachers of Saul of Tarsus interpreted Scripture in such a way as to keep him from seeing the truth until he met Jesus near Damascus. However, Paul's conversion experience quickly removed the veil, and he saw the Messiah in the passage, much as the Ethiopian eunuch had (Acts 8:32-35).

**17. Now the Lord is that Spirit:** . . . This is the God's Spirit at work, R–PNT . . . By the word 'Lord' is to be understood the Spirit, –TCNT.

**and where the Spirit of the Lord [is], there [is] liberty:** . . . there is freedom, –FNTN . . . freedom is enjoyed, –WEYM.

**3:17.** Like Jesus, Paul declared God is Spirit (John 4:24). Indeed, He is Father, Son, and Spirit. Those who worship Him must worship in the Spirit and according to truth. The illumination of the Spirit makes alive the truth of Scripture. The Spirit enables one to find liberty instead of bondage as he reads the Bible. The sincere Israelite discovers freedom from slavery to the ritual of the Law.

However, this liberty is not license to sin, as Paul made clear in addressing the Galatians. He explained, "For, brethren, ye have been called unto liberty; only use not liberty for an occasion to the flesh" (Galatians 5:13). Proctor expressed a similar sentiment in commenting on liberty in 3:17. He said it consists in the fact that "the consciousness of the restraining and condemning nature of the law is taken away. Christians no longer desire to break the law; they are imbued with the spirit of the law" (*The New Bible Commentary*, p. 992).

**18. But we all, with open face:** . . . with unveiled face, –YNG.

**beholding as in a glass the glory of the Lord:** . . . reflecting as in a mirror, –CNFT . . . reflecting the glory, –RTHM.

**are changed into the same image from glory to glory:** . . . are being transformed, –YNG . . . will be transformed into the same resemblance, –FNTN . . . the same likeness, –WEYM . . . from one degree of glory to another, –WUST.

**[even] as by the Spirit of the Lord:**

**3:18.** The face of the Christian is open, unveiled. He beholds (contemplates) the glory of the Lord which he sees as if looking in a mirror. Like mirrors of polished brass in Paul's day, the Bible offers the reader an image of Jesus.

As the believer contemplates Jesus through prayer and the reading of the Word, the Spirit of the Lord changes (Greek, *metamorphoumetha*, cf. English, *metamorphosis*) him into the likeness and appearance he beholds. He is transformed (Romans 12:2 where the same Greek verb appears) into that image from one glorious level to

another. The complete likeness to Jesus will come when he sees Him face-to-face (1 John 3:2).

## Chapter 4

**1. Therefore seeing we have this ministry:** . . . For this cause, –ALFD . . . Discharging therefore this ministry, –CNFT . . . being engaged in this service, –WEYM . . . having this service, –FNTN.

**as we have received mercy:**

**we faint not:** . . . I never give up, –WLMS . . . we do not get discouraged, –PNT . . . we shrink not back, –ALFD.

**4:1.** God put Paul in the ministry. He did not choose it for himself. He always considered he received that honor as an act of mercy and grace (1 Timothy 1:12, 13).

His ministry offered life for death (3:7f.), justification for condemnation (3:9), and something permanent for the temporary (3:11). The Law, given by Moses, provided far less. Accordingly, the apostle stood strong in the face of opposition at Corinth. He did not lose heart.

**2. But have renounced the hidden things of dishonesty:** . . . we have repudiated, –HNSN . . . put a ban on secret and disgraceful methods, –NORL . . . We use no hocus-pocus, –PHLP . . . the secrecy which marks a feeling of shame, –WEYM . . . the hidden things of shame, –ASV . . . the secret dealings of shame, –FNTN.

**not walking in craftiness:** . . . no clever tricks, –PHLP . . . not wandering in villainy, –FNTN . . . we avoid unscrupulous conduct, –CNFT . . . the sphere of craftiness, –WUST.

**nor handling the word of God deceitfully:** . . . no dishonest manipulation, –PHLP . . . nor yet counterfeiting, –RTHM . . . nor falsifying the word of God, –HNSN.

**but by manifestation of the truth:** . . . But, by an open statement of the truth, –NORL . . . but with openness of the truth, –FNTN.

**commending ourselves to every man's conscience in the sight of God:** . . . in presence of God, –RTHM.

**4:2.** The false teachers in the church at Corinth had stooped to low levels in their efforts to discredit Paul's ministry. All that they practiced he had renounced. These included hidden, secret, shameful things. He detested the basic dishonesty which motivated them. The craftiness (*panourgia*, literally, "readiness to do anything without scruples") they used was a stench in his nostrils. Paul's critics even handled the Word of God deceitfully, in a distorted manner. They adulterated it, as the wine seller of the day who weakened his merchandise by diluting it with water.

By contrast, Paul openly proclaimed the truth of the gospel. He stated its concepts plainly with no intent or attempt to deceive or trick anyone.

Paul's ministerial critics who sought to draw disciples to themselves acted as if the end justifies the means. He simply relied on the manifestation of the truth to accomplish the task. He used nothing deceptive nor secretive. As he explained in his defense before Agrippa, "This thing was not done in a corner" (Acts 26:26).

Sincere ministers of the gospel have nothing to hide. They preach no esoteric truths understood only by the initiated, as Paul's Gnostic enemies claimed. When the high priest asked Jesus of His teaching as if it were secretive, He replied, "I spake openly to the world; I ever taught in the synagogue, and in the temple, whither the Jews always resort; and in secret have I said nothing" (John 18:20).

The apostle needed to do no more to recommend himself to those of a sincere conscience. Certainly such ministerial conduct left him acceptable (commendable in the sight of, before the presence of) to God.

**3. But if our gospel be hid:**...the meaning of our Good News, —WEYM.
**it is hid to them that are lost:**

**4:3.** Though some of Paul's critics at Corinth accused him otherwise, he exerted every effort to see that men heard the unadulterated truth of the gospel. He was careful that his behavior did not nullify the message he preached. He presented its precepts as clearly as possible. Bold in the process, he wrote, "Seeing then that we have such hope, we use great plainness of speech" (3:12). In spite of this some said Paul's preaching was too difficult for the common person to comprehend. Even Peter declared that in Paul's writings there were "some things hard to be understood" (2 Peter 3:16). However, Paul acknowledged the fact with all due respect, unlike the opposition in Corinth.

In such a setting the apostle explained that any failure to receive his message was not due to any fault of his. If his gospel was hidden (*kekalummenon*, "veiled," from the same root as in 3:18), it was veiled from those who were lost, namely those who were already in a state of perishing.

**4. In whom the god of this world hath blinded the minds of them which believe not:**...the God of this aeon, —HNSN...blinded the understanding, —MNTG...darkened the thoughts with unbelief, —FNTN...their minds have been kept in the dark, —TEV...the conceptions of the unbelieving, —RTHM.
**lest the light of the glorious gospel of Christ, who is the image of God, should shine unto them:**...that they should not see, —HNSN...so as to shut out the sunshine, —WEYM...kept from seeing the radiant light, —NORL...to stop them seeing the light shed by the Good News, —JB...the illumination of

the evangel of the glory of Christ, —CNDT...to prevent the illumination of the gospel...from penetrating, —BRKL...should not dawn upon them, —MNTG...Who is the representative of God, —FNTN...who is the exact likeness of God, —TEV...should not shine forth, —ALFD...cannot dawn upon them, —NEB...from dawning upon them, —GDSP.

**4:4.** The fault was in the fact that Satan, the god of this world (*aiōnos*, "this present age"), had blinded those who refused to accept Paul's message. The adversary is always ready to darken the minds of those who resist the gospel. In his letter to the Ephesians Paul wrote of people who have their understanding darkened through the blindness of their hearts (Ephesians 4:18). However, they could not escape personal responsibility by blaming their sinful state on the devil. The apostle further described them as those "who being past feeling have given themselves over" to a wicked way of life (Ephesians 4:19). They would not see; therefore, they could not see. Willful blindness became penal blindness.

Thus spiritual forces hindered those at Corinth from seeing the light of the gospel. They failed to recognize Jesus as the very image (likeness, exact representation) of God.

**5. For we preach not ourselves, but Christ Jesus the Lord:**...For we have not heralded, —BRKL...For I am not proclaiming myself, —WLMS...It is not ourselves that we preach, —BRCL...is not about ourselves, —BB.
**and ourselves your servants for Jesus' sake:**...your bond-servants, —NOYS.

**4:5.** The false apostles at Corinth apparently promoted themselves to a shameful degree. They chose a poor substitute in focusing on their own example rather than that of Jesus. By way of contrast, Paul declared he preached (*kērussomen*, "publicly proclaimed") Christ, not self. Some preached Moses (Acts 15:21); the apostle preached Jesus (1 Corinthians 2:2).

Paul constantly identified himself simply as a servant (*doulos*, a "slave" in contrast to a hired servant) of the Lord and of His people. In his first letter to the Corinthians Paul wrote, "Let a man so account of us, as of the ministers of Christ, and stewards of the mysteries of God" (1 Corinthians 4:1).

**6. For God, who commanded the light to shine out of darkness:**
**hath shined in our hearts:**
**to [give] the light of the knowledge of the glory of God in the face of Jesus Christ:**...to enlighten the knowledge, —FNTN...which is radiant on the face of Christ, —WEYM.

**4:6.** The Lord had done too much for Paul for him to ever stoop to the low level of preaching himself. God had performed a miracle in Paul's life like that of the Creation. In the beginning God said, "Let there be light: and there was light" (Genesis 1:3). The great Creator had also commanded the light to shine in the darkness of the heart of the former Saul of Tarsus, symbolized by the bright light he saw the moment of his conversion (Acts 9:3). It brought him the knowledge of the glory of God which radiated from the face of Jesus who knew no covering of the face as did Moses (3:13). The countenance of the Saviour shone brightly.

7. **But we have this treasure in earthen vessels:** ... But we possess, *—FNTN* ... This priceless treasure we hold, *—PHLP* ... within utensils of mere clay, *—BRKL* ... in a fragile case of clay, *—WEYM* ... in bodies of clay, *—NORL.*
**that the excellency of the power may be of God, and not of us:** ... That the pre-eminence, *—HNT* ... the exceeding greatness, *—HNSN* ... the surpassing greatness, *—MNTG* ... the grandeur of the power, *—FNTN* ... not to originate in us, *—WEYM.*

**4:7.** The Lord committed the treasure of the gospel to the apostle for careful management as a steward of God. Men of that day sometimes kept priceless objects in earthen jars. Of all the things held in store, the truths of the gospel were the most valuable.

With that analogy Paul recognized the greatness of the message committed to him as standing in sharp contrast to his frailty as its container. God arranged it that way so men would realize the extraordinary quality of what Paul possessed was of the Lord and not of man. Paul ministered by the power (ability) which God gave, so the Lord was glorified in all (1 Peter 4:11).

8. **[We are] troubled on every side, yet not distressed:** ... We are hedged in, *—BRKL* ... We are handicapped on all sides, *—PHLP* ... In everything distressed yet not straitened, *—HNT* ... afflicted in every way, but not crushed, *NASB* ... pressed hard, but not hemmed in, *—RTHM* ... yet not suppressed, *—HNSN* ... but not overpowered, *—FNTN.*
**[we are] perplexed, but not in despair:** ... We were without resources, *—KLGS* ... we suffer embarrassments, *—BRKL* ... we are puzzled, *—PHLP* ... yet not over-perplexed, *—PNIN* ... not destitute, *—CNFT* ... we are never at a loss, *—NORL* ... yet never utterly baffled, *—WEYM.*

**4:8.** Among the many charges brought against Paul by the opposition at Corinth was the claim he lived a life of relative ease as a preacher. The defense which builds as this letter unfolds makes that increasingly clear. The false teachers told tales of their hardships to make themselves appear the true ministers and Paul the doubtful one.

To explain, the apostle used a series of paradoxes in which he revealed he knew some of the worst and some of the best of times in his ministry. He experienced trouble and was hard-pressed on every side. Yet he was never crushed by his afflictions. He was sometimes perplexed as to the exact course of action he should take. He had no ready solution to some of his problems. In spite of it all, Paul never came to the point of despair.

9. **Persecuted, but not forsaken:** ... We are hunted but not caught, *—KLGS* ... pursued, yet never left unsuccoured, *—WEYM* ... yet not deserted, *—HNSN* ... yet not abandoned, *—WORL* ... not left in the lurch, *—WUST.*
**cast down, but not destroyed:** ... prostrate, *—HNT* ... smitten down, *—PNIN* ... struck to the ground, *—WEYM* ... repulsed, but not exterminated, *—FNTN* ... we may be knocked down but we are never knocked out! *—PHLP* ... but we do not perish, *—CNFT.*

**4:9.** Further, Paul was constantly persecuted (*diōkomenoi*, with the original meaning of "chase after, drive away, drive out"). He was pursued and hunted like a wild animal. Yet he never felt deserted or abandoned. Shortly after his conversion he was driven out of Damascus to escape certain death. Later, enemies of the gospel chased him from Antioch of Pisidia to Iconium and then to Lystra where they stoned him and left him for dead. They hunted him from Philippi to Thessalonica to Berea and then to Athens.

He was often cast down, but he was not left in despair (ruined, lost, destroyed). In the figure of a boxer in the ring, he was knocked down but never knocked out. The servant of the Lord in the will of God is indestructible in the ultimate view.

10. **Always bearing about in the body the dying of the Lord Jesus:** ... always being exposed to death, *—WLMS* ... the mortification, *—DOUY* ... the marks of a death like that of Jesus, *—TCNT* ... the putting to death of Jesus, *—HNSN.*
**that the life also of Jesus might be made manifest in our body:** ... that it may be clearly shown, *—WEYM, —WLMS* ... Jesus may be displayed, *—FNTN* ... may be disclosed, *—HNT* ... may also be set forth in our lives, *—NORL.*

**4:10.** Paul always carried in his own body the stigma associated with the crucifixion of Jesus. To the Jewish person such a man was cursed of God (Galatians 3:13). Because Paul identified himself as one with Christ, men sought to kill him too. The abuse Paul's physical body took left him with scars to prove this identification to those who questioned whether or not he knew hardships in the ministry. He wrote to the Galatians, "I bear in my body the marks of the Lord Jesus" (Galatians 6:17). He proudly wore them because in a sense they identified him as belonging to the Lord much as the branding of cattle shows ownership.

However, just as God raised Jesus from the dead following His crucifixion, so He manifested (made known, showed in a visible way) life in the apostle's body following his suffering. The death was his, but the life was that of Jesus.

**11. For we which live are alway delivered unto death for Jesus' sake:** ... surrendered for the sake of Jesus, –*FNTN.*
**that the life also of Jesus might be made manifest in our mortal flesh:** ... that the living power of Jesus, –*NORL* ... may yet be evidenced, –*BRKL* ... may be revealed, –*NAB.*

**4:11.** Paul knew what it was like to be constantly handed over to the custody of the police or the court for the testimony of Jesus. He concluded, though, that such was necessary in order that the life of Christ might be demonstrated in his mortal (subject to death, destined to die) body. Without death there can be no resurrection. Where there is no cross there is no crown.

**12. So then death worketh in us, but life in you:** ... In us then death is active, –*HNT* ... death is active in us, –*SEB* ... So that the preaching of the Gospel procures sufferings and danger of death to me, –*LOCK* ... while death is wearing down my frame, a new life is animating you, –*WAY* ... Life is active within you, –*TCNT* ... energizes in us, Fenton ... is operating in us, –*CNDT* ... we are constantly dying, while you are in full enjoyment of Life, –*WEYM.*

**4:12.** In verses 10 and 11 the paradoxical existence of both death and life at the same time relates to Paul's personal experiences. He referred to what he described later in this letter where he concluded, "For when I am weak, then am I strong" (12:10). However, he changed the application of his analogy in verse 12. Death still worked in him, but the resurrection life which resulted worked in those to whom he ministered. No doubt the desire for this caused him to pray as he did in Philippians. He wrote, "That I may know him, and the power of his resurrection, and the fellowship of his sufferings, being made conformable unto his death" (Philippians 3:10).

Harris stressed the changed figure when he wrote, "Here his thought seems to be 'I suffer exposure to physical death for your sakes (cf. v. 15a); you enjoy more of the risen life of Christ as a consequence.' He apparently saw not only a causal but also a proportional relation between his 'death' and the 'life' of the Corinthian believers. The deeper his experience of the trials and sufferings of the apostolic life, the richer their experience of the joys and privileges of Christian existence (cf. Colossians 1:24; 2 Timothy 2:10). The 'middle term' between his experience and theirs was the divine comfort that, having received, he could then dispense (cf. 1:4)" (*The Expositor's Bible Commentary,* 10:343).

**13. We having the same spirit of faith:** ... In the same spirit of faith, –*TEV* ... We have the same kind of faith as David had, –*NLTG.*
**according as it is written:** ... that was recorded, –*BRKL* ... as he who said in the Scriptures, –*WLMS* ... in the Writings, –*BB.*
**I believed, and therefore have I spoken:** ... from the faith in my heart, –*BB* ... and consequently speak, –*FNTN* ... therefore did I speak, –*WORL* ... and therefore speak out, –*NEB.*
**we also believe, and therefore speak:** ... that is why we speak, –*SEB.*

**4:13.** Faith put Paul at ease even in the face of severe persecution. He declared he had the same spirit of faith as the Psalmist whom men subjected to similar mistreatment. David kept his confidence in God in spite of adverse circumstances. "The sorrows of death compassed me," he wrote (Psalm 116:3). He proclaimed his faith before men, and the Lord delivered him from certain destruction. He said simply, "He helped me" (Psalm 116:6). Even so the apostle believed and continued to declare his faith.

**14. Knowing that he which raised up the Lord Jesus:** ... Because we are certain, –*BB* ... knowing that he, who resuscitated our Lord Jesus, –*MRDK* ... assured that He, –*BRKL.*
**shall raise up us also by Jesus:**
**and shall present [us] with you:** ... will give us a place in his glory, –*BB* ... and will bring us into his presence along with you, –*BRCL* ... to stand in His own presence, –*WEYM* ... and bring me side by side with you, –*GDSP* ... into his presence, –*TEV.*

**4:14.** Thoughts of suffering repeatedly on the brink of death for the sake of the gospel brought to mind for Paul the certainty of death sooner or later for all men, even for believers (cf. Hebrews 9:27). The sole exception will be in the translation of Christians who still live at the return of Christ (1 Corinthians 15:51f.).

However, death holds no terror for the child of God. Paul declared Christ's resurrection from the dead guaranteed that of the believer. The One who raised His only begotten Son will just as surely raise all His spiritual children one day. The apostle wrote to the Romans, "But if the Spirit of him that raised up Jesus from the dead dwell in you, he that raised up Christ from the dead shall also quicken (make alive) your mortal bodies by his Spirit that dwelleth in you" (Romans 8:11).

Triumphantly Paul pictured the morning of the resurrection as leading to the presentation of all believers before God. He declared both he and the faithful Corinthians would be in the number. In view of the current problems in the Corinthian church, the confidence Paul expressed was a compliment to them.

**15. For all things [are] for your sakes:** . . . Everything happens for your good, *—SEB* . . . all things are ordered, *—NEB* . . . Everything is for your sakes, *—BRCL* . . . for your benefit, *—TCNT.*

**that the abundant grace might through the thanksgiving of many redound to the glory of God:** . . . it may result in an overflowing, *—ADAM* . . . the exuberant favour of God, *—LOCK* . . . the grace being multiplied, *—PNIN* . . . reaches greater and greater numbers, *—GDSP* . . . the favour abounding, *—RTHM* . . . being more richly bestowed . . . and more and more promote the glory of God, *—WEYM* . . . may overflow, *—FNTN.*

**4:15.** Again Paul noted God intended his ministerial trials to benefit believers such as those at Corinth. He wrote the Romans that "all things work together for good to them that love God" (Romans 8:28).

Hardships provide a perfect setting for the grace of God to become abundant (*pleonasasa,* "to grow, spread to more and more people"). At the same time thanksgiving increases as it arises to the Lord from the many (*pleionōn,* comparative of *polus,* thus "more and more") yet to be won to Christ. All will redound or cause to overflow to the glory of God.

**16. For which cause we faint not:** . . . That is why, *—BECK* . . . Wherefore we lose not heart, *—HNT* . . . Therefore we never flinch, *—WAY* . . . we are not discouraged, *—BRKL* . . . we do not get discouraged, *—PNT* . . . we never give up, *—SEB* . . . we never collapse, *—PHLP.*

**but though our outward man perish:** . . . our nature, *—TCNT* . . . our outer nature is wasting away, *—WLMS* . . . outer man is decaying, *—CNFT* . . . is impaired, *—CMPB* . . . is corrupted, *—DOUY* . . . is exhausted, *—FNTN.*

**yet the inward [man] is renewed day by day:** . . . is being renewed, *—CNDT* . . . receives fresh strength, *—PHLP.*

**4:16.** These glorious facts gave Paul sufficient reason not to faint or lose heart. True, the difficulties encountered in his ministry wore his physical strength away. He knew well his outward man was decaying. At the same time, though, his inward man was renewed day by day.

The apostle realized what all aging believers know. They too find comfort in the fact that both decay and renewal go on at the same time within their being. They receive the answer to the prayer of the Psalmist, "Cast me not off in the time of old age; forsake me not when my strength faileth" (Psalm 71:9).

**17. For our light affliction, which is but for a moment:** . . . We have trials, *—NORL* . . . For the fleeting trifle, *—FNTN* . . . transitory burden of suffering, *—WEYM.*

**worketh for us a far more exceeding [and] eternal weight of glory:** . . . preparing for us an everlasting weight of glory, greater than anything we can imagine, *—BECK* . . . is producing for us, *—BRKL* . . . an enormously erupting everlasting, *—KLGS* . . . weight of majesty, *—HNT* . . . burden of glory, *—CNDT* . . . great beyond expression, *—CMPB.*

**4:17.** The Spirit within Paul brought him to the conclusion that his relatively insignificant affliction which brought distress because of the pressure of outward circumstances actually worked for his good. As something which was momentary, it brought about for him a far more exceeding (*huperbolēn eis huperbolēn,* literally "excess to excess"), beyond all measure or comparison, weight or fullness of glory. That glory would be eternal and would never fade away. To the Romans he wrote, "For I reckon that the sufferings of this present time are not worthy to be compared with the glory which shall be revealed in us" (Romans 8:18).

**18. While we look not at the things which are seen, but at the things which are not seen:** . . . we aiming not at, *—WLSN* . . . *—CMPB* . . . we do not fasten our eyes on the visible, *—BRKL* . . . what is not being observed, *—CNDT* . . . not looking for the visible things, but the invisible, *—RTHM.*

**for the things which are seen [are] temporal; but the things which are not seen [are] eternal:** . . . For the seen is for a time, *—HNT* . . . things that are seen pass away, *—CNBR* . . . are transitory, *—PHLP* . . . What is seen is only temporary, but what is unseen lasts forever, *—SEB* . . . things that are unseen, *—WORL* . . . are everlasting, *—KLGS.*

**4:18.** One of the things which kept Paul true to his calling was holding the proper perspective in life. He did not look (*skopeō,* "to gaze upon," in contrast to *blepō,* "to see") or concentrate his attention upon the things which are seen. He had but little interest in the things of this world. Any who accused the apostle of being a materialist would be very wrong.

Instead, the apostle fixed his gaze on the things which are not seen. His reason was the things which are seen are transitory, lasting only for time, while the things which are not seen are eternal. Elisha's servant with his physical eyes saw only their city surrounded with horses and chariots of the enemy army that had come to arrest the prophet. The man of God prayed, "Lord, I pray thee, open his eyes, that he may see" (2 Kings 6:17). As the servant viewed the unseen, he discovered God had placed horses and chariots of fire all around the prophet to protect him. The reality of the unseen world contained a greater army for Elisha than the seen world held against him.

## Chapter 5

**1. For we know that if our earthly house of [this] tabernacle were dissolved:** . . . that if perchance, *—RTHM* . . . this earthly house of our soul, *—NORL* . . . if this poor tent, our earthly house, is taken down, *—WEYM* . . . terrestrial tabernacle house should be demolished, *—CNDT* . . . may be thrown down, *—YNG* . . . is torn down, *—BECK* . . . should be dismantled, *—BRKL* . . . be destroyed, *—CNFT*.

**we have a building of God:** . . . I have a mansion built, *—MNTG* . . . a mansion built by God, *—CNBR*.

**an house not made with hands:**

**eternal in the heavens:** . . . everlasting, *—CMPB* . . . It lasts forever, *—SEB* . . . age-abiding, *—RTHM*.

**5:1.** With knowledge of the eternal, Paul could say he knew (*oidamen*, "to have insight provided by intuition or revelation") what comes at the end of life for the Christian. He ceases to live in his tabernacle, the physical body which is like a tent. The apostle knew well just how transitory and fragile such temporary dwelling places were since he made tents with his own hands. Peter also spoke of the day when he would "put off" his tent (2 Peter 1:14). At death, man's physical body is taken down and folded up like a tent.

Just as certain as death for Paul was the fact that afterward he would live in a house not made with human hands. In that world where temporal things no longer exist, his dwelling would be an eternal one in the heavens.

Life in the world to come is no less real than this one. It is no imaginary existence in a fog where one drifts in and out of consciousness. John recognized regarding the afterlife that "it doth not yet appear what we shall be" (1 John 3:2). However, he quickly added, "But we know that, when he shall appear, we shall be like him." After His resurrection Jesus demonstrated He was as real as before (Luke 24:26-43). He was no ghostly person, but a real one.

**2. For in this we groan:**

**earnestly desiring to be clothed upon with our house which is from heaven:** . . . longing to be clothed, *—HNSN, —WORL* . . . to be endowed with our little cottage, *—FNTN* . . . to be invested with that habitation, *—WLSN* . . . with our heavenly mansion, *—CMPB* . . . with our dwelling, *NASB* . . . the cover of my heavenly habitation, *—MNTG* . . . to put on our heavenly dwelling, *—RSV* . . . the glorified body from heaven, *—NORL* . . . the Heavenly home, *—PHLP*.

**5:2.** In the meantime some discomfort remains for the believer. He experiences a certain groaning because of undesirable circumstances in this life. He is not really "at home" in this world. In his letter to the Romans Paul said, "We . . . groan within ourselves, waiting for the adoption, to wit, the redemption of our body" (Romans 8:23). As Abraham of old, the Christian is a sojourner rather than a permanent resident on earth. Abraham "looked for a city which hath foundations, whose builder and maker is God" (Hebrews 11:10).

With the apostle the child of God earnestly desires and longs for the day when he will be clothed upon (*ependusasthai*, from the same root as the English word *endue*) with his house from heaven. That house, of course, is the glorified body of the transfigured Christian. The resurrection body alone can provide a proper covering for the soul's nakedness.

**3. If so be that being clothed we shall not be found naked:** . . . we shall not be found destitute, *—WLSN* . . . be found naked [a disembodied spirit], *—WUST* . . . be found without bodies, *—TCNT*.

**4. For we that are in [this] tabernacle do groan, being burdened:** . . . we who are in this tent sigh, *—CNFT* . . . groaning in deep trouble, *—MNTG*.

**not for that we would be unclothed, but clothed upon:** . . . because we do not want to take it off, *—MRDK* . . . but rather to be invested with the other coverings, *—BRKL* . . . to be unclothed [divested of our mortal body] but clothed upon [invested with our heavenly body], *—WUST*.

**that mortality might be swallowed up of life:** . . . that this our dying nature might, *—CNBR* . . . what is mortal may, *—MNTG* . . . may be absorbed by immortal life, *—NORL* . . . may be absorbed in Life, *—WEYM, —MRDK*.

**5:3, 4.** For the person of modesty, nothing could bring greater distress than appearing naked in public. Even so the soul shies away from being unclothed, without a body. Paul used this fact to explain that his desire, along with all Christians who still abide in their present physical bodies, was not to be unclothed. They do not seek death as such, whether by ordinary means, accidental means, or suicide. Despite the teachings of Freudian psychology, the apostle expressed no "death wish" here.

The sting of death has been removed for the Christian, but he finds no pleasure in the prospects of dying. He has no morbid fear of death, but it is still repulsive to his flesh.

What the believer anticipates in connection with death is being clothed upon with a new body. He knows the joy of having a redeemed soul, but he must await the day when his redemption applies to his body in the resurrection (Romans 8:23). Come that day, both the body and soul will agree in the pursuit of the things of God. Fleshly appetites will no longer pull in an opposite direction. The spirit-flesh conflict will cease.

Besides all this, any dread of death will be forever gone in the resurrection. The present state of mortality where man bears the burden of being subject to death will be "swallowed up" in a life that is eternal for the Christian.

**5. Now he that hath wrought us for the self-same thing [is] God:** . . . And he that prepareth us for this thing, —MRDK . . . prepared us for this very end, —NORL . . . has prepared us for this change, —TCNT . . . this very thing, —HNSN.

**who also hath given unto us the earnest of the Spirit:** . . . as a down payment, —ADAM . . . as a guarantee, —RSV . . . a pledge and foretaste of that bliss, —WEYM . . . a guarantee that we will live again, —SEB.

**5:5.** Worshipfully Paul declared God has prepared believers for this selfsame thing (this very purpose). To demonstrate His plan for our future He has given us an earnest, a down payment or the first installment, as a guarantee of the rest that is to follow. The realities of experiences such as new birth by the Spirit and the baptism in the Spirit serve that purpose for believers. To the Ephesians Paul wrote that after they believed they "were sealed with that Holy Spirit of promise, which is the earnest of our inheritance until the redemption of the purchased possession" (Ephesians 1:13, 14).

**6. Therefore [we are] always confident:** . . . Having good courage, —RTHM . . . we always behave undauntedly, —WSLY . . . always courageous, —HNSN.

**knowing that, whilst we are at home in the body:** . . . while we are sojourning, —WSLY.

**we are absent from the Lord:** . . . I am in banishment from, —MNTG . . . is to be abroad from the Lord, —HNT.

**7. (For we walk by faith, not by sight:):** . . . we are living a life of faith, —WEYM . . . We live by trusting Him, without seeing Him, —BECK . . . is faith, not appearances, —HNT . . . not by appearance, —ALFD, —HNSN.

**5:6, 7.** The apostle found reason to be confident and courageous because of these truths. His faith rested on facts. He could face hardships and even the threat of death without flinching. He knew that as long as he remained in his physical body he was absent from the Lord. Sight may not say such things, but faith does; and Paul ordered his life by its realities.

**8. We are confident:** . . . We are cheerful, —NORL. **[I say], and willing rather to be absent from the body:** . . . we prefer to be, —BRKL . . . would prefer to leave the body, —ADAM.

**and to be present with the Lord:** . . . to be at home, —CLMT, —HNSN . . . and go home to be with the Lord, —ADAM . . . to come home unto the Lord, —RTHM.

**5:8.** So significant was it that the apostle repeated the fact of his confident and courageous attitude in the face of death. Strange as it may seem to some, he was actually willing and even wished to be absent from the body so he could be present with the Lord. In writing to the Philippians, the Spirit moved him to say, "For to me to live is Christ, and to die is gain" (Philippians 1:21). Except for his ministry, he thought it better to depart and be with Christ (Philippians 1:23, 24).

**9. Wherefore we labour:** . . . Therefore we are ambitious, —WSLY, —HNSN, —CLMT . . . we are desirous, —FNTN . . . I strive earnestly, —CNBR . . . we make it our ambition, —HNT, —ADAM.

**that, whether present or absent, we may be accepted of him:** . . . we always want to please God, —SEB . . . to please Him, —ADAM, —DOUY . . . to be well pleasing to Him, —CNDT . . . to please Him perfectly, —WEYM . . . we may be approved by him, —NOYS . . . we may be well pleasing unto him, —ALFD.

**5:9.** The choice of living or dying did not rest with the man Paul, of course. He committed his way to the Lord. His concern was that of pleasing the Saviour, whether present (*endēmountes*, "at home," same as in verses 6 and 8) or absent (*ekdēmountes*, "away from home," same as in verses 6 and 8) from the physical body. He labored, strived earnestly for, and held as his chief ambition that very thing.

The ambition of the false teachers at Corinth was to please people and gain a following. Paul wanted peace with men too, but he aspired more to be accepted of the Lord.

**10. For we must all appear before the judgment seat of Christ:** . . . all be reviewed, —FNTN . . . all be exposed, —HNT . . . all must needs be made manifest before the tribunal, —RTHM.

**that every one may receive the things [done] in [his] body:** . . . may be requited, —BRKL . . . the things practiced in the body, —KLGS.

**according to that he hath done:**

**whether [it be] good or bad:** . . . or worthless, —WEYM, —ADAM.

**5:10.** The prospect of having to give an account to God for his conduct in the ministry kept the apostle on the right track. He faced the fact that all believers must one day appear (*phanerōthēnai*, "to show or reveal," i.e., "reveal themselves, be made known, stand openly") before the Lord. Each will be summoned to appear before the judgment seat (*bēmatos*, literally "steps") of Christ, to be judged as to the quality of their Christian service on earth.

Paul pictured that judicial bench as being at the top of a set of steps such as was the case in his day. The Romans not only believed crime must be punished, but they also held the penalty must be administered publicly. Accordingly, the judge sat openly at the top of the stairs to a governmental building to hear cases that came before him.

The believer's hearing before Christ will examine the nature of his service to the Master during his earthly life. Ministers especially will be judged according to the quality of the work they have done. If the spiritual buildings they have erected were made of wood, hay, or stubble, they will stand before Jesus without reward (1 Corinthians 3:12-15).

The judgment seat of Christ concerns rewards for past service as well as assignments for future service to the Master during the Millennium and the Eternal Age. To those who have erected a quality building in Christian service the Lord will say, "Well done, thou good and faithful servant: thou hast been faithful over a few things, I will make thee ruler over many things" (Matthew 25:21). Those who appear at that tribunal will not be at the Great White Throne Judgment where unbelievers will answer to God regarding matters of sin and salvation (Revelation 20:11-15). A thousand years separate the two judgments (Revelation 20:5, 6).

**11. Knowing therefore the terror of the Lord, we persuade men:** ... Consequently, knowing how to reverence the Lord, *—FNTN* ... how greatly the Lord is to be feared, *—WEYM* ... the fear-fulness of the Lord's judgment, *—CNBR* ... we "try to win over men," *—HNT* ... we are trying to win our fellow men, *—TCNT* ... we try to win men for Him, *—NORL.*

**but we are made manifest unto God:**

**and I trust also are made manifest in your consciences:** ... we shine forth, *—FNTN.*

**5:11.** Paul feared coming before God unprepared, and he held an equal concern for others. He knew well the terror (*phobon*, "fear," here that which causes fear) of the Lord. As the author of Hebrews wrote, "It is a fearful thing to fall into the hands of the living God" (Hebrews 10:31). For this very reason Paul did his best to persuade men to turn from sin.

The apostle realized, of course, that already he himself stood openly before the Lord. His Master knew he was genuine, and he hoped his sincerity was equally clear at Corinth in the face of false accusations against him.

**12. For we commend not ourselves again unto you:** ... to your favour, *—WEYM.*

**but give you occasion to glory on our behalf:** ... but are giving you an opportunity, *—WLSN* ... a ground of boasting, *—CNBR* ... opportunity to exult, *—HNT* ... to be proud of us, *—SEB* ... who on the surface are proud, *—BRKL* ... respecting us, *—PNT.*

**that ye may have somewhat to [answer] them which glory in appearance, and not in heart:** ... may have an answer ready, *—MNTG* ... who are proud of outward things, *—SEB* ... with whom superficial appearances are everything, *—WEYM* ... rather than the inward qualification, *—PHLP.*

**5:12.** Here, as elsewhere in this letter, Paul emphasized his reasons for defending his ministry. He intended not to recommend himself personally to them. As he explained earlier (3:1ff.), surely that was not necessary. He did not defend his person but his ministry. He persuaded men of his integrity for the sake of the Church.

Persons attracted to preachers who opposed Paul were taking pride in external things rather than the internal realities of character. They boasted of the accomplishments of their favorite ministers who tried to remove the apostle from his position of honor in the Church.

Then out of concern for the welfare of sincere Christians at Corinth, Paul gave them an opportunity to respond to his critics in kind. He did not want them to feel they followed an inferior apostle and thus become discouraged along the way.

**13. For whether we be beside ourselves, [it is] to God:** ... For if we are extravagant, *—MRDK* ... if we are mad, *—FNTN* ... if we are transported beyond ourselves, *—WSLY* ... were out of our mind, *—CNFT* ... taken leave of our senses, *—ADAM* ... it was in God's service! *—TCNT.*

**or whether we be sober, [it is] for your cause:** ... if we are sane, *—CNFT, —BECK* ... are rational, *—FNTN* ... if we are discreet, *—MRDK* ... are "in our senses," *—HNT* ... be of sound mind, *—ALFD* ... or are sober-minded, *—RTHM.*

**5:13.** Some hinted Paul was mentally unbalanced. They suggested he went to such extremes that he even sought hardships. Only a religious maniac would do such. Festus suggested something similar (Acts 26:24). He thought much study drove the apostle to the border of insanity. Even Jesus' family feared He was losing His senses at one time (Mark 3:21).

Paul answered that any apparent fanaticism was for God and any sound thinking was for the Corinthians' good. He did all for the Lord and others, not self.

**14. For the love of Christ constraineth us:** ... Christ is our motivation, *—ADAM* ... Christ's love controls us, *—SEB* ... sustains us, *—FNTN* ... overmasters us, —WEYM ... overmasters me, —MNTG ... impels us, —CNFT, —BRKL ... that urges us, —HNT ... controls us, NASB ... keeps us in harmony, —KLGS.

**because we thus judge, that if one died for all, then were all dead:** ... having concluded this, NASB ... the conclusion at which we have arrived being this, —WEYM ... consequently all died, —CNDT ... So, everyone died, —SEB.

**5:14.** Far from being motivated selfishly, Paul protested that the love of Christ compelled him. Since Jesus died for him, how could he live for himself?

Inspired by the Spirit, Paul declared the core of the gospel here. Christ died for all as a substitute; He was actually executed for the sins of others. It logically follows that everyone who accepts that substitute should view himself as dead.

**15. And [that] he died for all, that they which live should not henceforth live unto themselves:** ... should live no longer, —ALFD.

**but unto him which died for them, and rose again:** ... for their sakes, —CNDT ... on their behalf, NASB.

**5:15.** From the moment of conversion every believer should live for Christ, not self. Paul had written earlier, "Ye are not your own ... ye are bought with a price: therefore glorify God in your body, and in your spirit, which are God's" (1 Corinthians 6:19, 20).

**16. Wherefore henceforth know we no man after the flesh:** ... Consequently, —BRKL ... we esteem him no more on that account, —CMPB ... are acquainted with no one, —CNDT ... we do not evaluate a person from a worldly point of view, —NORL ... view no man carnally, —CNBR ... only as a human being, —BECK.

**yea, though we have known Christ after the flesh:** ... we know Christ personally, —FNTN ... as a man, —WEYM.

**yet now henceforth know we [him] no more:** ... we don't evaluate Him this way, —ADAM.

**5:16.** Those who viewed Paul as a self-seeking minister thought in human terms. They drew conclusions by the standards of worldly men. With spiritually blinded eyes people in general evaluate things falsely. They see through dark-colored, badly distorted glasses.

In contrast, the apostle had ceased to think in a worldly manner long before this. When he viewed Christ from a human point of view, he saw Him as a blasphemer. But after meeting the Master on the road to Damascus he knew Jesus as the Saviour of men.

As to the previous view of Paul and others concerning Jesus, Kent commented, "They thought of Him as a religious teacher from Galilee, untrained in any rabbinical school, who made messianic claims and was alleged to work miracles. Now, however, Paul no longer regarded Christ from this 'worldly point of view' (NIV)" (p. 88). He also noted that the apostle's remark here has nothing to do with the question of whether or not he saw Christ in flesh on earth.

After meeting Jesus personally near Damascus Paul also looked at all men with a different set of values. He judged them and knew them no longer as an unregenerate man knows them. He related to them no more as persons distinguished by color or of skin, country of origin, or station in life. He knew the truth that all equally need salvation.

**17. Therefore if any man [be] in Christ, [he is] a new creature:** ... there is a new creation, —MNTG ... a new creation altogether, —NORL.

**old things are passed away; behold, all things are become new:** ... The old is gone. Look! the new has come, —BRKL ... The old life has passed away, —MNTG ... the old state of things has passed away; a new state of things has come into existence, —WEYM.

**5:17.** Paul's radical change becomes the experience of all born-again believers. Once dead, now they are alive. Formerly blind, they see! Christ makes new creations of those who believe, as real as God made Adam in the beginning.

Biblical salvation not only brings something new, but it also subtracts something old. One's former set of values and his way of thinking disappear. His new outlook on life dictates a new lifestyle; the old becomes unworthy in his eyes.

The perfect tense of "become" (*gegonen*) indicates that the results of the new birth at some point of time in the past remain current for the Christian. Through an experience as real as life he has been translated from the old world to the new.

**18. And all things [are] of God:** ... This has all originated with God, —WLMS.

**who hath reconciled us to himself by Jesus Christ:** ... Who restored us to Himself, —FNTN.

**and hath given to us the ministry of reconciliation:** ... and gave to us the office of restoration, —FNTN ... the work of bringing people back to Himself, —SEB ... the ministry of peacemaking, NTPE.

**5:18.** That new life leads to the realization that all things are of God. Paul said reconciliation especially is by His initiative.

Man's sins alienated him from his Maker. Disobedience to God always brings distance in relationship with Him. Paul's good news was that God took the initiative to restore fallen man to fellowship with himself. If He had not, surely man would not. Indeed, he could not.

A gracious God gave this message to Paul to share with mankind. In a faithful ministry (*diakonia*, "service") he did what his Master told him to do.

**19. To wit, that God was in Christ:**
**reconciling the world unto himself:** . . . personally reconciling, *—PHLP* . . . getting rid of the enmity between Himself and the people of the world, *—BECK* . . . with his majesty, *—MRDK.*
**not imputing their trespasses unto them:** . . . not reckoning to them, *—YNG,* *—HNT* . . . not counting to them their offences, *—WLSN* . . . not invoicing against them their falling aside, *—KLGS* . . . not counting people's trespasses against them, *—ADAM* . . . not charging men's transgressions, *—WEYM* . . . their offences, *—RTHM* . . . not counting up their sins against them, *—BRKL* . . . instead of debiting men's offenses against them, *—WLMS.*
**and hath committed unto us the word of reconciliation:** . . . He has entrusted, *—WEYM,* *—NORL,* *—TCNT* . . . deposited with us, *—FNTN* . . . the message, *—CNFT.*

**5:19.** Having declared the doctrine of reconciliation as the center of Christian theology, Paul, directed by the Spirit, returned to the subject. The Corinthians, and indeed all men, must clearly understand the truth of the teaching.

The gospel begins with the fact that God was in Christ even while He was on earth. The fullness of the Deity dwelt in the body of Jesus (Colossians 2:9). Jesus was no ordinary man. If He had been, His death would have paid the penalty for His sins alone.

As it is, the Incarnation made reconciliation possible. Because Christ died for man's sins, his fellowship with God can be restored. The Father's righteousness demands each man pay the penalty for his sins. Since Jesus had none, He offered himself as a substitute for others. God accepted His death as such. Then God can stop imputing (counting against them) the sins of those who believe and still be true to His nature. In rebellion mankind committed many trespasses (took many false steps) on the road to destruction. Now because of Christ's obedience the record of all the believer's trespasses has been erased.

The Lord committed or deposited this message with Paul for careful handling. Paul managed this word of reconciliation as a steward of an estate entrusted to his care.

**20. Now then we are ambassadors for Christ:** . . . We are representing Christ, *—SEB* . . . we are envoys, *—HNT* . . . We are Christ's missionaries, *—NLTG* . . . I am an envoy to represent Christ, *—WLMS.*
**as though God did beseech [you] by us:** . . . God making his appeal through us, *—RSV.*

**we pray [you] in Christ's stead:** . . . So we plead, on behalf of Christ, *—NORL* . . . we implore you, *—FNTN* . . . on Christ's behalf, *—HNSN.*
**be ye reconciled to God:** . . . Come and be God's friends, *—BECK* . . . be gathered again to God! *—FNTN.*

**5:20.** Being a steward of the gospel treasure, the apostle was also an ambassador (from *presbeuō*, "travel [or] work as an ambassador") for Christ. The Greek "for Christ" (*huper Christou*) appears first in the sentence for the sake of emphasis. Paul had the full authority any ambassador on earth does. He was the personal representative of the Majesty who sent him from the heavenly kingdom to the earthly one. Jesus said to the 12 apostles, "He that receiveth you receiveth me" (Matthew 10:40). Any contempt or injury toward the apostle was an offense against the Head of State who dispatched him. His message was not his own but that of his Sovereign. When he shared it with men it was with the same authority as if God spoke.

Paul realized God pleaded directly with men through him. In Christ's place he begged men to be reconciled to God. The Lord provided for man's fellowship with Him to be restored, but he must accept that offer.

**21. For he hath made him [to be] sin for us:** . . . was regarded as sin, *—FNTN* . . . a sin offering, *—WSLY* . . . actually to be sin for our sakes, *—PHLP* . . . in our behalf, *—YNG,* *—HNSN.*
**who knew no sin:** . . . Christ never sinned, *—SEB* . . . who knew nothing of sin, *—CNFT.*
**that we might be made the righteousness of God in him:** . . . that we might be changed into the righteousness of God, *Cony-beare* . . . receive justification from God, *—NORL.*

**5:21.** To further explain the doctrine of reconciliation, the apostle declared it involved Jesus' becoming sin for mankind. The One who knew no sin (*hamartia*, to miss the mark, to be in error) God reckoned as bearing the sins of man at Calvary. As Isaiah said, "The Lord hath laid on him the iniquity of us all" (Isaiah 53:6).

As to the fact that Jesus knew no sin Meyer observed: "This does not merely mean that Christ never committed a sin in thought, word, or deed; that every thought which He ever conceived, every pleasure that He ever felt, every desire that ever stirred in His heart, was absolutely without stain of sin, sweet and pure; not merely that He was free from every stain of original sin: it means that He was the One whom sin could not reach, the One who could not be tempted with sin, as St. James expresses it (James 1:13), the One who was 'holy, harmless, undefiled, *separate from sinners,* and higher than the heavens' (Hebrews 7:26)" (pp. 118, 119).

Unthinkable as it was, God accounted such an One a sinner because it was necessary to make possible man's becoming righteous. Man's sins were charged to Christ's account. Christ's righteousness was credited to the account of all who would believe on Him. Paul announced this truth in 1 Corinthians 1:30.

Then under the inspiration of the Spirit the apostle pronounced history's greatest double paradox. God arranged both for Jesus to be made sin and for man to be made righteous!

## Chapter 6

1. **We then, [as] workers together [with him]:** . . . As God's co-workers, —SEB.

**beseech [you] also that ye receive not the grace of God in vain:** . . . Don't let God's love be wasted on you, —BECK . . . we further appeal to you, —BRKL... the gift of God in vain, —FNTN . . . to no purpose, —WEYM.

**6:1.** Paul was not only a steward or manager and an ambassador, but he was also a worker together with God. He used the same analogy in his earlier letter (1 Corinthians 3:9). There he pictured himself as a worker with God on a farm.

In such a responsible partnership the apostle pleaded with those in the church he founded not to receive the grace of God in vain or to no purpose. He feared they might depart from the Faith and surrender their confidence in his message because of what his critics said against him.

2. **(For he saith, I have heard thee in a time accepted:** . . . In a favourable season, —FNTN . . . At a time of welcome I have listened to you, —WEYM . . . I listened to you at the right time, —NORL . . . In an approved season, I hearkened to thee, —RTHM, —ASV.

**and in the day of salvation have I succoured thee:** . . . I aided thee, —HNSN . . . I assisted thee, —WLSN . . . I have helped thee, —CNFT, —HNT.

**behold, now [is] the accepted time:** . . . the present is a very favourable time, —FNTN . . . the highly acceptable time! —HNT . . . Now is the right time, —SEB . . . the time of loving welcome, —WEYM.

**behold, now [is] the day of salvation.):**

**6:2.** With the words of Isaiah to the Gentiles (Isaiah 49:8), Paul reminded the Corinthians God had heard them in an acceptable or favorable time (*kairos*, "fitting season," contrasted with *chronos*, which usually refers to time itself). In the day of salvation the Lord had succored (*eboēthēsa*, of its eight times in the New Testament, it is translated "help" six times) them. They must never take these things lightly.

3. **Giving no offence in any thing:** . . . Giving no cause of offence, —ALFD . . . We do not want to give offense, —NORL . . . we put no obstacle whatever in anyone's way, —BRKL . . . no single occasion of stumbling, —RTHM.

**that the ministry be not blamed:** . . . may not be impugned, —HNT . . . may not be discredited, —BRKL . . . should fall into discredit, —WEYM.

**6:3.** Indeed, let all at Corinth beware lest they cause any to stumble (*proskopēn*, "make a misstep," used here only in the New Testament). Paul declared he did his best to avoid such a tragedy lest the ministry be discredited.

4. **But in all [things] approving ourselves as the ministers of God:** . . . commending ourselves, —ASV.

**in much patience, in afflictions:**

**in necessities, in distresses:** . . . in straits, —RTHM . . . by helplessness, —WEYM . . . or even disasters, —PHLP . . . amid troubles, —HNT . . . calamities, —NORL.

**6:4.** Not only did Paul's motives and message validate his ministry, but so did his conduct. He related specifically how he labored to keep from contributing to the backsliding of anyone and to maintain the integrity of the ministry. In all things he sought to demonstrate he was a worthy preacher of the gospel.

He did so with much patience (steadfastness, endurance). The way he faced up to ministerial hardships indicated his genuineness. This was true in the affliction or difficulty he encountered because of outward circumstances. The various necessities and dire straits (*stenochōria*, "narrowness") he faced provided further opportunities for God to manifest His grace to Paul. So did the distresses and calamities he knew.

5. **In stripes, in imprisonments:** . . . in lashes, —BRKL.

**in tumults, in labours:** . . . in riots, —FNTN . . . in the midst of political instability, —WUST . . . by facing riots, —WEYM . . . mobbings, —BRKL . . . being mobbed, having to work like slaves, —PHLP . . . in toilings, —RTHM.

**in watchings, in fastings:** . . . in sleepless nights, —CNFT.

**6:5.** Further, the apostle understood what it means to suffer stripes or blows for Jesus' sake. He had even been imprisoned because he preached the gospel. He and Silas were both beaten and placed behind bars at Philippi. The jailer sensed their suffering so that immediately upon his miraculous conversion he "took them the same hour of the night, and washed their stripes" (Acts 16:33). Later Paul spent long periods in jail at Caesarea and Rome. Sometimes he barely escaped, and at other times he was left for dead in tumults or riots caused by enemies of the gospel where he preached.

None except the truly called and fully dedicated would labor as hard as Paul did. By day he toiled at his tentmaking trade to support himself and those with him. By night he shared with men the Bread of Life. When his long day ended, even what remained of some of his nights was sleepless because his prayer burden had him watching over the souls of men. He knew what it was to fast too, both voluntarily and involuntarily, when he had no food to eat.

**6. By pureness, by knowledge:** ... though innocence, –BRKL ... in innocence, –CNFT ... in chastity, –RTHM.

**by longsuffering, by kindness:** ... in patience, NASB ... in forbearance, –HNSN, –NORL ... when conferring benefits, –FNTN.

**by the Holy Ghost, by love unfeigned:** ... by sincere love, –WEYM ... in unaffected love, –CNFT ... unpretended love, –BRKL ... in genuine love, NASB ... by unpretended love, –FNTN ... a love devoid of hypocrisy, –WUST.

**6:6.** By pureness (the word includes sincerity and integrity) the apostle proved himself a genuine servant of the Lord. The knowledge God had imparted to him demonstrated it also. He learned it through the study of Scripture, but God revealed the correct understanding where his Jewish teachers had incorrectly interpreted the Word to him (Galatians 1:11, 12).

Through the power and fruit of the Spirit Paul showed longsuffering or forbearance toward weaknesses and wrongs of others, even when at times he could have retaliated. By the Holy Spirit he was full of kindness and generosity to others. He possessed that all-important attribute of love that was unfeigned, genuine and without hypocrisy.

**7. By the word of truth, by the power of God:** ... by true reason, –FNTN ... the proclamation of the truth, –WEYM.

**by the armour of righteousness on the right hand and on the left:** ... with the armor of justice, –CNFT ... the weapons of righteousness, –RTHM ... our only weapon is a life of integrity, –PHLP.

**6:7.** The apostle always spoke the word of truth in the power of God. As a warrior he wore the whole armor of God with weapons of defense in his left hand and offense in his right.

**8. By honour and dishonour:** ... ignominy, –WEYM ... and disgrace, –FNTN.

**by evil report and good report:** ... through blame and praise, –BRKL ... through calumny and praise, –WEYM.

**as deceivers, and [yet] true:** ... They call us imposters, –NORL ... looked upon as impostors, –WEYM.

**6:8.** Paul continued his list in discussing his conduct stating several paradoxes he had experienced as a preacher. He was honored by his friends and dishonored by his enemies. Some spread evil reports about him and slandered him while others gave good reports. However, Paul knew he always spoke the truth.

**9. As unknown, and [yet] well known:**
**as dying, and, behold, we live:** ... Never far from death, –PHLP.
**as chastened, and not killed:** ... as punished, NASB ... seemingly crushed, –FNTN ... and not put to death, –YNG.

**6:9.** Sometimes the apostle experienced human sorrow, but in it all he had cause for rejoicing. From his prison cell in later years he wrote, "Rejoice in the Lord always: and again I say, Rejoice" (Philippians 4:4).

**10. As sorrowful, yet alway rejoicing:** ... yet our joy is inextinguishable, –PHLP.
**as poor, yet making many rich:** ... as destitute, –RTHM ... as indigent but making many wealthy, –BRKL ... but we bestow wealth on many, –WEYM.
**as having nothing, and [yet] possessing all things:** ... we have everything worth having, –PHLP.

**6:10.** Paul knew poverty too. He could feel with those who went hungry and suffered need (Philippians 4:12). In fact, it was in discussing times of need he declared, "I can do all things through Christ which strengtheneth me" (Philippians 4:13). However, the apostle was willing to be in financial want at times if through devotion to duty regardless of circumstances he could make others rich spiritually. In this he was like Christ. Later in this second letter to the Corinthians Paul wrote that "though he (Christ) was rich, yet for your sakes he became poor, that ye through his poverty might be rich" (8:9). The apostle could say he had nothing, yet he possessed all things.

**11. O [ye] Corinthians, our mouth is open unto you:** ... We keep nothing back from you, –HNT ... I am unsealing my lips to you, –MNTG ... we address you frankly, –BRKL ... We have spoken freely to you, –NORL.
**our heart is enlarged:** ... is expanded, –WEYM ... is wide open to you, –CNFT.

**6:11.** Suddenly, with great feeling the apostle shouted out the address, "O ye Corinthians!" Only twice elsewhere did he do such a thing in his letters. After crying "O foolish Galatians," he chided them for having turned away so soon from a faith in Christ to the ritualistic worship of Judaism again (Galatians 3:1). He addressed the

Philippians by name while commending them for sending him a missionary offering (Philippians 4:15).

The expression showed deep emotion as he wrote these words. With a passion one can feel as he reads these lines, the apostle cried out he had opened wide his mouth to them. He had spoken freely and honestly to them on all occasions. He had opened his heart toward them also. His was no mere professional relationship. He loved them with all his heart.

**12. Ye are not straitened in us:** ... In us there is no lack of room for you, —CNFT ... Our affections toward you are not restricted, —NORL ... There is no narrowness in our love to you, —WEYM ... You are not restrained by us, NASB.

**but ye are straitened in your own bowels:** ... in your own affections, —FNTN ... in your own souls, —SAWR ... in your hearts' afflictions, —RTHM.

**6:12.** Paul made clear there was no distance between him and his audience as far as he was concerned. The relationship was not straitened (restricted, strained) on his part. They had broken the fellowship. If they continued to remain apart from him, the trouble was in their own "bowels." The word is a synonym for heart. Paul used it to speak of the seat of the emotions or affections.

**13. Now for a recompense in the same:** ... now as a return of benefits, —SAWR ... you should widen your affections toward us, —NORL.

**(I speak as unto [my] children,) be ye also enlarged:** ... let your hearts also be wide open to me, —MNTG ... open wide your hearts, —BRKL ... with the same complete candor! —PHLP.

**6:13.** With as strong a plea as it is possible for man to make, the apostle begged the Corinthians who had turned against him to return his steadfast love for them. He urged a recompence of the same affection he had shown them. He asked only for a fair exchange of enlarged hearts. He wanted a return of their confidence, to be sure, but more than that, he wanted their love.

In all this Paul spoke tenderly to his readers as his children in the Faith. He reminded them in his earlier letter they had many teachers but only one father (1 Corinthians 4:15).

**14. Be ye not unequally yoked together with unbelievers:** ... Do not be mismated, —NORL, —RSV ... Don't be mismatched, —SEB ... Don't be hooked up with, —KLGS ... Be not getting diversely-yoked, —RTHM, —PNT ... unequally connected, —FNTN ... Share no incongruous yoke, —HNT ... Don't link up with unbelievers, —PHLP ... like oxen yoked with asses, —WEYM.

**for what fellowship hath righteousness with unrighteousness?:** ... What participation,

—WLSN ... How can right and wrong be partners? —BECK ... for what common ground, —BRKL ... what partnership, —NORL ... for what partaking is there to righteousness and lawlessness? —YNG ... and iniquity, —ALFD, —PNIN ... what do righteousness and lawlessness share in common? —ADAM.

**and what communion hath light with darkness?:** ... what partnership, —WEYM ... what in common, —PNT.

**6:14.** Concern for evil in the hearts of the critical faction at Corinth caused Paul to call for a separation between them and true Christians in the church. His plea was for a pure congregation divorced from the sins of society, whether in the lives of pagans about them or in the professing believers in their fellowship.

He began with a command that genuine disciples not be unequally yoked with unbelievers. Under the Law the Lord did not allow the mismatching of uneven teams of animals. No one should plow an ox and an ass together (Deuteronomy 22:10). How much less should unequal men be yoked?

In his first letter to Corinth the apostle instructed that fellowship cease between sincere and hypocritical Christians. Real disciples should keep no company with any man who was called a brother who practiced fornication or who was covetous, an idolater, a railer, a drunkard, or an extortioner (1 Corinthians 5:11). Paul likewise told Titus to withdraw from a factious person who constantly caused division in the body (Titus 3:10, 11).

To further make his point Paul asked a series of rhetorical questions. What do righteousness and lawlessness have in common to share with each other? What fellowship can light and darkness have together?

**15. And what concord hath Christ with Belial?:** ... What harmony is there, —CNFT

**or what part hath he that believeth with an infidel?:** ... what partnership, —BRKL ... or what portion, —HNSN ... who can classify faith with unbelief? —FNTN.

**6:15.** What concord (*sumphōnēsis*, "agreement" here only in the New Testament) does Christ have with Belial ("worthlessness")? What part or portion does a believer share with an infidel (*apistos*, same as in verse 14) or unbeliever?

**16. And what agreement hath the temple of God with idols?:** ... What common ground, —PHLP ... What connection, —WLSN ... what compact, —WEYM ... what alliance, —NORL ... has God's sanctuary, —HNT ... the sanctuary, —YNG.

**for ye are the temple of the living God; as God hath said:**

**I will dwell in them, and walk in [them]:** ... live and walk among them, —BECK ... move among them, —CNFT ... travel with them, —FNTN.

**and I will be their God, and they shall be my people:**

**6:16.** What agreement or union does the temple (*naos*) of God have with idols? In regard to the communion service Paul wrote earlier, "Ye cannot drink the cup of the Lord, and the cup of devils: ye cannot be partakers of the Lord's table, and of the table of devils" (1 Corinthians 10:21).

The apostle declared Christians are the temple of God, again using *naos*, the abiding place of Jehovah. From Leviticus 26:12 he quoted the promise that the Lord would both dwell with and walk among His people.

What relationship can there be then between each of these items in the five questions? The obvious answer is none. In every case the two stand as opposite because they belong to different realms. The logical conclusion is believers and unbelievers can have no close communion, whether in the church, in marriage, or in business. Any association a believer has with an unbeliever should have the goal of winning him to Christ.

**17. Wherefore come out from among them, and be ye separate, saith the Lord:** ... So, come away, —SEB ... Come out of company with them, —WLMS ... depart from the midst of them, —WLSN ... from the heathen, —TCNT.

**and touch not the unclean [thing]:** ... touch nothing impure, —WEYM ... Touch nothing that is sinful, —NLTG.

**and I will receive you:** ... Then I will accept you, —SEB ... I will give you welcome, —RTHM ... I will welcome you with favor, —HNT.

**6:17.** To "come out from among them" should be an automatic reaction in view of the above reasoning. Still, Paul used the aorist imperative to issue his call for separation to indicate urgency. His words are from Isaiah 52:11. Once they leave the world behind, God's children should then touch no unclean thing. If they "come out" and "touch not," the Lord will receive (*eisdexomai*, here only in the New Testament) or welcome them.

**18. And will be a Father unto you, and ye shall be my sons and daughters:**
**saith the Lord Almighty:** ... The Lord the Ruler of all, —WEYM ... the All-Ruling Lord, —FNTN ... the All-powerful God, —NLTG ... The Lord Omnipotent speaks, —BRKL.

**6:18.** The apostle had one more promise for the faithful at Corinth. As they lived in faith and obedience to Him, God would be their Father and they would be His sons and daughters. This

promise is specifically from the Lord Almighty (*pantokratōr*, used as a part of God's name 10 times in the New Testament and always translated "Almighty").

## Chapter 7

**1. Having therefore these promises, dearly beloved:** ... Dear friends, —SEB ... In possession, —BRKL ... As we possess these promises, —HNT.

**let us cleanse ourselves from all filthiness of the flesh and spirit:** ... let us purify, —SAWR ... we should purify ourselves, —FNTN ... from all defilement, —WEYM ... every pollution, —YNG, —CNDT ... all contamination, —WUST ... from all polution of flesh, —RTHM.

**perfecting holiness in the fear of God:** ... Let us be completely holy, showing respect for God, —SEB ... and complete our dedication by reverence, —BRKL ... progressively accomplishing holiness, —WUST ... secure perfect holiness, —WEYM ... completing our holiness, —ADAM ... perfecting purity in reverence, —FNTN ... by consecrating ourselves to him completely, —PHLP.

**7:1.** On the basis of these promises Paul had a new appeal for the converts at Corinth. It concerned the doctrine of sanctification. The doctrine has both its positive and negative aspects. It involves separation from the secular on the one hand and dedication to the sacred on the other. Neither a legalistic separation from sin nor an empty profession of dedication to God constitutes sanctification. Here the apostle's emphasis is on the separation side of the doctrine. He exhorted a cleansing of self from sin.

In one sense it is God who sanctifies (1 Thessalonians 5:23, 24). However, man must participate in it as Paul made clear here. In Leviticus 20:7, 8 Jehovah instructed the people of Israel to sanctify themselves, though a moment later He declared, "I am the Lord which sanctify you."

With an emphasis on man's responsibility in sanctification Paul stated he must rid himself of filthiness, that which defiles the flesh in outward acts such as drunkenness, stealing, and murder. He cannot afford to take less care as to what soils his spirit, the inner sins of pride, envy, and jealousy.

When the believer accepts what Christ did for him, he is immediately sanctified (1 Corinthians 6:11). However, he has a continuous duty of perfecting (maintaining, completing) holiness in his life. He is under obligation to do so in the fear of God, with appropriate awe and respect for Him.

**2. Receive us:**... Make room for us, *—PNIN*... Take us into your hearts, *—HNT*... Open your hearts to us, *—ASV*... Give us a favorable hearing, *—CNBR*.

**we have wronged no man:**... We injure no one, *—CNDT*.

**we have corrupted no man:** ... ruined, *—PHLP, —HNT*.

**we have defrauded no man:** ... We tricked no one, *—KLGS*... we took advantage of no one, *NASB, —ASV, —PNT*... we didn't take advantage of anybody, *—ADAM*... we have imposed on no one, *—GRBR*... we have plundered none, *—FNTN*... cheated, *—PHLP*... gained any selfish advantage, *—WEYM*... we have exploited no one, *—BRKL*.

**7:2.** Continuing his plea of 6:11-13, the apostle again begged the Corinthians to receive or make room for him in their hearts. Thus he had not departed from the overall discussion of his relationship with them. His earlier treatment of the subjects of sins and holiness showed the Corinthians' attitude toward them affected their fellowship with him as well as with God.

In renewed defense of his ministry Paul protested that he had not wronged or treated any man unjustly. Nor had he corrupted or defrauded (taken advantage of, cheated) anyone. Possibly some whispered he had misused church funds, a charge he would soon answer in detail in chapters 8 and 9. At the direction of the Spirit Paul used the aorist tense with each of the three verbs to say he had never at any time done any of these things.

**3. I speak not [this] to condemn [you]:**
**for I have said before:**... I have previously said, *—HNSN, —WLSN*.

**that ye are in our hearts to die and live with [you]:**... are ready to live and die with you, *—GRBR*.

**7:3.** Anticipating possible misunderstanding of his purpose in writing as he did, the apostle declared his aim was not to condemn all the Corinthian believers with the few who had made the false charges. Justifiably he hated evil, without or within the church in the Greek city, but he was angry at no person. He repeated again that those of the congregation in Corinth were his very life. He would live with them, sharing their joys and sorrows, and if necessary he would even die with them. Along with his converts elsewhere, the hope of seeing them stand acceptably before the Lord on judgment day was the major reward he anticipated. His converts were his joy and crown (1 Thessalonians 2:19, 20). No wonder they filled his heart.

**4. Great [is] my boldness of speech toward you, great [is] my glorying of you:**... I trust you; I am proud of you, *—NORL*... Great is my confidence, *—CNFT*... is my freedom, *—YNG*... very loudly do I

boast of you, *—WEYM*... To your face I talk to you with utter frankness, *—PHLP*... on your behalf, *—RTHM*... for I am very proud of you, *—FNTN*.

**I am filled with comfort:**... I'm very much encouraged, Beck... I am quite content, *—FNTN*.

**I am exceeding joyful in all our tribulation:**... I'm overjoyed, *—BECK, —RSV*... Overbound with, *—YNG*... I am overloaded with joy, *—KLGS*... I am thoroughly delighted, *—ADAM*... supremely delighted, *—FNTN*... greatly superabounding with the joy, *—RTHM*... filled with good cheer, *—PNT*... I overflow with joy in all our affliction, *—HNSN*... my heart overflows with joy amid all our affliction, *—WEYM*.

**7:4.** Precisely because he loved the Corinthians so much Paul felt he could be fearless in his speech toward them. In case any among them counted his straightforward preaching as harshness, he wanted them to know also that he was just as forward in praising them among Christians wherever he went. As a faithful father, he showed great boldness in correcting them, but he took great pride in them too.

In fact, thoughts of them brought him much comfort. The inspiration he drew from their lives caused his joy to overflow even in the distress brought on by outward circumstances he experienced. True ministers always draw much strength from those they serve.

**5. For, when we were come into Macedonia:**
**our flesh had no rest:**... our bodies had no rest at all, *—SEB*... enjoyed no respite at all, *—BRKL*... no relief at all had our flesh, *—RTHM*... such as human nature craves, *—WEYM*.

**but we were troubled on every side:**... in utter distress, *—HNT*... oppressed, *—PNT*.

**without [were] fightings, within [were] fears:**... it was wrangles without, *—HNT*... wranglings outside, *—BRKL*... contentions without, *—FNTN*... conflicts without, *—KLST*... and anxiety within, *—PHLP*.

**7:5.** Among the troubles he experienced were those he had in the province of Macedonia just before he wrote this letter. At Ephesus he wrote 1 Corinthians and sent it with Titus as his personal messenger. Paul was so anxious to know how they had received it he started toward Corinth to meet Titus on his return. Taking the land route, he stopped briefly at Troas. When the young minister did not arrive as soon as expected, the apostle hastened to Macedonia. All this he explained earlier in 2:12, 13.

Of course Paul ministered while he waited. He found no rest for his weary body. Outwardly he dealt with quarreling and strife in Macedonia as in other places. Inwardly he wrestled with anxieties and concerns as to the condition of the church at Corinth.

**6. Nevertheless God, that comforteth those that are cast down:** ... who consoleth the lowly, −WORL . . . who comforts the downhearted, −MNTG, −WLMS . . . who encourages the weary, −KLGS . . . who lifts up the downcast, −NORL . . . those who feel miserable, −BECK . . . the disconsolate, −WLSN . . . the depressed, −MRDK.

**comforted us by the coming of Titus:** ... has encouraged us, −TCNT.

**7:6.** However, the God of all comfort, He who provides consolation for all the humbled, met Paul's personal needs. God providentially arranged for Titus to arrive just at the right time with priceless encouragement. His personal presence (*parousia*) wonderfully refreshed the apostle.

**7. And not by his coming only:** ... not only in his presence, −YNG.

**but by the consolation wherewith he was comforted in you:**

**when he told us your earnest desire:** ... narrating to us, −WLSN . . . rehearsing to us, −RTHM, −WORL . . . declaring to us your longing desire, −CLMT . . . how much you yearned to see me, −SEB.

**your mourning, your fervent mind toward me:** ... of your penitence, −TCNT . . . your deep sorrow, −SAWR . . . your lamentation, your zeal for me, −YNG . . . how loyal you were to me, −WLMS.

**so that I rejoiced the more:** ... was happier still, −MNTG . . . so that my sorrow has been turned into joy, −CNBR . . . I was gladder still, −WLMS.

**7:7.** While renewed fellowship with a much-loved brother meant a lot to Paul, Titus' arrival brought news which strengthened him more than ever. The young preacher himself had been greatly refreshed through his visit to the Corinthian church. The grace of God he saw in their lives comforted him to no small extent. The fire of this enthusiastic report warmed Paul's heart immediately.

However, the apostle was interested in more than just the welfare of Titus. Imagine the thrill as his youthful partner rehearsed events at Corinth which spoke loudly of the believers' earnest desire, their longing to see the apostle. Titus told also of the love for Paul they manifested with tears of sorrow. The old warrior listened intently as Titus told him about the believers' fervent mind or zeal for him. With the load of not knowing how they might respond to his earlier letter lifted, Paul rejoiced greatly.

That the Corinthians earnestly desired to see him, mourned because they had pained him, and remained devoted friends though false teachers exerted so evil an influence to the contrary, meant a great deal to Paul.

**8. For though I made you sorry with a letter:** ... For even though I hurt your feelings, NTPE ... I caused you pain, −ADAM.

**I do not repent:** ... I am not regretting it, −CNDT ... and now I am glad I sent it, −PHLP.

**though I did repent:** ... Even if I was inclined to regret it, −TCNT.

**for I perceive that the same epistle hath made you sorry:** ... that I grieved you by the letter, −WSLY.

**though [it were] but for a season:** ... temporarily, −FNTN ... even for an hour, −RTHM ... though only momentarily, −BRKL ... only for a while, −RSV ... only for a time, −HNT.

**7:8.** The apostle referred to the earlier letter in 2:4. He said he shed many tears as he wrote it. Its corrective content caused fears he might overburden the Corinthians with grief when his intent was simply to demonstrate his love and concern for them. As a matter of fact, Paul even wrote a letter before that one. He mentioned it in 1 Corinthians 5:9 where he revealed a small portion of its subject matter.

Of the extent to which Paul went previously, and again here to close the distance between himself and the Corinthians, Carver wrote, "In a most delicate manner Paul attempts to perfect his reconciliation with the church. If all the misunderstandings, suspicions, and bitterness are to be removed from their relationship, the past must be opened up, not just covered over only to rise again in some future circumstances. Love that is spiritual seeks a reconciliation so real that the relation can actually be the same again even though the healed wound will ever bear a scar" (*Beacon Bible Commentary,* 8:569, 570).

Titus truthfully reported the second letter made the Corinthians sorry and caused them pain. In spite of that the apostle declared he had not repented (*metamelomai*, not the usual word for repent), i.e., he did not regret he had sent it. However, he experienced the human emotion of regretting temporarily the corrective tone of his message. Any who have duties in discipline, parents included, understand what he felt. Without it, the disciplinarian should examine his motives. Paul was glad after it was all over that the letter had caused pain for only a season (a short while, even a moment).

**9. Now I rejoice, not that ye were made sorry, but that ye sorrowed to repentance:** ... you were sad enough to change your hearts, −SEB ... brought you to repentance, −TCNT ... led you to repentance, −CNFT ... to reformation, −YNG, −HNSN ... to change of thinking, −KLGS ... had a salutary effect, −WEYM.

**for ye were made sorry after a godly manner:** ... grieved unto a return to God, −FNTN ... grieved after a godly sort, −HNSN ... such as God intended you to have, −GRBR.

**that ye might receive damage by us in nothing:**...that ye might suffer loss, —CLMT, —ASV...might suffer no loss through us, —HNT...no detriment from us, —MRDK...so that you were not punished by it uselessly, —FNTN...not merely to make you offended by what we said, —PHLP...you were not in the least damaged by us, —BRKL.

**7:9.** Now Paul could rejoice, though he found no pleasure in causing them pain. The happiness he experienced was over their sorrow which led them to repentance (*metanoia*, "change of mind or attitude," the more usual word for repentance). It relieved him to know the Corinthians had not sustained injury through the corrective ministry of his letter.

**10. For godly sorrow worketh repentance to salvation not to be repented of:**...For, sorrowing on account of God worketh a conversion, —MRDK...There are no regrets, —SEB...a repentance not to be regretted, —WEYM...never to be regretted, —NOYS.

**but the sorrow of the world worketh death:**...results in death, —HNT...produces death, —CNFT, —WEYM.

**7:10.** The apostle revealed much about the doctrine of repentance here. He stressed that sorrow is not repentance. In fact, only godly sorrow works toward repentance. It is from God, produced by the Holy Spirit. It is also directed toward Him for having offended Him through sin. In his farewell to the Ephesian elders Paul declared he regularly preached repentance toward God and faith toward Jesus (Acts 20:21).

King David experienced godly sorrow after his sin with Bathsheba. He recorded his prayer of repentance in Psalm 51:4: "Against thee, thee only, have I sinned, and done this evil in thy sight." With that attitude he found pardon from God.

By contrast, the sorrow of this world regrets only sin's discovery and leads merely to dread of the consequence of sin. Since it does not work repentance, it ends in eternal death in the lake of fire. It can also adversely affect a person's health in this life and lead to physical death. Depression flowing from worldly sorrow can result in suicide.

King Saul sensed only the sorrow of this world at his rejection by Jehovah. It caused him concern lest he lose respect in the eyes of the men of the army he commanded. When the prophet Samuel refused to help him keep up appearances, Saul sought to physically restrain the man of God (1 Samuel 15:22-30). In the end he committed suicide (1 Samuel 31:4).

**11. For behold this selfsame thing:**...Look at this very fact, —HNT...For mark the effects of this very thing, —WEYM.

**that ye sorrowed after a godly sort:**...your Divine grief, —FNTN...God's type of sorrow, —SEB...suffered in accordance with the will of God, —WLMS.

**what carefulness it wrought in you:**...what earnestness, —CNFT...how great diligence it produced in you, —SAWR.

**yea, [what] clearing of yourselves:**...what explanations, —TCNT...what eagerness to defend yourselves, —NORL.

**yea, [what] indignation:**...What strong feeling! —TCNT.

**yea, [what] fear:**...what alarm, —WEYM.

**yea, [what] vehement desire:**...earnest longing! —TCNT...longing affection, —WEYM...what yearning, —CNFT.

**yea, [what] zeal:**...what fervor, —MNTG...what enthusiasm, —ADAM.

**yea, [what] revenge!:**...You wanted to make it right, —SEB...you punished the guilty, —GRBR...what concern for justice, —ADAM...what exacting of punishment! —ALFD...what a decision it produced from you! —FNTN.

**In all [things] ye have approved yourselves to be clear in this matter:**...In every respect, —PNT...Upon the whole, —CMPB...You have completely wiped away reproach, —WEYM...you demonstrated yourselves, NASB...ye evinced yourselves to be chaste, —RTHM...to be innocent, —MNTG...to be pure in the matter, —HNSN...from every stain of guilt, —CNBR.

**7:11.** Paul experienced a worshipful spirit as he contemplated the fact that the Corinthians had known godly sorrow. He knew that is what produces true repentance. The change of mind it involves is by no means a surface action. Rather, it is a deep-seated alteration in the inner man. Its product is a basic change of attitude. It brings a totally new outlook on life.

With repentance comes a change of mind about God and His holy demands. It alters a person's attitude about sin. The penitent comes to realize he has greatly offended the Lord by his wicked deeds. That sense, that knowledge becomes so real the repentant one weeps over his sins. True repentance is so radical in experience it is part of the process of the new birth.

Godly sorrow leads to repentance; repentance plus faith in Christ culminates in regeneration; and regeneration produces conversion where the believer turns from sin to live a new life. The apostle illustrated this truth as he marveled at what repentance produced at Corinth.

Paul noted that repentance produced a strong desire to correct the wrongs at Corinth. It produced in the believers an eagerness to clear themselves, to present a true defense (*apologia*) by attending to the problem of sin in their ranks. It brought indignation or anger against the sin of the member of their church who had an incestuous affair with his stepmother (1 Corinthians 5:1).

Further, repentance stirred fear (reverence, respect) for God in the hearts of the Corinthians. Pondering truth as to the judgment of the Lord on sin brought about a wholesome awe in His presence. It gave them a vehement desire for restoration to full fellowship with the Lord and the apostle Paul. The zeal they felt in repentance caused them to adminster discipline on the offender.

In the end repentance propelled the believers at Corinth into such action that they demonstrated they were now clear and innocent in the matter. They responded very differently to the apostle's original letter of instruction that they attend to the problem. Instead of weeping over the sin among them then, they had proudly declared their conduct acceptable to God (1 Corinthians 5:2). After all, didn't they have all the gifts of the Spirit in operation in their services?

**12. Wherefore, though I wrote unto you:**...Consequently, even if I write to you, —*CNDT.*

**[I did it] not for his cause that had done the wrong:**...not to punish the offender, —*WEYM*...not on account of the profligate, —*FNTN.*

**nor for his cause that suffered wrong:**

**but that our care for you in the sight of God might appear unto you:**... our diligent care over you, —*WSLY*...how deep your devotion to us really is, —*TEV.*

**7:12.** With deep appreciation for the way the Corinthians had responded to the ministry of correction in his letter, Paul had a final word of explanation. He had not written with any ill will toward the one who had done the wrong, even though that one had treated another, his father, unjustly. Nor had Paul addressed the issue just to defend the one who had suffered the injustice to his wife. Paul's cause was more basic. He intended to show the care and devotion to them that he maintained before God.

**13. Therefore we were comforted in your comfort:**...On this account, —*BRKL*...That is why we have been so comforted and encouraged, —*BRCL*...your own concern for us, —*JB.*

**yea, and exceedingly the more joyed we for the joy of Titus:** ... We were more than delighted, —*BRCL*...we were especially delighted to see, —*NIV*...by the happiness of Titus, —*TCNT*...we had the even greater happiness of finding Titus so happy, —*JB*...also delighted beyond everything by seeing how happy Titus is, —*NEB.*

**because his spirit was refreshed by you all:** ...This is what comforts me, —*MNTG*...because all of you had cheered him up, —*BECK*...you have all

helped to set his mind completely at rest, —*NEB*...his spirit has been refreshed, —*NIV*...his spirit had been made glad by you all, —*BB* ... his spirit has been made stronger, —*NLTG*...was soothed by all of you, —*BRKL*...the way in which all of you helped to cheer him up! —*TEV* ... by the good disposition he found you all in towards me, —*LOCK*...he has no more worries, —*JB.*

**7:13.** Returning to the matter of Titus' report, Paul said once more it brought him much encouragement. He wrote again also of the blessing those at Corinth were to Titus. Above his own comfort, the apostle was even more pleased at what he saw in his young partner. Titus' spirit was refreshed, his mind set at rest through his visit to the troubled church. He had gone, wondering how the believers would receive him as a disciplinarian. Their reception soon relieved him of all anxiety over the matter.

As Paul's associate, Titus knew controversy from the beginning (Galatians 2:1, 3). Both his experience and gifts from God appeared to suit him for ministry to churches with problems. His service to Corinth as Paul's partner on this occasion suggests that. Later, he was also sent to Crete to handle administrative difficulties in the churches there (Titus 1:5). The apostle dispatched him on a mission to Dalmatia while he, Paul, was confined to prison at Rome (2 Timothy 4:10). For these reasons scholars often picture Titus as being a more forceful figure in church matters than Timothy.

**14. For if I have boasted any thing to him of you:**...I had bragged about you, —*SEB.*

**I am not ashamed:**...you have not let me down, —*PHLP*...and you have not disappointed me, —*TEV*...I was not disgraced, Fenton, —*CNDT*...my pride in you has been justified, —*NEB*...I have had no reason to be ashamed of it, —*GDSP*...I am specially gratified by this, —*BRCL.*

**but as we spake all things to you in truth:**...bore the mark of truth, —*NEB.*

**even so our boasting, which [I made] before Titus:** ... just so the proud claims we made, —*BRCL* ... our boasting to Titus has proved to be as true, —*JB.*

**is found a truth:** ... turned out to be truth, —*KJII*...is verified, —*CMPB.*

**7:14.** Paul had often boasted to Titus of the wonderful believers at Corinth. His "if I have boasted" here could be read "since I have." The personal attack against Paul by the few did not blind him to the greatness of the many. As the youthful minister departed on his unpleasant journey, no doubt Paul assured him genuine Christians in the church would prove true though things looked dark at the moment.

As to his use of compliment in ministry to men, Hughes saw Paul "not hesitating to reprove what is amiss, but yet warmly and sympathetically encouraging them in the true emotions of those whose hearts are regenerate, which is the best way of ensuring that their past errors will not be repeated. A minister who keeps the main end in view, the glorious goal to which he wishes to guide his people, will realize that to be truly faithful in his dealings with them means to encourage them lovingly in that which is good as well as to correct and discipline them when they fall into sin" (*The New London Commentary,* p. 280).

The founder of the church at Corinth had not overstated the case. He thanked its members in this follow-up letter for not humiliating him before Titus. What he had told his traveling companion about them proved to be true, just as everything he had preached to them about Jesus was true. As he wrote earlier, he was not among those ministers who dilute the gospel in the way some wine merchants cheapen their product by mixing it with water (2:17).

**15. And his inward affection is more abundant toward you:** . . . His heart goes out all the more to you, *—GDSP* . . . his tender affection, *—YNG* . . . are especially favourable towards you, *—FNTN.*
**whilst he remembereth the obedience of you all:** . . . as he continues recalling, *—WLMS* . . . when he calls to mind, *—RTHM* . . . the obedience which all of you manifested, *—WEYM.*
**how with fear and trembling ye received him:** . . . with respect and reverence, *—NORL* . . . by the timidity and nervous anxiety with which you welcomed him, *—WEYM.*

**7:15.** Upon Titus' return Paul learned he loved the Corinthians more than ever. His former respect for them was based on hearsay evidence. Now he had an abundant inward affection (*splanchna*, English "spleen," the verb form of the word is always translated "compassion") for them based on firsthand acquaintance.

Two things about the faithful at Corinth impressed Titus. Though he was younger and a stranger, they welcomed him with fear and trembling. Such a respect for the ministry spoke well of the founding father of the church. He also took special note of their obedience. First, they were most cooperative with him. Second, they carefully followed every instruction of the letter from Paul he delivered to them in disciplining the sinning member. Third and most of all, they had a strong determination to do the will of God in every area of responsibility.

**16. I rejoice therefore that I have confidence in you in all [things]:** . . . I have good courage

concerning you, *—WORL* . . . I do celebrate the fact that in all your affairs, *R—PNT* . . . you have justified my good opinion of you in every way, *—NORL* . . . because I relied upon you in everything, *—FNTN.*

**7:16.** Paul concluded his discussion of the disciplinary case by repeating the fact that the Corinthians' behavior had brought him joy. Furthermore, they had renewed his confidence in them. He knew he could depend on them under every circumstance.

## Chapter 8

**1. Moreover, brethren, we do you to wit of the grace of God:** . . . we make you acquainted with, *—WLSN.*
**bestowed on the churches of Macedonia:**

**8:1.** The apostle had a new subject to discuss at this juncture in his letter. In this section he dealt with the matter of worshipful giving. He used the whole of chapters 8 and 9 for this major division of the epistle.

Paul informed the church at Corinth of the grace of giving which God had granted to Christians in the churches of Macedonia. At least the congregations at Philippi, Thessalonica, and Beroea were included. He used the affectionate term "brethren" to address the Corinthians.

**2. How that in a great trial of affliction:** . . . how, under ordeal of terrible affliction, *—BRKL* . . . much proof of tribulation, *—PNIN* . . . while passing through great trouble, *—WEYM* . . . Amid a severe ordeal of distress, *—HNT.*
**the abundance of their joy:** . . . because of the overflow of their kindness, *—FNTN* . . . their boundless joy, *—WEYM.*
**and their deep poverty abounded unto the riches of their liberality:** . . . have had an abundant issue in rich generosity upon their part, *—HNT* . . . in the wealth of their liberality, *NASB.*

**8:2.** The apostle told the Corinthian believers that Macedonian churches had given an offering for needy brethren in Jerusalem. They did this in spite of the great trial of affliction they themselves had endured. Zahniser wrote, "This region had suffered the ravages of civil war between Caesar and Pompey, between Brutus and Cassius and the triumvirs, and finally between Augustus and Antonius. They actually made a petition for a surcease of their burdens of taxation in the reign of Tiberius and were granted the favor as a depleted area" (The *Wesleyan Bible Commentary,* 5:298).

Yet they had abundant joy despite their need. Their abundant liberality or generosity matched their joy. In their giving they followed the example of the widow who gave out of her poverty while others gave of their surplus (Mark 12:43, 44).

Then how can the apostle write of "the riches of their liberality"? As Hughes asked, "How could the Macedonians have wealth if they lived in deep poverty? They gave from their ability (defined in 8:11-12)—that is, their giving was commensurate with their resources, small though they were. But the Macedonians also gave *beyond* their ability. They gave until it hurt. For that reason, Paul used them as a model for the Corinthians when he discussed equality and heart-level giving" (*Everyman's Bible Commentary,* p. 75).

3. **For to [their] power, I bear record, yea:** ... I can testify that to the utmost of their power, *—WEYM* ... and I give evidence beyond their ability, *—FNTN.*
**and beyond [their] power [they were] willing of themselves:** ... yes, beyond their means, they gave, *—CNFT* ... gave of their own accord, *—ASV* ... they voluntarily have given, *—BRKL* ... of their own free will, *—NORL.*

**8:3.** Paul bore them record (was their witness, *marturia*) that they gave in the offering beyond their ability. They did so willingly of themselves with no appeals from the apostle for contributions.

4. **Praying us with much entreaty:** ... In fact they simply begged us, *—PHLP* ... they insistently begged, *—KLST.*
**that we would receive the gift, and [take upon us] the fellowship of the ministering to the saints:** ... that they might participate in the beneficence, *—MRDK* ... to accept their gifts, *—PHLP* ... to convey the gift, *—FNTN* ... being rendered to God's people, *—WEYM* ... supporting their fellow-Christians, *—NORL* ... the fund for their fellow-Christians, *—TCNT.*

**8:4.** In fact, they had asked Paul earnestly for the privilege of participation in the project. Paul did not beg them, but they begged him! They insisted that he accept their money and take it with him to pass on to the Christians in financial straits in Jerusalem. They urged him to take on the true fellowship of such a ministry (service, *diakonias*). Being poor themselves they knew how to feel with others in great need.

Of course the apostle was not opposed to the effort. Nor was he unconcerned about brethren short of life's necessities in Jerusalem. He and Barnabas had already taken a similar offering for needy Christians to Jerusalem (Acts 11:27-30). The money came from the young Gentile church at Antioch of Syria. The Jerusalem church itself had demonstrated generosity toward needy members from the start (Acts 4:34, 35).

5. **And [this they did], not as we hoped:** ... And they surpassed our expectations, *—HNT* ... not according as we expected, *—YNG* ... beyond our expectations, *—CMPB* ... more than we expected, *—BECK* ... a mere cash payment, *—PHLP.*
**but first gave their own selves to the Lord, and unto us by the will of God:**

**8:5.** The way the Macedonians went about presenting their offering was beyond anything the apostle could have hoped for. They exceeded all his expectations. First, they gave themselves in full devotion to the Lord. Giving of money to God apart from that would be pointless. Their worshipful giving was certainly in the will of God.

6. **Insomuch that we desired Titus, that as he had begun:** ... We therefore encouraged Titus, *—FNTN* ... so that I insisted that, *—WLMS* ... so that we exhorted, *—HNSN* ... the one who commenced the work, *—WEYM.*
**so he would also finish in you the same grace also:** ... he should also see to the completion of this expression of your sympathy, *—TCNT* ... to bring it to successful completion, *—NAB* ... to get this bounty completed, *—HNT* ... to complete this gracious arrangement, *—BRKL* ... this gracious work, *—RSV.*

**8:6.** With thanksgiving in his own spirit at the grace of giving in the hearts of the Macedonians, Paul responded to their request to head up the project. It fitted with his burden and some preliminary preparations he had made earlier to collect funds for the same purpose at Corinth and in Galatia. Titus was instrumental in assisting the apostle in that he took his previous letter to the Corinthians. It contained instructions on how to raise the funds (1 Corinthians 16:1-3).

Since Titus had already worked on the project at Corinth, Paul requested him to return there to finish what he had started. It may be the apostle's critics and the trouble they caused in the Corinthian church had slowed the effort. Regardless, Paul was anxious that God perfect the grace of giving in the hearts of Corinthian believers as they completed collecting funds for the needy.

7. **Therefore, as ye abound in every [thing, in] faith:** ... You are rich in so many things, *—NORL* ... you are already very rich in faith, *—WEYM.*
**and utterance, and knowledge:** ... and discourse, *—RTHM* ... of eloquence, of spiritual illumination, *—WAY* ... and doctrine, *—PNT* ... and a ready exposition, *—WUST.*
**and [in] all diligence, and [in] your love to us:** ... perfect enthusiasm, *—WLMS* ... enthusiasm in every form, *—WAY* ... all earnestness, *—HNSN, NASB* ... every kind of zeal, *—BECK* ... unwearied zeal, *—WEYM* ... and in complete eagerness, *—ADAM* ... and all careful work, *—KLGS.*
**[see] that ye abound in this grace also:** ... in this gracious work also, *NASB* ... this grace of liberal giving also flourishes in you, *—WEYM* ... in this work of kindness, *—BECK.*

**8:7.** Their spiritual father praised the Corinthians that they abounded in possessing many of God's gifts and graces. In the gifts of faith and knowledge they ranked high among the churches. In their meetings the Spirit often granted utterances, tongues, interpretation, and prophecy. They showed much diligence (eagerness, zeal) about the things of God. Above all they were full of love which they had frequently manifested toward Paul. In his first letter to them he offered similar commendation saying, "Ye come behind in no gift" (1 Corinthians 1:5-7). In like manner, he now wanted them also to abound in the grace of giving.

**8. I speak not by commandment:** ... Not by way of injunction, —RTHM ... I don't want you to read this as an order, —PHLP ... I do not speak imperatively, —FNTN ... I am not issuing an order, —BRKL.

**but by occasion of the forwardness of others:** ... but as testing the sincerity, —CNFT ... through the earnest zeal of others, —PNT.

**and to prove the sincerity of your love:** ... but to test the genuineness of your love, —NORL ... want a genuine proof of your friendship, —FNTN ... the reality of your Love, —WLSN ... the dependability of, —KLGS ... the good disposition of your charity, —DOUY.

**8:8.** Paul preferred not to speak by commandment on the matter of this offering even though in his apostolic office he could have. He wrote the same to Philemon whom he chose to beseech rather than to enjoin (Philemon 8, 9). God is more pleased when His people give on some other basis than obedience to law, though the grace of giving should provoke one to give more than the law requires.

Paul had better ways of appealing to the believers at Corinth for these funds. For one, he challenged them by the forward, zealous example of others in giving, namely, the Macedonians. Then he appealed to their love for God and the brethren. The offering allowed them to demonstrate its sincerity and genuineness.

**9. For ye know the grace of our Lord Jesus Christ:** ... the graciousness of, —CNFT ... the condescending goodness, —WEYM ... the bounteous grace of our Lord, —HNT.

**that, though he was rich, yet for your sakes he became poor:** ... Who, when existing in wealth, impoverished Himself for you, —FNTN ... he became destitute, —RTHM.

**that ye through his poverty might be rich:** ... you might be made wealthy, —WUST.

**8:9.** Another basis of appeal Paul used in stirring Christians at Corinth to give was the example of Jesus. It, of course, was the greatest of all. The apostle declared it was grace even on His part that caused Him to surrender His riches in becoming poor that all who believe on Him might be rich.

A more complete account of what Jesus left behind to come to earth is in Philippians 2:5-8. Possessing the wealth of the universe in His pre-incarnate state, He gave it all up to be born a man. He experienced that birth in abject poverty. The humble inn in the town of His birth had no room as a decent place for Him to come into the world. His mother bore Him, attended only by Joseph. She lay on a straw-covered dirt floor of a stable. His only crib was the feeding trough for the animals who shared the place of His birth, probably a cave stable in Bethlehem.

During His stay of 30 years on earth He never owned a place to lay His head (Matthew 8:20). When He came to the end of His earthly life the only provisions He could offer for the care of His mother came through the kindness He requested of a friend with His dying breath (John 19:26, 27). Before they crucified Him they stripped Him of the meager clothing He wore. Soldiers gambled to see who would get the garments of pitifully small value He left behind (Mark 15:24).

In death they buried Him in a borrowed tomb (Matthew 27:60). Others provided the customary burial cloths and spices, and they were relative strangers (John 19:38-42). Thus He lived and died owning nothing of this world's goods.

**10. And herein I give [my] advice:** ... In this matter, then, I offer my counsel, —NORL ... But in this matter I give you an opinion, —WEYM ... Still, on this subject, —HNT ... I give judgment, —HNSN.

**for this is expedient for you, who have begun before:** ... It is to your interest, —CNFT ... for this thing is profitable, —PNT ... for this is beneficial for you, —WLSN ... this is to your advantage, NASB ... who not only originated the work, —FNTN.

**not only to do, but also to be forward a year ago:** ... also to do it willingly, —WSLY.

**8:10.** Paul appealed to the most noble motives as godly reasons for worshiping the Lord through giving. Instead of giving orders, he offered advice and presented his opinion. He concluded that approach was expedient (advantageous, better) for the Corinthians. His suggestion was that since they were eager to start the worthy project of collecting funds for needy brethren in Jerusalem "a year ago," now they should complete it.

**11. Now therefore perform the doing [of it]:** ... So now finish, —KLGS ... also complete what you must do, —ADAM ... complete the doing, —HNSN ... complete the enterprise, —BRKL ... complete the deed, —HNT.

**that as [there was] a readiness to will:** ... to purpose it, —PNT.

**so [there may be] a performance also out of that which ye have:** ... so there may be the completion, —CLMT ... your desire to carry it through, —CNFT ... so [shall be] the completion also, —HNSN ... the completion out of what ye have, —WORL ... in proportion to what ye have, —WSLY ... to what you possess, —HNT.

**8:11.** The apostle commended the Corinthians for their readiness of mind to raise money for the needy. However, it was more than a mental assent toward a worthy cause. It moved them to will (*thelein*) to work on the project.

Now Paul exhorted them to complete it. Each should give according to what he had. In his earlier letter he stated the same principle. Every believer at Corinth was to contribute to this offering according as God had prospered him (1 Corinthians 16:2). From the first, such offerings in the church were in keeping with each one's ability to give (Acts 11:29).

**12. For if there be first a willing mind:** ... For if the desire exists, —FNTN.

**[it is] accepted according to that a man hath:** ... it is acceptable according to what one may possess, —FNTN.

**[and] not according to that he hath not:**

**8:12.** As the Spirit moved on him, the apostle emphasized that the attitude of the heart is the important thing in Christian giving. That is what God accepts as worship rather than the money presented. Certainly the amount given is not what the Lord looks for. Instead, He receives any servant who approaches Him in giving on the basis of what he has to offer. If in his heart he would give much but has little, heaven's record shows a large offering. God expects no one to give what he does not have. None must be asked to give above his ability.

Of course, those who have much and offer little find small favor with the Lord. They make the mistake of trying to worship grudgingly with the hand rather than in spirit and in truth. With them God is not well pleased.

As Ironside explained, "It was not a question of saying, 'Well, I would do something but am not able,' but a question of doing what they could. If you can give only a little to the Lord, give that, and He will multiply it. If you can give a great deal, give it to Him. He looks into the heart. Many a one puts in a dime, and on the books of heaven it goes down as though it were a dollar, but do not put in a dime if you could give the dollar, for that won't go down at all!" (p. 199).

**13. For [I mean] not that other men be eased, and ye burdened:** ... and ye pressured, —YNG ... and

you loaded down, —KLGS ... and you distressed, —CNBR.

**8:13.** The apostle declared it was not his intent that those who received this offering should be relieved financially while at the same time those who gave it were burdened by it. God's plan does not call for some to give to the extent they do without basic necessities so others may live in abundance.

**14. But by an equality, [that] now at this time your abundance [may be a supply] for their want:** ... You have a surplus right now, —KLGS ... Your present abundance, —ADAM ... but to make your burdens equal, —CNBR ... by the rule of equality, —ALFD ... at the present time, —CNFT ... for their deficiency, —RTHM, —WLSN.

**that their abundance also may be [a supply] for your want:** ... what they will not need will relieve your need, —BECK ... for your deficiency later on, —WEYM.

**that there may be equality:** ... rather share fairly, —KLGS ... and so it will be fair, —BECK ... so that there may be equalization of burdens, —WEYM ... and thus conditions become equalized, —BRKL.

**8:14.** What the apostle preached here about sharing with others was the principle of equality. It seemed reasonable that at a time when Christians in Jerusalem suffered want, their brethren in other parts of the world should share their abundance with them. At another time (*kairos*, "season," rather than *chronos*, measured time) the situation would be reversed. Then those in Jerusalem would have the opportunity to return the favor.

**15. As it is written, He that [had gathered] much had nothing over:** ... had no surplus, —HNSN, —WLSN ... had not more than enough, —RTHM ... were not over-fed, —FNTN.

**and he that [had gathered] little had no lack:** ... had not less, —RTHM.

**8:15.** Instead of communism, the apostle's instructions encouraged a certain thermostatic principle of equality as illustrated in Israel's gathering of the manna in the wilderness. If a person collected much or little, it all measured the same (Exodus 16:18)! The greedy person found his surplus weighed no more than the one who tried to honestly bring in his share. The individual who was unable to collect his due portion discovered it measured what God allowed anyway.

No one was to save any manna gathered as the day's supply for the day following. Those who disobeyed the command found what they kept over spoiled (Exodus 16:20). In the same way corruption always accompanies the hoarding of wealth.

**16. But thanks [be] to God:**
**which put the same earnest care into the heart of Titus for you:** ... Who is imparting the same diligence, –*CNDT* ... who kindles in the heart of, –*WLMS* ... who has put an equal zeal for you, –*NAB* ... who has inspired Titus, –*CNFT* ... who putteth the same diligence for you, –*PNIN* ... the same devotion for you, –*BRKL*.

**8:16.** This offering presented as an act of worship provoked other praise to the Lord. For one thing, Paul thanked God for putting the same zealous concern for the Corinthians in the heart of Titus.

**17. For indeed he accepted the exhortation:** ... has responded to my appeals, –*TCNT* ... he accepted the call, –*KJII* ... welcomed our request, –*WEYM* ... welcomed my request, –*BECK* ... our appeal, *NASB*, –*NORL*, –*ADAM*.
**but being more forward:** ... and, impatient to begin, –*FNTN* ... being already more diligent, –*RTHM* ... but was so enthusiastic about it that, –*NORL* ... because he is so enthusiastic for you, –*WLMS* ... but being very earnest, –*NOYS*, –*WLSN* ... and being extremely diligent, –*SAWR*.
**of his own accord he went unto you:** ... by his own volition, –*BRKL*.

**8:17.** Titus readily welcomed Paul's "exhortation" (request) (8:6) to proceed to Corinth to assist in completing the giving project there. Indeed Titus felt a sense of special urgency toward the matter. In reality he went to the Greek city voluntarily, even more than in response to the apostle's appeal.

Hughes has noted the oneness of the apostle and his associate and wrote: "'The same earnestness' (8:16) linked Titus' heart to Paul's. Not only did Titus share the same earnestness for the offering, but he went of his own accord (8:17). Titus was a true self-starter and was motivated first by his own desire and, second, by Paul's appeal. Paul stressed that fact to support the genuineness of Titus' ministry" (*Everyman's Bible Commentary*, p. 81).

**18. And we have sent with him the brother:**
**whose praise [is] in the gospel throughout all the churches:** ... whose fame in the service of, –*TCNT* ... who is so well known for his preaching, –*KLGS* ... whose applause in the evangel, –*CNDT* ... whose fame as a herald of the Glad-tidings has spread through all the churches, –*WAY*.

**8:18.** Wisdom dictated that Paul ask others to join Titus in this money-raising project. That was his plan from the beginning. In a previous letter to Corinth he stated, "Whomsoever ye shall approve by your letters, them will I send to bring your liberality unto Jerusalem" (1 Corinthians 16:3).

Paul included a letter of recommendation for these brethren within his letter to the Corinthians. Such documents were an important part of the world of the First Century just as they are today. Paul referred to their prevalent use earlier (3:1-3). Ministerial credentials serve the purpose of letters of recommendation.

The apostle commended one he sent with Titus as a "brother" known well among the churches of the area. Everyone spoke highly of his work in the gospel, perhaps as a preacher.

**19. And not [that] only:**
**but who was also chosen of the churches to travel with us with**
**this grace:** ... he was also appointed, –*HNT* ... he was also ordained by, –*DOUY* ... had been expressly chosen ... to accompany me with this beneficence, –*MRDK* ... as appointee, –*BRKL* ... who was also appointed by vote by the assemblies, –*YNG* ... has been selected, –*ADAM* ... as our fellow-traveller, –*RTHM*.
**which is administered by us:** ... which we are undertaking, *NTPE* ... we're doing, –*BECK*.
**to the glory of the same Lord:** ... to honor the Lord, –*BECK*.
**and [declaration of] your ready mind:** ... demonstrates also the willingness, –*PHLP* ... and to our cordiality, –*MRDK*.

**8:19.** Further, this "brother" had been chosen by the churches for this particular assignment. The election process involved voting by a show of hands (*cheirotoneō*, "to stretch out the hand"). His duty was to "travel with us with this grace." *Charis* is usually translated "grace," but here and in verse 4 it means "gift," referring to the financial offering being collected.

Of this "brother" Meyer observed, "Evidently this man was not one of Paul's regular assistants" (p. 183). The churches of Macedonia chose him. As earlier, churches near Timothy recommended him to Paul, "So now the congregations of Macedonia had engaged the services of this brother, and on the basis of their observation had elected him as a traveling companion for Paul to deliver the collection in Jerusalem" (ibid., p. 184).

Paul took seriously the charge to administer (*diakoneō*) these funds. The offering accomplished purposes other than just meeting the needs of brethren in financial straits. Everyone participating did so in worship, to the glory of God. The offering also demonstrated the grace of giving the Lord had worked in the hearts of believers at Corinth. It showed their ready mind and willingness to love their brethren in Christ in deed as well as word.

**20. Avoiding this, that no man should blame us in this abundance which is administered by us:** ... Thus we shall avoid any criticism, –*NORL* ... We take this precaution, *—BRKL* . . . guarding against this, *—SAWR* . . . We are taking precautions to prevent anyone from impugning us in reference to this munificence, *—HNT* . . . We're trying to avoid any criticism of the way we're handling this great gift, *—BECK* . . . that no one should discredit us, *NASB* . . . that no one should cast censure on us, in [respect to], *—MRDK* . . . of this generous amount, *—CNFT* . . . which is being dispensed, *—WLSN.*

**8:20.** The sacredness of the assignment produced carefulness in administrative procedure for the apostle. He determined to avoid anything that might lead someone to find fault with what was done. He had already suffered enough unjust criticism from his enemies at Corinth. They were always ready to suggest he intended to personally profit from the money in this offering. He needed no more such censure.

Nor did the apostle want anyone to credit him as the source of this lavish gift. God's people gave it all. He simply administered (*diakoneō*, "served") in it.

21. **Providing for honest things:** . . . for we take forethought, *—NOYS* . . . providing honourable things, *—RTHM* . . . for in forethought, *—PNT* . . . we are attentive to things commendable, *—MRDK* . . . for we take thought for things honorable, *—ASV* . . . so we plan ahead to do good, *—ADAM* . . . and to be absolutely aboveboard, *—PHLP.*

**not only in the sight of the Lord:** . . . God's approval of our integrity, *—WEYM* . . . not only before God, *—MRDK.*

**but also in the sight of men:** . . . but also before men, *—MRDK* . . . but man's also, *—WEYM.*

**8:21.** Some preachers conclude they do not care what people think as long as they know their ministry is acceptable with God. Paul was of a different opinion. His carefulness as a church administrator led him to plan ahead with due consideration for things honest before men and God. Of course, he and the others must first actually be praiseworthy before God; but he felt they must also appear that way in the presence of men. This was especially true regarding church finances. He determined that everything would be both honest and open. He left no room for suspicion or criticism.

22. **And we have sent with them our brother:** **whom we have oftentimes proved diligent in many things:** . . . we have frequently put to the test on various occasions, *—BRKL* . . . and found dependable, *—KLGS.*

**but now much more diligent, upon the great confidence which [I have] in you:**

**8:22.** Paul had already named Titus as the chairman of the finance committee as well as one of its members (8:6, 16). He added another and

wrote a recommendation of him here also. He is called simply "our brother." Often challenging circumstances had tested him, and in every case they proved him diligent, zealous for the cause of Christ. Sensing Paul's love for Corinth, he was eager to serve there.

23. **Whether [any do inquire] of Titus:** **[he is] my partner and fellow-helper concerning you:** . . . he is my comrade, *—HNT* . . . my mate, *—CNDT* . . . he is my intimate companion, *—TCNT* . . . my associate, *—BRKL* . . . and assistant, *—MRDK* . . . in your behalf, *—WORL.*

**or our brethren [be inquired of, they are] the messengers of the churches:** . . . and both the brothers are official messengers, *—PHLP* . . . they are missionaries, *—WUST* . . . they are delegates, *—WEYM* . . . the apostles of the ecclesias, *—CNDT* . . . apostles of assemblies, *—RTHM.*

**[and] the glory of Christ:** . . . a credit to Christ, *—HNT.*

**8:23.** Next the apostle wrote his letter of recommendation for Titus. He was a full partner in the apostle's work. He shared (*koinōnos*) totally in all responsibilities. He was a fellow helper, a true working companion.

Titus and the other two brethren were messengers (*apostoloi*, "sent ones") of the churches. They were missionary representatives of their congregations. Their lives radiated the glory of Christ. Their ministerial conduct brought honor to His name.

24. **Wherefore show ye to them, and before the churches:** . . . Indicate therefore to them, *—HNSN* . . . Display to them, *—NOYS* . . . exhibit ye to them, *—MRDK* . . . demonstrate to the churches, *—ADAM.*

**the proof of your love:** . . . the exhibition of, *—RTHM.*

**and of our boasting on your behalf:** . . . and the truth of our boasting, *—ADAM* . . . and a justification of our boasting, *—WEYM* . . . and justify my boasting, *—CNBR* . . . ground for my praising you so highly, *—WLMS* . . . respecting you, *—MRDK.*

**8:24.** With such impressive credentials, it is little wonder the apostle recommended these men to the church at Corinth without reservation. Obviously, the congregation must give them an appropriate reception.

Paul called for a proper demonstration of Christian love toward these traveling ministers upon their arrival at Corinth. No doubt he also expected the people to attend to their needs for room, board, and other expenses while they were there assisting in the money-raising project. He had taught the church about adequate support for the ministry in his first letter to its members (1 Corinthians 9:6-14). His masterful treatise argued that logic, the Law, and the Lord Jesus all instruct proper care for the ministry. Paul's concluding statement was, "Even so hath the Lord ordained that they which preach the gospel should live of the gospel" (1 Corinthians 9:14). The apostle expressed confidence that the church would at this time set a good example "before the churches" as to the way ministers should be treated.

Once more Paul asked believers at Corinth to justify all the favorable things he had been saying about them. They had not disappointed him during Titus' visit (7:14). No doubt he was more concerned for their reputation than his embarrassment.

## Chapter 9

1. **For as touching the ministering to the saints:**... For, respecting the, —WORL...concerning the ministration by the saints, —MRDK...as regards giving or withholding relief from the members of the church, —WAY.

**it is superfluous for me to write to you:**...It may seem a waste of time for me to write to you, —NORL...it is really unnecessary for me, —WEYM...it is needless that, —CNBR.

**9:1.** As if to pause yet renew his discussion of the project for the needy in Israel, the apostle spoke of it as a "ministry" to the saints. He no longer referred to it as a "collection" as in his first letter (1 Corinthians 16:1). In this epistle he constantly wrote of it in connection with the "grace" of giving. The Spirit inspired Paul to keep the subject of money in the church on a high plane. Ministers today would do well to follow his example.

Confidently, the apostle said it was really unnecessary for him to write about the offering. Everything he said about it was already in their hearts. He wrote in the spirit of Peter who wanted to put his audience in remembrance, though they were already established in the truth he presented (2 Peter 1:12).

2. **For I know the forwardness of your mind:**...for I have known your readiness of mind, —YNG...I know your readiness, —WORL...I know your willingness, —CMPB.

**for which I boast of you to them of Macedonia:**...you in Greece, —WEYM.

**that Achaia was ready a year ago:**...was prepared, —FNTN...has been prepared for a year back, —HNT...has been prepared since last year, —NORL...hath been prepared for a year, —PNIN.

**and your zeal hath provoked very many:**...and the zeal of you did stir up the more part, —YNG...has stimulated the majority, —HNSN...has consequently been a stimulus, —PHLP...through your zeal many were aroused, —FNTN...your enthusiasm has stimulated more than yourselves, —WAY...has excited many, —WLSN...stirred up the majority, —RTHM...a goodly number, —BRKL.

**9:2.** Paul knew well the Corinthians' willingness in the matter of the offering. In fact he had boasted of their attitude about it to the Macedonians. He declared those of Achaia, Greece, were prepared to give to the fund the year before. Complimenting them, he told the Corinthians their zeal had provoked (aroused, stirred) many others to contribute.

Then the apostle praised the Corinthians to the Macedonians, and he praised the Macedonians to the Corinthians (8:1-6). He had a wholesome rivalry going between the churches. Sometimes congregations today enjoy friendly competition as a means of stirring themselves to do their best in supporting worthy causes.

True, as Hughes noted, Paul elsewhere condemned glorying in men (*The New London Commentary*, p. 323). In his first letter to the Corinthians he said "that no flesh should glory in his (God's) presence" (1 Corinthians 1:29). The instruction came in the form of condemnation because various factions in the church had been picking favorite preachers solely on the basis of differing personalities. Their choice bore no relation to differences in doctrine or practice. To end the discussion he declared, "Therefore let no man glory in men: for all things are yours" (1 Corinthians 3:21). God gave different ministers with various abilities and talents. Believers need them all.

However, Hughes explained, "Paul's glorying here is neither in men nor in human achievements as such, but in the grace of God manifested in and through the lives of men. Thus he has already gloried to the Corinthians of the amazing liberality of the Macedonians, but in doing so he has attributed everything to 'the grace of God which hath been given in the churches of Macedonia' (8:1). True Christian giving flows from the prior giving of God's grace, and Paul's glorying in the goodness of God" (*The New London Commentary*, p. 323).

3. **Yet have I sent the brethren:**...My reason for sending our Brothers, —TCNT.

**lest our boasting of you should be in vain in this behalf:**...may not be made void in this respect, —ALFD, —ASV, —HNSN...in this particular be proved empty, —PNT...in this particular matter an empty boast, —TCNT...may not be made empty in this case, NASB...you may not turn out to have been an idle one, —WEYM...turned into an empty boast, —CNBR...you should be found empty in this instance, —CNFT...should be made void in this respect, —RTHM.

**that, as I said, ye may be ready:**...ye may be prepared, —MKNT.

**9:3.** Still, the apostle did not want the pace of the project to slow. So he appointed a "finance committee" and sent its chairman and members to Corinth. Again he expressed mild concern that his boasting about his converts in Corinth might prove to be in vain. He wanted to make sure that his talk of their being ready with their offering was completely true. Certainly they were prepared to give the year before, as he had said. Now he desired their readiness to include money in hand.

**4. Lest haply if they of Macedonia come with me, and find you unprepared:** . . . accompany me, *—HNT* . . . and find that you are not ready, *—WLMS.*

**we (that we say not, ye) should be ashamed in this same confident boasting:** . . . we would feel humiliated, *—BRKL* . . . not to say yourselves, *—CNFT* . . . ashamed in this matter, *—DOUY* . . . in this assertion, *—FNTN* . . . should be put to shame for that glorying, *—MRDK.*

**9:4.** Sending the brethren on ahead, Paul himself planned to go to Corinth later. He foresaw the possibility that some Macedonian believers might accompany him. If they arrived with him and found the church unprepared with its offering, what a source of embarrassment that would be to the apostle. He thought of all the boasting he had done to the Macedonians about how aggressive the Corinthians were when it came to giving! He shuddered to think of how humiliated he would be to find their offering incomplete.

The apostle made a parenthetic comment about his not mentioning the possibility of embarrassment for the believers at Corinth in case they had not completed the fund-raising project. Modestly, he would rather speak of the possibility of his failure than theirs. Either way, an appeal to avoid humiliation is an acceptable motivation to Christian service.

**5. Therefore I thought it necessary to exhort the brethren:** . . . I have therefore considered it needful, *—HNT* . . . I was careful to request these my brethren, *—MRDK* . . . necessary to urge, *—ADAM* . . . to entreat, *—ASV.*

**that they would go before unto you:** . . . so that they might proceed to you, *—FNTN.*

**and make up before hand your bounty:** . . . arrange in advance, *—BECK, —RSV* . . . and get your promised love-offering ready beforehand, *—WLMS* . . . your previously promised blessing, *—HNSN* . . . this your before-promised blessing, *—RTHM* . . . your afore-promised bounty, *—PNIN* . . . your long-promised liberality, *—HNT* . . . this previously announced gift, *—WLSN.*

**whereof ye had notice before, that the same might be ready:**

**as [a matter of] bounty, and not as [of] covetousness:** . . . be spontaneous, *—FNTN* . . . as a free gift, *—SAWR* . . . as a blessing, *—YNG* . . . as money that was gladly given and not forced out of you, *—BECK* . . . to be a spontaneous gift, and not money squeezed out of you, *—PHLP* . . . and not of grudging

avarice, *—HNT* . . . but gives grudgingly under pressure, *—WUST* . . . not a matter of stinginess, *—KLGS* . . . and not something extorted from you, *—BRKL* . . . not as something exacted under pressure, *—ADAM.*

**9:5.** Paul's tact in handling the delicate financial project in the church at Corinth is evidence he was clothed by the Spirit as he wrote and as he engaged in the administrative functions of the pastor. With the remote prospect that the congregation was not ready with its offering, he explained he thought it necessary (considered it his duty, felt a compulsion) to send the brethren on ahead. They would arrange to receive the offering in advance of his arrival. Their aim was to guide the people in gathering their contribution beforehand (*prokatartizō*, here only in the New Testament).

The apostle reminded the Corinthians they had received notice of this offering well in advance. This gave ample time for everyone to give his fair share without placing a hardship on any. The tithing system fits perfectly into Paul's teaching here on the grace of giving. It provides for both equitable and systematic giving. True worshipers paid tithes from grateful hearts long before the law of Moses required it, as did Abraham (Genesis 14:20) and Jacob (Genesis 28:20-22).

Paul was concerned that the offering be one of bounty (*eulogias*, "good words"), a gift of blessing. He did not want it to be one of covetousness or miserliness. Take note that covetousness manifests itself in many, subtle ways. Men usually associate it with amassing wealth, but Paul shows here it can reveal itself in hoarding wealth, giving grudgingly in an offering. For him the offering was a means of enhancing their relationship with God. Right attitude meant everything in view of that purpose.

**6. But this [I say], He which soweth sparingly shall reap also sparingly:** . . . Mark this! *—HNT, —CNFT* . . . he that sows thinly, *—KLGS.*

**and he which soweth bountifully shall reap also bountifully:** . . . But if you sow generously, *—BECK* . . . who sows liberally, *—BRKL* . . . and the generous sower will also reap, *—FNTN* . . . with blessings also shall reap, *—RTHM.*

**9:6.** Though the apostle was determined not to encourage any to give above his ability, he did promote generosity of heart. To do so he recalled the law of harvest. Sow sparingly, and reap accordingly; sow bountifully, and reap plenteously.

Under God Paul selected powerful words to encourage generous giving. He employed *eulogias*, "blessing," with a play on words here. His message, then, was that those who sow seeds of blessing will reap a harvest of blessing. To warn against stinginess he recalled words of the wise man: "There is that scattereth, and yet increaseth; and there is that withholdeth more than is meet, but it tendeth to poverty" (Proverbs 11:24).

The apostle applied the law of harvest to giving in his epistle to the Galatians also. He instructed support of the ministry saying he that was taught must "communicate" or share with "him that teacheth in all good things" (Galatians 6:6). Then he spoke of reaping what is sown as true whether the sowing is to the flesh or Spirit.

**7. Every man according as he purposeth in his heart:** . . . what he has decided upon in his own mind, —*WEYM* . . . as he has predetermined, —*RTHM* . . . he had planned, —*BRKL.*

**[so let him give]:**

**not grudgingly, or of necessity:** . . . not of grief, —*HNSN* . . . not regretting his gift, as if it were wrung from him, —*WAY* . . . not sorrowfully, —*WLMS* . . . and not do it reluctantly or under compulsion, —*WEYM* . . . not with sadness, not by constraint, —*MRDK.*

**for God loveth a cheerful giver:** . . . loves a hilarious, —*BRKL.*

**9:7.** Paul's next principle on giving is basic. Let each man contribute to worthy causes as he purposes or decides in his heart and makes up his mind before the Lord to do. Elsewhere Paul emphasized giving according to financial blessings God has granted (1 Corinthians 16:2). In short, ability for sharing equals responsibility to give.

The apostle advised against giving grudgingly or reluctantly. Certainly Christ did not give His all with that attitude. Paul wanted none to contribute to this offering with a feeling of necessity or compulsion.

Paul never employed high-pressure methods in raising church funds. In his former letter to Corinth he asked that monies be given systematically, on a regular weekly basis, specifically so that there would be no pressure to collect an offering when he arrived (1 Corinthians 16:2). If one contributes in the excitement or pressure of the moment, he may later regret it. The apostle realized that such an attitude kills worship.

On the other hand, a cheerful (Greek *hilaros,* English *hilarious)* spirit enhances worship. God loves those who give gladly.

**8. And God [is] able to make all grace abound toward you:** . . . God has power to shower upon you every kind of blessing in abundance, —*TCNT* . . . able to lavish all grace, —*CNDT* . . . give you every free gift in full measure, *NTPE* . . . to make your every spiritual blessing overflow for you, —*WLMS* . . . to reward you abundantly for every gift, —*GRBR.*

**that ye, always having all sufficiency in all [things]:** . . . under all circumstances, —*BRKL.*

**may abound to every good work:** . . . you may have ample means for all good works, —*WEYM* . . . you may have a surplus, —*KLGS.*

**9:8.** The apostle not only declared God loves a cheerful giver, but he promised the Lord would make it possible for His children to give generously. Writing of "grace" (*charis*) abounding so as to provide a sufficiency for every good work, he used the word in a new sense. The promise implies an ability to contribute to every cause. Grace works in financial matters so that the believers will have sufficient to make giving possible.

God's blessings rested on Israel to give both cheerfully and generously at the building of the tabernacle. The people actually gave so much they had to be restrained (Exodus 36:5-7). This is one of the unusual instances in history when people gave "more than enough for the service" of the Lord.

**9. (As it is written, He hath dispersed abroad:** . . . The Bible says of such a person, —*BECK* . . . He distributed freely, —*GRBR.*

**he hath given to the poor:** . . . He has lavished his gifts on the needy, —*NEB* . . . gave generously, —*BRCL.*

**his righteousness remaineth for ever:** . . . His almsgiving remains, —*WEYM* . . . His acts of love last forever, —*NLTG* . . . abides to the remotest age, —*RTHM* . . . continues for ever, —*TCNT* . . . his good deeds will never be forgotten, —*JB* . . . his kindness lasts forever, —*BRCL.*

**9:9.** Paul spoke next of spiritual blessings which accompany generous giving. He took the words of Psalm 112:9 as a text for his comments. The Psalmist sings the praises of the man of means who freely disperses abroad and shares generously of his goods with others. He especially distributes what he has among the poor and needy. Consequently, God's favor is upon him so his righteousness remains forever, literally "unto the age."

Jesus spoke the same beautiful truth in the Sermon on the Mount. He exhorted men to lay up treasures in heaven rather than on earth. Thus they concentrate on that which remains forever.

**10. Now he that ministereth seed to the sower both minister bread for [your] food:** . . . may He who is supplying seed to, —*YNG* . . . he who gives seed for putting into the field, —*BB.*

**and multiply your seed sown:** . . . shall multiply your store, —*WAY* . . . your store of seed, —*NIV* . . . will furnish you with plenteous store of seed, —*CNBR* . . . will take care of the growth of your seed, —*BB.*

**and increase the fruits of your righteousness;):** . . . at the same time increasing the fruits of your righteousness, —*BB* . . . he will multiply it and swell the harvest of your benevolence, —*NEB* . . . to yield a plentiful harvest, —*WEYM* . . . increase the products, —*CMPB* . . . and he will make it grow into a plentiful harvest, —BRCL ... increase your generous yield, —NAB ... and make your righteousness grow into a fine harvest, —SEB ... make the harvest of your good deeds a larger one, —JB ... and enlarge the harvest of your uprightness, Goodspeed ... and produce a rich harvest, —TEV.

**9:10.** Paul's meditation on the truth of the Psalmist stirred a prayer in his heart. Remembering what Isaiah said, he addressed the One who gives seed to the sower and bread for food (see Isaiah 55:10). He asked that One to multiply the seed sown, both of the natural and the spiritual kind. Multiplying natural seed supplies the sower's need and makes it possible for him to share with others. Then Paul prayed that God would increase the fruits of righteousness for all of His people, in keeping with the song the apostle quoted in verse 9.

11. **Being enriched in every thing to all bountifulness:** ... You will grow rich in every way, —GDSP ... He will always make you rich enough to be generous at all times, —TEV ... in every respect, —BRKL ... to every kind of generous giving, —KJII ... for all liberality, —CMPB ... so that you can be generous on every occasion, —NIV.
**which causeth through us thanksgiving to God:** ... so that through me you can show perfect liberality, —GDSP ... will evoke thanksgiving, —BRKL ... wakes a chorus of thanksgiving to God, —WAY.

**9:11.** Again the apostle promised the Lord will enrich the believer to all bountifulness or generosity. As he gives to meet the needs of others, such as ministers like Paul, the apostle declared in turn, "My God shall supply all your need according to his riches in glory by Christ Jesus" (Philippians 4:19). However, in a word specifically for the rich, the apostle said God not only gives them all things richly to enjoy, but He also intended they be ready to distribute and willing to share what they have with others (1 Timothy 6:17, 18).

Good things follow spiritually when one relates to God financially according to Paul's teaching. Experiencing the realities of the promises the apostle recalled here caused him to offer thanksgiving to God. Giving in worship then is not a temporal matter only but an eternal one. It relates not only to material but to spiritual things. It belongs in the sanctuary and is vital in all that transpires in the life of the Church.

12. **For the administration of this service not only supplieth the want of the saints:** ... For the rendering of a public service like this, —TCNT ... It is like a serving ministry which does two things, —SEB ... not

only is replenishing the wants, —CNDT ... filling up the deficiencies of the saints, —RTHM.
**but is abundant also by many thanksgivings unto God:** ... but is also rich, —MRDK ... overflows also in much gratitude, —CNFT ... also results in abundant thanksgiving, —TCNT ... Many people will thank God, —SEB.

**9:12.** At this point Paul reached the climax of his message. Certainly his concern in discussing the offering for the needy had been hungry people whom he wanted to see fed. Naturally he desired those dressed in rags to be properly clothed, and those without housing to have adequate shelter. He emphasized again one good from this service was that it would supply the needs of the saints. However, he finally focused on what his highest aims were.

What follows here fits the same mold of what the apostle wrote on church finances in a note of thanks to the Philippians (Philippians 4:10-19). Though he expressed appreciation for an offering they had sent, he was careful to show giving in the church does much more than just help pay the bills or feed the preacher. Their offering demonstrated their love for him, and the love behind it meant more than its contents. Through it they commendably shared the burden of his financial straits. But he did not write with a hint they send another offering soon. What he encouraged was their laying up treasure in heaven. They needed to have fruit credited to their account there. Most of all, though, the presentation of their gift resembled the worship of old when men burnt sacrifices before Jehovah. It was "an odor of a sweet smell, a sacrifice acceptable, well-pleasing to God" (Philippians 4:18).

Then in a similar way here, going beyond the important matter of meeting human need, the apostle first declared the offering would produce much thanksgiving to God. He had drawn attention to the fact that the giver is blessed and worships. Now he stated those receiving the offering also would respond with abundant thanksgiving.

13. **Whiles by the experiment of this ministration they glorify God for your professed subjection unto the gospel of Christ:** ... In the way that you stand the test of this service, —NORL ... they are praising God for your loyalty, —BRKL ... to your professed adherence to the Good News, —WEYM ... for your fidelity to your profession of faith, —TCNT ... for the alliance of your profession, —FNTN.
**and for [your] liberal distribution unto them, and unto all [men]:** ... and for the generosity of your contribution, —HNT ... and, by your generous sharing with them, —KLGS.

**9:13.** Paul understood the "experiment of this ministration," or better "the approved character of their service," would have a second desirable effect. It would inspire the recipients to glorify God at the evidence of the Gentiles' subjection to the gospel. The offering would provide tangible proof to the Jewish Christians that Gentile conversions were real. Theirs was no mere "professed," or more correctly merely an expressed subjection. It was genuine.

Thirdly, the recipients would thank God for the Corinthians' liberal distribution (*koinōnias*, here "unselfishness, devotion to others"). They would appreciate the gift, but more, they would recognize it came from hearts where a work of grace had been done.

**14. And by their prayer for you:** ... with warm affection, *—ADAM.*

**which long after you for the exceeding grace of God in you:** ... elicited by God's surpassing grace bestowed on you, *—KLST* ... who ardently love you, *—CMPB* ... because of the unusual measure, *—BRKL* ... because of the excellent grace, *—DOUY* ... surpassing grace which is resting upon you, *—WEYM.*

**9:14.** Fourth, the Jewish brethren would pray for the Gentile members of the body of Christ. Though miles separated them, they were united in a common spirit of prayer.

Fifth, the recipients of their gift would have a deep affection for their benefactors. The offering would serve to cement the bond of love between them. For Paul nothing was more valuable than unity in the Church. How he preached, taught, worked, and prayed for it, especially between Jewish and Gentile believers. Now it would be furthered through this gift.

The "longing" of the recipients of the offering toward those who gave would also include a desire to follow the example of the contributors. They would see the exceeding (*huperballousan*, one of Paul's several superlatives) grace of God in them. That would cause a burning desire for the Lord to do a similar work in their hearts.

In Romans 15:25, 26 the apostle gave the exciting conclusion of the matter discussed in Second Corinthians chapters 8 and 9. He wrote, "But now I go unto Jerusalem to minister unto the saints. For it hath pleased them of Macedonia and Achaia to make a certain contribution for the poor saints which are at Jerusalem."

**15. Thanks [be] unto God for his unspeakable gift:** ... for His indescribable gift! *NASB* ... His unexpected bounty! *—FNTN* ... for his indescribable bounty! *—RTHM* ... for his inexpressible free Gift! *—WLSN* ... for his inestimable gift! *—TCNT* ... for His indescribable gratuity! *—CNDT* ... more priceless than

words can tell! *—NORL* ... precious beyond description, *—WAY.*

**9:15.** Paul reached a peak experience in meditation on giving here. Stirred deeply, he exclaimed, "Thanks be unto God for his unspeakable gift!" "Thanks" is another meaning of *charis*. The superlative *anekdiēgētos* ("unspeakable, indescribable") appears only here in the New Testament.

## Chapter 10

**1. Now I Paul myself beseech you by the meekness and gentleness of Christ:** ... I personally make this appeal before you, *—GRBR* ... make a personal appeal to you, *—TCNT* ... appeal to you personally, *—NORL, —BRKL* ... advise you, *—FNTN* ... and yieldedness of Christ, *—CLMT* ... and considerateness of the Christ, *—RTHM* ... and clemency of Christ, *—MKNT* ... and modesty of Christ, *—DOUY* ... and leniency of Christ, *—CNDT.*

**who in presence [am] base among you:** ... am quiet in appearance, *—FNTN* ... who am humble when I'm face to face with you, *—BECK.*

**but being absent am bold toward you:**

**10:1.** Paul began a new section of his letter here. He returned to the matter of his relationship to the church at Corinth. Earlier he defended his office; now he defends more himself. This then is the most personal part of the most personal letter of the apostle.

The apostle emphatically identified himself anew, "I Paul myself." The pleas, the appeals, and the entreaties he was about to make rested on the meekness and gentleness of Christ. The fact that Paul followed Christ's example led his enemies to charge he appeared base, overly humble, and subservient as a preacher. They sarcastically said he was bold only when he was absent and writing letters to them.

**2. But I beseech [you], that I may not be bold when I am present with that confidence:** ... with the assurance, *—RTHM.*

**wherewith I think to be bold against some:** ... may not have to "make a brave front," *—HNT.*

**which think of us as if we walked according to the flesh:** ... who entertain the notion, *—BRKL* ... who regard us as if, *—HNSN, NASB* ... as working only for human satisfaction, *—NORL* ... who fancy we work for selfish ends, *—FNTN* ... we are guided by worldly principles, *—WEYM.*

**10:2.** However, they made the mistake of thinking Paul's meekness was weakness. They did not understand that the weak do hot have the strength to be meek. Meekness is strength under perfect control. In meekness Paul patiently besought and entreated the offenders to correct the error of their ways, or else the next time he was present he would demonstrate his confidence and boldness against his critics.

One offense they had committed against the apostle was to say he walked according to the flesh. Their fleshly behavior showed they were the ones who did so. They were wrong to conclude Paul thought and lived on a worldly plane just because they did. But they loudly, though falsely, proclaimed theirs was a walk in the Spirit in contrast to Paul.

**3. For though we walk in the flesh:** . . . though we are still living in the world, *—WEYM.*
**we do not war after the flesh:** . . . we do not war with carnal weapons, *—BRKL* . . . we do not fight our battles, *—NORL* . . . we do not contend for self, *—FNTN.*

**10:3.** Almost as if to throw back at them some of their words against him, the apostle stated he certainly did "walk in the flesh" in the sense that he lived as all human beings do. He grew tired, weary, and hungry as all men; therefore he needed food, clothing, and shelter as all others. And to be sure, Paul experienced the same physical hardships his critics gloried in.

However, he denied he warred "after the flesh." As a veteran soldier of the Cross he was too wise for that. He would no more go to battle with fleshly weapons than David would have dressed in Saul's armor (1 Samuel 17:38, 39).

**4. (For the weapons of our warfare [are] not carnal:** . . . are not of the flesh, *—HNSN.* **but mighty through God:** . . . but powerful through God,. *—PNT* . . . powerful with God, *—RTHM* . . . but divinely powerful, *NASB.*
**to the pulling down of strong holds;):** . . . for the purpose of destroying fortresses, *—FNTN* . . . in overthrowing strong fortresses, *—WEYM* . . . to upset defense lines, *—KLGS* . . . for the Demolition of Fortresses, *—WLSN.*

**10:4.** Paul emphatically denied his weapons, including any piece of his armor for spiritual warfare, were of a carnal, physical, or fleshly nature. He took no undue advantage of unsuspecting men through any misuse of personal charm. He refused to use dishonest flattery in attempts to manipulate men. No intellectually appealing philosophical discussion fell from his lips to draw people to himself personally. Disappointment came to those who sought "excellency of speech" (1 Corinthians 2:1) in his sermons. He purposely excited no one with merely psychologically stimulating material.

Instead, his implements of war were mighty because they were those supplied by God. With them he pulled down, overpowered, conquered, and destroyed spiritual strongholds. Such fortresses were prisons for the minds of men. Since the gods of this world guard the bars that hold them, only spiritual weapons more effective than theirs can set their captives free.

**5. Casting down imaginations:** . . . They upset reasonings, *—KLGS* . . . we tear down calculations, *—BRKL* . . . every deceptive fantasy, *—PHLP* . . . Destroying reasonings, *—WSLY* . . . defeating opponents, *—FNTN* . . . casting down [false] speculations, *—HNSN* . . . we overthrow arrogant 'reckonings,' *—WEYM.*
**and every high thing that exalteth itself against the knowledge of God:** . . . and every height elevating, *—CNDT* . . . and every imposing defense, *—PHLP* . . . and overthrowing every barrier raised against, *—TCNT* . . . and every rampart that erects itself, *—HNT* . . . that towers high in defiance of, *—WEYM* . . . the wisdom of God, *—NLTG.*
**and bringing into captivity every thought to the obedience of Christ:** . . . They make prisoners of every thought, *—KLGS* . . . I can make each rebel purpose my prisoner-of-war, *—WAY* . . . and subduing, *—FNTN* . . . and are bringing captive every intent, *—RTHM* . . . and bringing every intent, *—ALFD* . . . every understanding, *—DOUY* . . . bringing them into subjection to Christ, *—LOCK* . . . and make it yield to Christ, *NTPE.*

**10:5.** Indeed, the apostle's war instruments cast down (*kathairountes*, same as in "pulling down" in verse 4) imaginations. These included sophistries, philosophical reasonings with a surface and fallacious logic. Such had a basic appeal to a fleshly intellect. Embracing systems of thought of this kind fed an arrogant attitude that exalted itself in opposition to the true knowledge of God.

Paul's reference to "casting down imaginations" and "bringing into captivity every thought" does not encourage mental warfare for the believer. True, things in the mind often trouble the conscientious Christian, and he would like to rid himself of them. He feels condemned by them as the apostle did in Romans 7. But victory comes through the covering of the blood of Jesus, as Paul found in Romans 7:25 and 8:1.

The Christian experience was certainly not simply one of thought warfare for Paul. He determined to bring all non-Biblical teaching he encountered into captivity. He captured and led away as a prisoner of war every philosophical system which was contrary to the view of this world set forth in Scripture. All his conclusions on the great questions of life came into obedience to the gospel of Christ.

**6. And having in a readiness to revenge all disobedience:** . . . we shall make quick work of punishing, *—KLST* . . . and competent to expel every mutineer, *—FNTN* . . . and are prepared to punish, *—CMPB* . . . to administer justice, —BRKL . . . are prepared to punish all disobedience, —CMPB.

**when your obedience is fulfilled:** . . . is complete, —HNT . . . is fully shown, —BRKL . . . is made complete, —WLMS.

**10:6.** Paul was ready to take revenge on (to punish, to discipline in his apostolic office) every false teacher at Corinth. Their disobedience (*parakoē*, "unwillingness to hear") must be dealt with. However, he put the welfare of believers first. Only when their "obedience" (*hupakoē*, willingness to hear with the intent of obeying) was fulfilled or perfected did he intend to turn to troublesome teachers. Then he would attend to them as in the case of military officers who are court-martialed.

**7. Do ye look on things after the outward appearance?:** . . . Look at the facts as they are, NTPE . . . at the surface of things? —FNTN.

**If any man trust to himself that he is Christ's: let him of himself think this again:** . . . Let him reflect about it, —NORL . . . let him consider again, —SAWR . . . let him ponder this over in his mind, —BRKL.

**that, as he [is] Christ's, even so [are] we Christ's:**

**10:7.** Though the apostle earlier chided the Corinthians for looking at outward appearances (5:12), now he called on them to observe the obvious. Let them take note of those persons among them who boasted that they were in Christ and yet in so doing left the impression that others were not. They were convinced "in themselves" of that fact. They particularly questioned the spiritual standing of preachers like Paul.

The apostle called on these members of the "Christ Party" at Corinth (1 Corinthians 1:12) to think again. He belonged to the Saviour as much as they did. This should have been obvious to all even by outward appearances!

**8. For though I should boast somewhat more of our authority:** . . . we boasted excessively about our authority, —FNTN . . . to boast more loudly of our apostolic authority, —WEYM . . . about our authorization, —BRKL.

**which the Lord hath given us for edification:** . . . for building up, —YNG.

**and not for your destruction:** . . . and not for overthrowing it, —TCNT . . . and not for your ruin, —BRKL.

**I should not be ashamed:** . . . I shall never have to blush for doing so, —WLMS.

**10:8.** However, at this point Paul's modesty called forth a word of explanation. He sensed some might think he went too far in boasting of his authoritative position in Christ. Even if he bragged a little too much, he spoke only honestly of what the Lord had given him.

Besides, his ministerial gifts and graces came from the good hand of God with the intent that they be used to edify or build up believers in churches such as at Corinth. The Master never meant them for destruction (*kathairesis*, as in verse 4). With them the apostle tore down fortresses of the devil. On the other hand, false preachers in Corinth used their abilities to tear down churches!

Paul felt no shame in this defense of himself. His motives were pure. He knew that if the opposition should be able to discredit him personally, they would nullify his message. Actually, his enemies were the ones who stood in disgrace.

**9. That I may not seem as if I would terrify you by letters:** . . . I do not wish to intimidate you, —NAB . . . as if I were frightening you, —PNT . . . that I am trying to frighten you, —NORL . . . that I am scaring you, —KLGS . . . as if I wanted to frighten you by my letters, —WEYM . . . who writes you terrifying letters, —PHLP . . . that I am writing empty threats, —CNBR . . . to be frightening you, —ADAM . . . merely by my letters, —HNT.

**10:9.** To clarify things further, Paul stated that he wanted nothing he wrote in this letter to terrify (*ekphobeō*, here only in the New Testament) or frighten anyone. He did not want anything he said to seem that way or have that appearance. The Spirit inspired him to help rather than to hurt.

**10. For [his] letters, say they, [are] weighty and powerful:** . . . are impressive, —BECK . . . and forceful, —WLMS . . . and vigorous, —TCNT.

**but [his] bodily presence [is] weak:** . . . is unimpressive, NASB . . . is insignificant, —BRKL . . . he is feeble, —NORL.

**and [his] speech contemptible:** . . . he is hard to listen to, —NLTG . . . and people despise what he says, —BECK . . . and the speech despicable, —YNG . . . and the speech insignificant, —HNSN . . . and his rebukes who heeds them? —WAY . . . and rhetoric powerless, —FNTN . . . and there is nothing to his speeches, —NORL . . . of no account, —PNT, —PNIN.

**10:10.** Even the apostle's critics at Corinth recognized that his letters were weighty and powerful. They acknowledged their effectiveness, though their words contained no real compliment. Continuing their attack on the apostle, they said only when he wrote letters from a distance did he appear courageous. They claimed when he was in residence at Corinth his bodily presence (*parousia*) was weak and most unimpressive. Again they misinterpreted the meekness and gentleness of Christ which he possessed by the power of the Spirit (10:1).

Paul's ministerial enemies further declared his speech (*logos*, "word") was contemptible. In their opinion it amounted to nothing. They might have admitted the content of his sermons was acceptable, but they judged his delivery of the poorest sort. He had no polish such as they witnessed in the lectures of the graduates of the schools of rhetoric. What he said may have been presentable, but how he said it was almost repulsive to them. They had their eyes on the entertainment of form and cared little for the speaker's actual message.

In his first letter to Corinth (1 Corinthians 2:1-5), Paul had said he refused to cater to the demands of such an audience. No doubt he sought to clothe his message in an attractive form, but not to merely entertain men in the process.

**11. Let such an one think this:** . . . Such people should consider this, *—FNTN.*

**that, such as we are in word by letters when we are absent:** . . . in our epistolary discourse, *—MRDK.*

**such [will we be] also in deed when we are present:** . . . no less strong will I be in action, *—WAY* . . . are we in act, *—CNDT* . . . when we are there, *—KLGS.*

**10:11.** The apostle had a further word for the opposition to ponder. If they thought the words of his letters severe just because he was absent, he would change all that when he arrived. Once present at Corinth again, his actions would support the word he used in writing to them. He would soon dispel any charge of cowardice against him through the boldness he used in confronting his critics.

**12. For we dare not make ourselves of the number:** . . . For we presume not to equal, *—WSLY* . . . we dare not rank, *—HNSN.*

**or compare ourselves with some that commend themselves:** . . . persons distinguished by their self-commendation, *—WEYM* . . . who commend their own qualities, *—BRKL.*

**but they measuring themselves by themselves:** . . . by their own standards, *—PHLP* . . . by their own yardstick, *—BECK.*

**and comparing themselves among themselves:** . . . or by comparisons within their own circle, *—PHLP.*

**are not wise:** . . . are without understanding, *—ASV, —PNIN, —WORL* . . . they do not show good judgment, *—NORL* . . . they don't show good sense, *—BECK* . . . are without discernment, *—RTHM* . . . are guilty of folly, *—CNBR.*

**10:12.** To further prevent misunderstanding of the focus on himself, Paul declared he dared not join the crowd of preachers who wrote their own letters of recommendation. That was pure presumption. If any thought him lacking the courage to do so, he acknowledged guilt to that charge of cowardice with a touch of sarcasm. He was not brave enough to belong to that group.

Those ministers judged themselves successful by subjective, human standards. They evaluated themselves by themselves. In this they acted unwisely. They lacked insight and understanding in truly spiritual things. These were actually men of ignorance!

**13. But we will not boast of things without [our] measure:** . . . We are not going to make any extravagant claims, *—NORL* . . . ours will be no immoderate exultation, *—HNT* . . . as regards the unmeasured things, *—RTHM.*

**but according to the measure of the rule which God hath distributed to us:** . . . Our limit is the field of work to which God has bound us, *—BECK* . . . by the sphere of activity that God has assigned to us, *—ADAM* . . . rule God has set for us, *—KLGS* . . . which the God of measure, *—HNSN* . . . the province . . . apportioned to us, *—ASV* . . . allotted to us, *—PNT* . . . hath imparted to us, *—MRDK.*

**a measure to reach even unto you:** . . . a sphere which reaches even to you, *—MNTG.*

**10:13.** False teachers trying to unseat the apostle at Corinth even took credit for things to which they had contributed nothing. They refused to recognize they had entered into other men's labors. Not even the 12 apostles could claim their work was totally of themselves. Jesus said to them, "I sent you to reap that whereupon ye bestowed no labor" (John 4:38).

By contrast Paul said he determined never to boast of things outside his "measure," beyond the limits set by the call of God on his life. It established for him a sphere of responsible activity in gospel work. The Lord distributed or assigned this rule (*kanonos*, English *canon*) to him.

Paul's original call sent him to Gentiles and kings as well as to the Children of Israel, with emphasis on the former (Acts 9:15). Once in the early part of his ministry he thought he might do a profitable work among his own people in the Jerusalem area. To emphasize the intended direction of his missionary call, the Lord said to him, "Depart: for I will send thee far hence unto the Gentiles" (Acts 22:21).

The rule for him was clear. His mission was to preach the gospel in virgin territory, where Christ had never been named (Romans 15:20). God did not intend him to labor where other preachers had already worked. His assignment was that of planting new churches, not to build on another's foundation.

This designated sphere of influence had brought the apostle to Corinth. When he worshipfully recalled what the Lord did through him in founding the church there, he spoke justifiably of things within the limits God had set for him.

14. **For we stretch not ourselves beyond [our] measure]:** . . . we are not overextending ourselves, *NASB* . . . We are not claiming too much, *—NORL* . . . not going beyond our commission, *—CNFT* . . . not overstepping the limits of my authority, *—MNTG.*

**as though we reached not unto you:**

**for we are come as far as to you also in [preaching] the gospel of Christ:** . . . for we outstrip others, *—CNDT.*

**10:14.** Accordingly, Paul declared his ministry did not extend beyond the limits the Lord determined for him when he came initially to Corinth. It was not as if his territory did not reach that far, as some of the critics may have suggested. Indeed, he was living by the rule he had made for himself based on his missionary call.

He reminded the Corinthians he was the first to come (*phthanō*, "come before") to them with the gospel. He had the privilege of preaching and announcing the good news to them the first time they heard it.

15. **Not boasting of things without [our] measure:** . . . We are not boasting extravagantly, *—NORL.*

**[that is], of other men's labours:** . . . and take credit for other men's labours, *—WEYM* . . . about the work done by others, *—NORL* . . . in other person's hard work, *—KLGS.*

**but having hope, when your faith is increased:** . . . as your faith groweth, *—ASV* . . . by a growing of your faith, *—RTHM.*

**that we shall be enlarged by you according to our rule abundantly:** . . . shall enlarge our sphere of influence, *—BRKL* . . . we shall be magnified, ASV, *—SAWR* . . . to be magnified among you superabundantly, *—CNDT.*

**10:15.** Certainly then, Paul did not boast of things beyond his measure, his sphere of God-appointed influence or action. He did not take credit for what other men had done in the work of the Lord's kingdom. He did not boast of other men's labors as his critics did. They ignored the fact that the one whose influence they were doing their best to ruin was the very one who had founded the church they worked in. In sorrow Paul wrote these words to save the church they would destroy.

As a matter of fact, the apostle held a God-given hope that his sphere of influence would soon extend even further to the west, beyond Corinth. Believers in Corinth would actually assist him in that ministry. As their faith increased, as it matured in successfully resisting the opposition's attempts to destroy it, they would help make possible an increase in his territory. Their missionary support would greatly enlarge his area of action.

16. **To preach the gospel in the [regions] beyond you:** . . . shall tell the Good News in the districts beyond you, *—WEYM* . . . in places that lie beyond you, *—CNFT.*

**[and] not to boast in another man's line of things made ready to our hand:** . . . without having to take credit for work done in another's field, *—NORL* . . . work already done in another man's field, *—BECK.*

**10:16.** With the help of the Corinthians, Paul knew he would preach the gospel in the regions beyond them. He wrote the Romans a similar message. He said, "Whensoever I take my journey into Spain, I will come to you: for I trust to see you in my journey, and to be brought on my way thitherward by you" (Romans 15:24). Writings of Ancient Church fathers reveal the apostle did indeed minister the gospel in Spain. He went there probably during the period between his first and second Roman imprisonments.

Again Paul indirectly rebuked his critics who sought to steal the hearts of the Corinthians from him. He declared he was not as some who boast of "another man's line of things" or range of actions. Other workers made things ready for their hands, yet they took full credit for the whole project.

17. **But he that glorieth, let him glory in the Lord:** . . . the proud should be proud in the Lord, *—FNTN.*

**10:17.** However, no one should conclude the apostle fought on a fleshly plane with his enemies. It is not so much his person he defended as the gospel. He struggled not simply to keep certain Christians loyal to him. He wanted them to remain true to God. Accordingly, he turned back to the previously written Word of God. Jeremiah said none should glory (*kauchaomai*, "boast," as in verse 16 and throughout this passage) in his wisdom, strength, or riches, but men must glory only in the Lord (Jeremiah 9:23, 24). In his first letter to Corinth Paul included the same principle (1 Corinthians 1:31).

18. **For not he that commendeth himself is approved:** . . . the man of genuine character is not he who commends himself, *—HNT* . . . It is not self-commendation that matters, *—PHLP* . . . not who accredits himself, *—WAY* . . . it is not people who recommend themselves that win approval, *—TCNT.*

**but whom the Lord commendeth:** . . . but whom the Lord establishes, *—FNTN* . . . he whom the Lord praiseth, *—MRDK.*

**10:18.** To glory, boast, or commend oneself does not necessarily mean one is approved by God. Commendation from the Lord is all that matters. In his previous letter to the Corinthians the apostle said the judgment of others or even his own appraisal of himself was of no consequence

(1 Corinthians 4:3, 4). The Lord's judgment at the last day will determine all.

## Chapter 11

**1. Would to God ye could bear with me a little in [my] folly:** . . . Please, put up with a bit of foolishness of mine, —BRKL . . . I want you to put up with me while I indulge in a bit of foolishness, —ADAM . . . you would put up with a little folly from me, —NORL . . . with a little "senselessness" from me! —HNT . . . as to some little imprudence, —RTHM.

**and indeed bear with me:** . . . you will have to tolerate me, —BRKL.

**11:1.** Once more the Spirit moved the apostle to apologize for the focus on self. He asked his readers to bear with him in his folly (foolishness or seeming lack of sense) and then thanked them that they were already doing just that.

Paul disliked the role of the self-defender. It rubbed against the grain of his modesty. The trait of true modesty displayed itself repeatedly in his ministry. In First Corinthians he said, "I am the least of the apostles, that am not meet to be called an apostle" (1 Corinthians 15:9). In Ephesians he spoke of himself as one who was "less than the least of all saints" (Ephesians 3:8).

**2. For I am jealous over you with godly jealousy:** . . . for I am zealous, —YNG . . . I rave for you with a Divine madness, —FNTN . . . For I am ardently devoted to you, —WLSN . . . For I love you, —CNBR . . . I feel a divine jealousy for you, —WLMS.

**for I have espoused you to one husband:** . . . For I have betrothed you, —WEYM . . . I arranged your wedding, —KLGS . . . I promised you in marriage, —BECK . . . for I affianced you to one, —HNSN . . . to one Man, —NORL.

**that I may present [you as] a chaste virgin to Christ:** . . . a pure virgin, —YNG . . . like a faithful bride, —WEYM.

**11:2.** Paul offered a clear reason behind this self-defense which was distasteful to him. He was jealous over his converts at Corinth. Concern for their welfare forced his foolishness. Injured pride had nothing to do with it. It was not even a human emotion that moved him. Instead, it was a jealousy (*zēlos*), a zeal like that of God.

Nothing is more detestable than human jealousy. The author of The Song of Solomon rightly observed, "Jealousy is cruel as the grave" (Song of Solomon 8:6). It brings great strain to many a marriage. However, the Lord makes clear repeatedly in His Word that He is jealous over His people. For example, Zechariah declared, "Thus saith the Lord of hosts; I am jealous for Jerusalem and for Zion with a great jealousy" (Zechariah 1:14). Thus Paul said his was a "godly" jealousy.

Contrasting the two kinds of jealousy, Harris wrote, "Human jealousy is a vice, but to share divine jealousy is a virtue. It is the motive and object of the jealousy that is all-important. There is a place for a spiritual father's passionate concern for the exclusive and pure devotion to Christ of his spiritual children, and also a place for anger at potential violators of that purity (11:29)" (*The Expositor's Bible Commentary,* 10:385).

Behind Paul's feelings was the fact he had espoused (betrothed, engaged) them to be married to Christ. Fathers made full arrangements for marriages in ancient cultures, and this is so even among some societies today. The engagement was to one husband. A love and a relationship of that magnitude could be for only one Person, Christ.

The apostle was also fearful about his converts at Corinth. As any father he anticipated the day he could proudly present his daughter to her husband as a chaste, pure virgin (*parthenon*). Church purity is a valid concern for any pastor.

**3. But I fear, lest by any means:** . . . I am apprehensive, —WLMS.

**as the serpent beguiled Eve through his subtlety:** . . . as the snake tricked Eve by his cunning, —KLGS . . . by its trickery seduced Eve, —BECK . . . completely deceived Eve in his knavery, —RTHM . . . by his cunning, —NORL.

**so your minds should be corrupted from the simplicity that is in Christ:** . . . I am afraid that you will be fooled, —NLTG . . . your minds should be led astray, NASB . . . your thoughts may be turned aside, —WLMS . . . so your imaginations should be corrupted, —CNBR . . . should be seduced from your single-mindedness, —MNTG . . . led astray from their simple devotion, —NORL . . . from their single-heartedness and their fidelity to Christ, —WEYM . . . from that singleness of heart, —HNT . . . your simple and pure loyalty, —BECK.

**11:3.** However, Paul feared unfaithfulness at Corinth might deny him that privilege. He was not ignorant of the way the flesh and the devil work. Satan in the form of a serpent deceived Eve with his subtilty (*panourgia*, "craftiness, trickery," readiness to do anything). Then Paul's concern was that the minds of the Corinthians might be corrupted and led astray from the simplicity and sincerity that is in Christ.

**4. For if he that cometh preacheth another Jesus:** . . . if the newcomer, —FNTN . . . had proclaimed to you, —MRDK . . . a pseudo-Jesus, R—PNT.

**whom we have not preached:**
**or [if] ye receive another spirit:** . . . Spirit different from the One, —WEYM, —WLMS.
**which ye have not received:**
**or another gospel, which ye have not accepted:** . . . which you did not embrace, —WLSN . . . different from what you previously welcomed, —BRKL.

**ye might well bear with [him]:** ... you submit to it readily enough, —RSV.

**11:4.** The apostle was surprised at the ready response Corinthian believers had given to the newcomers (*erchomenos*). They preached or proclaimed another (*allos*, "another of the same kind") interpretation of the same Jesus. Their representation of Christ was different from that which Paul presented to them. They were of another (*heteron*, "another of a different kind") spirit too. It was not the same kind of spirit the apostle projected to them. Theirs was in fact another (*heteron*) gospel. It was not the good news they accepted when Paul, their father in the Faith, first came to them. Then how could they put up with such preachers so easily?

The apostle did not include "ye might well bear with him" in his remarks to the Galatians regarding similar false teachers. There he instructed, "If any man preach any other gospel unto you than that ye have received, let him be accursed" (Galatians 1:9).

**5. For I suppose I was not a whit behind the very chiefest apostles:** ... I consider myself to be deficient in nothing, —FNTN ... I consider myself not a single bit inferior to those surpassingly superior apostles of yours! —WLMS ... regard myself as nowise inferior, —CNFT ... behind the very foremost apostles, —NOYS ... to these extraspecial messengers of yours, —PHLP.

**11:5.** To make his point clear Paul felt compelled to declare he was of the opinion he was not a whit behind or not at all inferior to such chief or super apostles. Interestingly, his words differ markedly from some of his first letter to the Corinthians. In it he judged himself to be "the least of the apostles," and not at all worthy to be called an apostle (1 Corinthians 15:9). Earlier he had compared himself with true apostles while in his second letter he stands in contrast to false teachers.

Though the apostle acknowledged he may have seemed to have no sense in speaking of himself in such terms, instead, under the inspiration of the Spirit he was indeed wise. The sage of old advised at times it is necessary to "answer a fool according to his folly, lest he be wise in his own conceit" (Proverbs 26:5). In the same sense Paul replied to the false charges made against him by the "super apostles" at Corinth.

**6. But though [I be] rude in speech:** ... if in the matter of speech I am no orator, —WEYM ... If I am untrained in speech, —KLGS ... though I be unskilled in speech, —MNTG ... Even if I lack skill in rhetoric, —BRKL ... even uncultured in [my] discourse, —RTHM ... though I be a common man in my speech, —ALFD ... even if I am not a polished speaker, —NORL.

**yet not in knowledge:** ... I know what I'm talking about, —BECK ... yet I am not wanting in the gift of knowledge, —CNBR.

**but we have been thoroughly made manifest among you in all things:** ... we have made that perfectly clear to you in every way, —HNT ... at all events, among you! —FNTN.

**11:6.** As earlier (10:10), the apostle again responded to accusations against his speech. Some declared he was rude (*idiōtēs*, a layman as compared to a specialist), unskilled as a public speaker. Since the claim came from his critics, it was not necessarily a statement of fact. Certainly his sermons as recorded in Acts are reasoned, logical, lucid presentations. Nonetheless, he admitted he was not schooled as a polished lecturer in the art of Greek rhetoric. Such men of his day became popular entertainers and collected considerable sums from the crowds that flocked around them.

However, Paul gave no ground to the opposition when it came to knowledge. In that area he had thoroughly demonstrated his ability among them in every way. Presenting truth was his aim in a public address. His concern was the message, not the manner of its presentation.

**7. Have I committed an offence in abasing myself:** ... Or did I commit a sin, —HNSN ... did I commit a fault, —DOUY ... by humbling myself, —MRDK ... thereby degrading myself, —NORL.

**that ye might be exalted:** ... in order that you might be exalted, —NORL ... to push you forward? —KLGS.

**because I have preached to you the gospel of God freely?:** ... without charge, —ALFD ... without a fee, —PHLP ... without fee or reward? —WEYM, —CNBR ... to you for nothing? —HNT ... without compensation? —BRKL ... free of charge? —CNFT ... free of cost? —MNTG ... without accepting any pay? —WLMS ... without payment, —TCNT.

**11:7.** The itinerant lecturers who used their mouths to make a living charged sizable fees for every performance. People paid gladly to hear such "professionals." By way of contrast, while planting a church Paul did not ask the infant congregation to support him financially. Instead he worked with his hands as a tentmaker to supply his own needs (Acts 18:1-3). This caused his critics to say he was not a "professional."

Concerning this issue Hughes wrote, "Among the Greeks the accredited rhetorician or philosopher was a 'professional' man who charged for his services and lived by his art. For a speaker to refuse remuneration, or not demand it, would at once cause his listeners, such as the sophistication of their outlook, to suspect him of being spurious, a mere *poseur,* and his teaching as worthless" (*The New London Commentary,* p. 383). Socrates gained repute by standing alone against the Sophists in this practice.

In 1 Corinthians 9:6-14 Paul said established churches should meet the financial needs of their minister. He declared the Law, reason, and Christ all taught this principle. His conclusion was, "Even so hath the Lord ordained that they which preach the gospel should live of the gospel" (1 Corinthians 9:14).

Yet he asked for no such support in pioneering churches (1 Corinthians 9:15-18). He wanted to establish new congregations on a solid foundation. The apostle determined not to be classified with the traveling entertainers. He was not in the ministry for money (Acts 20:33, 34). Further, by word and deed he instructed young converts to shun the prevailing notion among Romans that it was beneath the dignity of a free man to work for a living (Acts 20:35). To be truly Christian they must work to meet their own needs and to have extra to give to those who could not supply their own needs.

With some accusing him of being unprofessional because he worked, Paul wondered if he had committed an offense (*hamartian,* "sin") in presenting the good news to them freely (without cost, as a gift). In the eyes of his enemies he degraded himself by doing so. Of course, he made them appear exalted by way of comparison.

8. **I robbed other churches:** . . . I stripped Other Congregations, –WLSN . . . I sponged on other churches, –WLMS.

**taking wages [of them], to do you service:** . . . receiving pay from them, –WEYM . . . when I took supplies from them to serve you, –KLGS . . . taking rations, –PNT . . . receiving supplies with a view to the ministering unto you, –RTHM . . . for ministering to you, –PNIN . . . to minister to you free of charge, –PHLP . . . for services to you, –FNTN.

9. **And when I was present with you, and wanted:** . . . and being deficient, –FNTN . . . and my resources failed, –WEYM . . . and very hard up, –PHLP . . . and ran short of funds, –BRKL . . . and had needs, –ADAM . . . and in need, –TCNT . . . when I lacked the actual necessities of life, –MNTG.

**I was chargeable to no man:** . . . I was not a burden on any man, –HNSN . . . I was burdensome to none of you, –MRDK.

**for that which was lacking to me the brethren which came from Macedonia supplied:** . . . supplied beforehand my deficiency, –WLSN.

**and in all [things] I have kept myself from being burdensome unto you, and [so] will I keep [myself]:** . . . so in every way, –HNT . . . free from troubling you for maintenance, –FNTN . . . and I shall continue to do so, –TCNT.

**11:8, 9.** As a matter of fact, at times he "robbed" (accepted wages, offerings) from churches he had previously established so he could minister to them. For example, after he left Macedonia and moved on south to plant the churches at Thessalonica and Corinth, the believers at Philippi sent several offerings to the apostle (Philippians 4:15, 16). Despite what his critics said, Paul determined to continue his financial policy in planting new churches.

10. **As the truth of Christ is in me:**
**no man shall stop me of this boasting in the regions of Achaia:** . . . that will not be silenced, –KLGS . . . will not be silenced anywhere in Greece, –BECK . . . within the boundaries, –MNTG . . . in the district, –FNTN . . . in the country of Greece, –NLTG.

**11:10.** Protesting by the truth of Christ which he held to, Paul emphatically declared nothing would change his mind in this matter. He would not allow criticism from his enemies to set the criteria for ministerial ethics in his life. Slander would not change his character. If he must boast to match the opposition, he would glory in the fact that he acted correctly concerning finances in planting new churches, especially in the regions of Achaia, Greece. As he wrote earlier, "It were better for me to die, than that any man should make my glorying void" (1 Corinthians 9:15). The false apostles may have made merchandise of the gospel, but he never would.

11. **Wherefore? because I love you not? God knoweth:**

**11:11.** Did Paul's personal policy on church finances show a lack of love for his converts in Corinth? No doubt his critics hinted if he really had their welfare at heart he would have treated them more "professionally." To the contrary, it was precisely because he loved them so much that he did not demand their support in pioneering the congregations in Corinth.

Writing another church he planted, and defending himself against the same charge, the apostle said he worked night and day so he would not be a burden to young converts. His conduct concerning ministerial support demonstrated he was "affectionately desirous" of them and that they were "dear" to him (1 Thessalonians 2:5-9). He loved them so much he treated them gently "as a nurse cherisheth her children."

12. **But what I do, that I will do:** . . . I will continue to do, NASB . . . But I will persist, –WEYM . . . to do what I am doing, –NORL.

**that I may cut off occasion from them which desire occasion:** . . . that I may cut off opportunity,

NASB, —CMPB ... that I may deprive them, —CNFT ... to eliminate the opportunity, —BRKL ... that I may take away any pretext for their boasting, —ADAM.

**that wherein they glory, they may be found even as we:**

**11:12.** Once more the founder of the church at Corinth declared his determination to continue doing what he had always done in the way he treated finances as a pioneer pastor. Inspired by the Spirit as he wrote, he aimed to catch those who slandered him in this matter in their own trap. His explanations snatched the occasion for glorying right out of their hands. He "pulled the rug from under their feet." He made them appear as human as the one they criticized, slandering him as the lowly preacher who had to work because his ministry was so poor it did not support him.

**13. For such [are] false apostles, deceitful workers:** ... They are counterfeits of the real thing, dishonest practitioners, —PHLP ... For these sham apostles tricksters, —FNTN ... false missionaries ... tricky workmen, —KLGS ... dishonest workmen, —WEYM ... cheating workmen, NTPE.

**transforming themselves into the apostles of Christ:** ... fashioning themselves, —PNIN ... assuming the garb of apostles of Christ, —WEYM ... clothing themselves in the garb of Christ's Apostles, —CNBR ... masquerading as, —HNT ... in disguise passing as, —NORL ... wearing the masks of Christ's apostles, —BRKL.

**11:13.** For the first time in his letter Paul plainly called his critics false apostles (*pseudapostoloi,* here only in the New Testament). They were deceitful, dishonest workers. They transformed and disguised themselves so as to appear to be the apostles of Christ. He warned the elders at Ephesus that such false teachers, wolves in sheep's clothing, would arise among them seeking to draw away disciples unto themselves (Acts 20:29, 30). Sadly, in the end they would devour the flock they pretended to care for.

**14. And no marvel:** ... It is no surprise! —NLTG ... and no wonder, —YNG ... And it is not surprising, —WLSN.

**for Satan himself is transformed into an angel of light:** ... can disguise himself as, —WEYM ... masquerades as, —BRKL ... pretends to be, —KLGS.

**11:14.** Paul, the true apostle, was not at all surprised at this problem caused by his critics at Corinth. He knew well what worked in the darkened hearts of wicked men. These false teachers were servants of Satan. As true children of the devil they acted like their father. He regularly disguises himself as an angel of light, never appearing as darkness.

**15. Therefore [it is] no great thing if his ministers also be transformed as the ministers of righteousness:** ... So it is nothing extraordinary, —BRKL ... So, it isn't any big thing, —SEB ... So it isn't surprising, —BECK ... his servants transform themselves, —FNTN.

**whose end shall be according to their works:** ... whose doom, —WLMS ... whose consummation, —CNDT ... correspond to their deeds, —RSV ... in accordance with their actions, —WEYM ... In the end they will get exactly what their actions deserve, —TEV ... in the end they will get what their conduct deserves, —BRCL ... will end up the same way they lived, —SEB ... so shall be their fate, —HNT ... be in keeping with their deeds, —ADAM.

**11:15.** Understandably, then, the apostle reasoned it is no great thing for the ministers (*diakonoi,* "servants") of Satan to disguise themselves as promoters of righteousness. They, like the devil, appear to be what they are not. Satan never approaches the Christian as Satan. He came to Eve as one who knew how to help her "be as gods" (Genesis 3:5). In the same way sin rarely tempts as sin. Once recognized for what it is, the temptation to sin loses much of its force. Likewise error often presents itself as truth.

So these false apostles seemed to advance just causes. However, as Paul wrote the Romans, "They that are such serve not our Lord Jesus Christ, but their own belly; and by good words and fair speeches deceive the hearts of the simple" (Romans 16:18).

Their true nature would appear at the end. Their reward would be according to their works. Paul implied they will be dammed on judgment day. He did not teach here contrary to his message elsewhere that men are saved by grace and not works (Ephesians 2:8, 9). Still, there is a Biblical sense in which people will be judged, "every man according to their works" (Revelation 20:13).

**16. I say again, Let no man think me a fool:** ... I repeat, —CNFT ... no one should presume me to be imprudent, —CNDT ... Let no one imagine me to be imprudent, —RTHM ... that I am vain, —NORL ... a Simpleton, —WLSN.

**if otherwise, yet as a fool receive me:** ... But, if you do, bear with me, —SEB ... then treat me as a fool, —JB ... put up with me as such, —BB ... accept me as a fool, —BRCL ... show me at least the patience you would show a fool, —GDSP.

**that I may boast myself a little:** ... Then I can brag a little as fools do, —SEB ... Give me a chance to do just a little talking about the claims I am proud of, —BRCL.

**11:16.** The list of charges against the apostle was long; therefore, he continued his defense. However, before turning to the next false claim against him he apologized more for his "foolishness." He did not want to appear as lacking in modesty. The behavior of the braggart was particularly distasteful to him. If he appeared as a fool, though, he asked for tolerance in boasting yet about himself.

Recognizing that modesty should prevail in the ministry of every preacher, Kent reasoned: "There are times, however, when personal explanations are necessary. In order to prevent distorted statements, unfounded gossip, or outright slander, or to protect the welfare or reputation of others, it may be one's duty to set the record straight, even when one must risk feelings of awkwardness. Surely it is essential to defend the truth and prevent the twisting of facts when the Lord's work is involved" (p. 173).

**17. That which I speak, I speak [it] not after the Lord:** . . . When I confidently brag like this, *—SEB* . . . When I boast in this reckless way, *—GDSP* . . . what I am saying now is not what the Lord would have me say, *—TEV* . . . is not prompted by, *—JB* . . . I am not speaking here as a Christian, *—NEB* . . . This isn't a Christian way to talk, *—BRCL*.

**but as it were foolishly:** . . . but as though in delirium, *—FNTN* . . . as if in a fit of folly, *—JB*.

**in this confidence of boasting:** . . . in the certainty that I have something to boast about, *—JB*.

**11:17.** Paul explained that his boasting was not a Christian characteristic. It was "not after the Lord." However, by this he offered no disclaimer to inspiration in writing this paragraph. Noting this Meyer observed: "When Paul in this verse says that he is not speaking *kata kurion*, he is not referring to inspiration. He does not mean to say that the Lord has nothing to do with the matter and is not giving him the very words by His Spirit" (p. 274). He concluded, "Paul is simply referring to his method of speaking in the given situation" (ibid., p. 274). Indeed, the Spirit directed him in a necessary vindication of truth in order to preserve the integrity of the gospel the apostle preached. On the surface what follows seems the greatest of all Paul's boasting, but in these prefacing remarks he never appeared more humble.

**18. Seeing that many glory after the flesh:** . . . since men generally boast of their personal affairs, *—NORL* . . . Since many boast about their position, *—FNTN*.

**I will glory also:**

**11:18.** Circumstances forced him to compare himself with those who gloried after the flesh or by human standards. Of course he knew the teaching of the wise man who advised, "Answer not a fool according to his folly, lest thou also be like unto him" (Proverbs 26:4). Yet he was also acquainted with the wise man's instruction to "answer a

fool according to his folly, lest he be wise in his own conceit" (Proverbs 26:5). Both exhortations are obviously good. The dilemma is when do you apply which? In this case the Spirit gave Paul the wisdom to know it was now time to apply the second part of the counsel of the sage of old.

**19. For ye suffer fools gladly:** . . . ye bear with, *—ALFD*, *—PNT* . . . being tolerant to fools, *—NORL* . . . will gladly tolerate fools, *—BRKL*.

**seeing ye [yourselves] are wise:**

**11:19.** With tongue in cheek the founder of the church at Corinth complimented those he won to Christ for suffering fools gladly. They not only tolerated those who bragged on themselves, but they apparently loved their boasting. This, he said sarcastically, indicated just how wise they were! At the moment he felt the same as Job who chided his "comforters" in saying, "No doubt but ye are the people, and wisdom shall die with you" (Job 12:2).

**20. For ye suffer, if a man bring you into bondage:** . . . You even put up with those who exploit you, *—NAB* . . . if he enslaves you, *—HNSN* . . . if a man takes away your liberty, *—PHLP*.

**if a man devour [you]:** . . . if anyone bites you, *—KLGS* . . . lives at your expense, *—WEYM* . . . spends your money, *—PHLP* . . . or imposes on you, *—BRKL*.

**if a man take [of you]:** . . . if a man seizeth you, *—ALFD* . . . if he takes advantage of you, *NASB* . . . when they prey upon you, *—NORL* . . . or traps you, *—BECK* . . . makes a fool of you, *—PHLP* . . . if they rob, *—FNTN* . . . or exploits you, *—BRKL*.

**if a man exalt himself:** . . . if anyone makes himself a tyrant, *—KLGS* . . . or lords it over you, *—BECK* . . . if any one is lifting himself up, *—RTHM* . . . or snubs you, *—BRKL*.

**if a man smite you on the face:** . . . if he beats you on the face, *—HNSN*.

**11:20.** Believers in Corinth even allowed these false teachers to bring them into bondage. They seemed to enjoy the fact that such leaders usurped authority over them. Apparently they liked being reduced to slavery.

These gullible Christians put up with preachers who devoured them (consumed them, ate them up). They tolerated men who took of their goods, demanding offerings for their support.

Simple as these believers were, ministers who exalted themselves before them appealed to their fancy. They liked the star on the stage. Men who used what we would call today the Hollywood approach to evangelism attracted and held their attention.

Strange as it seemed, they were so duped they even allowed these preachers to slap them in the face, the highest form of personal insult. By no means did Paul suggest they should do otherwise than "turn the other cheek" when attacked by a persecutor (Luke 6:29). However, the situation at Corinth was entirely different. People there willingly submitted themselves to be exploited.

**21. I speak as concerning reproach:** ... By way of disparagement I assume that, —ALFD ... by way of disparagement, —ASV ... —HNSN ... I say this to my discredit, —HNT ... I'm ashamed to admit it, —BECK.

**as though we had been weak:** ... because we have been insulted, —FNTN.

**Howbeit whereinsoever any is bold: (I speak foolishly,) I am bold also:** ... I will match him, —BRKL.

**11:21.** Paul reproached himself, admitted to his shame that he might have allowed some to think him weak. He might have appeared powerless because Spirit-produced character made him cautious in speaking out to defend himself. Yet immediately he declared he was ready to be as bold, as courageous as anyone. So he proceeded to boast even more forcefully than earlier of his ministerial experiences (see 6:4-10).

**22. Are they Hebrews? so [am] I:** ... Are they Jews? —BECK ... I also! —YNG.

**Are they Israelites? so [am] I:** ... I too! —RTHM.

**Are they the seed of Abraham? so [am] I:** ... descendants of, —WEYM ... the offspring of, —HNT ... the posterity, —SAWR ... from the family of, —NLTG.

**11:22.** The apostle found it necessary to defend against the charge his ministry was inferior to that of the false apostles. His critics questioned his birth and background. They probably pictured him as not being a "real" Jew. If so he would not have moved in Gentile circles as a minister. The Ebionites, a First Century Jewish sect, spread a rumor that Paul was a Gentile by birth.

In response, the apostle said he was as much a Hebrew, an Israelite (a seed, a descendant of Abraham), as they. As in writing to the Philippians, he reasoned if anyone had a right to brag about the nobility of his birth he had even more (Philippians 3:4-6).

**23. Are they ministers of Christ?:** ... Are they servants of, —WEYM.

**(I speak as a fool) I [am] more:** ... I [am] above [them], —PNT ... as if I were out of my mind, —WEYM ... like one out of his senses, —HNT ... (in defect of understanding, I say it,) I am superior, —MRDK.

**in labours more abundant:** ... Overflowing in hard work, —KLGS ... I have labored harder, —ADAM ... with measureless toils, —BRKL ... I have done more work than anyone else, —NORL.

**in stripes above measure:** ... suffered innumerable lashings, —ADAM ... in Scourges to excess, —WLSN ... by excessively cruel floggings, —WEYM.

**in prisons more frequent:** ... in bonds, —MRDK ... far more imprisonments, NASB.

**in deaths oft:** ... facing death so frequently, —BRKL ... often exposed to death, —CNFT ... in the jaws of death, —ADAM.

**11:23.** Paul said, "So they proudly proclaim they are the ministers, servants of Christ, do they? Well, I am even more so!" Yet immediately the apostle's modesty compelled him to apologize again. This time he termed such boasting of self sheer madness. He played the part of a fool (*paraphronon*, "one beside himself," stronger than *aphron* in verses 16 and 19).

If the opposition wanted a comparison between his ministry and theirs, he would oblige. Was their work demanding? He worked harder. Had they suffered stripes, felt the blows on their back for preaching? He had known the experience "above measure," to a much greater degree than his critics. If they had been behind bars for Jesus' sake, he had been imprisoned more frequently. He had even been near death often as he faced angry mobs.

**24. Of the Jews five times received I forty [stripes] save one:** ... Five times the Jews gave me a whipping, —NORL ... was I scourged, —MRDK ... less one, —WLSN.

**11:24.** Fellow Jews had beaten Paul with 39 stripes on 5 different occasions. The law of Moses limited such punishment to 40 blows, but Jewish custom permitted only 39 lest a miscount go beyond what the Law allowed (Deuteronomy 25:3).

**25. Thrice was I beaten with rods:** ... with Roman rods, —WEYM ... I have been scourged by the Romans, —MNTG.

**once was I stoned, thrice I suffered shipwreck: a night and a day I have been in the deep:** ... was floating on the open sea, —WEYM ... I have been adrift at sea, —BRKL ... in a swamp, —CNDT.

**11:25.** The apostle also suffered at the hands of the Gentiles. He had been sentenced (likely in a Roman court) to a beating with rods three different times. He knew one such experience as a pioneer pastor at Philippi, though the punishment he received was illegally administered (Acts 16:23-37).

Once the apostle was stoned by those of his own people. At Lystra Jewish rebels persuaded a mob to illegally stone Paul. Afterward they dragged him outside the city leaving him for dead (Acts 14:19). However, wondrously the Lord raised him up. He immediately returned to the city and the next day continued on his journey in ministry (Acts 14:20).

The apostle had also suffered shipwreck. In fact, once he spent a day and night (*nuchthēmeron*, literally 24 hours) adrift in the depth of the sea. Luke did not record the account of this incident in Paul's life in Acts. The story he told of the sea disaster during the voyage to Rome came some time after Paul wrote this epistle.

**26. [In] journeyings often:** . . . by frequent travelling, −WEYM . . . During frequent Journeys, −WLSN . . . I've traveled much, −BECK.

**[in] perils of waters:** . . . amid dangers in crossing rivers, −WEYM . . . which I was exposed to danger, −ADAM.

**[in] perils of robbers:** . . . of bandits, −MNTG.

**[in] perils by [mine own] countrymen:** . . . from kindred, −YNG.

**[in] perils by the heathen:** . . . from the people who do not know God, −NLTG . . . from the pagans, −KLGS.

**[in] perils in the city:** . . . in towns, −TCNT.

**[in] perils in the wilderness:** . . . in perils in desert, −RTHM . . . dangers in the country, −TCNT . . . in the open country, −KLGS . . . in lonely places, −WAY.

**[in] perils in the sea:**

**[in] perils among false brethren:** . . . dangers from spies in our midst, −WEYM . . . from traitors disguised as fellow-believers, −WAY . . . among sham brothers, −BRKL . . . from false friends, −BECK.

**11:26.** The apostle next listed several pairs of perils he faced in his many travels. These dangers that confronted him daily no doubt surpassed anything his critics at Corinth could brag about in their experience.

Paul risked his life when his travels demanded he cross swollen streams and rivers without bridges. The more sure footing of the journey on land brought the threat of robbers. He knew what it was to be in danger among his own countrymen, the Jews, as well as to face peril from the heathen, the Gentiles (*ethnōn*). He was not safe whether he was in the city or in the wilderness (uninhabited areas, the countryside). On board ship the storm could swallow him up at any time. The most painful thought of all to Paul, though, was the fact that he faced perils among false brethren.

**27. In weariness and painful-ness:** . . . I have experienced hard work, −NORL . . . in labor and travail, −ASV, −HNSN . . . in toil and hardship, −RTHM.

**in watchings often:** . . . often in sleepless watchings, −CNBR . . . in vigils many a time, −HNT.

**in hunger and thirst:**

**in fastings often:** . . . often without food, −RSV.

**in cold and nakedness:** . . . poorly clad and exposed to cold, −WLMS . . . and exposure, NASB.

**11:27.** Further, the apostle knew weariness from the toil of his labor. He suffered the pain of exertion and hardship. Sleepless nights caused by ministerial care forced their way into his place of sleep. Often he fasted of necessity due to lack of food. Sometimes he was even short of sufficient clothing.

No doubt Paul's fastings were often of a religious nature, though apparently not in this reference. Hughes wrote, "The 'fastings' should not here be taken to refer to self-imposed religious disciplines, but rather to the forgoing of meals in order that his work as a minister of Christ might not be interrupted. Inspired by the example of his Master, the will of God was paramount in his life, far more important than food and drink, for the impulse of his whole ministry was the realization that 'man shall not live by bread alone' and that his meat was to do the will of Him that had sent him, and to accomplish His work (Matthew 4:4; John 4:34)" (The *New London Commentary,* p. 413).

**28. Beside those things that are without:** . . . Apart from all the rest, −HNT . . . Besides these experiences, −BRKL . . . besides these outward trials, −ADAM.

**that which cometh upon me daily:** . . . which presseth upon, −ASV . . . is imposed on me, −RTHM.

**the care of all the churches:** . . . the anxious care, −WLSN . . . there is my concern for all the churches, −WLMS.

**11:28.** Surely none of the "super apostles" could claim they suffered more than Paul. He was at the forefront of the battle. However, in addition to those items of personal abuse that came from without, the apostle carried a heavy burden for all the churches (*ekklēsiōn,* "assemblies") under his care. No doubt the constant threat of disruption from the false teachers made the load heavier.

The apostle did not just establish congregations and forget them. For example, some time after returning from their first missionary journey he said to Barnabas, "Let us go again and visit our brethren in every city where we have preached the word of the Lord, and see how they do" (Acts 15:36). As Ironside noted, "Paul carried the people of God upon his heart. He could not go into a place and labor for a while and then be through with them. They were still on his heart, and if they got into trouble, into difficulty, into dissension, it burdened him, and he took it to God and wrote letters to them and tried to help and bless" (p. 249).

**29. Who is weak, and I am not weak?:** . . . Who is infirm, −YNG . . . but I share his weakness? −CNBR.

**who is offended, and I burn not?:** . . . Who is hindered, −HNT . . . Who is made to stumble, −CNFT . . . Who is led astray into sin, and I am not aflame with indignation? −WEYM . . . who is in danger of stumbling, −NOYS . . . without my suffering grief? −BRKL . . . but I burn with indignation, −MNTG.

**11:29.** Paul feared lest any become fainthearted and give up. He felt keenly with people in their weaknesses. If he learned of anyone who had been offended (*skandalizetai*, English *scandalized*) or caught in a trap, he burned with indignation against sin and its causes. Likely the false apostles at Corinth had wrecked the faith of some.

**30. If I must needs glory:** . . . If I must boast, —CMPB.

**I will glory of the things which concern mine infirmities:** . . . boast of what pertains to my weakness, NASB . . . the things which belong to my weakness, —NOYS . . . that show my weakness! —WLMS.

**11:30.** In his battle with the critics at Corinth Paul felt compelled to boast about his ministry. However, he again declared he would glory only of those things which revealed his infirmities. Circumstances which made clear his weakness forced him to lean on the Lord for strength. In this way God was glorified.

**31. The God and Father of our Lord Jesus Christ, which is blessed for evermore:** . . . who is blessed throughout the ages, —WEYM . . . to the remotest ages, —RTHM.

**knoweth that I lie not:** . . . is aware that I am not lying, —CNDT . . . knows That I do not falsify, —WLSN.

**11:31.** The opposition at Corinth had first accused Paul of doing little in the ministry in comparison to them. Now that the apostle had given a long list of his experiences to show them wrong, he realized the next plot to discredit him would probably include suggestions he had exaggerated his case.

Accordingly, he called God to witness that he was telling the truth. He declared the "God and Father of our Lord Jesus Christ" knew he did not lie. He tried to deceive no one in what he wrote. Earlier in this letter he had likewise protested, "I call God for a record upon my soul" (1:23). Elsewhere he affirmed he spoke the truth in Christ and did not lie (Romans 9:1; Galatians 1:20; 1 Timothy 2:7).

Contrary to the thinking of some, Jesus did not forbid the taking of such "oaths" in a legal setting when He said, "Swear not at all" (Matthew 5:34). God instructed His people early on that matter. Moses taught them to "swear by his name" (Deuteronomy 6:13). Then it is not wrong to sincerely say "so help me God" when testifying in court. When Pilate stated, "I adjure thee by the living God," Jesus knew He had been placed under oath and answered accordingly (Matthew 26:63).

Interestingly, as the apostle called upon God to witness his truthfulness, he could not help but insert an exclamation of worship to Him. "May He

be blessed (*eulogētos*, 'to speak well of), praised for evermore," he said.

**32. In Damascus the governor under Aretas the king:** . . . the big chief, —KLGS . . . the commander of the army, —MRDK.

**kept the city of the Damascenes with a garrison:** . . . had the gates of that city guarded, —TCNT . . . guarded the city, —FNTN . . . kept watch over, —ALFD.

**desirous to apprehend me:** . . . intending to, —CMPB . . . wishing to seize me, —YNG . . . wishing to capture me, —NORL . . . in order to catch me, —FNTN . . . wanting to arrest me, —CNDT.

**33. And through a window in a basket was I let down by the wall:** . . . through an opening, —HNSN, —WEYM.

**and escaped his hands:** . . . and fled out of his hands, —YNG . . . and ran away from his hands, —KLGS . . . and escaped from his grip, —BRKL . . . escaped from his clutches, —WLMS . . . slipped through his fingers, —WAY.

**11:32, 33.** Paul gave one final example of hardships through which God had been glorified in his life. The experience was from the early days of his ministry. The governor at Damascus sought to arrest him with an intent to turn him over to the Jews. In the attempt he posted guards at every gate of the city watching all who went out, day or night (Acts 9:24).

By the grace of God and the assistance of his fellow believers the apostle escaped. From a house built on the wall of the city through one of its windows they let him down in a hamperlike basket, no doubt under the cover of darkness.

## Chapter 12

**1. It is not expedient for me doubtless to glory:** . . . I must needs boast, —ALFD . . . I have to keep on boasting, —WLMS . . . although there is no advantage in doing so, —ADAM . . . there is nothing to gain by it, NTPE . . . I am forced to boast, though it is unprofitable, —MNTG . . . I am compelled to boast. It is not a profitable employment, —WEYM . . . It is not profitable, —HNSN . . . it is not proper, Mac-knight . . . It is necessary to glory, though it is not indeed profitable, —CLMT.

**I will come to visions and revelations of the Lord:** . . . I will pass on to a worthier subject, —WAY . . . to apparitions, —CNDT . . . what the Lord has shown and told me, —BECK . . . that I have had, —NORL.

**12:1.** Though Paul felt obligated to boast of some of his experiences as a preacher under the present circumstances, he knew the dangers involved. Generally, such was not expedient (helpful, profitable). However, he concluded he must speak further of some of the remarkable things the Lord had done for him. These included visions in which he saw genuine images of heavenly things. They also brought him revelations (disclosures, knowledge) from above. The risen Lord communicated to him his understanding of the gospel in this way (Galatians 1:11, 12).

**2. I knew a man in Christ above fourteen years ago:** . . . all this happened fourteen years ago, —WAY.

**(whether in the body, I cannot tell:** . . . I have not known, —YNG . . . I know not, —HNSN . . . whether it was an actual physical experience, —PHLP . . . I am not aware, —CNDT.

**or whether out of the body, I cannot tell: God knoweth;):** . . . that is known to God alone, —WAY.

**such an one caught up to the third heaven:** . . . was taken up, —NLTG . . . suddenly conveyed away, —WLSN, —CMPB . . . carried up as far as the third heaven, —FNTN . . . was snatched away to the third heaven, —ADAM, —CNDT . . . to the highest heaven, —WEYM.

**12:2.** Again, though, as Paul spoke of one of his most wonderful experiences he did so with extreme modesty. He talked about it in the third person. In that way he took himself out of the picture and gave all credit to the Lord. He rehearsed what happened to "a man" more than 14 years before. Apparently he had told no one of this event. Much less had he ever boasted about it.

Some wonder, though, if Paul was actually writing of himself. Harris responds: "Undoubtedly so, for several reasons: (1) He knew the exact time the revelation took place (v. 2) and that its content was beyond words even if it were permissible to try to communicate it (v. 4). (2) The revelation was directly related to the receipt of a 'thorn,' which was given, says Paul, 'to me' (v. 7). (3) The reference to a lack of awareness whether he was in the body or not (vv. 2, 3) points to a personal experience. (4) Paul would be unlikely to feel embarrassment (cf. 1) about boasting on another person's behalf (cf. v. 5a). (5) For Paul to relate a remarkable experience that happened to some Christian unknown to the Corinthians but known to Paul would scarcely fit the context" (*The Expositor's Bible Commentary,* 10:395).

He was not certain whether that man was in the body or out of the body during the experience. Only God knew for sure. At any rate, it was the most sacred and personal event of his life. It took him to the third heaven. The first heaven is the atmosphere. The second is that of outer space. It houses the sun, moon, and stars. The third is the place of God's abode. He later called it paradise (verse 4).

**3. And I knew such a man:** . . . But I know such a person, —SEB.

**(whether in the body, or out of the body:** . . . Again, I don't know, —SEB . . . whether in or outside, —NAB . . . or apart from, —MNTG . . . or separated from, —TCNT.

**I cannot tell: God knoweth;):**

**12:3.** Certainly, the apostle wrote not of his conversion here, as glorious as that was. That had happened 20 years before, and he often spoke of it. He may have been speaking of what took place at Lystra as he was stoned and dragged out of the city by the mob, "supposing he had been dead" (Acts 14:19). So twice in recalling the matter he declared whether "the man" was dead or alive at the moment, he knew not. Only God did.

To be certain, though, the experience gave him a taste of what all believers will know in eternity. When body and soul are separated at death, blessed consciousness continues. Even more wonderful, death does not interrupt fellowship with God. Actually, that fellowship becomes enhanced.

**4. How that he was caught up into paradise: and heard unspeakable words:** . . . inexpressible words, NASB . . . unutterable utterances, —RTHM . . . indescribable things spoken, —WLSN . . . unutterable ideas, —FNTN . . . secret words —CNFT.

**which it is not lawful for a man to utter:** . . . that it is not possible for man to speak, —YNG . . . and that man must not repeat, —NORL . . . must not, be translated into human speech, —PHLP . . . that it is not permissible, —ADAM . . . it is not permitted, —MRDK . . . it is not granted to man to utter, —DOUY . . . no human being is allowed to repeat, —BRKL . . . to relate, —WLSN.

**12:4.** This marvelous experience took the man into paradise. The word used spoke of a garden, a park. The Septuagint used it for the Garden of Eden. To the dying thief who believed, Jesus said, "Today shalt thou be with me in paradise" (Luke 23:43). Then Jesus himself went immediately there upon His death. To all who overcome, the Lord promised the privilege of eating of the tree of life which "is in the midst of the paradise of God" (Revelation 2:7).

While he was in that beautiful garden in the third heaven, the person of whom Paul wrote heard things too sacred to tell upon his return to earth. What he experienced was simply unspeakable. No human language could ever adequately describe what he saw and heard. Further, it was unlawful to speak of them. God did not permit a full account of it. What took place contained a message for "the man" alone.

**5. Of such an one will I glory: yet of myself I will not glory:**

**but in mine infirmities:** . . . save in weaknesses, —PNIN.

**12:5.** Paul's paradise experience was by grace alone. The apostle could not possibly boast about it as if he accomplished it. Under the Spirit's control, he could but modestly glory of what happened as if he spoke of some other person's heavenly venture. Again he declared he would take pride only in his weaknesses for they forced him to rely on God.

**6. For though I would desire to glory:** ... if I were disposed to glory, –MRDK ... should choose to continue boasting, –MNTG.

**I shall not be a fool:** ... it would not be vanity, –NORL.

**for I will say the truth:**

**but [now] I forbear, lest any man should think of me above that which he seeth me [to be]:** ... but I refrain, –HNSN, –MRDK ... in case anyone should esteem me beyond, –HNT ... than what you see and hear about great revelations, –KLGS.

**or [that] he heareth of me:**

**12:6.** On the other hand, if Paul were the kind of preacher who wanted to brag about himself, he could do so and not be as some fools were in the process. After all, he could relate some exciting things and just be telling the truth.

However, he refrained from writing of other heavenly experiences. He feared some might evaluate or esteem him more highly than they should. As with all men, to see Paul was to be aware of his humanity. If he spoke too much of wonders in his life and later some learned he was just another mortal, they might lose confidence in him and his gospel.

The apostle was determined that all should understand what he had explained before in this letter. He wrote, "We have this treasure in earthen vessels, that the excellency of the power may be of God, and not of us" (4:7). He wanted the faith of his converts to rest in the Lord, not man (1 Corinthians 2:5).

**7. And lest I should be exalted above measure through the abundance of the revelations:** ... keep me from feeling proud, –BECK ... be made overbearing by the sublimity of the revelations, –FNTN ... to prevent my becoming absurdly conceited, –PHLP ... including the superb fact of the revelations, –BRKL ... by the transcendancy, –WLSN ... by reason of the exceeding greatness, –HNSN ... were so surpassingly wonderful, –NORL ... lest I should be over-elated ... judging by the stupendous grandeur of the revelations, –WEYM.

**there was given to me a thorn in the flesh:** ... like the agony of impalement, –WEYM ... given a chronic pain in my body, –NORL ... a sting of my flesh, –DOUY ... a sharp spike was sent to pierce my flesh, –TCNT ... a splinter in the flesh, –CNDT.

**the messenger of Satan to buffet me:** ... It bothered me like a satanic angel, –NORL ... a messenger of the adversary, –HNSN ... an instrument of Satan, for my discipline, –TCNT ... the devil's messenger to plague me, –BECK ... to correct me, –FNTN ... that it

might afflict me, –WLSN ... to beat me up, –KLGS ... to maltreat me, –BRKL ... to slap me around, –ADAM.

**lest I should be exalted above measure:** ... but it kept me from becoming puffed up, –NORL ... so that I might not be haughty, –FNTN ... to keep me from being too much elated, –WAY ... that I might not be too much lifted up, –NOYS.

**12:7.** In Paul's life the Lord allowed events to combat pride. His eternal plan allows "that no flesh should glory in his presence" (1 Corinthians 1:29). With visions and revelations, there was a danger pride might raise its ugly head. To prevent this God permitted a thorn to come and remain in Paul's flesh. To stick a thorn in the foot is a most painful experience. Not to remove it to relieve the suffering is ordinarily unthinkable.

Many have speculated about Paul's thorn. One guess is it was some illness of the eyes because he wrote the Galatians with large letters and they were willing to give him their eyes if they could (Galatians 6:11; 4:15). Some liberals say the thorn was epilepsy and that his conversion experience on the road to Damascus was among his many seizures! This is unthinkable. Others think his problem was one of chronic attacks of malarial fever.

Paul said a messenger of Satan brought the thorn. The spirit buffeted (beat, struck as with the fist) and tortured him. The devil continuously slapped the apostle on the face, as the present subjunctive tense of the verb shows. Thus Paul followed the story of his most blessed experience in life (verses 2-4) with that of his deepest humiliation.

**8. For this thing I besought the Lord thrice:** ... Concerning this, Afford ... Three times I begged, –PHLP, –WLMS ... I implored the Lord, –FNTN ... I invoked the Lord, –BRKL.

**that it might depart from me:** ... to rid me of it, –NORL.

**12:8.** Little wonder, then, Paul talked to the Lord earnestly about removing such a thorn. He besought (intreated, implored, urgently appealed to) God three times for relief.

Even Jesus had three seasons of prayer for assistance in Gethsemane (Mark 14:35-41). Elijah petitioned for rain seven times before water fell from the sky (1 Kings 18:42-44). Daniel had to remain before the Lord for 21 days before his answer came (Daniel 10:12-14).

**9. And he said unto me:** ... but His reply has been, –WEYM ... He has protested to me, –CNDT.

**My grace is sufficient for thee:** ... My help is sufficient for you, –ADAM ... is enough, –HNT.

**for my strength is made perfect in weakness:** ... for my power is completed, –KLGS ... for power matures in weakness, *—WEYM* . . . my power is shown the more completely, *—PHLP* . . . My power is perfected in weakness, *—FNTN* . . . is made complete, *—RTHM* . . . in infirmity, *—DOUY* . . . in the forge of infirmity, *—WAY.*

**Most gladly therefore will I rather glory in my infirmities:**

**that the power of Christ may rest upon me:** . . . that the strength of, *—HNSN, —NOYS* . . . that Christ's power might overshadow me, *—ADAM* . . . may settle upon me, *—HNT* . . . may dwell in me, *—CNFT, —DOUY.*

**12:9.** God's answer to Paul's prayer did not remove the thorn. The Lord sometimes gives a negative response to the most earnest petition. Instead it gave him assurance God would provide sufficient grace and divine strength to sustain him regardless of his trials. As the apostle himself declared in 1 Corinthians 10:13, with every temptation the Lord always provides a way of escape making it possible to bear up under the difficulty.

More wonderfully, though, God's power reaches its perfection through human weakness. As the smallest of light shines most brightly in the darkest of nights, the Lord reveals His strength most completely in the face of man's helplessness. As someone has said, Christians are somewhat like tea; their real strength does not show until they are in hot water.

Having learned the lesson Jesus taught him through the thorn, Paul experienced an attitude change. He came to the place where he could gladly glory in his weakness. He knew it was necessary for him to realize his helplessness in order for the power of Christ to rest upon him and become an overshadowing tent to cover him.

Hughes has warned against misusing the apostle's words here in following "the errors of a later ascetic theology which encouraged men to think that by means of self-inflicted bodily sufferings and indignities they could accumulate forgiveness of post-baptismal sins and justifying merit before God. That was a joyless theology of insecurity; whereas Paul's theology is one of unclouded joy and impregnable security . . ." (*The New London Commentary,* p. 452). He concluded Paul's thorn was not self-induced but *given.*

10. **Therefore I take pleasure in infirmities:** . . . I am contented, *—WLSN* . . . That is why I delight in, *—TCNT.*

**in reproaches, in necessities:** . . . in outrage, *—CNBR* . . . in insults, in dire needs, *—KJII* . . . with injuries, *—SAWR* . . . with problems, *—KLGS.*

**in persecutions, in distresses for Christs's sake:** . . . and calamities, *—NORL* . . . in dire calamities, *—BRKL* . . . and hard pressed for Christ, *—BECK* . . . in behalf of Christ, *—NOYS.*

**for when I am weak, then am I strong:** . . . when I am consciously weak, *—WLMS* . . . then am I powerful, *—RTHM.*

**12:10.** The apostle declared again he delighted in and cheerfully accepted the fact of his human weakness. Then he revealed more of what the thorn involved. It included suffering reproaches (shame, insults, mistreatment) at the hands of his enemies. At times it brought necessities (privations and hardships). Periods of distress (difficulty, anguish) came with it.

Understandably, then, the apostle sought relief from such constant pressures. However, the lesson he learned by carrying a heavy burden was priceless. He came to know man's extremities are God's opportunities. As long as his suffering was for Christ's sake, he rested in the assurance that when circumstances pressed him to helplessness he would then, and only then, experience the help of the Lord. To say "when I am weak, then am I strong" sounds contradictory, but the paradox expresses a truth more valuable than gold.

Of course, not all suffering in the lives of Christians qualifies for such blessings as followed Paul's. As Peter warned, "Let none of you suffer as a murderer, or as a thief, or as an evildoer, or as a busybody in other men's matters" (1 Peter 4:15).

11. **I am become a fool in glorying:** . . . I have been guilty of folly, *—CNBR* . . . I have been talking like some imbecile, *—WAY* . . . a Simpleton, *—WLSN* . . . I am nutty, *—KLGS.*

**ye have compelled me:** . . . You have forced me, *—FNTN* . . . You drove me to it, *—KLGS* . . . You have constrained me to it, *—CMPB.*

**for I ought to have been commended of you:** . . . ought to have been my vindicators, *—WEYM.*

**for in nothing am I behind the very chiefest apostles:** . . . I am equal to your best missionaries, *—KLGS* . . . was I inferior to the most eminent apostles, *—WORL* . . . I am not a single bit inferior to your surpassingly superior apostles, *—WLMS* . . . have I fallen short of the most eminent apostles, *—CNFT* . . . to these super-apostles, *—ADAM.*

**though I be nothing:** . . . even if I am rated as a nobody, *—NORL* . . . though I be of no account, *—CNBR.*

**12:11.** As if coming down to earth from the heights of ministerial argument, Paul for a final time said he was a fool to boast about himself as he had. The conduct of the opposition at Corinth forced him to it.

Instead of being compelled to self-vindication through circumstances, the apostle reasoned the Corinthians should have been commending him. After all, in nothing was he the least inferior to the "super apostles" among them. In times of conflict Christians can be wrong in failing to take a stand on the side of righteousness.

The "chiefest apostles" with Paul should have engaged in an honest appraisal of themselves. In that case they would have joined in chorus with him in saying "I am nothing" and not have been guilty of any false humility.

**12. Truly the signs of an apostle were wrought among you in all patience:**...Certainly the criteria that distinguish the apostle, *−KLST* ... The credentials of, *−FNTN*...The signs that mark a true Apostle, *−TCNT*...tokens of my apostolate, *−BRKL*...were performed, *−SAWR*...in all endurance, *−RTHM.*

**in signs, and wonders, and mighty deeds:**...and miraculous powers, *−HNT* ... and by supernatural works, *−ADAM.*

**12:12.** Instead, the critics bragged of miracles in their ministry as if done by their own hands. Paul said he too wrought wonders among them, but not by his strength. God blessed the integrity of his patient, steadfast endurance. The risen Saviour worked with him confirming the Word he preached as with His early followers (Mark 16:20).

The Lord granted signs which pointed men heavenward. The Spirit performed wonders to attract and hold the attention of men. Christ did mighty deeds and miracles, as needed to accomplish good in the lives of people.

The apostle sent a similar message concerning his ministry to the Romans (Romans 15:18, 19). The writer of Hebrews also declared the Word "was confirmed unto us by them that heard him; God also bearing them witness, both with signs and wonders, and with divers miracles, and gifts of the Holy Ghost" (Hebrews 2:3, 4).

**13. For what is it wherein ye were inferior to other churches:**... ye were at disadvantage when compared, *−NOYS.*

**except [it be] that I myself was not burdensome to you?:**... except that I did not accept payment, *−FNTN*...did not burden you with my expenses? *−NORL* ... never hung as a dead weight upon you? *−WEYM*...except that I did not take up offerings among you? *−KLGS.*

**forgive me this wrong:**... My humblest apologies for this great wrong! *−PHLP*...Pardon me this unfairness, *−BRKL* ... Pardon my unfair treatment of you, *−WAY*...this injury, *−DOUY*...this injustice! *−YNG, −WLSN.*

**12:13.** The "super apostles" at Corinth said the church there was an inferior one until they came along. Paul asked for the specifics of the charge. In what way were they inferior? To answer his own question, with tongue in cheek he suggested perhaps it was in the fact that he had not asked for a salary while he pastored the Corinthian church. Thus he returned to the subject he discussed earlier at length (11:7-12).

The "I" is emphatic in the sentence. The question was, "Is it that I myself was not burdensome, dead weight on you while planting your church?" This distinguished him from his critics who would not have thought of preaching without pay.

With a touch of irony the apostle asked the Corinthians to forgive him this wrong. If not demanding they meet his financial needs stunted the growth of their church, he was sorry. But, of course, the whole idea was outlandish and nonsense.

**14. Behold, the third time I am ready to come to you:**...I am preparing, *−MNTG.*

**and I will not be burdensome to you:**... and I shall not be a nuisance to you, *NTPE.*

**for I seek not yours, but you:**...I desire not your money, *−WEYM*...I am not hunting for what you have, *−KLGS* ... this was my cunning, *−MNTG* ...I seek not your goods, *−HNT*...not your Property, *−WLSN*...It is you I want, *−PHLP.*

**for the children ought not to lay up for the parents:** ... should not accumulate wealth, *−BRKL* ... should not save up, *−CNFT*...ought not to be hoarding, *−CNDT.*

**but the parents for the children:**

**12:14.** At this point Kent wrote of the crucial conclusion of a letter saying, "Whether it will be accepted and will motivate the readers to appropriate action, or will simply irritate them and thus compound the problem, may depend on the tone of the final paragraphs. Paul had been writing about some sensitive matters. He had spoken of misunderstandings, mistreatment, wrong interpretations placed on his actions, and of a disturbing tendency at Corinth to tolerate wrong teaching. If his apostolic admonition were to be heeded, Paul must make every attempt to leave the impression that he was the Corinthians' friend and sought only their best interests" (p. 189).

In the beginning of this letter Paul defended himself against the charge he did not really love the Corinthians or else he would have returned to them by now. In response he explained God directed his way (1:17-23). He did not decide where he would or would not go as any man might. Besides, they needed to correct some errors before he came.

Now near the end of the epistle, the apostle spoke again of his next visit to Corinth. He said it was the third time he was ready to come. Had he made a second trip to Corinth already? Some think he did, but it was such a hurried, unprofitable visit the Bible does not record the details of it. Acts does not mention it. It may have been the "painful visit" Paul alluded to earlier in this letter (2:1).

Whatever the case, once more the apostle declared he would not change his financial policy toward them. He would not demand pay in coming to Corinth again. It was not their money he wanted but their hearts. He was their spiritual father, unlike the false teachers who had come after him (1 Corinthians 4:15). As a parent he did not expect his children to provide for him, but he wanted to store up treasure for them.

**15. And I will very gladly spend and be spent for you:** ... cheerfully will I both pay [my] expenses, —MRDK ... and be entirely spent for your souls, —YNG ... to invest and be invested for your souls, —KLGS ... spent out for the sake of, —PNT ... and be completely spent on behalf of your souls, —NORL ... be fully spent in behalf of your souls, —RTHM ... and be exhausted, for the sake of, —FNTN ... and be bankrupted for the sake of your souls, —CNDT ... for your welfare, —TCNT.

**though the more abundantly I love you:** ... If I love you excessively, —BRKL.

**the less I be loved:**

**12:15.** Paul's parental heart opened wide as he declared he would gladly spend all he had for his spiritual children. He was even willing to be spent, to pour out his own physical life to the last drop in sacrifice for them (*psuchōn*, literally, their "souls"). He felt as when he wrote the Philippians, "Yea, and if I be offered upon the sacrifice and service of your faith, I joy, and rejoice with you all" (Philippians 2:17).

He realized, of course, children do not always repay a parent's love in kind. Sometimes they hurt worst the ones who love them most. Even so, the more he loved the Corinthians the colder they seemed to feel toward him in return.

**16. But be it so, I did not burden you:** ... I was not a financial burden to you, —NORL.

**nevertheless, being crafty:** ... but you say that I was crafty all along, —TCNT ... was I a clever fellow, —BECK ... this was my cunning, —MNTG ... but yet you say that I was crafty, —NORL ... by being a trickster, —WLMS ... like the cunning knave he is, —WAY.

**I caught you with guile:** ... But some say I set a trap for you, —NLTG ... with which I caught you by a trick, —MNTG ... but, being a rascal, have taken pay of you by a trick! —FNTN ... and got the better of you by deceit, —NORL ... I cheated you by my cunning, —WLMS ... entrapped you, —WAY ... who trapped you with some trick? —BECK.

**12:16.** However, as far as his conduct toward his converts was concerned, their response to his deeds of kindness did not dictate his behavior. As a true spiritual father he loved, expecting nothing in return. Indeed, no wise parent gives of himself to a child just to be repaid in later years.

For that reason Paul had decided long before this not to be a financial burden to believers at Corinth. They were wrong in being influenced by what the critics said in a slanderous manner of the apostle. To drive the point home, he sarcastically put himself in a class with the opposition for a moment. He said, "Being crafty (clever, sly as they are), I caught you in a trap."

Of this Hughes wrote, "Craftiness was, of course, characteristic of the Apostle's detractors, just as it is pre-eminently characteristic of Satan, whose ministers they were (11:15). As Satan beguiled Eve with his craftiness, so too these deceitful workers (11:13) were seeking to delude and pervert the Corinthian Christians whom Paul had betrothed to Christ (11:2f.)" (*The New London Commentary*, p. 464). They said he received money with crafty intent. Then, "The fact was that they would dearly have liked to get their own fingers on that money; but, being unable to do this, they did the next most damaging thing, which was to ascribe to the one whose authority they wished to destroy the designs of their own evil hearts" (ibid., p. 465).

**17. Did I make a gain of you by any of them whom I sent unto you?:** ... Did I exploit you through anyone, NTPE ... I did not make any money out of you, —WLMS ... that I pilfered from you? —MRDK ... wrung fraudulent gain from you? —WAY ... whom I dispatched to you? —HNT.

**12:17.** Some of the apostle's enemies suggested that though he asked for no money in planting the church at Corinth, he no doubt profited from the offering he raised for needy brethren in Judea. He responded, "Did any of those I sent ever make a gain, take advantage of, cheat, or defraud you?" The negative particle *me* expects a "no" answer. Contrary to the charge against him, Paul never used his apostolic office as a "cloak of covetousness" (1 Thessalonians 2:5).

**18. I desired Titus, and with [him] I sent a brother:** ... I summoned, —BRKL ... I pleaded with Titus to go, —ADAM ... I urged Titus to go, —CNFT ... I besought Titus, and I sent forth in conjunction, —RTHM.

**Did Titus make a gain of you?:** ... Has Titus exploited you? —GRBR ... take any advantage of you? —ASV, —HNT ... plunder you? —FNTN.

**walked we not in the same spirit?:** ... Did he and I not proceed, —HNT.

**[walked we] not in the same steps?:** ... and in the same course? —FNTN ... Did we not act alike? —KLGS ... And do exactly the same things, —BECK ... in the same tracks? —BRKL.

**12:18.** Specifically, did Titus or the brother sent with him take advantage of them financially? (see 8:16-22). Did not Titus show the same attitude toward money that Paul did? Did they not tread the same footsteps? The *ou* in both of the last questions expects a "yes" answer.

**19. Again, think ye that we excuse ourselves unto you?:** . . . You are imagining, all this time, —*WEYM* . . . Do you think we are apologizing to you again? —*FNTN* . . . we are trying to justify ourselves in your eyes, —*NORL* . . . we have been defending ourselves before you? —*RSV.*
**we speak before God in Christ:**
**but [we do] all things, dearly beloved, for your edifying:** . . . for your spiritual welfare, —*NORL* . . . for the sake of benefiting you, —*FNTN.*

**12:19.** Did they think he had returned to excusing (*apologoumetha*, cf. English *apologize*), defending himself before them? With the Spirit moving on Paul as he wrote, he declared he spoke before God pleading the sacrifice of Christ for justification in his case. God was his judge, not men. Further, the cause Paul defended was the Lord's, not his.

Of course, he did minister to man in what he wrote. He intended his letter to edify or build up the Corinthians. He counted the recipients of his epistle as among the "dearly beloved" in spite of the note of rebuke in much of what he wrote. No doubt only a small group had caused his problems.

**20. For I fear, lest, when I come, I shall not find you such as I would:** . . . For I dread, —*MNTG* . . . for I am apprehensive that, —*WLMS.*
**and [that] I shall be found unto you such as ye would not:**
**lest [there be] debates, envy-ings:** . . . strifes, —*RTHM* . . . wranglings, —*NOYS* . . . finding arguments, —*PHLP.*
**wraths, strifes:** . . . animosities, —*CNFT* . . . **passions,** —*FNTN* . . . rivalry, slander, —*NORL* . . . intrigues, —*HNSN* . . . ugly temper, sectarianism, —*BRKL* . . . party spirit, —*MNTG* . . . hot tempers, selfishness, —*KLGS* . . . angry passions, —*HNT* . . . ill-natured talk, —*WEYM* . . . intrigues, —*CNBR* . . . and obstinacy, —*MRDK* . . . divided loyalties, —*PHLP.*
**backbitings, whisperings:** . . . detractions, —*CNFT,* —*DOUY* . . . bad talk, gossip, —*KLGS* . . . undue eulogy, —*WEYM* . . . slanderings, inflations, —*FNTN.*
**swellings, tumults:** . . . big heads, —*KLGS* . . . swollen heads, *NTPE* . . . haughty pride, —*WLMS* . . . disturbances, —*FNTN,* —*WLSN* . . . and insolence, —*MRDK* . . . unrest, —*WEYM* . . . arrogance, —*MNTG* . . . self-assertion, —*TCNT* . . . insurrections, —*YNG* . . . conceits, disorders, —*HNSN* . . . commotions, —*PNT* . . . seditions, —*RTHM* . . . and disharmony, —*PHLP* . . . and disorder, —*RSV* . . . disorderly behavior, —*BECK.*

**12:20.** The apostle was concerned about what might happen when he arrived at Corinth. He was apprehensive lest they not solve many of their remaining problems before he came. He would like all difficulties to be removed in advance of his arrival. Otherwise, his duty would be that of a disciplinarian. Then they would not find him as they would like either.

He hoped his letter would be enough. To follow Paul's example, today's pastors must also attend to problems rather than ignore them. However, like the apostle they would do well to try mild remedies before turning to more severe ones.

The apostle established another good pattern for ministers of all times in that he went beyond speaking in general terms. He listed specific evils. He feared lest he find the congregations engaged in debates (discord, contentions). He was concerned he would see the subtle sin of envy or jealousy in the assembly. Envy manifests itself in the form of hatred of others because they have something you wish you had.

The apostle was apprehensive lest conditions in the church would become so tense that some would lose control to wrath or outbursts of anger. Also, he did not want to see strifes (disputes, outbreaks of selfishness) which promoted factions in the congregation.

Certainly backbiting (evil speech, defamation of character, or slander) was out of place in a fellowship of believers. And few things are worse than whispering (talebearing, gossip).

With things at Corinth as they were Paul did not know but what he would also discover the sin of "swellings." The word refers to being puffed up through pride. After all, in his first letter to them the apostle had rebuked the congregation at Corinth for having spiritual pride (1 Corinthians 5:2). Such a church would be in a state of tumult (disorder, unruliness).

**21. [And] lest, when I come again, my God will humble me among you:** . . . may humiliate me before you, —*NORL,* —*WLMS.*
**and [that] I shall bewail many which have sinned already:** . . . and I should mourn over, —*WSLY* . . . and I shall lament many of those who had previously sinned, —*RTHM* . . . many whose hearts still cling to their old sins, —*WEYM.*
**and have not repented of the uncleanness and fornication and lasciviousness which they have committed:** . . . and gross sensuality, of which they have been guilty, —*WEYM* . . . and no self control, —*KLGS* . . . and whoredom . . . they did practise, —*YNG* . . . and prostitution, —*CNDT* . . . the wantonness, —*WAY* . . . impurity, immorality, and licentiousness, —*RSV* . . . and sensuality which they practised, —*HNT* . . . for the vice, and profligacy, and excess, which they have practised, —*FNTN* . . . which they perpetrated, —*RTHM* . . . in which they have indulged, —*TCNT.*

**12:21.** If Paul did discover sin like this in the Corinthian church, it would understandably break his heart. The shame and embarrassment would cause him to weep. He would mourn over the many who had sinned already. Obviously, he would rather God not permit him such a humiliating experience.

The tactfulness of this Spirit-led minister is inspiring. As he wrote of perhaps finding the Corinthians less than he wanted them to be, he softened the rebuke by adding he didn't want them to be disappointed in him either. Instead of talking of their embarrassment, he spoke of his. He rebuked "with all longsuffering" (2 Timothy 4:2).

The apostle's wisdom also shows in that he could have spoken of the existence rather than just the possibility of sin in the lives of members of the Corinthian assembly. Indeed he continued with a focus on those who had actually committed the sin of uncleanness or immorality. There were also those who had practiced fornication (*porneia*, which refers to all illicit sexual activity). Others were guilty of lasciviousness (licentiousness, sensuality). Even worse, they had not repented of their sins.

## Chapter 13

1. **This [is] the third [time] I am coming to you:** . . . This is my third visit to you, —BRKL.

**In the mouth of two or three witnesses shall every word be established:** . . . On the evidence of, —WEYM, —FNTN . . . each statement, —TCNT . . . Every fact is to be confirmed, NASB . . . Every charge must be established, —NORL . . . every matter shall be decided, NTPE . . . must be substantiated, —ADAM . . . shall every declaration, —RTHM . . . shall be confirmed, —BRKL . . . Everything must be proved, —BECK . . . be made to stand, —CNDT.

**13:1.** Again Paul informed the Corinthians of the anticipated trip to see them. It would be his third visit to their church (12:14). As such it should confirm the gospel he had shared with them in keeping with the validating laws of Moses. To protect the innocent, under God the leader of Israel decreed the court could convict only "in the mouth of two or three witnesses" (cf. Deuteronomy 17:6; 19:15).

Jesus said believers must use this principle in matters of church discipline (Matthew 18:16). Paul instructed elsewhere that it must apply in trials for ministers (1 Timothy 5:19).

2. **I told you before:** . . . I now forewarn you, —MNTG . . . the second time, —CMPB.

**and foretell you, as if I were present, the second time:** . . . and am saying beforehand, —RTHM . . . and I do say beforehand, —WORL.

**and being absent now I write to them which heretofore have sinned, and to all other:**

**that, if I come again, I will not spare:** . . . I will not let up on you, —KLGS . . . I shall have no mercy,

—JB . . . I will show no leniency, —NEB, —KLST . . . nobody will escape punishment, —TEV.

**13:2.** Thus the apostle warned when he arrived, if necessary, he would follow legal principles, scripturally founded, regarding witnesses in dealing with the offenders at Corinth. He had given them fair warning earlier when he was present with them during his second visit. This could have been the time he went there "in heaviness" (2:1). Once more in advance of his third arrival he made clear his determination to rid the church of evil.

Paul specifically addressed those who had already sinned (12:21). However, he wanted all others who might be tempted to follow their example to also know he would not spare them. He would practice strict discipline. With the congregation assembled he would dismiss them from membership in the church (1 Corinthians 5:4, 5), turning them out to the camp of Satan where they belonged. He would put away such evil persons from among the fellowship of believers (1 Corinthians 5:2, 13). Under God he would rid the lump of all leaven (1 Corinthians 5:7).

With such a disciplinary stance toward sin, one readily understands why the apostle was incensed that some said his theology allowed Christians to sin with impunity. To the Romans he wrote that was slanderous and declared those who misquoted him would meet a just damnation in the end (Romans 3:8).

3. **Since ye seek a proof of Christ speaking in me:** . . . You want proof, —JB . . . You will have all the proof you want, —TEV . . . since you are demanding proof, —NIV . . . You are looking for proof that Christ speaks through me, —BRCL.

**which to you-ward is not weak:** . . . When he deals with you, —TEV . . . he is no weakling, —BRCL.

**but is mighty in you:** . . . but is powerful in you, —ASV . . . makes his power felt among you, —NEB . . . powerful among you, —SEB.

**13:3.** Some at Corinth had demanded proof that Paul was a true apostle, that Christ really spoke through him. He announced he would give it when he arrived, though probably not the kind of evidence they would like. He would demonstrate his God-given authority to lead the church in matters of discipline.

As Christ came once as an advocate or defense counsel and will come the next time as Judge, so Paul's next visit would be as a disciplinarian. He might have appeared weak to some, but no more. He would show himself mighty (strong, courageous) for the sake of the gospel and those who truly believed it. The time for forbearance would be past. Further waiting would damage the Lord's cause too much.

**4. For though he was crucified through weakness:** ... For he was feeble, —BB ... he was a weak mortal when he was crucified, —GRBR ... in human weakness He died on the cross, —WAY ... True, it was in weakness that he died, —BRCL ... nailed to the cross, —SEB.

**yet he liveth by the power of God:** ... which gives him continuing life, —BRCL.

**For we also are weak in him:**

**but we shall live with him by the power of God toward you:** ... but in our relations with you, —TEV ... the source of our life, —BRCL ... we will live with Christ for you, —SEB ... for your benefit, —JB.

**13:4.** In the case of Christ, it is true He was crucified when He possessed the weakness of His human form. Those who looked on at the cross mocked at the idea He saved others when they thought Him so powerless He could not even save himself (Matthew 27:42). Little did they know what the truth really was. The fact is, if He saved himself, others He could not save. In the end, God bared His mighty arm toward Jesus in that He raised Him from the dead (Ephesians 1:19, 20). He demonstrated that Jesus is His Son through the miracle of the Resurrection (Romans 1:4). In like manner, children of the Lord, such as Paul, who may appear weak now will one day live by that same power of God.

**5. Examine yourselves, whether ye be in the faith:** ... Test yourselves to discover whether you are true believers, —WEYM ... to find out, —SEB ... whether you are continuing in the faith, —WLMS ... are you living the life of faith? —NEB.

**prove your own selves:** ... put your own selves under examination, —WEYM ... Prove it to yourselves, —SEB.

**Know ye not your own selves:** ... Or do ye not recognise yourselves? —RTHM ... Do you acknowledge, —JB ... Surely you recognize, —NEB ... You must be well aware, —BRCL.

**how that Jesus Christ is in you:** ... is among you? —SEB.

**except ye be reprobates?:** ... if you are sincere? —WEYM ... unless indeed you fail the test? NASB ... unless you are rejected ones, —KJII ... Or are you backsliders? —NORL ... you turn out to be, —ADAM ... unless you are counterfeits? —BRKL.

**13:5.** The Corinthians had been so quick to examine and judge Paul that he had a suggestion for them. They should be proving, putting themselves to the test, instead of him. The apostle placed "yourselves" and "your own selves" first in these two sentences for the sake of emphasis. Thus his first sentence began, "Yourselves examine."

Men analyze metal with respect to its purity. They try coins to determine their genuineness. Even more so, Christians ought to often take a careful look at the state of their souls. At least every time they approach the communion table they should examine themselves (1 Corinthians 11:28). With David they must pray, "Search me, O God, and know my heart: try me, and know my thoughts: and see if there be any wicked way in me" (Psalm 139:23, 24).

It is imperative for believers to assure their hearts that they are continuing in the Faith. Even when there appears no need to search the inner man, Paul warned, "Let him that thinketh he standeth take heed lest he fall" (1 Corinthians 10:12).

The apostle said believers at Corinth must know (know exactly, completely, through and through) that Christ lived within them. Otherwise they might end up as reprobates (not having passed the test, unqualified, rejected, worthless). With such clear instruction, those who say Paul taught Christians are unconditionally secure read something into his writings that is not there.

**6. But I trust that ye shall know that we are not reprobates:** ... I hope that we do not flunk out, —KLGS ... that we are not disapproved, —RTHM ... not unapproved, —NOYS ... are not without proof, —WLSN ... we haven't failed in our test, —BECK ... that we are not false Christians, —GRBR.

**13:6.** Since the Corinthians had spent so much time and effort in examining Paul, he was confident they had come to a correct conclusion of his standing before God. Certainly he was no reprobate. In saying so he was expressing no rash self-confidence. He was as careful in guarding the spiritual state of his own soul as he was to exhort them to be careful to examine themselves. In his first letter to them he wrote, "But I keep under my body, and bring it into subjection: lest that by any means, when I have preached to others, I myself should be a castaway" (*adokimos*, "reprobate") (1 Corinthians 9:27).

**7. Now I pray to God that ye do no evil:** ... make supplication to God, —BRKL.

**not that we should appear approved:** ... not in order that our sincerity may be demonstrated, —WEYM ... not so that we may appear superior, —FNTN ... not that we may appear as men of genuine character, —HNT.

**but that ye should do that which is honest:**

**though we be as reprobates:** ... though we may appear to have failed, —NORL.

**13:7.** As so often in his letters, from Paul's inner being flowed a spontaneous prayer for the Corinthians. He prayed they would do no evil. He wanted individual believers to live upright lives. He desired the church in Corinth to be free from sin.

Yet his prayer was for their sake instead of his. His motive remained pure. He was not asking that the church he pioneered at Corinth be trouble-free so he would appear approved (tried and true, genuine) as a successful preacher. In fact, he was willing to appear as a reprobate, as a failure, if that would contribute to their salvation. As he wrote the Romans, "I could wish that myself were accursed from Christ for my brethren, my kinsmen according to the flesh," if that would save their souls (Romans 9:3).

What the apostle prayed for was honest (morally good, noble, praiseworthy) living on the part of the Corinthians. He wanted them to stand approved not only before men but more so before God.

**8. For we can do nothing against the truth:** ... we have no power against, *—NOYS* ... we have no ability against the truth, *—BRKL.*

**but for the truth:** ... but only for the furtherance of the truth, *—WEYM* ... but only in defense of the truth, *—MNTG* ... in harmony with it, *—RPNT.*

**13:8.** Despite what Paul's critics at Corinth said about him, he was no hypocrite. Something within made it impossible for him to do anything against the truth. As John wrote of the genuine child of God, "His seed remaineth in him: and he cannot sin, because he is born of God" (1 John 3:9). To speak of a sinning Christian is like referring to an honest liar or a trustworthy thief. It is a contradiction of terms. Of course, the impossibility to sin is a moral rather than an absolute one. For both of these apostles, integrity within compelled them to do everything in life in keeping with the truth of God.

**9. For we are glad, when we are weak:** ... And so we rejoice, *—KLST.*

**and ye are strong:** ... but ye may be powerful, *—RTHM.*

**and this also we wish, [even] your perfection:** ... and we pray for this, *—FNTN* ... What we pray for is your improvement, *—RSV* ... it is your development that we pray for, *—HNT* ... even your restoration, *—HNSN* ... that you may be made perfect, *—NORL* ... the perfecting of your characters, *—WEYM* ... your complete restoration, *—WLSN* ... your perfect reformation, *—CNBR.*

**13:9.** Once more Paul's unselfishness came through. He did not promote self. His concern was the welfare of his converts. He was glad to be weak if that contributed to their being strong. He wished for (*euchometha*, "prayed for") their perfection, that they be complete in their Christian lives. Earlier in this letter he was concerned with their "perfecting holiness in the fear of God" (7:1). He was like the writer of Hebrews who exhorted, "Therefore leaving the principles of the doctrine

of Christ, let us go on unto perfection" (Hebrews 6:1). They must pursue maturity.

**10. Therefore I write these things being absent:** ... On this account, *—PNT.*

**lest being present I should use sharpness:** ... not have to treat you harshly, *—NORL* ... I may not employ severity, *—FNTN.*

**according to the power which the Lord hath given me to edification:** ... using the authority, *—BECK* ... in accordance with the authority, *—FNTN.*

**and not to destruction:** ... and not for casting down, *—YNG.*

**13:10.** Again the apostle declared his hope that his corrective letter would be all he ever needed to do to help them mend their ways. He preferred to rebuke while absent than when present after his arrival. He feared if he waited until then he might use sharpness (*apotomōs*, only here and in Titus 1:13 in the New Testament), proceeding in a more cutting way than he would desire.

Instead, their spiritual father desired to use his God-given abilities to build believers up. To use his authority to tear down gave him no pleasure.

**11. Finally, brethren, farewell:** ... To sum it all up, brothers, *—BRKL* ... In conclusion, *—CNFT.*

**Be perfect, be of good comfort:** ... Move on to the best, *—KLGS* ... Aim at perfection, take courage, *—MNTG* ... Mend your ways, pay attention to my appeal, *—ADAM* ... Reform what is amiss in yourselves, *—CNBR* ... be adjusted; receive admonition, *—BRKL* ... Keep on growing to be perfect, *—BECK* ... perfect yourselves, *—FNTN* ... be at harmony, be encouraged, *—HNT* ... be joyful, secure perfection of character, *—WEYM* ... rejoice ... take courage, *—NORL* ... be getting restored to order; be receiving consolation, *—RTHM* ... be of good cheer, *—PNT* ... be made complete, *NASB.*

**be of one mind, live in peace:** ... may harmony and quietness be among you, *—MRDK* ... agree in your thinking; preserve peace, *—BRKL* ... be like-minded, *NASB* ... cultivate peace, *—WLSN.*

**and the God of love and peace shall be with you:**

**12. Greet one another with an holy kiss:** ... a saint's kiss, *—HNT* ... a sacred kiss, *—WLMS* ... an affectionate hug, *R—PNT.*

**13. All the saints salute you:** ... All the holy people greet you, *—BECK* ... All God's people here send greetings to you, *—WEYM.*

**14. The grace of the Lord Jesus Christ:** ... The favour, *—RTHM* ... spiritual blessing, *—WLMS.*

**and the love of God, and the communion of the Holy Ghost, [be] with you all. Amen:** ... May you be joined together by the Holy Spirit, *—NLTG* ... the fellowship that is ours in the Holy Spirit, *—PHLP* ... the fellowship the Holy Spirit gives, *—BRCL* ... and the companionship of, *—TCNT* ... and the communication of, *—DOUY* ... and the sharing of, *—SEB* ... and the common sharing of, *—WLMS* ... and the joint participation of, *—WLSN* ... and the participation in the holy Spirit,

—*GDSP*... and the partaking of, —*NOYS*... as you share Him be with you all! —*BECK*.

**13:11-14.** At last the painful letter approached its close. In its final section the Corinthians were still called brethren. None of its chastisement should say otherwise. Its author bade them farewell (*chairete*, a word that exhorted them to rejoice).

Again Paul challenged those he loved to be perfect, complete. He wanted them to be comforted and assured that God cares. They needed to be of one mind, thinking, believing, and speaking in agreement. In his earlier epistle Paul wrote, "Now I beseech you, brethren, by the name of our Lord Jesus Christ, that ye all speak the same thing, and that there be no divisions among you; but that ye be perfectly joined together in the same mind and in the same judgment" (1 Corinthians 1:10). Now they still needed to live in peace, dwelling together in harmony.

All four of Paul's exhortations here are present imperatives, indicating these must go on with continuous action at Corinth. In that case the God of love and peace would abide in their fellowship. Paul wrote often of the God of peace; here he reminded the Corinthian believers that He is also the God of love.

Paul frequently ended his letters with a request that certain ones be greeted in the congregation. Here he merely asked that believers at Corinth greet one another with a holy kiss. The implication was that the salutation be a warm one and included approaching the fellow member of the body of Christ by name.

The custom of greeting with a kiss was prevalent in the ancient world as it is in many places yet today. Paul indicated its frequent use by mentioning it elsewhere (Romans 16:16; 1 Corinthians 16:20; 1 Thessalonians 5:26). Peter brought his first epistle to a close much as Paul did this one, calling it a "kiss of charity" (1 Peter 5:14).

Certainly, New Testament believers did not exchange kisses between the sexes in their meetings. Paul would never have encouraged anything that might possibly be sensuous. Indeed, in the synagogues from which many earlier Christians came, men and women occupied different parts of the building. In some cultures today they do not sit together in church, not even husband and wife. However, despite the fact that they gave the customary kiss with all discretion, the passing of the years saw outsiders accusing believers of promoting unwholesome relations through the practice. Thus it declined. It has been replaced by the handshake in a large part of the world.

Paul also usually closed his letters by sending greetings from those associated with him to the recipients of the communication. Here he simply said, "All the saints salute (*aspazontai*, 'greet,' from the same root as the verb in verse 12) you." This included the Christians of Macedonia where the apostle was when he wrote this letter.

As here, Paul frequently called believers saints. They occupied that position because they were sanctified, separated from sin and dedicated to God. This happened the moment of their conversion, though some were vile sinners an instant before. In the first letter to the Corinthians Paul took note of the "before" and "after" scene in the lives of many of them. The list of sins of which he wrote included fornication, idolatry, homosexuality, thievery, and drunkenness. Then he remarked, "And such were some of you: but ye are washed, but ye are sanctified, but ye are justified in the name of the Lord Jesus, and by the Spirit of our God" (1 Corinthians 6:9-11).

In closing the Roman letter Paul declared in Romans 16:16, "The churches of Christ salute you." He followed this short greeting with salutations from various brethren whom he mentioned by name (Romans 16:21-23). The scribe who wrote the words as the apostle dictated even added, "I Tertius, who wrote this epistle, salute you in the Lord" (Romans 16:22).

The benediction in verse 14 of 2 Corinthians is the most complete of Paul's letters. It includes each member of the Trinity, God the Father, the Lord Jesus Christ, and the Holy Spirit. From each it promised triple blessings, grace, love, and fellowship.

# GALATIANS

## Overview

### Background

#### The Recipients of the Epistle

The ethnic term *Galatian* comes from the same root as the word *Gaul*. It refers to some Celtic tribes that had for many centuries lived in the territory now known as Turkey (Asia Minor), near where Ankara, the capital of Turkey, is situated. Shortly before the birth of Christ the territory of the Galatians had come under the control of the Roman Empire. It was made a Roman province, together with other countries in Asia Minor, among them Pisidia (Acts 13:14) and Lycaonia (Acts 14:6).

#### The Activity of Paul Among the Galatians

Paul's first visit to Galatia must then have taken place during his second missionary journey. He was warmly received by the Galatians in spite of his "infirmity of the flesh" (4:13, 14) which did not hinder them from assisting him in every way. The apostle visited the Galatians a second time with the intent of securing and building up that which had been won during his first visit. However, a short time (cf. 1:6) after this second visit Paul received word that a serious heterodoxy was threatening the Galatian church. In order to counteract this heresy Paul wrote the Epistle to the Galatians. It was written perhaps during Paul's ministry in Ephesus (Acts 19), but it is also possible that it was written earlier from Corinth, perhaps almost at the same time as the Epistle to the Romans. Some scholars believe it was written from Antioch, just prior to the Jerusalem conference recorded in Acts 15.

#### The Purpose of the Epistle

The epistle was written to refute the dangerous teaching the Judaizers were seeking to promote. Their teaching had already caused problems in the church at Jerusalem (Acts 15:1-5), but it had been unanimously rejected by the apostles (Acts 15:6-12). However, the heresy was emerging in other places where there were Jews who would nourish it.

The Galatians had evidently been quick to listen to the arguments of the Judaizers who were seeking to convince the new Christians they must keep the Mosaic law concerning circumcision and observance of the Jewish feasts (5:2-6). Paul maintained that it is impossible to mix faith in Christ as the way of salvation and the Law as a means of salvation (2:16; 5:2). He insisted that circumcision inevitably involved an obligation to keep the entire Law (5:3).

The Judaizers were also seeking to undermine Paul's authority in the very churches he had founded. They sought to give the impression that Paul was a second class apostle, that he ranked far below the apostles in Jerusalem. Paul met this kind of attack everywhere even though he insisted there was the best possible relationship between him and the other apostles (Galatians 2:7, 9; Acts 15:1-29). He continually maintained that he had been called to be an apostle by the resurrected Lord Jesus, not through any action of the other apostles (1:1, 15-17).

Paul's refutation of the Judaizers' heretical teaching is the main issue of the epistle, but there are references to some of the effects false doctrine has on the daily lives of those who are led astray by it. The epistle mentions some indication of a backsliding into paganism (4:8, 9), to mutual disagreement (5:15), and an indecent lifestyle (5:17-21).

### The Distinctive Characteristics of the Epistle

Paul had no cowriter when he wrote the Epistle to the Galatians. Unlike some of his other epistles, it contains no personal greetings, nor does it give any indication of where it was written. Paul often dictated his epistles, adding his own personal greetings at the end, but the conclusion of Galatians is much longer than usual (6:11-18). However, there are three distinctive characteristics.

From its beginning this epistle is unusual. First, it is remarkable that there is no thanksgiving or intercession for the recipients of the letter. First Timothy and Titus do not have these distinctives either, but in the Epistle to the Galatians it almost seems sinister since they are replaced by the ill-boding words, "I marvel that ye are so soon removed from him that called you into the grace of Christ unto another gospel" (1:6).

The second distinctive mark is that the epistle is unusually impassioned in its language. In 10 places at least Paul used very sharp and blunt expressions: 1:8, 9; 2:11, 13; 3:1, 3; 4:11; 5:10, 12; 6:13. In addition, Paul interrupted his discussion of the main theme of the epistle by referring to the personal response of the Galatian believers to the heresy being taught by the Judaizers: 3:1-4; 4:8-20; 5:7-12. We see this kind of interruption in 2 Corinthians but with this difference: the spontaneous interruptions to the teaching being given in that epistle were due to joy and comfort, whereas the interruptions in Galatians were due to Paul's anger because of the heresy being promulgated by the Judaizers and his sorrow because the Galatian Christians had been enticed to forsake the doctrine of faith in Christ alone for their salvation.

The third distinctive mark of the epistle is that it contains the longest connected account of Paul's life in any of the Epistles: 1:15 through 2:15. Here we are given Paul's view of his life as recorded by Luke in Acts 7:58; 8:3; portions of chapters 9 and 11, and chapters 12-15. Paul's account in Galatians verifies his apostolic authority which the Judaizers were challenging.

It must be emphasized that in spite of Paul's wrath which is directed toward the heretics, the epistle testifies strongly of his love for the Galatian Christians. Many times he used the expression "brethren" (1:11; 3:15; 4:12, 28, 31; 6:1, 18). He spoke of the Galatians as "sons" (4:6, 7) in whom he wanted to have confidence (5:10), and he gave directions to those who were "spiritual" (6:1). He wrote of the good memories he had of his visits with them (4:12, 14, 15; 5:7), and he called them "my little children" (4:19). The epistle closes with Paul's desire that peace and mercy be upon those who accept his "rule" (6:16).

## Outline of Galatians

### I. Introduction (1:1-14)

This section contains Paul's greeting (verses 1-5), his reason for writing the epistle (verses 6-9), and his testimony that the gospel he preached was from God and had been given him by "the revelation of Jesus Christ" (verses 10-12), a gospel that was contrary to his earlier, self-chosen manner of life (verses 13, 14).

### II. Paul's Earlier Life (1:15-2:15)

Paul had been predestined to preach the gospel and called to be an apostle not by man, not even the original apostles or the Early Church. His calling and training came to him directly from the Lord Jesus Christ, and the apostles in Jerusalem were at last persuaded that he had been called by Christ to take the gospel to the Gentiles.

### III. Paul's Teaching (2:16-5:12)

Paul's main theme in the epistle is that justification comes through faith in Christ alone, not by works of the Law. The Law was given to unveil sin. It was the "schoolmaster to bring us unto Christ, that we might be justified by faith. But after that faith is come, we are no longer under a schoolmaster" (3:24, 25).

### IV. Admonitions (5:13-6:10)

Paul was careful to stress that the liberty which believers have in Christ is not to be used as an excuse for resorting to the works of the flesh. Rather, the true effect of Christian liberty which comes through justification by faith leads to a life of faith and good works which are motivated by love.

### V. Conclusion (6:11-18)

The epistle ends with a short summary of the main contents of the letter which Paul had written with his "own hand." He gave further testimony to the power of the Cross, refusing any additional means for salvation. The basic premise of the epistle is Jesus only, not Jesus plus anything else.

## Attack On the Heretics

After his initial greeting to the Galatians, Paul began immediately to deal with the heresy which was causing so much division and confusion. He marveled that the Galatian Christians had "so soon" turned away from the true gospel he had preached to them. He declared that the Judaizers were distorting the gospel. He felt it was necessary to vindicate his apostolic authority, since the Judaizers were seeking to discredit that authority.

Paul had once been a persecutor of the Church. He had been more zealous for the Jewish religion than any other person. But the day came when God revealed His Son and called him to preach the gospel to the Gentiles. Three years after his conversion Paul went to Jerusalem to see Peter, with whom he stayed for 2 weeks. It was at this time he met James, the brother of the Lord.

Fourteen years later he went to Jerusalem again, accompanied by Barnabas and Titus. The purpose of this visit was to present the Law-free gospel to them "of reputation" (2:2). The apostles to whom he referred enjoined nothing of importance on Paul and accepted his call to preach the gospel to the Gentiles. They gave him and Barnabas "the right hands of fellowship" as colaborers in the gospel.

Paul next related to the Galatians an incident when he had to withstand Peter to his face. In Antioch Peter had eaten with the Gentile Christians, thus expressing his emancipation from the Jewish manner of eating. However, when some Jewish Christians came in, Peter withdrew. Since Peter had agreed with the Law-free gospel Paul preached, Paul considered his actions hypocritical. It is interesting to note that in his epistle to the Galatians, written many years later, Paul did not hesitate to unveil Peter's weakness in Antioch. Nor did he spare Barnabas who "also was carried away with their dissimulation" (2:13). In chapter 1 Paul wrote, "But though we, or an angel from heaven, preach any other gospel unto you, than that which we have preached unto you, let him be accursed" (verse 8). These words indicate how serious Paul was in his desire that the gospel be kept clean. He spared neither himself nor any fellow apostle or close friend if there should be any deviation from the truth.

Christ had broken down, by His death on the cross, the division between Jew and Gentile (Ephesians 2:11-13). Peter had a practical part in breaking down the division by entering the house of Cornelius and preaching the gospel (Acts 10:28), and by maintaining in the circle of the apostles the truth that God had poured out upon the Gentiles the same Holy Spirit the Jewish believers had received (Acts 11:1-18; 15:7-11). By his action at Antioch, he rebuilt the wall which he himself had had a hand in breaking down.

When Paul did not retreat from attacking a fellow apostle who had shown weakness when he should have stood firmly, it is easy to understand that he did not show the real heretics any mercy. The so-called Judaizers whom Paul was opposing did not really deny the gospel, but they wanted to add something to the gospel. This distorted the gospel of Christ into "another gospel," a false gospel. The delusion of the Judaizers was that they mixed the Law and gospel together. They maintained that salvation is partly by faith, partly by works. With flaming zeal, Paul opposed this falsification of the gospel: "But though we, or an angel from heaven, preach any other gospel unto you than that which we have preached unto you, let him be accursed" (1:8).

Paul's argument was that this false gospel robbed God of the honor that belongs to Him because it implies that His grace is not great enough to forgive sin until the sinner deserves it. The argument continues: If faith is not enough for salvation, then it can only be because the redemptive work of Christ is not sufficient. If salvation can be obtained in whole or in part by works it disparages the work of Christ and maligns the character of God by doubting His free grace.

Such an attitude is a demonstration of unbelief. Therefore, Paul wrote to those who believed they could be justified by their works that they had fallen out of grace and that the work of Christ on their behalf would profit them nothing (2:21; 3:1-4; 5:2-4). The heterodoxy which they had accepted had robbed them of their salvation. That is why Paul opposed the heretics so strongly. They led men astray. Paul wrote, "Christ is become of no effect unto you, whosoever of you are justified by the law; ye are fallen from grace" (5:4). Paul feared that all the Galatian believers had experienced had been in vain (3:4). His only hope was that in their confusion they had not become real Judaists, that

they did not understand the real issues, and that they had kept their faith in Christ (3:26; 5:10).

The Judaism which penetrated the early Christian churches and which Paul opposed so strongly was the same distorted view of Jewish religion that Jesus fought against during His entire earthly ministry, that is, Pharisaism. Some Jews had joined the first Christian churches without being loosed from their Pharisaic attitude (Acts 15:5). Paul, who had been a Pharisee, knew how totally impossible it was to combine Christianity and Pharisaism. Paul's struggle against it wherever he found it was a continuation of the battle which Jesus had faced.

In addition to the Christianized form of Pharisaism which had its origin in the backslidden Jewish religion, another spiritual current which had its origin in paganism threatened to infiltrate the churches. The Gnostic mystery religions mixed myths of the Orient with Greek philosophy. The "Christian" forms of gnosticism mixed the gospel of Jesus Christ with so-called "wisdom," the worship of angels and an explanation of "man and the physical universe as resulting from a series of emanations from the supreme godhead," as well as an ascetic element with a strong emphasis upon mortification of the body (Colossians 2:23).

Paul warned that after his departure these forces would gain power in the churches which would cause a great backsliding and precede the revelation of the Antichrist. History shows that this was so. The main delusion was seeking to add something to the work of Christ in order to gain salvation. From this root all other delusions have grown up.

The Reformation is the great historical testimony to the doctrine of justification by faith alone in Christ's redemptive work. Forgiveness of sin comes only through faith in His atoning death. This expresses the Biblical doctrine of salvation: "Therefore we conclude that a man is justified by faith without the deeds of the law" (Romans 3:28). "It is God that justifieth" (Romans 8:33). "But to him that worketh not, but believeth on him that justifieth the ungodly, his faith is counted for righteousness" (Romans 4:5). "But for us also, to whom it shall be imputed, if we believe on him that raised up Jesus our Lord from the dead; who was delivered for our offenses, and was raised again for our justification" (Romans 4:24, 25).

The question could be asked, "What was the motive and intent of these Judaizers? What did they really want?" Perhaps their first and most important supposition was that the work, death, and resurrection of Jesus Christ could be incorporated into the Jewish religion. In the Gospels we find the disciples had the same line of thought. In Acts we see that in spite of repeated signs and events it was almost impossible for the first pure Jewish church in Jerusalem to understand that they had entered into a totally new covenant into which all nations are welcomed and who do not have to come through the Law.

Paul met their activity everywhere he went. They taught, "Except ye be circumcised after the manner of Moses, ye cannot be saved" (Acts 15:1). "There rose up certain of the sect of the Pharisees which believed, saying, That it was needful to circumcise them, and to command them to keep the law of Moses" (Acts 15:5). We can have some sympathy for these men who valued the old covenant so highly that they did not spare any effort in order to make the Gentiles join it. But we can also understand that the Spirit of God did signs and wonders in order to open their eyes to the truth. It is perhaps more difficult to understand that only a few of them received the truth.

Paul revealed the pride which lay behind their activities. Fallen, sinful man, "the flesh," would not give up its own honor, admit its total fall, and accept the preaching of the Cross as the only way to salvation. Paul recognized the deadly danger of adding anything to the gospel. Delusions of later periods have often consisted of the same kind of false doctrine: that of seeking to add something else to the work of Jesus on the cross. Regardless of what this other thing or things may be, it has always led to heterodoxy, and also has often led to a reprobate and sinful life with all kinds of excesses.

## Survey Comment

The genuineness of the Epistle to the Galatians has been almost undisputed. In it the apostle spoke of his Damascus experience. He spoke with authority, fully aware of the One who had sent him (1:1). He was confident that the same God who raised up Jesus from the dead had called him for His service, separating him from his mother's womb to preach the gospel to the Gentiles (1:15, 16). That God-given authority to go to the Gentiles meant also that he was bound. If he made any attempt to change the contents of the message, he himself would be accursed (1:8).

It is remarkable that in the opening section of the epistle, Paul did not present the contents of the gospel but rather its immutability. If it is altered, it is no longer the gospel (1:7). The gospel is not a work of man which can be presented today but becomes out of fashion tomorrow. It stands firm eternally because it came from God and was revealed by His Son. It is constantly called "the gospel of Christ" (1:7). This expression can be understood as the gospel which belongs to and descends from Christ (subjective genitive) as well as the gospel which concerns Christ and reveals Him as the central figure (objective genitive).

In 1:4 Jesus is presented as the One who gave himself in order to deliver us from our sins. This truth is referred to again in 4:3-5. Jesus is the deliverer from the powers of wickedness. The believer is plainly "called unto liberty" (5:13). Those who pervert the gospel are characterized as those who spy on the liberty believers have in Christ Jesus.

In 2:16-3:24 Paul dealt with the theme of justification by faith. What is meant by this expression? To justify means to pass a sentence of acquittal. This takes place when an individual gives his life to Jesus Christ. Jesus took upon himself our sins and gives us instead His righteousness. This involves a deep union with Christ which can best be expressed by Paul's words "I am crucified with Christ" (2:20). The result is the "I" lives no longer. Christ lives within the believer: He is formed within the Christian (4:19). That is why the phrase "in Christ" is used so often. It is a word which God speaks and man hears, and receiving involves faith, trusting that when God says it, it happens. Therefore, believing is a main point in the Epistle to the Galatians. Paul illustrated this by referring to a child's relationship with his father (5:4-6). The believer's faith is like the trust of a child and results in obedience (6:16).

This "obedience to the faith" (Romans 1:5) is not to be confused with keeping the Law. They are as different as night and day as the Epistle to the Galatians shows. When an individual seeks to be "justified by the works of the law" (2:16), he is relying on his own works, but this is a great illusion. If one prefers to follow the way of the Law and one's own righteousness, he must keep the entire Law without exception (5:3). No man can do this (3:10). "No man is justified by the law in the sight of God" (3:11).

These two terms, justification by the Law and salvation by grace are diametrically opposed. Where one is the other must give way; they are contradictory propositions. The delusion which the Galatians were facing was that they wanted it both ways. Paul said those who were seeking to make the Law the way of salvation were under a curse, a curse which Christ died to free us from (3:10, 13).

What is the Law then? "It was added because of transgressions," Paul said (3:19). There are different opinions as to what this means. Some feel that the works of the Law produce transgression. It is more likely that he meant the Law illuminates the transgressions which have already taken place, the transgressions which can no longer be hidden. Thus the Law works not only as a judge but as a protector.

Paul used the illustration of the pedagogue (schoolmaster, 3:24) and the tutor or governor (4:2). Their important work for the child lasted only "until the time appointed of the father" (4:2). Then the child became free. The holy commandment of the Law was fulfilled by God himself in Jesus Christ. His innocent suffering and punishment became an atonement for all our sins. The Law can no longer judge the believer. Its work was to conclude all under sin (3:22), so that grace is given by faith. Thus justification does not come through the works of the Law, but through "the obedience of faith." The believer receives the Spirit not by works of the Law but by "the hearing of faith" (3:2). He can only be taught to call God "Father" by the Holy Spirit (4:6). No one on his own can understand that he is a child of God. This understanding is a gift of the Spirit.

The doctrine of justification by faith is foretold in the Old Testament: "The scripture, foreseeing that God would justify the heathen through faith, preached before the gospel unto Abraham" (3:8). Jesus himself on the walk to Emmaus spoke to the two disciples of all that the Old Testament said "concerning himself" (Luke 24:25-27). The view that the Old Testament is totally irrelevant for Christians is completely foreign to the teaching of the Bible.

Paul used examples from the Old Testament in different ways. Abraham was an example of faith (3:6-9). Paul explained the expression concerning the offspring of Abraham as referring directly to Christ, who was of the family of Abraham (3:16). Paul used Sarah and Hagar as "types" of two different kinds of life. The son of the bondwoman was begotten "after the flesh" (4:23). Sarah's son was begotten by virtue of the "promise," corresponding exactly with the story in the Old Testament. Paul was certain that the story of these two women tells something which is of the greatest importance to the entire salvation history. Paul declared that the promise given to Abraham cannot be annulled by the Law which was given much later. The Law was never intended as a way of salvation. The Law could never justify, it could only judge (3:21).

The doctrine of justification by faith leads us to consider the liberty which believers have in Christ. Paul wrote of the believers' release from the curse of the Law (3:13; 4:5). Another important release which Paul mentioned is from "the elements" and from the gods "which by nature are no gods" (4:3, 8-10). Opinions differ among interpreters, but the most natural interpretation is to think of this as a reference to Gentile idols. Behind these the evil spirits of Satan hide (cf. 1 Corinthians 10:19, 20).

The Galatians who wanted to make the Law a way of salvation had a tendency to return to some of the paganism from which they had been delivered. This resulted in their turning away from Christ to something else. The result was bondage. They turned to the ways of "the flesh" (3:3). They flattered the old, evil man and nourished his pride. They provided for man's honor, not God's. This has been observed on many mission fields. Paganism is a dark spiritual power of great strength. If this spiritual power has the slightest opportunity, it will reenter an individual from whom it has been driven by Christ. There is a good reason why Paul used the expression "in vain" (4:11). We do not know the extent of the Galatians' backsliding into paganism, but Paul considered his short remark sufficient.

We now reach a new main theme in the epistle: the description of the work of the Holy Spirit in the Church and in the life of each individual. In matters great and small the apostles wanted to be guided by the Spirit, not only in those matters which concerned eternal things but also in temporal, for example, the agreement Paul wrote of in 2:7-10. It concerned a temporary matter, but the small word "saw" in verse 7 discloses that the Spirit influences and guides believers to the truth in temporary situations. Paul also called attention to the miracles which the Spirit works in the lives of believers (3:5). The Book of Acts witnesses to these miraculous acts of the Holy Spirit. But whether the Spirit works in miraculous ways or in quiet everyday ministry to the believers, it is still the Spirit who is at work.

The Epistle to the Galatians calls attention to what Paul called the "walk In the Spirit" (5:16), being "led by the Spirit" (5:18), bearing "the fruit of the Spirit" (5:22). All of these encompass the work of the Spirit in the life of the individual believer and in the life of the Church collectively.

To "walk in the Spirit" seems to indicate the initiative of each individual while on the contrary to "be led by the Spirit" reminds one of an irresistible force which comes from above. In this case, the individual does not himself decide the direction he will walk. Because of the work of the Holy Spirit, each believer can reach his full potential so that he can take the initiative, work, and live, but at the same time realize that he is no longer his own master. It is the Spirit that drives him. This becomes clear when one considers the Christian life as a child-or son-connection to God the Father by Jesus Christ (4:5, 6). This new dependence as a child of God leads to true liberty.

The expression "fruit" which Paul used to describe the work of the Spirit in the life of the Christian was used by Jesus himself in John 15:4, 5. It is difficult to find any better picture. The fruit is totally dependent on the tree and is typical for this special tree. The believer is united with the Father and the Son. Therefore the fruit the believer bears is of a certain kind (5:22, 23). Love is mentioned first. It is the meaning and fulfillment of the Law (5:13, 14). It is the secret behind all of God's work because He is love. The other fruit mentioned are included in the love that is the fruit of the Spirit.

The fruit of the Spirit is contrary to the works of the flesh (5:19-21). The words "the flesh" can indicate many different things. In 4:13, 14 it indicates the body in a totally neutral meaning. In other places it refers to man, or more definitely fallen, sinful man. When this word is used, the translator as well as the interpreter must be very careful. In the Epistle to the Galatians the word is used in the sense of that which is contrary to the Spirit (3:3; 4:29; 5:16f.; 6:8), the natural man in his sinfulness. The work of the Holy Spirit in each individual is exercised in the spirit of the individual, in the heart as Jesus said (Mark 7:19).

There is a distinct contrast between the works of the flesh and the fruit of the Spirit which Paul mentions by name. This is seen clearly when a comparison is made:

**Adultery, uncleanness—love**
**Lasciviousness—joy**
**Idolatry, witchcraft—peace (that which God gives, Ephesians 2:14)**
**Hatred—longsuffering**
**Variance, emulations, wrath—gentleness**
**Strife—goodness**
**Seditions, heresies—faithfulness**
**Envyings—meekness**
**Murders, drunkenness, revelings—temperance**

Individuals respond to persons, events, and problems according to whether or not they are following Christ. The non-Christian exhibits one type of behavior because he is doing the works of the flesh. The Christian who is bearing the fruit of the Spirit exhibits another type of behavior. It is not a matter of psychological difference which causes the two types of behavior. Flesh is flesh and can only produce the works of the flesh, although they can be embellished differently according to breeding and temperament. But behavior changes when Christ is Lord of the life. He and He alone can produce the fruit of the Spirit in the life of the individual who is born again.

Thus we see once more that it is the Holy Spirit in the life of the Church and the individual that creates this great difference. It is the difference between light and darkness, salvation and perdition. That is why Paul fought so strongly against those who were contending that salvation comes through doing the works of the Law. The Law is holy and good, and it will be fulfilled (5:14), but the "flesh" cannot fulfill it. The natural man cannot justify himself. It is arrogant to try to do so. Such individuals are seeking to "make a fair show in the flesh" (6:12). They are living in self-delusion (6:3).

Those who were telling the Galatians they must be circumcised according to the Mosaic law, saying that not until then could they consider themselves true Christians, were perverting the gospel. That is why Paul stood so strongly against them. It was a matter of eternal life or eternal death (1:6, 7).

But even though Paul stood firmly against the heresy of salvation through works, it does not mean that the gospel approves the works of the flesh. Christian liberty is not a "liberty for an occasion to the flesh" (5:13). In his epistles Paul gave many instructions which were taken directly from the Old Testament (5:14; 6:7, 8). The Lutheran fathers called this "the third use of the law." Just as the Holy Spirit throws light on the salvation history of the Old Testament, showing that it points to Christ, so He can throw light on the admonitions of the Law to be used in the Christian life. But never does He indicate that salvation can be built upon the works of the Law.

Galatians 5:5 is a short summary of all that the gospel gives to the believer: "We through the Spirit wait for the hope of righteousness by faith." "We wait" is the attitude of the Christian as he daily turns to God and when he looks forward to the return of the Lord Jesus. "Through the Spirit" involves a negative response to all the "works of the flesh." "By faith" indicates there can be no attempt to make oneself deserving of salvation, no compromise with the "works of the law." "The hope of righteousness" is the sentence of acquittal which God has pronounced because of the Cross and which will on that great Day free us from perdition and lead us into glory.

# The Epistle of Paul to the Galatians

## Commentary

### Chapter 1

**1. Paul, an apostle, (not of men, neither by man, but by Jesus Christ, and God the Father, who raised him from the dead;):** . . . a legate, —*MRDK* . . . I, Paul, who am appointed and commissioned a messenger, —*PHLP* . . . whose call to be an apostle did not come from man, —*TEV* . . . not from man or through man, but appointed by, —*FNTN* . . . not even through the intermediate agency of man, —*WUST* . . . not by human appointment or human commission, —*NEB* . . . whose authority is not derived from men and is due, not to man, —*TCNT* . . . I was not chosen by men, —*SEB* . . . nor commissioned by any man, —*MOFT* . . . Who rouses Him from among the dead, —*CNDT* . . . who made him come back from the dead, —*BB*.

**1:1.** In his letters Paul followed the usual ancient letter pattern: greetings, prayer for addressees, thanksgiving, the particular contents of the letter, special salutations and greetings. In Galatians, these divisions break down as follows: the greetings and prayer for the addressees, 1:1-5; the particular contents, 1:6-6:17; and the special salutations and greetings, 6:18. Paul has omitted the thanksgiving since the Galatian Christians were tempted to leave the way of grace for that of law, of works.

Some Jewish Christians in Jerusalem failed to understand the true meaning of salvation by grace alone; they thought that to believe in Jesus was only the beginning. Each believer was expected to live totally as a Jew in order to be saved. This included circumcision. Acts 15:1, 2 informs us that these Jews from Jerusalem had come to Antioch and caused havoc in the church. Some went on to trouble the new churches in Galatia.

These Jewish Christians, often termed Judaizers, had told the Christians of Galatia Paul had not been faithful to his instruction, that he had failed to tell them the complete requirements for salvation. Because of this, in his opening statements Paul stressed that he had received his commission as an apostle not *from* men nor *through the agency of* man. Rather, he had been personally called "by Jesus Christ, and God the Father." Then he added an important phrase: "who raised him from the dead." Christ's resurrection guaranteed the certainty of salvation by grace alone (1 Corinthians 15; Colossians 1:13-23).

**2. And all the brethren which are with me, unto the churches of Galatia:** . . . and the group of friends now with me, —*NEB* . . . all the Christians, —*BECK* . . . who are beside me, —*MOFT* . . . to the assemblies, —*RTHM*, —*WORL*, —*FNTN* . . . to the Communities of, —*HNT* . . . To the congregations in the Galatian area, —*FNTN*.

**3. Grace [be] to you and peace from God the Father, and [from] our Lord Jesus Christ:** . . . be kind to you and give you peace, —*FNTN* . . . will be good to you, —*EVRD* . . . spiritual blessing, —*WLMS* . . . favor to you, —*WLSN* . . . peace be granted to you from, —*WEYM*.

**4. Who gave himself for our sins:** . . . who according to the Father's plan, —*PHLP* . . . Jesus sacrificed himself for, —*FNTN* . . . who gave Himself to suffer for, —*WEYM*.

**that he might deliver us from this present evil world, according to the will of God and our Father:** . . . in order that he might rescue us, —*WLSN* . . . to rescue us from this present wicked age, —*TCNT* . . . take us for himself out of the present age, —*RTHM* . . . the present evil age, —*PNIN* . . . from the present evil world order, —*PHLP* . . . the present wickid world, —*WCLF* . . . evil life, —*SAWR*.

**1:2-4.** The Christians at Antioch, including Barnabas, joined Paul in greeting the churches which he and Barnabas had established during their first missionary journey (Acts chapters 13 and 14). "Grace" means God's unmerited love made possible through the atoning work of Jesus Christ. "Peace" with God is the blessed result of receiving God's unmerited grace. Peace is spiritual well-being (Romans 5:1, 2). Paul added, "and from our Lord Jesus Christ." Because He has paid the ransom price for the believer's salvation, He is their Lord and King. Christians belong to Him completely as their spiritual King (Romans 6). "Jesus" means "Saviour" as the angel explained to Joseph (Matthew 1:21).

To stress the certainty of grace, Paul carefully explained the true role of Christ (verse 4), namely, as the One who gave himself freely for the salvation of the world. The Jews viewed the present age as the wicked age, the age of the Evil One. In contrast, the age to come was to be an age of peace and prosperity for those who were truly members of God's covenant people. Paul stressed that such deliverance is the will of God who is also the Father. This tremendous statement reminds the believer of God's promise that the woman's Seed would crush the power of the Evil One (Genesis 3:15) and the prophecy of Isaiah 53 that Jesus would become the obedient suffering and then victorious Servant for man's salvation. Through the Spirit's work, all believers in Christ now belong to Him, yet are still in the present evil age (2 Corinthians 5:17-21).

**5. To whom [be] glory for ever and ever. Amen:** ... to the ages, –*RTHM* ... for the ages of the ages, –*WLSN*.

**1:5.** The beautiful doxology Paul added here is not found at the end of the greetings and prayers in his other letters. God's glory means the total radiance of His presence, all that God is. God is worthy of ongoing praise and adoration to the end of time into all eternity (Psalms 29:2; 96:8). Paul ended his doxology with "Amen," solemnly confirming what he had just said. In Hebrew *'amen* had the same emphatic force; the hearer (or writer) was strongly affirming the truth of the preceding statement. Other New Testament doxologies also end with Amen (e.g., Romans 16:27; 2 Peter 3:18), as do the Old Testament doxologies at the end of the first four sections of Psalms (Psalms 41:13; 72:19; 89:52; 106:48).

**6. I marvel that ye are so soon removed from him that called you into the grace of Christ unto another gospel:** ... I wonder, –*DOUY* ... I am astonished, –*WLSN* ... I am astonished ... deserting him, –*TCNT* ... that thus quickly ye are making a change, –*RTHM* ... so quickly deserting him, –*CNFT* ... ye are so sone turned from him, –*TNDL* ... you are transferred from him, –*RHEM* ... so soon turning from him, –*NOYS* ... so quickly turned away, –*SAWR* ... so quickly removing from him, –*PNIN* ... unto a different gospel, –*ALFD* ... forsaking him that had called you, –*GNVA*.

**7. Which is not another:** ... which is nothynge els, –*CRNM*.

**but there be some that trouble you, and would pervert the gospel of Christ:** ... except in this respect that, –*CNFT* ... certain persons are disturbing you, –*SCLT* ... people who are harassing you, –*TCNT* ... who disturb you, –*SAWR* ... would subvert, –*WSLY* ... wishing to change the joyful message of, –*RTHM* ... seeking to change entirely the gospel, –*NOYS*.

**1:6, 7.** Paul's style now became more terse. He went at once to the very heart of the Galatians' problem. Acts 14:21-23 records that Paul and Barnabas stopped at each of the new mission churches in Southern Galatia to strengthen, encourage, and organize them before returning to Antioch. Paul's use of the phrase "so soon" suggests that not much time had passed before he heard that the Galatians were being influenced by the message of the Judaizers. Paul expressed his utter amazement and astonishment.

The apostle used the verb "called." The Galatians had been called by the grace of Christ. The

Holy Spirit, working through the gospel which Paul and Barnabas had shared, had worked faith in their hearts (Titus 3:4-8).

But now they were being tempted by the Judaizers who stressed that salvation was by works, by living as Jews. In Acts 15:10 Peter said that to live according to the Law was too heavy a yoke for even Jews to carry, let alone requiring Gentiles to live that way. History informs us that before A.D. 70, the Jewish rabbis had added 341 rules for daily life.

Paul emphatically stated that the so-called "gospel" with which the Galatians were being tempted was "another" gospel. The Greek word translated "another" (*heteron*, verse 6) means "different in kind." Paul used this word to emphasize that the gospel which the Judaizers said was the true gospel was a totally false gospel. Then he went on to describe it as not being in any way a gospel at all.

**8. But though we, or an angel from heaven: preach any other gospel unto you than that which we have preached unto you, let him be accursed:** ... should announce glad tidings, –*WLSN* ... preach to you another Gospel, –*WSLY* ... contrary to what we have preached, –*SAWR* ... than that which we delivered to you, –*WORL* ... any other gospel than the one you have heard, may he be damned! –*PHLP* ... let him be anathema! –*CNFT*.

**9. As we said before, so say I now again, If any [man] preach any other gospel unto you than that ye have received, let him be accursed:** ... You have heard me say it before, and now I put it down in black and white, –*PHLP* ... and I repeat it now, –*TCNT* ... is delivering unto you, –*RTHM* ... preache vnto you otherwaies, –*GNVA* ... contrary to what, –*SCLT* ... any other gospel than the one you have already heard be a damned soul! –*PHLP*.

**1:8, 9.** To emphasize that he and Barnabas had shared the *genuine* gospel with them, Paul used a decisive illustration. He stated that even if an angel from heaven would bring a gospel different from what they had shared, God's eternal curse and condemnation would rest on him. He restated this fact in another way to emphasize most emphatically the fatal consequences of listening to the Judaizers and their false gospel. All who believed what these were promoting as the true gospel would experience God's wrath and His eternal damnation. What the Judaizers were promoting as the only way to salvation was in fact the certain path to damnation.

**10. For do I now persuade men, or God? or do I seek to please men? for if I yet pleased men, I should not be the servant of Christ:** ... Does that make you think now that I am serving man's interests or God's? –*PHLP* ... do I now obey, –*WLSN* ... am I now seeking the favor of men, *—ASV*...soliciting the favour of men, *—SCLT*...men's favor, *—PNIN*.

**1:10.** Paul went on to stress that his role as the called apostle of Jesus Christ was to be faithful to the true gospel. Seemingly the Judaizers had accused him of seeking to please the Galatians by not telling them they had to live as Jews in order to be saved. Paul carefully stressed that this accusation was totally untrue. The gospel which he preached was that which he had received from Jesus Christ himself. And this true gospel he had faithfully shared with them.

**11. But I certify you, brethren, that the gospel which was preached of me is not after man:**...But I assure you, *—NOYS*...For I give you to understand, *—DOUY, —CNFT*...I make known to you, *—WORL*...I would remind you...is not a human invention, *—TCNT*...not according to man, *—RTHM*.

**12. For I neither received it of man, neither was I taught [it], but by the revelation of Jesus Christ:**...No man gave it...no man taught it...it came to me as a direct revelation, *—PHLP*.

**1:11, 12.** Next Paul provided decisive information on how he had received the gospel. In doing so, he used the term translated "brethren" (*adelphoi*), fellow members of God's family. He used this affectionate term a number of times in this letter, especially when he had to use harsh words to emphasize that the true way of salvation is grace, not works. In this way he stressed that, despite their spiritual wavering, he still had a deep love for them as the sheep of God's flock. He also frequently used this affectionate term in other letters in which he had to take his readers to task for unchristian behavior or had to encourage them in the light of difficulties they faced. This is especially true of 1 and 2 Corinthians and 1 and 2 Thessalonians.

Paul informed them that the origin of the gospel he shared with them went back directly to a revelation of Jesus Christ himself. The Book of Acts records what happened, once in Luke's account (Acts 9:3-19) and twice in what Paul himself told two different sets of hearers. In Acts 22:3-16 Paul spoke to the temple mob which had almost killed him. In Acts 26:12-18 he spoke especially to Agrippa II, a part-Jew. In each of these instances, his listeners would understand that Paul had experienced a heavenly appearance of God's glory.

Each of these accounts stresses that on the Damascus Road an exceedingly bright glory-light shone down from heaven on Saul (Paul) and his companions. From the heavenly light came the voice of the risen and ascended Christ. Saul's

respectful reaction to that voice indicates that he understood it was the glorified Christ himself.

Acts 25:13ff. records that Herod Agrippa II made a state visit to the Roman governor Festus in Caesarea. He was reputed to be an expert in Jewish religious questions. He also had the right to appoint the high priest. In the words spoken to Agrippa II and Festus, Paul carefully informed them what Jesus had told him. He was called to share Christ as the fulfillment of the prophecies of old. This message of salvation by grace alone was to bring men, through the work of the Holy Spirit, from darkness to light and free them from the control of the devil (Acts 26:15-18). As the servant of Christ, Paul had faithfully shared this message in Galatia. The Greek term translated "servant" (*doulos*) in verse 10 actually means "slave," one who has been purchased and therefore totally belongs to the purchaser. Jesus had redeemed Paul with His precious blood from the power of the Evil One. Now Paul totally belonged to Christ, and this Paul never forgot. He remained faithful to Christ always.

**13. For ye have heard of my conversation in time past in the Jews' religion:**...ye have heard of my behaviour, *—WSLY*...of my former manner of life, *—CNFT*...my former course of life, *—MRDK*...way of life, *—ALFD*...my former conduct, *—MNTG*...my past career, *—PHLP*...as an adherent of the Jewish religion, *—WLMS*...as to my behaviour at one time in Judaism, *—RTHM*...when I was devoted to Judaism, *—TCNT*.

**how that beyond measure I persecuted the church of God, and wasted it:**...That I Exceedingly persecuted, *—WLSN*...with fanatical zeal, and, in fact, did my best to destroy it, *—PHLP*...I viciously persecuted, *—ADAM*...was persecuting the assembly of God, *—WORL*...how furiously I used to persecute the church, *—MNTG*...and made havoc of it, *—TCNT*...and ravaged it, *—CNDT*...tried to demolish it, *—ADAM*.

**1:13.** Paul reminded the Galatians that they knew of his earlier way of life. He had probably shared this with them when he and Barnabas brought them the gospel. In describing his attitude recorded in Acts 26:11, Paul used a strong Greek word (*eporthoun*) to show his religious fury toward Christ's followers. He had regarded them as blasphemers for believing in One condemned by the Council as a blasphemer and executed at their behest.

This word *eporthoun* was also used of a wild animal which mauls and devours its prey. Wild animals were often used in the arenas in the cities and towns of Galatia to entertain people. Unarmed humans were forced to face such wild animals and, as a result, were mauled to death and devoured to the glee of the crowds present.

**14. And profited in the Jews' religion above many my equals in mine own nation, being more exceedingly zealous of the traditions of my fathers:**... I progressed in Judaism, –CNDT...and I advanced in the Jews' religion, –ASV . . . I was far advanced in Judaism, –NORL...I outstripped many of my own, –MNTG ... above many of my years among my countrymen, –WSLY . . . above many contemporaries among my kindred, –RTHM ... I was ahead of most of my contemporaries...and had a greater enthusiasm for the old traditions, –PHLP...zealous for the doctrine, –MRDK...being an extreme fanatic for my ancestral traditions, –ADAM . . . for my ancestral instructions, –WORL.

**15. But when it pleased God:**... when the time came for God, –PHLP.

**who separated me from my mother's womb, and called [me] by his grace:** . . . Who gave me birth from my mother, –FNTN . . . who had chosen me from the moment of my birth, –PHLP . . . who had set me apart, –MNTG . . . from my very birth, –NOYS...reached me by his mercy, –TCNT... by His unmerited favor, –WLMS...He had special plans for me, –SEB.

**1:14, 15.** Paul reminded the Galatians that they knew of his life before Christ appeared and called him to be an apostle. He did this to emphasize that he knew the way of works and its implications far better than did the Judaizers. Paul had excelled his fellow Jews in his zeal for living totally as a Jew in accordance with the traditions of his fathers.

Paul's letter to the Philippians describes his former status as a Jew (Philippians 3:4-6). First of all, he noted that he was circumcised on the eighth day and thereby became a "son of the covenant." By descent he was an ethnically pure and true son of Israel, God's covenant people. As such, he was a descendant of Benjamin, the youngest son of Jacob and his beloved Rachel, who died soon after his birth. He was the only son of Jacob to be born in the land of Canaan, the covenant land. Because of the location of their small territory through which passed an important north-south road and several east-west roads, the Benjaminites were forced to be warlike. They were known to be first in battle. Psalm 68:24-27 states that they were also first in worship. Paul (Saul) was named after Saul of the tribe of Benjamin, the first king of Israel. The tribe of Benjamin remained faithful to David's dynasty.

Paul went on to say in Philippians that he was "a Hebrew of the Hebrews." The religious language of his pious home in Tarsus was Hebrew, the language of the inspired Scriptures. It was rather rare for this to be true of a Jewish family living in the Dispersion. In fact, in a synagogue service in the Dispersion, the Scriptures were first read in Hebrew if anyone present could read the Hebrew even if he did not understand what he was reading. This was then followed by a reading of the Scriptures in the Septuagint, in the Greek, the universal language of that day.

Paul was a Pharisee (see word study at number 5168 in *The Greek-English Dictionary*) trained by the illustrious Gamaliel, the successor of his famous grandfather Hillel who died about A.D. 20 (Acts 5:34-39; 22:3). In Philippians 3:6 Paul described himself as so excelling in righteousness that he was "blameless" from the Pharisaic viewpoint. A Jewish scholar has stated that before the year A.D. 70, 341 rules of the oral Law were added to what was already present in the written Law, the Torah (Pentateuch). These additional laws were to be followed by those zealous for living out their ancestral faith.

**16. To reveal his Son in me, that I might preach him among the heathen; immediately I conferred not with flesh and blood:**...He kindly decided to show me His Son, –BECK...was pleased to reveal, –ADAM . . . that I might proclaim him to the non-Jewish world, –PHLP . . . I did not confer, –WSLY...I communed not of the matter, –GNVA...I condescended not to, –DOUY, –RHEM...consult with, –WLSN...I didn't receive advice or get help from any human being, –SEB...I did not at once consult some human authority, –NORL . . . I did not immediately submit it to flesh, –CNDT...instead of consulting any human being, –TCNT... without consulting a human being, –MNTG...any human creatures, –WLMS.

**17. Neither went I up to Jerusalem to them which were apostles before me; but I went into Arabia, and returned again unto Damascus:**... I did not even go to Jerusalem to meet those who were God's messengers before me, –PHLP...but at once I went, –FNTN...rather, I went away to, –ADAM...I retired to Arabia, –WLMS...then came back to Damascus, –BECK.

**1:16, 17.** Like Jeremiah (Jeremiah 1:5) and John the Baptist (Luke 1:13-17), God had planned a special role for Paul before his birth. This included growing up in the cosmopolitan, international trade and cultural center of Tarsus. Historical references rank Tarsus after Athens and Alexandria as outstanding cultural centers.

All this was part of Paul's preparation for serving as a missionary to the Gentiles. Jesus' appearance to him on the Damascus Road totally changed his attitude and life, as he noted in Philippians 3:7-9. From the time of his call to the end of his life at the executioner's block, Paul lived in close association with the Gentiles as a humble servant of Jesus Christ. What he had cherished before as a dedicated and devout Pharisee, he now regarded as being sewage (*skubala*, Philippians 3:8).

Because of the false accusation of the Judaizers, Paul stressed that after his conversion he did not return at once to Jerusalem to receive further instruction and the approval of the apostles and the Church. Rather, as Luke informs us in Acts 9, he vigorously shared Christ in Damascus. This aroused the fury of the Jews. The one sent by the Council to arrest Christ's followers was now a forceful promoter of this blasphemous heresy. To save his life, Paul fled to Arabia, which can mean any place east of the Jordan and outside of Damascus. After 3 years he returned to Damascus and again very actively shared Christ with his fellow Jews. This resulted in their fierce anger against him.

**18. Then after three years I went up to Jerusalem to see Peter:** ... to get acquainted with, *—MNTG, —ADAM* ... to get to know, *—BECK* ... to become acquainted with Cephas, *—RTHM* ... to make the acquaintance of Peter, *—NORL* ... to relate my story to Cephas, *—CNDT* ... to question Kephas, *—FNTN.*
   **and abode with him fifteen days:** ... I only stayed with him just over, *—PHLP* ... I stayed a fortnight with him, *—TCNT* ... stayed in his company, *—BRKL* ... and remained with him, *—WLSN* ... and tarried, *—PNIN* ... and spent two weeks with him, *—MNTG, —WLMS.*

**19. But other of the apostles saw I none, save James the Lord's brother:** ... Yet I became acquainted with no one, *—CNDT* ... I did not meet any of the other messengers, *—PHLP* ... except James, *—CNFT* ... the Master's brother, *—TCNT.*

**20. Now the things which I write unto you, behold, before God, I lie not:** ... All this that I am telling you is ... the plain truth, *—PHLP* ... I do not falsely affirm, *—WLSN* ... in presence of God, *—RTHM* ... I call God to witness that I am telling the truth, *—MNTG* ... I am not falsifying, *—BRKL.*

**1:18-20.** Acts 9:22-25 and 2 Corinthians 11:32, 33 tell us that the Jews, in league with the Nabataeans, planned to kill Paul. (Secular history does not provide information on the exact relationship between the Nabataeans [Arabs] and the Romans at this time.) Paul was let down from the walls at night to permit him to escape to Jerusalem. When the Christians avoided Paul; Barnabas vouched for him (Acts 9:26, 27).

Paul explicitly stated that he went to Jerusalem to "see" Peter. The Greek term translated "see" (*historēsai*) means "to visit, to make someone's acquaintance." Although this term includes informal conversation, it does not permit any inference of formal training. Paul used this term to emphasize that he did not go to Jerusalem to be taught and formally certified for ministry by Peter and the leaders of the church in Jerusalem. He carefully made this point because the Judaizers said that he had been unfaithful to his training and certification.

While in Jerusalem, Paul also met James, the half brother of Jesus who served as the head of the mother church. Matthew 13:55 and Mark 6:3 give the names of four brothers of Jesus. They are also described as the sons of Mary. In actuality they were Jesus' half brothers.

While in Jerusalem Paul again vigorously shared the gospel for 15 days. Because of a plot against his life, he was taken by some Christians to the seaport of Caesarea and put on a ship bound for Tarsus in Cilicia (Acts 9:28-30). Paul closed this part of his account with an important legal phrase which included an oath: "Before God, I lie not." The Galatians understood the legal significance of this phrase. If used by someone in court to assure the correctness of his position, he won the case. But if the oath was thrown back by the other litigant, the swearer of the oath could lose his case. If used outside of court as a voluntary oath, it was a warning that the swearer was willing to proceed further.

Paul used this term to emphasize that the Judaizers had lied about him. He was truly an apostle, personally called by Jesus Christ. As he would emphasize again in Galatians 2, the gospel of salvation by grace alone, which he had faithfully shared with them, was the only true gospel.

**21. Afterwards I came into the regions of Syria and Cilicia:** ... After that I went into the regions, *—NORL* ... to the districts, *—TCNT.*

**1:21.** Paul stated that he left Jerusalem to return to the regions of Syria and Cilicia. He did not provide further information on his activity there; neither did Luke do so directly. Acts 15:41 tells us that at the beginning of his second missionary journey, Paul (and by implication, Silas) went through Syria and Cilicia, confirming and strengthening the churches. At this time Syria, together with the eastern part of Cilicia in which Tarsus was located, formed one large province. It is possible that Paul was actively engaged in sharing the gospel in Cilicia as well as in the Syrian area north of Antioch.

**22. And was unknown by face unto the churches of Judaea which were in Christ:** ... I was not known by sight, *—ADAM* ... they did not know me, *—BECK* ... did not know my face, *—SEB* ... but I was unknown personally, *—WLSN.*

**23. But they had heard only, That he which persecuted us in times past:** ... They knew only by hearsay, *—NORL* ... All they knew of me, in fact, was the saying, *—PHLP* ... our former persecutor, *—ALFD* ... who persecuted us formerly, *—SAWR* ... at one time, *—RTHM.*

now preacheth the faith which once he destroyed:...of which he once made havoc, *—PNIN*...he formerly made havoc, *—PNT.*

24. And they glorified God in me:...they praised God, *—TCNT*...And they thanked God for what had happened to me, *—PHLP*...on my account, *—WLSN.*

**1:22-24.** In summarizing this part of his letter, Paul carefully stressed that the churches of Christ in Judea did not know him personally. Judea here probably means Palestine. In about A.D. 44 the various sections of the west bank of Palestine came under the rule of Herod Agrippa I. Paul wrote of "the churches of Judea which were in Christ" to stress that these assemblies were Christian churches. In the Septuagint the word translated "churches" (*ekklēsiais*) is used several times as a religious term for God's covenant people gathered for worship. These churches were praising God that the former ferocious persecutor of the Faith was now actively sharing the gospel.

## Chapter 2

1. Then fourteen years after I went up again to Jerusalem with Barnabas, and took Titus with [me] also:

2. And I went up by revelation:... My visit on this occasion was by divine command, *—PHLP*...in consequence of a revelation, *—CNFT.*

and communicated unto them that gospel which I preach among the Gentiles, but privately to them which were of reputation, lest by any means I should run, or had run, in vain:... and I conferred with them, *—CNFT*...and submitted to them, *—WLSN*...I did this first in private conference with the Church leaders, to make sure that what I had done and proposed doing was acceptable to them, *—PHLP*...laid before them...those of eminence, *—SCLT*...to persons of distinction, *—SAWR*...before those who are thought highly of, *—TCNT*...particulerly with them which were counted chiefe, *—GNVA.*

**2:1, 2.** Saul's persecution and Stephen's stoning caused some Greek-speaking Jews, who had come from the Dispersion to Palestine, to flee. They scattered to the island of Cyprus and along the eastern coastline up to Antioch, the cosmopolitan capital of the Roman province of Syria. Antioch was the third largest city in the Roman Empire, surpassed in population only by Rome and Alexandria. It was known for its moral laxity.

Luke noted that among these Jewish Christians were some who had come from Cyprus and from Cyrene in North Africa. These not only shared their faith in the synagogues of Antioch but also with the Gentiles. This was most unusual, but God richly blessed their witness. When the church in Jerusalem heard about it, they sent Barnabas, who had been born in Cyprus, to minister to them.

Later, when God so richly blessed this outreach, he went to Tarsus to persuade Saul (Paul) to join him (Acts 4:36, 37; 9:27; 11:19-26).

About A.D. 44, Agabus came to Antioch and foretold a great famine in various parts of the Roman Empire. The Antioch church resolved to gather an offering for the poor Christians in Palestine. The Jewish historian Josephus records that this famine hit Palestine in A.D. 46 (*Antiquities,* 20:2:5). (The 14 years seemingly refers back to Paul's conversion in A.D. 32.) According to secular history, various parts of the vast Roman Empire suffered famine at different times during this period.

Paul, Barnabas, and Titus were sent to Jerusalem with the offering. They also discussed the gospel privately with Peter, John, and James as the leaders of the church at Jerusalem to make sure that they totally shared the same gospel, namely, that salvation is by grace alone for both Jew and Gentile alike. They did this, Paul wrote, "lest by any means I should run, or had run, in vain." The Greek word for "run" (*trechō*) is a verb which to the Galatians meant all the energy and effort which was necessary in running to win in a race. Athletic events in the amphitheater were an intimate part of the life experience of Paul's readers. Paul meant that both the mother and daughter churches had to agree that there was no difference in requirements for salvation between Jew and Gentile.

3. But neither Titus, who was with me, being a Greek, was compelled to be circumcised:...my associate, *—WLSN.*

**2:3.** The acid test came with Titus. Titus was a Greek, and therefore a Gentile Christian. As such, he had not been circumcised. In fact, circumcision for a Greek was considered unthinkable. To circumcise a man was thought to mutilate the body beautiful. Paul tersely stated that Titus was not compelled to be circumcised, despite the determined efforts of the "false brethren" (*pseudadelphous,* verse 4) to compel this.

Titus became one of Paul's stalwart helpers. When necessary for the sake of the gospel, he could be very firm. Later, perhaps in A.D. 55, Paul sent him to Corinth as his official representative to cope with the problems of that very difficult church. Titus was Paul's coworker in beginning the outreach on Crete; note what Paul says about the Cretians in Titus 1. Later Paul wrote the letter we know as the Epistle to Titus.

4. And that because of false brethren unawares brought in:...In fact, the suggestion would never have arisen but for the presence of some

pseudo-Christians, —PHLP . . . secretly introduced, —WLSN, —RTHM . . . introduced unawares, —WSLY.

**who came in privily to spy out our liberty which we have in Christ Jesus, that they might bring us into bondage:** . . . who wormed their way into our meeting . . . and then attempted to tie us up with rules and regulations, —PHLP . . . came in surreptitiously, —PNT . . . to spy upon our Christian liberty, —TCNT . . . the freedom we enjoy, —WLMS . . . in order to enslave us again, —MNTG . . . into servitude, —DOUY.

**5. To whom we gave place by subjection, no, not for an hour; that the truth of the gospel might continue with you:** . . . to whom we did not yield, —SCLT . . . by submission, —WLSN . . . But we did not yield to them even for a moment, —NORL . . . We did not give those men an inch, for the truth of the Gospel for you and all Gentiles was at stake, —PHLP . . . might abide unshaken among you, —MNTG . . . might prevail for you, —WLMS . . . might always be yours! —TCNT . . . might still abide with you, —RTHM.

**2:4, 5.** Paul described how this event took place. While the six leaders were meeting in private session, some of the Judaizing Christians *pareisēlthon* ("came in by stealth") to demand that Titus be circumcised. In very vigorous language, Paul stated that they had sneaked in "to spy out our liberty" which Christians have in Christ and to attempt to bring them back into the slavery of the Law. This would result in eternal condemnation. By the phrase "liberty . . . in Christ," Paul meant freedom from the demands of the Law which believers in Christ have because of their faith in Him. Paul called these men "false brethren" because they did not understand the gospel of grace.

Not for a moment did the six leaders permit these false brethren to dictate to them. To have done so would have denied the cardinal truth of the gospel. It would have meant that salvation was strictly by works and not by grace. It is not wrong to make concessions for the sake of harmony but only if it does not violate basic principles.

Some have questioned why Paul refused to circumcise Titus but did circumcise Timothy. Acts 16:1-3 records that Timothy's father was a Greek but his mother was a Jewess. In fact, 2 Timothy reveals that both his mother and grandmother were very pious Jews and carefully trained Timothy in the Scriptures (2 Timothy 1:4, 5; 3:15-17). Because his mother was a Jewess, Timothy was considered a Jew. So in good judgment, keeping in mind the work for which Timothy was to be trained, it was helpful to circumcise him. This did not in any way involve a compromise of the gospel. This was in line with Paul's principle to make himself "all things to all men."

**6. But of these who seemed to be somewhat, (whatsoever they were, it maketh no matter to me: God accepteth no man's person:) for they**

**who seemed [to be somewhat] in conference added nothing to me:** . . . they who undoubtedly were something, —WSLY . . . they which seemed great, —CRNM . . . what rank they held, —NORL . . . is of no consequence, —CNDT . . . as far as the leaders of the conference were concerned . . . God is not impressed with a man's office . . . they had nothing to add to my Gospel, —PHLP . . . it makes no difference to me . . . God is partial to no man, —SAWR . . . God is no respecter of persons, —MNTG . . . God pays no attention to outward appearances, —WLMS . . . does not recognise human distinctions, —TCNT . . . communicated nothing new, —NOYS . . . laid no further burden on me, —CNFT.

**2:6.** Paul emphasized a very important point, namely, that God is not a respecter of persons, a truth found throughout the Scriptures. As God's faithful servant, Paul followed His example. And so, in verse 6, Paul suggested that the Judaizers may have sought to pit the Jerusalem leaders against him and Barnabas. Paul agreed that the three men—Peter, James, and John—were men of reputation. But these men in no way tried to impose their judgment on Paul and Barnabas. Rather, they agreed that Paul and Barnabas had been faithful to the gospel in not circumcising Titus. Thereby they had safeguarded the proper understanding of the gospel, that of salvation by grace alone.

**7. But contrariwise:** . . . Rather, —NORL.

**when they saw that the gospel of the uncircumcision was committed unto me, as [the gospel] of the circumcision [was] unto Peter:** . . . they recognized that I had been commissioned, —NORL . . . they saw that I had been entrusted with, —TCNT . . . saw that I was entrusted with, —SCLT . . . seeing that I had been entrusted with, —RTHM . . . the Gospel for the uncircumcised was as much my commission as, —PHLP.

**2:7.** In this whole episode, Paul demonstrated his keen mind, developed also during his training by Gamaliel. All of the Epistle to the Galatians has the character of a carefully written legal document, especially the first two chapters.

The Judaizers had accused Paul of being unfaithful to his instructions by the key men of the Church. Paul carefully documented that his call and instruction came from Jesus Christ himself. He recorded that his special call as a missionary to the Gentiles was recognized by the leaders at Jerusalem. They recognized that Christ had entrusted the outreach to the Gentiles especially to Paul and the outreach to the Jews especially to Peter. It should be understood that in each case God's call was not categorical but each one was to concentrate his ministry on those to whom he had been called.

2:8. Paul restated the same truth in verse 8. The Greek word translated "wrought effectually" (*energēsas*) stresses that God was working equally in both Peter and Paul to enable them faithfully and effectively to carry out the mission for which God had chosen them.

**8. (For he that wrought effectually in Peter to the apostleship of the circumcision, the same was mighty in me toward the Gentiles:):** ... who had done such great work in Peter's ministry ... was plainly doing the same, *—PHLP* ... inwardly wrought in me, *—RTHM* ... operated also in me for the gentiles, *—SAWR.*

**9. And when James, Cephas, and John, who seemed to be pillars, perceived the grace that was given unto me, they gave to me and Barnabas the right hands of fellowship; that we [should go] unto the heathen, and they unto the circumcision:** ... who were reputed to be pillars, *—PNIN* ... who were manifest pillars, *—SAWR* ... and when they recognized, *—CNFT* ... the right handes of societie, *—RHEM* ... Recognizing the charge ... their hands in acknowledgement, *—TCNT* ... in full agreement that our mission was to, *—PHLP.*

**2:9.** Paul noted that Peter, James, and John were considered to be "pillars," the principal leaders of the mother church. These three men recognized the special role of Paul and Barnabas as given them by God and gave to them the right hand of fellowship (*koinōnia*). This important Greek word means Paul and Barnabas recognized that they were in total agreement with them on the cardinal doctrines of Scripture. In this instance, the focus was on salvation by grace alone through faith in Jesus Christ. This action again indicates that the Judaizers were wrong in their false accusations. Neither Jewish nor Gentile Christians had to be circumcised and live as Jews in order to be saved.

**10. Only [they would] that we should remember the poor; the same which I also was forward to do:** ... They make only one request of us ... that very thing I have diligently tried to do, *—NORL* ... I also gave diligence to do, *—PNIN* ... warnynge only that, *—TNDL* ... provided only that, *—CNFT* ... only urging, *—WLSN* ... be mindful of the destitute, *—RTHM* ... I was diligent to do, *—TNDL, —GNVA* ... I was careful to doe, *—RHEM* ... with this I was ... only too ready to agree, *—PHLP.*

**2:10.** The leaders asked Paul and Barnabas to remember the urgent needs of the poor Christians, particularly those of Jerusalem. History informs us that Jerusalem, a city of around 35,000, was never economically independent. Its population was always underemployed. It did have a system of helping the poor. Once a week the poor residents received a basket of food and clothing: bread and beans for lentil stew without meat, and

fruit in season. Special provisions were made for the poor to observe the Passover meal. It is unknown whether poor Jewish Christians were being excluded from such help because of their faith, but it might have happened.

Paul and Barnabas were most willing to ask the churches to gather such an offering. Doing so would also remind them of their ties with the mother church in Jerusalem. Paul and chosen representatives of churches founded by him brought such an offering to Jerusalem at the end of his third missionary journey (Acts 20:4; 21:15-19; 1 Corinthians 16:1-4; 2 Corinthians 8, 9). This was also an opportunity for the delegates and believers in Jerusalem to understand more fully the unity of the Church.

**11. But when Peter was come to Antioch, I withstood him to the face, because he was to be blamed:** ... I rebuked him, *—MRDK* ... I opposed him to his face, because he stood convicted, *—TCNT* ... I resisted him in face, because he was reprehensible, *—RHEM* ... I had to oppose him publicly, for he was then plainly in the wrong, *—PHLP* ... Because he was blameable, *—WLSN* ... he had become worthy of blame, *—RTHM* ... he had shown how wrong he was, *—BECK* ... because he was in the wrong, *—NORL* ... he was obviously wrong, *—ADAM* ... he stood condemned, *—WLMS.*

**2:11.** Some time after Paul, Barnabas, and Titus returned to Antioch, Peter came from Jerusalem to see for himself the vibrant life in this world missions church. He also joined in the fellowship meals of the church, at which Jewish and Gentile Christians ate together. This demonstrated the unity of their common faith in salvation by grace alone.

In practice Jews did not eat with Gentiles, whom they considered to be chronic sinners. In fact, of the 341 rules the rabbis had added for daily life (see note on 1:6, 7), two-thirds dealt with table fellowship. Several times during His ministry Jesus was reproached for eating with people whom the Pharisees considered "sinners" (Matthew 9:9-13; Luke 19:1-9).

**12. For before that certain came from James, he did eat with the Gentiles:** ... It happened like this, *—PHLP* ... he used to eat, *—NOYS* ... he was in the habit of eating, *—WLMS* ... with the converts from heathenism, *—TCNT.*

**but when they were come, he withdrew and separated himself, fearing them which were of the circumcision:** ... and hold aloof, for fear of offending, *—TCNT* ... out of sheer fear of what the Jews might think, *—PHLP.*

**13. And the other Jews dissembled likewise with him; insomuch that Barnabas also was carried away with their dissimulation:** ... Peter was two-faced, —SEB...the remaining Jews, —RTHM...carried out a similar piece of deception, and the force of their bad example was so great that even Barnabas, —PHLP... acted hypocritically, —ADAM... acted just as insincerely, —BECK...joined him in this pretense ... by their insincerity, —NORL ... was carried away by, —WORL ... led astray by their hypocrisy, —WLSN...influenced to join them in their pretense, —WLMS.

**2:12, 13.** God had prepared Peter to understand that such a distinction was not part of His plan. From his experience with the Samaritan Christians (Acts 8:14-17) and especially through the special training God had given him prior to sharing the gospel with Cornelius and his Gentile friends (Acts 10:1-11:18), Peter had learned God makes no distinction between Jew and Gentile. Peter used God's action to refute the attack of "false brethren" in Jerusalem. Table fellowship of Jewish and Gentile Christians was in keeping with their common faith in Christ.

But then some of the "false brethren" of verse 4 came to Antioch. They are described as "certain (men) from James." As Acts 15 underlines, James (Jesus' half brother) was the head of the church at Jerusalem. Here James is a term for the Jerusalem church. The earlier verses of this chapter show that these men were not official representatives or that James shared their narrow views (see also Acts 15:1-32). They are described as "them which were of the circumcision." This description singles out their view that both Jews and Gentiles had to be circumcised in order to be saved.

When Peter saw them and learned how determined they were to enforce their narrow and unchristian views, he became very much afraid. Whereas earlier, during this visit in Antioch, Peter had freely eaten with Gentile Christians, he now avoided having table fellowship with them. The Jewish Christians at Antioch were prompted to follow Peter's example and did not eat with their fellow Gentile Christians. This practice of joyful table fellowship between Jewish and Gentile Christians had been going on for a number of years. This reveals the seriousness of the situation and the gross offense it gave.

In time, Barnabas also became afraid of what these hard-nosed, mistaken Jewish Christians from Jerusalem might do and also avoided eating with his Gentile members. This was a crushing experience especially for the Gentile Christians as well as a very disquieting development for all.

**14. But when I saw that they walked not uprightly according to the truth of the gospel:** ... walked not correctly, —SAWR...they were not keeping to the straight path, —TCNT.

**I said unto Peter before [them] all, If thou, being a Jew, livest after the manner of Gentiles, and not as do the Jews, why compellest thou the Gentiles to live as do the Jews?:** ... in the presence of all, —WLSN ... in such a way that all the other Jews could hear what I said, —SEB...you, who are a Jew by nation, live like a foreigner and not like a Jew, how can you urge the foreigners to Judaize? —FNTN ... in front of everybody, —ADAM ... why on earth do you try to make Gentiles live like Jews? —PHLP ... hou constreynest thou hethen men to bicome, —WCLF ... adopt foreign ways of living ... to adopt Jewish ways? —TCNT ... to live like Jews, —ADAM...follow Jewish customs, —WEYM.

**2:14.** Called by the ascended Christ himself, Paul never forgot the great meaning of this call and its implications for his total life as Christ's apostle to the Gentiles. He never compromised the truth of the gospel and its tremendous possibilities for faith and life. This becomes very apparent in working through his 13 letters.

Paul's greatness and his firm refusal to compromise the truth of God's Word can be seen in his reactions to this very disturbing situation. By their actions, Peter, Barnabas, who had been sent to lead the church at Antioch, and the Jewish Christians were denying the cardinal truth of the gospel: salvation by grace alone. It was through this message that the Spirit had brought the Gentiles to faith, and now by the actions of Peter and the other Jewish Christians it was being grossly and openly denied.

In this tense scene Paul publicly rebuked Peter. (He used the name "Cephas," his Aramaic name, which Paul normally used in his letters to refer to Peter.) He singled out Peter who, in the eyes of those present, represented the mother church in Jerusalem. By his actions Peter was denying the cardinal truth of the gospel. The Greek word translated "walk uprightly" (*orthopodousin*) literally means "walking in a straight line" according to the truth of the gospel. Technically, as a Jew, by eating with Gentiles the bread and other food which had been dedicated through prayer to God, Peter had been living as a Gentile. Paul questioned how he could insist (by now separating himself from the Gentiles) that they had to live as Jews?

**15. We [who are] Jews by nature, and not sinners of the Gentiles:** ... We are natural Jews, and not sinners from among the heathen, —FNTN ... We Jews were not born non-Jewish or sinners, —SEB...by birth, —TCNT, —MNTG, —WEYM ... by race, —SAWR ... sinners from among the gentiles, —WORL.

**2:15.** Paul reminded Peter (and also all the Jewish Christians present) that by nature they were ethnically Jewish. By birth they were true descendants of Abraham, the father of God's covenant people (Genesis 12:1-3), and, as such, they were ethnically members of God's covenant people. The Gentiles were the exact opposite. Because of their ethnic origins, not being descended from Abraham, they were considered by the Jews to be habitual, chronic sinners. They were completely outside the covenant relationship with God. Therefore, they could not help but live in gross sin. They lived constantly under the eternal curse of God. This reflected the Jewish view of that day. Paul referred to this to demonstrate to the Jewish Christians the true meaning of their gross sinful act. Thereby they were denying that salvation is by grace alone.

**16. Knowing that a man is not justified by the works of the law, but by the faith of Jesus Christ, even we have believed in Jesus Christ:** ... being conscious that, −*BB* ... is not accepted as righteous, −*NOYS* ... not declared righteous, −*RTHM* ... but we know that a man is not made righteous by ritualism, except through a faith of, −*FNTN* ... a man is justified not by performing what the Law commands but by faith in, −*PHLP* ... a person is not made right with God by following the law. Committing oneself to Jesus Christ is what makes a person right with God, −*SEB* ... as the result of actions done in obedience to Law, −*TCNT* ... through obedience to Law that a man can be declared free from guilt, −*WEYM* ... but by simple trust in Christ, −*WLMS* ... we ourselves also have put our faith in Christ, −*MNTG.*

**that we might be justified by the faith of Christ, and not by the works of the law:** ... that we might stand right with God through dependence upon faith, −*TCNT* ... are justified by our faith and not by our obedience to the Law, −*PHLP* ... not by doing what the law commands, −*WLMS.*

**for by the works of the law shall no flesh be justified:** ... Observance of the Law, −*NORL* ... for, by the deeds of the law, −*MRDK* ... no one can achieve justification, −*PHLP.*

**17. But if, while we seek to be justified by Christ, we ourselves also are found sinners:** ... as we grasp the real truth, −*PHLP* ... to be declared righteous, −*RTHM.*

**[is] therefore Christ the minister of sin? God forbid:** ... does that mean that Christ makes us sinners? −*PHLP* ... would that make Christ an agent of sin? Certainly not, −*TCNT* ... does that make Christ a party to our sin? −*WLMS* ... By no means, −*CNFT* ... Absolutely not! −*NORL.*

**2:16, 17.** Paul reminded all present that no one, Jew or Gentile, can be justified by the works of the Law, i.e., by seeking to earn salvation through works. In so doing, he echoed the truth of Psalm 143:2: "And enter not into judgment with thy servant: for in thy sight shall no man living be justified."

Paul used the verb *justify* three times in verse 16. He used it in the legal sense of "being declared just and righteous." This verb is passive in this verse. It is God alone who can declare one to be righteous, but only if the requirements of God's justice and righteousness have been fully met. Man's sinful nature causes him to commit sins, so he cannot consider himself righteous before God. By nature all, both Jews and Gentiles, are under God's righteous wrath.

To Peter and the Jewish Christians Paul emphatically stated that no one can justify himself by avoiding table fellowship with Gentiles and meeting other requirements of the Law. Both Jews and Gentiles are sinful, regardless of ethnic origins, and hence are under God's judgment. Only by faith in Christ and His atoning sacrifice can anyone be saved. This included also those who by birth considered themselves to be ethnically members of God's covenant people and descendants of Abraham. Paul stressed that regarding salvation there are no privileged (Jews) or underprivileged (Gentiles) people. All by nature are under God's wrath as Paul emphasized also in his other letters, for example, Romans 3:23-26 and Ephesians 2. He restated this fact again in the closing words of this verse to stress the decisive nature of grace alone for man's salvation.

Paul asked a very important question to emphasize what he had said. The actions of Peter, Barnabas, and the Jewish Christians implied that they wanted to be righteous by what they did. Paul in essence said that by their action of not eating with the Gentile Christians, they placed themselves again under the curse of the Law. *Hamartia* ("sin") is used here in its proper meaning of conduct which is in violation of true righteousness.

Paul answered with an emphatic "God forbid!" (*mē genoito*). In Galatians Paul used this emphatic expression twice, once here and again in 3:21. In this very dramatic manner, Paul forcefully demonstrated the true meaning and implication of their sinful action.

The expression "God forbid" in the New Testament is used almost exclusively by Paul. The single non-Pauline use is that of Luke 20:16 in the reaction of members of the Jewish Council to the meaning of Jesus' Parable of the Dishonest Lessees of the Vineyard (Luke 20:9-16; see also Isaiah 5). They understood that God would take the covenant relationship away from them and give it to the Gentiles.

**18. For if I build again the things which I destroyed, I make myself a transgressor:** ... if I reconstruct, −*CNFT* ... if I rebuild those ... I constitute Myself, −*WLSN* ... if, what things I pulled down,

*—RTHM* . . . the things I had demolished, *—MRDK* . . . I proved myself to have done wrong, *—TCNT* . . . a prevaricator, *—DOUY.*

**2:18.** To impress on his Jewish hearers the seriousness of what they had done, Paul made another telling statement. He reminded them that when they had come to faith, they had destroyed the basis of their former hope of salvation, namely, that of works. They had been led to see and confess that salvation is only by grace through faith in Christ. By their action in avoiding eating with the Gentile Christians, Peter, Barnabas, and the Jewish Christians had actually denied the way of grace and returned to that of works. That which they had declared invalid when they came to faith, they now by their action declared to be the only way of salvation. Hence, they had become transgressors. Transgression implies a law transgressed (Romans 4:15; 5:13). And no one can keep the Law.

**19. For I through the law am dead to the law, that I might live unto God:** . . . I am dead to the Law's demands so that I may live for God, *—PHLP.*

**20. I am crucified with Christ: nevertheless I live; yet not I:** . . . I am nailed to the cross, *—DOUY* . . . I died on the cross with Christ, *—PHLP.*

**but Christ liveth in me: and the life which I now live in the flesh I live by the faith of the Son of God, who loved me, and gave himself for me:** . . . as for my present earthly life, *—TCNT* . . . The bodily life I now live, I live believing in . . . who loved me and sacrificed himself, *—PHLP.*

**21. I do not frustrate the grace of God: for if righteousness [come] by the law, then Christ is dead in vain:** . . . I cast not away, *—DOUY* . . . I do not abrogate, *—GNVA* . . . I despyse not, *—CRNM* . . . I do not cast away, *—CNFT* . . . I refuse to stultify the grace, *—PHLP* . . . I refuse to ignore, *—NORL* . . . I am not setting aside the favour of God . . . Christ needlessly died, *—RTHM* . . . I refuse to set aside the mercy of God . . . then Christ died for nothing! *—TCNT* . . . died for nought, *—PNIN, —ASV* . . . died unnecessarily, *—WLSN* . . . died without cause, *—WCLF* . . . died needlessly! *—WORL.*

**2:19-21.** Paul's words take on added meaning in view of the self-description he gave in Philippians 3:4-11. He, the proud Pharisee who considered himself to be totally blameless (*amemptos*) before God, realized when the exalted Christ appeared to him on the Damascus Road that his entire way of life and self-estimation was worthless. In fact, in Philippians 3:8 he used a very strong Greek word, *skubala*, properly translated "dung," "sewage." Through Christ's action, so beautifully and forcefully stated in Philippians 3:9-11, Paul died to the way of works of the Law, and empowered by the Spirit (Titus 3:4-8), began to live his life in grace to God.

Paul went on to say in one verse what he developed in much greater detail in Romans 3-8. In so doing he referred to a form of execution which was well known to his readers, namely, crucifixion. This was a very common form of execution in the Roman world, usually reserved for slaves and those of the lower classes of society. However, as history records, under certain circumstances a Roman citizen too could be, and was, crucified. Every larger town, such as the Galatian Antioch and Iconium, had its place of execution at a well-traveled place outside the town walls. The upright beam of the cross was always left in place, waiting for the next victim who would carry the crossbeam to the place of his execution.

Paul stressed that when Christ died on the cross, he was crucified with Him. When Christ rose from the dead, he rose with Him. Hence, it was not his life he lived, but that of Christ who lived in him—a truth which he so well restated in Romans 6:1-11. And so the life he now lived as a human being was lived by faith through the Spirit's work, a faith centered in Christ who gave himself for Paul and for all mankind (Romans 6 and 8).

In his notes on 2:20 the great expositor C.I. Scofield presented a basic truth: "Christianity is the outliving of an indwelling Christ" (*The Scofield Reference Bible*). Once a believer has captured this truth, he realizes that all he does must present a proper view of the Son of God reaching the world through him.

Paul closed with the words, "I do not frustrate the grace of God." The Greek word translated "frustrate" (*athetō*) actually means "make null and void." The action of Peter, Barnabas, and the other Jewish Christians had in fact nullified the true meaning of God's grace.

Paul had been accused of not sharing the full dimensions of the gospel by not carefully stressing that all had to live as Jews. And so Paul restated what this in actuality meant, namely, that if salvation is by works, then Christ had died in vain. Grace was nonexistent.

## Chapter 3

**1. O foolish Galatians, who hath bewitched you, that ye should not obey the truth:** . . . O senseless, *—DOUY* . . . O vnwitti galathianes, *—WCLF* . . . O Thoughtless Galatians, *—WLSN, —RTHM* . . . you dear idiots . . . who has been casting a spell over you? *—PHLP* . . . You let someone trick you, *—EVRD* . . . who has been fascinating you, *—TCNT.*

**before whose eyes Jesus Christ hath been evidently set forth, crucified among you?:** . . . who saw Jesus Christ the crucified so plainly, *—PHLP* . . . were told very clearly about the death of

Jesus, —EVRD . . . was previously represented as having been crucified, —WLSN . . . was openly set forth, —PNIN, —RTHM, —ASV, —WORL . . . was described before the eyes, —TNDL . . . was described in your sight, —GNVA . . . was depicted as crucified? —TCNT . . . has been depicted crucified? —CNFT . . . was portrayed among you, —PNT . . . clearly pictured before your eyes as the Crucified One? —NORL.

**3:1.** Chapters 3 and 4 stress the certainty of salvation by grace alone. Paul now shifted the tone of his letter to exclaim, "O foolish Galatians!" The Greek word translated "foolish" (*anoētoi*) refers to those who knew better but failed to use what they knew.

Paul went on to ask, "Who hath bewitched you?" or, "Who has confused, hypnotized you?" In the second part of this verse, Paul reminded the Galatians that he and Barnabas had dramatically stressed the significance of Christ's crucifixion in God's plan of salvation by grace alone.

**2. This only would I learn of you, Received ye the Spirit by the works of the law, or by the hearing of faith?:** . . . that I want to find out from you . . . or to your having listened with faith? —TCNT . . . by the dedes of the lawe, or by the preachynge of the fayth? —CRNM.

**3. Are ye so foolish? having begun in the Spirit, are ye now made perfect by the flesh?:** . . . Are ye so thoughtless? —WSLY . . . so void of understanding? —SCLT . . . beginning with what is spiritual, —TCNT . . . now you vvil be consummate with the flesh? —RHEM.

**4. Have ye suffered so many things in vain? if [it be] yet in vain:** . . . if indeed it was really to no purpose! —TCNT . . . it is for nothing, —WLSN.

**5. He therefore that ministereth to you the Spirit, and worketh miracles among you, [doeth he it] by the works of the law, or by the hearing of faith?:** . . . Who therefore supplieth you, —PNIN . . . and endows you with, —TCNT . . . he then who imparteth, —SCLT . . . worketh mighty works in you, —ALFD . . . that imparts to you . . . and exercises miraculous powers . . . by the doctrine of faith? —SAWR.

**3:2-5.** Paul went on to ask in a dramatic manner (following the Greek sentence structure), "This only would I learn of you, received ye the Spirit by the works of the law, or by the hearing of faith?" Paul repeated the two phrases "works of the law" and "hearing of faith" again and again in this chapter to emphasize the certainty of salvation by grace through faith alone.

In Romans 10:17 Paul stated: "Faith cometh by hearing, and hearing by the word of God." Titus 3:4-8 carefully stresses the role of the Holy Spirit in bringing people to faith. And this fact Paul stressed again and again.

Again he asked, "Are ye so foolish?" And then continued, "Having begun in the Spirit, are ye

now made perfect by (*epiteleisthe*, 'finishing in') the flesh?" Note the decisive tenses he used. He continued, "Have ye suffered so many things in vain?" Acts 13 and 14 shed some light on this question. Acts 14:2-5 indicates that Jews from Antioch stirred up people against the Christians in Iconium. Whether those in Antioch and Lystra suffered we are not specifically told.

Paul closed verse 4 with "if it be yet in vain." In other words, there was still hope! And then he restated in essence what he said earlier in verse 2. In verse 5 he again used a very strong word translated "worketh" (*energōn*). Acts 14:3 records that God used Paul and Barnabas to work "signs and wonders." Acts 14:8-10 records the healing of the man lame from birth, and verse 20 tells how Paul recovered after being stoned and left for dead.

**6. Even as Abraham believed God, and it was accounted to him for righteousness:** . . . and that was regarded by, —TCNT . . . and it was credited to him, —CNFT . . . and it was ascribed to him, —GNVA.

**3:6.** This verse goes back to Genesis 15:6. Abraham had obeyed God's gracious call (Genesis 12:1) and had led his clan to Mamre, just north of Hebron, in the land of Canaan. Some years had gone by. God still had not given him and his aged wife Sarah a son as He had promised in Genesis 12:1-3. When God appeared to him in a vision, Abraham, in indirect Middle Eastern fashion, reminded God that He had failed to keep His promise (Genesis 15:2, 3). God took him outside and asked him to count the stars in the heavens and told him, "So shall thy seed be!" (Genesis 15:5). Abraham's response was that he "believed God, and it was accounted to him for righteousness." Paul here quoted Genesis 15:6.

Humanly speaking, at the advanced age of Sarah, God's promise to give them a son seemed impossible. However, Abraham believed that God could and would keep His promise. This was fulfilled when Abraham was 100 and Sarah was 90 years old (Genesis 21).

The more important fulfillment of God's promises lay well in the future. The most important was that of sending the Seed, the Saviour. This Paul emphasized in the verses which follow. The Galatians had the privilege of living in the age when God's promises of the Saviour had been fulfilled.

**7. Know ye therefore that they which are of faith, the same are the children of Abraham:** . . . Know you, certainly, —WLSN . . . Ye perceive, then, —RTHM...those whose lives are based on faith, —TCNT...are the real sons of, —CNFT.

**3:7.** Paul used a very strong imperative ("Know!") to remind the Galatians that all who believe in the certainty of God's promises are true descendants of Abraham, regardless of their ethnic origins.

The Greek uses the term *sons* (*huioi*) translated as "children." The term *son* had a special legal meaning in the thought pattern of that day. A son was legally an heir, and through him the family line continued. Paul used the term here in the nongender sense; this is reflected in the translation of "children." He did the same in Romans 8:14-17.

**8. And the scripture, foreseeing that God would justify the heathen through faith, preached before the gospel unto Abraham, [saying], In thee shall all nations be blessed:**...because God knew beforehand, —MRDK...anticipating God's justification, —MNTG...that God would make the heathen righteous by means of a faith promised from the first, —FNTN...announced the good news beforehand, —ADAM...preached the gospel beforehand, —PNT...really proclaimed the Gospel centuries ago in the words spoken to Abraham, —PHLP...all the heathen shall be blessed, —TCNT.

**9. So then they which be of faith are blessed with faithful Abraham:**...All people who believe are blessed in the same way that Abraham was blessed for his faith, —FNTN...All men of faith share the blessing of Abraham, —PHLP...blessed as partners with trusting Abraham, —WLMS...with believing Abraham, —MRDK...with the faith of Abraham, —FNTN...Abraham who had faith, —ADAM.

**3:8, 9.** In verse 8 Paul made a very important statement. He said that Scripture foresaw God's plan of salvation. Second Timothy 3:16 and 2 Peter 1:20, 21 carefully state that the Scriptures are the inspired Word of God. This Paul firmly believed. Hence, he emphasized that God in the Scriptures foretold His gracious plan of salvation.

God promised Abraham at the time of his call that in him would "all families of the earth be blessed" (Genesis 12:3). In Genesis 18:18 and 22:18 the phrase "all the nations of the earth" is used. And Paul added a very important statement. To experience such a spiritual blessing, it is necessary to believe in the certain promises of God, just as Abraham did. Physical ancestry from the line of Abraham means nothing spiritually. By the Spirit working through the Word, to believe as Abraham did is all important for salvation.

**10. For as many as are of the works of the law are under the curse:**...Now, all who depend on works, —ADAM...For whoever are dependent on a law of rituals, —FNTN...but people who depend on following the law to make them right are under condemnation, —FNTN.

**for it is written, Cursed [is] every one that continueth not in all things which are written in the book of the law to do them:**...A person must do everything which is written in the book, —FNTN...every one who does not abide by all, —TCNT...all who do not continue in all the writings of the book, —FNTN...in the scroll of the law, —RTHM...to perform them, —CNFT...to fulfyll them, —CRNM...Everyone, however, who is involved in trying to keep the Law's demands falls under a curse, —PHLP.

**3:10.** To emphasize what he had said, Paul restated it in the negative. In 2:16 he used the phrase "works of the law" three times. Here he used it again to stress that what the Judaizers were saying as necessary for salvation would result in being eternally under God's curse, resulting in eternal damnation.

To undergird what he said, he quoted from Deuteronomy 27:26. These words were spoken by Moses to Israel at Abel-Shittim east of the Jordan shortly before his death on Mount Nebo. They were carried out when Israel renewed its covenant with God at Mount Ebal and Mount Gerizim (Joshua 8:30-35).

Moses had been instructed that six tribes were to stand on Mount Gerizim, the Mount of Blessing, and six on Mount Ebal, the Mount of Cursing. The Levites were to recite the 12 curses found in Deuteronomy 27:15-26. After each curse the people were to respond with "Amen." The curses emphasized pagan idolatry and gross immorality which God's covenant people were to avoid. Whereas the first 11 curses placed a ban on specific acts of disobedience, the 12th was more comprehensive, especially as found in the Septuagint. To make sure there could be no misunderstanding, Paul changed the reading "of this law" to "which are written in the book of the law." The term "book of the law" refers to the five books of Moses, which in the Hebrew are known as *Torah*. *Torah* means "revelation, instruction." It is important to remember that sometimes this term should be understood this way rather than "law," also in the New Testament. Sometimes it has reference to the Pentateuch, and it is also sometimes used as a term for the entire Old Testament Scriptures.

**11. But that no man is justified by the law in the sight of God, [it is] evident:**...none in law, —FNTN...no one stands right with God, —TCNT...is brought into right standing with God, —WLMS...It is made still plainer that no one is justified...by obeying the Law, —PHLP...it is manifest, —RHEM...is clear, —ADAM.

**for, The just shall live by faith:**...The Scriptures say, The person who is right with God by faith will live forever, —SEB . . . because the just person, —ADAM . . . The righteous, —PNIN, —FNTN, —PHLP.

**12. And the law is not of faith: but, The man that doeth them shall live in them:** . . . is not based on faith, —TCNT . . . has nothing to do with faith, —MNTG . . . is not a matter of faith, —PHLP . . . does not require faith, —ADAM . . . Instead, the law says, A person who wants to find life by following these things must do the things the law says, —SEB . . . the ritual did not come from faith; on the contrary, the performer of them must live, —FNTN.

**13. Christ hath redeemed us from the curse of the law, being made a curse for us: for it is written, Cursed [is] every one that hangeth on a tree:** . . . ransomed us, —TCNT . . . purchased us . . . for is it written: . . . cursed beyond measure, —FNTN . . . The law put us under condemnation, but Christ took that condemnation away. He changed places with us, —SEB . . . becoming in our behalf a curse, —RTHM . . . hanged on a beam of wood, —NOYS.

**14. That the blessing of Abraham might come on the Gentiles through Jesus Christ:** . . . Christ did this, so that God's promised blessing . . . could be given to all people, —SEB . . . might come to, —FNTN . . . might be realized by the Gentiles, —ADAM . . . might be extended to the heathen, —TCNT.

**that we might receive the promise of the Spirit through faith:** . . . the Annunciation of the Spirit, —WLSN . . . might become available to us all, —PHLP.

**3:11-14.** Everyone who seeks to earn salvation by his works is under God's curse, but those who believe in God's promises are declared righteous by Him. Paul quoted from Habakkuk 2:4: "The just shall live by his faith." Habakkuk served as God's prophet after the tragic death of King Josiah at Megiddo in the battle against Pharaoh-nechoh II of Egypt in 609 B.C., and the latter's defeat in 605 B.C. by Nebuchadnezzar of Babylonia. Judah then became a vassal state of Nebuchadnezzar (2 Kings 23 and 24). In 587 B.C. Jerusalem was destroyed and the people of Judah were taken into exile in Babylonia. Please note that even though there is some debate on this, possibly the better date for Jerusalem's destruction is 587 B.C.

In view of what the people of Judah viewed as stark tragedy, the emphasis of Habakkuk may be described as asking how God can permit evil so good may come out of it. God's answer is that this can only be understood from the vantage point of trusting in God and His righteous dealings. The key is to remember the crucial words: "The just shall live by faith," not by works.

Paul emphasized that believers can be just and righteous in God's sight only through the redemptive work of Christ. He quoted Deuteronomy 21:22, 23 which speaks of the execution of one guilty of a capital offense. He was first executed and then his dead body was hung up for all to see. From two of the Dead Sea Scrolls, the Nahum

Pesher (4QpHab, fragments 3 and 4, column 1, lines 5-8) and the Temple Scroll (column 64, lines 6-13), we know that by the Second Century B.C., anyone executed for certain religious crimes by crucifixion was understood to be under God's curse as found in Deuteronomy 21:22, 23. Paul's words reflected this understanding.

Paul noted in 1 Corinthians 2:2 that he was determined "not to know any thing among you, save Jesus Christ, and him crucified." In 1 Corinthians 1:23 he stated that for Jews, as those who considered themselves to be the religious elite, Christ's crucifixion was a "stumblingblock" (*skandalon*). For Greeks, as the cultured elite, it was "foolishness" or nonsense (*mōrian*). But in the next verse Paul stated, to those who are called, both Jews and Gentiles, "Christ is the power of God, and the wisdom of God" (1 Corinthians 1:24).

In verse 14 Paul concluded this part of his decisive argument. It is totally through Christ's redemptive work as a fulfillment of God's promise to Abraham that Gentiles will also be saved through faith in His atoning merit.

Paul ended this verse with the words: "That we might receive the promise of the Spirit through faith." Luke 24:49 records some of Jesus' final words to His disciples, shortly before His ascension. He reminded His disciples that He would send them "the promise of my Father." In Acts 1:4 Jesus told His disciples to remain in Jerusalem and "wait for the promise of the Father."

These words also recall words Jesus spoke to His disciples (John 14-17) which reveal the role of the Holy Spirit as Christ's Spirit, whom the Father would send in Jesus' name (John 14:26). The verbs which Jesus used in His description of the ongoing work of the Spirit are very important: teach and remind (John 14:26); tell the truth about Him (John 15:26); convince (John 16:8); lead, speak what He hears and tell what is coming, and glorify Christ (John 16:13, 14).

Crucial in Paul's argument is the fact that through the Spirit's work, Gentiles also are led to believe in the certainty of salvation by grace alone.

**15. Brethren, I speak after the manner of men:** . . . Let me take an illustration, Brothers, from daily life, —TCNT . . . Let me give you an everyday illustration, —PHLP . . . I speak humanly, —FNTN . . . in human fashion, —RTHM . . . according to what is practised among men, —NOYS . . . by an example from human relationships, —ADAM.

**Though [it be] but a man's covenant, yet [if it be] confirmed, no man disannulled, or addeth thereto:** . . . a man has made his will, —NORL . . . even a testament made by a man, —FNTN . . . Even a human contract, —WLMS . . . once it has been ratified, —ADAM . . . no one sets aside, —RTHM . . . no man doth abrogate it, —GNVA...no one setteth aside, or changeth any thing in it, —MRDK...or alters, —CNFT...or superadds conditions, —WLSN...or adds conditions to it, —TCNT...when it is established, —SAWR.

**3:15.** To emphasize what he has said before, Paul used a variety of illustrations, with special reference to life and thought patterns so intimately a part of life in Galatia.

The first illustration is that of a last will and testament, using the Greek word *diathēkē*, in its secular meaning. This was an important word in the world of that time. It was as important then for one to properly draw up such a document as it is today, to make sure that the inheritance would be passed on as desired. Paul also used a number of other legal terms which at that time were also an intimate part of dealing with such a document. He said that "if it be confirmed" ("ratified") in the proper manner, "no man disannulleth," that is, sets it aside and annuls it, or "addeth thereto," that is, adds a codicil. Such a will could be activated only when the testator's death was registered as Hebrews 9:16, 17 states. And the terms of the will had to be carried out exactly as stated in the document.

**16. Now to Abraham and his seed were the promises made. He saith not, And to seeds, as of many; but as of one, And to thy seed, which is Christ:** ... Note in passing that the scripture says not "seeds" but uses the singular "seed," meaning Christ, —PHLP...and to his heir, —FNTN... "and to your descendant," that is, Christ, —WLMS.

**3:16.** Paul used this illustration because a last will involves an inheritance as he now emphasized. God's promise was made to Abraham and his seed. To make certain there was no misunderstanding, "He saith not, And to seeds, as of many; but as of one, And to thy seed, which is Christ." The Greek word for "which" (*hos*) is exclusive; it can only refer to "seed" in the singular in this sentence. Paul's use of the term "seed" recalled God's words to Abraham in Genesis 22:18: "And in *thy seed* shall all the nations of the earth be blessed." This came through the redemptive work of Jesus Christ, the woman's Seed whose heel was bruised but who crushed the head of the Evil One by His crucifixion and His descent into hell (Genesis 3:15; 1 Peter 3:18, 19).

**17. And this I say, [that] the covenant, that was confirmed before of God in Christ:** ... Therefore, I argue, —NORL . . . And I assert this, —FNTN . . . Now this is what I am trying to say, —ADAM . . . Now this I affirm . . . previously ratified by God, —WLSN . . . My point is this: . . . An agreement already confirmed, —TCNT...already ratified by God, —ALFD.

**the law, which was four hundred and thirty years after, cannot disannul, that it should make the promise of none effect:** ... which came into existence...cannot render null...and thus rob the promise of its value, —PHLP...does not invalidate, —WORL...to be set aside, —TCNT...so as to cancel, —WLMS...to invalidate the promise, —WLSN...cannot abrogate the covenant previously established by God, —SAWR...maketh not void to frustrate the promise, —RHEM...so as to cancel the promise in it, —NORL.

**18. For if the inheritance [be] of the law, [it is] no more of promise: but God gave [it] to Abraham by promise:** ... For if our inheritance depends on the law, —WLMS...if the receiving of the promised blessing were not made...that would amount to a cancellation of the original, —PHLP...it ceaseth to be the consequence of the promise, —NOYS...so graciously bestowed, —WLMS.

**3:17, 18.** The term *diathēkē* is used in the Greek secular meaning of "last will and testament" only three times in the New Testament (Galatians 3:15; Hebrews 9:16, 17). Otherwise it is always used in the meaning of God's covenant of grace as a translation of the Old Testament Hebrew term *berîth*. In seeking to find a Greek word for the Hebrew *berîth*, the translators of the Hebrew Old Testament into Greek found this term to be the nearest in meaning to that of the Hebrew term.

Paul noted that God made His covenant of grace with Abraham 430 years before He formally received Abraham's descendants in covenant relationship at Mount Sinai (Exodus 19). God carefully emphasizes (especially in Exodus 19:4; 20:2; and Deuteronomy 7:6-10) that this was a tremendous grace event. Unfortunately as a result of their unfaithfulness before the Exile and the consequence of this traumatic experience, the Jews had made this grace event into a law event.

Important for Paul's argument is the fact that when God made His covenant of grace with Abraham, he was still an uncircumcised Gentile. In fact, it would be 24 years later that Abraham and all male members of his clan were circumcised (Genesis 17:23-27). This covenant was not annulled by the much later event at Sinai which the Jews had made into law.

In verse 18 Paul restated this important fact. They were the heirs of the promise of grace God had made to Abraham. As he had received the promise strictly in grace, the Galatians as his spiritual heirs had received it also in grace. The claim of the Judaizers that all had to be circumcised and live as Jews was totally without any scriptural basis. Their "gospel" was false. It had not come from

God. The gospel Paul had shared with them was the *true* gospel, the eternal truth.

**19. Wherefore then [serveth] the law?:** ... What ... was the use of, —*TCNT* ... To what end then was the Law? —*NOYS* ... To what purpose, then, —*MNTG* ... What then was the design of the Law? —*SCLT* ... Why then the Law? —*WLSN* ... Where then lies the point of the Law? —*PHLP.*

**It was added because of transgressions, till the seed should come to whom the promise was made:** ... It was a later addition, —*TCNT* ... It was enacted on account of, —*CNFT* ... It was to operate till, —*NORL* ... until the "Offspring" should come, —*MNTG* ... until the descendant to whom the promise was made should come, —*WLMS.*

**[and it was] ordained by angels in the hand of a mediator:** ... having been arranged through, —*WORL* ... having been instituted, —*WLSN* ... was inaugurated in the presence of, —*PHLP* ... being appointed by angels, —*SAWR.*

**20. Now a mediator is not [a mediator] of one, but God is one:** ... an intermediary between a single individual cannot be, —*FNTN* ... isn't needed when there is only one party, —*ADAM* ... The very fact that there was an intermediary is enough to show that this was not the fulfilling of the promise, —*PHLP* ... implies more than one person, —*MNTG* ... but God is only one, —*TCNT.*

**3:19, 20.** Paul then asked a very important question: "Why, then was the Law given? What purpose does it serve?" This question flows naturally from the argument of the preceding verses. And his answer: "Because (for the sake) of transgressions it was added" (Greek). The Greek word translated "transgressions" (*parabaseōn*) means that which happens when a law is made. Literally it means a law or a norm which is overstepped. So a sign reading "Keep off the grass" often results in the reaction of willfully walking on the grass. As Paul said in Romans 4:15, "Where no law is, there is no transgression." When a sinner meets the Law, he reacts by transgressing it, and this results in committing more sins.

To say this in another way: Prod a sleeping lion with a stick, and it at once reacts with anger. The stick does not make the lion a wild beast. That it already is. Prodding the lion merely results in *showing* what the lion truly is. So the Law exposes the innate sinfulness of man. Paul did not say "because of sin," since transgression is a violation of explicit law and results in the recognition of the sinfulness of such violation. In Romans 7:7 Paul said: "I had not known sin, but by the law: for I had not known lust, except the law had said, Thou shalt not covet." Transgression results in multiplying sin.

Paul continued: "Till the seed should come to whom the promise was made." The "seed" is

patently the same as in verse 16, namely, *the Seed* of Abraham, who is Jesus Christ. This thought is further developed in verses 23-25.

The last part of verse 19 seems to reflect a Jewish thought pattern. A careful reading of the Sinai event as described in Exodus and reflected in other parts of the Old Testament does not shed direct light on this sentence. Deuteronomy 33:2 has been suggested as the source of the role of angels. A close translation of the Hebrew text results in: "He came from His holy myriads; from His right hand came a fiery law for them."

The Hebrew phrase for "a fiery law" is *'ēshdat,* the meaning of this is uncertain. The Septuagint translates the Hebrew for "fiery law" as "at His right hand were angels with Him." This reading seems to be reflected in Stephen's comment: "Who have received the law by the disposition of angels" (Acts 7:53) and in Hebrews 2:2: "For if the word spoken by angels was steadfast. . . ." Josephus records Herod as saying: "We have learned the noblest of all our doctrines and the holiest of all laws through angels sent from God" (*Antiquities of the Jews,* 15:136).

The role of a mediator is clarified in verse 20. A mediator involves at least two parties. Paul emphatically said that God is *one.* God acted unilaterally for himself when He made His covenant of grace with Abraham, and this provides God's way of salvation for all, both Jew and Gentile alike.

**21. [Is] the law then against the promises of God? God forbid:** ... Does the Law, then, frustrate the promises, —*NORL* ... Is the Law then to be looked upon as a contradiction of the promise? —*PHLP* ... then opposed to, —*MNTG* ... contrary to, —*CNFT* ... in opposition to, —*TCNT* ... Be it not so, —*PNIN* ... Of course not! —*ADAM.*

**for if there had been a law given which could have given life, verily righteousness should have been by the law:** ... was able to make alive, —*WLSN* ... was able to impart life, —*WLMS* ... would have actually existed through Law, —*TCNT* ... then no doute ryghtewesnes, —*CRNM* ... then surely justification would have been, —*ADAM.*

**22. But the scripture hath concluded all under sin, that the promise by faith of Jesus Christ might be given to them that believe:** ... the Law makes all men guilty of sin, —*NORL* ... pictures all mankind as prisoners of sin, —*WLMS* ... locks up everybody under sins so that, —*ADAM* ... to those having faith, —*RTHM.*

**3:21, 22.** Paul went on to state that the Law cannot give life; it merely results in exposing the inborn sinfulness of man and his transgressions, going back to man's fall into sin (Genesis 3; Romans 3:23; 5:12). The Scriptures record both man's sin and God's promise of the woman's Seed, whom He would send to secure salvation for all, whether

Jew or Gentile. But only those who believe in this promise receive it as God's gift.

**23. But before faith came, we were kept under the law:** ... were we being guarded, –RTHM ... were kept in custody, –SCLT ... under restraints, –TCNT ... we were guarded under Law, –WLSN, –ADAM ... we were perpetual prisoners under the Law, –MNTG ... kept under the rule of the Law, –NORL.

**shut up unto the faith which should afterwards be revealed:** ... being locked up, –ADAM ... we were all imprisoned under ... with our only hope of deliverance the faith that was to be shown to us, –PHLP ... in preparation for the Faith, –TCNT, –WLMS ... which shuld afterwarde be declared, –TNDL.

**24. Wherefore the law was our schoolmaster [to bring us] unto Christ, that we might be justified by faith:** ... is become our tutor, –PNIN ... has become our child-conductor unto Christ, –RTHM ... was a monitor for us, –MRDK ... was like a strict governess in charge of us until we went to the school of Christ and learned to be justified, –PHLP ... has proved a guide to lead us ... we may stand right with God, –TCNT.

**25. But after that faith is come, we are no longer under a schoolmaster:** ... Once we had that faith we were completely free from the governess's authority, –PHLP ... no longer under a guardian, –ADAM ... no longer under the leader of our childhood, –FNTN.

**3:23-25.** When Paul said "before faith came," he meant "before the Seed came" (by Christ). So from the time of Sinai until Christ's actual coming, Christ was the One promised to come sometime in the indefinite future. The faith of those living in the Old Testament era was in the certainty that God would keep His gracious promises. The Law, as it were, kept man in confinement until God's promises were fulfilled in Christ.

To drive home this point, Paul used an illustration well known to his readers. The Greek term *paidagōgos*, translated "schoolmaster" or "guardian-trainer," was a slave, one who was put in total charge of his owner's son. This began when the boy was old enough to leave the care of his nurse. The slave-attendant's duty was to teach the boy good manners and even punish him, if necessary. He walked him to school, carrying his satchel. A special place in the school was reserved for such slave-attendants, where they waited until the school day ended. Then the slave-attendant took the boy home, quizzed him on what he was to have learned, had him recite his memory work, and the like. The son was under the total care of such an attendant from about the age of 6 to 16. Crucial for the boy and his future was the character and previous training of the attendant since the boy would reflect in life the training the slave-attendant gave him.

Thus the Law's role was to bring us to Christ, to teach us that by the Law salvation is impossible. Keeping the Law perfectly in accordance with God's will is impossible for man. The history of God's covenant people as recorded in the Old Testament tragically emphasizes this fact.

Already, before Sinai, they had demonstrated their sinfulness. When Pharaoh's military might came close to them at the Red Sea, they chided Moses. At Marah they grumbled because the water was bitter. They murmured bitterly against God in the Wilderness of Sin over food, and some ignored God's instructions with reference to the manna. During this time Moses also had to act as the mediator in disputes of which there were so many in Israel.

Soon after the solemn covenant event at Mount Sinai, Israel worshiped the golden calf and fell into gross immorality. At Kadesh-Barnea they believed the 10 spies who doubted they could defeat the peoples living in the land of Canaan, even though God had promised to give them the land. Many joined Korah, Dathan, and Abiram in their rebellion against God.

Israel failed to destroy all the inhabitants in the land of Canaan, and this resulted in unfaithfulness to God, as the Book of Judges faithfully records. Again and again God had to punish them to call them back to Him.

The history of the divided kingdoms shows their unfaithfulness. During the reigns of Omri and Ahab the Northern Kingdom fell into the immoral worship of the Canaanite fertility gods of Baal and Asherah. In time God took many of them into exile and later also the Southern Kingdom. After the return from exile, God's people again became unfaithful to Him. He had to send them men such as Nehemiah, Ezra, Haggai, Zechariah, and Malachi to seek to bring them back. The intertestamental history of the Jews reveals the same tragic fact.

**26. For ye are all the children of God by faith in Christ Jesus:** ... You are all God's sons through, –ADAM ... now that you have faith, –PHLP.

**27. For as many of you as have been baptized into Christ have put on Christ:** ... For all ye that are baptised, –TNDL ... as were immersed ... were clothed with, –WLSN ... clothed yourselves with, –TCNT.

**3:26, 27.** But now Christ had come. In Him God's promises through the centuries were fulfilled. Through His redemptive work the fence (partition) between Jew and Gentile had been removed. Christ's role as the suffering, obedient, and then victorious Servant guaranteed the certainty of salvation by grace alone for all. This blessing is experienced by all who through the Spirit's work believe in Him.

To emphasize this very important fact, Paul used an example from the life experience of the Galatians. Only a Roman citizen had the right to wear the garment of his special status, the toga. This white woolen garment with its purple stripe(s) was a cherished symbol of his exalted status. When the son of a Roman citizen became of age, he could exercise his right and put on the toga which symbolized his high status. So, when a person comes to faith, "he puts on Christ."

**28. There is neither Jew nor Greek, there is neither bond nor free, there is neither male nor female:** . . . there is neither servant, –SAWR . . . neither slave, –ADAM . . . nor one a slave, –FNTN.

**for ye are all one in Christ Jesus:** . . . All distinctions between . . . have vanished, –TCNT . . . for you all are united in Christ, –FNTN.

**29. And if ye [be] Christ's, then are ye Abraham's seed, and heirs according to the promise:** . . . if you belong to, –WLSN . . . ye are, consequently, Abraham's seed, –WORL . . . you are real descendants, –WLMS . . . then you are the descendants of Abraham, –MNTG . . . you are of Abraham's race, inheritors by the promise, –FNTN . . . sharers in the inheritance, –TCNT . . . in keeping with the promise, –ADAM.

**3:28, 29.** Paul closed this part of his argument with a very important statement. When he said, "There is neither Jew nor Greek," he made a very telling point. In the Jewish view, they of all people were the religious elite. They and they alone knew the true God and were His covenant people. All others were under God's curse. From the viewpoint of the Greeks, only those who were ethnically Greeks were the culturally elite. The rest were barbarians.

Paul went on to say "neither bond (slave) nor free." The Galatians understood the great difference of both the social and legal status of those who were either slaves or free. Paul continued, "neither male nor female." The Septuagint in Genesis 1:27 uses the same words which Paul used, when it says, "male and female created he them." It is of crucial importance that Paul here speaks of the universality of salvation. By nature all, regardless of gender, are under the curse of sin. Through Christ's redemptive work all who believe enjoy the blessings of grace.

Verse 29 restates and summarizes what Paul has said in this chapter. All who are in Christ are spiritually Abraham's descendants and hence are heirs with him of the blessings God promised him,

namely, salvation by grace alone, the gospel which Paul had faithfully shared with the Galatians.

## Chapter 4

**1. Now I say, [That] the heir, as long as he is a child, differeth nothing from a servant, though he be lord of all:** . . . What I mean is this, –MNTG . . . Again, let me illustrate . . . become master of the whole estate, –NORL . . . is a babe, –PNIN . . . is a litle one, –RHEM . . . is a minor he is no different from . . . though he is the owner of everything, –ADAM . . . though he be the owner of the whole inheritance, –MNTG.

**2. But is under tutors and governors until the time appointed of the father:** . . . is under guardians, –PNIN . . . and trustees, –MNTG . . . and stewards until the time that was set beforehand by, –ADAM.

**3. Even so we, when we were children, were in bondage under the elements of the world:** . . . when we were like infants, –TCNT . . . So too we, when we were minors, were enslaved by the world's presuppositions, –ADAM . . . were held in servitude, –PNT . . . were in subordination under the elements of the world, –MRDK . . . were enslaved under the rudiments, –WLSN.

**4:1-3.** In this chapter Paul used a number of other examples to reemphasize the certainty of salvation by grace alone. In verses 1-3 he used an illustration which was very much part of the life of the Galatians. As is true also today, a child whose parents had died was considered a minor even though he was the heir of the parental estate. According to Roman law, the heir as a minor was placed in the charge of a guardian (tutor) who had been nominated by the father, until he was 14 years old. The guardian was in total charge of the welfare of the minor, including also his education. The management of the estate was entrusted to an appointed manager(s) (governors) until the heir reached the age of 25. Only then could he take over his inheritance.

What was true of the minor was true of Paul and his fellow Jews. He used a strong Greek word translated "were in bondage" (*dedoulōmenoi*, "enslaved"). Paul referred back to the training period from the time of Sinai to Christ and His atoning work. The Jews were enslaved "under the elements of the world." The Greek word translated "elements" is *stoicheia*. This means primarily items placed side by side in a row, such as the ABCs, and hence the "first principles" or "rudiments" as in Hebrews 5:12. (See p. 546 for further discussion.) Here Paul referred to the time from Sinai till Christ came. In this way, he said that God's covenant people were living under the Law, learning that salvation was not by or through the Law.

**4. But when the fulness of the time was come, God sent forth his Son, made of a woman, made under the law:** ... but when the time was ripe for it, —*TCNT* ... when the right time came, —*SEB* ... when the proper time came God sent his son, born of a human mother and born under the jurisdiction, —*PHLP* ... when the completion of the time came ... born under a ritual, —*FNTN* ... produced from, —*WLSN* ... born of a woman, —*ADAM* ... born subject to law, —*WLMS*.

**5. To redeem them that were under the law, that we might receive the adoption of sons:** ... God did this, so that he could buy back the freedom of those, —*SEB* ... so that He might buy out those, —*FNTN* ... to redeem from captivity, —*MNTG* ... to ransom those, —*NORL* ... myght receaue the inheritaunce that belongeth vnto the natural sonnes, —*CRNM* ... receive the privileges of sons, —*TCNT*.

**4:4, 5.** The phrase "fulness of the time" is a very inclusive term. It refers to all that God in His eternal wisdom had seen necessary to take place before the *right time* could come for His Son to be born and the fulfillment of His promise to Abraham.

God's people had to learn that salvation is by grace even though the Pharisees stressed the way of law and obedience as crucial in prompting God to send the Messianic Age. Many pagans recognized the bankruptcy of their ancestral religion and were looking for some meaning in life. Many of the more educated went through the motions of the religious rites which were an intimate part of civic functions. Others joined various mystery cults, thereby to experience union with the god(s) in the rite and with fellow worshipers, regardless of their status.

More Jews lived outside of Palestine in the Dispersion than in Palestine. Many of these continued to worship God. The relative simplicity of the Jewish religion attracted many pagans to visit and worship in the synagogue. Some of these became serious "God-fearers" or even proselytes, i.e., full Jews.

The conquests of Alexander the Great resulted in Greek becoming the common, international language and brought in a common Hellenistic culture. The conquests of Rome in time brought the Mediterranean world under its control. The reign of Emperor Augustus finally brought peace to this extensive area after centuries of warfare. For many the Greek word *euangelia*, "good news," was a fitting term for the Roman peace.

The Roman navy swept pirates off the seas, making maritime commerce and travel safe. Already in the Second Century B.C. the empire began establishing well-built, long-lasting roads. This continued into the early centuries A.D. In time over 50,000 miles of such roads were

constructed. This facilitated not only governmental communications but also commerce. As a result of such activity in this glorious era of peace there came prosperity and high hopes of better things to come. The "fullness of time" was an era of great anticipation.

Isaiah 7:14 foretold the virgin birth of the Immanuel. Verses 15-25 in prophetic language speak of the sad events and turmoil which God's unfaithful covenant people would face before this prophecy would be fulfilled.

At the right time God sent His Son. Both Matthew and Luke carefully emphasize that Jesus was virgin born. In fact, Matthew 1:23 quotes Isaiah 7:14. Luke 2:21-24 records His circumcision and, as the firstborn, He was bought back through a sacrificial rite. The Synoptics record that He was tempted by Satan. Satan's direct confrontation failed, but he continued to try to entrap the woman's Seed through others. The agony in Gethsemane is an example of what Jesus faced in His role as the obedient and suffering Servant (Isaiah 53). His passion ended in that triumphant cry, "It is finished!" and His voluntary death (John 19:28-30). Hebrews 2:14-18 and 4:14-16 point out that Jesus faced genuine temptations but did not sin. All this was necessary "to redeem them that were under the law, that we might receive the adoption of sons." Adoption was also part of life at that time.

**6. And because ye are sons, God hath sent forth the Spirit of his Son into your hearts, crying, Abba, Father:** ... Who calls out, —*ADAM* ... The Spirit cries out, —*SEB* ... exclaiming, —*WLSN* ... Dear, dear Father! —*MNTG*.

**7. Wherefore thou art no more a servant, but a son; and if a son, then an heir of God through Christ:** ... So that no one is now a slave, —*FNTN* ... you are no longer a slave ... an heir by God's own act, —*WLMS* ... God's child, God's heir, —*SEB* ... an heire also, —*RHEM* ... an heir as well, —*ADAM*.

**4:6, 7.** Paul dramatically emphasized the full meaning of being "sons" and all this term means. As sons, through the Spirit's work, we may call God "Father" with all its implications. In Romans 8 Paul so beautifully enlarged in great detail on its full significance. As sons, God, in grace, made us His heirs, heirs of eternal life. As sons, we have the privilege of saying "Abba," Aramaic for *Father,* but with the loving filial overtones of what is meant by *Daddy.*

**8. Howbeit then, when ye knew not God:** ... Formerly, —*NORL* ... But at that former time, —*WLMS* ... Once, however, —*ADAM* ... at that time,

*—WLSN* . . . Yet formerly, in your ignorance of God, *—TCNT* . . . In the past, you didn't know God, *—SEB.*

**ye did service unto them which by nature are no gods:** . . . in bondage to them, *—ASV* . . . under the authority of gods who had no real existence, *—PHLP* . . . exist not, *—ALFD.*

**9. But now, after that ye have known God, or rather are known of God, how turn ye again to the weak and beggarly elements, whereunto ye desire again to be in bondage?:** . . . now that you have found God, *—TCNT* . . . having acknowledged, *—WLSN* . . . ye desyre afresshe, *—TNDL* . . . vnto impotent and beggerly ceremonies, *—GNVA* . . . how can you revert to dead and sterile principles and consent to be under their power all over again? *—PHLP* . . . poore elements, *—RHEM* . . . weak and helpless elemental false gods, *—NORL.*

**4:8, 9.** Paul specifically addressed those who were Gentiles. He reminded them that before their conversion they had worshiped gods which did not exist. Deuteronomy 32:21 uses a Hebrew term which means "no-god," a term echoed in Isaiah 37:19; Jeremiah 2:11; 5:7; and 16:20. In 1 Corinthians 12:2 Paul used the term "dumb idols." These had enslaved them. But now they were "known of God" as His redeemed children (Romans 8:29). Paul emphasized that what they had become in Christ was strictly God's doing, not theirs in any way. To emphasize his point Paul used a striking term—*slavery.* They knew well the meaning of slavery, since this was such an intimate part of life at that time. One could become a slave, a thing, as a result of war or through political or economic misfortune. And so Paul asked them if they wished again to become slaves, spiritual slaves. What was happening was so absurd, beyond all reason, if they would just stop to think what would happen to them. Once free through God's grace, they would again become enslaved to what Paul described as "weak and beggarly elements." He stressed these were completely devoid of any power whatsoever. In fact, they were nonexistent.

In this case, the Galatians were enamored with the legalism promoted by the Judaizers, namely, their insistence that whether a Jew or Gentile Christian, everyone had to be circumcised and live as a Jew in order to be saved. But, Paul stressed, the end result was the same: spiritual slavery and eternal condemnation. God's eternal curse would rest on them.

**10. Ye observe days, and months, and times, and years:** . . . Your religion is beginning to be a matter of observing certain days, *—PHLP* . . . scrupulously observing, *—WORL* . . . Seasons, *—WLSN.*

**11. I am afraid of you, lest I have bestowed upon you labour in vain:** . . . I am afraid, on your account, *—NORL* . . . Frankly, you stagger me,

*—PHLP* . . . lest I have expended, *—SAWR* . . . may have been wasted, *—TCNT.*

**4:10, 11.** What is the meaning of verse 10? Each of these occasions is part of the Jewish worship calendar. "Days" refers to Sabbaths and other holy days. "Months" probably refers especially to the new moons, observed at the beginning of every month (Numbers 28:11-15). The Greek word *kairous*, translated "times," means "seasons." It is an indefinite period of time in either length or frequency of observance, and hence may best refer to the great festivals: Passover, Firstfruits, and Harvest ("Tabernacles"). "Years" probably refers to the sabbatical year (every seventh year) or the year of Jubilee, the 50th year. All of these were of utmost importance in the thinking of the Judaizers.

**12. Brethren, I beseech you, be as I [am]; for I [am] as ye [are]: ye have not injured me at all:** . . . I entreat you, *—WLSN* . . . I also was as ye are, *—WORL* . . . become as I . . . Ye did me no wrong, *—PNIN* . . . Ye slighted me in no way, *—PNT* . . . In nothing did ye wrong me, *—RTHM.*

**4:12.** Again Paul used the loving term "brethren," brothers and sisters in Christ. For Paul this was an earnest term of endearment as he sought to persuade the Galatians that they were headed for condemnation. He wished to emphasize that he lovingly had their eternal welfare at heart. He was not concerned about himself or his own reputation. He basically said in summary form what he later wrote in 2 Corinthians 6: "My heart is wide open to you; let yours also be wide open to me!" He assured them that this was not in any way a personal matter with him.

**13. Ye know how through infirmity of the flesh:** . . . You remember that I was not well, *—NORL* . . . how handicapped I was, *—PHLP* . . . illness was the cause, *—TCNT.*

**I preached the gospel unto you at the first:** . . . I euangelized to you heretofore, *—RHEM.*

**14. And my temptation which was in my flesh ye despised not, nor rejected; but received me as an angel of God, [even] as Christ Jesus:** . . . And ye did not slight or disdain my temptation, *—WSLY* . . . You didn't shrink from me or let yourselves be revolted at the disease which was such a trial to me, *—PHLP* . . . that trial of mine, *—WLSN* . . . though I was a trial to you in my flesh, *—CNFT* . . . in my complaint, it did not inspire you with scorn or disgust, *—TCNT.*

**4:13, 14.** Paul reminded them of the fine response they had shown when he shared the gospel with them. He deeply appreciated their loving reaction when he experienced an attack of what he described as an "infirmity of the flesh." In 2 Corinthians 12:7 he called it "a thorn in the flesh." It is impossible to be sure what this malady was.

Fourteen different suggestions have been made as to what it might have been. Among the various possibilities are the following: pain in the head or ear; epilepsy; convulsive attacks; eye trouble; a speech impediment; malaria. This last one was proposed by the noted scholar William Ramsay. He suggested that Paul caught malaria in the mosquito-malaria ridden area of low-lying Pamphylia (pp. 422-425). Acts 13:13-20 states that Paul and his companions arrived at Perga from Cyprus and immediately left to climb through the rugged Taurus Mountains to Antioch, lying 3,600 feet above sea level. This involved a distance of about 100 miles.

In Antioch Paul was struck by what may best be recognized as a malarial attack, which, for both the victim and those present, can be a very unpleasant experience. Paul carefully notes that, rather than despising or scorning him, they "received (him) as an angel of God, even as Christ Jesus" himself.

**15. Where is then the blessedness ye spake of? for I bear you record, that, if [it had been] possible, ye would have plucked out your own eyes, and have given them to me:** ... Where, then, [is] your happiness? —RTHM ... What then [has become of] your high appreciation [of me]? —PNT ... is your self-congratulation? —CNFT ... that if it might haue be don, —WCLF ... you would have torn out, —TCNT ... you would have dug out, —SAWR, —WLSN.

**16. Am I therefore become your enemy, because I tell you the truth?:** ... the same truth, —PHLP.

**17. They zealously affect you, [but] not well:** ... People are courting your favour, but not honourably, —TCNT ... They are zealous for you in no good way, —PNIN ... thei louen (loveth) not you wel, —WCLF ... They court you from no good motive, —CNFT ... They love you ardently, not honorably, —WLSN ... but not in honesty, —NOYS ... but not rightly, —SCLT ... not nobly, —RTHM.

**yea, they would exclude you, that ye might affect them:** ... They want to isolate you, —TCNT ... What they desire is to exclude you from me, —NORL ... They would like to see you and me separated altogether, and have you all to themselves, —PHLP.

**18. But [it is] good to be zealously affected always in [a] good [thing], and not only when I am present with you:** ... Don't think I'm jealousit is a grand thing that men should be keen to win you, whether I'm there or not, —PHLP ... But do you emulate the good in good, —RHEM ... it is good to be an object of zeal, —NOYS ... to loue earnestly, —GNVA ... in a good matter, —ASV.

**4:15-18.** Paul contrasted the Galatian's reaction to him and the gospel message then and in their present uncertain state. The first part of verse 15 in this context is best translated, "Where is that sense of congratulation now? What has

happened?" Paul asked. The Greek goes on to say, "I bear witness" (*marturō*), a strong legal phrase as Paul contrasted their loving reaction then and their subsequent puzzling behavior. He reminded them that formerly they would have shared their eyes, if this would have helped him in any way. He added that in telling them the truth he was their friend, even if they considered him an enemy. He had their welfare at heart.

The opening words in verse 17, following the Greek, may well be translated, "They are courting you but not for honorable intentions." The purpose of the Judaizers was to gain the Galatians as their followers. They wanted the Christians in Galatia to actively court their favor, to shut themselves off from fellowship with Paul and the belief in the certainty of salvation by grace alone. Their intentions were dishonorable and would result in their eternal damnation. Paul restated this positively in verse 18, following the Greek, "It is always good to be courted for honorable intentions, and not only when I am present with you."

Paul and Barnabas had gone to the Galatians with very honorable intentions, namely, to share with them the glad news of the fulfillment of God's promises of salvation by grace alone. To return to the illustration Paul used earlier in this chapter, the time of the guardians and the managers had come to an end. The time set by the Father had come.

Acts 13:16-41 tells us what Paul said when he was asked to speak in the synagogue at Antioch on the Sabbath. How carefully he stressed that in Jesus Christ the prophecies in the Old Testament of the coming Messiah had been fulfilled. One Bible scholar has computed that the Old Testament contains 333 prophecies about Christ which were fulfilled during his sojourn on earth.

Acts 13:42, 43 records the response of the hearers. They heard the glad news of the fulfillment in Christ. They kept on pleading with Paul that on the next Sabbath he would speak to them again. Luke notes that many Jews and God-fearers (Gentiles) followed Paul and Barnabas, who instructed them and urged them to continue to believe in salvation by grace alone.

Acts 13:44-52 provides information on the reaction of the Jews to the presence of many Gentiles. Filled with envy, they vigorously contradicted and reviled Paul. Paul and Barnabas told them that they had brought the gospel of the fulfillment of the prophecies in Christ first to them as being ethnically God's covenant people. But now they would turn to the Gentiles. Working through devout Gentile women, the wives of the prominent men of Antioch, the Jews were able to force Paul and Barnabas to leave.

When Paul and Barnabas left at the end of the first missionary journey to return to Antioch, Syria, the Judaizers courted the Christians in Galatia with dishonorable intentions to seek to persuade them not to follow the way of grace but that of law.

**19. My little children, of whom I travail in birth again until Christ be formed in you:** . . . in pains of childbirth, *—NORL* . . . vntill Christ be fassioned in you, *—TNDL* . . . be imprinted in you, *—GNVA.*

**4:19.** Paul addressed them as "My little children!" in his fatherly affection for them. Then he used a dramatic word picture. When he and Barnabas first shared the gospel with the Galatians, they, as it were, went through the pains of giving birth to those who believed their message. Paul was asking if he had to do this again to be used of God in returning them to saving faith in Christ.

**20. I desire to be present with you now:** . . . How I wish I could be, *—NORL* . . . how I long to be with you now! *—PHLP.*

**and to change my voice; for I stand in doubt of you:** . . . and speak in a different tone, *—TCNT* . . . and to change my speech, *—SCLT* . . . and to change my tone; Because I am perplexed concerning you, *—WLSN* . . . Perhaps I could then alter my tone to suit your mood. As it is, I honestly don't know how to deal with you, *—PHLP* . . . for I am perplexed about you, *—PNIN* . . . I am ashamed for you, *—DOUY* . . . with you, *—RTHM.*

**4:20.** Paul faced the problem that as much as he would have liked, he could not return to Galatia to talk with the believers in person. The Judaizers had wreaked havoc also in Antioch. They claimed to speak for the leaders of the church in Jerusalem. As Acts 15 informs us, Paul, Barnabas, and others had to travel (probably walk) more than 300 miles from Antioch to Jerusalem to discuss this extremely serious problem.

Acts 15 records that after the Judaizers, followed by Peter, Barnabas, and Paul, had spoken, James stressed that God's plan of salvation by grace included also the Gentiles. Since the Judaizers had pretended to speak for the church (Acts 15:24), the official letter authorized by this meeting stated that they had *not* been official representatives. Their view of salvation was wrong. Salvation was by grace alone!

**21. Tell me, ye that desire to be under the law, do ye not hear the law?:** . . . ye who are wishing to be under law, *—WORL* . . . you who want the Law as

your master, *—NORL* . . . do you not listen to the Law? *—TCNT* . . . have you not read the Law? *—CNFT.*

**22. For it is written, that Abraham had two sons, the one by a bondmaid, the other by a free-woman:** . . . where it is written, *—FNTN* . . . by the slave, *—ADAM, —PHLP.*

**23. But he [who was] of the bondwoman was born after the flesh; but he of the freewoman [was] by promise:** . . . the son of the slave, *—ADAM* . . . the child of the slave-girl, *—WLMS* . . . the child of the slave-woman was born in the ordinary course of nature, *—TCNT* . . . was naturally produced, *—WLSN* . . . was born in a natural way, *—NORL* . . . was born to fulfill, *—WLMS* . . . was born in fulfilment of a promise, *—MNTG* . . . in virtue of the promise, *—CNFT.*

**4:21-23.** To reemphasize what he had said, Paul used an illustration from the life of Abraham. He introduced it just by the use of the term "law" in the legal sense; the second use means *Torah,* the Pentateuch. Paul asked, "Why don't you listen to Scripture, to the *Torah!*"

In this letter Paul drew heavily on the life of Abraham, the father of God's covenant people. Abraham was 75 years old when God called him at Haran in Upper Mesopotamia (Genesis 12:1-3). His wife Sarah was 65 years old, beyond the childbearing age. Some time went by; how much we are not told.

In Genesis 15:1-3 Abraham reminded God that He had not as yet kept His promise. Since he was the head of a large clan (see Genesis 14:14), he had to provide a leader to take his place after his death. His proposal of adopting Eliezer as his legal son and heir reflects a Mesopotamian legal pattern. In an acted out reply, God told Abraham that he would have more descendants than the stars in the heavens. And Abraham reacted in firm belief that God would keep His promise.

Some years later Sarah's faith faltered. She persuaded Abraham to have intercourse with her Egyptian slavegirl, Hagar. In Mesopotamian law, the issue of such a union would be considered Sarah's legal son. Abraham's faith also faltered. He listened to Sarah, and in due time Ishmael was born. At that time Abraham was 86 years old (Genesis 16). Fourteen years later when Abraham was 100 years and Sarah 90 years old, the true covenant son Isaac was born to Abraham and Sarah as God had promised. When he was weaned, Ishmael ridiculed Isaac. Sarah told Abraham to send Hagar and Ishmael away. At first Abraham was unwilling, but at God's command, he did so (Genesis 21). Because his faith led to obedience, God has honored him: "Abraham believed God, and it was counted unto him for righteousness" (Romans 4:3).

Paul drew on this incident to emphasize the certainty of grace. Since Abraham was the father of God's covenant people, this illustration would have a special effect on the Jewish Christians in Galatia.

Sarah was a free woman and the wife of Abraham, and hence part of God's covenant promise. As Sarah's slave, Hagar was not part of God's covenant plan. Isaac was freeborn as the fulfillment of God's covenant promise (Genesis 12:2, 3). Ishmael's conception was strictly due to a physical union and was not part of God's covenant plan. Isaac, not Ishmael, was the covenant son.

**24. Which things are an allegory: for these are the two covenants; the one from the mount Sinai, which gendereth to bondage, which is Agar:** . . . for these represent, *—WLSN* . . . these things may be allegorized . . . bearing children who will be slaves, *—ADAM* . . . Which thinges betoken mystery, *—TNDL* . . . have another meaning . . . bearing children unto bondage, *—ALFD* . . . one indeed, from Sinai Rock, born in slavery, *—FNTN* . . . who heareth children into bondage, *—NOYS* . . . which bringeth forth for bondage, *—MRDK* . . . produces a race of slaves, *—TCNT* . . . bearing children into slavery, typified by Hagar, *—PHLP.*

**25. For this Agar is mount Sinai in Arabia, and answereth to Jerusalem which now is:** . . . and it corresponds to the present, *—WLSN* . . . she resembles, however, *—RTHM* . . . Mount Sinai being in Arabia, the land of the descendants of Ishamael, *—PHLP* . . . and bordreth vpon the citie, *—TNDL* . . . and represents the present Jerusalem, *—SCLT* . . . Jerusalem now existing, *—NOYS.*

**and is in bondage with her children:** . . . for the Jews are still, spiritually speaking, "slaves," *—PHLP* . . . for she is in slavery with her children, *—ADAM* . . . she is enslaved with, *—FNTN* . . . all of its people are slaves to the law, *—SEB.*

**26. But Jerusalem which is above is free, which is the mother of us all:** . . . But the free woman typifies, *—PHLP* . . . the heavenly Jerusalem, *—SEB* . . . the exalted Jerusalem, *—WLSN* . . . the supreme Jerusalem is a free woman, *—FNTN* . . . who is our mother, *—ADAM.*

**4:24-26.** The Greek word sometimes translated "allegory" (*allēgoroumena*) is here better translated "illustration." In actuality, Paul's very effective but somewhat involved illustration is best identified as typology. Paul referred to an important Old Testament event to show its deeper meaning in God's overall covenant purpose.

Hagar and her son Ishmael were not part of God's covenant plan. Therefore, her descendants would be children "in bondage with her." She represents the covenant of the Law, given at Mount Sinai. Because the Jews misunderstood its purpose and expected to be justified by its works, they became in bondage to the Law. The "Jerusalem which now is" represents the present state of the Jews, still in bondage. The "Jerusalem which is above" represents the new covenant of grace.

Paul's readers would understand how this bondage was true of the Pharisees and their followers.

They brought their offerings and sacrifices to the temple in Jerusalem to fulfill the requirements of the Law. They, like the Judaizers, felt they could earn salvation by keeping the Law. But, Paul stressed, they would not experience salvation. They were and would continue to be in spiritual bondage.

Sarah, Abraham's wife, gave birth to Isaac, the son of the "free woman." He was the son of God's promise, part of His covenant plan of grace. Isaac's spiritual descendants are and will be "children of promise." The "Jerusalem which is above is free, which is the mother of us all," is the illustration Paul used for all who humbly and gratefully believe in God's promises of salvation by grace alone.

**27. For it is written, Rejoice, [thou] barren that hearest not; break forth and cry, thou that travailest not: for the desolate hath many more children than she which hath an husband:** . . . For the Scripture says, *—WLMS* . . . O childless woman, *—NORL* . . . break into shouts, thou who art never in labour, *—TCNT* . . . into shouting, you who feel no birth pangs, *—WLMS* . . . who has not given birth to children, *—FNTN* . . . the deserted one, *—RTHM* . . . the desolate woman has more children than the woman who has a husband! *—ADAM.*

**28. Now we, brethren, as Isaac was, are the children of promise:** . . . Now you, brothers, like Isaac, *—ADAM* . . . are children according to the promise through Isaac, *—FNTN* . . . was born in the normal way, *—SEB* . . . we are children born "by promise," *—PHLP.*

**4:27, 28.** Paul continued with a quotation from Isaiah 54:1. Isaiah spoke of an event to take place in the future. In 587 B.C. the Babylonians took Jerusalem, destroyed it, and carried its inhabitants away. The Jews thought this could never happen. Because of their self-centered misinterpretation of their covenant status they thought God would not dare let the Babylonians destroy the city and especially the temple. If He did, the enemy would believe their great Babylonian gods, such as Marduk and Ishtar, were more powerful than the true God of Judah. But God did permit the great destruction and in so doing taught the Jews an important lesson: He would not allow anyone, even His beloved people, to sin and escape punishment.

Unfortunately the lesson which God sought to teach them through Jerusalem's destruction and the exile of the people did not last. The closing chapters of 2 Kings and 2 Chronicles as well as the books of Ezra and Nehemiah and the prophets of their day—Haggai, Zechariah, and

Malachi—indicate that the full lesson had not been learned.

Israel had become spiritually barren. The Jews still counted too much on a special relationship with God, because they were of Abraham's ethnic line. But they did not have Abraham's faith. So the Jerusalem of Jesus and Paul's day was barren of spiritual life.

But the "barren" Jerusalem, in God's plan, would become a spiritual Jerusalem. There the Church would be born, and many spiritual children would be born, composed of those who put their trust in God's covenant of grace. So Paul could add: "Now we, brethren, as Isaac was, are the children of promise" (verse 28).

**29. But as then he that was born after the flesh persecuted him [that was born] after the Spirit:** . . . but just as in old times, —MNTG . . . born in the ordinary course of nature, —TCNT, —WLMS . . . born according to, —ADAM . . . he who was born naturally despised him who was by the Spirit, —FNTN.

**even so [it is] now:** . . . It is the same way now, —SEB . . . so it is today, —WLMS, —PHLP.

**30. Nevertheless what saith the scripture? Cast out the bondwoman and her son: for the son of the bondwoman shall not be heir with the son of the free-woman:** . . . But what does the Scripture say? —SEB . . . Yet what is the scriptural instruction? —PHLP . . . Send away, —TCNT, —NORL, —MNTG . . . the slave girl with her son; for the son of the slave girl shall not inherit, —FNTN . . . Throw out the slave . . . for by no means shall the son of the slave share the inheritance, —ADAM . . . The son of the free woman will receive everything that his father has, —SEB . . . shall not inherit with, —ASV . . . shall in nowise inherit, —WORL.

**4:29, 30.** Paul states, "Even so it is now." The Judaizers were spiritual descendants of Ishmael, the son of the slavegirl Hagar. As Ishmael had mocked Isaac, the true son of promise as the son of Abraham and Sarah, so Ishmael's true spiritual descendants were mocking the way of grace. They were slandering Paul by saying that he was not a true called apostle and that the gospel which he had shared was at best incomplete. They were persecuting the Galatian Christians, the true spiritual descendants of Isaac and the true heirs of God's promise of salvation by grace alone. They were telling the Galatians that salvation was one of works, of faithfully and totally living as a Jew to merit salvation. They were falsely claiming to be the official spokesmen for the Church, and any variation from what they said was wrong.

**31. So then, brethren, we are not children of the bondwoman, but of the free:** . . . by that libertie, —GNVA . . . we are not to look upon ourselves as the sons of the slave woman but of the free, not sons of slavery under the Law but sons of freedom under grace, —PHLP.

**4:31.** Paul once more emphasized the crucial significance of this passage for the Galatians. By their faith in salvation as God's gift of grace, like Isaac, they had become true children of Sarah, the free woman and wife of Abraham. He was summarizing what he had said, especially in verses 21-30. He wanted to be sure they understood that the message of the Judaizers was false. Salvation was not to be achieved by works, by living as a Jew and seeking to earn God's favor. The message of the Judaizers was one of damnation, not salvation. In the process of pointing out this truth Paul strongly demonstrated his deep concern about the salvation of these converts.

## Chapter 5

**1. Stand fast therefore in the liberty wherewith Christ hath made us free, and be not entangled again with the yoke of bondage:** . . . It was for freedom that Christ freed us; stand firm therefore, —ADAM . . . stand you firm, and do not again be held fast in a Yoke of Servitude, —WLSN . . . on the freedom with which Christ has freed us, and submit not again to a yoke of slavery, —FNTN . . . do not be caught again, —CNFT . . . and do not submit again, —NORL . . . be not again bound fast to, —NOYS . . . Don't turn and go back into slavery, —SEB . . . and wrappe not youre selves agayne in the yoke, —TNDL . . . stop letting your necks be fastened in the yoke of slavery again, —WLMS . . . be not again subject to a yoke of servitude, —SAWR.

**5:1.** Paul dramatically restated in this verse what he had said in the preceding two verses. The order of the Greek words expresses greater emphasis: "In freedom Christ us has freed, stand therefore, and not again in a yoke of bondage be held fast!" In three verses Paul used a form of the word *free* four times (4:30, 31; 5:1). He did this to state most emphatically that salvation is by grace, and not by works, as the Judaizers were teaching.

But Paul added another analogy to emphasize the grave danger confronting them in listening to the Judaizers. He wrote, following the Greek word order, "And not again in a yoke of slavery be held." Slavery was a basic part of life in the Roman Empire, including Galatia. Legally a slave belonged totally to his master who had complete control over him. Technically the slave was chattel: property that could be sold. His status was no greater than an animal. The Galatians were intimately acquainted with slavery and its implications. In fact, some among these Christians may well have been slaves or owners of slaves.

Paul's use of this analogy to express the real meaning of what would happen if the Galatians would listen to the Judaizers was very telling.

There was no possibility they could misunderstand what he was saying, namely, that by heeding the Judaizers they would come into a far worse (spiritual) bondage.

**2. Behold, I Paul say unto you, that if ye be circumcised, Christ shall profit you nothing:** ... Listen, *—PHLP* ... will be of no advantage to you, *—TCNT, —CNFT* ... will be of no benefit to you, *—WLSN* ... will avail you nothing, *—SCLT* ... will not be of any help to you, *—NORL.*

**3. For I testify again to every man that is circumcised, that he is a debtor to do the whole law:** ... to every one who becometh circumcised, *—NOYS* ... that he binds himself to obey, *—TCNT* ... That he is bound to perform, *—WLSN* ... to obey all the rest of the Law! *—PHLP.*

**5:2, 3.** Paul left nothing to chance. He showed how what the Judaizers had told them would affect their spiritual welfare. For the first time in this part of his argument he expressly mentioned circumcision. From the viewpoint of a Jew circumcision was absolutely necessary for salvation. Only through circumcision could one become a true son of Abraham, a son of the covenant. The Galatians knew that for one who was a Greek and for many who were part of the Hellenistic culture of that day, circumcision meant a mutilation of the body and brought a heavy negative stigma. In the men's section of the public baths circumcision became immediately apparent to all present.

Paul drew on his apostolic authority as Christ's chosen apostle when he said, "I Paul say unto you." He expressly addressed this to the uncircumcised Gentile Christians that if they allowed themselves to be circumcised, they would have to keep the Law completely. Then they would have no claim on Christ. There is no middle ground. Salvation is strictly by grace.

**4. Christ is become of no effect unto you, whosoever of you are justified by the law; ye are fallen from grace:** ... Ye are severed from, *—PNT* ... ye are fallen away from, *—PNIN, —NOYS* ... You have severed yourselves from Christ ... you have become outcasts from mercy, *—TCNT* ... you put yourself outside the range of his grace, *—PHLP.*

**5. For we through the Spirit wait for the hope of righteousness by faith:** ... are ardently waiting, *—RTHM* ... the righteousness we hope to see, *—PHLP.*

**6. For in Jesus Christ neither circumcision availeth any thing, nor uncircumcision; but faith which worketh by love:** ... there is no validity in either ... faith which expresses itself in love, *—PHLP* ... which by love is mighty in operation, *—TNDL* ... is all important, *—TCNT* ... Faith operating in us by Love, *—WLSN* ... strongly operating by love, *—SCLT.*

**5:4-6.** Paul stressed again the full implications of what he had said. The Judaizers taught that only by keeping the Law was it possible to be justified before God. Paul used a very strong Greek verb, prefaced by a preposition, to stress that all who wished to be justified by the Law were totally cut off from Christ; they had "fallen out of" (*exepesate*) grace. They had absolutely no hope of salvation.

Now Paul restated in the positive what he had said so emphatically in the negative. He described the way of grace: "For we *through the Spirit* wait for the hope of righteousness by faith" (verse 5; cf. Titus 3:4-8; Romans 5:1, 2; 6:1-12, 23; 2 Corinthians 5:16-21). Then he stated that in God's sight circumcision, or lack of it, makes no difference *as long as it is not considered necessary* for salvation. Acts 16:3 informs us that Paul circumcised Timothy as an act of good judgment since his mother was a Jewess and hence, he would be considered a Jew. But Paul refused to circumcise Titus, a Greek; this would have been a gross denial of salvation by grace alone (2:3-5).

Both Jews and Gentiles were numbered among the Galatian Christians. Their salvation, regardless of ethnic origins, came about because of true faith which "became effective" (*energoumenē*) by love. Through the Spirit's work, Christ's self-giving love (*agapē*) fills those who believe (Romans 5:5). And such love again expresses itself in the ongoing daily life of the Christian (see verses 22-26). In all his letters Paul always stressed that the faith that is alive is the faith that is lived in daily life (for example, Romans 12-15).

**7. Ye did run well:** ... You were once making good progress! *—TCNT* ... You were making progress, *—NORL* ... splendid progress, *—PHLP.*
**who did hinder you that ye should not obey the truth?:** ... who put you off the course you had set for the truth? *—PHLP.*
**8. This persuasion [cometh] not of him that calleth you:** ... Him inviting you, *—WLSN.*

**5:7, 8.** When Paul wrote, "Ye did run well," the imagery of the athletic events would flash before the eyes of the Galatians. As ruins and archaeological excavations reveal, larger towns had an amphitheater and other facilities for athletic events. These events played a very important role in both the community and individual lives of people. The Galatians knew well the tremendous physical exertion required for competitive running events.

Paul followed this with another athletic term translated "hinder" but better translated in this context as "cut you off," as often happens in such athletic events. Runners then as today tried to cut off a competitor and thereby seek to win the race.

Paul asked the Galatians a very striking and attention-getting question: "Who has cut you off from the way of grace?" To cut someone off in an athletic event was always for personal advantage. In verse 8 Paul stated emphatically that this was not the work of Christ, who *is calling* (*kalountos*) you. (The tense of the verb is important.) Through the ongoing work of the Holy Spirit, and also through Paul's letter, Christ was continuing to call them to stay on the way of grace. Those who were seeking to cut them off from grace for their own gain were the Judaizers (see 6:13).

**9. A little leaven leaveneth the whole lump:** ... Alas, it takes only a little leaven to affect, –*PHLP* ... ferments the whole mass, –*CNFT* ... corrupteth the whole paste, –*RHEM* ... all the dough, –*TCNT* ... the Whole Mass, –*WLSN.*

**10. I have confidence in you through the Lord, that ye will be none otherwise minded: but he that troubleth you shall bear hi s judgment, whosoever he be:** ... Still, I have faith in you ... will receive his condemnation, –*NORL* ... I have become persuaded, –*RTHM* ... you will not take any fatal step. But whoever it is who is worrying you will have a serious charge to answer one day, –*PHLP* ... the man who is disturbing your minds, –*TCNT.*

**5:9, 10.** Paul used a well-known illustration from their daily life to emphasize what he had said. The use of yeast in the bread baking process was an intimate part of their daily life experience. In promoting their false doctrine (leaven, yeast), the Judaizers had not told the Galatians the full story. Paul warned them that what these enemies of Christ had said would in the process destroy their hope of salvation. And the Judaizers would experience God's eternal wrath and suffer the consequences of eternal damnation.

In verse 10 Paul contrasted himself with those who were disturbing the Galatians. On his part he had been and still *is* confident (following the Greek perfect tense, *pepoitha*) that they will listen and in the end not accept the false doctrine of the Judaizers.

After the Jerusalem meeting which stressed grace as the only way of salvation, Silas (Roman name: Silvanus) joined Paul on his second missionary journey. As the official representative of the Jerusalem meeting (Acts 15:22), Silas could speak for the church to the Galatian Christians to stress that salvation was by grace alone. It seems certain that the Galatians were persuaded of this important truth (Acts 15:41-16:5). Paul also revisited these churches at the beginning of their third missionary journey (see Acts 18:22, 23; 19:1). The "upper coasts" (Greek: regions) is the area between Antioch in Galatia and Ephesus.

**11. And I, brethren, if I yet preach circumcision, why do I yet suffer persecution? then is the offence of the cross ceased:** ... then the hostility due to the cross, –*NORL* ... the scandal of the cross, –*WLSN*, –*DOUY* ... Then is the stumbling-block of the cross removed! –*CNFT* ... been done away, –*PNT*, –*ASV.*

**12. I would they were even cut off which trouble you:** ... I wish those who are so eager to cut your bodies, –*PHLP* ... would go the length of mutilating themselves, –*TCNT* ... would even cut themselves off! –*ALFD* ... who unsettle you, –*CLMT.*

**5:11, 12.** Seemingly it had been said that Paul was stressing the importance of circumcision. Paul took note of this. He again affectionately said, "Brethren." If this was true, he asked, why was he still being attacked, slandered, and persecuted? Then the Jews and Judaizers would have no reason to be offended at the Cross. For then salvation would be through works and not grace.

Paul's reference here to the offense (scandal) of the Cross was probably meant more in the sense of the Cross as a symbol of grace earned by Christ through His suffering and death. In 1 Corinthians 1:23 the same Greek word (*skandalon*) is used to mean "a cause for stumbling." God's curse was seen to rest on all who had been executed for a religious crime and hung up for all to see (Deuteronomy 21:22, 23).

**13. For, brethren, ye have been called unto liberty; only [use] not liberty for an occasion to the flesh, but by love serve one another:** ... invited to Freedom ... be you subservient to each other, –*WLSN* ... for freedom, –*CLMT* ... be careful that this freedom does not become an excuse for sinful gratifications, –*NORL* ... be careful that freedom does not become mere opportunity for your lower nature, –*PHLP* ... for self-indulgence, –*TCNT* ... for sensuality, –*CNFT* ... as an indulgence to the flesh, –*SCLT.*

**14. For all the law is fulfilled in one word, [even] in this; Thou shalt love thy neighbour as thyself:** ... the entire law, –*RTHM* ... can be summarized ... in one command, –*NORL* ... is comprised in one precept, –*SCLT* ... is summed up by this one command, –*PHLP* ... fulfilled in one saying, –*ALFD.*

**5:13, 14.** Paul next began to write about what it means to live the freedom which is the believer's through Christ. Christians have been called to be free. The Greek word *eklēthēte*, translated "called," is used here as a term for God's effort through the gospel to call them to the way of grace. But Paul warned the Galatian Christians that freedom in Christ does not mean license. A central facet of the Christian life is serving one another in self-giving love (*agapē*; see verse 6). By quoting Leviticus 19:18, Paul reemphasizes one of the central messages of Jesus (Matthew 19:19; 22:39; Mark 12:31; cf. Luke 10:25-37).

Paul's encouragement to "serve one another" calls to mind one of the great words of the New Testament—*doulos*. It is usually translated "servant" or "bondservant," but more precisely it means "slave." It is the word Paul used in Philippians 2:7 when he said Jesus took on himself the "form of a servant." It calls to remembrance the concept of the love slave of Exodus 21:1-6. The man had the right to become free, but because of his love for his master, he chose to become a slave forever. The man had his ear lobe pierced with an awl and became a marked man from that time on, for the scar would remain. Those who now serve Christ through love instead of duty are marked men and women. They are different!

**15. But if ye bite and devour one another, take heed that ye be not consumed one of another:** ... continually wounding and preying upon one another, *—TCNT* ... lest you destroy one another altogether! *—NORL* ... by each other, *—WLSN.*

**5:15.** The stress on salvation by works tended to promote controversy. Paul used very vigorous language to counter this. The strong verbs translated "bite" and "devour" suggest the imagery of wild animals preying on each other and engaging in deadly struggle. This too was part of the life experience of the Galatians. Each major town had its amphitheater which, among other entertainments, would feature the activities of wild animals. Sometimes condemned criminals would be executed by being forced to fight such animals and, in the process, be mangled and devoured by them. Paul warned the Galatian believers to be on guard, lest, in the process of senseless controversy brought on by the Judaizers, they would be devoured by such sinful activity.

**16. [This] I say then, Walk in the Spirit, and ye shall not fulfil the lust of the flesh:** ... Heed my advice, *—NORL* ... Let your steps be guided by the Spirit ... will not gratify the cravings of your earthly nature, *—TCNT* ... you shal not accomplish, *—RHEM.*

**17. For the flesh lusteth against the Spirit:** ... hath desires opposite to the Spirit, *—SCLT* ... lusteth contrary to the sprete, *—CRNM* ... are contrary to those of the Spirit, *—NORL.*

**and the Spirit against the flesh: and these are contrary the one to the other: so that ye cannot do the things that ye would:** ... while the whole power of the Spirit is contrary to the lower nature. Here is the conflict, *—PHLP* ... in opposition to those of our earthly nature, *—TCNT* ... for these are opposed to each other, *—CNFT* ... for they two are antagonistic, *—MNTG* ... these oppose one another, *—NOYS* ... for these ben aduersaries to gidre, *—WCLF* ... you cannot always do what you would or should, *—NORL* ... do not perform the things which you wish, *—WLSN* ... you cannot do anything you please, *—WLMS.*

**18. But if ye be led of the Spirit, ye are not under the law:** ... if you are habitually led by, *—MNTG* ... if you are guided by, *—WLMS* ... if you are following the guidance of the Spirit, *—TCNT* ... if you follow the leading of the Spirit, you stand clear of the Law, *—PHLP.*

**5:16-18.** To emphasize what he now added, Paul used the expression, "I say!" Grammatically the Greek is best translated, "Keep on walking by the Spirit." The Greek preposition translated "by" (expressed by the dative case, cf. *pneumati*) stresses that only through the Spirit's work is this possible. In this letter Paul emphasized the ongoing role of the Spirit in the lives of believers. It is only through His work in their hearts that they will not carry out and fulfill the lusts of their sinful nature, the flesh (the self-life), which seeks to satisfy its own sinful and destructive desires and reactions.

In verse 17 Paul contrasted the sinful flesh and its desires with the Spirit and His work. These are constantly clashing with each other. The Greek word translated "lusteth" (*epithumei*) perhaps is better understood as "strongly desires." What the sinful flesh, man in his sinfulness, desires is the opposite of what the Spirit, working in the believer's heart, desires. If a man chooses to do what is evil, the Spirit opposes this. If he chooses to do what is good, the sinful flesh seeks to hinder this. Some view Romans 7:18-25 as a description of this ongoing conflict: "O wretched man that I am! who shall deliver me from the body of this death?" (Romans 7:24).

Paul closed this part of his argument with the comforting statement of verse 18. To "be led of the Spirit" means "to walk by the Spirit," to be empowered by Him. To walk by the Spirit means freedom from the power of sin. "For sin shall not have dominion over you: for ye are not under the law, but under grace" (Romans 6:14). Sin and the devil have lost their power over the believer.

**19. Now the works of the flesh are manifest, which are [these]; Adultery, fornication, unclean-ness, lasciviousness:** ... The activities of the lower nature are obvious, *—PHLP* ... are evident, *—NORL* ... whoredom, *—MRDK* ... Impurity, *—WLSN* ... unchastity, *—TCNT* ... immodesty, luxury, *—DOUY* ... indecency, *—MNTG* ... wantonness, *—RTHM, —NOYS.*

**5:19.** Paul went on to give a list of vices. These fall into four categories. The *first* category is that of varying degrees of sexual immorality. The first vice mentioned is *porneia*, translated as "adultery" or "fornication." Although it primarily refers to immoral relations with harlots, it is also used of all kinds of immoral sexual relations. Our English word *pornography* comes from the root of this word. The second term, *akatharsia*, means "impurity" and has a wider meaning: the misuse of sex and indulging in other forms of immorality. It is used to show the tendency of vice to be contagious. The next term is *aselgeia*, "wantonness," flaunting of self without any restraint whatsoever. Immorality of all kinds, also as part of idol worship, was for many an intimate way of life in the time of Paul, and this was very true also of Galatia.

**20. Idolatry, witchcraft, hatred, variance, emulations, wrath, strife, seditions, heresies:** ... sorcery, quarrels, *—TCNT* ... magic ... discords, *—MRDK* ... Resentments, Altercations, *—WLSN* ... outbursts of wrath, *—NOYS* ... ill-temper ... divisions, *—NORL* ... party-spirit, *—MNTG* ... enchantment, enmities, strife, jealousy ... factions, divisions, *—RTHM* ... contentions, *—SAWR* ... sects, *—DOUY.*

**21. Envyings, murders, drunkenness, revellings, and such like:** ... Inebrieties, Revellings, *—WLSN* ... outbursts of passion, *—TCNT* ... carousings, *—CNFT* ... glottony, *—GNVA* ... and things like these, *—NOYS.*

**of the which I tell you before, as I have also told [you] in time past, that they which do such things shall not inherit the kingdom of God:** ... as I did forewarn you, *—ASV* ... which I forewarn you, *—PNIN, —CLMT* ... I solemnly assure you ... that those who indulge in such things, *—PHLP* ... that those practicing such things, *—WORL.*

**5:20, 21.** The *second* category is that of sinful worship of idols or any substitute for true worship. In some pagan religions of that time this also involved sexual immorality. The term "witchcraft" (*pharmakeia*) is literally translated "sorcery." This term can refer to the use of magic arts of any kind, which was very popular at that time. Acts 19:11-20 speaks of Sceva's sons and the magical documents. It can also refer to witchcraft which involved the use of drugs to harm others. This was a serious offense in Roman law and resulted in severe punishment.

The *third* category of vices involves interpersonal relations. The first is "hatred," normally translated "enmities." This term provides the keynote for the various expressions of negative interpersonal relationships in this category, such as, ill feeling or hatred against others, resulting in hostile acts. The next vice ("variance") is a Greek word best translated as "strife" or "quarrelsomeness."

The next vice is translated "emulations." In our idiom this word is best translated as "jealousy" or "envy," depending on the context of its use (Acts 5:17; 13:45; Romans 13:13; 1 Corinthians 3:3; James 3:14-16). Its expression easily results in "wrath," the next term Paul used. In its negative meaning, the Greek word stresses the outburst of rage.

The next three vices have a close relationship with each other. The first is translated "strife," and in New Testament usage is the result of a selfish ambition, giving rise to rivalry and a party spirit. From this come "seditions" (dissensions or "divisions") which result from a party spirit. This again describes those who hold set views and opinions. The term "heresies" is better translated today as "cliques." The final vices in this category— "envyings, murders"—are specific acts of an envying spirit, due to a grudging spirit which cannot bear someone else's prosperity.

The *fourth* category begins with "drunkenness," excessive drinking resulting in drunken orgies. The next term, "revelings," involves what accompanies such orgies. Paul stressed that the vices listed in verses 17-21 result in a loss of salvation.

**22. But the fruit of the Spirit is love, joy, peace, longsuffering, gentleness, goodness, faith:** ... produces in human life fruits such as these, *—PHLP* ... graciousness, *—RTHM* ... forbearance ... trustfulness, *—TCNT* ... kindness, *—PNIN* ... fidelity, *—WSLY, —WLSN.*

**23. Meekness, temperance: against such there is no law:** ... modesty, continency, *—CNFT* ... Mildness, *—DOUY, —RHEM* ... self-control, *—PNIN.*

**5:22, 23.** Paul next spoke of the *fruit* of the Spirit. Note that he said "fruit"; this is the result of the Spirit's work. The first fruit is that of love (*agapē*), self-giving, self-sacrificing love which has its source in Christ's self-giving love resulting in man's salvation (1 Corinthians 13:13). The result of love is "joy" and "peace," grounded in the believer's grace relationship with God (Romans 14:17; 15:13). These form a triad.

From this triad flow "longsuffering" or patience, the quality of being long-tempered, especially when others may seek to provoke the Christian. "Gentleness" in the original has the meaning of "kindness." Next is "goodness" with special reference to generosity. This is followed by the Greek word *pistis*, "faith," which in Paul's usage may be translated as "faithfulness," especially referring to one's relationship with others. In modern English the quality of "meekness" is best expressed with "gentleness" in dealings with others. The Greek meaning of "temperance" is best expressed as "self-control" of human desires. All of these virtues are the result of the Spirit's work.

**24. And they that are Christ's have crucified the flesh with the affections and lusts:** ... Note that it is those who belong to, *—NORL* ... they who belong to Christ, *—SCLT* ... have already crucified their earthly nature, with its passions and its cravings, —TCNT . . . with the vices and concupiscences, —DOUY, —RHEM . . . passions and desires, —WLSN.

**25. If we live in the Spirit:** . . . if we live by the Spirit, —NORL . . . If our lives are centered in the Spirit, —PHLP . . . is due to the Spirit, —TCNT.

**let us also walk in the Spirit:** . . . let us press on after, —MRDK . . . let us also keep step in, —MNTG . . . let us be guided by, —PHLP . . . by the Spirit, —NORL.

**26. Let us not be desirous of vain glory, provoking one another, envying one another:** . . . not become conceited, nor should we provoke, —NORL . . . Let us not be ambitious for our own reputations, for that only means making one another jealous, —PHLP.

**5:24-26.** All of the above are the fruits of Christ's redemptive work. Paul wrote that all who belong to Christ "have crucified the flesh with the affections (*pathēmasin*, 'sinful desires') and lusts (*epithumais*, 'passions')." Christ kept the Law for sinful mankind. The writer of Hebrews stressed that Jesus was tested as believers are, but He did not sin (Hebrews 2:18; 4:15). Through His crucifixion and death on the cross He paid the awesome penalty for man's sin. Toward the close of the 3 hours of darkness, He cried out, "My God, my God, why hast thou forsaken me?" (Matthew 27:46; Psalm 22:1). (The essence of eternal punishment consists in being forever separated from God.) And just before voluntarily giving up His life He cried out, "It is finished!" (John 19:30). The Greek word for "finished" (*tetelestai*) is in the perfect tense, which emphasizes that except for dying and rising again, Jesus' role as Redeemer was completed. Paul beautifully stressed Christ's redemption and its significance in Romans 6:1-13.

In verse 25 Paul reminded the Galatians what it means to live in the Spirit. Through the Spirit's work Christians are to "walk in a straight line" (*stoichōmen*) with the Spirit. In verses 22 and 23, Paul had carefully sketched what this means.

In verse 26 Paul warned his readers against the opposite of what it means to walk in the Spirit. The Greek term *kenodoxoi*, "vainglory," means to boast when there is nothing to boast about, to have a false estimate of self. "Provoking one another" was used for challenging one another in an athletic event or combat. Paul used it to refer to challenging others to do what they may hesitate to do or to envying others for what we dare not do. Against such temptations of the Evil One, Christians must always be on guard.

## Chapter 6

**1. Brethren, if a man be overtaken in a fault, ye which are spiritual, restore such an one in the spirit of meekness; considering thyself, lest thou also be tempted:** . . . should be surprised by, —WLSN . . . be preoccupied in any fault, —RHEM . . . be overtaken in any trespass, —PNIN . . . be caught in any trespass, —WORL . . . is caught in some wrongdoing, you who are spiritual should set him right, —NORL . . . should be caught in a guilty act . . . put the man right, —TCNT . . . helpe to amende him, —GNVA . . . instruct such a one in the spirit of, —DOUY . . . enfoorme ye such oon in spirit of softnesse, —WCLF.

**2. Bear ye one another's burdens, and so fulfil the law of Christ:** . . . Carry . . . and so live out, —PHLP . . . and so render full obedience, —TCNT . . . of the Anointed one, —WLSN.

**6:1, 2.** Paul began his final words with the endearing term "Brethren," brothers and sisters in Christ! He used this term 10 times in Galatians. Lovingly he reminded them that those who walk in the Spirit also need to express a loving concern for others. If a fellow Christian inadvertently becomes involved in a fault (the Greek word *paraptōmati* means "a false step"), those who walk in the Spirit will in a gentle, loving way, seek to restore him. They are to remember, Paul warned, that they too are equally as vulnerable to temptation (1 Corinthians 10:12). Believers are to treat their fellowman as lovingly as they would wish to be treated if they had fallen into sin. Paul reminded the Galatians, as do other passages in Scripture, that the Evil One keeps on tempting those who are in Christ, seeking to lead them to destruction. In 1 Peter 5:8, 9 Peter graphically describes him roaming about as a roaring lion, "seeking whom he may devour."

The Greek word *bastazete*, translated "bear," is a term which is often used for carrying a heavy burden. Paul used it to emphasize the responsibility of those who seek to walk in the Spirit to bear the burden of those who appear to be weak in the Faith (Romans 15:1). His words recall Jesus' loving invitation (Matthew 11:28-30). At the Last Supper Jesus told His disciples: "A new commandment I give unto you, That ye love one another; as I have loved you, that ye also love one another" (John 13:34). The "law of Christ" means the law of God as spoken and lived out by Jesus Christ.

**3. For if a man think himself to be something, when he is nothing, he deceiveth himself:** . . . fancies himself to be somebody, when he is really nobody, —TCNT . . . deceaueth hys awne mynde, —CRNM . . . he is mentally deceiving himself, —RTHM . . . he seduceth him self, —RHEM . . . he is fooling himself, —NORL . . . in his ymaginacion, —TNDL.

**6:3.** Paul warned against the Christian comparing himself to fellow Christians. This is the result of spiritual pride. The tendency is to imagine that he himself is something and pride himself in what he thinks he is. In the Greek Paul used the strong verb *phrenapata* which is used only here in the New Testament. It means "to deceive" or "delude" oneself. Such false estimation easily results in having no positive understanding and sympathy with others in their shortcomings and, as a result, failing to be loving and gentle.

**4. But let every man prove his own work, and then shall he have rejoicing in himself alone, and not in another:** ... examine his own conduct, —MRDK ... learn to assess properly the value of his own work and he can then be glad when he has done something worth doing without depending on the approval of others, —PHLP ... test his own work ... rather than comparing himself with another, —ADAM ... will have boasting, —WLSN ... and not in comparison with another, —NOYS.

**5. For every man shall bear his own burden:** ... must carry his own load, —TCNT, —WLMS ... must carry his own pack load, —MNTG ... bear his own load, —WORL, —ADAM ... shoulder his own pack, —PHLP.

**6:4, 5.** In verse 4 Paul used the Greek verb *dokimazetō* which means to "test or examine" (KJV: "prove"). This involves careful, discerning self-examination in the light of how God views the believer. Doing this will keep a Christian from assuming or even boasting about himself without honestly recognizing the true condition of his own spiritual state. He will recognize that all that he is in the sight of God is solely God's work, not his, and hence, he has nothing to boast about. Not to do so will result in that of which the Pharisee was guilty in Luke 18:9-14. Paul stressed that everyone is answerable to God for himself. In 1 Corinthians 4:4 he told the criticizing Corinthians: "He that judgeth me is the Lord."

The Greek term for "rejoicing," *kauchēma*, means "ground for boasting," "achievement." Any such ground for boasting is strictly the work of the Holy Spirit. Doing this through the Spirit's guidance keeps us from comparing ourself with "another." Note what Paul says in Romans 15:17-19 and 2 Corinthians 10:13-18. In the latter passage troublemakers were part of the context. It is possible that this was true also of the Judaizers and their troubling activity in Galatia.

Paul then quoted a common saying and in so doing used a strong Greek word for "burden" (*phortion*) which can mean the cargo of a ship (Acts 27:10). Everyone is responsible to God for what he is: that is his burden. The seriousness of this is emphasized in Philippians 2:12, 13 where Paul said, "Work out your own salvation with fear and trembling," and then he stressed that "it is God which worketh in you both to will and to do of his good pleasure."

**6. Let him that is taught in the word communicate unto him that teacheth in all good things:** ... him who is instructed, —SCLT ... him that is catechized, —RHEM ... him that is being orally-instructed, —RTHM ... minister vnto him, —GNVA ... should share with his teacher, —NORL ... share in all good things, —PNIN ... share everything good that he has with the one who instructs him, —ADAM.

**6:6.** At first glance the immediate connection between this verse and the preceding is somewhat puzzling. The Greek verb (*koinōneitō*) translated "communicate" ("share") may refer to the material or the spiritual. Many take it to mean that those who are taught the Word are to contribute toward the teacher's material support. However, it may also mean, because of the context, that Christians should share, take part in all good things, that is, the Word which is taught. Acts 14:23 records that Paul and Barnabas appointed elders to be in charge of each church in Galatia and its spiritual growth. These may or may not have served without remuneration.

**7. Be not deceived; God is not mocked: for whatsoever a man soweth, that shall he also reap:** ... Do not mistake, —MRDK ... God is not to be derided, —WLSN ... is not to be trifled with, —TCNT ... is not to be scoffed at, —WLMS ... is not scorned, —WCLF.

**8. For he that soweth to his flesh shall of the flesh reap corruption:** ... who sows for, —ADAM ... to gratify his own flesh, —NORL ... of their earthly nature will reap decay, —TCNT ... will reap destruction, —WLMS.

**but he that soweth to the Spirit shall of the Spirit reap life everlasting:** ... for the Spirit will reap eternal life, —ADAM ... enduring Life, —TCNT.

**6:7, 8.** Paul's vigorous comment is very much in order. The Galatians were to share in the "good things" which they were taught, namely, the message of salvation by grace alone. But the Judaizers were promoting a false gospel. Paul emphatically warned against listening to them. Do not be misled, he said; God is not mocked! The Greek word for "mocked," *muktērizetai*, means "to turn up one's nose." Both the Judaizers and those who were listening to them as well as also being boastful about themselves would receive God's judgment. To sow refers back to 5:16 and its expression of walking in the Spirit. To sow to the flesh means to do those sins which are listed in 5:19-21. To sow to the Spirit refers to the fruit of His work as listed in 5:22-26. Again Paul stressed the role of the Spirit and the blessed result of His work. (Paul's analogy of sowing and reaping was part of the annual experience of the Galatians.)

**9. And let us not be weary in well doing: for in due season we shall reap, if we faint not:** ... let us not lose heart, —PNT . . . let us not be faint-hearted, —NOYS . . . Let us stop getting tired of doing good, —WLMS . . . for, unless we throw in our hand, the ultimate harvest is assured, —PHLP . . . at the proper season, —WLSN . . . if we do not grow weary, —TCNT . . . if we do not give up, —WLMS . . . if we do not lose courage, —NORL . . . if we don't slacken, —ADAM.

**10. As we have therefore opportunity, let us do good unto all [men], especially unto them who are of the household of faith:** . . . let us treat every one with kindness, —TCNT . . . especially to the members of the family, —SAWR . . . especially those who belong to the Christian household, —PHLP . . . to those who are of one family with us in the faith, —NORL . . . the family of faith, —WLMS.

**6:9, 10.** The verb *to reap* provides the connection with the preceding. Paul reminded believers that, through the Spirit's work, to keep on walking in the Spirit is an ongoing process. To slow down or even to stop is never in order for a Christian. This temptation was and is a common one. Paul in his other letters stressed this ongoing need (1 Corinthians 15:58; 16:13; Philippians 1:27-30; 2:14, 15; 4:1, 4-9; 1 Thessalonians 3:12, 13; 2 Thessalonians 3:13). Paul added, "For in due season we shall reap, if we faint not." It is essential to remember that such reaping is again an expression of God's grace.

Paul restated in the positive what he had just said in the negative. The Galatians were reminded to do that which was beneficial, and especially spiritually beneficial to all men, "especially. unto them who are of the household of faith." The word "household" was an important legal and social term at that time. All who were part of a given household (family, servants, and slaves) were part of this inclusive unit. For example, when Lydia came to faith, she and her whole house (household) were baptized. The same metaphor is used in Ephesians 2:19, 1 Timothy 3:15, and 1 Peter 4:17. All who share faith in Christ form religiously a single unit, a household. Paul stressed an important principle of the Christian life. If believers ignore the spiritual welfare of their fellow Christians, less thought will be given to the spiritual welfare of the unbeliever.

**11. Ye see how large a letter I have written unto you with mine own hand:** . . . Notice the large letters, —ADAM . . . Look at these huge letters I am making, —PHLP . . . in how large letters, —SCLT . . . in my own handwriting! —MNTG.

**6:11.** Paul customarily dictated his letters. His purpose for the Galatians was to warn that they would fall from grace if they listened to the Judaizers. Now he himself took up the pen and graphically called their attention to it. He did this also at the close of several other crucial letters to churches facing grave problems (1 Corinthians 16:21; Colossians 4:18; 2 Thessalonians 3:17). His letter was to be read to all the churches in Southern Galatia.

**12. As many as desire to make a fair show in the flesh, they constrain you to be circumcised:** . . . who are disposed to glory, —MRDK . . . who wish to appear to advantage in regard to outward things, —TCNT . . . to make a fair appearance, —SAWR, —PNT . . . They want to present a pleasing front to the world, —PHLP . . . a fine outward show, —WLMS . . . compel you, —PNIN, —CLMT.

**only lest they should suffer persecution for the cross of Christ:** . . . for the simple reason, —BRKL . . . solely that, —FNTN . . . they want to avoid being persecuted, —PHLP . . . only that they may not be persecuted, —ASV . . . fearing they will be persecuted, —SEB . . . that they may escape persecution, —ADAM.

**13. For neither they themselves who are circumcised keep the law; but desire to have you circumcised, that they may glory in your flesh:** . . . For the circumcisers themselves never observe the ritual; but they wish you to be circumcised, so that they may boast about your body, —FNTN . . . These men who are circumcised do not obey the law themselves, —SEB . . . so that they can boast of your submission, —NORL . . . about your submission to their ruling, —PHLP . . . so that they may boast of your observance of the rite, —TCNT . . . boast of you as members of their party, —WLMS.

**6:12, 13.** In the verses which follow, Paul quickly summarized the basic points he had made previously. He began by noting the selfish motives of the Judaizers. Their concern was to "make a good showing" (*euprosōpēsai*) for themselves. They differed from their fellow Jews only in that they had accepted Jesus as the promised Messiah, but failed to understand His true mission and its saving significance. Seemingly they wished to remain in good standing with the main-line Jewish community. For them to be able to boast that they had persuaded Jewish and Gentile Christians to return to the way of the Law would give them a favorable reputation in Jerusalem. Then they would not face the disfavor and wrath of the Jewish opposition.

Paul stressed that the Judaizers desired to persuade the Galatian Christians to be circumcised so they could boast to Jerusalem about their zeal for the Law. In other words, the Judaizers were not concerned about the spiritual welfare of the Galatians, but rather about their own standing in the Jewish community. Their concern was to avoid persecution for the cross of Christ.

The value of a believer's actions are not marked by how much is done so much as it is by his reason for acting. What motivates him? Why does he act in a certain way? That is what counts.

**14. But God forbid that I should glory, save in the cross of our Lord Jesus Christ, by whom the world is crucified unto me, and I unto the world:** . . . But for me, perish the thought, *—BRKL* . . . But, may I never boast, *—SCLT* . . . But I myself will not become boastful, *—FNTN* . . . but fer be it fro me to haue glorie, *—WCLF* . . . I hope that I will never brag about something like that! *—SEB* . . . that I should glory in anything except in, *—MNTG* . . . that I should boast about anything or anybody . . . which means that the world is a dead thing to me, *—PHLP* . . . except about the cross, *—ADAM* . . . is dead to me, *—TCNT.*

**15. For in Christ Jesus neither circumcision availeth any thing:** . . . It doesn't matter whether a person is, *—SEB* . . . is of any account, *—ADAM* . . . has any value, *—WLMS* . . . is of any importance, *—TCNT* . . . that counts, *—PHLP.*

**nor uncircumcision, but a new creature:** . . . All that is important is, *—SEB* . . . What counts is a new birth, *—NORL* . . . but a new creation, *—PNIN, —WLSN, —FNTN* . . . but a new nature, *—TCNT* . . . but the power of new birth, *—PHLP.*

**6:14, 15.** In sharp contrast to the attitude of the Judaizers, Paul carefully set forth his own basis for boasting. His only basis was, and always would be, not self but strictly God's grace expressed in the cross of Christ. It must be remembered that even to speak of the cross in polite Roman society of that time was unthinkable. The cross in that culture was the symbol of the greatest ignominy and disgrace, normally used only as the form of execution for slaves and the lower levels of society. It was considered such a horrible, unthinkable form of execution that no cartoonist would even think of doing a cartoon of crucifixion. And thus far, no cartoon of crucifixion dating back to the First Century has been found.

Paul added: "By (through) whom the world is crucified unto me, and I unto the world." When the risen and ascended Christ appeared to him on the Damascus Road, it had a decisive effect on him. All that he had valued in the past was now seen to be mere sewage, the meaning of the Greek word *skubala* Paul used in Philippians 3:8. In direct contrast is "the world," which stands for the world at enmity against God. It includes also the desire to be justified by works. In the analogy Paul used, the Cross was the permanent barrier between him and the world, also between what he once had been as Saul the self-righteous Pharisee, and Paul, the humble and grateful missionary, personally called by the glorified Christ. This must always be true of all believers in Christ.

In Paul's past, circumcision made an effective distinction between Jew and Gentile. Only the circumcised could be true sons of Abraham, and therefore true members of God's covenant people. But now, through the cross of Christ, this physical distinction was no longer valid. Whether one was circumcised or not made no difference at all. Through the Cross, all who are led by the Spirit to believe in Christ have become a new creation (Titus 3:4-6; 2 Corinthians 5:17). No longer are they under the curse of the Law, but they have the great privilege and joy of living under grace with the certain hope of eternal life. In this way, Paul stressed again his faithfulness to the commission which he had received from Christ himself. And for this he paid the supreme penalty (2 Timothy 4:6-8).

**16. And as many as walk according to this rule, peace [be] on them, and mercy, and upon the Israel of God:** . . . Peace and mercy to, *—SEB* . . . And whoever follow, *—CNFT* . . . all who will govern their lives by this rule, *—MNTG* . . . on all who are in line with this rule, *—ADAM* . . . they who press forward in this path, *—MRDK* . . . And as many as discipline themselves by this rule, *—FNTN* . . . To all who live by this principle, to the true Israel, *—PHLP* . . . they are God's Israel, *—TCNT* . . . upon God's true Israel! *—NORL* . . . the true Israel of God, *—WLMS.*

**6:16.** The Greek word *kanon* translated "rule" has the meaning in classical Greek of the straight edge of a ruler used by masons and carpenters. It is used here metaphorically in the sense of that which sets a standard or principle. It is in keeping with this meaning that Paul used a verb which means "walking in a straight line" according to a rule. The Galatians understood this illustration from the use of a ruler in daily life. Paul thereby sought to impress on them that circumcision promoted by the Judaizers as necessary for salvation is meaningless to all who understand who they are through Christ; also, that to be led by the Spirit in their faith and life is imperative.

All who are led by the Spirit to live in grace are the true Israel of God. The term "Israel" is another title for those who through the Spirit's work are members of God's covenant people, regardless of ethnic origins. As such they experience spiritual peace and well-being and also His ongoing mercy as a gift. They are the *new* Israel through faith; they and they alone will experience God's gracious gift of eternal life. This verse concludes the paragraph begun in verse 11.

**17. From henceforth let no man trouble me: for I bear in my body the marks of the Lord Jesus:** . . . Finally, *—WLSN* . . . But from now let none of them trouble me; for I carry in my body, *—FNTN* . . . interfere with me after this. I carry on my scarred body the marks of my owner, *—PHLP* . . . let no one cause me trouble, since I bear on my body the brandmarks, *—ADAM* . . . From this time forth . . . of Jesus, my Master, *—MNTG* . . . For the future . . . branded on my body, *—TCNT* . . . let no man be troublesome to me,

—*DOUY* . . . the brandmarks, —*RTHM* . . . the tokenes of, —*WCLF* . . . I carry scars on my body which show that I belong to Jesus, —*SEB* . . . the scars that mark me as Jesus' slave, —*WLMS.*

**6:17.** Before his final benediction, Paul introduced a strong closing remark. The Judaizers in their attempt to enslave the Christians in "work-righteousness" had caused Paul much concern. In his closing appeal, he stressed that he carried on his body the "brand-marks" (*stigmata*) of Jesus Christ. This was language that the Galatians understood. Slaves were sometimes branded to identify them as slaves. This was especially true of a runaway slave, who upon being caught, could be branded as such for the rest of his life. He could also be branded by having to wear an inscribed metal band welded around his neck.

What were the marks (*stigmata*) of Christ? No specific answer can be given. Acts 14:19 records that Paul was stoned at Lystra and dragged out of the town. Second Corinthians, perhaps written in late summer of A.D. 55, records other painful experiences of Paul (2 Corinthians 11:23-27). However, he did not in each case say when he suffered them. His body bore scars from the ill treatment he had received.

**18. Brethren, the grace of our Lord Jesus Christ [be] with your spirit. Amen:** . . . Brothers, may the gracious love of, —*SEB* . . . May the blessing, —*TCNT* . . . The spiritual blessing, —*WLMS.*

**6:18.** Paul closed with a benediction which is almost the same as in Philippians 4:23 and Philemon 25. His closing words, "the grace of our Lord Jesus Christ" restate the emphasis of Paul in this letter, namely, grace alone! Paul went on to say "be with your spirit." Those who through the Spirit's work live in grace also enjoy spiritual peace. Paul closed with "Amen" as he did in the opening greeting in 1:5. "So let it be!"

# EPHESIANS

## Overview

Ephesians is the main epistle of the New Testament concerning Christ and the Church. The closely related Epistle to the Colossians has as its main theme the cosmic Christ. It declares His pre-existence, His coming in the flesh, and His inherent glory. The theme of the Epistle to the Ephesians is the universal Church which gathers together all the people of God, Jew as well as Gentile (2:11-19). The major feature of the epistle, however, is that it presents the most complete picture of the theology of the New Testament.

## Outline of the Epistle

I. PRAISE AND PRAYER (1:1-23)

A. Authorship and Greeting (1:1, 2)

B. Praise for Salvation (1:3-14)

1. Introduction: What was lost in Fall is regained in Christ (1:3).

2. God has chosen us in Christ before the foundation of the world (1:4-6).

3. In the crucified Christ we have redemption from guilt and death (1:7).

4. In Christ all are united (1:8-10).

5. In Christ both Jew and Gentile are united unto one Body (1:11-14).

C. Prayer (1:15-23)

1. Thanks to God that all believers are united in faith and love (1:15, 16).

2. Petition that God by His Spirit will give believers hope and strength (1:17-19).

3. Praise that the resurrected and ascended Christ is Lord and Head of His church (1:19-23).

II. THE PREACHING OF THE GOSPEL (2:1-3:21)

A. It is by the grace of God that believers are saved from death and given new life (2:1-10).

B. Though Israel has a special place in salvation history, there is now no division between Jew and Gentile. Both are saved by grace and are each part of the Body, the Church (2:11-22).

C. Paul is the apostle to the Gentiles (3:1-13).

D. Believers must be strengthened in the Faith and in their fellowship with other believers in their life in Christ, rooted in His love and kept in His hope until the day of completion (3:14-21).

III. THE FRUIT OF THE GOSPEL (4:1-6:18)

A. In the life of the Church the gospel produces the fruit of unity (4:3-6).

B. Each new believer receives his special gifts with which he is to serve others (4:7-16).

C. The new life in Christ must be lived out in the particulars of every day (4:17-6:9).

D. In the home man and wife are both under the dominion of the love of Christ, parents and children are under the education of Christ, and slaves and masters are both subject to the same Lord (5:21-6:9).

E. The new life in Christ is portrayed as a struggle against evil powers. However, in this struggle believers are to put on the whole armor of God, fight with His weapons, and in all situations support one another through prayer and supplication (6:10-18).

IV. CONCLUSION (6:19-23)

A. Paul asked the church at Ephesus to remember his work in prayer (6:19, 20).

B. Paul recommends Tychicus who brought the epistle (6:21, 22).

C. Benediction (6:23, 24)

## Authorship of the Epistle

Paul himself claimed to be the writer of the epistle (1:1; 3:1). The writer is obviously of Jewish descent (1:11; 2:3). He belonged to "the holy apostles" (1:1; 3:3, 5). He had been entrusted with the secret of God, His plan of salvation for the entire world through Christ, and he had been called to preach that good news (3:7), but he was aware that his calling was by grace, that indeed he was "less than the least of all saints" (3:8). All this points to Paul as the author.

Early Church history supports this fact. Irenaeus, Tertullian, and Clement of Alexandria were convinced Paul was the author of the epistle. Most of the apostolic fathers referred to the epistle or quoted from it directly. In his first epistle to the Corinthians (46:6), Clement of Rome referred to Ephesians 4:4-6. In a letter to Polycarp (chapter 5), Ignatius made reference to Ephesians 5:25. Polycarp himself alluded several times to the Epistle to the Ephesians (*Epistle to the Philippians* 1:3; 10:2; 12:1). It seems that it is the best attested of all Paul's letters.

## Place and Date of Authorship

When and where did Paul write this epistle? Though not directly stated, there are several indications. In 3:1 the author presented himself as "the prisoner of Jesus Christ for you Gentiles." In 3:13, he wrote of the tribulations he suffered "for you." In 4:1 he again characterized himself as "the prisoner of the Lord," and in 6:20 as "an ambassador in bonds." These words are most probably to be interpreted as from a prisoner in an actual prison. There are three possibilities to consider.

(1) In the beginning of this century some scholars felt these words of Paul referred to an imprisonment in Ephesus. One mentioned Paul's reference to his missionary sufferings in Ephesus (1 Corinthians 15:32; 2 Corinthians 1:8) which, according to the wording, could very well have referred to an arrest and a threatening sentence of death. Paul wrote that in the year 54 he had already been "in prison more frequent" (2 Corinthians 11:23). Clement of Rome mentioned in his letter to the church in Corinth (5:6) that Paul had a total of seven imprisonments. However, there is no direct knowledge of any imprisonment in Ephesus, even though archeology has unearthed a building in Ephesus which is shown as "the prison of Paul." Although Luke did not include all of the details of Paul's ministry, it is unlikely he would have failed to mention such an imprisonment of the apostle. If there was such an event it was more likely that it was of only a few days' duration.

(2) Another possibility is that the Epistle to the Ephesians was written during the 2-year-long period when Paul was in custody in Caesarea, from the summer of 55 to the fall of 57 (Acts 24-26). The only real argument for this hypothesis is that Paul was apprehended not many weeks after his farewell to the Ephesian elders at Miletus (Acts 20:17f.). Paul's words concerning his opportunities for ministry (6:19f.; Colossians 4:3) speak directly against the Caesarean hypothesis. So does his mention of the many friends and coworkers who surrounded him (Colossians 4:7f.).

(3) The nearly unanimous church tradition is that the Epistle to the Ephesians was written by Paul during his imprisonment in Rome from the spring of 58 to 60. Paul's mention (6:21f.) of Tychicus, "a beloved brother and faithful minister," as the bearer of the epistle speaks also for this point of view. Tychicus is mentioned also in the same way in Paul's epistle to the Colossians (4:7f.). Although he was in bonds (3:1; 4:1; 6:20; Colossians 4:18; Philippians 1:12f.), Paul was given liberty to receive guests, to preach, and teach those who came to him (Acts 28:30, 31). He could also write letters!

## The Readers

The epistle is obviously directed toward Gentile Christians (1:13; 2:1, 11f.; 3:1) who had recently entered the Christian community (1:13, 18; 2:5; 4:1, 4, 20; 5:14). Because of their recent past, there was a risk of backsliding. They must be strengthened and matured in the life of the Christian community (3:14; 4:13) and be admonished to live separated lives (4:17f.).

Where did these people live? The epistle indicates at Ephesus (1:1). Another hint is given in 6:21 where Tychicus is mentioned as the one who delivered the epistle. According to Colossians 4:7ff., he was also the one who carried Paul's letter to the church at Colossae which had a strong spiritual and geographic connection with the churches in Laodicea and Hierapolis (Colossians 2:1; 4:13f.). These three churches lay in the southeast part of Phrygia (Acts 16:6; 18:23). Politically they belonged to the Roman province of Asia as did Ephesus in the western section. In these territories the readers of the Epistle to the Colossians as well as the Epistle to the Ephesians lived.

## The Genuineness of the Epistle

As has been mentioned, Ephesians is among the best confirmed letters of Paul as far as "outward" testimony is concerned. But during the end of the 17th Century certain questions arose concerning its authenticity because of "internal" problems.

(1) The first concerned the language and style of the epistle. This question arose because there are about 50 words which are not found in the generally undisputedly genuine epistles of Paul. Some of those words are used only once in the New Testament. Also, there are long, involved sentences, and participle and genitive constructions which indicate a richness of language not usually found in Paul's writings.

However, this argument does not hold up. For instance, in the indisputable Epistle to the Galatians, of the same length as the Epistle to the Ephesians, there occur a similar number of "special" words which indicate Paul knew and used these words. There is absolutely nothing in the epistle which does not find a natural explanation in the purpose Paul had in writing.

(2) The second objection was that the doctrinal content of the epistle belonged to a later period. Especially mentioned was Christ's preexistence, His activity in the creation, and His dominion over the visible as well as the invisible world. Also attacked was the fully developed idea of the Church as well as the choice of words used to describe justification by faith and the Parousia. But, with no exception, all of these doctrinal teachings are found in the generally accepted epistles of Paul. Paul wrote of Christ the universal Lord especially in Romans 8:28f.; 1 Corinthians 8:5f.; and Philippians 2:6-11. It was the resurrected, glorified Lord who met Paul on the road to Damascus. The Church is something more than a series of individual church-

es. It is a literal, organic unity. First Corinthians 12:22f., as well as Romans 12:4f., characterize it as the body of Christ.

In the Epistle to the Ephesians we must allow Paul to use new expressions for indisputable truths of the Christian faith. The crucified and resurrected Christ is referred to as "our peace" (2:14). The return of Christ in the clouds, the resurrection of the dead, and the catching away of those still alive are described as our "hope" (1:18) "in the ages to come" (2:7) and "the day of redemption" (4:30). We find all of these ideas mentioned in the Epistle to the Colossians.

(3) The most important argument against the Pauline authorship of the Epistle to the Ephesians is that although Ephesians and Colossians are almost parallel epistles, Ephesians contains entire sections which do not appear in Colossians. Examples are the doxology (1:3-14), the development of the unity of Jews and Gentiles in Christ in the Church (2:11-22), the section concerning the unity of the Church and the multitude of gifts (4:3-16), and the wonderful words concerning the Church as the bride of Christ (5:22-33). Colossians contains a distinct argument against a particular heterodoxy being promulgated in Colossae, while the corresponding theme in the Epistle to the Ephesians is addressed by preaching and instruction rather than direct argument.

The Epistle to the Colossians contains a series of named persons who either sent greetings or who were greeted personally (4:9-17). It seems that the author of the Ephesian letter was not on close personal terms with most of his readers. This does not necessarily mean that the readers were total strangers to the author. (Some years had passed since Paul had visited them. He had spent 3 years ministering to the Christians at Ephesus and was on personal terms with them.) The twice repeated "heard of" (1:15; 3:2) and the fact that the epistle lacks personal greetings led to the argument concerning the authorship of the epistle.

The words "at Ephesus" (1:1) are not found in two of the oldest manuscripts (Sinaiticus and Vaticanus). Neither Origenes in Alexandria nor Basilius in Caesarea in Asia Minor found these words in any of the manuscripts placed before them. However, there must have been a place named. One cannot read the first sentence of the epistle without it.

The most probable explanation is as follows: Paul is a prisoner in Rome. He receives a visitor from the Colossian church and learns of problems there. Paul dictates his letter to the Colossians, dealing with the heterodoxy of which he has been informed. That is why this epistle has such a personal and polemic character. Tychicus is to take the epistle to Colossae, and the thought occurs to Paul that he could make a circular trip with epistles to all the churches in the province. So Paul writes another epistle. It is broader and clearer and less polemic. It expresses some of the matters discussed in his letter to the Colossians, but it is in a form which can meet the situation in all the churches in the province. Copies are made for the different churches. The name of each church is added in the opening of the letter along with Paul's blessing in his own handwriting.

It is not puzzling that the copy of the letter which was given to the church in Ephesus has been "kept" and has found its place in the New Testament. The original church grew until there was not enough space for it under one roof. Thus there were quite a few churches in the great city. Each church would naturally want a copy of Paul's letter for continual reading. When Ephesus became one of the leading centers of Christianity, the epistle spread from place to place and was best known as "The Epistle of Paul to the Ephesians." But originally it was "the circular of Paul, the apostle, to the church in the province of Asia."

The connection between the actual, personal, and polemic epistle to the church at Colossae and the circular letter to a larger group of churches (the Epistle to the Ephesians) can be compared to the connection between the Epistle to the Galatians and the Epistle to the Romans. The Epistle to the Galatians is the actual "real" epistle, written to correct a situation. The Epistle to the Romans is a systematized, precise theological explanation of the same gospel and its "problems."

## An "Epistle"

No matter how many personal greetings and actual problems were dealt with in the New Testament epistles, none of them are a "once only" epistle, still less a private epistle. They are all "official" letters intended for reuse, for continued reading in the churches (Colossians 4:16; 1 Thessalonians 5:27). Gradually they were given to an even larger group of churches and finally to the whole of Christianity.

But the Epistle to the Ephesians is, to a larger extent than any other, to be read in the church service. This is evident not only from 3:4, where Paul assumed such a reading (*anaginōskontes*, meaning to read with a loud voice), but also from the tone and disposition of the entire epistle.

Attention has been drawn to the fact that the Epistle to the Ephesians is a church service via an epistle! There is the greeting (1:2), the opening hymn (1:3-14), and thanksgiving and prayer (1:15-23). The sermon falls in two parts—preaching (2:1-3:21) and admonition (4:1-6:18). There are "announcements" (6:19-22), and finally there is the blessing (6:23).

Although this goes too far, there is no doubt about the liturgical tone and design of the epistle. This is evident not only in the preaching which is Christ-centered, but we listen also to the oldest Christian hymn. There is no doubt that 1:3-14 is a complete hymn. There are also well-known doxologies as quotations (1:20f.; 2:14-18; 5:14). Water baptism and the Lord's Supper have their place, and 5:28-30 speaks of Christ as the One who gives His church nourishment for their new life. The joyful "gloria" is sounded in 3:20, and the epistle ends with an "amen" and inheritance from the synagogue service. Intercession (1:15f.) has the same liturgical tone as the preceding hymn.

## Problems Addressed in the Epistle

The fact that because of its universality the Epistle to the Ephesians differs from the Epistle to the Colossians does not mean there are no problems addressed in its admonitions. One cannot think of the Epistle to the Ephesians so universally edifying that it floats in the air!

(1) Chapter 2 deals with the old problem of the Law versus grace. Certain Jewish Christians felt the death and resurrection of Jesus Christ were not sufficient for salvation. They insisted that circumcision and the commandments of the Law must be added to the preaching of salvation by grace.

(2) The well-known question concerning Paul's apostleship was also inescapable. Paul addressed this matter in 3:1-13.

(3) Backsliding into the old ways of paganism was such a threatening problem that it drove the apostle to his knees in prayer that God would keep, strengthen, and mature the believers so that they would not be "carried away with every wind of doctrine" (3:14f.; 4:13f.).

(4) Paul did not hesitate to deal with moral problems (4:17f.; 5:23-33).

(5) Paul had dealt strongly with the problem of gnosticism which was making inroads into the Christian community of Colossae. The apostle addressed the subject again in the Epistle to the Ephesians, but this time from a positive angle, presenting Christ as Lord of all. All in heaven and on earth are subject to Him (1:10, 20f.; 2:2, 7; 3:10, 21; 4:10; 6:12).

## Paul's Ministry in Ephesus

At the beginning of his second missionary journey, Paul intended to go to the Roman province of Asia. It seemed to the apostle that Ephesus was geographically and strategically the next place to establish a church. But the Holy Spirit led otherwise, and the fruitful ministry in Europe was the result. On the return journey, however, the apostle visited Ephesus (Acts 18:18-21). On the Sabbath Day he went to the synagogue and "reasoned with the Jews" who invited him to remain for a longer time with them. The apostle realized that the time had come for a rich ministry in Ephesus. It would be the bridgehead for the gospel in the province of Asia. Because of this, Paul left Aquila and Priscilla, a married couple of his working group, to arrange for the future work in Ephesus.

After a "stay at home" during the winter of 51-52, Paul began his third missionary journey. On his way to Ephesus, he visited the young churches in Galatia and Phrygia and arrived in Ephesus in the spring of 52. From the "upper coasts" (Acts 19:1), the apostle overlooked the city which would become his place of ministry for the next 3 years, a city which would become one of the centers of the Christian church during the next centuries.

## The City of Ephesus

Down in the broad valley where the river Kaystros flowed out into the Aegean Sea, the city lay before Paul's eyes. It was large and beautiful with its white houses and long streets, the great harbor, and the multitude of people, over 300,000 inhabitants. There were other cities too in this corner of the Roman Empire. The province was the richest of all the provinces. The seaport towns were Smyrna and Miletus. Pergamum was the residence of the governor of the province. Thyatira, Sardis, Philadelphia, Hierapolis, Laodicea, and Colossae were there, but Ephesus was the greatest and most important city.

In Paul's time Ephesus was already an old city. It was founded about 900 B.C. by Greek emigrants. By the time a Christian church was founded there, Ephesus had become the fourth largest city of the Roman Empire with a mixed population. Besides the descendants of the original Greek population there were people from Asia Minor, the Orient, and the Jews who had established a synagogue.

Ephesus was an important commercial city and shipping center. It was the transit trade route between Rome and the province of Asia. It was also a great tourist city. The great attraction which drew visitors from all parts of the then known world was the temple of Artemis. Artemis was originally a Greek goddess of the hunters. She became a symbol of fertility, a sex goddess, encircled and served by 1,000 temple prostitutes. Her temple, Artemision, was built about 700 B.C. It was burned in 356 B.C. by Herostrat. Fifty years later it was rebuilt by Deinokrates, the architect, and it was described as one of the seven wonders of the ancient world. This temple stood for 500 to 600 years until it was destroyed by the Goths in the migration period of A.D. 262. The Goths destroyed the city so totally that the English archeologist J.T. Wood took 7 years to confirm its location and recover artifacts. That it disappeared so completely is due to the fact that parts of the city were used for other construction purposes, for example, the church of Sophia in Bysants about A.D. 500.

The destruction and subsequent disappearance of the temple and the city changed the level of the land, filling the great harbor with sand. Not until recent decades have archeologists been able to uncover the streets and houses, squares and temples, the mighty amphitheater and other public buildings of the once prosperous city.

The Epistle to the Ephesians describes Gentile life in a city given over to paganism—its fascinating power (2:1-3), its emptiness and licentiousness (4:17-19), its lewdness, drinking, lust, and other darkness (5:3f.). Sex in Ephesus, as well as religion, had become big business. Among the buildings which have been uncovered is the great and distinguished bordello of the city. It was difficult for Christians to maintain a Christian lifestyle in such surroundings, and Paul warned of the danger of compromise.

## The Revival in Ephesus and the Province of Asia

According to Acts 19:1-7, Paul's first experience in Ephesus was his meeting with some of the disciples of John the Baptist. The revival which came as a result of John's preaching bore fruit not only among Jews in Palestine but also in the Diaspora, notably in the province of Asia and in Alexandria in Egypt (Acts 18:24f.). Paul preached the gospel to these disciples of John in Ephesus, baptizing them in the name of Jesus. And when Paul laid his hands upon these men, they received the baptism of the Spirit.

Paul also went to the synagogue and shared with the Jews the good news of the gospel of Christ. With frankness and persuasion he spoke concerning "the kingdom of God." For 3 months the apostle presented the gospel to the Jews. But division came. "(Many) were hardened, and believed not, but spake evil of that way before the multitude" (Acts 19:9). It had been Paul's experience everywhere (Acts 13:14f.; 14:1f.; 17:1f.; 18:4f.). Paul now had to separate himself and organize an independent Christian church. The meeting place at first was in the school of Tyrannus where lectures and conversations took place during the early hours of the forenoon before the noonday heat came. Ordinarily Tyrannus could rent his rooms to other similar purposes. Codex D adds in Acts 19:9 that Paul used the rooms "from the 5th until the 10th hour." In the morning Paul worked at his trade of tentmaking, along with his coworkers Aquila and Priscilla (Acts 20:33-35).

That Paul indulged in "disputing" ("dialogue," dialegomenos, Acts 19:9) does not mean that he tried to find a religious denominator. Paul preached Christ without any compromise, not as a way but as the Way (Acts 19:9, 23). In the Epistle to the Ephesians the same distinct testimony to Christ is given. Only through Him is there access to God (2:18; 3:12). Thus, the "dialogue" refers only to the Greek form of public speaking. Believers met for fellowship and worship in the largest Christian homes (Acts 20:20), for example, the home of Aquila and Priscilla (1 Corinthians 16:19). This type of ministry lasted without interruption for 2 years "so that all they which dwelt in Asia heard the word of the Lord Jesus, both Jews and Greeks" (Acts 19:10).

Epenetus was the first convert in Asia. Paul spoke highly of him (Romans 16:5). An extensive revival followed. Jews as well as Greeks heard the word of the Lord. The revival spread to all the towns of the province. Sick ones were healed and evil spirits cast out of those who were possessed (Acts 19:10-20). One of the distinguishing marks of the revival was joy. An outcome of this joy was obedience. The Christians burned the things connected with their pagan rituals. Their release from the evil spiritual powers was expressed in visible actions (1:21; 2:2; 6:12).

## Opposition and Departure

Paul now decided to leave Ephesus in order to visit some of the churches he had begun on his second missionary journey. The apostle was zealous in his service to the Lord and to those who had been won to Christ. He was already planning his fourth journey which he hoped would bring him to Rome, the capital of the world. However, something took place which caused Paul to send Timothy and Erastus ahead, while he himself remained in Asia "for a season."

The silversmiths in Ephesus had a lucrative business making small silver shrines to Artemis (Diana), but since so many in the city had become Christians their business was seriously affected. Something had to be done. Demetrius, a silversmith, summoned the workmen to discuss the matter. Income had diminished, unemployment threatened, and the honor of the goddess had been violated! Tempers began to boil. A great shout used at all the feasts of Artemis sounded: "Great is Diana of the Ephesians."

A demonstration march followed. The workers went to the greatest rallying place in the city, the theater. The inhabitants of the city, hearing the tumult, joined in the march. Two of Paul's coworkers were dragged along. Paul wanted to interfere, but he was stopped by members of the church and friends in the city council. The disturbance in the theater lasted for 2 hours. Finally the town clerk was able to speak to the people, warning them that unless they dispersed the Roman authorities would become involved, and they would have to account for their actions.

When the uproar ceased, Paul called the Christians together, bade them farewell, and departed for Macedonia.

## Retrospect and Anxiety

How did Paul himself judge his years of activity in Ephesus? We can ascertain some of his feelings from the epistles he wrote. In spite of the great results of his ministry, there were problems. In 1 Corinthians 15:32 we read Paul's words, "I have fought with beasts at Ephesus." The struggle was so difficult that it was only his faith in the Resurrection which upheld him. The apostle also wrote to the Corinthians about the trouble he and his co-workers had to endure in the province of Asia: "We were pressed out of measure, above strength, insomuch that we despaired even of life" (2 Corinthians 1:8). Paul could not have meant the Demetrius demonstration, since this took place after the Corinthian epistle was written. But his words unveil some of the tense and perilous conditions under which Paul labored in Ephesus.

In addition, Paul was concerned about the work in Ephesus. He longed for an opportunity to speak to the leaders of the Ephesian church. That opportunity came half a year later (Acts 20:15-21:1). In the spring of 55, after visiting Greece, Paul set sail for Syria. The ship harbored in Miletus. The apostle's friends in Ephesus were only a day's journey away, so he sent for them to come to him. Paul felt he would never again visit Ephesus, that "bonds and afflictions" awaited him. So his sermon to the Ephesian elders was full of admonition concerning their role as overseers in the church. He reminded them of certain facts concerning his ministry among them. He warned them that even in the midst of the church some would arise speaking perverse things which would draw some believers after them. Their motive would be gain. Paul exhorted the leaders of the church to be watchful, to remember the apostle's warning to the church when he was ministering to them. He reminded the leaders that during his 3 years among them he had not taken any remuneration from the church but had earned his own living by his craft. After praying with the leaders, the elders accompanied Paul to the ship and bade him farewell with tears.

## Major Themes of the Epistle

The Epistle to the Ephesians has been called the deepest book of the New Testament, where the "vision of the purpose of God stretches from eternity to eternity" (Hiebert, p. 269). It has been called "the most divine composition of man which includes each Christian doctrine" (Coleridge as cited by Bruce, *New International Commentary on the New Testament, Colossians, Philemon, and*

*Ephesians*, p. 230). In a few short chapters the fundamental truths of the gospel are concentrated.

Citing Peake who calls it "the quintessence of Paulinism," Bruce goes on to conclude that it sums up the leading themes of Paul's epistles (*New International Commentary on the New Testament, Colossians, Philemon, and Ephesians*, p. 229). The doctrines preached by the great apostle have been brought together in a completed unity. Harpur states that doctrines which in other places are presented in sentences are here placed together in a harmonious connection with the Christian faith as an entirety, each thing in its own place and context. The doctrine of the Epistle to the Romans concerning salvation by grace through faith, the appeal for Christian unity in the First Epistle to the Corinthians, the claim for apostolic authority in the Second Epistle to the Corinthians, matters concerning the Law and the gospel in the Epistle to the Galatians, the Christology of the Epistle to the Colossians, the eschatology of the First Epistle to the Thessalonians are all presented in the Epistle to the Ephesians. However, instead of the argumentative and polemic style of some of the other epistles, these doctrines are presented in a clarified style in the Epistle to the Ephesians.

The main themes of the epistle are not presented in a systematic or dogmatic form. The epistle is not a theological essay. The main contents are presented in a stream of inspiration. New thoughts come from the preceding ones in a network of sentences and subsidiary clauses, often connected by the small word *in*, (Greek, *en*) which is used not less than 120 times in the Greek text. N.B. Harrison calls the theme of oneness in Christ "the loftiest truth of the Bible" (p. 135). The continual theme is what Christians have and are in Christ. In a style which is at the same time plain and exalted, Paul describes the riches of salvation. Doctrine is lifted to praise, theology becomes worship. The epistle is a hymn concerning Christ and His holy bride (Schaff, *History of the Christian Church,* 1:780).

However, the apostle does not lose contact with the world of everyday realities. Along with the doctrinal teaching of the epistle, there is admonition and instruction for the daily life of Christians in the home and in the church.

## Christology

The Christology of the Epistle to the Ephesians (as well as that of the Epistle to the Colossians) is one of the most exalted in the New Testament. It includes:

### (1) Christ's Humility

"Now that he ascended, what is it but that he also descended first into the lower parts of the earth? He that descended is the same also that ascended up far above all heavens, that he might fill all things" (4:9, 10). This passage corresponds with the section concerning the humiliation and exaltation of Christ recorded in Philippians 2:5-11. What does the expression "the lower parts of the earth" mean? Does it refer to the earth itself (which is lower than the heavens) or the kingdom of death (which is lower than the earth)? John 3:13 speaks of the admission of the Son of Man into heaven, and it is contrasted to His coming to the earth, which strengthens the first interpretation. In Romans 10:6f. (cf. Deuteronomy 30:12f.) the ascension of Christ is contrasted with His descent to the kingdom of death. Both interpretations are thus possible.

### (2) Christ's Death On the Cross

It was through His bodily death on the cross that Christ won our redemption through His blood (2:7). The cross is the symbol of the substitutional death of Christ on our behalf, a death which was under the curse of God (Galatians 3:13). That is why the Cross expresses the totality of the gospel (1 Corinthians 1:18; cf. Romans 1:16). On the cross Christ received in our stead the sentence of God's wrath upon sin (Romans 3:24, 25; cf. 1 John 2:2).

### (3) Christ's Resurrection

In 1 Corinthians 15:5f., Paul gave the historical proof of the resurrection of Christ. In Ephesians Paul spoke of the resurrection of Christ as a demonstration of the power of God and a testimony that this power is "to us-ward who believe" (1:19, 20). As in the other epistles, as well as the whole of the New Testament, the resurrection of Christ has a central place in the Epistle to the Ephesians (see Acts 2:24; Romans 1:4; 4:25; 14:9; 1 Corinthians 15; 1 Peter 1:3; Revelation 1:18).

### (4) Christ's Exaltation

Christ's exaltation is a leading theme in the Epistle to the Ephesians. Christ was not only resurrected, He is seated at the right hand of God in heaven, elevated above every power and authority in this world and the one to come. All has been placed under His feet, and He has been made the Head of all things (1:20, 23). He ascended up above all heavens in order to fill all things (4:8-10). The Epistle to the Ephesians maintains a Christology which can be traced throughout the New Testament, from the earliest Christian preaching (Acts 3:20, 21) to the last book of the Bible (Revelation 1:13-18).

### Soteriology

The doctrine of salvation is presented in the Epistle to the Ephesians. Paul declared that salvation is in Christ. It is called "redemption through his blood" (1:7), and it is presented through the words of the gospel (1:13). Salvation consists of the forgiveness of sins (1:7), and believers are made partakers of His eternal life (2:1-5). Salvation is not of works (2:9). It is given by grace and must be received through faith (2:8) and brings about a new manner of life which results in good deeds (2:10).

Forgiveness of sin is called justification in Romans 4:5, 6, and it consists in the fact that sin is not imputed to us. Salvation makes us new creatures in Christ (2 Corinthians 5:17). It is "by grace through faith" (2:8), and the antithesis "not of works" and "unto good works" (2:9, 10) expresses the main principle in the doctrine of salvation in the New Testament.

### Ecclesiology

The doctrine concerning the Church is one of the most important themes in the Epistle to the Ephesians. Paul used the word *church* (*ekklēsia*) to refer to local churches and to the Church universal (1 Corinthians 12:28; 15:9; Galatians 1:13; Philippians 3:6; Colossians 1:18-24). In the Epistle to the Ephesians Paul wrote mainly of the Church universal, but when particular matters needed attention Paul wrote to the local churches.

The Church is the body of Christ. Christ himself is the Head (4:15, 16), and Christians are the members of that Body (4:25; cf. 1 Corinthians 12:12f.). The Church is also the temple of God, built on the foundations which the apostles and prophets laid, and Jesus Christ is the Cornerstone (2:20-22; cf. 1 Corinthians 3:9-17). Paul called the Church of the New Testament a "secret, a mystery." According to its usage in the New Testament, this word means a divine plan which has been made known through revelation. It was Paul's privilege as the apostle to the Gentiles to make known the mystery that Jesus Christ, the Messiah of Israel and the Son of God, now resides in the Church which consists of Gentiles as well as Jews (3:1-12). Gentiles are no longer strangers and foreigners, excluded from the household of God. Through faith they are now a part of the family of God and share in the promise in Christ.

Paul defined precisely the universality of the Church and its unity. The division between Jew and Gentile has been broken down forever: "He is our peace, who hath made both one, and hath broken down the middle wall of partition between us, having abolished in his flesh the enmity" (2:14, 15). The expression "middle wall" is probably a reference to the wall in the temple beyond which Gentiles could not pass. In Christ the barriers have fallen. Jews and Gentiles alike are made nigh by the blood of Christ, with access by one Spirit to the Father. The picture of the Church drawn by Paul in 3:10-12 has cosmic dimensions and opens up perspectives whose depths we do not fully understand at the present time. The future of the Church, that which God has prepared for those who love Him, exceeds all that the eye can see, the ear hear, or that which has entered into the heart of man. Even though it has been revealed, it still remains a mystery (1 Corinthians 2:9, 10).

## Eschatology

Ecclesiology now becomes eschatology. The glory which the Church now has will be exceeded by the glory of the world to come (Hebrews 6:5). The Church which is pictured as sitting "together in heavenly places in Christ Jesus" (2:6) is said now to be in battle with the devil and all his powers (6:12). But that Church is waiting for the return of Christ (4:30). The earnest of our inheritance is the Spirit He has given us (1:14). The Church has received the firstfruits of the Spirit (Romans 8:23) and awaits the new day which shall break with the return of Christ.

# The Epistle of Paul to the Ephesians

## Commentary

### Chapter 1

**1. Paul, an apostle of Jesus Christ by the will of God:** ... messenger ... by God's choice, –*PHLP* ... by the pleasure of God, –*MRDK* ... because that is what God wanted, –*EVRD.*
**to the saints which are at Ephesus, and to the faithful in Christ Jesus:** ... God's holy people, –*EVRD* ... even to Believers in, –*WLSN* ... sanctified, and believing, –*MRDK* ... faithful followers of, –*NORL* ... To "the holy people who live in the city of, –*SEB* ... to them which believe on Iesus, –*TNDL* ... to all faithful Christians ... and other places where this letter is read, –*PHLP.*

**1:1.** The name "Paul" comes from the Latin and means "small." Hebrew parents often gave their sons Gentile names in addition to Jewish ones. Because of the nature of this epistle, the Holy Spirit inspired Paul to introduce himself as an apostle. Much debate exists relative to the exact recipients of this letter. Three of the oldest manuscripts, the Chester Beatty Papyrus (dated circa 200); the Codex Sinaiticus; and the Codex Vaticanus (usually dated in the Fourth Century), do not contain the words "at Ephesus." The earliest extant manuscript containing the words "at Ephesus" is at least two centuries later than the last two manuscripts referred to above. This fact and others have led some scholars to believe the epistle actually was written as a cyclical letter to be read in all the churches of Asia Minor.

**2. Grace [be] to you, and peace:** ... Favour to you, –*RTHM* ... May gracious love and peace come to you, –*SEB* ... spiritual blessing, –*WLMS.*
**from God our Father, and [from] the Lord Jesus Christ:**

**1:2.** Paul greeted his readers in the normal fashion of the day. It was conventional first to mention the author's name, then refer to the recipients of the letter, and lastly to greet them in a pleasant way. What is different about Paul's approach is that, in addition to the fact that the Holy Spirit very definitely inspired him to do so, he constantly used the Greek idea of "grace" (*charis*) and the Hebrew idea of "peace" which was translated into Greek and became a very common word of that day (*eirēnē*). "Grace" contains the meaning of receiving something completely undeserved, and

"peace" contains the idea of enjoying inner tranquility, undisturbed by external circumstances.

**3. Blessed [be] the God and Father of our Lord Jesus Christ:** ... Praise be to, –*TCNT* ... Praise God! He is the Father, –*SEB* ... Let the God and Father ... be blessed, –*FNTN.*
**who hath blessed us with all spiritual blessings in heavenly [places] in Christ:** ... who, through our union with Christ, –*TCNT* ... for giving us through Christ every possible spiritual benefit as citizens of Heaven! –*PHLP* ... has given us every spiritual blessing in heaven, –*EVRD* ... in heuenly thynges, –*CRNM* ... among the celestials, –*CNDT* ... in the heavenly spheres, –*BRKL* ... that heaven itself enjoys, –*NORL* ... in the heavenly regions in Christ, –*NOYS* ... on high in Christ, –*CNFT.*

**1:3.** In many of his epistles Paul gradually built up to his major thesis, but in this letter he began with one of the most important of all theological truths: God's purpose for the New Testament Church. The position of the believer is "in the heavenlies in Christ"; this describes the sphere and the nature of our spiritual experiences. "In Christ" or its equivalent can be found 10 times from verses 3 through 13 of the first chapter, and the preposition "in" (en) is used approximately 120 times in the 6 chapters of Ephesians. Because verses 3 through 14 are one complete sentence in the Greek, it is obvious the passage should be treated as one complete thought. Some Bible scholars believe this passage was used as a hymn sung in the Early Church in praise to God.

**4. According as he hath chosen us in him before the foundation of the world:** ... consider what he has done, –*PHLP* ... before a foundation, –*RTHM* ... before the constitution, –*RHEM* ... before the casting down of the world, –*CLMT* ... bifor the makynge of the world, –*WCLF* ... were layd, –*GNVA.*
**that we should be holy and without blame before him in love:** ... intending that we, –*TCNT* ... and unspotted, –*DOUY* ... and immaculate, –*RHEM* ... blameless in his presence, –*WLSN*, –*RTHM* ... living within his constant care, –*PHLP.*

**1:4.** Now we come to the extremely important question, "How can God be sovereign and man be free at the same time?" Many take this verse, as well as verse 5, to teach the election by God of some to salvation and some to damnation. They understand the word "chosen" (*exelexato*) to mean God chooses some individuals to be spared to the exclusion of all others. An alternative to this position states that what God determined before the creation of the world was not who would be saved and who would be lost, but the institution of the New Testament Church.

The verb "chose" is a middle voice verb meaning "He chose us for himself." The "in him" in this verse, as well as the statement in verse 3, indicates that all God's blessings come to people "in Christ" (literally "in the sphere of Christ").

One of the main ideas behind the term *election* is that God has taken the initiative to provide salvation. This passage places more emphasis on the method of election than on the persons involved. Election is a choosing based upon God's grace, not upon man's merit. In addition the verse focuses not as much upon *whom* God has chosen (i.e., individuals or a Body), but upon *why:* that we should be holy and blameless ("without blemish") before Him.

Again, there are differing views of what the latter part of the verse means. Some say it teaches that holiness and blamelessness are imputed to the individual at the time of his election. Others believe it is a reference to progressive sanctification.

**5. Having predestinated us unto the adoption of children by Jesus Christ to himself:** ...having before appointed us, *—SCLT* ...having foreordained us, *—ASV* ...having in Love previously marked us out for Sonship, *—WLSN* ...for the privileges of his sons, *—TCNT.*

**according to the good pleasure of his will:** ...in fulfilment of his loving purposes, *—TCNT* ...to the purpose of his will, *—DOUY.*

**1:5.** This verse further describes why God has chosen believers: that through His Mediator, Jesus Christ, we may stand before Him as children. Whereas "election" looks back to discover whom God has chosen, "predestination" points forward to what God has determined shall be the destiny of those who are His. Because it pleased Him to do so, He predetermined that He would adopt us as His own children based on the merits of Christ alone. It is "not by works of righteousness which we have done, but according to his mercy he has saved us" (Titus 3:5).

Some interpret these passages to say that after God predestined believers to adoption, He elected them to be holy, etc. Others insist that election and adoption are accomplished simultaneously. Meyer points out that elsewhere in the New Testament predestination is not distinguished from election "as something preceding it; it rather substantially coincides with it" (*Meyer's Commentary,* 7:315). Only "foreknowledge" seems to be a prior activity on God's part (cf. Romans 8:29).

**6. To the praise of the glory of his grace:** ...to the praise of his glorious grace, *—SAWR, —SCLT* ...and so we praise His glorious mercy, *—NORL* ...that we might learn to praise that glorious generosity of his, *—PHLP.*

**wherein he hath made us accepted in the beloved:** ...he hath graced us in his beloved son, *—DOUY* ...by which He has made us the objects of His favor through His beloved, *—NORL* ...which He freely bestowed on us in the Beloved, *—CLMT* ...which has made us welcome in the everlasting love he bears toward the Son, *—PHLP.*

**1:6.** Salvation and all its benefits are the results of God's glorious grace (His unmerited favor). As such it deserves our praise. "Accepted in the beloved" introduces a transition to Christ who is the subject of the following verses.

**7. In whom we have redemption through his blood:** ...For by union with Christ, *—TCNT* ...at the cost of, *—PHLP.*

**the forgiveness of sins:** ...freely forgiven, *—PHLP* ...in the pardon of our offences, *—TCNT.*

**according to the riches of his grace:** ...through that full and generous grace, *—PHLP.*

**1:7.** If this total passage from verse 3 through verse 14 was used as a hymn by the Early Church, the second stanza focused on the redemptive work of Christ. The word "redemption" actually has a definite article before it in the original language, so it specifies "the redemption," indicating the one and only way of salvation. The language used here was very familiar to a person of that day to whom the slave market was a common sight, a place where human beings were offered for sale to the highest bidders. The mention of Christ's blood (*tou haimatos autou*) refuted the docetic Gnostic notion that Christ did not have a real body but only seemed to have one. The "riches of his grace" caused Christ to redeem us by the payment of a price (Greek, *lutron*; cf. *apolutrōsin*), the giving of himself as a sacrifice for our sins.

**8. Wherein he hath abounded toward us:** ...so abundantly did he lavish upon us, *—MNTG* ...heaped upon us, *—TCNT* ...moste plentifully, *—GNVA* ...which has overflowed into our lives and opened our eyes to the truth, *—PHLP.*

**in all wisdom and prudence:** ...by countless gifts of wisdom, *—TCNT* ...and all spiritual understanding, *—MRDK* ...and Intelligence, *—WLSN.*

**1:8.** What God did He performed "in all wisdom and prudence," or with wisdom and intelligence. Because He is omniscient, God never is without knowledge of what is transpiring, and He is able to apply that knowledge to make prudent decisions. The term "lavished" used by the NIV translators very appropriately expresses the idea contained in the Greek term Paul used here (*eperisseusen*) to refer to the way God's grace "abounded" toward us.

**9. Having made known unto us the mystery of his will:** ...the sacrament of his will, −RHEM...the secret purpose of his will, −MNTG...the secret of his plan, −PHLP.

**according to his good pleasure which he hath purposed in himself:** ...according to his fre be- neuolence, −GNVA.

**1:9.** The term "mystery" (*mustērion*) refers to something kept hidden until a certain time, something only God could reveal. It does not describe something mysterious, but something that remains hidden until God chooses to reveal it. Paul used it mainly in Ephesians to describe the fact that in the New Testament Church no distinction exists between Gentiles and Jews.

**10. That in the dispensation of the fulness of times he might gather together in one all things in Christ:** ...when the tyme were full come, −TNDL... for the government of the fulness of the ages, −MNTG... as regards the administration of, −PNT... the fulness of the seasons, −PNIN... to re- unite for himself, −RTHM... to re-establish all things, −CNFT... to re-unite under one head, −SCLT... the establishment of a New Order, −TCNT.

**both which are in heaven, and which are on earth; [even] in him:** ...everything that exists in Heaven or earth shall find its perfection and fulfill- ment in him, −PHLP.

**1:10.** The language used continues to express the purpose which God had in mind, that in this day in which we are privileged to live, all those people "in Christ" would be part of the same Body, with no distinctions. The scope of this verse, howev- er, cannot be limited just to the present age. The work of subjecting this universe totally to Christ will continue in the Millennium. The word trans- lated "dispensation" (*oikonomian*) comes from two Greek words placed together, one meaning "law" (*nomos*) and the other meaning "house" (*oi- kos*). It literally becomes "house-law" and often is translated "stewardship." Because the word can be used in different ways, the Bible student must look at it within the context where it is used. Here it obviously relates to the overall purpose of God to subject everything to Christ in an ultimate sense.

**11. In whom also we have obtained an inheri- tance:** ...we also are called by lot, −RHEM...that in all which will one day belong to him we have been promised a share, −PHLP.

**being predestinated according to the purpose of him:** ...previously marked out, −WLSN...being marked out beforehand,

−RTHM...chosen beforehand, −MNTG...according to the plan of Him, −NORL...foreordained, −PNIN.

**who worketh all things after the counsel of his own will:** ...is executing his own fixed purpose, −TCNT...who achieves his purposes by his sovereign will, −PHLP...agreeably to the counsel, −WLSN...the counsel of his pleasure, −MRDK.

**1:11.** It is almost beyond the human mind to fathom that God allows us to share the glory that belongs to Christ, the One to whom this total universe will be subjected ultimately. His will not only includes the exaltation of Christ, it also in- cludes our participation in His blessings because we are part of those who are "in Christ." This verse reminds us again that all this happens be- cause of God's design. In fact, in this verse Paul used three words that have the idea of "will" ex- pressed in them. *Prothesin* normally contains the idea of "purpose." *Boulēn* sometimes expresses the idea of "counsel," but usually relates to "purpose" or "will." The third term or last noun in the verse (*thelēmatos*) is a general Greek term for "will." This approach is very typical of Paul's epistles when he multiplied synonyms to amplify an idea.

**12. That we should be to the praise of his glo- ry:** ...that we should win praise for his glorious Name, −TCNT...bring praise to his glory! −PHLP.

**who first trusted in Christ:** ...we who had first put our hope in, −WLMS...before placed our hope in the Messiah, −NOYS...had before hoped in Christ, −ASV.

**1:12.** The phrase "praise of his glory" occurs in relation to each member of the Trinity: of God (verse 6), of Christ (verse 12), and the Holy Spirit (verse 14).

**13. In whom ye also [trusted], after that ye heard the word of truth, the gospel of your sal- vation:** ...And you too trusted him, −PHLP.

**in whom also after that ye believed, ye were sealed with that holy Spirit of promise:** ...you were signed with, −DOUY...have been stamped with the seal of, −WLMS...in him were marked as his by receiving the holy Spirit, −TCNT... even the holy [Spirit], −ALFD.

**1:13.** The finishing touches on this beautiful portrait show the work of the Holy Spirit in re- demption. Verse 12 says "we" (Jews) and verse 13, "ye" (Gentiles). The Holy Spirit is the One who, after we hear and believe the truth of the gospel, actually places a seal of ownership upon us. Seals were in common use in those days. A person often stamped his letters with a seal or a sign to prove they were sent by him. Pagan cults often stamped their devotees with seals in the form of tattoos. A seal indicated a document was genuine and au- thentic. We do much the same thing today when we brand steers, sheep, etc., or when we use the corporate seal of an organization to certify some statement or authenticate a document.

A person who is "in Christ" has been sealed as God's property. This does not happen until a person hears and believes the gospel message. This does not mean that God does the sealing first, and then the person hears the gospel message. "After that ye believed" actually comes from a Greek aorist participle (*pisteusantes*) which is used in an adverbial sense here and normally would be translated "after believing."

The original term for "heard" (*akousantes*) is also an aorist active participle and means "after hearing." According to the order used in the verse, "after hearing" comes first, followed by "after believing," and the whole process culminates with an aorist passive verb (*esphragisthēte*) meaning "you were sealed." This verb indicates that God performed the act of sealing, as well as indicating that it was a decisive act. To understand what is being said, it is absolutely crucial to look at this passage in its entirety from verse 3 through verse 14.

**14. Which is the earnest of our inheritance:** . . . the pledge of our common heritage, —*MNTG*. . . as a guarantee of purchase, —*PHLP*.

until **the redemption of the purchased possession:** . . . that we might be fully restored to libertie, —*GNVA* . . . for the recouering of the purchased possession, —*CRNM* . . . unto the complete redemption of his purchased property, —*MNTG* . . . until the redemption of them that are alive, —*MRDK*.

**unto the praise of his glory:** . . . vnto the laude of his glory, —*TNDL*.

**1:14.** This becomes even more obvious when one realizes the "in Christ" person has been given an *arrhabōn* ("earnest, down payment, deposit") as a pledge that the full payment will be given when Jesus returns to this earth. The down payment we have received is the Holy Spirit himself (Romans 8:9, 16). His indwelling presence is a guarantee that God will consummate all His promises to us when the proper time arrives.

The noun "redemption" (*apolutrōsin*) refers to the culmination of the process which will become a reality when Jesus returns to this earth and believers are resurrected.

All these promises should make us burst into praise as they did the apostle Paul. Now we can see a little more clearly why it is a mistake to take only a few statements out of this complete sentence from verse 3 through verse 14. God does not give us only part of the total picture and leave us confused. He has informed us clearly about the function of each member of the Trinity in the work of redemption. The Father planned, the Son provided, and the Holy Spirit protects the ones who accept God's provision!

**15. Wherefore I also:** . . . On this account, —*WLSN* . . . For this reason, —*ADAM* . . . Since, then, —*PHLP*.

**after I heard of your faith in the Lord Jesus:** . . . hearing about, —*ADAM* . . . that prevails among you, —*TCNT*.

**and love unto all the saints:** . . . and about your love, —*ADAM* . . . and the practical way in which you are expressing it toward fellow Christians, —*PHLP*.

**1:15.** The normal custom in writing letters was to include thanksgiving and prayer somewhere near the beginning of an epistle. This verse speaks of the believers' "faith in the Lord Jesus" and their "love unto all the saints." The word "heard" suggests that the apostle did not know personally many of the recipients.

Just as we saw one complete sentence in the Greek in verses 3-14, we again see one complete sentence in verses 15-23. "Wherefore" (*dia touto*) literally means "on account of this" and refers back to 3-14. It is as if Paul were saying, "Now that you are part of God's predestined elect, what is next?"

**16. Cease not to give thanks for you:** . . . do not omit giving thanks, —*WLSN* . . . thank God continually, —*PHLP*.

**making mention of you in my prayers:** . . . making constant mention, —*TCNT* . . . making a memorie of you, —*RHEM* . . . I never give up praying for you, —*PHLP*.

**1:16.** Therefore, Paul prayed constantly that believers would be recipients of the lasting benefits of salvation, or that they would mature in their spiritual experiences.

**17. That the God of our Lord Jesus Christ, the Father of glory:** . . . the Father most glorious, —*MNTG* . . . the Glorious Father, —*WLSN* . . . who is the all-glorious Father, —*NORL*.

**may give unto you the spirit of wisdom and revelation:** . . . may grant you, —*WLMS* . . . to inspire you with, —*TCNT* . . . give you spiritual wisdom and the insight, —*PHLP*.

**in the knowledge of him:** . . . in the full Knowledge of him, —*WLSN* . . . in the recognition of him, —*MRDK* . . . through an intimate knowledge, —*MNTG* . . . through a growing knowledge of Him, —*WLMS* . . . to know more of him, —*PHLP*.

**1:17.** Verse 17 begins with the Greek word *hina*, a very strong way of expressing purpose that normally is translated "in order that." It is followed by a verb (doe) which is in the optative mood. According to some grammarians, the optative mood is found only 67 times in the New Testament, most often to express a wish. It denotes the blessing Paul desired for believers: that they would comprehend fully what they had received in Christ. Paul's earnest prayer was that God would continue to bestow upon believers the gift of His Holy Spirit already imparted to them, with the result of making them wise in understanding the bestowments of His grace.

It should not be taken for granted that this would happen automatically. Even though they already knew God in a special way, he wanted them to know Him better. He emphasized a full knowledge, or a complete understanding of God's redemptive work in Christ. This could take place only with the help of the Holy Spirit. Even though the word for "spirit" here (*pneuma*) lacks a definite article in the Greek text, it likely refers to the Holy Spirit, the One who helps Christians grow spiritually. "Wisdom" probably refers to a continued condition of proper application of knowledge; while "revelation" most likely relates to the single glances afforded believers into the will of God in special circumstances.

**18. The eyes of your understanding being enlightened:** ... And that your mind, *−NORL* ... eyes of your heart, *−WORL* ... that your mental vision may be made so clear, *−TCNT* ... may be flooded with light, *−MNTG.*

**that ye may know what is the hope of his calling:** ... that you may receive that inner illumination of the spirit which will make you realize how great is the hope to which he is calling you, *−PHLP* ... of his invitation, *−WLSN* ... of his vocation, *−RHEM* ... to which He calls you, *−WLMS.*

**and what the riches of the glory of his inheritance in the saints:** ... the magnificence and splendor of the inheritance promised to, *−PHLP* ... of His glorious inheritance for the saints are, *−ADAM.*

**1:18.** Paul prayed that the "heart" (see variant) would have eyes (*opthalmous*) with which to look out toward Christ. After making the purpose of his prayer clear, Paul pinpointed three very important matters essential to Christian maturity, as if to say, "If you really want to grow spiritually, you must understand these matters."

Paul prefaced each of the three items with "what" (*tis, ti*). First, if believers are to grow properly in the Lord, they must understand "the hope of his calling." "Hope" (*elpis*) was a term Paul often used and refers to an "expectant attitude." The apostle had just explained in verse 14 that Christians receive at salvation only a down payment of all that God has promised them. A proper attitude of hope longs for and expects God to consummate all His promises to His people. This tremendous hope serves as a strong incentive to spur believers on to spiritual maturity.

Secondly, understanding "God's inheritance in the saints" will lead to growth in the Lord. The Bible speaks in many places about the inheritance God has promised His people, but in this verse there is a locative case expression in the Greek which literally means "in the sphere of the saints." Obviously, God does not "need" anything from us. However, He does "want" our praise (verses 6, 12, 14). When Christians truly realize they are the only part of God's creation that can praise God willingly because they have experienced salvation (Revelation 5:9, 10), it should give tremendous motivation toward spiritual maturity.

**19. And what [is] the exceeding greatness of his power to usward who believe:** ... and what is the excellence of the majesty of his power, *−MRDK* ... how tremendous is the power available to us, *−PHLP* ... the immeasurable greatness, *−ADAM* ... the surpassing Greatness, *−WLSN, −RTHM* ... and how surpassingly great is the power, *−TCNT* ... of his might in us who believe, *−MNTG* ... available to us who believe, *−NORL.*

**according to the working of his mighty power:** ... measured by His tremendously mighty power, *−WLMS* ... according to the operation, *−SAWR* ... as seen in the energy of that resistless might, *−MNTG* ... It is in keeping with the force of His mighty strength, *−ADAM* ... according to the efficiency of the strength of his power, *−MRDK* ... the strength of his might, *−PNIN, −WORL* ... the energy of his mighty strength, *−WLSN* ... the inward working of the strength, *−RTHM* ... to the energy of his mighty power, *−SCLT.*

**1:19.** Thirdly, understanding "the exceeding greatness of his power to us-ward who believe" will make possible growth in the Lord. The apostle explained this idea throughout the remainder of the chapter. To explain just how much power is available to believers, Paul used four different Greek terms in this verse. "Power" (*dunamis*) means "inherent ability, capability, potential." "Working" comes from the Greek word from which we get *energy* (*energeia*) and denotes "operative power." "Mighty" (*kratos*) refers to "manifested strength." The last word in the verse ("power," *ischus*) is "power as an endowment" or "the possession of power."

**20. Which he wrought in Christ, when he raised him from the dead:** ... Which he exerted, *−WSLY* ... which he performed, *−SAWR* ... demonstrated, *−PHLP* ... exerted for Christ, *−ADAM.*

**and set [him] at his own right hand in the heavenly [places]:** ... seated him, *−ADAM* ... gave him the place of supreme honor, *−PHLP* ... in the highest heaven, *−NORL.*

**1:20.** This power always operates "in Christ." In other words, believers cannot do with this power what they choose, but its use must conform to the direction given by Christ, the head of the Church. The proper exercise of this power requires continuous faith in Christ, just as we believed in Him at conversion. The resurrection of Christ was the greatest possible manifestation of God's power. "Set him at his own right hand" relates to the position of authority which He has. Notice the beautiful progression in Paul's description of the power of God available to help believers grow in Christ. First, he made a strong appeal about realizing the necessity. He continued by saying that the power must operate through Christ. Lastly, he used the greatest example of the power of God— the resurrection of Christ.

**21. Far above all principality, and power, and might, and dominion:** ... infinitely superior to any conceivable command, *—PHLP* ... exalting him above all angelic Beings, *—TCNT* ... far above all hierarchies, *—MNTG* ... far above every government, authority, *—WLMS* ... and authority ... and lordship, *—SAWR* ... all rule, and authority, and power, and lordship, *—ALFD.*
**and every name that is named:** ... above every name, *—CNFT* ... yea, far above every other title that can be conferred, *—WLMS* ... that can be mentioned, *—TCNT* ... that could ever be used, *—PHLP.*
**not only in this world, but also in that which is to come:** ... in the future age, *—WLSN.*

**1:21.** This verse continues to exalt Christ and indicates His position of superiority over all creatures, both in heaven and earth. Jews of Paul's day generally believed that angels controlled human destiny, so Paul used the normal Jewish hierarchy of terms to indicate that Christ is in control. He has absolute authority because He is infinitely superior. Gnostics also conceived of angels as being intermediary beings between the so-called "unknowable God" and mankind. Paul, of course, did not agree with any type of Jewish or Gnostic angelic hierarchy. Much to the contrary, this verse serves as a good example of the way the apostle used the very teachings of antibiblical groups to expose the heresy inherent in them. This verse is also an example of Paul's method of piling up expressions in order to prove the point that Christ is superior to all these beings, and He will be superior also to whatever authorities will exist in the coming age.

**22. And hath put all [things] under his feet:** ... subjected All things, *—WLSN, —MRDK* ... under the power of Christ, *—PHLP.* **and gave him [to be] the head over all [things] to the church:** ... and constituted Him, *—WLSN* ... set him up as head of everything, *—PHLP* ... as its supreme Head, *—TCNT* ... the heed of the congregacion, *—TNDL.*

**1:22.** This statement comes from Psalm 8:6 with special emphasis on the perfect man, Jesus Christ. The fact that God's plan included the incarnation of Christ still continues to be one of the most outstanding doctrines of the New Testament Church.

**23. Which is his body:** ... For the Church is, *—PHLP.* **the fulness of him that filleth all in all:** ... the full development of Him, *—WLSN* ... who is wholly fulfilled in all, Confraternity ... who in every respect and everywhere is perfect, *—NORL* ... who fills the universe, *—MNTG* ... who fills everything everywhere, *—WLMS.*

**1:23.** Paul's emphasis on the necessity of understanding the power of God available, to believers comes to a conclusion with a classic reminder that the Church is the beneficiary of that power. Because the Church is a living organism with Christ as its head, God manifests His power through it. "Fullness" (*plērōma*) was a favorite term of the Gnostics who used the word to refer to the so-called intermediary beings between God and people. Paul used the verb form here in a passive sense It contains the idea of the Church being not only Christ's body, but of its being filled by Him.

## Chapter 2

**1. And you [hath he quickened]:** ... And he filleth you, *—SCLT* ... did he make alive, *—ASV.*
**who were dead in trespasses and sins:** ... at one time spiritually dead, *—NORL* ... by reason of your offenses, *—CNFT.*

**2:1.** The first 10 verses in this chapter are among the most evangelistic in the Scriptures, explaining beautifully the actual steps which occur in salvation. Paul began by reminding believers of their wretched condition before God performed the miracle of redemption. "Were dead" comes from a combination of a participle and an adjective (*ontas nekrous*), so it literally means "being dead" and refers to spiritual death which is the state of separation from God. While some Bible scholars say it is impossible to make a distinction between the words "trespasses" and "sins," others claim "trespasses" refers to outward manifestations of sin and "sins" relates to the sinful nature of a fallen human being.

**2. Wherein in time past ye walked according to the course of this world:** ... For at one time you lived in sin, *—TCNT* ... in which you passed your lives after the way of, *—MNTG* ... you drifted along on the stream of this world's ideas of living, *—PHLP* ... to the worldliness of this world, *—MRDK.*
**according to the prince of the power of the air:** ... and obeyed its unseen ruler, *—PHLP* ... according to the pleasure of the prince potentate, *—MRDK* ... the governer that ruleth in the ayer, *—TNDL.*
**the spirit that now worketh in the children of disobedience:** ... now operating in, *—WLSN* ... which now operates, *—SAWR* ... who is still operating in

those who do not respond to the truth of God, —PHLP ... inwardly working in the sons of obstinacy, —RTHM ... children of unbelief, —DOUY.

**2:2.** This verse further depicts the lost condition of mankind by specifying the forces working against them. First, unbelievers walk "according to the course of this world." This is a way of saying that fallen creatures manifest their state of spiritual death by living lives of enslavement to the world's standard of values, values that are human-centered, not God-centered.

Secondly, the rest of the verse informs us of the power that works behind this "spirit" of the age, or the ways of this world. Satan takes advantage of man's lost condition. He is at work "in the children of disobedience" or he is "operating in the sons of disobedience."

Here the writer of this epistle depicts the forces which war against believers as they seek to live godly lives: the world, the flesh, and the devil. The world is an external foe, its evil influences surrounding the believer. The flesh (the self-life) is an internal enemy, its weaknesses making it susceptible to temptation. Satan is an infernal foe, going about like a roaring lion, seeking whom he may devour. He uses the influences of the world to seduce believers, and he takes advantage of believers by attacking them at their weakest points. But God has not left believers at the mercy of these enemies of the soul. He is the eternal Friend and Deliverer who will bring victory.

**3. Among whom also we all had our conversation in times past in the lusts of our flesh:** ... we all once passed our lives, indulging the passions of, —MNTG ... once lived while gratifying the cravings of our lower nature, —WLMS.
**fulfilling the desires of the flesh and of the mind:** ... doing the promptings, —CNFT ... the will of, —DOUY ... and followed the impulses and imaginations of our evil nature, —PHLP ... and of the thoughts, —PNIN, —WLSN.
**and were by nature the children of wrath, even as others:** ... children, by nature, of anger, —RTHM ... and by nature we were exposed to God's wrath, as the rest of mankind, —WLMS ... being in fact under the wrath of God by nature, like everyone else, —PHLP ... we were exposed to the divine judgement, like the rest of mankind, —TCNT ... like all the rest, —MNTG.

**2:3.** Here Paul uses the pronoun "we" (*hēmeis*) to show that the sinful condition he had just described applied to Jews as well as to Gentiles. In verse 1 he refers to "you," the Gentile believers to whom he was writing. Next, Paul specified the third force that works against unbelievers—their fallen sinful nature. The word for "lusts" (*epithumiais*) may be used in a good sense (Luke 22:15)

or in an evil sense, depending on its use in the specific context. Paul's use here obviously refers to evil desires. Unbelievers habitually yield to the cravings of the sinful nature with which they were born (Romans 5:12). As a result, they "were by nature the children of wrath." The word "wrath" speaks of God's abiding opposition to evil (Matthew 3:7; Romans 1:18), and it is a reminder that those individuals who continue to practice sin are facing the wrath of God.

**4. But God, who is rich in mercy: for his great love wherewith he loved us:** ... gave Life to us in, —TCNT.

**2:4.** After describing what believers were in the past, the apostle began his picture of the present condition of Christians with "but God" (*de theos*). Man does not have to continue to live on the lower plain described in the first three verses of this chapter; God made a higher level of life possible for those who would accept it. God intervened because of His great love (*tēn pollēn agapēn autou*), the motivating force behind all that He does. In 1 Corinthians 13, the great classic in which he described this marvelous love, Paul detailed very specifically many of the important aspects of love. At the same time, he reminded believers that this same love must be the motivating force behind all their deeds as Christians.

This love caused God to act in mercy (*eleeō*), which can be defined as love in action. Because He loves so much, God performs specific acts of mercy.

**5. Even when we were dead in sins:** ... when we were spiritually dead because of our sins, —NORL.
**hath quickened us together with Christ:** ... gave us life together, —PHLP ... made us live together, —MNTG ... he made alive together, —WLSN.
**(by grace ye are saved;):** ... It is by God's mercy, —TCNT ... remember, by grace and not by achievement, —PHLP ... and rescued us by his grace, —MRDK.

**2:5.** God's greatest act of mercy is explained in this verse. Even though we were dead spiritually, He "quickened us together with Christ" (*sunezōopoiēsen tō Christō*). This verb is the first of three in the context that has the prefix *sun-* ("with"). The second (*sunēgeiren*) was translated by the NIV "raised us *with* Christ," and the third (*sunekathisen*), "seated us *with* him." These verbs beautifully summarize what God does for believers in the Lord Jesus Christ. First, He implants spiritual life within; then He elevates them to a new level of life; and thirdly, He permits them to enjoy a continuous relationship with Christ in this present earthly life. He accomplishes all this "by grace," *chariti*, an instrumental case construction in the

Greek language which expresses the means by which something is accomplished.

"Grace" explains how God operates. It refers to "undeserved favor" and is a constant reminder that God does not manifest acts of mercy toward people because they deserve them. "Ye are saved" in this verse actually comes from a perfect tense participle ("having been saved," *sesōsmenoi*), showing a completed action with continuous results. Salvation is probably expressed this way because of the necessity of an initial act of conversion. However, God does not cease working in believers' lives after conversion.

**6. And hath raised [us] up together, and made [us] sit together in heavenly [places] in Christ Jesus:** ... has lifted us right out of the old life, *–PHLP* ... and reserved a seat for us near Him in the heavenly home, *–NORL* ... in the celestials, *–RHEM* ... in the heavenly realm, *–MNTG.*

**2:6.** The last verse in this section shows the marked contrast between the believers' former lost condition and their present situation in Christ. While believers still live in mortal bodies on earth, they also participate in the resurrection life of Christ. The emphasis in this context is the believer's identification with Christ in His death (verse 5), His resurrection (verse 6), and His ascension (verse 6).

**7. That in the ages to come he might show the exceeding riches of his grace:** ... he might exhibit, *–WLSN* ... the overflowing riches, *–CNFT* ... the amazing riches, *–MNTG* ... the boundless wealth of his mercy, *–TCNT* ... the magnitude of the riches of his grace, *–MRDK* ... the immeasurable wealth of His mercy, *–NORL.*
**in [his] kindness toward us through Christ Jesus:** ... in his bounty, *–DOUY* ... he has expressed toward us, *–PHLP.*

**2:7.** However, the story is not yet complete. Verse 7 shows why God has done all that verses 4-6 describe. This verse begins with a strong statement of purpose, "that" or "in order that" (*hina*). Throughout all eternity the Church will be a demonstration to all creation of God's grace. Believers will truly be "trophies" of God's grace forever. "He might show" (*endeixētai*) is a middle voice verb meaning "to show for one's self" or for His own glory. So, for eternity believers will be glorifying God.

**8. For by grace are ye saved through faith:** ... are ye made safe through fayth, *–GNVA* ... through your faith, *–TCNT.*
**and that not of yourselves:** ... It is not due to yourselves, *–TCNT* ... this is not from you, *–WLSN* ... this is not your own doing, *–NORL.*
**[it is] the gift of God:**

**2:8.** Verses 8-10 remind believers that they need to accept what God has provided them in Christ Jesus. We see an amplification of the statement in verse 5, "by grace ye are saved." In the original language this verse begins with the definite article "the" before "grace" (*tē ... chariti*). Also, the verse begins in the Greek with a postpositive "for" (*gar*) which could be translated "because." Grace is the "cause" for the total plan of God. On the one hand, grace is the objective, instrumental cause of salvation. On the other hand, faith is the subjective medium for the process of salvation, so it is a necessary condition. "It is the gift of God" refers to the whole process of salvation, not just to the granting of faith to believe.

**9. Not of works:** ... and cometh not of workes, *–CRNM* ... earning, *–PHLP.*
**lest any man should boast:** ... No one can pride himself upon, *–PHLP* ... in order that, *–ALFD* ... that no man may glory, *–DOUY* ... lest any one glory, *–MRDK.*

**2:9.** This is probably the reason Paul reminds us in the previous verse that salvation cannot be earned in any way. There is no possibility of self-achieved salvation, and no reason for boasting.

**10. For we are his workmanship:** ... what we are we owe to the hand of God upon us, *–PHLP* ... for we are his creation, *–SAWR,* *–MRDK* ... his handiwork, *–MNTG.*
**created in Christ Jesus unto good works:** ... having been formed in, *–WLSN.*
**which God hath before ordained that we should walk in them:** ... to do those good deeds which God planned for us to do, *–PHLP* ... which God before prepared, *–RTHM* ... afore prepared, *–CLMT,* *–ASV* ... made ready beforehand, *–CNFT* ... predestined us to make our daily way of life, *–MNTG* ... that we should devote our lives to them, *–TCNT.*

**2:10.** Even though it is not possible to earn salvation, this verse reminds us that work indeed is involved in the total process, that is, God's work. We are the result of that work. The total passage has come "full circle." Verse 2 reminds us that those in a lost state "walked" (*periepatēsate*) a certain way. The last word in verse 10 in the Greek language is the word "walk" (*peripatēsōmen*) again. Only here the walking as believers is as His "workmanship," as products of what God's grace can do in people. Christians are God's "work of art," His "masterpiece," so they may "walk about" in good works. In fact, believers were "created in Christ Jesus" for that very purpose. Good works do not bring salvation to a person; they are the result of salvation.

**11. Wherefore remember, that ye [being] in time past Gentiles in the flesh:** ... you were at one time heathen, *−NORL* . . . that ye formerly were carnal, *−MRDK* . . . formerly gentiles by birth, *−SAWR*.

**who are called Uncircumcision by that which is called the Circumcision in the flesh made by hands:** . . . performed by hand, *−NOYS* . . . performed upon the body by the hand of man, *−TCNT*.

**2:11.** These words were written to Gentile Christians who had been brought out of the darkness of paganism and into the light of God's love. "Remember" comes from a present imperative Greek verb (*mnēmoneuete*) and could be translated "keep on remembering." Notice the exclusiveness and contempt that most Jews ("the Circumcision") held for Gentiles ("Uncircumcision"). Circumcision was instituted by God himself (Genesis 17:10-14) as an external sign of the covenant He made with Abraham. This important rite signified externally what had happened to Abraham internally. However, by Paul's time this physical sign had become more of a sign of the difference between Jew and Gentile than of a person's relationship to God. Paul reminds people that internal—not external—circumcision is what really matters (Galatians 5:6; Colossians 2:11). The apostle certainly did not share the contempt most Jews held for Gentiles. Incidentally, most Gentiles at that time also looked at Jews with contempt.

**12. That at that time ye were without Christ:** . . . at that time you were separated from Christ, *−NORL* . . . in that season, separate from Christ, *−RTHM*.

**being aliens from the commonwealth of Israel:** . . . alienated from the polity of, *−SAWR* . . . from the regulations of, *−MRDK*.

**and strangers from the covenants of promise:** . . . you were outsiders, *−TCNT* . . . you knew nothing about the covenant that God had promised to make, *−NORL*.

**having no hope, and without God in the world:** . . . not possessing, *−WLSN* . . . had nothing to look forward to and no God to whom you could turn, *−PHLP* . . . and godless, in the world, *−RTHM*.

**2:12.** Paul reminds his Gentile readers of a far more important matter, their actual condition before they became united with Christ. Their former condition is summarized by a series of five descriptive statements. First, they previously "were without Christ." In the original language this consists of an ablative case construction which in itself normally indicates separation.

Secondly, they were "aliens from the commonwealth of Israel." The word translated "commonwealth" or "citizenship" (*politeias*) is used also in Acts 22:28 where it refers to Paul's Roman citizenship. These Gentiles had no rights of citizenship in "spiritual Israel" (Romans 9:6, 7; 11:1-5).

Thirdly, these Gentiles were "strangers from the covenants of promise." "Covenants" refers to God's promises to Abraham (Genesis 12:2, 3; 13:14-17; 15:1-5; 17:1-22; 22:15-18). "Promise," or literally "the promise," is a reminder that all the promises of God to Abraham, Isaac, and Jacob stemmed from that one great promise of the coming Messiah (Genesis 3:15).

Fourthly, the Gentiles to whom Paul was writing had been in a state of "having no hope," which is the natural consequence of being without Christ (1 Thessalonians 4:13). Lastly, they had been "without God."

**13. But now in Christ Jesus ye who:** . . . through the blood, *−PHLP* . . . But now you are in union with Christ, *−NORL*.

**sometimes were far off:** . . . who formerly were, *−WLSN* . . . who were formerly far off, *−PNT* . . . were once outside the pale, *−PHLP*.

**are made nigh by the blood of Christ:** . . . have been brought near by, *−MRDK* . . . are with us inside the circle of God's love and purpose, *−PHLP*.

**2:13.** What a definite contrast verses 13-22 show when compared with verses 11 and 12. In verse 12 these Gentiles were "in the world," but in verse 13 they were "in Christ Jesus." In verse 12 the words "at that time" are contrasted in verse 13 with "now." They once were "far off," but "are made nigh." All this took place, of course, "by the blood of Christ." Because the docetic Gnostics denied the humanity of Christ, Paul was very careful to specify that He was a real human with genuine blood. Redemption came through the death of Christ, and the means of cleansing was His shed blood. It was not an ordinary death. Those who opt for a "bloodless religion" do so outside the parameters of Scripture and manifest a modern form of gnosticism.

**14. For he is our peace:** . . . He Himself is, *−WLMS* . . . living peace, *−PHLP*.

**who hath made both one:** . . . made the two divisions of mankind one, *−TCNT* . . . He is the one who has made us both into one body, *−WLMS* . . . made a unity of the conflicting elements, *−PHLP*.

**and hath broken down the middle wall of partition [be\* tween us]:** . . . and hath demolished, *−MRDK* . . . and having removed the enmity, *−WLSN* . . . and dissoluing the middle wall, *−RHEM* . . . has broken down the party-wall, *−MNTG* . . . broke down the barrier which separated them, *−TCNT* . . . broken down the dividing wall that separated us, *−NORL* . . . broken down the barrier that kept us apart, *−WLMS* . . . the middle wall of separation, *−SCLT* . . . wall of the enclosure broke down, *−RTHM*.

**2:14.** Notice the shift here to "our," denoting that Jesus has brought both Gentiles and Jews into a body that is characterized by peace. The apostle used the term "peace" as the basis of unity in the body of Christ. The temple itself was divided into various courts: Holy of Holies, Holy Place, priests, Israel, women, Gentiles. A wall, about 3 or 4 feet high, ran through the temple area separating the Court of the Gentiles from the inner court into which Jews only were permitted. This wall contained an inscription which read: "No foreigner may enter within the barricade which surrounds the sanctuary and enclosure. Any(one) who is caught doing so will have himself to blame for his ensuing death." Paul himself nearly got into serious trouble because some people falsely accused him of taking an Asian Gentile, Trophimus, beyond this point (Acts 21:27-29).

**15. Having abolished in his flesh the enmity, [even] the law of commandments [contained] in ordinances:** ... He has put a stop to the hostility, —WLMS ... annulled the Law, —WLSN ... contained in decrees, —SCLT ... In abrogating through his flesshe the hatred, —GNVA ... the cause of hatred, —CRNM.

**for to make in himself of twain one new man:** ... that he might create of the two one new man, —NOYS ... and made in himself out of the two, —PHLP ... by uniting both to himself, —TCNT.

**[so] making peace:** ... thus producing peace, —PHLP.

**2:15.** Much of the language of this section, verses 13-18, is language that relates to a body. Comparing the Church to a human body was one of the New Testament's favorite metaphors. How did Jesus accomplish this unity of Gentiles and Jews into one body? This verse says He did so by "having abolished in his flesh the enmity" which was the "law of commandments."

Jesus "abolished" the Mosaic law in the sense that He fulfilled all its requirements. He himself said He had not come to destroy the Law or the Prophets, but to fulfill them (Matthew 5:17, 18). Therefore, Jesus was the only one qualified to remove all previous distinctions between Jews and Gentiles and "to make in himself ... one new man," a definite reference to the New Testament Church in which no distinctions exist.

**16. And that he might reconcile both unto God in one body by the cross:** ... united in one Body, —TCNT ... by the sacrifice of one body on the cross, —PHLP.

**having slain the enmity thereby:** ... destroyed the enmity, —WLSN ... and put an end to their antagonism, —NORL ... had killed the hostility through it, —WLMS ... made utterly irrelevant the antagonism between them, —PHLP.

**2:16.** Just as verse 15 indicates that Christ is the point of convergence for all people, so verse 16

shows that the Cross is the place of convergence. God is the great Reconciler. Even though it was man who had separated himself from God by his sins, God initiated the act of reconciliation by sending His Son. Now we are reconciled to Him and to one another because He has "broken down the middle wall of partition between us" (verse 14).

**17. And came and preached peace to you which were afar off, and to them that were nigh:** ... told both you who were far from God ... that the war was over, —PHLP.

**2:17.** This verse is a clear statement of the reason for Christ's coming to this earth. He "preached peace" (*euēngelisato eirēnēn*) to the ones "which were afar off," the Gentiles to whom Paul wrote this important epistle, and "to them that were nigh," the Jews.

**18. For through him we both have access by one Spirit unto the Father:** ... united in spirit, are now able to approach the Father, —TCNT ... we both have the introduction, —WLSN ... we both haue an open way, —GNVA.

**2:18.** As a result of the peace that Jesus' death on the cross provides for both Jews and Gentiles, both groups have access to the Father through Christ by the Holy Spirit. The term "access" comes from a Greek word (*prosagōgues*) which was the title used for the official in an oriental court who introduced visitors to the potentate. The word does not refer just to liberty of approach, but to an actual introduction.

Notice the involvement of the Trinity. Through Christ, or because of His sacrifice on the cross (Romans 5:2), the Holy Spirit introduces believers to the Father. The Bible is marvelously consistent about the total involvement of the Trinity in all that God does for us and through us as His people. All of God's blessings have always come to mankind through Jesus Christ, and the Holy Spirit has always been the member of the Trinity who performs the specific acts. This pattern can be seen in the Bible even from creation itself (Genesis 1:1, 2; John 1:1-3). The emphasis in this verse relates to the fact that access to the Father does not depend upon any value inherent in the believer, but is dependent upon the sacrifice of Christ on his behalf.

**19. Now therefore:** ... Take notice then, —MNTG ... So, —WLMS.

**ye are no more strangers and foreigners:** ... outsiders and aliens, —TCNT, —PHLP ... sojourners, —PNIN, —WLSN, —CLMT, —MRDK.

**but fellowcitizens with the saints:** ... with every other Christian, —PHLP.

**and of the household of God:**...you belong now to, *−PHLP*...You are members of God's own family, *−NORL*...the domestics, *−DOUY*...and members of God's Household, *−TCNT.*

**2:19.** Up to this point in this total passage which began in verse 11, we have seen the New Testament Church mainly has been compared to the unity of a human body, but now this verse begins a comparison of the New Testament Church to a beautiful temple with each stone occupying an important position in the total structure. Believers are no longer "strangers and foreigners" but members of this temple with all the rights and privileges of membership. The first term (*xenoi*) relates to short-term transients and the second (*paroikoi*) to aliens who have settled in a particular country but have no intrinsic rights because they are not citizens.

**20. And are built upon the foundation of the apostles and prophets:**
**Jesus Christ himself being the chief corner [stone]:** . . . being the highest corner stone, *−RHEM*...the actual foundation-stone being, *−PHLP.*

**2:20.** God is constructing a beautiful temple, the Church. Paul refers to "the foundation of the apostles and prophets." The Old Testament prophetic word and the New Testament apostolic word form the basis of our Christian faith and teaching. Through the preaching of the gospel, the apostolic ministry brought the New Testament Church into existence. The reference to "the chief corner stone" comes from Psalm 118:22, 23, a passage which Jesus related to himself (Mark 12:10, 11) and Peter ascribed to Christ (Acts 4:11; 1 Peter 2:7). It sometimes meant the stone placed at the extreme corner, so it could bind together the other stones in the structure. It was the most important stone in a building because the stability of all the others depended upon it. It also provided the standard to follow for straight lines both horizontal and vertical.

**21. In whom all the building fitly framed together:** . . . an entire building, in process of being fitly conjoined together, *−RTHM* . . . all the edifice is framed, *−MRDK*...the whole structure is closely fitted together, *−CNFT*...United in him, *−TCNT*...is harmoniously fitted together, *−WLMS*...being harmoniously cemented together, *−SCLT*...fitly compacted together, *−WLSN.*
**groweth unto an holy temple in the Lord:**...increases into, *−WLSN*...sacred through its union with the Lord, *−WLMS* . . . grows together into a temple consecrated to God, *−PHLP.*

**2:21.** This is another important reminder that Jesus is the One who holds the New Testament

Church together and in a state of unity. "Framed together" comes from a present participle in the Greek language (*sunarmologoumenē*) which literally means "being joined together" and shows that the work is continuous and progressive.

**22. In whom ye also are builded together:**...You are all part of this building, *−PHLP*...are continuously built together, *−MNTG..* you yourselves, in union with Him, in fellowship with one another, are being built up, *−WLMS.*
**for an habitation of God through the Spirit:**...for a dwelling-place, *−MNTG*...for God through the Spirit, *−WLMS* . . . so that God can find in you a dwelling-place for His Spirit, *−NORL*...for a spiritual habitation, *−SAWR, −WLSN.*

**2:22.** This verse contains Paul's personal note to the Ephesian believers. Perhaps some of them felt like second-class citizens because they did not live in Jerusalem and were not part of that important local body. The apostle reminded them that they were just as important to God as any other group of Christians.

## Chapter 3

**1. For this cause I Paul:**...This, then, is the reason why I, *−TCNT.*
**the prisoner of Jesus Christ for you Gentiles:**...in behalf of you nations, *−PNIN.*

**3:1.** "For this cause" probably refers back to Paul's statements in chapter 2 comparing the New Testament Church first to a human body and secondly to a temple. The apostle did not admit he was a prisoner of the Roman emperor, Nero. The genitive case used here in the Greek language does not signify merely a prisoner who belonged to Christ; rather, it refers to the fact that Christ, not Nero, had imprisoned him. In other words, Paul knew his stay in prison was part of God's will for his life.

This confinement resulted in benefit for the Gentiles. Had he never been imprisoned in Rome, Paul probably would not have had such a tremendous impact upon the believers in Rome (Philippians 1:14), an impact that touched the entire Roman Empire.

**2. If ye have heard of the dispensation of the grace of God:**...the responsible charge with which God entrusted me, *−TCNT*...a steward of His grace, *−NORL.*
**which is given me to you-ward:** . . . appointed me to be . . . intended for you, *−NORL* . . . entrusted to me for you? *−MNTG*...with respect to you, *−PNT.*

**3:2.** Paul felt compelled by the Holy Spirit to explain more thoroughly what he had mentioned only briefly about Jews and Gentiles being incorporated into the "one body" with no distinctions and with equal privileges and responsibilities (2:16). Paul had been given "the dispensation of the grace of God" or an "administration of God's grace." "Dispensation" (*oikonomia*) literally means "house manager" and could be translated "stewardship, economy, administration, arrangement, plan, task." In other words, God had given him the responsibility of making known to the world the meaning of the mystery God had revealed to him: the amazing unity of the New Testament Church, with no distinction between Gentiles and Jews.

**3. How that by revelation he made known unto me the mystery:** . . . by direct revelation, —*MNTG* . . . the secret, —*WLSN*.

**(as I wrote afore in few words:** . . . as I have already briefly told you, —*TCNT* . . . as I have briefly written before, —*WLMS* . . . written briefly of this above, —*PHLP* . . . wrote briefly before, —*WLSN*.

**3:3.** According to this verse, he had already mentioned this mystery. Perhaps he was referring to two previous statements in this epistle (1:9; 2:16). "Mystery" (*mustērion*) does not mean something mystical but something that is incomprehensible until God chooses to reveal it. The term for the "revelation" (*apokalupsis*) is the same word from which we derive the title of the last book in the Bible. In the New Testament it means something undiscoverable by humans unless God makes it known to them. It was a very common term to people of that day. For example, it was used of the unveiling of a statue the public had not seen until that time.

**4. Whereby, when ye read, ye may understand my knowledge in the mystery of Christ):** . . . ye may perceive my insight into, —*NOYS* . . . will explain to you, —*PHLP* . . . you can judge of my insight into that secret truth, —*MNTG*.

**3:4.** Some people minimize the written Word of God and emphasize the spoken word more than they should. While the spoken word certainly is important, it cannot supersede the written Scriptures. Paul apparently intended that the recipients of this letter spend time reading the Scriptures.

**5. Which in other ages was not made known unto the sons of men:** . . . was hidden to past generations of mankind, —*PHLP* . . . In former generations, —*TCNT* . . . in other generations, —*PNIN*, —*WLSN*.

**as it is now revealed unto his holy apostles and prophets by the Spirit:** . . . been made plain to God's consecrated messengers, —*PHLP*.

**3:5.** We do not know why God had not revealed this "mystery" before this time. Peter also made it clear in his first epistle that God did not choose

to manifest certain things to people nor even to angels (1 Peter 1:1-12). The Old Testament is full of examples of what is known in the science of hermeneutics as a "progressive revelation." God revealed certain matters to mankind in stages. Paul explained to the Galatians that Christ did not come to this world until "the fulness of time was come" (Galatians 4:4).

**6. That the Gentiles should be fellowheirs, and of the same body:** . . . the heathen are jointheirs, —*TCNT* . . . the Gentiles form one body with us, —*MNTG* . . . be co-heirs, —*SCLT* . . . should be sharers of his inheritance, —*MRDK* . . . and a Joint-body, —*WLSN* . . . and joint-partners, —*RTHM* . . . equal heirs, —*PHLP*.

**and partakers of his promise:** . . . and Co-partners, —*WLSN* . . . and are coheirs and copartners, —*MNTG* . . . and partners with us, —*WORL*.

**in Christ by the gospel:** . . . through the good news, —*WLMS*.

**3:6.** In this verse we see a clear example of Paul's use of the term "mystery" (the word may not have the same meaning in every context). The mystery was not that a Gentile finally could be saved. Paul himself quoted several Old Testament passages indicating God's redemptive work among Gentiles (Romans 9:24-33; 10:19-21; 15:9-12). Three terms are used in verse 6 which are prefixed by adding the preposition *sun-* ("with"). "Fellow heirs" (*sunklēronoma*), "same body" (*sussōma*), and "partakers" (*summetocha*) serve as excellent examples of Paul's common practice of reinforcement by compounding synonyms or phrases that are very close in meaning. Therefore, the mystery was that Gentiles and Jews would belong equally to the same body.

During the Old Testament period Gentiles had been allowed to become Jewish proselytes and to share in God's blessings, but a distinction always existed between them and those who were Jews by birth. Why did not Paul give this definition in chapter 2 when he started expounding the subject of Gentiles being "fellow heirs" with Israel? It often was his style to lead up to his theme.

**7. Whereof I was made a minister:** . . . for which I was called to serve, —*WLMS*.

**according to the gift of the grace of God:** . . . according to the free-gift, —*RTHM* . . . God's unmerited favor, —*WLMS*.

**given unto me by the effectual working of his power:** . . . which was imparted to me by the energy of, —*WLSN* . . . by the operation of, —*MRDK* . . . the exercise of his power, —*TCNT*, —*WLMS* . . . by the power with which he equipped me, —*PHLP*.

**3:7.** Verses 7-13 show clearly the attitude Paul had concerning the great responsibility God had given him to publish this mystery to the world. First, he realized that to be a servant (*diakonos*) of God is "the gift of the grace of God." His grace puts people into ministries in His church, and His power makes it possible for them to fulfill these ministries. Paul used two Greek terms to describe this ability. "Effectual working" comes from the word from which we get energy (*energeia*), and "power" comes from the familiar word *dunamis*. Unfortunately, many connect this second term only with the concept of power. Perhaps the noun *ability* would better indicate its meaning in most contexts. The same God who gave Paul the tremendous responsibility to reveal God's plan to the world also performed this act purely out of His grace and promised to give the ability or the power necessary to carry out the responsibility.

**8. Unto me, who am less than the least of all saints:** ... the very lowest, *—WLSN* ... less than the least, *—PHLP* ... the least deserving, *—TCNT* ... of all His people, *—WLMS.*

**is this grace given:** ... this unmerited favor was bestowed, *—WLMS.*

**that I should preach among the Gentiles:** ... to enable me to proclaim, *—PHLP* ... that I might preach as good news to the heathen, *—WLMS.*

**the unsearchable riches of Christ:** ... the unfathomable riches, *—NORL* ... the incalculable riches, *—PHLP* ... the boundless riches of Christ, *—WLMS* ... of the undreamt-of wealth that exists in the Christ, *—TCNT.*

**3:8.** Instead of boasting about his own abilities and the fact that God had given him such an important task, the apostle considered himself an unworthy servant, mainly because previous to his conversion he had persecuted Christ by persecuting His church (Acts 9:5; 1 Corinthians 15:9; Philippians 3:6; 1 Timothy 1:13). In spite of his previous position of violently opposing the New Testament Church, God gave Paul the privilege and responsibility of proclaiming to the world the mystery of that Church.

One should not get the impression from Paul's terminology about himself that he was putting himself down. That would have been false humility, which really is just another form of pride. People sometimes become "proud of their humility" by trying to manifest it to other people. No one can read Paul's writings and think he was like that. He did not boast about his abilities, even though he had many of them. Exceptional abilities and positions of prominence in themselves do not corrupt individuals, but the temptation to allow one's self to become proud definitely increases in such situations. The antidote to the danger is a very simple but effective one: allow God to keep

you humble. He certainly did it for Paul (2 Corinthians 12:1-10).

**9. And to make all [men] see what [is] the fellowship of the mystery:** ... and to enlighten all, *—SAWR, —RTHM, —ALFD* ... and to illuminate al men, *—RHEM* ... should show to all men what is the dispensation, *—MRDK* ... and to bring to light what is the dispensation, *—PNIN* ... and to make clear how is to be carried out the trusteeship of this secret, *—WLMS* ... the new dispensation of that secret purpose, *—MNTG* ... the meaning of that secret, *—PHLP.*

**which from the beginning of the world hath been hid in God, who created all things by Jesus Christ:** ... which has been concealed from the ages, *—WLSN* ... which has for ages been hidden away, *—WLMS* ... has been hidden from eternity, *—CNFT* ... has kept hidden from the creation until now, *—PHLP.*

**3:9.** "To make all men see" actually means "to bring to light" or "to turn on the light." This Greek infinitive comes from the word which translates into English as *photo* and serves as the prefix for many English terms. Paul did not picture himself in some small room turning on a light. His vision went far beyond that limited idea. The apostle pictured himself in the center of the earth, exposing to the entire world the revelation that God had made known to him.

The Lord made it very clear to His disciples in His commission to them (Matthew 28:19, 20) that believers have two main responsibilities relative to people in this world. One is to evangelize them. The apostle Paul took this challenge seriously.

The second responsibility Jesus gave His disciples was to help other believers to mature in their faith. Again, Paul took this matter seriously, and much of his ministry was involved in training people to minister to others.

**10. To the intent that now unto the principalities and powers in heavenly [places]:** ... And the object of this is, *—TCNT* ... The purpose is that all the angelic powers, *—PHLP* ... in order that now may be made known to the Governments, *—WLSN* ... to the rulers and authorities in heaven, *—WLMS* ... that now his manifold wisdom, *—MNTG* ... in the heavenly regions, *—SCLT.*

**might be known by the church the manifold wisdom of God:** ... in order that now his manifold wisdom should, *—MNTG* ... should now see the complex wisdom of God's plan, *—PHLP* ... many-sided wisdom, *—TCNT* ... so that the many phases of God's wisdom, *—WLMS* ... the much diversified Wisdom, *—WLSN.*

**3:10.** This verse should be compared with 1 Peter 1:12 which explains that even angels did not previously know what God had planned for the Church Age. Some people elevate angels to positions far beyond what the Bible gives them. God, on the other hand, elevates people to positions of importance in His kingdom, and He uses angels to help them (Hebrews 1:7). The Gnostics of Paul's day made the mistake of completely reversing the matter. Apparently even heavenly beings, described in this verse as "the principalities and powers," did not understand the "mystery" of the New Testament Church until God chose to reveal it through the apostle Paul.

**11. According to the eternal purpose which he purposed in Christ Jesus our Lord:** . . . to a plan of the ages, –PNIN . . . in conformity to that timeless purpose which he centered in, –PHLP . . . which he accomplished in, –CNFT . . . executed in the gift of Christ, –WLMS . . . our Master, –TCNT.

**3:11.** Even though God purposed from before the creation of the world (1:4, 5) that the New Testament Church would be brought into being in "the fulness of time," He did not reveal the fact until He allowed Paul the glorious privilege of making that truth known to the world.

**12. In whom we have boldness and access with confidence by the faith of him:** . . . this freedom of speech, –WLSN . . . By union with Him and through faith in Him we have a free and confidential introduction to God, –WLMS . . . we dare . . . to approach God, –PHLP . . . this fearless confidence, –MNTG . . . and entrance with confidence, –GNVA.

**3:12.** In fact, even the ability to know God comes to us through Christ. The NIV renders "access" (*prosagōgēn*) as "approach." The previous use of the term (2:18) is in a different context, that of comparing the New Testament Church to a human body.

The second use of the term tells believers they have access to God "by the faith of him" or "through faith in him (NIV)," that is, through faith in Christ, not faith in some angel or other creature. Believers can enter the Father's presence with "boldness" and "confidence" because they are covered with the righteousness of Christ. Those who have placed their faith in Him have done so because they realize He is the only One who met the requirements of God laid down in the Old Testament law. Therefore, when God looks at those people who live by faith in the Lord Jesus Christ, He sees the righteousness of Christ.

**13. Wherefore I desire that ye feint not at my tribulations for you:** . . . Do not, then, lose courage, –NORL . . . I beg you not to lose heart, –MNTG . . . beg you not to be dismayed at the sufferings, –TCNT . . . I entreat you not to be disheartened, –NOYS . . . pray, that I may not be discouraged by my afflictions, –MRDK . . . over the sorrows that I am suffering for

your sake, –WLMS . . . on account of my afflictions, –SAWR.

**which is your glory:** . . . they bring you honor, –WLMS . . . for they are an honour to you, –TCNT . . . Indeed, you should be honored, –PHLP.

**3:13.** A person in prison, as Paul was, might have a tendency to pity himself and to want other people to feel sorry for him. However, Paul asked his readers not to be discouraged because of his suffering for them. The word he used for "tribulations" normally refers to that narrow set of circumstances the person finds himself in at the moment. It could be compared to a person climbing a steep path that is very narrow. On the one side the path is bordered by mammoth rocks that would be impossible to scale. The other side of the path is bordered by a steep cliff. Therefore, the person traveling this path cannot swerve to the left, nor to the right. He has no choice but to press ahead or to turn around and go back. Of course, the idea of going back was not an acceptable option to Paul.

**14. For this cause I bow my knees unto the Father of our Lord Jesus Christ:** . . . For this reason I kneel before, –WLMS . . . fall on my knees, –PHLP.

**15. Of whom the whole family in heaven and earth:** . . . all fatherhood, earthly or heavenly, –PHLP . . . from whom every family, –WLMS.

**is named:** . . . derives its name, –WLMS, –PHLP.

**3:14, 15.** Here begins another of Paul's Spirit-inspired prayers. He is about to express his desires for the believers as he prays to the God who has a Father relationship with them.

Paul's first prayer (1:15-23) was concerned with the necessity of Christian growth, and this second prayer concerns the necessity of Christian service. This verse contains a statement about the fatherhood of God that confuses some people. They take this verse and others like it to mean that everyone is a child of God by virtue of being part of His creation. But there is a definite distinction between the fatherhood of God relative to creation and the fatherhood of God relative to conversion. Only those who have accepted Jesus Christ as Lord and Saviour are the children of God (John 8:44). It seems that in this verse Paul was referring to the fatherhood of God relative to creation.

**16. That he would grant you, according to the riches of his glory:** . . . the riches of His perfect character, –WLMS . . . the glorious richness of his resources, –PHLP.

**to be strengthened with might by his Spirit in the inner man:** . . . to be Powerfully strengthened, –WLSN . . . to be fortified by his Spirit, –RHEM . . . to be made mighty through his Spirit, –PNIN . . . by breathing his Spirit into your very souls, –TCNT . . . in the inward man, –ASV . . . in your inmost being, –MNTG.

**3:16.** Paul's actual prayer consists of five petitions. The first two are introduced in verse 16 in the original language by *hina* ("in order that"). The third and fourth are introduced by another *hina* in verse 18. The fifth petition is introduced by the third *hina* in the latter part of verse 19. It is as if the apostle was saying, "If you really want to serve God properly, these five items must be considered important matters."

First, he prayed that God would strengthen the believers or give them the power of the Holy Spirit. "To be strengthened with might" comes from two Greek words put together to state that no one can serve God adequately without the ability the Holy Spirit gives. *Dunamis* relates to "inherent ability" (as in Acts 1:8) to be witnesses unto Christ, and *kratos* relates to "manifested strength" and shows that power in action.

**17. That Christ may dwell in your hearts by faith:** . . . may make His permanent home, —WLMS . . . actually live in your hearts, —PHLP.

**that ye, being rooted and grounded in love:** . . . when firmly rooted and established, —TCNT . . . so deeply rooted and so firmly grounded, —MNTG . . . You must be deeply rooted, your foundations must be strong, —WLMS . . . and well-established, —WLSN . . . firmly fixed, —PHLP.

**3:17.** Secondly, Paul prayed that "Christ may dwell in your hearts by faith." This does not mean the believers were not already Christians and that Christ did not already dwell in them. The idea expressed is that of a permanent dwelling as opposed to a temporary experience. Paul wanted the believers to maintain a consistent experience so that Christ would indeed "feel at home" on a permanent basis. When He can "settle down and be at home," the Christian's witness for Him will be a consistent one.

Paul was also concerned that the believers should be "rooted and grounded in love." Both of these first two terms come from perfect passive participles in the Greek language, showing the necessity of the initial work of salvation being accomplished by God, and indicating the necessity of continued results.

**18. May be able to comprehend with all saints:** . . . that ye may be full mighty to grasp firmly, —RTHM . . . that ye may be able to explore, —MRDK . . . may receive power to grasp the dimensions, —NORL . . . may be strong enough to grasp the idea, —WLMS.

**what [is] the breadth, and length, and depth, and height:** . . . how wide and deep and long and high, —PHLP . . . and the depnesse, —WCLF.

**3:18.** Thirdly, Paul prayed that the believers would be able to comprehend "what is the

breadth, and length, and depth, and height," the overwhelming richness of the gospel and of the love of Christ. As long as we are here on earth, this knowledge can be only in part (1 Corinthians 13:9). We can know it and learn about it by experience as we share with other believers the spiritual insights and experiences God brings to us.

It is like exploring a diamond mine. The farther and deeper we go, the more treasures we discover and the more desire we have to acquire all that God desires to provide for us.

**19. And to know the love of Christ, which passeth knowledge:** . . . yes to come at last to know . . . although it far surpasses human understanding, —WLMS . . . the knowledge-surpassing love of Christ, —WORL . . . though it is beyond all understanding, —TCNT . . . so far beyond our comprehension, —PHLP . . . which transcends all knowing, —MNTG . . . which exceeds knowledge, —SAWR . . . more excellent thanne science, —WCLF.

**that ye might be filled with all the fulness of God:** . . . may be filled to the full with God himself, —TCNT . . . filled through all your being, —PHLP . . . with all the "plenitude" of, —MNTG . . . with the perfect fullness of, —WLMS.

**3:19.** Fourthly, Paul prayed for believers "to know the love of Christ, which passeth knowledge." This is not a repetition of the thought in verse 18, but is an appeal to experience personally this vast love of God. We shall not only have a theoretical and intellectual knowledge of this love, but also a real, personal experience of it. The Greek word used here (*gnōnai*) is often used in the New Testament for experiential knowledge.

Lastly, Paul prayed that Christians "might be filled with all the fulness of God." Christ was "full of grace and truth" (John 1:14), descriptive of the glory of God, His character. Further, "Of his fulness have all we received" (John 1:16). Believers have various levels of capacity (which can be increased), but they can be recipients of those qualities which constitute the "fulness of God."

**20. Now unto him that is able to do exceeding abundantly above:** . . . able to accomplish, —CNFT . . . to do infinitely more, —MNTG . . . by his almighty power, —MRDK.

**all that we ask or think:** . . . than we ever dare to ask, —PHLP . . . or conceiving, —RTHM . . . or imagine, —WLMS.

**according to the power that worketh in us:** . . . by his power within us, —PHLP . . . operating in us, —WLSN.

**3:20.** The possibility of always reaching out for more of the ability the Holy Spirit gives caused Paul to break forth into a doxology, expressing the fact that God does "exceeding" or "superabundantly" (*huperekperissou*) more than we can request or even imagine, according to His power (*dumamis*) that works (*energeia*) within us. This great promise is conditional. The degree that we allow God's power to work *in* us determines the extent of what He can do *for* us.

**21. Unto him [be] glory in the church by Christ Jesus:** ... through Christ, *—PHLP.*
   **throughout all ages, world without end:** ... for all generations, age after age, *—TCNT* ... down through all the ages of time without end, *—CNFT* ... to all the generations of eternal ages, *—ALFD* ... from tyme to tyme, *—CRNM* ... for ever and ever, *—PHLP.*
   **Amen:**

**3:21.** Because the ability and energy to accomplish the work of the New Testament Church really come from God, the glory must go to Him for what is accomplished. Even though he was in captivity, Paul's ability to praise God was not chained. Many of his most exuberant outbursts of praise are found in the Prison Epistles and came out of very trying circumstances.

The word "glory" in this verse comes from the Greek noun from which we derive *doxology* (*doxa*). According to Paul's instruction, this praise should come forth from the Church, a reminder of the main purpose for which the Church exists. The chapter ends with the truth that this praise will continue forever, an excellent reminder of our eternal vocation, praising God through Jesus Christ.

## Chapter 4

**1. I therefore, the prisoner of the Lord, beseech you:** ... I urge you, then, *—TCNT* ... I summon you then, *—MNTG* ... therefore plead with you, *—NORL* ... entreat you, *—WLMS* ... I am in prison because I belong to the Lord, *—EVRD.*
   **that ye walk worthy of the vocation wherewith ye are called:** ... live lives ... of your high calling, *—PHLP.*

**4:1.** This chapter begins the practical section of Ephesians. Paul normally balanced his epistles with a theological portion and a practical portion. The "therefore" of verse 1 serves as a bridge connecting all the apostle had written up to this point with what follows.

In the Greek text "beseech" (*parakalō*) is first in the sentence for emphasis. Paul was concerned that believers should cross the bridge from analysis to action, from theology to morality, from Christian faith to Christian life, from the revelation of doctrine to the development of practice. He made this very strong appeal as "the prisoner of the Lord."

Verses 1-16 describe the unity and diversity of the New Testament Church. Paul began his exhortation by appealing to the Ephesians to live lives worthy of the calling God had given them. "Worthy" (*axiōs*) is an adverb of manner used with scales. Basically it means "bringing up the other beam of the scales" or "bringing into equilibrium." It carries the idea of one thing being the equivalent of another thing. In other words, a Christian's practice should "weigh as much as" or "be equivalent to" his profession. If it truly does "weigh as much as," that person will be doing what the whole Book of Ephesians tells him to do.

**2. With all lowliness:** ... Accept life with, *—PHLP* ... vvith al humilitie, *—RHEM* ... with perfect humility, *—WLMS* ... lowliness of mind, *—RTHM.*
   **and meekness:** ... and mildenes, *—RHEM* ... and gentleness, *—MNTG.*
   **with longsuffering, forbearing one another in love:** ... sustaining each other in Love, *—WLSN* ... put up with one another in love, *—NORL* ... making allowances for one another, *—PHLP.*

**4:2.** Furthermore, it will be reflected in the three qualities mentioned in verse 2. The first two, "lowliness and meekness," refer to a person's attitude toward self. A person with a proper balance between profession and practice will be humble, will not be full of haughty pride. A truly humble individual will be in balance, not thinking too highly of himself, nor, at the other extreme, putting himself down. Such a person will also be meek, which is the opposite of self-assertion. The third quality, forbearance, is a social virtue, expressing the ability to be patient with the weaknesses of other people.

**3. Endeavouring to keep:** ... Make it your aim, *—PHLP* ... to preserve, *—MNTG.*
   **the unity of the Spirit in the bond of peace:** ... to be at one in the Spirit, *—PHLP.*

**4:3.** The absence of these three qualities will definitely jeopardize Christian unity. Unity does not just happen. Because this is a present tense idea, we must constantly work at it.

**4. [There is] one body, and one Spirit:** ... You all belong to one body, *—PHLP.*
   **even as ye are called L. one hope of your calling:** ... as you all experienced one calling to one hope, *—PHLP* ... just as there is but one hope resulting from the call you have received, *—WLMS.*

**4:4.** The apostle then gave the perfect example of unity—that which is exhibited among the members of the Trinity. They never disagree. Verse 4 describes the work of the Holy Spirit. There is one Body, and the Holy Spirit is the One who makes us members of it. As a result, we share "one hope," an expectant attitude concerning the second coming of Christ and all the benefits related to it.

**5. One Lord, one faith, one baptism:**...One Immersion, —*WLSN*, —*SCLT*.

**4:5.** Verse 5 reminds us that there is only one Lord. When Paul wrote these words, nearly every cult of mystery religion had its own lord. However, the New Testament has only one Head, the Lord Jesus Christ, and He is the only means of access into His church.

The term "faith" is used several different ways in the Scriptures. Sometimes it relates to the subjective placing of confidence in God; sometimes it refers to the body of doctrine that believers accept; sometimes it refers to a means of access. The last is the use in this context.

The statement concerning "one baptism" does not deny the reality of other types of baptism (in water, in the Holy Spirit, in suffering) but refers to the one baptism without which the others would not be possible—the baptism into the body of Christ (1 Corinthians 12:13).

**6. One God and Father of all, who [is] above all, and through all, and in you all:**...who is the one over all...and the one living in all, —*PHLP*...works through all, —*TCNT*...who pervades us all, —*WLMS*.

**4:6.** The Father is described as the One who originated all that verses 4 and 5 describe. The Father is sovereign ("above all"), the sustainer ("through all"), and the One who gives the energy for all that happens ("in . . . all").

**7. But unto every one of us is given grace:**...individually grace is given to us in different ways, —*PHLP*...to each one of us, —*WLSN*...has been entrusted with some charge, —*TCNT*.
**according to the measure of the gift of Christ:** . . . measured out as a gift from Christ, —*NORL*...donation of Christ, —*RHEM*.

**4:7.** Suddenly Paul moved from discussing the Church as a whole to the individuals comprising the Church in order to show that unity is not uniformity. In His work of developing unity among God's people the Holy Spirit does not obliterate their individuality. In fact, He uses their differences. Christ gives "unto every one of us" a function or ministry in His body, and these functions are diverse. It is inconsistent to say, "I am a Christian, but I do not have a ministry." Christ gives to every Christian a ministry.

**8. Wherefore he saith:** . . . Concerning this the Scripture says, —*WLMS*.
**When he ascended up on high, he led captivity captive:**...led a multitude of Captives, —*WLSN*...He led a host of captives, —*WLMS*.
**and gave gifts unto men:** . . . gave gifts to mankind, —*TCNT*.

**4:8.** In verse 8 Paul paraphrased Psalm 68:18 to show the qualifications of Christ to grant these "gifts" or ministries to His disciples. This psalm gives a description of what probably was a return of King David after a military conquest. At the same time it is a messianic psalm of victory describing the completed work of Christ in accomplishing the plan of salvation.

**9. (Now that he ascended, what is it but that he also descended first:** . . . implies that he also descended, —*MNTG*...except that He had first gone down into the lower regions, —*WLMS*.
**into the lower parts of the earth?:**...into the inferiour partes, —*RHEM*...to the under-regions of the earth? —*NORL*...to the depth of this world, —*PHLP*.

**4:9.** Three major possibilities exist about the meaning of this verse. A few commentators think these statements refer to the coming of the Holy Spirit on the Day of Pentecost (Acts 2), but this interpretation is not very plausible. Others believe they are a reference to the incarnation and subsequent ascension of Christ after He accomplished what He came to earth to do. Still others believe Jesus actually descended into Hades to proclaim that His work of redemption was complete.

**10. He that descended is the same also that ascended up for above all heavens:**...is identically the same person, —*PHLP*...up beyond the highest Heaven, —*TCNT*.
**that he might fill all things.):**...that he might fulfill, —*MRDK*...that the whole universe from lowest to highest might know his presence, —*PHLP*...to fill the whole universe with his presence, —*TCNT*.

**4:10.** While there may be disagreement concerning what Paul meant, it is clear that he was explaining Christ's right to give specific ministries to the Church. Here Paul used a word often found in his writings which usually is translated "fullness" (*plērōma*) but here is a verb that translates "might fill." This same word was used often by the Gnostics to refer to angelic beings they considered as intermediary beings between God and human beings. The apostle made it clear, however, that Christ is all in all. He is the One who fills the whole universe because He is omnipresent; angels are not.

**11. And he gave some, apostles; and some, prophets:** ... He appointed some men, *—MNTG* ... His "gifts unto men" were varied, *—PHLP.*

**and some, evangelists; and some, pastors and teachers:** ... Missionaries, *—TCNT* ... preachers of the Gospel, *—PHLP* ... shepherds, *—PNIN,* *—WLSN* ... and doctors, *—DOUY.*

**4:11.** Paul lists here various types of ministries. The apostolic ministry is carried on by leaders who take the gospel where it has not gone before. Sometimes missionaries have this type of ministry. The prophetic ministry is to forthtell (for the present) and sometimes foretell God's will and plans. Evangelists are individuals who constantly present the message of salvation through redemption accomplished at Calvary. Because the Greek text shows only one definite article (*tous*) before "pastors ... teachers," the two words may be referring to the same office. However, because the definite article here is plural, Paul may have been writing of two different offices. The pastor is the individual leader who shepherds God's people, while the teacher systematizes and teaches sound doctrine to believers. Yet the pastor might easily have a teaching function, as he surely needs in our present time. This list is not in order of importance, but in order of necessity. Each ministry is important for the proper functioning of the Church.

**12. For the perfecting of the saints, for the work of the ministry:** ... in order to equip, *—MNTG* ... to the consummation of the sainctes, *—RHEM* ... might have all thinges necessarie to worke, *—TNDL* ... with a view to, *—CLMT* ... to the fitting of, *—RTHM* ... for the complete qualification, *—WLSN* ... with a view to fitting his People, *—TCNT* ... for the immediate equipment of God's people, *—WLMS.*

**for the edifying of the body of Christ:** ... for the building up of, *—WORL.*

**4:12.** The remainder of the passage through verse 16 describes clearly the two basic reasons why God places some people into full-time ministry. Christ has given every Christian a ministry, but not every Christian is a full-time minister in the sense of it being an occupation. First, these occupational ministers exist "for the perfecting of the saints" or to equip the saints so they in turn can minister for Christ. Some scholars believe the comma after the word "saints" does not belong there and stress that every believer has a ministry to fulfill. The word used here comes from *katartismos* and normally refers to furnishing something. The body of Christ will be built up as all Christians are involved in ministry.

**13. Till we all come in the unity of the faith:** ... Until we all meet into, *—DOUY* ... until we all attain to that unity, *—TCNT* ... until we all advance into the oneness, *—RTHM.*

**and of the knowledge of the Son of God:** ... and common knowledge of, *—PHLP.*

**unto a perfect man, unto the measure of the stature of the fulness of Christ:** ... we arrive at real maturitythat measure of development which is meant by, *—PHLP* ... a full grown Man, *—WLSN.*

**4:13.** Secondly, God has called full-time, occupational ministers to help believers mature in the Lord, or to become more and more like Christ himself. As believers mature they will advance from the infancy state into full-grown adults. Some theologians enjoy emphasizing the similarities between natural birth and spiritual birth and natural growth and spiritual growth. They fail sometimes, however, to describe the differences between them. For example, in natural birth a person has no choice as to which family he will be part of in life. In spiritual birth an individual does make a choice to become part of the family of God. In natural life growth is nearly automatic, unless something is wrong organically with the child. However, spiritual growth is never automatic.

**14. That we [henceforth] be no more children:** ... We are not to remain as, *—PHLP* ... that we may no longer be, *—NOYS* ... be Infants no longer, *—WLSN.*

**tossed to and fro, and carried about with every wind of doctrine:** ... billow-tossed and shifted round, *—RTHM* ... fluctuating to and fro, *—WSLY* ... and whirled about, *—SCLT* ... backward and forward and blown about by every breath of human teaching, *—TCNT* ... not borun aboute with eche wynde of techynge, *—WCLF* ... wind of teaching, *—PNIN.*

**by the sleight of men, [and] cunning craftiness, whereby they lie in wait to deceive:** ... devised in the wickedness ... according to the wiles of error, *—CNFT* ... in the weywardnesse of men, *—WCLF* ... by the wickedness of men, *—DOUY* ... through the dishonest tricks of men, and their cunning in the wily arts of error, *—NOYS* ... which is in the trickery of men ... in systematic deception, *—WLSN* ... that leadeth to the system of error, *—ALFD.*

**4:14.** Instability is one definite sign of immaturity. Paul himself upbraided some Corinthians who were still "babes in Christ" after apparently being Christians for about 5 years (1 Corinthians 3:1-4). The writer of Hebrews dealt with the same basic problem in his letter (Hebrews 5:11-6:12).

"Cunning" comes from an interesting Greek word (*kubeia,* "cube") which was used literally of dice throwing. A clever trickster actually could hold two sets of dice in his hand and throw whichever set he desired. Tricksters who use crafty methods appeal to immature Christians who do not grow spiritually. These "babes in

Christ" seem always to be looking for something a little more sensational than the last thing that appealed to them. Unfortunately, these individuals help many religious hucksters to build their own kingdom, rather than concentrating on building God's kingdom.

**15. But speaking the truth in love:** ... But being followers of truth, —ALFD ... to hold firmly to the truth, —PHLP.

**may grow up into him in all things, which is the head, [even] Christ:** ... we shall grow into complete union, —TCNT ... to grow up in every way, —PHLP.

**4:15.** Instead of falling for trickery Christians should be obedient to Christ. Obedience to Christ and the ability to recognize religious charlatans are definite signs of Christian maturity. Christ is the source from which the ability to grow comes, and He is the object or goal of that growth. Immature Christians have a tendency to overly revere Christian leaders. Obviously, leaders should be respected. Sometimes, however, respect can turn into worship. Paul dealt with this tendency to exalt leaders when he wrote his first letter to the Corinthians (1 Corinthians 1:10-17). While Christian leaders do help us grow spiritually, we need to keep our concentration on Christ, the perfect example.

**16. From whom the whole body fitly joined together and compacted by that which every joint supplieth:** ... and united, —WLSN ... yf all the body be coupled and knet, —CRNM ... a harmonious structure knit together by the joints, —PHLP.

**according to the effectual working in the measure of every part, maketh increase of the body unto the edifying of itself in love:** ... gets each part to work properly, develops each part accordingly, —NORL ... to the proportionate Energy of Each single Part, —WLSN ... according to the functioning in due measure of each single part, —CNFT ... in proportion to the activity of each individual part, —TCNT ... makes continual growth, —MNTG ... for its building up in love, —WLMS.

**4:16.** In addition to the fact that a mature Christian will be stable and obedient, the last verse of the section shows this will result in a coordinated "body" with each member fulfilling his function. Just as the human body grows as a total organism with each part being involved, so the body of Christ grows as believers allow Christ His rightful place and as they do their part in the total process.

Unfortunately, many modern congregations have adopted the unscriptural philosophy of "hiring" a pastor to perform all the ministry for the congregation. These congregations can grow only to a certain point because one person can accomplish only so much. How refreshing it is, though,

to see a local assembly where most of the members are involved in some kind of ministry. That church will be a growing assembly, meeting the needs of people in the area and reaching the lost for Christ.

Believers need to be taught that full-time ministers are placed in the Church by Christ to help equip the saints so they in turn can minister and help others mature in the Lord. Even the first New Testament apostles were concerned about being able to give themselves to prayer and the ministry of the Word (Acts 6:4). A careful study of Acts chapter 6 will show that the apostles considered themselves "in the service of the Word" or "the deacon of the Word" (tē diakonia tou logou). The first obligation of occupational ministers must be to pray and to expound God's Word.

**17. This I say therefore, and testify in the Lord:** ... This is my instruction, then, which I give you from God, —PHLP ... and attesting in, —RTHM ... and give witness, —BB.

**that ye henceforth walk not as other Gentiles walk, in the vanity of their mind:** ... Do not live any longer as, —PHLP ... that you are to go no longer in the way of the Gentiles, —BB ... that you no longer walk, —WLSN ... as the heathen usually do, in the frivolity of, —WLMS ... in the perverseness, —MNTG ... in aimlessness of, —RTHM.

**4:17.** There is a long-standing debate about what happens to the fallen, sinful nature of a person who becomes a Christian. For example, some individuals think it is completely eradicated at conversion. Others take a "group encounter" approach in which through a "self-discovery" or "catharsis" method they attempt to bring the sinful nature under control. The Bible clearly expresses the fact that God does not remove the sinful nature at salvation, but its power is broken so a Christian need no longer be governed by it, though he still must grapple with it. Instead of removing the Adamic nature when a person becomes a believer, God places a new nature within the person, the indwelling Holy Spirit (Romans 8:9). Romans, chapter 7, Galatians 2:20; 5:13-26; Colossians 3:1-17, as well as many other passages, describe the constant internal warfare within the Christian between the "new nature of Christ" and the Adamic nature. Ephesians 4:17-32 is one of these passages.

Paul approached the matter by first explaining the negative aspect of the process and further showing how God broke the power of the sinful nature at the person's conversion. The apostle first encouraged the Gentile believers not to live as they had before their conversion to Christ. They formerly lived "in the vanity of their mind," the way pagans were living. They had lived in the sphere of the emptiness of their minds, denoting an ignorance of divine things, a lack of knowledge that involved moral blindness.

**18. Having the understanding darkened:** ...they live blindfold in a world of illusion, *–PHLP* ... their cogitation darkened, *–GNVA* ... their vnderstanding obscured, *–RHEM.*

**being alienated from the life of God:** ... they are cut off from the Life of God, *–TCNT* ... beynge farre from a godly lyfe, *–CRNM* ... estranged from the life of God, *–WLMS* ... the life of God is strange, *–BB.*

**through the ignorance that is in them:** ...of the stupidity, *–WLSN* ... that exists among them, *–WLMS.*

**because of the blindness of their heart:** ... because of the hardening, *–CLMT, –MNTG* ... because of the stubbornness of their hearts, *–WLMS* ... and insensitiveness, *–PHLP.*

**4:18.** They were ignorant because they had hardened their hearts against God. The "blindness of their heart" or hardening of their hearts led to a condition of callousness that made it impossible for them to experience true spiritual life that comes only from God. The apostle made these Gentiles personally responsible for what had happened to them. He certainly did not teach some fatalistic kind of approach that they had no responsibility for their actions. While Paul definitely believed in the sovereignty of God and constantly emphasized His grace, he balanced that view by stressing man's freedom of choice and the necessity for exercising faith.

**19. Who being past feeling have given themselves over unto lasciviousness:** ... For lost to all sense of shame, *–TCNT* ... They have stifled their consciences and then surrendered themselves, *–PHLP* ... who being without feeling have given themselves up to lewd-ness, *–SAWR* ... They have become callous, have abandoned themselves to sensuality, *–NORL.*

**to work all uncleanness with greediness:** ...and greedily practice any form of vice that lust can crave, *–NORL* ... practicing any form of impurity which lust can suggest, *–PHLP* ... with covetousness, *–PNIN* ... unto covetousness, *–DOUY.*

**4:19.** This hardening of their hearts led to a condition of "being past feeling." This latter term relates to losing all sensitivity to pain. This calloused condition prevented them from experiencing any moral consciousness. Just as thick callouses prevent people from feeling physical pain, willful rebellion against the work of the conscience eventually makes the conscience completely ineffective.

The description of a constant falling more deeply into sin is reminiscent of Romans 1:18-32 where Paul again characterized the Gentile world away from God. A careful search of that passage,

especially verse 20, will show the same general emphasis on human responsibility, so it is impossible for a person to justify his lost condition.

"Lasciviousness" refers to "sensuality" which leads to all types of impurity or uncleanness that goes deeper and deeper into sin because it never is satisfied. In Romans chapter 1 the apostle Paul also dealt with the subject of homosexuality that is described here in verse 19. Three times he said that God gave them over to something. First, "God gave them over in the sinful desires of their hearts to sexual impurity for the degrading of their bodies with one another" (Romans 1:24, NIV). Secondly, "God gave them over to shameful lusts" (Romans 1:26, NIV). Thirdly, "He gave them over to a depraved mind, to do what ought not to be done" (Romans 1:28, NIV).

**20. But ye have not so learned Christ:** ... you have learned nothing like that, *–PHLP.*

**21. If so be that ye have heard him, and have been taught by him:** ... you really listened to him, *–TCNT* ... if you have really heard his voice and ... that he has taught you, *–PHLP.*

**as the truth is in Jesus:** ... understood the truth, *–PHLP.*

**4:20, 21.** This verse begins with a very important "But." Because God had performed a miracle in the Ephesians, they no longer existed in this state of ignorance and separation from God. He said, "Ye have not so learned Christ."

Paul could write these words with assurance because he and the members of his evangelistic team had much to do with teaching the Ephesian Christians what they knew about Christ.

**22. That ye put off concerning the former conversation the old man:** ... you should lay aside your former mode of life, *–SAWR* ... respecting your former conduct, *–SCLT* ... the former Course of life, *–WLSN* ... and your former habits, *–NORL.*

**which is corrupt according to the deceitful lusts:** ... who perisheth, *–NOYS* ... owing to the passions fostered by Error, *–TCNT* ... according to the desire of error, *–DOUY.*

**4:22.** Even though the legal work of salvation had taken place in these lives, it was necessary for them to discard completely the old way of life. This passage contains one of the great paradoxes of Scripture because, after explaining the legal work of salvation God had performed in their lives, Paul went on to appeal for an experiential casting off of sin. The same verb appears in Colossians 3:8 with the same basic idea of putting off a former way of life. A person does this by denying the cravings of the sinful nature (Romans 6:13; Galatians 2:20; 5:13).

**23. And be renewed in the spirit of your mind:** ... undergo a mental and spiritual transformation, –TCNT ... in the spirit of youre soule, –WCLF ... must be renewed continually, –NORL.

**4:23.** Now we come to the positive aspect of the process. Because the Christian life is not a void, people need to "be renewed." This phrase comes from a present passive infinitive (*ananeousthai*). It is present because it is a continuous process. It is passive because God accomplishes the work only as believers yield to the Holy Spirit. It takes place "in the spirit of your mind," a probable reference to the fact that the will is involved in causing the process to continue.

**24. And that ye put on the new man:** ... put on the clean fresh clothes of the new life, –PHLP ... the man of new mould, –RTHM.

**which after God is created in righteousness and true holiness:** ... who, according to God, –WLSN ... created after God's likeness, –MNTG ... is shapen in ryghtewesnes, –CRNM ... and sacredness of the truth, –RTHM.

**4:24.** At the same time Christians must also "put on the new man," a reference to allowing the Holy Spirit to be the controlling force in their lives. If they are doing this it will manifest itself in "righteousness and true holiness." The Greek word for "new" (*kainos*) here refers to newness in quality. God is not only the pattern but also the author of this new life.

**25. Wherefore putting away lying:** ... Finish, –PHLP ... put away falseness, –MNTG ... leaving off falsehood, –WLSN ... stripping off what is false, –RTHM ... let falsehood be abandoned, –NORL.

**speak every man truth with his neighbour:** ... tell your neighbor the truth, –PHLP.

**for we are members one of another:** ... for we are all parts of the same body, –NORL.

**4:25.** The fruit that comes from a person's life—his actions—proves whether the person is yielding to the sinful nature or to the Holy Spirit. To illustrate his point Paul used four representative examples of problems that were very important in his day and still are today. Verse 25 deals with lying, an obvious manifestation of the fallen nature. By way of contrast, Paul encouraged Christians to "speak every man truth with his neighbor," because they are members of the same Body.

**26. Be ye angry, and sin not:** ... be sure that it is not out of wounded pride or bad temper, –PHLP.

**let not the sun go down upon your wrath:** ... Never go to bed angry, –PHLP ... upon your angry-mood, –RTHM.

**4:26.** In the second example there is also a negative and a positive. This admonition relates to the improper use of anger which results from yielding to the Adamic nature, and the proper use of anger which results from yielding to the Holy Spirit. "Be ye angry, and sin not" comes from the imperative verbs "be angry" and "do not sin" and is a quotation of Psalm 4:4.

The same word for anger (*orgē*) is used of God (Matthew 3:7; Mark 3:5; Romans 1:18; 12:19), so anger in itself is not sinful. Jesus certainly was angry when He cleansed the temple in Jerusalem (John 2:13-16). There are times when righteous anger should be manifested against injustice and other forms of sin.

"Let not the sun go down upon your wrath" also comes from a present imperative prohibition so it could be rendered, "Stop letting the sun go down on your wrath." Anger easily can lead to resentment or bitterness, the meaning of the second word (*parorgismos*) which is translated "wrath" in this verse. If a person becomes angry for some legitimate reason, whatever triggered the anger should be settled before the day is past, a way of saying it should be taken care of immediately.

**27. Neither give place to the devil:** ... don't give the devil that sort of foothold, –PHLP ... and do not give any opportunity, –TCNT ... give no case to, –MRDK ... give occasion to, –ALFD ... nor give an Opportunity for the Accuser, –WLSN ... the backbyter, –CRNM ... the adversary, –RTHM.

**4:27.** The devil will use anything he can to hinder God's people, and the improper use of anger is one of his greatest tools. Never give Satan an opportunity to take advantage of them.

**28. Let him that stole steal no more:**

**but rather let him labour, working with [his] hands the thing which is good:** ... in honest industry, –MNTG ... rather let him toil, –WLSN ... find employment, and do good work with his hands, –NORL.

**that he may have to give to him that needeth:** ... he may have something to share, –TCNT ... to distribute to the indigent, –SCLT ... that you may be able to give to those in need, –PHLP.

**4:28.** Stealing is another manifestation of yielding to the Adamic nature. Pilfering was a way of life for many of the Ephesian Christians before their conversion. Apparently some of them continued to practice it even after becoming Christians because Paul literally told them to "stop stealing." Working is the best practical antidote to stealing. Furthermore, the person who works hard will have something to share with others who are in need.

**29. Let no corrupt communication proceed out of your mouth:** ... Let no evil speech, −DOUY ... no evil word, −SAWR ... corrupt discourse, −WSLY ... no putrid discourse, −RTHM ... corrupt Word proceed, −WLSN ... Al naughtie speache let it not proceede out, −RHEM.

**but that which is good to the use of edifying:** ... good words instead, −PHLP.

**that it may minister grace unto the hearers:** ... that it may afford benefit, −SAWR ... it may confer a Benefit, −WLSN ... which God can use to help other people, −PHLP.

**4:29.** The fourth issue, "corrupt communication," really deals with "putrid, rotten, corrupt, filthy, rancid" speech. When Christians constantly work and live with other people who are not believers, they are often subjected to such ungodly language. However, they must not use that fact as an excuse for succumbing to that which is a normal way of life for the unsaved people around them.

**30. And grieve not the holy Spirit of God:** ... be not making sorrowful, −RTHM ... Never hurt, −PHLP.
**whereby ye are sealed unto the day of redemption:** ... He is ... the personal pledge of your eventual full redemption, −PHLP ... in whom ye were sealed, −PNIN, −ASV ... in whiche ye ben markid, −WCLF.

**4:30.** In addition to the four specific items mentioned, Paul warned the Ephesians literally to "stop grieving the Holy Spirit." His presence in a person's life is one of the most important proofs that he belongs to God. Because of this serious matter believers must be careful not to do anything that would grieve Him.

Sins of attitude are referred to in the closing verses of the chapter. Apparently these grieve the Holy Spirit as much as the four sins the apostle warned against. Among other things, this verse portrays the Holy Spirit as a Person with the ability to be grieved.

**31. Let all bitterness, and wrath, and anger, and clamour, and evil speaking:** ... indignation, −DOUY, −CNFT ... passion ... brawling, and abusive language, as well as all spite-fulness, −TCNT ... and outcry and defamation, −RTHM ... and cursed speaking, −GNVA.

**be put away from you:** ... Banish from among you, −TCNT ... be banished from, −SAWR.
**with all malice:** ... with all baseness, −RTHM.

**4:31.** Therefore, we need to "put away" all "bitterness" (*pikria*, resentfulness), "wrath" (*thumos*, a violent outburst of anger), "anger" (*orgē*, a settled feeling of anger), "clamor" (*kraugē*, shouting), "evil speaking" (*blasphēmia*, blasphemy), and "malice" (*kakia*, ill feeling).

**32. And be ye kind one to another:** ... You must practice, −WLMS.
**tenderhearted:** ... compassionate, −WLSN ... and merciful, −CNFT ... be understanding, −PHLP.
**forgiving one another, even as God for Christ's sake hath forgiven you:** ... Be as ready to forgive others as, −PHLP ... pardoning one another, −RHEM ... has generously forgiven you, −CNFT ... has graciously forgiven you, −WLMS ... freely forgave you, −CLMT.

**4:32.** This verse begins in the Greek language with an appeal to "keep on becoming kind to one another." The idea expressed is that of abandoning one attitude completely and replacing it with another attitude. Forgiving other people is not always easy, but Christians have the greatest of all incentives for doing so, the fact that Christ forgave them.

This total passage, along with many others, shows that the apostle Paul certainly did not believe the fallen, sinful nature was removed completely at salvation. Instead, at conversion the power of the Adamic nature is broken so a person is no longer a slave to it. At the same time God places within the person His Holy Spirit, so in a real sense he then has two natures. This results in a struggle that continues throughout this earthly life. But the more the Christian yields to the Holy Spirit, the easier it becomes. Also, the more a person resists the cravings of the Adamic nature, the easier it will be for his spiritual nature to dominate his way of life.

## Chapter 5

**1. Be ye therefore followers of God, as dear children:** ... Become therefore, −WLSN ... Learn then to imitate, −MNTG ... as moost dereworthe sones, −WCLF ... try to be like God, −EVRD.

**5:1.** Verses 1-20 serve as one of the most beautiful descriptions of the Christian life that can be found in the Bible. Paul first instructed Christians to be "followers of God" or "imitators of God." The English word *mimic* comes from the Greek term for "followers" (*mimētai*). This word normally is used of imitating people (1 Corinthians 4:16; 11:1; 1 Thessalonians 1:6; Hebrews 6:12) and churches (1 Thessalonians 2:14). Here, however, it is used of the imitation of God, which is the loftiest endeavor that could ever be placed before a person.

The appeal sounds very reminiscent of Jesus' appeal to His disciples in the Sermon on the Mount (Matthew 5:48). It is another way of saying, "Allow Christ to be your prototype." Just as growing from an infant into an adult consists of a long, gradual process, so the apostle told believers literally to "keep on becoming." There is no point in this earthly life when a person can afford to let up his effort in this matter. God's great love for His children makes it possible for them to constantly become more like Christ.

**2. And walk in love, as Christ also hath loved us:** ... Live your lives in, —*PHLP* ... Let love guide your footsteps, —*NORL* ... and practice living in love, —*WLMS*.

**and hath given himself for us an offering and a sacrifice to God for a sweetsmelling savour:** ... and which he perfectly expressed when, —*PHLP* ... and delivered himself up, —*WLSN* ... as a fragrant offering, —*WLMS* ... an oblation, —*RHEM*.

**5:2.** As believers do this, they will be constantly ordering their behavior in the sphere of love (*agapē*). Because "God is love" (1 John 4:8, 16), as believers imitate Him they will be living in a manner that manifests that same love (1 Corinthians 13). In the light of all that Christ did on the cross, that should not be too much to ask. That is what makes it possible for Christians to live lives of love. He acted not only as a priest but also as the very sacrifice himself. The Greek word for "sacrifice" (*thusia*) describes one who is innocent of crime shielding with his body the one who deserves the punishment. The expiatory character of Christ's death includes giving himself in our place as a sacrifice.

**3. But fornication, and all uncleanness:** ... As for sexual vice, —*MNTG* ... and every kind of impurity, —*TCNT* ... All impurity, —*WLSN* ... or sensual greed, —*WLMS*.

**or covetousness:** ... and avarice, —*MRDK* ... or unbridled Lust, —*WLSN* ... inordinate desire, —*SCLT* ... the itch to get your hands on what belongs to other people, —*PHLP*.

**let it not be once named among you:** ... don't even talk about such things, —*PHLP* ... these should not even be mentioned, —*NORL*.

**as becometh saints:** ... they are no fit subjects for Christians to talk about, —*PHLP* ... as Christ's People, —*TCNT* ... as becomes Holy persons, —*WLSN*.

**5:3.** In the light of the wonderful sacrifice of Christ, Paul warned believers in verses 3-7 to sever themselves completely from their former way of life. Obviously, he listed only some representative sins of people who were not walking in the sphere of the love of God. "Fornication" (sexual immorality) and "uncleanness" (any kind of impurity) were serious external sins in that day. However, the apostle considered "covetousness" (greed) just as improper for God's holy people. Any kind of sin is inconsistent with a life of love. God's love does not motivate us to sin!

**4. Neither filthiness, nor foolish talking, nor jesting:** ... The keynote of your conversation should

not be, —*PHLP* ... Neither obscenity, —*WSLY* ... and shamelessness, —*RTHM* ... nor double meanings, —*SCLT* ... with anything dishonourable, —*TCNT* ... nor indecent jesting, —*NOYS*.

**which are not convenient:** ... which is to no purpose, —*DOUY* ... which are beneath [you], —*RTHM* ... for these are not becoming to Christians, —*NORL*.

**but rather giving of thanks:** ... Substitute for them thanksgiving, —*TCNT* ... but a sense of all that we owe to God, —*PHLP*.

**5:4.** "Filthiness" (obscenity) literally means "filthy language." "Foolish talking" is talk that is characteristic of fools, people literally with "empty heads." The first type of verbal sin mentioned here needs very little explanation, except to emphasize that it takes a concentrated effort to avoid it, especially if a person lives in a non-Christian family or works in an environment where this type of language is a way of life. Good, clean jokes certainly have their place, even among God's people. But there is a difference between a joke that merely helps to lighten the atmosphere with good laughter and one that borders on that which is coarse or base.

"Foolish talking" probably is the most difficult of the three verbal sins mentioned here to define. The apostle did not imply that people always have to be serious in order to please God. "Foolish talking" is empty or vain conversation which does not contribute to the spiritual maturity of individuals. Such "talking," as well as obscenities and coarse joking, are out of place for believers. Instead, Christians should constantly verbalize thanksgiving.

**5. For this ye know, that no whoremonger, nor unclean person, nor covetous man, who is an idolater:** ... this ye know, assuredly, —*WORL* ... no Fornicator, —*WLSN* ... (which makes him an idolater), —*NORL*.

**hath any inheritance in the kingdom of Christ and of God:** ... can have any share in the kingdom, —*NORL*.

**5:5.** This verse could be misinterpreted very easily to mean that a person who commits a single sin suddenly loses his relationship to God. The emphasis here is the same as in many other scriptural passages; that is, if a person can consistently practice sin without repentance, it is obvious the person does not know God any longer. People who can constantly practice immorality, impurity, greed, or similar sins, are giving priority to these sins rather than to God. That is probably why Paul called such a person "an idolater." Anything that becomes more important than God himself has become a "god."

**6. Let no man deceive you with vain words:** . . . seduce you, —RHEM . . . with meaningless phrases, —TCNT . . . with empty words, —PNIN, —WLSN, —WORL . . . with worthless arguments, —NORL.

**for because of these things cometh the wrath of God upon the children of disobedience:** . . . It is these very things which bring down, —PHLP.

**5:6.** Verse 6 probably contains a warning against some kind of gnosticism which held that such practices as the apostle Paul condemned here were irrelevant to spiritual life, because they related to the body only and not to the spiritual nature of a person. Many of the Gnostics believed all matter was evil. Because the human body is matter, according to them, it also is evil. Some of them practiced extreme asceticism in order to control the "evil" body, while others went to the opposite extreme and practiced extreme licentiousness. Because the body supposedly was evil, whatever a person did with it would not influence him spiritually.

Paul warned against being deceived with such empty words. The term for "vain words" (*kenois logois*) literally relates to words without reality or substance. Listening and succumbing to this kind of suggestion is not only dangerous, it also brings the wrath of God upon those who practice this kind of lifestyle.

**7. Be not ye therefore partakers with them:** . . . Have nothing to do with men like that, —PHLP . . . do not become their Associates, —WLSN . . . Be not ye therfore companyons of them, —CRNM . . . become co-partners, —RTHM.

**5:7.** Paul's advice was not to partake with them. Because the construction here is a present imperative prohibition, it literally means "stop becoming partakers with them."

**8. For ye were sometimes darkness:** . . . once you were, —PHLP . . . you were formerly, —SAWR.

**but now [are ye] light in the Lord: walk as children of light:** . . . Live then as, —PHLP.

**5:8.** Again we see a definite contrast between the past and the present. Because these believers had been delivered from their former spiritual darkness, they were not to be content with living in some ambiguous twilight. Probably much of this section, from verse 8 through verse 14 is based upon Jesus' statement about himself (John 8:12) and His followers (Matthew 5:14) being the "light of the world."

**9. (For the fruit of the Spirit [is] in all goodness and righteousness and truth;):** . . . for the fruit of the light, —CNFT . . . consysteth in all goodnes, —CRNM.

**5:9.** Just as the rays of the sun help cause plants and flowers to grow, so the light of the Lord should bring to life in believers the qualities mentioned in this verse. Because God is good in the ultimate sense of the word, if a person allows His will to become important in his life, God's goodness will be reflected in him as well. "Righteousness" or "justice" basically means to do that which is right. The light of God should cause believers to treat other people fairly or with justice.

"Truth" normally is defined as "that which conforms to reality." Of course, the problem is determining what is reality. The Bible makes it clear that Christ is the personification of truth (John 14:6), and the Bible is the written expression of that truth (John 17:17).

**10. Proving what is acceptable unto the Lord:** . . . always be trying to find out, —TCNT . . . searching out, —WLSN . . . Accept that which is pleasinge, —TNDL . . . You must learn to do what is pleasing to the Lord, —NORL.

**5:10.** "Light" comes from the Greek term *phōtos* from which we get *photography* and several other terms. It is a very common expression in the Bible, normally depicting the drastic difference between "what is acceptable unto the Lord" and what is characteristic of a life of practicing sin.

**11. And have no fellowship with the unfruitful works of darkness:** . . . be not partakers, —SAWR . . . Steer clear of the activities of darkness, —PHLP.

**but rather reprove [them]:** . . . let your lives show by contrast how dreary and futile these things are, —PHLP.

**5:11.** According to this verse, Christians have two basic obligations with respect to sin: have nothing to do with it and "reprove" it. The idea contained in the first obligation is literally "stop participating with people who practice sin." The second obligation is even more drastic, because sinners usually do not like the light turned on when they are practicing evil in darkness.

**12. For it is a shame even to speak of those things which are done of them in secret:** . . . It is degrading, —TCNT . . . it is indecent ever to mention, —WLSN.

**5:12.** The writings of Paul always emphasize the exceeding sinfulness of sin, but never more evidently than here. Some of the sins committed by people under cover of darkness were so abhorrent to Paul that he hesitated even to mention them.

**13. But all things that are reproved are made manifest by the light:** . . . light is capable of "showing up" everything for what it really is, *–PHLP* . . . their true character made manifest, *–TCNT.*

**for whatsoever doth make manifest is light:** . . . for it is light that discouereth all things, *–GNVA.*

**5:13.** Societies may change, and methods of committing sin may change, but one truth does not change. When sin is exposed to the light of God's truth, something drastic happens. People who allow the Bible to have access to their lives will become very uncomfortable if they are practicing sin. The Holy Spirit is extremely faithful in reproving the world of sin (John 16:8). In other words, He proves the world, or nonbelievers, wrong about their attitudes toward sin, righteousness, and judgment. He seeks to bring them to the realization that the sacrifice of Jesus is the only sacrifice given for the sins of mankind.

**14. Wherefore he saith:** . . . The Scripture therefore says, *–NORL* . . . Thus God speaks through the scriptures, *–PHLP.*

**Awake thou that sleepest, and arise from the dead, and Christ shall give thee light:** . . . stande vp from death, *–GNVA* . . . will enlighten thee, *–CNFT* . . . vvil illuminate thee, *–RHEM* . . . shine upon thee, *–PHLP.*

**5:14.** This verse could be a loose paraphrase of Isaiah 26:19 and 60:1, or Paul could have been quoting an early baptismal hymn or some poem familiar to his readers. The metaphor is that of the morning, when the darkness of night is dispelled by the rising of the sun. The idea expressed in the Greek language literally is to "stand up out of the dead ones."

**15. See then that ye walk circumspectly:** . . . Be extremely careful, then, *–TCNT* . . . Take hede therefore, *–TNDL, –CRNM* . . . Look therefore carefully how ye walk, *–PNT.*

**not as fools, but as wise:** . . . not as men who do not know the meaning and purpose of life, *–PHLP.*

**5:15.** "See" (*blepete*) is another way of saying "watch out" or "take heed" or "be very careful." The old term "circumspectly" (literally "looking around") contains the idea of walking "strictly."

**16. Redeeming the time, because the days are evil:** . . . avoydyng occasyon, *–CRNM* . . . making the most of every opportunity, *–TCNT* . . . Make the best use of your time, *–PHLP.*

**5:16.** The present participle in this verse is in the middle voice and refers to purchasing for one's self or for one's personal benefit on a continuous basis. "The days are *evil*" (*ponēros*) speaks of evil "in

active opposition to that which is good." If Christians are not careful, the evil nature of this age will rob them of the opportunities to do God's will.

**17. Wherefore be ye not unwise:** . . . be not thoughtless, *–SCLT* . . . inconsiderate, *–WLSN* . . . vague, *–PHLP.*

**but understanding what the will of the Lord [is]:** . . . but firmly grasp what you know to be the will of God, *–PHLP.*

**5:17.** Doing God's will cannot become a reality in a person's life unless that person understands what God's will is. Actually, "be ye not unwise" in this verse comes from another present imperative prohibition, so it literally means "stop becoming those who are foolish."

**18. And be not drunk with wine, wherein is excess:** . . . Do not drink wine to excess, for that leads to profligacy, *–TCNT* . . . wherein is riot, *–PNIN* . . . *–ASV* . . . luxury, *–DOUY* . . . for in that is debauchery, *–CNFT* . . . by which comes Debauchery, *–WLSN* . . . rioteousnes, *–RHEM.*

**but be filled with the Spirit:** . . . let the Spirit stimulate your souls, *–PHLP.*

**5:18.** Above all else, that which makes the Christian life successful and pleasing to God is living in the power of the Holy Spirit. Quoting Proverbs 23:30, Paul warned against the folly of indulging in wine. Bacchus, the wine god, was one of the "gods" worshiped by pagans. Therefore, drunkenness was a normal part of pagan life. Apparently some of the Gentile Christians continued to follow their former practice, even though to them Bacchus was no longer a "god." The command comes from another present imperative prohibition, and it could be translated "stop being drunk with wine." Drunkenness only leads to "excess" or debauchery.

Instead of being filled physically, Paul encouraged Christians to be filled spiritually. The command here is from a present passive imperative verb, literally, "be being filled with the Spirit"; it is not optional. It is passive, denoting that God has to accomplish it. Thirdly, it is present, meaning it is an ongoing process.

**19. Speaking to yourselves in psalms and hymns and spiritual songs:** . . . Express your joy, *–PHLP* . . . speaking to one another, *–CNFT* . . . canticles, *–DOUY.*

**singing and making melody in your heart to the Lord:** . . . Keep on praying and praising, *–WLMS* . . . using your voice in songs, *–BB* . . . chaunting, *–RHEM* . . . and making music, *–WLSN, –ADAM* . . . and dancing in your hearts, *–FNTN* . . . for the ears of God! *–PHLP.*

**5:19.** This verse gives some excellent advice about staying full of the Holy Spirit. A person does so by worshiping God. Paul here mentioned only two of the many ways to worship God. We worship God through singing psalms set to music, through hymns which are songs of praise to God, and through spiritual songs. It is difficult to know exactly what is meant by this last type. Some Bible scholars think it refers to songs of testimony which are based upon spiritual experiences, while others think it refers to singing in other tongues (cf. 1 Corinthians 14:15). Our worship in song certainly should contain a balance among these three types of singing.

**20. Giving thanks always for all things:** ... Thank God at all times, *−PHLP* ... continue giving thanks for everything, *−WLMS* ... at all times, *−RTHM.*
**unto God and the Father in the name of our Lord Jesus Christ:**

**5:20.** Believers also worship God by constant thanksgiving. The Greek term from which we get the word *thanksgiving* comes from the word that translates into English as *eucharist* (*eucharisteō*), a term for the Communion service.

**21. Submitting yourselves one to another in the fear of God:** ... And "fit in with" one another, because of your common reverence, *−PHLP* ... keep on living in subordination, *−WLMS* ... being subordinate to each other, *−SCLT* ... be ruled by one another, *−BB* ... subjecting yourselves, *−PNIN* ... out of reverence, *−TCNT* ... out of respect, *−ADAM* ... reverence for Christ, *−MNTG.*

**5:21.** In the Greek language this important section of Ephesians begins with the statement, "subjecting yourselves to one another out of reverence for Christ" or "out of regard for His will and His glory." Paul reveals the most conspicuous of areas in which Christians should submit to one another. Marriage, family, and work are three areas in life where a person needs to have a peaceful relationship.

The structure of the entire passage from 5:21 through 6:9 stems from the participle *hupotassomenoi* which begins verse 21, occupying the emphatic position. Because it is a present participle it refers to an activity that must be continuous. Because it is middle voice (the middle and passive voices have identical endings in present tense verb forms) it indicates it must be voluntary. In Colossians 3:18 Paul used the verb form of the word, but the same participle occurs in Titus 2:5, and also 1 Peter 3:1, 5. In all these instances the middle voice is used, showing the necessity of voluntary submission.

**22. Wives, submit yourselves unto your own husbands, as unto the Lord:** ... must learn to adapt yourselves to, *−PHLP* ... live in subordination to, *−WLMS* ... be under the authority of, *−BB.*

**5:22.** These statements about wives and husbands were very radical in an age that definitely belonged to men. This passage of Scripture clearly establishes the fact there should be no sense of inequality among God's people.

In the ideal Christian family, the wife should voluntarily submit to the leadership role of her husband as "priest" of the family. He is responsible for the spiritual welfare of the family. He should not force his wife to submit to him, nor should she take a passive approach in submitting. A woman who voluntarily submits to the leadership of her husband will be the main recipient of benefits derived from the action.

**23. For the husband is the head of the wife:** ... since a husband, *−ADAM.*
**even as Christ is the head of the church:** ... just as, *−WLMS* ... in the same way as, *−TCNT, −PHLP* ... heed of the congregacion, *−TNDL, −CRNM* ... Head of the assembly, *−WORL.*
**and he is the saviour of the body:** ... He Himself is, *−ADAM* ... a Preserver, *−WLSN* ... the same is he that minystreth saluacyon vnto the body, *−CRNM.*

**5:23.** This verse should be considered in light of the phrase "as unto the Lord" in verse 22. God certainly does not expect a Christian wife to do unscriptural things out of obedience to her unsaved husband. The term "head" here again relates to the function of the husband as the spiritual leader of the family. In a family where the husband is not a Christian the wife may have to accept the position of spiritual leadership while she is doing what the Bible instructs her so that her husband will also become a Christian (1 Corinthians 7:10, 11).

**24. Therefore as the church is subject unto Christ:** ... The willing subjection of, *−PHLP.*
**so [let] the wives [be] to their own husbands in every thing:** ... so the married women, *−WLMS* ... should be reproduced in the submission of wives, *−PHLP.*

**5:24.** Again, this submission must be voluntary or it will not work. The term "every thing" also must be considered in the light of the qualifier in verse 22, "as unto the Lord." The wife has a supportive role, something like soldiers under the leadership of an officer. They need each other.

**25. Husbands, love your wives, even as Christ also loved the church, and gave himself for it:** ... But, remember, this means that the husband must give his wife the same sort of love, *−PHLP* ... and delivered Himself up for it, —WORL, —MRDK... delivered Himself up for her sake, —FNTN.

**5:25.** The rest of the chapter describes the husband's responsibility. Just as the wife's primary responsibility can be summarized in "voluntary submission," so the husband's special duty is "love" (*agapaō*). Just as the submission of the Church to Christ serves as the wife's model, the love of Christ for the Church reflects the husband's attitude toward his wife. Christ loved His church enough to die for it. If the genuine love of the husband (like that of Christ for the Church) balances the loving, voluntary submission of the wife, she will find it easy to fulfill her role. Real love will not take advantage of the partner.

If a man truly loves his wife, he will want to share with her in every possible way. The arrangement God established between a wife and a husband does not imply that he is to make all the decisions. If he truly loves her, he will share the decision-making responsibilities with her, as long as he does not abdicate his position as the spiritual leader of the family.

**26. That he might sanctify and cleanse it:** ... to consecrate her, —WLMS ... having purified her, —WLSN ... that after cleansing her, —MNTG ... so as to consecrate it, —NORL.

**with the washing of water by the word:** ... by the laver of water, —DOUY ... in the fountayne of water, —TNDL ... by the bath of the water in the word, —NOYS ... with the water of His message, —FNTN ... according to his promise, —TCNT ... in the word of liif? —WCLF.

**5:26.** Individuals are cleansed from their sins and become members of the body of Christ as they respond to the Word (*rhēma*, Romans 10:8; 1 Peter 1:25). Other passages describe the process of cleansing that occurs at conversion (John 3:5; Titus 3:5; Hebrews 10:22). Paul is here speaking of the cleansing power of the Word of God. The Scriptures often use water in a metaphoric sense, in relation to the work of regeneration. But the Word also continues to have a cleansing ministry throughout our Christian life.

**27. That he might present it to himself a glorious church:** ... and might constitute it, —MRDK ... the rectified church, —FNTN ... a Church full of splendor, —NORL ... gloriously arrayed, —ADAM.

**not having spot, or wrinkle, or any such thing; but that it should be holy and without blemish:** ... free from spots, wrinkles or any other disfigurements ... perfect, —PHLP ... or Blemish, —WLSN ... or any such blemish; but on the contrary holy and faultless, —MNTG ... and vndefoulid, —WCLF ... but holy and faultless in every respect, —NORL ... but to be consecrated and faultless, —WLMS ... nor anything like them, —FNTN.

**5:27.** Not only does Christ perform the initial work of cleansing at salvation, but He continues to work in believers to remove every stain and wrinkle. "Spot" or "stain" refers to impurity, and "wrinkle" is a sign of age or decay. Therefore Christ, through the work of the Holy Spirit, continues to purify those who are His, thereby removing from them the stains left by their former lives.

Furthermore, in a real sense, even though the body may be deteriorating, the work of Christ in the continuous sanctification process is making the soul "younger." It is difficult to know exactly why the word "wrinkle" is used in the context, but perhaps it carries the idea of reversing the inward process of deterioration that was occurring before conversion.

**28. So ought men to love their wives as their own bodies:** ... In like manner, —NOYS ... In similar way, —BRKL ... In the same way, —ADAM ... married men ought to, —WEYM ... ought to give their wives the love they naturally have for, —PHLP ... as being their own, —HNT.

**He that loveth his wife loveth himself:** ... The man who loves, —SEB ... The lover of, —FNTN ... his own wife, —HNT ... is the extending of his love for himself to enfold her, —PHLP ... does but love himself, —CNBR ... is thereby loving himself, —WAY.

**5:28.** This verse describes another reason for a husband to love his wife—the fact they are one flesh. No sane person destroys his own body, so for a husband to treat his wife merely as property means he is damaging himself in the process. The apostle already had used Christ's love for the Church as the model for the husband. Just as Christ never bullies His church, so the husband should not be guilty of that error.

The mystical union between a wife and a husband is one of the most marvelous relationships known to humans. Next to the spiritual relationship a Christian has with Jesus himself, the marital bond is no doubt the strongest tie any one person could have with another person. This is one reason the act of sexual intercourse is so sacred. It is the ultimate expression of two companions showing their love to each other. It should not be cheapened! Again, of course, the matter of voluntary submission comes into focus. Christians who truly follow Paul's instructions in verse 21 are people who will enjoy their marital relationship.

**29. For no man ever yet hated his own flesh:** ... his own body, —WEYM ... ever hated his own person, —WAY ... neglects, —PHLP.

**but nourisheth and cherisheth it:** ... nay, it is nourished, —HNT ... on the contrary, he feeds and warms it, —FNTN ... He feeds it and cares for it, —NORL ... feeds his body and takes care of it,

*−TCNT* . . . and looks after it, *−PHLP* . . . and cherishes it, *−WEYM* . . . carefully protects it, *−BRKL* . . . and provideth for it, *−MRDK.*

**even as the Lord the church:** . . . even as is the Community also by, *−HNT* . . . as Christ treats, *−BRKL* . . . as Christ does for the church, *−ADAM* . . . Christ does the same thing for his community, *−SEB* . . . for his body, *−PHLP.*

**5:29.** The fact that Christ "nourisheth and cherisheth" or "feeds and cares for" His church is one of the most prominent truths taught in Scripture. As its organic Head, He gives the orders in a manner that expresses true concern. He alone truly knows the needs of His people, and He operates in them through the Holy Spirit in the light of those needs. He gave the written Word of God so that Christians would have answers to the pressing problems of life. A person who consistently studies the Bible will gain an understanding of Jesus that is not possible in any other way.

**30. For we are members of his body, of his flesh, and of his bones:** . . . because we are, as it were, *−WEYM* . . . because we are parts of His body, *−FNTN* . . . we are his flesh and blood I *−PHLP.*

**5:30.** This verse encapsulates what the Bible teaches in detail in many other places. Notice how the institution of marriage is elevated throughout this passage by comparing it to the relationship between Christ and His body, the Church. Jesus is not just a figurehead; He truly is the operating Head of His church. As the "Vine," He is the One who possesses eternal life, but He shares it with the "branches" (John 15:5). Branches do not possess life in themselves, but draw upon the life that exists in the vine. In the same way the members of a body do not give orders to the head, just as the members of Christ's church should not presume to give orders to Him.

**31. For this cause shall a man leave his father and mother:** . . . On this account, *−WLSN, −BRKL* . . . For this reason, *−ADAM* . . . This is why, *−SEB* . . . Instead, *−HNT* . . . Therefore shall, *−MOFT* . . . a man is to leave, *−WEYM* . . . shall a man forsake father and mother, and shall be knit to his wife, *−WAY.*

**and shall be joined unto his wife:** . . . and adhere to, *−MRDK* . . . and be closely united, *−TCNT* . . . and shall cleave to, *−PNIN, −DOUY, −ADAM* . . . and so perfectly unite himself, *−WLMS* . . . united to his wife, *−WLSN, −RTHM, −FNTN.*

**and they two shall be one flesh:** . . . shall become one body, *−FNTN.*

**5:31.** The Scriptures reinforce the truth that husbands must love their wives as Christ loves the Church by referring to Genesis 2:24. This probably constitutes the most profound and fundamental statement in all Scripture relative to God's plan concerning marriage. It describes beautifully the leaving, cleaving, and weaving process through which people go as they leave their childhood homes and establish homes of their own (Mark 10:7-9).

First, there must be a definite leaving behind of the childhood family. While it may work in some cases, it probably would be much better for newly wedded couples not to live with their families, nor even extremely close to them. Secondly, they need to cleave to each other in every sense of the word. This means accepting the other person completely and not trying to reform each other. Thirdly, as they allow the process to work, the two will be experientially woven into one fabric. Legally this takes place when they are united in marriage, but experientially it takes an entire lifetime.

**32. This is a great mystery:** . . . There is a deep truth here, *−TCNT* . . . The marriage relationship is doubtless, *−PHLP* . . . a great secret, *−WLSN* . . . a great sacrament, *−DOUY, −RHEM.*

**but I speak concerning Christ and the church:** . . . I mean in reference to, *−CNFT* . . . now with reference to, *−TCNT* . . . but I give it as a picture of Christ and the Church, *−NORL* . . . with respect to, *−RTHM* . . . in regard to, *−FNTN* . . . of something deeper still, *−PHLP.*

**5:32.** Paul's reflection on Genesis 2:24 probably caused the apostle to exclaim, "This is a great mystery." The fact that people could become one with Christ as members of His body was almost too much to comprehend. The same wonder applies to the wife-husband relationship. Paul's own experience illustrated this truth. All of his life until he reached approximately 30 years of age, religion had been uppermost. He was so zealous for what he thought pleased God that he persecuted the Early Church severely. Suddenly, because of the manifestation of Christ to him, all this changed, and for the first time in his life he was able to enjoy an intimate relationship with Christ.

**33. Nevertheless let every one of you in particular so love his wife even as himself:** . . . And especially you, every individual, *−FNTN* . . . each one of you, individually, *−WLSN* . . . love his wyfe truely, *−TNDL* . . . in the same way that, *−ADAM.*

**and the wife [see] that she reverence [her] husband:** . . . must respect, *−WLMS, −ADAM* . . . show respect for, *−TCNT* . . . have proper respect for, *−NORL* . . . let the wife reverence her husband in the same way, *−FNTN.*

**5:33.** The entire passage concludes by again reminding the Ephesians of the total emphasis throughout, that husbands should love their wives, and wives should respect their husbands.

## Chapter 6

**1. Children, obey your parents in the Lord:** . . . be obedient to your parents, *—FNTN* . . . as those whom God has set over you, *—PHLP.*

**for this is right:** . . . the right thing for you to do, *—PHLP* . . . this is a just precept, *—WLSN.*

**6:1.** The fact that children are addressed directly indicates they must have been a part of local churches and attended public worship services. Children are told to "obey" their "parents." The qualifier "in the Lord" shows that God does not want children to do wrong just because their parents command them to do so. Paul was describing the ideal Christian family where parents had dedicated themselves to the Lord, and were bringing up their children "in the nurture and admonition of the Lord" (verse 4). Both Old and New Testaments condemn disobedience to parents (Proverbs 30:17; Romans 1:30; 2 Timothy 3:2).

**2. Honour thy father and mother:** . . . You must honor, *—WLMS.*

**which is the first commandment with promise:** . . . The first commandment to contain a promise, *—PHLP* . . . promise attached, *—MNTG.*

**6:2.** The apostle reinforced his imperative by quoting the fifth commandment of the Decalogue (Exodus 20:12; Deuteronomy 5:16). A puzzling statement is added calling it "the first commandment with promise." Some commentators take this to mean the first commandment of the second table of the Decalogue, if indeed there were two tables. The Jews, however, normally divided the Ten Commandments into two groups of five each. Other Bible scholars take the adjective "first" (*prōtē*) to mean "primary" or "chief." Still others understand the term "commandment" to refer to all the divine commandments, not just the ones recorded in the Decalogue. The third idea seems more consistent with the manner in which Jesus prioritized commandments (Matthew 22:37-40; Mark 12:28-31).

**3. That it may be well with thee:** . . . so that thou mayest prosper, *—TCNT* . . . That thou mayest be in good estate, *—GNVA.*

**and thou mayest live long on the earth:** . . . shalt be long-lived upon the land, *—RTHM.*

**6:3.** This verse contains the promise. It is a quotation of Deuteronomy 5:16 and expresses the fact that obedience to God's laws will bring God's blessings. In the context of the statement in Deuteronomy, many commandments were given to Israel. Obedience to these commandments would benefit in many ways, including the matter of enjoying longer life. Although many of the specific commandments given to Israel were not transferred into the New Testament, the basic philosophy behind them was.

**4. And, ye fathers:**

**provoke not your children to wrath:** . . . fret not your children to anger, *—ALFD* . . . do not irritate, *—WLSN* . . . do not exasperate your children, *—SCLT* . . . don't overcorrect your children or make it difficult for them to obey the commandment, *—PHLP.*

**but bring them up in the nurture and admonition of the Lord:** . . . but educate them, *—SCLT* . . . but rear them in the discipline, *—CNFT* . . . with Christian training and advice, *—TCNT* . . . with Christian teaching in Christian doctrine, *—PHLP* . . . in the techynge and chastisynge, *—WCLF* . . . in the instruction and discipline, *—WSLY* . . . and correction of the Lord, *—DOUY* . . . and information of the Lorde, *—TNDL.*

**6:4.** Verse 4 warns fathers against nagging their children to the point where they feel helpless to achieve parental expectations. This certainly was a revolutionary concept in a society where the father's authority was absolute. Actually the Greek term for "father" (*patera*) sometimes was used to mean "parent" (Hebrews 11:23), so Paul may have been addressing both parents. Parents who constantly goad their children may cause them to fall into a state of perpetual resentment. Instead, parents should train and instruct their children.

The first term, "nurture" (*paideia*), is the word from which we derive *pedagogy*. It can refer to discipline but normally contains a broad meaning of "education," the entire training and instruction of the young. The second term, "admonition" (*nouthesia*), is a narrower term, referring to training by word or instruction.

**5. Servants, be obedient to them that are [your] masters according to the flesh:** . . . be subject to, *—SAWR* . . . vnto your carnal masters, *—GNVA* . . . to your lordes, *—RHEM.*

**with fear and trembling, in singleness of your heart, as unto Christ:** . . . giving them undivided service, *—TCNT* . . . in the sincerity of, *—SAWR* . . . in the Integrity of, *—WLSN* . . . in the simplicity, *—DOUY.*

**6:5.** Most writers estimate that approximately 60 million people, or one-third of the population of the Roman Empire, were slaves at that time. Paul carefully encouraged these slaves who had become followers of Christ to obey their masters (*kurioi*) as they would obey Christ. In other words, they should not use their Christian freedom for an excuse not to render faithful service. While it may be stretching the passage too far, it is easy to make some comparisons between these statements about slave-master relationships and employee-employer relationships today. Christians should feel more obligated to do a good job.

**6. Not with eyeservice, as men-pleasers; but as the servants of Christ:**
**doing the will of God from the heart:** ... doing what you believe to be the will of God for you, *—PHLP* ... trying to carry out, *—WLMS* ... from the Soul, *—WLSN, —SCLT, —ADAM* ... out of [the] soul, *—RTHM.*

**6:6.** Whatever Christians do, they should do for the glory of God. While it may be important to want to impress the ones for whom they work, it is much more important to realize that Jesus is always cognizant of what they are doing. There is a definite connection between the responsibility to do a good day's work and the will of God. Paul had defined the Christian work ethic in 2 Thessalonians 3:6-15. Christians can bring reproach on the name of Christ by stealing time; some witness for the Lord when they are being paid to work. Paul made it clear to these Christian slaves that faithful service would be a testimony to their masters. Some of their masters were also Christians, but no doubt many of them were not.

**7. With good will doing service:** ... performing service kindly, *—SAWR* ... Give your service heartily and cheerfully, *—TCNT* ... serving as slaves with good will, *—ADAM* ... keep on working as slaves, *—WLMS.*
**as to the Lord, and not to men:** ... not for people, *—ADAM.*

**6:7.** These words may seem almost unfair when one considers that Paul was addressing people who were owned by other people. Slaves had no real rights of their own, which from a purely human viewpoint might seem justification enough to encourage them to shirk their responsibilities or at least not to put too much effort into them. Instead, they are advised to serve "with good will" or "wholeheartedly." While it is not certain why the inspired writer kept emphasizing the matter of serving as "to the Lord," it may have been because some of these slaves were having trouble with their own attitudes and therefore not being good Christian examples to their masters.

**8. Knowing that whatsoever good thing any man doeth, the same shall he receive of the Lord:** ... You may be sure that God will reward a man for good work, *—PHLP* ... will get his reward from the Lord, *—WLMS.*
**whether [he be] bond or free:** ... irrespectively of whether the man be, *—PHLP.*

**6:8.** The bottom line is the fact that a Christian's ultimate reward will come from the Lord, so service must be rendered as unto Him. At the judgment seat of Christ (1 Corinthians 3) all believers will stand on the same level. There will be no slave-master, employee-employer distinctions when we stand in His presence. Christians should

realize that He is the only One who knows whether what a person does is truly a "good thing." A master or an employer may have the wrong attitude about certain things and may not credit the slave or employee properly because of that improper attitude. There need be no fear of that happening with Christ. His motives are always good and right. More than that, He knows exactly what each believer's motives are, and He will judge rightly.

**9. And, ye masters, do the same things unto them, forbearing threatening:** ... You slave-owners, too must maintain the same attitude, *—WLMS* ... show the same spirit to your slaves, and stop threatening them, *—MNTG* ... Don't threaten, *—ADAM* ... be conscientious and responsible, *—PHLP.*
**knowing that your Master also is in heaven:** ... nor forgetting that you are responsible yourselves to a Heavenly employer, *—PHLP* ... knowing that in the heavens is One Who is both Lord of them and of you, *—ADAM* ... for you know that their real Lord and yours is, *—WLMS.*
**neither is there respect of persons with him:** ... he recognizes no distinctions between, *—TCNT* ... and that He never shows, *—WLMS* ... there is no favoritism, *—ADAM* ... there is no Partiality, *—WLSN* ... makes no distinction between master and man, *—NORL, —PHLP.*

**6:9.** Masters are warned to treat their slaves fairly, realizing their own ultimate responsibility and accountability to their own Master in heaven. Obviously, some of the Ephesian Christians were slave owners. In the light of the fact that slaves of that day normally had no rights, Paul's language was very revolutionary. The brief letter to Philemon shows how concerned Paul was for Christian slaves of the day. Even though neither he, nor the Early Church in general, spoke out forcefully against slavery, one should not get the impression that they favored it. In 1 Timothy 1:9, 10 Paul placed "mensealers" or "slave traders" (NIV) in some very bad company. He wrote, "We also know that law is made not for good men, but for lawbreakers and rebels, the ungodly and sinful, the unholy and irreligious; for those who kill their fathers or mothers, for murderers, for adulterers and perverts, for slave traders and liars and perjurers—and for whatever else is contrary to the sound doctrine" (NIV).

While this teaching about slavery may not seem very radical to the modern individual, it certainly was for Paul's day. No doubt this teaching helped mankind eventually to see the unscripturalness of slavery. It was not until later that Christianity made a concerted effort against this evil, but New Testament teachings laid much of the groundwork for later actions. Certainly no one can charge the apostle Paul with being in favor of slavery. Thank God for the progress we have made in this matter. There is still a long way to go.

**10. Finally, my brethren, be strong in the Lord:** ... In conclusion, —PHLP ... For the rest: ... Be getting empowered in, —RTHM ... get empowered in, —PNT.

**and in the power of his might:** ... of his boundless resource, —PHLP.

**6:10.** Verses 10-20 deal with the counterpart of the Christian's internal warfare described earlier (4:17-32). "Finally" literally means "for the rest" (*to loipon*). From a description of the ideal home the focus suddenly shifted to the battlefield. Paul's writings frequently speak of the Christian life in military terms. The language here, however, describes something that is more than just a figure of speech. This battle is real, difficult, and dangerous. Although salvation may be free to the person who receives it, it is not culminated ultimately without great effort. No true soldier of Jesus Christ can expect to be immune from the assaults of the enemy, and no Christian can afford to be neutral in the conflict.

In the light of the seriousness of this warfare, the Christian cannot be self-reliant. "Be strong" comes from a present passive verb, indicating a command to be strong "in the Lord" or "in the sphere of the Lord" or "to participate in the strength that is inherent in Him." It is present, indicating the necessity of continuous dependence upon Him. It is also passive, showing that strength must come from outside the believer, for without God's help he would never make it.

**11. Put on the whole armour of God:..** . the complete-armour, —RTHM.

**that ye may be able to stand against the wiles of the devil:** ... you can successfully resist, —PHLP ... be able to stand your ground, —TCNT ... that ye may stande stedfast against the craftie assaultes, —GNVA ... against the subtle ways, —PNT ... against the deceites of the Deuil, —RHEM ... against the spiritual [forces] of evil in the heavenlies, —RTHM ... so that you may be able to resist the devil's cunning tactics, —NORL.

**6:11.** Therefore, the inspired writer advised putting on the whole armor (*panoplia*) God has provided for Christians so they may stand victoriously in this battle. The emphasis on "to stand" can be found again in verses 13 and 14. It contains the idea of being successful in this spiritual battle.

Because "put on" comes from a middle voice verb, it contains the idea of "putting on for one's self." Christians must do this in order to counter the "wiles" or "schemes" or "strategies" of the devil. The original word here (*methodeias*) is

transliterated into English as *method* and would be an appropriate rendering of the idea expressed. The word for "devil" (*diabolos*) in this context literally means "slanderer."

The order in this passage about spiritual warfare cannot be overemphasized. While it is not wise to overemphasize the devil, neither is it wise to go to the other extreme and ignore him.

**12. For we wrestle not against flesh and blood:** ... for our conflict, Sawyer ... the struggle is not against, —WORL ... is not only with flesh, —SCLT ... is not against any physical enemy, —PHLP.

**but against principalities, against powers, against the rulers of the darkness of this world:** ... with the governments, with the authorities, —WLSN ... against the authorities, —PNIN ... against the potentates of the darkness of this world, —SAWR.

**against spiritual wickedness in high [places]:** ... against wicked spirits in heavenly places, —WSLY ... agaynst spretuall craftynes in heauenly thynges, —CRNM ... against the spiritual [hosts] of evil in the heavenly [worlds], —SAWR ... the spiritual forces of wickedness on high, —CNFT ... spiritual wickednesses, which are aboue, —GNVA ... against the wicked spiritual forces of the underworld itself, —NORL ... in the aerial regions, —SCLT ... in the celestials, —RHEM.

**6:12.** The conflict is serious because the battle is not against natural forces, but spiritual. Paul referred to "principalities" (*archas*), "powers" (*exousias*), "rulers" (*kosmokratoras*), and "spiritual wickedness." The language shows that these beings are spiritual and not like people whose bodies consist of blood and flesh, etc. "High places" or "heavenly realms" merely denotes the unseen realm in general and not the atmosphere.

Christians are not just shadowboxing in this spiritual warfare. The enemies are real, but thank God they can be overcome by His grace. When describing the reality of these enemies, some commentators add that sometimes in those days the loser in a Greek wrestling contest had his eyes gouged out with resulting blindness for the remainder of his life. That should give a little idea of the reality of these enemies.

**13. Wherefore take unto you the whole armour of God:** ... On this account, take up, —WORL ... On account of this take up the complete, —WLSN ... you must wear, —PHLP.

**that ye may be able to withstand in the evil day:** ... be able to resist, —WLSN, —SCLT ... resist evil in its day of power, —PHLP.

**and having done all, to stand:** ... having done all thoroughly, —PNIN ... having accomplished all, —ALFD ... when you have fought to a standstill, —PHLP ... to stonde perfect in all thinges, —TNDL ... and, when it is all over, you will still be holding your own, —NORL.

**6:13.** The word "wherefore" literally means "on account of this" (*dia touto*) and relates back to the earlier description of the conflict and the enemies. "Take unto you" refers to the decisive act of taking all the armor God has supplied so that a person can stand his ground when the evil days come, a probable reference to the time when the conflict becomes most severe. As a result, "having done all" or "after you have won the battle," the Christian can stand victoriously.

**14. Stand therefore, having your loins girt about with truth:** ... Stand firm, then, girt about with the belt of, —MNTG ... Take your stand then with truth as your belt, —PHLP.
**and having on the breastplate of righteousness:** ... and wearing, —MNTG.

**6:14.** Before the armor could be put on, the soldier had to bind the loose, flowing garments worn by people of that day, so he could enjoy freedom of movement. To tighten the belt meant a soldier was ready for duty, and to loosen it meant he was going off duty. In the Scriptures "loins" (*osphun*) were used often to signify strength. Girded loins meant the opposite of self-indulgence, ease, or carelessness. Paul compared the wide leather belt of the soldier to the belt of truth worn by the Christian who stands literally "in the realm of truth." The person who operates in the realm of the truth of God's Word will not be defeated in battle.

"The breastplate" usually was composed of metallic scales, but sometimes it was made of leather or bronze. It covered the torso, and so protected the vital organs of the body—the heart, the lungs, etc. The breastplate often saved the Roman soldier from being mortally wounded. Similarly, the person who is just or righteous, because he has accepted the righteousness of Christ, will not be mortally wounded in the spiritual warfare in which he is engaged. Putting on the breastplate of righteousness means an individual has come to grips with the basic tenets of the gospel.

**15. And your feet shod with the preparation of the gospel of peace:** ... with the firm foothold of the Good News of Peace, —TCNT ... shod with the stability of, —MNTG ... firmly on your feet, —PHLP.

**6:15.** Thirdly, the soldier needed sure footing to enable him to march and to move quickly when necessary. The Roman sandal or military shoe was bound by a thong over the instep and around the ankle, and the sole was studded with nails to permit surefootedness. "The preparation of the gospel of peace" is a fitting way of stating that a Christian must be prepared with the gospel which has peace as its message.

**16. Above all, taking the shield of faith:** ... in addition to all, —NOYS ... take to you the confidence of faith, —MRDK.
**wherewith ye shall be able to quench all the fiery darts of the wicked:** ... able to extinguish, —TCNT, —DOUY ... it can quench every burning missile the enemy hurls at you, —PHLP ... the fine dartes of the most wicked one, —RHEM ... the flaming darts of the Evil One, —MNTG ... all the fire-tipped arrows shot by the evil one, —WLMS.

**6:16.** "Above all" literally means "besides all." Believers should never be without the shield of faith. The large body-shield usually measured about 4 feet high by 2 1/2 feet wide. It normally was constructed of alternating layers of bronze and oxhide. Many of Rome's enemies used arrows dipped in pitch which would be set aflame and propelled toward the Roman soldiers. The shield would break the arrow's force and cause them to fall harmlessly to the ground. Just as the soldier could not afford to be without this protective shield at any time, the follower of Christ cannot for one moment afford to be without faith.

**17. And take the helmet of salvation:** ... And receive, —WORL ... take the helmet salvation provides, —WLMS.
**and the sword of the Spirit:** ... and in your hand, —PHLP ... the sword the Spirit wields, —WLMS.
**which is the word of God:** ... which is God's Truth, —TCNT.

**6:17.** The fifth item, the helmet, was made of bronze with leather attachments, or of leather strengthened with metallic plates. It protected the head of the individual. First Thessalonians 5:8 makes another reference to this piece of equipment, calling it "the hope of salvation." It seems to refer to the fact that a person's will, a very important part of his intellectual process, is involved in the hope of full salvation. Christians must continue to will to serve God if they expect the ultimate consummation of all His promises. The head may also symbolize the mind which needs protection. Finally, Paul spoke of the offensive weapon, the "sword of the Spirit, which is the word of God."

**18. Praying always with all prayer and supplication in the Spirit:** ... Continue to pray, —MNTG ... Do all of this with prayer and petition, —ADAM ... Keep on praying in the Spirit, —WLMS ... praying at all seasons, —CLMT ... at every Season, —WLSN ... at all times, —SCLT ... praying at every opportunity in [the] Spirit, —PNT ... Pray much, and at every opportunity, —NORL ... with every kind of spiritual prayer, —PHLP.
**and watching thereunto with all perseverance and supplication for all saints:** ... keeping alert and persistent, —PHLP ... and to that end stay alert ... concerning all of the saints, —ADAM ... be

vigilant in all perseverance, —CNFT ... and Entreaty, —WLSN ... and interceding for all the saints, —MRDK.

**6:18.** Because the proper attitude in battle is just as important as the proper equipment, Paul reminded the Ephesians of the need for prayer and watchfulness in this spiritual conflict. Prayer must be "in the Spirit" or "in the sphere of the Holy Spirit" in order to be effective. "Praying" comes from a more general word for prayer. It speaks of the necessity of always being in an attitude of prayer, of having a consistent prayer life. "Supplication" comes from a Greek term which relates to special times of need. If Christians truly practice prayer as a way of life, when the special times of need come they will be prepared for them.

"Watching" (*agrupnountes*) translated literally means "to be awake or alert." Having the proper attitude in this spiritual warfare cannot be overemphasized. It is dangerous to take a flippant attitude about something this serious. The conflict is a real one, the enemies are spiritual forces that are not limited to the physical realm, but God has provided sufficient necessary equipment for believers to be victorious in the battle.

**19. And for me, that utterance may be given unto me, that I may open my mouth boldly:** ... and on my behalf, —ASV ... particularly for me, —SCLT ... on my behalf, that Eloquence, —WLSN ... that I may be given the right words to say, —ADAM ... that I may be able to speak freely here, —PHLP.

**to make known the mystery of the gospel:** ... that I may courageously make known the secret truths, —TCNT ... the secret of the good news, —ADAM.

**6:19.** Because Paul practiced what he preached, he asked the Ephesians to pray that God would help him proclaim the gospel, even though he was in chains. The apostle's request teaches an important lesson about the purpose of prayer. While there is no doubt that Paul also prayed for his own needs, the main emphasis of this prayer request was that God would give him the enablement to present the gospel message with boldness. This is consistent with Jesus' words to His disciples that His children should seek His kingdom and His righteousness first, and depend upon Him to supply their needs (Matthew 6:33). Perhaps Christians would receive more answers to prayer if they followed Paul's example and prayed more for the power to proclaim the gospel, rather than always asking God for things for self.

**20. For which I am an ambassador in bonds:** ... of which I am an envoy in prison, —WLMS ... a messenger in chains, —MRDK ... an ambassador with a chain, —ADAM.

**that therein I may speak boldly, as I ought to speak:** ... have the courage, —TCNT ... speak as courageously as, —WLMS ... as it is necessary for me to speak, —PNT ... that I may speak out about it, —PHLP ... as is my duty, —NORL.

**6:20.** From the time of his conversion (Acts 9), Paul was consumed with one chief aim in life—proclaiming the gospel to the world. He considered himself a special appointee of Jesus Christ himself, much as a president of a country appoints an ambassador to represent him personally in another country. An ambassador does not speak for himself, but for the prominent person he represents. This gives a certain amount of boldness to the ambassador. How much more this should be true of a representative of Jesus Christ.

**21. But that ye also may know my affairs:** ... to know all that concerns me, —TCNT ... how I am faring, —NOYS ... what condicion I am in, —TNDL.

**[and] how I do:** ... and what I do, —TNDL ... and how I am getting on, —PHLP.

**Tychicus, a beloved brother and faithful minister in the Lord:** ... faithful Christian minister, —PHLP.

**shall make known to you all things:** ... will inform you, —SAWR, —NOYS ... will acquaint you, —MRDK ... will give you all the information, —WLMS ... will tell you personally, —PHLP.

**22. Whom I have sent unto you for the same purpose:** ... I am sending him to you bringing this letter, —PHLP ... that is the very reason I am sending him, —WLMS ... for this very thing, —WSLY ... for this very purpose, —CNFT, —MNTG.

**that ye might know our affairs:** ... to let you know how I am, —WLMS ... you may learn all about us, —TCNT ... that ye may know our state, —PNIN ... know about us, —MNTG.

**and [that] he might comfort your hearts:** ... he might console, —RTHM ... and that he may cheer your hearts, —MNTG ... may take fresh heart, —PHLP.

**6:21, 22.** Verses 21 and 22 are almost identical with Colossians 4:7-9. Tychicus was the "beloved brother" who took this letter to the Ephesians. The word for "brother" (*adelphos*) contains the idea of "coming from the same womb," and "minister" comes from the word *diakonos* from which we get *deacon.*

In our contemporary society where speedy travel from one part of the world to another is commonplace, it is hard to appreciate the importance of this comment. Tychicus traveled with Onesimus (Colossians 4:9) on this journey. Onesimus was a slave who had run away from his master, Philemon. Many slaves were killed for doing much less than Onesimus had done. By being with this slave, Tychicus was endangering his own life as well. Traveling the great distance from Rome to Asia Minor and placing his life in danger paled into insignificance when compared with his mission of reporting the welfare of Paul and his team and of encouraging the believers of Ephesus and the surrounding communities. The word "comfort" or "encourage" comes from the same Greek term (*parakaleō*) from which we get one of the names for the Holy Spirit—Paraclete.

The word "our" in the verse may refer to some or all of the people Paul listed in the closing statements of his epistle to the Colossians (Aristarchus, Mark, Jesus called Justus, Epaphras, Luke, and Demas). The Prison Epistles indicate that the apostle Paul normally had a sizable retinue of helpers with him or at least assisting him in some ways. He was a very secure man who was not threatened by other people. In fact, he seemed to enjoy elevating other people by referring to them at various times. Many of these younger and lesser-known associates received important recognition in the Christian world by the references of the apostle. The people of that day did not have an elaborate means of recommending people to congregations and to fellow Christians, so comments like Paul's concerning Tychicus and others were very important.

**23.** **Peace [be] to the brethren:** . . . to the brothers, —*WLMS* . . . to all Christian brothers, —*PHLP.*
**and love with faith:**
**from God the Father and the Lord Jesus Christ:** . . . our Father, —*WLMS.*

**6:23.** In his closing benediction there are some of the same terms Paul used to begin this classic letter. He wanted the Ephesians to enjoy the peace of God, that inner tranquility that is not disturbed by external circumstances. Furthermore, he emphasized the love of God that operates in a person through faith. In the Scriptures this word *agapē* consistently relates to the motivating force behind all that God does. As it operates in believers, whatever they do will have the same motivation (1 Corinthians 13). There is a relationship between faith and love. What many people call "love" really is not related to Biblical love. Unfortunately, an erotic substitute for Biblical love has become very prominent.

**24.** **Grace [be] with all them that love our Lord Jesus Christ in sincerity. Amen:** . . . May God's blessing be with all, —*TCNT* . . . Help be with all . . . with an incorruptible love, —*ADAM* . . . whose love to our Lord Jesus Christ is love imperishable, —*HNT* . . . who love our Lord Jesus, —*TEV* . . . who have true love for, —*BB* . . . who have a love unfailing for, —*CNFT,* —*GDSP* . . . with all who have an undying love for, —*WLMS,* —*BECK,* —*MOFT* . . . with all those people who love our Lord Jesus Christ with a love that never dies, —*SEB* . . . to their immortalitie, —*GNVA* . . . who sincerely love our Lord, —*PHLP* . . . in incorruption, —*PNIN,* —*DOUY,* —*RTHM,* —*RHEM* . . . with constancy, —*SAWR* . . . without corruptness, —*MRDK* . . . with perfect sincerity, —*WEYM* . . . with a love which will never die, —*BRCL.*

**6:24.** Paul's Prison Epistles place great emphasis upon the term "grace." The apostle was a "gracious" man because he was a recipient of God's grace, and one of his main desires was that other people would also receive this grace. Grace truly does come to "all them that love our Lord Jesus Christ in sincerity." When a person truly responds to the unmerited favor bestowed by God, how can he help but respond in sincere love?

The twin of "grace" is "gratitude." The two should be coupled in an inseparable manner in a Christian's life. They certainly were in Paul's. His constant praise from prison was an explicit manifestation of an important truth taught throughout the Bible: God's grace is not limited to our circumstances. When reading Ephesians, believers should not forget that Paul was in prison when he wrote it.

# PHILIPPIANS

## Overview

### Paul's Ministry in Philippi

At the beginning of Paul's second missionary journey (Acts 15:36-18:21) the apostle, accompanied by Silas, traveled from Antioch in Syria throughout Asia Minor. Timothy joined them in Lystra. The three men then journeyed to Philippi via Troas. They arrived probably in the year 49/50 (cf. Acts 16:9f.). Their stay at this time was short and quite dramatic. They were subjected to rough treatment from some of the citizens of Philippi and as a result were thrown into prison. However, they were delivered by direct intervention from God (Acts 16:25-28), and as a result of Paul's ministry a vigorous church was born, consisting mostly of Gentile converts.

Paul often mentioned the churches of Macedonia (Romans 15:26; 2 Corinthians 8:1-5; 11:9). He received economic assistance from the church at Philippi (4:10-16), even though normally he was reluctant to receive support from anyone (1 Corinthians 9:15f.). Even though the church at Philippi was not rich, the people participated willingly in the collection for the poor in Jerusalem (Romans 15:26; 2 Corinthians 8:1-5). Paul visited the church at Philippi whenever possible and again toward the end of his third missionary journey (Acts 20:3-6).

### The City of Philippi

The city of Philippi, which originally was called Krenides, was conquered in 360 B.C. by Philip II of Macedonia. He fortified the city, utilized its minerals, and renamed it Philippi. It was incorporated into the Roman Empire in 167 B.C. In 42 B.C., the territory around the city became the scene of the battle between the victorious armies of the emperor and the forces which were commanded by Brutus and Cassius, the murderers of Julius Caesar. After the battle quite a few of the veteran soldiers settled in the city. In 31 B.C., it became a Roman colony (Acts 16:12). The total name of the city became "Colonia Julia Augusta Philippensis."

Often a Roman colony was exempted from taxes and duties to the emperor. A Roman settlement was ruled according to the same laws which were in force in Italy. Because of this Roman citizens felt they were on "Italian soil" even though their city might be far removed from the native country. Roman patriotism was no doubt strong in Philippi. Notice the words of the accusation against Paul and his companions as recorded in Acts 16:21,

"(They) teach customs, which are not lawful for us to receive, neither to observe, being Romans."

### Content of the Epistle

Paul's letter to the Philippians was written at a time when he was in captivity in Rome (1:7, 13, 14, 16). The church at Philippi had heard of the apostle's imprisonment, and the believers were anxious to know how things were going with him. They had sent him economic assistance by their messenger Epaphroditus (2:30; 4:10, 14, 18).

In the first main section (1:12-26), Paul described his situation. It was his joy to tell the Philippians that his captivity had been a means of strengthening the gospel rather than repressing it. His bodyguards were convinced that he had been imprisoned because he was a Christian, not because he was guilty of any crime.

His imprisonment had given confidence to many of his "brethren in the Lord," so that they were preaching the gospel without fear. Paul even rejoiced that though some were preaching Christ out of envy and strife, at least Christ was being preached.

From the very beginning of the epistle, the keynote was joy—joy in spite of external tribulation and adversity (1:4, 18; 2:2, 17; 4:4). Paul was not certain as to the outcome of his imprisonment, whether he would be set free or be condemned and executed. Of vital importance to him was that Christ should be glorified whether by his life or by his death (1:20). From the introductory section, Paul moved into a series of exhortations concerning Christian conduct (1:27-2:18).

After speaking about his own situation, the apostle began to speak to the Philippians about theirs. He exhorted the believers to be of one mind, to show mutual humility and love. This admonition may have been in reference to an incipient schism in the church (4:2f.). It cannot be overlooked that this situation may have been the main reason for his writing the epistle. Paul often used the expression *all*. He constantly emphasized that he prayed for them all and that he longed for them all with the love of Christ (1:4, 7, 8, 25).

The section of admonition contains the famous Christ hymn which describes the humiliation of Christ, His obedience to death, and His subsequent resurrection and victory over the powers of evil.

In 2:19-30 Paul wrote of his plans for the future. He promised to send Timothy to Philippi as soon as possible to learn the exact situation there. In the meantime he had decided to send Epaphroditus immediately. It is possible also that he was the one who delivered Paul's letter to the Philippians. Paul often used Timothy as his special and trusted messenger (cf. 1 Thessalonians 3:2 and 1 Corinthians 4:17). In addition to correcting any possible disagreement, Timothy could add verbally to what Paul had written (see 1 Corinthians 4:17). First Corinthians 11:34 shows that Paul did not mention all matters in his epistles, that he sometimes preferred oral instruction. However, in 3:1 Paul wrote, "To write the same things to you, to me indeed is not grievous." The expression "the same things" may refer to what Timothy would tell them.

But suddenly Paul launched into a violent and vehement attack on the heretics who represented a great danger to the Philippian church. After this digression, Paul returned once more to a discussion of conditions in the church at Philippi and especially to the strife between Euodias and Syntyche. His exhortation to them was accompanied by an appeal to others to help these women who had labored with him in the gospel.

Not until the close of the epistle did Paul mention directly the economic assistance he had received from the church (4:10-20). His words in this passage bear testimony to the close and warm fellowship which existed between the apostle and this church. More than any other, the Epistle to the Philippians is characterized by personal warmth and love between the writer and the church.

## Outline

I. GREETING (1:1, 2)

II. THANKSGIVING AND INTERCESSION (1:3-11)

III. THE PRESENT SITUATION OF THE APOSTLE (1:12-26)

   A. The Progress of the Gospel (1:12-18a)

   B. Desire That Christ Be Glorified (1:18b-26)

IV. THE ADMONITION OF THE APOSTLE (1:27-2:18)

   A. Admonition to Unity (1:27-30)

   B. Admonition to Mutual Love and Humility (2:1-4)

   C. The Christ Hymn (2:5-11)

   D. Practical Consequences (2:12-18)

V. FUTURE PLANS OF THE APOSTLE (2:19-30)

   A. The Plan to Send Timothy (2:19-24)

   B. The Sending of Epaphroditus (2:25-30)

VI. WARNING AGAINST HERETICS (3:1-21)

   A. Introduction and Warning (3:1, 2)

   B. Loss of All for Christ's Sake (3:3-11)

   C. True and False Perfection (3:12-16)

   D. True and False Conduct (3:17-21)

VII. ADMONITION TO UNITY AND JOY IN THE LORD (4:1-9)

VIII. THANKSGIVING FOR THE PHILIPPIANS' GIFT (4:10-20)

IX. CLOSING (4:21-23)

## The Author of the Epistle

That Paul is the author of Philippians is generally accepted. However, there are some who do not agree that the epistle in its present form is from Paul's hand. It is the abrupt change of subject from 3:1-3:2 that is questioned. In 3:2 the theme and tone of the epistle changed radically when Paul made his sharp attack upon the heretics.

Quite a few investigators are inclined to believe this is an interpolation from an earlier or later epistle of Paul. It is not denied that chapter 3 was written by Paul. The question is whether it belongs to the present Epistle to the Philippians. Opinions differ also as to the length of the insertion. Either it begins with 3:2 and ends with 4:1 or 4:3, or that it continues to 4:9 or 4:20. Some investigators think 4:10-20 is the original letter of thanks to the Philippians.

As an argument that the Epistle to the Philippians consists of excerpts from a number of epistles of Paul there are those who cite the letters of Polycarp, bishop of Smyrna in the first part of the Second Century. Polycarp said that Paul wrote many letters to the Philippians. In regard to the radical change of tone and theme in 3:2, it is well to remember similar digressions in other epistles of Paul (see 2 Corinthians chapters 10 through 13).

If the Epistle to the Philippians was dictated (cf. Romans 16:22), it is possible that new information concerning the Judaistic heretics was received during a pause in the dictation. This would cause Paul to repeat either what he had previously written or to add to the instructions which he had asked Timothy and Epaphroditus to give the church orally. This would explain the sudden change of tone in 3:2.

As an argument that 4:10-20 originally formed an independent epistle, the following can be stated: (1) It seems strange that Paul would wait until the end of the epistle to mention his thanks for the assistance he had received from the Philippians. (2) The greatest problem is caused by the long interval between the receipt of the Philippians' gift and the sending of the epistle. Chapter 2:25-27 assumes that word was sent to the Philippians concerning the sickness of Epaphroditus during his stay with Paul and that the apostle had been told of the anxiety of the church. If the epistle was written from Rome, this could have been a period of up to 4 months.

It can generally be said that this discussion does not solve any of the matters of exegesis of the epistle. It is possible to link the different sections and give plausible explanations of the differences. It is best not to take these theories seriously until we face an exegetical difficulty that can be solved only by rethinking the possibility of fragments.

## The Christ Hymn

There can be no doubt that this hymn (2:5-11) is an integral part of the epistle even though it differs distinctly from the other text. It is a one-piece, poetic composition, characterized by many participle constructions, parallel expressions, and short, condensed sentences. The hymn consists of two main sections which are built up in parallel style. One section describes the debasement of Christ and the other emphasizes His exaltation. There is a natural pause between verses 8 and 9 ("Wherefore") where there is a distinct change of theme.

The traditional view of the hymn expresses the true humility and pure, devoted love of Christ. In this He is a model for believers. "Let this mind be in you, which was also in Christ Jesus" (2:5). The hymn describes how God's own being was manifested in Jesus. The borders of this world have burst because God revealed himself as a Man.

This redemptive wonder is described by the antithetical words, He who was "in the form of God . . . took upon him the form of a servant." The fact that Christ is described as a servant is because He totally accepted the conditions of man's existence in order to redeem man (cf. Galatians 4:3, 9; Colossians 2:8, 20).

But the hymn indicates further that though Christ became a man, that identification did not express His entire being. The Greek word *homoiōmati* contains, as in Romans 8:1, a contrasting element. This appears, among other things, in the subsequent description of His obedience. The obedience of Christ is contrasted to the disobedience of Adam. Christ, in contrast to Adam, accomplished something vital by His obedience (Romans 5:12-17; 1 Corinthians 15:20-49).

The obedience of Christ is often described in the New Testament as the final act of salvation (Romans 5:12; Hebrews 5:8). He took upon himself the body of a servant and as such became subject to the conditions of death. Thus the Incarnation and death are linked together. By humbling himself and entering the human situation He became subject to death (Hebrews 2:15, 16). The obedience of Christ indicates His humility and His deep union with man. But at the same time when He became obedient unto death He also became the Lord of death.

In verse 9 there is a change of subject. The word "Wherefore" indicates that that which follows is a direct result of that which precedes. The New Testament teaches that God exalts the one who humbles himself (Matthew 23:12; Luke 14:11). But the exaltation of Christ is not to be understood as a result of His humility but as a consequence of His obedience and death.

The obedience of Christ was something more than an ethical performance. It was His final act that made our salvation possible. That is why God exalted Him. The power of death was broken. He was not destroyed by death but gained the victory over it (Colossians 2:15; 1 Peter 3:22).

Jesus Christ is the Lord. The title of God in the Old Testament is thus ascribed to Jesus. Verse 10 quotes Isaiah 45:23 where the *Kurios* (Lord) title is ascribed to God. When the *Kurios* title which originally belongs to God is ascribed to Jesus we have a strong testimony to the deity of Christ. Jesus is the representative of God, and God acts through Jesus. The way to God is through Jesus. The hidden God has revealed himself through Jesus. To place oneself under the dominion of Christ is tantamount to the experience of true liberty.

## Time and Place of Writing

The epistle contains no exact information concerning the time or place of its writing. However, it is evident that Paul was a prisoner when he wrote the epistle (1:7, 13, 14, 16; 2:17). It is also clear that his captivity was one that could result in condemnation and execution (1:20; 2:17). The major possibilities are Rome, Caesarea, or Ephesus. According to Acts 23:11, 12 Paul was imprisoned in Jerusalem, in Caesarea (23:23f.), and in Rome (28:16f.). The imprisonment in Jerusalem was very short. The Epistle to the Philippians indicates a longer time of captivity. Second Corinthians, which was written at the end of the third missionary journey, indicates that Paul had been in prison many times (2 Corinthians 6:4-10; 11:23, 24).

### Rome

The traditional viewpoint is that the Epistle to the Philippians was written in Rome. The strongest evidences in favor of this viewpoint are as follows:

(1) Paul's imprisonment in Rome (Acts 28:16f.) lasted for 2 years. He was transferred to Rome from Caesarea when he appealed his case to the emperor (Acts 25:11). In that case the epistle was written toward the end of this period, about A.D. 60. The epistle presupposes an extensive, preceding correspondence between Paul and the church in Philippi.

(2) The mention of "all the palace" (1:13) and "they that are of Caesar's household" (4:22) point to Rome.

(3) The picture Paul painted of the rivaling groups, where some preached Christ out of envy and strife, intending to cause Paul pain and grief (1:14-18) also points to Rome. Such a situation is almost unimaginable in Ephesus where Paul ministered for so many years.

(4) The Epistle to the Philippians indicates a serious captivity where the possibility of appealing an unfavorable sentence was available to the prisoner. This points to Rome and the court of the emperor where Paul (Acts 25:11) had just pleaded his case.

(5) Paul wrote concerning the economic support he had received from the church in Philippi as he admitted his "affliction" (4:14). There would probably not have been any need of such support if he had been in captivity in Ephesus. Neither would the need for support have been so great in Caesarea. The believers in Jerusalem would not have forsaken the one who had brought the church the collected gifts of money.

## Other Views

Although there are many reasons to support the view that the Epistle to the Philippians was written in Rome, there are other points of view which can be mentioned:

(1) Before the Epistle to the Philippians was sent, there had evidently been an extensive period of travel and correspondence between Paul and the church at Philippi. They had been informed of Paul's arrest and imprisonment. A collection for him had been undertaken and the money had been sent with Epaphroditus who became ill while he was with Paul. The Philippians had learned of this serious illness, and their anxiety concerning Epaphroditus had been conveyed to the apostle. Paul had then decided to send Epaphroditus back to Philippi so that the church could see he was fully recovered (2:25-28). Thus it must be supposed that word was sent between Philippi and Rome four times before the Epistle to the Philippians was sent.

This extensive traveling seems to indicate that the writing place must have been near Philippi with possibilities for frequent and fast contact. If one accepts that Paul wrote the epistle from Rome, this traveling activity during the conditions of the time must have taken place within a period of about 10 months.

(2) Mention of "the palace" in 1:13 does not necessarily point to Rome. The palace was in fact the normal designation of the residence of a governor of the province with appurtenant administration premises for the soldiers who would be stationed there. The expression in 4:22 does not point absolutely to Rome. Civil employees might well be designated as employees of the emperor.

(3) It appears from the epistle that Paul expected to return to the church in Philippi and to spend some time there (2:24; 1:24-27). This could indicate that the epistle was written at a time when Paul was still ministering in these territories. However, these arguments against Rome as the place where Paul wrote the epistle are not conclusive. First, Paul's conditions as a prisoner had no doubt changed radically during the 5 years he had been in prison. Years of captivity can change a person so that he no longer has the strength to begin another work.

## Caesarea

Those who maintain that Caesarea was the place from which the epistle was written argue:

(1) The mention of "bonds" in 1:13 is best understood in connection with the conditions under which Paul lived as a captive in Caesarea. He was under military guard and without liberty to preach (Acts 23:35). The captivity mentioned in Acts 28 is described as a type of house custody where Paul was free to receive visitors and to preach the gospel.

(2) The Jews who made the charges against Paul (Acts 21:27) are the ones about whom Paul wrote in Philippians 3. However, the conditions of Paul's captivity cannot be conclusive as an argument against Rome or as an argument for Caesarea. This could not have been a real possibility if Paul was able to make an appeal. Paul did indeed make an appeal to the emperor (Acts 25:11). We know that Felix was willing to free Paul in Caesarea (Acts 24:26). In addition, Paul had a strong desire to go to Rome (Acts 23:11). There is no indication of this in the Epistle to the Philippians. Finally, Acts 24:26 indicates Paul had sufficient funds in Caesarea, while Philippians 4:12 shows he had suffered economic need.

## Ephesus

When Ephesus is proposed as the place where the Epistle to the Philippians was written, the following reasons are given:

(1) Paul's words in 2 Corinthians 1:8, 9 and 1 Corinthians 15:31, 32 correspond with the description he gave in the Epistle to the Philippians. The expression Paul used in 1 Corinthians 15:32 should no doubt be understood figuratively. It is probable that as a Roman citizen Paul could not have been sentenced to fight against wild beasts. But it is obvious that he had some experiences in Asia which endangered his life. This also corresponds with the description in the Epistle to the Philippians.

(2) Many of the difficulties which appear if Rome is taken as the writing place of the epistle are solved immediately if we suppose that Ephesus was the writing place. The short distance between Ephesus and Philippi makes the various journeys possible. The plans which are explained in Philippians 2:19f. correspond with the information given in Acts 19:22 (cf. 1 Corinthians 4:17; 16:10). Paul's desire to meet the Philippians once more (Philippians 1:26; 2:24) is also fulfilled (Acts 20:1; cf. 19:1).

(3) Acts 19:22 confirms that Timothy was with Paul in Ephesus. On the contrary there is no indication Timothy was in Rome. (4) The similarity of the contents of the Epistle to the Philippians on the one hand and the epistles to the Galatians, Romans, and 1 and 2 Corinthians points to Ephesus as the writing place. However, content similarity does not necessarily indicate the same period of writing. It must also be asked why Paul did not appeal his case if he was in Ephesus. The possibility for appeal was present in Ephesus just as it was in Caesarea. It is also strange that Paul did not receive assistance from the church if he was in Ephesus. It is also difficult to imagine men in Ephesus who preached the gospel with the intent to hurt Paul. There is also need to prove that Paul's captivity in Ephesus lasted for at least 3 months. During this period the traveling activity mentioned before could have taken place. There is another question: Was Paul at liberty to write and work as a missionary during his captivity in Ephesus? We know that he had this liberty during his captivity in Rome.

## The Heretics of Chapter 3

In 1:13-18 Paul wrote the Philippians about some of his "brethren in Christ" who were preaching Christ out of "envy and strife," hoping to cause Paul more grief. But Paul was filled with joy because Christ was being preached. But in chapter 3, when Paul wrote about those who were spreading error, the tone is quite different. Evidently these men had not yet penetrated the church but were a distinct danger.

The description Paul gave seems to indicate these men were the Judaizers he had written about in the Epistle to the Galatians. However, it is questionable if these were the same as those referred to in verse 18f. It appears that the men described in the first part of the chapter were men who thought they had received a special revelation. Perhaps they were Gnostics who boasted of their special revelation which they believed gave them a share of the heavenly glory in this life. That is why they did not expect a resurrection of the dead (cf. verse 11 and 1 Corinthians 15:12; 2 Timothy 2:18). They were enemies of the cross of Christ (verse 18; cf. 1 Corinthians 1:23; 2:2). The glory of which they boasted (verse 19; 2 Corinthians 3:7-4:17) was in reality their shame.

The expression "whose god is their belly" indicates these men thought only of themselves. The word "belly" in this context could refer to their selfish ego (cf. Job 15:35). Paul rejected their view of perfection (3:12f.). He himself did not feel he had reached such a state. His determination was to press on. Christian living involves faith in the righteousness of Christ which has been imputed to the believer. It implies community with Christ in His suffering and death (Romans 6:1-11). For the Christian the power of the Resurrection is a reality. By it a believer can overcome sin. His final resurrection is ahead when his true perfection will be completed (3:10-21).

# The Epistle of Paul to the Philippians

## Commentary

### Chapter 1

**1. Paul and Timotheus:**
**the servants of Jesus Christ:** ... true servants, *—PHLP*... bondmen, *—PNIN*, *—WLSN*... slaves, *—WLMS*.
**to all the saints in Christ Jesus which are at Philippi:** ... To all Christ's People, *—TCNT*... to alle the holi men, *—WCLF*... to all God's people in union with, *—WLMS*... all true Christians, *—PHLP*... who live in Philippi, *—EVRD*.
**with the bishops and deacons:** ... including the pastors, *—NORL*... with overseers, *—PNIN*, *—WLSN*... with the elders, *—MRDK*... and ministers, *—RTHM*, *—PNT*... with the Presidents and Assistant-Officers, *—TCNT* ... and assistants, *—WLMS*.

**1:1.** In the Epistle to the Philippians Paul followed the usual manner in his introduction, according to the pattern of letter writing which we discover from surviving papyri. Sometimes the apostle used an amanuensis (a person who writes what another dictates) (cf. Romans 16:22). However, there is no clear indication of an amanuensis here.

"Servants" (*douloi*) suggests submission without servility, slavery that is motivated by love, and service of a willing spirit. "Saints" (*hagioi*) means "set apart ones" who have confessed Christ as Saviour. Paul made no sharp distinction between clergy and laity. Rather, he emphasized the bond between them. Further, he did not use the title *bishop* in the sense Ignatius did in the Second Century in reference to a threefold ministry of bishops, presbyters, and deacons. Evangelicals generally recognize the same New Testament leader being addressed as "bishop, overseer, superintendent" (*episkopos*—Acts 20:28; Titus 1:7); "elder, presbyter" (*presbuteros*—Acts 20:17; Titus 1:5; 1 Peter 5:1); and "pastor, shepherd" (*poimēn*—Acts 20:28; 1 Peter 5:2).

**2. Grace [be] unto you, and peace, from God our Father, and [from] the Lord Jesus Christ:** ... spiritual blessing, *—WLMS*.

**1:2.** The apostle often coupled the terms "grace" and "peace" in his greetings. The term "grace" comes from the Greek word *charis* and generally refers to a favor done out of the pure generosity of the heart, expecting nothing in return. "Peace" (*eirēnē*) is a Hebrew concept (*shalōm*) which denotes the harmony and well-being of a life that has been reconciled to God through Jesus Christ.

**3. I thank my God upon every remembrance of you:** ... I thank God every time I remember you, *—EVRD*... in al memorie of you, *—RHEM*... in every entreaty, *—WLMS*... for all my memories of you, *—NORL*... at the constant recollection of you, *—MRDK*... whenever I think of you, *—PHLP*.

**1:3.** It was common for Paul to pray for the people to whom he wrote, and his prayers of thanksgiving and supplication usually go together. The basis of his thanksgiving was his overall remembrance of the believers in Philippi.

**4. Always in every prayer of mine for you all:** ... I always pray for all of you, *—EVRD*... My constant prayers for you, *—PHLP*... always making supplication, *—SCLT*... in every petition, *—MNTG*.
**making request with joy:** ... making supplication on behalf of you, *—WLSN*... are full of joy, *—TCNT*... are a real joy, *—PHLP*.

**1:4.** As he contemplated all that God had done for them and through them, Paul was filled with joy. Joy is the keynote of the entire epistle. Because joy is the by-product of something else, the apostle was not referring to some superficial happiness when he made this statement.

**5. For your fellowship in the gospel:** ... for they bring back to my mind how we have worked together, *—PHLP*... your communication, *—DOUY*... your communicating, *—RHEM*... because of your association with me in spreading the gospel, *—CNFT*... in furtherance of the gospel, *—ASV*... in forwarding the gospel, *—MNTG*.
**from the first day until now:** ... until the present, *—RTHM*.

**1:5.** This joy resulted from their fellowship (*koinonia*) with him in the gospel. People who refer to fellowship as "two people in a ship" certainly cheapen the idea expressed in the original term. It meant far more than just enjoying someone else's company. In the original sense it expressed a joint participation in a common ministry or interest. *Partnership* is a very appropriate contemporary term to express the idea. (See the word study on *koinonia* in the *Greek-English Dictionary*.) The Philippians had participated in Paul's ministry with their prayers and finances for approximately 10 years, from the beginning of the assembly until the writing of this epistle. In fact, there is a definite article before the adverb "now" (literally, "the now"), so Paul probably was pointing to the gift they just had extended to him through Epaphroditus.

The Philippians seem to have found a very special place in the heart of the apostle. His mind raced back to "the first day," when he became acquainted with them. The warm relationship between a true pastor and his people continues even after he has moved away.

**6. Being confident of this very thing:** . . . For of this I am quite sure, *−TCNT* . . . I am convinced of this, *−CNFT* . . . Of this I am fully persuaded, *−MNTG* . . . having become persuaded of, *−WORL* . . . being persuaded of this very thing, *−PNT*.

**that he which hath begun a good work in you:** . . . he who commenced, *−WLSN*.

**will perform [it] until the day of Jesus Christ:** . . . you will perfect it, *−PNIN*, *−ALFD* . . . will keep on perfecting it, *−NORL* . . . will accomplish them, *−MRDK* . . . will go on completing it, *−MNTG* . . . will bring it to perfection, *−CNFT* . . . will carry it on till, *−SAWR* . . . will continue to complete it, *−WLSN* . . . will be completing it, *−SCLT* . . . will fully complete [it], *−RTHM* . . . will go on developing it, *−PHLP*.

**1:6.** Conversely, even though he had much cause for thanksgiving as he remembered the Philippian saints, Paul was not entirely satisfied with their spiritual state. His desire for them was that God would continue the work He had begun in them.

Deists teach that God merely wound up the universe and withdrew from it, allowing it to operate by itself. Just as the Bible counters this kind of theory relative to creation, it also stresses that God is interested not only in the spiritual birth of His people, but also in their continued growth and maturity. A person certainly does not receive all of God's benefits at the conversion experience. That is only the starting point, the gateway to many benefits from God. Paul was "confident" that God would keep believers in this process until the day Jesus returns to receive His people unto himself.

**7. Even as it is meet for me to think this of you all:** . . . It is only natural, *−PHLP*.

**because I have you in my heart:** . . . I have an affectionate remembrance of you, *−TCNT* . . . because I hold you in heart, *−PNT* . . . you are very dear to me, *−PHLP*.

**inasmuch as both in my bonds:** . . . during the time I was in prison, *−PHLP* . . . in these fetters of mine, *−MNTG*.

**and in the defence and confirmation of the gospel:** . . . when I have been free to defend and vindicate the Gospel, *−NORL* . . . in the work of defending and establishing the Good News, *−TCNT*.

**ye all are partakers of my grace:** . . . being joint-contributors, *−WLSN* . . . as sharers in my joy, *−CNFT*.

**1:7.** The apostle's confidence in the Philippians was based upon the fact that they had shared God's grace with him for approximately 10 years. Even though he was in prison, God's grace was not imprisoned. Some of the greatest fruits of his ministry came while Paul was in prison. At least five of the Epistles the Holy Spirit inspired him to write were written while he was in prison. There the apostle's influence reached many, even in Nero's palace.

The term "defense" comes from the Greek word from which we derive *apologetics* (*apologia*). However, Paul used the word in connection with the "confirmation of the gospel." Too often we think of the term "defense" in a negative sense, as if we had to keep unbelievers from taking something from the gospel. Paul realized the process of defending would result in the confirmation of the gospel.

**8. For God is my record:** . . . God knows, *−PHLP* . . . is my witness, *−PNIN*.

**how greatly I long after you all:**

**in the bowels of Jesus Christ:** . . . with the tenderness of, *−TCNT* . . . with the tender Sympathies, *−WLSN* . . . in tender affections, *−RTHM* . . . in tender mercies of, *−PNIN* . . . in the tender heart of, *−ALFD* . . . with the deepest Christian love and affection, *−PHLP*.

**1:8.** Paul compared his longing for the Philippians to the straining of an athlete reaching forward to the goal set for him. This longing was motivated by the love Jesus has for His own people, an affection so great that He died for His people. In King James' day "bowels" referred to the seat of the emotions.

**9. And this I pray:** . . . My prayer for you, *−PHLP*.

**that your love may abound yet more and more:** . . . may grow yet stronger and stronger, *−TCNT* . . . may have still more love, *−PHLP*.

**in knowledge and [in] all judgment:** . . . and with perfect discernment, *−TCNT* . . . and all discernment, *−PNIN* . . . and in all spiritual sense, *−WSLY* . . . all Perception, *−WLSN*, *−RTHM*, *−ALFD* . . . and in all understanding, *−DOUY*.

**1:9.** Paul's actual prayer for the Philippians begins in this verse and includes two specific requests. His supplication for them was prefaced with one of the Greek terms expressing purpose (*hina*, "in order that"). He prayed that their love would abound more and more in knowledge and in perception. Thus it is possible for a believer's love (*agapē*) to increase. In like manner, "knowledge" (*epignōsis*) here denotes full or ever-increasing understanding.

"Judgment" or "perception" or "depth of insight," on the other hand, is concerned with practical application of love. Scriptural love is not indiscriminate love that is manifested in any manner a person chooses. The Christian experiences increasing love in his life and the ability to discern the proper application of it.

**10. That ye may approve things that are excellent:** . . . examine the differences of things, —WLSN . . . approve the better things, —CNFT.

**that ye may be sincere and without offence:** . . . you may be without fault, —SAWR . . . that ye may be incorrupt, —RTHM . . . that ye may be pure, —NOYS.

**till the day of Christ:**

**1:10.** According to this verse, this combination will enable Christians to discern what is best for them. A gullible love accepts anything, but a love manifested in full knowledge and in practical application distinguishes the genuine from the spurious.

The root word translated "approve" here was used of the assaying of metals, as well as of the approval of candidates for the degree of medicine. Therefore, it refers to the act of testing something for the purpose of approving it. God does not want Christians to accept everything, but He wants them to approve only what is "best" or "excellent." Some things may be "good" in the normal sense of the word but may not be "best." Paul wanted the Philippians to accept the approved things that would help them "be sincere and without offense."

The second request in Paul's prayers for the Philippians relates to the level of personal character and demeanor. This sincere and unoffending attitude will be manifested ultimately at the judgment of believers by Christ himself.

**11. Being filled with the fruits of righteousness, which are by Jesus Christ:** . . . that you may bear a rich harvest, —TCNT . . . produced by the power that Jesus Christ gives you, —PHLP.

**unto the glory and praise of God:**

**1:11.** Such an attitude also will yield a harvest of righteousness through Jesus Christ. In a real sense God is working in believers to make them more and more like the Lord Jesus Christ. When a person becomes a Christian and chooses to follow Jesus, that person accepts the righteousness of Christ as the only righteousness sufficient to satisfy the requirements of God. At the same time, a process begins in that life so that the righteousness of Christ becomes gradually imparted to that individual. Initially the righteousness of Christ is imputed at the time the person becomes a Christian, but the righteousness of Christ is imparted by the Holy Spirit throughout the believer's entire lifetime.

**12. But I would ye should understand:** . . . I want you to know, —PHLP.

**brethren, that the things [which happened] unto me:** . . . that my experiences, —CNFT.

**have fallen out rather unto the furtherance of the gospel:** . . . have resulted in the advancement, —SAWR . . . turned out to the advantage of, —PHLP . . . chaunced vnto the greate furtheraunce of, —CRNM . . . to the great furtheryng, —GNVA . . . unto the progress of, —ASV . . . rather unto an advancement, —RTHM . . . Advancement of the Glad Tidings, —WLSN . . . unto the progress of the gospel, —CLMT.

**1:12.** In verses 12-26 the apostle described his ambition more clearly than in any other place in his writings. Further, the passage expresses what the ambition of every Christian should be. It is summarized best in verse 20 with the statement, "Christ shall be magnified in my body, whether it be by life, or by death."

The apostle initially introduced the subject in verse 12 by indicating two factors which did not serve as the basis for his purpose in life. First, he said his ambition was not based upon circumstances. Literally, he was "not under the circumstances." He controlled them, not vice versa.

**13. So that my bonds in Christ are manifest in all the palace and in all other [places]:** . . . My imprisonment has been plainly seen, —TCNT . . . my imprisonment means a personal witness, —PHLP . . . are famous throughout all the, —GNVA . . . in the whole praetorium, —PNIN . . . in the whole of the praetorian camp, —RTHM.

**1:13.** Paul then proceeded to give examples which proved that his being in prison had not curtailed his work for the Lord, but rather, had advanced the cause of Christ. First, his circumstances had enabled him to witness to the palace guard (*praitōriō*). The term for "palace" could refer to at least four different things: (1) those forming the praetorian guard, (2) the emperor's palace, (3) the barracks of the praetorian guard, or (4) the judicial authorities. The context seems to support the first option. Emperor Tiberius concentrated 10,000 soldiers in Rome with the express purpose of guarding him and his court. They were handpicked soldiers with special qualifications and special privileges. To reach men of this caliber for Christ was a remarkable achievement for the gospel.

**14. And many of the brethren in the Lord, waxing confident by my bonds:** . . . gaining courage from my chains, —CNFT . . . beynge encouraged thorow my bandes, —CRNM . . . somehow taking fresh heart in the Lord from the very fact that I am a prisoner, —PHLP.

**are much more bold to speak the word without fear:** . . . now venture with far greater freedom,

—TCNT . . . should be much more abundantly bold, —RTHM . . . more abundant courage, —SAWR, —WLSN . . . in boldly proclaiming, —PHLP.

**1:14.** While serving as "chaplain" to this group, Paul also encouraged the Christians in Rome. "Many of the brethren" in Rome had been encouraged "to speak the word" because of Paul's circumstances. Perhaps the joy and contentment he manifested while in prison had a strong impact upon them. This example and the one expressed in verse 13 clearly show that Paul was not "under the circumstances." Too many times Christians allow opposing forces to discourage them from doing what God has called them to do. Circumstances sometimes can be changed, but sometimes they cannot be. If God does not see fit to change them, He must have some purpose for them.

**15. Some indeed preach Christ even of envy and strife:** . . . some actually proclaim the Christ out of jealousy and opposition, —TCNT . . . and contentiousness, —CNFT.
**and some also of good will:** . . . in good faith, —PHLP.

**1:15.** Paul knew opposition from false preachers even in prison. He had experienced it from the beginning of his ministry for Christ (Acts 9), and it continued until his earthly life was complete. Paul recognized that some people preached Christ out of pure motives and some others preached Christ out of impure motives. The latter group consisted of people who envied Paul's authority, position, and ministry. Perhaps while he was able to move freely in his proclamation of the gospel, they hesitated to move against him. However, when Paul was placed in prison, these jealous individuals probably felt unhindered in their activities. They preached Christ, but their real objective was to gain adherents for themselves.

**16. The one preach Christ of contention:** . . . in a spirit of rivalry, —TCNT . . . out of rivalry, —MNTG . . . of a factious spirit preach Christ with no pure intent, —NOYS.
**not sincerely:** . . . and not purely, —GNVA.
**supposing to add affliction to my bonds:** . . . to superadd Affliction to, —WLSN . . . adding bitterness to, —MNTG . . . hoping to make my chains even more galling than they would otherwise, —PHLP.

**1:16.** This verse begins the apostle's own commentary on the statement he made in the previous verse. The motive behind a person's actions may not always be known to other people, but God knows what it is. People who preach Christ "out of good will" do so out of love (*agapē*). However, another group preached Christ out of "contention." These individuals apparently thought they could enhance their own positions by degrading the apostle.

The term "affliction" (*thlipsis*) means "trouble involving direct suffering" (Louw and Nida, Lexicon, 1:243). One pictures the painful rubbing of iron chains on Paul's hands and legs.

Notice the marks of hypocrisy manifested by these individuals:

(1) envy, which makes a person want what belongs to someone else; (2) strife, or an attitude of competitiveness; (3) contention, which causes a person to resort to all kinds of intrigue in order to elevate self; (4) insincerity, or the opposite of doing something out of good will; and (5) pretense, which leads a person to cloak ulterior motives.

**17. But the other of love:** . . . out of their love for me, —PHLP.
**knowing that I am set for the defence of the gospel:** . . . God has set me here in prison to defend our right to preach, —PHLP . . . for the vindication of, —MRDK.

**1:17.** However, the worthy group manifested the following marks of honesty: good will, love, and truth. They did this because they knew Paul was defending the gospel in a scriptural manner.

**18. What then?:** . . . But what does it matter? —PHLP.
**notwithstanding, every way:** . . . However they may look at it, —PHLP . . . nevertheless, —SAWR . . . In one way or another, —NORL.
**whether in pretence, or in truth:** . . . or sincerely, —GNVA.
**Christ is preached:** . . . is being made known, —TCNT . . . is proclaimed, —PNIN.
**and I therein do rejoice, yea, and will rejoice:** . . . that fact makes me very happy, —PHLP.

**1:18.** To summarize, Paul responded, "What does it matter?" He, of course, did not condone preaching from false motives, but he knew the hearers could be saved when Christ is preached regardless. False ministerial motives cannot cancel the truth of the gospel as the power of God unto salvation.

**19. For I know that this shall turn to my salvation:** . . . this will result in, —SAWR . . . My Deliverance, —WLSN . . . will be for the good of my own soul, —PHLP.
**through your prayer:** . . . thanks to, —PHLP . . . through your intercession, —SCLT.
**and the supply of the Spirit of Jesus Christ:** . . . and the assistance of, —CNFT . . . and the subministration of, —RHEM . . . and because of the bountiful resources, —NORL . . . and a rich supply of the Spirit of Jesus, —MNTG.

**1:19.** Paul's ambition was not based upon his circumstances, nor upon the opinions of other people. He made it clear that his ambition to magnify Christ in his body was possible only because of his relationship to Christ. The chief priority in any believer's life is to keep Christ first in his life (Matthew 6:33).

The apostle was confident that he could count on two kinds of aid: human and divine. "Your prayer" shows how much Paul desired and depended upon the prayers of God's people. "The supply of the Spirit of Jesus Christ" indicates the divine aid that always comes to the person whose total trust rests in God. "Supply" or "help" comes from the term *epichorēgia* which means "help which undergirds and strengthens the object." This results from a proper relationship with Christ, where everything else will fall into place.

It is difficult to know exactly what Paul meant by the word "salvation" or "deliverance" (NIV) in this verse, but it certainly seems to indicate he expected to be released soon from prison. It could, of course, refer to "deliverance" from this earthly life, when he would have the privilege of being with Christ. His Master meant everything to him.

**20. According to my earnest expectation and [my] hope:** . . . As I hartely loke for, —GNVA . . . It all accords with my own earnest wishes, —PHLP.

**that in nothing I shall be ashamed:** . . . that I shall never feel, —MNTG . . . hope that I shall never disgrace myself, —WLMS.

**but [that] with all boldness, as always:** . . . but with All Confidence, —WLSN . . . but that with fearless courage, —MNTG . . . with the utmost boldness, —PHLP.

**[so] now also Christ shall be magnified in my body:** . . . will be honoured, —TCNT.

**whether [it be] by life, or by death:** . . . whether that means I am to face death or to go on living, —PHLP.

**1:20.** Paul stated his purpose in life with the term *apokaradokian*, which usually is translated "eager expectation," "earnest expectation," "deepest desire," "undivided and intense expectation." It consists of three Greek words combined into one, indicating the craning of a person's neck in order to catch a glimpse of what is ahead. The word was used in classical Greek of a watchman in the bow of a ship peering into the darkness, eagerly looking for a beacon of light.

Clearly the apostle's ambition was to glorify Christ in his body. He knew that whatever happened, God would not let him fall into a situation of hopelessness or abandon him in any way. Because Paul was one with the Lord he knew that nothing, even death, could break that union. In fact, death would only make the union more complete. If a person's life consists primarily in the acquisition of things, then death would mean a cessation of the chief reason for being. Such a

person would have to leave behind everything of importance to him.

**21. For to me to live [is] Christ:** . . . living means Christ, —WLMS. **and to die [is] gain:** . . . and deeth is to me a vauntage, —TNDL . . . and dying brings gain, —WLMS.

**1:21.** Here Paul clearly describes his concept of life. The personal pronoun "me" occupies the emphatic position in the original language, expressing more than just an opinion about life, but indicating Paul's actual situation. He knew he was ready for life or for death. Death would only give him more of Christ.

The word for "gain" (*kerdos*) was used in Paul's time to mean "interest, gains, profits." Death would be like cashing in the principal and the interest. Paul sounded like a bird in a cage; death would be liberation from that captivity, or the limitations of the flesh. Eternal life begins when one believes on Christ; however, he does not possess it in the sense of being able to do with it as he wills. Still, he maintains it as long as he is in vital relationship to Jesus. Jesus attempted to impress upon Martha that Lazarus really had not died in an eternal sense because the person who believes upon Him as Lord will never die.

**22. But if I live in the flesh, this [is] the fruit of my labour:** . . . But if to keep on living here means fruit from my labor, —WLMS . . . my labours bear fruit? —TCNT.

**yet what I shall choose I wot not:** . . . I do not exactly know, —WLSN . . . I cannot say, —NOYS . . . I cannot tell which to choose, —WLMS.

**1:22.** However, if Paul lived longer, he would be afforded more opportunity to work for God and harvest more fruit. While dying physically meant gain for him, continuing on this earth meant gain for those people who would hear the gospel message through him.

**23. For I am in a strait betwixt two:** . . . but am in a quandary, —MNTG . . . held in constraint, —RTHM . . . I am hesitating between two desires, —WLMS . . . I am hard pressed from both sides, —CNFT . . . For I am constrayned of these two thinges, —CRNM.

**having a desire to depart, and to be with Christ:** . . . I have a strong desire to break camp, —MNTG . . . to be dissolved, —DOUY.

**which is far better:** . . . obviously the best thing for me, —PHLP . . . far, far better, —RTHM.

**1:23.** Paul was torn between two alternatives. A definite article in the Greek makes the statement read "the two." The idea is that of strong pressure bearing upon him "from" or "by" (*ek*) two sources: his desire to be with Christ and his desire to work longer for Him. "To depart" is a euphemism for physical death and comes from a military term meaning "to strike camp" and from a nautical expression meaning "to release a vessel from its moorings."

**24. Nevertheless to abide in the flesh [is] more needful for you:** ... that I should stay here still, —TCNT ... is more necessary, —ALFD ... is necessary for your sake, —CNFT ... that I should stay here on earth, —PHLP.

**1:24.** This verse clearly expresses Paul's unselfishness. It reminds one of an elderly person who should be able to sit back in retirement and allow someone else to do the work. Instead, that person takes a position that entails much responsibility and works harder than ever. Many times older people have reached the zenith of their knowledge and experience, and their knowledge and experience can be of great assistance in God's kingdom. Apparently Paul felt that way. There was proper balance in his life. He knew the Church would continue to grow and expand without him, but he also realized his own value to the members of that church.

**25. And having this confidence:** ... That is why I feel pretty well convinced, —PHLP ... having become assured of this, —WORL ... with this conviction, —CNFT ... fully believing this, —WLSN.

**I know that I shall abide and continue with you all:** ... and stay behind, —RTHM.

**for your furtherance and joy of faith:** ... for your progress, —PNIN, —WLSN, —MNTG ... for your advancement, —NOYS ... to help you forward in Christian living, —PHLP.

**1:25.** Even though Paul had a great desire to be with the Lord, he knew his ministry on earth was not yet complete. The word for "confidence" (*pepoithōs*) is a perfect participle which indicates Paul's confidence in the matter was one which resulted from the past action of turning the matter over to the Lord, and it indicates he still maintained this confidence while he wrote this epistle. The apostle emphasized the "furtherance and joy" or "progress and exaltation" the Philippians would experience as the result of his release.

**26. That your rejoicing may be more abundant in Jesus Christ for me:** ... that your boasting respecting me may abound, —PNT.

**by my coming to you again:** ... when I come to see you, —PHLP.

**1:26.** So, Paul's ultimate goal of glorifying Christ in his body would be realized, whether in life or in death. He was confident of that fact because he determined to maintain his relationship with Christ as the basis for everything else in life. In his negative approach to the matter of a person's ambition in the beginning of this passage, Paul uncovered the two issues in life that probably give people the most problems—circumstances and the opinions of others. While God does at times use circumstances to show us His will, we cannot afford to be dominated by them. Sometimes we can change our circumstances, and sometimes we should. On the other hand, we should not rule out the providence of God in our circumstances.

It also is possible to go to two extremes with reference to the opinions of other people. Christians should not ignore the advice of godly people. Still, they must be careful not to be overly disturbed by the criticism of others who are not totally committed to God.

**27. Only let your conversation be:** ... No matter what happens, you must live lives, —NORL ... do lead lives, —MNTG ... let your lives be, —TCNT, —CNFT ... Let your conduct be, —MRDK ... let your behavior be, —WSLY ... Only conduct yourselves, —ALFD ... behave yourselves, —WLSN ... let your manner of life, —ASV ... lyue ye worthili, —WCLF.

**as it becometh the gospel of Christ:** ... in a manner worthy of, —NOYS ... worthily, —WLSN ... be worthy of, —ASV ... worthy of the Good News, —TCNT.

**that whether I come and see you, or else be absent, I may hear of your affairs:** ... or remain absent, —CNFT ... I may hear concerning you, —SCLT ... I maye yet heare of your condicyon, —CRNM ... hear about you from a distance, —PHLP.

**that ye stand fast in one spirit:** ... that you are standing firm, animated by one spirit, —TCNT ... that ye continue in, —GNVA ... in a united spirit, —PHLP.

**with one mind striving together for the faith of the gospel:** ... having one purpose, —NORL ... battling with a single mind, —PHLP ... with one soul striving together, —NOYS ... and in one soule, labouringe, —TNDL ... and that with one purpose you are continuing to co-operate in the fight for faith in the good news, —WLMS.

**1:27.** The bulk of Paul's epistle consists of a series of exhortations to these believers who meant so much to him. Some of the exhortations are especially local in their application, but all of them relate to all of Christianity in all ages and to all local churches. His first exhortation is an appeal for Christians to follow Christ's example. "Only" or "whatever happens" (NIV), from the Greek *monon*, appears first in the sentence and is in the emphatic position; it means "above all else," "whatever may happen," "at all costs." The matter of chief importance in Paul's mind was for God's people to use Christ as the model for the process in which they found themselves. If a believer's ambition truly is to magnify Christ in his body (1:20), that person will not only live for Christ (1:21), but will become more and more like the Son of God.

"Conversation" or "conduct yourselves" (*politeuesthe*) bears a relationship to two Greek terms (*polis*, "city"; *politēs*, "citizen"). The total idea then is to live as a citizen of God's kingdom, to have a deportment worthy of the gospel of Christ, to perform the duties of a citizen.

"Becometh" means to "weigh as much," to "have a value equal to," to "be worth as much." The word "spirit" here refers to the unity of spirit that a local body of believers will have if they have blended and fused themselves together to accomplish God's plan for them.

**28.** **And in nothing terrified by your adversaries:** ... and in nothynge fearinge youre adversaries, –TNDL ... in no way terrorized by its enemies, –MNTG ... not caring two straws for your enemies, –PHLP ... frightened by your opponents, –WLMS ... by the opposers, –WLSN.

**which is to them an evident token of perdition:** ... which to them is cause of, –RHEM ... this will be an indication of coming Ruin, –TCNT ... Your fearlessness will then be to them a sign of their own coming defeat, –NORL.

**but to you of salvation, and that of God:** ... but to you cause of helthe, –WCLF ... you yourselves are being saved, –PHLP.

**1:28.** When believers strive together for the gospel, there will be opposition. When Christ lives His life in them, there will be freedom from cowardice. This was beautifully illustrated in the early disciples (Acts 4:18-20; 5:40-42). The fact that the Philippians also were suffering persecution was like a two-edged sword. On the one hand, it served as a sign or pointer or proof that their persecutors were enemies of the gospel and were headed for eternal destruction. On the other hand, it confirmed the salvation of the Philippian saints. People reflect what they are by their actions. Those who oppose the simple message of the gospel indicate by their actions that they do not know the Author of the gospel message.

**29.** **For unto you it is given in the behalf of Christ:** ... it has been graciously granted to you, –WLMS ... the privilege, –PHLP.

**not only to believe on him:** ... not merely of believing, –PHLP ... of trusting in him, –TCNT.

**but also to suffer for his sake:**

**1:29.** It is not new for Christians who are proclaiming the message of salvation to attract the antagonism of the world. Jesus warned about it in John 15:18-25. Anyone who attacks evil will face opposition. The apostle connected believing on Christ with suffering for Him. Believers should not get the impression that somehow by suffering for the cause of Christ they can add to Jesus' sacrificial work on the cross. There is no way believers can add to the infinite sacrifice of Christ in their behalf, but they can share in the same kind of rejection that Jesus faced from people who did not want to accept Him. Because servants are not greater than their master, the followers of the Lord should expect the same kind of treatment He received.

**30.** **Having the same conflict which ye saw in me:** ... having the same contest, –RTHM ... that I am still having, –WLMS.

**and now hear [to be] in me:** ... and which you hear that I am maintaining still, –TCNT ... concerning me, –WLSN.

**1:30.** In his closing statement of this section, Paul referred to his experience as a struggle, and he reminded the Philippians that they were experiencing the same kind of struggle. He used the term *agōna* from which we get the word *agony*. It certainly expresses very well the nature of the battle in which believers find themselves. The apostle did not say he had experienced this struggle only before his imprisonment. He was still facing it. The agony of the spiritual battle was not lessened in captivity. It is difficult to know exactly what Paul meant by this statement, but no doubt agonizing in prayer must have been an integral part of the total matter.

## Chapter 2

**1.** **If [there be] therefore any consolation in Christ:** ... any exhortation, –PNIN ... Any Comfort, –WLSN ... any encouragement comes through Christ, –TCNT.

**if any comfort of love:** ... any solace, –RTHM ... Any Soothing of Love, –WLSN ... any persuasive power in love, –TCNT.

**if any fellowship of the Spirit:** ... if any participation of, –SAWR ... if any society, –DOUY ... if any communion, –SCLT ... if any partaking of, –NOYS.

**if any bowels and mercies:** ... if any tender mercies, –PNIN ... any tender-affections, –RTHM.

**2:1.** Christians are not only to be imitators of Christ in conduct, but also in humility. Paul's "therefore" here indicates a definite connection with his appeal for unity in 1:27-33. Humility is a very important requisite for unity, and without unity God's people cannot experience the joy of the Lord.

In the Greek grammar Paul's "if" here does not question the existence of what he is about to mention. Rather, it carries the meaning "since" or "in view of the fact." His first statement indicates that encouragement or consolation does exist. Secondly, God's love brings comfort as it flows among His people. Christians also enjoy fellowship, or joint participation, in the Holy Spirit. Lastly, "bowels and mercies" or tenderness and compassion do exist in God's church. By using this form of address the apostle not only was affirming the reality of these qualities, but he was also appealing for them to be exercised in the assembly.

**2. Fulfil ye my joy:** ... make my happiness complete, −TCNT ... complete My Joy, −WLSN.
**that ye be likeminded:**
**having the same love:** ... maintaining the same love, −SCLT.
**[being] of one accord, of one mind:** ... sympathizing with each other, having one opinion, −SAWR ... joined-in-soul, −RTHM ... united in soul, −WLSN.

**2:2.** The fourfold appeal listed in verse 1 immediately precedes a fourfold declaration of results in verse 2. The statement "fulfil ye my joy" shows that the Philippians fell somewhat short of Paul's expectations. Here we see a slight glimpse into the apostle's philosophy about spiritual progress in the believer's life. He probably commended the Philippian church as much or more than any other group to whom he wrote, but he realized they still had room for growth. "Be likeminded, having the same love, being of one accord, of one mind" are all terms that show an same love, being of one accord, of one mind" are all terms that show an intentional piling up of expression to emphasize the necessity of unity.

**3. [Let] nothing [be done] through strife or vainglory:** ... in a spirit of rivalry or from vanity, −TCNT ... from Party-spirit, −WLSN ... out of contentiousness, −CNFT ... by way of factiousness, nor yet by way of empty-glory, −RTHM.
**but in lowliness of mind:** ... but in humility, −NOYS.
**let each esteem other better than themselves:** ... regard the others as his superiors, −CNFT.

**2:3.** Verse 3 seems to imply that some egotism and boastfulness existed in the Philippian assembly. Each exalted self and his own group. Humility serves as an antidote to such a sinful spirit. Paul's statements about it indicate a humble person refuses to do anything for selfish ambition or vain conceit.
"Strife" (*eritheian*) contains the idea not only of strife but of rivalry, so a person who practices this approach does things at the expense of other people in order to elevate self. "Vainglory" (*kenodoxian*) contains the word for *glory,* but Paul amplified it by adding the word for *empty* or *vain,* implying that this kind of activity brings a kind of glory that has no substance and therefore is meaningless. "Let each esteem other better than themselves" does not mean putting down self, but

refers to being concerned about the needs of others before the needs of self.

**4. Look not every man on his own things:** ... None of you should think only of his own affairs, −PHLP.
**but every man also on the things of others:** ... but each should learn to see things from other people's point of view, −PHLP.

**2:4.** So, instead of following party spirit and promotion of self, Paul enjoined Christians to put the interests of other people first. A truly humble person encourages and helps others.

**5. Let this mind be in you, which was also in Christ Jesus:** ... Let the spirit of, −TCNT ... Let Christ himself be your example as to what your attitude should be, −PHLP ... this disposition, −WLSN.

**2:5.** Paul used the perfect example of humility to illustrate his point and appealed to believers to share the attitude of Christ. While verses 5-11 contain some of the most important Christological truths in the Bible, they were written in a context which should encourage Christians to emulate the example of Christ in humility. Thus, having the mind of Christ means "to think as Christ thought."

**6. Who, being in the form of God:** ... had the divine nature, −TCNT ... had always been God by nature, −PHLP ... beyng in the shape of God, −GNVA.
**thought it not robbery to be equal with God:** ... counted it no act of robbery, −WSLY ... deemed not his equality with God a thing to grasp at, −ALFD ... did not cling to his prerogatives as God's equal, −PHLP ... something to be clung to, −TCNT.

**2:6.** Many Bible scholars think verses 6-11 comprise the substance of a hymn early Christians sang in worship of Christ. This verse makes it clear that even though He possessed equality with the Father, Jesus did not cling to it. The term "form" or "nature" (NIV), from the Greek *morphē,* refers to possessing the essential attributes which belong to the essence or nature (*ousia*) of God. Jesus could not have possessed the essential attributes of God without being God. However, He did not hang onto what was rightfully His. (See *Overview,* p. 538, for further discussion.)

**7. But made himself of no reputation:** ... emptied himself, −WSLY, −CNFT ... but impoverished himself, −TCNT ... but he abased himself, Sawyer ... but divested Himself, −WLSN ... of no consideration, −NOYS.
**and took upon him the form of a servant:** ... by consenting to be a slave, −PHLP ... by taking the nature of, −TCNT.

**and was made in the likeness of men:**... became lyke vnto men, —CRNM... made into the similitude of men, —RHEM... as mortal man, —PHLP.

**2:7.** Instead of clinging to what was rightfully His, Christ emptied himself (*heauton ekenōsen*). Pondering this, theologians pose several questions. Did He empty himself of His divine nature? Did He cease to be deity for a short period of time? That would have been impossible. How could God cease to be God? How could a human cease to be a human? Therefore, He divested himself not of the nature nor attributes of deity, but of the prerogatives that belonged to Him. In other words, He emptied himself of the expression of deity, not the possession of deity.

It is important to note that His emptying was voluntary. He had to do this in order to take upon himself the essential attributes (*morphē*) of a servant. Perhaps scholars argue so much about what Jesus laid aside that they fail to see that He actually took something upon himself. Becoming a human, of course, necessitated that He lay aside the prerogatives of deity, so it was a true self-emptying. The term for "likeness" (*homoiōmati*) implies a true human likeness and not a mere phantom, as the docetic Gnostics suggested.

**8. And being found in fashion as a man:**... founde in his aparell, —TNDL... in condition, —WLSN.
**he humbled himself, and became obedient unto death:**... by submitting even to death, —TCNT.
**even the death of the cross:**

**2:8.** Jesus also took the "fashion" (*schema*) or "appearance" (NIV) of a man, which means His outward appearance was definitely that of a man. Further, He died as a criminal, therefore taking the curse (Deuteronomy 21:23) of the cross upon himself.

**9. Wherefore God also hath highly exalted him:**... This is why, —WLMS... for which thing god enhauncid him, —WCLF... raised him to the very highest place, —TCNT... has now lifted him so high, —PHLP... uplifted him far on high, —RTHM... supremely exalted Him, —WLSN.
**and given him a name which is above every name:**... and freely granted to him, —WLSN... and graciously bestowed upon him, —MNTG... which ranks above all others, —TCNT... which is more excellent than all names, —MRDK.

**2:9.** As a result of this obedience to the plan of the Father, the Son possessed something He did not have before His incarnation. What did Jesus have after His crucifixion, resurrection, and ascension that He did not have before all this transpired? What did He take back to heaven that He

did not have previously? His humanity has to be the only answer to these questions. He always was the Son of God, but He was not a human until His incarnation.

Because there is a definite article before "name" in verse 10, some scholars believe the reference must be to a specific name for God. Verse 11 ascribes to Jesus Christ the term "Lord" (*kurios*), the word used by the Septuagint translators when they translated the Old Testament into Greek. They consistently used this title for the Old Testament name Yahweh or Jehovah. This was the ineffable Name that Jews hesitated to write or say.

**10. That at the name of Jesus every knee should bow:**... so that in the name of Jesus everyone should kneel, —WLMS.
**of [things] in heaven, and [things] in earth:**... whether in, —PHLP... of beings, —SAWR... of the celestials, terrestrials, —RHEM.
**and [things] under the earth:**... and of hellis, —WCLF... and infernals, —RHEM... in the underworld, —WLMS.

**2:10.** So Jesus has been freely given all the attributes of deity ascribed to the Father in the Old Testament by the Hebrew name *Jehovah*. All creation will ultimately acknowledge the man Jesus as fully God (Lord), with a position equal to that of the Father.

**11. And [that] every tongue should confess:**... And that is why, in the end, —PHLP... everyone, —WLMS... every tongue should acknowledge, —TCNT.
**that Jesus Christ [is] Lord, to the glory of God the Father:**... vnto the prayse of, —TNDL.

**2:11.** "Lord" was the characteristic confession of the Early Church, and it should be the characteristic confession of all contemporary believers. The Greek word for "Lord" (*kurios*) is one of the terms meaning "master."

**12. Wherefore, my beloved:**... my moost dereworthe britheren, —WCLF... my dearly loved friends, —WLMS... my dearest friends, —PHLP.
**as ye have always obeyed:**... as you have always been obedient, —WLMS... as you have always followed my advice, —PHLP.
**not as in my presence only, but now much more in my absence:**... not only when I was present to give it, —PHLP... not only as though I were with you but much more because I am away, —WLMS.
**work out your own salvation with fear and trembling:**... be keener than ever to work out the salvation... with a proper sense of awe and responsibility, —PHLP... with reverence and awe, —TCNT.

**2:12.** Paul followed his profound description of the self-humbling of Christ with a practical application to the situation in the Philippian church.

The apostle was just as practical as he was profound. Furthermore, he did not divorce learning from living. The "wherefore" in verse 12 seems to be a return to the exhortation in 1:27-30 to emulate Christ's example in conduct. It sounds as if Paul was saying, "Because you have the example of Christ's humility to imitate, the example of His exaltation to encourage you, you need to obey Him and continue steadfastly in your faith." The example of Christ served as a much stronger incentive to good works than Paul's own physical presence with them.

The apostle carefully informed the Philippians that they were responsible before God for their own salvation. They could not lean upon him, so his absence should not make a difference in whether or not they were faithful to God. Paul, of course, did not tell the Philippians they should work *for* their salvation. A person cannot "work out" what he does not have. Nowhere in Scripture is the paradox of divine sovereignty and human responsibility more clearly shown than here. "Work out" contains the idea of carrying out to an ultimate conclusion. In this process, which obviously is a reference to the work of sanctification, the attitude must be one of serious caution.

**13. For it is God which worketh in you both to will and to do of [his] good pleasure:** . . . for God is he who is working effectually among you, —WLSN . . . and the performance, —CNFT . . . to accomplish according to his good will, —DOUY . . . and also the dede, euen of his fre beneuolence, —GNVA.

**2:13.** God, of course, not only gives the *will* to please Him, but also the *ability*. So, verse 12 delineates human responsibility and verse 13 divine responsibility. It is never "either/or." The scriptural approach is not "let go and let God," but "get in there with God." Paul exhorted the followers of Christ as if he were an Arminian. At the same time he prayed as if he were a Calvinist. Both approaches contain truth. In a sense Christians "were saved" the moment they believed; they "are being saved" as the Holy Spirit applies the sanctification process to their lives; and they "will be saved" at the resurrection.

**14. Do all things without murmurings and disputings:** . . . avoid discontent and dissension, —TCNT . . . and hesitations, —DOUY . . . and without questioning, —CNFT . . . without grucchingis and doutingis, —WCLF . . . and staggerings, —RHEM.

**2:14.** After carefully instructing the Philippians about the necessity of allowing the sanctification process to work, Paul added that they should do so without "murmurings" and "disputings." "Murmurings" is an onomatopoetic word (*gongusmōn*),

a word in which the sound resembles its meaning. It refers to undertone mumbling and is constantly used in the Septuagint for the prolific murmuring of the Israelites in the wilderness when they journeyed from Egypt to Canaan. "Disputings" relates to ill-natured controversies.

**15. That ye may be blameless and harmless:** . . . that ye may become faultless, —RTHM . . . that ye maye be faute lesse and pure, —TNDL . . . that ye maye be soch as no man can complayne on, —CRNM . . . and sincere, —SAWR.
**the sons of God, without rebuke:** . . . the simple children, —RHEM . . . without blemish, —PNIN, —ASV . . . unrebukable, —WSLY . . . and inoffensive, irreproachable, —WLSN.
**in the midst of a crooked and perverse nation:** . . . in the middes of a naughtie and wicked, —GNVA . . . of a depraved and, —CNFT . . . of an evil-disposed, —TCNT.
**among whom ye shine as lights in the world:** . . . appear as Luminaries, —WLSN . . . shining like stars in a dark world, —TCNT.

**2:15.** Instead of murmuring and disputing about the process through which the Holy Spirit takes us, Christians should become "blameless and harmless." "Become" (NIV) shows the progressive nature of the experience. "Blameless" literally means "free from defect," and "harmless" has the sense of "unadulterated." The latter term often was used in that day to distinguish wine that had been watered down. All this beautiful process takes place in a "crooked" or "wicked" and "perverse" generation. Christians live in a real world rather than growing in a "greenhouse" setting.

**16. Holding forth the word of life:** . . . exhibiting, —WLSN.
**that I may rejoice in the day of Christ:**
**that I have not run in vain, neither laboured in vain:** . . . that I did not live my life for nothing, nor toil for nothing, —TCNT.

**2:16.** In verse 15 Paul expressed a twofold purpose for the Philippians: their own spiritual development or maturity, and their witness to unbelievers. In verse 16 Christians are instructed to shine as "luminaries" in this sin-darkened age. It could be compared to two travelers proceeding in the darkness, one with a light and the other without a light. The one extends his light to the other person to help guide him on his journey. The "word of life," of course, is the gospel message.

The apostle connected the continuance of the Philippian believers with his own accountability on the Day of Judgment when all Christians will give account to Christ of the deeds performed in their earthly lives after becoming Christians. Paul was not concerned only with beginning a church in the city of Philippi; he wanted to see those believers stand faithfully in the Lord until their earthly life ended. As a result, "in the day of Christ," the judgment day for Christians (1 Corinthians 3:10-23), Paul would be able to glory in the fact that his labors in Philippi had not been wasted.

17. **Yea, and if I be offered upon the sacrifice and service of your faith:** . . . if I am even to be poured out, *−RTHM* . . . if I am even poured out on, *−NOYS.*

**I joy, and rejoice with you all:**

18. **For the same cause also do ye joy, and rejoice with me:** . . . for the selfsame thing, *−DOUY.*

**2:17, 18.** In the earlier part of the chapter Paul spoke of the perfect example of self-abnegation of Christ himself. In these verses there is another example of the same attitude, his own. Paul expressed his unselfish willingness to give his life as a martyr for the Lord. Several years later he used nearly the same terminology just before he actually did suffer martyrdom (2 Timothy 4:6). He used the metaphor of a cup of wine being poured upon a burnt offering. He wrote about the pouring out of his blood upon the sacrifice which was the Philippians' testimony and service for God. The Philippians understood very well this type of language. They often saw public ceremonies where animals would be sacrificed and wine would be poured on top of the sacrifice.

Just as the Philippians and Paul both had a part in the sacrifice, so they would all rejoice. In this there is a good reminder of the present blessing that comes from performing good deeds. Even though the ultimate reward will come at the judgment seat of Christ, a certain satisfaction comes to the individual at the time the deed is performed.

There is another reference to the main theme of this epistle, the joy of the Lord that believers experience. If Christians truly are to experience this joy on a continuous basis, they must be concerned about good deeds coming from their lives. While believers do not come to an experience of salvation because of their good works, good works should be the natural outgrowth of the conversion experience. James referred to this, stating, "Faith without works is dead" (James 2:26).

Verses 12-18 depict progression in the Christian life. No believer is satisfied just being saved. He works with God in the process of sanctification. Good works result. The unconverted take notice, believe, and rejoice.

19. **But I trust in the Lord Jesus to send Timotheus shortly unto you:**

**that I also may be of good comfort:** . . . that I may be refreshed, *−SAWR.*

**when I know your state:** . . . when I knowe what case ye stonde in, *−TNDL* . . . I know your circumstances, *−CNFT* . . . I know the things pertaining to you, *−RHEM.*

**2:19.** The reader encounters Paul's love for people here as elsewhere in his writings. In a study of his works, one frequently comes across associates whom Paul trusted and tried to help in the ministry. Timothy was one of the most outstanding. He certainly lived up to his name which means "good comfort."

20. **For I have no man like-minded:** . . . No one like disposed, *−WLSN.*

**who will naturally care for your state:** . . . who will care truly, *−ASV* . . . who is so genuinely solicitous for you, *−CNFT* . . . who would take a genuine interest, *−TCNT* . . . who will genuinely care, *−PNIN* . . . will be genuinely anxious as to, *−RTHM* . . . wyth so pure affection careth for your matters, *−GNVA* . . . who really will care for your interests, *−SAWR.*

**2:20.** After stating that he was sending Timothy to the Philippians to help guide them and to cheer him by advising him of their situation, Paul made a puzzling statement. Timothy was the only one who was "likeminded," or the only one who had the same kind of genuine interest in the Philippians that Paul had. This complaint should not be taken to mean Paul had no genuine Christian friends in Rome, but apparently Timothy was the only one Paul felt comfortable to send as his representative to Philippi.

21. **For all seek their own:** . . . seeking their own interests, *−MNTG.*

**not the things which are Jesus** Christ's: . . . . . . not for the interests of, *−WLMS* . . . do not really care for the business of, *−PHLP.*

**2:21.** However, the words "for all seek their own" must be taken seriously. Sometimes even well-meaning believers put their own interests before those interests that belong to the work of God. Where were Aristarchus, Mark, Jesus Justus, and Demas whom Paul mentioned in his closing remarks in his letter to the Colossians? Although this may be conjecture, perhaps Demas' problem began at this time. We know from the apostle's comment in his second letter to Timothy that Demas ultimately forsook him (2 Timothy 4:10). Apparently Timothy was so dedicated to the work of the Lord that Paul could depend upon him to lay aside his own interests and make time to visit Philippi.

**22. But ye know the proof of him:** . . . you have had proof of his worth, *—NORL* . . . you know his tested character, *—WLMS* . . . his worth, *—CNFT* . . . an experiment of him, *—RHEM.*

**that, as a son with the father:** . . . like a son helping his father, *—MNTG* . . . in fellowship with his father, *—WLMS.*

**he hath served with me in the gospel:** . . . working with me, *—PHLP* . . . toiled with me like a slave in preaching the good news, *—WLMS.*

**2:22.** Paul was so concerned about the Philippians that he was willing to give up Timothy's companionship and dispatch him to them. Timothy had proved himself over a period of time. The Greek word for "proof" (*dokimēn*) refers to putting someone or something to the test for the purpose of obtaining approval. The apostle had observed Timothy very carefully before making this statement concerning him. No one received Paul's approval without "having the goods."

**23. Him therefore I hope to send presently:** . . . to send immediately, *—WLSN.*

**so soon as I shall see how it will go with me:** . . . just as soon as I can see how my case is going to turn out, *—WLMS* . . . as soon as I can tell how things will work out for me, *—PHLP.*

**2:23.** Comments like "so soon as I shall see how it will go with me" cause some Bible scholars to think Paul sensed he was about to be released from prison. Several other comments in Philippians seem to suggest the same possibility though the apostle always made it clear he committed his future to the Lord regardless of what it held. Even so, reliable tradition indicates Paul was released from prison and experienced several more years of ministry.

**24. But I trust in the Lord:** . . . God gives me some hope, *—PHLP* . . . having confidence, *—WLSN.*

**that I also myself shall come shortly:** . . . I myself shall follow, *—TCNT* . . . that it will not be long before I am able to come, *—PHLP.*

**2:24.** In this verse we see the other side of the coin. While he was not positive what would happen in the future, Paul had placed his confidence in the Lord who is omniscient. The idea expressed in this verse is probably close to what a person would mean when saying, "I trust I will be able to do so and so." It indicates a goal orientation which is essential if a person ever is to accomplish anything worthwhile in life, but at the same time it expresses a realization that God may have other plans. Paul was a goal-oriented person. He normally made careful plans relative to what he wanted to do next, but at the same time he allowed for God to change the plans if He so desired.

**25. Yet I supposed it necessary to send to you Epaphroditus:** . . . I esteemed, *—WLSN, —RTHM* . . . I have considered it desirable, *—PHLP* . . . But I counted it necessary to, *—CLMT* . . . and I gessid it nedeful, *—WCLF.*

**my brother, and companion in labour, and fellowsoldier:** . . . fellow worker and comrade-in-arms, *—PHLP.*

**but your messenger, and he that ministered to my wants:** . . . your apostle, *—DOUY* . . . and minister to my need, *—CLMT.*

**2:25.** The man the Philippians had sent as their messenger to Paul was about to return home, and the apostle desired that they honor Epaphroditus in the Lord. His name means "charming," and he certainly lived up to his name. Even though the shorter form of Epaphroditus is Epaphras, this is not the same person referred to in Colossians 4:12. Paul used some very complimentary titles for this man. In addition to calling him a "messenger," he also was a "brother," a "companion" or "fellow worker" (NIV), and a "fellow soldier," a person in active combat against the enemy.

**26. For he longed after you all, and was full of heaviness, because that ye had heard that he had been sick:** . . . He has been homesick for all of you, *—NORL* . . . and was sore troubled, *—PNIN, —ASV* . . . and was much troubled, *—NOYS* . . . and was much depressed, *—WLSN* . . . and in great distress, *—RTHM* . . . and has been distressed, *—ADAM* . . . and was anxious, *—MRDK.*

**2:26.** While in Rome, Epaphroditus suffered the very common malady of homesickness, and the apostle did not try to cover up the fact. This seems to indicate to a certain degree what a strong tie Epaphroditus had with the Philippian church. Some Bible scholars conjecture that he was the pastor of the assembly and had left Archippus in charge during his absence (Colossians 4:17). In addition to being homesick, he actually contracted some serious physical illness while with Paul in Rome. Some writers think that he contracted the "Roman fever," an especially dangerous disease to unacclimated strangers. If he arrived at Rome during the hot season, this would have been even more likely. His condition must have been a protracted one, because enough time had elapsed for word of his condition to reach Philippi and for a return message to get back to Rome.

**27. For indeed he was sick nigh unto death:** . . . And I can assure you that his illness very nearly proved fatal, *—TCNT* . . . and came near to death, *—ADAM* . . . so sick that he was on the point of dying, *—WLMS.*

**but God had mercy on him:** . . . took pity on, *—WLMS* . . . pitied him, *—WLSN.*

**and not on him only, but on me also, lest I should have sorrow upon sorrow:**...to keep me from having one sorrow after another, —*WLMS*...leest I hadde heuynesse on heuyns, —*WCLF*...have grief upon grief! —*ADAM*...added to my other troubles, —*NORL*.

**2:27.** Even though his main mission seems to have been to take the financial gift to Paul, Epaphroditus himself became a gift of comfort and strength to the apostle who was awaiting trial. Whatever malady struck his life nearly killed him, but God healed him. In describing the healing of his friend on this occasion, the apostle used a common Greek word (*eleeō*) for "mercy." It stems from God's love (*agapē*) for people. In this miracle of healing the Lord showed mercy not only to Epaphroditus but to Paul as well. His explanation of it showed how tenderhearted he was.

**28. I sent him therefore the more carefully:**...I am particularly anxious, —*PHLP*...I am all the more eager to send him, —*ADAM*...therfor more haistli I sente him, —*WCLF*...the more diligently, —*PNIN*...the more speedily, —*NOYS*.
**that, when ye see him again, ye may rejoice:**...you may be glad of it, —*WLMS*.
**and that I may be the less sorrowful:**...and to know of your joy will lighten my own sorrows, —*PHLP*...and my own sorrow may be lightened, —*TCNT*...I may have less anxiety, —*NORL*...my grief may be lessened, —*ADAM*.

**2:28.** Having gone through this experience certainly made Epaphroditus more capable of glorifying the Lord. Whether or not a Christian receives lasting spiritual benefits from the trials of life depends to a great extent on the person's own attitude. No doubt Paul was able to help Epaphroditus maintain a proper attitude through this total experience. As a result both lives benefited spiritually.

Evidently Paul also wanted the entire assembly in Philippi to benefit from the experience. Therefore, the fact that God had healed Epaphroditus brought joy to himself, to Paul, and ultimately to the entire assembly at Philippi. The Bible makes it clear that physical healing is not an end in itself. God performs these acts of mercy so that as a result people will turn to Him. God was glorified through the healing of Epaphroditus.

**29. Receive him therefore in the Lord with all gladness:**...So give him a hearty Christian welcome, —*WLMS*...Welcome him in the Lord, —*PHLP*...with all joy, —*MNTG*.
**and hold such in reputation:**...You should hold men like him in highest honor, —*PHLP*...and such intreate with honour, —*RHEM*...show honor to men like him, —*CNFT*...make muche of such, —*GNVA*...have

such in estimation, —*SAWR*...such like persons, —*WLSN*...in honor, —*PNIN*...in esteem, —*SCLT*.

**2:29.** This verse contains another example of the way Paul loved to honor other people who deserved it. He certainly was an unselfish man who felt no compulsion to put down other people in order to elevate himself. He encouraged the Philippian assembly to welcome this man with open arms and honor him for his work for Christ. The honor Christians bestow upon other people needs to be "in the Lord" or "in the realm of the Lord" so that God receives the ultimate glory for all that is accomplished in His kingdom. He receives this ultimate glory if we truly honor Christian leaders in a scriptural fashion. Because the danger of self-elevation always is present, Paul's practice here can serve as a good example for all Christians to follow.

**30. Because for the work of Christ he was nigh unto death:**...his loyalty to Christ brought him very near death, —*PHLP*...at the point of death, —*TCNT*.
**not regarding his life:**...he risked his life, —*PHLP*...yelding his life, —*RHEM*...hazarding his life, —*ALFD*...imperiling his soul, —*WORL*.
**to supply your lack of service toward me:**...what distance prevented you all from doing, —*PHLP*...your deficiency of service, —*WSLY*.

**2:30.** It is highly possible Epaphroditus' sickness had resulted from overexertion. Perhaps his body was so weakened by all the work involved in helping at this time that he was sick and "nigh unto death."

## Chapter 3

**1. Finally, my brethren:**...As to what remains, —*RTHM*, —*SCLT*.
**rejoice in the Lord:**
**To write the same things to you, to me indeed [is] not grievous:**...To repeat what I have already written, —*TCNT*...to me surely it is not tedious, —*RHEM*...is not irksome, —*PNIN*, —*WLSN*, —*RTHM*.
**but for you [it is] safe:**...and to you it is necessarie, —*RHEM*.

**3:1.** "Finally" does not imply the apostle was about to close the epistle. Although the Greek term *to loipon* sometimes does mean "finally," it more likely means "for the rest" in this context.

At first glance, verse 1 may not seem to be connected to the verses that follow, but Paul's encouragement to "rejoice in the Lord" should be considered as a positive preventative to becoming entangled in the false teaching that he was about to expose and condemn. People who are constantly rejoicing in the Lord probably have less chance of succumbing to false teaching than those who do not seem to consider worshiping God very important. The Philippians stood in danger of being led astray by two types of false teachings: legalism, and its opposite, antinomianism.

**2. Beware of dogs:** ... Look out for the, *–PNIN.* **beware of evil workers:** ... evildoers, *–NORL.* **beware of the concision:** ... Beware of dissen-syon, *–CRNM* ... of the men who mutilate them-selves, *–TCNT.*

**3:2.** Verse 2 contains a threefold warning show-ing the gravity of the situation. Three times Paul wrote "beware" or "watch out for" to emphasize what he was about to say. In addition to a three-fold "beware," Paul also had a threefold epithet for these false teachers. He first called them "dogs." He labeled them such because their characteris-tics resembled those of the wild packs of scaven-gers roaming the streets at the time, causing hav-oc wherever they went, in addition to attacking people. Secondly, Paul called them "evil workers," which implies they actively opposed the gospel of God's grace. Thirdly, he designated them "the concision." While they claimed to be "the circum-cision," Paul said they were really only "mutilat-ed." In other words, their mechanical, unscriptur-al approach to the important rite of circumcision reduced it to mere laceration of the body. Mutila-tion of the body was practiced regularly in pagan religious rites, but this practice was forbidden in the Old Testament (Leviticus 21:5; 1 Kings 18:28).

**3. For we are the circumcision:** ... we are truly circumcised, *–NORL.* **which worship God in the spirit:** ... we who are serving, *–WLSN.* **and rejoice in Christ Jesus:** ... we find our joy in Christ Jesus, *–PHLP.* **and have no confidence in the flesh:** ... and trust not, *–ALFD* ... in such mutilation of the flesh, *–NORL.*

**3:3.** Paul used the true term for circumcision (*peritomē*) which is used in the New Testament for "circumcision of the heart" (Romans 2:25-29) and refers to the breaking of the power of the fallen nature (Colossians 2:11). The three characteristics listed in this verse describe the people who truly have been circumcised: (1) they "worship God in the spirit"; (2) they "rejoice" or "glory" in Christ Jesus (not in personal attainments); and, (3) they do not trust in the "flesh." The term for "flesh" here does not refer to the body, but to the unre-generate human nature. Paul, of course, was not being egotistical by using the pronoun "we" in this statement. Instead he was expressing the certainty of the personal relationship he had with Christ. This is a good definition of true circumcision.

**4. Though I might also have confidence in the flesh:** ... although I have ground of confidence, *–SAWR.*

**If any other man thinketh that he hath where-of he might trust in the flesh, I more:** ... can rely upon external privileges, *–TCNT* ... thinketh that he hath reason for confidence, *–NOYS* ... I rather! *–RTHM.*

**3:4.** In verses 4-6 we see a catalog of Paul's own attainments before his conversion. His purpose in giving this list of merits was certainly not to boast. In fact, the opposite is true. He did it deliberate-ly to show the folly of trusting in human merits. His inventory of attainments includes seven items which can be divided into two categories. The first category includes four involuntary privileg-es that belonged to him because of heredity and environment.

**5. Circumcised the eighth day:** **of the stock of Israel:** ... of the kinred of, *–GNVA* ... from Israel's race, *–RTHM* ... a true Jew, *–PHLP.* **[of] the tribe of Benjamin, an Hebrew of the Hebrews:** ... of Hebrew parentage, *–NORL* ... a full-blooded Jew, *–PHLP.* **as touching the law, a Pharisee:** ... As far as keeping the Law is concerned, *–PHLP.*

**3:5.** First, he was circumcised when 8 days old as required by the Law (Leviticus 12:3). By con-trast, proselytes were circumcised as adults. Ish-mael was 13 years old when he experienced this rite (Genesis 17:24-26).

Secondly, Paul was an Israelite. The term des-ignates God's chosen nation which He selected to represent Him and be His witnesses on earth (Isa-iah 43:1-10; Romans 11:1; 2 Corinthians 11:22).

Paul also claimed he was a member of a special tribe, that of Benjamin. This tribe alone was faith-ful to Judah when the other 10 tribes left to form their own kingdom (1 Kings 12:21), and after the Babylonian Exile it actually merged with Judah (Ezra 4:1).

Lastly, Paul was "a Hebrew of the Hebrews," which informs us that he was raised in a home where Hebrew and Aramaic were used (Acts 21:40; 22:2). Many Jews of the day spoke only the Greek language and followed Greek customs, and therefore they were designated "Hellenists."

The last three items in Paul's catalog of human merits belonged to him by choice. He chose to be a Pharisee, the strictest of the religious groups of the day.

**6. Concerning zeal, persecuting the church:** ... you can judge my enthusiasm, *–PHLP* ... the congregacion, *–TNDL.* **touching the righteousness which is in the law, blameless:** ... respecting the righteousnes,

—*SCLT* . . . as regards the, —*TCNT* . . . I don't think anyone could have found fault with me, —*PHLP* . . . I was irreproachable, —*WLSN* . . . having become faultless, —*RTHM* . . . I was vnrebukable, —*GNVA*.

**3:6.** He also chose to be extremely zealous for what he believed to be true. In fact, he was so zealous that he persecuted the followers of Jesus (Acts 9:1, 2), a practice for which he was sorry the rest of his earthly life. Thirdly, judged by legalistic righteousness, he was "blameless."

**7. But what things were gain to me:** . . . every advantage that I had gained, —*PHLP* . . . which once stood to my credit, —*TCNT* . . . the thynges that were vauntage vnto me, —*CRNM*.
**those I counted loss for Christ:** . . . esteemed as a Loss, —*WLSN* . . . esteemed for Christ, detriments, —*RHEM* . . . accounted a detriment, —*MRDK*.

**3:7.** However, what things were gain to Paul, or that he considered as profit, he suddenly reckoned as nothing when compared to knowing Christ. The Greek verb for "counted" (*hēgēmai*) is a perfect tense verb which could be rendered "I have counted" and speaks of an action with continuing results. The action part has to be a reference to his conversion recorded in Acts chapter 9. The progression implied in the verb relates to the fact that from the time of his conversion until the time of writing this statement, Paul continued to consider all that gain as nothing compared to knowing Christ in a personal way. The language here is very similar to a bookkeeper's ledger in which the accountant would erase the word "gains" or "credit" and write the term "loss" or "debit."

**8. Yea doubtless, and I count all things [but] loss:** . . . Yes, indeed, I certainly do count everything as loss, —*WLMS*.
**for the excellency of the knowledge of Christ Jesus my Lord:** . . . compared with the priceless privilege, —*WLMS* . . . because of the superiority of the knowledge, —*RTHM* . . . as compared to the priceless worth of knowing Jesus, —*NORL*.
**for whom I have suffered the loss of all things:** . . . For his sake I have suffered, —*MNTG* . . . I have lost everything, —*WLMS*.
**and do count them [but] dung:** . . . and esteem them, —*MNTG* . . . and value it all as mere refuse, —*WLMS* . . . reckon it all the merest refuse, —*TCNT* . . . account them as filth, —*SCLT* . . . and do iudge them but vyle, —*CRNM* . . . to be vile refuse, —*WLSN*.
**that I may win Christ:** . . . in order to, —*WLMS* . . . gain Christ, —*DOUY*.

**3:8.** Here Paul repeated his declaration for emphasis and added a few more details. He used the same word "count" twice, but this time in the present tense in the Greek language, mainly referring to something being progressive. Time relates only to this type of verb in a secondary sense;

progression is the primary factor emphasized. "Dung" or "rubbish" (NIV) refers to something thrown out as worthless. The apostle considered an intimate and continuous knowledge of Christ as his personal Saviour more important than all his former attainments mentioned in the context. It would be difficult to study Paul's writings in very much detail without seeing his constant emphasis upon the personal relationship between two persons, God and a human being. Christianity is more than just religion; it is relationship.

**9. And be found in him:** . . . and be actually in union with Him, —*WLMS*.
**not having mine own righteousness, which is of the law:**
**but that which is through the faith of Christ:** . . . that which spryngeth of the fayth, —*TNDL*.
**the righteousness which is of God by faith:** . . . the real right standing . . . which originates from Him and rests on faith, —*WLMS* . . . which is derived from God and is founded on faith, —*TCNT* . . . on the ground of faith, —*PNT*.

**3:9.** In his beautiful description of all God had accomplished in his life, Paul suddenly took his readers to the future judgment seat of Christ. He realized that every believer will stand before the Lord to be judged for his works after his conversion. The apostle did not want to stand in Christ's presence depending upon his own righteousness because he knew it would not suffice. Instead of his own righteousness that previously had meant so much to him, he wanted to be covered with the righteousness of Christ. He reminded the Philippian believers that this righteousness of Christ comes only from God as a gift, and faith is the medium through which it comes.

**10. That I may know him:** . . . My aim is to get to know, —*TCNT* . . . I long to come to know Him, —*WLMS*.
**and the power of his resurrection:** . . . and the efficacy of, —*MRDK* . . . the power shown by, —*PHLP* . . . and experience the power of His resurrection, —*NORL*.
**and the fellowship of his sufferings:** . . . now I long to share, —*PHLP* . . . and the participation, —*SAWR* . . . and the societie of his passions, —*RHEM*.
**being made conformable unto his death:** . . . even to die as he died, —*PHLP*.

**3:10.** Next the apostle returned to the present in his thoughts. He realized his earthly life had not ended, so he still had to live with present realities. He wanted to enjoy four realities in his earthly life: (1) to know Christ, or to have a richer experience in Him; (2) to know the power of His resurrection, or to experience constantly the same power that raised Christ from the dead; (3) to participate in the sufferings of Christ for the sake of righteousness; and (4) to be conformed to the death of Christ, or to experience the same self-emptying described of Jesus (2:7).

Verse 10 gives an excellent catalog of items that a Christian should want to be present realities on a continuous basis. Even though a Christian obviously knows Christ, that knowledge can increase and become more intimate as the person experiences spiritual growth. Paul related the power (*dunamis*) of the Resurrection to the necessity of experiencing spiritual strength to live an overcoming Christian life on a continuous basis. Many people quote this marvelous verse but leave out the segment relating to suffering and conforming to the death of Christ.

**11. If by any means I might attain:** . . . if possibly, —*WLSN* . . . I may advance into, —*RTHM.*

**unto the resurrection of the dead:** . . . that lifts me out from among the dead, —*WLMS.*

**3:11.** Paul next expressed his ultimate desire to be part of the physical resurrection of believers (Revelation 20:6). His comment in the previous verse about spiritual resurrection would only have shown half the picture had he not made this reference to the physical resurrection that Christians will enjoy one day. The Greek term here literally refers to "the out-resurrection from the dead" and vividly depicts the fact that some people will be snatched from among the dead long before the remainder are resurrected.

The term "attain" does not imply Paul viewed being part of the first resurrection a matter of works. However, he did emphasize the necessity of constantly maintaining an integral relationship with Christ, because only people definitely related to Jesus via conversion will be included in the first resurrection.

**12. Not as though I had already attained:** . . . nor do I consider myself, —*PHLP* . . . No, I have not yet reached that goal, —*NORL* . . . I do not say that I have already won, —*MNTG* . . . secured it, —*TCNT.*

**either were already perfect:** . . . or already have reached perfection, —*RTHM*, —*WLMS.*

**but I follow after, if that I may apprehend that for which also I am apprehended of Christ Jesus:** . . . But I am pressing on, —*TCNT* . . . but I pursue . . . I was laid hold on, —*WLSN* . . . I keep going on, grasping ever more firmly, —*PHLP* . . . I am pressing on to see if I can capture it, —*WLMS* . . . that I may attain that for which also I was arrested by, —*SAWR* . . . also I was laid hold on by Christ, —*ALFD* . . . I am also comprehended of Christ, —*RHEM.*

**3:12.** Paul again returned to the present and expressed the realization that he had not arrived at any pinnacle of perfection. Apparently some of the Philippians were making such a claim for themselves. First, he approached the matter with

an aorist verb (*elabon*) which was translated "attained," indicating that at the time of his conversion he did not receive everything God had for him. In addition, his statement "either were already perfect" indicates that from the moment of conversion until the writing of the epistle he still had not been perfected. This second verb is a perfect tense so it refers to an initial act followed by continuous action or results. In this case it probably refers to continuous action.

Thus Paul's two verbs both stress he did not claim to have yet reached perfection. Instead of feeling he had arrived, he said, "I follow after" or "press on" (NIV).

**13. Brethren, I count not myself to have apprehended:** . . . to have laid hold, —*RTHM*, —*ASV*, —*WORL* . . . that I haue gotten it as yet, —*CRNM* . . . to have fully grasped it even now, —*PHLP.*

**but [this] one thing [I do]:** . . . I do concentrate on this, —*PHLP.*

**forgetting those things which are behind:** . . . leave the past behind, —*PHLP* . . . what is behind me, —*MNTG.*

**and reaching forth unto those things which are before:** . . . I strain forward, —*CNFT* . . . and straining every nerve, —*TCNT* . . . and stretching forth, —*WLSN*, —*DOUY.*

**3:13.** Verse 13 contains even stronger language than verse 12. After carefully repeating the fact that he had not yet arrived at the goal set for him by God himself, Paul emphasized that what he did constantly was to stretch forward toward it. In order to keep pressing toward the goal, he had to forget what was behind. "Forgetting" in this context does not imply obliterating something from the mind, but refers to the constant necessity of pushing something out of the mind. It speaks of a continuous process rather than a momentary occurrence. Again, the language is that of a runner completely forgetting his opponents who are following him in a race. Even the slightest looking back will slow down his progress.

**14. I press toward the mark:** . . . I go straight for, —*PHLP* . . . to press on to the winning-post, —*TCNT* . . . toward the goal, —*SCLT*, —*ASV.* **for the prize of the high calling of God in Christ Jesus:** . . . my reward the honor of being called by God, —*PHLP* . . . of the heavenly calling, —*ALFD* . . . of the upward calling, —*PNIN* . . . the supernal vocation, —*DOUY.*

**3:14.** The culmination of Paul's testimony in verse 14 contains a statement about the goal and the prize God placed before him. To him Christ was both the goal and the prize. This is one of the amazing marvels of Scripture. In a human contest the goal and the prize could not, at least normally, be the same.

The Bible speaks often of the process of maturing through which God takes His followers. However, it does not take place automatically. Christians have a part, and God has a part (2:12, 13). Even so, full maturity will not be attained until the resurrection. Therefore, the glorified life in heaven is both the goal and the prize.

**15. Let us therefore, as many as be perfect, be thus minded:** . . . as [are] of full growth, let this be our resolve, *—RTHM* . . . attend to this, *—SCLT.*

**and if in any thing ye be otherwise minded:** . . . but if ye should think differently, *—SCLT* . . . if ye have a different mind, *—NOYS* . . . if at present you cannot see this, *—PHLP.*

**God shall reveal even this unto you:** . . . this is the attitude which God is leading you to adopt, *—PHLP* . . . will make that also plain to you, *—TCNT.*

**3:15.** At first verse 15 may seem to contradict verses 12 and 13. Paul had renounced the false idea that it is possible in this earthly life to reach a level of absolute sinless perfection. The language of the previous section might lead a person to say, "Since I cannot arrive at a level of absolute sinless perfection, why should I constantly put forth effort to become like Christ?" Paul immediately countered that tendency by making it clear that although it is impossible to reach a place of absolute sinless perfection in this life, it is possible to reach a certain level of Christian perfection.

The same idea expressed in the Greek term for "perfect" or "mature" (*teleios*) is also emphasized in 1 Corinthians 2:6; 14:20; Ephesians 4:13, 14; Colossians 1:28; 4:12; Hebrews 5:14; and 6:1. It does not contain the implication of being perfect in the sense of flawlessness; rather, it refers to having reached a level of completeness or maturity. In verse 12 Paul was speaking of a finished product, whereas in verse 15 he was referring to a relative spiritual maturity where there is room for development and growth. An apple serves as a good illustration of this matter. In June it is a perfect apple, but it is far from mature. In September it is far more mature, perfect, or complete.

**16. Nevertheless, whereto we have already attained, let us walk by the same rule, let us mind the same thing:** . . . walk on by the same path, *—ALFD.*

**3:16.** This verse shows the meaning of Christian perfection, or a state of Christian maturity. When we live up to what God has already shown us, He is able to lead us further on the route to perfection. However, if believers balk at the instructions written in the Scriptures, they hinder the process. We may never fully understand all of Scripture; God illuminates it to us by degrees. Still, we can learn to act like Christ, the Perfect One.

**17. Brethren, be followers together of me:** . . . join one another in copying my example, *—TCNT.*

**and mark them which walk so as ye have us for an ensample:** . . . as you have us for a Pattern, *—WLSN* . . . you have our model, *—DOUY.*

**3:17.** Paul encouraged the Philippians to follow his example in this matter. "Us" probably refers to Timothy, Silas, and Luke who assisted the apostle in his initial ministry in Philippi. The Greek word for "ensample" or "example" (*tupos*) sometimes refers to the impression left by a stroke, and it is the same word used for the nail prints left in Jesus' hands (John 20:25). It also can be used to mean "a pattern" (1 Corinthians 10:6, 11; 1 Thessalonians 1:7), and this is the meaning here. The Philippians were warned to mark the ones who did not follow that pattern.

**18. (For many walk, of whom I have told you often:**

**and now tell you even weeping, [that they are] the enemies of the cross of Christ:** . . . even with tears, *—PHLP* . . . who behave as though they hated the cross of, *—NORL.*

**3:18.** After warning the Philippians to mark certain people, Paul here described them as enemies of the cross of Christ. One cannot be sure whether he referred to false teachers within the Philippian church or to outsiders. Perhaps both groups existed. These were not the legalistic people described at the outset of the chapter. They no doubt were professing Christians who allowed their liberty to degenerate into license (Galatians 5:13). They could be called antinomians. They believed in no laws, no regulations. However, the extreme legalists and the antinomians Paul described in this chapter had one thing in common: they lived as enemies of the gospel of Christ.

**19. Whose end [is] destruction, whose God [is their] belly:** . . . Their end is ruin, *—CNFT* . . . whose ende is dampnacion, *—TNDL* . . . end is perdition, *—ALFD* . . . whos god is the wombe, *—WCLF* . . . their stomach, *—SAWR.*

**and [whose] glory [is] in their shame:** . . . They take pride in their shame, *—NORL* . . . their glorie in their confusion, *—RHEM* . . . their pride is in what they should be ashamed of, *—PHLP.*

**who mind earthly things.):** . . . who regard, *—SAWR* . . . who are engrossed with earthly things, *—WLSN* . . . which are wordeley mynded, *—GNVA* . . . this world is the limit of their horizon, *—PHLP.*

**3:19.** The people Paul described here were probably Gentiles with Epicurean tendencies. The Epicureans constituted a Greek school of philosophy with the basic views that satisfaction of the physical appetites was the highest purpose of mankind. In addition to describing these people as enemies of the Cross, Paul designated their end as destruction, a reference to eternal separation from God. A person's god is that to which he gives himself. These people had made their own unbridled lusts their gods. Although they gloried in their "freedom" to live as they pleased, their perverted actions only brought them shame. Paul's closing description of these false teachers is a very straightforward one—"who mind earthly things."

**20. For our conversation is in heaven:** ... For our enrollment as citizens, —*RTHM* ... For our place of administration, —*CLMT* ... our citizenship, —*PNIN* ... our country is in the heavens, —*ALFD.*

**from whence also we look for the Saviour, the Lord Jesus Christ:** ... we expect the, —*SAWR* ... are we ardently awaiting, —*RTHM* ... we are waiting with longing expectation, —*CLMT* ... we await [the] Saviour, —*PNT* ... we also are awaiting the return of, —*NORL.*

**3:20.** In contrast to false teachers, those people who choose to follow Christ recognize a standard based upon something far more important than earthly pursuits. Paul used the same word for "conversation" or "citizenship" that he used in 1:27, but there he used the verb *politeuomai,* and here the noun *politeuma.* The Christian is a citizen of heaven and he longs for the kingdom of heaven to become a present reality (Matthew 6:10; Ephesians 2:19). In a sense the Church is a "colony of heaven" much as Philippi was a Roman colony. The realization that the Saviour of believers one day will return for those citizens of heaven constitutes a powerful incentive for correct living.

**21. Who shall change our vile body:** ... who will refashion, —*CNFT* ... who shall fashion anew, —*PNIN* ... who will transform, —*WLSN,* —*WORL* ... our humble body, —*SAWR* ... the body of our humiliation, —*ALFD.*

**that it may be fashioned like unto his glorious body:** ... that it may be conformed, —*ASV* ... to resemble, —*PHLP.*

**according to the working whereby he is able even to subdue all things unto himself:** ... by the exertion of the power, —*WLMS* ... by the power that enables Him, —*ADAM* ... by the energy with which he is able even to subject all things to himself, —*MNTG* ... which makes him the master of everything that is, —*PHLP.*

**3:21.** When He returns for His church believers' bodies will be changed like His own (1 John 3:2). The term translated "change" (*metaschēmatisei*) refers to the outward change of these "vile" or "lowly" (NIV) bodies. Redeemed souls will occupy redeemed bodies such as Christ's after His resurrection. Then since doctrine determines conduct and destiny, Christians must avoid the extremes of both legalism and antinomianism.

## Chapter 4

**1. Therefore, my brethren, dearly beloved and longed for:** ... So, my brothers whom I hold dear and greatly desire to see, —*ADAM.*

**my joy and crown:** ... and winner's wreath, —*ADAM.*

**so stand fast in the Lord, [my] dearly beloved:** ... by the help of the Lord keep on standing firm, dearly loved friends, —*WLMS* ... who are very dear to me, —*TCNT* ... my deerest, —*RHEM* ... dear friends, —*ADAM* ... and remember how much I love you, —*PHLP.*

**4:1.** The first four verses of this chapter may seem unrelated to each other; however, if one remembers Paul's stress on joy, the association becomes clear. Verse 1 begins with another "therefore," which in this case comes from a Greek term literally meaning "so as" (*hōste*). This "so as" refers back to the entire first three chapters of the letter, to which Paul gives an excellent climax in this fourth chapter.

The term for "crown" (*stephanos*) is the word from which we derive the name *Stephen.* It relates to the laurel wreath placed around the neck or upon the head of the victor in an athletic contest. It was not at all like a diadem (*diadēma*) worn by a ruler or priest of the day. The laurel began to wilt shortly after it was picked from a tree, so it was only transitory. On the other hand, the Philippian saints consisted of Paul's permanent joy and crown, or his reward for his labors in Philippi.

**2. I beseech Euodias, and beseech Syntyche:** ... I exhort, —*PNIN* ... I beg you by name, —*PHLP* ... I urge, —*ADAM.*

**that they be of the same mind in the Lord:** ... to live in harmony as fellow-Christians, —*TCNT* ... to think alike in the Lord, —*ADAM* ... by the help of the Lord, —*WLMS.*

**4:2.** Perhaps the problem he pinpointed in verse 2 represented many such differences in the assembly. People cannot constantly experience joy if they are always bickering over minor matters. Paul therefore appealed to Euodias and Syntyche to settle their differences. While he could have *ordered* them to solve their problem, he instead *begged* them to do so. The Greek word behind the term "beseech" (*parakalō*) is the same word from which we derive *Paraclete,* one of the prominent New Testament names for the Holy Spirit, the One who is the master pleader.

It is unfortunate that the only thing we know about these two ladies, in addition to the fact that they labored with Paul when he ministered in Philippi, is that they could not get along and could not reconcile their differences. When Paul told them to "be of the same mind in the Lord," he used the same word as in 2:5 (*phronein*) where he instructed the Philippians to have the attitude of Christ.

These ladies certainly did not live up to their names. *Euodias* means "prosperous journey" and *Syntyche* means "pleasant acquaintance." Paul did not insist they think alike in everything, but if each had the selfless attitude of Christ, each would respect the other's viewpoint, and neither would be contentious.

**3. And I entreat thee also, true yokefellow:** ... I request you also, *—WORL* ... Yes, I also ask you, who have shown yourself to be genuine in bearing the yoke together with me, *—ADAM* ... genuine yokefellow, *—RTHM* ... my true comrade, *—WLMS*.
**help those women which laboured with me in the gospel:** ... assist those, *—WLSN* ... give them aid, *—NOYS* ... keep on cooperating with, *—WLMS* ... who struggled together with me for the good news, *—ADAM*.
**with Clement also, and [with] other my fellowlabourers, whose names [are] in the book of life:** ... the rest of my fellow-workers, *—WLMS*.

**4:3.** According to verse 3, these two women definitely had assisted Paul in his ministry in Philippi. From the very genesis of the assembly, women filled prominent places in the Philippian church (Acts 16:13ff.). It is a well-known historical fact that women held more prominent positions in the province of Macedonia, the province in which Philippi was located, than they did in most other parts of the Roman world. The apostle asked a third party to assist Euodias and Syntyche to settle their differences. Commentators disagree as to whether "true yokefellow" merely describes the person addressed or whether his actual name was Suzugos, the literal Greek noun from which "yokefellow" comes. Clement and other individuals not only helped Paul in his ministry in Philippi, but their names were known to God.

**4. Rejoice in the Lord alway:** ... Delight yourselves in God, *—PHLP*.
**[and] again I say, Rejoice:** ... yes, find your joy in him at all times, *—PHLP*.

**4:4.** People who actively serve God generally reflect the joy of the Lord, and this may explain Paul's sudden outburst in verse 4. Bible commentators generally agree that this verse reflects most clearly the theme of the letter.

**5. Let your moderation be known unto all men:** ... Let your gentleness, *—PNIN*, *—WLSN* ... Let your considerateness, *—RTHM* ... Let your yieldedness, *—CLMT* ... Let your forbearing spirit be plain to every one, *—TCNT* ... Let your modesty be known to

all men, *—DOUY* ... Have a reputation for gentleness, *—PHLP*.
**The Lord [is] at hand:** ... never forget the nearness of, *—PHLP* ... is near, *—WLSN* ... is nigh, *—DOUY*.

**4:5.** Because joy is the outward expression of some inward cause, Paul quickly moved from external matters to internal matters. If the peace of God truly abides within a person, it will reflect itself in outward joy. Joy is a wonderful by-product of the peace described in verse 7 which contains the central theme from verses 5-9. The rest of the passage describes what we must do in order to constantly experience this peace.

Verse 5 gives the first condition as "moderation" or "forbearance" (RSV). In other words, a person cannot enjoy the peace of God unless he can forbear other people. Paul buttressed his command by adding a solemn warning about the Lord's nearness. He may have had Psalm 145:18 in mind, or he may have been referring to the Aramaic expression *Maran atha* ("O Lord, Come"—1 Corinthians 16:22). In the light of Paul's constant references to the imminency of the Lord's return, the latter probably is what he meant.

**6. Be careful for nothing:** ... Do not be anxious about anything, *—TCNT* ... In nothing be anxious, *—PNIN* ... For nothing be anxious, *—RTHM* ... Have no anxiety, *—CNFT*.
**but in every thing by prayer and supplication with thanksgiving let your requests be made known unto God:** ... let your petitions, *—CNFT*.

**4:6.** Secondly, to know God's peace we must not worry, since that betrays a lack of trust in God. Paul's words can be translated, "Stop being anxious." Then the apostle offered prayer as the solution to worry.

Paul gave a complete picture of the process by using four different Greek terms. (1) "Prayer" (*proseuchē*) is used constantly in the New Testament of prayer in general. (2) "Supplication" (*deēsis*) concerns special times of need. (3) "Thanksgiving" (*eucharistia*) looks back to previous answers to prayer in which God helped in similar situations. (4) "Requests" (*aitēmata*) refers to specific requests for specific needs.

**7. And the peace of God, which passeth all understanding:** ... which surpasses every human conception, *—TCNT* ... which surpasses all Conception, *—WLSN* ... which rises above every mind, *—RTHM*.
**shall keep your hearts and minds through Christ Jesus:**

**4:7.** Then if anyone does the above things, God's peace will keep him. The apostle used a military term here: "keep" here literally means "to garrison, to guard, to keep, to arbitrate, to umpire" our hearts and minds. Because Philippi was a Roman colony and a military outpost, the garrisoning of the city by Roman soldiers was a very familiar sight. Since "hearts" (*kardias*) and "minds" (*noun*) suffer most at the lack of inner tranquility, God promises to guard both.

**8. Finally, brethren:** ... In conclusion, —*TCNT.*
**whatsoever things are true:**
**whatsoever things [are] honest:** ... as many as [are] dignified, —*RTHM* . . . are honorable, —*WLSN* ... modest, —*DOUY* ... chast, —*WCLF* ... are venerable, —*PNT.*
**whatsoever things [are] just:**
**whatsoever things [are] pure:** ... holy, —*PHLP.*
**whatsoever things [are] lovely:** ... are amiable, —*WLSN* ... whatever benevolent, —*SCLT* ... whatever lovable, —*CNFT.*
**whatsoever things [are] of good report:** ... are reputable, —*SAWR* ... or anything attractive, —*TCNT.*
**if [there be] any virtue, and if [there be] any praise:**
**think on these things:** ... the same be taking into account, —*RTHM* . . . attentively consider, —*WLSN* ... there let your thoughts dwell, —*TCNT* ... consider these things, —*SAWR.*

**4:8.** The third condition to enjoying the peace of God relates to a person's thought life. Christians cannot enjoy God's peace if they are always allowing unwholesome thoughts to fill their minds. Paul gave a representative list of six types of things on which believers should concentrate, but no doubt he could have continued the list.

"True" (*alēthē*) refers to truth in the widest sense. Jesus called himself "the way, the truth, and the life" (John 14:6), and He designated God's Word as truth (John 17:17). "Honest" (*semna*) relates to things worthy of honor, or things worthy of reverence, as opposed to a flippancy that lacks seriousness. "Just" (*dikaia*) has to do with what is right according to God's standard which is spelled out in the Scriptures; we have no excuse for not knowing what is right. "Pure" (*hagna*) means "stainless" or "chaste" and relates to things that encourage purity. "Lovely" (*prosphilē*) refers to things that incite true love, rather than erotic behavior. "Good report" (*euphēma*) relates to things attractive in character.

The "if" here is an indicative mood "if" (*ei*) in the Greek language and often is called "a condition of the first class." It often is translated "since." In other words, these attributes, and many similar ones, do exist and should be considered virtuous and worthy of praise.

**9. Those things, which ye have both learned, and received, and heard, and seen in me,**

**do:** ... you should continually put into practice, —*TCNT* ... these things practice, —*WLSN.*
**and the God of peace shall be with you:** ... and you will find, —*PHLP.*

**4:9.** The last and perhaps most important condition for enjoying God's peace is to practice (*prassete*) what we have heard and seen. The emphasis shifts from right thinking to right doing. The former verse enumerated the proper subjects of meditation; this verse encourages the proper course of action which naturally should follow right thinking. If a person will take seriously the four conditions given by the apostle Paul and put them into practice, God will prove himself faithful to His promise.

**10. But I rejoiced in the Lord greatly:** ... I was exceedingly glad, —*TCNT* ... It has been a great joy to me, —*PHLP.*
**that now at the last your care of me hath flourished again:** ... now at length, —*DOUY,* ... has revived, —*CNFT* . . . ye have revived your thoughtfulness for me, —*PNT* . . . your thought for me, —*ASV* ... in your care for my welfare, —*NOYS.*
**wherein ye were also careful, but ye lacked opportunity:** ... I don't mean that you had forgotten me, —*PHLP.*

**4:10.** In his application to the Philippian saints, Paul had one more topic to treat. He used the immediate occasion, which was his sincere expression of appreciation for their financial support, to teach them an extremely important lesson. The phrase "your care of me hath flourished again" may indicate a suspension of their financial support for a time due to the influence of false teachers.

**11. Not that I speak in respect of want:** ... under the pressure of want, —*TCNT.*
**for I have learned, in whatsoever state I am, [therewith] to be content:** . . . in whatever circumstances, —*SAWR* . . . in whatever condition, —*WLSN* ... learnt to be independent of circumstances, —*TCNT* ... to be self-sufficing, —*CNFT.*

**4:11.** Paul had learned the true secret of life, and he desired to share it with them. The verb "learned" here is an aorist verb and is a good example of what grammarians call a *resultative* or *culminative* aorist. "The culminative aorist views the act as having occurred but emphasizes the end of the action or the state of being resulting from the action" (Summers, p. 67). At some particular point in his life, Paul made a commitment to serve the Lord faithfully no matter what circumstances he had to face. The results of that decision still were evident in his life when he wrote this short letter to the Philippians. We know from

Acts chapter 9 that shortly after Paul's conversion, he faced persecution, and certain enemies of the gospel attempted to kill him. God protected him though, and some believers lowered the apostle to the ground in a basket (Acts 9:25). Perhaps it was then that he determined to serve God faithfully no matter what happened.

**12.** **I know both how to be abased:** . . . I am initiated both to be, *−PNT* . . . how to be brought low, *−RTHM* . . . how to live humbly, *−CNFT* . . . how to be in low estate, *−ALFD* . . . when things are difficult, *−PHLP.*
**and I know how to abound:** . . . how to have more than enough, *−RTHM* . . . when things are prosperous, *−PHLP.*
**every where and in all things I am instructed both to be full and to be hungry:** . . . I have been schooled, *−CNFT* . . . I have been well taught, *−NOYS* . . . have I learned the secret both, *−CLMT.*
**both to abound and to suffer need:** . . . I have learned the secret of facing either poverty or plenty, *−PHLP* . . . into prosperity and want, *−TCNT* . . . and to be in want, *−PNIN* . . . and to be destitute, *−WLSN.*

**4:12.** The idea expressed at the end of verse 11 and in verse 12 literally means "I have learned the secret" or "I have been initiated." It is the translation of a Greek word (*memuēmai*) used by the Stoic school of philosophy to mean a man should be self-sufficient for all things, or independent of external circumstances. The word also was used for the feeding of animals, so a fattened or satisfied animal was described this way.

Even though Paul used the very word Stoics used to boast about their self-sufficiency, his sufficiency was based upon his relationship to Christ. His sufficiency came not through the kind of mechanical self-discipline practiced by the Stoics, but because of his union with a personal God. In addition, verse 12 also clarifies the fact that his sufficiency was not based upon material possessions.

**13.** **I can do all things through Christ which strengtheneth me:** . . . I endure all things with him that strengthens me, *−SAWR* . . . I have strength for all things in him, *−ALFD* . . . I have strength for all circumstances, *−PNT* . . . of him who makes me strong! *−TCNT* . . . in him who empowers me, *−RTHM.*

**4:13.** Paul's sufficiency did not come from circumstances, but from Christ. Since the Greek text here contains the title "Christ," He obviously was the One empowering Paul so that he could accomplish "all things," or whatever God wanted him to do.

**14.** **Notwithstanding ye have well done:** . . . ye did well, *−NOYS.*
**that ye did communicate with my affliction:** . . . ye had fellowship with my tribulation,
*−CLMT* . . . in sharing with me, *−NOYS* . . . in sympathizing with, *−WLSN* . . . my tribulation, *−DOUY.*

**4:14.** One could get the impression from the writer's statements in verses 10-13 that he did not appreciate the Philippians' help as much as he should have. To counter this possible impression, verse 14 begins with the preposition *plēn* ("notwithstanding" [KJV]; "yet" [NIV]; "nevertheless" [NASB]). He truly did appreciate their faithful help from the early stages of his ministry in Macedonia (Acts chapters 16 and 17), about 10 years before the writing of this letter.

Even though his dependence rested in God, Paul was wise enough to know that God works through His people. In fact, in this verse he used a term related to the normal word for "partnership" (*koinōnia*). God used the Philippians to *share* in the problems the apostle faced at that time. Paul described these problems by using the Greek term *thlipsis* which normally means "tribulation." It was not an easy period of time for him, and he wanted them to know they had done well to share with him. In fact, their assembly seems to have been the only one that faithfully supported him over an extended period of time.

**15.** **Now ye Philippians know also, that in the beginning of the gospel:** . . . that in the early days of the Good News, *−TCNT.*
**when I departed from Macedonia:**
**no church communicated with me as concerning giving and receiving, but ye only:** . . . you were the only Church who shared with me the fellowship of, *−PHLP.*

**4:15.** The terminology here, and again in verse 17, suggests the Philippians actually kept records and had an account of their giving to Paul. "Giving and receiving" comes from a general expression used in that day of "debits and credits" and can be found in many references to business transactions of that period. They had shared with him in his affliction or troubles. The example of the Philippian church should serve as an incentive for contemporary assemblies to share in the ministries of ministers like the apostle Paul. He normally did not settle down in one place, so was dependent upon the Holy Spirit speaking to people in local churches to help support him, a practice that is still followed.

**16.** **For even in Thessalonica ye sent once and again unto my necessity:** . . . you twice sent me help, *−PHLP* . . . you sent money, *−WLMS* . . . you sent more than once to relieve my wants, *−TCNT* . . . for my need, *−WLSN.*

**4:16.** Generally, local churches that are truly evangelistic will also be strong missionary churches. Philippi must have been that kind of church. Even while Paul ministered in Thessalonica (Acts 17:1-9), the Philippian believers allowed their ministry to advance beyond their own geographic borders and assisted the apostle in his activities among the Thessalonians. During that period of ministry in Thessalonica Paul faced very trying circumstances. No doubt being able to depend upon the Lord using the Philippians to help him must have meant a lot to him.

**17. Not because I desire a gift:** ... It is really not the gifts that I crave, —*NORL* ... It isn't the value of the gift that I am keen on, —*PHLP.*

**but I desire fruit that may abound to your account:** ... but I do want the profits to pile up to your credit, —*WLMS* ... the profit accumulating to your account, —*CNFT* ... the abundant profit that accrues, —*MNTG* ... that increaseth, —*PNIN* ... I wish fruits may multiply unto you, —*MRDK.*

**4:17.** Paul was quick to add in this verse, however, that he was not writing in this way because he was asking for another offering. In these statements Christians see the attitude they should have with respect to financial help from other people. On the one hand, they must be grateful. On the other hand, they must always remember, as well as remind other people, that God is the One who meets their needs. The apostle considered their offerings to him as really "unto the Lord." Verse 17 indicates that the fruit which resulted from their joint participation with him would be added to their account. By investing in Paul's ministry they could expect to receive rich dividends from God.

**18. But I have all, and abound:** ... I have received your payment in full, and more too, —*WLMS* ... and to spare, —*TCNT* ... in fact I am rich, —*PHLP.*

**I am full:** ... I am amply supplied, —*WLMS* ... quite content, —*PHLP.*

**having received of Epaphroditus the things [which were sent] from you:** ... thanks to your gifts, —*PHLP* ... the gifts which you sent me, —*TCNT.*

**an odour of a sweet smell, a sacrifice acceptable, wellpleasing to God:** ... they are like sweet incense, —*WLMS* ... a Fragrant Odor, —*WLSN* ... lovely fragrance, —*PHLP.*

**4:18.** At the same time that the Philippians benefited spiritually from their acts of kindness to Paul, he was reaping the benefit as well. Paul considered the gift they sent via Epaphroditus as enough to make him "abound," and he assured them he was "full." Because these people certainly were not obligated to give to assist Paul, he looked at their gifts as if they had been given to God. The Philippians understood the kind of language Paul used here, because they often viewed public sacrifices of animals. Paul assured them their sacrifice

was accepted by God in the same manner a fragrant aroma would be accepted by a human.

**19. But my God shall supply all your need:** ... will fully supply, —*WLSN* ... will liberally supply, —*WORL* ... will fill up your every need, —*RTHM* ... will amply supply your every need, —*WLMS* ... all your necessity, —*MRDK.*

**according to his riches in glory by Christ Jesus:** ... according to his Glorious wealth, —*WLSN* ... so great is his wealth, —*TCNT* ... from his glorious resources, —*PHLP.*

**4:19.** The apostle went on to assure the Philippians that the same God who met all his needs also would meet all their needs. Many times people quote this verse by changing the "your" to "our" or "my." Paul wanted his friends in Philippi to enjoy God's divine supply just as he was. In a sense, God's treatment of the Philippians would correspond to their treatment of Paul. Paul wrote "my God" probably because he had tested and tried Him as his own provider. Some people interpret the King James' language here to mean riches in a specific place (heaven), but the statement refers to the glorious bounty of God's riches. God would recompense the Philippians because His resources are limitless. He does everything "in glory" (*en doxē*) or "in a glorious way" because of His limitless resources, and He manifests them "by Christ Jesus."

**20. Now unto God and our Father [be] glory for ever and ever. Amen:** ... Give glory to our God, —*SEB* ... be the honour for ever and ever, —*FNTN,* —*HNT* ... be prayse for euer more, —*GNVA* ... be glorie world without end, —*RHEM* ... the ages of the ages, —*PNIN,* —*WLSN,* —*WEYM.*

**4:20.** In the light of the insights Paul shared above and the wonderful promise specified in the previous verse, one can understand Paul's sudden outburst in verse 20. Contemplating all this, he broke forth in a beautiful doxology.

**21. Salute every saint in Christ Jesus:** ... Remember me to, —*WLMS* ... Greet, —*ADAM* ... Give my greetings, in the fellowship of Christ Jesus, —*NEB* ... Greetings to every true Christian, —*PHLP* ... Greet each believer who is in union with Messiah Jesus, —*WAY* ... My Christian greetings to every one of God's people, —*WEYM* ... everyone who is holy, —*BECK* ... euery holi man, —*WCLF* ... to all our fellow-Christians, —*TCNT* ... to every one of God's dedicated people, —*BRCL.*

**The brethren which are with me greet you:** ... The brothers beside me salute you, —*MOFT* ... send you their good wishes, —*TCNT* ... send their greetings, —*WEYM* ... wish to be remembered to you, —*WLMS* ... would like to send their best wishes, —*PHLP.*

**4:21.** The New Testament term *saints* relates to all Christians. In this verse the term literally reads "every saint" (*panta hagion*). The Greek word for the term normally is an adjective and indicates a quality of a person. It relates to being "holy" or "sanctified" and basically describes a person set apart for God's service. The word also can be used of objects dedicated to the service of the Lord, much like the furnishings of the Old Testament tabernacle or temple. Several "brethren" were with Paul at the time he wrote this epistle, and the apostle used the words *saints* and *brothers* interchangeably.

**22. All the saints salute you:** . . . All the holy, —*FNTN* . . . All God's people, —*WEYM* . . . people here greet you, —*SEB* . . . wish to be remembered to you, —*NORL*, —*WLMS.*

**chiefly they that are of Caesar's household:** . . . but especially, —*RTHM* . . . especially the Imperial slaves, —*MOFT* . . . those who belong to, —*HNT* . . . the members of the Emperor's household, —*WLMS* . . . those who belong to the imperial establishment, —*NEB* . . . of Caesar's court, —*BRKL* . . . of Caesar's family, —*SAWR.*

**4:22.** In this verse Paul switched his terminology to "all the saints" (*pantes hoi hagioi*). He must have been referring to all the believers in Rome, many of whom he had met during his 2-year imprisonment.

Paul's brief note about the saints within the household of Caesar in itself speaks volumes to the world. Nero, one of the most infamous of the Caesars, was ruling at that time. It is very doubtful that Nero had heard very much about Paul at the time Paul wrote these words. While we cannot be sure exactly what happened, Paul's case may have been dismissed because of the expiration of the statute of limitations. Apparently, if a case was not settled within 2 years, it was dismissed. Ironically, Paul who may have been obscure to Nero has won far more fame down though the centuries than all the Caesars combined.

**23. The grace of our Lord Jesus Christ [be] with you all. Amen:** . . . The spiritual blessing of, —*WLMS* . . . May the gracious love of, —*SEB* . . . be with your spirit, —*CLMT*, —*ADAM*, —*HNT.*

**4:23.** After exchanging greetings, Paul spelled out the reason it is possible for a person to cope with life and still possess the joy of the Lord. One word in the apostle's last statement serves as the answer—"grace." Invariably, Paul seemed to feel compelled to summarize his writings with some reference to God's grace. Perhaps the personal miracle God performed for him was the main reason for that practice. If anyone deserved the judgment of God, he knew he did, but instead God had manifested His grace to him.

# COLOSSIANS

## Overview

The city of Colossae, with its neighboring cities Hierapolis and Laodicea, was situated in the Lycus Valley in the south of Phrygia. During the time of the apostles this territory belonged to the Roman province of Asia. Colossae was the oldest of the three. Though it had once been a great city, now it was overshadowed by its sister cities.

Paul had not visited the churches in the Lycus Valley, but evidently many of the members of the Colossae church knew him personally from his ministry in Ephesus which was situated in the same province (see Acts 19:10). Epaphras, a native of Colossae and one of Paul's coworkers, founded the church in Colossae and perhaps others in neighboring cities as well.

What prompted Paul to write this epistle? First, Epaphras had visited the apostle while he was in prison and told him of problems the church was experiencing. Second, Paul was moved by the Holy Spirit to write a letter addressing these problems and the issue of false teachers in the church. (See the section below titled "The Colossian Heresy.")

According to the tradition of the Ancient Church, Paul wrote this epistle from Rome, as he did the letters to Philemon and the Ephesians. The close connection with these two epistles is obvious. In the Epistle to Philemon many names are repeated. And more than one-fourth of the Epistle to the Colossians' content is found in the Epistle to the Ephesians.

Apart from its opening and close, Colossians contains three main sections: teaching on the person of Christ in the second half of chapter 1; a polemic on freedom in Christ from human regulations in chapter 2; and admonition toward practical Christian living in chapter 3 and the early part of chapter 4. One main theme pervades the Epistle to the Colossians: Christ is presented as the supreme image and Head of all things—in the natural world and the spiritual realm. Christians, united with Him, are freed from sin and live out that freedom in holy behavior and loving relationships.

## Outline of the Epistle

I. GREETING AND PRAYER (1:1-14)

II. TEACHING (1:15-29)

    A. The Person of Christ (1:15-19)

    B. The Work of Christ (1:20-23)

    C. The Tool of Christ (1:24-29)

III. POLEMIC (2:1-23)

    A. The Mystery of God (2:1-5)

    B. The Wisdom of the World (2:6-8)

    C. The Complete Salvation (2:9-15)

    D. The Rudiments of the World (2:16-23)

IV. ADMONITION (3:1-4:6)

    A. Seek That Which Is Above (3:1-4)

    B. Mortify the Earthly Members (3:5-11)

    C. A New Life (3:12-17)

    D. Rules for Households (3:18-4:1)

    E. Prayer and Supplication (4:2-4)

    F. Those Who Are Without (4:5, 6)

V. CLOSING AND PERSONAL GREETINGS (4:7-18)

## The Colossian Heresy

Colossians was written as a polemic, and this is important to understanding it fully. Like Galatians, Colossians was sent to combat heresy that threatened to disrupt and possibly destroy the church. But Colossians is much milder than Galatians as a polemic. This is due, in part, to the Colossians' resistance to the heresy they faced, whereas the Galatian church had allowed the false teachers an entrance and were already being deceived. Paul could give thanks for the Colossians and praise them for their faith, hope, and love (1:3ff.). He commended them for their orderliness and firm faith (2:5). Yet the apostle was very concerned that the Colossian believers were in great danger of being taken captive by vain philosophy (2:8). So he wrote to instruct and encourage them.

Paul does not name or explain in any detail the heresy in the Colossian church. This suggests that we do not have to understand a delusion or heresy to know and believe the truth. The Christology of this epistle belongs to the highest form of polemics and preaching in the New Testament. It rises far above its polemic intent, however, and exalts Christ in a unique way. Paul combats the Colossian heresy in an edifying manner. He presents the "cosmic Christ" as the source and goal of creation and redemption. He opens perspectives far beyond the issue of correcting some heretics in a small church in Phrygia. And he gives to the believers in Colossae, and us, a view of Christ that no other book does.

It is wrong, however, to view the epistle without considering the heresy Paul addressed. Though the content does focus on the person of Christ, modern readers must understand the controversy to fully appreciate that focus. The "Colossian delusion," like the Galatian heresy, is alive and among us today. Though it may be disguised in different wrappings, the dogma of syncretism never changes. An admixture of religious beliefs threatened the church in Colossae; this is what the epistle addressed.

## Heresies Facing the Early Church

Two basic aberrations of Christian doctrine faced the Early Church. One came from the Jewish religion and consisted of a mixture of Law and gospel. In Galatians, written much earlier, Paul strongly opposed this delusion. He called it "another gospel" which was no gospel at all but a distortion of the true gospel of Christ. The second attack came from Gentile philosophy, the so-called "wisdom" of men. In First Corinthians Paul wrote that the infiltration of Gentile thoughts and ideas would oppose the power of the gospel. Faith and "wisdom" are just as incompatible as faith and works of the Law.

The church in Corinth was threatened by infiltration from Greek philosophy—the "wisdom of men." The Galatian churches had been invaded by Jewish legalists teaching salvation by "works of the Law." Here in Colossae the church was under attack by a form of heterodoxy that included both Greek philosophy and Jewish legalism. This is clear from Paul's description of the heresy—it consisted of a mixture of Jewish and Gentile elements.

The specific content of the Colossian heresy is difficult to determine. Judging from the content of the messages to the churches in Revelation 2 and 3, various heresies gradually penetrated the churches in Asia Minor before the end of the First Century. In Ephesus there were some who said they were Jews but really were the synagogue of Satan (Revelation 2:9). In Thyatira the woman Jezebel, who called herself a "prophetess," taught and seduced believers to "commit fornication, and to eat things sacrificed unto idols" (Revelation 2:20). In Pergamos, some held to "the doctrine of Balaam" and "the doctrine of the Nicolatians" (Revelation 2:14, 15). Long before this Paul had warned the elders in Ephesus that after his departure false teachers would appear. Some of these would come from outside, but others would arise from within the Church (Acts 20:29, 30).

Among the Jewish religious forms existing at this time in Asia Minor was a group of John's disciples. These imitators of John the Baptist can be traced far into the Christian Era. Paul met this group during his visit to Ephesus (Acts 19:1-3).

The First Century experienced a tremendous variety of religious transition and upheaval. Christianity was affected by many "voices." Some aided the Church's growth, while others threatened its existence as the true expression of Christ's body. Though there are distinct differences in the heresies in Corinth, the churches in Galatia, and that in Colossae, there are common elements as well. For example, the "delusion in Colossae" and the "delusion in Galatia" contain Judaistic elements that are similar. Greek philosophy found in the Corinthian "wisdom" parallels the "philosophy" that sought to invade the church in Colossae.

The form of Judaism which had become Christian and had penetrated the Galatian churches had its origin in Jerusalem (Galatians 2:4; compare Acts 15:24). But the Judaistic tendencies in Colossae had another source because they were not the same as the original Palestinian doctrine. They may have come from the immediate local situation. The Jewish colony in Colossae was old. Two centuries earlier Antiochus the Great had deported 2,000 Jewish families to Phrygia (Josephus, *Antiquities of the Jews,* 12:3:4). During the long exile these Jews had adopted some of the practices and doctrine of the Gentiles, and their orthodox Jewish brethren were displeased with this. The Talmud (*Shabbath,* 147b.) has sometimes been quoted to substantiate this orthodox dissatisfaction: "The wine of Perugitha and the water of Diomsith cut off the Ten Tribes from Israel!" The name Perugitha is understood as Phrygia, and if this is correct, the Phrygian Jews were considered as belonging to the 10 tribes.

The Jewish Diaspora was often influenced by the philosophies and beliefs of their environment. One example is the Jewish philosopher Philo from Alexander (circa 30 B.C. to A.D. 50). He attempted to form a synthesis of Hebrew faith in God and Greek philosophy. His disciples spread his ideas widely.

Lightfoot poses an interesting theory in his commentary (pp. 81-113). He suggests the Colossian heresy can be traced to the sect of the Essenes. Lightfoot says there are pre-Gnostic features found in the Essenes' beliefs, and that they displayed a Gnostic Judaism. He believes this special form of Judaism secured a foothold in this part of Asia Minor during the time of the apostle.

These theories have some support in the Qumran texts. W.D. Davies lists the similarities as: linguistic peculiarities, calendar correspondences, Sabbath rules, and decisions concerning food and asceticism. Also, there is a strong emphasis on wisdom and knowledge which includes a special worldview and angel doctrine. But we do not find in the Epistle to the Colossians any mention of the ritual bath of the Essenes. F.F. Bruce thinks the Qumran texts do not support a connection between the sect of the Essenes or the Qumran community and the Colossian heresy. He instead adopts Matthew Black's formulation of a nonconformist Judaism (*New International Commentary* on the New Testament, Colossians, Philemon, and Ephesians, p. 23).

It is evident there had existed a great variety of groups and beliefs in the Jewish religion, and not the least in the Diaspora. We discover in Acts traces of Judaism mixed with occultism. Acts 13:4-12 tells of a Jewish sorcerer and false prophet who opposed Paul's preaching of the gospel. Acts 19:13-16 describes Jewish conjurers who tried to use the name of Jesus as Paul had done (compare Matthew 7:22). Luke says these exorcists were sons of a Jewish high priest. When they were overcome by the evil spirit of a possessed man, many in Ephesus became Christians and confessed they had been occupied with the same practice of "curious arts." They brought their books of sorcery and burned them, disassociating themselves from all such things.

Occultism had gained admittance into certain Jewish groups and could also easily infiltrate the new and possibly naive Christian congregations. Magic was perceived as the ability to force evil beings to submit or flee by the use of superior means. Often that means was superior spiritual beings who had authority over the lower beings that roamed the earth and tormented or possessed men. This kind of necromancy was forbidden in Israel but was common in paganism. It was this heresy that seemed to be threatening the church in Colossae. Paul speaks of the "principalities and powers" and warns against the worship of angels (2:15, 18).

Here is an important feature of the possible heresy in Colossae. As already noted, there was probably an admixture of Jewish legalism and Gentile philosophy as the basis for the Colossian heresy. But each of these had unique characteristics. The Judaism that appeared in Colossae was not the Pharisaic orthodoxy that Jesus confronted in the Gospels. Likewise, the Gentile "wisdom" preached in Colossae was not the same as the rational, intellectual, Greek wisdom which appeared in Corinth. In the Colossian heresy we discern an element of mysticism that later became a dominant characteristic of gnosticism in the Second Century.

Such a fusion of different religious and philosophical elements had already taken place in some forms of Judaism and Gentile systems of thought. The First Century was characterized by syncretism. This mixture of religions was a product of the new age brought about by the removal of the East-West barrier. Alexander the Great marched his armies to the East. Later on the Roman Empire united the Occident and the Orient. When the old Greek and Roman gods lost their appeal, the time was ripe for a fusion of the East's religions and the West's philosophy. Mystery religions of the Orient made their entry into the religious life and thinking of the West. Because Colossae was situated on a commercial route between East and West, it was susceptible to "new" and "different" patterns of thought.

## Angel Worship and the Colossian Church

The new age had the distinctive stamp of an idolatry that had been "spiritualized." It was more insidious than the idolatry that worshiped graven images of stone or precious metals. This worship of spiritual powers replaced tangible idols with "principalities and powers" that were conjured in the mind. Many such "worshipers" shunned pictures and monuments of their gods. They sought to contact the "powers" directly.

This "worshipping of angels" threatened to penetrate and destroy the true worship of the church in Colossae (2:18). Paul wrote his polemic against this because it concerned a form of religion which was disguised by its spirituality. The old idolatry was clearly discerned by its use of tangible idols. The new idolatry was aimed toward spiritual beings and therefore appeared more legitimate.

Even the Jews, who turned away from image worship with disgust, could give the angels such an elevated position that it would be considered worship. Philo maintained that the angels participated in creation. Justin Martyr wrote of Jewish teachers who preached that man's outward form had been prepared by angels. These teachers maintained that when God said, "Let us make man," He spoke to angels (Genesis 1:26). Among the Nag Hammadi texts has been found a saying that some of the Jewish sects taught that God has created all which exists, while others said that "the multitude of the angels stood by him and they received from the powers the seven substances . . . in order to create" (The Apocryphon of John, 2:1:15).

It was a frightful and dangerous thought that man could see an angel as his creator. Such a view was no less dangerous when fitted into a Gentile philosophical train of thought in the First Century. It was an old Greek view that material substance was so unholy that God could have nothing to do with it. The false teachers in Colossae were saying the angels or "powers" created the material world, and man could only be delivered from his bodily imprisonment by these same powers (H.M. Carson, Tyndale New Testament Commentaries, 12:16).

One view held that these powers (angels) controlled the connection links between heaven and earth (Bruce, New International Commentary on the New Testament, Colossians, Philemon, and Ephesians, p. 26). Angels became the mediators for man, bringing men divine revelation and carrying their prayers to God. There was even an extreme view that Christ himself had to submit to the authority of the prince of angels on His way from heaven to earth. By extension, this same view would put Christ under the authority of this "power" when He returned to heaven.

A strong objection must be registered against this artificial product of fantasy. It is a doctrine that reduces the person and work of Christ. Instead of being the one and unique Son, Christ becomes one of the many. He who is the Creator is placed on a level with the creature.

Many of those who had listened with interest to the heretics in Colossae had very little understanding of the consequences which the new doctrine produced. But Paul was aware of them. He understood that the primary thing in jeopardy was their salvation; someone was about to "beguile" them of the "reward" (2:18). This was a serious matter. So when Paul wrote his epistle, he did not explain any details of the preaching of the heretics. His readers had a good understanding of it, but Paul did oppose the heresy in several particulars. He did this polemically by rejecting the heresy. But first and more importantly he addressed the heresy by teaching the supremacy of Christ.

This heresy confronting the Colossians, both in its contents and its consequences, was one of the most dangerous heterodoxies that ever attacked the Church. Though the heresy was first found in a special form and unique to Colossae, it represented something much more than a local phenomenon. First, it was a mixture of the Gentile doctrine of wisdom that threatened to infiltrate many of the Gentile churches. Second, this delusion contained the germ of the later Gnostic heresy which in the Second Century caused such havoc in the Church.

The characteristic feature of so many delusions is that they offer believers something more than that which they already have in Christ. They imply that what Christ has done is not enough and needs something additional. That was the teaching of the Judaistic seducers in Galatia. The heretics in Colossae seem to have presented the same falsehood that what Christ gives is not enough. The fullness of life in God could not, in their opinion, be achieved through Jesus Christ only. It must be sought through works of the Law, asceticism, worshiping of angels, and a special, secret knowledge. The Colossian heresy represented an attempt to achieve a higher level of spirituality than other believers had attained. Implied was the need for a total change of attitude concerning Christianity.

This was exactly what early gnosticism taught. The idea was that one could "improve" on Christianity. This later developed into a bitter controversy. But even in its early form, gnosticism was no less dangerous, though perhaps more disguised. During the First Century gnosticism was more of a religious-philosophical attitude than a system of belief in a finished form. That is why it could easily adapt to Gentile or Jewish groups and find admittance to Christian churches. Thus the "wisdom" in Corinth showed a face different from that seen in Colossae. Yet Corinth was not without certain features of the early Gnostic heresy. One example was the Greek idea of indifference to the body, which led to sexual immorality. The Gnostics taught that since the body was evil, what was done with the body was inconsequential. In Colossae the false teachers went to the opposite extreme and demanded asceticism and ill-treatment of the body.

In these two extremes the Gnostics attempted to solve the problem of physical embodiment: either they ignored the body as insignificant and consigned to licentiousness, or they tried to suppress the body with rigid asceticism. The Christian churches troubled by this heresy were in a twin danger; the extremes of the heresy were very confusing. Paul warned the church against both extremes. First he attacked the tendencies of the Colossian church to succumb to adding works of the Law and the wisdom of men to salvation. Then he listed in the admonition section of the Colossian epistle a comprehensive "vice-catalog" and warned the believers against the sins which bring God's wrath on the children of disobedience. But he made it clear that the Colossian Christians no longer lived in such practices. So there is no real indication of moral sin or ethical problems in the church at Colossae.

But this infiltration of Gentile "wisdom" and Jewish "law-keeping" was a matter of great concern. In the Colossian church there was significant evidence of these problems, and Paul addressed these with apostolic earnestness.

## "The Rudiments of the World"

It is obvious that Jewish teachers of the Law had gained access to the Colossian church. These legalists agitated for strict adherence to certain rules of the Mosaic law (2:16). They may have attempted to introduce the separation of clean and unclean animals (compare Leviticus 11). They sought to obligate others to keep the calendar of Jewish feasts (compare Leviticus 23) and the day of the new moon (see Numbers 10:10; 28:11). They taught that Gentile Christians should keep the Jewish Sabbath (compare Exodus 20:8-11; 31:14-16). Paul opposed all of this and showed that it was but a shadow of that which should come (compare Hebrews 8:5; 10:1). It belonged to the tradition of men (2:8), and Christ died to deliver believers from all this. Christians are no longer subject to "rudiments of the world" because they are "dead with Christ" (2:20). Paul asks, "Why, as though living in the world, are ye subject to ordinances, (touch not; taste not; handle not; which all are to perish with the using;) after the commandments and doctrines of men?" (2:20).

The Greek term behind "rudiments" is *stoicheion* which means "an element" or "first principle" and was used, for example, of the letters of the alphabet as basic elements of speech. As is usually the case, the meaning of *stoicheion* is controlled by its context. In Hebrews 5:12 *stoicheion* is used to mean the first principles or ABCs found in the Word of God.

Opinions differ as to what Paul meant when he used the expression "the rudiments of the world." The two most widely accepted positions which have surfaced in the discussion are: (1) that Paul used it in reference to the Law (Galatians 4:3, 9) or worldly philosophy (Colossians 2:8, 20). Adam Clarke suggests that Paul, in Galatians 4:3, is adapting a Jewish phrase concerning the Jewish teachers' explanation of the Law (*Clarke's Commentary*, 6:403). When this is called the "tradition of men" (2:8), Clarke thinks it must be understood against the background of the Hebrew expression *haolam hazzeh* which is translated literally by the Greek expression *tou kosmon toutou* (ibid., 6:523). This is often used to signify the Jewish system of rites and ceremonies. In Hebrews 7:16-18 the Law is characterized as "the law of a carnal commandment" which has "weakness and unprofitableness." Paul also refers to the "weak and beggarly elements" in Galatians 4:9.

Furthermore, some interpreters who promote this first position believe *stoicheion* stands for the Gnostic or proto-Gnostic philosophers' teaching. This view is found among other writers in antiquity. Tertullian (A.D. 145-220) wrote that Paul warned the Colossians they must beware of the seducing philosophy or *stoicheion* of this world "not understanding thereby the mundane fabric of sky and earth but worldly learning, and 'the traditions of men,' subtle in their speech and their philosophy" (*Against Marcion*, 5:19). Those commentators who understand *stoicheion* to be the rudimentary teachings of the Law or heathen philosophy, which would enslave believers and nullify the freedom of the gospel would include: A.T. Robertson (p. 117); J.B. Lightfoot (p. 180); C. F. D. Moule (p. 91); and W. Hendriksen (*New Testament Commentary, Colossians and Philemon*, pp. 109f.).

(2) In more recent times a second position has arisen which views *stoicheion* in the Epistle to the Galatians and the Epistle to the Colossians to mean "spiritual powers" which, according to the astrological views of that time, ruled over the heavenly bodies and the elements of earth, fire, air, and water. Such a view makes a connection between these "spiritual powers" and the angels which were worshiped in the church at Colossae. However, it is impossible to know for certain how

much of this was included in the Gentile philosophical teaching that was attacking the first-century Christian churches. It is true, however, that not one instance can be found of *stoicheion* being used to refer to demons or spiritual powers at this time. The silence of Clement of Alexandria and Tertullian on this point suggests they were unaware of this interpretation. Those scholars who hold to this view include: F.W. Beare (p. 101) and E.F. Scott (*Moffatt's New Testament Commentary, Colossians, Philemon, and Ephesians*, p. 43). As F.F. Bruce states, regardless of the precise nature of this heretical teaching, for the Colossian Christians to accept it would be a sign of "spiritual retrogression" (*New International Commentary on the New Testament, Colossians, Philemon, and Ephesians*, p. 99).

Although opinions differ as to the meaning of this special Greek term, all agree that the Colossian heresy involved worship of angels. This is one of the things Paul strongly argued against in this epistle. It is puzzling that he connected the worship of angels with humility. What relationship is found in the two? Perhaps it was because the false teachers said man was too insignificant and unworthy to appear before God directly. Any approach or appeal to God must be mediated through angels. This assumes the angels that were worshiped were good angels. But the practice was not more acceptable because of this.

Hendriksen calls on several witnesses to testify to the actual practice of angel worship in these times and territories. First, the church father Theodoret said in his commentary on Colossians 2:18: "The disease which Paul denounces, continued for a long time in Phrygia and Pisidia." Second, Irenaeus stated that the true church opposed this practice. In his work titled *Against Heresies*, Irenaeus assured his readers that one does not call on angels or use other evil tricks, but he directs his prayer to the Lord who has made all things. Third, in the year A.D. 363 the Synod in Laodicea, a neighboring city of Colossae, declared: "It is not right for Christians to abandon the church of God and go away to invoke angels." Fourth, according to W.M. Ramsey, the archangel Michael was worshiped widely in Asia Minor, and this went on for centuries. As late as A.D. 739 the victory over the Saracens was ascribed to the assistance of Michael. He was also given credit for miraculous healings (Hendriksen, *New Testament Commentary, Colossians and Philemon*, p. 126).

In occult circles there were many different concepts concerning spiritual powers worthy of worship. They were sometimes considered benevolent assistants, some kind of "fellow-redeemers" who made the work of Christ perfect. Others considered these spiritual powers as mighty opposers who had to be placated so they did not hinder men from reaching God. This was all done through "*gnosis*." Within "*gnosis*" is something far more than intellectual knowledge. It involves a secret insight that is won through mysterious and mystical experiences. In effect, this "*gnosis*" is the only way men can reach God and perfection. And it is aided by spiritual powers that guard admittance to God.

Paul wielded his full apostolic authority and spiritual power against this idea. His message was: There are no secret paths to God prepared for a select few. There is just one way, and it is open to all. The primary weapon Paul used against occult syncretism was the mighty preaching of Christ. Paul sets a convincing argument and positive teaching against the delusion that threatens the Colossian church.

Each age has its domineering form of occultism, whether it is the mystery religions of ancient time, the sorcery of the middle ages, or the pseudo-religious witchcraft of the present. Each age boasts its own intellectualism or science or philosophy. But during the changing epochs of time the Epistle to the Colossians has stood in sharp contrast with its unchangeable message focused on Christ, God's key to the secrets of the universe. Christ is the Creator and Sustainer of all things. He is Lord of and far above all powers in heaven and on earth. In Him are all the treasures of wisdom and knowledge.

## The Christology of the Epistle to the Colossians

In its purest essence the Epistle to the Colossians is a Christological discussion of cosmic dimensions. Inspired by the Spirit, Paul discussed the relationship between Christ and God, Christ's connection with creation, and Christ's headship of the Church. It must be said here that the expression "the cosmic Christ," a designation used by some, must not be misunderstood. Paul is not presenting a "Christ of the Philosophers." As he does in all his other epistles, the apostle presents the crucified Christ as the focus of God's plan for the universe.

The Christology of the epistle refutes the syncretistic delusion that had infiltrated the church at Colossae. This shows once more that Christian doctrine is often formed in the struggle against heresy. It was not just on a theoretical or theological basis that Paul wrote about these great themes in this letter. What kindled the inspired presentation was a real need in a small and vulnerable church, in danger of being seduced by clever propagandists. The preaching of Christ as the mystery of God—the center of creation and redemption—was the apostle's reply to the present need of the church. The church itself was stretching to see Christ as supreme. That such a tremendous presentation of the person and work of Christ could be made in a few short chapters is a wonder of inspiration.

## Christ's Deity

### The Preexistent Christ

Paul named Christ as the mystery of God and began his Christology by discussing Christ's relationship with God. What he presented had not even entered the heart and thought of man. Paul received it by revelation from the Holy Spirit who searches and knows the deep things of God (1 Corinthians 2:6-10). The eternal, Triune God unveiled the secrets of His being to His creation. The mystery is not that there is something hidden in God. What is most amazing is that we have such a clear knowledge of this Triune God! This knowledge, though far from perfect because of our limited human understanding, is revealed to us in Holy Scripture.

Paul reveals inter-Trinitarian relationship when he writes of Christ's place in the Godhead. Christ is the Son of God and the beloved of God (1:13). He is "the image of the invisible God," the perfect and completely valid expression of what God is (Colossians 1:15; compare Hebrews 1:3). He is the firstborn of all creation (1:15); He has no genesis; yet He is before all things (1:17). This echoes God's proclamation of His name to Moses, "I AM" (Exodus 3:14; compare John 1:1).

The allusion to the wisdom in Proverbs 8 and 9 is unmistakable. Here and elsewhere in the Wisdom literature wisdom is personified. It is more than a divine qualification. It is a divine Person. The wisdom of God has existed as long as God has existed—for all eternity. The Hebrew term *qānāh* has many shades of meaning. It can mean to buy or win something for oneself. It can mean create or take possession of something through a symbolic action. But *qānāh* can also mean to own, to have something in one's possession. It is obvious this is how the term should be understood in Proverbs 8:22. The Lord neither created nor bought this wisdom. He possessed it from the beginning, from eternity.

### The Incarnated Christ

The Son existed before He entered His human existence. All thought of Incarnation without preexistence is first without meaning and second without Biblical support. Incarnation did not mean that a new individual of mankind had arisen but that an eternal, divine Person had entered the sphere of human life. John 1:14 says, "The Word was made flesh." The Incarnation means God was revealed in flesh (see 1 Timothy 3:16).

Paul emphasized to the Colossians that God's fullness resides in Jesus Christ (1:19; 2:9). This is a mystery, and because of this Christ is called the "mystery of God" (2:2). Jesus Christ is all that God is. Secondly, Paul emphasized the true humanity of Jesus. Though the fullness of God dwells bodily in Him (2:9), reconciliation took place "in the body of his flesh" (1:22). The reference here is not to a body that seems to be or looks like a body; it is an actual physical body. The Incarnation involved the deity of Christ (the fullness of the Godhead) and the humanity of Christ (His entering the human race through natural birth). This is the true God (1 John 5:20), found in the body and nature of a man.

## The Glorified Christ

The preexistent and incarnated Christ is now the glorified Christ (3:1-4). Paul emphasized three things: (1) Christ is risen from the dead (3:1). (2) Christ is "above," He "sitteth on the right hand of God" (3:1). (3) At His return Christ will be revealed in glory (3:4). Christ includes His people in all this. They are dead with Him (3:3), risen with Him (3:1), hid with Him (3:3), and will be revealed with Him when He returns (3:4).

## Christ in Creation

Paul explained Christ's connection with creation by saying He is the firstborn of every creature (1:15). He is before everything in time and above all in authority. He created that which is visible as well as that which is invisible. This includes the principalities and powers which the heretics in Colossae wanted to place on an equal or even higher level than Christ. Paul used three phrases to describe the creation work of Christ.

## By Him Were All Things Created (1:16)

When speaking of Christ's connection with creation in Romans 11:36, Paul said, "For of him, and through him, and to him, are all things." Here in 1:16 it is changed to "by him" which is stronger yet. It is the same expression Paul used in his sermon at Athens: "In him we live, and move, and have our being" (Acts 17:28). Christ is the One who creates and sustains the creation. In the beginning He spoke everything into existence. Now He upholds everything by the power of His word (compare Hebrews 1:3). As Creator and Sustainer, Christ is the fountain of our existence.

## All Things Were Created by Him (1:16)

Christ is the mediator of creation. God said, "Let us make man." And Christ is the One who executed the command of God. John tells us: "All things were made by him; and without him was not any thing made that was made" (John 1:3). The word translated "by" in John 1:3 and Colossians 1:16 is *dia* and means "by, through, by means of." Creation was brought into existence through the action of Christ.

## All Things Were Created for Him (1:16)

He who is the beginning is also the end. Christ did not create to give the creation to someone else. It will be His eternal possession. He will never abandon it. When His creation was lost because of sin, He came to earth to win it back. One day the sacrificed Lamb will be handed the deed to the redeemed creation (Revelation 5:1-10; compare Jeremiah 32:11). Creation exists because of Christ. It is His by the first act of creation and His by the final act of redemption.

## Christ in Redemption

The third major point in this Christology of the Epistle to the Colossians is the place of Christ in redemption. This doctrine of Soteriology is remarkably complete.

## The Means of Redemption

Redemption was effected by "the blood of his cross" (1:20) and "in the body of his flesh" (1:22). Through this the demand of God's righteousness is satisfied and the handwriting of ordinances is blotted out because Christ nailed it to the cross (2:14). Because of this, we have redemption, the forgiveness of sins (Colossians 1:14; compare Ephesians 1:7). This redemption and forgiveness is received by faith and demonstrated in water baptism (2:12). Everyone who continues in the Faith will achieve the goal the gospel gives: to be presented "holy and unblamable and unreprovable in his sight" (1:22, 23).

## The Victory of Christ Over the Enemy

The victory of Christ over spiritual powers stands as a triumphant contrast to that which the heretics in Colossae obviously taught. It seems these heretics maintained that Christ had to give up part of His authority to rulers or powers in the heavens on His way from heaven to earth (at the time of the Incarnation). Later on these same powers forced the suffering of Christ on the cross. This argument was used as a proof that certain spiritual powers stood above Christ in authority and power. But Paul says that the opposite is the case. It was not the evil powers that were triumphant when Christ suffered and died on the cross. It was Christ who conquered the powers and authorities and made a show of them openly in their defeat (2:15).

## Christ in You

By the work of Christ the believer is delivered from the power of darkness and translated into the kingdom of the beloved Son of God (1:13). This means that Christ is now among and in believers (2:17). This life-changing experience has its origin in our union with Christ who is Saviour and Lord (2:19). As Paul moves into the admonition segment of the epistle, he has as its starting point that believers are dead and risen with Christ (3:1ff.).

Rather than giving a higher revelation of the truth or shedding light on the apostolic preaching, the heresy of the false teachers consisted of a worthless mixture of religious substitutes. It is but an apparent wisdom, something which may gain a reputation for wisdom, but which does not contain true values.

In Jesus Christ are hid all the treasures of wisdom and knowledge (2:3).

# The Epistle of Paul to the Colossians

## Commentary

### Chapter 1

**1. Paul, an apostle of Jesus Christ by the will of God:** . . . Paul-appointed through God's will, —WAY . . . messenger of, —PHLP . . . by the pleasure of, —MRDK . . . through the will of, —WEYM . . . God wanted me to be an apostle of Christ, —SEB.

**and Timotheus [our] brother:** . . . brother Timothy, —PHLP.

**1:1.** Colossians begins with the typical salutation of the day: the name of the writer or writers, the name of the recipient or recipients of the letter, and a few words of greeting. In the opening statement, Paul probably had at least two reasons for designating himself an apostle. Unlike the Philippians, the Colossians did not know him personally. Furthermore, he was writing to refute the serious unscriptural gnosticism that had crept into the assembly. As an apostle he was an official representative of the Saviour himself and was clothed with His authority.

At the very outset of this epistle Paul linked his office and call to the will of God. He had certainly not chosen this position for himself. Note also the manner in which he connected himself with Christ Jesus. He literally belonged to Christ as His representative.

The use of the term "Jesus Christ" at the very outset may have been a deliberate attempt to emphasize the exalted position of Jesus. The Gnostics constantly endeavored to denigrate the deity of Christ by seeking to rob Him of His full majesty. It is interesting to note that Paul did not use the name of Jesus by itself in the entire epistle. He would have nothing to do with the mentality that relegated Jesus to anything less than true God and true man. Although Paul mentioned Timothy as being with him, it is not certain that Timothy served as secretary on this occasion.

**2. To the saints and faithful brethren in Christ which are at Colosse:** . . . To Christ's People, —TCNT . . . to all faithful Christians, —PHLP . . . To the people of God, —WEYM . . . to God's consecrated ones in . . . to the brothers who are still true to their union with Messiah, —WAY . . . to the consecrated . . . who are in union with, —WLMS . . . holi and feithful brotheren, —WCLF . . . to the holy and faithful

fellow believers, —BECK . . . to the holy and believing brothers, —MNTG . . . believing brethren, —CNDT.

**Grace [be] unto you, and peace, from God our Father and the Lord Jesus Christ:** . . . Favor and Peace, —WLSN . . . Blessing, —FNTN . . . May gracious love and peace come to you from, —SEB . . . be granted to you from, —WEYM.

**1:2.** "To the saints" refers to the status of the recipients of this letter, rather than to a degree of holiness attained. The second half of the title could be translated either "faithful brothers" or "believing brothers," although the first makes more sense because the second would be redundant. The most important fact expressed is that they were "in Christ," or "lived in the realm of Christ," as people related to Him through the new birth. As he normally did, Paul combined the Greek greeting "grace" and the Hebrew greeting "peace."

**3. We give thanks to God and the Father of our Lord Jesus Christ:** . . . I want you to know by this letter, —PHLP . . . We constantly give thanks, —BRKL . . . I am continually thanking God, —MNTG.

**praying always for you:** . . . Every time we pray, —WLMS . . . We are always praying, —SEB . . . when we pray for you, —ADAM, —MOFT . . . constantly praying for you, —WEYM, —PHLP . . . at all times in your behalf praying, —RTHM.

**1:3.** Also, according to his normal custom, the apostle followed his greeting with a sincere thanksgiving to God for the believers to whom he was writing. He and his associates thanked God for the Colossians relative to four matters. This verse gives a good pattern for people to follow when they pray. It should be preceded by thanksgiving.

**4. Since we heard of your faith in Christ Jesus:** . . . whenever we do we thank God . . . because you believe, —PHLP.

**and of the love [which ye have] to all the saints:** . . . and of your love for all God's people, —WLMS . . . you are showing true Christian love toward other Christians, —PHLP . . . for all the fellow-Christians, —NORL . . . for all of the holy people, —SEB.

**1:4.** This verse introduces the specific items for which Paul thanked God when he thought of the Colossian Christians. First, he was grateful to God because they had placed their faith in Christ Jesus. Although there are many things for which Christians should thank God, none is more important than the one Paul listed first: faith in the Lord Jesus Christ. If a person does not have that, nothing else really counts for much. The apostle knew the Colossians had taken the first step, the step that definitely is the all-important one.

It is the Holy Spirit that makes faith in Christ possible, A person does not just decide to place his faith in the Lord. The Holy Spirit must first give the impetus. Even Jesus made it clear that a person cannot come to Him without this divine initiative (John 6:44). The whole process of salvation happens as a result of God's grace (Ephesians 2:8).

Secondly, the apostle and his associates thanked God always for the love the Colossians extended to all the saints. Their faith did not consist merely of verbal profession. They translated their confession of Jesus Christ into action, and this action was prompted by the love (*agapē*) that God alone is able to infuse into a person.

**5. For the hope which is laid up for you in heaven:** ... We know that you are showing these qualities because you have grasped the hope, *—PHLP* ... because of your hope of what is, *—WLMS* ... being preserved for you, *—WLSN* ... that is hidden away, *—SEB* ... which awaits fulfilment in Heaven, *—TCNT.*
**whereof ye heard before in the word of the truth of the gospel:** ... Long ago you heard of this hope through the message of, *—WLMS* ... that hope which first became yours when the truth was brought to you, *—PHLP* ... of which you previously heard in the plea for the truth of, *—FNTN* ... the truth of the joyful message, *—RTHM* ... in the Word of truth concerning the good news, *—ADAM.*

**1:5.** Thirdly, this faith and love results from hope which is based upon the gospel message received. "Hope" can either be subjective or objective, depending upon the context. As the word is used here, it is obviously objective. In other words, the salvation the Colossians already enjoyed also had a future aspect when God would consummate His promises to them. In a sense, they had received a down payment of God's blessings, but the remainder would be given in heaven.

Notice the manner in which Paul connected this hope with the gospel. From the very beginning (Genesis 3:15), people have cherished the hope that one day the Messiah would come to earth and remedy the sinful condition of mankind. Truly the simple gospel message that Jesus died, was buried, and rose again according to the Scriptures constitutes the greatest impetus to hope that mankind has ever known.

**6. Which is come unto you, as [it is] in all the world; and bringeth forth fruit, as [it doth] also in you:** ... which is present among you, *—SCLT* ... which reached you, and since it is bearing fruit and is growing among you, just as it is all over the world, *—WLMS* ... as also in the whole world it is bearing fruit and growing in the same way, *—ADAM* ... it produces Christian character, *—PHLP* ... It is producing fruit and increasing its influence, *—SEB.*

**since the day ye heard [of it], and knew the grace of God in truth:** ... from the day you first heard of God's favor and ... came to know it, *—WLMS* ... from the day you heard and truly recognised the Divine gift, *—FNTN* ... from the time you first heard and realized the amazing fact of God's grace, *—PHLP* ... and acknowledged the favor, *—WLSN* ... and truly knew, *—ADAM* ... and understood what that mercy really is, *—TCNT.*

**1:6.** Fourthly, the Colossians were producing fruit because they were permitting the gospel to work in them. Notice the beautiful progression in the four items for which the apostle and his associates always thanked God when they remembered the Colossians. Faith, love, and hope naturally should lead to fruit. Just as surely as a seed planted in soil will produce fruit if it is given the proper care, so the gospel will produce fruit where people allow it to do so. Paul made it clear in this verse that God's grace or unmerited favor is manifested to people as they accept the gospel and allow it to grow in their lives. Because all the benefits God bestows upon people come to them by grace through faith, continuous belief in the truth of the gospel is absolutely essential to the total process.

**7. As ye also learned of Epaphras our dear fellowservant:** ... You learned these things, we understand, *—PHLP* ... our dearly loved fellow-slave, *—WLMS.*
**who is for you a faithful minister of Christ:** ... who faithfully represents us as a minister, *—TCNT* ... who is in the same service as we are, *—PHLP.*

**1:7.** This verse is the first reference in this lovely epistle to the individual known as "Epaphras." The apostle designated him "our dear fellow servant" or "our beloved (*agapētou*) fellow slave." "Servant" or "slave" comes from the common New Testament word *doulos* which could denote a love-slave relationship. In other words, a person willingly dedicates himself to the Lord somewhat as a person would become a willing slave to another person. The term *bondslave* probably best expresses the idea. It is similar to the love-slave concept described in Exodus 21:1-6. Paul added the Greek preposition *sun* to the word "servant" that indicates being with someone, or being together in the sense of close relationship.

Epaphras also was a "faithful minister." "Minister" comes from the Greek term *diakonos* normally translated "deacon." Epaphras most likely was converted during the approximately 3 years Paul ministered in Ephesus (Acts 20:31), was trained in Paul's school, and returned to his hometown to begin a New Testament church.

**8. Who also declared unto us your love in the Spirit:** ... It is he who has told us about, *—NORL* ... who also related to us, *—WLSN* ... who also made evident to us, *—RTHM* ... it was from him that we heard about your growth in Christian love, *—PHLP* ... which is inspired by the Spirit, *—TCNT* ... who told me of the love awakened in you by, *—WLMS* ... hath manifested to us ... in the spirit, *—DOUY*.

**1:8.** There is a good possibility that Epaphras became the pastor of the assembly in Colossae. Epaphras was so in touch with the pulse of the assembly in Colossae that he was able to relate to the apostle what the latter called "your love in the Spirit." In the original language the term "Spirit" (*pneumati*) is not preceded by a definite article, but it still obviously refers to the Holy Spirit and not just to the human spirit.

**9. For this cause we also, since the day we heard [it], do not cease to pray for you:** ... This is why, *—WLMS* ... so you will understand that since we heard, *—PHLP* ... For this reason from the day I heard of it, *—MNTG*.

**and to desire that ye might be filled with the knowledge of his will:** ... and making request that, *—ALFD* ... and to ask that, *—NOYS* ... that ye myght be fulfylled, *—CRNM* ... and to ask that ye may be filled, *—NOYS* ... that ye may be filled up to the full-knowledge of, *—RTHM* ... as to the exact knowledge, *—WLSN*.

**in all wisdom and spiritual understanding:** ... with spiritual wisdom, *—TCNT* ... and spiritual insight, *—MNTG*.

**1:9.** Having expressed his gratitude to God for all these facts relayed to him by Epaphras, Paul then earnestly prayed for the Colossian saints. Paul's 218-word sentence in the original language begins at verse 9 and continues through verse 20. First, he prayed they would receive a greater knowledge of God's will. The term "filled" suggests the idea of filling to completeness. He wanted them to have a thorough or full knowledge (*epignōsis*) or an ever-increasing knowledge. Paul described a thorough knowledge which involved a deep, accurate, and comprehensive acquaintance with the way God expressed himself in the Bible.

Apparently the Colossians did not lack knowledge, but they were in need of help in the area of spiritual perception, without which they could be easily victimized by a system of thought that could undermine their whole experience with God. The Colossians already had some knowledge of God's will, but they needed more or a fuller development.

This full knowledge would consist of spiritual wisdom and understanding. The first of these two terms is a general word embracing the whole range of mental faculties, and the second term refers to insight which discriminates between the true and the false.

**10. That ye might walk worthy of the Lord unto all pleasing:** ... so that your manner of life may be, *—MNTG* ... that ye myght be fulfylled, *—CRNM* ... so as to please him, *—NOYS*.

**being fruitful in every good work:** ... by perennially bearing fruit, *—WLMS* ... by good actions of every kind, *—TCNT*.

**and increasing in the knowledge of God:** ... and growing in, *—WORL* ... may grow yet deeper, *—PHLP*.

**1:10.** Paul's second petition is a consequence of the first. The knowledge of God is not imparted to be an end in itself, but is given to enable believers to live in a manner worthy of the Lord. To "walk worthy of the Lord" means in general to live a life commensurate with what the Lord has done for a person. Doctrine and ethics were inseparable to Paul. Right knowledge should lead to right behavior. The Greek word translated "worthy" (*axiōs*) often was used in connection with a pair of scales in which the item on one side should weigh as much as the item on the other side.

Paul did not imply that believers can ever repay the Lord for what He has done for them. On the other hand, it would be a real affront to Him if Christians did not live in a worthy manner. Paul used four parallel participles in this passage to define precisely the ways a worthy life will be manifested. First, the believer who is walking properly will be "fruitful." Secondly, that person will be "increasing in the knowledge of God."

**11. Strengthened with all might, according to his glorious power:** ... May you be completely strengthened, *—CNFT* ... with a strength proportionate to the power displayed in God's majesty, *—TCNT* ... by the might of his glory, *—MNTG* ... from God's boundless resources, *—PHLP*.

**unto all patience and longsuffering with joyfulness:** ... so that you will find yourselves able to pass through an experience and endure it with courage, *—PHLP* ... with patience and good cheer, *—NORL*.

**1:11.** Thirdly, a person who is living a worthy life will experience being "strengthened with all might." In making this statement Paul purposely piled up expressions for emphasis. Both "strengthened" and "might" come from one of the common Greek words for power or "inherent ability" (*dunamis*), while the word "power" in the next part of the statement comes from a word basically meaning "manifested strength" (*kratos*).

This mighty power in turn will manifest itself in "patience," "longsuffering," and "joyfulness." The first term relates to perseverance in spite of all kinds of obstacles. The Greek word actually means more than "patience"; it especially contains the idea of holding to a course of action with steadfast determination. This kind of perseverance seems most difficult when affliction is present. "Longsuffering" basically means to forbear other people. It more closely denotes the idea of patience than does *hupomonē*. "Joyfulness" is self-explanatory, but is an ingredient not always present along with patience and longsuffering.

**12. Giving thanks unto the Father, which hath made us meet:** ... who has made us fit, *—SAWR* ... who enabled us to share in, *—NOYS* ... made us worthy, *—CNFT* ... and qualified us, *—WLSN* ... who is qualifying us, *—SCLT* ... who enabled us to share, *—MNTG*.
**to be partakers of the inheritance of the saints in light:** ... to share the lot of, *—CNFT* ... for a portion in the inheritance, *—SAWR* ... the lot of His people in the realm of light, *—WLMS* ... those who are living in, *—PHLP*.

**1:12.** The remainder of the passage through verse 14 contains the basis for wanting to live the right kind of life. God has qualified believers, or made them fit, to share in the inheritance of His saints by delivering them from the realm of spiritual darkness and placing them in His Son's kingdom through His wonderful sacrifice.

**13. Who hath delivered us from the power of darkness:** ... rescued us from the tyranny of Darkness, *—TCNT* ... rescued us from the empire of darkness, *—NOYS* ... delivered us out of the dominion of darkness, *—WORL, —MNTG, —WLMS*.
**and hath translated [us] into the kingdom of his dear Son:** ... and transferred us, *—CNFT* ... and reestablished us, *—PHLP* ... and transplanted us, *—MNTG* ... and has removed us, *—TCNT* ... of the Son of his love, *—SAWR, —RTHM*.

**1:13.** This verse makes the drastic nature of the experience of regeneration even more evident. The language is quite typical of the way Paul pictured the life of a person before accepting Jesus Christ as Lord. He constantly described the lost condition of people outside of Christ. He wrote about God's delivering believers from "the power of darkness." "Power" actually comes from a common Greek term (*exousia*) normally translated "authority." The language depicts a very drastic experience, being snatched out of one condition and placed in another condition. This second condition occurs when a person becomes part of Christ's kingdom or comes under His rulership.

**14. In whom we have redemption through his blood:** ... For it is by his Son alone that we have been redeemed, *—PHLP*.
**[even] the forgiveness of sins:** ... the remission of our sins, *—CNFT*.

**1:14.** Paul could not have closed his prayer in a more fitting manner than by reminding the Colossians of the redemptive work of the Messiah, the most important work of all history. In the original language the term "redemption" contains a definite article, literally meaning "the redemption." *Redeem* carries the idea of "buying back" something that had been sold. Possibly Paul was thinking of his own experience when he referred to "the forgiveness of sins." The entire prayer from verse 9 through verse 14 serves as an excellent reminder of the necessity of a proper balance between knowledge and experience. A person needs proper knowledge, it must be translated into experience.

**15. Who is the image of the invisible God:** ... who is the likeness, *—MRDK* ... He is a visible image of, *—MNTG* ... is the very incarnation of the unseen God, *—TCNT*.
**the firstborn of every creature:** ... and Head of all creation, *—TCNT* ... He existed before creation began, *—PHLP*.

**1:15.** This verse begins the main theme of the letter: the preeminence or supremacy of Christ. The Gnostic heresy which apparently had infected the Colossian assembly contained many unscriptural doctrines, but its main error was its depreciation of the person and work of Christ. Many Bible scholars believe this section of Scripture consisted of a hymn sung by the Early Church.

Paul first described Christ as "the image of the invisible God." The Bible states in several locations that the essence or substance of God is invisible to human beings (Romans 1:20; 1 Timothy 1:17; Hebrews 11:27). It also states that no man can ever see God, an obvious reference to the Father, but that Christ has made the Father known (John 1:18; 14:9).

"Image" expresses two crucial points. First, it suggests "representation, likeness." Hebrews 1:3 reflects the same idea through another Greek term that was translated "exact representation" in the New International Version. "Manifestation" is the second idea reflected in the term "image" (John 1:18; 14:9). Paul also described Christ as "the firstborn of every creature." "Firstborn" (*prōtotokos*) does not imply that Jesus is part of creation, but rather indicates His priority and sovereignty over all creation.

**16. For by him were all things created:** ... for it was through him that everything was made, *—PHLP.*

**that are in heaven, and that are in earth, visible and invisible:** ... all that is seen and all that is unseen, *—MRDK.*

**whether [they be] thrones, or dominions, or principalities, or powers:** ... whether they be Maiestie or Lordship, *—GNVA* ... or Lordships, or Governments, or authorities, *—WLSN* ... or sovereignties, *—MRDK* ... angelic Beings whatever their power or rank, *—TCNT.*

**all things were created by him, and for him:** ... Through him, *—PHLP.*

**1:16.** This verse reinforces this interpretation by emphasizing that Christ's relationship to creation is not that of being part of it but that of bringing all things into existence. Notice the progression in this passage. First, Paul showed Christ's relationship to deity, and then His relationship to creation. The words "by him" in this verse would be translated better as "in Him" because they express the fact that He was the agent through which everything was created (John 1:3). The tense of the verb "were created" is aorist in the first instance and perfect tense in the second, referring to the continuous result. (See *Overview,* pp. 548f.)

**17. And he is before all things:** ... He is both the first principle, *—PHLP* ... and he precedes, *—WLSN* ... he was prior to all, *—MRDK.*

**and by him all things consist:** ... and the upholding principle of the whole scheme of creation, *—PHLP* ... and all things depend upon him for their existence, *—TCNT* ... they all in him hold together, *—RTHM* ... all things have been permanently placed, *—WLSN* ... alle thingis ben made of nought bi him, *—WCLF* ... all things have held together, *—WORL* ... all things subsist, *—MNTG.*

**1:17.** Here Paul summarizes the previous affirmations of the supremacy of Jesus in creation. Not only did Jesus always exist (John 1:1; 8:58), but He holds all creation together. Thus, the Gnostic philosophy that matter is evil and was created by some being other than Christ is completely unscriptural.

**18. And he is the head of the body, the church:** ... which is composed of all Christian people, *—PHLP.*

**who is the beginning, the firstborn from the dead:** ... Life from nothing began through him, and life from the dead began through him, *—PHLP.*

**that in all [things] he might have the preeminence:** ... so that He alone should stand first in everything, *—WLMS* ... he is the source of its Life, that he in all things may stand first, *—TCNT* ... he might be prefident, *—SCLT* ... in al things holding the primacie, *—RHEM.*

**1:18.** Just as Christ is supreme over the natural creation, so is He sovereign over the new creation, the New Testament Church of which He is the Head. He is supreme in the spiritual realm as well as in the material realm.

The constant use of the term "body" for the Church suggests several important facts. First, it designates the Church as a living organism, composed of members vitally connected to one another. Secondly, it points to the Church as the means through which Christ accomplishes His purposes and performs His work in the world. Thirdly, it shows that the union between Christ and His church constitutes a very vital and intimate one.

Verse 18 establishes the ground for Christ's vital headship of the Church. He is the "beginning" (*archē*) or "source" or "origin." He is the "firstborn" (*prōtotokos*), the first to rise from the realm of the dead in a permanent fashion (Revelation 1:5). This implies the idea of opening the way for others to follow. Because of these achievements, Christ deserves recognition as the Preeminent One.

**19. For it pleased [the Father] that in him should all fulness dwell:** ... it was the divine choice that all the divine fullness should dwell, *—WLMS* ... that the divine nature in all its fulness should dwell in Christ, *—TCNT.*

**1:19.** God planned that His "fulness" (*plērōma*) would reside in Christ. *Fullness* was the very term used by the Gnostics for the totality of so-called divine emanations, or intermediary beings, which they believed controlled people's lives.

The Gnostic teachers parceled out deity among the many spirit beings, called "aeons," which they envisioned as filling the space between God and the world. According to them, any communication between God and the world and between the world and God had to pass through the spheres in which these intermediary beings exercised rule. They included Christ as one of many such "divine beings," but the apostle made it clear that Christ is the only mediator between God and men (1 Timothy 2:5).

**20. And, having made peace through the blood of his cross:** ... pacifying by the bloud, *—RHEM* ... through the blood He shed on His cross, *—WLMS.*

**by him to reconcile all things unto himself:** ... that through Him, *—WLMS.*

**by him, [I say], whether [they be] things in earth, or things in heaven:**

**1:20.** God willed that through Christ all reconciliation would occur. "Reconcile" literally means bringing back into proper relationship. Because

God was not the offender, the Bible uses the term relative to men being brought back into the proper relationship with God.

Reconciliation has both an objective and a subjective side. Objectively, God removed the barrier between himself and sinful man by the death of Christ on the cross, so sinners may experience a living relationship with God. Subjectively, people must accept the possibility for reconciliation that God has provided.

**21. And you, that were sometime alienated and enemies in [your] mind by wicked works:** ... because youre myndes were set in euyll worckes, –CRNM ... were once estranged, –TCNT ... that were once alienated, –NOYS ... formerly being Aliens, –WLSN ... and hostile in [your] intention, –RTHM ... hostile at heart in your evil deeds, –MNTG ... and hostile in disposition as shown by your wrongdoings, –WLMS ... because of your evil deeds, –MRDK ... in evil works, –WORL.

**yet now hath he reconciled:** ... to you, he hath now given peace, –MRDK.

**1:21.** Paul reminded the Colossians in a very straightforward manner of their condition before their reconciliation to God. The language is very reminiscent of Romans 1:18-32 and gives a vivid picture of heathenism at its worst. The apostle probably carefully pinpointed the Colossians' former evil behavior because many Gnostics taught that it mattered little how a person lived in the body, as long as he cultivated the spirit.

This approach serves as a very convenient justification for practicing sin. Paul connected the word "mind" with "wicked works." "Yet now" in this verse indicates God's intervention. Notice the obvious contrast between the frank statements "were sometime alienated and enemies" and "yet now hath he reconciled."

**22. In the body of his flesh through death:** ... by His death in His human body, –WLMS ... through the death of his body on the cross, –PHLP.

**to present you holy and unblameable and unreproveable in his sight:** ... that he might welcome you to his presence, –PHLP ... and without blemish, –PNIN ... without sin, –NORL ... and without offence, –MRDK ... and undefiled and irreproachable, –CNFT ... to present you consecrated, faultless, and blameless, –WLMS ... and unaccusable in his presence, –RTHM ... and unaccusable before Him, –CLMT ... irreproachable before his presence, –PNT.

**1:22.** Paul very carefully combined two Greek words in this verse (sōma, "body," and sarx, "flesh") to specify the actual humanity and genuine body of Jesus. The Gnostics generally taught that reconciliation could be accomplished only by spiritual beings, but Paul emphasized that it happened by the putting to death of Jesus'

physical body. "In the body of his flesh" indicates the sphere in which reconciliation took place, and "through death" specifies the instrument by which it happened.

Christ's ultimate purpose in this glorious process of reconciliation is to present believers before God at His second coming as those who have become Christlike through the sanctification process. This statement, as well as the following verse, should be enough to show that Christians are not perfected at conversion. Even though positionally believers are perfect because the perfection of Christ has been imputed to them, experientially they must go through the process of progressive sanctification in which the Holy Spirit works in them to make them actually like the Lord Jesus Christ.

**23. If ye continue in the faith grounded and settled:** ... Only you must remain firmly founded, –CNFT ... and established, –SAWR ... if, that is, you remain true to your Faith, –TCNT ... if indeed you continue well grounded and firm in faith, –WLMS ... and steadfast, –WORL.

**and [be] not moved away from the hope of the gospel, which ye have heard:** ... and that you do not shift away from, –NORL ... and immoveable from the hope, –DOUY ... the hope inspired by the good news, –WLMS.

**[and] which was preached to every creature which is under heaven:** ... which has been preached all over the world, –WLMS ... indeed, the whole world is now having an opportunity of hearing, –PHLP.

**whereof I Paul am made a minister:**

**1:23.** The last verse in this section about the supremacy of Christ in redemption contains a warning to the Colossians against relapsing into their former condition and an encouragement to continue to recognize Jesus as their all-sufficient Saviour.

The "if" here is the focal point of much controversy because it is an indicative mood "if" (ei) in the Greek language. Because of the mood involved, it often is translated "since," so it is used by some people to deny any element of condition in the context. Although certainly not all grammarians agree concerning this point, in the indicative mood "if" may denote the fact that the actor in a situation knows what decision he will make, but other people do not know. Therefore, "if ye continue" would mean the Colossians knew their own intentions, but other people may not have.

Obviously, just making the decision is not all that is involved in the matter. The Holy Spirit gives us the ability to continue in "the faith," but He cannot help us unless we permit Him to do so. The language of the entire verse seems to lend support to the conditional element involved in continuing to allow Christ to accomplish His work in our lives. He is not satisfied just to bring us to an initial experience with himself. He obviously wants that relationship to continue. The passage closes with a lovely statement showing the universality of the gospel which God manifested to mankind.

**24. Who now rejoice in my sufferings for you:** ... I am now glad to be suffering, —WLMS ... on your behalf, —TCNT ... on your account, —WLSN.

**and fill up that which is behind of the afflictions of Christ in my flesh:** ... I supplement the afflictions endured by the Christ, —TCNT ... and supply the deficiencies, —SAWR ... and am filling up the deficiencies, —RTHM ... that want of the passions of Christ, —RHEM.

**for his body's sake, which is the church:** ... in behalf of, —MNTG.

**1:24.** In his description of the supremacy or preeminence of Christ, Paul went from creation (1:15-17) to redemption (1:18-23) and then to his own ministry in the present passage through verse 29. Some people take the statement in verse 24 to mean that something is lacking in the atoning value of Christ's sacrifice and Paul was able to supplement the saving work of Christ through his own sufferings. The whole system of a treasury of merit consisting of the sufferings of Christ plus the afflictions of "the saints," and dispensed in the form of indulgences, comes from a false interpretation of this verse and from other statements.

While we cannot be positive about exactly what Paul had in mind, he probably was referring to the thought that the union between Christ and His church is so intimate that He suffers when they suffer. His personal sufferings may be over, but His people cannot suffer without its having an impact on Him as well.

The apostle surely did not believe Christians are exempt from suffering. A philosophy that teaches God exempts Christians from any form of suffering is dangerous because people who believe it will not be prepared when the difficulties of life arise.

**25. Whereof I am made a minister:** ... have been made, —WLMS.

**according to the dispensation of God which is given to me for you:** ... It was God who appointed me to this office, —NORL ... according to the administration, —RTHM ... according to the ordinance of God, —GNVA ... the stewardship entrusted to me, —MNTG ... that stewardship of God, —WLSN ... a commission granted to me for your benefit, —PHLP.

**to fulfil the word of God:** ... to complete the word of God, —SAWR ... fully to declare God's message, —MNTG ... that I might prove among you the universal message of God, —WLMS.

**1:25.** The word translated "dispensation" (*oikonomia*) literally means "house-manager" and could be rendered "stewardship, administration, economy." The apostle was keenly aware that God had given him a divine commission to preach the Word. Furthermore, he was always concerned about giving out the Word of God.

While Paul may have had something else in mind, it is possible he was referring to the necessity of people receiving the Word of God and practicing it. In other words, he was not pleased just to dispense the truth of the Scriptures in a manner similar to scattering seeds in a field. He was concerned that the seed of the Word of God would take root and produce fruit in people's lives.

Apparently the translators of the New International Version believed Paul was referring to presenting the totality of the Word of God. That idea is very consistent with the statement by the apostle to the Ephesian elders (Acts 20:27) in his farewell address to them. His constant intention always involved informing people of all the will of God, not just certain segments of it. Either interpretation seems consistent with the total teachings of the apostle. Whatever he meant, the verse obviously shows the apostle's intense determination to present the Word of God to other people.

Paul's chief concern in regard to his personal ministry was very clear. He wanted Christ to be supreme in it. He did not want to become sidetracked on some minor issue that did not emphasize the centrality of the gospel. A person who truly declares the gospel message as central is a person who will make Christ supreme in his ministry. This is the kind of ministry that truly touches and changes lives for Christ.

**26. [Even] the mystery which hath been hid from ages and from generations:** ... that sacred mystery which up till now, —PHLP ... the secret which was concealed, —WLSN ... the mystery concealed from ages, —SAWR ... from former ages, —TCNT.

**but now is made manifest to his saints:** ... but now is opened to his saynctes, —TNDL ... but is now revealed to his saints, —MRDK ... but now uncovered to God's people, —WLMS ... but which is now as clear as daylight to those who love God, —PHLP.

**27. To whom God would make known:** ... They are those to whom God has planned to give a vision, —PHLP.

**what [is] the riches of the glory of this mystery among the Gentiles:** ... the riches of this glorious mystery, —WSLY ... the glorious wealth of this secret, —WLSN ... of his secret plan for the sons of men, —PHLP ... when exhibited among the heathen, —TCNT.

**which is Christ in you, the hope of glory:** ... And the secret is simply this ... bringing with him the hope of all the glorious things to come,

*—PHLP* . . . Christ in union with you, your Hope of glory! *—TCNT.*

**1:26, 27.** Paul was faithful to the divine commission God had entrusted to him (Acts 9:15), but he made it clear in this passage that the revelation of this mystery was disclosed to the saints in general and not just to him. Paul had more to say about God's purpose for Christians in general in the first seven verses of chapter 2, but his brief reference here indicates the way he constantly reminded other people of their responsibility to proclaim the gospel. A careful search of the apostle's writings will reveal several passages where Paul first described his own responsibility to carry out the commission God gave to him, only then in turn reminded Christians of their responsibility to do the same. God will use anyone to propagate His message to the world. The obligation belongs to all believers. Truly the fact that Christ actually indwells believers constitutes one of the greatest mysteries the human race has ever known. He, of course, does so in the person of the Holy Spirit who indwells every believer (Romans 8:9).

**28. Whom we preach:** . . . whom we announce, *—WLSN* . . . We are proclaiming Him, *—WLMS.*
**warning every man:** . . . admonishing, *—WLSN,* *—DOUY,* *—CNFT.*
**and teaching every man in all wisdom:** . . . we teach everyone we can, all that we know about him, *—PHLP* . . . with ample wisdom, *—WLMS.*
**that we may present every man perfect in Christ Jesus:** . . . into God's presence perfected by union with Christ, *—TCNT* . . . every man complete in Christ, *—RTHM* . . . everyone mature through union with Christ, *—WLMS.*

**1:28.** This statement reflects beautifully the fact that Paul was not satisfied just to enjoy fellowship with the Lord personally. He wanted everyone else to enjoy this same experience. For that reason he proclaimed Christ, and his associates did the same. This proclamation consisted of "warning" unbelievers and "teaching" believers so the latter would mature in Christ. His ultimate goal was to present spiritually mature people to Christ at His second coming. He used the term "every man" three times in this verse, showing that he was not an exclusionist. This verse also shows that Christ always was central in his ministry.

One can see the proper balance Paul and his associates practiced in their ministries. First, they were concerned about the unconverted and warned them with the Word of God with the express purpose of helping them to turn to the Lord Jesus in order to find forgiveness for their sins. However, that concern did not end when people became Christians. It only changed to a different type of concern, that of helping individual believers become more and more Christlike. This is God's ultimate purpose for believers.

**29. Whereunto I also labour:** . . . to which end I also am laboring, *—NOYS* . . . whereunto I am also toiling, *—RTHM.*
**striving according to his working, which worketh in me mightily:** . . . ardently contending, *—WLSN* . . . with all the strength that God gives me, *—PHLP* . . . which operates in me with power, *—SAWR.*

**1:29.** This verse serves as an excellent culmination of Paul's comments about his own ministry. His ministry did not cease just because of his incarceration, but even while in prison he was able to "labor." "Striving" or "struggling" (NIV) comes from a Greek participle which has the word from which we get *agony* (*agōna*) as its basis. How could he agonize in prison? He must have been referring mainly to prayer. He also purposely used two Greek words relating to power. The first was translated "working" and comes from a Greek term which gives us our word *energy* (*energeia*). The second was translated "mightily" and comes from the word for *inherent ability* or *power* (*dunamis*). In this first chapter of Colossians, the apostle set forth Christ as supreme in every sense of the word, in creation, in redemption, in an individual's own ministry, and in his practical Christian living.

## Chapter 2

**1. For I would that ye knew what great conflict I have for you:** . . . I would ye knewe what fyghtyng, *—GNVA* . . . what a struggle I have, *—MRDK* . . . how great a contest I am waging for you, *—MNTG* . . . how great a struggle I have entered upon for you, *—TCNT* . . . how Great a Struggle I have about you, *—WLSN* . . . that I have struggled inwardly a great deal, *—NORL* . . . what great concern, *—CNFT* . . . what great wrestling, *—PNT* . . . what bisynesse I haue for you, *—WCLF.*
**and [for] them at Laodicea:**
**and [for] as many as have not seen my face in the flesh:** . . . and on behalf of those, *—ADAM* . . . yes, for all who have never known me personally, *—WLMS* . . . and whoever have not seen my bodily presence, *—FNTN* . . . for all who have never met me, *—PHLP.*

**2:1.** After carefully stating the supremacy of Christ in his own ministry, Paul made it clear that the Lord should be preeminent in every Christian's life. In fact, he struggled for them in prayer that God's purpose would be realized in their lives. The English word *agony* comes from the Greek term translated "conflict" in this verse. The language sounds as if he was in perpetual distress over them, and the possibility of their relapse into their former sinful ways brought him dismay and sorrow. Paul's statement also clearly demonstrates his loving concern for believers. He did not want them to stagnate, but to mature in their faith. Many commentators use this verse to prove that Paul did not start the churches in Colossae and Laodicea. Yet Paul had a concern for both churches. Notice that he asked the Colossian believers to pass the epistle along to the Laodicean church.

**2. That their hearts might be comforted:** ...may be consoled, *−RTHM, −FNTN* . . . may be confirmed, *−ALFD* . . . may be encouraged, *−WLMS, −ADAM, −PHLP.*

**being knit together in love:** ...find out more and more how strong are the bonds of Christian love, *−PHLP* . . . We want you welded together, *−BRKL* . . . as they are joined together in love, *−ADAM* . . . and bound together with love, *−SEB* . . . being closely united, *−SCLT* . . . united in love, *−SAWR.*

**and unto all riches of the full assurance of understanding:** . . . leading to, *−ADAM* . . . and by having attained to the full assurance, *−WLMS* . . . be ever so richly convinced, *−BECK* . . . and all the wealth of the full conviction of reason, *−FNTN* . . . for you to grow more certain in your knowledge, *−PHLP.*

**to the acknowledgment of the mystery of God, and of the Father, and of Christ:** . . . that in turn results in, *−ADAM* . . . in comprehending the secret of God, *−FNTN* . . . May they come to a perfect knowledge, *−MNTG* . . . so that they may finally reach the fullest knowledge of the open secret, *−WLMS* . . . more sure in your grasp of God himself, *−PHLP* . . . knowing God's secret Christ, *−SEB.*

**2:2.** Paul began in verse 2 to express the purpose for this struggle in prayer for them. He prefaced his comments with a very strong Greek term (*hina*) often used to preface statements of purpose and usually translated "in order that." First, Paul coveted for them encouragement, comfort, or inner strength. Second, he desired that they be united or "knit together" in love (*agapē*). While error is divisive, true love that emanates from God himself is the motivating force that binds God's people together. Thirdly, he wanted them to have a full knowledge, or constantly increasing knowledge of what it meant to have Christ indwelling them, what Paul labeled here "the mystery of God." It is a marvelous mystery that Christ does indwell His people, but the more we understand God's work in the believers, the clearer this "mystery" becomes. This is an excellent reminder that our knowledge of Christ improves progressively throughout the Christian life. While all Christians "know" Christ because of the living relationship that exists between the Lord and His people, Christian maturity enables them to know Christ in an ever-increasing manner.

**3. In whom are hid all the treasures of wisdom and knowledge:** . . . secret knowledge, *−FNTN* . . . and hidden wisdom are found in Christ, *−SEB* . . . in which are stored, *−WLSN* . . . are to be found stored up, *−TCNT* . . . are concealed, *−CNDT.*

**2:3.** This verse continues the idea and shows why it is so important for believers to progress in their knowledge of Christ as a result of their relationship with Him. The verse contains an obvious reply to the Gnostics who taught a limited and perverted kind of knowledge. It is absolutely necessary for Christians to have a proper knowledge of Christ, because in Him "are hid all the treasures of wisdom and knowledge." The Gnostics taught that knowledge was an end in itself and had to be parceled out through intermediary beings. Paul vehemently rejected this mentality, insisting that a full knowledge of God comes only through Christ. As well as countering Gnostic thought, this statement militates against any religious philosophy that claims people can come to salvation without Christ. As Peter said to the religious hierarchy in Jerusalem, "There is none other name under heaven given among men, whereby we must be saved" (Acts 4:12).

**4. And this I say, lest any man should beguile you with enticing words:** . . . that no one may impose on you, *−NOYS* . . . I write like this to prevent you from being led astray by someone or other's attractive arguments, *−PHLP* . . . may deceive You with Persuasive speech, *−WLSN* . . . that no one may reason you aside with plausible discourse, *−RTHM* . . . may delude you with persuasive speech, *−WORL* . . . deceiue you in loftines of vvordes, *−RHEM* . . . by loftiness of words, *−DOUY* . . . with persuasiveness of speech, *−CLMT.*

**2:4.** Fourthly, the apostle was concerned that the Colossians not be deceived with "enticing words" or "fine-sounding arguments" (NIV) or "persuasive speech." Apparently the Gnostics (as are most false teachers) were very adept at deluding people because they majored in persuasive speech. Their "fast talk" was a proof that the art of persuasion, although the height of oratory, can degenerate into trickery.

Paul sincerely hoped the Colossians would remain faithful to the truth of God's Word. They lived in an age when rhetoric was emphasized as a sign of an educated person. Obviously, both the ability to relate a message and having the proper message are extremely important to our effectiveness as Christian workers. One can tell quickly from the writings of the apostle that he not only was a profound writer, but he also knew well the art and science of proper rhetoric. However, he was always careful to depend upon the power of the Holy Spirit. He knew mere human ability could not meet the need of a lost soul (1 Corinthians 2:1-5).

**5. For though I be absent in the flesh, yet am I with you in the spirit:** ... I am not with you in person, *—TCNT* ... though I am a long way away from you in body, in spirit I am by your side, *—PHLP* ... in body, *—DOUY.*

**joying and beholding your order:** ... watching like a proud father, *—PHLP.*

**and the stedfastness of your faith in Christ:** ... the stability of your faith, *—WLSN* ... and the firm foundation, *—ALFD* ... of the solid front which you present through your faith, *—TCNT* ... and the solid structure of your faith towards Christ, *—RTHM.*

**2:5.** Paul's desire for the Colossian saints relative to the four items he mentioned in his letter was not dependent upon his physically being with them. In this verse he used two words in a military sense to express his desire that they stand in "order" and in "steadfastness," comparing them to the orderly array of a well-disciplined army. A certain beauty exists in an orderly array whether in a military unit or in something else. A military commander must experience a certain satisfaction from observing his unit at attention.

**6. As ye have therefore received Christ Jesus the Lord, [so] walk ye in him:** ... Now, therefore, just as you have accepted Christ Jesus as your Lord, *—NORL* ... live your lives in union with him, *—TCNT* ... so go on living in him, *—PHLP.*

**2:6.** Actually, this verse and verse 7 serve both as a conclusion to verses 1-5 and as an introduction to the rest of the chapter. The Colossians and their neighbors had begun their life in Christ, and Paul encouraged them to continue to live in Him. It is not enough to be converted. God wants His children to continue to grow until they reach maturity. This verse beautifully summarizes the total Christian life. It begins when a person accepts the provision God made through the sacrifice of Christ on the cross, and it continues by depending upon that same work of grace. Both occur through faith.

**7. Rooted and built up in him, and stablished in the faith:** ... founded, *—SAWR* ... May you become stronger and yet stronger in, *—NORL.*

**as ye have been taught, abounding therein with thanksgiving:** ... overflowing with, *—RTHM* ... may your lives overflow with gratitude! *—NORL* ... with joy and thankfulness, *—PHLP.*

**2:7.** Paul summarized the manner in which Christians should live by using four Greek participles: (1) "Rooted" comes from a perfect tense participle (*errhizōmenoi*) which normally would be translated "having been rooted" and expresses the initial experience of being connected to Christ, as well as the continuing result of that initial relationship. (2) "Built up" (*epoikodomoumenoi*) shows

Paul's change from an agricultural metaphor to one of construction, expressing the idea of allowing God to continue His work of construction in the believer's life. It is very encouraging to know God is not finished with the believer yet, but He patiently continues His work of construction in them. (3) "Stablished" (*bebaioumenoi*), or "being strengthened," refers to making firm or stable, expressing the ultimate purpose God has for working in our lives. (4) "Abounding" (*perisseuontes*) completes the cycle, because everything a Christian does should be permeated with thanksgiving.

Perhaps Paul emphasized the necessity of beginning in Christ and continuing in Christ just before his next message to the Colossians because if they did these two things they would not drift into false doctrine. Continuing to make Christ the central or focal point of the Christian life will serve as a positive preventive from drifting into false teachings.

**8. Beware lest any man spoil you through philosophy and vain deceit:** ... Take care, *—WLSN* ... that nobody spoils your faith through intellectualism or high-sounding nonsense, *—PHLP* ... See that no one leads you off as a prey, *—SAWR* ... some one who will capture you, *—TCNT* ... make you naked by philosophy, *—MRDK* ... drag you away captive, *—MNTG* ... captures you by the idle fancies of his so-called philosophy, *—WLMS* ... make a prey of you ... and empty deceit, *—SCLT* ... and disceatfull vanitie, *—CRNM.*

**after the tradition of men, after the rudiments of the world, and not after Christ:** ... according to the instruction of men, *—RTHM* ... following human tradition, *—WLMS* ... and the world's crude notions, *—MNTG* ... on men's ideas of the nature of the world, and disregards Christ! *—PHLP* ... not according to Christ, *—WLSN.*

**2:8.** This verse begins the main doctrinal section of this epistle. Paul made it very clear to the Colossians that Christ is always central in scriptural doctrine. Verse 8 contains a negative warning to Christians not to allow themselves to be taken captive by a philosophy that does not allow Christ the preeminence.

The term "spoil" in the King James Version sometimes contains the idea of kidnapping. In the original language "philosophy" (*philosophias*) is preceded by a definite article. Thus the reference seems to relate to a particular false teaching, probably gnosticism. In this verse *stoicheia* likely refers to elementary religious teachings (cf. 2:20). (For further discussion of *stoicheia*, see *Overview*, pp. 546f.)

**9. For in him dwelleth all the fulness of the Godhead bodily:** ... For it is in Him that all the fullness of Deity continues to live embodied, *—WLMS* ... the Deity bodily, *—WLSN* ... resided substantially in Him, –SCLT . . . in a bodily form, –TCNT . . . corporally, –RHEM.

**2:9.** This verse begins the positive side of the matter. While the Gnostics' view represented the fullness of deity as distributed among the angels, Paul was adamant about the fact that all physical manifestation of deity comes only through Christ. In fact, the Greek term for "dwelleth" (*katoikei*) is the same word used in 1:19 and means "permanently dwell." In several places the Bible emphatically states that the essence or nature of God is invisible to humans (John 1:18; Romans 1:20; Colossians 1:15; 1 Timothy 1:17).

**10. And ye are complete in him:** . . . and ye are filled full in him, –PNT . . . ye are made full, –ASV . . . you are in him replenished, –RHEM . . . through union with Him you too are filled with it, –WLMS.

**which is the head of all principality and power:** . . . who is the fountainhead of all authority, –NORL . . . He is the Head of all principalities and dominions, –WLMS.

**2:10.** Because of that important fact, believers have all they need in Christ. "Complete" or "fullness" (NIV) comes from a perfect passive participle and literally refers to "having been filled." Because of their relationship to Christ through regeneration, believers have all the completeness they need in Christ.

**11. In whom also ye are circumcised with the circumcision made without hands:** . . . through your union with Him you once received, not a hand-performed circumcision, –WLMS.

**in putting off the body of the sins of the flesh by the circumcision of Christ:** . . . even in putting off your sensual nature, –MNTG . . . in stripping you of your lower nature, –WLMS . . . the getting rid of the tyranny of the earthly body, –TCNT . . . you were set free from your sinful nature, –NORL . . . being set free from the sins of the flesh by virtue of, –PHLP.

**2:11.** The rest of the passage continues a masterful description of just what we do enjoy of this "completeness" or "fullness" in Christ. First, we have received true circumcision, defined here as "putting off of the sinful nature" (NIV). External circumcision occupied a very prominent position under the Old Testament economy (Genesis 17:9-14), but even under it God required that it be accompanied by circumcision of heart (Jeremiah 4:4). Apparently God instituted the rite of circumcision with Abraham as the outward manifestation of what God had done inwardly for Abraham. Here Paul labeled circumcision as the breaking of the power of the Adamic nature of a person that takes place at conversion. No longer is

the regenerated person a slave to that fallen nature which he possesses from natural birth.

**12. Buried with him in baptism:** . . . for you were buried, –WLMS . . . being jointly-buried, –RTHM . . . just as in baptism you shared in his death, –PHLP.

**wherein also ye are risen with [him] through the faith of the operation of God:** . . . sharing the miracle of rising again to new lifeand all this because you have faith in, –PHLP . . . and raised to life with Him through your faith in the power of God, –WLMS . . . in the working of God, –CNFT . . . through a belief of the energy of God, –SCLT . . . in the energy of that God, –MNTG.

**who hath raised him from the dead:**

**2:12.** This verse provides truth very similar to that found in Romans 6, where Paul likened the experience of water baptism to a spiritual death, burial, and resurrection. The water is a symbol of a grave, and the immersion of a believer represents burial. When he is brought out of the water again, it represents his "resurrection" to the new life. It is a picture of dying to the old life of sin, taking a public stand that he is dead to the old life. He has received a new nature, he is a child of God. He will live a different kind of life. It should mean something more than a mere ritual. The Holy Spirit has baptized the new believer into the body of Christ (1 Corinthians 12:13). Water baptism is an outward sign of an inward work. Dead to the old life and alive unto God, the believer is to walk in "newness of life" (Romans 6:4).

**13. And you, being dead in your sins and the uncircumcision of your flesh:** . . . dead in the offenses, –RHEM . . . of your sensual nature, –MNTG . . . who were spiritually dead because of, –PHLP . . . although you were dead through your shortcomings and were physically uncircumcised, –WLMS . . . and your uncircumcised nature, –TCNT.

**hath he quickened together with him, having forgiven you all trespasses:** . . . hath he given life, –NOYS . . . God made you live again through fellowship with Christ. He graciously forgave us all our shortcomings, –WLMS . . . He pardoned all our sins! –TCNT . . . having freely pardoned All our offences, –WLSN . . . pardoning you al offenses, –RHEM . . . forgiven us all our sins, –MRDK.

**2:13.** Paul here gave one of the best definitions of death that a person can discover anywhere in the Scriptures or elsewhere. Death basically relates to separation. Paul reminded the Colossians of their state of spiritual death or separation from God previous to their conversion to Christ. He explained it as being dead in their sinful practices, because the circumcision of which he wrote in verse 11 had not taken place in their lives. But God had raised them from the dead spiritually, so they were enjoying true resurrection, or spiritual resurrection, as well as true forgiveness. They had been separated from God because of sin, but now, through Jesus' death, there was no longer any separation. They were close to Him.

**14. Blotting out the handwriting of ordinances that was against us, which was contrary to us:** ...He cancelled the bond (consisting of rules and regulations), *–TCNT* ...He freely wiped out our lawbreaking and left out the unreasoning complaints written against us, *–KLGS.*
**and took it out of the way, nailing it to his cross:** ...and took it away out of the midst, *–RTHM* ...and has removed it from the midst, having nailed it, *–WLSN* ...fastening it to the cross, *–DOUY.*

**2:14.** Not only does God forgive, but He also forgets the charges against the one forgiven. Because of His omniscience God does not "forget" in the same way humans often speak of forgetting. Rather, He removes the charges and does not hold them against the one forgiven any longer. The entire Mosaic law, which Paul described as "the handwriting of ordinances," presents a condemnation of the entire human race. The law of Moses points out how God expects people to live, but Christ is the only one who fulfilled all the requirements of the Old Testament law. Because He fulfilled the requirement by taking the penalty of sin upon himself, God accepts the righteousness of Christ in the believer's behalf.

Ephesians 2:15 contains a statement very similar to the one in this verse. "Nailing it to the cross" (NIV) shows how truly Jesus identified with sinners, being made sin for us (2 Corinthians 5:21). It was customary under Roman law to write out a copy of the law that a criminal had broken and nail that inscription above the person's head on the cross on which he was impaled. Sometimes the placard also contained a description of the offense of the person being crucified.

**15. [And] having spoiled principalities and powers:** ...Disarming, *–CNFT* ...having disarmed, *–NOYS.*
**he made a show of them openly, triumphing over them in it:** ...He made an example of them openly, *–CLMT* ...made a public exhibition of them, *–WLSN* ...held them up to open contempt when he celebrated his triumph over them on the cross! *–TCNT* ...and led them captive in triumph, *–NOYS* ...celebrating a triumph over them thereby, *–RTHM.*

**2:15.** This verse carries further the explanation of the believer's completeness in Christ by describing the true freedom Christians enjoy as a result of being in Christ. Satan took advantage of mankind's helpless condition. Therefore, the drama of the Cross involves spiritual beings as well as human beings. By His wonderful sacrifice, Christ not only released His people from the guilt of sin and also its dominion.

The language used here suggests the homecoming parade called a triumph that was accorded a victorious Roman general who had conquered a foreign land (2 Corinthians 2:14). Just as the Roman general made a public spectacle of his enemies, Christ made a public spectacle of Satan and all his forces.

**16. Let no man therefore judge you in meat, or in drink:** ...judge you in eating, *–ALFD* ...therefore rule you as regards eating, *–PNT.*
**or in respect of an holyday, or of the new moon, or of the sabbath [days]:** ...of a Festival, *–WLSN.*

**2:16.** Not only do people become complete in Christ, but they also stay complete in Christ. The prohibition here, because it is a present active imperative form of the verb, probably prohibits the continuation of an action, so it could be translated: "Stop letting anyone judge you." The Colossians apparently were listening to false ideas and as a result were straying from their completeness in Christ. Because Christ had freed them from their former bondage to the requirements of the Mosaic law, they were to resist any attempt to ensnare them in a new bondage to legalistic requirements. They were told to stop allowing the use of the list of ceremonial matters that followed Paul's warning as a basis for judging their standing before God.

Commentators vary as to whether the regulations listed in verse 16 refer to the dietetic injunctions of the Mosaic law or to a form of asceticism taught and practiced by the Colossian Gnostics. Probably both are true. Jesus taught that foods themselves are neither moral nor immoral (Mark 7:18, 19). "Holyday" no doubt refers to the annual Jewish feasts, and "new moon" to the monthly Jewish celebration held in connection with their lunar calendar. The "sabbath" was a weekly festival held from sundown Friday until sundown Saturday.

**17. Which are a shadow of things to come:** ...of the future things, *–WLSN.*
**but the body [is] of Christ:** ...the substance is in the Christ, *–TCNT.*

**2:17.** Paul clarified the reason for not allowing such matters to be a basis for judgment concerning their standing in Christ. Such things were only a shadow (Hebrews 10:1) of what was to come. The transitory items should be discarded in favor of the "body" or reality they now knew in Christ.

**18. Let no man beguile you of your reward:**...seduce you, *—DOUY*...cheat you, *—CNFT*...defraud you of your prize, *—ALFD*...rob you of your prize, *—CLMT.*

**in a voluntary humility and worshipping of angels:** ... by persuading you to make yourselves "humble" and fall down and worship angels, *—PHLP*...and religion of Angels, *—RHEM.*

**intruding into those things which he hath not seen, vainly puffed up by his fleshly mind:**...defraud you as an umpire, *—WLMS*...speculating about the things, *—WORL*...prying into things, *—WLSN*...dwelling in the things which he hath seen, *—ASV* ... inflated by an unspiritual imagination, *—PHLP*...speculates about visions he has had, and is proud in his sensual mind, *—NORL*...is vainly inflated in his fleshly mind, *—MRDK*...by their merely human intellect, *—TCNT*...by his mere human mind, *—CNFT*...by his material mind, *—MNTG.*

**2:18.** For the believer to allow anyone to lead him away from his completeness in Christ could "beguile" or rob him of his reward. The imperative verb used in this verse (*katabrabeuetō*) is translated best in the New American Standard Bible as "Let no one keep defrauding you of your prize." Seemingly, Paul was encouraging the Colossians not to allow anyone to divert them with false teachings, because doing so would cause them to waste precious time that should be used in making spiritual progress, progress which ultimately would bring them reward at the judgment of believers. Normally Paul described humility as a virtue; consequently, here it must be a reference to false humility. Just what is the connection between false humility and the worship of angels? Perhaps this can best be answered by looking at the approach some people take toward the Lord. They feel they are too sinful and too unworthy to go directly to the Lord, therefore they must go through some intermediary being. This attitude may be very pious and may represent humility, but it often expresses a subtle kind of pride. (Cf. *Overview*, pp. 544-546 for a discussion of angel worship.)

**19. And not holding the Head:**...It is from the head alone, *—PHLP.*

**from which all the body by joints and bands having nourishment ministered, and knit together:** ... by means of the arteries, *—PNT* ... and compacted together, *—WLSN.*

**increaseth with the increase of God:**...grows with a divine growth, *—TCNT, —MNTG*...with a growth that God produces, *—WLMS*...is nourished and built up and grows according to God's laws of growth, *—PHLP*...wrought by God, *—NOYS.*

**2:19.** According to Paul's continued emphasis, the basic problem of that person related to "not holding the Head," or to losing "connection with the Head" (NIV), an obvious reference to Christ.

This phrase stresses the necessity of a continuous relationship with Jesus, the One who will cause every part of the Body to function properly as it remains connected to Him (Ephesians 4:15, 16).

**20. Wherefore if ye be dead with Christ from the rudiments of the world:**...you are dead to the principles of this world's life, *—PHLP*...from the elements, *—PNIN* ... to worldly ways of looking at things, *—NORL.*

**why, as though living in the world, are ye subject to ordinances:**...why do you now...submit to its rules, *—NORL*...to such rules as, *—TCNT*...are ye submitting to decrees, *—RTHM*...submit yourselves to dogmatisms founded on teachings and doctrines of men, *—MNTG.*

**2:20.** In concluding the matter, the apostle Paul summarized the issue of completeness in Christ by warning the Colossians against being led back into the basic principles of the world; he used the same term (*stoicheia*) in verse 8. It is used in 2 Peter 3:10 of the basic elements of the physical universe and in Hebrews 5:12 of the elementary truths of the Scriptures. It refers to anything in a row or series, like the letters of an alphabet.

The "if" in verse 20 could be translated "since." In other words, since they had rejected the way of the world in which they had lived before their conversion to Christ, why after being *in Christ* would they want to live by the world's standards? The world's rules or dogmas are based on the false idea that salvation can be obtained by "doing something" and often amounts to a list of negatives. Strangely enough, many times non-Christians accuse Christians of being negative, when actually the opposite is true.

Christianity does not consist of a list of "do's and don'ts." It begins with the positive step of committing one's life to Jesus Christ and gaining a relationship with Him. From the moment of conversion the Holy Spirit indwells the believer. Becoming a follower of Christ makes the grace and mercy of God available to that person. A plethora of spiritual benefits, including the fullness of the Holy Spirit, become available to the believer. In the process of giving these benefits to the Christian, God also removes undesirable habits from him. Salvation certainly does not come to an individual merely by "giving up" something.

**21. (Touch not; taste not; handle not:**...Don't touch this, Don't taste that and Don't handle the other? *—PHLP.*

**2:21.** Paul made it clear that nonbelievers are the negative ones. Non-Christians are the ones who mistakenly think salvation comes to an individual who does not do certain things or supposedly "gives up" certain habits. Paul summarized this kind of religious approach very accurately when he wrote, "Touch not; taste not; handle not." Asceticism is not true holiness.

**22.** **Which all are to perish with the using;):** . . . referred to cease to exist, *—TCNT* . . . are consumed, *—WLSN* . . . all perysshe thorow the very abuse, *—CRNM* . . . will all pass away after use! *—PHLP.*
**after the commandments and doctrines of men?:** . . . the precepts and teachings of men? *—CLMT* . . . these purely human prohibitions, *—PHLP.*

**2:22.** Besides, these things perish with use. Everything finally wears out. Furthermore, these dogmas are purely of human invention. Before drawing a conclusion that the apostle Paul was a very liberal man, the first 17 verses of chapter 3 of this letter need to be studied. He definitely believed in proper Christian standards, but standards that come from God, not standards that originate in the human mind. So, Paul's final appraisal of asceticism was that it is a dismal failure. One may punish the human body to the limit and still have a soul filled with ungodly lusts. Paul believed in the necessity of controlling the human body, but he warned that the real danger of asceticism is its avoidance of the real problem: that of dealing with the sinful, Adamic nature.

**23.** **Which things have indeed a show of wisdom in will worship:** . . . Which have an appearance of, *—SAWR* . . . shevv of vvisedom in superstition, *—RHEM* . . . in Self-devised worship, *—WLSN* . . . in a self-devised religious observance, *—CLMT.*
**and humility, and neglecting of the body:** . . . self-abasement and self-control of the body, *—NORL* . . . and humblenes, *—GNVA* . . . and harsh treatment of the body, *—TCNT* . . . and severe treatment of, *—WORL* . . . and severity to the body, *—NOYS.*
**not in any honour to the satisfying of the flesh:** . . . in no respect for the surfeiting, *—SAWR* . . . but are of no real value against the indulgence of our earthly nature, *—TCNT* . . . not of any value for perfecting of the flesh, *—PNT* . . . lead to the full gratification of, *—CNFT* . . . for a Gratification of the flesh, *—WLSN.*

**2:23.** If a person keeps his body under subjection and gloats over the fact, thinking he is superior to other Christians, he has become the modern counterpart of a Pharisee. In this verse the apostle summarized the activities of people who fail to accept Jesus as their Head, and instead attempt to satisfy God through their own efforts. First, he emphasized that their approach may seem to be a wise one. As a result, they probably will receive commendation from many people for the good moral lives they live. Secondly, they practice "will-worship" or "self-imposed worship" (NIV) rather than accepting the pattern God has given in the

Scriptures. Thirdly, Paul accused these individuals of a "false humility" (NIV). So, instead of developing a scriptural humility, these people substituted a self-manufactured one that glorified self, not God. Fourthly, Paul castigated these false teachers "neglecting of the body" as being ineffective relative to controlling the "satisfying of the flesh" or relative to "restraining sensual indulgence" (NIV). Genuine humility brings glory to God.

## Chapter 3

**1.** **If ye then be risen with Christ:**
**seek those things which are above:** . . . reach out for the highest gifts of Heaven, *—PHLP.*
**where Christ sitteth on the right hand of God:** . . . where your master reigns in power, *—PHLP.*

**3:1.** The Bible teaches true holiness and very clearly tells how to obtain it. It begins with the believer continuously centering his interest in Christ. If a person has truly been converted he is enjoying the resurrection life of Christ. Christ not only is the Author of his new life, but the constant source of it. The phrase "the right hand of God" indicates the position of supreme authority; so Christ, not some angel, must be the focal point for a proper system of ethics.

**2.** **Set your affection on things above:** . . . Fix your thoughts, *—TCNT* . . . Set your mind, *—ASV* . . . Mind the things, *—WLSN* . . . employ your minds, *—SAWR* . . . Keep thinking of the things, *—WORL.*
**not on things on the earth:** . . . not on earthly things, *—MNTG* . . . not to the passing things of earth, *—PHLP.*

**3:2.** "Set your affection" refers to a continuous experience and definitely denotes the place a person's will has relative to true holiness. God does not force His will upon people to make them conduct their lives in complete accordance with His plan. The basis for this new style of life comes from heaven itself, the same place from which the new birth originated (John 3:3). The same One who makes this new birth possible also makes a new standard of life possible. Christians are obligated to judge everything by the standards of this new life.

**3.** **For ye are dead:**
**and your life is hid with Christ in God:** . . . and your true life is a hidden one, *—PHLP.*

**3:3.** This is possible because they have died to the old order, to the world's way of thinking and doing. "Dead" comes from the Greek word *apethanete* that relates to a definite act, so believers are "hid with Christ in God" or live by God's power.

**4. When Christ, [who is] our life, shall appear:** ...the secret center of our lives, —*PHLP* ...shall be manifested, —*PNIN*, —*WLSN*, —*WORL.*

**then shall ye also appear with him in glory:** ... shall you also be made manifest in, —*SAWR* ...shall be manifested, —*MRDK* ...manifested in glory, —*ALFD* ...and you will all share in that magnificent denouement, —*PHLP.*

**3:4.** Verse 4 contains another very important reason for the Christian to constantly center his interests on Christ. One day He will return to receive His people unto himself. The Greek word used here for "appear" (*phanerōthē*) contains the idea of *manifestation*. At that time Christ will display to the world that there is only one way of salvation, through His sacrifice on the cross. Furthermore, there is only one way of true holiness: for the believer to allow the life of Christ to be manifested through him.

**5. Mortify therefore:** ...kill, —*TCNT* ...Put to death, —*PNIN*, —*WLSN* ...slay, —*MNTG.*

**your members which are upon the earth:** ...all your animal appetites, —*TCNT* ... your baser inclinations, —*MNTG.*

**fornication, uncleanness, inordinate affection:** ... Impurity, —*WLSN* ... passion, —*PNIN*, —*SAWR*, —*WORL* ...base coveting, —*RTHM* ...unnatural desires, —*MNTG* ...vnnaturall lust, —*CRNM* ...lustful passion, —*ALFD.*

**evil concupiscence, and covetousness:** ... evil desires, and especially greed, —*TCNT* ... inordinate lust, —*WLSN* ...and the greed, —*MNTG.*

**which is idolatry:** ...is as serious a sin as idolatry, —*PHLP.*

**3:5.** This verse gives another of the paradoxes, or seeming contradictions, in Paul's writings. He had just told the Colossians (verse 3) that they had "died," but in verse 5 he tells them to "mortify" or "put to death" (NIV) their "members which are upon the earth" or "whatever belongs to your earthly nature" (NIV).

Because Christ is the focal point or center of the Christian's life, he can depend upon His power to help him overcome the sinful nature with which he was born. Although believers died to the world's way of thinking when they became Christians, their fallen Adamic nature was not completely removed. While the power of the sinful nature was broken, they still have to contend with it.

Because Paul was not content to treat sin in an abstract way, he enumerated representative sins to be laid aside. "Fornication" relates to all illicit sexual activities, and in this context, "uncleanness, inordinate affection," and "evil concupiscence" probably also refer to sexual matters. "Covetousness" or "greed" (NIV) is idolatry because it means placing the affections on earthly rather than heavenly things.

**6. For which things' sake the wrath of God cometh on the children of disobedience:** ...of incredulitie, —*RHEM.*

**3:6.** This verse warns that such yielding to sin brings the wrath of God. Some people mistakenly have the idea that God dislikes sin only in the unbeliever, but He excuses sin in the Christian. God certainly does forgives sins (1 John 1:9), but that does not mean He condones it.

**7. In the which ye also walked some time:** ...And never forget that you had your part in those dreadful things, —*PHLP.*

**when ye lived in them:** ... when you lived that old life, —*PHLP.*

**3:7.** Paul reminded the Colossians that the sins he had just listed were representative of their lives before becoming Christians. Then he listed other sins that must be resisted so they would not question in their minds exactly what he meant. This reminder also served to counter the false teaching of many licentious Gnostics who taught that what was done with the physical body had no influence upon the spiritual nature of the individual because they considered the body, as well as all other matter, to be evil.

**8. But now ye also put off all these:** ...you also must renounce them all, —*MNTG* ...But now, put all these things behind you, —*PHLP.*

**anger, wrath, malice, blasphemy, filthy communication out of your mouth:** ...no more evil temper or furious rage, —*PHLP* ...passion, spite, slandering, and bad language, —*TCNT* ... and foul talk, —*NORL* ...shameful speaking, —*PNIN* ...shameful-talk, —*RTHM* ...vile conversation, —*SAWR* ...Evil speaking, —*WLSN* ...abusive language and foul-mouthed utterances, —*CNFT* ...foul language, —*ALFD* ...obscene discourse out of your mouth, —*SCLT.*

**3:8.** "Put off" contains the idea of laying aside, as a person would lay aside old worn-out clothing. They were to rid themselves of "anger" (*orgēn*), or "a settled attitude of anger." "Wrath" (*thumon*) refers to "a violent outburst of wrath." "Malice" (*kakian*) means "a tendency of mind that wants to harm other people." "Blasphemy" (*blasphēmian*) relates to "injuring other people with words." "Filthy communication" (*aischrologian*) or "abusive language" completes Paul's enumeration of terms descriptive of the Colossians before they became Christians, but the list certainly does not comprise an exhaustive one.

**9. Lie not one to another:**...Do not speak falsely, —WLSN...Stop these practices, —NORL.

**seeing that ye have put off the old man with his deeds:**...Get rid of your old self and its habits, —TCNT...but strip off the old self with its doings, —MNTG...with his practices, —WLSN, —RTHM, —MRDK.

**3:9.** Because the prohibition here consists of a present imperative one, it literally means "stop lying to each other." This type of activity, though a regular part of the old life, is not consistent with the new life in Christ. Paul included lying with a list of some very unsavory habits, apparently indicating that lying is just as terrible in the sight of God as the other matters.

Paul's basis for making this prohibitive statement about lying should be considered carefully. He used a Greek participle (*apekdusamenoi*) which literally means "after putting off" or "having put off." Therefore, the Colossians had rejected "the old man," or the old sinful nature, when they became Christians. Why then would they want to pick it up again and allow it to manifest itself in actions such as lying?

**10. And have put on the new [man]:**...and have begun life as the new man, —PHLP.

**which is renewed in knowledge after the image of him that created him:** ...which is in the process of being made new, —WLMS...who is being moulded afresh, —RTHM...in the likeness of the Creator, —NORL.

**3:10.** God encourages His people to actions that will help them progress in the sanctification process, the purifying process through which God is taking all Christians so He can make them more like Christ. The believer's new nature resembles a growing plant that grows stronger and stronger in a continuous, advancing process. Yielding to the fallen Adamic nature does not help the process. This verse serves as a marvelous reminder that God has reversed the process of degeneration that the Scriptures speak about. God knows how to recycle people.

**11. Where there is neither Greek nor Jew, circumcision nor uncircumcision:**...In which state, —WLSN.

**Barbarian, Scythian, bond [nor] free:** ...foreigner, —RTHM...or savage, —PHLP.

**but Christ [is] all, and in all:**...Christ is all that matters, for Christ lives in them all, —PHLP.

**3:11.** All types of bigotry are actually part of the old life. "Greek nor Jew" refers to racial prejudice; "circumcision nor uncircumcision" to religious bias; "Barbarian, Scythian" to cultural distinctions; and "bond nor free" to social barriers. Initially, the term "Barbarian" denoted a person

who could not speak Greek, but by New Testament times it had come to mean anyone who did not participate in the Greco-Roman civilization, a so-called "uncivilized person." Scythians were considered the lowest class of barbarians. As far as God is concerned all these distinctions are man-made and result from our fallen sinful condition. Christ abolishes all these sinful distinctions.

**12. Put on therefore, as the elect of God, holy and beloved:**...Clothe yourselves, —CLMT...picked representatives of the new humanity, purified and beloved of God himself, —PHLP.

**bowels of mercies, kindness, humbleness of mind:**...with the entrails of mercie, —WCLF...hearts of compassion, —SAWR ...with tender affections of compassion, —CLMT ...tenderness of heart, —TCNT...an heart of pity, —ALFD...lowliness of mind, —RTHM, —NOYS.

**meekness, longsuffering:** . . . . modestie, —RHEM...Patient endurance, —WLSN.

**3:12.** Paul next turned from the negative to the positive. God's people should not yield to the kinds of sins enumerated in verses 5-11. Instead, as they would replace old worn-out garments with new ones, they should "put on" the items he was about to mention. "Bowels of mercies" is an Old English way of saying "deeply felt affection" or "sensitivity to people in need." "Kindness" refers to "sweetness of disposition." "Humbleness" means "a proper estimate of one's self." "Meekness" is the opposite of being harsh, and "longsuffering" means to "forbear other people." "Put on" is located first in the sentence in the Greek and indicates the position of most emphasis. These are the "garments" of the new life.

**13. Forbearing one another, and forgiving one another:** ... Bear with one another, —CNFT...you must be tolerant with one another, —NORL ...supporting one an other:...and pardoning one other, —RHEM...and freely forgiving, —WLSN, —WORL.

**if any man have a quarrel against any:**...if any one has a charge, —SAWR...may have a Cause of complaint, —WLSN...if any of you have grounds for complaint against others, —TCNT...if you have a difference with anyone, —PHLP.

**even as Christ forgave you, so also [do] ye:**...forgive one another freely, —TCNT...as freely as the Lord has forgiven you, —PHLP.

**3:13.** The "garments" of the new life also include the ability to forgive one another as the Lord forgives the believer. As a result of the wonderful work of Christ on the cross, believers have experienced true forgiveness (2:13), and God has canceled the multitudinous charges that stood against them (2:14). In the light of this glorious fact, how can Christians harbor grievances against fellow Christians? Because every person in the world is different from every other person to some degree, each is bound to find characteristics in others that grate against his own characteristics. This does not change when individuals become Christians. Sometimes the differences among people seemingly become more than they can bear, and they say things they should not say to one another. In these cases the only recourse is to ask for forgiveness and to be quick to grant forgiveness to one another.

**14. And above all these things [put on] charity:** . . . and in addition to all these, *—SAWR* . . . put on the robe of love, *—NOYS* . . . be truly loving, *—PHLP.*
  **which is the bond of perfectness:** . . . the bond of the completeness, *—WLSN* . . . the golden chain of all the virtues, *—PHLP.*

**3:14.** "Charity" or "love" (NIV) (*agapē*) is the belt which keeps all the other virtues in place. It could also be compared to a lubricant that enables the parts of a complicated machine to function smoothly. It is the motivating force for a believer, uniting all the other qualities into a state of completeness.

The language of the verse comes from the type of garments worn by people in the day in which this statement was written. Because people normally wore loose-flowing outer garments, it often became necessary to "gird the loins" before moving into action. Having the "loins girded" indicated a state of readiness. For instance, a soldier could not move quickly against the enemy unless he tied his garments with his belt or girdle. Without a sincere love for other people it would be impossible to overlook the faults they manifest.

**15. And let the peace of God rule in your hearts:** . . . the peace that Christ can give keep on acting as umpire, *—WLMS* . . . arbitrate in, *—PNIN* . . . rejoice in your hearts, *—DOUY* . . . reign in your hearts, *—CNFT* . . . preside in your hearts, *—SCLT* . . . control your thinking, *—EVRD* . . . exult in your hartes, *—RHEM.*
  **to the which also ye are called in one body:** . . . for you were called to this state as members of, *—WLMS* . . . You were all called together in one body, *—EVRD* . . . as members of the same body you are called to live in harmony, *—PHLP.*
  **and be ye thankful:** . . . And practice being thankful, *—WLMS* . . . and never forget to be thankful, *—PHLP.*

**3:15.** As the Christian allows these virtues to abide within him and as he permits God's love to hold all these "garments" in place, the "peace of God" will serve as an umpire. This refers to the peace Christ gives to His people (John 14:27). Situations often arise in which a person must choose among various options. A wise Christian is one who does not allow any course of action to ruffle the peace within him.

This principle also could apply to a local congregation of believers. Some assemblies seem always to be at odds over some matters, usually very minor ones. On the other hand, some local churches do not allow such matters to upset the balance of peace that exists among them. "Peace" (*eirēnē*), or "inner tranquility," will reign supremely if given a chance to do so.

On the other hand, peace seems to be very delicate and can be frustrated very easily. This peace needs to be accompanied by thankfulness. If thankfulness becomes a way of life, it will make it much easier to maintain a state of peace. It helps us look on the bright side instead of focusing upon the events which can disturb our calm.

**16. Let the word of Christ dwell in you richly in all wisdom:** . . . Let the teaching of Christ, *—EVRD* . . . have its home in you, *—MNTG* . . . dwell in you abundantly, *—CNFT, —SCLT* . . . dwel in you plenteously, *—GNVA* . . . aboundantly, *—RHEM* . . . continue to live in you in all its wealth of wisdom, *—WLMS.*
  **teaching and admonishing one another in psalms and hymns and spiritual songs:** . . . keep on teaching it to one another and training one another in it with thankfulness, *—WLMS* . . . and help one another along the right road with your psalms and hymns and Christian songs, *—PHLP* . . . and spiritual canticles, *—RHEM.*
  **singing with grace in your hearts to the Lord:** . . . in [your] gratitude singing, *—RTHM* . . . in your hearts singing praise, *—WLMS* . . . with thankfulness, *—EVRD* . . . with gratitude in your hearts, *—WLSN* . . . singing God's praises with joyful hearts, *—PHLP.*

**3:16.** This verse contains another imperative about allowing the "word of Christ" to dwell within us. This probably has reference to the gospel message that should be central in all our teachings. If that is true, it will be "wise teaching" (*didaskontes*) and "admonishing" or "counseling" (*nouthetountes*).

Furthermore, the gospel message should be central in our singing, which here is described ideally as a balance among the Old Testament Psalms put to music, "hymns," which are songs addressing praise to God, and "spiritual songs," which probably are songs of testimony addressed to God. The last term also could mean singing in other languages as people worship God.

**17. And whatsoever ye do in word or deed:** . . . Everything you say and everything you do, *—EVRD* . . . whatever you say or do, *—WLMS* . . . or in work, *—SAWR, —RHEM* . . . or action, *—SCLT.*
  **[do] all in the name of the Lord Jesus:** . . . let it all be done with reference to, *—WLMS.*
  **giving thanks to God and the Father by him:** . . . and through Him continue to give thanks to God the Father, *—WLMS.*

**3:17.** The total passage closes in this verse with a summary of the fundamental principle of Christian ethics. While the New Testament does contain many negatives such as the ones listed in verses 5-11, it is not just a list of do's and don'ts. Rather, the main guiding principle for word and action is that we should not bring reproach on the name of the Lord Jesus. If we say and do everything in harmony with His revealed will and because we are His followers, it truly will be said and done by His authority.

The last part of verse 17 shows that this kind of lifestyle does not come out of a sense of duty, but out of gratitude to God the Father for all that Christ has done for us. It is very fitting that Christians should respond to God out of gratitude for His marvelous grace extended to them. The apostle Paul definitely believed in Christian standards, but standards that are Christ-centered and that emanate from the Scriptures.

18. **Wives, submit yourselves unto your own husbands:** . . . continue to live in subordination to, —WLMS . . . adapt yourselves to, —PHLP.
**as it is fit in the Lord:** . . . as is becoming, —RTHM . . . for that is your duty as Christians, —TCNT.

**3:18.** After describing Christ as the only all-sufficient Saviour for mankind and the source of the Christian's life, Paul applied the supremacy of Christ to particular groups of people. A correct understanding of the word "submit" (*hupotassō*) here can come only by realizing the verb is in the middle voice.

Because the verb is not active the husband cannot say, "You must submit to me," and because it is not passive, the wife cannot say, "I am forced to submit to you." The middle voice represents the actor in a sentence somehow participating in the results of the action. Here the verb is middle voice to show the necessity of this submission being voluntary. This does not imply he is any more important than she, nor that she is on any lower level (Galatians 3:28).

The Bible makes it clear that not every person fills the same function (Romans 12:3-8; 1 Corinthians 12:27-31; Ephesians 4:11). The same is true in the family that is true in the Church in general. The husband's role is to be the spiritual leader of the family, and the wife's is to support him in that role. The supportive role is just as important as the leadership role. Paul added, "as it is fit in the Lord," or "this is in harmony with His will."

19. **Husbands, love [your] wives:** . . . be sure you give your wives much love and sympathy, —PHLP.
**and be not bitter against them:** . . . and never treat them harshly, —TCNT . . . and do not behave harshly to them, —WLSN . . . and be not cross or surly with them, —MNTG . . . don't let bitterness or resentment spoil your marriage, —PHLP.

**3:19.** Husbands, on the other hand, are obligated to love their wives and not to treat them harshly. The fact that Paul wrote such terse statements in Colossians relative to the relationship between husbands and wives serves as one reason some think he wrote this letter first, then followed it with Ephesians.

20. **Children, obey [your] parents in all things:** . . . your duty is to obey your parents, —PHLP.
**for this is well pleasing unto the Lord:** . . . for at your age this is one of the best things you can do to show your love for God, —PHLP.

**3:20.** Christ also should be supreme in the relationship between children and parents. Children are instructed to obey their parents in everything. One should realize again that this is referring to a Christian family where the parents and children are believers. God, of course, does not expect a Christian child to sin just to obey the whim of an unbelieving parent. Paul added the qualifier "in the Lord" (Ephesians 6:1).

21. **Fathers, provoke not your children [to anger]:** . . . be not fault-finding, —SAWR . . . be not irritating, —RTHM . . . do not exasperate, —SCLT . . . do not harass, —MNTG . . . do not provoke your children to resentment, —NORL . . . to indignation, —RHEM.
**lest they be discouraged:** . . . or they may become disheartened, —TCNT . . . lest they be of a desperate mynde, —CRNM . . . lest you make them spiritless, —MNTG.

**3:21.** The term "fathers" here may actually refer to parents as it does in Hebrews 11:23. It is not clear whether Paul intended to give this instruction to both parents, but the apostle considered fathers the spiritual leaders of their homes. As such they ultimately were accountable for what happened in the home.

Paul warned fathers against becoming too severe with their children, lest the latter become discouraged because of the severity of the demands placed upon them. Sincere parents, of course, want their children to surrender their lives to Christ and do His will. Because of this they have a strong tendency to pressure their children to do right, and if they are not very careful, this pressure can take the form of constant nagging. While the Scriptures definitely instruct children to obey their parents, parents should not depend on force but administer discipline in love, justice, and moderation.

**22. Servants, obey in all things [your] masters according to the flesh:** . . . Slaves, practice obedience to your earthly masters in everything, *—WLMS.*

**not with eyeservice, as men-pleasers; but in singleness of heart, fearing God:** . . . not as though they were watching you and as though you were merely pleasing men, *—WLMS* . . . giving them undivided service, in reverent awe of the Master, *—TCNT* . . . with a sincere heart, *—SAWR* . . . in Sincerity of Heart, *—WLSN* . . . out of reverence for your Lord, *—MNTG* . . . in simplicity of heart, fearing the Lord, *—PNT.*

**3:22.** One should not assume from these comments that the apostle Paul favored slavery. Nowhere in his writings does he endorse this system. In fact, in 1 Timothy 1:10 "menstealers" or "slave traders" are classed with "whoremongers," "liars," and other evildoers. The Roman world at that time was full of slaves. Some Bible commentators estimate that approximately one-third of the population of the Roman world consisted of slaves. Paul did not recommend outright revolt by slaves against their masters but rather advocated faithful service, as unto the Lord.

**23. And whatsoever ye do, do [it] heartily:** . . . whatever ye are employed in, work from the heart, *—SCLT* . . . So no matter what the task, do your work heartily, *—NORL* . . . do it with all your heart, *—WLMS* . . . work it from the soul, *—WLSN* . . . put your whole heart and soul into it, *—PHLP.*

**as to the Lord, and not unto men:** . . . as doing it for the Lord, *—NORL* . . . as work for the Lord and not for men, *—WLMS* . . . as into work done for God, and not merely for, *—PHLP.*

**3:23.** "Do it heartily" actually comes from a Greek phrase containing the word for *soul* (*psuchē*). The statement serves as good proof that more than the body is involved. The terminology used shows that attitude is just as important as physical condition.

The attitude expressed in this verse certainly militates against the selfish approach often fostered by some people. Sometimes individual employees have become so selfish they keep seeking more and more from employers until eventually companies are forced to close. In other cases, employees have been willing to make wage concessions in order to save their company and their jobs. Whether slaves or employees, when a person looks at labor as working for the Lord, their total mental outlook changes.

**24. Knowing that of the Lord ye shall receive the reward of the inheritance:** . . . the recompense of the inheritance, *—CLMT* . . . for you know that it is

from the Lord that you are going to get your pay in the form of an inheritance, *—WLMS.*

**for ye serve the Lord Christ:** . . . so keep on serving, *—WLMS* . . . since you are actually employed by, *—PHLP.*

**3:24.** Paul could have encouraged the slaves to rebel against their owners. Instead he reminded them of the permanent reward they would receive from the Lord, providing they were laboring for His glory. The Bible promises God's people an eternal reward that will far outweigh the difficulties experienced in these few years upon this earth.

**25. But he that doeth wrong shall receive for the wrong which he hath done:** . . . but the delinquent will receive, *—MRDK* . . . he who acts unjustly, *—WLSN, —SCLT* . . . will be paid back, *—MNTG* . . . the wrong he has done, *—WLMS.*

**and there is no respect of persons:** . . . and human distinctions will not be recognised, *—TCNT* . . . and there will be no favoritism, *—MNTG* . . . and there are no exceptions, *—WLMS* . . . naturally no distinction will be made between master and man, *—PHLP.*

**3:25.** Interestingly enough, the apostle Paul included failure to fulfill our responsibilities in our vocations in the category of items considered wrong or unrighteous. The principle of sowing and reaping is emphasized in many places in the Scriptures. Just as a person who sows corn can expect to reap a harvest of corn, so a person who sows righteous acts can expect to reap righteousness. No one is foolish enough to think he can sow one type of seed and reap some other type of fruit, but many people seem to think they can sow unrighteousness without reaping the results. The reaping is just as sure as the sowing.

Paul reminded the Colossians that God does not show favoritism. The Greek term from which we derive "respect of persons" actually comes from the word for *face* (*prosōpon*). Therefore, Paul is saying that what a person's face looks like does not make any difference with God. Because of attractive physical features, some people are able to get away with things other people might not be able to get away with in their human relationships. God, however, does not make His decisions based upon the facial features of a person. He will reward according to the inner motives of the individual.

## Chapter 4

**1. Masters, give unto [your] servants that which is just and equal:** . . . you must practice doing the right and square things by your slaves, *—WLMS* . . . do equity, *—MRDK* . . . render justice and equity to, *—WORL* ... and equitable, *—PNT* ... deal justly and fairly with, *—MNTG.*

**knowing that ye also have a Master in heaven:** ... have a heavenly employer, *—PHLP.*

**4:1.** Paul's comments in this section seem to be rather one-sided, but he did not leave the subject without a stern warning that masters should treat their slaves properly, because they also had a Lord or Master. "Just" in this verse refers to providing justice, and "equal" relates to the necessity of being equitable in all transactions with slaves. Apparently these masters worshiped God in the local assembly alongside their own slaves. A tendency might develop to give preference to the masters.

**2. Continue in prayer:** ... Always maintain the habit, *—PHLP* ... Attend constantly, *—WLSN* ... Persevere in prayer, *—MRDK* ... Devote yourselves to prayer, *—TCNT.*

**and watch in the same with thanksgiving:** ... be both alert and thankful, *—PHLP* ... and by this means stay wide awake when you give thanks, *—WLMS.*

**4:2.** After showing in detail that Christ must be supreme in everything, from creation even to our actions at home, Paul exhorted the Colossians with respect to two very important matters: prayer and their conduct toward unbelievers. With respect to the first exhortation concerning prayer, the apostle first clarified the fact that God's will concerning prayer is that we devote ourselves to it, or that we continue in it. Although prayer is to be maintained as a regular habit, it should not become just a routine matter. It is to be accompanied with watchfulness, which denotes diligence and persistence. The term "watch" literally means "to be awake." Paul emphasized thankfulness as needed to accompany prayer.

**3. Withal praying also for us:** ... At the same time keep on praying for me too, *—WLMS.*

**that God would open unto us a door of utterance:** ... for the entrance of, *—PHLP.*

**to speak the mystery of Christ:** ... to announce, *—CNFT* ... to declare, *—SAWR* ... talk freely of, *—PHLP* ... that I may tell the open secret about Christ, *—WLMS.*

**for which I am also in bonds:** ... for which I am even confined, *—SCLT.*

**4:3.** The apostle certainly was not above asking other people to pray for him. However, this verse indicates his request was not for selfish ends. His statement reveals one of the most important purposes for prayer, liberty to proclaim the gospel message. No one can doubt that Paul's consuming desire was for the advancement of the gospel. The pronoun "us" no doubt includes his coworkers mentioned later in the chapter. He literally

requested the Colossians to pray that God would "open . . . a door" for the Word. He may have been expressing his desire that the obstacles standing in the way of the preaching of the gospel be removed (1 Corinthians 16:9; 2 Corinthians 2:12), or he may have been asking for the Holy Spirit's help (Ephesians 6:19, 20).

**4. That I may make it manifest, as I ought to speak:** ... that I may declare it plainly, *—SAWR* ... that I may unfold it, *—MRDK.*

**4:4.** This verse seems to indicate that Paul had in mind the necessity of having the Holy Spirit's assistance in proclaiming the gospel. He knew his efforts would be futile without that divine aid. The "it" comes from a personal pronoun (*auto*) that is neuter in gender, referring back to the phrase in verse 3, "the mystery of Christ," which also is neuter. The term probably means the same as it does in 2:2, that Christ does indeed indwell His people, and it is possible for a person to have a living relationship with Him. Helping people know this glorious fact was one of the most prominent passions of Paul's life.

For many years he lived a religious life. He was extremely zealous for what he thought was right (Galatians 1:14), but he exchanged all that for the privilege of knowing Christ, or having a personal relationship with Him through being born from above (Philippians 3:7). From the time of his personal conversion to Christ (Acts 9) until the time of his death, the apostle's consuming desire was to help other people know this same kind of experience.

**5. Walk in wisdom toward them that are without:** ... Be wise in your behavior toward non-Christians, *—PHLP.*

**redeeming the time:** ... and lose no oportunite, *—CRNM* ... buying up your opportunities, *—MNTG* ... make the best possible use of, *—PHLP.*

**4:5.** New Testament Christians used the term "them that are without" or "outsiders" (*tous exō*) for those people who were unbelievers (1 Corinthians 5:12, 13; 1 Thessalonians 4:12; 1 Timothy 3:7), but they did not use the term in a derogatory manner. Paul's instruction to "walk in wisdom toward them" shows his first reason for stating Christians should be "redeeming the time." They were to "buy up" every opportunity to be guided by wisdom, or to take every opportunity to live up to the light of God's will (1:9).

**6. Let your speech [be] alway with grace, seasoned with salt:** ... Speak pleasantly to them, but never sentimentally, *−PHLP* . . . be all wayes well favoured, *−TNDL.*

**that ye may know how ye ought to answer every man:** . . . that ye may know how it is necessary for you to answer each other, *−CLMT* . . . how to give every man a fitting answer, *−MNTG* . . . each one in a proper way, *−NORL.*

**4:6.** Paul's second area of concern was related to the speech of the Colossian saints. He encouraged them to have speech "with grace," or "gracious" (RSV) speech. The person who manifests gracious speech can do so because he has experienced the grace of God in a personal way. Having experienced this marvelous grace should make a person want to see other people also enjoy it. Therefore, gracious speech comes as a result of God's grace being manifested in a Christian.

"Seasoned with salt" comes from a perfect participle (*ērtumenos*) and literally means "having been seasoned," indicating something previously appropriated that continues to operate. The term could refer to the attractiveness of one's speech as salt enhances flavor, or to the idea that salt prevents corruption, from the common use of salt as a preservative. Paul probably had the latter idea in view.

**7. All my state shall Tychicus declare unto you:** . . . All my circumstances, *−PNT* . . . All my affairs, *−ASV* . . . will inform you of all things relating to me, *−SAWR.*

**[who is] a beloved brother, and a faithful minister and fellow-servant in the Lord:** . . . and Faithful Assistant, *−WLSN* . . . in the Master's work, *−TCNT.*

**4:7.** Paul's rather lengthy conclusion to the epistle gives a beautiful portrait of his fellow laborers in the gospel, in addition to referring casually to Barnabas. Paul was not a loner; he apparently enjoyed being with other people. More importantly, he was a very secure man who was not afraid to share his ministry with other people. He normally seemed to have several associates assisting him. He definitely had learned the important lesson of reproducing himself through other people. Paul called Tychicus a "beloved brother," a "faithful minister and fellow servant" (Acts 20:4; Ephesians 6:21; 2 Timothy 4:12; Titus 3:12).

**8. Whom I have sent unto you for the same purpose:** . . . This is partly why, *−PHLP* . . . for this very purpose, *−MNTG.*

**that he might know your estate, and comfort your hearts:** . . . The other reasons are . . . that he may put new heart into you, *−PHLP* . . . the things that concern you, *−DOUY* . . . that he might know your affairs, *−MRDK* . . . that he may know your condition, *−NOYS* . . . that he may give your hearts renewed courage, *−NORL* . . . to cheer your hearts, *−MNTG.*

**4:8.** Tychicus proved himself to be such a faithful associate of Paul that the latter was able to send him all the way from Rome to visit the Colossians. Paul knew these saints were concerned about his welfare, and he was concerned about their state of affairs. So, he sent a personal emissary at least 1,000 miles.

**9. With Onesimus, a faithful and beloved brother:** . . . our dear trustworthy Brother, *−TCNT* . . . well loved, *−PHLP.*

**who is [one] of you:** . . . who is one of your own number, *−WLMS* . . . of your own congregations, *−PHLP.*

**They shall make known unto you all things which [are done] here:** . . . They will tell You, *−WLSN* . . . will inform you of every thing here, *−NOYS* . . . of conditions and activities here, *−PHLP* . . . that is going on here, *−TCNT.*

**4:9.** Onesimus, Philemon's runaway slave who had been converted under Paul's ministry in Rome, was a native of Colossae and is described in detail in the apostle's letter to Philemon. Onesimus and Tychicus took the letter to the Colossian church. By the time Paul wrote his epistle to the Colossians Onesimus had become "a faithful and beloved brother."

**10. Aristarchus my fellow-prisoner saluteth you:** . . . my fellow-captive, *−WLSN, −MRDK* . . . sends you his good wishes, *−TCNT* . . . wishes to be remembered to you, *−WLMS.*

**and Marcus, sister's son to Barnabas:** . . . the first-cousin, *−RTHM* . . . the cousin of, *−PNIN, −MNTG.*

**(touching whom ye received commandments:** . . . I believe I told you before about him, *−PHLP* . . . about whom you received, *−MNTG* . . . received instructions, *−CNFT* . . . received directions, *−NOYS.*

**if he come unto you, receive him;):** . . . give him welcome, *−RTHM* . . . give him a hearty welcome, *−WLMS.*

**4:10.** Next, Paul mentioned three Jews who were assisting him at that time. Aristarchus (Acts 19:29; 20:4; 27:2) was a Macedonian from Thessalonica. While it is possible that this man voluntarily became a prisoner in order to assist Paul, the title "fellow prisoner" may be used in a metaphorical sense to denote a person's voluntary submission to Christ.

John Mark was Barnabas' cousin who had abandoned Paul and Barnabas during Paul's first missionary journey (Acts 13:5, 13). (Although the King James' translators referred to Mark as Barnabas' nephew, most commentators render the Greek term *ho anepsios* as "cousin." The word actually could mean either.)

When Barnabas wanted to take Mark on the second journey, a serious rift developed between him and Paul (Acts 15:37-39). The apostle eventually was reconciled to both men (1 Corinthians 9:6; 2 Timothy 4:11; Philemon 24). As far as we know, Paul's reference to Mark here is the first mention made of the latter since that separation. The apostle's attitude toward Mark had made a complete about-face. This same Mark was a companion to Peter (1 Peter 5:13) and wrote the second Gospel. The parentheses in verse 10 may indicate Paul had written previously to the Colossian church.

**11. And Jesus, which is called Justus:** . . . So does Jesus who is called, —WLMS . . . Joshua, —TCNT.

**who are of the circumcision. These only [are my] fellowworkers unto the kingdom of God, which have been a comfort unto me:** . . . Of the Jewish Christians, —NORL . . . another Hebrew Christian, —PHLP . . . though still holding to circumcision, —TCNT . . . These are the only converts from Judaism that are fellow-workers with me here for the kingdom of God, who have proved a real comfort to me, —WLMS . . . became to me an encouragement, —RTHM . . . which were vnto my consolacion, —TNDL.

**4:11.** Jesus Justus completed the trio of Jews who were a comfort to Paul at that time. "Jesus," the Greek form of *Joshua* or *Jeshua,* was a common Jewish name, but in this case it was coupled with the Latin surname Justus, meaning "the just" or "the righteous." This is the only reference to him in the Scriptures. Paul's comment in this verse does not imply these men were the only Jews to accept the gospel message. It just means that at that time they were the only Jews assisting him in his ministry. The statement probably relates only to Jews who were connected with Paul's ministry while he was in prison.

**12. Epaphras, who is [one] of you:** . . . one of your own number, —WLMS . . . another member of your Church, —PHLP.

**a servant of Christ, saluteth you:** . . . wishes to be remembered to you, —WLMS . . . sends his greeting, —PHLP.

**always labouring fervently for you in prayers:** . . . always striving, —SAWR . . . who is ever solicitous for you, '—CNFT . . . He works hard for you, —PHLP . . . always earnestly pleading for you in his prayers, —WLMS . . . always agonizing for you, —MNTG . . . striving for you, —PNIN . . . contending in your behalf, —RTHM.

**that ye may stand perfect and complete in all the will of God:** . . . that you may become mature, —PHLP . . . that you may hold out and perfectly carry out God's will in everything, —NORL . . . that you may stand fast as men mature and of firm convictions in everything required by the will of God, —WLMS . . . fully assured in, —PNIN, —RTHM, —ALFD, —NOYS . . . in the Whole Will of God, —WLSN . . . in all the good pleasure of God, —MRDK.

**4:12.** Paul also mentioned three Gentiles who were supporting him for the gospel at that time.

Epaphras, who probably started the churches in Colossae, Laodicea, and Hierapolis, had been sent by the Colossians to visit the apostle. He must have been converted during the 3 years Paul ministered in Ephesus (Acts 20:31), spent some time under Paul's tutelage, and returned to his home area to publish the good news about Jesus Christ to his family, friends, and others. In this verse Paul commended Epaphras for being a servant of Christ Jesus and for earnestly praying for the saints in Colossae, Laodicea, and Hierapolis because he wanted them to mature in Christ.

**13. For I bear him record:** . . . For I can testify, —WLMS . . . From my own observation I can tell you, —PHLP.

**that he hath a great zeal for you:** . . . to his deep interest in you, —MNTG . . . he has a real passion for your welfare, —PHLP . . . much labour for you, —DOUY, —ASV.

**and them [that are] in Laodicea and them in Hierapolis:** . . . and for the brothers, —WLMS . . . and for that of the Churches at, —PHLP.

**4:13.** This verse continues to emphasize how concerned Epaphras was that these three churches should be delivered from the Gnostic heresy. The fact that he traveled all the way from Colossae to Rome to seek Paul's advice and help certainly indicates the severity of the situation. Too often believers allow false doctrines to infiltrate church congregations without taking the matter seriously.

Much gnosticism under different names has infiltrated into some contemporary churches. Perhaps if more people were wrestling in prayer as Epaphras did, there would be less trouble with such heresy. People who are in constant communion with God in prayer certainly are more capable of detecting false doctrine when the devil tries to introduce it into an assembly. If he cannot keep people from believing the gospel, he will try to get them off track with false doctrine. Many modern assemblies seem to be troubled with some of the same false doctrines that Paul exposed in this epistle, especially in the second chapter where he specifically pinpointed certain views that were inconsistent with the completeness of believers in Christ.

**14. Luke, the beloved physician, and Demas, greet you:** . . . our much-loved doctor, —TCNT . . . the most deere, —RHEM . . . Our dearly loved . . . wish to be remembered to you, —WLMS.

**4:14.** Luke, the author of the third Gospel and Acts, was a physician who accompanied Paul on parts of his second and third missionary journeys, as well as on his voyage to Rome. He may have used his healing skills to help the apostle, but we know for certain he faithfully assisted Paul in the gospel ministry (2 Timothy 4:10, 11; Philemon 24).

Anyone who knows much about the Greek language will agree that Luke's writings reflect the knowledge of a highly educated person. That, of course, would have meant nothing without the help of the Holy Spirit. The way the Acts of the Apostles was written should be ample proof of Luke's dependence upon the Spirit. Incidentally, Luke wrote a larger part of the New Testament than even Paul did, although the latter wrote a greater number of books. Some people give the impression that education helps very little when a person dedicates himself to Christian ministry. They stress that inspiration is far more important than education. Obviously, education will not suffice by itself. However, when inspiration, or the help of the Holy Spirit, is coupled with education, a person often has a wider sphere of ministry.

**15. Salute the brethren which are in Laodicea, and Nymphas:** . . . greetings, —PHLP . . . Remember me to the brothers, —WLMS.

**and the church which is in his house:** . . . and the assembly, —PNT . . . the congregation, —PHLP . . . the church that meets at her house, —WLMS . . . which meets at her home, —MNTG.

**4:15.** During the first centuries of the Early Church, local bodies of believers normally met for worship in houses like this one. Many of them contained large upper rooms which lent themselves to large gatherings of people. Normally only people who were fairly wealthy could afford such houses, so Nymphas must have been relatively affluent. Later in church history, the crowds became too large to meet in individual homes, so buildings were constructed for worship. Of course, Jesus himself made it clear that true worship does not depend upon the physical location (John 4:21-24).

**16. And when this epistle is read among you:** . . . When this letter has been read to you, —WLMS . . . in your Church, —PHLP.

**cause that it be read also in the church of the Laodiceans:** . . . have it read to, —WLMS.

**and that ye likewise read the [epistle] from Laodicea:** . . . and see to it that you too read the one that is coming from, —WLMS . . . see that you read the letter I have written to them, —PHLP.

**4:16.** The "epistle from Laodicea" is a mystery. Some commentators think the statement is a reference to the letter we know as Ephesians. Ephesians probably was written as a cyclical letter to be circulated throughout the churches in Asia Minor, but it is very unlikely the author of the letter

would call it the "letter from Laodicea" (NIV). A spurious letter that claims to be this "letter from Laodicea" does exist, but even a novice can detect that it consists of plagiarism of some of Paul's writings. The most likely and simplest explanation of this problem is that Paul did indeed write a letter to the Laodiceans which was lost for some reason. The fact that Paul told the Colossians to have this epistle read also in the Loaodicean church seems proof enough of this latter theory.

**17. And say to Archippus:** . . . A brief message to, —PHLP . . . tell Archippus, —WLMS.

**Take heed to the ministry which thou hast received in the Lord, that thou fulfil it:** . . . Be attentive, —MRDK . . . Attend to . . . to perform it fully, —SAWR . . . Attend on the service, —WLSN . . . See to it that you continue until you fill full your ministry which you received in the Lord's work, —WLMS . . . be careful to discharge to the best of his ability the office to which he was appointed, —TCNT . . . God called you into his service Oh, do not fail Him! —NORL.

**4:17.** Although we cannot be positive, Archippus probably was the son of Philemon and Apphia (Philemon 2) and may have been selected by the church as interim pastor during the absence of the pastor, Epaphras. The language of this verse does seem to indicate that some ministerial responsibility had been assigned to Archippus. "Take heed" literally comes from a Greek word (*blepe*) usually translated "look to" in this type of construction, and "ministry" is derived from the term from which we normally get *deacon* (*diakonian*), often meaning "ministry." Paul seemed convinced that Archippus had received this ministry "in the Lord," so it was not assigned to him through the will of man alone.

**18. The salutation by the hand of me Paul:** . . . This farewell greeting is, —WLMS . . . add this farewell in my own hand-writing, —TCNT, —MNTG . . . My personal greeting to you written by myself, —PHLP.

**Remember my bonds:** . . . Be mindful of my bonds, —WSLY . . . be ye myndeful of my boondis, —WCLF . . . Keep in mind, —RTHM . . . My chains! —WLSN . . . Remember that I am still a prisoner, —WLMS . . . Don't forget I'm in prison, —PHLP.

**Grace [be] with you. Amen:** . . . Spiritual blessing, —WLMS . . . God's blessing be with you, —TCNT.

**4:18.** Apparently an amanuensis, a person who writes what someone else dictates, had written the epistle up to this point. Most of Paul's epistles seem to indicate this normal pattern. Some people argue that Paul's use of this procedure proves his sight had deteriorated to the point that he was forced to use a secretary. It also could stem from the possibility that he had very poor handwriting, so used someone whose handwriting would be more readable. It was customary for Paul to write a few words of greeting with his own hand to mark the autographed letter as genuine and to discourage the spread of spurious letters.

Finally, he reminded the Colossians of his physical chains, a fact he referred to several times throughout the Prison Epistles. He did not state this to elicit sympathy, but perhaps to remind believers that his circumstances had been sifted through the grace of God. Perhaps that is why he included his final benediction, "Grace be with you." He knew God did not show special favor to him, but would manifest His grace to all individuals who would depend upon it. That fact has never changed.

# 1 THESSALONIANS

## Overview

The epistles of Paul can be separated into four groups: (1) *Eschatological,* epistles which deal with last things. (2) *Soteriological,* epistles which deal with the doctrine of salvation. (3) *Ecclesiastical,* epistles which deal with matters concerning the Church. (4) *Pastoral,* epistles which contain direction for the coworkers of Paul, the men who were shepherding local bodies of believers.

The two epistles to the Thessalonians belong to the first of these groups. The first epistle gives one of the most complete presentations of the return of Christ and the events connected with it which we have in the New Testament. The second epistle contains one of the principal prophecies concerning the man of sin, the Antichrist. Paul did not give this teaching in the form of an essay. As was his custom, he wove it together with encouragement and admonition.

It is possible to consider the epistles to the Thessalonians only from a strict, eschatological point of view. The exhortation sections were then directed to those who had misunderstood some of Paul's teaching concerning the Lord's return. In 1 Thessalonians the apostle replied to the questions which had arisen concerning believers who had died. Second Thessalonians deals primarily with questions concerning the return of the Lord and the Day of the Lord. It is no doubt correct to say that eschatological matters are the dominant theme of these two epistles, but there are other elements, especially in the First Epistle to the Thessalonians.

First Thessalonians is strongly related to 2 Corinthians where Paul defended his apostolic ministry. It seems that during this entire period of Paul's ministry he was persecuted continually by Jewish opponents who slandered him and used every opportunity to undermine his authority. They attacked not only his doctrine and preaching but his character and manner of living. This forced Paul to defend his ministry. This is evident both in 2 Corinthians and 1 Thessalonians as well as other places in his epistles.

The accusations against the apostle in Thessalonica seem, at least partly, to be the same as those he faced in Corinth. He was obviously accused of intending to take advantage of the church economically. His opponents tried to make the church he had founded suspicious of his motives. The future of the church depended on whether or not these personal attacks were rejected. Paul was the first Christian they had met. He represented the Christian faith (Moffatt, *Expositor's Greek Testament,* 4:6, 7). If their trust in him personally was undermined, it would quite naturally have a destructive influence on their faith in the message he had brought them. Paul defended himself not for his own sake but for the good of the church. The first half of this epistle deals with his defense.

In addition to the personal and eschatological themes, Paul also dealt with ethical and ecclesiastical matters. When we consider these insertions, 1 Thessalonians falls into six different parts including the Opening and Closing. Thus the following outline:

I. OPENING (1:1-4)

II. HISTORICAL MATTERS (1:5-2:16)

III. PERSONAL MATTERS (2:17-3:13)

IV. ETHICAL MATTERS (4:1-12)

V. ESCHATOLOGICAL TEACHING (4:13-5:11)

VI. CLOSING (5:23-28)

Paul reminded the Thessalonians of his ministry among them. He rejected all the accusations of his opponents by reminding the Thessalonians of the good results from the preaching of the gospel among them. He called their attention to the holy and blameless lives he and his coworkers had lived among them. He called God himself as a witness to this (2:5, 10), but he appealed also to the believers themselves (2:1, 5, 9, 10, 11). The Christians should not be affected by the accusations which had been brought against Paul and his fellow workers when they themselves had witnessed the clean and unselfish lives the missionaries lived. Paul reminded the church that those who now opposed the apostles had earlier killed the prophets and the Lord Jesus.

In 2:17 through 3:13 the apostle continued his defense by assuring the Thessalonians of his deep, personal affection for them. He wrote of his keen desire to visit them again and of the hindrance of Satan to the many attempts he had made to come to them (2:18). The Thessalonians were not to believe that indifference had caused Paul to delay his visit to them. On the contrary, he prayed night and day that God would make it possible for him to visit his friends again (3:10, 11). In the meantime the apostle had sent Timothy to them and rejoiced because of the good news Timothy had brought back (3:2-7).

## Paul's Ministry in Thessalonica

Paul first came to the city of Thessalonica with Silas during his first missionary journey (Acts 17:1f.). Thessalonica, which corresponds to the present-day Salonika, was a large and important seaport town. It was one of the most important cities in the Roman province of Macedonia. It was named after the half sister of Alexander the Great. When the Romans divided the conquered Macedonia into four republics, Thessalonica became the capital of one of these. When the province was once more united, Thessalonica became the capital and residence of the Roman governor.

The majority of the population was Greek, with an infusion of Romans and Orientals. There was a large Jewish colony in the city. As was his custom, Paul began his ministry in the synagogue where he spoke to the Jews on 3 Sabbath days. Paul lived and worked with a man named Jason, probably a Jew who had the same trade.

Paul's ministry in Thessalonica did not last long, but it had results. Some Jews and "of the devout Greeks a great multitude, and of the chief women not a few" were won for the gospel. This made the Jews jealous, and they stirred up a tumult. Jason's house was stormed with the intent of bringing Paul and Silas out to the people so they could be accused on some political matter. But Paul and Silas had slipped away, and in order not to cause further difficulty for the church, they traveled on.

During their stay in Thessalonica, which perhaps lasted 2 or 3 months, or perhaps up to half a year, Paul received gifts of money from the church in Philippi (Philippians 4:15, 16).

From the account in Acts it appears that Paul and Silas first went to Beroea where they had a successful work. When the aggressive Jews from Thessalonica heard this, they went to Beroea and "stirred up the people" there (Acts 17:13). In order to avoid further trouble, the believers sent Paul and his traveling companions to Athens. Timothy and Silas remained in Beroea. After a short stay in Athens, Paul went on to Corinth where he ministered for quite some time.

Paul had sent Timothy back to Thessalonica, and it was through him that Paul later learned of developments in the church in that city. The church had shown remarkable progress. Word of their faith in God had spread. Paul wrote that they had become a model for all the believers in Macedonia and Achaia.

However, the church at Thessalonica was not without problems. It seems that some were not showing proper respect for their leaders (5:12f.). Some of the members had become idle (4:11f., 5:14). It is possible the reason for this was that they did not understand the eschatological preaching of the apostles. Their misunderstanding of these matters possibly caused them to feel there was no reason to be concerned unduly with earthly matters when the coming of the Lord was so close at hand.

One matter which caused uneasiness in the church was the thought of "those which are asleep," the dead in Christ. Paul answered their questions in 4:13f. It must be remembered that this was still early in the history of the Church. It is generally accepted that Paul's letters to the Thessalonians are the earliest of his epistles, with the possible exception of the Epistle to the Galatians. Paul was ministering in Corinth when Timothy brought him the report of the church in Thessalonica (Acts 18:5). This was during the time when Gallio was the deputy of Achaia (Acts 18:12f.). On the basis of Roman records this was the year A.D. 51. It was during this year that both epistles to the Thessalonians were written.

There have never been any serious objections to the genuineness of the First Epistle to the Thessalonians. It is accepted as a genuine writing of Paul. Internal as well as external evidences confirm this. With some justification it has been said that the epistle itself is its strongest testimony. The epistle fits exactly into the historical context where it is placed. The external evidences are also distinct. It is included in Marcion's as well as in Muratori's canon. It can be found in ancient Syrian as well as in Latin translations. Irenaeus mentioned it in his great work *Against Heresies.* Tertullian quoted it as written by the apostle. Clement of Alexandria as well as other leading men of the Early Church ascribed it to Paul.

## Eschatological Teaching

The distinctive mark of 1 Thessalonians is Paul's teaching on eschatological matters (4:13 through 5:11). This teaching falls naturally into three parts: (1) Anticipation of Christ's return; (2) The Second Coming; (3) Times and seasons.

## Anticipation of Christ's Return

"And to wait for his Son from heaven, whom he raised from the dead, even Jesus, which delivered us from the wrath to come" (1:10). In a few compressed words this verse gives us a picture of the early return of Christ as viewed by the Early Church. The Thessalonians did not wait for an event but for a Person. This Person is identified in several ways: He is the Son of God. He is "the man Christ Jesus" (cf. 1 Timothy 2:5). He is the deliverer from the wrath to come. He is "Jesus of Nazareth, which was crucified" (Mark 16:6), now risen from the dead. He is the One who by His resurrection from the dead proved He is the mighty Son of God (Romans 1:4). He is "this same Jesus" (Acts 1:11) for whom the Thessalonians were waiting.

However, this event which represented hope and deliverance will also be a time of God's judgment upon sin. Therefore, the message concerning the return of Christ is a paradox. Christ's return will deliver believers from "the wrath to come," the wrath which His coming precedes. His return is therefore a consoling as well as a fear-inspiring event.

This judgment of wrath must by no means be understood as an impersonal process of nature, a product of cause and effect. On the contrary, the coming wrath is God's holy reaction against all unrighteousness and evil. It is not blind causation which brings judgment upon sin, but a God who sees everything. God has not given judgment upon sin to the dead laws of nature but to His only begotten Son. The wrath which will come upon sinners is the wrath of the Lamb (Revelation 6:16).

The Word gives examples of those who were saved from God's wrath in the past: Noah and his family in the ark; Lot from wicked Sodom; Israel from Egypt's bondage, having first been delivered from judgment by the blood placed upon the houses. In like manner the people of God will be delivered from God's judgment of wrath when Christ returns. That deliverance will come as a result of the grace that "is to be brought unto you at the revelation of Jesus Christ" (1 Peter 1:13).

God has called believers "unto his kingdom and glory" (2:12). The kingdom of God, which is now hidden in those who believe (Romans 14:17; 1 Corinthians 4:20; Colossians 1:13), will be manifested visibly (Matthew 25:31; Luke 1:32, 33; Revelation 2:26, 27; 20:4). Believers enter into the kingdom of God through many tribulations (Acts 14:22; 2 Thessalonians 1:4, 5), but those who suffer with Christ will be glorified with Him (Romans 8:17; 1 Peter 4:13).

Paul wrote (2:19, 20) that those whom he had won for Christ were his joy and honor. He considered the Thessalonian believers as his wreath of victory. To see them at Christ's coming would be reward indeed.

The hope of the return of Christ is the supreme motive for holy living (1 Thessalonians 3:13; cf. 1 John 3:3). However, Paul was not speaking here of sanctification as a process but of the complete and perfect holiness of believers at the return of Christ: "unblamable in holiness before God, even our Father, at the coming of our Lord Jesus Christ with all his saints." The Greek word which is used for *holiness* (*hagiōsunē*) here is used only one other time in the New Testament (Romans 1:4), and in the Septuagint it is used only concerning the holiness of God himself. This holiness was Paul's highest aim for his fellow believers. It is the holiness which God himself will produce in His own. Thus the return of Christ means not only that believers will be glorified, but that they will be perfectly sanctified.

## The Coming of the Lord

Although Paul had given the Thessalonian church a thorough introduction to the doctrine of latter things, evidently his oral teaching had not touched upon the questions the believers had concerning those who were dead in Christ. This matter had caused unrest in the church. These newly converted believers had a vivid expectation of the Lord's return. Their entire manner of life was adjusted to waiting for the Son of God from the heavens (1:10). Therefore, it took them totally by surprise when some of the members of the church died. These Christians were waiting not for death but for the return of Christ. Had the believers who died lost that which was the real aim and completion of their salvation? And, if they had not lost salvation itself, had they lost the opportunity to participate in the glorious climax of salvation history which His return represents?

Paul replied to this question, and he did so in a context which gives the most complete presentation of the return of Christ in the New Testament. His explanation is short and terse, but it presents a detailed picture of the different phases of the second coming of Christ. Paul spoke with apostolic authority. He had received many revelations from the Lord ever since the beginning of his ministry (cf. Acts 9:5, 6; 22:17-21; 1 Corinthians 11:23; Galatians 1:12; 2:2). In 1 Corinthians 15:51-54 Paul spoke of a "mystery" revealed to him concerning the transformation of believers at the return of the Lord. It is reasonable to believe that in the same revelation the Lord had given him information concerning those who are "dead in Christ."

The "dead in Christ" (4:16) are referred to as "them which are asleep" (4:13). Sleep as a picture of death among the Jews, as well as the Gentiles, spoke especially of the inactivity and cessation of the mind. For the Christian the picture of death as sleep has a much deeper and stronger meaning. By His death and resurrection Christ has changed death for the believer. To die in Christ is to expire and awake. It must not be understood as any kind of soul sleep. It is the body that sleeps in the grave (cf. Daniel 12:2). The spirit, the conscious personality, is separated from the body by death (James 2:26) and goes to be with the Lord (2 Corinthians 5:8). Paul declared that whether believers wake or sleep, they are together with the Lord. That this means a fully conscious condition appears from Philippians 1:23 where Paul declared that to be with the Lord is "far better" than the life on earth.

Paul thus sets the church at Thessalonica at rest concerning their fear and sorrow for the dead in Christ. This does not mean Paul praised death.

He still considered death an enemy, even though it has lost its sting for the Christian (1 Corinthians 15:26, 55). The apostle wished to be "clothed upon with our house which is from heaven" (2 Corinthians 5:2). This transformation will occur at the coming of Christ. But if the coming of the Lord should be delayed, Paul said he would rather "be absent from the body, and to be present with the Lord," that is, by death to be moved from life on earth to heavenly life (2 Corinthians 5:8).

It was important for Paul to convince the Thessalonians that the believers who had died would not suffer any loss. First, they were already with the Lord. Second, they would by no means lose the triumphant glory of the Lord's return. When the believers who live at the return of Christ are transformed, the dead in Christ will rise incorruptible (1 Corinthians 15:22). They who are alive will not go ahead of those who sleep. The dead in Christ will rise first (4:15, 16). In this connection, although Paul gave a survey of the events at the return of Christ, he did not mention any time interval because 1 Corinthians 15:52 tells us all will take place in a moment, in the twinkling of an eye. But even though from a human point of view it seems it will all take place simultaneously, it has its divine order of occurrence.

Before Paul explained the succession of the events, he referred to that which is the basis of the Christian hope for the future: ". . . if we believe that Jesus died and rose again" (4:14). Christian belief and hope have a historical anchorage. Christians do not build on philosophical speculations but on divine revelation. The resurrection of Christ is a model and guarantee of the resurrection of His people. He himself is the firstfruits of those who are asleep (1 Corinthians 15:20). In Him the resurrection of believers is a reality already. That which will take place with them has been demonstrated in Christ's resurrection (cf. Ephesians 1:19, 20).

Paul began this section with the words, "I would not have you to be ignorant, brethren, concerning them which are asleep" (4:13). Paul used this expression many times when he wanted to draw attention to an important matter or to introduce a new theme (Romans 1:13; 11:25; 1 Corinthians 10:1; 12:1; 2 Corinthians 1:8). The negative form is positive in meaning: "But I would have you know" (1 Corinthians 11:3; Colossians 2:1). It does not imply an accusation, as for instance the words, "Do ye not know?" (1 Corinthians 6:2, 3; 9:13) which refer to things they should have known.

Thus the apostle did not reproach the believers in Thessalonica for the unrest they were feeling because of the believers who had died. He exhorted them not to sorrow "as others which have no hope." Paul was not talking about natural, human sorrow because of the death of a believer. Jesus himself wept at the tomb of Lazarus and He understands human feelings. But when a believer goes to be with Christ, the church should not sorrow as those who have no hope. The apostle encouraged Christians to remember two things: First, the dead in Christ are now with Him; second, the dead in Christ will be together with Christ when He returns.

In a series of concise, short statements Paul drew a rough draft of the events which would take place at the parousia of Christ. This Greek word, the *parousia*, which also can mean "presence," is one of the principal words of the New Testament used in connection with Christ's return.

The first thing Paul mentioned is that Christ personally will return. He will not send a deputation of angels to take His people from the earth. The Lord himself will come down from the heavens. It will be an official, royal arrival. It will be accompanied by a commanding shout, with the voice of the archangel and the trumpet of God. The people of the world will probably hear but not understand the shout and the sound in a similar manner as men heard the voice from heaven when God spoke to Jesus (John 12:28, 29) or when the companions of Saul on the road to Damascus heard the heavenly voice (Acts 9:7; 22:9). But those who believe in Christ will understand immediately when they hear the Lord's shout and the sound of the trumpet.

The dead in Christ will arise and they, together with those who are alive in Christ, will receive their resurrection bodies, similar to the glorious body of Christ himself. Without any process of death those who "are alive and remain" will be clothed upon with their new house from heaven.

The two groups of believers, the dead and they who are alive, will be caught up in the clouds to meet the Lord in the air. The new bodies which believers will receive will make it possible for them to move about in space without difficulty, just as Jesus himself. But the air is only the meeting place, not a permanent residence. Opinions differ as to what happens next. Paul gives no details. He simply says, "And so shall we ever be with the Lord. Wherefore comfort one another with these words" (4:17, 18).

## The Times and the Seasons

In the preceding section Paul dealt with matters concerning the return of the Lord of which the Thessalonians were "ignorant" (4:13). But it seems the believers at Thessalonica, like the apostles (Acts 1:6, 7), wanted further information concerning the "times and the seasons."

In this new section (5:1-11) Paul appealed to the knowledge which the Thessalonians had received from his oral teaching during his time of ministry among them. The apostle used two words for "times" and "seasons." Times (*kronon*) speaks of chronological order. Seasons (*kairon*), while synonymous, speaks of the quality of the times rather than the chronology (cf. 1 Peter 1:11). The expression "day of the Lord" has an Old Testament background. "Lord" as well as "day" is without the article, so the designation almost always must be considered as a proper name (Morris, *New International Commentary on the New Testament, 1&2 Thessalonians,* p. 151 note 5). The Day of the Lord is the judgment day when God will punish sin. It is just as inevitable as the travail which comes upon a woman with child. Paul discussed the Day of the Lord further in his second epistle to the Thessalonians.

Next, Paul contrasted the attitudes of two different groups concerning "that day." Sudden and inevitable perdition will come to the children of darkness, but deliverance will come to the children of light. "For God hath not appointed us to wrath, but to obtain salvation through our Lord Jesus Christ" (5:9). The basis for this deliverance is that Christ "died for us, that, whether we wake or sleep, we should live together with him" (5:10). Here the apostle refers again to the preceding section where he has assured believers that the dead in Christ and those who are alive and remain will be caught away together. But judgment will come to the children of darkness who have lived in self-deceit. Their false security, when they say "Peace and safety," will only bring upon them "sudden destruction" (5:3).

# The First Epistle of Paul to the Thessalonians

## Commentary

### Chapter 1

1. **Paul, and Silvanus, and Timotheus: unto the church of the Thessalonians:** ... to the ecclesia, *—CNDT* ... to the congregation, *—CMPB* ... to the [local] assembly, *—WUST.*

**[which is] in God the Father and [in] the Lord Jesus Christ:** ... assembled in God, *—LILY* ... in union with God, *—TCNT.*

**Grace [be] unto you, and peace, from God our Father, and the Lord Jesus Christ:** ... May you have His loving favor, *—NLTG* ... Blessing and, *—FNTN* ... Gracious love, *—SEB* ... Favor to you, *—KLGS* ... [Sanctifying] grace to you and [tranquilizing] peace, *—WUST.*

**1:1.** Silas and Timothy joined Paul in greeting the church at Thessalonica. Silas, a leader of the Jerusalem church (Acts 15:22), traveled with Paul on his second missionary journey. Both spread the news of the Spirit's word of wisdom that Gentile Christians were not required to become Jewish proselytes or to be circumcised. Like Paul, Silas was a Roman citizen, and he proved to be an ideal companion in their travels (Acts 16:20, 37).

Timothy, on the other hand, was a young man who had a Greek father but a godly Jewish mother and grandmother. The believers in his home church told Paul what an outstanding young believer he was. This led Paul to take Timothy along as a helper and student. Thus the churches sent both younger and older leaders who were well qualified into the work of missions. Both Silas and Timothy were with Paul when the church at Thessalonica was founded.

In saluting the church (the assembly of free citizens of heaven who are under Christ's rule), Paul combined the two greetings, grace (commonly used by the Greeks) and peace (used by the Jews). Many used these words casually, like our "hello," but Paul used them with deep meaning. Grace is given first place. All we have, are, and hope for as Christians comes through the grace ("unmerited favor") of God, shown us by the death of His Son in our place. Then, with our sins taken care of at Calvary, we become recipients of the peace (health, well-being, wholeness, spiritual prosperity) that is our heritage in Christ (John 14:27).

2. **We give thanks to God always for you all:** ... We offer thanks, *—BRKL* ... We always thank God, *—SEB* ... I am continually thanking God, *—MNTG.*
**making mention of you in our prayers:** ... regularly mentioning you, *—ADAM* ... incessantly remembering, *—CMPB* ... constantly mentioning you, *—RSV* ... continually making a remembrance of you, *—CNFT.*

**1:2.** Though the Thessalonians had needs, Paul did not begin immediately to counsel or exhort the believers. His first thought was to express genuine thanksgiving for them, reminding them of his faithful prayers for them.

3. **Remembering without ceasing your work of faith:** ... We cannot forget, *—NORL* ... as I call to mind, *—MNTG* ... we never fail to recall the efforts, *—TCNT* ... and without intermission recall your active faith, *—BRKL* ... remembering your work that comes from faith, *—ADAM* ... produced and characterized by the faith, *—WUST.*
**and labour of love:** ... and labor that comes from love, *—ADAM* ... and your toil motivated and characterized by your divine and self-sacrificial love, *—WUST* ... your loving labour, *—FNTN.*
**and patience of hope:** ... and your enduring hope, *—CNFT* ... and endurance of hope, *—KLGS* ... and steadfastness of hope, *—RSV* ... your hope that never gives up, *—NLTG.*
**in our Lord Jesus Christ:**
**in the sight of God and our Father:** ... in front of, *—CNDT* ... in the presence of, *—MNTG.*

**1:3.** It was never Paul's habit to look on the dark side. His prayers for the Thessalonian Christians were full of the memory of the work which was inspired by their faith, the labor (unremitting toil) that flowed from their love, and the patience (steadfastness, endurance) based on their hope. Though Paul was with them only a short time, the preaching of the Word in the power of the Spirit had established in them the central and most abiding principles of Christian life. As Paul later told the Corinthians, faith, hope, and love will remain when all other gifts and blessings have fulfilled their function and have faded into the past (1 Corinthians 13:13).

The order is different here from that in First Corinthians, however. Faith, love, and hope is the order of experience rather than of importance. The preaching of the gospel first becomes effective when it is received in faith. The truth of Christ then gives a confidence in God and brings us to a commitment that is expressed in obedient work. The word *pisteōs* carries the idea of "faith-obedience."

**4. Knowing, brethren beloved, your election of God:** . . . I know, O brothers, beloved of God, *—MNTG* . . . we know His choice of you, *—BRKL* . . . that He has chosen you, *—NORL, —WLMS.*

**1:4.** Paul's thanksgiving for the Thessalonians was tied not only to their faith, love, and hope but also to their "election." The Greek word *eklogēn*, from which comes the English word "election," means a choosing out, the manner of choosing, and the way in which the choice is made. Ephesians 1:4 states that believers are elected in Jesus Christ and that this election was from before the foundation of the world. It was not an arbitrary election but an election "according to the foreknowledge of God the Father" (1 Peter 1:2). The Bible speaks much of God's election and is equally clear concerning man's responsibility to make his calling and election sure by faith and faithfulness.

**5. For our gospel came not unto you in word only:** . . . for the evangel of our God, *—CNDT* . . . not merely reach you in talk, *—BRKL* . . . not in mere words, *—NORL* . . . not merely as so many words, *—TCNT.*
**but also in power, and in the Holy Ghost, and in much assurance:** . . . and in much fullness, *—CNFT* . . . and it carried with it full conviction, *—TCNT* . . . and with sound conviction, *—BRKL* . . . with full conviction, *—RSV* . . . with deep conviction, *—MNTG* . . . and in much confidence, *—KLGS* . . . and with absolute certainty, *—WLMS.*
**as ye know what manner of men we were among you for your sake:** . . . It was for your good, *—NORL* . . . the manner in which I behaved myself among you, *—MNTG.*

**1:5.** Verses 5 and 6 give two reasons Paul knew their faith was real and why he could recognize them as brothers loved by God (loved with a continuing, abiding, faithful, holy love).

First, Paul knew their faith was real because of the way the gospel was presented. It was not just a matter of reasoning or eloquence. Paul had not come with the ranting of a deranged leader, nor with the persuasion of some modern philosopher, nor with the high pressure methods of some of the modern cults. He presented the gospel in word. It had content and meaning. But it came also in mighty power (*dunamei*), and in the Holy Spirit, and in much assurance. (See Acts 1:8; John 15:26, 27.) The message clearly was not from men but from God. (See 1 Corinthians 2:4, 5.)

Paul was not like those promoters of products and ideas who know that much of what they say is pure fabrication. When he preached the necessity of Jesus' death and resurrection in order to satisfy God's justice and show His love, he did so with full confidence in the truth of his message (Acts 17:2, 3). The Thessalonians recognized also that Paul and Silas backed up the message by the kind of lives they lived. They knew the character of these men by their kindness toward them, in that all they did was for the sake of the believers. They saw how unselfish the messengers were. They also saw them growing and developing in the power of the Spirit, just as they expected the believers to do.

**6. And ye became followers of us, and of the Lord:** . . . You copied us, *—SEB* . . . followed our example, *—NORL* . . . And you imitated us, *—KLGS* . . . you began to follow the pattern, *—MNTG* . . . followed the example set by us, *—WLMS.*
**having received the word in much affliction:** . . . having embraced the word, *—CMPB* . . . in spite of great affliction, *—LILY* . . . in great tribulation, *—CNFT.*
**with joy of the Holy Ghost:** . . . with the delight of, *—FNTN* . . . with such joy in, *—BECK* . . . joy from, *—ADAM* . . . with joy inspired by, *—RSV* . . . with a gladness inspired by, *—TCNT* . . . joy that had its source in, *—WUST.*

**1:6.** Secondly, Paul knew their choice was real because of their response to the gospel. They became followers (imitators) of Paul and of Christ. This was seen in the way they received (welcomed) the Word and in the way they continued to welcome it with Spirit-given joy even when severe affliction (persecution) arose.

**7. So that ye were ensamples to all that believe:** . . . with the result that you became a model for all those, *—ADAM* . . . so that you become models to all, *—CNDT* . . . you became a pattern to, *—MNTG, —WUST.*
**in Macedonia and Achaia:** . . . and Greece, *—BECK.*

**1:7.** The word *hōste* introduces a result clause and links together verses 6 and 7. Because they had received and continued welcoming the Word joyfully in the midst of tribulation (verse 6), the believers in Thessalonica had become "patterns" (*tupous*) for Christians not only in their own province of Macedonia but in Achaia (Greece) as well. Originally the word *tupon* described the impression left by a blow. Here the word carries an ethical meaning; that is, they served as "patterns" for Christian conduct and "examples" others could follow (see Morris, *New International Commentary on the New Testament, 1&2 Thessalonians,* p. 60). In other words, the entire church became a model for what a Christian church or assembly of the citizens of the kingdom of God ought to be.

Even today the Christian is under careful observation, and his life serves as an example to others, for good or for bad. This is especially true when the believer is in the midst of tribulations. If he remains steadfast in the Faith and loyal to the Lord, his message and his Master are wonderfully proclaimed. If, however, he departs from the Faith and deserts the Saviour, the credibility of the gospel suffers. To the unbeliever in particular, one's actions speak louder than one's words.

**8. For from you sounded out the word of the Lord:** . . . it was from you that the Lord's Message resounded, –TCNT . . . there has been caused to sound forth in a loud, unmistakable proclamation the word, –WUST . . . Not only has the Lord's Word spread from you through, –BECK . . . The Lord's message rang out from you, –SEB . . . has rung out from you, –WLMS . . . ring out loud and clear throughout, –NORL . . . has been echoed abroad, –FNTN.

**not only in Macedonia and Achaia, but also in every place your faith to God-ward is spread abroad:** . . . the echo of which still rolls on . . . in every place your faith which is directed toward God has gone forth, –WUST . . . and its sound has been heard . . . in every place where the tidings of your faith toward God, –MNTG . . . but everywhere people have heard of your faith in God, –BECK . . . but in every place where your faith in God has become known, –ADAM . . . has gone forth, –LILY . . . has been broadcast everywhere, –BRKL . . . has spread far and wide, –TCNT.

**so that we need not to speak any thing:** . . . so that we are not under any necessity to be saying a thing, –WUST . . . we need not say another word, –NORL . . . so that we don't need to say anything about it, –ADAM . . . so that we need never mention it, –WLMS.

**1:8.** By pointing to them as an example Paul did not mean the church was without problems. That which made them a pattern for others was the fact that from them the Word of the Lord (the message concerning Christ) rang out and *continued* to ring out (expressed by the perfect tense verb *exēchētai*). The picturesque word translated "sounded out" in the KJV occurs but once in the New Testament. From the time of Chrysostom (ca. A.D. 347-407) it has been thought to symbolize the brilliant tone and dynamic resonance of a sustained trumpet blast (see "Homilies on Thessalonians" in *Nicence and Post-Nicene Fathers,* 13:327ff.). Chrysostom also makes this observation about the virtuous character of a true Christian: "As a sweet-smelling ointment keeps not its fragrance shut up in itself, but diffuses it afar, . . . so too illustrious and admirable men do not shut up their virtue within themselves, but by their good report benefit many and render them better" (ibid., 13:327). Their message was clear and loud, like the crashing of thunder or like the continuous, clear call of a trumpeter leading an army attacking an enemy.

Not only was their witness effective in Macedonia and Achaia, but their location on the Egnatian Way, a major Roman trade route, brought them in contact with travelers from all over the Roman Empire. The believers took advantage of their opportunities and won many to Christ. The report of the extraordinary faith they expressed to God was spreading in all directions.

**9. For they themselves show of us what manner of entering in we had unto you:** . . . For they voluntarily tell about us, –BRKL . . . For others, of their own accord, –MNTG . . . what a welcome we had among you, –RSV . . . tell about our coming to you, –KLGS . . . what sort of entrance, –CMPB.

**and how ye turned to God from idols to serve the living and true God:** . . . from false gods, –SEB . . . to be slaves of a true, –MNTG . . . the God who lives on and is real, –WLMS.

**1:9.** Thus it was that when travelers from various parts of the Roman Empire met Paul in Corinth they would immediately begin to tell what they had heard in Thessalonica. They knew that Paul had entered the city and established a church. They told how the Thessalonians had turned to God from idols. This was no mere switching of religious affiliation or changing of philosophies such as the heathen might do. The Thessalonian believers had made a complete and total change in their lives and worship. They were now serving (as love slaves) the living and true (real, genuine) God. By this, they made it clear that the gods they once worshiped were not real. (Compare Isaiah 40:19; 41:7; 44:15-19.)

**10. And to wait for his Son from heaven, whom he raised from the dead:**
**[even] Jesus, which delivered us from the wrath to come:** . . . Jesus, our deliverer from the punishment which is impending, –TCNT . . . our Deliverer from the terror of the future, –FNTN . . . will rescue us from the punishment that is coming from God, –SEB . . . who keeps us from the coming wrath, –KLGS . . . from the coming retribution, –BRKL . . . out of the coming indignation, –CNDT . . . from the anger of God that is coming, –NLTG.

**1:10.** As soon as the Thessalonians responded to the truth of the gospel preached in the power of the Holy Spirit, they knew God to be real, and they came to know and love Him. Thus they did not find it hard to serve Him and wait for His Son to come from heaven.

Central to the faith of the Thessalonians was the fact that God had raised Jesus from the dead. His resurrection guarantees the resurrection of the believer (1 Corinthians 15:20; John 11:25, 26; 14:19). It also gives the assurance that what Jesus did by His sacrificial death on Calvary makes Him the believer's Deliverer (Rescuer, Preserver) from the wrath which is sure to come on a sinful world.

Paul's preaching to the Gentiles in Thessalonica must have been similar to his preaching to Gentiles in Athens (Acts 17:22-31). Paul taught that God is holy. He cannot go against His own nature. Thus, He cannot bring in Christ's holy kingdom without dealing with sin. He made provision for removing sin at the Cross. But His wrath (which is against sin, not against people) must come. The present world order must be destroyed before Christ can introduce the promised new order (Daniel 2:34, 35, 44; 7:26, 27; John 3:36; Romans 1:18; 9:22; Ephesians 5:6; Colossians 3:6; Revelation 1:18; 14:10, 19; 15:7; 16:1; 19:15). In view of this, the believers were always working, always ready, always prepared to meet the Lord.

## Chapter 2

**1. For yourselves, brethren, know our entrance in unto you, that it was not in vain:**...You yourselves can testify, *—NORL*...did not fail of its purpose, *—MNTG*...was not futile, *—BRKL*...was by no means a failure, *—WLMS*...was not a failure, *—NIV*...was not wasted, *—NLTG*...was not without results, *—TCNT*...was not ineffectual, *—FNTN.*

**2:1.** What travelers were saying (1:9) about Paul's effective presentation of the gospel, the Thessalonians themselves knew to be true. His ministry was not "in vain" (empty). His preaching was neither foolish, worthless, nor ineffective. More important, the manner of his preaching and the nature of his ministry were not empty in the sense of being hollow, unreal, false, or pretentious.

**2. But even after that we had suffered before, and were shamefully entreated, as ye know, at Philippi:**...although I had already borne, *—MNTG*...having been injuriously treated, *—YNG*...and being outraged in, *—CNDT*...and had been insulted, *—SEB*...shamefully handled, *—CMPB*...had been ill-treated and insulted, *—NORL.*
**we were bold in our God:**...we had confidence in, *—CNFT*...we took great courage, *—BRKL*...we dared to tell you, *—NIV.*
**to speak unto you the gospel of God with much contention:**...in much conflict, *—YNG*...amidst a great combat, *—CMPB*...in spite of great opposition, *—TCNT*...in spite of the terrific strain, *—WLMS.*

**2:2.** These evangelists were not seeking comfort, ease, or the praise of men. The Thessalonians knew what had happened at Philippi (Act 16:19-24) where Paul and Silas were shamefully insulted and treated outrageously. Though they were Roman citizens, they were beaten and thrown into a dank, inner dungeon where they were placed in stocks.

But their suffering and abuse at Philippi had not caused Paul and Silas to be timid or wary in presenting the gospel when they came to Thessalonica. The message they preached was the gospel, the good news of God. God gave it, and Paul and Silas were bold, free, open, and fearless in presenting it. Even in the face of great opposition, with enemies contesting every move, they could not keep still. (Compare Jeremiah 20:9.) The greater the conflict, the more intense the struggle, the more courageous the apostles became.

**3. For our exhortation [was] not of deceit, nor of uncleanness, nor in guile:**...For our entreaty, *—CNDT*...For our appeal did not originate from, *—WLMS*...our appeal to you was not based on a delusion, *—TCNT*...we did not make our appeal by advocating false doctrines, *—NORL*...our appeal springs neither from delusion, nor from impure motives, *—BRKL*...was not from error, nor from impure motives, *—CNFT*...or tricky motives, *—SEB.*

**2:3.** There was nothing of pretense about Paul and Silas. However, a strong defense of their ministry was needed, comments F.F. Bruce, because there were so many "wandering chaHrlatans" peddling their religious and philosophical wares for profit (*Word Biblical Commentary,* 45:26). But Paul was not motivated by personal ambition, pride, or prestige. Instead, it was the "love of Christ" that constrained him (see 2 Corinthians 5:14). As a result, their preaching or exhorting did not have its source in deceit (error, delusion, a wandering from the path of truth). Nor did it come from uncleanness (impurity, immorality, vicious or unnatural motives). Paul's methods were also free from guile (cunning, craftiness, and falsity).

**4. But as we were allowed of God:**...for since we have been so approved by God, *—WLMS.*
**to be put in trust with the gospel, even so we speak:**...as to be entrusted with...we are now telling it, *—WLMS.*
**not as pleasing men, but God, which trieth our hearts:**...not to ingratiate ourselves with men, *—BRKL*...who looks at our hearts, *—NORL*...God tests and proves our hearts, *—NLTG.*

**2:4.** Paul and Silas knew in their own hearts that they were approved of God, no matter what people might say about them. God, in fact, showed His approval by the very tests He put them through. By approving them in testing and finding them worthy He allowed them to be entrusted with the gospel.

This God-given trust was their only reason for speaking to the people. Nothing they said in their preaching or in their attempts to persuade men to accept Christ came from any desire to please or accommodate men. Their only desire was to please God, knowing they could not deceive Him or "pull the wool" over His eyes. He tries (examines, tests) the heart. (See 1 Samuel 16:7; 1 Chronicles 28:9; 29:17; Psalm 11:4; Jeremiah 11:20; 17:10; Romans 8:27.) Thus Paul had to be true to the full gospel (1 Corinthians 9:16).

**5. For neither at any time used we flattering words, as ye know:** ... we never used smooth-sounding words, —*NLTG.*

**nor a cloak of covetousness; God [is] witness:** ... neither were we under some pretext after money, —*BRKL* ... or a pretext for, —*CMPB* ... or make false professions in order to hide selfish aims, —*TCNT* ... nor any pretext for avarice, —*CNFT* ... with a pretense for greed, —*CNDT.*

**2:5.** The preaching of Paul and Silas was free also from the flattery and covetousness so common among those who seek to persuade. Flattering words usually cover up ulterior motives. Those who flatter usually want something for themselves or they want to use another person for their own benefit. God himself, who sees all, was a witness that Paul's preaching was not a cloak for covetousness. The Bible warns us against false teachers who may seem very good, very pious, but whose religion is only a cover-up for avarice. Their real god is their belly (Romans 16:18; Philippians 3:19). They pay lip service to Christ, but their real concern is to satisfy their greed.

**6. Nor of men sought we glory, neither of you, nor [yet] of others:** ... neither did we seek plaudations from, —*BRKL.*

**when we might have been burdensome, as the apostles of Christ:** ... We might have acted with authority, —*CMPB* ... we could have made heavy demands, —*NORL* ... we could have claimed a position of honor among you, —*CNFT* ... I might have exercised authority as Christ's apostle, —*MNTG* ... as apostles we could have stood on our official dignity, —*WLMS.*

**2:6.** For others, religion is just an act by which they try to get glory, honor, praise, and approval from men. Paul and his companions were not like that. At no time did any of them try to build up their personal prestige or exalt themselves. Never did they say things just to get the "amens" of the people.

Most often, Paul delighted to call himself a servant (literally, *doulos,* "a slave") of the Lord Jesus. A slave did not spend his time contending for his rights or exalting his own dignity. He had none. He was completely at his master's disposal. This is in line with the very word *apostolos* ("apostle") which means "sent one," a person sent with an obligation to carry out the commission given by his superior. Jesus was sent by the Father, sent to serve, not to be waited on. He gave His life (Mark 10:45). He told His apostles, "So send I you" (John 20:21).

**7. But we were gentle among you:** ... On the contrary, —*MNTG* ... mild-mannered in your circle, —*BRKL* ... in your midst, —*YNG* ... with a childlike simplicity, —*TCNT.*

**even as a nurse cherisheth her children:** ... like a nursing mother tenderly fostering her own, —*BRKL* ... like a mother caring for, —*NLTG* ... who fondles her own children, —*NORL* ... when she tenderly nurses her own children, —*MNTG.*

**2:7.** Nor did Paul and Silas try to throw their weight around. They did not wield apostolic authority in a haughty way or insist on their own importance as apostles. Instead of declaring who they were, they declared who Christ is. They saw their apostleship as a burden on their own hearts, not as a burden to be placed on the people. Thus they were never dictatorial. Instead of being burdensome, they were gentle. This was more than an occasional act of kindness. Their kindness was like that of a nursing mother who cherishes her own children, suckling them, keeping them warm, comforting them with all kinds of tender, loving care.

**8. So being affectionately desirous of you:** ... We loved you very much, —*SEB* ... We liked you so much, —*KLGS* ... being ardently attached to you, —*CNDT* ... in my fine affection, —*MNTG.*

**we were willing to have imparted unto you, not the gospel of God only, but also our own souls, because ye were dear unto us:** ... it was my joy to give you, —*MNTG* ... to lay down our very lives too for you, —*WLMS* ... because you came to be beloved by us, —*CNDT* ... but also our lives ... You had become precious to us, —*SEB.*

**2:8.** The apostles were not cold, harsh announcers of doom, and the "gospel" is not simply a homily preached from a pulpit or a street corner. It also involves the testimony, character, and lifestyle of the one who calls himself a Christian. Best remarks, "The missionary is not someone specialized in the delivery of a message but someone whose whole being, completely committed to a message which demands all, is communicated to his hearers" (*Black's New Testament Commentaries,* 10:102, 103). They approached the Thessalonians with affectionate desire, with warm, kindly feelings. Though as Gentiles the Thessalonians were ungodly and undoubtedly had many bad habits, the apostles did not withdraw from them or look down on them but were well pleased to share the gospel of God. They continued to share with the same attitudes when the Thessalonians began to accept the gospel. Then the people became even more beloved, and Paul, Silas, and Timothy were pleased to pour out their very souls for them. They shared their innermost selves, their whole personalities, even to the point of being willing to give their lives for the believers. This was no pretense. They really cared.

**9. For ye remember, brethren, our labour and travail:** ... You recall, —*MNTG* ... our toil and hardship, —*NIV* ... We were exhausted, —*SEB* ... you remember our hard work and sweat, —*KLGS*.

**for labouring night and day:** ... we worked at our trades, —*TCNT* ... working at manual labor, —*WUST*.

**because we would not be chargeable unto any of you:** ... so as not to be burdensome, —*CNDT* ... that we might not become a burden, —*ADAM*.

**we preached unto you the gospel of God:** ... while we proclaimed, —*WUST* ... we heralded to you, —*BRKL* ... I proclaimed to you, —*MNTG*.

**2:9.** Paul and Silas proved they cared. Some people might declare they would die for another, but when put to the test they would not cross the street to give help. But the Thessalonians would well remember the apostle's toil (hard work and exertion) in the midst of hardship. Night and day they worked hard and struggled to overcome difficulties so they would not be a burden to any. By his tentmaking, Paul supported the whole evangelistic party (Acts 20:34). The general picture seems to be that he worked from dawn until noon or a little after at his trade. Then he spent the rest of the day preaching, teaching, and going from house to house exhorting and encouraging the people (Acts 18:3, 4; 19:9; 20:20, 31).

Paul did not have to work so hard at his tentmaking. Even Jesus recognized that the worker who is spreading the gospel should receive wages for that work (Luke 10:7). Paul told the Corinthians that the command of the Law not to muzzle an ox while it is treading out the grain (Deuteronomy 25:4) was written for believers. Those who sow spiritual seed by the preaching of the gospel have a right to reap a material harvest from those who receive the benefits of the gospel. Paul, however, did not use this right (1 Corinthians 9:3-18). He did not want to burden the new churches he was founding. He wanted to do everything possible to establish them in the Lord. He was not preaching the gospel for money but because of a divine commission that he could not escape. Yet he taught the churches to support their elders who directed the affairs of the church and were faithful in teaching and preaching (1 Timothy 5:17, 18).

**10. Ye [are] witnesses, and God [also], how holily and justly and unblameably we behaved ourselves among you that believe:** ... You can testify ... with what pure, upright, and irreproachable motives, —*WLMS* ... you are those who bear testimony ... how blamelessly we ordered our lives among you, —*WUST* ... and so is God, —*MNTG* ... how purely, righteously, and blamelessly, we were with you believers, —*FNTN* ... and righteous and irreproachable

we were in our relationships to you, —*ADAM* ... was our conduct towards you, —*CNFT* ... and beyond reproach, —*TCNT*.

**2:10.** Not only were the apostles gentle, kind, and considerate, they were also men of integrity both in their actions and in their inner thoughts and purposes. The Thessalonians were witnesses to their behavior, as was God also. They knew what a holy (God-pleasing), just (right, upright), and blameless way of life the apostles showed in all their relationships with the believers. None of them could point a finger of reproach or accusation against any of Paul's company. Every one of them were men and women of unimpeachable honesty and sincere devotion. What a contrast they were to the false teachers who were making accusations against them.

**11. As ye know how we exhorted and comforted and charged every one of you, as a father [doth] his children:** ... even as you know how as a father exhorts and encourages his own children, —*WUST* ... we urged and encouraged, —*ADAM* ... appealed to each of you and cheered you on, —*BRKL* ... how I was wont to treat each of you ... exhorting and imploring and adjuring each one, —*MNTG* ... as a father deals with his own children, —*NIV* ... treats his own children, —*SEB*.

**2:11.** To the gentleness of a mother, then, they added the continuous care, concern, and firm guidance of a father, treating the believers with the same faithful love that a good father shows toward his own children. In this they felt a responsibility to be the loving guardians of their spiritual children. They did not bring people to the Lord and then leave them to drift along or follow their own devices. They knew it would be all too easy in that environment for the new converts to be enslaved again by the sin and false religions around them. Like a good father, the apostles could not neglect their children.

**12. That ye would walk worthy of God:** ... that you should be habitually ordering your behavior in a manner worthy, —*WUST* ... to walk in a manner that is, —*ADAM* ... you should live to please God, —*NLTG*.

**who hath called you unto his kingdom and glory:** ... Who is calling you into His empire, —*ADAM* ... who summons you, —*WUST* ... to share in his Glory, —*TCNT*.

**2:12.** With fatherly concern, then, they exhorted and challenged, comforted and encouraged believers, in order to warn, instruct, and confirm each one of them. In this their whole purpose was to help the believers walk worthy of God.

God's kingdom and glory are closely intertwined here. The "kingdom" is not a topic discussed in great detail by Paul, although it is strongly emphasized in the Gospels. The New Testament teaches that the kingdom of God has both present (Matthew 13:38; Mark 1:15; 9:1) and future (James 2:5; Revelation 11:15) aspects. Some say that we must be working now to establish the kingdom of God on earth before the return of Christ. This teaching is not Biblical. Morris states, "In the Scriptures, it is clear that God and no other establishes the kingdom" (*New International Commentary on the New Testament, 1&2 Thessalonians*, p. 85).

God's kingdom has to do with His royal power and rule rather than with territory. His glory has to do with the revelation of His holy nature, not only in majesty and might but also in goodness, righteousness, love, and mercy. This is the same glory John says was revealed in Christ, a glory "full of grace and truth" (John 1:14). It includes gracious help that is the outflow of the divine nature, the practical effect of God's life and love as it is ministered to believers by the Holy Spirit. As Christians receive of this grace and glory they come to know the truth of God in all His faithfulness and reality. This makes it possible for believers to show they are in the Kingdom or under the rule of God by manifesting His rule in righteousness, peace, and joy in the Holy Spirit (Romans 14:17).

**13. For this cause also thank we God without ceasing:** ... On this account, *—CMPB* ... I am giving continual thanks, *—MNTG* ... we also thank God regularly, *—ADAM* ... constantly giving thanks ... unceasingly, *—WUST.*

**because, when ye received the word of God which ye heard of us:** ... when you heard from me, *—MNTG* ... because you welcomed the word, *—KLGS* ... when you took hold of the divine message, *—BRKL* ... having received a reason for listening to us concerning God, *—FNTN* ... because when you appropriated to yourselves the word, *—WUST.*

**ye received [it] not [as] the word of men:** ... you accepted it, *—SEB, —FNTN* ... you did not accept it as a human message, *—BRKL* ... not as a word finding its source in men, *—WUST* ... as a human Word, *—ADAM* ... not a human message, *—SEB.*

**but as it is in truth, the word of God:** ... but rather, for what it truly is, *—ADAM* ... but as it actually is, *—NIV* ... which in truth it is, *—MNTG* ... as it truly is, a Divine reason, *—FNTN.*

**which effectually worketh also in you that believe:** ... who himself is effectually at work in you, *—MNTG* ... And it is still working in you, *—KLGS* ... which is being constantly set in operation in you who believe, *—WUST* ... which is at work in you, *—ADAM* ... who have accepted the Faith, *—TCNT.*

**2:13.** The remainder of this passage (2:13-16) expresses Paul's continuous and increasing thanksgiving for the way the Thessalonians received the Word and continued in it.

In this verse two different Greeks words are used for the reception of the gospel. When the apostles came preaching their God-given message, the people accepted it, taking it into their hearts (*paralabontes*, "having received, accepted"). Why? Because they welcomed it (*edexasthe*, "welcomed, accepted") not as the clever or beautiful product of human thinking or human genius, but as the Word of God, which it truly is. (See Romans 10:13-17.) The Word thus accepted and welcomed could not help but work in them in an effective way, especially since they not only began to believe (expressed an initial faith) but kept on believing.

Notice that though Paul and Silas proclaimed the Word as God's agents, the Word itself was the instrument God used to do His work. The Word is God's hammer, the Holy Spirit's sword (Jeremiah 23:29; Ephesians 6:17). It is God's best tool by which He builds the Church, His best weapon for winning victories that glorify His name. However, the Word must be mixed with faith if it is to be effective (Hebrews 4:2). Even Jesus was hindered by an atmosphere of unbelief (Matthew 13:58).

**14. For ye, brethren, became followers of the churches of God which in Judaea are in Christ Jesus:** ... became imitators of God's churches, *—ADAM* ... began to follow the example of, *—MNTG* ... of the assemblies of God, *—YNG.*

**for ye also have suffered like things of your own countrymen:** ... the same sort of ill-treatment, *—WLMS* ... by your own fellow-tribesmen, *—CNDT* ... of your fellow-citizens, *—TCNT.*

**even as they [have] of the Jews:**

**2:14.** Part of the effective working of God in Thessalonica was seen in the way the new believers became imitators of the assemblies in Judea, the Jewish believers whose sphere of life was in Christ Jesus.

Paul reminded the believers of the way jealous synagogue leaders had stirred up mob violence against the new Thessalonian disciples, taking evil, malicious men from among the marketplace loafers and inciting them to cause a riot (Acts 17:5). Thus the Thessalonian believers suffered at the hand of their own countrymen, just as the believers in Judea had.

**15. Who both killed the Lord Jesus, and their own prophets:** ... who put to death, *—BRKL* ... and the early preachers, *—NLTG.*

**and have persecuted us:** ... and also drove us out, *—NIV.*

**and they please not God:** ... They still continue to displease God, *—NORL.*

**and are contrary to all men:** ... They hinder everybody, *—KLGS* ... and opponents of all people, *—BRKL* ... and are hostile to, *—CNFT, —NIV.*

**2:15.** Verses 15 and 16 may sound anti-Semitic on the surface. However, they refer not to Jews in general but to those Jews who were rebels against God. These were the Jews who killed the Lord Jesus and also their own prophets (Matthew 5:12; 23:29-37; Luke 13:33, 34; Acts 3:15). They do not include the mass of the Jewish people, nor even all of their leaders. Men like Nicodemus, Joseph of Arimathea, and even Gamaliel, certainly did not have any part in the killing of Jesus. The Jews in Judea as a whole respected the apostles at first and held the Church in high honor (Acts 2:47; 5:13). Even when the Sanhedrin stoned Stephen, devout Jews (who were not Christians) buried him and wept over him (Acts 8:2). The persecution was carried out by leaders like Paul himself who created an atmosphere of threats and murder (Acts 8:1; 9:1).

After his conversion, Paul also was persecuted by his former compatriots. They thought they were pleasing God and doing Him a service by persecuting Paul and hounding him from place to place. But the jealousy that made them do this did not please God. It only showed they were opposed and hostile to all men. They had built up such a prejudice against others because they knew nothing of the love of God.

**16. Forbidding us to speak to the Gentiles:** ... by trying to keep us from, *—WLMS* ... they try to prohibit us, *—NORL* ... they try to prevent us, *—TCNT* ... They try to stop us, *—SEB.*

**that they might be saved:**

**to fill up their sins alway:** ... All their sins have piled up upon them, *—KLGS* ... they are always piling up their sins, *—NORL* ... to fill to the brim the cup of their sins, *—WLMS* ... they always heap up their sins to the limit, *—JB* ... their iniquities, *—CMPB.*

**for the wrath is come upon them to the uttermost:** ... divine indignation has at last overtaken them, *—BRKL* ... is coming upon them at length, *—CMPB* ... God's judgment has overtaken them at last! *—TCNT.*

**2:16.** The unbelieving Jews in Thessalonica even went so far as to forbid (hinder, try to prevent) Paul and his friends from speaking or even talking to the Gentiles with a view to their salvation. The present participle (*areskontōn*, verse 15) emphasizes that this was a continual, ongoing activity of these Jews. They wanted to keep God, His love, and His promises to themselves! Instead, they were only filling up the measure of their own sins. Like the Canaanites who were driven out before Israel, the cup of their iniquity was finally full. (See Genesis 15:16.) The wrath of God would come on them "to the uttermost," that is, in the end, and forever.

**17. But we, brethren, being taken from you for a short time:** ... being bereaved of you, *—CNFT* ... our having been absent from you, *—TCNT* ... we were forced to leave you, *—SEB.*

**in presence, not in heart:** ... in person, *Fen ton* ... but not in spirit, *—NORL.*

**endeavoured the more abundantly to see your face with great desire:** ... out of great desire, *—ADAM* ... have striven very eagerly, *—FNTN* ... made eager efforts to behold you face to face, with strong longing, *—MNTG* ... longing to see you personally, *—BRKL* ... we made every effort to see you, *—JB.*

**2:17.** Paul used a strong word to show how he and Silas felt when they were forced to leave their new brothers in Christ. They were taken from them, made orphans as it were, by separation from them. The apostles felt bereaved (torn, desolate) when separated from them even for a brief time (more literally, a season of an hour). Yet, they wanted the people to know that the separation was only outward, only in person, not in heart.

Paul tried to help the believers realize how much it hurt him to leave them when he knew they needed teaching and encouragement. He certainly had no desire or intention to stay away. In fact, ever since he left them he had been making tremendous efforts to see their faces again "with great desire." It was not a case of "out of sight, out of mind" with him. To Paul, nothing took the place of personal contact with those converted under his ministry. The love of Christ that made him reach out to lost sinners made him reach out even more to them once they had believed.

**18. Wherefore we would have come unto you, even I Paul, once and again:** ... Accordingly, we wanted to, *—ADAM* ... for that reason I would fain have visited you, *—MNTG* ... we wished on two occasions, *—FNTN* ... did more than once, *—TCNT.*

**but Satan hindered us:** ... but the adversary, *—CMPB* ... but Satan got in the way, *—KLGS* ... interfered with us, *—BRKL* ... blocked our way, *—ADAM* ... prevented it, *—WLMS.*

**2:18.** On two specific occasions Paul wanted to come. In each case he would have come except that Satan hindered or thwarted him. Paul recognized that Satan (the adversary) is the real enemy behind all opposition to the gospel. As the adversary, Satan's purpose is to hinder the work of God and stop the forward march of the Church. As the god of this world, he blinds the minds of unbelievers, trying to keep out the light of the glorious gospel of Christ (2 Corinthians 4:4). As the prince or ruler of the power or domain of the air, he is the spirit who works in those who are disobedient to God (Ephesians 2:2). Believers are warned not to give any chance or opportunity to the devil to exert his influence (Ephesians 4:27). Though the shield of faith is sufficient to quench all the fiery darts he throws at them (Ephesians 6:16), he can still hinder. In spite of their intention, purpose, and desire, Satan can sometimes cause a setback for God's people. Apparently God permitted this hindrance without telling Paul why.

**19. For what [is] our hope, or joy, or crown of rejoicing?:** ... or winner's wreath about which I boast? —ADAM ... the victor's wreath in which I exult? —MNTG.

**[Are] not even ye in the presence of our Lord Jesus Christ at his coming?:** ... Isn't it you? —ADAM ... What but your own selves, —MNTG ... in his presence? —KLGS ... when He will appear? —FNTN.

**2:19.** Paul's delay in returning to Thessalonica, then, was due to Satan, not to any lack of loving care on his part. The Thessalonian believers meant everything to Paul. They were his hope, his joy, his victor's crown of rejoicing. This was a crown to be proud of when Paul and his fellow workers would stand before the Lord Jesus Christ at His coming, that is, when He returns in royal power and glory to judge the earth and bring in His kingdom.

**20. For ye are our glory and joy:** ... Yes, you are, —ADAM ... are already our pride and our delight! —TCNT ... our boast, —FNTN ... my pride and delight, —MNTG.

**2:20.** Very emphatically Paul repeated that the believers were indeed the glory and joy of those who led them to Christ.

Paul was not saying here that he was looking for some reward for winning the Thessalonians to the Lord. The very fact that they had accepted Christ filled Paul and his companions with joy. Just to see these believers stand in the presence of the Lord at His coming would fulfill the apostles' hope and would be all the glory and joy they wanted. They were like parents who rejoice to see their children have good success. They were like teachers who feel rewarded when their students go on to live a worthwhile life.

## Chapter 3

**1. Wherefore when we could no longer forbear:** ... when we could not stand it any longer, —BRKL ... enduring it no longer, —FNTN ... when I could no longer stand it, —KLGS ... when I could no longer bear it, —MNTG ... we could wait no longer, —NLTG.

**we thought it good to be left at Athens alone:** ... we thought it best, —NORL ... we decided to remain at, —CNFT ... I made up my mind to be left behind ... all alone, —MNTG ... to stay behind alone in Athens, —SEB.

**3:1.** Paul's concern for the Thessalonians weighed heavily upon him. Even though he had

no news from Thessalonica, he knew very well that the unbelievers who had pursued him to Beroea (Acts 17:13) would not cease putting pressure on the Christians in their own city. In those days there was no question about it. Those who became believers were sure to suffer; they were persecuted; they were attacked by Satan and by the people who were his willing agents. Satan has usurped authority that really belongs to God and claims the whole world as his territory. The Thessalonians were suffering, and Paul's concern caused him to stay in Athens alone.

**2. And sent Timotheus, our brother, and minister of God, and our fellowlabourer in the gospel of Christ:**
**to establish you, and to comfort you concerning your faith:** ... to give strength, —NLTG ... to hearten you, —MNTG ... to strengthen and encourage you, NASB, —FNTN ... to give you advice on matters of your faith, —BRKL ... to console you for the sake of, —CNDT.

**3:2.** Paul therefore sent Timothy to establish, confirm, and strengthen them by thoroughly grounding them in the Word of God. He was also to comfort, encourage, and challenge them to strengthen their faith. Notice how Paul encouraged them to accept Timothy and his ministry. Paul did not talk about Timothy as a novice or apprentice but as a true brother (in the Lord) to the apostles, a minister (servant and love-slave of God), and a fellow worker with the apostles in the gospel of Christ. The Thessalonian Christians could have confidence in the teaching and encouragement he would give them.

**3. That no man should be moved by these afflictions:** ... so that no one should be shaken, —MNTG ... may be disturbed, NASB ... didn't want anyone to be shaken by these troubles, —SEB ... might be deceived amid these difficulties, —WLMS ... by these sufferings, —FNTN ... by these distresses, —BRKL.
**for yourselves know that we are appointed thereunto:** ... to which you are aware that we are exposed, —FNTN ... appointed for this, —KJII ... that we are appointed to troubles, —MNTG.

**3:3.** Timothy's purpose was to strengthen them so none of them would be moved (shaken, disturbed) by those afflictions (troubles, tribulation, persecution) Paul knew they were enduring. In fact, the Thessalonian believers themselves already well knew that followers of Christ are appointed (destined, set) to suffer for the Lord's sake. (See Matthew 5:10-12.)

**4. For verily, when we were with you, we told you before that we should suffer tribulation:** ... We, too, had warned you of this, —NORL ... we told you in advance, —BRKL ... we predicted to you,

—CNDT . . . For even when I was with you I used to tell you beforehand that I was to suffer affliction, —MNTG . . . we were certain to encounter trouble, —TCNT . . . we were going to be pressed with difficulties, —WLMS.

**even as it came to pass, and ye know:** . . . And so it proved, —TCNT, —MNTG . . . and so it came to pass, NASB . . . exactly as you know it happened, —BRKL.

**3:4.** When they were first converted, Paul warned them in advance that they were about to suffer tribulation (trouble, persecution, affliction) because of their loyalty to Christ. Even before Paul left this actually began to take place.

Again and again the Bible foretells that suffering, testing, and persecution will become the lot of true believers. A hostile world says that real Christianity is perverse and unwholesome. The enemy still tempts believers to turn aside from the plain path of holiness and total dedication to Christ that God has set before them and seek an easier road.

In the light of what the Bible as a whole says about the end of the age, we should prepare ourselves to prosper in spite of suffering and persecution. We need to understand the real teaching of Scripture concerning prosperity and aim at entering the Kingdom through much tribulation (Acts 14:22). *Prosper* in the Bible means "to go well" or "do wisely" and usually refers to our final success. Joshua 1:7, 8 uses "prosper" in this sense and explains it by a word for success that really means "to do wisely" (as in 1 Samuel 18:5, 14). It is translated "deal prudently" (KJV) of the suffering Servant of the Lord (Isaiah 52:13). Yet His greatest success came when God "prospered" His purposes in Him by taking Him by the way of Gethsemane and the Cross (Isaiah 53:4-10). Paul knew what this meant and found God's grace sufficient (2 Corinthians 11:23-27; 12:9, 10).

**5.** **For this cause, when I could no longer forbear:** . . . Consequently when, —CNFT . . . without delay, —FNTN . . . That was why, —WLMS . . . so, it was for this reason, —ADAM . . . when I could no longer bear the suspense, —NORL . . . no longer endure the uncertainty, —TCNT . . . no longer concealing my anxiety, —CMPB.

**I sent to know your faith:** . . . to learn about, —ADAM . . . to find out about your faith, —MNTG.

**lest by some means the tempter have tempted you:** . . . fearing that, —MNTG . . . the Tempter had overtried you, —FNTN.

**and our labour be in vain:** . . . our toil might prove of no avail, —TCNT . . . come to naught, —CNFT . . . would be wasted, —NLTG . . . and our labor might be lost, —WLMS . . . and our work had been for nothing, —FNTN.

**3:5.** Paul was not sure, however, that the Thessalonians had learned the lessons he had learned.

(See Philippians 4:12.) The word *mēpōs* is often used with a verb in the subjunctive mood (see *genētia*, "should become") to express a feared result. Combined with the subjunctive it can also indicate anxiety "directed toward warding off something still dependent on the will" (Rienecker, p. 594). Paul recognized that while a peril existed, apostasy was not inevitable. The will of the believer was the determining factor. He knew, however, there was a definite danger that the tempter (Satan) might use their persecutions and troubles to tempt them to fall away. Should the tempter succeed, all the work Paul and his company had done in Thessalonica would go for nothing. Paul did not really expect this, yet he could not bear the thought. For this cause he sent Timothy to find out the state of their faith.

**6.** **But now when Timotheus came from you unto us:** . . . now that Timothy has returned, —MNTG . . . now returned to us from you, —NORL.

**and brought us good tidings of your faith and charity:** . . . has brought good news, —MNTG.

**and that ye have good remembrance of us always:** . . . you always think kindly of us, NASB . . . that you are still holding me in affectionate remembrance, —MNTG . . . how you retain us constantly in loving remembrance, —BRKL . . . that you always have good memories of us, —SEB, —ADAM.

**desiring greatly to see us, as we also [to see] you:** . . . always longing to see me as I also am longing, —MNTG . . . just as we are longing to see you, —TCNT.

**3:6.** Before Timothy returned, Paul left Athens and went on to Corinth, where more opposition and difficulty awaited him (Acts 18:6, 12). What joy it was, then, when Timothy returned and brought good news, first of the Thessalonians' faith and love, then of their good remembrance (including warm, kindly feelings) of Paul, and their desire, longing, and yearning to see him.

The verb used here of bringing good news (*euangelisamenou*) is the one used almost everywhere else in the New Testament of proclaiming good news concerning Jesus. Except for the angelic announcements of the birth of Jesus, it is used everywhere for the proclaiming or preaching of the gospel. But calling Timothy's report good news was appropriate in that it confirmed to Paul that the gospel was still being received and was still effective in the Thessalonian believers' lives. Their faith was the result of the gospel. The very word for faith used here (*pistin*) indicates a faith expressed by obedience to God and His Word. It was a faith that works or operates and is made effective by love (Galatians 5:6). Their love was also the result of the gospel, for it was the outflow of the love God revealed in Christ at the Cross.

Their acceptance of and continuance in the gospel was the cause of their regard for Paul and their desire to see him, a desire as strong as his was to see them.

**7. Therefore, brethren, we were comforted over you:** ... For this reason, —ADAM ... These things have cheered us, —NORL ... I have been comforted ... in regard to you, —MNTG ... I have been encouraged about you, —WLMS.

**in all our affliction and distress by your faith:** ... in your every distress and crushing affliction, this encouragement finding its source in your faith, —WUST ... for all our hardship and suffering, —FNTN ... over your faith, —MNTG.

**3:7.** Thus, after months of apprehensive concern, after all Paul's fears about what Satan might do to the Thessalonians through persecution and temptation, Timothy's report brought comfort and encouragement to Paul. The enemies of the gospel had not been able to turn the believers from the Lord or from Paul. Paul, now rejoined by Silas also (Acts 18:5), was in the midst of much affliction, with painful circumstances involving physical privation and distress caused by persecution, pressure, and crushing trouble. The report of the continuing faith of the Thessalonian believers not only cheered him and relieved the pressure of his passionate concern, it gave him new courage to go on.

**8. For now we live, if ye stand fast in the Lord:** ... now I am really living, —MNTG ... we enjoy living, —BRKL ... It brings to us renewed life, —NORL.

**3:8.** The word *stēkēte* emphasizes the idea of standing firmly. The anxiety expressed in verses 5 through 7 seems to fade as Paul recognized that it was their faith "in the Lord" that produced this firm stand. Notice also that the common but important Pauline theme of a believer's position "in Christ" is seen in the phrase "in the Lord." This verse, therefore, does not imply any further doubt about their condition. "If" here has almost the idea of *when* or *whenever.* What Paul meant was that the assurance they were standing firm in the Lord gave him a new burst of life. Paul could now throw himself into the work at Corinth with new energy. Life to Paul meant spreading the gospel. His consuming passion was to turn men to Christ and see them established in the truth.

**9. For what thanks can we render to God again for you:** ... How can we ever thank God adequately, —ADAM ... give back to God in return concerning you, —WUST ... in your behalf, —MNTG.

**for all the joy wherewith we joy for your sakes before our God:** ... for all of the joy that we have experienced because of you, —ADAM ... for all the delight with which we rejoice, —FNTN ... in return for all the joy which you cause me in the presence of, —MNTG ... with which we are rejoicing on account of you, —WUST ... the joy you give us? —NLTG.

**3:9.** Paul's troubles and sufferings for the gospel's sake were not even worth considering in comparison to the joy the good news of the Thessalonians' faith brought to him. His rejoicing in God's presence was pure and unselfish. Joyfully, he recognized what God had done and cried out, "What thanks can we render to God?" In other words, any thanks believers give Him is totally inadequate to express what is really due Him.

**10. Night and day praying exceedingly:** ... we pray early and late, —NORL ... most earnestly, NASB, —TCNT ... earnestly wishing, —FNTN ... earnestly requesting, —CMPB ... asking in prayer quite beyond measure and as earnestly as possible, —WUST ... to pray with deepest earnestness and keenest eagerness, —WLMS.

**that we might see your face, and might perfect:** ... to see you personally, —BRKL ... that I may see you face to face, —MNTG ... may supply, —CNFT ... and complete the things, —WUST ... We want to help your faith to be complete, —NLTG.

**that which is lacking in your faith?:** ... whatever is yet lacking in your faith, —MNTG ... anything that is missing, —SEB ... to adjust the deficiencies, —CNDT.

**3:10.** The joy and good news did not lessen Paul's concern for these new converts, however. It only increased it. Now that he knew how well they were getting along, he wanted all the more to see them in order to perfect or complete what was lacking in their faith, that is, in what they still needed to add to their knowledge and understanding of the gospel.

There is, of course, no insinuation here that there was any deficiency in their personal faith in the Lord. Paul simply recognized that the new converts needed further teaching. While rejoicing in what God had done, he knew God had much more for them. "Perfect that which is lacking" was a phrase often used in those days for the supplying of an army with provisions. Paul wanted to provide these new believers with spiritual food that would help them march on to greater and greater victories. The good food of God's Word would bring further spiritual growth.

As an apostle Paul had the responsibility to train the new believers who had turned their backs on the world to follow Jesus. It was God's purpose that all of them would come to the place where they could do the work of ministry and edify or build up the body of Christ both spiritually and in numbers. Then the whole Body, united to Christ, the Head, and to their fellow members in love, would be able to grow by what each individual believer received from Christ (Ephesians 4:11-16).

So intense was Paul's desire to do this that day and night he was praying (literally, begging) exceedingly (beyond all measure, with utmost earnestness) for God to permit him to minister to the Thessalonians again in person.

**11. Now God himself and our Father:**
**and our Lord Jesus Christ, direct our way unto you:** . . . facilitate our journey to you! —FNTN . . . prepare our way, —BRKL . . . guide my way to you! —WLMS . . . guide our steps to you! —NORL . . . lead us to you, —BECK . . . my path to you, —MNTG.

**3:11.** With the mention of prayer Paul actually broke out into a prayer: "Now God himself and our Father, and our Lord Jesus Christ, direct our way unto you." "Direct" includes the idea of making a straight path and removing obstacles. Satan had twice hindered Paul from coming. God alone could clear the way.

**12. And the Lord make you to increase and abound in love one toward another, and toward all [men]:** . . . And as for you, —WUST . . . Meanwhile, may the Lord cause you, —MNTG . . . make you grow in love and overflow with it for one another and for everybody, —BECK . . . make your love for one another and for all people, —ADAM . . . fill you to overflowing with love, —FNTN . . . and multiply in, —KJII.
**even as we [do] toward you:** . . . as my love for you does, —WLMS . . . even as also we have this divine . . . love for you, —WUST . . . just as ours does for you, —ADAM . . . just as we love you, —BECK.

**3:12.** Paul's prayer was primarily for the believers. He could teach them, but only God through Christ could cause them to increase and abound (excel and overflow) in love. "Love" here is "*the* love," Calvary love, not just brotherly love. God would make this kind of love overflow toward each other and toward all people.

God had caused that kind of love to pour out of the apostles' hearts toward the Thessalonians. It was the same love God showed "toward us, in that, while we were yet sinners" and really His enemies, "Christ died for us" (Romans 5:8, 10). No one can work up this kind of love by his own efforts or reasoning. It comes only as Christ fills believers' hearts, and His love in them overflows. This too is the work of the Holy Spirit as He strengthens His children with mighty power in their inner being so Christ may continue to dwell in their hearts by faith, and they, being rooted and grounded in love, may be strong enough to grasp and make their own the love of Christ (Ephesians 4:16-19).

**13. To the end he may stablish your hearts unblameable in holiness:** . . . that He might stabilize,

—WUST . . . and so may He give you inward strength to be holy and without a fault, —BECK . . . so that He may strengthen your hearts to be faultless in purity, —WLMS . . . you will be spotlessly holy, —BRKL . . . in spotless holiness, —FNTN . . . make your spirits strong, —SEB . . . irreproachable in holiness, —ADAM.
**before God, even our Father:** . . . in the presence of, —WUST . . . in the sight of, —WLMS.
**at the coming of our Lord Jesus Christ with all his saints:** . . . at the appearance of our Lord, —FNTN . . . when our Lord Jesus comes, —BECK . . . with all the holy ones, —KLGS . . . when our Lord Jesus comes back with all His consecrated ones, —WLMS.

**3:13.** The overflow of love is also the key to spiritual advancement and holiness. Creeds, doctrines, and rules may have a place and may be good in themselves, just as the law of Moses was holy, just, and good (Romans 7:12). Yet, they become deadly without superabundant love. Only as Christians love one another with Calvary love and reach out in that love to unlovely, rebellious sinners does the Lord establish their hearts (strengthening and confirming the purposes of their hearts) so they will stand blameless "in holiness before God, even our Father, at the coming of our Lord Jesus Christ with all his saints." "Holiness" here is holy dedication to the will and service of the Lord.

There is some controversy about whether "his saints" (holy ones) refers to angels, to believers, or both. In some cases *saints* does refer to angels. (See Zechariah 14:5 as interpreted by Jesus in Mark 8:38. See also Matthew 25:31.) Yet "the saints" in Paul's epistles are usually the believers who have turned their backs on the world to follow Jesus and who stand in His righteousness, not their own. Most take it that the word "all" removes restrictions and thus includes both angels and believers. The important thing is that the expression of Christ's love in and through believers prepares them to be part of the company who are in Christ at His coming.

## Chapter 4

**1. Furthermore then we beseech you, brethren:** . . . Finally then . . . I continue to, —MNTG . . . Therefore, for the rest, —FNTN.
**and exhort [you] by the Lord Jesus:** . . . and strongly advise you, —BRKL . . . and appeal to you, —JB.
**that as ye have received of us how ye ought to walk and to please God:** . . . as you learned of me, —MNTG . . . we gave you instructions, —SEB . . . as to what your daily life must be, —TCNT.
**[so] ye would abound more and more:** . . . So let it increase more, —KLGS . . . to keep on doing still better, —BRKL.

**4:1.** The practical section of this epistle now begins. What is said here was not new to the Thessalonians. Nor did Paul give them harsh or arbitrary commands. He knew the kind of society in which they lived, so he wanted to encourage them.

Those to whom Paul so tenderly addressed these exhortations were brethren. (*Adelphoi* often includes both brothers and sisters.) They had already received and accepted Paul's answer to the questions "How must we live?" and "How are we to please God?" They were indeed striving to please God. In fact, the assurance that it is possible to please God, and that God takes pleasure in His people, was a strong incentive to holy living. But no believer can rest on his laurels. So Paul urged the Thessalonian Christians to abound more and more.

**2. For ye know what commandments we gave you by the Lord Jesus:** . . . You have not forgotten the instructions, *−JB* . . . what charges I laid upon you, *−MNTG* . . . the directions that we gave you, *−TCNT* . . . by authority of, *−BRKL.*

**4:2.** The secret of this progress in excellence was to continue to follow the loving instructions already made known to them by Paul. These precepts were not Paul's, however. They came from God through Jesus.

**3. For this is the will of God:** . . . What God wants, *−JB.*

**[even] your sanctification:** . . . is for you all to be holy, *−JB* . . . that you be holy, *−NORL* . . . that you grow in holiness, *−NAB.*

**that ye should abstain from fornication:** . . . keep yourselves . away from lewdness, *−BRKL* . . . that you should practice abstinence from sexual immorality, *−WLMS* . . . Stay away from sexual sin, *−SEB* . . . from all prostitution, *−CNDT* . . . from whoredom, *−CMPB* . . . from sex sins, *−NLTG.*

**4:3.** The reason Jesus gave instructions instead of letting believers go their own way is that sanctification (holiness, consecration, dedication to God's plan and purposes) is God's will for every believer. Sanctification also means a separation from all that is unclean, specifically from fornication (immorality, sexual freedom).

**4. That every one of you should know how to possess his vessel:** . . . should see the duty of making one woman his wife, *−TCNT* . . . how to control his own body, *−SEB* . . . to win his own wife, *−BRKL* . . . should learn to take his own wife out of pure and honorable motives, *−WLMS* . . . see to it that he chooses for himself a wife to be held, *−NORL.*

**in sanctification and honour:** . . . in holiness, *−CNFT* . . . in purity, *−BRKL.*

**4:4.** Paul went on to say that for believers, keeping away from immorality involves knowing how to possess their vessels in sanctification (consecration, dedication to God) and honor (respecting its value).

Many take "possess his vessel" to mean "acquire a wife." They appeal to such passages as 1 Peter 3:7 which speaks of the wife as "the weaker vessel" and 1 Corinthians 7:2 which says that to avoid immorality each man should have his own wife and each woman her own husband. This view emphasizes that the purpose of marriage is greater than sexual indulgence. Unbridled lustful passion that treated the wife as a mere sex object characterized many heathen marriages. Marriage that does not show respect and honor to the wife is not likely to help a person avoid immorality.

Others point out that 1 Peter 3:7 looks at both man and wife as vessels. The body is spoken of as an earthen vessel (2 Corinthians 4:7). Moreover, in dealing with this same subject of immorality, Paul spoke of the body as the temple of the Holy Spirit (1 Corinthians 6:18, 19; see also Romans 6:12).

The Greek in this verse (4:4) is not conclusive. "Possess" is often used of acquiring land, or gold, or gifts, and could be used of acquiring a wife. However, the Biblical declaration is that in fornication or any sexual immorality the sin is against one's own body (1 Corinthians 6:18). This would seem to favor taking "vessel" as "body" here.

**5. Not in the lust of concupiscence:** . . . not in lack of self-control, *−KLGS* . . . not in passionate desire, *−NAB* . . . not in lustful passion, *−BRKL* . . . not in the passion of lust, *−CNFT.*

**even as the Gentiles which know not God:** . . . like the heathen, *−FNTN.*

**4:5.** Our "vessel," then, must be kept in honor, not in lustful passion in the manner of the Gentile pagans who did not know God. In other words, if one really knows God he will learn to gain control of his vessel in such a way as to maintain its dedication to God and its honor. However, if "vessel" does refer to a wife, a comparison between the Christian and the pagan is in view. (Although the term *ethnē* often refers to Gentiles or non-Jews versus Jews, here the term is used to contrast believers and nonbelievers.) Reflecting upon ideas conveyed in verses 4 and 5, Frame points out that "pagan marriage was marked by the absence of holiness and respect for the wife and by the presence of passionate lust" (*International Critical Commentary,* 38:151). On the other hand, the Christian marriage should demonstrate qualities which are an outgrowth of consecration to the Lord, i.e., "sanctification and honor" (verse 4).

The word *epithumias* by itself can simply mean a desire or a longing without a negative connotation (see Luke 22:15, for example, where Jesus said, "With *desire* I have desired to eat this passover with you before I suffer"). *Pathos,* however, always expresses a negative sense in Pauline writings (see Romans 1:26 and Colossians 3:5). The phrase *pathei epithumias,* therefore, describes someone who is "caught in the grip of lustful passions he is quite unable to control" (Morris, *New International Commentary on the New Testament, 1 & 2 Thessalonians,* p. 124).

**6. That no [man] go beyond and defraud his brother in [any] matter:** ... Let no one cheat or trick, —*KLGS* ... that no one transgress and overreach his brother, —*CNFT* ... take advantage of, —*BRKL* ... by taking advantage of a brother, —*JB.*
**because that the Lord [is] the avenger of all such:** ... is a punisher, —*BRKL.*
**as we also have forewarned you and testified:** ... as we said to you before also, and certify, —*CNDT.*

**4:6.** Another reason for keeping away from immorality is that what it does to our brother calls for divine punishment. Immorality will always "go beyond" or overstep and transgress proper limits in disregard of the rights of others. It defrauds a brother, cheating and taking advantage, not only of him but also the neighbor whom Christians are supposed to love as themselves (Luke 10:27). All sins cheat. Premarital sex cheats one out of virginity. Adultery cheats the true marriage partner. Homosexuality cheats one out of the kind of relationship between a man and a woman that God intended from the beginning (Matthew 19:4, 5).

**7. For God hath not called us unto uncleanness, but unto holiness:** ... to a life of immorality, but to one of personal purity, —*WLMS* ... but to a holy life, —*BRKL.*

**4:7.** God offers more than a fire escape from hell. His call is into a way of life that brings glory to the One who has called the individual out of darkness into His marvelous light (1 Peter 2:9). Not immorality but holiness brings a person into conformity with the will of God.

**8. He therefore that despiseth, despiseth not man, but God:** ... he who rejects these things, —*CNFT* ... whoever rejects this teaching, —*WLMS* ... he who is repudiating is not repudiating man, —*CNDT* ... is not objecting to a human authority, —*JB* ... the slighter of it does not slight man but God, —*BRKL.*
**who hath also given unto us his holy Spirit:** ... who continues to put His Spirit in you, —*WLMS.*

**4:8.** Those who reject the call to holiness and the warning against immorality, setting them aside as if null and void, are rejecting not man but God who is the giver of the Holy Spirit. They forget that

the Spirit is supremely holy, and a believer's body is His temple.

**9. But as touching brotherly love ye need not that I write unto you:** ... there is really no reason, —*NORL* ... you have no need of, —*WLMS.*
**for ye yourselves are taught of God to love one another:** ... are Divinely instructed, —*FNTN.*

**4:9.** Brotherly love will help Christians in their battle against immorality. Such love in that day was used by the Greeks and Romans to refer almost exclusively to love between blood brothers and sisters. It implied affection, kindness, and consideration for one another (Romans 12:10). But from the beginning believers felt a kinship with one another stronger than any natural blood tie. They were truly in one family with God as their Father in a very personal way. (See Romans 8:14-17.)

Paul did not want the Thessalonians to think his mention of brotherly love suggested any lack on their part, however. He did not really need to remind them. They were "taught of God" to love one another (John 6:45). The love that God teaches is something greater even than brotherly love. It is *agapē,* a love that usually refers to a high, holy, faithful, self-giving love. God taught it by demonstrating His love in sending His Son to die on Calvary (Romans 5:8). God wants to make believers channels of His love toward all by their love toward their brothers and sisters in Christ. He wants them to demonstrate this love in very practical ways. (See 1 Corinthians 13:4-8.)

**10. And indeed ye do it toward all the brethren which are in all Macedonia:** ... you practise it, —*CNFT.*
**but we beseech you, brethren, that ye increase more and more:** ... But I exhort you ... to abound in this yet more, —*MNTG* ... we beg you, love them even more! —*SEB* ... to make even greater progress, —*CNFT.*

**4:10.** The Thessalonians did not discriminate in their love. It was expressed to all throughout the whole country. They did not pick out only those who were nice to them, who agreed with them, or who were like them. God shows no partiality, no respect of persons in His love. Neither did they. But Paul still urged them to increase more and more in their love. God is still pouring out His love. He wants all believers to be ever-increasing channels for that love.

**11. And that ye study to be quiet:** ... and that you be ambitious, —*CNDT* ... to keep advancing in it, —*BRKL* ... make your ambition to be quiet, —*KLGS* ... to make a point of living quietly, —*JB.*
**and to do your own business:** ... and practice your own trade, —*KLGS* ... and attend to your own

affairs, *—NAB*...Mind your own business, *—SEB*...to mind your own affairs, *—BRKL*, *—CMPB*.

**and to work with your own hands:**

**as we commanded you:**...as we recommended to you, *—BRKL*...as I charged you, *—MNTG*...as we directed you, *—TCNT*.

**4:11.** Christians must be careful, however, lest love and concern for others turn them into spiritual busybodies, always poking their noses into other people's business. Paul asked the believers to do three things to balance their outgoing love.

First, they were to make it their aim to live a quiet life. Christians are not to try to be spectacular or flamboyant. They are not to seek to be the center of attention, demanding that the spotlight be focused on them.

Second, they are to busy themselves with their own affairs, minding their own business, their own concerns, taking care of their own homes. This will give them enough to do without meddling and trying to run other believers' lives.

Third, believers are to work with their own hands. Paul set an example in this (1 Corinthians 4:12). He instructed Christians to follow that example. Manual labor is good for all.

**12. That ye may walk honestly toward them that are without:**...Then outsiders will respect the way you live, *—SEB*...that you may be well conducted before the outsiders, *—FNTN*...that you are seen to be respectable, *—JB*...that you may be walking respectably, *—CNDT*...that you may live influentially with the outsiders, *—WLMS*...may win respect from outsiders, *—TCNT*.

**and [that] ye may have lack of nothing:**...won't need to be dependent, *—ADAM*...you need not depend on anyone, *—BRKL*...that you may not need help from any man, *—MNTG*...and will not be on relief, *—KLGS*.

**4:12.** Another reason for working with their own hands (including all productive work) was so they could walk honestly (behave decently) toward outsiders (nonbelievers). The able-bodied Christian is not to depend on others to support him and his family. Nor is he to expect continual supernatural supply. By his own labors he is to have no lack of anything he really needs.

**13. But I would not have you to be ignorant, brethren:**...We desire you not to be, *—FNTN*...we don't want you to be, *—ADAM*...to have any misunderstanding, *—WLMS*.

**concerning them which are asleep:**...those who have died, *—NLTG*...who have already died, *—SEB*...about those who sleep, *—ADAM*...who are falling asleep, *—MNTG*.

**that ye sorrow not, even as others which have no hope:**...that you may not be grieved, *—CMPB*...You must not sorrow like other men, *—MNTG*...You have

no reason to grieve like the rest, *—NORL*...so you may not grieve as others do, *—BRKL*...otherwise you might yield to grief, *—NAB*...lest you grieve as others who haven't any hope, *—ADAM*...who have no expectation, *—CNDT*...who are without a hope, *—FNTN*.

**4:13.** In Paul's concern for morals and behavior in this life, he did not forget the life to come. The Bible always looks ahead. It sees our behavior in this life in the light of God's great plan that will climax when Jesus returns.

At this point in this letter, Paul turned to answer a question which arose because some believers had already died. The Thessalonians were from a Greek background where they formerly supposed the dead went down into a dark underworld from which there was no return. Some of the new believers apparently felt that those who died before the return of Christ would miss that glory and joy.

This false impression or false teaching needed to be corrected. False teachers arose very quickly in the Early Church. But instead of destroying the truth, they only succeeded in causing it to be brought out more clearly and more powerfully by the apostles. Possibly the false teachers here suggested those who died would not share in the benefits of Jesus' coming. If so, this would bring sorrow to the believers who remained alive.

"Sorrow" here has the idea of distress, hurt feelings, and mental anguish. In this kind of sorrow they were coming very close to the black despair and empty hopelessness reflected on the tombstones of the heathen of the time. The present participle *echontes* denotes ongoing activity—in this instance, the unrelenting hopelessness experienced by a nonbeliever with respect to death. Paul wanted them to know the truth that would keep them from that kind of grief. Christians are not like the heathen who have no hope.

**14. For if we believe that Jesus died and rose again, even so them also which sleep in Jesus will God bring with him:**...in the same way, through Jesus, *—ADAM*...God will, by means of Jesus, restore with Him those, *—FNTN*.

**4:14.** The key to a Christian's hope is his belief in the fact that Jesus died and rose again. The word "if" does not imply any question of that belief. It introduces a "first class" conditional clause (a clause with *ei* and an indicative mood verb in the "protasis" or "if" side of an "if-then" statement) and is properly translated "since." It simply indicates that as surely as they believed, so surely will the dead believers be with Jesus when He returns. Their belief in Christ's death and resurrection was not a mere mental acceptance of the facts, however. It involved a personal identification with Jesus in His death and resurrection, as pictured in water baptism.

**15. For this we say unto you by the word of the Lord:** . . . I tell you, *—MNTG* . . . by the Lord's Word, *—ADAM* . . . as a message from the Lord, *—FNTN.*

**that we which are alive [and] remain unto the coming of the Lord:** . . . we who live, who survive until, *—CNFT* . . . we who may be still living when, *—NORL* . . . we who are left behind living, *—KLGS.*

**shall not prevent them which are asleep:** . . . shall not at all take precedence over those asleep, *—BRKL* . . . will not get ahead of the sleepers, *—KLGS* . . . will not go ahead of those who have died, *—NLTG* . . . will have no advantage over those who have passed to their rest, *—TCNT.*

**4:15.** Paul had a clear word from the Lord about this. Of course, all he wrote in his epistles was by inspiration of the Holy Spirit. But in this case Paul also had a definite saying of Jesus. Jesus himself, in giving Paul the gospel, made it clear that those who are alive and remain till the coming of the Lord will not precede, get ahead of, or have any advantage over those who died with their faith in Jesus. The fact Paul used "we" in this verse does not mean he was sure he would be alive. He simply meant whoever is alive at Christ's return.

**16. For the Lord himself shall descend from heaven with a shout, with the voice of the archangel, and with the trump of God:** . . . shall personally descend, *—BRKL* . . . with a loud summons, *—TCNT* . . . with a command, with the voice of the angel leader, *—SEB* . . . at a call from the archangel, *—NORL* . . . the voice of the archangel will call out the command, *—JB.*

**and the dead in Christ shall rise first:** . . . those who died in union with Christ, *—TCNT* . . . will rise again, *—FNTN.*

**4:16.** Those who die before the return of Christ will not miss a thing. The Lord will descend from heaven with a shout or command, with the voice of the archangel, and with the trumpet of God. Then the dead in Christ will immediately rise in response to His command. (See *Overview*, pp. 553-555.)

**17. Then we which are alive [and] remain shall be caught up together with them in the clouds:** . . . afterward we, the living . . . be instantly taken up in clouds, *—CMPB* . . . the survivors, *—NAB* . . . the living remnant, shall at the same time be carried up in clouds, *—FNTN* . . . at the same time be snatched away together, *—CNDT.*

**to meet the Lord in the air: and so shall we ever be with the Lord:** . . . in the sky! *—NORL, —NLTG* . . . for an introduction by the Lord into the eternal condition, *—FNTN.*

**4:17.** The moment after the dead arise, those who are alive and remain will join with them

to form one great body. Together we will all be caught up (snatched up in a powerful manner, carried up suddenly in great power) to meet the Lord (for a meeting with the Lord) in the air.

This sudden snatching away to meet the Lord is often referred to as the "rapture." Some try to belittle this word and say we should not use it because it is not in the Bible. In-depth study shows, however, there is justification for using it. The Greek word used here meant "to seize." Then, it came to mean "to snatch up forcibly." It was used of robbers snatching up whatever they wanted to steal, or of an eagle snatching up its prey. Paul used it of being caught up to the third heaven (2 Corinthians 12:2).

The Greek word was translated into the Latin by *raptus.* From this comes our English words *rapt* and *rapture.* Today these words usually speak of being carried away emotionally or spiritually. But one meaning of *rapt* in current dictionaries is "lifted up and carried away." Thus it is perfectly good English to translate this verse, "Then we which are alive and remain shall be rapt (or raptured) together with them in the clouds." A force far beyond gravity, a supernatural power far greater than the rockets that lift astronauts into space, will suddenly snatch us into the air for a meeting with Jesus. *Meeting* is a word often used in connection with the coming (*parousia*) of a king, emperor, or governor to visit a city. The people would go out to welcome the dignitary.

Paul said nothing here about the events of the meeting (which include the judgment seat of Christ and the Marriage Supper of the Lamb). Nor did he say anything of our return with Christ to destroy the armies of the Antichrist and set up His millennial kingdom. Paul concluded simply by saying that believers will always, forever, be with the Lord.

**18. Wherefore comfort one another with these words:** . . . Because of this, *—NLTG* . . . Encourage and console one another, *—NORL* . . . with this truth, *—WLMS.*

**4:18.** There is no greater comfort, encouragement, or exhortation that can be given to another than the fact that whether Christians live or die they will be caught up to be with Christ when He comes.

## Chapter 5

**1. But of the times and the seasons, brethren:** . . . Relative to periods, *—BRKL* . . . with regard to the exact time and date, *—TCNT* . . . about dates and times, *—SEB* . . . and dates, *—LILY* . . . and the eras,

−CNDT . . . when and at what kind of times these things will happen, −NLTG.

**ye have no need that I write unto you:** . . . there is no need for writing to you, −FNTN.

**5:1.** The fear that they might miss something if they died before the Rapture made the Thessalonian believers want to know how soon the Lord would come. Paul did not need to add to what Jesus had said (Acts 1:7).

**2. For yourselves know perfectly:** . . . for you are yourselves keenly aware, −BRKL . . . because you surely know, −KLGS . . . For you well know, −NORL.

**that the day of the Lord so cometh as a thief in the night:**

**5:2.** The believers knew perfectly well that the Day of the Lord will come as a thief in the night. The sudden, unexpected coming of the Day of the Lord had been explained to them. The present tense here means that it is sure to come. In other places Paul refers to signs which will indicate the time is approaching, but there will be no immediate warning so there will be time to get ready.

**3. For when they shall say, Peace and safety:** . . . Just at the moment when men are saying, −LILY . . . Things are peaceful and safe, −SEB . . . Peace and security, −KLGS, −FNTN . . . All is quiet and safe, −TCNT.

**then sudden destruction cometh upon them:** . . . destruction will strike them suddenly, −NORL . . . unforeseen is on them, −BRKL . . . then extermination is standing by them unawares, −CNDT . . . seizes them, −FNTN.

**as travail upon a woman with child:** . . . as the agony of, −FNTN . . . like birth pains, −WLMS . . . like the birthpangs of a pregnant woman, −BRKL . . . as birth pangs upon, −CNFT . . . on an expectant mother, −NORL.

**and they shall not escape:**

**5:3.** At the very time when the Lord returns, unbelievers will be rejecting the warnings of the Bible and crying, "Peace and safety" (security). But in the midst of their declarations that people do not need God to have peace (including health, well-being, and spiritual peace of heart and mind) or security (including the gaining of all that is certain and true), sudden destruction (ruin, death) will come upon them. (See Jeremiah 6:14.) Just as women have no way of stopping birth pangs once they start, even so once the Day of the Lord comes it will carry through to its conclusion. The words *ou mē* indicate strong negation and can be translated "by no means." There will be *no* possibility of escape.

**4. But ye, brethren, are not in darkness, that that day should overtake you as a thief:** . . . you are not in the dark, −SEB . . . that the day falls on you,

−KLGS . . . take you by surprise, −LILY . . . to surprise you like a thief, −RSV . . . That day will not surprise you as a robber would, −NLTG . . . take you by surprise as if you were thieves, −TCNT.

**5:4.** What Paul said about the Day of the Lord with its judgments catching men by surprise applies only to the wicked, the careless, the unbelieving, the spiritually unprepared. This verse makes a strong contrast between believers and unbelievers. Paul was confident in the reality of the believers' faith and their dedication to the Lord. The Day of the Lord will not overtake Christians to seize them and carry them into the vortex of judgment. It will, however, not be because they know when it is coming. The day and the hour will be hid from them the same as it will be from everyone else.

**5. Ye are all the children of light, and the children of the day:**

**we are not of the night, nor of darkness:** . . . We do not belong to, −WLMS.

**5:5.** But they will not be caught unprepared because they are not in darkness. Amos rebuked the people of his day who were talking about the Day of the Lord but doing nothing to prepare for it (Amos 5:18). For them, it would be a day of darkness and not light. This was because they were already walking in moral and spiritual darkness. God is light, and He has made provision for Christians to walk in the light (1 John 1:5-7).

Believers are not only walking in the light, they are "children of light." They are characterized by and share the nature and character of light. (See Luke 1:78, 79; 2:32; John 1:9; 8:12 where Jesus is the light.)

Believers are also "children of the day." Some take this to mean the Day of the Lord. But the context shows Christians are children characterized by "day." Thieves come in the night. True believers are always in the day, spiritually speaking. Light is their way of life. They do not belong to darkness (Ephesians 5:8-11).

**6. Therefore let us not sleep, as [do] others:** . . . So then, −ADAM . . . Consequently, then, we may not be drowsing, −CNDT . . . like the rest, −BRKL . . . as do the rest, −MNTG . . . the rest of mankind, −NORL.

**but let us watch and be sober:** . . . let us keep alert, −KLGS . . . alert and level-headed, −ADAM . . . but to be vigilant and alert, −LILY . . . be on our guard and composed, −BRKL . . . we should be awake and alert, −SEB . . . but we keep guard and are sober, −FNTN . . . watchful and self-controlled, −MNTG.

**5:6.** Since Christians are "day" people, Paul exhorts them not to keep on sleeping as do others. They must watch, be alert, be vigilant. They must also be sober in the sense of exercising self-control, well-balanced and avoiding excesses and extremes.

**7. For they that sleep sleep in the night:** ... the sleepers, —FNTN.

**and they that be drunken are drunken in the night:** ... the drunkards, —FNTN ... get drunk at night, —ADAM.

**5:7.** The world is like a drunken man whose liquor has deadened his sensibilities until he has fallen asleep and is unconscious of his true condition. Warnings against sin pass over him and bring no response. Those who are drunk become drunk in the night because they hope the darkness will cover their condition. But those who are of the day are willing to let the light of the Holy Spirit search their lives.

**8. But let us, who are of the day, be sober:** ... since we are of the day, —ADAM ... let us keep our minds awake, —NLTG ... be self-controlled, —MNTG.

**putting on the breastplate of faith and love:** ... clothed in, —FNTN ... outfitted with faith, —BRKL.

**and for an helmet, the hope of salvation:** ... the expectation of salvation, —CNDT.

**5:8.** The command to watch suggests the vigilance of a sentry on duty and facing danger. First, Christians must be light. They are of the day. They must be sober (self-controlled, well-balanced) and make the proper preparations. They must put on their armor.

They are to put on over their hearts the "breastplate of faith and love" to guard their emotions. For a helmet to guard their thoughts, plans, and aspirations, they need the "hope of salvation" (cf. Ephesians 6:10-17; 2 Corinthians 10:4). The breastplate is very significant. Faith needs to work by love if it is to be effective (Galatians 5:6). Plans and ideas also need to be focused in the right direction by the hope of salvation. Salvation here speaks of the believers' future inheritance, including everything that will be theirs when Jesus comes again (cf. 1 Peter 1:3-5).

**9. For God hath not appointed us to wrath:** ... For God's intention is not to punish us, —NORL ... has not destined us, —CNFT ... for indignation, —BRKL ... did not plan for us to be punished, —SEB ... to reap His wrath, —WLMS.

**but to obtain salvation by our Lord Jesus Christ:** ... for the acquisition of, —FNTN ... to secure salvation through, —ADAM ... but to win salvation through, —MNTG.

**5:9.** There is further assurance of the hope of salvation in that God has not appointed believers to wrath. Some take this to mean that they will not share the wrath that shall engulf the sinful world during the "Great Tribulation" because the Church will be taken out in the Rapture. God's *protection* of Noah during the flood and of Lot at the destruction of Sodom and Gomorrah illustrates how His people are sheltered from His wrath against sinners. The judgments indicated in Revelation are clearly stated to be wrath (Revelation 6:16, 17; 11:18; 14:10, 19; 15:1, 7; 16:1, 19; 19:15). This is the wrath Paul was referring to here.

**10. Who died for us:**

**that, whether we wake or sleep:** ... whether we remain alive or have fallen asleep, —TCNT.

**we should live together with him:** ... we may find life in union with him, —LILY ... we will be with Him, —NLTG.

**5:10.** Believers gain salvation, not by what they do, but by what Christ has already done. He died for all; but only those who accept His sacrifice will live together with Him. Here Paul gives the Thessalonian believers great comfort and encouragement, reinforcing what he wrote in 4:14-18. Not only is there great hope in knowing that believers will not suffer the wrath of God, but even death ("sleep") cannot separate them from being united with Christ for all eternity.

**11. Wherefore comfort yourselves together:** ... Continue building each other up, —SEB ... encourage one another, —RSV.

**and edify one another, even as also ye do:** ... and strengthening one another, —NORL ... as in fact you are doing, —BRKL.

**5:11.** With this in mind Paul urged Christians to comfort one another, to edify or build up each other. This is parallel to the exhortation of 4:18. Paul is either making a continuing reference to what he had just explained concerning the second coming of Christ, or else he is still attempting to renew the hope of those who were mourning the death of fellow believers.

**12. And we beseech you, brethren:**

**to know them which labour among you:** ... to appreciate those who toil, —LILY ... to respect those who work, —NLTG ... to show regard for those who toil among you, —TCNT.

**and are over you in the Lord, and admonish you:** ... and your advisers, —BRKL ... and presiding over you, —CNDT ... and teach you the way, —NORL.

**5:12.** Paul concluded this letter with a series of loving exhortations. Someone has called these a chain of pearls of practical wisdom.

Though it is the Christian's responsibility to edify others, he needs additional encouragement and guidance. Therefore God has called and chosen leaders, equipped by gifts of the Spirit, to work among them. They are over believers in the Lord. That is, they are concerned about believers, care for them, and give them aid. This includes elders, pastors, and deacons, as well as teachers who instruct. Paul asked his brothers (and sisters) to know (and appreciate) these teachers and leaders.

**13. And to esteem them very highly in love for their work's sake:** ... treat them with the greatest honor in love, —SEB ... lovingly in highest regard, —BRKL.

**[And] be at peace among yourselves:**

**5:13.** Christians should esteem these leaders very highly, recognizing their worth, and giving them thoughtful consideration and superabundant respect. This is not a matter of exalting an office or of conferring personal prestige, however. It is a matter of giving honor where honor is due, not merely as a duty, but in love "for their work's sake." This implies that these spiritual leaders are really working hard as servants of the Body, not as lords over them (cf. Matthew 20:25-28).

The next exhortation might seem to be a complete change of subject. Actually, it is not. There is no greater way for Christians to encourage spiritual leaders and teachers than to live at peace among themselves. Nothing is more frustrating than an atmosphere of dissension, quarreling, and murmuring (criticism that is said under your breath). God is able to give leaders grace in spite of any lack of peace and unity among their people. But so much more can be done when the people are in one accord.

**14. Now we exhort you, brethren:**
**warn them that are unruly:** ... warn the disorderly, —TCNT ... warn those who are lazy, —SEB ... reprove the idle, —LILY ... reprove the irregular, —CNFT.
**comfort the feebleminded:** ... cheer up the fainthearted, —BRKL ... comfort the fainthearted, —CNFT ... encourage the timid, —NORL.
**support the weak:** ... uphold the infirm, —CNDT.
**be patient toward all [men]:**

**5:14.** The remaining exhortations are directed to all the church. Paul never puts all the responsibility for good order, growth, and development of the church on the leaders. Love, courtesy, and respect for the ministry of the Spirit will bring order. (Compare 1 Corinthians 14:40 where Paul calls for moderation or self-control, not a moderator.)

All Christians have a responsibility to warn the unruly (including the idle or lazy). "Warn" here means more than rebuke or point a finger. It includes the idea of instructing. Believers must help the "unruly" to see they are going in the wrong

direction and show them how to get back on the right path (Galatians 6:1).

"Comfort the feeble-minded" in King James' day meant to encourage those who were irresolute, vacillating, too weak to have any real purpose or to overcome discouragements. It included those who were so despondent they were tempted to give up.

Supporting the weak implies holding on tightly or firmly to them to keep them from drifting away and to keep them in fellowship with the Church, never criticizing them for their weakness but helping them to feel they have the support of the Lord as well as of their fellow Christians. This means being patient and longsuffering with all believers (1 Corinthians 13:4; Ephesians 4:2; Colossians 3:13).

**15. See that none render evil for evil unto any [man]; but ever follow that which is good:**
**both among yourselves, and to all [men]:** ... and to everybody, —LILY.

**5:15.** This kind of loving patience will keep believers from holding grudges. The command is that no one takes revenge or tries to pay back evil with evil. (Compare Romans 12:9-21.) Christians can best do this by always pursuing the good, not only toward other believers but toward all (including those who oppose them).

**16. Rejoice evermore:** ... Always be joyful, —WLMS.
**17. Pray without ceasing:** ... pray constantly, —RSV.
**18. In every thing give thanks:** ... Always be grateful, —LILY ... give thanks in all circumstances, —RSV.
**for this is the will of God in Christ Jesus concerning you:** ... regarding you all, —CNFT.

**5:16-18.** The remaining commands are all in a plural form so they apply to the whole church both as individuals and as a body. These things are to mark collective worship. Even more important, they are to mark the believer's daily life. There is no alternative but to rejoice always and to keep on rejoicing at all times in obedience to God.

Very closely related to this joy is the fellowship Christians have with the Lord as they engage in constant, unceasing prayer. At every opportunity their hearts go out to God. The channel of communication is always open. They may express themselves in a variety of ways (1 Corinthians 14:13-15).

It is also the will of God for believers in Christ to give thanks in everything. Because of who God is and what He has done, He is worthy of praise whether the believer feels like praising Him or not. Often the Holy Spirit will envelope those who praise Him with the joy of the Lord, regardless of the circumstances. (See Acts 16:25.)

**19. Quench not the Spirit:** ... Do not extinguish, —LILY, —CNFT ... the Spirit's fire, —BRKL ... Dampen, —KLGS.

**5:19.** Believers must also be careful not to quench (suppress, extinguish) the fire of the Spirit. The form of the Greek verb actually means "to stop putting out" the Spirit's fire. Fear, carelessness, and sin can all dampen our response to the Spirit.

**20. Despise not prophesyings:** ... Scorn not, —CNDT ... prophetic utterance, —BRKL.

**21. Prove all things:** ... But test all things, —CNFT. **hold fast that which is good:** ... and retain what is good, —BRKL ... retaining the ideal, —CNDT.

**22. Abstain from all appearance of evil:** ... Keep away from evil in every form, —BRKL.

**5:20-22.** Of all the gifts, the one which most often brings edification is the gift of prophecy (1 Corinthians 14:1, 3). It brings spiritual strengthening, encouragement, challenge, and solace. Because it is so important Christians must not despise or treat it with contempt. There are counterfeits, however, so Christians must test everything and hold fast to what is good (noble, edifying). At the same time, believers are to "abstain from all appearance of evil."

**23. And the very God of peace sanctify you wholly:** ... sanctify you completely, —CNFT, —ADAM ... consecrate you wholly, —MNTG ... consecrate your whole being, —WLMS ... will make you completely holy, —SEB ... make you entirely holy, —KLGS ... make you perfect in holiness, —LILY ... purify you perfectly, —FNTN.
**and [I pray God] your whole spirit and soul and body be preserved blameless:** ... may your entire being, —ADAM ... may your whole person, —CMPB ... be without a flaw, —BRKL ... be kept sound, —RSV ... be kept perfect and faultless, —TCNT ... be kept altogether faultless, —MNTG.
**unto the coming of our Lord Jesus Christ:** ... for the coming, —ADAM.

**5:23.** In conclusion Paul commended the Thessalonians to God with a prayer. They could not fulfill all these exhortations in and by themselves. They needed help from God, who is the true Author of the Christian's peace (including spiritual health and well-being). He must come on the scene and sanctify (consecrate, dedicate) them completely (through and through). Paul prayed also that this sanctification would keep them blameless until the coming of our Lord Jesus.

**24. Faithful [is] he that calleth you:** ... He who calls you can be trusted, —NORL ... may be trusted, —TCNT ... is reliable, —BRKL.
**who also will do [it]:** ... and He will accomplish it, —BRKL, —ADAM ... he will fulfil my prayer, —MNTG ... and He will effect it, —FNTN:

**5:24.** Because God is faithful believers can depend on Him to do what He has promised and to act in carrying out His great plan and purpose of redemption. Thus Paul's prayer will be answered for all who respond in faith and heed the warnings he has given in this passage.

In writing to the Corinthians, Paul indicated he served a faithful God and he wanted to be just as faithful and trustworthy. So his word was not yes and at the same time no (2 Corinthians 1:18-20). That would be impossible, for in Christ there is only yes. In other words, Paul preached a positive gospel. He did not proclaim Christ as Saviour and say perhaps He would save them and perhaps He would not. He did not proclaim Him as Baptizer in the Holy Spirit and say perhaps He would fill believers with the Spirit and perhaps He would not. In Jesus Christ there is only "yes" to all the promises of God.

It is very important for Christians to recognize this positive nature of apostolic preaching. They spoke of positive proofs. They declared that what God was doing was according to the Scriptures. They constantly emphasized the fact that *gospel* means "good news" and is backed by the power, love, and faithfulness of the God who created this universe and who is determined to carry out His plan to its final consummation.

**25. Brethren, pray for us:** ... Brothers, keep us in mind in your prayers, —BB.

**26. Greet all the brethren with an holy kiss:** ... Give regards to, —FNTN ... Say hello to all the Christians with a kiss of holy love, —NLTG ... a sacred kiss, —BRKL, —WLMS.

**27. I charge you by the Lord:** ... I solemnly charge you, —CMPB ... I adjure you, —TCNT, —MNTG ... I order you, —SEB ... I urge you, —KLGS.
**that this epistle be read unto all the holy brethren:** ... to have this letter read to all, —MNTG ... to read this letter to all, —ADAM.

**5:25-27.** Paul brought this letter to an end by more brief exhortations followed by a benediction. First Paul asked them to pray for him and his fellow workers. Never did he suppose that the work of God could be done by his own faith, labor, or prayers alone. He was always conscious that the work of God must be done through a united body of believers with each contributing the gifts which the Holy Spirit distributes as He wills (1 Corinthians 12:11).

Next Paul asked that his love for them and their love for each other be expressed by the token of a "holy kiss" (probably on the cheek). This was acceptable in the culture of that day. It is still practiced by many Christians throughout the world. In other cultures a handshake or possibly a hug can be a holy greeting. "Holy" is the key word here.

Then Paul gave strict orders that this letter be read to all the "holy brethren," that is, to all the consecrated, dedicated Christians, both men and women. He did not want any of them to miss the message the Spirit had given him for them. The Early Church recognized that these letters were also needed by all the churches.

28. **The grace of our Lord Jesus Christ [be] with you. Amen:** . . . The love of our Lord, *—BECK* . . . The spiritual blessing of, *—WLMS* . . . The favour of, *—RTHM* . . . our Lord Jesus the Messiah, *—MRDK* . . . May the Grace, *—NAB* . . . The gracious care of, *—BKWD* . . . May the blessings of, *—HRBR.*

**5:28.** Paul's closing benediction called for the grace, the unmerited favor, of our Lord Jesus Christ to be with the believers in Thessalonica. This is the way he ended most of his letters.

# 2 THESSALONIANS

## Overview

The overview to 1 Thessalonians gives the background for both epistles. At the end of the Second Century 2 Thessalonians was commonly accepted as written by Paul. It was included in Marcion's canon and in the fragment of Muratoris.

Besides the general comparison of teaching and exhortation, a common pattern in Paul's epistles, 2 Thessalonians follows these chapter divisions:

I. OPENING (1:1, 2)

II. TRIBULATION AND WARNING (1:3-12)

III. THE DAY OF THE LORD AND THE LAWLESS ONE (2:1-17)

IV. ADMONITIONS (3:1-15)

V. CLOSING (3:16-18)

## The Day of the Lord and the Lawless One

The main part of the epistle (chapter 2) is an eschatological section concerning the man of sin. It is one of the most detailed prophecies in the Bible concerning Antichrist. No other prophetic passages totally cover the divine revelation Paul provided in this chapter. It is therefore of vital importance to the understanding of latter-time prophecies. Eschatological interpretation systems that do not take chapter 2 into account are suspect no matter how extensive or detailed they might be otherwise. Second Thessalonians chapter 2 stands as a test and corrective for any popular teaching concerning the return of Christ (Erdman, p. 85).

Even though this chapter gives information concerning the events of which we would have no knowledge otherwise, it also raises certain questions. It must be admitted this is no doubt one of the most difficult passages in the entire New Testament. It may be one of the passages which Peter wrote was "hard to be understood" (2 Peter 3:15, 16). This is partly because what Paul wrote was a supplement to the oral teaching he had given the Thessalonian church (2:5, 6). It is possible that, like us, even the Thessalonians did not fully understand all the apostle wrote in this chapter.

Paul's second letter to the Thessalonians was in response to certain questions which had arisen concerning "the coming of our Lord Jesus Christ, and by our gathering together unto him" (2:1). Some think the questions were a result of a misunderstanding of what Paul had written in his first letter to them. But such an interpretation is contradicted by the apostle's own words. It appears from what Paul wrote (2:2, 3) that false teachers had caused the Thessalonians to be "shaken in mind." It is obvious that those who were seeking to deceive the believers were accusing Paul of false doctrine, an accusation which the apostle rejected without hesitation (2:2).

Paul did not say definitely that a false epistle, supposedly to have come from him, was being circulated, but he did reckon with such a possibility. The troublemakers seem to have indicated that such a document existed. The first Christian churches had to take into account the possibility of false epistles and to learn how to differentiate between the false and the authentic (W.A. Stevens, *American Commentary on the New Testament*, 5:82).

What was the false doctrine and the misconception of the Thessalonians? The false assertion was that the Day of the Lord had already come. Paul did not deny that the Day of the Lord was at hand (Romans 13:12; Philippians 2:16); he did deny that it had come to pass already. Other New Testament passages maintain the same view (Hebrews 10:37; James 5:8; Revelation 1:1; 22:20). Could the Thessalonians really have thought the coming of Christ had taken place, that deceased believers were risen, and that they themselves had been left behind? If this had been the case, would not the apostle simply have rejected such a position by reminding the Thessalonians that he, as well as they and believers in other places, had not experienced the Rapture?

Instead of doing so, Paul wrote about two facts: The Day of the Lord would be preceded by "a falling away" and the revealing of Antichrist, "the son of perdition" (2:3). Many Bible scholars offer the explanation that the Day of the Lord with its mighty acts of judgment is something essentially different from the Parousia, the second coming of Christ. Even Bible interpreters who disagree with this explanation admit that the Day of the Lord represents a complex idea which includes many different events (Morris, *New International Commentary on the New Testament, 1&2 Thessalonians*, p. 217). But can one separate the Day of the Lord from the Parousia since Paul's opening statement binds the two events together? In 1:7-10 the apostle declared that the Day of the Lord would be for salvation and judgment.

Some interpreters have indicated there should be a contrast between the eschatological section in 1 Thessalonians 5:1-5, which speaks of the immediate coming of Christ, and 2 Thessalonians 2:1f., which indicates that certain events must precede the Day of the Lord. In this connection some say that the same tension between that which nobody knows and that which we all ought to know can also be found in the eschatological sermons of Jesus (Matthew 24:32-36) (Bruce, *Word Biblical Commentary,* 45:116). Others say Paul is speaking of two different events in the two epistles: In 1 Thessalonians, the Parousia, the coming of the Lord for His church; in 2 Thessalonians, the *apokalupsei*, the revelation of Christ to the world (Walvoord, pp. 108f.; Hiebert, p. 65). Opposing theological views will interpret this section from their own eschatological general viewpoint, and each of them will find support and face the difficulties which are rather evenly distributed.

## The Apostasy

Before the Day of the Lord the apostasy must take place. Jesus warned of this *hē apostasia* which will be characteristic of the latter days (Matthew 24:11, 12, 24; Luke 18:8). Paul foretold it and described it in detail (1 Timothy 4:1-3; 2 Timothy 3:1-5; cf. James 5:1-8; 2 Peter 2:1-22; 3:3-6; Jude 18). The apostasy made itself known in the days of the apostles. It has grown steadily worse during the intervening centuries, but it will reach its culmination in the latter days.

Paul defined this apostasy as a rejection of sound doctrine accompanied by ethical and moral decay. But this apostasy seems in fact to be combined with a false piety (2 Timothy 3:5). In classical Greek the word is used to indicate military or political revolt. In the Septuagint it is used in connection with revolt against God (Joshua 22:22). The apostasy of the latter days will not be limited to the Christian church, although Matthew 24:24 says that even some of the elect will be led astray. The apostasy of which Paul wrote will be a revolt against all divine law and authority and a general rejection of the truth of the gospel.

This last great revolt against God will have its origin in that part of the world that is called Christian. The nations that have had the light of the gospel for centuries will turn to the lie. This apostasy will be expressed in an active and aggressive hatred of all Christianity, and it will culminate in anti-Christian persecution (Matthew 24:9; Revelation 13:15). But this universal revolt against God will have its root within the nominal Christian church. It is when the salt loses its power and the light becomes darkness that cruelty is given unlimited power in the world (Matthew 5:13f.).

In passing it may be mentioned that some scholars have suggested that the word *apostasia* can be translated "snatching away." Liddell and Scott give a secondary meaning of the word as "departure,

disappearance" (*LSJ,* "*apostasia*"). If this were the correct translation, it could mean the rapture of the Church. However, there is not strong support for this view.

## The Man of Sin

As a consequence of the apostasy, the man of sin will appear. Although Paul did not use the name *Antichrist,* there is no doubt that he was describing this last great opponent of God and the people of God. This section of the Scripture (2:1-12) is one of the three major prophecies concerning this puzzling person (cf. Daniel 7 and Revelation 13).

Paul wrote that the man of sin will be "revealed," which emphasizes the supernatural aspect of his coming (Morris, *New International Commentary on the New Testament, 1&2 Thessalonians,* p. 221). The word is used three times (2:3, 6, 8). It stands as an antithesis to the revelation of Christ (1:7). It is not the existence, birth, or presence of Antichrist which marks the beginning of the anti-Christian period, but his revelation, the fact that he makes himself known and is revealed as he really is. His public appearance in the arena of history will unveil his identity. He will no doubt have lived many years on earth before his manifestation as Antichrist (Ryrie, p. 105). He will be revealed "in his time" (2:6), that is, when the time for his appearance has come, and the world is ripe for receiving its despot.

The appearance of Antichrist is also called his coming (*parousia,* 2:9) and is once more an antithesis to the coming of Christ (*parousia*) mentioned in 2:8. Paul wrote that the coming of Antichrist "is after the working of Satan with all power and signs and lying wonders" (2:9). The term "lying wonders" does not mean tricks or deceptions. These wonders will be genuine miracles that will support the preaching of lies. They will be the means of making men believe the lies (2:11). These wonders of the lie will be characterized by three words which are used to describe the miracles of Jesus (Acts 2:22) and the miracles which confirmed the ministry of the apostles (Hebrews 2:4). The term *dunamei,* "power" (here in the singular), refers to the supernatural power which will produce the works. The word *semeiois,* "sign," does not mean empty, aimless demonstrations of power, but rather supernatural events which will signify authority and confirm a message. The word *terasin,* "wonders," refers to the surprise and attention which these works will create in the spectators.

The power of God was behind the miracles which Jesus and the apostles performed, and they were signs of Jesus' deity and the truth of His message. Conversely, the wonders of the lie caused by satanic powers will give a false authority to the message of the lie, forming an integral part of the system of seduction. This system, this "mystery of iniquity" (2:7), which in due time will bring "that Wicked" (2:8) into power, that is, the Antichrist, was active in the time of the apostles. There had been many antichrists already (1 John 2:18), but the great Antichrist could not arise yet because there was a Power which kept him back.

Paul gave a distinct picture of the character of Antichrist. First, he called him the "man of sin" (2:3). Some manuscripts have "the man of lawlessness." This is accepted by UBS, which admits it is an uncertain translation. *Textus Receptus* follows the majority of texts and uses "the man of sin." These words express the evil character of Antichrist. He will be the embodiment of sin itself. He will be the contrast of Jesus Christ who did not know sin (2 Corinthians 5:21), who did no sin (1 Peter 2:22), and had no sin (1 John 3:5).

Paul also called Antichrist "the son of perdition" (2:3). The expression is a Hebrew idiom. It refers to the nature as well as to the destiny of Antichrist (cf. Revelation 17:8). Jesus used the same term for Judas Iscariot (John 17:12). This has caused some to think that Judas will come from the abyss as Antichrist in the latter days, a thought which is totally foreign to the New Testament. The mere fact that Judas committed suicide (Matthew 27:5), while Antichrist will receive his deadly wound from a sword (Revelation 13:14), makes the idea impossible.

The third term Paul used of Antichrist is the "Wicked" one (2:8). He will be the embodiment of the secret of lawlessness that has been active down through the ages. The word *lawlessness* in this instance stands for something more than anarchy in a social or political sense. Anarchy will not be a distinguishing mark of Antichrist's rule. When Antichrist gathers humanity under his dominion, it will be, among other things, because he will offer an alternative to anarchy and terrorism. The lawless one will become the absolute emperor, exponent of a totally unlimited willfulness (Daniel 7:25). Antichrist is called the "Wicked" one because he will oppose the law of God and introduce his own godless, lawless system founded on principles which are diametrically opposed to the law and will of God.

Paul mentioned two other characteristics of Antichrist. He will be the opponent of God and the people of God. The Hebrew word for *Satan* means the opponent or the enemy. Thus we see that Antichrist is mentioned here by the same name as his master. Antichrist will also be the one who exalts himself (2 Thessalonians 2:4), while Christ is the One who subjected himself (Philippians 2:5f.).

Paul did not say much about the career of Antichrist. Immediately after the apostle wrote about the revelation of the "Wicked" one, he spoke of Antichrist's destruction at the coming of the Lord (2:8). In an earlier part of the chapter (2:4) Paul wrote that the man of sin will sit down in the temple of God "showing himself that he is God." This will be a demonstration of the innermost characteristic of anti-Christianity, that of deifying man.

Does the expression "the temple of God" refer to a literal temple of God in Jerusalem, or must it be understood figuratively to refer to the Church as the temple of God? There might be a strong case for both views. One view does not necessarily exclude the other. Many interpreters throughout the ages have understood the temple metaphorically. The reformers believed the expression referred to the power of the pope. Modern interpreters maintain that it means the Antichrist will seek to dethrone God in men's hearts.

Those who maintain a literal understanding point to the close relationship with the words of Jesus concerning the abomination of desolation that shall stand in the holy place (Matthew 24:15f.). Jesus' words were distinctly connected with things that will take place in the future in Jerusalem and Judea and were literally understood by those who heard Him. The connection between the sermon of Jesus and that which Paul wrote is further strengthened because of the fact that the words of Jesus in Mark 13:14 concerning the abomination of desolation are rendered in a grammatical form which shows they refer to a person who then could be none other than the Antichrist.

As long as the temple in Jerusalem remained, it was natural to understand Paul's words literally. Later on, it was usual for the Early Church to suppose a rebuilt Jewish temple and a literal fulfillment of that which Jesus and Paul said. This view was maintained by many Early Church fathers, among others by Irenaeus in his work *Against Heresies* (5:30:4). If the Jews do rebuild their temple it will reinforce such a view. Whether or not these words refer to a literal fulfillment, it is evident that Antichrist will proclaim his deity and demand public worship (cf. Revelation 13:8, 12, 15).

## The Restraining Power

In chapter 2 Paul gave an important account of the succession of eschatological events. Preceding the Day of the Lord, the apostasy must come and the "Wicked" one must be revealed (2:2, 3). But before Antichrist can be revealed, that which "letteth" his revelation must be taken away (2:6, 7). This power which withholds cruelty and prevents the revelation of Antichrist is spoken of as a person (2:6) as well as a thing (2:7) and can then be understood as a person and the effect of this person. The Thessalonians knew who and what this power was (2:5, 6). This power must be something and someone stronger than Satan, because it prevents the devil from revealing the Antichrist. It must also be a power and a person who has been active during the entire Christian period and who continually restrains Antichrist.

The church in Thessalonica knew what Paul was referring to, but even the Early Church fathers had lost this knowledge. Among the interpreters of the Bible there have been a number of conjectures:

(1) The Roman Empire, embodied in the Emperor Nero. But that empire perished without any appearance of Antichrist.

(2) The authority at the time of Paul represented by the emperor. But although authorities can keep human cruelty in check to some extent, they cannot restrain Satan. Besides, the realm of Antichrist will not be without authority. On the contrary, it will be a totalitarian government. Those who accept this conjecture state that Paul used a veiled and mysterious language in order to hide the fact that he was speaking of the downfall of the empire.

(3) The Holy Spirit in the Church. The argument for this view is that God alone is stronger than Satan and can thus restrain him from revealing Antichrist. Those who maintain this view believe that when the Church is caught away and the Holy Spirit, has completed His work in and through the Church the hindrance to the revelation of Antichrist will be removed.

As we have stated, the question is a puzzling and difficult matter. It is hard to understand how a matter which was distinctly understood by the early Christians has been a problem for all later generations. Perhaps God wanted to keep it secret.

## Two Groups of Men

The last part of chapter 2 concerns two groups of men of a quite different situation and destination. At first, Paul spoke of those to whom God will send strong delusions so they will believe the lie and receive His sentence of judgment (2:10-12). Next Paul addressed those whom God had chosen "from the beginning" to receive "salvation through sanctification of the Spirit and belief of the truth" (2:13-17). Only those who will not receive the love of the truth will believe the lie (cf. Romans 1:24-28).

God did not harden the heart of Pharaoh until he had hardened himself (Exodus 8:32; 9:12). In like manner, those who will not believe the truth but who delight in unrighteousness will be sentenced and lost. But those who believe in the truth and in the saving message of the gospel will win "the glory of our Lord Jesus Christ" (2:13f.).

# The Second Epistle of Paul to the Thessalonians

## Commentary

### Chapter 1

1. **Paul, and Silvanus, and Timotheus:**
**unto the church of the Thessalonians:** ... To the congregation of, *−SEB* ... to the ecclesia, *−CNDT* ... in the city of Thessalonica, *−NLTG.*
**in God our Father and the Lord Jesus Christ:** ... in union with, *−TCNT.*

**1:1.** Paul's first letter to the Thessalonians was intended to encourage them to remain faithful and to give them practical exhortations for Christian living in the light of Christ's return. Every chapter contains some reference to the Second Coming. After delivering the epistle, Timothy returned to Paul with the report that the believers now had even more questions about the Lord's return. Paul then wrote to deal with these questions.

The greeting shows that Silas (called by his full name Silvanus) and Timothy were still with Paul and were cosenders of the letter.

Paul recognized the Thessalonian church as being in a right relationship with God the Father and the Lord Jesus Christ, who is the very source and sphere of the believer's life. Notice that Christ is presented as equal with the Father. Because of the Son's deity the Church can be said to be in God the Father, also in Christ.

2. **Grace unto you, and peace, from God our Father and the Lord Jesus Christ:**

**1:2.** On this verse Marshall remarks, "Whereas grace is particularly associated with Christ (2 Corinthians 13:14) and peace with God (Romans 15:33; Philippians 4:7) here God the Father and the Lord Jesus Christ are named together as the one source of both grace and peace" (*New Century Bible,* 43:168).

3. **We are bound to thank God always for you, brethren, as it is meet:** ... It is our duty, *−NORL, −TCNT* ... We must give thanks, *−NLTG* ... We have a sense of personal obligation to be constantly thanking God, *−WUST* ... It is fitting that we should, *−CNFT* ... We ought always to thank God for you, brothers, as is appropriate, *−ADAM* ... because it is right, *−KLGS* ... and rightly so, *−NIV.*
**because that your faith groweth exceedingly:** ... because of the abundant growth of, *−MNTG* ... your faith is flourishing, *−CNDT* ... is growing wonderfully, *−WUST* ... is growing so splendidly, *−BRKL* ... is growing so well, *−ADAM* ... is growing fast, *−SEB.*
**and the charity of every one of you all toward each other aboundeth:** ... and of the overflowing love with which every one of you is filled toward one another, *−MNTG* ... and the love that every one of you has for one another is increasing so much, *−ADAM* ... for each other is increasing, *−NIV* ... is also on the increase, *−NORL* ... is stronger all the time, *−NLTG* ... is continually increasing, *−TCNT* ... exists in great abundance, *−WUST.*

**1:3.** Even though there were problems, Paul first drew attention to what was good about their situation. He (along with Silas) felt under obligation to give thanks to God at all times concerning them, as was fitting and proper. Paul felt very strongly that what God had done for the Thessalonian believers deserved his thanks to God. But that was not all; the believers had proved worthy of this. They did not need to feel ashamed or belittle themselves in any way. Clearly, the report Timothy brought back showed they were a healthy church.

Growth is always the sign of life and health. Their faith was growing wonderfully, like a luxuriant, spreading tree. The faithful, Calvary love of each one of them was abounding, becoming greater and richer, increasing and spreading like a flood toward each other. The "faith," of course, was a faith in Christ which was deepened and strengthened through obedience to His Word. Their love was a self-giving love that reached out to others, even to people they did not like, especially to people who might not deserve love. It was shown in service, in humility, in courtesy, and in consideration for one another. Above all, it was shown without restrictions.

4. **So that we ourselves glory in you in the churches of God:** ... We are proud of you, *−NLTG* ... boast of you, *−CNFT* ... mention you with pride, *−BRKL* ... So that I myself am boasting about you among, *−MNTG* ... in the assemblies of God, *−FNTN.*
**for your patience and faith in all your persecutions and tribulations that ye endure:** ... we boast about your perseverance, *−NIV* ... regarding your obedience and fidelity, *−FNTN* ... concerning your endurance and faith, *−KLGS* ... in spite of your persecutions and crushing sorrows, *−WLMS* ... which you are displaying in all the troubles, *−MNTG* ... that ye bear, *−YNG* ... which you are bearing, *−CNDT.*

**1:4.** As a result, Paul and his company gloried in them (boasted of them, spoke of them in the highest terms among all the churches). They especially rejoiced to tell other believers of the Thessalonians' patience (steadfast endurance, fortitude, perseverance) and their faith in the midst of their persecutions and the tribulations, pressures, oppression, affliction, and trouble which they continued to endure. In fact, they put up with all these troubles willingly. What a powerful faith this was! Unbelieving Jews assaulted them because of their Christian testimony. Unbelieving Gentiles joined in with persistent persecution. But faith and love kept the Christians triumphant!

**5.** **[Which is] a manifest token of the righteous judgment of God:** ... They are evidence of God's fair verdict, –*BRKL* ... This is a clear proof, –*NORL* ... a proof of, –*CMPB* ... These persecutions will vindicate God's justice as a judge, –*TCNT* ... the right decision of God, –*FNTN.*

**that ye may be counted worthy of the kingdom of God, for which ye also suffer:** ... shows that you are fit for the Kingdom, –*KLGS* ... in behalf of which you are even now suffering, –*MNTG.*

**1:5.** Paul saw the patience and faith of the Thessalonians under persecution as a clear evidence of the righteous judgment of God. The very fact that God upheld them in the midst of all this suffering and testing was proof of His faithfulness. He could be counted on to reward them and to "recompense" their enemies as well (verse 6).

Their faith and brave endurance were also indications that they would be counted worthy of the future kingdom or rule of God. This was all the more true because it was on behalf of the Kingdom and in view of the Kingdom that they suffered and endured hardship.

Paul said he endured all things for the elect's sake, for the sake of those who had elected or chosen to follow Jesus. He wrote to Timothy, "That they may also obtain the salvation which is in Christ Jesus with eternal glory." Then he added, "It is a faithful saying: For if we be dead with him, we shall also live with him: if we suffer (endure), we shall also reign with him" (2 Timothy 2:10-12). Thus, whether Christians suffer physically or not, the important thing is to endure. This means that believers are to stand their ground when others are fleeing, to hold out when others are giving in, to remain steadfast to the end whatever others do.

**6.** **Seeing [it is] a righteous thing with God to recompense tribulation to them that trouble you:** ... He will pay back trouble, –*NIV* ... to repay with trouble, –*NORL* ... to repay affliction to those

afflicting you, –*CNDT* ... to repay your afflictors with affliction, –*FNTN* ... those who afflict you, –*CNFT.*

**1:6.** To encourage the Thessalonians further in their brave endurance of persecution and trouble, Paul pointed out that it was also a "righteous thing with God to recompense (repay) tribulation" (including affliction and trouble) to those who troubled (afflicted) them. This is still a moral universe. God will see to it that what troublemakers have sown, they will also reap.

**7.** **And to you who are troubled rest with us:** ... you, the afflicted, –*CMPB*, –*FNTN* ... rest, along with me, –*MNTG.*

**when the Lord Jesus shall be revealed from heaven with his mighty angels:** ... at the Appearing of, –*TCNT* ... comes down from heaven, –*NLTG* ... with his powerful angels, –*SEB.*

**1:7.** The present participle *thlibomenois* indicates that the Thessalonians were even then in the midst of suffering. To these who were "being oppressed," the promise of rest must have been most welcome. Eadie says, "This *anesis* is the immediate aspect of heaven to the suffering, rest to the weary and worn-out, release from all the disquiet, pain, and sorrow of the earth" (*Greek Text Commentaries*, 5:238).

This will take place in the revelation (unveiling, disclosure, revealing) of the Lord Jesus from heaven with the angels (messengers) of God's mighty power. This *unveiling* is a term used also of Christ's coming to destroy the present world system and set up His kingdom on earth (Daniel 2:35, 45). Then those now troubled (oppressed, distressed, and persecuted) will be free from toil and conflict.

**8.** **In flaming fire taking vengeance on them that know not God:** ... He will punish those, –*NIV* ... in a blaze of fire ... shall mete out retribution, –*BRKL* ... to inflict punishment, –*CNFT* ... handing out vengeance, –*KLGS* ... inflicting a just retribution on, –*CMPB* ... giving judgment to those not perceiving God, –*FNTN* ... to those who are not acquainted with, –*CNDT* ... who do not acknowledge God, –*SEB.*

**and that obey not the gospel of our Lord Jesus Christ:** ... who will not accept the Gospel, –*NORL* ... who do not listen to the good news, –*KLGS*, –*WLMS* ... upon those who turn a deaf ear to the Good News, –*TCNT.*

**1:8.** While the coming of Christ brings blessing to believers, it will be a time of judgment upon those who have been enemies of the gospel. Jesus will suddenly appear in "flaming fire" to take vengeance (in the sense of rendering justice) on those who know not God, those who "obey not the gospel of our Lord Jesus Christ."

Those who "know not God" include those who have willfully rejected knowledge that was available to them. (Compare Hosea 4:6; 8:12.) Paul also pointed out that the world once knew God, but men exalted themselves and began worshiping the created thing rather than the Creator (Romans 1:19-25).

Those who obey not the gospel are those who heard it but actively rejected it and took a course of disobedience. They are a specific group within the group that knows not God. They are even more guilty, for they know what they are doing.

**9. Who shall be punished:** ... who shall suffer justice, *—YNG* ... They will pay the penalty of everlasting ruin, *—BRKL.*

**with everlasting destruction from the presence of the Lord:** ... by being shut out forever from, *—KLGS* ... of eonian extermination, *—CNDT* ... and exclusion from the Lord's presence, *—NORL* ... and shut out from, *—NIV* ... with eternal ruin, *—CNFT* ... an enduring death, *—TCNT.*

**and from the glory of his power:** ... from the shining greatness of, *—NLTG* ... from the glory of his strength, *—SEB* ... and His glorious might, *—WLMS.*

**1:9.** Those who know not God and obey not the gospel will receive just judgment when Jesus appears in flaming fire and speaks the word that will destroy the Antichrist and his armies (Revelation 19:11-15). They will pay the full penalty, which will be eternal destruction, everlasting ruin, and eternal loss away from the presence of the Lord. They will be separated forever from fellowship with God, shut out from the visible glory of His power.

This banishment from the manifest presence of God will be the vindication of God's holy, righteous nature. The sinner imagines he can escape, but this is totally impossible by the very nature of things. It will be evident then that God has indeed created a moral universe. (See Luke 13:27; Matthew 8:12; 22:13; 25:30.)

**10. When he shall come to be glorified in his saints:** ... to be honoured in his People, *—TCNT* ... with his consecrated ones, *—WLMS.*

**and to be admired in all them that believe:** ... and to be marveled at in, *—CNFT.*

**(because our testimony among you was believed) in that day:** ... for you also believed our testimony, *—MNTG* ... has been confidently accepted among you, *—WLMS.*

**1:10.** The chief purpose of Christ's coming in glory is not simply to judge the wicked, however. They will be judged, for they failed to fulfill the very purpose for which they were created, and by their persecutions they attempted to hinder God. However, the real purpose of Christ's return and revelation is that He may be "glorified in his saints"; that is, in all the believers, including the Thessalonians to whom Paul was writing.

The emphasis may be that Jesus will be glorified and honored *among* His saints. As He returns in this revelation of flaming fire, He will be accompanied not only by the angels, but also by all the saints, by all true believers, all whose righteousness is in Christ. All who believe will be filled with awe as they see His supernatural power and glory revealed in His glorious appearing and in the just judgment of His enemies.

It is possible also to take this to mean that His marvelous character and glory will be reflected in the believers. Since this means, in either case, all believers, all who accept and obey the gospel, it will include the Thessalonians; they believed the testimony of Paul and his company when it was brought to them.

**11. Wherefore also we pray always for you:** ... With this in mind, *—NIV* ... With this in view, *—WLMS* ... To this end I am making my constant prayer for you, *—MNTG* ... we always pray this about you, *—ADAM.*

**that our God would count you worthy of [this] calling:** ... may consider you, *—ADAM* ... beseeching God to make you worthy of your calling, *—MNTG.*

**and fulfil all the good pleasure of [his] goodness:** ... and by His power fully satisfy your every desire for goodness, *—WLMS* ... also accomplish in a powerful way all of the good you want to do, *—SEB* ... fill you with all the benevolence of goodness, *—CMPB* ... and to fulfil mightily every desire of goodness, *—MNTG* ... fulfill every good intention, *—ADAM.*

**and the work of faith with power:** ... and complete every activity of your faith, *—WLMS* ... and effort of faith, *—MNTG* ... every faith-inspired effort, *—BRKL* ... and every faithful deed of yours by His power, *—ADAM.*

**1:11.** In view of all their suffering and faithfulness, and in view of Christ's return and the divine rest believers will enjoy with Him at that time, Paul prayed always and at all times for the Thessalonian believers.

His first request was that God would count (or make) them worthy of the call to which they were already responding.

Second, he asked that God would fulfill (perfect and complete) all the good pleasure, purpose, and delight of His goodness. God wants to bring believers to the place where, if they will let Him, their whole purpose and joy is to do what is good in His eyes.

Third, Paul asked that God would fulfill or perfect the work (activity) of faith, making it effective with power.

**12. That the name of our Lord Jesus Christ may be glorified in you:** . . . will be honored by you, –NLTG.

**and ye in him, according to the grace of our God and the Lord Jesus Christ:** . . . and you be glorified in him, –MNTG . . . and you by Him, in keeping with, –ADAM . . . and you through union with Him, in accordance with the favor of, –WLMS . . . through the mercy of, –NORL.

**1:12.** Only in connection with acts of faith could Paul's final petition in this prayer be fulfilled. Then, through the believers' worthy response to His call, their delight in goodness, and their activity of faith, the name of our Lord Jesus Christ will be glorified in them and they in Him.

"The name of our Lord" includes His whole person, character, and nature. "His name shall be called Wonderful (a supernatural wonder; He himself will be a miracle), Counselor, The mighty God, The everlasting Father, The Prince of Peace" (Isaiah 9:6). His name also speaks of His royal dignity and His supernatural power and majesty. (See Hebrews 1:4; Philippians 2:8-11; Acts 3:12-16.) It refers to all that God is.

The true and holy nature of Jesus is thus to be glorified in believers and they in Him (in close, personal union with Him, as in John 17:1, 10, 21-26). But Christians cannot do this in themselves or of themselves. There is no way Christians can bring glory to God apart from His grace. This grace was made manifest at Calvary.

## Chapter 2

**1. Now we beseech you, brethren, by the coming of our Lord Jesus Christ:** . . . We have a request to make of you, –NORL . . . we are asking you, –CNDT . . . we request you, NASB . . . I entreat you . . . concerning the coming of our Lord, –MNTG . . . relative to the coming of. –BRKL.

**and [by] our gathering together unto him:** . . . and our assembling to Him, –CNDT . . . to meet him, –MNTG . . . and our final muster before Him, –WLMS.

**2:1.** It is important to take note of the events which will take place at the second coming of Christ. There will be a rapture of the Church. There will be a Great Tribulation. There will be the return of Christ in judgment to judge His enemies.

The sequence of events is a matter of controversy, which often finds good people on opposite sides. Some believe Christ will come in the Rapture before the Tribulation, others in the middle of the Tribulation, and others at the close. A large segment of evangelical believers concur in the pre-Tribulation view.

When Paul speaks of the "coming of our Lord Jesus Christ," he is referring to the entire scope of the Second Coming. It is the reason for his advice in the following verses.

**2. That ye be not soon shaken in mind, or be troubled:** . . . Do not be alarmed, –NORL . . . to be readily unsettled or disturbed, –BRKL . . . not to allow your minds to be alarmed or quickly upset, –SEB . . . you may not be quickly shaken, –KJII . . . not to be hastily shaken, –CNFT . . . not to be quickly shaken out of your wits, –MNTG . . . be not suddenly shaken In mind, –CMPB . . . shaken from your composure, NASB . . . not lightly to let your minds become unsettled, –TCNT . . . or worried, –NLTG . . . nor even be excited, –WLMS . . . nor excited, –KLGS.

**neither by spirit, nor by word, nor by letter as from us:** . . . by the talk you hear, –NLTG . . . or by a message, –MNTG . . . or by letter attributed to us, –CNFT . . . or by a letter allegedly from us, –BRKL.

**as that the day of Christ is at hand:** . . . the Day of the Lord is here now, –KLGS . . . has already come, –NORL, –SEB . . . is already here, –WLMS.

**2:2.** Instead of acting like intelligent people with sound judgment, the Thessalonian Christians were departing from their senses like a ship blown from its moorings. Thus they were disturbed (frightened, agitated) and filled with feverish anxieties.

The cause of all this confusion was the false teaching spread by people who claimed to have authority both from the Holy Spirit and from Paul. They seem to have produced forged letters purporting to come from Paul upholding their new teaching, which was that the Day of Christ (the period of time in which Christ will bring His judgments) had already come. Thus they taught that the persecutions and tribulations the Thessalonians were then experiencing were part of the Day of Christ, and they could not therefore be encouraged by the prospect of a literal rapture of believers. It is possible also that these false teachers taught that Christ had already returned spiritually, thus ignoring the plain statement of Acts 1:11.

Some of the older manuscripts have "the day of the *Lord*" instead of *Christ*. This then refers to the Old Testament use of this expression as a period of divine judgment at the end time.

**3. Let no man deceive you by any means:** . . . Do not let anyone fool you, –NLTG . . . lead you into a mistake, –CMPB . . . by any method, –CNDT.

**for [that day shall not come], except there come a falling away first:** . . . for the apostasy is to come, –BRKL . . . unless the apostasy comes first, –CNFT . . . because the apostasy must first appear, –CMPB . . . there will be a falling away from the faith, –NORL . . . until after the Great Apostasy, –MNTG . . . until the great revolt occurs, –WLMS . . . departing, –TNDL (1526), –CVDL –GNVA (1557), –BEZA.

**and that man of sin be revealed, the son of perdition:** ... the son of destruction, –SEB, –KLGS ... and the appearing of that Incarnation of Wickedness, –TCNT.

**2:3.** No matter how logical the false teachers might have seemed, they were still wrong. The Day of the Lord could not have come because there must be a falling away first, and the "man of sin," the "son of perdition," must be revealed. Some take "first" in the sense of "prior," that is, before the Day of Christ. A more common meaning of "first," however, is first in sequence. That is, the first thing after the Day of the Lord begins will be the falling away and the revealing of the man of sin. Since these had not happened, the Day of Christ had not yet begun, and the Thessalonians could still expect the Rapture.

Some take the falling away to mean religious apostasy, a great abandonment of spiritual religion that will give the Antichrist opportunity to take over. Others take it to be a rebellion against truth and justice, a defiance of God's authority among all nations.

Dr. E. Schuler English suggests another possibility: that the word *apostasia* has a secondary meaning of "take away" and might point to the rapture of the Church. (See *Overview,* p. 558 and the word study at *apostasia,* number 640.)

Some ancient manuscripts have "man of lawlessness" instead of "man of sin." This person will put himself above the law and make his will supreme as an absolute dictator. His reign will be short however. He is also the son of perdition, that is, he is doomed to eternal loss just as Judas was (John 17:12). This does not mean Judas will come back as the Antichrist. (See *Overview,* pp. 558-560.)

**4. Who opposeth and exalteth himself above all that is called God, or that is worshipped:** ... He will lift himself above all of these things, –SEB.
**so that he as God sitteth in the temple of God, showing himself that he is God:** ... He will go into the temple of God and take his seat there, –NORL ... in the house of God, –NLTG ... he places himself in the temple of God, openly exhibiting himself, –CMPB ... he takes his seat ... displaying himself as being God, NASB ... setting himself out to be, –KJII ... with the acclaim that he himself is God, –BRKL ... displays himself as actually being God! –TCNT ... proclaiming himself to be, –WLMS ... claiming that he is God, –SEB.

**2:4.** Paul wrote that the man of sin will continue long enough to set himself up against "all that is called God" (everything divine) and against every object of worship. He will tear down all the established religions of the world and all the minor

religions and cults as well. He will claim to be God and will sit personally in the temple of God, claiming it as his possession. "Temple" (sanctuary) is used by Paul elsewhere of the Church or the Christians. Thus, some think the Antichrist's temple will be the apostate church. However, the sanctuary here is the Holy Place, and it is better to take it as a literal temple.

**5. Remember ye not, that, when I was yet with you, I told you these things?:**

**2:5.** Paul had already explained this in his preaching at Thessalonica, but his explanation is not given here.

**6. And now ye know what withholdeth that he might be revealed in his time:** ... you know now what the restraining influence is which prevents, –TCNT ... there is a power that is now holding him back, –NORL ... You know the power that is keeping the man of sin back now, –NLTG ... you know the power that is holding him back, –WLMS ... what impedes his being revealed, –BRKL ... what restrains him from being revealed, NASB ... in his proper time, –CNFT.

**2:6.** "What withholdeth" (or, "holds back") is neuter gender. Many commentators (both ancient and modern) take this to refer to the Roman Empire. Some ancient writers took it to be the preaching of the apostles. But since Paul uses the neuter to refer to the Holy Spirit (because the word *spirit* is neuter), many take it that the power that holds back the revelation of the Antichrist is the Holy Spirit. Having examined the structure of the Greek in this verse, Ellingsworth and Nida offer this translation: "You are experiencing the power which holds the Wicked One back now, so that he will be revealed at the proper time, and not before" (*Helps for Translators,* 17:169). However, they are not dogmatic about the precise interpretation of the verse. They agree with Best who states, "No theory can be held to be satisfactory and as Augustine realized long ago (*The City of God,* 20:19) we must acknowledge our ignorance" (*Black's New Testament Commentaries,* 10:301).

**7. For the mystery of iniquity doth already work:** ... The secret of lawlessness, –SEB ... is already operating, –CNDT ... secretly works, –CMPB.
**only he who now letteth [will let], until he be taken out of the way:** ... provided only that he who is at present restraining it, –CNFT ... only till he who now restrains, –CMPB ... Someone is holding it back, –SEB ... now must first be gotten out of the way, –BRKL.

**2:7.** The many contradictory views on this verse emphasize how little any know. Some interpreters of the "historic school" have held that the masculine "he" refers to the Roman emperor, others the apostle Paul, and still others the popes who stepped into the gap after the fall of Rome. Modern post-Tribulationists may think the withholding power is "law and order." Most pre-Tribulationists hold that the neuter form of verse 6 and the masculine form of verse 7, the power and character which "withholdeth" the Antichrist, is the Holy Spirit.

Some pre-Tribulationists believe the power is the Christian Church. During this age the Holy Spirit works through believers, whose bodies are His temples. As a unit believers comprise a temple of the Spirit (1 Corinthians 3:16; 6:19). Thus the masculine words of verse 7 are thought to refer to the "gathered" believers who are caught up in the Rapture.

At least this is clear: this passage speaks of a power and/or a person strong enough to withhold Satanic influences, so the man of sin cannot be revealed as long as this power is at work in the world.

**8. And then shall that Wicked be revealed:** ... the representative of lawlessness, —WLMS ... the lawless one, —KLGS, —MNTG.

**whom the Lord shall consume with the spirit of his mouth:** ... will despatch with, —CNDT ... will destroy him with, —WLMS ... with the breath of, —BRKL, —MNTG ... of his lips, —TCNT.

**and shall destroy with the brightness of his coming:** ... and rub him out, —KLGS ... and put a stop to his operations by, —WLMS ... by the appearance of, NASB ... the brightness of his appearing, —MNTG.

**2:8.** When this restraining influence is removed, the Antichrist, that wicked or lawless one, will immediately be revealed. But even at that very time his doom will already be sealed. When He comes in flaming fire (1:7, 8), Jesus will consume (destroy) him with the spirit (breath) of His mouth. The way Jesus will destroy the Wicked One parallels the actions of the Lord Jehovah in Isaiah 11:4: "He shall smite the earth with the rod of his mouth, and with the breath of his lips shall he slay the wicked." (See also Revelation 19:15.) One word from the Lord is all it will take.

Two closely related words are used to describe the coming of Christ, *epiphaneia* ("appearing") and *parousia* ("coming"). Marshall points out that *epiphaneia* was used in the Septuagint to describe an epiphany or revelation of God (2 Samuel 7:23; 2 Maccabees 2:21; 3:24). He further states that it was used in Hellenistic Greek to describe visits from emperors and other dignitaries (*New Century Bible,* 43:200). It was also applied to the Christ's first coming (see 2 Timothy 1:10). *Parousia* is the

common term used to describe the second coming of Christ.

The very brightness of Christ's coming, a glory which blesses the believers, will help bring violent destruction to the Antichrist and his armies.

**9. [Even him], whose coming is after the working of Satan:** ... Satan will use this man of sin, —NLTG ... whose coming is according to the energy of Satan, —MNTG.

**with all power and signs and lying wonders:** ... He will use all kinds of false powers, proofs, and miracles, —SEB ... in the shape of all kinds of deceptive miracles, —TCNT ... with his plenitude of power and pretended signs and wonders, —WLMS ... with pretended signs and miracles, —NORL ... many powerful works that will be false, —NLTG ... all of them false, —BRKL.

**2:9.** To the people who do not know the Antichrist is doomed, his coming will seem supernatural. It is also called a "coming" (*parousia,* presence). It will be according to the working or energizing of Satan in all sorts of deeds of power, miraculous signs, and amazing wonders. But all these will be lies. ("Lying" applies to all three. See John 8:44.) Satan will use these signs and lying wonders to get the attention of the people of the world.

**10. And with all deceivableness of unrighteousness in them that perish:** ... with all the deception of wickedness, NASB ... with every seduction of injustice, —CNDT.

**because they received not the love of the truth, that they might be saved:** ... because they did not welcome, —BRKL ... because they did not receive the love of the truth for their salvation, —MNTG.

**2:10.** These false signs and wonders will entice those who make pleasure or money their god. The Antichrist will tempt them with every kind of wicked deception. The connotation of this ties it in with the seduction that comes from wealth (Matthew 13:22), sin (Hebrews 3:13), reveling in deceptive pleasures (2 Peter 2:13), and every kind of deceitful lust (Ephesians 4:22).

This seductive deception will be effective in those who are *already* perishing, lost, gone astray, already on the broad road leading to destruction (Matthew 7:13).

Satan's false signs will also deceive those who did not welcome the love of the truth that they might be saved. That is, they did not become real disciples of Jesus but continued to follow their own ways. (Compare John 8:31, 32.)

"Saved" here does not refer to conversion, however, but to the salvation and inheritance which will be believers' when they are changed into Christ's likeness.

**11. And for this cause God shall send them strong delusion:** . . . It is because of this refusal, —NORL . . . a working of error, —KJII . . . a deluding influence, NASB . . . a deceiving power, —SEB.

**that they should believe a lie:** . . . resulting in their believing, —WUST . . . to believe the falsehood, —BRKL . . . for themselves to make the Falsehood credible, —FNTN . . . that they should put faith in a falsehood, —MNTG . . . till they actually believe what is false, —WLMS . . . that will cause them to believe the lie, —ADAM.

**2:11.** Because they have no love for the truth God will send them a strong, deluding influence. Bruce says that "a power is set in operation within them which makes them prone to embrace error" (*Word Biblical Commentary,* 45:174). This will lead them to "believe a lie" (literally *the lie,* not any lie that happens to come along, but the big lie, the false claims and pretensions of the Antichrist).

**12. That they all might be - damned:** . . . that all may be, —ADAM . . . they all should be condemned, —MNTG . . . might be judged, —WUST.

**who believed not the truth:** . . . who do not trust to, —FNTN . . . who are faithless to the truth, —MNTG.

**but had pleasure in unrighteousness:** . . . but delight in evil, —NORL . . . They enjoyed sin, —SEB . . . but take pleasure in injustice, —KLGS . . . in wickedness, —WUST.

**2:12.** The result will be that all who have not welcomed the love of the truth will "be damned" (judged, called to account, and condemned). The first and most important ground for their judgment will be the fact that they did not believe (and obey) the truth. Second, they took "pleasure in unrighteousness." They approved, considered good, took delight in, and sought satisfaction in wrongdoing, injustice, wickedness, and evil. In other words, they kept going along with sin, considered it normal, and promoted it as desirable. Strong delusion is already making many believe that those who practice the works of the flesh can still be acceptable to God. But the Bible clearly warns that "they which do such things shall not inherit the kingdom of God" (Galatians 5:19-21). God expects believers to cultivate the fruit of the Spirit and crucify the flesh with its affections and lusts or desires (Galatians 5:22-24). Those who do not do so will be well prepared to accept the Antichrist's false claims.

**13. But we are bound to give thanks alway to God for you:** . . . I ought to give thanks to God continually, —MNTG . . . we have a sense of moral obligation to be giving thanks to God, —WUST.

**brethren beloved of the Lord:** . . . brothers dear to the Lord, —ADAM . . . whom the Lord loves, —MNTG.

**because God hath from the beginning chosen you to salvation:** . . . from the rest of mankind, —WUST . . . planned for you to be saved, —SEB . . . for salvation, —ADAM.

**through sanctification of the Spirit and belief of the truth:** . . . in consecration of, —MNTG . . . and by faith in the truth, —ADAM.

**2:13.** Paul did not dwell long on the deceptions of the Antichrist. He quickly went on to say in a positive way how he felt bound (under obligation) to keep giving thanks at all times for his brothers (and sisters). They had received the love of the truth. They were loved not merely by Paul, but also by the Lord. In contrast to those who will be deceived by the Antichrist, they will be brought into salvation. God has chosen them for this end. God's purpose for believers is not only that they enjoy salvation but also reach Christian maturity.

God has not only chosen that believers be brought into ultimate salvation where they will be changed into Christ's likeness (1 John 3:2), He has also chosen the means to bring them to this goal. They only reach the goal through a continued sanctification by the Spirit and a steadfast belief of the truth. The Holy Spirit consecrates believers and separates them from sin, and at the same time He separates them to God and to obedience to His will. He also gives help and power to live a holy (dedicated) life. The believer's part is a continued faith in the truth, a faithful, obedient acceptance and practice of the truth.

**14. Whereunto he called you by our gospel:** . . . He summoned you, —WUST . . . through my gospel, —MNTG . . . by means of our good news, —ADAM.

**to the obtaining of the glory of our Lord Jesus Christ:** . . . that you might secure for yourselves, —ADAM . . . resulting in your acquisition of, —WUST.

**2:14.** The means by which God called the Thessalonians to this salvation was Paul's preaching of the one true gospel ("good news"). It was the same gospel preached by the other apostles (Galatians 1:16, 17; 2:2). Any other "gospel" can only bring a curse (Galatians 1:7-9).

The fulfillment of this salvation will be when Christians enter into the full possession of the glory of our Lord Jesus Christ. All who keep believing will enter the glory (Ephesians 1:4-10). Also implied here is the truth clearly expressed at Philippians 3:21 which says that Christ "shall change our vile body, that it may be fashioned like unto his glorious body."

**15. Therefore, brethren, stand fast:** . . . Consequently, then, —CNDT . . . So then . . . be constantly standing firmly, —WUST . . . stand steady, —KLGS.

**and hold the traditions which ye have been taught:** . . . and hold fast the teachings, —MNTG . . . and hold on to that which we have taught you, —KLGS . . . hold on to the instructions you learned, —BRKL . . . and keep a tight grip on the teachings, —WLMS . . . that you were taught by us, —ADAM . . . which you were taught either orally or through our letter, —WUST.

**whether by word, or our epistle:** . . . by word of mouth, —MNTG . . . or letter, —CMPB.

**2:15.** In view of the glory to come, Paul challenged the Thessalonians to stand fast and keep holding on to the traditions (teachings) taught them by the Word (in his preaching) and in his epistles. Human traditions are not meant here. The word "traditions" in this case speaks of teachings handed down from God through Jesus. Paul was emphasizing that his teachings did not come from his own mind. He was simply passing along the message handed down by the Lord. Like the Old Testament prophets who spoke for God, he was not free to change it or mix in any of his own ideas. (See 2 Peter 1:20, 21.)

For believers, this means taking a stand on and being true to the entire Bible. Careful examination of the Book of Acts and the Epistles shows that Paul and all the apostles preached the truths recorded in the four Gospels, truths Jesus repeated again and again in the many places where He preached and taught. They also preached the gospel from the Old Testament which was the only written Bible they had.

16. **Now our Lord Jesus Christ himself, and God, even our Father, which hath loved us:**

**and hath given [us] everlasting consolation:** . . . and has graciously given us, —WLMS . . . gave us unfailing comfort, —TCNT . . . and gives us ageless encouragement, —KLGS . . . eternal encouragement, —MNTG . . . everlasting encouragement, —WUST.

**and good hope through grace:** . . . and well-grounded hope, —BRKL . . . this gift having been given us in [His] grace, —WUST.

**2:16.** To his exhortation to stand firm, Paul added a prayer. In the final analysis, Christians cannot stand in their own strength or hold to the Scriptures through their own understanding. Believers need Jesus Christ himself and God the Father to help them. They can expect God to do this because of His love. He demonstrated and proved His love by giving His Son to die on Calvary (John 3:16). He pours that love into the believer's heart when He gives him the Spirit (Romans 5:5).

Believers have further assurance that God will always encourage and strengthen them because He has already given them everlasting consolation (eternal, unfailing, inexhaustible comfort and encouragement) and a "good hope" by His grace (His unmerited, undeserved favor).

17. **Comfort your hearts:** . . . encourage your hearts, —ADAM, —WUST.

**and stablish you in every good word and work:** . . . and stabilize them in the sphere of, —WUST . . . and support you, —ADAM . . . will make you strong in, —SEB . . . strengthen you in every good thing you do or say, —WLMS.

**2:17.** As Christians stand firm, holding on to the teachings of God's Word, they can expect God and Christ to comfort (encourage) their hearts and to strengthen and confirm or firmly fix them, not merely in their minds, but in every good word and work. (Here some important ancient manuscripts place "work" before "word." This is the correct order for the Christian witness. The believer's works must be established in the grace of God before his words can mean very much.)

# Chapter 3

1. **Finally, brethren, pray for us, that the word of the Lord may have [free] course:** . . . Furthermore, —CNDT . . . My last words to you, —NLTG . . . In conclusion, —CNFT . . . pray on . . . that God's word may run swiftly, —MNTG . . . may make progress, NAB . . . may rapidly spread, —CMPB . . . may spread quickly, and be received with honour, —JB.

**and be glorified, even as [it is] with you:** . . . as in your own case, —MNTG.

**3:1.** "Finally" indicates Paul was changing the subject and bringing this letter to an end with a variety of concluding exhortations.

First, he requested prayer for his situation. Paul and his evangelistic party were having difficulties in Corinth. Opposition was growing. But Paul's chief concern was not for himself, but that the Word of the Lord (the gospel) might have free course. He wanted to see it continue to spread rapidly and without hindrance. He wanted it to advance and be glorified (honored or received with honor). More than anything he wanted to see the gospel triumph. He knew the Thessalonians wanted this too.

2. **And that we may be delivered from unreasonable and wicked men:** . . . Pray that we will be rescued from unfair, evil men, —SEB . . . that we may be kept free from the snares of, —NORL . . . from confused and evil men, —NAB . . . from troublesome and evil men, —CNFT . . . from those unbalanced and malicious people, —BRKL.

**for all [men] have not faith:** . . . do not hold the faith, —MNTG.

**3:2.** Paul was not blind to the opposition. He knew he was surrounded by unreasonable (perverse, twisted) and wicked (evil, malicious) men. He wanted prayer that he might be delivered (preserved or rescued) from them. This prayer was urgent, "for all men have not faith" (literally, "the faith is not of all"); that is, the gospel had not been received by all. Thus, even in requesting deliverance, his chief concern was not mere self-preservation. He wanted more to hear and believe.

**3. But the Lord is faithful:**
**who shall stablish you, and keep [you] from evil:** . . . and guard you from, —MNTG . . . He will protect you from the evil one, —SEB.

**3:3.** In spite of the dangers, the evil men, and the difficult circumstances, Paul declared that "the Lord is faithful." He is worthy of trust. Believers can depend on Him and His promises. He will establish (support, confirm, and strengthen) believers. He will keep (guard, defend, protect, and preserve) them from evil (from the Evil One or from that which is evil). "Keep" is really a military term used of one who stands guard. "Evil" most likely means the Evil One, Satan, who instigates evil men to assault believers. What a picture this is: God standing guard for us against the devil, at the same time strengthening us for the battle and putting us on firm footing.

**4. And we have confidence in the Lord touching you:** . . . as regards you, —CNFT . . . fully fixed our faith on you, —MNTG.
**that ye both do and will do the things which we command you:** . . . and will continue to do, —MNTG . . . what we direct you, —TCNT . . . whatever we enjoin, —NAB . . . what we suggested, —BRKL.

**3:4.** Paul had no doubts about the faith of the Thessalonian believers. He had full "confidence in the Lord" for (toward) them. Their relation to the Lord as well as his own relationship to them made him confident that they were doing and would continue to do what he had commanded (instructed, directed) them to do. This command or instruction undoubtedly included the request to keep praying for him. But it also anticipates what he was about to command or instruct them to do.

**5. And the Lord direct your hearts into the love of God:** . . . May . the Lord guide your hearts, —SEB . . . incline, —MNTG . . . lead you to a heartfelt love for God, —TCNT.
**and into the patient waiting for Christ:** . . . and to a stedfastness like that of, —TCNT . . . and into a patient endurance like Christ's, —WLMS . . . and the fortitude of Christ, —JB.

**3:5.** Paul further prayed that the Lord would direct their "hearts into the love of God" and "into the patient waiting for Christ"; that is, into the patient endurance that Christ showed, or into Christlike fortitude and steadfastness. This direction would make their way straight and remove the obstacles which Satan had used to obscure their path (see Rienecker, p. 596, on the word *kateuthunai*).

**6. Now we command you, brethren, in the name of our Lord Jesus Christ:** . . . I summon you, brothers, —MNTG . . . we are giving you strict orders, —NORL . . . by the authority of, —SEB . . . on the authority, —WLMS.
**that ye withdraw yourselves from every brother that walketh disorderly:** . . . to keep away from, —JB . . . to shun any brother who leads an idle and disorderly life, —MNTG . . . stay away from every brother, —KLGS . . . who lives irregularly, —CNFT . . . any Christian who is lazy, —NLTG . . . who is a lazy person, a troublemaker, —SEB . . . who is living as a shirker,/ —WLMS.
**and not after the tradition which he received of us:** . . . which is not according to the rule you received from me, —MNTG.

**3:6.** First Thessalonians 5:14 urged the believers to warn the unruly (the indisciplined, the lazy, the idle, the truants from work and duty). Now it seems that Timothy's report had indicated that a considerable number were pious idlers, too "spiritual" to dirty their hands with manual labor. Instead of working they were busybodies, disorderly, and meddling. This cannot be tolerated in the life of Christians. With utmost seriousness and severity Paul commanded the rest of the Christians in the name of the Lord Jesus Christ not to associate with any who lived without working. Ellingsworth and Nida suggest that the phrase "in the name of the Lord Jesus Christ" is equivalent to saying "as representing our Lord Jesus Christ" or perhaps "on the authority of the Lord Jesus Christ." They state, "In this context, Paul is obviously asserting that he is speaking on behalf of the Lord Jesus Christ" (17:200). The very fact that they were Christians meant the rest of the believers could not ignore the lazy way they were living. The name (person, nature, and character) of Jesus is dishonored by such dereliction of duty. The name (authority) of Jesus as Lord and as Christ (God's Anointed) backed up Paul's command. They were living contrary to the tradition (teaching handed down from Jesus) which Paul had already given them.

**7. For yourselves know how ye ought to follow us:** . . . you know well how you must imitate me, —MNTG . . . copy our example, —TCNT.
**for we behaved not ourselves disorderly among you:** . . . I did not lead an idle or disorderly life, —MNTG.

**3:7.** Paul had also set an example which the Thessalonians knew they ought to follow, even imitate. Paul could make this bold command because he was "imitating" Jesus (see 1 Corinthians 11:1, "Be ye followers [i.e., 'imitators'] of me, even as I also am of Christ"). There was nothing lazy about Paul's way of life when he was among them. He never played truant when there was work to do. Neither did he sit around idly and let others do the work when he could help. Even when he was shipwrecked he was concerned about the needs of others and was the first one out to collect more wood for the fire (Acts 28:3).

**8. Neither did we eat any man's bread for nought:** . . . We were not indebted to anyone, —NORL . . . neither did we eat bread gratuitously from anyone, —CNDT . . . without paying for it, —NLTG . . . without pay, —BRKL . . . unless we paid for it! —SEB.
**but wrought with labour and travail night and day:** . . . instead, we did hard and heavy work, —BRKL . . . laboring to the point of exhaustion, —NAB.
**that we might not be charge-able to any of you:** . . . that we might not burden any of you, —CNFT . . . so that we would not be a load on any of you, —KLGS.

**3:8.** When Paul came to Thessalonica to preach the gospel, he did not accept any free meals. He paid room and board, not only for himself, but for his entire evangelistic party. He did this by laboring with constant exertion and hardship day and night. His trade of tentmaking was not an easy one. The purpose of all this toil and struggle to earn a living was that he and his fellow workers for the Lord might not be chargeable or be a burden to any of the believers. Actually, the love of Christ flooded his own heart and flowed out to them.

**9. Not because we have not power:** . . . Not that we had no claim on you, —NAB . . . Not that I have no right to be supported, —WLMS . . . we had not a right to receive support, —TCNT . . . Not that I have no right to such support, —MNTG.
**but to make ourselves an en-sample unto you to follow us:** . . . it was simply to give you an example for you to imitate, —MNTG . . . but to give you a pattern to imitate us, —KLGS . . . to give you in our conduct a pattern for you to imitate, —NORL.

**3:9.** By saying that he did not want to be a burden to them, Paul did not mean to give the impression that the work of the ministry should not be supported financially. He had the power (the authority and the right) to ask them to give him all the support he needed. But he waived that right for the sake of a greater spreading of the gospel in new areas. (See 1 Corinthians 9:3-18 where Paul deals with the same subject and shows his concern for the gospel.) In Thessalonica he waived that right also in order to provide believers with an example to follow or imitate. No doubt, there were Thessalonians who would have been glad to

contribute to the support of Paul and his fellow laborers, as the believers in Philippi actually did (Philippians 4:15, 16). But he knew some would use his example as a pretext for not working. He refused to give them that kind of excuse.

**10. For even when we were with you, this we commanded you:** . . . I used to charge you, —MNTG . . . I gave you this direction, —WLMS.
**that if any would not work, neither should he eat:** . . . if he refused to do any work, —JB . . . If a person refuses to work, —SEB, —WLMS.

**3:10.** In addition to setting an example, Paul had repeatedly commanded the Thessalonians that if anyone was not willing to work, neither should he eat. This work ethic was suggested by the fact that Adam was given work to do in the Garden of Eden and by the judgment on Adam that, "In the sweat of thy face shalt thou eat bread" (Genesis 3:19). The Book of Proverbs has many warnings against laziness and characterizes the wise both as fearing the Lord and as industrious. Rabbis in New Testament times insisted that every young rabbi learn a trade, just as Paul had.

**11. For we hear that there are some which walk among you disorderly:** . . . But we are informed, —WLMS . . . there are those of your number who are leading idle and disorderly lives, —MNTG . . . some of you are wandering dead beats, —KLGS.
**working not at all, but are busybodies:** . . . loafers, nosey about other people's affairs, —KLGS . . . busy in other folks' affairs, —BRKL . . . but are meddling, —CNDT . . . but prying into other people's affairs, —CMPB.

**3:11.** Again and again Paul had heard reports that there were those among the Thessalonian believers who were walking disorderly; that is, living in idleness, accepting no responsibility. Instead of being workers, they were meddlers. Instead of taking care of their own business, they were busybodies, poking their noses into everyone else's business.

Paul used the same word of young widows in writing to Timothy (1 Timothy 5:13). In those days it was practically impossible for widows to get jobs. The law of Moses made provision for them by commanding that gleanings of the harvest be left for them to gather (Deuteronomy 24:19-21). But among the heathen, widows often died of starvation. Thus, from the first, the Church accepted an obligation to support widows (Acts 6:1).

Paul found, however, that this kind of charity was not good for the younger widows. They learned to be idle (lazy, useless, and careless). With time on their hands they visited around and became tattlers or gossipers, spreading foolish chatter and nonsense, and sometimes malicious stories. They also became busybodies. They gave attention to things that were no concern of theirs and became meddlers. For this reason Paul encouraged them to marry again and accept the responsibilities of their own homes.

**12. Now them that are such we command and exhort by our Lord Jesus Christ:** . . . and entreat, by the authority, —MNTG.

**that with quietness they work, and eat their own bread:** . . . to work in quietness, —MNTG . . . and so earn, —TCNT . . . earn their own living, —NORL, —KLGS.

**3:12.** Jesus himself did not encourage idleness among His followers. His parables often call men to work in the harvest field. Paul therefore commanded and exhorted (challenged, encouraged) by the Lord Jesus Christ, that any who were idle or busybodies should go to work. Instead of going around imposing on the hospitality and good nature of other Christians, they were to work in quietness; that is, with a quiet restful spirit and with an inner tranquility.

**13. But ye, brethren, be not weary in well doing:** . . . never grow tired of doing what is right, —JB . . . don't become weary, —ADAM . . . should not be despondent in, —CNDT . . . never get tired of doing good, —SEB.

**3:13.** Paul recognized that the majority of the believers in Thessalonica were honest, hardworking people. The danger was that those who were neglecting their responsibilities might cause the rest to grow weary or lose heart. But whatever others do, Christians must never grow tired of doing what is right, honorable, noble, excellent, and fair to everyone concerned.

**14. And if any man obey not our word by this epistle:** . . . If any man does not give heed to what I have said in this letter, —MNTG . . . whoever doesn't obey what we say in this letter, —ADAM.

**note that man:** . . . mark that man, —MNTG . . . mark that person, —WLMS . . . remember who he is, —NLTG . . . single him out, —NAB . . . give him notice, —SEB.

**and have no company with him:** . . . Don't associate with him! —SEB . . . and avoid his company, —TCNT . . . don't mix with him, —ADAM . . . do not get mixed up with him, —BRKL . . . stop having anything to do with him, —WLMS . . . to be ostracized, —NAB.

**that he may be ashamed:** . . . so that he may become ashamed of himself, —ADAM . . . so as to make him feel, —MNTG . . . that he may be abashed, —CNDT.

**3:14.** For the most part, these lazy loafers would not recognize themselves as guilty of the kind of idleness and interference in the affairs of others

Paul was talking about. So Paul told the church to note them with disapproval and to cease to associate with them, with the intention of bringing them to their senses and making them ashamed of their idleness and meddling. The Greek implies also a hope of bringing them to the place where they would respect the Word given in this epistle.

**15. Yet count [him] not as an enemy:** . . . do not regard him, —CNFT.

**but admonish [him] as a brother:** . . . but warn him, —BRKL . . . but caution him, —TCNT . . . counsel him, —ADAM.

**3:15.** In withdrawing their fellowship, the believers must not withdraw their love. The disobedient person who persisted in habits of laziness and gossip was still a brother (or sister). The warnings must be given in a gentle loving way, not as scathing denunciations. The warnings should bring the sin home to the person in such a tender way that the lazy ones would be ashamed. Thus, the call was for a withdrawal of close fellowship, not a complete shunning or avoidance of the person. As members together of the local Body, Christians should gently try to bring the idler to a place where he will not only be ashamed of laziness, but will go to work in obedience to Paul's command. Then the rest of the believers will be able to give him fellowship again without being afraid that he will meddle, spread gossip, or stir up trouble in the church.

**16. Now the Lord of peace himself give you peace:** . . . who gives us peace, —WLMS . . . give you His peace, —ADAM.

**always by all means:** . . . everlasting . . . in every place, —CNFT . . . all the time and in every way, —JB . . . always, in every thing, —MRDK . . . in every way about everything, —KLGS . . . in every possible way, —NAB . . . in every event, —CMPB . . . in whatever circumstances you may be, —WLMS . . . in every form, —FNTN . . . continually, —PNT . . . at all times, —CLMT.

**The Lord [be] with you all:**

**3:16.** Paul brought this epistle to a conclusion with a prayer that "the Lord of peace" would give them peace at all times and by all means; that is, in every way possible and in all places. In other words, what they really needed was Jesus himself. He is the One who gives peace, a peace the world knows nothing about (John 14:27). Without Him believers are nothing. Without Him they have nothing that is really worthwhile or of eternal value. Thus, when Paul said, "The Lord be with you all," including those who were still disobedient to the commands of this letter, Paul expressed a fact, not a mere desire. The Lord was with them.

He would continue to be with them. Paul had no doubt about this.

It was good that the Thessalonians were excited about the prospect of Christ's second coming. But Paul saw that what they needed was not greater expectation but better habits of life. They needed less talk about the time of His return and more living in the light of His coming. He had given them work to do. When He comes He expects to find Christians busy doing His will and seeking to please Him.

**17. The salutation of Paul with mine own hand, which is the token in every epistle:** ... I append this signature to every letter I write, —*NAB* ... I, Paul, add this farewell, —*TCNT* ... write this greeting with my own hand, and this is the indication in every letter, —*ADAM* ... add this greeting in my own handwriting, which is my token in every letter, —*MNTG* ... This is the mark, —*CNFT* ... Paul's handwriting; which is a sign in, —*BRKL* ... which [circumstance, namely, that I wrote it personally, whereas the rest of the letter was dictated to a secretary] is the mark of genuineness in every letter, —*WUST* ... It is the way I finish all my letters, —*NLTG* ... This is the sign of all letters, —*KLGS* ... It is my signature on every letter, —*SEB* ... this a distinguishing mark in every letter, *NASB* ... the mark in every letter of mine, —*WLMS* ... my

sign in every letter, —*FNTN* ... which is the mark of genuineness, —*JB*.

**so I write:** ... Thus, —*MNTG* ... that I have written it, —*ADAM* ... In this manner am I in the habit of writing, —*WUST* ... This is my handwriting, —*BECK*, —*WLMS* ... am extending greetings, —*HRBR*.

**3:17.** At this point, Paul took the pen from the scribe and wrote the concluding benediction in his own handwriting. The Thessalonians could have assurance that this letter was no forgery but was indeed one of his. The mention of "every epistle" implies he wrote often. Some of those letters may have been very brief notes or exhortations, however. Not all of his letters were preserved. But we have the assurance that those which we do have were not only inspired by the Holy Spirit, but used by the Spirit to bless all the churches where they were circulated and read.

**18. The grace of our Lord Jesus Christ [be] with you all. Amen:** ... The love of our Lord, —*BECK* ... The favour of, —*RTHM* ... The spiritual blessing of our Lord, —*WLMS* ... of Jesus the Messiah, —*MRDK*.

**3:18.** Through this and the other epistles that have been preserved in God's divine providence, the "grace of our Lord Jesus Christ" that Paul wanted for the Thessalonians is still being ministered to Christians today.

# 1 TIMOTHY

## Overview

### Structure

The letter is the first of the so-called Pastoral Epistles, which also include 2 Timothy and Titus (see commentary). Timothy, the recipient of the letter, was the younger friend and coworker of Paul. He is mentioned in Acts and several of the other Pauline letters. One can presume that 1 Timothy was written sometime between A.D. 61 and 64, after Paul's first Roman imprisonment and prior to the Neronian persecutions.

Some have attempted to identify the structural outline of the letter; however, usually these constructions become somewhat artificial. Nonetheless, there are some interesting models. W.B. Wallis discerns a pattern of themes centering on task and poetic doxology: in the opening doxology (1:17), in the main body of the letter (3:16, the hymn), and in the closing doxology (6:15, 16). J. Sidlow Baxter finds two main sections, chapters 2 and 3, which concern the Church and the local assembly, and chapters 4 through 6, which addresses pastors (pp. 371-380). The structure of most other interpretations is either too rigid or too flexible.

The absence of agreement on structure may indicate that structure is limited in the letter; after all, it is a letter, not a treatise. The author's thought flows evenly and naturally from theme to theme, with pauses and interruptions much like those in a conversation. Obviously, little insight is gained by trying to force the letter's contents into some rigid or dogmatic framework. Actually, the chapter divisions in the epistle seem as useful as any other structural arrangement.

As with most of Paul's other letters, 1 Timothy has a theoretical teaching element and section which contains admonitions. There is one difference. Whereas normally the two elements are distinct, in 1 Timothy the material is subdivided into several subsections, which may contain both practical and theoretical parts.

The teaching section is of a polemic and dogmatic nature in which Paul discussed faith and the proclamation of the Church. It occurs in three smaller sections, chapters 1, 4, and 6. The practical admonition section, which addresses worship and conduct in the local church, appears in two subsections in chapters 2, 3, and 5.

If one accepts this kind of arrangement, the following structure reflects the contents of 1 Timothy:

I. TEACHING SECTION (1:1-20; 4:1-16; 6:1-21)

  A. The Law and the Gospel (1:1-20)

    1. Deceivers and False Teachers of the Law (1:3-11)

    2. Paul's Testimony and Gospel (1:12-17)

    3. Timothy's Task (1:18-20)

  B. False and True Doctrine (4:1-16)

    1. The Falling Away (4:1-3)

    2. Sound Teaching (4:4-11)

    3. Personal Admonition (4:12-16)

  C. False Teaching and the Profit Motive (6:1-21)

II. PRACTICAL ADMONITION (2:1-15; 3:1-16; 5:1-25)

  A. The Worship Service (2:1-15)

    1. Prayer and Intercession (2:1-7)

    2. The Conduct of Men (2:8)

    3. The Conduct of Women (2:9-15)

  B. Elders and Deacons (3:1-16)

    1. Elders (Overseers) (3:1-7)

    2. Deacons (3:8-13)

    3. The Church and Its Message (3:14-16)

  C. Support and Service (5:1-25)

    1. The Ministry of Admonition (5:1, 2)

    2. The Support of Widows (5:3-16)

    3. The Treatment of Elders (5:17-25)

## I. Teaching Section (1:1-20; 4:1-16; 6:1-21)

Paul opened this section with a reminder that he was an apostle of Jesus Christ. Although Paul was writing to one of his close friends, a fellow laborer in the gospel, the letter is something more than mere personal correspondence. The letter would be received as Holy Scripture and read in the church. The letter thus authorized Timothy to perform the charge given to him to oversee the church in Ephesus. Wielding apostolic authority, Paul reminded Timothy of the charge given to him on a former occasion. His words are instructive for the Church throughout all generations.

A central theme in this letter is "sound doctrine." Apostolic teachings, as reflected by the New Testament writings, were already fairly well defined by this time. All preaching and teaching were tested against the standard of the apostolic testimony. Paul's understanding of "sound" should be seen in light of this. The sense is probably not too far removed from the expressions "sound, healthy, whole" in our language. The sound teaching of the gospel is "whole, true, and correct." It brings restoration and healing, two essential ingredients of salvation. The term "sound," *hugiainō*, occurs in the New Testament only in the Pastoral Epistles. "Sound doctrine" (1 Timothy 1:10; 2 Timothy 4:3; Titus 1:9; 2:1) is evidently synonymous with "the 'healthy' words" of the gospel (1 Timothy 6:3), which Timothy heard from Paul (2 Timothy 1:13). Such "sound, healthy" teaching results in a "sound, healthy" faith (Titus 1:13; 2:2) and encourages "sound speech that cannot be condemned" (Titus 2:8).

In contrast to the sound teaching of the gospel stand the "unhealthy" doctrines of the false teachers (cf. 1 Timothy 6:4; 2 Timothy 2:17). It is Timothy's task to resist these false teachers and their useless and harmful teachings. False teachers do not create true faith in God, but make people "reprobate concerning the faith" (2 Timothy 3:8).

It appears that Paul left Timothy in Ephesus with the responsibility to "charge some that they teach no other doctrine (than the gospel)" (1:3), Timothy was to do the work of an evangelist (2 Timothy 4:5); and from the esteem Paul had for this rather young man, it appears that he was one of the most effective workers on Paul's team of ministers. Paul and Timothy saw the gospel spreading at an almost unbelievable rate during this time. But, while the gospel had the potential to spread as never before, it also came under attack by heretical doctrines that threatened to force their way into the churches and destroy the progress that had been made. That Paul would devote a letter to this problem speaks of the kind of leader he was. It shows how seriously the apostles took the task of keeping the gospel pure and unadulterated.

From what Paul wrote to Timothy, we have only partial knowledge of the nature of the heresy Timothy was to combat. The heresy in Ephesus apparently had some of the syncretistic features (i.e., a "mixed" conglomeration of religio-cultural ideas) found in the Colossian heresy (see commentary on Colossians), but it was probably not identical to this. Actually, Paul may have been attacking several kinds of deceptive teachings in his letters to Timothy. In some cases the problems had not yet occurred, while in others they had only begun. Some forms of the aberration involved useless "word-battles" (see 2 Timothy 2:14ff.) over foolish and trivial questions (2 Timothy 2:23). Other distortions of the principal teachings of the Christian faith, such as the resurrection, also were taking place (2 Timothy 2:18; cf. 1 Timothy 1:20).

Paul warned against "false knowledge" (6:20). This perhaps suggests some teaching similar to gnosticism had infiltrated the church, as it had in Corinth and especially Colossae. Paul advised that in the last days, false teachers would preach seductive doctrines that would deceive many. Part of their message would include a false asceticism and the forbidding of marriage (4:1f.).

## A. The Law and the Gospel (1:1-20)

### 1. Deceivers and False Teachers of the Law (1:3-11)

One major aspect of the heresy in Ephesus seems to have been Jewish in origin. Paul referred to those who desired "to be teachers of the law" (1:7). This suggests they were not qualified, legitimate teachers of Jewish law, but wanted to appear to be so as to gain the respect this knowledge would bring to them. Paul spoke with bitter irony of their ignorance and lack of perception. These so-called teachers did not even understand what they themselves were saying, not to mention their lack of understanding what they were talking about so confidently (1:7). They were focusing their attention on tales, endless genealogies, and myths, in much the same manner as ancient rabbis. Evidently they had created imaginative additions to the Old Testament genealogies, added fanciful stories about the characters, and then created wild, allegorical interpretations. Paul said their "genealogies" were "endless" (1:4) (Hiebert, p. 30).

Paul's description of these deceivers as teaching "false doctrines" (NIV; Greek, *heterodidaskalein*) is very striking. It suggests they were teaching something "other" than the gospel. It probably included material outside of the scope of the divine revelation of the Word of God. Indeed, much of what they were engaged in was entirely speculation and was even outside the realm of common sense. Latent in its "stupidity," therefore, was a kind of impenetrable nature. Fighting against speculation with common sense and logic is often useless; the very premise of reason is foreign to those obligated to their own speculations. Both Greek and Hebrew thought agree: one argues in vain with stupidity (see Proverbs 27:22). Any cogent response to speculations such as these is only wasted; thus, the very system supporting them must be rejected. Some false teaching deserves no other acknowledgment than dismissal without discussion.

Paul addressed the problem of those who were presuming to integrate the Law and the gospel. Over against the false teachers' prideful ignorance, he places a statement elementary and common to Christian teaching: "But we know that the law is good, if a man use it lawfully" (1 Timothy 1:8; cf. Romans 7:12). But this is precisely what the false teachers fail to do. They did not know or understand the proper use of the Law, so they perverted it and used it in ways neither intended nor appropriate. Paul exposed their error in both negative and positive terms.

First, the Law is *not* for the sake of the righteous, who do not violate it, but for the lawbreakers who break the commands not to steal or to murder. Neither did Paul view the Law as a restriction or a threat to Christian freedom. The judgments and penalties of the Law are irrelevant to the righteous man because he keeps the Law. The false teachers, therefore, were totally unjustified in using the Law to put the righteous under the slavery and fear of the Law. A motive much higher than fear keeps the Christian from sinning. "The goal of this command is love" (1:5, NIV); the motive of love is the fulfillment of the Law (cf. Romans 13:8-10).

Second, Paul showed who the Law *is* for by giving a list of sins which he considered as among the worst the ungodly can commit. The Law stands against all this. Moreover, at this point the Law is in complete agreement with the "sound doctrine; according to the glorious gospel" (1:10, 11). Whatever is condemned by the Law is condemned by the gospel too. Faith in the gospel does not abolish the Law; it confirms and fulfills it (cf. Romans 3:31).

## 2. Paul's Testimony and Gospel (1:12-17)

Unlike the heretics in Ephesus who wanted to be teachers (1:7), Paul had been entrusted with something greater than the Law—the "glorious gospel of the blessed God" (1:11). This was not something Paul deserved, or earned; on the contrary, he was himself formerly a "persecutor," "blasphemer," and a "violent man." He regarded himself as among the "worst" of sinners. However, he received God's grace, thereby becoming the very proof of the gospel that he was called to preach. Paul included both his being entrusted with the gospel and his experience of salvation in the powerful words, "This is a faithful saying, and worthy of all acceptation, that Christ Jesus came into the world to save sinners" (1:15). The words of Jesus (Matthew 9:13) are echoed in Paul's comments.

This is the first of the sayings in the Pastoral Epistles marked by the introductory words, "this is a faithful saying." On two occasions "and worthy of all acceptation" are added (1:15; 4:9). Its shorter form appears in 1 Timothy 3:1; 2 Timothy 2:11; and Titus 2:11.

## 3. Timothy's Task (1:18-20)

The gospel, which meant everything to Paul, must be preached to others. He must defend it and confirm it (Philippians 1:7), and he could not remain silent when it. was under attack or in danger of perversion, for that would be treason. In this "good struggle" he also included his spiritual son, Timothy.

Paul, now an elderly servant of the Lord, began transferring the responsibility for the gospel to his younger coworker. This explains why he asked— or rather commanded—that Timothy remain in Ephesus. Timothy was essentially there to defend the gospel and the local church from the heretics who threatened to take it over.

Paul passed on to Timothy a commandment, an order (*parangelian*; 1:18). The term fits nicely with Paul's military imagery: the higher ranking officer was passing on a command to the younger soldier of the Cross. The command or the task to which Timothy was entrusted was first and foremost to guard the truth of the gospel against the false teachers (1:3). But this involved supervising the conduct of believers in the house of God (3:15). Doctrinal instruction and practical teaching thus are joined in the Pastoral Epistles as integral components of successful pastoral work.

Next, with a series of personal encouragements and admonitions aimed at Timothy, Paul wove the practical and theological together. In 1:19 the apostle mentioned the two qualities that are necessary and inseparable: faith and a good conscience. Christian faith can never be divorced from Christian lifestyle. Hymeneus and Alexander forgot this and consequently made a "shipwreck" of their faith (1:20). The secret of faith can only be kept by a clean conscience (3:9).

## B. False and True Doctrine (4:1-16)

Whereas in chapters 2 and 3 Paul introduced a large section on worship in the church and the practical concerns associated with it, he resumed his discussion of doctrinal issues in chapter 4. The concluding statement of chapter 3, with its mighty declaration that summarizes the Christian proclamation, "God was manifest in the flesh," is the bridge to the doctrinal section. Paul continued to forewarn that in the coming times the church of Christ and its followers would be rejected and persecuted. The Church represents the essence of the truth. For this reason, all the powers of delusion and falsehood will come against it.

## 1. The Falling Away (4:1-3)

Throughout the New Testament there is the warning that in the last days there will be a great falling away. Jesus himself spoke of this (Matthew 24:11, 12; Luke 18:8), and the apostles Peter (2 Peter 2:1ff.) and John (1 John 2:18f.) described the coming apostasy in strong language. The apostle Paul often discussed the theme (see 2 Thessalonians 2:3f. and 2 Timothy 3:1f.). Paul appealed to a special revelation: "Now the Spirit speaketh expressly" (4:1-3). This is not some vague symbolic warning or sign. The Holy Spirit says expressly that apostasy will occur. It is essential that the Church be prepared to meet the challenge apostasy brings.

In the original language there is an interesting, subtle difference between the "coming" or "latter times" (1 Timothy 4:1) and the "last days" (2

877

Timothy 3:1). The first expression almost certainly includes the backsliding of the end times, but it is not restricted to the apostasy of the last days. The Church of the New Testament as an eschatological body actually lived in the circumstances of the last days (1 Corinthians 10:11). Throughout history, the church has had to combat apostasy, for its development seems to parallel the spread of the gospel.

Paul's comments in 1 Timothy 4:1f. strongly resemble those in 2 Thessalonians 2:3f. where apostasy takes on a concrete form. It is described as if the first recipients of the letter were familiar with it. It also seems to point to a larger, more extensive apostasy that is expressed in a variety of heresies and which climaxes at the coming of the Antichrist. It is obvious that this apostasy originated and had its source in the heretical teachings that confronted the Early Church. But the apostasy described in the New Testament also extends beyond the scope of those early heresies.

The kind of apostasy Paul envisioned in this epistle was characterized by a willing turning away of some from the revealed truths of the gospel. Paul recognized that full knowledge of the secrets of the Faith belongs to the future; the Church is only on the way to such knowledge (Ephesians 4:13). Even though he recognized the believer's understanding is only partial (1 Corinthians 13:9), he nevertheless maintained that he preached the whole counsel of God (Acts 20:27). Heralds of the gospel must hold this dual aspect of knowledge in tension. However, there is a substantial difference between possessing an incomplete knowledge of the divine plan and rejecting the fundamental truths of the Word of God. The latter is heresy, whether it adds to or subtracts from what is written (Revelation 22:18).

Paul suggested that the falling away from the Faith has a demonic as well as a human origin. The heresy he opposed is the "doctrines of devils" (4:1). But it is also "the tradition of men" (Colossians 2:8), championed and propagated by men. Paul described these false teachers as "hypocrites" whose consciences were "seared" or "cauterized" (4:2).

In describing the nature of the false teachings, Paul mentioned two things which were forbidden: (1) marriage, and (2) eating of certain foods (4:3). This is a remarkable as well as startling example of how seriously the apostle regarded false teaching. The false asceticism propagated by the false teachers was in no way viewed as some harmless by-product of religious zeal. Paul condemned the teachings as demonic and those endorsing them as false.

## 2, 3. Sound Teaching and Personal Admonition (4:4-16)

The opposite of the "other teachings" is the "good doctrine" (4:6). Timothy was to nourish himself and others with it. Paul joined warnings against succumbing to the false teachings with personal instructions to Timothy concerning his responsibility to preach the truth: "Take heed unto thyself, and unto the doctrine . . . for in doing this thou shalt both save thyself, and them that hear thee" (4:16).

## C. False Teaching and the Profit Motive (6:1-21)

The final chapter of this letter contains a warning to slaves and to the rich who were members of the church. For the most part, however, it continues to reflect Paul's concern about false teaching. In chapter 5 Paul had already admonished his readers about practical matters in the life of the church.

A characteristic feature of this last section is that Paul attacked not only the false teaching per se, but also the false teachers. Paul did not draw a distinction between the person and the problem, nor did Jesus (cf. Matthew 23:1-33; cf. 2 Corinthians 11:13-15; Philippians 3:2). The teaching and the teacher were judged together. A tree is known by its fruit (Matthew 7:15-20). From his evil treasure an evil man brings forth evil things (cf. Matthew 12:33-35).

Paul was not interested in having dialogue with every kind of false teaching under the sun. To take them seriously would in effect be dignifying them with a response they did not deserve (Hiebert). But he did characterize the false teaching. He called it "fables" (1:4), "vain jangling" (1:6), "the doctrines of devils" (4:1), and "old wives fables" (4:7). He described the false teachers too. He exposed them as arrogant and ignorant (1:7), moral reprobates, having their consciences seared with a hot iron (4:2). They were conceited and foolish, with a sick craving for conflict (6:4). Their minds were corrupt.

At the climax of his condemnation, Paul used familiar language to indict his opponents: They were preachers of the gospel for the sake of making a living. They were shysters who enslaved others and devoured the churches (2 Corinthians 11:20). They nullified the Word of God for their own profit (2 Corinthians 2:17). They served not the Lord but their stomachs! (See Romans 16:18.) Their stomach was their god (Philippians 3:18, 19). Paul had said this earlier, and Timothy had certainly heard it before, but the inspired apostle seemed to think it should be repeated: the false teachers thought that godliness was to be used as a means to financial gain (6:10). Unclean motives defile one's life and teaching. But Paul addressed Timothy: "But thou, O man of God, flee these things" (6:11).

He concluded the letter with a sincere personal appeal. First, he gave an admonition to keep the commandment pure (6:13-16). After adding a warning to the rich, he made another personal appeal to avoid all false teaching: "O Timothy, keep that which is committed to thy trust, avoiding profane and vain babblings, and oppositions of science falsely so called" (6:20, 21).

## II. Practical Admonition (2:1-15; 3:1-16; 5:1-25)

The section of practical admonition is composed of two sections, chapters 2 and 3 and chapter 5; however, the topic itself falls into three parts. The first gives guidelines for conducting the worship service (chapter 2). The second outlines requirements for elders and deacons (chapter 3). The third discusses how the church is to support some of its members and the responsibilities of those it serves (chapter 5). Woven throughout this material is a series of principles and personal admonitions to Timothy.

Actually, this practical section is why these letters came to be called the Pastoral Epistles. One of their characteristic features is that they contain guidelines for worship and leadership structure in the church. Jointly the Pastoral Epistles provide a practical resource for teachers. But it would be a total misunderstanding of the nature of the worship service as described in the New Testament to think that the letters are not relevant to the Church as a whole. It is fundamental to ministry that the Church is to insure that worship and proclamation take place properly and in accordance with the Scriptures (1 Peter 2:9). Leaders of the church are not to dominate over their "flock" (1 Peter 5:3). They are shepherds who lead the flock by their example.

## A. The Worship Service (2:1-15)

The believer's life of devotion is expressed in two ways. The Christian can seek fellowship with God in quiet and solitude, but he or she can also worship God in fellowship with those who share the same faith. This joining together around the Word and prayer has always been a trademark of genuine Christianity.

The apostle Paul offered guidelines (chapter 2) for the worship gatherings, just as he had done elsewhere. For example, 1 Corinthians chapters 11 through 14 are devoted to the worship service. Rules are given for men and women on how to conduct themselves during gatherings for prayer, and instructions are given concerning proper behavior at the love feasts and Lord's Supper. Further, Paul outlined how the gifts of the Spirit are to be used in the church services. The section falls into three parts: an admonition to pray, a warning to men about their behavior, and a word to women about their conduct in the worship service.

## 1. Prayer and Intercession (2:1-7)

The apostle underscored the importance of prayer: "I exhort therefore, that, first of all. . . ." He appealed to their love and conscience. Four words are used to denote the nature of public prayer. *Prayers:* this is the normal word for a "request." It comes from a verb meaning "to lack something"; it thus denotes prayer on the basis of need. *Supplications:* this is a decidedly religious term that is only used in connection with prayer to God. It emphasizes the reverence that must be shown during prayer. *Intercessions:* the Greek term denotes prayer for others, especially prayer for a leader or superior. It connotes trust and expectation. *Thanks:* this is the proper response in prayer. One is to be thankful for what has already been received and grateful for the answer to prayer that is forthcoming.

The Church is to pray for all men, since God wants all men to be saved. The intercession of the Church especially on behalf of those in high positions in society affects the life and circumstances of the Church, and consequently its impact upon society.

## 2. The Conduct of Men (2:8)

At issue here is not liturgical prayers offered by ministers, but the prayers of the entire congregation. The one who leads the entire Body to the throne of God must himself be fit for this. There is to be no wrath, strife, or quarrels among believers. Such conditions are an impediment to prayer.

## 3. The Conduct of Women (2:9-15)

Women played an active role in prayer in the Early Church (1 Corinthians 11:5). When they participated in the worship service, they were to dress modestly. Related to their role in the church Paul said the women must not exert authority over or teach a man (2:12). As a basis of this prohibition he appealed to the arrangement of creation and to the sentence of God upon the woman because she was deceived at the Fall (1 Timothy 2:13, 14; cf. Genesis 3:6). Nevertheless, it appears from 1 Corinthians 11:5 (cf. 1 Corinthians 14:3) that Paul acknowledged the right of women to prophesy and pray. From Titus 2:3, 4 and Acts 18:26 (cf. Philippians 4:2, 3), it seems that Paul was not excluding women from all kinds of teaching in the congregation.

## B. Elders and Deacons (3:1-16)

After Paul gave some rules for the kind of behavior expected in the worship service, it is natural that he should then discuss spiritual leadership. In chapter 3 he particularly spoke of overseers (elders) and deacons. He concluded this section by a further reminder of the role of the Church and the greatness of its message.

## 1. Elders (Overseers) (3:1-7)

Paul wrote (Ephesians 4:11) that it is God who gives pastors and teachers to the Church. But God does not give these gifts to disinterested parties. Paul suggested that those aspiring to the "office" of overseer "desire a good work." The Greek term used here for "aspire" denotes "seeking," "reaching for." There is no sense that such "yearning" is improper; on the contrary, it is viewed as commendable, provided one is qualified. The ability to be an elder does not depend on the opinion of the one seeking the position, but whether other believers find his character in keeping with the demands of the position of overseer and teacher.

Related to this accountability, the Scriptures provide certain requirements which must be met if one is going to serve as a leader in the Church. Paul lists 15 qualifications demanded of the candidate. There are certain expectations as to moral blamelessness, an ability to control one's temper, and spiritual maturity.

## 2. Deacons (3:8-13)

The same qualifications apply to those wanting to serve as deacons. If they meet the requirements, they may serve (3:10). Paul did not outline their duties. Most likely the elders had a position of spiritual oversight, while the deacons took care of the practical affairs of the church. Hard and fast distinctions cannot be drawn between the two ministries. Some might not have regarded the practical aspect of ministry as valuable as the more "spiritual" role of oversight. This may explain why Paul mentioned that the good deacon can acquire a "respected position."

Verse 11 could suggest that Paul also envisioned women in the role of deaconess. Romans 16:1 indicates that women did serve as deacons—whether the "office" was present or not—in the early churches. Without question there was a need for the ministry of women; their qualifications correspond, for the most part, with the requirements upon deacons.

## 3. The Church and Its Message (3:14-16)

Besides what Paul said about the nature of worship and leadership roles, Paul added some personal words to Timothy about the greatness of the Church and its message. The Church is God's house; it undergirds the presence of the truth in this world.

The truth and the message proclaimed and supported by the Church are united in what many regard as an ancient Christian hymn. In six brief sentences Paul summarized the life story of Christ, from His incarnation to His ascension. It is a magnificent proclamation of "God manifest in the flesh" (3:16).

## C. Support and Service (5:1-25)

Having discussed the question of false and genuine doctrine (chapter 4), Paul once again picked up the theme (from chapters 2 and 3) about the divine ministry of the Church and some unique ministries for which some are chosen. The apostle offered further instruction in practical local church life matters, using his personal instructions to Timothy as the means.

## 1. The Ministry of Admonition (5:1, 2)

First the apostle advised regarding each member's role of spiritual leadership. He listed the various groups according to sex and age. The young man Timothy was to show respect and honor to the older person, even when as the leader he must admonish them (cf. Leviticus 19:32). He was not to speak harshly or disrespectfully. Timothy was to treat younger men as brothers. Thus he was not to patronize them or lord it over them as a superior, even though he is the leader of God's people in Ephesus. To older women he was to speak with gentleness and respect worthy of his own mother.

The final group Paul mentioned were the young women. They were to be treated as sisters. Here the apostle added: "with all purity." Paul was fully aware of the temptations associated with being a pastor. Care must be taken when restoring an erring brother and even more so a sister. That Paul should caution one of his most trusted coworkers (Philippians 2:19-22) and close personal friends about this brings out Paul's understanding of basic human nature. Paul realized that one falling prey to sexual temptation will find it difficult to be restored in the eyes of men (Proverbs 6:33). How many scandals could have been avoided had young men and elders alike applied the warning "in all purity" to every thought, word, look, and deed (cf. Matthew 5:28).

## 2. The Support of Widows (5:3-16)

The first Jerusalem church took care of widows (Acts 6:1f.). Later, all Christian churches were taught to show such care. When Paul wrote that widows were to be respected (5:3), the same idea is conveyed as when Jesus quoted the fourth commandment to the Pharisees (Matthew 15:3-6). To honor and respect one's father and mother includes—as far as Jesus is concerned—providing for their basic needs.

It should be noted here, however, that Paul asked the recipients of such support to return the favor by serving the body of believers. It was the church's responsibility to see to it that poor churches were not exploited by shysters and undeserving needy. Paul has no pity for the lazy: "If any would not work, neither should he eat!" (2 Thessalonians 3:10).

The widows to be enrolled to receive support from the church must be over 60 years old (5:9). During their lifetime they must have demonstrated their fear of God in a variety of ways. They must be genuine widows—truly alone, without family. If they had children or grandchildren, it was their responsibility to care for their parents. There is no excuse for trying to pass this responsibility on to the church.

Younger widows were not to be included in the group to receive support. Of course this did not prevent them from receiving temporary assistance if necessary, but they were not exempt from the responsibility of caring for themselves. Paul did not want them to learn idleness by wandering from house to house spreading foolish talk (5:13). The support provided by the church was not to encourage laziness. Paul advised the younger women to marry and run their own house (5:14). This resembles his advice in 1 Corinthians 7:9 where he stated that those who do not have the gift of remaining unmarried should get married.

The word used here is *pistin*, the word usually translated "faith" in the New Testament. Apparently, Paul was referring here to the sad possibility that some younger women, who had become widows, had strayed from a path of righteousness and had married nonbelievers.

Paul was certainly not saying they must remain in celibacy, i.e., could not marry again, for in the next verse he recommends that the younger women marry. Since the elders and deacons of the church and the apostles themselves were married, it could not be said that these women sinned if they remarried. Earlier in this epistle Paul had written that forbidding to marry was heretical (4:3).

Some of the older widows were perhaps deaconesses. Possibly if their health allowed, they were assigned certain duties and tasks in exchange for assistance. Early fathers of the Church allude to "widows of the church" who were chosen to take care of administering charity, caring for orphans, and so on.

### 3. The Treatment of Elders (5:17-25)

Paul used the term "honor" ("double honor") in describing what is due the elders of the church. Here *time* refers to financial support, as the context makes plain, which contains a saying of Jesus found in Luke's Gospel: "The laborer is worthy of his reward" (1 Timothy 5:18; cf. Luke 10:7). The Church is obligated to support its elders, especially those who "labor in the word and teaching." A church must support those who devote all their time to its service.

Paul concluded this section by giving some principles for dealing with an elder who has sinned (5:19, 20). He warned against hastily installing someone in this spiritual position (5:22). Related to this, time must be allowed to prove or disprove the true nature of the man's character (5:24, 25). All of this, however, must be done without partiality or prejudice (5:21).

# The First Epistle of Paul to Timothy

## Commentary

### Chapter 1

1. **Paul, an apostle of Jesus Christ:** . . . Missionary, *—KLGS* . . . an ambassador of, *—WUST.*
**by the commandment of God our Saviour:** . . . by order of, *—ADAM* . . . by the appointment, *—FNTN* . . . according to the injunction of God, *—CNDT.*
**and Lord Jesus Christ, [which is] our hope:**

**1:1.** Paul began his letter to Timothy in the usual formal style of many of his epistles. He named himself and identified his relationship to God and Christ. Though this was a personal letter to Timothy, Paul made certain it was understood that his authority was equal to that of any of the original apostles Jesus appointed (2 Corinthians 11:5). After all, it was Jesus who had appointed him to his ministry (see Acts 9:15). Timothy would not doubt the authority of Paul, but some in Ephesus might.

The idea of authority is underscored by the phrase "by the commandment of God." From his conversion on the road to Damascus till the end of his earthly life, Paul understood he was under orders from God. His claim of authority was based on his call and divine commission as "an apostle of Jesus Christ."

"God our Saviour" is a title used by Paul in only six places (1 Timothy 1:1; 2:3; 4:10; Titus 1:3; 2:10; 3:4). The other New Testament writers who used it are Luke (Luke 1:47) and Jude (Jude 25). Its roots are in the Old Testament (see Deuteronomy 32:15; Psalms 24:5; 106:21; Isaiah 43:3; 45:15, 21; 63:8). The word *Saviour* appears 24 times in the New Testament, 10 of which are in the Pastoral Epistles.

2. **Unto Timothy, [my] own son in the Saith:** . . . my genuine child, *—WUST, —WLMS* . . . my true son, *—MNTG* . . . his true Child in the Faith, *—TCNT.*
**Grace, mercy, [and] peace:** . . . spiritual blessing, *—WLMS* . . . help, *—ADAM* . . . give you gracious love, *—SEB* . . . loving favor and loving-kindness, *—NLTG.*
**from God our Father and Jesus Christ our Lord:** . . . by the appointment of, *—TCNT.*

**1:2.** Paul addressed Timothy as "my own son in the faith." By this personal and intimate identification, the apostle might have been suggesting two things: (1) Timothy was converted under Paul's ministry, and (2) Paul "adopted" Timothy

as a spiritual son. In Philippians 2:19-22 Paul gave Timothy high commendation, ending with these words: "As a son with the father, he hath served with me in the gospel."

To the usual salutation of "Grace . . . and peace," Paul added the word "mercy." Grace contains two concepts in the New Testament: undeserved generosity and God-ordained universality (God doesn't play favorites). "Peace" is the usual greeting in Eastern countries. By adding "mercy," Paul reminded Timothy of the Old Testament concept of God's loving-kindness and steadfast love.

3. **As I besought thee to abide still at Ephesus:** . . . As I begged you, *—MNTG* . . . I requested you, *—FNTN* . . . As I urged you, *—ADAM* . . . As I entreated you to continue, *—CMPB* . . . I still beg you to stay on in, *—WLMS.*
**when I went into Macedonia:** . . . was setting out for, *—MNTG* . . . While I was traveling to the Macedonian area, *—SEB.*
**that thou mightest charge some:** . . . and instruct certain individuals there, *—MNTG* . . . so that you may give orders to certain persons, *—ADAM* . . . to warn certain teachers, *—WLMS.*
**that they teach no other doctrine:** . . . to stop teaching, *—ADAM* . . . some not to teach novel doctrines, *—CNFT* . . . not to teach any different doctrine, *—RSV* . . . not to be teaching things contrary to sound doctrine, *—WUST* . . . not to be teaching heterodoxy, *—MNTG.*

**1:3.** The purpose for Timothy's presence in Ephesus, and a key to the purpose of this letter, is found in the words, "That thou mightest charge some that they teach no other doctrine." The word "doctrine" is a key word of the Pastoral Epistles. Of the 50 occurrences in the New Testament, 17 are in the Pastorals.

4. **Neither give heed to fables and endless genealogies:** . . . to invented stories and interminable genealogies, *—BRKL* . . . or endless lists of ancestors, *—SEB* . . . to myths and endless pedigrees, *—NORL.*
**which minister questions:** . . . Such studies promote controversies, *—LILY* . . . which beget controversies, *—CNFT.*
**rather than godly edifying which is in faith: [so do]:**

**1:4.** False doctrine was endangering the Church, and Paul wanted Timothy to speak out against it. This heresy was known by two distinct characteristics: "fables" ("myths, idle tales") and "endless genealogies." False teachers used these to promote controversies among believers. Timothy was told to take a strong stand against these false teachers and command them to cease.

Some commentators see a reference here to the heresy of gnosticism. But it seems these false teachers were Judaizers, not Gnostics. Fables and genealogies were a favorite pastime of certain Jews who delighted in embellishing the text of the Old Testament and bringing others under condemnation with fabricated laws.

**5. Now the end of the commandment is charity:** . . . whereas the aim of our charge is love, *—RSV* . . . Love is the real reason, *—SEB* . . . The aim of all your instruction, *—TCNT* . . . Now the purpose of this charge is, *—CNFT* . . . The purpose of our instruction, *—BRKL.*

**out of a pure heart, and [of] a good conscience, and [of] faith unfeigned:** . . . a sincere faith, *—NORL.*

**1:5.** This verse introduces a basic precept of the gospel—love (translated "charity" here). The "end" or purpose of the "commandment" is love (see Romans 13:8-10). This *agapē* is to come from (1) a pure heart, (2) a good conscience, and (3) sincere faith.

"Pure heart" is *katharas kardias*. Originally, *katharos* meant "clean" as opposed to "soiled" or "dirty." Later it was used of something void of debasing admixture. A pure heart has motives that are absolutely pure and unmixed.

The word "conscience" appears 22 times in the New Testament. Paul wrote about consciences that are "good" (1 Timothy 1:5, 19); "pure" (1 Timothy 3:9; 2 Timothy 1:3); "seared" (1 Timothy 4:2); and "defiled" (Titus 1:15).

**6. From which some having swerved:** . . . Some people have failed to hit the mark, *—LILY* . . . Some going astray from, *—CNFT* . . . have wandered away, *—SEB.*

**have turned aside unto vain jangling:** . . . They are lost in empty talk, *—SEB* . . . turned off into empty talk, *—BRKL* . . . diverted to frivolous subjects, *—TCNT* . . . to nonsensical discussions, *—NORL.*

**7. Desiring to be teachers of the law; understanding neither what they say:**

**nor whereof they affirm:** . . . or the things about which they make assertions, *—RSV* . . . or that concerning which they are insisting, *—CNDT.*

**1:6, 7.** Note the verbs in this threefold description of "some": they had "swerved, . . . turned aside"; they were "desiring to be" but "(not) understanding." The "some" here are the same ones mentioned in verse 3, the false teachers. Paul said they had "turned aside unto vain jangling."

This is an interesting term. The context seems to show "vain jangling" to be the primary characteristic and activity of these false teachers. Paul pointed out that fables and endless genealogies were their stock in trade. It was all meaningless discussion, empty argument, and purposeless talk. He also said they had turned aside from the truth and were so ignorant they could not even understand their own words.

**8. But we know that the law [is] good:** . . . is admirable, *—BRKL.*

**if a man use it lawfully:** . . . uses it rightly, *—CNFT* . . . if legitimately used, *—TCNT* . . . in the right way, *—NORL.*

**1:8.** Verse 8 begins an extended sentence that does not end until verse 11. The initial verse is introductory; verse 11 is a bridge from "the law" to "the glorious gospel of the blessed God." In writing about God's law, Paul made two important points: (1) God's law is good if it is used properly, and (2) laws are not made for righteous men but for unrighteous people. The point he wanted Timothy to grasp was that the Law had a primary purpose—to restrain wickedness and evil behavior.

**9. Knowing this:**

**that the law is not made for a righteous man:** . . . is not laid down for an honest person, *—BRKL* . . . not for the person who is right with God, *—NLTG.*

**but for the lawless and disobedient:** . . . for the unjust and rebellious, *—CNFT* . . . for the immoral and profane, *—NORL* . . . and insubordinate, *—CNDT* . . . rebels, *—SEB.*

**for the ungodly and for sinners:** . . . for irreligious and wicked people, *—TCNT.*

**for unholy and profane, for murderers of fathers and murderers of mothers, for manslayers:**

**1:9.** Paul gave a long list of lawbreakers in verses 9 and 10. This list greatly resembles the Ten Commandments found in Exodus 20:1-17. Perhaps because Paul had just referred to the Law, the Holy Spirit directed him to list those people who correspond to and flagrantly break the "thou shalt nots" of the Old Testament.

The "lawless" deliberately break the law to satisfy their own desires and ambitions. The "disobedient" refuse to obey any authority; they are a law unto themselves. The "ungodly" have no reverence for God, and they defiantly withhold the praise and glory due Him. "Sinners" describes the character of those who miss the mark of God's law.

Note that all these descriptions are in pairs. "Unholy and profane" (*anosioi* and *bebēloi*) are precise and ugly words. The person who is *anosios* is worse than a mere lawbreaker. He violates the very decencies of life. The man who is *bebēlos* desecrates everything that is holy and dirties everything he touches.

**10.** **For whoremongers, for them that defile themselves with mankind:** ... for sexual perverts, −BRKL ... homosexuals, −LILY, −SEB ... for people guilty of sodomy, −TCNT ... for sodomites, −CNFT.

**for menstealers, for liars, for perjured persons:** ... slave traders, −SEB ... falsifiers, −BRKL.

**and if there be any other thing that is contrary to sound doctrine:** ... and against any other crime contrary to, −LILY ... against right teaching, −NLTG ... against the healthy teaching, −SEB.

**1:10.** This verse continues the list of lawbreakers that begins in verse 9. Two groups are similar in nature and conduct: the *pornoi* and *arsenokoitai.* "Whoremongers" are fornicators. "Them that defile themselves with mankind" are homosexuals. The culture of the First Century was replete with sexual sins. It was common practice in pagan religions to condone sexual immorality as behavior pleasing to the gods. At Corinth, the temple of Aphrodite, goddess of love, had 1,000 sacred prostitutes who plied their trade every day. "Liars" and "perjured persons" twist the truth to serve their own ends. They break the ninth commandment.

Finally, Paul concluded the list with the words "any other thing that is contrary to sound doctrine." The word "sound" here literally means "health-giving" and denotes the wholesomeness of true Christian teaching. This word occurs frequently in the Pastoral Epistles, but nowhere else.

**11.** **According to the glorious gospel of the blessed God, which was committed to my trust:**

**1:11.** The word "glorious" is appended to "gospel." Here and elsewhere it is in the genitive form and connotes content rather than quality. God's glory is revealed to men in the gospel that witnesses to Christ. (Compare John 1:14, 18; 2 Corinthians 4:4, 6.)

"Blessed" here describes God as experiencing within himself the perfection of bliss (Guthrie, *Tyndale New Testament Commentaries,* 14:62). Timothy was told to focus on the doctrine that is wholesome and the gospel that reveals God's glory. This gospel was committed to Paul's trust. The inference is that the same gospel was committed to Timothy's trust as well.

**12.** **And I thank Christ Jesus our Lord, who hath enabled me:** ... I am deeply grateful to, −TCNT ... has strengthened me, −CNFT ... who has qualified me, −CMPB ... Who invigorates men, −CNDT.

**for that he counted me faithful:** ... because he counted me trustworthy, −CNFT ... for thinking me trustworthy, −WLMS ... He deemed me worthy, −BRKL ... considered me reliable, −NORL.

**putting me into the ministry:** ... he appointed me for this work, −SEB.

**1:12.** Beginning with verse 12 the tone changes. From verse 12 to verse 17, Paul bursts forth in praise and thanksgiving for the grace of Christ and the mercy of God. Paul thanked Christ for three things: strength, trust, and a call to service. No doubt Paul was seeking to encourage Timothy by recounting his own reception of grace. The verbs in this and the following verses are in the aorist (past) tense. But Paul could not recount what Christ had done for him without breaking into thanksgiving and worship (see verses 12, 17).

**13.** **Who was before a blasphemer, and a persecutor, and injurious:** ... Before He chose me, −NLTG ... although formerly I defamed, −LILY ... and a bitter adversary, −CNFT ... and an oppressor, −BRKL ... and a man of violence, −SEB.

**but I obtained mercy:** ... was shown me, −WLMS.

**because I did [it] ignorantly in unbelief:** ... I didn't know what I was doing, −SEB.

**1:13.** Paul said he had been a "blasphemer." Blasphemy is the opposite of "blessing" the name of God. Three Hebrew words are translated "blaspheme": *gādhaph*—"cut, wound, revile, blaspheme"; *chāraph*—"speak sharply against, reproach"; and *bārakh*—"utter a curse against." *Blasphēmeō*, used in the New Testament, means "speak harmfully against." Paul used the noun form to describe his blasphemy and could very well have had the Old Testament's meanings in mind.

The word "injurious" is a strong, descriptive term. It refers to a violent, insolent man—a doer of outrage and injury to others. It could include the idea of *sadist*—one who inflicts pain on another for the sheer joy it brings.

Though Paul was all this, he said, "But I obtained mercy (see verse 16), because I did it ignorantly in unbelief." Paul did not excuse his sinful past, he exalted God's mercy!

**14.** **And the grace of our Lord was exceeding abundant:** ... and the spiritual blessing of, −WLMS ... was lavished superabundantly, −LILY ... has abounded beyond measure, −CNFT ... has superabounded, −CMPB ... There was no limit, −TCNT ... was overflowing, −KLGS.

**with faith and love which is in Christ Jesus:** ... inspired by union with, −WLMS.

**1:14.** The phrase "and the grace ..." is connected to and extends the previous verse where Paul said he was given "mercy." (Compare the greeting in verse 2.) For Paul, the "grace of our Lord" was not just an abstract concept but an active force dominating both his thoughts and actions. He wrote to the Corinthians, "By the grace of God I am what I am" (1 Corinthians 15:10; compare Romans 5:8,

10, 20, 21). Paul then defined this grace with the words "exceeding abundant" (*huperepleonasen*). The prefix *huper* expresses the superabundance of divine grace given to Paul.

The words "faith" and "love" provide a strong contrast to the sinful life of unbelief and hatred that Paul had just mentioned. Someone has said of verse 14 that Paul saw "grace" as providing for his salvation, "faith" appropriating it, and "love" applying it.

**15. This [is] a faithful saying:** . . . Reliable is the message, *—BRKL* . . . This statement is something you can trust, *—SEB.*
   **and worthy of all acceptation:** . . . and deserving of wholehearted acceptance, *—BRKL* . . . of all reception, *—CMPB.*
   **that Christ Jesus came into the world to save sinners:**
   **of whom I am chief:** . . . I am at the head of the list, *—LILY* . . . I am foremost, *—BRKL* . . . And I was the worst, *—NORL* . . . I myself am first! *—KLGS* . . . and I am the worst sinner, *—NLTG* . . . the worst one, *—SEB.*

**1:15.** The Pastoral Epistles have four "faithful sayings." They appear nowhere else. In two of them (1:15 and 4:9) Paul added the words "and worthy of all acceptation." (See 1:15; 3:1; 4:8, 9; 2 Timothy 2:11.) Most commentators see the words here as a "current, primitive creedal statement." That Christ came into the world to save sinners is the very heart of the gospel. Jesus said of himself, "The Son of man is come to seek and to save that which was lost" (Luke 19:10). No greater truth exists. Jesus came to save sinners! And Paul said he was "chief" (*prōtos*). Paul used superlatives to refer to himself, whether it was the least of the apostles (1 Corinthians 15:9), or less than the least of all saints (Ephesians 3:8), or the "chief" of sinners.

**16. Howbeit for this cause I obtained mercy:** . . . Yet for this very cause, *—MNTG* . . . for this reason, *—LILY* . . . for the express purpose, *—TCNT.*
   **that in me first:** . . . that in my case, *—WLMS* . . . so that in me, the chief of sinners, *—MNTG.*
**Jesus Christ might show forth all longsuffering:** . . . might display His unlimited patience, *—BRKL* . . . might display his perfect patience, *—RSV* . . . might display all his boundless patience, *—MNTG* . . . to demonstrate how vast is His patience, *—NORL.*
   **for a pattern to them:** . . . as an illustration for those, *—MNTG* . . . as an example to those, *—CNFT.*
   **which should hereafter believe on him to life everlasting:** . . . who should later believe in him, and so gain life eternal, *—MNTG* . . . to obtain eternal life, *—WLMS.*

**1:16.** The first part of this verse repeats the statement regarding Paul's reception of mercy. But here the purpose is revealed: "But for that very reason

I was shown mercy so that in me, the worst of sinners, Christ Jesus might display his unlimited patience as an example for those who would believe on him and receive eternal life" (NIV). Paul saw his former life and his present life as an illustration, pattern, example, and exhibit for all who "should hereafter believe."

"The Greek word rendered *pattern* (*hupotupōsis*) may be understood either as an outline sketch of an artist, or as a word-illustration expressing an author's burning purpose. . . . The construction (*epi* with the dative) after the verb *believe* indicates that Christ is the firm basis of faith. Such unshakable assurance serves not only in this life but in eternity" (Guthrie, *Tyndale New Testament Commentaries,* 14:66). Paul's life—both his former life as a zealous persecutor of Christians and his present life as an incarcerated apostle of Christ—was to be a "pattern" for others. What God did for and with Paul, He could do for others. There was no shame for Paul. God's grace had been abundant for him (verse 14); it could be the same for others.

The "first" here does not reflect preference or superiority. It connects with the concept of "pattern." Paul had been saved 30 or so years before, and God's mercy shown in Paul illustrated, exhibited, and patterned what is available for all who believe in Jesus Christ. Those who followed Paul's example of belief were also candidates for the superabundant grace of the Lord Jesus Christ.

**17. Now unto the King eternal, immortal, invisible, the only wise God:** . . . to the King Who lives forever . . . He is the One Who never dies, *—NLTG* . . . the King of the ages, *—LILY, —KLGS* . . . who cannot die or be seen, *—SEB.*
   **[be] honour and glory for ever and ever. Amen:** . . . throughout the endless ages! *—NORL* . . . Let it be so, *—NLTG.*

**1:17.** Paul began this section (verse 12) with thanksgiving; he closed it with praise. It is properly called a doxology (from *doxa*—"glory, brightness, majesty," and *logos*—"word, declaration"). This doxology burst forth as Paul remembered the mercy of God and the grace and patience of Christ. It contains five parts: God as (1) King, (2) eternal, (3) immortal, (4) invisible, and (5) the only God.

"King eternal" is literally "king of the ages." This is the only place where Paul used this term. Very likely he had the Jewish concept of two ages in mind: the age that is and the age to come. "Immortal" has the meaning of "not subject to death." "Invisible" means "unable to be seen." But the eye of faith sees God (compare Hebrews 11:27; John 14:9). Paul praised the "only wise God" (perhaps better read "only God") who is worthy of "honor and glory for ever and ever. Amen." (So be it!)

**18. This charge I commit unto thee, son Timothy:** ... This is the instruction, —WLMS ... I am laying upon you, —MNTG.

**according to the prophecies which went before on thee:** ... It is in harmony with prophecies, —NORL ... according to the predictions formerly made, —MNTG ... in agreement with the previous prophecies, —BRKL ... according to the inspired utterances which pointed to you, —LILY ... the prophetic utterances, —RSV, —WLMS ... once made concerning thee, —CNFT.

**that thou by them mightest war a good warfare:** ... Use them to fight the good fight, —SEB ... continue to fight the good fight, —WLMS ... that you might carry out a good campaign, —KLGS ... in the spirit of these predictions, —MNTG.

**1:18.** In this final paragraph of chapter 1, Paul picked up the "charge" he began at 1:3. He instructed "son Timothy" with two military metaphors. He charged (commanded) Timothy to "war a good warfare." As this first chapter has revealed, this warfare was on at least two fronts: doctrinal and moral. The situation in Ephesus was critical. If the church was to advance, a fight against false teaching and moral sins must be waged.

"The prophecies which went before on thee" probably refers to Timothy's ordination into the ministry and his induction into missionary work (cf. 1 Timothy 4:14 and 2 Timothy 1:6).

**19. Holding faith, and a good conscience:** ... keeping fast hold of faith, —MNTG.

**which some having put away:** ... they have discarded this, —TCNT ... have cast aside, —MNTG.

**concerning faith have made shipwreck:** ... made shipwreck of their faith, —MNTG.

**1:19.** Timothy was to fight the good fight with two offensive weapons: "faith, and a good conscience" (see verse 5). The Biblical word *conscience* is a compound and literally means "coperception." It is that within which enables a person to distinguish between right and wrong.

"Put away" (*apōtheomai*) implies a violent and deliberate rejection of one's personal conscience; the end result is shipwrecked faith. With the word "shipwreck" the metaphor turns from military to nautical.

**20. Of whom is Hymenaeus and Alexander:** ... Among them are, —MNTG.

**whom I have delivered unto Satan:** ... whom I have surrendered, —BRKL ... whom I handed over to, —TCNT ... whom I have given over, —MNTG.

**that they may learn not to blaspheme:** ... so that they could be corrected, —SEB ... as a punishment for blaspheming, —NORL ... to teach them not to speak against God, —NLTG ... to be so disciplined

that they will stop their abusive speech, —WLMS ... so that they may be taught not to blaspheme, —MNTG.

**1:20.** Paul mentioned two men who had turned from the truth and were blaspheming God by their words and conduct. Little is known of these two. Hymeneus was a false teacher and is mentioned in 2 Timothy 2:17, 18. Two Alexanders had connections with the city of Ephesus. One was a Jew (Acts 19:33, 34) and the other was a coppersmith who did a great deal of harm to Paul (2 Timothy 4:14). Perhaps the second Alexander is indicated in verse 20. These two men were spiritually bound over to Satan (see Job 2:6; Matthew 16:19; 1 Corinthians 5:3-5) as a disciplinary measure to teach them not to blaspheme. This very likely means they were excommunicated from Christian fellowship. The purpose was intended to be remedial, not punitive.

# Chapter 2

**1. I exhort therefore, that, first of all:** ... I am urging, —MNTG.

**supplications, prayers, intercessions, [and] giving of thanks;**

**be made for all men:** ... be offered regularly, —MNTG.

**2:1.** Chapter 2 contains two topics: instructions concerning public prayer (1-8) and women in the church (9-15).

The words "first of all" stress the priority of prayer. The four words that follow describe prayer in its various aspects. (1) "Supplications" (*deēseis*) has the basic meaning of "requests." It is not exclusively a religious word; it means a request made either to a fellowman or to God. But it does connote need. (2) "Prayers" (*proseuchas*) differs from the first. Supplications may be addressed either to man or God, but prayer is always and only addressed to God. (3) "Intercessions" (*enteuxeis*) has the sense of "petitions." It is the noun form of *entunchanō*, a word that had acquired a special meaning in Paul's day: "to enter into a king's presence and to submit a petition to him." God is the King of kings. (4) "Giving of thanks" (*eucharistias*) brings in a beautiful balance. Prayer is not only asking God for things, it also means thanking God for who He is and what He does.

**2. For kings, and [for] all that are in authority:** ... for all in high positions, —CNFT ... and all those being in a superior station, —CNDT ... all those in prominent places, —KLGS.

**that we may lead a quiet and peaceable life:** ... that with all reverence and dignity, —BRKL ... live quiet God-like lives, —NLTG.

**in all godliness and honesty:** ... in all piety and gravity, —YNG ... in all piety and worthy behavior,

—*CNFT*...in perfect piety and soberness, —*NORL*...and seriousness, —*WLMS*...in a truly religious and earnest spirit, —*TCNT*...and holiness, —*NIV*...and dignity, —*KLGS*.

**2:2.** As Paul continued his exhortation regarding prayer, he designated "kings, and . . . all that are in authority." Paul made no distinction as to whether or not governmental leadership is hostile to Christianity. Christians are to pray for civil leaders so "we may lead a quiet and peaceable life." The Greek adjective *ēremon* translated "quiet" occurs only here in the New Testament. The basic meaning is that of "restfulness unmarred by disturbance."

"Godliness" contains the dual meaning of reverence for God and respect for man. The Greek word translated "honesty" (*semnotēs*) contains the varied meanings of "reverence, dignity, seriousness, respectfulness, holiness." Perhaps the meaning here is "a proper sense of the seriousness of life."

3. **For this [is] good and acceptable in the sight of God our Saviour:**... This is the right thing to do, —*WLMS*...for this is ideal and welcome, —*CNDT*.

**2:3.** The placement of "for" and its meaning is uncertain. Most commentators think what follows refers back to the universal prayer of verse 1. Prayer for all is "good and acceptable in the sight of God our Saviour." Beginning with the title "God our Saviour" the emphasis shifts from the theme of prayer to that of salvation. This new theme extends through verse 7.

4. **Who will have all men to be saved:**... who is ever willing, —*WLMS*...who wants all men, —*NIV*.
**and to come unto the knowledge of the truth:** ... and come into a realization of the truth, —*CNDT*...to begin understanding the truth, —*SEB*...to an increasing knowledge of, —*WLMS*.

**2:4.** Much controversy has revolved around the meaning of this verse. Does God save all? Or does God *want* all to be saved. Peter's second epistle tells us God is "not willing that any should perish, but that all should come to repentance" (2 Peter 3:9). We know from other Scriptures that not everyone will believe the good news of God's provision for their salvation. Salvation has been provided for all, but only those who accept it are saved.

5. **For [there is] one God:**
**and one mediator between God and men, the man Christ Jesus:** ... and one go-between, —*BRKL*...and one intermediary, —*WLMS*.

**2:5.** First Timothy 2:5 makes two exclusive declarations: "There is one God, and one mediator

between God and men" (see Romans 3:29, 30; 10:12). "Mediator" means "someone who stands between." In order for Jesus to be a true representative of mankind, He became a man. The One who existed with God in eternity came to live with man in time and understands both sides (see Hebrews 4:14-16).

6. **Who gave himself a ransom for all:**...a purchase price, —*KLGS*.
**to be testified in due time:**...of which the testimony is in its proper season, —*CMPB*...in its proper time, —*NIV*...at the proper time, —*WLMS*.

**2:6.** The word "ransom" (*antilutron*) means "payment." In the First Century the word *lutron* was used for the ransom price paid to free a slave. The preposition *anti* ("instead of") suggests substitution (cf. Mark 8:37; 10:45).

"To be testified in due time" means "to be declared at the appointed time." God's appointed time for all men to be saved is "now" (2 Corinthians 6:2).

7. **Whereunto I am ordained a preacher, and an apostle:** ... for which purpose, —*WLMS*...that I was myself appointed a Herald, —*TCNT*.
**(I speak the truth in Christ, [and] lie not;):**
**a teacher of the Gentiles in faith and verity:**...of the heathen in the realm of, —*WLMS*.

**2:7.** Paul's threefold ministry seems a strange insertion at this juncture. But it is a logical summary of what he has just said about God and Christ. Paul was "ordained" ("by God" is understood) a preacher, apostle, and teacher of the Gentiles (see 2 Timothy 1:11). No doubt the semiprivate nature of this epistle prompted Paul to establish his authority. Paul's authority would have relevance for Timothy's authority. The churches in Ephesus would view Timothy as Paul's envoy.

8. **I will therefore:**...So I want, —*WLMS*.
**that men pray every where:**...to offer prayer, —*WLMS*.
**lifting up holy hands, without wrath and doubting:** . . . with hands reverently uplifted, —*TCNT*...which are kept unstained by anger and dissensions, —*WLMS*...and contention, —*CNFT*...without anger and disputing they lift up dedicated hands, —*BRKL*...without anger or argument, —*NORL*...They should not be angry or argue, —*NLTG*...No anger. No arguing, —*SEB*.

**2:8.** "I will" is a strong expression, meaning more than "I wish." It has the sense of "I command." This is a transitional verse. It refers back to the first verse and becomes a bridge to the next verse. Believers are to pray in all circumstances. "Every where" might be understood as "in every place"; that is, wherever Christians meet for worship.

Prayer was to be accompanied by "lifting up holy hands" (see 1 Kings 8:22; Psalms 28:2; 141:2; 143:6). These uplifted hands were to show the personal purity and freedom from improper motives of the worshiper. The word "doubting" is better rendered "disputing" or "dissension."

**9. In like manner also:**
**that women adorn themselves in modest apparel:** . . . that women should make themselves attractive by their discreet, quiet, and modest dress, *—TCNT* . . . to be decently dressed, *—CNFT* . . . to dress modestly, *—NIV.*
**with shamefacedness and sobriety:** . . . should use good sense and be proper, *—SEB* . . . decorously, with modesty and sanity, *—CNDT.*
**not with broided hair, or gold:** . . . avoiding fancy hairdos, *—SEB.*
**or pearls, or costly array:** . . . or expensive clothing, *—CNFT.*
**10. But (which becometh women professing godliness):** . . . as is appropriate for women, *—BRKL* . . . they should make themselves attractive, *—TCNT.*
**with good works:** . . . by their good actions, *—TCNT.*

**2:9, 10.** Verses 9 and 10 address a woman's appearance in public; verses 11 and 12 teach about women's place in the Church. Eve is used as an illustration of man's priority in creation and the woman's deception in the temptation (verses 13, 14). Verse 15 tells of a woman's salvation in childbearing.

A careful reading of verses 9 and 10 shows three positives and three negatives concerning women's dress. The three positives are (1) modest apparel, (2) decency, and (3) sobriety. In general, what Paul was saying is that women are to give a silent witness by their modest dress and active good works. The word "modest" means "orderly, decent." It reflects a correct attitude toward propriety. "Shamefacedness" carries the meaning of "modesty, decency, godly fear." "Sobriety" means "self-control." It connotes a balanced and discreet self-restraint.

The negatives are more explicit. They are (1) braided hair, (2) gold and pearls, and (3) expensive clothes. All three of these relate to the customs of the first-century church. Some women spent hours preparing their long hair in highly fashionable styles, fastening their plaits with ribbons and brightly colored bows. Rich women would interweave gold, silver, and pearls in their hairstyles. It is very likely that expensive clothes were outlandish in style and color, drawing undue attention to the wearer.

Paul wrote to Timothy that immodest or inappropriate dress distracts from the witness of a Christian woman. It may distract others from seeing her "good works" which are to be the true adornment of those who profess godliness.

**11. Let the woman learn in silence with all subjection:** . . . should be quiet when they learn, *—NLTG* . . . learn quietly and be under authority, *—NORL* . . . should listen quietly to their teachers, *—TCNT* . . . put herself completely under authority, *—SEB.*
**12. But I suffer not a woman to teach, nor to usurp authority over the man:** . . . I do not consent to women becoming teachers, *—TCNT* . . . or to exercise authority, *—CNFT* . . . nor to rule a husband, *—YNG* . . . neither to domineer over, *—BRKL* . . . or be leaders over men, *—NLTG.*
**but to be in silence:**

**2:11, 12.** Paul next discussed how a woman ought to behave in the church. His instructions here are nearly identical to those found in his first letter to the church at Corinth: "Let your women keep silence in the churches: for it is not permitted unto them to speak" (14:34; see also 14:35). (In 1 Corinthians the context was the public worship service.) Note that in this passage the subject "women" has changed to the singular "woman," which may indicate Paul was speaking of "woman" in the generic sense.

In verse 11 Paul exhorted women to learn and to be in full submission. This parallels the prohibitions recorded in verse 12, i.e., not to teach and not to have authority over the man (see "*authenteō*," number 825, in the *Greek-English Dictionary*). There may have been some very specific local problems Paul was addressing; however, if this is the case they are not identified in his Epistle. It appears that Paul was simply repeating instructions for rules of conduct. In verses 13 and 14 he appeals to principles put in place by God and His created order (cf. 1 Corinthians 11:9).

It is suggested that since Christianity had brought new freedom to women who had lived within an extremely male-dominated society, there may have been some localized abuses of this freedom by women who began to assert themselves more forcefully. Such conduct would have brought shame to the new churches and would have created a stumbling block to the people of that culture.

**13. For Adam was first formed, then Eve:** . . . was first molded, *—CNDT.*
**14. And Adam was not deceived:** . . . Adam was not fooled, *—NLTG* . . . was not seduced, *—SEB.*

**but the woman being deceived was in the transgression:** ... deluded, *−CNDT* ... and became a sinner, *−NIV* ... fell into sin, *−SEB.*

**2:13, 14.** Paul supported his teaching with an allusion to Genesis. He recounted God's purpose in creation and Eve's part in the first sin. In these verses Paul was not basing what he said on the social position of women in his time but on the universal principle of priority seen in the creation of man and woman (compare 1 Corinthians 11:2-16). Paul was not putting the total blame for the Fall on Eve. In other places the apostle clearly shows that Adam was to blame (see Romans 5:12-21).

**15.** **Notwithstanding she shall be saved in childbearing:** ... And yet, through her childbearing, salvation has come, *−NORL* ... through motherhood, *−SEB.*

**if they continue in faith and charity and holiness:** ... never abandon faith, *−TCNT* ... and sanctification, *−YNG.*

**with sobriety:** ... sanity, *−CNDT* ... good sense, *−SEB.*

**2:15.** Most commentators agree this is the most difficult text in the Pastoral Epistles. Who is the "she" and does becoming a mother save a woman? Some view the woman here as referring to Eve because of the context. Her "deliverance" would come through the pain of childbirth (Genesis 3:15, 16) because eventually the "seed of the woman" would come to bring salvation. Others see "she shall be saved in childbearing" as a reference to Mary's giving birth to the One who is the Saviour.

Still others take the statement "she shall be saved in childbearing" literally. The Greek word translated "saved" here has a wide variety of meanings. The primary rendering is "preserve or rescue from natural dangers and afflictions" (*BAGD*, "sōzō"). Paul followed that statement by mentioning the qualifications for claiming the promise: continuing in "faith and charity and holiness with sobriety." Many Christian women have claimed this promise when facing childbirth and have found special help.

## Chapter 3

**1.** **This [is] a true saying:** ... It is a trustworthy statement, *NASB* ... This is something you can trust, *−SEB* ... Faithful is the saying, *−CNDT.*

**If a man desire the office of a bishop:** ... If anyone is craving the supervision, *−CNDT* ... Anyone who aspires to be a Presiding-Officer, *−TCNT* ... wants to be a church leader, *−NLTG* ... is eager for, *−CNFT* ... aspires to, *−BRKL.*

**he desireth a good work:**

**3:1.** The first seven verses of chapter 3 list the qualifications of a "bishop." A bishop in the First Century was an overseer or spiritual leader of a local church. *Pastor, bishop,* and *elder* are interchangeable terms. Acts 20:17 and 28 use three Greek terms that show these words to be synonymous.

**2.** **A bishop then must be blameless:** ... a man of irreproachable character, *−NORL* ... must be a good man, *−NLTG* ... must be above suspicion, *−SEB.*

**the husband of one wife:** ... married but once, *−CNFT.*

**vigilant, sober, of good behaviour:** ... temperate, *−KJII, −WLMS* ... respectable, *NASB.*

**given to hospitality:**

**apt to teach:** ... skillful in teaching, *−WLMS.*

**3:2.** Verses 2-6 list 15 qualifications for the "bishop" (overseer, elder, pastor). Ten are positive and five are negative. A 16th in the list (verse 7) addresses the overseer's reputation as it relates to the world. Verse 2 sets forth seven positive characteristics. "Blameless" literally means "not to be laid hold of." Other translations are "above reproach" and "without fault." In 6:14 the same Greek term is translated "unrebukable."

"Husband of one wife" reflects the social and cultural situation of the First Century. Polygamy, easy divorce, and remarriage were prevalent. Paul taught that monogamy is God's requirement for a pastor. The spiritual leader must be a "one-wife man." Marital entanglements beyond the "one" can bring discredit to his position and reproach on the Church. (See Genesis 2:18-25; Matthew 19:3-9; Mark 10:2-12.)

"Sober" in general means "temperate" and specifically "free from excess, well-balanced, self-controlled." "Of good behavior" refers to conduct that is "orderly, respectable, honorable." "Apt to teach" means "able or competent to teach."

**3.** **Not given to wine, no striker, not greedy of filthy lucre:** ... not addicted to strong drink, *−WLMS* ... nor a fist-fighter, *−BRKL* ... not quarrelsome, *−CNDT* ... not greedy of ill profit, *−KJII* ... or pugnacious, *NASB* ... not after money, *−BRKL.*

**but patient, not a brawler, not covetous:** ... conciliatory, *−BRKL.*

**3:3.** Scholars disagree as to whether *oinos* ("wine") in this verse, verse 8, and 5:23 refers to grape juice or a fermented drink, and therefore, whether the apostle is advocating temperance or abstinence. Other Scriptures give guidance for believers and especially leaders. They take a strong stand against drunkenness (see Leviticus 10:8, 9; Proverbs 20:1; 23:19-21, 29-35). The awful consequences of traffic fatalities and ruined homes force a thinking believer to make his decision on the basis of the great principle stated in Romans 14:21, "It is good neither to eat flesh, nor to drink wine, nor any thing whereby thy brother stumbleth, or is offended." "Not greedy of filthy lucre" is "not a lover of money" in the New International Version. Money becomes dirty when it is viewed with greed or obtained dishonestly (cf. 6:10).

The only positive characteristic in this verse is the term "patient." Its basic meaning is "gentle, peaceable." This contrasts the following negative, "not a brawler." The literal meaning is "abstinence from fighting" and describes someone who is "disinclined to fight."

**4. One that ruleth well his own house:** ... controlling his own household ideally, –CNDT ... presiding beautifully over his own home, –BRKL.
**having his children in subjection with all gravity:** ... keeping his children, –WLMS ... under control, NASB ... and perfectly respectful, –CNFT.
**5. (For if a man know not how to rule his own house:** ... to manage, –BRKL.
**how shall he take care of the church of God?):**

**3:4, 5.** Verses 4 and 5 deal with the family relationships of the spiritual leader. He is to be "one that ruleth well his own house." The Bible views the father as the head of the marriage and the family (see Ephesians 5:22-33; 6:1-4). The parenthetic question in verse 5 is a strong argument for this qualification. "With all gravity" (verse 4) does not mean with strict reserve or somber sternness. The sense here is "with complete dignity" and in a manner that fosters respect.

**6. Not a novice:**
**lest being lifted up with pride:** ... or else becoming conceited, –WLMS ... being conceited, –CNDT.
**he fall into the condemnation of the devil:** ... he may incur the doom, –WLMS ... and incur the condemnation passed on the devil, –CNFT ... incurred by the devil, NASB.

**3:6.** Being a leader demands experience and wisdom for making decisions. The new convert or inexperienced Christian faces many pitfalls. The Greek word for "novice" is the root of the modern term *neophyte*. "Lifted up with pride" literally means "to wrap up in smoke."

**7. Moreover he must have a good report of them which are without:** ... enjoy a favorable reputation, –BRKL ... an ideal testimony, –CNDT ... with outsiders, –WLMS.
**lest he fall into reproach and the snare of the devil:** ... not fall into disgrace, –CNFT ... fall into the devil's trap, –WLMS.

**3:7.** The spiritual leader (overseer, elder, pastor) "must have a good report of them ... without."

Non-Christians in Timothy's locale should have been able to look at the churches, and especially the leaders, and find nothing wrong or even suspect. A good reputation brings an effective witness.

**8. Likewise [must] the deacons [be] grave:** ... In the same way, –KJII ... be men of dignity, NASB.
**not doubletongued, not given to much wine:** ... addicted to strong drink, –WLMS.
**not greedy of filthy lucre:** ... fond of sordid gain, NASB ... for base gain, –CNFT ... for ill-gotten gains, –BRKL ... dishonest gain, –WLMS.

**3:8.** This section (verses 8-13) lists the qualifications for the office of deacon. Several of those given for bishops (elders, pastors, overseers) are repeated. *Deacon, servant,* and *minister* all come from the Greek word *diakonos.* The collective term "deacons" is a special word for a class of helpers who were subordinate to bishops or elders (see Philippians 1:1). Acts 6 gives us a picture of the first deacons.

Deacons must first be "grave." The basic meaning here is "serious" or "worthy of honor and respect." Deacons are not to be "double-tongued" (*dilogos*). Two meanings are possible: (1) "saying different things to different people to suit the occasion" or (2) "given to repetition," i.e., a "talebearer." Either could be applied to the qualifications for this office. The words of a deacon are to be truthful and sincere. They are not to betray confidences or talk about others in derogatory terms.

**9. Holding the mystery of the faith in a pure conscience:** ... the open secret of faith, –WLMS.

**3:9.** In the New Testament the word *mystery* refers to a secret unknown to the masses but revealed to a believer or believers. For a parallel reading and an expansion of Paul's use of *mystery,* see Romans 16:25, 26. Connected with "faith" it means the truths of the gospel revealed in Jesus Christ. Deacons, knowing the tenets of faith (the truth found in the gospel), should hold these with a "pure (clear, clean) conscience" (see 1:5, 19).

**10. And let these also first be proved:** ... be put on probation, –BRKL.
**then let them use the office of a deacon, being [found] blameless:** ... if they are beyond reproach, NASB ... and then, if irreproachable, they may serve as deacons, –BRKL ... being unimpeachable, –CNDT.

**3:10.** The qualification here is similar to that for a bishop given in verse 6: "not a novice." The word "proved" (from *dokimazō*) means "to test in the hope of being successful," thus giving a positive result to the period or manner of proving. The idea is that of "careful scrutiny" (compare Acts

6:3). "Being found blameless" (*anenklētos*) carries the sense of "that which cannot be called to account, irreproachable."

**11. Even so [must their] wives [be] grave:** ... let the women be honorable, *—CNFT.*
**not slanderers, sober, faithful in all things:** ... not gossips ... and perfectly trustworthy, *—WLMS.*

**3:11.** Because the Greek word *gunē* is used for "woman" and "wife," it is uncertain whether Paul was writing about the wives of deacons or the office of deaconess. Since the context focuses on deacons, it is quite possible Paul extends their ministry as shared by their wives. Four qualifications are given. Two repeat those given to deacons. The other two involve discretion, self-control, and industry. "Not slanderers" (*diaboloi*) is translated "malicious talkers" in the New International Version. Gossip, out of control, can turn to slander. "Faithful in all things" may be translated "absolutely trustworthy."

**12. Let the deacons be the husbands of one wife:** ... should be men who have been married but once, *—CNFT.*
**ruling their children and their own houses well:** ... and good managers of, *NASB* ... controlling children, *—CNDT* ... and well-ordered households, *—NORL.*

**3:12.** As Paul returned to deacons, he repeated the qualifications he set forth for bishops (see verses 2, 4). Marital fidelity and parental control are as important for deacons as for pastors.

**13. For they that have used the office of a deacon well:** ... those who render good service, *—WLMS.*
**purchase to themselves a good degree:** ... win a good standing for themselves, *—WLMS* ... a very good position, *—SEB.*
**and great boldness in the faith which is in Christ Jesus:**

**3:13.** Verse 13 ends Paul's instructions regarding deacons. It commends those who serve well. They gain the esteem and respect of those whom they serve and find boldness or assurance in their relationship with Jesus Christ. The words "good degree" are best understood as "reputation." The "great boldness" deacons demonstrate is first toward man; it could, however, be toward God just as well (compare Hebrews 10:19).

**14. These things write I unto thee, hoping to come unto thee shortly:**

**3:14.** In the final paragraph of this chapter (verses 14-16) Paul gave the central focus and theme of the entire epistle. This key passage records Paul's purpose for writing and gives a creedlike statement that summarizes the gospel.

As discovered earlier (1:3), Paul left Timothy in Ephesus. Paul had probably given Timothy oral instructions and now was detailing them with written confirmation. The apostle hoped to come to Ephesus and see Timothy. It is unknown whether he did or not. Even at this writing Paul had serious doubts; note the words in the following verse, "But if I tarry long."

**15. But if I tarry long, that thou mayest know:** ... yet, if I should be tardy, *—CNDT* ... but in case I should be, *—TCNT* ... In case I am delayed, *—NORL* ... if I am detained, *—WLMS* ... if I am delayed, *—CNFT.*
**how thou oughtest to behave thyself in the house of God:** ... how we must live in God's family, *—SEB* ... how one ought to conduct himself, *NASB* ... how you should act among people in the church, *—NLTG* ... in the Household of God, *—TCNT.*
**which is the church of the living God:**
**the pillar and ground of the truth:** ... and base of the truth, *—CNDT* ... and support of the truth, *—CMPB.*

**3:15.** Many see in the words "that thou mayest know how thou oughtest to behave thyself in the house of God" the central purpose for this letter. Though addressed primarily to Timothy, it certainly would be read in a much wider circle (very possibly in the local congregations in and around Ephesus). So Paul's teaching in this entire epistle would guide many individual Christians in proper behavior. "To behave" is translated from the Greek verb *anastrephō*, "to conduct oneself," and includes both the walk and conversation of a Christian.

"In the house (*oikos*) of God" means "in God's household, in God's family." The next clause contains an expanded meaning in the words "the church (*ekklēsia*) of the living God." *Ekklēsia* means "a company of people who have been called out" and refers to a local congregation as a part of the Church.

This *ekklēsia* is "the pillar (*stulos*) and ground (*hedraiōma*) of the truth." The word "pillar" was sometimes used for the decorative column that often supported statues of famous citizens. "Ground" is the "support, bulwark, buttress" that supports the building. And "truth" refers to the gospel.

**16. And without controversy great is the mystery of godliness:** ... And without doubt, *—KJII* ... by common confession, *NASB* ... Very important indeed is the hidden truth of godliness, *—NORL* ... We must agree that the secret of our faith is great, *—SEB.*
**God was manifest in the flesh:** ... Christ appeared in a human body, *—SEB* ... Christ came to

earth as a Man, —NLTG... He was revealed in our nature, —TCNT.

**justified in the Spirit:** ...vindicated in, NASB...pure in His Spirit, —NLTG ... He was shown to be right by the Spirit, —SEB.

**seen of angels:** ...Appeared to angels, —CNFT.

**preached unto the Gentiles:** ... Proclaimed among, NASB ... heralded among, —BRKL ... The nations heard about Him, —NLTG.

**believed on in the world:** ... Men everywhere put their trust in Him, —NLTG.

**received up into glory:** ...He was taken up into heaven, —NLTG.

**3:16.** "Truth" carries over from verse 15 as the focus of the great creedal hymn of verse 16. This hymn begins with the preexistent Christ and ends with His glorious ascension. The phrase "mystery of godliness" occurs only here. (For comments on "mystery" see verse 9.)

In the hymn the first three statements are understood only by divine revelation. The last three are attested by historical records in the Gospel and Acts.

"God (He who = Christ) was manifest in the flesh (emphasizes the humanity of Christ), justified in (vindicated by) the Spirit (cf. Romans 1:3), seen of angels (cf. Ephesians 3:10; 1 Peter 1:12), preached unto the Gentiles (the nations), believed on in the world, received up into glory (the Ascension)."

## Chapter 4

1. **Now the Spirit speaketh expressly:** ... distinctly says, —NAB...has explicitly said, —JB...is saying explicitly, —CNDT...The Holy Spirit tells us in plain words, —NLTG.

**that in the latter times some shall depart from the faith:** ... that in subsequent eras, —CNDT... in future times some will apostatize, —CMPB...there will be some who will desert, —JB.

**giving heed to seducing spirits, and doctrines of devils:** ... deluding spirits and demonic teachings, —BRKL.

**4:1.** Chapter 4 continues the explicit instructions Paul gave Timothy in this pastoral letter. The first five verses predict an imminent apostasy and give a solemn warning regarding false teaching. "The Spirit speaketh expressly" ("in specific terms") indicates God was giving "directions" through prophets in the Church (compare Acts 20:23; 21:11).

"In the latter times" refers to the time following this letter, not "last days" as in 2 Timothy 3:1. It is quite possible this apostasy and false teaching was being given at the very time this epistle was being read. The "some (who) depart from the faith" are apostates. *Apostasy* is "renunciation, abandonment, defection, departure, withdrawal," and "a

falling away." An apostate is someone who does these things with regard to his religious beliefs. To "depart from the faith" means to willfully abandon belief in "the faith" ("the body of revealed truth") (compare Titus 1:13; Jude 3). "Faith" is an important word in 1 Timothy; it appears 19 times.

What these apostates do after abandoning "the faith" is incredible: they give heed to "seducing (misleading) spirits" and doctrines taught by demons. Having thrown off belief in the true God, they embrace and espouse the "doctrines" of supernatural evil beings (compare Ephesians 6:11ff.).

2. **Speaking lies in hypocrisy:** ...Like hypocrites they will tell lies, —SEB.

**having their conscience seared with a hot iron:** ... having their conscience branded, —CNFT... whose own consciences are burned out, —NORL...having been cauterized, —CNDT.

**4:2.** The human agents of these demons are found "speaking lies in hypocrisy." False teachers were foretold by Jesus (see Matthew 24:11; Mark 13:22). These hypocritical liars mentioned by Paul were probably early Gnostics who taught that *spirit* is altogether good and *matter* is totally evil (see verse 3). The word "seared" (*kautēriazō*) is the root for the word *cauterize*. "Conscience" is another important word in this first letter to Timothy; this is the fourth time it has appeared: 1:5, 19; 3:9; 4:2. The idea of a seared conscience may mean their consciences have been branded with a hot iron to indicate ownership by Satan (Guthrie, *Tyndale New Testament Commentaries*, 14:92).

3. **Forbidding to marry, [and commanding] to abstain from meats:** ...They prohibit marriage, —BRKL ... and they discourage marriage, —TCNT...to stay away from certain foods, —SEB.

**which God hath created to be received with thanksgiving:**

**of them which believe and know the truth:** ... and have a clear knowledge of the truth, —MNTG.

**4:3.** Two of these false teachings are given in verse 3: "They forbid people to marry and order them to abstain from certain foods" (NIV). This asceticism reflected the early evidence of gnosticism. The Gnostics taught that all matter is evil and only that which is spirit is good. One's abstinence from marriage and meat, they said, would make him holy and acceptable to God. Paul did not comment on the first teaching (Scripture deals with that, Genesis 2:18), but he did the second.

**4. For every creature of God [is] good:** ... everything that God has created, –*MNTG.*

**and nothing to be refused:** ... and no food is to be rejected, –*JB* ... and nothing is to be rejected, –*CNFT, MNTG.*

**if it be received with thanksgiving:** ... provided it is accepted with, –*WLMS* ... when gratefully received, –*BRKL.*

**4:4.** Regarding abstinence from certain foods, Paul repeated a principle of Scripture: "God saw every thing that he had made, and, behold, it was very good" (Genesis 1:31). In the second clause, "nothing to be refused" (*apoblētos*, "to be thrown away"), Paul was perhaps referring to God's command to Noah (Genesis 9:3). He added "if it be received with thanksgiving" to give the correct context in eating any kind of food (compare Romans 14:6). The words "received with thanksgiving" are repeated from verse 3.

**5. For it is sanctified by the word of God and prayer:** ... For it is made clean by, –*NORL* ... It is made holy, –*SEB* ... it is hallowed through the word, –*CNDT.*

**4:5.** This verse presents some difficulty in interpretation. Connected with "if it be received with thanksgiving" (verse 4), the "it" of verse 5 must refer to "every creature" used for food. The primary meaning is the need for having a thankful attitude toward the food God has provided.

Another significance is related to the phrase "by the word of God." The "word of God" is "divinely inspired utterance" and primarily refers to the Scriptures. Genesis 1:31 states that everything God made "was very good." Genesis 9:3 points out that God has given mankind both meat and plant life for sustenance.

**6. If thou put the brethren in remembrance of these things:** ... As you lay all these things before the brothers, –*MNTG* ... before the brotherhood, –*NAB.*

**thou shalt be a good minister of Jesus Christ:** ... a noble minister, –*MNTG.*

**nourished up in the words of faith and of good doctrine:** ... in the precepts of the faith and that noble teaching, –*MNTG* ... the fine teaching, –*WLMS.*

**whereunto thou hast attained:** ... to which you have been conforming your life, –*BRKL* ... which you have so faithfully practiced, –*NORL* ... which you have followed, –*MNTG, WLMS.*

**4:6.** The first verses define a problem; verses 6-16 give the solution. "Put ... in remembrance" (*hupotithēmi*) literally means "to point out or make known"; the term is a gentle, humble word. It is not "command" but "suggest, advise." Timothy was not to issue orders but to gently suggest the brothers consider "these things" (what Paul had just said in verses 4 and 5).

The words in the next clause, "a good minister of Jesus Christ," could be the title of this entire section (verses 6-16). A good minister is "nourished" by "words of faith" and "good doctrine." The NIV reads: "... brought up in the truths of the faith and of the good teaching that you have followed." "Attained" (*parakoloutheō*) can either be "which you have closely investigated" or "which you have followed as a standard" (see 2 Timothy 3:10).

**7. But refuse profane and old wives' fables:** ... But avoid, –*CNFT* ... But make it your habit to let worldly and old women's stories alone, –*WLMS* ... Have nothing to do with godless myths, –*JB* ... Stay away from unholy stories, –*SEB* ... old womanish myths, –*MNTG.*

**and exercise thyself [rather] unto godliness:** ... Train yourself spiritually, –*JB* ... Train yourself to lead a religious life, –*TCNT* ... Train yourself to be godly, –*SEB.*

**4:7.** First, Timothy was to "refuse profane and old wives' fables." "Refuse" carries the idea of strong rejection (compare 2 Timothy 2:23; Titus 3:10). "Profane" (*bebēlos*) was used in 1:9 to describe a certain type of sinner. "Old wives' fables" (*muthoi*, "silly myths") were stories old women told to children.

Second, Timothy was to "exercise ... unto godliness." The figure of athletics is introduced here and developed in the next verse (compare 1 Corinthians 9:25-27).

**8. For bodily exercise profiteth little:** ... For bodily training, –*CNFT* ... Physical exercise is profitable to some extent, –*NORL* ... Physical training has some importance, –*SEB* ... is beneficial, –*CNDT.*

**but godliness is profitable unto all things:**
**having promise of the life that now is, and of that which is to come:** ... of the future life as well, –*JB* ... and that which is impending, –*CNDT.*

**4:8.** Some have misread Paul's statement here. He did not say physical exercise is unprofitable. He said it is of some profit or value. But spiritual exercise ("godliness") brings value or profit to all things. Godliness brings "promise" of blessings in this life and in the next life too. The godly person has the best of both worlds.

**9. This [is] a faithful saying and worthy of all acceptation:** ... You can depend on this as worthy of complete acceptance, –*NAB* ... This teaching is reliable, –*TCNT* ... is true and absolutely trustworthy, –*NORL* ... it is worth complete acceptance, –*SEB* ... and they can be trusted, –*NLTG* ... worthy of all welcome, –*CNDT* ... of entire acceptance, –*CNFT.*

**4:9.** In this verse there is another one of Paul's "faithful sayings" (cf. 1:15; 3:1), but a puzzle confronts our attempt at understanding. Does the "faithful saying" go with verse 8 or verse 10? Most commentators are divided because the Greek construction can be understood either way. Here are the main arguments:

The contrast of verse 8 seems to be a "faithful saying." It reads like a proverbial statement—something that would likely be repeated and possibly taught to others.

Those who contend the "faithful saying" is found in verse 10 point out the evident theological content of this verse. It follows the pattern of two previous statements (1 Timothy 1:15; 3:1) and another found in 2 Timothy 2:11. In all these instances the content follows the word "saying."

**10. For therefore we both labour and suffer reproach:** . . . For this purpose, *—BRKL.*
**because we trust in the living God:**
**who is the Saviour of all men:** . . . of the whole human race, *—JB.*
**specially of those that believe:** . . . particularly of believers, *—BRKL.*

**4:10.** This appears to be the first time Paul resorted to the plural "we" in this letter. In this verse Paul wrote that he was giving the ministry his best efforts. The word for "labor" is *kopiōmen* and suggests vigorous work; it also continues the metaphor of "exercise" in verses 7 and 8. The other word Paul used is *oneidizō.* Matthew 27:44 uses the same term, stating, "The robbers who were crucified with him also heaped insults on him" (NIV). Paul understood as well as anyone what it means to know the fellowship of the sufferings of Christ. The word "trust" signifies "hope," and the perfect tense shows a continuous state of hope in the "living God."

**11. These things command and teach:** . . . Continue to give these orders and to teach these truths, *—WLMS.*

**4:11.** Beginning with verse 11 Paul gave Timothy practical advice concerning his public ministry. It related to Timothy's sound teaching and behavior. Timothy's earliest training had been in Judaism. As a young person he was converted to Christianity (very possibly by Paul himself). Timothy gained his spiritual strength and stature from the truths he absorbed and the sound teaching or doctrine he followed. These were to be the starting point of his ministry toward others.

**12. Let no man despise thy youth:** . . . Let no one look down on you, *—NAB* . . . because you are young, *—NLTG.*
**but be thou an example of the believers:** . . . but always set an example for, *—WLMS.*

**in word, in conversation, in charity, in spirit, in faith, in purity:** . . . in behavior, *—BRKL, —CNDT* . . . in chastity, *—CNFT.*

**4:12.** Though others might be older than Timothy, he was to allow no one to despise him because of his age. (It is very possible Timothy was about 30 at this time.)

Timothy was to become an example to other believers; he was to show exemplary characteristics and conduct. The first two in this list relate to his public life: "in word" = teaching, speech; "in conversation" = conduct, lifestyle. The final characteristics are inner qualities that motivate outward action.

**13. Till I come, give attendance to:** . . . Till I arrive, *—BRKL* . . . devote yourself, *—NAB, —WLMS* . . . be diligent, *—CNFT* . . . Make use of the time, *—JB* . . . spend time, *—SEB.*
**reading, to exhortation, to doctrine:** . . . the public reading of, *—WLMS.*

**4:13.** Here is another reference to Paul's hope of coming to Ephesus in the near future (compare 1:3; 3:14). Till that time Timothy was to give priority to a threefold public ministry.

"Reading" probably refers to the public reading of Scripture (the Old Testament). "Exhortation" refers to public proclamation of the gospel ("preaching"). "Doctrine" means Timothy was to have a teaching ministry that presented the basic tenets of the Faith.

**14. Neglect not the gift that is in thee:** . . . Make good use of this gift, *—NORL* . . . that was prophetically granted you, *—BRKL* . . . you received, *—WLMS.*
**which was given thee by prophecy:** . . . in fulfilment of the predictions, *—TCNT.*
**with the laying on of the hands of the presbytery:** . . . when the elders laid their hands upon you, *—WLMS* . . . with the imposition of the hands of the eldership, *—CMPB.*

**4:14.** Paul reminded Timothy of the gift (*charisma*) that had come to him. The gift was very possibly the spiritual abilities Timothy needed for the ministry. The Lord bestowed these when the elders ordained Timothy for the ministry. "No difficulty need be entertained over the fact that in 2 Timothy 1:6 Paul speaks exclusively of his own part in such a ceremony, for there are two possible solutions: either the elders were associated with Paul in the ceremony, . . . or else the two references to laying on of hands may refer to different occasions. The former, on the whole, seems the more likely explanation" (Guthrie, *Tyndale New Testament Commentaries,* 14:98).

**15. Meditate upon these things; give thyself wholly to them:** ... Care about these things, —SEB ... Think about all this, —NLTG ... Attend to your duties, —NAB ... Practise these things, —TCNT ... Continue cultivating these things; be devoted to them, —WLMS.

**that thy profiting may appear to all:** ... so that everybody will see your progress, —WLMS ... your progress may be apparent to all, —CNDT ... may be obvious to every one, —TCNT.

**4:15.** This summary verse refers to what Paul had just written in verses 13 and 14. The initial word translated "meditate" is the verb *meletaō* which can also mean "practice, attend to." This sense is given in the NIV: "Be diligent in these matters." The next clause, "give thyself wholly to them," is literally "be in them." "Profiting" (*prokopē*) may be translated "progress" or "advance." The purpose for Timothy's diligent and wholehearted involvement was to be an effective witness to everyone, thus giving no one grounds for "despising" or looking down upon him because of his youth.

**16. Take heed unto thyself, and unto the doctrine:** ... Take great care about what you do, —JB ... Paying special attention always to your conduct, —NORL.

**continue in them:** ... Stay true to what is right, —NLTG ... Persevere in these things, —MNTG, —WLMS.

**for in doing this:**

**thou shalt both save thyself, and them that hear thee:** ... and your hearers, —MNTG ... those who listen to you, —WLMS.

**4:16.** Here is a twofold challenge: "Take heed unto thyself, and unto the doctrine." The Greek for this clause is literally: "Give attention to yourself and to the teaching." No matter how correct Timothy's doctrine might be, if there was a flaw in his life, his ministry would be ineffective.

Donald Guthrie comments: "The danger of neglecting one's own salvation is greater in the Christian minister than in others, and even the apostle Paul himself could fear lest he became a castaway after preaching to others (1 Corinthians 9:27). Calvin suggestively comments that although salvation is God's gift alone, yet human ministry is needed, as is here implied" (*Tyndale New Testament Commentaries,* 14:99). Too often the minister expends all his energies toward others and neglects his own pursuit of spiritual vitality and daily communion with God.

If Timothy did this he would save himself and his hearers. This is not a proof text for salvation by works. What Paul was writing here correlates with his Spirit-inspired challenge to the Philippians: "Work out your own salvation with fear and trembling" (Philippians 2:12; cf. verse 13).

A.M. Stibbs supplies this comment: "Note how the minister not only fulfils his ministry by what he says (those he serves are described as *your hearers),* but also necessarily completes it, or spoils its effectiveness, by how he himself lives" (p. 1173). Often our character and conduct shout so loudly those listening cannot hear a thing we say. A godly character is a more important possession than great abilities or special talent.

## Chapter 5

**1. Rebuke not an elder:** ... Do not chide, —BRKL ... Do not rebuke sharply, —NORL ... Do not reprimand, —TCNT ... Don't criticize an older man, —SEB ... sharply rebuke an old person, —KLGS.

**but intreat him as a father:** ... but always appeal to him, —WLMS ... but exhort him, —CNFT.

**and the younger men as brethren:**

**2. The elder women as mothers:**

**the younger as sisters, with all purity:** ... with perfect chastity, —LILY ... with absolute purity, —BRKL.

**5:1, 2.** Chapter 5 begins a new section. Paul now addressed the subject of relationships. These are contained in 5:1-6:2.

First are age relationships (verses 1, 2). The word "elder" does not refer to church officials (as in 5:17) but to older men. Timothy was not to "rebuke" (a strong term meaning "censure severely") an older man. If correction was necessary, Timothy was to "entreat" ("exhort," a softer term) him as if he were Timothy's own father.

Younger men were to be treated as brothers. Timothy was to treat older women as he would his mother and younger women as his own sisters. Paul's instructions show a spirit of family relationships within the congregations. An added caution was to be observed with younger women: "with all purity." Timothy was to avoid impropriety or intimacy in ministering to young women. His relationship with women was to be above reproach.

**3. Honour widows that are widows indeed:** ... Always care for, —WLMS ... who are really widows, —CMPB.

**5:3.** This verse begins a section devoted to widows (3-16). Four classes of widows are mentioned: real widows (verses 3, 5, 9, 10), widows with relatives (verses 4, 8, 16), widows living in pleasure (verses 6, 7), and young widows (verses 11-15). The "widows indeed" ("real widows" who were without means or relatives and thus were truly destitute) were to be given "honor." This included proper recognition, value, and reverence. This "honor" might include material assistance, compensation, and care.

**4. But if any widow have children or nephews:** ... or grandchildren, −NLTG, −MNTG ... or descendants, −KLGS.

**let them learn first to shew piety at home:** ... toward their own household, −MNTG ... in the treatment of their own families, −WLMS.

**and to requite their parents:** ... to pay the debt they owe their parents, −WLMS ... should repay what they owe to their grandparents, −SEB ... and to make some return to their parents, −MNTG.

**for that is good and acceptable before God:** ... since this is pleasing to God, −LILY ... pleasing in God's sight, −MNTG.

**5:4.** Then there were widows with relatives who were able to support them. These relatives were instructed to "requite" ("repay, make return"). They were to support and provide for them. The word "nephews" (*ekgona*) means "descendants" and is better translated "grandchildren." The care of a female parent or grandparent "is good and acceptable before God" (see Exodus 20:12).

**5. Now she that is a widow indeed, and desolate:** ... who is really a widow, −WLMS ... and left solitary, −CNFT ... and is left all alone, −RSV.

**trusteth in God:** ... has fixed her hope on God, −WLMS ... relies on God, −CNDT.

**and continueth in supplications and prayers night and day:** ... devotes herself to prayers and entreaties, −WLMS.

**5:5.** The "widow indeed" (identified as the one "who is really in need" in the NIV text of verses 3 and 5) was the most destitute and desolate of persons. She had no children and no relatives to care for and support her. So the Church was to be her family. Though this kind of widow was desolate (*memonōmenē* = "left entirely alone") she maintained a strong faith in God as her Provider. The Greek verb translated "continueth" indicates this is an attitude rather than continuous action.

**6. But she that liveth in pleasure:** ... she who is self-indulgent, −RSV ... who lives voluptuously, −BRKL ... who gives herself up to luxury, −WLMS ... only for the joy she can receive from this world, −NLTG ... who is devoted to pleasure, −TCNT.

**is dead while she liveth:** ... she is spiritually dead, −NORL ... is a living death, −TCNT.

**5:6.** A unique class of widows was those living in pleasure. The verb here is *spatalaō* and literally means "live wantonly, live riotously." In Ephesus and elsewhere in the First Century, many single women resorted to immoral living as a means of support. Paul might have had this kind of widow in mind when he said, "But she that liveth in pleasure is dead while she liveth." Because these widows had chosen to support themselves in this unchristian manner, they were outside the sphere

of the Church's responsibility and care. The phrase "is dead while she liveth" indicates a condition when though the body's physical life is maintained, its spiritual life is dead.

**7. And these things give in charge:** ... Drive home these suggestions, −BRKL.

**that they may be blameless:** ... be without reproach, −WLMS.

**5:7.** As Paul often did in this pastoral letter, he reminded Timothy of the "charge" ("command") he was to give (compare 1:3, 18; 4:11). The purpose was "that they may be blameless." But the "they" is somewhat obscure. Are "they" the widows who lived in pleasure (verse 6) or the relatives of destitute widows (verse 8)? Some think verse 7 refers back to the widows living in pleasure. If Timothy commanded them to stop "living wontonly," then they would be blameless. But Guthrie says it "must refer to the responsibility of children to support their forbears (verse 4), and the responsibility of widows to fulfil the requirements mentioned in verse 5" (*Tyndale New Testament Commentaries,* 14:101).

**8. But if any provide not for his own:** ... for his own family, −RSV ... for his own relations, −TCNT ... does not support his relatives, −SEB.

**and specially for those of his own house:** ... of his immediate family, −LILY.

**he hath denied the faith:** ... he has disowned, −CNDT ... he shows that he does not believe, −SEB.

**and is worse than an infidel:** ... than an unbeliever, −BRKL.

**5:8.** Though the primary application is to widows in the Ephesian churches, the principle of caring for those in a person's immediate family applies universally. Christian families are obligated to provide for members of the family. "Worse than an infidel" suggests that even the unbeliever has this sense of family responsibility.

**9. Let not a widow be taken into the number under threescore years old:**

**having been the wife of one man:** ... having been married but once, −CNFT.

**5:9.** Having clearly defined who a real widow is, Paul now gave instructions regarding the local church's relationship to her. Because she was destitute and in need of care, she was eligible to be put on an official list ("taken into the number") of widows. But there were certain qualifications beyond need.

The second qualification, "having been the wife of one man," literally means "a one-man wife." It does not have to restrict the sense to "married only once." The main idea in "wife of one man" is monogamous fidelity.

10. **Well reported of for good works:** . . . She should have a reputation for good deeds, –*LILY.*

**if she have brought up children:** . . . bringing up, –*WLMS.*

**if she have lodged strangers:** . . . being hospitable, –*WLMS.*

**if she have washed the saints' feet:** . . . the feet of God's people, –*WLMS.*

**if she have relieved the afflicted:** . . . helping people in distress, –*WLMS.*

**if she have diligently followed every good work:** . . . and for showing kindness, –*NLTG* . . . in carefully pursuing, –*CNFT* . . . devoting herself to any sort of doing good, –*WLMS* . . . to every charitable cause, –*NORL.*

**5:10.** The qualifications for "official widows" (those recognized and supported by the churches) are listed. "Good works" begin and end this verse. The words "well reported" refer to the reputation of a Christian widow. She earns a good reputation by her good works which are: (1) child care, (2) hospitality, (3) humble service, and (4) benevolence. In the matter of child care she must have brought up her own children well (compare 3:4, 5 for the elder) and have taken in and cared for orphans. Historians tell us it was very common for children in ancient times to be orphaned because of their parents' divorce or death. Widows who took these children in were showing compassion.

"Washed the saints' feet" may be literal foot washing. But it can also be representative of any menial task. The general meaning is the widow's willingness to accept the humblest job.

Some see in these verses the earliest reference to an "order" of widows who were set apart by the local church for special duties. There was such an order in the Third Century, but whether it existed in A.D. 64 when Paul wrote to Timothy is uncertain. The Greek verb standing behind "taken into the number" (verse 9) is *katalegō* which can mean "reckon." If this is the case, real widows (see verses 3, 5) would be reckoned at the age of 60.

11. **But the younger widows refuse:** . . . Keep . . . off this roll, –*WLMS.*

**for when they have begun to wax wanton against Christ:** . . . become impatient of the restraint of Christ, –*CMPB* . . . when they grow restive under the yoke of the Christ, –*TCNT* . . . after their sexual desires become strong again, –*SEB.*

**they will marry:**

12. **Having damnation:** . . . and so deserve censure, –*WLMS.*

**because they have cast off their first faith:** . . . because they reject, –*SEB* . . . they become guilty of breaking their first promise, –*NORL* . . . for breaking their previous pledge, –*WLMS* . . . violated, –*RSV.*

**5:11, 12.** Beginning with verse 11 Paul gave instructions concerning a group called "younger widows." He dealt with them somewhat severely. The word "refuse" suggests younger widows were not to be put on the register as the others were. There was a special danger for them that might lead them into sin because of a desire to remarry. They were not being told they must not remarry at all. This would contradict Paul's teaching of verse 14 and 1 Corinthians 7:9. The danger Paul was warning against was that these widows might "wax wanton," that is, turn away from Christ and marry an unbeliever. This would be leaving their "first faith" and their pledge to serve Christ wholeheartedly. Also, younger widows might lack the spiritual maturity to devote themselves to prayer and good works and thus become lax in their devotion to the Lord.

13. **And withal they learn to be idle:** . . . Presently they acquire habits of idleness, –*BRKL* . . . they learn to be lazy, –*SEB.*

**wandering about from house to house:**

**and not only idle, but tattlers also and busybodies:** . . . but gossipers as well, –*CNFT.*

**speaking things which they ought not:**

**5:13.** Paul continued to list the characteristics of younger widows. They would "learn" to become idle busybodies who were social gadabouts and vicious gossips. William Barclay comments: "Because a woman had not enough to do, she might become one of those creatures who drift from house to house in an empty social round. It was almost inevitable that such a woman would become a *gossip;* because she had nothing important to talk about, she would tend to talk scandal, repeating tales from house to house, each time with a little more embroidery and a little more malice. . . . She would be very apt to be over-interested and over-interfering in the affairs of others" (*The Daily Study Bible, The Letters to Timothy, Titus, and Philemon,* p. 114). A *busybody* pays attention to affairs of others and is meddlesome. A *tattler* ("talebearer") betrays private confidences.

14. **I will therefore that the younger women marry:** . . . My advice is, –*NORL* . . . I think it is best for, –*NLTG* . . . young widows marry again . . . manage a home, –*BRKL* . . . and govern their house, –*KLGS.*

**give none occasion to the adversary to speak reproachfully:** . . . This will not give the enemy a chance to say bad things about us, –*SEB* . . . and avoid giving our opponents an opportunity for scandal, –*TCNT* . . . to criticize them, –*LILY* . . . for abusing us, –*CNFT.*

**5:14.** Paul, still addressing the topic of younger widows which he began in verse 11, expressed his "will" concerning them. (He used this same expression in 2:8 when he instructed men to pray everywhere.) He wrote to Timothy, "I will therefore that the younger women marry." Paul then listed the specific duties of the married woman: (1) she was to bear children, (2) guide or "rule" the house ("household"), and (3) by occupying her time and effort in these pursuits keep slander from her doorstep.

The word "occasion" is a military term and means "a base of operations" (compare Paul's use of this term in such passages as Romans 7:8, 11; 2 Corinthians 11:12; Galatians 5:13). The "adversary" here is not the devil but any human opponent who might take advantage of or bring an accusation against a young widow.

**15. For some are already turned aside after Satan:** . . . to follow, –*WLMS.*

**5:15.** The instructions in verse 14 are all the more imperative when Paul reminded Timothy that "some are already turned aside after Satan." It seems some young widows were appointed in the recent past to serve the churches in practical and benevolent ministry (see verse 10). Because they lacked the wisdom of age and experience, they fell prey to their own sexual desires (verse 11) and gave themselves over to immoral conduct. In doing so they removed themselves from the protection of the church and entered the domain of Satan.

**16. If any man or woman that believeth have widows:** . . . has widowed relatives, –*LILY,* –*CNFT.*
**let them relieve them:** . . . she should help them, –*WLMS* . . . let her take care of them, –*BRKL* . . . let him come to their aid, –*NORL* . . . you must care for them, –*NLTG.*
**and let not the church be charged:** . . . be free from the burden, –*WLMS* . . . be burdened, –*CNFT.*
**that it may relieve them that are widows indeed:** . . . so that it can help the widows who are really dependent, –*WLMS* . . . real widows who have no support, –*NORL.*

**5:16.** Before moving on to a new set of relationships, Paul summarized his instructions concerning widows. J.B. Phillips paraphrases it this way: "As a general rule it should be taken for granted that any Christians who have widows in the family circle should do everything possible for them and not allow them to become the church's responsibility. The church will then be free to look after those widows who are alone in the world" (Phillips).

**17. Let the elders that rule well:** . . . who preside well, –*CMPB.*
**be counted worthy of double honour:** . . . should be given twice as much pay, –*NLTG* . . . should be held

deserving of especial esteem, –*TCNT* . . . as deserving twice the salary they get, –*WLMS* . . . deserve double the pay, –*SEB.*
**especially they who labour in the word and doctrine:** . . . work hard at preaching, –*SEB* . . . in preaching and teaching, –*RSV.*

**5:17.** Spiritual leaders are the second major group treated in chapter 5. In verses 17-20 Paul covered several items: how much a pastor should be paid, how he should be protected from slander, and how he should be rebuked publicly if he has sinned.

The text uses the word "elders." This is different from its use in verse 1. Here it means the officials set over local churches, i.e., "pastors." The term "rule" (literally, "superintend") indicates general oversight. "Well" seems to be the condition laid down for special consideration regarding payment. These pastors are worthy of "double honor." No doubt this refers to remuneration, especially in the context of verse 18. "Double" may not mean "twice" in the strictest sense. "Ample" or "generous" is probably Paul's intent.

Paul singled out a special class of spiritual leaders in the last clause of verse 17. "They who labor in the word and doctrine" are the preachers and teachers of the Word and tenets of the Christian faith.

**18. For the scripture saith:**
**Thou shalt not muzzle the ox that treadeth out the corn:** . . . when he is treading out the grain, –*WLMS.*
**And, The labourer is worthy of his reward:** . . . A person who works should be paid, –*NLTG* . . . is entitled to his support, –*LILY* . . . deserves his wage, –*BRKL* . . . deserves to get his pay, –*NORL* . . . is worth his wages, –*TCNT* . . . of his wages, –*CNFT.*

**5:18.** To give strength to his instruction in verse 17, Paul quoted Deuteronomy 25:4 which says: "Thou shalt not muzzle the ox when he treadeth out the corn" (compare 1 Corinthians 9:9). The slight difference in the Deuteronomy passage and here is the words "when he." This is found in the Greek present participle here in verse 18; the meaning is "while it is treading." The idea is the ox may be muzzled at other times but not while it is working at the threshing floor. Paul probably quoted this to appeal to the moral principle behind the illustration rather than the letter of the Law.

Paul's second quotation from Scripture is from Jesus (Matthew 10:10 and Luke 10:7). Luke had already written his Gospel before he wrote Acts (Acts 1:1), was a close coworker with Paul during much of his ministry, and was with him when this epistle was written. Very likely Paul had read

Luke's Gospel and here was quoting from it. It is noteworthy that Paul recognized Luke's writings as Scripture, as Peter did Paul's (2 Peter 3:15, 16).

The meaning is clear. Applied to "the elders that rule well" (verse 17), they are "worthy of double honor" and "worthy of . . . reward." If the first is questionable as meaning remuneration, the second certainly cannot be taken any other way.

**19. Against an elder receive not an accusation:** . . . Do not entertain a charge against an elder, *—BRKL* . . . Make it a rule not to consider a charge preferred against, *—WLMS* . . . do not assent to an accusation, *—CNDT* . . . against a presbyter, *—LILY.*

**but before two or three witnesses:** . . . unless it is supported by, *—LILY, —CNFT, —BRKL.*

**5:19.** The Law was very clear that no man was to be condemned on the testimony of a single witness: "One witness shall not rise up against a man for any iniquity, or for any sin, in any sin that he sinneth: at the mouth of two witnesses, or at the mouth of three witnesses, shall the matter be established" (Deuteronomy 19:15).

Paul applied this principle to any accusation against an elder. This practice would protect spiritual leaders from unwarranted slander. Later on the rule was amended to require that the two witnesses should be Christians. This was to prevent untrue accusations from those who sought to slander church leaders.

**20. Them that sin rebuke before all:** . . . Rebuke habitual sinners, *—LILY* . . . Rebuke offenders publicly, *—TCNT* . . . Prove them wrong publicly, *—SEB.*

**that others also may fear:** . . . Then the others will show respect, *—SEB* . . . that the rest may be awed, *—BRKL.*

**5:20.** Paul told Timothy that if a leader was found to be guilty of sin, he was to be rebuked ("reproved, corrected") before all. Whether the "all" means before all the elders or before the entire church is not clear. But the reason for this public rebuke is plain: it would deter others from falling into the same sin.

These instructions have direct reference to spiritual leaders. It would be improper to apply them to Christians in general with the exception of the principle regarding witnesses (see verse 19; compare Matthew 18:16).

**21. I charge thee before God, and the Lord Jesus Christ, and the elect angels:**

**that thou observe these things without preferring one before another:** . . . carry out these directions uninfluenced by prejudice, *—TCNT* . . . without discrimination, *—NORL.*

**doing nothing by partiality:** . . . Don't pre-judge or give any special favors to anyone, *—SEB* . . . in no way favoring either side, *—LILY, —CNFT* . . . that you act with no favoritism, *—BRKL* . . . Show favors to no one, *—NLTG* . . . doing nothing from bias, *—CNDT.*

**5:21.** Although verses 21-25 continue the instructions regarding elders, they contain personal counsel to Timothy. In verse 21 Paul laid an especially strong "charge" ("I solemnly protest") on Timothy before three witnesses: God, the Lord Jesus Christ, and the elect angels (compare 2 Timothy 4:1). Paul told Timothy he was to "observe" ("guard, keep") and to apply all the rules without prejudice or partiality.

**22. Lay hands suddenly on no man:** . . . Impose hands hastily on no one, *—CMPB* . . . hands of ordination on no one hastily, *—BRKL* . . . Never ordain any one hastily, *—TCNT* . . . Do not be in a hurry about choosing a church leader, *—NLTG.*

**neither be partaker of other men's sins:** . . . nor participate in, *—RSV* . . . Don't share in the sins of others, *—SEB* . . . not to be responsible for the sins of others, *—WLMS.*

**keep thyself pure:** . . . Keep your life untarnished, *—TCNT.*

**5:22.** "Lay hands suddenly on no man" has been seen by some as referring to the discipline of an impenitent wrongdoer (a Christian). But it is better to conclude the reference is to ordaining elders. The treatment of elders is the immediate context and "laying on of hands" was used by Paul to mean the rite of ordination (1 Timothy 4:14; 2 Timothy 1:6). The meaning here is "ordain no one with undue haste" and connects with "partiality" in verse 21. If there is bias in the selection of elders, the ordination process may be hasty and regrettable.

Some believe that in the reference to "other men's sins" Paul was cautioning Timothy that ordaining others placed him as surety for their characters. Timothy might be implicated in any sins a newly ordained elder committed. At any rate it is wise to avoid involvement in other's misconduct. "Pure" here has the sense of honorable and upright conduct, though it also can mean "holy, chaste."

**23. Drink no longer water:** . . . Do not drink water only, *—NLTG.*

**but use a little wine:** . . . but be using a sip of wine, *—CNDT* . . . take a little wine, *—WLMS.*

**for thy stomach's sake and thine often infirmities:** . . . You are often sick, *—SEB* . . . to strengthen your stomach and relieve its frequent attacks, *—WLMS* . . . and your recurring illness, *—BRKL* . . . and your frequent illnesses, *—KLGS.*

**5:23.** This verse is a personal parenthesis. Paul was concerned for Timothy's health and gave him a prescription for his infirmity. It may connect with "keep thyself pure" in verse 22.

Timothy evidently was a total abstainer. Possibly his abstinence was based on the Nazarite vow (see Numbers 6:3, 4). His mother was a Jewess (Acts 16:1), so he may have received this teaching from her (2 Timothy 1:5; 3:15). "Drink no longer water" suggests Timothy was drinking water exclusively. Water in that day and throughout the eastern countries was polluted and unsafe. (For discussion about *oinos* see the commentary on 3:3.) Paul prescribed a "little wine" as medicine for Timothy's "often infirmities." Timothy had a weak stomach and the polluted water was aggravating his condition. So Paul suggested a remedy.

**24. Some men's sins are open beforehand:**... The sins of some men can be seen, —NLTG...before investigation, —LILY, —CNFT...are very evident, —WLMS...are conspicuous, —RSV, —TCNT.

**going before to judgment:**... clearly lead them on to, —WLMS... and pave the way for their judgment, —TCNT.

**and some men they follow after:**... their sins show up later, —NORL... The sins of others appear later, —SEB...the sins of others lag behind, —WLMS.

**25. Likewise also the good works of some are manifest beforehand:**... usually very evident, —WLMS.

**and they that are otherwise cannot be hid:**

**5:24, 25.** Verses 24 and 25 present a contrast of sins and good works and enlarge on Paul's caution, "Neither be partaker of other men's sins" (5:22). "Open beforehand" refers to sins that are "conspicuous, clearly evident, immediately obvious." The words "going before" mean "pointing, leading the way." "Judgment" refers to God's judgment of men.

The meaning of these contrasts is clear. Obvious sins lead the way to judgment. Hidden sins follow men to judgment. Obvious good works are noticed, applauded, and appreciated. Hidden good works are known to God and will be rewarded. God will deal with men in a fair and equitable manner.

"These parallel observations, viewing human potentialities both negatively and positively, bring out forcibly the complexities involved in selecting suitable candidates for God's work. Hasty action relies on first impressions, but these impressions are often deceptive. Unworthy men might be chosen, whose moral culpability lies deeper than the surface; and worthy men, whose good actions are not in the limelight, might easily be overlooked. The whole situation demands extreme caution" (Guthrie, *Tyndale New Testament Commentaries*, 14:109).

## Chapter 6

**1. Let as many servants as are under the yoke:**...who are owned by someone, —NLTG.

**count their own masters worthy of all honour:**...esteem their masters as, —MNTG...deserving of, —CNFT...of all respect, —BRKL...worthy of full respect, —NIV...of the highest **respect,** —WLMS.

**that the name of God and his doctrine be not blasphemed:**... and the teachings, —MNTG...may not be dishonored, —NORL...may not be maligned, —TCNT...is not slandered, —KLGS...may not be abused, —WLMS.

**6:1.** Chapter 6 continues the topic of relationships but introduces a new group: slaves. Verse 1 was addressed to Christian slaves with non-Christian masters. Christian slaves found equality in the Church but were still considered inferior in society. The words "under the yoke" reflect the attitude of non-Christian masters. They regarded slaves in the same category as cattle. If a Christian slave considered himself as an heir of salvation and his master as a son of perdition, a feeling of pious superiority on the part of the slave could result. This would put strain on the master-slave relationship and seriously hinder the slave's service to his master and witness for Christ. So a new attitude is needed. Paul says Christian slaves are to give full respect to these masters. This would bring glory to God and would not bring reproach on His name or the gospel.

**2. And they that have believing masters:**...if they have Christian masters, —NORL...whose masters are Christian believers, —MNTG.

**let them not despise them, because they are brethren:**...let them not slight them, —YNG...must not treat them with disrespect, —MNTG...should not look down on their masters, —SEB.

**but rather do them service:**... to serve them even better, —NIV...rather slave for them the better, —MNTG.

**because they are faithful and beloved partakers of the benefit:**...because those who get the benefit of their services are believing and beloved, —MNTG.

**These teach and exhort:**...Continue to teach and preach this, —MNTG...the things to teach and insist on, —TCNT.

**6:2.** Paul now addressed Christian slaves who were owned by "believing masters." Both were members of the same local church; a dilemma existed: equality in the spiritual realm but masters and slaves in the natural realm. Slaves with Christian masters were advised "not to show less respect for them because they are brothers" (NIV). Because a slave and his master were equal in the Church and brothers in Christ the tendency on the part of the slave would be to treat his master on an equal basis at home. The slave would forget his place and tend to show less respect to his master when he should "do them service," that is, serve them well.

Why did not the Church fight slavery by requiring Christian slave owners to free their slaves? When we consider that possibly half the population of the Roman Empire in the First Century was composed of slaves, we then understand what social and political havoc this would have brought. The spiritual fellowship and equality within the Christian church was the seed whose maturation, in the course of time, did away with slavery (see Galatians 3:26-28). The gospel brought to men a freedom which a revolutionary rebellion could never have accomplished.

"Partakers of the benefit" may refer to masters or slaves. If the master, he would receive benefit from the conscientious and joyful work of the slave. If the slave, he would benefit from the kindness and brotherly love of the master. So the benefit was mutual. "These things teach and exhort" introduces what follows.

**3. If any man teach otherwise:** . . . teaches heterodoxy, —MNTG . . . different doctrines, —WLMS.
**and consent not to wholesome words:** . . . and refuses to consent, —MNTG . . . to agree with, —WLMS.
**even the words of our Lord Jesus Christ:** . . . the wholesome messages of, —WLMS.
**and to the doctrine which is according to godliness:** . . . to the teaching that fosters godliness, —BRKL . . . and to the teachings of religion, —MNTG . . . and godly teaching, —SEB.

**6:3.** Verses 3-10 is a new section and contains further warnings to Timothy. False teachers is the subject of verses 3-5. The teaching here is similar to that found in 1:3-7.

These false teachers "consent not to wholesome words." The word "consent" (*proserchomai*) means "approach," with a derived sense of "attaching oneself to." "The words of our Lord Jesus Christ" could mean the sayings of Jesus or words about Jesus, i.e., the gospel. The latter is better suited to the context since "doctrine" ("teaching") immediately follows. Paul made "doctrine" one of the major themes of this letter to Timothy (see 1:3, 10; 4:6, 13, 16; 5:17; 6:1).

**4. He is proud, knowing nothing:** . . . Such a man is nothing but a conceited ignoramus, —NORL . . . he is boastful, —SEB . . . he is puffed up, —KLGS . . . though really he is utterly ignorant, —TCNT.
**but doting about questions and strifes of words:** . . . has an unhealthy interest in controversies, —NIV . . . about controversies and disputes, —CNFT . . . and verbal contentions, —CMPB . . . with a morbid appetite for, —WLMS.

**whereof cometh envy, strife, railings, evil surmisings:** . . . which lead to, —WLMS . . . bad suspicions, —BRKL . . . wicked suspicions, —CNDT . . . unjust suspicions, —CMPB.

**6:4.** Verses 4 and 5 describe the characteristics of a false teacher. "Proud" means "conceited, puffed up." "Knowing nothing" means "ignorant." "Doting" is a strange and unique word and possibly can be translated "being sick (mentally)" and by extension, "having a morbid craving for." "Questions" means "controversies," and "strifes of words" is "arguments." In a few words Paul said a false teacher is (1) conceited, (2) ignorant, (3) sick, and (4) argumentative.

Four negative results (a fifth is listed in verse 5) of this argumentative nature are: (1) "envy," (2) "strife" ("dissension, quarreling"), (3) "railings" ("blasphemies, slander, malicious talk"), (4) "evil surmisings" ("suspicions"). All of this is evil and disruptive and has no place in the company of believers.

**5. Perverse disputings of men of corrupt minds:** . . . and incessant wrangling, —TCNT . . . empty arguments from men of poisoned -minds, —KLGS . . . perpetual contention between people of depraved minds, —BRKL . . . who have polluted minds, —SEB.
**and destitute of the truth:** . . . They do not have the truth, —NLTG . . . who have lost all hold on the Truth, —TCNT.
**supposing that gain is godliness:** . . . They think religion is a way to get much for themselves, —NLTG . . . They think that religion is a way of making money, —SEB . . . that godliness is a means to financial gain, —NIV.
**from such withdraw thyself:** . . . Keep aloof from such, —NORL . . . Keep away from such, —KLGS.

**6:5.** "Disputings" are "constant frictions" or "incessant quarrel-ings." These are the stock-in-trade of "men of corrupt minds." This term means these men were incapable of moral judgment and therefore were "destitute of the truth." The false teacher believed the lies he spouted in foolish and perverse arguments. This had brought him to intellectual and moral deprivation.

Donald Guthrie questions the reading "supposing that gain is godliness." He says in his commentary: "The concluding clause should read 'supposing that godliness is a way of gain,' or as Moffatt translates it, 'they imagine religion is a paying concern'" (*Tyndale New Testament Commentaries*, 14:112). The Greek construction supports this, as does the context. The idea of using religion for profit is what Paul addressed next.

**6. But godliness with contentment is great gain:** ... is great prosperity, *–KLGS.*

**6:6.** Paul repeated what he had just written in verse 5 but with one significant difference, he added the word "contentment." "Contentment" is an inward sufficiency that comes from a full acceptance of and appreciation for God's provisions. This contentment is an inner possession and is unaffected by outward circumstances.

The word "gain" is *porismos* and means "good business, profit." Here in verse 6 it connotes more than material wealth. The possession of things is not the only measure of "gain."

**7. For we brought nothing into this world: and it is certain we can carry nothing out:** ... and, obviously, *–BRKL* ... it is manifest, *–YNG* ... it is evident, *–CNDT.*

**6:7.** Godliness with contentment is great gain because "we brought (absolutely) nothing into this world (when we were born), and it is certain we can carry (absolutely) nothing out (when we die)." This proverbial statement was not new with Paul. God inspired both Job and Solomon to speak and write this same truth (see Job 1:21; Ecclesiastes 5:15). Paul was saying that material possessions are of fleeting, secondary importance. They are not part of the true self which will abide. The words "carry nothing out" refer to a person's "exit" from this life.

Possessions are external; contentment is internal. Money is material; godliness is spiritual. Godliness and contentment will go with us when we depart. All the other things will be left behind.

**8. And having food and raiment let us be therewith content:** ... and sufficient clothing, *–CNFT* ... we will be satisfied with these things, *–SEB.*

**6:8.** "Having food and raiment" reminds us of Jesus' words in Matthew 6:25-34. "Food" ("nourishments, sustenance" [plural]) suggests a full supply for each day. "Raiment" (also in the plural, "coverings") includes both clothing and shelter. So Paul was certainly aware he was repeating what Jesus said. "Be therewith content" is in the future indicative tense and is not so much an exhortation to be content but an assertion that this is the path to real contentment.

**9. But they that will be rich:** ... But men who want lots of money, *–NLTG* ... men who keep planning to get rich, *–WLMS.*
**fall into temptation and a snare:** ... are tempted ... They are trapped into, *–NLTG.*
**and into many foolish and hurtful lusts:** ... and hurtful cravings, *–BRKL* ... and harmful ambitions, *–TCNT* ... hurtful desires, *–WLMS.*

**which drowned men in destruction and perdition:** ... which plunge men, *–CMPB* ... plunge people, *–BRKL* ... that sink men into ruin, *–YNG* ... These things drag them into sin and will destroy them, *–NLTG* ... into destruction and ruin, *–WLMS.*

**6:9.** The opposite of godliness with contentment is greed. This greed takes one in an ever-downward spiral. Verses 9 and 10 are not addressed to the already rich but to those who want to become rich. These people "fall," then "drown." The language vividly describes the destiny of the greedy: "temptation and a snare" (usually refers to the devil's snare), "foolish and hurtful lusts" (sensual desires), "destruction and perdition" (eternal loss, utter ruin).

**10. For the love of money is the root of all evil:** ... For covetous-ness, *–CNFT* ... Loving money is the root of all kinds of, *–SEB* ... of all kinds of evil, *–NIV* ... of every kind of evil, *–NORL* ... of all sorts of evil, *–WLMS.*
**which while some coveted after:** ... and in their eager desire to be rich, *–MNTG* ... reaching after riches, *–WLMS.*
**they have erred from the faith:** ... have been seduced from, *–NORL* ... have turned from the faith, *–NLTG* ... have wandered from the faith, *–WLMS.*
**and pierced themselves through with many sorrows:** ... and have been pierced to the heart by many a regret, *–TCNT* ... a pang, *–WLMS.*

**6:10.** Paul concluded his instructions regarding those who are greedy with the now oft-quoted phrase, "For the love of money is the root of all evil." Many, however, misquote it. They think it to be, "Money is the root of all evil." If this were so, only the rich would be capable of wrongdoing; the poor would not be bothered by evil. Actually, the reading is "a root of all evil," not the only root, for that would be an exaggeration. Rather, it is a root from which every kind of evil can grow.

The results of this greed are disillusionment, backsliding, grief, and heartbreaking remorse. The literal Greek for the word "erred" (passive form) is "were led astray." This suggests those who covet after money are victims in the grip of an unrelenting deception. "Pierced themselves through" means the "many sorrows" ("pains") were self-inflicted.

**11. But thou, O man of God, flee these things:** ... as a man of God, *–WLMS* ... must avoid all this, *–TCNT* ... run away from, *–SEB.*
**and follow after:** ... Hunt, *–KLGS.*
**righteousness, godliness, faith, love, patience, meekness:** ... uprightness ... steadfastness, gentleness, *–WLMS* ... integrity, piety, *–MNTG* ... endurance, *–ADAM* ... justice, *–KLGS* ... mildness, *–CNFT.*

**6:11.** Verse 11 begins the final section of this first letter to Timothy. It contains a personal charge that repeats and summarizes much of what Paul has already written.

The title "man of God" was given to Old Testament greats like Moses, Samuel, and many of the prophets (see Deuteronomy 33:1; 1 Samuel 9:6). Paul paid tribute to Timothy by addressing him with this lofty title. In his second letter, Paul used the same term to refer to every mature Christian (2 Timothy 3:17).

Timothy was told to "flee" and "follow" (cf. 2 Timothy 2:22). The "these things" are all Paul has just enumerated from verse 4 to the present point. Timothy was to focus his attention on six virtues. "Righteousness" means "giving God and men their due," i.e., "what is right." "Godliness" means "piety" (cf. Titus 2:12). This is godly faith, the devout and practical expression of Christianity.

"Faith" connotes "fidelity, faithfulness." "Love" (*agapē*) in this frame of reference means a high, holy love that seeks the best for others. "Patience" means "endurance, steadfastness" that perseveres in the worst of circumstances. "Meekness" is a "gentleness" that is the opposite of the argumentative, divisive, envious spirit of those who run after riches.

**12. Fight the good fight of faith:** . . . Keep contending in the noble contest of, *—MNTG* . . . Keep up the good fight of, *—WLMS*.

**lay hold on eternal life:** . . . seize hold, *—MNTG* . . . hold firmly on everlasting life, *—KLGS*.

**whereunto thou art also called:** . . . to which you were called *—MNTG*.

**and hast professed a good profession before many witnesses:** . . . you made the good confession, *—ADAM* . . . when you confessed the good confession in the presence of, *—MNTG*.

**6:12.** "Fight the good fight of faith" reflects the figure taken from the Olympic games where the contestant keeps on until the prize is won. The difference in the Greek tenses of the verbs here suggests "fight" as an ongoing process and "lay hold on" as a decisive act. The word "fight" (*agōnizomai*) means "contend for a prize." The prize or goal here is eternal life. This is not just unending life in the future, but eternal life that has its source in God. It is a present possession as well as a future promise.

The latter part of this verse probably refers to Timothy's baptism where he "professed (confessed) a good profession (confession)" (compare verse 13). This was "before many witnesses"; it was a "public" confession of his faith in Jesus Christ.

**13. I give thee charge in the sight of God:** . . . I urge you, *—TCNT* . . . I tell you this in front of

God, *—NLTG* . . . In the presence of, *—MNTG* . . . I instruct you with authority, *—ADAM*.

**who quickeneth all things:** . . . gives life to everything, *—NIV, —SEB* . . . gives life to all, *—MNTG* . . . who preserves the life of all His creatures, *—WLMS*.

**and before Christ Jesus:**

**who before Pontius Pilate witnessed a good confession:** . . . Who made the good confession, *—ADAM* . . . in testifying before, *—WLMS* . . . who bore witness to the good confession, *—MNTG*.

**6:13.** "I give thee charge in the sight of God . . . and before Christ Jesus" indicates the solemnity and authority of Paul's words. This was not just a casual correspondence letter; it was a communication of the very words of God. Beginning with this verse Paul, inspired by the Spirit, wrote one of those long sentences for which he is famous. It extends to the end of verse 16 and is 92 words in the King James Version. Much of this section is taken up with a praise doxology.

The words "who quickeneth all things" refer to God as Lifegiver, Creator. They imply His eternality and sovereignty, a theme repeated in the following verses. The references to "Christ Jesus" and His "confession" before Pilate are a reminder to Timothy that just as Christ made a good confession, so Timothy should also (compare verse 12). John records Jesus' "confession" in John 18:37: "Pilate therefore said unto him, Art thou a king then? Jesus answered, Thou sayest that I am a king. To this end was I born, and for this cause came I into the world, that I should bear witness unto the truth. Every one that is of the truth heareth my voice."

**14. That thou keep this commandment without spot, unrebukable:** . . . I solemnly charge you, *—WLMS* . . . I charge you, keep your commission spotless, *—MNTG* . . . and free from suspicion, *—ADAM* . . . keep the principles stainless and irreproachable, *—BRKL*.

**until the appearing of our Lord Jesus Christ:** . . . till the manifestation of, *—YNG* . . . unto the advent of, *—CNDT*.

**6:14.** The word "commandment" in this verse possibly refers to Timothy's baptismal commission. There he would have received directions to fulfill all the obligations and duties of the ministry. Then again it may refer to the charge Paul had just given him in verses 11 and 12. The "thou" here is emphatic. "Keep" means "guard, hold, reserve, preserve." This commandment was to be kept "without spot" and "unrebukable" ("without blame, irreproachable").

In the last clause of this verse Paul made reference to Christ's "appearing" (*epiphaneia*; "manifestation, showing"). The coming of Christ is constantly in focus in Paul's letters. (Compare 1

Corinthians 1:8; Philippians 2:15, 16; 1 Thessalonians 3:13; 5:23 for the concept of blamelessness at the coming of Christ.)

**15. Which in his times he shall shew:** ... At the right time, we will be shown, —NLTG ... For in his own good time this will be brought about by, —MNTG.
**who is the blessed and only Potentate:** ... that God is the One Who has all power, —NLTG ... Sovereign, —BRKL, —WLMS ... and only Ruler, —NORL, —KLGS.
**the King of kings, and Lord of lords:**

**6:15.** Verses 15 and 16 contain a doxology of praise. Some commentators see this as a doxology used in the synagogue worship because of its Jewish-sounding structure and words. Very possibly when Paul focused his attention on God's sovereignty, the Spirit brought these words to mind. The words "which in his times" reflects God's sovereignty: He holds the time in His own hands. "Potentate" (*dunastēs*) signifies "prince, chieftain, ruler, sovereign" (compare Acts 8:27). The word "only" preceding "Potentate" suggests power was not delegated but resident in God alone; this power is unique to God.

The title "King of kings, and Lord of lords" is found only here in all the writings of Paul. There are parallels of this title in the Old Testament— see Deuteronomy 10:17; Psalm 136:2, 3; compare Daniel 4:34—that may have prompted Paul to praise God using these words. John the Revelator is the only other New Testament writer to use this title (Revelation 17:14; 19:16).

**16. Who only hath immortality:** ... Only God never dies, —SEB ... who alone possesses immortality, —MNTG, —WLMS ... He only has everlasting life, —KLGS.
**dwelling in the light which no man can approach unto:** ... and dwells in light inaccessible, —CNFT ... in unapproachable light, —BRKL, —WLMS.
**whom no man hath seen nor can see:**
**to whom be honour and power everlasting. Amen:** ... and everlasting dominion! —NORL ... and eternal dominion, —WLMS.

**6:16.** Paul praised God for His "immortality." The word "only" signifies a unique kind of immortality: that which is "unending life" from beginning to end. The Christian will experience immortality (see 1 Corinthians 15:53, 54), but his will be the kind that extends a life that had a beginning. God had no beginning and will have no ending; He is the "immortal ... God" (1:17).

Paul then praised two attributes of God: first, His transcendence: "dwelling in the light which no man can approach unto" (literally, "unapproachable light"); second, His invisibility: "whom no man hath seen nor can see" (compare Exodus 33:17-23). The repetition of the word "see" may be of some significance. God can see men but men cannot see God. God is aware of all that men are doing but men are unaware of what God is doing. This brings the thought back to God's sovereignty just expressed in verse 15.

Finally, Paul ended this doxology with the words, "To whom be honor and power everlasting. Amen." The word "power" means "might, rule" and focuses again on the sovereignty of God. In Ephesians 1:19, 6:10, and Colossians 1:11 Paul wrote about God's power as it relates to Christians.

**17. Charge them that are rich in this world:** ... Command those, —NIV ... Continue charging, —WLMS ... the rich of this world, —MNTG.
**that they be not highminded:** ... not to brag, —SEB ... not to be elated in mind, —CMPB ... not to be haughty, —NORL ... not to be supercilious, —MNTG.
**nor trust in uncertain riches:** ... They shouldn't place their hope upon wealth, —SEB ... to rely on the dubiousness of riches, —CNDT ... and not to fix their hope on, —WLMS ... on such an uncertain thing as wealth, —TCNT.
**but in the living God, who giveth us richly all things to enjoy:** ... who richly and ceaselessly provides us with everything for our enjoyment, —WLMS ... who provides all things in abundance, —CNFT ... richly for our use, —MNTG.

**6:17.** If verses 11-16 are considered as parenthetic, the link can be seen between those who wish to be rich (verses 9, 10) and those who are rich (verses 17-19). Paul instructed Timothy to command the rich to avoid arrogance and a false trust ("hope") in perishable wealth. The words "in this world" contrast with "the time to come" in verse 19.

The rich are "to put their hope in God, who richly provides us with everything for our enjoyment" (NIV). In an age of rampant materialism (Paul's day and the present), the reminder of the uncertainty of riches may fall on deaf ears. But those who are wise will put their hope in God; those who are foolish will trust in this world's "uncertain riches."

**18. That they do good, that they be rich in good works:** ... Charge them to practise benevolence, —MNTG.
**ready to distribute, willing to communicate:** ... to be open-handed, —TCNT ... and generous-hearted, —WLMS ... to give generously, —NORL ... to be generous givers, —BRKL ... They must be generous and want to share, —SEB ... and willing to share, —NIV ... to be liberal in giving, glad for fellowship, —KLGS.

**6:18.** In this verse Paul gave Timothy several positive and practical demands for the rich to consider. Primarily, these are goodness and generosity. The words "be rich" mean "liberal." "Ready to distribute" means "generous." "Willing to communicate" means "willing to share."

So the charge to the rich involves at least three demands: (1) acquiring a sensitivity to the needs of others; (2) doing good works toward others; and (3) being generous and willing to share. This is difficult for many wealthy persons to follow. The danger of riches is that they blind the owner to the realities of life. The rich person is often unaware of those who are poor and destitute. He must be "charged" to do these things (verse 17).

**19.** **Laying up in store for themselves:** . . . laying up a reserve, *—KLGS.*

**a good foundation against the time to come:** . . . a sound foundation for the future, *—BRKL.*

**that they may lay hold on eternal life:** . . . Then they will have the only true life! *—NLTG.*

**6:19.** When the rich do the good works of verse 18, they are "laying up in store for themselves a good foundation against the time to come." This is not salvation by works. The rich who are addressed in verses 17-19 are Christians—they are already saved. So their good works provide treasure in heaven (compare Matthew 6:20). The words "time to come" refer to the future world; see the contrast of verse 17, "in this world." The words "eternal life" (*tēs aiōniou zōēs*) may be translated "life which is life indeed." The same expression is found in verse 12. This underscores the contrast of true life to an uncertain life wholly supported by earthly riches.

So Paul's instructions to Timothy regarding those who are rich are clear: they are to avoid the attitudes of arrogance and selfishness and to do good works and share their wealth with others. By doing these things the rich will.be laying a foundation for the future and an assurance for the life to come. They do not do these things to buy their way into heaven, however. They demonstrate their love for the Lord and their fellow human beings by using their wealth in ministry to others (compare Luke 12:15; 1 John 3:17).

**20.** **O Timothy, keep that which is committed to thy trust:** . . . guard what you were given I *—SEB* . . . guard the deposit in your trust, *—KLGS.*

**avoiding profane and vain babblings:** . . . Shun, *—MNTG* . . . Turn your back on, *—TCNT* . . . from the irreligious and empty discussions, *—BRKL.*

**and oppositions of science falsely so called:** . . . futile phrases and contradictions of, *—WLMS* . . . and the contradictions of so-called

knowledge, *—CNFT* . . . of falsely named knowledge, *—KLGS.*

**21.** **Which some professing:**

**have erred concerning the faith:** . . . Have erred from, *—MRDK* . . . have missed the mark, *—RTHM* . . . as regards the faith, *—NORL* . . . Have gone astray from, *—PNT* . . . Have deviated from, *—PNIN* . . . gone altogether astray, *—TCNT* . . . have fallen away from, *—CNFT* . . . but they have strayed away from the faith, *—SEB* . . . have missed the target of the faith, *—ADAM* . . . and have lost their faith, *—BECK* . . . have failed in the faith, *—WLMS.*

**Grace be with thee. Amen:** . . . May you have God's loving favor, *—NLTG* . . . Favour with you, *—RTHM* . . . God's love be with you all! *—BECK* . . . Spiritual blessing be with you all, *—WLMS.*

**6:20, 21.** In Paul's final words to Timothy in this first letter, no new note is struck. He repeated a challenge and a caution that have already filled the letter. But the words selected by the Spirit are significant. First, Paul called Timothy by name. *Timothy* is from two words: *timaō* = "to honor," and *theos* = "God." Literally this means "he who honors God."

Second, Timothy was to keep ("guard," see verse 14) what has been committed ("entrusted") to his trust (*parakatathēkē*, literally "deposit"). *Deposit* is the word for money deposited with a banker or a friend. When demanded, the entire sum is to be returned. The word *parakatathēkē* is used only here and in 2 Timothy 1:12, 14. A free translation of this clause might be, "Guard the deposit of the gospel that is committed to you."

Third, Timothy was to avoid "profane and vain babblings" ("godless, empty talk," cf. 1 Timothy 1:4; 4:7; 2 Timothy 2:16), "oppositions" ("objections, contradictions, word battles"), and "science falsely so called" ("science" here is the word *gnōsis* which means "knowledge"). Very likely this is a reference to an early form of gnosticism, a heresy of the Second Century that taught salvation through knowledge. The word translated "oppositions" is *antithesis*. Two possible meanings have been offered: (1) "controversies" and (2) "rival theses, opposing tenets," i.e., opposite views of an argument.

Those who have adhered to the above have "erred" ("missed the mark, wandered away," translated "swerved" in 1:6) from the Faith.

The Greek for "with thee" is singular. However, it is likely that Paul expected Timothy to share this letter and that it would be read to the entire Ephesian congregation, which could have been several churches.

# 2 TIMOTHY

## Overview

Imprisoned in Rome for the second time, the apostle Paul wrote a second epistle to Timothy, his friend and coworker. It is the most personal of all of Paul's letters. Despite its warm personal nature, the letter is also an apostolic "handing over" of the gospel into the care and supervision of Timothy, Paul's spiritual son and successor.

## Structure

Some of Paul's letters reflect a highly organized structure. This is most clear in Paul's letter to the Romans, which has a very systematic arrangement. Other letters also have a distinct separation between theological teaching and more practical advice. In the Pastoral Epistles (1 and 2 Timothy and Titus) it is difficult to differentiate between the didactic and practical portions of the letters. Doctrine, advice, warnings, and instruction all course in and out of the work. The Pastoral Epistles are furthermore not treatises of some kind, but are genuine letters, characterized by the open sharing of feelings and thoughts.

Nevertheless, they reflect a common theme. Aspects of teaching and revelation are integrated with a logical and orderly presentation. In spite of any digressions or parenthetic statements, the chief lines of thought are clearly traceable.

Second Timothy falls into three sections. The first consists mainly of practical advice and encouragement to Timothy as he carried out his spiritual ministry. The second part addresses Timothy's problem with false teachers. The third contains Paul's words of farewell, the final testimony of that great apostle.

The following outline surveys the letter's general contents:

## I. The Soldier of Jesus Christ (1:3-2:15)

Paul primarily wrote 2 Timothy to encourage his younger friend and coworker to labor fruitfully for the gospel. The epistle repeatedly encourages and challenges to action. This especially characterizes the first part of the letter, which is more personal and pertains to Timothy's ministry and role in the community.

## A. The Completion of the Former Covenant (1:3-5)

It is most remarkable that when Paul encouraged Timothy in his work, he began by reminding him of his spiritual ancestry and heritage. Because of his pious Jewish mother, Timothy shared in the sincere faith of his mother and grandmother (verse 5; cf. Acts 16:1ff.). Paul's, as well as Timothy's, ancestors were among those who in faith awaited the fulfillment of the messianic promises and prophecies (Hebrews 11:13, 39). Thus, Paul could claim that like his "forefathers" before him, he had served God with a clear conscience. He participated in a chain of servants offering holy service to God just as others had before him. This recalls what Jesus said His disciples would do. They would enter into the work of others and reap what others had sown (John 4:36-38). If those living in the time of promise served God faithfully, how much more should those who live in the time of fulfillment be faithful. Timothy was urged to prove himself worthy of the heritage of faith that had been in his family for generations.

## B. The Fulfillment of the New Covenant (1:6-2:13)

The heritage of faith of the old covenant carried over into the new. Gentiles can be "grafted" (Romans 11:17) into the family of God (Ephesians 2:19). There is a transmission of revealed truth, sacred knowledge, and gifts of grace. Timothy had shared in this chain. Through the laying on of the apostle's hands, the "good deposit" (NIV) of the revealed word had been committed to him (1:13, 14). It was his responsibility to hand over that truth to faithful men who would, in turn, instruct others (2:2).

What Timothy received from Paul was heard in the presence of many witnesses. Thus, it was not secret or esoteric knowledge intended for some special group. Christianity knows no special knowledge reserved for some elite few. Neither Jesus (John 18:20, 21) nor His apostles passed on anything other than what they proclaimed in public. It was this "good deposit" (NIV) Timothy was to "guard" (1:14). He was not to bury it (cf. Matthew 25:18). The gospel is not to be hidden, inaccessible, or unusable. As an influential force in the world it must be continually passed on from generation to generation until the end of time. "This is true, apostolic succession" (Lenski).

Timothy was vital to the transmission and administration of the gospel at this point in time. Therefore, he was to "fan into flame" (NIV) his gift of grace (1:6). He was to be strong in the grace that is in Christ (2:1), and he must endure hardship as a good soldier of Jesus Christ (2:3).

## II. The Apostasy (2:14-4:5)

The second section, which is perhaps the heart of the epistle's message, concerns the struggle against heresy, a problem that Paul continually dealt with in his letters. He had written earlier to Timothy warning him of the problem. Now he again broached the topic. First, he mentioned those deceivers who had already assaulted the Church (2:14-26). Second, he warned of future false teachings (3:13), and third, he noted that Scripture and the proclamation of the Word are the two weapons the Church has against such deception (3:14-4:5).

## A. The False Teachings of the Present Age (2:14-26)

The Church has battled false teaching and heresy since its inception. If the "profane and vain babblings" are not resisted by the leadership of the church, they will "eat as doth a canker" and pollute the entire Body (2:16, 17). Timothy was to have nothing to do with false teaching (2:16, 23); he was to give it no place whatsoever.

The second section opens with a solemn charge to Timothy to warn those who are "quarreling about words" (NIV). Such arguments do not benefit anyone and, in fact, only lead to further ungodliness (2:14). The apostle was not forbidding doctrinal discussions; neither was he ordering Timothy not to denounce false teaching. On the contrary, Paul was urging him to take action, to warn the false teachers to cease their useless "fighting over words" (logomachein). The prohibition is applied to those who encourage and propagate error. This is clear in light of 1 Timothy 6:3-5, which uses the same Greek word for "quarreling about words" (cf. verse 4). Timothy was to avoid disputes over fanciful Jewish legends, genealogical records, and philosophy. Such debate serves no purpose except to promote controversy and strife. A servant of the Lord is not to wage warfare in this manner (2:23, 24). And even when he defends the truth, he is to remain gentle. With humility and gentleness, he is to instruct his opponents. Only in this way will he have a chance to convert his challengers to Christ (2:25, 26).

Timothy was told to warn and instruct those flirting with false teaching, but only to a point. If he had warned them twice before and they still refused to listen, he was to sever any ties with them so as to keep himself from being defiled (2 Timothy 2:21; cf. Titus 3:10, 11). He was not to continue arguing with such men or attempt to disprove their silly contrivances (2:23). His duty was to preach "the word of truth" (2:15).

## B. The Apostasy of the End Times (3:1-13)

In spite of the fact that Paul lived during the greatest time of growth the Church has ever known, the Holy Spirit made him aware of the dangers of erroneous doctrines already present. He knew that the heretical inclinations he saw in his own day would only worsen. False teachings would always continue (2:16). The lure of the present age would evolve into the falling away of the last days (cf. 1 Timothy 4:1-3). Enemies of the truth would increase, while morality in general would decline at an alarming rate. The relationship between false doctrine and ethical/moral standards was repeatedly emphasized by Paul. Now he drew a frightening picture of some who would live in the last days. There are striking similarities between the vices listed in 2 Timothy 3:1-5 and the ones in Romans 1:21-32. The difference, however, is alarming and tragic: Whereas in the letter to the Romans Paul referred to the unenlightened ignorance of paganism, he referred here to the logical end of apostasy. This involves persons who sin knowingly against the light.

Even though Paul was confident that the particular false teachers against whom Timothy was struggling would not grow any stronger (3:9), he nevertheless realized that such false doctrines would flourish in the future (3:13). He warned Timothy of a time when people would not endure sound teaching, when they would turn away from what is true to what is false (4:3, 4). If Timothy was to face opposition and persecution, he must realize that everyone wishing to live a godly life in Christ Jesus will be persecuted (3:12). Whatever form enemies of the gospel take, the true Church must always endure their opposition.

## C. The Scripture and Proclamation (3:14-4:5)

Paul warned Timothy not to be carried away by all these false allurements. He was encouraged to stand fast in what he had been taught and in what he was convinced was true, because he knew from whom it had come: the pious and holy men and women whose moral uprightness far exceeded that of the false teachers. And most importantly, he was to remain faithful because of the "holy Scriptures," which he had learned from his childhood, which have the power to make one wise unto salvation through faith in Jesus Christ. All the Holy Scriptures (plural, verse 15), and the entire Scripture (singular, verse 16), was given by the inspiration of God and are "profitable" in the Church.

Timothy was to hold fast to the truth of Scripture for his own sake. But it was also to be his message: "Preach the word," commanded Paul (4:2). While people are still willing to listen, the truth must be proclaimed, because the time is coming when they will turn their ears away (verses 3, 4). Timothy labored under the constraint of time, as the Church has throughout the centuries. The very stubbornness of people to receive the Word will bring the day of grace to its close. The night will come when no one can work (John 9:4). Then the Lord will call His servants home from the harvest fields.

## III. Paul's Farewell Words (4:6-18)

Up to this point the letter has focused on Timothy. The first section encouraged him to be a good soldier of Jesus Christ. The second centered around the struggle Timothy had with the false teachers. But in this third section Paul moved to his own situation. His farewell words gave the letter as a whole a heightened sense of dignity, and they possess the kind of distinctive forcefulness the final words of a remarkable and noble person always have. The farewell words thus became Paul's "last will and testament," not only for Timothy but for the Church throughout the ages. For the final time the apostle to the Gentiles speaks to us.

## A. A Completed Course (4:6-8)

These verses contain one of the most poignant testimonies ever given in the face of death and the grave. Paul realized that his "departure" was drawing near. The Greek term for "departure" originally meant "a release." It was used of "loosening" tent cords when a military troop prepared to move on, or it referred to "hoisting" (i.e., "freeing") the anchor of a ship to get under way.

## 1. Retrospect (4:7)

Facing death, Paul reviewed his service. The unbelief and sin of his past were forgotten, hidden in the immeasurable grace and forgiveness of God. He summarized his pilgrimage as a Christian in three concise statements.

*a. "I have fought a good fight."* Paul's entire life and apostolic ministry were a struggle against the devil and the forces of evil, against blatant enemies and treacherous brethren. But he regarded it as the "good fight," the supreme and most noble struggle a person can undertake. He struggled for the sake of the gospel and for the salvation of men and women everywhere.

*b. "I have finished the course."* Throughout his ministry, in an effort to attain "perfection" and to secure the prize of victory, Paul had pressed toward the goal (Philippians 3:12-14). Now he was about to cross the finish line. He did not slow his pace as he neared the end; neither did he waver at the prospects of entering the judgment hall and the site of sentencing. He was not deterred from finishing the race by any of these (Acts 20:24). From his perspective the race was finished!

*c. "I have kept the faith."* Paul had maintained his personal faith and could joyfully affirm, "I know whom I have believed" (1:12). "Faith" here denotes more than personal faith, however. "Faith" is the essence of the truth of the gospel, the valuable "deposit" which had been entrusted to him and which he had passed on to Timothy in its purest form. This is the same faith once entrusted to the saints (Jude 3).

## 2. A Glimpse of the Goal (4:8)

The Lord, the just Judge, would give the crown of righteousness to His servant. Paul had stood before many judges, and he knew that an unjust judge would now pass the sentence of death on his physical life. But this was not the final word. Paul knew the judgment seat of Christ awaited him; he did not fear the judgment of men (1 Corinthians 4:3-5; 2 Corinthians 5:10). The judgment of Christ held no fear for Paul, for throughout his earthly pilgrimage he had kept the Faith. He was assured of reward; there would be no injustice in the Lord's judgment. But Paul knew others would share in the reward: "Not to me only," he wrote, "but unto all them also that love his appearing."

## B. Paul's Loneliness (4:9-13)

Despite the triumph of faith and the confidence of hope expressed by Paul, he was nonetheless tired and lonely. Just as he had spoken openly about his faith and confidence, so now he spoke frankly about his loneliness and hardship. He reflected no "otherworldly" attitude where his circumstances were concerned; unlike the fanatic, his feet were firmly planted on the ground. Thus, he was deeply grieved that so many had deserted him in his time of need. So many stalwarts of the Faith have shared in similar circumstances.

Paul had sent some of his coworkers on new missions. Others left for their own reasons. Perhaps most troubling was that Demas deserted him for the sake of the world which he loved. Luke alone remained. Now, one final time before he died, Paul wanted to see his spiritual son in the Faith. "Timothy, come soon," he pleaded. "Come before winter." Mark, once rejected by Paul as a coworker, was now welcome, having regained Paul's confidence (Colossians 4:10). Paul needed his scrolls and a cloak which he had left at Troas, the scrolls perhaps for his trial and his cloak for winter. This request places a stamp of authenticity on the letter. What pseudepigrapher would have thought of mentioning something so ordinary in a letter he hoped to pass off as sacred?

## C. The First Defense (4:14-18)

Paul had already faced trial when he wrote this last letter. He was at this point neither condemned nor acquitted. The trial had been postponed indefinitely, but there was every reason to believe it would continue. Paul did not doubt the outcome.

The New Testament's records of Paul (Acts 28) close with him being under house arrest at Rome, waiting for his case to be heard by the emperor, which was his right as a Roman citizen. After this there is no completely reliable information as to what happened. Many answers are offered, each having some degree of possibility, some more than others. There seem to be four basic possibilities:

(1) Paul was condemned and executed after being imprisoned in Rome for 2 years. This is perhaps the first impression one receives from comparing Acts with the Pauline letters. Against this argument is that such a scenario does not allow for any other visits to Asia Minor or Crete as the Pastoral Epistles imply took place. However, a question should be raised here: Can the brief records of the journeys of Paul recorded in Acts positively exclude an earlier dating of the Pastorals? The letters to the Corinthians contain evidence of travels not mentioned in Acts; why shouldn't the Pastoral Epistles reflect a similar condition? This possibility is not as easily dismissed as some would contend.

Related to this, the farewell address of the apostle to the elders in Ephesus (Acts 20:16-38) should be mentioned. Paul stated here, not as idle conjecture but with the confidence of a divine revelation, that he would not see them again (Acts 20:25; cf. Acts 20:38). He also described what would take place after his death (Acts 20:29), and his words implied again that this was more than idle speculation; it was revealed prophetic knowledge. Paul showed no intention of returning to Ephesus or of taking up any work in the eastern part of the Roman Empire (cf. Romans 15:23). He planned to go to Jerusalem (Acts 20:22), then to Rome and Spain (Romans 15:25, 28).

(2) The second possibility of Paul's situation in Rome is that after 2 years of relatively relaxed custody (house arrest), he was transferred to harsher conditions. After a time he was then sentenced to be executed (P. N. Harrison). From 2 Timothy 1:16-18 it appears that Paul no longer enjoyed the privilege of house arrest that Acts 28:16 reflects.

(3) A third possibility is that Paul was exiled from Rome. This view finds support in 1 Clement which mentions that Paul endured exile among other hardships (1 Clement 5:6). This theory opens some attractive prospects. Just as Paul's desire to visit Rome was fulfilled when he was sent there as a prisoner, it is possible that his plans to visit the south of Spain were realized when he was sent there in exile (J. J. Gunther). Such an outcome of his trial is not impossible. Apollonius of Tyana, for example, was exiled to Spain. The emperor's court may have found it expedient to forbid Paul from returning to his former labors in Jerusalem, where his presence often resulted in disturbances. Thus, they sent him to Spain where he would not be such a threat to "law and order."

(4) The most common view held is that Paul was released from his first imprisonment in Rome, perhaps after a sentence of acquittal or perhaps because his Jewish accusers did not appear within the length of time prescribed by Roman law. Paul may have then voluntarily fulfilled his desire to preach the gospel in Spain. This follows Ancient Church tradition, which claims that after his acquittal Paul visited other regions of the empire.

Numerous Scriptures can be appealed to as supporting this view. For example, Philippians, which was written while Paul was imprisoned in Rome, indicates that he was expecting to be released soon and to go to Philippi (Philippians 2:24). To Philemon he wrote: "But withal prepare me also a lodging: for I trust that through your prayers I shall be given unto you" (Philemon 22). Other facts imply that Paul traveled later to Rome, shortly before writing 2 Timothy. For example, in 4:20, Paul wrote, "Erastus abode at Corinth." This cannot refer to Paul's having left Erastus while he traveled to Jerusalem, for on that journey Timothy accompanied him and would have already known this (cf. Acts 20:4, 5). The same reasoning applies to the comment, "Trophimus have I left at Miletus sick." When Paul was sent as a prisoner to Rome, the ship did not stop at either Corinth or Miletus. If Paul did not make a later trip to Rome, he was telling Timothy something he already knew, which happened before his journey to Jerusalem. Another factor favoring a later imprisonment is that among others, Mark and Timothy were with Paul in Rome when he wrote Colossians (Colossians 1:1; 4:10). Now in

4:11, Paul asked Timothy to come to him and bring Mark along. Jointly these references are strong evidence that Paul was released from his first imprisonment and was in a second imprisonment in Rome when he wrote 2 Timothy.

Whether Paul was exiled or whether he was released after his first imprisonment, it is clear that later he was put in prison again. When he wrote the final letter to Timothy he was under strict confinement and knew the outcome of his case would be death. The "first defense" had occurred, but we are not told who his accusers were. Silence up to this point concerning their identity may be telling. If Jews from Jerusalem had traveled to Rome to testify against Paul, their presence would almost certainly have been noted; but it was not. However, in the immediate context, one "Alexander the coppersmith" is mentioned, which perhaps indicates that he was Paul's accuser and principal opponent. If this is true, it is very easy to see why Paul cautioned Timothy against him.

The charge against Paul appears to have been related to his activity in Asia Minor. He might have been trying to summon witnesses from that region to Rome in order to testify on his behalf. His coworkers could not be witnesses; they would only be considered accomplices. But, testimonies from respected individuals from the churches of Asia Minor might have some effect. But fearing consequences, none of those he called upon came to his defense. They might also have felt Paul's case was so prominent that their testimony would be useless. Paul states: "At my first answer no man stood with me, but all men forsook me" (4:16).

The statement in 1:15 that "all they which are in Asia be turned away from me" may be an allusion that at least some lacked sympathy for Paul's case. Some may have viewed his aggressive evangelistic activity as causing unnecessary hostility from opponents. Some may have leveled unjust charges against him, which further undermined his confidence in others. Paul was pained when his friends deserted him, but he forgave them just the same! "I pray God that it may not be laid to their charge" (4:16). He was naturally fully aware of the personal risk they would have had to take to be a witness for his defense.

From Paul's perspective, however, much more was at stake than his personal defense. He viewed his testimony at the trial as *kerygma*, i.e., preaching, proclamation of the gospel (4:17). This testimony thus completed Paul's "course" in this life as far as he was concerned. Death was now welcomed as a benefit and relief (Acts 20:24; Philippians 2:21-24). "The Lord shall deliver me from every evil work, and will preserve me into his heavenly kingdom" (4:18) was his final summation. He ended the letter with salutations similar to those in the other Pastoral Epistles.

The city of Rome contains many reminders of the life and ministry of the apostle Paul. In some ways he left his stamp upon the city at least as much as Peter did.

Near the site of the Roman Forum is a church which covers the traditional location of the Mamertine Prison where Paul was imprisoned before his death. It contains a plaque and a door which pay tribute to the great apostle.

The plaque asserts that both Paul and Peter were incarcerated here and makes an interesting claim. It names 2 guards of the prison, and 47 others who were won to Jesus Christ through the witness of these 2 men. Whether apocryphal or not, we can be sure that these early leaders of the Church improved every opportunity to win men to the cause of the Son of God, whom they loved supremely.

On the other side of the small prison cell is a huge iron door. It is claimed that behind it is a tunnel which terminates at the River Tiber. When prisoners died of natural causes or execution, their bodies were dragged through the tunnel and dumped in the river. If this was indeed the place of Paul's imprisonment, his comment in this epistle carries unusual significance: "God hath not given us the spirit of fear; but of power, and of love, and of a sound mind" (1:7).

The Ostian Gate is the traditional site of Paul's execution. Nearby is one of Rome's seven basilicas, St. Paul Outside the Walls. At the entrance to the church stands a statue of the apostle. Like most of the other statues of him in the city, if not all, he is shown with an upraised sword in one hand, and a scroll under the other arm. Undoubtedly the sculptor meant this to signify Paul's position as the human author of much of the New Testament and to honor him as a champion of the gospel.

Paul has been described as a "Christ-drunk agitator" who, wherever he went, had either a riot or a revival—and sometimes both. It appears accurate to say that aside from Jesus Christ he did more to shape the course of Christianity than any other man.

# The Second Epistle of Paul to Timothy

## Commentary

### Chapter 1

1. **Paul, an apostle of Jesus Christ by the will of God:** ... an ambassador, *—WUST.*
   **according to the promise of life:** ... because God promised life, *—BECK* ... in agreement with, *—ADAM* ... sent forth to proclaim, *—MNTG.*
   **which is in Christ Jesus:** ... that comes through union with, *—WLMS.*

**1:1.** Paul's greeting in this second letter is similar to that of his first epistle to Timothy. Here it is abbreviated and changed slightly (compare 1 Timothy 1:1, 2). It is accepted by most that 2 Timothy was Paul's final epistle, written about A.D. 67. Many see it as Paul's "last will and testament," written from a Roman prison shortly before his death (see the tone in 4:6-8).

As in most of his letters, Paul identified himself as "an apostle of Jesus Christ." "Apostle" means "one sent on a mission, a messenger, envoy." (See comments on 1 Timothy 1:1.) The words "by the will of God" indicate Paul was aware of the divine purpose in his life and ministry. He wrote in a similar manner in several other letters (cf. the first verses of 1 and 2 Corinthians, Ephesians, Colossians; see also Galatians 1:1, 15, 16). "The promise of life" in Jesus is eternal life that comes through faith in Him (cf. Titus 1:1-3).

2. **To Timothy, [my] dearly beloved son:** ... a child beloved, *—CNDT* ... my dear child, *—ADAM* ... my dearly loved child, *—WLMS.*
   **Grace, mercy, [and] peace, from God the Father and Christ Jesus our Lord:** ... give you love, *—BECK* ... spiritual blessing, *—WLMS* ... [tranquilizing] peace, *—WUST.*

**1:2.** Paul's fatherly affection for Timothy is indicated in the words "Timothy, my dearly beloved son" (see comments on 1 Timothy 1:2, compare 1 Corinthians 4:17). *Timothy* means literally "he who honors God." The word "son" is literally "child." Paul and Timothy had a very special relationship.

The greeting of "grace ... and peace" is very common in Paul's letters. Here he added "mercy" as he did in 1 Timothy; these are the only two times this word is appended to a greeting. "Peace" is a common Hebrew greeting (Hebrew, *shalōm*). But those who used it in the Christian context

meant more than a common greeting like "hello." When Jesus used this term in John 14:27 He meant the total well-being and inner rest of spirit that comes from fellowship with God.

3. **I thank God:** ... I feel grateful, *—BRKL* ... I constantly have a spirit of thanksgiving to God, *—WUST.*
   **whom I serve from [my] forefathers with pure conscience:** ... to whom I am rendering sacred service from the time of my forebears, *—WUST* ... whom I worship, *—WLMS* ... as my fathers did, *—MNTG* ... to Whom I give the service of worship as my forefathers did with a clean, *—ADAM* ... as my ancestors did, *—TCNT* ... with a clear conscience, *—SEB* *—KLGS.*
   **that without ceasing I have remembrance of thee:** ... as I ceaselessly remember you, *—WLMS* ... remember you ... as I never fail to do, *—BECK* ... as unceasingly I have you in my mind ... for needs, *—WUST* ... remember you regularly, *—ADAM.*
   **in my prayers night and day:** ... in my requests, *—ADAM* ... in my petitions. *—WUST.*

**1:3.** As in many of his letters, Paul began by thanking God. Then he wrote that he served God "as my forefathers did" (NIV). Paul cherished his Jewish heritage and later reminded Timothy of his own (1:5; 3:15).

Paul served God "with (a) pure (clear) conscience" (compare 1 Timothy 1:5). He had no ulterior motives; his mind and heart were untainted. The words "without ceasing" connect with "remembrance of thee in my prayers" but not with "night and day." The meaning is: "Whenever (or 'as often as') I remember you in my prayers, I give thanks." For similar wordings, see Romans 1:9; Philippians 1:3; Colossians 1:3.

4. **Greatly desiring to see thee, being mindful of thy tears:** ... I yearn to see you, *—BRKL,* *—SEB* ... longing to see you, even as I recall your tears, *NASB* ... When I remember, *—ADAM.*
   **that I may be filled with joy:** ... that I might be perfectly happy, *—BRKL* ... that my happiness may be complete, *—MNTG* ... that I may feel the fullest joy, *—WLMS.*

**1:4.** Many commentators and a few translations connect "night and day" with "greatly desiring to see thee." This seems to be the sense of what Paul was expressing (see 4:9, 21). Note the contrast between "tears" and "joy." Paul remembered the tears Timothy shed at their last parting (possibly when Paul left for Macedonia, 1 Timothy 1:3). But he knew that when they met again his heart would be "filled with joy."

In these expressions—and in this entire letter—we see the personal emotions of the aged apostle Paul. He knew his time on this earth was short. He wrote in affectionate terms with great intensity. In his first letter he addressed Timothy as "my own son in the faith." This reflected the spiritual relationship they had. In this second letter Paul called Timothy "my dearly beloved son." This set the tone for the warmth and affectionate reminiscence that fills the epistle. No other letter of Paul (with perhaps the exception of Philemon) is so personal as 2 Timothy.

**5. When I call to remembrance the unfeigned faith that is in thee:** ...I have been reminded of that sincere faith which is in your heart, —MNTG ...your genuine faith, —KJII ...your unalloyed faith, —BRKL ...your sincere faith, —ADAM.

**which dwelt first in thy grandmother Lois, and thy mother Eunice:** ...a faith that first found a home in the heart of, —WLMS.

**and I am persuaded that in thee also:** ...I am convinced, —TCNT ...I am fully persuaded, —MNTG ...and am sure is in you, —KLGS ...and I am sure that it is in you as well, NASB ...and dwells, I am certain, —CNFT ...dwells in you too, —ADAM.

**1:5.** The thought of verse 4 continues but turns to a new "remembrance" (this term is used three times in verses 3, 5, and 6). The Greek for "call to remembrance" is *hupomnēsin lambanōn*. It literally means "having received a reminder" and suggests that Paul had just received news regarding Timothy.

Paul commended Timothy for his sincere faith (compare 1 Timothy 1:5). According to Guthrie, "Scott supposes that 'faith' here means no more than religious feeling, since no question of sincerity could arise over the inner relation of the soul to God. Yet a profession of such faith could certainly be unreal, and where the sincerity of faith is transparent there is good reason for its special mention. It may be, as White suggests, that Timothy was deficient in other aspects of his conduct, but 'his unfeigned faith made up for much'" (Guthrie, *Tyndale New Testament Commentaries,* 14:124).

This same faith "dwelt" ("lived") in his mother and grandmother. The word "first" (*prōton*) could mean Lois was the first to believe, then her daughter Eunice, then Timothy. Acts 16:1 refers to Timothy's mother as a Jewess who "believed." Timothy's father is called a "Greek," a term used by Jews at that time to mean non-Jew. Nothing is said of his faith. Very possibly he was not a believer. It is clear that Timothy's faith was modeled by his maternal parent and grandparent.

**6. Wherefore I put thee in remembrance:** ...I am reminding you, —SEB, —TCNT ...For this reason let me remind you, —MNTG.

**that thou stir up the gift of God:** ...I remind you to kindle afresh, NASB ...to stir into flame, —TCNT ...I ask you to keep using, —NLTG ...to rekindle the inner fire which God gave you, —NORL ...to keep ever blazing that gift of God, —MNTG ...to rekindle into a flame God's gift, —ADAM ...the fire of the divine gift, —WLMS ...to keep the fire of God's spiritual gift burning, —SEB.

**which is in thee by the putting on of my hands:** ...which came upon you, —WLMS ...when I ordained you, —NORL ...through the laying on of my hands, —MNTG.

**1:6.** The word "wherefore" refers back to "unfeigned faith." Paul's use of the term "remembrance" in this verse is similar to that of 1 Corinthians 4:17. The New International Version gives this sense: "I remind you to fan into flame the gift of God, which is in you through the laying on of my hands." What was the "gift of God" in Timothy? This *charisma* was more than natural ability; it was a special empowering of the Holy Spirit, received at the time of Timothy's ordination (compare 1 Timothy 4:14). Timothy was urged to develop this gift through regular use. He did not need a new gift but was to "rekindle" the gift he already had.

**7. For God hath not given us the spirit of fear:** ...I say this because, —ADAM ...the Spirit that God has given us does not impart, —WLMS ...a cowardly attitude, —SEB ...of fearfulness, —KJII ...of timidity, NASB, —CNDT ...of being afraid, —KLGS.

**but of power, and of love, and of a sound mind:** ...and discipline, NASB ...and self-control, —BRKL, —KLGS, —WLMS ...and of self-government, —CMPB ...and of self-restraint, —ADAM ...and wise discretion, —NORL.

**1:7.** "For" connects this verse with verse 6 and extends the idea of God's gift. The Greek aorist of "hath not given" refers to a specific point in the past. God has not ever given "the spirit of fear" (*deilias*, used only here and meaning "timidity, cowardice"). The general idea could be "lack of confidence" (see 1 Corinthians 16:10, 11). When Paul used the plural "us" he was probably wanting to soften what Timothy could have felt was a personal criticism.

Following this negative reminder, Paul emphasized three qualities for effective service: power, love, and self-control. "Power" can be understood as authority and boldness that come from strength of character. "Love" is the *agapēs* that reaches out toward others in caring and effective ministry. The servant of God must be of "sound mind" ("self-disciplined, self-controlled") to be effective. This is a divinely given self-control. A person must rule himself first, then he will be able and worthy to rule others.

**8. Be not thou therefore ashamed of the testimony of our Lord:**...So then, don't be, —*ADAM*...So you must never be ashamed of, —*WLMS*... to bear witness for our Lord, —*MNTG.*

**nor of me his prisoner:**

**but be thou partaker of the afflictions of the gospel:** ... Nay, join with me in suffering for, —*MNTG*... but suffer for the good news in fellowship with me, —*WLMS*... but rather share with me my suffering for the good news, —*ADAM.*

**according to the power of God:**...as far as God enables you, —*TCNT.*

**1:8.** Although it had not happened yet, Timothy's timidity could have made him ashamed enough to stop testifying for the Lord. Paul added that Timothy might be tempted to be ashamed of Paul as a prisoner. Natural timidity could produce inaction that would be misunderstood as shame. Continued timidity would bring shame. Paul encouraged Timothy to be a "partaker of the afflictions of the gospel." This denoted a readiness to share in the sufferings the gospel might bring (compare 2:3). "According to the power of God" means that sharing in suffering is not done in human strength alone; God's power is always present to encourage and edify.

**9. Who hath saved us:**

**and called [us] with an holy calling:**...the One Who chose us to do His work, —*NLTG.*

**not according to our works:** ... This was not by our efforts, —*SEB* ... not because of our deeds, —*ADAM*...not dealing with us according to our works, —*MNTG.*

**but according to his own purpose and grace:** ... on account of, —*CMPB* ... because of His own design, —*NORL*...unmerited favor, —*WLMS.*

**which was given us in Christ Jesus before the world began:** ... from all eternity, *NASB* ... before this world existed, —*CNFT*...before the beginning of time, —*MNTG.*

**1:9.** The last word in verse 8, "God," is the subject of the next 22 English words. The word "grace" in verse 9 then becomes the subject for the following 22 words. Then "Jesus Christ" (verse 10) becomes the subject for the next 15 words. The final clause of 15 words (verse 11) has Paul ("I") as its subject. Those 110 words from verse 8 through verse 11 are all one sentence in the King James Version. (The Greek text goes on through verse 12 before the thought is concluded.)

The progression of verses 9 and 10 gives the essence of the gospel: believers are saved and called to holiness according to God's purpose and grace given and revealed in Jesus Christ who abolished death and brought life and immortality to light. Some commentators have suggested these verses form the basis of an early liturgical hymn much like that in 1 Timothy 3:16 (compare 2 Timothy 2:11-13).

The Christian's calling is to holiness. First Peter 1:15, 16 also says this same thing. Paul reiterated that "our works" do not save us (see Titus 3:5 where he emphatically stated this truth; compare Ephesians 2:8-10). Salvation and a call to holiness are purely at God's initiative; they are His "purpose and grace . . . given us in Christ Jesus" (see Romans 8:28; 9:11; Ephesians 1:11). This was "before the world began" (literally "before times eternal," compare Titus 1:2).

**10. But is now made manifest by the appearing of our Saviour Jesus Christ:** ... but has only recently been made known through, —*WLMS.*

**who hath abolished death:** ... who truly made death of no effect, —*KJII*... He has destroyed death, —*CNFT* . . . who has, indeed, vanquished death, —*CMPB*...He has made an end of Death, —*TCNT*...has put a stop to the power of death, —*WLMS.*

**and hath brought life and immortality to light:** ... yet illuminates life, —*CNDT*...and incorruption, —*CNFT.*

**through the gospel:**

**1:10.** Paul next moved from the idea of eternity back to time with the words "now made manifest" ("revealed"). The "appearing" (*epiphaneias*) of Christ refers to His first advent. The same word is used in Titus 2:11-13 of His second advent. The Jews used the word *epiphaneias* of God's saving acts during the Maccabean struggles. The Greeks used this word to refer to the coming of the emperor to his throne.

The word "abolished" is from the Greek *katargēsantos* which means "render inoperative." The aorist tense shows a completed action in the past (compare 1 Corinthians 15:26 which refers to a future event). The sense here is that in a onetime act Christ "abolished" death. He "rendered inoperative" the power that had previously held men in its grasp.

Christ "brought" (again the aorist tense) "life and immortality to light." The idea here is that life and immortality had been obscured, hidden. Christ, through His life, death, and resurrection, brought them out where they could be seen. The word "gospel" includes the full revelation of God in Christ.

**915**

**11. Whereunto I am appointed a preacher, and an apostle, and a teacher of the Gentiles:** . . . of which I am appointed a herald, *—CMPB.*

**1:11.** The words in this verse are very similar to those in 1 Timothy 2:7 (see comments there). "Preacher" is *kērux*, "herald," and denotes "one, with authority, who makes a public proclamation." "Apostle" is *apostolos*, "one who is sent; envoy, ambassador." Paul did not speak for himself but for the One who sent him. Paul's authority was not his own. He was a preacher and teacher sent by God.

**12. For the which cause I also suffer these things:** . . . On this account, too, *—BRKL* . . . This is why, *—WLMS.*
**nevertheless I am not ashamed:**
**for I know whom I have believed:** . . . in Whom I have put my trust, *—NLTG* . . . whom I have put my faith, *—TCNT.*
**and am persuaded that he is able to keep:** . . . I am convinced that He is able to guard, *NASB* . . . I am absolutely sure, *—WLMS* . . . has the power to guard, *—KLGS.*
**that which I have committed unto him against that day:** . . . what I have trusted to Him, *—SEB* . . . that which he has put in my care, *—KLGS* . . . entrusted to Him, *—BRKL* . . . my work which I have given back into His care, *—NORL* . . . until the day He comes again, *—NLTG.*

**1:12.** Paul was suffering imprisonment, privation, loneliness (and whatever else is included in "these things") for the sake of the gospel and his commitment to proclaim and teach its truths. He wrote, "I am not ashamed; for I know whom I have believed, and am persuaded." These verbs are significant. The Greek perfect tense of "I have believed" implies a continuing attitude of belief and trust. The present tense of "I am not ashamed" and "am persuaded" ("convinced") agree with "I have committed" to show Paul's present attitude and continuing action.

The Greek word behind "that which I have committed" is *parathēkēn* and equals "my deposit" (so also in verse 14, compare 1 Timothy 6:20). "That day" is the Day of Judgment at Christ's coming (so also in verse 18).

**13. Hold fast the form of sound words:** . . . Retain the standard of, *NASB* . . . Continue to be an example in wholesome instructions, *—WLMS.*
**which thou hast heard of me:** . . . you have heard from me, *—MNTG* . . . learned from me, *—WLMS.*
**in faith and love which is in Christ Jesus:** . . . that come from union with, *—WLMS.*

**1:13.** Verses 13 and 14 comprise a charge to Timothy and extend the thought of Paul's personal commitment (verse 12). Timothy was told

to "hold fast" and "keep." He was to hold fast the "form of sound words." "Form" (*hupotupōsin*) can mean "example" ("pattern" in 1 Timothy 1:16). Paul not only preached the gospel, he also lived it so others might follow him. "Sound" means "health-giving." "Words" means "teaching, doctrine" (compare Titus 1:9) and refers to the gospel in particular.

Timothy was to temper his teaching with "faith and love." It is also possible these words relate to the verb "hold fast"; he was to show a spirit and manner that reflected pure faith and love.

"Faith" includes the ideas of fidelity and hope. "Love" is the Greek *agapē*, a Godlike love that desires the best for others. The words "in Christ Jesus" emphasize union with Christ as needful for the above. Faith and love are not possible apart from Christ. These virtues issue from Him.

**14. That good thing which was committed unto thee keep:** . . . Guard what you were trusted with, *—SEB* . . . guard the good deposit, *—ADAM* . . . Guard the glorious trust, *—MNTG* . . . that precious entrusted deposit, *—BRKL* . . . this fine deposit of truth, *—WLMS* . . . that has been entrusted to you, *—NORL.*
**by the Holy Ghost which dwelleth in us:** . . . by the help of, *—BRKL* . . . by the aid . . . who has His home in our hearts, *—WLMS* . . . that lives in us, *—KLGS* . . . who makes his home in us, *—MNTG.*

**1:14.** "That good thing" means the gospel (compare 1 Timothy 6:20). Timothy was to "keep" ("guard") what had been "committed" (*parakatathēkēn*, again see verse 12) to him. "Keep by the Holy Ghost" implies that without the help of the Holy Spirit it would be impossible for Timothy to guard the deposit of the gospel.

Stanley Horton comments: "We must have a twofold commitment: to Christ and to the gospel. In Paul's commitment to Christ, he put his life and ministry in Christ's hands as a deposit for Christ to guard and keep. . . . The other side of our Christian commitment is the accepting of the gospel as a deposit which we must keep and guard. The very form of the words in which the gospel was originally given is important."

**15. This thou knowest:** . . . You are aware of the fact that, *NASB* . . . You already know that, *—MNTG.*
**that all they which are in Asia be turned away from me:** . . . who are in the province of, *—ADAM* . . . abandoned me, *—SEB* . . . forsook me, *—MNTG.*
**of whom are Phygellus and Hermogenes:** . . . among them, *—MNTG* . . . including, *—ADAM.*

**1:15.** Paul used hyperbole (a deliberate exaggeration) when he said "all" had deserted him. Not all had turned away, but there was a mass exodus and widespread desertion, perhaps led by Phygellus and Hermogenes. Nothing else is known of these two; that they are named suggests they were the leaders of this defection. The "all" may refer to all those who had been asked by the Roman authorities to vouch for Paul and failed to do so. "Asia" refers especially to the Roman province in western Asia Minor comprising Mysia, Lydia, Caria, most of Phrygia, and the islands off the coast.

**16. The Lord give mercy unto the house of Onesiphorus:**
**for he oft refreshed me:** . . . for many a time, —MNTG . . . He came often to comfort me, —NLTG.
**and was not ashamed of my chain:** . . . of my being a prisoner, —BRKL.

**1:16.** There was one who stood by Paul: Onesiphorus ("profitable, help-bringer"). He "oft refreshed" Paul by making personal visits and possibly giving material assistance. He also "was not ashamed" of Paul's imprisonment. Paul prayed that God would give mercy to the household of Onesiphorus (see 1:18).

**17. But, when he was in Rome:** . . . Indeed, when he arrived at Rome, —ADAM . . . when he came to Rome, —MNTG.
**he sought me out very diligently, and found [me]:** . . . But he hunted carefully for me, —KLGS . . . he sought for me, —MNTG . . . he searched and searched until he found me, —SEB . . . and finally found me, —WLMS.

**1:17.** Onesiphorus was commended for specific spiritual and practical ministry to Paul. A native of Ephesus, Onesiphorus traveled to Rome and "sought . . . out (Paul) very diligently." The circumstances of imprisonment in the First Century made it very difficult to locate and provide assistance to political prisoners. Onesiphorus no doubt had to risk his own safety in order to find Paul. Then, to visit him on several occasions would put Onesiphorus' life in jeopardy. But Paul said this Ephesian layman "searched hard for me until he found me" (NIV).

**18. The Lord grant unto him that he may find mercy of the Lord in that day:**
**and in how many things he ministered unto me at Ephesus:** . . . how great were the services, —WLMS . . . how many services, —MNTG . . . he rendered to me, —CMPB.
**thou knowest very well:** . . . you very well know, —WLMS . . . you know best, —KJII . . . you know better than I, —MNTG.

**1:18.** The commendation of Onesiphorus is continued in the context of a brief prayer. This verse repeats verse 16 with an important addition and a significant change. In verse 16 Paul mentioned "the house (household) of Onesiphorus." In verse 18 Paul used the personal pronoun and did not mention the household. Then Paul referred to the Day of Judgment ("in that day"). Comparing the two requests, it seems Paul was concerned with the household in verse 16 and the man in verse 18. Some commentators speculate that Onesiphorus was dead and cite 4:19 as further evidence. They then question whether Paul was praying for the dead in verse 18. There is no evidence at all to support the speculation that Onesiphorus was dead. Verse 18 could very possibly be understood as a spoken desire that Onesiphorus would find God's mercy in the day when all men will need that mercy. It is unwise to build a doctrine of prayer for the dead from a verse that needs 20th Century speculation about the demise of an individual.

Timothy was well aware of the ministry of Onesiphorus at Ephesus. This would have taken place either in Paul's third missionary journey (Acts chapter 19) or his fourth journey that ended with his imprisonment in Rome (1 Timothy 1:3).

## Chapter 2

**1. Thou therefore, my son, be strong:** . . . Do you then, my son, strengthen your heart, —MNTG . . . Accept the strength, my dear son, that comes from, —JB . . . be strengthened in, —CNFT . . . be invigorated, —CNDT.
**in the grace that is in Christ Jesus:** . . . in the favor, —KLGS.

**2:1.** The second chapter opens a new topic that involves personal encouragement to Timothy. He was encouraged to be a good soldier of Christ and to endure hardship (verses 1-13). He was to be an approved workman who correctly handled the Word of God (verses 14-26). "Thou" is emphatic. "Therefore" contrasts Timothy with the "all" (see 1:15) who took part in the defection from Paul. Paul called Timothy "my son," a very personal, affectionate term.

"Be strong" (*endunamou*) is in the present tense and passive voice. These project the meaning "be continually strengthened." "Grace" is qualified by "in Christ Jesus." This grace is divine help freely given to those who do not deserve it. But it is only available in and from Jesus Christ.

**2. And the things mat thou hast heard of me:** . . . The teachings which you, —MNTG.
**among many witnesses:** . . . attested by many witnesses, —MNTG . . . in the presence of many listeners, —TCNT.
**the same commit thou to faithful men:** . . . Pass these things on, —SEB . . . commend to trustworthy men, —CNFT . . . to reliable men, —BRKL . . . reliable people, —JB.
**who shall be able to teach others also:** . . . who shall be competent to teach, —CNDT.

**2:2.** Paul's instruction in this verse was for Timothy to be faithful as a teacher. He was to take the words heard from Paul and "commit" ("entrust") them to "faithful" ("reliable, trustworthy") men. These men were to be true believers who cherished the Christian faith and were full of faith themselves. They would not only be loyal to the gospel but would also become competent teachers who would pass the truth on to others.

**3. Thou therefore endure hardness:** ... Conduct thyself in work as, –CNFT ... Put up with your share of difficulties, –JB ... take your share of hard sufferings, –NORL.
**as a good soldier of Jesus Christ:** ... As a noble soldier, –BRKL ... A soldier on active service, –TCNT.

**2:3.** In verses 3-6 Paul used three illustrations from life to show Timothy the scope of his Christian calling. The first is that of a soldier. The word "hardness" means "hardship." The adjective "good" means "noble, excellent." A soldier is called upon to endure the hardship and rigors of battle. As a good soldier of Jesus Christ, Timothy would suffer hardship—which includes persecutions, misunderstanding, and opposition.

**4. No man that warreth:** ... No enlisted recruit, –BRKL ... No soldier, –SEB.
**entangleth himself with the affairs of [this] life:** ... is involved in, –CNDT ... gets mixed up with the world of business, –SEB ... gets himself mixed up in civilian life, –JB ... with the occupations of this life, –CMPB.
**that he may please him who hath chosen him to be a soldier:** ... to please his commanding officer, –NAB.

**2:4.** The New International Version renders this verse: "No one serving as a soldier gets involved in civilian affairs—he wants to please his commanding officer." The emphasis here is not a renunciation of family, friends, home, business, etc., but a caution against preoccupation with things that entangle. The Greek is *empleketai* (middle voice, "become entangled, involved"), used only here and in 2 Peter 2:20. The caution does not mean the affairs of this life are wrong; they are wrong when they entangle and keep believers from the priority of pleasing God (compare Mark 4:18, 19). Being a soldier demands sacrifice, discipline, obedience, and an uncompromising loyalty.

**5. And if a man also strive for masteries:** ... If someone competes as an athlete, –SEB.
**[yet] is he not crowned, except he strive lawfully:** ... unless he has competed according to the rules, –CNFT ... unless he competes fairly, –BRKL ... unless he has kept all the rules, –JB.

**2:5.** The second illustration is that of an athlete. "Strive for masteries" means "competes as an athlete" (NIV) and reflects what Paul wrote in 1 Corinthians 9:24-27. "Except he strive lawfully" is "unless he competes according to the rules" (NASB). The Greek *nomimōs athlēsē* refers to the professional athlete, not the amateur. Probably Paul was referring to the athlete who participated in the Olympic Games.

In Paul's time the Olympic Games were well known. Athletes trained long and hard. Winners of the various contests became national heroes. If a contestant cheated to gain advantage and was discovered, he was publicly shamed and barred from the games. Each athlete was to adhere strictly to the rules.

**6. The husbandman that laboureth:** ... The toiling farmer, –CNDT.
**must be first partaker of the fruits:** ... must have first share of the produce, –BRKL.

**2:6.** The third illustration is that of a hardworking farmer. "Laboreth" is the Greek verb *kopiōnta* which denotes hard, diligent toil. The farmer works hard because he expects to partake of his crops. He must plant, cultivate, water, weed, and wait. Then, in the time of harvest, he must toil long and hard. But his dedicated effort will be rewarded.

**7. Consider what I say:** ... Reflect on what, –NAB ... Think over what I say, –NORL.
**and the Lord give thee under-standing in all things:**

**2:7.** Paul summarized his three illustrations with a charge to Timothy. "Consider" means "put your mind on" and implies Timothy should grasp the meaning of what has just been said and how it applied to his own ministry. As Timothy did this the Lord would add "understanding" ("insight," i.e., the ability to make right judgments) that was beyond Timothy's human ability.

**8. Remember that Jesus Christ:**
**of the seed of David was raised from the dead:** ... Who was born from the early family of David, –NLTG ... with David as a human ancestor, –NORL.
**according to my gospel:** ... This is the Good News I tell, –SEB ... to the gospel I proclaim, –MNTG.

**2:8.** This verse begins a new thought that focuses on Jesus Christ. "Of the seed of David" points to the humanity of Christ and would thus encourage Timothy to "remember" that Jesus was a man tempted like everyone else (Hebrews 4:15). "Raised from the dead" focuses attention on the deity of Christ and God's power shown in the Resurrection (compare Romans 1:1-4). To Paul the Resurrection is the premier truth of the gospel which he called "my gospel" (compare Romans 2:16; 16:25; 1 Corinthians 15:1).

**9. Wherein I suffer trouble:** . . . I suffer punishment, *—BRKL.*

**as an evil doer, [even] unto bonds:** . . . as a criminal, *—CNFT* . . . as a malefactor, *—CMPB, —MNTG* . . . even to the extent of wearing chains, *—WLMS* . . . even to shackles, *—BRKL.*

**but the word of God is not bound:** . . . But God's message is no prisoner, *—MNTG* . . . but they cannot chain up God's news, *—JB* . . . But, God's message has not been confined, *—SEB* . . . is not chained, *—NLTG.*

**2:9.** The word "wherein" refers to the last word in verse 8: "gospel." Paul was in trouble and chains for preaching the gospel. "Evildoer" means a common criminal. The only other New Testament use of this word is in reference to the two criminals crucified with Jesus (Luke 23:32, 39). There it is translated "malefactors." "Bonds" means "fetters, chains." From his own present suffering and bondage, Paul could exclaim, "But the word of God is not bound!" The sense here is that Paul could still preach in prison, and the gospel was being proclaimed by many others.

**10. Therefore I endure all things:** . . . That is why, *—MNTG.*

**for the elect's sakes:** . . . for the sake of the chosen, *—MNTG.*

**that they may also obtain the salvation which is in Christ Jesus with eternal glory:**

**2:10.** "Therefore" means "on this account," i.e., "for the sake of the gospel and its proclamation." Paul endured (compare verse 3) everything "for the elect's sake." "Elect" means "chosen" or "choice." It does not refer to an elite group, but to all those who will yet believe on Christ, i.e., all Christians. The following phrases verify this. Note how the word "salvation" is connected with "in Christ Jesus." He added here the words "with eternal glory." This refers to the final state of salvation.

**11. [It is] a faithful saying:** . . . You can depend on this, *—NAB* . . . It is a trustworthy message, *—BRKL* . . . that you can rely on, *—JB.*

**For if we be dead with [him], we shall also live with [him]:** . . . As we have shared his death, we shall also share his life, *—TCNT.*

**2:11.** Verses 11-13 comprise a "faithful saying" that is considered by most scholars to be lines from an early Christian hymn. Of the five "faithful sayings" in the Pastorals (1 Timothy 1:15; 3:1; 4:9; here; Titus 3:8), this is the longest.

"If we be dead" is the Greek aorist tense that refers to a specific act in the past and could be rendered "if we died with him." These words could refer either to Christ's death on the cross (we were crucified with Him) or the act of Christian baptism where believers spiritually identify with Christ (see Romans 6:3, 4, 8). Some see in this reference to death and eternal life Paul's expression of his coming martyrdom. This may be possible.

**12. If we suffer, we shall also reign with [him]:** . . . If we hold out to the end, *—NAB* . . . If we hold firm, *—JB.*

**if we deny [him], he also will deny us:** . . . If we say we do not know Him, *—NLTG* . . . If we say no to him, *—SEB* . . . He will also personally go back, on us, *—BRKL* . . . he, too, will disown us, *—TCNT.*

**2:12.** "If we suffer" is better rendered "if we endure." The same Greek word is translated "endure" in verse 10. Here the verb is in the Greek present tense which indicates a sustained activity. Suffering is important, but endurance is more important. Endurance contains the idea of remaining steadfast and faithful when others are giving up.

"If we deny (disown) him" in the Greek suggests a remote possibility rather than a certainty. If we repudiate or disown Christ, He will disown us in the Day of Judgment. These words are reminiscent of Jesus' statement in Matthew 10:32, 33.

**13. If we believe not, [yet] he abideth faithful:** . . . We may be unfaithful, *—JB* . . . If we are not faithful, *—SEB.*

**he cannot deny himself:** . . . for he cannot disown himself, *—CNFT* . . . He cannot play false to Himself, *—BRKL* . . . He cannot go against what He is, *—NLTG* . . . he must remain true to himself, *—SEB.*

**2:13.** The idea of unfaithfulness underscores the first clause. It could be rendered "if we are faithless." This contrasts with God's utter faithfulness. He is trustworthy. He, because of His perfect nature, cannot deny himself.

**14. Of these things put [them] in remembrance:** . . . Remind them of this, *—JB* . . . Recall these things to their minds, *—CNFT.*

**charging [them] before the Lord:**

**that they strive not about words to no profit:** . . . about words for nothing useful, *—CMPB* . . . words that are not important, *—NLTG.*

**[but] to the subverting of the hearers:** . . . leading to the ruin of the listeners, *—CNFT.*

**2:14.** This verse opens a new topic that might be titled "An Approved Workman." It extends to the end of chapter 2. Paul entrusted Timothy to remind and charge others. He was saying, "Don't engage in word fights!" They result in "no profit" and "subverting" ("ruin"; Greek, *katastrophē*, literally, "turning upside down") of the hearers. This is similar to Paul's charge in 1 Timothy 1:3-7 and his description in 1 Timothy 6:4, 5.

**15. Study to show thyself approved unto God:** ... as one who has passed the test, —*SEB.*
**a workman that needeth not to be ashamed: rightly dividing the word of truth:** ... correctly analyzing, —*BRKL* ... as one who is correct in his analysis of, —*NORL* ... accurate in delivering the Message, —*TCNT.*

**2:15.** "Study" here is much broader than the meaning of the word as it relates to book learning. It means "be eager, be zealous, be diligent, make every effort, do your utmost." Timothy was to do his best to "show" (*parastēsai,* "present oneself for service") himself "approved" (*dokimon,* "accepted after testing") unto God.

This presentation to God involves two aspects: (1) a worker who is not ashamed (the Greek word used here has a passive force: "not to be put to shame," cf. Philippians 1:20) and (2) a worker who can rightly divide or correctly handle the truth. "Rightly dividing" (*orthotomounta*) is literally "straight cutting." The possible metaphor behind this phrase is the farmer who plows a straight furrow or the road builder who cuts a road across country in a straight direction. Timothy was to be a person who goes straight ahead, not veering to the right or to the left.

Another meaning is "correctly handling" and refers to Timothy's call to the correct exegesis of God's Word. He must not twist or change the truth. "The word of truth" refers to the "gospel." Paul also used this phrase in Ephesians 1:13 and Colossians 1:5.

**16. But shun profane [and] vain babblings:** ... Avoid worldly, idle talk, —*NAB* ... Have nothing to do with pointless philosophical discussions, —*JB* ... Stay away from unholy stories and empty talk, —*SEB.*
**for they will increase unto more ungodliness:** ... for they contribute much to, —*CNFT.*

**2:16.** Paul warned Timothy to shun godless chatter and empty sounds. Walter Lock paraphrases this first clause: "But to all these irreligious and frivolous hairsplittings give a wide berth" (*International Critical Commentary, Commentary on the Pastoral Epistles,* p. 97). "Vain babblings" is talk that is void of value and irreverent in substance and spirit.

The "they" in the second clause could have two meanings. It could refer to the profane and vain babblings that lead to increased ungodliness. "They" could also refer to false teachers who go on and on toward ungodliness. The next two verses refer to specific false teachers.

**17. And their word will eat as doth a canker:** ... the influence of their talk will spread like the plague, —*NAB* ... like cancer, —*SEB.*
**of whom is Hymenaeus and Philetus:**

**2:17.** "Their word (the false teachers' words) will eat (Greek, 'find pasture') as doth a canker (gangrene)." The Greek word *gangraina* was a medical term in Paul's day that described a malignant sore that eats away healthy tissue.

Twice Paul named Hymeneus as one who had departed from the truth (see 1 Timothy 1:20; 2 Timothy 2:18). Philetus was also named as a cohort of Hymeneus. Both their names occur separately among those of Caesar's household whose relics have been found in the Columbaria (vaults) at Rome.

**18. Who concerning the truth have erred:** ... missed out on the truth, —*BRKL.*
**saying that the resurrection is past already:** ... has already occurred, —*CNDT* ... already happened, —*CMPB* ... has already taken place, —*TCNT.*
**and overthrow the faith of some:** ... in consequence, they are upsetting, —*NORL* ... and are subverging the faith, —*CNDT* ... are undermining some people's faith, —*WLMS* ... This upsets the faith of some, —*KLGS.*

**2:18.** "Erred" is *ēstochēsan,* "wandered away" (see 1 Timothy 1:6; 6:21). Hymeneus and Philetus were probably teaching that there was no bodily resurrection, but only the spiritual resurrection, which Paul described in Romans 6:1-11. This "spiritualizing" destroyed the faith of some believers because the resurrection is one of the central truths of the gospel. The word "overthrow" can be rendered "overturn, upset, ruin, destroy."

**19. Nevertheless the foundation of God standeth sure:** ... God's solid foundation stone is still in position, —*JB* ... God's solid foundation stands firm, —*SEB* ... the truth of God cannot be changed, —*NLTG* ... still stands unmoved, —*TCNT* ... stands unshaken, —*WLMS.*
**having this seal:** ... bearing this seal, —*CNFT* ... with these inscriptions, —*WLMS* ... and this is the inscription on it, —*JB.*
**The Lord knoweth them that are his:** ... knows who belongs to him, —*SEB.*
**And, Let every one that nameth the name of Christ depart from iniquity:** ... who professes the name of, —*NAB* ... who bears the name of the Lord must abstain from evil, —*WLMS* ... stand aloof from wickedness, —*BRKL* ... quit sinning! —*NORL* ... must turn away from sin! —*NLTG* ... let him step aside from injustice, —*KLGS.*

**2:19.** The word "nevertheless" (*mentoi,* a particle of contrast) is a traditional term. Paul moved from a negative tone in the preceding verses to one of encouragement in the next few verses.

"Foundation" (*themelios*, variously translated "foundation stone, treasure, reserve") could refer to several things: Christ, the apostles, the Church, or the truth. Because of its clear use in Ephesians 2:20 (see verses 19-22 there), the Church seems the best choice (compare 1 Timothy 3:15).

"Seal" is *sphragida*, a term meaning "inscription." It carries the idea of ownership (compare Ephesians 1:13). The presence of God's seal identifies the true Christian. Two quotations from the Old Testament make up this "seal"; the first reflects God's ownership, the second speaks of man's responsibility. "The Lord knoweth them that are his" is a paraphrase of Numbers 16:5. That text comes from the narrative of Korah's rebellion. Moses told the people God would show them who was His and who was not. "Knoweth" means "is intimately acquainted with."

The second quotation, "Let every one that nameth the name of Christ ('the Lord' is found in all the uncials and versions) depart from iniquity," is a reflection of Moses' words in Numbers 16:26—again from the Korah narrative.

Both of these concepts were taught by Jesus (Matthew 7:22, 23; Luke 13:27). They present two principles regarding the Church. First, the Church consists of those who belong to God. Second, the Church consists of those who have departed from unrighteousness.

**20. But in a great house there are not only vessels of gold and of silver:** . . . there are different bowls, *—SEB* . . . articles, *—WLMS.*

**but also of wood and of earth:** . . . and clay, *—NAB, —CNFT* . . . and pottery, *—KLGS.*

**and some to honour, and some to dishonour:** . . . some are kept for special occasions, *—JB* . . . some for noble, some for ignoble uses, *—MNTG* . . . some for lowly uses, *—WLMS.*

**2:20.** In verses 20 and 21 Paul introduced an illustration to show the different functions of people in the Church. The "great house" is the Church and the "vessels of gold and silver" and "of wood and of earth ('clay, earthenware')" are the different kinds of people in the Church. Contrast is a secondary idea here; variety is the primary meaning.

"Some to honor" ("for noble purposes") and "some to dishonor" ("for ignoble purposes") should not be considered parallel to "gold and silver" and "wood and . . . earth." The idea of contrast is primary here and very possibly refers back to the false teachers mentioned above. The focus in this verse is on the cleanliness of each "vessel" (person).

**21. If a man therefore purge himself from these:** . . . will cleanse himself, *—WLMS.*

**he shall be a vessel unto honour:** . . . a distinguished vessel, *—NAB* . . . for honorable uses, *—WLMS.*

**sanctified, and meet for the master's use:** . . . He is special and useful for, *—SEB* . . . consecrated, *—MNTG* . . . and useful to the Lord, *—CNFT* . . . an article serviceable to its owner, *—TCNT* . . . made holy and pleasing to the big boss, *—KLGS.*

**[and] prepared unto every good work:** . . . and kept ready for any good work, *—JB* . . . fit for any good purpose, *—NORL* . . . ready for any good service, *—WLMS.*

**2:21.** "If a man therefore purge (*ekkatharē*, used only here and in 1 Corinthians 5:7) himself from these (probably the false teachings mentioned earlier), he shall be a vessel unto honor ('for noble purposes')." The obvious reference is to Timothy and the false teachers. The application is for all Christians.

Three results are clear: (1) he is "sanctified" ("set apart for a holy purpose"); (2) he is "meet (*euchrēston* ['useful, profitable'], cf. 2 Timothy 4:11; Philemon 11) for the master's use"; and (3) he is "prepared unto every good work" ("ready to do any and every good work"). Readiness is the emphasis in this last clause.

**22. Flee also youthful lusts:** . . . Run away from the evil desires, *—SEB* . . . Flee from the passions of youth, *—MNTG* . . . from the evil impulses of youth, *—WLMS.*

**but follow righteousness, Saith, charity, peace:** . . . Go in pursuit of, *—BRKL* . . . run after, *—MNTG* . . . fasten your attention on, *—JB* . . . ever strive for uprightness, *—WLMS* . . . and pursue integrity, *—NAB.*

**with them that call on the Lord out of a pure heart:** . . . in company with, *—MNTG.*

**2:22.** Here Paul began a direct address to Timothy. To the end of chapter 2, this text includes at least three imperatives: (1) flee youthful lusts (verse 22), (2) avoid arguments (verse 23), and (3) be gentle and teach (verse 24). Warnings as well as exhortations are found in verses 22-26.

"Flee" is *pheuge* ("flee from, avoid, shun"). "Youthful lusts" is variously translated "evil desires of youth" (NIV), "youthful passions" (RSV), or "turbulent desires of youth" (Phillips). Timothy is told to run away from these.

Then Paul commanded Timothy to "follow" (*diōke*, "to pursue without hostility, to follow after") four positive virtues: "righteousness, faith, charity, peace." This repeats what Paul wrote in his first letter (1 Timothy 6:11) with the exception of "peace." "Faith" includes the ideas of integrity, loyalty, reliability, faithfulness, and obedience. "Charity" is the kind of love that seeks the highest good for others. "Peace" denotes a right relationship with God and men. (See 1:2.)

**23. But foolish and unlearned questions avoid:** . . . Avoid these futile and silly speculations, *—JB* . . . Stay away from brainless arguments, *—KLGS* . . . and ignorant controversies, *—CNFT.*

**knowing that they do gender strifes:** . . . they breed quarrels, *—CNFT* . . . they beget contentions, *—CMPB* . . . It can only lead to trouble, *—NLTG.*

**2:23.** Paul cautioned Timothy: "Don't have anything to do with foolish and stupid arguments, because you know they produce quarrels" (NIV). Again, this was not a new instruction (see 1 Timothy 1:4; 4:7; 6:20; 2 Timothy 2:16). Timothy was told to make a conscious effort to sidestep the divisive, unprofitable, foolish, and ignorant questions that "gender (produce, breed) strifes" (*machas*, "quarrels," cf. Titus 3:9 where it refers to legal contentions).

**24. And the servant of the Lord must not strive:** . . . a slave of the Lord must not quarrel, *—WLMS.*

**but be gentle unto all [men]:** . . . on the contrary, to be courteous to every one, *—TCNT.*

**apt to teach, patient:** . . . skilled in teaching, *—BRKL.*

**2:24.** Here Timothy is called "the servant of the Lord" ("the Lord's bondservant"). This term could apply to any Christian (compare 1 Corinthians 7:22), but in this case it specifically refers to Timothy as one called to a special ministry. God's servant (1) "must not strive"—he doesn't get embroiled in quarrels or word battles; (2) must "be gentle" (*ēpion einai*, "kind")—even when he has to point out a fault in another; (3) must be "apt ('able') to teach"—he is skillful in the important position of Christian teacher; (4) must be "patient" (*anexikakon*, "forbearing, bearing evil without resentment," used only here)—he possesses an attitude of patient forbearance toward those who oppose him.

**25. In meekness instructing those that oppose themselves:** . . . He must gently correct people, *—SEB.*

**if God peradventure will give them repentance:** . . . God might grant them, *—WLMS.*

**to the acknowledging of the truth:** . . . that would lead them to a full knowledge of the truth, *—WLMS.*

**2:25.** God's servant (5) must in "meekness" instruct "those that oppose themselves"—the meaning here is a gentleness that corrects others with kindness, self-control, and a humility that is willing to forgive. "Those that oppose themselves" are people who set themselves up as opponents to God's servant by their false teachings and immoral conduct.

**26. And [that] they may recover themselves:** . . . they may come to their senses,

*—BRKL* . . . Then they will wake up and get away from, *—SEB.*

**out of the snare of the devil:**

**who are taken captive by him at his will:** . . . in which they have been caught by him to do his will, *—WLMS.*

**2:26.** The purpose of God's gift of repentance (verse 25) is seen in the words "that they may recover (*ananēpsōsin*, literally, 'that they may return to soberness') themselves out of the snare ('trap') of the devil" (compare 1 Timothy 3:7; 6:9). These people had been "taken captive" (*ezōgrēmenoi*, "to catch alive," used only here and in Luke 5:10) by the devil "to do his will" (NIV, RSV).

## Chapter 3

**1. This know also:** . . . But understand this, *—RSV* . . . You must understand that, *—NLTG.*

**that in the last days perilous times shall come:** . . . dangerous times, *—LILY* . . . there are troublesome times impending, *—BRKL* . . . the times will be dangerous, *—NORL* . . . There will be hard times during, *—SEB.*

**3:1.** The character of men in the last days is the theme of the first nine verses of chapter 3. "The last days" refers not only to the end of the Messianic Age, but to the times in which Paul was living as well. "Perilous" (*chalepoi*, "difficult, terrible, grievous, hard to live in") times were coming.

**2. For men shall be lovers of their own selves:** . . . selfish, *—TCNT.*

**covetous, boasters, proud, blasphemers:** . . . mercenary, *—TCNT* . . . arrogant, abusive, *—RSV.*

**disobedient to parents, unthankful, unholy:** . . . ungrateful, *—LILY, —CNFT* . . . irreverent, *—NORL.*

**3:2.** Verses 2-5 comprise one sentence. Eighteen evil characteristics of men in the last days are listed.

"Lovers of their own selves" (*philautoi*, "self-loving") and "covetous" (*philarguroi*, "lovers of money") are the twin sins from which flow all the others cataloged. The "boasters" and "proud" have similar traits. A boaster (*alazones*) is a braggart. *Alazones* was originally a "quack doctor" who wandered about with medicines and spells, boasting he could cure people. "Proud" is *huperēphanoi*, "to show oneself above," and denotes a person who is haughty, arrogant, and prone to swagger.

"Blasphemers" (*blasphēmoi*) are "evil-speaking, slanderous, abusive" people. They speak disrespectfully of God and their fellowmen. The "disobedient to parents" break the civil and moral laws. To strike one's father was as bad as murder in Roman law. Abusing a parent in the Greek culture caused disinheritance. Jews honored their parents because this is one of the Ten Commandments. The "unthankful" (*acharistoi*, "ungrateful") and the "unholy" (*anosioi*, "offenders of all that is holy") seem to be a pair. The sin of ingratitude often comes from the secular person who is out of fellowship with God.

**3. Without natural affection, trucebreakers, false accusers:** ... implacable, –*RSV* ... pledgebreakers, –*LILY* ... lacking in love for kinsmen, irreconcilable, –*WLMS.*

**incontinent, fierce, despisers of those that are good:** ... profligates, –*RSV* ... brutal, –*BRKL.*

**3:3.** The six sins listed in this verse are those (1) "without natural affection" (*astorgoi*, from *storgē*, "family love"); (2) "trucebreakers" (*aspondoi*, from *spondai*, "truce, agreement"); (3) "false accusers" (*diaboloi*, "slanderers"); (4) "incontinent" (*akrateis*, "without self-control"); (5) "fierce" (*anēmeroi*, "brutal, savage"—describes wild beasts); (6) "despisers of those that are good" (*aphilagathoi*, "haters of good"—i.e., all that is good, whether in people or things).

**4. Traitors, heady, high-minded:** ... treacherous, –*CNFT* ... swollen with pride, –*LILY* ... swollen with conceit, –*RSV* ... conceited, –*BRKL.*

**lovers of pleasures more than lovers of God:** ... pleasure-loving, –*BRKL.*

**3:4.** The final four in Paul's catalog of godlessness are (1) "traitors" (*prodotai*, "treacherous"—those in Paul's day who, because of hatred, turned Christians in to the Roman authorities); (2) the "heady" (*propeteis*, "rash, reckless, hasty"); (3) the "high-minded" (*tetuphōmenoi*, "conceited"); and (4) "lovers of pleasures more than lovers of God" (*philēdonoi mallon ē philotheoi*).

**5. Having a form of godliness:** ... They will have a semblance of religion, –*LILY* ... keeping up the forms of, –*WLMS* ... holding the form of religion, –*RSV.*

**but denying the power thereof:** ... but disowning its power, –*CNFT* ... they are strangers to its power, –*BRKL.*

**from such turn away:** ... These, also, shun, –*CNDT* ... Avoid such people, –*WLMS.*

**3:5.** All these people have a "form" (*morphōsin*, "outline, semblance") of godliness, but they deny the power. They go through the motions and maintain all the external forms, but they know nothing of true Christianity as a dynamic power to change lives. Timothy was told to "turn away" from such people.

**6. For of this sort are they which creep into houses:**

**and lead captive silly women:** ... captivate weak-natured women, –*BRKL.*

**laden with sins:**

**led away with divers lusts:** ... controlled by all sorts of impulses, –*BRKL* ... swayed by various impulses, –*RSV* ... by various lusts and gratifications, –*CNDT.*

**3:6.** After describing their character, Paul next warned Timothy about the actions of the "men" just mentioned. "For of this sort" refers to these men. They "creep" (*endunontes*, "worm one's way"—implies devious methods of entry) into houses described in terms of the female occupants. They are described as silly, sinful, and sensual. "Silly women" (*gunaikaria*) means literally "little women" and is a diminutive expressing contempt. It could be translated "weak-willed women, gullible women, foolish women."

These silly women are (1) led "captive" (the same Greek word used to describe prisoners of war), (2) "laden with sins" (the idea here is an acute state of guilt consciousness), and (3) "led away with divers lusts" ("swayed and led away by various evil desires and seductive impulses," *The Amplified Bible*).

**7. Ever learning, and never able to come to the knowledge of the truth:**

**3:7.** A fourth description of these "silly women" is that they are "ever learning, and never able to come to the knowledge of the truth." "Ever learning" does not mean they assimilate what they hear. It might better be translated: "Always listening, but never able to learn or know the truth." This suggests that they only hear the sensational and not the serious or sacred. Possibly they wish to pose as enlightened, learned females. But in truth they are ignorant of the truth.

**8. Now as Jannes and Jambres withstood Moses:** ... set themselves against, –*WUST* ... opposed Moses, –*TCNT.*

**so do these also resist the truth:** ... so also these people oppose the truth, –*ADAM* ... withstand, –*MNTG* ... set themselves against the truth, –*WUST.*

**men of corrupt minds:** ... they are persons with corrupted minds, –*ADAM* ... men of a depraved mind, –*CNDT.*

**reprobate concerning the faith:** ... and worthless in all that concerns **the faith,** –*MNTG* ... disapproved concerning the Faith, –*WUST* ... rejects when it comes to the faith, –*ADAM* ... and counterfeits, –*BRKL* ... They have failed the faith, –*SEB.*

**3:8.** Jannes and Jambres are not mentioned in the Old Testament. But Jewish tradition (Targum of Jonathan) says they were two of the Egyptian magicians who withstood Moses and Aaron when they came to Pharaoh (Exodus 7:10-13). Paul had three things to say about these false teachers who were like Jannes and Jambres: (1) They "resist the truth" (stronger than passive resistance, the Greek means "oppose"). "The truth" is the gospel.

(2) The phrase "men of corrupt minds" indicates depravity and utter corruption, describing those who can no longer understand the truth (compare Romans 1:21, 22; Ephesians 4:17, 18; 1 Timothy 6:5). (3) "Reprobate (*adokimoi*) concerning the faith" means "not standing the test, worthless, base, rejected." The RSV renders these two descriptions as "men of corrupt mind and counterfeit faith."

**9. But they shall proceed no further:** ... They will not, however, make very much progress, –TCNT ... But they will not get on, –MNTG ... they shall make no further progress, –WUST.

**for their folly shall be manifest unto all [men]:** ... their insane folly shall become evident to all, –WUST ... will be as plain to everyone, –ADAM ... will be obvious to all, –LILY, –CNFT ... will be made as openly manifest to all, –MNTG.

**as theirs also was:** ... as was that of, –MNTG.

**3:9.** The NIV translates this verse, "But they will not get very far because, as in the case of those men, their folly will be clear to everyone." Paul used the Old Testament contrast of truth and folly (see especially in Proverbs). Because these men oppose "the truth" and reject "the faith" (verse 8), their end is utter folly which will be evident to everyone. The word "manifest" is *ekdēlos*, "clearly evident, clear, plain." The words "as theirs also was" refer back to Jannes and Jambres (verse 8). Timothy was assured that truth will triumph in the end. The cover-up of sin is unwise. Those who profess to love and serve God but seek to hide their evil desires and sinful actions will suffer shame in the end. If their sin is not exposed in this life, they will face it in the next.

**10. But thou hast fully known:** ... You, in contrast, –ADAM ... But as for you, you were attracted as a disciple to me because of, –WUST ... closely followed, –CNFT ... have followed, –MNTG.

**my doctrine, manner of life, purpose, faith:** ... motive, –CNDT ... my teaching, my conduct, my aims, –MNTG.

**longsuffering, charity, patience:** ... my great concern, –KLGS ... patience, love, endurance, –MNTG.

**3:10.** Verse 10 begins a new section that might be titled "Paul's Final Advice to Timothy." It begins with the example of Paul's own experiences. His testimony would be an encouragement to Timothy who had an inclination toward timidity.

The "but thou" is emphatic and shows the contrast between Timothy and the men Paul had just been writing about. "Thou hast fully known" is the Greek word *parēkolouthēkas* which means

literally "to follow alongside." Here it could be translated "have observed, investigated" (compare Luke 1:3). Paul commended Timothy for his responsive discipleship (compare 1 Timothy 4:6).

Paul then enumerated nine qualities that showed his own experiences. "Doctrine" ("teaching") is first. This is a major theme of both letters to Timothy. "Manner of life" (*agōgē*, "conduct, way of life") denotes Paul's general behavior. "Purpose" is *prothesei* and means "chief aim." "Faith" (*pistei*) is the body of truth that constitutes the gospel. "Longsuffering" is *makrothumia* and denotes "patience," especially patience with people. "Charity" is *agapē*, a love that seeks the best for others. "Patience" is *hupomonē* and is better translated "endurance" or "steadfastness." This is not passive patience but active mastery of the ups and downs of life.

**11. Persecutions, afflictions, which came unto me at Antioch, at Iconium, at Lystra:** ... as well as the persecutions and sufferings which befell me, –MNTG ... the hurts, –KLGS ... and the sufferings that I underwent, –ADAM.

**what persecutions I endured:** ... You know all the persecutions, –MNTG ... what persecutions I went through, –TCNT ... I bore, –ADAM.

**but out of [them] all the Lord delivered me:** ... rescued me, –BRKL.

**3:11.** The list continues with "persecutions" and "afflictions" Paul received in his missionary work in Antioch (Acts 13:50), Iconium (Acts 14:5, 6), and Lystra (Acts 14:19, 20). These three cities in Galatia were visited on Paul's first and second missionary journeys. Lystra was Timothy's hometown (Acts 16:1).

Paul then declared, "But out of them all the Lord delivered (rescued) me." This deliverance included a premature death by stoning (Acts 14:19, 20). These triumphant words reflect the Psalmist's words in Psalm 34:17. Though in prison when he wrote, Paul was constantly aware of the hand of God in his life.

**12. Yea, and all that will live godly in Christ Jesus shall suffer persecution:** ... Yes indeed, –WLMS ... In fact, all who want to, –ADAM ... all who purpose to live a godly life, –MNTG ... will be persecuted, –SEB ... will have plenty of trouble, –KLGS.

**3:12.** Paul now moved from his own experiences to encourage Timothy and all who would read this letter. Paul wrote, "In fact, everyone who wants to live a godly life in Christ Jesus will be persecuted" (NIV). This Biblical principle is found throughout the New Testament (see Matthew 10:22; Acts 14:22; Philippians 1:29; 1 Peter 4:12, 13).

The "all that will" in the King James Version means "all who desire to, all who are so minded or determined." The idea of volitional choice is inherent in the Greek behind this phrase. The words "in Christ Jesus" mean more than "Christian." They stress the mystical union of the believer and Christ.

William Barclay comments: "It is Paul's conviction that the real follower of Christ cannot escape persecution. . . . If anyone proposes to accept a set of standards quite different from the world's, he is bound to encounter trouble. If anyone proposes to introduce into his life a loyalty which surpasses all earthly loyalties, there are bound to be clashes. And that is precisely what Christianity demands that a man should do" (*The Daily Study Bible Series, Letters to Timothy, Titus, and Philemon*, pp. 197, 198).

**13. But evil men and seducers shall wax worse and worse:** . . . wicked men, *—BRKL* . . . and swindlers, *—CNDT* . . . and pretenders, *—NORL* . . . and impostors will go from bad to worse, *—CNFT, —TCNT* . . . will go on to their worst, *—ADAM.*

**deceiving, and being deceived:** . . . deceiving others, and being themselves deceived, *—MNTG* . . . misleading others and misled themselves, *—WLMS.*

**3:13.** Some commentators see verse 13 as the start of a new section. But it seems more of a transitional sentence, linking Paul's experiences with his charge to Timothy that begins in verse 14. The "seducers" (*goētes*, "wizards, wailers") are "imposters" who "wax worse and worse" (*prokopsousin . . . cheiron*, "go from bad to worse"). The literal meaning of "wailers" refers to incantation by howling and implies these seducers/imposters were using black magic. While deceiving others, they deceived themselves.

**14. But continue thou in the things which thou hast learned:** . . . do you hold fast what you have learned, *—MNTG.*

**and hast been assured of:** . . . and are convinced of, *—ADAM* . . . and have held to be true, *—MNTG* . . . and been led to rely upon, *—WLMS.*

**knowing of whom thou hast learned [them]:** . . . You know those from whom you have learned it, *—MNTG.*

**3:14.** In Paul's charge to Timothy, the apostle reminded his son "in the faith" (see 1 Timothy 1:2) of the basics of the Christian faith. These verses (14-17) are key texts of the letter. They could be titled "The Value of the Scriptures." Timothy was told to "continue" ("abide, stay") in what he had learned and had been "assured" ("convinced") of. He knew those who had taught him. The final clause is no doubt a reference not only to Paul

as Timothy's spiritual "father," but to Timothy's mother and grandmother as well.

**15. And that from a child thou hast known the holy scriptures:** . . . from childhood, *—ADAM* . . . from thy infancy, *—CNFT* . . . you are acquainted, *—CNDT* . . . the Sacred Writings, *—TCNT.*

**which are able to make thee wise unto salvation:** . . . which are able to instruct you, *—RSV* . . . to make you wise about salvation, *—ADAM.*

**through faith which is in Christ Jesus:**

**3:15.** "From a child" means "from infancy, from a babe." "The holy Scriptures" refers to the Old Testament and can also be translated "the Sacred Writings." A Jewish boy began to study the Old Testament at the age of 5. Timothy was even younger when his mother Eunice and his grandmother Lois taught him at home (see 1:5). They taught him the Old Testament discipline of obedience to God and pointed him to the coming Messiah. As he responded in faith, Timothy received the salvation God had promised in the Old Testament and provided in the person of His Son Jesus Christ.

The words "able to make thee wise unto salvation" carry the idea of giving the ability to make the choice that results in salvation. "Able" is the present participle that means a permanent, enduring quality.

**16. All scripture [is] given by inspiration of God, and [is] profitable:** . . . Every Scripture, seeing that it is God-breathed, *—MNTG* . . . is breathed out by, *—ADAM* . . . is inspired by, *—NORL* . . . and useful, *—SEB* . . . is valuable for, *—KLGS.*

**for doctrine, for reproof, for correction:** . . . for teaching, *—SEB* . . . for conviction, *—ADAM* . . . for refuting error, for giving guidance, *—TCNT.*

**for instruction in righteousness:** . . . for disciplined training, *—ADAM* . . . for training in doing what is right, *—NORL* . . . for training others in the path of duty, *—TCNT.*

**3:16.** This verse is the "Golden Text" on the inspiration of the Word. "All Scripture" in this context (see verse 15) refers primarily to the Old Testament since much of the New Testament had not been written. Of course, the New Testament also has adequate support for believing it was divinely inspired. The phrase "given by inspiration of God" is one word in the Greek, *theopneustos*, which means "God-breathed." Inspiration was the process used to produce "all Scripture." By the in-breathing of the Holy Spirit, men spoke or wrote the actual words of God (see 2 Peter 1:21).

This inspiration applies only to the original documents we call autographs. Archaeological discoveries have not produced a single autograph. All we have today are copies of those originals.

**925**

Though there are minor differences in these copies, they are in perfect agreement concerning the major doctrines of the Christian faith.

The second half of verse 16 lists four profitable uses of Scripture. (1) "Doctrine" ("teaching") is important to a correct understanding of the truth and the reception of salvation. (2) "Reproof" ("rebuking" or "conviction of sin") from reading or hearing the Word of God is important to conviction, repentance, and confession. (3) "Correction" ("restoration to an upright position or a right state") brings man back to a proper relationship with God. (4) "Instruction ('training, discipline') in righteousness" is profitable because it gives God's view of life's priorities.

17. **That the man of God may be perfect:** ... may himself be complete, —MNTG ... will be right, —SEB.
**thoroughly furnished unto all good works:** ... well-fitted and adequately equipped for, —BRKL ... up to date, —KLGS ... completely fitted for, —CMPB ... fully equipped for, —NORL ... completely equipped for every good work, —MNTG ... fitted out for every good act, —CNDT ... and perfectly equipped for every good action, —TCNT ... for every good task, —ADAM.

**3:17.** All these uses of Scripture have a purpose: "that the man of God may be perfect, thoroughly furnished unto all good works." The word "perfect" means "fit, capable, complete." "Furnished" means "equipped." The result is "all good works."

## Chapter 4

1. **I charge [thee] therefore before God, and the Lord Jesus Christ:** ... I solemnly call on you, —ADAM ... I adjure you in the presence of God, —MNTG.
**who shall judge the quick and the dead:** ... the living, —WLMS.
**at his appearing and his kingdom:**

**4:1.** The central theme of Paul's final charge to Timothy comes into sharp focus at the beginning of chapter 4. Verses 1-5 are a key passage of the entire letter. Though Paul had written some very important words, his "charge" here is direct, brief, and emphatic. "Before God" means "in the presence of God."

When Paul referred to "the Lord Jesus Christ" he added "who shall judge the quick (living) and the dead." This idea of judgment is a primary theme of Paul's preaching and writing (see Acts 17:31; Romans 2:16; 1 Corinthians 4:5). Jesus Christ is the One to whom this judgment is given by the Father. It will happen "at his appearing and (the coming of) his kingdom." "Appearing" is *epiphaneian*, a Greek term used to refer to the Roman emperor's (1) ascension to the throne and

(2) visit to a province or town. In this application, both concepts fit Christ's appearing and kingdom.

2. **Preach the word:** ... Herald the message, —BRKL.
**be instant in season, out of season:** ... be prepared, —NIV ... be earnest, —YNG ... stay at it, —WLMS ... Preach it when it is easy and people want to listen and when it is hard and people do not want to listen, —NLTG ... in good times and bad times, —KLGS.
**reprove, rebuke, exhort:** ... convince, —TCNT.
**with all longsuffering and doctrine:**

**4:2.** Five exhortations in this verse comprise the focus of Paul's charge to Timothy. The aorist tense adds solemnity to the imperatives. Timothy was commanded to "preach the word"; this reference is to the gospel he heard from Paul.

"Be instant in season, out of season" is rendered in the *Amplified Bible,* "Keep your sense of urgency ... , be at hand and ready, whether the opportunity seems to be favorable or unfavorable, whether it is convenient or inconvenient, whether it be welcome or unwelcome." "Instant" is the verb *ephistēthi*, "to stand by, be at hand," i.e., "prepared, ready, urgent."

"Reprove" is the Greek *elenxon*, "correct, convince." Compare 1 Timothy 5:20; Titus 1:13; 2:15 for Paul's other uses of this term. "Rebuke" is *epitimēson*, a term denoting censure. "Exhort" is *parakaleson*, a term that may be translated "exhort" or "encourage" depending on the context. Either meaning may be used here. "Reprove" and "rebuke" are negative terms that denote correction and discipline. "Exhort/encourage" means to bring comfort and edification.

All of these imperatives are to be accompanied by "great patience and careful instruction" (NIV). Here are both the manner ("patience") and the method ("careful instruction") Timothy should use.

3. **For the time will come:** ... For the era will be when, —CNDT ... for there shall be a season, —YNG.
**when they will not endure sound doctrine:** ... when men will not put up with, —NIV ... they will not listen to, —WLMS ... when they will not tolerate wholesome instruction, —BRKL ... will not put up with healthy teaching, —SEB ... wholesome doctrine, —CMPB ... sound teaching, —TCNT.
**but after their own lusts:** ... to gratify their own evil desires, —WLMS.
**shall they heap to themselves teachers:** ... will surround themselves with, —WLMS ... many teachers, —SEB.
**having itching ears:** ... to say what they want to hear, —SEB ... that will tickle their ears, —BRKL ... tickle their itching fancies, —NORL.

**4:3.** Paul warned Timothy of a future time when opposition to the gospel would be flagrant. Men would not "endure (*anexontai*, 'bear with, put up with, have the mind or patience to receive') sound doctrine ('teaching')." Instead, they would "heap" (*episōreusousin*, "heap together, accumulate") teachers who would say things that would tickle their ears. The idea behind "itching ears" is that of entertainment. Such people want their ears tickled with sensational, stimulating oratory. So, opportunistic teachers take advantage of them and tell them what they want to hear.

**4. And they shall turn away [their] ears from the truth:** . . . They will not listen, —*NLTG.*
  **and shall be turned unto fables:** . . . to hear myths, —*BRKL* . . . to fairy stories, —*KLGS.*

**4:4.** Because some would not put up with sound doctrine, they would "turn away their ears from the truth." This suggests a deliberate refusal to hear the truth of the gospel. When they did this, then they would "be turned unto fables." "Turned unto" is from *ektrapēsontai*, a Greek verb that suggests a wandering from the true path without knowing it. "Fables" is *muthoi*, "myths."

**5. But watch thou in all things, endure afflictions:** . . . Use self-control in everything, —*SEB* . . . keep your head in all situations, —*NIV* . . . be always self-controlled, —*MNTG* . . . Face hardships, —*TCNT.*
  **do the work of an evangelist:** . . . do the work of a Missionary, —*TCNT, —MNTG.*
  **make full proof of thy ministry:** . . . Finish your ministry, —*SEB* . . . discharge all the duties of your ministry, —*NIV, —MNTG* . . . fully perform your ministry, —*CMPB* . . . of your Office, —*TCNT.*

**4:5.** Here are found four brief imperatives directed exclusively to Timothy. "Watch" (*nēphe*, "be sober") suggests moral alertness (compare 1 Thessalonians 5:6, 8). The meaning here is that of self-control and self-possession. "Endure afflictions" is similar to Paul's charge in 2:3. "Afflictions" may be translated "hardship, suffering." It is the same word used in 2:3; there it is translated "endure hardness."

"Evangelist" (*euangelistou*, literally, "a messenger of good") denotes a preacher of the gospel. It is used three times in the New Testament: here, Acts 21:8, and Ephesians 4:11. Though Timothy had important administrative duties in Ephesus, he was not to neglect bold, public declaration of the gospel.

"Make full proof (*plērophorēson*) of thy ministry (*diakonian*)" contains the idea of fulfillment. The *Amplified Bible* renders it: "Fully perform all the duties of your ministry."

**6. For I am now ready to be offered:** . . . I for my part am a libation, —*MNTG* . . . I am already being poured out in sacrifice, —*CNFT.*
  **and the time of my departure is at hand:** . . . the time of my release hath arrived, —*YNG* . . . and the time of my unmooring is at hand, —*MNTG.*

**4:6.** Verses 6-8 contain very personal remarks about Paul's view of his "departure" and beyond. Two illustrations show Paul's triumphant view of death. The first is the Old Testament "drink offering" (wine poured around the base of the altar, Numbers 15:1-10). Paul said, "I am now ready to be offered" ("poured out as a libation"). The verb tense indicates the action is already in process.

The second illustration is found in the word "departure." It is the Greek *analuseōs* which literally means "loosing" (as a ship from its moorings or an animal from its yoke) or "dismantling" (as of a tent). The loosing connotes freedom. The dismantling of a tent is reminiscent of the words in 2 Peter 1:14, 15.

**7. I have fought a good fight:** . . . fought in the glorious contest, —*MNTG* . . . the grand fight, —*BRKL.*
  **I have finished [my] course:** . . . I have finished my career, —*CNDT* . . . I have finished the work I was to do, —*NLTG* . . . I have finished the race, —*SEB* . . . I have run the race, —*MNTG.*
  **I have kept the faith:** . . . I have continued faithful, —*CMPB* . . . I have preserved, —*TCNT.*

**4:7.** The three illustrations in this verse relate to the Olympic Games. "I have fought a good fight" (*agōna*, "contest, struggle"). "I have finished my course" (*dromon*, "race"). Notice Paul did not say, "I have won my race." Rather, he said "finished."

Two meanings are possible in the phrase "I have kept the faith." The first is from the games: "I have kept the rules" (compare 2:5). The second is from the business world: "I have kept the conditions of the contract." Paul had "guarded the deposit of Christian truth" (compare 1:14). See *Various Versions* for a fuller meaning.

**8. Henceforth there is laid up for me a crown of righteousness:** . . . At last, —*SEB* . . . there is in store for me, —*NIV* . . . there is reserved, —*KLGS* . . . There is a prize, —*NLTG* . . . the garland of righteousness, —*MNTG.*
  **which the Lord, the righteous judge, shall give me at that day:** . . . will award to me, —*MNTG.*
  **and not to me only:** . . . me alone, —*ADAM.*
  **but unto all them also that love his appearing:** . . . who love His advent, —*CNDT* . . . who have longed for, —*SEB* . . . to all who desire His appearing, —*FNTN.*

**4:8.** "Henceforth (*loipon*, 'already') there is laid up (*apokeitai*, 'reserved, set aside') for me a crown of righteousness ('laurel wreath of honor')." Paul knew he would receive this crown "at that day" (the Day, when Christ will come again). Then he added that "the Lord, the righteous judge," will award a crown to everyone who loves His appearing. The perfect tense suggests they have loved and will continue to love His appearing.

**9. Do thy diligence to come shortly unto me:** . . . Do your best to come to me soon, –ADAM, –WLMS . . . Try to come to me soon, –FNTN . . . Make haste to visit me soon, –BRKL . . . to come to me speedily, –MNTG.

**4:9.** Verse 9 begins a new section that includes personal instructions, greetings, and a final testimony. Paul wanted to see Timothy before he died so he wrote, "Do thy diligence (do your best) to come shortly (quickly) unto me." He repeated this request a little later, implying that inclement weather might prevent Timothy from coming if he did not "come before winter" (verse 21).

**10. For Demas hath forsaken me:** . . . has deserted me, –TCNT, –MNTG . . . abandoned me, –SEB . . . has left me, –FNTN.

**having loved this present world:** . . . for love of, –MNTG . . . loving the present age, –FNTN.

**and is departed unto Thessalonica:** . . . and is gone to, –MNTG . . . and went off to, –ADAM.

**Crescens to Galatia, Titus unto Dalmatia:**

**4:10.** As Paul began his list of coworkers, a blight appears. "Demas hath forsaken (deserted) me, having loved this present world" (aiōna, "age, era, life"). Paul had mentioned Demas twice before. In Philemon 24 Paul called him a "fellow laborer." In Colossians 4:14 Paul merely mentioned Demas' name. And now the apostle called him a deserter. The charge was not that Demas had deserted the Faith or the Church; he had deserted Paul. This suggests Demas left Paul when Paul needed him most.

Crescens had departed to Galatia. Nothing else is mentioned in Scripture regarding Crescens. Galatia was either the northern area of Asia Minor (Gaul) or a Roman province in what is now central Turkey. Titus had been sent to Dalmatia. Titus had earlier been sent as an emissary to Corinth (2 Corinthians 8:16ff.), then was left on the island of Crete (Titus 1:4, 5).

**11. Only Luke is with me:** . . . Luke alone is, –ADAM . . . There is no one but Luke with me, –TCNT . . . is the only one who is now with me, –WLMS.

**Take Mark, and bring him with thee:** . . . Taking up Mark, –FNTN . . . Bring Mark when you come, –NLTG . . . Pick up Mark, –MNTG, –WLMS . . . Get Mark, –ADAM.

**for he is profitable to me for the ministry:** . . . for he is useful tome, –CNFT . . . he is useful for the work, –SEB . . . for he can be of great help to me, –NORL . . . He is a great help, –KLGS . . . he is useful

to me in my ministry, –MNTG . . . useful in serving me, –ADAM.

**4:11.** This verse includes information and instructions concerning two other coworkers. First, Paul wrote, "Only Luke is with me." Paul called Luke "the beloved physician" in Colossians 4:14 and listed Luke among the "fellow laborers" in Philemon 24. (Note that these references are the same as those mentioning Demas.) Possibly Luke stayed with Paul to care for the physical needs of the aged apostle.

"Take Mark, and bring him with thee: for he is profitable (euchrestos, 'helpful, useful') to me for the ministry (diakonian, a term meaning general 'service')." This service could either be in the gospel or to Paul's personal needs. John Mark had earlier deserted Paul and Barnabas (Acts 13:13), but later he proved himself and attended Paul in his first Roman imprisonment (Colossians 4:10; Philemon 24). Now Paul said Mark was useful in service.

**12. And Tychicus have I sent to Ephesus:** . . . I dispatch to, –CNDT.

**4:12.** Tychicus was a trusted emissary who carried at least two other epistles to their destinations. The Epistle to the Ephesians came via Tychicus from an earlier imprisonment of Paul in Rome (see Ephesians 6:21, 22). From that same imprisonment, the Epistle to the Colossians was delivered by Tychicus (see Colossians 4:7, 8). In addition, Tychicus may have brought this letter to Timothy since Paul was sending him to Ephesus. It is also possible that Tychicus delivered Paul's letter to Titus (see Titus 3:12).

This reference to Tychicus' departure for Ephesus may give reason for Paul's request that Mark be brought to Rome. Paul needed Mark to take Tychicus' place. Too, Tychicus could have been sent to replace Timothy in Ephesus.

**13. The cloak that I left at Troas with Carpus:** . . . I left a heavy coat with, –SEB.

**when thou comest, bring [with thee]:**

**and the books, [but] especially the parchments:** . . . and the scrolls, especially the vellums, –CNDT . . . especially the leather scrolls, –SEB.

**4:13.** In this verse Paul referred to personal belongings: his cloak, books, and parchments. The "cloak" (phailonēn) was a large outer garment that was sleeveless and circular in shape with a hole in the middle for the head. It resembled a poncho and extended to the ground. This cloak would help Paul cope with the cold, damp atmosphere of his prison cell.

The "books" (*biblia*, "scrolls") were of papyrus, an inexpensive writing material. The "parchments" (*membranas*) were made from animal skins (vellum). Some commentators speculate that the parchments were Paul's official papers such as his certificate of Roman citizenship. These same commentators also say the parchments could have been copied portions of the Old Testament and that Paul would want the Scriptures with him during the coming winter (verse 21).

Donald Guthrie comments: "It is impossible to say what either the books or the parchments (*membranai*) were, but the latter word suggests documents of some value, since vellum was too expensive to replace the common papyrus for general purposes. . . . But though there can be no more than speculation about their identity, the desire to receive them throws interesting light on Paul's literary pursuits, even while on missionary journeys. It is not impossible, at least, that Paul had in his possession some written account of the Lord's doings and sayings and that he wished to have them to hand (sic) in his present critical situation" (*Tyndale New Testament Commentaries*, 14:173).

**14. Alexander the coppersmith did me much evil:** . . . the metalworker, *—BRKL* . . . did me a great deal of harm, *—NIV* . . . showed much ill-feeling towards me, *—TCNT* . . . hurt me very much, *—SEB*.
**the Lord reward him according to his works:**
**15. Of whom be thou ware also:** . . . Do thou also avoid him, *—CNFT* . . . You, also, must be on your guard against him, *—TCNT*.
**for he hath greatly withstood our words:** . . . for he hath vehemently opposed, *—CNFT* . . . he is violent in his attacks on our teaching, *—NORL* . . . He fought against every word we preached, *—NLTG* . . . He was very much against our teachings, *—SEB*.

**4:14, 15.** Very little is known of the Alexander mentioned here. The name is given in two other references (Acts 19:33; 1 Timothy 1:20). It is uncertain whether these are the same individual. It is not stated what Alexander did to Paul. The only clue is in the words "did me much evil" and "greatly withstood our words." This might mean Alexander had argued with Paul when he sought to teach other Christians. Or it may mean Alexander had testified against Paul at his trial.

Paul said the Lord would "reward" ("repay") Alexander for what he had done. This reflects the Bible's teaching of divine "payment" in passages like Psalm 62:12, Proverbs 24:12, and Romans 12:19. Timothy was told to "be thou ware." The literal meaning is "be on your guard against" or "keep yourself away from" this "coppersmith" ("metalworker") named Alexander.

**16. At my first answer no man stood with me:** . . . At my first trial no one helped me, *—NLTG* . . . no one supported me, *—BRKL*.
**but all [men] forsook me:** . . . but everyone deserted me, *—NIV*.
**[I pray God] that it may not be laid to their charge:** . . . May it not be reckoned against them! *—CNDT* . . . May the Lord not hold this against them! *—SEB*.

**4:16.** "At my first answer" (*apologia*, "defense") probably refers to Paul's preliminary hearing prior to the formal trial. It may have been early in his stay in Rome (Acts 28:30, 31). That "no man stood with" him could be explained by the fact that Roman Christians were not acquainted with Paul's ministry, hence they could not appear as witnesses for the defense. Though "all men forsook" Paul, he did not hold it against them but forgave them. He asked for God's mercy on those who had deserted him. (For further discussion see *Overview*, pp. 574-76.)

**17. Notwithstanding the Lord stood with me, and strengthened me:** . . . the Lord stood at my side, *—NIV*.
**that by me the preaching might be fully known:** . . . the proclamation, *—TCNT*.
**and [that] all the Gentiles might hear:**
**and I was delivered out of the mouth of the lion:** . . . And I was drawn to His side, *—WUST* . . . was freed out of, *—YNG* . . . rescued from the lion's jaws, *—MNTG, —WLMS* . . . from the lion's jaw, *—BRKL* . . . from a lion's mouth, *—FNTN*.

**4:17.** The translation "notwithstanding" may be too strong for the Greek *de*. The normal "but" is probably more accurate: "But the Lord stood with me." "Stood" is from the verb *paristēmi*, "to stand by for help." The Greek verb *enedunamōsen* translated "strengthened" implies the giving of moral courage—in this case to proclaim the gospel in Rome.

Paul expressed his single objective in the words "that by me the preaching might be fully known." The verb *plērophorēthē* means "fully performed." "All the Gentiles" is *panta ta ethnē*, a phrase used in Romans to describe the scope of Paul's apostleship (Romans 1:15) and the extent of the revelation of the mystery of the gospel (Romans 16:26).

"I was delivered" is in the aorist tense which suggests Paul was reflecting on a past event. "Out of the mouth of the lion" adds an expression which was commonly used in Paul's day to express deliverance from extreme danger. Several interpretations have been proposed: (1) Paul was delivered from actual lions in the amphitheater; (2) this may be a metaphoric way for Paul to say his first hearing (verse 16) did not bring a guilty verdict or sentence of death; (3) the "lion" was Nero who could not convict Paul because of lack of evidence; (4) the "lion" was the devil (see 1 Peter 5:8). The first or second explanations seem most plausible.

**18. And the Lord shall deliver me from every evil work:** ... will keep me from every sinful plan they have, *—NLTG* ... will rescue me from every wicked act, *—ADAM* ... The Lord will draw me to himself away from every pernicious work actively opposed to that which is good, *—WUST* ... from all the evil that is done, *—BECK* ... from all the attempts of the wicked, *—FNTN* ... from every evil attack, *—NIV* ... from every wicked scheme, *—NORL* ... from every wicked work, *—WLMS* ... from every evil assault, *—MNTG* ... from every evil deed, *NASB.*

**and will preserve [me] unto his heavenly kingdom:** ... and will keep me safe and sound for, *—WUST* ... and save me to, *—WLMS* ... and will save me and take me to, *—BECK* ... will continue to rescue me from all attempts to do me harm, *—NAB* ... for His celestial kingdom, *—CNDT* ... for His heavenly empire, *—ADAM.*

**to whom [be] glory for ever and ever. Amen:** ... To him be, *—MNTG* ... be honor, *—FNTN* ... forever and forever, *—WUST* ... for the ages of the ages, *—WLSN.*

**4:18.** The future tense of "and the Lord shall deliver me" contrasts with the aorist of verse 17. Whether this future deliverance refers to a physical or spiritual deliverance is uncertain. However, it is probably better to see it as spiritual because of the words that follow. The verb translated "preserve" is *sōsei*, "save." Here it means "keep safe." "Unto" is the Greek *eis*, "into, for." This meaning makes more sense when used with "heavenly kingdom" than a physical meaning would. Paul's salvation would be completed when Christ brought Paul *into* the heavenly kingdom. Deliverance was not to be *from* death but *through* death.

**19. Salute Prisca and Aquila, and the household of Onesiphorus:** ... Greet, *—ADAM, —WUST* ... Give my love to, *—NORL* ... Give my good wishes, *—TCNT* ... Give my greetings to, *—MNTG* ... Remember me to, *—WLMS* ... Regards to, *—FNTN* ... and the family of, *—CMPB, —BECK.*

**4:19.** Paul's final greetings begin here and extend to the end of the letter. He names nine coworkers; some were in Ephesus with Timothy, some were in Rome, and two were elsewhere. First in the list are Prisca (Priscilla) and Aquila. This couple had assisted Paul in Corinth and accompanied him to Ephesus (Acts 18:2, 3, 18, 19). They had instructed Apollos (Acts 18:26) and had risked their lives for Paul (Romans 16:3, 4).

Onesiphorus had found Paul in Rome and "refreshed" him (see comments on 1:16, 17). It is possible that Onesiphorus may have lost his life

for his loyalty and service to Paul. Note the greeting was to Onesiphorus' household, not to the man personally.

**20. Erastus abode at Corinth:** ... Erastus hath stopped at, *—MRDK* ... remained at, *—MNTG* ... stayed in the city of, *—SEB.*

**but Trophimus have I left at Miletum sick:** ... I left behind me, *—MNTG* ... I left in Miletus infirm, *—YNG* ... being infirm, *—CNDT* ... being ill, I left behind, *—WUST.*

**4:20.** Acts 19:22 tells of an Erastus who was sent as an emissary of Paul to Macedonia. Romans 16:23 refers to a church member named Erastus who was city treasurer or director of public works. Although we cannot be certain of the identity of the man named here, Timothy knew him and would be interested in his whereabouts. Trophimus is mentioned in Acts 20:4 and 21:29. Miletus is a seaport on the coast of Asia Minor about 50 miles south of Ephesus.

**21. Do thy diligence to come before winter:** ... If possible, *—KLGS* ... Exert yourselves, *—MRDK* ... Do your best to get here, *—NIV, —WLMS* ... Do your best to come, *—SEB, —WUST* ... Try to come before, *—NLTG, —MNTG, —FNTN* ... Hurry to arrive, *—BRKL* ... Endeavor to come, *—CNDT* ... Hasten to come, *—CNFT* ... Make haste to come, *—CMPB.*

**Eubulus greeteth thee, and Pudens, and Linus, and Claudia:** ... There greet you, *—WUST* ... greets you along with, *—ADAM* ... say hello to you, *—NLTG* ... wishes to be remembered to you, *—WLMS* ... send regards to you, *—FNTN.*

**and all the brethren:** ... all the brotherhood, *—MNTG* ... and all the fellow Christians, *—BECK* ... and all the friends, *—FNTN.*

**4:21.** "Do thy diligence (best) to come before winter" is the second time Paul expressed his desire to see Timothy. The apostle said essentially the same thing in verse 9.

"Before winter" expresses Paul's urgency. Navigation on the Adriatic Sea would cease during the winter months. This fact suggests that Paul may not have expected to live until spring. Paul desperately wanted to see his "dearly beloved son" (1:2); whether he did or not is uncertain.

Paul sent greetings to Timothy from four unknown Christians: Eubulus, Pudens, Linus, and Claudia. Nothing else is known of these four except from tradition.

The name *Eubulus* means "good in counsel." *Pudens* is the Greek name from Latin that means "modest, bashful." He is commemorated in the Byzantine (Greek Orthodox) Church on April 14 and in the Roman Catholic Church on May 19. He has a fanciful and probably fictional connection with Claudia. Irenaeus and Eusebius, Ancient

Church fathers, reported that Linus was the first bishop of Rome (Kelly, p. 6).

*Claudia* is the feminine form of *Claudius.* "By some she is thought to have been the daughter of the British King Cogidunus, and the wife of Pudens (mentioned in the same verse), and sent to Rome to be educated; that there she was the protegee of Pomponia (wife of the late commander in Britain, Aulus Plautius) and became a convert to Christianity. On the other hand, it may be said that this attempt at identification rests on no other foundation than the identity of the names of the parties, which, in the case of names so common as Pudens and Claudia, may be nothing more than a mere accidental coincidence" (*Unger's Bible Dictionary,* "Claudia").

"And all the brethren" shows that Paul held no grudge against any who might have "deserted" him at the time of his first trial. A few sentences earlier he had said, "All men forsook me" (see comments on verse 16). Now he sends their greetings to Timothy.

**22. The Lord Jesus Christ [be] with thy spirit: Grace [be] with you. Amen:** . . . God's love be with you all! —BECK . . . Spiritual blessing be with you all, —WLMS . . . Blessing be with you, —FNTN . . . Favour [be] with you, —RTHM.

**4:22.** The benediction of verse 22 is in two parts. "The Lord Jesus Christ be with thy spirit" was directed personally to Timothy. The word "thy" is singular (compare Philemon 25). But the second part, "Grace be with you," is for all Christians. The word "you" is plural (similar endings are found in Paul's first letter to Timothy and his letter to Titus). This shows the present letter to Timothy was intended for public reading (compare Paul's closing in 2 Thessalonians 3:17, 18).

As Paul began this letter (and all his letters) with the salutation of grace, so he ended this final letter with, "Grace be with you (all). Amen."

# TITUS

## Overview

The Epistle to Titus, together with 1 and 2 Timothy, form the group of letters known since the middle of the 18th Century as the Pastoral Epistles. The name points to the idea that these letters provided detailed guidance for structuring and organizing church leadership. The letters are very closely related both in terms of historical circumstance and literary style.

## Authorship

Like the other two Pastoral Epistles, the letter to Titus claims quite explicitly to have been written by Paul the apostle. This appears expressly in the author's opening salutation (1:1) and finds further support in the personal elements within the letter. No one in the Early Church ever questioned Pauline authorship. It rightfully claims apostolic authority and validity for the entire Church.

The external witnesses to the Pauline authorship of Titus are quite strong. Many writers during the early Christian Era directly or indirectly confirmed its authenticity; for example, 1 Clement (ca. A.D. 96), Justin Martyr (ca. A.D. 155-161), Theophilus from Antioch (ca. A.D. 150-180), and Irenaeus (ca. A.D. 180). In addition, the Muratorian Canon (ca. A.D. 200) confirms the genuineness of the letter and its authority in the Church. That the heretic Marcion did not include any of the three Pastoral Epistles in his collection should not be afforded too much weight. His theology stands in direct opposition to many of the main points of these letters. He, therefore, had reason to reject the Pastorals (he also rejected three of the Gospels).

Serious objections against the letters' claim of authenticity only appeared in modern times. Since the middle of the 19th Century increasingly numerous interpreters reject Pauline authorship. It should be noted here there is agreement the letters stem from the same source. Thus it is impossible to say one epistle is genuine and another not, or vice versa.

The arguments most often used to question the authenticity of the Pastoral Epistles include:

## Personal Data

The letters contain certain personal data (e.g., travels, companions, circumstances) about Paul which do not fit with what is known about Paul from other sources, especially Acts. With respect to Titus, one especially thinks of the missionary efforts on Crete, which the letter presumes Paul

and Titus undertook jointly (1:5). To maintain the authenticity of the letter, therefore, it must be assumed that Paul was released from his incarceration in Rome mentioned in Acts 28. But this is not held to be very likely.

The counterargument: It must be admitted that Paul's personal circumstances described in the Pastorals demand that Paul be free from prison and on some type of journey. Evidence strongly suggests that this is precisely the case. Paul expected the trial of Acts 28 to end in his justification (Philippians 2:24, Philemon 22). Further, it is clear that neither Festus nor Herod Agrippa found any fault in Paul. In their eyes he should have been released. The account of Paul's imprisonment does not leave the reader feeling uncertain about Paul's fate; rather, it gives the impression that there was no real danger at the time. If Paul's trial had resulted in his death, we could expect a report to that effect. In addition, according to the most logical understanding of 1 Clement, Paul did indeed travel to Spain as he had planned (Romans 15:28). Later historical sources testify to this as well.

## Stylistic Reasons

A rather extensive analysis of the language and style of the Pastoral Epistles has been done which uncovers some noteworthy facts: An unusually high number of words not otherwise appearing in the New Testament occur in the Pastorals. Similarly, a significantly high percentage of words occur in the Pastorals which do not appear in the other Pauline writings. Moreover, some of the more characteristic features of Paul are absent in the Pastorals, and there is a remarkable similarity between the writings of the second-century "apostolic fathers" and that of the Pastoral Epistles.

Counterarguments assert that the linguistic analysis of the letters is less than reliable for settling the authorship question. Many factors could explain satisfactorily the linguistic and stylistic differences. Paul certainly was capable of adjusting or altering his style and vocabulary, and the occurrence of atypical Pauline themes could explain the presence of new vocabulary and the absence of old. The similarity between themes in the Pastorals could explain the similarity in language between the apostolic fathers of the early Second Century and the Pastorals. A significant number of the terms otherwise not found in the New Testament do occur in the Septuagint, which Paul used and with which he was certainly familiar. Furthermore, it is noteworthy that many of the linguistic arguments used to reject the Pastorals as authentic could also "prove" inauthentic those Pauline epistles whose authorship is not disputed! If authenticity depended on a percentage of "non-Pauline" words, then Romans could be rejected as Pauline. Also, within the remaining 10 Pauline letters there is an extraordinary number of fundamental Pauline words which are absent in part or in whole.

## Official View and Organization

Another argument against the authenticity of the Pastorals is the alleged presence of the so-called monarchial episcopate, i.e., church government by a single bishop. If this were true, it would suggest a kind of church structure that belongs to a later period. In addition, it is curious that Paul, who is otherwise so flexible on such matters, should be discussing church polity at all.

Counterarguments to this position concede that the monarchial episcopate does appear for the first time in the Second Century. Such a rigid structure first occurs in the writings of Ignatius. But such a later church structure does not necessarily occur in the Pastoral Epistles. Titus 1:5-9 shows clearly there is no precise distinction between an elder (*presbuteros*) (1:5), and a bishop (*episkopos*) (1:7). The terms are freely applied to the same persons. Earlier letters by Paul reflect a similar kind of church structure to that found in the Pastorals. For example, Philippians 1:1 mentions bishops (*episkopois*) as well as deacons (*diakonois*) and suggests Paul's interest in such matters (cf. 1 Corinthians 12 and Acts 14:23). That Christianity should develop in the direction of a leading elder or overseer should not seem strange. After all, James assumed a similar position in the Early Church in Jerusalem (Galatians 2:12). From Revelation 2 and 3, where almost certainly the leader of the church is called an "angel" of the church, the leader represents a special envoy to the church (cf. 1 Timothy 5:17). Thus, it is reasonable to assume that church structure developed rapidly in Paul's lifetime. In fact, even the Qumran writings show that an organized society with structured leadership was extant prior to Paul.

## Heresy Reflects Later Struggles

This position maintains that the heresy of the Pastoral Epistles reflects the more developed, emerging Gnostic systems of the Second Century. Some point especially to the "genealogies" and "myths" (cf. Titus 3:9; 1 Timothy 1:4).

Counterarguments to this position contend that "genealogies" should be understood as a reference to Jewish speculations concerning genealogies of the Old Testament (cf. 1:10). The term *genealogias* (Titus 3:9; cf. 1 Timothy 1:4) never occurs in Gnostic writings in reference to the Gnostic technical term "aeon." Myths (1:14) are distinctly identified

as Jewish myths; neither are these to be regarded as Gnostic speculations of the Second Century.

Conclusion: In spite of the intensive study of the problem regarding authenticity of the Pastorals, no one has proved that Paul could not have written them. The authority of Holy Scripture itself assures us that this will not take place in the future either.

## Date

The letter to Titus was written in the last year of Paul's life, in the period between his release from his 2-year imprisonment in Rome and his final martyrdom in Rome, which Paul himself anticipates in 2 Timothy. His release from prison must have occurred before the fire of Rome (A.D. 64, July 19-27), since after the fire it would have been unlikely that he would be freed. The first confinement took place either in 60-62 or 61-63. It is not clear whether Paul was martyred during the persecution of the fall of A.D. 64, or whether he—as Ancient Church tradition claims—was executed during the last year of Emperor Nero's reign (A.D. 67-68). The best date for the letter, therefore, is probably around A.D. 62 and 67.

## Purpose

The purpose of the letter is to offer guidance for organizing the church and for answering ethical questions. In addition, it serves to exhort Titus to come to Paul in Nicopolis as soon as possible (3:12) and to insure that Zenas and Apollos have what they need for their journey (3:13).

## Outline

I. SALUTATION (1:1-4)

II. DIRECTIVES FOR ELDERS OF THE CHURCH (1:5-9)

    A. Personal Qualifications (1:6-8)

    B. Spiritual Qualifications (1:9)

III. INSTRUCTIONS FOR DEALING WITH FALSE TEACHERS (1:10-16)

IV. ETHICAL INSTRUCTIONS (2:1-10)

V. THE POWER OF GOD'S GRACE TO TEACH (2:11-15)

VI. THE BELIEVER'S RELATIONSHIP WITH AUTHORITIES (3:1, 2)

VII. SALVATION AND REGENERATION PRESUPPOSED IN THE NEW LIFE (3:3-8)

VIII. FURTHER GUIDANCE FOR HANDLING THE FALSE TEACHERS (3:9-11)

IX. PERSONAL REMARKS AND GREETINGS (3:12-15)

## I. Salutation (1:1-4)

The salutation sheds light on Paul's ministry and affords some insight into what Paul's apostleship involved. Paul introduced himself as the "servant of God, and an apostle of Jesus Christ." He used the expression "servant (literally 'slave,' *doulos*) of God" only this one time. In using this epithet he was aligning himself with the prophets and patriarchs of old. In contrast to the false Jewish teachers who have infiltrated the church and who dismiss the truth of the gospel as having nothing to do with the old covenant, Paul considered himself as the final link in the chain of authoritative revelation extending from the Old Testament to the apostles of the Lord in the new covenant.

The goal of ministry (service) is faith and knowledge. Paul's entire efforts aimed toward this goal. He did not merely want to awaken faith in those who had not heard the gospel, he also wanted to strengthen the faith of God's elect.

## II. Directives for Elders of the Church (1:5-9)

The evidence suggests that there is no difference between "elders" (verse 5, *presbuterous*) and "bishops" (verse 7, *episkopon*). When Titus appoints elders, he must realize that not everybody is suited for such a task. Therefore, some guidelines for choosing elders are given.

### A. Personal Qualifications (1:6-8)

The qualifications for eldership take into consideration one's lifestyle. The home life of an aspiring elder is first to be examined. He must be the husband of one wife; his children are to exhibit proper behavior. The Christian home is a reflection of the church. The head of a household is responsible for directing the home and rearing the children. Similarly, those in charge of the church should manifest an exemplary home life before they are even considered fit to be church leaders.

The qualities not proper for a bishop are listed (1:7); such features are not to be part of Christian character. Such characteristics would render a professing Christian's testimony null and void. Titus 1:8 addresses those positive qualities a church leader *is* to have. A spiritual leader must not only impose certain requirements on others, he or she must exemplify proper behavior. First and foremost he must have pledged himself to God.

### B. Spiritual Qualifications (1:9)

Great emphasis is laid upon the fact that leaders hold fast to apostolic teaching. This is the last, and perhaps most important, requirement of a leader. Only when apostolic teaching is rigidly followed can genuine proclamation be assured. By living this way, the leader will be able to carry out two other functions of the bishop role. First, he will be able to bring the Word of God in comfort and admonition in every circumstance of life. Second, he will be able to dispute those who doubt or argue. At stake here is not only human talent, such as el-

oquence; rather, the ultimate issue is insight that is anchored in the Word of God, the foundation of the church.

## III. Instructions for Dealing with the False Teachers (1:10-16)

No one preaching the gospel should be surprised when opposition arises. It is a natural consequence, because the Word of God challenges the thoughts of the natural person (cf. 2 Corinthians 10:4, 5). It happens in Crete, though, that the opposition stems directly from the false teaching. Verse 10 reveals that Jewish Christians are involved, and verse 14 suggests that some have been swayed by certain Jews who directly oppose Christ. In the latter case the opponents are not Jewish Christians, but blatant enemies of the gospel who have turned away from the Faith. They revelled in Jewish legends (verse 14), i.e., legends based in part upon the Bible and in part on imaginative speculation. The result was non-Biblical teachings. From verse 15 we learn that included in these teachings was asceticism (cf. 1 Timothy 4:3). Jewish Christians were affected by such teachings and tried to incorporate them in the church at Crete.

Paul characterizes the teaching of the opponents as "vain talk" (verse 10). Nothing of what they say originates in God. Titus is advised to take two steps: (1) to silence the harmful, destructive talk of the false teachers, for it is more than absurd, it is dangerous. False teaching caused homes to split (cf. Matthew 12:25; contrary to the model in verse 6). (2) The opponents, whose faith was "diseased, sick," were to be "rebuke(d) sharply" (NIV) in an effort to turn them from their error (verse 13).

## IV. Ethical Instructions (2:1-10)

Various groups within the church are given ethical guidelines. Five groups are mentioned in this passage. Paul gives admonitions that will preserve and strengthen the family unit and which will assist it in functioning according to the creative power of God. The admonitions are related to sound doctrine (verse 1) and to the instructive grace of God (verse 10). The dynamic Word of God is active. Paul admonishes his readers to make room for the spiritual power intrinsic in the sound teaching of the gospel.

## V. The Power of God's Grace to Teach (2:11-15)

This section is grammatically linked to the preceding. It reiterates that Paul's admonitions are founded upon and sustained by the Word of God. Christian conduct and Christian doctrine are inseparable, just as fruit cannot exist apart from a tree.

This relationship between behavior and doctrine permeates the entire letter.

The grace of God which brings salvation to all men is the same grace that teaches us to reject ungodliness (verses 11, 12; cf. Colossians 1:6). It saves not on the basis of our works or on the condition that we satisfy some demand. (1) Grace is a continuous process. Our sanctification is not complete, and neither is salvation totally realized in this life. (2) Grace allows us to say *no* to ungodliness and *yes* to godliness. That grace teaches us to say no to the world's values does not imply some kind of ascetic attitude toward life. Instead, it means believers say no to anything, that encourages worshiping the creature more than the Creator. (3) A perspective that recognizes the reality of eternal life is part of the process of the sanctified life and it constantly governs one's motives.

## VI. The Believer's Relationship with Authorities (3:1, 2)

Even though believers are people of hope who live their lives looking to the coming of Christ, they must not neglect their responsibilities in this life. Such an eschatological perspective should, on the contrary, help believers to be faithful to carry out the responsibilities God gives them in this life.

Paul does not particularize the relationship believers are to have with authorities, but he admonishes Titus to warn the church to be subject, i.e., obey the laws of the land, and to be prepared to do any good work.

The advice is more general in verse 2. The important thing is to refrain from a critical and disruptive attitude, and to show instead an attitude of respect, gentleness, and meekness towards all men. The extent to which one yields is without measure ("all gentleness," "all men").

## VII. Salvation and Regeneration Presupposed in the New Life (3:3-8)

This passage reflects the basis and the relevance of the admonition given in verses 1 and 2. The ideas of "formerly" and "now" as well as the inclusive term "we" are typically Pauline (cf. Ephesians 2:3; 5:8). In contrast with the seven attitudes in verses 1 and 2 to which we are now called, verse 3 reminds us of seven conditions under which we were once enslaved. Verses 4-8 contain another aspect of the basis for this caution. God's work of salvation is being disclosed. The ethical implications of that salvation are now made plain.

## VIII. Further Guidance for Handling the False Teachers (3:9-11)

Time and authority must be used wisely. Paul warns Titus not to enter into a disruptive, time-consuming debate over the arguments of the false teachers. He is to use his authority to rebuke and reject them, having first thoroughly warned them of the consequences of their actions.

## IX. Personal Remarks and Greetings (3:12-15)

Obviously Paul needs Titus. But the situation at Crete is so unstable and critical that Titus cannot leave the island now. He must wait until he finds a replacement.

# The Epistle of Paul to Titus

## Commentary

### Chapter 1

**1. Paul, a servant of God:**...a slave of, *—MNTG*...a bondservant of God, *NASB.*

**and an apostle of Jesus Christ:**...but missionary of, *—KLGS.*

**according to the faith of God's elect:**...appointed to strengthen the faith of God's Chosen People, *—TCNT*...to stimulate faith in God's chosen people, *—WLMS*...to promote the faith of God's chosen people, *—ADAM.*

**and the acknowledging of the truth which is after godliness:**...and the full knowledge of the truth that brings about godliness, *—ADAM*...to lead them on to a full knowledge of religious truth, *—WLMS*...which goes with piety, *—MNTG.*

**1:1.** The formal salutation of the letter to Titus is longer than those in the other Pastorals. Beside length, additional significant differences are: (1) Paul called himself a "servant of God"—used only here and not in any of his other letters. (2) The content of this greeting is replete with doctrinal terms. The salutation is contained in the first four verses.

"Servant" is *doulos*, "slave" or "servant." The Greek means (1) "slave"—one who completely belongs to his master with no freedom of his own; or (2) "servant"—one who willingly chooses to serve his master (compare Exodus 21:1-6). Paul was both a "servant of God" and an "apostle of Jesus Christ." The claim to apostleship adds weight to the letter, since an apostle was especially commissioned by Christ.

Three important terms—faith, knowledge, godliness—focus on three practical truths. "Faith" in Scripture means absolute trust in God. Paul wrote of "the faith of God's elect." The elect are believers who make up the Church (compare Romans 8:33; Colossians 3:12). Added to faith is "acknowledging (*epignōsin*, 'knowledge') of the truth." "Godliness" is active reverence toward God. Clearly, faith in God and knowledge of the truth lead to godliness.

**2. In hope of eternal life:**...I write in hope of, *—MNTG*...in expectation of life eonian, *—CNDT*...of everlasting life, *—KLGS.*

**which God, that cannot lie, promised before the world began:**...who never lies, promised before times eternal, *—MNTG*...long ages ago,

*NASB*...before the ages began, *—CNFT*...before time began, *—BRKL, —SEB.*

**1:2.** Another virtue is "hope" (*elpidi*). In the Bible it is firm assurance and expectation, not wishful thinking. Here it is anchored in eternal life promised by God who "cannot lie" (*apseudēs*) (Numbers 23:19; Hebrews 6:18). He stands in strong contrast to the Cretans who were habitual liars (Titus 1:12). "Before the world began" is literally "before time eternal."

**3. But hath in due times manifested his word:**...At the proper time, *—NORL, —WLMS*...it is revealed in its own time, *—KJII*...at the proper season, *—CMPB.*

**through preaching, which is committed unto me:**...in proclaiming which I have been entrusted, *—MNTG*...through the message that I preach, *—WLMS.*

**according to the commandment of God our Saviour:**...by order of,. *—SEB*...according to the injunction of, *—CNDT.*

**1:3.** "Due times" contrasts with "before the world began" in the previous verse. The plural *kairois idiois* could refer to various times or as a collective singular to a particular time (Galatians 4:4). The NIV has "his appointed season."

"His word" is God's authoritative message that centers in Jesus Christ, i.e., the gospel. "Manifested" means "brought to light" and emphasizes the clear proclamation ("preaching") of the gospel. This ministry was "committed" (*episteuthēn*, "to be entrusted with") to Paul (compare Galatians 1:1; 2:7; 1 Timothy 1:11; 2 Timothy 1:11).

Three times in Titus Paul used the phrase "God our Saviour" (here; Titus 2:10; and 3:4; compare 1 Timothy 1:1; 2:3; 4:10).

**4. To Titus, [mine] own son after the common faith:**...his true Child in their one Faith, *—TCNT*...You are my true son, *—NLTG*...genuine child, *—WLMS*...my genuine son, *—CMPB*...my true son in a common faith, *—MNTG*...by the faith we share, *—SEB.*

**Grace, mercy, [and] peace:**...be spiritual blessing, *—WLMS.*

**from God the Father and the Lord Jesus Christ our Saviour:**

**1:4.** Titus was a Greek and a valuable coworker of Paul (see 2 Corinthians 2:12, 13; 7:5, 6; 8:6, 23; 12:18; Galatians 2:1-5). Paul called him his "own" (*gnēsiō*, "genuine, true") son. This word, used also of Timothy (1 Timothy 1:2), suggests Titus was converted under Paul's ministry. "The common faith" is the faith shared by all believers.

**5. For this cause left I thee in Crete:** ...for this reason, —MNTG ...for this express purpose, —WLMS ...The reason why I left you behind, —NORL.

**that thou shouldest set in order the things that are wanting:** ...that you might straighten out unfinished business, —BRKL ...to finish up the thing left undone, —KLGS ...to straighten out things that still needed to be done, —SEB ...anything that is defective, —CNFT ...the things left unfinished, —CMPB.

**and ordain elders in every city:** ...and constitute elders city by city, —CNDT ...and appoint presbyters, —MNTG ...and appoint Officers of the Church in the various towns, —TCNT.

**as I had appointed thee:** ...as I had instructed you, —MNTG ...as I gave you directions, —BRKL.

**1:5.** Paul gave Titus a twofold assignment for his work in Crete. The two had ministered together on the island, then Paul left Titus behind to (1) "set in order the things that are wanting" and (2) "ordain elders in every city."

Crete is a mountainous island southeast of Greece, approximately 160 miles long and 35 miles wide. An immoral, savage people populated numerous coastal cities. The Cretans had a bad reputation throughout the entire Mediterranean world.

The two objectives follow Paul's usual pattern for establishing churches. Perhaps because Paul's visit was brief he had not had time to "set in order (straighten out) the things that are wanting (unfinished, defective)." So Titus was to do what Paul had left undone. Second, Titus was to "ordain (appoint) elders (*presbuterous*) in every city." The term *elder* suggests maturity and experience. It is synonymous with "bishop" (verse 7). Appointing elders was Paul's usual procedure (see Acts 14:23).

**6. If any be blameless:** ...must be above suspicion, —SEB ...of irreproachable character, —TCNT.

**the husband of one wife:**
**having faithful children:** ...having believing children, —KLGS.

**not accused of riot or unruly:** ...not charged with being incorrigible or unruly, —BRKL ...and have never been charged with dissolute or unruly conduct, —TCNT ...of being wild or disobedient, —SEB ...of dissipation or rebellion, NASB ...or insubordination, —MNTG.

**1:6.** Verses 6-9 contain a list of qualifications for elders. It is similar to the list given in 1 Timothy 3:1-7. An elder must be *anenklētos* ("blameless, irreproachable"). (Note this is repeated for the "bishop" in verse 7.) Emphasis is placed on the family life of an elder. This seems to be a prerequisite to becoming a spiritual leader ("overseer") of the church.

"Husband of one wife" (1) assumes the elder is an older man who is married but does not categorically exclude a single man; (2) does not restrict marriage to a second wife if a previous wife is deceased; (3) has the primary meaning of a faithful, monogamous marriage (compare comments on 1 Timothy 3:2).

"Faithful" should be understood as "believing"; i.e., "having believing children." The two negatives here are meaningful because of the lifestyle of Cretans. An elder's children must not be accused of *asōtias* ("debauchery, dissipation, profligacy, wild extravagance"). This term is used in Luke 15:13 of the Prodigal Son. The elder's children must not be *anupotakta* ("unruly, undisciplined, disobedient, rebellious, insubordinate").

**7. For a bishop must be blameless, as the steward of God:** ...a pastor must be above reproach, —WLMS ...must be unimpeachable, —CNDT.

**not selfwilled, not soon angry:** ...not irritable, —CNDT ...nor full of passion, —KJII ...not quick-tempered, NASB.

**not given to wine, no striker, not given to filthy lucre:**

**1:7.** The term "bishop" (synonymous with "elders," verse 5) can be translated "overseer" and suggests responsibility. "Steward of God" conveys the idea of a manager of a household or estate. The overseer or steward of God's "household" (the local church) must not be (1) *authadē* ("overbearing, arrogant"), the idea here is a man of conceit, intolerance, arrogance, stubbornness, and contemptuousness; (2) *orgilon* ("quick-tempered, inclined to anger"); (3) *paroinon* (literally, "given to overindulgence in wine"); (4) *plēktēn* ("not violent, no striker"), not ready to come to blows. (5) *Aischrokerdē* ("fond of dishonest gain") denotes a man who does not care how he gets money so long as he gets it.

**8. But a lover of hospitality, a lover of good men:**

**sober, just, holy, temperate:** ...sensible, NASB, —WLMS ...continent, —CNFT ...self-controlled, —CNDT.

**1:8.** Next Paul lists positive requirements. First, he is to be *philoxenon* (literally, "a lover of strangers," in other words, "hospitable"). Next, he is to be *philagathon* ("a lover of good things" or "a lover of good people"). The Greek word is used only here in the New Testament. Probably the sense is "good things" or "goodness" more than "good men." An elder is to be *sōphrona* ("prudent, thoughtful, self-controlled, sober"). The sense here is the wise control of every thought and instinct.

As to the elder's spiritual requirements, he is to be *dikaion* ("upright, just, righteous"), giving respect to man and reverence to God, as well as *hosion* ("pious, devout, holy").

"Temperate" (*enkratē*) means "disciplined, in full control of oneself." It is similar to "sober" but has the added meaning of possessing inner strength to control one's desires and actions.

**9. Holding fast the faithful word as he hath been taught:** ... who continues to cling to the trustworthy message, *—WLMS* ... clinging to, *—KJII.*

**that he may be able by sound doctrine both to exhort:** ... able to entreat with sound teaching as well as to expose those who contradict, *—CNDT.*

**and to convince the gainsayers:** ... to refute those who contradict, *NASB* ... and to confute opponents, *—CNFT* ... the ones who speak against the truth, *—KJII* ... those who oppose him, *—WLMS.*

**1:9.** The leader (elder, overseer) must hold the "faithful (reliable, sure, trustworthy) word" he has been taught. By "sound doctrine" (occurring eight times in the Pastoral Epistles, it means "correct teaching") he will be able to "exhort" (encourage, edify) and "convince" (refute, convict, point out, rebuke in a convincing way) the "gainsayers" (those who oppose sound doctrine).

**10. For there are many unruly:** ... insubordinate people, *—WLMS.*

**and vain talkers and deceivers:** ... senseless talkers, *—BRKL.*

**specially they of the circumcision:**

**1:10.** Verses 10-16 describe false teachers whose character is totally opposite to that of the elder just described. False teachers were (1) *anupotaktoi* ("unruly, rebellious, insubordinate"). This rebelliousness is against God's Word and God's messengers, specifically those who were troubling Paul and Titus. They were (2) *mataiologoi*— "vain talkers, empty-headed babblers" (compare 1 Timothy 1:6). They were (3) *phrenapatai* ("deceivers, misleaders") who taught things without substance.

Paul then identified them as "of the circumcision." These Judaizers (Galatians 2:12ff.) believed circumcision and the keeping of Jewish ceremonial laws were necessary for salvation. They held to unscriptural Jewish myths (verse 14) and genealogies (Titus 3:9; see 1 Timothy 1:4). They were ascetics with scruples against things God considered good (Titus 1:14, 15; see 1 Timothy 4:3-5).

**11. Whose mouths must be stopped:** ... These ought to be silenced, *—BRKL* ... who must be gagged, *—CNDT.*

**who subvert whole houses:** ... who subvert whole families, *—CMPB* ... They are upsetting entire families, *—SEB.*

**teaching things which they ought not:** ... not to think, *—WLMS.*

**for filthy lucre's sake:** ... on behalf of sordid gain, *—CNDT* ... for the sake of dishonest gain, *—WLMS* ... to make money, *—NLTG.*

**1:11.** Paul wrote Titus that these Judaizers' "mouths must be stopped" (muzzled, silenced, bridled) because they were subverting (ruining, upsetting, overturning) "whole houses" (households, families). They were teaching what was wrong "for filthy lucre's sake"; that is, "for dishonest gain."

**12. One of themselves, [even] a prophet of their own, said:** ... By one of their own number, *—MNTG* ... their own countrymen, *—WLMS.*

**The Cretians [are] alway liars, evil beasts, slow bellies:** ... bad actors, lazy fatties, *—KLGS* ... idle gluttons, *—MNTG* ... lazy gluttons, *NASB, —CNFT* ... but they love to eat, *—SEB.*

**1:12.** Paul quoted Epimenides, a 6th-century, B.C., native of Knossos, Crete, and a philosopher held in high esteem. In Greek literature "to Cretanize" meant to lie and cheat. "Evil beasts" (brutes) suggests the maliciousness attributed to animals. The words "slow bellies" can be translated "lazy gluttons." This describes the Cretan's uncontrolled greed.

**13. This witness is true:** ... This testimony, *—MNTG* ... this opinion of them is true enough, *—NORL* ... this tendency is true, *—WLMS.*

**Wherefore rebuke them sharply:** ... correct them sternly, *—BRKL* ... be exposing them severely, *—CNDT.*

**that they may be sound in the faith:** ... that they may be healthy, *—CMPB.*

**1:13.** With the words "this witness (testimony) is true," Paul gave credence to the words of Epimenides (verse 12). Because Cretans were liars and lazy gluttons, Titus was to "rebuke them sharply." "Rebuke" is from the Greek verb *elenche* which has three basic meanings in the Pastorals: (1) "bring to light, expose, set forth" (Titus 2:15); (2) "convict, convince, point out" (Titus 1:9); and (3) "reprove, correct" (see 1 Timothy 5:20). The second meaning is the sense in this verse.

"Sharply" is the Greek adverb *apotomōs* ("severely, rigorously"). It occurs only here and in 2 Corinthians 13:10. "That they may be sound in the faith" is the purpose and objective of this sharp rebuke. Correction and restoration are the goals Paul set before Titus. "The faith" refers to the doctrine (accepted tenets of faith among the early Christians).

**14. Not giving heed to Jewish fables:**...and may pay no attention to Jewish legends, *–TCNT*...must not hold onto Jewish legends, *–SEB*...and not hang on to Jewish fairy tales, *–KLGS.*
**and commandments of men, that turn from the truth:**...and to injunctions of people who turn their backs on the truth, *–BRKL.*

**1:14.** This verse describes what the Cretan Christians were already doing. It shows the Judaistic influence, first toward fables, then toward asceticism. The Cretans were giving heed to "Jewish fables" (myths). (Compare Titus 3:9; see 1 Timothy 1:4 and comments there.) They were being turned from the truth of the gospel by the "commandments of men." This is reminiscent of the Colossian heresy that Paul addressed in Colossians 2:20-22 and is further delineated in Titus 1:15. The New International Version translates this last clause: "the commands of those who reject the truth." Compare Isaiah's words in Isaiah 29:13 and Jesus' teaching in Mark 7:6-9.

**15. Unto the pure all things [are] pure:**...all meats are pure, *–CMPB.*
**but unto them that are defiled and unbelieving [is] nothing pure:**...but nothing is clean to those, *–SEB.*
**but even their mind and conscience is defiled:**...are polluted, *–CMPB*...are alike filthy, *–TCNT.*

**1:15.** "The pure" (*katharois*, "clean," both ceremonially and morally) refers to believers who are a contrast to the next clause and the term "unbelieving." "Things" does not include actions; Paul was not saying, "Unto the pure all actions are pure." Jesus said, "Behold, all things are clean unto you" (Luke 11:41). Paul repeated this in similar words in Romans 14:20 and taught that God made everything good (1 Timothy 4:4).

But the "defiled and unbelieving" (*apistois*, "faithless") find nothing *katharon* ("pure"). The "unbelieving" could possibly refer to weak Jewish Christians who did not believe Christ abolished the ceremonial law (compare Romans 10:4; Ephesians 2:15; Colossians 2:14). Paul said their minds and consciences were defiled. Defilement begins in the mind and conscience (see Jesus' teaching in Matthew 15:10, 11, 16-20; Mark 7:14-23). The *Living Bible* renders this final clause: "for his dirty mind and rebellious heart color all he sees and hears." The word "defiled" (both places) means "corrupted."

**16. They profess that they know God:**...They claim, *–KJII, –SEB*...They are avowing an acquaintance with, *–CNDT.*
**but in works they deny [him]:**...they disown him, *–TCNT.*
**being abominable, and disobedient:**...being detestable, *NASB*...They are rotten, *–SEB.*
**and unto every good work reprobate:**...and are found worthless in every good task, *–NORL*...they are utterly unsatisfactory, *–TCNT.*

**1:16.** A strong contrast exists between the first two clauses: "They profess (claim)... but in works they deny (disown)." False teachers stood condemned by their own conduct. Paul said they were (1) *bdeluktoi* ("abominable, detestable, repulsive"); (2) *apeitheis* ("disobedient"); and (3) *adokimoi* ("reprobate, unfit, unqualified, worthless, useless, rejected after testing"). The mention of "every good work" introduces a key emphasis in Titus (see 2:7, 14; 3:1, 8, 14).

## Chapter 2

**1. But speak thou the things which become sound doctrine:**...let your speech be consistent with, *–NAB*...what falls in line with wholesome doctrine, *–BRKL.*

**2:1.** Chapter 2 opens with a shift in content. Paul addressed Titus with "But... thou." This is an emphatic pronoun contrasting Titus' work with that of the false teachers which Paul denounced in 1:10-16.

The word "speak" is also in contrast to the speech and conduct of the Cretan false teachers (see 1:10, 11). Titus was to speak about the things that "become (*prepei*, 'to be suitable, fitting') sound doctrine" (compare 1:9). Other translations for "become" are "in accord with, befits." The Greek word *prepei* was used by Paul in several different contexts: see 1 Corinthians 11:13; Ephesians 5:3; 1 Timothy 2:10.

**2. That the aged men be sober, grave, temperate:**...be reserved, *–CNFT*...venerable, sensible, *–BRKL*...be vigilant...prudent, *–CMPB*...worthy of respect, self-controlled, *–SEB*...and discreet, *–TCNT.*
**sound in faith, in charity, in patience:**...and constancy, *–JB*...and enduring, *–SEB.*

**2:2.** In his instructions to Titus, Paul indicated how behavior must line up with belief and illustrated how this applies to various age groups and sexes. In this verse Paul wrote about what the "aged men" must be. He listed six traits.

(1) They were to be *nēphalious* ("sober, temperate, practicing restraint"). This denotes refraining from wine and having moderation in general. (2) They were to be *semnous* ("grave, serious, worthy of respect, responsible"; compare 1 Timothy 3:8,

11). (3) They were to be *sōphronas* ("temperate, sensible, prudent, self-controlled, thoughtful, soberminded"; compare verse 8).

(4) Older men must be "sound" (*hugiainontas*), healthy in faith, love (*agapē*), and patience (*hupomonē* ["endurance, steadfastness, fortitude"]). Years should add strength to a man's faith, increase tolerance of others, and produce ability to endure whatever comes.

**3. The aged women likewise:** . . . that elderly women, *−CNFT* . . . in like manner, *−CMPB.*

**that [they be] in behaviour as becometh holiness:** . . . should be reverent in their behavior, *−NORL* . . . be reverent in their demeanour, *−TCNT* . . . be in deportment, *−CMPB* . . . in demeanor, *−CNDT* . . . behave in ways that befit those who belong to God, *−NAB.*

**not false accusers, not given to much wine:** . . . with no scandalmongering, *−JB* . . . not enslaved to much wine, *−CMPB.*

**teachers of good things:** . . . teachers of the right behavior, *−JB.*

**2:3.** "Likewise" (*hōsautōs*) stresses that the aged women should have the same moral fiber as older men. They must be reverent in behavior. The Greek behind "as becometh holiness" means "as befits a holy person." Slander and drunkenness are two vices that were common practices among Cretan women. Christian women are to resist these actions and conduct and instead be "teachers of good things." The Greek word is *kalodidaskalous* and may be translated "teach what is good." This teaching would take place primarily in the home and among the younger women, not in the church (compare 1 Timothy 2:11, 12).

**4. That they may teach the young women to be sober:** . . . that they may train, *−CNFT* . . . teachers of what is noble, *−BRKL.*

**to love their husbands, to love their children:** . . . to be affectionate wives and mothers, *−WLMS.*

**5. [To be] discreet, chaste, keepers at home, good:** . . . to control themselves, *−SEB* . . . domestic, *−CNFT* . . . pure-minded, *−TCNT* . . . good housekeepers, *−BRKL.*

**obedient to their own husbands:** . . . submissive to, *−BRKL* . . . subordinate to, *−WLMS.*

**that the word of God be not blasphemed:** . . . will not fall into disrepute, *−NAB* . . . be not reviled, *−CNFT* . . . so that the message of God is never disgraced, *−JB* . . . may not be maligned, *−TCNT* . . . suffer reproach, *−WLMS.*

**2:4, 5.** Older women were to teach the young women *philandrous* ("to love their husbands") and *philoteknous* ("to love their children"). Both Greek terms occur only here in the New Testament. The

base word is *phileō* ("to love, have affection for, like").

Five important teachings follow: (1) "to be discreet," *sōphronas* ("sensible, self-controlled, prudent"); (2) "chaste," *hagnas* ("pure"); (3) "keepers at home," *oikourous* (possibly "workers at home, busy at home, domestics"); (4) "good," *agathas* ("kind," i.e., not hard or mean in their management of the home); (5) "obedient (subject, submissive) to their own husbands." The purpose for all this was "that the word of God be not blasphemed" (maligned, discredited).

**6. Young men likewise exhort to be sober minded:** . . . exhort to govern their passions, *−CMPB* . . . to control themselves, *−SEB* . . . to behave prudently, *−BRKL* . . . to be sensible, *−NORL.*

**2:6.** Titus was to address the young men with one message: "Be soberminded!" He was to "exhort" (encourage, urge) them to this one objective. *Sōphronein* ("soberminded, self-controlled, prudent") is a word often found in this letter to Titus (see 1:8; 2:2, 4). It stresses the need for self-mastery.

**7. In all things showing thyself a pattern of good works:** . . . a model of ideal acts, *−CNDT.*

**in doctrine [showing] uncorruptness, gravity, sincerity:** . . . be serious and be sincere, *−SEB.*

**2:7.** Having given instructions regarding young men, Paul now charged Titus (who may be considered a "young man") to proclaim the gospel by his life. The word "pattern" is *tupon* ("example, model"). Literally it means "an impress of a die." The same charge was given to Timothy (1 Timothy 4:12). But here Titus was commanded to be an example of "good works" (a key term in this epistle). His life should show what the gospel is and can do.

But his talk was important too. His "doctrine" (teaching) was to show "uncorruptness" (untaintedness, integrity). This underscores the need for purity of motive. Titus' teaching was to show "gravity" (seriousness, reverence, dignity). This points out the need for dignity of manner. As a teacher, Titus should demonstrate both purity of motive and dignity of manner.

**8. Sound speech, that cannot be condemned:** . . . Offer a healthy message that cannot be criticized, *−SEB* . . . so wholesome that nobody can make objections to it, *−JB.*

**that he that is of the contrary part may be ashamed:** . . . that will shame the opponent, *−BRKL* . . . may be put to shame, *−WLMS.*

**having no evil thing to say of you:** . . . having nothing bad to say concerning us, *−CNDT* . . . and not open to criticism, *−NORL* . . . against us, *−SEB.*

**2:8.** "Sound speech" (soundness of speech or wholesome speech) that "cannot be condemned" (censured, reproached) would put his opponents to shame. If Titus was an example in the words he spoke, those who opposed him ("he that is of the contrary part") would find nothing they could gainsay. The final clause of this verse, "having no evil thing to say of you," carries the idea that Titus was to present no opportunity for his opponents to use an evil report against him. His "sound speech" was to be truthful, wholesome, and absolutely irreproachable. Anything his opponents might say would then be seen as false, fabricated, empty, and evil.

**9. [Exhort] servants to be obedient unto their own masters:** . . . Continue urging slaves to practice perfect submission, —WLMS . . . to be submissive, —TCNT.

**[and] to please [them] well in all [things]:** . . . to give them perfect satisfaction, —WLMS.

**not answering again:** . . . Tell them not to contradict, —TCNT . . . not contradicting them, —NAB . . . not to talk back, —BRKL . . . without argument, —NORL . . . They must not argue, —NLTG.

**2:9.** Next Paul addressed the subject of slavery as he did in 1 Timothy 6:1, 2. Titus was to "exhort" (teach, urge, bid) Christian slaves to be "obedient" (subject, submissive) to their masters. The Greek for "masters" is the root for the English word *despot* and shows the absolute authority the master had over his slave. Roman slaves had no legal rights whatsoever.

Slaves were to "please them well in all things," that is, give satisfaction in every respect. The verb translated "not answering again" is literally "to contradict" and can mean "to oppose, to show active enmity against."

**10. Not purloining:** . . . or pilfer, —TCNT . . . not pilfering, —CNFT . . . no petty thieving, —JB . . . not embezzling, —CNDT . . . not secretly stealing, —CMPB.

**but showing all good fidelity:** . . . but showing faithfulness, —CNFT . . . but prove they can be trusted in every way, —NLTG.

**that they may adorn the doctrine of God our Saviour in all things:** . . . they are in every way a credit to the teaching, —JB . . . they shall beautify the teaching of, —BRKL.

**2:10.** "Purloining" is literally "put on one side for themselves" and connotes petty stealing. This was easily done by household slaves. On the positive side, slaves were to show they could be trusted. In so doing they would "adorn" the gospel. *Kosmōsin* ("adorn, do credit to") is literally "put in proper order." The Greek verb can be used of the setting of a jewel to show its best features and full

beauty. Christian slaves could testify of the gospel by their willing obedience to their masters.

**11. For the grace of God that bringeth salvation hath appeared to all men:** . . . the saving grace of God made its advent to all humanity, —CNDT . . . with its offer of salvation to all mankind, —WLMS . . . for all people, —BRKL . . . to save all mankind, —SEB.

**2:11.** Verses 11-14 constitute one of the two doctrinal sections of this epistle (the other is 3:4-7). Paul here described God's grace and its effect on believers. It brings salvation and results in rejection of ungodliness and demonstration of holy living.

The word "for" introduces this new paragraph and the doctrinal basis for the ethical demands just given (verses 2-10). "Grace" is God's undeserved love (compare Romans 5:6-10) shown in Christ and independent from any human effort (see Titus 3:5; Ephesians 2:8, 9). "Hath appeared" is in the aorist tense which points to one definite act. In this case it is the Incarnation that brought Christ to us (compare 3:4).

**12. Teaching us that:** . . . instructing us, —CNFT.

**denying ungodliness and worldly lusts:** . . . to renounce impiety and evil passions, —MNTG . . . to give up godless ways and worldly cravings, —WLMS . . . and all our worldly ambitions, —JB.

**we should live soberly, righteously, and godly:** . . . and live temperately, —NAB . . . to live self-controlled, —SEB . . . we should live wisely, —KLGS . . . serious, upright, —WLMS.

**in this present world:** . . . in this present age, —MNTG.

**2:12.** "Teaching" here is more than instruction. The word in the Greek means the whole process of educating a child—instruction, encouragement, and discipline. The grace of God teaches that Christians should live differently. First, negatively, they deny or renounce "ungodliness" (lack of reverence for God, godlessness). Second, they give up "worldly lusts" (passions, desires).

Positively, Christians live "soberly" (self-controlled, prudently), "righteously" (upright, justly), and "godly" (reverently). A triad of relationships may be seen in these adverbs. A Christian lives right in relation to himself (self-controlled), to others (justly), and to God (reverently). He does this "in this present world" (age).

**13. Looking for that blessed hope, and the glorious appearing:** . . . While we look for, —MNTG . . . with expectation of, —BRKL . . . while we are waiting for the realization of, —WLMS . . . expecting the blessed hope, —CMPB . . . as we await our blessed hope, —NAB.

**of the great God and our Saviour Jesus Christ:**

**2:13.** The doctrinal emphasis now moves from the Incarnation to the Second Advent. Paul calls it "that blessed hope." It is not just a wish but divine assurance for life beyond this life. Paul referred to this event in his other pastoral letters (see 1 Timothy 6:14; 2 Timothy 4:1). Here he wrote of the "glorious appearing" (*epiphaneian*) of Jesus Christ. His first coming was with fullness of grace (Titus 2:11, compare John 1:14). His second coming will be in the fullness of glory.

The phrase "the great God and our Saviour Jesus Christ" can refer to both Father and Son. It can also be translated "our great God and Saviour Jesus Christ" and focus on the Son's deity. No matter which translation is accepted, the primary sense is that Jesus is coming again, and He will be seen in His true glory and majesty. This is our blessed hope!

**14. Who gave himself for us:**
**that he might redeem us from all iniquity:**...to buy us back from all lawlessness, *—KLGS*...to ransom us from, *—WLMS*...from every kind of sin, *—SEB*.
**and purify unto himself a peculiar people:**...to cleanse for himself, *—NAB*...a nation, *—SEB*.
**zealous of good works:** ... eager to do good deeds, *—SEB*...eager to do good works, *—BRKL*...good deeds, *—NORL*.

**2:14.** The doctrinal emphasis now focuses on Christ's atonement. He "gave himself for us" in order to "redeem" (*lutrōsētai*, literally, "to release on receipt of a ransom") us from all "iniquity" (wickedness, lawlessness) and "purify" (compare Ephesians 5:25, 26) us. Redemption and purification are the two great works involved in salvation.

"Peculiar" means "special, chosen, one's own possession" (1 Peter 2:9). Such people are "zealous" (eager, devoted) to do good work.

**15. These things speak, and exhort, and rebuke:** ... and expose with every injunction, *—CNDT*...use them to refute opponents, *—TCNT*.
**with all authority:** ... with absolute authority, *—TCNT*.
**Let no man despise thee:** ... and no one is to question it, *—JB*...Let no one slight you, *—CNDT*...Let no one disregard you, *—NORL*...Don't let anyone look down on you! *—SEB*...Let no one belittle you, *—WLMS*.

**2:15.** As a summary, verse 15 is transitional to 3:1 where Titus was to speak, exhort, and rebuke. "Speak" (teach) involves proclamation.

The command "exhort" involves encouragement (compare 2 Timothy 4:2). Titus was to encourage the Cretan Christians with positive and edifying words, but with the balance of the next command. "Rebuke" (reprove) involves the ministry of conviction. Titus was to convince

wrongdoers of their sins so that they might repent and seek God's forgiveness and cleansing.

Titus was to do all this "with all authority" (*epitagēs*). This Greek term is used only by Paul and always in the sense of a divine command. Titus was to recognize that his authority came from God. He then must not allow anyone to "despise" (disregard) him (compare 1 Timothy 4:12).

## Chapter 3

**1. Put them in mind:**...Constantly remind people, *—WLMS*.
**to be subject to principalities and powers, to obey magistrates:** ... to obey the leaders of their country, *—NLTG*...to respect government authorities, *—KLGS*.
**to be ready to every good work:**...for any honest work, *—RSV*...for any good enterprise, *—WLMS*.

**3:1.** Verses 1 and 2 open a new topic that might be titled "Practical Christian Living." The first verse addresses the Christian's obligation to earthly government. Verse 2 deals with the Christian's obligations to his fellowman. Both Paul (Romans 13:1-7) and Peter (1 Peter 2:13-17) addressed the issue of duty to civil government.

Christians are to be "subject" (submissive) to "principalities and powers" (rulers and authorities). These terms are meant to be inclusive; they refer to all levels of government. "To obey magistrates" is one part of this submission. "To be ready (for) every good work" is the other part. Good works is a major theme of this epistle (see 1:16; 2:7, 14; 3:1, 8, 14).

**2. To speak evil of no man, to be no brawlers:** ... not to slander anyone, *—BRKL* ... to avoid quarreling, *—LILY*, *—TCNT* ... stop abusing anyone, *—WLMS* ... not quarrelsome, *—CNFT* ... to be peaceable, *—SEB*.
**[but] gentle, showing all meekness unto all men:**...to be considerate, *—SEB*...but moderate, *—CNFT*...but equitable, *—CMPB*.

**3:2.** Outlined here are the Christian's obligations to his fellowman, whether or not he is a Christian. Four duties are listed; the first two are negative, the last two are positive. The Christian is not to "speak evil of" (slander) anyone. This was an especially favorite pastime of the beastly Cretans (1:12). The Christian is hot to be a "brawler" (*amachous*, "not a fighter"). The English word *macho* came from this root through the Latin and Spanish languages.

The positive duties are gentleness (considerateness, kindness) and meekness (*praotēta*—which describes the person whose temper is always under control and who bears wrongs done to him, showing humility and perfect courtesy).

**3. For we ourselves also were sometimes:**...once we too were, —WLMS.

**foolish, disobedient, deceived:**...were thoughtless, —BRKL...and deluded, —NORL...misled, —TCNT.

**serving divers lusts and pleasures:**...habitual slaves, —WLMS...slavishly serving divers inordinate desires, —CMPB...slaves to various lusts, —CNFT...to passion and all sorts of pleasures, —KLGS.

**living in malice and envy:**...spending our lives, —WLMS...wasting our time in, —BRKL.

**hateful, [and] hating one another:**...People hated us and we hated them, —SEB.

**3:3.** This verse provides a general description of unregenerate human nature. Paul expressed this in the past tense, and the list shows how great the grace of God really is. "Foolish" is *anoētoi*, literally, "senseless, without spiritual understanding." Disobedience is directed toward God and deception is related to man. A metaphor of slavery describes man's bondage to his passions and pursuit of pleasures. Malice and envy have but one result: being hated by others and "hating one another."

**4. But after that the kindness and love of God our Saviour toward man appeared:**...then there dawned on us the, —NORL...and philanthropy of God, —CMPB.

**3:4.** The "but" that begins this verse provides a strong contrast to that which has gone before. Man's degenerate human nature—the worst—is contrasted with God's kindness and love—the best. Verses 4-7 form the second doctrinal section of this letter (2:11-14 is the first).

Paul wrote to Titus that two wonderful characteristics of God have "appeared" (*epephanē*, compare 2:11). God's *chrēstotēs* ("kindness, goodness, generosity") has come to man. *Chrēstotēs* is not just a warm feeling on God's part, but His generous action toward man that is a part of His nature (and in contrast to man's nature described in verse 3). God's *philanthrōpia* ("love for mankind," the root of the English word *philanthropy*) means His love for all mankind (compare John 3:16). Paul built on these two characteristics in the next verses with such words as "mercy" and "grace." God's kindness and love are the beginning point of God's salvation of man.

The title "God our Saviour" has been used in this epistle twice before (1:3; 2:10; compare 1:4; 2:13; 3:6).

**5. Not by works of righteousness which we have done:**...not for upright deeds, —WLMS...not in consequence of any righteous actions, —TCNT...not because of any deeds that we had done in righteousness, —MNTG.

**but according to his mercy he saved us:**...but in agreement with His mercy, —BRKL...in virtue of his own mercy, —RSV...because of his own pity for us, —MNTG.

**by the washing of regeneration:**...through the bath, —CNFT, —WLMS...by the renovating power of, —TCNT.

**and renewing of the Holy Ghost:**...renewal, that come from, —ADAM.

**3:5.** Salvation is God's work. Paul said it is "*not* by works of righteousness (deeds prescribed by the law of Moses) which we have done, but according to *his* mercy he saved *us*" (italics supplied to show the emphasis in the Greek). Man cannot earn his salvation by good deeds.

Then Paul added the means of this salvation: "By the washing of regeneration (rebirth), and renewing (renewal) of the Holy Ghost." This is what Jesus taught Nicodemus (compare the wording in John 3:5). "Washing" is seen by most commentators as a reference to water baptism which is an outward seal and sign of regeneration. "Renewing" is that inner work of the Spirit Jesus was talking about in John chapter 3.

**6. Which he shed on us abundantly:**...which he poured out on us richly, —CMPB...who was given to us freely, —NORL...God generously poured out, —SEB...He poured out effusively, —ADAM.

**through Jesus Christ our Saviour:**

**3:6.** Verse 6 says God "shed" (*execheen*, "poured out"—the verb here is in the aorist tense and therefore looks back to a specific event, i.e., the Day of Pentecost) His Holy Spirit "abundantly" (generously, richly; compare Acts 2:33). "On us" refers to Paul and his associates' personal experience of being filled with the Holy Spirit. The mediator of this wonderful outpouring is "Jesus Christ our Saviour."

**7. That being justified by his grace:**...In order that, —MNTG...so that we might come into right standing with God, —WLMS.

**we should be made heirs according to the hope of eternal life:**...become possessors of enduring Life, —TCNT.

**3:7.** Paul moved from the doctrines of salvation and the Holy Spirit to those of justification and adoption. The past, present, and future can be seen in this verse. God's grace brings justification—past sins are forgiven. Then He adopts those who believe on Christ (Galatians 3:4, 5), and their present life is hid with Christ in God (Colossians 3:3). The hope of eternal life is yet future (compare Titus 1:2; Romans 8:11, 15-17).

The word "heirs" contains tremendous significance. Imagine a similar situation in the natural, of an urchin on the streets—homeless, unloved, with a bleak future. Then a rich man adopts him, gives him his name, and makes him his heir. That, in a small way, describes what God has done for believers. Heirs of all He has! Only eternity will reveal what that means.

**8.** **[This is] a faithful saying:** ... What I have just said is trustworthy, *—LILY* ... This saying is trustworthy, *—MNTG* ... It is a message to be trusted, *—WLMS* ... This word is dependable, *—KLGS*.

**and these things I will that thou affirm constantly:** ... Now, I want you to insist on these things with assurance *—ADAM* ... I want you to be emphatic about these things, *—WLMS* ... on these subjects that I desire you to lay especial stress, *—TCNT* ... On this I want you to firmly insist, *—MNTG*.

**that they which have believed in God:**

**might be careful to maintain good works:** ... may be anxious to excel in good deeds, *—LILY* ... to devote themselves to doing good deeds, *—SEB* ... may be careful to take the lead in doing good, *—WLMS*.

**These things are good and profitable unto men:** ... which is excellent and beneficial for all people, *—BRKL* ... and render service to mankind, *—WLMS*.

**3:8.** This verse is transitional. "This is a faithful saying" refers to the doctrinal statement of verses 4-7. Titus was to keep on affirming "these things" (compare 2:15). The purpose is given in the next clause. Carefulness to "maintain" (*proistasthai,* literally, "to be forward in, to devote themselves before all else to") good works is good and profitable for everyone.

**9.** **But avoid foolish questions, and genealogies:** ... from foolish issues, *—SEB* ... controversies, *—WLMS* ... pedigrees, *—BRKL*.

**and contentions, and strivings about the law:** ... strife, and wranglings about, *—BRKL*.

**for they are unprofitable and vain:** ... they are useless and futile, *—LILY, —CNFT* ... for they are futile and purposeless, *—BRKL* ... These are useless and without purpose, *—SEB* ... and unsatisfactory, *—TCNT*.

**3:9.** Paul closed this letter with a summary instruction to Titus. What he wrote he also wrote to Timothy (1 Timothy 1:4; 6:4, 20) and would do so again (2 Timothy 2:23). From all this we know the situation in Ephesus and that on Crete were similar. Paul was greatly concerned about false teachers who were challenging sound doctrine and the practice of Christian good works.

Titus was told to avoid four things. "Avoid" is *periistaso,* literally, "to turn oneself about so as to face the other way." (1) "Questions" may be translated "controversies, speculations." (2) "Genealogies" refers to Old Testament genealogical lists. Jewish false teachers would insert stories and myths between the names, attributing fictitious exploits to people in the lists. (3) "Contentions" may be translated "arguments, dissensions." (4)

"Strivings (quarrels) about the law" refers to "legalistic battles" centered on the Mosaic law. This phrase summarizes what Paul wrote in Titus 1:10-16 (cf. 1 Timothy 1:3-7). These are unprofitable and "vain" (useless, futile).

**10.** **A man that is an heretic:** ... who is factious, *—RSV, —WLMS* ... A sectarian man, *—CNDT*.

**after the first and second admonition reject:** ... stop having anything to do with him, *—WLMS*.

**3:10.** "Heretic" (*hairetikon,* "contentious man, factious man") describes a divisive person. Originally this term described someone who took legitimate doctrine to the extreme. Not until later did it mean "holding false doctrine." Titus was to admonish (warn) such a person once, admonish him the second time, and have nothing to do with him on the third occasion. "Reject" is *parakou* ("to leave out of account," different from "avoid," verse 9). Admonition, not argument, is called for. Rejection severs fellowship.

**11.** **Knowing that he that is such is subverted:** ... you may be sure that such a man is crooked, *—WLMS*.

**and sinneth, being condemned of himself:** ... He is sinning and he knows it, *—NLTG* ... he knows he's wrong, *—SEB*.

**3:11.** "He that is such" refers to the one in verse 10 who will not listen and stubbornly refuses any correction. He is (1) "subverted" (warped, perverted), (2) sinful, and (3) self-condemned. The idea of this last description is that Titus need not spend time either in contention or condemnation. The heretic is self-condemned by his perverted mind and sinful actions.

**12.** **When I shall send Artemas unto thee, or Tychicus, be diligent to come unto me to Nicopolis:**

**for I have determined there to winter:** ... for I have arranged, *—TCNT*.

**3:12.** This verse begins the final personal instructions and greetings so characteristic of Paul's letters. Nothing is known of Artemas. Tychicus was a trusted coworker who traveled with Paul and on occasion was Paul's emissary who carried letters to certain churches (see Acts 20:4; Ephesians 6:21, 22; Colossians 4:7, 8; 2 Timothy 4:12). Either one or the other of these men would probably take over the work in Crete so Titus could meet Paul in Nicopolis. There were three cities of this name (which means "city of victory"): one in Cilicia, one in Thrace, and one in Epirus. The Nicopolis Paul referred to here is probably the last one and was on the western shore of Greece in the Roman province of Dalmatia.

Paul wrote he had "determined" (decided) to winter there. By his use of "there" instead of "here" Paul showed he was not yet in Nicopolis when he wrote this epistle. Further, he was still free to travel. This places the time of writing between Paul's first and second imprisonments in Rome.

**13. Bring Zenas the lawyer and Apollos on their journey diligently:** . . . Equip Zenas, the jurist and Apollos carefully for their journey, –BRKL . . . the Teacher of the Law, –TCNT . . . diligently set forward on their journey, –WUST.

**that nothing be wanting unto them:** . . . Let them want nothing, –MNTG . . . Do your best to supply everything that Zenas . . . and Apollos need for their trip; be sure they lack nothing, –ADAM . . . in order that not even one thing be lacking to them, –WUST . . . see that they lack nothing, –RSV.

**3:13.** Titus was asked to bring two men with him to Nicopolis. Zenas the lawyer (*nomikon*—the Greek word does not indicate nationality) is mentioned only here. If he was a Jewish convert, "lawyer" could mean he was an expert in the Mosaic law, i.e., a scribe. If he was a Gentile convert, it could mean he was a Roman lawyer. It is quite possible Paul wanted Zenas to come for some legal reason. Did Paul know he would soon be imprisoned again? Was he wanting legal advice concerning his rights as a Roman citizen? These questions are only speculative, but the historical situation makes them probable.

Apollos was a Jew, a native of Alexandria, and a well-known coworker (see Acts 18:24-28; 1 Corinthians 1:12; 3:4-6, 22; 16:12). In his early ministry he was counseled by Aquila and Priscilla who taught him "the way of God more perfectly" (Acts 18:26). Acts 18:28 says that after this "he mightily convinced the Jews, and that publicly, showing by the Scriptures that Jesus was Christ."

"Bring . . . on their journey diligently" could mean Zenas and Apollos were in Crete or they would be picked up by Titus on his way to Nicopolis. The last phrase may be translated "see that they have everything they need." Titus was to provide material assistance to Zenas and Apollos. This suggests the practice of Christian hospitality in which itinerant workers such as evangelists and missionaries were given room and board plus traveling expenses (compare Romans 15:24; 1 Corinthians 16:6; 3 John 5-8).

**14. And let ours also learn to maintain good works:** . . . let our people learn to devote themselves to honest work, –MNTG . . . to engage in good deeds, –ADAM . . . learn . . . at good works, –KLGS . . . learn to busy themselves constantly in good works, –WUST.

**for necessary uses:** . . . to supply the necessities of their teachers, –MNTG . . . to meet pressing needs, –ADAM . . . the right use of their hands, –KLGS . . . for necessary needs, –WUST.

**that they be not unfruitful:** . . . In this way they will not be destitute of good deeds, –LILY . . . in order that, –WUST . . . so that their lives may not be barren of results, –TCNT . . . may not be unproductive, –BRKL . . . Then they will not be useless, –KLGS . . . They must learn to be productive, providing for real needs, –SEB.

**3:14.** In this verse Paul gave a general exhortation. "And let ours (our people) also learn to maintain (the idea of this Greek verb is priority, i.e., devoting oneself before all else to) good works" (a main theme of this epistle, see 1:16; 2:7, 14; 3:1, 8).

Paul added the phrase "for necessary uses." This is the practical side of good works. Two concepts are inherent in these words: (1) The Cretan Christians were to "maintain good works" so they might be independent and provide for their own needs. (2) They were to give priority to good works so they would be able to help those who were in need.

**15. All that are with me salute thee:** . . . All my companions greet you, –LILY . . . All those with me send greetings to you, –WUST.

**Greet them that love us in the faith:** . . . greet our affectionate friends in the faith, –ADAM . . . those who are fond of us in the Faith, –WUST.

**Grace [be] with you all. Amen:** . . . The grace, –WUST . . . Favor be with you, –CMPB . . . Help be with all of you, –ADAM.

**3:15.** The closing benediction is very similar to most in Paul's epistles. "All" refers either to those in Paul's traveling party or possibly to those seen on his trip whom Titus knew.

"Love" in this greeting is *philountas* and denotes Christian love, not natural love. It is this uniquely Christian love that unites believers. The Greek behind "in the faith" has no article. *En pistei* could mean "faithfully," i.e., "those who love us faithfully as Christians."

The closing blessing is similar to the other Pastorals (see 1 Timothy 6:21; 2 Timothy 4:22). "AH" begins and ends this verse. As in Paul's letters to Timothy, the plural closing indicated this letter was to be read to the churches.

# PHILEMON

## Overview

### The Authenticity of the Letter

The Pauline authorship of the letter to Philemon is virtually undisputed. Since it was first known it has been included in the letters of the apostle Paul. Only a few maintain that it is a "Christian social treatise" on the master-slave relationship placed on the lips of Paul for effect. If that were the case, however, the argument for social equity would have appeared much more vividly.

### A Private Concern or a Letter for the Whole Church?

It may seem that Philemon is only a private correspondence to a specific individual about a particular, confidential matter. Were that the case, why was it included in the canon of the New Testament? Everything indicates that it is an apostolic letter to a church; only formally does it appear as a private correspondence. The more one examines the letter, the more obvious its relevance for the Church of all times becomes.

The circumstances pointing in this direction are as follows:

(1) It is true that the personal term "you" (singular) recurs in the main body of the letter. These instances are referring to Philemon, but not only him. A woman, Apphia, is also mentioned, who may be Philemon's wife (cf. 1 Corinthians 9:5) or a female servant of the church (cf. Romans 16:1). The letter is also addressed to Archippus who, according to Colossians 4:17, was also entrusted with a ministry in the Lord. But primarily, as mentioned in its opening words, the letter is aimed at the church in the house of Philemon (verse 2). Thus, it is a letter for the church, but because of a unique problem it is addressed to the host of the church (cf. Romans 16:23).

(2) Timothy is a cosender. He regularly accompanied the apostle Paul in his duties, not the least in the Asian province where Colossae was located.

(3) Paul does not describe himself as an apostle as he usually does; nevertheless, his apostolic call and authority shine through. Paul's authority as apostle would allow him to give Philemon specific commands concerning the present problem (verse 8); however he does not. Neither does he doubt that Philemon would respond to such commands (verse 21).

### Philemon—Host of the Church

The name Philemon does not appear anywhere else in the New Testament. Almost certainly he is from Colossae in Phyrgia. The generally acknowledged relationship between this letter and the letter to the Colossians is obvious. Onesimus is mentioned in both letters (Colossians 4:9; Philemon 10), and those named in verses 23, 24 also send their greetings in Colossians 4:10-15.

Philemon is called "our dearly beloved" (*agapētō*) (verse 1). Whether this means a dear friend or one beloved by God is not clear. Paul and Philemon are apparently good friends (verse 17). The description of Philemon as a coworker (verse 1) shows that he was involved in Christian ministry. He opened his home for worship services (verse 2), and he invited guests like Paul and his coworkers to attend (verse 22). Philemon demonstrated his Christian faith in acts of charity. He also helped the poor in the church (verses 5-7). From verse 19 we note that Paul was the instrument through whom Philemon became a Christian. How or when this occurred is not recorded.

### Onesimus and His Confession

Philemon was a "master" (*kurios*), in other words a "slave-owner." Slavery was seen during that time period as an inevitable by-product of the structure of society. Slaves often received humane treatment. Some, however, worked in chains, as in the silver mines, while others were "household slaves" in the houses of the well-to-do. The latter were entrusted with a great deal of responsibility in caring for the children.

There were slaves in Christian households as well. The issue here is not that slavery existed, but how the slaves were treated. Among the earliest Christians many were slaves, but in the relationship between God and the individual, there was no difference between a slave and a master (1 Corinthians 12:13; Galatians 3:28; Colossians 3:11). At the Lord's table they sat side by side.

*Onesimus* means "one who benefits another"; that is, "profitable." Paul made a play on words with this in verses 11 and 20. It is stated expressly that Onesimus was a slave (verse 16), and Colossians 4:9 describes him as faithful, dear, a brother, one of their own, and thus a member of the church.

Verse 10 indicates that Onesimus became a Christian when he met Paul. Onesimus was associated with Paul in a unique way during the latter's confinement. It is virtually certain that the imprisonment spoken of was Paul's confinement in Rome. Ephesus would be too close to Colossae, and Caesarea too small for the runaway slave to hide. Rome, though, would be well suited.

## Paul As a Sponsor

We are not told all the circumstances, but Onesimus had deserted his master Philemon, stealing some money while doing so. There is much missing in the story as it is recorded in the Scriptures. We are not told the sum of the money, how he was able to reach Rome, how he happened to contact Paul, and the steps by which Paul was able to lead Onesimus to salvation. It is sufficient to learn all this occurred.

Now Onesimus faced a difficult problem. He had wronged his master, he must confess. His restitution required that he return to Philemon putting himself back into slavery. Wishing to help in the reconciliation, Paul wrote this letter, interceding for Onesimus who had become like a "son" to him.

The apostle asked Philemon to receive Onesimus as if he were Paul himself (verse 17). The stolen funds were lost, but Paul requested that they be charged to his account. Paul tried to open Philemon's eyes to the fact that something good could come from all this misfortune.

## What "More" Did Paul Expect?

What did the apostle mean when he stated he was sure Philemon would "do more than I say" (verse 21)? It could have been just a general expression of confidence, but some students give a greater significance to the term. (1) He was asking for Onesimus' release from being a slave. But this could cause a problem if Philemon's other slaves were kept in servitude. (2) He was asking Philemon to send Onesimus back to him to minister to him in his own bondage. But if this were so, why did Paul request lodging be prepared for him in a soon-coming visit (verse 21)? At any rate, it is apparent from verse 16 that Paul expected Philemon to receive Onesimus in a special relationship: "Not now as a servant, but above a servant, a brother beloved."

## The Double Citizenship of Believers

Paul did not claim Onesimus must be freed. The abolition of slavery was not an issue of that time. It is obvious that for Paul Christians were to be obedient to civil law as far as was possible. They lived in a world with masters and slaves, but they were not of this world. Christ was their real Master.

Life in this dual existence meant that Christian slaves served their masters from a willing heart. They served sincerely and were obedient as if their service to their master was service to Christ. For Christian slave owners, the dual citizenship of Christian slaves meant they were not harshly treated or overworked (Ephesians 6:9). Slaves were to be treated reasonably and with justice (Colossians 4:1).

Joined with every other loyal citizen group throughout history and within various social structures, Christians have worked to improve social conditions, even in the employer/employee relationship. The Christian must carefully discriminate between the private and political consequences of his actions as a believer. He or she must realize that though the "more" cannot always be explicitly identified, it is nevertheless always present.

## Christian Love—Always in Process

As we have seen, the letter to Philemon is not a Christian social treatise with a specific answer for a specific social problem. Rather, it is an apostle's teaching of faith and trust in Christ and an apostolic admonition to a Christian and his church to discern the proper response of love. On this occasion the issue concerned a slave/master relationship; today it could be the employee/employer—the essence is the same. The response is the same: love has no limit; it is always in the process of realization.

If the letter to Philemon were only intended for private consumption, it would have never made the canon or the body of Pauline letters. It has been read throughout the churches of the ancient world as an "epistle" to be read in the worship service, just as the other letters of Paul.

## Later Traditions and Their Significance

The young Church took this letter to heart. The multiplicity of traditions associated with the characters of the letter attest to this. A great deal could be said about any of them. Philemon became the bishop in his town, and his entire family was martyred under Nero's reign. Onesimus became a prominent member of the church at Colossae. When the martyr and bishop Ignatius wrote around A.D. 110 to the church in Ephesus, he gave thanks because he had received encouragement from a delegation of elders from Ephesus, led by the bishop named Onesimus. There is good reason to accept these traditions. This is almost certainly the Onesimus from the Book of Philemon. Some, however, think that Onesimus became the bishop of Beroea of Macedonia. Others think he followed Paul on a missionary journey to Spain. Finally, some contend that he was martyred in Italy. Whatever the case, all of this reflects how highly the Early Church regarded the letter to Philemon.

# The Epistle of Paul to Philemon

## Commentary

**1. Paul, a prisoner of Jesus Christ:** ... for Jesus, —*WLMS*, —*FNTN*.
**and Timothy [our] brother:** ... brother Timothy, —*MNTG* ... my fellow worker, —*BECK*.
**unto Philemon our dearly beloved, and fellowlabourer:** ... to our dear friend, —*ADAM* ... our dear fellow worker, —*BECK* ... To my beloved friend and coworker, —*MNTG*.

**1.** Rather than identify himself as an apostle since he wrote to a friend, Paul called himself a "prisoner of Jesus Christ," not of Nero. He named Timothy as an associate. The definite article (*ho*) specified him as *the* brother. The addressee is Philemon whom the apostle called "dearly beloved" and "fellow laborer."

**2. And to [our] beloved Apphia:** ... the dear Apphia, —*FNTN* ... to my sister Apphia, —*MNTG*.
**and Archippus our fellow-soldier:** ... our fellow Christian, —*BECK*.
**and to the church in thy house:** ... the group that meets, —*SET* ... and to the ecclesia, —*CNDT* ... the [local] assembly, —*WUST* ... to the congregation, —*FNTN* ... that meets at your home, —*BRKL*.

**2.** The address continues with the mention of Apphia and Archippus, possibly the other members of the family to which Paul wrote the epistle. Archippus is called a "fellow soldier." The title suggests he was a church leader, perhaps interim pastor in Epaphras' absence. The address closes with a reference to the assembly that met in the house of Philemon. He opened his home to believers as a place for worship and study.

**3. Grace to you, and peace:** ... spiritual blessing be with you, —*WLMS* ... help and peace, —*ADAM* ... [Sanctifying] grace to you and [tranquillizing] peace, —*WUST* ... love you and give you peace, —*BECK*.
**from God our Father and the Lord Jesus Christ:** ... May God, —*BECK*.

**3.** Paul's greeting concludes with the normal combination of the Greek idea of "grace" and the Hebrew concept of "peace." Since "grace" (*charis*) occupies the emphatic position in Paul's statement, it definitely points to the necessity of depending upon it in our Christian lives. "Peace," or inner tranquility that does not depend upon external circumstances, naturally follows the reception of God's grace by a human being. This grace and peace come from "God our Father and

the Lord Jesus Christ" (compare Romans 1:7; 1 Corinthians 1:3; 2 Corinthians 1:2; Galatians 1:3; Ephesians 1:2; and all of Paul's letters; note he adds "mercy" to the greetings in the Pastoral Epistles).

**4. I thank my God:** ... I always thank, —*ADAM*, —*WLMS* ... and giving thanks to God, —*MNTG*.
**making mention of thee always in my prayers:** ... I am ever mentioning you, —*MNTG* ... every time I mention you, —*WLMS* ... remembering you on the occasions of my seasons of prayer, —*WUST*.

**4.** In the Greek the verb translated "I thank" occupies the first position, the position of emphasis, and comes from the term (*eucharistō*) from which we get *eucharist*, one of the outstanding terms describing the communion service which the Scriptures teach should be a time of thanksgiving. God never intended for the Lord's Supper to become a ceremony full of empty formality and devoid of His presence. Neither did He intend for people to think He automatically conveys His grace to them just because they keep this ceremony religiously. As usual, Paul allowed his inner being to express itself in praise before he took his petitions to God. Commentators disagree as to whether the term "always" (*pantote*) should go with the thanksgiving expressed in this verse or with the prayer request he was about to express to God.

**5. Hearing of thy love and faith, which thou hast:** ... because I hear of ... faithfulness that you show, —*ADAM* ... you practice, —*BRKL* ... which you hold, —*MNTG*.
**toward the Lord Jesus, and toward all saints:** ... and for all the Christians, —*NORL* ... and all His people, —*WLMS*.

**5.** Now we begin to see why Paul always thanked God and always prayed for Philemon. This believer certainly enjoyed a good balance between his relationship with God and man. Paul expressed this proper balance he detected in Philemon by referring to his "love and faith" which he had toward the Lord Jesus and the saints. It is very possible that Paul was thanking God for the love and faith that Philemon had "toward" (*pros*) the Lord Jesus and for the love and faithfulness he expressed "to" (*eis*) all the saints. The horizontal expression should stem from the vertical relationship.

**6. That the communication of thy faith:** ... I pray that the generosity which springs from your faith, —*LILY* ... praying that this sharing of your faith,

**949**

—ADAM...that your participation, —MNTG...that you will actively share your faith, —SEB...in sharing, —NIV.

**may become effectual by the acknowledging of:** ...that you may be active, —NIV...may result in their recognition in us, —WLMS...may become operative in the realization of, —CNDT...may have the effect of bringing about a full knowledge of, —ADAM...as you come to acknowledge, —MNTG.

**every good thing which is in you in Christ Jesus:** ...all the good things that we have, —ADAM...everything that is right with reference to Christ, —WLMS.

**6.** After thanking God for what he saw in his friend Philemon, Paul prayed that this man always would be active in sharing his faith with other people. "Communication" comes from the Greek noun (*koinōnia*) from which we get the English word *fellowship*. The word, however, carries the idea of participating with someone or participating in some kind of ministry. Verse 7 makes clear that in Philemon's case "fellowship" included sharing with brethren who were in need. The apostle knew that as Philemon would share his faith with other people in this practical way, it in turn would help him to become more and more effectual in his witness for Christ. "Become" indicates something that definitely is progressive in nature. Paul believed in the possibility of improving in one's witness for the Lord. This fact becomes even more evident by the Greek word (*epignōsei*) that the NIV translators rendered "full understanding." Therefore, as a person shares his faith in the Lord Jesus Christ, the person who receives the message not only benefits from it, but the person who gives the message also comes to a more complete understanding of all the good things that God has promised to His people. All these benefits, of course, come to us only "in Christ Jesus" or "through Christ" because we belong to Him.

**7. For we have great joy and consolation in thy love:** ...I have enjoyed much happiness and encouragement from, —ADAM...and comfort, —MNTG.

**because the bowels of the saints:** ...The hearts of the Christians, —NLTG.

**are refreshed by thee, brother:** ...have refreshed the hearts of, —NIV...you have revived the hearts of, —ADAM...and you have likewise cheered the hearts of, —NORL.

**7.** Not only did Philemon's expression of love (*agapē*) help him to gain a more complete understanding of what he possessed in Christ, but it also brought "joy and consolation" to Paul. Philemon literally "refreshed the bowels (*splanchna*) of the saints" by his activities. This interesting phrase expresses the way people of that day spoke of the innermost being of a person. Because the bowels, or intestines, of a person occupy a position of depth in the human body, this type of terminology speaks very fittingly of the deepest emotions a person can express. Often translators use the word *heart* to try to capture the idea expressed in the term. Therefore, Philemon obviously practiced a ministry of Christian relationships in which he allowed the Holy Spirit to make him a definite encouragement to people.

**8. Wherefore, though I might be much bold in Christ:** ...Christ gives me full liberty, —TCNT...I have plenty of freedom, —SEB...So then, although I am quite free, —ADAM.

**to enjoin thee that which is convenient:** ...to order you to do what you should do, —SEB...that I might charge thee, —CNFT...to give you directions as to your duty, —BRKL...to lay down the course you should adopt, —TCNT...as to what is proper, —CNDT.

**8.** The heart of the epistle, of course, consists of a passionate appeal for Philemon to accept Onesimus back into his household. The appeal was based upon several matters that are expressed in the next few verses. First, instead of using bold authority, Paul appealed to the mutual love shared by him and his friend. Church leaders today would do well to follow Paul's example.

**9. Yet for love's sake I rather beseech [thee]:** ...I prefer in the interests of love, —LILY...I prefer to make my appeal on the basis of love, —BRKL...yet the claims of love make me prefer to plead with you, —TCNT...my argument will be that you do it for love's sake, —NORL.

**being such an one as Paul the aged:** ...an old man, —CMPB.

**and now also a prisoner of Jesus Christ:**

**9.** Instead of using boldness to command Philemon to acquiesce to the apostle's wishes, he appealed to his friend on the basis of love. The Greek word for "beseech" (*parakalō*) is a very strong word, so the use of this verb shows even more the humility and tact of the person who used it. Again Paul reminded his friend that he was a prisoner of Christ Jesus, another way of affirming that he had been incarcerated in accordance with God's will, not just at the whim of the evil Nero. More importantly, Paul added the fact he was an aged man at the time of making this passionate appeal. The Greek noun (*presbutēs*) Paul used here also is translated a number of times in the New Testament as "elder" or "presbyter." However, here it obviously refers to an aged man.

**10. I beseech thee for my son Onesimus:** ...I plead with thee, —CNFT...I appeal to you, —WLMS...for my child, —SEB.

**whom I have begotten in my bonds:** ...for I have become his spiritual father here, —NORL...during my imprisonment, —LILY...I have given Life, —TCNT.

**10.** Furthermore, Paul attested that Onesimus had experienced a true conversion to Jesus Christ, so he appealed to Philemon on the basis of this important bond they enjoyed. "My son" literally comes from a phrase meaning "my child" (*tou emou teknou*). It would be difficult to mistake this terminology to mean anything but the fact God had permitted Paul to lead Onesimus to an experience of true regeneration. It must have occurred during Paul's 2-year imprisonment in Rome (Acts 28:30, 31).

**11. Which in time past was to thee unprofitable:** ... He once was useless to thee, —*CNFT* ... Formerly he was useless to you, —*NIV.*

**but now profitable to thee and to me:** ... now he is useful, —*WLMS.*

**11.** In fact, Onesimus' life had so changed that now he was "profitable" whereas he previously had been "unprofitable." This is a very vivid description of the results of true salvation. Paul used a form of the Greek word *chrēstos* twice. First, by adding an alpha to the term (*achrēston*), he negated the word. Then, he added *eu*, or the adverb "well." It expresses the dramatic change Christ can make in a person's life. "Onesimus" means "profitable." He had not lived up to his name before. Now he could.

**12. Whom I have sent again: thou therefore receive him:** ... whom I have sent back, —*CMPB* ... I sent him ... back to you, —*SEB.*

**that is, mine own bowels:** ... as though he were my very heart, —*CNFT* ... as an object of my tenderest affection, —*CMPB* ... though it is like tearing out my very heart, —*TCNT.*

**12.** As he continued his letter it is clear Paul believed in making restitution whenever it was possible to do so; he knew Onesimus owed a definite obligation to Philemon. Again Paul used the Greek term for "bowels" to express the emotional connection that being able to lead Onesimus to the Lord had knit between them. It was not easy to send back this man who meant so much to him. Can you picture the emotional response Philemon must have experienced as he read these words? The fact Paul manifested his sincere respect for Philemon must have elicited an even greater respect from the heart of Philemon for the apostle. People in leadership positions should always realize that respect does not come because it is demanded. It is generated by actions such as the one exhibited by the famous apostle on this occasion. He is a good example to follow.

**13. Whom I would have retained with me:** ... I would have liked to, —*NIV* ... I would have preferred

to keep him with me, —*LILY* ... I should like to retain him for myself, —*BRKL.*

**that in thy stead he might have ministered unto me:** ... so that in your place, —*KLGS* ... to serve me on your behalf, —*NORL* ... to wait on me, —*WLMS.*

**in the bonds of the gospel:** ... while I wear these chains for the good news, —*WLMS.*

**13.** Paul had every right to request Onesimus' assistance in gospel ministry, but the apostle respected his friend Philemon too much to take advantage of the circumstances. What did Paul mean by "in thy stead"? In verse 19 the apostle reminded Philemon that the latter owed the former his very life. This no doubt refers to Philemon's spiritual life, although we cannot be positive about all Paul meant by the statement. Onesimus had ministered to Paul as Philemon would have done if he had been present. He had been Philemon's substitute.

It was not easy for Paul to send Onesimus back to his master Philemon. Paul used a very descriptive phrase here: "the bonds of the gospel." Paul was a prisoner at the time, enduring hardship for the sake of the gospel. Onesimus had been a great blessing to the aged prisoner. Now he would no longer have the comfort and assistance of the one he had led to the Lord.

**14. But without thy mind would I do nothing:** ... without your consent, —*ET* ... unless you knew about it, —*SEB* ... I would not do a single thing about it, —*WLMS.*

**that thy benefit should not be as it were of necessity:** ... your kind action may not be compulsory, —*BRKL* ... Then your goodness would not be forced, —*SEB* ... not be as of compulsion, —*CNDT* ... and not forced, —*NIV.*

**but willingly:** ... but voluntary, —*CNFT*, —*CNDT*, —*WLMS* ... will be spontaneous, —*NIV* ... because you wanted to, —*NLTG.*

**14.** Paul would not take the liberty to assume Philemon would go along with Paul's desire to keep Onesimus as his assistant. He did not want to act without his friend's consent, even though he probably had the authority to do so. Then Paul gave the main reason for his approach relative to this matter. He did not believe in manipulating people into positions so they would have to do him favors—what he called "of necessity" (*kata anankēn*). Paul preferred for people to act "willingly" (*kata hekousion*).

**15. For perhaps he therefore departed for a season:** ... Perhaps this is why he was briefly separated from you, —*LILY.*

**that thou shouldest receive him for ever:** ... that you might get him back permanently, —*NORL.*

**15.** This verse seems a little puzzling when one realizes that God certainly did not will for Onesimus to desert his master. However, God did permit it to happen. He made an evil circumstance "work together for good." As a result, Onesimus heard the message of salvation, gave his life to the Lord Jesus Christ, and became a new creature in the Lord. "Season" literally refers to "an hour" (*hōran*), that is, for a short time; and the phrase "for ever" means for eternity (*aiōnion*).

**16. Not now as a servant:** ... for he is not only your property, —NORL ... not as a slave any longer, —WLMS.

**but above a servant, a brother beloved:** ... but better than, —BRKL.

**specially to me, but how much more unto thee:**

**both in the flesh, and in the Lord?:** ... both as a man and as a Christian, —LILY, —TCNT.

**16.** There is a definite relationship between the thought expressed in verse 15 and the one in verse 16. But there is a slight shift from the previous basis of Paul's sincere respect for his friend Philemon to an emphasis upon the spiritual relationship they both had shared for some time and that now Onesimus also shared with them. Did Paul mean by the words "not now as a servant" that he expected Philemon to free Onesimus and grant him a completely different social status from what he previously had? Although we cannot be sure about the apostle's intentions, it sounds as if he was not in favor of slavery for Onesimus. There is at least a hint that Philemon should consider the possibility of changing Onesimus' status as a slave.

**17. If thou count me therefore a partner:** ... if you consider me a comrade, —WLMS ... as a true friend, —NLTG.

**receive him as myself:** ... accept Onesimus as you would accept me, —SEB ... welcome him as me, —KLGS ... take him to your bosom as you would me, —WLMS.

**17.** As a result of the spiritual bond among the three now, the apostle knew he could depend upon his "partner" (*koinōnon*) to accept Onesimus as he would Paul himself. Obviously, God had not called Philemon to fulfill the same function in the New Testament church that He had called Paul to fulfill, nor had He given to Philemon the same responsibility He had placed upon Paul. Still, they were "partners."

**18. If he hath wronged thee, or oweth [thee] ought:** ... if he cheated you at all, —BRKL ... if he have injured you, —CMPB.

**put that on mine account:** ... charge it to me, —CNFT, —TCNT ... put it on my bill, —KLGS.

**18.** Here we come to the heart of the matter of restitution in Paul's letter to Philemon. This fifth basis for Paul's appeal to his friend to accept Onesimus stands in stark contrast to the fourth one, showing that the spiritual should not be separated from the practical. Paul's promise to make any necessary restitution certainly would have been a meaningless offer unless he had the funds to back up his statement. We do know that he lived in his own rented house (Acts 28:30), so he must have had some material means. In a spiritual sense the apostle's example here gives us a beautiful picture of what Christ did for humans when He took the penalty for our sins upon himself. We owed a debt that we never could have paid to God, but Jesus took the debt upon himself and paid a debt He really did not owe.

**19. I Paul have written [it] with mine own hand:**

**I will repay [it]:** ... I will refund it, —CNDT ... I will pay it in full, —WLMS.

**albeit I do not say to thee:** ... not to mention, —WLMS.

**how thou owest unto me even thine own self besides:** ... you, yourself, are indebted to me, —NORL ... you owe me your life, —NLTG ... your very life, —SEB ... your very soul, —TCNT.

**19.** If the apostle indeed dictated the epistle to an amanuensis as was his normal custom (Romans 16:22), he must have taken the writing instrument suddenly from the writer and with his own hand wrote, "I will repay it." Just as suddenly, though, he reminded the recipient of the letter of the reciprocal debt Philemon owed him. As was noted previously, this reminder must have referred to the spiritual debt Philemon owed to the apostle because he probably heard the gospel message through Paul's ministry, either during the time the apostle spent in Ephesus (Acts 19) or on some other occasion, or by some indirect means. Possibly Epaphras, or someone else who received training under Paul in Ephesus, preached the gospel of salvation to Philemon, resulting in his conversion to Christianity. The statement, though, may mean even more than that.

**20. Yea, brother, let me have joy of thee in the Lord:** ... I would like some return myself from you, —WLMS.

**refresh my bowels in the Lord:** ... Comfort my heart, —LILY ... Console my heart, —CNFT ... Refresh my inmost being, —KLGS ... you will lift up my heart in Christ, —SEB ... buoy up my deepest feelings in Christ, —BRKL.

**20.** The sixth and final basis for Paul's appeal was his confidence in his friend Philemon. Paul was not above asking other people for help when special needs existed. Besides, his request was not for himself, but for a friend whom God had blessed in a special way by bringing him into the family of God. For the third time in this short letter Paul used the Greek neuter term (*ta splanchna*) that expresses the deepest emotions possible for a person to feel.

**21. Having confidence in thy obedience I wrote unto thee:** ... Confident of your compliance, —*LILY* ... Trusting in thy compliance, —*CNFT.*

**knowing that thou wilt also do more than I say:** ... I am sure that, —*WLMS* ... knowing that thou wilt do even beyond, —*CNFT* ... knowing full well that you will do by me what I am asking, —*MNTG* ... I know you'll do even more than I ask, —*BECK* ... do even more than I have suggested, —*ADAM* ... even beyond the things I say, —*WUST* ... more than I request, —*BRKL.*

**21.** The apostle was sure Philemon would do even more than he asked. Paul must have known Philemon well enough to realize he would respond positively to such a request. How could anyone turn down a request couched in the terms of this passage? It would be interesting to know exactly what Philemon's response was. It would not be too difficult, though, for a spiritually minded individual to conclude that the recipient of the letter must have acquiesced to Paul's request without any hesitation. All of us need to make serious requests at times. If we would allow it to do so at such times, Paul's pattern in making his crucial request of Philemon could be a great help to us.

**22. But withal prepare me also a lodging:** ... One thing more, Bed: ... Please also prepare for me, —*MNTG* ... At the same time get a room ready for me, —*ADAM* ... be putting in readiness a guest room for me, —*WUST* ... get the guest room ready, —*KLGS* ... have a guest-room ready for me, too, —*WLMS.*

**for I trust that through your prayers:** ... for I am expecting, —*WUST* ... for I am hoping by your prayers, —*MNTG* ... through your prayers, —*ADAM.*

**I shall be given unto you:** ... I shall have the gracious privilege of coming to you, —*WLMS* ... being restored to you, —*LILY* ... to be given back to, —*BECK* ... granted to you, —*WUST.*

**22.** As in the other Prison Epistles, here again Paul indicates an expectation of imminent release from his first Roman imprisonment. His request of Philemon to prepare a guest room for him makes it clear. It also shows early believers provided for traveling ministers. But even while making this request, showing tact once more, Paul commended his future host for his prayers for him.

**23. There salute thee Epaphras:** ... sends you his best regards, —*NORL* ... sends you greetings,

—*MNTG* ... greets you, —*ADAM* ... wishes to be remembered to you, —*WLMS.*

**my fellowprisoner in Christ Jesus:** ... my cellmate, —*SEB* ... my fellow captive, —*CNDT* ... in the cause of, —*WLMS.*

**23.** The Colossian correspondence contains added information about Epaphras, and the reference in this verse no doubt concerns the same person. What did Paul mean by calling Epaphras "my fellow prisoner in Christ Jesus"? Was he using the phrase metaphorically to mean Epaphras also had become a bondslave of Jesus Christ, or had this man actually been placed in prison for some reason? Maybe Epaphras became a prisoner voluntarily in order to assist Paul.

**24. Marcus, Aristarchus, Demas, Lucas, my fellowlabourers:** ... along with, —*ADAM* ... so do ... my fellow workers, —*MNTG*, —*WLMS.*

**24.** The reader should notice that the same five people are mentioned in this passage as in Colossians 4:10, 12, 14. This fact helps lend credence to the belief of many commentators that Paul wrote Colossians and Philemon at approximately the same time. Mark was a relative of Barnabas, a very close friend and associate of the apostle Paul. Fortunately, Barnabas had shown more patience than Paul, and it seems that Barnabas was right, and that Paul realized this fact at a later time. Mark not only became an associate of Paul and a definite help to him, but he also assisted the apostle Peter in his ministry (1 Peter 5:13), as well as being privileged to write the Gospel that bears his name. Aristarchus also became one of Paul's trusted associates and traveled with him many times (Acts 19:29; 20:4), even on his journey as a captive to Rome (Acts 27:2). At this time even Demas served as a trusted assistant of Paul. Luke, a Gentile physician who dedicated his life to the Lord Jesus Christ, completed the entourage of people with Paul at that time, people that Paul honored by calling them "fellow laborers."

**25. The grace of our Lord Jesus Christ [be] with your spirit. Amen:** ... The help of, —*ADAM* ... The love of the Lord, —*BECK.*

**25.** Paul's closing statement serves as another excellent reminder of his dependence upon God's grace and his consuming desire that other people do the same. "The grace of our Lord Jesus Christ" is that operating principle which caused Christ to sacrifice himself on the cross for the sins of mankind.

# HEBREWS

## Overview

The literary style of the Epistle to the Hebrews is immediately striking. Without any greeting or opening, the author introduces his main theme: Christ is the fulfillment and completion of the revelation of God which began in the Old Testament. The letter does, however, close in keeping with epistolary style and custom, with a series of personal greetings and wishes for the recipients' well-being.

One notes the absence of any biographical opening comments about the author of the letter to the Hebrews. Although almost certainly the author was known and respected by his recipients, his identity has nonetheless been forgotten. Even the Early Church had to be content with speculating as to his identity. Some thought it was Paul (e.g., Clement of Alexandria, died ca. 215), while others contended it was Barnabas or another of Paul's coworkers.

Despite the inclusion of Hebrews in the Pauline corpus as early as the Third Century by the Eastern church, it was not until the Fourth Century that the West included it in the New Testament Scripture collection as the 14th letter of Paul. Even as late as the Reformation, however, questions concerning the canonicity of Hebrews persisted. When Luther resisted placing Hebrews among the "correct certain main books" of Scripture, his decision was linked to a particular doctrinal issue, one that had been debated in the Church since ancient times. Some believe 6:4-6 teaches there is no possibility of being saved after once falling from faith. Such a strong viewpoint greatly affected the general attitude and practice of the Church towards repentance. It further led to a decrease in the letter's reputation. By virtue of its own immanent truth, however, the letter to the Hebrews did manage to survive and has proved to be one of the pillars of New Testament revelation.

The question of authorship is unanswerable. One of the best hypotheses is Luther's theory that it was Apollos. According to Acts 18:24-28, Apollos, who worked in Ephesus, was a Jewish Christian from Alexandria: "an eloquent man . . . mighty in the Scriptures." Both of these qualifications, knowledge of the Scriptures and eloquence of speech (a by-product of his Hellenistic culture) could be applied to the author of Hebrews. But as readers of the Bible we must be content with what the letter itself tells us, and it does not tell us its author's name. Some scholars aver that although the style is different from Paul's other writings he may be the author of this book.

We do learn that he knows Timothy (13:23) and that he was with believers from Italy (13:24). From this some have concluded that the letter was sent to the church in Rome or to a group within it.

Since portions of the letter to the Hebrews appear in 1 Clement, it is clear that it was written before A.D. 95. Perhaps it was penned as early as the midsixties, since we read nothing in it about the destruction of the temple.

The letter indicates that the writer was disturbed by the spiritual condition of some of his readers. At a time when they should have been prepared to teach others, it was still necessary to teach them the fundamental truths of the Faith (5:12). Their problem was that they were "dull of hearing" (5:11). The seriousness of the situation is reflected in the author's repeated warnings of the risk of backsliding (6:4-8; 10:26-31; 12:15-17). There was apparently some tendency towards schism (10:25), as well as a spiritual weakening and faintheartedness (12:3). The main issue was that second generation Christians (2:3) needed to be strengthened in their faith.

As the Greek title (*pros hebraious*, added in the Second Century) indicates, the letter probably was addressed to a church body largely made up of Jewish Christians. Under the pressure of persecution and discouragement because the coming of the Lord had not occurred (10:32-39), they were being enticed to return to Judaism. In light of this, the author admonished them to hold fast to their profession of faith (4:14-16). They must not throw away their confidence, which held a promise of great reward (10:35). The warnings are so general, though, they can apply to Christians of all generations.

## The Distinct Trait of the Epistle to the Hebrews

In order to understand properly the Epistle to the Hebrews, one must scrutinize the text and read it in connection with the rest of the New Testament. No New Testament writing stands alone, isolated from the rest. The great contribution of the New Testament Scriptures is their united testimony to Jesus Christ as Lord and Saviour. Their dependence on one another, though, varies considerably.

Of all of the epistolary literature, the Epistle to the Hebrews stands apart as the one most distinctly referring to the earthly life of Jesus. Here we encounter a clear recognition that Jesus is God incarnate, that He was tempted, that He agonized in Gethsemane (5:7), that He suffered and died. We also detect some doctrinal correspondence with the Gospel of John: (1) the preexistent Jesus takes part in creation (cf. John's prologue); (2) Jesus is portrayed as the priestly intercessor (John 17, the high priestly prayer); and (3) like John, the author of Hebrews is concerned about properly worshiping God in spirit and truth (cf. John 4:23).

In the same way the letter shares a close affinity with Paul's theology. Both emphasize the inability of the Law to save or atone for sin (Romans 3:20; Hebrews 10:1f.). Both contrast Sinai and the heavenly Jerusalem (Galatians 4:24f.; Hebrews 12:18f.), and both understand Jesus' death to be a sacrifice. Paul, however, does not portray Jesus as the High Priest. This is an important distinction that characterizes the Epistle to the Hebrews.

More than any other letter in the New Testament, Hebrews is oriented around the cultic, ritualistic system of Judaism. The presentation builds upon images of sacrifice and atonement. Taking the Old Testament's guidelines for ritual sacrifice and priestly service as a starting point, the author portrays Christ to his readers as the One who makes atonement, the ultimate High Priest, whose self-sacrifice secured, once and for all, our eternal redemption (9:12).

The Epistle to the Hebrews shows how the old covenant and its temple cultus had attained its end and fulfillment in Christ. The chain of logic here is reminiscent of Paul's dispute with Judaism over the proper understanding of the Law. Now the ritual of the Old Testament sacrificial system is being exposed as just as inadequate as the Old Testament Law to atone and redeem mankind from its sin. Such redemption requires a far superior sacrifice than that which the high priest offered on the Day of Atonement. Instead of taking away sins, these offerings only succeeded in being a reminder of sin (10:1-4). But, because Christ offered himself as a pure sacrifice to God (9:14), He cleansed us from our sins (1:3). He has given us the ability to approach the Holy of Holies with boldness (10:19) and to serve God (12:28).

Hebrews provides a proper understanding of the two covenants. It is handled in such a way that the old covenant is not consequently viewed as superfluous. God is the source of both covenants. That there should be two covenants is also according to the counsel of God; it is part of His plan of salvation. Hebrews also emphasizes that believers, even of that era, were living in the last days (1:2) when God in a decisive way had graciously intervened in the history of His people, in accordance with His promises. All the promises were fulfilled in Christ, God's Son. Therefore, solely because

Christ had come, the inspired writer could challenge the most time-honored institutions of the Jewish religion—the tabernacle, the priesthood, and the sacrificial system.

The Old Testament, however, retains its significance, since it forms the background for the ultimate revelation of God in Christ. So the entire thesis is constructed on the Old Testament, which is viewed from a messianic perspective.

Hebrews must be viewed in light of first-century circumstances, especially in reference to Judaism outside of Palestine, i.e., Hellenistic Judaism, which flourished in the Greek culture. Perhaps the foremost representative of Hellenistic Judaism would be Philo, who lived in Alexandria from around 20 B.C. to A.D. 45. But Hebrews does not follow Philo, as the altogether different use of Scripture makes plain.

Even though Philo considered the Old Testament to be divine Scripture and knew its contents, he used an allegorical method to interpret it. This enabled him to interpret Scripture according to his own philosophical premises rather than according to Biblical teachings. In contrast to Philo, Hebrews does not interpret Old Testament texts philosophically, but messianically. In company with the other witnesses of the New Testament, it proclaims the message of the Bible as a record of God's saving act in Christ. Each quotation from the Old Testament is carefully interpreted in light of its fulfillment in the new covenant.

Typically, this reflects a typological method according to which persons and institutions of the Old Testament are interpreted as "types" or "patterns" that occur in the New Testament. Melchizedek is thus presented as a type of Christ, as the true High Priest (chapter 7); the tabernacle a picture of the heavenly sanctuary (chapter 9). The main point is that the realization or fulfillment of the types began with Christ; the Law was just a shadow of the good things to come, not the things themselves (10:1).

## The Outline of the Epistle to the Hebrews

The arrangement of this epistle is precise and clear-cut. The first major section extends to chapter 5 and discusses the superiority of the revelation of the new covenant over the old. Christ surpasses the angels (chapter 1) as well as Moses (chapter 3). The second major section extends from 4:14-10:31 and gives a thorough description of the high priestly office of Jesus and His work of atonement. The third and final main section is made up largely of admonitions (10:32-13:17). This is not to imply that admonishing is limited to only the final three chapters; on the contrary, the letter's entire structure of sections of instruction interspersed with pastoral advice suggests this is a prime concern.

The structure of the letter does not alter its primary goal: to encourage the readers to persevere in and better understand their faith.

## Outline

I. THE NEW, FINAL REVELATION OF GOD (1:1-4:13)

  A. God Has Spoken by His Son (1:1-4)

  B. Christ's Superiority to the Angels (1:5-14)

  C. Warning Against Falling From Salvation (2:1-4)

  D. The Temporary Humbling of Christ (2:5-18)

  E. Christ's Superiority to Moses (3:1-6)

  F. Warning Against Stubbornness (3:7-19)

  G. Continuation of the Sabbath Rest (4:1-10)

  H. Praise of the Word of God (4:11-13)

II. CHRIST AS THE TRUE HIGH PRIEST (4:14-10:31)

  A. Christ the Compassionate High Priest (4:14-16)

  B. In the Manner of Melchizedek (5:1-10)

  C. Renewed Rebuke of Readers (5:11-6:8)

  D. God's Covenant Faithfulness (6:9-20)

  E. Jesus Is High Priest Just Like Melchizedek (7:1-28)

  F. Jesus Is High Priest in the Heavenly Sanctuary (8:1-13)

  G. The Perfect Sacrifice of Jesus (9:1-10:18)

  H. The Danger of Apostasy (10:19-31)

III. STANDING FIRM IN THE FAITH (10:32-13:25)

  A. Keeping One's Confidence (10:32-39)

  B. The Power of Faith in the Lives of the Patriarchs (11:1-40)

  C. Christ the Author and Finisher of the Faith (12:1-11)

  D. Warning Against Rejecting the Grace of God (12:12-17)

  E. The Glory of the New Covenant (12:18-29)

  F. Social Responsibilities (13:1-6)

  G. Religious Gatherings (13:7-17)

  H. Personal Applications (13:18-25)

## The New, Final Revelation of God (1:1-4:13)

Understanding the significance of the names of Jesus is essential for understanding the Book of Hebrews. The name characterizing the human nature of the Lord, "Jesus," is used no less than nine times:

"But we see Jesus, who was made a little lower than the angels" (2:9). By virtue of His incarnation Jesus was restricted in time and space; He had to comply with the restrictions of His humanity and at last was handed over to certain men and the powers that stood behind them. The fact that He humbled himself and became obedient unto death (Philippians 2:8) is the basis for His being crowned with glory and honor.

"Consider the Apostle and High Priest of our profession, Christ Jesus" (3:1). Jesus brought together in His person the roles of both Moses and Aaron under the old covenant. As the "one sent" (*apostolon*, "apostle") from God, Jesus relates to us the Word of God. As the true High Priest, He has covered our sins and given to us the grace of God.

Jesus entered behind the veil (i.e., into the Holy of Holies) as a forerunner for us (6:20). In His ministry as High Priest He retains His true humanity, thus He is not inferior to the Aaronic high priest who alone was allowed to enter the Most Holy Place.

Jesus represents a better covenant (7:22). He became the guarantee of a new and better covenant as a true man.

Because of the sacrifice of Christ, we are given confidence ("boldness") to enter the Holy of Holies (10:19). By virtue of the sacrifice of the One who shared our nature, we have gained access to God (cf. Romans 5:1ff.).

As we fix our eyes on Jesus, the author and finisher of our faith, we see that looking to Him is the source of our strength (12:2). Through His obedience, He provided the perfect model of faith.

We have come to the mediator of a new covenant, Jesus (12:24, see 7:22).

Christ suffered outside the gate (13:12). Once again we see how the name *Jesus* is related to His suffering and death.

The God of peace brought the Great Shepherd of the flock, even our Lord Jesus, up from the dead (13:20). The Resurrection, which is otherwise not mentioned in Hebrews, is explicitly mentioned here. Its truth is affirmed by the presence of the earthly name, Jesus, in reference to it. We should observe here that the name Jesus has a unique relationship to the bodily appearance of the Lord, His humbling of himself, His suffering, and His death. The redemptive act on history is not based on some pagan myth of redemption.

## God has Spoken by His Son

A fundamental event for the Hebrews' argument is the reality of the Incarnation. God became man in Jesus. This view closely corresponds with the one found in the "Christ hymn" of Philippians 2:6-11. As the Son, Jesus learned obedience, and in every way Christ subjected himself to the will of God (5:8). Only after He had suffered everything necessary in the plan of God could He become the source of our eternal salvation (5:9). By suffering Jesus demonstrated that through the cross He was the perfect offering for sin. Obedience marked His service to God and made available forgiveness of sins and salvation.

The Book of Hebrews takes very seriously the need for humanity to be saved. All human beings are subject to death. Death is not regarded as natural, however, but an unnatural consequence of the power of sin. There is no escaping death's power as long as the devil has authority over death and over all those subject to death. If there is to be any salvation, the devil must be conquered on his own terms: on earth by a human being. This is why Christ had to come as a man and share in "flesh and blood" (2:14).

Christ's incarnation and subsequent death has a twofold sense: (1) Through His death as a man He overcame the ruler of death, the devil (2:14). (2) Christ redeemed mankind, which has always been enslaved to the fear of death (2:15). Because Christ submitted willingly to every consequence of being human, including being tempted, He is able to be a true high priest, who is merciful and faithful (2:17,18).

In explicit statements Hebrews provides a rough draft of the life of Christ. Christ calls men His brothers (2:11); He partakes of flesh and blood (2:14). His being "made like his brethren" expresses an identification with humanity, including things common to men—temptation, suffering, and death. It is as the One who was tempted and who suffered that Jesus offers comfort to those who are tempted (2:18).

Also descriptive of the work of Jesus are names like "Christ," "Lord," "Son of God." The title *Son* especially permeates the Book of Hebrews, as does *Son of God*. The opening verses reflect this fact: "God, who at sundry times and in divers manners spake in time past unto the fathers by the prophets, hath in these last days spoken unto us by his Son" (1:1,2).

All of God's former saving work among the people of Israel pointed toward the final revelation of the Son. Incarnation, thus, was the goal of God's revelation. The new age could begin; the time of fulfillment had arrived, just as the prophets foretold. Once again God was speaking, now through His Son, "whom he hath appointed heir of all things, by whom also he made the worlds; who being the brightness of his glory, and the express image of his person, and upholding all things by the word of his power, when he had by himself purged our sins, sat down on the right hand of the Majesty on high" (1:2,3).

This opening description of the nature and work of the Son shows how exalted this position is in the history of salvation. Christ is not just the Redeemer who "had by himself purged our sins," He is also the One by whom all of creation came into existence. To the same degree as other New Testament writings, Hebrews emphasizes that Christ participated in the creation of the universe (as well as in maintaining its existence; cf. John 1:3; Colossians 1:17).

But first and foremost, Christ is the Redeemer. He has cleansed us from our sins (1:3). Sin prevents men from approaching God; it is only removed when purification is made. Christ provided such cleansing by His perfect sacrifice. By virtue of His saving work, Christ has been exalted to the right hand of God. Moreover, it is noteworthy that as early as this introduction Christ is portrayed in His threefold role of Prophet (God has spoken to us by His Son), Priest (He, by himself, cleansed us from sin), and King (He sat down at the right hand of the Majesty).

Whether Christ is called by His earthly name, Jesus, or His divine title, Son of God, He is one person. The divine will is disclosed in one person, according to Hebrews, the Son (2:10). God speaks to us through His Son, and it is the Son, who having cleansed us from sin, sits at the right hand of God (1:1-4).

Although Hebrews repeatedly refers to the "Son," God is called "Father" on only one occasion (Hebrews 1:5, a quote from 2 Samuel 7:14). God is the exalted Majesty from whom Christ receives all. God installed Christ as heir (1:2). Christ also receives the office of High Priest, since He did not presume such honor for himself (5:5).

The essential relationship between the Son and God comes through in the following statement: "Who being the brightness of his glory, and the express image of his person" (1:3). The divine status of Christ is not based on adoption, but on His nature. Christ reveals the Father. He is a reflection (*apaugasma*) of His glory and a perfect image, representation (*charaktēr*) of the nature of God, i.e., what God is really like (cf. John 5:19,30; 14:9).

In virtually the same breath Hebrews presents the Son's relationship to the world. He participated in creation—"by whom also he made the worlds"—and in the providence of God—"upholding all things by the word of his power." Finally Christ is the heir of all things. The created world did not only come into existence through Christ, it would fall into utter chaos without Him. Because Christ became heir, it is further implied that creation first attains consummation in Him (cf. 1:13; 10:13).

Corresponding to the aforementioned titles, Christ's work is viewed from a twofold perspective: His earthly life and His service in heaven, in the heavenly sanctuary.

Since the "children" have "flesh and blood," He partook of their nature as well (2:14; cf. 7:14). Hebrews stresses that as representative of all mankind, Christ's humanity was total; in every way He had to be like His "brothers and sisters" (cf. 2:17). His tasting of death was to the advantage of all (2:9). Although He is fully human, this in no way detracts from His being fully God. The Incarnation began a brief temporary period during which Christ willingly submitted to the will of the Father. For a little while He was made a little lower than the angels (Hebrews 2:7,9; cf. Philippians 2:7).

Temptation, tears, and suffering are characteristics of any human life. Except for the Gospels, it is the Epistle to the Hebrews which most realistically captures the earthly life of Jesus (4:15; 5:7f.; 7:26). Christ's being subject to earthly trials enables Him in His glorified humanity to have compassion upon the weak (4:15). But Christ is different from humankind in one distinct way: He is without sin (4:15; 7:26). Moreover, the book adds some other virtues: Jesus trusted God (2:13; 5:7ff.); He was faithful (2:17; 3:2); He was merciful and compassionate (2:17; 4:15); and He had great faith (12:2).

At no time, however, is the human nature of Jesus stressed in reference to His sacrificing of himself. He is God and man in one and the same person, Jesus Christ. In a passage resembling the testimony of John the apostle that Christ has the power to lay down His life and to take it up again (John 10:18), the Epistle to the Hebrews stresses that it was by virtue of the eternal Spirit that Christ offered himself up as a spotless offering (9:14; cf. 7:16).

The Epistle to the Hebrews draws a close relationship between the earthly obedience of Christ and His exaltation to the right hand of God in heaven (cf. 2:9; 12:2). The book looks back on the humility and suffering that took place in the past, and at the same time looks forward to the worldwide dominion of Christ which is yet to be revealed.

Unlike the writings of the apostle Paul, Hebrews gives themes like the Resurrection (13:20) and Second Coming (9:28; 10:37) only a moderate role. It attaches much more significance to the Ascension (4:14; 6:20; 7:26; 9:11f.,24) and to Christ's being seated on the throne at the right hand of God in heaven (1:3; 8:1; 10:12; 12:2). This is where Christ exercises His role as eternal High Priest on our behalf (9:24; cf. 7:25). From here He also encourages those who are tempted (2:18). The consummation of the work of atonement makes possible Christ's ascension to the heavenly throne (1:3).

## Warnings in the Epistle

One distinguishing feature of the Epistle to the Hebrews is that its teaching is often interrupted by warning sections (3:1-4,16; 5:11-6:20; 10:19,39; 12:1-13,17). Based on what he knew was occurring among his readers, the author offered some practical advice and warning. But rather than appearing to be "interruptions," they may reflect key passages for unlocking the meaning of the letter as a whole. One is immediately struck by the elaborate explanations of the priesthood and sacrificial system. This presentation, it should be realized, is addressing a particular, definite problem of believers. The actual situation is best reconstructed by looking at the warning sections.

The heart of the Book of Hebrews is that Christ is sacrificed, once and for all, and through this He has provided cleansing for our sins and access to God's throne (9:19,22). In keeping with this theme, Christ is the forerunner who leads His people into the heavenly land of promise (6:20; 11:13-16). The Christian is responsible to strive by faith and perseverance for this heavenly goal, according to the pattern provided by Christ's own life and death (12:1-3; 13:12,13).

## Christ's Superiority to the Angels

Many Scripture references are presented in 1:5-14 to show Christ's superiority to the angels. Chapter 2 opens with an admonition not to be lured away from salvation. The Holy Spirit intends to divert believers from such disaster by reminding them that Christian revelation is proclaimed, not by angels, but by the Lord himself. Moreover, it is confirmed by mighty deeds (2:3,4) and has an explicit relationship with the world to come (2:5).

According to Jewish thinking the law of Moses had been mediated by angels (cf. Galatians 3:10; Acts 7:53). This undoubtedly had influenced some of the believers; they were thus in jeopardy of forfeiting their salvation and denying the revelation of God in Jesus Christ. In the world to come dominion belongs solely to Christ.

## Warning Against Backsliding

The believer's lifestyle should be governed by an awareness of the powers of the coming age (3:1ff.). As those having a share in the heavenly calling, they are obligated to hold fast to their Christian hope with confidence and conviction (3:1,6). And once more, Christ is their pattern for this.

Certainly Moses' faithfulness is an encouraging example, but as the Son of God, Jesus has an authority that exceeds that of Moses by far (3:2-6).

## Warning Against Stubbornness

The crisis facing the believers was best compared with the situation Israel experienced in the wilderness. In actuality, the Christian life is itself an "exodus" whose goal is to experience the Scriptures' promise of rest (3:7-11). Psalm 95:7-11 offers a sharp caution. The "today" of the Psalms did not lose its relevance for the readers of Hebrews. It summoned the hearer to seize the eternal moment announced by Jesus, and to complete the journey that began by believing in Him. The risk consists in the fact that like ancient Israel, some will harden themselves and will not attain "rest" because of their unbelief (3:12-19).

## Continuation of the Sabbath Rest

The writer offers a more encouraging word in chapter 4. The promise of entering God's rest is still in force. No one should think that it is too late (4:1). Again the author recalls Psalm 95, which is essentially the invitation given to the wilderness generation and which is now given to us. The Israelites forfeited the promise because of unbelief. But the Word of God is not ineffective. Even though they declined the invitation, the invitation is still in effect (4:6-9). Therefore, no one should think that he or she will be abandoned if by faith one seizes God's promise for his or her own.

Nevertheless, the author does not deny that the call for decision is urgent. He warns his readers against the danger of backsliding so they too do not become an example of disobedience (4:11). Note that throughout the letter the threat of falling was viewed as very present (cf. 6:4-6; 10:26-31; 12:15-17).

An interesting "digression" occurs in 5:11-6:20. Here the author pauses to shift his teaching to the spiritual level of his listeners. Having frequently referred to Christ as the true High Priest, the writer is ready to give a basic description of Christ's role as High Priest. This is difficult, though, for the readers are "dull of hearing" (5:11). He reproaches them, because instead of making progress in Christian understanding, they have to be instructed in the most basic principles of the Faith (Hebrews 5:12-14; cf. 1 Corinthians 2:6ff.; 3:1ff.; 1 Peter 2:2).

The "basic foundations" ("elementary teachings," NIV) of faith are listed in 6:1,2. There are six aspects, paired in three groups: "repentance and faith," "teaching on baptisms and laying on of hands," and "the resurrection of the dead and eternal judgment." The first two are linked to the basic articles of the Gentile mission (Windisch), and are probably indicative that the author is first thinking of Gentile Christian readers. However, nothing would prevent them from being Jews either. "Repentance and faith" belong together and represent the response to the preaching demanded by Jesus himself (cf. Matthew 5:20; Mark 1:15; John 14:1). "Teachings concerning baptisms and the laying on of hands" also belong together. "Baptisms" here probably refers to "absolutions, washings, or other ritual purifications, such as Jewish proselyte baptism or the baptism of John.

Christian baptism may be meant, although the plural is used (cf. the use with Apollos in Acts 18:24-26). The Book of Acts frequently depicts the Spirit as being given through the laying on of hands at baptism or by an apostle. It was critical that Jewish converts be instructed about the res-

urrection of the dead and eternal judgment, since Christian revelation gave these events new significance (Manson, pp.62,63).

The writer is reaching a climax in his argument. His readers should have grown in their faith, but instead they are still immature. As a result of their immaturity the threat of backsliding is even greater. But the author is not totally discounting their possibility of salvation (6:9). They once demonstrated their Christian faith and love in their actions (6:10; cf. 10:32). The critical issue now is that they show a similar zeal and enduring faith so the promises of God might be realized (6:11,12). With warning as well as encouragement the Scriptures have awakened the spiritual sensitivity of the believers.

We encounter the same combination of encouragement and admonition in the second large admonishing section (10:19-39). On the one hand, the writer urges his readers to enter boldly into the Holy of Holies and to carry out the priestly duties to which they have been called. On the other hand, he warns them against falling into (i.e., being judged by) the hands of the living God. The shift in the voice of the verb reflects the pastoral concern of the writer. By virtue of Christ's sacrifice access to God is made possible. The potential for worshiping God and loving one's neighbor is made available. Therefore, there is a repeated invitation to enter the Holy of Holies (10:19), to draw near to God (10:22), and to encourage one another toward love and good deeds (10:24). But the readers must also be aware of the terrible judgment that awaits them if they ignore God's promise of grace in Christ (10:26f.).

Finally, chapter 13 contains a series of admonitions that first involve relations with society (13:1-6) and then congregational concerns (13:7-17). Among the social obligations of believers one finds hospitality (Hebrews 13:2; cf. Romans 12:13; 1 Peter 4:9), care of prisoners (Hebrews 13:3), and respect for marriage (Hebrews 13:4; cf. 1 Corinthians 6:9).

In later verses the readers are urged to remember the example left to them by the patriarchs and their forebears. They are not to be "carried away by all kinds of strange teachings" (13:9, NIV). Of the utmost importance is that they—because of their total dependence on Christ—offer the sacrifice of praise which pleases God (13:15,16).

The closing chapters give some important clues as to the background of the letter. It seems that the author is especially concerned about some divisiveness that is threatening the church. He thus warns against neglecting the assembling together for common worship (10:25). He also warns them not to succumb to false teachings (13:9). In conjunction with this he advises them to pay close attention to their leaders (13:17; cf. 13:7).

## "Salvation" in the Hebrews Epistle

Salvation is deliverance from the power of death; indeed, it is a rescue from every power or force that opposes God (5:7). But this is the negative side of salvation. Positively, salvation means a realization of the promises of God. This can be experienced in the present (6:9), but it will reach its total fulfillment in the eschatological consummation (1:14; 9:28).

Based upon the overall understanding of the Epistle to the Hebrews, the concept of salvation might best be described as "rest" (4:9,10). Rest is the fulfillment of God's promises. Especially is this so in the eschatological sense of physical and spiritual blessing. The expression *Sabbath rest* is best understood in relation to the Jewish concept that the Sabbath was a prototype of the future age to come.

If it is legitimate to describe salvation in terms of location, salvation is one's "homeland" (11:14,16); it is a "city" (11:10,16; 12:22; 13:14). Christian hope is thus directed toward an eternal heavenly goal. As a background to this, all the earthly institutions, such as the tabernacle, the Law, and the temple, are only shadows of the future heavenly reality. Abraham waited patiently for a "city which hath foundations, whose builder and maker is God" (11:10). This is why Abraham became a model of the Christian pilgrim, "For here have we no continuing city, but we seek one to come" (13:14).

The Old Testament shows that God is faithful. Some of the patriarchs and forebears were allowed to see the promises fulfilled. Abraham and Sarah were two such heroes of the Faith (6:15; cf. 11:11). But, in relation to the sending of the Son in the last days, any notion of fulfillment of the Old Testament promises can only be interpreted as models for the much more glorious fulfillment of the coming consummation (11:40). Against this backdrop the urgency of the author to the Hebrews is better appreciated. Salvation is infinite in scope from God's point of view. To reject it will inevitably lead to judgment (2:3).

Even though the Epistle to the Hebrews does not contain the word *Saviour* (*soter*), Christ is explicitly presented as the "pioneer of salvation" (2:10) and the "author of eternal salvation" (5:9). The life and work of Christ create the possibility of salvation for mankind. Through His obedience He clears a path for His "brothers and sisters" to approach God.

## Christ As the True High Priest (4:14-10:31)

What sets the Son apart: from all others, and what typifies His role in salvation, is that having offered a cleansing sacrifice for our sins, He placed himself at the right hand of the Majesty on high (1:3). With this saying the Epistle to the Hebrews succeeds in combining in a unique way the priestly and kingly offices of the ministry of Christ. This unique perspective has its most distinct form in the presentation of Christ as our High Priest.

## The Ministry of the High Priest

Humanity exists for the purpose of having fellowship with God. God created mankind in His own image (Genesis 1:27) to share a relationship based on love with his Creator and to enter into His rest (Hebrews 4:9). But humanity rebelled against God and rejected the Creator through acts of sin and disobedience.

Fallen humanity works hard trying to reestablish the severed ties with God, to rediscover the fellowship with and access to God that was lost because of Adam's fall. It is the duty of the priest to be the instrument of this "reconnection." Hebrews reflects the longing for perfection (7:11; 9:9) that is the basis for the high priest's service. The priest is the intermediary between God and man. The Jewish high priest represented the people to God and at the same time represented God to the people.

The revelation at Sinai held the promise that Israel would one day become a kingdom of priests and a holy people for God (Exodus 19:6). The people were thus concerned about such a relationship, but the priesthood was only performed by members of the priestly tribe, Aaron, his sons, and the Levites (Numbers 3:6-13).

The priest had several responsibilities. The Bible describes a few of the priestly duties that were linked to the Law, to teaching, and to the authority to judge (Leviticus 10:8-11; Deuteronomy 17:8,9). It also describes those duties centering around the tabernacle service, such as placing the showbread (Leviticus 24:5-9), burning incense (Exodus 30:7,8), sacrificing (especially the sprinkling of the blood, Leviticus 1:5), and blessing (Numbers 6:22-27).

The high priest represented all the people. This role was especially evident on the great Day of Atonement when he entered into the most holy area of the temple to make atonement for himself as well as for the sins of all Israel (Leviticus 16). The chain of reasoning was that through the person of the high priest the people themselves appeared before God in the very place (Holy of Holies) where His divine presence appeared in such a special way.

The Epistle to the Hebrews pays particular attention to the sacrifice offered on the Day of Atonement, because this event serves as a model for the work of Christ. At the same time, it was unmistakable proof of the inadequacy of the old covenant (10:1-4). In contrast to the sacrifice of the high priest, which had to be performed on a yearly basis, the sacrifice of Christ was "once for all" (10:10). The eternal sacrifice bears witness to the end of the old age and the establishment of the new covenant (9:15).

In 5:1-4 the writer explains the nature of the high priestly office, including its duties and place in the covenant arrangement. To be qualified to be a high priest, one must be chosen among men (5:1); he must understand human problems (5:2,3); and he must be called by God (5:4). The verses that follow show that Christ more than fulfills these requirements (5:5-10; cf. 2:17; 3:1; 4:14,15). The requirement that the high priest be a descendant of Aaron is not discussed here but is given special attention in chapter 7.

## The Eternal Priesthood of Christ

The fundamental text proving the high priestly status of Christ is Psalm 110:4: "Thou art a priest for ever after the order of Melchizedek." This passage is cited in Hebrews 5:6,10; 7:17,21 and is united with Psalm 2:7, a key text for interpreting the Epistle to the Hebrews.

The citations from the Psalms demonstrate the legitimacy of Christ's claim to the high priesthood, even though the Book of Hebrews is the only New Testament book to make such an assertion. The context for this unique witness of the Book of Hebrews must be sought in Jesus' own intimation that His death was a sacrifice (Mark 10:45; 14:24). Sacrifice is naturally connected with a priest who sacrifices (cf. John 17:19). In the same way, there is a close connection between Jesus' saying that He would build a temple not made by hands (Mark 14:58; 15:29; Matthew 26:61; John 2:19) and the concept in Hebrews of Jesus as the High Priest who enters into the heavenly sanctuary (9:24).

It is crucial to realize that everything implied in the concept of high priest—historically as well as theologically—is fulfilled once and for all in Christ. Christian confession since ancient times stands on this statement: Jesus is the true High Priest who has opened the way for us to the Most Holy Place (6:20; 10:19,20).

This explains why the high priestly office assumed by Christ is modeled not only after the Levitical priesthood, but also from the superior priesthood of the priest-king Melchizedek. Beginning with a Biblical promise: "Thou art a priest for ever after the order of Melchizedek" (Psalm 110:4; cf. Hebrews 5:6,10), the writer of Hebrews repeats in the early verses of chapter 7 what the Bible says concerning Melchizedek. This serves as the background for the perfect priesthood of Christ.

Who was Melchizedek? Point by point the writer lists what the Bible says about him in Genesis 14:17-20. He begins with Melchizedek's name and titles. Melchizedek is a messianic name, literally meaning "king of righteousness" (cf. Zechariah 9:9), as well as "king of peace" (cf. Isaiah 9:6). In connection with this king of Salem (i.e., Jerusalem), it is told that after the battle he met with Abraham with bread and wine and blessed him as a priest of the Most High. Abraham gave Melchizedek his tithe, thus signifying his acceptance of the God of this stranger and his authority as a priest.

When Melchizedek is described as being "without father, without mother, without descent, having neither beginning of days nor end of life, but made like unto the Son of God" (7:3), it appears to refer to the Jewish religion. According to Judaism, only one with a spotless and pure descent could become a priest (Ezra 2:61-63; Nehemiah 7:63-65). Thus Melchizedek did not meet the requirements. He was "unfit" for priestly service! But, it is perfectly clear that Melchizedek is a priest of a heavenly, unexplainable order. The logic of Hebrews does not always rest on Psalm 110:4. Melchizedek is a priest eternally; he thus lives continually and does not have a beginning or end.

One might ask whether the author of Hebrews detracts from Jesus by emphasizing the uniqueness of Melchizedek. But the contrary is true. The more he relates about Melchizedek, the more the glory of the Son of God shines through. Those numerous sayings about this ancient priest all have a messianic fulfillment and all point toward the Son of God. What occurred in ancient time is a prelude to what "in the last days" had become a reality in Christ. It is proper to say that because of Christ, new light is shed on the ancient, mysterious story of Melchizedek in Genesis 14.

That the priesthood of Melchizedek is superior to the Levitical priesthood is brought out by the writer's observation that Abraham offered a tithe to Melchizedek. Obviously the one who receives the tithe is superior to the one who gives it (7:4-8). We also find here a thought of great significance in the Scriptures. When Abraham met Melchizedek and gave him a tenth of his goods, in a unique way, as a descendant of Abraham, Levi was present too. The offspring is affected by his ancestor's actions. Thus Levi indirectly acknowledged the superior priesthood of Melchizedek (7:9,10).

The same kind of reasoning occurs on a higher plane. Adam was the first member of the human family. This made his fall even more catastrophic, because Adam is a corporate expression of all mankind to come. The many are going to be disobedient because of the fall of the one (Romans 5:17). This is why salvation had to be accomplished by one who could represent all humanity. Christ's duty was to restore what Adam had forfeited. Through His obedience He established a totally new race of people justified through His blood (Romans 5:9).

The account of Melchizedek serves as the first indication of the end of the old priesthood and the beginning of the new order. The Levitical priesthood was inadequate. The fact that Scriptures speak of a priest of another kind (other than those before), like Melchizedek, shows this. Undeniably a reorganization of the priesthood has occurred; the office is now the responsibility of the tribe of Judah. Scripture does not speak of priests from that tribe, but Christ did not acquire His status as High Priest through the Law, which required a certain parentage. Rather, He is the One with eternal existence. He alone is worthy of the testimony: "Thou art a priest for ever after the order of Melchizedek" (7:13-17).

Chapter 7 concludes the critical discussion of the superiority of Christ's priesthood to the Aaronic service (7:20ff.). The writer earlier showed that Christ has the qualifications of the ideal high priest. He is faithful, merciful, and compassionate (2:17,18; 4:15; 5:8; 7:26), and He received His position by virtue of a divine calling (5:5).

Moreover, as High Priest, Christ has several advantages over the Aaronic priesthood: (1) He was installed by an oath (7:21). (2) His priesthood cannot perish because He remains forever (Hebrews 7:23,24; cf. Psalm 110:4). (3) He is not affected by evil; He is perfect, unlike the Aaronic priest (7:26-28). (4) His sanctuary is not on earth, but in heaven (8:1; 9:11). (5) His sacrifice was given once and for all (*ephapax*); in contrast, the Jewish high priest had to offer sacrifice every year (9:12; 10:11). (6) The sacrifice of Christ reflects His total consecration (7:27; 10:10).

The writer reaches a brief climax in 8:1 when he states that we "have such a high priest, who is set on the right hand of the throne of the Majesty in the heavens." On a par with what is said in 1:3, this text shows how Christ unites the two offices of priest and king in His person. Having provided one offering for sins and thereby placing himself forever at the right hand of God, Christ now waits for the dominion that He secured to be finally established (10:11-14). These statements unite the priestly and kingly offices.

That Christ is forever at the right hand of God further signifies that His royal priesthood is eternal: "Jesus Christ the same yesterday, and today, and for ever" (13:8). As High Priest He stands between humanity and God; as King He represents God to humanity. Both roles are in effect eternally, because in perfectly fulfilling the will of God, Christ has taken His place at the right hand of the throne of God (12:2).

As our eternal and true High Priest, Christ can intercede to God on our behalf (7:25; 9:24; cf. Romans 8:34). We may ever bring God offerings of praise through Him (13:15). Christ provides access to the throne of God. "Let us therefore come boldly unto the throne of grace, that we may obtain mercy, and find grace to help in time of need" (4:16). We have this confidence through the sacrifice of Christ (10:19-22). Thus Christ fulfilled and surpassed the model provided by the Levitical priesthood. Eternal redemption was won by the One who is both sacrifice and priest.

## The Earthly and Heavenly Sanctuary

It is natural that in conjunction with the priesthood of Christ the Book of Hebrews discusses the sanctuary. The high priest and sanctuary are closely connected. Christ is said to serve in the sanctuary, the true tabernacle (8:2). With the additional comment that the sanctuary was not constructed by human hands but by the Lord himself, a contrast is obviously being drawn between the heavenly and earthly sanctuaries. Earthly priests serve in the earthly sanctuary, which is only a pattern and a shadow of the heavenly (8:5).

The reference is almost certainly to the portable, Mosaic tabernacle of Israel's wilderness journeys. The tabernacle sanctuary that Moses ordered to be built is the pattern of the coming perfect sanctuary (Exodus 25:9; 25:40; Hebrews 8:5).

The earthly sanctuary is described as a "tabernacle" (*skēnēn*; 8:5; 9:21; 13:10). The two parts of the tabernacle were the first room, called the Holy Place, and the second room, called the Most Holy Place (Holy of Holies; 9:2ff.). The Epistle to the Hebrews closely adheres to the language of the Septuagint at this juncture. Accordingly, *skēnēn* refers to the tabernacle as a whole. Besides *skēnēn*, the Book of Hebrews also utilizes the expression *to hagion* in connection with the earthly sanctuary (9:1). The Septuagint as well as Josephus and Philo also use this expression in this way.

Of decisive importance for the Epistle to the Hebrews is the idea that the heavenly sanctuary was a model for the earthly sanctuary. This idea is expressed as early as Exodus 25:40 (cf. Hebrews 8:5). Christ carries out His priestly duties in the heavenly sanctuary, in the true tabernacle. Hebrews 9:11 and 24 further emphasize that the heavenly sanctuary is not made by hands; in other words, it does not belong to this world. The heavenly temple is the true temple; the earthly tabernacle is just a reflection, a shadow of this. The logical outcome of such reasoning is fully realized in Christ.

Hebrews 9:1-5 gives the floor plan of the earthly tabernacle. The various parts are listed according to the information in Exodus 25 and 26. This provides a realistic background for the later description of the sacrificial service.

In the first room (Holy Place) the lampstand stood, as did the table and the bread of Presence (showbread). Behind this front room, separated by a veil, was the place of God's presence. There too was located the ark of the covenant containing the tables of the Decalogue. Inside the Most Holy Place cherubim watched over the mercy seat, the cover for the ark of the covenant and the place of atonement. Here atonement was made for the sins of the people. "There I will meet with thee, and I will commune with thee from above the mercy seat, from between the two cherubim which are upon the ark of the testimony, of all things which I will give thee in commandment unto the children of Israel" (Exodus 25:22; cf. 30:6). This is why this room was the most holy of all places.

## "Sacrifice" in the Hebrews Epistle

As is the case with other themes in the Epistle to the Hebrews, our understanding of sacrifice will be enhanced by recognizing the contrast between the old and new covenants. The Levitical sacrificial offering has its counterpart in the atoning sacrifice of Christ the High Priest. Hebrews reveals something majestic and significant in the Mosaic rituals of divine worship. Christians need not think otherwise; rather, if they acknowledge the beauty and significance of the Law, they will understand the gospel even better (Westcott).

It is important to recognize the time frame associated with the rituals and commands of the old covenant. They were in effect "until the time of the new order" (9:10, NIV). The nature of worship under the first covenant was not counter to the will of God. God had specifically overseen their implementation through Moses. However, because of its inability to secure complete atonement (i.e., including one's conscience; 9:9), the order of worship under the old covenant proved its own inadequacy. Since under the first covenant the priests had only limited access to the sanctuary—and the people had none at all—it had to be admitted that access to the heavenly sanctuary was not truly open (9:6-8). Through the Holy Spirit, we have a better understanding of the nature of the old covenant (Michel).

The Book of Hebrews views the Christ event as initiating and completing the transition from one age to the next. Until Calvary the place of sacrifice was in the earthly tabernacle. The new age involves worship of God in the heavenly sanctuary, where Christ has entered as forerunner. In the same manner, under the leadership of Christ, believers are able to enter the Most Holy Place (10:19; 13:14). The signs of the new age to come are present already; it is up to men and women to prepare themselves (8:13; 9:9; 13:12ff.).

The new covenant coming through Christ is spoken of in 9:11-14. Just as the earthly high priest entered the Holy of Holies on the Day of Atonement (e.g., especially Leviticus 16), Christ as High

Priest has entered heaven itself. And just as the high priest brought the sacrificed blood of goats and oxen, Christ has presented a sacrifice too—His own blood.

Similarities between the Aaronic high priest and Christ our High Priest are obvious, but Christ's role as High Priest is distinctive: (1) Christ has not entered an earthly but a heavenly sanctuary (9:11). (2) He has not presented the blood of bulls and goats, but His own blood (9:12). (3) He does not enter the sanctuary every year, but did so "once for all" (10:10; cf. 9:12, 26, 28). (4) Through His sacrifice, Christ has secured eternal redemption for those who believe in Him. Through the Cross, sin as the force which separates humanity from God has been overcome; access to the throne of God has been made freely possible (9:26).

The sacrificial system of the Old Testament was unable to secure any permanent atonement. That it had to be repeated each year proves this. Rather than removing the transgressions of the people, the Day of Atonement only reminded them of their perpetual sinfulness (10:1-4).

Naturally, the author of Hebrews regards the sacrificial system of the old covenant as typical of the perfect atoning work of Christ. When he associates Christ's offering of His blood with that of the various sacrifices of the old covenant, we should realize that the former sacrifices can only appear as ineffective, imperfect (10:1-14). But we must have a proper understanding of this effect. The old covenant sacrifices pointed to something beyond themselves. They were a model for the perfect atoning sacrifice that Christ would bring. That is why the old sacrificial system is described in such negative terms; it is to highlight the superiority of Christ's sacrifice, which began on the "night in which he was betrayed" (1 Corinthians 11:23). The old rituals of course served their purpose in their day, until the new covenant could be introduced. They thereby helped prepare God's people for their total fulfillment in Christ.

Under the former sacrificial system there was a sharp distinction between the offering of an animal and the presentation of its blood. Usually the sacrifice was butchered by the one on whose behalf the sacrifice was made; or, if it was a public sacrifice, by the representative of the people (i.e., the priest). But the sprinkling of blood on the altar could only be performed by a high priest. Under the new covenant Christ is both the sacrifice as well as the High Priest. Thus when He presents himself as a spotless sacrifice to God, He fulfills both roles by virtue of the Spirit (cf. 9:14). He consequently also fulfilled in His dual nature as God-man the purpose of human existence. He purified our conscience from dead works and enabled us to serve the living God. He is therefore the Mediator of a new covenant, so they which are called might receive the promise of eternal inheritance (9:14,15).

Before leaving the Book of Hebrews' teaching on sacrifice, we will outline in detail the ritual that took place on the Day of Atonement, because, as it was noted, it plays a significant role in preparing for the work of Christ.

The Day of Atonement was celebrated on the 10th day in the 7th month (tishri, equivalent to October). It is described in detail in Leviticus 16 (cf. Leviticus 23:26ff.; Numbers 29:7ff.; Ezekiel 45:17ff.). The rituals on the Day of Atonement reflected an understanding of the many views of sacrifice, which according to divine decree were established to afford mankind entrance to God (Westcott).

The central figure was the high priest. All general priestly duties were performed on this day by the high priest. He prepared himself to fulfill these obligations a full 7 days in advance. On the day itself, after cleansing himself he dressed in sacred garments (Leviticus 16:4). The sacrificial animals were prepared: "And he shall take of the congregation of the children of Israel two kids of the goats for a sin offering, and one ram for a burnt offering. And Aaron shall offer his bullock of the sin offering, which is for himself, and make an atonement for himself, and for his house" (Leviticus 16:5,6).

Then the high priest entered the Most Holy Place and sprinkled some of the blood of the bullock on the lid of the mercy seat. As he did this, smoke from the lighted incense veiled the lid of the mercy seat covering the ark of the testimony. This prevented him from dying as he performed the ritual (Leviticus 16:12-14). The high priest was to do the same thing as he offered the goat as a sin offering for the people. He thus provided atonement for all the sins of the Israelites (Leviticus 16:15,16).

When the high priest had obtained atonement for his house, himself, and the entire congregation of Israel, a general confession of sins followed. When the high priest put his hands on the head of a live goat and confessed the sins and transgressions of the people, by faith the sins were transferred to the goat, which was then led into the desert (Leviticus 16:20-22).

The ritual concluded when the high priest took off his linen clothes, washed himself, and sacrificed a burnt offering for himself and for the people. He thereby obtained atonement for himself and for them (Leviticus 16:23-25). Finally the corpses of the animals that had been sacrificed were burned outside of the camp (Leviticus 16:27). Each year this event was repeated in an effort to reestablish the covenant relationship with God that had been destroyed because of the sins of the people.

The points of similarity between the high priest of the old covenant and that of the new are obvious. It is not necessary to review the several differences again. The differences remind one of the stars, whose light pales when the sun rises. The Epistle to the Hebrews testifies to the perfect nature of Christ's atoning sacrifice.

## Conscience and Perfection

The deficiency of the old covenant lay first and foremost in the inability of its offerings to "make him that did the service perfect, as pertaining to the conscience" (9:9). We come face-to-face here with a major concern: conscience and perfection. Both terms occur rather late in the Scriptures.

The expression "conscience" does not occur in the Old Testament. An individual might recognize his wrongdoing (e.g., David, 2 Samuel 12), but the Old Testament does not advance any dogmatic theory that man is intrinsically equipped with a moral awareness or ethical principle. From the Biblical perspective, humanity stands guilty in the presence of the will of God as it is revealed in the Law. As far as the Gospels are concerned, a similar idea is presented. The term "conscience" does not occur, but when Jesus taught He appealed to the personal discernment of His listeners (Luke 12:57; cf. Luke 10:36,37).

Now, outside the Gospels we find the term "conscience" (suneidēsis) in Acts, Romans, 1 and 2 Corinthians, the Pastoral Epistles, Hebrews, and 1 Peter. Paul's writings reflect a somewhat classical understanding of "conscience" as the inner voice that guides individuals concerning what is right and wrong. The Gentiles give evidence, suggests Paul in Romans 2:15, that what the Law requires is written on the hearts of the Gentiles, as their conscience bears witness to it. Men are obligated, therefore, to submit to authorities "not only for wrath, but also for conscience' sake" (Romans 13:5). Thus, Paul writes, conscience can be a witness or a judge between himself and others (cf. 2 Corinthians 1:12; 4:2; 5:11).

In the Pastoral Epistles, conscience plays a special role as a characteristic of proper Christian faith. Paul's coworker, Timothy, is admonished to fight the good fight, holding faith and a good conscience (1 Timothy 1:18,19; cf. 4:2; Titus 1:15). It is the apostle's duty to promote "charity out of a pure heart, and of a good conscience, and of faith unfeigned" (1 Timothy 1:5; cf. 3:9; 2 Timothy 1:3).

In the Epistle to the Hebrews conscience also plays a significant role. It is the response of the conscience which lays bare the insufficiency of the old sacrificial system (9:9; cf. 10:2). Conversely, the perfect sacrifice of Christ purifies the conscience and allows the believer to praise and serve God

(9:14; 10:22). Now one can know for sure that he or she has a good conscience (13:18).

The expression *perfection* or *completion* (*teleiōsis*) is equally important. Like the term *conscience*, *perfection* occurs five times in the Epistle to the Hebrews; in addition one finds the related term *finisher* (*teleiotēs*) applied to Christ. From the Biblical point of view, *perfection* involves undivided devotion to God, especially in the covenant relationship. Therefore, the prayer in Psalm 119:80 reads: "Let my heart be sound in thy statutes." This idea of undivided devotion to God is the background for Jesus' words in Matthew 5:48, "Be ye therefore perfect, even as your Father which is in heaven is perfect."

The expression *completion* acquired a new and unique dimension when used in conjunction with the revelation in Christ. The hidden counsel of God, His plan of salvation, was on the brink of fulfillment. With the birth of the Son of God that fulfillment, the "fulness of time," came (Galatians 4:4; cf. Ephesians 1:10). Jesus' work was a carrying out of the will and plan of God (John 4:34). It culminated in His death (John 19:28,30). "It is finished," He cried out.

From such a viewpoint the author of Hebrews testifies to the perfection of Christ and to humanity's "perfection" or "completion" by faith in Christ (cf. Colossians 1:17,18). A fundamental prerequisite to Christ's saving death was His following the path of suffering. "For it became him, for whom are all things, and by whom are all things, in bringing many sons unto glory, to make the captain of their salvation perfect through sufferings" (2:10). That Christ had to suffer and debase himself poses no inconsistency with the fact of His honor and authority as God. There was no other way to salvation than incarnation and suffering (cf. 2:14-18). Through this, Christ became the "pioneer" of salvation and the source of eternal salvation (5:10).

The life and work of Christ determine our salvation. Christ is the author of faith as well as the One who perfects it (12:2). As the One who has been made perfect forever, Christ can lead others to perfection (5:9; cf. 11:40; 12:23).

## A New Covenant

On several occasions the author uses the term *covenant*. Christ is the guarantor of a "better covenant" (7:22); specifically, the "better" covenant is based upon "better" promises (8:6). The expression "covenant" (*diathēkēs*) in Hebrews, as in the Septuagint, reflects the Hebrew term *berîth*. *Berîth* and *diathēkē* indicate God's initiative in making an agreement with humanity. According to the common Hellenistic-understanding, *diathēkē* denotes a "last will." The decisive factor is that *diathēkē* is used with both meanings in Hebrews.

As a mediator (*mesitēs*), Christ is contrasted with Moses, who was a mediator between God and His people under the old covenant (Hebrews 8:6; cf. Galatians 3:9). The writer emphasizes the reality of the new covenant. The idea that the new covenant is based on better promises is merely the logical outcome of the fact that the Biblical promises are fulfilled in Christ.

The promise of a new covenant goes back to Jeremiah 31. There it is prophesied that the days would come when the Lord would establish a new covenant with the house of Israel and the house of Judah. Then He would write His commands in their minds and hearts and create a totally new relationship with God. God would also blot out all their sins (Jeremiah 31:31f.; Hebrews 8:8-12).

These "better promises" are superior to those promises of God which depended on the obedience of the people. If they failed, the promises were nullified (8:9). But, on one critical point the old and new covenants agree: covenants are sealed with the offering of sacrifices (and offering meals; Hebrews 9:15ff.; cf. Genesis 15:17,18; 31:43-54; Exodus 24:1-11).

The term *covenant* or *testament* presupposes that the one who initiated the agreement must die before the agreement is put into effect (9:16,17). The old covenant was also established with the shedding of blood, since Moses sprinkled blood on the people, the scroll of the commandments, the tabernacle, and all the vessels of the divine worship (9:18-22).

Nonetheless, the sacrifice of Christ is different from and superior to the offerings of the old covenant. Again the Scripture shows the effect of Christ's perfect sacrifice (9:23-28). He offers His own blood in the heavenly sanctuary (9:24,25) and does away with sin, once and for all (9:26).

The idea of covenant does not merely guarantee a link to Israel's history; it also offers a new plan of salvation that builds on the perfect redemptive work of Christ. By virtue of this, men and women can stand before God and serve Him as He desires (10:19f.; 12:28).

## Standing Firm in the Faith (10:32-13:25)

### "Faith" in the Hebrews Epistle

Hebrews 11 is rightfully called the "Faith Chapter." In it one receives a basic introduction to the nature of faith. But there is more. One also sees the power of faith manifested in terms of heroes of faith under the old covenant.

The "Faith Chapter" is designed to support and to encourage the readers to enduring faith. The appeal to persevere in faith occurs immediately prior to this section (10:36ff.). The writer presents a rough draft of the sacred history of the Old Testament from one unique vantage point. He presents the most well-known characters of the Old Testament as models of faith and faithfulness.

But what is faith? Our writer tells us: "Look at the ancestors of the Faith." The forebears include the heroes of Israel's faith. These models can teach us two things: (1) how great and valuable is the gift of faith, and (2) the power that faith exhibits.

Those trusting and believing in God never turned to Him in vain. Because they received God's help and blessing, it is obvious for later generations that the exploits of the heroes of faith were done according to God's will. Why did they receive grace? Because they believed God. In other words, they trusted in God's promises; they clung to the promise in hope, despite the fact they never saw the realization of their faith. The line of reasoning in Hebrews is similar to Paul's testimony of the Christian hope. "We are saved by hope: but hope that is seen is not hope: for what a man seeth, why doth he yet hope for? But if we hope for that we see not, then do we with patience wait for it" (Romans 8:24,25).

Israel's relationship with God was always intended to be by faith. None of the patriarchs could serve God half-heartedly; they could only serve fully trusting Him by faith. Just a glance at the ancestors of faith tells that they always trusted in what was not seen and that God rewarded them. Everything significant and wonderful in Israel's history was received by faith as God's gift to those who believed.

Hebrews 11:1 defines faith: "Faith is the substance of things hoped for, the evidence of things not seen." Once again we notice a close relationship between faith and hope. If there is no human hope, there is little chance for man to be stirred to believe. That is why the word and promise of God lay the foundations for human faith. Faith and hope are directed toward the invisible God, His word, and His promises. In faith, those things in question are precisely those things that are not seen, "for we walk by faith, not by sight" (2 Corinthians 5:7).

"Faith is the substance of things hoped for." Here there is help in distinguishing between faith and illusion. Faith is the full assurance of something and is reflected in everything we do. Thus faith is a power in our lives, a power that leads us to action.

Faith also involves conviction. The power and influence of the visible world is actually much less than the voice of the invisible. The tangible and concrete do not have the ability to support us, carry us, and give us a share in the riches of Christ. It is encouraging to know that the invisible comes to us and convinces us of the truth of God.

With this definition of the nature of faith, not only is the history of heroes of the Faith illuminated, but also the road which believers must travel—by faith not sight—is brought into perspective. In the natural we see only that God has summoned Christ to heaven where He is exalted to the right hand and installed as High Priest. There He helps us. We cannot see this, but we believe it by faith.

Faith in what is not seen and in the future are the main point. "For by it the elders obtained a good report" (11:2). The Word of God often expressly describes an individual as "righteous" or as having "found favor with God." This indicates that he or she trusted God and His promises.

We marvel at God's visible hand throughout Creation; what we see in Creation causes us to praise God. However, what we see as "visible" was created out of the invisible through the power of the Living Word. Hebrews 11:3 attaches a special significance to this understanding of creation. We should not be astonished that God wants us to fix our desires and heart on what is invisible, since what is seen originates in the invisible Word of God. We are to find fulfillment not in the visible, material world, but in the invisible.

A long list of the heroes of faith follows this introduction. The first true example of faith is Abel. We are told that he placed his offering on the altar. If the point is that only the visible is important, Abel acted unreasonably. Why sacrifice his animal? The answer: he longed for the invisible and sought blessings which he could only hope to attain. The sacrifice of Abel (and his entire life) are a testimony to his faith (11:4).

The second example of faith is Enoch (11:5). The Bible only tells us that he "walked with God" (Genesis 5:22-24). But the author of Hebrews sees a new relationship in this comment. Enoch possessed a faith that was pleasing to God. "Without faith it is impossible to please him" (11:6). Literally, he *set himself* to walk with God. His will was involved.

The story of the life of Noah was still well known in the time of Jesus (cf. Matthew 24:37ff.). The ancient account also shows how Noah built his ark in the midst of an unconcerned and faithless generation. What caused him to take such a "strange" action? From a human vantage point there was no immediate danger, but Noah listened to God's warning and did not pay attention to the jeering world. He "condemned the world, and became heir of the righteousness which is by faith" (11:7).

More than anyone else in history, the ancestors testify of the nature and character of faith. All the patriarchs, Abraham, Isaac, and Jacob demonstrated faith. They had received the promise of the land, but they nonetheless never actually possessed it. All the time they patiently looked forward to the heavenly land that they had not yet entered (11:8-16).

Abraham is a particularly noteworthy example. The New Testament clearly shows him as the greatest Old Testament example of faith (Romans 4:3; Galatians 3:6; James 2:23; cf. Acts 7:5). Abraham demonstrated his faith early in his career, when he left his homeland and people in order to go to the land God had promised to show him (11:9).

Perhaps even more thrilling than this, however, is the account of his offering of Isaac (11:17-19). We recall that Abraham was commanded to offer his only son, the son given as the realization of the promise of God (11:11,12). During this episode it seems as if God had reneged on His promise to Abraham. This brought Abraham into the strongest struggle of faith; indeed, it was his greatest test. He realized, however, that under the circumstances there was no alternative but to trust God, believe on Him fully to fulfill His promise, even though Isaac should die. Consequently, Hebrews pictures Abraham's offering of Isaac as a figurative foreshadowing of the Resurrection. Here, for the first time we have the idea that God can "raise" from the dead (11:19).

The next name on the roll call is Moses. His life story is also a tremendous testimony to his faith (11:23-29). Five examples from his life are given: (1) His being delivered at his birth from the infanticide ordered by the evil pharaoh (11:23); (2) his willingness to share the fate of God's people (11:24-26); (3) his faithfulness toward the invisible God rather than the visible and powerful pharaoh (11:27); (4) his institution of Passover (11:28); and (5) the crossing of the Red Sea together with the Israelites (11:29).

The following verses contain an additional series of examples of faith from Israel's history. By faith the walls of Jericho fell (11:30). According to Joshua 6, the walls fell on the seventh day of the siege, when, following the divine command, Israel walked around the city seven times, the priests blew their trumpets, and the people gave a loud shout. Their faith was exhibited in the conviction that their extraordinary actions would indeed accomplish what God said they would. Rahab, a prostitute, is also mentioned because of her great faith (cf. Matthew 1:5).

Under the heading of the prophets and those who gave their lives for their faith, the list of heroes of the Faith draws to a close. Now the writer gives other examples without elaborating on the nature of their faith. The power of faith and faith expressed in trial are the primary subjects discussed in this section (11:32-38). Victory as well as "defeat" (death, torture) are by-products of the same faith. Triumph and God's intervention are not the only criteria of genuine faith. The courage to suffer, even a willingness to die, are not in any way inferior demonstrations of faith.

The way God related to men and women of old varied greatly. At times He visibly intervened on their behalf; on other occasions it appeared as if He did not help at all. Some saw mighty miracles; others did not. Nonetheless, both groups were faithful. Some glorified God through their lives; others did so through their deaths. We observe that faith enables one to overcome but also to be overcome; to live but also to die. Faith follows wherever God leads.

The concluding verses of chapter 11 underscore even further that faith looks toward the future. This is reflected in the statement: "And these all, having obtained a good report through faith, received not the promise" (11:39). They waited until "now," "that they without us should not be made perfect" (11:40).

The Old Testament is repeatedly seen as a document of promise. Faith was indeed present in Old Testament times, but it was directed toward what occurs in Christ. God's plan concerns all His chosen ones (9:15). Therefore, one group cannot attain perfection without the other.

## The Life of the Church

The Book of Hebrews gives the impression that it is speaking to a church in danger of giving up the Faith (cf. 12:12,13). This explains the constant attempt to stir up, encourage, and warn believers.

As in the writings of the apostle Paul, Hebrews depicts the life of the Christian believer as a race (cf. 1 Corinthians 9:24,25; Philippians 3:13,14; 2 Timothy 4:7). The goal lies ahead, hidden in the Word and promises of God. Therefore, it is necessary to lay aside anything that might keep one from running or finishing the race (i.e., sin; 12:1). We must also accept the available help. The Old Testament heroes of faith were mentioned in chapter 11. How much more help is there when we fix our eyes upon Jesus, the author and finisher of our faith (12:2,3)! His invitation is this: "Come unto me, all ye that labor and are heavy laden" (Matthew 11:28). He is able to give the soul new courage.

Having described the life of the Church as a race, the Scripture now turns to the image of a struggle (12:4). With the expression, "You have not yet resisted to the point of shedding your blood" (NIV), the readers are given brief warning that even more perilous times may lie ahead. They have endured great trials and suffered loss of property and honor (10:32-34), but they have not yet given their lives. This possibility must be acknowledged; believers should not be surprised if hardships come to that point (cf. 1 Peter 4:12). Instead of being ashamed of such a fate, believers must come to understand that it is because they are children (cf. Proverbs

3:11,12). An earthly father who loves his children will indeed discipline them (12:4-8).

The analogy between the earthly father and the Heavenly Father (here "Father of spirits"), is elaborated on in 12:9ff. in an effort to show that the goal of divine discipline is to promote holiness (12:10), righteousness (12:11), and peace (12:14).

Believers are particularly portrayed as having free access to God through the sacrifice of Christ. Christ thus opened a new and living entrance to God through the "veil" ("curtain," NIV) which is His body (10:20). The imagery comes from the temple. A veil or curtain separated the outer sanctuary from the Holy of Holies. The veil is allegorically understood to represent the body of Christ. Figuratively, His body was "torn in pieces" at His death when His blood was shed. The giving of His life enables us to enter the presence of God.

That believers now have free access to God is a main theme in the Epistle to the Hebrews. Under the old covenant entrance was not possible. Now, however, because of the sacrifice of Christ, an entrance free of all obstacles has been provided. Now we can truly worship God.

## The Meaning of Worship

The Epistle to the Hebrews shows that the Old Testament's rituals and priesthood were fulfilled in Christ. In the Early Church there was no high priest. Christ was the true, eternal High Priest.

But what does the Epistle to the Hebrews say about the Early Church's understanding of worship? In what practical ways does the letter show that "the way to the sanctuary," thanks to the work of Christ, is open?

Believers are people of the new covenant. Their worship is not a return to the former arrangement under the old covenant given at Sinai. On the contrary, they approach heaven itself, the place where God has chosen to establish His name (Deuteronomy 12:5). This is the true Mount Zion, the heavenly Jerusalem. There, in a sense, the earthly people of God join the crowds which stand before the Ancient of Days (Daniel 7:10). They also join with the Church of the Firstborn who are able to stand before the Son of Man (Luke 21:36). There they encounter the eternal God and the mediator Jesus Christ, who bears the blood of the new and eternal covenant. In the presence of God they receive an unshakable kingdom, one more reason why they owe thanks and acceptable service to God (12:28).

Here we catch a glimpse of the meaning of worship as revealed in Hebrews. Worship under the new covenant takes place in heaven (12:22). This is a consequence of Christ's having once and for all entered the Holy of Holies; of His offering His own blood as a sacrifice for our sins; and of His having obtained our eternal redemption (9:12). This is

the basis for understanding the priestly access to God the people of the new covenant enjoy: "Having therefore, brethren, boldness to enter into the holiest by the blood of Jesus, by a new and living way, which he hath consecrated for us, through the veil, that is to say, his flesh; and having a high priest over the house of God; let us draw near with a true heart" (10:19-22).

This may be why the reader's attention is constantly directed to the riches that belong to those in Christ Jesus. They need to understand also the value of being able to worship God. They have an altar from which they who serve at the tabernacle had no right to eat. This suggests that their worship, even in its sacrificial meal, was in every way superior to the old covenant. We also do not lack an altar; we have one from which we receive strength and power.

The following verses show that the suffering of the Lord "outside the camp" had a sanctifying effect (13:12). Christians can partake of this holiness if they are willing to go with Him "outside the camp" and bear His reproach (13:13). There is a distinct, vital relationship between the sacrifice of Christ and the "sacrifice" of believers in choosing the way of self-denial and rejection of the world's values. The "sacrifices" the believer has to offer to this relationship are shown: "By him therefore let us offer the sacrifice of praise to God continually, that is, the fruit of our lips, giving thanks to his name. But to do good and to communicate forget not: for with such sacrifices God is well pleased" (13:15,16).

The key to the church's worship is contained in the phrase "by him." It emphasizes the unique privilege of believers. It is "by Christ"—"the Way" that we have access to God. It is only "by Him" that we can offer anything pleasing to God (cf. 1 Peter 2:5; Romans 1:8; 16:27; Colossians 3:17).

When 13:14 emphasizes that we seek a coming city, it also reflects a certain view of worship. While believers wait for the time when they join Christ in heaven, where He has ascended (4:14; 8:1), they are already experiencing the heavenly glory anticipated by the signs Christ has given. Thus, in a certain sense the altar of 13:10 is in heaven, where Christ has offered His own blood, the eternal sacrifice for redemption. But, precisely because the issue is one of sacrifice, Christians approach this altar as they gather around the table of the Lord in the Communion service.

## Use of the Old Testament in Hebrews

The Book of Hebrews makes extensive use of the Old Testament. There are many direct quotes and even more allusions. Portions from the Pentateuch are cited 12 times; the Psalms, 11; the Prophets, 4; and there is 1 quotation from Proverbs. Of the

29 quotations, 23 are from either the Pentateuch or Psalms. It is odd that there are not more references to the prophetic writings, especially in those passages where he speaks of the Old Testament sacrificial system. The person and work of Christ is primarily illuminated from passages in the Psalms.

Most of the quotations in Hebrews do not occur elsewhere in the New Testament. This holds true for 21 out of 29 of the quotations. Of the remaining eight, one is cited in the Synoptic Gospels, while the others appear in Acts, Paul's epistles, and Revelation.

Hebrews presents the Old Testament as a divine oracle from start to finish. The Biblical account is the voice of God's word; the Word is thus alive in Scripture (4:12f.). Scripture, therefore, is not merely a "book"; it is a living word from God to people of all time. The words of the Bible and its promises also extend beyond the time of their writing. The consistent use of the present tense in the citations also underscores this truth: "He is not ashamed to call them brethren, saying . . ." (2:11,12); "as the Holy Ghost saith . . ." (3:7); "ye have forgotten the exhortation which speaketh unto you as unto children" (12:5).

There is no parallel in the New Testament to this style of quotation. Usually when the present tense of "says" appears, it is connected to the name of the prophet (e.g., Isaiah "says," Romans 10:16) or to Scripture (Romans 9:17). This feature verifies that the Book of Hebrews views God as speaking personally and precisely in the Old Testament.

Further investigation reveals that the writer regularly relies upon the Septuagint translation. Many citations, however, do follow the Hebrew text. On eight occasions the citation differs from the Hebrew but corresponds with the Greek. Finally, some quotations do not correspond with either the Septuagint or the Hebrew (6:13,14; 9:20; 10:30). Here perhaps a later, traditional form is being used. This reveals a view that Scripture contains a deep spiritual meaning. Scripture is handled very carefully, and the deeper meaning of passages appear.

The final revelation of God—in His Son—is totally perfect, "but the word of the oath, which was since the law, maketh the Son, who is consecrated for evermore" (7:28). It is therefore a serious offense to neglect such a great salvation (2:3) or to refuse Him who speaks (12:25). The saying, "Today if ye will hear his voice," (3:15) is thus applicable to Christians of all time.

The numerous Old Testament quotations also illuminate the theme "fulfillment of promise" (cf. the story of Abraham, Genesis 22:16, 17; Hebrews 6:13,14; 11:8f.). Abraham is a unique example of obedience (Hebrews 11:8), patience (Hebrews 11:9f.), and faith (Hebrews 11:17f.; cf. Romans 4:18). The patriarchs who also received the prom-

ise demonstrated the same kind of faith as Abraham (11:9).

The next step in the history of revelation is the account of the giving of the Law at Sinai. The Epistle to the Hebrews records this in 3:7ff. and in 4:1ff., using words from Psalm 95:7ff.: "Today if ye will hear his voice." The word of God is alive and speaks even to this day. Even though the disobedient wilderness generation fell, the promise of God was still in effect. The fulfillment of the promises awaits those who are repentant: "Today if ye will hear his voice, harden not your hearts" (4:7).

The giving of the Law is referred to in Hebrews 12:18ff. (cf. Exodus 19:12,13; Deuteronomy 4:11,12). The concluding of the giving of the covenant is also mentioned in Hebrews 9:19,20 and 10:29 (cf. Exodus 24:8). The occupation of Canaan is mentioned as a sign of the true and lasting rest (4:8; cf. 11:30,31).

The religious institutions of the Old Testament, e.g., the tabernacle and the worship therein, and especially the Day of Atonement, are given special attention (Hebrews 8:5f.; 9:1f.; cf. Exodus 25:40; 26:33; 30:10). All of this was merely a foreshadowing of the heavenly temple and its ritual, which was to be finalized when the new order was introduced.

The fulfillment of the promise of a new covenant is the final step in the ancient revelation (Jeremiah 31:31ff.; cf. Hebrews 8:8f.; 10:15f.). The new fellowship between God and mankind is based on God's forgiveness and presupposes personal acknowledgment of God. What remains to be fulfilled is the promise of Haggai 2:6 (cf. Hebrews 12:26f.).

The declaration that Christ is the Son of God rests first and foremost on Psalm 2:7 and 2 Samuel 7:14 (cf. Hebrews 1:5; 5:5). In the light of this confession, Christ stands as unique from any other of God's messengers.

That Christ is King is demonstrated from Psalm 45:7,8 (cf. Hebrews 1:8,9). The people of God's new covenant build the certainty of inheriting an unshakable kingdom on this fact (Hebrews 12:28; cf. Daniel 7:27). A more elaborate understanding of Christ's work is provided in the model of the priest-king Melchizedek (Hebrews 5:6,10; 6:20; 7:11f.; cf. Psalm 110:4). This unusual king shows that the work of Christ extends to others besides Israel.

Finally, according to Psalm 8:4ff., Christ is the Son of Man (Hebrews 2:6ff.). In Him humanity discovers its true potential. Christ is not ashamed to call men His brothers (Hebrews 2:11,12; cf. Psalm 22:23). His faithfulness exceeds that of Moses (Hebrews 3:1f.; cf. Numbers 12:7). Through His total obedience Christ summons a new humanity. These are those who because of their faith and obedience to Him will inherit salvation (5:9).

The Old Testament was written for our instruction. The reality of this fact is driven home by the Epistle to the Hebrews. It makes a call to leave comfortable, secure positions and participate in the soon coming perfect joy. We see this plan realized best in the history of the people of Israel. There we find solace to endure the tension between the difficulties of the present and the future bliss.

# The Epistle to the Hebrews

## Commentary

### Chapter 1

**1. God, who at sundry times and in divers manners spake in time past, unto the fathers by the prophets:** ... Long ago God spoke, −BECK ... It was bit by bit ... in olden times, −WLMS ... It was in a number of stages and in a variety of ways, −ADAM ... in ancient days spoke to our ancestors ... at many different times, −MNTG ... and many modes, −CNDT ... by various methods, −WLSN ... to our early fathers, −NLTG.

**1:1.** The majestic opening words of this epistle set the tone for the entire book. They subtly contrast the former ancient revelation, the Mosaic covenant, with the final, present revelation in Jesus Christ, the new covenant. Under the old covenant God spoke to the Hebrew fathers by the prophets. This self-disclosure was periodic and partial in nature. It was spread out over at least 10 centuries and given by various means. Sometimes God directly intervened in history; sometimes the Holy Spirit worked internally in the minds of the prophetic writers; sometimes God revealed himself through visions or dreams; often God's message was delivered by angels. Such revelations were preparatory and piecemeal. And they were given in the past.

**2. Hath in these last days spoken unto us:** ... in these latter days, −WLMS.
**by [his] Son:** ... in One who by nature is, −WUST ... through a Son, −WLMS.
**whom he hath appointed heir of all things:** ... And He has been given everything for a heritage, −NORL ... appointed lawful owner of everything, −WLMS.
**by whom also he made the worlds:** ... of whom also he constituted the ages, −WLSN ... It was through him that God made the universe, −TNT.
**3. Who being the brightness of [his] glory:** ... He radiates, −TNT ... who shines with God's glory, −BECK ... as he is the reflection of his glory, −KLGS ... being an emanation of God's glory, −MNTG ... being an Effulgence, −WLSN.
**and the express image of his person:** ... the perfect representation of, −ADAM, −WLMS ... and the exact image of God's nature, −NORL ... and an exact Impress of his substance, −WLSN ... the exact picture of God's real being, −SEB ... the exact reproduction of His essence, −WUST ... The Son is as God is in every way, −NLTG ... and stamp of his substance, −MNTG ... and the embodiment of the divine nature, −TCNT.

**and upholding all things by the word of his power:** ... He sustains everything by His powerful word, −ADAM ... continues to uphold, −WLMS ... upholds the universe, −TNT ... besides carrying on all by his powerful declaration, −CNDT ... and sustaining, guiding, and propelling all things by, −WUST ... sustaining the Universe by the expression of His mighty Will, −WADE ... through the powerful mandate of God, −NOLI.
**when he had by himself purged our sins:** ... He made an expiation for the sins of men, −MNTG ... After he had provided a cleansing from sin, −SEB ... procured man's purification from sins, −WLMS.
**sat down on the right hand of the Majesty on high:** ... has taken his seat, −MNTG ... he sat at the right of the Greatness in the Highest, −KLGS ... of Almighty God in heaven, −TNT.

**1:2, 3.** But the divine disclosure which has been made in Jesus Christ is substantially different. First of all, it is current. It has taken place "in these last days," and it has been given to believers. Secondly, it is cumulative. It completes what was begun in the Old Testament. The phrase "in these last days" is messianic and points out that in the Son there is the fulfillment of what was only promised by the old covenant. It is the equivalent of saying that in the Son God has spoken His final message of salvation. All that is needed for salvation has been revealed in the Son. Finally, the inspired writer emphasized the Christological nature of this revelation. By omitting the article on the word "Son" (*huiō*) he pointed to the essential characteristic of the messenger. It is in such a person as His Son that God has spoken His ultimate word of salvation. Only such a One could bring redemption to a lost race.

The text enumerates nine factors which demonstrate the superiority of the Son as the divine messenger. (1) He is "heir of all things." These words echo the commission given to Adam (Genesis 1:28), ring with the promise of Psalm 2:7, 8, and sparkle with the dignity of man described in Psalm 8:5,6. Certainly they resound with overtones of the Cross. Jesus told of the vineyard owner (Matthew 21:37,38) who finally sent his son, saying, "They will reverence my son," only to hear the evil tenants reply, "This is the heir; come, let us kill him, and let us seize on his inheritance." This reflects the attitude Jesus faced while here on earth. (2) The Son is the agent by whom God created the universe and the ages of time through which it passes.

(3) Christ is the flashing forth of the Father's glory; like a brilliant ray from the sun, He reveals God's perfections. (4) Like the impression made in wax by a signet ring, He is the exact expression of God's character in human form. There is not one feature of God's character that is not displayed in His Son. (5) By His powerful utterance, He upholds the universe, that is, He carries it along to its final destiny. He is the Lord of history. But He is more than a revealer of knowledge. (6) He has already by himself effected the cleansing and removal of the believer's sins. He is the Redeemer. (7) He sits and rules as absolute Sovereign and (8) as Intercessor at God's right hand.

**4. Being made so much better than the angels:** ... being thereby shewn to be, *—WADE* ... proving Himself to be as much, *—WLMS* ... He became as much superior, *—ADAM* ... became as much greater than, *—BECK.*

**as he hath by inheritance:** ... that he has inherited, *—MNTG.*

**obtained a more excellent name than they:** ... a greater name than theirs, *—NLTG* ... has received a title, *—SEB* ... having shown himself as much greater than the angels as the Name that he has inherited surpasses theirs, *—TCNT* ... a name far beyond them, *—KLGS* ... far greater than the angels with their inferior name, *—TNT* ... is more exalted than theirs, *—WADE* ... is more distinguished than theirs, *—NOLI.*

**1:4.** The ninth characteristic of the Son used to emphasize His superiority is His name, "Son." The name *Son* is inherently superior to the name *angel*. It was as the Son of Man that Jesus entered into the messianic office through His incarnation, suffering, and resurrection. The eternal deity of Jesus as the Son of God and His human sonship is not the consideration at this point, but rather His messianic sonship which is dependent on His divine-human personhood. To be Messiah He had to be the God-man.

The rest of chapter 1 elaborates on the superiority of the Son to the angels. Some recent interpreters think this argument is directed at the influence of the Essenes of the Qumran community on the Jewish Christian readers of this letter. This is possible, but the argument in the context emphasizes the superiority of the gospel to the Law. In the light of Psalm 68:17, Galatians 3:19, Acts 7:38, and the Septuagint rendering of Deuteronomy 33:2, it is clear that the Jews heavily emphasized the mediation of the angels in the giving of the Law. To professing Jewish Christians who might be tempted to revert to Judaism, the Son's superiority to the angels was an important matter.

Angels were so prominent in ancient Israel's history, its people were tempted to worship them, but to do so would be to worship the creature rather than the Creator (Romans 1:25). Paul warned the Colossians not to show devotion to angels (Colossians 2:18). John said of the heavenly messenger who showed him many things, "And when I had heard and seen, I fell down to worship before the feet of the angel which showed me these things. Then saith he unto me, See thou do it not: for I am thy fellow servant" (Revelation 22:8,9).

**5. For unto which of the angels said he at any time:** ... God never said to any, *—TNT* ... did he ever say, *—WLSN.*

**Thou art my Son, this day have I begotten thee?:** ... I have fathered you, *—SEB* ... I am Your Father, *—BECK* ... today I have become your Father? *—WLMS.*

**And again, I will be to him a Father, and he shall be to me a Son?:** ... I will become His Father, and He shall become my Son, *—WLMS.*

**1:5.** Psalm 2:7 is quoted to point out the contrast between the Son and the angels. Although the angels as a group are called the "sons of God" in the Old Testament (Genesis 6:2; Job 1:6; 2:1; 38:7), no angel ever is called "Son." The Father, however, calls Jesus "Son" at His baptism and at the Transfiguration. God promised David a son who would establish David's house, throne, and kingdom forever (2 Samuel 7:13,14). And David knew about and looked for a greater Son than Solomon (Psalm 89).

**6. And again, when he bringeth in the first begotten into the world:** ... And further ... into the habitable world, *—MNTG* ... when he introduces this ... into the universe, *—NOLI* ... when God is about to send, *—TNT* ... when He brings the First-born into the world of men, *—WADE* ... His Firstborn, *—ADAM* ... into the inhabited earth, *—CNDT.*

**he saith, And let all the angels of God worship him:** ... He declares ... all God's angels must worship Him, *—WADE* ... will bow before him, *—NOLI.*

**1:6.** Here the third Old Testament quotation is taken from the Septuagint. This form of the Deuteronomy 32:43 quotation has also been discovered in a Hebrew fragment of the passage found among the Dead Sea Scrolls (Cross, pp.182-184). The context of Deuteronomy is one of judgment, vengeance, and reward, and the angels are worshiping Jehovah. Since Jesus Christ the Son will execute the Father's final judgment, the reference in Deuteronomy implies the deity of the Son and shows His superiority to the angels, because they are commanded to fall down and worship Him.

In this verse the Son is called "first-begotten" (*prōtotokon*). Paul said Christ was the first begotten or "firstborn from the dead" (Colossians 1:18). John wrote the same (Revelation 1:5). Here "firstborn" is an expression meaning Christ's resurrection from the dead. In 12:23 the word "firstborn" is used for the perfected Christian church in heaven. There it appears in the plural and includes all the believers who are a firstfruit for God.

*Prōtotokon* refers to either superiority in rank or first in time. Hebrews 1:5 spoke of Christ as the "begotten" in a quote from Psalm 2:7. The Father said to the Son, "This day have I begotten thee," but the statement refers not to a literal birth. Rather, it points to a position of rank. God later declared of the Messiah, "Also I will make him my firstborn, higher than the kings of the earth" (Psalm 89:27). Here "firstborn" suggests being "supreme in rank" rather than "first in time." In other words, God would make His Son as the Messiah higher than all other kings of the earth. Hebrews had a similar message as to His being superior to angels.

**7. And of the angels he saith:** ... Now referring to the angels He says, −*ADAM* ... when speaking of angels, −*TNT* ... speaking of their mutability, −*WADE.*

**Who maketh his angels spirits:** ... He makes the winds his angels, −*TCNT* ... He turns His angels, −*WLMS* ... into winds, −*MNTG.*

**and his ministers a flame of fire:** ... And His attendants, −*WLMS* ... and his servants, −*TNT* ... And his public officers flaming fire, −*KLGS* ... His Ministrants into lightning-flame, −*WADE* ... and the lightnings are his servants, −*NOLI.*

**1:7.** The fourth quote comes from Psalm 104:4 and is contrasted with the fifth quotation given in verse 8. These words depict the angels as the messengers and ministers of God. They are beings created to perform His service. By portraying them in this capacity, the Psalmist likens them to wind and flames. This imagery stresses the fleeting, temporary, and changeable character of the angels' service to God.

**8. But unto the Son [he saith]:** ... But referring to, −*ADAM* ... regarding, −*WLMS* ... when speaking of the Son, −*TNT* ... Who is unchanging, −*WADE.*

**Thy throne, O God, [is] forever and ever:** ... Thy throne is God's throne, lasting for ever, −*WADE* ... will last, −*TNT* ... will stand forever, −*WLMS* ... is from everlasting to everlasting, −*NORL.*

**a sceptre of righteousness [is] the sceptre of thy kingdom:** ... and the rod of Your empire, −*ADAM* ... the scepter of equity, −*WUST* ... an equitable rule is Thy rule of Thy Dominion, −*WADE* ... Your royal sceptre stands for, −*TNT* ... the scepter of justice, −*MNTG* ... You rule your kingdom fairly, −*SEB.*

**9. Thou hast loved righteousness, and hated iniquity:** ... loved justice, −*WADE* ... loved right and hated wrong, −*BECK* ... hated lawlessness, −*MNTG*, −*KLGS* ... and hated wickedness, −*TCNT* ... and hated what is wrong, −*SEB.*

therefore God, [even] thy God, hath anointed thee:** ... This is why God, your God, called you, −*TNT* ... hath welcomed Thee, −*WADE.*

**with the oil of gladness above thy fellows:** ... with the sacred oil above your companions, −*NOLI* ... with the festal oil more abundantly than, −*TCNT* ... with the oil of Exultation beyond thy associates, −*WLSN* ... the oil of rejoicing above your friends, −*KLGS* ... With tokens of joy beyond the Angels Thy associates, −*WADE* ... gave you the joy of being anointed king ... and not your companions, −*TNT* ... has made you king over your friends, −*SEB* ... beyond Your companions, −*ADAM* ... beyond thy comrades, −*MNTG* ... Thy partners, −*CNDT.*

**1:8, 9.** To spotlight the Son's position over against the subservience of the angels, the inspired writer next cited Psalm 45:6,7. This prophetic and messianic psalm speaks about the God-man, the Son. He was to come from the house of David, a dynasty with which God had made an extraordinary covenant (2 Samuel 7:13,14), a covenant which would only be fulfilled in Jesus the Messiah. In Psalm 45, the Messiah is designated "God." He is promised an eternal throne. His rule is described as just. He is portrayed as One who is personally committed to righteousness. He has been anointed royally and crowned with joy.

Later, 12:2 describes the way this joy came—through suffering. The joy of believers can come this way also, as 12:3-11 points out. The word *metochous*, translated "fellows" in 1:9, is translated "partakers" in 12:8. By sharing in Christ's sufferings we share also in His joy. Because of salvation believers have been endowed with an inexpressibly glorious joy (1 Peter 1:8), but the joy brought by sharing in the sufferings of Christ is even greater. The same truth is expressed in 1 Peter 4:13, though the word "partakers" comes from a different Greek word: "Rejoice, inasmuch as ye are partakers of Christ's sufferings; that, when his glory shall be revealed, ye may be glad also with exceeding joy."

**10. And, Thou, Lord, in the beginning hast hud the foundation of the earth:** ... founded the earth, −*WLMS.*

**and the heavens are the works of thine hands:** ... With your own hands you made, −*TNT* ... the sky, −*WADE.*

**11. They shall perish; but thou remainest:** ... They will be destroyed, −*ADAM* ... you remain permanently, −*WUST* ... You will always be here, −*NLTG* ... yet Thou art continuing, −*CNDT* ... but you will continue, −*SEB.*

**and they all shall wax old as doth a garment:** ... all will grow time-worn, −*WADE* ... will grow old, −*WLMS* ... and worn out as a garment, −*WUST* ... as clothes become old, −*TNT.*

**1:10, 11.** Next the inspired writer of Hebrews hurled a long quote from Psalm 102:25-27 at his readers with scarcely any introduction. He used only the word "and." Since the Son is the Father's agent in creating the universe and the ages through which it progresses (see 1:2), these words about Jehovah the Creator are fittingly used of Jesus Christ the Son.

Once again the Septuagint version is employed. There are some minor differences between Hebrews 1:10-12 and Psalm 102:25-27. The meaning and substance, however, are the same. In Psalm 102:24 it is "God" who is addressed, but in 102:22 He is identified as "Lord," which is the translation of the Hebrew word for *Jehovah*. In the Septuagint He is addressed as "Lord," that is, *kurion*. Consistent with his understanding of the Old Testament the writer to the Hebrews recognized Jesus is God and freely used passages of Scripture which speak about Jehovah in talking about Him. In the reference in Psalms these words were addressed by the Lord to the one who offered the prayer at the beginning of the psalm. Yet the Lord addressed part of His answer to the Lord. To whom else could such words be directed? Who else but the Son is both Creator and Lord? In contrast with the creation and the angels, He is the eternal, unchanging Son.

He existed before the universe because He created it. It is not everlasting; He is. It is affected by the process of aging. Like a fragile garment susceptible to humidity, sunlight, and the jaws of the moths, the physical creation will shrivel, decay, dry out, and crumble. But Jesus Christ our Lord, the eternal Son of God, creator of all, shall remain forever and ever. Since He is Jehovah God, there is no reason to puzzle or wonder why created beings like the angels will bow down and worship Him, confessing Him Lord of lords.

**12. And as a vesture shalt thou fold them up:** ... You will roll them up like a robe, —ADAM ... like a blanket, —BECK ... like a cloak, —TNT ... like a mantle, —WADE.

**and they shall be changed:** ... like the changing of one's coat, —WLMS ... you will change them, —NOLI.

**but thou art the same:** ... you remain, —TNT ... Thou continuest the same, —WADE.

**and thy years shall not fail:** ... will not come to an end, —ADAM ... your years have no end, —NOLI ... your years will never cease, —WLMS ... You will never get old, —SEB ... will never end, —BECK ... you will never die, —TNT.

**1:12.** The imagery continues here in the quotation. The sky and the earth will be collapsed like clothing in the hands of the Lord. He is unchangeable. He does not lose His strength in an aging process.

**13. But to which of the angels said he at any time:** ... God never said to any angel, —NLTG.

**Sit on my right hand:** ... Just keep your seat, —WLMS.

**until I make thine enemies thy footstool?:** ... make your foes a footstool for your feet? —WLMS.

**1:13.** Finally, the inspired writer employed his favorite passage from the Old Testament, Psalm 110:1. The question is asked: To what angel did Jehovah ever offer the place of favor and blessing in absolute sovereignty over His conquered enemies? To what angel was the office of king in the messianic kingdom ever given? Undoubtedly this passage was in mind back in verse 3 when the Son was described as having "sat down on the right hand of the Majesty on high."

The warrant for understanding this text as a reference to the Son comes from Jesus Christ himself. In His confrontation with His enemies during Passion Week after He had turned all their trick questions back on them, He inquired of them, "What think ye of Christ? whose son is he?" (Matthew 22:42). After they replied that the Messiah was a descendant of David, Jesus asked how it could be that David called the Messiah "Lord" in Psalm 110:1. They of course did not reply. Logically, since the Messiah could be both "Lord" and a human descendant of David, He would have to be both God and man at the same time. This psalm's implications for the Son are used here to underscore His exaltation, power, royal station, and sovereignty as supports for the superiority and finality of the divine revelation which centers in Him. At the same time, the idea that the Son is now sitting in heaven waiting for His ultimate victory is introduced.

**14. Are they not all ministering spirits:** ... are simply spirits in the service of God, —TNT ... all attending spirits, —WLMS.

**sent forth to minister:** ... sent to help, —TNT ... commissioned for service, —CNDT ... sent on a commission, —WUST ... sent off to serve for the benefit, —ADAM ... to minister to their needs? —TCNT.

**for them who shall be heirs of salvation?:** ... those who are going to be saved? —BECK ... those who are to enter into salvation, —TNT ... for the sake of those who are going to be unceasing possessors of salvation? —WLMS.

**1:14.** Here the final touch to the argument was added. The angels are not only inferior to the Son; they might also be considered inferior to believers, at least in the sense that they are sent out continually to serve human beings who are destined to inherit salvation. The arguments in verses 4-14 show that Jesus the Son is better than the angels because: (1) God has designated Him individually as His messianic Son and declared Him to be His Son in power by resurrection from the dead; (2) angels are commanded to worship the Son; (3) He is God; (4) He is eternal and unchanging; (5) He is personally righteous and rules in absolute equity; (6) He is the Creator; (7) He is seated securely at the right hand of God, awaiting the day when He will rule the universe in absolute sovereignty.

## Chapter 2

**1. Therefore we ought to give the more earnest heed:** . . . On this account it behoves us to attend more earnestly, *—WLSN* . . . That is why we should listen all the more carefully, *—BECK* . . . we ought to give, *—TCNT* . . . we have to pay much closer attention, *—KLGS* . . . we must pay all the more attention, *—ADAM* . . . even closer attention, *—TNT* . . . listen all the more to, *—NLTG.*

**to the things which we have heard:** . . . to the message once heard, *—WLMS.*

**lest at any time we should let [them] slip:** . . . to keep from drifting to one side, *—WLMS* . . . we won't drift away from it, *—ADAM* . . . for fear we should drift away, *—MNTG* . . . so that we do not drift from our course, *—TNT.*

**2:1.** On the basis of the Son's superiority to the angels, the first of several stern warnings is issued. Because God has spoken in such an exalted way of His Son, Christians must be careful lest they drift away from the sure anchorage of revelation in the Son. The picture is one of a ship slipping by its anchorage in a protected harbor.

**2. For if the word spoken by angels was stedfast:** . . . if the message spoken through, *—WLMS* . . . the word of the Law . . . was so binding, *—TNT* . . . had its authority confirmed, *—TCNT* . . . was certain, *—ADAM* . . . proved to be valid, *—NORL.*

**and every transgression and disobedience:** . . . and every violation and infraction of it, *—WLMS* . . . that anyone who broke it or disobeyed it, *—TNT.*

**received a just recompense of reward:** . . . received its full punishment, *—ADAM* . . . met with its just retribution, *—MNTG* . . . received fair punishment, *—SEB.*

**2:2.** As was shown in the commentary on 1:4, angels were present on Mount Sinai and mediated in the giving of the Law. That Law fixed a firm penalty for transgression and disobedience. That is the "word spoken by angels." Under it sin incurred the penalty of physical death.

**3. How shall we escape:** . . . how is it possible for us to escape, *—WUST*

**if we neglect so great salvation:** . . . if we disregard, *—TCNT.*

**which at the first began to be spoken by the Lord:** . . . It was at the outset declared, *—ADAM.*

**and was confirmed unto us by them that heard [him]:** . . . the people who heard him showed us that it was true, *—SEB* . . . guaranteed its truth to us, *—BECK.*

**2:3.** If the Mosaic covenant firmly fixed the death penalty and it was mediated only by angels, what about the penalty for neglect of the new covenant which has been established by the Son who is himself God, eternal, unchanging, righteous, the Creator, and the sovereign Judge? If the greater message is neglected will there not be a greater penalty? The words are emphatic—those who live in this final age of human history when God himself was revealed in the Son—how shall they escape? Those who neglect the message of the Son face a fate worse than physical death; they will endure the spiritual death of eternal torment and separation from God. The description of Revelation 14:11 is graphic: "And the smoke of their torment ascendeth up for ever and ever: and they have no rest day nor night." Jesus spoke more about hell than all of the apostles and prophets combined. He, the Lord, brought this gospel message, and His words were attested by eyewitnesses.

**4. God also bearing [them] witness:** . . . testified to it by signs, *—ADAM* . . . God also bearing joint-testimony, *—WUST* . . . God proved what they said was true, *—NLTG* . . . co-attesting both by, *—WLSN* . . . corroborating their testimony, *—MNTG* . . . has also confirmed their testimony, *—NORL.*

**both with signs and wonders:** . . . by showing us special things, *—NLTG* . . . amazing things, *—SEB.*

**and with divers miracles:** . . . by various powerful deeds, *—CNDT* . . . and different kinds of powers, *—SEB* . . . and many great powers, *—KLGS.*

**and gifts of the Holy Ghost:** . . . as well as by imparting the holy Spirit, *—TCNT.*

**according to his own will?:** . . . measured out according to, *—KLGS* . . . imparted in accordance with, *—MNTG* . . . distributed as He wished, *—ADAM* . . . as he saw best, *—TCNT* . . . as He saw fit, *—NORL.*

**2:4.** Furthermore, these eyewitnesses have been attested by God the Father who put His stamp of approval on their testimony by pouring out the miraculous events which accompanied the apostolic preaching in the founding and establishment of the Church on the Day of Pentecost: in Samaria, in the home of Cornelius, in Ephesus upon the conversion of John the Baptist's disciples, and on many other occasions recorded in Acts. The Messianic Age is the age of the fullness of the Holy Spirit. Those who put their trust in

Jesus Christ drink of the fullness of the Spirit. The apostolic message came from the Son who has sent the Spirit to fill and empower believers and to distribute spiritual gifts in the body of Christ sovereignly as He wills.

**5. For unto the angels hath he not put in subjection the world to come:** ... did not put the future world, —SEB ... the control of that Future World, —TCNT.

**whereof we speak:**

**2:5.** Having sternly warned his audience of the dire consequences facing those who disregard the gospel of God's beloved Son, the writer returned to the theme of the Son's present seating at the Father's right hand. He did this in order to further advance his comparison of the Son and the angels, but also to show that the full exaltation of the Son had not yet been completed. It will be shown that the world to come will not be put in subjection to angels but to the exalted Son of Man.

**6. But one in a certain place testified, saying:** ... Instead, the Holy Writings say, —NLTG ... There is a Scripture passage that says, —NORL ... But somewhere someone had declared, —BECK.

**What is man, that thou art mindful of him?:** ... that You remember him, —ADAM, —KLGS ... that thou should'st remember him? —TCNT ... that you should think of him, —WLMS.

**or the son of man, that thou visitest him?:** ... Or any man, that thou carest for him? —MNTG ... in order to come to his aid? —WUST ... that You look out for him? —NORL ... That thou dost regard him? —WLSN ... that you should care for Him? —WLMS ... that you should show concern for him? —TNT.

**2:6.** Only in Christ, as sitting with Him on His throne, can man rise to a position higher than the angels. At present he has a lower status than the angels, and since any superiority of mankind to angels is not readily apparent, and since the Son became a man, there would be some questions arising in the minds of those who received this epistle: In the light of His becoming flesh and experiencing hunger, exhaustion, pain, suffering, and crucifixion, how can the Son be superior? Are not the angels superior to men and so to Him?

With these objections in mind, Psalm 8:4-6 was cited. Here David proclaimed the dignity, nobility, and greatness of man. He was awestruck by the splendor of the heavens and felt dwarfed by their majesty (Psalm 8:3). He marveled that the Lord should have any concern for mankind and was amazed that He should visit the feeble human race for the purpose of healing their weaknesses. As Asaph put it in Psalm 80:17, men pray, "Let thy hand be upon the man of thy right hand, upon the son of man whom thou madest strong for thyself."

The term "son of man" is freighted with significance. It speaks of the ideal man. It was Jesus' favorite self-designation and visualizes Him as the ideal man, the last Adam who has come to undo the consequences of Adam's fall.

**7. Thou madest him a little lower than the angels:** ... inferior to angels, —WLMS.

**thou crownedst him with glory and honour:**

**and didst set him over the works of thy hands:** ... And hast set him to govern, —MNTG ... Thou hast appointed him over, —WADE.

**2:7.** God created the human race in His own image. He created mankind a little lower than the angels and ordained them to rule over the earth (Genesis 1:26-31). Instead, they sinned and now find themselves degraded. The emphasis is upon the humiliation of man. As a result of Adam's disobedience, men have been cursed. Even though God gave this dominion to man and not to the angelic hosts, the Lord expelled him from Eden's paradise and subjected him to sorrow and suffering (Genesis 3:14-24).

**8. Thou hast put all things in subjection under his feet:** ... You put everything under his control, —SEB ... Thou hast reduced all things, —WADE ... and subjected everything beneath his feet, —ADAM.

**For in that he put all in subjection under him:** ... Subjected ... means that, —TNT ... by reducing, —WADE ... when He gave Him authority over everything, —WLMS.

**he left nothing [that is] not put under him:** ... He left nothing outside His control, —BECK ... did not leave a single thing that was not put under His authority, —WLMS ... not even the angels—exempt from subjection to his control, —WADE.

**But now we see not yet all things put under him:** ... But as conditions are ... we do not yet see all things reduced to subjection under him, —WADE ... we do not see everything actually under His authority, —WLMS.

**2:8.** Man's situation is tragic. He does not have dominion over the earth. His efforts to master the earth are cursed by sweat and drudgery. He is subject to the destructive powers of natural disasters: hurricanes, tornadoes, tidal waves, floods, volcanic eruptions, and earthquakes. He is ravaged by disease and grows old. In the end he is conquered by death. What a tragedy!

By application and practice of his God-given abilities, by conscious deliberation, by systematic calculation based on his powers of observation, by employing his creative powers, man is supposed to exercise dominion in the service of God for His glory. Yet he does not. He is staring down the barrel of nuclear destruction and radiation sickness. Millions starve to death. Everywhere man is confronted by wretchedness, depravity, misery, despair, and sinfulness. At the present time, he does not see the nobility and dignity of the human race evident in the subjugation of all his enemies. There are many foes left to conquer.

It is a sad scene: man, created with such dignity and such a noble destiny, ruined by the Fall and degraded by the ravages of sin. But, thankfully, the last chapter has not been written.

**9.** **But we see Jesus, who was made a little lower than the angels:** . . . though we do behold Him, *—WADE* . . . What we do see is Jesus . . . made for a little while, *—TNT* . . . Who for a short time was, *—ADAM* . . . who was made inferior, *—WLMS* . . . a little lower than heavenly messengers, *—KLGS.*

**for the suffering of death:** . . . because of the death he suffered, *—TNT.*

**crowned with glory and honour:** . . . wreathed with, *—CNDT.*

**that he by the grace of God:** . . . By God's gracious love he did this, *—SEB* . . . that by God's favor, *—WLMS.*

**should taste death for every man:** . . . He might experience death, *—WLMS* . . . tasted the bitterness of death, *—NORL* . . . might die for everyone, *—TNT* . . . for all sorts of people, *—ADAM* . . . for the sake of everyone, *—CNDT* . . . for every person, *—KLGS.*

**2:9.** The original readers of this epistle did not see a triumphant human race ruling in dignity over the earth. Nor did they see a victorious Messiah when they looked about. Indeed, they saw the Son, Jesus, who had recently been crucified in a criminal execution. It is not only the race which has been humbled by God; the Son has also been humiliated. In His death He was "made a little lower than the angels."

But the epistle looks beyond the Son's temporary humiliation to the objective which God the Father pursued in the Son's death. The results of Jesus' death are "glory and honor," the same crown which the Lord intended for mankind (Psalm 8:5). By suffering the particular death which He experienced at Calvary, the Son became a channel for the grace of God. His death is described as a "taste" because it was a real but temporary experience. Jesus did not remain dead. His death, moreover, had purpose and significance for the whole human race. It was a death which He died for others. It was substitutionary. The text says Jesus died "for every man." The phrase *huper pantos* means "in the place of every man."

**10.** **For it became him:** . . . For it befitted him, *—MNTG* . . . It fitted Him well, *—BECK* . . . It was appropriate for Him, *—WLMS.*

**for whom [are] all things, and by whom [are] all things:** . . . by Whom everything exists, *—ADAM* . . . created all things for his own purposes, *—TNT* . . . who is the Final Goal and the First Cause of the universe, *—WLMS.*

**in bringing many sons unto glory:** . . . in conducting Many Sons, *—WLSN* . . . many children to glory, *—WLMS.*

**to make the captain of their salvation:** . . . to make Jesus a perfect Leader, *—NLTG* . . . to perfect the Inaugurator, *—CNDT* . . . him who leads them to salvation, *—TNT* . . . the Pioneer of their salvation, *—MNTG.*

**perfect through sufferings:** . . . achieve perfection through suffering, *—NORL* . . . through the process of suffering, *—WLMS.*

**2:10.** Here we are introduced to the great heart of God. It is entirely appropriate for the Creator and Sustainer of all things in the universe to direct His Son along a path of suffering in pursuit of His objective for mankind. The "many sons" whom He is glorifying are the human beings who will be restored from the effects of the Fall and will exercise dominion over the earth. This restoration will be achieved by the "captain," that is, the *archēgon,* the pioneer of their deliverance—Jesus the Son. Because of God's love, He became a trailblazer in respect to man's salvation. He opened up the way to God in heaven. The perfection spoken of here is not a moral perfection. There is no suggestion that Jesus had moral defects which were remedied by His suffering. As will be seen in the following verses and in 5:8, 9, it is His qualification for entrance into the high priesthood as a man which is in view.

**11.** **For both he that sanctifieth and they who are sanctified:** . . . he who purifies, *—TCNT* . . . the one who cleanses them from sin, *—TNT* . . . and those who are being hallowed, *—CNDT.*

**[are] all of one:** . . . all spring from, *—WLMS* . . . all one common origin, *—NORL* . . . all have one Father, *—BECK.*

**for which cause he is not ashamed to call them brethren:** . . . That is why, *—TNT.*

**2:11.** Both the priest who sets apart the people and the people who are set apart must be "all of one," that is, out of the same group. To represent the human race, the Son had to become flesh. Since He came to sanctify believers as their priest, the humiliation involved in His becoming one of them and dying for them did not stop Him. Identifying with sinners as brothers caused Him no shame. His suffering as one with them and for them was prophesied.

What a beautiful statement: "He is not ashamed to call them brethren." Christ had many reasons to be ashamed of the race to which He belonged. In His own line were murderers, adulterers, liars. Again we see the grace of God demonstrated.

**12. Saying, I will declare thy name unto my brethren:** . . . when He says, *–WLMS* . . . I will announce, *–ADAM* . . . I will proclaim, *–TNT.*

**in the midst of the church will I sing praise unto thee:** . . . I will join the congregation in singing your praise, *–TNT* . . . in the midst of the congregation, *–NORL, –WLMS* . . . I will sing a hymn to You, *–ADAM* . . . shall I be singing hymns, *–CNDT* . . . I will sing to You in the middle of the congregation, *–SEB.*

**2:12.** Here Psalm 22:22 is cited. As the source of Jesus' agonized cry, "My God, my God, why hast thou forsaken me?" (Psalm 22:1), the first part of this psalm is a lament and a cry for deliverance. In the second part, beginning with 22:22, the lament is followed by words of thanksgiving. The same Jesus, who lamented His abandonment by the Father while on the cross bearing our sins, is seen in this messianic psalm praising God for deliverance in the midst of His brethren, the assembled saints.

**13. And again, I will put my trust in him:** . . . I myself, like others, *–WADE* . . . I will confide in him, *–WLSN.*
**And again, Behold I and the children which God hath given me:** . . . Here I am and the children, *–WLMS.*

**2:13.** Next the inspired writer cites words from Isaiah 8:18. In the context of Isaiah 8, the prophet spoke these words to the nation of Israel which had rejected the message he brought from Jehovah. In the face of his rejection, Isaiah declared that he had put his trust in the Lord. This same attitude and these same circumstances were true in the life of Jesus. He came to His own people, Israel, and they crucified Him. In the hour of His trial, Jesus identified himself with other men by putting His trust in the Lord. Psalm 22:24 indicates that the Lord did not turn from the afflicted, "But when he cried unto him, he heard." As a man, in His loneliest hour, Jesus the Son put His trust in the Father.

This verse continues to quote from Isaiah 8:18: "Behold, I and the children whom the Lord hath given me are for signs and for wonders in Israel from the Lord of hosts, which dwelleth in mount Zion." Even though the people rejected Isaiah, his preaching and his children and their symbolic names stood as a continuing witness to the unbelieving Jews: *Isaiah* means "Jehovah is salvation"; *Shear-jashub* means "a remnant will return"; *Mahershalalhashbaz* means "hasten booty, speed plunder." Likewise, the professing Jewish Christians who were in danger of rejecting the Son were to look to the meaning of His name. *Jesus* means "Saviour." The Son and His children are those who put their trust in the Lord.

**14. Forasmuch then as the children:** . . . Since then, *–WLMS.*

**are partakers of flesh and blood:** . . . since human nature is the common heritage, *–TCNT* . . . share our mortal nature, *–WLMS.*

**he also himself likewise took part of the same:** . . . in like manner, participated in the same, *–WADE* . . . also shared in their humanity, *–SEB* . . . took on Himself a full share of the same, *–WLMS* . . . shared their human nature in the same way, *–TNT.*

**that through death:** . . . in order that He by His death, *–WLMS* . . . His purpose was, *–TNT* . . . which His possession of the same physical nature rendered possible, *–WADE.*

**he might destroy him that had the power of death:** . . . he might vanquish, *–WLSN* . . . might put a stop to the power of, *–WLMS* . . . he might render powerless, *–MNTG, –TCNT* . . . to depose, *–TNT* . . . by death cancel out him who has the strength of death, *–KLGS* . . . He might render inoperative the one having the dominion of, *–WUST* . . . who has the might of death, *–CNDT* . . . who has in Death the instrument of his sway, *–WADE.*

**that is, the devil:**

**2:14.** Having argued that the Son needed to become a man in order to qualify for the priesthood by identifying with the race He came to represent, the inspired writer stated the fact simply: the Son has actually become a man.

The incarnation! What an event! What a concept! Only an all-wise God could have conceived such a plan, to stoop down as it were, in order to raise man from his hopelessness.

In the second half of the verse there begins the examination of the consequences of Christ's qualifying for the priesthood. Three powerful results of Christ's high-priestly work are presented. One is given in verse 14, another in verse 15, and the third in verses 17 and 18. First of all, Jesus Christ shattered the power of the devil (1 John 3:8; Colossians 2:15). Jesus marched into Satan's fortress of death, disarmed him, chained him, and robbed him of his captives.

**15. And deliver them who through fear of death:** . . . and set at liberty . . . because of their dread of death, *–WLMS* . . . that He might set free those, *–NORL* . . . and release those, *–TNT* . . . terrified by death, *–BECK* . . . were subject to the fear of, *–WADE.*

**were all their lifetime subject to bondage:** . . . held in Slavery, *–WLSN* . . . were subjected to slavery throughout their entire lifetime, *–ADAM* . . . lived their whole lifetime in bondage, *–NORL* . . . We no longer need to be chained to this fear, *–NLTG.*

**2:15.** Secondly, the sufferings and death of Jesus save the prisoners of fear. The fear of death enslaves. Men who fear death will force themselves to do things that nothing else could force them to do. For sinful men the fearful judgment of the living God stands beyond the grave. But Christ delivers believers.

**16. For verily he took not on [him the nature of] angels:** . . . For of course it is not angels, —WLMS . . . It is clear He didn't come to help angels, —BECK.

**but he took on [him] the seed of Abraham:** . . . but descendants of Abraham, —WLMS.

**2:16.** The work of Christ influences the whole universe (Ephesians 1:10), but His redemptive work was not done for angels but for mankind. The author pointed out that the Son identified himself not with angels but with the nation of Israel, the descendants of Abraham and for those who have his faith.

**17. Wherefore in all things it behoved him:** . . . And consequently it was necessary, —TCNT . . . This is why he had to, —TNT.

**to be made like unto [his] brethren:** . . . He had to be made like His brothers, —WLMS . . . had to be made in all respects, —TNT.

**that he might be a merciful and faithful high priest in things [pertaining] to God:** . . . that he might serve God . . . with compassion and faithfulness, —TNT . . . become a compassionate, —MNTG . . . a sympathetic High Priest, —WLMS . . . in what is related to God, —ADAM.

**to make reconciliation for the sins of the people:** . . . in order to, —WLSN . . . make propitiation, —ADAM . . . and pay for the sins, —BECK . . . for the purpose of expiating the sins of his People, —TCNT . . . to atone for the people's sins, —TNT.

**2:17.** Finally, by His death and resurrection, Jesus Christ has *secured the priesthood for sinners.* The text presents two aspects of that priesthood. Jesus Christ the "merciful and faithful high priest" has by His death provided a *covering for sins.* Believers have been covered by His blood and His righteous life. He has paid the penalty for their sins. The word *hilaskesthai* looks at the propitiatory aspect of Christ's work. It refers to the satisfaction of God's wrath by Christ's sacrifice. The wrath of God due to the sinner has been diverted from the sinner and fallen on Jesus. The word is loaded with the imagery of the sacrifice and blood sprinkled on the lid of the ark of the covenant on the Day of Atonement. As that blood ceremonially covered the sins of Israel on a yearly basis, so the blood of Jesus actually and effectively covers "the sins of the whole world" (1 John 2:2). God the Son was sent by the Father to take the wrath of the Father upon himself in order that sinners who put their trust in Him might be declared righteous and reconciled to their God.

**18. For in that he himself hath suffered being tempted:** . . . It is because he himself has been tested by suffering, —TNT.

**he is able to succour them that are tempted:** . . . is also able instantly, —MNTG . . . He is able to help those, —ADAM . . . to give immediate help to any, —WLMS . . . those who are now being tested in the same way, —TNT.

**2:18.** The propitiation secured by Jesus' sacrifice does not, however, exhaust the effects of His priesthood. Christians have only begun to experience its benefits when they enjoy forgiveness.

The Son provides *comfort in suffering.* In becoming a priest, Jesus blazed a trail by obeying the Father's will in His sufferings. Believers cannot experience anything that He has not already experienced. He endured all the hardships that mankind can suffer. Having been tempted, He knows the force of the temptations which assail them. He suffered and triumphed over His sufferings. He comforts His own and gives them grace sufficient to overcome their strongest temptations.

## Chapter 3

**1. Wherefore, holy brethren:** . . . My fellow-Christians, —NORL . . . For these reasons, —KLGS . . . my Christian brothers, —WLMS.

**partakers of the heavenly calling:** . . . you who share in God's calling, —SEB . . . partners of a celestial calling, —CNDT.

**consider the Apostle and High Priest of our profession, Christ Jesus:** . . . contemplate, —NOLI . . . think carefully on, —KLGS . . . attentively regard Jesus, —WLSN . . . fix your eyes on . . . the Apostle and High Priest of our Religion, —TCNT . . . fix your thoughts then upon Jesus, —MNTG . . . the Messenger and High Priest whom we profess to follow, —WLMS . . . in our confession of Faith, —WADE.

**3:1.** After concluding his discussion of the relationship between Jesus' sufferings and His superiority to the angels, the inspired writer began a brief presentation of the Son's superiority to Moses. The assertion that the message of the Son is superior to the message of the angels delivered on Mount Sinai (2:1-3) raises questions about the place of Moses who was also associated with the Law given at Sinai. Therefore, the readers of the epistle are asked to consider Jesus the Messiah who is designated "the Apostle and High Priest of our profession." As Apostle He was sent by the Father to reveal the Father to men; as High Priest He represents men to the Father.

Jesus the Christ, the Messiah, is a two-way mediator. In this twofold mediation, He parallels Moses who was sent by Jehovah to deliver the Law to Israel and who also on several occasions interceded with Jehovah on Israel's behalf as their representative. Just as Israel acknowledged Moses as a mediator between themselves and the Lord, so believers confess Jesus Christ as the Mediator between themselves and the Father.

**2. Who was faithful to him that appointed him:** . . . to see how faithful He was to God, *–WLMS.*

**as also Moses [was faithful] in all his house:** . . . in all the house of God, *–WLMS* . . . all God's household, *–TNT.*

**3:2.** A further point of likeness between Jesus and Moses is singled out here: both were "faithful" to God in the responsibilities which He gave to them. The sphere of their work is identified by the term "house" which is picked up in the next verse when the inspired writer moved away from points of similarity.

**3. For this [man] was counted worthy of more glory than Moses:** . . . is held in greater regard, *–TCNT* . . . is judged to be worthy of, *–WLMS* . . . has been considered worthy of greater honor, *–ADAM* . . . of greater glory, *–MNTG.*

**inasmuch as he who hath builded the house:** . . . just as the founder of a household, *–TNT* . . . as He Who constructs it, *–CNDT* . . . A builder, *–SEB* . . . he who has organized a household, *–WADE.*

**hath more honour than the house:** . . . has greater glory than, *–WLMS* . . . deserves more praise, *–SEB* . . . is more than the household itself, *–TNT* . . . enjoys more honour than the household, *–WADE.*

**3:3.** "For" introduces the reason the readers of the epistle should set their minds upon Jesus. Jesus surpasses Moses. "Counted worthy" conjures up pictures of a balance scale. The parallels between Moses and Jesus now move from comparison to contrast. The weight of Jesus' glory is greater than Moses' to the same degree that the contractor who constructs a house has greater honor than the house.

**4. For every house is builded by some [man]:** . . . is organized by, *–WADE* . . . is built by somebody, *–WLMS* . . . is founded by someone, *–TNT.*

**but he that built all things [is] God:** . . . he who built the universe, *–MNTG* . . . but the builder and furnisher of the universe, *–WLMS* . . . but God is the founder of everything, *–TNT* . . . organized the Universe, *–WADE.*

**3:4.** "For" in this verse ushers in the explanation of the "house" illustration. Houses do not materialize from nothing; each has been built by someone. The house in view here is *panta*, the totality of all existing things, the entire universe. God is its builder. He is clearly greater than Moses. The context provides clear interpretation of these words. The Son is the Father's agent in creation (1:2). He is addressed as God (1:8). He is portrayed as

**982**

Creator (1:10-12). Jesus' glory far surpasses the glory of Moses, because He is the builder of the house, the Creator of the universe.

**5. And Moses verily [was] faithful in all his house, as a servant:** . . . The loyalty of Moses was, *–NOLI* . . . as an attendant, *–CNDT* . . . it was as a servant that Moses was faithful, *–TNT* . . . in the administration of the whole of God's Household, *–WADE.*

**for a testimony of those things which were to be spoken after:** . . . being included among its members for the purpose of bearing testimony to the Truths that were afterwards to be communicated, *–WADE* . . . bore witness to what God would say, *–TNT* . . . that would be disclosed in the future, *–ADAM* . . . to a Message still to come, *–TCNT.*

**3:5.** Moses' status and significance were not examined. His faithfulness (introduced in verse 2) was addressed. This is not the writer's personal opinion; it is the judgment of the Lord. Numbers 12 gives the account of Miriam and Aaron complaining against Moses. In response to them, Jehovah spoke in Moses' defense. He declared that Moses was superior to the prophets because he received God's words directly, not in visions and dreams. In proclaiming Moses' superiority, He says, "My servant Moses is not so, who is faithful in all mine house" (Numbers 12:7). The passage is almost cited verbatim here. "Mine house" is changed to "his house" because the writer was reporting God's evaluation indirectly.

In the last part of the verse, two contrasts are drawn. Moses is classified by the Lord as "a servant." The term *therapōn* does not carry the connotations of slavery or menial service; rather, it is associated with dignity and personal service. Yet it does indicate that Moses was responsible and accountable to the Lord as a subordinate not born in the family. Finally, Moses testified of "things which were to be spoken after." The revelation which he received from Jehovah was inferior to the revelation spoken in the Son because that word was God's final message of salvation (1:1,2).

**6. But Christ as a son over his own house:** . . . but Christ was faithful as a son, *–TNT.*

**whose house are we:** . . . We are His family, *–BECK* . . . we are that house, *–WLMS* . . . ruling over God's household, *–TNT.*

**if we hold fast:** . . . if we hold firmly, *–ADAM* . . . if we should be retaining the boldness, *–CNDT* . . . if only we keep, *–TNT* . . . keep up our courage, *–NORL.*

**the confidence and the rejoicing of the hope:** . . . our confidence and pride in the hope that is ours, *–TNT* . . . and the joy that hope inspires, *–WLMS.*

**firm unto the end:** . . . unshaken to, *–TCNT* . . . unto the consummation, *–CNDT* . . . the very end, *–WLMS.*

**3:6.** Christ's superiority to Moses is stated simply. He is not a servant; He is "a son." He is not "in" the house; He is "over" it. It is not someone else's house; it is "his own house," the one He himself created. Those who profess faith in Jesus Christ are His creation, if their confidence is strong enough to boldly maintain their hope in Jesus' future restoration of mankind's lost "glory" and "honor."

7. **Wherefore (as the Holy Ghost saith:**
**To day if ye will hear his voice:** . . . Listen to his voice today, *–TNT* . . . if you hear Him speak, *–BECK.*

**3:7.** Verse 6 introduced a long section of application which consists of encouragement, exhortation, and warning. It extends to 4:13. Those who received this epistle were professing Jewish believers who were under great pressure to abandon their profession of faith in Jesus as the Messiah. Their exact situation is not known, but it is fairly easy to imagine some of the trials that pressured them: family and religious ties to Judaism, ostracism by their peers, economic sanctions, famine, poverty, loneliness, religious persecution, and perhaps the threat of martyrdom.

To underscore the danger of their turning back, the inspired writer pointed out the parallel between their situation and that of those who were with Moses in the wilderness. Moses was a great servant of the Lord, but almost all who followed him died in the wilderness and never entered the Promised Land. Jesus is the Son and the revealer of a superior message. Those who fail to follow Him by faith wherever He leads them will also fail to enter into the realization of that which He has promised to them.

As a foundation for this extended warning, the writer fully quoted Psalm 95:7-11. First of all, he introduced the quote in a notable manner. "Wherefore" indicates that the passage is cited in support of the conditionality of hope. Secondly, the introductory phrase "as the Holy Ghost saith" reveals his high view of the Old Testament. The words of Psalm 95 are presented as the work of God the Holy Spirit, and they spoke with divine authority to the professing Hebrew Christians of the First Century, even though they were written to their ancestors several centuries beforehand.

8. **Harden not your hearts, as in the provocation:** . . . don't close your minds as it happened when the people provoked me, *–BECK* . . . don't let your hearts become stubborn, as you did during the rebellion, *–SEB* . . . Do not be stubborn as you once were when you rebelled against him, *–TNT* . . . as

they did in provoking me, *–WLMS* . . . as in the revolt, *–ADAM* . . . when they turned against Me, *–NLTG.*

**in the day of temptation in the wilderness:** . . . during the day of testing in the desert, *–ADAM* . . . that day when you put him to the test in the desert, *–TNT.*

9. **When your fathers tempted me, proved me:** . . .Where your forefathers found I stood their test, *–WLMS* . . . tried my forbearance, *–MNTG* . . . when they tried my patience, *–TCNT* . . . and tested Me, *–NORL.*

**and saw my works forty years:** . . . they watched me at work, *–TNT* . . . were acquainted with My acts, *–CNDT* . . . my marvellous deeds during so many years, *–WADE.*

**3:8, 9.** Since the interpretation and application of these words is drawn out in 3:12-4:13, only a few historical notations are given here. Psalm 95 begins with a call to worship Jehovah followed by the quotation in this verse, a warning against disobedience to the Lord. The words just prior to the quote include the statement, "We are the people of his pasture" (Psalm 95:7), an idea in line with the inspired writer's application: this is the way believers must behave, if they are to be God's house. The "if" clause of verse 7 recalls Exodus 19:5 and Deuteronomy 5:25. "Harden not" evokes images of Pharaoh's and Israel's rebellions. "The provocation" hints at the incident in Exodus 17 which occurred at a place Moses called Massah and Meribah, meaning "temptation" and "strife," "because they tempted the Lord . . ." (Exodus 17:7). In spite of God's goodness in always providing their needs, such events were repeated for 40 years (e.g., Numbers 20:1-13).

10. **Wherefore I was grieved with that generation:** . . . That is why I became angry with the people of that time, *–TNT* . . . I am disgusted with, *–CNDT* . . . I was sore displeased, *–MNTG* . . . I was indignant with, *–WLMS.*

**and said, They do alway err in [their] heart:** . . . Their hearts are always going astray, *–ADAM, –WLMS* . . . They always think wrong thoughts, *–NLTG* . . . Their hearts always wander away, *–SEB* . . . They are always wandering, *–MNTG* . . . Their hearts are always straying, *–TCNT.*

**and they have not known my ways:** . . . but they did not acknowledge my ways, *–WLSN* . . . they have never come to know, *–WLMS* . . . they do not understand, *–TNT* . . . and never have learned My paths, *–BECK.*

**3:10.** Murmurings against Jehovah characterized the entire wilderness generation. The Lord continually punished the guilty, and eventually His patient longsuffering ended. Israel did not focus her heart on Him; as a result they did not obey Him.

**11. So I sware in my wrath:** . . . As I shewed when I swore, −WADE . . . in my indignation, −WLSN . . . So in My anger I took oath, −NORL, −WLMS . . . while I was angry, I made a vow, −SEB . . . I swore, −TNT.

**They shall not enter into my rest):** . . . that they would never come in and rest with me, −TNT . . . not be admitted to, −WLMS.

**3:11.** Israel had grieved God by their murmurings and disobedience. Finally, His grief changed to anger, when they turned back from entering Canaan at Kadesh-barnea. The Lord swore an oath prohibiting them from ever setting foot in the "Promised Land" of rest (Numbers 14:23). They wandered for a total of 40 years until all that generation had perished in the wilderness.

**12. Take heed, brethren, lest there be:** . . . Consequently, I repeat, −WADE . . . Watch out, brothers, −ADAM . . . Brothers, be careful, −SEB . . . See to it, −WLMS.

**in any of you an evil heart of unbelief:** . . . a wicked and faithless heart, −TCNT . . . no wicked, unbelieving heart is found, −WLMS.

**in departing from the living God:** . . . as shown by your turning away from, −WLMS . . . by apostatizing, −WLSN . . . should fall away from, −TNT . . . "that pulls away from, −SEB . . . manifesting itself in apostasy from, −MNTG . . . that would turn you away from, −ADAM.

**3:12.** Addressing the professing Jewish Christian readers as "brethren," the writer began to apply Psalm 95 by telling them to watch out in case any of them had an "evil heart" which he identified as a heart characterized by unbelief. In using the word "heart," he was not talking merely of their emotional nature. "Heart" referred to the core of their being. The action of such an evil heart is described by the phrase *en tō apostēnai* which speaks of their turning aside from God. Unbelief abandons God and rebels against Him. The God they were in danger of leaving was not some idol; He is the "living" God. The whole tenor of the argument to this point argues that if they abandoned their belief in the Son, they would be rebelling against God as the wilderness generation did in Moses' day.

**13. But exhort one another daily:** . . . On the contrary, −WADE . . . What you should do . . . is to encourage one another every day, −TNT . . . continue to encourage, −WLMS.

**while it is called To day:** . . . as long as there lasts the interval which is called, −WADE . . . as long as "Today" shall last, −WLMS.

**lest any of you be hardened:** . . . made stubborn against God, −TNT.

**through the deceitfulness of sin:** . . . by the seduction of sin, −CNDT . . . by a Delusion of sin, −WLSN . . . by the trickery of sin, −KLGS . . . by sin's deceiving ways, −WLMS.

**3:13.** The danger of rebellion was so great that the writer asked the believers to admonish and encourage each other on a daily basis. The verb *parakaleite* echoes both the negative and positive elements associated with exhortation. Its meaning can be illustrated by picturing someone running alongside a long-distance runner and exhorting him to finish the course in the face of his fatigue and exhaustion. There is a warning about the effects of quitting, but there is a sense of unity and a spirit of hope which comes to the fore. In his comments on Psalm 95, the writer emphasizes the sense of urgency and immediacy attached to the word "Today." The danger of turning from the Son must be attended to on a daily basis, because the sin of unbelief sneaks up on a believer. Little by little an individual can be hardened and become unaware.

**14. For we are made partakers of Christ:** . . . We have become Companions of, −TCNT . . . We share in Christ, −BECK . . . we shall have become Christ's partners, −TNT . . . become real sharers, −WLMS.

**if we hold the beginning of our confidence stedfast unto the end:** . . . we only remain so, provided we retain unshaken to the end the confidence which we had at first, −WADE . . . if we hold our first title deed firm, −MNTG . . . the assumption confirmed unto the consummation, −CNDT . . . if we keep firm to the end the faith we had at first, −WLMS.

**3:14.** The prize in a race does not go to those who start out quickly. Those who finish are the ones who are honored. Over the centuries some controversy has arisen over the meaning of the phrase *metochoi gar . . . tou Christou* ("partakers of Christ"). Most interpreters have taken it to mean "companions with Christ," seeing it as a reference to the believer's participation with Christ in the Kingdom. Some, however, have interpreted it as a reference to the Christian's union with Christ. The context seems to argue in favor of the first meaning. The participation under consideration is something in the future. When a believer maintains the faith that brought salvation until the end of this life, either until death or the Second Coming, he will most certainly participate with the Son in His kingdom. Participation in the promised kingdom of God is not dependent upon a profession of faith alone; it is conditioned upon displaying the reality of that profession by living a life which continues following after God.

History has often recorded the failure of those who seemingly started out well but dropped out along the way. The history of the kingdom of Judah illustrates this. Time after time a king would begin his reign seeking to please God, but because of evil influences would turn away from Jehovah.

Only those who persist in finding and obeying the will of God can expect to achieve the prize which God has designed for them. "Steadfast" must be the watchword for the follower of Christ.

**15. While it is said:** ... With regard to the declaration, *—WLSN* ... Scripture says to us also, *—TNT* ... This warning is still being uttered, *—WADE* ... and yet the warning continues to be spoken, *—WLMS*.

**To day if ye will hear his voice:** ... Listen to his voice today, *—TNT*.

**harden not your hearts, as in the provocation:** ... Do not continue to harden your hearts, *—MNTG* ... Do not be stubborn as you once were when you rebelled against him, *—TNT* ... as in the revolt, *—ADAM* ... as in the embitterment, *—CNDT* ... as in the rebellion, *—NORL* ... as they did in provoking me, *—WLMS* ... as when ye exasperated me, *—WADE*.

**3:15.** Returning to Psalm 95:7, 8, the inspired writer continued his theme of the urgency and immediacy of the danger of unbelief. The implication both here and in verse 13 is that the time will come when the opportunity for genuine belief will be past. Belief must be exercised while the gospel invitation stands open.

**16. For some, when they had heard, did provoke:** ... who was it that heard and yet provoked Him? *—WLMS* ... Who listened to his voice and rebelled? *—TNT* ... For who were they who, after hearing God speak, exasperated Him? *—WADE*.

**howbeit not all that came out of Egypt by Moses:** ... Was it not all, *—WLMS* ... under the leadership of Moses? *—WADE*.

**3:16.** Some who heard God's promise and warnings bitterly rebelled against Him anyway. Not all who experienced God's gracious deliverance from Egypt rebelled against Him in the wilderness. Failure was not inevitable; it was the result of personal choice.

**17. But with whom was he grieved forty years?:** ... with whom was God incensed, *—NORL* ... was God angry, *—TNT* ... was He deeply displeased during so many years? *—WADE*.

**[was it] not with them that had sinned:**

**whose carcases fell in the wilderness?:** ... whose dead bodies, *—MNTG* ... whose corpses fell, *—ADAM* ... whose bodies dropped dead in the desert? *—BECK*.

**3:17.** A series of rhetorical questions begins to drive home the lesson of Israel in the wilderness. Which Israelites disgusted and angered Jehovah during those 40 years of trial in the desert? The account written by the eyewitness Moses is clear. The corpses strewn across the pages of the Pentateuch and the Sinai peninsula are the corpses of the Children of Israel who tested God's patience by repeated acts of sin. Their bleaching bones testified to their disobedience.

**18. And to whom sware he:** ... To whom did He take oath, *—WLMS*.

**that they should not enter into his rest:** ... that they should not be admitted to, *—WLMS* ... that they would never come in and rest with him? *—TNT*.

**but to them that believed not?:** ... except to the stubborn? *—CNDT* ... Those who did not obey God! *—SEB* ... to those who disobeyed? *—BECK*, *—TNT*.

**3:18.** The verse begins with another question with an obvious answer. This time the focus is on the penalty and the nature of the sin which led to the death of so many in the wilderness. Those who died are characterized as those who were prohibited from entrance into Canaan by the oath of the living God. The essence of the sin which brought down the wrath of God upon them was unbelief. Instead of zeroing in on the rebellion, backbiting, complaining, grumbling, murmuring, and defiance which fill the pages of the Old Testament record of Israel's wilderness experience, the writer looked at the source of these acts of sin: deep inside, underneath it all, was their refusal to believe God.

**19. So we see that they could not enter in:** ... could not be admitted to it, *—WLMS* ... they were precluded from entering, *—WADE*.

**because of unbelief:** ... because they did not believe, *—TNT* ... it was through mistrust, *—WADE*.

**3:19.** In case some did not get the point, it was repeated forcefully. God drew a line, and the disobedient Children of Israel were not able to cross it. They could not leave the wilderness and enter Canaan because they did not take God at His word. It was their unbelief which kept them from entering into the rest which the Lord had promised.

# Chapter 4

**1. Let us therefore fear, lest:** ... the one thing we should fear, *—TNT* ... be on our guard, *—MNTG* ... we must be apprehensive, *—WADE*.

**a promise being left [us] of entering into his rest:** ... as long as God's promise that we should go in and rest with him still stands, *—TNT* ... though there is a promise still standing, *—TCNT* ... The same promise of going into God's rest is still for us, *—NLTG* ... the promise for us to be admitted, *—WLMS* ... still remains open, *—NORL*.

**any of you should seem to come short of it:** ... may be found, *—WLMS* ... seeming to be deficient, *—CNDT* ... some of you might not make it, *—SEB* ... failed to satisfy the conditions governing entrance, *—WADE* ... may be judged to have missed, *—BECK* ... one of you should think he has missed his chance, *—TNT*.

**4:1.** Since God keeps His word and punishes unbelief by denying "rest" to those who do not trust Him, those who profess faith in the Son ought to fear God. This is what the Son himself taught His disciples (Matthew 10:28) when He said: "And fear not them which kill the body, but are not able to kill the soul: but rather fear him which is able to destroy both soul and body in hell." After all, it was the Son who promised rest to those who would come unto Him: "Come unto me, all ye that labor and are heavy laden, and I will give you rest. Take my yoke upon you, and learn of me; for I am meek and lowly in heart: and ye shall find rest unto your souls" (Matthew 11:28,29).

At this juncture, the inspired writer began to ring the changes on the word "rest" which appeared in the last verse of his citation from Psalm 95 (Hebrews 3:11). He used the word *katapausin* which is found in the Septuagint translation of the psalm and is related to the word *anapausin* employed in Matthew 11:29. In this verse he was concentrating on the danger which threatened some of those to whom he was writing the epistle. Like the Children of Israel in Moses' day, they might never experience God's promised rest.

**2. For unto us was the gospel preached:** ... For we have had the good news, *—WLMS* ... communicated to us, *—WADE.*

**as well as unto them:** ... just as it was to those men of old, *—TNT* ... they received the Gospel, *—NOLI* ... even as they had, *—WADE.*

**but the word preached did not profit them:** ... the proclamation of the Gospel, *—NOLI* ... the preaching that they heard, *—TNT* ... but the message heard did them no good, *—WLMS* ... was of no service to them, *—WADE.*

**not being mixed with faith in them that heard [it]:** ... because when they heard it, *—NOLI* ... it was not inwardly assimilated through faith by the hearers, *—WADE* ... not having been blended, *—CNDT* ... of those who were attentive to it, *—TCNT* ... they did not believe it, *—NORL* ... they were not by faith made one with those who heeded it, *—WLMS* ... in their hearts, *—TNT.*

**4:2.** Once again a section of explanation begins with the word "For." The writer specifically drew a parallel between his readers and the Hebrews in the wilderness. Both groups had good news preached to them. Obviously, Israel had been delivered from slavery in Egypt and was to gain entrance to the land of Abraham, Isaac, and Jacob. The good news preached to the readers of this epistle was spoken by God in His Son (1:2; 2:3). The fact that the Israelites heard the message with their own ears, however, did not do them the slightest bit of good. Physical hearing was not enough to bring the experience of the reality of Canaan to fruition. The seed of that promise had to fall into good ground where it was received in faith before it could bear fruit in their lives. But, sad to say, even though they heard the words, and the meaning of the words may have entered into their understanding, there was no enjoyment of the promise in actual experience, because the message was not united with faith in the Children of Israel who heard it. They needed faith as well as hearing.

**3. For we which have believed do enter into rest:** ... are being admitted to, *—WLMS* ... into that promised Rest we who have reposed faith in God are in the course of entering, *—WADE* ... are going into rest with him because we are believers, *—TNT* ... We enter his rest only if we believe, *—NOLI.*

**as he said:** ... Scripture says, *—TNT* ... just as He has implied in the words, *—WADE.*

**As I have sworn in my wrath, if they shall enter into my rest:** ... As in my anger I took oath, *—WLMS* ... In my anger I swore that they would never come in and rest with me, *—TNT.*

**although the works were finished from the foundation of the world:** ... even though His works had been completed, *—ADAM* ... All His works had been planned before, *—NORL* ... at the creation, *—WLMS* ... though ever since the creation of the world God's work had been finished, *—TNT* ... after the foundation, *—WADE.*

**4:3.** For those who believe today, the opposite is true. Believers are in the process of entering into rest. The linear action of the verb *eiserchometha* emphasizes the process in those who "have believed." The tense of *pisteusantes* ("having believed") refers to the moment of genuine conversion. Here the writer repeats the part of Psalm 95 already cited in Hebrews 3:11. Although the English text of 3:11 and the part of 4:3 containing the quote are different, the Greek text is exactly the same. The "if" appears in 4:3 because here the Greek has been translated more literally and shows the idiomatic form of an oath made in the Hebrew language. The rather cryptic ending of verse 3 seems to heighten the sense of tragedy. Israel was, by their own sin and God's punishing oath, kept from entering into the divine rest which had been available ever since God himself had rested from His work in creation. They brought judgment upon themselves.

**4. For he spake in a certain place of the seventh [day] on this wise:** ... For this is what Scripture says somewhere, *—TNT* ... somewhere He speaks of, *—WLMS* ... as you know, concerning the Seventh Day the Divine Spirit has spoken thus, *—WADE.*

**And God did rest the seventh day from all his works:** ... from all He had done, *—BECK.*

**4:4.** Here (as in 2:6) is demonstrated complete trust in the divine authority and authorship of the Old Testament. The human author of this passage is not specifically identified. This approach shows respect for the readers' familiarity with the contents of the Pentateuch and other Old Testament Scriptures. They were well aware of the source of this quotation from Genesis 2:2. "For," which introduces this verse, indicates that the inspired writer is clarifying the previous sentence.

Anyone who knew the Genesis account of creation knew that after 6 days of creative activity God had completed His work and rested on the seventh day. Most people had not recognized the implications of God's rest other than in regard to its relationship to Israel's resting on the Sabbath. Apparently the inspired writer of Hebrews had given it a great deal of thought, and he was about to tie in the idea of God's resting with Psalm 95 and Canaan's conquest.

**5. And in this [place] again:** ... while in this passage again He says, *—WLMS* ... But Scripture also says, *—TNT* ... in the passage just quoted, *—WADE.*

**If they shall enter into my rest:** ... They shall never come in and rest with me, *—TNT.*

**4:5.** For a fourth time the writer refers to God's oath prohibiting the wilderness generation's entrance into Canaan (3:11,18; 4:3). Undoubtedly, this emphasized that it was God's judgment which kept them from entering the Promised Land, but there is something further: "my rest" focuses on it as a rest which comes from and belongs peculiarly to God. It is, moreover, a rest which He makes available to those who determine to follow after Him.

**6. Seeing therefore it remaineth that some must enter therein:** ... It still remains true that some will enter it, *—NORL* ... Clearly then it is still open for some to go in and rest with him, *—TNT* ... there is still in reserve an opportunity for some to enter, *—WADE* ... some are being admitted to it, *—WLMS.*

**and they to whom it was first preached:** ... and those who previously had the good news announced, *—ADAM* ... who first had the good news told, *—WLMS* ... to whom the Good News was formerly communicated, *—WADE.*

**entered not in because of unbelief:** ... were precluded from entering on account of their disobedience, *—WADE* ... disbelieved and did not go in, *—TNT* ... were not admitted because of disobedience, *—WLMS.*

**4:6.** Since it is God's rest and not man's rest, it still exists and is available for others (*tinas,* "some," an indefinite pronoun) to experience. Those to whom the invitation was originally extended did not experience God's rest because they did not believe the promises which God made to them. They wanted to go back to Egypt. They couldn't trust God to conquer the giants in Canaan. The word translated "preached" (*euangelisthentes*) means to announce good news or news of a victory. It points out the parallelism between the Christian gospel (*euangelion*) preached to the Hebrew readers of this epistle and the promise of conquest over the Canaanites given to their forefathers in the wilderness.

**7. Again, he limiteth a certain day:** ... He is again specifying, *—CNDT* ... He again ... makes definite reference, *—WADE* ... once again God appoints a day, *—TNT* ... marks out a certain day, *—ADAM* ... so He sets another day, *—BECK* ... He again fixes a definite day, *—WLMS.*

**saying in David, To day, after so long a time:** ... speaking after a long interval, *—TCNT* ... saying long afterward through, *—WLMS* ... after ever so long an interval, *—WADE* ... many years later, *—TNT.*

**as it is said:** ... using the words quoted above, *—TNT* ... in words that have been quoted before, *—WADE.*

**To day if ye will hear his voice, harden not your hearts:** ... you must listen to his voice, *—TNT* ... You must not harden, *—WLMS* ... don't let your hearts become stubborn, *—SEB.*

**4:7.** This verse refers again to the quotation from Psalm 95 and points out that God *is* (present tense) setting a limit (*horizei*) on His offer of rest. It will not always be available. Yet it was not a one-time offer of rest made only to the Jews in the wilderness. To prove this point, the writer reminded his readers that the words he has quoted were written by David, not by Moses; that is, they were written over 400 years after the time of the Exodus and wilderness wanderings. Although David wrote the psalm, it was God who was speaking "in David."

Most important of all, God is still speaking (the participle *legōn* is in the present tense), and the time limit which He sets is expressed in the word "Today" (*Sēmeron*). The implication is clear. God is still speaking and offering His rest through the words of David in Psalm 95, even "after so long a time." More than 400 years after Moses and the Children of Israel perished in the wilderness, God in David offers His rest, saying, "Today."

**8. For if Jesus had given them rest:** ... if Joshua had really given them, *—WLMS.*

**then would he not afterward have spoken of another day:** ... God would not have continued to speak of another day, *—TNT* ... of another and later Day, *—WADE.*

**4:8.** It would be hard for first-century believers to accept this truth. After all, they were not wandering around in the wilderness murmuring against God's miraculous provision of water, manna, and quail. What did God's oath, swearing to keep the wilderness generation from the Promised Land, have to do with first-century Hebrew Christians?

To meet this response, a further explanation was given of the analysis of Psalm 95. Since God through David says "Today," it is necessary to conclude that the Israelites who entered Canaan under Joshua did not experience God's rest either. Otherwise, God would not still be offering His rest through David by saying "Today." (*Joshua* and *Jesus* are the same name, and the reference here is to the Old Testament Joshua, not to Jesus Christ. See the NIV translation of 4:8.)

**9. There remaineth therefore:** . . . At any rate, —NORL . . . There is still in reserve, then, —WADE . . . is still open for, —TNT.

**a rest to the people of God:** . . . there is a keeping of sabbath still open for God's people, —SEB . . . a sabbath of rest is still awaiting God's people, —WLMS.

**4:9.** With great confidence, the inspired writer drew the conclusion and marked it off by the word "therefore," a logical connective that hints at the inescapability of the logic used. Beyond the time of Israel's conquest of Canaan under Joshua, a Sabbath Day's rest remains for "the people of God." This term links God's offer of rest with His rest on the Sabbath or seventh day referred to in verse 4 (cf. Genesis 2:2). This rest is available not just to Israelites, but to all who may be designated "people of God," Jew and Gentile alike.

**10. For he that is entered into his rest:** . . . if anyone goes in and rests with God, —TNT.

**he also hath ceased from his own works, as God [did] from his:** . . . has rested from his works, —WLMS . . . himself rests altogether from his works, —WADE . . . just as God stopped working, —ADAM.

**4:10.** This verse offers some explanation of the use of the term "his rest" (*katapausin autou*). The person who experiences God's rest is the one who has "ceased from his own works, as God did from his." God's rest was not a cessation of all His activity. He ceased His creation, but He continued to sustain it and take an active part and interest in it, as is seen in His relationship with Adam and Eve (Genesis 3:8ff.). God created the human race and placed it upon earth so He could maintain a unique relationship with those whom He had created in His own image. God's rest certainly included the maintenance of His fellowship with mankind.

**11. Let us labour therefore to enter into that rest:** . . . So let us be alert, —KLGS . . . let us make every effort, —ADAM . . . be earnest to enter, —MNTG . . . then strive diligently, —NORL . . . We should be eager, therefore, to enter that perfect Rest, —WADE . . . Let us do our utmost then to enter that rest, —TNT . . . let us do our best to be admitted to, —WLMS.

**lest any man fall:** . . . so that not one of us may fail, —WLMS.

**after the same example of unbelief:** . . . through being disobedient as they were, —TNT . . . through such disobedience as is illustrated by the example just given, —WADE . . . through the same sort of, —WLMS . . . by the same pattern of disobedience, —ADAM.

**4:11.** A restoration to fellowship between human beings and their Creator is the result of the Son's work, but, as is seen in 2:8, 9, this yet remains to be fully accomplished. Entrance into God's rest is still in the future. It is the consummation of Jesus' work. It is neither the new birth nor entrance into heaven at death. It is entrance into and full participation in the eternal kingdom of God established at the second coming of Jesus Christ. (For a full discussion of this interpretation consult Kaiser, pp. 153-175.) The verb "labor" (*spoudasōmen*) issues a strong exhortation for the readers to diligently apply themselves by doing everything they possibly can to secure their entrance into God's eternal rest, lest they die in unbelief as the Israelites did in the desert.

**12. For the word of God [is] quick, and powerful:** . . . God's Message is a living and active power, —TCNT . . . the Divine Reason, —WADE . . . is alive and full of power in action, —WLMS . . . lives and is active, —BECK . . . and workable, —KLGS . . . and energetic, —WLSN.

**and sharper than any twoedged sword:** . . . and keener than any two-edged blade, —WADE . . . and more cutting than Any two-edged Sword, —WLSN . . . any double-edged sword, —WLMS . . . a sword that cuts both ways, —NLTG.

**piercing even to the dividing asunder of soul and spirit:** . . . It can slice between, —SEB . . . It is a judge of, —KLGS . . . penetrating deeply enough to split soul and spirit, —ADAM . . . cutting through even to a Separation of Life and Breath, —WLSN . . . even to the severance of soul from spirit, —MNTG.

**and of the joints and marrow, and [is] a discerner of the thoughts and intents of the heart:** . . . It is keen in judging the thoughts, —NORL . . . It can tell the difference between the desires and the intentions of the human mind, —SEB . . . and detecting the inmost thoughts, —TCNT . . . and is a sifter and analyzer of the reflections and conceptions of the heart, —WUST . . . is a judge of the sentiments and thoughts of the heart, —CNDT . . . the very thoughts, —MNTG.

**4:12.** God's warning from Psalm 95 is still in force. The Word is "quick," meaning "alive" (*zōn* emphatically stands first in the verse). It is "powerful," meaning "active." It is "sharper than any two-edged sword" because it penetrates more than the physical body. It is comprehensive in its effects. It reaches into all the various parts and functions of the individual and makes judgments. The emphasis is not upon the separation of one part from another, but upon the penetration of all the individual parts, even down to the innermost secrets and purposes which are hidden in the core of an individual's consciousness, away from the eyes of other people.

**13.** **Neither is there any creature that is not manifest in his sight:** ... No created being can escape God's notice, —NORL ... before Him no creature can hide, —ADAM ... can hide from Him, —BECK.

**but all things [are] naked and opened unto the eyes of him:** ... Everything is exposed and laid bare, —TCNT ... and vulnerable to, —ADAM ... and helpless before the eyes, —BECK ... and laid prostrate before, —MNTG.

**with whom we have to do:** ... We must give an answer to God, —SEB ... to Whom we are accountable, —CNDT.

**4:13.** As has been evident throughout this epistle, virtually no distinction has been made between God and the Scriptures. When the Scriptures speak, God is speaking. In this verse the dynamic, living quality of God's Word in Psalm 95 is attributed to God himself. The challenge to believe and not harden one's heart "Today" while there is still time relates to the powerful all-encompassing authority of that Word to sit in judgment on every creature.

The term "opened" (*tetrachēlismena*) is full of illustrative potential. Literally, it refers to bending the neck backward so the face is looking upwards. It is used sometimes to describe the act of falling prostrate naked before someone. In its figurative use it means to lay bare. Any of these usages fit the context of this verse. God has the power and authority to sit in judgment over all human behavior: each person must grovel helplessly before Him in judgment. His judgment is efficient and inescapable.

**14.** **Seeing then that we have a great high priest:** ... We have a great Religious leader, —NLTG.

**that is passed into the heavens, Jesus the Son of God:** ... who has gone through the heavens, —BECK.

**let us hold fast [our] profession:** ... we should firmly retain the confession, —WLSN ... Let us keep our trust in Jesus Christ, —NLTG ... hold fast to our faith in Him, —NORL ... cling to, —BECK.

**4:14.** Having come to the end of his warning which began in 3:7, the inspired writer applied its

challenge to the theme of the superiority of Jesus the Son as it is displayed in His high-priestly ministry. He is not an ordinary, run-of-the-mill high priest. He is "great" because He is the Son, exalted and sitting at the Father's right hand until He returns victorious over all of His enemies to establish His eternal rest.

Here there is a foreshadowing of an argument that will be stated explicitly later on (9:11,24; 10:20): Jesus did not pass through the cloth veil of the temple into a sanctuary built by men; indeed, He has entered into God's heavenly sanctuary and is seated there until His return. In light of these facts, Christians must hold on to their profession of faith in Him unto the very end in spite of all the trials that surround them. He is Jesus—our Deliverer.

**15.** **For we have not an high priest which cannot:** ... who isn't able, —ADAM.

**be touched with the feeling of our infirmities:** ... suffer with, —KLGS ... sympathize with our weaknesses, —ADAM.

**but was in all points tempted like as [we are:** ... but One Who has been tried in all respects, —CNDT ... tested in every spot that we are, —KLGS ... and in every respect, —NORL ... in every way just as we are, —BECK.

**yet] without sin:** ... yet He never sinned, —NORL ... yet without committing any sin, —WLMS ... but he did not sin, —TNT.

**4:15.** The reason Christians must cling to their profession of Jesus as their Messiah and God is given here. He is one with us. He became a man and is, therefore, able to understand human frailties and weaknesses. The word "infirmities" (*astheneiais*) includes both moral and physical weaknesses. The verb used (*sumpathēsai*) indicates that Jesus is able to empathize with believers because He has experienced the limitations and feelings that are common to all humans.

Furthermore, although He never succumbed to any temptation and never sinned, He was subjected to the full gamut of temptations to evil. This means that He was tested and tried but that He never committed a sin or was enticed by evil in His mind to the extent that He approved of it. He understands the power of temptation, and He also knows the stratagems by which it is successfully resisted.

**16.** **Let us therefore come boldly unto the throne of grace:** ... let us approach, —TNT ... let us continue coming with courage to the throne of God's unmerited favor, —WLMS.

**that we may obtain mercy:** ... we may receive, —TNT.

**and find grace to help in time of need:** ... just when we need it, —ADAM ... for seasonable help,

—WUST . . . and to find His spiritual strength, —WLMS . . . and get help for the days ahead, —NORL . . . and we may find favor for needed help, —KLGS . . . and find help through his grace, —TNT.

**4:16.** Because the Son knows the power of sin and the means of success over temptation, believers can come to Him in prayer with confidence in His wisdom and ability to help when they are confronted with temptation. The readers of this epistle were facing the temptation to abandon their profession of faith in the face of ridicule and persecution. Most assuredly, the Son, who was abandoned by His disciples and forsaken by the Father while on the cross, understands the needs of those who are tempted to forsake Him in the hour of trial.

The word "boldly" (*parrhēsias*) conveys a sense of openness, freedom, and confidence. When Christians come to God in prayer through the Son, they receive not justice, but God's grace and mercy. This is available because of Jesus Christ's sacrifice on the cross. The help that is available through such prayers is timely (*eukairon*), that is, it exactly fits the need at the right moment.

## Chapter 5

**1. For every high priest taken from among men:** . . . who is chosen from, —NORL . . . selected from men, —BECK.

**is ordained for men in things [pertaining] to God:** . . . is appointed to officiate on behalf of men, —WLMS . . . is appointed to represent men in matters related to God, —ADAM . . . to serve before God, —TNT.

**that he may offer both gifts and sacrifices for sins:** . . . and sin-offerings, —WLMS.

**5:1.** Having hinted at Christ's priesthood in the prologue (1:3) and having mentioned it explicitly in 2:17, the inspired writer began to argue in earnest for the superiority of Jesus' priesthood over the Aaronic priesthood. He began by presenting the qualifications for the priesthood in 5:1-4 and then proceeded to point out how Jesus Christ has met these qualifications. In verse 1 he noted that, first of all, a high priest must be human (he had already underscored Christ's humanity in 2:10-18). Secondly, a high priest was ordained to represent men in their relationship to God, more specifically in regard to the offering of sacrifice in connection with sins (another truth already introduced but not yet elaborated; see 1:3 and 2:17).

**2. Who can have compassion on:** . . . Such a one is capable of dealing tenderly with, —WLMS . . . He can bear gently, —TNT . . . he can gently handle people,

—SEB . . . He must also have patience, —KLGS . . . is able to deal gently with, —MNTG.

**the ignorant, and on them that are out of the way:** . . . the ignorant and erring ones, —WLMS.

**for that he himself also is compassed with infirmity:** . . . is troubled with weakness, —BECK . . . is inextricably involved in weakness, —ADAM . . . encompassed with moral weakness, —MNTG . . . is subject to weakness, —WLMS.

**5:2.** The third essential for qualification to the high priesthood related to the character of the high priest. He was a special kind of human being. The verb translated "have compassion" (*metriopathein*) means to deal gently with someone. The Aaronic high priests were able to offer sacrifice for those who committed sins in ignorance or who sinned without premeditation or presumption, but no provision was made for those who sinned deliberately (Numbers 15:28-30). This provision for the ignorant and wandering involved the Aaronic high priest in magnanimous treatment of these two groups because the high priests themselves were also encircled (*perikeitai*) by the same chains of weakness.

**3. And by reason hereof he ought:** . . . and because of that weakness, —TNT . . . being feeble, he has to make sin-offerings, —BB . . . he is obligated, —ADAM . . . he obliged himself, —NOLI.

**as for the people, so also for himself, to offer for sins:** . . . to offer sin-offerings, not only for the people but for himself as well, —WLMS . . . for himself also, just as he does for the people, —TNT . . . on behalf of himself, just as he does on behalf of the People, —WADE.

**5:3.** Because the high priests of the Aaronic priesthood were guilty of wandering and committed sins of ignorance, they found it necessary to offer sacrifices not only for the sins of the Children of Israel but also for their own personal acts of sin. These personal sacrifices offered up by the high priests were not something done voluntarily. They were absolutely necessary; the word "ought" (*opheilei*) indicates their obligation. In the use of the present infinitive "to offer" (*prospherein*), there may be a foreshadowing of the later emphasis on the daily necessity of such sacrifices (7:27). Daily sinning required that they seek forgiveness each day.

**4. And no man taketh this honour unto himself:** . . . No one of his own accord assumes this honor, —NORL . . . And no one presumes to take for himself this honourable office, —WADE . . . no one takes this office upon himself, —TNT.

**but he that is called of God, as [was] Aaron:** . . . unless he is called . . . as Aaron was, —NOLI . . . but, on the contrary, —ADAM . . . is called to it by God, —WLMS . . . given authority by God, —BB.

**5:4.** The fourth essential qualification for the high priesthood was that the appointment was divine. Aaron did not elect himself to be the high priest. Self-initiative did not qualify one for the priesthood. It was an office and honor that only God could bestow. The background of Aaron's appointment as the high priest for Israel was God's choice of the tribe of Levi to be the priestly tribe. All the Levites stood in a special relationship to God, with special responsibilities. They had certain assigned duties in relation to the tabernacle. Aaron was the logical choice then for the office of high priest.

5. **So also Christ:** ... In the same way, —SEB, —BB...Even Christ, —NOLI...Thus also the Messiah, —FNTN.

**glorified not himself to be made an high priest:** ... didn't exalt Himself, —ADAM ... did not Himself decree, —FNTN...did not of himself assume the dignity of, —TCNT...did not take upon Himself, —WLMS...did not invest himself with the glory of the high priest, —NOLI ... did not claim for Himself the dignity of being made, —WADE...the honour of becoming, —TNT.

**but he that said unto him:**...On the contrary, he was invested by God, who said, —NOLI...but He was raised to that dignity by Him Who said, —WADE...but on the contrary, —MNTG...he was made high priest by God who said to him, —TNT...but it was God who said, —WLMS.

**Thou art my Son, to day have I begotten thee:**...I have today become your Father, —WLMS.

**5:5.** So Christ's appointment was not from any ambition or self-initiative on His part. He did not thrust himself forward or lobby for the position. His elevation to the office of High Priest came from the Father, the One who said, "Thou art my Son, today have I begotten thee." These words hark back to the first argument for the Son's superiority to the angels. In Hebrews 1:5 these same words from Psalm 2:7 are quoted. At Jesus' baptism the Father identified Him as "my beloved Son, in whom I am well pleased" (Mark 1:11). The same words were spoken by the Father at the Transfiguration (Matthew 17:5). The reference seems to be to the Father's launching Jesus in His messianic sonship, not to His eternal generation or human birth. Eternally, He is the Son of God, the Second Person of the Trinity. From a human standpoint He was the son of Mary, born in Bethlehem. Messianically, He became the Messiah once He had met the qualifications for the priesthood.

6. **As he saith also in another [place]:**...just as He says likewise in a second passage, —WADE...as

in a different place, —CNDT...in another passage, —WLMS.

**Thou [art] a priest for ever after the order of Melchisedec:**...a priest for all time, —TCNT...according to the ordination of, —KLGS...to the order of, —WLSN...in the category of Melchizedek, —SEB...Belonging to the rank of, —WLMS.

**5:6.** Here the inspired writer introduced his favorite Old Testament quotation from Psalm 110:4—the psalm he cited the most. He referred to it again and again. The purpose was to introduce the Melchizedekian priesthood as the messianic priesthood which stands in contrast to the Aaronic priesthood. The eternality of this priesthood as indicated by the words "for ever" will be drawn out later on in the epistle (7:24-28).

7. **Who in the days of his flesh:**...in the days of his earthly life, —TCNT...In His humble life on earth, —BECK...For during His human life, —WLMS.

**when he had offered up prayers and supplications:**...He offered specific requests, —ADAM...offered up special, definite petitions, —WUST...offering both petitions and, —CNDT ... and entreaties, —NORL, —WLMS.

**with strong crying and tears:** ... crying aloud with tears, —WLMS.

**unto him that was able to save him from death:**...who had power to save him, —KLGS...out of death, —WLMS.

**and was heard in that he feared:**...because of His reverence, —ADAM ... because of His beautiful spirit of worship, —WLMS...Because of His reverent submission to God, —NORL.

**5:7.** At this point the epistle abruptly alludes to a historical incident in the life of Jesus with the phrase "in the days of his flesh." The allusion relates to the discussion of the essential qualifications for the high priesthood. It offers an example of the humanity and weakness of the Son which qualifies Him as a compassionate Person who is able to offer up effective prayers to God in heaven.

The situation alluded to is graphically described. It was a situation in which Jesus did face suffering unto death. His prayers were not normal petitions but "entreaties" (*hikētērias*) for the deliverance of His life, and they were uttered with strong emotion, loud cries, and tears. The incident which seems to fit this description is the prayer offered in Gethsemane when Jesus sweat "as it were great drops of blood" (Luke 22:44). The emphasis here is on Jesus' humanity and oneness with men in His agony.

The final words "was heard in that he *feared*" refer to Jesus' reverential piety and trust of God, because the word for *fear* is *eulabeias*, not *phobos*. Jesus was heard in His being strengthened to do His Father's will.

**8. Though he were a Son:**... although he was the Son of God, —NOLI... Son though he was, —WADE.

**yet learned he obedience by the things which he suffered:**... He found out from what He suffered what it means to obey, —BECK... He learned from what He suffered how to, —WLMS.

**5:8.** This verse presents an extremely difficult statement. In spite of Jesus Christ's divine messianic sonship, in spite of His being God and the promised blessed Deliverer-King, He was subjected to the humiliation, shame, fear, pain, instruction, and discipline of suffering as a human being. But what does it mean that He "learned . . . obedience by the things which he suffered"?

As God, the Son was omniscient. When He became flesh, He set aside the independent use of His divine attributes and the independent exercise of His will. Thus Luke could describe Him as growing "in wisdom and stature" (Luke 2:52). He did not increase in knowledge as God, but, as the God-man, He grew physically and mentally. So as the God-man, Jesus learned experientially what it means to obey the Father's will, when He suffered as a human in Gethsemane and at Calvary.

**9. And being made perfect, he became:**... And when He was finished, —BECK... and because He was perfectly qualified for it, —WLMS.

**the author of eternal salvation unto all them that obey him:** ... responsible for, —KLGS ... the source of, —NORL... the Origin of, —ADAM... of endless salvation, —WLMS.

**5:9.** The obedience experienced in Jesus' suffering is here described by the past participle "being made perfect" (teleiōtheis). This verb is used in the Septuagint to describe the consecration of the hands of the high priest (Exodus 29:9, 29, 33, 35; Leviticus 4:5; 8:33; 16:32) and once of the consecration of the high priest to service (Leviticus 21:10). After being consecrated to the high priesthood by experiencing the sufferings common to humanity, Jesus then became the cause (aitios) of everlasting deliverance to all of those who, unlike the Children of Israel in the wilderness, obey Him. In the New Testament obedience is often used as a synonym for belief (as in "obeying the truth" [1 Peter 1:22] and "they have not all obeyed the gospel" [Romans 10:16]).

**10. Called of God an high priest:**... and He was introduced by, —ADAM... God has pronounced him, —NORL... having been declared by God, —WLSN... being proclaimed by God, —BECK... since He had received from God the title of, —WLMS.

**after the order of Melchisedec:**... with the rank of, —WLMS.

**5:10.** Now comes the reminder, on the basis of the quotation from Psalm 110:4 introduced in Hebrews 5:6, that the Son's eternal high priesthood is not Aaronic but patterned after that of Melchizedek. The emphasis in verses 6, 9, and 10 falls on the eternality of His high-priestly work.

**11. Of whom we have many things to say:**... I have much to say to you about Him, —WLMS... our discourse will be long, —WADE.

**and hard to be uttered:** ... of difficult interpretation, —WLSN... but it is difficult to make it clear to you, —WLMS... hard to make intelligible to you, —WADE.

**seeing ye are dull of hearing:**... so slow to learn, —TCNT... seeing that you seem sluggish in spiritual understanding, —NORL... since you have become so dull in your spiritual senses, —WLMS... slow of apprehension, —WADE.

**12. For when for the time ye ought to be teachers:** ... in view of the time that has elapsed, —WADE... You should have become teachers a long time ago, —SEB... although you ought to be teachers of others because you have been Christians so long, —WLMS.

**ye have need that one teach you again:**... you actually need someone to teach you over and over again, —WLMS.

**which [be] the first principles of the oracles of God:** ... what are the rudimentary elements, —CNDT... to teach you the ABC of God's Word again, —BECK... the very alphabet of the Divine Revelation, —TCNT... the elementary principles of God's revelation, —ADAM... the very elements of the truths that God has given us, —WLMS.

**and are become such as have need of milk, and not of strong meat:** ... you have come to need milk, —TNT... you are in constant need of milk instead of, —WLMS... not solid food, —ADAM... solid nourishment, —CNDT.

**5:11, 12.** In these verses the inspired writer indicated that he desired to expand on Christ's Melchizedekian priesthood, but that the spiritual condition of his readers prevented him from doing so. The information he wished to convey was difficult to interpret and explain (dusermēneutos), and they were sluggish and slothful (nōthroi) in their listening.

The implication is that a grasp of deep spiritual truth is dependent in part on the diligence of the believer in listening. The readers of the epistle had been believers long enough to have advanced to the function of teaching, but they had not. Instead, they found themselves in need of being once again taught the stoicheia, the ABCs of God's self-disclosure. They had not advanced normally in their spiritual growth. They should have been chewing on tough meat like mature adults, but instead they were retarded. They had to be taught the baby lessons designed for new Christians.

Paul instructed the Corinthians as Hebrews does here: "I have fed you with milk, and not with meat: for hitherto ye were not able to bear it, neither yet now are ye able" (1 Corinthians 3:2). The sad thing is those of both groups were not the only ones who suffered from their lack of spiritual maturity. Recognizing this, Pfeiffer wrote, "Immature Christians not only hurt themselves, by robbing themselves of the spiritual benefits which accompany maturity, but they rob others also. Christians should be 'teachers' (5:12), sharing their spiritual blessings with others, both within and without the Church. It is the entire Church that has been called to a teaching ministry, although some individuals have special gifts (Ephesians 4:11-12). The Great Commission includes the command, 'teach all nations' (Matthew 28:19)" (pp.46,47).

**13. For every one that useth milk:** ... anyone who lives on milk, —TNT.
**[is] unskilful in the word of righteousness:** ... is inexperienced in the message of right-doing, —WLMS ... has no experience of the message of righteousness, —TNT.
**for he is a babe:** ... he is only an infant, —WLMS.

**5:13.** The vivid imagery of verse 12 is expanded here. They needed milk; that is, to have the basic principles of the gospel message explained to them. Because they had not fully grasped these first principles, they were unable to comprehend the deeper truths of the Word of God. The term "unskilful" translates *apeiros* which means "not tested," the idea being that the Hebrews were not able because they did not have enough experience.

**14. But strong meat belongeth to them that are of full age:** ... Solid food is for mature people, —ADAM ... belongs to full-grown men, —WLMS ... is for advanced Christians, —TCNT ... for grownup people, —BECK.
**[even] those who by reason of use have their senses exercised:** ... Their minds are exercised by habit, —KLGS ... whose senses are habitually in training to distinguish between, —NORL ... for those who by constant practise have their faculties trained, —MNTG ... who on account of constant use have their faculties trained, —WLMS.
**to discern both good and evil:** ... to tell the difference between right and wrong, —SEB ... for discriminating between the ideal, —CNDT.

**5:14.** The other side of the coin is examined in this verse. Tough meat is for the *teleiōn*, those who have matured, who in turn are described as "those who by reason of use have their senses exercised to discern both good and evil." The imagery here switches to the gymnasium. The development of Christian discernment is likened to the training of an athlete's skills by the discipline of practice.

The Hebrew believers had not received spiritual insight because they had not been wrestling with spiritual truths. Hence they were not able to separate good from evil.

## Chapter 6

**1. Therefore leaving the principles of the doctrine of Christ:** ... Let us now dismiss the question of elementary Christian instruction, —NORL ... let us once for all quit the elementary teaching, —WLMS ... leaving the elementary teachings, —ADAM.
**let us go on unto perfection:** ... and continue progressing toward, —WLMS ... we should progress towards maturity, —WLSN ... go on to completion, —KLGS ... go on to more mature things, —SEB ... toward maturity, —ADAM.
**not laying again the foundation:** ... let us stop relaying a foundation, —WLMS ... We do not need to teach these first truths again, —NLTG.
**of repentance from dead works, and of faith toward God:** ... turning away from depending on dead human efforts, —SEB ... from works that mean only death, —WLMS.

**6:1.** In the light of their situation, the Hebrew believers were challenged to do what they had been avoiding: to leave *ton tēs archēs tou Christou logon*, the word of the beginning of the Messiah. This phrase is the equivalent of the *stoicheia*, the first principles of God's self-revelation mentioned in 5:12. They needed to go beyond an elementary understanding of the difference between Judaism and Christian messianic teaching. The challenge was to go on to a deep, mature understanding of the implications of their confession of faith in Jesus as the Messiah.

There are great depths of truth to be discovered. They were not to lay "again the foundation." These basic gospel truths are the foundation for Christian living and should not be forgotten. However, our Christian knowledge should not be limited to a few truths found in the Word of God. In 1 Corinthians 3:10 Paul states that we should build upon this foundation—the same thought expressed in these verses.

In 6:1,2 the inspired writer identified the six ABCs of messianic teachings upon which the superstructure was to be built. The first foundational truth mentioned is "repentance from dead works." The phrase "dead works" appears again in 9:14. In both places it seems best to take it as a reference to reliance upon good works as the means or cause of one's salvation. Repentance would then be the recognition that one's good works have no power to save because they are dead. They cannot produce eternal life. Those who have truly repented have stopped relying on their own good works for salvation. On the contrary, they have discovered

993

the second of the messianic ABCs. They have turned away from their own works and trusted God to give them eternal life. Their faith is not in themselves but in the power of the living God.

**2. Of the doctrine of baptisms, and of laying on of hands:** ... the Doctrine of Immersions, —WLSN ... of teaching about baptisms, —ADAM ... about ceremonial washings, —WLMS ... besides the imposition of hands, —CNDT.

**and of resurrection of the dead, and of eternal judgment:** ... and a final judgement, —TCNT.

**6:2.** This verse lists four more of the initial doctrines of messianic faith: baptism, laying on of hands, resurrection, and judgment. All six of the doctrines listed in verses 1 and 2 are not distinctives of Christianity as opposed to a true messianic Judaism. A Jew who carefully read his Old Testament would have understood all six of these teachings.

**3. And this will we do, if God permit:** ... And we will progress, —WLMS.

**6:3.** At this point, the inspired writer professed the expectation that both he and his readers would advance beyond the ABCs if God allowed them to live long enough, provided their hope and professions were genuine.

**4. For [it is] impossible for those who were once enlightened:** ... Some people once had the light, —SEB.

**and have tasted of the heavenly gift:** ... tasting the celestial gratuity, —CNDT ... have experienced the gift from heaven, —WLMS.

**and were made partakers of the Holy Ghost:** ... and have become sharers of, —ADAM, —NORL ... and have become companions of, —WUST ... and came to share in, —TCNT ... who had the Holy Spirit just as others did, —BECK.

**5. And have tasted the good word of God:** ... and have experienced how good God's message is, —WLMS.

**and the powers of the world to come:** ... and the miracles of the coming age, —ADAM ... and the mighty powers of the age to come, —WLMS ... of the Future Age, —MNTG ... the future world, —SEB.

**6. If they shall fall away:** ... have fallen by the wayside, —WLMS.

**to renew them again unto repentance:** ... to keep on restoring them to their first repentance, —WLMS.

**seeing they crucify to themselves the Son of God afresh:** ... since they continue ... to their detriment, —WLMS ... they repeatedly crucify, —MNTG ... they nail the Son of God to the cross again, —SEB.

**and put [him] to an open shame:** ... and have exposed Him publicly to shame, —NORL ... and expose him to, —MNTG ... all over again and publicly

disgrace Him, —ADAM ... exposing him to open contempt, —TCNT ... and hold Him up for mockery, —BECK.

**6:4-6.** Once again the importance of perseverance in the Faith is repeated. The word "for" (*gar*) indicates that Christian maturity is the hope but is not a certainty. The reason that they were to pursue maturity and not seek once again to lay the foundation of basic principles is now made clear: those who commit apostasy are beyond redemption. This is not to say that God's grace is not able to reclaim these, but as Bruce points out, "... as a matter of human experience the reclamation of such people is, practically speaking, impossible," (*New International Commentary on the New Testament, Hebrews,* p. 118).

The writer describes these individuals in four participial phrases. (1) *"Were once enlightened."* Some see this as a reference to water baptism. Whatever event is being alluded to, at some particular time these individuals understood Jesus was the Messiah. (2) *"Have tasted of the heavenly gift."* While some take this to be a reference to the eucharist (ibid., p. 120), others believe it is a reference to the Holy Spirit (cf. 1 Corinthians 12:13; Montefiore, *Black's New Testament Commentaries, Hebrews,* p. 109).

(3) *"Were made partakers of the Holy Ghost."* (For "partakers" see 3:14.) These had received the laying on of hands (cf. Acts 19:6). Some have argued that the absence of the definite article with "Holy Ghost" indicates that this is a broad reference to some activity or gift of the Spirit. However, whether it is the Spirit or the gifts of the Spirit which are in question cannot be determined solely from the presence or absence of the article. As Bruce points out, "It is precarious to argue that the personal Holy Spirit is not intended here," (*New International Commentary on the New Testament, Hebrews,* p.121).

(4) *"Have tasted the good word of God: and the powers of the world to come."* The parallel of the "good word of God" (the use of *rhēma* indicates a specific utterance and not the gospel message in its entirety) with "the powers of the world to come" appears to be a reference to an experience of the supernatural powers and signs that the kingdom of God had come.

Some have minimized the power of this warning by stating that it is simply a hypothetical case and never occurred. Others have overstated the writer's intent by trying to make a case against the possibility for the forgiveness of any post-baptismal sin. What must be kept clearly in view is that this irretrievable falling away (*parapesontas*) is the specific sin of apostasy, i.e., a complete rejection of one's confession of Christ (cf. 10:26,37f.)

**7. For the earth which drinketh in the rain that cometh oft upon it:**...a piece of ground, *–WLMS.*

**and bringeth forth herbs:** ... and produces plants, *–BECK*...bears vegetation, *–ADAM.*

**meet for them by whom it is dressed:**...that is useful to, *–ADAM*... for those who have tilled it, *–NORL* ... for the people who farm it, *–SEB* ... for whom also it is cultivated, *–WLSN.*

**receiveth blessing from God:** ... shares a blessing, *–WADE.*

**8. But that which beareth thorns and briers:**...if it continues to yield, *–WLMS*...if that soil produces, *–TNT*...But land which produces thorny weeds and thorn bushes, *–SEB*...But if it gives nothing but weeds, it is worth nothing, *–NLTG*...and thistles, *–ADAM.*

**[is] rejected, and [is] nigh unto cursing:**...it is regarded as, *–TCNT*...considered worthless, *–MNTG, –WLMS*...disqualified, *–CNDT*...has no value, *–NORL* ... verging on the state of a land accursed, *–WADE*...under God's curse, *–TNT.*

**whose end [is] to be burned:** ... its end is, *–WADE*...its final fate is burning, *–WLMS*...and will finish in flames, *–TNT.*

**6:7, 8.** Most likely the Lord's Parable of the Sower and the kinds of ground (Matthew 13:18-23; Luke 8:4-15) is the background of the illustration. Those whose profession endures and produces fruit are the good ground. Fruit is blessed and weeds are cursed by God. The application seems clear enough. Not all who initially hear the message of God spoken in His Son actually have the roots of faith.

**9. But, beloved, we are persuaded better things of you:**...But in your case, my dearly loved friends...we are sure of, *–WLMS*...we have no doubt about you, *–TNT*...are convinced, *–WADE.*

**and things that accompany salvation:** ... You know what is good and leads to your salvation, *–TNT*...conditions conducing to, *–WADE*...that point to, *–WLMS.*

**though we thus speak:**...even though we speak in such a tone, *–WLMS* ... though we speak thus gravely, *–WADE.*

**6:9.** Having confronted believers with the terrible end awaiting those who turn back (apostatize) from their profession of faith in the Son, the inspired writer declared that he did not think the readers of this epistle were the kind of ground that only produces thistles and weeds. Even though he had issued a stern warning about God's judgment upon those who turn back from Jesus Christ, he indicated confidence that their lives showed evidence of real faith which produces the genuine fruits of salvation and maturity in Christ. Although he is concerned about the possibility of some in their midst apostatizing, his basic anxiety relates to their failure to reach maturity.

**10. For God [is] not unrighteous to forget your work:**...is not so unjust as to forget the work you have done, *–WLMS.*

**and labour of love, which ye have showed toward his name:**...the love you have shown His name, *–WLMS*...the love which you have evinced, *–WADE*...for him, *–TNT.*

**in that ye have ministered to the saints, and do minister:**...in the service you have rendered for your fellow-Christians, and still are doing, *–WLMS*...when you serve the saints, *–CNDT*...by serving His saints in the past and at present, *–ADAM*...in your past and present service to his people, *–TNT.*

**6:10.** Once again, the word "For" which begins the verse indicates that the inspired writer was offering an explanation of the statement which he had just made. He had stated the basis for confidence in the reality of their salvation. It was grounded in two realities: the nature of God and the characteristics of faith displayed in their lives.

First, God is righteous and just. He keeps His promises. He declares those who trust in Jesus Christ to be righteous. He covers their sins and delivers them from the consequences of their transgressions. He promises life eternal to all who believe in Jesus Christ His Son, and He will make good His promise. Second, in spite of the spiritual immaturity of the believers who received this epistle (5:11-14), they displayed the fruits of genuine faith by their actions. They displayed love by exhausting themselves in deeds of love (*tou kopou tēs agapēs*) directed toward their fellow believers. What they have done for God's children has, of course, been done for Him and for the Son (Matthew 25:40). Their works sprang not from a desire to gain merit in God's sight, but out of love for Him and His people, from a genuine desire to please Him.

This lifestyle of giving was not a onetime thing. It continued to characterize their behavior, for they "have ministered to the saints" in the past, and even now they "do minister." The continuation of their labor of love was an evidence of their enduring faith.

**11. And we desire that every one of you:**...Now we are yearning, *–CNDT*...We are very eager that each one of you, *–TNT.*

**do show the same diligence:**...to continue to show the same earnestness, *–WLMS*...you should go on showing the same zeal, *–TNT.*

**to the full assurance of hope unto the end:** ... until the consummation, *–CNDT* ... to the very end, *–WLMS*...until your hope is fully and finally realized, *–TNT.*

**6:11.** Having taken note of their love, the inspired writer pointed out other areas of their lives where they needed to work hard on the cultivation of other Christian virtues which are indicative of maturity. It is imperative that believers display the same careful concern and painstaking effort in the development of full assurance in regard to the Christian's hope—the victorious reign of Jesus Christ at the end of this age. There is high emotional intensity in the words "desire" (*epithumoumen*) and "diligence" (*spoudēn*). The latter term indicates that believers are to make every effort to display their confidence in the promised but as yet unrealized subjugation of the universe to the Son (2:8,9). Apparently some of the Christians at that time had begun to waver in their "full assurance of hope" concerning the glorious second coming of Christ to rule over His kingdom. The display of confidence in the Lord's second coming is a hallmark of Christian maturity.

**12. That ye be not slothful:** ... Then do not become slack, *—MNTG* ... Do not be lazy, *—KLGS* ... so that you may not grow careless, *—WLMS*.

**but followers of them who through faith and patience:** ... We want you to be like those who, *—TNT* ... follow the example of those who through their faith and patient endurance, *—WLMS*.

**inherit the promises:** ... are now possessors of the blessings promised, *—WLMS* ... are now taking possession of God's promises, *—TNT*.

**6:12.** The inspired writer charged these believers with a sluggish laziness, calling them *nōthroi* (see also 5:11). He urged them to put an end to such sloth by observing and imitating the patriarchs of Genesis, who "through faith and patience inherit the promises" of God after an earthly pilgrimage characterized by faith in the midst of lives marked by longsuffering (*makrothumias*) without reward.

**13. For when God made promise to Abraham: because he could swear by no greater, he sware by himself:** ... He took the oath by Himself, *—NORL*.

**6:13.** The ground of Christian confidence in the face of as yet unrealized promises from God is found in the patriarchs' experience of God's character. First, God based His promise to Abraham on an oath. Oaths are not lightly undertaken. They are solemn matters of business and courtroom procedure, designed to emphasize the seriousness of the matter and to secure honesty between parties to an agreement or testimony. Since God can swear by no one greater, He swore by His own character and greatness when He made His promise to Abraham (Genesis 22:16) concerning the blessing and numbering of his descendants. God takes His promises seriously.

**14. Saying, Surely blessing I will bless thee:** ... declaring, Assuredly, *—WADE* ... I will certainly bless you, *—TNT*.

**and multiplying I will multiply thee:** ... For sure, I will give you many children, *—NLTG* ... I will increase you, and increase you, *—MNTG* ... I will certainly bless you over and over again, *—WLMS* ... and increase thy numbers, *—TCNT* ... I will surely give you many descendants, *—SEB*.

**6:14.** This particular promise of God to Abraham was cited as the writer quoted Genesis 22:17. The reference is to God's promise to richly bless the descendants of Abraham and Isaac while at the same time increasing their number incalculably.

**15. And so, after he had patiently endured:** ... in reliance upon this pledge ... through his patience, *—WADE* ... after patiently waiting, *—TCNT*.

**he obtained the promise:** ... he got what was promised, *—ADAM* ... Abraham got what God promised, *—BECK*.

**6:15.** God kept this mind-staggering promise. Because of their advanced ages and Sara's history of barrenness, both parents laughed at God's promise. But, according to that promise, Sarah conceived and bore Isaac, and through Isaac's son Jacob the Lord increased and enriched Abraham's descendants, the nation of Israel—after Abraham had suffered long (*makrothumēsas*).

**16. For men verily swear by the greater:** ... For it is a custom among men to take oath by something greater than themselves, *—WLMS* ... Men swear by one who is greater than themselves, *—TNT*.

**and an oath for confirmation [is] to them an end of all strife:** ... to silence anyone who opposes them, *—BECK* ... the oath is final for confirmation, *—MNTG* ... This confirms agreements, *—SEB* ... ends all arguments, *—ADAM* ... puts an end to further questioning, *—NORL* ... settles any dispute, *—WLMS* ... terminates Every Dispute among them, *—WLSN*.

**6:16.** Continuing the explanation of the grounds of a believer's confidence in God's promises, the writer analyzed the purpose of an oath in human affairs. In matters over which there is some strife, i.e., in disputes (*antilogias*), oaths are introduced to end or mark the boundary (*peras*) for the purpose of establishing and confirming agreement. In taking oaths, men swear by God who is greater than they are. They do so in order to convince other men that they are truthful and intend to abide by their promises.

**17. Wherein God, willing more abundantly to show:** ... because God wanted to make the strongest demonstration of, *—WLMS*.

**unto the heirs of promise the immutability of his counsel:** ... the unchangeable nature of,

−ADAM . . . the unchangeableness of, −TCNT . . . the unchangeable character of His purpose, −WLMS.

**confirmed [it] by an oath:** . . . He interposed with an oath, −WLMS.

**6:17.** The implication here is that God, even though He is not like men, confirmed His promise to Abraham and his descendants by an oath. That oath underscored God's unchangeableness, "the immutability of his counsel." To do this He accommodated himself to the human custom of emphasizing one's word by means of an oath, thus communicating the solemnity and import of His promise. His oath was to grant assurance to Abraham's heirs.

**18. That by two immutable things:** . . . so that by Two unalterable Things, −WLSN . . . that through the instrumentality of two immutable facts, −WUST . . . two unchangeable things, −BECK, −WLMS.

**in which [it was] impossible for God to lie:** . . . for God cannot possibly tell a lie, −NORL . . . to break faith, −MNTG . . . to prove false, −WLMS.

**we might have a strong consolation:** . . . may have strong encouragement, −KLGS.

**who have fled for refuge:** . . . fled for shelter, −KLGS . . . who have taken refuge with Him, −WLMS.

**to lay hold upon the hope set before us:** . . . to make us seize upon the hope that lies ahead of us, −WLMS.

**6:18.** This assurance flows from two unchanging realities. The first is clearly stated: God cannot lie. The certainty of a promise is rooted in the nature of the one who makes it. In this case it is the Lord, the all-powerful Creator, the righteous Judge of all men, who made the promise. His word is His bond. If He says it, without doubt, it will be accomplished.

The second unchanging reality is implied in the oath. Even though God cannot lie, He has taken the additional step of interjecting an oath based on His own unchanging nature. The purpose of the oath was to strengthen the assurance of those who are to inherit the promises. God's promise and His oath are true because He cannot deny His own righteous character. It does not change.

The result of God's promise and oath is our "strong consolation." The unchanging character of God assures the believer of the fulfillment of everything which He has promised. Christians who have fled from the wrath due them because of their sins have seized upon the hope which God the Father has offered in His Son, Jesus Christ. Since it is not yet fully realized, it is hope. It is "set before us" as the promise was to the patriarchs. It is grounded in God's immutability, even though it is unfulfilled as yet. The promise of the subjection of the universe to Jesus at the end of this current

age provides believers with admonition and encouragement to endure in the midst of current trials and sufferings.

**19. Which [hope] we have as an anchor of the soul:** . . . like an anchor for our lives, −BECK.

**both sure and stedfast:** . . . both secure and confirmed, −CNDT . . . secure and strong, −MNTG . . . and safe, −WLMS . . . It will never move, −NLTG.

**and which entereth into that within the veil:** . . . which reaches up behind the heavenly veil, −WLMS . . . on the inner side of the curtain, −ADAM.

**6:19.** The hope that all things will be subordinated to the Son serves as an anchor for the believers' lives. It is a source of stability in the seas of life. Circumstances change, but Christians have a firm, unchanging hope. It is both certain and steady because it partakes of the eternal; it "entereth into that within the veil," a reference to the Son's priesthood.

**20. Whither the forerunner is for us entered, [even] Jesus:** . . . Jesus has gone there as, −NOLI . . . where Jesus has blazed the way for us, −WLMS . . . where Jesus went in before us on our behalf, −TNT . . . has entered for us, −FNTN.

**made an high priest for ever after the order of Melchisedec:** . . . for he has become, −TNT . . . having become, as we have seen, −PHLP . . . becoming Chief Priest, −CNDT . . . with the rank of, −WLMS . . . according to the order of, −NOLI, −FNTN.

**6:20.** The allusion to the sanctuary, the Holy of Holies which existed beyond the veil of both the tabernacle and the Jerusalem temple, directs attention to the high priestly work of Jesus Christ. Once a year on the Day of Atonement, the high priest sprinkled the blood of sacrifice upon the lid of the ark of the covenant. This reference provides a transition from the warning and explanation (5:11-6:19) back to the subject of Jesus' superiority to the Aaronic high priesthood, begun in 5:1.

As High Priest, Jesus has entered into the Holy of Holies in heaven as our forerunner (prodromos). Like a scout or pioneer He has gone on before, and believers are to follow His path. On the basis of His entrance, believers can follow Him into the very presence of God. According to Romans 8:34, He is there making intercession for us. He has met all the requirements for a high priest (5:1-10). His work, however, is not effective only from one annual Day of Atonement to another; instead, it is "for ever." It is not patterned after the work of Aaron and his descendants, but (as has already been pointed out by the citation from Psalm 110) it is modeled after the priesthood observed in the instance of Melchizedek found in Genesis 14:18-20.

## Chapter 7

1. **For this Melchisedec, king of Salem: priest of the most high God:** ... of the Highest God, —*FNTN*.

**who met Abraham returning from the slaughter of the kings:** ... when he returned from the defeat, —*ADAM* ... on his way back after, —*TNT* ... returning from the combat with, —*CNDT* ... when the latter was returning from smiting the kings, —*WADE* ... coming back from beating the kings, —*KLGS* ... from defeating the kings, —*BECK* ... after putting the kings to death, —*BB*.

**and blessed him:** ... bestowed his blessing, —*WADE* ... put his blessing on him, —*WLMS*.

**7:1.** The sentence begun in this verse is completed in verse 3. Essentially it declares that Melchizedek remains a priest in perpetuity. Verses 1 and 2 add several other observations about Melchizedek. Before commenting on this, a few words are to be said about the relationship between this epistle and intertestamental Jewish literature. In the *Testaments of the Twelve Patriarchs* (ca. 135- 105 B.C.) there is an expectation of two messianic figures: one royal from Judah and one priestly from Levi. Fragments from cave 11 at Qumran (ca. A.D. 50) represent Melchizedek as the champion and deliverer of the Jewish remnant and attribute to him functions that are elsewhere in Qumranic literature ascribed to the archangel Michael. It is possible that a combination of teachings like these are being combated by the teaching in this part of Hebrews. The inspired writer began by identifying Melchizedek as the priestly king of Salem who met Abraham after his defeat of Chedorla-omer and his federation of kings (see Genesis 14).

2. **To whom also Abraham gave a tenth part of all:** ... So Abraham gave him, —*TNT* ... set apart a tenth, —*FNTN* ... apportioned a tithe of all the spoil, —*MNTG* ... contributed a tenth of all his spoils, —*WLMS* ... gave him a tribute, —*PHLP* ... As a tribute, —*NOLI* ... of everything which he had, —*BB*.

**first being by interpretation King of righteousness:** ... this is the translation of his name, —*WADE* ... being first named, —*BB* ... whose name is interpreted as, —*FNTN* ... who first of all, in accordance with the meaning of his name, —*WLMS* ... His name means "first king of righteousness," —*NOLI* ... king of what is right, —*SEB* ... of Justice, —*KLGS*.

**and after that also King of Salem, which is, King of peace:** ... And secondly, —*WADE* ... and his other tide, —*PHLP* ... and then in addition ... that is to say, —*BB* ... By translation of this name, —*NORL* ... he is also, —*TNT* ... which means, —*WLMS*.

**7:2.** Verse 2 indicates three things about Melchizedek. First, Abraham paid a tithe of all the spoils of his victory to Melchizedek. Second, the etymology of the name Melchizedek is

**998**

*melek*, Hebrew for "king," and *tsadîq*, Hebrew for "righteousness." Literally, the name is "king of righteousness" or *righteousness* is king. Third, he was the "King of Salem." "Salem" is Hebrew for "peace." So Melchizedek was also the "King of peace." These facts are significant because Jesus' high priesthood is patterned after the priesthood of Melchizedek who was a type of Christ.

3. **Without father, without mother, without descent:** ... There is no record ... There is no genealogy, —*NORL* ... or ancestral lineage, —*ADAM* ... no ancestry, —*WLMS* ... without a genealogy, —*CNDT* ... without a family tree, —*KLGS* ... or line of ancestors, —*BECK* ... designated by name, no recorded genealogy, —*WADE*.

**having neither beginning of days, nor end of life:** ... we don't know when he was born or how long he lived, —*SEB* ... no reference to, —*TNT* ... no specified beginning of existence, —*WADE* ... no date of birth or death, —*NORL* ... nor termination of life, —*WUST* ... no end to his life, —*WLMS*.

**but made like unto the Son of God:** ... In this he resembles, —*TCNT* ... but resembling the Son of God, —*MNTG*.

**abideth a priest continually:** ... remains a priest perpetually, —*ADAM*, —*WLSN* ... remains a priest continually, —*WUST* ... is remaining a priest to a finality, —*CNDT* ... he remains a priest for all time, —*TNT* ... he stays a priest without ending, —*KLGS* ... as priest continues on and on with no successor, —*WLMS*.

**7:3.** Melchizedek is mentioned in only two places in the Old Testament (Genesis 14; Psalm 110). No mention is made of his origin, his parents, or his descendants. There is no record of his birth or his death. He simply appears in the Biblical text as a priest from Salem who appeared before Abraham, praising God. He is likened to the Son of God whose perpetual priesthood is eternal by divine decree. Some interpreters have seen Melchizedek as a preincarnate appearance of the Second Person of the Trinity, but it seems best to let the text stand in its most natural sense. "Made like unto the Son of God" means that a parallel exists between Melchizedek and Jesus.

4. **Now consider how great this man [was]:** ... observe how great was the dignity of this man, —*WADE*.

**unto whom even the patriarch Abraham gave the tenth of the spoils:** ... the Old Father Abraham gave a tenth of what he captured, —*KLGS* ... of all he had taken in the war, —*NLTG* ... the best of the booty, —*CNDT*.

**7:4.** The writer calls attention to the greatness of Melchizedek: namely, that Abraham—the father of the Jewish nation, and the spiritual father of all who believe, the one whose seed was to be multiplied and blessed materially—paid tithes to someone else, to Melchizedek, who must have been a great man indeed.

**5. And verily they that are of the sons of Levi:** ... those of the descendants of Levi, *−WLMS.*
**who receive the office of the priesthood:** ... who accept, *−WLMS.*
**have a commandment to take tithes of the people according to the law:** ... are authorized by the Law, *−MNTG* ... are commanded to exact tenths, *−WADE* ... to collect a tenth from the people, *−WLMS.*
**that is, of their brethren:** ... from other Israelites, *−BECK* ... from their fellow-Israelites, *−TNT* ... from their own brothers, *−WLMS.*
**though they come out of the loins of Abraham:** ... they are Abraham's descendants, *−ADAM* ... they have sprung from, *−WLMS.*
**6. But he whose descent is not counted from them:** ... but He whose pedigree is not derived, *−WLSN* ... this man who had no Levitical genealogy, *−MNTG* ... the man whose ancestry is not traced from them, *−WLMS* ... was not a descendant of Levi, *−SEB* ... was outside their line of descent, *−BECK.*
**received tithes of Abraham:** ... collected a tenth, *−WLMS* ... a tenth part from, *−TNT.*
**and blessed him that had the promises:** ... and put his blessing on the man who had, *−WLMS.*

**7:5, 6.** According to the Mosaic law which governed Jewish life, it was the descendants of Levi whom Jehovah designated to receive the tithe offerings of the nation of Israel (Numbers 18:21,26). These Levitical priests were descendants of Abraham through Isaac and Jacob and, as is pointed out in 7:11, they were the priesthood associated with Moses' brother Aaron.

All of this shows the superiority of the priesthood of Melchizedek to that of Aaron, in part, because of priority in time. Besides this, though, the account demonstrates tithing existed before the Law. Abraham paid a tithe of the spoils of victory in battle to show his gratitude, and not because some law required it of him. Jacob vowed to tithe financial blessings from God long before the law of Moses demanded it. In response to a promise of the Lord's goodness that would come to him, he said, "Of all that thou shalt give me I will surely give the tenth unto thee" (Genesis 28:22).

*Akrothinion* for "spoils" in verse 4 here suggests a high view of tithing. It refers literally to "firstfruits." Thus Abraham gave "the first of spoils" to Melchizedek. So tithing is in keeping with the ancient exhortation, "Honor the Lord with thy substance, and with the firstfruits of all thine increase" (Proverbs 3:9).

Melchizedek, however, was not a member of the Aaronic, Levitical priesthood. That priesthood was given to men who were descendants of Abraham. Melchizedek, being a contemporary of Abraham, therefore, possessed some other kind of

priesthood. Moreover, that priesthood obviously preceded the formation of the Aaronic priesthood which was not established until the time of Moses, hundreds of years after Abraham. By some other authority than that of the Mosaic law, Abraham, the father of the Children of Israel, had tithes levied on him by this stranger, the mysterious Melchizedek, a priest of unknown origin and of an unknown priesthood.

Furthermore, this inscrutable personage possessed the power to issue blessings to Abraham. Genesis 14:19 says, "And he blessed him, and said, Blessed be Abram of the most high God, possessor of heaven and earth." God had made Abraham exceedingly rich. He had just been blessed by God in his attempt to liberate Lot and the possessions of the kings of Sodom and Gomorrah from Chedorla-omer and the kings who were with him. This Abraham was blessed by Melchizedek. Melchizedek must have been very great indeed.

**7. And without all contradiction:** ... Everyone would agree, *−SEB* ... it is beyond all dispute, *−ADAM* ... all controversy, *−MNTG* ... Unquestionably, *−TNT.*
**the less is blessed of the better:** ... that a more important person, *−SEB* ... the inferior, *−TNT* ... blessings come down from the superior ones to the inferior, *−NORL* ... it is the superior who blesses the inferior, *−TCNT* ... by the greater, *−ADAM.*

**7:7.** There is no dispute. The man who receives a blessing is the lesser of the two. The man who does the blessing is greater than the one who is blessed. On the basis of this argument, although Abraham was very great, since Melchizedek blessed Abraham, it logically follows that Melchizedek was the greater of the two.

**8. And here men that die receive tithes:** ... mortal men collect the tenth, *−WLMS* ... are receiving the tenth part, *−TNT.*
**but there he [receiveth them], of whom it is witnessed:** ... it is attested, *−MNTG.*
**that he liveth:** ... a man affirmed by Scripture to be still living, *−TNT* ... lives on, *−WLMS.*

**7:8.** This verse contrasts the Old Testament record concerning Melchizedek and the Levitical priests. "Here" refers to the record of the Levitical priests. They were dying men. The Old Testament contains the genealogical records of the Levitical priesthood. One high priest succeeded another, replacing the one who had just died. "There" refers to the record of Melchizedek given in Genesis 14. That record mentions only that he is living; it does not record his death. There is no definite record of his predecessor or of his successor. The

Scripture still testifies of this to those who read it (*marturoumenos*).

**9. And as I may so say:** . . . I might almost say, *—WLMS* . . . Indeed it might be said, *—TNT.*

**Levi also, who receiveth tithes, payed tithes in Abraham:** . . . who now collects the tenth, through Abraham paid the tenth, *—WLMS* . . . the man who received a tenth part, has paid it, *—TNT.*

**7:9.** Indeed, since Levi was a descendant of Abraham, he in some way could be considered to have paid tithes to Melchizedek. The phrase "as I may so say" does not indicate that the writer of Hebrews was indicating that Levi actually paid tithes to Melchizedek. Only in a nonliteral way of looking at the situation, it could be said that he did so. Abraham was the spiritual and physical progenitor of Levi; in this respect he was greater than Levi. Since Abraham paid a tithe to Melchizedek who was greater than himself, then in a manner of speaking, Melchizedek was greater than Levi.

**10. For he was yet in the loins of his father:** . . . he was in the body of his ancestor, *—BECK* . . . he was a vital part of his forefather though yet unborn, *—WLMS.*

**when Melchisedec met him:**

**7:10.** The unique line of argument begun in the previous verse is concluded here. Since Levi was seminally descended from Abraham through his son Isaac and his grandson Jacob, Levi was in this manner present and paying tithes with Abraham his great-grandfather.

**11. If therefore perfection were by the Levitical priesthood:** . . . the spiritual perfecting of men had been possible through the functions of, *—WADE* . . . had been attainable through, *—TCNT* . . . had fulfilled its purpose, *—TNT* . . . had been reached through, *—WLMS.*

**(for under it the people received the law,):** . . . for on it as a basis even the law was enacted for the people, *—WLMS* . . . was the basis on which a Legal system for the Jewish People was constituted, *—WADE* . . . with which the giving of the Law to the people was closely linked, *—TNT.*

**what further need [was there] that another priest should rise:** . . . what . . . need would there have been for another kind of, *—TNT* . . . why did another priest still need to come, *—BECK* . . . of appointing a different priest, *—WLMS.*

**after the order of Melchisedec:** . . . with the rank of, *—WLMS.*

**and not be called after the order of Aaron?:** . . . and for him not to be described as, *—TNT* . . . instead of designating one with the rank of, *—WLMS* . . . rather than to be named after, *—ADAM* . . . described as having a different rank from, *—WADE* . . . after the ordination of, *—KLGS* . . . instead of through Aaron's priesthood? *—SEB.*

**7:11.** At this point the writer began to move from the contrast between Melchizedek and the Levitical priests to the goal of his whole argument: the contrast between the Levitical priesthood and the high priestly accomplishments of Jesus the Son of God. If the Levitical priesthood had been able to effect perfection, there would have been no need "that another priest (Jesus) should rise after the order of Melchizedek." This reasoning assumes that the priesthood needed to be perfect if it was to be efficacious. It also assumes that the Levitical priesthood was imperfect.

Perhaps most important of all to the line of argument, there is the assumption that the Mosaic law and the Levitical priesthood were inextricably linked. If the Aaronic high priests and their ministrations could not bring in the age of perfection and the messianic restoration of Eden's paradise, neither could the statutes, rites, ceremonies, and penalties of the Mosaic code establish a basis for the promised age.

The word *teleiōsis* ("perfection") means the completing or finishing of anything, so nothing imperfect is left and nothing has been omitted. In reference to the Levitical priesthood, it means fulfilling the purpose for which the priesthood was established; that is, providing a system whereby the people could come to God in an acceptable way and find full pardon. This "perfection" the Levitical law could never accomplish.

**12. For the priesthood being changed:** . . . When a different person is made priest, *—BECK* . . . when a change in the priesthood takes place, *—WLMS* . . . being transferred, *—CNDT.*

**there is made of necessity a change also of the law:** . . . a change in its law necessarily takes place, *—WLMS* . . . there should also be a change of the Law, *—TNT.*

**7:12.** Since the Mosaic covenant and its legislation are so closely intertwined with the Levitical priesthood, a change of priesthood (from Levitical to Melchizedekian) also necessitated a change of legal systems. At this point the new legal system or new covenant was not identified. That was held in abeyance until the development of the contrast between the Aaronic priesthood and the priesthood of Melchizedek, exemplified in Jesus Christ. The new covenant was explicitly introduced in 8:6.

**13. For he of whom these things are spoken:** . . . of whom this is said, *—WLMS.*

**pertaineth to another tribe:** . . . became a member of, *—WLMS* . . . are said belonged to a different tribe, *—ADAM.*

**of which no man gave attendance at the altar:** . . . from which no one has come to serve at the altar, *—TNT* . . . no member of which ever officiated,

—WLMS...has ever attended as priest, —WADE...could serve, —SEB.

**7:13.** Under the Mosaic covenant the priests were to come from the tribe of Levi and the line of Aaron, but the new High Priest of whom this epistle speaks, Jesus Christ, did not come from the tribe of Levi. Jesus Christ, therefore, is by necessity a Priest under a different system from the one instituted by Moses. Under Moses no one from Judah, Jesus' tribe, was eligible to perform priestly duties at the altars of the temple or tabernacle. Jesus, a new kind of Priest, works under a new system.

**14. For [it is] evident that our Lord sprang out of Judah:** ...For it is taken for granted that, —CNDT...for it is very plain, —WLSN...it is quite clear that our Lord descended from, —TNT.

**of which tribe Moses spake nothing concerning priesthood:** ...Moses said nothing about priests in connection with this tribe, —TNT.

**7:14.** The evidence provided by the genealogy of Jesus in both Matthew and Luke traces His human ancestry back to the house of Judah on both the side of Joseph and His mother, Mary. It demonstrates that He is a legitimate claimant to the throne of David and that He is qualified by birth to be the Messiah. At the same time, however, that human genealogy disqualified Him from any possibility of serving as a priest in the Jewish temple. That was the right of Levites.

**15. And it is yet far more evident:** ...The matter is, TNT ...still more superabundantly sure, —CNDT ...yet more abundantly clear, —MNTG ...it becomes even plainer, —SEB ...That point is much clearer still, —BECK...it is still more overwhelmingly clear, —WLMS...appears still more manifest, —WADE.

**for that after the similitude of Melchisedec:** ...one analogous to, —WADE...in the likeness of, —WLMS.

**there ariseth another priest:** ...different type, —WADE...another kind of priest...arises, —TNT.

**7:15.** Beyond the silence of the Mosaic legislation in regard to a priestly Messiah or a royal priesthood out of the descendants of Judah, there is something even more evident. It was so plain that it had been noticed and had led to some of the speculation noted earlier (7:1). There were some Jews among the Essenes of Qumran and elsewhere who understood some of the messianic implications of Psalm 110. For they did expect some kind of an angelic Melchizedek to appear and deliver the holy Jewish remnant at the end of the age. Of him it is written, "And Melkizedek will avenge the vengeance of the judgments of God" (G. Vermes, p.267). In the *Testaments*

*of the Twelve Patriarchs* 18:2, Levi predicts "then the Lord will raise up a new priest." Psalm 110:4 speaks of the Messiah as a priest like Melchizedek, but on the basis of the Mosaic law the Jews had not been able to understand how Messiah could be both King and Priest. Hebrews 7 shows how Jesus can be both.

**16. Who is made:** ...is appointed, —WLMS.

**not after the law of a carnal commandment:** ...not appointed according to a Law, —BECK...of a transitory enactment, —MNTG...does not depend on a system of earthly commandments, —TNT...not on the basis of a physical qualification, —WLMS...not because of human rules and laws, —SEB...that required fleshly qualifications, —ADAM...of a fleshly precept, —CNDT.

**but after the power of an endless life:** ...but rather according to the power of an indestructible life, —ADAM...according to the energy of an indissoluble life, —MNTG...flowing from a life that cannot end, —WLMS...but by the power of a life that cannot be destroyed, —SEB...a life that nothing can destroy, —TNT...of immortal life, —NORL...of an imperishable Life, —WLSN.

**7:16.** In this verse the inspired writer described the other (*heteros*) priest, i.e., another of a different type. This new priest's elevation to the priesthood was according to the statutes of another kind of law. Strong emphasis is placed on the permanency and current efficacy of this new priest. First of all, the verb "who is made" translates the Greek word *gegonen* which by its tense refers to a past action that has results enduring to the time of the writing. Through His incarnation and suffering Christ became a Priest and He remains a Priest. The Levitical priests under the Mosaic law were determined according to *sarkikēs*, a term which relates to the flesh. Here it is used not in reference to the sin nature but in regard to the fact that Aaronic priests were determined by their descent. There is the implication that the priesthood passed from one generation to another. Levitical priests died and were succeeded by their descendants. The "new priest," however, exists not by commandment but by power. And what a power it is: the power not of death and succession, but "the power of an endless life." Not just any life, but life which is *akatalutou*, life which cannot be dissolved. He lives forever!

**17. For he testifieth:** ...For the Psalmist testifies, —NORL...For the Scripture bears witness, —WLMS...for Scripture affirms, —TNT...for his possession of this is evidenced by the statement, —WADE.

**Thou [art] a priest for ever after the order of Melchisedec:** ...with the rank of, —WLMS.

**7:17.** The proof adduced for the eternal life of this "new priest" was taken from Psalm 110:4. The Lord himself had said that the Messiah is eternally a priest of the Melchizedekian order. For all who trust the Lord, His Word settles the issue. No further proof is needed.

**18. For there is verily a disannulling of the commandment going before:** ... The old rule was done away with, *−SEB* ... The earlier rule is canceled, *−BECK* ... For indeed an Abrogation of the Preceding Commandment, *−WLSN* ... of a prior Code of commands, *−WADE* ... the rescinding of a previous regulation, *−WLMS* ... The previous commandment has been set aside, *−TNT* ... a former commandment is set aside, *−ADAM* ... there is coming to be a repudiation of the preceding precept, *−CNDT* ... there is a setting aside, *−MNTG*.

**for the weakness and unprofitableness thereof:** ... because it was weak and ineffective, *−NORL, −WLMS* ... because of its ... futility, *−WADE*.

**7:18.** This verse begins a contrast which is completed in verse 19. A contrast is made between the ineffectiveness of the Law and the hope offered by the new covenant (7:22). On the one hand, the previous commandment, i.e., the one "going before," is canceled. The term *athetēsis* is found frequently in the legal papyri of the New Testament period. It refers to cancellation or annulment of contracts for various causes. Often it is associated with inefficiency, inability, and unfitness. In this verse it refers to the just mentioned weakness of the dying Levitical priests. Their humanity made them inadequate.

**19. For the law made nothing perfect:** ... the Law completely failed to fulfill its purpose, *−TNT* ... brought nothing to spiritual perfection, *−WADE*.

**but the bringing in of a better hope [did]:** ... is brought to us, *−WLMS* ... the introduction of, *−WADE*.

**by the which we draw nigh unto God:** ... in the strength of which, *−WADE* ... through which we have approach to God, *−WLMS* ... it brings us close to God, *−BECK*.

**7:19.** "The law made nothing perfect" is a startling statement. It could not remedy the consequences of Adam's fall. It could not eradicate sin, conquer death, or cleanse consciences from moral guilt before the Lord. It could provoke sin, reveal it, and condemn it. It could deal with sin only in an external ceremonial way, but it was powerless to overcome sin and its results. Its priests entered into an earthly sanctuary once a year, but they died eventually because of sin's unbroken sway. Jesus, the new, undying Priest of the Melchizedekian order, however, brought in a much better hope—a hope by which believers are now actually drawing near to God himself. Through the Son

Christians are able daily and continuously to enter into the very presence of God.

**20. And inasmuch as not without an oath [he was made priest]:** ... by so much as He was not appointed without God's taking an oath, *−WLMS*.

**7:20.** As with God's promise to Abraham (6:13), this new priesthood is doubly certified because it was established by an oath. The value of an oath depends on the character of the one making it. Since the maker of this covenant was God, who is completely holy and righteous, the oath is sure.

**21. (For those priests were made without an oath:** ... were appointed, *−WLMS*.

**but this with an oath by him that said unto him:** ... He became a priest with an oath, through the One who says to him, *−TNT*.

**The Lord sware and will not repent:** ... took oath, *−WLMS* ... He will never change it, *−SEB* ... and will not change His mind, *−ADAM, −WUST* ... will not change His decision, *−WADE* ... will not be regretting it, *−CNDT* ... and will never be sorry for it, *−KLGS* ... and he will not go back on his word, *−TNT*.

**Thou [art] a priest for ever after the order of Melchisedec:):**

**7:21.** For the first time the writer cited all of Psalm 110:4, revealing that the Melchizedekian priesthood of the Messiah was established by a divine oath. The implication seems to be the same as the argument articulated previously in his presentation of the Abrahamic covenant (6:13-20). God himself has singled out the importance of the Melchizedekian order by underscoring its establishment with an oath. He did not do this when He established the Levitical priesthood.

**22. By so much:** ... this implies that, *−WADE*.

**was Jesus made a surety of a better testament:** ... This makes Jesus a guarantee of, *−NORL* ... the Covenant for which Jesus has become Surety, *−WADE* ... become the guarantee of a better covenant, *−ADAM, −WLMS* ... has Jesus become a Pledge, *−WLSN* ... become the sponsor of a better covenant, *−CNDT*.

**7:22.** This verse gives the name of this undying, oath-established Priest—Jesus (last named in 6:20). The emphasis upon this identification is inescapable. Literally, the word order of the verse is: "In proportion to the degree that this is a better covenant, He is become a guarantee, Jesus" (author's translation). The term "surety" (*enguos*) speaks of a bond for bail or a marriage dowry. The certainty of the efficacy of the new and better covenant is linked to the superiority of the new covenant, which in turn is inherent in the nature of the Son, Jesus. Everything He touches is better: His name and inheritance (1:4); the hope which

He offers (7:7); the covenant which He established (7:22); the sacrifices which He offers (9:23); and the benefits which He brings (10:34; 11:16, 35, 40; 12:24).

**23. And they truly were many priests:** ... There is another point, −*TNT* ... there was a succession of priests, −*NORL* ... Many priests were needed to continue the line, −*SEB* ... have become numerous, −*WLMS.*

**because they were not suffered to continue by reason of death:** ... they have been prevented by death from continuing, −*MNTG,* −*WLMS* ... for death stopped them from staying on, −*NORL* ... on account of being hindered by Death, −*WLSN* ... from remaining in office, −*TNT.*

**7:23.** This verse begins to spell out the things implied by *sarkikēs* in verse 16. The one undying Priest, Jesus, is superior to the many dying priests of the Levitical order. Because they were mortal, there were continual changes in the priesthood. Because Jesus is alive forevermore, His priesthood is an unchanging one.

**24. But this [man], because he continueth ever:** ... in consequence of His continuing to exist for ever, −*WADE.*

**hath an unchangeable priesthood:** ... holds his priesthood inviolable, −*MNTG* ... has an inviolate priesthood, −*CNDT* ... he has a priesthood which cannot pass to another, −*TNT* ... because He Himself lives on forever, −*WLMS* ... He never passes on his priestly work to others, −*SEB* ... which is untransferable, −*WUST.*

**7:24.** Although Jesus died, He did not remain dead. He lives. His priesthood is a permanent priesthood. Because of His indissoluble life (7:16), His ministry remains *aparabaton.* This term may have both meanings in view: Jesus' priesthood is both unchangeable and nontransferable because He himself is eternal.

**25. Wherefore he is able also to save them to the uttermost:** ... and hence, −*WADE* ... he is also able for all time, −*TNT* ... makes Him able to save completely, −*ADAM* ... any and all, −*WLMS.*

**that come unto God by him:** ... who approach God, −*NORL.*

**seeing he ever liveth to make intercession for them:** ... because he is alive always to turn to God on their behalf, −*TNT* ... He lives forever to pray for them, −*NLTG* ... to intercede for them, −*MNTG* ... to interpose on their behalf, −*WLSN.*

**7:25.** At this point the writer emphasized the staggering relevance of Jesus' eternal priesthood. Since Jesus is alive forever, He is able to function as the believers' Priest eternally. His chief purpose as Priest is summed up by the word *entunchanein.* This term means that Jesus meets with God the Father in order to represent believers and to ask Him to act graciously on their behalf. As a living, eternal Priest He intercedes for believers. The power of His indissoluble life enables Him to keep on delivering those who are His because, unlike the priests who stopped functioning at death, His ministry continues on.

The phrase "to the uttermost" translates *eis to panteles.* This phrase could be rendered by the English word *finally.* It includes the idea of completeness and totality, but it also has connotations of time. The deliverance effected by Jesus' intercession is both thorough and final. At the end of time the believer's salvation will be total. None of a Christian's needs are beyond the scope of His deliverance. But the inspired writer was careful to maintain a proper perspective on the necessity of faith. Deliverance is for those who keep on coming to God through Jesus alone.

**26. For such an high priest became us:** ... This was the High Priest we needed, −*TCNT* ... Such was the divine High priest we needed, −*NOLI* ... We needed just such a High Priest, −*NORL* ... A high priest of such a kind does indeed meet our need, −*TNT* ... was appropriate to our needs and conditions, −*WADE.*

**[who is] holy, harmless, undefiled:** ... innocent, unstained, −*ADAM,* −*WLMS* ... saintly, −*WADE* ... immaculate, −*NOLI.*

**separate from sinners:** ... sinless, −*NOLI* ... sundered from the sinful, −*WADE* ... is different from sinful men, −*NLTG* ... far removed from sinful men, −*WLMS.*

**and made higher than the heavens:** ... raised higher than, −*NORL* ... and exalted above the heavens, −*MNTG* ... and elevated far above the very heavens, −*WLMS.*

**7:26.** Verse 26 continues to summarize the superiority of Jesus as a Melchizedekian High Priest. It is fitting for Christians to have a High Priest with such qualifications. Unlike the Levitical priests, He is holy, sinless, and innocent in His own person. In His relationships with others, He is perfect. In His humanity He was unlike other men because He is sinless. He has moral perfection. Exalted, He ministers in heaven.

**27. Who needeth not daily, as those high priests:** ... has no need, like those human high priests, −*NOLI* ... is not daily under the necessity, −*WADE* ... as did the Levitical priests, −*WLMS.*

**to offer up sacrifice, first for his own sins:** ... offer sacrifices daily, −*TNT.*

**and then for the people's:** ... and next for those of, −*WADE.*

**for this he did once, when he offered up himself:** ... For this sacrifice was made once for all, −*MNTG* ... this latter is just what He did once for all, −*WLMS* ... He made one sacrifice for all mankind, −*NOLI* ... for all time, −*SEB.*

**7:27.** Unlike the Levitical priests, Jesus does not have to offer sacrifices for His own sins. His sinless perfection eliminates any need for atonement for himself. But there is something more important. The power of His indissoluble life renders His sacrificial death for others far more efficacious than any of the animal sacrifices offered by Aaronic priests. They offered sacrifices for themselves and their people day after day. Jesus had to offer himself only once.

**28. For the law maketh men high priests which have infirmity:**... appoints to the high priesthood men full of imperfections, —*NOLI*... men high priests who have weakness, —*ADAM*... human beings subject to weakness, —*TNT*... men who are subject to moral and physical infirmity, —*WADE*... these men are not perfect, —*SEB*.
**but the word of the oath, which was since the law:** ... but the assertion about the taking of an oath, which was spoken after the time of the law, —*WLMS*... the declaration in God's oathtaking, which occurred later than the Law, —*WADE*... which came later than the Law, —*TNT*.
**[maketh] the Son, who is consecrated for evermore:** ... appoint for ever the perfected Son, —*TNT*... appoints as High Priest a Son who has been rendered perfect for ever, —*WADE*... appoints a Son who is perfectly qualified to be High Priest forever, —*WLMS*.

**7:28.** The Mosaic law established priests with sinful weaknesses, but the divine oath of Psalm 110:4, which came after the Mosaic covenant, established the Son as an eternal Priest. Seated at the right hand of God and addressed as Son, His priesthood is perfect—without limits. This is the One to whom we can come with our needs, knowing He is completely able to provide help.

Jesus' intercession for believers can be aptly illustrated by an incident from antiquity. In classical Greece in a certain city state there were two brothers. They were as different as night is from day. Amyntas was the hero of the city. He had led them to victory in battle. He had defended them at the jeopardy of his own life. His brother Aeschylus was a ne'er-do-well and a blackguard. Aeschylus' double-dealing and treacherous ways caught up with him. He was brought to trial before the assembly of citizens. The evidence against him was both overwhelming and undisputed. There was no doubt: Aeschylus was guilty of treason. He would be banished from the presence of the citizenry and his family forever.

The laws, however, entitled him to a defense, and he had chosen his brother Amyntas for his advocate. The prosecution rested its case, and it was time for Amyntas to defend Aeschylus. Every eye was upon him as he took his place on the stage in the center of the town's amphitheater. What would he say? What could he say in defense of his guilty brother? He said nothing. As all the citizens anxiously waited, Amyntas withdrew his right arm from his cloak and slowly raised its scarred stump for all to see, reminding them of the price he had paid in defense of their freedom. When he returned to his seat, the citizenry, stunned and stirred, acquitted Aeschylus. So it is when Jesus pleads the believer's cause. His very life intercedes. It is Christ, crucified and risen, who makes intercession.

## Chapter 8

**1. Now of the things which we have spoken [this is] the sum:** ... Now the important thing is this, —*NLTG*... to crown what we have been saying, —*WADE*... The chief thing, however, —*WLSN*... The pith of all, —*MNTG*... This is the point of what is being said, —*SEB*... the main point in what I am saying is this, —*WLMS*.
**We have such an high priest:**... a Religious Leader Who had made the way for man to go to God, —*NLTG*... such as I have described, —*TCNT*.
**who is set on the right hand:** ... one who has taken His seat, —*WLMS*... has sat down, —*WADE*.
**of the throne of the Majesty in the heavens:**... of God's majestic throne in heaven, —*WLMS*.

**8:1.** Chapter 8 begins with a clarification of the argument the inspired writer has been presenting by singling out the main thrust of that argument up to this point. The divine oath of Psalm 110:4 which prophesied of the establishment of an eternal Melchizedekian priesthood had now, in the lifetime of those to whom the Epistle to the Hebrews was written, been fulfilled. Such a Priest is not a figment of wishful thinking or speculation. He is now a reality. He is the believer's possession. The waiting is over. Jesus has risen and sits exalted on the right hand of God. He has completed everything necessary for the atonement of the sins of the whole human race and has sat down in God's heavenly sanctuary in the place of preference and blessing. All of God's favor and authority are His to command. He does not stand or bow in the presence of God as a sinful priest must. He is seated, because He is the Son, and His sacrifice is completed. Although He represents men who are upon the earth, He is not ministering in an earthly temple or tabernacle; He deals with spiritual realities in God's heavenly abode.

**2. A minister of the sanctuary:** ... where he serves in the sanctuary, —*TNT*... and acts as Officiating Minister in the Heavenly sanctuary, —*WADE*... as officiating Priest, —*WLMS*... who ministers now in the sanctuary, —NORL . . . to serve as priest in the holy place, —BECK.

**and of the true tabernacle, which the Lord pitched, and not man:** . . . the genuine one, —WUST . . . this being the Real Tabernacle, —WADE . . . which is also the true tent of worship, —WLMS . . . which the Lord, not man, set up, —TNT.

**8:2.** Christ's priestly service (*leitourgos*) occurs in the Holy of Holies and the true (that is, genuine) tabernacle. This is not the tent which Israel pitched in the wilderness of Sinai; it is a tabernacle which has been set up by the Lord himself. The contrast is between the earthly and the heavenly, the temporal and the eternal, the human and the divine, the external physical and the spiritually real.

**3. For every high priest is ordained to offer gifts and sacrifices:** . . . is appointed, —WLMS . . . to present both bloodless Offerings, —WADE.

**wherefore [it is] of necessity that this man:** . . . and accordingly it is essential that Jesus, too, —WADE . . . our high priest too must, —TNT.

**have somewhat also to offer:** . . . should have an Offering to present, —WADE.

**8:3.** All high priests appointed by God had certain common responsibilities and tasks to perform. They were all appointed to offer gifts and sacrifices to God on behalf of the people whom they represented. This aspect of priestly service has been alluded to and hinted at previously (2:17) and expressly mentioned but not commented upon (5:1).

It is important to understand the necessity of sacrificial offerings and gifts as the principal function of any priesthood. To this point, however, the writer has compared and contrasted the personal qualifications of the Son with the personal qualifications of the descendants of Aaron who formed the Levitical priesthood under the aegis of the Mosaic covenant. He has demonstrated the personal superiority of the Son to these priests and their priesthood. Now it is imperative that he demonstrate the superiority of Jesus' priestly ministry over the ministry performed by the Levitical priesthood. It was broached at the end of the previous section (7:27), but in this chapter he begins a presentation in minute and painstaking detail.

**4. For if he were on earth:** . . . However, if He were still on earth, —WLMS.

**he should not be a priest:** . . . He wouldn't be, —ADAM . . . He would not even be, —CNDT.

**seeing that there are priests that offer gifts according to the law:** . . . since there exist Priests who present the gifts prescribed by Law, —WADE . . . there are those who officiate in accordance with the law in offering the gifts, —WLMS . . . demanded by the Law, —BECK.

**8:4.** It has been demonstrated that Jesus was not qualified as a priest under the Mosaic code. The earthly priesthood was assigned to the descendants of Aaron (7:5,6). Other than His sacrifice on the cross, Jesus' incarnation and suffering have already been presented as preparation for priestly service (2:9-18; 5:7-9). His priestly service is performed not on earth but in heaven.

This verse has some bearing on attempts to date the writing of the epistle. Since there is reference to the ministry of the Levitical priests, they would still have been serving. This ministry ceased after the Romans destroyed the Jerusalem temple in A.D. 70, so it would seem logical to believe this letter was written before A.D. 70.

**5. Who serve unto the example and shadow of heavenly things:** . . . They are performing a service, —TNT . . . yet they officiate in a sanctuary that is a mere copy, —WLMS . . . a mere sketch and outline, —WADE . . . of the heavenly reality, —MNTG.

**as Moses was admonished of God:** . . . This is evident from the warning, —ADAM . . . Moses has been apprized, —CNDT . . . as Moses . . . was warned, —WLMS.

**when he was about to make the tabernacle:** . . . when about to be completing the tabernacle, —CNDT . . . when he was about to make the tent of worship, —WLMS . . . when he was about to erect the tent was instructed to do, —TNT.

**for, See, saith he, [that] thou make all things:** . . . Be careful to make all of it, —BECK . . . See to it that you make it all, —WLMS . . . that you do everything, —TNT.

**according to the pattern showed to thee in the mount:** . . . after the model shewn to thee, —WADE . . . just like the pattern shown you on the mountain, —WLMS.

**8:5.** This verse presents and examines the nature of the ministry of the Levitical priests. Their priestly service was secondary to the heavenly. It was only a copy (*hupodeigma*) and shadow of the heavenly realities. The evaluation of their service was based upon the Old Testament record. When Jehovah instructed Moses to begin the construction of the tabernacle, He said, "And look that thou make them after their pattern, which was showed thee in the mount" (Exodus 25:40). The tabernacle was patterned after heavenly realities revealed to Moses. The Levitical tabernacle, therefore, was not the real thing but only a copy of the heavenly reality.

The basic appeal of ritualistic religion is to the flesh rather than to the spirit of man. Its pageantry stirs his human emotions. That which he sees holds aesthetic meaning for him. He likes the beauty and grace of the routine its ministers go through. It is all a work of art to him. Soon after God instituted it, Israel had reduced the forms of worship in Judaism to mere ritual.

To warn the Hebrews against turning back to the pageantry of Judaism, the writer played down the splendor of its temple and referred to the tabernacle, *skēnēn*, literally "tent," instead. He said worship there was but a shadow of the real. To focus on it was like following the shade of a man walking in the sun rather than the person himself. In Hebrews that Person was Jesus. Why return to the shadow of a man when you have the Man? This was his question.

**6. But now hath he obtained a more excellent ministry:** ... But as it is, Jesus has obtained a far superior ministry, –*TNT* ... But Christ has a more perfect work, –*NLTG* ... Jesus has received a ministry that is better than theirs, –*SEB* ... He has entered upon a priestly service as much superior to theirs, –*WLMS* ... a Superior Service, –*WLSN*.

**by how much also he is the mediator of a better covenant:** ... as the covenant of which He is the Mediator is superior to theirs, –*WLMS* ... in proportion as the "covenant" of which He is the Intermediary is superior to the earlier, –*WADE*.

**which was established upon better promises:** ... which has been enacted upon, –*MNTG* ... it has been established on the basis of, –*TNT* ... being constituted on the basis of better Promises, –*WADE* ... which rests upon better promises, –*NORL* ... God has based it on better promises, –*BECK* ... it has been enacted upon superior promises, –*WLMS* ... based on nobler promises from heaven, –*NOLI*.

**8:6.** To the degree that Jesus has been established as "the mediator" of a better covenant set up on the basis of better promises—to that same degree He has obtained a "more excellent" priestly ministry. The inspired writer has shown Jesus to be a messenger who is superior to the angelic messengers of the old covenant, and he has shown Him to be a superior priest because of His indissoluble life. The implication has been all along that a superior messenger and a superior priesthood mean a superior covenant.

In order to demonstrate the superiority of the new covenant the inspired writer next identified and analyzed the new covenant. He laid bare the promises of that covenant in order to compare them with the promises of the Mosaic covenant. In this way he showed the promises of the new covenant were superior—not because they were more reliable (both came from God who cannot lie) but because the goals which they were designed to accomplish were superior to the objectives set up for the Mosaic law.

**7. For if that first [covenant] had been faultless:** ... if the former covenant, –*TNT* ... if the carrying-out of that first Covenant ... had afforded no ground for censure, –*WADE* ... had been perfect, –*NORL* ... had been unimpeachable, –*NOLI*.

**then should no place have been sought for the second:** ... God would not have been seeking a place for a second, –*TNT* ... there would have been no need for, –*MNTG*, –*NOLI* ... there would have been no occasion, –*NORL* ... could have been no room for a second one, –*WLMS*.

**8:7.** The very fact that God set up a second covenant indicates that the first covenant was indeed lacking something. The second covenant provides clues to this weakness.

**8. For finding fault with them, he saith:** ... For, blaming them, –*CNDT* ... because He was dissatisfied with His people, –*WLMS* ... He finds fault with his people, saying, –*TNT* ... God himself impeached it and denounced our forefathers for its invalidation, saying, –*NOLI*.

**Behold, the days come, saith the Lord:** ... Lo, –*WADE* ... the time is coming, –*WLMS*.

**when I will make a new covenant:** ... when I will complete, –*ADAM* ... when I will conclude, –*TNT*, –*WADE* ... a new agreement, –*SEB*.

**with the house of Israel and with the house of Judah:**

**8:8.** The purpose of quoting the new covenant from Jeremiah 31:31-34 is manifold. For one thing, it was necessary to show that the temporary nature of the Mosaic covenant was known to the prophets. It was also the divine intention to supersede the law of Moses. An analysis of the provisions of the new covenant was necessary in order to prove its superiority to the Sinaitic code.

In introducing the Old Testament quotation the inspired writer set the stage with an introductory formula which identified the context in which the new covenant was given by the Lord. It also highlights the contention that the old covenant was seriously deficient. The announcement of the new covenant arose in a situation where Jehovah was excoriating Israel for its sinfulness and pronouncing judgment upon the nation because of its failure to keep the Law. Immediately after giving a death sentence for sin, Jehovah announced that at some time in the future He would establish a new covenant with both Israel and the house of Judah, thus reuniting the divided kingdom.

Though Jehovah made the new covenant with Israel, its provisions belong to any who meet its conditions. National Israel refused to accept it in the First Century by rejecting Jesus as the Messiah. Regardless, His death put His covenant or will into effect. Individual Jews believed and received, including the recipients of this letter (Romans 11:5). However, they constituted only a "remnant." In the future so many Jewish people will believe on Jesus that one might even say "all" Israel will be saved (Romans 11:26). In the meantime, any who receive Jesus partake of the benefits of the covenant.

**9. Not according to the covenant that I made with their fathers:** ...It won't be like the covenant that, *—ADAM* ... Not on the lines of the covenant which, *—WADE* ... will be different from the covenant, *—NOLI* ... unlike the one that I made with their forefathers, *—WLMS.*

**in the day when I took them by the hand:**

**to lead them out of the land of Egypt:** ... to bring them, *—TNT* ... lead them forth, *—WADE.*

**because they continued not in my covenant:** ...they did not follow the Old Way of Worship, *—NLTG* ... did not abide by, *—BRCL* ... on their part, did not adhere to my covenant, *—WADE* ... But they did not stick to their agreement, *—NORL* ... they did not keep the agreement with me, *—BB* ... they themselves repudiated my old covenant, *—NOLI* ... they have not been loyal to My covenant, *—BECK* ... they did not abide by their covenant with me, *—WLMS* ... they remained not in My plan, *—FNTN.*

**and I regarded them not, saith the Lord:** ...And I would not listen to them, *—KLGS* ... and I left them alone, *—ADAM* ... So I, on my side, paid no regard to them, *—WADE* ... I also did not take care of them, *—SWAN* ... I let them go their own way, *—BRCL* ... I was sorry for them, *—FNTN* ... paid no attention to them, *—SEB* ... So I did not care for them, *—WLMS* ... I ceased to care, *—TNT* ... So I had to repudiate them also, *—NOLI* ... I gave them up, *—BB.*

**8:9.** In this verse the quotation contrasts the nature of the new covenant with the old and brings forward at least one reason why the Lord determined to create a new covenant with His people Israel. Jehovah said the new covenant would be different. It would not operate according to the same standard as the covenant which He established with the Children of Israel when He led them out of Egypt through the Red Sea on dry land. This new covenant would be set up because of Israel's failure to keep the Sinaitic covenant. They did not abide in the covenant of the Lord. Since they did not dwell in His covenant, He left them to their own devices and allowed them to suffer the consequences of their rebellion.

**10. For this [is] the covenant that I will make with the house of Israel:** ...this is the agreement, *—BB* ... This, then, is the settlement I will make, *—FNTN* ... that I will contract, *—ADAM* ... to which I will commit myself for, *—WADE.*

**after those days, saith the Lord:** ...in the future, *—SEB, —NOLI* ... In those days, *—WLMS.*

**I will put my laws into their mind:** ... I will impress, *—WADE, —NOLI* ... to their comprehension, *—CNDT* ... into their understanding, *—FNTN.*

**and write them in their hearts:** ...I will inscribe them, *—WADE.*

**and I will be to them a God:** ... Then I will be their God, *—NOLI.*

**and they shall be to me a people:** ...they will be my people, *—NOLI.*

**8:10.** At this juncture Jehovah began to outline the provisions of the new covenant. The nation of Israel was identified as the second party to the covenant. The new covenant would be established "after those days" which (in the context of Jeremiah 31:29) refers to the time when Jehovah would pour out His judgment on Israel because of their sins. This identifies it as sometime after the Babylonian captivity and return to Palestine.

Having indicated when and with whom He would make His new covenant, the Lord enunciated its terms. The first of these was very different from any provision found in the Mosaic law. He said, "I will put my laws into their mind, and write them in their hearts." These laws were not to be external as were those given to Moses on tablets of stone. They would be internalized in the mind, consciousness, and emotional center of the entire nation. The end result would be that Israel would actually become what God had always desired them to be: His people (Exodus 6:7).

Ezekiel joined Jeremiah in promising a day when God would internalize Israel's religion (Ezekiel 36:25-27). He promised cleansing from moral filthiness. The Lord would give a new heart, a tender one of flesh, to replace a hard one of stone. Thus both prophets promised an experience of heartfelt religion. Ezekiel further declared God would put a new spirit within. This makes possible a walk according to God's laws. With the Psalmist one can say, "I delight to do thy will, O my God: yea, thy law is within my heart" (Psalm 40:8). We can live by internal constraint, not external restraint.

Ezekiel and Jeremiah use "spirit," "heart," and "mind" as synonyms. Rather than finding a distinction between "putting laws in the mind" and "writing them on the heart," it is more correct to see the expressions as forming a Hebrew parallelism. Taylor wrote, "In 10:16 the two terms are inverted; this suggests that the writer thinks of the two clauses as a simple parallelism, and *mind* and *heart* as synonyms. In 8:10 the laws are inscribed in the heart, while they are put into the mind; but in 10:16 they are inscribed on the mind and put into the heart" (*Beacon Bible Commentary,* p.98).

**11. And they shall not teach every man his neighbour:** ... No man shall teach, *—TNT* ... there will be no need, *—BB* ... there will be no necessity, *—BRCL* ... nevermore will each one need to teach, *—WLMS* ... Then they will not have to teach their neighbors, *—NOLI* . . . to instruct, *—TCNT* . . . his fellow citizen, *—MNTG* . . . his friend, *—FNTN.*

**and every man his brother, saying, Know the Lord:** . . . each one teach his brother, *—WLMS* . . . Acquaint thee with the Lord, *—WADE.*

**for all shall know me, from the least to the greatest:** . . . because from small to great, *—TNT* . . . all shall be acquainted with Me, *—CNDT* . . . From the lowest to the highest, *—WLMS.*

**8:11.** The personal relationship which God desires with His people, "to them a God" and "to me a people" (verse 10), was further heightened by the description of the covenantal terms revealed in this verse. The need for mediation between God and men found in the priests and teachers of the old covenant would be eliminated under the new agreement. No longer would people need to admonish one another to come to know the Lord, because all of them would have firsthand experience knowing the Lord. In having access to the Lord, all, from the most powerful and influential to the least important, would be on an equal basis.

**12. For I will be merciful to their unrighteousness:** . . . will pardon their misdeeds, *—NORL* . . . upon their wrong-doings, *—MNTG* . . . to their deeds of wrong, *—WLMS* . . . to their iniquities, *—WADE.*

**and their sins and their iniquities will I remember no more:** . . . never, never any more will I recall their sins, *—WLMS.*

**8:12.** Jehovah next declared the greatest provision of the new covenant, something not found in the Mosaic law—provision for the forgiveness of sins. Under the new covenant He promised to show mercy to their unrighteousness. He also declared that He would not hold their lawlessness against them.

The intention was not to deny there could be an experience of forgiveness in the time of the old covenant. Obviously David knew the blessing of forgiveness, and the knowledge of justification by faith was available since the time of Abraham. Yet these things were not based on any provisions which God had built into the Mosaic covenant. They grew out of the covenant which the Lord had made with Abraham. The sacrificial system administered by the Levitical priesthood did not cleanse consciences of moral guilt or deal with the penalty of sin. They only provided ceremonial cleansing on an annual basis. God does not change. His merciful and gracious character are seen in the Old Testament Scriptures (Micah 7:18) and revealed in the Mosaic law, but in the new covenant there is a complete forgiveness, only foreshadowed in the old. Along with this comes a freedom from fear and from the power of man's fallen nature not known under the old covenant.

**13. In that he saith, A new [covenant]:** . . . In speaking of a new covenant, *—WLMS* . . . By saying 'new,' *—TNT* . . . a covenant of a new type, *—WADE.*

**he hath made the first old:** . . . He has pronounced, *—WADE* . . . made the first obsolete, *—ADAM.*

**Now that which decayeth and waxeth old:** . . . and whatever is obsolete and antiquated, *—WLMS* . . . growing old and decrepit, *—CNDT* . . . that which grows old and creaky, *—KLGS* . . . and feeble, *—NORL.*

**[is] ready to vanish away:** . . . is about ready to disappear, *—NORL* . . . is fast disappearing, *—KLGS* . . . It will never be used again, *—NLTG* . . . is not far from disappearing, *—TNT* . . . is on the point of disappearing, *—TCNT* . . . is on the verge of vanishing, *—WLMS* . . . disappearing altogether, *—WADE.*

**8:13.** Verse 13 gives the writer's concluding remarks on his citation of the new covenant text from Jeremiah 31:31-34. But this only serves as a launching pad for the main discussion of its superiority which is developed in chapters 9 and 10. The main contention at this point was that the announcement of a new covenant and the introduction of the Son necessitated the cancellation of the Mosaic covenant (7:11,18; 8:7). The new and the old are incompatible. They cannot coexist. The new antiquates the old. Being obsolete, the old was near its vanishing point. It was gone—in A.D. 70.

## Chapter 9

**1. Then verily the first [covenant] had also:** . . . So indeed, *—WLMS.*

**ordinances of divine service:** . . . There were special ways of worship and a special holy place, *—NLTG* . . . regulations of worship, *—ADAM* . . . for divine worship, *—TCNT* . . . of public worship, *—MNTG.*

**and a worldly sanctuary:** . . . and it had its sanctuary, an earthly one, *—TNT* . . . and the earthly holy place, *—BECK* . . . one that shared the nature of the material world, *—WADE.*

**9:1.** This verse begins with the Greek word *eichen* which means "had." It is significant that the Mosaic covenant is referred to in the past tense, for it has just been depicted as being on the verge of disappearing. Exodus 25:40 was cited in Hebrews 8:5, and chapter 9 proceeds to describe the copies which Moses was commanded to make for the wilderness tabernacle. This was in order to describe the Levitical priesthood's divine service in the offering of sacrifice on the Day of Atonement. Verse 1 refers to the old covenant as "the first." It had regulations (*dikaiōmata*) which governed the service performed by its priests. It possessed not the genuine heavenly sanctuary but the holy place which was worldly (*to te hagion kosmikon*); its sanctuary was an earthbound, man-made copy of the heavenly original shown to Moses (9:24).

**2. For there was a tabernacle made; the first:** ... The sanctuary was built, —SEB ... there was constructed a Tabernacle—consisting, first, of a Front Tent, —WADE ... outer part of the tent, —WLMS ... a tent was constructed, —TNT.

**wherein [was] the candlestick, and the table, and the show-bread:** ... containing, —WADE ... where the lampstand and the table with the Bread of the Presence were, —TNT ... was equipped with the lamp and table, —WLMS ... and the presentation bread, —ADAM ... and the holy bread was on it, —NLTG ... the oblation bread, —NOLI.

**which is called the sanctuary:** ... which is termed the holy place, —CNDT ... The Holy of Holies, —WADE.

**9:2.** Here the inspired writer recounts for Jewish believers the details of worship at the tabernacle. The intent is to show God provided a better approach through Jesus. Previously he had shown Christ as a better messenger than the prophets or angels; a better apostle than Moses or Joshua; as our High Priest, better than Aaron; and offering a better covenant to Israel. Now he emphasizes Jesus brought better provisions for worship.

He had respect for worship in Judaism, but by the Spirit he said some shocking things to prevent believers in Israel from turning back to the old means of access to God. As Carter observed, "The tabernacle was intended of God as a *means* of worship, *not* as an *object* of worship. It was intended as a symbol to direct their thoughts and devotion to the realities of the coming Messiah which it symbolized" (*The Wesleyan Bible Commentary,* p. 109).

Verse 2 describes the furniture found in the outer sanctuary or Holy Place which was designated as "the first." With the Old Testament Scriptures as his authority and its record of the institution of tabernacle worship in the Mosaic law, the writer portrayed not the temple but the *skēnē* i.e., the tabernacle or tent which was moved around with Israel in their wanderings. Since the Hebrews were familiar with this setup, the contents of the outer sanctuary or Holy Place were merely itemized without further commentary. The first sanctuary of the tabernacle housed a lampstand, a table, and the bread known as shewbread or the "bread of the Presence." Details concerning their specifications, construction, and placement are found in Exodus 25, 37, and 40.

**3. And after the second veil:** ... Behind the second curtain, —BECK, —WADE ... beyond which was, —TNT.

**the tabernacle which is called the Holiest of all:** ... there came a Rear Tent, —WADE ... is the tent that is called the holy of holies, —WLMS ... known as the Inner Sanctuary, —TCNT.

**4. Which had the golden censer:** ... This room contained the golden altar, —SEB ... In it were a golden altar for burning incense, —TNT ... golden incense-altar, —WLMS ... where special perfume was burned, —NLTG.

**and the ark of the covenant overlaid round about with gold:** ... the chest for the covenant, —WLMS ... covered all over, —MNTG ... completely covered, —BECK ... covered on all sides with gold, —NOLI ... with gold plating, —WADE.

**wherein [was] the golden pot that had manna:** ... a golden jar, —WLMS, —TNT ... the Golden Casket containing, —WADE ... it contained the golden urn with the manna, —NOLI.

**and Aaron's rod that budded:** ... staff which germinates, —CNDT ... which blossomed, —WLSN ... which sprouted, —TNT.

**and the tables of the covenant:** ... the tablets on which the covenant was written, —WLMS ... the stone tablets of the covenant, —TNT ... inscribed with the Covenant, —WADE.

**9:3, 4.** These verses describe the inner sanctuary's contents. The words used are *Hagia Hagiōn*, the Holy of Holies. The entrances to both the inner and outer holy places were covered by veils. The gold censer or altar of incense (*thumiatērion*) was not in the Holy of Holies. It stood before the entrance to the inner sanctuary and thus was in the Holy Place. But the smoke of the incense burned upon it was designed to penetrate the veil and permeate the Holy of Holies as it ascended before the ark of the covenant.

Since this intimate association existed between the altar of incense and the ark of the covenant, they are tied together by the use of the same participle (*echousa* translated "which had") in reference to both. The ark was "overlaid round about with gold" (*perikekalummenēn pantothen*), meaning it was overlaid with gold both on the outside and the inside.

Three items were kept inside the ark of the covenant: a golden urn filled with manna as a reminder of God's provision in the wilderness, Aaron's rod which had budded, and the tablets of the Decalogue. By the time of the dedication of Solomon's Temple, two of these items had disappeared (see 1 Kings 8:9). We are not told when this occurred, but it may have happened during the period of 7 months when the ark was in exile in the land of the Philistines (see 1 Samuel 5 and 6).

**5. And over it the cherubims of glory:** ... And above it, —ADAM ... above the chest were the winged creatures, the symbols of God's glorious presence, —WLMS ... were the angels of glory, —BECK ... who revealed God's glory, —TNT.

**shadowing the mercyseat:** ... overshadowing the propitiatory shelter, —CNDT ... the place of reconciliation, —TNT.

**of which we cannot now speak particularly:** ... But now is not the time to talk about every detail of these things, —SEB ... it isn't possible to speak in detail about these things, —ADAM... of which I cannot now speak in detail, —WLMS.

**9:5.** Fashioned on the lid of the ark of the covenant were the "cherubim of glory," angelic guardians. Their function was to guard the presence of Jehovah. For the Lord was indeed *the* "Glory." The lid which these figures overshadowed was called the mercy seat.

The Septuagint term *hilastērion*, used here for "mercy seat," reminded believers of the sacrifices and rituals performed once a year on the Day of Atonement. On that day when the high priest entered into the Holiest of Holies and sprinkled sacrificial blood on the lid of the ark, it ceremonially covered the sins of the nation of Israel until the next Day of Atonement.

Later on in the epistle this imagery brings into sharper focus the contrast between it and the sacrificial death of Jesus at Calvary. This seed so deftly planted by the Holy Spirit will be harvested later.

6. **Now when these things were thus ordained:** ... Under these arrangements, —TNT... Such then were the arrangements, —MNTG ... But that is how it was arranged, —BECK ... With these arrangements completed in this way, —WLMS.

**the priests went always into the first tabernacle:** ... continually enter the outer tent, —TNT. ... regularly go into the outer part of the tent of worship, —WLMS.

**accomplishing the service [of God]:** ... in conducting their official services, —WLMS ... when they carry out the duties of their service, —TNT ... performing the divine service, —CNDT ... in the discharge of their sacred duties, —TCNT.

**9:6.** The opening words of this verse clearly indicate that only a cursory treatment will be given to the physical aspects of the tabernacle's furniture and sanctuaries in the light the previous citation of Exodus 25:40 (Hebrews 8:5). They were inferior copies of the heavenly realities.

The first four words of this verse (*Toutōn de houtōs kateskeuasmenōn*) could be translated "Now when these things were constructed thus," that is, when Moses had carried out the Lord's command and built the tabernacle and its furnishings according to the pattern which had been shown to him on Mount Sinai. So, after the copies were made, the priests began to perform their priestly duties. The service which they provided continually on a daily basis (as signified by *diapantos*) was, however, only performed in the first or outer sanctuary.

7. **But into the second:** ... but into the inner tent, —MNTG ... into the inner room, —NORL.

**[went] the high priest alone once every year:** ... nobody but the high priest may go, —WLMS ... once annually, —WLSN.

**not without blood, which he offered for himself:** ... and never without blood which he offers for himself, —WLMS ... He always takes blood with him, —TNT.

**and [for] the errors of the people:** ... and the people's sins of ignorance, —ADAM ... and for the sins committed in ignorance by the people, —WLMS.

**9:7.** Entrance into the inner sanctum, the Holy of Holies, the place where the cherubim overshadowed the lid of the ark as guardians of the Shekinah glory that symbolized Jehovah's presence, was limited to only the high priest. Ordinary priests were not allowed to enter. Moreover, even the high priest was rigidly restricted in his access to the innermost sanctuary of the tabernacle. He could not march into the presence of the Lord anytime he felt like it. Only once a year, on the 10th of Tishri—the Day of Atonement—was the high priest allowed to enter "the holiest of all" (verse 3). (See Exodus 30:10 and Leviticus 16:34.) Before he could do so, he had to observe the sacrificial rites and ceremonies outlined in Leviticus 16. Blood had to be shed for him and the people.

8. **The Holy Ghost this signifying:** ... making it evident, —CNDT ... teaching by this, —MNTG ... was showing, —WLMS.

**that the way into the holiest of all was not yet made manifest:** ... there was as yet no access to the real sanctuary, —WLMS ... the way into the sanctuary was not revealed, —TNT ... was not made plain, —KLGS ... had not yet been opened, —SEB ... has not yet been disclosed, —MNTG.

**while as the first tabernacle was yet standing:** ... as long as the outside tent and its Old Way of Worship were being used, —NLTG ... while the old covenant was still in force, —NORL ... while the outer tent was still in existence, —WLMS, —TNT.

**9:8.** The word "this" refers back to the description in the previous verses of the once a year ministry of the high priest on the Day of Atonement. The ceremonies performed on that day were intended by the Holy Spirit to indicate that entrance into the very presence of God in heaven was severely limited. As long as the Levitical rites and ceremonies were practiced, access into the presence of God "was not yet made manifest." Men were not free to come to God at any time; they were restricted to the once a year, symbolic rites.

9. **Which [was] a figure for the time then present:** ... This is symbolic for today, —SEB ... for it is

merely a symbol of the present time, –*WLMS*...pointing to the present, –*TNT*.

**in which were offered both gifts and sacrifices:** ... it means, –*TNT*... in connection with which gifts and sacrifices are repeatedly offered, –*WLMS*.

**that could not make him that did the service perfect:** ...they cannot make ... the worshiper perfect, –*WLMS*.

**as pertaining to the conscience:** . . . inwardly, –*TNT*.

**9:9.** Controversy has arisen over the meaning of the first statement in this verse. The King James translators saw the Levitical rites as a "figure" (*parabolē*) for the Children of Israel. They indicated this by translating the participle *enestēkota* as "the time then present." It is possible that this refers to the time period after the establishment of the new covenant, *the time now present.* If it has the first meaning, the text would be saying that the ceremonies had a parabolic significance to those who practiced them. If it is the latter, then it means that they have parabolic significance to those under the new covenant. This latter sense seems to fit the argument better. The thrust of the rest of the verse is clear: the rites performed by the high priest under the Levitical system had no power to consecrate or cleanse the consciences of the high priest or those he represented.

God meant conscience to serve man well. It is not self-imposed or man would rid himself of it. To the Romans Paul wrote, "I lie not, my conscience also bearing me witness in the Holy Ghost" (Romans 9:1). Still, it can become defiled (1 Corinthians 8:7) as well as seared and leave one insensible (1 Timothy 4:2). Since to a degree it is fallible, "Let your conscience be your guide" is not a safe maxim. It needs cleansing; God has provided for that through Jesus.

**10.** **[Which stood] only in meats and drinks, and divers washings:** . . . since they were concerned only with food and drink and ritual washings of different kinds, –*TNT*... since they deal only with food and drink and various washings, –*WLMS*.

**and carnal ordinances:** ...that is, with mere material regulations, –*WLMS*... and other things to do with the body, –*NLTG*... external ceremonies, –*TCNT*.

**imposed [on them] until the time of reformation:** . . . which are in force only until the time of setting things straight, –*WLMS* ... until the time of correction, –*ADAM*... the time set up for making all things right, –*KLGS*... when things would be set right, –*BECK*.

**9:10.** Indeed, the Levitical offerings were limited to physical, external practices. They were only intended to be temporary. The extent of their power dealt "only" with food (*brōmasin*) and drink, and various ritual ablutions, and other regulations

(*dikaiōmasin*) for the physical body (*sarkos*). These are mentioned in contrast to the conscience (9:9). The final phrase appears nowhere else in the Septuagint or New Testament. In its context, however, *mechri kairou diorthōseōs* can only refer to the fact that these regulations were set up temporarily until the divinely appointed time of the reconstruction of things under the new covenant.

**11.** **But Christ being come an high priest of good things to come:** ...when Christ came as the High Priest of good things that have already taken place, –*WLMS*.

**by a greater and more perfect tabernacle:** ...He went by way of that greater and more perfect tent of worship, –*WLMS*...through the Superior and more Perfect Tabernacle, –*WADE*.

**not made with hands:** ...reared by, –*WADE*...not made by human hands, –*WLMS*.

**that is to say, not of this building:** . . . I mean, no part of, –*WADE* ... not of this material creation, –*MNTG* ... not belonging to this physical creation, –*NORL*...not a part of this world, –*SEB*...not a part of our created world, –*BECK*.

**9:11.** This verse begins a sentence which is not completed until verse 12. It expressly declares the result of the Son's high priestly ministry is the completion of eternal redemption. Since Christ has been placed in the office of High Priest, not on earth as Aaron but as a Melchizedekian priest in the genuine sanctuary of heaven (9:24), He has inaugurated the "good things" promised by the new covenant. They are no longer future ("things to come"). The sanctuary in which He performs His priestly ministry is not part of the physical creation ("this building") nor is it something which like the Levitical tabernacle was constructed by human effort, "made with hands" (cf. Acts 7:44-49).

**12.** **Neither by the blood of goats and calves: but by his own blood he entered in:** ...with the accompaniment ... of His own Blood, –*WADE*...with His own blood He ... went into, –*WLMS*.

**once into the holy place:** ...once for all ...the real sanctuary, –*WLMS*.

**having obtained eternal redemption [for us]:** . . . and pay a price that frees us forever, –*BECK* . . . and secured our eternal redemption, –*WLMS* . . . eternal deliverance, –*TNT* . . . everlasting forgiveness, –*SEB*.

**9:12.** The comparison pointing out the superiority of Christ the Son's priestly offering is continued in this verse. He did not offer the blood of animals in His sacrifice. Rather, by His very own blood, the blood of the Son, described in verses 11-14, He entered into the holy sanctuary—heaven itself. And He did not do this year after year; He did it only "once." So powerful was His blood that it effected an everlasting redemption from the curse of sin.

**13. For if the blood of bulls and of goats:**
**and the ashes of an heifer sprinkling the unclean:** ... sprinkling those who are ceremonially unclean, —WLMS ... the latter being sprinkled on those who have incurred physical defilement, —WADE ... of polluted persons, —ADAM ... the contaminated, —CNDT.
**sanctifieth to the purifying of the flesh:** ... is hallowing to the cleanness of, —CNDT ... were sufficient to make the body pure again, —NORL ... become sanctifying agencies for effecting ceremonial purification, —WADE ... purifies them with physical cleansing, —WLMS ... and free them from ritual uncleanness, —TNT.

**9:13.** The sacrifices of animals under the old covenant were not useless. After all, they were appointed by God. The sacrifices commanded to be performed annually on the Day of Atonement (Leviticus 16:14-16) and the ceremonies in which the ashes of a sacrificed heifer were mixed with water and sprinkled by the priest upon those ceremonially unclean (Numbers 19:2,17-19) provided sanctification, that is, ritual cleansing for the external, physical body ("flesh").

The point is not that these sacrifices had no power whatsoever, but that their power was restricted and small in contrast to the power displayed in the single sacrifice of the Lord Jesus Christ. The argument then is from the smaller to the greater, from the weaker to the more powerful. If these earthly sacrifices had earthly consequences, then the sacrifice of the Son offered in heaven has heavenly, eternal consequences.

**14. How much more shall the blood of Christ:** ... more effectively, —WADE ... of the Anointed one, —WLSN.
**who through the eternal Spirit:** ... Who by means of, —ADAM ... eternal in its potency, —WADE.
**offered himself without spot to God:** ... He gave Himself as a perfect gift to God, —NLTG ... offers Himself flawless to God, —CNDT ... a spotless offering to God, —WLMS.
**purge your conscience from dead works:** ... purify your consciences, —WLMS ... cleanse your conscience, —MNTG ... from dead human efforts, —SEB.
**to serve the living God?:** ... the ever-living, —WLMS.

**9:14.** By a rhetorical question then, the inference is drawn concerning the superiority of the Son's sacrifice. To the degree that His blood is superior, to that same degree His sacrifice is more powerful in its effects. Christ, the Messiah, offered himself to God the Father as a perfect, unblemished sacrifice, for He was sinless (4:15). His sacrifice was not passive. The animals in the Old Testament were in every sense victims, but Jesus voluntarily laid

down His life for the sheep (John 10:17,18), indicating the greatness of His love. He was a victor!

This tremendous sacrifice was accomplished through the agency of the "eternal Spirit." Interpreters have disputed the exact meaning of this phrase. Many take it as a reference to some ministry of the Holy Spirit to Jesus during His crucifixion. Others see it as a reference to Jesus' eternal nature in His sonship as Second Person of the Trinity. The Greek phrase *dia pneumatos aiōniou* has no article with it and literally means "through eternal spirit." Since the argument is for the superior effects of Christ's sacrifice on the basis of His personal superiorities, it seems best to understand this as a reference to the indissoluble life inherent in the eternal Son (7:16).

By means of offering His eternal life, i.e., "Spirit," He was able to cleanse (*kathariei*) the believer's conscience from "dead works," that is, reliance on one's own efforts to obtain merit before God (6:1). They are freed from bondage to this guilt.

**15. And for this cause he is the mediator of the new testament:** ... So, because of this, —ADAM ... this is why, —WLMS ... he is a go-between, —KLGS.
**that by means of death, for the redemption:** ... in order that, after He had suffered death for securing redemption, —WLMS ... was the price to set them free from sin, —SEB ... He paid the ransom to free people, —BECK.
**of the transgressions [that were] under the first testament:** ... from the offenses committed under the first covenant, —WLMS.
**they which are called might receive:** ... those who had been invited to share it might obtain, —WLMS.
**the promise of eternal inheritance:**

**9:15.** Because Jesus Christ is the Son of God, His blood is superior to the blood of animals and makes the new covenant superior to the old. A superior sacrifice was needed to establish a superior covenant. His death made Him the Mediator (*mesitēs*) of the new covenant. Generally, the term *mesitēs* is taken in the sense of go-between, but in this context as well as those of 8:6 and 12:24 it may be interpreted as referring to Jesus as a surety or guarantee of the new covenant. Because His blood is superior to that of animals, He was able to become the surety for God's new and superior covenant.

Interpreters dispute the use of the term *diathēkēs* ("testament") in 9:15-18. Some say it means "will" in all these uses. Others say it means "covenant." Most recent interpreters think there is a play upon both meanings of the word. In the Septuagint and in one instance in Aristophanes' comedy *Birds* (414 B.C.), it is used of a compact between two parties, one of whom clearly dominates and fixes the terms of agreement. In the Septuagint it refers to God's "treaties" or covenants with men. By the time the New Testament was written, however, the term *suntheke* was generally used by the Greeks to describe contracts, and *diatheke* was universally used to speak of a man's last will and testament.

The blood of animals could not bring salvation; the shedding of the Son's blood did. It made possible "the redemption of the transgressions" of those who sinned under the Mosaic law. Because of Christ's sacrifice it was possible for them to receive the eternal inheritance which they had been promised in the covenant God made with their forefather Abraham. By linking the discussion to the promise made to Abraham, the idea of an inheritance was introduced and paved the way for the play on the use of the term *diatheke* as a last will and testament.

**16. For where a testament [is]:** ... Where there is a will, *—ADAM* ... For when a will is made, *—WLMS*.

**there must also of necessity be the death of the testator:** ... That will is worthless, unless someone can prove that a person died, *—SEB* ... it is necessary that the death of him who makes it be proved, *—WLMS*.

**9:16.** An inheritance is what is passed on to the heirs after the one who promises it to them in his will dies. The heirs do not receive what is promised until the one who makes the will passes away.

**17. For a testament [is] of force after men are dead:** ... That piece of paper, *—NLTG* ... For a will goes into force only, *—NORL* ... For a will is valid only after a man is dead, *—WLMS*.

**otherwise it is of no strength at all while the testator liveth:** ... it is never valid when that which ratifies it is alive, *—WLSN* ... means nothing as long as he is alive, *—NLTG* ... as long as the one who made it is still living, *—BECK* ... is still alive, *—ADAM*.

**9:17.** The effectiveness (*bebaia*) of a will is dependent upon the death of the one who made it. The promise is not carried out while he is alive. Although it is not expressly stated here, the imagery points to Jesus as the testator who made the promise to Abraham and who activated it by His own death.

**18. Whereupon neither the first [testament] was dedicated without blood:** ... That is why, *—TNT* ... As a matter of fact, *—NOLI* ... Consequently, *—WADE* ... It was for this very reason, *—BRCL* ... the first Agreement of God's will was not put into force, *—PHLP* ... neither the former was renewed without blood, *—FNTN* ... neither was the first testament inaugurated without blood, *—WUST* ... not even the

first covenant was ratified without the use of blood, *—WLMS* ... was not in effect until blood sealed it, *—SEB*.

**19. For when Moses had spoken:** ... having been repeated by, *—FNTN* ... had announced, *—BRCL* ... had been communicated ... by Moses, *—WADE* ... had been proclaimed by Moses, *—TNT* ... had promulgated, *—NOLI*.

**every precept to all the people according to the law:** ... had given all the rules of the law, *—BB* ... every regulation in the law ... to all the people, *—WLMS* ... told the people of every command, *—PHLP* ... every commandment comprised in the Law, *—WADE*.

**he took the blood of calves and of goats:** ... of the sacrificed calves, *—NOLI* ... young oxen, *—BB*.

**with water, and scarlet wool, and hyssop:** ... together with the water, *—WADE* ... crimson wool, and a bunch of, *—WLMS* ... red wool, *—BB*.

**and sprinkled both the book and all the people:** ... put it on the book itself, *—BB* ... the Lawbook, *—WADE* ... both the scroll itself and the entire people, *—CNDT* ... the book containing the law and all the people, *—WLMS*.

**9:18, 19.** The necessity of a death in the carrying out of any settlement based upon a divine *diatheke* is illustrated by the procedures used when God established the first covenant, that is, the Mosaic covenant, with the Children of Israel at Sinai. The record found in Exodus 24:5-8 is clear. When the Lord inaugurated (*enkekainistai*) the Mosaic covenant, animals were sacrificed, and their blood was used in the ceremonies and rites accompanying the ratification of the compact.

To speak vividly, in type, of the death of Christ which was to come, Jehovah instructed Moses that animals must lose their lives at the institution of His first covenant with Israel. To stand in solemn assembly and watch them die for their sins, knowing they had done no wrong, must have had a sobering effect on the worshipers. They may have wept as eyes focused on the cutting of each creature's throat while a priest caught his blood in an appropriate container. Exodus says, "Moses took half of the blood, and put it in basins; and half of the blood he sprinkled on the altar" (Exodus 24:6). It was a dramatic picture of redemption.

Silence settled over the congregation of Israel as Moses read from the book of the old covenant. Then the great leader of God's people placed the scroll in a conspicuous place and sprinkled some of the blood from the bowl on it. The rest of the second half of the blood Moses used in a ceremony one would have to experience to sense its full impact. Scripture says, "And Moses took the blood, and sprinkled it on the people, and said, Behold the blood of the covenant, which the Lord hath made with you concerning all these words" (Exodus 24:8). Understandably, those present responded, "All that the Lord hath said will we do, and be obedient" (Exodus 24:7).

**20. Saying, This [is] the blood of the testament:** . . . declaring This is the Blood making binding the Covenant, *—WADE* . . . This blood seals the agreement, *—SEB* . . . is the sign of the agreement, *—BB* . . . that ratifies the covenant, *—WLMS.*

**which God hath enjoined unto you:** . . . that God commanded you to obey, *—SEB* . . . commanded me to make with you, *—WLMS* . . . has prescribed for you, *—NORL* . . . ordered you to keep, *—ADAM* . . . which God has concluded with you, *—FNTN* . . . which God makes for you, *—PHLP.*

**9:20.** The description of the inauguration of the Mosaic covenant given by the writer was not a word-for-word or step-by-step quotation from the Old Testament account. The basic purpose in alluding to the inauguration of the Mosaic covenant seems to be found in the words "the blood of the testament." They come directly from Exodus 24:8 which uses the word "covenant." They form the proof of the argument. When God establishes a covenant (*diathēkē*), blood must be shed. The inspired writer links the establishing of the first covenant with the new covenant by combining the words of Exodus 24:8 with words spoken by our Lord Jesus Christ when He was about to inaugurate the new covenant: "This" and "which God hath enjoined unto you." Compare Hebrews 9:20 with Mark 14:24; Matthew 26:28; Luke 22:20; 1 Corinthians 11:25. The word "this" (*touto*) appears in all the records of Jesus' establishment of the Lord's Supper. The other words are a paraphrase of Exodus 24:8.

**21. Moreover he sprinkled with blood:** . . . In the same way, *—NLTG.*

**both the tabernacle, and all the vessels of the ministry:** . . . the tent and all the utensils of the priestly service, *—WLMS* . . . and all the vessels of worship, *—ADAM* . . . all the vessels of service, *—MNTG* . . . and all the tools for service, *—KLGS* . . . All the utensils of the public service, *—WLSN* . . . utensils used in divine worship, *—NORL.*

**9:21.** This verse moves beyond the inauguration of the Mosaic covenant to describe events that occurred later: the consecration of the tabernacle and its sacred vessels. No specific references are cited. The emphasis is on the place of sacrificial blood in the rites associated with the Mosaic law. By divine commandment blood was pervasive in the observance of the old covenant.

**22. And almost all things are by the law purged with blood:** . . . under the law, *—WLMS* . . . purified by Blood, *—WLSN.*

**and without shedding of blood is no remission:** . . . and without an Effusion of Blood no

Forgiveness takes place, *—WLSN* . . . there is not forgiveness of sins, *—ADAM* . . . Sins are not forgiven unless blood is given, *—NLTG* . . . no sins are forgiven, *—BECK* . . . no forgiveness is granted, *—WLMS* . . . is coming no pardon, *—CNDT* . . . no forgiveness was to be obtained, *—TCNT.*

**9:22.** Two more pieces of evidence are here presented for the contention concerning the preeminence of blood sacrifice under the old covenant. The use of blood sacrifice in ceremonial rites of cleansing and in sacrifices for the ceremonial remission of sin is cited. In almost all cases of ritual cleansing of ceremonially defiled persons and objects a blood sacrifice was commanded.

Scholars point out three exceptions to this law: (1) Poor people were allowed to bring a meal offering for their sin offering (Leviticus 5:11); (2) Metal weapons taken as the spoils of war were to be cleansed by fire (Numbers 31:50); (3) When the nation of Israel was cleansed after the rebellion of Korah, incense is mentioned but not blood sacrifice (Numbers 16:46). Otherwise, all instances of cleansing involved animal sacrifice of some kind.

The second evidence, found in Leviticus 17:11, says the Lord has given sacrificial blood to make atonement for human lives. There may be ritual cleansing that is bloodless, but there can be no forgiveness of sin without sacrificial bloodshed. These sacrifices typified the death of Jesus, the Lamb of God, who gave His life for the whole world.

**23. [It was] therefore necessary:** . . . on the one hand, *—WLMS.*

**that the patterns of things in the heavens:** . . . that the copies of the heavenly things, *—MNTG* . . . the copies of the original things in heaven, *—WLMS* . . . But the highest things needed, *—KLGS.*

**should be purified with these:** . . . by these rites, *—NORL* . . . with such sacrifices, *—WLMS.*

**but the heavenly things themselves with better sacrifices than these:** . . . the original things themselves in heaven, *—WLMS* . . . required nobler sacrifices, *—MNTG.*

**9:23.** Moses only copied the tabernacle and its furnishings after the heavenly articles revealed to him on Mount Sinai; therefore, it was appropriate for the sacrifices offered on these earthly altars to be sheep and bulls and goats. The ceremonial cleansing of the Law only cleansed earthly and physical things. Heaven needed a sacrifice that was better.

**24. For Christ is not entered into the holy places made with hands:** ... a sanctuary made by human hands, —WLMS.

**[which are] the figures of the true:** ... and just a copy of the real thing, —BECK ... that is a picture of, —ADAM ... representations of, —CNDT.

**but into heaven itself:** ... it was into heaven itself that He went, —WLMS.

**now to appear in the presence of God for us:** ... on our behalf, —ADAM.

**9:24.** That the heavenly realities shown to Moses on Mount Sinai needed to be cleansed with better sacrifices than the blood of bulls and goats was demonstrated by the ascension of Jesus Christ into heaven itself. He is seated in the heavens at the right hand of God the Father. It is there that He makes priestly intercession for His people. He did not enter into the Holy of Holies here on earth. He did not deal with the earthly figures and copies. He had to do with the genuine articles. His high priestly ministry takes place in "heaven itself." Moreover, what He does in heaven is "to appear in the presence of God for us." And He is doing it "now." So the contrast with the ministry and sacrifices of the Aaronic high priesthood advances. Not animals, but the Son; not on earth in a tent, but in heaven in the very presence of God.

**25. Nor yet that he should offer himself often:** ... Nor has He done so for the purpose of offering himself in sacrifice frequently, —WADE ... offer Himself repeatedly, —ADAM ... has not given Himself many times, —NLTG ... He did not have to make an offering of Himself again and again, —NORL ... not to sacrifice Himself over and over again, —BECK.

**as the high priest entereth into the holy place every year:** ... enters the sanctuary, —TNT.

**with blood of others:** ... with an offering of, —TNT ... with blood that is not his own, —WLMS, —WADE.

**9:25.** Another element of contrast is that Jesus did not have to offer himself as a sacrifice on more than one occasion. The high priests of the Levitical order were commanded by the Lord to enter into the sanctuary once every year (Leviticus 16). Furthermore, this annual sacrifice did not involve the sacrifice of themselves; they instead offered the blood shed by other victims, the animals previously mentioned. In every way this epistle proves that the work and sacrifice of God's Son, Jesus Christ the Lord, is definitely superior to those of the old covenant.

**26. For then must he often have suffered:** ... if that had been the case, He would have had to suffer over and over again, —WLMS ... seeing that otherwise Christ would have had to suffer death repeatedly, —WADE.

**since the foundation of the world:** ... from the time of the creation, —NORL ... from the beginning of the universe, —KLGS.

**but now once:** ... as it is, once, —WLMS ... for all time, —NLTG.

**in the end of the world hath he appeared:** ... He has manifested Himself once for all at the Consummation of the World's successive Ages, —WADE ... He has appeared, —ADAM ... at the perfect completion of the ages, —KLGS ... at the end of the ages, —MNTG ... at a Completion of the Ages, —WLSN ... he has been revealed, —TNT.

**to put away sin by the sacrifice of himself:** ... get rid of sin, —BECK ... that sin may be set aside, —TNT ... to abolish sin through the sacrifice of Himself, —WADE.

**9:26.** If Jesus had been on the same level as the Levitical priests, it would have been necessary for Him to have suffered many times "since the foundation of the world." This statement is a bit puzzling and, in the end, mind-boggling. Since the Son is also the Creator, He was also available at the foundation of the world. Yet this does not seem to be the intended meaning. The argument is the value of Christ's self-sacrifice contrasted to the value of the animal sacrifices required by the Mosaic law. Obviously, the self-sacrifice by its very nature could only be performed once. If it had only the same power as the annual sacrifices, it would have had to be repeated over and over from the beginning of time to equal the value of the animal sacrifices.

This, however, has not been the case. Because He is the eternal Son of God, Jesus accomplished more than all of the sacrificed animals by sacrificing himself only once. In Him the Father has spoken finally "in these last days" (1:2). His single sacrifice has ushered in "the end of the world" (literally the Greek says "the end of the ages"). He has by His atonement begun the final age of human history. By offering himself, He has accomplished what all of the animal sacrifices failed to do: the annulment (*athetēsin*) of sin. For as Horatius Bonar declares in his hymn, "Richer blood has flow'd from nobler veins to purge the soul from guilt and cleanse the reddest stains."

**27. And as it is appointed unto men once to die:** ... Indeed, just as men must die but once, —WLMS ... Men are destined once, —NORL ... inasmuch as the destiny in store for men is to die only once, —WADE.

**but after this the judgment:** ... they face judgment, —ADAM ... be judged, —WLMS.

**9:27.** Since Jesus has "put away sin," there remains no more need for sacrifice. He does not need to sacrifice himself over and over again, and believers do not need to continue to offer blood sacrifices. The ritual sacrifices of the Mosaic system served God's intended purpose. The old covenant was "ready to vanish away" (8:13). Shortly after this epistle was written, the animal sacrifices of Judaism ceased with the destruction of the Jerusalem temple in A.D. 70. (The Jews did offer sacrifices on the ruins of the temple for a short while until the Romans stopped them.) Christ died once for all, and the next item on His agenda is "the judgment." But He will be the Judge.

**28. So Christ:** ...so too, —TNT.
**was once offered to bear the sins of many:** ...once for all to take away the sins, —WLMS.
**and unto them that look for him:** ...those who are eagerly waiting for Him, —WLMS . . . to those who are awaiting him, —TNT.
**shall he appear the second time without sin:** ...again He will appear, without having anything to do with sin, —WLMS . . . not as a sin-bearer, —NORL . . . not to deal with sin, —TNT . . . no longer burdened by human sin, —WADE.
**unto salvation:** ...but to bring salvation to, —TNT . . . to bring them final salvation, —WLMS . . . for the accomplishment of their Salvation, —WADE.

**9:28.** So Jesus Christ, God's Son, was offered once in death. And what a death it was: a substitutionary death. The words used here are graphic. He was offered "to bear the sins of many." God placed upon Him "the sins of many." He carried away, bore the burden, and removed (*anenenkein*) sins for the many. The sins of all who will believe were laid on Him. He has borne the penalty for sin (i.e., for the many of those who believe), and they do not have to look forward to judgment. Instead, believers, those who look for Him, discover that for them Jesus will "appear the second time without sin unto salvation." By His one sacrifice, He has removed believers' sins forever. When He returns He will not come as a sacrifice, nor will He come to condemn and remind believers of their sins; He will come to bring what He promised: the inheritance secured and guaranteed by His atoning death—the believers' eternal salvation.

## Chapter 10

**1. For the law having a shadow of good things to come:** ...since the law cast only a shadow of the blessings to come, —WLMS . . . is like a picture, —NLTG . . . only a shadow of the benefits in store for the godly, —NORL . . . having only a dim outline of the good things in the future, —BECK . . . since it provides only an outline of, —WADE . . . It only foreshadows blessings that are to come, —TNT.
**[and] not the very image of the things:** ...and not a perfect reproduction of the Reality of those Blessings, —WADE . . . is not identical with actual realities,

—TNT . . . and not their very substance, —MNTG . . . did not possess the reality itself of those blessings, —WLMS.
**can never with those sacrifices:** ...by a repetition of the same sacrifices, —WADE.
**which they offered year by year continually:** ...by a constant repetition of the same sacrifices, —TNT . . . repeated endlessly year after year, —BECK . . . that are perpetually offered, —WLMS.
**make the comers thereunto perfect:** ...make worshippers perfect, —TNT . . . make perfect those who come to worship, —WLMS . . . can never . . . render perfect those who approach to worship, —WADE.

**10:1.** In the first four verses of chapter 10, the argument for the superiority of Jesus' once-for-all sacrifice is emphasized by the references to the inadequacies of the Levitical sacrifices. Added to the reiteration of points made previously, fresh insights are given.

First of all, the inspired writer put the two covenants in their proper relationship. The new was portrayed as "the very image of the things" (*autēn tēn eikona tōn pragmatōn*); that is, it is the reality, the embodiment of the real thing. The old, the Mosaic law, was but the shadow cast by the new covenant. In the Law there was only the rough outline of the new covenant but not all its colors and details. The new covenant was also called "good things to come." This emphasized its quality as "good" and underscored the fact that it brought into existence things that did not exist under the old covenant.

The chief point of contrast was made in regard to the sacrificial system enacted by the Mosaic law. The phrase "those sacrifices" refers to the animal sacrifices mentioned in chapter 9, particularly those offered annually on the 10th of Tishri, the Day of Atonement. They were inadequate because they could not perfect those who offered them.

**2. For then would they not have ceased to be offered?:** ...otherwise, would not such sacrifices (I ask) have ceased to be presented, —WADE . . . If that were possible, the sacrifices would no longer be offered, —TNT.
**because that the worshippers once purged:** ...because those who offered them, having once been purified, —WLMS.
**should have had no more conscience of sins:** ...They would not feel guilty, —SEB . . . would have had no further consciousness, —WLMS . . . and would no longer have a sense of guilt, —TNT.

**10:2.** The inadequacy of the Levitical sacrifices is obvious. They did not deal with sin in any final sense. The fact that they had to be offered over and over again on an annual basis is proof of this contention. If they had been effective in a final sense, they would not have been repeated year after year. Having made this point clear, the writer then proceeded to identify further the nature of their inadequacy. If those who offered sacrifices under the Levitical system had actually been once for all (*hapax*) purified (*kekatharmenous*), literally had been cleansed and remained cleansed of their sins, they would not still have had any awareness of their sinful guilt before God. It is clear, however, that they were continually aware of their guilt before God because their consciousness of guilt forced them to keep on offering animal sacrifices, not only on Yom Kippur, the Day of Atonement, but on various occasions between the annual Day of Atonement.

3. **But in those [sacrifices:** . . . in fact the opposite happens, *–TNT* . . . On the other hand, through these sacrifices, *–WLMS.*
**there is] a remembrance again [made] of sins every year:** . . . there is given a real reminder of their sins, *–WLMS* . . . only serve to remind people every year, *–TNT.*
4. **For [it is] not possible that the blood of bulls and of goats:** . . . the blood . . . is unable to, *–WLMS.*
**should take away sins:** . . . to be eliminating sins, *–CNDT* . . . can never take sins away, *–TNT.*

**10:3, 4.** Verse 3 comments on the effect of the sacrifices offered in the annual ceremonies of Yom Kippur. Unlike the new covenant's Lord's Supper, the sacrifices of the Day of Atonement did not provide a remembrance of forgiveness. Instead they provoked remembrance of sins committed. They were not designed to instill gratitude; they served to create guilt feelings.

The reason the animal sacrifices of the Levitical system created guilt feelings was inherent in their very nature. They did not possess the power necessary to remove the moral guilt of mankind's offense against God.

5. **Wherefore when he cometh into the world, he saith:** . . . Consequently, *–ADAM* . . . It is for this reason, *–MNTG* . . . This is why, when Christ was coming . . . he said to God, *–TNT.*
**Sacrifice and offering thou wouldest not:** . . . It was not a sacrifice and an offering that you wanted, *–TNT.*
**but a body hast thou prepared me:** . . . Yet a body dost Thou adapt to Me, *–CNDT.*
6. **In burnt offerings and [sacrifices] for sin thou hast had no pleasure:** . . . You weren't pleased with, *–ADAM* . . . No, you never cared for, *–NORL* . . . you never took delight, *–WLMS* . . . You found no pleasure in, *–TNT.*
7. **Then said I, Lo, I come:** . . . See, I have come, *–WLMS* . . . Here I am, O God, *–TNT.*
**(in the volume of the book it is written of me,):** . . . the writing in the scroll, *–BECK* . . . In the roll of, *–ADAM* . . . In the summary of the scroll, *–CNDT* . . . in

the first part of the scroll, *–SEB* . . . just as the Scripture writes about me, *–WLMS.*
**to do thy will, O God:** . . . what you want, *–BECK.*

**10:5-7.** Much controversial discussion has been generated by the quotation of Psalm 40:6-8 in Hebrews 10:5-7. It revolves around three questions: (1) how the psalm is used, (2) the meaning of the psalm; (3) the differences between the Hebrew of the Masoretic text and the Greek language of the Septuagint and that which is used in the Epistle to the Hebrews. The differences can be explained by recognizing the Greek as a paraphrase rather than a direct quotation of the Hebrew. In the English version of the Old Testament, Psalm 40:6 reads, "Mine ears hast thou opened," while Hebrews 10:5 says, "A body hast thou prepared me." Most contemporary commentators think the quotation in Hebrews substitutes "body" for "ears" as a whole for the part. However, this interpreter feels both Psalm 40 and Hebrews refer to the custom described in Exodus 21:6 and Deuteronomy 15:17.

In those verses there is a description of a slave who has been set free by his master but who wants to continue to serve him out of love. As a sign of his voluntary servitude, he has his ears digged or pierced. This fits the argument of Hebrews at this point quite well. It also explains the paraphrase and its use of "body" for "ears." In Koine Greek the word *body* is often used as a synonym for *slave* (see M-M, "soma"). The point is that God did not prefer an animal sacrifice; He preferred the voluntary, loving servitude of Israel's obedience as a living sacrifice as opposed to empty ritual sacrifices.

The paraphrased citation of Psalm 40:6-8 is offered as an illustration of the attitude exhibited by Jesus Christ. In His incarnation He displayed the attitude which the Lord sought in Israel. He wanted the sons of Abraham to demonstrate voluntary obedience. In laying down His life as an atonement for the sins of mankind, Jesus displayed the attitude of voluntary servitude exhibited in Psalm 40:6-8, Exodus 21:1-6, and Deuteronomy 15:12-17. This willingness to serve God voluntarily by sacrificing himself (along with His superiority as God's unique, one-of-a-kind Son) makes Jesus' sacrifice superior to the sacrifice of bulls and goats.

This attitude was exemplified by Jesus after His entrance into the world as a man, for the word *hēkō* means that He had already entered into the world when He echoed the words of Psalm 40:7 (*hēkō* could be translated "I have come").

The phrase "volume of the book" refers to the requirements of the law of God revealed in the Mosaic covenant. It does not refer to the external rituals and ceremonies of the Law but to its spiritual demands upon the Children of Israel. In Psalm 40:8 David made this clear by adding, "Thy law is within my heart," words reminiscent of the promise of the new covenant (Jeremiah 31:33). Jesus came voluntarily to meet the requirements of the Law's precepts and of its messianic prophecies. Most specifically He came to die as the Seed of the woman who crushes Satan's head (Genesis 3:15).

**8. Above when he said:** . . . First He says, —BECK . . . Although at first, —WLMS.

**Sacrifice and offering and burnt offerings and [offering] for sin:** . . . and sin-offerings, —TNT . . . offerings for sin which are prescribed by the Law, —NOLI.

**thou wouldest not, neither hadst pleasure [therein]:** . . . neither desires nor takes pleasure in, —NOLI . . . you neither wish nor enjoy, —KLGS . . . You did not want or find pleasure in, —TNT . . . You were not pleased with these things, —SEB . . . You never wished or took delight in, —WLMS.

**which are offered by the law:** . . . all of which are repeatedly offered in accordance with the law, —WLMS . . . which are prescribed by the Law, —NOLI.

**10:8.** Parts of the quotation from Psalm 40 were repeated for the purpose of clearly contrasting the old covenant with the new covenant. As in the previous citation, the emphasis falls upon the Lord's lack of pleasure in the ceremonial sacrifice of animals as offerings for sin. God had required them, but not for the purposes Israel had supposed. As noted already (10:3), they reminded Israel of sin without removing the guilt of sin.

**9. Then said he, Lo, I come to do thy will, O God:** . . . He afterward said, —WLMS . . . Here I am, O God, ready to do, —TNT . . . I have come to do what You want, —SEB.

**He taketh away the first, that he may establish the second:** . . . He is despatching the first, —CNDT . . . He negatives the first kind of sacrifice in order to substitute the second, —WADE . . . So Jesus Christ abolishes the first . . . to establish the second, —TNT . . . He is taking away the first to let the second take its place, —WLMS . . . The former statement is set aside to be replaced by the latter, —TCNT . . . God took away the first group of sacrifices, —SEB.

**10:9.** But when the Son entered into the human condition saying, "Lo, I come to do thy will, O God," the situation was changed dramatically. That which existed under the old Mosaic law began to pass away; in its place the Lord established the new covenant prophesied by Jeremiah and Ezekiel. Willing to carry out the will of God, the Son of God, Jesus Christ, replaced the Mosaic covenant established at Mount Sinai and set up the new covenant instituted at Mount Calvary.

**10. By the which will we are sanctified:** . . . In accordance with this divine will, —NOLI . . . it is by the fulfilment of this Will of God that we have been

Hallowed, —WADE . . . It is by this will of God that we are consecrated, —WLMS . . . we are cleansed and set apart for his service, —TNT.

**through the offering of the body of Jesus Christ once [for all]:** . . . once, and once only, —ADAM . . . Because he did what God wanted him to do and offered his body, —TNT . . . by the sacrifice of the body, —NOLI.

**10:10.** This verse specifically identifies the will of God and clearly sets forth the results of the Son's obedience to that will. In no uncertain terms, the death of Jesus Christ is described as "the offering of the body of Jesus Christ once for all." These words highlight the voluntary, sacrificial nature of His death and underscore its superiority and permanence. He offered one sacrifice, and its consequences are permanent. The phrase *hēgiasmenoi esmen* is also emphatic. It means that by Christ's death believers have been and remain sanctified.

**11. And every priest standeth daily ministering:** . . . Every other priest stands officiating, —WLMS . . . is celebrating his service daily, —NOLI . . . Every Jewish priest stands, —TNT . . . day after day, —MNTG.

**and offering oftentimes the same sacrifices:** . . . offering repeatedly, —TNT . . . over and over again, —WLMS.

**which can never take away sins:** . . . although they are unable to take away our sins, —WLMS . . . which can never actually take away sins, —NORL . . . can never remove, —TNT.

**10:11.** Verses 11-18 summarize the arguments concerning the superiority of the Son's high priestly sacrifice. The contrasts given in this passage have all been stated before either directly or by implication. The priests of the Levitical order stood. Jesus is seated in heaven. Their service was daily, but Jesus sacrificed only once. They repeatedly offered the same kind of animal sacrifices which did not even possess the remotest possibility of taking away sin and its consequences.

**12. But this man:** . . . this One, —WLMS . . . this priest, —TNT.

**after he had offered one sacrifice for sins for ever:** . . . having offered One Enduring Sacrifice, —WLSN . . . for sins for all time, —TNT . . . offering for all time, —ADAM . . . once for all and for all time, —WLMS . . . availing in perpetuity, —WADE.

**sat down on the right hand of God:** . . . sat down in perpetuity on, —WUST . . . has taken His seat, —WADE . . . took His seat at God's right hand, —WLMS.

**10:12.** In contrast to the descendants of Levi and Aaron, "this man," the Son of God, offered one sacrifice—himself. It took care of sins forever. When His sacrifice was completed, He had no need of offering another. It could not be repeated; it did not need to be. It was not offered to the Lord in some earthly sanctuary. Rather, His sacrificed and resurrected body ascended to the heavenly sanctuary where He is sitting at the right hand of the Father in honor of His finished work.

**13. From henceforth expecting:** ... Since then He has been awaiting the day, —*NORL* ... waiting henceforward, —*WADE* ... from that time waiting, —*WLMS.*
**till his enemies be made his footstool:** ... may be placed underneath his feet, —*WLSN* ... made the footstool of His feet, —*WLMS,* —*WADE.*

**10:13.** These words allude to the often quoted beginning of Psalm 110. Jesus is seated at God's right hand because the Father has asked Him to sit there until all of His enemies have been subdued. So Jesus, who is an eternal Melchizedekian priest, sits in heaven, eagerly looking forward to the time when His enemies shall become "his footstool." Then He shall be not only the believers' High Priest but King of kings and Lord of lords.

**14. For by one offering he hath perfected for ever:** ... by that one sacrifice, —*WLMS* ... by one single offering, —*TNT* ... He has brought to completion forever, —*WUST* ... he has permanently perfected, —*WLSN* ... perfected in perpetuity, —*WADE.*
**them that are sanctified:** ... those who are consecrated to Him, —*WLMS* ... those who are being set apart, —*ADAM* ... *those* whom he cleanses and sets apart for his service, —*TNT* ... for Godlike living, —*NLTG.*

**10:14.** Jesus is able to sit in the heavenly sanctuary because there is nothing more for Him to do in regard to making offering for human sin. He could truly announce, "It is finished!" By His one sacrifice He accomplished what all the offerings of lambs, bulls, and goats sacrificed under the Mosaic law could never accomplish. The Law and its sacrifices could not perfect those who worshiped under their aegis (7:19; 9:9; 10:1), but the solitary offering of the Son has perpetually perfected believers, that is, *tous hagiazomenous* (the ones who are being sanctified). The work of Christ's one sacrifice continues to sanctify believers; there is no need for a repetition of His sacrifice.

**15. [Whereof] the Holy Ghost also is a witness to us:** ... assures us of this, —*BECK* ... gives us the testimony, —*WLMS.*
**for after that he had said before:** ... First he says, —*TNT* ... after saying, —*WLMS* ... after affirming, —*WADE.*

**10:15.** To close the doctrinal argument for the superiority of the atoning sacrifice of Jesus Christ, the inspired writer returned to Jeremiah 31 and the prophecy of the new covenant. The comments in this verse are dependent upon the sequential order of the statements made in Jeremiah 31. First, it is noted that Jeremiah's words were divinely inspired. The Holy Spirit was their ultimate Author.

Second, the words quoted in verse 16 (Jeremiah 31:33) were written before the words alluded to in verse 17 (Jeremiah 31:34). The point made in this verse is that the Spirit promised *both* the internalization of the Law *and* the forgiveness of sin.

**16. This [is] the covenant that I will make with them:** ... to which I will commit myself, —*WADE.*
**after those days, saith the Lord:** ... In those last days, —*WLMS.*
**I will put my laws into their hearts:** ... I will impress my laws on their hearts, —*WADE.*
**and in their minds will I write them:** ... And will inscribe them, —*MNTG* ... upon their mind, —*WADE.*

**10:16.** Jeremiah 31:33 was cited to remind believers that the divinely instituted new covenant promised to internalize God's laws, and that God himself promised to write His laws in the minds and hearts of His people sometime after their Babylonian captivity.

**17. And their sins and iniquities:** ... Then he adds, —*NOLI* ... and lawless ways, —*NORL* ... and their lawless acts, —*TNT* ... and deeds of wrong, —*WLMS* ... and their offences, —*WADE.*
**will I remember no more:** ... I will never, never any more recall, —*WLMS* ... I will forget, —*NOLI* ... I will keep no more memory of, —*BB.*

**10:17.** Third, there is the reminder that in the institution of the same covenant God promised to forgive Israel's sins and never to remember them (Jeremiah 31:34).

**18. Now where remission of these [is:** ... Consequently, when sins are remitted by God, —*NOLI* ... When these people are forgiven, —*SEB* ... where there is a pardon of these, —*CNDT* ... forgiveness of these, —*WADE* ... Where these have been forgiven, —*TNT.*
**there is] no more offering for sin:** ... no more need of an offering, —*WLMS* ... there is no longer any need for, —*TNT* ... there is no longer any room for any sacrifice for sin, —*NOLI.*

**10:18.** Finally, there is the conclusion of the whole argument as far as Jewish Christians' continuance in the practices of the old covenant is concerned. If sins have been remitted, there is no further need for any sacrifices. The Old Testament sacrifices continued as a reminder of sin (10:3). Christ's one self-sacrifice has taken care of sins forever. Therefore, there is now no more need for sacrifice.

The implication is that the ritual sacrifices offered in the temple at that time were unnecessary and would soon cease. They were on the brink of extinction (8:13). Why should Jewish Christians persist in offering animal sacrifices? Christ put an end to animal sacrifices for sins. The stirring melody and opening words of Horatius Bonar's magnificent hymn comes to mind: "No blood, no altar now, the Sacrifice is o'er! No flame, no smoke ascends on high, the lamb is slain no more."

**19. Having therefore, brethren:** ... Since then, my brothers, *—WLMS* ... So now, brothers, *—TNT* ... being able, *—BB.*
**boldness to enter into the holiest by the blood of Jesus:** ... to go into the holy place without fear, *—BB* ... we can boldly enter the sanctuary through the blood of Jesus, *—NOLI* ... we may with complete freedom pass through the curtain into the sanctuary, *—TNT* ... we have free access to the real sanctuary, *—WLMS* ... we have a cheerful confidence, *—MNTG* ... we have ... confidence for approaching, through the Blood of Jesus, the entry into the Holy of Holies, *—WADE.*

**10:19.** This verse begins the final section of the epistle—an extended section of application and warning which basically argues that since Christ is a superior messenger who mediates a superior message through His superior high priestly atonement, believers ought to do the following things lest they apostatize and suffer damnation. The first of a series of exhortations begins in verse 22. Verses 19-21 summarize the grounds upon which the entreaties are founded.

Christians are in a different position than Israel was under the old covenant. The access which they had to God was extremely limited. Their high priestly representative could enter into the "holiest" only once a year, and his efforts achieved only ceremonial results. Believers live under the new covenant, however, because of the blood shed by Jesus the Son, and they have access to the inner sanctum of heaven itself. They may enter into the very presence of God with "boldness" (*parrhē-sian*). This word has connotations of freedom, frankness, openness, and confidence. Believers have been set free from fear. They recognize that the divine Judge is their Father, who loves and forgives and comes to their rescue because of Jesus' shed blood.

**20. By a new and living way, which he hath consecrated for us:** ... an entry which, *—WADE* ... that He inaugurated for us, *—ADAM* ... He opened for us, *—BECK, —WLMS.*
**through the veil, that is to say, his flesh:** ... through the curtain, *—ADAM* ... the Rent Curtain ... which separated Him from the immediate Presence of God and which was rent on the Cross, *—WADE* ... He opened the curtain, which was His own body, *—NLTG* ... His physical nature, *—WLMS* ... by means of his own body, *—TNT.*

**10:20.** Access into the presence of God through the atoning death of Jesus is called "a new and living way." As once a year the veil opened to admit

the Levitical high priest, so the veil of His flesh has opened to provide access to God at any time.

**21. And [having] an high priest over the house of God:** ... and since in Him we have a Great Priest, *—WLMS* ... over God's household, *—TNT.*

**10:21.** Furthermore, the One who serves as High Priest is not an underling called to *serve in* the house of God (3:1-6). Indeed, He is the Son who by right of His divine inheritance *rules over* the house of God.

**22. Let us draw near with a true heart in full assurance of faith:** ... let us continue to draw near ... with sincere hearts and perfect faith, *—WLMS* ... let us now approach Him ... with unwavering faith, *—NORL* ... approach God with our guilty consciences cleansed, *—TNT* ... sincere in our hearts and convinced in our faith, *—BECK.*
**having our hearts sprinkled from an evil conscience:** ... with our hearts cleansed from the sense of sin, *—WLMS* ... to rid us of, *—ADAM* ... should be made pure from a guilty conscience, *—SEB.*
**and our bodies washed with pure water:** ... bathed in clean water, *—CNDT, —WLMS.*

**10:22.** There is no more need to offer animal sacrifices. The believers' sins are forgiven permanently. Jesus' blood allows them to enter into God's presence at any time. Jesus is God's sovereign soon-to-be-ruling Son. Christians should live lives that are characterized by three activities: prayer (10:22), perseverance (10:23), and encouragement(10:24,25). These three activities are enjoined on Christians by three cohortative subjunctive verb forms which appear in our English text following the words "let us." By the verb *proserchōmetha*, believers are entreated to keep on coming near to God in prayer. A believers' life should be consistently characterized by doing this. This is a high privilege. Unlike those under the Levitical system whose high priestly representatives could only have direct contact with God once a year on the annual Day of Atonement, believers through Jesus Christ have access to God at any time.

Christians should make the most of their unique opportunity, because they have a cleansing that is both ceremonial (in the ordinance of baptism) and actual (in the removal of the moral guilt of their consciences). Since they are thus cleansed by Christ's blood, they can come to God with a genuinely open heart, with no pretense, absolutely confident that He will welcome them and hear them because they have trusted His Son Jesus Christ as their atoning sacrifice.

**23. Let us hold fast the profession of [our] faith without wavering:** ... keep on holding to the hope that we profess, —WLMS... the hope which we have professed and never turn away from it, —TNT... without swaying, —ADAM... never in doubt, —NORL... without twisting, —KLGS.

**(for he [is] faithful that promised;):**... and He is dependable, —SEB... God has given his promise and he can be trusted, —TNT.

**10:23.** Christians are enjoined by the verb *katechōmen* to keep on possessing the confession of their *elpidos aklinē*, that is, to persevere in maintaining their unwavering hope. Jesus who suffered and died for them is now seated at the right hand of God the Father. They do not yet see Him in all His power and kingdom glory (2:8), but they look for Him to return as King of kings and Lord of lords. They must persist in this hope because God is trustworthy. They can rely upon Him to keep His Word. He cannot lie, and He has sworn by oath that Jesus is an eternal Melchizedekian priest-king.

**24. And let us consider one another:**... We must try to think, —TNT.

**to provoke unto love and to good works:**... let us take one another into our thoughts with the aim of stimulating mutual love and good deeds, —WADE... how we can stimulate one another, —BECK... so as to arouse one another, —NORL.... as to stimulate one another to love, —WLMS... and do good, —TNT.

**25. Not forsaking the assembling of ourselves together:**...We must not abandon our practice of meeting together, —ADAM... Do not quit meeting together, —SEB... Let us not neglect meeting together, —KLGS... stop neglecting our meeting, —WLMS.

**as the manner of some [is]:**... according as the custom of some is, —CNDT... as some have the habit, —KLGS... as some do, —WLMS.

**but exhorting [one another]:**... but rather let us encourage one another, —NORL.

**and so much the more, as ye see the day approaching:**... as you behold, —MNTG... as you see the day drawing near, —ADAM... the day of His return coming near, —NLTG.

**10:24, 25.** Christians are exhorted by the verb *katanoōmen* to be constantly aware of one another and the need to stimulate one another to loving behavior and good works. The word translated "provoke" is *paroxusmon*. It refers to sharp contention and argument, suggesting that believers must sharply confront one another with their responsibility. If such admonition is to take place, Christians must meet together on a regular basis. A Christian cannot profit from the gifts of others unless he fellowships with them. Apparently those receiving this epistle were withdrawing from the fellowship of the whole congregation in favor of their miniflock. In the light of the approaching day (a reference to the return of the Lord in

judgment with some implications for the nearness of Jerusalem's destruction), the gathering of all was urged.

**26. For if we sin wilfully:**... If we deliberately go on sinning, —ADAM... if we should voluntarily sin, —WLSN... if we go willfully sinning, —WLMS.

**after that we have received the knowledge of the truth:**

**there remaineth no more sacrifice for sins:**... there is no sacrifice left to be offered for our sins, —WLMS.

**10:26.** Having strongly admonished believers to prayer, perseverance, and provocation, the inspired writer now added a stern warning. If believers fail to appropriate the blessings of the new covenant, they are placing themselves in jeopardy of a worse fate than the fate of unbelieving Israelites in the wilderness. If Christians sin willfully (*hekousiōs* means "freely, without coercion") after having experienced the full knowledge of the truth concerning the superiority and finality of revelation and redemption in God's Son Jesus Christ our Lord, then there is no other sacrifice available for the forgiveness of sins.

This verse has been misused to buttress the teaching that there is no forgiveness of deliberate sins committed after one has become a Christian. The writer is dealing with apostasy, not backsliding. In the context it was addressed to Hebrew Christians who were in danger of apostatizing from their profession of Jesus as Messiah. The inspired writer assured them that if they turned aside from Calvary's atoning sacrifice and returned to Judaism, they would not be able to procure forgiveness of sins and have free access to heaven. Christ's sacrifice is the only one that removes sin and secures access to the Throne of Grace. Through Him we may come to the Father in prayer.

**27. But a certain fearful looking for of judgment:**... but only a fearful anticipation, —ADAM... only a terrible waiting for judgment, —SEB... only a terrifying prospect of judgment, —WLMS... expectation of, —MNTG.

**and fiery indignation, which shall devour the adversaries:**... the hot fires of hell will burn up those who work against God, —NLTG... and a fiery hatred which eventually will consume those who hate Christ, —NORL... which is going to devour God's enemies, —WLMS.

**10:27.** For those who deliberately reject Christ's atoning sacrifice only judgment remains. It is vividly described as *phobera*, terrifying, "fiery indignation," a judgment which is destructive because it literally eats up (*esthiein*) those who are against Jesus Christ.

**28. He that despised Moses' law:**...Anyone repudiating Moses' law, −CNDT...Any one who set at naught, −MNTG...Anyone who violates, −BECK.
**died without mercy under two or three witnesses:**

**10:28.** As in the previous warnings issued (2:2,3; 3:7-4:11), comparisons and contrasts between the judgments under the Mosaic law and those under the new covenant are drawn. Those who ignored and broke the Law given through Moses found no mercy when their trespasses were verified by the testimony of two or three eyewitnesses (Deuteronomy 17:2-6). The crime specifically mentioned in the Deuteronomy 17 passage is that of idolatry. Turning aside from the Son of God and His atoning sacrifice is certainly a form of idolatry. It is turning from the true God to a powerless substitute.

**29. Of how much sorer punishment, suppose ye:**...How much worse do you think, −ADAM...how much Worse Punishment, −WLSN.
**shall he be thought worthy:**... will he be adjudged to deserve, −WADE...a man will deserve, −TNT...one deserves, −WLMS.
**who hath trodden under foot the Son of God:**...who have trampled, −TCNT.
**and hath counted the blood of the covenant, wherewith he was sanctified, an unholy thing:**...treated the blood of the covenant as of no account—the very blood which had cleansed him, −TNT...and has attached no sacred significance to the Blood, −WADE...counts as a common thing, −WLMS...and has profaned that covenant blood, −MNTG...by which he is hallowed contaminating, −CNDT...is worth nothing? −NLTG.
**and hath done despite unto the Spirit of grace?:**...and outrages, −CNDT...and have heaped insults on the gracious Spirit, −TCNT...insults the Spirit of love? −BECK...the Spirit that grants God's unmerited favor? −WLMS.

**10:29.** In the light of the severity of punishment given to idolators under the old covenant, how much greater punishment will God mete out to those who have trampled God's Son under their feet? Moses was only a servant, but Jesus is the Son and heir over the house of God (3:1-6). To apostatize is to treat the blood of Jesus, the blood of the new covenant, as a common thing (*koinon*, defiled or profane, something which everyone has access to; for example, a threshold). Finally, it is to treat the Holy Spirit, "the Spirit of grace," in an insolent and arrogant manner (*enubrisas*). The implication of the question "shall he be thought worthy," which is embodied in the verb *axiōthēsetai*, is: what magnitude of punishment fits the crime? When Christ put forth this same idea in parable form to His enemies, He said the Father would

"miserably destroy those wicked men" (Matthew 21:41).

**30. For we know him that hath said:**
**Vengeance [belongeth] unto me, I will recompense, saith the Lord:**...To me is justice, −KLGS...I have the right to punish, −BECK...Revenge belongs to Me, −SEB...Retribution is Mine, −WLSN...I will repay, −ADAM...I will pay back! −WLMS...To me belongs the infliction, −WADE.
**And again, The Lord shall judge his people:**...will be His people's judge, −WLMS...will pass judgment, −WADE.

**10:30.** The answer to the question of verse 29 is evident. The God of the old and new covenants has not changed. The God of the new covenant is the same God who spoke through Moses and the prophets. In warning Israel about the consequences of disobeying the Mosaic law by turning aside to worship idols, He told them that vengeance and repayment were His prerogatives (Deuteronomy 32:35). He also declared that He would judge Israel for their departure from the Sinaitic covenant (Deuteronomy 32:36).

**31. [It is] a fearful thing to fall into the hands of the living God:**...The very worst thing that can happen to a man, −NLTG...a fearful experience, −ADAM...It is a terrifying thing, −WLMS.

**10:31.** To be caught in the web of God's active judgment is a terrifying prospect. (The word *phoberon*, "terrifying," is used also in verse 27.) But that is the only fate that awaits those who turn aside from the new covenant blessings procured by the blood of God's beloved Son, rejecting His sacrifice.

Some people find it difficult to believe a loving God would send judgment. But the One who is the very essence of love is also holy and righteous. When the limits of His mercy have been exceeded, nothing is left but to receive His just judgment. His hands of blessing are beyond description, but when His hands are used in judgment, the expression "fearful thing" is most appropriate.

**32. But call to remembrance the former days, in which:**...Remember what happened in those earlier days, −TNT...you must continue to remember, −WLMS.
**after ye were illuminated:**...when first you received the light, −WLMS...after having been enlightened, −MNTG...after you had received the light of God, −TNT.
**ye endured a great fight of afflictions:**...You suffered much, −NLTG...You won a great contest of suffering, −SEB...endured so great a struggle with persecution, −WLMS...Though it was a hard and painful struggle, you remained steadfast, −TNT.

**10:32.** In the face of the prospect of fiery judgment from the hands of the living God, Hebrew believers were asked to reflect on the time when they were initiated into the Christian community after having been enlightened concerning the claims of Jesus the Son. Their profession of faith embroiled them in a great struggle (*athlēsin*). In that struggle they were subjected to many different kinds of suffering. Intense as that experience was, they had managed to endure it to the end. In their early experience of suffering for the sake of Jesus Christ they had borne up well under pressure.

33. **Partly, whilst ye were made a gazing-stock:**... You were not only made, −*TNT*... by being exposed as a public spectacle, −*WLMS*.

**both by reproaches and afflictions:**... to insults and violent sufferings, −*WLMS*.

**and partly, whilst ye became companions of them that were so used:**... having become Joint-participators, −*WLSN*... you deliberately shared the lot of others who were being treated in this way, −*TNT*... by showing yourselves ready to share with those who were living in this condition, −*WLMS*.

**10:33.** The description of the Hebrew Christians' first subjection to religious persecution is now made even more specific. They had become a spectacle for others to mock. The verb *theatrizomenoi* carries connotations of being abused in public. It is further qualified by the terms *thlipsesin* (which refers to being narrowly confined by pressure) and *oneidismois* ("abuse, reproach, insult, and shame"). They had experienced this suffering because they had become *koinōnoi* ("partners") with those who were already being persecuted in his way. The implication is that those who evangelized them were already being persecuted and that by responding to their message these believers were also receiving similar public castigation.

34. **For ye had compassion of me in my bonds:** ... For you took pity on the prisoners, −*NORL*... you showed sympathy with those who were in prison, −*WLMS*... You suffered with those in prison, −*TNT*.

**and took joyfully the spoiling of your goods:** ... you took it cheerfully, −*BECK*... and cheerfully accepted the plundering of your goods, −*NORL*... submitted to the violent seizure of your property, −*WLMS*... the confiscation, −*MNTG*... the seizure of your possessions, −*WLSN*.

**knowing in yourselves that ye have in heaven:**... because you knew you owned, −*SEB*... you possessed, −*TNT*.

**a better and an enduring substance:** ... have better and permanent property, −*CNDT*... better things which last, −*SEB*... even lasting possessions, −*MNTG*... one that was lasting, −*WLMS*.

**10:34.** At this juncture the inspired writer revealed that he himself was in prison at the time of their conversion. The implication is that he had something to do with their conversion also. The thrust of his purpose in asking them to recall the time of their conversion and the persecution which followed it is then made clear. He wished them to remember two things: (1) the way in which they responded to that persecution; (2) the knowledge which helped them to respond in such a manner. They had sympathized with him in his imprisonment, and they had experienced joy when robbed of their possessions. They had been able to do this because they possessed in heaven something which was both better and more permanent than what they lost.

Their patience in persecution was a great thing; enduring it without murmuring, still greater; their rejoicing in it greatest of all.

35. **Cast not away therefore your confidence:** ... So then, don't throw away, −*ADAM*... do not fling away, −*MNTG*... Then don't lose your courage, −*BECK*... you must never give up your confident courage, −*WLMS*... your trust, −*NLTG*.

**which hath great recompense of reward:**... for it holds a rich reward for you, −*WLMS*.

36. **For ye have need of patience:**.. .You need to have endurance, −*SEB*.

**that, after ye have done the will of God:**... to carry out the will of God, −*WLMS*.

**ye might receive the promise:** ... you may obtain, −*ADAM*... the blessing, −*WLMS*.

**10:35, 36.** Since the atoning sacrifice of Jesus Christ provided them with confidence (*parrhēsian*, this is the same "boldness" referred to in 10:19), they were admonished not to throw it away because it had the prospect, not of fiery judgment, but of great reward. Those who trust in the Son will enter into eternal rest as recipients of God's eternal salvation. Such an inheritance should not be abandoned. Nothing should be done to jeopardize it.

In order for believers to be certain about receiving this "great recompense of reward," one thing is needed: patience. *Hupomonēs* describes one particular aspect of patience, the quality of endurance. It speaks about enduring the afflictions and trials until those troubles are ended. Patient endurance to the end will receive the reward. Believers must respond to the current crises in their lives in the same way they reacted when they first professed faith in the Son of God (10:32-34). With the eyes of faith, they must look beyond their present circumstances to the glory of their future inheritance. Just as Jesus came to do the Father's will and knew it would involve Him in suffering and death, so believers discover that for them God's will also involves suffering. When they have "done the will of God," however, they will actually go beyond their knowledge of God's promise and receive it for themselves in their personal experience.

**37.** **For yet a little while:** . . . It is just a short time, —ADAM.

**and he that shall come will come, and will not tarry:** . . . God will come. He will not be late, —SEB . . . will be arriving and not delaying, —CNDT . . . will not put it off, —KLGS.

**38.** **Now the just shall live by faith:** . . . Meantime my righteous servant will live on by faith', —WLMS.

**but if [any man] draw back, my soul shall have no pleasure in him:** . . . If anyone turns back, —NLTG . . . And if he shrinks back, —NORL . . . I won't be pleased with him, —ADAM . . . has no delight in him, —WLMS.

**10:37, 38.** To fix his admonition firmly in their minds, the inspired writer turned to another quotation from the Old Testament. With the words "For yet a little while," he alluded to Isaiah 26:20 which has a parallel context to that of Hebrews. In both cases believing Jews were suffering hardship and being encouraged to wait patiently for the fulfillment of God's promise.

The rest of the quotation comes from the Septuagint text of Habakkuk 2:3,4. Just as the Lord told Habakkuk not to worry about the Babylonians escaping judgment but to trust Him and wait for the coming of the messianic fulfillment, so verses 37 and 38 admonish and encourage believers.

They may think the Son's coming has been delayed, but this is not so: His return is certain and will take place according to God's schedule. If a believer turns back (*huposteilētai* is here used with the meaning "apostatize"), God is displeased. The one who apostatizes, i.e., abandons his profession of faith in the Son to return to Judaism and its animal sacrifices, will not receive the promised inheritance in glory.

**39.** **But we are not of them who draw back unto perdition:** . . . of those shrinking back, —CNDT . . . not of a disposition to draw back so as to perish, —WLMS . . . into destruction, —ADAM . . . to their Ruin, —TCNT.

**but of them that believe to the saving of the soul:** . . . has faith that leads to the preservation of the souls, —ADAM . . . unto the gaining of the soul, —MNTG . . . in order to a Preservation of Life, —WLSN.

**10:39.** After firmly issuing the fourth warning (10:26-38), the inspired writer again indicated that the majority of those to whom the epistle was written were not included in the group who actually would apostatize. By using the pronoun

"we" throughout this section, he included himself with them (9:24; 10:10,22-24,26,30). They were not such as those who turned back to destruction. The word translated "perdition" is *apōleian*; it occurs 17 other places in the New Testament where it is translated as "damnation," "destruction," "perdition," "pernicious way," "waste," and "damnable." The end of those who turn back from faith in Jesus Christ the Son is eternal damnation. The inspired writer, however, indicated that he and those to whom the epistle was written were true believers.

## Chapter 11

**1.** **Now faith is the substance of things hoped for:** . . . is a Basis of things hoped for, —WLSN . . . is the real part of things, —KLGS . . . is the assurance of, —WLMS . . . is a solidly grounded certainty about, —ADAM . . . is the title-deed, —MNTG . . . is an assumption of what is being expected, —CNDT . . . is confidence in the realization of one's hopes, —TCNT.

**the evidence of things not seen:** . . . the proof of the reality of the things, —WLMS . . . It is being sure of what we cannot see, —NLTG . . . It is the proof we do not see, —KLGS . . . a conviction regarding things which are not yet visible, —TCNT.

**11:1.** The danger about which the inspired writer warned springs from the sin of unbelief. The antidote for this dread poison is faith. First of all a brief description of faith is given in verses 1-3. The word translated "substance" is *hupostasis*; it could also be translated "essence" or "confidence." It is modified by the phrase "of things hoped for." Its best meaning seems to be that faith is that which *underlies* the inheritance which believers expect to receive. Secondly, the writer declares that faith is the evidence which gives proof of the existence of the unseen world.

**2.** **For by it the elders obtained a good report:** . . . It was for their faith that our ancestors won God's approval, —TNT . . . The elders had this kind of faith long ago. It pleased God, —SEB . . . the Ancients were attested, —WLSN . . . The men of long ago won approval for their faith, —BECK.

**3.** **Through faith we understand:**
**that the worlds were framed by the word of God:** . . . that the universe, —ADAM . . . was fashioned by, —MNTG . . . the worlds were created, beautifully co-ordinated, and now exist, —WLMS . . . made by God's word, —TNT.

**so that things which are seen were not made of things which do appear:** . . . the things that we see did not evolve out of existing matter, —NORL . . . so that what we see came into being from what we cannot see, —TNT . . . did not develop out of mere matter, —WLMS . . . not made out of what is visible, —MNTG . . . that are apparent to us, —ADAM.

**11:2, 3.** In these verses two more characteristics of faith are given:

(1) It is the means by which the elders (the Old Testament heroes of faith discussed in this chapter) gained their favorable testimonies.

(2) It is the means by which believers are able to understand the world which is seen and to grasp its relationship to the unseen world.

**4. By faith Abel offered unto God a more excellent sacrifice than Cain:** ... brought to God a better sacrifice, *−BECK* ... a greater sacrifice, *−TNT* ... more acceptable to God than Cain did, *−WLMS.*
**by which he obtained witness that he was righteous:** ... by it he was approved as an upright man, *−WLMS.*
**God testifying of his gifts:** ... by accepting his gifts, *−MNTG* ... showed approval of, *−TNT* ... since God approved him for the offering he made, *−WLMS.*
**and by it he being dead yet speaketh:** ... by it he still continues to speak, though dead, *−WLMS.*

**11:4.** Verses 4-7 present faith as the means by which Abel, Enoch, and Noah were declared righteous. This brief section emphasizes the necessity of faith as the means of pleasing God and stresses the resultant righteousness displayed in the lives of these three men of faith.

As to Abel, many have inferred that his sacrifice was acceptable because it was a blood offering. He brought an offering from his flock while Cain presented one from his field.

However, this difference in the two sacrifices stands out as only one among others. Further, God later permitted even a sin offering that was bloodless. The poorest of the poor could sacrifice a handful of flour for his sins and find favor with the Lord. As God explained to Moses, "But if he be not able to bring two turtledoves, or two young pigeons, then he that sinned shall bring for his offering the tenth part of an ephah of fine flour for a sin offering" (Leviticus 5:11). Recognizing this, the writer of Hebrews declared, "And almost all things are by the law purged with blood" (9:22). Under the inspiration of the Spirit, though, he went on to rightly place the emphasis on blood sacrifice. He wrote, "And without shedding of blood is no remission" (ibid.).

The offerings of Cain and Abel also contained qualitative differences. *Pleiona*, translated "more excellent," simply means "more" in some qualitative sense. Genesis indicates Abel carefully selected "of the firstlings of his flock and of the fat thereof" (Genesis 4:4) while Cain simply "brought of the fruit of the ground" whatever his hand happened to find (Genesis 4:3). Still, the most important difference between Cain and Abel in their worship to God concerns the element of faith. Hebrews makes clear what Genesis only implies. The significant things is Abel offered his sacrifice

"by faith." That faith demonstrated itself as he presented a first-class blood offering. The Lord counted his faith as righteousness. The inspired record of this incident still testifies to Abel's life of faith. That life serves as an example for others of all times.

**5. By faith Enoch was translated:** ... Faith caused Enoch to be taken up, *−NORL* ... was transferred, *−CNDT* ... was removed to another place, *−ADAM* ... was transplanted from earth, *−WLMS* ... was taken up from the earth, *−NLTG* ... was taken away, *−TNT.*
**that he should not see death:** ... without dying, *−NLTG* ... so that he did not experience dying, *−WLMS.*
**and was not found, because God had translated him:** ... no remains of him could anywhere be found, *−WADE* ... had conveyed him, *−WUST* ... because God had taken him to heaven, *−SEB* ... taken him away, *−TNT.*
**for before his translation he had this testimony:** ... We know that this was due to his faith, *−TNT* ... before he was transplanted from earth evidence was given him, *−WLMS* ... stands in the Scriptures his good record, *−WADE.*
**that he pleased God:** ... he was well-pleasing to God, *−BB.*

**11:5.** These comments on Enoch follow the Septuagint, not the Hebrew Masoretic text. In Genesis 5:24 the English Old Testament translated from the Hebrew reads: "He was not; for God took him." The Septuagint says Enoch "was not found, because God had translated him" and "he pleased God." Neither text expressly mentions faith. Since faith is the only means by which sinful men can please God, Enoch must have lived a life characterized by faith, because the Scriptures declare his life was pleasing to God. Both the Hebrew text and the Septuagint indicate that God did not take Enoch in death but by a miraculous removal from this life which changed him from a mortal man to an immortal. Since the Bible says "Enoch walked with God" (Genesis 5:22,24), it is clear that he was a man of faith. God's Word testifies to Enoch's God-pleasing obedience. Habakkuk 2:4 provides the link between faith and God's being pleased with men (Hebrews 10:38).

The Bible never separates faith from obedience. Indeed, Paul wrote of the "obedience of faith" (Romans 16:26). When a sinner is genuinely converted, his changed lifestyle indicates the reality of his faith. Then through the years his confidence in God causes him to walk softly before the Lord in obedience to His commandments. He stands in awe at Jesus' words, "Why call ye me, Lord, Lord, and do not the things which I say?" (Luke 6:46). Keeping the commandments of God gives him "the answer of a good conscience toward God" (1 Peter 3:21).

Enoch's experience fit this pattern. Commenting on it Taylor wrote, "God's Spirit witnessed that all was well; no last-minute adjustments were needed. Here again the part faith played was indirect—faith, in itself, cannot translate anybody to heaven. But Enoch's walk with God was by faith, and the translation was God's sovereign reward for his faithfulness in so walking" (*Beacon Bible Commentary*, p. 140).

**6. But without faith [it is] impossible to please [him]:** ... it is not possible to be well-pleasing to him, —*BB*.

**for he that cometh to God must believe:** ...anyone who approaches God must believe, —*WLMS*...who comes near to God, —*NOLI*... First, to believe, —*NORL*...must have faith, —*TNT*.

**that he is:** ...that He exists, —*ADAM*, —*TNT*... that there is a God, —*WLMS*.

**and [that] he is a rewarder of them that diligently seek him:** ... and proves a Rewarder, —*WADE*...that He gives rewards to all who earnestly try to find Him, —*WLMS*... of those who are seeking Him out, —*CNDT*...to the one who keeps on looking for Him, —*NLTG*... to the people who are searching for Him, —*SEB*.

**11:6.** This verse enunciates the principle drawn from the Septuagint version of Habakkuk 2:4 ("the just shall live by faith") and is demonstrated by the Biblical account of Enoch's life. Apart from faith no man can receive God's approval. Whoever comes to God, i.e., prays and worships, must do two things if his worship is to be accepted as were the sacrifice of Abel and the life of Enoch. They must believe *both* that God exists *and* that He rewards those who earnestly seek Him. The Hebrews to whom this epistle was written believed in God's existence, but some of them apparently were wondering whether or not Jesus was truly the Messiah and if He was going to return to set up the kingdom of God. They were assured that if they continued to walk with God, they would also obtain a testimony to their own righteousness before God. The same is true for believers today.

**7. By faith Noah:** ...Through his faith, —*WADE*.

**being warned of God of things not seen as yet:** ... having been divinely admonished, —*WLSN*...received God's warning about events which at the time belonged to the future, —*TNT*...being divinely warned about a catastrophe which was not yet within sight, —*WADE*...of the impending disaster, —*NOLI*.

**moved with fear, prepared an ark to the saving of his house:** ... proceeded conscientiously to construct an Ark for the preservation of his household, —*WADE*...He listened carefully to what God said, —*TNT*... with reverential care prepared, —*WUST*...in reverence prepared an ark for saving his

family, —*WLMS*...he built a large boat, —*NLTG*...constructs an ark, —*CNDT*.

**by the which he condemned the world:** ...and by his faith, —*WLMS*...His faith was a judgement on the world, —*TNT*.

**and became heir of the righteousness which is by faith:** ... By means of it he entered into possession of, —*TNT*... an heir of the justification that comes by faith, —*NORL*...and became possessor of the uprightness that results from faith, —*WLMS*.

**11:7.** Noah, after receiving a divine admonition (*chrēmatistheis*, used also of Moses in 8:5), responded obediently in faith out of his reverence for God (*eulabētheis*). Noah's building the ark displayed faith as a response to God's instructions. God spoke and Noah obeyed Him. His obedience was remarkable. It clearly displayed one of the main characteristics of faith described in verses 1-3. God's admonition to Noah described things which had not yet occurred, but since Noah knew and trusted God, he built the ark in the face of mockery and opposition. The absurdity of building a huge ship far from the sea in preparation for a worldwide flood daunted Noah not in the least. His trust in God informed and undergirded him. The coming deluge was not a laughing matter; it was a certainty. So it is with the second coming of Jesus Christ. The world may mock, but the King will come and all will acknowledge that He is Lord. By his faith Noah accomplished three things: (1) He delivered his family from the flood; (2) His obedience contrasted with the unbelief of his contemporaries who died in the flood; (3) He became a recipient of the by-faith righteousness of God.

**8. By faith Abraham, when he was called:** ...It was faith that enabled, —*TCNT*... on being called, —*WLMS*.

**to go out into a place which he should after receive for an inheritance, obeyed:** ...obeyed God's call to go out to a country which one day God would give him to be his own, —*TNT*...in starting off for a country which he was to receive as his own, —*WLMS*.

**and he went out, not knowing whither he went:** ...He left his home, —*NLTG*...and he did it in spite of the fact that he did not know where he was going, —*WLMS*...not having the faintest idea about where he was going, —*ADAM*.

**11:8.** The second section of Old Testament heroes begins here; 11:8-22 presents the patriarchs from Abraham to Joseph. They are all represented as pilgrim-sojourners who "all died in faith, not having received the promises" (11:13). The emphasis is upon their endurance and hope in the face of life's trials.

Most appropriately the section begins with Abraham who is the "father of all them that believe" (Romans 4:11). As in the case of Noah, Abraham's faith was demonstrated by his response to a word from the Lord. He was living in Ur, but God "called" him to leave for an unknown destination. His by-faith response was obedience. Interestingly, there is no mention of Abraham's hesitations or miscues. The emphasis is upon Abraham's long term adherence to the principle of believing and obeying God. When all is said and done, even though he was ignorant of his final destination, Abraham believed God would finally bring to pass all the things included in His promise. On the basis of this trust in God, Abraham acted. He knew by faith that the things which he could not see were realities dependent upon God's faithfulness.

**9. By faith he sojourned in the land of promise:** . . . Faith kept him there in the promised land, —NORL . . . he made his temporary home in the land that God had promised, —WLMS.

**as [in] a strange country:** . . . lived as a stranger, —BECK . . . lived as a foreigner, —SEB . . . as an alien, —MNTG . . . he settled, like a stranger in a foreign land, —TNT . . . as in an alien land, —CNDT . . . although a land inhabited by others, —WLMS.

**dwelling in tabernacles with Isaac and Jacob:** . . . living merely in tents, —WLMS . . . as Isaac and Jacob did, —TNT.

**the heirs with him of the same promise:** . . . who were to share the promise with him, —WLMS . . . to whom God had also made the same promise, —TNT.

**11:9.** Abraham did get to see the land of Canaan which the Lord had promised to give to him and his descendants, but he never actually settled there or received title deed to it as his personal possession. He traveled within its borders as a nomad. He was a foreigner; *allotrian* refers to the fact that the land where he "sojourned" was "a strange country" to him. This fact is underlined by his lifestyle: he and his family lived in tents and followed their herds. His son and grandson lived in the same manner. In the light of these facts, it is apparent that all three of these patriarchs died without actually receiving the land which had been promised to Abraham as part of his inheritance from God. Therefore, all of them were only heirs in prospect, not actual inheritors while they lived upon the earth.

**10. For he looked for a city which hath foundations:** . . . he continually looked for, —MNTG . . . he was confidently looking forward to, —WLMS . . . was waiting for the city, —TNT . . . that could not be moved, —NLTG.

**whose builder and maker [is] God:** . . . that had God for its Architect, —ADAM . . . and Constructor, —WADE . . . is the Designer and Architect, —WLSN . . . the city designed and made by, —TNT.

**11:10.** These patriarchs were richly blessed by God. They possessed vast wealth, and their family was large and powerful. They walked with the Lord and were obviously blessed by Him. Yet they did not receive all which He had promised. In spite of this they remained faithful to the Lord. Why? Since they were men of faith, they were able to gaze beyond the world which they experienced through their senses. They understood that the world in which they lived was not their ultimate home. Abraham eagerly anticipated (*exedecheto* means "to welcome, to look forward to something") something far superior to the things which he observed in the Canaan of his day. He expected a way of life (*polin* means far more than "city") that was permanently designed and created by God, the divine craftsman (*technitēs*). He expected not *high tech* but *divine tech*!

**11. Through faith also Sara herself received strength to conceive seed:** . . . also obtained power, —CNDT . . . received power, —MNTG . . . for Conception, —WLSN . . . to become pregnant, —WLMS.

**and was delivered of a child when she was past age:** . . . and actually gave birth to a child, although she was past the time of life for it, —WLMS . . . though she was unable to have children and was in any case, —TNT . . . beyond the period of her prime, —CNDT . . . though she was past the normal time of life for motherhood, —WADE.

**because she judged him faithful who had promised:** . . . because she considered Him Who promised trustworthy, —ADAM . . . she thought that He who made her the promise was to be trusted, —WLMS . . . could be trusted to redeem His promise, —WADE.

**11:11.** Abraham's wife Sarah was not exposed for her frailties (laughing at God's promise of a child or giving Hagar to Abraham so that he might have a son). She is remembered because of what she accomplished through her faith in the Lord. Her initial response to the divine declaration that she would give birth to a son in her advanced age may have been laughter, but in the end she conceived and bore Abraham the son whom God had promised. Through her act of obedience she was empowered by God to become pregnant in spite of her age and her lifelong barrenness. Her behavior flowed from her faith in God. After God had reiterated His promise to Abraham and Sarah, she considered who God was and what He had already done for them. He had always kept His promises in the past, so she trusted Him to keep this promise and by her obedience conceived and bore the miracle child Isaac.

**12. Therefore sprang there even of one:** ... and consequently from a single individual, –*WADE* ... from one man, –*WLMS*, –*TNT*.

**and him as good as dead:** ... him practically dead, –*MNTG* ... and that dead as to any prospects for offspring, –*WLMS* ... and that, too, one whose physical vigour had decayed, –*WADE*.

**[so many] as the stars of the sky in multitude:** ... there sprang descendants, –*WADE* ... came descendants as numerous as, –*TNT* ... a people as numberless as the stars in the sky, –*WLMS*.

**and as the sand which is by the sea shore innumerable:** ... as countless as the grains of sand on the seashore, –*TNT* ... that nobody can count, –*BECK*.

**11:12.** This verse emphatically stresses the astronomical results of Abraham and Sarah's trusting God for the promised son. The best way to emphasize their faith is to render a literal translation of the word order found in this verse: "Wherefore even from one man they were being born, even from one who had died in regard to such things, even as the stars of the heaven in their multitude and as the sand beside the shore of the sea, the sand innumerable!" (translation by the author). Faith in God's promises brings amazing results.

**13. These all died in faith:** ... all died victoriously as a result of their faith, –*WLMS* ... died having faith, –*SEB* ... dominated by faith, –*WUST* ... still believing, –*NORL* ... sustained by their faith, –*WADE*.

**not having received the promises:** ... although they had not yet received in full, –*NORL* ... without getting what was promised, –*BECK* ... the blessings promised, –*WLMS*.

**but having seen them afar off:** ... that is, because they really saw them in the far-off future, –*WLMS* ... but perceiving them ahead, –*CNDT* ... but they did see them from a distance, –*ADAM* ... but having seen and saluted them from a Distance, –*WLSN* ... those things were far in the future, –*SEB*.

**and were persuaded of [them], and embraced [them]:** ... and hailed them, –*MNTG* ... and welcomed them, –*WLMS*.

**and confessed that they were strangers and pilgrims on the earth:** ... They openly acknowledged, –*TNT* ... and so professed to be only foreigners and strangers here, –*WLMS* ... that they were only strangers and exiles here, –*NORL* ... who had no permanent home, –*BECK*.

**11:13.** Without exception, all of these patriarchal figures died *kata pistin* (in accordance with the standards of a life of faith) without ever having actually received the promise which God had made to Abraham (Genesis 12:1-3). They never possessed Canaan as their own property. They were blessed by God, but they never saw the greatness of the nation of Israel or the countless numbers of their descendants. Nor did they live to see the whole world blessed in the seed of Abraham: Jesus Christ, God's Son.

Yet they did have an inkling, a clue as to what was happening and what was going to happen. Dimly through the eyes of faith, although they were far, far away (*porrhōthen* means "a long way off"), they had a faint understanding of the great things God would do. And the little understanding which they had was "embraced" (*aspasamenoi* literally means "greeted") by them.

God gave them a glimmer of light, and they received it warmly and respectfully. They understood and believed that at some time in the future God was going to fulfill His spectacular promises. They had convictions; they "were persuaded" that God would in the future, as He always had done in the past, keep His promises—all of them. He was trustworthy. Thus they willingly and consciously acknowledged the truth of the old spiritual: "This world is not my home; I'm just a passin' through. My treasures are laid up somewhere beyond the blue."

**14. For they that say such things declare plainly:** ... When people say such things as that, –*TNT* ... people who make such a profession as this show, –*WLMS*.

**that they seek a country:** ... they are looking for, –*TNT* ... they seek a homeland, –*ADAM* ... they are seeking a Fatherland, –*MNTG* ... are in search of a country of their own, –*WLMS*.

**11:14.** The next three verses expatiate the theme of the patriarchal pilgrimage. Verse 14 begins with the particle *gar* ("for") which serves as an indication that the verse is designed to explain what was said in the previous verse. The people who admitted they were strangers and temporary residents on the earth revealed (*emphanizousin*) something about themselves. Their confession was an open declaration that they were searching for a fatherland (*patrida*). They felt rootless from an earthly viewpoint because they were not at home. Their roots were in heaven. That was their real home. That is where they would spend eternity.

**15. And truly, if they had been mindful of:** ... If their hearts had been in, –*BECK* ... been cherishing the memory of, –*WLMS*.

**that [country] from whence they came out:** ... the country they left, –*BECK*.

**they might have had opportunity to have returned:** ... they might have gone back, –*NLTG* ... they might have had a chance to go back, –*KLGS*.

**11:15.** The patriarchs of Israel never settled down in Canaan, but it was not because their hearts were in Mesopotamia where Abraham began his wanderings. If that had been the case— that they preferred Mesopotamia to Canaan— they had many opportunities to return. For instance, instead of going down into Egypt, they could easily and more profitably, from a purely human standpoint, have returned to the land of their forefathers and received a more hospitable welcome. To their credit it can be reported they never returned to Ur. They knew they had left in obedience to God's command. To return would be contrary to God's will.

**16. But now they desire a better [country], that is, an heavenly:**...as it is they are reaching out for, −TNT...The better country that they longed for was nothing less than heaven itself, −NORL...they were yearning for, −SEB...longing for a better homeland, −MNTG.

**wherefore God is not ashamed to be called their God:**... This is why, −WLMS...Consequently, −WADE...it is no shame to God to be named their God, −BB...was proud to be called their God, −NOLI.

**for he hath prepared for them a city:**...has prepared for them a home in heaven, −NOLI...he has made ready a town for them, −BB.

**11:16.** This verse draws a contrast between what they might have done but did not and the implications of what they actually did do. The "now" (nun) is not used in a temporal sense but in a logical sense meaning "since" or "as it is." Instead of settling in Canaan or returning to Mesopotamia, what they actually longed to do (oregontai) was to inhabit a city-state (polin, verse 10) which had a lifestyle that had come from heaven itself. They wanted something better spiritually than what they had observed in either Ur or Canaan. There was an empty longing in their lives which could only be filled with spiritual reality. Because they possessed this spiritual insight and established their values by it, God was pleased with them. He identified himself with them. He was not afraid to call himself "the God of Abraham, the God of Isaac, and the God of Jacob" when He identified himself to Moses (Exodus 3:6). He was pleased because they had been correct in looking for the heavenly city He had "prepared for them."

**17. By faith Abraham, when he was tried, offered up Isaac:**...Through his faith, −WADE...when he was put to the test, −WLMS.

**and he that had received the promises:**...he who had welcomed, −WADE.

**offered up his only begotten [son]:**...he was ready to offer up, −TNT...was prepared to offer, −WADE...was starting to offer as a sacrifice, −WLMS...the only son of his body, −BB.

**11:17.** In addition to their sojourning lifestyle there were two other important aspects of their faith: their endurance of trials and their obedience to the Word of God. The two themes are highlighted one against the other. In their pilgrim attitude, which grew out of their faith, they were confronted with hardships and tribulations, but their faith enabled them to keep their eyes on the future which God was preparing for them. With their eyes on that hope, they were able to keep their equilibrium in the midst of the shifting storms of life. God tested Abraham by asking him to sacrifice Isaac who was his monogene, his uniquely born son of the promise, and by faith Abraham proceeded in obedience.

**18. Of whom it was said:**...and though he had been told, −TNT.

**That in Isaac shall thy seed be called:**...Your descendants will come through Isaac, −ADAM, −SEB...that your posterity will be traced, −MNTG...Your posterity will arise through, −NOLI...shall there be traced a posterity that shall bear thy name, −WADE.

**11:18.** These words explain the word monogene as it is used of Isaac. In his willingness to sacrifice Isaac, Abraham was letting go of the son of God's promise. Abraham had complained to God because he feared he would die childless and that his servant Eliezer would inherit all of his possessions according to the customs of that day (Genesis 15:2,3ff.). Having an heir was so important to Abraham that he had fathered a son by Sarah's handmaiden Hagar (at Sarah's instigation). Giving up Isaac was no easy thing. God was taking away what He had promised, that which Abraham cherished the most—God's promised son (Genesis 21:12). Abraham had waited and almost given up hope that the promise would be realized. God's demand was costly.

**19. Accounting that God [was] able to raise [him] up, even from the dead:**... For he considered the fact that God was able to raise people, −WLMS...was able even to raise the dead to life, −TNT.

**from whence also he received him in a figure:**...And in a way he did get him back from the dead, −BECK...Indeed, figuratively, he received him back from death, −NOLI...and in a sense he really did receive his son back from death, −TNT...and so from the dead, in a figure, −WLMS...in a figurative sense it was from the dead that he recovered him, −WADE.

**11:19.** But Abraham's trust in the Lord was equal to the Lord's demand. The participle logisamenos indicates that Abraham thought carefully about his experiences with God and concluded that since He could make a barren Sarah give birth to a child, He also was able to resurrect Isaac after he had been sacrificed. The narrative in Genesis 22 testifies to Abraham's faith in this matter. He assured his servant that both he and Isaac would return, and he was confident that the Lord would furnish a sacrifice on the mountain

(Genesis 22:5,8). Abraham believed God could raise Isaac from the dead because Abraham had already received Isaac figuratively from the deadness of Sarah's womb.

**20. By faith Isaac blessed Jacob and Esau:** ... Through his faith, —WADE ... put his blessings, —WLMS.

**concerning things to come:** ... gave news of things to come, —BB ... even in connection with things still in the future, —WADE ... for the future, —WLMS.

**11:20.** Reliance on God's fulfillment of all which He had promised was also characteristic of Isaac. He had observed the faith of his father Abraham and had seen the faithfulness of the Lord. So, even though he did not experience the complete fulfillment of the promise in his own lifetime, he blessed Jacob and Esau concerning future blessings.

**21. By faith Jacob, when he was a dying:** ... when his end was nigh, —MNTG ... when about to die, —WLMS.

**blessed both the sons of Joseph:** ... put his blessing on each of Joseph's sons, —WLMS.

**and worshipped, [leaning] upon the top of his staff:** ... he bowed in worship, —TNT ... leaning on the top of his walking cane, —SEB.

**11:21.** Jacob, who had valued the blessing associated with the promise so much that he had schemed and cheated Esau out of his firstborn rights, also died without gaining all of God's promised blessings. Nevertheless, before he died, he passed on the blessing by skipping over his eldest son Reuben and giving the rights of the firstborn to Joseph's younger son Ephraim instead of the elder son, Manasseh (Genesis 48:1, 5, 16, 20). This follows the Septuagint account instead of the Hebrew Masoretic text's account of Genesis 48.

There was a prophetic element in Jacob's blessing upon the sons of Joseph. Even though Manasseh was older than Ephraim, Jacob placed his right hand (signifying the greater blessing) upon the head of Ephraim. It was fulfilled in their later history.

**22. By faith Joseph, when he died:** ... at the end of his life, —ADAM ... at his decease, —CNDT ... as he was dying, —NORL ... when his end was near, —BECK, —TNT ... at the closing of his life, —WLMS.

**made mention of the departing of the children of Israel:** ... referred to, —TNT ... remembered the exodus of the sons of Israel, —WUST ... made mention of the future migration of the Israelites, —WLMS.

**and gave commandment concerning his bones:** ... gave instructions, —ADAM ... and gives directions, —CNDT ... and said what was to be done

with his bones, —TNT ... as to the removal of his bones, —NORL ... what to do with his body, —WLMS.

**11:22.** Likewise, Joseph, when he passed away, exhibited the same faith in God's promises that his fathers had displayed. He was so certain the Lord would give Canaan to his descendants for their possession that he instructed them to carry his bones from Egypt so they could be buried in Canaan. By faith he looked forward to the momentous events of the Exodus by which the Lord would miraculously deliver his progeny from Egypt and mold them into the nation of Israel.

**23. By faith Moses, when he was born:** ... at his birth, —WLMS ... after his birth, —TNT.

**was hid three months of his parents:** ... the parents of Moses hid him for three months, —TNT.

**because they saw [he was] a proper child:** ... was a delightful child, —ADAM ... he was a handsome child, —NORL ... they saw he was a fine baby, —BECK ... he was a beautiful child, —WLMS ... he was a very lovely child, —TNT.

**and they were not afraid of the king's commandment:** ... they refused to respect the King's order, —TCNT ... were not afraid to disobey, —SEB ... did not fear the edict of the King, —WLSN ... the mandate of, —CNDT ... the king's decree, —MNTG.

**11:23.** At this point the account moves into the third and final section of chapter 11 from the patriarchal era to the national era. In doing so the emphasis moves from the faith of those who lived with an unfulfilled promise to the mighty deeds of faith accomplished by the heroes of Israel.

Verse 23 begins with the parents of Moses. Their faith led them to fearlessly disobey Pharaoh's edict to kill all male Hebrew infants. Moses' parents were prompted to risk the penalty for breaking the law because of the striking appearance of the baby. The word *asteion* found here also appears in the Septuagint account (Exodus 2:2) and in Stephen's narrative (Acts 7:20).

**24. By faith Moses, when he was come to years:** ... when he had grown up, —WLMS.

**refused to be called the son of Pharaoh's daughter:** ... refused to be known as, —WLMS ... to decline the title of, —TCNT.

**11:24.** The insight of Moses' parents was vindicated by Moses when he reached adulthood. Moses was raised with all the material and cultural advantages available to a member of the royal family of Egypt. He lived at a time when he himself might have become king (if the Pharaoh's daughter mentioned was Hatshepsut who ruled as Pharaoh and died childless). However, Moses possessed a true understanding of God's promise to his forefathers which enabled him by faith to deny the daughter's claims that he was her son. He had a sense of values which allowed him to reject the temptations of wealth, prestige, influence, and power offered to him by Egypt.

**25. Choosing rather to suffer affliction with the people of God:** . . . he preferred to suffer hardships, *—WLMS* . . . and preferred being mistreated, *—BECK* . . . preferring rather to be maltreated, *—CNDT* . . . having chosen for himself, *—WUST* . . . to share ill-treatment, *—MNTG* . . . to be mistreated along with God's people, *—ADAM.*

**than to enjoy the pleasures of sin for a season:** . . . than to be having sin's enjoyments temporarily, *—WUST* . . . instead of having fun doing sinful things for awhile, *—NLTG* . . . rather than to have temporary enjoyment of sinful pleasures, *—NORL.*

**11:25.** Moses could have accepted a role in the court of the king of Egypt as the Pharaoh's grandson. He could have disassociated himself completely from his Hebrew kinsmen, but he made a conscious choice not to do so. He observed the affliction and oppression of his own people and decided to identify himself with them. He did this because he knew they were "the people of God." He had heard the promises of God, and he had believed them to be true. It was out of this faith that he reacted when he saw an Egyptian abusing one of his kinsmen (Exodus 2:11,12). It was his faith that God would keep His promise to Abraham and his descendants that led Moses to an understanding of the temporary nature of the things he enjoyed in Egypt. His hope for the fulfillment of all of God's promise enabled him to endure the sufferings he experienced when he identified himself with the Hebrew people.

**26. Esteeming the reproach of Christ:** . . . He considered, *—ADAM* . . . and thought the reproach endured for the Christ, *—WLMS* . . . he thought that the stigma which attaches to the Christ, *—TCNT.*

**greater riches than the treasures in Egypt:** . . . was of greater value, *—TCNT* . . . was greater wealth than all the treasures, *—WLMS.*

**for he had respect unto the recompense of the reward:** . . . He examined the pay, *—KLGS* . . . he was looking ahead to the reward, *—ADAM, —SEB, —BECK* . . . for he fixed his eyes on the reward, *—MNTG* . . . for he was looking ahead to the promised reward, *—NORL* . . . kept his eye upon the reward, *—WLMS.*

**11:26.** Moses was not fooled by the material culture of Egypt. He saw through and beyond it. This was no small accomplishment, as anyone who has seen the King Tut exhibit in the Cairo Museum or visited the Egyptology section of the Louvre can testify. The world is still dazzled by the splendor and wealth accumulated by the royal families of Egypt. Moses was not. He took it all in and concluded that there was greater wealth available in

the abuse which he would suffer for the sake of Christ. Moses knew of the promise made to Adam and Eve (Genesis 3:15) and looked for the Christ, i.e., the Anointed One, the promised Deliverer. In the light of the eternal reward promised by the Lord, Moses was able to renounce the promises of Egyptian glory and to endure the reproach and abuse associated with the Hebrews.

**27. By faith he forsook Egypt:** . . . he abandoned Egypt, *—WUST* . . . he left Egypt, *—WLMS.*

**not fearing the wrath of the king:** . . . because he was not afraid of the king's anger, *—WLMS.*

**for he endured, as seeing him who is invisible:** . . . for he persevered, *—WLMS* . . . he "saw" the One Who is unseen, *—ADAM* . . . as though he could see Him, the unseen King, *—NORL* . . . for he understood the invisible as seen, *—KLGS.*

**11:27.** The flight of Moses from Egypt after he killed the Egyptian overseer and was seen by one of his Hebrew kinsmen is not the subject of this verse. It refers rather to the time of the Exodus when he led the Children of Israel out of Egypt in the face of the Pharaoh's protestations. Exodus 2:14 is clear. When Moses left Egypt the first time, he was afraid, but when he led the entire nation at the Exodus, he was bold and unafraid: at that time he was clearly operating by faith. Earlier, he had identified with his people out of faith, but his flight was motivated by self-interest, not faith. His fearless behavior at the time of the Exodus was the result of his newly acquired vision of faith. Having encountered the Lord in the burning bush, he was then able to endure Pharaoh's wrath because he knew the living God who is genuine but unseen.

**28. Through faith he kept the passover:** . . . he celebrated, *—BECK* . . . he instituted the Passover, *—WLMS.*

**and the sprinkling of blood:** . . . and put the blood on the doorposts, *—BECK* . . . and the pouring of blood upon, *—WLMS.*

**lest he that destroyed the firstborn should touch them:** . . . the Angel who was destroying, *—WADE* . . . so that the destroyer of the first-born might not touch them, *—WLMS* . . . to protect the firstborn of Israel from the Angel of destruction, *—NOLI* . . . would not touch the first-born of Israel, *—TNT.*

**11:28.** Moses' newly reinforced faith erased his fear of the king. He delivered the Lord's ultimatums and stood up to the king. He rallied the Hebrews, and instead of fearfully sneaking off, he boldly led Israel to freedom. By faith, he obeyed God and convinced the people to obey God in the observance of the Passover sacrifice and meal. As a result they were delivered while the Egyptians were thrown into disarray by the slaughter of their firstborn children.

**29. By faith they passed through the Red sea as by dry [land]:** . . . Through their faith . . . as over dry ground, *—WADE* . . . they crossed the Red Sea, *—TNT* . . . as though it were, *—WLMS.*

**which the Egyptians assaying to do were drowned:** . . . The Egyptians tried it, too, *—BECK* . . . who tried to do the same, *—NORL* . . . in attempting it, *—WLMS* . . . they were swallowed up, *—MNTG* . . . they were engulfed, *—WADE.*

**11:29.** Furthermore, it was by the obedience of faith that Moses led the Hebrew people to their triumph over the wily Pharaoh. Seemingly trapped between the army of Pharaoh and the waters of the Red Sea, they were again the ones who benefited from Moses' implicit trust in the Lord. In the face of almost certain disaster, they were delivered by the Lord. The wind blew, the sea parted, and under cover of the divine cloud they passed through the waters on dry ground while the pursuing army drowned. The deliverance of the Hebrew people was accomplished through the unwavering faith of Moses in the face of the powerful Egyptian army and in spite of the cringing fear of the Israelites (Exodus 14:10-12).

**30. By faith the walls of Jericho fell down:** . . . Through faith on the part of Israel, *—WADE* . . . collapsed, *—NORL.*

**after they were compassed about seven days:** . . . after the Israelites had marched round them for seven days, *—TNT* . . . they had been encircled, *—ADAM, —MNTG* . . . being surrounded on, *—CNDT* . . . after it had been surrounded, *—SEB* . . . after a siege of seven days, *—NOLI* . . . each of seven days, *—WLMS* . . . for six days, *—WADE.*

**11:30.** The same kind of deliverance continued to follow the nation of Israel whenever they trusted the Lord. Under the leadership of Joshua, they experienced the remarkable victory over Jericho in their campaign to vanquish the Canaanites and take possession of the land promised to Abraham's descendants. By the apparently foolish tactic of marching around the fortress walls of the city for 7 days in obedience to the Lord's commandment, then shouting in faith, they conquered the well-fortified city.

**31. By faith the harlot Rahab:** . . . the prostitute, *—ADAM.*

**perished not with them that believed not:** . . . escaped, *—NOLI* . . . did not die, *—KLGS* . . . was preserved from perishing along with those who had been defiant, *—WADE* . . . didn't perish with her disobedient people, *—BECK* . . . was not destroyed with the unbelievers, *—TNT* . . . with those who disobeyed God, *—WLMS.*

**when she had received the spies with peace:** . . . she had welcomed the scouts as friends, *—WLMS* . . . she had given the spies a friendly welcome, *—TNT* . . . with friendliness, *—TCNT* . . . peaceably, *—WADE.*

**11:31.** At the same time Israel was trusting God to fight for them at Jericho, within the walls of that same city lived Rahab the prostitute. She had heard of the Lord's exploits on behalf of His people. As a result, she believed that the Lord was the true God. When confronted by Joshua's spies, she cooperated with them and asked for deliverance. She is a prime example of saving faith (James 2:25) and an ancestress of both King David and the Saviour, our Lord Jesus Christ.

**32. And what shall I more say?:** . . . What further example do I need? *—NORL* . . . why should I continue to mention more? *—WLMS* . . . What more need I say? *—TNT.*

**for the time would fail me to tell of Gedeon, and [of] Barak, and [of] Samson, and [of] Jephthae:** . . . Time does not allow me, *—SEB* . . . There will not be time enough, *—BECK* . . . to discourse concerning, *—WLSN.*

**[of] David also, and Samuel, and [of] the prophets:** . . . and of the early preachers, *—NLTG.*

**11:32.** The inspired writer has already made three points concerning the results of faith, and "time" would not allow more expanded analyses of faith in the lives of individuals, so he said, "And what shall I more say?" But verses 33-40 do say more, without identifying individuals, indicating that, even after entrance into the land of Canaan, faith was necessary during the eras of the judges, kings, and prophets. It is noteworthy that Gideon, Barak, Samson, Jephthah, and David all had glaring weaknesses recorded in Scripture. But with all their faults, their faith was eventually displayed in doing what God called them to do. By faith they all accomplished great things for God.

**33. Who through faith subdued kingdoms, wrought righteousness:** . . . they won wars, *—NLTG* . . . conquered kingdoms, brought about justice, *—ADAM* . . . administered justice, *—WLMS* . . . established justice, *—NORL* . . . They did what was right, *—SEB* . . . did righteous works, *—BECK.*

**obtained promises, stopped the mouths of lions:** . . . received new promises, shut the mouths, *—WLMS.*

**11:33.** Verses 33-38 provided a summary of the great deeds of faith accomplished during the time of the judges, kings, and prophets. The descriptions offered are applicable to many Old Testament heroes, not only those named in the previous verse. Most of the judges and many of the kings of Judah and Israel would be among those who "subdued kingdoms." David would of course head the list because he forged a mighty kingdom. He and Solomon ruled over the greatest near-eastern kingdom in their time. Gideon routed the Midianites. Barak (though Deborah was the judge at that time) overthrew the Syrians. Samson harassed the Philistines, and Jephthah smote the Ammonites.

All of these victories came about through faith in the Lord. In setting up the rule of Jehovah in Israel and Judah, those who trusted the Lord performed righteous deeds by setting up equity and justice as standards in governing. Like Abraham, David was singled out by God to be the recipient of special promises: his family, throne, and kingdom were to be established forever (2 Samuel 7:14ff.). Daniel was cast into a den of lions and emerged unharmed because he trusted God to deliver him (Daniel 6). Both David (1 Samuel 17:34f.) and Samson (Judges 14:5,6) were also given power over lions.

**34. Quenched the violence of fire:** ... stopped the force of fire, –WLMS ... quenched the power of fire, –MNTG ... put out raging fires, –BECK.

**escaped the edge of the sword:** ... from dying by the sword, –WLMS.

**out of weakness were made strong:** ... were invigorated from infirmity, –CNDT ... found great strength, –WLMS.

**waxed valiant in fight:** ... grew mighty, –WLMS ... became mighty in war, –ADAM ... they became mighty warriors, –NORL.

**turned to flight the armies of the aliens:** ... and rounted armies, –MNTG ... They completely defeated foreign armies, –SEB ... overturned the Camps of Foreigners, –WLSN.

**11:34.** Daniel 3 gives the account of Shadrach, Meshach, and Abednego being cast fully clothed into the flames of Nebuchadnezzar's furnace and emerging unscathed. Countless numbers of believing Jews were delivered from death in battle when they faced overwhelming odds. As a boy David slew the giant Goliath. The blind Samson grew his hair, regained his strength, and pulled the temple of Dagon down on himself and his Philistine tormentors. A timid Gideon and 300 Israelites routed the Midianite armies. By God's power human weakness prevailed over strength. Jonathan single-handedly defeated a Philistine garrison. David surrounded himself with mighty men who fought valiantly for him in the wars which built the kingdom of Judah. The fearful host of Assyria was annihilated in the days of Hezekiah through the faith of the king and angelic intervention (2 Kings 19:35).

**35. Women received their dead raised to life again:** ... by a resurrection, –WLMS.

**and others were tortured, not accepting deliverance:** ... Others chose to be beaten, –NLTG ... were broken on the wheel, –MNTG ... they were tortured to death, –SEB ... others endured tortures, because they would not accept release, –WLMS ... were beaten to death, not accepting the deliverance offered, –WLSN ... refusing to be delivered, –ADAM ... not anticipating deliverance, –CNDT ... they refused to be freed, –BECK.

**that they might obtain a better resurrection:** ... that they might gain, –WADE ... that they might rise to a better life, –WLMS, –TNT ... they wanted to inherit a better life after their resurrection, –NOLI.

**11:35.** Through the faith of the prophets Elijah and Elisha, the widow's son was raised from the dead (1 Kings 17:17ff.) and the Shunammite's son was resurrected (2 Kings 4:18ff.).

In the period between the Old and New Testaments, during the Jewish revolt against the Seleucid king, Antiochus IV, seven brothers were captured and tortured to death because they refused to be released on condition of violating the Mosaic dietary and sacrificial laws. By faith they remained true to their God in anticipation of resurrection in the messianic kingdom where they would be allowed to please and obey God rather than man (2 Maccabees 6:18-7:11).

Many others suffered at the hands of the Persians, Egyptians, Syrians, Greeks, and Romans during the intertestamental period. Some interpreters feel that the verb "tortured" which is *etumpanisthesan*, which means "to beat a drum," refers to the martyrdom of Eleazar who was stretched on a drum and beaten to death (2 Maccabees 6:18-30).

**36. And others had trial of [cruel] mockings and scourgings:** ... had experience of, –WADE ... Others knew what it was to be taunted, flogged, –TNT ... endured derision, –NOLI ... stood the test of taunts and tortures, –WLMS ... had to face taunts and blows, –TCNT.

**yea, moreover of bonds and imprisonment:** ... others were chained and imprisoned, –ADAM ... and even chains and prisons, –WLMS.

**11:36.** In addition to the martyrs of the Maccabean revolt, others were tested by persecution. The prophet Jeremiah was threatened by priests and prophets because of his prophetic word concerning judgment upon Jerusalem. Later he was imprisoned and beaten by King Zedekiah. Others suffered similar fates when they spoke to Israel concerning the judgment of God. The prophet Urijah, a contemporary of Jeremiah, was executed by King Jehoiakim for preaching the same message as Jeremiah (Jeremiah 26:20-23). All were examples of the endurance made possible by faith in God.

**37. They were stoned:** ... stoned to death, –WLMS. **they were sawn asunder:** ... sawn in two, –WLMS, –TNT.

were tempted, were slain with the sword:...they were tortured to death, —*WLMS* ... murdered with, —*BECK*...slaughtered by the sword, —*NORL*...put to death by the sword, —*TNT*...butchered by the sword, —*WADE*.

they wandered about in sheepskins and goatskins: ... they had to roam about, clad only in, —*WADE* ... With nothing on their bodies but skins of sheep or goats they wandered here and there, —*WLMS*.

being destitute, afflicted, tormented: ... They had nothing left, were oppressed, evil treated, —*KLGS* ... suffering poverty, oppression and misery, TNT ... suffering from destitution, distress, and ill-usage, —*WADE* ... poor, oppressed, —*NORL* ... ill-treated, —*ADAM*...persecuted, ill-used, —*TCNT*...mis-treated, —*WLMS*.

**11:37.** The description of the hardships suffered by believers continues in this verse. As is seen in the Gospel of John, the Jews were apt to stone people in mob action, and many of God's servants died before an angry crowd. The "sawn asunder" refers to the tradition that the prophet Isaiah died in this gruesome way (The *Ascension of Isaiah the Prophet* 5:1). Execution by sword was common in the ancient world. In 1 Kings 19:10 there is a reference to Elijah's words that Israel had slain many of the Lord's prophets with the sword.

The declaration that God's people "were tempted" (*epeirasthēsan*) is possibly a play on words since the Greek verb referring to sawing in two is *epristhēsan*. Some Greek manuscripts omit *epeirasthēsan*. Those who wandered about lacking food and water, and clothing themselves in animal skins, would include Elijah when he fled from Jezebel and a host of prophets whose messages of judgment were rejected by Israel.

**38. (Of whom the world was not worthy:):**...by the world which was not worthy of them, —*NOLI*.

they wandered in deserts, and [in] mountains: ... wandered about in lonely places, —*TNT*...straying in wildernesses, —*CNDT*.

and [in] dens and caves of the earth:...and hiding in caverns and underground cavities, —*WADE*...caves, and holes in the ground, —*WLMS*, —*TNT*.

**11:38.** Before finishing the list of indignities and horrors suffered by the prophets, the inspired writer injected an editorial comment that "the world was not worthy" of these heroes of faith. The people of power, influence, prestige, and wealth who persecuted these saints were in no way equal to them. These persecuted ones understood the invisible and eternal world. They knew that its value was far beyond the wealth of the entire world which surrounded their senses. While they hid from their oppressors in the wilderness

and caves, they trusted God and kept their eyes fixed upon the unseen realities of God's kingdom.

**39. And these all, having obtained a good report through faith:**... by their faith won God's approval, —*WLMS*.

received not the promise:... did not obtain the promised blessing, —*WLSN*...none of them received what He had promised, —*WLMS*.

**11:39.** Like the patriarchs before them, the judges, kings, and prophets who believed God gained a reputation for righteousness by faith while they lived, but they all died without seeing the Lord fulfill His promise. As was previously argued in 4:8, 9, God's promised rest did not arrive when Israel entered Canaan; it is still future for His people.

**40. God having provided some better thing for us:**... for us God had something still better in mind, —*NORL* ... With us in mind God had an even better plan, —*TNT*.

that they without us should not be made perfect:... in order to have them reach their goal with us, —*BECK*...apart from us might not attain perfection, —*WLMS*...Only with us should they be brought to perfection, —*TNT*.

**11:40.** This lack of fulfillment of promise was not a failure on God's part. It was part of the divine plan. God actually foresaw (*problepsamenou*) this situation, that is, that there was "something better for us" (NASB). According to God's plan, the age in which He began to fulfill His promise would follow the times of the patriarchs, judges, kings, and prophets. That time began when the eternal Son of God became flesh—"in these last days" (1:2). The Lord spoke His final word through His Son Jesus Christ.

The conclusion is obvious. Since the first coming of Jesus Christ, believers live not in promise but in the age of fulfillment, the new covenant age. It was in God's purpose to make the Old Testament saints wait for the coming of the messianic Son, the establishment of the new covenant, and the exploits of Christian believers, before He establishes His eternal kingdom at the time of the second coming of Jesus Christ. There is a unity between the saints of the two covenants, and it is to be discovered in the person of Jesus, "the author and finisher of our faith" (12:2).

## Chapter 12

**1. Wherefore seeing we also are compassed about with so great a cloud of witnesses:**... figuratively encircled by a great crowd, —*NORL* ... we are encircled, —*MNTG* ... by such a large number of witnesses! —SEB ... of those who are bearing testimony, —WUST ... so vast a crowd of spectators, —WLMS.

**let us lay aside every weight:** ... let us throw off, —WLMS ... let us get rid of every burden, —BECK ... we must put off every, —ADAM ... putting off every impediment, —CNDT.

**and the sin which doth so easily beset [us]:** ... the sin that clings about us, —MNTG ... the sins that cling to us so closely, —NORL ... Sin can easily tie us up, —SEB ... that is so readily found all around us, —ADAM ... cleverly places itself in an entangling way around us, —WUST ... that easily entangles our feet, —WLMS.

**and let us run with patience the race that is set before us:** ... run with endurance, —WLMS ... the Course marked out for us, —WLSN ... that God has planned for us, —NLTG.

**12:1.** The first two verses of chapter 12 apply the principles of faith presented in chapter 11. The vast multitude of saints described as heroes of faith were witnesses to the first-century Jewish believers who may have been wondering whether or not they could finish the course which they began when they confessed Jesus as their Messiah. Some of them might have been wondering whether or not their confession was worth all the trouble it was causing them. The testimony of the witnesses marshaled from the Old Testament assures all believers that it is possible to be justified by faith, gain a reputation for righteous living, endure suffering and death without seeing the promise completely fulfilled, and accomplish great things for God. Since they did it, all believers can do it. For the race of life, believers are to trim down, that is, get rid of the sin of unbelief which will impede their progress. Forsaking all other impediments to faith, they are to run the race "with patience," i.e., "endurance" (NASB) (hupomonēs). They are to finish what they have begun.

**2. Looking unto Jesus the author and finisher of [our] faith:** ... keeping our eyes, —WLMS ... our eyes fixed upon, —TCNT ... the pioneer and perfecter, —MNTG ... the Inaugurator and Perfecter of, —CNDT.

**who for the joy that was set before him:** ... instead of the joy which lay before, —WLMS.

**endured the cross, despising the shame:** ... and scorned its shame, —NORL ... disregarding the Shame, —WLSN ... with no regard for its shame, —WLMS ... and cared nothing for its shame, —TNT ... making light of the ignominy of it, —WADE.

**and is set down at the right hand of the throne of God:** ... and since has taken His seat at, —WLMS.

**12:2.** Like a runner, believers are encouraged not to look back but to fix their gaze upon (aphorōntes) Jesus because He is the trailblazing pioneer (archēgon), the One who brings faith to completion (teleiōtēn). He set an example for believers under persecution. He endured the agony

and suffering of crucifixion and discounted the shamefulness of a criminal execution because He set His gaze on the joys of the Resurrection and His eternal rule at God's side.

**3. For consider him:** ... Yes ... just think of the examples set by Him, —WLMS ... Think of Jesus, —TNT ... consider the steadfastness of Him, —WADE.

**that endured such contradiction of sinners against himself:** ... and the way he bore the bitter enmity of sinful men against himself, —TNT ... such opposition from, —ADAM ... such hostility, —MNTG ... so great opposition aimed at Him by sinful men! —WLMS.

**lest ye be wearied and faint in your minds:** ... It will help you not to, —BECK ... Then you will not grow tired and lose heart, —TNT ... so that you won't get tired and give up, —ADAM ... to keep from growing weary and fainthearted, —WLMS.

**12:3.** These words reemphasize the exhortation given in the previous verse. The word "for" (gar) could well be translated "indeed" in this situation. The word translated "consider" is unusual. In the papyri it was used in reference to the careful comparison of accounts; here it is metaphoric. The Hebrew believers were asked to carefully examine the example set by Jesus in His endurance of the verbal hostility and abuse (antilogian) of sinful men. The perfect tense of the verb "endured" stresses the abiding results of His endurance. It is not just a matter of historic interest; it is significant for all believers. Careful consideration of Jesus' endurance of persecution has the power to encourage believers and keep them from gradually fading and dropping out of the race when things get rough.

**4. Ye have not yet resisted unto blood, striving against sin:** ... So far, in your struggle against sin, you have not had to face death itself, —TNT ... as you have struggled on against sin, resisted to the point of pouring out your blood, —WLMS ... when contending against sin, —CNDT.

**12:4.** The Jewish believers to whom the epistle was written were reminded that even though they had "resisted" (antikatestēte, "stood against") the sin of unbelief because of their identification with Jesus, they had not yet been asked to die while struggling (antagōnizomenoi, "wrestling against") with the temptation to apostatize. Jesus and the Old Testament saints are reminders to all believers that it is possible to endure such persecution even to the point of dying. The eternal nature of the reward is far superior to anything that can be gained by "giving up in the struggle." To continue living in the present age at the expense of forsaking Christ and His eternal kingdom is to squander the greatest treasure for a mere pittance.

**5. And ye have forgotten the exhortation:**...Have you forgotten that Scripture, –TNT...these words of comfort, –SEB...the encouragement, –WLMS...the appeal, –WADE.

**which speaketh unto you as unto children:**...which reasons with you, –WADE...which is addressed to you as sons, –WLMS.

**My son, despise not thou the chastening of the Lord:**...do not despise the training of the Lord, –MNTG...think not lightly of the Lord's discipline, –TCNT...don't take it lightly, –SEB...refrain from thinking lightly of the discipline the Lord inflicts, –WLMS...of the Lord's training, –BECK.

**nor faint when thou art rebuked of him:**...Do not give up, –NLTG...nor get weary, –NOLI...do not lose heart when he reproves you, –TNT...when you are corrected by Him, –WLMS.

**12:5.** The fact that some of the Jewish Christians who were recipients of this letter may have been thinking about giving up their confession of Jesus as Messiah indicates they had lost sight of a very important Old Testament teaching. They needed to be reminded of a spiritual truth which they had forgotten. The exhortation given was from Proverbs 3:11,12. The Greek word *paraklēseōs* carries a double-edged impact. It has both the idea of admonition and a sense of comfort and encouragement. Whenever this word is used, it not only confronts believers with their failure to behave in the proper way, but it also reminds them of the provisions which God has made to enable them to do what He desires them to do. And so it is here in Hebrews 12.

This Scripture verse is particularly appropriate because it speaks to members of the family of God, to "children" (literally *huiois*, "sons," NASB). It is a gentle reminder that those who are not mature often lose sight of long-range goals in the panic of present difficulties. The Greek word for "despise" is *oligōrei*, and it means "to belittle." So the first part of the admonition is not to belittle the "chastening of the Lord" (*paideias*, the disciplinary instruction given to *paidion*, an infant or child).

**6. For whom the Lord loveth he chasteneth:**...he disciplines, –WLSN...everyone He loves, –WLMS...every child he loves, –NOLI.

**and scourgeth every son whom he receiveth:**...and whips every, –ADAM...he acknowledges, –TCNT...chastises...whom He heartily receives, –WLMS.

**12:6.** The reason believers are not to belittle God's disciplinary instruction nor fade away in response to His showing them the error of their ways (*elenchomenos*, 12:5) is set forth in the second half of the quotation. The disciplinary instruction of the Lord is a result of His love for

His sons. This discipline is described by the verb "scourgeth" (*mastigoi*) which means "to punish by whipping." Without exception, each son whom the Lord "receiveth" (*paradechetai*, "welcomes, accepts") is subject to such discipline. God's love does not overlook the sins of His children; it disciplines them.

**7. If ye endure chastening:**...You must submit to discipline, –WLMS...endure suffering, –NOLI...Your steadfastness serves to discipline you, –WADE...for discipline's sake, –TNT.

**God dealeth with you as with sons:**...is treating you as, –NOLI.

**for what son is he whom the father chasteneth not?:**...Is there any son whom his father does not discipline? –TNT...who is the son, –WLMS...that a father doesn't discipline? –ADAM...who does not at times punish his sons? –NORL...whose father does not train? –KLGS...doesn't correct? –BECK.

**12:7.** The Greek text does not have an "if" here. It says "you are enduring unto disciplinary instruction." The "ye" is plural and looks at the group as a whole. Since believers are recipients of divine discipline, God is dealing with them as His children. "For what son is he whom the father chasteneth not?" On the basis of the previous statements, the conclusion is obvious. Since "every son" (12:6) is disciplined, those who are not disciplined are not being treated as sons.

**8. But if ye be without chastisement:**...If you do not have the discipline, –TNT...If you lack the discipline, –NOLI...without discipline, –CNDT.

**whereof all are partakers:**...in which all true sons share, –WLMS...of which all men have their share, –WADE.

**then are ye bastards, and not sons:**...your sonship is not legitimate, –NOLI...you are Spurious, –WLSN...illegitimate children, –ADAM...base-born, –WADE.

**12:8.** This verse graphically describes those who never experience God's disciplinary instruction: to be without God's discipline is to be a "bastard." When God recognizes someone as His own child, He exercises His discipline in their lives because He loves them. The statement "whereof all are partakers" seems to indicate that the Jews to whom the epistle was sent were for the most part genuine members of the family of God.

**9. Furthermore we have had fathers of our flesh which corrected** [us]:...We had human fathers, –TNT...Remember that our fathers on earth punished us, –NLTG...from our natural fathers, –WLSN...in our earthly fathers we have had disciplinarians, −WADE . . . our natural fathers used to correct us, −BECK . . . who disciplined us, −ADAM.

**and we gave [them] reverence:** . . . we held them in respect, −TNT . . . we used to treat them with respect, −WLMS.

**shall we not much rather:** . . . how much more cheerfully should we, −WLMS . . . Should we not be even more willing to, −TNT.

**be in subjection unto the Father of spirits, and live?:** . . . submit to, −WLMS . . . our spiritual Father and so gain life? −TNT.

**12:9.** This verse reflects on the comparison inherent in the father/ son metaphor which Proverbs 3:11,12 applies to God. There is not only a similarity between God and human fathers, there is also a stark contrast, and it needs to be emphasized. Earthly fathers discipline their children, and they are respected for their efforts. Their training and guidance has the purpose of leading their children into patterns of behavior that are profitable and will keep them out of trouble. Should it not be even more true in regard to the response to the discipline which believers receive from God who is "the Father of spirits"? This title is used for God to heighten the contrast with "fathers of our flesh."

A contrast is also made between the kinds of response made to an earthly father and the Heavenly Father. The response to the human father is *enetrepometha*, "have regard or respect for"; the response to the Heavenly Father is *hupotagēsometha*, "subjection, subordination." Verse 9 closes by clearly declaring that "subjection" to the Heavenly Father's discipline will produce life in His sons.

**10. For they verily for a few days chastened [us]:** . . . Our human father disciplined us, −TNT . . . for a short time, −NORL.

**after their own pleasure; but he for [our] profit:** . . . as it seemed right to them; but He for our advantage, −WLSN . . . but he does it for our good, −WLMS.

**that [we] might be partakers of his holiness:** . . . so that we may share, Adams . . . His holy character, −WLMS.

**12:10.** Human fathers are fallible. The prevalence of child abuse makes it necessary to emphasize this. Some new believers wrestle with the image of God as their Father because they had earthly fathers who abused them. Verse 10 explicitly says that the discipline of a person's earthly father is limited; it is for "a few days." In addition, their discipline is "after their own pleasure." The Greek here could be translated "according to the standard which seems good to them." The discipline exercised by human fathers varies in its effectiveness. It may be too harsh; it may be too lenient; it may be designed to reach goals which are at odds with what God desires. This is not true of God's disciplinary instruction. Whatever He does by way of discipline is for the believer's benefit.

**11. Now no chastening for the present seemeth to be joyous:** . . . All punishment seems terrible at the time, −SEB . . . never seems at the time to be pleasant, −TNT . . . for the time being no discipline seems to be pleasant, −WLMS.

**but grievous: nevertheless afterward:** . . . it always seems unpleasant and painful, −BECK . . . it is painful; later on, however, −WLMS . . . yet subsequently, −CNDT.

**it yieldeth the peaceable fruit of righteousness:** . . . produces . . . lives of peace and goodness, −TNT . . . yields a return, −WUST . . . the fruit of peace, −WLMS.

**unto them which are exercised thereby:** . . . those who have been trained by it, −ADAM . . . trained under it, −MNTG.

**12:11.** Keeping the nature of God's discipline clearly in mind, along with its superiority to the discipline given by human fathers, a basic principle is given. First, there is the acknowledgment that even the discipline of the Heavenly Father has an unpleasant side. Discipline is arduous and sometimes painful. When believers are in the midst of discipline, they are not enjoying themselves. Discipline is not gladness; it is grief. Some children aspire to be Olympic stars, but few are willing to give up their playtime for the rigorous discipline of training, hour upon hour, away from other enjoyable pursuits. There is a sacrifice involved in discipline.

The principle, however, is clearly stated in two significant words: "nevertheless, afterward." After the grief and pain of discipline's sacrifice comes the reward. In the case of God's discipline, the reward is "the peaceable fruit of righteousness." In the end the pursuit of God's righteousness will result in peace and rest from hostility and labor. This result, however, is not the automatic product of divine discipline. The response and attitude of God's children to His discipline is all important. The desired fruit is enjoyed only by "them which are exercised" by God's discipline. The word translated "exercised" is *gegumnasmenois*; it triggers images of athletes training in the gymnasium.

**12. Wherefore lift up the hands which hang down:** . . . So tighten the grip of your slipping hands, −WLMS . . . lift your listless hands, −ADAM . . . brace up the wearied hands, −WLSN . . . your drooping hands, −TNT.

**and the feeble knees:** . . . stiffen the stand of your knocking knees, −WLMS . . . the paralyzed knees,

−CNDT... and the shaky knees, −KLGS... strengthen your weak knees, −TNT.

**13. And make straight paths for your feet:**... keep your feet in straight paths, −WLMS... make level Paths, −WLSN... for your feet to tread in, −WADE.

**lest that which be lame be turned out of the way:** ... Then lameness will not cause your limb, −TNT... so that your lame ankles may not be twisted, −ADAM... that the lame limb may not be dislocated through irregularities in the road, −WADE.

**but let it rather be healed:** ... but instead be cured, −WLMS.

**12:12, 13.** The athletic image is continued in this verse. In view of the "nevertheless, afterward" principle just stated, believers are to fix their eyes on the goal and to encourage one another when they see discouragement and dispirited living. Verse 13 speaks to the goal of pursuing righteousness on "straight paths." It entails an exhortation to healing through doing what is right. Behaving unrighteously is likened to tripping and twisting or dislocating (ektrapē) a joint.

**14. Follow peace with all [men]:**... Make it your aim to be at peace with everyone, −TNT... the maintenance of peace, −WADE... Run swiftly after peace, −MNTG... Try hard to live in peace, −BECK.

**and holiness, without which no man shall see the Lord:** ... Seek holiness, −TNT... and strive for that consecration without which no one, −WLMS.

**12:14.** The figurative language of the previous verse is made explicit here. In line with the heroes of the Faith whom they are to imitate, those who "obtained a good report" (11:2), believers are encouraged to diokete, that is, "pursue, follow hard after" peace. They are also admonished to do the same in regard to holiness because it is absolutely essential for those who will see God. Living by faith in pursuit of a righteous life is not optional; for the Christian it is a necessity.

**15. Looking diligently:**... See to it, −TNT... Continue to look after one another, −WLMS ... supervising, −CNDT... looking carefully, −WLSN... Keep a watchful eye, −WADE.

**lest any man fail of the grace of God:**... that no one be wanting of, −CNDT... lest any one fall back from the favor of God, −WLSN... that no one fails to gain God's spiritual blessing, −WLMS... that no one falls away from God's grace, −TNT.

**lest any root of bitterness springing up trouble [you]:**... or some evil like a bitter root, −WLMS... no bitterness springs up to cause trouble, −TNT.

**and thereby many be defiled:** ... and be poison to many, −NORL ... and many be stained by it, −KLGS... and spoil everybody's life, −TNT... be contaminated by it, −WLMS.

**12:15.** The responsibility for self and others is clearly laid on the line by these words. Believers are to oversee one another (episkopountes) in order to prevent anyone from falling short (husterōn, the same verb found in Romans 3:23) of God's grace. The emphasis here, as it has been throughout the epistle, is on perseverance and endurance. When God's disciplinary instruction comes into believers' lives, some are tempted to become bitter. To complain and rail against His discipline is an improper response. It does not allow for the training and exercise which in the end produces righteousness and peace. Indeed, it is likened to a bitter weed which causes trouble and annoyance; it is a weed which spreads a poisonous contagion. It defiles or stains (mianthōsin) many by its presence.

**16. Lest there [be] any fornicator, or profane person, as Esau:**... Let no one be immoral or irreverent, −NORL... Don't let anyone become a sexual sinner, −SEB... See to it that there is no immoral or worldly person, −TNT... or scorner, −MNTG... some immoral or godless person like Esau, −WLMS.

**who for one morsel of meat sold his birthright:**... who for a single meal, −ADAM... for one feeding, gave up, −CNDT... bartered his birthright, −WADE... he sold his inheritance rights for just one meal! −SEB.

**12:16.** This verse begins a warning which extends to the end of the chapter (12:29). The seriousness of coming short of God's grace (12:15) evokes the image of Esau. Esau is one of the saddest figures in Bible history. He had so much in his favor, but he failed because he succumbed to fleshly desires—a warning for us against carnality. Believers are to diligently exercise the oversight enjoined in the previous verse in order to keep the immorality and irreligious behavior of Esau from corrupting their congregation.

In one hasty decision, Esau revealed his true character. He was shortsighted. Genesis 25 records how he returned home from the field hungry and for a single meal bartered away his rights as the firstborn son. His exact words were, "Behold, I am at the point to die: and what profit shall this birthright do to me?" (Genesis 25:32). He was not only trading legal privileges and rights of an earthly, material nature, but he was also trampling under foot the covenant of promise which God had made with Abraham. Esau was born as the son of the promise. In trading away his birthright he discounted the spiritual realities inherent in the covenant. In this he was parallel to any of the professing Hebrew believers who were yielding to the pressures around them and abandoning their profession of faith in Jesus as Messiah. In forsaking that profession, they also were abandoning all hope for their eternal future.

17. **For ye know how that afterward:** ... later, —WLMS.

**when he would have inherited the blessing, he was rejected:** ... though he wished afterwards, —WADE ... he afterward desired to inherit, —MNTG ... wanted to claim, —TNT ... he was most anxious to inherit, —NORL ... he wanted to get possession of, —WLMS ... he was refused, —WLSN ... he was turned down, —KLGS ... his appeal was rejected, —WADE.

**for he found no place of repentance:** ... no opportunity to change his mind, —ADAM ... he never found an opportunity for repairing his error, —TCNT ... He could find no way of undoing what he had done, —TNT ... no opportunity of reversing his choice, —WADE.

**though he sought it carefully with tears:** ... though he sought it earnestly, —MNTG ... he tried to get the blessing, —WLMS.

**12:17.** The folly of Esau's evaluation and decision is driven home by the reference to his remorse as described in Genesis 27:34, 36, 38. He did not fully appreciate the uniqueness of the rights which he traded so easily. There was only one birthright. It could not be shared, and Jacob would not give it back because he prized it. Esau's decision was irreversible. Esau gave away a spiritual as well as an earthly inheritance, that is, that the messianic promise might be fulfilled through his line. His loss was irrevocable, he found no place for repentance. Here is a clear warning for us to escape Esau's fate by giving priority to spiritual concerns.

18. **For ye are not come unto the mount that might be touched:** ... tangible in nature, —WADE.

**and that burned with fire:** ... ablaze with fire, —WADE ... with its blazing fire that could be felt, —TNT.

**nor unto blackness, and darkness, and tempest:** ... there is now no gloom, or pitch-darkness, or storm, —NORL ... and a whirlwind, —ADAM ... and to murk, —WADE.

**12:18.** This verse returns to the same argument used in chapter 2: since believers have received a superior revelation in Jesus Christ, they are subject to a more severe punishment than those who rejected the instructions given when the Lord met with Moses on Mount Sinai. The awesome phenomena and warnings that accompanied the giving of the Law are vividly described. The description depicts the events recorded in Exodus 19:12-25; 20:18. The basic point in Hebrews is in the contrast of verses 18-21 and 22ff. Verse 18 declares, "For ye are not come unto the mount that might be touched." Verses 22-24 stress that believers have come to the heavenly realities associated with Jesus and instituted by Him. The basic thrust then is that disobedience to the heavenly realities will bring a far greater judgment than rejection of the earthly realities that accompanied Moses' institution of the Law. The effect of this contrast is

spectacular because of the experience of Israel at Sinai where they were terrified by the fire, smoke, impenetrable darkness, and howling winds.

19. **And the sound of a trumpet, and the voice of words:** ... and the blare of a trumpet and an audible voice, —MNTG ... and trumpet-blast, —WLMS ... and oracular voice, —TNT ... a Speaking voice, —WADE.

**which [voice] they that heard entreated:** ... so alarming, —WADE ... and a voice whose words made the hearers beg, —WLMS.

**that the word should not be spoken to them any more:** ... that not a word more should be added, —WLMS ... that they should not have to hear any more, —TNT.

**12:19.** In a rising crescendo of trumpets, the thunderous voice of the Lord spoke to Moses, and the people of Israel were filled with dread. In their fear they cried out to Moses, "Speak thou with us, and we will hear: but let not God speak with us, lest we die" (Exodus 20:19).

20. **(For they could not endure that which was commanded:** ... They could not stand what was ordered, —SEB ... they did not try to bear the order, —WLMS ... could not endure the injunction, —WLSN.

**And if so much as a beast touch the mountain:** ... that even an animal which touched, —TNT ... if a wild animal, —WLMS.

**it shall be stoned, or thrust through with a dart:** ... it shall be pelted with stones, —CNDT ... must be stoned to death, —WLMS.

21. **And so terrible was the sight:** ... as he looked at the apalling sight, —NORL ... so terrifying, —WLMS ... was the scene, —MNTG.

**[that] Moses said, I exceedingly fear and quake:):** ... I am trembling with fear, —ADAM ... I am terrified, —BECK ... and terror-stricken! —WLMS.

**12:20, 21.** Death by stoning or arrow was the penalty for merely touching Mount Sinai during the time the Lord was speaking to Moses. It was applied to both men and beast. The contrast here is the difficulty of approaching God under the old covenant as compared with the easy access through Jesus Christ. The experience was so frightful that even Moses, the peerless leader, feared "exceedingly."

22. **But ye are come unto mount Sion:** ... No, you stand before, —TNT.

**and unto the city of the living God, the heavenly Jerusalem:**

**and to an innumerable company of angels:** ... to myriads of angels, —ADAM, —WLSN ... to countless hosts of angels, —TCNT ... and its mighty host of angels, —TNT.

**12:22.** Verse 22 contrasts God's revelation in the new covenant with the terror and unapproachability of the Lord as He revealed himself in the wilderness. The city which the patriarchal nomads sought had now come. First-century Christians had come to it. They lived at the beginning of the age of fulfillment, not in the age of promise. They entered into the very presence of God in the heavenly sanctuary through Jesus Christ (9:24); they were no longer limited to the annual representation of a dying high priest in an earthly tabernacle or temple. In Christ Jesus they had direct access to the living God at any time. The angels, whom so many of them may have been concerned about because they felt they were a part of the Jewish religious system, were in the presence of the living God by the myriads (tens of thousands). They are still in the service of God for His people (1:14). There is no dread and terror for believers in approaching God. The fire, blackness, smoke, trumpets, and thunderous voice have been replaced by light and splendor. The "do not even touch" has become "come and see."

**23. To the general assembly and church of the firstborn:** . . . You are in the presence of the joyous assembly, –*TNT* . . . to a universal convocation, –*CNDT* . . . to the festal gathering and assembly of God's firstborn sons, –*WLMS* . . . enrolled in heaven, –*KLGS*.

**which are written in heaven:** . . . whose names are written, –*TNT* . . . enrolled as citizens in heaven, –*WLMS* . . . registered in heaven, –*MNTG*.

**and to God the Judge of all:** . . . to a Judge who is the God of all, –*WLMS* . . . of all men, –*TNT*.

**and to the spirits of just men made perfect:** . . . who have been brought to completeness, –*WUST* . . . of just ones completed, –*KLGS* . . . of upright men who have attained perfection, –*WLMS* . . . and the spirits of good men who have been made perfect, –*TNT*.

**12:23.** The first word of this verse (*panēgurei*) sets the tone of the contrast most specifically; it could be translated "festal assembly." It sets a scene of joy and celebration which easily overshadows the darkness and terror of Sinai. The gathering is styled *ekklēsia prōtotokōn*, "church of the firstborn." This is a picture of the true Church Universal. It is more than an organization, no matter how effective and blessed its ministry may be. It is an organism, composed of all true believers, born into the family of God.

This portrayal has staggering implications. It indicates that all believers are on an equal basis in Jesus Christ. And what a basis it is: they are all firstborn heirs, those to whom a double portion of the inheritance is due. This was no vague hope. Their names were already enrolled in the lists of those who possess citizenship in the heavenly Jerusalem. This was quite a mind-boggling image to Christians in the Early Church who lived in

an empire that had many cities composed of 80 percent slaves and only 20 percent citizens. Their God, the living God, is also the One who in the end will judge every man. Christians may be discouraged and downtrodden by the corruption and injustice they are experiencing in this life, but they can be assured of justice in the heavenly city. When they look around Zion, they will meet "the spirits of just men made perfect." They are numbered among the righteous who have been made complete in the Son.

**24. And to Jesus the mediator of the new covenant:** . . . Now you meet Jesus, –*NOLI* . . . through whom the new covenant has been made, –*TNT* . . . of a fresh covenant, –*CNDT*.

**and to the blood of sprinkling:** . . . you are sprinkled with his blood, –*NOLI* . . . to his sprinkled Blood, –*MNTG* . . . and whose shed blood, –*TNT*.

**that speaketh better things than [that of] Abel:** . . . has far better things to say to us than Abel's, –*TNT* . . . which is more powerful than, –*NOLI* . . . that speaks in nobler accents, –*WADE* . . . whose message cries louder, –*MNTG* . . . which speaks a better message than even, –*WLMS*.

**12:24.** Here, by direct and explicit statement, the inspired writer returned to the previous argument concerning the superiority of Jesus as the Mediator of God's promised new covenant. The words of verse 24 evoke memories of all the blessings secured by the high priesthood of One who has been made an eternal Melchizedekian priest. The blood of Abel, shed by his brother Cain, still cries out in condemnation of Cain; the blood of Jesus, shed by His brethren, still cleanses the consciences of sinners and covers them when they come to God in prayer.

**25. See that ye refuse not him that speaketh:** . . . Take care that you do not refuse to hear, –*TNT* . . . Be sure you listen to the One Who is speaking, –*NLTG* . . . lest you should reject Him, –*WLSN*.

**For if they escaped not:** . . . if there was no escape for those, –*WADE* . . . have paid the penalty for their disobedience, –*NOLI*.

**who refused him that spake on earth:** . . . when they refused to listen to their instructor, –*MNTG* . . . because they refused to listen to him who warned them here on earth, –*WLMS* . . . uttered His warnings from an earthly Height, –*WADE*.

**much more [shall not] we [escape]:** . . . What chance have we of escaping, –*TNT* . . . how much less can we, –*WLMS* . . . We are going to be punished more severely, –*NOLI*.

**if we turn away from him that [speaketh] from heaven:** . . . if we reject, –*WLMS* . . . if we turn our backs on the one, –*TNT* . . . who turn a deaf ear to Him, –*WADE* . . . who warns us from heaven, –*BECK*.

**12:25.** Since these tremendous benefits belong to those who embrace Jesus the Son, they ought not to reject the message which God is yet delivering through Jesus' "blood of sprinkling" (verse 24). Since the Children of Israel, wandering in the desert with limited access to the Lord, were not able to escape the God of Sinai when they rejected His message, it will be even more impossible for Christians to escape God the Son who came from heaven (John 3:31; 6:38) if they turn aside from Him.

Pondering all this Carter wrote: "A comparison is employed to make vivid and emphatic the distinction between the Mosaic and the Christian eras (cf. Hebrews 2:2, 3). The author reveals that the greater responsibility rests upon the Christian believers because of their higher privileges in Christ. Grace makes the Christian's moral and spiritual responsibility to God greater than was the Jew's under the law. The meaning of the word refuse here appears not to be a stubborn and rebellious rejection of Christ, but rather a sort of begging-off (cf. Luke 14:18; Hebrews 12:1), or excuses and withdrawals (cf. Hebrews 10:38). Such an excusing, evasive, withdrawing, responsibility-shunning attitude is almost certain ultimately to lead the soul to turn away from him that warneth from heaven. When the believer begins to deprecate the blessings and benefits of Christ and the Christian religion, he will end in departing from the living God, unless he experiences a radical change of attitude (cf. Psalm 1:1)" (*The Wesleyan Bible Commentary,* pp.168,169).

**26. Whose voice then shook the earth:** ... God's voice shook the earth then, —*TNT* ... made the earth to rock, —*WADE* ... at the time, —*NOLI.*

**but now he hath promised, saying:** ... whereas now He has given an assurance in these words, —*WADE* ... Now he has warned us again, —*NOLI.*

**Yet once more I shake:** ... Once more I will make ... to tremble, —*WLMS* ... again, once for all, I will cause ... to quake, —*WADE.*

**not the earth only, but also heaven:** ... not only the Earth but also the very Heaven, —*WADE* ... but heaven as well, —*TNT.*

**12:26.** God thundered from Sinai and the earth shook, but the days of dread and doom are not all past. The promise of future judgment of heaven and earth, referred to here, was spoken to the remnant of Jews who were building the temple after they had returned from Babylon (Haggai 2:6). They were few in number and beset on every side by enemies—Arabs, Ammonites, Samaritans, and the governor of the neighboring province. They were discouraged because some of the old-timers remembered the glory of Solomon's Temple and thought the new temple was insignificant in comparison. But through Haggai, the Lord promised

the future glory of their temple and His judgment of their enemies. This same promise is yet to be fulfilled and speaks hope to discouraged Christians who think of quitting.

**27. And this [word], Yet once more:** ... Now that expression, "Once more," —*WLMS* ... Yet again, —*WADE.*

**signifieth the removing of those things that are shaken:** ... implies the final passing away of all that can be shaken, —*WADE* ... the final removal, —*WLMS.*

**as of things that are made:** ... the whole order of created things, —*TNT* ... as being created and material, —*WADE.*

**that those things which cannot be shaken may remain:** ... in order that the realities which are incapable of being shaken (since they are immaterial) may alone remain, —*WADE.*

**12:27.** Chapter 12 closes with an explanation of the significance of the quotation from Haggai 2:6 for professing Christians and then draws pointed attention to the value of fear as a deterrent to apostatizing from the Faith. The certainty of God's justice has relevance for the Christian's value system. In the judgment, the Lord will remove everything that is not of lasting value: His enemies, the enemies of believers, pain, death, sickness, drudgery, poverty, famine, disease, sorrow, suffering, and persecution. That which remains will be unshakable. The implication is that if anyone turns aside from his profession of faith in Jesus, he is like Esau—nearsighted. He will be trading short-range fulfillment of desire (escape from his sufferings for Jesus' sake) at the expense of an "eternal weight of glory" (2 Corinthians 4:17), citizenship in God's unshakable kingdom.

**28. Wherefore we receiving a kingdom which cannot be moved:** ... Accordingly let us who are to receive a Dominion which is proof against any shock, —*WADE* ... accepting an unshakable kingdom, —*CNDT* ... which is unshakable, —*MNTG.*

**let us have grace:** ... Let us, therefore, be thankful, —*WLMS.*

**whereby we may serve God acceptably:** ... let us offer him the worship he can accept, —*TNT* ... this will enable us to offer acceptably to God, —*WADE.*

**with reverence and godly fear:** ... with conscientiousness and awe, —*WADE* ... with holy awe, —*MNTG.*

**12:28.** Since Christians are citizens in God's eternal kingdom, they are exhorted to "keep on holding on" (*echōmen*) to God's grace. His grace will see them through their current trials. More importantly, it will enable them to worship and serve God as priests (*latreuōmen*) whose sacrifices, like those offered by Abel, are acceptable to the Lord, because they are offered out of an attitude of reverence (*eulabeias*, recognition of God's greatness, righteousness, and sovereignty).

**29. For our God [is] a consuming fire:** ... is a fire that destroys everything, —*NLTG* ... is destroying fire, —*KLGS* ... is indeed an all-devouring fire, —*TNT.*

**12:29.** The alternative to pious service and endurance by God's grace is apostasy which incurs God's wrath. His wrath is a fire which devours everything in its path. Believers ought to heed the words of Jesus not to fear men but to fear God who is able to destroy them spiritually in hell (Matthew 10:28).

## Chapter 13

**1. Let brotherly love continue:** ... As brothers in Christ, never cease loving one another, —*TNT* ... Christians, keep on loving one another, —*BECK* ... must be maintained, —*ADAM* ... continue to love one another, —*NORL.*

**13:1.** The first 19 verses of chapter 13 consist of a series of exhortations instructing Christians how to live in obedience to the new covenant by offering their lives as living sacrifices in their priestly service and worship. The first exhortation (verse 1) goes to the heart of the new covenant. Jesus wrapped up the whole Law in commandments by enjoining complete love for God and love for neighbor. In the Upper Room as He prepared His disciples for His imminent death, He declared that the mark which would distinguish believers was a new commandment: loving one another.

Verse 1 is not a random exhortation disconnected from the rest of the epistle; it is a timely reminder of the essential sign of true discipleship. James's epistle says that those who do not live by Jesus' "royal law" (James 2:8) are guilty of living a lie "against the truth" (James 3:14).

**2. Be not forgetful to entertain strangers:** ... Do not neglect to show hospitality, —*MNTG* ... Don't forget to welcome strangers, —*SEB* ... to open your homes, —*TNT* ... Do not remain neglectful of hospitality to strangers, —*WLMS.*

**for thereby some have entertained angels unawares:** ... have had angels as their guests, —*NORL* ... heavenly messengers without knowing it, —*KLGS* ... without realizing it, —*ADAM* ... unconsciously, —*WLSN.*

**13:2.** Hospitality (*philoxenias*, "love of strangers"), according to Jesus' Parable of the Good Samaritan, is included in love of neighbor. Moreover, the patriarchs Abraham and Lot (Genesis 18:2ff.; 19:1ff.) entertained strangers who turned out to be angels sent from the Lord.

**3. Remember them that are in bonds, as bound with them:** ... remember those who are in prison, as though you were in prison with them, —*WLMS.*

**[and] them which suffer adversity:** ... of those maltreated, —*CNDT* ... and those mistreated, —*KLGS* ... ill-treated, —*WLMS.*

**as being yourselves also in the body:** ... since you, too, are liable to similar physical punishment, —*WLMS.*

**13:3.** The admonition here was for the Hebrew Christians to continue to identify themselves with those who had been imprisoned because of their faith in Jesus. They were not to abandon these fellow believers out of fear for their own safety. They were one with those who were "in bonds" and must continue to feel their sufferings and needs as their own (6:10; 10:32-34). Since they themselves had not yet entered eternity but remained in their earthly bodies, they could yet face the same sufferings.

**4. Marriage [is] honourable in all:** ... The married state should be regarded as, —*TCNT* ... must be honored by everybody, —*ADAM* ... should be respected by everyone, —*NLTG* ... should think highly of marriage and keep married life pure, —*BECK.*

**and the bed undefiled:** ... and the marriage bed must be unpolluted, —*ADAM* ... and the marriage relations kept sacred, —*WLMS.*

**but whoremongers and adulterers God will judge:** ... Persons who are sexually vicious and immoral God will punish, —*WLMS.*

**13:4.** While on the subject of love, the inspired writer spoke of the value of marriage. It is not to be disdained but held in high regard. Perhaps this declaration was necessary because of the influence of the Hellenistic culture which surrounded the early Christians. Many Greek philosophers taught that the body and its sexual functions were either evil or inferior.

This verse places a high value on the marriage relationship. The word *timios*, "honorable," could be translated as "costly." The Christian is to value his relationship with his spouse so highly that he will avoid defiling the *koitē* or marriage "bed" by keeping himself from any kind of sexual relationship outside of the marriage union and from adulterous relationships while married. Premarital sex, sodomy, prostitution, and homosexual acts are all included in the term *pornous*, and, like adultery, they will fall under the judgment of our holy God.

**5. [Let your] conversation [be] without covetousness:** ... You must not be lovers of money, —*NORL* ... You must have a turn of mind that is free from avarice, —*WLMS* ... May fondness for money not be your manner, —*CNDT* ... Let your life be untainted by love of money, —MNTG . . . Don't be greedy, —BECK . . . Be not of an avaricious disposition, —WLSN.

**[and be] content with such things as ye have:** . . . being satisfied with your present circumstances, —WUST.

**for he hath said:**

**I will never leave thee, nor forsake thee:** . . . nor will I ever abandon you, —TCNT . . . or desert you, —BECK.

**13:5.** Since Christians look for a future kingdom which is both unshakable and heavenly, they are not to concentrate their affections and efforts upon the accumulation of worldly wealth. The believer's *tropos*, "lifestyle," should be "without covetousness," i.e., *aphilarguros*, "without love of silver." A Christian should be satisfied with the things which he already possesses. The primary focus here is not on worldly possessions, but on the spiritual wealth possessed in Jesus Christ, particularly focused in the Lord's promise never to leave His people (Joshua 1:5; also Matthew 28:20).

**6. So that we may boldly say:** . . . say with complete confidence, —ADAM.

**The Lord [is] my helper, and I will not fear:** . . . I will dismiss all fear, —WADE.

**what man shall do unto me:** . . . What harm can man do, —WADE.

**13:6.** The result of the Lord's abiding presence in the midst of His people is courage. Knowing that He is with them, they are filled with confidence and boldness. They echo the words of Psalm 118:6 which is quoted here. In the middle of distress and suffering, their confidence rests with the Lord. They do not have to be afraid of the pain, injury, or death which men may inflict. This was a strong encouragement and exhortation to any of the Hebrew Christians who may have been disposed to abandon their faith in the face of adversity.

**7. Remember them which have the rule over you:** . . . Remember your pastors, —NORL . . . You must not forget your former leaders, —WLMS.

**who have spoken unto you the word of God:** . . . for it was they who brought you the message of God, —WLMS.

**whose faith follow, considering the end of [their] conversation:** . . . Consider how they closed their lives, —WLMS . . . take a look at the results of their behavior and imitate their faith, —ADAM . . . Think of the way they lived and died, and imitate their faith, —TNT.

**13:7.** In the midst of their temptation to apostatize, the Hebrews were also encouraged to continue remembering their former leaders who guided them and spoke God's words to them. They were to imitate (*mimeisthe*, "follow") the example of

their leaders' faith. This may be a reference to the heroes mentioned in chapter 11, or it may refer to the founders of their church who had died. Their lives of victorious faith proved that the Hebrew Christians could also persevere.

**8. Jesus Christ the same yesterday, and to day, and for ever:** . . . in the past, in the present, and for all time to come, ever the Same, —WADE.

**13:8.** Not only do the lives of the heroes and saints witness to the ability of human beings to live by faith in the face of opposition and overwhelming odds, but the example and promises of the Lord Jesus Christ also provide evidence and encouragement to Christians who waver before the enemy. The One who "endured the cross" sits at God's right hand in power and glory (12:2). The One who promised to be with His disciples unto the end of this age (Matthew 28:20) is still the same. Everything else in the life of the believer may change—his job, his family, his self-esteem, his influence, his popularity, his wealth—but Jesus is always the same, and He is always with the believer, encouraging and empowering him to live the life of faith and obedience.

**9. Be not carried about with divers and strange doctrines:** . . . Do not be led astray by them, —NORL . . . stop being carried away with varied and strange teachings, —WLMS . . . with different kinds of, —BECK . . . by high sounding and strange teachings, —KLGS.

**For [it is] a good thing:** . . . the right course is, —WADE . . . it is an Excellent thing, —WLSN.

**that the heart be established with grace:** . . . to have our resolution braced by a sense of Divine Favour, —WADE . . . for the heart to be strengthened by God's spiritual strength, —WLMS . . . It is God's grace which strengthens our souls, —TNT.

**not with meats:** . . . and not by regulations regarding food, —MNTG . . . not by special kinds of food, —WLMS . . . not by restrictions about particular foods, —WADE.

**which have not profited them that have been occupied therein:** . . . those who make the observance of such restrictions a rule of conduct have not been benefited thereby, —WADE . . . from which those adhering to them have gotten no good, —WLMS . . . which never helped anyone who followed them, —TNT.

**13:9.** Because Jesus is unchanging, the one fixed point in a world of change, the believer has an anchor in the midst of changing circumstances. Because of the stability the Christian has in Jesus, he can stop being blown around by the novel and alien teachings which constantly arise to oppose the Christian faith. The living, eternal Son continuously channels the grace of God to those who trust Him. Dependence on the Son of God is the source of strength which enables the believer to be courageous when afflicted and persecuted.

The writer is here contrasting the entire gospel economy, under the title "grace," with the Levitical system under the title of "meats." The latter term is appropriate because after certain sacrifices worshipers could have a meal using part of the offering. Instead of being carried away by error and apostatizing, they should become established in the truth of the gospel. Salvation comes only through the grace manifested at Calvary.

**10. We have an altar:** . . . As for us, —NOLI . . . Ours is a spiritual altar, —NORL.

**whereof they have no right to eat which serve the tabernacle:** . . . but of the Oblations presented on it they who perform Divine worship in the Tabernacle have no right to eat, —WADE . . . from which those who officiate in the tent, —TNT . . . at which the ministers of the Jewish tent of worship, —WLMS . . . the worshipers of the old tabernacle are not allowed, —NOLI.

**13:10.** The inspired writer now pointed to the mutually exclusive nature of the new covenant sacrifice and the sacrifices offered under the Mosaic Covenant. Christians do not need to identify themselves with the animal sacrifices offered under the Jewish system. Those who continue offering under the old system, which only foreshadowed the reality of Christ's sacrifice, do not possess the *exousian* ("power, right, privilege, authority") to "eat" from the new covenant sacrificial altar.

**11. For the bodies of those beasts:** . . . That reminds me that, —NOLI . . . those animals, —WLMS . . . For (to draw a parallel from the Mosaic Law) the bodies of the victims, —WADE.

**whose blood is brought into the sanctuary:** . . . is taken . . . into the Holy of Holies, —WADE.

**by the high priest for sin, are burned without the camp:** . . . as a sin-offering, —WLMS . . . are not eaten by the worshippers but are burnt, —WADE . . . outside the precincts of, —NOLI . . . outside the camp, —TNT.

**13:11.** In order to accentuate the point about the powerlessness of preoccupation with meats, the writer directed attention to the rites of the Day of Atonement. The bodies of the animals which had been sacrificed were not eaten nor taken into the innermost sanctuary. They were taken outside of the Israelites' camp and burned. It was the blood that was taken "into the sanctuary" and sprinkled on the lid of the ark of the covenant. It was blood, not flesh, that provided ceremonial cleansing under the old covenant.

**12. Wherefore Jesus also:** . . . That is why, —TNT . . . Consequently, —WADE . . . For this reason, —NOLI.

**that he might sanctify the people with his own blood:** . . . in order that he might make the people holy, —TNT . . . purify, —TCNT.

**suffered without the gate:** . . . and died, —NOLI . . . outside the City-gate, —WADE.

**13:12.** The fact that sin offerings and burnt offerings were burned outside the Israelite camp (Exodus 29:14; Leviticus 4:21) leads to another parallel with the sacrifice of Jesus on the cross. Just as those offerings were burned outside the camp, so the death of Christ occurred outside the walls of Jerusalem. It is the shedding of Jesus' blood which cleanses. Emphasis is placed on the idea that His sacrifices took place *exō tēs pulēs* (outside the gate of the city).

**13. Let us go forth therefore unto him without the camp:** . . . let us follow him outside the old camp, —NOLI.

**bearing his reproach:** . . . enduring the reproach that He endured, —WLMS . . . the same stigma as he, —TCNT . . . and bear the abuse He suffered, —BECK . . . and share his disgrace, —TNT . . . enduring the same obloquy as He endured, —WADE.

**13:13.** There is a symbolism in the location of the sacrifice of Jesus and that of the animals. Those who go to Calvary, to the altar of Jesus, can no longer serve and worship at the altar of the temple or tabernacle. They must leave Israel, that is, go outside of the camp and away from the Jewish system. Therefore, professing Jewish Christians had to leave the Jewish altar and rites and identify themselves clearly with Jesus. In doing this they accepted the "reproach" (*oneidismon*, see also 11:26) which comes upon those who identify themselves with Christ.

The situation faced by the Hebrew Christians was not new. Moses and all true believers who have come after him suffered because of their allegiance to the Messiah (John 15:19; 16:33; 2 Timothy 3:12). There is a stigma associated with true faith; believers must be prepared to bear it: they cannot be friends with Jesus and partners with the world at the same time.

**14. For here have we no continuing city:** . . . we have no permanent city here below, —NORL . . . our permanent home is not here on earth, —NOLI . . . there is no city here on earth that will last forever, —NLTG . . . an abiding city, —MNTG . . . no lasting City, —WADE.

**but we seek one to come:** . . . we are looking for the city that is yet to come, —TNT . . . we are searching for that city which is to be ours, —WLMS.

**13:14.** Building upon the imagery of the patriarchs which was presented in 11:1,16 and 12:22, the writer explained that believers must be willing to bear the shame of identification with Jesus because they recognize they do not have a permanent city upon earth and look, therefore, for the establishment of God's eternal, heavenly city in the future. Just as the heroes of faith (chapter 11) looked beyond this world in their pilgrimage, so Christians also must break away from the value system of the world and endure persecution because they seek God's approval and reward—not man's.

**15. By him therefore:** ... So then, through Christ, –WLMS.

**let us offer the sacrifice of praise to God continually:** ... let us never cease to offer up, –TNT.
**that is, the fruit of [our] lips giving thanks to his name:** ... the speech of lips, –WLMS ... praise that springs from lips which acknowledge his name, –TNT ... that confess his name, –MNTG.

**13:15.** Believers have priestly responsibilities under the new covenant. All Christians are priests (1 Peter 2:5). As such they are called upon to offer up sacrifices. But the sacrifices offered under the new covenant are not animal sacrifices; they are spiritual sacrifices. Instead of offering the fruit gathered in the harvest in worship and sacrifice, believer-priests are to worship the Lord by continuously praising Him and giving thanks to Him for their eternal salvation.

**16. But to do good and to communicate forget not:** ... Do not forget to do good and fellowship, –KLGS ... do not forget to be beneficent and to Distribute, –WLSN ... to be kind, –TNT ... stop neglecting to do good, –WLMS ... and to share, –ADAM ... and to speak the Good Word to others, –NORL.
**for with such sacrifices God is well pleased:** ... highly pleased, –WLMS.

**13:16.** This verse continues to identify some of the spiritual sacrifices Christians are called upon to offer as believer-priests. The first term used here, *eupoiias*, means "doing good." It refers to works of mercy and benevolence which spring from the kindness and generosity of the believer's heart. Those who have received God's grace in forgiveness know what it is to be in need. Their gratitude for God's help in their time of need overflows and leads them to reach out to help others, specifically sharing their material substance with others (*koinōnias*). True Christian religion manifests itself in action. It helps those who cannot help themselves. It opens up both its heart and its wallet (James 1:22-27; 2:15-17; 4:17). God is satisfied and very pleased with sacrifices which possess the qualities presented in these two verses: praise, thanksgiving, helping, giving, and sharing.

17. **Obey them that have the rule over you, and submit yourselves:** ... Obey your pastors and submit to their will, –NORL ... Continue to obey and to be submissive to your leaders, –WLMS ... put yourself under their authority, –SEB.
**for they watch for your souls:** ... Day and night they take care of you, –TNT ... for they are vigilant for the sake of your souls, –CNDT ... they are ever watching in defense of your souls, –WLMS.
**as they that must give account:** ... as men who will have to give account of their trust, –WLMS ... for they are responsible to God for you, –TNT.
**that they may do it with joy, and not with grief:** ... Make this a joy to them and not a burden, –TNT ... with lamentation, –MNTG ... and not groaning, –KLGS.
**for that [is] unprofitable for you:** ... that wouldn't be to your advantage, –ADAM ... it is no help to you, –NLTG ... For that would be worthless to you, –KLGS ... That would not do you any good, –TNT.

**13:17.** The love for God and for one another which has been under consideration in this section is to be directed also to local church leadership. Because of their position and the relationship of trust which exists, Christians are to "obey" those who are leading (*hēgoumenois*) them. They are to place themselves under ("submit" to) their leaders in a spirit of yieldedness (*hupeikete*). These leaders are alertly watching over the "souls" (*psuchōn*, "lives," "persons") under their care as those who are responsible and who will have to give an account of their guardianship. The reference here is to the general watchful care of local church leaders over the congregation of saints.

The members of the congregation are admonished to follow their leaders in a quiet and gentle manner so the leaders will find the responsibility of oversight art enjoyable task. The alternative is groaning (*stenazontes*)—laborious chafing and struggling under the unpleasant task of shepherding a flock of wayward strays. It is far better for a congregation to follow its leadership peaceably. When there is resistance and rebellion, joy turns into *alusiteles*, something which is confining, inferior, unprofitable, and disadvantageous.

18. **Pray for us:** ... Continue to pray, –WADE ... Keep on praying, –TNT ... for me, –WLMS.
**for we trust we have a good conscience:** ... since we are becoming more and more persuaded, –WADE ... We are sure that we have a clear conscience, –TNT ... I am sure that my own conscience is clear, –NOLI.
**in all things willing to live honestly:** ... since it is our wish to conduct ourselves honourably in every respect, –WADE ... that I do my best to live a righteous life in every respect, –NOLI ... we want to

behave well in everything, —ADAM . . . in everything I want to live a noble life, —WLMS . . . we want to do what is right in all circumstances, —TNT.

**13:18.** As a leader, the inspired writer requested prayer for himself and other leaders. In keeping with the responsibilities of love, all Christians can engage in this positive action on behalf of their leaders. The assembly of believers that prays earnestly and continually for its leadership will be a happily united congregation. Faithful leaders are worthy of the prayers of their congregations because they have a "good (*kalēn*, 'noble, worthy of emulation') conscience, in all things willing to live honestly." In all the areas of their lives they conduct themselves in a way that demonstrates they are open and willing to live exemplary lives before their brethren.

19. **But I beseech [you] the rather to do this:** . . . And more especially do I beg you to do so, —WLMS . . . I beg you most earnestly for your prayers, —TNT . . . And I appeal to you all the more earnestly to carry out this request of mine, —WADE.

**that I may be restored to you the sooner:** . . . so that God may bring me back, —TNT . . . so I may be brought back to you the more quickly, —KLGS . . . that I may return to you, —NOLI.

**13:19.** To the general call to prayer for himself and their leaders, the writer added an urgent appeal. He wished to be present with those to whom the epistle was written, but something was hindering him from doing so. He encouraged them *perissoterōs* ("more earnestly," RSV) to pray for him in order that he might be restored to them at once. The exact cause of this separation was not revealed. But whether it was sickness, imprisonment, bad weather, a change in financial situation, poor traveling conditions, or the pressure of his responsibilities in connection with some other church's problems, it made no difference. He was convinced that prayer could alter his situation and bring him into their midst once again. What a magnificent testimony to the power of prayer in the Church!

20. **Now the God of peace:** . . . who gives us peace, —WLMS.

**that brought again from the dead our Lord Jesus:** . . . Who brought up from among the dead, —WADE.

**that great shepherd of the sheep:** . . . The Great Sheep Herder of the flock, —KLGS.

**through the blood of the everlasting covenant:** . . . with the marks of the Blood shed by Him to make binding an Eternal Covenant, —WADE . . . the blood by which He ratified the everlasting covenant, —WLMS . . . in the blood of the ageless agreement, —KLGS.

**13:20.** Verses 20 and 21 compose a closing benediction. The blessings of "the God of peace" were invoked upon this group of embattled Hebrew Christians. Nothing could be a more appropriate reminder of God's power to overcome the turmoil in their lives and the surrounding world. His power was demonstrated convincingly in the resurrection of our Lord Jesus Christ. He came back from the dead. He is the Leader whom the sheep follow. Even though the sheep go down into the valley of death, they have nothing to fear because Jesus, the Great Shepherd, will lead them through and out of death. He has been there before them and triumphed. He knows the way and has defeated the foe. Jesus has become the eternal High Priest who always lives to secure the believers' deliverance. The shedding of His blood made possible an eternal covenant. It is a covenant that will never be superseded, because it rests on the final, once-for-all, sin-covering sacrifice of God's unique Son. Christians have nothing to fear.

21. **Make you perfect in every good work to do his will:** . . . may God (I repeat) equip you thoroughly with every good quality, for the accomplishment of His will, —WADE . . . perfectly fit you, —WLMS . . . knit you together, —WLSN . . . be adapting you to, —CNDT . . . equip you, —MNTG.

**working in you that which is wellpleasing in his sight:** . . . so that you may do his will, —TNT . . . accomplishing through you what is pleasing to Him, —WLMS.

**through Jesus Christ:** . . . May he do in us through Jesus Christ, —TNT.

**to whom [be] glory for ever and ever. Amen:** . . . have all the shining greatness forever! Let it be so, —NLTG.

**13:21.** The inspired writer prayed that God would, through Jesus Christ, restore and equip (*katartisai*) the Hebrew Christians so they could carry out His will in the performance of the good deeds described in verses 1-19. He also prayed that their performance would gain the approval of God, just as the heroes of faith referred to in chapter 11 obtained a good testimony from God concerning their righteousness, faithfulness, and mighty exploits. Such behavior is possible only through the grace mediated by Jesus Christ; therefore, all of the praise and glory will be given to Him as the eternal ages unceasingly roll on.

22. **And I beseech you, brethren, suffer the word of exhortation:** . . . Now I encourage you, —KLGS . . . I beg you, brothers, to listen patiently to this message, —WLMS . . . I urge you, fellow Christians, listen patiently to what I say, —BECK . . . be patient with my word of, —NORL . . . bear patiently with this word of exhortation, —TNT . . . put up with my word of encouragement, —ADAM . . . bear with the word of

entreaty, —CNDT . . . bear with these words of advice, —TCNT.

**for I have written a letter unto you in few words:** . . . for I have written to you briefly, —MNTG . . . for I have written you only a short letter, —WLMS.

**13:22.** After the benediction, the epistle concludes with a few personal remarks and greetings. The Hebrew Christians to whom the epistle was written were asked to bear the exhortations of the epistle with patient endurance (*anechesthe*). The letter was called *tou logou tēs paraklēseōs* (the word of consolation), a strong word of encouragement. The believers were insistently asked to focus their attention on the finality of Jesus' work and encouraged to rest completely in Him.

**23. Know ye that [our] brother Timothy is set at liberty:** . . . I want you to know, —TNT . . . You should know that Brother Timothy has been released, —NORL . . . Let me inform you that our Brother, —WADE . . . is out of prison, —NLTG . . . is free again, —BECK.

**with whom, if he come shortly, I will see you:** . . . if he comes in time I will bring him with me when I come, —TNT . . . If he comes soon, he and I will see you together, —WLMS . . . we will visit you together, —TCNT.

**13:23.** Apparently Timothy had been confined in prison and only recently been set free. This seems to throw light on the writer's own circumstances mentioned in 13:19. The matter of the identity of the writer of the Epistle to the Hebrews is debated by Biblical interpreters. On the basis of this verse many would argue that Paul was the inspired writer of this epistle. On the basis of the great differences observed between Hebrews and the letters of the New Testament known to have been written by the apostle Paul, many evangelical scholars are reticent to attribute Hebrews to him. The ideas and themes of the epistle certainly are in agreement with Paul's teachings, but the vocabulary, style, and other linguistic features are quite different from those found in Paul's epistles. Barnabas, Luke, Silas, and many other names have been put forward as suggested writers of Hebrews. Obviously, if Paul did not write this epistle, someone in the Pauline circle did, someone who was associated with Timothy.

Since the writer whom the Spirit used is nowhere identified in the epistle by name, it seems wisest to conclude with the second-century church father, Origen of Alexandria, that "as to who actually wrote the epistle, God knows the truth of the matter." (Cited from the fourth-century church historian, Eusebius, in *Church History,* 6:25:11-14.) But whoever the writer was, he expected Timothy to join him soon, and they planned then to travel and visit the recipients of the epistle.

**24. Salute all them that have the rule over you, and all the saints:** . . . Greet all your leaders, —ADAM, —CNDT . . . Give my warm greetings to, —TNT . . . Remember us to all your leaders and to all the Christians, —WLMS . . . Greet all the officials, —KLGS . . . all the Christian lay-members, —NORL.

**They of Italy salute you:** . . . The Immigrants from Italy send you their kind remembrances, —WADE . . . Christians from Italy wish to be remembered to you, —WLMS . . . Our Italian friends also send you their greetings, —TNT.

**13:24.** The greetings of this verse are as enigmatic as the reference to Timothy in verse 23. There is first the standard epistolary greetings to the leaders of the church to whom the epistle was sent and to the "saints," that is, to the whole assembly of believers. The final sentence is, however, not clear. The words "they of Italy salute you" indicate the greetings were from some natives of Italy. This may mean the epistle was written from Italy and greetings were sent from all the Italian Christians. But it may also mean that he was somewhere other than Italy, and the Italian greetings indicate he was writing to people who resided in Italy. There is no easy way to decide the issue. This is one reason Hebrews is called a general epistle. The arguments propounded seem to make the most sense if they are thought of as being directed to professing Jewish Christians.

**25. Grace [be] with you all. Amen:** . . . God's loving favor, —NLTG . . . Gracious love, —SEB . . . God's spiritual blessings, —WLMS . . . God bless you all, —LBCH . . . May the favor of God, —MKNT . . . God's favor and spiritual blessing, —AMPB.

**13:25.** The magnificent epistle ends with the standard epistolary close used in Christian letters. The full meaning of the word "grace" was artfully presented as the case for the permanent superiority of Christ's saving work as it was argued throughout the epistle. This is a final prayer that the Hebrew Christians would all experience it.

# JAMES

## Overview

### Opening

The Epistle of James belongs to the so-called General (Catholic) Epistles. The books were given this designation because most of them are not addressed to any specific individual or local church. The author presents himself as James; the epistle is sent "to the twelve tribes which are scattered abroad." This phrase is thought to address a group of Jewish-Christian readers living in the Diaspora (the regions of the dispersion). Since the epistle was written in Greek, it is plain that it spoke to Greek-speaking Jews who believed Jesus to be the Messiah.

On the Day of Pentecost, many Jews from other parts of the Roman Empire visited Jerusalem. These, believing in the proclamation of the apostles, carried the gospel back to their homeland in the Diaspora (cf. Acts 2:9-11; 9:2; 11:19; 13:1).

The author describes himself simply as "James, a servant of God and of the Lord Jesus Christ." This is enough for his readership to recognize him. During the early Christian Era there was only one James who could consider himself that familiar to the Jewish Christian constituency, namely James the brother of Jesus, leader of the church in Jerusalem (cf. Galatians 2:12). The Jews of the Diaspora were used to receiving religious advice and guidance from the church in Jerusalem. This made it easy for them to accept instruction from James. Because of his location in the holiest city of Judaism and the hub of the Christian faith as well, James could contact Jewish Christians throughout the Roman Empire, especially during the pilgrimage feasts when travelers would come to Jerusalem (e.g., Acts 2). Thus, there may have been some personal contact between James and his readers. The authoritative as well as brotherly tone of his letter shows James was a highly esteemed and beloved Christian leader.

There is a strong argument from tradition that James the brother of the Lord authored this epistle. Some contend for two other apostles of the same name. James the son of Alpheus was probably too unrecognized to claim such authority for himself. John's brother, James the son of Zebedee, died as a martyr as early as A.D. 44. However, this need not exclude him from having authored the epistle, since much of the evidence suggests that it was written before the apostolic council in Jerusalem (A.D. 49-50). It could have been written in the midforties.

Nevertheless, in all probability the author is the Jerusalem church leader James, the brother of our Lord. The unique style and manner of the epistle itself support this position, especially when compared with the correspondence from the council recorded in Acts 15. (1) Both have the same form of greeting (cf. James 1:1; Acts 15:23). (2) Both use the same Greek word for "to visit" (cf. James 1:27; Acts 15:14). (3) Both have the same Greek expression for turning back to God (James 5:19,20; Acts 15:19). (4) The idea that "by the name of the Lord believers are 'called'" is the same in James 2:7 and Acts 15:17.

The Epistle of James was known relatively early in the Early Church, but it was included among the "disputed letters" for a time. Origen first attributed the letter to James the brother of the Lord and accepted it as Holy Writ. Athanasius, Jerome, and Augustine also acknowledged the epistle as genuine. At the councils of Hippo (A.D. 393) and Carthage (A.D. 397) the epistle was accepted as canonical. One of the chief reasons for the delay in its inclusion was almost certainly its appeal to Jewish Christians. Gentile Christians, who largely controlled the Church in later years, were perhaps reluctant to include books other than those used by their own missionaries and apostles. An apparent contrast between Paul and James may have also contributed to the delay.

Even as late as the Reformation the question of the canonicity of the epistle was raised again. Since more than 400 years of evangelical Christianity have preceded us, the question may seem superfluous. But to the Reformers, who in effect "rediscovered" the Scriptures, the issue was quite different. Should the canon of the Roman Catholic Church be adopted wholesale? As we learn from history, they did not adopt such a policy; some books of the Roman Catholic canon are not in the Protestant Bible. When the Synod of Trent accepted the apocryphal books into the canon, Protestants did not. But the Epistle of James was retained, in keeping with the process of canonization in the Early Church. With respect to the question of the authenticity of the epistle today there is almost no strong difference of opinion.

It is not easy to outline this epistle; some even consider it impossible. Those structures that have been attempted usually are lists of themes. James has a somewhat loose structure, arranged around one central theme. Its message is crystal clear and forms the background for interpreting the entire letter. Its central theme comes to the fore in 2:14-26, the main section of the letter: Faith and obedience are inseparable.

## The Literary Style of the Epistle

Knowing the literary style of the epistle is a vital step towards understanding its message. The epistle reflects a particular type of literature known as paraenesis. During the First Century paraenetic writings were commonplace in the Jewish and Greco-Roman cultures (Dibelius Hermeneia, James, p.3). This kind of writing is characterized by ethical instruction and rules for living. Normally these are somewhat loosely joined together according to major themes. It is important to keep in mind the relationship to these themes.

This type of writing is reminiscent of Jewish wisdom writings; for example the short, pithy style and the frequent use of the imperative mood. Furthermore, useful illustrations and applications are interspersed; vices and virtues are listed. Often dialogue takes place between imagined opponents. This technique, known as diatribe, was also used by the Greeks.

Many places in the New Testament show evidence of this paraenetic style, especially the writings of Paul and James. They both employ paraenetic lists (Galatians 5:19-23; James 3:13-18), and both hold debates with imagined opponents whom they drive into a corner during the course of debate (Romans 3:1-20; James 2:14-26). The admonition sections of Paul's letters often contain paraenesis; James, also, contains paraenetic instruction.

## The Relationship with Other Scriptures

Numerous similarities between the contents of the Epistle of James and contemporary Jewish and Greek writings can be demonstrated. There are also some striking similarities between James and Old Testament sayings, Gospel passages, and other New Testament letters. James, however, was no "compiler" of tradition; rather, he was an independent and original inspired writer, guided by the Holy Spirit in what he wrote.

In his brief letter James makes a number of citations or allusions to the Old Testament, including the Pentateuch, Joshua, 1 Kings, Job, Psalms, Proverbs, Ecclesiastes, Isaiah, Jeremiah, Ezekiel, Daniel, Hosea, Joel, Amos, Jonah, Micah, Zechariah, and Malachi. Thus we see in James a beautiful illustration of the unity of the Bible and of the hermeneutics of the Holy Spirit. The deity of Jesus is emphasized as His words are accorded the same authority as those of God in the Old Testament Scriptures.

The parallels with the Gospels is one of the most distinctive features of the Epistle of James. If one compares one of Paul's letters with James, their differences in style and content will be readily apparent. There would be a different response if one compared James with the Gospels, especially Matthew. Then their similarities would be striking. Ryrie finds no less than 15 references to the Sermon on the Mount alone (p. 137). Mussner points out 12 points of contact with the Gospels. He goes on to cite G. Kittel's finding of some 26 similar points of contact with the Gospels (pp.47f.). E. Thidemann has compiled the correspondences: James 1:2 and Matthew 5:11; James 1:4 and Matthew 5:48; James 1:5 and Matthew 7:7; James 1:6 and Matthew 9:29; James 1:17 and Matthew 7:11; James 1:22 and Matthew 7:24; James 1:23 and Matthew 7:26; James 2:5 and Matthew 5:3,5; James 2:6 and Luke 18:3, 20:47, Mark 12:40; James 2:8 and Matthew 22:39; James 2:11 and Matthew 5:21; James 2:13 and Matthew 5:7; James 2:14f. and Matthew 25:21-46; James 2:15 and Matthew 6:25; James 3:1f. and Matthew 5:9; James 4:2 and Matthew 5:21; James 4:3 and Matthew 7:7; James 4:4 and Matthew 12:39; James 4:9 and Luke 6:25; James 4:10 and Matthew 23:12; James 4:11 and Matthew 7:1; James 4:13-15 and Matthew 6:34; James 4:17 and Luke 12:47; James 5:1 and Luke 6:24; James 5:2 and Matthew 6:19; James 5:5 and Luke 16:19; James 5:6 and Luke 6:37; James 5:7 and Mark 4:26-29; James 5:9 and Mark 13:29, Matthew 24:33; James 5:10 and Matthew 5:12; James 5:12 and Matthew 5:34; James 5:17 and Luke 4:25; James 5:19 and Luke 17:3, Matthew 18:15.

These parallels indicate a close relationship with the events described in the Gospels. Not all of these parallels are equally significant, but collectively they cannot be dismissed outrightly. It is virtually impossible that these similarities occurred by chance. The writer was intimately associated with Jesus and had the advantage of personal observation. This also supports the view that the writer was the brother of Jesus.

It is evident that James had extensive knowledge of Jesus' sayings, both from his own memory and from common knowledge among those who had been with Him. The Holy Spirit could recall Jesus' teachings to James, according to His purpose in this epistle. It may have been written prior to any of the Gospels, and perhaps, as some contend, it is the earliest document of the New Testament.

Apart from the four Gospels, no other New Testament writings contain such a clear echo of the Gospel words of Jesus. In reality the whole epistle is knit together with sayings of Jesus. These form the background for the Christology and soteriology (doctrine of salvation) of the Epistle of James.

## Christology

The Epistle of James is very clear in its presentation of those doctrines it is concerned with. It was not intended to cover every doctrine of the Christian faith. However, this is not as unique as some have tried to argue; other New Testament writings are similar. The Bible is not designed so every document repeats what every other one says. The doctrine of the sufficiency of Scripture concerns Scripture as a unit, not each book.

Since the beginning of Christianity the Church followed the teachings of the apostles (Acts 2:42). In this epistle the essential apostolic teaching about divine revelation and redemption are presumed to be known by believers. Thus, we see why Jude, without any explanation, challenges his readers to strive for "the faith which was once delivered unto the saints" (Jude 3). If this holds true for Jude, which deals with Christian doctrine, why is it strange to some that James—a letter concerned about Christian life-style—should do the same?

In commenting on James in this way it should be emphasized that the epistle does have an abundance of Biblical advice that is unique in its Christian content, but which modifies Jewish material. The very concept of God in James is "Christianized." God is "Father" (2:17; 3:9); He has revealed himself in the Son, Jesus Christ. The letter further has a rather sophisticated Christology and soteriology.

James proclaims Jesus Christ is Lord (1:1; 2:1; 5:8). This is called the first Christian symbol (Romans 10:9; Philippians 2:11), and we find it as early as James. When the first Christians called Jesus "Lord," kurios, they adopted the Old Testament's language (cf. John 20:28). James interchanges the name Lord with God the Father and the Son; at times it is difficult to determine just which is meant (e.g., 5:7-15). And when in his opening James referred to himself as a "servant of God and of the Lord Jesus Christ," it was an equation of Jesus with God. This was asserting the deity of Jesus Christ. Furthermore, we note that James presented Jesus Christ as the object of faith; He is the One in whom we trust (2:1). Like the rest of the New Testament authors, according to James the faith that saves us is faith in Christ. Of course, this includes faith in God (2:23).

James refers to this Jesus in whom we trust as "Jesus Christ the Lord of glory" (2:1). Particularly for James, as brother to the Lord and as a witness of Jesus' humanity and humbleness during their days in Nazareth, this designation must have been among James' most natural expressions for his faith in Jesus Christ. But from other New Testament passages we see that Christ's death, resurrection, and ascension are the heart of the Christian faith (Acts 4:33). The death of Christ—the Cross—is implicit in the preaching of His resurrection (cf. 1 Corinthians 1:18; 15:3-5). In Ephesians 1:19 and 2:10 the message of the resurrection and ascension of Christ capture the entire message of the gospel. Salvation is there described as being "made alive in Christ" (2:5). Paul adds in Ephesians 4:9 the comment that the exaltation of Christ would have been of no consequence to us had He not first humbled himself in His humanity.

It is precisely because Christ died for our sins that in Romans 10:9 Paul can state that faith in the resurrection of Jesus is saving faith (cf. 1 Thessalonians 1:10). James' understanding of "the faith of our Lord Jesus Christ, the Lord of glory" must have included the dimension of faith in the person and work of Jesus Christ. The phrase thus summarizes the Christian faith. The glorified Lord in whom the Church believes is none other than the Lord who answers prayers (James 5:14,15; cf. Mark 16:17; Acts 3:16; Colossians 3:17).

Connected to the Christology of the epistle is an eschatology that places the return of Christ in the center of the events of the last days: "The coming of the Lord draweth nigh" (5:8). This reflects the vibrant expectation of the Early Church (cf. John 21:23; 1 Thessalonians 1:10; Hebrews 10:37). Believers saw themselves as living in the last days (1 Corinthians 10:11; Hebrews 1:2); Christ's return was imminent. During trials and persecutions the coming of the Lord was the sustaining hope of the Church. They anticipated the coming of Christ the Saviour. The eschatology and soteriology of the epistle are founded on its Christology.

## Soteriology

Soteriology, or the doctrine of salvation, is proclaimed by the Epistle of James in much the same language and terms as in the rest of the New Testament. It can be described as justification (2:23), with the corresponding concepts of grace (4:5) and forgiveness of sins (5:15). Likewise, the idea of a new birth is discussed (1:18). God is said to be mighty to save (4:12). With reference to the new birth, it is said to take place by faith. The idea of faith in James is especially faith in Jesus Christ (2:1). The believer belongs to the name that called him (James 2:7; cf. Acts 4:12, where the name of Jesus is the only name given whereby men can be saved). These unique elements comprise the background for understanding some difficult passages in the letter.

At issue in the Epistle of James is the concept of justification. James speaks of justification by faith as well as justification by works (2:21-25). If one hopes to comprehend this paradox, the letter's teaching about the way to salvation must be understood. Then the reader will discover that James does not allow humanity the least hope of self-justification. James' view of the fallen nature of humankind forbids any such notion.

The prime difference between the Mosaic law and the gospel of Christ was that the former was based on works and the latter on grace. Under both systems individuals had to choose for themselves whether to serve God or not. Men are born with a corrupt, sinful nature, because of Adam's sin. This imposes on them a tendency toward unrighteousness and sin. Unless they find a means of atonement, only judgment can be their lot.

God has always provided a way for men to obtain forgiveness. Under the Law there was an elaborate system of sacrifice, with the great one on Yom Kippur, the Day of Atonement. On that occasion, once a year, the high priest offered a bullock for the sins of the entire nation, sprinkling the blood on the mercy seat in the Holy of Holies. Then a scapegoat was brought, and laying his hands on its head, the high priest confessed over the goat "all the iniquities of the children of Israel, and all their transgressions in all their sins" (Leviticus 16:21). Then the goat was sent into the wilderness, never to return, symbolizing God's forgiveness.

Note that the atonement was made for all the sins of all the people; however, individuals had to enter by faith into the reality of that atonement by their own decision, by an act of their own will. The other sacrifices provided this opportunity.

In Jesus' day some of the Pharisees had the idea they could be justified by fully keeping the Law. This is why they developed a detailed collection of rules, the "traditions of the elders," to interpret the Law. But Jesus revealed they could not even keep the first commandment, to love God wholly. Paul, a former Pharisee, could testify that he had reached the point of being "blameless" as far as the "righteousness which is in the law" was concerned (Philippians 3:6)—but he had not found salvation!

The same principle holds true concerning salvation under the gospel. Christ died for the sins of the whole world, so atonement has been made for all mankind. "God is not willing that any should perish" (2 Peter 3:9). But each individual must choose for himself. By the Holy Spirit, God is seeking to draw all men, but He does not force men to accept. Neither does he arbitrarily reject any. Man has a free will by which he may choose.

The Scriptures say, "There is none righteous, no, not one" (Romans 3:10). James emphasizes this truth by his discussion of the tongue (3:1-12). "The tongue can no man tame. It is an unruly evil, full of deadly poison" (verse 8). And back of the tongue stands the heart. Whatever the tongue says reflects the voice of the heart. It is impossible to "tame" the tongue, because man cannot control

his sinful nature. Only by acquiring a new nature can victory come. And this is what God does for men through the new birth, making them "partakers of the divine nature" (2 Peter 1:4).

Jesus stated that a bad tree cannot bring forth good fruit. This is a central theme in His teaching; it is also one proclaimed by the apostles who followed Him. Peter wrote of an empty way of life received by tradition from their fathers (1 Peter 1:18). John wrote: "If we say that we have no sin, we deceive ourselves" (1 John 1:8). Paul tells us that the "carnal mind is enmity against God: for it is not subject to the law of God, neither indeed can be" (Romans 8:7). Skimming a series of passages in James shows that he totally agreed with this viewpoint which challenged the Jewish understanding of justification. Consequently, we see that there is no basis for thinking that James believed one can be justified by works. Such a notion is just as unthinkable as believing a bad tree could bear good fruit or that a bitter fountain could provide fresh water (3:12).

Such a radical but Biblical view of the sinful nature of humanity forms the backdrop for all that James—in concert with the other New Testament authors and Jesus—understood to take place at salvation. Salvation is the unmerited forgiveness of sin and the justification (i.e., pronouncing as righteous) of the guilty party (2:23; 5:15). Moreover, it involves such a radical transformation of the individual's personality and disposition that it is called "rebirth, regeneration, or re-creation." It is part of Jesus' own message: "Ye must be born again(!)" (John 3:7). Paul put it this way: "If any man be in Christ, he is a new creature: old things are passed away; behold, all things are become new" (2 Corinthians 5:17). Peter said that God "according to his abundant mercy hath begotten us again unto a lively hope by the resurrection of Jesus Christ from the dead" (1 Peter 1:3). John wrote: "Whosoever believeth that Jesus is the Christ is born of God" (1 John 5:1).

James joined in this harmonious proclamation: "Of his own will begat he us with the word of truth that we should be a kind of firstfruits of his creatures" (1:18). The original wording of the Greek is an emphatic expression, which in the New Testament uniquely denotes regeneration. It signifies the new birth from above; "that which is born of the Spirit is spirit" (John 3:6). We were dead spiritually, separated from the life of God, but have been made alive in Christ (Ephesians 2:1,5).

Because James opened his epistle with this understanding of salvation as regeneration, a clear light is shed on his later comments about justification. When the nature of the tree is altered, should it then be able to produce fruit of a different kind? When the fountain is cleansed, should it not be able to give fresh water? When a person becomes a new creature in Christ and has partaken of the very divine nature, should this not lead to a new lifestyle (cf. Romans 6:4)?

Justification cannot be divorced from regeneration. What kind of faith could possibly justify without regenerating? None. The faith that justifies also brings new birth and the transformation of the individual. That is why any faith not expressed in good works is dead and useless (i.e., not faith at all). Faith that does not cause renewal will neither cause righteousness. James brings his discussion to a climactic close with the formulation: "justified by works." The one justified by faith will also be justified by his works.

## Against Antinomianism

The Epistle of James is also a polemical document directed against antinomianism (lit., "antilaw," a rejection of the law which leads to immorality). It is a grand monument to the moral sensibility and integrity of the Early Church.

Within the Jewish-Christian and Gentile churches of the early Christian Era, many shared common struggles. The Gentile believers were confronted by their own heritage of Greek philosophies and "wisdom," while the Jewish Christians felt pressure from their Jewish heritage. These influences circulated throughout the Diaspora. Jewish Christians as well as Gentile Christians had to make a fundamental break with their past. It is easy to understand, though, that many brought with them the mind-set and habits of their days outside of Christ. Related to this tendency is the curious fact that both Jewish and Gentile elements eventually manifest themselves in the area of practical living.

Even more strangely, they appear in two diametrically opposed forms. On the one hand, there is the false asceticism and on the other, licentious libertinism. Jewish Christians were prone to both excessive legalism and overt rejection of all laws. Legalism was an attempt to attain righteousness through the works of the Law; lawlessness appealed to a salvation solely based on faith and void of any obedience.

The New Testament Scriptures combat both legalists and antinomians, whether they originated in Jewish legalism or Gentile philosophical systems. The Epistle to the Galatians is the strongest attack on a Jewish righteousness-by-works mentality, while the Epistle of James is a confrontation with the problem of antinomianism. It may seem that James contrasts with Galatians and argues for the validity of works, but upon closer scrutiny we see that the New Testament as a whole endorses obedience (i.e., "works"). John the Baptist demanded "fruits meet for repentance" (Matthew 3:8). Jesus himself concluded His Sermon on the Mount by

underscoring the necessity of both hearing and acting on His Word (Matthew 7:24ff.). Paul the apostle shaped his preaching to both Jews and Gentiles so "that they should repent and turn to God, and do works meet for repentance" (Acts 26:20.). Peter exhorted his audience to maintain good behavior so the Gentiles could see their good deeds (1 Peter 2:12). John wrote: "Let us not love in word, neither in tongue; but in deed and in truth" (1 John 3:18).

James too calls for works. Christian character becomes manifest in works and vice-versa. Patience must lead to works (1:4). To listen to the Word must promote good deeds (1:22). Faith also leads to works (2:14), as does compassion (2:15,16). Wisdom is to make itself known through works (3:13). Such required good deeds are not exactly the converse of "bad deeds," but of a faith in God that is expressed only in words. "Therefore to him that knoweth to do good, and doeth it not, to him it is sin" (4:17).

## James and Paul

The contrast that some have maintained exists between James and Paul is usually supported by setting certain texts over against others. For example, what Paul said in Romans 3:28: "We conclude that a man is justified by faith without the deeds of the law," is contrasted with what James said in 2:24: "Ye see then how that by works a man is justified, and not by faith only." It must be admitted, if this were the only comment either of these authors wrote, it would be difficult to reconcile them. But both of these detached texts fall in unique contexts; both are conclusions to a certain chain of logic, and they are intelligible only in light of their immediate context. Paul rejected works of the Law as "dead works" (cf. Hebrews 9:14) as far as justification is concerned. James rejected faith without works, "dead faith," as a means of justification.

It is important to understand what the two authors did not mean. James could not possibly have meant that a person becomes righteous in God's eyes through his own efforts to fulfill the Law. He consistently asserted in his letter that all of us fail in many things (3:2). Moreover, he noted explicitly that a single violation of the Law means one is guilty of violating all of the Law (2:10). Thus James dismissed any notion that righteousness is attained through keeping the Law as vigorously as Paul did in Galatians 3:10 and 5:2-4. James knew no way to salvation other than rebirth through the word of truth, i.e., the gospel (1:18), and through justification by faith (2:23).

Paul, for his part, was not saying that the faith which justifies is a faith unrelated to works (obedience). Did he not conclude his comments in Romans 3:21-31 by asking: "Do we then make void the law through faith? God forbid: yea, we establish the law"?

The phrase "God forbid" surfaces throughout the Epistle to the Romans. In many instances it functions precisely to reject the notion that a Christian can "continue in sin" (6:1, 2,15). Paul indignantly opposed any who twisted his message in such a manner (3:8). For Paul, faith that justifies is faith that "worketh by love" (Galatians 5:6), and although one may have all faith, it is nothing without love (1 Corinthians 13:2). Thus, Paul and James fully correspond in their understanding of justification. James does not teach salvation without faith, and Paul does not teach salvation without the works of faith.

A contrast between James and Paul can actually be contrived only if one adopts an interpretation of salvation that places both of them in opposition to what is otherwise taught by the rest of the New Testament., Moreover, such an interpretation would make them inconsistent within their own writings. It is plain that Paul understood "works" in two different senses: there are "works of the law" and "good works." It is equally obvious that James understood works in only one sense—as the fruit of faith.

Of course, it is rather easy to create a false contrast between the two if these distinctions are not maintained. If one compares what Paul said about works of the Law with James' comments about works of faith; and if one also places what Paul said about true faith alongside what James said about dead faith, then it is possible to make it appear as if the two are diametrically opposed to one another.

However, it would be just as easy to make them appear to contradict themselves. The same Paul who said in Romans 3:28 that man is justified by faith without deeds, said in 1 Corinthians 7:19 that keeping the commandments of God is essential to faith. Moreover, James wrote in 2:21 that Abraham was justified by works, but in verse 23 James goes on to say Abraham was justified by faith. Neither Paul nor James, however, seemed to see any contradiction in their words. On the contrary, it appears as if Paul took it for granted that those saved by grace, not works, are saved to do good works (Ephesians 2:9,10). Likewise, James viewed justification by works not in contrast to, but as a confirmation of and in fulfillment of justification by faith (2:21-24).

Some of those who do not agree that the Epistle of James is a response to Paul, still think that the letter may be a correction to a misunderstood "Paulism" similar to the kind Paul himself combated. This should probably be viewed as anachronistic, since there is much to indicate that James was written prior to Galatians and Romans. The kind of antinomianism James attacked does not necessarily have to be a result of some misunderstanding of Paul.

What James might call justification by works is actually the practical outworking of the doctrine of justification by faith. The Epistle of James uses both the notion of faith and works in the same context; one does not negate the other. In this connection it is important to recognize that James is neither the first nor the last to speak of righteousness by works. Jesus himself did, as did Paul. Jesus said that on the day of judgment a person will be condemned or justified according to his works (Matthew 12:37). Similarly, Paul referred to a judgment according to works (Romans 2:16; 14:10; 1 Corinthians 4:4,5; 2 Corinthians 5:10).

Two possibilities are latent in the expression "judgment according to works," either condemnation or justification. The term *justification* comes from the language of the courts and denotes a decision of "innocent" by a judge. At the last day the sentence will be passed according to works; this does not nullify that we are justified by faith. No. James notes that when Abraham was justified by works it was the fulfillment (practical outworking) of justification by faith (2:22,23).

The same holds true for justification by works on judgment day. James says that faith was made perfect by works. The faith that is demonstrated in deed becomes perfect. When faith is manifest through works the tension between faith and works disappears. Then our being justified by faith and judged by works is consistent.

We are saved apart from anything we might do, but we receive what we deserve at the Judgment. Justification by faith is the basis of salvation; justification by works is the fruit of salvation. Though Abraham was justified by faith (Genesis 15:6), he was justified by works 30 years later when he offered Isaac in sacrifice (Genesis 22:12). At that time Abraham had lived as the friend of God (Genesis 18:17). He lived a holy life (Genesis 17:1). Through his life he confirmed the pronouncement of justification given to him by God because of his faith.

# The Epistle of James

## Commentary

### Chapter 1

1. **James, a servant of God and of the Lord Jesus Christ:** ... bondman, *—DRBY* ... slave, *—MNTG* ... I am a workman owned by God, *—NLTG.*

**to the twelve tribes which are scattered abroad, greeting:** ... that are in exile, *—TCNT* ... scattered over the world, *—LBCH* ... that are in the Dispersion, *—CNFT* ... Rejoice! *—FNTN* ... Health, *—CMPB.*

**1:1.** From the earliest days of church history it has been believed that the writer of this epistle was James, a brother of Jesus (Matthew 13:55; Galatians 1:19). He was the leader of the infant church (Acts 12:17; 15:13; 21:18; Galatians 2:12).

The writer introduced himself modestly, simply referring to himself as a servant, meaning a bondslave. See Exodus 21:5,6 for the background of this practice. The submission to God and also to the Lord Jesus Christ reminded Jewish believers that Jesus is the Messiah, coequal with God the Father.

The epistle was addressed to Christians (2:1) who were scattered abroad. The dispersion of the 12 tribes of Israel began in Old Testament times through deportations by foreign powers (2 Kings 18:9-12; chapters 24,25). Christians were scattered as a result of persecution following the martyrdom of Stephen (Acts 11:19).

2. **My brethren, count it all joy:** ... esteem it all, *—CNFT* ... consider it entirely a happy situation, *—ADAM* ... Consider it all pleasure, *—FNTN.*

**when ye fall into divers temptations:** ... when you are encompassed by various trials, *—SWAN.*

**1:2.** The Christians to whom James wrote were having problems not of their own making. They fell into them. These various kinds of problems very likely included severe persecution from both Jews and Gentiles (2 Timothy 3:12). The word translated "temptations" can also have the meaning of trials. That which was an external trial of faith could become an internal temptation to sin. Christians were not to react negatively, but to consider it "all joy" (pure joy, free of bitterness) when times of testing came.

3. **Knowing [this], that the trying of your faith:** ... well aware, *—BRKL* ... these prove, *—NLTG.*

**worketh patience:** ... begets, *—CNFT* ... develops, *—TCNT* ... is working out endurance, *—NORL* ... brings out steadfastness, *—BRKL.*

**1:3.** The reason believers were to rejoice when their faith was tested was that the right attitude would result in steadfastness or endurance. Trials are not intended to destroy, but to strengthen.

4. **But let patience have [her] perfect work:** ... let endurance have, *—MNTG* ... So let the work of testing go on, *—NORL* ... have a perfect effect, *—CMPB* ... have full play, *—BRKL.*

**that ye may be perfect and entire:** ... until your endurance is perfect in every way, *—NORL* ... that you may be fully developed and perfectly equipped, *—WLMS* ... may be completed and rounded out, *—BRKL* ... unimpaired, *—CNDT.*

**wanting nothing:** ... not lacking in anything, *—MNTG* ... no defects whatever, *—BRKL.*

**1:4.** Endurance was not an end in itself. Its perfect work was to make believers "perfect and entire." Perfection or maturity was a progressive product of endurance. See Hebrews 6:1. Entirety or completeness indicated symmetrical development of character; no virtue of the fruit of the Spirit (Galatians 5:22,23) was to be lacking.

5. **If any of you lack wisdom, let him ask of God:** ... are deficient in, *—TCNT.*

**that giveth to all [men] liberally, and upbraideth not:** ... He is eager to help you, *—LBCH* ... who gives to all men freely and without upbraiding, *—MNTG* ... who generously gives, *—WLMS* ... to all without begrudging anyone, *—NORL* ... unreservedly, *—ADAM* ... who gives freely to all people, *—SEB* ... and reproaches not, *—DRBY* ... and does not censure, *—WLSN.*

**and it shall be given him:** ... Ask, then, and you will receive, *—NORL.*

**1:5.** "Wanting nothing" (verse 4) is a very high goal. It might still be a future attainment. James followed this statement by saying that if anyone lacked wisdom he could ask God for it. In the process of godly living there will be trials and challenges for which human wisdom is totally inadequate. In addition human wisdom may at times be evil and contrary to Biblical principles (3:15) and the will of God.

When wisdom is lacking, the believer is to ask God who gives generously. Divine wisdom is a gift of God. But the wisdom which is in view here is what God will give to all believers, not only the spiritual gift which Paul refers to as a "word of wisdom" (1 Corinthians 12:8). They who pray to God will act with more wisdom than they have themselves.

Wisdom can be imparted in various ways. God spoke to Saul of Tarsus in an audible voice (Acts 9:3-6), while He gave Ananias instructions by means of a vision to go and minister to Saul (Acts 9:10). God is sovereign and communicates wisdom in any way He considers appropriate.

The word "ask" as in Matthew 7:7 is in the present tense and means to keep on asking. Lest believers fear that God will become weary with our excessive asking, James indicates He is liberal (gives without reluctance or restraint) and does not upbraid (rebuke or embarrass) the asker for coming often.

**6. But let him ask in faith, nothing wavering:** ... ask with confidence, *—TCNT* ... for there can be no doubting, *—NORL.*
**For he that wavereth is like a wave of the sea:** ... because the doubter, *—FNTN* ... he who hesitates, *—WLSN* ... he who is irresolute, *—CMPB* ... like a surge of the sea, *—MNTG.*
**driven with the wind and tossed:** ... tossed to and fro by, *—NORL* ... driven hither and thither at the mercy of the wind, *—TCNT* ... blown about and broken, *—FNTN.*

**1:6.** Prayer for wisdom must be in faith which is untainted by doubt. Doubt indicates an unwillingness to rely completely on God. Because of this reluctance the believer is deprived of inner peace. He tosses like a wave between trusting human wisdom and trying to rely on divine wisdom.

**7. For let not that man think that he shall receive any thing of the Lord:** ... Such a man need not suppose, *—MNTG* ... cannot expect to get, *—NORL.*
**8. A double minded man [is] unstable in all his ways:** ... a hesitating man, *—FNTN* ... vacillating men, irresolute at every turn, *—TCNT* ... turbulent in all his ways, *—CNDT* ... unstable at every turn, *—MNTG* ... does not himself know what he wants, *—LBCH* ... His heart is divided into two parts, *—SEB.*

**1:7, 8.** In writing about faith, James made a distinction between mental assent and a firm conviction. Demons believe in the existence of God (James 2:19), but the believer who asks of God must not only believe that He exists, but "that he is a rewarder of them that diligently seek him" (Hebrews 11:6).

"That man" indicates a slight contempt for the person who vacillates in trusting God. He is double-minded, trying to look in two directions for help. See Matthew 6:24.

**9. Let the brother of low degree:** ... A Christian brother who has few riches, *—NLTG* ... in humble circumstances, *—MNTG* ... of humble rank, *—FNTN* ... in lowly circumstances, *—ADAM* ... who is poor, and tested, *—NORL.*
**rejoice in that he is exalted:** ... glory in his exaltation, *—MNTG* ... be proud of the honor, *—NORL* ... boast about his high circumstances, *—ADAM.*

**1:9.** In the early days of the Church, members were from all classes of people including slaves (Ephesians 6:5) and the destitute (Acts 2:45; 1 Corinthians 11:21). In contrast to those unstable in faith, rather than being filled with resentment, these new believers were encouraged to be delighted because of their exalted position as "fellow citizens with the saints, and of the household of God" (Ephesians 2:19).

**10. But the rich, in that he is made low:** ... the wealthy of his humble place, *—BRKL* ... but a rich brother, in his humiliation, *—MNTG* ... Let also the one who is rich, but humbled, rejoice, *—NORL* ... in his lowliness, *—CLMT* ... his low condition, *—CNFT.*
**because as the flower of the grass he shall pass away:** ... for he too will fade away, *—NORL* ... like a flower that will die, *—NLTG* ... here for only a short while, *—SEB.*

**1:10.** At the Cross all believers whether rich or poor are on an equal footing. The person the world considers disadvantaged is elevated to a high standing in Christ, and the person the world considers to be in the upper class of society is brought low to the place where his trust is in Christ instead of in riches. People cannot earn a position in the family of God through either poverty or wealth. All are saved by grace through faith apart from works (Ephesians 2:8,9).

Jesus indicated it is hard for a person of wealth to enter into the Kingdom (Matthew 19:16-26). Hard, not because of the wealth, but because of the attitude a desire for wealth can create (1 Timothy 6:9,10). Jesus taught: "Blessed are the poor in spirit: for theirs is the kingdom of heaven" (Matthew 5:3). This is why the rich brother is to rejoice. When he is "made low," that is, becomes so poor in spirit that he makes a complete commitment to Christ, he becomes a fellow member of the household of God (Ephesians 2:19).

The rich brother who is made low has an eternal perspective concerning life and wealth. He has come to see that "the things which are seen are temporal; but the things which are not seen are eternal" (2 Corinthians 4:18). He recognizes that life with all its possessions constitutes a stewardship which brings blessing to the cause of Christ (Acts 4:34-37; 11:27-30).

**11. For the sun is no sooner risen:** ... as the sun comes up, –MNTG.

**with a burning heat:** ... with its glowing heat, –BRKL ... and brings a scorching wind, –NORL ... with scorching heat, –WLSN.

**but it withereth the grass, and the flower thereof faileth:** ... The grass dries up from it, and the flowers wither one by one, –NORL ... parches the grass, –CNFT ... the herb, –BRKL.

**and the grace of the fashion of it perisheth:** ... All that lovely sight must go! –NORL ... and all its beauty is gone, –TCNT ... It is no longer beautiful, –NLTG ... The sun's heat destroys their beauty, –SEB ... the beauty of its appearance is destroyed, –ADAM ... the comeliness of its look has perished, –DRBY ... the beauty of its form disappears, –FNTN ... its lovely appearance is ruined, –BRKL.

**so also shall the rich man fade away in his ways:** ... despite his money, will also come to nothing, –NORL ... he will come to an untimely end, –TCNT ... will the rich man wither, –CNFT ... amid his pursuits, –MNTG ... in the middle of his efforts, –LBCH.

**1:11.** The mention of quickly withering grass and flowers to illustrate the transitory nature of life was a figure the readers of James' letter could understand. In that part of the world the brief season of green grass and colorful flowers is often followed by a time of great heat which produces a sudden transformation from beauty to drabness. Jesus also referred to a south wind, the sirocco, which increases the effects of the intense heat (Luke 12:55). Jesus illustrated the suddenness with which life can terminate with the Parable of the Rich Man (Luke 12:16-20). At the time he was concerned with plans for increasing his wealth, his life came to a sudden end.

**12. Blessed [is] the man that endureth temptation:** ... Happy the man, –WLSN ... who holds out in case of trials, –NORL ... who stands firm, –TCNT, –LBCH ... who sustains trial, –CMPB.

**for when he is tried:** ... when he has stood the test, –MNTG ... having been approved, –CLMT ... becoming qualified, –CNDT.

**he shall receive the crown of life:** ... the prize of life, –NLTG.

**which the Lord hath promised to them that love him:** ... that is promised, –BRKL.

**1:12.** The truly blessed or happy believer in this life is not one who is free of trials but the one who endures them and is steadfast during the testings. The structure in the Greek translated "when he is tried" indicates the testing has been concluded and the person has been approved as genuine. After the testing this person receives a crown of life which is promised to those who love God. "Of life" in the expression "crown of life" stands in apposition to "crown." It indicates the believer will receive "the crown, the life." The article "the"

before the word "life" refers to the quality of life which follows physical death.

Jesus spoke of the nature of this life when He said to those who are persecuted for righteousness' sake, "Rejoice, and be exceeding glad: for great is your reward in heaven" (Matthew 5:12). Paul referred to this new quality of life when he wrote: "Eye hath not seen, nor ear heard, neither have entered into the heart of man, the things which God hath prepared for them that love him. But God hath revealed them unto us by his Spirit" (1 Corinthians 2:9,10).

**13. Let no man say when he is tempted:** ... he should never say, –NORL ... in the hour of temptation, –TCNT.

**I am tempted of God:**

**for God cannot be tempted with evil:** ... is incapable of, –WLSN ... to do wrong, –LBCH.

**neither tempteth he any man:** ... He Himself tempts no one to do evil, –NORL.

**1:13.** Apparently some believers whose faith was being tested allowed the testing to become an occasion of yielding to sinful impulses. Instead of accepting personal responsibility for their failure they were blaming God. This tendency began in Eden when Adam blamed Eve, and God indirectly, and Eve blamed the serpent (Genesis 3:12,13). James was emphatic. Believers were wrong in blaming God.

Because God is absolutely holy, He cannot be tempted with evil. Sometimes He tests believers, but He in no way tempts them to sin. In fact, God will not allow temptation that is greater than the believer can withstand and always provides a way of escape (1 Corinthians 10:13).

**14. But every man is tempted, when he is drawn away of his own lust, and enticed:** ... Now each one is undergoing trial when, –CNDT ... Rather, each one is tempted by his own evil desires by which he lets himself be enticed and lured, –NORL ... tempted by their own passions— allured and enticed by them, –TCNT ... when he is allured by his own evil desire, –WLMS ... by his own inordinate desire, –WLSN ... lusts that allure and entice him, –MNTG ... His selfish desire pulls him away from God, –SEB ... by the longing and seducing of his own lust, –FNTN.

**1:14.** In this verse James took away every excuse anyone might use for not accepting personal responsibility for sin. A person is tempted when he is drawn away by his own lust. Inherent in this statement is recognition of the fact of original sin. Every offspring of Adam and Eve is born with the impulse to sin (Psalm 51:5). It is not external circumstances but the wrong kind of internal desires which lead to sin (Matthew 15:17-20).

Legitimate desires can be drawn out beyond legitimate bounds, and when this happens the person is enticed or trapped. For example, the desire for food is proper, but it is wrong when it becomes gluttony. The same can be said of other God-given desires.

**15. Then when lust hath conceived, it bringeth forth sin:** ... evil desire, –NORL ... When he does what his bad thoughts tell him to do, –NLTG ... and gives birth to sin, –MNTG ... having conceived produces sin, –WLSN.

**and sin, when it is finished:** ... when it is mature, –MNTG ... when it has run its course, –NORL ... is fullgrown, –LBCH ... fully consummated, –CNDT ... the sin grows, –SEB.

**bringeth forth death:** ... and results in death, –SEB ... ends in death, –NORL.

**1:15.** When desire becomes illegitimate it gives birth to sin, and sin results in death. (See Romans 6:23.) This death can be physical or spiritual. God chastens the sinning believer. While not all sickness is the result of sin, in the case of the Corinthians it was, and God even allowed some to die so their souls might be saved (1 Corinthians 11:28-30). On the other hand, death can be spiritual, that is, resulting in separation from God (Isaiah 59:2; 1 Timothy 5:6).

**16. Do not err, my beloved brethren:** ... Do not be deceived, –MNTG ... Make no mistake about it, –SEB ... let no one mislead you, –NORL ... do not be fooled about this –NLTG.

**17. Every good gift and every perfect gift is from above:** ... Every desire to give, –NORL ... and every perfect boon, –MNTG ... every perfect endowment, –TCNT ... Every beneficent gift, –FNTN.

**and cometh down from the Father of lights:** ... the Maker of the Lights in the heavens, –TCNT.

**with whom is no variableness:** ... there is not a change of position, –FNTN ... not a single change, –ADAM ... God never changes, –LBCH ... is always consistent, –SEB.

**neither shadow of turning:** ... and in His light there are no shadows, –LBCH ... nor shadow of eclipse, –MNTG ... neither shadow that is cast by turning, –CLMT ... nor shadow of alteration, –CNFT ... or the least Variation, –WLSN.

**1:16, 17.** James commanded believers to cease from the error of blaming God. He made it clear that rather than being the source of temptation to sin, God is the source of nothing but good. "Every good gift" seems to refer to the manner in which God gives. It is liberal, without reluctance or ulterior motives (cf. verse 5). "Every perfect gift" emphasizes the completeness of the gift; nothing is lacking.

To illustrate God's greatness and unchangeableness James used the figure of light. Not only is God the Creator of sun, moon, and stars, but unlike lights of the universe which cast changing shadows or can be obscured by such things as clouds, God never changes (Malachi 3:6). He is light, and "in him is no darkness at all" (1 John 1:5).

**18. Of his own will begat he us with the word of truth:** ... Because he willed, –MNTG ... He brought us into being, –NORL.

**that we should be a kind of firstfruits of his creatures:** ... in order that we might be a sample of what He created for Himself, –FNTN ... an earnest of still further creations, –TCNT.

**1:18.** After pointing out in verse 17 that God is the giver of every good gift, James called special attention to the gift of salvation. This was provided of "his own will." God took the initiative. After Adam and Eve sinned God promised a plan of redemption (Genesis 3:15). Jesus made it clear that His followers were the result of divine initiative when He said, "Ye have not chosen me, but I have chosen you" (John 15:16). Paul pointed out that God's plan of salvation was not an afterthought. Man's need of salvation was in God's mind before the foundation of the world (Ephesians 1:4).

"Begat he us" speaks of the new birth, of regeneration. Jesus told Nicodemus, "Except a man be born again, he cannot see the kingdom of God" (John 3:3). Paul pointed out the absolute need of becoming a new creature (Galatians 6:15).

An agency in regeneration is "the word of truth." Peter wrote that believers are born again by the Word of God (1 Peter 1:23). The Holy Spirit is also active in regeneration (John 3:5; Titus 3:5). He works through the Word, reproving man of sin, righteousness, and judgment (John 16:8-11). When man believes the gospel (1 Corinthians 4:15) and accepts Christ as Saviour (John 1:12,13; Galatians 3:26), he becomes a new creature.

"Firstfruits" speaks of the beginning of a harvest which is to follow. James' readers were among the beginning of the great gospel harvest which continues to this day. Paul used the expression in the same way (Romans 16:5).

**19. Wherefore, my beloved brethren:** ... Mark this well, –MNTG.

**let every man be swift to hear, slow to speak, slow to wrath:** ... be quick to listen ... slow to lose your temper, –NORL ... tardy to speak, –CNDT ... in growing angry, –MNTG.

**20. For the wrath of man worketh not the righteousness of God:** ... Anger is not the way to arrive at the justice God demands, –NORL ... a man's anger does not further the righteous purpose of God,

*—MNTG*...does not work the justice of, *—CNFT*...is not conducive to Divine righteousness, *—FNTN*.

**1:19, 20.** Believers are begotten "with the word of truth" (1:18), and because of the importance of the Word believers should be "swift to hear." The Word is not only an agent in regeneration but in sanctification as well (John 17:17; 2 Timothy 3:16,17).

Early congregations of believers were small and often met in homes (Philemon 2). In such informal gatherings there were undoubtedly discussions of Biblical truth. James warned against quick, ill-considered comments which would only lead to confusion.

The word here translated "wrath" seems to imply a continuing resentment. It is tragic but true that ill-considered observations sometimes lead to resentment which does not demonstrate righteousness.

**21. Wherefore lay apart all filthiness and superfluity of naughtiness:** . . . strip yourselves of everything impure, *—WLMS* . . . Remove every evil, *—SEB* . . . suppress ill-will and all wickedness within you, *—NORL* . . . stripping off all vicious filth, *—FNTN* . . . put aside all filthy habits, *—TCNT* . . . all that is dirty and wrong, *—NLTG*...superabundance of evil, *—CNDT*...evil excesses, *—ADAM*.

**and receive with meekness the engrafted word:**...accept the Word which is planted in you, *—NORL*...in a gentle heart, *—BRKL*...the implanted Word, *—MNTG*.

**which is able to save your souls:**...that contains the power to save your souls, *—BRKL*.

**1:21.** Believers are to lay aside like a garment all moral filth, all that is sordid. "Superfluity of naughtiness" might also be translated "the remains of wickedness." They had already given up some pagan practices and were urged to give up what still remained.

Eager reception of the Word would result in ultimate salvation. Salvation includes deliverance from the penalty of sin (past), from the power of sin (present), and ultimately from the presence of sin (future).

**22. But be ye doers of the word:** . . . Obey the message that you hear, *—NORL* . . . Put that Teaching into practice, *—TCNT* . . . Obey the Word of God, *—NLTG*...Do whatever God tells you to do, *—LBCH*.

**and not hearers only:** . . . not merely hearers, *—MNTG*...by merely listening, *—BRKL*.

**deceiving your own selves:** . . . beguiling yourselves, *—CNDT* . . . you are only fooling yourselves, *—SEB*...not deluders of yourselves, *—BRKL*.

**1:22.** James here began an emphasis on what the believer should do with the "engrafted word" (1:21). It was not enough to be hearers; they were to make sure they became doers of the Word. Hearing is important because faith comes by hearing (Romans 10:17). But unless hearing is followed by obedience, the consequences can be tragic. In the Parable of the Two Builders (Matthew 7:24-27) Jesus emphasized the difference between hearers who acted upon what they heard and those who did nothing about what they heard.

The word translated "deceiving" carries the idea of false reasoning. The "nondoers" rationalized their lack of conformity to the Word. Like the priest and Levite in the Parable of the Good Samaritan who probably justified their disregard of the injured man, "hearers only" were rationalizing their failure to obey what they heard.

**23. For if any be a hearer of the word:** . . . Any man who listens to the Word, *—NORL* . . . whoever hears the message, *—BRKL*.

**and not a doer:**...but does not carry out its message, *—NORL*...without obeying it, *—WLMS*...without acting upon it, *—BRKL*.

**he is like unto a man beholding his natural face in a glass:**...is similar to the man who observes his own face, *—BRKL*...looking at, *—CNFT*...contemplating, *—FNTN*...in a mirror, *—MNTG*.

**24. For he beholdeth himself, and goeth his way:** . . . he takes a look at himself and goes off, *—BRKL*...after he has looked carefully at himself, he goes away, *—MNTG*.

**and straightway forgetteth:** . . . and presently, *—CNFT*...immediately forgets, *—CMPB*...at once forgets, *—MNTG*...then promptly forgets, *—BRKL*.

**what manner of man he was:**...what he is like, *—MNTG*...what he looked like, *—SEB*.

**1:23, 24.** James compared the casual hearer of the Word with a man who looks into a mirror and does nothing to improve his appearance. The person who does nothing more than hear the Word disregards changes He needs in character. The word translated "glass" would better be translated "mirror" since it was made of polished metal.

**25. But whoso looketh into:** . . . The truly wise man, *—LBCH* . . . the man who looks closely, *—MNTG*...he who has looked carefully, *—CNFT*...looks seriously into, *—BRKL*.

**the perfect law of liberty:**...the Law of Freedom, *—TCNT*.

**and continueth [therein]:**...continues looking, *—MNTG*...and perseveres, *—CMPB*...and is faithful to it, *—BRKL*.

**he being not a forgetful hearer:**...who is not a forgetful listener, *—BRKL* . . . a heedless listener who forgets the message, *—NORL*...don't merely listen and forget, *—BECK*.

**but a doer of the work:**...but an active worker, *—BRKL*...a doer who does, *—MNTG*.

**this man shall be blessed in his deed:**...you'll be happy as you do it, *—BECK*...blessed as a doer, *—NORL*...in his practice, *—BRKL*.

**1:25.** The word translated "looketh into" (*parakupsas eis*) is in contrast to the casual beholding of 1:24. It pictures a person stooping over to see something better. It means intent looking and careful examination because the subject under consideration is very important. The same word describes how John and Mary stooped down and looked into the open tomb in which Jesus had been placed (John 20:5,11) because this was a matter of tremendous significance to them.

The person who seriously continues looking "into the perfect law of liberty" is the person who is blessed. The perfect law is described as "the law of liberty."

The Old Testament law was not perfect. It could not give life or righteousness (Galatians 3:21). It was only a shadow of good things to come (Hebrews 10:1). It was only a schoolmaster to lead to Christ so that believers might be justified by faith (Galatians 3:24).

In the Old Testament God promised a new covenant in which He would place His law within the human heart (Jeremiah 31:33). Jesus introduced this new covenant with His atoning death (1 Corinthians 11:25). This perfect law or new covenant was the "engrafted word" (1:21) James' readers had received. This is the law of liberty which sets believers free from the Law as a means of righteousness (Romans 10:4) and also from sin (Romans 8:1-4). The law of liberty is not a freedom to sin (Romans 6:1,2; Galatians 5:13) but a freedom to serve God (Romans 6:22). The person who continues in the perfect law and acts accordingly will be the happy person.

**26. If any man among you seem to be religious:** . . . Whoever supposes he is religious, —BRKL . . . thinks that he is, —NORL.

**and bridleth not his tongue:** . . . who does not restrain, —WLSN . . . but does not control what he says, —SEB.

**but deceiveth his own heart:** . . . but deludes his own Heart, —WLSN.

**this man's religion [is] vain:** . . . his religious worship, —WLMS . . . a man's religious observances are valueless, —TCNT . . . is empty, —MNTG . . . is worthless, —NORL . . . is useless, —BRKL . . . does him no good, —LBCH.

**1:26.** "Seem to be religious" may be translated "thinks of himself as being religious." Self-deception has often been a problem with people who associate with true believers. The words translated "religious" and "religion" refer to the external aspects of a relationship with God. Jesus dealt with this matter when He warned against wrong motives in giving, praying, and fasting (Matthew 6:1-18).

An unbridled tongue is one indication that a person's inner life does not match his outward profession. Just as a horse needs a bridle to control and direct it, the tongue of the believer needs proper control and direction.

The bridled tongue presupposes bridled thinking. The way to bridle the mind and the tongue is to continue to meditate on the Word of God (1:25). Philippians 4:8 gives guidelines for proper thinking: thinking about that which is true, honest, just, pure, lovely, of good report, virtuous, and praiseworthy.

Critical people are often motivated by resentment, jealousy, or bitterness. They fail to speak "the truth in love" (Ephesians 4:15). Their religion is vain. It does not honor God.

**27. Pure religion and undefiled before God and the Father:** . . . What God the Father accepts as pure unpolluted service, —SEB . . . Your way of worshiping is pure and stainless before God the Father if, —BECK . . . and without blemish, —NORL . . . in agreement with, —BRKL.

**is this, To visit the fatherless and widows:** . . . are things like this, —SEB . . . to give aid to, —CNFT . . . to care for children who have no fathers, —LBCH . . . to look after orphans, —MNTG . . . help orphans, —NORL.

**in their affliction:** . . . in their need, —NORL . . . in their hour of trouble, —TCNT . . . in their distress, —FNTN . . . in their tribulation, —CNFT.

**[and] to keep himself unspotted from the world:** . . . to keep one's own self unstained, —WLMS . . . to keep personally free from the smut of, —BRKL . . . from the contamination of the world, —TCNT . . . unstained, —NORL . . . keep yourself clean from the world's evil ways, —LBCH.

**1:27.** The words "pure" and "undefiled" present the qualities which should characterize the believer. See Mark 7:3, 5, 15-23. "Before God and the Father" may be translated "before our God and Father" or "before God who is our Father." Believers are to be more concerned about God's approval than man's.

One example of pure religion is to "visit the fatherless and widows in their affliction." God had expressed a special concern for orphans and widows in His earliest instructions to Israel (Exodus 22:22). In the early days of the Church, deacons were chosen to care for the widows (Acts 6:1-3).

The word "visit" implies more than just making a contribution of material assistance. The church was to support and sustain the orphans in their problems. The less fortunate were to be included in the social life of the church.

Believers should also jealously watch that they do not become spotted or stained by the world. They are in a world of people who are enemies of God. Jesus did not pray that they should be removed from the world but kept from the evil (John 17:15). But believers also have a responsibility. They must guard against conformity to the world. Through meditation on the Word they are to be transformed (Romans 12:2; also see James 1:25).

## Chapter 2

**1. My brethren, have not the faith of our Lord Jesus Christ:** ... since you believe in, *—NORL* ... do not join faith in, *—CNFT* ... do not hold the faith, *—MNTG* ... do not combine faith, *—BRKL* ... stop trying to maintain your faith, *—WLMS.*
**[the Lord] of glory, with respect of persons:** ... do not show anyone partiality, *—NORL* ... don't treat people differently, *—SEB* ... don't prefer one person to another, *—BECK* ... in a spirit of caste, *—MNTG* ... with the worship of rank, *—TCNT* ... while showing favoritism, *—ADAM.*

**2:1.** James here continued his emphasis on "pure religion" (1:27) by stating that partiality or favoritism of persons should not be tolerated among believers. The world has always been guilty of partiality, and this form of worldliness can also be carried over into the lives of God's people. This evil was forbidden in Israel's earliest days (Leviticus 19:15; Deuteronomy 1:17). Jesus' critics recognized that He did not show favoritism (Luke 20:21). This was a lesson even Peter had difficulty learning (Acts 10:34; Galatians 2:11-14).

There are various opinions as to the significance of the words "the Lord of glory." Some hold it might mean that Christ now reigns in glory (Luke 24:25), while others see it as an adjective and interpret it "our glorious Lord Jesus Christ."

**2. For if there come unto your assembly a man with a gold ring:** ... For should there enter into your meeting a gold-ringed man, *—BRKL* ... Thus, two men may come into your congregation, *—NORL* ... into your synagogue, *—MNTG, —WLSN.*
**in goodly apparel:** ... and dazzling clothes, *—MNTG* ... is well-dressed, *—NORL* ... in showy clothing, *—SWAN* ... in splendid apparel, *—DRBY* ... fine apparel, *—CNFT.*
**and there come in also a poor man in vile raiment:** ... shabbily clad, *—BRKL* ... shabby clothes, *—NORL* ... wearing ragged old clothes, *—SEB* ... in Dirty Clothing, *—WLSN* ... with sordid apparel, *—CMPB* ... mean attire, *—CNFT.*

**2:2.** James here gave an illustration of what might have happened in an assembly setting. Then as now there were extremes of wealth and poverty. It was even possible that both a slave holder and his slave(s) would be present. This is why Paul dealt with the responsibilities and relationships of both masters and slaves (Ephesians 6:5-9).

The contrast between rich and poor would have been obvious. "Gold ring" is more literally "gold-fingered." Wealthy Greek and Roman men wore many rings on the fingers of the left hand. Wearing them on the right hand was considered less than masculine. The poor man on the other hand not only lacked fine clothes but was described as wearing vile clothing. In classical Greek the word translated "vile" indicated dry dirt. Apparently some were so poor they had to wear soiled work clothes as they gathered with believers.

The use of *sunagōgē*, "synagogue, assembly," here for a gathering of Christians is unique in the New Testament. Some have conjectured that the reason *sunagōgē* was used and not the more common *ekklēsia* is that James represents a stage of Christianity before there was a clear break from Judaism. Others point out that *sunagōgē* was used well into the Second Century by Christian writers. As such it could designate either the place of worship or the congregation. Here it is a less specific term denoting a special gathering that was noncultic in character (Davids, *New International Greek Testament Commentary, James,* p. 108).

**3. And ye have respect to him that weareth the gay clothing:** ... you are deferential to the man, *—TCNT* ... you pay special attention, *—NORL* ... you look up to him, *—MNTG* ... him who is clothed in fine apparel, *—CNFT* ... to the one well-dressed, *—BRKL.*
**and say unto him, Sit thou here in a good place:** ... Here is a fine chair, please be seated, *—NORL* ... in this fine place! *—MNTG* ... this place of honor, *—WUST* ... this good seat, *—ADAM.*
**and say to the poor, Stand thou there:** ... You stand back there, *—LBCH.*
**or sit here under my footstool:** ... Sit on the floor at my feet! *—MNTG* ... sit lower than my footstool, *—SWAN* ... or crouch under my footstool, *—FNTN.*

**2:3.** James here shifted attention from the hypothetical rich and poor visitors to the reaction of the believers. "Ye have respect" means literally to "look upon" and in this case to give special respectful consideration to the rich man.

In reproving scribes and Pharisees, Jesus indicated they loved the "chief seats in the synagogues" (Matthew 23:1-6). Apparently even in Christian gatherings there were seats of privilege. The rich visitor was courteously invited to occupy such a choice place.

In contrast, the poor person was treated carelessly, if not rudely. He was told either to stand in a given place or sit on the floor at some believer's footstool. The believer did not even offer him a seat. Both men should have received a similar welcome into the gathering where both might have accepted Christ as Saviour.

**4. Are ye not then partial in yourselves:** ... do you not make improper distinctions, *–WLMS* ... Are you not contradicting yourselves? *–SEB* ... haven't you discriminated among yourselves, *–ADAM* ... Do you not see that you are making class-distinctions among yourselves, *–TNT* ... It is all wrong to make such differences between, *–LBCH* ... do you not make a split among yourselves, *–KLGS* ... within your own group? *–NORL.*

**and are become judges of evil thoughts?:** ... become men who are wrong in their judgment? *–BECK* ... your standards of judgement are all wrong? *–TNT* ... is there not some evil motive back of such discrimination? *–NORL* ... from evil Reasonings? *–WLSN* ... with evil deliberations? *–BRKL* ... of bad ideas? *–KLGS.*

**2:4.** "Are ye not then partial in yourselves" could be translated, "Do you then not doubt or waver within your thinking?" The same Greek verb here translated "partial" is used in 1:6 where the idea is doubting or wavering, double-mindedness. When these believers made prejudicial distinctions between classes of people they wavered between the thinking of the world which made class distinctions and the faith they claimed to possess which forbade showing partiality.

In making the distinction between the rich and poor, the believers were setting themselves up as judges. "Judges of evil thoughts" may better be translated "judges with evil thoughts." They had wrong motives and false standards. These standards were not God's, but the world's. They were looking at outward appearances, while God looks on the heart. In anointing a successor to Saul as king of Israel, Samuel was made aware of God's method of evaluating people (1 Samuel 16:7).

**5. Hearken, my beloved brethren:** ... Listen, *–MNTG* ... Dear Christian brothers, *–NLTG* ... dear fellow Christians, *–BECK.*

**Hath not God chosen:** ... didn't God choose, *–BECK.*

**the poor of this world rich in faith:** ... the outcast of the world, *–KLGS* ... those whom the world regards as poor, *–TNT* ... to be wealthy in the sphere of faith, *–WUST.*

**and heirs of the kingdom:** ... inheritors of the Kingdom, *–KLGS* ... to take possession, *–TNT* ... should come to possess, *–TCNT.*

**which he hath promised to them that love him?:**

**2:5.** The plea to "hearken" or "listen" indicated the intensity of James' appeal. The problem of partiality was not unimportant.

James then pointed out that God had chosen the poor whom the believers were insulting. Jesus said, "Him that cometh to me I will in no wise cast out" (John 6:37). While God welcomes all

who come to Him, these believers were making the poor feel less than welcome (2:6).

The poor were not chosen because they were poor but because they accepted Jesus as Saviour (John 3:16,18). They were chosen before the foundation of the world (Ephesians 1:4), not arbitrarily, but on the basis of what God knew as to how they would respond to Jesus (1 Peter 1:21).

God chose those whom the world classified as poor in order that He might make them rich—not as the world considers riches, but rich in faith. See Luke 12:21; 16:11; 2 Corinthians 8:9. The richness included future blessing as "heirs of the kingdom." There are present (Romans 14:17) and future (Matthew 26:29) blessings of the Kingdom.

**6. But ye have despised the poor:** ... you insult, *–TCNT* ... you have humiliated, *–TNT* ... you have dishonored the poor man, *–MNTG* ... you have beaten down the outcast, *–KLGS.*

**Do not rich men oppress you:** ... use their power to oppress you, *–CNFT* ... who make things hard for you? *–LBCH* ... exploit, oppress, and dominate you, *–WUST* ... gang up on you, *–KLGS.*

**and draw you before the judgment seats?:** ... and drag you to court? *–MNTG.*

**2:6.** The people the world considered rich were next brought into focus. They were not evil or lost because of their wealth but because they had not accepted Jesus as Saviour (John 3:18). The readers of this letter were not only wrong in flattering the rich because it was incompatible with the Christian faith but because these were the people who oppressed and persecuted them (5:1-6). See Acts 13:50; 16:19; 19:23-41.

**7. Do not they blaspheme that worthy name:** ... good, *–CNFT* ... glorious, *–MNTG* ... excellent, *–DRBY* ... noble, *–BRKL* ... Are not they the ones who scoff at the beautiful name, *–WLMS* ... slander the fine Christian name, *–NORL.*

**by the which ye are called?:** ... you bear, *–NORL* ... by which you are distinguished? *–FNTN* ... by which you were called the Lord's own, *–BECK.*

**2:7.** The believers' partiality was further ill-advised because the people they honored were the very ones who dishonored the Christ after whom Christians were named (Acts 11:26). Paul himself at one time had been one of the world's elite who persecuted the Church (Acts 26:9-11).

**8. If ye fulfil the royal law according to the scripture:** ... If you are keeping, *–MNTG* ... If you really observe, *–BRKL* ... If you really do everything the royal law demands, as it is written, *–BECK* ... The royal command is found in, *–SEB.*

**Thou shalt love thy neighbour as thyself, ye do well:** ... you do right, *–NORL* ... you are doing what is right, —TCNT . . . you are doing splendidly, —WUST . . . you behave beautifully, —BRKL.

**2:8.** "If ye fulfill" is stronger in the Greek and can be translated "if you really fulfill." Some think believers were claiming to fulfill the "royal law" by honoring the rich, but in reality, they were disobeying the Law by not showing equal honor to the poor.

"The royal law according to the Scripture" is identified as loving a neighbor as oneself. See Leviticus 19:18. Paul showed that this law was a summary of God's moral law (Romans 13:8-10; Galatians 5:14). It is probably called "the royal law" because it presupposes loving God without reservation (see Matthew 22:40 with 1 John 4:20) and because it encompasses all aspects of the moral law.

9. **But if ye have respect to persons, ye commit sin:** . . . If you have the spirit of caste, —MNTG . . . show partiality to persons, —NORL . . . go in for external show, —SWAN . . . show favoritism, —ADAM . . . treat anyone differently, —SEB . . . prefer one to another, —BECK . . . you are practicing sin, —BRKL.

**and are convinced of the law as transgressors:** . . . the Law convicts you, —BECK . . . you stand convicted, —BRKL . . . and you are judged as evil-doers by the law, —NORL . . . being offenders against it, —TCNT . . . as culprits, —FNTN.

**2:9.** James made some strong statements concerning the practice of favoritism. He made it clear as in 2:4 that prejudice is not a trifling matter, and here he labeled it sin. The etymology of the Greek word translated "sin" means to miss the mark or target. Those wishing to practice the "royal law" missed the mark completely when showing prejudice or favoritism.

"Convinced of the law" may better be translated "convicted by the law." Discrimination against the poor was condemned in Scripture on several occasions (Leviticus 19:15; Deuteronomy 1:17; 16:19). When believers violated this law they were without excuse; they were convicted by the Law as being guilty of transgression.

The Greek word translated "transgress" means to go beyond. It is a strong word which indicates not inadvertent slipping, but deliberately crossing the clearly marked line of Scripture, in this case, regarding partiality.

10. **For whosoever shall keep the whole law, and yet offend in one [point]:** . . . This is the way the law works . . . but breaks one commandment, —NORL . . . yet stumbles, —MNTG . . . slips, —BRKL . . . shall fail in one point, —WLSN.

**he is guilty of all:** . . . may become entangled with all, —FNTN . . . becomes guilty in every respect, —BRKL . . . you're guilty of breaking all of it, —BECK.

**2:10.** The Pharisees of Jesus' time were rebuked for picking which laws they wished to consider important while neglecting others (Matthew 23:23). It is possible some worldly believers were guilty of the same attitude. James made it clear that no believer had the right to exempt himself from any part of God's law. To deliberately disregard one of God's commandments was to disregard the whole, even though all commandments were not transgressed.

11. **For he that said, Do not commit adultery, said also, Do not kill:** . . . Do not sin with another man's wife, —LBCH . . . You must not commit murder, —WLMS . . . Thou shalt not murder," —TCNT.

**Now if thou commit no adultery, yet if thou kill:** . . . So, in case you commit no adultery, but you kill, —BRKL . . . wilt commit murder, —CNFT.

**thou art become a transgressor of the law:** . . . you are guilty of breaking the Law, —NLTG . . . you have become a breaker of, —BRKL . . . you are a wrongdoer, —SEB.

**2:11.** James here used an extreme illustration of adultery and murder to show how wrong it was to choose which commandments one would keep. The application must have been obvious. Believers who obeyed most of God's commandments, but deliberately disobeyed by showing partiality, were still transgressors.

12. **So speak ye, and so do:** . . . So speak and act, —MNTG . . . In your speech and in your actions, —NORL . . . Let both your talk and your action be such, —SWAN . . . in such a way, —BRKL.

**as they that shall be judged by the law of liberty:** . . . as are on the verge of being judged by, —SWAN . . . as befits people who are to be, —BRKL . . . as men about to be judged by, —CNFT . . . by the Law that makes men free, —NLTG . . . the Gospel law, —NORL.

**2:12.** "So speak ye, and so do." In the hypothetical case of the rich man and the poor man (2:2), believers manifested improper speech and action. The believers had become judges with evil motives (2:4). Now James reminded them that they themselves faced coming judgment. See 1 Corinthians 3:11-15; 2 Corinthians 5:10. They should speak and act accordingly.

The New Testament speaks of liberty the believer enjoys (Luke 4:18; John 8:32,36; Romans 8:21; 2 Corinthians 3:17). But this liberty is not freedom to indulge in improper conduct (Romans 6:1- 4). It is freedom to allow the Holy Spirit to manifest Himself in daily life (Romans 8:2-4; Galatians 5:22,23). Believers will be judged on the basis of what they did with this enabling.

13. **For he shall have judgment without mercy, that hath showed no mercy:** . . . For merciless judgment will be the portion of the merciless man,

—WLMS . . . merciless judgment is meted out to the merciless offender, —NORL . . . for judgment is merciless for him who has not practised Mercy, —WLSN.

**and mercy rejoiceth against judgment:** . . . mercy glories in the face of judgment, —MNTG . . . mercy triumphs over judgment, —ADAM . . . Mercy asserts her superiority to Justice, —TCNT.

**2:13.** The "royal law" includes showing mercy, which has its own reward (Matthew 5:7). Some early Christians seemed to adopt the attitude of the Pharisees who were meticulous in observing laws and traditions they liked, but disregarded others. They showed no mercy in wanting to impose judgment even when true repentance was demonstrated (John 8:3-11 with Micah 6:8). Failure to show mercy will be a factor in the Day of Judgment (Matthew 7:1,2).

To show mercy is not to condone evil. Paul instructed the church at Corinth to turn an immoral man over to Satan for the destruction of his flesh (1 Corinthians 5:5). The motivation for administering this discipline was to be redemption—"that the spirit may be saved." Then when repentance became evident, Paul in his second letter urged the church to forgive (2 Corinthians 2:5-8).

"Mercy rejoiceth against judgment" is better translated "glorieth" or "triumphs" over judgment. The believer who has received God's mercy and in daily life fulfills the "royal law," which includes mercy, can face coming judgment with confidence.

**14. What [doth it] profit, my brethren, though a man say he hath faith, and have not works?:** . . . What is the use, —BRKL . . . what good is it if any one says that he has faith, if he has no deeds? —MNTG . . . if a person claims he has faith, —SEB . . . if he has no good deeds to prove it? —WLMS . . . but fails to bring it into practice? —FNTN.

**can faith save him?:** . . . This sort of faith can't save him, can it? —ADAM.

**2:14.** James pointed out the uselessness of claiming to have faith if it is not supported by works. Jesus taught that the person who has genuine faith will do the will of God (Matthew 7:21; see also Matthew 25:41-46; Luke 6:46). Lack of love and mercy indicates a lack of true faith. "Can faith save him?" may be translated "Can that faith save him?" There is a difference between claiming to possess faith and true possession.

**15. If a brother or sister be naked:** . . . They lack both the needed clothing, —NORL . . . is poorly clad, —BRKL.

**and destitute of daily food:** . . . in need of, —MNTG . . . in want of daily food, —CNFT . . . and lacks the day's nourishment, —BRKL . . . has nothing to eat, —KLGS . . . has not enough food for one day, —TNT.

**2:15.** The expression "brother or sister" has two implications. Christianity elevated the status of womanhood above that of the existing cultures. The needs of suffering women were recognized along with that of suffering men. It also emphasized the care believers should have for hurting members of the Christian community (Galatians 6:10).

**16. And one of you say unto them, Depart in peace, be [ye] warmed and filled:** . . . Oh, I am so sorry for you! —FNTN . . . Go your way, and good luck to you! May you keep warm and get a good, square meal! —NORL . . . Goodbye, keep yourself warm and eat well, —NLTG . . . find enough to eat, —LBCH . . . find warmth and food for yourselves, —MNTG . . . have a good dinner, —TNT . . . eat heartily, —BECK.

**notwithstanding ye give them not those things which are needful to the body:** . . . Then suppose, too, that you do not give them these very things they need, —NORL . . . but at the same time you do not give the necessaries of the body, —MNTG . . . without supplying them with their bodily needs, —BRKL . . . does nothing at all to make it possible, —TNT . . . gives nothing the body needs, —KLGS.

**what [doth it] profit?:** . . . what is the good of that? —TNT . . . what good would that do them? —MNTG . . . What does such talk amount to? —NORL . . . what is the use? —BRKL . . . what is it worth, —KLGS.

**2:16.** The ill-clad and hungry brother or sister in James' illustration (2:15) seemed to make people uncomfortable if they had only a profession of faith. One of the group became the spokesman who tried to ease the embarrassment by urging the needy to leave the gathering rather than helping them. It was the common problem of not wanting to get involved.

"Depart in peace" was a customary Jewish parting expression. It had deep meaning when used sincerely, expressing a wish for total well-being. See Mark 5:34; Luke 7:50. When used as a formula for asking someone to leave it was hypocritical and in this case utterly heartless.

"Be ye warmed and filled" indicated an intentional decision not to do anything to provide help. It was expecting that someone else would respond to the need, making the destitute person responsible for finding such a generous person.

The change from the singular "one of you" to the plural "ye" indicates that the entire congregation was guilty of the action even though just one person was the spokesman.

"What doth it profit" indicates the uselessness of an empty profession of faith. When a selfish condition exists, the needy are not cared for, and the able but unwilling persons lose an opportunity to be a blessing and in turn to be blessed. See

Psalm 112:9 with 2 Corinthians 9:6-11; Proverbs 19:17; 28:27.

**17. Even so faith, if it hath not works:** ... Faith is like that. If there is nothing to show for it, *—TNT* ... the faith that issues in no works, *—BRKL* ... without deeds to show for it, *—NORL*.

**is dead, being alone:** ... is by itself a lifeless thing, *—MNTG* ... it is just a word, *—TNT*.

**2:17.** James here applied the truth of his illustration in 2:15,16. Faith which does not result in works is dead. It is like a lifeless corpse. It does not respond to human need.

While James emphasized the uselessness of faith without works, he was not in conflict with Paul's emphasis on salvation by faith. Paul expressed the importance of works following faith in such passages as Ephesians 2:8-10. Believers are God's workmanship "created in Christ Jesus unto (for) good works." Faith that is genuine will result in good works.

**18. Yea, a man may say, Thou hast faith, and I have works:** ... Some one indeed may say, *—MNTG* ... and I am a man of action, *—TCNT* ... I have good deeds, *—WLMS*.

**show me thy faith without thy works:** ... I answer, *—MNTG* ... Prove to me you have faith without any works, *—BECK* ... can you show me your faith apart from, *—NORL* ... without its practices, *—BRKL*.

**and I will show thee my faith by my works:** ... and I will prove to you, *—WUST* ... by my actions, *—TCNT* ... by the loving deeds that I do, *—LBCH* ... through the practices, *—BRKL* ... I'll prove to you I have faith, *—BECK*.

**2:18.** It seems that in objection to James' emphasis on the inseparability of faith and works, some were taking the position that faith and works were separate entities. In essence the objectors were saying, "Some have the gift of faith and others have the gift of works." It is possible they based their view on teaching such as "there are diversities of gifts" (1 Corinthians 12:4).

James forcefully rejected this attempt to separate faith and works and challenged objectors to give one example of true faith which did not result in good works. This, of course, was impossible. James was not teaching that saving faith is earned by good works, but that true faith results in godly action. A faith which does not result in a change in a believer's life is not truly faith (2:14).

Verse 18 is another way of stating what Jesus taught when He said, "By their fruits ye shall know them" (Matthew 7:16-20).

**19. Thou believest that there is one God;** ... Do you believe, *—BRKL* ... that there is only one God? *—TNT*.

**thou doest well: the devils also believe, and tremble:** ... So far, so good, *—NORL* ... That's fine! *—BECK* ... That is good, but it is not enough, *—LBCH* ... the demons believe, and they shudder, *—MNTG* ... and tremble at the thought, *—TCNT* ... and because they do, they shake, *—NLTG* ... shake with fear, *—SEB*.

**2:19.** Here James dealt further with the kind of faith he criticized in 2:17,18. These people were orthodox in doctrine. They believed there is one God as opposed to the polytheism of pagans. Orthodox Jewish readers of this epistle had very likely reaffirmed Deuteronomy 6:4 every morning and evening. Gentiles among the readers could have been influenced by their Jewish friends.

James did not criticize the belief in monotheism; he commended the readers for it ("Thou doest well"). What James criticized was the mere intellectual assent without a commensurate change of lifestyle. In answering the scribes concerning the first of all the commandments, Jesus quoted Deuteronomy 6:4 and taught that this belief should affect the believers' relationship with God and man (Mark 12:28-31). Faith must be followed by action.

The writer stated that "the devils also believe, and tremble." This illustrates the tragic result of a correct belief without a proper alignment of life with that belief. The demons have a correct belief about God but do not change their conduct. They recognized Jesus as "the Holy One of God" but trembled or shuddered at the prospect of their ultimate destiny (Mark 1:24). See Matthew 8:29; Mark 5:7; Luke 4:41.

**20. But wilt thou know, O vain man:** ... do you really need proof, *—NORL* ... do you really want to understand, *—TCNT* ... do you want to be convinced, O foolish man, *—MNTG* ... O senseless man! *—WUST* ... you worthless person, *—ADAM* ... O unproductive man, *—BRKL* ... you foolish fellow, *—BECK* ... You silly man! *—TNT* ... empty person, *—KLGS*.

**that faith without works is dead?:** ... faith apart from deeds is barren? *—MNTG* ... is empty talk, *—LBCH* ... is worth nothing? *—SEB* ... is unproductive? *—WUST* ... is useless? *—CNFT* ... is delinquent? *—BRKL*.

**2:20.** "But wilt thou know ..." has the meaning of "Do you desire to know?" The writer here shifts the emphasis to supporting Scripture with which Jewish readers were very familiar. Abraham was claimed as father of the Jews (John 8:39). His faith was prominent in their theological discussions.

The adjective translated "vain" has the thought of being empty, ignorant, lacking in good sense. The word was also used at times to indicate a person trying to make an impression. The King James translators seem to follow this implication by using the word "vain."

**21. Was not Abraham our father justified by works:** ... Think of, —*TNT* ... our ancestor, —*MNTG* ... made just, —*KLGS* ... get to be righteous on the basis of works, —*BECK* ... vindicated by works, —*WUST* ... made righteous due to his works, —*BRKL.*
**when he had offered Isaac his son upon the altar?:**

**2:21.** There is no contradiction here between Paul and James. Paul in Romans 3:28; 4:3,19-22, and elsewhere refers to the method of justification. When Abraham was 100 and Sara 90 years old (Genesis 17:17), Abraham believed God would fulfill His promise (Genesis 15:1-6). James (2:21) taught that Abraham's obedience in offering Isaac many years later was the proof of genuine faith (Genesis 22). The context makes it clear that James taught a person is justified by the kind of faith which is genuine and results in obedience.

**22. Seest thou how faith wrought with his works:** ... His deed, you see, proved that his faith was active and real, —*LBCH* ... see how faith was co-operating with deeds, —*MNTG* ... You see his faith was active with works, —*BECK* ... how in his case faith and actions went together, —*TCNT* ... faith was spurring him on to do good works, —*NORL* ... faith worked along with his works, —*CNFT.*
**and by works was faith made perfect?:** ... the works, in turn, carried his faith on to perfection, —*NORL* ... and how faith reached its supreme expression through his works, —*BRKL* ... by works reached its goal, —*BECK* ... was completed by works, —*ADAM.*

**2:22.** "Faith wrought with his works" is literally "worked with his works." His actions were an indication that his faith was at work in all he did. As Phillips points out in his paraphrase, his faith and actions were partners.

"By works was faith made perfect." The goal of true faith is a life in conformity to that faith. The genuineness of Abraham's faith was proven when it reached the goal of obedience to God.

**23. And the scripture was fulfilled which saith, Abraham believed God:** ... And what is written, —*BECK* ... the Scripture came true, —*BRKL* ... put his trust in, —*NLTG.*
**and it was imputed unto him for righteousness:** ... it was accounted to him, —*BRKL* ... it was credited to him, —*NORL, WLMS* ... and so God declared him, —*SEB* ... it was reckoned to him as justice, —*CNFT.*
**and he was called the Friend of God:** ... God's friend, —*MNTG* ... God's beloved, —*SEB.*

**2:23.** At the time when Abraham was still childless he believed God's promise that his seed should be as innumerable as the stars of heaven (Genesis 15:5). There must have been many occasions when this faith in God's promise was tested. Willingness to offer Isaac (Genesis 22) was undoubtedly the greatest evidence of this faith. It was not only an act of obedience, but of faith that God could raise his son from the dead if the sacrifice should be required (Hebrews 11:19). When Abraham was willing to offer up the only means by which the promise could be realized, the Scripture was fulfilled that he believed God. In this act it was shown that his faith and works were one. This was faith in full development.

Abraham was called the "Friend of God" (2 Chronicles 20:7; Isaiah 41:8). Jesus indicated the significance of friendship with God when He said: "Ye are my friends, if ye do whatsoever I command you. Henceforth I call you not servants; for the servant knoweth not what his lord doeth; but I have called you friends; for all things that I have heard of my Father I have made known unto you" (John 15:14,15). In Genesis 18:17 there is an example of God revealing to His friend Abraham His intentions concerning Sodom.

**24. Ye see then how that by works a man is justified:** ... This shows, as you must understand ... by a faith that works, —*NORL* ... a person is pronounced righteous due to his works, —*BRKL* ... a man gets to be righteous on the basis of his works, —*BECK* ... on the principle of works, —*DRBY.*
**and not by faith only:** ... not merely by his faith, —*WLMS* ... not on account of faith alone, —*BRKL.*

**2:24.** In 2:14 James asked if faith without works can save. Here he gives the answer. No one is saved by the kind of intellectual belief which does not result in appropriate actions. Saving faith is more than mental assent to orthodox doctrine.

**25. Likewise also was not Rahab the harlot justified by works, when she had received the messengers:** ... Similarly, too, was not Rahab ... due to her works, —*BRKL* ... with the prostitute, —*TCNT* ... In the same way, too, was not Rahab the innkeeper ... after having entertained the spies, —*NORL.*
**and had sent [them] out another way?:** ... sent them back safely, —*NORL* ... sending them off by a different road? —*WLMS.*

**2:25.** Some readers might have questioned the use of Abraham as an illustration of faith and works because he was such an outstanding person. James next used Rahab the harlot as an illustration. She was as bad as Abraham was good, but she too was justified by a faith (Hebrews 11:31) which resulted in good works. See Joshua 2:8-14. She believed in the God of whom she had heard, and because of this faith she hid the spies and then assisted them in escaping. What was said of

Abraham who was at one end of the spectrum was also said of Rahab who was at the other end. They were both justified by an active faith. Their works were evidence of their faith. One indication of the standing Rahab received as a result of her faith is that she was one of only four women listed in the genealogy of Joseph, the husband of Mary of whom Jesus was born (Matthew 1:4,5).

26. **For as the body without the spirit is dead:** . . . which does not have the breath of life, −LBCH . . . apart from, −CLMT . . . when separated from its spirit, −NORL . . . without breath is lifeless, −FNTN.
**so faith without works is dead also:** . . . faith is dead without deeds, −MNTG . . . Faith is dead when nothing is done, −NLTG . . . apart from works, −NORL.

**2:26.** In chapter 2 James emphasized that mental assent alone is worthless. Now in conclusion he compares faith without works to a body without the spirit. It is like a corpse—dead. To be meaningful, faith and works must go together like spirit and body.

## Chapter 3

1. **My brethren, be not many masters:** . . . my fellow Christians, −BECK . . . not many of you should become, −NORL . . . many teachers, −MNTG.
**knowing that we shall receive the greater condemnation:** . . . we are assuming the more accountability, −BRKL . . . are criticized all the more severely, −NORL . . . we teachers shall be judged by a severer standard than others, −MNTG . . . will receive stricter judgment, −ADAM . . . a severer sentence, −CMPB . . . a greater judgment, −CNFT . . . those of us who teach will be judged very carefully, −SEB.

**3:1.** The word "masters" means literally "teachers." Problems existed in the early days of the Church because of false teaching. The conflict concerning faith and works (chapter 2) is a case in point. It seems it was popular to be a teacher, and unqualified, self-righteous people were appointing themselves to this role. They failed to recognize that those endowed by the Spirit with a teaching ministry (1 Corinthians 12:28) are the gifts of Christ to the Church (Ephesians 4:11), as in the case of Acts 13:1. Teachers themselves should have a teachable attitude (Romans 2:1,2) rather than being autocratic and schismatic.

Scripture recognizes that false teaching can come both from without and within the Church (Acts 20:29; 1 Peter 2:1). In this case James spoke to unqualified teachers as "my brethren."

The writer here identified himself as a teacher, and indicated that teachers will have to give an account of their ministry in the future (see Hebrews 13:17). All believers will appear before the judgment seat of Christ (2 Corinthians 5:10; see

also 1 Corinthians 3:13-15), and there will be degrees of judgment. More will be required of those who have received much (Luke 12:48). Teachers will be evaluated on a stricter basis because they have had greater opportunity to receive and understand truth.

2. **For in many things we offend all:** . . . For we all are likely to stumble, −NORL . . . in many respects we often stumble, −MNTG . . . We all make many mistakes, −NLTG, −SEB . . . All of us sin much, −BECK . . . we all often offend, −DRBY . . . we all make many a slip, −BRKL.
**If any man offend not in word:** . . . One who does not make any slip of the tongue, −NORL . . . if any man never stumbles in speech, −MNTG . . . If a man controls his tongue, −LBCH . . . If anyone never slips in speech, −WLMS . . . doesn't sin in what he says, −BECK.
**the same [is] a perfect man:** . . . is perfect indeed, −TNT.
**[and] able also to bridle the whole body:** . . . A man like that can keep his whole self, −TNT . . . able as well to control his entire body, −BRKL . . . and has control over his whole body as well, −NORL . . . able also to lead round by a bridle the whole body, −CNFT . . . able to rule, also, −CMPB.

**3:2.** James here shifted attention from teachers only and included all believers. James pointed out that without any exception everyone offends or stumbles (same word as in 2:10). This is a strong statement indicating that believers often offend. James 2:10,11 indicates these offenses are blameworthy.

In the previous sentence James had referred to offenses in general. Now he brought offenses of speech into focus. Those who deny that good works accompany true faith are prone to sin in talking. This offending includes attitudes of speech such as sarcasm and impatience (1:19) as well as content.

A person who does not cause stumbling by the wrong use of the tongue "is a perfect man." This does not mean absolute perfection; rather, it means he is a believer of spiritual and moral maturity (see 1:4). The writer goes on to state that such a person is able to "bridle the whole body." He is using the illustration of the way a rider is able to control a horse.

3. **Behold, we put bits in the horses' mouths, that they may obey us:** . . . When we control their mouths, −SEB . . . so that we can make them, −SEB.
**and we turn about their whole body:** . . . we guide, −NORL . . . we control their whole body also, −MNTG . . . so that they are yielding to us, −CNDT.

**3:3.** A bit is a small object, but it controls the entire animal. Likewise, a person who can control his tongue can control his entire being. What is in the heart determines speech content and attitude

(Matthew 12:34). If there is genuine faith in the heart, the accompanying works will be both appropriate speech and conduct.

**4. Behold also the ships, which though [they be] so great, and [are] driven of fierce winds:** ... Notice the ships ... driven by violent winds, —BRKL ... Look at the ships, too! No matter how big they are or how strong the wind that drives, —NORL ... though they are so large, —MNTG ... being of such proportions, —CNDT ... Sailing ships are driven, —NLTG ... great as they are, and driven by boisterous, —CNFT.

**yet are they turned about with a very small helm:** ... how they are steered, —BRKL ... tiny rudder, —WLMS.

**whithersoever the governor listeth:** ... wherever the impulse of the helmsman wills, —MNTG ... turned about in whatever direction the will of the pilot directs, —NORL ... wherever the touch of the steersman pleases, —CNFT ... to whatever point the impulse of the pilot chooses, —SWAN ... wherever the helmsman's whim determines, —BRKL.

**3:4.** James further illustrated the relationship of the activity of the tongue to the activity of the entire body with the rudder of a ship. A slight pressure on the rudder of the ship controls its course.

The illustration of the ship and rudder added another dimension—fierce winds. James pointed out that no matter how adverse the circumstances, if the rudder can be controlled by the pilot, the entire ship can be controlled. The point of the illustration is that if a believer can maintain control of his tongue in adverse circumstances, he can maintain control over his entire being.

**5. Even so the tongue is a little member, and boasteth great things:** ... It is the same with our tongue ... it brags about, —SEB ... True, the tongue is only a very small member of the body, —NORL ... is a small organ and can talk big, —BRKL ... can boast of great achievements, —WLMS ... but it boasts mightily, —CNFT.

**Behold, how great a matter a little fire kindleth!:** ... See how a tiny flame can set a mighty forest afire! —NORL ... Behold, how small a fire—how great a forest it kindles! —CNFT.

**3:5.** Here the inspired writer emphasizes how important the tongue is though it is a small member of one's body. Just like the bit which is small in relationship to the size of a horse and the rudder which is small in relationship to a ship, the little tongue can do great things. Some interpret "boasteth" to mean that the tongue is haughty, while others interpret it as reference to accomplishment of great achievements. Peter's proper use of the tongue resulted in the conversion of about 3,000 souls being added to the Church (Acts 2:41).

James has been pointing out that small things can have a beneficial effect. A small bit can be used to guide a horse. A rudder can affect the course of a large ship. Now he goes on to show that small things can also be destructive in their effect.

The word "matter" can refer either to a forest or stacks of lumber. Fire can either have a good or disastrous effect. The point here is that if the tongue is not controlled, careless or evil words, no matter how few, can produce a catastrophe.

**6. And the tongue [is] a fire, a world of iniquity:** ... is like a spark, —TCNT ... a universe, —FNTN ... of wickedness, —NORL ... of injustice, —CNDT.

**so is the tongue among our members, that it defileth the whole body:** ... it contaminates, —TCNT ... it pollutes, —SEB ... it taints, —BRKL ... It can poison the whole body, —NORL.

**and setteth on fire the course of nature:** ... enflames, —BECK ... fires up the whole order of beginnings, —KLGS ... every power in man's makeup, —NORL ... the whole machinery of existence, —BRKL ... the wheel of nature, —MNTG ... the course of our life, —CNFT ... it sets the whole round of our existence ablaze, —TNT ... the entire cycle of our life, —NOLI.

**and it is set on fire of hell:** ... Its own fire comes from hell itself, —TNT ... It turns our existence into an infernal torture, —NOLI ... as it gets its fire from hell, —BECK ... while it is kindled by, —BRKL ... set afire by the junk pile, —KLGS ... is set on fire by Gehenna, —WLSN ... by the flames of the Pit, —TCNT

**3:6.** These are strong words used to describe the tongue's activities if it is not curbed. The Holy Spirit is striving to stress how much damage an unbridled tongue can cause. The NIV translates it this way: "The tongue also is a fire, a world of evil among the parts of the body."

The tongue is "a world of iniquity." The entire unrighteous world system can find expression through the tongue. See Psalms 10:7; 12:3,4. The use of the tongue affects the whole body. When the tongue becomes an instrument of evil, the entire personality is stained and polluted. Jesus used a different word (signifying to make ceremonially unholy) to teach the same truth when He said, "That which cometh out of the mouth, this defileth a man" (Matthew 15:11).

"The course of nature" (literally, "the wheel of birth") probably is referring to the entire sphere of human existence. Phillips in his paraphrase suggests an uncontrolled tongue makes "a blazing hell" of life.

"Hell," *gehenna* (from *Gē Hinnōm*, "the valley of the sons of Hinnom," a dump south of Jerusalem used for pagan sacrifices [2 Kings 23:10]) was used as an image for the divine punishment of Israel (Jeremiah 19). By the New Testament period it was known as the place of punishment after the final judgment. As the abode of Satan (Davids, *New International Greek Testament Commentary, James*, p. 143), *gehenna* is identified as the source of the tongue's evil.

**7. For every kind of beasts, and of birds, and of serpents, and of things in the sea, is tamed, and hath been tamed of mankind:** ... For Every Species both of Wild beasts and of Birds, *—WLSN* ... of reptiles and sea animals, *—WLMS* ... creatures in the sea, *—BECK* ... can be tamed by the human genius, *—FNTN*.

**3:7.** If there were those who might claim it is impossible to control the tongue, James refers them back to the creation record where God indicated the four categories of creatures over which man was to have dominion (Genesis 1:26,28).

The word here translated "tamed" might more accurately be translated "subdued" (same word as in Mark 5:4). The word can include the idea of domestication. Many animals ranging in size from those smaller than dogs to those as large as elephants have been domesticated and trained to serve mankind. But the word goes beyond domestication and includes the idea of domination over creatures which cannot be domesticated.

**8. But the tongue can no man tame; [it is] an unruly evil:** ... no man has as yet been able to tame the human tongue, this unrestrainable evil, *—NORL* ... an evil thing, uncontrollable, *—TNT* ... restless evil that it is, *—MNTG* ... It is a restless plague! *—TCNT* ... a reckless evil, *—ADAM* ... an undisciplined evil, *—FNTN* ... this undisciplined mischief, *—BRKL* ... a turbulent evil, *—CNDT* ... this unruly fiend, *—NOLI*.

**full of deadly poison:** ... It is a store-house of, *—TCNT* ... distended with death-carrying venom, *—CNDT*.

**3:8.** However, the tongue presents a greater problem than the animals. Man who has the power to control the wild nature of animals, apart from God, cannot control his own tongue. "No man" is a strong expression and might be translated "no one of men."

The tongue is an "unruly evil," literally, an evil which cannot be held back. It is like a wild animal restlessly wanting to make an attack. It is like an enemy that cannot be contained by military force. Phillips translates it, "It is an evil always liable to break out."

The tongue is "full of deadly poison." In describing the activities of his enemies, David wrote, "Adders' poison is under their lips" (Psalm 140:3). The untamed tongue prefers speaking evil rather than good (Psalm 52:2-4). It prefers destroying rather than helping (Psalm 64:2-5). It seeks to destroy reputation and morale through slanderous gossip.

**9. Therewith bless we God, even the Father:** ... with our tongue, *—BECK* ... With it we bless, *—CNFT* ... We use it to praise, *—TNT* ... We praise, *—NORL* ... the Lord and Father, *—BRKL*.

**and therewith curse we men:** ... we are accustomed to, *—MNTG* ... and yet curse human beings, *—SEB* ... with it, we bawl out people, *—KLGS* ... other people, *—BECK* ... our fellow men, *—NOLI*.

**which are made after the similitude of God:** ... born in the likeness of, *—KLGS* ... who are made in the image of God, *—NORL* ... who once were made like God, *—BECK* ... made in God's likeness, *—TCNT*.

**3:9.** In the previous verse James dealt with the nature of an evil tongue. The tongue, however, is capable of speaking both evil and good. (See Proverbs 10:11, 19, 31, 32; 18:21; Matthew 12:34-37.) In this verse the writer dealt with the inconsistency of the tongue, first blessing God and then cursing man.

To bless means to praise, to extol. Blessing God is the highest function of the tongue, described in Scripture as good and comely (Psalms 33:1; 147:1). But it is absolutely inconsistent for the Christian to bless God and then curse man made in the likeness of God. Believers should not only refrain from cursing but also bless those who curse and persecute them (Luke 6:28; Romans 12:14).

The reason cursing man is evil is that he was made "after the similitude of God," that is, in His likeness. (See Genesis 1:26,27.) The likeness of God in man was not physical or material. Jesus said, "God is a Spirit" (John 4:24), and "a spirit hath not flesh and bones" (Luke 24:39).

The likeness was natural, consisting of intelligence, emotions, and will; and moral, a tendency toward God, though accompanied with the power to make wrong choices. The tendency of fallen man is now away from God, to go his own way. When man sinned in Eden, the likeness to God was severely marred but not lost. Because man retains likeness to God, human life is sacred. To curse man is to curse the likeness of God in man.

**10. Out of the same mouth proceedeth blessing and cursing:** ... praise and cursing come from, *—BECK* ... pour forth, *—MNTG*.

**My brethren, these things ought not so to be:** ... It is not right, *—NORL* ... We mustn't do that, my fellow Christians, *—BECK*.

**3:10.** Others have pointed out that the tongue is capable of both good and evil expression (Proverbs 18:21). Here, however, the writer points out that it is unnatural for both good and evil to come from believers. James is emphatic, "These things ought not so to be."

James was not writing to unsaved people but to "brethren." A mixture of good and evil speaking can be expected from the natural man, but it is totally out of place for the believer. It should not happen.

**11. Doth a fountain send forth at the same place:** ... Does a spring pour forth from the same opening, —MNTG ... The spring does not well up ... from the same cleft, —BRKL ... discharge, —NORL ... from the same spring mouth? —KLGS.

**sweet [water] and bitter?:** ... fresh, —BECK ... and salt, —KLGS.

**3:11.** People in Palestine were familiar with the reference to fountains and springs. They were dependent on them for their water supply. Towns were built around springs which provided adequate water in an arid country. The woman of Samaria indicated that her town of Sychar was near the well first used by Jacob (John 4:12).

The people to whom James wrote understood that a spring does not alternate between yielding sweet and bitter water. It was either one or the other, but not both. The reason towns were not built around the Dead Sea is because springs in that region were known to yield only brackish water.

In man, though redeemed and regenerated, the tongue is capable of both good and evil, because he retains his fallen nature along with the new nature. In Galatians 5:17 Paul describes the conflict between the old and new natures. While man cannot tame his own tongue, he can turn the control of it over to the Holy Spirit. When he does this, the Holy Spirit becomes a well of living water in his life (John 7:37,38). When the believer quenches the Spirit, the bitterness of his fallen nature expresses itself.

**12. Can the fig tree, my brethren, bear olive berries?:** ... Nor is it possible, is it, my brothers, —BRKL ... Friends, —NORL ... Do you pick olives from a fig tree? —KLGS.

**either a vine, figs?:** ... a grapevine, —MNTG.

**so [can] no fountain both yield salt water and fresh:** ... Of course not, —TNT ... it is impossible to have, —SEB ... a salt spring, —BECK ... Neither can salt produce, —BRKL ... No more can salt water yield fresh water, —MNTG ... pour out fresh water, —KLGS.

**3:12.** Just as it is not the nature of the fig tree to bear olives, nor of the vine to bear figs, it is not the nature of the regenerate spirit to speak evil. Whichever nature man allows to dominate his life—the old or the new—determines what his speech will be. This is why it is important to be filled with the Spirit continually (Ephesians 5:18).

**13. Who [is] a wise man and endued with knowledge among you?:** ... who is truly wise? —SEB ... intelligent, —MNTG ... instructed,

—CNFT ... discreet among you, —WLSN ... understanding, —BRKL ... and knows what is going on, —KLGS ... in your company? —TNT.

**let him show out of a good conversation:** ... Let him show his deeds by his good life, —MNTG ... he who lives a good life, —NORL ... by good behavior, —CMPB ... Let him exhibit it by the nobility of his conduct, —FNTN ... Let his life ... be an example, —TNT.

**his works with meekness of wisdom:** ... does his deeds in humility? That is wisdom, —NORL ... his actions are carried on with unobtrusive wisdom, —BRKL ... In a gentle spirit of wisdom, —BECK.

**3:13.** Now James returned to the responsibility of teachers mentioned in verse 1. Those equipped to be teachers were not only to be knowledgeable but to demonstrate their wisdom with a good conversation, a "good life" (RV).

The teacher is not to use his good conduct to draw attention to himself. This was the sin of hypocrites (Matthew 6:1-5). Jesus demonstrated the true spirit of the teacher when He said, "I am meek and lowly in heart" (Matthew 11:29). The godly teacher will not be selfishly ambitious and arrogant, but mild and gentle.

**14. But if ye have bitter envying and strife in your hearts:** ... if you cherish, —WLMS ... jealousy and faction, —MNTG ... bitter jealousy and selfish aims, —NORL ... and rivalry, —ADAM.

**glory not, and lie not against the truth:** ... don't brag about it, —SEB ... do not pride yourselves in it and play false to the truth, —BRKL ... and be liars against the truth, —CNFT.

**3:14.** "Envying" is here used to translate *zēlon* which does not have a bad connotation in itself. It is used in a good sense in 2 Corinthians 11:2. Paul calls it "godly jealousy." The adjective "bitter" indicates James was referring to evil jealousy which carnal teachers can harbor. This same Greek word appears in Galatians 5:20 where it is translated "emulations."

"Strife" is translated as "selfish ambition" in the Revised Standard Version. This evil is also listed as a work of the flesh in Galatians 5:20.

If a teacher is dominated by jealousy and selfish ambition, he is instructed to stop being boastful and to stop lying against the truth. He repudiates the truth of the gospel by ungodly attitudes regardless of how wise he claims to be.

**15. This wisdom descendeth not from above, but [is] earthly, sensual, devilish:** ... Such wisdom does not come down from above; instead it is earthly, animalistic, —BRKL ... terrestrial, soulish, —CNDT ... natural, —DRBY ... the wisdom of demons, —SEB ... demoniacal, —WLSN.

**3:15.** This wisdom is "earthbound" (*NEB*); it "comes from the world" (Phillips). Earthly wisdom originates with man and has only an earthly perspective. "Sensual" means literally "natural, belonging to the soul." It originates in the mind of natural man and stands in contrast to the wisdom of God's Word (2 Timothy 3:16) which is spiritually discerned (1 Corinthians 2:13,14).

Demonic power is the source of some kinds of wisdom. Paul warned that some people would give "heed to seducing spirits, and doctrines of devils" (1 Timothy 4:1; cf. 1 John 4:1).

**16. For where envying and strife** [is]:...... wherever jealousy and faction exist, *—MNTG*...and selfishness, *—NORL*...and rivalry, *—TCNT*...and partyism are, *—SWAN*...and self-seeking exist, *—ADAM.*
**there** [is] **confusion and every evil work:**...disorder, *—TCNT*...instability, *—CNFT*...all sorts of evil practices, *—WLMS*...everything base, *—BRKL.*

**3:16.** James has referred to the evils of envy and strife in verse 14. Now he shows the harm they can produce if allowed to remain—"confusion" (*akatastasia*). It is related to the word translated "unstable" (*akatastatos*) in 1:8. Earthly wisdom results in confusion and instability, while godly wisdom results in harmony and stability.

**17. But the wisdom that is from above is first pure, then peaceable, gentle:**...comes from God, *—SEB*...comes from on high, *—MNTG*...is first of all chaste...moderate, docile, *—CNFT*...lenient, *—CNDT*...courteous, *—BRKL.*
[and] **easy to be entreated:**...compliant, *—ADAM*...listens to reason, *—LBCH*...open to conviction, *—TCNT*...conciliatory, *—MNTG*...willing to yield, *—WLMS*...easy to be persuaded, *—SWAN*...congenial, *—BRKL.*
**full of mercy and good fruits:**...overflowing with, *—MNTG*...bulging with, *—CNDT*...rich in compassion, *—TCNT*...good deeds, *—NORL.*
**without partiality, and without hypocrisy:**...free from doubt, *—WLMS*...free from favoritism, *—ADAM*...impartial and sincere, *—NORL*...without judging,...dissimulation, *—CNFT*...unpretentious, *—BRKL.*

**3:17.** It must be understood that God's wisdom is pure from all that is earthly, sensual, and devilish. The wisdom which is from below, from the world, is the complete opposite.

Divine wisdom is "peaceable" in contrast to earthly wisdom which creates confusion. It is peace-loving and produces "peacemakers" (Matthew 5:9). It is "gentle"; that is, it is fair, forbearing and considerate, in contrast to the arrogant spirit produced by earthly wisdom. It is "easy to be entreated," that is, reasonable as opposed to harsh or stubborn. It is "full of mercy and good fruits." God's wisdom results in compassion for the suffering, and produces good works as opposed to the evil work (3:16) resulting from human

wisdom. The wisdom from above is "without partiality" (literally "undivided"). There is no indecision about commitment to God. It is "without hypocrisy." There is no attempt to pretend or to make a good impression.

**18. And the fruit of righteousness is sown in peace:**...And the harvest, which righteousness yields...comes from a sowing in peace, *—BRKL*...of justice, *—CNFT*...grows peacefully within, *—SEB.*
**of them that make peace:**...by those who are working peace, *—MNTG*...those who practise Peace, *—WLSN*...the peacemakers, *—BRKL.*

**3:18.** In verse 16 James showed that the product of earthly wisdom is confusion and every evil work. In verse 18 he showed that the product of divine wisdom is righteousness. Those endued with divine wisdom are peaceable (3:17). Righteousness is the crop which is then reaped.

## Chapter 4

**1. From whence** [come] **wars and fightings among you?:**...What causes wars and feuds, *—NORL*...the conflicts and quarrels, *—MNTG.*
[come they] **not hence,** [even] **of your lusts that war in your members?:**...Do they not come from your passions which are always making war among your bodily members? *—MNTG*...from your inordinate passions, *—WUST*...from your own selfish desires, *—SEB*...your own sensual desires, *—NORL*...from your vices fighting in your organs? *—FNTN.*

**4:1.** James here dealt with the source of the hostility which existed among some Christians. "Wars and fightings" are plural and indicate that conflict was a continuing condition.

People often blame environment and circumstances for conflicts. But it is not only external conditions but internal inordinate desires which ignite conflicts.

The word "lusts" is used to translate the Greek word *hēdonōn* from which we get the word *hedonism*. James identified personal pleasure and bodily desires at the cost of neighbors' interests as the cause of conflict. Jesus taught that the seeking of the pleasures (same Greek word) of life choked the seed of God's Word (Luke 8:14), and when God's will is ignored, human conflicts result.

People who live only to please themselves cause their own problems. Their desires war against the soul (1 Peter 2:11). Carnal desires strive for supremacy in the believer's life at the cost of displacing Christ's lordship.

**2. Ye lust, and have not: ye kill, and desire to have:**...You continually crave, *—MNTG*...You covet...and envy, *—CNFT*...You desire, but do not possess, –SWAN... There is something that you want but you do not have it, so you get it by killing, –NORL.

**and cannot obtain:**

**ye fight and war, yet ye have not, because ye ask not:** ... You engage in conflicts and quarrel, –WUST... You quarrel and wrangle, –CNFT... You do not possess, because you do not pray, –FNTN.

**4:2.** In the original Greek manuscripts there was no punctuation or even separation of words. For this reason commentators have differed as to the correct punctuation in this verse. The NASB translates it as follows: "You lust and do not have; so you commit murder. And you are envious and cannot obtain; so you fight and quarrel."

The reason some people find no satisfaction in life is that they lust after and fight for the things they want instead of asking God for His good and perfect gifts (1:17).

**3. Ye ask, and receive not, because ye ask amiss:** ... You continue to ask and do not receive, because you are asking with a wrong purpose, –MNTG... ye ask evilly, –CLMT.

**that ye may consume [it] upon your lusts:** ... to waste it on, –ADAM ... you want the things for your own lustful pleasures, –NORL... that you may expend upon your vices, –FNTN... your passions, –CNFT... dissolute pleasures, –BRKL.

**4:3.** There is another reason some people do not receive an answer to their prayers. They ask of God, but their motives are wrong. They are not praying according to God's will (1 John 5:14) but according to their own selfish lusts.

**4. Ye adulterers and adulteresses, know ye not:** .... Do you not realize, you apostates, –BRKL... renegades, –SWAN... faithless wives! –WLMS.

**that the friendship of the world is enmity with God?:** ... loving this world is hating God? –SEB... is [thereby] constituted an enemy, –WUST... is hostility to God? –FNTN.

**whosoever therefore will be a friend of the world:** ... whoever determines to be, –BRKL... wishes to be, –CNFT.

**is the enemy of God:** ... becomes, –CNFT... takes his stand as, –BRKL ... is [thereby] constituted, –WUST... you are against God, –NLTG.

**4:4.** The metaphor of adultery is used in Scripture to describe unfaithfulness to God (Deuteronomy 31:16; Jeremiah 3:20). Hosea's marriage to an adulterous wife was an illustration of Israel's unfaithfulness to God. Jesus spoke of an "evil and adulterous generation" (Matthew 12:39). It is strong language, but a believer who turns away from God is committing spiritual adultery.

The "friendship of the world" is a desire for a relationship with those who reject God and His Word. When it comes to allegiance there can be no gray area in a believer's life. Either he takes

God's point of view (John 15:14) or that of the world. For the believer friendship with the world is more than incompatible; it is enmity, that is, hostility toward God. One of the worst crimes a person can commit is to be a traitor to his country. It is even worse for a believer to give his allegiance to the forces which oppose God.

"Whosoever" in the Greek is emphatic. It indicates a deliberate choice to give allegiance to the world rather than to God. Demas is an illustration of one who chose to desert the cause of Christ because of love for the world (2 Timothy 4:10). Those who choose the world constitute themselves enemies of God.

**5. Do ye think that the scripture saith in vain:** ... do you think it is mere empty talk when the Scripture says, –NORL... speaks falsely? –WLSN... unmeaningly, –FNTN... to no purpose? –BRKL.

**The spirit that dwelleth in us lusteth to envy?:** ... When God put His Spirit in us He is a jealous lover, –LBCH... which has its home in us yearns over us unto jealousy? –MNTG... that took His abode in us longs for us with holy jealousy, –NORL... covets unto jealousy, –CNFT.

**4:5.** James was not quoting any single passage when he said, "Do ye think that the Scripture saith (speaks) in vain ... ?" It seems he was referring to the general import of various passages dealing with this subject. Either allegiance to the world and God at the same time is impossible, or Scripture is vain, that is, without value.

The word "lusteth" here means to have a strong yearning for what others are or have. There are various translations of this difficult passage. Some hold it is the natural spirit which lusts to envy (see 4:1,2). Others hold it is God who yearns jealously for undivided affection.

**6. But he giveth more grace:** .... But He affords the more, –BRKL ... He keeps on showing us mercy, more and more, –NORL ... gives us more loving favor, –NLTG ... bestows Superior Favor, –WLSN... gives a more valuable gift, –FNTN... greater grace, –WUST... greater favor, –CMPB.

**Wherefore he saith:** ... For this reason it says, –CNFT... as Scripture says, –NORL.

**God resisteth the proud, but giveth grace unto the humble:** ... against, –SEB ... opposes, –NORL... sets himself in opposition to the Haughty, –WLSN... in battle array against the arrogant, –WUST.

**4:6.** But God "giveth more grace." If the position in verse 5 is taken that it is the natural spirit of man which envies, it follows that regardless of how inordinately man does so, God will give abundant grace to control the desires. If the position is taken that God yearns for the believer's undivided loyalty, it follows that God's grace is sufficient to help the believer be completely loyal. Either way, the believer has no excuse for compromising his loyalty to God. He has a great promise: "Where sin abounded, grace did much more abound" (Romans 5:20).

Believers have a choice to make. The believer's attitude determines whether he will be the object of God's opposition or grace. (See also 1 Peter 5:5.) Those who in arrogant pride reject God's claim of undivided allegiance will find that God opposes them. Pharaoh's experiences illustrate this well. He refused to recognize or give allegiance to God in spite of many evidences of His sovereignty. As a result he found God opposed him over and over again (Exodus 5-14). Those who come to God in humility, however, will receive His abundant grace.

**7. Submit yourselves therefore to God:** ... ever be subject to God, *—MNTG* ... put yourselves under God's authority, *—SEB.*
**Resist the devil, and he will flee from you:** ... Stand up to, *—TNT* ... Stand opposed to the enemy, *—WLSN* ... repel, *—FNTN* ... and he will run away, *—NLTG.*

**4:7.** This verse reveals the two actions which will bring victory: submitting to God and resisting the temptations of Satan. To submit is to place or arrange oneself under, as a good soldier places himself under an officer of higher rank. It is a voluntary act of humility to submit to God.

It is the humble who will receive God's help, not those who proudly try to resist Satan in their own strength. Satan often causes believers to fail by appealing to their pride. He did so in the Garden of Eden when he told Eve, "Ye shall be as gods" (Genesis 3:5), and Eve did not resist him. When Jesus was tempted by Satan in the wilderness, He provided an example of how believers can triumph. He resisted Satan with Scripture (Luke 4:4, 8, 12).

**8. Draw nigh to God, and he will draw nigh to you:** ... draw near, *—MNTG* ... come close, *—NORL* ... Get close to, *—SEB* ... come near, *—TNT.*
**Cleanse [your] hands, [ye] sinners:** ... Wash your hands, *—NORL.*
**and purify [your] hearts, [ye] double minded:** ... cleanse your hearts, *—TNT* ... you vacillating men! *—TCNT* ... you who have divided hearts, *—SEB* ... you of divided interests, *—BRKL* ... you doubters, *—BECK.*

**4:8.** In Old Testament times priests were to approach the symbols of God's presence only at prescribed times. Now, believers are invited to come boldly to the Throne of Grace (Hebrews 4:14-16). They can do this through meditation in the Word and prayer.

Washing was an important ritual of Old Testament priests (Exodus 30:20,21). Today all believers are priests (1 Peter 2:9), and while they abhor sin, they cannot say they never sin (1 John 1:8). They need the cleansing of the blood and "the washing of water by the word" (Ephesians 5:26). Purity of life is important for the believer (Psalm 24:3,4).

A double-minded person is two-faced, trying to look to God and also to the world (cf. 1:8). This person is guilty of spiritual adultery. There is personal responsibility to remove worldly inclinations (1 John 3:3). Notice that it is a matter of the heart. Our love for God determines our relationship with Him.

**9. Be afflicted, and mourn, and weep:** ... Become miserable, *—SWAN* ... Lament, *—MNTG* ... Feel your misery, *—BRKL* ... Now is the time for sorrow, mourning and lamentation, *—TNT* ... Be sorry on account of your sins; grieve over them, *—NORL* ... and cry for your sins, *—LBCH.*
**let your laughter be turned to mourning:** ... your worldly laughter give way to, *—NORL* ... to sorrow, *—BRKL.*
**and [your] joy to heaviness:** ... your enjoyment, *—BRKL* ... your gayety be turned to sadness, *—NORL* ... your gladness to dejection, *—ADAM* ... into gloom! *—MNTG.*

**4:9.** Those who boasted of human wisdom (3:14-16) were guilty of wretched behavior (4:1-4) and pride (4:6). James urged them to give evidence of repentance (2 Corinthians 7:9-11). This was not a time for laughter and lighthearted behavior.

**10. Humble yourselves in the sight of the Lord:** ... Take a low position, *—BRKL* ... before the Lord, *—MNTG* ... in the presence of the Lord, *—WLSN.*
**and he shall lift you up:** ... and He will honor you, *—BECK* ... will raise you up, *—MNTG* ... exalt you, *—CNFT* ... set you high, *—BRKL.*

**4:10.** Some readers of this epistle believed exaltation comes through envy, strife, and self-seeking. It is people who humble themselves that will be exalted (Matthew 23:12; Luke 18:14; cf. Matthew 5:5). The opposite is also true. Those who try to promote themselves usually fail.

**11. Speak not evil one of another, brethren:** ... Do not be talking against each other, *—MNTG* ... do not slander, *—NORL* ... Do not malign, *—BRKL* ... Stop defaming, *—WUST* ... Do not disparage one another, *—TCNT* ... my fellow Christians, *—BECK.*
**He that speaketh evil of [his] brother, and judgeth his brother:** ... He who gossips about his brother, *—KLGS* ... Anyone who talks against his fellow Christian, *—BECK* ... if you disparage, *—NOLI* ... says evil against his brother or makes himself his brother's judge, *—BB* ... condemning his brothers, *—MNTG* ... or

criticizing his brother, —WLMS...or who passes judgement on him, —TNT.

**speaketh evil of the law, and judgeth the law:**...talks against...and condemns, —BECK...maligns the Law, —BRKL...in fact, he is speaking against the law and judges the law, —NORL...the Law of God, —NOLI.

**but if thou judge the law, thou art not a doer of the law, but a judge:**...If you sit in judgement on the Law, —TNT...by criticising the law, —NORL...If you condemn the Law, you're not doing what it says but you're being its judge, —BECK...you are not a follower of the law, —SEB...you are not an observer, —NOLI...you are not its practicer, —BRKL...you are not a doer of the law, but a critic, —KLGS.

**4:11.** James urged the believers, "Speak not evil one of another." They needed to be reminded of Psalm 133:1: "Behold, how good and how pleasant it is for brethren to dwell together in unity!" It reflects badly upon the Christian faith when believers do not live in peace with one another. A slanderer puts himself above the Law (2:8,10). He acts as though He knows better than the edicts of God's law and in so doing constitutes himself a judge of the Law rather than a doer (1:22-24).

**12. There is one lawgiver, who is able to save and to destroy:**...You well know that God is the only law-giver...to save and condemn, —NOLI...and Critic, —KLGS...only one Lawgiver and Judge, —BECK...He who has the power, —BRKL...who has the power of salvation and of destruction, —BB...and to punish with death, —NORL.

**who art thou that judgest another?:**...who are you, to be condemning your neighbor? —MNTG...that you should pass judgment on your fellow man? —NORL...that you presume to judge, —WLMS.

**4:12.** Readers of this epistle who were slandering their brethren were motivated by pride. They were assuming the prerogative of God in passing judgment on others. By doing this they were rejecting the royal law, "Thou shalt love thy neighbor as thyself" (2:8). They then replaced this with their own law by which they felt justified to judge others. It was necessary for James to remind his readers that God alone is the Judge.

God gave the moral law to Israel at Sinai. Exodus 20:1-17 records the Ten Commandments. Other aspects of the moral law are recorded in subsequent writings of Moses, in Exodus, Leviticus, and Deuteronomy. It is possible James referred to this law, but more likely he referred to what is known as the royal law (see above). Jesus summed up the essence of the Jewish law in two commandments: loving God with all the heart, soul, mind, and strength and loving one's neighbor as himself (Mark 12:28-33).

References to God's power to judge righteously and in turn to save or destroy are found in the Old Testament (Deuteronomy 32:39; 1 Samuel 2:6-10; 2 Kings 5:7). God's power to save or destroy was also demonstrated in New Testament times. Christ brought Lazarus back from the dead (John 11), and Herod was destroyed as a judgment from God (Acts 12:20-23). It would seem, however, that the primary application of this statement is future. When Jesus spoke of persecution to His disciples He said: "Fear not them which kill the body, but are not able to kill the soul: but rather fear him which is able to destroy both soul and body in hell" (Matthew 10:28).

In the Greek the word "you" is in a place of emphasis. It is as though James asked, on the basis of what had just been stated, "And you, who do you think you are to place yourself above this God?"

**13. Go to now, ye that say:**...Stop a moment, you who say, —NORL...Behold now, —CNFT...Come on now, —FNTN...Look out, now, you who are saying, —KLGS...Some of you are in the habit of saying, —TNT...How foolish it is to say, —BB.

**To day or to morrow we will go into such a city:**...we shall proceed to this city, —WUST...into some city, —KLGS...to this or that town, —TNT.

**and continue there a year, and buy and sell, and get gain:**...spend a year there, and trade and make money, —MNTG...and do business, —LBCH...and traffic in merchandise, —CMPB...and make a good profit, —NORL...and become rich, —FNTN.

**4:13.** In the previous verses James dealt with those who placed themselves above the Law by judging others. In verse 13 he dealt with those who disregarded God in the process of making plans. The folly of these people was not that they planned but that they planned without God. They had no right to say "tomorrow," for they had no assurance of surviving till then. To plan for a year was even worse presumption. It is all right to plan if we include God. Paul made plans, but he did so with full recognition of God's prerogative to change the plans (Acts 16:6-10).

Some of the believers to whom this epistle was written apparently believed that they and they alone would make their life plans. They would determine when they would go ("Today or tomorrow"), where they would go ("into such a city"), and why they would go (to "sell, and get gain"). Instead of looking to God for guidance in the process of planning, they acted as though God did not exist.

**14. Whereas ye know not what [shall be] on the morrow:**...you who do not know, —CNFT...what will become of your Life on the morrow, —WLSN...when all the time you do not know what will happen,

—MNTG . . . What do you know about tomorrow? Nothing, —NORL.

**For what [is] your life? It is even a vapour:** . . . of what character is your life, —WUST . . . but a mist, —MNTG . . . It is like fog, —NLTG . . . a smoke, —CMPB.

**that appeareth for a little time, and then vanisheth away:** . . . visible for awhile, —FNTN . . . that can be seen for a little while, and then it is gone, —NORL . . . appearing for a brief time, —MNTG . . . and then disappearing, —TCNT.

**4:14.** The problem with these itinerant merchants was that they acted as though they had ultimate control over their future. They ignored the warning of Scripture, "Boast not thyself of tomorrow; for thou knowest not what a day may bring forth" (Proverbs 27:1). They acted like the man Jesus described in the Parable of the Rich Fool (Luke 12:16-21). He boasted that he had enough wealth to last many years and planned on a hedonistic lifestyle. That night he died. He had become wealthy in this life but was not rich toward God. He had the wrong kind of riches.

James challenged these readers to consider the transitoriness of life. He said it is like steam which can be seen for a few moments, then vanishes. It is certain life will end, but when this will happen is uncertain.

Throughout the Scriptures figures of speech are used indicating the brevity of life. It is like a "handbreadth" (Psalm 39:5), a "dream" (Psalm 73:20), "a shadow that declineth" (Psalm 102:11), "a flower" (Job 14:2), and like "grass" (1 Peter 1:24). James compared life to a "vapor," something that is visible for just a brief period.

**15. For that ye [ought] to say, If the Lord will, we shall live, and do this, or that:** . . . You ought rather to say, —CNFT . . . and we are alive, —NORL.

**4:15.** The writer emphasized the need for considering the will of God in making plans. At one time when Christians wrote of future plans in correspondence they used the letters *D.V.* They stand for the Latin words Deo volente, that is, "God willing." Paul recognized that any future plans he might have were subject to God's will. To the Ephesian believers he said, "I will return again unto you, if God will" (Acts 18:21). To the Corinthians he wrote, "I trust to tarry a while with you, if the Lord permit" (1 Corinthians 16:7). Some readers of James' epistle in their pride did not acknowledge any dependence on God.

**16. But now ye rejoice in your boastings:** . . . as matters stand, you are proud and you boast, —NORL . . . But instead you are proud, —NLTG . . . you are glorying in these insolent boastings, —MNTG . . . you pride yourselves on your presumption, —TCNT . . . you glory in empty presumptions,

—SWAN . . . you boast in your proud speeches, —WLSN . . . in your arrogance, —CNFT.

**all such rejoicing is evil:** . . . All such pride, —NLTG . . . All such bragging, —SEB . . . boasting, —CNFT . . . is sin, —NORL.

**4:16.** Instead of recognizing dependence on God, these merchants gloried in their arrogant self-confidence. Like the hypocritical Pharisees they were concerned with impressing others with their human ability, rather than humbly pleasing God. This bragging was evil. Boasting is bad at all times, but it is even worse when people do it arrogantly.

**17. Therefore to him that knoweth to do good:** . . . The principle is this, that whoever knows what is right to do, —NORL . . . to do right, —MNTG.

**and doeth [it] not, to him it is sin:** . . . and does not perform it, —WLSN . . . but does not do it, is guilty of sin, —NORL . . . commits a sin, —CNFT.

**4:17.** Definite acts of sin are deplorable, but they are not the only kind. Here James emphasized the sinfulness of "sins of omission." The merchants (James 4:13-16) failed to walk humbly with God (Micah 6:8). This was as much sin as any positive acts of sin they might have committed. Jesus denounced the Pharisees for the things they had left undone (Matthew 23:23). The priest and Levite who disregarded the needs of the injured traveler were guilty not of a sin of commission, but of omission (Luke 10:30-37). The rich man sinned against Lazarus, not by mistreating him in some aggressive manner, but by neglecting him (Luke 16:19-31).

## Chapter 5

**1. Go to now, [ye] rich men, weep and howl:** . . . Look out now, —KLGS . . . Come on you wealthy, weep with loud wailings, —BRKL . . . Come now, you rich people, —BECK . . . you men of wealth, take heed! —NORL . . . mark my words, —TNT . . . Cry out and be very sad, —SEB.

**for your miseries that shall come upon [you]:** . . . for the troubles coming upon you, —KLGS . . . that are sure to overtake you, —WLMS.

**5:1.** The inspired writer now proceeds to present stern warnings to those who are rich, because of calamities which they will experience. We must remember, however, that in Scripture people are not denounced because of wealth but because of its misuse and abuse. Abraham, a man of great wealth, was a friend of God (2:23). God called Job a perfect and upright man (Job 1:8).

The rich mentioned here, like those in 2:2-6, were apparently not members of the congregations. They were not called to repentance, but rather to "weep and howl" for their coming judgment.

It is assumed they will remain unrepentant. The warning came to believers who might be tempted to make wealth their chief object.

**2. Your riches are corrupted:** . . . Your hoarded wealth is rotten, *—FNTN* . . . riches lie rotting, *—MNTG* . . . have wasted away, *—TCNT* . . . are worth nothing, *—NLTG* . . . is ruined, *—BRKL* . . . corrode, *—CNDT.*

**and your garments are moth-eaten:** . . . your clothing has become, *—MNTG* . . . eaten by insects, *—LBCH.*

**5:2.** In Bible times objects of wealth included foodstuffs, costly clothing, and precious metals. The corrupted riches here probably refer to grain which had rotted while in storage. The rich fool stored up vast quantities of crops (Luke 12:16-21). While people starved, heartless men allowed food to spoil.

Their beautiful apparel would become spoiled. Elegant, embroidered clothes were prized possessions of the wealthy. The fact that Paul said he "coveted no man's . . . apparel" (Acts 20:33) is an indication that luxurious clothes were objects of envy.

**3. Your gold and silver is cankered:** . . . covered with rust, *—BRKL* . . . eaten away, *—DRBY* . . . tarnished, *—BECK.*

**and the rust of them shall be a witness against you:** . . . and their canker, *—DRBY* . . . tarnish, *—BECK* . . . will be for a testimony, *—MNTG* . . . evidence against you, *—BRKL* . . . is witness against you, *—KLGS.*

**and shall eat your flesh as it were fire:** . . . consume, *—BRKL* . . . eat your bodies, *—KLGS* . . . devour . . . as fire does, *—CNFT.*

**Ye have heaped treasure together for the last days:** . . . hoarded riches, *—ADAM* . . . been storing up fire, *—MNTG* . . . You have piled up treasures in these last days, *—BECK* . . . You have heaped up as for a fire at the end of your days, *—FNTN* . . . that you have stored up against the last days, *—BRKL* . . . You piled up security in last days, *—KLGS* . . . while the world is coming to an end, *—TNT.*

**5:3.** Their silver and gold would lose their value. They would become as worthless as thoroughly rusted iron. In the Day of Judgment, whatever the nature of the wealth possessed, it would have absolutely no positive value. In fact, the wealth they had dishonestly acquired and selfishly hoarded, and which they valued so highly, would become a witness against them in the Day of Judgment. It would insure their condemnation and intensify the fires of judgment (see Romans 2:5). Only treasures of righteousness will stand the test.

"Ye have heaped treasure together *for* the last days" reads *"in* the last days" in the NIV. At a time when people should be laying up treasures in heaven (Matthew 6:19-21), they were spending

time and effort to accumulate inappropriate wealth to live in selfish extravagance.

**4. Behold, the hire of the labourers:** . . . the pay of, *—BRKL* . . . wages of, *—MNTG* . . . the workmen, *—NORL.*

**who have reaped down your fields:** . . . who mowed, *—MNTG* . . . harvested, *—NORL* . . . gathered your harvests for you, *—TNT.*

**which is of you kept back by fraud, crieth:** . . . You have stolen, *—LBCH* . . . you cheated them out of the pay that they deserved, *—SEB* . . . you never paid the men, *—BECK* . . . which you have withheld from them, *—BRKL* . . . which have been kept back by you unjustly, cry out, *—CNFT* . . . shout out at you, *—ADAM.*

**and the cries of them which have reaped are entered into the ears of the Lord of sabapth:** . . . and the complaints of, *—ADAM* . . . the outcries of the harvesters, *—NORL* . . . of the reapers, *—BRKL* . . . the groans of those who cut grain have come to the ears, *—BECK* . . . of the Lord of Hosts! *—TCNT* . . . of the Lord of Armies, *—WLSN.*

**5:4.** In those days there were no labor laws, and the rich often treated workers very unfairly. It appears they had cheated these people out of their just wages. Now, like the blood of Abel (Genesis 4:10), which cried out for vengeance, the defrauded wages in a sense cried out for condemnation of the rich. A just God would not ignore the cry that came from the defrauded workers and defrauded wages. This is why those who had obtained their riches in a way that was illegitimate should weep, because they can anticipate certain judgment (5:1-3).

"Saba-oth" is a transliteration from the Hebrew and means "hosts." It is a powerful expression of God's omnipotence. In the Old Testament He was seen not only as the God of Israel's army, but of heavenly bodies and angelic forces (Judges 5:20; 2 Kings 6:17).

**5. Ye have lived in pleasure on the earth, and been wanton:** . . . have lived luxuriously, *—MNTG* . . . have feasted upon earth, *—CNFT* . . . indulged yourselves, *—DRBY* . . . in luxury and self-gratification, *—NORL* . . . an easy life in the land, *—BRKL* . . . a life of extravagance, *—TCNT* . . . and been licentious, *—WLSN* . . . and been profligate, *—CLMT* . . . and squander, *—CNDT.*

**ye have nourished your hearts, as in a day of slaughter:** . . . fattened your hearts, *—MNTG* . . . on dissipation in the day of slaughter, *—CNFT* . . . as in a day of festivity, *—CMPB.*

**5:5.** James says, "Ye have lived in pleasure on the earth and been wanton." Weymouth translates this sentence, "Here on earth you have lived self-indulgent and profligate lives." The living here on earth is in sharp contrast with what these people will face at the judgment.

Without concern about life after death, these rich people lived in selfish luxury. "Wanton" suggests waste. Like the Prodigal Son, they squandered their substance (Luke 15:13) rather than administering it judiciously as a stewardship.

Some understand "ye have nourished your hearts, as in a day of slaughter" to mean unrestrained feasting after a victorious battle. Others, like the RV, omit the word "as" and understand the "day of slaughter" as the Day of Judgment and in contrast to "on the earth." The rich, by presumptuous, unrestrained living, were preparing themselves for the Day of Judgment like animals gorging themselves for the day of slaughter.

**6. Ye have condemned [and] killed the just:** . . . you have murdered, *—TCNT* . . . and put to death, *—CNFT* . . . killed the One right with God, *—NLTG* . . . the upright, *—BRKL* . . . the righteous man, *—MNTG* . . . an innocent man, *—SEB*.

**[and] he doth not resist you:** . . . unresisting, *—MNTG* . . . who did not even oppose you! *—NORL*.

**5:6.** The rich were not satisfied with cheating workers out of their wages. They went so far as to use their influence to condemn and kill righteous people in violation of God's command not to pervert justice (Exodus 23:6; Deuteronomy 24:17). Some who were wrongfully drawn "before the judgment seats" (2:6) were through harsh treatment put to death.

The situation of the poor was so hopeless that they could not or would not resist those who mistreated them. It is possible that they reacted according to the guidance of Paul in Romans 12:19: "Avenge not yourselves." God would avenge them.

**7. Be patient therefore, brethren, unto the coming of the Lord:** . . . So, endure patiently, *—BRKL* . . . fellow Christians, *—BECK*.

**Behold, the husbandman waiteth for the precious fruit of the earth, and hath long patience for it:** . . . Note how the farmer awaits the precious produce of the soil, keeping patient about it, *—BRKL* . . . crop on the ground, *—BECK*.

**until he receive the early and latter rain:** . . . till it has had the spring and summer rains, *—TCNT* . . . until the early and late rains come, *—TNT, —KLGS* . . . to get the fall and the spring rains, *—BECK* . . . the early and latter harvest, *—WLSN* . . . getting the early and late fruit, *—CNDT*.

**5:7.** The Greek word translated "be patient" (*makrothumēsate*) basically means "be longsuffering." Just as God suffers long with difficult people (Psalm 86:15; Jonah 4:2; 2 Peter 3:9), believers are to do likewise (1 Thessalonians 5:14). Longsuffering is a fruit of the Spirit (Galatians 5:22).

Believers were assured that oppression would not continue indefinitely. The coming of the Lord would bring about a change. The second coming of Christ is a "blessed hope" for believers (Titus

2:13) and a source of comfort (1 Thessalonians 4:18).

The writer used the work of a farmer to emphasize the need for patience. He would prepare the soil, plant the seed, and wait for the crops to mature. Most of all, he would wait for the rain.

God had promised two rainy seasons in Palestine (Deuteronomy 11:14). The "early rain" came in late October or early November and provided moisture needed for sowing the seed. The "latter rain" usually came in the early months of the year and was essential for maturing the harvest.

**8. Be ye also patient; stablish your hearts:** . . . So you keep waiting patiently, *—BRKL* . . . have great patience, *—KLGS* . . . You, too, be patient, and keep your courage, *—BECK* . . . Fortify your hearts, *—NORL* . . . Firm up your hearts, *—ADAM* . . . Make your hearts strong, *—SEB* . . . strengthen your hearts, *—CNFT*.

**for the coming of the Lord draweth nigh:** . . . because the Lord will soon be here, *—BECK* . . . because the Lord's coming will soon take place, *—TNT* . . . the presence of the Lord has come, *—KLGS* . . . is at hand! *—MNTG*.

**5:8.** Here James applied the previous illustration to suffering believers and said, "Be ye also patient." Just as the farmers showed patience because they had learned to trust in God's providential provision, believers were to be patient in their difficult circumstances.

To "stablish your hearts" means to strengthen, make fast, to set firmly so the heart will be unshakable. God through His divine intervention works in believers' lives that "he may stablish your hearts unblamable in holiness before God, even our Father, at the coming of our Lord Jesus Christ with all his saints" (1 Thessalonians 3:13). But believers have a personal responsibility to establish their own hearts. The means by which this is done is the truth of God's Word (1 Peter 2:2).

Believers were not only assured that God heard their cries (5:4), but the Lord was coming to do something about world conditions. When problems exist, time seems to drag by. But time seems shortened for those who have the heavenly perspective.

**9. Grudge not one against another, brethren:** . . . Do not make complaints against each other, *—MNTG* . . . Don't blame your troubles on one another, fellow Christians, *—BECK*.

**lest ye be condemned:** . . . or you will be, *—BECK* . . . that you may not be judged, *—CNFT* . . . so you may not come under judgment, *—BRKL*.

**behold, the judge standeth before the door:** . . . You know, *—BECK* . . . Look, *—KLGS* . . . is here, standing at the door, *—TNT* . . . is standing just outside, *—SEB* . . . has already stationed Himself at the gates! *—FNTN*.

**5:9.** The word translated "grudge" literally means "groan." When people have severe problems, the "groaning" can become murmuring or grumbling, criticizing others for real or imagined grievances. This judging of others is the opposite of the patience James wrote about in the previous verse.

In the Sermon on the Mount Jesus taught, "Judge not, that ye be not judged. For with what judgment ye judge, ye shall be judged: and with what measure ye mete, it shall be measured to you again (Matthew 7:1,2). Sometimes the judgment of those who are critical of others comes in this life. Paul warned the Corinthians, "Neither murmur ye, as some of them also murmured, and were destroyed of the destroyer" (1 Corinthians 10:10). Murmuring deserves no place in a believer's life.

The phrase "the judge standeth before the door" has serious implications. The Judge now stands knocking at the door of hearts seeking redemptive admission (Revelation 3:20); then He will open the door in judgment.

**10.** **Take, my brethren, the prophets, who have spoken in the name of the Lord:** . . . brothers, think of the prophets, *—TNT* . . . fellow Christians, take the prophets who spoke in the Lord's name, *—BECK.*
**for an example of suffering affliction, and of patience:** . . . as an example of labor and patience, *—CNFT* . . . for your example of ill-treatment that was patiently endured, *—BRKL* . . . of patiently suffering wrong, *—BECK* . . . the patience of the prophets, *—MNTG* . . . of great suffering and great patience, *—KLGS.*

**5:10.** The experiences of those who have gone before us, and their examples of godly perseverance can be like a beacon to guide us. As these suffering Christians were told to consider the prophets as examples of endurance, they might have thought of people such as Moses (Deuteronomy 18:18), Elijah (1 Kings 17:1), Elisha (1 Kings 19:16), and Jeremiah (Jeremiah 1:1,2). The fact that they had "spoken in the name of the Lord" did not mean they were free from suffering.

**11.** **Behold, we count them happy which endure:** . . . Remember, we call those happy, *—BECK* . . . we count those that were stedfast, *—MNTG* . . . we admire those who have patience, *—SEB* . . . we call them blessed who have endured, *—CNFT* . . . who remains faithful to the end, *—LBCH* . . . for their way of enduring, *—BRKL.*
**Ye have heard of the patience of Job, and have seen the end of the Lord:** . . . stedfastness, *—MNTG* . . . how Job endured, and you saw how the Lord finally treated him, *—BECK* . . . seen the purpose of, *—CNFT* . . . noticed what conclusion the Lord effected, *—BRKL.*

**that the Lord is very pitiful, and of tender mercy:** . . . because the Lord is very tenderhearted, *—BECK* . . . compassionate and merciful, *—SWAN* . . . full of tenderness, *—MNTG* . . . tender compassion, *—DRBY* . . . deeply sympathetic, *—BRKL.*

**5:11.** "Behold, we count them happy which endure" is better translated "which *endured.*" This is another element in the encouragement of those presently suffering affliction. Those who have already endured are considered happy or blessed.

The experiences of the patriarch Job and how he came through successfully are a great encouragement to believers. The word here translated "patience" is different from the word so translated in 5:7. There the meaning is longsuffering. Here the meaning is endurance. Job was not always longsuffering with his friends, but he endured. His affirmation, "Though he slay me, yet will I trust in him" (Job 13:15) testified to his steadfastness.

The readers who had heard of Job's endurance were also aware of his vindication. They saw the end which the Lord brought about. Readers could learn from Job's experience that even though believers have much affliction, the final outcome is happy. If the outcome is not always happy in this life, as in the case of Stephen, the heavenly welcome and reward will be of indescribable blessedness (Acts 7:55,56).

The way God dealt with Job reveals His character. It only *seemed* that God had forsaken him; all was well at the last. "Pitiful," very compassionate, refers to God's feeling for man. "Tender mercy" speaks of how He acts toward man.

**12.** **But above all things, my brethren, swear not:** . . . More than anything else, *—SEB* . . . my fellow Christians, *—BECK* . . . do not take oaths, *—LBCH.*
**neither by heaven, neither by the earth, neither by any other oath:** . . . any other kind of oath, *—FNTN.*
**but let your yea be yea; and [your] nay, nay:** . . . If you mean yes, say yes, *—NLTG* . . . let your "yes" mean yes, *—NORL* . . . be just yes, *—BECK.*
**lest ye fall into condemnation:** . . . so you will not fall under, *—MNTG* . . . will escape being judged, *—NORL* . . . may incur no judgment, *—BRKL* . . . or you will be condemned for it, *—BECK.*

**5:12.** Here James comes back to the matter of the believer's speech (see 1:26; 3:2,8; 4:11). As in the words of Jesus to which James referred, the emphasis is on total honesty. It seems dishonesty had become so prevalent that in interpersonal conversation people would affirm statements with an oath. Matthew 23:16-22 indicates how oaths were dishonestly manipulated by the Pharisees so commitments would not be binding.

Some understand that not swearing by an oath applies to all situations including official oaths. Others understand it as calling for total honesty in communication and not applying to legal matters. Alfred Plummer in holding that this verse does not extend to legal matters points out that the Mosaic law "not only allowed, but enjoined the taking of an oath in certain circumstances: and Christ would hardly have abrogated the law, and St. James would hardly have contradicted it without giving some explanation" (*The Expositor's Bible*, 24:305). (See Deuteronomy 6:13; 10:20; Isaiah 65:16; Jeremiah 12:15,16.) Jesus dealt with this matter also (Matthew 5:34-37).

**13. Is any among you afflicted?:** ... When any one of you is, –*TCNT*... in trouble? –*MNTG*... in distress? –*FNTN*... suffering, –*SWAN*... sad, –*CNFT*... suffer evil? –*DRBY*... ill-treatment, –*WLMS*.
**let him pray:**
**Is any merry?:** ... when any one feels cheerful, –*TCNT*... in good spirits? –*MNTG*... in a happy mood? –*WLMS*.
**let him sing psalms:**... sing hymns, –*TCNT*... praises, –*WLSN*... play music, –*CNDT*... unto his harp, –*MNTG*.

**5:13.** As he comes to the close of the epistle, James deals with a series of very personal matters. If believers are afflicted, he says, the answer is to pray instead of complain. If, on the other hand, they are in a happy mood, they should sing unto the Lord. As in the case of Paul and Silas, praying and singing can be combined (Acts 16:25). See also Ephesians 5:19,20.

**14. Is any sick among you?:** ... any one of you ill? –*MNTG*.
**let him call for the elders of the church:**... Let him summon, –*FNTN*... send for, –*MNTG*... bring in the presbyters, –*CNFT*... of the congregation, –*SEB*.
**and let them pray over him anointing him with oil in the name of the Lord:** ... pouring on oil, –*BECK*... rubbing him with olive oil, –*CNDT*.

**5:14.** Here believers have instructions as to what to do in the case of sickness. The word translated "sick" has the idea of being weak. It is the opposite of the word used for strength. The reference seems to be to a feebleness which results in inability to work.

When this sickness develops, the suffering believer is to call for the elders of the church. One title of church leaders in Bible times was *elder*. Apparently they were also known as bishops. See Acts 20:17 with 20:28 where the Greek word for *bishop* is translated "overseer." Because of the debilitating nature of the illness, the elders were to be called to the home rather than have the suffering person come to the congregation. Jesus

himself went to the homes of those who were sick (Matthew 8:14; Luke 8:41, 42, 51).

The elders were not only to pray but to anoint with oil. Anointing the sick with oil was instituted by the Lord. The oil in Scripture is often a type of the Holy Spirit. It is by His power that miracles occur. It was to be done in Jesus' name, that is, by His authority. The Twelve "anointed with oil many that were sick" (Mark 6:13).

**15. And the prayer of faith shall save the sick:** ... if you believe, your prayer will make the sick person well, –*BECK*... that is offered in faith, –*WLMS*... will restore the sick, –*MNTG*... heal the sick man, –*NLTG*... save the distressed one, –*CLMT*.
**and the Lord shall raise him up:** ... restore him to health, –*TCNT*... make him well, –*LBCH*... make him healthy, –*BECK*.
**and if he have committed sins, they shall be forgiven him:** ... if he feels guilty of sins, –*BECK*... it shall be removed from him, –*FNTN*.

**5:15.** The writer assures his readers that there will be results, that healing will occur. It is not always known who it is that prays the prayer of faith. It might be the sick person as in the case of two blind men who followed Jesus into a house (Matthew 9:27-29); or the faith of sympathetic friends as in the case of the servant of the Roman centurion (Matthew 8:5-13); or the faith of an "elder" as in the case of Dorcas (Acts 9:36-43; 1 Peter 5:1). While there are different ways in which healing comes, it is not man, but the Lord, who raises them up.

In some cases there will be spiritual results also. There are times when sickness is the result of sin. Because of abuses in connection with the Lord's Supper at Corinth, Paul wrote: "For this cause many are weak and sickly among you, and many sleep (die)" (1 Corinthians 11:30). On the other hand, there are times when illness is unrelated to sin. Jesus made it clear there was no sin involved in the case of the man born blind (John 9:1-3). If sin is involved, there is forgiveness (1 John 1:9).

**16. Confess [your] faults one to another:**... Admit, –*SEB*... your sins, –*MNTG*.
**and pray one for another, that ye may be healed:** ... pray for one another to be healed, –*BECK*... may be saved, –*CNFT*... be cured, –*BRKL*.
**The effectual fervent prayer of a righteous man availeth much:** ... The energetic supplications, –*SWAN*... The Earnest Supplication, –*WLSN*... by praying vigorously, –*BECK*... fervent supplication, –*DRBY*... The operative petition of the just, –*CNDT*... the unceasing prayer of a just man, –*CNFT*... the earnest prayer of a good man can do much, –*TCNT*... from the heart of a man right with God has much power, –*NLTG*... The inwrought prayer of a righteous man exceedingly prevails, –*CLMT*... Very powerfully productive is the

prayer of, —FNTN . . . the power of his sincere prayer is tremendous . . . When a person is right with God, —SEB . . . is mighty in its working, —MNTG . . . has great effect, —BRKL . . . very powerful effects, —ADAM.

**5:16.** We are to confess our faults (sins) and pray for one another that we may be healed. Here the matter of sin, sickness, and healing moves beyond the case where elders are called. The confession of sin is to one another. This might be a reference to Jesus' teaching concerning the importance of reconciliation between believers (Matthew 5:23,24). Sickness can be caused by harboring resentment, and it is difficult to pray with ill will in the heart. Removing resentment is a factor in spiritual healing.

Here are stated principles to follow if we desire to have an effective prayer ministry. The prayers of a man who is right with God can accomplish much. The righteous person is the one who practices right living (1 John 3:7). Believers who tolerate sin in their hearts cannot pray effectively (Psalm 66:18).

**17. Elias was a man subject to like passions as we are:** . . . with feelings just like ours, —WLMS . . . like ourselves, subject to the same infirmities, —CNFT . . . of like nature with us, —CLMT . . . of similar weakness with us, —BRKL.
**and he prayed earnestly that it might not rain:** . . . but when he prayed fervently, —TCNT . . . he kept on praying, —KLGS.
**and it rained not on the earth by the space of three years and six months:** . . . there fell no rain on the ground, —BRKL.

**5:17.** Here is a statement which should boost the spiritual morale of every believer. It was anticipated that some would feel it was natural for a man of heroic achievement to be able to pray effectively, but effective prayer could not be expected of ordinary persons. James made it clear that Elijah was a man with a nature exactly like theirs. The same person who seemed to be so in control on Mount Carmel (1 Kings 18:25-46) was the one who would desire to have God take his life after he heard of Jezebel's threats (1 Kings 19:4). The readers of this epistle could not excuse themselves from praying effectively by elevating Elijah to an exalted status.

The word "earnestly" interprets a Hebrew idiom which means "he prayed with prayer." This Hebraism indicated intensity. While the words he spoke are not recorded, there was an indication of his intensity in his physical posture. "He cast himself down upon the earth, and put his face between his knees" (1 Kings 18:42).

This reference mentions his prayer *for* rain, but he undoubtedly prayed just as earnestly it

would *not* rain. There is no discrepancy between the statement "the space of three years and six months" and 1 Kings 18:1 which states "the word of the Lord came to Elijah in the third year." The two rainy seasons in Palestine were about 6 months apart. For the first 6 months Ahab undoubtedly ridiculed Elijah's announcement that there would be no rain. This prophecy would not be verified until the 6-month period between rains had passed and it failed to rain. Jesus also had stated that it did not rain for 3 years and 6 months (Luke 4:25).

**18. And he prayed again, and the heaven gave rain:** . . . Again he prayed earnestly, —BRKL . . . heaven sent rain, —BECK . . . the sky gave, —MNTG . . . gives a shower, —CNDT . . . rain fell from heaven, —NOLI.
**and the earth brought forth her fruit:** . . . the ground, —BECK . . . the soil yielded its produce, —BRKL . . . germinates her fruit, —CNDT . . . the soil again produced, —TNT . . . produced its crops, —WLMS.

**5:18.** The lesson for readers was that if the earnest prayer of a right-living person could become the instrument by which God controls the weather, this kind of prayer can also be the means by which He grants healing.

**19. Brethren, if any of you do err from the truth:** . . . My fellow Christians, —BECK . . . if anybody among you, —KLGS . . . one of you strays, —MNTG . . . wanders from, —LBCH . . . fallen away from the true religion, —NOLI.
**and one convert him:** . . . if anyone turns him around, —KLGS . . . some one brings him back, —MNTG . . . one can turn him back, —FNTN . . . try to bring him back, —LBCH.

**5:19.** James clearly addresses his next exhortation to anyone within the community of faith who apostatizes. The term here for "err" (*planēthē*) means to "no longer believe what is true, to start believing what is false"; "to wander or stray from the truth," (Louw and Nida, *Greek-English Lexicon*, 1:374). This could either be the result of a willful decision or the deceit of Satan. The "truth" is not merely an intellectual reality but a way of life. This one who apostatizes through disregarding the ethical and moral norms of the community is in need of someone to bring them back (*epistrepsē*), i.e., to turn them back to the truth. Here the writer affirms the Biblical principle of personal accountability among the members of the body of Christ.

**20. Let him know, that he which converteth the sinner:** . . . Remember this, —SEB . . . be sure of this, —TNT . . . let him be assured, —BRKL . . . know that he who turns the one missing it, —KLGS . . . he ought to know that he who causes a sinner to be brought back, —CNFT . . . brings a sinner back, —MNTG . . . who turns back a Sinner, —WLSN.

**from the error of his way:** . . . from the wandering of his way, —BRKL . . . his Path of Error, —WLSN . . . his misguided way, —CNFT . . . his wrong way, —BECK . . . from his wandering road, —KLGS.

**shall save a soul from death:** . . . keeps a soul, —BB . . . will save his soul, —CNFT . . . will save that man's soul, —TNT . . . he has reserved a soul, —PHLP.

**and shall hide a multitude of sins:** . . . and veil from God's sight, —WADE . . . and is the cause of forgiveness for sins without number, —BB . . . and prevent a multitude of sins, —FNTN . . . covers up a great number of sins, —BRKL . . . and many sins will be forgiven, —NLTG . . . and will cause many sins to be forgiven, —TNT . . . cover many sins, —BECK . . . will be covered, —SEB . . . will "cover a multitude," —PHLP . . . and will draw a veil over a host of, —BRCL . . . and bring about the forgiveness of many sins, —TEV . . . and cover an uncounted number of, —WMCK

**5:20.** The one who seeks to turn the erring one back to the truth is now reminded of the teaching of the church on this issue. The willingness of believers to confront sin in an attitude of humility and love, and their conscious efforts to restore the erring brother or sister have eternally redemptive results. Death, usually considered here to be eternal death, is the result of sin for the "soul" or individual that lives in a state of apostasy. When believers take responsibility for one another, forgiveness and atonement are extended. Believers become channels of grace to one another in the body of Christ. This final phrase describes the extent of the forgiveness and not the state of the sinner (Davids, *New International Greek Testament Commentary, James,* p.200).

# 1 PETER

## Overview

Peter is often referred to as the apostle of hope, Paul the apostle of faith, and John the apostle of love. In his epistles Peter addressed particular problems, as did Paul and John. Together these apostles dealt with the entire spectrum of the Christian faith.

Peter's epistles contain a wealth of doctrine and encouragement. The flow of 1 Peter is smooth and even; 2 Peter is somewhat more uneven. In many ways the differences in form and style remind one of the differences between Paul's epistles to the Romans and Galatians. First Peter is didactic and gives warning. Second Peter is quite polemic. Nonetheless, in both letters the predominant concern is the care of the believer.

## Canonicity

Christians of the First Century were actively engaged in determining the authenticity and apostolicity of the epistles. Peter's first epistle satisfied the two main criteria for acceptance as Holy Scripture: It was apostolic and it had since the outset been accepted as Holy Scripture by the Early Church.

It is among the best attested documents in the New Testament. The first witness to its authenticity comes from the Bible itself. Peter himself referred to it when he used the words "second epistle" (2 Peter 3:1).

According to the church historian Eusebius of Caesarea the epistle was commonly regarded as genuine. Some believe there is an echo of 1 Peter in 1 Clement (ca. A.D. 96), Ignatius (ca. A.D. 110), the Shepherd of Hermas, and the Epistle of Barnabas. Papias (A.D. 125) also used 1 Peter. From that same time (A.D. 125) there are probable allusions to 1 Peter in Polycarp. Other Second Century writers also appear to refer to the letter and ascribe it to Peter the apostle (e.g., Basil [125], Theodotion [160], and Irenaeus [180]).

It was not until more recent times that the authenticity of the epistle was questioned. Modern Biblical criticism based the objection to the authenticity of 1 Peter on historical and dogmatic questions as well as on the linguistic style.

Historical objections culminate for the most part in the supposed improbability that Peter, the apostle to the Jews, would write a letter to churches in Asia Minor, the supposed "jurisdiction" of Paul. But Paul himself endorsed Peter's authority or perhaps "popularity" among his churches (1

Corinthians 1:12). It is further argued that the letter presupposes a persecution in Asia Minor (ca. during the reign of Domitian, 81-96), which did not actually occur until after Peter's death. However, nothing in the epistle itself suggests that such a state-backed persecution of Christians was under way. The contrary is true (cf. 2:13,14). But still it is clear from the Book of Acts and the Epistles that Christians faced opposition from the very beginning, much like Peter wrote about in his letter.

Arguments against the authenticity of the letter based on linguistic style question the ability of a Galilean fisherman to write such excellent Greek. Peter understood and used Greek, but it is very likely that Silas (Silvanus; cf 1 Peter 5:12), the old friend and coworker of Paul and the coauthor of the letters to the Thessalonians, also coauthored 1 Peter.

Objections raised because the First Epistle of Peter used the Septuagint rather than the Hebrew Bible (Masoretic Text) are of little consequence, since the Qumran texts have shown other texts which could have been the basis here. On the other hand, it is still quite likely that the Septuagint did indeed serve as the basis of the Scripture citations in 1 Peter. Peter simply used the text of his audience.

Dogmatic objections to Petrine authorship concern the distinct similarities between some of Paul's writings, particularly Ephesians and Romans. Without question there are similarities, but this only proves that in the Early Church there was a unified doctrinal foundation as well as fruitful dialogue among leaders. Peter acknowledged the letters of Paul and knew them well (2 Peter 3:15,16). His first epistle also indicates some points of contact with Hebrews and the Epistle of James.

The objections raised against the authenticity of Peter's first epistle are of even less consequence in light of the stronger external and internal witnesses to its authenticity. The external witnesses mentioned above are so reliable that it seems no book of the New Testament has an earlier, stronger, or better attestation. Furthermore, we have the epistle's own testimony and some strong internal reasons for accepting it as genuine.

## Authorship

Peter, the apostle of Jesus Christ, introduced himself as the author (1:1). He asserted his apostolic authority and claimed equal status with the leaders of the Church by describing himself as "also an elder" (5:1). When he admonished those guarding the "flock" of God, his words implied that such action was his duty—a reminder of the pastoral calling given to Peter by the Lord following His resurrection (John 21:15-17).

One interesting feature is that the words used to describe the sufferings of Christ correspond more closely to Mark's Gospel than to any of the other Synoptics. It is a well-known and ancient tradition that Mark relied on Peter as his principal source.

There is a striking similarity between the sermons and speeches of Peter recorded in the Book of Acts and his words in the epistle. Related to this is the consistent understanding that the Christ-event was the fulfillment of Old Testament prophecies (1 Peter 1:10,12; cf. Acts 3:18-24). Further, both relate that God makes no distinction between people (1 Peter 1:17; cf. Acts 10:34) and that Christ is the stone rejected by the builders (1 Peter 2:7,8; Acts 4:10,11). Finally, there is similar importance attached to the name of the Lord (1 Peter 4:14,16; cf. Acts 3:6,16; 4:10,12; 10:43).

Suffering is a central theme in 1 Peter, especially the suffering of Christ. It is interesting to compare what the letter says with what Peter said as reported in the Gospels and Acts. The Gospels relate that Peter resisted the fact that Jesus had to follow the way of suffering (Matthew 16:21f.). However, in the Book of Acts, a focal point of Peter's preaching is that "Christ should suffer" (3:18; cf. 2:23). In his first epistle Peter equated "suffering" with "the death of Christ." He described himself as a "witness of the sufferings of Christ" (5:1). He wrote that Christ was "put to death in the flesh" (3:18), but his tendency was to emphasize the suffering aspect of that death (cf. 2:21; 3:18; 5:1). He stressed the fact that the prophets "testified beforehand the sufferings of Christ" (1:11).

The epistle indicates that believers are to share in these sufferings; it is the way to glory (4:13). They are to enter this glory "after that ye have suffered a while" (5:10; cf. 1:6,7). Peter was a man traveling in the shadow of the Cross. Like his Master, he knew a cross awaited him at the end of his journey. Peter differed in this respect from his fellow apostles. During most of their apostolic service their personal hope was for the return of Christ. Of John it was said: "that disciple should not die" (John 21:23). Paul could say that he did not wish to be unclothed, but clothed with his heavenly dwelling (2 Corinthians 5:4). He felt it better to remain until the coming of the Lord than to die a natural death. He could say: "We which are alive and remain unto the coming of the Lord" (1 Thessalonians 4:15). But paradoxically, the very one known as the apostle of hope could not entertain a personal hope that he would escape death. Peter knew he would glorify God through his death (John 21:18,19); he also knew it would not be long

in coming (2 Peter 1:14). It was the Peter who approached the day when he would be led where he did not want to go who wrote these epistles.

After he met Jesus, Peter's life fell into three sections: (1) the years when he accompanied Jesus; (2) after the Resurrection, until he left Jerusalem—during this time (ca. A.D. 45-48), he was the major leader of the Church (Acts 1-12); (3) very little is known of the third period during which he was one of the pillars of the Church until his death (Galatians 2:9). The legacy of these two letters are the apostle's last will to Christianity.

## Recipients of the Epistle

The epistle is addressed "To God's elect, strangers in the world, scattered throughout Pontus, Galatia, Cappadocia, Asia and Bithynia" (1:1, NIV). These words indicate the initial readers lived in the Roman provinces in the northwestern section of Asia Minor. The term "strangers" is understood by some to refer to Christian Jews of the Diaspora. Others regard the term as a symbol for the believer's status as a "stranger" in the world. Many references in the epistle indicate that the latter interpretation is preferred. For example, formerly believers lived in ignorance (1:14) and shared in abominable idolatries (4:3). Perhaps the most vivid illustration is that they were formerly "not a people" (2:10). Most likely the churches that received the letter were of mixed, Jewish-Gentile congregations.

Apparently the believers were facing strong harassment from outsiders. Peter used the terms "suffer" or "suffering" no less than 16 times. Although the outsiders had slandered the believers as evildoers, there is no evidence that this was a state-sponsored persecution. The authorities were not seen in a hostile light but rather as a police force to punish the evildoers and praise those who did well. Evidently the Christians were still being protected by the authorities (2:13-17), but the opposition was beginning. Peter wrote to encourage his brothers and sisters (cf. Luke 22:32).

## Time and Place

The closing words of the epistle (5:13) indicate that it originated in "Babylon." If this is to be taken literally, it probably refers to Babylon on the Euphrates. There was a Roman military outpost in Egypt with this name, but it is unlikely that this obscure defense post was the place referred to by Peter. In Mesopotamia there was an ancient, rather large Jewish settlement, and even though the city of Babylon was largely destroyed, some Jews still lived in this region. It would not be out of the question to assume that Peter, the apostle to the Jews, had visited this place. If his letter originated here it would account for the east-to-west listing of regions in the opening greeting.

If Babylon is to be understood figuratively, the meaning is without question "Rome." It is not easy to understand why the apostle would choose such cryptic language, but the two other figurative expressions in the verse favor such an understanding. The text literally reads: "She, that is at Babylon, elected together with you, salute you, and so does Marcus my son" (5:13). The word "she" is understood figuratively as the church. "Marcus" was undoubtedly, like Silas, "Mark," Paul's coworker. He was the "son" of Peter only in a spiritual sense. When the two expressions are taken figuratively, it makes good sense to take Babylon in the same way. If this is the case, as in Revelation 16:19; 17:18; 18:2, 10, "Babylon" refers to Rome. An ancient tradition indicates Peter was martyred at Rome during Nero's persecution of Christians in the fall of A.D. 64. The time of the apostle's death is therefore established sometime between 64 and 67; the two letters sometime before this. During this time, Paul was imprisoned in Rome; in Jerusalem, earlier, James had been put to death by the Jews. Peter must have thought his own death was drawing near, and he must have wanted to reach his friends with a word of warning and encouragement.

## Survey and Structure

As we find in Paul's writings, there are distinct teaching portions and encouragement sections in 1 Peter. In the first section (1:1-2:11), doctrinal matters are presented. The remainder of the letter is devoted primarily to practical admonition and advice. Nonetheless, there is no truly sharp distinction between teaching and advice. Peter described his writing as an encouragement and a testimony (5:12). Doctrine is the basis for encouragement and admonition. Because God has begotten us again (1:3), we should live holy lives "as obedient children" (1:14-17). Believers are to follow Christ's example, walking in His footsteps (2:21). Because Christ took our sins, we are to be dead to them (2:24). The thought of reward can be motivation to holy service (5:2-4). Thus the Christian is to seek God's acceptance.

The strong emphasis on humility and submissiveness was virtually at odds with the Greek notion of human dignity. The manner in which good works are portrayed in this epistle did not coincide with either Jewish or Greek thought. It is a unique Christian ethic, modeled on Christ's example presented in this epistle.

Because teaching and advice are so interwoven, it is not easy to distinguish a clear-cut structure or outline. Interpreters have used their own points of view and different thematic interests to create a structure. Many are useful and insightful; many are similar. One should not force the epistle into some rigid arrangement. However, the following outline should be helpful in seeing the main content:

I.      Salvation in Christ (1:1-2:10)

II.     The Conduct of the Christian (2:11-3:12)

III.    The Sufferings of the Christian (3:13-4:19)

IV.     Final Encouragement (5:1ff.)

## The Theology of Peter

Since Peter was one of the closest followers of Jesus during His public ministry, it is reasonable to assume much of what he wrote echoes the teaching of the Lord. At the same time there is a strong undercurrent of Pauline theology. This suggests that during the apostolic period much of the teaching was shared by the body of Christ as a whole (cf. Galatians 2:1ff.). There is a significant amount of theology in 1 Peter. In this Overview only the main points can be mentioned.

### (1) The Trinitarian View of the Godhead

The epistle opens with a clearly expressed faith in the Trinity: "Elect according to the foreknowledge of God the Father, through sanctification of the Spirit, unto obedience and sprinkling of the blood of Jesus Christ" (1:2). The great trinitarian doxology of 1:3-12 delineates the role of each of the three Persons of the Godhead in salvation. These verses give one of the clearest trinitarian statements in the New Testament.

### (2) God the Father

Peter used the phrase "God the Father" (1:2) in much the same way John's Gospel speaks of God as "Father" in the absolute sense, i.e., as a member of the Godhead. This is markedly underscored in 1:3: "the God and Father of our Lord Jesus Christ." Here faith in God is linked to Christology. The God preached by Peter is the One who beforehand spoke through the prophets and who anticipated the coming of Christ (1:10,11). In these last times God the Father has revealed himself in the Son (1:5). God is the "faithful Creator" (4:19). He is holy and expects holiness from His people (1:15). He judges without respect of persons (1:17). Believers have been brought "to God" and into right relationship with Him through the suffering and death of Christ (3:18). It is through Christ that believers have faith in God, and this faith means hope in God for eternal glory (1:21).

### (3) Christology

Peter's theology is fundamentally Christological. It is so comprehensive that it covers virtually every main element of the New Testament's teaching about the person and work of Christ. First Peter includes most of the major soteriological (doctrine of salvation) and eschatological (doctrine of last things) teachings as well. Within this brief letter the apostle Peter emerges as one of the great teachers of the Christian faith. The following can be mentioned:

## Preexistence of Christ (1:20)

Before the foundation of the world Christ was. This was an actual preexistence and a real manifestation in time (cf. John 1:1-14). Even in His preexistence Christ was the spotless Lamb who was to redeem mankind with His blood (1 Peter 1:19; cf. Revelation 13:8).

## Prophecy of His Coming (1:11)

Old Testament prophets prophesied that Christ would come. They testified to His sufferings as well as to His humiliation and subsequent glorification. Actually, through the Holy Spirit (here the Spirit of Christ), Christ himself testified to His coming. That the Spirit bore witness as the Spirit of Christ centuries, indeed thousands of years, before the coming of Christ is reminiscent of Hebrews 11:26. Long before Christ's coming, Moses considered the dishonor of associating with Christ of more value than the treasures of Egypt.

## Christ—Messiah

The most often used title for the Lord in 1 Peter is simply "Christ" (1:11,19; 2:21; 3:15, 16, 18; 4:1, 13, 14; 5:1, 10, 14). The combination "Jesus Christ" is not used as often (1:1, 2, 3, 7, 13; 2:5; 3:21; 4:11). Although Peter used the title "Christ" as a proper name, he could not have done so without being fully aware that the name meant "Messiah," the "anointed one." Peter's dramatic confession at Caesarea Philippi, "Thou art the Christ, the Son of the living God" (Matthew 16:16), indicated that awareness. Such a messianic proclamation was also a distinct feature of Peter's sermons in Acts (Acts 2:14-16; 3:12-26, etc.).

## The Incarnation

Peter viewed Jesus' birth as well as His return as a "revelation" (1:20; cf. 1:7,13; 4:13; 5:4). At His birth the preexistent Christ entered the human sphere. This corresponds with Paul's use of the phrase "manifest in the flesh" (1 Timothy 3:16). Other New Testament writers took the same position (e.g., Paul, 1 Timothy 3:16; cf. 2 Thessalonians 1:7; the author of Hebrews, 9:26; cf. verse 28; John, 1 John 3:5,8; cf. 2:28; 3:2).

## Christ's Sinlessness

The apostle Peter was an eyewitness to the words and ministry of the only sinless Person ever to live on earth. Christ is the only One who could ever issue the challenge: "Which of you convinceth me of sin?" (John 8:46). Peter repeatedly emphasized that Christ was free from sin ("who did no sin," 2:22). Christ was the "lamb without blemish" (without innate sin) and "without spot" (without

external sin). He alone could offer sacrifice for others (1:19), the "just for the unjust" (3:18).

## Christ's Example

God's holiness was revealed and demonstrated in Jesus Christ as He lived out His perfect life among men. Peter presented Christ's holiness as the model for believers, "Leaving us an example, that ye should follow his steps" (2:21). He argued (1:15,16) that God's own holiness should be incentive for holy lives among His people.

## Substitutionary Death

Not for one minute did Peter entertain the idea that merely by example Christ secured salvation for the believer. As soon as he presented Christ as example (2:21-23), he moved on to write of Jesus as the One who atoned for sin, "who his own self bare our sins in his own body on the tree" (2:24). Christ's death was a substitutional death, "the just for (*huper*) the unjust" (3:18). The Greek term *huper*, here means "instead of," "in place of," "for." It functions in much the same way as it does in Philemon 13, "that in thy stead he might have ministered unto me." The issue, then, is full substitution. Christ takes the place of the sinner.

Peter further underscored this in 1:19, where he referred to Christ as the blameless sacrificial Lamb. This recalls the symbolic, substitutional nature of the Levitical sacrifices. However, in contrast to the repeated sacrifices of the priests, Christ "hath once suffered" (3:18), i.e., "once and for all" (cf. Romans 6:9,10; Hebrews 9:28; 10:10-12). Christ offered the perfect sacrifice for our sins. It does not have to be repeated. He offered himself in our place to "bring us to God" (3:18), to grant us access to God (cf. Hebrews 10:19,20). He gave himself that "we, being dead to sins, should live unto righteousness" (2:24).

In the original language the term for "redeemed" is *lutroō*, which implies a redemption based on a ransom. (Cf. Matthew 20:28, where Jesus said the Son of Man would give His life as a ransom for many [*lutron anti*, "ransom instead of" to be precise]; cf. also 1 Timothy 2:6: "Who gave himself a ransom for all" [*antilutron huper*, literally "ransom instead of"].)

## Descent to the Realm of the Dead (3:18-20)

Most interpreters unite these verses with those texts referring to Christ's descent to the kingdom of death following His death on the cross. Jesus promised the repentant thief he would join Him in paradise (Luke 23:43), which is understood as the habitation of the righteous after death. Peter mentioned Christ's descent into the kingdom of death, but he emphasized the fact that Christ did not remain there (Acts 2:27,31). Paul also wrote of Christ's visit to the kingdom of the dead during the time between His death and resurrection (Romans 10:7). The context of 3:18-22 concerns Christ's death, resurrection, and ascension. If one takes this to mean that as a part of salvation history Jesus departed and preached to the spirits in prison (cf. 1 Peter 4:6; 2 Peter 2:4-9; Jude 6), it raises a number of questions. These will be addressed later in a separate section.

## The Resurrection

Three times in his first epistle Peter mentioned the Resurrection. He wrote that the basis of the believer's hope is that God raised Jesus from the dead and gave Him glory (1:21). He stated (1:3) that God has "begotten us again unto a lively hope by the resurrection of Jesus Christ." Possibly, the expression "quickened by the Spirit" (3:18, i.e., "made alive") refers to the Resurrection.

## Ascension

Christ's ascension into heaven is portrayed in Scripture as a visible, tangible event (Acts 1:9). Peter was an eyewitness of the Ascension (Acts 1:22; 3:22). His words in his first epistle echo his sermon in Solomon's Porch in which he declared that Christ will remain in heaven until the time of His return and the restoration of all things (Acts 3:20,21).

## Exaltation

Christ did not have to wait until His return to receive glory (1 Peter 1:11,21; 4:13; cf. 1 Timothy 3:16). He has already entered "into his glory" (cf. Luke 24:26). Peter reported that He now "is on the right hand of God, angels and authorities and powers being made subject unto him" (3:22). He is a "living stone, disallowed indeed of men, but chosen of God, and precious" (2:4). God's response to the world's rejection of His Son (2:21ff.; 3:18) is that He exalted Christ and gave Him the name "Lord" (1 Peter 1:3; cf. Philippians 2:9-11). Christ is also to be honored in the Church of God in this way (3:14).

The concept of Christ seated at the right hand of God is central to New Testament teaching. Peter concluded his sermon on the Day of Pentecost with this picture (Acts 2:33-36). Paul united it with the exaltation of Christ above all authorities (Ephesians 1:20ff.). In Hebrews 8:1ff., and 1 John 2:1, 2, this concept is joined with the truth that Christ is High Priest and Advocate for His people.

## The Return of Christ

Christ's glory is closely associated with His exaltation and will be revealed when He returns (4:13). Peter encouraged believers to set their hope fully on the grace that will become their portion at His revelation (1:13). His return is called the "salvation ready to be revealed in the last time" (1:5). The trial of their faith will result in praise and honor (1:7). Faithful servants of the Lord will receive the unfading crown of glory (5:4). But the Lord's return will also mean judgment, for He will be "ready to judge the quick and the dead" (4:5). Judgment has already begun at the house of God, "and if the righteous scarcely be saved, where shall the ungodly and the sinner appear?" (4:17,18).

These strong words warn of the eschatological judgment Peter wrote about in his second epistle. But in 1 Peter the apostle encouraged believers who were experiencing persecution and opposition. Their trials were only for "a season" (1:6). When the Lord returns, believers will receive joy in exchange for their sufferings (4:13), and delight in the incorruptible inheritance reserved for them in heaven (1:4).

## (4) the Holy Spirit (Pneumatology)

In keeping with the trinitarian understanding of God in this letter, the unity of the Godhead is strengthened by Peter's reference to the Spirit as the Spirit of God (4:14), the Spirit of Christ (1:11), and the Holy Spirit (1:12). During the time of the old covenant, the Spirit of Christ through the messianic prophecies (1:11) testified of the sufferings of Christ and the glory that would follow. In the present age the Spirit works through the preaching of the gospel (1 Peter 1:12; cf. 1 Thessalonians 1:5). He performs a sanctifying work in believers (1 Peter 1:2; cf. the fruit of the Spirit, Galatians 5:22). In times of trial, when believers are scorned because of the name of Christ, the Spirit watches over and strengthens them (1 Peter 4:14; cf. Matthew 5:11).

## (5) Holy Scripture

There are several pertinent comments relevant to Holy Scripture in 1 Peter. The apostle used the expression "the scripture" (2:6) as synonymous with "the word" (2:8), "the word of God" (1:23), or "the word of the Lord" (1:25). This Word is the divine seed which gives new birth (1:23; cf. 1:3). Those who reject Christ do not believe the Word (1 Peter 2:8; cf. John 5:46,47). Those who refuse to believe the Word will "stumble," "whereunto also they were appointed" (2:8). God will judge those who reject His Word by handing them over to their own unbelief (cf. Luke 16:31; 2 Thessalonians 2:10-12). The Word of God is alive; it can therefore give new life (1:23). The Word of the Lord is the true, spiritual "milk" that allows the new believer to grow in the knowledge of their salvation (2:2). The Word of the Lord endures forever (1 Peter 1:25; cf. Matthew 5:18; Luke 21:33; John 10:35).

First Peter points out that the Old Testament prophecies were not the result of mechanical dictation, but were both a divine and human effort. The prophets inquired and searched diligently concerning what the Spirit revealed to them (1:10-12). The authority of Scripture is emphasized in 4:11 in that those who speak in the church are to do so as if speaking the Word of God.

## (6) Personal Salvation

The objective side of salvation is an integral part of the Christology of the letter and was discussed earlier in that section. Here it will only be noted that Peter explicitly pointed out that personal salvation is "by grace." The people of God are those who have obtained mercy (2:10) and who stand in the grace of God (5:12). The humble are given grace (5:5). Unlike those who stumble because of unbelief, the faithful will not be confounded (2:6-8). Believers are chosen by God (1:1) and called (1:15). They have returned to God (2:25). They believe in Christ (1:8; 2:7) and have been born again (1:23). They testify to their salvation by water baptism (3:21). They are to pattern their lives after Christ's example (2:21). The consummation of their salvation will be experienced in the eternal kingdom of God (1:9).

## (7) the Church (Ecclesiology)

Peter wrote to "churches" (plural) which were cared for by elders (5:1,2). This presupposes local church structure. "The church that is at Babylon" was very likely a local church (5:13). Elsewhere, the Church universal was in the mind of the apostle. The Church is the flock of God scattered throughout the land (5:2). Believers are compared with living stones that are part of a "spiritual house" (commonly understood as temple imagery, 1 Peter 2:5; cf. 1 Corinthians 3:16,17). Believers are also called a "holy priesthood" (2:5,9). They are the new people of God (2:9,10), a concept peculiar to the New Testament.

The wide range of Peter's theology cannot be limited to what has been discussed above. Only the most significant aspects could be presented. Such a concentration of "theological doctrine" in one place is perhaps paralleled only in Ephesians and 1 John. These three small documents illustrate the depth of apostolic preaching.

## The Spirits in Prison

First Peter 3:19 is a frequently debated text. It refers to Christ's having "preached unto the spirits in prison." Since ancient times a variety of interpretations have been offered. Three have become especially prominent and deserve our attention. A short survey of each will be of value.

## (1) the View of the Early Church

During the first two centuries, the Early Church apparently viewed 3:19 as a reference to Christ's descending to the kingdom of death during the time between His death and resurrection. There,

announcing the victory of the Cross, He redeemed the righteous who lived under the old covenant. For example, the Shepherd of Hermas and Irenaeus both refer to an apocryphal saying about Jeremiah: "With Jeremiah he makes his death and his descension to Hades (the kingdom of death) known by saying: 'The Lord, the Holy One of Israel, did remember his dead ones, they who earlier did sleep in the dust of the earth, and descended to them in order to preach glad tidings and to deliver them'" (Irenaeus). "I will penetrate all the lower parts of the earth and I will visit all those who are asleep (i.e., the dead), and I will inform all those who are waiting for the Lord" (Shepherd of Hermas, *Similitude* 9:16:6, 24, 25).

The primary thrust of this view is that Christ was not idle during His visit to the realm of the dead like His counterpart Jonah the prophet. Instead, Christ subdued the kingdom of death and assaulted and conquered the forces of Satan. He took the "keys of hell and death" (cf. Revelation 1:18), and thereby attained power to release death's prisoners. This viewpoint is expressed in the creedal phrase, "went down to the kingdom of death."

Whether or not one accepts this interpretation as valid, however, it does not explain why Christ preached to the stubborn and rebellious of the generation of the Flood, i.e., Noah's contemporaries. Many attempts have been made to overcome this inadequacy.

## (2) the View of Augustine

Augustine's interpretation of 3:19, later followed by theologians of the Middle Ages, was already implicit in the Latin translation (Vulgate) of the verse. According to the Vulgate, Christ's "preaching" is understood to have taken place during the time of Noah, while God waited patiently. This view is accepted by many theologians today.

To support this view many appeal to the fact that the grammatical form of the sentence concerning those who "sometime were disobedient" refers to the period in which the action took place. According to this view, Christ's preaching then did not take place in hell but, by virtue of His preexistence, He preached by the Spirit (Genesis 6:3) through Noah, "the preacher of righteousness" (2 Peter 2:5). This preaching as well as the resistance to it took place "when once the longsuffering of God waited in the days of Noah, while the ark was a preparing" (3:20). Since only eight were saved, it is evident that most refused to heed Noah's message. By referring to this in verse 21, Peter hoped to stimulate the Christians to work fearlessly, even though there might be little result.

The fact that the gospel was preached to the dead (4:6) can then be understood in the same way. Even those who died had the opportunity to hear the "gospel" through God's messengers before they died, as Christ preached through Jonah (see above). Those who died, who were no longer "in the flesh," could not be judged as if they were "in the flesh." Thus the preaching of the gospel had to have taken place in times past. To be "judged according to men in the flesh" probably refers to their death (cf. Hebrews 9:27).

Theologians who reject the Augustinian interpretation find it too "artificial." They believe it is exegetically arbitrary. The Greek term *poreutheis* occurs twice in this passage. First, in 3:19 it is used of Christ's descent into hell. Second, in 3:22 it refers to Christ's ascension. This leads many to disagree that the expression "he went" (*poreutheis*) in verse 19 refers to the preexistence of Christ.

## (3) the Hypothesis Concerning Angels

In 1890, F. Spitta introduced a theory which gained many followers. His hypothesis had its origins in Jewish pseudepigrapha and other writings of the pre-Christian period, such as the Book of Enoch, the Apocalypse of Baruch, the Testaments of the Twelve Patriarchs, and Jubilees. Some of these apocryphal writings indicate that, according to Genesis 6:2ff., fallen angels had sexual relations with women of the human race. The Biblical text refers to "sons of God" who had relations with the "daughters of men" (Genesis 6:2; cf. Jude 6,7). Their offspring were the "Nephilim," or "giants" (Genesis 6:4). The hypothesis is that the Flood came as a result of this intercourse between fallen angels and humankind. According to the Book of Enoch, the fallen angels and their offspring were the origin and source of all paganism. They became sort of evil "guardian angels" to kings and powerful world figures. Enoch indicates that such "giants" were imprisoned in the deepest darkness.

Those interpreters who contend for this "angel hypothesis" think Peter's first epistle express-es the view that Jesus, following His death, went and announced His victory to these demonic spirits. Therefore, they state, paganism's power was thereby shattered, causing the princes of the spiritual realm to admit Christ's dominion. More recent interpreters have frequently united such a view with the doctrine of the "restoration of all things" (*apokatastatis*). This teaching maintains that eventually even the evil spirits will be saved. But this view goes too far.

Many of those who accept this theory believe Christ's preaching in hell was a proclamation of judgment, a demonstration of His triumph. They contend that Peter used this to remind and encourage Christians to proclaim the gospel boldly, to men and women presently controlled by these forces. They cite 3:22 as a proof text of their theory.

However, many interpreters reject any theory along these lines. They consider such theories "fables of Jewish Gnostic Haggadah." They maintain that any "angel theory" is inconsistent with Jesus' words that angels neither marry nor are given in marriage (Mark 12:25). Those who insist that Christ preached salvation to evil spirits in hell encounter the direct opposition of Scripture.

## Summation

There is little hope of making some definitive choice among these various options; the problem is simply too complex. Nevertheless, it is helpful to be aware that differing views exist. This should encourage careful study of the choices before making a decision. One need not feel compelled to understand completely everything in Scripture.

One conclusion can be drawn: this passage gives no basis for any such universalistic teaching or for salvation after death.

# The First Epistle of Peter

## Commentary

### Chapter 1

**1. Peter, an apostle of Jesus Christ:** ... From Peter, –SEB ... a missionary of, –NLTG ... an ambassador, –WUST.

**to the strangers scattered throughout Pontus, Galatia, Cappadocia, Asia, and Bithynia:** ... To the exiles, –NOLI ... to the foreign-born Jews, –WLMS ... to the elect sojourners, –CLMT ... to those who dwell as strangers, –SWAN ... To God's chosen, homeless people, –SEB ... to the chosen expatriates, –CNDT ... to the chosen strangers of the Dispersion, –FNTN.

**1:1.** Peter was one of the Twelve whom Jesus called and ordained (1) to be with Him, and (2) to go forth to preach, heal, and cast out devils (Mark 3:14-16). He was a dynamic leader, a spokesman for the Twelve. Three times the New Testament lists the Twelve (Matthew. 10:1-4; Mark 3:16-19; Luke 6:12-16), and in each case Peter is mentioned first. However, he never claimed supremacy over the others.

The epistle is addressed to the believers, chiefly Jewish Christians, scattered throughout five Roman provinces of Asia Minor. Peter called them "strangers" (*parepidēmois*, sojourners) because earth is but their temporary home; their permanent abode is heaven. The term "scattered" suggests they were clustered in little church groups here and there.

**2. Elect according to the foreknowledge of God the Father:** ... chosen-out ones ... having been determined by the foreordination, –WUST ... chosen in accordance with, –WLMS ... according to the predetermination, –FNTN.

**through sanctification of the Spirit:** ... the setting-apart work of, –WUST ... in their spiritual consecration, –SWAN ... in holiness of spirit, –CNDT.

**unto obedience and sprinkling of the blood of Jesus Christ:** ... resulting in obedience of faith, –WUST ... in order to obedience, –CMPB ... has washed you clean with His blood, –LBCH.

**Grace unto you, and peace, be multiplied:** ... May God bless you more and more, and give you still greater peace, –TCNT ... May blessing and peace be abundant to you! –FNTN ... May you have complete peace and gracious love, –SEB ... Sanctifying grace ... and tranquilizing peace, –WUST ... peace to you be increased! –ADAM ... be to you in increasing measure! –NORL.

**1:2.** The believers are "elect" (*eklektois*, chosen) according to the foreknowledge of God the Father, through sanctification of the Holy Spirit. Only once does *prognōsin* appear elsewhere in the New Testament, and that is in Peter's sermon (Acts 2:23) where he said the arrest of Christ was foreknown by God. The words "sanctification of the Spirit" also appear in 2 Thessalonians 2:13.

The result of the believers' election should be "obedience" (*hupakoēn*, see verse 22) and "sprinkling of the blood of Jesus Christ." *Rantismos* also appears in Hebrews 12:24 in reference to the "blood of sprinkling, that speaketh better things than that of Abel." The "sprinkling" recalls an event recorded in Exodus 24:7,8. On that occasion the people told Moses, "All that the Lord hath said will we do, and be obedient." After they had made this declaration, Moses "took the blood, and sprinkled it on the people." Their pledge of obedience preceded the sprinkling of the blood; similarly Peter's mention of "obedience" comes before "sprinkling of the blood of Jesus Christ," signifying that atonement through His blood is for the obedient.

Peter's wish was that the believers might enjoy "grace" (*charis*, favor) and "peace" (*eirēnē*, tranquility) in abundance.

**3. Blessed [be] the God and Father of our Lord Jesus Christ:** ... be eulogized, –WUST.

**which according to his abundant mercy hath begotten us again unto a lively hope by the resurrection of Jesus Christ from the dead:** ... impelled by ... caused us to be born again so that we have a hope which is alive, –WUST ... His boundless pity, –FNTN ... given us a new Life of undying hope, –TCNT ... born anew into a living hope, –MNTG ... regenerated us through the Resurrection, –WADE.

**1:3.** Peter honored God the Father as the source of salvation. Out of His abundant "mercy" (*eleos*, compassion) the believers have been begotten again so they have a lively "hope" (*elpida*, expectation) because God raised Jesus Christ from the dead. Peter used the thought of "living" quite often (see 1:23; 2:4, 5, 24; 4:5,6). No doubt he remembered when his hope was dashed by the Crucifixion; but hope is no longer dead. Due to the Resurrection, believers now have a living hope through the living Christ.

**4. To an inheritance incorruptible, and undefiled:** ... for the enjoyment of an allotment,

*—CNDT* . . . so that we may share in that imperishable, stainless, *—TCNT* . . . will never decay, spoil, *—SEB*.

**and that fadeth not away:** . . . They will never fade or spoil, but will last for ever, *—LBCH*.

**reserved in heaven for you:** . . . They are being kept safe in heaven for us, *—NLTG* . . . guarded in safe deposit in heaven, *—WUST*.

**1:4.** The believer's inheritance is incorruptible and undefiled unlike some earthly inheritances that disappear before they can be obtained, or that prove to be flawed or defective in their titles. This inheritance is failproof; it "fadeth not away" (*amaranton*, is perpetual). James 1:11 says the rich man shall "fade away" (*maranthēsetai*, pass away, be extinguished), and this word appears in the inscriptions on some ancient tombs. Even these inscriptions will fade away, they are not perpetual; but this inheritance in Christ is "a crown of glory that fadeth not away" (5:4).

**5. Who are kept by the power of God through faith:** . . . are garrisoned, *—CNDT* . . . constantly being kept guarded by, *—WUST*.

**unto salvation ready to be revealed in the last time:** . . . at the end of time, *—FNTN* . . . at the final Hour of reckoning, *—WADE* . . . in the last era, *—CNDT* . . . in a last season which is epochal and strategic in its significance, *—WUST*.

**1:5.** The inheritance is reserved for those who are "kept" (*phrouroumenous*, protected) by the power of God "through faith." God's power protects the believers as they exercise faith. Both the heirs and the inheritance are being guarded; the protective work continues as the believers keep on believing. The outcome is "salvation" (*sōtērian*, deliverance) which is ready to be revealed in the "last time" (*kairō eschatō*, end time). The believers were under great pressure; the persecution instigated by Nero at Rome was spreading in their direction. But Peter assured them that deliverance lay ahead and an eternal inheritance was in their future.

**6. Wherein ye greatly rejoice:** . . . Exult in this, *—MNTG* . . . you are to be constantly rejoicing with a joy that expresses itself in a triumphant exuberance, *—WUST* . . . be exceedingly glad, *—FNTN*.

**though now for a season, if need be, ye are in heaviness through manifold temptations:** . . . if conditions require it, *—SWAN* . . . briefly at present, if it must be, being sorrowed by various trials, *—CNDT* . . . you are distressed, *—WLSN* . . . grieved by numerous trials, *—FNTN*.

**1:6.** "Wherein" probably relates to the ultimate deliverance to which Peter referred in verse 5. "Ye greatly rejoice" is not imperative but merely a statement of fact. The believers could "greatly rejoice" (from *agalliaō*, exult) even though "if need

be" they had to endure persecution, because their "heaviness" was only "for a season." Though they should encounter "manifold temptations" (*poikilois peirasmois*, various adversities) they could "think it not strange" (4:12), for it was leading to "praise and honor and glory" (1:7).

**7. That the trial of your faith, being much more precious than of gold that perisheth:** . . . the testing of, *—CNDT* . . . the proof of, *—WLSN* . . . the genuineness of your faith, *—TCNT* . . . for gold can be destroyed, *—LBCH*.

**though it be tried with fire:** . . . be approved by fire-testing, *—WUST* . . . yet, being tested by, *—CNDT*.

**might be found unto praise and honour and glory at the appearing of Jesus Christ:** . . . may redound, *—MNTG* . . . may be discovered after scrutiny to result in, *—WUST* . . . may be found in approval, rectification, and honour and distinction, *—FNTN* . . . may be found for applause and glory, *—CNDT* . . . when Jesus Christ is revealed, *—BRKL*.

**1:7.** Peter said the believers' faith is much "more precious" (*timiōteron*, most valuable, "of great price" as in Matthew 13:46) than gold, for gold "perisheth" (*apollumenou*, is destroyed). Although gold perishes (wears away), it is tested by fire until it proves to be unalloyed. Similarly the believers' faith must undergo testing to remove all the baser elements (impurities) so it may bring praise, honor, and glory to God and to them at the "appearing" (*apokalupsei*, revelation) of Jesus Christ.

Peter himself knew something about persecution, both religious and political. He had suffered at the hands both of the Sanhedrin and of Herod Agrippa I, and he had failed the test on one occasion (Luke 22:54-62). But he had recovered, and he was able to strengthen his brethren through this epistle, encouraging them and exhorting them that their "faith fail not" (Luke 22:32).

**8. Whom having not seen, ye love:** . . . You never met him, *—NOLI* . . . although you have never seen Him, *—WLMS* . . . not perceiving, *—CNDT* . . . because of His preciousness, *—WUST*.

**in whom, though now ye see [him] not, yet believing:** . . . not seeing at present, *—CNDT* . . . have faith in him, *—LBCH*.

**ye rejoice with joy unspeakable and full of glory:** . . . you feel a joy and a glory beyond words to tell, *—LBCH* . . . and exult with a triumphant happiness too great for words, *—TCNT* . . . inexpressible and glorious, *—WLSN* . . . anticipating delight, *—FNTN* . . . exalted, *—NORL* . . . glorified, *—WUST*.

**1:8.** The believers had not seen Jesus, but their faith was in Him and they loved Him, so they shared the blessing Jesus promised when He said to Thomas, "Blessed are they that have not seen, and yet have believed" (John 20:29). Since Peter was present when those words were spoken, it is not surprising that he should mention their love for Him whom they have never seen and their belief in Him whom they could not see now.

Peter spoke approvingly of their rejoicing in Jesus Christ. They were jubilant with joy unspeakable and full of "glory" (*dedoxasmenē*, brightness, radiance, splendor, majesty). This word is used of the "glory" of Moses' countenance which shone so brightly the people could not gaze upon it (2 Corinthians 3:7). The joy of salvation is unutterable, indescribable; the Greek word *aneklalētō* does not appear elsewhere in the New Testament although the Authorized Version translates two other words as "unspeakable" in 2 Corinthians 9:15 and 12:4.

**9. Receiving the end of your faith:** . . . upon the occasion of you receiving, —WUST . . . being requited, —CNDT . . . obtaining the issue of, —WLSN . . . which is the purpose of, —ADAM . . . the goal of believing, —SEB . . . the promised consummation, —WUST . . . of your faith, —CNDT.

**[even] the salvation of [your] souls:** . . . which is the final salvation of, —WUST.

**1:9.** The "salvation" (*sōtērian*, deliverance, preservation, wholeness) Peter wrote of is not conversion but the ultimate fullness of redemption. His readers were already receiving a foretaste of this final salvation of their "souls" (*psuchōn*, whole beings), which is the "end" (*telos*, goal, culmination) of their faith. It is "the grace that is to be brought unto you at the revelation of Jesus Christ" (1:13). This full salvation, which their faith would lead to in the end, actually was theirs all the way to that end, while they appropriated it by faith.

**10. Of which salvation the prophets have inquired and searched diligently:** . . . Concerning which salvation the prophets seek out, —CNDT . . . prophets conducted an exhaustive inquiry and search, —WUST . . . sought out and investigated, —WLSN.

**who prophesied of the grace [that should come] unto you:** . . . who predicted in advance, —WADE . . . concerning the grace which is for you, —CNDT . . . the particular grace destined for you, —WUST . . . of the blessing intended for you, —BRKL.

**1:10.** Peter said the prophets wrote of this salvation. This would reassure the believers, especially the converted Jews who had a profound trust in the Old Testament. The prophets spoke of "the grace that should come unto you" (the grace meant for you), but they did not know what this meant. They were puzzled to understand this gospel of grace which seemed to make their religion of good works and sin offerings outdated, though they "inquired" (*exezētēsan*, sought out, investigated) and "searched diligently" (*exēreunēsan*,

explored carefully). John Wesley says of their inquiry, "like miners searching after precious ore, (they searched) after the meaning of the prophecies which they delivered."

**11. Searching what, or what manner of time the Spirit of Christ which was in them did signify:** . . . made inquiry and research to find out, —BRKL . . . searching as to what season or character of season the Spirit . . . was making plain, —WUST . . . searching into what or what manner of era the spirit of Christ in them made evident, —CNDT.

**when it testified beforehand the sufferings of Christ:** . . . when it predicted the sufferings that were destined for, —BRKL . . . surrounding the Messiah, —FNTN.

**and the glory that should follow:** . . . which would come after these sufferings, —WUST . . . along with them, —BRKL.

**1:11.** The Spirit of Christ in the Old Testament prophets was the Holy Ghost, as made clear in 2 Peter 1:21 (they spoke "as they were moved by the Holy Ghost"). The Third Person of the Trinity has many names, including Spirit of God, Spirit of the Lord, Spirit of His Son, Spirit of Truth, Holy Spirit of God, Comforter, and Promise of the Father. The Spirit within the prophets foretold the sufferings of Christ and the glories (plural) that should follow His sufferings. The prophets sought to know "what (time), or what manner of time" (*eis tina ē poion kairon*) the Spirit "did signify" (*edēlou*, did disclose, point toward). They knew what they were prophesying but not at what time these messianic prophecies would be fulfilled. God only reveals to His servants what they need to know in order that they might be able to trust Him for what they do not know. His faithfulness in the past gives assurance that He will provide all they need in the present and in the future. Like the prophets of old, we do not know all the details of the future, but in His own time God will reveal it unto us, when we no longer "see through a glass, darkly, but then face to face" (1 Corinthians 13:12).

**12. Unto whom it was revealed, that not unto themselves, but unto us they did minister the things:** . . . that it was not for their own advantage, —WADE . . . to you they dispensed them, —CNDT.

**which are now reported unto you by them that have preached the gospel unto you with the Holy Ghost sent down from heaven:** . . . were now informed through, —CNDT . . . who was sent down on a commission from heaven, —WUST.

**which things the angels desire to look into:** . . . into which messengers are yearning to peer, —CNDT . . . have long wanted to know, —LBCH . . . have a passionate desire to stoop way down and look into [like the cherubim above the mercy seat who gazed at the sprinkled blood and wondered at its meaning], —WUST.

**1:12.** The prophets could not discover what they sought by searching, but it was revealed to them that their prophecies "did minister" (*diēkonoun*, served), not to themselves but to future believers—to Peter and his peers. Peter reassured believers that the message they had received from preachers like Paul and John was the same gospel the prophets foretold. They prophesied of the things which are now reported to believers by those who have preached the gospel with the same Spirit (whether called Holy Spirit or, as in verse 11, Spirit of Christ) who inspired the prophecies. The Spirit was "sent down from heaven" at Pentecost (see Acts 2:2).

This good news is so wonderful the angels "desire" (*epithumousin*, eagerly long for) to "look into" (*parakupsai*, stoop down and peer into) it. Angels intently watch the plan of redemption unfold, but they cannot participate in it because "Christ died for the ungodly" (Romans 5:6), not for angels.

13. **Wherefore gird up the loins of your mind:** . . . having put out of the way once for all everything that would impede the free action of your mind, —WUST . . . of your comprehension, —CNDT . . . as a means of spiritual preparation, —WLMS . . . get your minds set for action, —NORL . . . brace up your minds, and exercise the strictest self-control, —TCNT . . . keeping level-headed, —ADAM . . . loins of your understanding, —FNTN.
**be sober, and hope to the end for the grace that is to be brought unto you:** . . . being vigilant, —WLSN . . . calm and collected, —SWAN . . . in spirit, —WUST . . . expect perfectly, —CNDT . . . set your hope, —CLMT . . . with perfect stedfastness, —DRBY . . . which will be offered, —NOLI.
**at the revelation of Jesus Christ:** . . . upon the occasion of the revelation, —WUST . . . at the unveiling of Jesus Christ, —WLMS, —CNDT.

**1:13.** In view of their spiritual privileges, Peter called believers to holy living. In those days people wore long, loose robes, and in order to run or do manual work, they had to lift their robes and tuck them in their belts. So Peter directed believers to gird up the "loins" (*osphuas*, hips) of their "mind" (*dianoias*, understanding, comprehension). Since "loins" often denotes procreative powers (as in Acts 2:30; Hebrews 7:5,10), the reference to "loins of your mind" suggests the mind is the procreator of human actions. The thought is father to the deed. Therefore believers should fortify their minds—"having your loins girt about with truth" (Ephesians 6:14). They should "be sober" (*nēphontes*, be alert, self-controlled) and they should "hope" (*elpisate*, expect) "to the end"

(*teleiōs*, fully, completely) for the grace that is to be brought to them at the revelation of Jesus Christ.

14. **As obedient children, not fashioning yourselves:** . . . Do not obey those low passions, —LBCH . . . let your lives be shaped, —TCNT . . . not configuring, —CNDT . . . stop molding your character, —WLMS . . . assuming an outward expression, —WUST.
**according to the former lusts in your ignorance:** . . . you formerly had in the ignorance of your passionate desires, —WUST . . . desires you used to cherish, —WLMS . . . cravings, —SWAN . . . passions which once swayed you, —TCNT . . . ruled you when you did not know what was right, —LBCH.

**1:14.** As "obedient children" of their Heavenly Father (*hōs tekna hupakoēs*, children of obedience, in contrast to "the children of disobedience" in Ephesians 2:2), believers are to be holy, no longer "fashioning" themselves (from *suschēmatizō*, to conform, as in Romans 12:2) according to the former "lusts" (*epithumiais*, strong desires). Formerly in their "ignorance" (*agnoia*, lack of knowledge) they indulged their natural cravings, but now they are enlightened.

15. **But as he which hath called you is holy:** . . . but, according as, —CNDT . . . after the pattern of the One who called you, —WUST.
**so be ye holy in all manner of conversation:** . . . become holy persons in every kind of behavior, —WUST.

**1:15.** "Be ye holy" is an imperative, a solemn command. Peter told believers that God who called them is "holy" (*hagion*, pure, blameless), and He is to be their standard or pattern in all "manner of conversation" (*anastrophē*, manner of life, behavior).

16. **Because it is written:** . . . This is exactly what Scripture teaches, —NORL . . . and is on record, —WUST.
**Be ye holy; for I am holy:** . . . Become holy, —FNTN . . . You must be holy, —SEB . . . You be holy individuals, because, as for myself, —WUST.

**1:16.** Peter called upon believers' reverence for the Old Testament by referring to Leviticus 19:2, "Ye shall be holy: for I the Lord your God am holy." He says, "It is written" (*gegraptai*, it stands written). The written Word has special force, particularly the Scriptures. This was Christ's defense when tempted by the devil: "It is written" (Luke 4:4).

17. **And if ye call on the Father:** . . . be careful to approach Him reverently, —NORL . . . invoking, —CNDT.
**who without respect of persons:** . . . impartially judges, —WLSN . . . fair to each, —SEB.
**judgeth according to every man's work:** . . . impartially by their actions, —NOLI.

1094

**pass the time of your sojourning [here] in fear:**...you may behave, for the time, –*CNDT*...during your residence as aliens, –*ADAM* . . . your homelessness, –*SWAN* . . . your service in reverence, –*FNTN*...your fleeting stay, –*WLMS*.

**1:17.** The Father, "without respect of persons" (*aprosōpolēptōs*, without partiality), judges "according to every man's work" (*kata to hekastou ergon*, according to the deed of each one). Therefore, if believers wish to call on God the Father, they should monitor their conduct and spend the time of their "sojourning" (from *paroikeō*, dwell as strangers as in Acts 13:17, reside as foreigners) here "in fear" (*phobō*, reverence). As a son fears his father and obeys him, knowing he will be disciplined if he fails to do so, believers should fear the Lord and keep His commandments; but they do not obey Him simply because they are afraid to do otherwise. They keep His commandments because they love Him (John 14:15), and they love Him because He first loved them (1 John 4:19).

Peter emphasized that believers are only "sojourning" on this earth as "strangers and pilgrims" (2:11). They are mere visitors on this planet, passing through as pilgrims en route like Abraham to their permanent home in that "city which hath foundations, whose builder and maker is God" (Hebrews 11:10). Since they are bound for a holy place they should be holy people. They should not fix their hearts on worldly things or copy the people of this world, for it is not their native country.

**18. Forasmuch as ye know that ye were not redeemed with corruptible things, [as] silver and gold:** . . . knowing as you do, that not by means of perishable things, little coins, –*WUST*...it was not by perishable valuables, –*WADE*...you were not bought and made free, –*NLTG*.
**from your vain conversation [received] by tradition from your fathers:** . . . from the useless behavior patterns, –*ADAM*...your useless ways such as traditionally came down from your forefathers, –*BRKL* . . . from the slavery of your ancestral follies, –*FNTN* . . . from your foolish behavior, –*CMPB*...vain behavior, handed down, –*CNDT*...transmitted to you from, –*WADE*...your futile manner of life handed down from generation to generation, –*WUST*...your ancestors, –*MNTG*.

**1:18.** Peter pointed to a further incentive to holy living beyond the holiness and justice of God by stressing the high cost of redemption. He reminded believers they were not redeemed with "corruptible" things (*phthartois*, decayed, perishable) such as silver and gold. If silver and gold were the ransom price, Peter would not have been set free, for he said, "Silver and gold have I none" (Acts 3:6). Slaves were set free by silver and gold, but a greater price was required to redeem believers

from the "vain" (*mataias*, empty, profitless) "conversation" (*anastrophēs*, lifestyle, behavior) they had received by tradition from their fathers. Christ and His apostles taught a lifestyle superior to that followed by any non-Christians, whether they were Jews or Gentiles.

**19. But with the precious blood of Christ:**...with Christ's valuable blood, –*ADAM* . . . the costly blood, –*WUST*.
**as of a lamb without blemish and without spot:** . . . like that of a perfect lamb, –*SEB* . . . without stain, –*NORL* . . . unblemished and immaculate, –*NOLI*...a flawless and unspotted lamb, –*CNDT*.

**1:19.** The ransom price was the "precious" (*timiō*, most valuable) blood of Christ. As a lamb brought to the slaughter (Isaiah 53:7), He was "without blemish" (*amōmou*, faultless, without blame) and "without spot" (*aspilou*, unstained), fitting the requirements of the Paschal Lamb (see Exodus 12:5). The "Lamb of God" (John 1:29,36) must be perfect. Any lesser sacrifice would be unacceptable (see Leviticus 22:20).

**20. Who verily was foreordained before the foundation of the world:**...provided, –*BRKL*...designated in advance, –*WADE* . . . foreknown, indeed, before the disruption of the world, –*CNDT*...before the foundation of the universe was laid, –*WUST*.
**but was manifest in these last times for you:** . . . disclosed at the end of times, –*BRKL*...visibly manifested at the closing years of the times for your sake, –*WUST*...for your sakes He has been revealed, –*NORL*...at the extremity of the ages, –*FNTN*.

**1:20.** The messiahship of Jesus was foreordained (or foreseen by God) before the "foundation" (*katabolēs*, founding) of the "world" (*kosmou*, world order). Christ's advent was no afterthought (see Revelation 13:8). It was known from the beginning by both the Father and the preincarnate Son, but they waited for "the fulness of the time" (Galatians 4:4) to put the great plan of redemption into action. Peter said Christ was "manifest" (*phanerōthentos*, made apparent, incarnated) in these "last times" (*eschatōn tōn chronōn*, at the end of time) for the sake of believers ("you"). Jesus was chosen for this mission before the world began, and the believers to whom Peter wrote were "a chosen generation" (1 Peter 2:9).

**21. Who by him do believe in God, that raised him up from the dead, and gave him glory:** . . . who rouses Him . . . and is giving Him glory, –*CNDT*.
**that your faith and hope might be in God:** . . . and expectation is to be, –*CNDT* . . . rest in God, –*BRKL*.

**1:21.** Through Christ they have been believers in God, the One who "raised" (*egeiranta*, awakened, lifted up) Jesus from the dead and who gave Him "glory" (*doxan*, honor, acclaim). Peter emphasized repeatedly how God raised His Son and restored to Him the glory and full expression of His deity He enjoyed before the world was and for which He prayed in the Garden (John 17:5). In his address in Solomon's Porch Peter told how God had glorified His Son Jesus (Acts 3:13). He elaborated on this in his Pentecost sermon (Acts 2:33-36) and mentioned it again when brought before the Council (Acts 5:31). Because Christ was raised and glorified, their "faith" (*pistin*, reliance, assurance) and "hope" (*elpida*, confident expectation) is in God.

**22. Seeing ye have purified your souls in obeying the truth:** . . . With your souls purified by obeying the truth, —*BRKL* . . . by means of, —*WUST* . . . the obedience of truth, —*CNDT.*

**through the Spirit unto unfeigned love of the brethren:** . . . resulting in not an assumed but a genuine affection and fondness, —*WUST* . . . that issues into unpretended love of the brotherhood, —*BRKL* . . . unfeigned fondness, —*CNDT* . . . a genuine brotherly affection, —*TCNT* . . . without hypocrisy, —*MNTG* . . . with sincere brotherly affection, —*FNTN* . . . Love one another intensely, —*SEB.*

**[see that ye] love one another with a pure heart fervently:** . . . out of a true heart earnestly, —*CNDT* . . . intensely, —*WLSN* . . . you should most cordially and consistently love one another, —*BRKL* . . . from the heart love each other with an intense reciprocal love that springs from your hearts because of your estimation of the preciousness of the brethren, and which is divinely self-sacrificial in its essence, —*WUST.*

**1:22.** Believers have "purified" (*hēgnikotes*, sanctified, made clean) their souls in obeying the truth through the Spirit (see 1:2), as evidenced by their "unfeigned love of the brethren" (*philadelphian*, fraternal affection, brotherly kindness). There is cleansing power in God's truth as it is believed and obeyed. "Brotherly kindness" (*philadelphian*) is mentioned again in 2 Peter 1:7. Peter also mentioned a greater kind of love. He urged them to "love" (*agapēsate*) one another "fervently" (*ektenōs*, intently, earnestly, as also in 4:8). Whereas *philadelphia* is a love based on sentiment, *agapē* is a love based on principle and duty.

Believers love Christ (1:8), and they also love their brethren. In doing this they fulfill God's original purpose for His people: "Thou shalt love the Lord thy God with all thy heart . . . and thy neighbor as thyself" (Luke 10:27).

**23. Being born again, not of corruptible seed, but of incorruptible:** . . . having been regenerated, —*CNDT* . . . not from a germ that perishes, —*WLMS* . . . not of perishable seed but of imperishable, —*WUST* . . . an imperishable sperm, —*BRKL.*

**by the word of God, which liveth and abideth for ever:** . . . living and permanent, —*CNDT* . . . through God's Living and Lasting Message, —*WADE.*

**1:23.** Peter's statement that the Word of God "liveth and abideth for ever" is repeated in 1:25. Believers are born of that incorruptible Word (as stated also in James 1:18). They have been "born again" (*anagegennēmenoi*, begotten again, as in 1 Peter 1:3), not by "corruptible seed" (*sporas phthartēs*, parental seed that is perishable), but by the everlasting Word (*logou*, utterance, communication, particularly the Divine Expression as in John 1:1,14; 1 John 1:1; 5:7; Revelation 19:13). They can obey the truth and love one another (1:22) because they have had this new spiritual birth. They no longer have empty, worthless lives like their natural fathers (1:18), for they have been born again into a new family and now they are the children of God.

The holy Scriptures are also the Word of God. When a sinner comes seeking salvation, his faith must be based on what they promise. "Faith cometh by hearing, and hearing by the word of God" (Romans 10:17).

**24. For all flesh [is] as grass:** . . . The life of all men, —*TCNT* . . . All human life is just like, —*WLMS.*

**and all the glory of man as the flower of grass:** . . . and all its glory as a grass flower, —*BRKL.*

**The grass withereth, and the flower thereof faileth away:** . . . was caused to wither away, —*WUST* . . . the bloom, —*BRKL* . . . The flowers drop off, —*WLMS.*

**1:24.** Peter contrasted the frailty of human nature with the enduring character of God's Word by referring to Isaiah 40:8: "The grass withereth, the flower fadeth: but the word of our God shall stand for ever." All "flesh" (*sarx*, physical being, human nature) is as grass, and all the "glory" (*doxa*, dignity, honor) of man as the "flower" (*anthos*, blossom) of grass. The grass "withereth" (*exēranthē*, shrivels, dries up) and its blossom "falleth away" (*exepesen*, drops off).

**25. But the word of the Lord endureth for ever:** . . . the Lord's message remains forever, —*SEB* . . . the declaration . . . is remaining for the eon, —*CNDT* . . . abides for eternity, —*DRBY* . . . lives on forever, —*WLMS.*

**And this is the word which by the gospel is preached unto you:** . . . which in the declaration of the good news was preached, —*WUST.*

**1:25.** The life of grass is very brief and the life of its blossom is even shorter. That is what man is like, even if he be rich (see James 1:11). But the "word" (*rhēma*, utterances, sayings) of the Lord "endureth" (*menei*, abides, remains) forever. This imperishable Word finds its expression in the "gospel that has been preached" (*euangelisthen*, good news that has been announced, declared) to them.

## Chapter 2

1. **Wherefore laying aside all malice, and all guile:** ... Putting off, then, *–CNDT* ... cast off all wickedness, *–NOLI* ... Free yourselves, then, from, *–TCNT* ... So once for all get rid of all, *–WLMS* ... having stripped from you, *–SWAN* ... abandoning all vice, and deceit, *–FNTN* ... Put out of your life hate and lying, *–NLTG* ... and every craftiness, *–WUST*.
**and hypocrisies, and envies, and all evil speakings:** ... vilifications, *–CNDT* ... slanderings, *–WUST*.

**2:1.** In view of the transitory quality of human life and the permanence of the divine Word, Peter exhorted believers to change their lifestyle. Instead of giving expression to the elements which characterize carnal nature they should hunger for the Word. They should put away all "malice" (*kakian*, badness, trouble-making) and all "guile" (*dolon*, deceit, subtlety) and "hypocrisies" (*hupokriseis*, pretense) and "envies" (*phthonous*, jealousies, grudges) and all "evil speakings" (*katalalias*, backbitings, defamation).

2. **As newborn babes, desire the sincere milk of the word:** ... as newborn infants do, intensely yearn for, *–WUST* ... recently born ... the unadulterated milk, *–CNDT* ... long for, *–MNTG* ... crave for pure spiritual milk, *–TCNT*.
**that ye may grow thereby:** ... by it you may be nourished and make progress in [your] salvation, *–WUST*.

**2:2.** Peter called believers to be like newborn babes in their desire or craving for milk. He did not say they should *act* like babes, for the Scriptures repeatedly censor believers who act like children rather than grown men (see 1 Corinthians 3:2; 14:20; 16:13; Ephesians 4:14; 6:10). However, believers should never stop growing toward spiritual maturity. They need the "sincere" (*adolon*, without deceit or subtlety) milk "of the word" (*logikon*, of the utterances, sayings).

Some ancient manuscripts add "unto salvation" at the end of 2:2. This seems to indicate that craving for the milk, the unadulterated Word of God, will produce continuous growth until believers receive the inheritance that will be theirs when Jesus returns.

Peter was not contrasting milk with meat or solid food. Instead he was contrasting the pure milk of the Word with food that is mixed (adulterated) with harmful things. Every false cult needs some

other book, tradition, dream, or revelation to establish its doctrines. Believers should continually crave the Word in its simplicity and purity, instead of going off into the speculations of false teachers (Horton, pp.23,24).

3. **If so be ye have tasted that the Lord [is] gracious:** ... in view of the fact that you tasted that the Lord is ... loving and benevolent, *–WUST* ... kind, *–CNDT*.

**2:3.** Peter said believers have "tasted" (*eguesasthe*, experienced) that the Lord is "gracious" (*chrēstos*, good, kind). Therefore they should lay aside their old lifestyle and feed their souls on His Word (2:1,2). They should not be content with a taste but should crave it constantly and keep on growing. Fullness of Christian maturity is a goal for the future.

4. **To whom coming, [as unto] a living stone:** ... toward whom we are constantly drawing near, himself in character, *–WUST* ... approaching, *–CNDT*.
**disallowed indeed of men:** ... rejected indeed, *–MNTG*, *–CNDT* ... cast away ... as worthless by men, *–DRBY* ... repudiated after they had tested Him, *–WUST*.
**but chosen of God, [and] precious:** ... but in the sight of God a chosen-out One and highly honored and precious, *–WUST* ... distinguished in the presence of, *–FNTN* ... choice and valuable, *–TNT* ... held in honor, *–CNDT*.
5. **Ye also, as lively stones, are built up a spiritual house:** ... into a spiritual Edifice, *–WADE*.
**an holy priesthood:** ... in which you, like holy priests, *–PHLP* ... for a consecrated Priesthood, *–TCNT* ... a dedicated priesthood, *–BRKL*.
**to offer up spiritual sacrifices:** ... bringing up to God's altars, *–WUST*.
**acceptable to God by Jesus Christ:** ... through the mediator-ship of, *–WUST* ... are well-pleasing to, *–BRKL*.

**2:4, 5.** The metaphor now changes from a growing child to a growing building of which Christ is the foundation stone. Peter spoke of Christ as a living stone. The Jews considered Him as being dead by crucifixion; and as builders might reject an imperfect stone, so they "disallowed" (*apodedokimasmenon*, disapproved, repudiated, rejected) Christ in constructing their religious system. But believers have come to Him knowing He is alive and knowing He is "chosen" (*eklekton*, elect, favorite) of God. He is "precious" (*entimon*, prized, highly esteemed) to God and to them.

God uses what man rejects and often rejects what man approves. Peter brought out this idea in his Pentecost sermon, saying, "God hath made that same Jesus, whom ye have crucified, both Lord and Christ" (Acts 2:36). Jesus himself mentioned the fact when He quoted Psalm 118:22, saying, "The stone which the builders rejected, the same is become the head of the corner" (Matthew 21:42).

God is building a spiritual "house" (*oikos*, dwelling, household, as in 4:17, "house of God") and believers, as living stones, are the material with which He is constructing it. They compose God's house and they also compose the "holy priesthood" (*hierateuma hagion*, sacred body of priests) that ministers in His house. Peter understood that all believers are priests and can approach God directly, as in Hebrews 4:16. All can offer spiritual sacrifices (see also Romans 12:1; Ephesians 5:2; Philippians 2:17; 4:18; Hebrews 13:15,16) which God accepts through His Son.

Paul used the same metaphor of a growing spiritual building in Ephesians 2:21,22. Peter indicated this "spiritual house" includes believers in the five Roman provinces (1 Peter 1:1), recognizing that the church Christ is building (Matthew 16:18) is not merely a localized group but a universal Body.

6. **Wherefore also it is contained in the scripture:** ... For there is a passage of Scripture that runs, —*TCNT* ... There is a passage to this effect, —*PHLP* ... it is included in the scripture, —*CNDT.*

**Behold, I lay in Sion:** ... I place in Zion, —*BRKL.*

**a chief corner stone, elect, precious:** ... a keystone of great value, —*WADE* ... one that is choice, —*NORL* ... a choice stone, —*TNT* ... one chosen out ... highly honored and precious, —*WUST* ... a chosen, honored cornerstone, —*BRKL* ... a corner capstone, chosen, held in honor, —*CNDT.*

**and he that believeth on him shall not be confounded:** ... whosoever trusts in it, —*CMPB* ... the one who rests his faith on Him, —*WUST* ... shall never be put to shame, —*MNTG* ... will never meet with disappointment, —*WADE* ... will never be made ashamed, —*SEB* ... may by no means be disgraced, —*CNDT.*

**2:6.** Peter referred to Isaiah 28:16: "Behold, I lay in Zion for a foundation a stone, a tried stone, a precious corner stone, a sure foundation." He mentioned only "corner stone." Actually the cornerstone is also a foundation stone and might also mean the keystone at the center of an arch. Christ is the "chief corner stone," and he who builds on Him will never be "confounded" (*kataischunthē*, put to shame, dishonored).

7. **Unto you therefore which believe [he is] precious:** ... To you, then, who trust, —*CMPB* ... He is the Distinguished, —*FNTN* ... is of great value, —*TNT* ... is the honor and the preciousness, —*WUST.*

**but unto them which be disobedient:** ... to the unbelieving, —*CNDT* ... disbelievers, —*WUST* ... to those who refuse to believe, —*NORL.*

**the stone which the builders disallowed:** ... which the workmen put aside, —*NLTG* ... rejected by the builders, —*CNDT* ... did not think was

important, —*SEB* ... threw away, —*WLMS* ... repudiated, —*WUST.*

**the same is made the head of the corner:** ... this came to be for, —*CNDT.*

**2:7.** In his speech at the Beautiful Gate, Peter told the rulers of the Jews, "This is the stone which was set at nought of you builders, which is become the head of the corner" (Acts 4:11). Here he made a similar statement, quoting Psalm 118:22.

He divided mankind into two great classes. To the believers Christ is "precious" (time, most valuable, of high price; like the merchant in Matthew 13:46 who recognized the value of the "pearl of great price" and traded all his possessions for this one great treasure). But to the "disobedient" (*apeithousin*, disbelieving, unpersuadable) Christ is like the stone which expert builders disallowed; they deemed it imperfect and fit only for the rubbish heap. God raised Him from the dead and made Him the head of the "corner" (*gōnias*, angle). Christ is the cornerstone on which the spiritual building rests and which holds the building together.

8. **And a stone of stumbling, and a rock of offence:** ... a rock of entrapment, —*SWAN* ... that will make them fall, —*SEB* ... a Rock that trips the foot, —*WADE* ... a snare rock, —*CNDT* ... an obstacle stone against which one cuts, —*WUST.*

**[even to them] which stumble at the word, being disobedient:** ... even to those who because they are non-persuasible, —*WUST* ... are stumbling also at the word, being stubborn, —*CNDT* ... because they reject the Gospel, —*NOLI* ... refusing obedience to it, —*WADE.*

**whereunto also they were appointed:** ... and this is their appointed doom, —*WLMS* ... as they had been predestined to do, —*NOLI.*

**2:8.** Quoting Isaiah 8:14, Peter said Christ is a "stone of stumbling" (*lithos proskommatos*) to unbelievers. They "stumble" (*proskoptousin*, cut against, as also in Matthew 4:6) at the Word, being unwilling to obey it. He said Christ to them is a "rock of offense" (*petra skandalou*, a rock set to trip someone, as also in Romans 9:33). Whereas *lithos* means a loose stone in the path, *petra* means a ledge rising out of the ground.

Peter said the Jews were "appointed" (*etethēsan*, ordained, as in 1 Timothy 2:7; consigned) to stumble. He could not mean they were predestined to disobey, for God has not appointed anyone to suffer His wrath (1 Thessalonians 5:9); but He has appointed the disobedient to stumble. No one has to be in the category of the disobedient, but those who are cannot avoid the results.

**9. But ye [are] a chosen generation, a royal priesthood:**...select race, *—FNTN*...elect, *—MNTG*...a race chosen out, king-priests, *—WUST.*

**an holy nation, a peculiar people:** ... a set-apart nation, a people formed for [God's own] possession, *—WUST* ... a consecrated class of people, *—NOLI*... purchased people, *—MNTG* ... an acquired people, *—SWAN*...a procured people, *—CNDT*...a People for a purpose, *—WLSN*... for action, *—FNTN.*

**that ye should show forth the praises:** ... in order that you might proclaim abroad the excellencies, *—WUST*... so that you should be recounting the virtues, *—CNDT* ... commissioned to tell forth, *—WADE*...declare the perfections of him, *—CMPB.*

**of him who hath called you out of darkness into his marvellous light:** ... called you into participation, *—WUST.*

**2:9.** Those who stumble are not Israel as a nation but those, both Jews and Gentiles, who do not believe. As Israel was God's special treasure (Exodus 19:5,6), so now all who believe share in these privileged positions. In contrast to the fate of the "disobedient" (2:8), Peter said believers are a "chosen generation" (*genos eklekton*, an elect nation) and a "royal priesthood" (*basileion hierateuma*, kingly fraternity of priests). They are a "holy nation" (*ethnos hagion*, sacred race) and a "peculiar people" (*laos eis peripoiēsin*, a people purchased for God's own special possession). "Peculiar" in Old English had this idea of possession.

The purpose of believers' calling is that they might "show forth" (*exangeilēte*, tell out, publish) the "praises" (*aretas*, excellencies) of the Lord who has called them out of "darkness" (*skotous*, shadiness, obscurity) into His "marvelous light" (*thaumaston phōs*, wonderful illumination).

In the Scriptures darkness is often used to symbolize the state in which unbelievers find themselves, under the control of Satan, while light represents God and His kingdom. It is therefore a fitting description of conversion to refer to it as leaving darkness behind and coming into the light of the gospel.

**10. Which in time past [were] not a people, but [are] now the people of God:** ... who formerly, *—CMPB*...you were disinherited, *—NOLI.*

**which had not obtained mercy, but now have obtained mercy:** ... Once you were outside his mercy, *—TNT* ... have now secured compassion, *—FNTN*... enjoyed mercy, *—CNDT.*

**2:10.** Once believers were "not a people," but now they are the "people of God" (see Hosea 2:23). Hosea's words originally dealt with the Jews and their restoration, but Peter applied them to all believers (as Paul did in Romans 9:24-26). Once believers (when disobedient, like the Jews) "had not obtained mercy," but "now have obtained mercy" (*nun de eleēthentes*, now have received compassion).

**11. Dearly beloved, I beseech [you] as strangers and pilgrims:** ... Divinely loved ones...I beg of you, *—WUST*...I am entreating you, *—CNDT*...I implore you ... as lodgers and travellers, *—FNTN*... as only temporary dwellers *—WADE*... and Sojourners, *—WLSN*...as resident aliens and refugees, *—ADAM.*

**abstain from fleshly lusts, which war against the soul:** ... be constantly holding yourselves back from the passionate cravings which are fleshly by nature, *—WUST.*

**2:11.** Peter used the term "dearly beloved" (*agapētoi*, well-loved) often (see 2 Peter 1:17; 3:1, 8, 14, 15, 17). He wrote to implore believers as "strangers" (*paroikous*, sojourners, alien residents, non-citizens, as in Ephesians 2:19) and "pilgrims" (*parepidēmous*, temporary residents, as in 1 Peter 1:1) to "abstain" (*apechesthai*, refrain, as in 1 Thessalonians 4:3; 5:22) from "fleshly lusts" (*sarkikōn epithumiōn*, carnal desires, longings for gross sins of the flesh). He said these "war" (*strateuontai*, mobilize to fight, carry on a campaign, as in James 4:1) against the "soul" (*psuchēs*, the whole being).

His readers are followers of Christ, but Peter indicated the war was and is not over. Carnal desires keep arising so they must keep resisting. This struggle between the flesh and the Spirit is pictured vividly by Paul, who wrote, "Walk in the Spirit, and ye shall not fulfil the lust of the flesh" (Galatians 5:16).

**12. Having your conversation honest among the Gentiles:**...holding your manner of life among the unsaved steadily beautiful in its goodness, *—WUST* ... your behavior among the nations ideal, *—CNDT.*

**that, whereas they speak against you as evildoers:** ... in order that in the things in which they defame you as those who do evil, *—WUST.*

**they may by [your] good works, which they shall behold, glorify God:** ... by being spectators of ideal acts they should be glorifying God, *—CNDT*... attracted by your brilliant conduct, praise God whilst witnessing it, *—FNTN*... because of your works beautiful in their goodness which they are constantly, carefully, and attentively watching, they may glorify God, *—WUST.*

**in the day of visitation:** ... when He returns to take care of us, *—SEB*...when he is revealed to them, *—NOLI*...on the judgment day, *—WLMS*...in the day of His overseeing care, *—WUST.*

**2:12.** Peter said they should guard their "conversation" (*anastrophēn*, behavior, lifestyle) to keep it "honest" (*kalēn*, honorable, virtuous) among the "Gentiles" (*ethnesin*, nations, unconverted people, as also in 2:9; 4:3).

False charges were being leveled against them. Neighbors called them enemies of their society. Romans considered them hostile to emperor worship. Many "speak against" them (*katalalousin*, slander, speak evil, as also in 3:16) and call them "evildoers" (*kakopoiōn*, criminals, malefactors). However, by observing believers' "good works" (*kalōn ergōn*, honest and virtuous deeds) they will change their opinion and will glorify God in the "day" (*hēmera*, time) of "visitation" (*episkopēs*, checkup, inspection, confrontation, as in Luke 19:44).

**13. Submit yourselves to every ordinance of man for the Lord's sake:** ... Put yourselves in the attitude of submission ... giving yourselves to the implicit obedience, –WUST ... to every human creation because of the Lord, –CNDT.

**whether it be to the king, as supreme:** ... to the Emperor as supreme ruler, –MNTG ... as one who is supereminent, –WUST.

**2:13.** Although believers are citizens of heaven, they should obey civil laws while on earth. They should "submit" themselves (*hupotagete*, subordinate, be in subjection, as in 3:22) to every "ordinance" (*ktisei*, institution) of man for the Lord's sake, and should honor the king as being "supreme" (*huperechonti*, prime authority, having superiority) in his earthly realm. Christians should obey their earthly king, Peter said, as long as it did not require disobeying their heavenly King. Sometimes Christians have to choose between the two loyalties (see Acts 4:19,20), but Peter made it clear that Christians should be on the side of law and order.

**14. Or unto governors, as unto them that are sent by him for the punishment of evildoers:** ... as commissioned by him to bring criminals to justice, –BRKL ... sent by him to inflict punishment upon those who do evil, –WUST ... for vengeance, –CNDT.

**and for the praise of them that do well:** ... the commendation, –WADE ... the applause of doers of good, –CNDT ... encourage the well-behaved, –BRKL.

**2:14.** "Governors" (*hēgemosin*, chief rulers) are dispatched by the king not only for the "punishment" (*ekdikēsin*, vengeance, retribution) of "evildoers" (*kakopoiōn*, malefactors, criminals) but also for the "praise" (*epainon*, commendation) of those who "do well" (*agathopoiōn*, are virtuous). Therefore, believers should be in subjection as a good testimony for their Lord, so the rulers will commend them (see also Romans 13:3,4).

**15. For so is the will of God, that with well doing ye may put to silence the ignorance of foolish men:** ... intention of ... the senselessness

of ignorant men, –FNTN ... by doing good you might be reducing to silence ... men who are unreflecting and unintelligent, –WUST ... by behaving well you should silence the foolishness of thoughtless people, –BRKL ... muzzle the ignorant talk, –ADAM ... imprudent men, –CNDT.

**2:15.** It is God's "will" (*thelēma*, purpose, desire, pleasure, as in Revelation 4:11) that believers should "put to silence" (*phimoun*, muzzle, make speechless, as in Matthew 22:12) their slanderers by "well-doing" (*agathopoiountas*, being virtuous, of good reputation; see also 1 Peter 2:20; 3:16,17). Peter called the slanderers "foolish" men (*aphronōn*, stupid, egotistic, unwise, as in 2 Corinthians 11:16). A believer's only protection against slander is a transparently godly life. This may not save them from trouble but it is its own witness to the truth.

**16. As free, and not using [your] liberty for a cloak of maliciousness:** ... Live like free men, –WLMS ... doing all this as those who have their liberty, and not as those who are holding their liberty as a cloak of wickedness, –WUST ... veil for evil, –SWAN ... cover-up, –SEB ... some wickedness, –NORL ... as a pretext for vice, –NOLI ... misconduct, –MNTG.

**but as the servants of God:** ... as God's slaves, –CNDT ... but as those who are God's bondmen, –WUST.

**2:16.** Peter told believers to submit to civil authority willingly (not of compulsion) as men who are "free" (from *elutheria*, freedom from bondage) and not using that freedom as a "cloak" (*epikalumma*, veil, covering) of "maliciousness" (*kakias*, evil, spite, wickedness, as in 2:1). Instead of using their liberty as a pretext to do evil, they should use it as "servants of God" (*douloi theou*, bondservants of God). Peter and other apostles liked to call themselves slaves of God (see 2 Peter 1:1; Romans 1:1; James 1:1). Everyone is either a servant of God or a slave to sin (see 2 Peter 2:19). No one has absolute personal freedom. To be free indeed the believer must subject himself to the Word of Christ (John 8:31,32).

**17. Honour all [men]:** ... Pay honor, –WUST ... Show respect to everyone, –NORL ... Treat all men, –CMPB ... honorably, –BRKL.

**Love the brotherhood:** ... be loving, –WUST.

**Fear God:** ... Respect God, –SEB ... revere God, –BRKL.

**Honour the king:** ... Respect the head leader of the country, –NLTG ... deferential to the king, –TCNT.

**2:17.** Peter gave four directives which are brief in expression but broad in implementation. He told believers to (1) "honor" (*timēsate*, esteem, respect) all men, whether they deserve it or not; (2)

"love" (*agapate*, love much) the "brotherhood" (*adelphotēta*, the Christian fraternity); (3) "fear" (*phobeisthe*, be in awe, revere) God; (4) "honor" (*timate*, esteem, respect) the "king" (*basilea*, sovereign). Though he directed believers to honor all men, Peter specifically mentioned the king; the language used in his first directive indicates that some men deserve more honor than others. In each of the three latter directives the Greek verb denotes continuous action: believers should keep on loving the brotherhood; they should keep on fearing God; they should keep on honoring the king.

18. **Servants, [be] subject to [your] masters with all fear:** ... Domestics may do it by being subject to your owners, –CNDT ... Household slaves, put yourselves in constant subjection with every fear in implicit obedience to your absolute lords and masters, –WUST ... showing all respect, –SEB.

**not only to the good and gentle, but also to the froward:** ... the benevolent and considerate, –FNTN ... who are good at heart and sweetly reasonable, satisfied with less than their due, –WUST ... lenient, but to the crooked also, –CNDT ... those who are unfair, –TCNT ... of cruel disposition, –NORL ... unreasonable, –MNTG ... perverse, –CLMT ... arrogant, –NOLI.

**2:18.** Many of the believers to whom Peter was writing were slaves, so verses 18-25 are directed to them. He called them "servants" (*oiketai*, a menial domestic, household bondservant, as distinguished from *doulos*, the general term for slaves).

Peter's statements are imperatives. He directed them to be "subject" (*hupotassomenoi*, obey, be submissive) to their masters with all "fear" (*phobō*, alarm, awe), not only to the "good" (*agathois*, benevolent) and "gentle" (*epieikesin*, moderate, patient, as in James 3:17), but also to the "froward" (*skoliois*, unfair, crooked, as in Philippians 2:15). Some slave owners were kind, others were not. The test of obedience is to believers whose masters are oppressive (see Matthew 5:44-46). Similar directions to bondservants are given in Ephesians 6:5-7; Colossians 3:22-25; 1 Timothy 6:1,2; Titus 2:9.

It was not easy to be a slave in the First Century, even under the best of circumstances. It must have been a great test of a Christian slave to be submissive to a cruel master.

19. **For this [is] thankworthy:** ... this is grace, –CNDT ... is something which is beyond the ordinary course of what might be expected and is therefore commendable, –WUST.

**if a man for conscience toward God endure grief, suffering wrongfully:** ... if, because of conscience ... anyone is undergoing sorrows, –CNDT ... when a person because of the conscious

sense of his relation to God bears up under pain, –WUST ... unjust ill-treatment, –NOLI.

**2:19.** Peter said "this" (obedience to oppressive masters) is "thankworthy" (*charis*, gratifying, cause for thanks, as in Romans 6:17 and 2 Corinthians 2:14). God is pleased if a man or woman will "endure" (*hupopherei*, stay under, bear up, as in 1 Corinthians 10:13 and 2 Timothy 3:11) "grief" (*lupas*, heaviness, sorrows; the word is plural). This must be with a "conscience" (*suneidēsin*, moral consciousness, sense of duty; also in 3:16,21) toward God, "suffering" (*paschōn*, to experience sensation, feel pain) "wrongfully" (*adikōs*, unjustly). If the suffering arises from the servant's faith in the gospel, his patient endurance is all the more "thankworthy."

20. **For what glory [is it], if, when ye be buffeted for your faults, ye shall take it patiently?:** ... What credit can you claim, –TCNT ... what sort of fame is it when you fall short of the mark and are pummeled with the fist, –WUST ... you are beaten, –NLTG ... sinning and being buffeted, –CNDT ... you endure, –WLSN ... endure a beating, –SEB.

**but if, when ye do well, and suffer [for it], ye take it patiently:** ... when you are in the habit of doing good and then suffer constantly for it, –WUST ... if, doing good and suffering, you will be enduring, –CNDT.

**this [is] acceptable with God:** ... this is an unusual and not-to-be-expected action, and therefore commendable, –WUST ... beautiful in God's eyes, –TCNT ... brings honour, –FNTN.

**2:20.** What kind of "glory" (*kleos*, renown, praise) is there if, when a person is "buffeted" (*kolaphizomenoi*, beaten physically, as in Matthew 26:67) for his own "faults" (*hamartanontes*, repeated shortcomings, trespasses, sins, offenses), he shall "take it patiently" (*hupomeneite*, stay under, bear up, endure, as in Matthew 10:22 and James 1:12)? Christians may suffer because of misconduct, but only those who suffer for righteousness' sake are martyrs (Matthew 5:11,12). But if a person shall "do well" (*agathopoiountes*, be virtuous, as in 2:15; 3:16,17) and suffer, and if he takes it patiently, this is "acceptable with God" (*charis para theō*, thankworthy, cause for thanks as God looks at it, as in 2:19).

21. **For even hereunto were ye called:** ... For this, –CNDT ... to this very thing, –WUST.

**because Christ also suffered for us:** ... seeing that, –CNDT ... suffered on your behalf, –TCNT.

**leaving us an example, that ye should follow his steps:** ... leaving you a copy, that you should be following up in the footprints of Him, –CNDT.

**2:21.** "For even hereunto" (to suffer patiently) were they "called" (*eklēthēte*, summoned, as in

1 Peter 1:15; 2:9; 3:9; 5:10; 2 Peter 1:3) because Christ also suffered for them, "leaving" (*hupolimpanon*, to bequeath) them an "example" (*hupogrammon*, something to copy, a writing-copy for others to imitate) that they should follow his "steps" (*ichnesin*, tracks, footprints, as in Romans 4:12 and 2 Corinthians 12:18). One of the great guidelines a believer may adopt as a standard for behavior in any situation is to ask himself, "What would Jesus do?"

**22. Who did no sin, neither was guile found in his mouth:** . . . Nothing false was ever found, —*SEB* . . . He was guilty of no sin or the slightest prevarication, —*PHLP* . . . neither was Deceit found, —*WLSN* . . . He never did anything wrong, nor was anything deceitful ever heard from his lips, —*TCNT* . . . who never in a single instance committed a sin . . . after careful scrutiny, there was found not even craftiness, —*WUST* . . . did not commit sin and never uttered a lie, —*TNT*.

**2:22.** As prophesied in Isaiah 53:9, Christ "did no sin." Peter had already pointed to His sinlessness in 1:19. Neither was "guile" (*dolos*, deceit, subtlety, trickery, as also in 1 Peter 2:1; 3:10) "found" (*heurethē*, perceived, discovered after close scrutiny) in His "mouth" (*stomati*, implies speaking, as in 2 Corinthians 13:1).

**23. Who, when he was reviled, reviled not again:** . . . When they insulted Christ, —*SEB* . . . who when His heart was being wounded with an accursed sting, and when He was being made the object of harsh rebuke and biting, never retaliated, —*WUST* . . . did not revile in return, —*CMPB* . . . did not return the insult, —*BRKL*.
**when he suffered, he threatened not; but committed [himself] to him that judgeth righteously:** . . . did not threaten when abused, —*BRKL* . . . made no threats of revenge . . . committed his cause to the one who judges fairly, —*PHLP* . . . yet gave it over to Him Who is judging justly, —*CNDT* . . . kept on delivering all into the keeping of the One, —*WUST*.

**2:23.** The natural reaction to abuse is to retort in anger, trade insult for insult, and threaten to get even. Christ's example is the opposite. When "reviled" (*loidoroumenos*, slander, insult; the language denotes repeated incidents) He reviled not. (See 1 Corinthians 4:12.) When He "suffered" (*paschōn*, experience pain) He did not threaten or menace anyone in return. To follow such an example will require an attitude of forgiveness toward our opponents and of trust toward God. Christ's suffering was undeserved, but He simply "committed himself" (*paredidou*, as an accused man is handed over to a judge) to Him who judges (decides) "righteously" (*dikaiōs*, justly, equitably).

**24. Who his own self bare our sins in his own body on the tree:** . . . who personally in His own body, —*BRKL* . . . carries up our sins in His body on to the pole, —*CNDT* . . . on the cross, —*WLMS*.
**that we, being dead to sins, should live unto righteousness:** . . . having died with respect to our sins, —*WUST* . . . coming away from sins, —*CNDT* . . . so that we might abandon our sins, —*BRKL*.
**by whose stripes ye were healed:** . . . by whose scars, —*WLSN* . . . by Whose welt, —*CNDT* . . . By his bleeding wounds, —*SWAN* . . . by his trickling bruises, —*BRKL* . . . bleeding stripe, —*WUST* . . . His bruising was your healing, —*TCNT*.

**2:24.** Christ himself "bare" (*anēnenken*, carry, offer up, a verb commonly used of bringing sacrifices to an altar, as in 1 Peter 2:5) their sins in His own "body" (*sōmati*, as Isaiah 53:12 states, "He bare the sin of many") on the "tree" (*xulon*, timber, not a live tree). The cross became the altar, and Jesus became the perfect sin offering (Hebrews 9:28).

Peter here explained the purpose of Christ's death and resurrection, as Paul did also in Romans 6:1-23. It is that believers, being "dead" to sins (*apogenomenoi*, departed, absent, having renounced all sins) should "live" (*zēsōmen*, vital existence) unto "righteousness" (*dikaiosunē*, equity, doing right, as in Hebrews 1:9; also in 1 Peter 3:14; 2 Peter 1:1; 2:5,21; 3:13).

Referring again to the Crucifixion, Peter said that by Christ's "stripes" (*mōlōpi*, black bruise, bloody wound) they were "healed" (from *iaomai*, heal, make whole). Numerous believers to whom Peter was writing were slaves who may have received such stripes. Usually *iaomai* denotes physical healing, but sometimes, as in Hebrews 12:13, it means spiritual healing. Peter's meaning here is restoration as the context indicates. Christ healed their waywardness and sin so they could be restored to the sheepfold, live righteously, and not be as sheep going astray (2:25).

**25. For ye were as sheep going astray:** . . . You had wandered away like so many sheep, —*PHLP* . . . then you strayed like sheep, —*BRKL*.
**but are now returned unto the Shepherd and Bishop of your souls:** . . . you turned back to . . . the Supervisor of, —*CNDT* . . . and Guardian, —*MNTG* . . . and [spiritual] Overseer, —*WUST* . . . of your lives, —*WLSN*.

**2:25.** Before being healed they were as sheep "going astray" (*planōmena*, seduced, roaming into danger, as in 2 Peter 2:15). Peter was recalling Isaiah 53:6. Now, however, they have "returned" (from *epistrephō*, turn about, convert, come back; used negatively in 2 Peter 2:21,22) unto the "Shepherd" (from *poimēn*, keeper of sheep; translated "pastors" in Ephesians 4:11) and "Bishop" (*episkopon*, overseer, supervisor) of their souls. Here alone is Christ called the believers' Bishop who faithfully watches over His people. This verse recalls Jesus' words in Luke 15:4-7, the Parable of the Lost Sheep. Jesus called himself the Good Shepherd (John 10:11).

## Chapter 3

**1. Likewise, ye wives, [be] in subjection to your own husbands:** ... you married women, —TCNT, —WLMS ... be subordinate to your respective husbands, —WADE ... with implicit obedience, —WUST.

**that, if any obey not the word:** ... if any are stubborn also, as to the word, —CNDT ... even though certain ones obstinately refuse to be persuaded by, —WUST.

**they also may without the word be won by the conversation of the wives:** ... they will be gained without a word, —CNDT ... the behavior, —MNTG.

**3:1.** After writing about a servant's duty to be subject to an ungodly master, Peter wrote of a wife's duty toward an unbelieving husband. He directed "wives" (*gunaikes*, a woman, particularly a wife) to be in "subjection" (*hupotassomenai*, submission, under obedience) to their own husbands. *Hupotagēte* is used of submission to God (James 4:7) in contrast to yielding to Satan and again of submission to God's will as a son submits to the authority of his father (Hebrews 12:9). The word implies a voluntary adjustment to authority that is recognized as proper.

The object is that if any husbands are unbelievers—that is, if they "obey not" (*apeithousin*, refuse to believe) the "word" (*logō*, utterance, communication, message; likely means preaching)—they also without a word may be won to God by the "conversation" (*anastrophēs*, behavior) of their wives.

**2. While they behold your chaste conversation [coupled] with fear:** ... being spectators of your pure behavior in fear, —CNDT ... having viewed attentively your pure manner of life which is accompanied by a reverential fear, —WUST ... and deferential bearing, —WADE.

**3:2.** Though unbelieving husbands may not listen to gospel preaching, Peter said the pure and respectful conduct of their wives is a silent message they cannot easily ignore. They will be won over as they "behold" (*epopteusantes*, inspect, watch, as in 1 Peter 2:12) the wives' "chaste" (*hagnēn*, modest, pure, as in 1 Timothy 5:22) behavior combined with "fear" (*phobō*, awe, reverence; see Ephesians 5:33).

**3. Whose adorning let it not be that outward [adorning]:** ... let it not be that external one, —WLSN ... which is from without and merely, —WUST.

**of plaiting the hair:** ... of braiding aught into, —CNDT ... an elaborate gathering of the hair into knots, —WUST ... the outer beauty of fancy hairdos, —SEB.

**and of wearing of gold:** ... a lavish display, —WUST ... of decking with gold, —CNDT ... golden trinkets, —FNTN.

**or of putting on of apparel:** ... the donning of, —WUST ... the wearing of beautiful dresses, —MNTG ... garments, —CNDT.

**3:3.** Wives who wish to win their husbands for Christ should not depend on outward adornment such as braiding their hair, wearing gold trinkets, or putting on fine clothes, as worldly women do. *Kosmos* ("adorning") here has its old meaning of ornament, not the common meaning of the world (Robertson, *Word Pictures in the New Testament*, 6:108). Their adorning should not be that outward adorning of "plaiting" (*emplokēs*, elaborate braiding, interweaving; translated "entangled" in 2 Timothy 2:4 and 2 Peter 2:20) the hair. Nor should it be the "wearing" (*peritheseōs*, put around, wrap) of gold (ornaments of gold worn around the hair as nets, as well as on fingers, arms, and ankles) or of putting on of apparel. Peter was not forbidding the use of jewelry any more than the wearing of clothes but was contrasting outward display with inward beauty.

**4. But [let it be] the hidden man of the heart, in that which is not corruptible:** ... the unseen woman, —FNTN ... hidden human of the heart, —CNDT ... let that adornment be the hidden personality in the heart, imperishable in quality, —WUST ... unfading loveliness, —NOLI.

**[even the ornament] of a meek and quiet spirit, which is in the sight of God of great price:** ... a meek and quiet disposition, —WUST ... in the incorruptibility ... is costly, —CNDT ... something of surpassing value in God's sight, —BRKL.

**3:4.** Their adorning should be the "hidden" man (*kruptos*, secret, concealed, private) of the "heart" (*kardias*, innermost part of the being) in that which is "not corruptible" (*aphthartō*, imperishable, immortal, as also in 1:4,23). This should include the ornament of a "meek" (*praeos*, humble, mild, gentle) and "quiet" (*hēsuchiou*, peaceable, undisturbed) "spirit" (*pneumatos*, here meaning disposition, temper, as in 1 Corinthians 4:21) which is "of great price" (*poluteles*, very precious, as in Mark 14:3 and 1 Timothy 2:9) "in the sight" of God (*enōpion*, before, in the face of, as in James 4:10). God sees "in secret" (Matthew 6:4,6). He looks not on the outward appearance but on the heart (1 Samuel 16:7). Outward adornments are perishable, but a meek and quiet spirit is a very precious ornament in God's estimation.

**5. For after this manner:** ... thus formerly, —WUST... in this way, —BRKL. ·

**in the old time:**

**the holy women also, who trusted in God, adorned themselves:** ... whose expectation was in God, —CNDT... who fixed their hope on God, —BRKL ... sought to make themselves attractive, —NORL.

**being in subjection unto their own husbands:** ... submissive as they were, —BRKL ... and obeyed their husbands, —NOLI.

**3:5.** This is how the holy women of ancient times used to adorn themselves. They "trusted" (*elpizousai*, hoped, fixed their expectation, placed their confidence) in God and were "in subjection" (*hupotassomenai*, submissive, under obedience) to their own husbands.

**6. Even as Sara obeyed Abraham, calling him lord:** ... Sarah, for instance, —BRKL... was in the habit of rendering obedience to, —WUST.

**whose daughters ye are, as long as ye do well:** ... whose children you became, doing good, —CNDT... Her genuine daughters you become insofar as you do right, —BRKL... if the whole course of your life is in the doing of good, —WUST.

**and are not afraid with any amazement:** ... and let nothing upset you, —NORL ... fearing no intimidation, —ADAM ... not fearing dismay in anything, —CNDT... not being caused to fear by even one particle of terror, —WUST... not being frightened by any passionate emotion, —FNTN ... yield to no agitating fears, —WADE... are not terrorized by any fear, —BRKL.

**3:6.** As a prime example Peter pointed to Sarah who "obeyed" (*hupēkousen*, heed, pay attention to, do as commanded) Abraham, calling him "lord" (*kurion*, master, see Genesis 18:12; this was a general term of respect as in Genesis 23:6, 11, 15; 31:35; 32:4). Peter said they were true descendants of Sarah if they "do well" (*agathopoiousai*, be virtuous, have a good reputation, as in 1 Peter 2:15) and "are not afraid" (*phoboumenai*, be put in fear) with any "amazement" (*ptoēsin*, terror); that is, are "not afraid of sudden fear" (Proverbs 3:25). Hart suggests that "perhaps Peter regarded Sarah's falsehood as the yielding to a sudden terror for which God rebuked her" (5:64)

**7. Likewise, ye husbands, dwell with [them] according to knowledge:** ... You married men, —WLMS... live in the proper relation, —TCNT... let your home life with them be governed by the dictates of knowledge, —WUST.

**giving honour unto the wife, as unto the weaker vessel:** ... awarding honor, —CNDT... assigning honour to their feminine nature, —FNTN... as you would for a fragile vase, —ADAM.

**and as being heirs together of the grace of life:** ... fellow-inheritors with you, —WUST... who are also joint enjoyers of the allotment of the varied grace of life, —CNDT.

**that your prayers be not hindered:** ... and this, in order that no [Satanic] inroads be made into your prayers, —WUST... may not be denied, —NORL.

**3:7.** Having described the duties of wives, Peter next turned to husbands. They should "dwell" (*sunoikountes*, reside together) with their wives "according to *knowledge*" (*gnōsin*). Peter did not use the word *ginōskō* which appears in Matthew 1:25 in reference to carnal knowledge but used *gnosin* which indicates a mental understanding. Husbands should understand their wives and show respectful consideration toward them, realizing (1) that wives are "weaker" (*asthenesterō*, more feeble) than their husbands, and (2) that husbands and wives are joint heirs of the "grace" (*charitos*, benefit, favor) of life. Both husband and wife are essential in the marriage partnership; each needs the other, as indicated by Paul: "Neither is the man without the woman, neither the woman without the man" (1 Corinthians 11:11).

Prayers may be "hindered" (*ekkoptesthai*, cut off, hewn down) by wrongdoing or shortcomings in the life of any believer. As examples, Jesus mentioned such problems as a grievance between friends (Matthew 5:23) and an unforgiving spirit (Matthew 6:15). Peter indicated a husband's failure to respect his wife as an equal partner may block his prayers and make them ineffective. This warning may apply not only to private prayers but also to a household's united prayers. Family members cannot pray together effectively if there are strained relationships between them. This is particularly true if the misunderstanding or hostility is between husband and wife.

**8. Finally, [be ye] all of one mind, having compassion one of another:** ... Last of all, —NLTG... Now, to come to a conclusion, —WUST ... Now the finish: ... Be all of a like disposition, —CNDT... you should all be united, sympathetic, —TCNT ... have unity of spirit, —NOLI... be harmonious, —MNTG... have sympathy, —NORL... sympathising, —DRBY... you must be together in your thinking, —SEB.

**love as brethren, [be] pitiful, [be] courteous:** ... full of brotherly love, —DRBY ... fond of the brethren, tenderly compassionate, of a humble disposition, —CNDT ... tender-hearted ... humbleminded, —WUST.

**3:8.** Peter then addressed all, whether masters or servants, husbands or wives, and exhorts the entire body of believers to be "of one mind" (*homophrones*, like-minded, harmonious). Their attitude toward each other should be one of "compassion" (*sumpatheis*, sympathy, a fellow-feeling), and they should always show brotherly love, be "pitiful" (*eusplanchnoi*, tender-hearted), and "courteous" (*philophrones*, kind and friendly). Whether the believers were failing on these points or not, the instruction probably was not new—for these things were taught very generally by Christ and His apostles—but Peter wished to stir up their pure minds by way of remembrance (2 Peter 3:1). His exhortation would reinforce the teaching and encourage them to obey it.

**9. Not rendering evil for evil, or railing for railing:** . . . not paying back, −MNTG . . . not returning wrong for wrong, −FNTN . . . not giving back evil in exchange for evil, or verbal abuse in exchange for verbal abuse, −WUST . . . or abuse for abuse, −TCNT . . . nor insult for insult, −NOLI . . . reviling for reviling, −CNDT.
**but contrariwise blessing; knowing that ye are thereunto called, that ye should inherit a blessing:** . . . be constantly blessing, −WUST . . . speaking pleasantly, −FNTN . . . you should be enjoying the allotment of blessing, −CNDT.

**3:9.** Peter said the believers are called to receive a blessing, and in order to receive it they should invoke blessing on others, even those who injure them and revile them. They should not return "evil for evil" (*kakon*, wicked and injurious talk) nor "railing for railing" (*loidorian*, slander, reproach). Instead they should render "blessing" (*eulogountes*, commendation, benediction). As a reward, they will inherit a blessing which is explained in verse 10. This earthly blessing is in addition to their eternal inheritance which is "reserved in heaven" (1:4). Peter is echoing Christ's teaching: "Love your enemies, bless them that curse you, . . . that ye may be the children of your Father which is in heaven: for he maketh his sun to rise on the evil and on the good, and sendeth rain on the just and on the unjust" (Matthew 5:44,45).

**10. For he that will love life, and see good days:** . . . Whoever wants to enjoy life, −WLMS . . . be acquainted with good days, −CNDT . . . experience happy days, −TCNT.
**let him refrain his tongue from evil, and his lips that they speak no guile:** . . . the natural tendency of his tongue, −WUST . . . cease from evil, −CNDT . . . speaking deceit, −WLSN . . . annoyance, −FNTN.

**3:10.** In verses 10-12, Peter explained the "blessing" of verse 9 by quoting David's words in Psalm 34:12-16. He spoke of loving "life" (*zōēn*, life, either literal or figurative; probably he means a prolonged natural life, though he could mean spiritual life) and of seeing good "days" (*hēmeras*, either a 24-hour day or, figuratively, an extended period). To enjoy this full and satisfying life, Peter said

the believer should "refrain" (*pausatō*, restrain, quit, cease; as in 4:1, "He that hath suffered in the flesh hath ceased from sin") from speaking "evil" (*kakou*, wicked, harmful talk) and let no words of "guile" (*dolon*, craftiness, subtilty, deceit) escape his lips.

**11. Let him eschew evil, and do good:** . . . He must turn away from, −SEB . . . avoid evil, −CNDT . . . let him turn aside from vice, −FNTN . . . do right, −BRKL.
**let him seek peace, and ensue it:** . . . make it his aim, −WADE . . . and follow after it, −TCNT . . . pursue it, −CNDT . . . search for peace and keep after it, −BRKL.

**3:11.** The believer should not entertain evil thoughts nor expose himself to temptation. On the contrary, he should "eschew" evil (*ekklinatō*, avoid, go out of the way), that is, get out of its way when he sees temptation coming. "Eschew" is from a Norman word (*eschever*) meaning to shun or avoid. The believer should "lean away from" evil; he should bend over backward to avoid it.

More than that, he should take positive steps to do "good" (*agathon*, good, beneficial deeds; as in Galatians 6:10, doing "good" unto all men). Good deeds and good words should mark the believer, and he should be known for good relationships also. He should "seek" peace (*zētēsatō*, desire, seek after; as in Matthew 2:13 where Herod sought the young child to destroy Him). Peter's words echo Hebrews 12:14, "Follow peace with all men." Earnest effort is indicated; the believer should "ensue" peace (*diōxatō*, pursue, follow hard after, as in Philippians 3:14, "I press toward the mark"). The word "ensue" is obsolete; a proper translation is "pursue."

**12. For the eyes of the Lord [are] over the righteous:** . . . are directed in a favorable attitude towards, −WUST . . . are on upright men, −WLMS . . . on the just, −CNDT.
**and his ears [are open] unto their prayers:** . . . are inclined, −WUST . . . and he is listening to their prayers, −SEB . . . listen to their pleading cries, −WLMS . . . attentive to their prayer, −FNTN . . . towards their supplications, −DRBY . . . for their petition, −CNDT.
**but the face of the Lord [is] against them that do evil:** . . . the Lord frowns upon those who do wrong, −TCNT . . . those who practice, −WUST.

**3:12.** Peter said the Lord's eyes are *upon* the righteous (not "over" as in the Authorized Version). God looks upon them with favor, and His ears are always open to their prayers. He will faithfully fulfill His promises to grant their petitions; but He will be equally faithful to fulfill His warnings of judgment against evildoers also, for His "face" (*prosōpon*, face, visage, countenance) is against them that do evil. God cannot countenance wrongdoing (Habakkuk 1:13, Berkeley), nor will

He listen to the prayers of those who cherish iniquity in their hearts (Psalm 66:18, RSV).

**13. And who [is] he that will harm you:**...will injure you, –WLSN...will be illtreating you, –CNDT...do you evil, –WUST.

**if ye be followers of that which is good?:**...if you should become zealous of good? –CNDT...if you become eager for the right? –BRKL.

**3:13.** The word "and" shows cause and effect, basing verse 13 on the preceding verse. Peter indicated that since the believers are righteous and God is watching out for them, no one can "harm" them (*kakōsōn*, injure, damage, hurt; as in Acts 18:10, "No man shall set on thee to hurt thee") as long as they continue to be "followers" (*mimētai*, imitators; as in 1 Corinthians 11:1, "Be ye followers of me, even as I also am of Christ") of that which is good. Peter did not want the believers to feel overwhelmed by persecutions. Though such may come, God will never allow the testing to be more than His servants are able to bear (1 Corinthians 10:13).

**14. But and if ye suffer for righteousness' sake, happy [are ye]:**...if even you should perchance suffer...you are spiritually prosperous ones, –WUST...on account of righteousness, you are blessed, –BRKL.

**and be not afraid of their terror, neither be troubled:**...Do not let man frighten you; and do not allow yourselves to be distressed, –TCNT...Do not be dismayed, –NOLI...do not be affected with fear of them by the fear which they strive to inspire in you, neither become agitated, –WUST...you may not be afraid with their fear, nor yet be disturbed, –CNDT...nor be alarmed, –WLSN...or be disturbed at it, –WADE...by their threat, –BRKL.

**3:14.** Peter said that if the believers, for righteousness' sake, should "chance to suffer" (as Alford translates it), they are "happy" (*makarioi*, supremely blessed, fortunate; same word as in Matthew 5:10). So they should not fear their enemies' threats; they should not be made "afraid" (*phobēthēte*, alarmed, frightened) by their "terror" (*phobon*, alarm, fear). They need not be "troubled" (*tarachthēte*, disturbed, agitated) nor live in fear of what might possibly happen. The Greek construction ("but and if") suggests that suffering pain for righteousness' sake will be a rare thing; it may happen, but probably not. Believers should be prepared whatever happens.

**15. But sanctify the Lord God in your hearts:**...But consecrate Christ in your hearts, as Lord, –MNTG...hallow the Lord Christ, –CNDT...Make

a special holy place in your hearts for Christ, –SEB...but set apart Christ, –WUST.

**and [be] ready always to [give] an answer to every man that asketh you a reason of the hope that is in you:**...always being those who are ready to present a verbal defense to everyone who asks you for a logical explanation concerning, –WUST...ever ready with a defense for everyone who is demanding from you an account concerning the expectation, –CNDT.

**with meekness and fear:**...but give it calmly and respectfully, –TCNT...in a humble and reverent manner, –NORL...Be gentle as you speak and show respect, –NLTG...and a wholesome serious caution, –WUST.

**3:15.** Peter told the believers how to deal with opposition. "Sanctify" (*hagiasate*, hallow, make holy) is a word the pagan Greeks used to describe the setting apart of a temple to be used only for sacred purposes. "The Lord God" (*kurion...ton Theon*, God as Lord) might be changed to "Christ as Lord" (*kurion...ton Christon*, on the basis of very reliable Greek texts). Peter directed the believers to set Christ apart as Lord in their hearts—as their only Master—and be ready always to give verbal defense of their inner hope. "Be ready" (*hetoimoi*, prepared, adjusted) at all times with an "answer" (*apologian*, a clearing of oneself, defense; as in Acts 22:1, "Hear ye my defense"). They should be able to give the "reason" (*logon*, word, utterance, verbalization) of their inner "hope" (*elpidos*, happy anticipation, expectation).

The Greeks liked to debate issues of all kinds. Peter indicated the believers should be ready to discuss their faith openly. This calls for a clear understanding of their beliefs and for skill in presenting it. It does not negate the need for guidance and inspiration by the Holy Spirit which Jesus promised (Matthew 10:19). On the contrary, Peter said they should give their witness not in a high-handed, cocksure manner but with "meekness" (*prautētos*, humility, mildness) and "fear" (*phobou*, terror, fear, not of man but of God; that is, with reverence and dependence on divine guidance and inspiration).

Believers should not be surprised if they suffer in spite of the fact they are living godly lives. They should be prepared to give the right kind of answer in the face of rejection or persecution. They should not retaliate in self-defense or seek revenge. The best "answer" they can make is to live in such a way no one will believe the accusations.

**16. Having a good conscience:**...keep your conscience clear, –WLMS, –WADE...having a conscience unimpaired, –WUST.

**that, whereas they speak evil of you, as of evildoers:**...in the very thing in which they defame you, –WUST...in what they are speaking against you as of evildoers, –CNDT . . . who slander Your good Conduct in Christ, –WLSN.

**they may be ashamed that falsely accuse:** . . . will be ashamed of their slanders, –NOLI . . . they may be put to shame, those who spitefully abuse, insult, –WUST . . . they may be mortified, who traduce, –CNDT.

**your good conversation in Christ:** . . . when they see the good way you have lived as a Christian, –NLTG . . . your good manner of life, –CLMT . . . due to your union with Christ, –WADE . . . your good behavior in Christ, –CNDT.

**3:16.** In order to give an effective witness, Peter said they need a "good conscience" (*suneidēsin . . . agathēn*, guiltless moral consciousness). This sense of innocence will result from their good "conversation" (*anastrophēn*, manner of life) in Christ. There will be nothing in their lives to make them ashamed; but those who "speak" (*katalalōsin*, speak against, as in 2:12) evil of them will be "ashamed" (*kataischunthōsin*, dishonored, confounded) in the very matter wherein they falsely accuse the believers. "Whereas" may be translated "wherein." Their accusers will be "put to silence" (2:15). "Falsely accuse" is the same strong word (*epēreazō*) used in Luke 6:28; it means revile, insult, slander, spitefully abuse. The answer to false accusations is a godly life.

17. **For [it is] better, if the will of God be so:** . . . God may be willing, –CNDT . . . if perchance it be the will of God, –WUST.

**that ye suffer for well doing, than for evil doing:** . . . it is better when doing good . . . rather than when doing evil, –WUST . . . for doing right, than for doing wrong, –TCNT.

**3:17.** If perchance the believers have to suffer, it is "better" (*kreitton*, nobler) to suffer for well-doing than for wrongdoing. This will not happen, however, unless it is within God's "will" (*thelēma*, desire, choice, determination).

18. **For Christ also hath once suffered for sins:** . . . once died concerning sins, –CNDT . . . died once for all in relation to sins, –WUST . . . once died for sinners, –BRKL.

**the just for the unjust:** . . . the Innocent for the guilty, –WLMS . . . on behalf of, –WUST . . . for the sake of the unjust, –CNDT.

**that he might bring us to God:** . . . in order that, –WADE . . . that He may be leading us to God, –CNDT . . . that He might provide you with an entree into the presence, –WUST.

**being put to death in the flesh:** . . . in His body, –NORL . . . put to death as He was physically, –BRKL.

**but quickened by the Spirit:** . . . yet vivified, –CNDT . . . but raised to life, –WMCK . . . but made alive in Spirit, –MNTG . . . spiritually, –BRKL.

**3:18.** Peter pointed to Christ to illustrate the nobility of suffering according to "the will of God"

(verse 17) which was rewarded with resurrection. Though He was "just" (*dikaios*, innocent, righteous) He suffered "once" (*hapax*, a single time) for the sins of the "unjust" (*adikōn*, wicked, unrighteous). "Bring us to God" (*prosagagē*, approach, conduct) pictures Christ leading sinners to the Father's throne and presenting them there on the basis of His atoning death which has opened the way (Hebrews 10:19,20). Though put to death in the "flesh" (*sarki*, physical body), Christ was "quickened" (*zōopoiētheis*, vitalize, make alive) by the "Spirit" (*pneumati*, ghost, spirit). There is no capitalization in the Greek and some believe Peter was referring to Christ's human spirit, in contrast to His "flesh"; but in view of what follows it seems likely the reference is to the Holy Spirit.

19. **By which also he went and preached unto the spirits in prison:** . . . having proceeded, He made a proclamation to the imprisoned spirits, –WUST . . . being gone to the spirits in jail also, He heralds, –CNDT . . . and made proclamation, –WMCK

**3:19.** By the Spirit (or, as some prefer, in spirit) Christ went to the "spirits in prison" and "preached" unto them. Presumably this was between His death and His resurrection. Some believe the "spirits in prison" were the fallen angels mentioned in 2 Peter 2:4 and Jude 6. Others speculate that Christ preached to the wicked dead and gave them a second chance to be saved. However, "preached" may mean simply that He reported to the "saints in prison," whoever they be, His vicarious suffering and impending resurrection, the thought being not of appeal but of announcement. The Scriptures offer no "second chance" for those who have died without Christ. (For a full discussion see *Overview*, pp.509f.)

20. **Which sometime were disobedient:** . . . who were formerly apathetic, –FNTN . . . They did not obey in the past, –SEB . . . those once stubborn, –CNDT . . . who had refused to believe, –NOLI . . . who were at one time rebels, –WUST.

**when once the longsuffering of God waited:** . . . when the patience of God awaited, –CNDT . . . God's patience was delaying, –BRKL . . . was very patient with them, –NORL.

**in the days of Noah, while the ark was a preparing:** . . . This was when the ship was being built, –SEB . . . was being made, –WUST . . . was being got ready, –WADE . . . being constructed, –CNDT.

**wherein few, that is, eight souls were saved by water:** . . . were brought . . . through the time of deluge, –WUST . . . were carried safely through the Water, –WLSN . . . from the flood, –NORL.

**3:20.** Nearly all the people of Noah's day were "disobedient" (*apeithēsasin*, refuse to believe) and perished in spite of God's "longsuffering" (*makrothumia*, patience, forbearance). The relationship between verses 19 and 20 is not clear. In fact, the entire passage (verses 19-22) is difficult to interpret. "Men through the ages have struggled with this passage, and still it seems shrouded in mystery. Perhaps it is better to leave it that way. Our own salvation does not depend on our interpretation of this passage, and however we take it we can rejoice in the fact that it reflects the triumph of Christ" (Horton, p.52).

This verse reminds us of God's extreme patience and Noah's remarkable faithfulness. God waited 120 years before sending judgment, giving men a full opportunity to repent—how merciful He is! And Noah, despite ridicule and opposition, preached to his generation. At least he had this satisfaction—his family was saved.

Although Peter raised these questions, they are not answered here. However, the entire passage teaches an important truth. It is that God always gives a full opportunity to men to accept His mercy. He does not send people to hell; they go in spite of all the provisions He has made for their redemption.

**21. The like figure whereunto [even] baptism doth also now save us:** ... the antitype, immersion, *—CMPB* . . . a perfect illustration this is of the way you have been admitted to the safety of the Christian ark, *—PHLP* . . . as a counterpart now saves, *—WUST* . . . saves you nowadays, *—BRKL.*

**(not the putting away of the filth of the flesh** . . . not as removal of filth from the physical body, *—NORL* . . . does not mean we wash our bodies clean, *—NLTG* . . . not being intended for the removal of bodily uncleanness, *—WADE* . . . far more than the mere washing of a dirty body, *—PHLP.*

**but the answer of a good conscience toward God,):** . . . the inquiry of, *—CNDT* . . . the witness of, *—WUST* . . . by the earnest seeking of a conscience that is dear in God's presence, *—BRKL.*

**by the resurrection of Jesus Christ:** . . . the virtue of Christ's rising, *—PHLP.*

**3:21.** From the final words of verse 20 Peter launched into a discussion of water baptism and made it clear that baptism, like the Flood, is only a "figure" (*antitupon*, counterpart, representation; as in Hebrews 9:24, "Which are the figures of the true"). It takes more than washing in water ("the putting away of the filth of the flesh") to cleanse from sin. There are various views about the meaning of the phrase "saved by water," but all agree that it is not the water itself which saves, but Christ, who is symbolized by the ark. Cleansing comes by the shed blood of the Son of God. "Answer" (*eperōtēma*, inquiry) is a word the Romans used of the senate's approval after inquiry into a matter. God looks beyond the act of baptism and

searches to see whether the believer has truly repented and dedicated his life to divine service.

**22. Who is gone into heaven, and is on the right hand of God:** ... For he ascended into heaven, *—NOLI.*

**angels and authorities and powers being made subject unto him:** ... there having been made subject to Him, *—WUST* . . . where angelic Beings of every rank yield submission to him, *—TCNT* . . . are obeying Him, *—NLTG.*

**3:22.** The disciples saw Christ "go into heaven" (Acts 1:11), and now He is on the "right hand" (*dexias*, right as opposed to left, the right being the hand that usually takes) of God's throne (see Hebrews 8:1). "Angels" (*angelōn*, messenger, either holy or wicked) and "authorities" (*exousiōn*, mastery, jurisdiction) and "powers" (*dunameōn*, might, miracle power) are "made subject" (*hupotagenton*, under obedience, subordinated) unto Christ.

That Christ is now in heaven in a position of power at God's right hand has been a source of encouragement to believers in every century since the Ascension. Having overcome, He now has supreme authority and is able to supply believers with all that is necessary for them to overcome also.

# Chapter 4

**1. Forasmuch then as Christ hath suffered for us in the flesh:** ... having suffered for our sakes in flesh, *—CNDT* . . . in his human body, *—SEB* . . . physically, *—BRKL.*

**arm yourselves likewise with the same mind:** . . . put on as armor the same mind, *—WUST* . . . with the same attitude, *—NORL* . . . with the same resolve as he did, *—TCNT* . . . with a similar intention, *—FNTN* . . . with the same determination, *—WLMS* . . . with the same thought, *—CNDT* . . . you should take this same attitude as your weapon, *—SEB.*

**for he that hath suffered in the flesh hath ceased from sin:** ... has done with sin, *—WUST* ... has gained relief from sin, *—BRKL.*

**4:1.** Peter next identified himself with the believers. In the light of how Christ has suffered "for us," he told them to "arm yourselves" (*hoplisasthe*, equip yourselves with armor) with the same "mind" (*ennoian*, intent, thinking) as Christ. He "endured the cross, despising the shame" for "the joy that was set before him" (Hebrews 12:2). This same attitude of sacrificing self, enduring patiently, and rejoicing in tribulation will equip the believers to face false accusations and to resist sinful temptation. Peter indicated the reason they suffered persecution was that they had "ceased" (*pepautai*, stop, come to an end) from sin. If they had approved the loose living of their heathen neighbors, they would not have "suffered in the flesh."

**2. That he no longer should live the rest of [his] time in the flesh to the lusts of men, but to the will of God:**... in future, *—MNTG*... by no means still to spend the rest of his lifetime in the flesh in human desires, *—CNDT*... live the remaining Time, *—WLSN*... satisfying human appetites, *—NORL*... under the influence of human cravings, *—WADE*... but for a Divine purpose, *—FNTN.*

**4:2.** Peter showed that the change salvation brings into a person's life is very real, a complete about-face. No longer will the believer "live" (*biōsai*, spend an existence) the remainder of his "time" (*chronon*, while, season of time) in the "flesh" (*sarki*, physical body) catering to the "lusts" (*epithumiais*, strong desire, craving) of men. Instead he will yield himself to the "will" (*thelēmati*, desire, pleasure) of God. Man is self-centered by nature and is under great pressure to be concerned with his own comfort, pleasure, and security; but the believer who copies Christ is concerned with pleasing God, not himself.

**3. For the time past of [our] life may suffice us:**... the time which has passed by, *—CNDT.*
**to have wrought the will of the Gentiles:**... effected the intention of the nations, *—CNDT.*
**when we walked in lasciviousness, lusts:**... gave your life to sex sins and to sinful desires, *—NLTG*... having gone on in wantonness, *—CNDT*... you lived in shameless lewdness, evil passions, *—WMCK*... leading lives that are steeped in sensuality, *—WLMS*... living in sexual excess, having evil desires, *—SEB*... sensuality, *—NORL.*
**excess of wine, revellings:**... hard drinking, *—MNTG*... drunkenness, wild partying, *—ADAM*... wild sex parties, *—SEB*... debauches, revelries, *—CNDT*... disorderly dancing, *—WMCK*
**banquetings, and abominable idolatries:**... dissipation, *—WLMS*... drinking contests, *—SEB*... drinking bouts, and illicit idolatries, *—CNDT*... and forbidden idolatries, *—ADAM.*

**4:3.** The time before the believers became Christians, Peter said, was long enough and should "suffice" (*arketos*, be sufficient) for them to have "wrought" (*katergasasthai*, work, perform) the pleasures of the "Gentiles" (*ethnōn*, nations, heathen, non-Jewish people). Prior to conversion they "walked" (*peporeumenous*, go, journey) in "lasciviousness" (*aselgeiais*, shocking indecency, unbridled lustful indulgence, as in 2 Peter 2:7), "lusts" (*epithumiais*, strong desire, craving), "excess of wine" (*oinophlugiais*, winebibbing, drunkenness), "revelings" (*kōmois*, rioting, wild parties), "banquetings" (*potois*, carousal, drinking bout), "abominable idolatries" (*athemitois*

*eidōlolatreiais*, lawless, wanton acts that were part of the lewd orgies connected with pagan image-worship). There is no allowance here for Christians to "exercise personal liberty" to drink and carouse. Peter described the lewd idolatries as *athemitois* (abominable, unlawful), the same word he used in Acts 10:28 to describe a Jew's association with a non-Jew. In that case he was referring to Mosaic law, but here he may have been referring to Roman law also, for this lewd behavior was so abhorrent it was forbidden by Roman law as well as God's law.

**4. Wherein they think it strange that ye run not with [them]:**... people are astonished at your not running, *—TCNT*... they deem it extraordinary, *—WADE*... thinking it strange of you not to race together, *—CNDT.*
**to the same excess of riot:**... indulge in the same wild orgies, *—NORL*... same sink of corruption, *—DRBY*... same loose living and excess, *—WMCK*... the same puddle of profligacy, *—CNDT.*
**speaking evil of [you]:**... say terrible things, *—SEB*... abuse you, *—WLMS, —WMCK*... calumniating, *—CNDT.*

**4:4.** When believers refuse to take part in the world's pleasures, their unsaved neighbors think it "strange" (*xenizontai*, unfamiliar, foreign). They are astonished because the believers do not "run" with them (*suntrechontōn*, go along with the crowd) to the same "excess" (*anachusin*, effusion, overflowing) of "riot" (*asōtias*, profligacy, abandonment; as in Luke 15:13 where the prodigal's dissolute life is called "riotous living"). "Speaking evil" (*blasphēmountes*, defame, slander) is a strong word; it is used in Luke 22:65 of the treatment Christ endured. Believers are misunderstood and slandered.

**5. Who shall give account to him that is ready to judge the quick and the dead:**... rendering an account to Him Who is holding himself in readiness to judge the living, *—CNDT.*

**4:5.** But Peter said unbelievers will have to give account one day to God who is "ready" (*hetoimōs*, holding himself in readiness) to "judge" (*krinai*, call in question, decide, sentence) every human being whether presently "quick" (*zōntas*, living) or "dead" (*nekrous*, deceased, as in 2 Timothy 4:1, "Who shall judge the quick and the dead"). Peter at Cornelius' house said Christ was ordained "to be the Judge of quick and dead" (Acts 10:42), although in 1 Peter 1:17 he seems to say God the Father will be Judge. The apparent contradiction may be explained by the close association between the Father and the Son, as Christ points out in John 5:19-23.

**6. For for this cause was the gospel preached also to them that are dead:** ... for this purpose, —WUST ... this an evangel is brought to the dead, —CNDT.

**that they might be judged according to men in the flesh:** ... while judged with men physically, —BRKL ... with respect to their physical existence, —WUST.

**but live according to God in the spirit:** ... they might live with God spiritually, —BRKL ... with respect to their spirit existence, —WUST.

**4:6.** The inevitability of judgment is not only an incentive to holy living but also an important reason for preaching the gospel. Peter said the gospel was preached to persons now "dead" (*nekrois*, deceased) so that, although ungodly men may have condemned them for their godly way of life, they have received spiritual life from God. All through the epistle Peter was contrasting two classes and telling how the godly should react when persecuted by the ungodly. In 4:14 he contrasted the two classes, believers and unbelievers. In 4:17,18 he contrasted the fate of the one class with that of the other. Here in 4:6 he contrasted being judged by men and being judged by God.

Various interpretations of this verse have been offered. Scholars from Augustine to Luther have said "dead" should be taken spiritually (as in Ephesians 2:1, "dead in trespasses and sins"); but Peter had just used the term literally in the previous sentence. Other scholars suggest some of those to whom Peter was writing may have been concerned over the fate of believers who had died (see 1 Thessalonians 4:15-17) since he said the dead will be judged. Peter reassured them that the deceased will be judged on the same basis as "men in the flesh" (those still living) because the gospel was preached to them while they lived.

**7. But the end of all things is at hand:** ... Now the consummation of all, —CNDT ... the completion of all, —FNTN ... has approached, —WLSN ... has drawn near, —WADE.

**be ye therefore sober, and watch unto prayer:** ... Therefore exercise self-restraint, —TCNT ... Be self-controlled, —WMCK ... Be sane, then, and sober for prayers, —CNDT ... Be of sound mind therefore, and be calm and collected in spirit, —WUST ... be wise-minded, and wide awake about prayers, —SWAN.

**4:7.** Peter said the "end" (*telos*, culmination) of all things "is at hand" (*ēngiken*, approaching, drawing near). The same word is used in Matthew 3:2 by John and in James 5:8. How near the "end" Peter did not say, but he urged readiness. Believers need to be "sober" (*sōphronēsate*, sane, sound of mind) and "watch" (*nēpsate*, be watchful,

discreet) unto "prayers" (*proseuchas*, earnest petitions; the word is plural).

**8. And above all things have fervent charity among yourselves:** ... before all things in order of importance, —WUST ... love each other extensively, —ADAM ... having earnest love among yourselves, —CNDT ... cherish intense love for one another, —BRKL.

**for charity shall cover the multitude of sins:** ... for love veils, —MNTG ... throws a veil over, —WADE ... love makes up for a great many faults, —NORL ... hides an uncounted number of sins, —WMCK ... a mass of sins, —BRKL.

**4:8.** Readiness for the end calls for constant communion with God through prayers, but also for loving relationships with fellow believers. Above all else, the believers should have "charity" (*agapē*, self-giving love) one toward another, and this Christlike love should be "fervent" (*ektenē*, intense, stretched out). They should extend their love especially toward believers who offend. This forgiving love will cause believers to "cover" (*kalupsei*, conceal, hide) other people's sins rather than expose them.

**9. Use hospitality one to another without grudging:** ... Be hospitable, —CNDT ... welcome one another to your homes without grumbling, —WMCK ... without complaint, —NORL ... complaining about it, —SEB ... without murmuring, —WUST.

**4:9.** Peter said believers should extend this same love to travelers and other believers who need food and shelter. They should show "hospitality" (*philoxenoi*, kindness to visitors) and do it without "grudging" (*gongusmōn*, grumbling, murmuring).

**10. As every man hath received the gift:** ... according as he obtained a gracious gift, —CNDT ... In whatever quality or quantity each one has received a gift, —WUST.

**[even so] minister the same one to another:** ... Let each one serve the group, —BRKL ... dispensing faithfully, —TCNT ... among yourselves, —CNDT.

**as good stewards of the manifold grace of God:** ... like a good manager, —SEB ... ideal administrators of the varied grace, —CNDT ... God's many mercies, —NORL ... many-sided grace, —WMCK

**4:10.** "Every man" (*hekastos*, every one, male or female) has received a "gift" (*charisma*, favor, spiritual endowment). Paul wrote in Romans 12:8 of gifts of giving, of ruling, and of showing mercy which should be exercised cheerfully (without grudging, as Peter said in verse 9). Showing hospitality may be construed as the gift of doing deeds of mercy and kindness. But all believers have not the same gift. As Paul stated in 1 Corinthians 7:7, "Every man hath his proper gift of God, one after this manner, and another after that." Whatever gift one has, he should "minister" it (*diakonountes*, serve) to fellow believers, not neglecting it through carelessness or selfishness, but sharing it for the benefit of others. As good "stewards" (*oikonomoi*, overseer, manager) believers should faithfully dispense God's "grace" (*charitos*, favor, liberality) which is "manifold" (*poikilēs*, diverse) and therefore fits all situations. Whatever we have received we are responsible to use for God's glory.

11. **If any man speak, [let him speak] as the oracles of God:** . . . If a man preaches, *—NLTG*. . . . If speaking, let it be as God's suggestions, *—BRKL*. . . let it be with the power which God has bestowed, *—FNTN*. . . one who utters God's truth, *—MNTG*.

**if any man minister, [let him do it] as of the ability which God giveth:** . . . If a man helps others, *—NLTG* . . . If serving, let it be with the strength, *—BRKL* . . . dispensing, as out of the strength which God is furnishing, *—CNDT* . . . let him do so in reliance on the power which God supplies, *—TCNT*.

**that God in all things may be glorified through Jesus Christ:**

**to whom be praise and dominion for ever and ever. Amen:** . . . belong Glory and Sovereignth, *—WADE* . . . glory and the might for the eons of the eons, *—CNDT*.

**4:11.** The two kinds of gifts mentioned by Peter correspond to the twofold division of service in Acts 6:2-4. One is the speaking kind, the other a less public kind. If a person's gift is to "speak" (*lalei*, talk, preach, give utterance), he should speak as the "oracles" (*logia*, divine utterance, revelation) of God. That is, if he has a speaking gift such as tongues, interpretation, prophecy, the word of wisdom, the word of knowledge, teaching, exhorting, or preaching, he should speak in harmony with God's Word and depend on the Holy Spirit to inspire and guide. If a person's gift is to "minister" (*diakonei*, serve, as in Acts 6:2, "serve tables"), he should do it according to the "ability" (*ischuos*, strength, power) which God gives him. The purpose in all things is that God may be "glorified" (*doxazētai*, honor, magnify, render glorious). "Praise" (*doxa*, honor, worship) and "dominion" (*kratos*, vigor, power, strength) are ascribed to Christ (as in 2 Peter 3:18) for ever and ever. "Amen" (verily, so be it).

12. **Beloved, think it not strange:** . . . Dear friends, *—TCNT* . . . Divinely loved ones . . . stop thinking, *—WUST* . . . Do not be surprised, *—NLTG* . . . astonished, *—FNTN* . . . wonder not, *—CMPB*.

**concerning the fiery trial which is to try you:** . . . because of the fierce struggle you're in, *—SEB* . . . conflagration . . . which is becoming a trial, *—CNDT* . . . test by fire is coming upon you, *—WLMS* . . . smelting process . . . which has come to you

for the purpose of testing, *—WUST* . . . being applied to you, *—BRKL*.

**as though some strange thing happened unto you:** . . . an unexpected affair had surprised you, *—FNTN* . . . as if you were experiencing something odd, *—BRKL* . . . unexpected misfortune were befalling you, *—NOLI* . . . a thing alien to you, *—WUST*.

**4:12.** Returning to the subject of suffering for righteousness' sake, Peter said believers should not be surprised or think it "strange" (*xenizesthe*, alien, foreign) that they are undergoing a "fiery trial" (*purōsei*, ordeal; literally, a burning, but the word is used here to refer to a smelting furnace by which gold and silver are purified). He said the purpose of the "fiery trial" (persecution) is to "try" them (*peirasmon*, prove, tempt; as in 2 Peter 2:9, "The Lord knoweth how to deliver the godly out of temptation"). What is happening to them is nothing "strange" (*xenou*, alien, foreign). Christ did not promise His servants a life of ease or immunity from suffering. If the world persecuted Him, it will persecute His followers (John 15:20). But there may be comfort in the salutation "Beloved." It is *agapētoi*, the Greek word which speaks of God's self-giving and infinite love. It may be translated "divinely loved ones," a title that would remind the persecuted believers that they are dear to the heart of God.

13. **But rejoice, inasmuch as ye are partakers of Christ's sufferings:** . . . You should be glad, because it means that you are called to share, *—PHLP* . . . insofar as you share in common with, *—WUST* . . . be cheerful for sharing to some degree, *—BRKL* . . . you are participating, *—CNDT*.

**that, when his glory shall be revealed:** . . . the unveiling of His glory, *—CNDT* . . . when he shows himself in full splendor to men, *—PHLP*.

**ye may be glad also with exceeding joy:** . . . you may rejoice exultingly, *—WLSN* . . . rejoice triumphantly, *—WLMS* . . . rejoice, that you may be rejoicing, *—CNDT* . . . you may be thrilled with, *—WADE* . . . the most tremendous joy, *—PHLP* . . . with triumphant gladness, *—MNTG* . . . triumphantly cheerful, *—BRKL*.

**4:13.** Instead of thinking it a thing alien to them, the believers should expect persecution and should even "rejoice" (*chairete*, be glad, shout for joy; as in Luke 6:23, "Rejoice ye in that day, and leap for joy"). Insofar as the persecution is for the gospel's sake, they can find joy because they are "partakers" (*koinōneite*, share as partners) in Christ's sufferings. No matter how great their sufferings may be, they can look forward to the time of Christ's coming when His glory shall be revealed. At that time they will be glad "with exceeding joy," for since they are suffering with Him in this life, they will reign with Him in the life to come (2 Timothy 2:12). Peter wanted the believers to realize it is an honor to be fellow sufferers with Christ. He had not forgotten the day when he and the other apostles "departed from the presence of the council, rejoicing that they were counted worthy to suffer shame for his (Christ's) name" (Acts 5:41). Living with eternity in view will help us endure hardship.

**14. If ye be reproached for the name of Christ:**... If men speak bad of you, —NLTG... If someone insults you, —SEB... you are defamed, —BRKL... you have cast in your teeth, as it were, —WUST... for being Christ's followers, —PHLP.

**happy [are ye]:**... you are blessed, —MNTG... spiritually prosperous, —WUST... that is a great privilege, —PHLP.

**for the spirit of glory and of God resteth upon you:**... and power... has come to rest, —CNDT... is resting with refreshing power upon you, —WUST.

**on their part he is evil spoken of, but on your part he is glorified:**

**4:14.** "If" does not indicate a hypothetical case. The believers were indeed being "reproached" (*oneidizesthe*, defame, taunt, revile) for the name of Christ; therefore Peter said they were "happy" (*makarioi*, supremely blessed) "for the Spirit of glory and of God" (the Holy Spirit) "resteth" upon them (*anapauetai*, take ease, refresh). A special anointing or refreshing seems to rest upon those who are bearing reproach or suffering for Christ. This has been evident in the deaths of Stephen (Acts 7:55-60) and other martyrs. The Spirit rested on Christ in a special way (see Isaiah 11:2 which Peter quoted here). Peter added, "On their part he is evil spoken of, but on your part he is glorified." There will always be foes of the Christian faith, but we have a special opportunity. Jesus died for our salvation, now we can live in such a way as to bring glory to Him.

**15. But let none of you suffer as a murderer, or [as] a thief:**... none of your number, —PHLP... should have to be punished, —NORL.

**or [as] an evildoer, or as a busybody in other men's matters:**... or a poisoner, —WADE... as a profligate, or as a libeller, —FNTN... or a criminal or a meddler, —BRKL... or a troublemaker, —NORL... as a spy upon other people's business, —MNTG... or as a Meddling person, —WLSN... as a self-appointed overseer in other men's matters, —WUST... an interferer in other's affairs, —CNDT.

**4:15.** Whatever reproach a believer may suffer, it should result from serving Christ and not from doing wrong. Peter mentioned two specific crimes, murder and thievery, and adds the general classification "evildoer" (*kakopoios*, criminal, malefactor; the same word as in 2:12,14). After the lofty descriptions he had given of the believers' spiritual situation, it may seem incongruous

to warn them against such wickedness, but Peter realized they were still human and capable of lapsing back into the flesh, especially since they lived in an extremely immoral society. He also admonished against being "a busybody in other men's matters" (*allotrioepiskopos*, a word not used elsewhere, meaning meddler, one who spies out the affairs of other men). In view of the pressures of persecution, this may be a prohibition against spying or informing on others, something Jesus said some people would do (Matthew 10:21).

**16. Yet if [any man suffer] as a Christian, let him not be ashamed:**

**but let him glorify God on this behalf:**... let him give honor, —NORL... for bearing this name, —WLMS.

**4:16.** The term "Christian" is used in only two other New Testament verses (Acts 11:26; 26:28). It was originally a term given by Gentiles at Antioch; the Jews, who would not acknowledge Jesus to be the Christ (Messiah), would certainly not want to give recognition to that title. By the time this epistle was written, the name *Christian* had become one of reproach and generally used to describe Jesus' followers. The name exposed believers to shame, though systematic persecution had not yet developed. If a man suffers reproach as a Christian, he should not be "ashamed" (*aischunesthō*, feel disgraced) but should thank God for the privilege. Peter had once been ashamed and had denied his Lord (Mark 14:68), but now he had been converted into a man who could strengthen these believers (Luke 22:32).

**17. For the time [is come] that judgment must begin at the house of God:**... for punishment to begin, —TCNT... for judging starts with God's family, —SEB.

**and if [it] first [begin] at us, what shall the end [be] of them that obey not the gospel of God?:**... and if it starts with us, —WADE... who refuse to accept, —NOLI... who will not accept God's Good News? —NORL... who disobey God's good news? —ADAM... who are disobedient to the glad tidings of God? —WLSN... who are rejecting God's good news? —WLMS.

**4:17.** Peter evidently was referring to Ezekiel 9:6 where the Lord, in calling for judgment against the evildoers in Jerusalem, said, "And begin at my sanctuary." He said the time had come that "judgment" (*krima*, condemnation, sentencing) should begin at the "house of God," meaning no doubt God's "spiritual house" described in 2:5. Since he realized the coming judgment would be by fire (2 Peter 3:7), he may have been thinking of the believers' "fiery trial" as the beginning of the judgment; and if it "begin" at God's house, what shall be the "end" (*telos*, termination, final destination) of those who reject the gospel!

**18. And if the righteous scarcely be saved:**...with difficulty escape, *—CMPB.*

**where shall the ungodly and the sinner appear?:**... where will the irreverent, *—SWAN.*

**4:18.** Verse 18 is quoted from the Greek (Septuagint) version of Proverbs 11:31. Peter said it is only "scarcely" (*molis*, with difficulty) that the "righteous" (*dikaios*, just, holy, innocent) are "saved" (*sōzetai*, rescue, preserve) in the time of judgment. Since this is so, the fate of the "ungodly" (*asebēs*, irreverent, wicked) and the "sinner" (*hamartōlos*, transgressor) will be dire indeed. The Lord chastens those He loves in order to correct them (Proverbs 3:11,12). If the saved need correction, how much more will the unsaved merit the wrath of God whom they spurned!

**19. Wherefore let them that suffer according to the will of God:**

**commit the keeping of their souls [to him] in well doing, as unto a faithful Creator:**...confide their souls to a Reliable Builder, *—FNTN.*

**4:19.** Those who are experiencing the "fiery trial" are urged to "commit" (*paratithesthōsan*, put forth, consign) the keeping of their "souls" (*psuchas*, life, heart, mind) to God. The verb form denotes a continuous committing. The Greeks used this word in banking; it means to make a deposit. Peter urged the believers to place their lives in God's safe keeping. Their suffering is "according to the will of God" who has allowed it in order to purify their lives. Therefore they can commit themselves to Him with confidence, knowing He who created them will be faithful to fulfill His plan for their lives through all their ordeals.

## Chapter 5

**1. The elders which are among you I exhort:**...to those among you who are pastors, *—NORL.*

**who am also an elder, and a witness of the sufferings of Christ:** .... one who actually saw, *—TNT*...of the Passion of Christ, *—NOLI.*

**and also a partaker of the glory that shall be revealed:**...that is to be uncovered, *—WLMS.*

**5:1.** Peter concluded his epistle with solemn exhortations, first to church leaders, then to the general membership. He addressed the "elders" (*presbuterous*, presbyter, senior officer) saying he too was an "elder" (*sumpresbuteros*, copresbyter). He did not call himself pope, nor did he dictate. He identified himself with the local leaders and simply exhorted them (*parakalō*, entreat, beseech). An elder was a pastor or chief administrator in a

local assembly. Some evidently were teachers, and others simply saw that teaching was done (1 Timothy 5:17). The terms *elder, presbyter,* and *bishop* were used interchangeably in the Early Church.

Peter was a "witness" (*martus*, martyr, one called to bear witness) for Christ. The word refers not to the act of seeing but the act of testifying to what has been seen, as in Acts 1:8. (In 2 Peter 1:16, where he called himself an eyewitness, the apostle used a different Greek word.) Furthermore, he said he was a "partaker" (*koinōnos*, sharer, partner) of Christ's glory, referring probably to the Transfiguration (Matthew 17:1-9); but he indicated the "glory" (*doxēs*, radiant splendor, honor) was yet to be "revealed" (*apokaluptesthai*, uncover, disclose) so all believers would have the privilege of partaking as he did.

**2. Feed the flock of God which is among you:**... Be shepherds to, *—MNTG*... tend the flock, *—WLSN*...that is committed to your charge, *—WADE.*

**taking the oversight [thereof], not by constraint, but willingly:**... not through compulsion, *—MNTG*... not out of obligation, *—ADAM*... but voluntarily, *—WLSN*... by their own free will, *—NOLI.*

**not for filthy lucre, but of a ready mind:**...not out of eagerness to make a personal profit, but out of eagerness to serve, *—ADAM*...but of your own free will, *—TCNT, —WMCK*...but for the love of the cause, *—NORL*...but enthusiastically, *—SWAN*...but in a spirit of enthusiasm, *—WADE*... but because your heart is in it, *—TNT.*

**5:2.** Peter exhorted the elders to shepherd the believers. Probably he remembered when Christ said to him, "Feed my sheep" (John 21:17). "Feed" (*poimanate*, supervise, tend as a shepherd) includes the duties of guiding and guarding, as well as feeding. The "flock" (*poimnion*, group of sheep) is God's, not theirs. "Taking the oversight thereof" (*episkopountes*, care for, oversee, watch diligently; as in Hebrews 12:15, "Looking diligently lest any man fail"), they are to do it "willingly" (*hekousiōs*, voluntarily, with good will) and not for the sake of "filthy lucre" (*aischrokerdōs*, greedy or dishonest gain). "Lucre" itself is a good word meaning gain, profit, reward. It is not "filthy" unless the gain is ill-gotten. The motive of ministry should be a loving concern for people.

**3. Neither as being lords over [God's] heritage:**... Do not domineer, *—TNT*...not as domineering over the charge entrusted to you, *—FNTN*...not as masters of those in your keeping, *—WMCK*

**but being ensamples to the flock:**... but being Patterns, *—WLSN* ... proving yourselves models for the flock to imitate, *—WLMS.*

**5:3.** Elders should not be autocrats, ruling in highhanded fashion. The "heritage" (*klērōn*, allotment, portion, inheritance) they have been called to serve is God's. He has an inheritance (*klēronomias*) in His saints (Ephesians 1:18), and He expects the elders to care for them as faithful overseers. Peter said they should continually be "ensamples" (*tupoi*, type, pattern, model, example; as in 1 Timothy 4:12, "Be thou an example of the believers"). As undershepherds the elders should be living models or patterns of Jesus, the Chief Shepherd (5:4).

**4. And when the chief Shepherd shall appear:**... is manifested, *—CNDT.*
**ye shall receive a crown of glory that fadeth not away:**... you will win no fading wreath, *—TCNT*... you shall be requited with an unfading wreath of glory, *—CNDT*... crown of victory, *—TNT.*

**5:4.** Peter spoke of Christ, the "chief Shepherd," in a way that recognized the elders as undershepherds. When He shall "appear" (*phanerōthentos*, be made manifest) at His second coming, the Chief Shepherd will reward His faithful undershepherds with a crown, like the Greeks who bestowed crowns on victorious athletes or military heroes. However, the Greeks had crowns made of oak or ivy leaves which would fade, whereas the elders will receive a crown of "glory" (*doxēs*, honor, radiant splendor) that "fadeth not away" (*amarantinon*, fadeless like the *amaranth*, a flower that would not wither quickly like other flowers). The amaranth would revive if moistened with water, so it became a symbol of immortality.

**5. Likewise, ye younger, submit yourselves unto the elder:**... In the same way, *—NLTG*... you younger communicants, must obey the presbyters, *—NOLI*... may be subject, *—CNDT*... be in subjection to the elders, *—WUST*... accept the authority, *—TNT.*
**Yea, all [of you] be subject one to another, and be clothed with humility:**... all wear the servile apron of humility with one another, *—CNDT.*
**for God resisteth the proud:**... is against those, *—SEB*... opposes the proud, *—NORL*... is opposed to the Haughty, *—WLSN*... resists the arrogant, *—WADE*... opposes himself to those who set themselves above others, *—WUST.*
**and giveth grace to the humble:**... to those who are lowly, *—WUST.*

**5:5.** Proverbs 3:34 states God "giveth grace unto the lowly." Peter said He shows His favor to the "humble" (*tapeinois*, of low degree, lowly in heart; as in Matthew 11:29, "I am meek and lowly in heart"). On the other hand, God "scorneth the scorners" (Proverbs 3:34). He scorns the "proud" (*huperēphanois*, self-exalting) and "resisteth" them (*antitassetai*, oppose). This is a military term used of an army drawn up for battle. It means God's armies are set in opposition

to persons who are proud; so it is in the interest of young and old alike that all believers should be "clothed with" humility (*enkombōsasthe*, gird oneself). The apron worn by servants was called *enkombōma*. Peter may have been thinking of the time Jesus girded himself with a towel to teach the disciples a lesson in humility (John 13:4). If the younger believers are humble they will "submit" (*hupotagēte*, be subject, be under obedience) to the older believers. In fact, all should be subject one to another, all esteeming others better than themselves, and all looking for ways they can serve others rather than for ways others can serve them.

**6. Humble yourselves therefore under the mighty hand of God:**... Be humbled, *—CNDT*... Permit yourselves therefore to be humbled, *—WUST*... the powerful hand, *—FNTN.*
**that he may exalt you in due time:**... He should be exalting you in season, *—CNDT*... when His time comes, *—NORL*... in an appropriate season, *—WUST.*

**5:6.** The Greek for "humble yourselves" (*tapeinōthēte*) is passive ("be ye humbled") and indicates they should permit God to humble them. The process He is using to humble them is persecution, and Peter exhorted them to accept it willingly without resentment or rebellion. They are safe in putting themselves under the mighty hand of God, for He is abundantly able to "exalt" (*hupsōsē*, lift up, elevate) them in "due time" (*kairō*, due season, as in Matthew 24:45, "to give them meat in due season"). Humility is not a loss but a gain, for it puts the believer in God's favor and saves him from pride that would destroy him and rob him of future glory.

**7. Casting all your care upon him:**... tossing your entire worry, *—CNDT*... having cast all, *—WLSN*... having deposited with Him, *—WUST*... Throw all your anxieties upon him, *—TCNT*... Throw all your worries onto, *—SEB*... Cast every worry you have, *—WLMS*... all your anxious care on him, *—CMPB.*
**for he careth for you:**... for he makes you his care, *—TCNT*... He is caring concerning you, *—CNDT*... to Him it is a matter of concern respecting you, *—WUST.*

**5:7.** Pride makes one self-sufficient, whereas humility is a recognition of one's dependence on God. The believers can show their humility by "casting" (*epirrhipsantes*, throw upon, commit) all their "care" (*merimnan*, concern, anxiety) upon the Lord. Persecution and cares would tempt them to worry, but they have a Good Shepherd who "careth" (*melei*, is concerned) for them.

**8. Be sober, be vigilant:** .... Be temperate, —MNTG ... Be level-headed, —ADAM ... of a sober mind, be watchful, —WUST.

**because your adversary the devil, as a roaring lion, walketh about:** ... your plaintiff, —CNDT ... is working against you, —NLTG ... always prowling, —WLMS.

**seeking whom he may devour:** .... looking for someone to swallow up, —WMCK ... as his prey, —NORL ... to devour you, —WADE.

**5:8.** The believer who is too proud to feel his utter dependence on God is in grave peril, so Peter admonished everyone to be "sober" (nēpsate, watchful, mentally calm) and "vigilant" (grēgorē-sate, alert, awake). An enemy is seeking after them to "devour" them (katapiē, swallow), and one of his most effective weapons is pride. Jesus warned Peter against this enemy when He said, "Satan hath desired to have you" (Luke 22:31). Another name for this enemy is the "devil" (diabolos, false accuser, slanderer). Peter called him an "adversary" (antidikos, opponent in a lawsuit, as in Matthew 5:25). Satan is the great enemy of all the righteous and holy. He is a deceiver and varies his approach, coming sometimes as an "angel of light" (2 Corinthians 11:14) and sometimes as a "roaring lion" (the Greek describes the howl of a wild beast in fierce hunger). When a lion "walketh about" it is time for caution at the sheepfold. The lion's roar creates fear, and a frightened sheep may bolt from the flock to become easy prey. Therefore the shepherd and the sheep need to be on guard. Each sheep needs to stay with the flock and keep close to the shepherd for safety. A sheep is no match for a lion, and we are no match for the devil. But just as David protected his sheep, Jesus will come to the rescue of His people.

**9. Whom resist stedfast in the faith:** ... Stand firm against, —TCNT ... stand up to him, —TNT ... withstand, solid in the faith, —CNDT.

**knowing that the same afflictions are accomplished in your brethren that are in the world:** ... having perceived the same sufferings being completed in your brotherhood, —CNDT ... experiencing the same sort of sufferings, —WLMS.

**5:9.** A cowardly shepherd may flee when the lion roars, but a courageous one will "resist" (antistēte, withstand, as in James 4:7, "Resist the devil, and he will flee from you"). The believer can ward off Satan's attacks if he remains "steadfast" in his faith in God. The Greek stereoi, translated "steadfast," means firm, strong, sure, as in 2 Timothy 2:19, "The foundation of God standeth sure." The word was used of a Greek army unit or phalanx presenting a solid front; the soldiers stood in ranks and files that were close and deep, forming a strong defense against the weapons of their day. Peter reminded the believers their fellow Christians in other parts of the world were undergoing as much suffering as they. This would not make their pain any less, but it should keep them from dissipating their strength through self-pity.

**10. But the God of all grace:** ... from whom all help comes, —TCNT.

**who hath called us unto his eternal glory by Christ Jesus:** ... His eonian glory, —CNDT.

**after that ye have suffered a while, make you perfect:** ... by briefly suffering, He will be adjusting, —CNDT ... restore you, —TNT.

**stablish, strengthen, settle [you]:** ... make you firm, —TNT ... founding you, —CNDT.

**5:10.** Believers can find comfort in knowing the "God of all grace" is with them. His grace is "manifold" (4:10) or variegated. God has called them to salvation, and this is "unto" (with a view to) His eternal glory. First they must suffer "a while" (oligon, brief period, "a season," as in 1:6), but this will develop their spiritual lives. Peter foretold that through their present suffering God would make them "perfect" (katartisai, adjust, putting parts into right relationship and connection, fit together; as in 1 Corinthians 1:10, "That there be no divisions among you; but that ye be perfectly joined together"). He said God would establish them in unity, He would confirm them in spiritual power, and He would put them on a firm foundation.

**11. To him [be] glory and dominion for ever and ever. Amen:** .... Power belongs to Him, —SEB ... might for the eons of the eons, —CNDT ... through endless ages! —NORL.

**5:11.** Peter burst into an exclamation of praise as he contemplated the perfection of God's plan for His people. This doxology is similar to that given to the Son in 4:11.

**12. By Silvanus, a faithful brother unto you, as I suppose:** ... with the help of, —TNT ... I respect very much, —SEB ... I reckon him, —TCNT ... as I regard him, —WLMS.

**I have written briefly, exhorting, and testifying:** ... entreating and deposing, —CNDT.

**that this is the true grace of God wherein ye stand:** ... Hold on to it, —NORL ... unmerited favor, —WLMS.

**5:12.** Since we read of only one Silvanus in the Early Church, we may conclude this is the same man who assisted Paul in his missionary travels. In Acts he is called Silas. Due to his prominence among the church leaders in Jerusalem, he was chosen for the important mission to Antioch (Acts 15:22). Silvanus was well acquainted with

**1115**

the churches in Asia Minor to whom Peter was writing, for he helped to establish them; and he was a "faithful brother" to them, "as I suppose," Peter said. This is not conjecture on Peter's part; it is a positive appraisal, for the Greek (*logizomai*) means impute, reckon—not imagine or guess.

Peter had written "briefly"—that is, the epistle is comparatively short, and he was sending it by Silvanus. Possibly it was through Silvanus he had learned about the difficulties these churches were then experiencing, causing him to see the need of "exhorting" them (*parakalōn*, beseech, intreat) and "testifying" (*epimarturōn*, corroborate, attest further) that what they had been taught is "the true grace of God." He admonished them to "stand" in this grace (*histemi*, continue, abide, take a stand; as in Ephesians 6:11, "Stand against the wiles of the devil").

**13. The [church that is] at Babylon, elected together with [you], saluteth you:** ... sends you greetings, –SEB.
**and [so doth] Marcus my son:**

**5:13.** What is the city called Babylon here? Some believe Peter was speaking symbolically of Rome. There are many testimonies from the early centuries of the Christian Era to the effect Peter visited Rome and was crucified there. St. Peter's basilica stands above the apostle's supposed burial spot. Our Roman Catholic friends especially hold to this view.

Other scholars, however, believe Peter was writing from Babylon on the Euphrates. Though reduced from its former greatness, the city still had a large population in Peter's day, including many Jews.

Since Peter was the apostle to the Jews, it is understandable that he should have journeyed to that city to preach Christ to them. He said this church at Babylon was "elected together with"

them (*suneklektē*, chosen in company with, coelect in Christ) and "saluteth" them (*aspazetai*, greet). And so did "Mark my son," meaning John Mark, his son in the gospel. Early Christian writers state that after leaving his uncle Barnabas, Mark became helper to Peter under whose influence Mark wrote his Gospel.

**14. Greet ye one another with a kiss of charity:** ... Embrace one another, –FNTN ... with an affectionate kiss, –ADAM ... a loving kiss, –SEB ... kiss of love, –CNDT.
**Peace [be] with you all that are in Christ Jesus. Amen:** ... Peace be to all true Christians, –PHLP ... Every blessing be on you all who belong to Christ, –BRCL ... Grace be to you all, –CNFT ... to all of you, –EVRD ... are in union with, –TCNT, –WADE, –GDSP ... Peace to all those in Christ, –KLGS ... Happiness be to all among you who are steadfast in the belief and profession of the gospel, –MKNT ... who are in the Messiah, –MRDK ... may there be peace—every kind of peace (blessing), especially peace with God, and freedom from fears, agitating passions and moral conflicts. Amen—so be it, –AMPB.

**5:14.** Peter's admonition here is almost identical with Paul's comments in 1 Corinthians 16:20; 2 Corinthians 13:12; Romans 16:16. It was customary in the Early Church, after prayers, for the believers to welcome one another with a holy kiss. However, the custom gave rise to problems; as indicated by Clement of Alexandria, who said, "Love is judged not in a kiss but in good will. Some do nothing but fill the church with noise of kissing. There is another—an impure—kiss full of venom pretending to holiness." So the practice became regulated: men kissed only men, and women kissed only women, and the custom gradually dwindled, though it is still found in some Eastern and European churches. The benediction is peace to all who are committed to Christ Jesus and trusting in Him. "Amen" (verily, so be it).

# 2 PETER

## Overview

Simon Peter introduced himself as "a servant and apostle of Jesus Christ." He addressed the letter to "them that have obtained like precious faith with us"—i.e., a faith equally precious. This unique form emphasized that the faith of the recipients, which had come to them through the hearing of the gospel, was no less precious than the faith of those who had been eyewitnesses of Christ and His ministry (cf. John 20:29). Gentiles who were accepting Christ were in no way deficient or inferior to Jewish believers.

The author referred to an earlier letter (3:1). The most obvious and natural understanding of this is that it refers to 1 Peter. If so, it means that the recipients were a group of churches in Asia Minor. The apostle Peter's death was rapidly approaching (1:14). Perhaps he was already in prison. Based on this, it is reasonable to assume the letter was written in the midsixties, shortly before Peter was martyred. Second Peter 3:15,16 suggests the apostle Paul was still alive; this also supports an early dating of the letter.

No mention is made of the geographic origin of the letter. The "Babylon" of 1 Peter 5:13 probably applies to the second letter as well (see *Overview* for 1 Peter). If this is the case, not much time elapsed between the writing of the two letters.

## Canonicity

The authenticity of 1 Peter is among the best attested in the New Testament. It was accepted by the Early Church without any doubt. Second Peter, however, belongs to a group of writings which were disputed for a long time before they were included in the holy canon. Initially, it seems as if the letter was not widely known. It is difficult to determine where it first appeared. There are some indications it was known by 1 and 2 Clement (ca. A.D. 95), Aristedes, Valentinus, Hippolytus, Irenaeus, Justin Martyr, Barnabas, Polycarp, and Hermas. While these are uncertain allusions, the letter was cited as Holy Writ by Theophilus of Antioch who died in 183. Origen, around the year 240, first attributed the letter to Peter although he mentioned it was disputed by others. However, long before Origen, it was used in Egypt since it was included in the Sahidic version.

It is also significant that both 1 and 2 Peter appear in the Bodmer papyrus designated p72, dated sometime around A.D. 200. It is among the oldest uncials (a manuscript written in cap-ital letters) in

existence. It should also be pointed put that p72 includes only portions of 1 and 2 Peter and Jude. No other New Testament book is part of this manuscript. In light of its inclusion in p72, it is probable that it was read in some churches in certain regions of the world. This agrees with what church historian Eusebius wrote concerning Clement of Alexandria (died ca. 220) including 2 Peter in his Bible. This represents the ancient Egyptian tradition. A few Old Latin manuscripts dating from the 6th to the 11th centuries include parts of 2 Peter.

The external witnesses to the letter are thus not as weak as is sometimes asserted. Some suggest that on the basis of external testimony alone one would be compelled to accept the book as highly valued by early writers.

In the years immediately preceding the canonization of Scripture there was a wide acceptance of the epistle, e.g., Cyril of Jerusalem, Athanasius, Augustine, etc. Jerome included the letter in his Vulgate version. The epistle was also accepted as canon by the church councils at Laodicia (366), Hippo (393), and by the two councils at Carthage (397 and 419). As a result of the decisions of the last councils the Western Church accepted the same canon as had Athanasius in 367.

Not everyone is fully aware of how seriously the Early Church viewed the difficult task of determining the canon of the New Testament. Their intense and persistent debates only indicated their thoughtful concern. Acceptance by an ecclesiastical council did not in any way "make" a book Holy Scripture. The councils' decisions only acknowledged the immanence of the document, its apostolic origin, and its place in the Church. The process of canonization was final and irreversible. No one in a later era of church history would have the knowledge or sources available to the Early Church. The body of sacred writings accepted by the Early Church as canon was passed on to later generations as Holy Scripture.

## Questions Concerning Authorship

The following is a survey of recent objections to the authenticity of 2 Peter as well as the responses to these arguments. The issues can be divided into five main groups.

### (1) the Self-Testimony of the Author

The letter itself claims to be written by Simon Peter, the apostle of Christ (1:1). The author testified that he had been an eyewitness of Christ's majesty and that he had seen His glory on the "holy mount" (2 Peter 1:16-19; cf. Matthew 17:1f.). He reminded his readers that Jesus had told him ahead of time that he would die within a short time (2 Peter 1:14; cf. John 21:18). He also referred to a previous letter addressed to his readers (2 Peter 3:1; cf. 1 Peter 1:1). All of this seems to confirm the authenticity of the epistle. However, some seem to use such information as an argument against the genuineness of the letter. They accuse the author of being a pseudepigrapher who intentionally introduced these facts into the text in order to give it the appearance of Petrine authorship.

One thing is clear: The only alternative to being genuine is being false. Either the book was written by the apostle of Christ, or it was written by someone claiming to be him. Such a pretense was a literary form that was common in antiquity. In late Judaism numerous works were ascribed to individuals who could not have possibly written them. Likewise, many "gospels," "acts of apostles," "letters," and "apocalypses" which purported to be from apostles circulated in the Early Church.

It is asserted by some that during this time such falsification was harmless "pious fiction." Such an opinion is doubtful. It is one thing to say that literary falsifications occurred and that men were deceived; it is an entirely different matter to assert that such forgeries were accepted as authentic and ethically proper. Not even the Greeks tolerated such falsification. One Greek actor was fined 10 talents for inserting a line in a play. Herodotus reported that one Onamachritus was exiled because he added a verse to a poem by Musaeus. How can one suggest that Christians would be any more tolerant?

There are many examples of the church fathers distancing themselves from such practices. Irenaeus indignantly reproached the heretics for using forged epistles they had manufactured themselves. Tertullian wrote of a presbyter in Asia Minor who had authored the apocryphal "Acts of Paul and Thecla." Because this man had improperly used Paul's name in a document that represented his own fancies and thoughts rather than the words of Paul, he was promptly removed from his post. His excuse that he had done it out of love for Paul fell on deaf ears. Bishop Serapion of Antioch (ca. 180) responded similarly when he learned that one of the churches in his care was interested in the "Gospel of Peter." Immediately he placed a prohibition against using it and said, "For our part, brethren, we do receive Peter and the other apostles like Christ. But the epistles which falsely carry their name, we reject as experienced men because we know that they were not presented us by them."

It is not at all correct to say that the Early Church accepted literary forgeries. Even less correct is the view that such spurious writings were canonized! Writing letters in the name of someone else was not acceptable. The canonization process involved refusing to accept those writings not considered apostolic. How can anyone argue, then, that forgeries were commonly accepted? Of course false apostolic letters circulated in the Ancient Church. The apostle Paul warned against false apostolic letters that were being circulated in the Early Church (2 Thessalonians 2:2). Perhaps one of the reasons Paul signed his letters with his own hand was to prevent such forgeries (2 Thessalonians 3:17,18).

False epistles represented a twofold deceit. First, the author's name was false; second, he published his forgery as an apostolic word from God. Such deceit brought him under God's judgment of false prophets (Deuteronomy 18:20-22; Jeremiah 23:21). If 2 Peter is a forgery of this kind, what right would the author have to rebuke the false teachers (2:1)?

## (2) Inconsistencies Between 1 and 2 Peter

One argument used against the authenticity of 2 Peter is that its form and style are different from 1 Peter. First Peter contains some of the most sophisticated Greek of the New Testament. The same cannot be said for 2 Peter. Early theologians realized this. Jerome offered a possible explanation. Silvanus was Peter's scribe for his first letter (1 Peter 5:12). For his second letter he used another scribe or wrote it himself.

However, the gap between the two epistles is not as great as some would make it appear. Not everything is inconsistent. Some points have extraordinary similarities. The wording in 1 and 2 Peter is just as much alike as 1 Timothy and Titus, for example. To use linguistic differences as a basis for rejecting Petrine authorship of 2 Peter is therefore absurd.

## (3) the Reference to Paul

Another argument directed against the authenticity of 2 Peter concerns the mention of Paul in 3:15,16. Some find it unthinkable that Peter would refer to his fellow apostle as "our beloved brother Paul." But this should not seem so strange. New Testament epistolary literature regularly named persons. Paul did so in his letters (e.g., Romans 16). So did the apostle John (3 John 9,12). The same can be said of the letter to the Hebrews (Hebrews 13:23). Paul named Peter several times (1 Corinthians 3:22; 9:5; 15:6; Galatians 1:18; 2:7ff.). Why, then, should Peter's mention of Paul be disallowed? This is not a valid argument against the genuineness of the letter.

Some contend there was rivalry between Paul and Peter. Peter had been corrected by Paul in Antioch (Galatians 2:11ff.). But Peter had defended Paul before the apostolic council in Jerusalem

(Acts 15:7) and extended to him the right hand of fellowship (Galatians 2:9). Those who assert it is unlikely Peter would speak so kindly of Paul in his second epistle (3:15) underestimate the character of this apostle.

Some think the very mention of Paul's letters suggests 2 Peter belongs to a later time period. These assume that Peter knew of a collection of Paul's letters, but a *Corpus Paulinium* ("body of Pauline writings") was not an issue until late in the First Century. This was long after the death of Peter. But Peter did not say anything about a "collection" of Paul's writings. He spoke only of "all of his (Paul's) epistles" (3:15), noting only that he and Paul shared similar understandings concerning Christ's return. It is true that Peter values Paul's letters as "other Scriptures." The reference to "other scriptures" (3:16) refers to the Old Testament as well as to other New Testament writings used in the church gatherings. The early Christians considered the teaching of the apostles of equal value to the Old Testament. Thus it is no anachronism to equate apostolic Scriptures with the rest of Holy Writ.

## (4) the Relationship with the Epistle of Jude

Most of the content of the Epistle of Jude bears a striking similarity with portions of 2 Peter (Jude 5-19; cf. 2 Peter 2:1-3:3). There are similar vocabulary, concepts, and illustrations. Although copying is not implied, the correspondences are so evident that it seems there is some kind of relationship between the two epistles. Explanations for these similarities vary. Some contend the author of Peter borrowed material from Jude; others take the opposite view. Some regard the differences as a consequence of a revision. Others assert that one of the authors merely repeated the other from memory. Several interpreters believe the similarities and differences can be explained best by presuming a common source. For example, there might have been a common "catechism" or teaching condemning heretics (e.g., Reicke, *The Anchor Bible*, 37:147; Wheaton, 1251). Great debates have raged over "who used whom?" or "did anybody use anybody?"

The resolution to these interesting problems is a "toss-up." It is difficult to see how any of this affects the authenticity of the Scriptures. Both writers took responsibility for what they had written. Neither made any attempt to conceal his identity. The content may be similar but it is not identical. Jude claimed the apostles stood behind some of what he wrote (Jude 17,18; cf. 2 Peter 3:3). Both books were received by the Early Church as Holy Scripture. In essence they both say the same thing, exemplifying the scriptural principle that by "the mouth of two witnesses, or at the mouth of three witnesses, shall the matter be established" (Deuteronomy 19:15; Matthew 18:16; cf. Genesis 41:32).

## (5) the Anti-Gnosticism of the Epistle

One of the more serious objections to the authenticity of 2 Peter is that the letter opposes the kind of heresy belonging to a later period. However, it should be noted that the letter addresses a future problem. It speaks against false teachers who are to come (2:2). Like Paul, Peter wrote of the seductions of the "last days" (cf. 1 Timothy 4:1-3; cf. Acts 20:29-30). Church history confirms how accurate these predictions were and how important were the warnings.

Paul, as well as Peter, understood that seductions belong not only to the future. Both men were aware that the "mystery of lawlessness" was already at work (cf. 2 Thessalonians 2:7). Paul merged his prophetic word for the future with a description of the present (2 Timothy 3:1-9). The same combination of present and future tenses appears in the second chapter of 2 Peter. The apostle John wrote of antichrists already present in the world and the Antichrist who was to come (1 John 2:18). It is no coincidence that prophetic passages break the bonds of time; on the contrary, it is the nature of prophetic speech.

The assertion is unfounded that the kind of heresy opposed by Peter in his second epistle was not present during the early years of the apostle's life. Also, the heresies he described involved aberrations in both life and teaching. It is quite possible that there are Gnostic elements in the opposition's teaching in both 2 Peter and Jude. Peter's emphasis on Christian knowledge may be in response to this. It has been acknowledged for a long time that "protognostic" strains existed in some first-century churches. Colossians especially evidences this. The unique features of second-century gnosticism are not reflected in 2 Peter's attacks against its opponents. The polemic elements of 2 Peter cannot be used to undermine the authenticity of the letter.

## The Content of the Epistle

According to the custom of that day, the epistle opens with the author introducing himself and greeting his readers (1:1,2). Next he admonished believers to live a life of godliness according to the divine power given them in salvation. Through the power available in Christ, believers can escape the corruption of the world. They can become partakers of the divine nature and gain admittance into the eternal kingdom of Jesus Christ. Peter reminded his readers (1:12-21) he was an eyewitness of the glory and majesty of Jesus at the "holy mount." He emphasized the truth that it was the Holy Spirit who inspired the prophecies of Scripture.

Over against the Spirit-inspired prophecies stand the false prophecies of the heretics and their followers. The apostle commented on the inevitable destruction towards which they were heading (2:1-3). A warning was sounded in 2:4-22 of how the condemnation of these false prophets was anticipated by Holy Scripture. God did not spare the angels that sinned, but placed them in prison in caverns of darkness until the judgment. Neither did He spare the "ancient world" (pre-Noahic), except for Noah and seven others. Sodom and Gomorrah also faced certain destruction. Only "righteous Lot" was delivered from God's judgment on the immoral people around him. These examples show how the Lord delivers the righteous from trial. They also show how the ungodly, especially those who revile the Lord and slander heavenly beings, are kept for the Day of Judgment. The ungodly will perish as "irrational beasts." As those who "revel in daylight" they are full of adultery and greed, and are "accursed." They are like Balaam who wanted to be paid for unrighteousness. They are arrogant, rude, and have fallen back into the corruption from which they were delivered by Christ. Their final fate is worse than their first.

The apostle denounced those who mock the message of the Lord's return and say He is not coming (3:1-10). Just as the first flood overcame the world's inhabitants, so too will the coming of the Lord—the flood of fire—overcome the ungodly. New heavens and a new earth will come (3:12). That time is postponed only because the Lord is patient towards the ungodly. His desire is that all would repent.

Second Peter falls into three natural divisions which are reflected in the modern chapter breaks. The following outline can be made:

I. "The True Knowledge" (chapter 1)

    1. Admonition to fear God (1:3-11)

    2. An eyewitness (1:12-18)

    3. The prophetic word (1:19-21)

II. The False Teachers (chapter 2)

    1. False teachers will come (2:1-3)

    2. Judgment of false teachers (2:4-9)

    3. The character of false teachers (2:10-22)

III. The Return of Christ (chapter 3)

    1. The mockers of the last days (3:1-4)

    2. The Day of the Lord (3:5-10)

    3. The call for holiness (3:11-18).

# The Second Epistle of Peter

## Commentary

### Chapter 1

**1. Simon Peter, a servant and an apostle of Jesus Christ:** ... a slave, *—CNDT* ... a bondslave and an ambassador, *—WUST* ... and messenger, *—PHLP.*

**to them that have obtained like precious faith with us:** ... sends this letter to those who have been given a faith as valuable as ours, *—PHLP* ... to those who have been divinely allotted, *—WUST* ... to them who have reached a faith equally as honorable as ours, *—SWAN* ... obtained our common sacred faith, *—NOLI.*

**through the righteousness of God and our Saviour Jesus Christ:** ... by the equitable treatment of, *—WUST.*

**1:1.** The authorship of 2 Peter is questioned by some scholars who believe an unknown follower of Peter wrote it some years after his death. However, we can be confident that the epistle is the work of an apostle. It is full of orthodox and edifying teaching, and there is abundant reason to accept Peter as the author. Evidently this second epistle is an addition to the first and is addressed to the same churches in Asia Minor. It is a kind of farewell message. Peter perceived his death was near and he offered encouraging admonitions. He warned believers against false teachers who deny Christ's redeeming work.

The apostle's name is Simon (Acts 15:14 has Simeon, the Jewish form of the word). Jesus gave him a new name, Peter (*Petros,* "a rock"), which is the Greek form of *Cephas* (from the Hebrew *Kēph*).

Peter called himself a "servant" (*doulos,* bondslave) and an "apostle" (*apostolos,* delegate, ambassador, messenger, one who is sent) of Christ. The "faith" (*pistin,* belief, persuasion, assurance) believers have received and shared in is "like precious" (*isotimon,* similarly precious, of equal value or privilege) with that of Peter and the apostles. They have received this blessed assurance through the "righteousness" (*dikaiosunē,* equitable justification, innocence imputed to all without partiality) of "God and our Saviour Jesus Christ."

**2. Grace and peace be multiplied unto you:** ... spiritual blessing and peace be to you in increasing abundance, *—WLMS* ... be yours in plenty, *—WMCK*

**through the knowledge of God, and of Jesus our Lord:** ... as your knowledge ... grows deeper,

*—PHLP* ... through intimate acquaintance, *—BRKL* ... in the sphere of and by the experiential knowledge, *—WUST* ... in an ever-increasing knowledge, *—TCNT* ... in the recognition of, *—CNDT.*

**1:2.** Peter's wish was that they enjoy "grace" (*charis,* gift, favor of God) and "peace" (*eirēnē,* quietness, harmony, well-being) in "multiplied" measure. This will happen through their "knowledge" (*epignōsei*) of the Lord; that is, intimate acquaintance, full discernment, recognition, acknowledgment. This is not merely an intellectual knowledge of Biblical facts, but an experiential knowledge, a personal acquaintance with Jesus Christ as our Saviour and Lord.

**3. According as his divine power hath given unto us:** ... He has by his own action, *—PHLP* ... has bestowed on us, *—BRKL* ... gives it through His great power, *—NLTG.*

**all things that [pertain] unto life and godliness:** ... every requisite, *—BRKL* ... everything that is necessary for living the truly good life, *—PHLP* ... everything we need for our physical and spiritual life, *—NORL* ... for leading a good Christian life, *—LBCH* ... tends to life and devoutness, *—CNDT* ... for true religion, *—TCNT.*

**through the knowledge of him that hath called us to glory and virtue:** ... through the recognition, *—CNDT* ... through the experiential knowledge, *—WUST* ... in allowing us to know the one who has called us to him, through his own glorious goodness, *—PHLP.*

**1:3.** It is possible for believers to have a multiplied measure of grace and peace, seeing that God's divine power has "given" (*dedōrēmenēs,* grant generously, bestow freely) them all the things necessary for "life and godliness." Peter wanted believers to enter into all these potential blessings. They have the capability to "live godly in Christ Jesus," as 2 Timothy 3:12 describes it. The Lord has "called" (*kalesantos,* bid, summon personally, call by name) believers to His own "glory" (*doxēs,* honor, radiant splendor) and "virtue" (*aretēs,* manliness, holy excellence), thereby to manifest the divine character of Christ in their daily lives.

**4. Whereby are given unto us exceeding great and precious promises:** ... On account of which, *—CMPB* ... through which have been presented to us, *—CNDT* ... the greatest promises of all, *—ADAM* ... most honourable promises, −FNTN...and glorious promises, −WLMS...promised blessings, −BRKL.

**that by these ye might be partakers of the divine nature:**...become participants, −CNDT...to share God's essential nature, −PHLP.

**having escaped the corruption that is in the world through lust:** ...having fled away from, −WLSN...fleeing from the corruption which is in the world by lust, −CNDT...making it possible for you to escape the inevitable disintegration that lust produces in the world, −PHLP...having escaped by flight the corruption which is in the world in the sphere of passionate cravings, −WUST...that arises from passion, −BRKL...from the corrupting influences, −TCNT...owing to depraved desire, −FNTN...because of evil desires, −WLMS.

**1:4.** In giving believers "all things" (verse 3), the Lord has granted them "promises" (*epangelmata*, pledge, self-committal, assurance) that are very valuable and exceedingly great. If believers will claim these precious promises they may, even now, be "partakers" (*koinōnoi*, sharer, partner) in Christ's "nature" (*phuseōs*, genus, lineal descent, native disposition, constitution). Peter was speaking hereof regeneration, as in 1 Peter 1:3. This divine nature implanted within the believer by the new birth becomes the source of his new lifestyle. The new lifestyle does not come automatically; the believer must make an effort. He must flee away from "lust" (*epithumia*, passionate desire, strong craving—usually for what is forbidden) or he will experience "corruption" (*phthoras*, decay, ruin). "Having escaped" (*apophugontes*) means "escape by flight." God helps those who flee the old life to develop the new life if they cooperate with Him.

**5. And beside this, giving all diligence:** ...employing all diligence, −CNDT...concentrate all your endeavors upon, −WADE...having added on your part every intense effort, −WUST...do your utmost, −BRKL.

**add to your faith virtue:**...provide lavishly in your faith the aforementioned virtue, −WUST...supplement your faith with moral character, −WLMS...fortitude, −WLSN.

**and to virtue knowledge:** ...intelligence, −FNTN...spiritual knowledge, −WADE...experiential knowledge, −WUST.

**1:5.** Spiritual life either grows or dies. Believers should not be content to hold their "faith" (*pistei*, belief, assurance, persuasion, as in verse 1) but should "add" (*epichorēgēsate*, amply furnish, contribute nourishment) to it with wholehearted "diligence" (*spoudēn*, carefulness, intense effort). Peter listed seven supplements needed to round out the believer's faith. Two affect the believer's relationship to God (knowledge, godliness) and five affect his relationship to other people (virtue, temperance, patience, brotherly kindness,

love). "Virtue" here is not *dunamis*, the miracle-working power that went out of Jesus (Mark 5:30; Luke 6:19; 8:46). It is *aretēn*, meaning valor, holy excellence, moral power; as in Philippians 4:8, "If there be any virtue . . . think on these things." The word translated "knowledge" is *gnōsin*, meaning awareness, intelligent insight; as in John 15:15, "All things that I have heard of my Father I have made known unto you." As the believer opens his being to the Spirit and the Word, he begins to see truth in its proper perspective.

**6. And to knowledge temperance:** ...besides knowledge you must have self-control, −LBCH...self-restraint, −FNTN.

**and to temperance patience:** ...endurance, −CNDT.

**and to patience godliness:**...piety, −WLSN...devoutness, −CNDT.

**1:6.** "Temperance" (*enkrateian*; cf. Galatians 5:23) relates to the believer's entire lifestyle, not just drinking. It means self-control, mastery over one's temper, and over all physical appetites. It is the exact opposite of the self-expression and self-indulgence so prevalent in the world. "Patience" (*hupomonēn*) is not a quiet resignation to one's fate; it is a heroic perseverance in serving Christ in spite of opposition, as in James 1:3, "The trying of your faith worketh patience." "Godliness" (*eusebeian*; cf. 1 Timothy 6:11) speaks of piety, devoutness, holiness.

Peter had informed the believers that by the new birth they had become partakers of the divine nature; next he showed them how to develop divine character. It means adding those traits which reflect the presence of Christ in our lives.

**7. And to godliness brotherly kindness:** ...brotherly fondness, −CNDT...an affection for the brethren, −WUST.

**and to brotherly kindness charity:**...unselfish concern to, −SEB...with universal love, −WLMS...comprehensive, −WADE...divine, −WUST.

**1:7.** "Brotherly kindness" (*philadelphian*) is fraternal affection, fondness for a brother or sister in Christ; "charity" (*agapēn*) is a wider and deeper love. The latter is the kind that enables the believer to love his enemies (Matthew 5:44). The believer is to love others not because he likes them but because they need his love. It is volitional rather than emotional, a love that operates by deliberate choice. It is Calvary love (John 3:16), the love pictured in 1 Corinthians 13:4-7. Believers are to extend to others the kind of love God has shown to them.

**8. For if these things be in you, and abound:** ...if you possess and progress in these, *—FNTN* ... If you possess such virtues, *—NORL* ... who possess these virtues abundantly, *—NOLI* ... if these things are your natural and rightful possession, and are in super-abundance, *—WUST* ... and have them in increasing measure, *—WMCK* ... and continually increasing, *—WADE.*

**they make [you that ye shall] neither [be] barren nor unfruitful:** ... to be neither slothful, *—CMPB* ...is constituting you not idle nor yet unfruit-ful, *—CNDT* ...they will make you active and produc-tive, *—SEB* ... they prevent your being indifferent, *—TCNT* ... they will not permit you to be inactive, *—WLSN* ...neither be dilatory nor ineffective, *—FNTN.*

**in the knowledge of our Lord Jesus Christ:** ...in the recognition of, *—CNDT* ...the experiential knowl-edge of, *—WUST.*

**1:8.** Peter indicated the characteristics he enu-merated in verses 5-7 should be in them and "abound" (*pleonazonta*, increase exceedingly, overflow). This speaks of the Spirit-filled life which is an overflowing kind, spilling over so others are blessed. It also speaks of Christian character which is formed by developing all these qualities until they are ingrained in one's life. The believer's Christian character is either strong or weak depending on the extent to which he co-operates with the Holy Spirit in developing these qualities in his life.

The goal is to be neither "barren" (*argous*, use-less, ineffective) nor "unfruitful" (*akarpous*, un-productive). Believers' "knowledge" (*epignōsin*, intimate acquaintance, full discernment) of Christ should make them active in serving Him, and if they possess these qualities their service will be effective and fruitful.

**9. But he that lacketh these things is blind, and cannot see afar off:** ... Whoever does not prac-tice these things, *—LBCH* ... he in whom these are not present is blind, closing his eyes, *—CNDT* ...lacks these qualities, *—WLMS* ...he sees only what is under his nose, *—WMCK* ...shutting his eyes, *—CMPB* ...short-sighted, *—NORL.*

**and hath forgotten that he was purged from his old sins:** ... getting oblivious of the cleansing from the penalties of his sins of old, *—CNDT* ...having taken forgetfulness of the cleansing of, *—WUST* ...choosing to forget the pruning he has received from his old errors, *—FNTN* ...his former sinful ways, *—NORL.*

**1:9.** If a believer does not develop these charac-teristics he is "blind" (*tuphlos*, sightless, or partly so) and "cannot see afar off" (*muōpazōn*, blink when a light is too bright). In ancient Greek liter-ature *muōpazōn* was used for a nearsighted man. The nearsighted person who lacks these things "hath forgotten" (*lēthēn*, willfully forgotten) that he was "purged" (*katharismou*, cleansed, purified)

of the sins he committed prior to his conversion. If he would look back to the life of sin from which he was delivered, and look ahead to the eternal blessings God has promised, he would see the great advantage of developing his Christian char-acter to the fullest extent possible.

**10. Wherefore the rather, brethren, give dil-igence:** ... Consequently devote your attention, *—WADE* ... exert yourselves the more, and bend ev-ery effort, *—WUST* ... endeavor through ideal acts, *—CNDT* ...spare no effort, *—TCNT.*

**to make your calling and election sure:** ...to confirm your calling and choice, *—CNDT* ...to make for yourselves your divine call [into salvation] and your divine selection, *—WUST.*

**for if ye do these things, ye shall never fall:** ...if you practice these things, *—BRKL* ... you will never stumble, *—WUST* ... you should under no circum-stances be tripping at any time, *—CNDT.*

**1:10.** Because of what Peter said in verses 5-9, believers should show all the more diligence in developing these characteristics to assure them-selves not only of their "calling" (*klēsin*, invitation, summons) but also of their "election" (*eklogēn*, selection, being chosen).

All are called to be saved, but not all respond by trusting in Christ and living for Him. As Jesus said, "Many are called, but few are chosen" (Mat-thew 22:14). Jesus made this statement after tell-ing of a guest at the wedding who was ejected; he had accepted the invitation but was not wearing the wedding garment that was required.

Peter said that if believers "do" these things (and keep on doing them, as the Greek indicates), they shall never "fall" (*ptaisēte*, stumble and fall, be tripped up), and their election will be "sure" (*bebaian*, enduring, guaranteed). The word was used by the Greeks in a legal sense to indicate a warranty that protected a buyer.

**11. For so an entrance shall be ministered unto you abundantly:** ... you will be triumphantly ad-mitted, *—NOLI* ...the entrance shall be richly provid-ed for you, *—WUST* ... you will find a glorious door opening for you, *—LBCH* ... will be richly supplied to you, *—MNTG.*

**into the everlasting kingdom of our Lord and Saviour Jesus Christ:** ... into the eonian kingdom, *—CNDT* ...eternal, *—WUST.*

**1:11.** In this way believers will have an entrance into the everlasting kingdom of our Lord (the inheritance of 1 Peter 1:4), and it will be "min-istered" (*epichorēgēthēsetai*, amply furnish, con-tribute) to them "abundantly" (*plousiōs*, copious-ly, richly). "Ministered" is the same Greek word translated "add" in verse 5. If believers will add the Christian characteristics to their faith, God will add the abundant reward. Only an unmindful and nearsighted person could fail to appreciate such a future.

**12. Wherefore I will not be negligent:** ... I shall ever be about, *—CNDT* ... take care always, *—BRKL.*

**to put you always in remembrance of these things:** ... I think it is right for me to refresh your memory, *—SEB* ... be reminding you concerning these things, *—CNDT.*

**though ye know [them], and be established in the present truth:** ... even though you are aware of, *—CNDT* ... and have become firmly established ... which is present with you, *—WUST* ... and stand firm in the revealed truth, *—FNTN* ... and are steady-minded in the truth now available, *—BRKL.*

**1:12.** The sense of responsibility Peter felt throughout his ministry was intensified as he saw death approaching. He was determined not to be negligent. He knew a minister cannot safely assume his hearers will remember what he has taught them and that it is necessary to repeat familiar truths again and again. He did not condemn them or question their experience; on the contrary, he said they knew ("know," *eidotas*, be aware, perceive) the things he had been telling them, and they were "established" (*estērigmenous*, set fast, make stable) in the truth they now possessed. However, he intended to "put (them) in remembrance" of these things (*hupomimnēskein*, remind quietly), and he would do this "always" (*aei*, ever). He said he would keep on reminding them, for he wanted them to remain firmly fixed in the "truth" (*alētheia*, verity, as in 2:2).

**13. Yea, I think it meet, as long as I am in this tabernacle:** ... Yet I consider it right, *—FNTN* ... I think it my duty, *—TCNT* ... this is the right thing to do, *—NORL* ... Now I am deeming it just, *—CNDT* ... Indeed, I consider it due you as long as I am in this tent, *—WUST.*

**to stir you up by putting [you] in remembrance:** ... to excite you, *—WLSN* ... to be rousing you by a reminder, *—CNDT* ... to keep you wide-awake by reminding you, *—BRKL.*

**1:13.** Peter thought it "meet" (*dikaion*, right) to do this. In other words, it was his duty; he was under obligation "to stir (them) up" (*diegeirein*, awaken, arouse) by reminding them of the truth they had been taught, and he felt he must keep doing this as long as he was in this "tabernacle" (*skēnōmati*, dwelling, tent, tabernacle). Peter described his body as a temporary dwelling.

**14. Knowing that shortly I must put off [this] my tabernacle:** ... being aware, *—CNDT* ... knowing that very soon there is the putting off of my tent,

*—WUST* ... the time for me to strike tent comes swiftly on, *—MNTG.*

**even as our Lord Jesus Christ hath showed me:** ... declared to me, *—WLSN* ... made clear to me, *—BRKL* ... disclosed to me, *—FNTN* ... makes evident to me, *—CNDT* ... gave me to understand, *—WUST.*

**1:14.** Peter was aware that "shortly" (*tachinē*, impending, coming swiftly) he must "put off" (*apothesis*, lay aside, put away) his body. The language corresponds to Christ's statement in John 10:18, "No man taketh it from me, but I lay it down of myself." Peter indicated he would not die under protest; he was willing to lay down his life for the sake of his Lord. He said Christ had made this plain to him. No doubt he was recalling the prophecy (John 21:18,19) that he would die as a prisoner and not as a free man.

**15. Moreover I will endeavour that ye may be able after my decease to have these things always in remembrance:** ... Indeed, I will do my best also that on each occasion when you have need after my departure you will be able to call these things to remembrance, *—WUST* ... I will make every effort to enable each one of you to keep these things in mind after I am gone, *—BRKL* ... at any time ° after my departure, *—TCNT* ... to make mention of these things, ever and anon, also, *—CNDT.*

**1:15.** Peter wanted believers to have a written account of his teaching to help them after his death. He was an eyewitness of the life and teachings of Christ. He could testify firsthand to His death, burial, resurrection, and ascension. He could describe the Transfiguration for he was present. Once his generation passed, there would be no eyewitness testimony unless it was preserved in written form. So he said he would "endeavor" (*spoudasō*, be diligent, make every effort) to see that believers have a permanent reminder ("always in remembrance") of these things. His epistles will help meet this need. So will the Gospel of Mark written with his help. In describing his impending death, Peter used two words from the conversation on the Mount of Transfiguration (Luke 9:28-33); namely, *skēnōmatos* (tabernacle, verse 14) and *exodon* (decease, departure, as used in Hebrews 11:22 to describe the Exodus).

**16. For we have not followed cunningly devised fables:** ... we did not follow out to their termination, *—WUST* ... We had nothing to do with man-made stories, *—NLTG* ... we did not depend on invented stories, *—WMCK* ... This is no clever invention, *—LBCH* ... cleverly devised stories, *—TCNT* ... wisely made myths, *—CNDT* ... cleverly invented myths, *—NORL, ADAM* ... skilfully invented fables, *—WADE* ... fictitious stories, *—SWAN.*

**when we made known unto you the power and coming of our Lord Jesus Christ:** ... when we acquainted you with the power and coming, —BRKL... and presence, —CNDT... and personal coming of, —WUST.

**but were eyewitnesses of his majesty:** ... were Beholders of that Greatness, —WLSN... we saw his greatness! —SEB ... by becoming spectators of His magnificence, —CNDT... of His grandeur, —FNTN.

**1:16.** Peter's authority as a teacher depended on his authority as a witness, so he stated his qualifications again. Evidently there were false teachers who were saying the miracles attributed to Christ were only allegories, not facts. Peter emphatically denied this. He said he and the other apostles were not simply following through with "fables" (*muthois*, a fictitious tale, myth) which had been "cunningly devised" (*sesophismenois*, make wise in a good sense, or frame artfully in a bad sense). They were being truthful about Christ's "power" (*dunamin*, might, miracle-working power) and "coming" (*parousian*, advent). This word also appears in 3:4 which states: "Where is the promise of his coming?"

Some may be thinking such a spectacular event as the Second Coming is inconceivable, but Peter entertained no doubts, for he had already glimpsed Christ's glory. He was an "eyewitness" (*epoptai*, spectator, observer) of Christ's "majesty" (*megaleiotētos*, grandeur, mighty power); as Luke 9:43 says: "They were all amazed at the mighty power of God." He had seen the divine aura, and his testimony could not be shaken. The Greek *parousian* is the word used repeatedly by Christ and the apostles to refer to the Second Coming. The same word appears in ancient literature of the coming of any royal visitor.

**17. For he received from God the Father honour and glory:** ... from the God of Glorious Majesty, —LBCH ... The honor of his glorification was conferred upon him, —GRBR... and splendour, —FNTN.

**when there came such a voice to him from the excellent glory:** ... there was borne along by the sublime glory such a voice, —WUST... the Greatest Glory, —EVRD ... being carried to Him in such a way, —CNDT... such a voice was borne to Him from the supreme glory, —BRKL... brought to him by the magnificent Glory, —WLSN... from the Supreme Majesty, declaring, —FNTN ... from the Majestical Glory, —WADE... out of the sublime glory of Heaven, —PHLP.

**This is my beloved Son, in whom I am well pleased:** ... This is My much-loved Son, —NLTG... My Son, the beloved One, —WUST... in whom I delight, —TCNT, —MNTG ... am delighted, —BRKL ... toward Whom I am well disposed, —ADAM... and I love him. I am very pleased with him, —EVRD.

**1:17.** The voice described by Peter is also recorded in Matthew 17:5; Mark 9:7; Luke 9:35. According to Matthew, the voice also said, "Hear ye him," but the other Gospels omit these words.

This is not the first time such a message had come from heaven. It was heard at the baptism of Jesus: "This is my Son, whom I love; with him I am well-pleased" (Matthew 3:17, NIV). To Peter (also Paul) the voice from heaven had done more to authenticate Christ's deity than His miracles. No other apostle had seen more miracles than Peter, and he had seen some the other apostles had not seen and yet he offered the voice from heaven rather than the miracles as proof of Christ's authenticity. In the case of Paul (Saul of Tarsus) it was the voice from heaven, not miracles, that convinced him of Jesus' deity (Acts 9:4). When Christ was "transfigured" (Matthew 17:2) He was enveloped in a bright cloud (shekinah) which Peter called "the excellent glory," similar no doubt to the glory cloud which accompanied Israel through the wilderness journey (Exodus 40:34); when the glory cloud filled the temple to such a degree the priests could not minister (1 Kings 8:10); Ezekiel speaks of the cloud that filled the temple so that "the court was full of the radiance of the glory of the Lord" (Ezekiel 10:4, NIV). At the Transfiguration Peter spoke of the voice that came out of the bright cloud which marked God's presence.

**18. And this voice which came from heaven we heard:** ... We actually heard that voice speaking, —PHLP... we heard borne along, out from heaven, —WUST... we hear being carried out of heaven, —CNDT... sounded in our ears, —GRBR.

**when we were with him in the holy mount:** ... being together with Him, —CNDT... upon the holy hill, —FNTN ... on that sacred mountain, —WLMS.

**1:18.** The voice was heard by Peter, James, and John who were with Christ in "the holy mount." The latter words suggest a contrast between the old and new covenants. Sinai was a holy mount where God first revealed himself in His glory. Now there was another "holy mount," the Mount of Transfiguration, made holy by God's manifest presence. Peter remembered the occasion when he, James, and John heard that voice from heaven. They had seen not only Jesus but Moses (the representative of the Law) and Elijah (representing the prophets). Overwhelmed at the magnificent sight, Peter had suggested building three booths for Jesus and the others. But God had said about Jesus, "Hear ye him." A new order had come, the old was passing away. At Sinai God authenticated the law of Moses by fire and smoke, thunder and lightning. On the Transfiguration mount He authenticated the gospel of Christ by the radiant cloud of glory. The contrast is expressed in John 1:17, "For the law was given by Moses, but grace and truth came by Jesus Christ."

**19. We have also a more sure word of prophecy:** ... The word of prophecy was fulfilled in our hearing! *–PHLP* ... This makes us more sure about the message the prophets gave, *–EVRD* ... we have the message of the prophets more certainly guaranteed, *–WLMS* ... we have the prophetic word as a surer foundation, *–WUST* ... Spoken as they were by the Spirit of God, we consider them absolutely trustworthy, *–GRBR* ... we have the prophetic message reaffirmed, *–BRKL* ... more confirmed, *–CNDT* ... more firmly established, *–SWAN* ... which is a still surer guide, *–NORL.*

**whereunto ye do well that ye take heed, as unto a light that shineth in a dark place:** ... Pay attention to their words, *–LBCH* ... you, doing ideally ... as to a lamp appearing in a dingy place, *–CNDT* ... a lamp which is shining in a squalid place, *–WUST* ... in a gloomy place, *–TCNT* ... in a dismal place, *–WLMS.*

**until the day dawn, and the day star arise in your hearts:** ... till the day should be breaking and the morning star should be rising, *–CNDT* ... and the Light-bringer may arise, *–WLSN.*

**1:19.** Vivid and valuable though Peter's personal experience with Jesus had been, he said there was something more "sure" (*bebaioteron*, firm, steadfast) and that is the word of "prophecy" (*prophētikon*, foretelling). Old Testament prophecies are a more reliable foundation for faith than signs and wonders. Peter said believers should "take heed" (*prosechontes*, keep in mind, pay attention to) to them for they are like a lamp that lights up a squalid, forbidding place during the long hours before dawn. "Day-star" (*phōsphoros*) means morning star, a reference to Jesus (Revelation 22:16). The morning star is a harbinger of daybreak, welcoming the sun; that is, the "Sun of righteousness" (Malachi 4:2). So they had better pay attention to the lamp of prophecy, without which they will be in the dark.

**20. Knowing this first, that no prophecy of the scripture:**
**is of any private interpretation:** ... does not originate from any private explanation, *–WUST* ... is becoming its own explanation, *–CNDT* ... may be explained by any man's private meaning, *–WMCK* ... ever came about by a prophet's own ideas, *–SEB* ... ever originated as a private solution to someone's problem, *–ADAM* ... can be interpreted by man's unaided reason, *–TCNT* ... was ever made up by any man, *–NLTG* ... is not of its own Solution, *–WLSN* ... is of a single meaning, *–FNTN* ... is of private impulse, *–CMPB.*

**1:20.** They should heed it, knowing this first, that no prophecy is someone's personal, private idea. "Private" (*idias*) means one's own. "Interpretation" (*epiluseōs*) means solution, explanation. It comes from the verb *epiluō*, to untie, release. In other words, prophecy is of divine, not human, origin. "The interpretation here is not that of the

student of scripture, but of the inspired prophet or writer of the scriptures himself, since verse 20 speaks of the method by which these prophecies came with relation to these writers" (Wuest, *Word Studies in the Greek New Testament,* 2:35). As 1 Peter 1:11 states, the prophets did not fully understand what the Spirit within them signified when He "testified beforehand the sufferings of Christ, and the glory that should follow." Now the first part has been fulfilled, and it is like a lamp in the night. When dawn comes, His glory will be seen and the prophecy will be fully understood.

**21. For the prophecy came not in old time by the will of man:** ... no prophecy originated from man's own thinking, *–NORL* ... has ever yet originated in man's will, *–WLMS* ... never spoke by their own free will, *–LBCH* ... was never a result of human design, *–FNTN* ... not by the desire of man did prophecy come aforetime, *–WUST.*

**but holy men of God spake [as they were] moved by the Holy Ghost:** ... and so spoke at the prompting of God, *–TCNT* ... men spoke words from God who is the ultimate source, *–WUST* ... while they were being influenced by, *–SEB* ... were inspired by, *–NOLI.*

**1:21.** Here is one of the most definitive descriptions of Biblical inspiration. These writers were not inspired like a poet or an artist. They did not decide what or how to write. The Holy Spirit was the divine Author. They were not puppets, with no will of their own. Using their background, personality, and vocabulary, the Third Person of the Trinity moved with them and upon them to bring into being the sacred Scriptures which reveal God and His purposes and plans to man.

The Old Testament prophecies came not by human "will" (*thelēmati*, choice, determination, desire); but dedicated men of God "spake" (*elalēsan*, utter words, talk at length, preach) as they were "moved" (*pheromenoi*, carried, borne along) by the Holy Spirit. Since the Spirit inspired the prophecies, they require His illumination to be understood.

## Chapter 2

**1. But there were false prophets also among the people:** ... there arose also, *–WUST.*

**even as there shall be false teachers among you:** ... as there will be pretended teachers, *–TCNT* ... will rise up in your midst, *–NORL.*

**who privily shall bring in damnable heresies:** ... will stealthily introduce, *–WADE* ... secretly bring in destructive sects, *–MNTG* ... try to introduce abominable heresies, *–NOLI* ... destructive opinions, *–SEB* ... bring in teaching that will destroy you, *–WMCK* ... smuggling in destructive sects, *–CNDT* ... shuffle in destructive errors, *–FNTN* ... insidiously introduce destructive heresies, *–WLMS.*

**even denying the Lord that bought them:**...denying the sovereign Lord, *—WLSN*...disowning the Owner who buys them, *—CNDT.*

**and bring upon themselves swift destruction:**...sure destruction, *—NORL*...swift ruin, *—MNTG.*

**2:1.** After speaking of the true prophets of the Old Testament (1:21), Peter next warned against false ones. There were false prophets in Jeremiah's day, for example. They shouted, "Thus saith the Lord," but encouraged self-righteousness, denied the truth, and were proved wrong by the events that followed (Jeremiah 14:13-16). Peter warned there would be false teachers who would bring in "heresies" (*haireseis*, sect, division). Heresy means choosing a position contrary to generally accepted belief and thereby causing disunity. Such heresies would be brought in "privily" (*pareisaxousin*, stealthily, smuggled in disguise, perhaps as a mixture of truth and error). They are "damnable" (*apōleias*, ruinous, destructive, deadly), and the false teachers may even deny the Lord who redeemed them; but by so doing they would bring swift "destruction" (*apōleian*, ruin, destruction, damnation) upon themselves.

**2. And many shall follow their pernicious ways:** ... licentious courses, *—TCNT* ... disgusting ways, *—SWAN*...immoral ways, *—WLMS*...follow them into sexual excess, *—SEB* ... following out their wantonness, *—CNDT.*

**by reason of whom the way of truth:**...because of whom the glory of the truth, *—CNDT.*

**shall be evil spoken of:**...maligned, *—ADAM*...calumniated, *—CNDT.*

**2:2.** Peter compared the false teachers to false prophets of the past. The Lord said His people were "taken away for nought" so His name was "blasphemed" (Isaiah 52:5). Peter foretold that a large number would follow or imitate the "pernicious ways" (*apōleiais*, destructive) of the false teachers and, as a result, the "way of truth" (Christ and His gospel) would be "evil spoken of" (*blasphēmēthēsetai*, slander, revile). "Way" is *hodos* (road, route). "The way of truth" is Jesus, who said, "I am the way (*hodos*), the truth, and the life" (John 14:6).

**3. And through covetousness shall they with feigned words make merchandise of you:** ... In their avarice they will exploit you with invented tales, *—WMCK*...in their libertinism they will exploit you by means of, *—WADE*...suave words, *—CNDT*...fabricated stories, *—ADAM*...false arguments, *—NOLI*...make money off you, *—SEB.*

**whose judgment now of a long time lingereth not:** ... Their conviction, long recorded, will not be deferred, *—FNTN* ... whose judgment of old is not idling, *—CNDT.*

**and their damnation slumbereth not:** ... nor their Ruin slumbering, *—TCNT* ... on their trail destruction is awake, *—MOFT.*

**2:3.** The root of the problem is "covetousness" (*pleonexia*, greed, avarice) which would motivate the false teachers to defraud believers. The words of their teaching would be "feigned" (*plastois*, fabricated, formed as from clay or wax; this is where we get our word *plastic*). They would mold words at will to suit their greedy purposes. With fictitious talk they would "make merchandise" of believers. The word *emporeusontai* is the root for *emporium,* our word for a store with a large variety of goods for sale. Jesus used this word concerning the merchants in the temple who were doing business for selfish gain: "Make not my Father's house a house of merchandise (*emporiou*)" (John 2:16). Peter was warning against teachers who are not true servants of God but mere professionals. They make a business of their false teaching to gain something for themselves from the believers. He said "judgment" (*krima*, punishment) is in store for these people. For a long while the judgment "lingereth" not (*argei*, delay, slow down). In other words, they had been ripe for punishment for a long time, and Peter said their damnation (see verse 1) "slumbereth" not (*nustazei*, nod, fall asleep). Their sentence would not be postponed indefinitely.

**4. For if God spared not the angels that sinned:**...when they sinned, *—NOLI.*

**but cast [them] down to hell:** ... He plunged them down into hell, *—NORL*...but flung them into Tartarus, *—WADE*...thrusting them into the gloomy caverns of Tartarus, *—CNDT.*

**and delivered [them] into chains of darkness:** ... and locked them in dark prisons, *—LBCH*...Thick darkness, *—WLSN.*

**to be reserved unto judgment:**...to be kept for chastening judging, *—CNDT* ... delivered them over into custody for Judgment, *—WLSN.*

**2:4.** The downfall of false teachers is inevitable. Since God did not spare the angels that sinned, He will not spare human beings who are of a lower order of creation. Probably the reference is to the angels who fell when Satan fell (Jude 6). God cast these angels down to "hell" (*tartarōsas*, the deepest abyss of hades). Tartarus for the pagan Greeks was a place of punishment for evil, corresponding to the Gehenna of the Jews. It was the dark and doleful abode of the wicked dead. Peter said the sinning angels were given over into chains of "darkness" (*zophou*, blackness, gloom, mist). The sinning angels are being held in the black pit of "hell" (*tartarōsas*) to face "judgment" (*krisin*, tribunal) at the Great White Throne, at which point they will be consigned to the lake of fire (Revelation 20:10) which is prepared for the devil and his angels (Matthew 25:41).

**5. And spared not the old world:** . . . the ancient world, –NORL.

**but saved Noah the eighth [person], a preacher of righteousness:** . . . but preserved Noah, a herald of, –MNTG.

**bringing in the flood upon the world of the ungodly:** . . . bringing a Deluge on a World of Impious men, –WLSN . . . the irreverent, –CNDT . . . to destroy a godless world, –NORL.

**2:5.** As a second example of divine judgment, Peter cited the "flood" (*kataklusmon*, deluge, inundation; source of our word cataclysm) recorded in Genesis 6 and 7. God destroyed all the people of the ancient world except eight persons (see 1 Peter 3:20). Judgment fell upon the "ungodly" (*asebōn*, irreverent, impious), but Noah, a proclaimer of righteousness, was "saved" (from *phulassō*, preserve, keep safe under guard). Noah warned of the Flood coming upon the people by his example and by his preaching. His obedience in building the ark "condemned the world" (Hebrews 11:7). He warned them of judgment, but they went on with life as usual (Matthew 24:37). He told them God required righteousness, but they despised his preaching. The people perished, but Noah was spared.

**6. And turning the cities of Sodom and Gomorrha into ashes condemned [them] with an overthrow:** . . . God also completely destroyed, –LBCH . . . He burned them up, –SEB . . . condemns the cities . . . reducing them to cinders by an overthrow, –CNDT.

**making [them] an ensample unto those that after should live ungodly:** . . . having placed them as an example for those about to be irreverent, –CNDT.

**2:6.** A third example is the fate of Sodom and Gomorrah (Genesis 19:24,25). According to Jude 7 there were other nearby cities which also were destroyed by fire. The cities of the plain were "turned into ashes" (from *tephroō*, incinerate, consume). Strachan prefers to translate it "covered up with ashes," the wording found in a description of the eruption of Vesuvius (*Expositor's Greek Testament,* 5:135). God condemned the wicked cities with an "overthrow" (*katastrophē*, demolition, turning upside down, the word we spell catastrophe) thus making them a tragic "ensample" (*hupodeigma*, example, exhibit, specimen) to all who would follow. It shows what is in store for those who live in an "ungodly" manner (*asebein*, act impiously, irreverently, wickedly; as in Jude 15, "To execute judgment upon all, and to convince

all that are ungodly among them of all their ungodly deeds").

**7. And delivered just Lot:** . . . he rescued righteous, –TCNT . . . rescued the good man, –WMCK

**vexed with the filthy conversation of the wicked:** . . . who was worn out by the lascivious life, –MNTG . . . harried by the behavior of the dissolute in their wantonness, –CNDT . . . sick and tired of the immoral behavior, –ADAM . . . was very upset about the wild sex life, –SEB . . . being grievously harassed with the lewd conduct, –WLSN . . . distressed with the abandoned conversation of the godless, –DRBY.

**2:7.** But Lot was delivered from Sodom because he was "just" (*dikaion*, righteous, innocent, holy), and he abhorred the "conversation" (*anastrophēs*, behavior, conduct) of the "wicked" (*athesmon*, outlaw, rebel against God's law). Their conduct was so "filthy" (*aselgeia*, shameless, lascivious, unrestrainedly lustful) that it "vexed" him (*kataponoumenon*, sore distressed, exhaust with toil). It wore him down until he was weary. His soul rebelled against it until he was exhausted.

**8. (For that righteous man dwelling among them, in seeing and hearing:** . . . observing, –CNDT.

**vexed [his] righteous soul from day to day with [their] unlawful deeds;):** . . . he felt tortured in his righteous soul, –SEB . . . was tortured by their wicked doings, –TCNT . . . tormented his just soul by their lawless acts, –CNDT.

**2:8.** Lot was not just a visitor in Sodom; he was "dwelling" there (from *enkatoikeō*, settle down, reside). It was a wicked city when he chose it (Genesis 13:11-13). As he watched the shameless abandonment of the people and as he listened to their filthy talk, he "vexed his righteous soul." "Vexed" here is *ebasanizen* (torture, torment). Whether he was tortured with a sense of guilt for failing to correct such evil or to protest against it, we are not told, but he must have chastised himself severely for ever choosing to live in such a wicked city.

**9. The Lord knoweth how to deliver the godly out of temptations:** . . . is acquainted with the rescue of the devout out of trial, –CNDT . . . a pious man from, –NORL.

**and to reserve the unjust unto the day of judgment to be punished:** . . . keeping the unjust for chastening, –CNDT . . . to be cut off, –WLSN.

**2:9.** Here Peter made an application from the observations made in verses 4-8. The Lord will always find a way to deliver godly people (like Noah and Lot) out of "temptation" (*peirasmou*, enticement, adversity, trial; as in 1 Peter 4:12, "fiery trial"). Meanwhile He is holding the unjust (like the fallen angels, Noah's wicked neighbors, and the Sodomites) under guard awaiting the day of "judgment" (*kriseōs*, damnation, decision, tribunal) when they will be "punished." The Greek is *kolazomenous* (from *kolazō*), as in Matthew 25:46, "These shall go away into everlasting punishment." The verb form indicates the punishment is continuous. As surely as God delivered Noah and Lot, He will deliver tested believers. Noah's test was to keep believing in the midst of unbelief. It lasted many years but the Lord brought him through. Lot's test was to continue to trust God while enduring great trials. God brought him through successfully.

**10. But chiefly them that walk after the flesh in the lust of uncleanness, and despise government:** . . . especially those who satisfy their lower nature . . . who despise authority, —*WLMS* . . . seek after sensuality, —*FNTN* . . . through polluting lust, —*WADE* . . . are slaves of low sex habits, —*LBCH* . . . indulge in the lust of defiling sensuality, —*NOLI* . . . the lust of defilement, and in despising all authority, —*MNTG* . . . indulging their polluting passions and despising all control, —*TCNT* . . . more especially . . . who despise Dominion, —*WLSN* . . . oppose authority, —*NORL*.
**Presumptuous [are they], self-willed:** . . . Audacious, —*FNTN* . . . given to self-gratification, —*CNDT* . . . Daring, headstrong men! —*WLMS*.
**they are not afraid to speak evil of dignities:** . . . not afraid to curse the very angels in heaven, —*LBCH* . . . do not tremble when they abuse persons of majesty, —*WLMS* . . . defame Glorious Beings, —*WADE* . . . say bad things about the powers in heaven, —*NLTG* . . . scoff at the glories of the unseen world, —*NOLI*.

**2:10.** Peter used strong adjectives to describe false teachers. They are "presumptuous" (*tolmētai*, audacious, brazen, bold) and "self-willed" (*authadeis*, arrogant, self-pleasing). Their independent spirit often strikes out at organization. They "despise" (*kataphronountas*, look down on, scorn) any "government" (*kuriotētos*, dominion, authority). They especially resent the lordship of Christ which is the central theme of all apostolic teaching and practice. To "speak evil of dignities" indicates a rank skepticism regarding the supernatural. "Dignities" is *doxas* (glory, honor, radiant splendor) and probably refers to the angels.

**11. Whereas angels, which are greater in power and might:** . . . messengers, being greater in strength and power, —*CNDT*.
**bring not railing accusation against them before the Lord:** . . . bring no abusive charge against them, —*WMCK*.

**2:11.** Angels are greater in strength and ability than the false teachers, yet they do not bring any scurrilous accusation into God's presence against "dignities," not even against Satan or his fallen angels. Jude 9 explains in clearer detail: "Michael the archangel, when contending with the devil he disputed about the body of Moses, durst not bring against him a railing accusation, but said, The Lord rebuke thee" (as in Zechariah 3:2). Even the archangel Michael, who is greater in power and might than other angels, held Satan in such awe he refrained from rebuking him personally.

**12. But these, as natural brute beasts, made to be taken and destroyed:** . . . are irrational animals, —*NORL* . . . guided only by instinct, —*SEB* . . . to be caught and killed, —*BRKL* . . . born naturally for capture and corruption, —*CNDT*.
**speak evil of the things that they understand not:** . . . uttering blasphemies in the sphere of those things concerning which they are ignorant, —*WUST* . . . while maligning what they do not know, —*BRKL* . . . that in which they are ignorant, —*CNDT*.
**and shall utterly perish in their own corruption:** . . . They will die in their own sinful ways, —*NLTG* . . . shall in their . . . destroying surely be destroyed, —*WUST*.

**2:12.** Indulgence in pride, self-will, contempt for authority—which might be called sins of the spirit—often lead to indulgence in sins of the flesh. Peter said these false teachers act as mere animals born for capture and destruction. Their real desire is to satisfy their physical passions and get material gain. This verse is almost identical with Jude 10 which speaks of ungodly men who creep in secretly to turn liberty into license and deny Christ Jesus the Lord. Jude says they "speak evil of those things which they know not: but what they know naturally, as brute beasts, in those things they corrupt themselves." In their destroying, they themselves shall surely be destroyed. This is often the fate of evil men. Those who choose such a life eventually discover that in the end even that in which they found such pleasure fails to satisfy.

**13. And shall receive the reward of unrighteousness:** . . . being requited with the wages of injustice, —*CNDT* . . . as the hire, —*WUST* . . . rewarded by their own wickedness, —*BRKL*.
**[as] they that count it pleasure to riot in the day time:** . . . They esteem luxurious festivity, —*WLSN* . . . Deeming gratification by day a luxury, —*CNDT* . . . deeming luxurious living in the daytime a pleasure, —*WUST* . . . enjoying their deceitful ways, —*ADAM*.
**Spots [they are] and blemishes, sporting themselves with their own deceivings while they feast with you:** . . . They are a blot and a disgrace, —*NOLI* . . . moral blemishes and disgraceful blots, reveling in their deceitful cravings, —*WUST* . . . and flaws, —*CNDT* . . . and running sores in our society, —*LBCH* . . . they stuff themselves, —*SEB*.

**2:13.** There is a tragic "reward" (*misthon*, wage) for "unrighteousness" (*adikias*, wrongdoing), and the false teachers will "receive" it (*komioumenoi*, obtain). One charge against them is that they "riot in the daytime." Daylight hours are for productive activity, not revelry; as 1 Thessalonians 5:7 suggests, "They that be drunken are drunken in the night." The false teachers use the day to "riot" (*truphēn*, revel, live in luxury). This is their "pleasure" (*hēdonēn*, hedonism, sensual delight, lust). Peter called them "spots" (from *spilos*, spoil, stain, disfigure) and "blemishes" (*mōmoi*, blot, fault, flaw) that bring disgrace on the Church. "Sporting themselves" is *entruphōntes* (revel, live in luxury). "Deceivings" is *apatais*, but the context suggests it should be *agapais*, meaning love feasts, which would agree with Jude 12.

The Christians customarily ate a meal together before celebrating the Lord's Supper. The purpose was to promote fellowship and express love one for another, so it was called a love feast (feast of charity). The wealthier believers provided the food, but rich and poor ate together. Evidently the false teachers gorged themselves and turned the love feast into a travesty of what God intends this sacred service to be.

The Book of Jude (verses 12,13), almost a parallel passage, says, "These men are blemishes at your love feasts, eating with you without the slightest qualm—shepherds who feed only themselves. They are clouds without rain, blown along by the wind; autumn trees, without fruit and uprooted—twice dead. They are wild waves of the sea, foaming up their shame; wandering stars, for whom blackest darkness has been reserved forever" (NIV).

**14. Having eyes full of adultery, and that cannot cease from sin:** . . . having the distended eyes of an adulteress, —*CNDT* . . . are full of lust, —*NORL* . . . full of harlots, —*MNTG* . . . and are insatiable for sin, —*SWAN* . . . and unrestrained sin, —*FNTN* . . . They never stop sinning, —*SEB* . . . that never have enough of sinning, —*WMCK* . . . incessantly sinning, —*CMPB*.

**beguiling unstable souls:** . . . catching unstable souls with bait, —*WUST* . . . entice persons of weak character, —*TCNT* . . . unsteady souls, —*MNTG* . . . alluring unestablished, —*DRBY*.

**an heart they have exercised with covetous practices; cursed children:** . . . their hearts are trained to exploit, —*WMCK* . . . exercised with insatiable desires, —*CMPB* . . . practised in greed, —*FNTN* . . . accursed generation, —*MNTG* . . . Children of a Curse, —*WLSN*.

**2:14.** Another charge against them is their insatiable lust. They have "eyes full of adultery" (illicit sexual intercourse) and they "cannot cease" from it. Peter painted a vivid picture of a man "who cannot see a woman without lascivious thoughts arising in his heart" (Mayor, p. 135). This reminds us of Christ's words about the adultery in a lustful gaze (Matthew 5:28). "Beguiling" is *deleazontes* meaning to entrap, catch by bait, entice. "Exercised" is *gegumnasmenēn* (exercising in a gymnasium, training). The false teachers had trained their heart in the practice of "covetousness" (*pleonexiais*, avarice, fraudulency, greediness) and had become children of cursing. They were under a curse and headed for divine judgment.

**15. Which have forsaken the right way, and are gone astray:** . . . Leaving the straight path, they were led astray, —*CNDT* . . . Abandoning the straight road, —*WUST* . . . and have taken the wrong road, —*LBCH*.

**following the way of Balaam [the son] of Bosor, who loved the wages of unrighteousness:** . . . in the steps, —*TCNT* . . . followed in the tracks, —*BRKL* . . . liked to take a bribe for wrongdoing, —*NORL* . . . the money he got for his sin, —*NLTG* . . . profits of, —*WLMS*.

**2:15.** Balaam has become known in history as a man who sought to make personal gain at the expense of his ministry (see Numbers 22-24). He is a perfect example of what Peter was dealing with. Balaam sought to manipulate truth so as not to deny it, but to use it for his own advantage. He was not all bad, and much of his message was true; however, he finally lost out completely. He became numbered with the enemies who, according to his own prophecy, were marked for destruction, and his sad end is told in Numbers 31:8. Peter said the false teachers had abandoned the right road. They had gone astray by following in the footsteps of Balaam, the prophet who commercialized his gift. He sought the reward offered by Balak, "the wages of unrighteousness." He loved earthly things more than heavenly things. "Loved" is from *agapaō*, an intense kind of love, the word used in 2 Timothy 4:10: "Demas hath forsaken me, having loved this present world." The final wages of sin is death, though the present pay may seem desirable.

**16. But was rebuked for his iniquity:** . . . exposed for his own outlawry, —*CNDT* . . . the recipient of an effectual rebuke, —*WUST* . . . convicted by his own misdeed, —*BRKL* . . . for his own transgression, —*WADE*.

**the dumb ass speaking with man's voice forbad the madness of the prophet:** . . . a voiceless yoke-beast, uttering with a human voice, forbids the insanity, —*CNDT* . . . speaking with, —*FNTN* . . . the inarticulate beast of burden . . . restrained the insanity of, —*WUST* . . . reprimanded, —*CMPB* . . . prevented him from carrying out his mad purposes, —*LBCH* . . . put an end to the prophet's madness, —*WMCK*

**2:16.** Balaam's "iniquity" (*paranomias*, transgression) was exposed when his donkey spoke with a human voice. Actually the ass was "dumb" (*aphōnon*, voiceless), and yet it talked to Balaam and restrained him from doing something that was "madness" (*paraphronian*, foolhardy). Balaam had been hired by Balak, king of Moab, to try to turn God against the Israelites so they would not be able to defeat Moab's army. He knew that as long as God was helping the Israelites, his soldiers could not stand against them. So Balaam set out to curse Israel, which was madness indeed. But later he found a way to earn a reward from Balak. He succeeded in luring men of Israel to commit whoredom with women of Moab (see Numbers 25:1-3; 31:16), and this turned God against Israel and brought judgment upon them.

**17. These are wells without water:** . . . waterless fountains, —*NORL* . . . springs, —*MNTG* . . . dried up water holes, —*LBCH*.

**clouds that are carried with a tempest:** . . . mists driven before a gale, —*TCNT* . . . fogs driven by a hurricane, —*ADAM* . . . blown by a storm, —*SEB* . . . driven along by a Whirlwind, —*WLSN* . . . tempest-tossed, —*FNTN*.

**to whom the mist of darkness is reserved for ever:** . . . for whom the gloom of darkness has been kept, —*CNDT* . . . the blackness, —*WUST*.

**2:17.** Peter said the false teachers made an empty profession of faith. He compared them to "wells" (*pēgai*, fountain, spring) without water and to clouds that, instead of giving rain, are "carried" away (*elaunomenai*, driven) by a "tempest" (*lailapos*, squall, hurricane; as in Mark 4:37, the sudden "storm of wind" on the Sea of Galilee that threatened Christ and His disciples). What a disappointment to a thirsty traveler in the desert when he sees a patch of green ahead, only to find when he reaches it that the spring has dried up! Even worse is the plight of spiritually thirsty people who look for the living water, only to be disillusioned by false teachers.

**18. For when they speak great swelling [words] of vanity:** . . . They speak their folly in pompous oratory, —*NORL* . . . they say stupid, boastful things, —*SEB* . . . uttering extravagant things, —*WUST* . . . make loud foolish boasts about their wicked pleasures, —*LBCH*.

**they allure through the lusts of the flesh, [through much] wantonness:** . . . by using sensual cravings, —*NORL* . . . by an appeal to fleshly desires, —*ADAM*.

**those that were clean escaped from them who live in error:** . . . those who are just about escaping from those who are ordering their behavior in the sphere of error, —*WUST* . . . those who are scarcely fleeing from those who are behaving with deception, —*CNDT*.

**2:18.** New converts are special targets of false teachers. They "allure" (*deleazousin*, beguile, entrap, entice) those who are just escaping from the ranks of unbelievers who live in error. The false teachers talk in grandiose terms to do this. They are extravagant in their verbosity, and they sway the people with their "great swelling words," but Peter says their words are "vanity" (*mataiotētos*, empty, profitless, insincere). They appeal through carnal desires and through much "wantonness" (*aselgeiais*, lewdness, unrestrained immorality). By encouraging the new converts to compromise, they draw them back into the very lifestyle from which they recently fled.

Jude's description of the false teachers is even more devastating than Peter's. He said: "These are murmurers, complainers, walking after their own lusts; and their mouth speaketh great swelling words, having men's persons in admiration because of advantage" (Jude 16). Jude further stated: "Clouds they are without water, carried about of winds; trees whose fruit withereth, without fruit, twice dead, plucked up by the roots" (Jude 12). Jude called them "ungodly men, turning the grace of our God into lasciviousness, and denying the only Lord God, and our Lord Jesus Christ" (Jude 4). He stated: "These filthy dreamers defile the flesh, despise dominion, and speak evil of dignities" (Jude 8).

**19. While they promise them liberty:** . . . They talk about being free, —*LBCH* . . . promising them freedom, —*CNDT*.

**they themselves are the servants of corruption:** . . . they are inherently, —*CNDT* . . . are slaves to corrupt habits, —*TCNT* . . . are slaves of rottenness! —*MNTG*.

**for of whom a man is overcome, of the same is he brought in bondage:** . . . A person is a slave to whatever has defeated him, —*SEB* . . . anyone is discomfited, to this one he has been enslaved also, —*CNDT* . . . whom a person has been overcome with the result that he is in a state of subjugation, to this one has he been enslaved with the result that he is in a state of slavery, —*WUST* . . . is the slave of anything which masters him, —*MNTG*.

**2:19.** The false prophets promised "liberty" (*eleutherian*, freedom), but it is not the freedom Christ offered when He said, "The truth shall make you free" (John 8:32). Christ offers freedom from sin, not freedom to sin; and freedom from the Mosaic law, not freedom from the law of divine love. What the false teachers promised was a presumed liberty that amounts to license—a freedom to please oneself regardless of any restraining law. They would use liberty "for an occasion to the flesh" (Galatians 5:13). They would encourage people to sin saying God's grace will cover whatever sins they commit (see Romans 6:1). But Peter said these false teachers themselves really did not enjoy liberty, for they were "servants" (*douloi*, slave) of "corruption" (*phthoras*, depravity, defilement). They had been "overcome" (*hēttētai*, vanquish) by it and therefore were in bondage to it. All who yield themselves to sin are the servants of sin (Romans 6:16).

**20. For if after they have escaped the pollutions of the world through the knowledge of the Lord and Saviour Jesus Christ:** . . . having escaped from the defilements, *—FNTN* . . . while fleeing from, *—CNDT* . . . the corrupting ways, *—WLMS* . . . by an experiential knowledge, *—WUST.*
**they are again entangled therein, and overcome:** . . . they are again recaptured, *—FNTN* . . . they got involved again and were defeated, *—SEB* . . . defeated all over again, *—PHLP* . . . with the result that they are in a state of subjugation, *—WUST* . . . and succumb to them, *—WADE.*
**the latter end is worse with them than the beginning:** . . . their last state, *—DRBY, —WMCK* . . . their last position is far worse, *—PHLP* . . . the last things have become to them, *—WUST* . . . their last condition is worse, *—WLMS* . . . worse than the first, *—CNDT.*

**2:20.** Victims of false teachers will end up in a worse state than they were in before they were saved. Jesus made a similar statement in reference to a man from whom an unclean spirit had been cast out: "The last state of that man is worse than the first" (Matthew 12:45). He said the uncleanness becomes seven times worse when the evil spirits return. Similarly believers who, through acknowledging Jesus Christ as Lord and Saviour, have escaped (run away) from worldly "pollutions" (*miasmata*, defilement, uncleanness), if they should become entangled again in those pollutions and be conquered by them, will plunge into sin more deeply than before they were saved and be more helpless to free themselves from its grip. "Entangled" is *emplakentes*, meaning entwine, involve. It is the word used of braiding or plaiting the hair, a very deliberate process, and indicates their return to their former immoral lives is not a rash act but a willful choice on their part.

**21. For it had been better for them not to have known the way of righteousness:** . . . to have recognized, *—CNDT* . . . to have known the way of goodness at all, *—PHLP.*
**than, after they have known [it], to turn from the holy commandment delivered unto them:** . . . recognizing it, to go back to what was behind, *—CNDT* . . . after knowing it to turn their backs on the sacred commandments given to them, *—PHLP* . . . than to know it and later turn away, *—LBCH* . . . the sacred injunction, *—BRKL* . . . the sacred command committed to their trust, *—WLMS* . . . transmitted to them, *—WADE.*

**2:21.** There is another way in which those who turn back are worse off than before. It is because

they are abandoning or refusing the truth, the holy commandment, God's Word, apart from which they cannot hope for help. In the beginning the truth was new to them, and they were not hardened against it. Now they have become almost immune to its power. Jesus, using the eye as a metaphor, warned against this: "If therefore the light that is in thee be darkness, how great is that darkness" (Matthew 6:23). No one is so blind as he who shuts his eyes to truth! Another warning, that of apostasy, is given in Hebrews 10:26,27. If one willfully rejects God's provision of salvation after receiving the knowledge of the truth, there is no way left by which he can find forgiveness since he is deliberately rejecting Christ's sacrifice, the only sacrifice for sins. The "way of righteousness" is the message John the Baptist preached (Matthew 21:32). It is the way all must follow (1 Timothy 6:11) if they wish to lay hold on eternal life.

**22. But it is happened unto them according to the true proverb:** . . . Alas, for them the old proverbs have come true, *—PHLP* . . . In their case the true proverb becomes realized, *—BRKL* . . . these old sayings, *—SEB* . . . true saying, *—WUST* . . . has befallen them, *—CNDT.*
**The dog [is] turned to his own vomit again:** . . . A cur turning to, *—CNDT.*
**and the sow that was washed to her wallowing in the mire:** . . . A bathed sow, *—CNDT* . . . having been bathed, *—WUST* . . . scrubbed, *—BRKL* . . . went back to roll, *—SEB* . . . in the mud, *—TCNT* . . . in the muck, *—PHLP.*

**2:22.** Peter followed the familiar example of Jesus in using homely and vivid illustrations. He described what happens when a believer forsakes the ways of God by the illustrations of a dog and a pig. In each case the point is obvious: the false teachers had "escaped the pollutions of the world" (verse 20) but had not remained in the way of righteousness. When the opportunity arose, they reverted to their old nature and filthy ways. The first illustration is from Proverbs 26:11. The second does not appear in the Old Testament. In view of the Jews' repugnance for swine, it probably is from a Gentile source. There is a story in ancient literature about a hog that went to the public bath with people of high status. However, when coming out he saw a stinking drain and went and rolled himself in it. Peter could not have expressed contempt for false teachers more strongly than to class them with dogs and swine. By using these shocking comparisons, it is hoped believers will recognize deceivers for what they really are and will reject them.

# Chapter 3

1. **This second epistle, beloved, I now write unto you:** . . . This already, —CNDT . . . the second letter, —NORL . . . I have written to you, dear friends of mine, —PHLP . . . divinely loved ones, —WUST.

**in [both] which I stir up your pure minds by way of remembrance:** . . . in which I am rousing your sincere comprehension by a reminder, —CNDT . . . stir you up to remember with clear intelligence, —FNTN . . . in both of them I have tried to stimulate you, as men with minds uncontaminated by error, by simply reminding you of what you really know already, —PHLP . . . revive, —BRKL . . . to stir up your unsullied minds, —WLMS.

**3:1.** This, Peter's final letter to believers, stresses the need to keep the Second Coming in mind. It has been mentioned before (1 Peter 4:7), but now it is dealt with more fully. Peter did not tell them anything new but wished to "stir up" (*diegeirō*, arouse them to be wide awake, as in 1:13) their understanding by reminding them of what they had been taught. This was his purpose "in both"— that is, in this second "epistle" (*epistolēn*, letter) as well as the first. "Pure" is *eilikrinē*, meaning sincere, as in Philippians 1:10: "That ye may be sincere and without offense till the day of Christ." It means genuine; the word speaks of something being examined in full sunlight.

2. **That ye may be mindful of the words which were spoken before by the holy prophets:** . . . I want you to remember the words spoken of old, —PHLP . . . so that you may recall, —WADE . . . to recollect the words previously spoken, —WLSN . . . to remind you of the declarations which have been declared, —CNDT . . . of the sayings, —BRKL.

**and of the commandment of us the apostles of the Lord and Saviour:** . . . as well as the commands, —PHLP . . . of the precept of, —CNDT . . . also of the commands of the Lord, —BRKL.

**3:2.** In this chapter Peter emphasized two important issues. One is that the Word of God is true and dependable; it means just what it says. The other is that the purpose of prophecy is not to satisfy human curiosity regarding the future but to provide the incentive for holy living. He wanted believers to remember the Old Testament prophecies as well as the teachings of the apostles. "Commandment" does not mean any single precept but the entire gospel—all the teachings of the apostles. A.T. Robertson says a better translation of the Greek is "the commandment of the Lord and Saviour through your apostles" (*Word Pictures in the New Testament,* 6:172). The apostles were not teaching a message of their own but the message they received from Christ.

3. **Knowing this first, that there shall come in the last days scoffers:** . . . Recognise this fact first, —TCNT . . . First of all you should understand that . . . scoffers will come on the scene with their scoffing, —BRKL . . . You should never forget that in the last days mockers will undoubtedly come, —PHLP . . . will make fun, —SEB . . . will come and mock you, TNT . . . and will make sport of our faith, —LBCH . . . mockers with mockery, —WUST.

**walking after their own lusts:** . . . behaving in line with, —BRKL . . . men who live only for their selfish interests, —TNT . . . men whose only guide in life is what they want for themselves, —PHLP . . . ordering their manner of life according to their own personal desires, —WUST . . . going according to their own desires, —CNDT . . . their own evil desires, —NORL.

**3:3.** The reason the believers needed to be stirred up and constantly keep sound teachings in mind was that scoffers would arise in the Church. "Scoffers" is *empaiktai*, translated "mockers" in Jude 18, referring to the false teachers. The Greek phrase for "in the last days" is translated in various forms. John 6:39 has "on the last day." James 5:3 gives "for the last days." The Greek literally means "upon the last of the days." Peter was speaking about a future time beyond his own day and ministry.

4. **And saying, Where is the promise of his coming?:** . . . and they will say, —PHLP . . . What about his promised coming, —BRKL . . . of His appearing? —FNTN . . . of His presence? —CNDT.

**for since the fathers fell asleep, all things continue as [they were] from the beginning of the creation:** . . . Since our ancestors died, —SEB . . . Since the first Christians fell asleep, —PHLP . . . went to their rest, —NOLI . . . were put to repose, —CNDT . . . all things are remaining permanently in that state in which they were since the beginning of the creation, —WUST . . . everything has remained exactly, —WLMS.

**3:4.** Scoffers would ask about the "promise" (*epangelia*, pledge, assurance) of His coming. The reference is to Christ (verse 2). Peter was speaking of the "coming of our Lord Jesus Christ," as in 1:16. "Coming" is *parousias*, Greek for *presence*, meaning His personal arrival, a glorious event. Peter knew that if time went on, some would grow impatient, and scoffers would take advantage of the opportunity to mock the teaching. But the scoffers would be wrong when they said that ever since the forefathers "fell asleep" (passed away) all things remained just as they were from the date of creation.

To correct this mistake Peter referred to the Flood and the change it made in the earth. God had already intervened once, and He will intervene again. But unregenerate men and women do not want any intervention. They wish to pursue their sinful pleasures without interruption.

"Fathers" is *pateres*, meaning parent or ancestor. It may refer to the Old Testament prophets who spoke of the Day of the Lord, or to the apostles like Peter who would have died by that time. Peter preached about the second coming of Christ (Acts 3:20), as Jesus himself did repeatedly (Matthew 24:34) and as the angels promised at the Ascension (Acts 1:11).

**5. For this they willingly are ignorant of:**... They willfully ignore the fact, *—NORL* ... They deliberately ignore, *—TNT* ... they want to be oblivious of this, *—CNDT*... They are deliberately shutting their eyes to a fact that they know very well, *—PHLP* ... they willfully forget, *—WUST.*

**that by the word of God the heavens were of old:**... that there were heavens of old, *—CNDT* ... by God's command ... in the old days, *—PHLP* ... that heavens existed from ancient times, *—WUST.*

**and the earth standing out of the water and in the water:**... become solidified, emerging out of water, *—WADE* ... cohering out of water and through water, *—CNDT*... and land [standing] out of water, and by means of water, *—WUST.*

**3:5.** The scoffers would purposely forget the account of the Flood recorded in Genesis 6-8. "Willingly" is *thelontas*, meaning gladly, choice, preference. They would close their eyes to the Biblical account of how God, by the word of His power, created the "heavens" (*ouranoi*, sky, as in Matthew 16:3, "Ye can discern the face of the sky") and the "earth" (*gē*, land, ground). In the beginning all was water. God created the firmament to divide the water in the clouds from the water in the universal sea. Then He caused the sea to "be gathered together unto one place, and let the dry land appear" (Genesis 1:9). The water served to give consistency and coherence to the land; this is one interpretation of Peter's words, though there are others. By this interpretation, "out of the water" refers not to the position of the land but rather to the effect of the water upon the land. "Standing" is from *sunistēmi*, meaning set together, compacted, consist; as in Colossians 1:17, "By him all things consist" (are held together). Water keeps the earth moist and holds it together. Scholars are agreed only on the fact that the meaning is obscure.

**6. Whereby the world that then was, being overflowed with water, perished:** ... through which the ordered world of that time, having been deluged by water, was ruined, *—WUST* ... was also overwhelmed and destroyed, *—TNT.*

**3:6.** "Whereby" indicates the Flood occurred by means of God's command. By Him the earth was created, and by Him it was inundated (covered with water) so the earth and its inhabitants "perished" (*apōleto*, ruin, destroy fully).

**7. But the heavens and the earth, which are now:**... this present heaven, *—WMCK*

**by the same word are kept in store, reserved unto fire:**... also by God's command, *—PHLP*...stored with fire, *—CNDT* ... reserved for annihilation by fire, *—WADE.*

**against the day of judgment and perdition of ungodly men:**... maintained for the fire of the day of judgment, *—PHLP* ... and destruction of the godless, *—TCNT* ... of irreverent men, *—CNDT.*

**3:7.** Divine judgment upon human sins is inevitable, though the earth will never again be destroyed by a flood (Genesis 9:11). This verse says it will be by fire. "The same word" that created the world and that sent the Flood is now saving up the present heavens and earth, holding these elements in store for the fiery judgment which lies ahead. "Kept in store" is *tethēsaurismenoi*, to amass, to treasure up; as in Romans 2:5, "Treasurest up unto thyself wrath against the day of wrath." "Reserved" is *tēroumenoi* (to withhold, to keep in protective custody). "Perdition" is *apōleias* (ruin, loss, perishing). This same Greek word is translated "damnable" and "destruction" in 2:1, and as "pernicious" in 2:2. It is used in the case of Judas, whom Jesus called the "son of perdition" (John 17:12). In applying the word *perdition* to people, the New Testament always makes it clear that the one who is destroyed is responsible for his situation. There is never a fatalistic doom suggested. Even in Judas' case, the Gospels show that as late as the Last Supper, Jesus tried to help Judas to change his mind and purpose.

**8. But, beloved, be not ignorant of this one thing:** ... Do not forget, *—MNTG* ... we must not ignore this lesson of the ages, *—LBCH* ... don't let this fact escape you, *—SWAN* ... you are not to be oblivious, *—CNDT.*

**that one day [is] with the Lord as a thousand years, and a thousand years as one day:** ... may be equivalent to, *—WADE* ... as a single day, *—FNTN.*

**3:8.** "Beloved" (dearly loved) appears six times in Peter's second epistle. He cautioned believers not to forget "this one thing," that God is very longsuffering. He quoted from Psalm 90:4 to show a thousand years is not very long to the eternal God. When the Bible says "the end of all things is at hand" (1 Peter 4:7), it may mean tomorrow or it may mean a thousand years from now. So believers should not grow impatient if Christ's coming is not as soon as they expect. God's timetable is not synchronized with any earthly clock. Scoffers are ignorant of this. They view time from the standpoint of their own short lives and not from God's standpoint. However long it might be "since the fathers fell asleep" (verse 4), it is not very long in God's sight. Paul evidently expected Christ to return in his own lifetime. He wrote, "We which are alive and remain . . ." (1 Thessalonians 4:17). When it became apparent that he would die prior to Christ's coming, it did not trouble him. He still rejoiced in the crown of righteousness reserved for him and for all those who "love his (Christ's) appearing" (2 Timothy 4:6-8).

**9. The Lord is not slack concerning his promise:** . . . not slow in fulfilling, *—NORL* . . . about keeping, *—NLTG* . . . does not loiter over his promise, *—MNTG* . . . does not delay, *—FNTN* . . . is not tardy, *—CNDT* . . . to fulfil his promise, *—TNT* . . . to do what he has promised, *—WMCK*

**as some men count slackness:** . . . as some people consider him slow, *—TCNT.*

**but is longsuffering to us-ward:** . . . is very patient, *—LBCH* . . . is patient with you, *—SEB* . . . because of you, *—CNDT.*

**not willing that any should perish, but that all should come to repentance:** . . . does not want anyone to be lost, *—TNT* . . . that everyone should be prevailed on to repent, *—NORL* . . . but all to make room for, *—CNDT* . . . have an opportunity to repent, *—WLMS* . . . should come to Reformation, *—WLSN.*

**3:9.** There is a good reason why Christ has not yet returned. He does not wish for anyone to perish. Some will perish (verse 7), but that is not His desire. He patiently provides time and opportunity through the preaching of the gospel, and this is the only reason for the seeming delay in coming as He promised. He is not "slack" (*bradunei*, slow, remiss, tardy) in doing so, but is "longsuffering" (*makrothumei*, forbearing, enduring patiently) toward mankind. Instead of "us-ward," the Greek should be translated "you-ward." "Willing" is *boulomenos*, meaning choice, preference, being so minded; as in 2 Corinthians 1:15, "I was minded to come unto you."

**10. But the day of the Lord will come as a thief in the night:** . . . will approach like, *—FNTN* . . . will be arriving, *—CNDT* . . . will come suddenly and unexpectedly, *—NOLI* . . . as a robber comes, *—NLTG.*

**in the which the heavens shall pass away with a great noise:** . . . the heavenly bodies will burn up and be destroyed, *—WMCK* . . . with a crash, *—TCNT* . . . in a roaring crash, *—NORL* . . . a shrieking noise, *—ADAM* . . . rushing, *—DRBY* . . . whizzing, *—SEB* . . . booming, *—CNDT.*

**and the elements shall melt with fervent heat:** . . . and their constituents will be dissolved, *—FNTN* . . . by combustion, *—CNDT.*

**the earth also and the works that are therein shall be burned up:** . . . the works in it shall be found, *—CNDT* . . . utterly, *—CMPB.*

**3:10.** The Day of the Lord will certainly come (the Greek verb carries a positive emphasis). Believers need to remember this and be ready at all times; unbelievers need to realize it also, or they will suffer at the hands of a "thief in the night." Paul used this same expression in 1 Thessalonians 5:2 concerning the Lord's coming. Jesus warned of it, admonishing His disciples to be ready always, "for in such an hour as ye think not the Son of man cometh" (Matthew 24:44). "The day of the Lord" is not a single event but the period of time including the Second Coming, the tribulation period, and the establishment of Christ's kingdom. Peter skipped over all the intervening events and dealt with the final scene when the heavens shall pass away and the earth be burned up. "Elements" is *stoicheia* (basic parts, components). Some say it refers to stars and planets, others to the four elements of which the universe is composed (fire, air, earth, water). Although the atomic structure of chemical elements was not understood in Peter's day, his language may be interpreted in the light of these elements of which all matter is constituted. The picture is one of total destruction of the heavens and the earth.

**11. [Seeing] then [that] all these things shall be dissolved:** . . . In view of the fact that all of these things, *—PHLP* . . . Since the world will end like this, *—LBCH* . . . If the whole universe is to be dissolved in this way, *—TNT* . . . All these things in this manner being in process of dissolution, *—WUST.*

**what manner [of persons] ought ye to be in [all] holy conversation and godliness:** . . . Surely men of good and holy character, *—PHLP* . . . to what manner of men must you belong in holy behavior and devoutness, *—CNDT* . . . what exotic persons is it necessary in the nature of the case for you to be in the sphere of holy behaviors and pieties, *—WUST* . . . in conduct, *—NORL.*

**3:11.** Peter was more concerned with believers' spiritual condition than with details of what will happen to the heavens and earth. Since this judgment by fire is coming, he says they need to examine their hearts and lives. "Conversation" is *anastrophais* (manner of life, behavior). "Godliness" is *eusebeiais* (holiness, piety, reverence, devoutness). "Dissolved" is *luomenōn* (loosen, disintegrate, melt). It is the New Testament word that best describes atomic disintegration. It is also translated "melt" in 3:12. Since we have become familiar with nuclear power, we know something of "meltdowns," and we can imagine what will take place when all the atoms are smashed. Our knowledge of atomic explosions gives us some idea of the "great noise" (verse 10) which will result from the breakup of all matter.

**12. Looking for and hasting unto the coming of the day of God:** . . . who live expecting and earnestly longing for, *—PHLP* . . . expecting, and earnestly desiring, —CMPB...hoping for and hurrying the presence of God's day, —CNDT.

**wherein the heavens being on fire shall be dissolved:**...this day will mean that the heavens will disappear in fire, —PHLP.

**and the elements shall melt with fervent heat?:**...and the stars to melt in the heat, —TNT...elements burning up are being melted, —WUST...decompose by combustion! —CNDT...through intense heat, —WADE.

**3:12.** The Flood destroyed the earth but not the heavens. Here it says that when the earth is destroyed by fire, the heavens also will be affected: "The heavens being on fire shall be dissolved." So the scoffers are in for an even bigger surprise: there will be a complete destruction by fire, as compared with the partial judgment of the Flood. "Hasting" is *speudontas*, meaning eagerly awaiting as well as speeding. It also carries a sense of hastening His coming. We can do this by going into all the world and preaching the gospel to every creature (Mark 16:15). The purpose of the longsuffering of the Lord (3:9) is to give opportunity for every person on earth to hear the gospel and be saved. This challenge that faced Peter's generation has faced every generation since.

**13. Nevertheless we, according to his promise:**...but our hopes are not set on these, —PHLP.
**look for new heavens and a new earth, wherein dwelleth righteousness:**...are hoping for, —CNDT...new in quality, —WUST...will reign, —NOLI...in which nothing but good shall live, —PHLP.

**3:13.** Believers should not be preoccupied with the flaming destruction of the present heavens and earth but should be looking for new heavens and a new earth in which "righteousness" (*dikaiosunē*, holiness, innocence, equity) "dwelleth" (*katoikei*, reside, make its home). "New" is from *kainos*, meaning fresh. The new heavens and new earth will have a new quality. Some say the heavens and earth will be renewed, rather than being replaced with something brand new. On this question Stanley M. Horton states: "A good case can be made here (verse 10) for taking this as a renovation of the heavens and earth rather than an annihilation. The Bible does speak of 'everlasting hills' (Genesis 49:26; Habakkuk 3:6); the earth 'established forever' (Psalms 78:69; 104:5; 125:1,2), and 'abiding forever' (Ecclesiastes 1:4)" (p. 118). Horton goes on to say: "Since fire is often used in the Bible of cleansing or purifying, it may be taken that the heavens and earth are simply renovated, renewed, and restored to a better state by going through the fire" (ibid.).

**14. Wherefore, beloved, seeing that ye look for such things:**...So, dear friends, —TNT...On which

account, divinely loved ones, —WUST...while you are waiting, —NORL...in expectation of these things, —TCNT...whilst you are awaiting these events, —WADE...hoping for these things, —CNDT...for this transformation, —NOLI.

**be diligent that ye may be found of him in peace:**...do your best, —WUST...endeavor to be found by Him in peace, —CNDT.

**without spot, and blameless:**...irreproachable, —WUST...spotless, —BRKL...unspotted and flawless, —CNDT...clean and blameless in his sight, —PHLP.

**3:14.** Peter exhorted, "Be diligent" (*spoudasate*, eager, zealous, earnest, prompt). The word speaks of intense effort, as in 2 Timothy 2:15, "Study (*spoudason*) to show thyself approved unto God." Since believers are expecting a new heaven and new earth pervaded with righteousness, they should prepare themselves to be occupants of such a home so when Christ comes He will find them living in peace, "without spot" (*aspiloi*, unblemished, unstained, undefiled) and "blameless" (*amōmētoi*, faultless, without flaw or blot, untainted by the world).

The second coming of Christ was the great incentive for holy living among believers in the First Century. Peter referred to it here, and Paul often did in his writings. In 1 Corinthians 1:8 he urged believers to be "blameless in the day of our Lord Jesus Christ." In Philippians 1:10 he spoke of being "sincere and without offense till the day of Christ." He also expressed the need for being blameless at Christ's coming in 1 Thessalonians 3:13 and 5:23.

**15. And account [that] the longsuffering of our Lord [is] salvation:**...consider it as, Wuest...the continued patience of our Lord for your salvation, —BRKL...Meanwhile, consider that God's patience is meant to be man's salvation, —PHLP...be deeming the patience of our Lord salvation, —CNDT.
**even as our beloved brother Paul also according to the wisdom given unto him hath written unto you:**...Paul pointed out in his letter to you, written out of the wisdom God gave him, —PHLP.

**3:15.** Believers should refuse to be upset by scoffers, false teachers, or date setters, counting that the longsuffering of the Lord (His patience in granting more time before His coming) is due to His desire that all might repent and obtain salvation. Peter reminded them that Paul said the same thing in his writings. In Romans 2:4, for example: "Despisest thou the riches of his goodness and forbearance and longsuffering; not knowing that the goodness of God leadeth thee to repentance?"

**16. As also in all [his] epistles, speaking in them of these things:**...in his inspired wisdom wrote to you, —TNT...as also in all his letters, speaking in them concerning these things, —WUST...indeed in all his letters, he referred to these matters,

—PHLP . . . and as well in all the letters in which he mentions these subjects, —BRKL.

**in which are some things hard to be understood:** . . . there are some obscure passages, —NOLI . . . things difficult of being understood, —WUST . . . difficult to comprehend, —WADE . . . hard to apprehend, —CNDT . . . are hard to think through, —BRKL.

**which they that are unlearned and unstable wrest:** . . . which, unhappily, ill-informed and unbalanced people distort, —PHLP . . . which the Uninstructed and Unstable pervert, —WLSN . . . those who are unlearned and lacking stability distort, —WUST . . . The untaught and unsteady twist those writings, —BRKL . . . of weak character twist, —TCNT . . . the fickle distort, —FNTN . . . pervert their meaning, —TNT.

**as [they do] also the other scriptures, unto their own destruction:** . . . to their own ruin, —BRKL.

**3:16.** Peter did not say he could not understand some things in Paul's epistles. He was thinking of people who are "unlearned" (*amatheis*, ignorant) and "unstable" (*astēriktoi*, unfixed, vacillating), who take Scripture passages that seem unclear and "wrest" them (*streblousin*, twist out of context, strain, stretch). They "pervert the gospel of Christ," as Paul said (Galatians 1:7). They even teach people to "continue in sin, that grace may abound" (Romans 6:1), twisting the doctrine of grace. Peter said such teachers bring destruction upon themselves.

This is an important passage, for it shows that Peter considered Paul's writings, like the other Scriptures, to be inspired of God.

**17. Ye therefore, beloved, seeing ye know [these things] before:** . . . my friends whom I love, are forewarned, —PHLP . . . dear friends, forewarned as you are, —BRKL . . . my loved ones, having knowledge of these things before they take place, —BB . . . since you have been warned, —GRBR . . . you already know about this, —EVRD . . . now that you are forewarned, —NORL . . . before they happen, —LBCH . . . knowing in advance, —SWAN.

**beware lest ye also, being led away with the error of the wicked:** . . . be on guard, —SWAN . . . be careful not to be carried away, —WMCK . . . be constantly . . . lest having been carried away by the error of unprincipled men, —WUST . . . Do not let those evil people lead you away by the wrong they do, —EVRD . . . Do not be led astray by idle fancies arising from the errors of godless people, —GRBR . . . take care that you are not turned away by the error of the uncontrolled, —BB . . . so that you may not be carried away by the stray wanderings of, —BRKL . . . by the deceit of the lawless, —CMPB . . . with the deception of the dissolute, —CNDT . . . by the errors of lawless men, —WLMS . . . wicked men, —PHLP.

**fall from your own stedfastness:** . . . and so lapsing from your present stedfastness, —TCNT . . . so that you may not lose your firm stand, —GRBR . . . so that you will not fall from your strong faith, —EVRD . . . Never let them shake your solid faith, —LBCH . . . and so

lose your proper foothold, —PHLP . . . slip from your own moorings, —BRKL . . . from your true faith, —BB.

**3:17.** Peter summed up his appeal three times in his final chapter: in verse 11, "Seeing then that all these things shall be dissolved"; in verse 14, "Seeing that ye look for such things"; and verse 17, "Seeing ye know these things before." He saw the need to keep emphasizing basic truths and to keep fortifying believers. Peter had told them many things and had also reminded them of the things Paul taught them. Since they had been forewarned and forearmed with truth concerning all these matters, they were without excuse if they should "fall" (*ekpesēte*, drop away, fall out of, as in Galatians 5:4, "Ye are fallen from grace") from their "steadfastness" (*stērigmou*, stability, firmness); so they needed to "beware" (*phulassesthe*, be on guard, a military term). Believers never outlive their need of watchfulness. Paul reminded the Corinthians how Israel failed time after time, and added, "Wherefore let him that thinketh he standeth take heed lest he fall" (1 Corinthians 10:12). Peter indicated the danger is that believers may be "led away" (*sunapachthentes*, seduced, carried off) by the "error" (*planē*, straying, wandering) of the "wicked" (*athesmōn*, lawless). Those who "live in error" (2:18) are those who indulge the lusts of the flesh. Peter suggested that people who are weak along this line can be trapped again and again. He warned against these carnal people in the Church and indicated the believers would be carried away with them unless they remained firm in their faith and commitment to Christ.

It is not easy to breast the tide of compromise when others lower their standards and follow the ways of the world; but "God is faithful, who will not suffer you to be tempted above that ye are able; but will with the temptation also make a way to escape, that ye may be able to bear it" (1 Corinthians 10:13).

**18. But grow in grace, and [in] the knowledge of our Lord and Saviour Jesus Christ:** . . . But progress in goodness, —FNTN . . . be constantly growing in the sphere of grace and an experiential knowledge, —WUST.

**To him [be] glory both now and for ever. Amen:** . . . Glory be to him, —EVRD . . . and unto the Day of Eternity, —MNTG . . . as well as for the day of the eon, —CNDT . . . and until the dawning of the day of eternity! —PHLP . . . from now until an appointed day in a future era, —GRBR.

**3:18.** Rather than that they should fall from their steadfastness, Peter admonished them to keep on growing in grace and in the personal, experiential knowledge of Christ. They could know Him not only as "Jesus" (*Iēsou*, Jehovah-saved, the

**1137**

One who saves His people from their sins) and as "Christ" (*Christou*, the Messiah, the One anointed of God to lead His people), but also as "Lord" (*kuriou*, Master, Controller, the One supreme in authority) and as "Saviour" (*sōtēros*, Deliverer, Protector, Preserver, Healer, the One who makes a person whole in body, mind, and spirit). They needed to keep growing in this knowledge, for the best defense against falling is to keep growing

stronger. To Christ be "glory" (*doxa*, praise, honor, radiant splendor) both now and for "ever" (*aiōnos*, perpetually, "unto the day of eternity"). If believers follow Peter's instructions and keep growing in virtue, knowledge, temperance, patience, godliness, brotherly kindness, and charity (1:5-7), they will indeed bring glory to Christ. "Amen" (verily, so be it).

# 1 JOHN

## Overview

Although First John is commonly called an "epistle," it does not have some of the features that were typical of Greek letters of that period. It does not indicate the writer or the persons to whom the letter was sent. There is no greeting or closing. However, there is much throughout the epistle that reveals the type of community to whom the letter was sent. In addition, one can discern the personal and intimate bond between the writer and his readers.

Some scholars believe the epistle was a circular letter written to several churches in a particular region. In this respect it could be compared to 1 Peter and perhaps Ephesians. Such a theory might also explain the general tone of the letter as well as the intimate relationship implied between the writer and the recipients. Some describe 1 John as a tract, a homily (sermon), or a treatise of some kind.

## The Writer

The language, style, theological concepts, and thought world of the writer of 1 John indicates a close relationship to the Gospel of John. Because of this, the question of authorship must be resolved in connection with the discussion of the authorship of the Gospel. Attempts to demonstrate that a different person wrote the three letters and the Gospel have been vigorously challenged. First John is actually anonymous since the writer did not mention his name. However, the first readers of the epistle had no doubts as to the identity of the writer.

Second and Third John only indirectly identify the writer as "the elder" (*ho presbuteros*). This is probably not some official title (the "presbyter" being an elder on a council of elders). The definite article (*ho*) argues against it being an official title. Some interpreters hold that it denotes a person who bears apostolic tradition or a disciple of the apostle. Ancient tradition tells us the apostle John lived for a long time. As the only surviving apostle he might have chosen to call himself "the elder" or, in other words, the "chief elder."

The three most common solutions to the identity of the author are: (1) John the apostle, the son of Zebedee; (2) an otherwise unknown elder named John; (3) a former disciple of John who was the "editor" of the material.

The least viable option is solution number 2. The traditional solution, which clearly does not find much endorsement from contemporary scholarship, is that John the apostle was the author.

## Place and Time of Writing

The First Epistle of John gives no indication of its geographic origin. According to Irenaeus, the apostle John spent his last years in Ephesus. It is possible, therefore, that the epistle was written from somewhere in Asia Minor. This was the ancient tradition.

The letter can probably be dated sometime between A.D. 75 and 100. Since it was known in the first quarter of the Second Century, it cannot have been written any later. Some think it was composed prior to A.D. 70. That a Palestinian Jew should be familiar with the thought world of a different culture should not necessarily be surprising. A parallel is found in the Qumran writings (Dead Sea Scrolls).

On the other hand, some expressions are best explained as the author's turning his opponents' language to his own purposes while rejecting their theology. For example, the language shows some affinity with Gnostic thought, but the writer has thoroughly "Christianized" his understanding of those concepts. The author's shaping of Hellenistic Judaism's language and Gnostic concepts in no way implies that he endorsed such systems. He used the language of his hearers and interpreted their concepts, thoughts, and theology in a Christian light. The language thus became a weapon against his opponents.

## Structure

It is difficult to structure 1 John since the writer interwove the two themes of faith and love throughout the letter. The two basic themes were examined from different vantage points. This interrelationship between the various sections of the epistle has been described as "concentric circles." Perhaps a better description would be a "spiral," since there is movement and progression in each section. It is difficult to determine where one section ends and another begins. Moreover, one stylistic trait of the author was to introduce a series of associated ideas as the letter progressed. This might explain the seemingly "illogical"—or at least "surprising"—transitions and shifts of thought.

Without suggesting that the author had such a plan in mind when he wrote, we can still offer a brief outline illuminating the content of the letter.

I. THE PROLOGUE: THE OBJECT OF PREACHING, ITS BASIS AND PURPOSE (1:1-4)

## The Crises in the Church

First John was addressed to one or more churches in serious crisis. The struggle was not between Judaism and Christianity or between paganism and Christianity, but between true and false believers. The activity that had generated the crisis was that a group of prominent members—including teachers and prophets—of the church or churches were spreading their syncretistic version of Christianity. This mixture of Greek, Jewish, and Christian concepts was the source of the problem.

The comment in 2:19, "They went out from us but did not belong to us," is best interpreted as a schism within the church. Possibly those with whom John was contending had been excommunicated from the community. It is also possible they had willingly left the church. How many the "many" antichrists were cannot be determined (2:18; 4:1). As this quasi-Christian group which had left the church attempted to promote its ideals, another group still within the church community were sympathizing with these "heretics." The crisis was not only in the church, it was in the hearts of some believers.

First John speaks to this crisis. The author's main purpose was pastoral and positive. He reminded his readers of all they possessed in Jesus Christ, the Son of God. He encouraged them to remain in the true faith. The polemic leveled at the heretics was not against them but against their false theology which was nearly fatal to the church. Prior to 2:18 the polemic against the heretics is indirect; after that it takes on a more direct nature.

## The Heretics

The heretics were falsifiers of the Christian faith. They did not teach the truth, but a lie, since they had been seduced by the spirit of delusion. They were not of God but of the world. They were nothing other than antichrists and false prophets. They considered themselves "true" Christians, "superior" to those in the church who had not "advanced" as they had. It is not clear whether John was combating a unified group or whether there were several factions with a variety of common false theologies.

John began his attack on two fronts: one Christological, the other ethical. The apostle emphasizes that Jesus is the Word of Life (1:1); Christ (2:22; 5:1); the Son of God (4:15; 5:5; cf. also 2:23; 3:23; 5:11-13,20). He stressed that Jesus is the Christ, come in the flesh (1 John 4:2; 2 John 7); He came by water and blood (1 John 5:6). From 2:22 it seems that the heretics' Christology derived from the Jewish denial that Jesus was Messiah.

The main issue, however, was not whether Jesus was Messiah, but the relationship between the humanity of Jesus on the one hand, and the divinity of the Son of God on the other. Possibly, the false teachers did not directly deny the Incarnation, but from John's point of view they rejected it. They may have accepted the Incarnation without incorporating it into a doctrine of atonement. John, however, stressed the truth that the atoning sacrifice of Christ was the climax of God's love.

The heretics may have thought the Messiah, the Son of God, was united with the human Jesus only for a period. But this view in effect denied the Incarnation. Thus they had said "No" to God's salvation. The Christological understanding of the heretics is perhaps most clearly outlined in 5:6. They could agree that Jesus "came by water," which refers to Jesus' baptism. But John emphasized that Jesus came "not by water only, but by water and blood."

The ultimate heresy from John's perspective was to say the unity between the human and the divine was only temporary in Christ. It was not only the man Jesus who died on the cross but the God-man Jesus Christ, the Son of God. For the false teachers, Jesus' death did not matter at all.

Often the name *Cerinthus* appears in connection with the heretics John opposed. Cerinthus lived in Ephesus at the same time tradition says John lived in that city. Cerinthus denied the Virgin Birth and asserted that the "Christ nature" descended on Jesus at His baptism and departed before He was crucified.

Any actual docetic system in which Jesus was only a shell for the divine nature was *not* Cerinthus' position nor that of John's opponents. This development can be found only in the Second Century. For example, Ignatius of Antioch combated such Docetists who scorned the idea that God became flesh (*sarx*). Even though it is not possible to make a positive identification of the heresy opposed in 1 John, it does seem closely related, although not necessarily identical, to the teaching of Cerinthus. John insisted that to speak falsely of Christ was to be labeled a heretic. Any dissolution of the union between Jesus and Christ—even at His death—nullifies God's gospel of love.

Ethics, the Christian's relationship to his fellow believers, was John's other main concern. That relationship will be governed totally by his Christology. To walk in the light, to keep God's commandments to love one another, to do righteousness, and so on, are all expressions showing that faith in Jesus is inextricably bound to one's ethical lifestyle. They are not the cause of one's relationship with God, but they do characterize it.

Faith and ethics are inseparable elements of the Christian life. The commandment in 3:23 to exercise faith in Jesus and brotherly love toward others summarizes the entire Christian faith. To know God is to keep His commands (2:3). Faith in Christ and love for fellow believers are inseparable. Those who put aside faith in Jesus as the Christ are also rejecting the love of God. Those who fail to love the community of God are also neglecting to love God.

The manifestation of love is the sign of the genuine Christian. The love John wrote about is divine love, not love on a human level. Divine love is denied when one sets aside loving God's people. The sign of the world—and the heretics—is hate. The world cannot do otherwise (3:13)!

First John teaches that faith must manifest itself in the mundane affairs of day-to-day living, such as when a fellow believer is in need (3:16f.). The New Testament usually applies the term *brother* to Christians, not neighbors in general. The brotherly love of which John wrote involves love for fellow believers especially (3:11,23; 4:7, 11, 12).

However, love of all people—the world—was strongly underlined by John. In demonstration of this principle, John did not show hatred for those opposing and persecuting the Christian community to whom he wrote. There is insufficient evidence for calling them "amoral" or "libertines." Perhaps at best they should be understood as "elitist pneumatics," whose arrogance led them to moral indifference. For the most part they were well-satisfied with their so-called knowledge (*gnōsis*).

# The First Epistle of John

## Commentary

### Chapter 1

**1. That which was from the beginning, which we have heard:** ... We are writing to you about something which has always existed, *—PHLP* ... Christ existed before time began, *—LBCH.*

**which we have seen with our eyes, which we have looked upon:** ... discerningly seen ... gazed upon as a spectacle, *—WUST* ... something which we had opportunity to observe closely, *—PHLP* ... we have watched it, *—WMCK* ... we contemplated, *—DRBY.*

**and our hands have handled, of the Word of life:** ... even to hold in our hands, *—BRKL* ... touched with our own hands, *—MNTG* ... the very message of life, *—WLMS* ... Who is the Disclosure of the True life, *—WADE.*

**1:1.** First John is a gateway to the New Testament, presenting the deepest truths in the simplest terms.

The book omits the usual greeting, perhaps because it was intended for a general audience, traditionally the churches in the area of Ephesus. Instead, John opened with a prologue (as in the Gospel of John) which presents his credentials as an eyewitness of Christ and explains his purpose for writing.

John began with a sentence that is not completed until verse 3. His first topic is the Word of life. As in John 1, "the Word" is a title for Jesus Christ, the One who reveals the mind of God to men.

The Word existed from "the beginning," all the way back into eternity (cf. John 1:1). John and the other apostles had both heard and seen the Word, an experience that had given them knowledge which still remained with them (as shown by the Greek perfect tense of the verbs). They could even look back on specific incidents when they inspected the Word carefully; "looked upon" describes an intense scrutiny, and "handled" describes the type of physical contact recorded in John 20:27.

**2. (For the life was manifested, and we have seen [it]:** ... That Life was actually made visible, *—TCNT* ... it was life which appeared before us, *—PHLP* ... has been revealed, *—BRKL* ... seen it with discernment and have it in our mind's eye, *—WUST.*

**and bear witness, and show unto you that eternal life:** ... We can prove it, *—SEB* ... are testifying and reporting to you the life eonian, *—CNDT* ... are eyewitnesses of it, *—PHLP* ... are witnessing and are announcing to you, *—BRKL* ... and bringing back to you a message concerning the life, *—WUST.*

**which was with the Father, and was manifested unto us;):** ... which was face to face with, *—MNTG* ... who existed with the Father, *—BRKL* ... which is of such a nature as to have been in fellowship with the Father and was made visible to us, *—WUST.*

**1:2.** The second verse is a parenthesis, describing the "life" more fully. John asserted that his ministry of witness was based on the historical event of Christ's appearance as a man. God became man, and the apostles simply testified to what they had experienced. They declared the truth, making an official announcement of what God had done.

The verse gives a more detailed description of "the life." Jesus displayed the kind of endless, glorious life which God himself possesses. After all, He exists "with the Father," a term with a root meaning of "face-to-face with." This intimate relationship was then made known to mankind through witnesses such as John.

**3. That which we have seen and heard declare we unto you:** ... That which we have seen with discernment and at present is in our mind's eye, and that which we have heard and at present is ringing in our ears, we are reporting, *—WUST* ... We repeat, we really saw and heard what we are now writing to you about, *—PHLP* ... We saw Him and we heard Him and are telling you, *—BRKL* ... we are announcing to you, *—MNTG.*

**that ye also may have fellowship with us:** ... We want you to be with us in this, *—PHLP* ... that you may share the dear friendship with Him, *—LBCH* ... you may be participating jointly in common with us, *—WUST.*

**and truly our fellowship [is] with the Father, and with his Son Jesus Christ:** ... this fellowship of ours is with, *—BRKL* ... and our partnership is, *—MNTG* ... The fellowship we share together is, *—EVRD.*

**1:3.** After John finished his parenthesis, he repeated part of the first verse to help his readers pick up the threads of thought which began there. In the phrase "declare we unto you" John finished the main statement of the first verse. The purpose of the epistle was to make known the truth so the readers, as well as the apostles, could benefit from it.

Such a proclamation has a purpose: to enable the readers to have fellowship with one another. The present tense of "have" (*echēte*) implies continual fellowship, the relationship based on things shared or held in common like the property of a married couple. For more detail see "*koinōnia*" in the *Greek-English Dictionary*. This concept of

**1143**

fellowship with other Christians is one of the two major themes of 1 John. The other is introduced in the latter part of the verse: true fellowship among Christians involves fellowship with God as well, both the Father and the Son.

Of all the believers John probably was the one who could understand and appreciate what this kind of fellowship could mean. He was one of the "inner circle," along with Peter and James, who had enjoyed special privileges; for example, witnessing the transfiguration of Jesus. He was very close to Jesus, possibly more than the other apostles (note in 1:1 how he refers to that relationship). He is referred to as "one of his disciples, whom Jesus loved" (John 13:23) and sat next to the Lord at the Last Supper. But he had enjoyed that fellowship for only a little more than 3 years; now he could enjoy it continually through the Spirit.

**4. And these things write we unto you, that your joy may be full:**... We must write and tell you about it, because the more that fellowship extends, the greater the joy it brings to us who are already in it, *−PHLP*... to make your joy complete, *−NORL*... our joy, having been filled completely full in times past may persist in that state of fullness through present time, *−WUST.*

**1:4.** The prologue climaxes with one of the goals of the epistle (see also 2:1; 5:13)—overflowing joy. While the first three verses deal with John's lifelong work of witness, verse 4 refers specifically to the purpose of this epistle.

John was writing to cause joy (as in John 16:24). He wanted joy for the readers, as some versions suggest. And he wanted to share that joy himself, rejoicing as he saw his spiritual children walking in fellowship with God (3 John 4).

The joy will be "full," a Greek idiom for joy that is filled to the brim and continues to stay full to the point of overflowing.

**5. This then is the message which we have heard of him:** ... Here, then, is the message we heard him give, *−PHLP*... at present is ringing in our ears, *−WUST.*

**and declare unto you:** ... and are proclaiming to you, *−SWAN*... We are passing it on to you, *−NLTG*... and announce to you, *−ADAM, −WLSN*... are informing you, *−CNDT*... bringing back tidings to you, *−WUST.*

**that God is light, and in him is no darkness at all:** ... God as to His nature is light, and darkness in Him does not exist, not even one particle, *−WUST*... in any measure, *−SWAN*... no darkness whatever, *−BRKL*... not the faintest shadow of darkness, *−PHLP.*

**1:5.** John moved smoothly from the prologue into the first major strain of thought

(1:5-2:11)—the truth that God is light, and those who want to have fellowship with Him must live in light. Jesus himself had taught this truth in general terms (cf. John 1:4-9; 3:19-21; 8:12; 9:5; 12:46). Because God is light, the believer must live a life of holiness and of transparency and openness toward God.

The verse concludes with a contrast. Darkness is the opposite of light and thus symbolizes moral evil. Since God is light, John used a double negative to state emphatically that there is no darkness in Him.

**6. If we say that we have fellowship with him, and walk in darkness:**... Consequently, *−PHLP*... If we assert that, *−WADE*... If we claim communion with God, *−NOLI*... if we say we are friends with God, *−SEB*... we are His dear friends, *−LBCH*... we enjoy fellowship... while we are walking about in the dark, *−BRKL*... things in common we are having with Him, and thus fellowship, and in the sphere of the aforementioned darkness are habitually ordering our behavior, *−WUST.*

**we lie, and do not the truth:**... we speak falsely, *−WLSN*... we are falsifying and we are not practicing the truth, *−BRKL*... we should be both telling and living a lie, *−PHLP*... and not living in the truth, *−WMCK*

**1:6.** The apostle John developed his basic premise with a series of "if" statements that alternate between right and wrong ways of responding to God's light.

Verse 6 presents the first such approach: a man who claims fellowship with God yet habitually walks in darkness, hidden from the light of God. Both the claim to have fellowship with God and the walk that avoids His light are in the present tense, showing habitual action. Such a claim is absurd because the two claims are incompatible.

Such a contradictory combination of words and deeds reveals a deep-seated problem of falsehood. The person is a liar in word as well, for his actions are in stark contrast to the claim he has made.

**7. But if we walk in the light, as he is in the light:** ... if we really are living in the same light in which he eternally exists, *−PHLP* ... if within the sphere of the light we are habitually ordering our behavior, *−WUST* ... If, however, we walk about, *−BRKL.*

**we have fellowship one with another:** ... we have unbroken fellowship, *−WLMS*... we enjoy mutual fellowship, *−BRKL*... things in common and thus fellowship we... are having with one another, *−WUST.*

**and the blood of Jesus Christ his Son cleanseth us from all sin:**... and the sacrifice of, *−TCNT*... keeps continually cleansing us from, *−WUST*... continues to cleanse us from all sin, *−SEB*... will make us clean, *−LBCH*... will cleanse us from every sin, *−NORL*... purifies us from every form of sin, *−WADE*... every kind of sin, *−WMCK*

**1:7.** In contrast to one who merely claims to have fellowship with God, John put forward the case of one who demonstrates the reality of his fellowship with God by a righteous manner of life. This person continually (present tense) walks in the light. God expects each believer to stay on a path of life that is in the sphere of His light, in line with His holy character.

The result of such a holy life is twofold. First, we have fellowship—not only with God, as one might expect, but with each other. Both kinds of fellowship are tied together, as 1:3 declares, and genuine intimacy with God is the only possible basis for deep fellowship with other Christians.

Second, openness to the light cleanses sins, not only through admission to heaven, but as a continual cleansing process in the present life—one needed for any sin.

**8. If we say that we have no sin:** . . . indwelling, *—WUST.*

**we deceive ourselves, and the truth is not in us:** . . . we are only fooling ourselves, *—SEB* . . . we are deluding ourselves, *—BRKL* . . . ourselves we are leading astray, *—WUST* . . . has no place in us, *—TCNT* . . . the truth is not in our hearts, *—WLMS.*

**1:8.** A second group of people claims to have no sin, declaring the sin is not a continuing part of their life or their human nature. They may fall into an occasional misstep, but nothing serious enough to deserve the epithet "sinner."

Anyone who believes such a statement is more than a liar; he is deluding himself. "Ourselves" holds an emphatic position, because such people are not innocent victims; they take the lead in deceiving themselves. The New Testament uses "deceive" (Greek, *planōmen*) for serious error, not incidental mistakes. Such a claim demonstrates that the truth of the gospel has not become part of the person's life.

**9. If we confess our sins:** . . . if we freely admit that we have sinned, *—PHLP* . . . continue to confess, *—WUST* . . . avowing our sins, *—CNDT.*

**he is faithful and just to forgive us [our] sins:** . . . He is to be depended on, *—WLMS* . . . we find God utterly reliable and straightforward—he forgives our sins, *—PHLP* . . . be pardoning us our sins, *—CNDT.*

**and to cleanse us from all unrighteousness:** . . . and makes us thoroughly clean from all that is evil, *—PHLP* . . . from all wrongdoing, *—MNTG* . . . all injustice, *—CNDT.*

**1:9.** Rather than denying sin, believers are asked to acknowledge it freely. When we admit our sin, we find, paradoxically, that God removes it. "Confess" (Greek, *homologōmen*) implies we must acknowledge that our sin is sin and admit that we

committed it. The plural "sins" shows that confession includes specific acts of sin.

Once we confess sin, the character of God guarantees forgiveness. He is a faithful God who can be trusted to keep His promises (cf. Jeremiah 31:34). He is a righteous God who will forgive our sins because the death of Christ has already paid the penalty for them.

God's character leads to forgiveness and cleansing. He forgives sin, as one might release a debtor from his obligation to pay. And He cleanses from all unrighteousness, not only by imputing righteousness to the sinner's account but by gradually producing holy character in daily life.

**10. If we say that we have not sinned:** . . . if we take up the attitude, *—PHLP* . . . are now in a state where we do not sin, *—WUST.*

**we make him a liar, and his word is not in us:** . . . we make Him out to be, *—BRKL* . . . we challenge his truthfulness, *—NOLI* . . . we flatly deny God's diagnosis of our condition and cut ourselves off from what he has to say to us, *—PHLP* . . . and his Message has no place in us, *—TCNT* . . . Then God's Word does not rule our lives, *—LBCH* . . . has made no impression upon us, *—WADE.*

**1:10** Some say that the group mentioned in verse 10 is the same as the one in verse 8. Other say it speaks of a group who claimed they never committed even a single act of sin. The perfect tense of "have not sinned" implies that they have maintained complete freedom from sin to now.

Such a statement defames the character of God and presents Him to the world as a liar, because the whole gospel message rests on the fact that mankind is sinful and needs a Saviour. The claim of sinlessness shows an absence of the Word of God in the speaker's life.

## Chapter 2

**1. My little children, these things write I unto you:** . . . bairns, *—WUST* . . . the reason I write this to you, *—NORL.*

**that ye sin not:** . . . to keep you from sinning, *—TCNT* . . . that you may not continue to sin, *—MNTG* . . . in order that you may not commit an act of sin, *—WUST.*

**And if any man sin, we have an advocate with the Father, Jesus Christ the righteous:** . . . if anyone commits an act of sin, One who pleads our cause we constantly have facing the Father, *—WUST* . . . we have a patron, *—DRBY* . . . we have a Pleader for us, *—WADE* . . . a Counsel for defense in the Father's presence, *—BRKL* . . . Who stands face to face with, *—ADAM* . . . to help defend us before God, *—SEB* . . . will ask the Father to forgive you, *—LBCH* . . . an Entreater with . . . Christ, the Just, *—CNDT.*

**2:1.** John changed his format from hypothetical cases involving nonbelievers, and moved to the actual situation of his beloved "little children," a tender greeting to family members. He began by explaining that he did not intend to imply that sin is inevitable. No, he was writing to help them avoid committing even a single act of sin (see aorist tense).

Sin does occur, however, and God has provided a way for believers to respond to it. If anyone sins, Jesus is present to serve as his "advocate," a term often used for one who would testify in a person's favor in court. Christ is face-to-face with the Father making intercession for the Christian on the basis of His own righteousness granted to the believer. What an advantage, to have the Judge's Son as our Advocate!

**2. And he is the propitiation for our sins:** ... the means of washing away, –WMCK ... is the satisfying-sacrifice, –SWAN ... is the atonement for, –NORL ... the propitiatory shelter concerned with, –CNDT ... an expiatory satisfaction, –WUST.

**and not for ours only, but also for [the sins of] the whole world:** ... of all mankind, –NOLI.

**2:2.** This verse expands on the work that Christ did to provide a basis for the intercession mentioned in verse 1. He himself (emphasized in Greek) stands as a propitiation for the believer's sins. "Propitiation" (Greek, *hilasmos*) was used in secular writing for a sacrifice that appeased the wrath of an angered god. Some suggest that the New Testament uses it simply to describe a payment for sin; but the usage seems to include the idea that God is justifiably angry at sin. Christ is the divine sacrifice, provided by God himself, which makes it possible for the Lord to meet man without wrath.

This sacrifice is available to all believers as the basis for dealing with sin, but not just to John and his circle of believers. The verse declares strongly that the benefits of Christ's death are available to the entire world.

**3. And hereby we do know that we know him, if we keep his commandments:** ... By this token we recognize that we know Him, if we observe His commands, –BRKL ... this we know experientially that we have come to know Him, –WUST ... when we obey God's laws, –PHLP ... His precepts, –CNDT.

**2:3.** John stated the theme of his next segment in verse 3—there is a test by which one can demonstrate the reality of his relationship to God. The person who truly knows God will keep His commands.

Classical Greek used at least two words for "know": *oida*, which often referred to knowledge gained by abstract learning; and *ginōskō*, often referring to knowledge gained through experience.

John used *ginōskō* twice in this verse in order to describe ones knowledge of God as a Person, not merely an object of philosophical or theological speculation facts.

"We know him" is perfect tense, which John often used to describe the believer who has come to know God and still retains a personal relationship with God because of the initial encounter with Him. Such a relationship can be tested by looking for consistent obedience to God's commands.

**4. He that saith, I know him, and keepeth not his commandments:** ... but does not obey, –NORL ... his laws, –PHLP.

**is a liar, and the truth is not in him:** ... truth of God, –CNDT ... in this one the truth does not exist, –WUST ... but he lives in self-delusion, –PHLP.

**2:4.** The apostle took aim at one of the imposters who were plaguing the Early Church, a person who claimed to have the knowledge of God just described. But the promising words were linked with a life of disobedience to God's commands. The verdict is obvious. This person had failed the test of 2:3 and was a liar. His problem went beyond mere confusion; he was actively deceiving others and had no trace of the truth.

**5. But whoso keepeth his word, in him verily is the love of God perfected:** ... In practice, the more a man learns to obey God's laws, the more truly and fully does he express his love for him, –PHLP ... whoever observes His message, in him the love of God has truly reached maturity, –BRKL ... whoever habitually with a solicitous care is keeping His word, truly, in this one the love of God has been brought to its completion, –WUST ... God's love has accomplished its purpose, –ADAM ... truly in this one, –CNDT.

**hereby know we that we are in him:** ... In this way we recognize that we are in Him, –BRKL ... This is how we know that we are following God, –EVRD ... we have an experiential knowledge, –WUST.

**2:5.** Any Christian may qualify for the contrasting picture in this verse. Whoever habitually keeps the word of God is truly in fellowship with Him, despite the claims of some to be spiritually elite. "Love" appears here for the first of many times in the epistle. It could refer to the love which God has for us, but the context suggests that it means the love we should show toward God. Human love for God is imperfect in this life, but the verse uses a word (Greek, *teteleiōtai*) which means completeness rather than absolute perfection. This is love which becomes complete when it results in loving action (cf. 3:16-18). The final phrase repeats the test of any claim to fellowship with God: obedience to His commands.

**6. He that saith he abideth in him:** ... Whoever claims, −WLMS ... He who says, "I live in Christ," −LBCH ... saying that he is remaining in Him, −CNDT ... The life of a man who professes to be living in God, −PHLP ... saying that he as a habit of life is living in close fellowship with and dependence upon Him, −WUST ... God lives in him, −EVRD.

**ought himself also so to walk, even as he walked:** ... is morally obligated just as that One conducted himself, −WUST ... ought personally to live the way He lived, −BRKL ... must bear the stamp of Christ, −PHLP ... ought to live as Christ lived, −LBCH.

**2:6.** Intimacy with Christ inevitably produces a daily walk that mirrors the pattern of Christ's life. John used the word "abideth," a strong term, to describe a permanent relationship with Jesus, a concept probably drawn from the picture of vine and branches in John 15. Any person who claims to abide in Christ is under obligation to behave in the same way as his Lord. "Ought" and "walk" are both present tense, emphasizing the need to behave in this way continually.

John simply referred to "that one" (*ekeinos*; "he," KJV) without explaining that it referred to Jesus. Christ held such a central place in his thought that no further description was necessary (cf. 3:3, 5, 7, 16; 4:17).

**7. Brethren, I write no new commandment unto you, but an old commandment which ye had from the beginning:** ... Divinely loved ones, no commandment new in quality, −WUST ... Dear friends, I am writing ... only the old command which you have had, −BRKL ... My loved ones, I do not give you a new law ... which you had from the first, −BB ... this is no new doctrine ... one which you accepted, −GRBR.

**The old commandment is the word which ye have heard from the beginning:** ... It is just the old, original command, −PHLP ... is identical with the Message, −TCNT ... is the word which came to your ears, −BB ... is the truth that you have just heard, −GRBR.

**2:7.** Some may have protested that John was adding his own commands to the Christian faith. But he replied that all he said came directly from the words of Christ himself.

Since verses 9-11 move directly to a discussion of love, it is clear that John was speaking of Christ's command to love other Christians (John 13:34,35). John could speak with conviction, for he had been present when Jesus himself told His disciples He was giving them the commandment. "New" (Greek, *kainēn*) means "new in kind, novel." So the apostle was certainly not inventing new demands; on the contrary, he was repeating standards which the believers had known ever since they began their relationship with Christianity.

**8. Again, a new commandment I write unto you, which thing is true in him and in you:** ... On the other hand ... one that is real in Him and in you, −BECK ... In turn I write ... realized in Him, −BRKL ... But in one sense I am sending you a new doctrine. It runs thus, −GRBR ... I know that it is always new and always true, −PHLP ... which fact is true, −WUST ... you can see its truth in Jesus and in yourselves, −EVRD.

**because the darkness is past, and the true light now shineth:** ... I know this because the darkness is passing away and the real light, −BECK ... is being caused to pass away, and ... the genuine light, −WUST ... for the night is near its end and the true light is even now shining out, −BB ... the darkness must yield, and the ray of the true light must shine, −GRBR ... is beginning to lift, −PHLP ... is passing by, and ... already is appearing, −CNDT ... is already shining, −NORL.

**2:8.** A second look, however, shows that there is a sense in which the commandment is new, in relation to Christ because His death gave new meaning to the word "love." And it has become new to Christians as they experience it in their own lives.

This amazing revolution of love had even begun changing the face of the world. The darkness of sin and hate which was mentioned in 1:5 was passing off the scene, like a column of men disappearing in the distance. The verb should probably be taken in the middle voice, suggesting that the darkness was dissipating of its own accord. In the same way, the genuine light of the gospel was already in the process of shining to dispel the darkness, like a rising sun chasing the shadows.

**9. He that saith he is in the light:** ... A person may claim, −SEB ... He who professes, −WADE ... Whoever claims to be, −SWAN.

**and hateth his brother:** ... and nevertheless harbors hatred of his fellow-man in his heart, −GRBR ... is habitually hating, −WUST.

**is in darkness even until now:** ... is still in the darkness, −NORL ... in complete darkness, −PHLP ... to this very hour, −TCNT ... hitherto, −CNDT ... all the while, −BRKL.

**2:9.** John then moved to another test by which we can discover whether our fellowship with God is genuine. As he did in earlier tests, he shifted back and forth between positive and negative statements (cf. 1:6-10; 2:3-6). This verse introduces a person who claims to exist in the sphere of God's light, yet hates his brother. John's verdict is blunt: the man is in the dark, not the light. In fact, he has existed in the darkness all the way to the present moment. There is no room for intermediate attitudes between love and hate in the discussion; a person can either choose to show love by serving others, or refuse to meet their needs.

The test applies specifically to fellow Christians, as shown by the mention of "brother."

**10. He that loveth his brother abideth in the light:** ... is remaining, *–CNDT* ... is continually in the light, *–BRKL* ... lives and moves in the light, *–PHLP.*

**and there is none occasion of stumbling in him:** ... he will not fall down, *–LBCH* ... has no reason to stumble, *–PHLP* ... there is no stumbling-block in him, *–SWAN* ... he is no hindrance to others, *–WLMS* ... there is nothing within him to occasion stumbling, *–BRKL* ... there is no cause for falling, *–WMCK* ... there is no snare in him, *–CNDT.*

**2:10.** Love for fellow Christians is an evidence of a person's position in fellowship with God. And it is significant that the statement begins "He that loveth" rather than "He that saith," since it is describing a person who loves in action, not merely with words. "Abideth" (Greek, *menei*) refers to permanent residence in a location, rather than the temporary stay of a transient. And the present tense of the verb strengthens the emphasis on a permanent relationship.

Such a person is in the light, and there is no "occasion of stumbling" (Greek, *skandalon*) in him. *Skandalon* referred to an animal snare, then to an object that would cause one to trip himself up. The person who loves has nothing in his character that will cause him to stumble into sin.

John Wesley made an interesting comment: "He that hates his brother is an occasion of stumbling to himself. He stumbles against himself, and against all things within and without; while he that loves his brother has a free disencumbered journey" (John Wesley, et al., 1 John 2:10).

**11. But he that hateth his brother is in darkness, and walketh in darkness:** ... the brother-hater is in the dark and moves in the dark, *–BRKL* ... as a habit of life hates, *–WUST* ... and are living in, *–TCNT* ... is shut off from the light and gropes his way in the dark, *–PHLP* ... and is spending his life in the darkness, *–MNTG.*

**and knoweth not whither he goeth, because that darkness hath blinded his eyes:** ... he has to grope about, *–NORL* ... he cannot see in the dark, *–LBCH* ... without seeing where he is going. To move in the dark is to move blindfold, *–PHLP.*

**2:11.** On the other hand, one who hates his brother demonstrates that he is in darkness. First, he exists in darkness (2:9). Second, he walks around in darkness, open to the risk of stumbling over unseen obstacles. Third, he is going away in darkness, not knowing his direction (cf. John 12:35). The obscurity is complete because darkness has blinded his eyes. The aorist tense of "blinded" pictures the decisive moment when the darkness finally overtakes the sinner.

**12. I write unto you, little children, because your sins are forgiven you for his name's sake:** ... as my dear children, *–PHLP* ... have been put away from you permanently, *–WUST* ... because of the authority of Jesus, *–SEB* ... on account of his name, *–CMPB* ... through His name, *–CNDT.*

**2:12.** John opened a new section of the epistle by assuring his readers of their identity in Christ. Because they were genuine members of God's family, they could successfully cope with the spiritual dangers around them. Because of their conversion they had been born into the family of God, having become partakers of His nature. An earthly father considers it his duty to guide and protect his family. God assumes the same responsibility.

Verses 12-14 are a highly structured segment, with the symmetry and repetition of poetry. John presented his point in a pair of triplets, switching from the present tense to aorist at the midpoint, for reasons which are not completely clear.

He wrote first to "little children" (Greek, *teknia*), a term he often used as an affectionate description of all believers. He said he wrote to them because their sins had been forgiven, a fact already accomplished (perfect tense) through the name of Christ.

**13. I write unto you, fathers, because ye have known him [that is] from the beginning:** ... I write to you who are now fathers, because you have known him who has always existed, *–PHLP* ... come to know experientially, *–WUST* ... the Christ who lived before the world began, *–LBCH.*

**I write unto you, young men, because ye have overcome the wicked one:** ... Young children, *–CMPB* ... youths, *–CNDT* ... to you vigorous young men I am writing because you have been strong in defeating the evil one, *–PHLP* ... you have mastered, *–TCNT* ... conquered, *–NORL* ... gained the victory over the Pernicious One and as a present result are victorious over him, *–WUST.*

**I write unto you, little children, because ye have known the Father:** ... Yes, I have written these lines to you all, dear children, *–PHLP* ... children under instruction, *–WUST* ... you have come to know, *–BRKL.*

**2:13.** Next John addressed the fathers, the more mature believers, and wrote that they had received his message because they had come to know Christ (as in 2:3). He described the Lord as the One who is "from the beginning," the eternally existing One.

The triplet closes with a word to the younger men, a term generally used for those in the 25-40 age group. He wrote to these because they had already encountered Satan, the "wicked one," and had overcome his onslaughts.

Some versions begin verse 14 at this point. But John moves into his second triplet with another statement to "children" (Greek, *paidia*). The new word for children still refers to all believers but emphasizes their immaturity and need of guidance. John acknowledged that these too had come to know the Father.

**14. I have written unto you, fathers, because ye have known him [that is] from the beginning:** ... older men, —WADE ... to you fathers because of your experience of the one who has always existed, —PHLP ... have learned to know, —BRKL.

**I have written unto you, young men, because ye are strong:** ... strong with endowed strength, —WUST ... you have all the vigor of youth, —PHLP.

**and the word of God abideth in you:** ... God's Message is always in your thoughts, —TCNT ... you have a hold on God's truth, —PHLP ... stays in your hearts, —BRKL ... you have kept the divine Gospel, —NOLI ... treasured in your hearts, —NORL ... lives in you, —LBCH ... is always in, —WLMS ... remains in your thoughts, —WADE.

**and ye have overcome the wicked one:** ... you have gained the victory, —WUST ... You have power over the devil, —NLTG ... you have conquered the evil one, —BRKL ... you have defeated, —PHLP.

**2:14.** The apostle continued his message to the believers, speaking to the "fathers," the more mature members. He repeated the same message he gave them in verse 13.

Then he turned to the younger converts, the "young men," again giving almost the same message as in the prior verse. This time, however, he developed the thought more fully. Strength (Greek, *ischuroi*) is a trait naturally associated with the prime of young manhood, and the word used implies physical strength and ability. Not only did these young men possess great strength, but they also had the Word of God dwelling permanently in them. They had overcome Satan because they were strong. The source of their strength was the Word of God abiding in them. A believer's relationship to the Scriptures invariably determines the quality of his Christian experience. The Bible is called "the sword of the Spirit." Those who have hid God's Word in their hearts have the resources necessary to live an overcoming life and to defeat Satan. When He was tempted, Jesus himself used the Scriptures to defeat the devil.

**15. Love not the world, neither the things [that are] in the world:** ... Do not love the ways of the world, —LBCH ... Stop considering the world precious with the result that you love it, —WUST ... or what the world has to offer, —TCNT.

**If any man love the world, the love of the Father is not in him:** ... as a habit of life is considering the world precious, —WUST ... Whoever loves the world has not the Father's love in his heart, —BRKL.

**2:15.** An abrupt warning now follows. Christians enjoying such privileges must not center their affections on the world; only God is worthy of their highest devotion.

The command not to love is in the present tense, implying, it appears, that the people have already been developing an affection for the world and need to quench that interest.

The "world" (Greek, *kosmon*) is a word with the general meaning of an orderly arrangement, even used for a woman's adornment in 1 Peter 3:3. It also denotes the universe or the inhabited world. Here, however, it carries an evil connotation, describing the world system which Satan has arranged in his attempt to establish a kingdom without God. Believers are to love neither the world nor the things in it, a concept explained in the following verse. Such love is wrong because God demands we deliberately choose to focus our love on Him.

**16. For all that [is] in the world:** ... because everything in the world, —BRKL.

**the lust of the flesh, and the lust of the eyes, and the pride of life:** ... the passionate desire of the flesh ... the insolent and empty assurance which trusts in the things that serve the creature life, —WUST ... the passions of the flesh, the desires of the eyes and the proud display of life, —BRKL ... the desire seated in the flesh, —WADE ... the things that our lower nature and eyes are longing for, —WLMS ... wanting sinful things to please our bodies, —SEB ... the desire of the flesh, and the desire of the eyes, and the ostentation of living, —CNDT ... the glory and glamor of life, —NORL ... and a pretentious life, —TCNT ... the proud glory of life, —MNTG ... the pride of possessions, —ADAM ... the vainglory of life, —CLMT ... the vain ambitions of life, —NOLI.

**is not of the Father, but is of the world:** ... have their origin not from, —BRKL ... from the world as a source, —WUST.

**2:16.** John next explained why it is impossible to love both God and the world. The key issue is the fact that a person's attitudes will come from one source or another, either God or the world. Even seemingly neutral items become worldly if they spring from an attitude rooted in the world system, rather than one dependent on God.

John gave three examples of attitudes that come out of the sphere of the world. First comes the "lust of the flesh," the impulsive desire that originates in the sinful human nature and results in sensuality and other illicit cravings. The second attitude is the "lust of the eyes," the greedy craving that wants whatever it sees. Finally, the "pride of life." John's term for pride is a strong one, carrying the idea of boastful pretensions and bragging beyond the limits of reality. "Life" (Greek, *biou*) refers to mere physical or animal life rather than spiritual or eternal life. It is also used (as in 3:17) to describe the physical possessions that sustain life. The third sin mentioned, then, is that of overconfident pride because of one's possessions. Materialism is always a detriment to spiritual progress.

**17. And the world passeth away, and the lust thereof:** ... and its desire, –CNDT ... with its passions is passing away, –LBCH ... and its passionate desire, –WUST.

**but he that doeth the will of God abideth for ever:** ... whoever perseveres in doing God's will, –WLMS ... will live, –LBCH ... will endure, –NOLI ... is remaining, –CNDT.

**2:17.** A further reason why one should not love the world is that it is temporary. In fact, the present tense of "passing away" shows that the world system had already begun the process of decay that would eventually lead to its disappearance. The middle voice of the verb suggests that the world carries within it the seeds of its own destruction (*paragetai* can be translated as passive or middle voice).

Not only is the world passing away, but so is the "lust" or urgent desire connected with it. The world system only promotes items and values which are part of itself, and since the world is temporary, the things which worldly people want are also temporary.

In contrast, the person who follows the will of God is aligned with something eternal. Both the meaning of "abideth" and the mention of "for ever" underscore the permanence of the godly person. The Greek idiom for "for ever" (literally "into the ages") is a reminder that God's will extends beyond the current age into all the ages yet to come, into the expanse of eternity.

**18. Little children, it is the last time:** ... children under instruction, it is a last hour in character, –WUST ... it is the final age of the world, –NORL ... the last hour, –MNTG ... the final Period in the world's history, –WADE.

**and as ye have heard that antichrist shall come:** ... the false-christ is coming, –NLTG ... have arisen, –WUST.

**even now are there many antichrists:** ... now also there have come to be many antichrists, –CNDT ... many antichrists have already appeared, –WLMS ... and are here, –WUST.

**whereby we know that it is the last time:** ... from which we gather certainly that this is, –BRKL ... which confirms my belief that we are near the end, –PHLP ... a last hour in character, –WUST.

**2:18.** A new section of the epistle begins here, explaining the fact that God is truth. The rest of the chapter unfolds the need for those who claim

fellowship with God to pursue truth, not false teaching.

John addressed his readers as "little children" (Greek, *paidia*), a term emphasizing their immaturity and need to pay attention to the apostle's instructions.

"It is the last time" begins the section, a phrase that only occurs here in the New Testament. Similar terms are used often to describe the age just before Christ's return. The absence of "the" in Greek may suggest that John was not declaring that Christ's coming would certainly be soon; he did observe that his situation was similar to that foretold for the days just prior to the return of Christ.

Several passages in the New Testament describe a specific individual called the Antichrist, who has not yet appeared. Just before the return of Christ to set up His kingdom on earth an individual will arise, called the Antichrist. He will combine in one man to an ultimate degree all the hatred for God and opposition to Him. In John's day a number of people displaying traits like the future Antichrist had already appeared, and the "spirit of antichrist" was already present in the world. Only John used the word "antichrist" (in 1 John 2:22; 4:3; 2 John 7), and the prefix *anti* can mean either one who stands openly against the Lord or one who tries to present himself as a substitute for Him, a more subtle form of opposition.

The spirit of Antichrist includes all false teachers and enemies of the truth. This opposition to God may be expected to increase and intensify as time goes on, culminating in the person and activities of one who will gather together under his banner all the anti-God forces in a final attempt to dethrone God. The Book of Revelation depicts his activities and defeat.

**19. They went out from us, but they were not of us:** ... Out of us they come, –CNDT ... went out from our company, it is true, –PHLP ... they departed ... but they did not belong to us as a source, –WUST ... but they left us, –SEB ... never really belonged to us, –LBCH.

**for if they had been of us, they would [no doubt] have continued with us:** ... had they been ours, –BRKL ... If they had really belonged to us they would have stayed, –PHLP ... they would have remained with us, –WLSN.

**but [they went out], that they might be made manifest:** ... Because they left, –NLTG ... but their departure was designed to make it clear, –WADE ... it had to become clear, –BRKL ... In fact, their going proves beyond doubt that men like that, –PHLP ... they departed in order that they might be plainly recognized, –WUST.

**that they were not all of us:** ... were revealed as not being of us, –SWAN ... that all do not belong to us as a source, *—WUST*... that it might be shown that none of them belongs to us, *—WMCK*... they did not belong to our group, *—NORL*... were not "our men" at all, *—PHLP.*

**2:19.** The antichrists of whom John spoke came from the ranks of the believers. John used a play on words when he pointed out that they went out "from us" (Greek, *ex hēmōn*) but were not really "of us" (same Greek phrase). The first use refers to their physical location—they had been in the local churches but had left. The second use refers to the source from which they came—their separation showed that they had never really shared in the same spiritual fellowship as the others. John laid down the rule—those who desert show openly that none of them were truly one with the church.

**20. But ye have an unction from the Holy One:** ... Besides, you hold your anointing from, *—BRKL*... were anointed by, *—NORL*... have been consecrated by, *—TCNT*... you have received an appointment from, *—WMCK*

**and ye know all things:** ... all of you have the capacity to know [spiritual truth], *—WUST*... you all know the truth, *—LBCH*... you all are aware, *—CNDT.*

**2:20.** Unlike the false brethren, the true believers to whom John wrote had an "unction" or anointing which provided them with the ability to hold to the truth. "Unction" (Greek, *chrisma*) is a play on words—the false "christs" of verse 19 are contrasted with the "chrisma" (empowered saints) of verse 20. In the Old Testament, kings, priests, and prophets were anointed with oil to symbolize the Holy Spirit was empowering them for their task (cf. 1 Samuel 16:13; Isaiah 61:1). This verse speaks of how the Holy Spirit anoints the believer so he will have knowledge which comes from God, the Holy One. Gnostic false teachers claimed to be the sole source of truth, but the Holy Spirit makes it possible for all believers to know the truth.

**21. I have not written unto you because ye know not the truth:** ... The reason I wrote you was not that you do not know the truth, *—BRKL*... you are not acquainted with, *—CNDT.*

**but because ye know it, and that no lie is of the truth:** ... but that you know it and that from truth nothing false originates, *—BRKL*... is not out of the truth as a source, *—WUST.*

**2:21.** John did not write to convey hidden truths which had been concealed from his hearers; his letter was sent to people who simply needed to be reminded of things they already knew. They already knew the gospel, and when they recalled that no lie springs from that source of truth, they would recognize that truth and falsehood cannot coexist.

**22. Who is a liar but he that denieth that Jesus is the Christ?:** ... Who is the pre-eminent liar, *—WADE*... And what, I ask you, is the crowning lie? Surely the denial that Jesus is God's anointed one, *—PHLP*... Who is the liar whom I have in mind? *—GRBR* ... if it is not the denier that Jesus is the Christ? *—BRKL*... the man who rejects, *—TCNT.*

**He is antichrist, that denieth the Father and the Son:** ... I say, therefore, that any man who refuses to acknowledge the Father and the Son is an antichrist, *—PHLP*... is the enemy of Christ, *—EVRD*... even he who disowns, *—MNTG* ... because he repudiates both, *—NOLI* ... This person is the enemy of Christ, *—SEB.*

**2:22.** The believer's anointing is based on the teachings of the gospel which Christ and His apostles preached. Thus John asked them to use the truth they already knew to evaluate the message of new teachers. John attacked the heretics who taught that Jesus was a mere man who was indwelt temporarily by the Christ, a divine spirit who left Him just before the Cross. He who denies that Jesus is the Christ is denying the incarnation of Christ, undercutting the truth that God became man. No wonder John declared that such a person is *the* liar (emphatic in Greek)—this teaching would nullify the entire message of the New Testament!

The doctrine of the Incarnation may be considered the foundation stone for all other New Testament truth. "The Word was made flesh, and dwelt among us" (John 1:14) is the great statement which proclaimed God's plan for nullifying the effects of the Fall. If Jesus was not born of a virgin, He was not the Son of God. And He could not be the promised Messiah—Christ. He was not just divine, like God; He was deity himself, the very essence of God in human flesh. To deny this is heresy of the grossest sort.

Those who preached such doctrines evidently claimed to believe the same truths as other teachers concerning the Father, but John warned that anyone who denied the work of Christ was denying the Father as well.

**23. Whosoever denieth the Son, the same hath not the Father:** ... If anyone does not believe in the Son, *—EVRD* ... The man who will not recognize the Son cannot possibly know the Father, *—PHLP*... who is disowning... neither has, *—CNDT.*

**[but] he that acknowledgeth the Son hath the Father also:** ... he who confesses, *—MNTG, —LBCH* ... whoever accepts the Son has the Father, too, *—EVRD* ... who is avowing, *—CNDT* ... yet the man who believes in the Son will find that, *—PHLP* ... has the Father as well, *—BRKL*... is also in communion with the Father, *—GRBR.*

**2:23.** No one who denies the Son can claim to have a family relationship with the Father; both persons of the Godhead are together inseparably, and both must be accepted together. On the other hand, anyone who acknowledges Jesus as God's Son who became man shows that his Father is God.

This was a very important point to emphasize, especially for the apostle John. In the Gospel he wrote under the inspiration of the Holy Spirit, he had referred to the close relationship between the Father and the Son. When he pointed out that Jesus was the only One who could reveal God to mankind, he wrote, "The only begotten Son, which is in the bosom of the Father, he hath declared him" (John 1:18). To deny this would destroy the truth of the gospel.

**24. Let that therefore abide in you, which ye have heard from the beginning:** ... For yourselves I beg you to stick to the original teaching, *—PHLP* ... Be sure that you continue to follow the teaching that you heard from the beginning, *—EVRD* ... live in your heart, *—LBCH* ... be remaining in you, *—CNDT* ... let that stay with you, *—BRKL.*

**If that which ye have heard from the beginning shall remain in you:** ... If you do, *—PHLP* ... If you continue in that teaching, *—EVRD* ... let that remain in you, *—WMCK* ... stays with you, *—BRKL.*

**ye also shall continue in the Son, and in the Father:** ... you will abide, *—WUST* ... you will stay, *—EVRD* ... will be remaining in, *—CNDT* ... remain in union with, *—BRKL* ... you will be living in fellowship with, *—PHLP.*

**2:24.** How should a Christian respond to the false teachings of these antichrists? By continuing to believe the truths already learned. The Greek begins with "you," an emphatic contrast with the apostates. Rather than accepting novel ideas, the readers were to hold permanently to the doctrines which they learned in the beginning, when they first heard the gospel.

By obeying, they could remain in a living relationship with God. Abiding permanently with the Son allows us to have fellowship with the Father.

**25. And this is the promise that he hath promised us, [even] eternal life:** ... And that means sharing his own life for ever, as he has promised, *—PHLP* ... This is the message that he himself brought us, the message of the life hereafter, *—GRBR* ... And this is what the Son promised to us— life forever, *—EVRD* ... the life eonian, *—CNDT.*

**2:25.** God promises eternal life to all who remain in the Son. "This" refers to eternal life, as shown by the feminine forms of both words. And eternal life is more than infinitely continued existence; it is a quality of life which can be experienced now. Christ himself (note the emphatic

"he," Greek *autos*) promised eternal life in such passages as John 3:15,16; 6:40; 17:3.

This is no idle promise. Jesus often showed the relationship between eternal life and the resurrection. At the tomb of Lazarus He told Martha, "I am the resurrection, and the life" (John 11:25). Later in this epistle John states, "He that hath the Son hath life" (5:12). Therefore believers never really die. They are awaiting the resurrection.

**26. These [things] have I written unto you concerning them that seduce you:** ... It is true that I felt I had to write the above about men who would dearly love to, *—PHLP* ... about those people who are trying to lead you the wrong way, *—EVRD* ... those who want to mislead you, *—NORL* ... those who are deceiving you, *—CNDT* ... who are leading you astray, *—WUST.*

**2:26.** In the next two verses the apostle repeated some of his major points. First he described the character of the false teachers who were attempting to disturb the churches. He had written "these things" before, primarily in verses 18-25, describing the troublemakers as opponents of Christ and promoters of lies. Now he added the fact that they were deceivers. "Seduce" (Greek, *planōntōn*) means to cause someone to go astray. Since the rest of the letter envisions a situation where believers are being approached, but have not succumbed, this present participle may be describing action which is attempted but not completed. The heretics were trying to pull church members off the path but had not yet succeeded in large numbers.

**27. But the anointing which ye have received of him abideth in you:** ... Yet I know that the touch of his Spirit never leaves you, *—PHLP* ... Christ gave you a special gift. You still have this gift in you, *—EVRD* ... which Christ poured upon you, *—LBCH* ... is remaining in you, *—CNDT.*

**and ye need not that any man teach you:** ... having that anyone be constantly teaching you, *—WUST* ... you stand in no need of teaching from anyone, *—BRKL* ... and you don't really need a human teacher, *—PHLP.*

**but as the same anointing teacheth you of all things:** ... The Holy Spirit is able to teach you, *—NLTG* ... The gift he gave you teaches you about everything, *—EVRD* ... instructs you about everything, *—BRKL.*

**and is truth, and is no lie:** ... The Holy Spirit teaches only the truth, *—LBCH* ... This gift is true, *—EVRD* ... and is no falsehood, *—BRKL.*

**and even as it hath taught you, ye shall abide in him:** ... be constantly abiding, *—WUST* ... remain in Him, *—CNDT* ... continue to live in Christ, as his gift taught you, *—EVRD* ... hold faithfully to that which it has taught you, *—GRBR.*

**2:27.** Next John reviewed the anointing which enables the Christian to recognize truth. He began with an emphatic "you," as in verse 24, showing how different the true believers are from the false teachers. Earlier John asked us to let the anointing remain (2:24); here he asserted that it actually does remain in the believer.

This anointing implies the presence of the Holy Spirit, who makes it possible for us to escape dependence on human teachers. Of course John did not want to abolish teachers; he was functioning as a teacher when he wrote his book! But a Spirit-led Christian can detect truth and error without aid from any new breed of teacher.

The rest of the verse develops the command to abide in Christ. The Holy Spirit teaches the things a Christian needs to know, and His instruction is always true, not a lie. Then John repeated the fact that this anointing teaches the Christian, this time using the aorist tense to refer to the teaching ministry of Christ. The final phrase gives a command, "Abide in him." This is a reference to Christ, as shown by verse 28.

**28. And now, little children, abide in him:**...his teaching urges you to live in Christ, *—PHLP*...remain in union, *—WADE.*

**that, when he shall appear, we may have confidence:**...So that if he were suddenly to reveal himself we should still know exactly where we stand, *—PHLP*...if he is manifested, we may have boldness, *—SWAN*...in order that whenever He is made visible, we may have instant freedom of speech, *—WUST*...we can face him proudly, *—NOLI.*

**and not be ashamed before him at bis coming:** ... without shrinking from him in shame, *—NOLI*...and not hide from him in shame, *—WMCK*...and not be put to shame by Him, *—CNDT*...not be made to shrink away from Him in shame at His coming and personal presence, *—WUST.*

**2:28.** As John began another new section, he added a new concept to the command to abide: the second coming of the Lord. Christians should maintain an abiding relationship with Jesus so they can stand before Him unashamed when He returns. "Confidence" (Greek, *parrhēsian*) was used to describe the free citizens of Athens who were permitted to speak their minds boldly in the assembly. In contrast, a person with no abiding tie to God will shrink away in shame when the Monarch of the universe arrives.

**29. If ye know that he is righteous:** ... If you know in an absolute manner that, *—WUST* ... you should be perceiving that He is just, *—CNDT*...God is really good, *—PHLP.*

**ye know that every one that doeth righteousness is born of him:** ... who practices, *—BRKL* ... is begotten of Him, *—CNDT* ... a true child of God, *—PHLP*...from Him has been born, with the present result that that one is a born-one, *—WUST.*

**2:29.** John began a new cycle of teaching here, which took the same themes he had already handled, and developed the thoughts a little further. For instance, he deepened the thought of fellowship to the concept of sonship (3:9; 4:7; 5:1, 4, 18). After establishing our identity as family members, he moved on to show that the tests of true sonship are holiness, love, and truth.

The first topic is holiness (2:29-3:10). If we know the doctrinal fact that the character of God is righteous, we will be able to learn by experience the practical truth that those in His family must also have righteousness.

In context, it appears that the "he" of the first part of the verse refers to Jesus who has a righteous character. In the second part, "him" refers to the Father as the source of the new birth. Anyone who continually practices the righteousness which Christ displayed is demonstrating that he has received birth from God, stamping him with the divine likeness.

# Chapter 3

**1. Behold, what manner of love the Father hath bestowed upon us:**...Perceive, *—CNDT*...Consider the incredible love that, *—PHLP* ... See what amazing love, *—ADAM* ... what transcendent love, *—WADE* ...what a wealth of love the Father has lavished on us, *—BRKL*...what exotic [foreign to the human heart] love the Father has permanently, *—WUST.*

**that we should be called the sons of God:**...in allowing us to be called, *—PHLP*...to the end that we may be named children, *—WUST*...children, *—CNDT.*

**therefore the world knoweth us not, because it knew him not:** ... does not recognize us, *—TNT*...because it has not come into an experiential knowledge of Him, *—WUST* ... it did not know Him, *—BRKL.*

**3:1.** When John considered our place as children of God, he burst out in excitement. "Behold!" is a sharp command to pay attention to the marvelous kind of love which God has permanently bestowed. "What manner of" originally meant "from what country," and later became an exclamation of surprise and wonder (cf. Mark 13:1). This love (Greek, *agapē*) is God's way of showing mercy to man, not merely an emotional reaction. It is a special kind of love. The Greek language contains other words which may be translated "love," but they are less in meaning than agape love. They can mean just physical love, on an animal level. Another is best translated "affection," which can be strong. But God's kind of love is given without measure, does not ask for reciprocation. As a result of His love, we enjoy the status of God's children. And not in word only; many manuscripts add "we are," to show that the title is real.

Belonging to God's family implies suffering the world's misunderstanding. Opposition often arises, because men and women in the world system find God a mystery. They feel ill at ease and develop hostility toward God and His people.

**2. Beloved, now are we the sons of God:** . . . Divinely loved ones, now born-ones of, *—WUST* . . . we are God's children now, *—BRKL.*

**and it doth not yet appear what we shall be:** . . . not yet has it been made visible what we shall be, *—WUST* . . . We don't know what we shall become in the future, *—PHLP* . . . has not yet been shown, *—BRKL.*

**but we know that, when he shall appear, we shall be like him:** . . . We are aware that, if He should be manifested, *—CNDT* . . . We only know that, if reality were to break through, we should reflect his likeness, *—PHLP* . . . whenever it is made visible, like ones to Him we shall be, *—WUST* . . . when He has been revealed we shall resemble Him, *—BRKL.*

**for we shall see him as he is:** . . . according as, *—CNDT.*

**3:2.** Here John compared the present and future of God's people. Our present reality is the privilege of a position as children of God (not "sons," as in KJV). The future is still obscure, but we can know something about it. One great fact stands out—we will be like Christ. The great transformation will take place when He returns, and the Christian will be able to look upon the Lord just as He is in reality. The view of Christ is the secret to Christlikeness. Of course no one achieves perfect likeness, but "like" denotes a marked similarity of attributes.

Because believers have been made "partakers of the divine nature" (2 Peter 1:4), they possess a potential for manifesting the attributes of the Christ who dwells within them by His Spirit. In a sense the Son of God can live himself out of their lives by helping them act as He himself would in given situations. They are His representatives.

**3. And every man that hath this hope in him purifieth himself, even as he is pure:** . . . who has this expectation, *—CNDT* . . . resting on Him, *—BRKL* . . . continually set on Him is constantly purifying himself, *—WUST* . . . lives a pure life, *—LBCH* . . . Everyone who has at heart a hope like that keeps himself pure, for he knows how pure Christ is, *—PHLP.*

**3:3.** This future hope produces holy behavior. Without exception, a Christian who maintains his hope of being made righteous like Jesus will discipline himself to seek purity. When John began a verse with "every man" (Greek, *pas ho*), he was often refuting some group like the early Gnostics who set themselves up as a special class above the need for holiness. But the apostle showed that holiness brooks no exceptions.

**4. Whosoever committeth sin transgresseth also the law:** . . . who habitually commits sin, also habitually commits lawlessness, *—WUST* . . . practices law-breaking, *—BRKL* . . . is guilty of lawlessness, *—NORL* . . . is doing sin is doing lawlessness, *—CNDT* . . . is also acting in defiance of Law, *—TCNT* . . . breaks the law, *—WMCK*

**for sin is the transgression of the law:** . . . That is what sin is— breaking the law, *—LBCH* . . . by definition—a breaking of God's law, *—PHLP* . . . for sin is lawlessness, *—NORL* . . . is the violation of divine Law, *—NOLI.*

**3:4.** A person who is born from God habitually lives a righteous life; logically, a person living in sin is demonstrating that he has *not* been born into the family of God. A literal rendering of the first clause would be, "Everyone who commits sin also commits lawlessness." John went on to conclude the verse by pointing out that sin *is* lawlessness. The two words are virtually interchangeable.

Why belabor these definitions? "Sin" (Greek, *hamartian*) has a root idea of "missing the mark," while "lawlessness" (Greek, *anomian*) implies a more serious offense of purposely disregarding the law of God. The false teachers John mentioned may have been playing down the seriousness of "minor" offenses. But the apostle insisted that any form of sin is rebellion against God.

**5. And ye know that he was manifested to take away our sins:** . . . you are aware, *—CNDT* . . . you know absolutely, *—WUST* . . . He appeared, *—WLMS* . . . that He came in visible form, *—BRKL* . . . Christ became man for the purpose of removing sin, *—PHLP.*

**and in him is no sin:** . . . sin in Him does not exist, *—WUST* . . . and that he himself was quite free from sin, *—PHLP.*

**3:5.** How can a Christian tolerate sin when the very purpose of Christ's coming was to do away with sin? John's readers were well aware that the Lord became a man for the purpose of doing away with sins. The plural "sins" indicates that John was thinking not only of Christ's atonement for sin, but also of His power to remove acts of sin from the lives of His people.

Beyond that, Christ's very nature is sinless. John denied that sin had any place in the life of Jesus. The verb "is" portrays Christ as sinless in past, present, and future. Thus His people must abstain from sin.

**6. Whosoever abideth in him sinneth not:** . . . No one who keeps in union with Him, *—NORL* . . . constantly abiding, *—WUST* . . . who remains in Him does not sin, *—BRKL* . . . does not habitually sin, *—MNTG.*

**whosoever sinneth hath not seen him, neither known him:** . . . whoever lives in sin, *—MNTG* . . . The regular sinner has never seen or, *—PHLP* . . . practices sinning has neither looked on Him nor, —BRKL ... has not with discernment seen Him, —WUST.

**3:6** Next the writer makes a bold statement—everyone who abides in Christ does not sin. John often used the word abide in discussions of regeneration; he who abides is a child of God. Now he claimed that no child of God is going to sin. "Sinneth" is in the present tense, which normally emphasizes the continuing nature of an action. As 1:8-2:1 teaches, believers may commit an act of sin, but an individual genuinely born of God will not make it a continued practice.

The opposite also holds true. No one who continually sins has come to know God in a permanent relationship. The secret for overcoming is abiding in Christ.

**7. Little children, let no man deceive you:** ... Little born-ones, stop allowing anyone to be leading you astray, —WUST ... You, my children, are younger than I am, and I don't want you to be taken in by any clever talk just here, —PHLP ... lead you astray, —NORL, —TNT ... into the wrong way, —NLTG.

**he that doeth righteousness is righteous, even as he is righteous:** ... practices righteousness, —BRKL ... who lives a consistently good life is a good man, as surely as God is good, —PHLP ... who habitually does righteousness, —WUST.

**3:7.** Some were trying to twist the concept of holiness and lead believers astray, so John gave a direct warning against such predators. Regardless of any contrary teaching, it remains true that only the person who actually lives a righteous life deserves the title "righteous." Words are insufficient; we must live according to Christ's pattern.

**8. He that committeth sin is of the devil:** ... The person who keeps on sinning belongs to, —NLTG ... the man whose life is habitually sinful is spiritually a son of, —PHLP ... under the control of, —LBCH ... is of the enemy, —WLSN ... is doing sin is of the Adversary, —CNDT ... is out of the devil as a source, —WUST.

**for the devil sinneth from the beginning:** ... devil is behind all sin, as he always has been, —PHLP.

**For this purpose the Son of God was manifested:** ... On this account, —NORL ... came to earth, —PHLP ... appeared, —BRKL.

**that he might destroy the works of the devil:** ... should be annulling the acts, —CNDT ... with the express purpose of liquidating the devil's activities, —PHLP ... to break up, —BRKL ... bring to naught, —WUST ... undo the devil's deeds, —ADAM.

**3:8.** Sin is serious because of its source. Much as he earlier spoke about Christians who were born "from God," John now declared that the source of life for the habitual sinner is "of (from) the devil." From the dawn of earth's history, the adversary has continued his career of revolt against God.

And God is so opposed to Satan's activity that one of the chief reasons for Christ's incarnation was to break up the devil's works. Jesus Christ came to do away with sins (3:5).

**9. Whosoever is born of God doth not commit sin:** ... who is begotten of God is not doing sin, —CNDT ... When God makes someone his child, that person does not go on sinning, —EVRD ... does not practice sin, —PHLP.

**for his seed remaineth in him:** ... God's nature is in Him, —LBCH ... The new life God gave that person stays in him, —EVRD ... for a sperm divine remains within him, —BRKL ... because the God-given life-principle continues to live in him, —WLMS ... is in him, for good, —PHLP.

**and he cannot sin, because he is born of God:** ... is not able, —WUST ... can't go on sinning, —ADAM ... and such a heredity is incapable of sin, —PHLP ... he cannot practice sinning, —BRKL ... Because he has been begotten by God, —WLSN ... he has become a child of God, —SEB.

**3:9.** The writer here makes his strongest statement about the standard of holiness expected in children of God. The verse follows his common pattern of stating truth both in a negative and positive form. The first half of the verse makes a blanket declaration: no one who has been born of God commits sin. The perfect tense of "born" is used once again as a synonym for regeneration, and "of God" refers to Him as the source of spiritual life, just as in earlier verses.

The problem arises when this verse is placed alongside other verses which declare that no one is free from sin (1:8,10; 2:1). In addition, even the saintliest believers have testified that they could not live completely free from sin. How can these facts be reconciled?

Some have suggested that John referred to a special class of believers or a particular kind of sin. Others think that he spoke only of the ideal of the Christian life, or was actually giving a veiled command. But such interpretations require one to read meanings into the text beyond what it actually says. The explanation which adheres closest to the text is the one that points to the present tense used in the verbs. This and all the other passages dealing with the topic use the present tense, which normally describes habitual or continued action. In contrast, 2:1 uses the aorist tense, describing an isolated act of sin. God has provided a means of dealing with an occasional act of sin, but anyone who belongs to God's family will be unable to maintain a continual practice of sin.

A believer cannot remain in sin because "his seed remaineth in him." Some think that "seed" means God's offspring, and that His children remain in Him. But the context makes better sense when the verse is understood as God's seed remaining in the believer. As a parent's sperm passes on the family resemblance, the Father passes His nature on to His children.

Scientists who specialize in the field of genetics report that genes, passed on from generation to generation, greatly determine the nature and characteristics of offspring. If this is true in the natural, how much more so is it true in the spiritual realm. It might be said that when believers are born into the family of God, they receive, with the new nature, divine characteristics. It is the believer's responsibility, then, to develop these traits until he reaches spiritual maturity.

**10. In this the children of God are manifest:** ... This is the way to distinguish God's children from the devil's, *—WLMS* ... Here we have a clear indication as to who are, *—PHLP* ... we can see who God's children are, *—EVRD* ... are plainly distinguished by this, *—WADE* ... distinguished from, *—TCNT* ... are known apart, *—NORL* ... are distinguished in this way, *—TNT* ... are apparent, *—CNDT* ... are discovered, *—CMPB.*

**and the children of the devil:** ... and who the devil's children are, *—EVRD.*

**whosoever doeth not righteousness is not of God:** ... Anyone who does not practice righteousness, *—BRKL* ... The man who does not lead a good life, *—PHLP* ... Those who do not do what is right are not children of God, *—EVRD.*

**neither he that loveth not his brother:** ... who fails to love, *—PHLP* ... with a divine and self-sacrificial love, *—WUST.*

**3:10.** This verse sums up the preceding section on holiness (2:29-3:9) and makes a transition to the next section on love (3:11-24). By means of "this," namely, the test of holiness, it is possible to distinguish the children of God from the children of the devil. The hidden nature of a person's heart reveals itself in two symptoms: if a person fails to continually do what is righteous or if he fails to habitually love his brother, he is not connected to God as the source of life.

**11. For this is the message that ye heard from the beginning, that we should love one another:** ... this is the basic commandment, *—NOLI* ... This is the teaching, *—EVRD.*

**3:11.** The closing phrase of verse 10 leads into a discussion of love as a trait of God's children. The command to love is nothing new; it dates back to the beginning of their Christian experience (cf. John 13:34,35). Believers are to love all, but 1 John focuses specifically on love for other Christians. In the First Century, believers were an "endangered species." Since the Roman emperors were considered gods, Christians were considered

"atheists" and were to be exterminated. Only by demonstrating love could believers survive.

**12. Not as Cain, [who] was of that wicked one, and slew his brother:** ... Do not be like Cain who belonged to, *—EVRD* ... We are none of us to have the spirit ... who was a son of the devil, *—PHLP* ... whose motivation was from the evil one and he murdered his brother, *—BRKL* ... was out of the Pernicious One, and killed his brother by severing his jugular vein, *—WUST* ... and butchered his brother, *—WLMS.*

**And wherefore slew he him?:** ... And for what reason did he murder him? *—BRKL* ... Have you realized his motive? *—PHLP* ... on what account, *—WUST* ... on behalf of what, *—CNDT* ... And why did he kill him? *—NORL.*

**Because his own works were evil, and his brother's righteous:** ... It was just because he realized the goodness of his brother's life and the rottenness of his own, *—PHLP* ... his own deeds were wicked, *—LBCH* ... his acts were wicked, yet those of his brother, just, *—CNDT* ... those of his brother were virtuous, *—BRKL.*

**3:12.** John argued for the need to love one another by citing the bad example of Cain (Genesis 4). Cain's character was based on a relation to Satan, much as Christians are "of (from) God." His character expressed itself when he violently slaughtered his brother. Jesus linked hatred with murder (Matthew 5:21-28), naming Satan as a murderer (John 8:44). To hate someone is sinful and murderous, for the one who hates requires only opportunity before he actually commits the crime.

Next, John described Cain's motive (and at the same time hinted at the motivation for the persecution of believers in his own age). Cain's works were evil, while his brother's were righteous—so Cain killed Abel. Similarly, a Christian's good example is a standing rebuke to the one who cannot claim a lifestyle of righteousness. It reminds him of what he is like in comparison with what he ought to be. His attitude is irrational, like the king in ancient times who killed a messenger who brought him bad news.

**13. Marvel not, my brethren, if the world hate you:** ... You must not be surprised, *—WLMS* ... do not be, *—NORL, —NLTG* ... Do not feel, *—BRKL* ... Stop marveling, *—WUST* ... when the people of this world, *—EVRD.*

**3:13.** Cain showed the attitude characteristic of most members of the world system, and John immediately applied the principle to his audience.

The present tense of the command to stop being amazed suggests that the readers were surprised by the opposition they met, and John explained that hatred is the standard reaction of the world toward Christianity. Even the form of "if" implies that such a hatred is a fact.

**14. We know that we have passed from death unto life:** ... we have crossed the frontier, —PHLP ... we have proceeded, —CNDT ... we have made the transfer out of, —BRKL ... we have passed over permanently out of the death, —WUST.

**because we love the brethren:** ... the brothers, —BRKL.

**He that loveth not [his] brother abideth in death:** ... The man that does not love, —WMCK ... The man without love for his brother is living in death already, —PHLP ... loving in this manner is abiding in the sphere of the death, —WUST ... remains in death, —NORL.

**3:14.** The next two verses return to the test of faith which he set forth in 2:9-11—love for the brethren. "We" (Greek, *hēmeis*) is emphatic, marking the contrast with the world. The believer loves other Christians, while the world hates them.

John introduced a new description of salvation, picturing Christians as people who have "passed from death unto life." The verb *metabebēkamen* means a move from one location to another and is an apt description of the way salvation transfers a person from the sphere of darkness to the realm of light. The perfect tense once again describes the past conversion which introduces a person to a continuing relationship with Christ.

Continued love for other believers demonstrates that this transfer is genuine. Anyone who does not display that love is giving evidence that he has never come out of the sphere of death into which he was born.

**15. Whosoever hateth his brother is a murderer:** ... who actively hates his brother, —PHLP ... commits murder in his heart, —LBCH ... is a potential murderer, —NOLI ... is a man-killer, —CNDT ... manslayer, —CMPB.

**and ye know that no murderer hath eternal life abiding in him:** ... no man-killer at all has life eonian remaining, —CNDT ... has everlasting life remaining in him, —WMCK ... continuing within him, —BRKL.

**3:15.** This verse shows why hatred is a valid test of whether a person is unregenerate, though it may seem like a harsh standard. A person who continues to hate someone else (note the present tense) is actually a murderer. *Anthrōpoktonos* occurs only here and in John 8:44 where Jesus said that the devil is also a murderer. Elsewhere the Lord equated hatred with murder (Matthew 5:21,22), since the one who hates another actually has the same desire as a murderer but lacks the opportunity to carry out his wish. For John there

was no middle ground. Anyone who carries such an attitude around is demonstrating that eternal life does not reside in him.

**16. Hereby perceive we the love [of God], because he laid down his life for us:** ... We understand the meaning of love from this, that He laid down his own life on our behalf, —BRKL ... In Christ we saw what real love is, —LBCH ... we know what love is and can do, —NORL ... He, for our sakes, lays down His soul, —CNDT.

**and we ought to lay down [our] lives for the brethren:** ... as for us, we have a moral obligation on behalf of our brethren, —WUST ... our souls for the sake of, —CNDT.

**3:16.** Since love is a test of true Christianity, it is important to describe the characteristics of the love that passes the test.

The question is not difficult to answer, for every Christian has already come to know by experience the sort of love which God requires. The perfect tense of "perceive" points both to the cross, where Christ performed the supreme act of love, and to the experience of His love in our lives.

When John spoke of the One who "laid down his life for us," he made it obvious that he meant the death of Christ. This idiom describes a voluntary act of self-sacrifice. The death of Jesus was no accident, as He himself had said in John 10:17,18 and 15:13.

Just as the Lord laid down His life for mankind, believers have a moral obligation to lay down their lives for other Christians, following His example (John 15:12). This, of course, does not mean that a Christian dies to atone for the sins of others; rather, it shows the extent of the sacrifices that love may demand.

**17. But whoso hath this world's good, and seeth his brother have need:** ... whoever has as a constant possession the necessities of life, —WUST ... is rich enough to have all the things he needs, —SEB ... whoso may have the world's substance, —DRBY ... possesses the world's resources, and notices that his brother suffers need, —BRKL ... whoever may be having a livelihood in this world, and may be beholding his brother, —CNDT ... the life-sustaining things, —SWAN.

**and shutteth up his bowels [of compassion] from him:** ... and snaps shut his heart from, —WUST ... shuts up his pity against him, —WMCK ... steels his heart against him, —TCNT ... yet he closes his heart against him, —NORL ... stifles his emotions toward him, —ADAM ... and then locks his deep sympathies away from, —BRKL ... locking his compassions from, —CNDT.

**how dwelleth the love of God in him?:** ... can have no divine love in his heart, —NOLI ... is abiding in him? —WUST ... lodging in him? —BRKL.

**3:17.** The perfect example of Jesus is contrasted with the example of one who falsely claims to follow the Lord. The writer condemns the one who claims to be ready to die for a brother in an emergency, yet refuses to show practical love in the routines of life.

Such a person "hath this world's good(s)." "Whoso" is a broad expression, including anyone who fits the criteria. The word "good" comes from the Greek *bios* which describes the sort of physical life which an animal possesses, and it was later used, as here, to describe the physical possessions necessary to sustain life. The person has ample material resources. Second, the person "seeth his brother have need." The verb for seeing (Greek, *theōrē*) describes the careful gaze that makes one fully aware of the brother's difficulty. The present tense verbs show a continuing knowledge of a continuing need. Third, the person closes his heart against the needy brother. There is a change to the aorist tense when speaking of the man who "shutteth" his heart and chooses not to help. The "bowels" are mentioned because ancient writers thought of the internal organs such as the heart, lungs, and liver as the seat of the emotions, much as modern man uses the word *heart*.

Anyone who fits all three of these descriptions has failed the test of love. John asked his readers to be the judge: how can a person claim to have God's love as part of his person and react in such a calloused manner?

**18. My little children, let us not love in word, neither in tongue:** ... Dear children, —*BRKL* ... we should not be loving, —*CNDT* ... our love must not be, —*TNT* ... we must not manifest our love only in fine words on the tongue, —*GRBR* ... in the sphere of word, —*WUST* ... do not let our love be mere words, —*TCNT* ... or talk, —*SEB* ... or speech only, —*NORL* ... in theory, —*NOLI*.

**but in deed and in truth:** ... in act, —*CNDT* ... and in reality, —*NOLI* ... let us love in sincerity and in practice! —*PHLP* ... we should show that love by what we do, —*EVRD* ... as divine truth teaches us, —*GRBR*.

**3:18.** John urged his beloved children in the Lord to avoid such hypocrisy. They must avoid the kind of love that is only talk. Instead, their love should show itself in actions. And since even good deeds can be done with a hypocritical attitude or false motives, he added that the works of love should be done in truth. Sometimes "works" have received a bad name, but there is nothing wrong with them if done with the right motive.

**19. And hereby we know that we are of the truth, and shall assure our hearts before him:** ... If we live like this, we shall know that we are children of the truth and can reassure ourselves

in the sight of God, —*PHLP* ... In this way we shall become fully aware that to the truth we owe our lives, and in His presence our hearts shall be at peace, —*BRKL* ... we belong to the way of truth, —*EVRD* ... persuading our hearts in front of Him, —*CNDT* ... in His presence shall tranquilize our hearts in whatever our hearts condemn us, —*WUST*.

**3:19.** This verse begins by looking back at the message just given—that love for other Christians is a test of genuine membership in God's family. It goes on to assert that this love enables the believer to know with certainty that he is indeed "of the truth," one whose life originates in the truth of the gospel. In addition, the presence of love for other Christians allows us to pacify our troubled conscience and stand in the presence of God with confidence. Verse 22 connects this boldness to prayer.

**20. For if our heart condemn us, God is greater than our heart, and knoweth all things:** ... our heart should be censuring us, —*CNDT* ... even if our own hearts make us feel guilty ... God is infinitely greater, —*PHLP* ... is wiser than, —*LBCH* ... our conscience, —*NORL* ... He knows everything, —*BRKL*.

**3:20.** The grammar of this verse is difficult because of the two uses of the Greek term *hoti*, translated "for" and then left untranslated in the KJV. The opening phrase could be rendered "whatever our heart condemns" or "because, if our heart condemns, *we know* that God is...." In either case, the thought is that an oversensitive conscience can plague a Christian with unjustified guilt feelings, even though he passes such tests as the demand to love. In such a case, we can still come to God with confidence, even though our conscience condemns us. God is greater in knowledge than our conscience, and He is the final authority (cf. 1 Corinthians 4:3-5).

**21. Beloved, if our heart condemn us not, [then] have we confidence toward God:** ... Divinely loved ones ... a fearless confidence we constantly have facing God the Father, —*WUST* ... if we do not feel that we are doing wrong, we can be without fear when we come to God, —*EVRD* ... when we realize this our hearts no longer accuse us, we may have the utmost confidence in God's presence, —*PHLP* ... in case our hearts do not condemn us, then we draw near to God with confidence, —*BRKL* ... we can face God fearlessly, —*NOLI* ... we have boldness, —*CNDT*.

**3:21.** On the other hand, a person who does not suffer from an accusing conscience can have boldness toward God. "Confidence" (Greek, *parrhēsian*) means freedom and openness in speech, and though it referred to the return of Christ in 2:28, here it leads naturally into the topic of prayer in verse 22. "Toward God" (Greek, *pros ton theon*) often implies face-to-face intimacy, as one would enjoy in prayer to the Father.

**22. And whatsoever we ask, we receive of him:** ... whatsoever we may be requesting, we are obtaining, *—CNDT* ... And God gives us the things we ask for, *—EVRD* ... And he gives us all our requests, *—BB* ... and get from Him anything we ask, *—BECK.*
**because we keep his commandments:** ... we are keeping His precepts, *—CNDT* ... we observe His injunctions, *—BRKL* ... we are obeying his orders, *—PHLP* ... because we obey God's commands, *—EVRD* ... because we keep all his laws, *—BB* ... with solicitous care, *—WUST.*
**and do those things that are pleasing in his sight:** ... and practice what pleases him, *—NOLI* ... which are pleasing in His penetrating gaze, *—WUST* ... in his eyes, *—BB.*

**3:22.** When a Christian is confident of his place in God's family, regardless of any emotions of guilt or unworthiness, he can communicate with his Father in prayer with the assurance that he is being heard. The truth that God will answer that believer's prayer, whatever may be requested, is a strong promise.

The rest of the verse, however, adds restrictions to the promise. The reason one can ask and receive is because he has fulfilled the conditions given: keeping God's commandments and doing the things which please Him. The "commandments" refer to the explicit demands made by God, while "things that are pleasing" covers a broader range of acts that may not be directly mentioned in the Bible. Both "keep" and "do" are present tense verbs and imply a habitual obedience to God's will as a prerequisite for answered prayer. (See also 5:14,15.)

A life lived in yieldedness to the will of God is the secret to a successful Christian experience. The reason believers can expect answers to prayer is that as far as they know they are asking in accordance with the will of God (they certainly would not ask for anything contrary to His will). The result is that God gives them what they ask for, and if not, something better. There are many occasions in this life when we do not receive the answer we have expected. But our heavenly Father knows best, and when on the other side we know as we are known, we will learn that every time God answered in a way which was best for us. When our faith seems weak, we can always trust God to do what is right.

**23. And this is his commandment, That we should believe on the name of his Son Jesus Christ:** ... His orders are that we should put our trust in, *—PHLP* ... And this is his law, that we have faith in the name of his Son, *—BB* ... And this is His

injunction, that we put our faith in, *—BRKL* ... Put your trust in, *—NLTG.*
**and love one another, as he gave us commandment:** ... as he himself instructed us, *—NOLI* ... as He enjoined us, *—BRKL* ... as we used to hear him say in person, *—PHLP* ... as he taught us, *—GRBR* ... even as he said to us, *—BB* ... as He has ordered us to do, *—BECK.*

**3:23.** If answered prayer depends on keeping God's commands, then what are those commands? They can be summed up in the twin pillars of the epistle: faith and love. God wants man to believe in the name (and thus the Person) of His Son, and the aorist tense points to initial conversion. This is to be accompanied by a continual (present tense) practice of loving one another, just as Christ himself instructed in John 13:34; 15:12. Since, as John states in the next chapter, the very nature of God is love, and by the new birth believers receive of that nature, love should characterize them.

**24. And he that keepeth his commandments dwelleth in him, and he in him:** ... the one who as a habit of life exercises, *—WUST* ... He who obeys His commands remains in Him, *—BRKL* ... who does what He orders, *—BECK* ... will remain in communion with God, and God in communion with him, *—GRBR* ... lives in God, *—EVRD.*
**And hereby we know that he abideth in us:** ... We know that He really lives in us, *—LBCH* ... How do we know that God lives in us? *—EVRD* ... that God is in communion with us we know, *—GRBR* ... By this we know that He remains in us, *—BRKL* ... the guarantee of his presence within us, *—PHLP* ... our witness that he is in us, *—BB.*
**by the Spirit which he hath given us:** ... from the Spirit as a source whom He gave to us, *—WUST* ... by the spirit-world that He has granted to us, *—GRBR.*

**3:24.** This verse returns to a discussion of the significance of keeping those commandments. The person who habitually observes the requirements which God has laid down is the one who genuinely abides in God. "Him" in verse 24 refers to God the Father, as it did in verses 22 and 23.

The relationship goes in two directions—the believer abides in God and God abides in the believer—to underscore that intimacy with God can exist. Keeping God's commands is not the prerequisite for a relationship, but it does provide evidence of such a relationship.

A person who rests his assurance of salvation on an imperfect obedience to God's commands is likely to suffer from frequent doubts. So a second witness confirms the believer's standing with God. We can know in experience that God abides in us because of the presence of the Holy Spirit which comes only as a gift from Him (Romans 8:14-16). John did not explain how the Spirit's presence becomes obvious. His indwelling can be detected by spiritual people.

## Chapter 4

**1. Beloved, believe not every spirit:** ... dear friends of mine, *—PHLP* ... do not put trust in every Inspired Utterance, *—WADE* ... do not trust every inspiration, *—TCNT* ... do not put faith in, *—BRKL* ... every so-called spiritual utterance, *—WLMS*.

**but try the spirits whether they are of God:** ... test the spirits, *—CNDT* ... put the spirits to the test, *—BRKL* ... to see whether they are of Divine origin, *—WADE* ... to discover whether they come from, *—PHLP* ... for the purpose of approving them if they are, and finding that they meet the specifications laid down, *—WUST*.

**because many false prophets are gone out into the world:** ... the world is full of false prophets, *—PHLP* ... many false preachers, *—NLTG* ... have been traveling over the world, *—LBCH* ... have been let out into the world, *—BRKL*.

**4:1.** At this point the epistle begins a new strain of thought, arguing that sonship can be demonstrated by adherence to truth, particularly the truth about the person of Christ. Evidently false teachers who were harassing the churches with doctrines characteristic of the Gnostic heresy.

The opening command asks believers to stop putting faith in "every spirit," referring to people claiming to get their message from a supernatural source. Christians need to realize that not every spirit represents God. Instead of being gullible, they need to "try" (*dokimazete*, test) any prophet who claims to speak as a mouthpiece for the Spirit of God (cf. Deuteronomy 18:20-22). It was foolish to assume that all claimants truly have their origin in God, because a large number of false prophets were already in circulation, promoting their teachings throughout the world.

No one would deny that believers can receive guidance from the Holy Spirit. Jesus said of Him, "He will guide you into all truth" (John 16:13). But the human spirit may be involved, or even an evil spirit. This is the reason we have the right and the obligation to "try (test) the spirits," to see if their guidance conforms to the Word of God.

**2. Hereby know ye the Spirit of God:** ... In this you know, *—CNDT* ... By this we recognize, *—BRKL* ... Here is the way in which to recognize, *—TCNT* ... You can test them in this simple way, *—PHLP*.

**Every spirit that confesseth that Jesus Christ is come, in the flesh is of God:** ... which is avowing, *—CNDT* ... says, "I believe that Jesus is the Christ who came to earth and became a man," *—EVRD* ... who agrees ... that Jesus Christ has come in the sphere of the flesh ... and still remains incarnate, *—WUST* ... as having come incarnate, *—BRKL* ... actually became man, *—PHLP* ... that man speaks for God, *—LBCH*.

**4:2.** The question is, How does one test such people? The inspired writer gave a practical way to determine the truth—by examining the content of the prophet's message. If a spirit-inspired utterance is truly from God, it will be an open acknowledgment of Jesus, the Christ or Anointed One who became human. Gnostic teachers asserted that the divine Christ was separate from the man Jesus and merely indwelt Him temporarily. John opposed their view by demanding that genuine Christians accept Jesus and Christ as the same person. He also specified that Christ came "in flesh," omitting any article to emphasize the kind of nature He assumed. And the perfect participle "is come" shows that Christ's action in becoming man was more than a temporary arrangement.

**3. And every spirit that confesseth not that Jesus Christ is come in the flesh is not of God:** ... Another spirit refuses to say this, *—SEB* ... who denies that, *—NOLI* ... refuses to say this about Jesus, *—EVRD* ... that does not acknowledge Jesus, *—BRKL* ... this aforementioned Jesus, *—WUST* ... has come in a human body, *—NLTG* ... does not come from God, *—PHLP*.

**and this is that [spirit] of antichrist:** ... it is the utterance of Antichrist, *—WLMS*.

**whereof ye have heard that it should come; and even now already is it in the world:** ... which you were warned would come, *—PHLP* ... of whose coming you have heard. Right now he is in the world, *—BRKL* ... Now he and his agents are, *—NOLI* ... and it is now active in the world, *—WADE*.

**4:3** The test of truth is continued in negative form. If a person claims to reveal truth, yet refuses to acknowledge the apostolic doctrine of Christ, he is a deceiver. The present tense of "confesseth" (Greek, *homologei*) speaks of a habitual practice, and the meaning implies a personal conviction openly expressed. The definite article before Jesus (or "Christ," as many manuscripts indicate) refers back to the fuller statement of faith previously given in verse 2; the false spirits are those which deny that Jesus is the divine Christ who became man.

If such speakers were not inspired by the Holy Spirit, their message must come from a different spirit. This spirit is identified as the "spirit of antichrist" (cf. 2:18). The italicized word *spirit* (meaning it was supplied by the KJV translators) is the most logical way to translate the Greek construction. The very spirit which will empower the future "man of sin" was already at work in these false teachers.

Such subtle deception should have been no surprise to these believers, for the problem had already begun in John's day.

**4. Ye are of God, little children, and have overcome them:** ... As for you, out of God you are, little born-ones, and you have gained a complete victory over them and are still victors, –WUST ... you belong to God, –SEB ... and you have successfully resisted such men as these, –TCNT ... you have refuted these false teachers, –NORL ... You have won a victory over the false spirits, –LBCH ... you have conquered them, –CNDT ... and have defeated them, –BRKL.

**because greater is he that is in you, than he that is in the world:** ... He who is in our hearts is greater, –WLMS ... is mightier than, –NORL ... is far stronger than the antichrist, –PHLP.

**4:4.** The genuine believers who received the letter stood in strong contrast to those deluded by the spirit of Antichrist. They had God as the source of their spiritual life. These "little children" had been born into God's family. In addition they had overcome "them," namely, the false prophets of verse 1. The perfect tense of "overcome" shows that they had withstood the lure of false doctrine in the past and were still standing firm at the time of the epistle's writing. But they still needed to be on guard to maintain their purity in the future.

The reason they could overcome the power of evil was because the One who indwelt them was greater than the one indwelling the world. This phrase continues the contrast between the Holy Spirit and the "spirit of antichrist."

It is a great encouragement to be reminded of the power available to believers. Satan is an active force in the world, he has great power and many ways of attacking the people of God. It is good, then, to remind ourselves that though the devil is mighty, God is almighty. Satan may be powerful, but God is all-powerful.

**5. They are of the world: therefore speak they of the world:** ... The agents of the antichrist are children of the world; they speak the world's language, –PHLP ... so they talk from a worldly point of view, –BRKL ... out of the world as a source they are constantly speaking, –WUST.

**and the world heareth them:** ... and the world listens to them, –WUST, –BRKL ... of course, pays attention to what they say, –PHLP.

**4:5.** The false teachers who had harassed the churches based their work on a different source. They were creatures of the satanic world system, thoroughly at home in this view of life. Since their thoughts were in tune with the world, they found a ready audience when they spoke to other world-dwellers. They spoke the world's language and found easy acceptance.

**6. We are of God: he that knoweth God heareth us:** ... We are God's children and only the man who knows God hears our message, –PHLP ... Whoever has acquaintance with God, –BRKL ... will listen to us, –NORL.

**he that is not of God heareth not us:** ... what we say means nothing to the man who is not himself a child of God, –PHLP ... will turn a deaf ear to us, –NORL ... doesn't listen to us, –ADAM.

**Hereby know we the spirit of truth, and the spirit of error:** ... By this we may distinguish, –MNTG ... This gives us a ready means of distinguishing the true from the false, –PHLP ... This is the way to distinguish a true spiritual utterance from one that is false, –WLMS ... the inspiration that is Real and the inspiration that is delusive, –WADE ... has the true spirit or the false, –LBCH ... spirit of deception, –CNDT.

**4:6.** John spotlighted the readers in verse 4 and the heretics in verse 5. Here the focus is on the teachers of the truth. Like you, he claimed, "we are of God." And those who were in tune with God would listen to men like the apostles who had received their message from Him. Those who thought in the world's thought patterns would, of course, not care to hear the truth.

In conclusion one may see that there is another test of truth—the type of people who welcome a message give a clue to its nature. People who love truth will respond to a spirit characterized by truth; those who are already deluded will respond to a spirit of delusion.

**7. Beloved, let us love one another: for love is of God:** ... Dear friends, –EVRD ... To you whom I love I say, let us go on loving, –PHLP ... we should be loving, –CNDT ... because love springs from, –BRKL ... with a divine and self-sacrificial love, because this aforementioned love is out of God as a source, –WUST ... because love originates with God, –WLMS ... our love is of divine origin, –GRBR.

**and every one that loveth is born of God, and knoweth God:** ... has been born with the present result that he is regenerated and knows God in an experiential way, –WUST ... is God's son and has some knowledge of him, –PHLP ... has become God's child, –EVRD ... and possesses the true conception of God, Greber.

**4:7.** An abrupt change in theme marks the beginning of a new section here, one which focuses on the requirement that a genuine Christian must display love. The apostle had listed love before as a test of faith (2:7-11; 3:10-24); now the logic behind the test is explained.

John began by calling his readers "beloved," people who have experienced love. The opening phrase may be translated as a statement ("we love") or an exhortation ("let us love"). The later seems to fit better, for it was used in that way in 3:18. The present tense of the verb demands a continual practice of love toward one another.

The second part of the verse explains why Christians should exhibit such love. The love which was being discussed comes only from God; anyone who is habitually marked by this distinctive kind of love gives evidence of a relationship with God. He has been given a place in the Father's family which he still holds; in addition, he has a knowledge of God which is fed by personal experience of His presence.

**8. He that loveth not knoweth not God; for God is love:** ... He who is not loving, —BRKL ... He who is lacking in love has no understanding of God's nature, —GRBR ... cannot know him at all, —PHLP ... has not come to know God, because God as to His nature is love, —WUST.

**4:8.** The opposite case also holds true: if a person has a pattern of life which does not include *agapē*-type love, he shows that he never made the initial acquaintance of God. The aorist tense of "knoweth" is evidently an ingressive aorist which describes the beginning of a relationship.

The reason for such a sweeping statement is then explained. God is love; love is part of His essential nature. The lack of a definite article before "love" shows that the inspired writer was emphasizing the quality of love rather than attempting to define God's nature. Since love is an integral part of the divine nature, a person devoid of love shows that he has not been affected by contact with God. He is separate from God.

**9. In this was manifested the love of God toward us:** ... As for us, the love of God was revealed by the fact that, —BRKL ... the greatest demonstration of God's love for us has been, —PHLP ... was clearly shown the love of God in our case, —WUST ... among us, —CNDT.

**because that God sent his only begotten Son into the world:** ... that God has dispatched, —CNDT ... the uniquely begotten One, God sent off into the world on a mission in order, —WUST.

**that we might live through him:** ... to give us life through him, —PHLP, —EVRD ... so that through him we might obtain spiritual life, —GRBR.

**4:9.** A statement reminiscent of John 3:16 describes the way in which God has expressed His love in action. "In this" refers to the sending of the Son which is described in the balance of the verse. Love had always been part of the divine attributes, but it was not until the incarnation of Christ that God's love was fully revealed. The definite article before "love" identifies it as the particular love which characterizes the Lord. The phrase "toward us" (Greek, *en hēmin*) may be rendered "in us," or more appropriately, "among us." Jesus' coming displayed God's love among the members of the human race.

The second phrase of the verse begins with "his only begotten Son" in the Greek word order, stressing the marvelous nature of this gift. Jesus is the divine Son, the unique One (Greek, *monogenē*) unlike any other. He was sent (Greek, *apestalken*) with a mission to perform, one which has continuing results, as shown by the perfect tense of the verb. God's purpose was to make eternal life possible for His people.

**10. Herein is love, not that we loved God, but that he loved us:** ... We see real love, —PHLP ... His love for us was not occasioned by our having loved God first, —GRBR ... which love exists in this, —BRKL ... True love is God's love for us, not our love for God, —EVRD.

**and sent his Son [to be] the propitiation for our sins:** ... dispatches ... a propitiatory shelter concerned with our sins, —CNDT ... sent off His Son, an expiatory satisfaction concerning our sins, —WUST ... to make personal atonement for, —PHLP ... to be the atoning sacrifice for our sins, —NORL ... to be the way to take away our sins, —EVRD.

**4:10.** The discussion of love moves forward by explaining what love really is. It is found "herein" or "in this," the facts described in the remainder of the verse. The specific kind of love described thus far may be seen in its pure form, not in human affection, but in the love displayed by God himself.

The "we" in "we loved God" is emphasized in the Greek and placed in contrast with "he," the great Lover. The love which believers must have is not love which man originates. It is more than any affection which we have felt toward God. On the contrary, love originates with God. He is the initiator, the One who not only loved mankind, but translated love into deed by sending His Son on a mission to provide propitiation (see 2:2) as a way of making reconciliation with God possible.

**11. Beloved, if God so loved us, we ought also to love one another:** ... Loved ones, —BRKL ... dear friends! —EVRD ... If God loved us as much as that, surely we, in our turn, should love one another! —PHLP ... since in that manner and to that extent did God love us, also, as for us, we are under moral obligation to be constantly loving one another, —WUST.

**4:11.** God's love stands as an example for His children. He demonstrated His love through the Incarnation and by His provision of salvation (4:9,10), and "so" points back to this fact. "So" is a small word, but note how much it includes here. Think of the suffering of the Father in letting Jesus suffer. Think of the honor He bestows in making us part of His family. Amazing love! The form of "if" used in this verse assumes the truth of the statement; God has indeed loved us.

God's love places a moral obligation on all believers to maintain a pattern of love for one another.

**12. No man hath seen God at any time:** ... No one has ever seen God, *—WMCK* ... It is true that no human being has ever had a direct vision of God, *—PHLP* ... God in His [invisible] essence no one has ever yet beheld, *—WUST* ... has ever gazed upon God, *—CNDT.*

**If we love one another, God dwelleth in us:** ... In case we love one another, God remains in us, *—BRKL* ... Yet if we love one another God does actually live in us, *—PHLP* ... makes His abode in us, *—NORL* ... has full sway in us, *—SWAN.*

**and his love is perfected in us:** ... and only then does our love for Him become complete in our hearts, *—GRBR* ... and His love runs its full course in us, *—BRKL* ... and his love grows in us toward perfection, *—PHLP* ... has reached its goal. It is made perfect in us, *—EVRD.*

**4:12.** At this point John inserted the well-known fact that God is invisible; in fact, no one has ever seen His essence. The word "God" appears first in the Greek word order for emphasis, and it appears without a definite article to refer to the nature of God's being. The statement appears to be an abrupt shift in thought but actually sets the stage for a discussion of the way in which God may actually be known. Some might have been claiming to have visions in which they received special knowledge of the Lord, but the apostle denied their claims. Rather than revealing himself to a select few, God makes himself available to all who trust Him and show their faith by loving one another.

When a person habitually shows love to other Christians, it gives evidence that God has taken up a lasting relationship with that person. In addition, it demonstrates that the love which God gives has accomplished its intended purpose by producing a person who gives love to others. The combination of verbs emphasizes the existing result of God's past work in the person's life.

**13. Hereby know we that we dwell in him, and he in us, because he hath given us of his Spirit:** ... From this we know, *—BRKL* ... This is how we know ... He has given us some of His Spirit, *—BECK* ... we are remaining in Him, *—CNDT* ... the guarantee of our living in him and his living in us is the share of his own Spirit which he gives us, *—PHLP* ... we recognize from the fact that He has sent us spirits from His kingdom, *—GRBR* ... a portion of, *—ADAM* ... has given us a share in his Spirit, *—WMCK*

**4:13.** Another thought is added to this discussion of love: the believer can be confident of his relationship with God because of the presence of the Holy Spirit in his life. As usual, "hereby" looks toward the following phrase and shows the test by which one can know by experience that he is in a reciprocal relationship of fellowship with God.

The evidence is that God has given some measure of the work of the Holy Spirit, perhaps in the form of spiritual gifts, or simply His indwelling presence (contrast John 3:34).

**14. And we have seen and do testify:** ... Besides, we ourselves have seen and we are bearing witness, *—BRKL* ... are eyewitnesses able and willing to, *—PHLP* ... we have gazed upon Him, *—CNDT* ... and can tell the truth, *—BECK* ... we testify to that fact, *—NORL* ... as for us, we have deliberately and steadfastly contemplated, *—WUST* ... That is what we teach, *—EVRD.*

**that the Father sent the Son [to be] the Saviour of the world:** ... as the world's Savior, *—BRKL* ... to save the world, *—PHLP* ... the universe, *—GRBR.*

**4:14.** The epistle has just been discussing the truth that man can live in intimate relationship with God—and not merely a privileged few, but anyone who comes to Him in faith. Such an opportunity is almost too good to be true, and John paused briefly to declare that his words are indeed reliable. He opened with an emphatic "we" to underscore his personal knowledge of Christ's work. In words that recall 1:1, he declared that he and his fellow eyewitnesses had seen the great work of God which they testified about. The incarnation of Christ stands as an objective proof that we do indeed have the privilege of "abiding" in God.

Though no one has seen God directly (verse 12), John had seen (Greek, *tetheametha*) His work; the perfect tense shows that the sights were still registered in his mind. He could confidently claim accuracy as he now gave testimony.

The core of his message was the fact that the Father had sent His Son to become the "Saviour" of the world. *Saviour* (Greek, *sōtēra*) was used in various ways in secular Greek but occurs in Scripture primarily as a title for judges who rescued Israel from oppressors, and as the description for Jesus who came to deliver mankind from eternal death.

**15. Whosoever shall confess that Jesus is the Son of God:** ... Whoever acknowledges, *—TCNT* ... Everyone who says openly, *—BB* ... If someone says, *—EVRD* ... If anyone will acknowledge, *—NORL* ... whoever agrees with the statement that, *—WUST* ... should be avowing, *—CNDT.*

**God dwelleth in him, and he in God:** ... finds that God lives in him, *—PHLP* ... has God in him, *—BB* ... with him God remains in union, *—BRKL.*

**4:15.** Although verse 14 makes it clear that Christ provided salvation which is available to the world as a whole, it is not automatically applied to the whole population. So verse 15 follows with a statement that throws the doors wide open to any who will approach on God's terms—acknowledging that Jesus Christ is the Son of God.

The word for "confess" (Greek, *homologēsē*) implies a personal acceptance, not merely verbal assent. And the aorist tense describes a simple act of confession, perhaps the initial decision of accepting Jesus as the Son of God. The formula given (as in 4:2,3) would effectively eliminate from the body of believers the Gnostic heretics who denied that the human Jesus was either the Christ or truly the Son of God.

**16. And we have known and believed the love that God hath to us:** ... and have trusted, —*ADAM* ... we have seen and had faith in the love, —*BB* ... We have perceived the love that God cherishes for us and placed all our trust in it, —*GRBR* ... So we have come to know and trust the love God has for us, —*PHLP* ... And so we know the love that God has for us, and we trust that love, —*EVRD* ... put faith in the love which God cherishes in us, —*BRKL* ... we have believed and at present maintain that attitude, —*WUST.*

**God is love; and he that dwelleth in love dwelleth in God, and God in him:** ... who is remaining in love is remaining in God, —*CNDT* ... he who continues in love, —*BRKL* ... the man whose life is lived in love does, in fact live in God, —*PHLP.*

**4:16.** Although this verse sounds similar to verse 14, the words used ("known" and "believed") are different. So the "we" in verse 16 undoubtedly refers to John and his readers, rather than to the apostles. They had learned the facts of God's love shown in the gospel and had then trusted the message for themselves. This gospel announces the love which God has "to us" (Greek, *en hēmin*); the phrase goes beyond a mere description of the Father's love toward man and could be rendered "love which God has in us," a love which the believer can experience in his own life.

John repeated his statement (4:8) that God is love and used it to summarize this segment explaining the source of love. Since love is bound up with the essential nature of God, a person who dwells in that kind of love must also be dwelling in God, since He alone is the source of that love.

Note that the inspired writer did not say "love is God," for there is much which goes under that description which is not true love or the highest kind of love. Rather, since God is the very essence of love, all that He does issues from that nature. And since in the new birth believers are caused to share the divine nature, love will be their chief trademark.

**1164**

**17. Herein is our love made perfect:** ... So our love for him grows more and more, —*PHLP* ... this has been brought to completion the aforementioned love which is in us ... which love exists in its completed state, —*WUST* ... perfected with us, —*CNDT.*

**that we may have boldness in the day of judgment:** ... filling us with complete confidence for the day, —*PHLP* ... we can wait without any fear, —*LBCH* ... that we face the judgment day confidently, —*BRKL* ... resulting in our having unreservedness of speech at the day, —*WUST.*

**because as he is, so are we in this world:** ... because we are living His way in this world, —*BRKL* ... for we realize that our life in this world is actually his life lived in us, —*PHLP.*

**4:17.** One of the results of experiencing God's love is confidence in our relation to Him, a theme which the next verses explore. The mutual indwelling of God and the believer described in verse 16 is the means for God's love to reach a state of completion. "Made perfect" (Greek, *teteleiōtai*) does not mean absolute perfection; it generally describes that which is complete or fully developed, reaching its intended goal. As the child of God lives in intimacy with the Father, God's love eventually reaches the place where it has its intended effect (cf. 4:12).

Divine love will enable a believer to stand before God with confidence at the Day of Judgment. At the future day when we are evaluated by the Lord, we can know that there is no danger of condemnation. We can have this assurance because of the certain similarity between Christ and His people. In this context, the point of likeness is probably the fact that a Christian loves, just as Christ loves.

**18. There is no fear in love; but perfect love casteth out fear:** ... On the contrary, —*TCNT* ... Love contains no fear—indeed fully developed love expels every particle of fear, —*PHLP* ... instead, perfect love expels fear, —*BRKL* ... love which exists in its completed state throws fear outside, —*WUST* ... Love knows no fear. Perfect love drives out fear, —*NORL* ... pushes out fear, —*SEB* ... banishes fear, —*WADE.*

**because fear hath torment:** ... for fear implies punishment, —*TCNT* ... involves torture, —*BRKL* ... Restraint, —*WLSN* ... suggests painful punishment, —*NORL* ... carries a penalty, —*SWAN* ... has chastening, —*CNDT* ... always contains some of the torture of feeling guilty, —*PHLP.*

**He that feareth is not made perfect in love:** ... So long as a man is afraid that God will punish him, he shows that his love is not yet perfect, —*LBCH* ... has not reached love's perfection, —*BRKL* ... has not been brought to completion in the sphere of this love, and is not in that state at present, —*WUST.*

**4:18.** Turning to the opposite side of the subject, the apostle John stated that there is no kind of fear (no definite article) in the type of love he had been describing. The two attitudes counteract each other.

Instead of coexisting with fear, love expels it. The apostle was careful to specify that he is talking about the love which has become complete by learning to give love (cf. 4:12). When a person finds God's love being expressed through his deeds, he has no reason to fear God, as verse 17 mentions. After all, fear comes from the knowledge that punishment is coming. "Torment" (Greek, *kolasin*) consistently refers to punishment of various kinds, and John's description seems to include fear itself as part of the punishment. One who lives in fear of facing God shows that God's love has not taken its proper place in his heart.

**19. We love him, because he first loved us:** ... As for us, let us be constantly loving, —WUST ... We have the power of loving, because he first had love for us, —BB.

**4:19.** In contrast, genuine believers habitually show love, not because of their innate ability to show affection, but because God himself loved them, giving them the potential of displaying love in their own lives. The aorist tense of "loved" points back to the great demonstration of God's love: the incarnation and sacrifice of Christ.

This is a concept almost too great for the human mind to fathom. There is, in God, so much to love, and in us so little. The normal order would be to love Him. But, like a human parent, yet to a greater degree, God looks beyond our imperfections and loves us, not merely as a sentiment but demonstrating it by His actions.

**20. If a man say, I love God, and hateth his brother:** ... If someone says, —BRKL ... I am constantly loving God, —WUST ... and yet habitually hates his brother, —WLMS ... and yet hates his fellow-man, —GRBR.

**he is a liar:** ... his words are false, —BB.

**for he that loveth not his brother whom he hath seen:** ... for how can any one who does not love his neighbor whom he sees with his physical eyes, —GRBR ... whom he has seen with discernment and at present has within the range of his vision, —WUST ... He can see his brother, but he hates him, —EVRD ... who has no love for his brother whom he has seen, —BB ... before his eyes, —PHLP.

**how can he love God whom he hath not seen?:** ... is not able to, —BRKL ... cannot possibly love God, —WADE ... at present does not have within the range of his vision he is not able to be loving, —WUST ... the one beyond his sight? —PHLP.

**4:20.** The idea already introduced in 3:16-18 is further developed. A person who genuinely possesses God's love will express it toward others. John presented the hypothetical case of a person who claims to love God, yet acts in a way that contradicts his words. He habitually hates one who should have been considered his brother. There is no need to waste time analyzing the problem; this fellow is a liar, one who intentionally deceives others. The logic is simple: no one can love an invisible God when he cannot do the easier task of loving a brother whom he is able to see.

**21. And this commandment have we from him, That he who loveth God love his brother also:** ... we have this conclusion from, —SWAN ... this is the word ... he who has love for God is to have the same love for his brother, —BB ... And this is the order He gave us: ... If you love God, love your brother, —BECK ... it is his explicit command that the one, —PHLP ... It is from God that we have received the command that he who would love God must love his fellow-man also, —GRBR ... that the lover of God, —BRKL ... should constantly be loving also, —WUST.

**4:21.** As he had done previously in this epistle (2:7,8; 3:23), the apostle John declared that the command to love is nothing new, nothing that he had dreamed up himself. It is the very command which the Church already has received from God himself.

"This commandment" refers to the demand given in the latter part of the verse—to love one's brother as well as God. The "him" from whom we receive the command could be Jesus, as in some earlier parts of the epistle. However, God the Father appears in the immediate context, so it is likely that the commandment is one that comes from the Father. It may be a reference to the two great commands related by Jesus in Matthew 22:37-40.

While verse 20 asked how a person could love God and hate His children, verse 21 shows that one who loves God should love others simply because the God he claims to love has commanded love for brothers and sisters.

## Chapter 5

**1. Whosoever believeth that Jesus is the Christ is born of God:** ... Everyone who has faith that, —BRKL ... that Jesus is the Messiah is one of God's children, —GRBR ... is the promised Savior, —BECK ... is a child of God, —WMCK ... is God's child, —EVRD ... is the Christ begotten of God, —CNDT ... out from God has been born, —WUST ... proves himself one of God's family, —PHLP.

**and every one that loveth him that begat:** ... every one who loves the Father, —MNTG ... whoever loves the Parent, —ADAM.

**loveth him also that is begotten of him:** ... loves the child born of Him, —ADAM ... loves the Father's children, —EVRD ... has love for his child, —BB.

**5:1.** The new chapter continues the same line of thought, demonstrating that genuine love for

God inevitably produces love for other Christians. First, all who maintain a belief in Jesus as the divine Christ are born of God. The same doctrinal test had been used earlier (2:22; 4:2, 3, 15) to distinguish true believers from false Gnostic teachers. The man Jesus is the divine Anointed One who had been promised in the Old Testament, and those who believe this truth show they have been born from God. The perfect tense of "born" shows that this believer has entered God's family at a point in the past and still enjoys that family relationship. When a person is born again, he becomes a member of God's family, with God the Father and His Son the Elder Brother. Other believers are part of that family, and often that relationship becomes closer than natural family ties, because of a common bond.

If everyone who believes in Christ has a relationship with God by birth, then it is impossible to separate the child from the parent. And that is precisely the point in the second half of the verse. Anyone who loves God, the parent, must have a special place of affection for God's child. The aorist tense of "begat" is used to describe the act of God in producing a new child, then a switch is made back to the perfect tense of the same verb (Greek, *gegennēmenon*). This describes the believer's experience of the new birth with its abiding results.

**2. By this we know that we love the children of God:** ... The test of the genuineness of our love for God's family lies in this question, *—PHLP* ... In this way, we are certain that we have love for, *—BB* ... How do we know that we love God's children? *—EVRD* ... we are habitually loving the born-ones, *—WUST.*

**when we love God, and keep his commandments:** ... do we love God himself and do we obey his commands? *—PHLP* ... and keep his laws, *—BB* ... and practise, *—WLSN.*

**5:2.** This verse summarizes the discussion of the link between love for God and love for fellow Christians. There is a tightly-woven connection between three ideas that were featured in the previous verses: love for the children of God, love for God, and obedience to the commands of God.

The inseparable joining of these ideas may be learned from "this"—the teaching of 4:21-5:1 about God's command and the believer's place in God's family. When we know these truths, we also know that people who love God's children are the very ones who love God himself and do what He commands.

**3. For this is the love of God, that we keep his commandments:** ... For true love of God means this, *—BRKL* ... loving God means obeying his commands, *—PHLP, —EVRD* ... and with solicitous care

guarding and observing, *—WUST* ... means to obey His Word, *—NLTG.*

**and his commandments are not grievous:** ... they are not hard to keep, *—LBCH* ... are not burdensome, *—NORL, —WLSN* ... are not irksome, *—MNTG* ... aren't annoying, *—ADAM* ... not too hard for us, *—SEB* ... are not heavy, *—WMCK*

**5:3.** In verse 2 obedience is linked with love; now we learn that one leads to the other. The definite article identifies "love" here as the distinctive love (Greek, *agapē*) which has been discussed all through the epistle, and "of God" specifies the love which a believer has toward the Father (as in 5:2). When we love God in the way this epistle requires, we will habitually obey His commands.

These commands are not "grievous" (*bareiai*, heavy, difficult to carry). Jesus contrasted the heavy loads that Pharisees put on people (Matthew 23:4) with the light burden He would give (Matthew 11:30).

**4. For whatsoever is born of God overcometh the world:** ... This is the power that has mastered the world, *—TCNT* ... Everyone who is a child of God has the power to win against the world, *—EVRD* ... Anything which comes from God is able to overcome the world, *—BB* ... for God's "heredity" within us will always conquer the world outside us, *—PHLP* ... continues to conquer, *—WLMS* ... defeats the world, *—ADAM* ... is constantly coming off victorious over the world, *—WUST* ... overcome the power of the world with ease, *—GRBR.*

**and this is the victory that overcometh the world, [even] our faith:** ... It is our faith which conquers, *—SEB* ... In fact, this faith of ours is the only way in which the world has been conquered, *—PHLP* ... What gives us our victory over the powers of the world is our faith, *—GRBR* ... And this is the conquest, *—CNDT* ... that has come off victorious, *—WUST* ... that has triumphed over, *—BRKL* ... is victorious over the world, *—WADE.*

**5:4.** Note that God's commands are simple. They are easy to bear because of the new birth. The neuter "whatsoever" (*pan*) is used to stress that victory comes from the fact of regeneration, not the strength of the reborn person. The perfect tense of "born" is used to describe the new life that a believer now has as a result of being born of God.

This power to overcome the world comes from "our faith." The aorist "overcometh" points to a past victory, either the finished work of Christ on the cross (cf. John 16:33) or the moment when a person places faith in Christ's work in order to become part of the Christian family. There is also a continuing aspect of this victorious life. The faith which enables a person to receive Christ as Saviour will also enable him to maintain his Christian experience.

**5. Who is he that overcometh the world:**...The only one who triumphs over the powers of the world is, –GRBR...who could ever be said to conquer the world, –PHLP...who is conquering, –CNDT...Who is the world's victor, –BRKL...who is constantly coming off victorious, –WUST...the one who wins against the world, –EVRD.

**but he that believeth that Jesus is the Son of God?:**...except the man who really believes that the Jesus who entered the world is, –PHLP...is the person who believes that Jesus is the Son of God, –EVRD.

**5:5.** The emphasis switches from the general fact to a very specific rhetorical question: Who can overcome the world other than one who believes the truth about Jesus? Obviously, no one. Continued victory over the world and its temptations comes not from vague faith in an unspecified direction, but faith in the Jesus who is the "Son of God." Again, the apostle John contends for the combination of humanity and deity in Jesus, in opposition to the Gnostic heresy.

**6. This is he that came by water and blood, [even] Jesus Christ:**...came with the double sign of, –PHLP...through the instrumentality, –WUST...with the testimony of, –GRBR.

**not by water only, but by water and blood:**...the water of his baptism as man and the blood of the atonement that he made by his death, –PHLP...and in the blood, –BRKL...both bore witness to him, –GRBR.

**And it is the Spirit that beareth witness, because the Spirit is truth:**...which is testifying, –CNDT...endorses this as true, –PHLP...appeared as an unimpeachable witness on his behalf, –GRBR.

**5:6.** Verses 6-12 focus on the truth concerning the person of Christ. The discussion begins with the somewhat obscure declaration that Jesus Christ came by both water and blood. Some have taught that these two terms refer to baptism and the Lord's Supper, or to the water and blood flowing from Christ's body at the Crucifixion (John 19:34). But John was more likely referring to the baptism and death of Jesus. The apostle may well have been opposing the Gnostic idea that the divine Christ merely came upon the human Jesus at the Baptism, departing before the Crucifixion. On the contrary, it was Jesus the Christ who experienced both the water of baptism and the blood of death—not baptism alone.

Greek New Testaments often divide the verses at this point. The writer went on to show that the Holy Spirit acts as witness to this truth. The Spirit descended on Jesus at His baptism in the form of a dove, and Christ himself said that the Spirit's work was to bear witness of Him (John 15:26).

And who could be a more reliable witness than the One who is the Spirit of Truth?

**7. For there are three that bear record in heaven:**...The witness therefore is a triple one, –PHLP...three witnesses, –BRKL...three there are that are constantly bearing testimony, –WUST...are in one accord, –SWAN...that bears convincing witness, –WADE...that are testifying, –CNDT...that tell us about Jesus, –EVRD.

**the Father, the Word, and the Holy Ghost: and these three are one:**...the three support one conclusion, –WADE.

**8. And there are three that bear witness in earth:**...There is a threefold testimony, –TCNT...Thus we have three witnesses for him, –GRBR.

**the Spirit, and the water, and the blood: and these three agree in one:**...the Spirit in our own hearts, the signs of the water of baptism and the blood of atonement, –PHLP...The aforementioned three concur, –WUST...These three speak the same thing, –NLTG...and the three are in unison, –BRKL...and these three agree in their testimony, –GRBR...and these three have one purpose, –BECK.

**5:7, 8.** The key thought of 5:6-12, the final section on Christ's person, is that of witness. The writer explains how God has provided testimony to the true identity of Jesus Christ. Verse 6 introduces the Holy Spirit as the first witness, then verses 7 and 8 add two others—water and blood.

The fact that there are three witnesses is the main point of the sentence. Jewish law required two or three witnesses before a person could be convicted of a serious crime (Deuteronomy 17:6; 19:15; Matthew 18:16), so John presents three witnesses who are called upon to attest to the point. The present tense of "bear record" shows that all three testify continually.

Some writers have understood "water and blood" to refer to the ordinances of baptism and the Lord's Supper, pointing to the present participle as evidence that historical events cannot be meant. But since the same terms in verse 6 seem to mean the baptism and crucifixion of Jesus Christ, it would seem unwise to change the meaning so quickly. The three witnesses are all based on events in the life of Christ which continue to testify to His person whenever they are proclaimed (compare John's use of such testimony in 1:1-3).

The Spirit may refer to the descent in the form of a dove at the baptism of Jesus, since John the Baptist took this as proof of Jesus' deity (John 1:32-34). The water is likely a reference to His baptism again, particularly to the voice from heaven declaring Jesus to be God's beloved Son. And the blood refers to the death of Christ, a clear demonstration of His humanity that simultaneously showed Him to be more than merely a man. John took the pivotal events in the Gnostic version of Jesus' life and used them to bear witness to the divine-human Son of God. He added that all three witnesses agree in their testimony—literally, "the three are unto the one."

The King James Version contains an additional statement in these verses, calling on the Father, Son, and Holy Spirit as witnesses. Modern versions omit this segment because it did not appear in any Greek manuscripts prior to the 14th Century and did not exist in the Latin Vulgate translation until A.D. 800. The truth of these statements, however, are indubitable.

**9. If we receive the witness of men, the witness of God is greater:** . . . If we accept the testimony of men, −NORL . . . We believe people when they say something is true. But what God says, −EVRD . . . We accept human evidence on these terms, and surely the evidence of God has still greater weight, −BRCL . . . If we are prepared to accept human testimony, God's own testimony . . . is surely infinitely more valuable, −PHLP . . . we accept the evidence of men, −LBCH, −WMCK . . . If we welcome the witness of men the witness of God is greater, −KLGS . . . as authentic, how much more highly must we regard the testimony of God! −GRBR . . . more important, −NLTG . . . of still greater weight, −WADE.

**for this is the witness of God which he hath testified of his Son:** . . . And such testimony is available in the words with which God testified to us concerning His Son, −GRBR . . . because God's testimony is the truth He told about His Son, −BECK . . . This is the evidence that he has given in regard to his son, −BRCL . . . that He has borne testimony concerning His Son, −WUST . . . And he has told us the truth about his own Son, −EVRD . . . which God has given about his Son, −BB . . . that he witnessed about his son, −KLGS . . . that he has borne witness concerning his Son, −CNFT.

**5:9.** Evaluating such testimony, the writer called on his readers to move from the lesser to the greater. They accepted testimony from human witnesses (the form of the "if" clause assumes the statement to be true). Two or three witnesses were all that were required for legal proof. Therefore, they should accept the even better testimony of God himself. His word is more trustworthy than any human witness, and the triple testimony of Spirit, water, and blood is God's testimony. And since it is God's witness concerning His own Son, who could be better qualified to give testimony?

The writer has already mentioned, in verse 7, the three who "bear record in heaven" (the "Word," of course, refers to Jesus the Son of God). Jesus' life on earth was a testimony to His deity. Twice the Father testified to His Son, at His baptism and at the Transfiguration. And now the Spirit "beareth witness with our spirit, that we are the children of God" (Romans 8:16).

**10. He that believeth on the Son of God hath the witness in himself:** . . . Consequently, whoever believes in the Son of God can defend his faith by appealing to God's testimony, −GRBR . . . He who has faith in, −BB . . . The believer in the Son of God possesses the witness within himself, −BRKL . . . has the proof right in his heart, −LBCH . . . possesses this testimony in his heart, −NOLI . . . will find God's testimony in his own heart, −PHLP . . . has the truth that God told us, −EVRD.

**he that believeth not God hath made him a liar:** . . . He who disbelieves God, −BRKL . . . but whoever does not believe even the testimony of God, brands God as a liar, −GRBR . . . made Him a liar, and as a result considers Him to be such, −WUST . . . makes him false, −BB.

**because he believeth not the record that God gave of his Son:** . . . Such is the case with him who refuses to believe God's own testimony on behalf of His Son, −GRBR . . . he is deliberately refusing to accept the testimony concerning his own Son that God is prepared to give him, −PHLP . . . because he has not faith in the witness which God has given about, −BB . . . he has put no faith in the evidence, −BRKL . . . by not accepting the testimony, −NORL . . . with the result that he is in a settled state of unbelief, −WUST . . . does not believe what God told us about his Son, −EVRD . . . which God has testified concerning His Son, −CNDT.

**5:10.** In the last few verses the writer presented objective witnesses to the truth of the gospel. Now the text presents the subjective side of the issue: the necessity for each person to place faith in the Jesus who has been presented. All that God the Father has done to provide redemption, and all that God the Son has done by His death to make salvation possible will be of no value unless the individual acts to receive God's gift.

The person who places trust in Christ receives a confirming inner testimony to support the external proofs. The Holy Spirit chose words carefully here to specify faith that goes beyond a mere whim. In 3:23 the aorist tense of "believe" refers to the initial moment of accepting Christ as Saviour; here the present tense describes a faith that continues to trust in God's Son as a pattern for living. The phrase used for faith is *believe in* (Greek, *pisteuōn eis*), an expression which occurs numerous times in the Gospel of John and appears in the epistle here and in 5:13. While one might *believe* a person simply by accepting one of his statements, *believing in* a person implies a settled confidence in his overall trustworthiness. The phrase describes a faith that commits itself to Jesus, relying on Him to provide salvation and obeying His dictates as Lord.

Anyone who places such faith in Jesus as the Son of God finds that an inward testimony joins the outward evidences already mentioned in verses 8 and 9. These are the three witnesses—Spirit, water, and blood—which look to the historical events of Christ's life that prove His divine-human nature. Faith may begin by looking at factual evidence; it is confirmed by an inner conviction of truth which comes from the Holy Spirit.

The alternative is presented as well. Refusal to believe God is tantamount to calling God a liar (cf. 1:10). "Believeth" in the phrase "he that believeth not God" occurs without an accompanying "in" (Greek, *eis*) and means that the person refuses to accept the truth of the statements which God has made concerning His Son. This person does not even reach the point of personal trust in Christ. One who refuses to believe God has made Him out to be a liar; the perfect tense reminds the readers that such an insult to God's character continues as long as the man's decision to reject Christ remains unchanged. God has not changed His testimony, and the one who persists in rejecting it is impugning the Lord's truthfulness.

**11. And this is the record, that God hath given to us eternal life:** . . . And his witness is this, —BB . . . the evidence . . . God has granted us, —BRKL . . . This testimony also contains the truth that God has restored to us the life hereafter, —GRBR.
**and this life is in his Son:** . . . this real life is to be found only in, —PHLP . . . only in communion with His Son, —GRBR.

**5:11.** This verse focuses on the internal witness which the apostle mentioned in verse 10. It is the fact that God gave us eternal life. The aorist tense of "given" joins with the lack of a definite article for "eternal life" to show that a believer enjoys eternal life now. It is not merely a never-ending extension of our current existence; it is a quality of life which belongs properly to the God who inhabits eternity—but He chooses to give it to us at the moment we trust His Son who came as the sole source of this life.

**12. He that hath the Son hath life:** . . . It follows naturally that any man who has genuine contact with Christ has this life, —PHLP . . . Those who find the Son find Life, —TCNT . . . Accordingly, he who is in close communion with the Son has Spiritual life, —GRBR.
**[and] he that hath not the Son of God hath not life:** . . . and if he has not, then he does not possess this life at all, —PHLP . . . and he who lacks this communion with the Son of God also lacks spiritual life, —GRBR.

**5:12.** The apostle John summarized his discussion of the witnesses to Christ's person by drawing a simple, inescapable conclusion—since eternal life comes solely from the Son of God, he who has the Son is the one who possesses life.

"Having the Son" (cf. 1 John 2:23; 2 John 9) is used as a synonym for having a personal relationship with Jesus Christ. The one who has Christ also has life, and the present tense of the verb *echei* indicates once more that this life is a present reality, not merely a future possibility. This is one of the most simple, yet profound, statements of what salvation means. In John 1:12 Christ speaks of receiving Him, and in Revelation 3:20 He speaks of standing at the door and knocking and coming in at a sinner's invitation. When we have Him we have life, His life.

The latter part of the verse presents a strong contrast with the first statement. It is an illusion to believe anyone can have eternal life apart from the Son of God.

**13. These things have I written unto you that believe on the name of the Son of God:** . . . to have you see that you, who have faith in the name of God's Son, —BRKL . . . so as to make you aware, —GRBR . . . who already believe, —PHLP . . . in the authority of, —SEB . . . in the Self-revelation, —WADE.
**that ye may know that ye have eternal life:** . . . may be perceiving, —CNDT . . . in order that you may know with an absolute knowledge, —WUST . . . so that you may be quite sure that, here and now, you possess eternal life, —PHLP . . . obtain life in the beyond, —GRBR.
**and that ye may believe on the name of the Son of God:** . . . if you believe, —GRBR.

**5:13.** This verse begins the conclusion to the epistle. As he did in his Gospel (John 20:31), John closed his letter by stating his purpose for writing. While John's Gospel intended to bring people to faith, his epistle aims to help believers besieged by opposing views of Christianity, to enable them to know confidently that they have followed the truth. The word for "know" (Greek, *eidēte*) was often used for knowledge characterized by certainty.

"These things" refers most directly to the immediately preceding verses but also embraces the themes of the whole letter. The tests of faith presented throughout the epistle give the believer a basis for assurance that his relationship with God is a reality. The final phrase of the verse underscores the test most recently put forward: belief in Jesus as the Son of God. (See 5:10 for "believe on.")

**14. And this is the confidence that we have in him:** . . . Our hearts are filled with great confidence, —GRBR . . . this is the boldness, —DRBY, —CNDT . . . the assurance, —WUST . . . we have resting on Him, —BRKL . . . We can come to God with no doubts, —EVRD.
**that, if we ask any thing according to his will, he heareth us:** . . . we are certain that he hears every request that is made in accord with his own plan, —PHLP . . . if we make request for anything, —WADE . . . if we petition anything in agreement with, —BRKL . . . for

ourselves, —*WUST*...This means that when we ask God for things (and those things agree with what God wants for us), then God cares about what we say, —*EVRD*.

**5:14.** When we know that we are children of God, it is natural to have confidence when we approach Him in prayer. A believer may have the "confidence" (Greek, *parrhēsia*) that allows him to speak openly (the original meaning of the word). The phrase "in him" (Greek, *pros auton*) might be translated more clearly as "toward Him," since *pros* has a root meaning of "face-to-face" and often describes intimate personal relationships, as in John 1:1.

The believer knows that God hears any request with a favorable attitude, as long as it is in accord with His will. This passage is one of several that describe conditions for answered prayer (1 John 3:22; cf. John 14:14; 15:7).

**15. And if we know that he hear us, whatsoever we ask:**...He listens to us whatever we may petition, —*BRKL*...And since we know that he invariably gives his attention to our prayers, whatever they are about, —*PHLP*...God listens to us every time we ask him. So we know that he gives us the things that we ask from him, —*EVRD*...whatever we may be requesting, —*CNDT*.

**we know that we have the petitions that we desired of him:**...then the requests we ask of Him are assured us, —*BRKL*...we can rest assured that He will give us, —*NORL*...we can be quite sure that our prayers will be answered, —*PHLP*.

**5:15.** When we know that God has heard our request favorably, His power and love assure us that we have the answer we have asked. An unusual construction is used here for "if we know," linking *ean* with an indicative verb (but the combination did occur in some secular writings) which assumes that the condition is true. We know God has heard, thus we know that He will answer. In fact, the present tense of "have" is used because God's promise is as certain as the actual event would be.

**16. If any man see his brother sin a sin [which is] not unto death:**...In case someone sees his brother commit a sin, not fatal, —*BRKL*...which has not killed his soul, —*LBCH*...which does not lead to eternal death, —*SEB*...that is not deadly sin, —*WMCK*...which is not in its tendency towards death, —*WUST*...I don't mean deliberately turning his back on evil and embracing evil, —*PHLP*.

**he shall ask, and he shall give him life for them that sin not unto death:**...he should pray to God for him and secure fresh life for the sinner, —*PHLP*...he will petition and will obtain life for him, —*BRKL*.

**There is a sin unto death: I do not say that he shall pray for it:**...There is a deadly sin, —*MNTG*...True, there are mortal sins, —*NOLI*...a sin that means death; I advise no prayer for that, —*BRKL*...that leads to spiritual death—that is not the sort of sin I have in mind when I recommend prayer for the sinner, —*PHLP*...I do not urge you to make intercession for that, —*NORL*...make a request about that, —*ADAM*...Not concerning that one [sin] do I say that he should ask, —*WUST*.

**5:16.** Although most discussion of verses 16 and 17 focuses on the "sin unto death," it is important to note that the primary emphasis of the passage is on the other side of the question, the "sin not unto death." In view of verses 13-15, these two verses are primarily an example of one area in which Christians can pray confidently according to the will of God.

When a person sees a brother sinning, he can pray for that brother knowing that his prayer is in line with God's will. The term "brother" consistently refers to fellow Christians, so the "sin not unto death" is one which a believer might commit. It is a sin which other Christians can see. And it is a sin which is repeated (note the present tense of "sin"). The epistle has consistently declared that a genuine Christian cannot continue a pattern of sin; God will not allow it to keep on. Thus a person can pray for a sinning brother, and God will answer by giving that brother life, a restored life of fellowship with God.

There is such a thing as a sin which leads to death, and John did not instruct his readers to pray for forgiveness in such a case, because this would not be in accord with God's will. The sin unto death is not described, but it has been much discussed by later commentators. It may refer to the sin of a believer who persists in sin to the point where God judges him or her by physical death (cf. Acts 5:1-11; 1 Corinthians 11:30). Or it may refer to the sin of unbelievers such as the apostate teachers and their faction, who habitually committed sins which John cataloged as the marks of an unbeliever. In this case, the death involved would be spiritual death. Neither option would be a situation where a person would pray for God to forgive apart from repentance on the sinner's part.

**17. All unrighteousness is sin: and there is a sin not unto death:**...Any wrongdoing is sin, —*WLMS*...Every failure to obey God's laws is sin, of course, but there is sin that does not preclude repentance and forgiveness, —*PHLP*...there is sin which does not involve death, —*BRKL*.

**5:17.** There is no implication that sin is condoned by saying that some sins are less serious than others. Rather, like the statement in 3:4, there is the declaration that all unrighteousness is sin. "Unrighteousness" (Greek, *adikia*) refers to any behavior which does not measure up to God's standard. Thus any deviation from God's will or character is sin. If a believer sins, to avoid physical or spiritual death—or both, he must repent and find forgiveness.

**18.** **We know that whosoever is born of God sinneth not:** . . . We know absolutely, *—WUST* . . . that every one, *—SWAN* . . . who has derived his Life from God, *—TCNT* . . . the true child of God, *—PHLP* . . . is not habitually committing sin, *—MNTG* . . . does not continue to sin, *—SEB* . . . practices no sinning, *—BRKL*.
**but he that is begotten of God keepeth himself:** . . . guards himself, *—WLSN* . . . knows how to protect himself, *—NOLI* . . . maintains a watchful guardianship, *—WUST* . . . retains hold on him, *—BRKL* . . . he is in the charge of God's own Son, *—PHLP* . . . The Son of God keeps him safe, *—EVRD*.
**and that wicked one toucheth him not:** . . . the Pernicious One, *—WUST* . . . and the Evil One cannot hurt him, *—EVRD* . . . and the evil one must keep his distance, *—PHLP* . . . does not lay hold on him, *—CMPB* . . . does not get a grip on him, *—BRKL*.

**5:18.** The apostle closed his letter with a triple "We know," a threefold statement of bedrock truths.

First, we know that everyone who has been given birth from God does not keep on sinning—a restatement of 3:9. On the contrary, he is guarded from the "wicked one." The aorist tense of "he that is begotten" may well refer to Christ rather than the believer, and the most common rendering of "himself" is "him" (Greek, *auton*). The Son of God guards the believer so Satan cannot take hold of him to drag him into sin.

**19.** **[And] we know that we are of God, and the whole world lieth in wickedness:** . . . we ourselves are children of God, and we also know that the world around us, *—PHLP* . . . We know that we belong to God. But the Evil One controls the whole world, *—EVRD* . . . is under the power of, *—WLMS* . . . lies in the grip of the evil one, *—ADAM* . . . lies under the dominance of, *—BRKL*.

**5:19.** The second truth that a Christian may know with absolute certainty is the fact that he is connected to God and in opposition to the devil. Whereas verse 18 spoke of the theological principle that believers could overcome sin, verse 19 shifts to a more personal statement—"we" are from God. John placed himself with his readers as those who have God as the source of their life. Regardless of any doubts that their opponents may have kindled, they can be assured that they belong to the Father.

This is in sharp contrast to a second relationship, the tie between the world and Satan. The world (Greek, *kosmos*) refers to the entire system of society which Satan has built up in opposition to God. The entire civilization lies in "the wicked one," a standard translation of *tō ponērō*, resting passive and helpless in his control.

**20.** **And we know that the Son of God is come, and hath given us an understanding, that we may know him that is true:** . . . has actually come to this world, and has shown us the way to know the one who is true, *—PHLP* . . . with an absolute knowledge . . . given us a permanent understanding in order that we may be knowing in an experiential way the One who is genuine, *—WUST* . . . has given us a comprehension, *—CNDT* . . . has given us discernment to recognize the True God, *—TCNT* . . . has given us insight to recognize the true One, *—BRKL* . . . Who is the Real God, *—WADE*.
**and we are in him that is true, [even] in his Son Jesus Christ:** . . . We know that our real life is, *—PHLP* . . . our lives are in that true God, *—EVRD* . . . in union with the true One, *—BRKL* . . . we are in the Genuine One, *—WUST*.
**This is the true God, and eternal life:** . . . the genuine God and life eternal, *—WUST* . . . This is the real God and this is real, eternal life, *—PHLP*.

**5:20.** The third foundation truth which we know is that God has provided a way for us to escape from Satan's realm. Jesus Christ, the Son of God, has come and has given us understanding—both statements use verbs which look back to the historical event of Christ's incarnation and couple it to the benefits which His coming still provides. The Son not only became man, He revealed the truth. He gave "understanding" (Greek, *dianoian*), the capacity to receive spiritual truth.

It is good to have a certainty about our relationship with God. A believer does not practice sin. He has confidence that he is a child of God. And he knows he is a part of God, like a vine and its branches.

The goal of His coming was to make it possible to know truth personified, God the Father. The Gnostics could offer no secrets that could compare with this. The word "true" (Greek, *alēthinos*) emphasizes the fact that Jesus introduced the genuine God, in contrast to the pseudodeities of the cults.

Not only does the believer come to know the true God, but he also enjoys such an intimate relationship with Him that John can say "we are in him." And this bond to the Father comes from the fact that we are likewise "in" the Son. Knowing Jesus is the introduction to knowing His Father.

The sum of the whole matter is that the One whom John declared is the genuine God and the fountain of eternal life.

**21.** **Little children, keep yourselves from idols. Amen:** . . . Dear children, *—BRKL* . . . My children, keep yourselves from, —*NOYS* . . . put yourselves beyond the reach of, —*WLMS* . . . guard yourselves, —*MNTG* . . . But be on your guard . . . against every false god! —*PHLP* . . . away from, —*SEB* . . . beware of false gods! —*NORL* . . . guard yourselves from symbols, —*KLGS* . . . from false divinities, —*NOLI* . . . from misrepresentations of God, —*WADE* . . . from idolatry, —*MRDK* . . . from communication with evil spirits, —*GRBR* . . . false gods, [from anything and everything that would occupy the place in your heart due to God, from any sort of substitute for Him that would take first place in your life], —*AMPB* . . . My sons, avoid all idolatrous imitations, —*WAND* . . . keep yourselves from worshipping false gods and images, —*MKNT.*

**5:21.** The final statement is a warning. John prefaced it with his term of affection, "Little children," because he was deeply concerned for them with fatherly love. But the command itself is stern. "Guard yourselves from idols!" The aorist tense makes the tone even sharper. The idols meant could have been the actual idols which filled every Roman city, but were more likely to have been the false gods presented by Gnostic teachers.

Though John's readers faced great pressure from those who claimed to have the truth, he provided them with tests of holiness, love, and truth by which they could be confident that they truly belonged to the family of God.

# 2 JOHN

## Overview

### Author and Date

This epistle can best be described as a letter to the Church. Its length resembles that of the private letters of that day. The style, language, and thought world of 2 and 3 John prove both were written by the same person. Both also bear a relationship with 1 John. In both there is an abundance of Johannine expressions and concepts. Some of these are terms like "love, truth, to witness, testimony, commandment, a new commandment, and antichrist," as well as concepts like "to abide in, to walk in, to be of God, to see God." Those who have attempted to show two different authors of 1 John, and 2 and 3 John cannot be taken seriously.

Both 2 and 3 John can be dated around the same time (ca. A.D. 80-100). There is virtually no justification for identifying the epistle mentioned in 3 John 9 as 2 John. The church mentioned in 2 John is entirely different from the one to which Gaius (the recipient of 3 John) belonged. It can be surmised that both churches were located in Asia Minor. Comments concerning the "elder" can be found in the overview of 1 John.

### Canonicity

It is more noteworthy that these two short apostolic letters were included in the canon than that some placed them among the antilegomena, the disputed epistles.

As late as the beginning of the Fourth Century, Eusebius classified 2 and 3 John as among the "disputed." Sometime around the beginning of the Fifth Century, the Peshitta, the Syrian translation of the Bible, included 1 John but not the other two.

However, these two short letters were known and used in the Church, and they are included among the most ancient manuscripts in existence. Numerous theologians of the Early Church either paraphrased, cited, or interpreted verses or passages from all three epistles of John. Apparently 2 John was more widely used than 3 John. Further, it is difficult to imagine anyone putting himself in the awkward position of trying to honor the apostle by writing something that was directly against that which the letters themselves speak out against!

Even though they were disputed for a long time, those two letters did become part of the canon. Men of the Third and Fourth Century were convinced that 2 and 3 John were of apostolic origin.

The Second Epistle of John can be outlined in the following manner:

1. The opening (verses 1-3)
2. The children of the church—the joy of the elder (verse 4)
3. The challenge to mutual love (verses 5-6)
4. The warning against heretics (verses 7-9)
5. A "no" to heretics (verses 10,11)
6. Conclusion

### The Central Teaching of the Epistle

The conceptual framework and mode of expression in 2 John is strongly reminiscent of 1 John. Both speak of the relationship between genuine confession of Christ and loving one another. Also, in both texts although the writer spoke with authority, he did so with a warm and fatherly warmth. Nevertheless, there are some differences. Whereas the church mentioned in 1 John was experiencing a crisis because of the threat of false teachers, it appears as though the church addressed by 2 John had not yet undergone attack (verse 10) although the author cautioned that many deceivers had gone out into the world.

Verse 4 commends some of the members of the church whom the author knew. Their Christian walk caused him to rejoice "greatly." Their practical Christian living led him to believe the general situation of the church was good. However, he emphasized that walking in the truth and keeping the commandment cannot be divorced from faith in Christ and confessing His name. The close relationship between ethics and Christology was again stressed as "from the beginning" (cf. verses 5,6). Jesus had given the commandment, the apostles preached it, and those to whom the epistle was sent had heard it "from the beginning," i.e., from the first time they heard the gospel of love. The false teachers were denouncing this relationship. These "transgresseth" (verse 9). Perhaps the writer was using the opponents' own vocabulary in a sarcastic manner. Any so-called "progress" of the heretics was actually "regression." Their "enlightenment" was actually "darkness." They had "advanced" so far they had left God entirely.

These "deceivers" (verse 7) rejected the Incarnation as well as the Atonement. As a result they undermined the Christian commandment— indeed the power of—to love one another. They were probably confessing Jesus as "Lord," but at the same time were denying His lordship and His true nature as God-man. Therefore, the apostle wrote they were to be rejected immediately if they surfaced in the church and attempted to propagate their "faith." Their denouncement must be seen in the light of the love of God. Because they were actually spurning the love of God revealed in Jesus Christ "come in the flesh," the apostle of love had to correct them. Not to do so would have been unloving.

The apostle gave explicit instructions concerning those who attempted to enter the church but rejected apostolic doctrine (verse 10). They were not to be welcomed. "Into your house" here most certainly refers to the local church gathering, not someone's home. There is no disparity between

what John taught in this epistle and what Jesus taught concerning loving one's enemies. Jesus' own definition of love rejected sharply any twisted concepts concerning God. His conflicts with the Pharisees aptly illustrate this (e.g., Matthew 23). The decisive "no" directed at the heretics was equally a "yes" to the love of God. If the heretics had been given free rein under the pretense of love for God it would not have shown love for God or His children.

The heretics had threatened the relationship between God the Father and His children. This explains John's harsh reaction. He closed his epistle with an expression of hope that he would be able to visit them and elaborate more fully on the teaching he had given in the letter.

# The Second Epistle of John

## Commentary

1. **The elder unto the elect lady and her children:**... From the pastor, —NORL...I, a Ruler in the church, —BB... The Presbyter to a Mother Church, —WADE... The old man to the Chosen Lady, Fenton... The Lady whom God called, —LBCH... selected out by sovereign grace for salvation, —WUST...to Electa Cyria, —CMPB...From the Officer of the Church, —TCNT...This letter comes to a certain Christian lady and her children, —PHLP.

**whom I love in the truth; and not I only:**...as for myself, I love in the sphere of the truth, —WUST...I love all of you in the truth, —EVRD....of whom I am truly fond, —GRBR...held in the highest affection not only by me, —PHLP.

**but also all they that have known the truth:**...at present possess a knowledge of it, —WUST...all those who recognize, —BRKL ... all who have attained to knowledge of, —GRBR.

**1.** Second John provides an opportunity to observe the way the apostle John applied the principles taught in 1 John to a concrete situation. As usual, he chose to remain unnamed, simply introducing himself as "the elder." At the probable date of this epistle John would be the last surviving apostle and would need no elaborate introduction. His choice of "elder" refers both to his advanced age and to his position in the church.

The epistle is addressed to "the elect lady." Many have concluded that the "lady" was a local church, addressed figuratively as a woman. Her "children" would be the church members and the "elect sister" in verse 13 would be a sister church. Others believe the letter was intended for an individual Christian woman and her family. Either view is possible. The admonitions would be appropriate for either a person or for a congregation of believers.

The apostle declared that he loved this lady and her children in truth. The plural "whom" shows that the entire family was included in his love. He strengthened his statement by adding that she and her children also enjoyed the affection of all believers. Believers are described as "all they that have known the truth." The perfect tense is used to describe those who have gained a knowledge which produces a lasting relationship. *Ginōskō* often refers to the knowledge of God gained by personal experience of salvation.

2. **For the truth's sake, which dwelleth in us:**... Because of this true knowledge, —BB...that remains in us, —BRKL...We love you because of the truth—the truth that lives in us, —EVRD.

**and shall be with us for ever:**...which even now we know and which will be our companion for ever, —PHLP...which will remain united with us for all time to come, —GRBR...will exist with us, —FNTN...to eternity, —DRBY.

**2.** John went on to explain why Christians love this lady. It was not merely because of her unusual personality, but because "the truth" of the gospel had become part of every believer's life. Once the truth comes to reside in a person's life, it produces love for other Christians. It is the driving force of the Christian life, and the woman addressed in 2 John shared in that love. The Greek phrase "to the age" is the usual idiom for "for ever."

3. **Grace be with you, mercy, [and] peace, from God the Father:** ... Loving favor and lovingkindness, —NLTG.

**and from the Lord Jesus Christ, the Son of the Father, in truth and love:**...the Father's Son, —PHLP... with whom you are united by truth and peace, —GRBR.

**3.** Second John follows the customary letter format, first listing the writer and the recipient, then giving a greeting. Early Christians often used distinctively meaningful greetings like the one used here. Unlike other writers, who express their greetings as a wish, John stated his greeting in the future tense as a prediction. This woman and her household would enjoy grace, mercy, and peace. "Grace" refers to undeserved favor from God, "mercy" describes help bestowed on the helpless, and "peace" is both the fact of blessing and the subjective calm that springs from it.

These blessings come from a divine source: both Jesus Christ and God the Father. The apostle may have stressed this connection because of the tendency of some false teachers to separate the Father from the Son. The final phrase shows that the three blessings are administered with a balance between truth and love, which the rest of the letter strives to maintain. Both qualities are necessary. Truth which is not administered in love is too harsh to be fully effective. On the other hand, love which operates without a proper regard for truth can be mere sentimentality.

4. **I rejoiced greatly that I found:**... It has made me very happy, —NORL...I was very happy to find, —WMCK ... was greatly delighted, —FNTN ... I feel

extremely happy to have found, —BRKL . . . I am happy to find, —WLMS . . . I was delighted that I found, —ADAM . . . I was filled with joy when I met, —LBCH.

**of thy children walking in truth:** . . . among your children those who live in a true way, —BRKL . . . conducting themselves, —WUST . . . living in the truth, —WMCK

**as we have received a commandment from the Father:** . . . instruction, —BRKL . . . from the presence of, —WUST . . . the Father himself, —PHLP.

**4.** Like many letter writers of his day, John moved to a word of commendation. He declared that he rejoiced to discover good news about some of the lady's children. They were walking in truth. The perfect tense of "found" shows that his information remained true, and the present participle "walking" implies a continued pattern of healthy spiritual life. As a spiritual parent to many believers, John was always concerned about their welfare. The fact that only some are mentioned does not imply that the others were unfaithful, merely that John had not heard reports about them. These younger believers were walking or carrying out their daily actions in the sphere of the truth.

The next phrase forges a link between the lives of these believers and the command of God. Their walk in the truth was the kind of life which God demands. This phrase refers to the overall teaching of Scripture, rather than a specific verse.

**5. And now I beseech thee, lady:** . . . now I entreat you, —WUST . . . now I beg of you, Princess, —FNTN . . . I beg you now, dear lady, —PHLP.

**not as though I wrote a new commandment unto thee:** . . . not by way of writing you a new injunction, —BRKL . . . not as though I were issuing any new order, —PHLP . . . which is new in quality, —WUST.

**but that which we had from the beginning:** . . . but instead, —BRKL . . . simply reminding you of the original one, —PHLP.

**that we love one another:** . . . with a divine love sacrificial in its essence, —WUST.

**5.** At this point John turned to the immediate reason for the letter, the need to regain a proper balance between the demands of truth and love. He phrased his message as a formal request, not a command or a plea.

The apostle asked nothing new; he simply reaffirmed the command which Christians have obeyed since the Church began—to love one another. Christ gave the command in John 13:34, 35, and John repeated it in 1 John 3:11.

**6. And this is love, that we walk after his commandments:** . . . You must live in love, —LBCH . . . that we keep on living in accordance, —WLMS . . . consists in our behaving in agreement with His suggestions, —BRKL . . . we should be ordering our behavior

dominated by his commandments, —WUST . . . according to His precepts, —CNDT.

**This is the commandment, That, as ye have heard from the beginning:** . . . the very same command . . . the way you heard from the first, —BRKL . . . which you learnt from the first, —FNTN.

**ye should walk in it:** . . . to behave exactly, —BRKL . . . in its sphere you should be ordering your behavior, —WUST . . . live in love, —TNT.

**6.** Love, however, must be exercised within the guidelines of obedience. The first phrase here defines love more narrowly, as behavior that continually moves according to the standard of God's commands. Love is more than an uncontrollable emotion. It is action for the good of another, functioning within the limits of all God's other commands. The second part of the verse reiterates that this was the original intent of Christ's command to love.

**7. For many deceivers are entered into the world:** . . . For the world is becoming full of, —PHLP . . . there are many impostors, —TCNT . . . Many false teachers, —NORL . . . went forth, —WUST . . . have gone out, —BRKL.

**who confess not:** . . . They won't admit, —SEB . . . do not agree, —WUST.

**that Jesus Christ is come in the flesh:** . . . as having come incarnated, —BRKL . . . came as a human being, —TNT . . . sphere of flesh, —WUST . . . really became man, —PHLP.

**This is a deceiver and an antichrist:** . . . the misleader and the antagonist of Christ, —FNTN . . . the very spirit of deceit, —PHLP . . . what I call the work of the impostors, —NOLI.

**7.** There is a reason the explanation of verses 5 and 6 was necessary. Many deceivers had appeared, hoping to take advantage of the hospitality and love shown by unsuspecting Christians. Believers are indeed to love one another, but they must love discriminately.

These false teachers had already spread out into the world and posed a serious threat to the truth. John provided a test by which to detect such deceivers. These men did not acknowledge that Jesus Christ came in the flesh. They represented early gnosticism, a heresy which started from the position that all physical matter is inherently evil. The Gnostics could not accept a genuine Incarnation, in which God became man and took on human flesh. So John selected this key doctrine as the test of the false teacher. Anyone who denied the Incarnation was a representative of the deceiver par excellence, an antichrist who opposed the true Christ with an alternative message.

**8. Look to yourselves:** . . . Ever be keeping a watchful eye upon, *−WUST* . . . Look out for, *−BRKL* . . . Take care of, *−PHLP.*

**that we lose not those things which we have wrought:** . . . Don't lose the reward, *−SEB* . . . so you may not lose the results of, *−BRKL* . . . that which you have worked for, *−ADAM* . . . that we are working for, *−LBCH* . . . the things we accomplish, *−WUST.*

**but that we receive a full reward:** . . . instead, make sure of a full reward, *−BRKL* . . . but may receive full wages, *−DRBY* . . . you may be getting full wages, *−CNDT* . . . but persevere till God gives you your reward, *−PHLP.*

**8.** Here in verse 8 we find the first command in the letter: a warning to beware, to be on guard. This serves as the focus of John's message. *Blepete* is present tense and demands continual watchfulness to prevent disaster. Its plural form shows that both the woman and her household needed to watch themselves, to keep from being led astray by false teachers.

The purpose of John's warning was to prevent two harmful results from taking place. First, he wanted to forestall the destruction of his work. *Eirgasametha* carries the idea of work that involves labor and exertion; the people who had brought the gospel invested much time and energy in the task of winning converts such as the family addressed in this letter, and John did not want that work to be destroyed. He used a word that means to ruin or make useless; it is also used to describe the fate of unbelievers who perish eternally. Second, John did not want these believers to lose their rewards. His words do not suggest that they will lose everything, but they may fail to receive their full wages.

**9. Whosoever transgresseth, and abideth not in the doctrine of Christ:** . . . Everybody who goes beyond, *−ADAM* . . . Whoever wanders away, *−NOLI* . . . The man who is so "advanced" that he is not content with what Christ taught, *−PHLP* . . . Whoever assumes leadership, and does not remain in the doctrine, *−BRKL* . . . beyond the limits [of true doctrine] and does not remain in the aforementioned teaching with reference to the Christ, *−WUST.*

**hath not God:** . . . does not possess God, *−WUST* . . . has repudiated God, *−NOLI* . . . has in fact no God, *−PHLP.*

**He that abideth in the doctrine of Christ:** . . . The one who remains, *−WUST* . . . keeps moving in the sphere of, *−BRKL* . . . bases his life on Christ's teaching, *−PHLP.*

**he hath both the Father and the Son:** . . . this one possesses both, *−WUST* . . . as his God, *−PHLP.*

**9.** The next verse lays down general principles which explain the importance of the issues. Even though the men who came asking for hospitality

all claimed to be representatives of the gospel, not all of them deserved that status.

He began with a negative statement. Any person who showed certain characteristics was a person who did not have God. Such a person kept running forward, adding his own ideas to the teachings of Christ. The Gnostic teachers loved to boast of the hidden truths of salvation which they alone could reveal. They showed no desire to remain "in the doctrine (teaching) of Christ." Whether this phrase refers to the things which Christ taught or the things which His apostles taught about Him, these deceivers refused to stay within the framework of the original gospel. They insisted on adding their own concepts. John's verdict on all such people: they do not have God.

The verse moves on to state the positive side of the contrast. One who remains within the boundaries of the original teachings of Christ is the one who truly has God. In. fact, he has both the Son and the Father (cf. 1 John 2:23,24).

**10. If there come any unto you:** . . . In case anyone approaches you, *−BRKL* . . . If any teacher comes to you, *−PHLP.*

**and bring not this doctrine:** . . . who is disloyal to what Christ taught, *−PHLP* . . . is not bearing, *−WUST* . . . this teaching, *−SEB.*

**receive him not into [your] house:** . . . do not receive him in your home, *−BRKL* . . . don't have him inside, *−PHLP.*

**neither bid him God speed:** . . . Do not even say hello to him, *−NLTG* . . . And stop giving him greeting, *−WUST* . . . or wish him well, *−TCNT* . . . nor wish Him success, *−WLSN* . . . nor extend him your greeting, *−BRKL.*

**10.** John applied the general command to the particular situation which his friend now faced. The form of "if" used assumes that the sentence is a statement of reality. False teachers actually were coming to this home, men who did not carry with them the genuine teaching of Christ. When this happened, John's command was clear. Do not receive them! The present tense suggests that the lady may have been welcoming such people indiscriminately in the past, so John called on her to stop doing so. She was not to bring them into her home, and she was not to provide them with the hospitality and help that went with a formal greeting in that culture.

**11. For he that biddeth him God speed:** . . . who gives him a friendly greeting, *−NORL* . . . who bids him prosperity, *−SWAN* . . . he who wishes him success, *−CMPB* . . . bids him welcome, *−BRKL.*

**is partaker of his evil deeds:** . . . unless you want to share in the evil that he is doing, *−PHLP* . . . makes himself a sharer of those, *−BRKL* . . . partakes in his wicked works, *−DRBY* . . . is a partner in his works which are pernicious, —WUST... himself participates in his wicked doings, —FNTN ... shares in his evil works, —SWAN... his wicked acts, —CNDT.

**11.** John concluded by giving the reason it is wrong to provide loving hospitality for such people. More is involved than mere obedience to the command to love. It may seem harmless to speak words of greeting. But when such a greeting becomes participation in the evil deeds of an apostate, it is wrong. *Koinōnei* means "to share, participate" and implies close union and active participation, not just a superficial involvement. John forbade any variety of love that makes a believer a coworker with a false teacher. Opening one's home to such a person simply provided a heretic with a base for operations.

The overall message is clear. Christians are expected to display love for one another, but that love must be tempered by discriminating regard for truth. Harboring apostates is never approved by God.

**12. Having many things to write unto you:** ... Although I have, —BRKL... I have much to communicate to you, —WADE ... I have a lot that I could write to you, —PHLP.

**I would not [write] with paper and ink:** ... I would rather not use, —BRKL... did not, after giving the matter mature consideration, desire to do so with, —WUST.

**but I trust to come unto you:** ... but I hope to come, —FNTN, —TNT ... I am expecting to come, —CNDT ... am hoping to be present with you, —WUST... but I hope to have a visit with you, —BRKL.

**and speak face to face:** ... and talk with you, —BRKL... and speak by word of mouth, —FNTN.

**that our joy may be full:** ... our happiness may be complete, —BRKL ... our joy, having been filled completely full, might persist in that state of fullness through present time, —WUST... and our joy will be all the greater, —GRBR ... so that you may be very happy, —BECK ... for then our joy will be complete, —BRCL... your joy may be complete, —KLST... so that your joy might run over, —KLGS... and how we shall enjoy that! —PHLP... That will make us very happy, —EVRD ... that your happiness may be complete, —GDSP.

**12.** The epistle comes to a close in almost the same way as 3 John. John had many items he would have liked to discuss with his friend, topics not specified in the text. But when he composed the letter, he decided not to pursue them in writing.

He mentioned his writing materials, paper and ink. The letter was probably written on a single sheet of papyrus, the most common writing material of the time, manufactured from the stem of the papyrus reed. The ink was made of lampblack or soot mixed with water and gum, then hardened into sticks, to be cut and moistened for use as needed.

Rather than trust all his thoughts to writing, John hoped to make a visit to the household. At that time they would be able to talk face-to-face. The literal Greek idiom "mouth to mouth" is even more intimate than the English rendering. The result of this personal encounter would be an opportunity for both to experience a thoroughly joyful meeting. The combination of perfect tense and a form of the verb "to be" pictures a joy that is brought to fullness, then continues to be full to the point of overflowing. The same construction appears in 1 John 1:4.

**13. The children of thy elect sister greet thee. Amen:** ... There greet you the born-ones of your sister, the selected-out one, —WUST... of your beloved sister, —CMPB... your noble sister, who is of God's selection, —BB ... Your sister's children send their love, —PHLP... thy sister, Elect, —CNFT... whom God has chosen, —BECK... of your chosen sister send you their love, —EVRD ... chosen by God, send you their good wishes, —BRCL... send their hearty greetings, —GRBR... salute thee, —NOYS... sends you regards, —FNTN... send you greetings, —BRKL... wish to be remembered to you, —WLMS, —GDSP... Grace be with you, —MRDK.

**13.** In John's closing statement, he passed on greetings from the woman's nieces and nephews. "The children of thy elect sister greet thee." There is no greeting from the sister herself, who may have been absent or deceased. Some commentators have taken the position that the verse describes members of a sister church, probably the one where John resided. In any case, the "sister" is known as a "chosen" one, called by God to be a member of His family.

This epistle offers a powerful corrective to the tendency to overlook the importance of truth in our zeal to show love.

# 3 JOHN

## Overview

Third John is a personal letter written by "the elder" to an individual named Gaius. However, instead of addressing personal concerns, the letter deals with life in the church. In all of John's writings the term *ekklēsia*, "assembly," often used for the "church," occurs only in this little letter (verses 6,9,10). (Concerning the date and the place the epistle has in the canon, see the discussion in the overview of 2 John.)

In contrast to the First and Second Epistles of John, 3 John makes no mention of heretics, unless the resistance of Diotrephes is a result of his sympathizing with the deceivers. This, however, cannot be verified by the letter.

Even though 3 John does not discuss any deep theological issues, it remains valuable for the Church since it offers lucid insight into some of the difficulties facing a late First Century church (probably in Asia Minor). The epistle also presents a picture of lively missionary activity and a glimpse of how the gospel was supported financially.

## Third John can be outlined as follows:

1. Opening (verse 1)

2. Gaius—the Joy of the Elder (verses 2-4)

3. The Challenge to Support Missionaries (verses 5-8)

4. Diotrephes—the Perpetrator of Strife (verses 9,10)

5. The Recommendation of Demetrius (verses 11,12)

6. Closing (verses 13,14)

## The Main Theme of the Epistle

The letter centers around three persons: Gaius, Diotrephes, and Demetrius.

(1) Gaius, to whom the letter was addressed, must have been an influential person in the church. Fellow Christians or itinerant preachers had brought "the elder" the good report concerning Gaius' Christian lifestyle. The writer praised Gaius for welcoming the traveling brethren, and for his "walk in the truth." He let Gaius know he was depending on him to welcome his own "evangelists." They were to be shown hospitality and supported materially so that those to whom they ministered would not have to pay to hear them. This was the case among many Hellenistic itinerant philosophers and preachers. Because missionaries go forth in the name of Jesus, without asking for financial support from their listeners, those who send them must support them. The author included himself in this responsibility. He and Gaius were coworkers in the truth.

(2) Diotrephes was the ringleader of the opposition. He was the exact opposite of Gaius. He did not acknowledge the authority of the elder, so letters were of little consequence. Almost certainly John had written before but with little effect. Because of Diotrephes, the letter may not even have been read to the church.

Diotrephes' position in the church is not known. However, he certainly had significant influence. He had tried to oust those in the church who supported the traveling preachers (verse 10). No doubt he was a very self-reliant individual. Perhaps he was the leader of a group of elders. A close examination of the text indicates he was not a theological threat but a threat to authority.

Because Diotrephes did not accept the authority of the writer of the epistle, he spoke "malicious words" against him, but John promised that when he arrived he would remind the church of Diotrephes' works. It is not clear whether the strife was resolved. However, the fact that 3 John has survived through the centuries seems to indicate that "the elder" did achieve the desired results.

The situation may be summarized in three points: (a) Diotrephes was slandering "the elder." He disagreed with the missions strategy of "the elder." (b) He would not receive traveling missionaries. His negative attitude was hindering the spread of the gospel. (c) He was excluding some from the church. The present tense of "forbiddeth" and "casteth" may indicate what he was trying to do.

(3) Demetrius, the third main character, was probably one of the leaders of the itinerant missionaries. Perhaps he delivered the epistle. Gaius could address him candidly. Just as Gaius received a positive testimony from the itinerant missionaries, Demetrius also was spoken well of by all. His positive recommendation is a contrast to the false confessors of Christ (2 John 10,11), who were not to be received. Even though the "good report" concerning Demetrius widened the rift between Diotrephes and Gaius, the writer of the epistle indicated no action was to be taken for the wrong reasons.

## Closing

The greeting which closed the epistle reflects its private character. The greeting was from friend to friend, not from one church to another. The ab-

sence of a greeting to the church was probably because of the position Diotrephes had usurped for
himself.

# The Third Epistle of John

## Commentary

**1. The elder unto the well-beloved Gaius:** ... The Presbyter, —NOLI ... The old man to his friend, —FNTN ... My dear friend, —LBCH ... to the esteemed, —BRKL.
**whom I love in the truth:** ... whom, as for myself, I love in the sphere of the truth, —WUST ... with sincere love, —PHLP.

**1.** Even though 3 John is a short book, it teaches some crucial concepts of Christian life. As in his other letters, John remained anonymous, introducing himself simply as "the elder," referring both to his age and his status as the last surviving apostle.

The Gaius who received this letter remains unknown apart from the letter itself. The verse emphasizes John's love for Gaius. Even the word "I" is emphatic.

John loved Gaius "in the truth." The repeated use of "truth" here, as in his other writings, shows that truth was a central idea in the apostle's thoughts. He repeated the phrase both with the Greek definite article (verses 3,4,8,12) and without it (verses 1 and 3). Secular writings often used the phrase as a synonym for "truly," but the usage in 2 and 3 John suggests that here it refers to the specific truth that comes from God.

**2. Beloved, I wish above all things that thou mayest prosper and be in health:** ... My heartfelt prayer for you, my very dear friend, is that you may be as healthy and prosperous, —PHLP ... I pray that you may have good success, —LBCH.
**even as thy soul prospereth:** ... in the same way that your soul is prospering, —ADAM.

**2.** John used verses 2-4 to compliment Gaius for Christian virtues; the rest of the letter encouraged him to keep displaying those same virtues.

It opens with the warm greeting "beloved," which begins almost every paragraph (verses 2,5,11). Then John shared his prayer for Gaius—that he would be as prosperous in all areas of life as he had been in his spiritual life. The word "prosper" carries images of a successful journey, while the other verb describes good physical health.

**3. For I rejoiced greatly:** ... I felt extremely happy, —BRKL ... I was delighted, —PHLP.
**when the brethren came:** ... constantly coming, —WUST ... brothers arrived, —PHLP.

**and testified of the truth that is in thee:** ... and bearing witness of, —WUST ... and testified to your fidelity to the Truth, —TCNT ... and spoke so highly of the sincerity of your life, —PHLP.
**even as thou walkest in the truth:** ... obviously you are living in, —PHLP ... as for you, in the sphere of the truth you are conducting yourself, —WUST ... as indeed you are living the true life, —BRKL.

**3.** John knew of Gaius through the reports of traveling Christians who had passed through Gaius' hometown and brought word to John's location (traditionally Ephesus). These travelers consistently testified that Gaius was living in a way that matched the pattern set forth by God's truth. The verse closes with an added confirmation. The reality of the man's life matched the reports, for he actually walked in the truth.

**4. I have no greater joy:** ... Nothing pleases me more than, —ADAM ... Nothing affords me more enjoyment, —BRKL ... no greater satisfaction, —WADE.
**than to hear that my children walk in truth:** ... are habitually ordering their behavior, —WUST ... conduct themselves, —FNTN ... follow the truth, —LBCH.

**4.** Nothing gave John greater joy than to hear that his spiritual children continued to walk in line with the truth of the gospel. "My children" is emphatic and suggests that Gaius may have come to Christ through the ministry of John. And John wanted all the believers within his family to live godly lives.

**5. Beloved, thou doest faithfully whatsoever thou doest:** ... Beloved friend, you are acting faithfully when you do anything, —BRKL ... You practise faith, friend, when you bestow benefits, —FNTN ... You are acting loyally, my friend, —WMCK ... you are doing a work of faith, whatever you are performing, —WUST.
**to the brethren, and to strangers:** ... for the brothers, and specially for the strangers, —BRKL.

**5.** John next encouraged Gaius to maintain the specific virtue of hospitality. The opening phrase confirms the fact that God approved the ministry Gaius had already carried out.

John used two words to describe the deeds of Gaius. *Poieis* simply states that he actually carried out tasks, and the present tense shows that hospitality was a habit with him. *Ergasē* adds the idea of wearying labor, with an aorist form that sums up Gaius' whole history of service. His home had been open to Christian brothers, even those who were strangers to him.

Hospitality was one of the accepted virtues of the ancient world, as well as a command of Scripture (Titus 1:8; Hebrews 13:2). Christian workers traveled long distances, and public inns were expensive and primitive. So the Early Church developed an informal hospitality network, aided by believers' generosity.

**6. Which have borne witness of thy charity before the church:** ... bore testimony of your love before the assembly, —WUST ... They have testified before the church about your friendship, —BRKL.

**whom if thou bring forward on their journey after a godly sort, thou shalt do well:** ... whom you are doing well to provide with the necessities of travel ... on their journey in a manner worthy of God, —WUST ... to forward them on their journey in a way befitting God's service, —BRKL ... on their trip in a manner that is worthy of God, —ADAM.

**6.** More than one itinerant Christian had confirmed not only the truth (verse 3) but the love displayed by Gaius. *Agapē* means more than emotion or words; it is action.

The verb changes to future tense—"thou shalt do well" if you continue to show such love. This common phrase was a polite idiom like the English *please*. Gaius should continue to help those who came to him. *Propempsas* includes receiving a person, entertaining him for the night, and providing the supplies needed for the next stage of the journey. Gaius was to do this in a manner worthy of God, welcoming them in a manner appropriate for one who represents the Lord.

**7. Because that for his name's sake they went forth:** ... for the sake of that Name, —FNTN ... on behalf of that Name they have gone out, —BRKL ... they have started out, —MNTG.

**taking nothing of the Gentiles:** ... without accepting anything from, —BRKL ... taking not even one thing from the pagans, —WUST ... from their heathen converts, —TCNT ... they refused help from any one except Christians, —LBCH.

**7.** John explained the reasons these brothers deserved help. Their purpose was worthy; they went forth for the sake of the Name, either the name of Christ or of God the Father. They were missionaries, proclaiming the glorious person of God.

In addition, they did not take money from their hearers, as the typical religion-peddlers of the day did.

**8. We therefore ought to receive such:** ... Hence we ought to support such, —MNTG ... as a moral obligation to underwrite such as these, —WUST ... we owe it to support such as these, —SWAN ... ought to

entertain such, —WLSN, —WADE ... to show hospitality to such men, —WLMS.

**that we might be fellowhelpers to the truth:** ... in order to be ... in the truth, —BRKL ... fellow workers, —WUST.

**8.** This verse states a principle: believers must support such men. The unsaved need not pay for the gospel; instead, Christians are obligated to undertake the task of providing protection and resources. Such a ministry allows believers to become fellow workers with the truth. God's truth moves forward, and Christians have the privilege of sharing in the progress.

**9. I wrote unto the church:** ... I have written, —BRKL ... the assembly, —WUST.

**but Diotrephes, who loveth to have the preeminence among them:** ... the one who is fond of being the pre-eminent one among them, —WUST ... who is eager to be a leader, —NORL ... wants to be the head of the church himself, —LBCH ... likes to make himself prominent among them, —FNTN.

**receiveth us not:** ... declines to recognize us, —TCNT ... refuses to acknowledge my authority, —NORL ... is not accepting us, —WUST ... refuses to listen to me, —WLMS ... does not accept what we say, —SWAN ... doesn't recognize our authority, —ADAM ... rejected us, —SEB.

**9.** This verse marks an abrupt shift in mood, descending with a jolt to deal with a difficult situation. John had written a prior letter, now lost, to Gaius' church.

Surprisingly, the letter was rejected. Opposition was led by Diotrephes, whose aristocratic name meant "nurtured by Zeus." John introduced him as one who loved to have preeminence, to enjoy first place. In contrast, Colossians 1:18 declares that only Christ rightly holds first place.

**10. Wherefore, if I come, I will remember his deeds which he doeth:** ... On this account, if I should come, I shall bring to remembrance, —WUST ... I will denounce his actions, —NOLI.

**prating against us with malicious words:** ... all his noisy talk against us, —WMCK ... sneering at us with vile expressions, —FNTN ... talking wicked nonsense about us, —WADE ... in making empty charges against us with evil words, —SWAN ... pernicious words, —WUST ... in ridiculing us with his wicked tongue, —TCNT ... the evil words that he babbles about us! —ADAM.

**and not content therewith, neither doth he himself receive the brethren:** ... He does not stop with that, —LBCH ... accept the brethren, —WUST.

**and forbiddeth them that would:** ... and those who after mature consideration desire to do so, he prevents, —WUST ... he interferes with those who wish to welcome them, —WLMS.

**and casteth [them] out of the church:** ... excludes them, —WADE ... and out of the assembly he throws them, *—WUST*...expels them from the assembly, *—NORL*.

**10.** The apostle intended to make a visit and deal with the situation. Though he used the word "if," only the timing is uncertain. When John arrived, he would show Diotrephes' actions in their true light—as rebellion.

The indictment against Diotrephes falls into two categories. First, he spoke against John and his associates. *Phluarōn* pictures empty or foolish speech like a pot that boils over, throwing up a froth of bubbles. But more than mere foolishness was involved. These unjust accusations were aggressive, evil attacks. Second, Diotrephes went beyond words to actions. He refused to accept the Christian workers who came from John. He moved to prevent any other Christians in the assembly from helping the itinerants. And he expelled any who refused to be intimidated.

**11. Beloved, follow not that which is evil, but that which is good:** ... don't copy what is bad, *—SEB* . . . do not follow bad examples, *—WLMS*, *—NOLI* ... do not have the habit of imitating the evil, *—WUST*.

**He that doeth good is of God:** ... is out of God, *—WUST*.

**but he that doeth evil hath not seen God:**

**11.** Verses 11 and 12 focus on an important point of the letter. Verse 11 gives the first command contained in the letter. In the face of opposition from Diotrephes, Gaius must have been tempted to stop helping the missionaries. So John encouraged Gaius to imitate the good, not the evil.

*Agathon* describes that which is morally and spiritually good. *Kakon* is a weaker word, used for something inferior, lacking the qualities it should have.

The reason for John's command is that the only source of genuine good is contact with God (1 John 2:29; 3:9; 4:7; 5:1,18). In contrast, a person with habitually bad behavior shows that he has never come to know God. John often used such terms to distinguish saved and unsaved people. Diotrephes did not show the evidence of being a regenerate man.

**12. Demetrius hath good report of all [men], and of the truth itself:** ... Everyone has a good word to say for Demetrius, and the very truth speaks well of him, *—PHLP*...says good things about...And the truth agrees with what they say, *—EVRD*...there has been borne testimony by all, *—WUST*...has won a good reputation, *—WADE*...enjoys a good reputation from everyone and from truth itself, *—BRKL*...is being praised by every one, *—LBCH*.

**yea, and we [also] bear record; and ye know that our record is true:** ... We add our testimony too, *—BRKL*...Also, we say good about him. And you know that what we say is true, *—EVRD*...He has our warm recommendation also, and you know you can trust what we say about anyone, *—PHLP*...you know that our evidence is reliable, *—FNTN*...and this testimony still holds true, *—WUST*...is trustworthy, *—WADE*.

**12.** A new character abruptly appears. At the end of a discussion on the duty of hospitality and a warning to do what is right rather than following the bad example of Diotrephes, John now introduced Demetrius. The immediate purpose of the letter was evidently to introduce Demetrius as the bearer of the letter, a man worthy of Gaius' hospitality.

John provided a threefold recommendation for Demetrius who does not appear elsewhere in the New Testament. The first two testimonies are in the perfect tense, showing that he had a reputation that went back into the past. The first testimony is the general witness of those who know Demetrius. This is seconded by the testimony of the truth itself; his life matched the truth of the gospel so well that the resemblance was obvious. John offered his personal testimony as the third witness, giving assurance that Demetrius' exemplary character was still being maintained in the present. Gaius no doubt knew from past experience that John's recommendations were reliable, and Gaius could confidently offer help to Demetrius.

**13. I had many things to write:** ... There is a great deal I want to say to you, *—PHLP*...I want to tell you, *—EVRD*.

**but I will not with ink and pen write unto thee:** ... but I can't put it down in black and white, *—PHLP*...but I am unwilling to communicate to you, *—FNTN* ... but I do not desire to be writing to you, *—WUST*.

**13.** John ended the epistle quickly after he had made his request for the hospitality Demetrius needed. The closing verses of the book are remarkably similar to the end of 2 John.

Like so many writers, John had much to say, but neither the time nor inclination to put it on paper. The imperfect tense of *eichon* refers to the time when he was writing the letter and had many matters which could have been included. But when he had completed the epistle, there were several topics which he deliberately chose to omit, reserving them for a later date when he could say them more effectively in person.

John's writing instruments were ink and pen. The ink (literally "black") was made of soot and water thickened with gum, while the pen was actually made from the sharpened stem of a reed. Though writers of the day often used secretaries, the mention of ink and pen may hint that John wrote the letter in his own hand—perhaps a reason for its brevity.

**14. But I trust I shall shortly see thee:** ... I am hoping shortly, *—WUST* ... I hope to see you before long, *—PHLP* ... I hope to visit you soon, *—EVRD*.

**and we shall speak face to face:** ... and we will have a heart-to-heart talk, *—PHLP* ... Then we can be together and talk, *—EVRD*.

**Peace [be] to thee. [Our] friends salute thee:** ... All our friends here send love, *—PHLP* ... The friends here with me send their love, *—EVRD*.

**Greet the friends by name:** ... Remember the friends, *—FNTN* ... Remember us to, *—WADE* ... Remember me to our friends individually, *—WLMS* ... please give ours personally to all our friends at your end, *—PHLP* ... Please give our love to each one of the friends there, *—EVRD* ... to the friends one by one, *—WMCK*

**14.** John hoped to visit Gaius soon and speak more fully. The use of the word "hope" does not imply wavering; it merely acknowledges the fact that God is the One who controls our plans. The apostle planned to arrive soon to deal with the problems of the church and to speak personally to Gaius. The literal Greek rendering, "mouth to mouth," is the equivalent of the English idiom *face-to-face*.

John closed with "Peace be to thee," a traditional Jewish blessing that had been adopted by the early Christians. As usual, he selected a form suited to the situation. Peace was the blessing needed by the church in Gaius' city.

The last two greetings follow customary patterns. John first passed on greetings from believers in his own area who were friends of Gaius. Then he took the opportunity to ask Gaius to pass on his good wishes to mutual friends in the area. John made a point of asking that they be greeted by name, a phrase used elsewhere in the New Testament, only in John 10:3, to describe the good shepherd calling his sheep by name. John had a shepherd's heart, caring enough to pen this letter to one believer who faced a difficult situation.

Third John provides a case study in Christian living, showing how the broad principles outlined in 1 John may be applied to a specific problem. While 2 John is a warning against an unthinking kind of fellowship which extends hospitality to false teachers, 3 John gives guidance for the opposite problem: the temptation to retreat from the responsibility of offering fellowship when such a ministry leads to opposition.

# JUDE

## Overview

The epistle of Jude is the seventh and last of the so-called General Epistles. It concludes the epistolary literature of the presently arranged New Testament. Although no particular addressee is identified, its contents suggest it was directed to a certain church or group of churches facing a particular problem. As is often the case in the New Testament, the letter was intended to oppose false teaching which threatened the Church.

## Author and Date of Composition

The author called himself "Jude," the "servant (literally, 'slave') of Jesus Christ and brother of James." Doubtless, he was the Jude, who (in Matthew 13:55 and Mark 6:3) with *Jacob* (James) was identified as the brother of Jesus. Even though Jude was the only writer in the New Testament who referred to such a relationship, he did so in humility. He not only avoided directly calling himself Jesus' brother, he also placed himself in the shadow of his more well-known brother, James.

James was so well known by the recipients of the letter that no further explanation was needed. At that time there was only one James who fit this description, James the brother of Jesus and overseer of the church in Jerusalem (Galatians 1:19; 2:12; cf. Acts 12:17; 15:13).

Some have asserted this Jude was Judas Thaddeus or "the brother of James" (Luke 6:16; Acts 1:13). The genitive case, however, is ordinarily taken to mean the "son" of James, not "brother." Besides, it is out of the question that the apostle Jude is meant, for the writer placed himself out of the apostolic group (verse 17).

Jesus' brothers and sisters did not believe in Him during His earthly ministry (John 7:5). Following the Resurrection, Jesus revealed himself to James (1 Corinthians 15:8), and after the Ascension Jesus' brothers were with His mother and the apostles (Acts 1:14). Paul wrote that the brothers of the Lord became heralds of the gospel (1 Corinthians 9:5). Other than this there is little known about Jude.

In Eusebius' Church History, he explained that according to Hegesippus (ca. A.D. 180), two of the grandchildren of Jude had to appear before Emperor Domitian because they were from the royal lineage of David. It was feared they might lead some kind of Jewish rebellion. The emperor released them as harmless. His concerns were eased when he saw their hands marked by hard work and when he learned they lived as poor farmers in the land of the Jews. It is told, though, that they eventually became bishops in the Church.

The Epistle of Jude was strongly attested in the Early Church. Portions of it may appear in 1 Clement, the Shepherd of Hermas, the Epistle of Barnabas, the Didache, and in the writings of Polycarp. All of these are dated around the end of the First or beginning of the Second Century. The Muratorian Canon included Jude. Athenagoras and Tertullian knew it, and Clement of Alexandria referred to it in his book *Hupotuposes* ("Sketches"). Didymus defended its genuineness. A tract by Cyprian cited a verse from Jude as Holy Scripture. Origen appealed numerous times to the letter as a work by the brother of the Lord. He commended it as "certainly short," but dressed in a vigorous language by divine grace.

There seems to be little question that the epistle is authentic, but there was a question as to whether or not it should be included in the canon of the New Testament. Later scholars doubted the authorship and asserted it was written in the post-apostolic period. It is virtually impossible, however, to imagine a pseudepigrapher in the Second Century choosing the obscure name of Jude in an effort to give his writing credibility. Nothing in the content of the letter supports that idea. On the contrary, it can be observed that the writer, rather than appealing to his own authority, appealed to the words of the apostles (verse 17).

The origin of the epistle and its destination cannot be definitively determined. The time of writing is also uncertain. If Jude worked chiefly in Jewish regions it is more likely that he addressed churches in the Jewish regions of Syria. But, since Paul's words in 1 Corinthians 9:5 seem to indicate that the brothers of the Lord were known by the church there, it is possible and even likely, that their territory covered a wider range. Since the epistle is written in Greek it could have had a wide audience.

Even though the date of the writing of this epistle cannot be established with certainty, its contents seem to indicate it belongs to the later writings of the New Testament, probably between A.D. 65 and 80. Jude could still have been alive at this time. He appears among the last in the lists of Jesus' brothers, perhaps indicating he was one of the youngest.

The Epistle of Jude cites a text from the Apocrypha. This would have been acceptable during the First Century, but it caused uncertainty in later centuries. Eventually this led to its being a disputed letter. However, it was accepted into the canon at the Council of Laodicia in A.D. 364 and later at the Council of Carthage in A.D. 397.

Apparently Jude used at least two sayings from the Old Testament Apocrypha. Material from the Book of Enoch occurs in verses 6 and 13, and in verse 15 it is almost verbatim. Verse 9 contains some material from the Assumption (ascension) of Moses. It is also possible that something from the Testament of Naphtali appears in verse 6, and from the Testament of Asher in verse 8. Much of the Jewish apocrypha and pseudepigrapha were highly regarded during this time. Ancient Jewish traditions were embedded in these writings. Moreover, Jude was not the only Biblical writer to use sources outside of Scripture. The Old Testament refers to other historical works. Paul alluded to pagan poets (Acts 17:28; 1 Corinthians 15:32,33; Titus 1:12). He also alluded to a rabbinic midrash on the "rock in the desert" (1 Corinthians 10:4). He identified "Jannes and Jambres" as the Egyptian sorcerers who opposed Moses; that information did not come from the Biblical account. The use of other sources occurs in Acts 7:22; Galatians 3:19; Hebrews 2:2; 11:37; and James 5:17. This is not to say that pagan philosophers or Jewish pseudepigrapha were given canonical authority.

Another striking feature of Jude is its resemblance to 2 Peter, especially chapter 2. Much of the content is the same. There are too many differences to speak of "copying," but at the same time, the two epistles are so obviously related that some kind of dependency is undeniable. There are basically three theories purporting to explain this.

Some assert that 2 Peter used Jude; others take the opposite view. A third option is that both epistles came from a common source. These options have little impact on an understanding of the letter. Many interpreters point out that Peter wrote of "coming" ("shall be") false teachers (2 Peter 2:1), whereas Jude wrote of false teachers who had "crept in unawares" (verse 4). This might suggest that Peter viewed the danger as future, but Jude saw it as already present. Such an argument might have some validity, but it must be remembered that Peter often shifted between present and future tenses. Moreover, in verse 18 Jude spoke of the apostles warning that scoffers would come in the last days. Perhaps he was alluding to Peter's words in 3:3. That would indicate 2 Peter preceded Jude; however, this cannot be determined for certain.

## Contents

The Epistle of Jude is both a defense of the gospel and a polemical treatise. The author explained that his purpose was to write about their "common salvation." Compelled by circumstances, however, Jude forfeited that goal and instead he admonished his readers to "earnestly contend for the faith which was once delivered unto the saints." He gave a prophetic word, not from the will of men but the God of Scripture who inspired him to write (cf. 2 Peter 1:21).

The occasion for Jude's writing was that heretics had infiltrated the Church and were spreading their damaging doctrines. Just as it is useless for a farmer to continue sowing if the weeds have not been pulled, so it is fruitless to announce the truth if the lie is not confronted. These two factors go hand in hand.

The Epistle of Jude is the only book in the Bible whose sole objective is to combat the apostasy that will come prior to Christ's return. Its placement in the Bible makes it an introduction to the Book of Revelation. This provides the spiritual rationale for the apocalyptic judgments unveiled in the final book of the Bible. The Biblical teaching about apostasy is epitomized by Jude. With panoramic immensity this tiny epistle of only 25 verses surveys the history of apostasy in heaven and earth. Jude recalled the backsliding of angels and men. He gave examples from before the Flood as well as from Israel's history. He addressed the problem of apostasy in his contemporary Church and spoke of the falling away of the last days. In the latter, he particularly corresponds with the teaching of Jesus and His apostles.

Jesus said the last days would be characterized by seductions: "When the Son of man cometh, shall he find faith on the earth?" (Luke 18:8). Paul referred to the "falling away" (2 Thessalonians 2:3; cf. 1 Timothy 4:1), and he described the last days as a time when "sound teaching" would not be endured (2 Timothy 4:3). The apostle Peter wrote that false teachers would appear who "privily shall bring in damnable heresies" that would lead to destruction (2 Peter 2:1). Jude added his final, urgent appeal to the Church to "contend for the faith which was once delivered unto the saints."

This faith was delivered "once" (verse 3), that is, "once and for all," totally, completely. Sacred truth and the divine history of salvation are transmitted by Holy Scripture. When the apostolic canon was completed, nothing could be added or subtracted.

Jude is unique in both form and content. Two features of its composition are particularly exceptional. First, it is based on groups of three that are interspersed throughout the letter. Second, its argumentation is based on contrasts between "these" and "you."

The first and most significant main section describes the false teachers: their doctrine, character, and the judgment facing them. Against the continual "these" (i.e., the false teachers, verses

8,10,11,12,14,16,19) stands the antithetical "but beloved" (verses 17,20). The first section is characterized by "these," while the second largely features "you."

The following outline can be made:

I. OPENING (1-3)

1. Sender and Addressees (verse 1)

2. Blessing Wish (verse 2)

3. Motive (verse 3)

II. HERETICS DESCRIBED (4-19)

1. Three Distinguishing Features (verse 4)

   a. Ungodly

   b. Lawless

   c. Denying the Lord

2. Three Examples of Judgment (5-7)

   a. Israel in the Desert (verse 5)

   b. Angels That Sinned (verse 6)

   c. Sodom and Gomorrah (verse 7)

3. Three Main Sins (8-10)

   a. "Dreamers" (verse 8)

   b. Defilers of the Body (verse 8)

   c. Arrogant Mockers (verses 8-10)

4. Three Examples of Error (11)

   a. The Way of Cain

   b. The Error of Balaam

   c. The Rebellion of Korah (Core)

5. Five Images From Nature (12,13)

   a. A Submerged Reef (verse 12)

   b. Clouds Without Rain (verse 12)

   c. Trees Without Fruit (verse 12)

   d. Wild Waves of the Sea (verse 13)

   e. Wandering Stars (verse 13)

6. The Prophecy of Enoch (14-16)

7. The Prophecies of the Apostles (17-19)

III. BELIEVERS EXHORTED (20-23)

1. Three Exhortations (20,21)

   a. Build Yourselves Up (verse 20)

   b. Pray in the Spirit (verse 20

   c. Abide in God's Love (verse 21)

2. Three Prescriptions for Helping (22,23)

   a. With Sympathy (verse 22)

   b. With Boldness (verse 23)

   c. With Fear (verse 23)

IV. CLOSING DOXOLOGY (24,25)

## Heretics Described

The kind of violence the Biblical writers directed against opponents and deceivers may be shocking to some. But Jesus himself used vigorous condemnation of the Pharisees and scribes. He called them "serpents," a "brood of vipers," and those following them "children of hell" (Matthew 23:15,33). The apostles did not exercise restraint in condemning their opponents. Paul pronounced a curse upon those who preached another gospel (Galatians 1:8,9). He called his opponents "dogs" and "workers of evil" (Philippians 3:2). Peter compared the false teachers to "brute beasts" and called them "cursed children" whose judgment was certain (2 Peter 2:1, 3, 12, 14). Jude expressed the same harsh attitude when he attacked the false teachers who had infiltrated the church.

## 1. Three Distinguishing Features (Verse 4)

First, Jude described the false teachers as "ungodly," that is, without reverence or fear of God. Their godlessness was not passive, it was active, willful, and shameless. Furthermore, the heretics were lawless and mocked God's grace (cf. Romans 6:1f.) instead of allowing His grace to train them in living a holy life (Titus 2:12). Jesus' brothers, James and Jude, both stated explicitly that faith must be demonstrated in works. James showed that good works testify to a saving faith. Jude maintained that evil works are a sign of falling away from the Faith. The third feature of the heretics was that they denied Christ.

## 2. Three Examples of Judgment (Verses 5-7)

Jude continued by reminding his readers how the Lord had previously executed judgment over sinners. He gave three examples: first, *Israel in the desert* (verse 5; cf. Numbers 14:26-38; 1 Corinthians 10:1-13; Hebrews 3:7; 4:11). Next he referred to God's judgment on the *fallen angels* (verse 6). Once these angels sang the praises of God; now they are chained in utter darkness. Two types of sin caused their fall—pride and lust. The third warning example is *Sodom and Gomorrah* (verse 7). The kind of judgment portrayed here is not for a godless world but for religious deceivers.

## 3. Three Main Sins (Verses 8-11)

Jude went to the root of the false teachers' error when he called them *dreamers;* they were fanatics without spiritual sobriety. Their visionary experiences led them astray by diverting them into a spiritual realm of delusion; they were under the control of evil forces. They believed these experiences condoned their ungodly lifestyle. While they took pride in their false spirituality, they *corrupted themselves* with immorality in a way resembling some later Gnostic practices. Jude described them as having an *arrogant attitude*. They did not submit to higher authorities and even derided them.

## 4. Three Examples of Error (Verse 11)

Verse 11 pronounces a woe upon these false teachers (cf. Matthew 11:21; 23:13ff.). They are compared with three tragic figures of the Old Testament. They were following the *way of Cain,* who rejected true worship of God and tried to approach Him with an unacceptable offering. Cain was of the Evil One and killed his brother. The errorists were also like *Balaam,* who thought fear of God was a means of monetary gain (cf. 1 Timothy 6:5), and who led Israel into sin (cf. Revelation 2:14). The *gainsaying of Core* refers to Korah's rebellion against Moses' and Aaron's God-given authority, and he, and "they and all that appertained to them, went down alive into the pit" (Numbers 16:33). Korah's destruction presents a picture of the judgment awaiting Antichrist, the last ultimate deceiver (Revelation 19:20).

## 5. Five Images From Nature (Verses 12,13)

Heaven, earth, and sea all give vivid descriptions of these deceivers. They were like *submerged reefs* (*The Amplified Bible*) which, unseen, by sailors, cause their destruction. They were also like *clouds without water* which pass overhead without giving rain. They were like *unfruitful trees,* lacking any life or root (cf. Luke 13:6-9). Like *wild waves of the sea,* the false teachers brought garbage and debris onto the "shore" of the Faith. They were like *wandering stars* which have strayed from their courses and wander aimlessly in the night sky.

## 6. the Prophecy of Enoch (Verses 14-16)

According to the Scriptures, Enoch did not die but was translated to heaven by the Lord (cf. Hebrews 11:5). He is a pattern for those who will be "caught up" at the coming of the Lord. Jude 14 explains that Enoch prophesied about the coming of the Christ, thereby confirming the ancient tradition written in the Book of Enoch. Enoch's prophecy concerned the judgment of the ungodly. They are to be judged not only because of their ungodly works, but also because of the bitter and rebellious words they have spoken against the Lord.

## 7. the Prophecies of the Apostles (Verses 17-19)

Believers are not to be discouraged or disappointed because of persecutions; these must come (cf. Matthew 18:7). The apostles foretold that mockers would emerge during the last days (2 Peter 2:l; 3:3). But they also prophesied of the victory of God's kingdom. God's people are to hold fast and cling to the admonition of the Word and to be patient (cf. Revelation 3:10). Jesus offered words of encouragement to believers undergoing trials and the deceptions of the last days: "But he that shall endure unto the end, the same shall be saved" (Matthew 24:13).

## Believers Exhorted

Most of the epistle addressed the problem of deceivers, but in closing Jude added a short section encouraging believers to continue in the Faith. He concluded with resounding praise to God.

## 1. Three Exhortations (Verses 20,21)

While the children of God wait for Christ's coming, they must take care of their spiritual well-being. They must *build themselves up* in their holy faith through the truth revealed in Jesus Christ and passed on by the apostles. Furthermore, they are to *pray in the Holy Spirit*. The Word and prayer belong together, and through them the believer can *keep himself in the love of God* (cf. John 15:9). They are *sanctified by the Father* (verse 1), but they must stay within the bounds of God's love.

## 2. Three Prescriptions for Helping (Verses 22,23)

Believers are not merely to concern themselves with their own spirituality. They are to care for others also. Some who had been enticed by the false teachers were in desperate need of help. Help must be administered according to each situation. Some need compassion and understanding; others must be "snatched" from the "fire" of heresy, just as one might save someone from a burning building. Others had drifted so far from the truth as to give themselves over to sin and impurity. They could be helped only with extreme caution (cf. Galatians 6:1). Love for the sinner must be joined with an uncompromising hatred for the sin, so the impurity of the sin would not infect the believer.

Following these exhortations, Jude closed his epistle with praise to God to whom belongs all "glory, majesty, dominion and power, both now and ever."

# The Epistle of Jude

## Commentary

**1. Jude, the servant of Jesus Christ, and brother of James:** ... I am a workman owned by, –NLTG.
**to them that are sanctified by God the Father:** ... To those who accepted the heavenly invitation, –NOLI ... have been loved and are the permanent objects of His love, –WUST.
**and preserved in Jesus Christ, [and] called:** ... and are safeguarded through union with, –WADE ... in a position of being carefully guarded, to those who were divinely summoned, –WUST.

**1.** The Book of Jude has been called the Acts of the Apostates because it provides such a graphic description of the false teachers who plagued the Christian community in the First Century.

Jude's name was literally *Judas*. He was one of several men by that name in the New Testament. The second phrase, "servant of Jesus Christ," is a fascinating display of humility in light of the final identification, "brother of James." The only James prominent enough to stand without further identification was the writer of the Epistle of James, the brother of Christ himself (James 1:1; Galatians 1:19). Thus Jude was the brother of both James and Jesus himself (Mark 6:3).

The book was addressed to a general audience, defined by spiritual condition rather than a physical location. The recipients were described in three phrases. They were "loved by God the Father (NIV)," positioned within the sphere of God's love. The perfect tense of "loved" (see variant in *Interlinear*) describes a love based on God's past love which continues to the present. They were "preserved in ('kept by,' NIV) Jesus Christ." This phrase is also in the perfect tense, showing that they were safe now because Christ long before had taken up the task of keeping them. *Teterēmenois* implies close attention and watchful care. Jude addressed his readers as "called." The word may be used for a summons to a feast or a call to judgment, but in this verse it describes the way God calls men and women to come to Him for salvation.

**2. Mercy unto you, and peace and love, be multiplied:** ... and love—abundantly, –SEB ... be yours increasingly, –WADE.

**2.** Jude's greeting contains three elements. He prayed that believers might experience God's mercy, peace, and love (*eleos*, *eirēnē*, and *agapē*).

Jude wanted believers to be filled to their capacity with all three graces.

**3. Beloved, when I gave all diligence to write unto you:** ... although I was making all haste, –MNTG ... I was anxious to write to you, –WMCK ... I have been striving hard to write to you, –NORL.
**of the common salvation:** ... about the salvation we share, –SEB ... possessed in common by all of us, –WUST.
**it was needful for me to write unto you:** ... I was impelled, –FNTN ... I found it necessary, –WLMS ... had constraint laid upon me, –WUST.
**and exhort [you] that ye should earnestly contend for the faith:** ... beseeching you to contend with intensity and determination, –WUST ... to exhort you to fight earnestly, –NORL ... urge you to carry on a vigorous defense of, –WLMS ... to strive energetically, –FNTN ... to be strenuous in defence of, –WADE.
**which was once delivered unto the saints:** ... that was delivered to the saints in a full and final way, –ADAM ... entrusted into the safe-keeping of the saints, –WUST ... to God's people, –WLMS.

**3.** In verse 3 Jude explained the reason for his writing the epistle. It was vital that he write a letter urging these Christians to struggle to defend the Faith. *Epagōnizesthai* comes from the fierce competition of the athletic field. Believers must fight with all their strength to preserve "the faith" which has been handed down to them. *Hapax* means "once for all," because the message of Christianity was given to the Church at the beginning; it had not come in installments. The content of the apostolic gospel is fixed, not to be revised for each new era.

**4. For there are certain men crept in unawares:** ... entered, –WUST ... have slipped in surreptitiously, –ADAM ... have sneaked in, –WLMS ... into the Church, –NOLI ... by secret means, –LBCH ... furtively, –WADE.
**who were before of old ordained to this condemnation:** ... of whom in the long ago this condemnation was set forth in advance, –BRKL ... men predestined in ancient prophecies, –MNTG ... their doom was written down long ago, –WLMS ... predicted with reference to this judgment, –WUST.
**ungodly men, turning the grace of our God into lasciviousness:** ... godless persons, –WLMS ... impious ones, who pervert the grace of our God into unbridled lust, –BRKL ... men destitute of reverential awe ... perverting the grace of our God into moral anarchy and lack of self-restraint, –WUST ... they twist the mercy of God to mean that they can practice sex vice, –LBCH ... twisting

the grace of our God into a reason for debauchery, —ADAM . . . into license for debauchery, —WADE . . . giving us an excuse to live in uncontrolled immorality, —NORL . . . into what is disgusting, —SWAN . . . into profligacy, —FNTN . . . to orgies, —SEB.

**and denying the only Lord God, and our Lord Jesus Christ:** . . . and denying the only absolute Master, —WUST . . . disown our only Master, —WMCK

**4.** Here Jude began to go into detail. He had learned of a serious threat to the Church. A new breed of leader had slipped into the congregations. They appeared attractive but posed serious dangers. In 2 Peter 2, a parallel passage, the threat was still future, but by Jude's time the apostasy had begun. *Pareisedusan* was used for one who entered a place without being noticed. Like thieves, heretics were making a stealthy entrance through the side door. Jude wrote to warn his fellow Christians of the true character of these men.

This was not a new problem. Jesus had a Judas among His followers. Paul had found it necessary to warn the church about this danger. When he met with the elders of Ephesus on his way to Jerusalem, he told them, "I know this, that after my departing shall grievous wolves enter in among you, not sparing the flock" (Acts 20:29). The Book of Galatians was written to deal with the heresy of the Judaizers. And the danger is not diminished in our day. Leaders need to be on guard against heresy and teach believers so they will not be led away and "devoured" by false teachers. Satan is so subtle in his approach that believers must be aware of his tactics and be prepared to resist him.

Verse 4 summarizes the major themes expounded in the rest of the book. First, such men were under the judgment of God. Their doom was determined long before Jude wrote his epistle (see Isaiah 8:19-22; Zephaniah 3:1-8). Second, they were degraded in character and conduct. *Asebeis* is a central concept of the epistle, occurring five times. It describes one who fails to treat God with the worship and reverence He deserves. Beyond this ungodliness, false teachers distort Christian teaching. They twist God's grace into a license to sin (ignoring Titus 2:11-13). The final step in their shameful path is to deny Jesus as their Lord and Master. *Kurion* is a title of honor; *despotēn* emphasizes a master's power over his subjects. The apostates about whom Jude wrote denied the lordship of Christ.

**5. I will therefore put you in remembrance:** . . . I desire to remind you, —BRKL . . . I must remind you that God's patience has a limit, —LBCH . . . after mature consideration I desire to remind you, —WUST.

**though ye once knew this:** . . . although you have a full and final knowledge about it, —ADAM . . . since once you were quite familiar with all the facts, —BRKL.

**how that the Lord, having saved the people out of the land of Egypt:** . . . after rescuing the people, —BRKL.

**afterward destroyed them that believed not:** . . . destroyed at the next occasion those who practiced on faith, —BRKL.

**5.** In the next three verses Jude moved into a series of examples from the Old Testament, each demonstrating the fact that God deals with such rebellion. (Compare a similar set of illustrations in 2 Peter 2.)

First, believers were asked to remember Israel's experience during the Exodus. The story was familiar to them. They knew the details. But Jude extracted the main points. The Lord rescued His people from their bondage in Egypt, but when they reached the threshold of Canaan, they refused to believe God could give them possession of the land (Numbers 13). So God turned them back to the desert to wander until they died (Numbers 14:20-35; cf. 1 Corinthians 10:1-11). Despite their privileges, God judged them when they rebelled.

**6. And the angels which kept not their first estate:** . . . who did not stay in their appointed place, —NORL . . . who did not keep their first domain, —MNTG . . . had not kept their own original state, —DRBY . . . who kept not their own Principality, —WLSN . . . that did not remain in their own high office, —WMCK . . . who did not preserve their original rank, —WLMS . . . did not keep their first position, —SEB . . . did not guard their own dominion, —FNTN.

**but left their own habitation:** . . . and left their proper home, —TCNT . . . but left their proper dwelling place, —ADAM . . . abandoned their proper duty, —FNTN . . . deserted their heavenly homeland, —NOLI.

**he hath reserved in everlasting chains under darkness unto the judgment of the great day:** . . . He reserves in custody, —FNTN . . . kept in perpetual chains, —NORL, —WLSN . . . of the lower world, —SWAN.

**6.** Jude's second illustration came from the angels who rebelled. The exact Old Testament source for the verse is debated: some teach that it refers to the sin of angels ("sons of God," Genesis 6:2) or to the original fall of Satan and the angels, while others say it refers to an event preserved only in tradition. In any case, Jude declared that a group of angels sinned by refusing to keep the original position of authority and power given to them by God. Instead, they deserted their own assigned dwelling place. Despite their high rank, God judged them. They would not keep their place, so He has kept them imprisoned, waiting for the great Day of Judgment at the end of time. The darkness mentioned here is a deep, dense blackness, a fit picture of separation from God.

The fate of these angels teaches us a solemn lesson: They had been created holy by the hand of God and loved as His creation, for He who is holy loves holiness. But the relationship changed when by their own voluntary will they turned away from the God who created and loved them. They have lost their high place of privilege, and now await judgment. There are none so holy they cannot fail and fall.

**7. Even as Sodom and Gomorrha, and the cities about them:**
**in like manner, giving themselves over to fornication:** . . . glutted themselves in sensuality, —*MNTG* . . . gave themselves over to sexual sin, —*SEB* . . . indulged in grossest immorality, —*WLMS*.
**and going after strange flesh:** . . . even perversion, —*SEB* . . . after foul sensuality, —*FNTN* . . . and homosexuality, —*NORL* . . . and unnatural vice, —*MNTG*.
**are set forth for an example, suffering the vengeance of eternal fire:** . . . enduring the retributive justice of an aionian Fire, —*WLSN*.

**7.** Jude's third example came from the account of Sodom and Gomorrah which included three smaller towns in the vicinity: Admah and Zeboim, as well as Zoar, which was preserved at Lot's request (Genesis 19:1-25; Deuteronomy 29:23).

The text draws a close comparison between Sodom and the angels of verse 6. Both groups shared the same judgment; it is possible that they may have committed similar sins.

Sodom's specific sin was sexual immorality. *Ekporneusasai* is an intensified form of the usual word for sexual sin, and the seriousness of their sin is underlined by the phrase that follows: "going after strange (of a different kind) flesh," a clear reference to the homosexual sin practiced in Sodom.

Like other sinners described in these verses, Sodom and Gomorrah felt God's wrath. They are a perpetual demonstration of God's judgment on sin. They underwent doom by fire, a fire described by Jude as eternal because it corresponds to the fires of hell.

**8. Likewise also these [filthy] dreamers:** . . . by their dreamings, —*ADAM*.
**defile the flesh, despise dominion:** . . . make their flesh foul with sin, —*LBCH* . . . pollute our human nature, reject control, —*TCNT* . . . disgrace their bodies, defy their creator, —*NOLI* . . . discard authority, —*WLMS*.
**and speak evil of dignities:** . . . and scoff at, —*MNTG* . . . and speak disparagingly, —*TCNT* . . . and insult glorious beings, —*ADAM* . . . and deride the majesties, —*WLMS* . . . and revile their angels, —*NOLI*.

**8.** This verse begins a section that moves from rebels of the past to a description of the deceivers about whom Jude was troubled. He used several words to emphasize the shift in thought. *Homoiōs*

draws a parallel between the Old Testament sinners and the ones about whom Jude was writing. These men shared several unsavory characteristics. First, they "defile the flesh"—their immorality caused a moral stain. Second, they "despise dominion" (reject lordship)—they deliberately rejected any form of established authority that hindered their impulses. Third, they "speak evil of dignities" (blaspheme glories)—they condemned beings who possess high degrees of glory. The connection with verse 9 suggests that angelic beings may be meant here. Beyond these traits, the apostates were dreamers. Their distorted view of reality caused their rebellious attitudes.

**9. Yet Michael the archangel, when contending with the devil he disputed about the body of Moses:** . . . when in his encounter with the devil, —*BRKL* . . . in his controversy with, —*WADE* . . . when he was arguing, —*TCNT* . . . he reasoned about, —*WLSN*.
**durst not bring against him a railing accusation:** . . . did not dare to bring a reviling judgment, —*SWAN* . . . did not venture to pronounce sentence on his blasphemies, —*BRKL* . . . bring a sentence of judgment that would impugn his [original] dignity, —*WUST* . . . indulge in an abusive defence, —*FNTN* . . . an insulting accusation, —*ADAM* . . . in defamatory terms, —*WADE*.
**but said, The Lord rebuke thee:** . . . but simply said, —*FNTN*.

**9.** Jude illustrated the depth of their arrogance by pointing to an encounter between the two highest angels, Michael the archangel and the devil himself. The name of Michael, the chief angel, means "Who is like God?" He has the task of opposing Satan and defending Israel (Daniel 10:13,21; 12:1; Revelation 12:7-9). Satan began his career as perhaps the highest of all angels (cf. Isaiah 14:12-20).

The incident Jude described in verse 9 is not mentioned in the Old Testament, and no further details are known about it. Whether Jude knew of it through oral tradition or an apocryphal writing, the Holy Spirit guided his selection of facts, and its historicity need not be doubted.

Michael and Satan were involved in a dispute regarding the body of Moses which had been buried by God himself. Despite his high rank, Michael did not dare lay down a condemnation using blasphemous or slanderous words. Instead, he merely replied that God himself would rebuke Satan.

**10. But these speak evil of those things which they know not:** . . . sneer at anything they do not understand, —*BRKL* . . . are cursing anything they cannot understand, —*LBCH* . . . on the one hand, revile as many things concerning which they do not have absolute knowledge, —WUST.

**but what they know naturally, as brute beasts:** . . . while whatever they do know sensually as reasonless brutes, —BRKL . . . on the other hand, revile as many things by instinct like the unreasoning animals, which they understand, —WUST.

**in those things they corrupt themselves:** . . . by these they are being brought to ruin, —WUST . . . by those things they are corrupted, —BRKL . . . they can understand only sensual lusts, —NOLI . . . they destroy themselves, —NLTG . . . they ruin themselves, —ADAM.

**10.** Jude was dealing with blasphemers who coupled arrogance with ignorance. When they slandered beings higher than themselves (note verses 8,9), they did not know the seriousness of their offense.

They understood very little, and the knowledge they did have was the kind that would destroy them. *Epistantai* is the knowledge that comes through instinct or the five senses; it is no better than the capacity of an animal. These men only understood their own physical lusts, and they were headed for ruin as a result of indulging those desires. These men were a clear example of the saying, "A little knowledge is a dangerous thing." The only dependable knowledge is that which comes from God's Word.

**11. Woe unto them! for they have gone in the way of Cain:** . . . Alas for them! —WLSN . . . Terrible will be their end, —LBCH . . . they have marched the way of, —FNTN.

**and ran greedily after the error of Balaam for reward:** . . . led astray by Balaam's love of gain, —TCNT . . . they abandoned themselves for a reward, —WUST . . . They think of nothing but making money, —LBCH.

**and perished in the gainsaying of Core:** . . . have destroyed themselves in Korah's rebellion! —ADAM.

**11.** Jude wrote, "Woe unto them!" He then referred to three Old Testament characters to show how such sin leads to destruction.

The false teachers had followed "the way of Cain" who tried to approach God on his own terms and found his offering rejected (Genesis 4). He lacked an attitude of faith (Hebrews 11:4) and may have refused to offer the blood sacrifice God demanded.

Like the rushing waters of a breached reservoir, these false teachers hurried to follow Balaam's deceiving ways. When the prophet found himself unable to curse Israel, he earned his fee by suggesting a plan to destroy the people by luring them into sexual relations with pagan women (Numbers 22-25).

The false teachers were like Korah who led a revolt against Moses and Aaron (Numbers 16),

refusing to recognize the authorities God had placed over them, just as the apostates despised any higher power. The result was judgment; Jude's word "perished" goes beyond physical death to describe eternal separation from God.

**12. These are spots in your feasts of charity:** . . . These are like hidden rocks, —NORL . . . the stains, —BRKL . . . are blots on your love feasts, —ADAM.

**when they feast with you, feeding themselves without fear:** . . . in your company they shamelessly gorge themselves, —BRKL . . . carousing shamelessly, and feasting gluttonously, —NOLI . . . feast sumptuously without scruple, —MNTG . . . banqueting with you without a qualm, —ADAM . . . without reverence, —FNTN . . . as shepherds leading themselves to pasture, —WUST.

**clouds [they are] without water, carried about of winds:** . . . rainless clouds, —BRKL . . . carried past by the tempests, —SWAN . . . but they have no rain, —SEB.

**trees whose fruit withereth, without fruit:** . . . trees that are leafless, —TCNT . . . leafless autumn trees, devoid of fruit, —WADE . . . dead trees which bear no fruit, —LBCH . . . fruitless, —BRKL.

**twice dead, plucked up by the roots:** . . . doubly dead! —ADAM . . . having died twice, rooted up, —WUST . . . pulled up by, —WMCK . . . uprooted, —BRKL.

**12.** The next two verses contain a cluster of vivid descriptions of the apostates, all drawn from nature.

These men were like rocks (see *Interlinear*) submerged just below the surface, ready to tear the hull of a ship. The danger was real, even though hidden. Such men took part in the love feasts, the fellowship meals which accompanied the Lord's Supper in the first-century Church, and eventually abused it to the point that it was discontinued. Some versions translate *spilades* as "spots," but this definition did not develop until after the New Testament period. The deceivers feasted without any fear they would be called to account for their sins.

They were shepherds who took care of their own needs, rather than the needs of the sheep (cf. Ezekiel 34:8). They were like clouds carrying the promise of rain for a parched land, but with not a drop of water in reality. They had no stability, but went wherever the winds blew them. They were like trees "without fruit" in the late autumn when fruit was expected. They were doubly dead, dead all the way to the root; their fate was to be uprooted. Similarly, the false teachers promised great benefits, but produced no legitimate results.

**13. Raging waves of the sea:** . . . Their sins are like the dirty water along the shore, —NLTG . . . are wild waves, —NORL . . . wildly raging, —BRKL . . . untamed sea waves, —WUST.

**foaming out their own shame:** . . . waves which throw on the shore the foul smelling things beneath the sea, −LBCH . . . foaming out their shameful debris, −ADAM . . . throwing up to the surface their own shameful desires, −WMCK . . . their own disgrace, −BRKL.

**wandering stars:** . . . straying, −BRKL . . . wandering meteors, −WUST.

**to whom is reserved the blackness of darkness for ever:** . . . for whom the gloom of the abyss has been reserved, −NOLI . . . the gloom of darkness is forever reserved, −BRKL . . . doomed to utter darkness, −WLMS.

**13.** The apostates were like the turbulent waves of a polluted lake, casting up seaweed and rubbish on the beach. They spewed out openly the things most people would hide with shame.

The final comparison from nature pictured them as "wandering stars," shooting stars that flash for a moment and are then engulfed in darkness. *Planētai* refers to that which leads astray or causes one to wander from the path.

**14. And Enoch also, the seventh from Adam, prophesied of these, saying:** . . . seventh generation, −BRKL . . . there prophesied also with respect to these, −WUST.

**Behold, the Lord cometh with ten thousands of his saints:** . . . with myriads, −MNTG . . . holy myriads, −WUST . . . of His people, −WLMS . . . holy angels, −CMPB.

**14.** Jude described the troublemakers by using Old Testament examples and by metaphors from nature. Next he quoted an ancient prophet to show their doom was sure. The prophecy cited in verse 14 appears nowhere in the Old Testament. The text is quite close to a passage in the Book of Enoch. But whether Jude was quoting from the Book of Enoch or citing information he had received from some other source, the fact that it is included in the letter demonstrates its historic accuracy.

Enoch was seventh in line in the genealogy of Adam (Genesis 5). The record says Enoch was a man who walked so close to God that he was taken to heaven without passing through death. He also provides the only example of prophecy in the era before the Flood. His prophecy proves that rebels against God will be punished.

Enoch prophesied, "Behold, the Lord cometh." He employed the aorist tense of *come* (*ēlthen*) to describe an event still future, because its accomplishment is certain. From a New Testament perspective, it is clear the prophecy refers to the Second Coming.

The Lord will come accompanied by myriads of holy ones. "Myriads" (see *Interlinear*) was often used to denote 10,000 soldiers but could also refer to an indefinite large number. The "saints" (holy ones) mentioned in verse 14 may include angels

(as in Matthew 25:31) or human believers (as in Colossians 3:4) or both.

**15. To execute judgment upon all:** . . . He will judge the world, −LBCH.

**and to convince all that are ungodly among them:** . . . and to convict all, −NORL . . . effectually convict all those who are destitute of a reverential awe towards God, −WUST.

**of all their ungodly deeds which they have ungodly committed:** . . . concerning all their works of impiety which they impiously performed, −WUST . . . of which they have been notoriously guilty, −FNTN.

**and of all their hard [speeches]:** . . . all the harsh things, −SEB.

**which ungodly sinners have spoken against him:** . . . which impious sinners spoke against Him, −WUST.

**15.** Verse 15 continues the quotation from the prophecy of Enoch. One purpose of the Lord's coming is to mete out judgment against all and end the planet's rebellion. This judgment will be directed against sinful men and may also include the evil angels mentioned elsewhere in Jude. God will not only perform an act of judgment, He will also convict ("convince") all the ungodly of their wickedness.

The rest of the verse catalogs the depth of evil that will be judged. The world at Christ's return will be "ungodly," lacking in reverence for God and living in defiance of His will. Their deeds are ungodly, the manner in which they do the deeds is ungodly, and their harsh words against God are ungodly.

**16. These are murmurers, complainers:** . . . These wicked men are always complaining, −LBCH . . . complaining against their lot, −WUST . . . grumblers, malcontents, −ADAM . . . inveterate faultfinders, −FNTN . . . blaming others, −SEB.

**walking after their own lusts:** . . . pursuing their way at the prompting of their own passions, −WADE . . . ordering their course of conduct in accordance with their own passionate cravings, −WUST . . . proceeding in accordance with their own inordinate desires, −FNTN . . . They live to satisfy their evil passions, −WLMS.

**and their mouth speaketh great swelling [words]:** . . . they have arrogant words upon their lips, −TCNT . . . talk arrogantly, −NOLI . . . speak arrogantly, −ADAM . . . speaks immoderate, extravagant things, −WUST.

**having men's persons in admiration because of advantage:** . . . catering to personalities for the sake of advantage, −WUST . . . flattering people to gain favor, −ADAM . . . flatter men for their own advantage, −WMCK . . . for the sake of profit, −DRBY.

**16.** Jude concluded with a final list of phrases describing the seducers who had crept into the churches. The verse expands on the sins of speech that are mentioned at the end of Enoch's prophecy.

These men were grumblers ("murmurers"), much like the Israelites during their sojourn in the wilderness (cf. 1 Corinthians 10:10). By its pronunciation the word *gongustai* suggests a low rumbling of discontent, and it describes smoldering discontent that has not come out into the open. Such an attitude is one of the distinguishing marks of the godless person.

Such individuals are faultfinders, dissatisfied with their lot in life. The man who always cursed his luck was a standard character in classical Greek literature, and these apostates fit that stereotype. Like the angels mentioned in verse 6, they forgot to be grateful to God and wanted a role different from the one allotted to them.

They lived according to their own lusts, just as the people of Sodom and Gomorrah followed their sensual cravings. The present tense shows a continual pattern of life governed by the dictates of physical desires rather than the will of God. They speak puffed-up words. Their speech is pompous, bombastic oratory designed to impress, but empty of value. Hoping to gain an advantage for themselves, they pay excessive attention to influential people. *Thaumazontes* literally means "to be amazed." The false teachers are described here as flatterers, fawning on anyone who can help them reach their coveted places of honor. In setting themselves above the need to worship God, they worshiped men.

The central section of Jude, from verse 8 to verse 17, gives a chilling description of the apostates. In the beginning few of these traits would be obvious, and believers might welcome men of such seeming importance. But the rottenness beneath the surface must be uncovered. That was Jude's task.

**17. But, beloved, remember ye the words:** . . . do remember, dear friends, *—PHLP* . . . you must recollect, *—TCNT* . . . remember the predictions of, *—NOLI* . . . remember the suggestions, *—BRKL.*
**which were spoken before of the apostles of our Lord Jesus Christ:** . . . that the messengers of Jesus Christ gave us beforehand, *—PHLP* . . . what was foretold, *—TCNT* . . . that were given heretofore by, *—BRKL.*

**17.** A new section begins here. How should the Church respond to this terrible threat? Jude gave a series of instructions for dealing with the problem.

He began with "But, beloved," a dramatic switch from the renegades to the faithful Christians. Jude instructed believers to remember the warnings they had already heard. "Remember" is the first

command given in the letter. The believers' first line of defense was the realization that the original apostles had predicted such an invasion of heretics.

Though Jude did not quote a particular passage from the New Testament, he gave the general sense of the apostolic teaching recorded in Scripture in such passages as Acts 20:29,30; 1 Timothy 4:1; 2 Timothy 3:1-9; 4:3,4; and 1 John 2:18. God is not surprised; believers should not be taken by surprise either.

**18. How that they told you there should be mockers in the last time:** . . . At the end of this period there will be scoffers, *—ADAM* . . . when they said, *—PHLP.*
**who should walk after their own ungodly lusts:** . . . whose lives are guided by their own impious passions, *—BRKL* . . . who will live to satisfy their own godless passions, *—WLMS* . . . who live according to their own Godless desires, *—PHLP* . . . guided by their own sinful desires, *—NORL.*

**18.** Jude next quoted the specific warning which the apostles had given. The imperfect tense shows that this warning was given repeated emphasis in the early teaching.

The phrase "the last time" refers to the period before the return of Christ. Since that return can occur at any time, Jude applied it to his own era. At that time, "mockers" were predicted, as in 2 Peter 3:3. Mockers are those who ridicule God's Word and laugh at those who refuse to follow their lustful lifestyle. Despite their claims of freedom, "mockers" walk around enslaved by their desires for ungodly things.

**19. These be they who separate themselves:** . . . They are men who will create factions, *—NORL* . . . These are the agitators, *—BRKL* . . . These are the men who split communities, *—PHLP* . . . who are making trouble, *—SEB* . . . that set up divisions, *—WMCK* . . . who are causing divisions among, *—LBCH.*
**sensual, having not the Spirit:** . . . They are only physical, *—SEB* . . . for they are led by human emotions and never by the Spirit of God, *—PHLP* . . . living an animal life, *—WMCK* . . . they ignore their human spirit which has to do with the spiritual, religious part of a person's life, *—WUST* . . . mere animals, destitute of any spiritual nature, *—WLMS* . . . the worldly, who lack the Spirit, *—BRKL.*

**19.** These false teachers were the real cause of division, though they probably accused any protester of being unloving.

The apostates considered themselves spiritual and called common Christians *psuchikoi*, limited to the level of life that even plants shared. But Jude turned the tables and declared that *they* were the ones on the lower level.

Such individuals do not have the Spirit. In the light of Romans 8:9 the phrase shows these false teachers were not regenerate.

**20. But ye, beloved, building up yourselves on your most holy faith:** . . . you, dear friends of mine, build yourselves up on the foundation of your most holy faith, *—PHLP*. . . building yourselves up constantly in the sphere of and by means of, *—WUST.*

**praying in the Holy Ghost:** . . . and as constantly, *—WUST*. . . and are worshiping by, *—BRKL* . . . praying with a holy spirit, *—FNTN.*

**20.** Jude turned next to positive commands. Verses 20 and 21 declare the Christian's responsibility toward himself.

Jude again began with "But ye, beloved" to draw a contrast between genuine Christians and the false teachers. The primary command appears in verse 21, surrounded by three secondary instructions.

First, a believer should build himself up in the "most holy faith" rather than tearing it down as the apostates did. "Most holy faith" pictures the objective truth of the gospel as something utterly separate from any human doctrine.

Second, believers must pray in the Holy Spirit. Christians can claim the aid of the Holy Spirit in prayer (Romans 8:26,27) as they oppose the enemies of God (Ephesians 6:18).

**21. Keep yourselves in the love of God:** . . . with watchful care, *—WUST*. . . Cling to, *—NOLI*. . . within the shelter of God's love, *—WADE.*

**looking for the mercy of our Lord Jesus Christ unto eternal life:** . . . Wait patiently for . . . which will bring you to, *—PHLP* . . . all the while awaiting, *—BRKL*. . . Wait for the Lord Jesus Christ with his mercy to give you life forever, *—EVRD*. . . expectantly looking for . . . resulting in life eternal, *—WUST.*

**21.** The primary command of the sentence appears next: "Keep yourselves in the love of God." Verse 1 describes God's part in keeping the believer, verse 21 the human side. The Christian is to keep himself in the sphere of God's love, the place where His blessings are available.

Finally, the believer must wait eagerly for the mercy of God to be displayed. This is probably a reference to Christ's return.

**22. And of some have compassion, making a difference:** . . . For some of these men you can feel pity and you can treat them differently, *—PHLP*. . . on some . . . be showing mercy, on those who are in doubt, *—WUST*. . . Convince certain ones who separate themselves, *—BRKL.*

**22.** Verses 22 and 23 move to a different area: the Christian's duty toward others in the face of apostasy. In the situation Jude envisioned, some people

will be doubters, open to truth, but confused. In dealing with a sincere doubter, the believer must show mercy, leading him gently to truth.

**23. And others save with fear, pulling [them] out of the fire:** . . . Try to save them from hell fire, *—LBCH* . . . Others you must try and save by fear, snatching them as it were, *—PHLP*. . . show mercy to others with caution, *—ADAM*. . . by dragging them out of, *—MNTG.*

**hating even the garment spotted by the flesh:** . . . on still others have pity mingled with great caution, loathing even the clothing that has been, *—BRKL* . . . hating even the undergarment, *—WUST*. . . Pity those who are slaves to animal passions, *—LBCH*. . . while hating the very garments their deeds have befouled, *—PHLP*. . . even if you hate to touch their sin-soaked garments, *—NOLI*. . . Hate even their clothes which are dirty from sin, *—EVRD*. . . stained with their evil nature, *—SEB* . . . befouled by their lusts, *—NORL*. . . polluted with sensuality, *—FNTN.*

**23.** There are others who are more deeply committed to a false teaching than those mentioned in verse 22. In dealing with such people, a Christian may need to use a more direct approach. *Harpazontes* has the idea of "snatching" with some violence, just as you would snatch a child away from a flame. Lot's experience at the destruction of Sodom is an illustration. The "fire" in this verse probably refers to eternal fire, as in verse 7.

A third type of person mentioned in this verse calls for very careful treatment. Confirmed sinners must be approached with a combination of pity and fear. Their sin is so deep that believers must be aware of the danger of being defiled themselves. Believers are to hate even the "garment spotted (polluted) by the flesh." The picture comes from the Old Testament laws concerning lepers (Leviticus 13:47-59). The *chitōna* was the inner garment, the one next to the body. A leper's disease could cause his very clothing to be infected, and the garment would be burned to prevent the spread of infection. In the same way, some sinners seem to defile all who even touch them.

**24. Now unto him that is able to keep you from falling:** . . . can help you not to fall, *—EVRD*. . . to guard you, *—FNTN* . . . without stumbling, *—DRBY* . . . from stumbling, *—MNTG.*

**and to present [you] faultless:** . . . and to make you stand, *—WLMS* . . . without fault, *—PHLP* . . . can bring you before his glory without any wrong in you, *—EVRD.*

**before the presence of his glory with exceeding joy:** . . . exultant before the radiant glory of His eyes, *—GRBR*. . . before His glory, *—WAND*. . . give you a place in his glory, *—BB* . . . great joy before His glory, *—BECK*. . . to stand you before his glory, *—KLGS*. . . the manifestation of his glory at the day of judgment, *—MKNT*. . . his majesty, *—MRDK*. . . his glorious presence, *—WLMS*. . . the presence of His glory with abounding joy, *—BRKL* . . . in his presence irreproachable and triumphant, *—GDSP* . . . in gladness, *—CNFT* . . . with glad rejoicing, *—BRCL* . . . in triumphant joy, *—NORL* . . . with exquisite delight, *—FNTN* . . . with rejoicing, *—WMCK* . . . and with unspeakable joy, *—PHLP* . . . with unspeakable, ecstatic delight, *—AMPB* . . . and give you great joy, *—EVRD*.

**24.** The epistle concludes with a magnificent benediction and doxology. In the face of distressing problems, it is vital to know the God who is able to keep the Christian from falling. God is able to keep the believer "from falling" in the same way a sentry keeps watch to warn an army against attack. The Lord's watchcare over His children can enable them to walk surefootedly, like a horse picking its way through uneven terrain. With God on guard, no believer need be ambushed by temptations to immorality or by doctrinal deceptions.

Because He guards the believer from stumbling, God will also carry the process to completion. Christians can stand before Him in the presence of His glory in heaven and shout with excited joy, because they come to the Throne blameless. *Amōmous* is used in 1 Peter 1:19 to describe Christ, the spotless Lamb sacrificed to enable the believer to stand blameless before God.

This does not mean believers have never had a fault, for only Jesus lived a faultless life. Rather, it means that the faults of the past have been repented of and have been brought to the Cross where the blood of God's Son cleanses from all sin. What joy there will be to know that all has been forgiven, and now the faults are not imputed to our account. The faults which filled us with despair, doubts, and apprehension are now forgiven and forgotten. Matthew Henry says, "Where there is no sin there will be no sorrow; where there is the perfection of holiness, there will be the perfection of joy" (p.1117).

**25. To the only wise God our Saviour:** . . . namely, the only God . . . by means of Jesus the Messiah, *—MRDK* . . . to the only omniscient God, *—NOLI* . . . to God alone, *—WLSN* . . . He is the One who saves us, *—EVRD* . . . Who is our Deliverer through our Lord Jesus Christ, *—GRBR*.

**[be] glory and majesty, dominion and power:** . . . belong, *—CNFT* . . . be praise, *—MRDK* . . . be ascribed the glory of infinite perfection, and the majesty of empire absolutely universal; strength to govern that empire, and right to do whatever seemeth to himself good, *—MKNT* . . . let us give . . . honour, *—BB* . . . great honor, strength, *—KLGS* . . . might, and authority, *—MNTG* . . . greatness, *—EVRD*.

**both now and for ever. Amen:** . . . for all time past, *—EVRD* . . . before every aeon, *—HNSN* . . . before all time, *—WUST, —CNFT* . . . as in time immemorial, *—GRBR* . . . before time was, now, and in all ages, *—PHLP* . . . and now, and to all ages, *—ALFD* . . . from everlasting, so be it now and forever, *—BECK* . . . and now, and forever more, *—BRKL* . . . before time began, is now, and shall be for all time to come, *—TCNT* . . . both now and all time to come, *—KLGS* . . . until time ends, *—BRCL*.

**25.** Such a God deserves all praise. The epistle ends with a doxology. Jude addressed it to God the Father, who is the Saviour of man. Salvation comes through Jesus Christ who serves as the divine channel through whom man comes to the Father, thus bringing praise to the Father.

Jude ascribed four glories to God. "Glory" is the term for the visible display of God's attributes, His excellence. "Majesty" pictures the royal dignity of the King of the universe. "Dominion" describes the infinite control God exerts over the world. "Power" (authority) speaks of God's right to do as He pleases with His creation.

These characteristics belong to the Lord eternally, in eternity past, in the present, and throughout the eternal future.

# REVELATION

## Overview

### The Crown of the Bible

The Revelation of Saint John has been called the "crown" of the Bible. With this prophetic writing Holy Scripture draws to a complete and perfect end. It establishes the relationship of many of the prophecies of both the Old and New Testament writings. By means of this final, ultimate beacon of prophecy, the believer's attention is directed to the coming eternity. More than any other book in the Bible, the Book of Revelation is about the Christian hope. Within this tremendous prophecy of Christ's return is a picture of the last days. It describes those events which will precede His coming as well as those which will accompany and follow it.

Ever since the period of the Early Church, the Book of Revelation has been regarded as one of the most difficult books in the Bible to interpret. Many great scholars of the past, who may have had much to say on other books of the Bible, often remained silent or had very little to say on the last book. For many readers of the New Testament, Revelation is an unintelligible conglomeration of figurative images and literal language.

The method followed in the *Overview* will be to offer some helps for interpreting Revelation rather than giving a fixed interpretation. This will include the structure of the book, the most relevant background information, an examination of the significance of the symbolic language, and an investigation of its relationship to other documents of the Bible. A survey of the major schools of interpretation may also prove useful.

It is probable that no two students of the Bible agree on the meaning of all the details of prophecies relative to the last days, especially the events described in the Book of Revelation. Even in the *Complete Biblical Library* on occasion differing views are expressed in the verse-by-verse commentary and in this *Overview*. It is for this reason the editors have established as a general guideline that when sizable numbers of reputable scholars hold differing views on major matters, it is a fair approach to present those various views and the reasons for them. So when there are differences of opinion among conservative theologians, readers will be left to decide for themselves.

## Authorship and Date of Writing

The Book of Revelation is a letter sent to seven churches in the Roman province of Asia. The book itself claims to be written by John. He was apparently so well known to the recipients that no further elaboration of his identity was needed. A virtually unanimous tradition of the Early Church ascribes the book to the apostle John. Justin Martyr and Irenaeus, who were from Asia Minor, confirmed this. Moreover, church fathers like Melito, Hippolytus, Tertullian, Clement of Alexandria, Origen, and others supported this position.

The Greek style of the book suggests it was written by a Palestinian Jew. The style of writing and many of the words appear in the recognized writings of the apostle John. Linguistic and stylistic differences are no doubt intentional. As a prophecy the Apocalypse (from the Greek for "revelation") resembles the prophecies of the Old Testament.

The Book of Revelation was composed during a time of persecution. John was in exile on the Isle of Patmos when he received his visions. Those churches receiving his letter were beleaguered by severe persecutions. Recognizing this as the background for the book is crucial for a proper interpretation. In a unique sense Revelation is for Christians of all times who are undergoing persecution.

Many interpreters of Scripture think the book was written toward the end of the First Century during the Domitian persecution. Irenaeus and other church fathers also maintain this. Some scholars think it may have been written as early as the Neronian persecutions (A.D. 64); however, the picture we are given, together with external circumstances elsewhere in the world, more accurately fit a later time period.

Almost certainly a particular situation was being addressed by the writer, and this forms the background for the message of the overall work. But the book is not only a word of encouragement and admonition to believers in distress. It yields a prophetic message, exposing a glimpse into the future and pointing toward the consummation of all things—the eternal hope of the Church.

## Prophecy and Apocalypse

The writer identifies the book in two ways. His opening words describe it both as a "revelation" (*apokalupsis*, 1:1) and a "prophecy" (1:3). The terms are probably interchangeable, as they are, for example, in 1 Corinthians 14:30, 31. This, therefore, provides the Biblical framework for understanding the term *apocalypse*. Later the word acquired a unique theological sense, but at first it denoted every kind of speculative literature about the future that was so widespread in Judaism after the true prophetic spirit departed from the people.

Highly speculative and imaginative apocalyptic literature flourished in one or two centuries on either side of the beginning of the Christian Era. Predominantly it was a Jewish phenomenon, although some had Christian elements. Almost certainly the literature was originally patterned after the Book of Daniel. Typically, apocalyptic literature contains alleged visions and trances; often they are written in the name of some great, godly individual. Technically these are called pseudepigraphic writings. If one allows these traits to determine one's understanding, one comes to the rather paradoxical conclusion that the Apocalypse, the Book of Revelation, is not an apocalyptic writing at all! This recalls the well-known dilemma of the Old Testament of distinguishing between genuine and false prophecy. The apostle John wrote under his own name and claimed his visions were legitimate. In other apocalyptic writings the content is at best a mixture of truth and fantasy.

If, however, one adopts the meaning of "apocalyptic" based on Revelation rather than the other books, the term is more useful. Then we observe there are elements of Biblical prophecy whose form and contents resemble closely the final book of the Bible. This applies to many of the Old Testament prophets, especially Daniel, which, with a certain amount of justification can also be called "an apocalypse" of the Old Testament. Symbolic language and visions are especially common in the apocalyptic genre. Furthermore, the future time frame—last days, consummation of all things, age to come—is also typical of apocalyptic literature.

The Book of Revelation originated in Old Testament prophecy. Its language and imagery come from there, and in large measure its contents. But Revelation is much more than a repetition or recalling of Old Testament prophecies. The prophetic word concerning the consummation of the kingdom of God reaches a new clarity and depth in Revelation. The messianic prophecies about the coming of Messiah in lowliness and humility are realized. In the light of this fundamental fact of salvation history a great distinction is drawn between the first and second coming of Christ. The major theme of Revelation is the return of the Lord.

The great eschatological Olivet discourse of Jesus (Matthew 24 and parallels) stands as a bridge between the Old Testament prophecies and the Book of Revelation. When He speaks about the coming end-time tribulation He expressly points back to the prophet Daniel and thus links Old and New Testament prophecy.

## Main Interpretations

Perhaps no book in the Bible is so difficult to interpret as Revelation—and no other book has so many interpretations! The greatest obstacle lies essentially in the figurative language. As is true of the parables, the figurative language of the Apocalypse has a twofold function: to reveal and to conceal. The mystery of the kingdom of God is only revealed to those to whom it has been given.

Even though the symbols lack any fixed interpretation, certain rules of interpretation can be developed from the book's own explanation of its imagery and from a comparison with related Old Testament passages.

Differentiating between what should be understood figuratively and what should be taken literally is perhaps the greater problem. Two schools of interpretation reflect this. First, some interpret the book allegorically. Second, others maintain the best approach is to follow the usual principle of Bible interpretation: that is, everything is to be understood in its concrete sense. There are also two different attitudes toward whether the book should be seen as cyclical, that is, as a series of recapitulations, or as linear, that is, progressive.

The various schools of interpretation can be broken down into four main groups:

### 1. Spiritualist

The basic tenets of this view of interpretation can be traced to the Alexandrians, e.g., Justin Martyr, Irenaeus, and others. For example, Augustine identified the Millennium as the spiritual kingdom in this present Church Age. The spiritualistic interpretation contends that the book is not designed to teach the Church about the future age or coming events, but that it is intended to offer instructions concerning the spiritual principles of God's oversight of the world. The spiritual history of the Church is thus presented. The book gives the spiritual struggle that will continue throughout all ages and peoples. Revelation, thus, is supposed to afford believers a message of hope and comfort and the assurance of final victory.

### 2. Preterist

This interpretation arose in the 17th Century with Hugo Grotius and the Jesuit theologian Alcazar. It contended that the "prophecies" of the Apocalypse had already been fulfilled, and it had no room for future prophecies. It asserted that everything pertained to the writer's own situation in time and nothing beyond that. Some holding this interpretation, for example, interpret the ruler with a mortal wound who is healed as Nero, or that the beast of chapter 13 is Domitian. Every event in the book is believed to have occurred in the First Century A.D. or within the immediate future of that time.

## 3. Historicist

This interpretation predominated during the Middle Ages and in the time following the Reformation. This view advocates that Revelation is an allegory of church or world history written in advance. This view attempts to identify certain events in history with those recounted in the Apocalypse. These interpreters regard Revelation as a continual recounting of time in between the first coming of Christ and His return at the end of the world. Each group of visions cover a particular time frame.

This *Historicist* interpretation is often combined with the so-called *Recapitulation Theory* which holds that each group of visions in the Book of Revelation can cover the entire Church Age.

## 4. Futurist

This view prevailed during the Early Church, up till the time of Constantine. During the last two centuries this view has again surfaced, especially in so-called evangelical, conservative circles.

The eschatological or futuristic interpretation asserts that the visions of Revelation concern future events, for the most part occurring at the end of this age. The main theme is viewed as the return of Christ and those events surrounding it. Prophecies concerning the last days and the fulfillment of the promises of the kingdom of God are manifold in Scripture. Now, these are gathered into a single, chief prophecy in the last book of the Bible.

Each of these interpretive approaches has the support of significant persons in Church history. One could also say that the variety of views has to a certain extent enhanced our understanding. Undoubtedly the *spiritualist* interpretation is correct when it says the battle of the ages is reflected in the visions of Revelation. The *preterist* interpretation shows the relationship between this age and prophecy. It underscores the importance of the book for the struggling churches during the period of martyrdom. The most crucial contribution of the historical interpretation is not that it shows correspondences between secular history and prophecy, but that the typical message of prophecy can be rediscovered in history.

It might justifiably be said that Biblical prophecies have their fulfillment at many levels, which correspond to the ambiguous message of prophecy. But, irrespective of what degree of fulfillment one perceives prophecies to have had already, one cannot ignore that there will be a final, eschatological fulfillment. Neither a spiritualized interpretation nor a purely historical interpretation show the benefit of the Apocalypse as a prophetic book for the future. The historical interpretation overemphasizes the symbolic character of the book, and it allows too many defeats for it to be regarded as the ultimate fulfillment.

Without question there will be an eschatological fulfillment. But a one-sided futuristic interpretation is equally inadequate. The time of composition as well as later history is reflected in the visions. These become the background for the eschatological fulfillment. This is a historical development which culminates in the last days.

## Structure and Chronology

Even without a preliminary survey of Revelation, reading it will be profitable. Many of the details and sayings are immediately intelligible and are edifying to the believer. A more profound understanding of the book, however, depends on whether one grasps the main thrusts of the book, its structure, and chronological arrangement. This enables fitting the details into a larger framework and opens up the potential for a broader understanding of them which would otherwise be impossible.

Such a survey can be obtained through patient, thorough study. This does not come solely through self-study; only in the context of community can one hope to understand the height and depth of Revelation (cf. Ephesians 3:18). Interpreting the Book of Revelation calls for more than one person. It is the task of God's church throughout the age of the gospel. We need help in order to understand what we read (cf. Acts 8:31). We must continue to build on what others have laid as foundation.

The historical context, the meaning of the symbolism, and the various principles of interpretation have already been mentioned. The structure of the book is very plain. On the basis of 1:19, the book falls into two distinct parts: "the things which are" (chapters 2 and 3) and the main eschatological section, "the things which shall be hereafter" (chapter 4ff.). This basic introduction, though, is the only time one can find much consensus.

Two major views about the significance of the visions in the eschatological part of the book dominate. Some interpreters regard the different groups of visions as recapitulating and yet expanding the themes of the preceding visions. Others contend that the presentation is progressive and linear. In this view each group of visions picks up from the preceding one and adds its view.

For instance, the theory of recapitulation maintains that the visions of the seven seals, the seven trumpets, and the seven cups of wrath concern the same event from different points of view. The progressive view, however, contends that each part of that series refers to a different event, succeeding another in time.

The interpretive outcome depends ultimately on which approach is taken. If one understands the visions to be independent cycles which restate a preceding event, one can, for example, spiritualize the Millennium. If, though, one argues that the presentation is successive, it is difficult to ignore the fact that there must be a golden age between Christ's return and final judgment (chapters 19 and 20).

Almost certainly some parallels exist among the various series of visions. Nevertheless, it is doubtful whether or not this only reflects an escalation of judgment. When the seals are broken the plagues hit a fourth part of the earth (6:8); during the sounding of the trumpets a third of the earth is struck (8:8; 9:18); and when the cups of wrath are poured out the entire earth is affected.

It may seem as if the breaking of the seventh seal incorporates the sounding of the seven trumpets (8:1ff.), and that the seventh trumpet includes the seven cups of wrath (cf. the summary of future events in 11:18). If this is correct, there is a clear chronological progression in the presentation, which of course does not preclude there being sections which work backward and explain a matter more fully from its beginning.

As was previously noted, 1:19 distinguishes between "the things which are" and the "things which shall be hereafter." The present—or "part one"—is covered in the initial three chapters. These chapters reflect the historical occasion of the letter and include the writer's admonition of his readers. Part one includes the opening vision and the sending of the seven letters to the seven churches.

The distinct shift to future visions takes place in chapter 4:1: "I will shew thee things which must be hereafter." The future visions can be naturally broken down into two major groups: first, those events preceding the return of Christ are described; second, the Millennium, final judgment, and eternity are depicted.

It is helpful to survey the book according to three major sections: (1) The present (chapters 1-3); (2) the final time (chapters 4-19); (3) the condition of eternity (chapters 20-22). The second section contains the largest amount of material; with some justification it can be called the real focus of the book. The Book of Revelation is reluctant to describe eternity, but it gives a more detailed portrayal of the events of the last days. The second section of the book, apart from some minor detours, concentrates on three series of visions: the seven seals, the seven trumpets, and the cups of wrath. (See below for the structure.)

In addition to this structural arrangement, the section containing chapters 4-9 is set in a chronological framework. The events described herein take place in a seven-year period, or a "week of years" divided into half. Chapter 11, verses 2 and 3, seems to mention both halves of the "week of years." The first half covers the time of the two witnesses; the second is dominated by the period of the Antichrist.

The prophetic framework for the last days comes directly from the book of the prophet Daniel, chapter 9:24-27 (cf. 7:25; 12:7). Time in Revelation is referred to in *days* (e.g., 1260 days, 11:3; 12:6), *months* (e.g., 42 months, 11:2; 13:5), and in *years* (e.g., a time, times, and half a time, 12:14).

The last 3 1/2 years are a time of divine punishment for the world, just as the 3 1/2 years of drought during the time of the prophet Elijah were punishment for a backslidden Israel (Luke 4:25). At the same time, it is a time of persecution for believers. This is modeled after the time of tribulation Israel experienced at the hands of Antiochus IV Epiphanes, who perhaps typifies the Antichrist.

If this chronology is correct, it seems as if the opening of the seals and the first six trumpets belong to the first half of the week, even if the events announced by the seals and trumpets fall outside of this period. The seventh trumpet, which includes the seven vials (cups), belongs to the last half of the week. The entire 7 years is a time of affliction, but the last 3 1/2 years is the "Great Tribulation." During these 42 months Antichrist will have unlimited reign.

When it is stated in relation to the seventh trumpet that time will be no more (10:6, 7), this is not to say that time per se will cease; rather, it is a declaration that any postponement or delay of judgment is no longer possible. The last half of the week of years comes under the sign of the seventh trumpet; with the seventh trumpet the purposes of God are brought to their fulfillment, and the mystery of God is disclosed.

Opinions differ about whether the week of years time frame should be interpreted literally as "seven years," or whether it should be interpreted symbolically. Regardless of which option one chooses, a chronological framework is useful. But, since the Daniel prophecy—which forms the basis for Revelation—understands the week of years in a literal sense, there is scant evidence to support a figurative interpretation of the final 7-year period. Antichrist's short reign is limited to this period (cf. the words of Jesus in Matthew 24:22).

## Structure

SECTION 1: THE PRESENT TIME

  (Chapters 1-3)

Prologue (1:1-8)

  **A.** Opening vision (1:9-20)

  **B.** The letters sent to the seven churches (chap-

## The Opening Vision

The most prophetic book of the New Testament opens with the declaration that it is "the Revelation of Jesus Christ, which God gave unto him." This very declaration implies that the content was originally a revelation of God's future plans which were given to Jesus Christ. It is difficult to even begin to grasp how the omniscient Father reveals something—His plan and will—to the omniscient Son. This belongs to the realm of the divine mystery of the Trinity.

Some Scripture passages, though, do shed some light on this relationship. Jesus said (Mark 13:32) that the day of His return was not known to the Son—at least during His earthly life and humiliation. But there are several texts in John's Gospel that seem to indicate this involves something intrinsic to the interrelationship among the Godhead. The Son came from heaven and testified to what He had seen and heard (John 3:31, 32). What the Son heard from the Father, He spoke to the world (John 8:26) and announced to His disciples (John 15:15; cf. 5:30; 8:40). The central role of the Father in this trinitarian interrelationship appears to be confirmed also by Paul's words that God is the head of Christ (1 Corinthians 11:3). The Son does what He sees the Father doing (John 5:19) and knows what the Father tells Him.

The Apocalypse opens by announcing that the contents of the book are a revelation from God to His Son. This invests the book with a unique authority. It involves a disclosure of the plan of God whose import is so great that it originated in the eternal councils of the Godhead. Just as after His ascension Christ received the Holy Spirit from the Father and bestowed it on the Church (Acts 2:33), so too, as the Head of the Church He received this revelation of the future from God and gave it to His servants. What we share in is of such great value that the Father himself gave His own Son a unique revelation about it.

This divine revelation, therefore, came through many channels. First the Father gives it to the Son. Then Christ passed the revelation on to His angel. The angel gave the revelation to John in the form of "signs," i.e., symbols and images. What John saw and heard he wrote down under the inspiration of the Holy Spirit (22:6; cf. 2:7). Behind the message of Revelation stands the Triune God—Father, Son, and Holy Spirit. The message is proclaimed by the angel and written down by an apostle.

No one can be indifferent to a message of this origin and background. Nonetheless, this is unfortunately often the case. The Book of Revelation has been called the most neglected book in the Bible. As if to counteract this neglect, the Lord has given a unique promise to those who read the book or listen to it. This last item suggests that the Book of Revelation is to have its place in the reading of Scripture in the churches (cf. 1 Timothy 4:13).

When such a promise of blessing is associated with reading this book it reflects the crucial message it contains. Few books of the Bible have a more complete theology. All of the great Biblical themes are addressed, but the theme of Christian hope predominates. Revelation comprises the eschatological section of the New Testament. More than any other book in the Bible, Revelation and its visions of the future show the eternal existence in the new heavens and new earth awaiting the believer.

Revelation is the book of the consummation of the kingdom of God. With power God will bring His kingdom through to victory. Sin's revolt—on the cosmic scale—will be conquered. God will triumph over the enmity and power of the devil. Not the beast but the Lamb will receive royal power. Whereas the Gospels portray Christ in His suffering, Revelation depicts Him in His glorious body, an image which confronts us as early as the opening vision of the book. In his Gospel John described the glory which the Son received from the Father, when the "Word was made flesh." Now he described the Son of Man who walks in the midst of the lampstands; He who is the First and Last; He who was dead and is alive forever. Upon receiving this revelation of divine majesty, the disciple who once leaned on Jesus' bosom now fell as a dead man before the presence of his Lord.

The central episode in Revelation is not broken seals, blown trumpets, or empty cups of wrath, but that which opens and closes the book: "Behold, he cometh" (1:7; 22:7, 12, 20). The main figure in this prophecy is not the dragon nor the beast, but the Lamb who was slain and who now is before the throne of God. The opening and its first vision introduce key themes which will continue throughout the book.

## The Seven Letters Sent to the Seven Churches

Revelation falls into two parts. The first concerns "the things which are" and the latter the "things which shall be hereafter" (1:19). The first section contains much admonishment, while the second focuses mostly on apocalyptic visions of the future. The so-called Book of the Present Age (chapters 2, 3) is distinctly separated from the "Book of the. Future" by the vision of the throne in chapter 4, where it is said explicitly that John would be shown "things which must be hereafter" (4:1). The integral place of the section on the present age is further confirmed by the fact that it is connected with the opening vision in chapter 1. The present age division consists of seven letters sent to seven churches in Asia Minor. These seven churches are symbolized by seven lampstands; the "angels" of these churches by seven stars. The sender of the letter is the Son of Man, who in the opening vision appears among the lampstands. In several of the letters the Lord identifies himself by certain descriptions taken from the initial vision (Ephesus, 2:1; cf. 1:13 and 16; Smyrna, 2:8; cf. 1:18; Sardis, 3:1; cf. 1:16; Philadelphia, 3:7; cf. 1:18; Laodicea, 3:14; cf. 1:18, as the first one He is the "beginning of the creation of God").

The letters are addressed to the "angels" of each of the respective churches. Early interpreters understood the expression "angel of the church" to mean the "overseer." A few modern exegetes have posited that it refers to the "guardian angel" of the church, but this idea has little to commend it. First, nothing in the New Testament suggests that each church has its own "guardian angel," who oversees the spiritual status of the church. Furthermore, it is impossible to think that John addressed his seven letters to Asia Minor churches to spiritual beings, or that he was urging these angels to repent from their lukewarmness, lack of love, and spiritual depravity. Other interpreters have taken the "angel of the church" in a spiritual sense, as some kind of personification of the church. Note, however, that the seven stars, or angels, stand as something apart from the lampstand, which symbolizes the church. The letters are also addressed to individuals, not personifications.

It seems obvious, therefore, that the most ancient view that the angel was an overseer of the church is correct. The Greek term *angelos* corresponds to the Hebrew term *mal'āk*, "messenger." This latter expression especially is used of prophets (e.g., Haggai 1:13) and priests (Malachi 2:7). *Angelos* is applied in the New Testament to John the Baptist (Matthew 11:10), his messengers (Luke 7:24), and to messengers Jesus sent ahead of Him (Luke 9:52). Later Judaism called the intercessor in the synagogue "the messenger of the assembly," a title which corresponds to the phrase "angel of the church." "The angel of the church" translates the Hebrew expression *shaliach zibbor*, which was used to denote an important person in the Jewish synagogue. When a certain individual is addressed as the angel of the church, it indicates that during the apostolic age churches already had responsible overseers who brought the Word and teaching. These were in distinction to other elders or overseers.

There must have been churches in Asia Minor other than those mentioned here. But these seven were set apart to receive, guard, and pass on this prophetic book. The application of the respective letters becomes to each of the churches a direct message which connects the present condition of the church with the future. The content of the letters range from disclosure to disappointment, from warning to encouragement. Where failure and backsliding are pointed out, the path to renewal and restoration is also shown. The letters apply the larger message of the book to particular churches. One might also argue that the letters afford Revelation a historical quality, which is the distinctive stamp of the New Testament writings. In form the seven letters differ from any other epistolary literature of the New Testament. They more resemble prophetic words.

The structures of these letters are uniform. The addressee is given first: "And unto the angel of the church in . . . write." Next, the addresser identifies himself: "These things saith. . . ." The message follows next, and then the end, in two parts, comes. The two-part ending occurs in inverted order in the last four letters. The final section has an admonition to listen to what the Spirit is saying to the churches and a promise to those who overcome.

With regard to how the seven letters to the seven churches are to be understood, it is generally held that they had actual significance for the receiving churches. Such "divine analysis" on the internal condition of these churches tells us quite a bit about Christianity in the First Century. There is shocking evidence of how soon backsliding began to take place and how seriously the Lord views this, even though it is only in the earliest stages.

The letters sent to the churches continue to be a message for the Church of all time. This may explain their presence in Scripture. The message also has a personal appeal: "He that hath an ear, let him hear!" The letters depict some of the most ardent admonition concerning Christian life and doctrine in the New Testament. Surprisingly, however, the Church seems to have paid little attention to the letters' message, and it has paid a high price for its neglect. Each letter is like a standard against which the Church can assess itself. These seven churches were probably chosen because they are explicit examples of the various conditions in the Church. There were hundreds of towns in Asia Minor at this time. Other cities, almost certainly having churches, were larger and more important than Thyatira or Philadelphia, for example. But these seven churches reflect the Church at that time and for all time.

Up to this point most interpreters are in agreement. On the other hand, opinions differ greatly over whether the seven churches represent the successive types of churches throughout Church history. Some interpreters think the letters should be taken as some kind of prophecy of Church history. Different results will almost naturally come from taking this approach. If one examines the results of the various interpreters who take this view, one finds they are so divergent that they undermine the very thesis on which they build. Some think this approach "fanciful"; others however, think the alleged correspondences between Church history and these letters are more than coincidence. Those who take this view believe the seven churches in Revelation were divinely chosen to give prophetically the major directions in Church history.

One might be puzzled over how interpreters could be of such differing opinions in this matter. Two things seem obvious. First, at a very basic level the letters may resemble the pattern of Church history. Second, any detailed comparison is not possible.

## The Rapture

A major concern for interpreters of Revelation is the question of the timing of the "rapture" of the Church in the larger scheme of the last days. There are some theologians who are not even interested in such a question, but this should be an important issue for Bible-believing Christians. If the New Testament speaks of the Rapture as an actual, future event, it cannot be passed off as irrelevant.

There are three main New Testament texts that speak of believers being "caught up" to meet the Lord at His return. The first comes in a word from Jesus himself: "And if I go and prepare a place for you, I will come again, and receive you unto myself; that where I am, there ye may be also" (John 14:3). The Jews were waiting for Messiah to come and reestablish the kingdom of Israel on earth; thus, Jesus' words bring in an entirely new hope.

A second Scripture passage speaking of the Rapture is 1 Corinthians 15:51, 52: "Behold, I show you a mystery; We shall not all sleep, but we shall all be changed, in a moment, in the twinkling of an eye, at the last trump: for the trumpet shall sound, and the dead shall be raised incorruptible, and we shall be changed."

The third text is 1 Thessalonians 4:13-18, where, among other things, it is said that "the dead in Christ shall rise first: then we which are alive and remain shall be caught up together with them in the clouds, to meet the Lord in the air."

Paul described the Rapture as a "mystery." Thus it is a truth not previously revealed, but which has now been made known to the apostles and prophets of the Lord (cf. Ephesians 3:3-5). Those living by the old covenant expected a resurrection of the dead (e.g., Daniel 12:2), but that those alive at the coming of Messiah should be changed was unheard of. This truth reflects the greater disclosure of the New Testament.

One of the most puzzling facts of the New Testament is that the Book of Revelation does not mention the Rapture, at least not in an unmistakable manner. Nothing about believers being "caught away" is said either in the description of Christ's coming in chapter 19 or in any of the preceding visions. This is all the more puzzling since Revelation does speak of the "translation" of the two witnesses in chapter 11 and the male child in the symbolic language of chapter 12.

We cannot hope to resolve a problem that has so plagued interpreters in the past; neither can we offer any hard and fast arguments in favor of a particular view. However, it is important to summarize the various interpretations and their goals and bases.

Interpretations of the "rapture of the Church" can be divided into four main groups. (1) Some believe it will take place before the so-called Great Tribulation and before the 70th week of Daniel. (2) Some contend that the rapture of the Church will occur in the middle of the Tribulation. (3) Still others maintain that it will take place after the time of tribulation, when Christ returns with His heavenly multitudes (chapter 19). (4) Finally, some think it will take place after the Millennium. Before surveying, these main interpretations, two important elements that influence the interpretation of Revelation must be pointed out.

First, it is unmistakably clear there are believers on earth during the Great Tribulation described in the major section of Revelation. It is said that Antichrist will wage war against the saints (13:7). This involves a group of martyrs who endure in patience and faith (13:10). They refuse to worship the image of the beast (13:15). These believers are exhorted to remain "awake" and to be prepared for the return (16:15). A voice from heaven calls out to these people of God: "Come out of her (Babylon), my people, that ye be not partakers of her sins" (18:4).

As far as we are able to tell, there are only three alternatives for interpreting this: (1) The Rapture has not taken place and the Church is still on earth during the Great Tribulation. (2) A partial rapture has just taken place; some of the Church endures the Tribulation. (3) There may be a group of people converted after the rapture of the Church.

The second element influencing how one interprets Revelation is that conversion during the Tribulation is understood in Revelation as entirely possible. It seems as if one of the main reasons for the earth's afflictions is that God wants to bring people to repentance. In the midst of the Antichrist's reign an eternal gospel is preached to those who live on earth, "to every nation, and kindred, and tongue, and people" (14:6). When the two witnesses have been transported to heaven the people become frightened and give God the glory (11:13). When the trumpets of judgment sound and the cups of wrath are poured out, the refrain resounds: "They repented not" (9:20, 21; 16:9-11). This would be totally irrelevant if there were no call to repent or possibility of it.

Since it is obvious that conversion is possible during this time of tribulation, there is only one conclusion. If the rapture of the Church takes place before the Great Tribulation, the implication is that conversion is possible after Jesus' return and the Rapture. As should be noted, the interpretation chosen will cause great and serious consequences.

Below we will survey the four major interpretations of the Rapture:

## Pre-Tribulation Rapture

As a dogmatic teaching the belief that the Church will be "caught away" before the Great Tribulation is rather new. But the view of the imminence of Christ's return, which lies at the heart of this teaching, can be traced to the Early Church and the fathers of the Church. The Early Church lived in watchful anticipation of the coming of the Lord to take His church.

It was in the 19th Century that J.N. Darby advocated the eschatological system and theory of the pre-Tribulation Rapture (see *The Rapture of the Saints*). Those who adopt this position insist this is the revival of one of the great Biblical truths. The Early Church determined the foundation Christological doctrines. The soteriological doctrines of salvation, for example, the doctrine of justification by faith—which Martin Luther called the main doctrine by which the Church stands or falls—came out of the 16th Century Reformation. The eschatological teachings of the Church belong to those in the last days (cf. Daniel 12:4, 10). But it should be mentioned that these doctrines are not fully fixed in place. The details are still in the process of development.

The interpretation of the prophecies germane to the Rapture emerges out of a certain view of the Church, the Tribulation, and the Second Coming.

# 1. The Church

(a) *The Identity of the Church.* This theological viewpoint considers the Church of the New Testament as totally independent from and unrelated to Israel and believers of other ages. If the term *church* includes saints from all ages, then it is obvious that the Church will pass through the Tribulation, since everyone agrees that saints will be around during the Tribulation. It will be different if *church* denotes only believers of the present age. Then it is possible, even probable, that the Church of this age is exempt from the days of God's wrath.

(b) *The Mission of the Church.* A characteristic feature of the Church during the age of grace is that it is the temple of the Holy Spirit. Because the Spirit within believers is much stronger than the spirit in the world (1 John 4:4), sin and cruelty do not have free rein. From 2 Thessalonians 2:6-8 it is clear that only after that (neuter noun) which is holding the Antichrist back is removed can the man of sin, Antichrist, be revealed. The Greek term for "spirit," *pneuma*, is actually a neuter noun, but it may be taken as masculine when used of the Spirit. Thus "it" (what) should be understood in verses 6 and "he" in verse 7. The Holy Spirit works through the Church and opposes the spirit of Antichrist which is in the world already (1 John 4:3). When the Rapture removes the Church's influence from the world the powers of Antichrist will become manifest; he himself will appear. According to this view, the Church's presence in the world hinders the influence of evil in the world. The rapture of the Church becomes essential if any time of tribulation and Antichrist's reign is to occur.

(c) *The Disappearance of the Church.* A very puzzling feature of Revelation is that the word *church* suddenly disappears from the text after the third chapter. The expression reappears only in the final words of the book. Whereas the early chapters focus exclusively on the Church, it is apparently not part of the discussion of the Tribulation and Antichrist.

On the other hand, other groups of God's people do appear. The distinction between Israel and the Gentiles is marked; Israel is called "Israel," and Gentiles, "Gentiles." The situation seems clearly different from the Church that does not distinguish between Jews and Greeks. The Jewish character of this book cannot be explained if one takes this to be the period of the Church. If, however, this is a prelude to what Paul termed the admittance of Israel, the focus on Israel is understandable. It is further understandable that the Church of the age of grace drops from sight if the age of the Church is past.

(d) *The Church in Heaven.* Several texts are offered in support of the theory that the Church is in heaven during the Tribulation described in Revelation 4–19. For one, the extraordinarily sharp line drawn between "the things which are" (up to and including chapter 3) and "the things which shall be hereafter" (chapter 4) may suggest this. Even in the first section the discussion hints to future things, including trials to come and blessings. There are also allusions to the return of the Lord. Nevertheless, it is clear that a future entirely new age is in view in chapter 4. At the same time there is a connection: chapter 3 ends with the Lord's promise to the overcomers that they will sit on His throne. Chapter 4 opens with the 24 elders sitting on their thrones around the throne of God himself as His coregents.

Followers of this view take the 24 elders as symbols of the Church. "Elder" is an expression used in both the Old and New Testaments for leaders. Twenty-four is 2 times 12; this recalls the 12 patriarchs of Israel and the 12 apostles of the Early Church. The New Jerusalem, explicitly called the "Bride," the betrothed of the Lamb, also reflects this double 12 number: the names of Israel's 12 tribes and the 12 apostles are written on the gates and foundation stone of the city (21:12-14).

Revelation 13:6 states that the Antichrist mocks "them that dwell in heaven," the dwelling place of God. Paul employed a similar image in 1 Corinthians 3:16, 17, as did Peter (1 Peter 2:5). This text expressly states that during the reign of Antichrist the Church dwells in heaven.

The theory that the Church is in heaven during the time of Antichrist seems also reflected in 19:11, which speaks of the coming of Christ after the time of tribulation. It is stated that the armies of heaven follow Him on white horses. This cannot be any angelic army, because Paul wrote that when He comes on that day, "he shall come to be glorified in his saints, and to be admired in all them that believe" (2 Thessalonians 1:10). Not merely angels will be revealed with Him, but, "When Christ, who is our life, shall appear, then shall ye also appear with him in glory" (Colossians 3:4). Therefore, it is noteworthy that those accompanying the Lord in His return after the Tribulation come with Him from heaven. Nothing is mentioned here about an earthly multitude being caught up to join Him in this triumphant procession. Thus, the old argument that the Lord must first come *for* His own before he can come *with* them surely has some support. The same can be said about the Bride, the New Jerusalem, which comes down from heaven (21:10).

(e) *The Complete Church.* The doctrine of the pre-Tribulation Rapture is founded on the theory that the Church is a certain group of believers, an eschatological body belonging to the dispensation of Grace. It is possible that this group includes the saints of the old covenant, who cannot attain completion "without us" (Hebrews 11:40; cf. Romans 11:17; Ephesians 3:6). Not only this church but the entire Church, not just a part, will be caught away at the coming of the Lord.

The doctrine of the pre-Tribulation Rapture thus fundamentally differs with the view that only part of the Church will participate in the Rapture, and that the remainder of the Church will be taken later. A partial rapture runs counter to the doctrine of the unity of the Church. When the fullness of the Gentiles—all those to be saved—is reached, the age of the Church will be past (Romans 11:25). This is the consummate Church, complete in number, which will be caught up to meet the Lord.

Any theory of a partial Rapture concerns not only a particular view of the prophecies, but the entire gospel. Salvation is by grace. This applies to justification as well as final salvation in the eternal kingdom of God. The admonitions to stay awake and to keep one's robe spotless are not to be understood as somehow making one eligible for salvation; it is the free gift of God.

## 2. The Tribulation

(a) *The Nature of the Period of the Tribulation.* The advocates of a pre-tribulation rapture do not contend that the Church is exempt from the general trials the people of God have to endure. Jesus himself said: "In the world ye shall have tribulation" (John 16:33). Paul taught the newly converted that the Church will always undergo such trials: "through much tribulation enter into the kingdom of God" (Acts 14:22). He wrote that "all that will live godly in Christ Jesus shall suffer persecution" (2 Timothy 3:12). It is not, therefore, "much tribulation" that the Church will be rescued from, but the "Great Tribulation."

The "Great Tribulation" refers to a tribulation during the last days, unique both in form and intensity from any other previous time of distress. Both Old and New Testaments confirm it has no parallel in human history (Daniel 12:1; Matthew 24:21). Prophetic writings often call this time of tribulation the "day of the Lord, the day of the judgment of the Lord." It will be universal and will affect Jew and Gentile alike (Jeremiah 30:7; Ezekiel 30:3). The Day of the Lord is depicted in dramatic images. It will come like a whirlwind (Jeremiah 30:23, 24), like a burning oven (Malachi 4:1). It will be a day of clouds and thick darkness (Zephaniah 1:15); it will be darkness and not light (Amos 5:18). This kind of prophecy forms the backdrop in the New Testament for John the Baptist's preaching of the coming wrath, for Jesus' eschatological discourse, and for the visions of judgment in the Book of Revelation.

Different factors come together in the Great Tribulation. It will be a time of wrath. The devil will "come down," and he will be filled with wrath (12:12). The nations will be angry as the day of the fury of God comes (11:18). The Lord will visit the hosts of heaven on high and the kings of the earth below (Isaiah 24:21, 22; cf. Ephesians 6:12 and Revelation 12:9; 20:2). God's judgment of sin will have cosmic dimensions. The revolt of Satan and sinful humanity will reach its climax in Antichrist. The cup of God's wrath will be poured out over the fully ripened sin of mankind. God's patience will be ended when that day of vengeance comes (Isaiah 61:2). "The wrath of God, who liveth for ever and ever" (Revelation 15:7) "is poured out without mixture into the cup of his indignation" (14:10). God will "recompense tribulation" (2 Thessalonians 1:6) upon a world which has for hundreds of years persecuted God's people—His church.

The final tribulation will be unlike any other time of affliction ever experienced by the people of God. Without question the affliction of God's people will increase as time moves toward the end of the age. But those who espouse a pre-tribulation rapture contend that the Church will be spared from the time of God's wrath, when His judgment will fall on a rebellious and hardened humanity.

(b) *Examples of Deliverance.* The concept that the righteous will not undergo the tribulation of the last days can be traced back to Judaism (*The Babylonian Talmud, Sanhedrin* 98). To the Jewish listener, Jesus was reflecting a common understanding when He said, "Watch ye therefore, and pray always, that ye may be accounted worthy to escape all these things that shall come to pass" (Luke 21:36).

There are numerous Old Testament examples in which God removed His holy ones before He sent judgment (cf. Isaiah 57:1). Noah did not perish in the Flood like his ungodly contemporaries. Lot, too, was delivered from Sodom before God let fire and brimstone rain on the city (cf. 2 Peter 2:5-9). The people of Israel were not struck by the plagues that fell on the Egyptians (Exodus 8:22, 23), and Rahab was spared when the walls of Jericho fell (Joshua 6:25). Note that Jesus used Noah and Lot to illustrate conditions prior to His return (Luke 17:26-32).

The New Testament reports that Jesus warned His disciples about the impending destruction of Jerusalem; He gave them signs so they would know when to flee the city (Luke 21:20f.). Because the early Jerusalem church paid attention to these warnings many believers were saved. Those who insist that the Church will be taken away before the tribulation period and the coming of Antichrist contend that Scripture (e.g., Genesis 18:23-25) shows that God, according to such a principle of justice, will take His people from the world before He executes His judgment of wrath over the kingdom of Antichrist (Revelation 16:20) and over a hardened humanity that refuses to repent (Revelation 9:20, 21; 16:11).

(c) *Promises of Deliverance.* Proponents of a pre-tribulation rapture assert they have explicit scriptural support for the promise of deliverance. The judgment of wrath cannot be for believers, it is asserted, because, "God hath not appointed us to wrath, but to obtain salvation by our Lord Jesus Christ" (1 Thessalonians 5:9). Believers will be "saved from wrath through him" (Romans 5:9). God has called those who belong to Him to "wait for his Son from heaven, . . . Jesus, which delivered us from the wrath to come" (1 Thessalonians 1:10).

When the great day of God's judgment does come (Revelation 6:17), harsh punishments will afflict the earth and all its inhabitants. Famine, pestilence, violence, war, and natural catastrophes will wrack the earth. It is hard to imagine any other way for the Church to escape these catastrophes other than its being "raptured" before the Tribulation. If this were not so, the Church would have to go through the wrath of God's judgment and the persecutions of Antichrist. If the day of God's fury and the time of Antichrist occur before the Rapture, it is hard to imagine how the Early Church could view being among the "clothed upon" as more desirable than being "unclothed" (2 Corinthians 5:4). In other words, they saw being transformed at the Lord's coming more desirable than dying and being raised.

If the return of Christ is regarded as an event of the distant future, and if the most catastrophic time of human history is between the present and that return, then it must be far better to die and be with Christ (cf. Philippians 1:23; Revelation 14:13). Furthermore, this position implies that should the Church have to pass through the Great Tribulation most believers would have to suffer martyrdom. This would mean that the hope for the Lord's coming for His church of the last days is only a hope for future resurrection.

Even though the earliest Christians expected and endured persecution, nothing seems to indicate they viewed the approach of the Day of the Lord as nearer than His return. When Jesus spoke of the signs of the last days, He did not say that judgment was drawing near for believers, but that redemption was at hand (Luke 21:28). He said this because believers will escape the judgment to come (Luke 21:36). The message to the church in Philadelphia is a promise to the entire Church: "Because thou hast kept the word of my patience, I also will keep thee from the hour of temptation, which shall come upon all the world, to try them that dwell upon the earth" (Revelation 3:10). The Church will be delivered from the "hour of temp-

tation," not merely the afflictions endemic to the present age.

## 3. The Return

If one were to identify one consistent comment of the New Testament on the return of Christ, it would have to be that the return will come unexpectedly and suddenly. Jesus himself said that no one knows the day or the hour—He will come unexpectedly. This aspect of His return is why believers are to be like servants who are waiting for their master (Luke 12:36), like virgins waiting for the bridegroom (Matthew 25:1ff.), or like the "goodman of the house" who watches during the night because he expects a thief will break into his home (Matthew 24:43).

The epistolary literature of the New Testament clearly shows this was indeed the attitude of the Early Church: "Ye turned to God from idols to serve the living and true God; and to wait for his Son from heaven, whom he raised from the dead, even Jesus, which delivered us from the wrath to come" (1 Thessalonians 1:9, 10). The first generation of believers and apostles were anticipating Christ's return even in their lifetimes. Among early Christians the saying circulated about John: "That disciple should not die" (John 21:23). Paul identified the living Church with the dead in Christ: "The dead shall be raised incorruptible, and we shall be changed" (1 Corinthians 15:52). "We which are alive and remain unto the coming of the Lord shall not prevent them which are asleep" (1 Thessalonians 4:15). In addition to this there are the New Testament passages which exhort the people of God to be awake and prepared for His return. It is virtually impossible to reconcile these appeals for watchfulness and preparedness with the notion of a distant, future return of Christ. Daily anticipation of the Lord's return would be senseless.

Traces of the eager expectation of the Early Church appear in the apostolic and church fathers. For example, in his *First Epistle to the Corinthians* Clement of Rome wrote: "Of a truth, soon and suddenly shall his will be accomplished, as the Scripture also bears witness, saying, 'Speedily will He come, and will not tarry'; and 'the Lord shall suddenly come to His temple'" (*Ante-Nicene Fathers,* 1:11).

Scripture's strong emphasis on the unexpected and sudden return of the Lord, as well as its earnest appeals for preparedness (Matthew 24:42, 44; 25:13; Mark 13:33; Luke 21:36), can hardly be interpreted in any way other than that the Church must regard Christ's return as imminent. However, this does not nullify those texts which are equally clear that the return of Christ will occur after the time of Antichrist and the Great Tribulation

(Matthew 24:29; 2 Thessalonians 2:8; Revelation 19:11).

Scripture's paradoxical portrait of the return of Christ seems to indicate it will not be a single event but a series of events. The Rapture, thus, will take place suddenly, in a moment's time (1 Corinthians 15:52). But the Parousia implies that the arrival of the Lord will culminate finally in what Scripture calls "the brightness of his coming" (*epiphaneia parousias*; 2 Thessalonians 2:8). This may be called the *days* of the Son of Man (Luke 17:26) as well as the *day* of the Son of Man (Luke 17:30).

Following this view, the Parousia or return will begin when the Lord—prior to the Great Tribulation—descends in the clouds of heaven and catches up His church (1 Thessalonians 4:16f.). The return will be finalized when the Lord—after the Great Tribulation—is revealed from heaven, together with His saints, in glorious splendor (19:11ff.). However, this is not to suggest there are two returns. It is only one return in different stages of development and revelation. This seems to explain the similarities and contrasts in the Scripture's teaching on the return.

## Mid-Tribulation Rapture

Some interpreters of prophecy argue that the Church will remain on earth during part of the end-time distress, but that it will be caught away before it reaches its climax. This view represents a compromise between the two opposing views—pre- and posttribulation rapture. A rather strong, worldwide contingency of Christians faithful to the Bible accept this view.

The essential points of this position are that the Church will be on earth during the first half of the Tribulation, when hunger, pestilence, war, and natural catastrophes afflict humanity. The Church will not, however, go through God's wrath, which is instead directed against Antichrist and his kingdom. When the Great Tribulation—in the ultimate sense of that phrase—begins, Christ will return, the Church will be caught up with Him, and it will be removed from the Tribulation (cf. 7:14: "These are they which came out of great tribulation").

Some proponents of this view think Christ will return at the sounding of the seventh trumpet (11:15). They identify this as the "trump of God" (1 Corinthians 15:52; 1 Thessalonians 4:16). Some also see the rapture of the Church symbolized in the "rapture" of the two witnesses (11:12) and the male child (12:5).

According to this position the return of Christ and the Rapture are future events which do not occur until after the Antichrist has appeared and the judgments depicted in the visions of Revelation have begun to be fulfilled.

## Post-Tribulation Rapture

This position can be traced back to the Early Church, and it has been a prevailing view within most of Christendom. The view that the Church will go through the Tribulation is quite widespread.

Some proponents of this viewpoint, however, interpret the Tribulation not as some special time of future distress, but as the general affliction the Church has always experienced. The expectation of the imminent return of Christ present in the Early Church and to some extent later is explained as a consequence of having interpreted the visions of Revelation as having been fulfilled in the persecution of Christians in the First Century or later.

Several examples from the Early Church show that expecting the imminent return of the Lord could be combined with the view that Antichrist's appearance will precede the Parousia. The *Didache,* dated around A.D. 120, reads: "Watch over your life; your lamps must not go out, nor your loins be ungirded; on the contrary, be ready. You do not know the hour in which Our Lord is coming" (16:1). Christ's return, thus, was seen as imminent. Nevertheless, the author continued in that same section to predict that "the deceiver," i.e., Antichrist, will appear and humanity will endure its greatest trial. After this the trumpet will sound and the dead arise. Many theologians detect here an allusion to 1 Thessalonians 4:16. They assert that the *Didache* expressly witnesses that in the earliest years of the Church—some 20-30 years after the writing of Revelation—Christ's return and the Rapture were thought to occur after the Great Tribulation and Antichrist's appearance.

The basic view of post-Tribulationalism argues that the rapture of the Church will not take place until the return of Christ that occurs before the Millennium but after the Great Tribulation and Antichrist's rule. A series of arguments supports their position:

(a) *The Return is Not in Two Stages.* If the coming of the Lord occurs in two stages, with an interval of several years in between stages, it would be more accurate to speak of two returns. But such a notion is foreign to Scripture. It only knows of the first coming of Christ in humility and His second coming in glory.

Thus only one return is mentioned. The Greek terms used to describe this return are used synonymously: *parousia,* "coming," and *apokalupsis* and *epiphaneia,* "revelation." The proponents of this view state a secret coming is not mentioned; on the contrary, Jesus warned against believing rumors of a secret coming (Matthew 24:26). His return will be visible to everybody; every eye will see Him (Matthew 24:27; Luke 17:24; Revelation 1:7).

The hope of believers is to be revealed in glory with Christ when He returns (Colossians 3:4). Then the trial of their faith will be for praise and honor (1 Peter 1:7). The faithful love His appearing (2 Timothy 4:8), expect His appearing (1 Corinthians 1:7), and trust in the grace that is theirs at His manifestation (1 Peter 1:13). Their duty in this world is to keep the commandment pure until His appearing (1 Timothy 6:14).

(b) *The Interval Between the First and Second Comings.* The New Testament clearly speaks of certain *personal events* which must transpire between the first and second coming of Christ. Jesus foretold that Peter would become old and then suffer martyrdom (John 21:18, 19). Paul likewise received a revelation about his death as a martyr (2 Timothy 4:6). He warned leaders of the Ephesian church about what would happen after his departure (Acts 20:29f.).

Furthermore, there are certain *historical events* which must occur before Christ's return. Jesus foretold the destruction of Jerusalem (Luke 19:41-44; 21:20) and that Gentiles would overrun it until the last days (Luke 21:24ff.).

It is also plain that a period of *church history* continues between the ascension of Jesus and His return. God has a plan for the Church which will be realized in this age. The parables suggest a "long time" will elapse before His return (Matthew 25:5, 19). Especially important in this connection is that the command to spread the gospel, the Great Commission, is to be accomplished. "This gospel of the kingdom shall be preached in all the world for a witness unto all nations; and then shall the end come" (Matthew 24:14).

(c) *Signs of the Last Days.* The historical progress that will mark this age will reach its climax in a dramatic crisis immediately prior to the return. Certain eschatological signs will appear. "These things must come to pass" (Matthew 24:6). In 2 Thessalonians 2:1-8 two such signs are mentioned: A great falling away is to occur and the man of sin is to be revealed. Neither apostasy nor the activity of the Antichrist are unrelated to the Church. Backsliding is regarded as belonging to the future, but it emerges while the Church is still on earth, since apostasy can only take place when there is something to apostatize from (1 Timothy 4:1). And, in this view, when the Church is cautioned against Antichrist, this seems to imply that he will appear before the Church is caught up (cf. 1 John 2:18).

Furthermore, Jesus offered a series of signs of His coming (Matthew 24:3ff., with parallels). They proclaim it is obvious that such signs must precede the return. When such signs appear believers are not to think the end has come. Jesus' own words, "The end is not yet" (Matthew 24:6), suggest that for a time the Church must exist while these signs of the end, which He calls the "beginning of sorrows," are manifest.

(d) *The Great Tribulation.* When Jesus mentioned the "beginning of sorrows" in His great eschatological discourse, He was using an expression from Jewish apocalypticism which refers to the tribulations that precede the establishment of the messianic kingdom. These afflictions will in some way always be a part of human existence, but in such an augmented form they will be the "birth pangs" of the end. The Church will experience these trials both in their general form during the entire Christian Era as well as in their eschatological form in the end time. They reflect the "sufferings of Christ" the Church will endure; they are the measure of affliction it will undergo for the sake of the name of Christ in order to share in His glory (Romans 8:17, 18; Colossians 1:24; 1 Peter 4:13). This goal is attained during the tribulations of the last days, when the number of those martyred is complete (Revelation 6:11). The Church cannot be raptured as long as there is an aspect of the sufferings of Christ to be fulfilled. That is why the multitude of martyrs under the heavenly altar keep silence until this occurs. The Church receives its "reward" only on "that day" (cf. 2 Timothy 4:8).

Throughout the age of the gospel the Church has had to suffer for its faith; there is no reason things should be any different for the Church of the last days. Only those holding fast to the word of the Lord to be patient (3:10) will be preserved and rescued. Thus, endurance as well as strength is required. If the New Testament Church is a chosen people with spiritual maturity and the specific promises of God, it is difficult to understand how some other group of less spiritually mature believers could endure the harshest of afflictions. To suffer for Christ was considered by the New Testament writers to be a privilege: "For unto you it is given in the behalf of Christ, not only to believe on him, but also to suffer for his sake" (Philippians 1:29). This raises the question whether escaping affliction makes the Church privileged at all.

One fact is certain: the eschatological discourse of Jesus as well as the visions of Revelation indicate that there are many saints on earth during the tribulation of the last days. Those who maintain a posttribulation view take those saints to be none other than the Church.

The Book of Revelation is a word of encouragement to God's people who will go through this time of distress, and both the introduction (1:1-4) and the conclusion of the book (22:16) seem to indicate that it is a message to the Church. It would also seem quite strange if the major prophetic writing of the New Testament should not apply to the New Testament Church but to a totally different group.

(e) *No Pre-Tribulation Rapture.* Those who advocate a posttribulation rapture view state that when so much evidence seems to suggest that the Church will go through the Great Tribulation, it seems almost unthinkable how a doctrine should emerge which advocates a pre-tribulation rapture. The church fathers did not endorse such a view. Likewise, the reformers did not advocate it.

Neither Jesus' eschatological discourse nor the Book of Revelation propose a pre-tribulation rapture. Nor is there any explicit statement in any of the New Testament Scriptures about such a rapture. Most of the "evidence" offered in support of this view is only conjecture or the result of allegorical interpretation. It is certainly not enough on which to build a doctrine.

(f) *Post-Tribulation Rapture.* Those who maintain the view that the Rapture will occur after the Tribulation refer to the words of Jesus in Matthew 24:29-31, "Immediately after the tribulation of those days shall the sun be darkened . . . and then shall appear the sign of the Son of man in heaven: and then shall all the tribes of the earth mourn, and they shall see the Son of man coming in the clouds of heaven with power and great glory. And he shall send his angels with a great sound of a trumpet, and they shall gather together his elect from the four winds, from one end of heaven to the other." In addition to this Jesus proceeded (verses 40, 41) to tell of a "snatching away" when one will be taken and the other left (note, *paralambanō*; cf. Luke 17:34, 35; in contrast to those taken [*ēren*, Matthew 24:39] by the Flood or destroyed [*apōlesen*], Luke 17:27, 29).

Paul's teaching in 1 Thessalonians 4:16, 17 (cf. 2 Thessalonians 2:1) about the Rapture at the coming of the Lord appears to view the gathering of the elect of God in Matthew 24:31 and Mark 13:27 as its prototype. The parallel text, Luke 21:27, says that redemption "draweth nigh" at the onset of the signs, but even here redemption is connected with the coming of the Son of Man in the clouds of heaven with power and great glory. Further, the significant issue is to "stand before the Son of man" (Luke 21:36).

At the coming of the Son of Man the angels will gather together the chosen "with a great sound of a trumpet" (Matthew 24:31). Paul explained that the resurrection and "transformation" will take place "at the last trump" (1 Corinthians 15:52), and that the Lord will come "with the voice of the archangel and with the trump of God" when the Rapture occurs (1 Thessalonians 4:16, 17). The Book of Revelation states that when the seventh angel blows the last of the seven trumpets the mystery of God will be complete (10:6, 7). The seventh trumpet introduces and extends through those events leading up to the return of Christ and the establishment of the kingdom of God. The time then arrives when the dead will be judged

and the servants of the Lord will receive their reward (11:15-18). This reward will be given "at that day" (2 Timothy 4:8).

(g) *The Last Day.* Scripture associates the consummation of the kingdom of God with a fixed point in time, a certain day. Many designations are applied to this day. Among other things it is called the "day of Christ" (Philippians 2:16), the "day of our Lord Jesus Christ" (1 Corinthians 1:8), "the day of redemption" (Ephesians 4:30), "that day" (2 Timothy 1:12), or simply "the day" (1 Corinthians 3:13).

Jesus referred to this day as the last day and declared that on the last day all those believing in Him will be raised (John 6:39, 40, 44, 54; cf. 11:24). This final day must therefore be the day on which Christ returns, since Scripture explicitly states that the dead in Christ will rise when the Lord comes. The resurrection of the dead is the first event occurring at the Lord's return (1 Thessalonians 4:16). But the resurrection is not pictured as occurring before the Tribulation. On the contrary, one can see that a myriad of martyrs must wait (Revelation 6:11). Immediately following the Great Tribulation, when the Lord comes with His holy ones (19:11ff.), the first resurrection will take place (20:4, 5).

## Post-Millennium Rapture

The viewpoint that the coming of Christ and the Rapture will occur after the Millennium is, of course, closely connected with how one views the Millennium. This issue will be addressed with respect to 20:1-9.

Those who hold to the post-Millennium Rapture view must distinguish between a spiritual, symbolic understanding of the Millennium as the Christian Era and a literal understanding, which views the Millennium as an actual, future period in time. The latter view then holds that a millennial kingdom will be established as a result of the victorious advance of the gospel.

Both views, however, maintain that toward the end of the "thousand years" Satan will be released for a time and will deceive mankind. Then, Christ will appear in order to judge His enemies and to bring salvation to His people, who by virtue of the resurrection begin to participate in their eternal existence.

Those contending that the Millennium is synonymous with the age of the gospel normally think we are nearing the end of the Millennium. They think the Lord will soon come, immediately after the earth has endured a time of severe tribulation. This view in part corresponds with the post-Tribulation Rapture of the saints and return of Christ.

To a certain extent the futuristic view of the Millennium also resembles post-Tribulationalism. The triumph of the gospel still lies between the present and the future time of great conflict. The coming of the Lord and the Rapture are seen as being "a thousand years" (often figuratively) in the future.

## Conclusions

It is not possible to come up with any hard and fast conclusions. The matter is too complex, and opinions are too varied. The issue is probably not resolvable either theoretically or theologically. We will probably never understand the mystery of His coming "this side of glory," apart from the glimpses we have "through a glass darkly." We must rest in the fact that God allows us to know just as much as we need. We must keep in mind Jesus' words, "Now I tell you before it come, that, when it is come to pass, ye may believe that I am he" (John 13:19). Our imperfect understanding should not create doubt or uncertainty, but rather stir us to watchfulness. We do know this much at least—we must watch and wait for our Lord.

Since we understand only in part, we prophesy only in part (1 Corinthians 13:9). It is the task of prophetic preaching to explore the Biblical paradox which can say "The Lord will come!" (Hebrews 10:37) as well as "Antichrist shall come!" (1 John 2:18). This is what the apostles preached, and it is how we should.

The major interpretations of the prophecies cited here all have their strengths and weaknesses. The one who is truly convinced of his position should also be able to look at his own arguments from another's point of view. We should use the insight and work of others in studying Revelation, a book which holds such great promises of blessing for its readers.

## The 70th Week of Daniel

The line of distinction between what "is" and what "will be" appears to be drawn quite sharply in the early verses of chapter 4. Similarly, there is a clear transition at the beginning of chapter 20 from the tribulation period to the Kingdom Age, the Millennium. Thus the largest portion of the book, which concerns the tribulation period, falls between these two milestones and includes chapters 4 through 19.

The events described in this section apparently take place during a fixed time period. The time is given in *days,* 1260 (11:3; 12:6), *months,* 42 (11:2; 13:5), and *years,* time, times, and half a time, which means 1 year and 2 years and 1/2 year (12:14). From 11:2, 3, it seems as if the end time consists of two such periods of 3 1/2 years, i.e., a 7-year period. The two witnesses of God are active during the first 3 1/2 years (11:3), while the last 3 1/2 years are the time of Antichrist (11:2; cf. 13:5).

The opinions of interpreters are mixed regarding whether these divisions are literal or figurative. No matter how one interprets them, it is certain this is a chronological framework around which the central section of Revelation is structured. An understanding of these time periods, therefore, will influence how one interprets the book.

The chronology of the last days found in Revelation is taken from the book of the prophet Daniel. Daniel 7:25 mentions the 3 1/2-year period and refers to it in the same way as Revelation 12:14: "time, times, and half a time." Both texts say this will be a time when the people of God will be delivered into the hands of the enemy, when a fierce, cruel king of the end times will wage war against the saints and will rule without opposition. The same time period in 13:5 is the time of Antichrist, who wages war against the holy ones of God and gains dominion over the whole earth. The relationship between Daniel and Revelation, therefore, is unmistakable at this point.

Nonetheless, it is obvious from the Book of Daniel that the 3 1/2 years is the concluding phase of a much larger time period mentioned in Daniel 9. There we have the well-known prophecy of the 70 weeks of years, that is, 70 periods of 7 years. From Daniel 9:27 it is clear that the last of these 7-year periods is divided into two parts, each half equal to 3 1/2 years. The prophecy of the 70 weeks of years is one of the central prophecies of Scripture about the first coming of Christ as well as His return.

Daniel and his countrymen lived in exile in Babylon. Jeremiah the prophet had prophesied the Jews would spend 70 years in a foreign land before returning to their homeland. When the 70 years of captivity drew to a close, messianic expectations among the Jews heightened. Many thought the Messianic Age would break through with their return to their home. Then Daniel had this unique revelation which indicated that though the exile would last 70 years, there was to be a special period of 70 weeks of years before the Messiah. Gabriel the angel gave Daniel the message of the coming Messiah; he would again come to announce the birth of Jesus to the virgin Mary (Luke 1:26).

The prophecy states Daniel's people would see 70 weeks pass in order to atone for their sin and before they would see the realization of those prophecies (Daniel 9:24). A "week" here is not a week of days but of years. The original wording says "seventy sevens." Furthermore, Jewish people understood a week in many senses. There were "weeks of *days,*" such as from Sabbath to Sabbath; there were "weeks of *weeks,*" such as between Passover and Pentecost. "Weeks of *months*" passed before the Feast of Tabernacles, "weeks of *years*" until the Sabbath year (Leviticus 25:1-7), and "weeks of *year-weeks*" until the Jubilee (Leviticus 25:8).

A fixed point in time was established for the beginning of the 70 weeks. When the command was given to rebuild Jerusalem and to make it a fortified city, this was a signal that Israel's time of preparation had begun. The Jews received permission to return to their homeland in Daniel's day; some did. But the Persian king, Artaxerxes, did not order Jerusalem rebuilt until around 458 B.C. This occurred during about half a century under the direction of Ezra and Nehemiah.

Furthermore, Daniel was told by the angel that the 70 weeks of years would fall into three sections. The first part would last for 7 weeks of years; during this period Jerusalem would be rebuilt and streets and moats constructed. This would take place during the "troublous times" recorded in Ezra and Nehemiah.

The second section would consist of 62 weeks of years, i.e., 434 years. Added to the first 7 weeks of years, or 49 years, this became the "time unto the Messiah" (Daniel 9:25). Some translations do not translate the word, but render it as a name or title: Messiah.

If one calculates 483 years from the time of Ezra, one arrives at the time of Jesus. However, there is more. Daniel 9:26 reads: "After threescore and two weeks shall Messiah be cut off, but not for himself: and the people of the prince that shall come shall destroy the city and the sanctuary." Both of these prophecies were fulfilled. When Messiah came no earthly kingdom of glory was established; on the contrary, He was "cut off" (cf. Isaiah 53:8) and did not have any earthly dominion. The Jews expected a messiah who would deliver them from external enemies, but this astonishing prophecy prophesied that Messiah would die. After this Jerusalem and its temple were destroyed by the "people of the prince that shall come." This happened at the hands of a people not well known in Daniel's time.

Daniel 9:26 seems to suggest that an unknown interval of time would pass between the 69th and 70th weeks of years, as often happens in Biblical prophecies. This becomes even clearer in the light of fulfillment. This verse addresses two distinct events which will take place, not within the 69 weeks of years, but afterward. One event is the death of Messiah. The other is the destruction of Jerusalem upon the completion of the 69th week but before the 70th week begins. This demands a time lapse between the 69th and 70th weeks.

Concerning this indefinite time period it is further stated, "unto the end . . . desolations are determined" (Daniel 9:26). Nothing is said about how long this will last, but it will extend till the end, till the final 70th week. Then this will happen: "He shall confirm the covenant with many for one week: and in the midst of the week he shall cause the sacrifice and the oblation to cease, and for the overspreading of abominations he shall make it desolate, even until the consummation" (verse 27).

That sacrifice should be eliminated is always the word of a reprobate from Daniel's point of view. The last, ultimate enemy of God will be guilty of laying violent hands on what is holy. Further, we see from Daniel 12:11 that the elimination of the sacrifice and the erection of the abomination of desolation occur at the same time.

Jesus referred to Daniel's prophecy in His great eschatological discourse: "When ye therefore shall see the abomination of desolation, spoken of by Daniel the prophet, stand in the holy place, (whoso readeth, let him understand,) then let them which be in Judea flee into the mountains: . . . for then shall be great tribulation. . . . Immediately after the tribulation of those days shall the sun be darkened . . . and they shall see the Son of man coming in the clouds of heaven with power and great glory" (Matthew 24:15-30 [verses 15, 21, 29, 30]).

Daniel's prophecy places the erecting of the abomination of desolation in the center of the 70th week of years (Daniel 9:27). When Jesus recalled the prophecy of Daniel He stated that the abomination of desolation would take place in the end times, at the beginning of the Great Tribulation and immediately before the coming of the Son of Man with the clouds of heaven. Thus the 70th week of years must be part of the end times, the conclusion of this age. It is understandable how the final week of years becomes the time frame for the vision of the Book of Revelation of the Great Tribulation and the time of Antichrist. The Book of Daniel has already set the stage.

Interpreters differ as to how literally one should take the passages in question or what is meant by the cessation of the sacrifice, the abomination of desolation, etc. But most generally they agree that the 70th week of Daniel forms the chronological framework for interpreting Revelation.

## The Dragon

A central theme in Revelation is the triumph of the kingdom of God over the kingdom of Satan. The battle which will take place occurs on a universal, even cosmic, scale. Those evil powers suffering defeat are: (1) the dragon (chapter 12); (2) the beast (chapters 13, 19); and (3) the harlot (chapters 17, 18). An understanding of each of these three symbolic figures and their respective roles in the great drama of the end times is fundamental for interpreting Revelation.

The *dragon* is Satan (20:2). The *beast* and the *harlot* form a double symbol; they belong together but are not identical. These enemies of God represent two great powers of the end times. They both are figures who originate in history, but they are eschatological beings who do not manifest themselves fully until the end times. Revelation devotes a significant amount of space to describing these archenemies of the Kingdom. The beast stands in contrast to the Lamb, while the harlot Babylon is the antithesis to the Bride, the New Jerusalem.

The conflict between Michael and the dragon in 12:7f. reflects the spiritual and cosmic background for the battle fought on earth. Just as the story of Job can be understood only in light of Satan's role as accuser (Job 1, 2), the great battle of Revelation is intelligible only in light of Satan's role as the opponent of God. The personality of Satan, his interest in and relationship with humanity throughout history, is one of the most unexplained phenomena of our existence. Revelation, unlike any other book we possess, sheds some light on this powerful, mysterious enemy. His final, desperate battle and his ultimate judgment are told, and in chapter 12 Satan's past history is studied. Similarly, the emergence of the beast in history is recounted in 17:8-11.

The dragon is described as that "old serpent, called the Devil" (12:9). He was still in the heavens before he swept along with him a third of the stars of heaven and was cast to the earth. Some have pointed to Daniel 8:10 in this connection, which states that the small horn—Antiochus IV Epiphanes—threw some stars to the earth. The reference there was to the people of God. But it appears to have a different meaning in Revelation 12:4 where it appears as if a prophecy of the future and a prophecy of the past flow together, thus symbolizing the fall of the angels in sin. In his downfall the devil carried along a third of the multitudes of angels. In 9:1, 2 an angel is equated with a star. The Jews believed a fall had occurred among the angelic powers, and the New Testament confirms this. Peter, the apostle, wrote, "God spared not the angels that sinned" (2 Peter 2:4; cf. Jude verse 6). The devil led this rebellion. He is the Father of Lies and a murderer from the beginning (John 8:44). With him sin had its origin. The mystery of the dragon is the evil mystery of sin.

Two passages in the Old Testament seem to speak of Satan's fall. In each case figurative language, similar to that found in the messianic Psalms, is used. In these psalms there are passages which at first glimpse seem to refer to a Jewish king, but suddenly the image extends beyond this narrow frame and obviously refers to a greater personality. The two Scripture passages providing some background for understanding the devil are the taunting of the king of Babylon in Isaiah 14 and the eulogy sung of the king of Tyre in Ezekiel 28. The titles of the songs themselves reflect God's dual attitude toward sin. He mocks those who rise to question His almighty power (cf. Psalm 2:4). At the same time, however, He mourns over His lost and fallen creatures (cf. Genesis 6:6). In the song of the king of Babylon the subject is a brilliant star, the day star and son of the dawn, who ascends above the stars in an effort to make himself godlike. The song about the king of Tyre tells of one who was created as an "anointed," i.e., "princely," cherub and who lived in Eden. Again the discussion concerns one who wanted to be God (Ezekiel 28:2). In both Isaiah and Ezekiel the person or being in question will be humiliated or destroyed. One stage in this humiliation is witnessed by Revelation 12.

But this does not take place until the proper time. Sin must have its time of increase and maturity until eventually its true character will be disclosed before the entire cosmos. When the devil is cast down it will not be without a fight. This is somewhat strange, since God certainly did not have to fight with Satan in order to destroy his power. But apparently God is reluctant to use His divine power to crush the devil. Seemingly God instructs the angels to drive Satan from heaven. In this way the angels demonstrate convincingly their allegiance to either God or Satan.

Apparently the expulsion of the devil from heaven does not transpire until Satan is thoroughly exposed. The kingdom of the devil is the kingdom of the lie; his most important weapon is falsehood, and any progress he makes depends on deceit. That is why it is vital to expose his true character. The "unmasking" of Satan did not occur through God's divine omnipotence, but through the "weakness of God"—the cross of Christ (1 Corinthians 1:25). He who was the Son of God from all eternity humbled himself and became obedient, even unto dying on the cross (Philippians 2:8). The self-humiliation of Christ is a contrast to Satan's self-seeking. In the light of Christ's love and humility Satan's pride and hate are vividly exposed.

Christ's victory over the enemy is now visible, for "having spoiled principalities and powers, he made a show of them openly, triumphing over them in it" (Colossians 2:15). As the means of salvation, the Cross affects only humanity, for "he took not on him the nature of angels" (Hebrews 2:16). But as the revelation of the wisdom and nature of God, the cross of Christ has cosmic dimensions (Ephesians 1:10; 3:10). After Calvary Satan cannot have any hope of overthrowing the throne of God. His continuing to fight is only to revenge himself for his defeat and to drag as many as possible along with him in his fall.

The last stage of this ultimate battle is described in Revelation. The end times spoken of by Daniel the prophet are now at hand; the great prince of the angels, Michael will come to protect Israel (Daniel 12:1). The conflict between the angels of God and the fallen angels has gone on through the ages. Satan is prince of the powers of the air (Ephesians 2:2), and he has organized his "counter-kingdom" of sin. Satan is also called the "prince of this world" (John 14:30), indeed, even the "god of this world" (2 Corinthians 4:4). He seeks to build his own kingdom before God establishes His. The idea of an earthly kingdom without God is of satanic origin; it is an essential element in the strategy of the prince of the fallen angels. The earth is the last stronghold of Satan. For thousands of years Satan has sought to create his own totalitarian dominion over humanity. Just as the kingdom of God was present in seed form in Israel, so too, the kingdom of Antichrist has been latent in Israel's oppressors. Underlying these empires have been evil spiritual powers, Satan's "underlords" such as the prince of Persia or the prince of Greece (Daniel 10:20). When John in vision saw the dragon, the prince of evil spirits, he saw him with 7 heads and 10 horns (12:3). This corresponds precisely with the beast, who symbolizes the kingdom of the Antichrist. The 7 heads represent the 7 manifestations in history; the 10 horns stand for the 10 kings who will align themselves with Antichrist.

Even though Revelation does not reflect any fatalistic notion of history, what will occur on earth is seen as past in heaven. Moreover, each earthly event has its heavenly or spiritual counterpart. The last tremendous conflict will begin when Michael and his angels attack the dragon and his army of fallen angels. The dragon and his entire army will be overthrown. Satan will never again set foot in heaven; because of this the heavenly multitudes break out in praise. The downfall of Satan foreseen by Jesus (Luke 10:18) will occur in three stages. First, he will be thrown down from heaven to earth (12:9). Second, he will be cast into the abyss for a thousand years (20:3); and third he will be cast into the lake of fire (20:10).

John heard a voice telling the heavens to rejoice because of the demise of the dragon, but a pronouncement of woe was made over the inhabitants of the earth (12:12). There are two reasons for this. First, Satan will be restricted to earth, and he will concentrate all his efforts there. Secondly, knowing that his time is short, Satan will try to make the most of it. He will descend in great fury and intensify the persecution and great deception of the last days. He will select a willing human tool to carry out his attack on the kingdom of God: the beast, Antichrist; and the dragon will give him his power and dominion (13:2).

## The Beast

Even during the final battle, the devil apparently prefers to stay in the background. As he always has, he works through instruments. Actual contact with this fallen prince of the angels would undoubtedly frighten potential supporters. So, the devil must resort to deception and seduction. His final representative will be Antichrist.

In a number of texts Scripture foretells that in the last days a great and powerful opponent of God's ways will appear. Besides more isolated passages, there are three significant related prophecies that jointly provide a detailed picture of this strange person. Many titles are used. He is called the "man of sin," "the son of perdition" (2 Thessalonians 2:3), "the lawless one" (2 Thessalonians 2:8, NIV), the liar (1 John 2:22), the seducer and Antichrist (2 John 7), the beast, the first beast, the beast from the sea (Revelation 13:1, 4, 12), the beast from the abyss (Revelation 11:7), and so on. His most familiar title today is "Antichrist." This name is used four times in John's letters (1 John 2:18-22; 4:3; 2 John 7). Revelation calls him the "beast"; more precisely, the "wild beast." This expression is highly suitable for this prophetic book, since it can symbolize Antichrist as a person or his realm, just as any king is a symbol of his kingdom (cf. Daniel 2:38). The beast, therefore, is a person, and at the same time it represents the kingdom of Antichrist and the world throughout the ages. The various terms shed light on one another and together give a composite picture of what Scripture says about Antichrist.

## The Kingdom of the World Throughout the Ages

The kingdom of Antichrist has a historical background. It is the natural consequence of something that has evolved throughout history. It is the realization of the plan of the devil and the ambition of humanity to establish a world empire. But this dream will become a nightmare. It is a demonically inspired distortion of God's plan to rule all peoples under the kingship of Christ. It is reflected in every human effort to rule and govern the world apart from Christ.

The world imperialism differs significantly from a national government. While the "state" is legally obligated to maintain and ensure the liberty of its population, satanic dominion seeks to abolish the borders God has put between peoples and to put all nations under one rule (cf. Acts 17:26). Such rule is a perversion of ordinary government. It might be compared with a cancerous tumor which grows wildly. Demonically controlled empires have a cancer-like need to expand and conquer; their goal has always been to subjugate the entire world to their system; The demonic empire thus is not merely government in general.

To an even greater extent the kingdom of this world contrasts with the kingdom of God. The kingdom of the beast in the end times is a counter-kingdom to the kingdom of the Son of Man (Daniel 7:11-14), just as formerly world empires often contrasted with the theocracy of Israel. Here only those kingdoms which oppressed Israel are in view. The men God used to write the Scriptures were well aware there was more to the world than what their limited geographic knowledge told them. They knew of "kings from the east" (Revelation 16:12), and they knew there was a powerful kingdom in the north, which in the end times would attack restored Israel (Ezekiel 38:15). But these powers did not become of concern to them until their actions affected Israel. The earthly powers mentioned in Scripture which are forerunners of the kingdom of Antichrist are those kingdoms that have oppressed Israel, and only those. Daniel lists four: Babylon, Medo-Persia, Greece, and Rome (Daniel 2, 7). But Daniel was speaking prophetically about the future; he did not include Israel's former two oppressors, Egypt and Assyria (e.g., Isaiah 52:4).

Daniel's interpretation of Nebuchadnezzar's dream (chapter 2) and his own vision of the four beasts (chapter 7) are the basic ingredients of John's two visions of the beast (Revelation 13 and 17). Daniel spoke of four kingdoms that would appear one by one. In the dream of Nebuchadnezzar different metals symbolized the different powers. Daniel saw a lion, a bear, a leopard, and a beast with teeth of iron, claws of copper, and horns. The first beast, the lion, corresponded to the head of gold on the statue; it symbolized the kingdom of Babylon (Daniel 2:38). The bear corresponded to the silver breastplate and symbolized the Medo-Persian kingdom. It seems from many places in Daniel that the Medes and Persians were not two separate kingdoms but the second in the list. Daniel 5:28: "Thy kingdom is divided, and given to the Medes and Persians"; and Daniel 8:20 (cf. verse 3): "The ram which thou sawest having two horns are the kings of Media and Persia." This is corroborated by history. Media never single-handedly overthrew the kingdom of Babylon. The king of Persia, Cyrus, an ally of Media, conquered Babylon.

The third beast Daniel saw was a leopard with four heads. This corresponded to the copper belly and thighs on the statue of Nebuchadnezzar and represented the Greek kingdom, i.e., Alexander and his successors. Scripture verifies that these are likewise one and the same kingdom: The leopard had four heads, which showed the Greek empire would have four independent kingdoms (Daniel 7:6). The identical imagery is used in chapter 8 where the Greek empire is symbolized by a ram. First, the ram had one horn that stood for the first king, i.e., Alexander the Great (verses 5 and 21). This horn was broken off and four others grew up.

This meant that "four kingdoms shall stand up out of the nation" (verse 22). This was therefore still the Greek empire, even though now it is divided into parts (cf. the fourth kingdom which is divided into 10 parts; Daniel 2:41-44; 7:24). The Greco-Syrian empire of Antiochus IV Epiphanes belonged to the third world empire and was the extension of the Greek empire.

The fourth world empire in Daniel's vision was the Roman empire. Daniel's vision involved four world empires; the last, most powerful, and most terrible of these would "devour the whole earth" (Daniel 7:23). This statement cannot apply to the Greco-Syrian empire, which was insignificant in comparison to the former world powers. However, it does apply to Rome, and very aptly. Rome surpassed the former world kingdoms in power, domain, and duration. Furthermore, the Greco-Syrian empire did not manifest "ten horns," or "ten kings," but only four (Daniel 8:8). On the other hand, the 10 horns of the beast mentioned in John's vision do stand for the Roman empire. There the 10 horns are said to belong to the future (Revelation 17:12). In addition, this explicitly confirms that the fourth kingdom of Daniel would be the last of the world empires. It will be crushed by divine intervention, "without hands" (Daniel 2:34), at the coming of the Son of Man. Immediately it will be replaced by the kingdom of the Son of Man (Daniel 7:9-14), the eternal kingdom of God (Daniel 2:44). Nothing even remotely like this applies to the Greco-Syrian empire; in fact, it was conquered and succeeded by Rome. But the Book of Revelation foretells the same fate that befell the *fourth* kingdom of Daniel awaits the beast's empire rule by Antichrist. Antichrist and his kingdom will be destroyed at the return of Christ and replaced by the kingdom over which Christ will reign (Revelation 19-22).

The logical deduction from all this is that the beast with 10 horns in Daniel—the fourth beast in the list in chapter 7—must represent the Roman empire. In Revelation 13 and 17 this empire is symbolized by the beast with 10 horns. This concerns not merely likeness but identity. The fact is further substantiated by the fact that the small horn signifying Antichrist springs up from among the 10 horns on the fourth beast of Daniel. Moreover, the beast seen by John is thoroughly shaped by his predecessors and is a composite of the four beasts of Daniel. It resembles a leopard (the Greek empire). Its feet are like the bear (the Medo-Persian empire), and its mouth is like the lion's (the Babylonian empire). It is noteworthy that these three characteristics are listed in reverse order from the list in Daniel. It is as if the prophet and the apostle each saw the beast from a different side. Daniel lived during the time of the first beasts, during the

Babylonian captivity and Medo-Persian empire, and he anticipated the future. John lived in the time of the fourth beast, during the Roman empire; in this respect he looked backwards.

Thus, Daniel, and apparently the Book of Revelation, present the Roman empire as the kingdom of Antichrist. Until the Lord comes and establishes the kingdom of God, this empire will remain unchallenged. But this poses the problem of reconciling certain facts with the survival of the fourth kingdom of Daniel until the consummation of the world. Daniel 2:41-43 states that this kingdom will be "partly broken." It will be divided: "they shall not cleave one to another." This likewise conforms with later history. The Roman empire has not existed intact since its dominion in antiquity. But while Rome was still at its zenith, John foresaw this division. The angel spoke to him of the beast that "was," and "is not," and "yet is" (17:8). The solution to that enigmatic statement is tied to the seven heads of the beast (17:9-12). The heads symbolize seven kings. Five have fallen, the sixth is now, and the seventh is not yet begun. When the seventh comes he will only last a short time.

Some have tried to explain the seven heads of the beast as seven successive forms of the government or emperors of the Roman empire. Others have equated the 10 horns with the number of Gothic tribes which later overran the Romans. The most obvious answer is that none of these answers would have ever been offered apart from someone's trying to equate certain prophecies with historical events.

The seven heads of the beast are only a counterpart to the heads of the dragon. This involves something spiritual and closely tied to the nature of the beast itself. Since it is specifically stated that there are seven kings, and since kings are depicted as representatives of their kingdoms (Daniel 2:38), it seems logical to conclude that this refers to the various manifestations of those empires in history that oppressed Israel: Egypt, Assyria, Babylon, Medo-Persia, and Greece are the five which have fallen. Rome was the sixth kingdom in existence when John received his revelation; it would soon collapse. The seventh kingdom is a kingdom which will appear for a brief period of time. The eighth king is Antichrist and his rule. Because the eighth kingdom comes from the seventh, it probably means that he will come from the shortlived empire of the last days, which is depicted by the seventh head of the beast. Antichrist will assume dominion over this kingdom and transform it into his own domain. But since Daniel 7:8 and 24 clearly depict the little horn, Antichrist, as springing up among the 10 horns on the fourth beast, this shows that the kingdom of the end times—symbolized by the seventh head of the beast—is

the revived Roman empire: the beast which "was, and is not" will return.

This seems to be the most natural exegesis of these difficult Scripture passages and the most likely resolution of this mysterious puzzle. Whether this should be understood as some kind of literally resurrected Roman empire or something else is disputed. Nonetheless, many think this is exactly what will occur. Perhaps this anticipates ultimate manifestation of evil—Antichrist. In any case, the beast is more than a resurrection of ancient Rome, a point which almost all concede. The kingdom of Antichrist will become a cruel terror reaching far beyond the confines of ancient Rome. Furthermore, it will differ greatly from the revived Rome from which it evolves.

Whatever position one adopts concerning the restoration of the Roman empire in a geographic sense—and is this really all that unimaginable?—most interpreters probably would agree that the end-time reign of Antichrist is the ultimate form of that world empire which has appeared repeatedly throughout history. The theory that the Roman empire will be reestablished goes back a long way. The first proponent of this view may have been Hippolytus (ca. A.D. 160-235), who lived in Rome and was accepted by some as the bishop of Rome. He was one of the foremost theologians of his age and was the author of, among other writings, *"Treatise on Christ and Antichrist."* He predicted the Roman empire would perish but be revived. The revived Roman kingdom which he foresaw, would be divided into 10 kingdoms, and from one of these Antichrist would emerge. It is also interesting to note that Hippolytus maintained that there is an interval between the 69th and 70th weeks of Daniel 9:26, 27. He saw the 70th week as belonging to the end times immediately before the return of Christ.

The beast in Revelation 13 and 17 represents a person as well as a kingdom; a spirit as well as a system (cf. 1 John 4:3). This system is realized more or less in all the kingdoms of the world; ultimately, however, it will adopt its final form in the regime of Antichrist, who will organize all of humanity to battle God (16:13, 14), and who will deceive them into worshiping Satan and the beast (13:4, 14, 15). Only those who are led astray into this brotherhood of the devil and are marked with the mark of the beast on their foreheads will be allowed to buy and sell and to earn a living.

At the head of this system will be a person who encapsulates in himself all the apostasy, cruelty, and ungodliness the world has ever known. Before exploring more closely what Scripture has to say about this mysterious person, it may prove beneficial to examine the history of the interpretation of Antichrist.

## The History of Interpretation

Both Paul and John in their preaching and teaching reflect early Christianity's concern with Antichrist. Paul reminded his friends in Thessalonica that he had told them about the "man of sin," the "son of perdition," when he stayed with them (2 Thessalonians 2:3-5). John reminded his readers that they had "heard that antichrist shall come" (1 John 2:18). Actually, the apostles picked up on an ancient Jewish apocalyptic tradition. Judaism knew from the Old Testament that an "anti-Messiah" would appear. It is striking that the Psalms of Solomon, perhaps written around the year 60 B.C., identify Pompey, the commander of the Roman army, as an "anti-Messiah."

Thus, very early on, the Church was concerned about the identity of Antichrist. Before the New Testament canon was completed two Roman emperors had been identified as Antichrist: Caligula and Nero. Caligula planned to erect an image of himself in the temple in Jerusalem. This is precisely what Antiochus IV Epiphanes did. It was therefore an "obvious" reference to the prophecies of Daniel and to the words of Jesus concerning the abomination of desolation that would stand in the Holy Place. Even more thought that Nero was Antichrist. When that tyrant committed suicide, rumors began that he was not really dead but had fled to Asia and would return with a great army. Several arose pretending to be this "pseudo-Nero," but none were successful. After the time of what would have been his natural life span had passed, the legend became that Nero would rise from the dead. This thought is perhaps reflected in the *Ascension of Isaiah.* The legend of a Nero Redivivus (Nero revived), persisted for centuries, even until the time of Augustine, some 300 years later. The legend of Nero's return did not stem from Christian speculation but from the general populace, but it did have some effect on the Church.

Some of the early Christian writings contain references to the Antichrist. The *Epistle of Barnabas* claims that the Roman empire is the fourth in Daniel's series of visions and that it will be followed by 10 kingdoms. Antichrist was believed to come from one of these. *Irenaeus* thought Antichrist would be a Jew from the tribe of Dan. He appealed to Jeremiah 8:16 and to the fact that the tribe of Dan is not mentioned in the list in Revelation 7:4-8. A Jewish Midrash (interpretation) on Genesis 49:14-17 declares that from Dan darkness will spread over the earth. In spite of Irenaeus' belief that Antichrist would be a Jew, he strangely thought the number of the beast equalled *Lateinos,* "Latin" or "the Latin." *Tertullian* thought that Antichrist would appear very soon, but in his opinion he did not have to be a Jew. *Cyprian* also thought that the time of Antichrist was near. He wrote to priests and encouraged them that although Antichrist was coming, so too was Christ.

*Victorinus,* a bishop, was among the first systematic interpreters of the Book of Revelation. Fragments of his works show he felt Antichrist would be one of the Roman emperors. *Athanasius* and *Hilarius,* both strong defenders of the doctrine of the Trinity, regarded Antichrist more as the "seducer, deceiver." They perceived his forerunners as being within the Church. Athanasius stamped Emperor Constantine as a forerunner of Antichrist and thought he was the little horn of the Book of Daniel. *Jerome* preached that the breaking up of the Roman empire signaled the time of Antichrist was close at hand.

Throughout the Middle Ages the study of Antichrist was greatly influenced by two highly speculative propheticlike documents, *Tiburtine* from the Fourth Century and the so-called *Pseudo-Methodius* from the Seventh Century. The court official *Adso's* small essay on Antichrist, written around 954 and which incorporated the first of these two "oracles," also had a tremendous impact on thought in the Middle Ages. Despite the lack of Biblical substance and their deliberate attempts to deceive, they enjoyed great success. With the invention of the printing press they were among the first printed materials.

By that time, however, another view had emerged, especially in pre-Reformation piety groups. With the deep decline of the Church and the papal persecution of believers, many concluded the Antichrist was none other than the pope. The Reformers adopted this viewpoint, and in Protestant circles it was a dominant theory for a long time. (See section on chapter 17.)

It might be tempting to hold up to ridicule early interpreters of prophecy whose guesses as to the identity of Antichrist long since have been proved impossible. But it should not be forgotten that many of these theories had some valid elements. There have been many antichrists, although the final Antichrist has not yet appeared. The spirit of Antichrist is woven in and out of the fabric of human history.

## The Kingdom and Person of Antichrist

Some might be surprised that Antichrist should receive any attention at all. Some may think that such a topic of study is tasteless sensationalism. However, Antichrist plays a significant role in the drama of Biblical revelation of the end times. Apparently those whom God used to write the Scriptures themselves were interested in the last world empire and its strange emperor. Daniel wanted to know the "truth" of all this (Daniel 7:16), and as mentioned above, the end times formed one aspect of apostolic preaching. Obviously it is wrong to be indifferent to something that receives such serious consideration both in the Old and New Testaments. The significance of the subject is highlighted by the solemn "if any man has an ear, let him hear" (Revelation 13:9). How do people avoid being deceived? Or how do they survive the life-threatening persecutions unless they heed the prophetic admonition?

A precise survey of what the Scripture has to say about Antichrist, his kingdom, and his effect is truly significant for understanding Revelation. Below will be a sketch of the larger picture.

## (1) The Kingdom of Antichrist

The king and his kingdom are symbolized by the same beast. Antichrist and his domain cannot be separated. Nebuchadnezzar the king and Babylon were one (Daniel 2:38). Louis XIV, king of France, is alleged to have said, "I am France!" To an even larger extent this applies to Antichrist and his kingdom. Daniel 7:8 shows the Antichrist as one of the horns of the beast. Revelation 13:3 portrays him as one of the *heads of the beast,* but in later verses he is referred to as the *beast itself* (verse 4).

It is remarkable that one verse can speak of the seven heads (plural) of the beast and in the next verse refer to the "mouth" (singular) of the beast. But this shows that only one head was in power during the time of the vision: Antichrist and his kingdom. The kingdom of the beast will be the manifestation of what the former world empires only attempted; the kingdom of this world contrasts with the kingdom of the Son of Man. The kingdom of Antichrist will be the sum of all previous earthly empires. It will be the ultimate, final world empire, and it will be governed by the ultimate dictator—Antichrist. It will have the splendor of the statue (Daniel 2:31), and the horror of the beast (Daniel 7:7). The cruelty which sometimes lay hidden in previous world empires will be concentrated and disclosed fully (cf. Matthew 4:8). Just as the kingdom of God was present in its King, Jesus Christ, the kingdom of the beast will be realized in Antichrist. Here worship of the state, worship of man, and worship of Satan will come together; a world dictatorship will merge with a world religion.

## (2) The Person of Antichrist

The kingdom of this age will come under the authority of one political leader, who at the height of his career will obtain power unlike anyone before him. The beast represents a literal person, not a personification of some figurative, abstract world power; he is the "prince that shall come" (Daniel 9:26) in the last days. The Greek describes the beast in masculine terms: they "shall worship *him*" (13:8). This also implies that Antichrist should not be regarded as some supernatural being or some

physical incarnation of Satan. He is the "man of sin" (2 Thessalonians 2:3). This expresses the potential for sin that is intrinsic to the fallen human nature. If one speaks of a satanic incarnation, it is one in an already existing individual, such as when Satan entered into Judas Iscariot (John 13:27).

Prior to Antichrist's full manifestation, he almost certainly will be recognized as uniquely talented and skilled in leadership. One might question how someone so controlled by evil could have any depth of personality. If one draws his portrait based on his Old Testament era model, Antiochus IV Epiphanes, then he appears as a despicable and horrible man (Daniel 11:21): "In the latter time . . . a king of fierce countenance, and understanding dark sentences, shall stand up" (Daniel 8:23). He may be wise, but it is an evil wisdom (cf. James 3:15) which will express itself in cunning and deceit (Daniel 8:25; 11:23). In the area of religion he will be a "deceiver" (2 John 7) and a "liar" (1 John 2:22). The lie will be part of his arsenal (2 Thessalonians 2:9), and as the beast he will not hold back any of his evil, cruel power in accomplishing his goals (Revelation 13).

Two descriptions of Antichrist recur: his self-exaltation and his blasphemy. Like Antiochus Epiphanes he will "magnify himself in his heart" (Daniel 8:25); "he shall exalt himself, and magnify himself above every god, . . . he shall magnify himself above all" (Daniel 11:36, 37). Paul reiterated this with his warning that he "exalteth himself above all that is called God, or that is worshipped; so that he as God sitteth in the temple of God, showing himself that he is God" (2 Thessalonians 2:4). Antichrist will be blasphemous in word as well as deed. His type of blasphemy will resemble the kind of blasphemy of which Jesus was unjustly accused when He announced His messianic authority (Matthew 26:63-65) and equated himself with God (John 10:33). Jesus' claim was divine and true; Antichrist's will be satanic and false. The devil's desire to make himself equal to God will reside in Antichrist.

Nonetheless, it is noteworthy that the heads of the beast carry the names of blasphemy, not the heads of the dragon (12:3; 13:1). The beast, not the dragon, opens its mouth to blaspheme God. The devil, knowing God's power, trembles (James 2:19); he would not dare blaspheme openly. But the ignorant "brute beasts" of humanity blaspheme what they do not know (Jude 10). The comment that the heads of the beast have the name of blasphemy are a reminder that the heads represent those empires in which the emperor was revered as god and allegiance to the state was demanded and received. But the beast in 17:3 has the name of blasphemy all over his body; the kingdom of Antichrist will be even more blasphemous than its predecessors. Blasphemy will lie at the very root of Antichrist's nature; human arrogance will be joined with satanic pride.

Of the blasphemous and arrogant men of the last days, he is best characterized by his great oratory skill (Daniel 7:8, 11, 20). He will speak against the Most High (Daniel 7:25), and he "shall speak marvelous things against the God of gods" (Daniel 11:36). He will blaspheme God, His name, and His dwelling place; he will blaspheme those dwelling in heaven, angels, and men (Revelation 13:6). Those who follow Antichrist and his followers will all blaspheme (16:9, 11, 21). The God against whom no charge can be brought will allow this accusation to continue for 42 months (13:5).

Coinciding with the escalation of his attacks against God, Antichrist will increase his allegiance to Satan. As the viceregent of the devil, he will be chosen by the dragon to rule his earthly domain and to exercise his awful power. But Antichrist must pay for this by totally succumbing to Satan's authority. What Jesus refused on the Mount of Temptation—the kingdoms of this world and their glory—the "man of sin" will wholeheartedly accept (cf. Matthew 4:9ff.).

### (3) Why Does Antichrist Come?

Why does Antichrist come? Why does such an evil, godless person even have such an opportunity to lead humanity into such eternal destruction? This is a serious question needing careful reflection.

### (a) Antichrist Will Be the Choice of Humanity

Human beings receive what they choose. The kingdom offered by Antichrist will be the ideal kingdom of fallen and sinful men and women. They will prefer this to the lordship of Jesus Christ. Moreover, the world will be enticed by Antichrist because he will seem to be the only escape from a desperate situation. It will become increasingly apparent that mankind cannot control its world, that it is not the master of its own fate. The world desperately seeks a leader to control the chaos and resolve the world's problems. The fallen world relies only on human power to solve its problems, and when the time is right for a human leader like Antichrist to take control, he will become the symbol of humanity's self-worship and self-reliance.

### (b) Antichrist Will Be the Representative of the Dragon

Antichrist represents the last ditch effort of the devil to prevent the establishment of the kingdom of God. He will deceive humanity into worshiping and swearing allegiance to the devil. He is the key to the devil's plan, and he will be a special instrument for his closing moments (12:12).

### (c) Antichrist Represents a Judgment of God

No less than six times Revelation 13 says "there was given" (*edothē*) power to the first beast (verses 5, 7) or to the second beast (verses 14, 15). Despite the beast's having been equipped with the power of the dragon, he will be unable to do anything unless God allows it (cf. John 19:11). Antichrist can do his work only within the parameters and time limits imposed by God. This should comfort the persecuted people of God. But it also reflects God's just judgment on the earth; His instruments of judgment will be assigned their duties (cf. 6:2, 4, 8). God will give cruelty free rein so that it might render its own punishment. Indeed, God will permit it such latitude that He will allow Antichrist to set up his empire so Satan can make his offer to humanity.

### (4) Where Does Antichrist Come From?

Antichrist has a dual origin. One is human, historical; the other is spiritual. The first is from the "sea"; the second from the "pit." John described the beast as it ascended from the sea: first the horns, then the heads, and finally the body (13:1). The text is a glance backward at Daniel 7:1ff. where Daniel saw the four world empires emerging from the sea in the form of four beasts. The sea in antiquity was regarded as dangerous and unstable. As elsewhere in Scripture, here the sea is an image of the restless, anxious peoples of the world (Isaiah 17:12; 57:20; Jeremiah 6:22, 23; Luke 21:25). The political and social unrest of the multitudes of the earth will form the backdrop for the entrance of Antichrist. Since the sea and the beasts which emerge from it represent Gentile kingdoms, it most likely means that Antichrist will not be Jewish but Gentile. From Daniel 7:8 it seems that Antichrist will come from the fourth beast. He will not be one of the 10 kings represented by the 10 horns but the single, "little" horn which grows among the 10. The word "little" does not refer to his personality but to his political power. This suggests Antichrist will come on the scene as a relatively insignificant power or political leader in the domain of the fourth beast. Apparently this will be the first human appearance of Antichrist.

Antichrist's reign as a world dictator apparently will begin when he ascends from the abyss. This is a reference to his spiritual origins as the "son of perdition" (2 Thessalonians 2:3). This appearance is called a "revelation" in this passage; it is a manifestation of the diabolic character of his person and rule. The expression "son of perdition" is a Hebraism similar, for example, to "children of darkness."

## (5) How Does Antichrist Appear?

Antichrist will emerge as a political and military leader and religious deceiver. A characteristic feature of the end times before the Tribulation will be a false sense of security among the people. "When they shall say, Peace and safety; then sudden destruction cometh upon them" (1 Thessalonians 5:3). Antichrist will probably be behind this false sense of peace and safety. The world desperately needs peace and will readily welcome anyone who can create order in a hopelessly chaotic situation. But the new world "emperor" will actually be a military despot who worships the gods of power (Daniel 11:38). Paradoxically, Antichrist will gain world dominion through two avenues: war and peace.

A peculiar feature of Antiochus IV Epiphanes, the Old Testament prototype of Antichrist, is that he gained authority only over a few (Daniel 11:23). With the emergence of Antichrist, the potential to rule millions, indeed billions, of people will become a reality. The military leader who is cruel enough to employ the weapons of fear and terrorism at his disposal does not need any great armies to conquer an opponent. A large army can even become a handicap. To speak of peace and then threaten war is an ancient and widely used tactic.

In addition to diplomatic cunning and military might, Antichrist will use religious pressure, one of the most powerful weapons in human existence, to obtain his goals. Although misleading and perverted, it does exist and affects men and women everywhere. Antichrist will exploit his religious power; he will ally himself with Babylon the prostitute. Next he will delegate power to the false prophet who will be more like a minister of religious affairs and propaganda. Antichrist himself will become a religious figure who will unite the world under one world religion.

## (6) When Will Antichrist Come?

Do we know anything about when Antichrist will appear? To some extent, yes; it is possible to locate Antichrist within the scheme of the end times.

### (a) The Spirit of Antichrist

Just as the Spirit of Christ anticipated through the Old Testament prophets the coming of Christ (1 Peter 1:11), the spirit of Antichrist will incite the apostasy which will prompt the coming of Antichrist (1 John 4:3). Any revolution needs a time of preparation. Epoch-making events of the end times may seem to occur without notice, but actually they will be the result of lengthy, unobserved planning and development. The rule of Antichrist can only be possible in a morally and religiously corrupt society. Paul put it this way: "That day shall not come, except there come a falling away first,

and that man of sin be revealed" (2 Thessalonians 2:3). Antichrist will emerge out of the apostasy and will himself be the culmination of that backsliding. The spirit of Antichrist will precede his actual coming.

### (b) Many Antichrists

During the apostolic period antichrists had already begun to appear (1 John 2:18). Antichrists have always been present, but the last days will be especially characterized by the appearance of false prophets and false christs (Mark 13:22). There are two types of antichrists: religious and political. The many antichrists are a prelude and warning, leading to the last great Antichrist.

### (c) The Dragon

Satan will not hand over his authority and rule to Antichrist until after he has been vanquished in the heavenly realms and thrown down to earth. Never before has Satan—the dragon—handed his power over to a human being. This is his last desperate attempt to avoid his ultimate defeat in the spiritual realm. Because the devil will be denied access to heaven he will no longer be able to accuse God's saints before Him. A radical and wonderful change will occur in the conditions for God's people. Some think that this can occur only after the close of the Church period. At this point in time Satan raises up Antichrist as the last great persecutor of the saints.

### (d) The 10 Horns

As was previously noted, the "little horn" sprang up amid the 10 horns on the fourth beast of Daniel. These 10 horns were also part of John's vision of the beast. The 10 horns are said to be 10 kings. Thus Antichrist will be a somewhat later contemporary who will seize power. First will come the 10 horns and then the little horn.

### (e) The Progress of the World

The kingdom of Antichrist will be universal. He will exert authority over "all kindreds, and tongues, and nations" (13:7). At the same time, his kingdom is said to be limited in duration to 42 months (13:5). An empire such as his would only be possible in a world with modern means of communication and transportation. In ancient times the most remote countries would have never even heard of Antichrist before his time of reign was past. To use an expression not commonly found in theological discussions, it would be "technically impossible" for the prophecies of the Book of Revelation to be fulfilled prior to the development of modern technology.

### (f) That Which Restrains

When apparently questioned about why Antichrist had not appeared, Paul responded that something "restrained," "hindered," his coming.

"And now ye know what withholdeth that he might be revealed in his time. For the mystery of iniquity doth already work: only he who now letteth will let, until he be taken out of the way" (2 Thessalonians 2:6, 7). In verse 6 the subject of "withholdeth" is "what," a neuter which would ordinarily be understood as some abstract principle or force. However, in verse 6 the subject of "letteth" is "he," a masculine form which is ordinarily taken to mean a person. Paul had explained to the Thessalonians in person what he meant, so they knew what "withholdeth" Antichrist. But Christians of later times have not been privy to such information, which has resulted in great consternation. The various opinions can probably be reduced to two. One view contends that the "withholding" force is the civil authority which prevents lawlessness. The other interpretation argues that it is the influence of the Holy Spirit who restrains lawlessness and thus prevents the appearance of "the lawless one."

## The False Prophet

Antichrist will have coworkers. Early on he will seemingly join forces with the great prostitute (17:3). In addition he will work closely with the 10 kings under him who will champion his views totally and put their power and influence fully at his disposal (17:13). Antichrist will cooperate most intimately with the false prophet, who in chapter 13 is called the "second beast." The unity that will prevail between these two is rather unique for two representatives of evil. They will be united in hatred of God and His people. The false prophet will receive all his power from Antichrist (13:12) as the beast will receive its authority from the dragon (13:2). Therefore, the false prophet will be the assistant and servant of Antichrist. He apparently will not have any personal ambitions but will devote his entire attention to making men worship Antichrist.

### (1) His Personality

Revelation 13 portrays the false prophet as a beast coming up from the earth. This "second beast" displays none of the terrifying traits of the "first beast." It has two horns, but they are like the horns of a lamb. Such a gentle and innocent appearance, though, is a trick, because it speaks like a dragon. The lamb and the dragon are ordinarily symbols of Christ and the devil (respectively) in Revelation. Perhaps the use of the lamb here may be to indicate that the false prophet will appear in a form like Christ. He looks like Christ but is like Satan.

Jesus warned against false prophets and false christs, who were certain to come in the last days (Matthew 24:5, 11; 24:24). The false prophet, despite his appearance as a lamb, is actually a beast (*thērion*), who is just as bloodthirsty and cruel as the first beast. The false prophet will carry out the execution of those who fail to worship the image of the beast and those who do not take the mark of the beast in order to buy and sell.

### (2) His Prophetic Message

That he speaks like a dragon indicates that he brings the message of Satan. Throughout history false prophets have been among the main tools of the devil. The devil led humanity into the darkness of idolatry through false prophets; he led Israel astray through them; and he infiltrates churches in false prophecy. False prophecy will reach its climax in the second beast, the coworker of Antichrist.

The false prophet will appear as the only and ultimate authority in religious matters. He will represent the climax of human philosophy, and he will be a spokesperson for the supernatural demonic forces that infiltrate as teachers (1 Timothy 4:1). Therefore, he will gain total control over men's faith and thought; this is precisely the goal of the dragon.

The authority over the hearts and minds of mankind is solely for the purpose of exalting Antichrist, for proclaiming a man as God, and for making an entire world kneel in worship to him. The false prophet will have only one message; as the Christians preach only Christ, he will preach only Antichrist.

### (3) His Miracles

His message will be confirmed by miracles. He will call down fire from heaven "in the sight of men" (13:13). Even before Antichrist makes his entrance signs and wonders will prepare the way for his acceptance by the people. "Even him, whose coming is after the working of Satan with all power and signs and lying wonders" (2 Thessalonians 2:9). "Lying wonders" does not mean these are not actually miracles; that would only be trickery; these are actual wonders worked to support the lie itself. Miracles are not always necessarily performed through God's power. The divine and the satanic both belong to a supernatural order of reality that cannot be explained in human terms.

Throughout history both the kingdom of God and the actions of Satan have manifested themselves in supernatural activity. When God empowered Moses to work great wonders in order to instill the Israelites with faith (Exodus 4:8), the magicians of Egypt competed with him (Exodus 7:11, 22; 8:7). God warned His people about the miracles of the false prophets (Deuteronomy 13:1-5). Obviously God has limited Satan's activity on earth, but in the end times Satan will employ *"all power and signs and lying wonders."* "For there shall arise false Christs, and false prophets, and shall show great signs and wonders; insomuch that, if it were possible, they shall deceive the very elect" (Matthew 24:24). And the greatest of these lying wonderworkers will be known as the false prophet.

The Bible does not record the miracles performed by the false prophet, but it provides a couple of examples. It states that he makes fire come down out of heaven in the sight of men (13:13). This is reminiscent of Elijah's contest with the prophets of Baal on Mount Carmel, when he proposed that the one who answered by fire should be regarded as the true God (1 Kings 18:24f.).

Shortly before speaking of the false prophet, the Book of Revelation records how God's two witnesses perform a similar sign (Revelation 11:5, cf. 2 Kings 1:10). When the people refuse to repent in spite of the miracle demonstrated by the two witnesses, God permits the false prophet to imitate the divine sign and perform the miracle He had not allowed Baal's prophets to perform. And men who rejected the miracles of God will accept the miracles of the devil.

## The Image of the Beast

The false prophet performs another miracle. At the instruction of the false prophet "an image to the beast, which had the wound by a sword, and did live" is made (13:14), and the image comes alive (verse 15). This is an imitation of the miracle of creation. Man now claims he can do that of which only God is capable: to create life. The image is given spirit (*pneuma*). Unlike false idols of the past, which "have mouths, but they speak not" (Psalm 115:5), this idol will even be able to speak. Giving life (literally: spirit) to an inanimate image seems to be the false prophet's most spectacular feat.

The beast's image plays an important part in the description of the time of Antichrist. Daniel the prophet wrote of the erection of the "abomination that maketh desolate" (Daniel 12:11; cf. 9:27). Jesus himself explicitly said that this belongs to the end time (Matthew 24:15ff.). The erection of the image will mark the beginning of the Great Tribulation. Statues of emperors were well known in antiquity. Daniel 3 tells of Nebuchadnezzar's making an image of gold which he commanded his subjects to worship. Roman emperors, likewise, demanded worship; Christians were martyred because they refused to sacrifice or burn incense to the image of the emperor. In the end times the cultic practices of idolatry will be revived, and Satan's desire for worship will be given to Antichrist. Worshiping him will not be an option; those who refuse to worship the beast will pay with their lives.

## The Mark and Number of the Beast

The kingdom of the beast will be characterized by its totalitarian rule. This demand for total obedience to the state will result in social and religious slavery. Ultimate and total submission will be required from all; "all" (13:16), regardless of their social status, will be required to be "marked" with the "brand" of their owner—the beast. This is reminiscent of the time when slaves were marked with the names of their master, or when soldiers put the name of their commander on their bodies.

The mark of the beast will be a religious symbol. Because the mark will be visible, it will be a public declaration that one belongs to Antichrist and that one is a member of his devilish brotherhood. No room for remaining neutral will exist. It is a well calculated part of Antichrist's plan that he should choose the number *666* as a mark. Secret believers will not dare to take a mark which is mentioned in the Scripture, and this will eliminate any pretenders; all opposition will be brought to light. Scripture passionately describes the judgment that will come upon those who take the mark of the beast (14:9-13).

Those refusing to take the mark of the beast will be excluded from society. They will not be allowed either to buy or sell, even to sustain their lives. This suggests that some kind of universal boycott on those without the mark will be enforced; that would demand some kind of world economy. Today there are many organizations having the power to force whole societies "to their knees." Under the rule of Antichrist all such power will be under the control of the government; all personal liberty will cease.

The mark of the beast will consist of the name of the beast or the number of its name. A name can be translated into numbers since different alphabets have different numeric values. By adding up the sum of the numeric values of the numbers of the letters in a name one gets the number of that name. When Revelation was written it was quite common to use the number of a name if one wished to keep it a secret. Examples of this practice have been recovered in excavations at Pompeii. If a name was known, its numeric value was quite easy to figure out. On the other hand, if the name was not known, finding the name behind a sum of numbers could be difficult, if not impossible. The number of the beast, therefore, is given not for identification purposes, but for affirmation. When Antichrist appears and makes his name known, the number of the beast will confirm who he is.

From this it follows that it is impossible to discover beforehand the name behind the number of the beast. There are numerous strange instances in history where appearances of antichrists have been associated with the number *666*. At the same time there have been times when such speculation was farfetched and contrived.

## The Career of Antichrist

Chronologically arranging what Scripture says about the plight of Antichrist is difficult. Opinions, as usual, are diverse. Nonetheless, a summary of the prominent ideas should prove valuable for those wishing to become somewhat familiar with the issue.

Antichrist's activity seems to be divided into two distinct periods corresponding to the time frame in Revelation based on Daniel's 70th week of years. During the first of the 7-year periods, which may be even before this "week," Antichrist seems to be involved in what might be termed his period of normal human activity and development.

His path to power during this time is more closely depicted in Daniel. At first he will emerge among the 10 kings as a small political force. Then, conquering 3 of the 10 kings, he will become more and more powerful, until eventually his power will exceed the others (Daniel 7:8; 7:20-24).

When Revelation picks up the story, Antichrist is depicted as the leader of the seventh world empire, symbolized by the seventh head of the beast. The great harlot, Babylon, is seen riding on the back of the beast (13:1f.; 17:4, 9-11). But then one of the heads of the beast is mortally wounded (13:3). This may have both a personal and corporate impact. Both Antichrist the man and his evil empire are mortally wounded, but the larger context of chapter 13 suggests a person. When 13:14 says Antichrist is injured by the sword, it probably means the wound was received in a battle with his enemies. There is a strange parallelism between the beast and the Lamb. When the issue concerns the head of the mortally wounded beast the original text employs the same word used for the Lamb slain (13:8; cf. 5:6). The word translated in 13:14 as "did live" is also the same Greek word (*ezēsen*) which in chapter 20:4 is translated "lived." Thus it might seem as if the mortal wound and reviving of Antichrist is an imitation of the death and resurrection of Jesus.

The spectacular healing of the mortal wound seems to be of the utmost significance since it is mentioned three times in this chapter (verses 3, 12, 14). Satan does everything possible to downplay Jesus' sacrifice as unique. The beast can also claim, "I was dead, but I am alive" (1:18). Because of His obedience unto death, and His subsequent resurrection, Christ stands as the omnipotent head of all creation, worthy of all honor and blessing. Heaven's song will be to the Lamb who was slain. Antichrist will be only an imitation of Christ; but if this view is correct he will claim honor because he will die and then live again (Seiss, pp. 337-339).

If such an understanding is correct, the statement that Antichrist is the beast which comes from the pit (11:7; 17:8) and Paul's description of Antichrist as the "son of perdition" can be understood as something very concrete. Apparently the devil has some limited control over death (Hebrews 2:14); under certain circumstances he is allowed to use this power. It is the fact that the mortal wound is healed and Antichrist returns to life which will cause the world to follow the beast (13:3). Men will worship the dragon because it gives the beast power. Their praise for the beast: "Who is like unto the beast?" comes as a blasphemous antithesis to the Old Testament cry, "Who is like unto thee, O Lord?" (Psalm 35:10; cf. Exodus 15:11).

The healing of the beast's mortal wound will initiate the second phase of Antichrist's activity, the 42 months in which he will rule over all of humanity. His image now erected, the only religion permitted will be worship of Antichrist. He will attack any competing religion. He will kill the two witnesses (11:7) and wage war against the saints (13:7; cf. 12:17). With his 10 "under-kings" he will lay waste to Babylon (17:16). After this tremendous punishments will afflict the kingdom of the beast (the visions of the trumpets and the cups of God's wrath). Toward the end of this period the dragon, the beast, and the false prophet—the "unholy trinity"—will summon all the peoples of the earth "to the battle of that great day of God Almighty." The march to Armageddon will begin (16:13, 14).

Then, at the coming of Christ the beast and his kingdom will be destroyed (Revelation 19; cf. 2 Thessalonians 2:8). The world system of the kingdom of Antichrist will be judged in space and time. But as an individual Antichrist will be punished in eternity. Together with the false prophet he will be thrown alive into the lake of fire (19:20). Similar expressions are used for the great sinner who "goes down quick into the pit" (cf. Numbers 16:30-33). But Antichrist will not go to the realm of death. He and the false prophet will be thrown into the lake of fire. These two will precede the devil by a thousand years (20:10).

## Babylon the Great Harlot

The name of the harlot or prostitute Babylon is said to be a secret (17:5) and the harlot herself an evil mystery. The image drawn of this evil enemy of God is very complicated. Even the best of competent interpreters differ widely in their opinions here. Still, there are some fundamental points of agreement which can help in interpreting the most important elements of this figure.

First, it must be recognized that the harlot stands in contrast to the woman clothed with the sun in chapter 12. Furthermore, Babylon is the antithesis to the bride of the Lamb, the New Jerusalem (21:9ff.; cf. 19:7f.). Second, the beast and harlot should be taken together; they belong to the same image (17:7) and represent one and the same "mystery of iniquity" (2 Thessalonians 2:7). The events in chapter 13 concerning Antichrist and those in chapter 17 concerning Babylon interplay with one another.

What, then, does the great prostitute represent?

## (1) The Harlot Is a City

Whereas the beast symbolizes a kingdom, the harlot represents a city. It is given the name of the city of Babylon. To John a woman would have been the natural image for a city. The Old Testament sets one precedent for this. A pure and holy city is compared with a virgin or faithful wife, while a corrupt idolatrous city is called a harlot or adulteress (cf. of Jerusalem, Isaiah 1:21; of Tyre, Isaiah 23:17; of Nineveh, Nahum 3:4).

The city the prostitute stands for is also given. The name Babylon is a "mystery" and does not merely denote the ancient city on the banks of the Euphrates. In some ways Rome seems to be the city behind the image. The harlot is said to sit on seven mountains; Rome was situated on seven hills (cf. 17:9). Furthermore, the woman is depicted as "that great city, which reigneth over the kings of the earth" (17:18). First-century readers of this book would not have had any question about the identity of "Babylon"; it was Rome.

Chapter 18 expressly shows that an actual city is in question; the image accurately reflects the corrupt, self-indulgent, proud populace of Rome. Nevertheless, the image goes beyond this. Imperial Rome is not the only image present; the Babylon of the future, the capital city of Antichrist, is also in view.

## (2) The Harlot Is a Religious and Political System

Obviously Babylon represents a literal city, but it is no less obvious that it stands for much more. To apply this solely to Roman history would be an oversimplification of the highly symbolic language of Scripture. Babylon denotes a religious, cultural, economic, and political system which exercises worldwide influence and which is centered in a world capital. Two features characterize this system: deception and persecution.

Babylon's power will come from *deception*. This is reflected in the figurative language: "The inhabitants of the earth have been made drunk with the wine of her fornication" (17:2). In more explicit terms it is stated, "By thy sorceries were all nations deceived" (18:23). This therefore concerns not only the temptations of the world, but religious deception. Fornication is association with evil spirits, and the allurement of the last times will come because of lies and false miracles (2 Thessalonians 2:9). Scripture compares these deceptions to those false wonders performed by the Egyptian magicians Jannes and Jambres in their opposition to Moses (2 Timothy 3:8).

The great apostasy the apostle warned against involves giving "heed to seducing spirits, and doctrines of devils" (1 Timothy 4:1f.). Certainly demons are behind idols (1 Corinthians 10:20), but the greatest threat of the last days is more than primitive or modern idolatry. Rather, it is the false prophets who come in the name of Jesus and who can even jeopardize the security of those chosen by God (Matthew 24:4, 5, 11, 23-26). Babylon must be viewed in light of the eschatological discourses of Jesus and the comments of the apostolic letters on the end times.

The "abominations" in the cup of the harlot (17:4) may mean moral decay, but it is more probable they refer to religious corruption. Alford says that of the 21 times adultery is mentioned in Scripture, 18 pertain to the religious unfaithfulness of God's people, Israel, or the Church (*Greek Testament*, 4:704). Some suggest the three exceptions may be more apparent than real.

Babylon will also be a *persecuting force*. The inhabitants of the earth are made drunk by the seducing wine of the harlot's cup, but the harlot herself is made drunk by the blood of the saints and the martyrs of Jesus (17:6). In Babylon "was found the blood of prophets, and of saints, and of all that were slain upon the earth" (18:24). Babylon thus will share in the inheritance of punishment and judgment backslidden Israel had once heaped upon itself (Matthew 23:29ff.). Among the Jewish people a generation arose who "filled the measure of the guilt of their fathers." These thus became responsible for all the murders of the past. Similarly Babylon of the end times will "fill the measure" of the guilt of the past and become liable for the deaths of God's people (cf. Revelation 6:11).

The question of the identity of Babylon should be briefly restated: It will be an actual city, characterized by luxury and indulgence and thoroughly colored by sin and ungodliness. The city will be the world capital. In the end times, Rome, or another city resembling Rome, will become the center of Antichrist's empire. The great city will stand for a religious and political system marked by two traits: it will deceive and seduce the inhabitants of the earth, and it will persecute the saints. If history produces such a city and system, then it will be Babylon the great whore.

At this juncture a glimpse of the history of interpretation may prove useful. Some have advocated a literal interpretation of Babylon as the ancient Babylon of Chaldea on the Euphrates. This is a rather modern interpretation. No one seems to have understood prophecy in this way either in antiquity or in the Middle Ages. Nevertheless, some prominent interpreters maintain this view. They point out that Babylon was the first world empire (Genesis 10:8-12; 11:4), and it has always been regarded as a center of idolatry. This literal understanding then proceeds to postulate ancient Babylon will be rebuilt in the end times and become the residence of Antichrist. The Old Testament's prophecies of the destruction of Babylon will then have their final fulfillment in Babylon's fall as it is described in Revelation 18.

Objections to this viewpoint include the fact that Babylon is explicitly said to be a "secret," a cryptogram that is not to be taken literally (17:5). Neither was Babylon built on seven hills, but on the Plain of Shinar (17:9). Most importantly, Babylon never was a part of the Roman empire, a connection that the Babylon of Revelation seems to imply.

Another view contends that Babylon is a code word for Jerusalem (cf. 11:8, where Jerusalem is called "die great city, which spiritually is called Sodom and Egypt, where also our Lord was crucified"). Earlier in 3:9, John wrote of those claiming to be Jews but who were really from the synagogue of Satan. Now the holy city of the Jews is no longer the true Jerusalem, but has become a Babylon. Paul took a similar approach in Romans 2:28, 29 and Philippians 3:3. Even though the motif is well known, only a very few interpreters agree that John was here referring to Jerusalem. Everything else we read concerning Babylon seems to point in another direction.

The most popular interpretation as to the meaning of Babylon is that it represents Rome. The early church fathers believed this, and it was also accepted by such men as Tertullian, Jerome, Ambrosius, Ecumenius, Augustine, and Eusebius. Roman Catholic scholars such as Beda, Thomas Aquinas, Solmeron, Bellarmine, Lapide and Ribera agreed with this view. Many Protestant expositors concur. The basic question to be decided, then, is which Rome is meant—imperial (Gentile) Rome or papal Rome?

## (a) Imperial Rome

The Roman Catholic view is that Babylon refers to Imperial Rome. This is still their official church view. However, if this is correct, why would John be so astonished when he saw the woman drunk with the blood of the witnesses of Jesus (17:6)? After all, he lived during the era of the bloody Domitian persecutions. Besides, the events described will take place during the reign of the Antichrist, not during the time of the emperors (17:11-16). Nor was the city of Rome ever destroyed in such a way as chapter 18 describes, never to rise again.

## (b) Papal Rome

In medieval times and up to the time of the Reformation among those disillusioned by the papacy, the view developed that the harlot Babylon referred to papal Rome and represented backsliding and apostate religion. Among the strict monastic order of the Franciscans the belief spread that the papacy was the great harlot Babylon and the pope was the Antichrist. Most of the Reformers, Luther, Melancthon, Calvin, Zwingli, Knox, Tyndale and the English Reformers taught this. During the bloody days of the Inquisition and the religious wars in which millions died and great parts of Europe became waste, it was not difficult for many to accept this view.

Many other views have emerged. Some Roman Catholic theologians have proclaimed Luther the Antichrist and the Reformation as Babylon. In his commentary of 1614 the Spanish Jesuit Alcazar revived the old Catholic view that the judgment of the great harlot, the destruction of Babylon, was accomplished by Constantine and his successors.

A major view among evangelical scholars today is that the woman really represents all false religion. It will culminate in the days when Antichrist rules, when there will be a diabolical union between godless political power, under the leadership of Antichrist, and false, apostatizing religion. One seldom hears the papacy-Babylon view expressed.

The Babylon of the last days will become a religious-political system which will gather in itself all false religion. In a sense the beast and the harlot have been present throughout the Christian Era. In the First Century there were already antichrists (1 John 2:18). The writings of Paul (2 Thessalonians 2:3; 1 Timothy 4:1-3) deal with the dangers of backsliding. Even the letters to the churches of Revelation 2 and 3 indicate spiritual declension was already taking place.

The woman of 17:3 sits on the beast. This must mean that to some extent she will control and guide the beast. If this were not so, she could not reign over the kings of the earth (17:18). This may explain why the beast and the 10 kings aligned with it hate the harlot and at last kill her (17:16). At first Antichrist will need the assistance of the harlot and form an alliance with her. But after he has consolidated his position of power, he will reject and rob her. He "exalteth himself above all that is called God" (2 Thessalonians 2:4; compare Daniel 11:36, 37). He will deify himself and demand worship; no other kind of religion will be tolerated (13:15). It has been said that history is the key that unlocks prophecy. Since this is so, the safest course is to let the events of the future reveal the full meaning of this highly symbolic and controversial passage.

## The Consummation

### (1) The Millennium

Revelation 19 closes with the judgment of the beast and false prophet. Chapter 20 continues to describe the judgment of Satan himself. Verses 1-3 explain that Satan will be bound and thrown into the abyss for 1,000 years. After being released for a short time, he will be recaptured and thrown into the lake of fire, where the beast and the false prophet are (verse 10).

A thousand years, i.e., the Millennium, will pass in between the time Satan is thrown into the abyss and into the lake of fire. This period will begin the time of the resurrection of those who have died in the Tribulation because they would not receive the mark of the beast. The period will close when the final revolt against the kingdom of God is crushed and fire falls from heaven. Then will come the judgment of the entire world, and the eternal ages will be ushered in. This section is recognized as one of the most difficult passages in Scripture, and there are three main lines of interpretation.

During the first three centuries this text was largely understood as the time when an earthly kingdom of Christ would be established. It was believed it would last 1,000 years. After Christianity overcame paganism in the Roman empire, and after it became the "state religion," the opinion prevailed that the Millennium would occur during the history of the Church. Some held that the Millennium began with Constantine and his declaration of Christianity as the state religion. Others contended that the foundation of the Kingdom was laid when Christ was victorious on the cross. The Millennium, thus, included the entire Christian Era.

The view that the Millennium occurred figuratively in history via the Church is known as amillennialism (Latin: a, "not"; mille, "thousand"; annus, "year").

Those maintaining there will be a literal kingdom of God established on earth in the end times, in the time between the temporal and eternal existence, are split into two camps. There are, first, those who think the kingdom of God will be established through the victories of the gospel and conclude when Christ returns. This theory is called postmillennialism (from Latin, post, "after"). Second, others contend that the return of Christ will signal the beginning of the Millennium. This theory is called premillennialism (Latin, pre, "before"). It is beneficial for every reader of Scripture to have a basic grasp of these various positions, so a short survey will be given:

### (a) Amillennialism

The position that the time of the Church is the Millennium—called amillennialism—had its first significant champion in Origen, who rejected a literal interpretation of the Millennium. However, Augustine was the one who made this theory a Church doctrine. He interpreted the Millennium spiritually and taught that the Church is the Kingdom where saints reign. He associated the establishment of the Kingdom with the first coming of Christ and maintained that Satan and his forces were bound by the victorious Cross. When Revelation 20:4, 5 declares that the first resurrection will occur in connection with the establishment of the Kingdom, Augustine interpreted this symbolically and said it applies to conversion.

Augustine's stance became official Catholic doctrine. His view was also accepted by the Reformers Luther and Calvin. The position was further endorsed by the Augsburg Confession. This document rejected those who tried to teach a Jewish doctrine that prior to the resurrection the holy and devout would govern a holy, world empire where all ungodliness was subdued. However, we must be aware that it was an extreme form of chiliasm the Reformers rejected.

Initially amillennialists interpreted the thousand years in a literal sense. Around A.D. 1000 this caused excited expectation that Christ would return and the world would end, which, of course, did not happen. Still, the Augustinian view dominated throughout church history. Amillennialism does not allow for any literal kingdom of God on earth. It maintains the description of Revelation 20, like any other related passage in Scripture, must be considered figuratively, that the kingdom of God is solely spiritual in nature; anything less would take away from their belief that the spiritual nature of the kingdom of God has replaced the old covenant. The time of the gospel is, therefore, the "millennium." The promises to Israel concerning a kingdom are spiritually fulfilled in the Church and its history. Amillenialists believe the devil is bound with the "chain of the gospel" and does not have free rein where the Word of God is preached. They maintain we now live in the Millennium—perhaps on the brink of the devil's being released from prison and his deceiving the peoples of the earth.

Amillennialism has taken a variety of shapes throughout history. As has been mentioned already, some schools of thought argue that certain phases of church history are the Millennium. Others, however, claim that the entire Church Age is the Millennium. This latter view, which sees Satan as bound and the earth ruled by saints, is difficult to reconcile with the New Testament as a whole, and with history. The Book of Revelation, too, has much to say about the circumstances of the Church in the world; it is consistently portrayed as enduring tribulation, persecution, and attacks by the enemy (e.g., Ephesians 6:12; 1 Peter 5:8; Revelation 12:11).

The theory that the Millennium began with the start of the "state church" of the Roman empire (Constantine) is unrealistic. Those adopting this view contend that Babylon is Gentile Rome and the beast (Antichrist) is the Gentile world power. The Millennium then becomes the glorious period following the destruction of the beast and Babylon. This would mean the Middle Ages were the Millennium, a position not defensible at all. The kingdom of peace under the government of Christ would then include the Spanish Inquisition, the Crusades, etc. Other options for dating the Millennium fare no better; one strange view is that the Millennium extended from Charlemagne to the end of the German empire in 1806.

Such far-out interpretations caused many to abandon any interpretive approach which sought to compare church history systematically with the visions of the Revelation of John. The end result was that interpreters began to follow their own personal theories and speculations.

To counteract these rigid systematic approaches some took a more spiritualized approach to interpretation and contended that the Book of Revelation is not concerned about events per se, but is speaking of general conditions throughout church history. Some have strongly resisted this interpretation.

For an amillennialist position ever to have a chance of success, the so-called "recapitulation theory" must lie at the basis of one's interpretation of Revelation. The immediate, natural impression one receives from reading the Book of Revelation for the first time is that the writer considered the Millennium as a segment of time between the tribulation of Antichrist and the final judgment before the white throne. Only with the help of the recapitulation theory could one avoid this natural understanding. In this view 20:1-3 is said to refer to the first coming of Christ, and by virtue of His victory over Satan, Christ has bound Satan and thrown him into the abyss for 1,000 years. One difficulty with this approach, however, is that Christ's victory over Satan is for all time, not merely for a long or short period of time.

Another thing that makes it difficult to endorse the recapitulation theory are the comments of 20:4-6, which state distinctly that those raised at the beginning of the Millennium are the ones who gave their lives during the tribulation of Antichrist. This does not refer to ungodly, spiritually dead men who are given new spiritual life; on the contrary, this refers to holy martyrs from the Tribulation. Their resurrection is expressly called the first resurrection, and thus it belongs to the resurrection of which Christ is the firstfruits (1 Corinthians 15:20, 23). The first resurrection (Revelation 20:4, 5) stands in contrast to the resurrection of the ungodly, which will not take place until the close of the thousand years.

To circumvent the "problem" of a resurrection at the beginning of the Millennium, some amillennial theologians say an actual resurrection is not being spoken of at all. They interpret the text to mean those who are dead in Christ are not dead at all; they live and rule with Him. Most can probably see this is rather dubious exegesis.

The strange fact is that whereas amillennialism is the mainstream historical teaching of the Church, many competent exegetes dismiss it. Modern interpreters have returned to a prophetic understanding of the end times. These view the Millennium as truly belonging to the future. Not all are convinced of this, but quite a number admit that a sound exegesis of the text virtually demands one adopt the view that it is a prophecy of the coming Millennium.

## (b) Postmillennialism

A second main interpretation of 20:1-6 is postmillennialism. This view represents a medium between the other two (premillennialism and amillennialism). Postmillennialism is identical to premillennialism in that the Millennium is understood literally and eschatologically as the kingdom of God in the end time. The prophecy of the Millennium is not considered to be fulfilled in the presence of the Church on earth.

But postmillennialism approximates amillennialism in that it regards the Millennium as a natural result of the victory of the gospel in the present age. The miraculous aspect of a coming earthly kingdom of God is rejected, at least in part, by most postmillennialists. They contend the Kingdom will be first and foremost a spiritual and social force which will alter and improve existing world conditions.

This is combined with the view which gives the theory its name. Whereas the premillennialists teach that the establishment of the Kingdom will take place as a result of divine intervention, postmillennialists maintain that the return of Christ will not occur till the end of the Millennium.

They believe the Millennium will be a time of the greatest missionary impact of the gospel ever known. This spiritual evangelistic thrust prevails, and no expectation of a visible revelation of divine glory exists.

Some of the various problems that arise in connection with postmillennialism are both exegetical and dogmatic. Thus, objections leveled against the amillennialist's understanding of the first resurrection mentioned in 20:1-6 also apply to the postmillennial view. How can a "first resurrection" be understood apart from being part of Christ's return (cf. 1 Corinthians 15:23)? Moreover, both postmillennialism and amillennialism require that the link between chapters 19 and 20 be broken; this view is even harder for the postmillennialist to defend.

In addition to these exegetical difficulties, a postmillennialist position also poses the unresolvable problem: How could the first Christians expect the return of Christ in their own time if they already knew there was going to be a period of 1,000 years between their own time and the time of Christ's return?

## (c) Premillennialism

Premillennialism denotes an interpretation that acknowledges the Millennium as the real kingdom of God on earth, established at the return of Jesus Christ.

Premillennialism thus differs from amillennialism in its understanding that God's kingdom is real rather than symbolic. Furthermore, premillennialism differs from those who regard the time of the Church as the Millennium in its holding that the Millennium is God's future, eschatological kingdom.

Premillennialism is unlike postmillennialism in its contention that the Millennium will be established at the return of Christ.

A principal objection raised against premillennialism is that the teaching of an earthly kingdom stands in contrast to the spiritual nature of the Kingdom in the teaching of Jesus. Jesus refused to be any kind of political Messiah. His kingdom is not of this world. The establishment of a visible, national, or international kingdom was never His goal. The essential nature of the Kingdom Jesus preached is spiritual. Therefore, it is natural that the New Testament interprets the Old Testament prophecies of a coming Kingdom in spiritual terms. Many of the prophecies usually applied to the Millennium are actually clear references to the age of the Church; others point to the eternal Kingdom of glory.

Moreover, the doctrine of the Millennium is itself constructed from a single passage of Scripture in a book which is thoroughly symbolic and whose revelations are given through signs (1:1). Can such a doctrine be justifiably built on such an isolated passage of Scripture, especially since neither the Gospels nor the apostolic letters have any explicit teaching about an earthly kingdom of God in between the time of Jesus' return and the judgment of the world? However, a series of arguments can be put forth for an eschatological premillennial view of the Millennium.

It should first be noted that this position builds upon the most natural and plain understanding of chapter 20. The relationship to the return described in chapter 19 is unmistakable. The beast and the false prophet will be seized and thrown into the lake of fire (19:20). The prophecy continues by declaring that the master of the beast, Satan, will be thrown into the abyss (20:1-3). The account also tells of the saints martyred during the Tribulation who will rise and reign with Christ (20:4-6). After the devil is released for a short time, he will be captured once more; this time he will be thrown into the lake of fire. Note well: he will not be thrown into the lake of fire at the same time as the beast and false prophet. He will join them there (20:10). The passage refers directly back to 19:20 and confirms that the thousand years will occur between the judgment of the beast (Antichrist) and the judgment of Satan. The chronological progression appears clear and unbroken.

In his vision John saw the martyrs who had been beheaded for their witness of Jesus living and reigning with Christ a thousand years (20:4). The Greek verb *ezēsan*, "lived," is an aorist meaning "became alive, came to life." The verb occurs in two other noteworthy passages in Revelation. In 2:8 it is used of Christ who "was dead, and is alive"; and in 13:14 it refers to the beast who "had the wound by a sword, and did live." It seems that in both of these passages the word means "to come alive, to come alive from the dead." *Ezēsan* distinctly refers to resurrection in 20:4, 5: "This is the first resurrection." The same meaning occurs in Matthew 9:18 where it is applied to Jairus' daughter; and in Romans 14:9 it refers to Jesus' bodily resurrection.

The fact that 20:4 also involves a bodily resurrection seems obvious. When John wrote that he "saw their souls," his words are undoubtedly an allusion to the souls beneath the altar mentioned in 6:9-11. These martyrs had been resurrected. Revelation 20:4 states these saints were "beheaded." This probably denotes they received the death penalty. Since the issue is physical death here, "life" almost certainly refers to bodily—resurrection—life.

In addition it should be noted that this first resurrection contrasts with the second resurrection at the end of the thousand years. The most logical conclusion is that the verb *ezēsan*, "became alive," means the same thing in verses 4 and 5. The language is not being allowed to speak for itself if the first resurrection is taken as spiritual and the second physical. Those who reign with Christ are like Him in life; that is, their body is a resurrection body. Premillennialism thus enjoys strong support from a natural and reasonable exegesis of the Scripture on which the doctrine of the Millennium is largely based. This becomes even more crucial because the passage itself is not particularly symbolic in character. It contains some explicit, prophetical sayings which must be understood for what they are and for what they say.

Against this background it is understandable that some assert the modern rejection of chiliasm is ordinarily based on dogmatic considerations rather than on Biblical interpretation.

With respect to the principles of interpretation that must be taken into consideration, some have rightly said the basic error committed by those interpreting this passage in a nonliteral sense is their misunderstanding of the peculiar nature of apocalyptic prophecy. Such interpreters further assign a meaning to apocalyptic vision which goes against the plain meaning of the text. Apocalyptic prophecy is not allegory; neither can the battles of the Church throughout history be equated with the millennial reign of risen martyrs.

An objection consistently raised against the idea of an eschatological, earthly kingdom of God is that the Millennium is spoken of in only one New Testament passage; otherwise the New Testament is silent concerning it. One can respond to this challenge, however, by noting that the doctrine is in no way based on some casual side remark. Rather, the doctrine of the Millennium is founded on an overall scriptural framework which acknowledges the establishment of the Kingdom and its consummation. The new aspect of this revelation—in comparison with earlier visions of the end time messianic kingdom—is that the duration of the Kingdom is stated. This is dramatically underscored by the fact that the "thousand years" is mentioned no less than six times.

This last fact should not be misinterpreted to mean the truth or reliability of a particular Scripture depends on how many times it appears in the Bible. But it should be carefully noted that the prophecy of the kingdom of God in 20:1-10 is by no means an isolated saying. It is related to a series of similar prophetic passages in both the Old and New Testaments.

The doctrine of a temporary earthly kingdom of God, nonetheless, is not one of the foremost themes of Scripture. It should not be allowed to overshadow such basic truths as the doctrine of Christ's return, the doctrine of the last judgment, or the doctrine of the eternal state of glory. Thus, it is understandable that the Millennium does not receive a greater place in the prophetic glimpse into the future. It is in keeping with the spiritual nature of the gospel that we do not have some elaborate, detailed outline of Old Testament prophecies concerning Israel's kingdom.

However, this is not to say the doctrine of the Millennium does not correspond with what the Old Testament has to say about the end time kingdom of God. The universal scope of the prophecies is reinforced and deepened. At the same time, the

Book of Revelation distinguishes sharply between the earthly, temporal kingdom of God and the eternal Kingdom, although the Old Testament often treats these two as one. Prophetic perspective at times blends separated events into a single picture.

The passage referring to the Millennium thus forms only a portion of what Scripture teaches about the kingdom of God, the basic theme of the Bible. During the period of the old covenant the restoration of the kingdom of Israel was the golden hope of the prophets (Isaiah 65:17-25; 66:19-22; Daniel 2:44; 7:14, 18, 22; Amos 9:11-15; Micah 4:1-4).

Indeed, the heavenly and universal dimensions of the Old Testament's prophecies are woven with a strong thread of Israelite nationalism. However, the Israel which received central attention in these glimpses of the future is the redeemed spiritual Israel. The hope of Israel is the kingdom of Messiah.

The announcement of the kingdom of God receives a central place in the New Testament. It is critical to the message of John the Baptist (Matthew 3:2), and Jesus himself opened His ministry by proclaiming, "The kingdom of heaven is at hand" (Matthew 4:17). Likewise, the apostles preached the gospel of the kingdom of God (Acts 8:12; 19:8; 20:25; 28:31). The final goal of Christian hope is the eternal kingdom of God (2 Timothy 4:18; 2 Peter 1:11). Clearly it is this eternal spiritual aspect of the Kingdom that dominates the preaching of the New Testament although some attention is given to the earthly, messianic kingdom, such as the one the apostles would have been familiar with from the Old Testament and the tradition of the synagogue.

Jesus himself said, "Ye which have followed me, in the regeneration when the Son of man shall sit in the throne of his glory, ye also shall sit upon twelve thrones, judging the twelve tribes of Israel" (Matthew 19:28). Acts 1:6 and 7 seem to suggest that the apostles, even after spending several years with the Master, were waiting for the "kingdom of Israel." When they asked when the establishment of the kingdom would take place, Jesus, in one sense, confirmed the relevance of their question with His reply: "It is not for you to know the times or the seasons, which the Father hath put in his own power." Therefore, in the counsels of God a time has been set for the reestablishing of the kingdom of Israel.

There are other texts in the New Testament which allow for the establishment of an earthly kingdom in the interval between the return of Christ and the consummation of the world. James' sermon at the Jerusalem Council could be understood as signifying that God will first choose a people from the Gentiles during the age of the gospel.

Then, national Israel will be reestablished and its repentance will result in "life from the dead" (Romans 11:12-15) for all Gentiles (Acts 15:14-18). The restoration of Israel and the blessing which this will bring on all the peoples of the earth becomes, therefore, a realization of the Old Testament promises of an earthly messianic kingdom.

Paul's substantial comments on the resurrection also allow for an interim period between the return of Christ, when those belonging to Him will be made alive, and the consummation, when He will hand the Kingdom over to the Father, and death will be destroyed (1 Corinthians 15:23-28).

Revelation 20 is not entirely unique. It is in keeping with the expectation and preaching of the Kingdom that runs throughout Scripture. This is by no means the only passage that speaks of an earthly kingdom, although it is the only text which explicitly associates a time period with the Kingdom. It should be pointed out adamantly that it is not the kingdom of God which will be destroyed after the thousand years, but the enemies of the Kingdom. God's kingdom will never be destroyed (Daniel 2:44). The earthly kingdom of God is one step in the realization of the eternal Kingdom, the new heavens and new earth.

Old Testament prophecies of a messianic kingdom had generated vibrant eschatological expectations within Judaism. This led to the production of apocalyptic literature, and it is in this literature that the concept arose of an end-time kingdom, sandwiched in between present reality and the future, eternal condition. The writings attributed to Enoch, for example, contain a number of references to such a kingdom. Second Enoch 32:3ff. states that the present world or age will last for 7 days, with each day being a thousand years, the seventh day with a 1,000-year Sabbath; this will be followed by an eighth, eternal day.

Apparently early Christians accepted such concepts. The Epistle of Barnabas, for instance, says the course of this world will be completed in 6 days, each lasting 1,000 years. Then the Son will return for judgment of the ungodly, and the seventh day of 1,000 years, the day of rest, will occur.

Obviously the idea of a visible kingdom of God that will be established at the return of Christ was part of the general understanding of the Early Church. The *Didache,* or "Teaching of the Twelve Apostles" (ca. A.D. 120), makes no mention of the Millennium, in spite of the fact that this document concludes with comments on the last things. But many of the church fathers, especially in the first three centuries, did believe in an earthly kingdom of God.

Papias (ca. A.D. 140) spoke of the teaching on the Millennium as an apostolic tradition. Justin Martyr (ca. A.D. 100-150) viewed the Millennium as the fulfillment of the Old Testament prophecies of an earthly, messianic kingdom for the Jewish people: "But I and others, who are right-minded Christians on all points, are assured that there will be a resurrection of the dead, and a thousand years in Jerusalem, which will then be built, adorned, and enlarged, [as] the prophets Ezekiel and Isaiah and others declare. . . . And further there was a certain man with us whose name was John, one of the apostles of Christ, who prophesied, by a revelation that was made to him, that those who believed in our Christ would dwell a thousand years in Jerusalem" (*Ante-Nicene Fathers, Dialogue with Trypho,* 1:239f.).

Irenaeus (ca. 130-200) considered the Millennium as a transitional period from the present to the ultimate, eternal happiness. He adopted the view of the Jewish synagogue that the present world order would last 6,000 years (corresponding to the 6 days of creation). Toward the end of this period ungodliness would increase, and persecution of the righteous would worsen, until eventually evil would become incarnate in the person of Antichrist. When he had completed his mission of evil and had placed himself in the temple of God, Christ would be revealed in heavenly glory and would conquer all His enemies. At that time the saints of God would be raised from the dead, and the kingdom of God would be established on earth. This kingdom, lasting for 1,000 years, would be equivalent to the sabbath rest which followed the creation. Jerusalem would be rebuilt; the earth would produce fruits and crops abundantly, and peace and justice would reign. After 1,000 years final judgment would come. Then a new creation would come in which the redeemed would live forever in the presence of God.

In a general sense this view resembles what premillennialism teaches, but for obvious reasons there is a wide variety of opinion when it comes to working out the details. Among the chiliasts of antiquity, some held the Millennium would be a re-creation of the earth and heavens (cf. Isaiah 65:17f.). In figurative language, which to some extent conveyed literal meaning, the glory of paradise recreated is told. Millennarians of a later period are normally more reserved here, but it is argued that the kingdom of God on earth will be a kingdom of righteousness and peace, where war is not known. The Millennium will also be a time of great evangelism; the knowledge of the glory of the Lord will fill the earth as water covers the bottom of the ocean (cf. Habakkuk 2:14). The Gentiles will unite with one another and with Israel to worship the living Lord (cf. Isaiah 2:3). Nonetheless, the Millennium does not reflect the perfection of the final consummation. Sin will still exist, and after the 1,000 years the devil will roam the earth seeking to seduce its inhabitants (20:7, 8). The eternal kingdom of God—the new heavens and new earth—will not come until this last rebellion by the devil is destroyed.

The basic premise of millennialism is that the kingdom of God will be realized, not only in the hereafter, but on earth, following the end of this age. The Millennium is the peaceful evening of the life of the earth, an evening of peace just prior to the eternal sabbath rest.

## (2) The Judgments and Hell

The doctrine of an eternal judgment is fundamental to the Christian faith (cf. Hebrews 6:2). God's role as Judge courses throughout the history of mankind and finds its last and greatest expression at the judgment of the world at the Great White Throne. This act of judgment will be God's final dealings with sin.

Judgment is intended to remove sin from the cosmos. Sin must be totally exposed and punished. God may indeed be patient with the sinner for a time in hope that repentance might occur, but as the guardian and guarantor of moral order in His created world, He cannot tolerate sin.

Throughout the ages God's judgments have been hidden and unsearchable (Romans 11:33), but the Day of Judgment will reveal God's just judgment (Romans 2:5). The judgment of the world will occur in order to bring to light that which is hidden. At the judgment the cosmic revolt against the Creator will be unmasked and laid bare for all to see. The judgment therefore will justify God and His rule over the world (Sauer, p. 174).

Although God's acts of judgment throughout history have often been provisional and corporate (affecting entire groups), the Last Judgment will be final and individual. At that time God's judgment will not concern nations, realms, or systems—such as occurred during the judgments of the tribulation period. On judgment day each individual will have to answer for himself. The eternal destiny of each person will be declared on that day.

It should be emphasized that this is the *last* judgment. It is apparent there has already been a special judgment of the believers and their works, often called the Bema Judgment or the "judgment seat of Christ" (2 Corinthians 5:10). Even if the Book of Revelation does not present any doctrinal statement about such an earlier judgment, there may be some hints of it.

For example, if the elders mentioned in 4:4 are men, not angels, they must at that time have already received the crowns which Paul states will be given "at that day" (2 Timothy 4:8). And 20:4 shows saints from the tribulation period resurrected and sitting upon thrones, to reign with Christ for a thousand years.

It seems obvious that these crowned and enthroned servants of Christ, who already have appeared at the Bema and have received their reward, will not now, after a thousand years in glory, be brought before the Great White Throne to have their eternal destiny decided. Jesus said that they who believe in Him will not come into condemnation (John 5:24). However, to say that only ungodly persons will appear at the Great White Judgment seems to be more than the Scripture itself says. When the text says "If any" (literal) were not found "written in the book of life," it seems implicit that some were found written there.

A possible solution is that this is not an actual trial. John 3:18 says that "he that believeth not is condemned already." The Great White Throne Judgment is the occasion of announcing the verdict for all mankind. The book in which works are recorded is read, for the guilty have a right to know the reasons for their sentence. The "deed" which has brought salvation to believers is their repentance and asking forgiveness. The reading of the names in the Book of Life is then a glorious formality. The sentence for both sinners and saints has been pronounced, and the judgment has been concluded.

John's presentation of the judgment of the world is solemn and serious, but it is also amazingly short and to the point. No effort is made to show the majesty and loftiness of the Judge. The reaction of the ungodly to the wrath of God has already been described in 6:14-17, where it states that sinners try to hide from the face of the One sitting on the throne and from the wrath of the Lamb, calling for the mountains and rocks to fall on them.

The description of the final judgment centers around a courtroom scene, including a judge, the accused, the facts of the case, and the judgment itself. The judgment scene is reminiscent of the judgment described in Daniel 7:9ff. In that passage the Ancient of Days takes his seat in the court as the participants are seated and the books are opened.

This will be the final event of world history. It will be God's final word concerning sin. It will be the last word the unrepentant sinner will ever hear from God. The Creator and Redeemer is now the Judge.

The throne seen by John was great and white. Its "greatness" testifies to the superiority and majesty of the One seated upon it. Its "whiteness" speaks of the holiness and justice which come from it. But it is also a reminder that the blood of the atonement, which covered the mercy seat—God's throne on earth—in the temple and thus atoned for the broken law of God, will no longer be available for the offender.

The throne John saw was probably not the heavenly throne he saw earlier (4:2). The sinner would hardly be allowed into heaven, even for judgment. The Great White Throne will probably be a special throne, erected for this last act of judgment.

The thought of one sitting on a throne is an expression that elsewhere in Revelation refers to God the Father (4:2, 9; 5:1, 7, 13; 6:16; 7:10, 15; 19:4; 21:5). However, it should be noted that Christ sits on the throne beside His Father (3:21). This highlights the unity between the Father and Son (John 10:30; 14:7-11), which does not exclude the one, although the work might be attributed to the other. If the Father is seated on the throne of judgment, then the Son is also there. That the Son has an active role in the judgment is confirmed by many texts (Matthew 19:28; 25:31; Luke 19:11-27; John 5:22, 27; Acts 10:42; 17:31; Romans 14:9, 10; 2 Corinthians 5:10).

In his vision John saw the dead standing before God; he also observed the opened books (20:12). The books represented divine records of deeds (the "book of works") and a listing of the redeemed (the Book of Life). On several occasions Scripture refers to divine books and records of human deeds and words, as well as a list of those belonging to God. The concept is also attested in extra-Biblical Jewish sources.

The "book of works" is a collection of legal documents. This underscores the Biblical principle that judgment will be carried out according to works. The paradox is that men are saved by faith alone, without works (Romans 3:28), and yet they will still be judged according to their works (Romans 2:6-8). The explanation for this is that saving faith cannot exist apart from works (James 2:17). Jesus declared that the tree would be known by its fruit, and it is the fruit of faith that will be examined on the Day of Judgment.

God has a record of each individual's life (Daniel 7:10; Malachi 3:16; cf. 2 Ezra 6:20; 2 Baruch 24:1; 1 Enoch 47:3). In one way it could be said each person writes his own life history with words and deeds. Each person will be judged by his own testimony. Woe to the one who faces a list of unforgiven sin on the Day of Judgment! When these books are opened all secret things will be revealed (Romans 2:16; Ecclesiastes 12:14).

The words, deeds, and motives of men will be reviewed and judged (Matthew 12:36; 2 Corinthians 5:10; Revelation 20:12). An especially serious sin to be judged is the sin of omission (Matthew 25:41-46), that is, failing to do good when the opportunity presented itself (James 4:17). Those who have neglected the salvation of God will not escape (Hebrews 2:3).

Equally important as the "book of works" is the Book of Life, the divine list of the redeemed. These are the ones who belong to God and who have their citizenship in heaven (Luke 10:20; Philippians 4:3; Hebrews 12:23). The Old Testament anticipates such a concept (Exodus 32:32; Psalm 87:6; Isaiah 4:3; Daniel 12:1). Also, in Jewish apocalypticism the idea was well known (1 Enoch 104:1; Jubilees 30:22).

The Book of Revelation devotes a significant amount of space to the Book of Life. Revelation 3:5 states that the one who overcomes will not have his name blotted out from the Book of Life. Revelation 13:8 and 17:8 both speak of those inhabitants of the earth whose names are not written in the Book of Life. Those whose names are not in the Book of Life will be thrown into the lake of fire (20:15). Only those having their names written in the Book of Life will receive permission to enter the heavenly city (21:27). In 13:8 and 21:27 the Book of Life is called the "book of life of the Lamb."

The Book of Life has been called the "main book" of the judgment, but this overlooks the fact that the "book of works" and the Book of Life will be in total harmony on the Day of Judgment. The two books will independently testify to the same matter. Whether or not one's name is written in the Book of Life will determine whether or not one enters heaven. Those not listed in the Book of Life will find an explanation for their omission in the "book of works." But the "book of works" will determine the degree of judgment. Nothing will be judged casually or with discrimination; everything will be carried out according to circumstances. It will be more bearable for Sodom than for those cities that rejected the words and works of Jesus (Matthew 11:24). In the Parable of the Unfaithful Servant Jesus taught that the one failing to put into action the will of his master, in spite of the fact that he knew it, will receive greater punishment than the one not knowing it (Luke 12:47, 48). Every useless word must be accounted for (Matthew 12:36). But even so small an action as giving a cup of water in His name will be rewarded (Matthew 10:42).

The dead will be judged. For men death means the end of life, but not the end of existence. The soul uniquely bears the personality of a person and is responsible for his behavior. But the entire personality of an individual will be judged; thus, judgment will take place following the resurrection. Those who are raised at this time are "the rest of the dead," in other words, those who did not participate in the first resurrection (20:5). Now they, too, will stand body and soul before God to be repaid for the deeds of their bodies. The comment that the sea will give back its dead underscores the fact that all people will be raised. In Jewish thought how those who perished in the ocean—without burial—could participate in the resurrection was somewhat problematic.

Death and hell (Hades) will be cast into the lake of fire (20:14). This inseparable team appears together elsewhere in Revelation (6:8). They symbolize death's impact upon the whole world; their destruction signals the complete and final victory over sin and its results. Death will be conquered and rendered powerless for the people of God. It has no place in the perfect kingdom of God. That death and Hades are thrown into the lake of fire, the site of God's eternal wrath, is the guarantee that it will never again exist in God's creation. Death's rulership in the world will be over.

This does not, however, mean death will no longer have control over those outside of the kingdom of God. On the contrary, it will join them in the lake of fire, where it becomes the "second death," the final horrible, eternal death. The second death will result in complete separation from God. Just as another, higher life exists with God, so too, there is another, even worse death. The second death will be a death without return, without any chance of resurrection. Just as rigor mortis makes the body stiff in death, it seems as if a kind of spiritual rigor mortis occurs in the spiritual life of those who die without having fellowship with God. The process of death is thus only finally complete after the second death. It is perhaps best explained as the consequence of God's total withdrawal from those who choose sin as their companion.

To be eternally separated from God is to be beyond His grace and His love. In this existence the lost do not even receive the spiritual or temporal benefits the ungodly receive during their earthly lives.

God is the origin and source of life. Any existence without a relationship with God is death, not life. Because knowing God involves both the knowledge of the Father and His messenger Jesus Christ (John 17:3), it is eternal death to be excluded from fellowship with this life itself. Just as a principal teaching of the New Testament is that salvation anticipates eternal life and that the two go together, likewise, death and perdition, eternal punishment, belong together (cf. 2 Corinthians 2:15, 16).

Perdition means eternal punishment, not the end of existence. Neither spiritual death (Ephesians 2:1), physical death (Luke 16:22, 23), nor eternal death (Revelation 20:14; cf. 14:11) are understood to be the termination of a person's mind. An understanding of death which is totally foreign to the Bible should not be imposed on Scripture. Nowhere in Scripture does death refer to the obliteration of man. Numerous passages in the New Testament show to the contrary that eternal death does not mean the end of existence, but "a tormenting condition of death which never ends."

The sentence of punishment which God will bring on the lost is an exercise of His sovereign power and right as Creator. But what God will punish has, in effect, already been punished by sin, for sin is often its own punishment. Only the one who has chosen to be lost will be judged as lost.

Hell is the judgment of full-blown sin (James 1:15). The power of evil must be stripped and rendered harmless. God's righteousness demands that the spread of sin be stopped. Gehenna will become a "prison" (Matthew 5:25, 26; 18:30, 35) where the lost are bound hand and foot (Matthew 22:13). This elicits the question, "How can God be just and good and still overlook all the evil and oppression that rules this present age?" Two factors may apply here. One, sin must be allowed to "ripen" so its true nature will become known to the whole universe. Two, God's patience with sinners is an invitation and opportunity for them to repent. In the present economy grace is in effect. For a time God is tolerant with those who refuse His grace and the forgiveness it brings (Acts 17:30; Romans 3:25). But once God's patience no longer serves its purpose, His forbearance will end. The Creator will not overlook the fact that the Evil One incites God's creatures to violence. When the time comes for judgment, He shall "destroy them which destroy the earth" (11:18). God is the foundation of existence and thus the guarantor of right, truth, and love. The doctrine of eternal punishment is the ultimate statement that evil has no more future.

God will totally destroy the kingdom of Satan. The devil has not created anything; his kingdom only exists as an aberration within God's creation, and all his power and success are achieved only through his abuse of the gifts of the Creator. If God allowed this abuse to continue forever, such an eternal kingdom of sin might be approved by Him. But such could never be. This reflects the bitter necessity of perdition. The one who refuses to be saved *must* be judged (2 Thessalonians 2:10-12). The Lord *must* "gather out of his kingdom all things that offend, and them which do iniquity" (Matthew 13:41), otherwise His kingdom would be corrupted. Neither as Creator nor Redeemer can the Lord be made a "servant of sin" (Galatians 2:17). Redemption's work is intended to be the basis for the forgiveness of and deliverance from sin, not an excuse for continued sinning. The Creator cannot tolerate His creation being used as an operation base for the spread of sin.

The second death will therefore be God's ultimate weapon in the war against sin. Eternal is the consequence of God's judgment and wrath. Sin is the only reason for condemnation. Eternal punishment will not only be an existence whereby the sinner will reap the inevitable consequences of sin, although certainly this is one aspect, but perdition is also God's judgment of sin and the sinner.

No doctrine of the Christian faith can be as troubling as the doctrine of eternal punishment. The idea that the condemned suffer for all eternity is very painful. It is easy to understand why this teaching encounters objection and even rejection, and why alternative interpretations of the Biblical evidence are offered. A close examination of the New Testament, however, shows there are few teachings which have as much support as the doctrine of eternal punishment.

Scripture plainly recognizes that coming under God's eternal damnation will be painful. Expressions such as "there will be weeping and gnashing of teeth" (in sorrow and despair) confirm this. The nature of this suffering is impossible to determine from a human standpoint. Just as the extent of eternal joy has not "entered into the heart of man" (1 Corinthians 2:9), so too, the suffering of the lost escapes comprehension. Such suffering surely will include the pain of a condemning and accusing conscience. The kind of anxiety and turmoil of conscience the ungodly experience in this life when they are hit by "the curse of the Law" (Galatians 3:13) might give an idea of the agony they will encounter in eternity.

It is perhaps more difficult here than in any other area to refrain from "taking away from the words of the book of this prophecy" (22:19). Even among Bible-believing Christians some may try to tone down the strong Biblical warning concerning perdition. Very often this is accomplished by spiritualizing and softening what the Bible intends to be taken literally. One must recognize, however, that even though the Bible uses symbols to teach about perdition, reality stands behind them. There is no guarantee there is any ultimate difference between the physical and spiritual in a phrase like "the lake of fire."

The thought of eternal damnation is just as difficult to understand as it is to explain away. Sin itself is an unsolvable riddle as far as its origin and nature are concerned; so too, is its development as the ultimate rebellion against God. For those who accept Scripture's revelation that sin has its end in eternal damnation, this is obvious. When the Bible speaks so seriously about the matter it is because God wants no one to perish (2 Peter 3:9). He wants all men to be saved (1 Timothy 2:4). God's alternative to eternal damnation is salvation and eternal bliss. Christian proclamation cannot abolish or hide the doctrine of eternal perdition, but it can preach that God has given His Son in order to save man from such destruction.

## The Eternal State

"In the beginning God created the heaven and the earth." These are the opening words of the Bible. God spoke the universe into existence by His command and omnipotence. The Bible concludes with the One sitting on the throne again speaking creative words: "Behold, I make all things new." When John at Patmos recorded his last magnificent visions he exclaimed: "And I saw a new heaven and a new earth."

Eternity thus makes a full circle. In eternity past God alone was all; in eternity future God will be all in all. It is this that God's people will share with Him. Actually, the Bible has no end—it ends with a new beginning!

Nevertheless, one aspect of existence must be brought to a close before the new can appear. Heaven and earth must pass away, and the sea will be no more (21:1). The old things must pass away in order to make room for the new. The fallen, sin-affected world will perish so that a newly created, perfect world can appear.

The Bible affords a realistic view of the world's future. On the one hand, it does not allow any room for Utopian visions of humanity successfully reconstructing this broken planet into a new paradise. On the other hand, the prophetic Word teaches that the good will ultimately be triumphant. God himself will make a new and better world.

This new world will involve what "eye hath not seen, nor ear heard, neither have entered into the heart of man" (1 Corinthians 2:9). Opinions about this new existence that are simply the product of imagination and fantasy are worse than useless, they are misleading. Listening to the words of the apostle John therefore becomes critical: "And I saw! And I heard!" Knowledge about the coming eternal world has been given only by revelation.

Some have experienced revelations related to this, but they are incomplete. There are "unspeakable words" which cannot be conveyed by human tongue. Also, there are things which "it is not lawful for a man to utter" (2 Corinthians 12:4). A double lock has been placed on the door; access is impossible as well as prohibited.

But, if the hidden things belong to God, then what is manifest belongs to men (Deuteronomy 29:29). The concept of eternal life is of great import for our spiritual life, for our sanctification (1 John 3:3), endurance (Hebrews 11:25, 26), joy (Luke 6:22, 23), and expectation (Philippians 3:20). Recognizing the reality of eternal life gives one different and more Godlike priorities (Matthew 6:20, 21).

Consequently, it becomes imperative that believers have Biblically based concepts of heaven. The most exhaustive Biblical treatment of this matter of our eternal home occurs in 21:1-22:5. John received this in a vision. Under some circumstances his visions were explained to him. In the company of John the seer we are, in the final chapters of Revelation, allowed to ascend to the summit of prophetic insight and catch a glimpse of the never-ending land of eternity.

## (1) Symbol or Reality

One major battleground of interpretation concerns whether the final revelation of the Bible should be understood literally or figuratively. There is a wide range of literal and figurative interpretation spanning across even the most conservative lines. One can find differences of opinion on all fronts.

This portion of Scripture also contains some expressly prophetic segments which cannot be understood apart from a literal understanding. When it is said that eternity will know no sorrow or torment, it should not be taken to mean anything other than simply that. Most people, likewise, understand the "new heavens and new earth" to be precisely that—a new creation.

Of major concern for some is whether the New Jerusalem that comes down from heaven is to be taken literally or figuratively. Some will argue that a city with a breadth half the size of Europe and a height as great as its length and breadth can in no way be a physical reality. This view contends the city is only emblematic of a spiritual reality, perhaps the Bride herself, i.e., the Church (cf. Psalm 48; Ephesians 5:32). Some think the New Jerusalem represents the people of God rather than standing for some actual city. Many authorities hold this latter view.

Over against a spiritual understanding stand a number of equally competent interpreters who maintain the vision describes a literal city. Some believe it is the city of the redeemed where the saints reside in eternity. Others contend it is the heavenly city anticipated by Abraham (Hebrews 11:10, 16). If the earthly city is real; the ocean real; why not the heavenly city? One interpreter regards the heavenly Jerusalem as the link between the new heavens and the new earth. The alternative, symbolic interpretation finds no support among members of this view, who argue that such a spiritualizing is not in keeping with how the remainder of prophetic texts in Revelation are understood. The list of this camp is endless.

When so many Bible-believing Christians fail to reach a consensus, and indeed arrive at opposing conclusions, it is a reflection of how even the arguments are on both sides. The value in such diversity is that both groups may contribute to our fuller understanding. A careful study of the last two chapters in the Bible seems to lead to the con-clusion that the visions are not to be taken either entirely literally or entirely figuratively. Several interpreters adopt this mediating position. The two perspectives complement rather than offset one another. In fact, both a purely literal approach and a totally figurative understanding are fraught with difficulties.

One might assume that taking a very literal approach to what Scripture teaches about the life to come is a sign of tremendous faith. The imprecise region of eternity is suddenly cloaked with earthly reality; clarity, color, and precision give it a true lifelike quality. The danger, however, is that such a "lifelike quality" is entirely "this-world-oriented"; it becomes little more than an improved version of this existence. In actuality a narrow literalistic interpretation reduces the magnitude of the prophecies. When the tree of life is discussed, certainly this involves more than a fruit-bearing tree. The "water of life," likewise, must involve more than ordinary water. Similarly, many of the other things John saw must have a symbolic quality as well.

Both the Old and New Testaments employ the highly symbolic imagery and color of the ancient Near East. Jesus taught in parables; Paul referred to the Church as the temple of God. The apostle Peter called Jesus Christ a "living stone," and believers "lively stones," which are built into a "spiritual house" (1 Peter 2:4-7). What would keep the apostle John from employing figurative language in this highly symbolic book whose message is "signified" (1:1).

The Bible declares that the profound and indistinct things of eternity are seen "through a glass, darkly" (1 Corinthians 13:12). We only catch glimpses of it in "images and signs." God speaks to us only in terms we can understand. Symbolism acknowledges the difference in God's order and ours; symbols become a kind of "Jacob's ladder" extending from heaven to earth. In the case of Biblical symbolism, the originals are in heaven.

For this reason eschatological symbols are more than mere symbols. Just as the heavenly is a forerunner of the earthly, the earthly prophetically foreshadows the coming heavenly. The Jerusalem seen by John the seer is real, indeed, but at the same time it spiritually symbolizes the glorified life in the hereafter.

A symbolic meaning does not necessarily do away with the concrete reality underlying the image. When the discussion concerns a new heaven and new earth, most believe this involves actual realities. Would it be reasonable for John, in describing the New Jerusalem, to introduce into this universe an event whose effects are solely symbolic? If a literal understanding has obstacles, it must also be admitted that a strictly symbolic interpretation seems strained.

All existence must be expressed in some form, including eternal life and existence. There is no better "probable view" of what reality in eternity consists than the portrait drawn by the final vision of Revelation. The most balanced and complete approach to this prophetic word seems to be one which incorporates the literal with the symbolic. Only the future will truly show what is literal and what is figurative. It is impossible to determine exactly what is symbolic and what is literal. Quite possibly the magnificence of the city will find literal fulfillment; on the other hand, the description unquestionably has symbolic elements.

Such a fusion of the symbolic and the literal is a popular approach among many interpreters. The new earth has a new city of God, the New Jerusalem, already spoken of in Revelation 3:12 (cf. Galatians 4:26; Hebrews 11:10; 12:22; 13:14; Revelation 21:10). The New Jerusalem is one with the Church triumphant which dwells within it.

## (2) Time and Corporality

Eternal life is an existence in eternity and in space, in time and at a place. God takes man into His own eternity and allows him to share in His eternal life. But such existence will not be without a body or outside of time and space. It is virtually impossible for human beings to escape the concept of time and space. Nor does the Bible offer any help concerning this. It says nothing of a "timeless eternity," but it does make it clear that eternity is unlimited time. God is himself described in terms of time when He is called the "Ancient of days" (Daniel 7:9). The Bible does not say that God lives in an "eternal present"; on the contrary, as the One who is, who was, and who is to come, He has a past and a future (1:4). Concerning Messiah it is said that His "goings forth have been from of old, from everlasting" (Micah 5:2). The Book of Revelation uses an earthly time frame without hesitation when it speaks about eternity. The unsaved have no rest day or night (14:11). The saints serve God day and night in His temple (7:15). The tree of life bears fruit each month (22:2). Time does not end; it is the "stuff" of which eternity is made.

The real contrast for eternity is not time but temporality. Here the contrast is drawn between what perishes and what is everlasting. Time will not rest until absorbed by eternity. Therefore, we can speak of eternity as the glorification of time. In eternity time will unfold in successive never-ending ages. Paul described eternity as the "ages to come" (Ephesians 2:7), at which time God will demonstrate His great kindness toward us.

Time and its passing belong to eternity; it will never cease. When 10:6 declares time will be no more, the idea is one of postponement or delay. Following the tribulation period time will still continue (13:5; 20:2-5; 22:2). But, even though time is part of eternity, almost certainly eternity will possess a quality greater than the sum of its time past; in the same way eternal life will be more than unending existence. God is the eternal God (Romans 16:26). This is not to say He is subject to eternity in the same way we are subject to time. On the contrary, God is the source and origin of eternity. Eternal life flows only from Him (1 Timothy 6:16; cf. John 5:25, 26). Men are invited to participate in this eternal life.

Just as the eternal existence of mankind is linked to time, it is also involved with corporeality. Eternal existence will be both spiritual and physical in nature. To spiritualize eternal existence to the point that the believer is viewed as having some kind of "spiritual" bodiless existence is wholly unfounded.

The redeemed will have bodies in a different sense. The children of God will not be simply spirit; they will have spiritual and glorified bodies. The Holy City of God will be suited to such bodies.

In both time and eternity the physical nature of human existence is integral to reality. Greek philosophy led to the mistaken conclusion that the physical body is somehow sinful. Such a concept is entirely foreign to the Bible. Scripture does not teach redemption *from* the body but redemption *of* the body (Romans 8:23). The resurrection of believers and the redemption of the body are assured by virtue of Jesus' own resurrection. He is the firstfruits, the first to be raised from the dead (Acts 26:23; 1 Corinthians 15:23). Just as Christ rose bodily from the dead, His people will also rise bodily (Philippians 3:21). True, His body had supernatural qualities, but it was still flesh and bone (Luke 24:39-42). Jesus encouraged His disciples to touch Him and to see He was no ghost or spirit. He ascended to heaven in this body (Acts 1:9-11), and the heaven spoken of here is not "castles in the air" or hollow allegories. The nature of the resurrection of Jesus gives us some insight into the nature of heavenly existence.

The Bible takes a rather firm stance regarding heaven. An existence without a physical body is not what awaits the people of God. A universe of physical substance existed prior to sin's arrival, and this same universe will again exist when sin is eternally abolished. The substance of this universe is God's creation; it is a building block of the universe. God will not allow His "glorious creation" to fall into the hands of the enemy to be destroyed. It will be glorified since every physical thing contains a germ of the spiritual.

The new physical body given to the people of God will be of the same kind as Christ's. This resurrection body is called a "spiritual body" (1 Corinthians 15:44) and stands in contrast to the present, natural body. The original language suggests it is spiritual rather than natural (Greek *psuchikos*) in quality; however, this is not to say the natural body is made of soul and the spiritual body of spirit. But just as the physical body is controlled by the soul (*psuchē*), the spiritual body is controlled by the spirit (*pneuma*). The spiritual body is perfectly suited for spirit. Paul explained this thoroughly in 1 Corinthians 15:35ff. (see commentary).

In his vision of the new heaven and new earth—and the New Jerusalem (chapters 21, 22)—John saw the new or the newly restored creation; the new, eternal home for the new race of those who have been born again. The creative power of God is not only at work when He creates out of nothing, as He did in the first creation, He also recreates what sin has destroyed.

Resurrection means the redeemed will receive bodies like the glorious resurrection body of our Lord. This body will be corporeal without being restricted by physical laws or space. But Scripture makes it plain this new body will not be of the same kind as our earthly bodies. Here we find the paradox that although Jesus' resurrection body was "flesh and bones" (Luke 24:39), Paul declared that "flesh and blood cannot inherit the kingdom of God" (1 Corinthians 15:50). The resurrection body, in other words, will be a glorified and transformed body.

The change in mankind's physical makeup will be similar to the transformation that will happen to the rest of the world. Our humanity prevents us from being able to envision adequately what will actually occur. It is clear, though, that earthly matter can change from one state to another—and back again—under certain temperature conditions. For example, an ice cube can be liquified, heated into steam, and if trapped can be refrozen to make an ice cube once again. This may afford a faint hint of how the Creator can transform His creation.

Modern physics is evidence of just how little is known of our world. If matter and entities of an invisible world existed in an "ether body," modern science would have to acknowledge that not only would such a form be invisible, it would also be able to walk, float, and fly throughout our earth without ever being recognized.

The invisible world spoken of by Scripture is as real as the visible and temporal world in which we live (2 Corinthians 4:18). This is true of the heavenly realm today, and it will hold true for the future and eternity. That is why any presentation of the world to come as an unreal existence of vapors, mists, and shadows is so misleading. It is indeed a remarkable paradox that many in some present-day churches are so consumed with materialism, yet are put off by the teaching of a tangible kingdom of Christ. Under the guise of spirituality they have been duped by fleshly philosophy. A vain prospect for an earthly future is entertained, while the underlying motives are faulty. When life beyond is obscured, present life acquires an import and meaning not attested in Scripture.

Man is not just a spiritual being; he never will be. He lives in a body and always will. The new creation, of which the Book of Revelation gives a glimpse, will be a world perfectly suited to mankind's spiritual/corporeal nature.

### (3) The New Creation

The miracle of creation will recur and a new world appear. The distinction between heaven and earth will remain intact in eternity, but their interconnectedness will be reinforced. God will unite everything in the heavens and the earth (Ephesians 1:10). This new, redeemed creation will be the eternal habitation of redeemed humanity.

The earth plays a role in man's fallen state as well as in his condition of being saved. As long as the earth serves the purposes of God, He will sustain it. But His love is such that it will not allow such a world to continue forever. It was not designed for a purpose like that.

The promise of a new heaven and a new earth is an ancient promise given to Israel (Isaiah 65:17; 66:22). Isaiah's prophecy of the new creation is tied to his prophecies of the coming messianic kingdom of the end times. The promises were recognized by Judaism and often appear in extra-Biblical sources. The purification of the entire universe was a common subject in apocalyptic sources. Jubilees 1:29 speaks of a "new creation when heaven and earth shall be renewed." First Enoch 45:4, 5 says heaven and earth will be transformed into a dwelling place for God's chosen (cf. 72:1; 91:16). Second Ezra 7:75 declares that in the end times God will "renew creation" (cf. 2 Baruch 32:6; 44:12; 48:50; 51:3).

The New Testament often attaches great importance to what is purely spiritual in the heavenly realm. In Jesus' sermons, as well as in the apostolic epistles, the concept of the eternal kingdom of God is consistent throughout. The idea of a restored creation is particularly fundamental to the Book of Revelation. All of creation has been affected by the Fall; consequently, heaven and earth must pass away (Matthew 5:18; 24:35).

The comment that "heaven" will pass away should probably not be taken to mean God's dwelling place will be destroyed. Apparently "heaven and earth" here denote the universe itself. "The powers of the heavens shall be shaken" so that the sun and moon will become dark and the stars will fall from heaven (Matthew 24:29). "The heavens shall pass away with a great noise, and the elements shall melt with fervent heat, the earth also and the works that are therein shall be burned up" (2 Peter 3:10). This almost certainly refers to some cosmic catastrophe in the visible universe. The things that are destroyed in the world fire are the "things that are shaken," but "those things that cannot be shaken" will remain (Hebrews 12:26-28). The kingdom of God and His throne in heaven will not be moved (Psalm 45:6).

Even the creation destroyed will not be annihilated. The God of the Bible is a good God. There is no trace of dualistic thought that matter is somehow evil. On the contrary, the Biblical writers considered sin as an aberration of God's good creation. God will destroy those who destroy the earth (11:18). The work of redemption is necessary for God to restore His creation.

Peter's comments that the heavens will be dissolved in fire and the elements melted with fervent heat (2 Peter 3:12) is not a reference to total annihilation. In fact, Romans 8:21 says there is hope that "the creature itself also shall be delivered from the bondage of corruption into the glorious liberty of the children of God." That is why creation longs for the revelation of the children of God (Romans 8:19). Creation, that is, the earth and everything on it, will thus share in the eternal glory. It will be transformed and changed.

Annihilation is not in question; rather, it concerns a purification of the universe. In a great heat the elements will dissolve (2 Peter 3:10); the earth will be reborn (Matthew 19:28); all things will be restored to the pre-Fall state (Acts 3:21); and, the world will be delivered from its bondage of corruption (Romans 8:21). It may be said the *form* of the earth and heavens as we now know it will be destroyed, and the result will be the making of the new heavens and earth.

The earth's own foundations will pass through the cleansing fire. Every spot of sin, every hint of the Evil One, every trace of death will be removed. A new universe will be born out of the fire of the world. The original wording suggests that it is "new" but not "different." It is the same heaven and same earth, but both have been wonderfully recreated. Nature has been recreated into the form God intended: no weeds, nor thorns or thistles. Those possibilities which have for so long lain dormant will be fully realized.

Many interpreters agree with such a position as outlined above. But it must be stressed that this involves more than a simple renovation of the former existence. Something will happen to the old order of creation; it will become entirely new and involve something beyond our limited understanding of reality. Obviously the new heaven and the new earth are not simply the old heaven and earth rejuvenated; they are new creations. Nothing less would suffice for the new creation's deliverance

from the bondage of corruption. Just as each person will experience salvation of the body through a miracle of transformation at the resurrection, all creation will experience this kind of transformation also. A new world will be created for a new people of God.

This will be a unique work of God. God himself will announce His new creation and proclaim himself the Alpha and Omega, the beginning and the end (21:5, 6). God as the beginning does not only mean He was the first one in time, He is the source and origin of all existence. When He is called the "last," the "end," it indicates that He determines the purpose and goal of life. He is that goal, and all of creation is created for Him (Colossians 1:16).

At the completion of anything a cry is given, "It is done!" This occurs three times in the New Testament: by Jesus on the cross (John 19:30); at the pouring out of the last cup of wrath (Revelation 16:17); and upon entrance into the eternal kingdom (21:6). God's words, "It is done," mark the realization of everything He has promised and foretold. His marvelous plan of salvation for both humanity and His creation will finally be realized.

## (4) The New Jerusalem

"And I, John, saw the holy city, new Jerusalem." Just as the pilgrim en route to Jerusalem for a feast might have rejoiced to see the city in the distance, so too, John rejoiced at the sight of his eternal home. What John saw in his vision will be seen by the entire Church at the dawn of the eternal day.

It seems as if John was seeing at first from a distance (21:2). Then, he apparently was taken to a high mountain to get a closer look (21:10). Often in Scripture mountains symbolize the presence of God. From mountaintops many revelations were given: Ararat, Moriah, Sinai, Carmel, and in the New Testament the mount on which the Sermon on the Mount was given and the Mount of Transfiguration. Jewish apocalyptic writings frequently associated mountains with the throne of God and heaven (1 Enoch 18:8; 24:1-3; 25:3; cf. Isaiah 2:2; Micah 4:1). In this passage in Revelation the mountain represents a sacred contrast to the desert where John saw the great harlot, Babylon. Both events were shown to John by one of the angels with the seven cups of wrath. Probably this was the same angel (cf. 17:1-3). God's punishments have achieved their purpose: Babylon has been destroyed; the New Jerusalem is revealed.

John's vision was of the new heavens and new earth. The new earth corresponds to a new capital city. And it is striking that perhaps the city is the most central image in the picture of the eternal state in the kingdom of God. Another common theme in Jewish apocalyptic was that a new Jerusalem would be revealed when Messiah came. The

Testament of Daniel (5:12) from the late Second Century B.C. made allusion to a new Jerusalem in which the saints would rejoice forever in the glory of God. Second Ezra 7:26 says the city, which is now invisible, will be revealed one day.

The New Testament confirms the conceptualizations of the synagogue. Paul referred to the "Jerusalem which is above" (Galatians 4:26). God is the architect and creator of the city (Hebrews 11:10; cf. Hebrews 12:22; 13:14; Philippians 3:20). The overcomers will be inscribed with the "name of my God, and the name of the city of my God, which is new Jerusalem, which cometh down out of heaven from my God" (Revelation 3:12). Against such a background the vision of John must be examined.

One maxim of the rabbis said that, in effect, all earthly things have their heavenly counterparts. The idea that the earthly Jerusalem was a model of the heavenly Jerusalem is older than the New Testament. Precisely because a heavenly original model is thought to be behind the earthly Jerusalem, it can serve as a pattern for the Jerusalem to come. In the original language of the Book of Revelation the Hebrew form of "Jerusalem" is retained (i.e., it is transliterated). This underscores the continuity between the earthly city and the heavenly one. A new and holy Jerusalem will appear, but it will still be Jerusalem.

The description of the coming of the New Jerusalem at the consummation is a picture of the abundance of eternal life. The Holy City will not be identified with heaven, but it comes from heaven. It will form the bridge between heaven and earth. Through it the two spheres will be united.

John saw the New Jerusalem coming down from heaven out of heaven (cf. 3:12). To the modern mind this stretches all of the knowledge we have concerning the universe and space. This creates the unavoidable assumption that there is a particular location where God dwells—a canopy where, surrounded by cherubs and holy angels, He reigns. The Biblical writers alluded to several heavens, and apparently they viewed the heavens as layered spheres. Acts 1:11 says Christ was taken up into heaven; according to Ephesians, He ascended far above all heavens (Ephesians 4:10). Now He dwells in the heavens (Hebrews 4:14) and in heaven itself (Hebrews 9:24). With the arrival of the New Jerusalem, and the throne of God, and the Lamb, the barrier between heaven and earth will be removed.

As said above, opinions vary as to how literally this should be understood. Some contend that when the Holy City descends from heaven, it symbolizes the Church. Others, however, argue for a strict literal interpretation. Some think it is possible this is a satellite city which is suspended above the earth during the millennial reign of Christ. Supposedly it is the dwelling place of the resurrected and transformed saints, who thus also have access to the earthly sphere. This may help explain another difficult dilemma: where do the resurrected saints stay in a period when earthly mankind continues to go about its daily existence?

According to human understanding the concept of a city which is as long as it is high is incomprehensible. But we are seeing it from heaven's viewpoint. Seiss says that the city will come down and have a close connection with the earth, but nowhere is it stated that it will "land" on the earth and become a part of it. The city will always continue to be the "Jerusalem which is above" (pp. 496f.). The people on earth will walk in its light, and this implies it is above them.

The Holy City is described in very plain, concrete terms. Its size and extent are given, as are the construction materials for the walls, gates, streets, etc. Some reject any literal understanding here and argue instead that John was more concerned with the spiritual features than with physical realities. Others are more cautious and suggest it is possible that although the new order may not primarily be of a physical character, it remains that the New Jerusalem will be the dwelling place of God's people. The people of God are called the "bride" in 19:7 (NIV), and they reside in the heavenly Jerusalem.

How large is this city? According to 21:16 it is "twelve thousand furlongs. The length and the breadth and the height of it are equal." Since a furlong is 220 yards, the total is 2,640,000 yards. Since there are 1,760 yards in a mile, the length, breadth, and height will each be 1,500 miles. The city will then cover an area of 2,250,000 square miles, about half the size of the continent of Europe.

The measurements given are so immense that some have argued they must be taken symbolically, not literally. However, this is not a convincing argument. After all, this is to be the capital city of the universe, where myriads of angels and the redeemed will live.

What will be the shape of the New Jerusalem? As usual, there are differences of opinion among scholars. Quite a few think it will be in the form of a pyramid (Lilje, p. 267). If this be true it is easy to visualize the throne of God placed at the top, while the river and street wind around the pyramid on their way down. A basic objection to this view is that we lose the symbol of a temple with the city a large Holy of Holies. In Solomon's Temple, as well as the one described by Ezekiel, the Holy of Holies is described as cube-shaped, equal in length, breadth, and height.

Mounce endorses the idea of a cube shape for the New Jerusalem: "The city that appears to John is said to be foursquare. This could mean it is laid out in a square pattern, but more likely it refers to a three-dimensional form—a cube whose length, breadth, and height are all equal. Not only are the terms in which the city is described most naturally interpreted as a cube, but the Greek word itself is used of huge rocks in the shape of a cube and of stones appropriate for building blocks." (See Mounce, *New International Commentary on the New Testament, Revelation*, p. 380.)

Heavenly Jerusalem stands in part as the perfected earthly Jerusalem. But first and foremost the heavenly Jerusalem will be the antithesis of Babylon. One author has suggested the contrast is so strong the Book of Revelation might be characterized as "A Tale of Two Cities." The subtitle "The Harlot and the Bride" might be fitting. Babylon will personify the evil forces of the world as the dominant city during the time of Antichrist. The New Jerusalem will be the glorious manifestation of the purity and glory of the kingdom of God. Compared to the splendor of Jerusalem, all the pomp of Babylon will be cheap glitter and makeup, such as a prostitute might wear.

The fact that both the kingdom of Antichrist and the kingdom of God are symbolized by cities in the Book of Revelation is quite remarkable. C. Anderson Scott writes: "A city is first the ambition of man and then the despair of man. The great lesson of this vision is that it remains the ideal of God. Babylon in all its incarnations, from the first on the Euphrates, through that set upon the Tiber, to those we know on the Seine or on the Thames, stands for the human instinct of fellowship and mutual cooperation, but also for the reiterated human experience that a great city is a great evil. In vain do we try to stem the steady tide of population setting from the country to town. In vain do we deplore the growth of these enormous communities. 'Back to the land' is a kind of despairing watchword, for the simple reason that so few wish to go. . . . And yet in the hands of men the city has become a monster which devours its children" (*Expositor's Library, Revelation*, pp. 308f.).

In spite of the seemingly intrinsic evil in the city, God still is preparing a city for His followers (Hebrews 11:16). Despite the terrifying examples of earthly cities gone awry, a city remains God's ideal for human existence in eternity. Even in paradise it is not good for the individual to be alone, without family and friends. One day the redeemed will be gathered into God's family, which can be both intimate and yet all-inclusive at the same time. In this life, although there are some intimate relationships, human beings are essentially strangers to one another. That will not be the case in eternity. There the redeemed will experience community in a way far beyond what is possible in the present world. The instinct of humans to commune with one another in all aspects of life is indeed significant.

New Jerusalem will be simultaneously a city and a garden. This reflects an ideal combination of culture and nature. The walls are described as "great and high" (21:12), but the city will not be a prison. Its gates will always be open. The idea of "going in and out" appears as early as John 10:9. The people of the New Jerusalem will not live only within the confines of the city. God's entire universe will be theirs to enjoy. "The nations of them which are saved" and kings of the earth will carry the glory and honor of the nations into the city (Revelation 21:24-26; cf. Isaiah 60:11; Haggai 2:7). Enormous debates have been waged over the identity of these "nations." Some think they include people and kings who belong within the city and who go out for different reasons. Others contend that only the chosen ones actually inhabit the city, while others live on the new earth. Some more cautious exegetes leave the question open. They reason that the meaning of 21:24ff. may be that only a certain segment of the redeemed live in the city, while more (Christians) live in its light which shines over the entire earth. Such a viewpoint seems to coincide more closely with Old Testament prophecies such as Isaiah 2:2-4; Micah 4:1-3; and Zechariah 8:20f. (though these are usually considered to refer to the Millennium). Furthermore, the Revelation's own discussion of "firstfruits" (Revelation 14:4; cf. James 1:18), which is then followed by a later harvest, tends to agree with this approach. At least there is no internal conflict between the inhabitants of New Jerusalem and the other peoples of the earth. In this view the resurrected saints are not only the populace of the kingdom but they are its government. If they reign they must have someone to reign over. In that case these subordinates are the "nations of them which are saved."

On the other hand, interpreters like P. Madsen, Fausset, Lange, Walvoord, Mounce, Beckwith, Eritsland, and others reject this view. They object that such a castelike division is in conflict with the spirit and letter of the Book of Revelation. The only division in the age to come will be between the saved within the city and the unsaved without (21:27; 22:14, 15).

This is no doubt a strong argument. However, it appears to be much weaker if one tries to explain this difficult passage by referring to the fact that John's language is taken from the descriptions of a perfect place found in the Old Testament, and there is nothing there which covers this point. As for other matters, we must wait for the answer until the time we have perfect knowledge.

John has given a rather detailed description of the Holy City. Even the most literal interpretation must admit that symbolism permeates his message. The prophet enlisted the most valuable earthly items—gold, pearls, and precious stones—to tell of the glory of the city. The riches Babylon attained through gross sin now belong to the Bride as a gift.

The angel escorting John showed him a city where the walls were "great and high" (21:12), 144 cubits. A cubit was figured to be the distance from the elbow to the tip of the middle finger of the hand, about 18 inches. Using this measurement, the wall will be 216 feet high. The walls of the New Jerusalem, therefore, are extremely high and thus insurmountable. But, when compared with the city's height the walls themselves will seem low. They will not shield the brilliance of the city (21:24). Moreover, they are of crystalline jasper, which will allow the glorious beams of light to shine through. The former promise to Jerusalem will receive its eternal fulfillment: "O thou afflicted, tossed with tempest, and not comforted, behold, I will lay thy stones with fair colors, and lay thy foundations with sapphires. And I will make thy windows of agates, and thy gates of carbuncles, and all thy borders of pleasant stones" (Isaiah 54:11, 12).

John saw the foundation stones of the walls of the city were precious stones, each with a different color and brilliance, and each probably extending from gate to gate. On the 12 foundation stones were written the names of the 12 apostles of the Lamb. Through their testimony and preaching the foundation of the Church was laid: Jesus Christ and His work. Through them believers have come to faith (Ephesians 2:20).

The gates John saw were constructed of enormous pearls. Many Jewish writers of the days immediately after the arrival of Christianity tell of city gates made of a single pearl. Either this is a reference to pearl fragments which are made to cover an entire gate, or the pearl is the gate itself (cf. the stone before the opening of Jesus' tomb). On the gates the names of the 12 tribes of Israel were written (see Ezekiel 48:30-34), a reminder of the place Israel has had in the history of salvation. Through the gates of Israel all the nations of the earth have been granted entrance to salvation (John 4:22). The true Israel of God, those who waited for Messiah, will have their place in the eternal city. The gates to the Holy City will always be open, and the angel who guards the gate will stand there as a blessed contrast to the cherubs whose flaming swords guarded the entrance to paradise (Genesis 3:24).

John testified that not only the street but the entire city was made of pure gold, clear and transparent. The city will shine with God's glory. The Bible gives us some other glimpses of this glorious light that shines from God. The reflection of this glory radiated from the face of Moses as he came down from Sinai (Exodus 34:29f.). It shone from Jesus when He was transfigured on the Mount (Matthew 17:2). An imprisoned Peter saw it shine in his cell (Acts 12:7), and Saul the persecutor was knocked to the ground and blinded by its brilliance on the road to Damascus (Acts 26:13). The glory of the Lord will illuminate the city because the "Lord is there" (Ezekiel 48:35). The word in Revelation 21:3 denoting God's having lived among men is *skēnē* (cf. John 1:14). This is a reminder of God's dwelling place in the old covenant (Leviticus 26:11; Ezekiel 37:27). The expression is also used to mean that the Son of God took up His dwelling, raised His tabernacle, among men (John 1:14). When *skēnē* is used like this it may be because it recalls the revelation of God's glory in the tabernacle (*mishkān*, "dwelling place"; *skēnē*, Septuagint) of the old covenant.

A main feature of the New Jerusalem is that paradise is regained. The tree of life and the river of life have been restored (Revelation 22:1, 2; cf. Genesis 2:8-10). The river flows from the throne of God and the Lamb. This is the fulfillment in eternity of the vision Ezekiel saw (Ezekiel 47:1-12), Zechariah's vision (Zechariah 14:8) of the stream which flowed through Jerusalem, and the streams which make glad the city of God (Psalm 46:4).

Once again man has access to the tree of life (22:2), thus to eternal, immortal life. Some scholars, such as Mounce, believe that the emphasis here is on the richness of the fruit as well as its variety (*New International Commentary on the New Testament, Revelation,* p. 387). Weymouth translates the passage as saying the tree of life "produces twelve kinds of fruit and brings forth a new harvest month after month."

Obviously the descriptions of the tree of life and the river of life contain much symbolism. If these symbols are interpreted in physical terms, the images take on a definite sacramental character. This is no less true of the leaves of healing, which suggest that total health and well-being are a mark of life eternal. The river and tree of life suggest a life complete in every way. He who eats of the tree of life will never hunger; He who drinks of the water of life will never thirst again.

## Eternal Life

God has irrevocably given all human beings some form of eternal existence, but eternal "life" is experienced only in fellowship with God. Eternal life is a gift of God (Romans 6:23). This is something believers already possess (1 John 5:13), but it is also something that has been promised to them in the future (1 John 2:25). Believers possess eternal life in faith as well as in hope; it is a present reality and a future hope.

Eternal life cannot be fully realized until eternity; and compared to eternity, life on earth is almost "embryonic." Paul contrasted present understanding as the difference between the immature understanding of a child and that of a mature adult (1 Corinthians 13:11). Believers do not presently know the abundance of the hope of His calling (Ephesians 1:18). Those who are eternally lost will never fully understand what they have rejected and missed.

The difficulty in explaining the glorious life in eternity is intrinsic to its being something beyond human experience. Human language lacks any point of reference with which to compare it. Moreover, eternal life is a spiritual reality, and the natural man does not receive things which belong to the Spirit or the kingdom of God. What God has prepared for those who love Him can only be appreciated by spiritual persons (1 Corinthians 2:9-14).

Holy Scripture seems reluctant to describe the eternal state. At this juncture the Bible stands in stark contrast to other religious writings. This brings to mind the fanciful myths of the Greeks and the earthly descriptions of paradise by the Muslim Koran. Jewish apocalypses, familiar to the apostle John, painted the delights of heaven in very earthly colors. Often the description shows the righteous fully enjoying earthly joys which were denied them on earth. The restrained Biblical portrait of eternal life is free of such details; it resists describing the indescribable as merely "earth revisited."

Still Scripture does tell us much about eternal life. The information comes from a variety of passages, most especially in the New Testament, where it often is spoken of in indirect terms. More elaborate explanations do occur, such as in Paul's discussion of resurrection and the consummation (1 Corinthians 15) and John's last vision of eternity (Revelation 21, 22). Some negative terminology is employed, that is, terms which tell what the saints will *not* experience; and some is in positive terms, that is, what the redeemed *will* experience.

From a negative perspective a basic quality of eternal life is that *there is no sin*. "And there shall in no wise enter into it any thing that defileth, neither whatsoever worketh abomination, or maketh a lie" (21:27). For those loving sin eternal life holds no attraction. But to the saints such a prospect is inviting; no longer will sin afflict the people of God. So much of earthly existence is infested with sin's effects. With good reason sin has been called the principal means of worldly amusement. The Bible comments that this "lust of the world" will pass away (1 John 2:17), and the "pleasures of sin for a season" (Hebrews 11:25) will come to an end. The believer must also be careful not to be "overtaken in a fault" (Galatians 6:1) or "hardened through the deceitfulness of sin" (Hebrews 3:13). The tempter was allowed to visit mankind in God's Adamic paradise, but in the new, eternal paradise nothing unclean will be allowed entrance. Sin will never again tempt the redeemed. Throughout the created order, nothing will ever again invoke God's divine wrath or punishment.

Not *only will sin be dispelled, its effects will also be banned forever.* The "former things," sorrow and torment, tears and weeping, and death, will be forever "passed away" (21:4). Life as it is now known will be totally changed in the new order. God's vanquishing of death will be a tremendous miracle, but that every tear will be wiped away is almost unbelievable. Believers can only wait for the day when all sorrow is gone, when the darkness of night will be replaced by the clear light of God. Sin's evil secret will be exposed; the riddle of existence will be solved.

The promise of 22:3 is: "And there shall be *no more curse*." No longer will there be any foundation for the curse, since the reason for it—sin—will be gone. The curse followed closely on the heels of sin; because of it the earth became perishable (Genesis 3:17). Even believers who acknowledge "there is therefore now no condemnation to them which are in Christ Jesus" (Romans 8:1) must continue to agonize or "groan" under the burden of earthly existence—upon which the judgment of God rests (Romans 8:22, 23). Indeed, even in the glorious millennial kingdom described by the prophet Isaiah there will be sinners afflicted by the curse (Isaiah 65:20). But John envisioned a day when there will no longer be a curse.

The Holy City will also *have no temple*. "And I saw no temple therein: for the Lord God Almighty and the Lamb are the temple of it" (21:22). There will no longer be a need for a *place* to worship, for the One the redeemed worship will be in the midst of His people. Sacrifice too will be obsolete, for He himself who is the Supreme Sacrifice will always be among them. Not only will the sacrificial system be abolished, but the temple itself will be done away with. It was only a shadow of the coming reality (cf. Hebrews 9:8). The Lord himself will be the temple of the city, and the entire city a Holy of Holies. The ancient prophecy in Zechariah 14:20, 21 will receive its total and ultimate fulfillment: "Holiness unto the Lord" will be written on every article in Jerusalem, even on the bells of the horses. Worship will no longer be something done at a set time and place, it will be life itself.

This is also stated in positive terms: *"his servants shall serve him"* (22:3). To serve God lies at the heart of Christian life (1 Thessalonians 1:9; Hebrews 9:14); it will not cease after present existence. Jesus said the servant who was faithful over a few things would be placed over much (Matthew 25:21). God himself is active. "My Father worketh hitherto, and I work" (John 5:17). Believers are called "laborers together with God" (1 Corinthians 3:9), and this cooperation will continue into eternity. Eternal life will be full of activity, a fact not at odds with the promise of eternal "rest" (Hebrews 4:1). The "rest" of Israel in the Promised Land, which is an image of the eternal sabbath of God's people, did not involve inactivity.

In serving the Lord in eternity the various natural gifts will flow. Each person has certain useful, learned, or acquired talents. They are part of each individual's physical makeup; therefore, such characteristics will accompany him into eternity. Those traits which were restricted or suppressed will blossom. Then each person will "become what he or she is"; he or she will be as the Creator intended. One's full potential will be realized. There will be no more restrictions or limits to potential. Physical limitations such as weakness or sickness that have "strangled" potential will be removed. Social limitations—lack of opportunity, human prejudice—will also be removed. Above all, the spiritual limitations imposed by sin will be absent.

*"And they shall reign for ever and ever"* (22:5). The service of saints in glory will be to reign. Since the beginning man was created to reign (Genesis 1:28), but because of the Fall he forfeited that privilege. "The crown is fallen from our head: woe unto us, that we have sinned" (Lamentations 5:16). A slave of sin is not fit to rule. To rule one must have both intellectual ability and moral and ethical integrity. A good leader needs a sense of justice, sound discernment, a sense of responsibility, love, compassion, and integrity. Such qualifications are not passed on genetically. They are developed through experience and through distinguishing between good and evil (Hebrews 5:14).

Since the beginning of creation God intended human beings to develop their moral consciousness. Part of this development process involved letting them choose between good and evil. The first instance of choosing between good and evil occurs in the account of the tree of knowledge. This "knowledge" was not "knowledge" of any ordinary kind, but a very special kind of knowledge, the knowledge of good and evil. "Good" meant obeying God's commands; "evil" was to disobey. At the point of moral decision man developed an ethical consciousness. Christ, as the Second Adam, experienced the same kind of choice when He was tempted by the devil. And although He was the Son of God, He did so to learn obedience (Hebrews 5:8; cf. Isaiah 7:16). In order to go through this trial and gain this experience the Son of God put on flesh and blood and became the Son of Man. Because He is the Son of Man, He received authority

to execute judgment (John 5:27; cf. verse 22 and Acts 17:31). He was tempted in the same way that human beings are so that He might become the ruler and judge of all (Hebrews 2:17, 18; cf. Deuteronomy 17:15; 18:15-18). If believers hope to rule with Him, they must be victorious like Him and by Him (3:21).

Even the Son of God who reigns from eternity, according to the Father's will, was made "perfect through sufferings" (Hebrews 2:10). This occurred prior to His being cloaked with the robe of a magistrate that at the end times He might judge the world. How much more important is it then that those who will reign with Him become "perfect" (Ephesians 4:13; cf. Hebrews 12:23). Something is required of those who will one day "judge angels" (1 Corinthians 6:3) and eternally rule with Christ on the throne of the universe. This honor—to rule—must be won. "If we suffer, we shall also reign with him" (2 Timothy 2:12; cf. Romans 8:17).

That God should invite people to share His throne is an almost unbelievable elevation of humanity. This involves more than an assignment of power, although that in itself is staggering. Actually, it is implicit in the power given to rule and in authority to judge that the saints will oversee vast dimensions of God's creation, including angels and men. The people of God are to obtain knowledge in this life so they can "approve things that are excellent" (Philippians 1:10). But one day they will obtain "the full assurance of understanding" (Colossians 2:2), i.e., the eternal counsel of God in Christ. "Then shall I know even as also I am known" (1 Corinthians 13:12). Everything will be explained, exposed for all to see. The saints will judge perfectly and will consult with God in His judgments. They will further cooperate in the realization of His plans. They will not exist in childlike, oblivious joy; rather, they will possess the deep abiding joy that comes from a mature understanding of God's salvation. Limited knowledge will be transformed—not into omniscience, but into a full knowledge that will enable them to rule in God's perfect kingdom.

In another instance of positive comment 21:7 says, "He that overcometh *shall inherit all things.*" Accordingly, the believer will not merely be God's coworker and Christ's coregent, he will also be Christ's fellow heir and co-owner of everything God has created. Paul said, "Whether . . . things present, or things to come, all are yours" (1 Corinthians 3:22). All things will belong to the believer because he belongs to Christ.

Saints will not rule as uninvolved "hired help." True, they are servants; but they are also God's children and the bride of Christ. The joy of ownership and the desire to own something are innate in human nature. Much of the strife and conflict in this world comes out of the realization that one can possess something in this life, if even for only a short time. In the end all must leave "naked as we came." But Jesus wants to reshape human desire to possess. He said, "Lay up for yourselves treasures in heaven, where neither moth nor rust doth corrupt, and where thieves do not break through nor steal: for where your treasure is, there will your heart be also" (Matthew 6:20, 21).

What finally makes heaven "worth it all," however, is this: "they shall see his face" (22:4). To experience God's presence and fellowship is the essential ingredient to eternity. Now Jesus Christ is He "whom having not seen, ye love; in whom, though now ye see him not, yet believing" (1 Peter 1:8). But when the redeemed see Him they will be like Him (1 John 3:2). While on earth the people of God must "walk by faith, not by sight" (2 Corinthians 5:7). But in eternity they will see the very face of God, a privilege not even the great lawgiver Moses was granted (Exodus 33:20; cf. 33:23).

Jesus declared the pure in heart would see God (Matthew 5:8); only they have this hope. The Old Testament attests to an ancient custom in which criminals were denied access to the king and were not allowed to see even his face (2 Samuel 14:24; Esther 7:8; Proverbs 25:5). This practice probably forms the backdrop for Psalm 24:3ff.: "Who shall ascend into the hill of the Lord? Or who shall stand in his holy place? He that hath clean hands and a pure heart." Every person has been given a secret longing for fellowship with the Creator which cannot be removed. Even when a person lives outside the community of the Lord he may still be at peace because of hope that eventually he can find refuge in God. To be excluded forever from the presence of God is such a tragedy that Scripture uses the most urgent appeals to induce man to comprehend its seriousness.

The eternal bliss of heaven consists first and foremost in the fact that the community of God will be totally and finally in order. Finally the pre-Fall condition will be restored; God will dwell among men. This will involve more than a "restoration" of something old. Mankind will experience deep fellowship and communion with the God of holiness. In the Garden of Eden the Creator walked with His creation in the cool of the evening's twilight. In the new paradise He will dwell among it in the full light of the eternal day. The redeemed will see His face, and He will reveal His eternal secrets to them; they will be privy to the secrets of God (1 Corinthians 2:10; Colossians 2:9)—to His thoughts and plans, His power, and glory, and love. They will know the One who surpasses knowledge itself. They will be His worthy company (made worthy by His grace) throughout eternity. They will offer thanksgiving for what He gives, praise for what He has done, and worship for who He is.

## The Ending of the Book

The theme of eternity dominates the end of the book (22:6-21). The chords of heavenly praise still resound. Three times it is said: "Behold, I come quickly" (verses 7, 12, 20). Once again there is a reminder of the Holy City: "Blessed are they that do his commandments, that they may have right to the tree of life, and may enter in through the gates into the city" (verse 14). The admonition also sounds once more: "For without are . . ." (verse 15). Nothing must be added here; nothing taken away (verses 18, 19).

The offer of eternal life is made repeatedly and distinctly in the final two chapters of the Bible: "I will give unto him that is athirst of the fountain of the water of life freely" (21:6). "Let him that is athirst come. And whosoever will, let him take the water of life freely" (22:17). That is the nature of God's free gift of salvation. So freely is the gift of salvation given. So freely can man receive it.

# Revelation

## Commentary

### Chapter 1

1. **The Revelation of Jesus Christ:** ... This is a Revelation, –BECK ... The unveiling [apocalypse] of, –MNTG ... received, –KLST.

**which God gave unto him:** ... granted Him, –BRKL.

**to show unto his servants things which must shortly come to pass:** ... to reveal, –KLST ... to inform ... what must speedily happen, –FNTN ... show his slaves, –MNTG ... to make known, –TCNT ... to point out ... what things must needs come to pass with speed, –RTHM ... what must shortly take place, –BRKL.

**and he sent and signified [it] by his angel unto his servant John:** ... disclosed it, –NOLI ... communicated it through, –WLMS ... tells the truth, –BECK ... shewed by signs, sending through his messenger, –RTHM ... made it known to, –NORL.

**1:1.** The true title of this book and the key to its message is "The Revelation of Jesus Christ." Each of the four Gospels presents a picture of Jesus, and His continued working through the Church is recorded in the Acts and the Epistles. He is still continuing that work through the Holy Spirit today. The Book of Revelation, however, gives us a new picture of Jesus. The first part of the book shows His concern over the churches at the time John was writing, about A.D. 95. The major part of the book gives a revelation or unveiling of some of the events of the end time which will lead to His coming in triumph as King of kings and Lord of lords.

As a fitting climax, the book ends by describing the glorious New Jerusalem and the new heavens and the new earth. All through the book, Jesus—not the Antichrist, not Satan—is the key Person. Thus the book is an unveiling of truths, many of which were hidden until this revelation or disclosure was given.

The book is addressed to the servants of Jesus (all true believers) and was sent by an angel who made known its truths to His servant John. It reveals things Jesus said must begin to take place quickly, without delay. It is, however, not a fortune-telling book. Those who use it as a means of trying to discover what is going to happen next have been disappointed again and again. Nevertheless, the book has been a blessing all through the Church Age. Its inspired vision of Jesus as the

coming One, the triumphant One, still thrills the believer.

2. **Who bare record of the word of God:** ... He in turn testifies to, –NORL ... bare witness as, –RTHM ... attests, –KLST ... who vouches for everything, –BECK ... who gave testimony of the message, –FNTN.

**and of the testimony of Jesus Christ:** ... the evidence of, –FNTN ... witness of, –RTHM.

**and of all things that he saw:** ... telling both what he heard and what he saw, –NORL ... omitting nothing of what, –TCNT ... as an eye-witness, –NOLI ... about everything he saw, –BECK ... which things he had seen, –FNTN ... whatever he perceived, –KLST.

**1:2.** Early Church tradition confirms that the John who bore witness to the things he saw concerning the Word of God (John 1:1, 14) and the testimony of Jesus was the apostle John, "the disciple whom Jesus loved" (John 21:20). Early Church writers testify that he ministered in Ephesus and eventually died there (Eusebius *Ecclesiastical History* 3.20.9; 3.23.4; 3.31.2).

3. **Blessed [is] he that readeth:** ... Happy are you, –BECK ... Happy is the person, –SEB ... who reads this, –NORL ... in public, –KLST.

**and they that hear the words of this prophecy:** ... and the hearers, –FNTN ... the messages of this prophecy, –WLMS.

**and keep those things which are written therein:** ... who observe what is recorded in it, –BRKL ... who take heed to do the things, –NORL.

**for the time [is] at hand:** ... For the appointed time is drawing near, –NOLI ... for the season, –RTHM ... For the Crisis is, –MNTG ... is near, –BECK.

**1:3.** Blessing and happiness are promised to those who read this book aloud, to those who hear the words of this prophecy, and to those who "keep" what is "written therein." This implies a practice of reading Scripture aloud in the assemblies, and it indicates the need to pay attention to what is being read. The blessing will come to those who obey the commands and injunctions found in the book.

4. **John to the seven churches which are in Asia:** ... From John, –NORL ... the seven congregations, –KLST ... the seven assemblies, –RTHM ... in the province of, –BECK ... in Asia-Minor, –FNTN ... the Roman Province, –MNTG.

**Grace [be] unto you, and peace:** ... Love and peace, –BECK ... Favour to you, –RTHM ... Blessing, –FNTN.

**from him which is, and which was, and which is to come:** . . . from the eternal God, —NOLI . . . from him whose name is, —KLST . . . is coming, —BECK, —BRKL, —RTHM . . . and will be, —TCNT . . . Who comes, —FNTN . . . and is to be, —MNTG.

**and from the seven Spirits which are before his throne:** . . . in presence of, —RTHM.

**1:4.** John sent greetings (along with the entire Book of Revelation) to the seven churches in the Roman province of Asia which was located in western Asia Minor, now part of Turkey. Most of these churches were probably founded during Paul's ministry in Ephesus (Acts 19:10, 20). Geographically the churches were located at about 50-mile intervals from Ephesus. These seven were not the only churches in the province, but they were in key cities. They were representative of the totality of the churches (which may be why the number seven was chosen) and of the various problems which had developed in what was probably the third generation of believers. In fact, each message to a specific church is followed by an exhortation addressed to all churches.

John combined the New Testament greeting of grace and the Old Testament greeting of peace, both coming from the one true and eternal God, who is, and was, and is to come; that is, who has no beginning and no ending but who ever lives. The grace and peace also come from the seven Spirits; that is from the sevenfold manifestation of the Holy Spirit. This may be a reference to the revelation of the Spirit on the prophesied Messiah (Isaiah 11:2) as well as to the sevenfold lamp in Zechariah 4:2, 6, 10. Revelation 4:5 and 5:6 give more information about this manifestation of the Holy Spirit.

**5. And from Jesus Christ, [who is] the faithful witness:** . . . the Witness whom we can trust, —BECK . . . the trustworthy Witness, —BRKL . . . the expounder of the true faith, —NOLI . . . True Witness, —FNTN.

**[and] the first begotten of the dead:** . . . the First-born, —WLMS . . . the Bringer-forth, —FNTN . . . the pioneer of the resurrection, —NOLI . . . the First of the dead to live again, —BECK . . . and the first to arise from the dead, —LAMS.

**and the prince of the kings of the earth:** . . . the One who rules over the kings of the world, —BECK . . . the Ruler of the kings, —NORL . . . the Commander of, —FNTN . . . the Sovereign of the kings of the earth, —WLMS.

**Unto him that loved us:** . . . He has loved us, —NORL.

**and washed us from our sins in his own blood:** . . . setting us free from, —SEB . . . released us from, —FNTN . . . has freed us from our sins, —BECK . . . washed away our sins, —NORL . . . has loosed us from, —MNTG.

**1:5.** More specifically, this grace and peace comes through the work of Jesus Christ who is identified in three ways in this verse. First, He is the faithful witness. He declared (or unfolded) the Father and His grace and truth (John 1:14, 18). He came to bear witness to the truth (John 18:37). He communicates the fullness of divine love to His followers (Romans 5:5).

Second, He is the firstborn from the dead. That is, He was the first to be resurrected with a new body that is immortal and incorruptible, never to decay, deteriorate, or die. The term "first-begotten," or "firstborn" (*prōtotokos*), also speaks of rulership. He takes the place of leadership which, according to ancient custom, belonged to the heir. (See Psalm 89:20, 26, 27 where God promised to make David His firstborn "higher than the kings of the earth." See also Colossians 1:15-18 where the Bible uses the same terminology to declare the priority and lordship of Jesus as the highest Ruler and Lord of all; compare 1 Corinthians 15:20; Exodus 4:22; Deuteronomy 28:1; Romans 14:9.) Through His grace and truth He makes believers joint heirs with Him (Romans 8:17) and sharers of His triumph.

Third, He is the Prince of the kings of the earth, for He is King of kings and Lord of lords (1 Timothy 6:15; Revelation 17:14; 19:16).

His grace and the reality of His truth is also seen in the praise John next gave for Christ's cleansing believers from their sins by His own blood that was shed on Calvary. As believers walk in the light, His blood keeps on cleansing them (1 John 1:7).

**6. And hath made us kings and priests unto God and his Father:** . . . has established us, —FNTN . . . has made us into royalty, —BRKL . . . a spiritual kingdom, —LAMS . . . has made us a kingdom and priests serving His God, —BECK . . . before His God, —NORL. **to him [be] glory and dominion for ever and ever. Amen:** . . . belong, —KLST . . . be ascribed, —TCNT . . . and power, —BECK . . . the majesty and the might, throughout the ages, —FNTN . . . to the ages of ages, Rother-ham.

**1:6.** Jesus is worthy of praise because He not only cleanses believers from sin, but He also makes them what God has always wanted His people to be: kings and priests unto God. When God delivered Israel out of Egypt and brought them to himself, He told them He wanted them to be His own people in a special way. Believers are to be a spiritual temple, a holy priesthood, a chosen generation (a choice race or people whose characteristics depend on what they receive from God, not on what they inherit from their parents), a royal priesthood (a body of kings who minister as priests to God, even the Father of our Lord Jesus), a holy nation (including both saved Jews and saved Gentiles; Ephesians 2:11-20), a people who are God's own possession in a special way (1 Peter 2:5, 9). By His grace through faith they enter into this royal priesthood of all believers and have access to the very Holy of Holies of God's presence (Hebrews 10:19, 20). This is the believers' position now, and they will reign with Christ when He returns (2 Timothy 2:12). No wonder John cried out that the Lord deserves "glory and dominion for ever and ever" (1:6)!

**7. Behold, he cometh with clouds:** ... Take note, *—KLST* ... See, *—WLMS* ... Look, He is coming in the clouds, *—BECK* ... to come among, *—MNTG.*
**and every eye shall see him:** ... He will be manifested to every eye, *—NOLI* ... shall look on Him, *—FNTN.*
**and they [also] which pierced him:** ... even of those, *—BRKL, —KLST.*
**and all kindreds of the earth shall wail because of him:** ... He will bring consternation to, *—NOLI* ... the people on earth will mourn over Him, *—BECK* ... shall beat the breast over Him, *—BRKL* ... will lament over Him, *—WLMS* ... smite themselves for him shall all the tribes of the land, *—RTHM* ... on account of Him, *—NORL.*
**Even so, Amen:** ... So it will be, *—BECK* ... So shall it be, *—TCNT, —MNTG* ... So it is to be, *—NORL* ... Yes, certainly, *—FNTN* ... Truly so, *—BRKL* ... Yea! *—RTHM.*

**1:7.** Along with the thought of Christ's power and dominion, John immediately interjected the hope of the Church. Most of those to whom he was writing were former Gentiles who, like the believers in Thessalonica, had "turned to God from idols to serve the living and true God; and to wait for his Son from heaven" (1 Thessalonians 1:9, 10). Though John was old, that hope was still bright.

John looked ahead in this verse to the point which he saw in more detail in chapter 19, the time at the end of the tribulation period when Jesus will come with clouds. At this coming the kindreds (nations, peoples, tribes) of the earth will beat their breasts in terrible mourning because of Him. This is not God's desire or purpose. The promise to Abraham was that in him and in his seed (the greater Seed, Jesus) all the families, tribes, and nations would be blessed. But because of the world's rejection of God's way and plan, Jesus will have to return "in flaming fire taking vengeance on them that know not God, and that obey not the gospel of our Lord Jesus Christ" (2 Thessalonians 1:7, 8).

Now, in this age, everyone has the privilege of obtaining salvation and receiving the baptism in the Holy Spirit. But once Jesus returns in His final triumph over the armies of the Antichrist, there will be nothing left for unbelievers but a baptism of the fires of judgment. Then John added a "Yes, truly!" It is not that he wanted that judgment to come upon the world, but he confirmed that the prophecies are indeed true.

**8. I am Alpha and Omega:** ... the A and the Z, *—BECK, —SEB, —RTHM.*
**the beginning and the ending, saith the Lord: which is, and which was, and which is to come, the Almighty:** ... the All-Sovereign, *—BRKL* ... Who exists, *—FNTN* ... whose name is 'He is,' and 'He was' and 'He is coming,' *—KLST* ... the Sovereign Supreme, *—WADE.*

**1:8.** Verse 8 concludes the salutation of the book. In verse 4 God the Father is described as the coming One, the eternal One. Here, Jesus so describes himself. He is the Alpha and the Omega (the first and last letters of the Greek alphabet, therefore, the beginning and the end, and thus himself without beginning or end). There is a sense also in which He is always the coming One. In the Old Testament the word translated "visit" (*pāqad*), is often used of God coming in blessing or in judgment. The New Testament says the Lord Jesus is the one Mediator between God and man, and He still comes to His followers (1 Timothy 2:5). In fact, Jesus told His disciples that wherever two or three gather in His name, He is there with them (Matthew 18:20). But this passage gives special emphasis to His future coming in triumph. He is coming again as the full revelation of the Almighty, the all-powerful, omnipotent God. All that God revealed himself to be in the Old Testament is revealed in Jesus in the New Testament. It is clear why this final book of the New Testament is called "the Revelation of Jesus Christ."

**9. I John, who also am your brother:** ... your fellow Christian, *—BECK.*
**and companion in tribulation:** ... and joint-sharer ... in the afflictions which you sustain, *—WADE* ... who share with you in the woes, *—MNTG* ... share with you suffering, *—BECK* ... fellow-partaker, *—RTHM* ... and fellow sharer in the distress, *—BRKL* ... participator in the affliction, *—FNTN.*
**and in the kingdom and patience of Jesus Christ:** ... and ruling and enduring, *—BECK* ... and the patient endurance which Jesus gives, *—WLMS* ... in the Dominion which you are to inherit, and in the steadfastness which you manifest through your union, *—WADE* ... and perseverance in union with, *—KLST* ... and kingship, and suffering of Jesus, *—FNTN* ... stedfastness of Jesus, *—MNTG.*
**was in the isle that is called Patmos:** ... found myself in the island, *—MNTG* ... came to be in, *—RTHM* ... known as, *—FNTN.*
**for the word of God:** ... on account of, *—FNTN* ... loyalty to God's Message, *—WADE* ... the

word, —RTHM . . . sake of God's Message, —TCNT . . . my preaching, —NORL.

**and for the testimony of Jesus Christ:** . . . Jesus' witness to it, —WADE . . . and witnessing about, —NORL . . . the truth told by Jesus, —BECK . . . testifying to Jesus, —WLMS . . . and my testimony for Jesus, —FNTN.

**1:9.** John received this wonderful revelation of Christ while he was an exile and a prisoner, not for any guilt of his own but because of his faithful proclamation of God's Word and his determined witness to Christ. This witness he shared with others who were enduring persecution and distress but who remained under the rule of Jesus with a steadfast patience. The presence of Jesus enabled him and them to bear up under Roman persecution.

Several different time periods have been suggested for the writing of Revelation and John's persecution. The most common of these suggestions include the reigns of Claudius (41-54), Nero (54-68), Vespasian (69-79), Domitian (81-96), and Trajan (98-117). The three early emperors have been suggested based on a literal interpretation of passages such as 6:9; 11:1ff.; 17:10. Others take the number *666* to refer to Nero if his name and title are put in Hebrew characters. The Book of Revelation, however, was written in Greek. The use of the first and last letters of the Greek alphabet (alpha and omega) show that the Greek alphabet was in mind, not the Hebrew. Furthermore, the persecution of Nero was not as widespread as was once supposed, and the general situation of the book fits the end of the reign of the emperor Domitian (A.D. 81-96), not Nero. The condition of the churches, the spread of the Nicolaitans, the pressure of the times—all indicate a time about A.D. 95.

Patmos is a rocky, treeless, 10-mile-long island, about 60 miles southwest of Ephesus. John may have been sentenced to hard labor in the quarries.

**10. I was in the Spirit on the Lord's day:** . . . The Spirit of prophecy came upon me, —LAMS . . . under the Spirit's power, —BECK . . . became Spirit-possessed, —BRKL . . . inspired, —FNTN . . . a trance, —TCNT . . . prophetic ecstasy, —KLST.

**and heard behind me a great voice, as of a trumpet:** . . . I hear, —CNDT . . . loud voice, —BECK, —MNTG . . . resembling a trumpet-blast, —FNTN . . . a voice as resounding as a trumpet, —KLST . . . a great sound like, —KLGS . . . like the calling of a war trumpet, —AMPB . . . like the loud sound of a horn, —NLTG . . . at my back, as of a horn, came to my ears, —BB . . . clear as the blast of, —WADE.

**1:10.** The "Lord's day" may mean Sunday, but this verse more probably means that the Holy Spirit projected John into the future Day of the Lord that is ahead of us. While experiencing this special move of the Spirit, a voice came like a trumpet blast.

**11. Saying, I am Alpha and Omega, the first and the last:** . . . It said, —NORL . . . The voice said, —EVRD . . . directing me, —WADE.

**and, What thou seest, write in a book:** . . . What thou beholdest, —RTHM . . . What you are observing write into, —CNDT . . . That which you see, —KLGS . . . put in, —BB . . . write on a scroll, —BECK.

**and send [it] unto the seven churches which are in Asia:** . . . Send it to these seven congregations, —SEB . . . send that book, —EVRD . . . and dispatch to, —FNTN . . . the seven assemblies, —RTHM . . . ecclesias, —CNDT.

**unto Ephesus, and unto Smyrna:** . . . They are in the cities of, —NLTG . . . at Ephesus, —KLST.

**and unto Pergamos, and unto Thyatira:** . . . Pergamum, —CNDT, —TNT . . . Thyatyra, —KLGS.

**and unto Sardis, and unto Philadelphia, and unto Laodicea:** . . . Laodikea, —HNSN.

**1:11.** The loud voice John heard was the voice of Jesus, again proclaiming himself as the Alpha and the Omega, the first and the last. The churches in the Roman province of Asia were Greek speaking. They would understand the use of the Alpha and the Omega to mean the beginning and the end and at the same time to mean His eternalness. As the first, He is the most prominent and more important in God's plan. As the last, He will never be replaced. No other messiah will ever take His place. No one else will ever be King of kings and Lord of lords after Him. His throne will be eternal. All others who claim to be Christ or Messiah are false. Jesus himself warned against them. He also gave the assurance that He will come suddenly. Thus, if anyone claims to be Messiah or Christ or a manifestation of Jesus, and believers are still on the earth, they can know that person is a false christ (1 Thessalonians 4:17).

John was not only to hear but to see and to write what he saw in a book, probably meaning on a roll of writing material made from the inner bark of the papyrus reed grown in the marshes of Egypt. Once the book was complete he was to send it to each of the seven churches of Asia. The order in which they are named is geographical. On the map they appear in a sort of circular progression. Ephesus, in Lydia, was the chief city of the Roman province of Asia, and the church there was established by Paul. Smyrna was a beautiful city on the Mediterranean coast about 45 miles north of Ephesus. Pergamos, the ancient Pergamum, modern Bergama, was the most important city of Mysia and was once the ancient capital of a wealthy kingdom. It was about 70 miles north of Smyrna. Thyatira, founded by Macedonian Greeks, was about 40 miles southeast of Pergamum on the Lycus River in Lydia. It was a busy industrial city noted for the dying of purple cloth. Sardis, the ancient capital city of Lydia, was a very wealthy city because of trade and the manufacture of textiles, dyes, and jewelry. It was about 30 miles southwest of Thyatira. Philadelphia (which means "love of brothers"), in Lydia, was about 30 miles east-southeast of Sardis and was a center of Greek culture. Laodicea, in Phrygia, had a large colony of Jews and was about 50 miles southeast of Philadelphia.

**12. And I turned to see the voice that spake with me:** . . . I accordingly turned to see, *—FNTN* . . . turned round, *—WADE* . . . I turn about to look for the voice which spoke, *—CNDT* . . . to look in the direction of the voice, *—ADAM* . . . to find out whose voice was speaking, *—NOLI* . . . turning to see the voice which said these words to me, *—BB* . . . to behold the voice, *—RTHM* . . . who was talking to me, *—BECK, —EVRD* . . . whose voice was addressing me, *—BRKL* . . . which was speaking to me, *—MNTG.*

**And being turned, I saw seven golden candlesticks:** . . . and as I turned, *—NORL* . . . I observed, *—FNTN* . . . lampstands, *—BECK.*

**1:12.** When John turned to see whose voice it was that was speaking to him, the first things he saw were seven golden "lampstands" (NIV). These were seven separate lampstands, not the seven-branched lampstand made by Moses (Exodus 25:31-37). These lampstands represented the seven churches of Asia which had just been named. The gold speaks of Christ in all His deity and glory, for the Church is the body of Christ. The olive oil burning in the lamps typifies the Holy Spirit. Thus, even though persecuted, the seven churches still had the power of the Spirit and the light of Christ to give to the world.

**13. And in the midst of the seven candlesticks; [one] like unto the Son of man:**
**clothed with a garment down to the foot:** . . . clad, *—FNTN* . . . wearing a long vestment, *—LAMS* . . . dressed in a robe, *—BRKL* . . . He wore a long robe, *—NORL* . . . wore a robe reaching down to his feet, *—BECK.*
**and girt about the paps with a golden girdle:** . . . fastened at the waist, *—FNTN* . . . towards the breasts, *—RTHM* . . . with a golden belt around His breast, *—BECK* . . . with a band of gold across, *—TCNT* . . . and He had a gold band around His chest, *—NORL* . . . across the breast, *—BRKL.*

**1:13.** The seven churches needed to know that Christ was still in their midst as their compassionate High Priest and conquering King. The attention here is not on the churches, however, but on Jesus in the midst. The Book of Revelation is first and foremost a revelation of Jesus Christ.

Jesus is described as "one like unto the Son of man." This is another example of the use of Old Testament language in the Book of Revelation. The phrase identifies Jesus with the One prophesied in Daniel 7:13. This Jesus, whom John saw, is the triumphant One who will come to receive "dominion, and glory, and a kingdom, that all people, nations, and languages, should serve him" (Daniel 7:14).

His clothing indicated both priestly dignity and royal office. The garment or long tunic was like that worn by priests and kings. The belt or band of pure gold around His chest (see Daniel 10:5) was a mark of triumphant royalty in contrast to the worker or servant who wore a belt of cloth or leather about the loins. Christ, the King-Priest identified as Jesus by the Book of Hebrews, is now at the right hand of the Father interceding on the believer's behalf (Hebrews 4:14-16; 1 John 2:1).

**14. His head and [his] hairs [were] white like wool, as white as snow:** . . . Both His head and, *—NORL.*
**and his eyes [were] as a flame of fire:** . . . His eyes blazed like, *—NOLI* . . . like coals, *—WLMS.*

**1:14.** The language of the descriptions given in verses 14 and 15 apply to God himself, especially as the mighty Judge and Ruler of the universe. Thus, John made it clear that all the attributes of the Father which the Old Testament visions described are also attributes of the Son. To the Son has been given all power and authority both to reign and to be the world's Judge (Matthew 28:18; John 5:22, 27).

The whiteness of the hair (see Daniel 7:9) represents absolute purity and the dazzling splendor of His holiness. The eyes like a flame of fire (see Daniel 10:6) speak of His penetrating wisdom and His righteous judgment.

**15. And his feet like unto fine brass, as if they burned in a furnace:** . . . His feet were like polished brass, glowing as if in a furnace, *—NORL* . . . as bright as when the metal has been smelted in a furnace, *—TCNT* . . . like white-glowing bronze refined in, *—BECK* . . . like precious ore as it glows in, *—BRKL* . . . like shining brass, when melting in a crucible, *—FNTN* . . . refined to white heat, *—WLMS* . . . glowing in an oven, *—SEB* . . . as in a furnace fired, *—RTHM.*
**and his voice as the sound of many waters:** . . . His voice resounded like the cataract of mighty waters, *—NOLI* . . . like the rushing of much water, *—SEB.*

**1:15.** The feet of the finest burnished, fire-refined, bronze (such as was used in censers for incense) speak not only of strength but of the brazen altar and thus of the sacrifice of Christ. Some believe that this bronze, instead of being the ordinary alloy of copper and tin, was an alloy of copper and gold (Ford, *The Anchor Bible,* 38:383).

The voice John heard was the voice of God, coming like the sound of many waters, loud and clear (see Ezekiel 1:24; 43:2). Thus, in this vision Jesus presented himself as the one Mediator between God and man as well as the One in whom dwells "the fulness of the Godhead bodily" (Colossians 2:9).

**16. And he had in his right hand seven stars:** . . . held, *—NORL* . . . holding, *—FNTN* . . . control of, *—WADE.*

**and out of his mouth went a sharp twoedged sword:** . . . double-edged, *—BECK* . . . going forth, *—RTHM* . . . from His mouth came forth, *—NORL* . . . came out of, *—EVRD* . . . issued speech that cut like a . . . broadsword, *—WADE* . . . a sharp two-edged blade is issuing, *—CNDT* . . . that cuts both ways, *—NLTG* . . . drawn from its sheath, *—FNTN.*

**and his countenance [was] as the sun shineth in his strength:** . . . His face was like the sun when it shines very brightly, *—BECK* . . . while his face shone, *—TCNT* . . . his face [glowed] as the sun shines, *—HNSN* . . . He looked like the sun shining at its brightest time, *—EVRD* . . . shone like the sun at its full strength, *—NORL* . . . shines in its full strength, *—BRKL* . . . his face shone like the sun at mid-day, *—TNT* . . . is as the sun appearing, *—CNDT* . . . bright as the sun shines at noon, *—NLTG* . . . shining in full power at midday, *—AMPB* . . . like the sun at noonday, *—NOLI* . . . shining in his power, *—RTHM* . . . in. his strength, *—FNTN* . . . in full splendor, *—KLST* . . . like the sun at its brightest, *—NAB.*

**1:16.** The seven stars in Jesus' right hand most probably represented the leaders or pastors of the seven churches. Being in His hand means protection and much more. The right hand is the hand of action. Thus, they were ready for Him to use them. No persecutor, no enemy of the Church, could stop them from leading the churches to do the will of the Lord and win victories for Him. In His hand—what a good place to be!

The sharp sword that came from Christ's mouth was also their sword, the sword of the Spirit, the powerful Word of God. (See Isaiah 11:4; 49:2; Ephesians 6:17; Hebrews 4:12; Revelation 19:15.) It may be that the sword also speaks of reproof and punishment to the churches, judgment beginning in the house of God (1 Peter 4:17). (See also 19:15 where the sword means judgment on the nations.)

Christ's face was like the sun in its strength, that is, in its full, summertime, noonday brilliance. In His resurrection appearances, though the body of Jesus was changed and was free from our limits of time and space, yet its full glory was veiled. It may be that the full restoration of that glory did not take place until after the Ascension (see John 17:5). At least, on the Damascus Road the light of

His glory was enough to blind Saul who became the apostle Paul (Acts 9:3, 8). What John saw here was the fullness of the glory of God in the face of Jesus—a fullness of glory that even Moses was not permitted to see (Exodus 33:18-23, especially verse 22; compare Exodus 34:29; Judges 5:31; Matthew 13:43; 17:2).

Believers can worship Christ now, and the Holy Spirit makes them very conscious of His presence. Yet, it is not until they are changed at the resurrection and the rapture of the Church that they will be able to see Him in the fullness of the glory "as he is" (1 John 3:2; see also 1 Corinthians 15:51, 52).

**17. And when I saw him, I fell at his feet as dead:** . . . when I perceived Him, I fall, *—CNDT* . . . When I caught sight of him, *—NAB* . . . I went down on my face at his feet as one, *—BB* . . . fell towards, *—RTHM* . . . like a dead man, *—BECK, NLTG* . . . as if dead, *—NORL.*

**And he laid his right hand upon me, saying unto me:** . . . He put, *—EVRD* . . . He places, *—CNDT* . . . touched me with his right hand, *—NAB.*

**Fear not; I am the first and the last:** . . . Don't be afraid, *—BECK* . . . Do not fear, *—KLGS* . . . Cease to fear, *—WADE* . . . Have no fear, *—WADE* . . . Do not be afraid any more, *—WLMS* . . . There is nothing to fear, *—NAB* . . . I am before all and after all, *—TCNT.*

**1:17.** John had already seen a glimpse of Christ's glory on the Mount of Transfiguration. There the face of Jesus shone like the sun, and His clothes glistened and glittered like lightning flashes from the outshining of inner glory (Matthew 17:2). But that was only a foretaste. The disciples were awed, but not struck down. John on Patmos, however, was not able to stand the full impact of the glory of God in Christ and fell into what must have been an unconscious state, a coma.

Then the same right hand that had held the seven stars was laid on John. He felt the same gentle touch and heard the same "Fear not" that had so often encouraged the disciples while Jesus ministered to them during His life on earth. What peace John must have felt, the peace that Jesus gives (John 14:27)!

Along with the "Fear not," Jesus gave John wonderful assurance. He has not changed. He is still the first and the last; the eternal, unchanging Christ; the same yesterday, today, and forever (Hebrews 13:8). He wants to be the most important Person in believers' lives so they can be prepared for that day when He shall come again.

**18. I [am] he that liveth, and was dead:** . . . the ever-living One, *—WLMS* . . . the Living One; and I became dead, *—RTHM* . . . I experienced death, *—BRKL* . . . I died, *—NORL.*

**and, behold, I am alive for evermore, Amen:** . . . but how wonderful, I live for ever and ever, −*KLST*...but see! I am alive again, −*NORL*...living am I to the ages of ages, −*RTHM*...I am living in the eternities of the eternities, −*FNTN*.

**and have the keys of hell and of death:**...I possess the keys, −*BRKL*...and hold, −*MNTG*...and the underworld, −*WLMS*...of hades, −*RTHM*...of the spirit land, −*FNTN*...the nether world, −*KLST*.

**1:18.** Jesus gave the further assurance that He is the same living Christ who rose from the dead and inspired new faith in His followers after the terrible ordeal of the Cross. He lives forever, and the future is in His hands.

"The Living One" ("I am he that liveth") is actually a title of God. (See Joshua 3:10; 1 Samuel 17:26, 36; 2 Kings 19:4, 16; Psalms 42:2; 84:2; Isaiah 37:4, 17; Jeremiah 10:10; 23:36; Hosea 1:10; John 5:26.) As the Living One He is the source of life and healing. The armies of Israel were the armies of the Living God. As the Living God He will bring wrath on the nations that they cannot endure. But the heart and soul of the believer thirsts for Him.

He also has the keys of death and Hades. Hades (*hadēs*) in the New Testament is the Greek name of the place of punishment where the wicked and the unbelievers suffer in the time between death and the final Great White Throne Judgment when death and Hades will be cast into the lake of fire. In the Old Testament it seems that God had the keys of death and therefore of Hades (in the Hebrew, Sheol). Satan did not have the keys; for God, not Satan, had control of what Satan could do to Job (Job 2:6). Jesus now has the keys because God has given Him all power and authority in heaven and in earth (Matthew 28:18). God has also "set him at his own right hand in the heavenly places, far above all principality, and power, and might, and dominion, and every name that is named, not only in this world, but also in that which is to come: and hath put all things under his feet" (Ephesians 1:20-22). This means nothing shall prevail against His church (Matthew 16:18).

**19. Write the things which thou hast seen:**...So write down now what you see, −*NORL*...what things thou sawest, −*RTHM*.

**and the things which are:** ... both what is, −*NORL*...what is now, −*BECK*.

**and the things which shall be hereafter:**...what is going to happen later, −*BECK* ... what shall occur, −*BRKL*...what is to take place, −*WLMS*...what things are about to be coming to pass after these things, −*RTHM* ... are about to happen after the present time, −*SEB* ... what will come after these, −*FNTN*...later, −*KLST*.

**1:19.** Jesus touched John, not just to revive him but to commission him to write the revelation he had just received and the revelation he was about

to receive. This seems to indicate a threefold division of the Book of Revelation: first, the preliminary vision in chapter 1; second, the messages to the churches in chapters 2 and 3; and third, the future events which are described beginning in chapter 4. God intended this revelation to be a means of blessing and revival for others, not only for the seven churches of Asia but also for believers throughout the Church Age.

**20. The mystery of the seven stars which thou sawest in my right hand:**...As for the mystery of, −*KLST*...The hidden meaning of, −*BECK*...The secret...that you see on My right hand, −*NORL*...saw upon, −*FNTN*.

**and the seven golden candlesticks:** ... lampstands, −*RTHM*.

**The seven stars are the angels of the seven churches:**...are the Bishops, −*NOLI*...messengers of, −*RTHM*...the seven congregations, −*KLST*.

**and the seven candlesticks which thou sawest are the seven churches:** ... the seven lights, −*WADE* ... the seven lamps, −*TNT* ... lampstands, −*BECK* ... assemblies, −*RTHM* ... congregations, −*KLST*...Churches themselves, −*WADE*.

**1:20.** Jesus next explained the mystery, that is, the secret meaning, the inner meaning of the symbol of the seven stars and the seven golden lampstands. The seven stars are the angels or messengers of the seven churches. The Greek word (*angelos*) can mean either "angel" or "messenger." Some Bible students take these angels to be patron angels of the churches even though they are identified with the churches (Harrington, pp. 80f.; Morris, p. 45). (Compare Daniel 10:13; 12:1.) Others take them to be the pastors of the churches since John was to write the message to them (Barnhouse, p. 32). Still others take the angels to be visitors or delegates from the churches who would take the Book of Revelation back with them (Ramsey, p. 98). (See 2 Corinthians 8:23 where the messengers are delegates.)

## Chapter 2

**1. Unto the angel of the church of Ephesus write:**...To the messenger of, −*WLMS*...the Guardian Angel, −*WADE*...of the assembly, −*RTHM*...of the congregation, −*KLST* ... in the city of, −*NLTG* ... say, −*BB*.

**These things saith he that holdeth the seven stars in his right hand:** ... has this to say, −*KLST*...are the words of Him, −*MNTG*...This is what He declares, −*WADE*...holds fast, −*RTHM*...the Controller of, −*FNTN*...the Omnipotent One, −*LAMS*.

**who walketh in the midst of the seven golden candlesticks:**...Who moves to and fro amidst, −*WADE*...walks about amid, −*RTHM*...walks among, −*BECK*, −*TCNT*...in the centre, −*FNTN*...in the middle of the seven gold lights, −*BB*...seven lights made of gold, −*NLTG*...lampstands, −*SEB*.

**2:1.** Though the leaders of the seven churches were stars in Christ's right hand under His direction and protection, He moved on feet of burnished bronze and subjected the churches to rigid inspection. His purpose, however, was to encourage and challenge them. Each letter begins with a revelation of Christ and a commendation, usually followed by a warning and a challenge. However, He commended their virtues even more than He warned them of their faults. He knew exactly what was going on in each church. He knew their successes, their failures, their victories, their problems, their difficulties. More than that, He knew exactly what each one needed.

In addition to the geographical sequence of the churches, many see a historical significance. The church at Ephesus corresponds, in a remarkable way, to the conditions of the Church as a whole in the First Century. The message to various churches ends with the Laodicean church, a church which had the general characteristics of the nominal church at the end of the age.

But the primary message of these letters was to the churches at the end of the First Century where all these conditions already existed. It is important also to recognize the valuable lessons of encouragement and warning for every person who is dedicated to God and who desires to live and work for Him in the present time.

The letter to the leader of the church at Ephesus drew attention first to the fact that Jesus held the seven stars firmly and with full authority in His right hand. He also kept walking in the midst of all the churches. He not only knew them; He was also very much concerned about them.

**2. I know thy works, and thy labour, and thy patience:** . . . I know about your deeds, —NORL . . . I have knowledge of, —BB . . . your achievements, —NOLI . . . your position, your industry, —FNTN . . . your conduct . . . your patience, —KLST . . . what you have done . . . how long you can wait and not give up, —NLTG . . . your doings, —WADE . . . your activities, your fatiguing toil, —BRKL . . . how hard you have worked, —BECK . . . your hard work and patient endurance, —WLMS . . . and long waiting, —BB . . . and stedfastness, —MNTG.

**and how thou canst not bear them which are evil:** . . . you can't tolerate wicked people, —BECK . . . you cannot endure those who are ungodly, —LAMS . . . you will not put up with, —BB . . . cannot bear evil men, —KLST, —WMCK . . . bad [men], —RTHM . . . evildoers, —TCNT . . . evil people, —SEB . . . wicked men, —NOLI.

**and thou hast tried them which say they are apostles, and are not:** . . . didst try those affirming themselves apostles, —RTHM . . . you have tested, —BECK . . . put to the test, —FNTN . . . those who claim to be, —NORL.

**and hast found them liars:** . . . you have found them to be impostors, —BRKL . . . and didst find them false, —RTHM . . . you have discovered them, —NORL.

**2:2.** The fact that Jesus knew their works and their labors (their Christian service involving difficulties and hardship) implies not only His personal knowledge of the facts but also indicates that He honored and remembered their works. He commended them for their patient endurance. It was not easy to be a faithful witness for Christ in the midst of the opposition and persecution from the world which they had to endure. He commended them for not allowing themselves to put up with evil. They were surrounded by a society and a culture that was full of evil practices and evil people. It would have been easy for them to ignore the evil and say nothing. But by their words and by their lives they showed they would not put up with evil. Above all, they put false apostles to the test of the Scriptures. Already many false teachers and false prophets had arisen, some of them right out of the churches. Most of them tried to give authority to their false teachings by calling themselves apostles. But the church at Ephesus did not tolerate them or their clever sermons. This church remained pure in its doctrine, holding to the body of teaching given to the genuine apostles of the Lord by Christ himself. Since Jesus honored the Old Testament and gave His teaching directly to Paul, the entire Bible must be our standard.

**3. And hast borne, and hast patience:** . . . I know, too, that you are patient, —NORL . . . You show that you possess, —TCNT . . . You have endurance, —BECK . . . have suffered, —FNTN.

**and for my name's sake hast laboured, and hast not fainted:** . . . and didst bear because of my name, —RTHM . . . you have endured much . . . and that you have not grown weary, —NORL . . . and aren't tired out, —BECK . . . you have not been exhausted, —BRKL . . . and have not wearied, —LAMS . . . have not failed, —FNTN.

**2:3.** As a final commendation Jesus recognized that the believers in Ephesus were untiring in their labors for the Lord. They had fortitude or steadfast endurance. For Christ's name's sake they had borne patiently whatever burdens came their way. They had worked hard and struggled, not only physically, but mentally and spiritually. Difficulties and opposition had not caused them to lose their zeal.

**4. Nevertheless I have [somewhat] against thee:** . . . I hold it against you, —BECK . . . I have this complaint, —NOLI . . . a charge, —FNTN.

**because thou hast left thy first love:** . . . you have given up, —BRKL . . . abandoned, —TCNT . . . forsaken, —FNTN, —NORL . . . your love isn't what it was at first, *—BECK* . . . you do not love me as you did at first, *—WLMS* . . . you no longer love me as you did in the beginning, *—SEB* . . . that thy first love thou didst let go, *—RTHM.*

**2:4.** However, in spite of their zeal and hard work for the Lord, the Ephesians had one serious flaw. They had left or forsaken their first love. The Greek here (*phēkas*) usually is used of willful abandonment, a deliberate giving up, though it also includes the results of long neglect. They were giving the Lord their service but not giving Him themselves. They were outstanding in their work for the Lord, but they no longer had the intimate fellowship with Him they once had.

"Love" here is the same word translated "charity" in the King James Version of 1 Corinthians 13. Once they had been channels for Calvary love. Once they had responded to Christ's love by pouring out their hearts in fervent love and praise to Him. Now they were satisfied to have right doctrine and fulfill what they considered their duty to the Lord. But their work for Him no longer showed Christlike compassion. Their lives were very busy but terribly barren.

**5. Remember therefore from whence thou art fallen:** . . . Be calling to remembrance, *—RTHM* . . . what you have fallen away from, *—NORL.*

**and repent, and do the first works:** . . . Change your heart! *—SEB* . . . and be sorry, and do as you did at first, *—BECK* . . . practice what you did previously, *—BRKL* . . . your former works, *—FNTN* . . . work as you did at first, *—NORL.*

**or else I will come unto thee quickly:** . . . Otherwise, *—NORL* . . . failing which, *—FNTN* . . . if not, I am coming, *—RTHM.*

**and will remove thy candlestick out of his place:** . . . remove, *—WADE* . . . take away your lampstand, *—NOLI* . . . to move your lampstand from its place, *—KLST.*

**except thou repent:** . . . except perchance, *—RTHM* . . . if you aren't sorry, *—BECK* . . . unless you alter your mind, *—FNTN.*

**2:5.** The Ephesian Christians needed to correct their lack of the high, holy love that had marked them when they first turned to the Lord. Three words are significant here: "remember, repent, do." By thinking back to their first response to Calvary love, they would realize from what state and from what height they had fallen and how much they needed to repent. By remembering how their love flowed out in the first years of the church's existence so that other churches were founded in nearby towns, they would realize the change that had come in their attitudes in the work they were doing for the Lord. Repentance means to change the mind in the sense of changing basic attitudes.

They needed to return, to change back to their former attitudes of love.

They also needed to do their first works over again. Some take this to mean that they were to go back and resume religious observances such as baptism and the Lord's Supper, which they had neglected. But this would only lead to more formality if their attitudes did not change. The first works here refer to works of love, works done in response to the outpouring of Christ's love in their hearts, works full of compassion. (See John 15:8-13, 17; 1 Peter 1:22; 1 John 4:7, 11, 20, 21; 2 John 5, 6.) If they did not repent they could expect a special, sudden act of judgment. Their lampstand would be removed out of its place. That is, the church would no longer be in a place where Jesus walked in their midst.

**6. But this thou hast, that thou hatest the deeds of the Nicolai-tanes, which I also hate:** . . . But this is in your favour, *—TCNT* . . . Still, you have this, *—NORL* . . . Yet you have this merit, *—WADE* . . . you have it to your credit, *—WLMS* . . . Yet I must give you credit, *—NOLI* . . . that you hate the doings of . . . just as I also do, *—KLST* . . . the corrupters of the people, *—FNTN.*

**2:6.** One thing the Ephesian church had in its favor was that they did not tolerate the Nicolaitans, a cult which was guilty of immoral teaching and practices (cf. 2:15). Irenaeus, one of the church fathers who wrote about 100 years later, said they were followers of Nicolas who was mentioned in Acts 6:5, and who backslid into a life of "unrestrained indulgence" (*The Ante-Nicene Fathers, Against Heresies* 26:3). There is no proof, however, that this was the Nicolas of Acts 6:5. A sect of Nicolaitans did exist among the Gnostics of the late Second Century A.D. They taught that Christians were free to indulge in any of the lusts of the flesh that they might desire. If the Nicolaitans of the First Century promoted that kind of sin, it is no wonder the Lord hated their deeds.

**7. He that hath an ear, let him hear what the Spirit saith unto the churches:** . . . let him listen, *—FNTN, —MNTG* . . . to what the Divine Spirit says, *—WADE* . . . is saying to the assemblies, *—RTHM* . . . to the congregations, *—KLST.*

**To him that overcometh will I give to eat of the tree of life:** . . . Be victorious, *—BECK* . . . To him that conquers, *—RTHM* . . . I will reward the victor with, *—NOLI* . . . I will grant, *—KLST* . . . the privilege of eating the fruit of, *—WLMS* . . . the right to eat of . . . the Life-sustaining Tree, *—WADE* . . . grant to eat of the fruit of, *—NORL.*

**which is in the midst of the paradise of God:** . . . that stands in, *—BECK* . . . which grows in the garden of, *—FNTN.*

**2:7.** After the message to the church at Ephesus, Jesus gave an exhortation that was a promise and a challenge for every believer who is willing to respond and obey. Jesus has a special reward for every person who overcomes. The word "overcome" is a strong one. The overcomer is a victorious believer. These victories are won only through Christ, as the believer remains in Him. Through Him Christians can be more than conquerors (Romans 8:37; see also 1 John 5:4).

Because of Adam's sin, mankind was cut off from the tree of life, and physical death became the universal fate. But because Christ lives, believers will once again partake of the tree of life, and there shall be no more death. (See 22:2-4, 14.)

The opposite is also implied. If a believer draws back and fails to accept Christ's provision for victory, the result will be eternal loss (Hebrews 10:35, 39). There is no middle ground. Believers either win or lose. This does not mean that "overcomers" are perfect, for only Jesus lived a perfect life, and even those who have been saved a long time have weaknesses against which they must strive. Rather, they have pledged allegiance to the great Overcomer, Jesus, who helps them overcome.

**8. And unto the angel of the church in Smyrna write:** . . . the messenger of the assembly, —*RTHM* . . . Guardian Angel, —*WADE* . . . of the congregation at, —*KLST.*

**These things saith the first and the last, which was dead, and is alive:** . . . This is the message of, —*NOLI* . . . died and became alive, —*BECK* . . . who became dead and lived, —*RTHM* . . . who tasted death and became alive, —*BRKL* . . . who died and has returned to life, —*MNTG* . . . who was dead but lives, has this to say, —*KLST* . . . but is restored to life, —*TCNT* . . . and came back to life, —*SEB* . . . yet lives, —*FNTN.*

**2:8.** The letter to the church at Smyrna begins by reminding them of Christ's eternity and of His death and resurrection. Some believe this was appropriate because of the history of the city itself. It had been destroyed and ceased to exist as a Greek city for several centuries and then was restored. But this verse indicates rather the compassion of Jesus for those who were partakers of His sufferings. The Christians at Smyrna needed this reminder of His nature, His salvation, and His victory.

**9. I know thy works, and tribulation, and poverty:** . . . I know your pressing trouble, —*WLMS* . . . I know your persecution, —*MNTG* . . . about your deeds, your afflictions, —*NORL* . . . how you have to suffer and how poor you are, —*BECK* . . . and destitution, —*RTHM.*

**(but thou art rich):** . . . still you are, —*KLST* . . . nonetheless, you are truly rich, —*NORL.*

**and [I know] the blasphemy of them:** . . . the reviling of those, —*MNTG* . . . the slanders proceeding from, —*TCNT* . . . the defamation from, —*RTHM* . . . the insolence of those, —*BRKL.*

**which say they are Jews, and are not:** . . . affirming themselves, —*RTHM* . . . who assert themselves to be, —*FNTN* . . . claim to be, —*NORL* . . . though they are not, —*KLST.*

**but [are] the synagogue of Satan:** . . . are, on the contrary, —*FNTN* . . . an assembly of, —*WMCK*

**2:9.** The Christians in Smyrna were workers for the Lord, but they were suffering a great deal of tribulation in the form of persecution. These persecutions affected their jobs and reduced them to poverty.

They were also persecuted by Christ-rejecting Jews who claimed to worship God but who really were under the control of Satan. Like the Jews who sought to kill Jesus, they were of their father the devil. (See John 8:34, 41, 44.) They were actually dishonoring God by their treatment of believers. (Compare Romans 2:23, 24.) A short time after this, Polycarp, who lived about A.D. 69 to A.D. 156, became bishop (or pastor) of the church in Smyrna. He was taught by several of the apostles, especially the apostle John at Ephesus. He pastored in a very dangerous period, but he was faithful in teaching the truths of the gospel which had been passed on to him. When he was finally martyred by the Romans, he refused to save his life by denouncing Christ. Then the Christ-rejecting Jews of Smyrna broke the Sabbath in order to bring the wood needed to burn him to death (*The Ante-Nicene Fathers, The Martyrdom of Polycarp,* 13).

**10. Fear none of those things which thou shalt suffer:** . . . Have no fear at all, —*NORL* . . . Be not afraid as to what, —*RTHM* . . . Never fear what you are about to endure, —*FNTN.*

**behold, the devil shall cast [some] of you into prison:** . . . You see, —*BECK* . . . the adversary is about to throw, —*RTHM* . . . is indeed going to put some of you, —*MNTG* . . , about to imprison, —*FNTN* . . . the devil is about to throw some of you, —*KLST.*

**that ye may be tried:** . . . This is to test you, —*BECK* . . . to test you there, —*NORL* . . . that you may be tested, —*MNTG.*

**and ye shall have tribulation ten days:** . . . you will be oppressed, —*LAMS* . . . you will be tortured for, —*NOLI* . . . will have to suffer, —*BECK* . . . you will be in suffering there, —*NORL* . . . tortured by affliction, —*FNTN* . . . you will undergo a brief time . . . as it were a mere ten days, —*WADE.*

**be thou faithful unto death:** . . . Be loyal, though it means your death, —*BRKL* . . . Show yourself faithful, —*WADE* . . . till you die, —*BECK* . . . even if you have to die, —*WLMS* . . . even till death, —*KLST.*

**and I will give thee a crown of life:** . . . I will grant, —*FNTN* . . . the crown which belongs to life, —*KLST* . . . as the wreath of victory, true Life, —*WADE.*

**2:10.** The afflictions and persecutions the believers in Smyrna suffered caused them to fear. The implication here is that they were growing more and more fearful or apprehensive of the future. Jesus therefore told them not to be afraid of what they were going to suffer, but He did not give them any false encouragement or false hopes of peace and prosperity. Persecution would get worse. The devil would see to it that soon some believers would be cast into prison and their faith put to a severe test. Some would die for their faith. But they would be able to face the future without fear if they kept two things in mind. Their sufferings would soon come to an end (after "ten days"). More important, physical death could not rob them of the life they had received in Christ. Beyond death a crown of life was waiting for them. This would be the victor's crown which consists of life. The word "crown" here (*stephanon*) was used of a king's crown or of a crown or wreath placed on the head of the winner in a race or athletic contest. Thus, even if Christians die, they win.

Satan was behind the persecutions that followed in the Second and Third Centuries A.D. There were at least 10 periods of persecution under the Roman emperors. Most were short, and some did not reach far into the provinces. Yet, millions of Christians were burned at the stake, thrown to hungry lions, tortured and killed in many terrible ways. But death and the forces of hell were not able to stop the spread of the gospel and the growth of the Church. By the time of Emperor Constantine (288-337) there were so many Christians that he made Christianity the official religion of the Roman Empire. Persecution under the Romans ceased, except for one short period later.

11. **He that hath an ear, let him hear what the Spirit saith unto the churches:** ... You have ears; then listen, —BECK ... Let him who has ears listen to ... the congregations, —KLST.
**He that overcometh shall not be hurt of the second death:** ... He who is victorious will not be hurt at all by, —KLST ... The victor will suffer no hurt from, —BRKL ... He that conquers in no wise may be injured in consequence of, —RTHM ... will escape all hurt from, —WADE.

**2:11.** At the conclusion of this letter the Spirit reminded all the churches that there is something worse than physical death. There is a second death or final separation (20:11-15). It will mean separation forever from God's plan, God's promises, God's love, God's mercy, and God's grace. There will be no faith or trust in God or in anyone else. There will be no hope for change, no hope for the future. There will be no fellowship with God or with anyone else. Those in the lake of fire will undoubtedly be filled with hatred for themselves and for all who helped to send them there. On the other hand, overcomers need never fear that second death. God has a place reserved for them in heaven.

The implication is also that if we do not remain faithful, the result is the second death, the lake of fire. There is no hope of anything else if one does not stay true to Christ. In Matthew 25:41 Jesus pointed out that the everlasting fire (of the lake of fire) was prepared, not for people, but for the devil and his angels. But those who refuse, rebel, or turn away in unbelief will share Satan's doom. If they do not change, after death there is nothing ahead but the judgment (Hebrews 9:27).

12. **And to the angel of the church in Pergamos write:** ... of the congregation, —KLST ... Per-gamum, —NORL.
**These things saith he which hath the sharp sword with two edges:** ... has this to say, —KLST ... Thus speaks, —NORL ... These are the words, —MNTG ... is wielding, —WLMS ... speech is effective as, —WADE ... possessor of the sharp double-edged, —FNTN ... who holds the ... two-edged, —TCNT.

**2:12.** Jesus drew the attention of the church in Pergamos to His sharp sword with its two edges. The two edges may imply His ability and power to win victories over all His enemies, human and demonic. It may also imply that He is able to use the sword in the other direction to deal with those in the church who do not continue to be faithful. The Bible teaches that judgment must begin in the house or household of God (1 Peter 4:17). This does not contradict God's promises of blessing. God promised blessings to Israel, but He brought judgment on Israel and Judah before punishing the Assyrians and Babylonians (Isaiah 10:5, 12; Ezekiel 9:6; Amos 3:2; Habakkuk 2:4-20). God is faithful to bless believers, but He is just as faithful to test them, judge them, deal with them, chasten and discipline them, not to destroy but to bring them to glory.

Peter shows that the sinner's road is far harder. For if the righteous (those who have accepted the cleansing of the blood of Christ and who continue to stand in Christ's righteousness) scarcely (with difficulty) are saved (1 Peter 4:18), it is certain the ungodly and the sinner will not escape the judgment of the Great White Throne and the lake of fire, which is the final state of the wicked.

13. **I know thy works:** ... what you have done, —NORL.
**and where thou dwellest:** ... I know where you live, —BECK.

[even] where Satan's seat [is]: . . . The devil is there on his throne, —BECK . . . you live in the capital of Satan, —NOLI . . . the throne of Satan [is], —RTHM . . . even where Satan has his throne! —NORL.

and thou holdest fast my name: . . . cling to, —BECK . . . yet you hold to my Cause, —TCNT . . . You are loyal, —NOLI . . . have preserved My Name, —FNTN . . . have been true to, —NORL.

and hast not denied my faith: . . . deny your faith in me, —BECK . . . you did not renounce your faith in Me, —NORL . . . not disowned your faith, —WMCK

even in those days wherein Antipas [was] my faithful martyr: . . . my faithful one, —RTHM . . . witness, —NORL.

who was slain among you: . . . He was taken from you and killed, —SEB . . . who was killed near you, —RTHM.

where Satan dwelleth: . . . you have the devil living there! —BECK . . . where Satan reigns, —NOLI.

**2:13.** Pergamos (properly called Pergamum) at that time was the capital of the Roman province of Asia. Jesus recognized it as a place where Satan dwelt and had his seat (or "throne," as the same word is translated in other places in this book). This probably refers both to the idolatry of the city and the severe persecution of the church. On the city's acropolis stood a great altar to Zeus, the chief Greek god. Nearby was an elegant temple dedicated to the goddess Athena. Outside the city wall was a shrine to the Greek god of medicine, Asklepios, with his symbol in the form of a serpent. Thus, the city was a center for both idolatry and persecution of Christians.

In spite of satanic opposition, the Christians showed their faith by their works. As the persecution became more severe, the whole church, in the face of death, held on to Christ's name, bearing witness to His character, nature, and work of redemption. They refused to deny the Faith. That is, they refused to water down or compromise the truths of the gospel. One of their number had already been slain as a martyr for his witness to Christ. His name, Antipas, "instead of all," may be a contraction of Antipater, "instead of a father" or "in place of a father." He is not mentioned anywhere else, but his name is to be remembered because of his faithful witness. Jesus called him "my faithful martyr" (the Greek word translated "witness" is also translated "martyr"). He not only bore witness to the truth about Jesus, but he had a personal relationship with Jesus and belonged to Him.

**14.** But I have a few things against thee: . . . Still, I have some few things against you, too, —NORL . . . a few complaints, —NOLI . . . I have nevertheless a little against you, —FNTN.

because thou hast there them that hold the doctrine of Balaam: . . . You have some there who

accept, —NORL . . . hold fast, —RTHM . . . what Balaam taught, —BECK . . . who are clinging to the teaching of, —WLMS . . . some adherents of the heresy of, —NOLI.

who taught Balac to cast a stumblingblock before the children of Israel: . . . who instructed, —FNTN . . . to trap the people of, —BECK . . . to put temptations in the way of, —TCNT . . . a temptation in front of, —SEB . . . ensnare, —NORL . . . to entice them, —WLMS . . . to throw a snare in presence of the sons, —RTHM.

to eat things sacrificed unto idols: . . . idol-sacrifices, —RTHM . . . idol-offerings, —FNTN.

and to commit fornication: . . . indulging in, —FNTN . . . participating in abominable orgies, —NOLI . . . and sin sexually, —BECK . . . and to practice lewdness, —BRKL . . . and commit licentious acts, —TCNT . . . to practise immorality, —MNTG . . . commit whoredom, —NORL.

**2:14.** Though this church as a whole was faithful to Christ and the truths of the gospel, there were some in their midst who needed the Lord's rebuke. They were compromising with the lax morals and the heathen social customs of the day. They were doing what some of the Israelites did not long before Moses' death. On the advice of the soothsayer and false prophet Balaam, King Balak of Moab used the women of Moab to entice men of Israel to come and take part in idolatrous feasts which encouraged immorality in the name of religion (Numbers 25:1-5; 31:16). Jesus called what they did prostitution. God does not accept religious rites and ceremonies as an excuse for breaking the Ten Commandments.

This does not contradict what the apostle Paul wrote about eating meat offered to idols (1 Corinthians 10:25-30). He was dealing with meat that had been bought in the marketplace and brought home to eat. These church members in Pergamum were joining in with the crowds who were worshiping false gods and committing sexual acts with heathen priests and priestesses, all supposedly to honor their gods. It may be that the Christians who did this were saying that since the idols were nothing, they could participate in these heathen rites without harm. Or they may have said, "Since God's grace abounds, we can go ahead and sin in this way, and we will be automatically forgiven." But the Bible makes it clear that believers are not to continue in sin that grace may abound (Romans 6:1, 2). Those who partake of the Lord's table must not have close fellowship with His enemies (1 Corinthians 10:21).

**15.** So hast thou also them that hold the doctrine of the Nicolai-tanes, which thing I hate: . . . Thus, you too have some, —KLST . . . the teaching of, −NORL . . . in like manner, −RTHM . . . like that of the corrupters of the people, −FNTN.

**2:15.** Some propose that Balaam's name is a rough equivalent in Hebrew of the Greek Nikolaos and identify the Balaamites and the Nicolaitans (Johnson, *Expositor's Bible Commentary,* 12:441). However, they seem to be two different groups here. It may be that the Nicolaitans encouraged the same kind of unrestrained indulgence without being involved in idolatry. It is clear that both took a wrong view of love and Christian liberty that leads to compromise of principles and even to licentiousness. They were like those today who claim to be Christians and yet do not condemn but rather encourage many of the sins the Bible condemns. The New Testament warns against legalism, it is true, but it also makes it very clear that Christians must not use their Christian liberty as an occasion for the flesh (Galatians 5:13). Believers are to walk, live, and conduct themselves in the Holy Spirit. Then they will not fulfill, carry out, or satisfy themselves with the lusts, cravings, or desires of the flesh or the old, sinful nature (Galatians 5:16). Jesus hated the doctrine of the Nicolaitans because it promoted a soft attitude toward sin and discouraged holy living.

16. **Repent; or else I will come unto thee quickly:** . . . So you must repent! If you do not, −NORL . . . failing which, −FNTN . . . Otherwise I will shortly visit you, −BRKL . . . but, if not, I am coming to thee speedily, −RTHM.

**and will fight against them with the sword of my mouth:** . . . and I will contend with such men, −TCNT . . . will wage war with them, −RTHM . . . make war against them with the sword of My mouth! −NORL . . . with the sword which is in my sheath, −FNTN . . . that is in my mouth, −KLST.

**2:16.** Just how much Jesus hates encouragement to sin instead of holiness is seen by the severity of His call to repentance. Unless those who embraced this doctrine changed their basic attitudes toward God, truth, and holiness, Jesus promised to fight against them with the sword of His mouth. By their compromising spirit, even though they still claimed membership in the church, they were putting themselves on the side of Christ's enemies whom He will come to destroy. Unless they repented, they would meet the same fate as the Antichrist and his false prophet who will be defeated and cast into the lake of fire prepared for the devil and his angels.

17. **He that hath an ear, let him hear what the Spirit saith unto the churches:** . . . listen to what, −WLMS . . . to the congregations, −KLST.

**To him that overcometh will I give to eat of the hidden manna:** . . . To him who is victorious, −KLST . . . the sacred manna, −NOLI.

**and will give him a white stone:** . . . a white ballot, −NOLI . . . a white token, −FNTN . . . (the colour betokening felicity), −WADE.

**and in the stone a new name written:** . . . a new name inscribed upon the token, −FNTN . . . a freshly-acquired name engraven . . . expressing a changed character, −WADE . . . upon the stone, −MNTG.

**which no man knoweth saving he that receiveth [it]:** . . . that is known only to him who gets it, −BECK . . . no one has knowledge but he to whom it is given, −BB . . . none but the receiver can understand, −FNTN . . . except the recipient, −BRKL.

**2:17.** In view of the warning to the church at Pergamum, all believers must listen to the Holy Spirit as He speaks to all the churches of all time. Then, instead of partaking of heathen feasts, they will eat of the hidden manna and partake of Christ's own nature. (See John 6:48-51, 58, 63 where Jesus says He is the true manna, the true bread from heaven. Believers eat His body and drink His blood, not by going through forms and ceremonies but by continually believing on Jesus and feeding on His Word. As bread He was given, broken, and must be taken as Lord and Saviour in order to receive His life. As bread He sustains the believer's spiritual life as he continually partakes of Him.)

Instead of being drawn into the immorality, lusts, and desires of the world, the believer will have the white stone of forgiveness and acquittal. In those times a white pebble was used to cast a vote calling for a verdict of "not guilty." Believers' sins are blotted out, and they become just as if they had never sinned. They will also receive a new name, which in the Bible means a new nature and a full inheritance.

18. **And unto the angel of the church in Thyatira write:** . . . messenger, −RTHM . . . of the congregation, −KLST . . . say, −BB.

**These things saith the Son of God:** . . . These are the words of, −MNTG . . . speaks as follows, −NORL . . . has this to say, −KLST . . . This is what the Son of God declares, −WADE.

**who hath his eyes like unto a flame of fire:** . . . like fiery flame, −WADE.

**and his feet [are] like fine brass:** . . . like white-glowing brass, −BECK . . . like white-hot metal, −BRKL . . . like burnished brass, −FNTN −MNTG . . . like burnished bronze, −KLST . . . like polished brass, −NORL . . . resemble fine copper, −WADE.

**2:18.** To the church in Thyatira Jesus first drew attention to the fact that He is the Son of God.

Though He took His place on the human scene as a real man, He was always fully God as well as fully man. He emptied himself of the outward signs of His glory while ministering here on earth, but He always retained His divine nature and divine power.

Second, His eyes were like a flame of fire. They were ready to burn away any covering for sin or wrongdoing that the church at Thyatira might be trying to hide from His searching gaze. Those who think they can ever hide anything from God or His Son are deceiving themselves.

Third, His feet were like the finest burnished bronze. There was no contamination in them. In His walk and ministry on earth and in heaven, He has always been completely free from sin. Thus, He is able to bring judgment on sin.

19. **I know thy works, and charity:** ... I have knowledge of, *—BB* ... your achievements, *—NOLI* ... your doings, *—WADE* ... deeds, *—NORL* ... position, *—FNTN* ... love, *—BECK.*

**and service, and faith:** ... your loyalty, your helpfulness, *—NOLI* ... and ministry, *—RTHM* ... help, *—BB.*

**and thy patience, and thy works:** ... endurance, *—RTHM* ... steadfastness, *—WADE* ... and strength in trouble, *—BB.*

**and the last [to be] more than the first:** ... I know that your last works are more than the first, *—MNTG* ... your latest achievements which outnumber the early ones, *—KLST* ... lately you've done more than at first, *—BECK* ... You are doing more now than you did in the beginning, *—SEB* ... your latter efforts are in advance of the first, *—FNTN* ... to be more abundant than, *—LAMS.*

**2:19.** Jesus knew many good things about the church at Thyatira. He knew their works and implied they were indeed commendable. It is evident these Christians did not come behind the other churches in their service to God and their fellow human beings.

Unlike the church at Ephesus, they had not left their first love. Rather, they showed the kind of steadfast, loyal love that was a response to and a reflection of the love of God, the love shown at Calvary. They were outstanding channels for the love which is the key fruit of the Spirit, the fruit that sums up and includes all the other fruit.

They were noted for service or ministry. The Greek word is used of the ministry of the prophets, apostles, deacons, and other church leaders. It is also used of the ministry of the gifts of the Spirit through whomever He wills. It is used of giving aid, support, and contributions to the needy. Their worship services must have brought glory to God and edification to all who were present. They must also have had a heart for the poor, the downtrodden, the widows, the orphans, and the foreigners.

Their Christianity was evident every day of the week.

Their faith and faithfulness were outstanding. Not only did they maintain their faith in God and His Word, not only were they manifesting the gift of faith, they were developing faith and faithfulness as the fruit of the Spirit.

They were noted for their patient endurance, fortitude, steadfastness, and perseverance in the midst of toil and suffering. This fortitude was Christlike and could only have come from constant communion and fellowship with Christ in the Holy Spirit. Christ's presence in their midst must have been a constant reality.

Furthermore, their works were steadily increasing from the first. There was an increasing devotion to Christ and continuous growth in their faithful service. This was indeed an outstanding commendation for this church.

20. **Notwithstanding I have a few things against thee:** ... I have to say, *—FNTN* ... But I have this against you, *—NORL, —MNTG* ... But I have this ground of complaint, *—WADE* ... Nevertheless I hold it against you, *—KLST.*

**because thou sufferest that woman Jezebel, which calleth herself a prophetess:** ... that you leave unchecked the woman ... who terms herself, *—WADE* ... that you tolerate that, *—BRKL* ... that thou dost let alone, *—RTHM* ... the self-styled prophetess, *—NOLI* ... who palms herself off as, *—FNTN* ... let the woman Jezebel go free, *—WMCK* ... you let the woman ... say she is a prophet, *—BB.*

**to teach and to seduce my servants to commit fornication:** ... and by her teaching, *—WADE* ... is permitted to teach and to mislead ... to commit adultery, *—NORL* ... and give false teaching, making my servants to go after the desires of the flesh, *—BB* ... and mislead them, *—BECK* ... is misleading my slaves, *—WLMS* ... and pervert, *—FNTN* ... teaches them to participate in abominable orgies, *—NOLI* ... and deceives my servants, *—RTHM* ... leading them to practise immorality, *—MNTG.*

**and to eat things sacrificed unto idols:** ... to partake of, *—WADE* ... to eat food, *—KLST* ... idol-offerings, *—FNTN* ... and take food offered to false gods, *—BB.*

**2:20.** In spite of all these good things Jesus said about the church in Thyatira, He had a few things against them. The compromise in Pergamum seems to have had its origin in pressures from the heathen forces ("Satan's throne") outside the church. In Thyatira there was the same compromise initiated and fostered by an apostate woman inside the church. Instead of "that woman," some ancient manuscripts read "your woman," which would mean "your wife," that is, the pastor's wife. The pastor and church tolerated her because she called herself a prophetess. Jesus, however, called her Jezebel. Actually, she was worse than the Old

Testament Jezebel, the wife of the king of Israel, who tried to root out the worship of the Lord by enticing Israel to worship Baal and even make Baal their national god.

This Jezebel, by claiming to be a prophetess, was putting her words and her teaching above the teachings of Christ and the apostles. Not only did she teach the people that it was acceptable in God's eyes for them to commit the spiritual adultery of mixing with idolatrous worship and idolatrous immorality, she cleverly seduced true servants of the Lord and led them astray from what was true and right. These were believers who really wanted to serve the Lord and had been faithful to Him. The good things that Jesus said about the church could be said of them. But since they had come under the influence of the prophecies and teachings of this Jezebel, they looked up to her and became her victims.

Prophecies should be put to the test of the Scriptures, not depending on a verse or half a verse here and there, but searching the Scriptures to see if the prophecy really agrees with the great teachings of the Bible. Others in the body of Christ should judge (1 Corinthians 14:29). Then, as believers stand steady and hold fast, the Lord himself will search hearts and bring the truth to light.

**21. And I gave her space to repent of her fornication:** . . . I gave her time to change, *—BECK* . . . have given her time, *—BRKL* . . . given her an opportunity, *—FNTN* . . . given her a respite, *—WADE* . . . time for repentance, *—MNTG* . . . to change her heart, *—SEB* . . . to repent of her impurity, *—NORL* . . . of her immorality, *—KLST.*

**and she repented not:** . . . but she refuses to turn from her sexual sins, *—BECK* . . . does not wish to repent, *—KLST* . . . refuses to repent out of, *—RTHM* . . . but she is determined not to turn from her licentiousness, *—TCNT* . . . has no desire to give up her fornication, *—FNTN* . . . from her immorality, *—MNTG.*

**2:21.** Jesus had already dealt with this woman and given her a period of time to repent. But she would not repent of her spiritual and moral adultery. This means she did not change her basic attitudes. She still maintained that mixing heathen worship and heathen practices with true worship was not really sin.

Even in the Old Testament God pronounced His most severe judgment on those who tried to worship Him and other gods as well. The Church in the Dark Ages of its history degenerated because they brought heathen ideas and practices into the churches. At first they resisted bringing even pictures into the churches. But in time they brought in images. Like the heathen, they gave attention to shrines and sacred relics. The false prophets of today are even worse, because they give more attention to human ideas and human philosophies than to the Word of God. Or they twist the Word of God to fit their human ideas and false teachings. It is sad that too often they, like this Jezebel, do not repent. They only proclaim more loudly that their prophecies or teachings are to be taken as authoritative.

**22. Behold, I will cast her into a bed:** . . . Look! *—FNTN* . . . See! I will put her on a sickbed, *—NORL* . . . lay her, *—MNTG* . . . on a bed of sickness, *—WLMS* . . . I throw her into a couch, *—RTHM.*

**and them that commit adultery with her into great tribulation:** . . . those who commit adultery with her into great tribulation, *—NORL* . . . will make those who live in sexual sin with her suffer much, *—BECK* . . . bring great distress upon those, *—MNTG* . . . with severe affliction, *—FNTN.*

**except they repent of their deeds:** . . . except perchance they shall repent out of her works, *—RTHM* . . . if they will not turn away from what she's doing, *—BECK* . . . unless they repent of their misdeeds, *—NORL* . . . turn away their minds, *—FNTN* . . . unless they turn away from her works, *—MNTG.*

**2:22.** Jesus promised to judge both this Jezebel prophetess and those who committed spiritual adultery with her by their mixed worship and their participation in heathen rites and ceremonies. Jesus said He would cast or throw her into a bed, probably a bed of sickness that could lead to physical death. Those who followed her prophecies and teachings Jesus said He would cast or throw into great tribulation, that is, into great distress and affliction that would bring anguish of heart and soul. It is not implied that Jesus wanted to do this. What He really wanted was for them to repent of their deeds or works done under the influence of these false teachings and false prophecies. He was being patient with them, and even with this Jezebel, by giving further opportunity for repentance.

**23. And I will kill her children with death:** . . . moreover, her children will I kill with pestilence, *—MNTG* . . . her children I will thoroughly extinguish, *—BRKL* . . . kill her followers, *—FNTN* . . . I will slay her children outright, *—NOLI* . . . I will smite, *—LAMS* . . . and I will surely strike her children dead, *—WLMS* . . . put her children to death, *—NORL* . . . will I surely destroy, *—WMCK*

**and all the churches shall know that I am he which searcheth the reins and hearts:** . . . shall get to know, *—RTHM* . . . will recognise, *—FNTN* . . . searches minds, *—BECK* . . . men's inmost hearts, *—WLMS* . . . the deepest human thoughts and feelings, *—SEB* . . . the secret thoughts, *—NORL.*

**and I will give unto every one of you according to your works:** . . . will reward each one, *—FNTN* . . . each of you according to what you have done, *—BECK* . . . to your deeds, *—NORL.*

**2:23.** Jesus continued the warning and made it even more severe. He said He would "kill" the spiritual children, that is, the followers of this Jezebel, "with death." This may mean He would bring some kind of fatal illness or pestilence upon them. This would be physical death. In 20:14 there is a reference to a spiritual death, the "second death." Whichever death is meant, this is a serious warning.

The false prophets who sought money, fame, or power in the Old Testament probably taught that it did not matter to God if people worshiped false gods as long as they brought their sacrifices to the temple. This Jezebel was ignoring the fact that Jesus knew her motives even though she tried to hide them and probably succeeded in hiding them from others, even from herself. The churches needed to know that Jesus is more than the gentle Saviour. He is also the Judge. He searches, examines, investigates the kidneys ("reins") and the hearts; that is, the innermost parts of their beings—their minds and hearts, their thoughts, motives, and feelings. He knows what is really within the heart. He knows what is behind the works, the deeds, the actions. He, as the impartial Judge, will give to each one according to his works, not as the individual sees them but as He sees them. (See John 5:22, 30.)

**24. But unto you I say, and unto the rest in Thyatira:** ... to the rest of you, −NORL.
**as many as have not this doctrine:** ... to as many of you as do not have, −NORL ... have not embraced, −FNTN ... hold not, −RTHM ... this teaching, −BECK.
**and which have not known the depths of Satan, as they speak:** ... and have not been initiated into the so-called deep mysteries of, −NOLI ... have not explored, −FNTN ... did not get to know the deep things of Satan (as they say), −RTHM ... the devil's deep things, as they call them, −BECK.
**I will put upon you none other burden:** ... I thrust not on you, −RTHM ... I will impose no other, −FNTN ... I have no extra burden to lay on you, −WLMS.

**2:24.** Jesus recognized that not everyone in the church at Thyatira had listened to the false prophecies and seductive teachings of this Jezebel. Thus, He had a word of comfort for those believers who had not been deceived by this false teaching and who had not experienced or fallen into its hidden satanic depths. Undoubtedly, this false prophetess Jezebel had claimed that she was giving them deeper teaching. She may have claimed to have reached into the depths of divine truth, the depths of God. But in reality she had led people into the depths of Satan. She may have said they must enter Satan's territory in order to defeat him. But Jesus said He would not impose any other burden

on those who rejected her teachings and refused to follow her example.

**25. But that which ye have [already] hold fast till I come:** ... Only thishold fast to what you have until I come! −NORL ... nevertheless, −RTHM ... cling to, −BECK ... keep it safe, −FNTN ... until I return, −NOLI.

**2:25.** Those who were still faithful to the gospel and to Christ needed only to hold fast to what they already had until Jesus returned. They were to be like the Thessalonians who "turned to God from idols to serve the living and true God; and to wait for his Son from heaven" (1 Thessalonians 1:9, 10). This serving while waiting included continuing the good works they were already doing.

**26. And he that overcometh:** ... To him who wins the victory, −NORL.
**and keepeth my works unto the end:** ... and who does My bidding to the end, −NORL ... keeps as far as an end my works, −RTHM ... continue to do, −BECK ... keeper of My institutions, −FNTN.
**to him will I give power over the nations:** ... I will grant authority over the Gentiles, −BRKL ... a governorship, −FNTN ... to rule, −NORL ... over the heathen, −WLMS.

**2:26.** Jesus is here emphasizing the need for perseverance. It is not enough for a person to begin the Christian life, the believer must continue to follow Jesus, learning of Him and serving Him "to the end." To those who overcome in this way He will give power and authority over the nations. That is, He will cause them to share His kingly rule.

**27. And he shall rule them with a rod of iron:** ... He shall shape them, −FNTN ... you will rule them, −BECK ... he shall shepherd ... with an iron sceptre, −RTHM.
**as the vessels of a potter shall they be broken to shivers:** ... He will smash them like earthen pots, −NOLI ... as vessels of clay are tempered together, −FNTN ... as the vessels of earthenware are dashed to pieces, −RTHM ... shattering them like pottery, −BECK.
**even as I received of my Father:** ... just as I have received power from my Father, −KLST ... even as I was disciplined, −LAMS ... was instructed by, −FNTN ... the same authority that I Myself have received from, −NORL.

**2:27.** Those who overcome will share in Christ's triumph and join Him in His work of a shepherd with a rod of iron. The shepherd's rod was used to break the bones of the enemies of the sheep. The rod of iron will shatter Christ-rejecting nations or peoples just as a pottery jar would be shattered into small pieces. The picture here ties in the prophecy of Psalm 2:8, 9 with that of Daniel

2:34, 35, 44, 45. (See also John 5:22 for the Father's part.)

Psalm 2 shows that God will give His messianic Son the nations or peoples of the earth as His inheritance. Faithful believers in Christ are heirs of God and joint heirs with Christ, so they will share in this inheritance and be with Him when He comes to establish His kingdom on earth (Galatians 4:7; Titus 3:7).

Daniel chapter 2 pictures the sequence of empires as a giant image with a head of gold representing Babylon, breasts and arms of silver representing Medo-Persia, belly and thighs of copper representing the Greek empire of Alexander the Great; legs of iron representing Rome, and feet of iron and ceramic clay representing nationalistic states that do not stick together. One empire gave way to another, but it was still the same image, the same old world system. Babylonian astrology, Medo-Persian ethics, Greek art and philosophy, and Roman law, with the idea that might makes right, all still have their influence in the world system today. There never has been a really new world order.

Daniel saw a stone "cut out without hands." It hit the image in the feet, and the gold, silver, copper, iron, and clay were all ground to powder and blown away. Then the stone "became a great mountain," a kingdom that filled the whole earth. The point of this prophecy is that Christ's kingdom will only come in its fullness on earth through judgment. Even the good things of the present world system must be removed and destroyed so that the better things of the Kingdom can come in.

28. **And I will give him the morning star:** ...present to him, —FNTN ... myself, who am the Morning Star, —WADE.

**2:28.** To the overcomers of all churches and all times who share in Christ's triumph, He will give more than power and authority over the nations. He will give them the morning star. Jesus is here saying that He will give of himself to the overcoming believer in a new and more wonderful way than ever before.

29. **He that hath an ear, let him hear what the Spirit saith unto the churches:** ... Now, let him, —NORL ... who has ears listen, —KLST ... is saying to the congregations, —SEB ... assemblies, —RTHM.

**2:29.** As before, Jesus emphasized that this message is not for one church only but for all the churches. It is the Spirit's message, but the Spirit takes the written Word and applies it to the hearts of all who will listen. Those who have ears will

have no excuse. All those who do not listen will be shattered by the judgment to come.

## Chapter 3

1. **And unto the angel of the church in Sardis write:** ... messenger, —RTHM ... of the congregation, —KLST.

**These things saith he that hath the seven Spirits of God, and the seven stars:** ... This is what He declares, —WADE ... has this to say, —KLST ... the Master of, —FNTN.

**I know thy works, that thou hast a name that thou livest, and art dead:** ... I know what you're doing, that people say you're living but you're dead, —BECK ... your conduct, —KLST ... You enjoy the reputation, —NOLI ... a name thou hast that thou art alive, —RTHM ... you are reputed to live, —FNTN ... seem to be living, —NORL ... have the reputation of being alive, but in reality, —WLMS ... you have the name of being alive, but are really dead, —MNTG ... lifeless, —WADE.

**3:1.** Jesus drew the attention of the church at Sardis to the fact that He has the sevenfold Spirit of God (see Isaiah 11:2-5). The Holy Spirit was and is available to do His work. Jesus also has or holds the seven stars that are the messengers or pastors of the seven churches. Even though He was about to give a more severe rebuke to the church at Sardis, He still had their leaders in His hands and was concerned about them and the churches they led.

The church at Sardis was a lively, active church. It had a name, a reputation. People on the outside considered it a spiritual church; full of life. But Jesus saw beneath the surface and declared it was dead (spiritually dead). It may be that the church was no longer depending on the Holy Spirit and was failing to follow the leadership God had given them. Paul had told Timothy that a time would come when men would be guilty of "having a form of godliness, but denying the power thereof" (2 Timothy 3:5). Sardis was fulfilling that prophecy.

2. **Be watchful, and strengthen the things which remain:** ... Wake up, —BECK ... Be alert, —WADE ... Be awake and invigorate remainders, —BRKL ... Be continually on the watch, and establish the things, —MNTG ... and henceforward stand firm, —FNTN ... those who are still alive, —NORL ... the rest, —KLST.

**that are ready to die:** ... the rest that are dying, —BECK ... that were about to die, —RTHM ... but on the point of death, —NORL.

**for I have not found thy works perfect before God:** ... I do not find your conduct, —KLST ... are not finished before My God, —BECK ... none of your actions perfected, —FNTN ... fulfilled in presence of my God, —RTHM ... in the sight of My God, —NORL.

**3:2.** The Christians at Sardis were depending on past experiences, but what little remained from the past was ready to die. None of their works were perfect, complete, or fully performed. Everything done in and by the church lacked the anointing of God which alone could bring God's work to its full expression. They needed to wake up, to strengthen those things that remained but were about to die. There was still hope that they could do this.

**3. Remember therefore how thou hast received and heard:** . . . Call to mind, then, —BRKL, —MNTG . . . Be calling to remembrance, —RTHM . . . Be mindful, then, —NORL . . . how you once accepted and listened to, —BECK . . . how you were instructed and taught, —FNTN . . . heard the message, —KLST.

**and hold fast, and repent:** . . . Take it to heart, —BECK . . . Follow that, —NORL . . . and observe, —RTHM . . . hold to it, —MNTG . . . and reform! —FNTN.

**If therefore thou shalt not watch:** . . . If you don't wake up, —BECK . . . not watchful, —FNTN.

**I will come on thee as a thief:**

**and thou shalt not know what hour I will come upon thee:** . . . you will in no way know, —NORL . . . you will not have the least idea, —KLST . . . in nowise mayest thou get to know during what kind of hour, —RTHM . . . the time, —FNTN . . . I will visit you, —NOLI.

**3:3.** Christ's purpose in giving this warning was to urge the church in Sardis to repent. In this verse Jesus used the promise of His second coming to reinforce that challenge. There is no greater encouragement to holiness and purity of life than the blessed hope of Christ's return (see 1 John 3:2, 3).

They needed to remember not *what* they had received and heard but *how* they had received and heard. This implies they had once received the truths of the gospel with joy. They had taken Christ as their Lord and Saviour with enthusiasm. Perhaps they were like the stony places in the Parable of the Sower and the Soils (Matthew 13:20, 21). They needed to look back and recapture some of the joy in the Lord they once knew. They needed to keep what they had received, to hold fast to the teaching given them, and to pay attention to it once more. It was not enough for them to rest on their past reputation. If they did not repent, wake up, and be on their guard, Jesus said He would come as a thief, that is, without warning. They would not know in advance the hour or the time He would come. The implication is that He would come in judgment, and once He came it would be too late for them to repent.

This seems to indicate Jesus would not wait until His second coming before bringing judgment on this church. He would be coming upon *them*; not on the world, not on all people. The church at Sardis would be the specific object of this judgment. Believers must always be on guard against sin and carelessness, no matter *when* the Lord may come.

**4. Thou hast a few names even in Sardis which have not defiled their garments:** . . . On the other hand, you have a few persons, —KLST . . . a few individuals, —SEB . . . soiled their clothes, —BECK . . . who have kept their robes clean, —NORL.

**and they shall walk with me in white: for they are worthy:** . . . Clothed in white, —KLST . . . white garments because they deserve it, —BECK . . . because they are deserving, —BRKL . . . deserve to do so, —WLMS.

**3:4.** Neglecting the hope of Christ's coming and failure to depend on the Holy Spirit to illuminate the truth and give them power for holy living had led many in Sardis to defile their garments. They were no longer cooperating with the Spirit in His work of sanctification. They were not obeying the injunction to keep themselves "unspotted from the world" (James 1:27). They needed to cast aside everything that might stain them with sin, especially all the malice, evil, spite, greed, and vicious wickedness that so characterizes the world. They needed to welcome and submit to God's Word with a teachable spirit (James 1:21).

But there were a few exceptions, and those Jesus counted worthy to walk with Him in white. The white clothing is a general word for clothes or robes made white. That is, made "white in the blood of the Lamb" (7:14) and thus white because of Christ's righteousness, not their own. (See also 19:8.) It seems that these believers were already walking with the Lord, keeping close to Him, and that is why they had not defiled their garments. Those who walk with the Lord in this life will be counted worthy to keep on walking with Him, having close fellowship with Him in the Kingdom to come.

**5. He that overcometh, the same shall be clothed in white raiment:** . . . The conqueror, —FNTN . . . He who is victorious shall be, —KLST . . . and that's how you will be dressed, —BECK . . . The one who defeats the enemy will be clothed in this way, —ADAM . . . Everyone who has power and wins will wear white clothes, —NLTG . . . thus array himself in white garments, —RTHM . . . will be clothed like them, —TNT . . . will be clad thus, —NORL . . . garments of purity, —WADE.

**and I will not blot out his name out of the book of life:** . . . will in no wise blot out, —MNTG . . . will not erase, —BECK . . . will not take his name from, —BB . . . I will not wipe his name out of, —TNT . . . out of the scroll, —RTHM.

**but I will confess his name before my Father, and before his angels:** . . . but I will own him as mine, —WLMS . . . I will acknowledge him, —NOLI, —NORL . . . and I will give witness to his name,

—BB...I will speak of his name in front of, —NLTG...for what he is, —WADE...in the presence of...his messengers, —RTHM.

**3:5.** Jesus here makes several promises to the one who overcomes. First He says he will be clothed in white. According to the commentator Adam Clarke, this may refer to an ancient Hebrew custom in regard to the priests, who were dressed in white. If it was thought a priest had sinned or was not of the seed of Aaron, he was brought before the great council of Israel to be tried. If they found he was guilty, he would be stripped of his white garment and instead given a black garment to wear and sent away. If a priest was found innocent, his white garment was restored to him, and he took his place again among the other priests. As always in Scripture, white symbolizes holiness, righteousness.

God keeps books. In Daniel's vision of the last days he saw that "the judgment was set, and the books were opened" (Daniel 7:10). In Daniel 12:1 the angel told of deliverance for "every one that shall be found written in the book." Malachi 3:16 tells of the blessings for those who revere God: "The Lord hearkened, and heard it, and a book of remembrance was written before him for them that feared the Lord, and that thought upon his name."

It is good to have one's name on a church roll, or listed with a worthwhile organization, but to have our names in the Book of Life is the best of all. Overcomers' names will remain there.

Finally, Christ makes the great promise that He will honor the overcomer by recognizing him before God the Father and all the holy angels. It would be considered a high honor for a person to be honored by an earthly head of state before a Congress or the Parliament, but consider what this will mean. Jesus will bring the believer out before His Father, with the myriads of angels standing around. Then the One who has redeemed us by His blood will take the believer by the hand and acknowledge him as His faithful follower. Such an honor will make all the trials of life seem as nothing. This is an honor to be desired, one for which a believer should strive with all his might.

**6. He that hath an ear, let him hear what the Spirit saith unto the churches:**...You have ears! —NLTG...who has ears, —KLST...let him give ear, —BB...let him listen, —FNTN...what the Divine Spirit says, —WADE.

**3:6.** Again Jesus called on all believers to give heed to what the Spirit was saying in these letters to all the churches.

**7. And to the angel of the church in Philadelphia write:**...the Guardian Angel, —WADE...of the congregation, —KLST...in the city of, —NLTG...say, —BB.

**These things saith he that is holy, he that is true:**...These are the words of, —TNT...has this to say, —KLST...This is what He declares...the Reliable, —WADE...the Holy One, the Real, —RTHM...the True One, —NORL.

**he that hath the key of David:**...the Holder of, —FNTN...who carries the keys, —WLMS...the symbol of authority, —WADE.

**he that openeth, and no man shutteth:**...When He opens a door, nobody will shut it, —BECK...has no superior to reverse what He does, —WADE.

**and shutteth, and no man openeth:**...no one will open it again, —NORL.

**3:7.** Of the seven churches, the church of the city of "brotherly love" was the most nearly perfect, and Jesus had no condemnation for them. Jesus drew their attention to His holiness. He is the Holy One, which is a title of God. He is true—the true One, the genuine One. Jesus is divine and shares the holiness of God the Father. (See Psalm 16:10; Isaiah 6:3; 40:25; 43:15; Acts 2:27; 13:35.)

Jesus is also the genuine messianic King who makes David's throne eternal. (See Acts 2:30, 32, 36; 3:14, 15; 1 John 5:20.) "The key of David" represents the authority of His royal office. (See Isaiah 22:22.) He already has that authority and was and is already manifesting His royal authority and power by using the key to open doors that no one can shut and shutting doors that no one can open. (See Matthew 28:18.)

**8. I know thy works:**...what you're doing, —BECK...I know your life, —TCNT...your position, —FNTN...your conduct, —KLST.

**behold, I have set before thee an open door:**...See! —NORL...Take notice. I have placed before you a door which has been opened, —KLST...mark! I have set before you an opportunity, like, —WADE...given before thee a door set open, —RTHM.

**and no man can shut it:**...and which, —KLST...none can close, —WADE.

**for thou hast a little strength:**...Although you have only a little strength, —BECK...Though you don't have much strength, —SEB...I know how weak you are, —NORL...the power you have is small, —WADE...though your strength was insignificant, —NOLI...hast little power, —RTHM.

**and hast kept my word:**...yet you have guarded My message, —FNTN...kept in mind, —WADE...and yet you have been true to My Word, —NORL.

**and hast not denied my name:**...you have not renounced, —BRKL...have not disowned, —WLMS.

**3:8.** Jesus knew the good works of the church in Philadelphia. He was already exercising His royal authority by setting an open door before them. Actually, He began exercising that authority when He commissioned His church and began His working with them. (See Matthew 28:19, 20; Mark 16:20.)

Adversaries might try to close that open door of ministry, but they would not succeed. When our work and our motivation are acceptable to the Lord we can expect to receive His help. No earthly power can stand against Him.

Some have thought that the phrase "little strength" means the believers at Philadelphia had only a small degree of spiritual power, but we must remember that generally Jesus speaks very favorably about this church. Scholars such as Robert Mounce (*New International Commentary on the New Testament, Revelation,* p. 117) assert that apparently this was a rather small congregation, and because of being limited in size they had not been able to make a major impact upon the city. However, in spite of this handicap, they had kept Christ's Word and refused to deny His name in the face of satanic persecution from the unconverted Jews. They were an obedient and faithful church that maintained its witness to Christ and the truth of the gospel. Even their little power was commended by the Lord.

**9. Behold, I will make them of the synagogue of Satan:** ... Listen! There are some belonging to the synagogue, *–NORL* ... Mark well, I will bring some of the synagogue of Satan, *–KLST* ... I will give those, *–FNTN* ... members of Satan's synagogue, *–WADE.*
**which say they are Jews, and are not:** ... that affirm themselves, *–RTHM* ... who assert themselves, *–FNTN* ... who declare themselves, *–NORL.*
**but do lie:** ... but are instead impostors, *–BRKL* ... speak falsely, *–RTHM* ... are lying, *–MNTG.*
**behold, I will make them to come and worship before thy feet:** ... I say that I will make them come and lie prostrate, *–KLST* ... bow down, *–BECK* ... bow in reverence before, *–MNTG* ... in presence of thy feet, *–RTHM.*
**and to know that I have loved thee:** ... and learn, *–BECK* ... and find out, *–WLMS* ... so that they may know, *–NORL.*

**3:9.** There was a serious conflict between the church at Philadelphia and the synagogue of the Jews, but Jesus told His followers they would be victorious. That the Jews would bow down before the believers and acknowledge Christ's love for them has an interesting Old Testament background. Many passages refer to Israel's triumph over her enemies in the end times. Then the Gentiles will come and bow down before her (see Isaiah 45:14; 49:23; 60:14; etc.).

But now Jesus announces that before that prophecy can be fulfilled, Israel herself will have to come and bow down and acknowledge that

Christ loves His church. So the apostate Jews who had become the synagogue of Satan will have to repent and humble themselves before God and the New Testament saints who have become part of His family.

When will this occur? Barclay takes this to refer to the time when every knee shall bow before Christ (*Daily Study Bible, Revelation,* 1:165). Or it may be that this is a promise to be fulfilled when the Jews as a whole accept Christ as their Messiah and Saviour at His second coming. As is often true, history is the key that unlocks the mysteries of prophecy.

**10. Because thou hast kept the word of my patience:** ... you have followed the example of my patient suffering, *–KLST* ... you have waited patiently for Me as you were told, *–BECK* ... You have guarded my doctrine, *–NOLI* ... guarded my message resolutely, *–FNTN* ... you have kept in mind my Message enjoining steadfastness, *–WADE* ... of my endurance, *–RTHM.*
**I also will keep thee from the hour of temptation:** ... I will keep you safe when the time of testing, *–BECK* ... I in turn will preserve you, *–KLST* ... of trial, *–FNTN, –RTHM.*
**which shall come upon all the world, to try them that dwell upon the earth:** ... which is about to come, *–MNTG* ... the whole world of men, to put to the test, *–WADE* ... for the testing of all the inhabitants of, *–NORL* ... the whole of the inhabited [earth], *–RTHM.*

**3:10.** This church kept the word or teaching about the patient endurance of Christ. They kept looking to "Jesus the author (leader, example, pacesetter) and finisher (perfecter who brings believers to maturity and completion because He has already reached the goal toward which believers strive) of our faith." For the joy (a joy believers will share) that was set before Him, He "endured the cross, despising the shame (caring nothing for the shame and unafraid of it), and is set down at the right hand of the throne of God" (Hebrews 12:2). This implies that they laid aside every weight (or encumbrance) and sin, and then, by running with patient endurance the race set before them, they kept their eyes on Jesus.

What did Jesus mean when He promised He would keep these believers from the "hour of temptation"? There are two principal and conflicting views concerning this matter about which there is much dispute. They deserve to be compared with each other.

First of all, it should be noted that the verse should be viewed from an end-time perspective, for Jesus immediately says, "Behold, I come quickly." Obviously, the temptation or trial in view is not a personal distress or a local persecution. It belongs to the eschatological time of temptation "which shall come upon all the world."

Such an early theological writer as Dr. Edwin Hatch says in his "Essay on Biblical Greek" that 3:10 has an "evident reference to the tribulations which are prophesied later on in the book" (p. 73). Most exegetes agree that it refers to what is called the Great Tribulation. This must mean that Philadelphia and the other churches are representative of the whole Church in this age.

Now, what does Christ mean when He says, "I will keep you from the hour of temptation"? Will the Church be kept *in* and *through* the Tribulation, or will she be kept from coming into it at all? One school of thought holds the Church will go through the Tribulation, but that Christ promised special protection here, pointing to John 17:15, where the same phrase "kept from" is found. Other expositors see in this verse a promise that the Church will be kept from enduring this trial, which is a time of God's righteous judgment upon sin, that the contexts of John 17:15 and Revelation 3:10 are quite different. See the *Overview* of this book for a more thorough treatment of this question.

**11. Behold, I come quickly:** . . . I will come, *—NORL* . . . I am coming soon, *—BECK* . . . I am coming speedily, *—RTHM.*

**hold that fast which thou hast, that no man take thy crown:** . . . Secure what you possess, so that none may rob, *—FNTN* . . . what you have that no one may snatch away your crown, *—KLST* . . . no one receive, *—RTHM* . . . cling to, *—BECK* . . . none may take away your wreath of victory, *—WADE.*

**3:11.** The hope of Christ's coming was to encourage the Philadelphian believers to hold fast to what they had, to what they received from Christ, lest they lose their crown. (The word "man" should not be emphasized here. The Greek is just a pronoun meaning "no one.") Because Christ promised to keep them did not mean they could let down their guard or become careless. They must avoid false teachers. They must keep fighting the only fight worth fighting, the fight of faith. (See Colossians 2:18, 19; 3:1-4; 2 Timothy 4:7, 8.)

**12. Him that overcometh will I make a pillar in the temple of my God:** . . . Him who is victorious, *—KLST* . . . Whoever defeats the enemy, *—ADAM* . . . I will make him who conquers, *—NORL* . . . I will make the one who has power and wins an important part that holds up the house, *—NLTG* . . . The one who is conquering, him will I be making, *—CNDT* . . . the one who wins the victory, *—EVRD* . . . I will make him a buttress in, *—WADE* . . . sanctuary, *—FNTN* . . . in the house of, *—BB.*

**and he shall go no more out:** . . . you will never leave it, *—BECK* . . . will never have to leave, *—EVRD* . . . and he may be coming out, *—CNDT* . . . and

there he shall stay for ever, *—TNT* . . . outside in no-wise may he go forth, *—RTHM* . . . shall never be put out of it, *—FNTN* . . . will never go out from it again, *—ADAM* . . . no more go in nor go out, *—KLGS* . . . never-more, *—MNTG.*

**and I will write upon him the name of my God:** . . . I will be writing on him, *—CNDT* . . . inscribe upon him, *—WADE.*

**and the name of the city of my God:** . . . of my divine commonwealth, *—NOLI* . . . of the town of, *—BB.*

**[which is] new Jerusalem, which cometh down out of heaven from my God:** . . . This city is, *—EVRD* . . . she who is to descend, *—RTHM.*

**and [I will write upon him] my new name:** . . . as well as My own new Name, *—FNTN* . . . and My fresh new Name, *—ADAM.*

**3:12.** For all those who are faithful followers of Jesus Christ there is a place of high honor, a place of permanence and stability as a pillar in the divine inner sanctuary. The word "temple" here (*naō*) is the inner sanctuary, the Holy of Holies. It is a word also used of the Church in Ephesians 2:20-22, but here it is used of the believers' place in the final state, that is, in the New Jerusalem where God will dwell with His people forever.

When the tabernacle of Moses existed, and later the temple of Solomon, the Holy of Holies was the most sacred place of the entire complex. Only one person, the high priest, dared to enter it, and he only once a year on the Day of Atonement. In it were resident the ark of the covenant crowned by the mercy seat. This sacred room represented the presence of God, for it was from there the pillar of cloud and of fire emanated. So for Christ to give a believer such a position in the very presence of God will be an honor surpassing any ever achieved by mortal man. This is the final blessing which Jesus announced to the churches, an honor which all believers should desire to attain.

Then Jesus will write on every overcomer the name of God, the name of the New Jerusalem which will come down to the new earth from the new heaven, and also Christ's own new name. The word "name" here stands for the authority, character, and person. It reminds Christians of 1 John 3:1, 2, which speaks of their being called the sons of God and as such bearing His name and character. John pointed out that believers are now the sons of God, but it does "not yet appear what we shall be: but we know that, when he shall appear, we shall be like him; for we shall see him as he is."

**13. He that hath an ear, let him hear what the Spirit saith unto the churches:** . . . Every person . . . should listen, *—EVRD* . . . who has ears . . . to the congregation, —KLST...listen to what, —WADE...give ear, —BB.

**3:13.** Once again the Scripture emphasizes that this promise is for anyone who will hear in all the churches of all times. The hearing ear is one of faith and obedience. Believers need to let the Spirit make these truths real in their hearts and lives.

**14. And unto the angel of the church of the Laodiceans write:**... for the messenger from the church in, —ADAM...the Guardian Angel, —WADE...the assembly in, —RTHM...the congregation, —KLST...in the city of, —NLTG...say, —BB...write this, —KLGS.

**These things saith the Amen, the faithful and true witness:**...Thus speaks, —NORL...This is what He declares Who is the very Truth...and Reliable Witness, —WADE...the expounder of the true faith, —NOLI...He who is absolutely faithful, the trustworthy...witness...has this to say, —KLST...the Veritable, —FNTN...certain witness, —BB...Real Witness, —RTHM.

**the beginning of the creation of God:**...the Origin of God's creation, —BECK...the source of God's creation, —SEB...the head of God's new order, —BB.

**3:14.** To the Laodiceans Jesus gave no commendation whatsoever. He called their attention to the fact that He is the Amen. 'Āmēn is a Hebrew word meaning "truly." It is a great word of response to the promises of God. Its root idea is firmness, certainty, and the assurance of faith. In Isaiah 65:16 it describes the Lord himself. Jesus is the revelation of all this means. As the Amen, He guarantees the truth of God's promises—promises that were still available even in Laodicea—promises that are available to every believer today. (See 2 Corinthians 1:20.)

Jesus is also "the faithful and true witness." He bears witness to the Father, to the truth of the gospel, and to His own nature and being as the unique Son of God, the second member of the Trinity. He will always be true to His Word. He is faithful, He will never fail to be faithful.

He is also the beginning, origin, first cause, and ruler of all God's creation. Christ as God the Son was not created. He always was, is, and will be. He was the Mediator in God's creation. All things were created through Him, and apart from Him nothing was created (John 1:3, literal). The world was made by Him (John 1:10). Now that He has ascended to the Father's right hand in heaven, He has a place "far above...every name that is named, not only in this world, but also in that which is to come" (Ephesians 1:20, 21). He is the One through whom all things were begun, and He will bring God's plan to its final consummation. He is still the one Mediator between God and mankind.

**15. I know thy works, that thou art neither cold nor hot:**...your conduct, —KLST...and find that you are, —NORL...nor fervid, —WADE...or warm, —BB.

**I would thou wert cold or hot:**...I wish that you were either, —FNTN...it would be better if you were, —BB...cold thou hadst been, —RTHM...either the one or the other! —NORL.

**3:15.** Apparently the Laodiceans had forgotten who Jesus really is and why He died. They were neither cold nor hot, and Jesus gave them a very sharp rebuke. They were cold before they were saved. When they accepted Christ, they were changed into zealous followers of the Lord. But now they had relapsed into a lukewarm condition. They were not cold enough to realize their need, so they were indifferent to challenges to service and calls to repentance. They were not hot enough to respond to the Spirit's moving, so nothing was really being accomplished for God. Jesus wished they were either cold or hot, for then He could do something with them.

**16. So then because thou art lukewarm, and neither cold nor hot:**...Therefore, since you are, —NORL...because lukewarm thou art, —RTHM...you are not one thing or the other, —BB.

**I will spue thee out of my mouth:**...I am ready to spit, —TCNT...I am about to, —NORL...I am going to vomit, —KLST, —WLMS...I am about to eject you out of, —WADE...spit you out, —BECK...I will repudiate you, —NOLI...I will have no more to do with you, —BB.

**3:16.** The Lord is disturbed when He is dealing with a people He can neither use nor bless. The Laodiceans did not oppose Him, but neither did they draw near to Him. Lukewarm water is not pleasant in the natural. Neither are lukewarm people. Because the Laodiceans were neither hot nor cold, Jesus said He would spew them out. They were like the second son in the Parable of the Two Sons. The father asked that son to go and work in his vineyard, and he said, "I go, sir; and went not" (Matthew 21:30). The Laodiceans claimed to be Christians, but they were not doing the will of their Heavenly Father.

**17. Because thou sayest:**...For you keep saying, —MNTG.

**I am rich, and increased with goods:**...I have grown, —BRKL...having become, —FNTN...and wealthy, —BECK...and prosperous, —NOLI...I have made money, —NORL...have acquired wealth, —WADE.

**and have need of nothing:**...am in want of, —WADE...have no need of anything, —KLST.

**and knowest not that thou art wretched, and miserable:**...pitiable, —WLMS...pitiful, —BECK...and destitute, —RTHM.

**and poor, and blind, and naked:**...beggared, —MNTG.

**3:17.** There are two schools of thought concerning the cause of the Laodicean lukewarmness. One is that it was their prosperity. They had become rich and used their money to multiply their possessions. They were so taken up with material things that they were neglecting spiritual realities. This church suffered no persecution. It was not troubled by false doctrine or false apostles. To the other churches, their situation must have seemed to be enviable, even ideal. But the Laodicean Christians had allowed themselves to become so self-satisfied in the enjoyment of riches and the things money can buy that they lost their desire for the things of God. They had not learned "how to abound" (Philippians 4:12). Thus, they were not only self-satisfied, they were self-deceived.

Another view as to the cause of their lukewarmness is that they had deceived themselves as to the degree of their spiritual life. They considered themselves more spiritual than others. They needed nothing.

This can be said: these people did not see themselves as God saw them—wretched, miserable, poor, blind, naked. They were not laying up true riches in heaven. They trusted in their prosperity as evidence of the blessing of God. They were self-righteous.

**18. I counsel thee to buy of me:** . . . So I advise you, *–BECK* . . . My counsel to you, therefore, is to come to Me and buy, *–NORL.*

**gold tried in the fire, that thou mayest be rich:** . . . tested, *–NORL* . . . gold-coin fired out of fire, *–RTHM* . . . that has been refined by, *–TCNT* . . . purified in fire, to make you rich, *–BECK.*

**and white raiment, that thou mayest be clothed:** . . . white clothes to put on, *–BECK* . . . and get white garments to clothe you, *–NORL* . . . that thou mayest be arrayed, *–RTHM* . . . to clothe yourself, *–MNTG.*

**and [that] the shame of thy nakedness do not appear:** . . . to keep your shameful nakedness from showing, *–BECK* . . . so as to cover up, *–NORL* . . . to hide your shameful nakedness, *–WLMS* . . . of your nudity, *–BRKL* . . . prevent the shame of your nakedness being visible, *–FNTN* . . . not be made manifest, *–RTHM, –MNTG.*

**and anoint thine eyes with eyesalve, that thou mayest see:** . . . and ointment for, *–TCNT* . . . to apply to your eyes, *–FNTN* . . . in order that, *–MNTG.*

**3:18.** There was still hope for the church at Laodicea. Instead of seeking this world's wealth, they could buy from Jesus pure gold, tested and refined with fire and therefore free from impurities. This gold is the gold of faith, which is worth far more than all the gold of this world, no matter how pure or how valuable that material gold might be (1 Peter 1:7). God wants believers to be rich in faith.

The Laodiceans could also receive from Christ white clothing, garments of triumphant righteousness (19:8). This would be theirs through the blood of the Lamb, a righteousness not their own but Christ's imputed to them, a righteousness made real in their lives through the sanctification of the Holy Spirit.

They needed also to buy of Christ a special ointment in order to anoint their eyes with spiritual eye salve so they might see their true state. They needed the help of the Spirit and the Word in order to have a clear vision of Christ, of heaven, and of the things of the Spirit. (See John 16:13 where Jesus promised the Holy Spirit would guide believers into all truth; that is, the truth of the gospel, the truth of God's Word.)

**19. As many as I love, I rebuke and chasten:** . . . I correct and discipline all whom, *–BECK* . . . I reprove, *–MNTG* . . . and punish those, *–SEB* . . . as I tenderly love, I convict and put under discipline, *–RTHM* . . . I examine and instruct, *–FNTN.*

**be zealous therefore, and repent:** . . . Be eagerly concerned then, *–BECK* . . . Therefore be in earnest, *–TCNT* . . . Be fervent, then, *–NORL* . . . Be serious. Change your heart! *–SEB* . . . burn with zeal and change your attitude, *–BRKL.*

**3:19.** The very fact that Jesus rebuked and disciplined the Laodiceans showed He still loved them. His love here is the love of affection. "I" is emphatic. The Father chastens and disciplines every son He receives (Proverbs 3:11, 12; Hebrews 12:5, 6). Jesus' love is like the Father's love in this.

"Rebuke" is the same word translated "reprove" used of the Holy Spirit's work in John 16:8. It includes the ideas of "expose, rebuke, refute, and show to be guilty." The Spirit convicts and convinces by proof. Jesus rebuked the Laodiceans just as the Holy Spirit rebukes the world and lukewarm or carnal Christians today.

There was hope for the Laodiceans if they would repent. Jesus urged them to rouse themselves out of their lukewarmness and be zealous. If they delayed, if they continued in their spiritual lethargy, Jesus would indeed spew them out of His mouth. Repentance would mean a change of attitude, a change of heart. They must become hot, on fire for the Lord, instead of lukewarm. They must recognize their true condition and heed the warning and the challenge the Lord was giving them. They must commit themselves to a continuing zeal, as the Greek present tense shows.

**20. Behold, I stand at the door, and knock:** . . . Here, *–KLST* . . . Mark these words of mine, *–WADE* . . . Listen, *–SEB* . . . Attend! *–FNTN* . . . See!

−NORL...I am standing...and knocking, −MNTG...See, I am waiting at the door and giving the sign, −BB.

**if any man hear my voice, and open the door:**...If you will listen, −BECK...listens to my call, −KLST...if perchance any one hearken to my voice, −RTHM...makes the door open, −BB.

**I will come in to him:**

**and will sup with him, and he with me:**...have supper with, −KLST...and dine with him, −BRKL...and eat with you, −NOLI...and will feast with, −WADE...will take food with him, −BB.

**3:20.** Christ's final words to the church in Laodicea are another wonderful demonstration of His love. Because of His love He rebuked and disciplined this church, but He did more. He took His stand outside the church door and kept knocking and knocking, waiting for someone to open the door. Though He had given severe warnings, His real desire was not to spew them out of His mouth but to sup, dine, have a meal. He longed to fellowship with them.

This is Christ's invitation still to all churches that no longer have the fires of revival, that have become institutions instead of movements. If someone, even one person, will open the door and enter into this renewed fellowship which Jesus offers, it may be the key to revival for the entire church.

This invitation can surely apply to individuals also. Christ does not force himself upon anyone. But if hearts are opened to Him, He will accept the invitation and bring His blessing and a wonderful fellowship in the Spirit as well.

**21. To him that overcometh will I grant to sit with me in my throne:**...As for him that is, −WADE...I will grant the victor, −NORL...him who is victorious...grant the favor of being seated beside me, −KLST...I will give a place with me on my high seat, −BB...give the privilege of sitting with Myself, −FNTN...to take his seat, −RTHM.

**even as I also overcame, and am set down with my Father in his throne:**...as I myself triumphed, −NOLI...as I have won the victory, −BECK...as I also conquered, −BRKL...even as I became the Victor, −NORL...as I too was victorious and am seated, −KLST...and have taken my seat with, −MNTG.

**3:21.** The letters to the seven churches conclude with another challenge to all believers. After the victory of the Cross and the Resurrection, Jesus ascended to His Father's throne (Ephesians 1:20, 21). There He "sat down on the right hand of the Majesty on high" (Hebrews 1:3; Mark 16:19). He is there now as High Priest and Advocate, interceding for believers (Hebrews 8:1; 1 John 2:1). He will be there until the time God the Father proceeds to make His enemies His footstool; that is, defeat them completely (Psalm 110:1). Then He

will come back in triumph to reign on earth in fulfillment of the Bible's prophecies of the Kingdom to come. The overcomers, who have shared with Christ in His triumph over sin and Satan, will share His throne.

**22. He that hath an ear, let him hear what the Spirit saith unto the churches:**...who has ears listen...says to the congregations, −KLST...listen to what the Divine Spirit says, −WADE.

**3:22.** This challenge is what the Spirit continues to say. The Spirit wants all churches of all ages to hear the message. It is for today, and it is individual and personal. It is not enough that spiritual victories were won in the past. The promises are to the overcoming believers. The overcomer, the winner, may have problems, battles, difficulties, or even defeats at times. But the overcomer remembers that Christ's victory is the secret of the believer's victory. He must keep his faith in Jesus (1 John 5:5). If a Christian sins, he must be quick to confess his sin and trust in Christ's faithfulness, not only to forgive but to cleanse and give victory (1 John 1:9; 2:1). Then he must keep on walking with Christ (1 John 1:7).

## Chapter 4

**1. After this I looked:**...After these things I saw, −BB...I had another vision, −WLMS...in a vision, −NORL...I saw, −RTHM.

**and, behold, a door [was] opened in heaven:**...and saw, −FNTN...on a sudden there appeared, −WADE...saw an open door to heaven, −NORL...which had been set open, −RTHM...standing open, −KLST.

**and the first voice which I heard [was] as it were of a trumpet talking with me:**...and the former Voice, −WADE...which I had previously heard, −KLST...that had spoken to me before, loud as a trumpet, −NORL...like a blast, −FNTN.

**which said, Come up hither:**...spoke to me, −KLST...up here, −RTHM.

**and I will show thee things which must be hereafter:**...point out to thee, −RTHM...what must happen after this, −BECK...what must occur in the future, −NOLI...which must come to pass, −LAMS...what must take place later, −KLST.

**4:1.** "After this" indicates a passage of time. John on Patmos did not see one continuous vision. There may have been days between the different sections of the book as they were revealed to him (see 7:1, 9; 15:5; 18:1). Thus, this verse brings us a change in scene and a change in time. John saw a door that stood open in heaven. Then the same voice which he heard in the previous vision (1:10) spoke to him with a sound like a trumpet telling him to "Come up hither" (to heaven). He was about to be shown things which would take place in the future fulfillment of God's plan. Chapters 4 and 5 deal with the events taking place at the throne in heaven and are introductory to all that follows in the Book of Revelation.

The phrase "I will show thee things which must be hereafter" takes us back to verse 19 of chapter 1. There Jesus told John he was to write about the past, present, and future. John had seen Christ revealed in great glory; he had written Jesus' letters to the messengers of the churches as described in chapters 2 and 3. Now it was time to reveal the full scope of God's plan as He would describe the last scenes of the history of the world and His blueprint for the ages to come.

**2. And immediately I was in the spirit:** ... Straightway, *–RTHM* ... At once, *–NORL* ... Suddenly I was thrown into an ecstasy, *–KLST* ... I came under the Spirit's power, *–BECK* ... Upon this I fell at once into a spiritual trance, *–WADE* ... became inspired, *–FNTN.*

**and, behold, a throne was set in heaven, and [one] sat on the throne:** ... and there before me was a Throne placed, *–WADE* ... there stood a throne, *–MNTG* ... To my surprise ... someone was seated, *–KLST* ... and observed ... upon the throne an Occupant, *–FNTN.*

**4:2.** Immediately John was in the Spirit and was caught away to the throne in heaven. Walvoord sees this as symbolic of the catching away of the Church (p. 103). Other scholars have also. The phrase "in the Spirit" is a key phrase. It occurs in 1:10 as an introduction to the first section of the book with John's vision of Christ in the midst of the golden lampstands. Here, in 4:2, it is an introduction to the vision of Christ on the throne, breaking the seven seals and administering the seven trumpets and the seven vials or bowls of judgment. It is found again in 17:3 where there is another change of scene followed by three concluding events: the fall of Babylon, the defeat of the Antichrist, and the end of Satan's deceptions. Much of the language in these chapters is symbolic, and there is a great deal of controversy over the meaning of these chapters as well as the order of events. However, it must be recognized that the symbols represent realities, not vague generalities. The Antichrist, for example, is called a beast, but the symbol represents a real man.

As John, in the Spirit, was caught away into heaven, his attention focused first on the throne of God which was already set or standing there. The Person seated on the throne was obviously God the Father.

**3. And he that sat was to look upon like a jasper and a sardine stone:** ... The occupant of the throne, *–KLST* ... was in splendour of aspect like, *–WADE* ... resembled, *–LAMS* ... had the appearance of a jasper stone, *–NORL* ... was in appearance like, *–MNTG, –TCNT* ... in brilliancy, *–FNTN* ... an opal stone, *–WMCK* ... carnelian, *–BECK.*

**and [there was] a rainbow round about the throne:** ... Over the throne there was a halo of the color of, *–NOLI* ... encircling, *–RTHM.*

**in sight like unto an emerald:** ... looked like, *–BECK* ... like, in appearance, *–RTHM* ... like the sparkling of, *–FNTN* ... appearance to an emerald, *–NORL* ... like an emerald to look upon, *–MNTG* ... like those of an emerald stone, *–NLTG* ... like a vision of emerald, *–KLST* ... emerald-green, *–WADE.*

**4:3.** John did not attempt to describe God, however. He was aware of God's presence, but the glory was too great for him to describe as having a shape or form. All he could do was to speak of the diamond brilliance and the fiery red presence that glowed with the red of the sard or carnelian. The "jasper" (KJV) is said in 21:11 to be crystal clear and thus was not the jasper of today which is opaque. It was more likely the diamond. The "sardine stone" (or sard, sardius, or carnelian) was a beautiful red precious stone or gem symbolizing redemption.

God often manifested himself in fire in the Old Testament, but this appearance was more glorious than anything ever seen before. Around the throne was a brilliant rainbow or halo of red's complementary color, a shining emerald green. (See 1 Timothy 6:16; James 1:17.)

**4. And round about the throne [were] four and twenty seats:** ... Also surrounding the throne, *–BRKL* ... were twenty-four smaller places to sit around the place where the King sits, *–NLTG* ... in a circle around, *–WADE* ... encircling, *–RTHM* ... the high seat, *–BB* ... 24 thrones around, *–SEB* ... other thrones, *–BECK, –TCNT.*

**and upon the seats I saw four and twenty elders sitting:** ... seated on these thrones, *–NORL* ... on these places twenty-four leaders were sitting, *–NLTG* ... twenty four Presbyters, *–WADE* ... rulers, *–BB.*

**clothed in white raiment:** ... clad, *–FNTN* ... arrayed, *–RTHM* ... dressed in white clothes, *–BECK, –NLTG* ... robes, *–NORL.*

**and they had on their heads crowns of gold:** ... golden crowns, *–KLST* ... golden circlets, *–WADE* ... headbands of gold on their heads, *–NLTG.*

**4:4.** God's throne was not the only throne John saw. In a circle around it were 24 seats or thrones (the word is same) for 24 elders. *Elder* or *presbyter* was used by the Early Church as a synonym for the bishop (overseer, pastor) of a local church. The Jews used it for members of the Sanhedrin, their senate and high court.

The Bible does not explain who the elders were. Modern writers such as Ladd insist they were angels, saying that 7:9-11 and 19:1-4 group the various ranks of heavenly beings together (p. 75). Ladd goes on to say that the bowls full of incense (5:8) indicate they were angelic messengers presenting the prayers of the saints before the throne in heaven (p. 89).

There are, however, a number of things which distinguish them from the angels. Nowhere in the Bible are angels called elders. The crowns the elders were wearing were victors' crowns or wreaths, and the word is used for crowns prepared for believers, not angels. The crowns, however, speak of royalty also. When the soldiers crowned Jesus with the crown or wreath (the same word) of thorns, their purpose was to mock Him as "the King of the Jews" (Matthew 27:37). In the text (4:4) the word is used in connection with the elders who were sitting on thrones and having royal power (5:10). The white clothing is also the same as that promised to the believers who are overcomers, winners (2:10; 3:4). Thus, there seem to be good reasons for believing the elders in some way represent the Church.

It is noteworthy also that in the record of Old Testament visions of the throne of God, where seraphs and cherubs are mentioned, there are no elders. This may indicate that the elders John saw were a new group that will be before the throne of God in the events of the latter time which John was shown in this vision. Their number, 24, might be a counterpart of the 24 clerical divisions of the temple (1 Chronicles 24:1f.). Some scholars think it stands for the total Church in the old and the new covenant with its 12 patriarchs and 12 apostles who have their names on the gates and base stones of the New Jerusalem (21:12-14). Then these 24 elders symbolize, or perhaps represent, the entire redeemed Church throughout all ages. (Note that they talked with John in 5:5; 7:13.)

5. **And out of the throne proceeded lightnings and thunder-ings and voices:** ... From the throne, −KLST ... coming forth, −RTHM ... came flames, −BB ... came flashes of lightning, rumblings, and peals of thunder, −BECK ... issued ... the sound of voices, −NORL ... and noises, −LAMS ... came from the place where He sits, −NLTG.
**and [there were] seven lamps of fire:** ... seven lights of fire, −BB, −NLTG ... blazing lamps, −MNTG ... flaming torches, −BECK ... fiery lamps, −FNTN ... torches of fire, −NORL.
**burning before the throne:** ... in presence of the throne, −RTHM ... in front of the throne, −BECK ... were before the high seat, −BB.
**which are the seven Spirits of God:** ... These were, −NLTG ... which symbolize, −NOLI.

**4:5.** John next noticed the throne and the seven lamps of fire in front of it. The lightnings,

thunderings, and voices are a reminder of Old Testament expressions of God speaking, as at Sinai (Exodus 19:16; 20:18). They added to the awe and majesty of the throne and were indicative of the judgments which were to come. The seven lamps of fire represented the sevenfold Spirit of God (Isaiah 11:2, 3).

6. **And before the throne [there was] a sea of glass like unto crystal:** ... Also in front of, −WLMS ... the place where He sits ... shining and clear, −NLTG ... in presence of the throne, −RTHM ... something like a sea, −KLST ... it seemed, −MNTG ... it looked like, −SEB ... transparent as crystal, −BRKL ... resembling, −FNTN, −TCNT ... a clear sea of glass, −BB ... crystal glass, −NORL ... crystal in lustre, −WADE.
**and in the midst of the throne, and round about the throne, [were] four beasts:** ... In front of and around the throne, −KLST ... in the middle of each side ... were four living beings, −BECK ... encircling it ... Creatures, −MNTG ... Around that place and on each side, −NLTG ... of the high seat, and ... about it, −BB ... in circuit of ... creatures, −RTHM ... Four Bodyguards, −NOLI ... were four animals, −LAMS.
**full of eyes before and behind:** ... had eyes everywhere, −BECK ... covered with eyes, −NORL ... dotted with eyes in front and behind, −WLMS ... full of intelligence as to what is before and what is behind, −FNTN ... round about, −BB ... and in back, −NLTG.

**4:6.** Between John and the throne, John saw something like a great sea of glass. He described in human terms something far more beautiful, clear, and sparkling with reflected glory than any human words can express. M. Kiddle sees this as a symbol of the distance and separation between the Creator and the creation (*Moffatt New Testament Commentary, Revelation*, p. 89).

Because the "sea" of glass is in the heavenly sanctuary, it may be considered analogous to the bronze laver in the earthly tabernacle (Exodus 30:18-21) and to the molten "sea" or giant laver in the temple of Solomon (2 Chronicles 4:2-6). The priests washed there before they appeared before the Lord for service, but the heavenly priesthood is already clean, already sanctified, already holy— thus the sea there is a sea of glass.

Four beasts or living beings around the throne completed the picture. (The word "creatures" here is not the same as that of the wild beasts used in other passages, such as 13:1.) They were full of eyes on the front and on the back. These eyes represented intelligence, alertness, understanding.

7. **And the first beast [was] like a lion:** ... the first creature, −WMCK ... the first living being like, −BRKL ... resembled, −FNTN.
**and the second beast like a calf:** ... looked like, −NOLI ... like a young bull, −BECK ... bullock, −FNTN ... like an ox, −KLST ... a young cow, −NLTG.

**and the third beast had a face as a man:** ... a human face, *—BECK.*

**and the fourth beast [was] like a flying eagle:** ... like an eagle flying, *—MNTG* ... like a very large bird with its wings spread, *—NLTG* ... in flight, *—BB, —WADE.*

**4:7.** The language describing the four living beings is drawn from the Old Testament, especially from the description of the cherubim in Ezekiel. Cherubim are mentioned first as guardians of the road to the Garden of Eden after the Fall (Genesis 3:24). There were sculptures of them in the tabernacle and the temple. There were two cherubim of gold above the mercy seat, the solid gold cover of the ark of the covenant (Exodus 25:18). God in His manifestation in the temple was often referred to as He who dwells between the cherubim (1 Samuel 4:4; 2 Samuel 6:2; 2 Kings 19:15; Psalms 80:1; 99:1; Isaiah 37:16). (The "im" in *cherubim* is the Hebrew plural ending; thus, *cherubim* is the plural of *cherub.)* In Ezekiel the cherubim were all alike. In Revelation 4 the living beings are each different and distinct.

On the basis of the Old Testament passages it would seem that they represented all God's creation: the lion as the king of the wild animals, the ox-calf as the chief domesticated animal in those days, the man created in the image of God, and the eagle as the king of birds. Thus, together they indicate that all nature joins in praising God. They indicate also, by honoring the One on the throne, that God is sovereign over all His creation.

In the early history of the Church it became popular also to connect these living beings with Christ and the four Gospels. Augustine, about A.D. 400, for example, saw Jesus in Matthew as the lion of Judah, in Mark as the man, in Luke as the ox-calf being sacrificed for all people everywhere, and in John as the eagle reaching the highest heights of spiritual revelation (*Nicene and Post-Nicene Fathers, The Harmony of the Gospels* 6.9).

**8. And the four beasts had each of them six wings about [him]:** ... each of the four living creatures has, *—NORL* ... living beings, *—ADAM* ... the four animals ... having six wings apiece, *—CNDT* ... these four living things, *—EVRD* ... each of the four living ones, *—KLGS* ... each individually, possessed, *—FNTN* ... having severally six wings, *—RTHM.*

**and [they were] full of eyes within:** ... these are covered with eyes both on top and underneath, *—NORL* ... round about, *—MNTG* ... around and inside are replete with, *—CNDT* ... were covered all over, *—EVRD* ... with eyes circling and on both sides, *—KLGS* ...all around and under, *—BECK* ...on their inward side, turned toward the Throne, *—WADE* ... around and within, *—RTHM* ... all over them, inside and out, *—NLTG.*

**and they rest not day and night, saying:** ... Day and night, without resting, *—TNT* ... without stopping they were saying, *—BECK* ... they never cease saying, *—WLMS* ... they sing ceaselessly, *—NOLI* ... exclaiming, *—FNTN* ... they are chanting, *—MNTG* ... they never stop saying, *—ADAM* ... they continually repeat, *—KLST* ... They take no rest, *—KLGS.*

**Holy, holy, holy, Lord God Almighty, which was, and is, and is to come:** ... Ruler of all, *—BB* ... the Sovereign Supreme, *—WADE* ... the All-powerful One, *—NLTG* ...is coming, *—BECK, —RTHM* ...and who will manifest himself, *—NOLI* ... Who comes, *—FNTN, —KLGS* ...Who art coming! *—CNDT.*

**4:8.** Each of the four living beings had six wings like the seraphim Isaiah saw in his inaugural vision where their wings spoke of both humility and quickness (Isaiah 6:1, 2). Seraph means "burning one," and they were so full of the reflected glory of God that they seemed to be on fire. Like the seraphim also they never cease crying "Holy, holy, holy," but they refer to God as the Lord God Almighty instead of the Lord of hosts. Instead of speaking of the earth being full of His glory, they speak about His eternality as the One who always was, always is, and always is to come. That they are full of eyes all around and within emphasizes their understanding and wisdom.

Though they praise God continually, they also perform the will of God and effectuate His judgments (6:1). Thus they are real beings, rational beings, not just symbolic. It seems they not only represent all creation before God, like the cherubim Ezekiel saw, but are also the leaders of all creation. They speak in unison as they praise God. They also speak individually (6:1, 3, 5, 7). Scholars such as Ford have proposed that these are the same beings of the heavenly court which Isaiah and Ezekiel saw, but each saw them from a different point of view and in different circumstances (*Anchor Bible,* 38:76-79). This, however, is not clear.

The threefold repetition of "holy" emphasizes God's supreme holiness. Holiness in the Bible is always twofold. Its basic idea is separation, but it includes both a separation from and a separation to. To put it another way, the two aspects may be characterized by the two words difference and dedication. God is totally separated from sin. His holiness makes Him completely different from His creation and also from the fallen world order that has been marred by sin. He is also completely dedicated to the carrying out of His great will and plan. The heathen considered their gods as fickle, changeable. But believers can afford to put their lives in God's hands for He is utterly dependable.

As the Almighty One, God has all power. He is omnipotent. He not only is dedicated to carrying out His plan but has the power to do it. Satan, who has always tried to thwart God's purposes, is mighty, but God is almighty. Men have tried to achieve great power, but compared to God the mightiest is a weakling. No king, no dictator, no demon or Satan himself can withstand Christ or prevent His final triumph.

His eternality means that by His very nature God cannot die or be destroyed. Atheists, communists, and rebels of all kinds may turn against Him. They will pass, but He remains. The expression of His eternality applies to the Triune God (compare 1:4 and 1:8) but is here directed to the Father.

**9. And when those beasts give glory and honour and thanks to him that sat on the throne:** ... And every time the living things do this, —EVRD ... These living creatures then offer, —NORL ... The four living beings speak of His shining greatness ... Who sits on His place as King, —NLTG ... when the living ones give praise, —KLGS ... to the Occupant of, —BRKL ... on the high seat, —BB.

**who liveth for ever and ever:** ... It is He who lives, —NLTG ... who is living, —BB ... that lives to the ages of ages, —RTHM.

**4:9.** This threefold praise is no mere form. The indication here is that the praise of the living beings is not continually on the same level. The Greek *hotan* ("when, whenever") means here that from time to time, over and over again, these living beings overflow in a great outpouring of glory, honor, and thanks to the One on the throne. This and similar phrases occur eight times in the Book of Revelation: 4:9, 11; 5:12, 13; 7:11, 12; 19:1; 21:24, 26.

**10. The four and twenty elders fall down before him that sat on the throne:** ... leaders get down in front of Him, —NLTG ... rulers go down on their faces before ... the high seat, —BB ... kneel before him, —NOLI ... bow down before, —EVRD ... fall prostrate before, —FNTN ... throw themselves before Him, —WADE ... in presence of, —RTHM ... the occupant, —KLST.

**and worship him that liveth for ever and ever:** ... give worship to him who is living for ever and ever, —BB ... render worship to him that lives to the ages of ages, —RTHM.

**and cast their crowns before the throne, saying:** ... taking off their crowns before the high seat, —BB ... put their crowns down, —EVRD ... throw their crowns before, —KLGS ... they lay their crowns down in front of the throne, as they sing, —TNT ... They lay their headbands in front of Him, —NLTG ... throwing down, —BECK ... cast their circlets ... exclaiming, —WADE ... They chant, —KLST.

**4:10.** At the same time these living beings break out with an overflow of homage to God, and every time they do, the 24 elders rise simultaneously from their own kingly thrones, descend from

them, and go and prostrate themselves before the throne of God, casting down their crowns before Him as they do. Thus they show their reverence, their dependence on God, and their subjection to Him. They also show that their authority is a delegated authority. Their royal power does not represent an opposing or separate kingdom but is subject to the throne of God and has its source in Him alone. It is said four times that the elders fall down worshiping (4:10; 5:8, 14; 19:4). They worship God as "him that liveth for ever and ever," the eternal "I Am" (Exodus 3:14, 15), in the same way as the four living beings (Revelation 4:9).

**11. Thou art worthy, O Lord:** ... It is right, our Lord, —BB ... Our Lord and God, You deserve, —BECK ... even our God, —RTHM ... it is right for You to have the shining greatness, —NLTG.

**to receive glory and honour and power:** ... to have, —BB ... to reserve for yourself, —KLST ... praise, —KLGS ... the majesty ... and the might, —FNTN.

**for thou hast created all things:** ... For you created everything, —WLMS ... you have created the universe, —NOLI ... because it was Thou that didst create, —WADE ... by you were all things made, —BB ... because you have made everything, —KLGS.

**and for thy pleasure they are and were created:** ... And because of thy will they came into being, —MNTG ... and Your will caused them to be created and to be, —BECK ... for Your purpose, —FNTN ... by reason of thy will they were in existence, —RTHM ... and to thy will they owe their existence and their creation, —TCNT ... they came into existence, —WLMS ... and exist only by Your will, —NORL.

**4:11.** In their praise the 24 elders recognize God as their Lord, which in the Old Testament language would refer to His covenant-keeping name (YHWH, sometimes spelled as Yahweh or Jehovah. Originally, the Hebrew language had no vowels, so it is difficult to ascertain the correct spelling.).

They ascribe their praise directly to God, recognizing that He is also their Creator and thus the Giver of all the good things His creation enjoys. Truly He is worthy to receive glory, honor, and power. There are two truths here. First, human beings cannot create something out of nothing. But God did at a specific point in the beginning of time. Mankind can only discover, use, and rearrange what has been given by God when He created all things. Second, all created things are not merely for mankind's benefit but for God's. He is honored only as created things are used for His glory.

The Roman emperors in triumphal entry were greeted with the words: "Worthy art thou!" And the title "Lord and God" was introduced in the cult of emperor worship by Domitian. The prayer of the elders is a contrast and a protest to the worship of the emperor and to the exaltation of any human being, man or woman.

This doxology of creation is the first song of praise of these 24 elders representing God's redeemed people. Their song corresponds with the first and most fundamental claim of God on His intelligent creatures, that they recognize His power and glory as Creator (Romans 1:19, 20). It is also the first subject revealed in the Bible (Genesis 1:1; compare Hebrews 11:3). To this almighty Creator-God every creature owes its very existence. God's sovereign, creative will is the sole reason that they came into being, in contrast to their previous nonexistence. That is, before Genesis 1:1 they existed only as an idea in the mind of God. He made them real by actually creating them.

The eschatological hope is founded upon this revelation of the Creator. It is a drama of creation and redemption. In chapter 4 there is a vision of the Creator. In chapter 5 there follows a vision of the Redeemer. He who created the world has the power, ability, and will to bring it to its proper goal and consummation.

## Chapter 5

1. **And I saw in the right hand of him that sat on the throne:** . . . lying upon, —MNTG . . . upon the right hand of the Occupant, —FNTN.

**a book written within and on the backside:** . . . a scroll, —BRKL, —RTHM . . . written inside and outside, —FNTN . . . a book with writing inside and on the back of it, —NORL . . . on both sides, —BECK, —WLMS.

**sealed with seven seals:** . . . close sealed, —MNTG . . . sealed down, —FNTN.

**5:1.** As John looked again, he saw in the outstretched hand of the Holy One on the throne a book in the form of a roll or scroll of papyrus. The papyrus pages were formed of two sheets of papyrus sewn together. On one of the sides the strips of the inner bank were horizontal. On the other side the strips were vertical. They were rolled up to form a scroll. Along the outer (leading) edge of the roll were seven seals that sealed it shut so that it would be necessary to open all seven seals before the book could be unrolled. Another view is that there were a series of seals, each opening a part of the scroll.

Everything in the scene emphasizes the importance and significance of this roll or book. The hand of God indicates the divine source of the book. Ordinarily, only one side of the papyrus sheets (the one with horizontal strips) was used (the pen would catch in the cracks on the side where the strips were vertical). But this book was full and its message important, so both sides

were used. The seals showed the importance of the message.

The Bible does not expressly say what was written in the book. One opinion is that it is God's book of the future (Mounce, *New International Commentary on the New Testament, Revelation,* p. 142; cf. Psalm 139:16; Ezekiel 2:9, 10; Zechariah 5:2, 3; Revelation 10:9; see also Daniel 12:4 with Revelation 22:10). The closed scroll would then indicate the plan of God yet unrevealed. To break the seals and open the scroll would mean to reveal and to carry out God's plan.

Beasley-Murray points out there is no indication the book was read. Ancient wills under Roman law were sealed with seven seals. This opinion would understand the scroll as a will or title deed (*New Century Bible, Revelation,* pp. 120-123). (Compare Jeremiah 32:6-15 where the prophet through a symbolic, prophetic action made known that the people of Israel would have their land back.)

2. **And I saw a strong angel proclaiming with a loud voice:** . . . I observed, —FNTN . . . a mighty messenger, —RTHM . . . mighty angel, —BECK, —BRKL . . . of mighty strength who asked with a loud voice, —NORL . . . He was announcing this loudly, —SEB. **Who is worthy to open the book, and to loose the seals thereof?:** . . . Is there no one worthy, —TCNT . . . Who deserves to, —WLMS . . . Who is qualified, —NOLI . . . and break the seals on it? —BECK.

**5:2.** With a loud challenge that rose above the sound of the worship around the throne a mighty, powerful angel (as in 10:1 and 18:1, 21) indicated his great concern over the message of the book. Many believe this may be God's revelation-angel Gabriel whose name is usually taken to mean "man of God" but may mean "strength of God" or "mighty one of God." Gabriel was the angel who ordered Daniel to close and seal his book (Daniel 12:4). This angel, in the manner of a herald, asked, "Who is worthy to open the book, and to loose the seals?" The final and decisive factor in history is moral and spiritual.

3. **And no man in heaven:** . . . no one in the heavens, —MNTG.

**nor in earth:** . . . on the earth, —MNTG.

**neither under the earth:** . . . beneath, —RTHM.

**was able to open the book, neither to look thereon:** . . . could open the scroll and read it, —NOLI . . . or to look into it, —MNTG . . . nor yet to gaze upon it, —FNTN . . . or to inspect it, —BRKL.

**5:3.** After a search was made of the three realms of creation (Philippians 2:10) no one was found worthy to open the book or even look into it. This means no created being is worthy to claim the Kingdom or take care of the future of the world.

No one is worthy to establish the kingdom of God on earth. Many have tried to solve the world's problems but without success.

**4. And I wept much:** ... I cried bitterly, —BECK ... began to weep, —WLMS.

**because no man was found worthy to open and to read the book, neither to look thereon:** ... Since no one was found worthy to open the book, or to read it or to look into it, —NORL ... to open the scroll or to look into it, —KLST ... or even to gaze at it, —FNTN.

**5:4.** At this John began weeping and could not stop. He recognized the importance of the revelation contained in the book. He, no doubt, connected it with the promise given in 4:1, "I will show thee things which must be hereafter." Now it seemed that no one was worthy, and John was surely conscious of his own unworthiness. He felt disappointment, thinking that the revelation could not be given after all.

This sets the book or roll apart from other books of prophecy. Even in the Old Testament God made it His practice to reveal His will and plan to the prophets (see Amos 3:7; 2 Peter 1:20, 21). Those prophets could receive the message, not because they were worthy in themselves, but because they were open to the Holy Spirit and moved or were led along by the Spirit. Spiritual things cannot be received by the ungodly (1 Corinthians 2:14, 15). But in this case John was in the Spirit and still was not worthy to open the book.

**5. And one of the elders saith unto me, Weep not:** ... one from among the elders ... be not weeping, —RTHM ... Don't cry! —BECK ... Cease to weep, —WADE.

**behold, the Lion of the tribe of Juda, the Root of David:** ... see! —FNTN ... here is One, —NORL ... listen ... the Scion of David, —WADE ... the Descendant of, —BECK ... the Offspring of, —BRKL ... who sprang from, —WLMS ... out of the tribe, —RTHM.

**hath prevailed to open the book:** ... has succeeded in opening, —FNTN ... has won a victory, —BECK ... has won the right to open, —WADE ... has been victorious, —SEB ... he conquered, —RTHM ... who has conquered and can open the book, —NORL ... and so he can open the scroll, —KLST.

**and to loose the seven seals thereof:** ... and break, —NORL ... can open the scroll and its seven seals, —BECK.

**5:5.** As John continued weeping, one of the elders came and told him to stop. His tears were unnecessary. One had prevailed, conquered, won a great victory. This One, the elder said, was "the Lion of the tribe of Judah." (See Genesis 49:9, 10. Judah was the leader of the tribes, and his symbol was a lion. Jesus is the Lion of Judah.) He is also the Root (shoot or scion growing from the root) of David.

The reference to the Lion of Judah indicates that His victory would bring fulfillment of the promises made to God's ancient people, Israel. The reference to the shoot out of the "Root of David" indicates His victory would also bring fulfillment of the promises given to David. After David, out of love for God, had decided to build a temple for Him, God made a covenant with the king. "Thine house and thy kingdom shall be established for ever before thee" (2 Samuel 7:16). The Davidic dynasty would always continue. (See also Isaiah 11:1, 10; compare 53:2; Ezekiel 19:11, 12, 14; Romans 15:12.) His great victory is the victory of the Cross (John 16:33), and His victory at Calvary has given Him the right to open the scroll.

**6. And I beheld, and, lo, in the midst of the throne:** ... I also saw in the intervening space, —FNTN ... Then I saw standing in front of, —KLST ... Then, right between the throne, —NORL ... standing midway between, —BRKL.

**and of the four beasts:** ... and in the midst of the four living beings, —KLST ... living creatures, —RTHM ... Beings, —FNTN ... on the one hand, —WADE.

**and in the midst of the elders:** ... among, —NORL ... Presbyters on the other hand, —WADE.

**stood a Lamb as it had been slain:** ... I saw a Lamb standing. It appeared to have been slain, —NORL ... in the middle of the high seat ... a lamb in his place, —BB ... not a Lion but a Little Lamb, —WADE ... standing, that looked as if it had been sacrificed, —ADAM ... as if slain, —KLST ... a Lamb placed, as having been sacrificed, —FNTN ... as though He had been, —WLMS ... as if He had been killed, —NLTG ... as though it had been butchered, —KLGS ... slaughtered, —BECK.

**having seven horns and seven eyes:** ... possessing, —FNTN.

**which are the seven Spirits of God:** ... These are, —NLTG ... which are God's seven spirits, —ADAM.

**sent forth into all the earth:** ... that He sends forth into all the earth, —ADAM ... sent on messages into, —WADE ... dispatched over, —BRKL ... who were given a mission to the whole earth, —KLST ... sent on duty to every portion of the earth, —WLMS ... who have been sent out into, —TNT ... to all parts of, —NOLI ... throughout, —FNTN ... all the world, —NLTG.

**5:6.** When John looked, he saw not a lion but a Lamb, still bearing the marks of having been slain. It was as God's Lamb that Christ conquered.

Terrible judgments must precede the coming of the Kingdom. The present world order with all its historic roots must be swept away to make room for it (Daniel 2:34, 35, 44, 45). The breaking of the seals and the opening of the book will bring the judgments. The opener of the seals thus will become the administrator of the judgment. He alone is worthy, for those who fall under this judgment cannot say to God's spotless Lamb, "You deserve this judgment too." Neither can they say, "You did not do enough to save us from this judgment." He gave His life.

As the Lamb stood in the middle of the throne, the four living creatures, and the four elders, John saw that He had seven horns and seven eyes. The sevenfold Spirit, which in chapter 4 burned as seven lamps of fire before the throne, had now become the active agent to take the wisdom and power of the Lamb into all the earth.

**7. And he came and took the book out of the right hand of him that sat upon the throne:**...The Lamb took the scroll, —KLST...he went, and now he has taken the book, —MNTG...from the right hand of the One Who sits on, —ADAM...of the Occupant, —FNTN, —NORL...of the One Who sat there as King, —NLTG.

**5:7.** The Lamb with the seven horns and seven eyes took the book out of the hand of the One who sat on the throne. Thus He received the title deed. It was the legal act by which He was given the authority to reign on this earth over this earth. That action will be the fulfillment of Daniel 7:13, 14. In that vision Daniel saw the Son of Man come before the throne and receive the Kingdom from the hand of the Ancient of Days.

As the Lion of Judah Christ will occupy His property which He created and bought, and He will powerfully bring in the new Kingdom Age. As the sacrificial Lamb He paid the price for it all by shedding His own precious blood.

The fact that John saw the sevenfold Spirit as now actively going forth into all the earth indicates that the Lamb is concerned about the earth and about carrying out God's will in all the earth. When He takes the book, things are about to happen.

**8. And when he had taken the book:**... When the Lamb took the scroll, Kliest.
**the four beasts and four [and] twenty elders fell down before the Lamb:**...the four creatures, —TNT...living beings, —ADAM...Senators prostrated themselves, —TCNT...fell prostrate, —FNTN...leaders got down in front of Him, —NLTG...went down on their faces, —BB...threw themselves before the Little Lamb, —WADE...in presence of, —RTHM.

**having every one of them harps, and golden vials full of odours:**...holding, each...incense-compounds, —RTHM...an instrument of music, and gold vessels, —BB...a lyre and golden bowls full of incense, —BECK...golden censers full of perfumes, —FNTN.

**which are the prayers of saints:**...which represent, —WLMS...symbolize, —KLST...of the holy people, —BECK...of the Christians, —NORL...of God's Hallowed People, —WADE.

**5:8.** Up to this point all the worship and praise was given to the One on the throne, God the Father. But when the Lamb took the scroll there was a great outburst of praise, starting at the throne and spreading until the 4 living creatures and the 24 elders fell down in worship before the Lamb. It is not clear whether or not the four living beings participated in the offering. The emphasis seems to be upon the elders. The parallel (4:9-11) shows the elders giving praise to the Creator. Here they gave the same praise to the Lamb, the Redeemer. It was praise and worship that belongs only to God (22:9). Thus they recognized the deity of the Lamb. He who became fully human was then and is now and always will be fully God. On earth Jesus was 100 percent God and at the same time 100 percent man. He kept within His person the attributes of deity and at the same time a full set of human attributes in such a way that they did not interfere with each other. Thus, He felt what human beings feel, yet without sin (Hebrews 4:15).

Instead of presenting their own crowns before Him, however, the 24 elders had harps, and they came before the Lamb, worshiping Him and presenting to Him golden bowls full of incense which are the prayers of the saints. (The "vials," KJV, were large, flat bowls. Here they are used as golden censers or fire pans such as were used to present offerings of incense before the Lord in Old Testament times.)

The saints, that is, the dedicated believers who "love his appearing" (2 Timothy 4:8), are praying above all else for the coming of the Kingdom when they shall reign on the earth.

The bowls of incense represent the fact that the book must be opened and the judgments of the Great Tribulation must take place before the prayers of the saints can be answered.

The harps indicate actual Greek-type lyres, not the Egyptian or even Davidic harps. The Greek word *kitharas* is the root of our word *guitar*. They probably sounded like guitars.

**9. And they sung a new song, saying:**... They sang a new canticle, —KLST...are sounding in a new song, —BB...a Song of an unfamiliar strain, in these words, —WADE.

**Thou art worthy to take the book, and to open the seals thereof:**...It is right for you...to make it open, —BB...qualified, —BECK...break its seals, —WADE.

**for thou wast slain:**...because Thou wert sacrificed, —BRKL...because You were sacrificed, —BECK...for you were put to death, —BB...slaughtered, —RTHM.

**and hast redeemed us to God by thy blood:**...You bought them, —BECK...didst purchase us, —RTHM...used your blood to buy back, —SEB...and have made an offering to God of your blood for men, —BB...didst ransom, —MNTG...didst buy for God, —TCNT...bought us and gave us to God, —NORL.

**out of every kindred, and tongue, and people, and nation:**...Men of every, —KLST...some out of every, —WADE...tribe, language, —BECK.

**5:9.** To the accompaniment of their musical instruments they sang a new song, a song to the Lamb, praising Him for His great work of redemption that made Him worthy to take the little book and open its seals. They sang the song because, as Paul indicated in Romans 8:21-23, all creation is groaning for that day when the curse will be lifted and the saints' redemption (resurrection) bodies will be received at Christ's appearing.

Singing "a new song" celebrated God's New Testament act of deliverance through Christ. The song emphasized Jesus' redemptive act—He literally purchased believers by His atonement on Calvary—so believers now belong to Him.

It is clear here that Jesus died for all. The redeemed ones will be from every kindred, that is from every tribe or racial group; some from every tongue or language; some from every people, a term used both of the tribes of Israel and the Gentiles; and some from all the nations (a term often used of foreigners considered to be religiously or morally inferior). The Bible could not be more precise or inclusive here. The blood of Jesus paid the price for the redemption of every human being of every race and color. God wants all to belong to Him, but they must accept His gift.

**10. And hast made us unto our God kings and priests:** ... You have consecrated them as royal priests, —NOLI ... and didst constitute them for, —WADE ... to be God's own, —BECK ... a kingdom and priests for, —KLST ... kingdom of priests, —NORL, —WLMS.

**and we shall reign on the earth:** ... They will rule over, —SEB ... rule as kings, —BECK ... they shall reign over the earth, —NORL.

**5:10.** This verse is one of the rather few instances where variations in the readings of ancient manuscripts of the New Testament make an important difference in interpretation. It is mainly a matter of three pronouns: "us" in verse 9, "us" and "we" in verse 10. If these words are in the original text, the 24 elders are redeemed people. If not, this question is left open. A few older manuscripts have no "us" in verse 9, so some translations read, "You purchased men for God." (See NIV.) Then in verse 10 they read "them/they" instead of "us/we." It may be, however, that the reading "them/ they" came because the four living beings joined in this song, and they were considered to be angelic beings. It seems clear, however, that the 24 elders

were indeed joining in the song as redeemed persons.

Those from every tribe, language, people, and nation who are now the purchased possession of God have also been made unto God kings, or rather, a kingdom and priests. This was God's desire for Israel (Exodus 19:6). It is what God accomplished and will accomplish in the Church (1 Peter 2:5, 9). Furthermore, believers will reign on the earth. That is, they will share Christ's throne as He promised the overcomers, not only in the heavenly kingdom, but also on earth.

**11. And I beheld, and I heard the voice of many angels round about the throne:** ... Then I looked, —BRKL ... In my vision I heard a chorus...who encircled the throne, —KLST ... And I saw, and there came to my ears the sound of a great number of angels, —BB ... many thousands of, —NLTG ... messengers in circuit of the throne, —RTHM ... encircling, —MNTG ... who stood round, —TNT ... surrounding the throne, —WLMS.

**and the beasts and the elders:** ... and also the sound of the living creatures, —NORL ... the Beings, —FNTN ... and rulers, —BB.

**and the number of them was ten thousand times ten thousand, and thousands of thousands:**...their number was, —TNT...myriads of myriads, —BRKL...thousands on thousands, —KLST.

**5:11.** As John continued looking, myriads of myriads of angels joined the 24 elders and the 4 living beings in a chorus that made a wonderful climax to this part of John's vision. A myriad (10,000) was the largest number used in the ancient Greek language. Thus the myriads of myriads plus thousands of thousands indicates that the number of angels was beyond the possibility of any human counting them.

**12. Saying with a loud voice:** ... singing aloud, —MNTG ... who called out loud, —BECK ... They shouted, —SEB ... They cried, —NORL ... with a great voice, —BB ... repeating in loud tones, —WADE.

**Worthy is the Lamb that was slain:** ... It is right to give to the Lamb who was put to death, —BB ... is the slaughtered Lamb, —RTHM ... is the Little Lamb, that has been slain as a Sacrifice, —WADE ... who was sacrificed deserves, —BECK ... Who was killed has the right, —NLTG.

**to receive power, and riches:** ... to get, —BECK ... wealth, —KLST, —NOLI.

**and wisdom, and strength, and honour, and glory, and blessing:** ... might, —NOLI ... and praise, —BECK, —TNT ... and celebrity! —FNTN ... and shining greatness and thanks, —NLTG.

**5:12.** The angels did not sing the song of redemption sung by the 24 elders in verses 9 and 10. They cannot sing the song of the redeemed. But they can join in giving praise to the Lamb, who still bears the marks of having been slain, and in declaring that He is worthy.

Here they declare that Christ is worthy to receive seven things, the first of which is power, mighty power. He had power on earth to do miracles, cast out demons, and raise the dead; but He never used His power to make things easier for himself. After His resurrection He declared, "All power (power and authority) is given unto me in heaven and in earth" (Matthew 28:18). Indeed He is worthy!

Second, He is worthy to receive riches. The wealth of the universe in boundless abundance is His by right doubly; first by creation, then by redemption.

Third, He is worthy to receive wisdom. His wisdom is the wisdom of God. In fact, He himself is the embodiment of God's wisdom (1 Corinthians 1:24).

Fourth, He is worthy to receive strength, not merely physical strength, but strength and might as the power of truth and as an attribute of God.

Fifth, He is worthy to receive honor, including the reverence and respect due Him for all He is and all He has accomplished in the plan of God.

Sixth, He is worthy to receive glory, including the brightness, splendor, and radiance of God who dwells in the light and who is Light. He left behind that glory, emptying himself of it when He came to be born in a manger. But His prayer in John 17:5 was, "Glorify thou me with thine own self with the glory which I had with thee before the world was." He now has that glory and will return in that glory.

Seventh, He is worthy to receive blessing. The first meaning of this word in Greek is "praise." That is the meaning when believers bless the Lord. They speak good words of thanks and praise for all He is, for all He has done, for all He has given, for all He has promised. He is worthy! He is exalted because He humbled himself (in contrast to the pride of Satan and human dictators).

**13. And every creature which is in heaven:** ... In the same way every creature, —KLST ... every created thing, —RTHM ... every living thing, —NLTG ... existing in the heaven, —FNTN ... which is in the sky, —WADE.
**and on the earth:**
**and under the earth:** ... beneath, —RTHM ... under the ground, —JB ... [in Hades, the place of departed spirits], —AMPB ... in the world below, —TEV.
**and such as are in the sea, and all that are in them, heard I saying:** ... on the sea, —BECK ... I heard every thing in all these places, —EVRD ... all living beings in the universe, —TEV ... And I heard him who sat on the throne say, —MRDK ... I heard exclaiming, —FNTN ... and all that they contain ... I heard the voice of, —NORL ... I hear also saying, —CNDT ... crying out together, —AMPB.

**Blessing, and honour:** ... All praise, —AMPB ... belong the fame, —FNTN.
**and glory, and power, [be] unto him that sitteth upon the throne, and unto the Lamb:** ... and the majesty, —AMPB ... and might, —BECK, —TEV ... and dominion, —LAMS, —RTHM.
**for ever and ever:** ... to the ages of ages, —RTHM ... through the eternities of the eternities! —AMPB ... For the eons of the eons! —CNDT ... for timeless ages! —PHLP.

**5:13.** John heard every created being in heaven, on the earth (on the land), under the ground, and upon the sea join in a grand chorus that echoed the truth of the preceding song. It ascribed blessing (praise), honor, glory, and power (another word indicating the strength, might, power, rule, and sovereignty of God shown in mighty deeds) to both God the Father, on the throne, and to the Lamb—"for ever and ever."

**14. And the four beasts said, Amen:** ... The four living creatures answered, —TEV ... The four Bodyguards answered, —NOLI ... The four animals said, —GDSP ... so be it! —AMPB.
**And the four [and] twenty elders fell down and worshipped him that liveth for ever and ever:** ... while the Elders, —PHLP ... elders [of the heavenly Sanhedrin] prostrated themselves, —AMPB ... bowed down, —BECK ... fall and worship, —CNDT ... and adored, —MRDK.

**5:14.** The cycle of praise is now shown back at the throne where it began, and the four living beings added their "Amen" to the universal worship and adoration of Him that sits on the throne and the Lamb. Seven times in this book there is a form of the expression "him that liveth for ever and ever"; six times concerning God (4:9, 10; 5:14; 10:6; 11:15; 15:7) and once concerning Christ (1:18).

# Chapter 6

**1. And I saw when the Lamb opened one of the seals:** ... Next I watched, —TCNT ... the lamb broke, —WLMS ... I perceived when the Lambkin opens one of the seven seals, —CNDT ... I saw the Lamb break open, —TEV ... the first of the seven, —BECK ... one out of the seven, —RTHM.
**and I heard, as it were the noise of thunder:** ... and I hearkened, —RTHM ... in my vision, —NOLI ... crying with a voice like thunder, —TCNT ... saying ... as of thunder, —LAMS ... thunder-peal, —FNTN.
**one of the four beasts saying, Come and see:** ... one of the four living creatures say, —TEV ... one of the four Animals say, —MRDK ... call with a voice, —BECK ... Be going! —RTHM.

**6:1.** In chapter 6 John is still viewing the heavenly scene. The Lamb is at the throne as He opens the seals. Some Bible students take it that the chronology of the Book of Revelation begins at this point. Within a period of 7 years the events of the latter time are described up to and including chapter 19. (Compare the *Overview* comments concerning the 70th-year week of Daniel.) The first four seals introduce "the four horsemen of the Apocalypse." The four horsemen are personifications, possibly representing a series of partly overlapping and increasing judgments which are included in the description of the fourth horseman. Some take it that with the opening of each of these seals the Lamb will release a judgment act that will continue throughout the 7-year period. Some take it that the seven seals will lead into the seven trumpets, and the seven trumpets will lead into the seven vials or bowls. Others take it that the seven seals, the seven trumpets, and the seven bowls all occur at the same time.

Still others point out that the fifth seal is clearly anticipatory of what will happen later. Also it is hardly likely that there will be conquest for a while, then war for a while, then famine for a while, then death for a while. Thus, it may be that when the seals were opened what John saw in each case was a vision there at the throne, with the sixth seal an overview of the whole period of divine judgment. Thus, by this series of visions John was made aware of some of the things God would use in the judgments to follow, judgments that will smash the present world system and bring in God's kingdom on earth. According to this view, nothing happens on earth when each seal is opened; instead, there is a vision John himself sees in heaven. This seems to fit the fact that when the seventh seal was opened there was silence in heaven. Up to that point all the attention was around the throne, and there was constant praise, song, and worship, with the tremendous angelic chorus joining in. But when the seventh seal was opened there was silence, because all attention was then directed toward the earth and to the events that were about to begin when all the seals were opened and the book unrolled. Some believe the trumpet judgments (partial judgments) are on one side, and the bowls (more complete judgments) are on the other.

When the first seal was opened the word "Come," uttered by one of the four living beings, sounded like a great crash of thunder. Some manuscripts read "Come and see!" This was an appeal to John. Some ancient manuscripts simply read "Come!" This might be understood as an order to the first of the four horsemen to appear.

**2. And I saw, and behold a white horse:** ... Then I looked, *—WLMS* ... I perceived, and lo! *—CNDT* ... and before my eyes was, *—PHLP* ... there before me, *—EVRD* ... Immediately a white horse appeared, *—JB.*

**and he that sat on him had a bow:** ... its rider, *—BECK* ... holding, *—BRKL* ... carried, *—PHLP.*

**and a crown was given unto him:** ... a coronet was given, *—MRDK* ... he was given the victor's crown, *—JB* ... a wreath, *—CNDT.*

**and he went forth conquering, and to conquer:** ... He rode out, *—TEV* ... and he went away, to go from victory to victory, *—JB* ... that he might, *—RTHM* ... as a conqueror, *—BECK* ... rode out, defeating the enemy. He rode out to win the victory, *—EVRD* ... and bent on conquest, *—PHLP* ... conquering hero, *—NOLI.*

**6:2.** John saw a white horse with someone on it carrying a bow as a symbol of battle. He was given a victor's crown and went out to win victories. Conquerors in those ancient times usually rode white horses to symbolize their triumph.

The Bible does not say who was riding on the white horse. Commentators have suggested a variety of possibilities. Chief among them are:

(1) Christ himself (Morris, p. 112). Christ, however, is at this point the Lamb breaking the seals. In 19:11-13 Christ is indeed pictured on a white horse, but all the details are different. The color of the horse is the only thing they have in common.

The phrase "there was given" is used rather often in the Book of Revelation. It is used to indicate God's permission for evil powers to carry out their nefarious work (9:1, 3, 5, with regard to the beast, the Antichrist; and 13:5, 7, with regard to his false prophet). The last three horsemen are definitely evil, and it seems a bit unlikely that Christ would be presented as one of the four horsemen in such a company.

(2) The "prince that shall come" (Daniel 9:26), that is, the Antichrist, the counterfeit Christ (Bullinger, pp. 252f.). In the term *antichrist* the *anti* in the Greek really means "instead of" or "in place of." Thus, the beast will not call himself the Antichrist. He will either claim to be the real Christ; or else he will say that Buddha, Jesus Christ, Muhammad, and others were all forerunners; and he is the final fulfillment of all that has gone before. He will also be the one who personifies the anti-Christian political and religious ideologies which will characterize the great end-time apostasy. Thus, it is possible that this rider is the Antichrist, and some have seen the bow without arrows as a symbol of temporary victory. This would also fit with the fact that no one will be able to make war successfully with the beast (13:4). He will even make war with the saints and overcome them (13:7).

**3. And when he had opened the second seal:** ... Then the Lamb broke open the second, —TEV .... when It opens, —CNDT.

**I heard the second beast say, Come and see:** ...I hearkened to... Be going! —RTHM ...the second living creature say, —TEV ...living thing, —EVRD ...the second Animal say, —MRDK ...cry, —PHLP.

**6:3.** When the Lamb broke and opened the second seal, the second living being said "Come," or "Come and see." Again, the command may have been addressed either to John or the second horseman.

**4. And there went out another horse [that was] red:** ...a second horse, —NORL ...another horse came forth, —MNTG, —WLMS ...This one was, —NLTG ...came out, fiery red, —BECK ...red like fire, —SEB ...a red one, —KLST ...the hue of blood, —WADE ...another horse that was fiery red rode off, —ADAM.

**and [power] was given to him that sat thereon to take peace from the earth:** ...he who was mounted upon it, —WADE ...Permission was given to its rider, —TNT ...his rider was empowered, —FNTN ...Its rider was commissioned, —KLST ...it was allowed to, —MNTG ...out of the earth, —RTHM.

**and that they should kill one another:** ...in order that, —TNT ...to make men, —WLMS ...permit men, —NORL ...and to have people slaughter one another, —BECK ...that people might put one another to death, —BB ...so that people would butcher one another, —BRKL ...they should murder each other, —FNTN ...to slay, —WADE.

**and there was given unto him a great sword:** ...was handed to him, —KLST ...was given a long sword, —NLTG.

**6:4.** Some have supposed that the rider on the fiery red horse is the Antichrist's cohort, the false prophet. But, in line with the interpretation of the rest of the seals, it seems better to take the rider as the personification of war, or of the lust for war, and the great sword as a symbol of war's destruction. Notice that the rider does not do the killing. He will simply take peace from the earth and cause men to slaughter, butcher, and murder each other. (The Greek word for "kill" here is not one for death in battle but for violent killing of all kinds.)

In His prophecy of the future from the Mount of Olives (Matthew 24) Jesus told His disciples that wars would characterize the present age, but He also emphasized that they would not necessarily be a sign of the end. "Ye shall hear of wars and rumors of wars: see that ye be not troubled: for all these things must come to pass, but the end is not yet" (Matthew 24:6). There have been very few years in the history of mankind when the earth has been free from war. It seems that one war has always led to another war. For example, World War I left seeds of hatred which led to World War II, and that war has led to numerous conflicts since.

Paul warned of a time coming when the forces restraining evil would be gone. "He who now letteth (hinders) will let, until he be taken out of the way" (2 Thessalonians 2:7). Whether one considers the one who "now letteth" to be the Holy Spirit or the Church, the prophecy tells of a time coming when that which restrains the full manifestation of evil will be gone. Peace will be displaced by strife, and love will be displaced by hate. Violence will become rampant throughout the earth.

The Scriptures indicate that the Antichrist will be a master at maneuvering people and will achieve power by flattery and deceit. He will promise peace, but he will not be able to bring it. The longing for peace will be superseded by a warring mood. Crime and violence will run rampant throughout the earth. Thus, conquest and war will bring part of the judgment of God on the earth. With peace taken from the earth, it will not be given back until the Prince of Peace returns, brings an end to the Antichrist's dominion, and establishes God's kingdom on earth.

**5. And when he had opened the third seal:** ...When the Lamb, —KLST ...when the third stamp was undone, —BB ...He broke open the third lock, —NLTG.

**I heard the third beast say, Come and see:** ...third living creature say, —NORL ...the voice of the third beast came to my ears, —BB.

**And I beheld, and lo a black horse:** ...So when I looked I saw, —NORL ...and there was, —TNT ...in my vision on a sudden there appeared ...the livid hue of the starved, —WADE ...suddenly I saw, —KLST.

**and he that sat on him had a pair of balances in his hand:** ...his rider, —FNTN ...a scale, —BECK ...held, —TNT ...had a pair of scales in his hand, —BRKL ...had something in his hand with which to weigh things, —NLTG.

**6:5.** Then the third living being said, "Come and see." The third horse John saw was black (compare Zechariah 6:2, 6). Black is the color which represents evil, suffering, and hunger (compare Lamentations 5:10). The rider had in his hands unusual equipment for a horseman: scales for weighing, such as a merchant would use. This rider seems to personify famine. Notice, the black horse followed the red. All through history, the aftermath of war has so often been inflation and famine. There may well be class warfare, the "Have Nots" fighting against the "Haves." Governments will have to make and enforce strict measures. It is not an exaggeration to say there will be multitudes of starving people. The scales may well symbolize the careful weighing out of food and possibly general rationing because of scarcity and famine (compare Leviticus 26:26; Ezekiel 4:16), all the result of beating their plowshares into swords. It is also divine judgment.

**6. And I heard a voice in the midst of the four beasts say:** ... heard the semblance of a voice, —*MNTG* ... that seemed to come from the middle of, —*BECK* ... in the centre of, —*FNTN* ... the four living beings, —*KLST* ... exclaiming, —*WADE*.

**A measure of wheat for a penny:** ... A choenix, —*FNTN* ... An eighth of a peck of wheat (the daily allowance for a man), —*WADE* ... quart, —*BECK* ... for a day's wage, —*BRKL* ... for a denary, —*RTHM* ... for a silver piece, —*KLST*.

**and three measures of barley for a penny:** ... quarts, —*RTHM* ... will cost not less than, —*WADE* ... for a shilling, —*MNTG*.

**and [see] thou hurt not the oil and the wine:** ... but don't damage, —*BECK* ... thou mayest not wrong, —*RTHM* ... yet you must not interfere with, —*FNTN* ... But you must not spoil, —*NORL* ... do not harm, —*MNTG* ... and thereby raise the price of them, —*WADE*.

**6:6.** Instead of prosperity, a person will have to give a whole day's wages for a little food. A "measure" was about a quart (considered 1 day's ration for an adult). A denarius was a silver coin (similar in size and weight to the Greek drachma) and was the average day's wage for a soldier or laborer at that time. These were famine prices inflated to about 12 times the normal price. A person who had a family to support would have to buy the cheapest possible food (represented by barley, the food of the poor and of slaves) and still would not have any of his wages left over for anything else. "Hurt not the oil and the wine" seems to mean that luxuries will be available, but only for the rich and powerful. "Hurt" (or damage, spoil) may imply injustice, that the rich or the powerful are taking advantage of the poor. Oil and wine were not considered luxuries in those days, however. Starvation is already spreading throughout the world today, and governments are not able to control it. The coming world dictator, the Antichrist, will not be able to deal with it either.

**7. And when he had opened the fourth seal:** ... broke, —*NORL*.

**I heard the voice of the fourth beast say, Come and see:** ... the fourth Living Creature calling, —*MNTG*.

**6:7.** With the opening of the fourth seal the fourth living being said, "Come and see." Each of these living beings thus introduced a new vision to John.

**8. And I looked, and behold a pale horse:** ... pale-green, —*BECK* ... an ash-colored horse, —*BRKL* ... pale

yellow, —*KLST* ... cream-coloured, —*TCNT* ... livid, —*FNTN*, —*RTHM* ... (the hue of a corpse), —*WADE*.

**and his name that sat on him was Death:** ... of his rider, —*FNTN* ... Pestilence, —*WADE*.

**and Hell followed with him:** ... And the king of the grave came with, —*WMCK* ... and Sheol followed after him, —*LAMS* ... The nether world was following him, —*KLST* ... followed along, —*RTHM* ... came close behind, —*BECK* ... the Grave accompanied him, —*FNTN* ... following after, —*MNTG*.

**And power was given unto them over the fourth part of the earth:** ... given control over, —*WADE* ... over a quarter of, —*FNTN* ... Authority was granted, —*BRKL* ... against the fourth, —*RTHM* ... over one quarter of, —*WLMS*.

**to kill with sword, and with hunger:** ... to slay, —*RTHM* ... to murder, —*FNTN* ... famine, —*BECK*, —*NOLI* ... to put to destruction ... and by taking away their food, —*BB*.

**and with death, and with the beasts of the earth:** ... with disease, as well as by means ... of the field, —*FNTN* ... pestilence, —*NOLI* ... by means of beasts, —*KLST* ... by the animals on the earth, —*BECK* ... the wild animals, —*WLMS*.

**6:8.** The ghastly pale, yellowish-green horse of the fourth seal which John saw speaks of pestilence and death. Death itself is pictured here as if it were a person riding the horse, and hell or Hades following after. Though Hades to the ancient Greeks was a general term for the abode of the dead, here, as in the rest of the New Testament, it is the place of punishment and fits the common idea of hell. Death and hell were given power and authority over those who died at this time. The dead are receiving their wages (Romans 6:23). They have been the servants of sin, slaves of sin, and death and hell have a rightful authority over them (see Romans 6:16-21). Death takes the body; hell, the soul.

It may be understood, then, that in this part of the Great Tribulation one-fourth of the world's population will die. Death will not be from natural causes but from a combination of the results of the first three seals plus the ravages of beasts. These are literal wild animals (a different word from that used in verse 1 or in chapters 4 and 6). They will undoubtedly multiply during these chaotic times and will be driven by disease and hunger. It is hard to conceive of anything like 1 or 2 billion people dying in such a short period of time.

The Bible does not specify exactly when this destruction will take place. However, since this is the last of the horsemen, the severity of the judgment seems to indicate it will take place when the world is well into the Great Tribulation. Some put it at the beginning of the last half of the Tribulation when the judgments will become more and more severe, until comparatively few people will remain alive.

**9. And when he had opened the fifth seal:**...the Little Lamb broke, −WADE...the fifth stamp was undone, −BB.

**I saw under the altar:**...underneath, −MNTG...beneath, −RTHM...at the foot of, −WADE.

**the souls of them that were slain for the word of God:**...of the martyrs, −NOLI...who had been killed, −BECK...who had been slaughtered for the sake of, −BRKL...slaughtered for being faithful to God's message, −WLMS...had been put to death for, −BB...had been sacrificed on account of, −FNTN...on account of the revelation made and attested by God, −KLST...for loyalty to God's Message, −WADE.

**and for the testimony which they held:**...because of the stand they had taken, −NORL...and the truth they were telling, −BECK...and the witness they bore, −BRKL...which they had borne, −TCNT...they maintained, −FNTN...and received by them, −KLST...and for loyalty to Jesus' testimony...which they preserved, −WADE...which they kept, −BB.

**6:9.** The opening of the fifth seal directed John's attention away from visions of what is going to happen on the earth. Now he saw souls under the altar in the heavenly temple. This indicates that part of the judgments recorded in 5:7 have to do with bringing judgment on a world that so often has martyred true witnesses for Christ.

Because they have shed their blood, these martyrs are pictured as "under the altar" just as the blood of the victims of the Old Testament sacrifices was poured out under the altar of burnt offering (Exodus 29:12; Leviticus 4:7). They did not contribute in any way to Christ's work of redemption, for He alone could die for sin, but they shared in the fellowship of His suffering and were conformable to His death (Philippians 3:10; Revelation 12:11). Like the apostle Paul, they were willing to sacrifice their lives for the Word of God and for the witness to which they firmly held in the face of death. Thus, their lives were poured out as a sacrifice before the Lord (2 Timothy 4:6).

**10. And they cried with a loud voice, saying:**...They pleaded loudly, −SEB...they cried, exclaiming, −FNTN...gave a great cry, −BB...kept crying out, −NORL...in loud tones, −WADE.

**How long, O Lord, holy and true:**...How long will it be, −BB...Until when...Real One! −RTHM...O Master, −MNTG...O Sovereign Lord, −TCNT...O Almighty Ruler, the Holy One, −NORL...O Sovereign Master...and Reliable, −WADE.

**dost thou not judge and avenge our blood on them that dwell on the earth?:**...How long will You wait, −NORL...will you refrain from charging and avenging, −WLMS...before you take your place as judge and give punishment for our blood to those, −BB...will you delay to judge, −FNTN...and inflicting vengeance for, −WADE...and punish them for killing us? −BECK...from the inhabitants of, −BRKL...and pay them back for killing us? −SEB.

**6:10.** M. Kiddle sees the phrase "how long" as the cry of apocalyptists as far back as Zechariah (Zechariah 1:12) and Daniel (Daniel 12:6). Thus the martyrs would include all the martyrs of past ages (*Moffatt New Testament Commentary, Revelation,* p. 119). Others take the word "dwell" to mean that those who killed these martyrs were still dwelling on the earth. This would make the martyrs those killed in the first part of the Tribulation, possibly by the whore Babylon (17:5, 6). Perhaps they are killed during the terrible calamities of the fourth seal. However, it is probably better not to be dogmatic. Notice they are in heaven, not in a condition of any sort of "soul sleep."

They addressed God as Lord, using a word that means "master" or "owner" and thus they recognized His divine authority and majesty. They appealed to God's character, that He is holy and true, as the basis for their prayer. Their cry was not for personal revenge, however. Jesus prayed for His executioners; so did Stephen. But, though prayer for lenience has its time, so has the prayer for justice, and now the hour of God's judgment is about to come. "Avenge" has the idea of securing justice for them. (Compare Luke 18:1-9.) Justice was not merely their personal desire. They were martyred because men rejected the Word of God and their testimony to Christ. As long as these rebels run rampant over the world, they hinder the work of God and must be judged before the Kingdom can be established and right and righteousness rebuilt on the earth.

What the martyrs cried out for is the fulfillment of the prophecy given in 2 Thessalonians 1:4-10. At the close of the Tribulation Jesus will appear "in flaming fire taking vengeance on them that know not God, and that obey not the gospel of our Lord Jesus Christ" (verse 8). At that time Christ will be glorified or honored and seen to be splendidly glorious in or among the saints who will be with Him and share His glory (verse 10). The martyrs under the altar long for the glory of that day and for the victory they will then share.

**11. And white robes were given unto every one of them:**...each of them, −KLST...White clothes, −NLTG...(the colour of victory), −WADE.

**and it was said unto them:**...they were ordered, −BB...it was bidden them, −RTHM...they were told, −NORL.

**that they should rest yet for a little season:**...to take their rest, −BB...be patient, −NORL...wait patiently, −KLST...to wait quietly a little longer, −BECK...yet a little time, −MNTG, −RTHM...a short time longer, −FNTN.

**until their fellowservants also and their brethren:**...They were to wait until all the other workmen owned by God, −NLTG...until the completion of their fellow-servants, —FNTN...was complete of the other servants, —BB...until the number... by their fellow slaves, —MNTG.

**that should be killed as they [were]:** ...who were about to be put to death, —MNTG...about to be slain, —RTHM...to be murdered, —FNTN...all to be slain as also they themselves had been, —NORL...just as they had been, —KLST.

**should be fulfilled:** ...until their number should be filled up, —NORL...were present, —BECK...Then the group would be complete, —NLTG.

**6:11.** For their encouragement and assurance these martyrs under the heavenly altar were given white robes, symbolizing righteousness. This assured them they would be among the number who would be with Christ in His glorious coming to establish His kingdom, and they would be sure to share that glory.

They were also told to rest or remain quiet for "a little season." The appointed time for Christ's return in judgment had not come. Others who were fellow servants and brethren (the word "and" can mean "even") must yet be martyred and join their number. Then all would see their cries for justice fulfilled.

Some commentators, such as R.H. Mounce, believe the white robes might symbolize spiritual or glorified bodies given to the martyrs, ahead of those mentioned in 19:8 (*New International Commentary on the New Testament, Revelation,* p. 159). Others, such as Wolvoord (pp. 134f.), understand it literally and consider it as a hint that souls in the intermediate state have provisional bodies which can be clothed. Still others emphasize the spiritual meaning of white robes, either as "symbols of blessedness and purity" (Mounce, *New International Commentary on the New Testament, Revelation,* p. 160), or the symbol of justification (Seiss, p. 148).

Even though these martyrs asked God to avenge their blood, they were more concerned with vindication. They had died as warriors in the battle against evil, heroes in a war which would make God's kingdom a reality. In heaven as well as on earth the redeemed pray, as in the Lord's Prayer, "Thy kingdom come." That time had not yet come, however. They were told they must wait yet a little while until the number of those who would yet die for their testimony was complete. The period of the Tribulation will be a blood bath for the world. Many will die through warfare and the plagues. In addition, to confess the name of Christ will almost certainly result in martyrdom. It is not pleasant to contemplate the horrible conditions which will prevail upon the earth, but from its very beginnings sin has produced terrible consequences. No wonder the "whole creation groaneth" (Romans 8:22) while waiting for the time of release.

**12. And I beheld when he had opened the sixth seal:** ...When the Lamb had opened, —KLST...I also saw, —FNTN...I looked, —MNTG...And I was in my vision when He broke, —WADE.

**and, lo, there was a great earthquake:** ...I had a vision of, —KLST...there occurred, —WADE...saw a tremendous earthquake occur, —BRKL.

**and the sun became black as sackcloth of hair:** ...haircloth, —FNTN...dark as sackcloth woven of black goats' hair, —WADE.

**and the moon became as blood:** ...whole moon, —RTHM...the full moon, —BRKL...full disc of the moon, —WADE...in its entirety became as red as, —KLST.

**6:12.** The opening of the sixth seal brought John's attention sharply back to the earth. As he looked, the vision revealed catastrophic signs of the end of the age taking place as prophesied in both the Old and New Testaments. (See Isaiah 34:4; Joel 2:31; Mark 13:24, 25.)

Many Bible interpreters tend to take these events as symbols of the political, moral, and spiritual breakup which will accompany the end of the age. (See 2 Timothy 3:1-5.) The other seals speak of actual events, however. The conquest, war, famine, death, and martyrdoms of the tribulation period will be real. Thus, there seems no reason to think these signs will not be real.

There is scientific evidence that the earth beneath the rock of the apparently solid crust of the earth is plastic basalt. Parts of the crust are in motion even now. It could be that the various parts of the crust will all break loose and bring this tremendous earthquake which would break out multitudes of volcanoes sending dust, gas, and ash to obscure the sun and the moon.

**13. And the stars of heaven fell unto the earth:** ...in the sky, —NORL...on the earth, —KLST.

**even as a fig tree casteth her untimely figs:** ...drops its unripe fruit, —BRKL, —TCNT...casts its green figs, —LAMS...just as the unripe winter figs fall from the fig tree, —KLST...sheds her winter-figs, —RTHM...sheds its unripe fruit, —NORL.

**when she is shaken of a mighty wind:** ...shaken by a violent wind, —BRKL...when it is swept, —KLST...by a gale, —MNTG...strong, —FNTN...before the force of a high wind, —NORL.

**6:13.** Anything great enough to produce such an earthquake would probably be accompanied by cosmic disturbances. Most take the stars falling as old-time language for tremendous showers of meteorites. The comparison to a fig tree dropping its late summer figs when shaken by a mighty wind indicates the large number. (These figs probably refer to figs that did not ripen and thus are still hanging on the tree when the winter storms arrive.)

**14. And the heaven departed as a scroll when it is rolled together:**...disappeared, *−TCNT, −SEB*...The sky was swept away just like, *−WLMS*...The sky receded, *−KLST*...were split in two, *−WMCK*...parted asunder like a rolled-up scroll, *−MNTG*...withdrawn, as a scroll rolling itself up, *−RTHM*...vanished like a scroll being rolled up, *−BECK*...folding up like a scroll, *−NORL*...rolled separately, *−LAMS*.

**and every mountain and island were moved out of their places:** ... moved from its place, *−WMCK*...was dislodged, *−BRKL, −KLST*.

**6:14.** The language here describing the heavens is the language of appearance. To the Old Testament Israelites the heavens looked like a tent outstretched above the earth (Psalm 104:2; Isaiah 40:22). The heavens departing—that is, the sky splitting and separating and curling to each side like a scroll—may also refer to atmospheric disturbances among the clouds (called the "first heavens" by the Jews), or perhaps there may be cosmic disturbances in the heavens beyond.

These phenomena in the aerial heavens which John "beheld" were followed by fearful changes in the configuration of the earth, drastic changes in the topography of the planet, all natural effects of the great earthquake (verse 12). This is no figure of speech. It refers to a literal catastrophe embracing the whole earth. Such cataclysmic events may indicate that the earthquake or breaking of the sixth seal will last up to the very end of the tribulation period. This seal seems to encompass a vision of the beginning as well as the culmination of the end-time judgments.

No place on earth is safe now from a possible earthquake. Though there are earthquake zones around the Pacific Ocean and through the Middle East and the Mediterranean, there have been and can be earthquakes in any part of the world. The description given in connection with the opening of the sixth seal shows a cataclysm that affects every mountain and every island. The only sure way to safety is to accept Christ now and find security in Him.

**15. And the kings of the earth, and the great men:** ... the important men, commanders, *−SEB*... the generals, *−BRKL, −TCNT*... the military leaders, *−WLMS* ... magnates, *−RTHM* ... nobles, *−FNTN*...the rulers, *−BB*.

**and the rich men, and the chief captains:**...the wealthy, the powerful, *−BRKL*...the rulers of thousands, *−RTHM*...and the princes, and the generals, *−MNTG*...their men of wealth and of might, *−NORL*.

**and the mighty men, and every bondman, and every free man:**...and the powerful, *−KLST*...and the strong, *−WADE* ... In fact, everyone, slave and

free, fled, *−NORL*...every servant, *−BB*...and every slave, *−BECK*...and freemen, *−MNTG*.

**hid themselves in the dens and in the rocks of the mountains:**...took cover in the holes, *−BB*...in caves and in clefts of, *−LAMS*...the rocks of the hills, *−FNTN* ... and among the crags of, *−WADE* ... and among the rocks in the mountains, *−NORL*.

**6:15.** Verses 12-14 have described the fearful physical convolutions of nature. The remaining verses of this chapter reveal the impact these have upon mankind, men from all walks of life who have witnessed what is happening. Vanished now is all arrogance and haughtiness. The voice of boasting falls silent. Nor is it just the convulsions of nature which terrify them. It is the realization that it is God himself, the ruler of the universe, whom they have seen in action. It is the hand of the Creator which is now shaking His creation. No wonder mankind trembles.

The seven classes mentioned here include all the leaders and all the common people of the world. The leaders are mentioned more specifically. There will still be kings. The great men include presidents, dictators, and other leaders. The rich men are mentioned because they have power. The chief captains, or literally "tribunes," is used here as a general term for all high military officers.

This universal recognition of a divine intervention in man's affairs is very remarkable. They knew the Day of the Lord had arrived. Atheism is as much out of fashion today as it was when God spoke from Sinai. As the Egyptians of Moses' time knew it was the God of Israel who had sent His judgments upon them, so the end-time generation will know (see 11:13; 16:9, 21).

The first reaction of all who are still alive, and have been left behind after the rapture of the Church (the rich and powerful as well as the poor and the slaves), will be fear as they try to hide themselves in the dens or caves and rock cliffs or rocky grottoes of the mountains.

**16. And said to the mountains and rocks:**...are saying, *−RTHM* ... began to say, *−MNTG* ... called to, *−FNTN*...exclaiming to the...crags, *−WADE*.

**Fall on us, and hide us from the face of him that sitteth on the throne:** ... Come down on us, covering us from, *−BB*...conceal us from the sight of, *−WLMS*...sight of the Lord, *−NOLI*...from the presence of the Occupant, *−FNTN*.

**and from the wrath of the Lamb:** ... the indignation of, *−BRKL* ... from the judgement of, *−TCNT* ... from the anger of, *−RTHM* ... of the Little Lamb, *−WADE* ... from the lamb's punishment, *−SEB*...displeasure, *−FNTN*.

**6:16.** Their first reaction will be followed by deep despair as they realize they cannot hide sufficiently in their caves and grottoes, and they call on the rocks and mountains to fall on them. It seems that the glory of the face or presence of the One who sits on the throne and the wrath of the Lamb are somehow revealed to them.

Now people begin to pray. Until now they had neglected many an opportunity to pray, but now the entire population of earth, those from every level of society (see verse 15), unite in a worldwide prayer meeting.

But sad to say, their absurd prayers, born of terror, are made not to God but to the rocks and the mountains. "Fall on us," they cry, "and hide us from the face of him that sitteth on the throne, and from the wrath of the Lamb." A lamb is known for its meekness, but this Lamb is also the "Lion of the tribe of Judah" (5:5, 6), and the world is now seeing the lion side of His character. The language here is reminiscent of the apocalyptic prophecy of Isaiah 2:9-21.

17. **For the great day of his wrath is come:** ... because the Day ... the great Day, —WADE ... of their retribution, —BRKL ... of their anger came, —RTHM.

**and who shall be able to stand?:** ... who can stand it? —WLMS ... No one can escape their anger, —NOLI ... and who can stand before it? —NORL ... and who can stand his ground? —KLST ... and who is able to stand and face it? —WADE ... and who has power to stand? —KLGS ... and who may keep his place? —BB ... and who can stand? —ADAM ... to stand against it? —NLTG.

**6:17.** The people of the earth who had ignored the multiplied warnings of coming judgment, now know that day has arrived.

They already know the answer to their question, "Who shall be able to stand?" Nobody.

It is significant that so early the Revelation states that the day of divine wrath has come. This seems to confirm the view that the seal judgments cover the entire tribulation period, and the seventh seal includes the trumpets and the vials.

## Chapter 7

1. **And after these things:** ... Following this, —BRKL ... After this, —WADE.

**I saw four angels standing on the four corners of the earth:** ... four messengers, —KLGS ... stationed at, —FNTN ... in their places at the four points of the earth, —BB ... the four quarters, —WADE.

**holding the four winds of the earth:** ... holding back, —BECK ... holding in check, —NORL ... holding fast, —RTHM ... keeping back ... in their hands, —BB ... restraining, —BRKL, —FNTN.

**that the wind should not blow on the earth:** ... that there might not be blowing a wind, —RTHM ... so that there might be no moving of the wind, —BB ... that no wind might blow on land, —TNT ... to prevent any wind, —WADE ... from blowing on, —MNTG ... upon the land, —FNTN.

**nor on the sea, nor on any tree:** ... nor against any tree, —NORL, —WADE ... nor any tree stirred! —FNTN.

**7:1.** In chapter 7 John records two visions during an interlude between the sixth and seventh seals. "After these things" means after the visions that accompanied the opening of the first six seals.

In the first of these visions John saw four angels standing on the four corners of the earth, powerfully holding back the four winds of the earth. They prevented any stormy wind from blowing destructively on the earth, the sea, or any tree. This was a calm before the storm, however.

"The four corners of the earth" does not mean the Bible indicates the earth is square. The Book of Job reminds us that God hung the earth on nothing (Job 26:7). Isaiah saw the Lord sitting above the circle or sphere of the earth (Isaiah 40:22). Even today people speak of "the four corners of the earth," meaning the four directions from the point of view of the surface of the earth, just as the four winds are the winds that come from the four directions.

2. **And I saw another angel ascending from the east:** ... I also observed, —BRKL ... arise from, —KLST ... coming up, —BB ... he ascended from the direction of the rising sun, —LAMS ... from [the] sun's uprising, —RTHM ... from the rising of the sun, —ADAM.

**having the seal of the living God:** ... holding, —FNTN ... having the mark, —BB ... carrying the mark of, —NLTG.

**and he cried with a loud voice to the four angels:** ... said with a great voice, —BB ... in a loud tone he cried thus, —WADE ... he called to, —FNTN.

**to whom it was given to hurt the earth and the sea:** ... who were empowered to punish, —FNTN ... to injure, —TCNT ... to harm, —KLST ... to do damage to, —BB ... both land and sea, —NORL.

**7:2.** Next John saw another (a fifth) angel rising up or ascending from the rising of the sun, that is from the east. He carried the seal of the living God. He called out urgently and loudly to the four angels to whom was given the responsibility to injure, harm, or damage the earth and the sea (as part of God's divine judgment, thus these four angels were messengers of doom).

Solomon's temple faced the east. The word *orient* means east, so that proper orientation originally meant facing east. Proper orientation for the Israelites, however, was to face west toward the Holy of Holies as they entered the temple court. Nevertheless, Ezekiel saw the glory departing from the temple by way of the Mount of Olives on the east (Ezekiel 11:23). In a later vision he saw the glory returning "from the way of the east" (Ezekiel 43:2; compare Zechariah 14:4). In view of this it seems appropriate that this fifth angel came from the east.

The seal was a signet that stamped or impressed a mark on something. A seal on something was a sign or stamp of approval or identification. A seal confirmed, attested, certified, or authenticated, thus assuring its ownership and genuineness, and sometimes its destination. The seal was often stamped in clay or wax on the outside of an envelope, package, or scroll. It was not something that in itself could not be broken, but it bore the mark of its owner, and therefore it was his authority that made it secure, not the seal itself. The seal or signet of verse 2 was the seal of the living God, and there is no higher authority. So those who were sealed were identified as belonging to Him and under His care and protection.

Then, because this angel bore the seal he had the authority to give a command to the other four angels who were holding back the four winds.

3. **Saying, Hurt not the earth:** ... The angel from the east said, —NLTG ... exclaiming, —FNTN ... He said, Waitdo not harm, —NORL ... Ye may not, —RTHM ... Do not injure, —WLMS ... Do no harm to, —MNTG ... damage, —BB.

**neither the sea:** ... the ocean, —SEB.

**nor the trees:**

**till we have sealed the servants of our God in their foreheads:** ... until we mark, —NOLI ... put a mark on, —BB ... put the mark of God on the foreheads of the workmen He owns, —NLTG ... until we have stamped ... to ensure their safety in the Coming Woes, —WADE ... the slaves, —MNTG ... upon their brows, —LAMS.

**7:3.** Though it was given to the four angels to hurt or damage, the fifth angel commanded them not to begin to injure or damage the earth, the sea, or the trees until "we have sealed the servants of our God in their foreheads." It is not clear who the fifth angel meant by "we" unless he was including the four angels. The Greek *doulous* normally means "slave," not servant. Most slaves in those days were captives taken in war. The apostle Paul delighted to call himself a slave of the Lord Jesus Christ. He had indeed been taken captive by the risen Jesus (Acts 9:3-6; compare Ephesians 4:8, 11). By calling himself a slave of Jesus, he emphasized that Jesus was indeed his Lord and Master.

The sealing described in 7:3 identifies the true slaves of God who are subject to Him and are His to command and therefore ready to carry out His will. (Compare Ezekiel 9:2-6.) Even in Old Testament times when God gave an outward sign He also gave the inner reality. When Samuel anointed David with the outward sign of the holy anointing oil, "the Spirit of the Lord came upon David from that day forward" (1 Samuel 16:13; literally,

"upward," for it was a growing, continuing experience). Those sealed must escape the wrath also.

4. **And I heard the number of them which were sealed:** ... there came to my ears ... those who had the mark on their brows, —BB ... how many there were who received the mark of God, —NLTG ... who were stamped with the seal, —TCNT.

**[and there were] sealed an hundred [and] forty [and] four thousand:** ... were stamped, —TCNT ... who were marked, —BB ... stamped as belonging to God, —WADE.

**of all the tribes of the children of Israel:** ... with representatives from every tribe, —KLST ... out of every tribe of the sons of, —NORL ... of the twelve family groups of, —NLTG ... of the people of, —BB ... of Israel's sons, —RTHM.

**7:4.** After they were sealed, and were in the condition of having been sealed, John heard their number, 144,000. They were sealed out of every tribe of the sons (people, descendants) of Israel. That is, not every person who claimed descent from Israel or membership in one of the tribes of Israel was sealed, but there were some from every tribe.

Because there are some changes in the way these tribes are named in the following verses, some believe the list is symbolic and really refers to the Church as the true Israel (Beckwith, p. 535; Ladd, *Revelation,* p. 114). However, though Christian believers are spiritual sons of Abraham if they share the faith of Abraham, the Church is never called sons of Israel, nor is it ever divided into tribes. In the Church all former divisions are meaningless (Galatians 3:28). The New Testament recognizes the Jews as the 12 Tribes. The 144,000 were Jews sealed for service.

5. **Of the tribe of Juda [were] sealed twelve thousand:** ... were stamped with the Seal, —WADE ... were marked, —BB.

**Of the tribe of Reuben [were] sealed twelve thousand:** ... from the family group of, —NLTG.

**Of the tribe of Gad [were] sealed twelve thousand:** ... from the tribe of, —TNT ... were marked with the sign, —EVRD.

**7:5.** Judah, the leading tribe, is mentioned first. Reuben was Jacob's firstborn, but he lost his rights due to sin. As a result the birthright went to Joseph (1 Chronicles 5:1, 2). But the leadership went to Judah because of spiritual strength. Gad was the first son of Leah's handmaid, and so had a place of leadership among the sons of the concubines.

6. **Of the tribe of Aser [were] sealed twelve thousand:** ... Asher, —BB.

**Of the tribe of Nephthalim [were] sealed twelve thousand:** ... Naphtali, —BB.

**Of the tribe of Manasses [were] sealed twelve thousand:** ... Manasseh, —BB ... were stamped with the Seal, —WADE.

**7:6.** Asher was the second son of Zilpah, Leah's handmaid. Naphtali was the second son of Bilhah, Rachel's handmaid. Manasseh was the older son of Joseph, Rachel's older son. There does not seem to be any reason for the order given here. It is different from any other Biblical list of the tribes.

Before Jacob died, he placed Joseph's sons, Ephraim and Manasseh, on the level of his other 11 sons, thus guaranteeing the double portion to Joseph. Ephraim and Manasseh became full tribes. Later, when they settled the Promised Land, Ephraim was given a full portion west of the Jordan River. But half of the tribe of Manasseh decided to stay east of the Jordan. The other half was given a portion on the west side.

**7. Of the tribe of Simeon [were] sealed twelve thousand:** ... from the tribe of, —ADAM.
**Of the tribe of Levi [were] sealed twelve thousand:** ... from the family group, —NLTG.
**Of the tribe of Issachar [were] sealed twelve thousand:** ... out of the tribe, —CNDT.

**7:7.** Simeon and Levi were the second and third sons of Leah. Issachar was her fifth son. In the division of the land under Joshua, Simeon was given an allotment within the territory of Judah (Joshua 19:9). But here Simeon has its own place distinct from any connection with Judah.

That Levi is listed here as one of the tribes seems very significant. Under the old covenant, the tribe of Levi was singled out as representative of the other 12 tribes for service in the sanctuary. It was not allotted a separate tribal territory of its own but was given cities scattered among the other tribes. (See Joshua 21:1-42.)

Thus, Levi was not numbered among the 12 tribes of Israel in Old Testament times (Numbers 2:33). But in this sealing of John's vision the Levites were given their place with the other tribes. This seems to mean they were not singled out as the priestly tribe. There may be a confirmation here that the sealing was under the new covenant, for the old covenant was no more (Hebrews 8:13).

In order to maintain the total of 144,000 with 12,000 out of each tribe, meant that with Levi in the 12, one tribe must be left out. The tribe not included in this list is Dan. There may be a reason for this. Dan was the only tribe that did not claim their God-assigned inheritance in the Promised Land. Their portion was on the edge of Philistine territory. When the Philistines became too warlike, the Danites went north. They found a place, Laish, that was easy to capture. They destroyed

Laish and built their own city there, naming it Dan (Judges 18:27-29). At the same time they turned to idolatry and persuaded a grandson of Moses to go with them as an idol priest. Yet Ezekiel 48:1 sees restoration for Dan.

**8. Of the tribe of Zabulon [were] sealed twelve thousand:** ... Zebu-lun, —MNTG.
**Of the tribe of Joseph [were] sealed twelve thousand:** ... (that is, Ephraim), —WADE.
**Of the tribe of Benjamin [were] sealed twelve thousand:** ... were marked, —BB.

**7:8.** Zebulon, the youngest son of Leah, is followed by tribes descended from the sons of Rachel: Joseph and Benjamin. Since Manasseh was already listed, it must be that Ephraim was recognized as the chief Joseph tribe and so deserved the name of Joseph. When the elderly and blind Jacob adopted Ephraim and Manasseh as full sons, Joseph brought his eldest son Manasseh opposite Jacob's right hand, and Ephraim opposite Jacob's left hand.

However, Jacob crossed his arms and placed his right hand (symbolizing superior blessing) on Ephraim and his left on Manasseh. Joseph was displeased and tried to move Jacob's right hand to Manasseh's head, but Jacob refused. He knew what he was doing and proceeded to prophesy that Ephraim would be greater than Manasseh. In the course of Israel's history this proved to be true. Ephraim became the leader of all the northern tribes, known as Israel, which was sometimes referred to as Ephraim. Indeed, Ephraim deserved to be called the Joseph tribe.

Benjamin was the smallest tribe, but like the others had 12,000 sealed. As mentioned before, the identity of the 144,000 who are sealed has been the subject of much discussion. The basic viewpoints of commentators as to Israel's standing in the New Testament and its future destiny cannot help but influence their view. Many consider those sealed as symbolic of the New Testament Church. Many others, however, who hold to a literal interpretation, believe they are a first-fruit of Israel's national and spiritual restoration. This view is commonly held by dispensational writers, but it is interesting that John F. Walvoord can point to a postmillennialist such as Charles Hodge and an amillennialist like William Hendricksen who also hold this view.

**9. After this I beheld, and, lo:** ... Later I looked, —SEB ... After this in my vision there appeared to my view, —WADE ... After that I saw, —KLGS ... After these things I looked and there was, —ADAM ... I had a

1286

vision. Suddenly, —*KLST*...and behold! —*RTHM*...and saw, —*FNTN*.

**a great multitude, which no man could number:** ... there appeared, —*KLST*...there was a vast host, —*BRKL*...a great innumerable crowd, —*NOLI* ... many people. No one could tell how many there were, —*NLTG*...a vast crowd was there, —*TNT*...a great army of people more than might be numbered, —*BB* ... vast throng that no one could count, —*WLMS*...great number ... so many people that, —*EVRD*...a great crowd that nobody was able to count, —*ADAM*...too great for any one to count, —*TCNT* ... which, to number it! no one was able, —*RTHM*.

**of all nations, and kindreds:**...they were from, —*TNT*...came from every nation, —*SEB*...and from tribes, —*FNTN*...every family, —*NLTG*.

**and people, and tongues:** ... every kind of, —*NLTG* ... and languages, —*TCNT*...language of the earth, —*EVRD*.

**stood before the throne, and before the Lamb:**...in presence of, —*RTHM*...standing in front of the place where the King sits, —*NLTG*...taking their places before the high seat, —*BB*...the Little Lamb, —*WADE*.

**clothed with white robes:** ... dressed in, —*BB* ... arrayed, —*RTHM* ... wearing white garments, —*NOLI* ... white clothes, —*NLTG* ... white clothing, —*KLGS*.

**and palms in their hands:** ... palm-branches, —*FNTN*, —*KLST*...branches, —*BB*, —*NLTG*.

**7:9.** In the second vision of this interlude the scene changes from earth to heaven; and John saw an innumerable multitude, countless thousands of people from every nation, kindred (tribe), people, and language, standing before God's throne. This multitude has to be different from the 144,000, for "no man could number" it. Those sealed were from Israel; these were from all nations. To understand this literally means that the 144,000 are included, since there is no longer a dividing line between Jews and Gentiles within the New Testament Church. Some regard them as tribulation saints, saved after the Rapture, but most understand them as Christ's church, now appearing in glory (see verse 14).

All the people in this "great multitude" were already clothed in long, flowing white robes which indicate they shared the righteousness of Christ, and that, like Abraham, their faith has been counted for righteousness. The Greek word is the same as the white robes given to the martyrs under the altar (6:11). It reminds us also of the white clothing promised to the overcomers in 3:5. All this white clothing appears to be identical.

The palm branches in their hands symbolize victory and show they share His triumph. As in the Triumphal Entry, the palm branches also indicate Jesus is their Lord and messianic King (John 12:13). The palm branches may also speak of the

Feast of Tabernacles as a type pointing to our dwelling forever with the Lord.

**10. And cried with a loud voice, saying:**...With a great voice they shouted these words, —*PHLP*...shouted, —*SEB*...chanted, —*FNTN*...They called out, —*TEV*...they cried, —*AMPB*...aloud,

**Salvation to our God which sitteth upon the throne:** ... Our salvation, —*WLMS* ...Victory to our God, —*JB*...Our deliverance is the work of our God who is seated, —*GDSP*...is from, —*FNTN*...is due to, —*BRKL*...is with, —*SWAN*...comes from, —*TEV*...belongs to, —*EVRD*...seated on the throne, —*NORL*.

**and unto the Lamb:**...And from, —*FNTN*, —*TEV*...to Them [we owe our] deliverance! —*AMPB*...And the Lambkin's! —*CNDT*.

**7:10.** This great multitude John saw before the throne kept crying out in unison and in total harmony, "Salvation to our God ... and unto the Lamb." Salvation belongs to our God as the only Source, and to the Lamb as the only One who could pay the price and make salvation available to us. Saying or singing this gives praise to God the Father on the throne and to the Lamb who is in the midst of the throne. "Salvation to our God" is a Hebraistic expression which is translated in Psalm 3:8, "Salvation belongeth unto the Lord (Jehovah)." This multitude understood fully that only from God and the Lamb had come their salvation from sin, from guilt, and from the wrath and judgments that were about to fall on the earth. They were full of joy as they stood before the throne.

**11. And all the angels stood round about the throne:**...all the messengers, —*CNDT*...standing in circuit of, —*RTHM* ... in a circle, —*SWAN*...encircling the throne, —*PHLP* ... were standing around them and around the throne, —*EVRD*.

**and [about] the elders and the four beasts:**...the four living things were there, —*EVRD* ... living creatures, —*RTHM* ... round the elders, —*AMPB*...and the four animals, —*CNDT*.

**and fell before the throne on their faces, and worshipped God:** ... Then they threw themselves face downward in front of, —*TEV* ... fell prostrate, —*AMPB*...bowed down on their faces, —*EVRD*...fall on their faces, —*CNDT*...and prostrated themselves with heads bowed before the throne, —*PHLP*...touched the ground with their foreheads, —*JB* ... rendered worship to, —*RTHM*...and paid homage, —*FNTN*.

**7:11.** Then John saw an outer circle of thousands of thousands of angels who had already taken their stand around the throne outside of the 24 elders and the 4 living beings. These all proceeded to fall on their faces, prostrate themselves before the throne, and worship God.

Notice the position of these angels. They were standing around the throne, ready to respond to the commands of the Father. At His bidding they also minister to the saints (see Hebrews 1:14). Notice also their humility, they fall before God in worship. If these glorious creatures who have never sinned do so, how much more should redeemed sons of men humble themselves before God.

These angels are created beings who have never sinned, who have always served God. Yet, they are in an outer circle. The multitude John saw from every nation, tribe, people, and language who were before the throne were inside that circle. Everyone in that multitude had sinned and come short of the glory of God (Romans 3:23). Yet they now had white robes and possessed the righteousness of Christ, so they were closer to the throne than the angels were.

12. **Saying, Amen: Blessing, and glory:** ... with these words ... Praise, —JB ... (So be it!) they cried, —AMPB.
**and wisdom, and thanksgiving, and honour:** ... thanks, —CNDT.
**and power, and might, [be] unto our God for ever and ever. Amen:** ... majesty and splendor ... [be ascribed], ... the eternities of the eternities! —AMPB ... belong to, —TEV ... strength be, —BECK, —WLMS ... to the ages of ages, —RTHM ... throughout eternity, —FNTN ... for the eons of the eons, —CNDT ... for timeless ages! —PHLP.

**7:12.** In their worship these angels joined in unison to say or sing: Amen (Truly, Verily), the blessing (the praise), the glory, the wisdom (not only the wisdom shown in creation, but especially the wisdom shown by God in carrying out His great plan of redemption), the thanksgiving, the honor (the reverence), the power (shown in His miraculous acts), and the might (shown in His plan of redemption) belong to our God for ever and ever. The Greek shows the article "the" belongs here, and its use is important, for it means all praise, all glory, all wisdom, all thanksgiving, all reverence, all power, and all might belong to our God. They always have and they always will.

Though these angels were not able to join in the song of the redeemed, that is, to apply it to themselves, they were full of praise to God and recognized His wisdom, power, and grace. We can be sure they too were full of joy, for "there is joy in the presence of the angels of God over one sinner that repenteth" (Luke 15:10). How more must it be true that the angels rejoice at the sight of this multitude of redeemed sinners who have repented and have found salvation through the Lamb of God who takes away the sin of the world (John 1:29).

13. **And one of the elders answered, saying unto me:** ... there answered one from among, —RTHM ... addressed me and said, —GDSP ... spoke to me, —NORL, —SWAN ... then spoke, and asked me, —JB ... turned to me and asked, —BECK.
**What are these which are arrayed in white robes?:** ... These who are clothed in white robes, —MRDK ... Do you know who these people are, —JB ... in the long white robes? —AMPB ... As for these dressed ... who are they? —FNTN.
**and whence came they?:** ... where do they come from? —FNTN, —TEV.

**7:13.** Next, one of the elders came to John. Apparently he wanted John to think, so he asked who these were who were clothed in long white robes and from whence they had come. He seemed to think John ought to know who they were. Perhaps he had in mind the promise given to the overcomers, that is, to the faithful believers in all churches, in 3:5.

14. **And I said unto him, Sir, thou knowest:** ... I replied, —FNTN ... And I have declared to him: ... My lord, you are aware, —CNDT ... answered him, My lord, you must know, —NORL ... I don't know, sir. You do, —TEV ... You know, —WLMS ... You can tell me, —JB.
**And he said to me, These are they which came out of great tribulation:** ... Then he told me: ... These are those who have come through the great oppression, —PHLP ... They are the people who came through, —GDSP ... who came from, —MRDK ... These are the people who have come safely through the terrible, —TEV ... who have been through, —JB ... These are they who are coming up out of the great tribulation, —SWAN ... suffering, —BECK ... Persecution, —TCNT ... ordeal, —NOLI.
**and have washed their robes:** ... because they have washed, —JB ... rinse their robes, —CNDT.
**and made them white in the blood of the Lamb:** ... through the blood-shedding of the Little Lamb, —WADE.

**7:14.** John very respectfully suggested that the elder knew. In this way he indicated he did not want to speculate. He wanted the elder to tell him, then he would know for sure who they were.

The elder replied, "These are they which came out of great tribulation." Interpreters such as Caird take the present participle "coming" (see *Interlinear*) to mean that some of the great multitude were already coming out of great tribulation in John's own day in the First Century (*Harper's New Testament Commentaries, Revelation*, p. 102).

Others believe it is continuous and refers to all those who are the saved during the entire Church Age. These think "the great tribulation" is a way of including all the tribulations of the ages. In most cases Acts 14:22 is cited as evidence of the "many tribulations" through which believers must pass. They refer to the fact Jesus said that in the world, that is, in this age, we shall have tribulation, a word that includes pressure, suffering, and persecution (John 16:33; compare Romans 12:12; 2 Corinthians 1:4; 7:4; 2 Thessalonians 1:4; Revelation 1:9; 2:9). Consequently, "these" would refer to the whole number of the redeemed who have finished their time of testing on earth and now stand before God (Lenski, pp. 260f.; Poellot, p. 111).

Others understand the participle to mean "these" are just coming out of the Great Tribulation at this time, just before the opening of the seventh seal. They indicate that this vision is of the time of the end, and they take the article *the* to mean this is the final Great Tribulation at the end of this age (Beasley-Murray, *New Century Bible, Revelation,* p. 147). (See 3:10, the hour of trial which is to come on the whole inhabited world, to test those dwelling on the earth. Compare Daniel 12:1.) It is true that there has always been pressure and persecution. But "these" points to a great increase of persecution along with a terrible outbreak of evil at the end of the age.

Some believe this part of John's vision is another side of what will be going on during the time of the seven seals. Others believe it is another side of what will be going on during the time of the seven trumpets.

The important thing is that "these . . . have washed their robes, and made them white in the blood of the Lamb." While they were on earth they put their faith in Christ and accepted His redemptive work on the cross. They may also include the full complement of the martyrs mentioned in 6:11. But the Bible does not say here that they are all martyrs or that they were slain. However, it is clear they are all born-again believers.

**15. Therefore are they before the throne of God:** . . . For this reason, *—RTHM* . . . It is on account of this, *—WADE* . . . Because of this, *—FNTN* . . . they are now, *—MNTG.*
**and serve him day and night in his temple:** . . . and render divine service to him, *—RTHM* . . . in His sanctuary, *—FNTN.*
**and he that sitteth on the throne:** . . . that is seated upon, *—WADE.*
**shall dwell among them:** . . . will shelter them in His tent, *—WLMS* . . . will spread a tent over them, *—RTHM* . . . protects them, *—FNTN* . . . spread his tabernacle over them, *—MNTG* . . . will spread over them His pavilion to shelter them, *—WADE* . . . will diffuse his glory on them, *—KLST.*

**7:15.** Because everyone in this multitude is clothed in long white robes of Christ's righteousness, washed in the blood of the Lamb, they are continually before the throne of God. Their sins have all been forgiven. There is nothing standing between them and the Lord. Day and night they

continually serve or worship Him in the Holy of Holies of His heavenly sanctuary. They never cease to praise and adore Him. They have become the fulfillment of what God wanted when He called Israel and then the Church to be a holy nation, a nation of king-priests for Him.

God on the throne continually spreads His tent or tabernacle over them. The latter is possibly a reference to the Shechinah glory (Exodus 40:34-38). Because God dwells in their midst and spreads His glory over them, He will shelter and protect them. They will never again have to be afraid of anything.

**16. They shall hunger no more, neither thirst any more:** . . . No longer, *—KLST.*
**neither shall the sun light on them, nor any heat:** . . . neither shall they be stricken by, *—LAMS* . . . Nor will the sun strike them, nor any scorching heat, *—NORL* . . . nor in anywise may the sun fall on them, or any intense heat, *—RTHM* . . . beat upon them, *—FNTN* . . . strike upon them, *—MNTG* . . . to scorch them, *—WADE.*

**7:16.** This multitude, composed of believers from every nation on earth, is coming out of the Great Tribulation. They seem to represent those arriving in heaven during the entire tribulation period. The language here is reminiscent of the promise of the Kingdom restoration to Israel described in Isaiah 49:10. They have thirsted when the water became bitter as wormwood and was turned to blood. They have hungered because they did not accept the mark of the beast and were forbidden to buy or sell. They have been scorched by the heat of the sun. Now none of these afflictions will ever come upon them again.

Many see here a spiritual fulfillment of the promises of Matthew 5:6 and John 6:35. This "multitude" will not only be satisfied with Christ's righteousness but also with the continuing fullness of the Holy Spirit.

**17. For the Lamb which is in the midst of the throne shall feed them:** . . . who has ascended the center of, *—BRKL* . . . before the throne, *—KLST* . . . will take care of them, *—SEB* . . . will be their shepherd, *—NOLI, —NORL* . . . shepherd them, *—MNTG, —RTHM.*
**and shall lead them unto living fountains of waters:** . . . guide them, *—RTHM* . . . to life-giving springs of water, *—TCNT* . . . to the springs of living waters, *—NORL.*
**and God shall wipe away all tears from their eyes:** . . . God will make glad their eyes for ever, *—BB* . . . will take away, *—NLTG* . . . will wipe out every tear out of their eyes, *—RTHM* . . . every tear shall God be brushing away from their eyes, *—CNDT.*

**7:17.** The Lamb who is in the midst of the throne, and therefore sharing the power and authority of the One on the throne, will feed (shepherd) them by springs of living water, and God will remove their sorrow, wiping every tear from their eyes.

Here there is a strong contrast with the use of the exact same verb *poimanei* in 2:27; 19:15; see also 12:5. In those passages, acting the part of a shepherd indicates the shattering of the nations with a rod of iron in terrible judgment that will bring an end to the present world system, climaxing in the reign of the Antichrist. Here, acting the part of the shepherd means bringing the fulfillment of all the Good Shepherd is to His sheep (Psalm 23; Isaiah 40:11; John 10:1-30; 21:15-17).

The springs of living water are the final fulfillment and fullness of what was promised in John 4:14 and 7:38. The waters of life will forever abundantly satisfy.

This is a great promise, since for mankind tears symbolize sorrow. Many events of life cause tears, even for the children of God. It is blessed to know a time is coming when a loving Heavenly Father will himself wipe away all tears.

## Chapter 8

**1. And when he had opened the seventh seal:** ... Then when the Lamb, —*TNT* ... broke open, —*NORL* ... stamp was undone, —*BB* ... the seventh lock, —*NLTG*.

**there was silence in heaven about the space of half an hour:** ... there followed, —*MNTG* ... there was quiet, —*BB* ... a silence came, —*FNTN* ... in the sky, —*ADAM* ... there was not a sound in heaven, —*NLTG* ... for a very short interval, as it might be half an hour, —*WADE*.

**8:1.** After the interlude of chapter 7, John saw the Lamb opening the seventh seal. Suddenly all the music, the singing, the shouting around the throne stopped. Silence reigned for about half an hour. Up to this time all the attention was on the throne and the persons and what was happening around it. Great events were about to take place. It was the silence of expectation. All creation, in heaven and earth, stood at attention. The attention is about to be focused on the earth and the horrors about to come. The seventh seal leads into the judgments of the trumpets which follow.

**2. And I saw the seven angels which stood before God:** ... saw the seven messengers, —*KLGS* ... standing before, —*NORL* ... who had their place before, —*BB* ... in the presence of, —*KLST* ... in front of, —*NLTG*.

**and to them were given seven trumpets:** ... were delivered, —*FNTN* ... seven horns, —*BB*, —*NLTG* ... were given to them, —*ADAM*.

**8:2.** Now John saw seven angels which had been standing and were still standing before the throne

of God in readiness to do His will. They are not named or otherwise identified, but they had already been selected to receive the seven trumpets which were now given to them. The trumpets here were probably straight silver trumpets like those used in the tabernacle (Numbers 10:2) and the temple (2 Chronicles 5:12). They were also used in battle (Numbers 10:1-10; 31:6; Hosea 5:8).

**3. And another angel came and stood at the altar:** ... another messenger came and stood before the throne, —*KLGS* ... stood over, —*RTHM* ... stood by, —*KLST* ... took his place, —*BB* ... took his stand at the Altar of Incense, —*WADE*.

**having a golden censer:** ... carrying, —*KLST*, —*TNT* ... holding, —*NORL* ... held a cup made of gold full of special perfume, —*NLTG* ... a gold vessel for burning perfume, —*BB* ... having a golden bowl, —*KLGS* ... had a golden pan, —*EVRD*.

**and there was given unto him much incense:** ... A vast quantity, —*BRKL* ... and he was given many sorts of incense, —*ADAM* ... great quantity, —*KLST*, —*MNTG*, —*TNT* ... an abundance, —*FNTN* ... incense-compounds, —*RTHM* ... much perfume, —*BB*.

**that he should offer [it] with the prayers of all saints upon the golden altar which was before the throne:** ... to mingle with, —*NORL* ... so that he might put it with the prayers of all the saints on the gold altar which was before the high seat, —*BB* ... so he could mix it in with the prayers of those who belonged to God, —*NLTG* ... [throwing them] upon, —*RTHM* ... to aid the prayers of all God's Hallowed Ones, —*WADE* ... of all God's people, —*TNT* ... which is in sight of, —*FNTN*.

**8:3.** Not only does the heavenly temple have a throne and a sea or laver; it also has a golden altar of incense before the throne. It is a reminder that the earthly tabernacle was built according to the pattern God showed Moses in Mount Sinai (Exodus 25:9). As Hebrews 9:3, 4 recognizes, "the holiest of all," that is, the inner sanctuary, had the golden censer, and even though in the tabernacle and temple the golden altar of incense was in the Holy Place, it was at the entrance of "the holiest of all," and belonged to the Holy of Holies. Hebrews also says "Christ is not entered into the holy places made with hands, which are figures of the true; but into heaven itself" (Hebrews 9:24). Thus, what John saw in heaven is the reality of which the earthly tabernacle was just a type.

John saw another angel, not one of the seven, who came at this point and stood at the altar holding a golden censer or fire pan. He was given "much incense" that he might "offer it with the prayers of all saints upon the golden altar." "Much incense" indicates a great number of prayers, probably the prayers of the saints of all ages, primarily prayers that included the petition, "Thy kingdom come." It indicates that the judgments of God's wrath are necessary for the fulfillment of the hopes and desires of the saints for the fullness of their inheritance in Christ. As Daniel 2:34, 35, 44, 45 prophesied, the present world order and all it has inherited from the past must be destroyed before Christ's kingdom can fill the earth. Satan knows this. He also knows his time is short, and he is behind the false religions, false cults, false ideas of toleration of sin, and the false "new age" ideas. All of these are trying to destroy Christianity. But Christ is victor.

**4. And the smoke of the incense, [which came] with the prayers of the saints:** . . . Smoke from burning the special perfume, *—NLTG* . . . of the perfume, *—BB* . . . together with, *—KLST* . . . of the holy, *—FNTN.*

**ascended up before God out of the angel's hand:** . . . rose together, *—NORL* . . . rose up, *—MNTG* . . . went up in front of God, *—NLTG* . . . in the sight of . . . from the hand, *—FNTN* . . . to the presence of God, *—KLST.*

**8:4.** Kiddle insists the incense here symbolizes the prayers of the saints, as in 5:8 (p. 146). Ladd on the other hand believes that since the incense was given to this angel, it was mingled with the prayers of the saints (*Revelation*, p. 125). The angel's action shows that the prayers must come before God by way of the altar. The cloud of sweetsmelling smoke that arose when the angel poured the incense on the altar symbolizes God's acceptance of the prayers. Jesus, of course, made the way, for He "loved us, and hath given himself for us an offering and a sacrifice to God for a sweetsmelling savor" (Ephesians 5:2). Now these prayers, stored up throughout the centuries, are about to be fulfilled.

**5. And the angel took the censer:** . . . took the vessel, *—WMCK* . . . the cup of gold, *—NLTG.*

**and filled it with fire of the altar, and cast [it] into the earth:** . . . made it full of the fire . . . and sent it down on, *—BB-* . . . filled it with live coals . . . and it was hurled, *—KLST* . . . and poured it on the earth, *—BECK* . . . and flung it to the earth, *—WLMS* . . . and threw it upon, *—FNTN* . . . down on the earth, *—NORL.*

**and there were voices, and thunderings:** . . . and there followed, *—FNTN* . . . there came thunders, *—BB* . . . noises, *—NORL* . . . and there ensued thunderpeals, *—WADE* . . . explosions, *—NOLI* . . . peals of thunder, rumblings, *—KLST.*

**and lightnings, and an earthquake:** . . . flashes of lightning, *—KLST* . . . and flames and a shaking of the earth, *—BB* . . . and the earth shook, *—NLTG.*

**8:5.** The same fire on the altar that made the incense and the prayers of the saints sweet and acceptable to God was now poured out on the earth. The angel filled the fire pan, which indicates the severity of the coming judgments of God's wrath.

When the fire hit the earth, John, who in vision was still in heaven at the throne, heard sounds similar to those that accompanied the giving of the Law at Mount Sinai (Exodus 19:16, 18, 19; 20:18). Here, however, these sounds indicated God was about to pour out judgments on the earth.

We are not told what the voices are, but the same word is used of the sound (or "voice") of a trumpet (cf. Zephaniah 1:14-16, which speaks of the great Day of the Lord). Thunder and lightning are used frequently in the Old Testament to show God is bringing a storm of judgment on sinners (1 Samuel 2:10; 7:10; Job 26:14; Psalms 18:13, 14; 77:18). Isaiah also prophesied, "Thou shalt be visited (in judgment) of the Lord of hosts with thunder, and with earthquake, and great noise, with storm and tempest, and the flame of devouring fire" (Isaiah 29:6). All these things John heard, along with the earthquake, must have had an effect like the sights, sounds, and the shaking at Sinai. They would surely cause the people on earth to tremble, just as the ancient Israelites did (Exodus 19:16).

**6. And the seven angels which had the seven trumpets prepared themselves to sound:** . . . the seven horns made ready for sounding them, *—BB* . . . now made preparations to sound their trumpets, *—NORL* . . . got ready to blow them, *—BECK, —NLTG* . . . made ready, *—WMCK*

**8:6.** Now the interlude is over. The prayers of the saints have been offered, the earth has been warned by the storms and the earthquake. The time of fulfillment has come. The seven angels have fully prepared themselves, and they lift their trumpets ready to sound them, undoubtedly waiting until God gives the signal to each in turn. (See Psalm 103:20, 21.)

The plagues which follow the sounding of the trumpets are partial judgments with one-third of the world affected. They are poured out on a sin-hardened world. We are not told whether this percentage means one-third of the earth's surface will be so devastated, or whether the plagues will affect all the world with the total equaling one-third. Whichever is the case, consternation will sweep around the world as the news of the disasters spreads. The media will use all their resources to relate what has taken place.

As in the case of the seals the first four trumpets form one group, followed by two that are distinct, and then by one final trumpet.

**7. The first angel sounded:** ...at the sounding of the first, *−BB*...blew his trumpet, *−NORL*...sounded his trumpet, *−KLST*...his horn, *−NLTG*.

**and there followed hail and fire mingled with blood:** ...there followed a rain of, *−NORL*...mixed with, *−FNTN*...with water, *−LAMS*...ice and fire, *−BB*.

**and they were cast upon the earth:** ...This fell on the earth, *−NORL*...it was hurled, *−KLST*...was sent on the earth, *−BB*...was poured upon, *−FNTN*...and they fell with violence upon, *−WADE*...came down on the earth, *−NLTG*.

**and the third part of trees was burnt up:** ...and a third of the woods, *−KLST*...of the earth, and of the trees, *−BB*.

**and all green grass was burnt up:** ...all green herbage, *−RTHM*...were destroyed by fire, *−KLST*.

**8:7.** The language used to describe the hail and fire mixed with blood is like that used in connection with the seventh plague God brought on Egypt through Moses (Exodus 9:13-35), but this plague is far more serious. The mention of blood reminds us of Joel's prophecy (Joel 2:31; Acts 2:19).

It seems this hail and fire were already mingled with blood when they appear in the heavens and are cast down upon (or, into) the earth. The chief effect will come from the fire which will burn up a third of the trees and all the green grass. In this it will be different from an ordinary forest or grass fire which usually comes when the grass or trees are parched and dry, not green. Though God will use hail and fire, there is no explanation of how it came to be mixed with blood. It is clearly a supernatural judgment.

A large segment of the population will be touched adversely by this plague. It will certainly affect agriculture, for many crops will be destroyed. This in turn will have an effect upon prices and lead to economic ruin for many. Nothing is said about any people being hurt or killed, though it is a dreadful possibility. It should be a warning to the entire world.

**8. And the second angel sounded:** ...When the second angel sounded his trumpet, *−NORL*...at the sounding of the second angel, *−BB*...blew the trumpet, *−BRKL*...his horn, *−NLTG*.

**and as it were a great mountain burning with fire was cast into the sea:** ...Then it seemed a great mountain was all afire and was hurled into the sea, *−KLST*...something like a great mountain, *−MNTG*...great mountain-like mass...fell with violence into the sea, *−WADE*...a great burning fiery mountain, *−FNTN*...it was as if a great mountain burning with fire was sent into the sea, *−BB*...like an immense mountain ablaze with fire was hurled, *−BRKL*...It was thrown into, *−NLTG*...was blown into, *−NORL*.

**and the third part of the sea became blood:** ...turned to, *−WADE*.

**8:8.** After the fire consumed on the land, the second angel blew his trumpet and something that looked like a great mountain mass appeared, and it was aflame with fire. It seems this also appeared in the heavens and was cast down into the sea. Morris speculates that this might be an asteroid or some mass of rock and combustible gases from outer space that ignites when it hits the earth's atmosphere (pp. 146f.). Again, it is not an accidental happening. God will direct it. It will fall into the sea at His timing when the second trumpet sounds. Its mighty impact might shake the earth, and certainly all will know about it.

As the initial result a third part of the sea is affected and becomes blood. (Compare the first of the 10 plagues on Egypt where the River Nile became blood. Exodus 7:17-21.) Some understand this to mean that the water will be transformed by God's creative power into actual blood. Others think the blood of dead sea creatures will make it bloody. Still others compare it to the "red tides" filled with dead and poisonous microorganisms which have sometimes appeared in the oceans even in modern times.

**9. And the third part of the creatures which were in the sea, and had life, died:** ...the created things that is, the things, *−WADE*...everything living in the sea, *−KLGS*...of the living creatures, *−TNT*...destruction came on a third part of the living things, *−BB*...creatures in the sea died, *−ADAM*...that had souls, *−RTHM*...all sea life died, *−NLTG*...perished, *−WLMS*.

**and the third part of the ships were destroyed:** ...part of the sailing vessels was destroyed, *−WADE*...were wrecked, *−BRKL, −FNTN*.

**8:9.** With a third of the sea turned to blood a further result was that a third of all fish, whales, and other sea creatures died. Then a third of all the ships were destroyed, totally ruined. It may be that the impact of the mountainous mass hitting the sea causes tremendous waves which will sink some ships and destroy those at anchor near the shore. This will have a disastrous effect on the world's food supply and the world's commerce as well. Though it is not stated, the destruction of the ships must bring a great loss of human life as well.

**10. And the third angel sounded:** ...Next, the third angel blew his trumpet, *−NORL*...a third messenger sounded, *−KLGS*...at the sounding of the third angel, *−BB*.

**and there fell a great star from heaven, burning as it were a lamp:** ...a large star...was burning with a fire that kept burning like a bright light, *−NLTG*...there went down from heaven a great star, burning like a flame, *−BB*...star fell out of the sky, *−NORL*...a burning star, like a great lamp,

*—FNTN* . . . flaming like, *—TNT* . . . blazing like a torch, *—BRKL, —WLMS.*

**and it fell upon the third part of the rivers:** . . . it came on, *—BB* . . . landing on, *—NORL* . . . it dropped upon, *—WADE.*

**and upon the fountains of waters:** . . . and on the places where water comes out of the earth, *—NLTG* . . . springs, *—ADAM, —FNTN, —MNTG.*

**8:10.** At the sounding of the third trumpet John saw a great star fall from heaven. It too was burning, with the appearance of the flame of a lamp or a torch; that is, with the flame streaming behind it as it fell. It apparently does not affect the land, but poisons the rivers and fountains (including ever-flowing springs and wells).

The Greek word for star was also used for planets, meteors, and any other heavenly body. It is also used metaphorically for angels, men, and even Christ. Commentators such as Lang view this and the preceding mountainous mass to be fallen angels cast out of heaven to wreak havoc on the earth (p. 169). But there is nothing in the passage to indicate anything other than a physical heavenly body, possibly a meteorite set on fire by friction with the atmosphere; though, in contrast to the preceding mountainous mass, this may be mostly liquid. It could be that this bitterness will be specially created by God to break up and dissolve in the rivers, springs, and wells, turning them into the bitterness of wormwood.

**11. And the name of the star is called Wormwood:** . . . Now the name of the star is called, *—ADAM* . . . Apsinthus, meaning, *—NORL* . . . is Bitterness, *—SEB* . . . Bitter-root, *—WMCK*

**and the third part of the waters became wormwood:** . . . for one-third of the waters turned to, *—NORL* . . . to the taste, *—WADE* . . . became bitter, *—BB.*

**and many men died of the waters, because they were made bitter:** . . . a number of men came to their end because, *—BB* . . . people died of the waters after they turned bitter, *—NORL* . . . in consequence of, *—RTHM* . . . it was poison, *—SEB* . . . they had been rendered so bitter, *—WADE* . . . embittered, *—FNTN.*

**8:11.** Wormwood, the name of the star, is taken from the name of a plant with very bitter juice. It is used in the Old Testament to represent the bitter results of sin (Proverbs 5:4, 5; Jeremiah 9:15), and is sometimes connected with gall (Deuteronomy 29:18; Lamentations 3:19). The plant is also called hemlock in the King James Version (Amos 6:12), but it is probably not the Greek hemlock, but a plant of the genus *Artemisia*. The star has its name because it makes the water in a third of the rivers, springs, and wells bitter as wormwood. Ordinary wormwood from the plants known by that name does not usually cause death. But this star does cause many human beings (*anthrōpōn*) to die. Thus, the star does make the water poisonous. The Greek (*ek*) indicates that drinking the poisoned water will be the cause of their death.

Since a third of the waters will be poisoned, the "many men" will probably include a large percentage of the population. This repetition of judgment on a third part of the trees, grass, sea creatures, ships, waters, and now people, should let the people who remain on earth know these judgments are not by chance or by accident, but are divine warnings. If they had not been deceived by the Antichrist, they would repent and cry out to God for forgiveness.

**12. And the fourth angel sounded:** . . . at the sounding of, *—BB* . . . blew his trumpet, *—NORL.*

**and the third part of the sun was smitten:** . . . was cursed with a plague, *—WLMS* . . . was eclipsed, *—LAMS* . . . were blasted, *—NORL* . . . was made dark, *—BB* . . . was struck, *—KLST.*

**and the third part of the moon, and the third part of the stars:**

**so as the third part of them was darkened:** . . . a third of their light, *—NORL* . . . should be darkened, *—MNTG* . . . lost their light, *—KLST.*

**and the day shone not for a third part of it:** . . . The day lost a third of its light, *—KLST* . . . there was no light, *—WLMS* . . . was darkened for, *—LAMS* . . . for a third part of its duration, gave no light, *—WADE.*

**and the night likewise:** . . . in like manner, *—RTHM* . . . as also the night, *—KLST* . . . the night, had no light, *—NORL* . . . at night it was the same, *—MNTG.*

**8:12.** John saw in his vision that the first three trumpets affected the earth. The fourth brought a mighty blow that struck the sun, moon, and stars, so that they were darkened. This does not mean merely a lessening of their light, however, for in a third part of the day the sun did not shine at all, and in a third part of the night, the moon and stars gave no light at all. This was to be a temporary situation, however, for later on the heat of the sun is increased.

The Bible gives no indication of what it was that struck such a blow. Darkness was often used by God as judgment. Joel spoke of the "day of the Lord" as a day of darkness (Joel 2:2). Amos warned the sinning Israelites of his day that, for them, the "day of the Lord" would be darkness and not light (Amos 5:18). Zephaniah 1:14, 15 called it a day of wrath as well as darkness and thick darkness. (See also Isaiah 13:10; Mark 13:24.) Jesus also used darkness to describe the final state of the wicked (Matthew 8:12).

Darkness was also one of the plagues in Egypt. The use of the language of the plagues in Egypt probably is meant as a reminder that these judgments are the fulfillment of promises to judge the enemies of God's people. But this darkness is quite different from the plague of darkness that fell on Egypt. In this judgment God will somehow cause the light to be lessened. He will also cause the sun to be totally obscured for the third part of the day, and He will totally obscure the moon and stars for the third part of the night. Most agree there is no naturalistic explanation of how this could take place. The God who created the universe controls it. This judgment is, like the others, supernatural. The Bible does not say anything here about the effect on the earth. It will undoubtedly cause a drop in the earth's temperature and upset the ordinary course of the winds and the weather. God's purpose here, as before, will be to let the world know this is not by chance, that there is still opportunity to repent. Though a holy God must judge, He does not really will any to perish (2 Peter 3:9).

**13. And I beheld, and heard an angel flying through the midst of heaven:** ... Then, in my vision, I heard an angel, as he was flying, —NORL . . . I looked and I heard a solitary eagle, —MNTG . . . I heard an eagle, —NOLI . . . a lone eagle flying in midheaven, —BRKL . . . as it flew in the middle of the sky, —KLST . . . as it flew in the zenith, —WADE.

**saying with a loud voice:** . . . cry out, —NORL . . . screaming loudly, —NOLI . . . with a great voice, —BB.

**Woe, woe, woe, to the inhab-iters of the earth:** . . . Alas, alas, alas, —BRKL, —WLMS . . . Perdition, perdition, perdition, Kliest . . . Trouble, trouble, —BB . . . It is bad! It is bad for those who live on the earth, —NLTG . . . Sorrow, sorrow . . . for all that live on, —WMCK . . . How horrible! How horrible! —SEB . . . awaits those who dwell on, —WADE . . . for those that dwell on, —RTHM.

**by reason of the other voices of the trumpet of the three angels, which are yet to sound!:** . . . because the three other angels are about to blow their trumpets! —NORL . . . because of the rest of the trumpet blasts . . . who are going to sound their trumpets, —KLST . . . Because of the rest of, —MNTG . . . when the sound comes from the horns that the other three angels will blow! —NLTG . . . the other voices of the horns . . . whose sounding is still to come, —BB . . . from the remaining utterances of the trumpet-blast, —FNTN . . . in consequence of the remaining, —RTHM . . . who are about to sound, —BRKL . . . who are about to blow, —TCNT.

**8:13.** The fourth trumpet of John's vision was followed by a brief interlude where an angel flying (probably flying back and forth) in midheaven brings further warning to the earth. Many ancient manuscripts and most of the ancient Latin and Syriac translations have "eagle" instead of "angel" in this verse. The Greek word for "eagle" is also used to mean "vulture." Thus, Caird sees this as a vulture symbolizing judgment and pronouncing these woes upon the inhabitants still living on the earth (*Harper's New Testament Commentaries, Revelation,* p. 117).

Whether it is an angel, eagle, or vulture, or possibly a cherub or seraph in the form of an eagle, the threefold repetition of "Woe!" is for emphasis. God wants the world to know that though the first four trumpet judgments were bad, what follows will be worse. The effects on the physical universe will be striking, unusual, and demonic. The seventh trumpet will also lead into the seven vials or bowls of God's wrath, which will be more complete judgments. They will be calamities from which no one can hide.

## Chapter 9

**1. And the fifth angel sounded:** . . . When . . . his trumpet, —NORL . . . blew, —MNTG . . . at the sounding of, —BB.

**and I saw a star fall from heaven unto the earth:** . . . an Angel, bright as a star, —WADE . . . that had fallen from the sky to the earth, —KLST . . . from the sky on to the land, —FNTN . . . from heaven upon the earth, —MNTG.

**and to him was given the key of the bottomless pit:** . . . the pit of, —BRKL . . . the shaft of the abyss, —BECK, —RTHM . . . was given to the angel, —NORL . . . of the great deep, —BB . . . the hold without a bottom, —NLTG.

**9:1.** When the fifth angel blew his trumpet, John saw a star which had already fallen or had just fallen out of heaven. This star was given the key to the pit or shaft of the abyss. Nearly all commentators agree that this is not a literal star but rather an intelligent being. Most think it was an angel.

However, there are contrasting views as to the identity of this angel. When the fall occurred is not stated. John saw the star only as a fallen one. Some think the star is Satan, others that it is one of his subordinates in the kingdom of darkness. Possibly, it could be Abaddon, the angel of the abyss mentioned in verse 11.

The star did not have the inherent authority to open the abyss (Christ is the One who has this), but it was given to him. The abyss is the abode of demons (Luke 8:31), where many of them are kept in custody.

The pit, in the Septuagint of Psalm 54:24 (55:23 in the English versions), is called the pit or shaft leading to (the place of) corruption, where the place of corruption means the depths of hell, the place of punishment for sinners.

The abyss was considered by the Jews to be a great hollow place deep within the earth. It is another name for the place of the dead (see Romans 10:7, where the King James Version translates it as "the deep," and it is parallel to the mention of hell in Acts 2:27). It is also the place where demons dread to be sent (Luke 8:31). The beast who is the Antichrist will also come out of the abyss (11:7), and Satan will be locked up and imprisoned there for 1,000 years while Christ reigns on earth (20:3). The King James translators called it "bottomless" because no human eye can plumb the darkness of its depths.

**2. And he opened the bottomless pit:** . . . he made the great deep open, —BB . . . the pit of the abyss, —FNTN . . . the hole, —NLTG.

**and there arose a smoke out of the pit:** . . . went up, —BECK . . . came out, —NLTG.

**as the smoke of a great furnace:** . . . like smoke belching from, —LAMS . . . a gigantic, —BRKL . . . huge furnace, —ADAM . . . from a mighty furnace, —NORL . . . big, —EVRD . . . of a great oven, —BB . . . from a place where there is much fire, —NLTG.

**and the sun and the air were darkened by reason of the smoke of the pit:** . . . grew dark, —MNTG . . . It darkened the sun, —KLGS . . . in consequence of, —RTHM . . . because of the smoke from, —NORL . . . the shaft, —ADAM, —TNT . . . the hole, —NLTG.

**9:2.** The shaft leading to the abyss is locked on the outside, so that whoever or whatever is inside cannot escape. However, when this star angel opened the pit or shaft of the abyss John saw a cloud of smoke come out of it, great enough to darken the air and the sun. Though the Bible does not say so, this would seem to indicate there was fire in the abyss. So it is possibly the same as the Hebrew Sheol (as in Numbers 16:30, 33; Job 17:16) and the Greek Hades, which in the New Testament is always a place of punishment. Jesus described it as a place where flames of fire torment sinners (Luke 16:23, 24). Some, however, believe there are several compartments and that Hades and the abyss are separate but connected.

**3. And there came out of the smoke locusts upon the earth:** . . . From the smoke came forth locusts, —KLST . . . came locusts that streamed upon the ground, —ADAM . . . Grasshoppers came from, —SEB . . . came down to earth, —NLTG . . . came onto the earth out of the smoke, —TNT.

**and unto them was given power:** . . . they were endowed, Fen ton . . . they were given the same sort of "authority," —ADAM . . . granted, —WADE . . . licence, —RTHM.

**as the scorpions of the earth have power:** . . . to sting like, —EVRD . . . as that possessed by scorpions, —TCNT . . . as authority of the earthly, —KLGS . . . like that of earthly scorpions, —KLST . . . like small animals that sting, —NLTG.

**9:3.** Coming out of the smoke that spread across the world was a terrifying cloud of locusts. God used locusts as a terrible plague on Egypt, but again, this locust plague will be much worse than that in ancient Egypt where God used locusts as His judgment (Exodus 10:4-6).

These locusts, though given power like that of the earth's scorpions, come out of the abyss, the bottomless pit. Thus, they are not ordinary locusts, but demons, released at this time to let people know a holy God demands judgment on sin. John's description in verses 7-10 shows they were not like locusts as we know them. It must be that they are called locusts, not because of their form, but because it is their nature to devour and destroy. Neither were they in the form of the scorpions that are so common in the land of Israel, often hiding under stones in the fields. These "locusts" have power to cause pain, torment, and misery like that of scorpions. The Bible mentions the power of their poisonous stings and uses them as a symbol of evil, especially spiritual evil (Ezekiel 2:6; Luke 10:19; 11:12).

**4. And it was commanded them that they should not hurt the grass of the earth:** . . . They were authorized to attack, —NOLI . . . they were told not to harm, —EVRD, —WADE . . . ordered to do, —BB . . . ordered not to harm the grass, —ADAM . . . bidden them that they should not injure the herbage, —RTHM . . . not to damage, —NORL.

**neither any green thing, neither any tree:** . . . any grass, —FNTN . . . or any plant, —EVRD, —TCNT . . . any green plant, —KLST . . . nor any green growth, —ADAM.

**but only those men which have not the seal of God in their foreheads:** . . . They were to harm only such of mankind as did not have, —NORL . . . on their brows, —LAMS.

**9:4.** Ordinary locusts destroy grass, green plants, and strip trees of their leaves. They come in a cloud that settles down on cultivated land and moves through the fields and orchards denuding all vegetation (Exodus 10:15). The fact that these locusts are told not to do so shows even more clearly that they are different from any other locusts that have appeared on earth.

Their purpose will be to injure, hurt, and damage human beings. The Bible does not say who gives them their orders. But the orders also limit their activity. They are not to hurt those who have the seal of God on their foreheads. This limitation is a reminder of how God limited Satan's power over Job (Job 1:12; 2:6). God who is almighty has ultimate control always, and therefore control of all He allows during this period of tribulation judgments.

John has already identified those who have the seal of God in their forehead as the 144,000 of the tribes of Israel (7:3). At this point they are protected from the torments of these demonic locusts. Therefore, they are still present on the earth. Some believe they have made converts to the Lord Jesus

Christ, and these converts have either been raptured, or martyred, or have also been sealed with the same sealing on the forehead.

**5. And to them it was given that they should not kill them:** . . . The locusts had orders not to kill, —NORL . . . it was granted, —FNTN . . . They were not permitted, —WLMS . . . They had no power to kill them, —NOLI.

**but that they should be tormented five months:** . . . but to keep on torturing, —NORL . . . to torture them, —BRKL.

**and their torment [was] as the torment of a scorpion:** . . . They inflicted a torture similar to the pain, —NOLI.

**when he striketh a man:** . . . when he has been stung, —NOLI . . . whensoever it may smite a man, —RTHM . . . when it stings a man, —FNTN, —NORL.

**9:5.** Two further limitations are put upon these demonic locusts. They are limited in what they can do. They cannot kill anyone. They are limited as to the time they can stay on earth. They can only torment and torture mankind with a sting like that of scorpions for 5 months. Ladd speculates that the 5 months may refer to the dry season in Palestine (May through September) (p. 132). Others believe it refers to the life cycle of ordinary locusts (Charles, *International Critical Commentary, Revelation*, 1:243). However, the only point here seems to be that the One who is in control gives them 5 months to do their work of judgment. It seems probable that at the end of that time they will be sent back into the abyss and imprisoned there until the final judgment.

**6. And in those days shall men seek death, and shall not find it:** . . . When those days come, —NORL . . . will look for, —BECK.

**and shall desire to die:** . . . they will be anxious to die, —BRKL . . . long to die, —BECK, —TCNT, —WLMS . . . covet to die, —RTHM.

**and death shall flee from them:** . . . fly from, —FNTN . . . death ever flees, —MNTG . . . but they will never find it, —NORL.

**9:6.** In the Bible repetition of the same idea in different words is a common means of emphasis. Not only are these demonic locusts commanded not to kill anyone, but people will seek death with a desire to die and bring an end to their dreadful pain and agony. But they will not be able to do so. This seems to mean that even attempts at suicide will not succeed. Death keeps fleeing from them, keeps running away from them. They escape death because death escapes from them. It seems also there is no place to hide from the stings of these demon locusts. As spirit beings no wall can stop them, no man-made lock can keep them out. Their sting is not arbitrary or senseless torture,

however. It is rather another warning and another opportunity for people to repent and turn to God. God always wants people to repent and receive forgiveness and salvation (2 Peter 3:9). But 9:20, 21 shows these people do not respond.

**7. And the shapes of the locusts [were] like unto horses prepared unto battle:** . . . In appearance, —NOLI . . . took the appearance of cavalry disciplined for war, —FNTN . . . the likenesses of . . . horses made ready for war, —RTHM . . . grasshoppers, —BECK . . . armed for battle, —NORL, —WLMS . . . equipped for, —MNTG.

**and on their heads [were] as it were crowns like gold:** . . . They seemed to have crowns, —NORL . . . were something like, —MNTG . . . what seemed to be, —KLST . . . circlets resembling gold in colour, —WADE.

**and their faces [were] as the faces of men:** . . . their faces resembled human faces, —TCNT . . . like men's faces, —MNTG.

**9:7.** Joel 2:4 describes the locust plague in terms of an army where they appear like horses. Joel, however, was talking about real locusts, which God identified as "my great army" (Joel 2:25), so the language Joel used to describe them is symbolic. The demonic locusts which John saw looked like war horses arrayed and prepared for battle. This seems to mean also that they were quite large. Some believe their appearance will entice people with a false promise of power and victory.

On their heads John saw something like crowns that looked like gold. But they are not real crowns, nor are they real gold. Mounce suggests they are symbolic and point to the fact that they will succeed in what they are allowed to do (*New International Commentary on the New Testament, Revelation*, p. 196). Others suggest that these are false crowns symbolizing the way demonic powers entice people with false promises, just as Satan tempted Jesus with a promise of the kingdoms of this world. However, there is no indication of such promises here. People only seek death (cf. Barnhouse, pp. 169-171).

Their faces, quite unlike the faces of real locusts, had the appearance of intelligent human beings. Their intelligence must be evil and demonic, however. Also, such a combination of the animal and the human in their appearance will be terrifying.

**8. And they had hair as the hair of women:** . . . like a woman's, —KLST.

**and their teeth were as [the teeth] of lions:** . . . like a lion's, —KLST . . . like lions' fangs, —WADE.

**9:8.** John further described the locusts as being covered with hair like a woman's hair. Some see this as an allusion to the long antennae of the locusts. Others, especially among older commentators, suppose it means these demonic creatures will stir up sins against women.

Their teeth like a lion speaks of destruction. That is, these demon locusts will be capable of rending and destroying like a lion, but they are not allowed to do so. The hurt comes from their scorpionlike tails. Nevertheless, the lionlike teeth add to the fierceness and terror of their appearance.

**9. And they had breastplates, as it were breastplates of iron:** . . . they had corslets, *−WADE* . . . that seemed to be made of steel, *−WLMS* . . . something like, *−MNTG* . . . were like iron, *−NORL.*

**and the sound of their wings [was] as the sound of chariots of many horses running to battle:** . . . the noise of their wings, *−MNTG* . . . the whirring of their wings was like the rattling of a number of war-chariots as they rush, *−WADE* . . . the noise of many chariots, drawn by horses, *−NORL* . . . as the sound of carriages, like an army of horses rushing to the fight, *−BB* . . . the roar of chariots . . . charging in battle, *−FNTN* . . . galloping into, *−TCNT* . . . rushing into battle, *−BECK, −KLST.*

**9:9.** The invincibility of these demon locusts is further indicated by their breastplates of iron. No ordinary weapon, no weapon available to mankind can stop, kill, or destroy them. They have no vulnerable spot.

The language is like that of Joel 2:4-8 where the prophet described the locusts in that plague as having the appearance of horses and "Like the noise of chariots on the tops of mountains shall they leap, like the noise of a flame of fire that devoureth the stubble, as a strong people set in battle array." Remember, Joel prophesied about the Day of the Lord.

The beating of the wings of these thousands of demon locusts makes such a great whirring noise that John can only describe it as the sound of chariots with many horses running to battle.

**10. And they had tails like unto scorpions:** . . . have pointed tails like, *−BB.*

**and there were stings in their tails:** . . . stings also, *−WADE.*

**and their power [was] to hurt men five months:** . . . in their tails they possessed their power, *−FNTN* . . . to torture men, *−MNTG* . . . to harm human beings for a period of, *−KLST* . . . is their power to give men wounds for, *−BB* . . . four months, *−WADE.*

**9:10.** The tails of these demon locusts have stings and are able to inflict pain in the same manner as real scorpions. Again John drew attention to the fact that the poison will hurt, injure, torture, and damage but not kill, and emphasized that their power and authority to do this will continue for 5 months. Then they will be gone, undoubtedly back to the abyss.

Some believe that since these are demons from the pit of the abyss, their strange appearance is a special creation of God for the purpose of using them for judgment. Others believe that as demons they are spirit beings invisible to the people on earth. However, John was using this language as a way of describing their spirit character and nature, and as a way of impressing on the readers the terrible suffering these demons impose on mankind. The language here indicates this is the way John saw them in his vision. If the language is symbolic, it represents reality, and the reality it represents will indeed come upon people who do not have the seal of God in their foreheads.

**11. And they had a king over them:** . . . These locusts, *−NLTG* . . . They had as their king, *−NORL.*

**[which is] the angel of the bottomless pit:** . . . the fiend of the abyss, *−NOLI* . . . He is the head angel of the hole that has no bottom, *−NLTG* . . . of the great deep, *−BB.*

**whose name in the Hebrew tongue [is] Abaddon:** . . . the Hebrew language, *−NLTG* . . . Destruction, *−WADE.*

**but in the Greek tongue hath [his] name Apollyon:** . . . and in the Greek language, *−BB* . . . he is called, *−MNTG* . . . that is, Exterminator, *−NOLI* . . . It means the one who, *−NLTG* . . . Destroyer, *−RTHM.*

**9:11.** That these are not real locusts is further indicated by the fact that they have a king over them, in contrast to locusts that have no king (Proverbs 30:27). The king is the angel of the abyss. Some have thought this angel is the one who presides over the pit or shaft of the abyss or bottomless pit (Beckwith, p. 563). Perhaps the best explanation is that this "king," as well as the angel of verse 1, is Satan, the destroyer of John 10:10.

The angel king of these demon locusts is named in the Hebrew 'avaddôn. This name is found in Job 26:6; 28:22; Psalm 86:13; Proverbs 15:11. In all these places it means destruction, the place of destruction, the realm of the wicked dead. In the Septuagint it is usually translated by *apōleia*, the Greek word for destruction. But John gave it a translation that applies to this angel that rules over these demon locusts, Apollyon, meaning "the destroyer."

**12. One woe is past:** . . . The first calamity is past, *−BRKL* . . . The first Trouble is past, *−BB* . . . this first woe, *−NORL* . . . time of trouble, *−NLTG* . . . One horror has gone, *−SEB* . . . departed, *−RTHM.*

**[and], behold, there come two woes more hereafter:** . . . Take note, two more woes are to come after this, *−KLST* . . . but mark! there come afterwards two Woes besides! *−WADE* . . . But listen, there are two more times of trouble coming after this, *−NLTG* . . . still two Troubles to come, *−BB* . . . follow after, *−LAMS* . . . are yet to come! *−NORL.*

**9:12.** John now moved in his vision to the end of the 5 months of torture by the demon locusts. They are gone. Their ultimate destination will be the lake of fire that is prepared for the devil and his angels (compare Matthew 25:41). The first of the three woes foretold in 8:13 by that flying angel is now past. Two more are to come, and it is implied they will be even worse. The second woe will be introduced by the sixth trumpet. The third woe will be introduced by the seventh trumpet which will lead into the seven vials or bowls of God's wrath. As we look ahead, it seems that the increase in the severity of the judgments matches the increase in the stubborn rebelliousness of mankind against God.

**13.** **And the sixth angel sounded:** ... The trumpet of the sixth angel, *—NORL* ... blew his trumpet, *—MNTG* ... at the sounding of, *—BB* ... his horn, *—NLTG.*

**and I heard a voice from the four horns of the golden altar which is before God:** ... a solitary voice, *—BRKL* ... came to my ears, *—BB* ... coming from the corners, *—SEB* ... from the projecting corners of, *—WADE* ... in the sight of, *—FNTN* ... standing before, *—NORL.*

**9:13.** At the sound of the sixth angel's trumpet John heard a voice from the four horns or projections at the corners of the golden altar that is before God. The incense poured out on the altar (8:3) represented the prayers of the saints. Thus, the judgment that followed was a further expression of God's divine justice and His holy wrath against sin and against the rebellion that brought suffering, torture, and death to His saints. Some believe the voice John heard was that of God or of an angel in response to the prayers offered at the altar (Beasley-Murray, *New Century Bible, Revelation*, p. 163). Others believe it was the united voice of the souls of the martyrs under the altar (6:9, 10) (Ladd, *Revelation*, p. 135). Still others believe it was the voice of the Lamb or the avenging angel in a pronouncement of judgment against those who had rejected the death and atoning blood of Christ (cf. Morris, p. 165).

**14.** **Saying to the sixth angel:** ... The voice said, *—KLST* ... one saying to, *—MNTG* ... It gave orders to the sixth, *—NORL.*

**which had the trumpet, Loose the four angels which are bound in the great river Euphrates:** ... who had the horn ... Make free ... who are chained, *—BB* ... Set free, *—TCNT* ... Free the four, *—BECK* ... Release the four angels ... imprisoned at, *—NORL* ... Liberate ... who are held captive, *—FNTN* ... the four fiends who are imprisoned by, *—NOLI* ... that are shackled, *—BRKL* ... that are kept under restraint, *—WADE.*

**9:14.** In Old Testament times God used the robber kings of the Euphrates valley to bring His judgment. The kings of Assyria made war and sought conquest to bring wealth and tribute every year of their reigns (except for the last years of Sennacherib after God's angel destroyed the major part of his army). Babylon, the great city on the Euphrates, was used by God in Jeremiah's day in the same way. Even though these nations did not know God was using them, God called them a rod in His angry hand to punish His sinning and rebellious people (Isaiah 10:5-7).

Thus, with this Old Testament background, the Euphrates River becomes a symbol of the spirit of conquest which God uses to bring His judgment. The sixth angel was told to loose the four angels who had been bound and were still bound at the Euphrates River (on its banks). This great river of the Old Testament world (about 1,700 miles long) was the northern limit of the territory God promised to Abraham and his descendants (cf. Genesis 15:18; Deuteronomy 1:7; Joshua 1:4). It was also the eastern boundary of the Roman Empire in John's day, and it seems to be the boundary of the Antichrist's kingdom. The four angels are different from those mentioned in 7:1, but they seem to be evil angels who are over demonic hosts. (Holy angels are never bound.)

**15.** **And the four angels were loosed:** ... they liberated, *—FNTN* ... were released, *—NORL* ... were made free, *—BB.*

**which were prepared for an hour, and a day, and a month, and a year:** ... that were held in readiness, *—MNTG, —TCNT* ... who had been held ready for this, *—KLST* ... waiting for, *—NORL* ... pending the appointed hour, *—WADE.*

**for to slay the third part of men:** ... that they might kill, *—FNTN* ... that they were to go out and kill, *—NORL* ... to destroy, *—MNTG* ... that they might put to death, *—BB* ... a third of the people, *—BECK* ... of mankind, *—KLST, —TCNT.*

**9:15.** While the demon locusts could only torture people, these four angels were commissioned to kill one-third of the entire human race. They had been fully prepared and held in readiness for a precise hour, day, month, and year. They must have been full of fury, but up to this time they were held back. Whether they knew when the time would come for them to be loosed we are not told. But God always knows the times and seasons (Acts 1:7), and He knew the exact time. When the command was given, these destroying angels were set free to bring this terrible judgment on a corrupt and rebellious world. Thus, they were overruled by God to accomplish His purpose. God is the One who is in control.

**16. And the number of the army of the horsemen:** ... the sum of the mounted forces under their control, —WADE ... of the regiments, —FNTN ... of the hosts of, —MNTG ... of the cavalrymen under their command, —NOLI ... of the troops of horseman, —KLST.

**[were] two hundred thousand thousand:** ... 200 million, —SEB ... two hundred millions, —WADE ... twenty thousand times ten thousand, —KLST ... twice ten thousand times ten thousand, —NORL ... two myriads of myriads, —RTHM.

**and I heard the number of them:** ... (I overheard the number), —SEB ... heard the sum, —WADE ... the number of them came to my ears, —BB.

**9:16.** When the four angels were loosed John saw troops of cavalry suddenly spread out before him in his vision, stretching as far as he could see. There were so many John obviously was not able to count them. But he heard their enormous number: two myriads of myriads. A Greek myriad was 10,000, so the total number was 200 million. These were entirely different from the demon locusts of the previous trumpet judgment. But they also seem to be demonic powers that were now to be used by the four angels to kill one-third of mankind. Nothing more is said about these four angels, however, but it is through the demonic hordes that they do their work. (Some do take them to be human armies.)

**17. And thus I saw the horses in the vision:** ... This is how the horses appeared in my vision, —KLST ... this was the aspect of, —WADE.

**and them that sat on them, having breastplates of fire, and of jacinth, and brimstone:** ... The men had pieces of iron over their chests ... blue like the sky, —NLTG ... and of those who were mounted upon them: ... the riders had corslets ... smoky-blue and sulphurous-yellow, —WADE ... They had fiery red, yellow, and blue armor, —SEB ... [the colour] of, —RTHM ... fiery breastplates, and purple and yellow, —FNTN ... that were fiery red, sapphire blue, and sulphur yellow, —ADAM ... hyacinth, Kliest ... fiery red, reddish blue, —NORL ... red as fire, dark blue as jacinth, and yellow as sulphur, —MNTG ... and glass and of burning stone, —BB.

**and the heads of the horses [were] as the heads of lions:** ... The horses' heads, —TNT ... looked like, —NLTG ... were like those of, —KLST.

**and out of their mouths issued fire and smoke and brimstone:** ... from their mouths came forth, —KLST ... and sulphur kept pouring out of their mouths, —WLMS ... belched from, —ADAM ... leaped from, —FNTN ... and a smell of burning, —BB.

**9:17.** John described what he saw as a vision. The Greek word *eidon* usually refers to something actually seen, however. Some take these descriptions to be highly symbolic. But all through the Book of Revelation where symbols are used they always represent something or someone very real.

The demonic hordes John saw are real, and the destruction they bring is real.

In describing what he saw in this vision John gave most of his attention to the horses, for they accomplished the destruction. The horses had riders, but they did not seem to be human. Their breastplates were fiery, and jacinth- or hyacinth-colored (bluish), and sulfurous. Because of its color the name was also given to a gem, a precious stone. It may signify how hard and impervious the breastplates were and how strongly they protected the riders. Brimstone is an old name for sulfur, which burns with a hot, blue flame and gives off a sulfur dioxide gas which is extremely unpleasant.

Some see the horses as having the same sort of breastplates. However, it seems better to see the riders as having them, with their colors like that of the fire, smoke, and sulfur that poured forth from the horses' mouths. (The Bible does not make clear whether all the horsemen had three-color breastplates, or whether some were fiery red, some smoky blue, and some sulfurous yellow.) The riders, however, did not seem to have weapons. Perhaps they simply guided the horses in such a way as to make them most effective in their destruction and judgment upon people.

The steeds upon which these creatures rode had bodies like horses but heads like lions, again emphasizing their strength, ferociousness, and destructiveness. Out of their mouths they continually spewed fire, and smoke, and sulfur. Thus, they must constantly generate these plagues within themselves. In this they seem to be embodiments of hell or the lake of fire itself.

**18. By these three was the third part of men killed:** ... By means of these three plagues, —FNTN ... A third of mankind was killed, —TNT ... third of the human race was killed by these three plagues of, —ADAM ... By these evils a third part of men was put to death, —BB.

**by the fire, and by the smoke, and by the brimstone, which issued out of their mouths:** ... in consequence of, —WADE ... by the sulphur that streamed out of, —BRKL ... and the burning smell which came out of their mouths, —BB ... that came forth from, —KLST ... which leaped from, —FNTN.

**9:18.** The fire, the smoke, and the sulfur that keep coming out of the mouths of the horses are all lethal. They become the demonic means by which one-third of mankind is killed. They are distinguished in this verse as three separate plagues, each bringing death to some. This may mean some of the horses spew out fire; some, smoke; and some, sulfurous gases. In the first woe rebellious sinners have been tortured by the demon locusts. Now in this second woe demonic horses cause some to be burned by the flames, some to be suffocated by the smoke, and some to be poisoned by the sulfur dioxide gas until the full third have been executed.

The use of fire, smoke, and sulfur is a reminder of God's judgment on Sodom and Gomorrah (Genesis 19:24, 28; cf. Jude 7). It should be a reminder that a world that is going the way of Sodom and that thinks the Bible is joking when it talks about judgment (Genesis 19:14) cannot escape the wrath of God.

**19. For their power is in their mouth:** ... Now the "authority" of these horses was in, *—ADAM* ... the licence of the horses, *—RTHM* ... The power of the horses is, *—NORL* ... seated in their mouths, *—WADE.*
**and in their tails:**
**for their tails [were] like unto serpents:** ... Their tails are like snakes, *—TCNT* ... resembled snakes, *—ADAM.*
**and had heads, and with them they do hurt:** ... possessing heads, *—FNTN* ... with heads by which they hurt, *—ADAM* ... like the heads ... and with them they could bite and kill, *—NLTG* ... with heads, and with them they work woe, *—MNTG* ... by means of which they make wounds, *—NORL* ... they give wounds, *—BB* ... with which they wounded people, *—BECK* ... with these they did harm, *—TNT* ... they caused harm, *—KLST* ... with these they inflict, *—WADE* ... doing injury, *—RTHM.*

**9:19.** The emphasis of this verse is, first, that the power of death is in the mouths of these horses with heads like lions. Second, they have power, not only to kill, but to torture, hurt, and damage. Like the locusts, they have power to hurt in their tails. But instead of being like scorpions, their tails are like snakes with heads that can give poisonous bites. Caird sees the snakes as evidence of the demonic nature of the horses and their relationship to Satan who is called "that old serpent" (12:9) (*Harper's New Testament Commentaries, Revelation,* p. 123).

Some surmise that this horde refers to the invasion of Rosh described in Ezekiel 38 and 39. It is the opinion of some that it will occur prior to the Great Tribulation. Others believe the Ezekiel passage refers to the Battle of Armageddon, recorded in 16:12-16. In either case, however, these are human armies, while those John saw are clearly demonic.

**20. And the rest of the men which were not killed by these plagues yet repented not of the works of their hands:** ... Yet in spite of this ... forsake what their hands had fashioned, *—WADE* ... the rest of humanity, *—BRKL* ... The rest of mankind ... still did not turn in repentance from what their hands had made, *—TNT* ... The men that were still living after these troubles were past, *—NLTG* ... the rest of the human race who were not killed in these plagues

didn't even then repent of, *—ADAM* ... the remainder of mankind who were not cut off by these ... failed to turn from the works of their own hands, *—FNTN* ... that escaped being killed by these, *—NORL* ... the rest of the people, who were not put to death by these evils, were not turned from, *—BB* ... not slain ... repented not out of, *—RTHM* ... They did not change their hearts, *—SEB* ... did not repent of the idols that their hands had made, *—KLST* ... of their misdeeds, *—NOLI.*

**that they should not worship devils:** ... kept on worshiping, *—NORL* ... would not turn away from worshiping demons, *—NLTG* ... They would not give up the worship of demons, *—MNTG* ... but went on giving worship to evil spirits, *—BB* ... or cease worshiping them, *—KLST.*
**and idols of gold, and silver, and brass:** ... They would not turn away from false gods made from, *—NLTG* ... images of, *—BB* ... copper, *—BECK* ... bronze, *—TNT.*
**and stone, and of wood:** ... stone and wooden idols, *—ADAM.*
**which neither can see, nor hear, nor walk:** ... None of these false gods can, *—NLTG* ... which have no power of, *—BB* ... nor have power to hear, *—KLGS* ... things that can, *—NORL.*

**9:20.** Evidently there was still opportunity to repent when these plagues came down on them, but the Bible states that the survivors did not do so. "Men" here (*anthrōpōn*) means all mankind, the population of the earth.

It is a sad commentary upon mankind that even the most horrible of judgments does not cause sinners to repent. Even though his country was devastated by 10 horrible plagues, the pharaoh of Egypt in Moses' time did not repent. Throughout history the same stubborn determination to cling to their sins has characterized unbelievers. Like a foolish driver who ignores the warning sign that a bridge has collapsed and speeds heedlessly on, people persist in the habits which are sure to destroy them, such as alcohol, tobacco, and drugs, not reckoning the cost.

God has done everything possible to cause men to turn to Him. He has sent faithful messengers to warn of impending doom. In one sense, even His judgments are acts of mercy, efforts to dissuade people from continuing their downward course. He does not take pleasure in the death of the wicked. His heart of love grieves over those who reject His call. Sin is a kind of insanity, for only the utterly foolish would persist in a course which will inevitably lead to eternal damnation.

John drew attention to the fact that the rest of mankind did not repent of the works of their hands, that is, man-made objects of worship. Like the Gentiles in Romans 1:21, 22, they persisted in their refusal to glorify the one true God, and they turn to idols. They are hardened rebels who want their own way at any cost. In fact, now that one-third of mankind is killed by this one judgment, they are more hardened than ever.

John specified demons at the head of the list of what people were worshiping, for all heathen worship of gods and goddesses is really the worship of demons (1 Corinthians 10:20, 21; Deuteronomy 32:17). This is true today in the humanistic and oriental philosophies that are spreading across the world. Then, like the Old Testament prophets, John condemned all images or idols that people worship or give homage to, no matter what type of material earthly craftsmen use to make them. (Brass is an old word for copper and copper alloys, especially bronze. Brass used today was unknown in Bible times.) Again, like the Old Testament prophets, John drew attention to the fact that these idols can neither see, nor hear, nor walk (Deuteronomy 4:28; Psalms 115:4-7; 135:15-18; Daniel 5:23). They are all "do nothing" gods. But whenever people reject the true God and put self on the throne, they soon turn to the worship of false gods.

**21. Neither repented they of their murders:** ... neither did they abandon, —FNTN ... Nor did they repent about, —ADAM ... These men were not sorry for their sins and would not turn away from all their killing, —NLTG ... change their hearts and turn away from, —EVRD ... They did not change their mind from, —KLGS ... And they had no regret for putting men to death, —BB.

**nor of their sorceries:** ... nor their poisonings, —FNTN ... or for their use of secret arts, —BB ... or their magic rituals, —ADAM ... evil magic, —EVRD ... and their witchcraft, —NLTG ... neither from their dope peddling, —KLGS.

**nor of their fornication:** ... immoralities, —NORL ... or for the evil desires of the flesh, —BB ... They would not stop their sex sins, —NLTG ... or their sexual immorality, —ADAM ... their sexual vice, —TNT.

**nor of their thefts:** ... or their robberies, —SEB ... or for taking the property of others, —BB ... and their stealing, —NLTG, —BECK.

**9:21.** As in Romans 1:24-32, those who turn away from the true God to a false worship soon turn away from righteousness and fall into all kinds of sin and immorality. Thus, those who do not repent of their false worship after the sixth trumpet, the second woe, do not repent of their murders, sorceries, immorality, and thefts either. Murders (willful, deliberate killings of individuals by individuals) apparently are so much on the increase that they characterize this generation. Sorceries probably include not only magic and the occult, but the use of magic potions, drugs, and other poisons as well. The heathen used drugs, especially hallucinatory drugs, to produce a false

sense of well-being, as well as a false religious ecstasy. Thus, the Bible uses fornication to include all kinds of false religious practices and satanic deceptions. "Fornication" here includes adultery, homosexuality, and all kinds of immoral sexual practices, whether practiced before or after marriage. Thefts accompany these things, because sooner or later the cost of these sins escalate.

## Chapter 10

**1. And I saw another mighty angel come down from heaven:** ... another strong angel, —KLST ... powerful, —EVRD ... descending out of, —RTHM ... from the sky, —WADE.

**clothed with a cloud:** ... clad with, —MNTG ... robed in, —FNTN ... dressed in, —EVRD ... arrayed, —RTHM ... covered with, —NLTG.

**and a rainbow [was] upon his head:** ... had a rainbow around, —NORL ... and an arch of coloured light was round, —BB ... He had many colors around his head, —NLTG ... encircled, —FNTN ... over, —RTHM.

**and his face [was] as it were the sun:** ... was like, —MNTG, —NORL.

**and his feet as pillars of fire:** ... his legs like, —KLST ... and his legs from the feet up were like fiery pillars, —ADAM ... like long flames, —NLTG ... like fiery columns, —WADE.

**10:1.** Just as there was an interlude between the sixth and seventh seals, there is one between the sixth and seventh trumpets, which seems to be preparatory for the seventh trumpet. The seventh trumpet is not blown until 11:15.

In the first of these intervening visions John saw another strong, mighty, powerful angel coming down out of heaven. He is "another" because he has not appeared on the scene before this time, but he is "another of the same kind" (Greek, *allos*), like those angels from heaven that have already been mentioned.

Because John saw this angel coming down from heaven, it appears that he saw this vision, not from heaven where he was caught up in 4:1, 2, but from the point of view of the earth. When this change took place, the Bible does not explain. Chapter 10:8 also indicates that John was now on earth and heard the voice from heaven.

The angel's description is unusual. He was wearing a cloud, a rainbow crowned his head, his face was as bright as the sun, and his feet were like columns of fire. Because the language is similar to the description of Jesus in chapter 1, and some of the phrases are used in other places of God, some theologians identify this angel as Jesus coming down to claim the earth as His possession (Barnhouse, p. 179). However, other theologians take a contrasting view. No one worships this angel. The manner in which he makes an oath by God in 10:6 would be appropriate for an angel, but not for Christ Jesus. Actually, the description of this angel simply draws attention to his heavenly glory. Beasley-Murray suggests John may be alluding to the angel Gabriel whose name can mean "the mighty one of God" (*New Century Bible, Revelation,* p. 170). The cloud and the bow signify God's faithfulness to His promises. The pillars of fire speak both of protection and judgment.

**2. And he had in his hand a little book open:** . . . he held, —*TNT* . . . holding . . . a very small, —*FNTN* . . . a little scroll, —*KLST* . . . he had a small scroll that was open, —*ADAM* . . . lying open, —*WADE*.
**and he set his right foot upon the sea:** . . . he put, —*BB* . . . he planted his, —*WADE* . . . he placed, —*TNT* . . . he stood with, —*KLGS*.
**and [his] left [foot] on the earth:** . . . land, —*MNTG, Rother-ham*.

**10:2.** The angel had in his hand a little book (document, scroll). This one was not fastened and had no seals. It had already been unrolled and was open in his hand. A different word in the Greek (*biblaridion*) indicates that this little book is not the book of chapter 5 that Jesus opened.

This angel is not only great in power but also great in size. As soon as he came down to earth he put his right foot on the land and his left foot on the sea. He and his message affect the whole world. There is a tremendous contrast here between the unrepentant rebels of chapter 9 and this glorious, colossal, and authoritative angel.

**3. And cried with a loud voice, as [when] a lion roareth:** . . . gave a loud cry, like the angry voice of a lion, —*BB* . . . in a loud tone, —*WADE* . . . he shouted with a great voice as a lion roaring, —*KLGS* . . . he shouted with a mighty voice that was like, —*ADAM* . . . just as a lion roars, —*KLST* . . . like the sound of, —*NLTG* . . . shouted as a lion roars, —*MNTG* . . . resembling the roaring, —*FNTN* . . . like the roar of a lion, —*NORL, —TNT*.
**and when he had cried, seven thunders uttered their voices:** . . . When he shouted, the seven thunders echoed his roar, —*NOLI* . . . at his cry the voices of the seven thunders were sounding, —*BB* . . . the seven peals of thunder spoke, —*TCNT* . . . spake with their own voices, —*RTHM* . . . gave forth their sound, —*KLST* . . . gave utterance, —*WADE*.

**10:3.** This mighty angel had a mighty voice, and he cried out with a deep, resonant sound that echoed loudly across the world like the roar of a lion. (Cf. Amos 3:8; Hosea 11:10 where God's voice is compared to that of a lion.) At the angel's shout, seven thunders uttered their own voices. (Cf. Psalm 29:3 where God's voice is like thunder.)

**4. And when the seven thunders had uttered their voices:** . . . had rumbled, —*WLMS* . . . had spoken, —*FNTN* . . . had sounded, —*NORL* . . . had given out

their voices, —*BB* . . . When the seven thunders spoke, —*KLGS*.
**I was about to write:** . . . I was ready, —*NORL* . . . write down what they had said, —*WADE* . . . I was about to put their words down, —*BB* . . . I began to write, —*KLGS*.
**and I heard a voice from heaven saying unto me:** . . . from the sky, —*MNTG* . . . came to my ears, —*BB* . . . which said, —*TNT*.
**Seal up those things which the seven thunders uttered:** . . . Keep secret, —*BECK, —NORL, —TCNT* . . . Lock up the things, —*NLTG* . . . Seal up the words that the seven thunders spoke, —*ADAM* . . . what the seven thunders have spoken, —*FNTN* . . . said, —*BB*.
**and write them not:** . . . don't write it down, —*BECK* . . . do not put them in writing, —*BB* . . . you may not write them down, —*ADAM* . . . do not write it, —*KLGS*.

**10:4.** The seven thunders did not just roar. They had an intelligible message. Since the seven seals and seven trumpets involve a sequence of events, it is reasonable to assume the thunders also reveal a sequence of events, perhaps a series of plagues giving further warning of worse judgment to come. In all other passages that mention thunder (8:5; 11:19; 16:18), they indicate the wrath and judgments of God. Barclay suggests that this refers back to the seven voices of God in Psalm 29:3-9 (*Daily Study Bible, Revelation,* 2:66). Both the angel's voice and the voice of the thunders, even apart from their message, speak to the world of God's power and majesty.

John had been given a command to write (1:19), and he was about to write what the thunders said when a voice out of heaven commanded him to seal up their messages and not write them down. The voice is not identified, but it speaks with divine authority. Some think it was the voice of God or Christ. The sealing seems to indicate a sense of urgency.

Sealing them means that "those things which the seven thunders uttered" contained a revelation God did not want the people to know. Daniel was told to seal the book until the time of the end (Daniel 12:4, 9). Though these messages were not to be revealed, the very fact that the Bible speaks about these seven thunders is important. It indicates that some things are going to happen during the end times that have not been revealed. This should make believers very careful not to be overly dogmatic about the sequence of events in the Book of Revelation. Certainly, it is not wise to speculate about the message of the seven thunders. Those who have done so have said many foolish and ridiculous things.

**5. And the angel which I saw stand upon the sea and upon the earth:** . . . the messenger whom I saw standing, —*KLGS* . . . saw stationed, —*FNTN* . . . taking his position, *−BB* . . . upon the land, *−MNTG* . . . upon the shore, *−WADE.*

**lifted up his hand to heaven:** . . . put up his right hand, *−BB* . . . raised his right hand to heaven, *−KLST, −KLGS, −WLMS* . . . heavenward, *−FNTN* . . . to the sky, *−ADAM.*

**10:5.** John accepted the words of the voice telling him not to write what the thunders said, and his attention turned back to the angel he saw standing on the sea and the earth. At this point the angel lifted his right hand toward heaven, not merely into the sky but with a gesture that declared he recognized God was on the throne. This was the gesture of one about to take an oath (Deuteronomy 32:40; Daniel 12:7). (The little book must have been in his left hand.)

**6. And sware by him that liveth for ever and ever:** . . . He vowed by the One, *−SEB* . . . He made a promise in the name of God, *−NLTG* . . . took his oath by him who is, *−BB* . . . living in the eternities of the eternities, *−FNTN.*

**who created heaven, and the things that therein are:** . . . who created the sky, *−NORL* . . . and whatever is in it, *−ADAM* . . . EVERYTHING IN IT, *−KLGS* . . . all that is in it, *−WMCK*

**and the earth, and the things that therein are:** . . . the earth . . . and everything in them, *−NORL* . . . and all that it contains, *−WLMS* . . . whatever is in it, *−ADAM.*

**and the sea, and the things which are therein:** . . . all that is in it, *−MNTG* . . . everything in them, *−TNT.*

**that there should be time no longer:** . . . He promised, *−NLTG* . . . There will be no more delay, *−BECK* . . . should be no more reckoning of time, *−LAMS* . . . should no longer intervene, *−FNTN* . . . no further respite, *−WADE* . . . no more waiting, *−BB.*

**10:6.** In a most solemn voice, it is certain, the angel swore his oath in the name of the One who lives for ever and ever, the Creator of everything in the universe, that is, in the name of God and the Lamb (4:10, 11; 5:13). By specifying the heaven and what is in it, the earth and what is in it, and the sea and what is in it, the angel contrasted the false worship of a rebellious unrepentant world mentioned in 9:20, 21. Their judgment is about to come because the eternal God and His Christ (who also shared in all God's work of creation, John 1:3), in their sovereign right of creation and by their eternal power, are in control. God had a plan in creation, as to sequence, balance, correspondence, and climax found in the days of creation as Genesis 1 shows. He also has a plan for redemption and to bring in the Kingdom, and He will faithfully carry it out to its final completion.

The content of the angel's oath was a message to all peoples and languages, whether they are on the sea or on the land. The angel wanted the whole world to know there would be no more delay before the seventh trumpet. The interlude was over. The final unfolding of God's purpose for the end of this age was about to take place. "Time" (*chronos*) usually means a period of time, but it may also mean "delay." The corresponding verb *chronizō* often means to delay or to delay by taking a long time in doing something. Thus, "delay" here is the proper meaning. The events that follow will rapidly come to pass. This may imply also that the time when it is possible for sinners to repent is getting very short.

Some have interpreted the angel's statement to mean that "time" as such is about to come to an end and a timeless eternity is about to begin. Actually, not enough is revealed about eternity to be sure whether it is timeless or not. The idea of a timeless eternity seems to have its origin in human philosophy rather than in the Bible. The New Testament often refers to the Church Age as "this age," and calls the future, "the age to come" (Mark 10:30; Luke 20:34, 35; Ephesians 1:21). Even the Greeks looked at eternity as the ages of the ages without end. This would seem to indicate some kind of progressive existence. Also, in the New Jerusalem the tree of life bears its fruit every month (22:2). Certainly, at the time the angel made this oath there was in view a considerable time ahead, for the thousand years of the Millennium are still in the future at this point.

**7. But in the days of the voice of the seventh angel:** . . . but that at the time when the seventh angel sends out his call, *−KLST* . . . is heard, *−WADE.*

**when he shall begin to sound:** . . . whensoever he may be on the point of, *−RTHM* . . . when he is ready to proclaim, *−FNTN* . . . at the sound of his trumpet, *−KLST* . . . is about to blow his trumpet, *−NORL* . . . when the sound of his horn is about to come, *−BB.*

**the mystery of God should be finished, as he hath declared to his servants the prophets:** . . . God's secret purpose, *−BECK* . . . then God's mysterious message, *−WLMS* . . . God's secret plan will be finished, *−SEB* . . . God will put His secret plan into action . . . as He told it to the early preachers He owned, *−NLTG* . . . then the Secret Purpose of God is brought to a conclusion, *−WADE* . . . will be accomplished, just as he proclaimed by his servants, *−KLST* . . . according to the Good News which he told unto his slaves, *−MNTG* . . . the secret of God will be completed, *−FNTN* . . . the foreordained dispensation of God would be fulfilled, *−NOLI* . . . as he declared the joyful message, *−RTHM* . . . as he announced to, *−TNT* . . . which He had told his servants the prophets, *−NORL.*

**10:7.** "But" indicates a strong contrast. Instead of any further delay, during the days of the sounding of the seventh trumpet (which was about to sound and which would continue sounding), the mystery of God, the good news about himself, which He announced to His servants the prophets, will be carried out, fulfilled, completed. Thus, the sounding of this trumpet will continue through a period of time, probably through the period of the outpouring of the seven bowls of God's wrath, the final defeat of the Antichrist, and the initiating of the millennial kingdom.

Some understand the "mystery of God" to mean salvation (Ladd, *Revelation,* p. 145). The simplest way to take it is that it refers to a new understanding of the nature, plan, and purpose of God. The word "mystery" is often used in the Bible of something that is not fully revealed in the Old Testament, but in New Testament times was made clear.

"Declared" or "announced" are the most common words in the New Testament for preaching the gospel, announcing the good news of salvation in Christ. This salvation includes the believer's entire inheritance which they are to receive in its fullness when Jesus comes to earth again. Therefore, it includes all the prophets foresaw, including the future Kingdom and even the new heaven and the new earth. As these things occur the complete fulfillment of the Old Testament prophecies will take place.

The prophets of the Old Testament made it clear that sin and corruption must be purged from the earth before God's kingdom can be established here. That the Kingdom must be brought in through judgment is therefore good news, for it means all that falls short of the glory of God in the present world system will be gone, replaced by the better things of the coming kingdom of Christ.

**8. And the voice which I heard from heaven spake unto me again, and said:** . . . I heard again, speaking, *—MNTG* . . . talking with me, *—RTHM* . . . then spoke to me once more, *—NORL* . . . And the voice came to me again from heaven, *—BB.*

**Go [and] take the little book which is open in the hand of the angel which standeth upon the sea and upon the earth:** . . . Withdraw! *—RTHM* . . . take the book opened in the hand of the messenger, *—KLGS* . . . take the open scroll that is in the hand of, *—ADAM* . . . take the scroll which lies open, *—TNT* . . . get the tiny scroll open in the hand of the messenger, *—CNDT* . . . containing a revelation of the future, *—WADE* . . . the angel who has his place on, *—BB* . . . whose feet are planted on both sea and land, *—PHLP* . . . stationed upon the sea, *—FNTN* . . . and on the land, *—NORL* . . . and on the dry land, *—KNOX.*

**10:8.** For the third time John heard a great voice from heaven. (Compare 4:1; 10:4.) This time he was commanded to go to the angel that was still standing with one foot on the sea and one on the earth and take the little book that was in the

angel's hand. Again it is clear John was now on earth, not in heaven.

There is much speculation about the contents of this little book. Some think it is the same as the book with the seven seals, though this is unlikely. Some take it as a message of woe to unbelievers. Some believe it is a message to the Church. Some think it is a further revelation of the events in chapters 11-19, or, perhaps, just the revelation given in chapter 11. Since it is in the hand of this mighty angel, it must be in some way representative of the Word and purposes of God.

**9. And I went unto the angel, and said unto him:** . . . So I went up to, *—AMPB* . . . So I went off toward, *—PHLP* . . . Going to the angel then, *—NORL* . . . I came away to the messenger, *—CNDT* . . . went to the messenger, saying to him, *—KLGS* . . . asking him, *—FNTN* . . . and told him, *—MNTG* . . . telling him to, *—HNSN, —KLST, —MRDK* . . . bidding him, *—KNOX.*

**Give me the little book:** . . . give me the little scroll, *—KLST, —TEV* . . . very little, *—FNTN* . . . tiny, *—CNDT.*

**And he said unto me, Take [it], and eat it up:** . . . Yes, take it, but eat it up, *—NORL* . . . Put it in your mouth, *—BB* . . . and devour its contents, *—WADE* . . . and swallow it, *—WMCK*

**and it shall make thy belly bitter:** . . . it will turn sour, *—TEV* . . . will be sour, *—EVRD, —SEB* . . . sour your stomach, *—TNT* . . . make your stomach sour, *—NLTG* . . . embitter, *—FNTN, —HNSN* . . . will be making your bowels bitter, *—CNDT* . . . you will find them painful to digest, *—WADE* . . . It will seem bitter in your stomach, *—NORL.*

**but it shall be in thy mouth sweet as honey:** . . . but in your mouth it will taste as sweet, *—ADAM* . . . though the absorbing of them will be as pleasant as eating honey, *—WADE* . . . but sweet as honey in your mouth, *—NORL, —PHLP.*

**10:9.** In obedience John went quickly to the great angel and asked for the little book. He was told to "eat it up," that is, completely. In his belly it would be bitter, but in his mouth it would be sweet as honey.

The meaning of eating the book is fairly obvious. It is similar to that of Ezekiel 2:8-3:3 where Ezekiel's call included the command to take and eat a book full of lamentation and mourning, yet in his mouth it was sweet. This pictured the fact that the prophet must digest the God-given message and make it part of him before going out to proclaim it to the people. Jeremiah spoke also of finding and eating God's Word and having it become the joy and rejoicing of his heart, which in the Hebrew would include his mind and innermost thoughts (Jeremiah 15:16). The psalmists also compared the teachings of God's Word to honey (Psalms 19:10; 119:103). Those whose hearts are open to receive God's Word find the Holy Spirit anointing it and bringing with it a sense of the nearness and presence of God that is indeed sweeter than honey. But believers too must eat it, digest it, and allow the Holy Spirit who inspired it to illuminate it and apply it to their own hearts and lives.

The Word of God is not all sweetness, however. The gospel speaks of both mercy and judgment. As Ezekiel proclaimed the Word of God, he had some bitter experiences. So did Jeremiah. At one time he felt like quitting, but the Word went beyond sweetness. It became like a burning fire shut up within his bones, and he could not stop giving it out (Jeremiah 20:8, 9). So also, the book John ate went beyond sweetness. It became bitter in his belly, that is, in his inner being. There was still a sweetness in receiving God's Word, and that continued in his mouth. The ingested Word affected him deeply. The belly the Bible often speaks of is the heart and the emotions.

The bitter feelings John experienced came after he digested the message and realized what he was required to proclaim. John, the apostle of love, would be telling out of a broken heart that even more terrible judgments must come. In this John experienced something of the broken heart of Jesus as He wept over Jerusalem, knowing what would happen to it and its people (Luke 19:41-44).

**10. And I took the little book:** ... the little scroll, —BRKL ... the very small book, —FNTN.

**out of the angel's hand:**

**and ate it up; and it was in my mouth sweet as honey:** ... and did as he said, —BB ... and devoured its contents, —WADE ... and ate it all, —WLMS ... It tasted sweet, —NORL.

**and as soon as I had eaten it, my belly was bitter:** ... when I had taken it, —BB ... But it turned bitter in my stomach, —NOLI ... my stomach was upset, —ET ... my stomach was in torture, —FNTN ... but it made my stomach sour after I had eaten it, —NLTG.

**10:10.** When John obeyed he found the book sweet in his mouth, but it turned bitter as soon as it was eaten, just as the angel had said it would. The anticipation of Christ's return and the establishment of His kingdom on earth is sweet. But the realization that the nations must be shattered like a potter's vessel (Psalm 2:9; Daniel 2:35, 44) is bitter. No one who has had the love of Christ fill his or her heart rejoices at the thought of judgment to come. God himself does not will that any should perish.

**11. And he said unto me, Thou must prophesy again before many peoples, and nations, and tongues, and kings:** ... And I am told, —WADE ... You are to give word again of what is coming in the future to, —BB ... You must tell what will happen again in front of ... families, —NLTG ... prophesy regarding, —RTHM ... And they said to me ... prophesy again

about, —KLST ... against races ... and many kings, —FNTN.

**10:11.** John's eating the little book was followed by a reaffirming of God's call to John to prophesy. There was a divine necessity laid on him to prophesy, not just for the seven churches of the Roman province of Asia, not just for the people of his own day and time, but for many peoples, nations, languages, and kings.

The meaning here is not necessarily that John was about to be sent personally before all these peoples and kings. The Greek *epi* with the dative case here can mean against, over, for, upon, as to, or about (cf. Blass and Debrunner, p. 123). Considering the period of time that immediately followed (since the book immediately became bitter), probably "against" is the best meaning. This fits the fact that the seven bowls were more complete judgments and have a wider effect over the world. Others understand it to mean "about" or "over" in a more general sense.

## Chapter 11

**1. And there was given me a reed like unto a rod:** ... like a measuring rod, —BRKL ... like a staff, —WLMS ... a long measuring stick, —SEB ... a wand, —WADE ... that is used to see how big things are, —NLTG.

**and the angel stood, saying:** ... Someone said, —NLTG ... with the message, —KLST ... and a voice said to me, —MNTG ... and I received the following command, —NOLI ... The orders followed, —NORL ... and was told, —WADE.

**Rise, and measure the temple of God, and the altar:** ... Go, —MNTG ... and take the measure of the house of God, —BB ... Measure God's temple sanctuary, —SEB ... measure for preservation, —WADE ... find out how big it is. Find out about the altar also, —NLTG.

**and them that worship therein:** ... See how many people are worshiping, —NLTG ... and count those worshiping in it, —BRKL ... those who worship there, —KLST, —NORL.

**11:1.** Chapters 10 through 14 include a series of interludes or parentheses that come before the seven last plagues introduced in chapter 15 and described in chapter 16. Chapter 11:1-13 continues the interlude or parenthesis between the sixth and seventh trumpet. It deals primarily with the two witnesses, whose identity has caused and still causes a great deal of controversy among Bible students.

First, John was given a large measuring rod like a shepherd's or traveler's staff. Since there were no chapter divisions in the original manuscripts, the verse seems to connect with the preceding one and suggests that it was given by the mighty angel who had just been talking to him. This same angel then told him to measure the temple proper, that is, the sanctuary containing the Holy Place and the Holy of Holies, the altar, and the worshipers (who would be in the Court of Israel and the Court of the Women). Measuring in the Bible is often a symbol of preparation either for destruction or preservation. Here preservation is indicated.

This can hardly be Herod's temple, for in fulfillment of Jesus' prophecy (Matthew 24:2), it was destroyed by the armies of Titus in A.D. 70, 25 years before the Book of Revelation was written. Rather, it indicates a temple built in Jerusalem in the time of the end, possibly after the Antichrist makes a covenant with the Jews. Ladd, however, sees that there are symbolic elements in this chapter and take the measuring of the temple, the altar, and the worshipers to be symbolic of God's preservation of the Jews (*Revelation*, pp. 150-152).

2. **But the court which is without the temple leave out, and measure it not:** . . . But omit, −*TCNT* . . . But exclude the court outside the temple from your measuring, −*KLST* . . . But do not take the measure of the space outside the house, −*BB* . . . Do not find out about the porch of the house, −*NLTG* . . . the outer court, −*FNTN* . . . the court within the temple, −*NORL* . . . omit, −*MNTG*.

**for it is given unto the Gentiles:** . . . given over, −*KLST* . . . given up to the heathen, −*TCNT* . . . given to the nations, −*FNTN* . . . the nations who do not know God, −*NLTG*.

**and the holy city shall they tread under foot forty [and] two months:** . . . and the holy town will be under their feet, −*BB* . . . they will trample over, −*NORL* . . . they shall frequent, −*FNTN* . . . have under their heels, −*WADE* . . . will walk over all the Holy City to wreck it, −*NLTG*.

**11:2.** John was commanded not to measure the court outside the temple proper, that is, the Court of the Gentiles. It was to be "cast out." God's holiness demands that these Gentiles be judged, not preserved and protected. "Gentiles" (*ethnesin*) is exactly the same word translated "nations" in the King James Version of 10:11. Thus, these are the rebel nations who did not repent when warned by the trumpet judgments (9:20, 21).

Though they are headed for judgment, the Gentile nations are given not only the Court of the Gentiles, but the Holy City, Jerusalem, to trample it down for 42 months, one-half of the 7-year period foretold in Daniel 9:27.

3. **And I will give [power] unto my two witnesses:** . . . will give permission, −*TCNT* . . . will give orders to, −*BB* . . . empower, −*KLST* . . . will give authority to, −*TNT* . . . my two men, −*NLTG*.

**and they shall prophesy a thousand two hundred [and] threescore days:** . . . they will continue teaching, −*TCNT* . . . who shall preach for a period

of, −*FNTN* . . . to be my spokesmen, −*KLST* . . . will be prophets for, −*BB* . . . who tell what they know, −*NLTG*.

**clothed in sackcloth:** . . . clad in, −*BRKL* . . . dressed in, −*TCNT* . . . hair-cloth, −*BB* . . . clothes made from the hair of animals, −*NLTG*.

**11:3.** Two witnesses appeared for a number of days that is equal to the 42 months. These are God's witnesses and prophesy clothed in sackcloth; that is, they speak for God. Sackcloth often indicates mourning. They are not vindictive. Though they bring further warnings of judgment, they do so with broken hearts.

There has been much speculation about the identity of these two witnesses. Kiddle sees them as two companies, two groups of Christians (*Moffatt New Testament Commentaries, Revelation,* pp. 193f.), but the description here seems too specific for anything but two individuals. In view of the statement that "it is appointed unto men once to die" (Hebrews 9:27), Morris sees them as Enoch and Elijah coming back to die since they escaped death (pp. 194f.). However, all who are in Christ and who are alive at His coming for the Church will be caught up to meet the Lord and will be changed. Their new bodies will be immortal and cannot die. Thus, Hebrews 9:27 is only a general statement that rules out a second chance after death (as well as any possibility of reincarnation).

Other suggestions are Moses and Elijah (Beasley-Murray, *New Century Bible, Revelation,* p. 183), or John the Baptist and Elijah, or God's continuing witness to Israel that climaxes in two great witnesses in this final period of great tribulation (Beckwith, p. 591).

4. **These are the two olive trees:** . . . These are symbolized by, −*KLST*.

**and the two candlesticks standing before the God of the earth:** . . . the two lampstands present before, −*KLST* . . . lights, −*BB* . . . lamps placed in the sight of, −*FNTN* . . . that stand before the Lord, −*NORL*.

**11:4.** In Zechariah chapter 4 the two olive trees are Zerubbabel the prince of David's line and Joshua the high priest. They are two anointed leaders who minister "not by might, nor by power, but by my Spirit, saith the Lord" (Zechariah 4:6). The two witnesses of Revelation are not the two witnesses of Zechariah 4, but by using this language John identified the two witnesses of verse 3 as Spirit-filled leaders.

Zechariah 4:2 also describes a golden lampstand supporting a large reservoir bowl that feeds oil into seven lamps. The two witnesses of 11:3 are both described as lampstands standing before the true God who is Lord over all the earth. When they prophesy they give from God such a fullness of light that no one can deny the truth and clarity of their message.

**5. And if any man will hurt them:**... When any one wishes, —MNTG... hates them and tries to hurt them, —NLTG... if anyone should want to harm them, —NORL... purposes to, —WADE... desires to harm them, —LAMS... would do them damage, —BB... attempts to injure, —FNTN.

**fire proceedeth out of their mouth:**... issues from, —FNTN... shoots out of, —ADAM... comes out of, —NORL.

**and devoureth their enemies:**... and consumes, —ADAM, —BECK... destroys, —NORL... puts an end to those who are working against them, —BB... their foes, —NOLI... kills those who try to hurt them, —NLTG.

**and if any man will hurt them, he must in this manner be killed:**... In just that way anyone who wishes to harm them will be killed, —KLST... has a desire to do them damage, —BB... wants to hurt them, in this way he must be killed, —ADAM... should wish to injure them, —FNTN... he must be killed just that way, —BRKL... is doomed to be killed, —NOLI... he would be killed in that way, —NORL.

**11:5.** If any person makes it his or her purpose to hurt or injure these witnesses in any way, fire goes out of their mouths and devours their enemies. This is the way God has ordained that those who want to hurt them must be killed. It probably means that all they have to do is speak the word, and the fire appears as if from their lips. Fear will be a strong part of their ministry, nullifying any opposition.

This reminds us of Elijah calling down fire from heaven on two groups, each with a captain and 50 men, sent to bring him before King Ahaziah (2 Kings 1:10, 12). But the power of both witnesses goes beyond what Elijah was able to do. The language actually may be more related to Jeremiah 5:14 where God said concerning Jeremiah, "Because ye (the people of Judah) speak this word (a word of treacherous rebellion against God and His prophets), behold, I will make my words in thy mouth fire, and this people wood, and it shall devour them." By this God meant the judgments Jeremiah prophesied would be carried out in spite of the false prophets who said they would not.

**6. These have power to shut heaven:**... They have authority to shut up the sky, —TNT... empowered to close up the sky, —KLST... possess the power to close up, —FNTN... to control the sky, —LAMS... to restrain the sky, —WADE... to keep the heaven shut, —BB.

**that it rain not in the days of their prophecy:**... so that it may not rain, —ADAM... so that no rain will fall during the days when they are prophesying, —NORL... during the days of their prophetic mission, —KLST... During the time they speak for God, —NLTG... in the days when they are

prophets, —BB... during the period of their preaching, —FNTN... while they are prophesying, —TNT.

**and have power over waters to turn them to blood:**... They have authority also over, —TNT... They can also turn water into blood, —NORL... to convert them into, —FNTN... to make them into, —BB... power to change all waters into, —NLTG.

**and to smite the earth with all plagues, as often as they will:**... to strike at will the earth with every kind of, —KLST... to scourge... as often as they may desire, —FNTN... with any Curse, —TCNT... They can send every kind of trouble to the earth whenever they want to, —NLTG... to send every sort of disease on the earth as their pleasure is, —BB... as oft soever as they may choose, —RTHM... as often as they please, —WADE.

**11:6.** Both witnesses have the power and authority to shut heaven to keep it from raining during the 1, 260 days of their ministry. Because Elijah prayed and it did not rain for the same period of 3 1/2 years (James 5:17), some take this as further evidence that one of the two witnesses is Elijah. There is a long tradition down through Church history of preachers and writers identifying one of the witnesses with Elijah, often connecting this with the prophecy of Malachi 4:5 where God said He would send Elijah "before the coming of the great and dreadful day of the Lord." Both witnesses have this power, and their authority seems to be even greater than Elijah's.

Like Moses, both witnesses have power and authority to turn the waters into blood and to smite the earth, that is, strike down the people of the earth, with plagues. On this basis, some believe the second witness must be Moses. Moses and Elijah did appear together on the Mount of Transfiguration, probably representing the Law and the Prophets. They spoke of Christ's "exodus," and it was evident they knew the importance of Christ's cross, resurrection, and ascension. Both of these witnesses have power and authority beyond that given to Moses. Both of them can strike the people of the earth with every plague as often as they wish. A great deal seems to be left to their will and judgment.

God has never left any period of history without a witness. Thus, He has His witnesses even during this time of great tribulation. Hardly anything in the Book of Revelation has stirred up more controversy than the identification of these two witnesses. Many have become very dogmatic about their choices of who they are. It is probably more important to recognize there are two of them, they work together, their agreement further establishes the truth of their prophetic warnings, and their message and the plagues they bring will leave the world without excuse.

**7. And when they shall have finished their testimony:** ... when they have completed their witnessing, —NORL ... concluded, —WADE ... come to the end of their witness, —BB ... giving their evidence, —SEB ... speaking for God, —NLTG.

**the beast that ascendeth out of the bottomless pit:** ... the wild animal ... will come up out of the hole without a bottom, —NLTG ... the monster that comes up, —BRKL ... arising, —KLST ... out of the great deep, —BB ... out of the abyss, —WLMS.

**shall make war against them:** ... make war on them, —NORL.

**and shall overcome them, and kill them:** ... will have power over them, —NLTG ... conquer them, and slay them, —FNTN ... put them to death, —BB.

**11:7.** The two witnesses will have the specified, limited time of 3 1/2 years to complete their testimony, that is, their prophetic witness as speakers for God. At the end of that time, the beast who will come up out of the abyss will make war with them, conquer them, and kill them.

It seems also that when their testimony is complete their power to bring fire on their enemies to devour them, and their power to smite the earth with all kinds of plagues will be at an end also. They will no longer have the protection they enjoyed for 3 1/2 years. The Book of Revelation does not go into detail and describe just how the beast will make war with them, but he will be victorious. It will appear that once again evil has triumphed. However, it will be only a temporary victory. The last pages of any book reveal who has really won.

"Beast" (*thērion*) is a term that means a wild animal. The Greek meaning is different from that of the living creatures of chapters 4 and 5. The use of the term is like that in Daniel 7, except the beastly nature in Daniel applies to empires, while here it applies to a person. This beast has not been mentioned up to this point, but the Bible seems to assume the readers will understand who he is. Some say he is the angel of the abyss, called Abaddon-Apollyon in 9:11. Walvoord believes he is Satan himself, forming a satanic trinity with the two beasts of chapter 13 (p. 181). Morris insists that though he comes up from the abyss, and thus derives his power from Satan, he is a man, undoubtedly the same as the first beast in chapter 13 (pp. 199-201). The same word is used of the beasts in chapter 13, which can be identified as the Antichrist and his false prophet. The first beast in chapter 13 can also be identified as the little horn of Daniel 7:8, 20, who makes war with the saints. Paul called him the man of lawlessness in 2 Thessalonians 2:3-10. He was foreshadowed by Antiochus Epiphanes (175- 163 B.C.) who sacrificed a pig in the temple and was the initial fulfillment of the little horn in Daniel 8:9-12, 23-25.

**8. And their dead bodies [shall lie] in the street of the great city:** ... Their corpses lay in the market place, —NOLI ... their lifeless bodies, —WLMS ... lie exposed, —SEB ... upon the broadway, Rother-ham ... in the open street of the great town, —BB ... in the Square, —WADE.

**which spiritually is called Sodom and Egypt:** ... called in prophecy, —KLST ... that is figuratively called, —WLMS ... whose mystical name is, —MNTG ... named, —FNTN.

**where also our Lord was crucified:** ... their Master, —FNTN ... was nailed to the cross, —SEB ... put to death on the cross, —BB.

**11:8.** To show their disrespect, the people will leave the bodies of the two witnesses exposed on the wide road or main street of the great city. The city is not named, but it is identified as a spiritual Sodom and Egypt, and is clearly identified as Jerusalem, because it is the city where our Lord was crucified.

Jerusalem is the great city, not because of its size or population, but because it has had a great and important place in the plan of God. Yet, at this time it has become a city of great sin. Because of its moral and spiritual degradation, Isaiah in his day had to call its rulers Sodom rulers and its people Gomorrah people (Isaiah 1:10). To the Jews Egypt represented the place of bondage. Here, it seems the people are under the slavery of sin. Some believe that at this time the Jews had already fled to a place in the wilderness, which some have identified as Petra, south of the Dead Sea in Edom.

It is significant that the bodies of these witnesses lie in the street of this city where their Lord was crucified. In a very real sense they now share in His sufferings.

**9. And they of the people and kindreds and tongues and nations shall see their dead bodies three days and an half:** ... persons from, —ADAM ... Men from, —KLST ... some will come from the peoples, tribes ... look at, —KLGS, —NORL ... from every people and from every family, —NLTG ... look upon, —MNTG ... shall gaze at their, —BRKL ... gazed at their corpses, —NOLI.

**and shall not suffer their dead bodies to be put in graves:** ... and refused to bury them, —NOLI ... refuse to let, —MNTG ... they will not allow the bodies to be entombed, —BRKL ... will not let anybody, —KLGS ... will not let them be buried, —NORL, —WLMS ... they will not allow their corpses, —TNT ... be put in the earth, —BB ... be laid in a sepulchre, —WADE ... into a tomb, —RTHM.

**11:9.** Some suppose that television will enable the people to see the bodies of these two witnesses lying in the wide street of the city. This may be so, but also many "out of" (*ek*) the various peoples, tribes, languages, and nations of the world will also come as representatives of the world's population. Some will perhaps already be in the city, either on business, or as emissaries stationed in the city. They crowd in around these dead bodies to view them. But they can do this for only 3 1/2 days, a very short period compared to the 3 1/2 years of their ministry.

During this period the people continue their despicable treatment and scorn of the two witnesses by refusing to allow their bodies to be placed in tombs. The differences between what happens to them and what took place at the crucifixion of Jesus are significant. Jesus alone was the sinless Lamb of God who shed His blood and died for our sins. No one can add anything to that. What God did for our redemption was finished on the cross. Then Jesus was placed in a tomb for 3 days and was raised for our justification.

10. **And they that dwell upon the earth shall rejoice over them, and make merry:** ... The inhabitants of the earth, *—TNT* ... those who then live here on earth will gloat over them, *—NORL* ... will have pleasure and delight over them, *—BB* ... will be very happy, *—SEB* ... because of the death of these two men, *—NLTG* ... will gloat over them and celebrate with feasts, *—WLMS* ... and be jubilant, *—ADAM* ... the inhabitants ... will also exult over them and make merry, *—FNTN.*

**and shall send gifts one to another:** ... exchange, *—NORL* ... send and receive gifts, *—KLGS* ... presents, *—FNTN* ... offerings, *—BB* ... They will do things to show they are happy, *—NLTG.*

**because these two prophets tormented them that dwelt on the earth:** ... these two spokesmen of God, *—KLST* ... these two men brought much trouble and suffering to the people, *—NLTG* ... were a source of, *—WADE* ... had been a torment to the inhabitants of, *—NORL* ... gave great trouble to all, *—BB* ... irritated the dwellers, *—FNTN* ... who troubled those living upon the earth, *—KLGS* ... to those who live in the land, *—ADAM.*

**11:10.** The news of the death of the two witnesses will undoubtedly be flashed around the world. All those dwelling on the earth will rejoice over them. They will gather together to make merry with great celebrations and feasting (and probably drinking). They will make it a time of sending gifts to one another as expressions of their gladness and joy. It will be like a great, worldwide, worldly, Christmas celebration but without Christ (compare also John 16:20 where Jesus said the world would rejoice at His death). Or, it might be considered like a devilish Feast of Purim where instead of rejoicing in what God had done to defeat the plans of the wicked Haman (Esther 9:19, 22), they will rejoice because they think God's representatives have been defeated forever. They will not know how short the period of their rejoicing will be.

All those who are still alive on the earth and who were tormented by these two prophets are glad because they are dead. The fact that they are called prophets here draws attention to their message which they spoke for God. Many of the people must have been tormented by the plagues. But the word "tormented" (*ebasanisan*) also includes the idea of mental torture, anguish, and harassment. God's message through the witness-prophets must have cut through to the hearts of many and made them feel the guilt of their sins. Now the witnesses were dead. The people felt relieved. The beast had won, and they undoubtedly took this to mean the message of the prophets was defeated as well, so they could rejoice, eat, drink, and be merry. They could go on in their wicked ways and feel comfortable about their godless lifestyle.

11. **And after three days and an half:** ... three and one-half days, *—NLTG.*

**the Spirit of life from God entered into them:** ... the breath of life, *—BRKL, —SEB* ... the living spirit ... will go into them, *—KLGS* ... from God came into them again, *—NORL.*

**and they stood upon their feet:** ... they got up on their feet, *—NORL.*

**and great fear fell upon them which saw them:** ... who watched them were terrified, *—BECK* ... then great terror, *—FNTN* ... great awe, *—WADE* ... and consternation seized those who saw them, *—WLMS* ... were seized by terror, *—NOLI* ... were very much afraid, *—NLTG* ... will fall upon those who see them, *—KLGS.*

**11:11.** After 3 1/2 days the celebration and rejoicing of the people left on earth will come to a sudden end. The Spirit of life from God will enter the bodies of the two witnesses, and they will stand up on their feet. The words for "spirit" and "breath" are the same in both Greek (*pneuma*) and Hebrew (*rûach*), thus, "The Spirit of life" is parallel to the "breath of life" God breathed on the first man He created (Genesis 2:7).

During the 3 1/2 days their bodies will lie in the broad street of Jerusalem, there may probably be those who will disfigure them. Decay will probably set in. But the Spirit of life is a creative, life-giving Spirit that comes out from God, full of His power. Thus, the two witnesses will be restored not only to life, but also to full health and vigor. They will be infused with spiritual life as well, and they will stand up full of the power of the Holy Spirit. What a witness to the fact that the victories of the beast will be shortlived! God is and always will be the Victor.

Those who observe their resurrection will be overwhelmed with a great fear, a sudden terror. Undoubtedly, they will remember the plagues and divine judgment brought by these two witnesses. They will suppose death and judgment will be their immediate portion. However, that part of the witness of these two prophets is over. More judgment is to come, but not through them.

**12. And they heard a great voice from heaven saying unto them:** ... Then the two men who told what they knew, *—NLTG* ... loud voice, *—NORL* ... heard a mighty voice from the sky, *—ADAM* ... calling to them, *—FNTN* ... came to their ears, *—BB* ... exclaiming, *—WADE* ... which said, *—TNT.*
**Come up hither:** ... Ascend, *—WADE* ... up here! *—KLST, —NORL, —TNT.*
**And they ascended up to heaven in a cloud:** ... went up to heaven on, *—MNTG* ... And they arose to the sky in, *—ADAM.*
**and their enemies beheld them:** ... saw them, *—TNT* ... All those who hated them watched them go, *—NLTG* ... in the view of their enemies, *—NORL* ... looked on as spectators, *—WLMS* ... watched them, *—FNTN, —MNTG* ... and were seen by those desiring their death, *—BB.*

**11:12.** The two witnesses will hear a great voice out of heaven calling them to come up, and immediately, while their enemies watch, they will go up to heaven in a cloud. It is probable that their enemies also will hear the voice, and it will gain their attention. But only the two witnesses ascend. The people who are left behind will only gaze into heaven as the disciples did when Jesus ascended (Acts 1:11).

What an important witness this will be! Though the details of the death and resurrection of the two witnesses are quite different from the death and resurrection of Jesus, the fact of their resurrection cannot help but remind their enemies of the resurrection of Jesus. Their ascension in a cloud will certainly remind them of the ascension of Jesus and of the prophecies of His return. Ever since the so-called period of Enlightenment of the 18th Century many have denied the supernatural and have proposed destructive critical theories intended to destroy the authority of the Bible. Many have denied that Jesus rose from the dead. But the people left in the world will not be able to deny the fact of this resurrection. Neither will they be able to deny this ascension, for the two witnesses will go up in full view of all, almost certainly seen worldwide on television. Their ascension will also connect their resurrection with the resurrection of Jesus. His resurrection is the guarantee of the resurrection, not only of these two witnesses, but of all believers. (See 1 Corinthians 15:3-57; John 11:25, 26.)

**13. And the same hour was there a great earthquake:** ... At that very moment, *—TNT* ... in that hour, *—MNTG* ... And during that very hour there was a

violent earthquake, *—ADAM* ... mighty, *—FNTN* ... the earth shook, *—NLTG* ... earthshock, *—BB.*
**and the tenth part of the city fell:** ... Ten percent of the city, *—SEB* ... the buildings of the city fell down, *—NLTG* ... causing the destruction of, *—NORL* ... came to destruction, *—BB.*
**and in the earthquake were slain of men seven thousand:** ... persons, *—KLST* ... were killed, *—NORL* ... came to their end, *—BB.*
**and the remnant were affrighted:** ... the survivors grew awe-stricken, *—BRKL* ... the rest were stricken with awe, *—WLMS* ... were in fear, *—BB* ... became over-awed, *—WADE* ... who were overcome with fright, *—KLST* ... were frightened, *—MNTG* ... became terrified, *—FNTN, —NORL.*
**and gave glory to the God of heaven:** ... and gave honor to, *—NLTG.*

**11:13.** In that hour, perhaps while the people are still watching the witnesses ascend, a great earthquake will destroy a 10th of the city and 7,000 people will be killed. This too is a reminder of the resurrection of Christ (Matthew 28:2). Those who are not killed will become terribly afraid. In their fear, probably realizing that greater judgments could come, they give glory to the God of heaven. "The God of heaven" is terminology used by Daniel and is parallel to the Lord of heaven and the Most High God in that book.

To give glory to God means to praise Him, recognizing His majesty, power, and might. At this point, at least, the rest of the people of the city will acknowledge that the power of God is greater than that of the beast who came out of the abyss. Perhaps some of those who give glory to God will turn to Him in genuine repentance, and become martyrs who refuse to take the mark of the beast. It is clear that the world as a whole does not repent, however, for they blaspheme God in the plagues that follow.

**14. The second woe is past:** ... The second horror is gone, *—SEB* ... Trouble, *—BB* ... is passed, *—MNTG* ... came to an end, *—NORL.*
**[and], behold, the third woe cometh quickly:** ... I warn you, *—KLST* ... But look, the third time of trouble is coming soon, *—NLTG* ... mark! the Third Woe comes shortly, *—WADE* ... But see, the third woe will soon cornel *—NORL* ... is speedily approaching, *—BRKL* ... soon to follow! *—MNTG, —TCNT* ... soon to come, *—WLMS.*

**11:14.** John, or the angel who spoke to him, now announced that the second woe was past. The third woe was about to come quickly, not immediately, but after a short time (as the Greek can mean, see *Bauer,* "*tachus*"). In fact, the third woe seems to be the seven vials or bowls of God's wrath which are introduced in chapter 15 and take place in chapter 16. In the intervening chapters a series of visions give further information about the events leading up to the final judgments of the tribulation period.

**15. And the seventh angel sounded:** ... at the sounding of, —BB ... blew the trumpet, —BRKL.

**and there were great voices in heaven, saying:** ... there ensued ... declaring,. —WADE ... there followed, —MNTG ... at which loud voices in heaven began to say, —NORL ... and strong shoutings, —BRKL.

**The kingdoms of this world are become [the kingdoms] of our Lord:** ... The reign over this world has passed to, —KLST ... The sovereignty of the world has come into the possession of our Lord, —WLMS.

**and of his Christ:** ... and His Messiah, —FNTN.

**and he shall reign for ever and ever:** ... and the Christ will reign, —WADE ... He will be the Leader, —NLTG ... He will have rule, —BB ... in the eternities of the eternities, —FNTN.

**11:15.** The seventh trumpet includes the seven bowls and the victory that follows. When it sounded John's attention was shifted back to the scene in heaven where he was taken in his vision in chapter 4. John heard loud voices in unison shouting out a victorious cry stating that the kingdoms of this world (the entire earth) have become the kingdom of our Lord and of His Christ (Jesus); and He shall reign as King into the ages of the ages, which is the Greek way of saying He will reign as King forever and forever, and His reign will never end. It will continue on through the Kingdom and into the new heavens and the new earth. Handel made this the theme of his masterpiece, "The Messiah."

It is evident also that the seventh trumpet of judgment is not the "last trump" of 1 Corinthians 15:52 and 1 Thessalonians 4:16. The trumpet that calls for the Rapture will be the last one to precede the wrath of God, and it is evident that wrath both precedes and follows this seventh trumpet of judgment.

The shout John heard was in anticipation of the coming victory. It is stated positively as if the total victory had already taken place. Yet verse 14 states that the third woe was yet to come. Thus, the shout of triumph was given in faith. Those in heaven saw the victory as good as won. Because God had said it, because God is in control, they could shout the victory in advance, giving honor to God the Father and His anointed Son.

**16. And the four and twenty elders, which sat before God on their seats:** ... Presbyters, who are seated, —WADE ... rulers, who are seated ... on their high seats, —BB ... in the sight of God, —FNTN ... on their thrones, —NORL ... who sat on the places given them in front, —NLTG.

**fell upon their faces, and worshipped God:** ... went down on their faces and gave worship, —BB ... fell to the ground, —NLTG ... paid homage, —FNTN ... prostrated themselves, —KLST ... and rendered, —WADE.

**11:16.** John, still in heaven as in chapter 4, saw for the eighth time the 24 elders who sat before God on their thrones. In response to the great shout of victory they fall prostrate on their faces before God and worship Him.

**17. Saying, We give thee thanks, O Lord God Almighty:** ... exclaiming, —BRKL ... give you praise ... Ruler of all, —BB ... the all-powerful One, —SEB ... Sovereign Supreme, —WADE.

**which art, and wast, and art to come:** ... whose name is 'He is,' —KLST ... who are and who were, —NORL.

**because thou hast taken to thee thy great power:** ... you have taken possession of, —KLST ... you have assumed your supreme authority and inaugurated your reign, —NOLI ... You are using Your great power, —NLTG.

**and hast reigned:** ... And begun to reign, —MNTG ... and didst become king, —RTHM ... and are sovereign, —NORL ... have begun to, —KLST ... and hast exercised Thy Rule, —WADE ... and are ruling your kingdom, —BB.

**11:17.** Their worship began with a song of thanksgiving, recognizing who God is. He is Lord, not only Lord and Master, but divine Lord. The Greek *kurios* is used for the divine name given in the Old Testament as YHWH, possibly pronounced Yahweh. (Modern writers combined the consonants of this personal name of God with the vowels from the Hebrew title meaning "Lord" and came up with a made-up name, Jehovah.) No one knows for sure how YHWH should be pronounced.

He is God, not only God, but literally "the God," that is, the one true God, the God of all.

He is Almighty, not only all-powerful, but literally "the Almighty." He is the Omnipotent One. The Greek word here is used in Jewish literature and in the New Testament only of God. It often translates two Hebrew titles of God: *tsevā'ôth* and *shaday*. As the Almighty He is *YHWH Tsevā'ôth*, the Lord of hosts. The hosts of heaven, the angels, all the forces in the universe, are under His supreme control. In the Psalms David points out again and again that God is the Creator and owner of the universe and therefore He is indeed the Lord of hosts. Psalm 24:1 draws attention to the fact that the earth is the Lord's. Verse 8 goes on to declare that He is strong and mighty, especially mighty in battle, and this identifies Him as the Lord of hosts.

He is also El Shaddai, God Almighty, the all-powerful, all-sufficient One. Shaddai is one of the oldest names of God, found in Genesis and often in Job. God made himself known in a special way to Abraham, Isaac, and Jacob, as El Shaddai. They experienced His power, His provision, His all-sufficiency. But those who are heirs of the same promise can experience His power and sufficiency too (Galatians 3:29). All the titles man can give still fall short of describing His glory and majesty.

He is also the One who continually is, who always was, and who is ever the coming One. There is no time limit to His eternal being. (Most early manuscripts leave out "the coming one" with the idea that they are looking at Him as having already come and entered in upon His reign.)

The 24 elders recognized that God has already taken His great power and now has begun to demonstrate His reign. The fact that judgments had begun showed He is indeed on the throne. The resurrection of the two witnesses showed He is in control, reigning in mighty power. No enemy will be able to stand against Him. The judgments about to come will accomplish His purposes and bring in the Kingdom. Christ on the throne has already shown himself to be King. In a sense He too is now beginning His reign over the kingdoms of this earth. Neither man, Satan, nor the Antichrist is really in control.

**18. And the nations were angry:** ... the heathen, —FNTN ... The nations raged, —BRKL, —MNTG ... grew, —WADE ... enraged, —WLMS ... had aroused themselves to anger, —KLST.

**and thy wrath is come:** ... Then the day of your anger, —KLST ... Now it is time for You to be angry with them, —NLTG ... came, —MNTG.

**and the time of the dead, that they should be judged:** ... the fitting Hour for, —WADE ... the time for the trying of the dead, —FNTN ... has come for the judging of the dead, —NORL ... It is time for the dead to stand in front of You and to be told they are guilty, —NLTG.

**and that thou shouldest give reward unto thy servants the prophets, and to the saints:** ... and for the regarding of Your servants, —NORL ... for the bestowal of the due reward upon, —WADE ... The time for rewarding thy slaves, —MNTG ... It is time for the workmen You own who are the early preachers and those who belong to you to get the pay that is coming to them, —NLTG ... the holy, —FNTN.

**and them that fear thy name, small and great:** ... those that reverence thee, —TCNT ... those who revere your name, —KLST ... those who hold in awe Thy Self-revelation both low and high, —WADE ... important people and those not important who honor, —NLTG.

**and shouldest destroy them which destroy the earth:** ... the time to destroy, —MNTG ... for the destroying of the destroyers, —NORL ... you will exterminate the exterminators, —NOLI ... the time of destruction for those who made the earth unclean, —BB ... who corrupt the earth, —LAMS ... who despoil the earth, —RTHM ... have made every kind of trouble on the earth, —NLTG.

**11:18.** The song of the 24 elders is also a song of anticipated victory covering the whole of the Day of the Lord without taking into account the time intervals in between some of the events. The elders see the anger of the nations, just as David foretold in Psalm 2:1-3. They see also the wrath of God, as the Old Testament prophets, Jesus, and the New Testament inspired writers did. They also see a time of judgment which will continue and find its final fulfillment in the consummation of God's plan (20:12-15). It is also a time of reward. The suffering servants of God will be both rewarded and avenged.

Those rewarded include the prophets. The reward is the salvation (including the inheritance) the prophets "inquired and searched diligently" about (1 Peter 1:10, 11). The saints are also rewarded. These must include all those dedicated servants of God of all ages. As Hebrews 11:39, 40 points out, the Old Testament saints, who "having obtained a good report through faith, received not the promise: God having provided some better thing for us, that they without us should not be made perfect."

To emphasize the fact that all the saints, that is, all who give themselves to the worship and service of the Lord, are included, they are further defined as all, whether small or great, who fear or reverence the Lord's name. All will be rewarded, including those who are saved and martyred during the Tribulation. God's judgments are sure. He keeps records of how people live. Those who have done wrong will be punished according to their deeds. Those who have served God faithfully will also be judged for their deeds and will receive a just reward.

The Lord's name stands for His character, nature, and person (including the three Persons in the Trinity). Those who destroy the earth include Satan and his followers. Satan is the great destroyer. He is also behind the greed that is polluting the atmosphere and physically destroying the earth.

**19. And the temple of God was opened in heaven:** ... God's house, —NLTG ... there was thrown open, —WADE ... the sanctuary, —FNTN ... God's temple in heaven was then thrown open, —NORL.

**and there was seen in his temple:** ... was seen inside, —MNTG ... within, —WADE ... in his house, —BB.

**the ark of his testament:** ... the ark containing, —NORL ... The special box which held the Old Way of Worship, —NLTG ... covenant, —FNTN, —LAMS ... agreement, —BB.

**and there were lightnings, and voices, and thunderings:** ... and there followed flashes of lightning, rumblings and thunder crashes, —NORL ... peals of thunder, —KLST.

**and an earthquake, and great hail:** ... and a terrific hailstorm, —BRKL ... a great hailstorm,

−LAMS, −NORL . . . and large hailstones, −KLST . . . a heavy hailstorm, −WADE.

**11:19.** Though the earthly temple in Jerusalem had been destroyed, and was not in existence when John saw these visions, the true temple of God has never been destroyed. It is eternal in the highest heaven where the throne of God is. In it is the ark of God's testament or covenant. This is not the ark of the old covenant that was in the tabernacle and in Solomon's Temple. That covenant was broken. Jeremiah prophesied that in the restoration that ark of the covenant would not come to mind or even be remembered (Jeremiah 3:16). In spite of later legends that say it was preserved, it was undoubtedly destroyed when Nebuchadnezzar destroyed Solomon's Temple in 586 B.C. When the temple was rebuilt the Holy of Holies remained empty and was empty in New Testament times. Consequently, this ark in the heavenly temple must be an ark symbolizing what Hebrews indicates is a new and better testament or covenant put into effect by the blood of Christ who "offered himself without spot to God" (Hebrews 8:6, 12; 9:11-14, 24-28).

Out from this heavenly temple and the true ark, and therefore from the presence of God, come thunderings, an earthquake, and great hail. These disturbances fall on the earth as indications of more judgment yet to come.

## Chapter 12

**1. And there appeared a great wonder in heaven:** . . . An illustrious portent then appeared, −BRKL . . . a great portent, −TCNT . . . a great miracle, −NOLI . . . a great sign, −RTHM . . . was seen, −MNTG, −WADE . . . appeared in the sky, −NORL.

**a woman clothed with the sun:** . . . clad, −FNTN . . . arrayed, −RTHM . . . enveloped in the sun, −NOLI . . . with the splendour of, −WADE.

**and the moon under her feet:** . . . beneath, −WADE.

**and upon her head a crown of twelve stars:** . . . a diadem, −MNTG . . . a circlet, −WADE.

**12:1.** John's attention has been on the events around the throne. But now comes an interlude where seven personages and four conflicts are introduced. First, in the heaven (which seems to mean in the sky, see verse 4) there appears a vision of a great wonder, actually, a sign pointing to an important truth by looking back in retrospect. The description of this sign is symbolic, but like the other symbols in the Book of Revelation, it represents a reality. What John saw was a woman clothed with the sun, standing on the moon, and having a crown of 12 stars on her head. In Psalm 104:1, 2, God is pictured as clothed with honor

and majesty, covering himself with light as with a garment. Also, Christ is the "Sun of righteousness," the light of the world (Malachi 4:2; John 8:12). But the language here is more reminiscent of Joseph's second dream where the sun was Jacob, the moon, Leah, and the 12 stars were the 12 sons of Jacob (Genesis 37:9). Thus, the woman most probably is Israel, pictured as a royal mother (cf. Isaiah 54:1; Galatians 4:26), with dominion over lesser things (standing on the moon), with the faithful among her 12 tribes (or their angel representatives) as majestic stars in her crown.

**2. And she being with child cried:** . . . was expecting to become a mother, −WADE . . . was pregnant, −BRKL . . . and screamed, −NOLI . . . cried out, −MNTG.

**travailing in birth, and pained to be delivered:** . . . and she cried out in anguish in giving birth to a child, −WLMS . . . because of the pain and anguish of childbirth, −KLST . . . and cried, agonized and tormented to bring forth, −FNTN . . . in the torturing pain of child-birth, −WADE . . . in agony in her birth-pangs, −NORL . . . in her pangs of birth, −NOLI.

**12:2.** The woman, with a child in her womb, was suffering severe birth pangs, crying out in agony, ready to give birth. Israel, that is, the godly remnant in Israel expecting the Messiah, finds that expectation bringing her through a long history of painful experiences (cf. Isaiah 26:17). The preparation for the first coming of Jesus (John 1:9) began long before Mary became the final representative of the godly women in Israel who hoped they might become the mother of the Messiah.

**3. And there appeared another wonder in heaven:** . . . another sign was seen, −FNTN . . . another Portent, −WADE . . . in the sky, −NORL.

**and behold a great red dragon:** . . . lo, −MNTG . . . Suddenly there appeared a huge, −KLST . . . a great fiery-red Dragon, −WADE . . . a monstrous red dragon, −NORL . . . a gigantic, fiery dragon, −BRKL.

**having seven heads and ten horns, and seven crowns upon his heads:** . . . possessing, −FNTN . . . diadems, −RTHM . . . there was a headband on each head, −NLTG.

**12:3.** Another wonder or sign appeared in heaven (or, in the sky). As a sign, it also pointed to something. What was seen was a great red dragon in the form of a serpent with 7 heads, 10 horns, and a crown or royal diadem on each of his heads. This serpent is not identified here, but in verse 9 he is called the devil, Satan. Just as the fiery red of the horse in 6:4 signified blood and death, so the fiery red of this serpent speaks of the fact that the devil is a murderer and has been a murderer from the beginning (John 8:44). In fact the conflict between Satan and the people of God really began back in the Garden of Eden. It was there the promise of victory over the old serpent was given (Genesis 3:15).

The seven heads symbolize, not wisdom, but satanic cunning. The 10 horns picture his claim of a completeness of power, a claim that is actually false, but which does mean he has been allowed to have power on earth (cf. Daniel 7:7, 24). Some see his power working through 10 kings. The seven crowns or royal diadems signify the completeness of authority over earth's kingdoms that he claims as "the god of this world" (2 Corinthians 4:4).

**4. And his tail drew the third part of the stars of heaven:** ... drags, —*RTHM* ... cut off a third of, —*LAMS* ... swept down, —*FNTN* ... was pulling, —*BB* ... swept away one third, —*NOLI* ... swept ... out of the sky, —*NORL*.

**and did cast them to the earth:** ... and dashed them down, —*MNTG*, —*WLMS* ... it hurled them, —*RTHM* ... threw them, —*FNTN* ... down on the earth, —*NORL*.

**and the dragon stood before the woman which was ready to be delivered:** ... This snake-like animal stood, —*NLTG* ... took his place, —*BB* ... took his stand in front of the woman who was about to give birth to a child, —*NORL* ... on the point of childbirth, —*KLST* ... placed himself before, —*FNTN* ... in the presence of, —*RTHM*.

**for to devour her child as soon as it was born:** ... in order that, —*NORL* ... when the birth had taken place he might put an end to her child, —*BB* ... so that when she was delivered, —*FNTN* ... waiting to eat her child, —*NLTG* ... that he might devour her son as soon as she had been delivered of him, —*KLST*.

**12:4.** With one sweep of the serpent's tail he drew (dragged away by force) a third of the stars of heaven and threw them down to the earth. Charles believes this is a look back at what Satan did when he first fell and drew a third of the angels with him (*International Critical Commentary, Revelation*, 1:320). Others take it simply as a terrible demonstration of his power (Walvoord, p. 189). This action is like that of the little horn (Antiochus Ephiphanes, Daniel 8:10). It is part of the symbolic "sign" of this vision. It shows the immensity of this serpent's strength and power. The struggle with Satan is no laughing matter.

The serpent who has all this power is then pictured as standing in front of the woman who was about to bear the child. He intends to devour the child as soon as it is born. He has known what this child would do ever since the promise of Genesis 3:15.

**5. And she brought forth a man child:** ... She gave birth to a Son, a Boy, —*BECK* ... She had a baby

boy, —*SEB* ... a masculine son, —*RTHM* ... an Infant, a male, —*WADE*.

**who was to rule all nations with a rod of iron:** ... destined to shepherd all nations with an iron staff, —*BRKL* ... to be the Leader of the world using a piece of iron, —*NLTG* ... with a scepter of iron, —*WLMS* ... an iron mace, —*WADE*.

**and her child was caught up unto God:** ... at once, —*WADE* ... was conveyed up towards, —*FNTN* ... was taken up to God, —*BB*.

**and [to] his throne:** ... towards, —*FNTN* ... and to his high seat, —*BB* ... the place where He sits, —*NLTG*.

**12:5.** The woman gave birth to a man-child, literally "a son, a male." In the opinion of this writer the apposition here of the words "son" and "male" shows that an individual is meant, not a group, not a company of people, not the Church, though the Church will share in the victory. The man-child represents Jesus. However, many scholars believe the man-child may represent the Church, for Christ was not raptured to escape the devil.

This son is identified as the one who is going to shepherd all the nations with a rod of iron. Chapter 2 (verses 26, 27) tells us Jesus will give power over the nations to the overcomers, not just to those of Thyatira but to all who remain faithful to the end. The overcomers will shepherd the nations with a rod of iron, breaking them in pieces as a potter's vessel is broken. But Jesus added that this is "as I received of my Father." In other words, the Father has appointed Jesus to be the One to shepherd the nations, shattering them in judgment with a rod of iron. But He will invite the faithful believers to share with Him in that victory. Psalm 2 also makes it clear that Jesus is the primary One whom God recognizes publicly as His Son and gives power over the nations. (See also 19:15.)

Satan would like to prevent that judgment by devouring the man-child who is born. He has shown that desire by his opposition to Israel down through the centuries, and finally by his attempts against Jesus during His life on earth. But Satan was thwarted in that desire by the Resurrection.

Some writers wonder why the life, ministry, death, and resurrection of Jesus are not mentioned in this picture. There is good reason for this. The focus of John's vision is not on salvation but on the judgment to come. That judgment is pictured in Daniel 2 as a shattering by a huge stone of the great image with the head of gold. It is assured because Jesus is now at the right hand of the Father at the throne, where He is waiting for that time when His enemies will be totally conquered (Hebrews 10:13).

**6. And the woman fled into the wilderness:** ... escaped into the wilds, —*WMCK* ... went in flight to the waste land, *−BB* ... ran away into the place where no people live, *−NLTG* ... into the desert, *−MNTG*.

**where she hath a place prepared of God:** ... she found, *−NORL* ... where God had a retreat, *−FNTN* ... a place of refuge, *−WADE* ... a place of safety made ready, *−WLMS*.

**that they should feed her there a thousand two hundred [and] threescore days:** ... He will care for her there, *−NLTG* ... where she could be fed, *−NORL* ... in which she is to be nourished, *−MNTG* ... they may be nourishing her, *−RTHM* ... that there she might be tended, *−WADE* ... so that there they may give her food, *−BB*.

**12:6.** John first saw the woman and the dragon or serpent as great signs in heaven. But the birth of the man-child took place on earth. In verse 6 the woman, Israel, is seen on earth. Just as the Old Testament often jumps from the first to the second comings of Christ in the same verse, so here the Book of Revelation leaps ahead to the end times where the woman, Israel, flees to the desert or wilderness. There she has a place already prepared for her by God. There she will be fed or nourished for 1, 260 days; that is, for 3 1/2 years of 360 days each, which seems to refer to the last half of the tribulation period. The repetition of this number in the Book of Revelation seems to mean the time is to be taken as literal rather than symbolic.

Some think the wilderness is symbolic of all the nations of the world, but the mention of a place prepared seems to mean something more specific. Some note that in Daniel 11:36-45, Edom Moab, and Ammon (the present country of Jordan) escape destruction. Isaiah 16:1-5 also speaks of Sela (now called Petra) and Moab. The Edomites thought Sela was impregnable, but Obadiah (verse 4) prophesied God would bring them down. Nabataean Arabs made Sela a mighty fortress again, and eventually the Romans conquered it. But it soon became lost to civilization, and its ruins were rediscovered in the early 1800's. Thus some think Petra might become the prepared place in the wilderness. The important thing, however, is not the location but the fact that wherever it is, God himself will see that the woman is nourished and protected there.

**7. And there was war in heaven:** ... Then war developed, *−BRKL* ... Now war broke out in heaven, *−NOLI*.

**Michael and his angels fought against the dragon:** ... had to fight, *−KLST* ... went out to fight against, *−NORL* ... went forth to war, *−MNTG* ... going out to the fight with the dragon, *−BB* ... making war with, *−RTHM* ... waging war, *−FNTN*.

**and the dragon fought and his angels:** ... his henchmen, *−NOLI* ... fought back, *−NORL* ... warred, *−WADE* ... made war, *−BB* ... so did his angels, *−KLST*.

**12:7.** The scene now shifts back to heaven to a great battle between Michael (whose name means "Who is like God?") and his angels on one side and the dragon or serpent and his angels on the other. It is Satan's last supreme effort to defeat God's angels and God's purpose and plan. Up to this time Satan and his demons have had principalities (spheres of influence) and have been powers (rulers of authority in the spirit world), as well as the rulers of the darkness of this world (world rulers of this darkness, the darkness of a sinful world). The Greek indicates, however, that the attack is launched by the archangel Michael. The forces of righteousness are in action. The rulership and dominion of the devil and his angels are about to come to an end.

**8. And prevailed not:** ... but they couldn't win, *−BECK* ... but they were defeated, *−KLST, −WLMS* ... but they were conquered, *−WMCK* ... But the dragon was not strong enough, *−SEB* ... but they failed, *−MNTG* ... they did not win, *−NORL* ... And they were overcome, *−BB*.

**neither was their place found any more in heaven:** ... and therefore there was no longer, *−NORL* ... and there was no room for them in heaven, *−WLMS* ... thrown out of heaven, *−NOLI*.

**12:8.** The dragon could not win this conflict with heaven. Satan has power, but his power cannot match the power of God's mighty chief angel Michael and his army of angels. As a result, whatever access Satan and his angels have had in heaven was no longer available. There was no more place for them in the heavenlies. Whatever happens of evil or wrong today, believers can be encouraged, for they know Satan is an enemy doomed to defeat.

**9. And the great dragon was cast out:** ... The snake-like animal, *−NLTG* ... thrown out, *−FNTN* ... was forced down, *−BB* ... thrown down, *−MNTG* ... That huge dragon ... was hurled down, *−KLST*.

**that old serpent, called the Devil:** ... This animal is, *−NLTG* ... he who is called, *−MNTG* ... the old snake, who is named the Evil One, *−BB* ... the Serpent of ancient days, *−WADE* ... the ancient, *−KLST, −RTHM*.

**and Satan, which deceiveth the whole world:** ... the Accuser, the deceiver of the whole of the habitable world, *−FNTN* ... the deceiver of all humanity, *−BRKL* ... he who leads the whole world astray, *−KLST* ... who seduces, *−WADE* ... by whom all the earth is turned from the right way, *−BB* ... He is the one who has fooled the whole world, *−NLTG* ... of all mankind, *−NOLI* ... the whole inhabited [earth], *−RTHM*.

**he was cast out into the earth:** ... was hurled, *−BECK, −WLMS* ... was thrown, *−FNTN* ... forced, *−BB*.

**and his angels were cast out with him:**...thrown down, *—MNTG*...hurled down with him, *—KLST.*

**12:9.** The great dragon or serpent, now called that old (ancient, from the beginning) serpent or snake because he was the one who tempted Eve in the Garden of Eden, is identified as "the Devil, and Satan." The basic meaning of *devil* is "slanderer." But even as the devil he is the "adversary," which is the meaning of the word "Satan." (See 1 Peter 5:8.) He is further identified as the deceiver who has led astray the whole inhabited world. He began his deceptions with Eve, and he is still trying to deceive both the world and the Church (2 Corinthians 11:3). But when Michael and his angels defeat him, he will be cast out into the earth and all his angels will be cast out with him.

When the 70 disciples returned to Jesus and told Him even the demons were subject to them, Jesus knew those minor victories were in anticipation of a greater victory to come, and He looked ahead to this time when Satan would fall from heaven. This defeat by Michael and his angels is, however, not Satan's final defeat. Though no longer able to enter the heavenlies, he still has power on earth. But his time will be short. As soon as the judgments of the bowls begin, all of them will follow in rapid succession, and after the final defeat of the Antichrist, Satan will be bound and cast into the abyss. Then the earth will be free from his temptations and evil schemes.

**10.** **And I heard a loud voice saying in heaven:**...a great voice, *—MNTG*...came to my ears, *—BB*...exclaiming, *—FNTN*...declaring, *—WADE.*

**Now is come salvation, and strength, and the kingdom of our God:**...Now the salvation which God brings about...his power and royalty, *—KLST*...Now have been secured the Victory and the Power and the Dominion, *—WADE*...Now God has saved from the penalty of sin! *—NLTG*...Just now came the salvation and the power, *—RTHM*...and Dominion of our God, *—TCNT.*

**and the power of his Christ:**...the authority of, *—WMCK*...and the sovereignty of His Christ, *—WLMS*...and the Rule of his Christ, *—TCNT*...of his Messiah, *—NOLI.*

**for the accuser of our brethren is cast down:**...have been established because the accuser of our brothers has been hurled down, *—KLST*...who kept accusing them day and night in the presence of our God, *—BRKL*...has been thrown out, *—BECK, —SEB*...who slandered our brethren, *—NOLI*...thrown down, *—MNTG.*

**which accused them before our God day and night:**...the one who kept accusing them, *—NORL.*

**12:10.** After Satan and his angels were cast out, John, still in heaven, heard a loud voice in heaven. The voice was the voice of those who are brothers to those tempted by Satan. Thus, it might be

the voice of the people of God who are there, or perhaps of the 24 elders as their representatives. Whoever they are, the casting out of Satan causes them to look ahead and rejoice in the final victory which is soon to come.

The voice proclaimed that now the salvation, mighty power, and kingdom or kingly rule of our God had come, even the authority and power of His Christ, His anointed One. Up to this point the accuser of our brothers had been accusing them before our God day and night. An example of this is in the first two chapters of Job where Satan accused Job of serving God for personal advantage. Zechariah 3:1-5 gives another picture of Satan resisting Joshua the high priest of the Jews who had returned from Babylon. He represented the returning Israel before God, but he was clothed in filthy, soiled garments. Satan was probably slandering them, saying their sins were too filthy to be forgiven. The Lord rebuked Satan then and restored and cleansed Joshua. But Satan's accusations are coming to an end. After the battle described in 12:7-9 he was cast down out of heaven. This victory was the assurance that nothing could now hinder the full carrying out of God's plan. It anticipates the establishment of God's kingdom and Christ's authority, which is already as good as done, even though some things must still take place before the earth sees Jesus bringing in its complete fulfillment.

**11.** **And they overcame him by the blood of the Lamb:**...Their victory was due to the sacrifice of, *—TCNT*...But they have defeated him, *—SEB*...they have conquered him, *—LAMS, —MNTG*...by means of, *—KLST.*

**and by the word of their testimony:**...through the might of their faith, *—NOLI*...by the fact of their evidence, *—FNTN*...by the preaching of the Word, *—NORL*...of their confession, *—WMCK*

**and they loved not their lives unto the death:**...For they preferred death to apostasy, *—NOLI*...because they did not cling to life but courted death, *—WLMS*...they did not spare themselves even to death, *—LAMS*...because they despised life even to the point of being willing to die, *—KLST*...and not by loving their own lives; they were willing to die, *—NORL*...in the face of death, *—BRKL*...better than death, *—FNTN.*

**12:11.** Verse 11 is a parenthesis to let us know that the believers, both men and women, were not defeated by Satan. Those brothers whom Satan continually accused before God had the secret of victory. They conquered Satan because the blood of the Lamb had power to defeat him and his accusations. Every victory over Satan down through the centuries, as well as the final victories in the end time, are all won because Jesus shed His blood and gave His life for us on the cross. The Cross and the Resurrection were really the greatest defeats of Satan. They guarantee victories for believers now as well as the great victory of their future resurrection and entrance into the joys of the Kingdom prepared for them by the Father (Matthew 25:34).

Believers are victorious over Satan also because of the word of their testimony. They do not allow anything or anyone to stop them from speaking for Christ. Furthermore, they do not love their own lives unto death. They are determined to serve Christ at any cost. Satan will try, but he cannot win this conflict with believers. Their faith conquers even their fear of death.

**12. Therefore rejoice, [ye] heavens, and ye that dwell in them:** ... So celebrate your triumph, —WLMS ... Exult therefore ... you who are sheltered in them! —FNTN.

**Woe to the inhabiters of the earth and of the sea!:** ... Woe to the earth and the sea! —MNTG ... to those who inhabit the land, —NORL.

**for the devil is come down unto you, having great wrath:** ... gone down, —MNTG ... descended to you, in great fury, —FNTN ... His fury is great, —NORL ... being very angry, —BB ... in a great rage, —KLST.

**because he knoweth that he hath but a short time:** ... having the knowledge, —BB ... knowing that the opportunity which he has is brief, —WADE ... only a little time left, —BECK ... his time is short, —FNTN, —NORL ... since he knows how brief is the time he has, —KLST.

**12:12.** The loud voice John heard in heaven then drew attention to the results of Satan's being cast out of heaven. It called on heaven and its inhabitants (including all those around the throne) to rejoice. The Greek speaks of the inhabitants "tenting" or "tabernacling" in heaven where God has His tabernacle (13:6). The inhabitants of heaven are thus "dwelling" with Him.

Because of the victory of Michael and his angels heaven will never again hear Satan's accusations against God's people. They are to rejoice also because God's kingly rule or power and Christ's authority was manifest in that victory. This means too that Christ, instead of giving so much of His attention to being the believers' advocate with the Father (1 John 2:1), will be looking to see the Father make His enemies His footstool as preparation for establishing the millennial kingdom.

But there is another result of Satan's being cast out of heaven. The voice continued with a pronouncement of woe to those inhabiting the earth and the sea. No one on earth, either on land or on the sea, will be able to escape the effects of what is to follow. The devil, the slanderous adversary,

has come down to them fuming with great fury, not only because he was cast out of heaven, but also because he knows he has but a short time to do anything on the earth. Satan is well aware of his final doom because he knows what is in the prophecies of the Bible. He knows God's Word is sure, but he remains a rebel.

Satan's activity thus continues through the remaining time of the tribulation period. He will be active through the Antichrist and his false prophet. God will also bring further judgments, pouring out His wrath on a world that is also rebelling.

**13. And when the dragon saw that he was cast unto the earth:** ... realised, —WADE ... was hurled down, —TCNT ... thrown, —FNTN ... down upon the earth, —NORL.

**he persecuted the woman which brought forth the man [child]:** ... he made cruel attacks on, —BB ... went in pursuit of the woman, —BRKL, —FNTN, —NOLI ... who had given birth to, —NORL ... the male Child, —WADE.

**12:13.** As soon as the dragon or serpent, the old devil, Satan, "saw he was cast unto the earth," he continued his conflict with Israel, pursuing the woman with renewed zeal. Jewish people have long known persecution, but the worst is yet to come. Many see this as the fulfillment of the time of Jacob's trouble prophesied in Jeremiah 30:7.

**14. And to the woman were given two wings of a great eagle:** ... was, however, supplied with, —FNTN ... the two pinions of, —WADE.

**that she might fly into the wilderness, into her place:** ... go in flight into the waste land, —BB ... to the desert, to her retreat, —FNTN ... to her dwelling, —KLST ... to her place of refuge, —WADE.

**where she is nourished for a time, and times, and half a time:** ... where she is tended, —WADE ... was fed, —FNTN ... given food, —BB ... where she was to get her meals for a time of twelve hundred and sixty days, —NORL ... during a period, —BRKL ... for three and a half years, —BECK ... during her foreordained period away from the presence of, —NOLI.

**from the face of the serpent:** ... far from, —KLST ... out of reach of, —WADE ... away from the presence of the serpent, —FNTN ... being safe from the snake, —NLTG ... of the snake, —BB.

**12:14.** Satan is not able to stop the woman from reaching the place God prepared for her in the wilderness, for she is given the two wings of a great eagle so she might fly there to be nourished for a time, times, and half a time; that is, 3 1/2 years.

The Book of Revelation is still using Old Testament language and typology. The two wings of the great eagle reflect the figure used in Exodus 19:4 where God told Israel, "I bare you on eagles' wings, and brought you unto myself." The eagle's wings are powerful, and the eagle's wings are symbolic of a mighty move of power. God did bring His people out of Egypt with a mighty move of His power, even though they had to walk. (See also Deuteronomy 32:10, 11; Isaiah 40:31.) Just what the two wings of the eagle mean, or what the eagle itself is here, may be controversial. However, it is clear that God will protect and preserve a godly remnant of His people.

That God will nourish the woman means He will provide her with food. The implication may be some supernatural provision of food God provided for Israel during their 40 years in the wilderness, or as He did for Elijah by the Brook Cherith.

The repetition of the facts given in verse 6 shows that verses 7 through 13 are a parenthesis. They did not have parentheses marks in Bible times, and this type of repetition is used to show that verse 14 takes up where verse 6 left off.

There, in the place God prepared for her, the woman is kept from the face or presence of the serpent or snake. The old devil that has caused so much trouble down through the centuries will not be able to touch her.

However, the "time, times, and half a time" according to Daniel 12:7 is the time the Antichrist will have dominion on the earth (cf. Daniel 7:25). The phraseology used here is in anticipation of the revelation of the Antichrist as the beast from the sea in the next chapter. Thus it is clear that his later efforts against Israel will be in vain.

**15. And the serpent cast out of his mouth water as a flood after the woman:** . . . sent out of, —BB . . . spit water from his mouth, —NLTG . . . poured water from, —MNTG . . . vomited water like a river, —BRKL . . . emitted from his mouth water, in volume like . . . behind the woman, —WADE.

**that he might cause her to be carried away of the flood:** . . . to drown the Woman, —NOLI . . . that she might be drowned in the stream, —FNTN . . . so that she might be taken away by the stream, —BB . . . to sweep her away with its torrent, —WLMS . . . with the flood, —NLTG.

**12:15.** Satan, that ancient serpent or snake, does not give up when he sees the woman fleeing. Out of his mouth he throws out water like a river with the intention of washing her away like a river in flood, to her destruction.

Some take the river to be a literal flood that is somehow sent into the wilderness in an attempt to drown the people. Even in desert areas of the Middle East sudden rainstorms can produce dangerous floods. As stated earlier, some students of the Bible have conjectured that the ancient rose-red city of Petra will be the place of refuge for God's people. The Siq, the mile-long narrow canyon

which leads into the valley which is the site of Petra, has been known to have sudden floods which have caused the death of people.

Since the water of the river comes out of the dragon's mouth, and since the word "dragon" has been identified in verse 9 as the ancient snake, the one who was in the Garden of Eden in the beginning, and further identified as the devil, even Satan, the word "dragon" is symbolic, and his mouth and the water can also be symbolic. Thus, others take the river to be a flood of false teachings, a "river of lies," coming from the mouth and out of the heart and mind of Satan. (Compare 2 Thessalonians 2:9-11.)

Still others point to the figure of a flood used in Jeremiah 46:8 and other passages where it represents an army. If this takes place when the Antichrist breaks his covenant with Israel and Israel flees, it would be logical for him to send a great army after them, just as Pharaoh sent after the Israelites when they left Egypt.

**16. And the earth helped the woman:** . . . gave help to, —NORL . . . came to the help of, —TNT . . . came to the rescue of, —MNTG.

**and the earth opened her mouth, and swallowed up the flood:** . . . came to her aid by opening, —KLST . . . with open mouth took up the river, —BB . . . caused a yawning chasm to open, and drank up, —WADE . . . It drank in the flood of water, —NLTG . . . swallowed the river, —WLMS . . . sucked up the river, —FNTN.

**which the dragon cast out of his mouth:** . . . that this snake-like animal spit, —NLTG . . . vomited from the mouth of, —FNTN . . . had emitted, —WADE . . . had disgorged from, —BRKL . . . had poured forth from his mouth, —MNTG . . . had sent out of his mouth, —TNT.

**12:16.** Satan's attempt to destroy the woman by a flood of water fails. "The earth helped the woman" by opening up its mouth and swallowing up the river. The language here is like that in Numbers 16:32, where God brought judgment on Korah and his company because of their rebellion and mutiny against God's chosen leaders, Moses and Aaron. There it is recorded that "the earth opened her mouth, and swallowed them up." Several other passages emphasize the supernatural character of this judgment as an act of God even though God used the earth to do it (Deuteronomy 11:6, 7; Psalm 106:17). Thus, we can take it that God is the true cause of the earth's opening its mouth. An earthquake can often cause wide and deep cracks to appear in the earth's surface, some extensive enough to absorb a large stream or at least divert its course, so the threat of a flood is nullified.

**17. And the dragon was wroth with the woman:** . . . was enraged at, —TCNT, —LAMS, —NORL . . . furious,

—FNTN . . . was angered at, —KLST . . . became angry, —TNT . . . was very angry with, —NLTG . . . on account of her escape, —WADE.

**and went to make war with the remnant of her seed:** . . . He went off to fight with, —NLTG . . . to wage war against, —WADE . . . went away . . . upon the rest of her children, —MNTG . . . with the rest of her descendants, —WLMS . . . of her offspring, —WMCK

**which keep the commandments of God:** . . . kept God's commandments, —TNT . . . those who keep, —ADAM . . . as many as keep God's commandments, —NORL . . . They are the ones who obey the Laws, —NLTG . . . who keep in mind, —WADE . . . keep the orders of, —BB.

**and have the testimony of Jesus Christ:** . . . and adhere to, —BRKL . . . and hold fast, —MNTG . . . and are faithful to the teachings of, —NLTG . . . and cling to the evidence, —FNTN . . . to bear testimony to Jesus, —WLMS . . . preserve the testimony borne thereto by Jesus, —WADE . . . and who have a testimony for, —ADAM . . . and possessed the testimony given by, —TNT . . . and profess the religion of Jesus, —NOLI . . . and as have the Gospel of Jesus Christ, —NORL . . . and the witness of Jesus, —BB . . . concerning Jesus, —KLST.

**12:17.** What the earth did in swallowing up the river made the dragon or serpent even more angry with the woman. Since he could not touch her in the place God had prepared for her, he went away from her and proceeded to make war with the rest of her seed. Her seed is identified as those who continually keep the commandments of God and keep on holding to the testimony or witness of Jesus Christ. (The commandments of God here are the witness that Jesus Christ gave.) This indicates that those of Israel who accept Christ as their true Messiah, Saviour, and Lord, and obey Him during this period will be persecuted by Satan as well as by the Antichrist and his followers. They are a godly remnant who may be martyred during this period, or survive until the Kingdom is established.

**12:18.** Many printed Greek New Testaments make this verse part of chapter 12, i.e., "And I stood upon the sand of the sea." Most ancient manuscripts have "I stood," meaning John stood on the sand of the sea, indicating a change in his location. This would connect this verse with 13:1, and on this basis this verse is part of 13:1 in most English versions. Other ancient manuscripts have "he stood," meaning the serpent, Satan, stood on the sand of the sea in anticipation of what was about to happen, but perhaps connecting this with his warfare with the rest of the woman's seed.

## Chapter 13

**1. And I stood upon the sand of the sea:** . . . And he stationed himself upon, —FNTN . . . he stood on the

sand by the sea, —KLST . . . took his place on, —BB . . . the seashore, —NORL, —TNT . . . on the sea strand, —WADE.

**and saw a beast rise up out of the sea:** . . . a wild beast, —FNTN . . . a wild animal, —NLTG . . . saw an animal coming up, —BECK . . . coming out of, —KLST . . . out of the waves, —NOLI.

**having seven heads and ten horns:** . . . which had, —WADE.

**and upon his horns ten crowns:** . . . with ten diadems on his horns, —WLMS . . . with a headband on each horn, —NLTG.

**and upon his heads the name of blasphemy:** . . . There were names on each head that spoke bad words against God, —NLTG . . . on his heads were blasphemous names, —BECK . . . a blasphemous name on each head, —NOLI . . . unholy names, —BB . . . titles, —MNTG . . . there was a filthy name on each, —SEB.

**13:1.** This chapter is still part of the interlude between the seven trumpets and seven seals. It begins to describe the reign of the Antichrist. John, either while standing on the sand of the seashore, or looking at a vision seen while he was in heaven, saw a wild animal rise up out of the sea. The "sea" represents the people or nations of the world (cf. 17:15). The beast represents the Antichrist and his government, the world government described in Daniel 7 in its final form. It is the same government pictured by the little horn in Daniel 7:8, 24, 25. This beast, like the great red serpent of chapter 12:3, has 7 heads and 10 horns. But instead of having the crowns on its heads, it has 10 crowns or royal diadems on its 10 horns. On its heads, instead, are the name (or names) of blasphemy; that is, a blasphemous name.

This name is not given here, but it is undoubtedly a name claiming deity or divinity. Though John does not use the name "Antichrist" here, the Greek *anti* primarily means "instead of." He is Satan's substitute for the real Anointed One of God. In other words, the Antichrist will not admit he is the Antichrist. He will claim that he is the real Christ. He may say, "Forget about Jesus, I am the one you are looking for." Or, he may say, "I am the fulfillment of a long line of anointed ones including Buddha, Muhammad, and the founders of all the other false religions of the world." In either case, in God's eyes that is blasphemy.

**2. And the beast which I saw was like unto a leopard:** . . . the wild beast, —LAMS . . . of my vision, —KLST . . . beast before me, —NORL . . . The wild animal I saw was covered with spots, —NLTG . . . resembled, —BRKL.

**and his feet were as [the feet] of a bear:** . . . It had feet, —NLTG . . . with feet like those of, —NORL.

**and his mouth as the mouth of a lion:**

**and the dragon gave him his power:** . . . gave this wild animal, —NLTG . . . also invested him with his power, —FNTN . . . gave to it its own power, —KLST.

**and his seat:** ... his throne, —BECK, —NORL ... and his own place to sit as king, —NLTG.

**and great authority:** ... and a wide-spread dominion, —TCNT ... his sovereignty, —NOLI ... extensive authority, —WADE ... given much power, —NLTG.

**13:2.** The wild animal John saw was a strange combination of all the four beasts in Daniel's dream (Daniel 7). It looked like a leopard, yet its feet looked like a bear's feet, and its mouth was like a lion's mouth. So the beast seems to represent not only the Antichrist's kingdom but the Antichrist himself. He represents a very real and terrible person whose cruelty and destructiveness is like a wild animal's. His purpose will be to gain religious, political, and economic power over the entire world when he appears in the tribulation period (cf. Daniel 7:4-6; 8:25; 9:27; Revelation 17:13).

The dragon or serpent was ready for him and gave him his satanic power, his throne, and his authority. Thus, he is Satan's representative on earth to do Satan's work.

**3. And I saw one of his heads as it were wounded to death:** ... His mortal wound, —BRKL ... one of the heads received a fatal wound, —KLST ... One of the heads of the wild animal looked as if it had been killed, —NLTG ... seemed to have been, —MNTG ... as I saw it, had been, —NORL ... appearing as though it had been mortally stricken, —WADE ... as though mortally wounded, —LAMS ... given a death-wound, —BB.

**and his deadly wound was healed:** ... but when the fatal wound, —KLST ... But this mortal wound healed, —NORL ... But the bad cut given to kill him was healed, —NLTG ... had been cured, —WADE ... was made well, —BB.

**and all the world wondered after the beast:** ... The whole world was amazed as it followed the animal, —BECK ... was surprised and wondered about this, —NLTG ... so amazed that they followed the wild beast, —WLMS ... followed after the beast in adoration, —NORL ... following ... wondering, —MNTG ... in admiration, —KLST ... admired the Monster, —NOLI ... the wild animal, —SEB.

**13:3.** It seems God will permit Satan to give the appearance of duplicating the Resurrection. One of the heads of the beast seemed to be mortally wounded. But its mortal wound was healed. Then the whole world was full of wonder, indicating they venerated or even worshiped the beast.

Earlier God revealed to the apostle Paul that the Antichrist's coming would be according to the working or energizing of Satan in all sorts of deceptive deeds of power, deceptive signs, and deceptive wonders, but all will be lies (2 Thessalonians 2:9).

Satan has power, but he is a liar and the father or source and promoter of lies (John 8:44). Everything he does is saturated with lies. His purposes

are false. His methods are wrong. But he will use these miracles and lying wonders to gain the attention of the people. As a result the people who do not know the Antichrist is doomed will think his coming is supernatural.

In the second chapter of 2 Thessalonians Paul made it clear that those who are convinced by Satan's deceptive miracles are first of all those who themselves are involved in every kind of wicked deception, especially the deception and seduction that comes from seeking wealth (cf. Matthew 13:22), the deceitfulness of sin (cf. Hebrews 3:13), reveling in deceptive pleasures which involve sin (cf. 2 Peter 2:13), and every kind of deceitful lust or deceptive desire (cf. Ephesians 4:22). Satan's deceptive miracle here (13:3) will be accepted by those who are already perishing, lost, gone astray, and already on the broad road leading to destruction (cf. Matthew 7:13).

Strong satanic delusion today is already leading many to believe homosexuality, premarital sex, abortion, adultery, and many other sins are normal and even desirable patterns of life. The Bible warns that those who practice such things will not inherit the kingdom of God (Galatians 5:19-21). Those who listen to Satan's lies now will become easy prey to his deceptive miracles, miracles intended to make the world believe the Antichrist is the real Christ. They will be filled with amazement and will acclaim him to be worthy of worship.

**4. And they worshipped the dragon:** ... Men did homage to the dragon, —NORL ... gave worship to, —BB.

**which gave power unto the beast:** ... he had transferred his authority to the beast, —FNTN ... because he had given authority to, —NORL.

**and they worshipped the beast, saying:** ... worshiped the beast, too, and kept on saying, —NORL.

**Who [is] like unto the beast?:** ... Who matches the beast, —BRKL ... is a match for this beast? —NORL ... Who is equal, —FNTN ... Who can compare with, —TCNT.

**who is able to make war with him?:** ... is there anyone who can fight with him? —BECK ... Who could fight it? —SEB ... who can fight against it? —KLST ... who can go to war against him? —NORL ... wage war, —FNTN.

**13:4.** In worshiping the beast people really will be worshiping the serpent who has given his power and authority to the beast. They will be involved in Satan worship. Actually, their words of praise do not mention Satan but exclaim, "Who is like the beast?" These words are similar to the Old Testament cry of Israel and the prophets who said, "Who is like the Lord?" (Exodus 15:11; Micah 7:18). They will not only be worshiping the beast, they will be making him their supreme god.

Their exclamation, "Who is able to make war with him?" indicates their belief that the beast is invincible but also greater than any god, even than the true God. The world will recognize the power of the Antichrist, both material and spiritual. They will be captivated by his personality and his apparent wisdom and ability.

**5. And there was given unto him a mouth speaking great things and blasphemies:** . . . a mouth with power to boast mightily and to blaspheme, *—NORL* . . . permitted to utter loud boasts, *—MNTG* . . . to utter arrogant blasphemies, *—NOLI* . . . to utter haughty words, *—KLST* . . . speaking boastfully and blasphemously, *—FNTN.*
    **and power was given unto him:** . . . endowed with authority, *—FNTN* . . . and also freedom to exercise authority, *—NORL.*
    **to continue forty [and] two months:** . . . to carry on its activities, *—KLST* . . . to work for, *—FNTN.*

**13:5.** "A mouth speaking great things" means eloquence. Note it is *given* to him. Back of all the Antichrist says will be Satan himself. He will use this power to exalt himself, but it will last only 42 months, evidently the last 3 1/2 years of the Tribulation. Apparently the Antichrist will gain power at the beginning of the Tribulation, make a covenant with Israel (Daniel 9:27), and gain control over 10 nations. But it will not be until the middle of the 7 years that he will break that covenant, demand worship, and take control over all the nations of the world. He will then reign for 3 1/2 years before Jesus comes again in flaming fire and in triumph as described in 2 Thessalonians chapter 1 and Revelation chapter 19.

Daniel's vision recorded in Daniel 7:8, 20, 25 describes the little horn which will eventually arise from the fourth beast and represent the Antichrist as having "eyes like the eyes of man, and a mouth speaking great things." Then it is explained to Daniel that "he shall speak great words against the Most High, and shall wear out the saints of the Most High." (See commentary on 13:7.)

**6. And he opened his mouth in blasphemy against God:** . . . He did so, *—NORL* . . . to slander God, *—BECK.*
    **to blaspheme his name:** . . . to curse God's name, *—NORL.*
    **and his tabernacle:** . . . His home, *—BECK* . . . and his dwelling place, *—LAMS* . . . His tent, *—FNTN* . . . and His heaven, *—NORL* . . . and the place of his glory, *—WMCK*
    **and them that dwell in heaven:** . . . those sheltered, *—FNTN* . . . those who dwell therein, *—NORL* . . . who live in his tabernacle in heaven, *—MNTG.*

**13:6.** The blasphemies of the beast are further defined as against God, against God's name and His heavenly tabernacle, and against those

dwelling with Him in heaven. Blaspheming God's name means he will speak against His nature and character, denying God's holiness, righteousness, faithfulness, love, mercy, and grace.

Blaspheming the heavenly tabernacle means he will deny that God is manifesting His glory in the Holy of Holies of heaven. It also means he will deny that the blood of Christ was presented before God once for all as the full atonement for our sins.

Blaspheming those dwelling with Him in heaven means he will defame the saints of all ages. He will mock their faithfulness to God and their dedication to His service.

All of this blasphemy will be the climax of the blasphemies inspired by the spirit of the Antichrist that is already in this world. John's first and second epistles do not deny that there will be a future Antichrist. But they recognize there are many antichrists in the world already, all of whom deny Jesus is God manifest in the flesh. They include all the cults as well as the self-styled "liberals" who deny what the Bible reveals about the divine-human nature of Jesus.

**7. And it was given unto him to make war with the saints:** . . . He was also permitted, *—NORL* . . . He was also allowed to wage war against, *—NOLI* . . . It was empowered to, *—KLST* . . . was allowed to fight against the people who belong to God, *—NLTG* . . . upon, *—MNTG* . . . with the holy, *—FNTN* . . . against God's Hallowed People, *—WADE.*
    **and to overcome them:** . . . and to conquer them, *—TCNT* . . . had power to win over them, *—NLTG.*
    **and power was given him:** . . . he was allowed authority, *—WADE* . . . there was given him authority, *—MNTG* . . . authority was granted, *—FNTN* . . . This authority given him extended to, *—NORL.*
    **over all kindreds, and tongues, and nations:** . . . every tribe, people, language, and nation, *—BECK, —WADE* . . . family and every group of people, *—NLTG.*

**13:7.** The beast will also be granted permission to make war with the saints and to conquer them. Power and authority will also be granted to the beast over every tribe, language, and nation. In each of these statements it is emphasized that the beast will not be acting on his own authority. He will be able to accomplish only what is given him to do. In this he will first of all be the agent of the old serpent, Satan, carrying out his devilish plans. But Satan will be able to go only as far as God allows him to go. Ultimately, God will have the final word.

It is evident from Daniel 7:3-8, 19-25; 11:45; and 12:6, 7 that the Antichrist will gain this control of all nations at or near the beginning of the last 3 1/2 years of the Tribulation.

Daniel 7:21 refers to the way the Antichrist will make war with the saints and prevail against them, meaning they will be killed. The saints here seem to be those who will reject the new religion controlled and made popular by the Antichrist. They will remain faithful to the Word of God and to the Lord Jesus Christ even in the face of persecution and death. The beast will conquer them, but this does not mean their faith is destroyed. Rather, most, if not all of them, will be added to the company of martyrs. Thus, they are the real overcomers, for their reward will be great.

The authority and rule of the beast will be extended, not just to the 10 nations he first controls, but to the entire world.

**8. And all that dwell upon the earth shall worship him:** ... each one, —*MNTG* ... the whole of the inhabitants ... shall pay him homage, —*FNTN* ... All the inhabitants of the earth will bow down to him, —*NORL* ... must render worship to him, —*WADE.*
**whose names are not written in the book of life of the Lamb:** ... all except those whose names had been written, —*NORL* ... everyone whose name has not been from the first in the book, —*BB* ... not recorded in, —*BRKL* ... is unrecorded in the Little Lamb's Book, —*WADE.*
**slain from the foundation of the world:** ... who was put to death, —*BB* ... was sacrificed since the world was made, —*BECK* ... from the founding of, —*BRKL* ... before the foundation, —*NORL* ... from the creation of, —*WMCK* ... foundation of the world onward, —*WADE.*

**13:8.** This verse makes it clear who will worship the beast. All those dwelling on the earth will bow down and worship him, for their names have not been written (previously or ever) "in the book of life of the Lamb who was slain" from the founding of the world.

Satan seeks worship. He tempted Jesus to bow down and worship him. But Jesus won the victory in our behalf (Matthew 4:8-10). However, during the last part of the Tribulation, the whole world will worship the beast, and through him they will in reality be worshiping Satan. It seems they will come to believe the beast is greater even than the true God.

There are two interpretations of the phrase "before the foundation of the world": one, that it refers to the names that were written; the other, that it refers to the sacrificial death of Christ on Calvary as God's Lamb. His substitutionary death for the sins of the world was something foreseen in the plan of God from the very beginning of creation. (See Genesis 3:15; 1 Peter 1:18-20.) Only through Him can believers have eternal life and have their names written in the Lamb's Book of Life. The saints are those who place their faith in

Jesus. They may include godly Israelites who have accepted Him as their Messiah, Lord, and Saviour.

**9. If any man have an ear, let him hear:** ... Let those who have ears listen, —*TCNT* ... So let him who has an ear, hear this, —*NORL* ... who has ears to hear, listen, —*MNTG* ... let him give ear, —*BB* ... listen to this, —*WADE.*

**13:9.** Jesus often used language like this in His exhortations and warnings. The verse draws attention to the importance of what follows. What is being said here in the Book of Revelation is not something intended to satisfy curiosity. Neither was it written just for the benefit of those in the end times. It was intended as a warning to everyone in the entire Church Age, and as an encouragement to all those going through troublous times.

**10. He that leadeth into captivity shall go into captivity:** ... Whoever leads others into, —*WLMS* ... Whoever is destined to go into, —*MNTG* ... If any one would capture, —*FNTN* ... He who takes others captive must himself go to prison, —*NORL* ... into captivity he goes, —*KLST* ... is to be taken prisoner, —*BECK.*
**he that killeth with the sword must be killed with the sword:** ... If any one murders, —*FNTN* ... if any is to be killed with the sword, —*WADE* ... Whoever is destined to be killed, —*NOLI* ... shall ... inevitably be killed, —*TCNT* ... with the sword he must be killed, —*KLST* ... will himself be slain by the sword! —*NORL.*
**Here is the patience and the faith of the saints:** ... This calls for the, —*KLST* ... In this is a reason for the patience and faith of the Christian saints, —*NORL* ... Here is needed the steadfastness ... of God's Hallowed People, —*WADE* ... to display patience and faith, —*TCNT* ... the endurance ... of the holy, —*FNTN* ... the fidelity of God's people, —*WLMS* ... This means that holy people must endure and be faithful, —*SEB.*

**13:10.** Those who lead others into captivity will be led captive themselves. Whoever kills with the sword must be killed with the sword. (See Matthew 26:52 for the words of Jesus concerning this.) This law of sowing and reaping will not be abrogated and the forces of Satan and the beast will not be able to escape it. The agents of the beast who capture and kill those who refuse the mark of the beast will themselves be defeated. As 19:15 shows, there is a greater sword, the sword of the Spirit, the sword of the living Word of God. Jesus will destroy the Antichrist and all his forces with the sword of His mouth, that is, by simply speaking the Word. These words are a reminder of this. They are also given to encourage believers' faith and trust in the Lord, and to help them endure with patience and steadfastness. (See also 14:12.)

The word "Here" is emphatic. It draws attention to the extreme trial of their faith tribulation saints will undergo. Yet they are not to take the sword to try to defend themselves. They must endure, for the period of the Antichrist's power will be short, and their reign with Jesus will be eternal.

**11. And I beheld another beast coming up out of the earth:** ... Then I noticed, *−BRKL* ... rising, *−NORL* ... ascending from the land, *−MNTG* ... out of the ground, *−BECK.*
    **and he had two horns like a lamb:** ... like those of, *−KLST* ... like a little lamb's, *−WADE.*
    **and he spake as a dragon:** ... he talked like, *−WADE* ... but it was wont to speak like, *−KLST.*

**13:11.** The first beast rose out of the sea (that is, out of the peoples of the world) and became a world ruler. John now saw a second beast rise out of the earth. Quite clearly he does not come from heaven although he will claim supernatural powers. He is "another" of the same kind as the first beast. His appearance is in sharp contrast to his words, for he has the two horns of a lamb, yet he keeps speaking like a serpent. He will try to give the impression of being a lamb, gentle and caring, full of great love, but it will be just an act. He is really a snake like that old serpent, the devil, and his words are deceitful, though clever. He will become a terrible part of the triad that is a false imitation of the Trinity. The true Trinity is a Triunity, with three divine Persons in the one eternal Being. But this evil trio will be made up of separate beings united only in their devilish plans.

**12. And he exerciseth all the power of the first beast before him:** ... he exerts the full authority, *−MNTG* ... of the former beast, *−KLST* ... and all the authority of the first Wild Beast he exercises in the latter's presence, *−WADE* ... all the authority of the first beast in his presence, *−NORL.*
    **and causeth the earth and them which dwell therein to worship the first beast:** ... It forced the earth, *−SEB* ... He also subdued the earth, *−FNTN* ... makes the earth and its inhabitants, *−MNTG* ... He makes the whole world and its people give worship to the first beast, *−NORL* ... worship the former beast, *−KLST* ... Wild Beast, *−WADE.*
    **whose deadly wound was healed:** ... whose deathstroke, *−MNTG* ... whose fatal wound, *−KLST* ... who had recovered from his death wound, *−NORL* ... mortal wound has been cured, *−WADE.*

**13:12.** This second beast will exercise all the authority and power of the first beast. The ancient serpent, Satan, will be the source of the second beast's power as he was of the first. With its power it will assist the first beast and force the earth and all its inhabitants to worship the first beast, drawing attention to its fatal wound that was healed. It is clear that not just one of the heads of the beast was wounded. The beast itself was wounded and restored. The concern of this second beast, who is also called the false prophet (16:13; 19:20; 20:10), will be with religion. Some believe he will already be the head of the apostate church during the first half of the Tribulation. When that church is destroyed, he will become the leader of the world religious system the Antichrist will establish in the last half of the Tribulation. By glorifying the beast and the beast's false resurrection, he will parody the Holy Spirit who glorifies the risen Christ.

**13. And he doeth great wonders:** ... produced, *−FNTN* ... performs impressive miracles, *−BRKL* ... works great miracles, *−NORL.*
    **so that he maketh fire come down from heaven on the earth in the sight of men:** ... to the extent of actually, *−WADE* ... even causing fire to come down, *−NORL* ... before men's eyes, *−WMCK*

**13:13.** The second beast will perform many great sign-miracles. ("Wonders" in this verse translates the same Greek word *sēmeia*, "signs," which is also used in John's Gospel for the miracles of Jesus.) In the presence of the people this second beast will even make fire come down out of heaven to the earth. This is clearly in imitation of the great miracle when Elijah called the people of Israel to a decision between the Lord and Baal. Elijah, at God's instruction, called fire down from heaven, something the priests of Baal could not do (1 Kings 18:22-39). This second beast, however, by Satan's power will bring down fire from heaven as a sign-miracle. As in the case of Elijah, and unlike the fire from the mouths of the two witnesses of 11:5, no one will be burned by the fire. But the people will be impressed. Even in a scientific age there are gullible people who follow false prophets and are deceived by false miracles that do not glorify God.

Chapters 19:20 and 20:10 refer to the second beast as the false prophet. His deceptive miracles are intended to mislead mankind. (See 2 Thessalonians 2:9-12.) Israel was warned that even if a prophet performed miracles and signs, if he turned people away from the worship of the true God, he was still a false prophet (Deuteronomy 13:1-3). True prophets speak for God and encourage people to serve Him and follow Christ.

It may be that the second beast who is the false prophet will encourage an ecumenical church which will draw together all religions and make them worship the first beast, the Antichrist. His deceptive miracles which will counterfeit Biblical miracles and even attempt to counterfeit the supernatural ministry of the Holy Spirit will help accomplish this. (See 2 Thessalonians 2:9, 10 where the Bible says the coming of the man of sin or lawlessness will be accompanied by the working [energizing] of Satan with all sorts of deeds of mighty power and miraculous signs and lying wonders, and with every kind of wicked deception [especially seduction from wealth and from the deceitfulness of sin] in them that are already perishing; because they received not the love of the truth, that they might be saved.)

**14. And deceiveth them that dwell on the earth by [the means of] those miracles:** ... Beguiling those, −LAMS ... It led astray the inhabitants of the earth because of the wonders, −KLST ... The people of the earth are deceived because of the signs, −NORL ... he deludes, in virtue of the Signs, −WADE.

**which he had power to do in the sight of the beast:** ... which he is permitted to perform, −MNTG ... that he was allowed to perform before the beast, −NORL ... was empowered to perform in the presence of the First Monster, −NOLI ... has been allowed to produce, −FNTN ... allowed to work under the eyes of the first Wild Beast, −WADE.

**saying to them that dwell on the earth:** ... He tells those who live, −MNTG ... and because of his order, −NORL ... directing those, −WADE ... telling the inhabitants of, −KLST ... Commanding those that live, −WMCK

**that they should make an image to the beast:** ... to erect a statue, −BRKL ... make a statue in honour of, −TCNT ... to make a god that looks like, −NLTG ... to the wild beast, −WLMS.

**which had the wound by a sword, and did live:** ... had been wounded by, −KLST ... who had received the sword-thrust, −FNTN ... who had the sword-stroke, −MNTG ... cut by the sword, −NLTG ... smitten ... lived again, −WADE ... and yet lived, −BECK, −NORL ... and came to life, −BB.

**13:14.** By means of the sign-miracles it will be permitted to work, the second beast will deceive (mislead) the inhabitants of the earth (that is, the unbelievers who are on the earth), for they are already on the broad road to destruction. Jesus warned that false prophets and false christs would arise (Matthew 24:24). The Antichrist and his false prophet will be the climax of all of that kind of deception, but the people will not realize the miracles of the false prophet are deceptive. They will accept his miracles as proof of the beast's claims that he is a god, the real Christ. In fact, he will talk the people into making an image of the beast (or to be dedicated to the beast) who had the sword wound and lived (was healed or maybe was resurrected). It will probably be a giant statue like that made by Nebuchadnezzar for the worship of himself (Daniel 3:1). The people will probably place the image of the beast (the Antichrist) in the temple to be rebuilt in Jerusalem (Daniel 9:27; Matthew 24:15; 2 Thessalonians 2:4). Thus the image will become a focal point for the false worship of the beast.

**15. And he had power to give life unto the image of the beast:** ... It was permitted to breathe life into, −TCNT ... It was enabled, −KLST ... Permission was granted him to infuse breath into, −FNTN ... to give breath to, −NORL ... give life to the false god, −NLTG.

**that the image of the beast should both speak:** ... so that the animal's statue could talk, −BECK ... so that words might come from, −BB ... so that it even spoke, −KLST ... and even make him speak, −NOLI ... actually spoke, −WADE.

**and cause that as many as would not worship the image of the beast should be killed:** ... cause to be put to death whoever, −FNTN ... all those who refused to worship the image of the beast, −NORL ... would die, −NLTG.

**13:15.** The second beast will receive power (evidently from Satan) to give life to the image of the beast (is it possible it is by trickery?). By doing this the false prophet will be able to claim divine power for himself and for the first beast, the Antichrist. This will be his greatest deception, for the gullible people will consider him deity. Then the prophecy of 2 Thessalonians 2:10, 11 will be fulfilled, that "because they received not the love of the truth, ... God shall send them strong delusion, that they should believe a lie."

By an indwelling breath or spirit the image will speak. This will surely encourage the people left in the world to continue believing that Antichrist is what he claims to be. The image will give a decree demanding that all who refuse to worship the image of the first beast, the Antichrist, are to be killed. This further reinforces the demand of the false prophet and shows that those who resist the Antichrist and continue to worship the Lord Jesus will be martyred for their faith. (See 6:9; 14:12, 13; 17:9-17.) Thus, it is clear that Antichrist will not follow a secular, humanistic, atheistic philosophy. He will want religion, but he will use religion to exalt himself as a god, as did the ancient kings of Egypt, Assyria, Babylon, and Rome.

**16. And he causeth all, both small and great:** ... The second wild animal made every person ... important men and to those not important, −NLTG ... It forced everyone, −SEB ... he compelled everyone, −NOLI ... And he makes all men, low and high, −MNTG ... all alike ... This applies to, −NORL ... the little, −KLST.

**rich and poor:** ... those who have wealth, −BB ... rich men and poor men, −NLTG.

**free and bond:** ... to those who are free and to those who are owned by someone, −NLTG ... freemen, −MNTG ... slaves, −FNTN ... bondmen, −WADE ... those who are not free, −BB.

**to receive a mark in their right hand, or in their foreheads:** ... to be branded, −BECK ... to have a brand put upon ... their brows, −MNTG ... have a mark stamped on, −WLMS.

**13:16.** The second beast will make no exceptions in his demand that all receive the mark of the first beast on their right hands or on their foreheads. Everyone, no matter what his wealth or social position, will be forced to submit. By the series of contrasts "small and great, rich and poor, free and bond (slave)" the Bible emphasizes all are included, and no one is left out.

This mark of the beast will be Satan's substitute for the mark put on the forehead of the 144,000 in 7:3. The 144,000 were sealed to identify them as belonging to the Lord. The mark of the beast will identify those who take it as followers of the beast and therefore under Satan's control.

The word "mark" (Greek *charagma*) was used of a mark or stamp which could be engraved, etched, branded, cut, or imprinted. It was used of brands on camels and stamped marks on documents as well as impressions on coins (Bauer). There is no known evidence, however, that any such mark, brand, or stamp was used in John's day or in the persecutions that continued to occur until the time of the emperor Constantine (for an extensive treatment of *charagma* see Deissman, pp. 240-247). No such mark of loyalty was placed on those who submitted to the worship of any of the emperors of Rome. This is an objection against the preterist view that claims the Book of Revelation was fulfilled in the First Century.

The nature of the mark of the beast or the method by which it will be applied is not described. However, once it is applied it is permanent and cannot be removed. Those who accept it will do so because they have rejected Christ and His righteousness and are deceived by the Antichrist and his false prophet.

17. **And that no** man **might buy or sell:** ... This means that no one can, —*NORL* ... It also prevented all, —*KLST* ... be allowed, —*FNTN* ... to do trade, —*BB*.

**save he that had the mark, or the name of the beast:** ... except those possessing that mark, —*FNTN* ... except such as bear the brand, —*WADE* ... the brand of the beast, —*MNTG* ... unless he has the mark, which is either the name of the beast, —*NORL*.

**or the number of his name:** ... or the code number, —*LAMS* ... the number corresponding to, —*BRKL* ... another way to write his name, —*NLTG* ... or the numerical cypher representing his Name, —*WADE* ... indicated by the letters of his name, —*TCNT* ... the number that represents the name, —*WLMS*.

**13:17.** By means of the mark of the beast the Antichrist will be able to control the economy of the entire world, for no one will be able to buy or sell without the mark. Nothing like this happened during the Roman persecutions. Nor has this happened throughout history, which is an objection

against the historicist interpretation of the Book of Revelation.

This domination of world economy will be used as a further incentive to take the mark of the beast. Since it is identified with the name of the first beast and the number of his name, the mark seems to be identified with his nature and character. It may be that taking the mark will also symbolize submission to both the Antichrist and the false prophet, and thus to both the government and world religion of the Antichrist. It would seem also from verse 15 that if anyone refuses to take the mark of the beast he will be sought out, discovered, and martyred. The result will be complete control of the entire world by the Antichrist.

18. **Here is wisdom:** ... Here we need to be wise, —*BECK* ... Here intelligence comes in, —*BRKL* ... Here there is needed insight, —*WADE* ... Wisdom is needed for the following, —*KLST* ... Here wisdom is needed, —*NORL* ... This was a wise provision, —*NOLI* ... Here is an opportunity to show discernment, —*TCNT*.

**Let him that hath understanding count the number of the beast:** ... Let whoever has intelligence adjudge the number, —*FNTN* ... him that has knowledge, —*WMCK* ... who has the mental keenness calculate the number of, —*WLMS* ... learn the meaning of the other way to write the name of the first wild animal, —*NLTG* ... should figure out the number, —*SEB* ... decipher the code number, —*LAMS* ... let him get the number of, —*BB* ... work out the significance of the cypher standing for the Name of the Wild Beast, —*WADE*.

**for it is the number of a man:** ... which really is, —*KLST* ... is a human one, —*FNTN* ... it is a number such as is used by man, —*WADE* ... This name is a man's name, —*NLTG*.

**and his number [is] Six hundred threescore [and] six:** ... Its number, —*CNDT, —KLGS, —TNT* ... their value as numbers is, —*BRCL* ... is 666, —*ADAM, —BRKL, —HNSN, —NLTG* ... six hundred and sixty-six, —*NORL, —WADE*.

**13:18.** This verse indicates God-given wisdom is necessary for understanding the meaning of the mark, and the "name" or character of the beast. However, the number *666* has become very controversial and has stirred more speculation than almost anything else in the Bible.

Before the invention of Arabic numbers (1, 2, 3, etc.) the Jews and Greeks often used letters of the alphabet for numbers. The first 10 letters were used for the numbers 1 through 10. The next letter, 20; the next, 30; and so on. It has been a popular pastime to add up the letters in names to try to come out with a total of 666. Some have taken Nero Caesar, put it into Hebrew letters (*Neron Kaisar,* which is not the normal way of spelling it), and have obtained a total of 666. However, the Book of Revelation is Greek in the original,

so this system is incorrect. Thus, there are no real grounds for applying it to Nero.

Throughout history people have tried to find 666 in almost every dictator or evil emperor that has come along. By various systems the number has been applied to men such as Hitler, Mussolini, and Stalin, even to some United States presidents. Some have assigned this number to the Pope. They came up with the correct figure by using the inscription, dedicated to the Pope, which is inscribed around the top of the wall inside St. Peter's Basilica in Rome. It is said that adding up just the letters that represent Roman numerals, the total comes to 666. The *Overview* section of this volume provides additional information concerning this custom. There is nothing in the Book of Revelation, however, that specifically tells us to add up the numbers in the name of the beast.

The key, however, seems to be the phrase that says "it is the number of a man" (literally, a number of mankind). Many Bible expositors believe the number *6* is the number standing for mankind. They also think *3* is the number of the Trinity. The threefold repetition, 666, could therefore simply mean the Antichrist is a man who believes he is a god or who declares himself to be a god. (See Revelation 13:8; 2 Thessalonians 2:4.)

## Chapter 14

**1. And I looked, and, lo, a Lamb stood on the mount Sion:** . . . I had a vision, *—KLST* . . . I saw, and consider this, *—WUST* . . . and behold, *—HNSN* . . . I perceived, and lo! the Lambkin standing, *—CNDT* . . . And I saw. And look, *—KLGS* . . . and there before me was, *—EVRD* . . . in my vision there appeared on a sudden the Little Lamb, *—WADE* . . . Then I looked, and there was the Lamb, *—ADAM* . . . saw the Lamb standing, *—NORL* . . . lo, there was the Lamb, *—MNTG* . . . on the mountain, *—BB* . . . the Mountain of Zion, *—NLTG.*

**and with him an hundred forty [and] four thousand:** . . . He was surrounded by, *—NOLI* . . . people with Him, *—EVRD, —NLTG* . . . 144,000, *—ADAM.*

**having his Father's name written in their foreheads:** . . . They all had, *—EVRD* . . . His name and His Father's name, *—NLTG* . . . bearing, *—WADE* . . . permanently inscribed on, *—WUST* . . . marked on their brows, *—BB.*

**14:1.** Before dealing with the final judgments of the tribulation period, the Book of Revelation presents a positive note. Chapter 14 brings a striking contrast to chapter 13. It goes to a mountaintop with a glorious picture of victory. It moves ahead to give a preview of the time when Jesus, as God's Lamb, will stand in victory and triumph on Mount Zion in Jerusalem, the capital of Christ's millennial kingdom. While the Antichrist is setting himself up as a god in Jerusalem, it seems the Bible cannot wait to let us know the kingdom and

glory of the beast is as nothing compared with that of the Lamb. The forced worship which he will demand is as nothing compared with the new song the followers of the Lamb will sing before the throne.

With Him are 144,000. In contrast to those who will take the mark or name of the beast, these saints will have the name of the Father of our Lord Jesus Christ on their foreheads. Their minds and hearts are identified as belonging to Him. They have been changed, glorified, and made like Jesus. They are overcomers.

There is a great deal of controversy about who these saints are. Some believe they are the same 144,000 mentioned in chapter 7. Others think they are faithful believers of all history. Some believe the number 144,000 does not represent a limited number but that it means fullness here, so that it includes all true believers.

**2. And I heard a voice from heaven, as the voice of many waters:** . . . And I heard a sound out of the sky that was like the roar of, *—ADAM* . . . a volume of sound proceeding out of . . . in loudness like the roar of many waters, *—WADE* . . . a sound from heaven, *—KLST* . . . I heard a sound, *—TNT* . . . came to my ears, *—BB* . . . resembling, *—FNTN* . . . like the noise of, *—NORL* . . . like the sound of rushing water, *—NLTG* . . . of flooding water, *—EVRD.*

**and as the voice of a great thunder:** . . . like the roll of heavy thunder, *—WADE* . . . and like the rumble of, *—ADAM* . . . echoed like a mighty cataract, *—NOLI* . . . like the sound of a loud peal of thunder, *—TCNT* . . . like a great peal, *—TNT* . . . of heavy thunder, *—CNDT, —NORL* . . . the sound of loud thunder, *—BB, —EVRD* . . . great thunders, *—KLGS.*

**and I heard the voice of harpers harping with their harps:** . . . It was followed by a melody of harpers, *—NOLI* . . . though the sound which I heard was in sweetness like the music of harpers, *—WADE* . . . And I heard also a sound like that of, *—NORL* . . . The voice I heard was like people playing music from boxes with strings, *—NLTG* . . . harpists, *—KLST* . . . players, playing on instruments of music, *—BB* . . . playing on their harps, *—BRKL.*

**14:2.** John seems to be on the earth at this time, for he hears a voice coming from heaven. The sound like many waters and like a great peal of thunder are reminders of 1:15 where the voice of Jesus sounds like many waters and 6:1 where the first seal is opened and one of the living creatures speaks. The plural used here, however, seems to indicate these are the combined voices of many in heaven.

Then John heard the sound of a multitude of harpists playing their harps to accompany their singing. The harps are the Greek *kitharais* or lyres. The sound of the music also comes from heaven just as the sound of the great voice did. It seems

to be the combined voices and music of a mighty choir and orchestra.

**3. And they sung as it were a new song before the throne:** ... This large group sang, —*NLTG* ... they made as it seemed, —*BB* ... they sang what seemed to be, —*NORL* ... a song of an unfamiliar strain, —*WADE*.
**and before the four beasts, and the elders:** ... before the living creatures, —*NORL* ... and rulers, —*BB*.
**and no man could learn that song but the hundred [and] forty [and] four thousand:** ... no man might have knowledge of the song, —*BB*.
**which were redeemed from the earth:** ... those from the earth whom God has made his for a price, —*BB* ... They had been bought by the blood of Christ and made free from the earth, —*NLTG* ... that were purchased from, —*BRKL* ... redeemed from earthly sins, —*NOLI* ... who had been ransomed from, —*NORL* ... at a Price, —*WADE*.

**14:3.** The harpists John heard were singing what seemed to be a new song. However, like the "new songs" in the Old Testament, it was a song of God's goodness and His salvation (Psalms 33:3; 40:3; 96:1; 98:1; 144:9).

This verse indicates the sound of their singing was not only coming out of heaven, it was coming from harpists-singers who were in front of the throne and before the 4 living creatures and the 24 elders that John saw first in chapter 4.

The harpist-singers are not angels. No one could learn that new song but the 144,000 who were redeemed from the earth. Therefore, the harpist-singers are the 144,000. At this point they are singing their new song before the throne in heaven. Verses 2-5 give the background to help identify the 144,000 who will appear with Christ on Mount Zion after He returns in glory and triumphs over the Antichrist and his armies.

Some consider the 144,000, "redeemed from the earth," to mean all believers who have been purchased by the blood of the Lamb who died for them. Other scholars believe this multitude is the firstfruits of Israel, mentioned in chapter 7.

**4. These are they which were not defiled with women:** ... who preserved complete virginity, —*KLST* ... had never allowed their virginity to be defiled by the pleasures of the flesh, —*NOLI* ... not polluted, —*FNTN* ... have not made themselves unclean with women, —*BB* ... in their intercourse with women, —*TCNT* ... who have kept themselves pure by not being married, —*NLTG*.
**for they are virgins:** ... they are pure, —*BECK* ... for they are celibates, —*BRKL*, —*MNTG*.
**These are they which follow the Lamb whithersoever he goeth:** ... the Little Lamb, —*WADE*.
**These were redeemed from among men:** ... They were bought from, —*SEB* ... were taken from among men, —*BB* ... purchased from among, —*FNTN* ... ransomed, —*NORL* ... At a Price from mankind, —*WADE*.

**[being] the firstfruits unto God and to the Lamb:** ... for God, —*KLST*.

**14:4.** The 144,000 are further identified as virgins who have not defiled themselves with women. The word "defiled" speaks of something impure, polluted, filthy. Therefore, it can hardly mean that all these 144,000 have never been married. The Bible makes it clear that "marriage is honorable in all, and the bed undefiled" (Hebrews 13:4). On the other hand, many Canaanite, Greek, and Oriental shrines were all around the seven churches of Asia. Many of these promoted fertility cults where sexual prostitution was carried on in the name of religion. Along with this was astrology, spiritualist mediums, and the occult. The Bible, in both the Old and New Testament, considers all these things as defiling. Some Bible scholars, therefore, understand "defiled with women" to refer to spiritual and moral defilement. That is, the 144,000 have not defiled themselves with the false cults and false religions that have arisen from time to time and are multiplying in the last days of this age. Rather, they are faithful followers of Jesus who have been redeemed through Christ and have been cleansed by His blood and made completely free from their old sins and guilt. Then, as they have walked in the Spirit in sanctification and submisssion, their lives have been characterized by holiness and obedience.

These 144,000 have separated themselves from the world and the apostate church (see 2 Corinthians 6:17). They have left all to follow God's Lamb, the Lord and Saviour (Mark 8:34; John 14:21). They are completely dedicated to Christ, for they put no limits on how or where they will follow. They go wherever He goes.

Again John emphasized that they have been redeemed from among mankind. This time he added that they are firstfruits unto God and to the Lamb. "Firstfruits" came to mean "the very best," or, "the highest quality." They are all made firstfruits, special, because they are redeemed. The price has been paid. They are cleansed.

**5. And in their mouth was found no guile:** ... They've never been known to tell a lie, —*BECK* ... They always despised falsehood, —*NOLI* ... no falsehood was found, —*FNTN* ... No lie was found on their lips, —*KLST*, —*NORL* ... there was not found a lie, —*WADE* ... no false word, —*BB*.
**for they are without fault before the throne of God:** ... and they stand, —*NORL* ... they are blameless before, —*WLMS* ... spotless, —*MNTG*, —*SEB* ... without blemish, —*KLST* ... they are untouched by evil, —*BB*.

**14:5.** The 144,000 who will be with Christ on Mount Zion are further identified as virgins because in their mouths was found no guile, no lies, none of the deception so characteristic of the devil. (Compare 21:27-22:15.) The redeemed 144,000 are also without fault, unblemished, blameless as they accompany themselves on their harps and sing their new song before the throne of God. The same word is used to describe Jesus. But it is also used to describe true believers whose sins and guilt are gone. (See 1 Thessalonians 5:23.) Because sins and guilt that are forgiven are gone, white as snow (Isaiah 1:18), purged away (Isaiah 6:7), blotted out (Isaiah 44:22), in the depths of the sea (Micah 7:19), cast behind God's back (Isaiah 38:17), separated from the believer as far as the east is from the west (Psalm 103:12), the redeemed are justified and in God's sight just as if they had never sinned.

**6. And I saw another angel fly in the midst of heaven:** . . . flying in mid-air, *—BRKL* . . . flying in the zenith, *—WADE* . . . between heaven and earth, *—BB.*

**having the everlasting gospel to preach:** . . . having to announce the good tidings of an everlasting reward to those sitting upon the earth, *—FNTN* . . . good news to proclaim, *—KLST* . . . to give to, *—NORL* . . . had an eternal evangel, to evangelize, *—MNTG* . . . having an eternal gospel to impart, *—WADE.*

**unto them that dwell on the earth:** . . . to announce to those, *—TCNT* . . . those sitting upon, *—FNTN* . . . among those who have their seat upon the earth, *—WADE.*

**and to every nation, and kindred, and tongue, and people:** . . . tribe, language, *—SEB.*

**14:6.** The Bible now returns in another vision to the theme of judgment. John, from where he was on earth, and in vision saw another angel (a good angel of the same kind he had seen before). This angel was flying in midheaven, with one purpose: to preach the good news of the eternal gospel to all on the earth, so no one left will be able to say on the judgment day that he has never heard.

The everlasting gospel is the same gospel proclaimed by the apostles and recorded in the New Testament. There is no other gospel. The apostle Paul said, "But though we, or an angel from heaven, preach any other gospel unto you than that which we have preached unto you, let him be accursed" (Galatians 1:8, 9). Even in the midst of the Tribulation God will still be seeking people who will turn to Him. The message of the gospel is always redemptive, and it calls people to a recognition of God's love, His sovereignty, His holiness, and is an appeal to worship Him. God alone is the One who created the universe, and He alone deserves the worship of those He has created.

**7. Saying with a loud voice:** . . . With a loud voice he proclaimed, *—NORL* . . . he cried, *—MNTG* . . . and directing in loud tones, *—WADE.*

**Fear God, and give glory to him:** . . . Respect God, *—SEB* . . . Have fear of, *—BB* . . . Reverence God, and give him praise, *—TCNT* . . . honour! *—FNTN.*

**for the hour of his judgment is come:** . . . the fitting moment for the execution of His judgment, *—WADE* . . . the time has come for Him to judge, *—BECK* . . . has arrived, *—FNTN.*

**and worship him that made heaven, and earth:** . . . therefore pay homage to the Maker, *—FNTN* . . . render worship to Him Who made the sky, *—WADE.*

**and the sea, and the fountains of waters:** . . . and water-springs, *—BRKL* . . . springs of waters, *—MNTG.*

**14:7.** The message of the angel will emphasize that God is not only the Creator but also the Judge, so it is well suited to the time of judgment during which it is given. It is the same genuine gospel preached by the apostles and has the same object: to influence people to repent. Even at this late hour of the Great Tribulation there will be an invitation to receive God's grace and salvation.

**8. And there followed another angel, saying:** . . . A second angel followed, and he said, *—NORL* . . . came after, *—BB* . . . exclaiming, *—FNTN* . . . crying, *—MNTG* . . . declaring, *—WADE.*

**Babylon is fallen, is fallen, that great city:** . . . Fallen, fallen is Babylon, *—NORL* . . . she has fallen, *—KLST* . . . Destruction has come to, *—BB.*

**because she made all nations drink of the wine of the wrath of her fornication:** . . . who intoxicated and infuriated all, *—NOLI* . . . who made all the heathen drunk with the wine of her furious fornications! *—FNTN* . . . drink the wine of vengeance due her immorality! *—WLMS* . . . with the maddening wine of her fornication! *—NORL* . . . the wine of the frenzy of, *—MNTG* . . . of her immoral passion, *—BECK* . . . her passionate unchas-tity, *—BRKL* . . . of her whoredom, *—LAMS* . . . of her passion for sexual vice, *—WADE* . . . wrath of her evil ways, *—BB* . . . which merits God's anger, *—KLST.*

**14:8.** Still in the same vision John saw that after the angel finished his work of proclaiming the good news of the everlasting gospel and warning all the people on earth, another angel followed, probably also flying in the midheaven. He proclaimed that the great city Babylon had fallen. The words of this angel are the same as that of the messenger who brought to Isaiah the news that the Babylon of his day had fallen, suddenly and totally destroyed by Sennacherib, in the manner Isaiah had prophesied, thus bringing a fulfillment that Isaiah saw as a harvest (Isaiah 21:9, 10).

The words "that great city" are a reminder of Daniel 4:30 where Nebuchadnezzar in his pride said, "Is not this great Babylon, that I have built for the house of the kingdom by the might of my power, and for the honor of my majesty?" In ancient times Babylon was the great city, the center of religion and commerce for Mesopotamia. The Assyrians made it one of their capitals in Isaiah's day before Sennacherib destroyed it. When it was rebuilt it soon assumed its place of leadership in heathen religion and world economy. It became a type pointing ahead to the Babylon of Revelation.

In John's vision the reason for Babylon's fall was that she had caused all nations to drink the fury of her sexual immorality. "Giving to drink" was used in Bible times of irrigating a field or saturating something with a liquid. So these words refer to Babylon's having saturated the nations of the world with such an appetite for sexual immorality and sexual deviation of all kinds that the desire for such things became a fury. Though the preceding angel preached or proclaimed the everlasting gospel and showed that even the judgments were intended to encourage people to worship God, most did not do so.

The Babylon of Daniel's day called on his three friends to join others in the worship of the golden image and threw them into a fiery furnace when they refused to worship anyone but the true God. The Roman Babylon of John's day persecuted Christians who refused to worship the emperor of Rome. The Babylon of Revelation refers to a worldwide political and religious system of the Antichrist that will torment and kill those who do not worship him.

This is not a different fall of Babylon from that prophesied in chapters 17 and 18. Those chapters give more details of this Babylon, which seems to be more than a city. It either heads or represents the whole world system in its political, religious, and commercial aspects. It is a message of warning and mercy, declaring that the religious system mankind has accepted has fallen. Note that it is a call to repentance but of short duration.

**9. And the third angel followed them, saying with a loud voice:** . . . Next came a third angel, −NORL . . . came after them, −BB . . . crying, −MNTG . . . declaring in loud tones, −WADE.

**If any man worship the beast and his image:** . . . Whoever worships, −ADAM . . . It will be bad for the person who, −EVRD . . . This is a word to anyone who worships, −NORL . . . the wild beast, −CNDT . . . and its statue, −KLST . . . and his false god, −NLTG.

**and receive [his] mark in his forehead, or in his hand:** . . . to anyone who gets the mark, −NORL . . . receives a brand, −MNTG . . . getting an emblem, −CNDT . . . the brand-mark, TNT . . . on his brow, −BB.

**14:9.** As the vision continued John saw a third angel with a further warning of the severity of the judgment to come. He too spoke with a loud voice

for all to hear. His message was that there will be no escape from the judgment to come for anyone who worships the beast and his image and takes a mark (of the beast) on his forehead or on his hand. By taking the mark and worshiping the beast and its image, they will seal their doom forever and ever. What a contrast this is with the temporary torment and death the Antichrist will bring on those who do not take the mark of the beast.

**10. The same shall drink of the wine of the wrath of God:** . . . To him will be given, −BB . . . Such a one, too, shall drink of the wine of God's anger, −NORL . . . of God's indignation, −BRKL . . . God's punishing wine, −SEB . . . of the fury of, −FNTN.

**which is poured out without mixture into the cup of his indignation:** . . . It is mixed in full strength, −NLTG . . . which is ready, −BB . . . unweakened, −KLGS . . . poured undiluted into His cup of wrath, −ADAM . . . that has been mixed undiluted in, −BRKL . . . unmixed in the cup of his anger, −MNTG . . . This wine is prepared with all its strength in, −EVRD . . . and made potent, −WADE . . . has been poured full strength into God's cup of punishment, −SEB . . . from the cup of His vengeance, −NORL . . . of His punishment, −BECK . . . of his wrath, −TNT.

**and he shall be tormented with fire and brimstone in the presence of the holy angels:** . . . They will be punished, −NLTG . . . will suffer torment by, −TNT . . . He will be put in pain with burning sulfur, −EVRD . . . he will be troubled . . . before the holy messengers, −KLGS . . . he will have cruel pain, burning with fire, −BB . . . he shall be tortured with Divine fire in the sight of, −FNTN . . . and sulphur before the eyes of, −WADE . . . before, −ADAM.

**and in the presence of the Lamb:** . . . before the eyes of the Little Lamb, −WADE . . . in front of, −NLTG.

**14:10.** The whole world that has been permeated with Babylonish immorality and corruption and that has drunk of Babylon's wine of passionate immorality and then worshiped the beast and its image and took its mark, will drink another type of wine. They will drink the wine of God's fury, mixed in the cup of His wrath, and they will drink it undiluted. "Fury" (Greek, *thumou*) is used of anger, wrath, and rage, and its outpouring is a common figure in the Old Testament. "Wrath" (Greek, *orgēs*) is the outpouring of God's anger against sin and evil. Both words indicate how serious God regards sin. The two words together bring emphasis to God's holy and righteous judgment against sin. Because God loves the world and because He knows what sin does, He hates sin, and His holiness demands that sin be judged. For that reason, those who practice sin and evil, who make sin their lifestyle, must suffer the wrath of God in judgment.

The pronouncement of this third angel is probably the most terrifying message found anywhere in the Bible concerning the fearful and final destiny of the lost. Throughout history believers have been held up as objects of public derision. Even so, the damned in the world to come must bear their judgment of "shame and everlasting contempt" (Daniel 12:2). It will be in the view of the entire universe as a demonstration and warning of the final results of sin. The Lamb who was slain for our sins and who was once judged by men will now himself be the Judge (cf. Matthew 26:64).

Let it be said, however, that there is no hint here of the attitude described in Jewish apocalyptic writings that the saints will gloat and triumph over the ungodly in their misery. For a Christian to do this would be unchristian. Remember Jesus' forgiveness of His enemies even as He hung in torment on the cross.

**11. And the smoke of their torment ascendeth up for ever and ever:** ... of their pain, –BB ... of their torture, –NORL, –WLMS ... of their being punished will go up, –NLTG ... goes up, –TNT ... shall rise up to the eternities! –FNTN.

**and they have no rest day nor night:** ... have no relief, –WADE ... have no respite, –TNT.

**who worship the beast and his image:** ... It is because they have worshiped the wild animal and his false god, –NLTG ... pay homage to, –FNTN ... his statue, –WLMS.

**and whosoever receiveth the mark of his name:** ... and have on them, –BB ... and all who carry, –NORL ... the brand-mark, –TNT ... the brand of his name, –MNTG.

**14:11.** Those who worship the beast and its image and receive or take the mark of its name will never have any rest day or night, for the smoke of their torment will go up for ever and ever. Some have taught that the torment of the wicked is only temporary. But the Bible says the fire is unquenchable (Matthew 3:12; Mark 9:43, 45; Luke 3:17). By its very nature it can never be extinguished. Its purpose is for eternal punishment.

One group teaches that the lake of fire will annihilate the sinners, so they will go out of existence. Still another group teaches that the purpose of the lake of fire is for purification, so that sinners and even Satan will be purified and saved in the end. But if it were possible for the lake of fire to bring salvation to sinners, why did Jesus have to die? This doctrine denies the necessity of the Cross. The entire Bible shows that the Cross and the resurrection of Jesus are central in God's plan. If there is salvation through the lake of fire, then Peter was wrong when he said concerning Jesus, "Neither is there salvation in any other: for there is none other name under heaven given among men, whereby we must be saved" (Acts 4:12). That their smoke goes up unto the ages of the ages is

the Greek way of saying forever and forever. No wonder Jesus asserted there will be weeping and gnashing of teeth when those in outer darkness realize they have missed the indescribable joys of heaven (Matthew 25:30, 41).

**12. Here is the patience of the saints:** ... Here is an opportunity for, –NOLI ... Here is the quiet strength, –BB ... In this situation the saints ... have the opportunity for patient endurance, –KLST ... Here is a call for the saints, –NORL ... in the endurance of, –BRKL ... This means that holy people must endure, –SEB ... there is consolation for the holy, –FNTN ... there is need for, –TNT ... there is needed the steadfastness of God's Hallowed People, –WADE.

**here [are] they that keep the commandments of God:** ... This is why God's people need to keep true to God's Word, –NLTG ... who always cling to, –WLMS ... those who obey God's commands, –NORL ... who faithfully keep, –KLST ... who keep in mind, –WADE ... the orders of, –BB.

**and the faith of Jesus:** ... and their faith in, –TNT ... and hold to faith in Jesus, –NORL ... and stay faithful to, –NLTG.

**14:12.** Why did the Lord have John record the messages of these three angels? It was not simply for the benefit of the people who will still be alive during the Tribulation. Rather, these messages are intended to give encouragement for the endurance of the saints, saints who continue to keep the commandments of God and the faith of Jesus. They are saints because they are born-again believers who have dedicated themselves to the worship and service of God. They make the will of God as revealed in His Word their lifestyle. The faith of Jesus is undoubtedly an objective genitive here and means they keep their faith in Jesus.

There were saints in John's day who needed to be encouraged by the fact that God will finally bring judgment on the world that rejects Christ and the gospel. All through the Church Age persecuted saints have been encouraged to endure suffering by what they read in the Book of Revelation. Christians in many parts of the world are being persecuted today. They need this message that encourages them not to give up, even in the face of possible martyrdom, for God will judge those who refuse the gospel. His justice will prevail.

**13. And I heard a voice from heaven saying unto me:** ... came to my ears, –BB ... directing, –WADE.

**Write, Blessed [are] the dead:** ... Put in writing, There is a blessing on, –BB ... Write ... From now on, blessed, –KLST ... Happy, –WADE.

**which die in the Lord from henceforth:** ... who from this time die as Christians, –WLMS ... from now on, –NORL, –TNT ... from henceforth die in union with, –WADE ... those who are dead who died belonging to the Lord, —NLTG...come to their end in the Lord, —BB.

**Yea, saith the Spirit, that they may rest from their labours:** ... Yes, says the Spirit, they are to have rest from their toils, —KLST...declares the Spirit, —WADE ... from their hard work, —BECK ... from their troubles, —BB...from their bruisings, —KLGS.

**and their works do follow them:** ... Their good deeds go with them, —TCNT...for the record of their deeds goes with them, —TNT...for their works will go with them! —NORL...All the good things they have done, —NLTG ... accompany them, —FNTN ... follow with them, —WADE.

**14:13.** Again in this vision John heard a voice from heaven. This time it was directed to him personally, and he was given the command to write. The final message of this vision is a word of encouragement. Some expositors do not apply this message to the people living during the Tribulation, saying it was a message for the Christians of John's time and also for all believers throughout Church history. From John's day on to the time of the end the dead who die in the Lord (that is, in fellowship with the Lord and in spiritual union with Him) are blessed or happy. The word is plural to indicate a fullness of blessings. The same word is used in the Beatitudes in Matthew 5. It means a happiness that does not depend on circumstances, because it comes from the fullness of the blessings of the Lord. These blessings and the happiness and joy that goes with them are eternal and will be wonderful beyond anything that can be imagined today.

The confirmation from the Holy Spirit is that those who "die in the Lord" will indeed rest from their labors. Their labors on earth are over, but since their works were in line with God's plan of redemption they will be treasures in heaven that will bring great reward at the judgment seat of Christ. This was an encouragement for those in John's day and also for believers today.

However, even if the admonition applies to believers of any era, other scholars adopt a different view because of the context, e.g., the term "from henceforth." They aver the meaning is that the trials will be so great it would be better to be martyred than to live through the Tribulation.

**14. And I looked, and behold a white cloud:**...I had a vision, —KLST ... and saw, —TNT ... I saw. And look, —KLGS...in my vision there appeared on a sudden, —WADE...a bright cloud, —WLMS.

**and upon the cloud [one] sat like unto the Son of man:** ... seated on the cloud, —NORL ... a seated figure like that of, —TNT ... sitting on the cloud was Someone like a Son of man, —ADAM ... was a Figure like a man, —WADE.

**having on his head a golden crown:**...a golden circlet, —WADE...having a golden wreath, —ADAM...had a headband of gold, —NLTG.

**and in his hand a sharp sickle:** ... scythe, —BRKL, —FNTN...a sharp curved blade, —BB...He had a sharp knife for cutting grain, —NLTG.

**14:14.** Now John saw a new vision. This time the vision was undoubtedly a prophecy of the judgments which will occur at the end of the Tribulation as described in 16:12-16 and 19:11-20. As John looked up from the earth he saw a white cloud. Sitting on the cloud was one "like unto the Son of man." This is language that refers back to Daniel 7:13 where Daniel in night visions saw "one like the Son of man" who came with the clouds of heaven. Jesus identified himself to His disciples as this Son of Man whose coming in power and great glory will cause all the tribes of the earth to mourn (Matthew 24:30). Later, when He was on trial before the Jewish Sanhedrin He told them the time would come when they would see the Son of Man sitting on the right hand of (God's) power and coming in the clouds of heaven (Matthew 26:64). Jesus identified himself with Daniel's vision of the Son of Man. The high priest called His words blasphemy. But John's vision confirms that Jesus is Daniel's Son of Man who will receive the Kingdom. He will come in victory and triumph.

The golden crown on His head indicates His royal power and glory. In Zechariah 6:9-13 crowns were put on the head of the high priest. It pointed to the fact that Christ would first do His priestly work and afterward would be crowned as King and Judge. He accomplished His priestly work of atonement on the cross. Now He is at the right hand of the Father interceding for believers.

When He returns the sickle in His hand will be for the purpose of judgment. John's vision is a reminder of what Jesus said in John 5:22, 23, "The Father judgeth no man, but hath committed all judgment unto the Son." He is still the Lamb who offered himself for the sins of all people of all times and places. But He warned that sinners will find Him coming as Judge when He returns.

**15. And another angel came out of the temple:** ... Another messenger came out of the Holy Place, —KLGS...from the sanctuary, —FNTN, —TNT...from the house of God, —BB, —NLTG...went forth from the temple, —ADAM.

**crying with a loud voice to him that sat on the cloud:** ... shouting, —MNTG ... called to Him with a loud voice, —NLTG ... in loud tones, —WADE ... to the one who was seated, —TNT.

**Thrust in thy sickle, and reap:**...Swing Your sickle, —BECK...Stretch forth, —WADE...Put your sickle to use, —KLST...Lay hold of Your sickle, —NORL...Use your sickle, —NOLI...Send out your scythe, —FNTN...Take your sickle and begin to reap, —TNT... Use Your knife and gather in the grain, —NLTG... Put in your blade, and let the grain be cut, —BB.

**for the time is come for thee to reap:**... for the hour to reap, —KLST... because the fitting time for reaping, —WADE... hour for cutting, —BB... for harvest time has come, —BRKL... the time to reap is here, —NORL... The time has come to gather the grain, —NLTG.

**for the harvest of the earth is ripe:**... the earth's harvest is fully ripe, —TNT... the grain of the earth is over-ready, —BB... because the earth is ready, —NLTG... was fully dried, —RTHM... has grown, —WADE... is overripe, —FNTN, —MNTG.

**14:15.** In his vision John saw still another angel (of the same kind as before) appear. This one came out of the sanctuary in heaven. This indicates He was an emissary representing the holiness of heaven's Holy of Holies, the holiness and righteousness of God himself. He too cried out with a loud voice, apparently loud enough for those on earth to hear, but he addressed the one sitting on the cloud. The one like the Son of Man must send out his sickle and reap. There can be no more delay. The time of reaping has come. The harvest of the earth is not merely ripe, it has literally dried up and withered. So this is not a harvest of good fruit. It is rather like the cutting off of dried up branches that have no life in them. The people it affects are all spiritually dead. They have been deceived by the Antichrist. They are ripe for this harvest of judgment that will come at the end of the Tribulation.

**16.** **And he that sat on the cloud thrust in his sickle on the earth:**... sent in his blade, —BB... plied his sickle over, —WADE... took his sickle to the earth, —TNT... swung His sickle over the earth, —WLMS... raised His knife over, —NLTG.

**and the earth was reaped:**... the harvest, —TNT... and its grain was cut, —BECK... was gathered in, —NLTG.

**14:16.** Now that the time for the judgment has come, the Son of Man sitting on the cloud does not hesitate. With one decisive move the sickle will reap the earth. This does not mean that He will do it all himself. Other passages show He will use angels for at least part of the work of judgment. (See Matthew 25:41.)

Too many have pictured Jesus only as meek, mild, and gentle. He is indeed filled with love, and as the Good Shepherd He is gentle. But He is not weak. He is tender and longsuffering. But when the time comes, He will not fail to bring the judgments of a holy God. The harvest of the earth will be reaped, and when He puts in the sickle it will be too late to repent.

**17.** **And another angel came out of the temple which is in heaven:**... house of God, —BB.

**he also having a sharp sickle:**... and he, too, had, —NORL... a sharp curved blade, —BB... knife for cutting grain also, —NLTG.

**14:17.** John saw still another angel coming out of the sanctuary in heaven, the glorious presence of God in the Holy of Holies. He also had a sharp sickle. This draws attention to the fact that angels will have a part in the final judgments of the Tribulation. It may be that this angel describes in a general way what will be accomplished by the seven last plagues which will be poured out by the seven angels described in the next two chapters. These plagues are the outpouring of the wrath of a holy God against sin and evil.

**18.** **And another angel came out from the altar:**... And still, —NORL.

**which had power over fire:**... had authority over, —FNTN, —NORL... over the fire, —KLGS.

**and cried with a loud cry to him that had the sharp sickle, saying:**... And he called out in a loud voice, —NORL... This angel called to the angel with, —EVRD... and he spoke with a mighty voice to the one, —ADAM... in loud tones... exclaiming, —WADE... to the angel who had the sharp knife, —NLTG.

**Thrust in thy sharp sickle, and gather the clusters of the vine of the earth:**... Swing out, —FNTN... Put your sharp sickle to use, —KLST... Send forth... of the land, —ADAM... Use your sharp sickle, —NORL... your knife, —NLTG... Take your sharp sickle and gather the grape-harvest of, —TNT... the bunches of grapes from the earth's vine, —WLMS... let the grapes of the vine of the earth be cut, —BB... in the vineyard of, —SEB.

**for her grapes are fully ripe:**... because, —ADAM... The earth's grapes are ripe, —EVRD... they are dead ripe, —KLGS... overripe, —BRKL... came to perfection, Rother-ham... fully ready, —BB... they are ready to gather, —NLTG.

**14:18.** Next, John saw another angel coming out from the altar with power and authority over fire. He too will be involved in the carrying out of the judgments. Which altar is not stated, but the altar of incense is most probable. It speaks of the prayers of the saints. Those prayers will be answered by the outpouring of the fires of God's wrath on the sinful world.

This angel cried out with a loud voice to the previous angel who had the sharp sickle. He must put in his sharp sickle. He must gather the bunches of grapes of the vine (or vineyard) of the earth, because its grapes are ripe. That they are ripe means there can be no more delay. The time of judgment has come. The day of salvation has passed.

Even though they are ripe, it does not mean any of them are good fruit. Isaiah used the figure of a vineyard when speaking of Judah and Israel in the love song of the vineyard (Isaiah 5:1-7). God had done His part in preparing the vineyard and in planting the very best vines. Yet, instead of bringing forth good grapes they produced bad grapes, literally, stinking grapes. God looked for Israel and Judah to produce justice (Hebrew, *mishpāt*), instead, there was oppression (Hebrew, *mispāch*). He looked for righteousness (Hebrew, *tsedāqāh*), instead, there was a bitter cry for help (Hebrew, *tseʻāqāh*). This called for judgment on Israel and Judah. He would allow the wall of His protection to be broken down. Enemies would come in and bring His judgment.

The figure of rotten, stinking grapes also fits the earth as a whole at the end of the age. The harvest of grapes as a picture of judgment that must precede restoration and salvation is also found in Isaiah 63:1-6. There Isaiah spoke of One who "speaks in righteousness, mighty to save." Then Isaiah asked the question, "Wherefore art thou red in thine apparel, and thy garments like him that treadeth in the winevat?" The answer came, "I have trodden the winepress alone; and of the people there was none with me: for I will tread them in mine anger, and trample them in my fury; and their blood shall be sprinkled upon my garments, and I will stain all my raiment. For the day of vengeance is in mine heart, and the year of my redeemed is come." Thus, the prophecy is not without hope. The time of the judgment is compared to a day, and the time of the redeemed is compared to a year.

Joel 3:11-15 also pictures this in connection with the judgment of the heathen nations at the valley of Jehoshaphat ("the valley where Jehovah judges"), the valley where God's decision of judgment will be manifest. Thus, Joel prophesied the command "Put ye in the sickle, for the harvest is ripe: come, get you down; for the press is full, the vats overflow; for their wickedness is great." God brought partial judgments in the past. They were warnings. But now more complete judgments must come.

**19. And the angel thrust in his sickle into the earth:** ... plied his sickle, –WADE ... swung his sickle down to the earth, –NORL ... sent his blade, –BB ... threw his sickle into, –KLGS ... took his sickle to, –TNT ... toward the land, –ADAM ... over the earth, –EVRD.

**and gathered the vine of the earth:** ... and stripped the earth's vine, –BRKL ... gathered the vintage, –NOLI ... the clusters of the vine, –MNTG ... the fruit of the vine of, –TNT ... gathered the earth's grapes, –EVRD ... was cut, –BB ... of the land, –ADAM.

**and cast [it] into the great winepress of the wrath of God:** ... this he threw into, –NORL ... and flung them into, –WLMS ... put the fruit into the large place for making wine. It was full, –NLTG ... put it into the great wine-crusher of, –BB ... of the anger of, –FNTN ... of God's anger, –KLST ... of the Great God, –KLGS.

**14:19.** The angel that comes out of the heavenly sanctuary will swing his sickle into the earth and gather the entire vine of the earth and throw it into the great winepress of the wrath (fury) of God.

In Bible times a farmer would hew out a vat or trough in a stone outcrop near his vineyard and use it as a winepress. The grapes would be put in the vat and people would jump up and down on them with their bare feet. The Old Testament (Isaiah 63:2, 3) used the treading out of the wine as a figure of speech for God's bringing of judgment and the fury of His wrath on the ungodly.

This vision looks ahead to the judgment at the end of the Tribulation when Christ returns. It is another way to picture what 2 Thessalonians 1:7-9 describes as the time "when the Lord Jesus shall be revealed from heaven with his mighty angels, in flaming fire taking vengeance (that is, render justice) on them that know not God" (including those who are willfully ignorant because they reject the truth).

**20. And the winepress was trodden without the city:** ... with its grapes, –NORL ... the grapes were crushed down in this tank, –SEB.

**and blood came out of the winepress, even unto the horse bridles:** ... issued from, –FNTN ... gushed out ... even to the bridles of, –MNTG ... in a stream so high, –NOLI ... streamed from, –WLMS ... reaching up as high as the bridles, –NORL ... came up as high as the mouth of a horse! –SEB.

**by the space of a thousand [and] six hundred furlongs:** ... and reaching out, –NORL ... and the circumference of, –LAMS ... for a distance of, –TCNT ... as far as, –MNTG ... for two hundred miles, –BRKL.

**14:20.** Several passages in the Old Testament compare the wrath of God to the use of a winepress. One of them is Jeremiah 25:15-38 where Jeremiah described God as emptying the cup of His wrath on Babylon and on all nations that had rebelled against God. They were all overripe for judgment. God is not mocked (Galatians 6:7, 8). The prophets warned many nations of their day of terrible judgments of God that would come upon them. These judgments on human lust for power that denied God's power point ahead to a future judgment of the world, the Antichrist, and his kingdom. No one knows how close the Day of the Lord is, but it will come in God's time. The Old Testament indicates that past judgments were indications of God's holy wrath and assurance that judgment will come when the time is ripe. Surely that time is soon to come, for a world that rejects

God is inviting disaster. See Psalms 97:3-5; 110; Proverbs 2:21, 22; Isaiah 34:8; 63:1-6; 66:15-17; Jeremiah 25:30-33; Matthew 13:40; Luke 17:34; Revelation 19:15.

The treading of the winepress will take place outside the city. This seems to mean outside the city of Jerusalem. The place may be what the Old Testament prophet Joel called the Valley of Jehoshaphat, which means the valley where Jehovah judges. (See Psalm 110:6; Matthew 25:31.)

The "wine" that comes from the grapes of the vineyard of the earth is human blood. Thus the treading out of the grapes speaks of tremendous slaughter. It may be another way of picturing the battle of Armageddon. (See Zechariah 14:1-4; Revelation 16:16; 19:17-19.)

The blood will flow (or some take it to mean the blood spatters) as it comes out to the height of horses' bridles, and it gradually diminishes until the flow ends at a distance of 1,600 furlongs (220 yards each). This figures out to 352,000 yards or 200 miles, which equals 320 kilometers.

## Chapter 15

1. **And I saw another sign in heaven, great and marvellous:** . . . I beheld, —MNTG . . . in the sky, a great . . . sign, —NORL . . . another great and amazing warning, —SEB . . . another symbol, —WLMS . . . and wonderful, —FNTN.
**seven angels having the seven last plagues:** . . . last Curses, —TCNT . . . These were to be the last, —NORL.
**for in them is filled up the wrath of God:** . . . for with the infliction of them the wrath of God is spent, —TCNT . . . with them God in His anger has finished what He intends to do, —BECK . . . God's indignation was completed, —BRKL . . . with them God's wrath is completely expressed, —WLMS . . . God's punishment will be finished, —SEB . . . by which the wrath of God was finally completed, —NOLI . . . has come to complete expression, —NORL . . . is ended, —WMCK

**15:1.** In John's next vision a great and wonderful sign appeared in heaven—seven angels having the seven last plagues. These are called the "last plagues" because in them the wrath and fury of God is "filled up," completed against the sins of the world that has come under the rule of the Antichrist during the Tribulation. In verse 7 these plagues are called the judgments of the "seven golden vials." The "vials" were not small vials but great large bowls.

John described these judgments beginning in chapter 16. They seem to be the outflow of the judgment of the seventh trumpet (11:15).

2. **And I saw as it were a sea of glass mingled with fire:** . . . the semblance of, —MNTG . . . something

that seemed to be . . . mixed with, —NORL . . . a glassy sea, —FNTN . . . tinged with fire, —NOLI.
**and them that had gotten the victory over the beast:** . . . who had defied the Monster, —NOLI . . . And those who had conquered the beast, —NORL . . . who came off conquerors from, —MNTG.
**and over his image:** . . . its statue, —KLST.
**and over his mark:** . . . and with, —NLTG.
**[and] over the number of his name:** . . . from the cipher of, —MNTG . . . representing his name, —WADE . . . and its numerical name, —KLST.
**stand on the sea of glass having the harps of God:** . . . were in their places by the sea of glass, —BB . . . were standing on the glassy sea, holding gold harps from God, —ADAM . . . holding harps given them by God, —NORL . . . All of them were holding music boxes with strings, —NLTG . . . with God's harps in their hands, —TNT . . . dedicated to the service of God, —WADE.

**15:2.** Now the scene changed again and John saw into heaven before the throne as in chapter 4. Standing on a sea or lake of glass or crystal, mingled with fire, were those who were victorious over the beast, over his image, over his mark, and over the number of his name. They had kept their faith when threatened by the demand to worship the beast and its image and by the demand to take the mark of the beast. All of them had harps of God, which probably means God-given harps or supernatural harps.

3. **And they sing the song of Moses the servant of God:** . . . they give the song, —BB . . . God's slave, —ADAM . . . the slave of, —MNTG . . . who was a workman owned by, —NLTG.
**and the song of the Lamb, saying:** . . . the Song of the Little Lamb, chanting, —WADE . . . as follows, —NORL.
**Great and marvellous [are] thy works, Lord God Almighty:** . . . Your actions are great and amazing, —SEB . . . The things You do are . . . powerful, —NLTG . . . full of wonder . . . Ruler of all, —BB . . . and wonderful, —FNTN, —TNT . . . are your deeds, —KLST . . . Sovereign Supreme, —WADE.
**just and true [are] thy ways:** . . . Righteous, —MNTG . . . You are always right . . . in everything you do, —NLTG . . . and reliable, —WADE . . . full of righteousness, —BB . . . and genuine, —ADAM.
**thou King of saints:** . . . King of the ages, —BECK, —NORL . . . King of the nations, —ADAM, —BRKL . . . of all nations, —NLTG . . . Thou King of kings! —MNTG . . . Everlasting King, —WADE . . . Eternal King, —BB, —TCNT . . . of the Eternities! —FNTN.

**15:3.** Moses was the faithful servant of God (Hebrews 3:5). He was used by God to bring plagues on Egypt, and through him God accomplished Israel's great deliverance. After God brought the Israelites through the Red Sea and destroyed the army that was pursuing them, Moses led them in a great song of praise (Exodus 15:1-18). His sister Miriam led the women as they danced for joy, playing their tambourines and singing a response to each of the verses of the song (Exodus 15:20, 21). The keynote to the song was the Lord's triumph and the fact that He had become their salvation (Exodus 15:1, 2). The song sung in heaven anticipates God's final victory over the beast and celebrates believers' triumphal joy in heaven.

It is also the song of the Lamb, because He is the Judge of all the enemies of God's people, and He is the One who brings eternal salvation to His saints. It is a song that both the saints of the Old Testament and the saints of the New Testament will now be able to sing.

The song first glorifies the great, wonderful, marvelous works of the Lord God Almighty. He is the same El Shaddai who revealed himself to Abraham and who has been powerfully fulfilling His covenants and promises throughout the ages. His ways as well as His acts are just or righteous and true or faithful. Even His acts in judgment reveal His holy character and His genuine righteousness. As the psalmist David recognized, "The Lord is righteous in all his ways, and holy in all his works. The Lord preserveth all them that love him: but all the wicked will he destroy" (Psalm 145:17, 20).

**4. Who shall not fear thee, O Lord:** . . . What man is there who will not have fear before you, —BB . . . who would not respect You, —SEB . . . Who will not honor You, —NLTG.

**and glorify thy name?:** . . . Who should not give glory to Your name? —NORL . . . praise, —FNTN . . . the Revelation of Thyself? —WADE.

**for [thou] only [art] holy:** . . . only You are, —NORL.
**for all nations shall come and worship before thee:** . . . in Your sight, —FNTN.

**for thy judgments are made manifest:** . . . Thy sentences of judgment have been made known, —BRKL . . . for Your righteousness has been shown! —NORL . . . Your just retributions have now been revealed, —NOLI . . . Your righteous deeds have become clear, —SEB . . . deeds of vindication have been disclosed, —WADE . . . For thy righteous acts have been made evident, —MNTG . . . are displayed! —FNTN.

**15:4.** The persecuted saints who are now glorified have a right to sing their song of victory. Their cause is just. Though the fullness of the victory has not yet come, they anticipate it, knowing that nothing can stop the Holy God from carrying out His purposes. His holiness not only means He is separated from all sin and evil, it also means He has separated himself to the task of bringing in the final victory and eventually the new heaven and the new earth.

Their song also anticipates the fact that "all nations" (that is, the saved out of all nations) will come and worship before the same Lord God Almighty they are now worshiping. (Compare Isaiah 2:2-4 where many people will come to learn from the Lord in order to walk in His paths.) This too was made possible by the Lamb. Jesus left the glory He enjoyed with the Father in heaven, humbled himself by taking the form of a servant, and was made in the likeness of men. He humbled himself even further and became obedient to death, to the most shameful kind of death ever known, the cross-kind of death. This is why God has exalted Him (see Philippians 2:9-11).

At the same time "all nations" will also recognize that God's judgments are righteous and are in line with true holiness and justice. (See Psalm 98:2, 3, 9.) Because of this they will humble themselves and give Him all the praise and glory due to Him.

**5. And after that I looked, and, behold:** . . . After this I had a vision, —KLST . . . in my vision, —WADE.

**the temple of the tabernacle of the testimony in heaven was opened:** . . . the house of the Tent of witness, —BB . . . the sanctuary of the tent, —FNTN . . . the inmost shrine of, —TCNT . . . thrown open in heaven, —NORL . . . which contains the tabernacle of the revelation, —NOLI.

**15:5.** Next John in a new vision saw the sanctuary of the tent of the testimony (the tent of witness) in heaven was opened. The language used here is like that used of the tabernacle in the wilderness with its inner sanctuary or Holy of Holies (holiest place of all) where stood the ark of the covenant which was the receptacle for the Ten Commandments. The "testimony" or witness in the earthly tabernacle referred to the tablets of stone that were the essence of the covenant (Exodus 32:15; Deuteronomy 10:5).

"Temple" in the King James Version is the Greek *naos*, a word here meaning the "heavenly sanctuary" (*Bauer*). Another word, *hieron*, is used of the entire temple with its courts. The temple in Jerusalem was built on the same plan as the tabernacle, but the picture here is given in terms of the tabernacle. But the people were familiar with the Pentateuch and that the tabernacle was built according to the pattern God gave to Moses on Mount Sinai. The tabernacle and its service were the "shadow of heavenly things" (Hebrews 8:5). But Jesus is now our High Priest, who is now interceding for believers. However, this vision indicated the situation was about to change.

Usually the open sanctuary speaks of access to God. Actually, the sanctuary was opened forever when the veil of the temple was torn in two from top to bottom when Christ died on the cross. For believers, Jesus is still the new and living (resurrected) way into the presence of the Father in the very Holiest of All (Hebrews 10:19, 20). But here John saw the sanctuary was open so the judgments of God might come out against mankind's sins and their rejection of His holy Word.

**6. And the seven angels came out of the temple:** . . . there came out of the sanctuary, *—MNTG* . . . from the house of God, *—BB.*

**having the seven plagues:** . . . that have charge over, *—WADE* . . . possessing, *—FNTN* . . . holding, *—NORL* . . . the seven punishments, *—BB.*

**clothed in pure and white linen:** . . . They wore clean, shining linen, *—BECK* . . . dressed in clean white linen, *—NORL* . . . pure and bright, *—MNTG.*

**and having their breasts girded with golden girdles:** . . . bound, *—FNTN* . . . encircled with golden sashes, *—KLST* . . . with golden cinctures, *—WADE* . . . with bands of gold about, *—BB.*

**15:6.** As John continued to observe this vision he saw a great procession. Seven angels came out of the sanctuary, that is, out of the very presence of the glory and throne of God. As angels, they were powerful spirit beings who are God's messengers. The white robes speak of their sinlessness. But the white robes combined with the golden belts around their breasts are also identified with the dress reserved for priests and kings. These angels, representatives of God and Christ, will be sent from heaven to bring more of God's righteous judgment on the earth. They will bear the seven plagues, the last series of judgments of the Tribulation.

**7. And one of the four beasts gave unto the seven angels seven golden vials:** . . . one of the four animals gives to the seven messengers, *—CNDT* . . . living ones, *—HNSN* . . . living creatures gave . . . seven golden bowls, *—NORL* . . . seven cups of gold, *—MRDK.*

**full of the wrath of God:** . . . brimming with, *—CNDT* . . . fury, *—FNTN* . . . the fierce anger, *—SWAN* . . . indignation, *—AMPB.*

**who liveth for ever and ever:** . . . Who is living for the eons of the eons, *—CNDT* . . . of Him Who lives in the eternities of the eternities, *—FNTN* . . . who lives for timeless ages, *—PHLP.*

**15:7.** Now one of the four living creatures that John saw first in chapter 4 comes forward. As a guardian of God's throne and as a representative of God's creation that longs for the coming Kingdom, it is appropriate that he take part in the events which prepare the way for that Kingdom— He comes with seven golden vials, not small vials but great, large bowls full of the wrath of God. There seems to be a contrast here to the golden vials or bowls of 5:8, where the bowls were full of incense that represented the prayers of the saints. Some see a connection here and take this to mean that the bowls of God's wrath are necessary in

order to make possible the fulfillment of the prayers of the saints.

The living creature gives the golden bowls of divine wrath to the seven angels. They will become God's agents to bring the last series of judgments on the remaining sinners of the world before Jesus comes back to earth. He will then win a triumphant victory over the Antichrist and his armies before establishing His kingdom on earth.

**8. And the temple was filled with smoke from the glory of God:** . . . And the inner sanctuary, *—WUST* . . . is dense with the fumes, *—CNDT* . . . majesty, *—CNFT, —FNTN* . . . the radiance, the splendor, *—AMPB.*

**and from his power:** . . . might, *—FNTN, —NORL.*

**and no man was able to enter into the temple:** . . . no one could go into, *—NORL* . . . the shrine until, *—NOLI.*

**till the seven plagues of the seven angels were fulfilled:** . . . until the completion of, *—FNTN* . . . afflictions, *—AMPB* . . . the seven troubles of, *—EVRD* . . . brought by the seven angels, *—TEV* . . . until the seven calamities of the seven messengers should be consummated, *—CNDT* . . . were at an end, *—NORL* . . . were finished, *—CNFT, —HNSN* . . . were accomplished, *—MRDK* . . . were past and over, *—PHLP* . . . should be brought to an end, *—WUST* . . . ended, *—AMPB.*

**15:8.** In his vision John saw smoke that was a revelation or manifestation of God's glory and mighty power filling the sanctuary. A similar manifestation of the glory of God once made it impossible for Moses and Aaron to enter the tabernacle in the wilderness (Exodus 40:34, 35; compare Isaiah 6:4; 1 Kings 8:10, 11; the clouds and smoke are parallel in meaning). This smoke represented the glory and holiness of God and made it impossible for anyone to enter the sanctuary until after the seven angels completed their work of pouring out the seven bowls of the seven plagues. Since no one could enter the sanctuary, it meant there could be no intercession to stop the judgment. God had been patient and longsuffering, but the time for these righteous judgments had come, as it must. There could be no more postponement.

## Chapter 16

**1. And I heard a great voice out of the temple saying to the seven angels:** . . . call out aloud to, *—BECK* . . . a loud command, *—NOLI* . . . from the sanctuary, *—FNTN.*

**Go your ways, and pour out the vials of the wrath of God upon the earth:** . . . Go and empty the seven bowls, *—TCNT, —WLMS* . . . Be going on your ways and be pouring out, *—WUST* . . . pour out . . . God's anger, *—TEV* . . . of the fury, *—FNTN* . . . fierce anger, *—SWAN.*

**16:1.** This chapter describes the outpouring of the seven last plagues John saw in this vision. The seven angels waited until a loud voice out of the sanctuary commanded them to go and pour out the seven bowls of the wrath or fury of God upon the earth. (Compare Isaiah 6:6.) The voice John heard seems to be the voice of God or Christ, since no one else will be allowed to enter the sanctuary until the bowl judgments are over. The Greek word order also seems to emphasize the power and authority of the voice.

Evidently these judgments follow in rather rapid succession shortly before Jesus returns to bring an end to the Antichrist and his rule. The trumpet judgments will be partial judgments, limited in their effect (8:7-12). The bowl judgments will be more severe, more complete judgments, without the limits placed on the trumpet judgments. In fact, they are stated in such a way that no one left on earth, even in the deepest caves or the most hidden valleys, will be able to escape the effects of at least some of them. These unprecedented plagues of divine wrath, sent by God himself, indicate that the tribulation period is sweeping onward to its final climax.

**2. And the first went, and poured out his vial upon the earth:** ... went off, −WUST ... the first departed, −BRKL ... The first angel left, −SEB ... and emptied his bowl, −PHLP ... poured out his bowl on the earth, −TEV ... on the land, −EVRD.
**and there fell a noisome and grievous sore:** ... which caused, −NORL ... Whereupon loathsome and malignant ulcers attacked, −PHLP ... Terrible and painful sores appeared, −TEV ... a loathsome and malignant ulcer attacked, −BRKL ... a sore bad and painful, −SWAN ... ugly ... sores came upon, −EVRD ... there came a foul and pernicious suppurated sore, −WUST ... foul ulcer appeared, −FNTN ... and horrible, painful sores, −WLMS.
**upon the men which had the mark of the beast:** ... who were branded with, −FNTN ... all those who bore the mark of the animal, −PHLP ... who have the mark of identification of the Wild Beast, −WUST.
**and [upon] them which worshipped his image:** ... his idol, −EVRD ... its statue, −PHLP.

**16:2.** When the first of these seven angels pours out his bowl on the earth those who had accepted the mark of the beast receive marks of a different sort. They had turned their backs on the worship of the true God and chosen to worship the beast and his image with all its satanic involvements. Now, this plague brings a bad, foul, and angry sore on them, men and women alike.

It is not an ordinary sore, but is abscessed, ulcerated, and malignant. Such sores were called "a sore botch that cannot be healed" (Deuteronomy 28:35). Job's "boils" (Job 2:7) were probably ulcerous sores of an infectious nature. They not only itched and hurt, but had a terrible odor, darkened his skin, and so disfigured him that his friends

hardly recognized him (Job 2:8, 12; 7:5; 17:1; 30:30) (see Pope, *The Anchor Bible,* 15:21; and Dhorme, p. 18).

The same word used of the sores caused by the outpouring of the first golden bowl is used in the Septuagint translation of Exodus, of the plague of boils "breaking forth with blains (blisters full of corrupt matter)" in the plagues of Egypt (Exodus 9:8-11). Thus this plague is similar, but it is even worse and more painful than those suffered by Job and by the Egyptians. Some interpreters wish to treat this plague as speaking of moral corruption, but the results and the pain show literal sores are meant.

**3. And the second angel poured out his vial upon the sea:** ... emptied his bowl, −NORL ... into the sea, −WUST.
**and it became as the blood of a dead [man]:** ... turned into blood like that of, −NORL ... which turned into a fluid like, −PHLP ... as of a corpse, −BRKL ... like a dead man's blood, −WADE ... became like the blood of a dead person, −TEV ... blood like it is in one who is dead, −SWAN.
**and every living soul died in the sea:** ... every spirit of life, −FNTN ... every living thing, −NLTG, −NORL ... every living creature died ... everything in the sea, −MNTG ... came to an end, −BB.

**16:3.** The outpouring of the second bowl will bring a second plague which will cause the sea to become as the blood of a dead person. This may mean it is not actual blood, but is like the corruption, stench, and appearance of the blood which has drained out of a corpse and is in the process of coagulating and decaying. This judgment of God will come on water that is so important to life, just as it did in the trumpet judgments, but in a more widespread form. The blood which under the Law represented the life (Leviticus 17:11) here will become the means of judgment and death.

This was similar to the first of the 10 plagues that came upon Egypt when Moses lifted up his rod and struck the waters of the River Nile (Exodus 7:20-25). There, all the fish in the river died. But this plague will be far worse than the plague in Egypt. John saw that every living soul (soul of life) that was in the sea died because of the terrible pollution. "Living soul" is the same phraseology translated "living creature" in Genesis 1:21, 24. It is used of fish, animals, and people, because all creatures have individuality and physical life. "Soul" in this verse is therefore not used in a theological sense.

Some interpreters wish to limit the "sea" in this verse to the Mediterranean (Beasley-Murray, *New Century Bible, The Book of Revelation*, p. 241). However, in view of the fact that these seven last plagues are severe and are not limited, the word "sea" seems to be more general, including all the oceans and seas.

Some interpreters wish to treat this plague as symbolic, with the sea representing the nations in general. However, this would mean every person in the world would die in this plague, and that is not the case, for other plagues follow. Consequently, the plague must affect literal seas and oceans and sea creatures.

**4. And the third angel poured out his vial upon the rivers and fountains of waters:** ... emptied his bowl, *—WLMS* ... let what was in his vessel come out into, *—BB* ... poured out his jar ... where water comes out of the earth, *—NLTG* ... into the water-springs, *—FNTN* ... springs of waters, *—MNTG.*
**and they became blood:** ... and they turned into blood, *—WLMS.*

**16:4.** When the third angel pours out the third golden bowl of God's wrath, the third plague will cause the rivers, streams, and springs to become blood also. There is no limit here as there was with the third trumpet judgment. All the sources of water for drinking and for washing are turned to blood. The Bible does not tell us the results, but this plague must bring suffering and death, for a human being cannot live long without water. The only possible solution to the problem will be finding a means of filtering out the water. But only relatively few will benefit from this, so there must be great suffering for humans and beasts alike.

**5. And I heard the angel of the waters say:** ... the voice ... came to my ears, *—BB* ... who has charge over waters, *—LAMS* ... exclaiming, *—WADE.*
**Thou art righteous, O Lord, which art, and wast, and shalt be:** ... You are fair, *—SEB* ... You are just ... O Holy One, You who are and were, *—NORL* ... True and upright, *—BB* ... Your retributions are, *—NOLI* ... you are just, *—KLST* ... The Existent, *—FNTN.*
**because thou hast judged thus:** ... the Holy, because Thou hast executed these judgments, *—WADE* ... in pronouncing these judgments, *—KLST* ... in inflicting this judgement, *—TCNT* ... thou hast condemned them, *—LAMS* ... In these Your decisions! *—FNTN* ... in Your judgments, *—NORL.*

**16:5.** John now heard the angel of the waters interject a justification for this terrible plague. Previously the Book of Revelation has spoken of angels who have power over winds (7:1) and power over fire (14:18). Now another angel is introduced. This is the only place where he is mentioned. Some suppose this angel is one who has been given control over the waters of the earth. Others suppose this angel is the third of the seven angels, the angel who will pour out this bowl of God's wrath on the waters.

This angel does not complain about the judgment of God. Instead, he recognizes that God is righteous. He knows also that God is the Eternal One, who always is, was, and shall be. Because of who He is He will be true to His own righteous nature, and the angel recognizes that God has demonstrated His nature by judging the followers of the Antichrist who are still left on the earth.

**6. For they have shed the blood of saints and prophets:** ... For men, *—MNTG* ... they made the blood ... come out like a stream, *—BB* ... because those whom Thou hast judged ... of Thy Hallowed People, *—WADE* ... poured out the blood, *—BRKL* ... of Your saints, *—NORL.*
**and thou hast given them blood to drink:**
**for they are worthy:** ... They are getting justice, *—NORL* ... as they deserve, *—BECK* ... They have had their deserts, *—TCNT* ... And this they deserved, *—MNTG* ... It is their due, *—NOLI* ... for they deserve it, *—LAMS* ... are deserving of it, *—WADE.*

**16:6.** God's righteousness and justice are seen also by the fact that these who have nothing left but blood to drink were themselves shedders of blood. They were all part of a world system that has shed the blood of saints and prophets. The saints refer primarily to the New Testament believers who lived lives consecrated to God and dedicated to His worship and service. Stephen was the first martyr. Many thousands of believers have been faithful unto death throughout the centuries from that day to this. Many more are yet to be added to their number.

Prophets are speakers for God. Primarily, this seems to refer to New Testament prophets who have been used regularly by the Spirit to strengthen, edify, and encourage believers in the local churches. Like the Old Testament prophets, they risked their lives, and many lost their lives for the sake of Christ and the gospel.

**7. And I heard another out of the altar say:** ... I heard the altar too, *—KLST* ... the Altar of Incense, *—WADE* ... the attendant of, *—FNTN* ... heard the altar saying, *—MNTG* ... heard an echo from the altar, *—NORL.*
**Even so, Lord God Almighty, true and righteous [are] thy judgments:** ... Yes, *—NORL* ... Your decisions are true and fair! *—SEB* ... are appropriate and righteous, *—NOLI* ... and just, *—KLST* ... Sovereign Supreme, *—WADE.*

**16:7.** John heard another voice out of the altar confirming the message of the angel of the waters. The speaker is not identified, but he is probably another angel. He affirmed also that no one can question God's acts of judgment for they are true and righteous. (Compare Psalm 19:9.) He is the Lord God Almighty. He is who He is, and He has the power to carry out judgments that show the kind of righteous and holy God that He is. The same El Shaddai who provided for the needs of Abraham and gave him promises is also the Mighty to save, and the Almighty Judge.

The world does not understand the "exceeding sinfulness of sin." (See Romans 7:13.) Nor does it understand the holiness of God that separates Him from all sin and evil so that He has an intense hatred of sin. Though God is also loving, His love must work in line with His holiness. Those who reject His provision for salvation through the blood of Jesus must be punished. In other words, sin must be dealt with. Those who do not deal with their sin at the Cross by confessing it and accepting God's forgiveness, must have their sin dealt with in judgment. (See John 3:19; Hebrews 1:9; Psalm 119:137.) This is not something arbitrary. It is part of the nature of reality.

**8. And the fourth angel poured out his vial upon the sun:** ... emptied, *−FNTN* ... his bowl, *−NORL.* **and power was given unto him to scorch men with fire:** . . . the sun was permitted, *−MNTG* ... and it was strengthened to scorch men with fire, *−KLST* ... and permission was given it ... with its fiery heat, *−WLMS.*

**16:8.** The first three plagues will affect the earth, air, and water. The fourth plague will be poured out on the sun. The God who created the sun has power over it as well. He can use it also to bring part of these final judgments. So the sun is given power to scorch the earth. This does not mean that by some natural process the sun will begin to give out more energy. This miracle of judgment will be accomplished by the power of God. Fire in the Bible often speaks of judgment (Isaiah 24:6; Malachi 4:1; and Matthew 3:10-12, for example). The fire here will aggravate the suffering caused by the ulcerated sores on the skin of those who have taken the mark of the beast. It may be also that this heat will melt the ice at the poles, raising the sea level and causing further devastation to many parts of the earth. (Compare Amos 9:5, 6.)

**9. And men were scorched with great heat:** ... When they were badly burned, *−BECK* ... by the intense heat, *−TCNT, −SEB* ... with terrific heat, *−BRKL* ... by the terrible heat, *−NORL.* **and blasphemed the name of God:** ... and they cursed, *−WMCK* ... They maligned the name of God, *−TCNT* ... reviled, *−FNTN.* **which hath power over these plagues:** ... who controlled these, *−BECK* ... Who possessed power, *−WADE* ... who tortured them with, *−NOLI* ... these Curses, *−TCNT.* **and they repented not to give him glory:** ... but they wouldn't change their hearts, *−SEB* ... changed not their minds, *−FNTN* ... nor did they give Him any

praise, *−NORL* ... they were not turned from their evil ways, *−BB.*

**16:9.** The great heat of this plague will burn mankind like fire or like a terrible fever. The pain will drive them, not to repentance, but to a vile blaspheming of the name of God. They will realize that God, not Satan, not the Antichrist or his false prophet, has control over these plagues. But they will give God no glory, for they will stubbornly refuse to recognize their sin against Him, and they will refuse to repent. By choosing to follow Satan, the Antichrist, and his false prophet, they will believe the big lie of the Antichrist's claims (2 Thessalonians 2:10). They will continue to love darkness and reject the light of God's truth.

**10. And the fifth angel poured out his vial upon the seat of the beast:** ... emptied his bowl, *−WADE* ... let what was in his vessel come out on the high seat of, *−BB* ... on the animal's throne, *−BECK* ... upon the throne of the beast, *−MNTG.* **and his kingdom was full of darkness:** ... was plunged in, *−BRKL* ... his dominion became, *−WADE* ... was shrouded in, *−WLMS* ... its kingdom was darkened, *−KLST* ... plunged his kingdom into darkness, *−NOLI* ... became darkness, *−MNTG* ... made dark, *−BB.* **and they gnawed their tongues for pain:** ... men bit their tongues, *−WMCK* ... And men chewed their tongues in consequence of their pain, *−WADE* ... because of the pain, *−KLST* ... in anguish, *−BECK, −NOLI* ... in their distress, *−NORL.*

**16:10.** The fifth angel will pour out his golden bowl on the headquarters of the beast. The Bible does not say where the throne of the beast is. Some suppose it will be Babylon, some think it will be Jerusalem or Rome. As a result the kingdom of the Antichrist will become totally dark. It will be like the plague of darkness on Egypt (Exodus 10:21-23). Darkness as judgment is mentioned a number of times in the Bible (Isaiah 60:2; Joel 2:2; Nahum 1:8; Mark 13:24, 25). This darkness will bring a disruption of the Antichrist's rule. It will also prevent those who are suffering from the previous plagues from getting any relief for their pain. In fact, their pain will be so intensified they will gnaw their tongues in agony.

**11. And blasphemed the God of heaven:** ... reviled, *−FNTN* ... said evil things against, *−BB* ... cursed God in heaven, *−NORL.* **because of their pains and their sores:** ... on account of their anguish and their wounds, *−FNTN* ...their sufferings, *−NORL.* **and repented not of their deeds:** ... did not turn from, *−FNTN* ... of their practices, *−BRKL* ... of what they had done, *−NORL* ... and abandon their doings, *−WADE* ... were not turned from their evil works, *−BB.*

**16:11.** For the second time during these bowl judgments of the seven plagues Revelation records that the people "blasphemed the God of heaven" and refused to repent of their wicked deeds. They will recognize their pain (suffering) and their sores are God's judgment on them, but this knowledge will only harden their hearts and minds against Him. They are still under the terrible deception of the Antichrist and his false prophet. But the phrase "God of heaven" reminds us of the promise in Daniel that the God of heaven will set up a Kingdom that will shatter and consume the kingdoms of the present world system and will be a Kingdom that will stand forever (Daniel 2:44, 45).

It is implied that repentance could stop the judgments, but no one will repent. Not only is there physical darkness because of this plague, the sufferers' minds are also darkened; they will not perceive the truth. The righteous judgments of God will only increase their rebellion. It should be clear also that no judgment, no purgatory, not even the lake of fire will bring repentance to those who have rejected the mercies of God and His great salvation.

12. **And the sixth angel poured out his vial upon the great river Euphrates:** . . . emptied, —WADE . . . poured his bowl, —NORL . . . mighty river, —FNTN.

**and the water thereof was dried up:** . . . its waters were dried up, —KLGS, —WADE . . . it became dry, —BB.

**that the way of the kings of the east might be prepared:** . . . In this way, the kings of the countries . . . could cross over, —NLTG . . . in order that the road for the kings from the East might be made passable, —WADE . . . so as to make ready the way, —MNTG . . . so that a way was made ready for, —KLST . . . to prepare the way for the kings from, —ADAM . . . prepared for the invasion of, —NOLI . . . a road might be prepared for the kings from the rising sun, Fenton.

**16:12.** The Euphrates was considered the great river of the Middle East during all of Old Testament times. It was the northeastern limit of the land promised to Abraham and his descendants (Genesis 15:18), and it was the eastern limit of the Roman Empire in New Testament times. When the sixth angel pours out his golden bowl the Euphrates will dry up. The Old Testament prophets drew attention to the drying up of waters as a means of divine deliverance, especially in connection with the crossing of the Red Sea and the Jordan. But occasionally they spoke of a drying up of waters as divine judgment (Isaiah 11:15; 42:15; Zechariah 10:11). In this case, however, the drying up of the Euphrates will mean it is no longer

1340

a barrier for the kings of the East (the Orient) to come with their armies in the direction of Israel and the valley of Megiddo. Satan with his power will drive them into joining together and taking part in a great conflict at the end of the Tribulation. (See Isaiah 11:15; Genesis 15:18; Joshua 1:3, 4.)

The sixth bowl then is part of the preparation for the Battle of Armageddon described in chapter 19. It will be a great struggle, but it will end in victory for the Lamb.

13. **And I saw three unclean spirits like frogs [come] out of the mouth of the dragon:** . . . I next saw proceeding from . . . resembling, —FNTN . . . three demons that looked like, —NLTG . . . hop like frogs from, —ADAM . . . three foul spirits leap like, —WLMS . . . three loathsome spirits, —NOLI . . . coming out of, —BB.

**and out of the mouth of the beast, and out of the mouth of the false prophet:** . . . the snake-like animal and the second wild animal and the false preacher, —NLTG . . . the pretended Prophet, —TCNT.

**16:13.** After the way is prepared for the kings of the east to come, the serpent, the beast, and the false prophet will be ready to go into action. The serpent is undoubtedly the seven-headed dragon or serpent described in chapter 12 and identified with the devil and Satan in 12:9. The beast is the Antichrist. Now the second beast, the beast out of the earth or the land (13:11-17), is named for the first time as the false prophet. Out of each of their mouths comes a foul, unclean spirit, each like a frog. They are not frogs, but frogs are their symbol. What a contrast to the Holy Spirit who came like a dove from heaven upon Jesus and then into Him!

Because "the unclean spirits like frogs" come out of the mouths of the unholy trio, they seem to represent the sending forth of some means of communication to the world. They are to make known the lying message of this trio in a deceptive but persuasive way.

14. **For they are the spirits of devils, working miracles:** . . . These are the demonic spirits, —KLGS . . . of demons, —WLMS . . . They were satanic spirits, —NOLI . . . demon spirits that perform miracles, —NORL . . . producing signs, —FNTN . . . working wonders, —KLST . . . working Signs, —WADE . . . who work miraculous signs, —ADAM . . . that do powerful works, —NLTG.

**[which] go forth unto the kings of the earth and of the whole world:** . . . which issue forth for the purpose of going to, —WADE . . . which they cause to be sent out to the kings of the whole habitable world, —FNTN . . . to assemble, —NOLI . . . and the peoples of the whole world, —NORL . . . all the kings of the earth, —NLTG . . . to the kings of the whole inhabited earth, —ADAM.

**to gather them to the battle of that great day of God Almighty:** . . . to muster them,

—*WLMS* ... to the war on the Day, —*WADE* ... for the war of, —*FNTN* ... when that great Day of God the Almighty comes, —*NORL* ... the Ruler of all, —*BB*.

**16:14.** These frogs are far worse than the plague of frogs that came upon Egypt (Exodus 8:2-11; Psalm 105:30). Frogs were unclean animals under the Law. These frogs are loathsome, unclean spirits, demon spirits who keep performing miraculous signs. They go out unto the kings of the earth, that is, of the entire inhabited world (including the kings of the east mentioned in connection with the plague described in verse 12), to gather them to the battle of that great day of God Almighty. Through their miracles and through the tremendous influence they exert on the minds of the rulers of the world, they will convince them to join with the Antichrist in the final battle of the Tribulation, a holocaust that will involve the whole world.

The miracles performed by these demon spirits seem to be the climax of what Jesus warned against when He said, "There shall arise false Christs, and false prophets, and shall show great signs and wonders; insomuch that, if it were possible, they shall deceive the very elect" (Matthew 24:24). But, as 2 Thessalonians 2:8-10 states: "And then shall that Wicked be revealed, whom the Lord shall consume with the spirit of his mouth, and shall destroy with the brightness of his coming: even him, whose coming is after the working of Satan with all power and signs and lying wonders, and with all deceivableness of unrighteousness in them that perish; because they received not the love of the truth, that they might be saved."

These demon spirits will concentrate on winning over the kings or rulers of the world. Their miracles will stir them with a bloodthirsty zeal for war. There will be no nations neutral in this war, this final battle of the Tribulation, a battle that will be part of the great day of God's judgment.

**15.** **Behold, I come as a thief:** ... It is written, —*NORL* ... See! I approach like, —*FNTN* ... Mark well, —*KLST* ... I am coming suddenly, like a robber, —*SEB* ... I am coming unexpectedly, —*NOLI*.

**Blessed** [is] **he that watcheth:** ... Happy the watcher, —*FNTN* ... is the alert one, —*BRKL* ... who stays awake, —*BECK* ... keeps watch, —*NORL* ... who is vigilant, —*KLST* ... who is on the watch, —*MNTG*.

**and keepeth his garments:** ... who clings to his clothing, —*FNTN* ... retains possession of his clothes, —*KLST* ... and guarding his clothing, —*MNTG* ... holds on to his garments, —*NORL* ... his robes, —*BB*.

**lest he walk naked, and they see his shame:** ... so that he does not have to walk about, —*KLST* ... that he may not go naked and be put to shame, —*NORL* ... so that he may not go unclothed, and his shame be seen, —*BB* ... and they gaze on, —*MNTG*.

**16:15.** At this point Jesus interjects a warning that is in line with His warnings given in the Gospels. "Coming as a thief" means coming unannounced and at an unexpected time. This is the third "blessed" in Revelation. Believers must watch, be on guard, be alert. "Keepeth his garments" means avoiding the stains of sin. "Naked" can mean "without outer garments, without proper covering," so in this passage it means without the white robes of Christ's righteousness. The sins that people try to hide will then be apparent to all. Instead of rejoicing with Christ and sharing in His triumph, they will shrink back in shame.

**16.** **And he gathered them together:** ... So they mustered them at the place, —*BRKL* ... accordingly, —*FNTN* ... So they assembled them, —*NORL* ... the spirits collected the kings, —*TCNT* ... they got them together, —*BB*.

**into a place called in the Hebrew tongue Armageddon:** ... which in Hebrew is called, —*NORL* ... in the Hebrew language, —*SEB* ... is named Har-Megeddon, —*FNTN* ... Mount of Megiddo, —*WADE*.

**16:16.** The rulers of the whole world will be gathered together to the place called Armageddon, which is the Greek transliteration of the Hebrew *Har Megiddôn*, "the Mountain of Megiddo." Although Joshua captured the king of Megiddo, the tribe of Manasseh failed to occupy the city or the surrounding area (Judges 17:11, 12). It guarded the pass used by ancient caravans and armies as they moved from the central valley or plain of Esdraelon to the coastal plain of Sharon on their way to Egypt. Deborah and Barak, whose story is told in the Book of Judges, won a great victory in this area (Judges 4:12-23). Many other battles in ancient times were fought here also (2 Kings 9:27; 23:29, 30). Even in modern times it has been the scene of great battles.

Armageddon will become the center for the battle of that great day of God Almighty, the battle at the end of the Tribulation. At the battle's end Jesus will return to earth in power and glory, with flaming fire to destroy the wicked (2 Thessalonians 1:7-10; compare Revelation 19:11-16).

This final battle will fulfill many Old Testament prophecies (Deuteronomy 32:43; Jeremiah 25:31; Joel 3:2, 7-17; Zephaniah 3:8; Zechariah 12:11; 14:2-5).

This battle will end when Jesus returns in power and glory and with a word defeats the Antichrist and his armies (Revelation 19:19-21; Zechariah 14:1-5). (See also Psalm 110:5; Isaiah 66:15, 16; 2 Thessalonians 1:7-10.) Earthquakes will also bring destruction on the whole world at this time (Revelation 16:18, 19; Jeremiah 25:29-33).

**17. And the seventh angel poured out his vial into the air:** . . . Lastly, *–KLST* . . . emptied his vial upon, *–FNTN* . . . poured out his bowl upon, *–MNTG.*

**and there came a great voice out of the temple of heaven, from the throne, saying:** . . . proceeded a loud voice, *–FNTN* . . . came out of the sanctuary, *–WLMS* . . . from the house of God, *–BB* . . . from the place where the King sits in, *–NLTG* . . . from the Throne within it, a loud Voice, declaring, *–WADE* . . . It said, *–NORL.*

**It is done:** . . . All is over, *–TCNT* . . . It has come! *–FNTN* . . . It is finished! *–MNTG* . . . It has all come to pass, *–WADE.*

**16:17.** When the seventh angel pours out the last bowl of God's wrath upon the air, thus filling the atmosphere with God's judgment, a loud voice from heaven's temple, from the very throne of God, will cry out, "It is done." The voice is that of God or Christ. The meaning is that the seventh plague will finish this sevenfold outpouring of the wrath of God upon the earth. Actually, the following verses describe what this plague brings upon the earth.

**18. And there were voices, and thunders, and lightnings:** . . . flames, *–BB* . . . lightning flashes, the sound of voices, thundering, *–NORL* . . . rumblings, peals of thunder, *–KLST.*

**and there was a great earthquake, such as was not since men were upon the earth:** . . . and the earth shook . . . much more than it had ever shaken before, *–NLTG* . . . There has never been such an earthquake since men peopled this earth, *–NORL* . . . had not occurred from the time, *–TCNT* . . . since man first existed on, *–WLMS* . . . in the history of mankind, *–NOLI* . . . since man began to be upon, *–MNTG* . . . since men came into being on the earth, *–WADE.*

**so mighty an earthquake, [and] so great:** . . . so extensive and so severe, *–BRKL* . . . It was tremendous! *–SEB* . . . it was so great! *–NORL* . . . so great an earthquake was it, *–KLST* . . . so violent, *–WADE* . . . earthshock, so full of power, *–BB.*

**16:18.** Voices, lightning, and thunder preceded the seals, the trumpets, and the bowls (4:5; 8:5; 11:19). The sixth seal also pictured a great earthquake that seemed to involve the entire crust of the earth (6:12-14), and may be a preview of this same earthquake. Earthquakes will also precede the trumpets and the bowls. With this final plague of the seven angels there will come voices, then a terrible storm with continuing thunder and lightning, followed by a great earthquake. The voices will probably repeat the judgment of God on the world system now dominated by Satan who is the prince of the power of the air (Ephesians 2:2), and especially the divine judgment about to fall on the Antichrist and his kingdom. God used storms to bring judgment in Old Testament times. The prophets spoke of thunder and lightning bringing

further judgments (Psalm 50:3, 4; Isaiah 24:17-21; 29:6; Joel 3:16; Haggai 2:6, 7).

The severity of the earthquake is emphasized by a fourfold repetition. It will be great, greater than any earthquake since mankind was on the earth, so mighty, and so great. There have been many great earthquakes in past history. In this century the 1908 earthquake in Messina, Italy, killed 76,483 people. The 1920 quake in Kansu Province, China, killed about 200,000 people. The 1923 quake in Tokyo, Japan, killed 99, 331. The 1911 New Madrid earthquake in Missouri was felt as far away as Savannah, Georgia. But this earthquake will affect the whole world. This prophesied earthquake will exceed all of these and will undoubtedly change the topography of the entire earth. In view of the shocking effect of recent earthquakes, it is hard even to imagine what this will do to the people left on the earth.

**19. And the great city was divided into three parts, and the cities of the nations fell:** . . . the great town was cut, *–BB* . . . The big and strong city, *–NLTG* . . . was shattered, *–MNTG* . . . rent, *–FNTN* . . . broke into three pieces, *–KLST* . . . split into three parts, *–BECK* . . . torn in three, *–TCNT* . . . was riven . . . the cities of the heathen nations collapsed, *–WADE.*

**and great Babylon came in remembrance before God:** . . . remembered in the sight, *–FNTN* . . . recalled to God's mind, *–WADE* . . . came to mind before the face of God, *–MNTG.*

**to give unto her the cup of the wine of the fierceness of his wrath:** . . . for Him to give to her the cup filled with the wine of His furious Wrath, *–WADE* . . . He made her drain the winecup . . . of His anger, *–NORL* . . . to receive the wine-cup of the fury, *–FNTN* . . . the passion of his anger, *–MNTG* . . . furious indignation, *–BRKL* . . . raging wrath, *–WLMS* . . . fierce anger, *–KLST.*

**16:19.** Commentators have given various interpretations as to the identity of "the great city." Because the name "Babylon" appears here, some believe that a rebuilt Babylon will become a world center for commerce and religion and will meet the fate described in chapter 18 (Bullinger, p. 492). Others believe it is Rome which was the center of world power in John's day (Charles, *International Critical Commentary, Revelation,* 2:52).

Still others consider it to be Jerusalem, which has been identified as "the great city" (11:8). It has already been one-tenth destroyed by an earthquake (11:13), and it is felt this is a literal earthquake which divides Jerusalem (cf. Barnhouse, p. 307). They consider it could be the fulfillment of the Zechariah 14:4 prophecy.

Babylon the Great being remembered before God does not mean God had forgotten it. This is Old Testament phraseology which means God now comes into the situation to do something about it (see Eising, "zākhar," *Theological Dictionary of the Old Testament,* 4:69-72). To that end it will be given the cup of the wine of the fury of God's holy wrath. The focus of all God's judgment here is on the "great Babylon." This is so important that both chapters 17 and 18 give more details of its fall. The world will see a demonstration that God's universe is a moral universe, for God will pour out His wrath on a world system that has rejected Him.

**20. And every island fled away:** . . . vanished, —BECK . . . disappeared, —SEB . . . went in flight, —BB.

**and the mountains were not found:** . . . not a mountain could be seen, —WLMS . . . disappeared, —TCNT . . . no trace was found, —WADE . . . sank from sight, —MNTG . . . were seen no longer, —BB.

**16:20.** The removal of islands and mountains seems to mean the topography of the earth will be changed in preparation for the coming kingdom. Some believe it means a restoration to conditions like those before the worldwide flood of Noah's day.

**21. And there fell upon men a great hail out of heaven:** . . . Huge, —NOLI . . . great drops of ice, —BB . . . Hailstones, —BRKL . . . Large, —KLST . . . descends from the sky, —WADE . . . mighty, —FNTN . . . poured down on men from the skies, —NORL.

**[every stone] about the weight of a talent:** . . . heavy as, —KLST . . . of immense weight, —NOLI . . . big as hundredweights, —BRKL . . . weighed about 100 pounds, —SEB.

**and men blasphemed God because of the plague of the hail:** . . . and men cursed God, —WLMS . . . men said evil things against God because of the punishment of the ice-drops, —BB . . . on account of, —FNTN . . . in consequence of, —WADE.

**for the plague thereof was exceeding great:** . . . awful, —SEB . . . destructive, —LAMS . . . terrible, —NORL . . . grievous, —KLST . . . exceedingly distressing, —WADE . . . for it is very great, —BB.

**16:21.** In addition to the great earthquake a plague of hail will bring another part of nature into use for judgment and further destruction. Hail has been used by God, as described in Exodus 9:24 and Joshua 10:11. It is prophesied in Isaiah 28:2 and Ezekiel 38:22. But this hail will be far worse than any hailstorm in the past, for the hailstones will weigh a talent, that is, about 75 pounds each. Again, there is no repentance, for the human beings left on earth will blaspheme God because of the hail.

## Chapter 17

**1. And there came one of the seven angels which had the seven vials:** . . . who had the seven bowls of wrath, —NORL.

**and talked with me, saying unto me, Come hither:** . . . spoke, —FNTN.

**I will show unto thee the judgment of the great whore that sitteth upon many waters:** . . . the sentence passed upon, —MNTG, —TCNT . . . the condemnation of, —LAMS . . . how judgment falls on the great harlot who sits where many waters meet, —NORL . . . the doom of the great Courtesan whose capital is located at the meeting-place of many rivers, —NOLI . . . the great prostitute, —BECK . . . the evil woman who is seated on the great waters, —BB . . . the doom of the great harlot, —BRKL . . . the condemnation of the famous whore, —SEB . . . who is seated at the confluence of many streams, —WADE.

**17:1.** Chapters 17 and 18 give details about the fall of Babylon the Great, a fall already announced in 14:8 and 16:19.

As mentioned above (16:19) some identify this Babylon with the ancient city rebuilt as a headquarters for the Antichrist. Others identify it with Rome, or Jerusalem, or with some other city. It may well symbolize the entire world system which opposes God. In this it is similar to the picture of the world system represented by the Babylon image seen by Nebuchadnezzar in Daniel chapter 2.

Verses 1-5 comprise the first section of this chapter. One of the seven angels used to pour out the seven bowls of God's wrath now spoke with John. The angel told John he would show him the judgment, that is, the condemnation and punishment of the great whore (harlot, prostitute) who sits upon the many waters.

The Bible often uses adultery and prostitution figuratively to represent false worship, worship of heathen gods, or other types of unfaithfulness to the true God or rebellion against Him (Isaiah 1:21; Jeremiah 3:9; Ezekiel 16:14-18, 32; James 4:4). Therefore, many believe this is figurative language for the religious Babylon that includes all false religions, false cults, and apostate churches. Its final form during the Tribulation will be the worship of the Antichrist.

Waters are used of Assyria (Isaiah 8:7, 8). "The many waters" of 17:1 are believed by some to refer to the system of irrigation canals which surrounded ancient Babylon on the Euphrates (Beasley-Murray, *New Century Bible, The Book of Revelation,* p. 251). However, verse 15 identifies them as the many peoples, crowds, nations, and languages of the world. This could mean that Babylon will be a city that dominates and controls all the nations or is supported by all the nations. Or, more probably, it means that Babylon represents the world system that includes the peoples of the world. Thus it refers to the world system from Babylon through the centuries to the time of the final judgments at the end of this age.

**2. With whom the kings of the earth have committed fornication:** . . . she with whom, *—FNTN* . . . lived in sexual sin, *—BECK* . . . committed adultery, *—NORL* . . . have had immoral relations, *—WADE*...made themselves unclean, *—BB.*

**and the inhabitants of the earth have been made drunk with the wine of her fornication:** . . . and the peoples of the earth have become intoxicated with the wine of her impurities, *—NORL* . . . with the wine of whose immorality the inhabitants of the earth have become drunken, *—WADE*...of her sexual vice, *—BECK*...of her unchastity, *—BRKL*...of her sexual sin, *—SEB*...of her pagan orgies, *—NOLI*...of her immorality, *—KLST, —MNTG*...of her evil desires, *—BB.*

**17:2.** It is possible that this vision does not follow the seven vials or bowl judgments. Rather, it may go back to give further details of the message of the angel given in 14:8. That angel announced the fall of Babylon as a result of making all nations drink of the wine of the wrath of her fornication. Now chapters 17 and 18 enlarge on what that means. It is emphasized that not just the nations in general but the kings of the earth have committed prostitution with her, primarily spiritual prostitution and idolatry. This may mean the rulers of this world enter into partnership with the Babylon religious system and its immorality and corruption.

The inhabitants of the earth are led astray by this great whore (harlot, prostitute). Hypocrites and false prophets encourage those of the world to follow her false doctrines. She requires no real holiness, no dedication to God. Instead, she intoxicates people with the wine of her fornication. Instead of following the one true God and worshiping Him in the Holy Spirit and in line with the truth of His written Word, they follow the philosophies of human thinkers and of the false religions of this world. As the first chapter of Romans indicates, instead of worshiping the true God, they put self on the throne, and soon are worshiping gods of their own making, gods they think they can manipulate. This leads to the practice of all the lusts of the flesh that Galatians 5:21 says will make it impossible for them to inherit the kingdom of God. These lusts of the flesh, along with involvement in false philosophies and false doctrines, false cults, and false rituals, deaden spiritual sensitivities just as wine deadens the mind and poisons the body.

**3. So he carried me away in the spirit into the wilderness:** . . . by him I was rapt in a spiritual trance to a lonely spot, *—WADE*...in spiritual rapture, *—WLMS* . . . took me away in the Spirit into a waste land, *—BB* . . . he conveyed me, *—FNTN*...he bore me away, *—MNTG* . . . carried me away in ecstasy to a, *—KLST*...into a desert, *—BRKL, —NORL* . . . to a lonely place, *—TCNT.*

**and I saw a woman sit upon a scarlet coloured beast:** . . . And he showed me a woman, *—KLGS*...where I observed, *—FNTN*...a woman riding, *—ADAM* . . . seated upon a scarlet Wild Beast, *—WADE*...on a bright red beast, *—BB*...on a red wild animal, *—NLTG.*

**full of names of blasphemy:**...having the name of Slander, *—KLGS*...full of evil names, *—BB*...inscribed with many words of blasphemy, *—LAMS*... covered with blasphemous titles, *—BRKL, —WLMS*...was written bad names which spoke against God, *—NLTG*...that was filled with, *—ADAM* . . . blasphemous names, *—NORL.*

**having seven heads and ten horns:**...possessing, *—FNTN.*

**17:3.** The angel carried John "away in the spirit" to a wilderness or desert. In 1:10 John was in the Spirit and saw a vision of Christ. In 4:2 he was in the Spirit and saw the vision of the throne of God in heaven. This time his experience is something like Ezekiel's for he was conscious of being carried away. There in a new vision he saw a woman sitting on a scarlet beast full of blasphemous names, that is, names that blasphemed the holiness and glory of the true God. This beast is obviously the same as the beast described in 13:1. The beast had 7 heads and 10 horns which are further identified in 17:10-12. The heads seem to indicate a sequence, so the beast has one head controlling it at a time. The 10 horns seem to act together at the same time. (See verse 12.)

Sitting on the beast is parallel to sitting on the many waters of verse 1. The woman John saw dominates, and her influence infiltrates the peoples and nations of the entire world.

Writers such as Barnhouse identify the scarlet beast with Rome and with a sequence of seven emperors (p. 320). But that limits it to the past, and the beast is present in the end times. The beast can better be identified as the world system or political Babylon that will support the apostate world religious systems and which will climax in the kingdom of the Antichrist.

The fact that she is carried by the beast indicates she will compromise with political power, tolerate unrighteousness, and seek the favor of an ungodly world.

**4. And the woman was arrayed in purple and scarlet colour:** . . . was bedecked with, *—NOLI* . . . dressed, *—FNTN* . . . was enwrapped,

—MNTG ... was clothed in, —KLST ... and bright red, —BB.

**and decked with gold and precious stones and pearls:** ... and bejewelled, —WADE ... bedecked with, —NORL ... decorated with, —KLGS ... trimmed with gold and valuable gems, —ADAM ... gilded with gold, —RTHM ... was glittering with, —TCNT ... ornaments of gold and stones of great price, —BB ... was encrusted with, —MNTG ... jewels, —FNTN ... and adorned with golden jewellery, —TNT ... and stones worth much money, —NLTG.

**having a golden cup in her hand full of abominations and filthiness of her fornication:** ... held in her hand, —KLST ... she held a golden cup full of things accursed, the filth of her lewd-ness, —NORL ... full of evil things and her unclean desires, —BB ... and unclean things pertaining to her sexual immoralities, —ADAM ... full of the sinful things from her sex sins, —NLTG ... the offenses and impurities of her lewdness, —BRKL ... of her sexual vice, —TNT ... the filthy fruits of her licentiousness, —TCNT ... the filth of her prostitutions, —FNTN ... and sacrilegious cravings, —NOLI ... and of the pollutions of, —WADE ... of her immorality, —MNTG.

**17:4.** This woman is a strong contrast to the woman of chapter 12 who was clothed with the sun. In contrast to Israel, the great whore is and has been clothed with the symbols of the riches and power of this world. Purple and scarlet were the colors of royalty and magnificence in Bible times (Judges 8:26; Daniel 5:7; Nahum 2:3). The dyes were extremely expensive, and only the wealthy could afford them. Thus the woman's clothes and the gold, jewels, and pearls that adorn her speak of all the external signs of success that the world seeks. The adornment is only on the surface, however, and her character is the opposite of the beauty she presents to the world that is under her influence. How different this is from the pure white garments of the those who have been washed in the blood of the Lamb! (Compare 3:5; 7:14; 19:8.)

The "golden cup" brings a further contrast, for it is quite different from the cup of the Lord. Her gold cup may look beautiful on the outside, but on the inside it is full of the abominations and filthiness of her fornications, her religious and moral corruption. Instead of offering the world the cup of salvation and the cup of suffering for Christ's sake, she offers carnal satisfaction in the name of religion.

**5. And upon her forehead [was] a name written:** ... on her brow, —BB ... a symbolic title was inscribed, —BRKL ... with a symbolical meaning, —WLMS ... a mysterious name, —KLST ... her name, —WADE.

**MYSTERY, BABYLON THE GREAT, THE MOTHER OF HARLOTS AND ABOMINATIONS OF THE EARTH:** ... a name of secret import, —WADE ... A SECRET, —FNTN ... with a hidden meaning, —BECK ... THE FILTHY THINGS OF THE WORLD, —SEB ... MOTHER OF THE EVIL WOMEN, —BB ... and all that is abominable on earth, —NORL.

**17:5.** The name written on her forehead indicates her character. "Mystery" may mean that up to this time her true nature and character have not been fully revealed.

According to Oates, the name "Babylon" was once thought to have originated from the earlier Sumerian name Ka-dinga. This Sumerian name was translated by the Akkadians as Bab-ilim and by the Hebrews as *Bābēl*. The city's earlier Akkadian name is now believed to be a secondary, popular spelling of Babil, the meaning of which is uncertain. In a later period the name appears in the plural form Bab-ilani, "gate of the gods." The Greeks then translated it *Babulōn*, thus the modern name Babylon (*Ancient People and Places* 94:60). It came to symbolize false religion, sorcery, astrology, the occult, human pride, and rebellion against the one true God. In 17:5 Babylon is the name given to the entire godless religious system that has dominated the world and that will climax in the religious system of the Antichrist and his false prophet.

Not only is her cup full of abominations, but she is the mother of harlots and of the abominations of the earth. From her has been spawned all the false religions and false cults that have arisen from the time of the tower of Babel until now. The word "abomination" is used of anything that is detestable in the sight of God, especially everything connected with idolatry, astrology, fortune telling, spiritualist mediums, heathen magic, witchcraft, drug-induced experiences, and the occult. It can well be applied also to all the secular, humanistic, satanic, and new age philosophies and teachings that are spreading today.

**6. And I saw the. woman drunken with the blood of the saints:** ... I took a look at the woman, drunk as she was, —NORL ... overcome, —BB ... of the holy people, —BECK ... of God's Hallowed People, —WADE.

**and with the blood of the martyrs of Jesus:** ... of those put to death because of Jesus, —BB.

**and when I saw her, I wondered with great admiration:** ... And I was very much surprised to see her, —BECK ... overcome, —BB ... on seeing her, —WADE ... I marveled and was filled with great wonder, —NORL ... I was utterly amazed, —BRKL ... utterly astonished, —WLMS ... amazed beyond measure, —TCNT ... I was deeply shocked, —NOLI ... with great amazement, —LAMS ... with a great wonder! —FNTN.

**17:6.** John saw the woman drunk with the blood of the saints and the blood of those martyred for Jesus. This again identifies the woman as personifying the entire anti-God world religious system. There is nothing in this passage that limits her lust to those who were martyred by Rome or to those who will be martyred during the Tribulation. Throughout history she has pursued and persecuted the followers of God.

Though she is dressed in royal colors and decorated with gold, jewels, and pearls, on the inside she is a "habitation of devils, and the hold of every foul spirit" (Revelation 18:2; Isaiah 47:12, 13). The false religions of this world have and will continue to persecute true followers of Christ. There have been martyrs all through the Church Age. Those who kill believers may give no outward indication of the demonic power that motivates them. Some may and some may not realize that demonic power is compelling them. But the desire to destroy Christian faith and deny the truth of the Bible is of satanic origin. The whole anti-God system will reach its climax in the religion of the Antichrist and his false prophet.

The vision of the woman on the scarlet beast filled John with great amazement (see *Various Versions* for several meanings). He wondered what this could mean.

**7. And the angel said unto me, Wherefore didst thou marvel?:**... But the angel asked, *—NORL*... Because of what do you wonder? *—FNTN*... Why were you amazed? *—WADE*... Why were you surprised? *—BB*.

**I will tell thee the mystery of the woman:**... I will explain, *—MNTG*... I shall disclose to you what the mystery about this woman is, *—NORL*... the mystic import of, *—WADE*.

**and of the beast that carrieth her:**... and of the Wild beast, *—WADE*... on which she is seated, *—NOLI*... on which she rides, *—NORL*.

**which hath the seven heads and ten horns:**... the seven-headed and ten-horned, *—KLST*.

**17:7.** The vision was no mystery to the angel. He assured John that he would explain to him the meaning of the woman and the wild beast that was carrying her. This was one mystery, not two. The beast and the woman are inseparably related. One cannot be understood apart from the other.

The angel also said he would explain the meaning of the 7 heads and 10 horns. Special attention is drawn to them because of their importance to the understanding of the sentence of judgment on the great harlot.

**8. The beast that thou sawest was, and is not:**... As to the beast you saw, he was, but is no more, *—NORL*... The red wild animal you saw... is now dead, *—NLTG*... existed at one time, *—SEB*... existed

once, now has ceased to be, *—KLST*... but exists no longer, *—WADE*.

**and shall ascend out of the bottomless pit, and go into perdition:**... Yet, *—KLST*... is about to come up, *—MNTG*... about to come up from the hole without a bottom, *—NLTG*... is destined to ascend... and is to go again, *—WADE*... he is to come out of... and then go back to perdition, *—NORL*... out of the great deep, *—BB*... proceed to, *—FNTN*... to go on to destruction, *—BRKL*... But it will finally be destroyed, *—NOLI*... go to be destroyed, *—LAMS*.

**and they that dwell on the earth shall wonder:**... the inhabitants, *—KLST*... shall be astonished, *—FNTN*... will be full of wonder,' *—BB*... will also marvel, *—NORL*... will be surprised, *—NLTG*.

**whose names were not written in the book of life from the foundation of the world:**... whose names have never been inscribed in, *—NOLI*... are not recorded... from the foundation of the world onward, *—WADE*... since the beginning of the world, *—SEB*... have not been put in the book of life from the first, *—BB*.

**when they behold the beast that was, and is not, and yet is:**... as they look at the red wild animal... but it will come back again, *—NLTG*... when they gaze on the beast; how he was, *—MNTG*... when they witness... and yet confronts them, *—FNTN*... because it was, then was no more, and is to come, *—NORL*... though it existed once but exists no longer, will nevertheless come again, *—WADE*... because it existed, then ceased to be, yet will come back to life, *—KLST*... but he will come back, *—SEB*... and now whose end has come, *—LAMS*... and still will be, *—BB*.

**17:8.** This passage is one of the most difficult to interpret in the entire Book of Revelation. What is the identity of the beast? Some think it refers to the Antichrist. Chapter 13 speaks of him as a beast. The description also seems to apply to a kingdom. The best exegesis seems to be that the beast is both a kingdom and a man (cf. Daniel 2:38 where Nebuchadnezzar is identified with his kingdom).

Many think of the beast "that was, and is not, and yet is" as referring to a revived Roman Empire, ruled by Antichrist in the end times. At the same time, it seems to point to a person who was (existed) "and was not" ("wounded to death," 13:3), "and yet is" (seemingly resurrected, so "all the world wondered").

The beast may also represent the Antichrist's kingdom. It has not existed as a political entity since the fall of the Roman Empire, but as a humanistic, anti-God system it has continued to dominate the world throughout the "times of the Gentiles." During the Tribulation it will emerge "out of the bottomless pit," the abyss, to be the empire of the beast, the Antichrist. In other words, it will be inspired, dominated, and indwelt by Satan.

Later the beast will be "cast alive into a lake of fire burning with brimstone" (19:20). A kingdom cannot be cast into a lake of fire, only a person can, so the beast of chapter 19 has to be the Antichrist. But a kingdom, a system, can be judged here on earth, and this will occur toward the end of the Great Tribulation.

Many leaders—Charlemagne, Napoleon, Hitler—have tried to establish a world empire, and Mussolini dreamed of one, saying he would make the Mediterranean Sea a Roman lake. But they all failed. The World Court, the League of Nations, and the United Nations have all tried to bring the nations together. They too have failed. But the spirit which will bring it to pass is still active in the world. The spirit of Antichrist is preparing mankind for it, and when its time has come, it will be accepted.

Neither the Antichrist nor his kingdom, symbolized by the beast, will last for very long, however. Their destiny is perdition and destruction. The Greek word *apōleia* was used of loss, then of total ruin or eternal destruction. It is used in the New Testament especially of the final punishment of the wicked in the lake of fire. Since a kingdom is composed of people, it means that both the Antichrist and his followers will suffer the same fate. The end then is eternal loss. Choices determine destiny. Those who reject God's offer of life are choosing eternal death.

Those dwelling on earth are the ones who will wonder at the beast, implying they will be attracted to him and accept him. It is said of them their "names were not written in the book of life." This must be in contrast to those who are living in heaven. For one group the future holds only eternal woe, for those in heaven there will be eternal happiness and joy.

**9. And here [is] the mind which hath wisdom:** ... Here is something for an intelligent person to think about, *–BECK* ... A wise mind is needed to interpret this, *–KLST* ... Here is a task for a mind with wisdom, *–NORL* ... Here is needed the understanding that has insight, *–WADE* ... Approach, you who have intelligence and understanding! *–FNTN* ... for the intelligent to ponder, *–BRKL* ... Here is an intelligent explanation, *–NOLI.*
**The seven heads are seven mountains, on which the woman sitteth:** ... the seven hills ... the woman is seated, *–NORL.*

**17:9.** The mind of wisdom means there is something here to help interpret John's vision. The seven heads have a twofold symbolism. They represent seven mountains or (as the Greek can also mean) seven hills. Some commentators have tried to find seven hills in Jerusalem. But there are not seven hills there. Actually, in New Testament times Rome was known everywhere as the city

of seven hills. All of John's readers in the seven churches would have thought of it as Rome.

This seems to mean that Christ and the Holy Spirit wanted the people of John's day to know they were in the Roman stage of the history of the world system. This would correspond with the legs of iron in the great image Nebuchadnezzar saw in Daniel chapter 2. Rome and its emperors were united in John's day against the true believers in Jesus Christ.

**10. And there are seven kings: five are fallen:** ... and they are, *–MNTG* ... are seven Emperors, *–WADE.*
**and one is:** ... One is now reigning, *–NOLI* ... is still alive, *–NORL* ... exists, *–FNTN.*
**[and] the other is not yet come:** ... has not yet made his appearance, *–KLST* ... has not appeared, *–FNTN.*
**and when he cometh, he must continue a short space:** ... and when he does he will stay only a little while, *–NORL* ... he must remain a short time, *–MNTG* ... his stay must be short, *–KLST.*

**17:10.** The seven heads also represent seven kings, each probably representing a kingdom in the sequence of the world system of which Rome was a part. One view sees these as five prominent kings of the Roman empire who preceded Domitian, or five kings who had the spirit of Nero and Domitian (Harrington, pp. 210f.; Charles, *International Critical Commentary, Revelation,* 2:69). The one that "is" would then be Domitian, and the one who "was not yet come" would be the Antichrist at the end time. Lilje links the one to come with a later tradition that Nero would come back as the Antichrist (p. 227). However, it is not possible to link these five kings clearly with any particular sequence of Roman emperors. It seems better to accept the interpretation of many who believe the five "fallen" empires to be Egyptian, Assyrian, Babylonian, Medo Persian, and the Greek empire of Alexander the Great (Barnhouse, p. 329; Morris, p. 337). Rome would thus be the one that is. The one not yet come would compare with the feet of iron and clay in the great Babylon image of Daniel chapter 2; that is, our present world arrangement of nationalistic states, some strong, some weak or brittle, and all failing to be able to stick together. That Rome was in the picture would be important for Christians of John's day. But it is stated in such a way that Roman officials would not be able to use it against Christians.

**11. And the beast that was, and is not:** ... that existed, then ceased to be, *–KLST* ... which existed once but exists no longer, –WADE … and then was no more, –NORL.

**even he is the eighth, and is of the seven:** … is himself an eighth king, although he belongs to the seven, –NORL … himself reckoned as an eighth, and yet is included among, –WADE.

**and goeth into perdition:** … and must go to, –KLST … goes on to ruin, –BRKL … is on his way to destruction, –TCNT … but destruction will be his lot, –NORL … destined to be destroyed, –LAMS … he is to go to, –WADE.

**17:11.** The beast not only has seven heads, but he himself is the eighth. He is "of the seven," that is, he belongs to the same Babylon world system that preceded him, even though he is not part of those seven. The Antichrist is not in the picture of chapter 2. But Daniel 7 introduces him as the little horn that arises out of the fourth beast. Revelation identifies him with the beast itself because he will be the climax and sum of all the ungodly world systems that precede him.

The beast, the Antichrist, will go into perdition or eternal loss at the end of the Tribulation. He will be cast into the lake of fire which was prepared for the devil and his angels.

12. **And the ten horns which thou sawest are ten kings:** … Then, as to the ten horns you saw, –NORL.

**which have received no kingdom as yet:** … who as yet have inherited no kingdom, –FNTN … who have not yet obtained a kingdom, –NORL … not yet received kingly rule, –WADE.

**but receive power as kings one hour with the beast:** … but they are to get authority as kings along with, –NORL … in conjunction with, –TCNT … invested with kingly authority for a single hour, –FNTN … for the briefest period, as it might be an hour and no more, –WADE … together with, –MNTG … allied with the wild beast, –WLMS.

**17:12.** The 10 horns represent 10 kings, that is, 10 kingdoms or nations that will have great political power for 1 hour, that is, for a short period of time. The Bible specifically states that these kingdoms or nations were not yet in existence in John's day. Therefore, they cannot refer to nations related to the old Roman Empire. They will come into existence at the end of the Church Age and will have power in the time of the end when the Antichrist appears. Three popular suggestions of the identity of these include: they will make up a world confederacy, or possibly a United States of Europe; they are a revived Roman Empire with Italy again as the leader (Barnhouse, p. 330); they are an empire with a rebuilt city of Babylon as their capital. However, Daniel 2:34, 44 shows that the image representing the sequence of world empires will be hit in the feet, not the legs, not the

head. Others interpret the number 10 as a number of completion and believe the 10 horns represent the fullness of all the kingdoms and nations at the end of the age, for they will all give their power and authority to the Antichrist (Ladd, *Revelation*, pp. 231f.). However they are interpreted, it is clear they will eventually oppose the Lord Jesus and the Bible and will be ready to follow the Antichrist. (See Daniel 7:7, 23, 24.)

13. **These have one mind:** … These have one purpose, –BRKL … All these, being of the same mind, –NORL … These are of one accord, –LAMS … They have one common policy, –WLMS … They have one goal, –SEB … have a single purpose in common, –WADE.

**and shall give their power and strength unto the beast:** … give their might and authority over to, –NORL … depute their power and authority to, –FNTN … surrender to, –WADE.

**17:13.** These 10 nations will be united in their mind and purpose and surrender their own power and authority in order to give all their support and loyalty to the beast, that is, to the Antichrist and his kingdom which will be the final manifestation of the godless world systems that have dominated the world since human government began.

Daniel 7:7, 8 tells of 10 horns that rise out of the fourth beast that Daniel saw, a beast representing the Roman Empire and all the nations that come from it. These 10 horns are not in unity at first. Three of them are uprooted before the little horn who represents the Antichrist. That is, they have to be forced into giving their power and authority over to the Antichrist. But the other seven willingly delegate their powers to him.

14. **These shall make war with the Lamb:** … wage war, –FNTN … They will fight against, –KLST … war against, –WADE.

**and the Lamb shall overcome them:** … the Lamb will defeat them, –SEB … will conquer them, –LAMS … will be victorious over them, –WADE.

**for he is Lord of lords, and King of kings:** … because He is, –WADE.

**and they that are with him [are] called, and chosen, and faithful:** … his foreordained … followers, –NOLI … those who are on his side, –TCNT … picked, and loyal, –BRKL … have been called chosen and found faithful, –NORL … Chosen by Him, and faithful to Him, –WADE.

**17:14.** The Book of Revelation now moves forward (with a preview of the events of chapter 19) to the final battle of the Tribulation where the Antichrist and his forces (including the 10 kingdoms or nations represented by the 10 horns) make war with the Lamb. This shows the completeness of their loyalty to the Antichrist and also indicates how they have been blinded by his deceptions.

But Christ will overcome them. He will win the war, for He is and always will be Lord of lords and King of kings. He is the rightful Ruler of this world, and in this battle He will win the victory that will bring in the millennial kingdom.

In this final battle Jesus will be accompanied by those who are "called, and chosen, and faithful." They have responded to the call to salvation and have faithfully served their Lord in the ways He has chosen.

**15. And he saith unto me:** ... Continuing, he said, —NORL ... He also said, —KLST.

**The waters which thou sawest:** ... you observed, —FNTN.

**where the whore sitteth, are peoples, and multitudes, and nations, and tongues:** ... where the harlot sits, are races, and crowds, —FNTN ... the woman who sold the use of her body, —NLTG ... where the harlot was seated, represent peoples, —NORL ... takes her seat, —MNTG ... and armies, —BB ... and languages, —SEB, —WADE.

**17:15.** The angel (17:1) who was showing this vision to John now clearly identified the symbolism of the waters where the great whore or harlot woman sat. They are peoples, multitudes, nations, and languages; that is, they are all the people of the world. They have all been influenced through the centuries by these false religious systems that will culminate in the state religion of the Antichrist. They have all been part of the Babylon world system represented by the image with the head of gold in Daniel chapter 2 and by the sequence of the four wild beasts in Daniel chapter 7. Those still existing in the end of the age will become part of Antichrist's kingdom.

**16. And the ten horns which thou sawest upon the beast:** ... as well as the beasts, —KLST ... and the red wild animal, —NLTG.

**these shall hate the whore:** ... will together hate, —WADE ... will rise against, —NOLI ... will be turned against the evil woman, —BB ... the harlot, —KLST.

**and shall make her desolate and naked:** ... They will abandon her, —SEB ... They will take everything from her and even her clothes, —NLTG ... make her poor, —NORL ... will render her isolated and stripped, —BRKL ... waste and uncovered, —BB ... and exposed, —WADE.

**and shall eat her flesh, and burn her with fire:** ... take her flesh for food, —BB ... devour her flesh and burn her up with fire, —NOLI ... burn up the remains with, —NORL ... consume her, —FNTN ... destroy her with, —TCNT ... by fire, —SEB.

**17:16.** At some point during the reign of Antichrist the 10 nations who support him will come to hate the harlot woman which will include false churches that may have the name of being "Christian," as well as all the other religions and cults of the world. Probably, they will see that if the Antichrist is to be worshiped, there is no room for any other religion. So they will destroy her completely with all of her institutions. The language here is like that of Ezekiel 23:11-25. They will make her desolate, without property or buildings. They will make her naked. That is, they will strip her of the purple and scarlet, the gold, jewels, and pearls. All the outward signs of power, wealth, beauty, and influence will be gone. Then they will eat her flesh, that is, consume and destroy the religious organizations with their priests and all their functionaries. Finally, whatever is left they will destroy with fire. The one who was drunk with the blood of martyrs will herself become a victim.

When will this take place? It is difficult to determine. This we know, it will occur after the Antichrist has declared himself to be god, and the kings have delivered their authority over to him.

**17. For God hath put in their hearts to fulfil his will, and to agree:** ... God put into their minds a plan that would carry out His desire, —NLTG ... to do what He has decided, —BECK ... to carry out His purpose, —KLST, —WLMS ... do to his purpose, and to be of one mind, —BB ... to accomplish, —SEB ... put it into their minds ... to execute in common a single purpose, —WADE ... to execute his purpose, in executing their common purpose, —MNTG ... to effect His own purpose, —FNTN.

**and give their kingdom unto the beast:** ... act in harmony in surrendering their royalty, —FNTN ... to give the beast their power to rule, —EVRD ... by handing over their authority to the animal, —PHLP ... giving up ... authority, —WLMS ... to the wild beast, —CNDT.

**until the words of God shall be fulfilled:** ... until what God has said is completed, —EVRD ... intentions ... are completed, —FNTN ... executed, —TCNT ... are accomplished, —CNFT ... come true, —SEB.

**17:17.** By their actions they will actually be carrying out the sentence of judgment mentioned in 17:1, even though they will not realize what they are doing is fulfilling God's judgment on the harlot woman. God is able to use the wrath of man to praise Him (Psalm 76:10). He used the Assyrians as a rod of punishment in His angry hand, even though the Assyrians did not know God was using them. They were just out to rob other nations in order to get wealth and power for themselves. But God used them, and then judgment came upon them in due time (Isaiah 10:5-12). God also used the Babylonians, even though He knew how wicked they were, but He brought an end to their empire in due time (Habakkuk 1:5-11).

What these 10 horns or nations and kingdoms do will help to prepare them also for their own judgment. They will be united in their worship of the beast. They will follow him into the final battle where all nations will be gathered together. But Jesus will return in flaming fire taking vengeance on those who know not God (Joel 3:2; Zechariah 14:2; 2 Thessalonians 1:7, 8).

**18. And the woman which thou sawest is that great city:** . . . whom you perceived, –CNDT.
**which reigneth over the kings of the earth:** . . . that rules over, –EVRD . . . which dominates, –PHLP . . . she that has a kingdom over, –RTHM . . . which has kingship over, –CNFT . . . is Empress, –TCNT . . . has dominion, –WLMS . . . dominates, –FNTN.

**17:18.** Now the harlot woman is identified with the great city that has dominion over the kings of the earth. In Daniel's time this was Babylon. In John's time it was Rome. In the Middle Ages it was the Roman Church that was crowning kings. However, none of these ever had dominion over all the kings or kingdoms of the earth. Thus, even though she is called a city, the woman remains the entire anti-God religious system that began at the tower of Babel and has dominated the kings and kingdoms of this world through the ages. It will be the Babylonish church or religion of the Antichrist and his false prophet in the first part of the Tribulation.

## Chapter 18

**1. And after these things:** . . . Later, –PHLP . . . Then, –EVRD.
**I saw another angel come down from heaven, having great power:** . . . I perceived another messenger descending, –CNDT . . . armed with, –PHLP . . . entrusted, –TCNT . . . possessed . . . authority, –BRKL.
**and the earth was lightened with his glory:** . . . illuminated, –BRKL . . . majesty, –FNTN . . . splendor, –NOLI.

**18:1.** "After these things" probably indicates a period of time passing before the final vision of God's judgment on the Babylon world system was given to John by still another angel. Apparently this angel has not yet had a part in the judgments of the Tribulation. He comes down out of heaven with great authority and power, and with a brightness of glory that lights up the earth. John also is on the earth. (In much of chapters 15 and 16 and in 17:1 it seems he was in heaven.)

**2. And he cried mightily with a strong voice, saying:** . . . voice of strength he proclaimed, –FNTN.
**Babylon the great is fallen, is fallen:** . . . The great city of Babylon is destroyed! –EVRD . . . It falls! It falls! –CNDT . . . She has fallen, –CNFT.
**and is become the habitation of devils:** . . . became the dwelling place, –CNDT . . . a home for, –EVRD . . . abode, –TCNT . . . den, –WLMS . . . refuge, –FNTN . . . resort, –BRKL . . . those possessed with, –LAMS . . . become a haunt of devils, –PHLP.

**and the hold of every foul spirit:** . . . a city for every evil spirit, –EVRD . . . nest, –NOLI . . . the jail, –CNDT . . . a prison for, –PHLP . . . haunt for every malign spirit, –FNTN . . . a dungeon . . . unclean spirit, –BECK.
**and a cage of every unclean and hateful bird:** . . . a stronghold, –CNFT . . . a city for, –EVRD . . . every foul, –PHLP . . . filthy, –FNTN . . . spiritually unclean, –SEB . . . loathsome, –WLMS.

**18:2.** This powerful and glory-filled angel then makes a loud proclamation, again declaring that Babylon the great has fallen. The emphasis in chapter 18 is on the commercial and political aspects of the great Babylon.

It may be this Babylon is a literal city or nation embodying the aspects of the city described here. Some believe this is the Babylon of the Old Testament times rebuilt (Bullinger, p. 550). Ancient Babylon, even in Assyrian times, was the economic, political, and religious center of the great Mesopotamian area. It is still in a central location with respect to the rest of the world. Others think it is some other city of worldwide economic and political influence, such as Rome or New York.

More likely, even if it might be a literal city, this Babylon seems to symbolize and represent the economic and political world system that in the end time will be brought under the rule of the Antichrist.

The total destruction of the city of Babylon by Sennacherib in 689 B.C. becomes a symbol of this future destruction. His army filled the city squares of Babylon with the corpses of the slain. He ordered his soldiers to smash all the idols except the two great idols of Bel and Nebo. He then leveled the city and dug trenches from the river making a swamp out of it, "pools of water." (See Isaiah 13:19-21; 14:22, 23; 21:9, 10; 46:1, 2; 47:1-15.)

Like the destruction of Babylon by Sennacherib, the destruction of 18:2 will make the political Babylon of the tribulation period a desolation, and its inhabitants will become the food for unclean birds. (See 19:17, 18 where the followers of the Antichrist become a feast provided by God for the birds.)

It is worth noting here that the verbs in Isaiah 13:20 are active in the Hebrew, not passive. Therefore, the translation should be, "It (Babylon) will not sit forever and it will not continue to dwell undisturbed from generation to generation." The end of Isaiah 13:22 reads "her time is near to come and her days shall not be prolonged."

Nothing in this passage says Babylon would not be rebuilt. Rather, it is a prophecy that was soon fulfilled in 689 when Sennacherib leveled Babylon to the ground. Therefore, Isaiah 21:9, 10 is not a prophecy. Rather, it is a record of how Isaiah received the news of Babylon's fall in 689 B.C. It was the thrashing, the result of the harvest of what Isaiah had been prophesying.

Actually, Babylon was rebuilt by Esarhaddon, Assyria's next king, and was later built up and greatly enlarged by Nebuchadnezzar. Cyrus did not destroy it. In fact, he destroyed no cities. He was actually welcomed into Babylon in 539 B.C. and given a triumphal entry complete with palm branches.

Thus, the Book of Revelation borrows from the language of Isaiah chapters 13 and 21 as well as from other prophecies dealing with Edom, Nineveh, and Babylon. The total desolation which will be brought by God's judgment will make it a place where nothing exists but demon spirits and unclean animals.

Actually, the inner nature of the Babylon world system is and has always been full of demon spirits and uncleanness. Judgment will strip away its veneer of beauty and glory and show it for what it really is.

**3. For all nations have drunk of the wine of the wrath of her fornication:** . . . All the peoples of the earth have drunk the strong wine of her sexual sin, —*EVRD* . . . as a result of the wine of the fury of her prostitution have all the nations fallen, —*CNDT* . . . the wine of her passionate unfaithfulness and have fallen thereby, —*PHLP* . . . fury, —*FNTN* . . . of her immorality, —*CNFT*.

**and the kings of the earth have committed fornication with her:** . . . have debauched themselves with her, —*PHLP* . . . sinned sexually with her, —*EVRD* . . . been corrupted by her, —*NOLI* . . . commit prostitution with her, —*CNDT*.

**and the merchants of the earth are waxed rich through the abundance of her delicacies:** . . . businessmen, —*WLMS* . . . of the world have grown rich from the great wealth of her luxury, —*EVRD* . . . enriched, —*NOLI* . . . as a result of her power to indulge, —*CNDT* . . . from the extravagance of her dissipation! —*PHLP* . . . of her trade, —*LAMS*.

**18:3.** The sins of Babylon have already been mentioned in 14:8 and 17:1, 2. She is doomed to destruction because all nations have drunk of the wine of the fury of her habitual immorality, both literal and spiritual. As 14:8 indicates, she made the nations do this. Yet they also chose to join in her religious apostasy by turning away from the true God and cultivating the same lusts. They were not forced to do so. It was by an act of their free will.

The merchants of the earth have been enriched by the power of her luxury. The excessive luxury that makes everyone want more and more luxury exerts a powerful effect and has become the means of enriching the merchants of the world. But it also leads to downfall. This was true in ancient Babylon where Belshazzar feasted and defied

God with a thousand of his lords. But in the same night the people threw open the gates to the army of Cyrus, and Belshazzar was slain. It was true in ancient Rome where a once frugal and powerful city gave itself over to luxury and pleasure and it finally fell.

**4. And I heard another voice from heaven, saying:** . . . another voice from the sky, —*ADAM* . . . came to my ears, —*BB* . . . directing, —*WADE*.

**Come out of her, my people:** . . . Go out from her, —*KLST* . . . Come forth, —*WADE* . . . out of that city, —*EVRD*.

**that ye be not partakers of her sins:** . . . Do not be a part of her sins, —*NLTG* . . . So you will not share her sins, —*BECK* . . . so that you may not participate in, —*TCNT* . . . so that you may not share in, —*WLMS* . . . that you have no fellowship with, —*MNTG* . . . may not be accomplices in, —*KLST* . . . have no part in her sins, —*BB*.

**and that ye receive not of her plagues:** . . . so as not to suffer, —*NORL* . . . that you may not share . . . along with her, —*KLST* . . . and lest you receive some of her plagues, —*ADAM* . . . and suffer from, —*WLMS* . . . and in order that you may not undergo any of her impending plagues, —*WADE* . . . Get away from the plagues which come upon her! —*SEB* . . . so you will not share her troubles, —*NLTG* . . . you will not receive the terrible things that will happen to her, —*EVRD* . . . may not become recipients, —*FNTN* . . . in her punishments, —*BB*.

**18:4.** John was still on the earth as he heard another voice from heaven, not of an angel this time, but either the voice of God or of one speaking for Him. The voice was not directed to John, but to God's people in general. It was a prophetic call to all true believers to come out of "Babylon the great." It was a call appropriate in John's day, and it has been appropriate through the Church Age. It is also a prophetic call to believers before and during the Tribulation. It is a call to separate themselves from participation in the sins and false religion of the Babylon world system.

Believers are to come out of her because if they remain in her they will yield to the temptation to have fellowship with her and will share not only in her wealth and prestige but inevitably in her sins. The result will be to receive upon themselves the same terrible plagues that John had already seen in visions of what will come on the world system during the Tribulation.

The Bible shows God has always wanted His people to be separate from the world with its lust of the flesh, lust of the eye, and pride of life. He has also wanted separation from false religious systems, rites, and institutions. The Old Testament prophets show that, even more than the heathen religion itself, God detests mixed religion that compromises with heathen ideas and heathen worship.

The New Testament also warns believers against being unequally yoked with unbelievers: "Come out from among them, and be ye separate, saith the Lord, and touch not the unclean thing; and I will receive you, and will be a Father unto you, and ye shall be my sons and daughters, saith the Lord Almighty" (2 Corinthians 6:17, 18).

**5. For her sins have reached unto heaven:** ... The city's sins, —EVRD ... are piled clear up to, —WLMS ... piled up as high as, —NOLI ... have piled up to the sky, —TNT ... have been heaped to, —MNTG ... have followed her to heaven, —KLGS ... to high heaven, —NORL.

**and God hath remembered her iniquities:** ... and God has not forgotten her misdeeds, —TCNT ... is now denouncing her iniquities, —NOLI ... is ready to punish her for her sins, —NLTG ... recalled to mind, —WADE ... has taken not of her evil-doing, —BB ... remembers her sinfulness, —NORL ... her crimes, —BRKL, —TNT ... her injustices, —KLGS ... wickedness, —FNTN ... the wrongs she has done, —EVRD.

**18:5.** The angel declared Babylon's sins had reached to heaven or to the sky (as the Greek word also means). This may mean they had piled up like an incredibly high tower of Babel. (Compare Jeremiah 51:9.)

That God "remembered" Babylon's unrighteousness does not mean God had forgotten it. The phrase "God remembered" is a Hebrew expression meaning God had been remembering it all along and now was about to go into action to do something about it. The same phrase is found in Genesis 8:1 where God remembered Noah and caused the rain to stop and the waters of the flood to recede. It is found in Genesis 19:29 where God remembered Abraham and sent Lot out of Sodom, for God knew of Abraham's loving concern for his nephew. Genesis 30:22 states that God remembered Rachel and answered her prayers by opening her womb so she conceived and had a son. Thus, God's remembering Babylon's unrighteousness means He had been considering it all along and now was about to bring His righteous divine judgment on it.

**6. Reward her even as she rewarded you:** ... Repay ... what she has given, —FNTN ... Pay her back in her own coin, —BECK, —WLMS ... Treat her as she treated others! —SEB ... Do to her as she has done to you, —NORL ... Render to what she rendered, —MNTG.

**and double unto her double according to her works:** ... yes, pay her double for what she has done, —NORL ... redouble it in accordance with her doings, —FNTN ... Yes, pay double what her deeds deserve, —MNTG ... in keeping with her deeds, —KLST.

**in the cup which she hath filled fill to her double:** ... The cup which she has poisoned, —FNTN ... a double portion, —KLST ... mix twice as much for her, —WLMS ... mix it double for her! —SEB ... Mix a double dose for her in the cup she has mixed for others, —NORL.

**18:6.** The theme changes now with a call for agents of God's judgment to do their work on Babylon. Some think this call is a response to the angel's call for the people of God to leave Babylon. As they leave, they call for retribution for what Babylon has done to them and to the many martyrs who died for their witness to Jesus. More likely, the voice here is still the voice of the same angel mentioned in verse 4.

The call is for God or His agents to act in divine justice and render or recompense to Babylon as she herself has rendered to others. True followers of Christ will not try to avenge themselves. As long as they are permitted to serve Christ in the Church Age, the love of Christ will cause them to forgive those who mistreat and malign them. But the time will come when those who have rejected God's loving provision of salvation through Christ must face God's holy and righteous judgment. (See Romans 12:19.)

Babylon will be judged double the double according to her works. This does not mean that her punishment will be double what she deserves. The judgment will still be according to her works. Doubling the double may be a way of saying she will receive a full measure of all she deserves. That is, she deserves punishment, not only for the suffering she has caused the saints, but also for the corruption, greed, and immorality behind what she did to them. She will drink the wrath of God from the same cup she used to pour out her fury on the people of God.

**7. How much she hath glorified herself, and lived deliciously:** ... and committed excess, —RTHM ... and luxuriated, —FNTN ... in which she lived in pride and luxury, —NORL ... and waxed wanton, —MNTG.

**so much torment and sorrow give her:** ... Visit on her, —KLST ... Pay her back with torture and pain, —SEB ... give her a like measure of torment and grief, —NORL ... in the same way ... anguish, —FNTN ... and tears, —MNTG.

**for she saith in her heart:** ... She claims, —NOLI ... she is always boasting, —WLMS.

**I sit a queen, and am no widow, and shall see no sorrow:** ... to be enthroned like, —NOLI ... I shall never know misery, —TCNT ... I will never feel pain, —SEB ... never see suffering, —FNTN ... shall in no wise see mourning, —MNTG.

**18:7.** The voice continued with further reasons for divine vengeance. Torment and sorrow, suffering and misery will be appointed for commercial and political Babylon. It will be given to the extent that they have glorified themselves and lived in greedy, self-serving, sensual luxury.

Part of the reason given for her judgment is that she was always thinking in her heart she was sitting as a queen, not a widow. She expected always to rule, to be in control. She did not believe the plagues of God's judgment would ever come upon her. Babylon of Isaiah's day felt the same way, but in fulfillment of Isaiah's prophecy it was leveled to the ground and made a swamp, "pools of water" (Isaiah 14:22, 23, as archaeological records of Sennacherib confirm). It is also sure that the Babylonian world system will come to a total end.

**8.  Therefore shall her plagues come in one day:** . . . will overtake her, —NORL . . . in a single hour, —FNTN . . . shall these plagues come upon her, —MNTG.
**death, and mourning, and famine:** . . . anguish, —FNTN.
**and she shall be utterly burned with fire:** . . . shall she be burnt, —WADE . . . completely, —BB.
**for strong [is] the Lord God who judgeth her:** . . . For the Lord God . . . is the One Who says she is guilty, —NLTG . . . because God her judge is mighty! —FNTN . . . Who has brought her to judgment, —WADE . . . is powerful, —NORL . . . is mighty, —KLST . . . who has condemned her, —TNT.

**18:8.** Because of Babylon's self-exaltation, taking glory to herself that belongs only to God, and because of her greedy, sensual luxury, the plagues of divine judgment will come on her suddenly in 1 day. This fits with the picture given in 2 Thessalonians 1:7, 8 and Daniel 2:34, 35, 44, 45. Death, mourning, and famine will be part of the judgment. Fire will complete it.

The judgment will show that God is strong, not weak. Babylon apparently treated God's delay in bringing judgment as a sign of weakness. They did not recognize the love behind His patience.

**9.  And the kings of the earth, who have committed fornication and lived deliciously with her:** . . . They are the ones who did sex sins with her and lived as rich people, —NLTG . . . who were lewd and wanton with her, —BRKL . . . who had immoral relations with her, and revelled, —WADE . . . who have practised sexual vice with her, —TNT . . . made themselves unclean with her, and in her company gave themselves up to evil, —BB . . . and shared her luxury, —TCNT, —SEB . . . lived luxuriously, —NORL.
**shall bewail her, and lament for her:** . . . shall weep and wail over her, —FNTN . . . and bewail her, —NORL . . . and mourn over her, —KLST . . . and crying over her, —BB . . . and be filled with sorrow, —TNT . . . and wring their hands over her, —WADE . . . and be sorry, —NLTG.
**when they shall see the smoke of her burning:** . . . When they behold, —MNTG . . . the smoke rising from the fires that burn her, —TNT . . . of her conflagration, —NOLI . . . as she is burning, —KLST.

**18:9.** The lamentation that begins here is the first of three. The first is a lamentation by the

kings of the earth (verses 9, 10). The second is by the merchants of the earth (verses 11-17). The third is by all the shipowners, all the sailors, and all those who make their living by the sea trade (the export/import trade). Much of the language describing their laments is taken from Ezekiel's lamentation over the city of Tyre (Ezekiel 27:12-36), but the situation here is different, and the application is different. In his vision John saw that those who witnessed the fall of the Babylon world system were terrified and filled with horror. They had trusted in it. Now it was suddenly being destroyed.

The kings and rulers of the earth will lament for Babylon because they have used their power and position for their own luxury and the gratification of their own pleasures. God hates the oppression caused by selfish rulers who exalt themselves and have no concern to help those under their rule. Their relations with the Babylon world system have been illicit. They have lived together in a voluptuous, sensual, godless manner, full of the lusts of the flesh.

The kings of the earth in this verse are not the 10 kings or kingdoms that are closely allied to the beast (the Antichrist). By God's sovereign direction, perhaps in spite of themselves, the beast and the 10 kings who have been taken over by him are the ones used to bring about Babylon's destruction (17:12-17). The kings of the earth in 18:9 are the rest of the kings and rulers of the world who fear that they too will share Babylon's torment. Archaeology shows that the kings of the Old Testament world were horrified when Sennacherib destroyed Babylon, leveled it to the ground, and made a swamp out of it in 689 B.C., in fulfillment of Isaiah's prophecies. This probably provided a typology pointing to the destruction of the Babylon world system described in Revelation. But the kings in Isaiah's day did not have as much fear as that which will envelop the kings left in the world as the end of the Great Tribulation approaches.

**10.  Standing afar off for the fear of her torment:** . . . Watching from far away, —BB . . . Standing at a safe distance for fear of sharing her punishment, —NOLI . . . They stand a long way from her because they are afraid of her sufferings, —NLTG . . . Frightened by her torture, —BECK . . . in terror at her torment, —TNT.
**saying, Alas, alas that great city Babylon, that mighty city!:** . . . and exclaiming, —WADE . . . They say, It is bad! It is bad for the big and powerful city, —NLTG . . . they will say, Woe, woe, —KLST . . . Sorrow, sorrow for . . . the great town, the strong town, —BB . . . the strong city, —MNTG.
**for in one hour is thy judgment come:** . . . Your condemnation came, —SEB . . . Retribution has overtaken you, —NOLI . . . How has your judgment come

in a single hour! —*FNTN* . . . you have been judged, —*BB* . . . has come to pass! —*NORL* . . . in a moment, —*KLST* . . . she is destroyed, —*NLTG*.

**18:10.** The kings of the earth make no attempt to come to the aid of the great city Babylon. Fear of its torment, fear that they too might be tortured, has already caused them to move far off where they are standing, observing the destruction of the city. It is described not only as a great city but as a strong city, a mighty city, with the implication that it considered itself secure. For many generations it had filled itself with the blood of the martyrs and seemed able to continue defying God and His people. Thus these kings of the earth probably thought they would keep on forever sharing the luxury and licentiousness of the city. But now all that hope is gone. The cry of these kings is a cry of displeasure, even of horror. The Greek may be translated either "Woe!" or "Alas!" In this case, it seems they keep saying "Alas, alas!" However, their cry is very emphatic and is like a hopeless wail. They recognize also that what is happening is judgment, sudden judgment, terrible punishment. Whether they understand that it is divine judgment is not specified in this verse. The fact that Babylon is described as so great and so mighty implies that God who is mightier is the One who has decreed the judgment.

**11. And the merchants of the earth shall weep and mourn over her:** . . . the traders . . . wail, —*WADE* . . . The men of the earth who buy and sell are sorry for her and cry, —*NLTG* . . . and grieve for her, —*FNTN* . . . and crying over, —*BB*.

**for no man buyeth their merchandise any more:** . . . They cry because there is no one to buy their things anymore, —*NLTG* . . . since no one will buy, —*NORL* . . . no one can buy their cargoes, —*WLMS* . . . because no man has any more desire for their goods, —*BB* . . . of their cargo none buys any more, —*FNTN*.

**18:11.** The merchants of the earth here are primarily the wholesalers, the people who have built up great wholesale and import/export businesses. They have cargoes of goods stockpiled, but there is no one buying them anymore. All trade and commerce has stopped. Thus these great merchant princes weep and mourn because of the destruction of the great Babylon world system. Their sorrow is not really for Babylon itself, however. Rather, it is for themselves because of the loss of their business and their hope for material gain.

This seems to imply that the fall of Babylon is accompanied by a worldwide economic collapse. Suddenly, all the currencies of all the nations of the world have no value. Apparently, the banks are closed, for everything in their vaults is now worthless. It may be that even before this happens

the world will move to a cashless society, and the whole system will be broken down.

**12. The merchandise of gold, and silver, and precious stones:** . . . This included, —*KLST* . . . no cargoes of gold, —*NORL* . . . stones of great price, —*BB*.

**and of pearls, and fine linen, and purple:** . . . fine cotton, purple dye, —*SEB* . . . delicate linen, —*BB* . . . robes of, —*BB*.

**and silk, and scarlet, and all thyine wood:** . . . and red; and perfumed wood, —*BB* . . . scarlet fabrics . . . none buys any aromatic timber, —*WADE* . . . every kind of, —*KLST* . . . their many chests of choicest wood, —*TCNT* . . . no kind of scent or costly wood, —*NORL* . . . sweet wood, —*FNTN* . . . All citron wood, —*MNTG*.

**and all manner vessels of ivory, and all manner vessels of most precious wood, and of brass, and iron, and marble:** . . . every kind of ivory product, —*KLST* . . . all sorts of ivory articles, —*BRKL* . . . ivory toys . . . all products of costly wood, —*FNTN* . . . And vessels of rare wood, —*MNTG* . . . made of fair wood . . . and stone, —*BB* . . . expensive woods, —*SEB* . . . of copper, —*WADE*.

**18:12.** The fall of Babylon seems to be preceded by a time of great prosperity, economic activity, and excessive luxury. To emphasize this, the angel whom John heard proclaim this prophecy gives specific details about the nature of the merchandise that is stockpiled and they have no buyers. The kinds of things mentioned are a reminder of the wealth of Tyre when it was the merchant capital of the Mediterranean world (compare Ezekiel 27:5-24). They were present in Rome in John's day. They represent the material things which the present world also considers so important.

They include cargoes of gold and articles made of gold, cargoes of silver and beautiful articles made of silver, cargoes of precious stones such as diamonds, and cargoes of pearls.

They include cargoes of fine linen such as was worn by prominent people in those days, cargoes of brilliant red or red-purple cloth, so expensive it was the clothing of royalty; cargoes of cloth and garments of silk, and cargoes of red-scarlet such as was worn by the Roman officers.

There are other cargoes: thyine (citron) wood, articles of ivory, all kinds of articles made from the most costly kinds of wood; articles and vessels made of copper, iron and articles or vessels and weapons made of iron; and cargoes of the finest and most precious kinds of marble and carved art objects made of marble.

**13. And cinnamon, and odours, and ointments:** . . . Likewise, no shipments of, —*NORL* . . . balsam and spices and myrrh, —*MNTG* . . . spice, incense, perfume, —SEB . . . cloves, and scents, —FNTN . . . and amomum, —KLST.

**and frankincense, and wine, and oil:** . . . and precious spices, —SEB.

**and fine flour, and wheat, and beasts:** . . . finest flour, —NORL . . . cattle, —FNTN . . . beasts of burden, —KLST.

**and sheep, and horses, and chariots:** . . . and hides, —LAMS . . . and wagons, —SEB . . . carriages, —FNTN.

**and slaves, and souls of men:** . . . the lives of, —WLMS . . . even human beings, —BECK . . . human lives, —KLST . . . bodies and souls, —BRKL, —SEB.

**18:13.** The list continues by itemizing cargoes of spices and perfumes, cargoes of food, and cargoes of property. Cinnamon is mentioned first among the spices and perfumes. The list continues with odors (incense to be burned for its pleasant odor), ointments, and frankincense.

Cinnamon not only includes the fragrant wood of the tree, *Cinnamomum zeylanicum* from Sri Lanka, but also the golden yellow, pleasant-smelling oil from its bark, an oil used in perfume (compare Proverbs 7:17 and Song of Solomon 4:14). Some ancient Greek manuscripts also have amomum spice (Greek, *amōmon*) as an additional commodity at this point in the list. Incense (odors) is in the plural and would include a variety of materials that could be used and burned as incense. Ointment is a general word for ointments and perfume, including myrrh and also the strongly aromatic perfumes that were kept in alabaster flasks (Luke 23:56). Frankincense is a white resinous gum from several varieties of a tree grown in Arabia. It had uses in medicine and in religious ceremonies.

The list of foods starts with wine. Then comes oil (that is, olive oil), the finest grade of wheat flour, wheat (the word sometimes includes other grains), cattle (the word was originally used of beasts of burden, pack animals and riding animals, but by New Testament times came to include various other domesticated animals, especially cows and oxen), and sheep.

This is followed by horses and chariots (actually, four-wheeled carriages here) representing the means of transportation available to the rulers and the wealthy aristocracy. It ends with slaves (literally, bodies) and souls (persons, including both men and women, since the word "men" here means humankind) who are possessed body and soul by their masters. In Roman times there were about 60 million slaves in the empire, and they were treated as merchandise. That kind of slavery is no longer common, but treating people as merchandise is still done in many ways.

This is a very impressive list of commodities. It seems to be intended to draw attention to the materialism of the Babylon world system, to their love of luxury, and to a vast amount of commerce and trade generated by the desires of the people of Babylon.

**14. And the fruits that thy soul lusted after are departed from thee:** . . . The profit . . . coveted, —KLST . . . The ripe fruits your soul longed for are gone, —NORL . . . the season for delighting in the lusts your soul desired is gone from you, —FNTN . . . are no longer within your reach, —TCNT.

**and all things which were dainty and goodly:** . . . Her luxury and splendor have perished forever, —NOLI . . . your dainties and your good things, —NORL . . . all your fat and your splendor have perished, —BECK . . . All of your wealth and glamor, —SEB . . . dazzle, —FNTN . . . and sumptuous, —MNTG.

**are departed from thee, and thou shalt find them no more at all:** . . . are lost to you, —LAMS . . . have disappeared, —SEB . . . have perished from your hands, —WLMS . . . and never again will they be experienced, —BRKL . . . nor shall they be found again, —FNTN . . . and you will never again find them, —NORL.

**18:14.** This verse is a general statement of how the ripe fruits the souls of the people of Babylon desired and longed for, along with the dainty (fat, costly, rich) things (including imported foods) and the goodly things (bright, shining things, including their expensive clothes and all their rich decorative objects and jewelry), are all gone, lost to them never to be found again (that is, never again to be possessed by them). This indicates a collapse of the present world order, both economic and political. It will be a final collapse. The present world order will never be restored. Instead, Christ will return and bring in the Kingdom. The reign of Christ will bring in a far better world order, free from the results of the curse that came because of the fall of man. People who are full of the materialistic desires of this present world always want more. But the creation itself is groaning for deliverance from the effects of the curse and so are true believers (Romans 8:22, 23).

**15. The merchants of these things:** . . . The businessmen who dealt in, —WLMS . . . The traders in them, —FNTN . . . The dealers in these wares, —NORL . . . commodities, —KLST.

**which were made rich by her:** . . . grew rich, —KLST . . . who were enriched by her, —FNTN . . . who had riches through her, —NORL . . . grew wealthy, —WADE . . . from her trade, —BRKL.

**shall stand afar off for the fear of her torment:** . . . will stand back at a distance, —NORL . . . frightened by her torture, —BECK . . . in terror of, —FNTN . . . but now they were afraid, —SEB . . . for fear of sharing her torment, —WADE.

**weeping and wailing:** . . . crying, grieving, —FNTN . . . and mourn aloud, —NORL.

**18:15.** The repetition in this verse connects back with the lament of the merchants of verse 11. This repetition is the Bible's way of showing that the verses in between which give the list of the cargoes of merchandise are a parenthesis. Thus this verse takes up where verse 11 left off.

The lists given in verses 12-14 are important because they draw attention to the merchants who were made rich by these things. They did not care about the people. They had no concern for what would be good for others. All they wanted was money, wealth. Verse 15 indicates they still have no real concern for the people who have bought their goods and made them rich. They fear only for themselves, lest they be drawn into the same destruction and torment that has fallen on Babylon. Consequently, they get as far away from Babylon as they can, leaving it to its destruction. They only watch the terrible conflagration from afar.

16. **And saying, Alas, alas, that great city:** ... and will cry, —WADE ... and exclaiming, —FNTN ... Woe, woe, —MNTG ... Alas! they will say. Alas for, —NORL.

**that was clothed in fine linen, and purple, and scarlet, and decked with gold, and precious stones, and pearls!:** ... adorned with, —NORL ... arrayed in ... and bejewelled, —WADE ... clad in cotton, —FNTN ... precious jewelry, —SEB ... glittered in gold, —KLST ... gilded with gold, —BRKL.

**18:16.** In their weeping and wailing the merchants cry out "Alas, alas" for the great city (repeating the cries of verse 10). The city (that is, the people of the city) was "clothed in fine linen, and purple, and scarlet, and decked (adorned) with gold, and precious stones, and pearls!"

All of these things are external adornment. There is no recognition of the inner adornment of the spirit. The great Babylon world system was full of all kinds of corruption, crime, and sin. But they covered it up with fancy clothing and jewels. This has been characteristic of the aristocrats of the world system from ancient Babylon to today. Even before that, the wealth buried with King Tut of Egypt was a cover-up for the corruption of the priests who murdered him. The astrology of Babylon set a pattern for those who still would rather look to the stars than to God. The ethics of Medo-Persia set a pattern for those who think a few good deeds will cover or make up for all their bad deeds. The art and philosophies of Greece set a pattern that glorified mankind rather than God. The Roman idea that the way to keep peace was to have the biggest army set a pattern for politics ever since. It is all still the same world system today, and it must be destroyed before the better things of the Kingdom can come in. But the merchants of this world are still so full of greed that they mourn at any sign of the loss or potential loss of their opportunities for material gain.

17. **For in one hour so great riches is come to nought:** ... your vast wealth vanished, —TCNT ... all this wealth has been laid waste, —BECK ... this great wealth has been destroyed! —NORL ... such great wealth as this! —RTHM ... Such wealth was destroyed, —SEB ... all this wealth is wiped out, —BRKL ... has all this wealth withered! —FNTN ... in a single hour! —NOLI ... is made desolate! —MNTG.

**And every shipmaster:** ... Every helmsman, —BRKL ... All ship pilots, —WLMS ... every shipowner, and pilot, —FNTN ... every sea-captain, —NORL.

**and all the company in ships:** ... and all who travel by sea, —WLMS ... everyone who makes journeys, —KLST ... and every one who sails to any port, —MNTG ... sea traveler, —SEB.

**and sailors:** ... the mariners, —KLST ... and seamen, —WADE ... all who traveled on ships, —NLTG.

**and as many as trade by sea:** ... sea merchant, —SEB ... and all whose trade is by way of the sea, —NORL ... and all that make their living by the sea, —WADE ... all the men who work at sea, —KLST ... all who worked on ships, —NLTG ... and all seafaring folk, —MNTG.

**stood afar off:** ... were watching from, —BB ... held back afar off, —NORL ... far away, —SEB ... at a distance, —FNTN ... a long way back, —NLTG.

**18:17.** The lamentation of the merchants continued by emphasizing again that in 1 hour the great riches, the entire wealth and the gorgeous decorations of the city, was laid waste, totally ruined. How foolish they were to trust in material things! They do not last. Though they attract people and fill them with desire for more of material things, they never satisfy.

Again, it is the shipmasters (captains, owners, pilots, helmsmen), the whole company or throng of those traveling by ship, the sailors, and all who work on the sea who stand afar off. These are the people who are involved in trade between nations.

18. **And cried when they saw the smoke of her burning, saying:** ... cried lamenting, —WADE ... as the city was, —KLST ... from the burning city, —MNTG.

**What [city is] like unto this great city!:** ... What town is like the great town? —BB ... Has there ever been such a city as powerful as this one? —NLTG ... can compare with, —TCNT ... can be compared to, —NOLI ... was comparable, —WADE ... was ever like this great city? —NORL.

**18:18.** The Bible again emphasizes the continued cries of the merchants of the earth, especially those connected with the sea trade, that is, with international trade and commerce, as well as those from whom they obtain the things they offer for sale. As they keep watching the burning of Babylon, they exclaim repeatedly, "What is like the great city?" There is amazement and astonishment in their cries. The language here is somewhat like the lamentation over the city of Tyre recorded in Ezekiel 27:25-36, especially verses 30 and 32.

**19. And they cast dust on their heads:** . . . threw, —MNTG.

**and cried, weeping and wailing, saying:** . . . and were sad, —BB . . . They were yelling and feeling sorry, —SEB . . . and bewailed, —NORL . . . and mourning, —MNTG . . . as they wept and grieved, they cried thus, —WADE.

**Alas, alas, that great city:** . . . Woe, woe, —MNTG . . . Sorrow, sorrow for the great town, —BB . . . for the great City, —WADE.

**wherein were made rich all that had ships in the sea by reason of her costliness!:** . . . in which was increased the wealth of all who had their ships on the sea because of her great stores! —BB . . . where all who have vessels on the sea grew wealthy in consequence of her possessions of value, —WADE . . . were enriched from her treasures! —FNTN . . . get rich through her extravagance, —NORL . . . out of her wealth, —KLST . . . Grew rich through her luxury! —MNTG.

**for in one hour is she made desolate:** . . . For in a single hour, —BRKL, —WLMS . . . in a moment she has been laid waste! —KLST . . . it has vanished, —TCNT . . . she is destroyed, —LAMS . . . has she become a desert, —FNTN.

**18:19.** The merchants of the earth threw dust on their heads as they kept crying or shouting out the lamentation of verse 18. In Bible times scattering dust on one's head was a common expression of great grief. (Compare Joshua 7:6; Lamentations 2:10.) At the same time they kept on weeping and mourning with loud wailing.

They also kept saying, "Alas, alas," or "Woe, woe!" (Greek, *ouai, ouai*). The repetition gives emphasis to their intense woe. Again, their concern and their feeling of woe was not really about the great city or over the fact that in 1 hour she was made desolate. Their central concern is totally selfish. They are really weeping over the fact that all those having ships in the sea were enriched by her costliness, that is, by the abundance of costly things that she bought. The destruction of the city means all their hope of wealth is gone. They are ruined financially. They brought the city what the *people* wanted. But now they have no way of getting what *they* want.

Jesus warned against the materialism that makes the pleasures of this world the sole object of life. If believers seek the kingdom of God, everything they really need will be added unto them (Luke 12:31). He also told His own disciples, the "little flock," not to be afraid "for it is your Father's good pleasure to give you the kingdom. Sell that ye have, and give alms; provide yourselves bags which wax not old, a treasure in the heavens that

faileth not, where no thief approacheth, neither moth corrupteth. For where your treasure is, there will your heart be also" (Luke 12:32-34).

All the wealth and all the glory of this present world order will be burned up or consumed by mighty manifestations of God's wrath before Jesus establishes the Kingdom. But believers do not need to be afraid, nor will they participate in the mourning of the merchants of the earth. The believers' concern is to seek the Kingdom, that is, the rule of God, first of all in their own lives, then in the Church, then through the influence of the Church on those around them.

Believers have the assurance also that they will not suffer during the destruction that is to come on the world during the Tribulation, for God's good pleasure is not only to give them the Kingdom but to give them a salvation and an inheritance that will preserve them from the wrath to come (1 Thessalonians 5:9).

**20. Rejoice over her, [thou] heaven:** . . . Celebrate over her, —BRKL, —SEB, —WLMS . . . Make merry over her, —KLST . . . Be glad at the sight of her ruin, —WADE.

**and [ye] holy apostles and prophets:** . . . saints, —FNTN . . . God's Hallowed People, —WADE.

**for God hath avenged you on her:** . . . has decided to execute the judgment upon her for you, —FNTN . . . has decided in your favour your suit against her, —WADE . . . judged your case against her, —KLST . . . has punished her for you, —BECK . . . because God condemned her for the way she treated you, —SEB.

**18:20.** In contrast to the weeping and wailing of the kings, merchants, and all the wealthy people of the world, all heaven, and especially the holy apostles and prophets, are commanded to rejoice over the destruction of Babylon because its destruction is God's vengeance in their behalf. Both the Old and New Testament remind us that vengeance belongs to the Lord. Believers are not to seek revenge for the mistreatment and persecution the world heaps upon them. The apostles and prophets have always suffered. Now the godly are to rejoice over God's righteous judgment on the world system that has been dominated by Satan and has been full of evil in its pleasures, luxury, government, and business affairs. (See 19:1 for further description of the celebration in heaven.)

The apostles and prophets and all heaven have good reason to rejoice because they have always been brokenhearted over the sin, the evil, the idolatry, the immoral conduct, and all the pride, greed, and murderous lusts of the flesh that have spread through human society since the fall of man. If Lot was distressed and disturbed by the immoral lifestyle of the people of Sodom (2 Peter

2:7, 8), how much more should the children of God be distressed by all the corruption in the world around them today!

**21. And a mighty angel took up a stone like a great millstone:** . . . a single powerful, *—FNTN* . . . strong, *—NORL* . . . size of a grinding stone, *—SEB* . . . lifted . . . like a millstone in size, *—WADE* . . . as great as, *—KLST.*
**and cast [it] into the sea, saying:** . . . threw, *—KLST* . . . hurled, *—NORL* . . . exclaiming, *—WADE.*
**Thus with violence shall that great city Babylon be thrown down:** . . . With this violence, *—KLST* . . . So shall Babylon . . . be overthrown, *—MNTG* . . . with a crash . . . dashed down, *—FNTN* . . . With such force shall Babylon . . . be hurled to destruction, *—NORL.*
**and shall be found no more at all:** . . . and disappear forever! *—NOLI* . . . and no trace of her shall be found any more, *—WADE.*

**18:21.** Then a strong and powerful angel performed a symbolic action by taking up an enormous millstone and throwing it into the sea where it disappeared. He prophesied that in the same way, that is, with the same sort of violence, the great city Babylon would be thrown down and disappear forever. The Bible is emphatic. Babylon will never, ever, be found any more at all. Its fall will be final and irreversible.

Along with political Babylon, the entire world order that is in opposition to God will come to an end. Then the Antichrist will make his final attempt to defeat the plan of God, and his rule will come to its final end when Christ returns to earth. Daniel 2 describes it as the Babylon image being hit in the feet by the stone cut out of the mountain without hands. This causes the gold of Babylon, the silver of Medo-Persia, the copper of Greece, the iron of Rome, and the iron and clay of the nationalistic states and countries since the fall of Rome and in our time, all to be reduced to powder and blown away. The kingdom of God will bring a brand new order such as the world has never seen before. Human imagination has never even dreamed of what it will really be like. But God revealed glimpses of it to the prophets in the Bible, especially to the prophet Isaiah.

**22. And the voice of harpers, and musicians, and of pipers, and of trumpeters, shall be heard no more at all in thee:** . . . No longer will the sound of harpists . . . and flutists, *—KLST* . . . minstrels . . . flute players, *—NORL.*
**and no craftsman, of whatsoever craft [he be], shall be found any more in thee:** . . . a skilled artisan, *—BRKL* . . . No workman doing any kind of work, *—NLTG* . . . in any art, *—WADE* . . . no worker, expert in art, will ever again be living in you, *—BB.*
**and the sound of a millstone shall be heard no more at all in thee:** . . . the sound of the grinding

mill, *—WLMS* . . . of a grinding stone, *—SEB* . . . of the crushing of grain, *—BB.*

**18:22.** The voice or sound of harpists (lyre players) who accompany their own singing, of musicians, of pipers (flute players), and trumpeters will no more be heard. All their celebrations are at an end. All the craftsmen will be gone. Neither will there be the sound of a millstone (probably including all the work of factories).

**23. And the light of a candle:** . . . No light of any lamp, *—NORL* . . . the shining of lights, *—BB.*
**shall shine no more at all in thee:** . . . will never shine there again, *—SEB* . . . be seen in you, *—BB.*
**and the voice of the bridegroom and of the bride shall be heard no more at all in thee:** . . . There will be no more happy voices from a wedding heard, *—NLTG* . . . the voice of the newly-married man . . . be sounding in you, *—BB* . . . will never be heard in you again, *—WLMS.*
**for thy merchants were the great men of the earth:** . . . because your traders, *—WADE* . . . were the magnates, *—RTHM* . . . the earth's prominent men, *—BRKL* . . . were very important on earth, *—SEB* . . . the princes of, *—FNTN, —MNTG* . . . were once the great lords of the earth, *—NORL.*
**for by thy sorceries were all nations deceived:** . . . You fooled people over all the world by your witchcraft, *—NLTG* . . . all the nations of the world were led astray by your sorcery, *—NORL* . . . by your magic charms, *—BRKL* . . . by your poisonous charm all nations were deluded, *—FNTN* . . . by your evil powers were all the nations turned out of the right way, *—BB.*

**18:23.** Not only will the sound of music and the sound of workmen never again be heard in the city, the light of a candle (lamp) will never again shine in it. (The Greek here means an oil-burning lamp made of metal or clay; tallow and wax candles were not known in New Testament times. The Bible uses the names of things familiar to John, but it must also be recognized that everything else in the same categories would be included.)

Finally, the voice of the bridegroom and of the bride will never again be heard in Babylon. The entire list given in verses 22 and 23 draws attention to the fact that not only will Babylon be thrown down and never again be found, everything in it will also come to a total and final end. The reason for Babylon's destruction is summarized by saying, first, that her merchants were the great ones of the earth. Their greatness was not good; rather, it was full of arrogance and pride. The political and economic Babylon of this chapter achieved its domination by controlling the economy and the markets of the world. But now this is at an end.

Second, Babylon is destroyed because by her sorceries were all the nations deceived (see also 18:3). Her sorceries included the use of magic arts, the occult, and drugs. By such means she led astray, deluded, and deceived the nations, that is, the people of the earth. She led them to believe that in wealth, luxury, and sensual pleasures they could find security and fullness of life. This kind of deception has always been a part of heathen religions. Much of it crept into the churches in the Dark Ages. Much of it is being popularized again through philosophies of some modern movements. But none of this is new. It is still the same old Babylon world system that exalts self, as did those who built the tower of Babel (Babylon). (See Genesis chapter 11.)

**24.** **And in her was found the blood of prophets, and of saints:**...was seen, *–BB*...of God's Hallowed People, *–WADE*.
**and of all that were slain upon the earth:**...and of all who have been put to death here on earth, *–NORL*...murdered upon, *–FNTN*.

**18:24.** The third reason for Babylon's destruction became apparent when there was found in her the blood of prophets, and of saints, and of all that were slain (killed with violence or in a violent manner) upon the earth.

Since the prophets are not identified as belonging to a particular group, it seems they include both Old Testament and New Testament prophets. The saints must also include all the saints who were martyred, not only during the Tribulation, but all down through history. Babylon is also said to be responsible for all those who have been slaughtered.

From this verse it is apparent that Babylon symbolizes more than any one city could be. Certainly, it was more than Rome or any city in existence today. It is representative of all the cities, possibly from the first city built by Cain (Genesis 4:17) to the present, and of the world system itself.

## Chapter 19

**1.** **And after these things:**...After this, *–MNTG*.
**I heard a great voice of much people in heaven, saying:**...there came to my ears a sound like the voice of a great band of people, *–BB*...I heard something like the sound of an enormous crowd in the sky, *–ADAM*...the semblance of, *–MNTG*...what sounded like, *–KLST*...the mighty shout of a great multitude, *–NOLI*...a great sound of voices from a vast multitude, *–WADE*...the mighty voice...exclaiming, *–FNTN*...what sounded like a large crowd, *–BECK*...the great shout of a vast crowd, *–TNT*...of a great throng, *–BRKL*...saying loudly, *–NORL*.
**Alleluia:**...Praise the Lord! *–BECK*...Praise ye Jehovah, *–WADE*...Thanks to our God, *–NLTG*.
**Salvation, and glory, and honour, and power, unto the Lord our God:**...the One Who saves from the penalty of sin...belong to Him, *–NLTG*...the majesty, and the might of our God! *–FNTN*...come

from our God, *–KLST*...are our God's, *–ADAM*...belong to our God, *–TNT*.

**19:1.** "After these things" indicates another vision is being presented. Chapters 17 and 18 deal primarily with the fall of the Babylonish world system. Chapter 19 deals with the final defeat of the Antichrist at the end of the Tribulation in connection with Christ's triumphant return in glory and power. He will bring judgment on the Antichrist and his armies and reign on earth with the believers.

This vision is introduced, not by an angel, but by the loud voices of a combined choir in heaven saying or singing a Hallelujah chorus, sung in response to 18:20, the just overthrow of Babylon. *Alleluia* is from the Greek form of the Hebrew *halelûyāh*. (The Hebrew *halelû* is a command to praise. *Yāh* is the abbreviation for the personal name of God, for which the Jews in New Testament times substituted the title "Lord." Thus, hallelujah simply means "praise the Lord!") It occurs here for the first time in the New Testament and occurs four times in this chapter (verses 1, 3, 4, 6). The "people in heaven" begin by singing praise to God, recognizing Him as their God in a personal way, attributing to Him salvation, glory, honor, and power. He has manifested them all.

**2.** **For true and righteous [are] his judgments:**...For the way He punishes people is right and true, *–NLTG*...are genuine, *–ADAM*...reliable, *–WADE*...just, *–KLST*...are his decisions, *–BB*.
**for he hath judged the great whore:**...He has sentenced, *–BECK*, *–BRKL*...by him has the evil woman been judged, *–BB*...convicted, *–FNTN*...brought to judgment, *–WADE*...passed judgment on the notorious prostitute, *–WLMS*...God has condemned the famous whore, *–SEB*...has punished the powerful woman, *–NLTG*.
**which did corrupt the earth with her fornication:**...who was corrupting the earth by, *–WADE*...who by her prostitution brought ruin upon the earth, *–TNT*...her immorality, *–WLMS*...who used her sexual sin to spoil the world, *–SEB*...who sold the use of her body...making the earth sinful with her sex sins, *–NLTG*...who made the earth unclean with the sins of her body, *–BB*.
**and hath avenged the blood of his servants at her hand:**...She killed those who worked for God, *–NLTG*...and He has punished her for, *–NORL*...forced her to make payment for, *–WMCK*...the death of, *–TNT*...his slaves, *–MNTG*...which her hands have shed, *–KLST*...from her hand, *–KLGS*...spilled by her hand, *–ADAM*.

**19:2.** Praise is given to God for His judgments which, in line with His nature, are always true, righteous, and just. The Babylon of Old Testament times was a wicked city, but it was also an empire and a world power that worshiped false gods and persecuted God's people. In New Testament times Rome was also a city and an empire, a world power that stood against God and persecuted God's people. In the Middle Ages the Roman church attempted to step into the place of a political power and persecuted those who rejected its unscriptural doctrines and practices.

Some believe that during the Tribulation the great whore or harlot Babylon will be a revived Roman Empire. Others prefer to understand it as a rebuilt Babylon on the Euphrates River. Still others see it as some great religious and commercial center which will take leadership at that time. Most likely it includes the whole Babylonish world system represented by the image in Daniel 2 and the wild beasts in Daniel 7. The important thing to notice is that it will be necessary to judge and destroy the great whore or harlot Babylon in order to make room for the reign of Christ and His pure and spotless bride, the Church.

God's judgment of the great whore or harlot Babylon brought divine vengeance on its fornication or moral and spiritual prostitution, by which it corrupted (seduced and destroyed) the earth (that is, the people on the earth). It also avenged the blood of all God's servants martyred by the anti-God world system. When the fifth seal was opened, the martyrs under the altar in heaven cried out for just vindication. They were given white robes and told to remain quiet for a little season until other martyrs would be added to their number (6:11). Now the little season has come to an end. The multitude of people in heaven rejoice that the divine judgment of Babylon has vindicated and avenged them with justice. But they served a God who said, "Vengeance is mine; I will repay" (Romans 12:19; Deuteronomy 32:35).

**3. And again they said, Alleluia. And her smoke rose up for ever and ever:** ... A second time they shouted, —WLMS ... Thanks to our God, —NLTG ... The smoke from her goes up, —TNT ... went up, —KLGS ... they cried, Praise ye Jehovah; and the smoke from her ruins ascends, —WADE ... shall go up through the eternities of the eternities, —FNTN.

**19:3.** The second hallelujah also comes from "much people in heaven." It seems even more emphatic and dramatic. It is prompted by the completeness of the just overthrow and judgment of the great Babylon world system. Though this overthrow is accomplished by the beast (the Antichrist) and the 10 kings (rulers, kingdoms, vassals) who are joined with the Antichrist, the judgment is from God. God used them just as He used Assyria (Isaiah 10:5-12) and Babylon (Habakkuk 1:6). As a reminder of God's justice and of the total destruction of the city, the smoke of Babylon

goes up for ever and ever. When Isaiah was dealing with Edom as a representative of the nations who were against God, the prophecy against Edom (Idumea) also called for a judgment where the smoke would go up forever (Isaiah 34:2, 5, 6, 9, 10). Thus the same thing is said of Babylon as a representative of the world system, or as the world system itself. (Some take the idea of the smoke ascending forever to mean even though Babylon disappears the smoke of its destruction keeps on going further and further from the earth into the distant galaxies and on and on forever.)

**4. And the four and twenty elders and the four beasts fell down and worshipped God that sat on the throne:** ... Presbyters ... threw themselves down and rendered worship, —WADE ... the four living creatures, —TNT ... living ones, —KLGS ... leaders ... got down and worshiped, —NLTG ... bowed, and paid homage to, —FNTN ... prostrated, —KLST ... went down on their faces and gave worship, —BB.

**saying, Amen; Alleluia:** ... exclaiming ... Praise ye Jehovah, —WADE ... Even so, praise to the Lord, —BB ... So be it! Praise the Lord! —BECK ... Let it be so. Thanks to our God! —NLTG.

**19:4.** The 24 elders and the 4 living beings in heaven respond to the hallelujahs of the "much people in heaven" by falling down before the throne of God and worshiping Him, saying "Amen," and by adding their own "Hallelujah" as they honor God for His justice and the righteousness of His judgment. They are still worshiping God in this last mention of them.

'Āmēn is another Hebrew word, a great word of positive response that can be translated "truly" in most cases. It comes from a root word that carries the basic idea of certainty or support. It is the response of faith that recognizes what has been said is sure, absolutely certain. Some today look at these prophecies as something which is only possible. They might hope that God will fulfill them, but they are not sure. The "Amen" of the 24 elders and the 4 living creatures shows that they put their full approval on what God has done and on the certainty that His judgment is just and all He does is right.

**5. And a voice came out of the throne, saying:** ... came forth from, —WADE ... from the high seat, —BB ... the place where the King sits, —NLTG.

**Praise our God, all ye his servants:** ... Give praise to our God, —BB, —TNT ... revere him, —KLST ... his slaves, —MNTG ... Give thanks ... you workmen who are owned by Him, —NLTG.

**and ye that fear him, both small and great:** ... both high and low, —TCNT ... those who respect Him, unimportant and important people, —SEB ... who honor Him with love, —NLTG ... in whom is the fear of him, —BB.

**19:5.** Again John heard a voice coming out of the throne with the command that all the servants of God are to keep on praising Him. Ladd believes the voice is that of one of the four living creatures who are there at the throne (*Revelation*, p. 245). Others think it is another angelic voice (Walvoord, p. 269).

The servants (slaves) of God are further identified as all those who fear Him, that is, who reverence, worship, and serve Him. "Servants" here is the ordinary Greek word for slaves. They are love slaves devoted to Him.

**6. And I heard as it were the voice of a great multitude:** . . . Then I heard again what seemed like the song of, *–NORL* . . . there came to my ears the voice of a great army, *–BB* . . . a sound of a vast multitude, *–WADE* . . . a great throng, *–FNTN* . . . like that of a great crowd, *–KLST.*

**and as the voice of many waters:** . . . like the roar of, *–NORL* . . . like the sound of, *–BB.*

**and as the voice of mighty thunderings, saying, Alleluia:** . . . like the roll of violent thunderings, *–WADE* . . . the peal of mighty thunders, *–WLMS* . . . the roar of terrific thunders, *–BRKL* . . . and the crash of many thunder-peals. These are the words, *–NORL* . . . sound of loud thunders, *–BB.*

**for the Lord God omnipotent reigneth:** . . . Now the Lord our God, *–KLST* . . . the Almighty, is King, *–BECK* . . . has become sovereign King, *–BRKL* . . . has now begun to reign! *–WLMS* . . . He is all-powerful, *–SEB* . . . our God, Ruler of all, is King, *–BB* . . . has shown Himself to be King, *–WADE* . . . has inaugurated his Kingdom! *–NOLI.*

**19:6.** The fourth hallelujah comes in response to the command from the throne to praise our God. Praise is deserved because He is the Lord, because He is omnipotent (all powerful), and because He is on the throne and now is about to begin the reign on earth through Christ.

Some think this fourth hallelujah (as well as the third) is the voice of the angelic hosts. But because they mention salvation (verse 1) it is more likely that the believers are meant. All the faithful will thus be in that number who respond to the angel's call to keep on praising our God. The praise here is louder and more joyful than the previous praise. The sound of this fourth hallelujah is like the sound of many waters and like the sound of mighty peals of thunder. He is worthy of praise for He is the Lord, He is our God in a personal way, He is almighty.

**7. Let us be glad and rejoice, and give honour to him:** . . . rejoice and exult, *–TCNT* . . . and triumph, *–MNTG* . . . and be delighted, *–BECK* . . . Let us celebrate,

*–NOLI* . . . glad with delight, *–BB* . . . be exceeding glad. Let us give him glory, *–NORL.*

**for the marriage of the Lamb is come:** . . . for the time of the marriage, *–KLST* . . . the time is come for the Lamb to be married, *–BB.*

**and his wife hath made herself ready:** . . . and his bride, *–LAMS* . . . and His destined wife, *–WADE* . . . has prepared herself, *–FNTN.*

**19:7.** A further and most important vindication of God's people will be the Marriage Supper of the Lamb, a great wedding banquet fulfilling the parables, prophecies, and typology of the relationship of the Church to Christ. This is a further reason for rejoicing. When this takes place all the universe will know that the Church is what the Bible says the Church is, the bride of Christ. It will bring great honor and give great glory to God the Father as a culmination of His great plan of redemption.

It will be a time for gladness that is full of joy and delight. There will be great rejoicing and shouting for joy. The anticipation of this great event causes believers to rejoice even now. The reality will be joy beyond our present imagination.

The Bride here is called the "wife" as a recognition that she has already entered into a close, loving, personal relationship with Christ. The same relationship is also symbolized by calling Christ the Head and the Church the body of Christ (Ephesians 1:22, 23; 4:15, 16; 1 Corinthians 12:12-27). When the Marriage Supper of the Lamb is ready the "wife" has already made herself ready. This is a very important point.

Note that the time is after the judgment of "the great whore," the false woman who is here contrasted with the true Church. This is also just at the close of the Tribulation. Thus the Lamb's wife includes all the redeemed, including those martyred during the Tribulation.

**8. And to her was granted that she should be arrayed in fine linen, clean and white:** . . . She was permitted to be dressed in, *–NORL* . . . Hers was the privilege of clothing herself in, *–KLST* . . . to put on dazzling . . . linen, *–BECK* . . . to be robed in a pure radiant robe, *–FNTN* . . . fine pure linen, *–LAMS* . . . bright and pure, *–MNTG.*

**for the fine linen is the righteousness of saints:** . . . for linen signifies the upright deeds, *–WLMS* . . . represents, *–NORL* . . . symbolize the righteous deeds, *–NOLI* . . . the good deeds of Christ's People, *–TCNT* . . . is the holy deeds of her saints, *–KLST* . . . of the holy, *–FNTN.*

**19:8.** In heaven the "wife" is already fully clothed in fine linen, clean and white, thus free from all impurity. The fine linen represents the "righteousnesses" of the saints. The Greek for righteousness is plural here and thus speaks of the righteous deeds of the saints (all believers). That is, these robes do not represent the imputed righteousness of Christ in which we stand justified before God, although it influences us to act righteously. They rather represent the acts of faith and righteousness that we do as the result of our relationship with Christ. They are the outworkings of the gift of salvation and the gifts of the Spirit which we receive freely from Him. These are empowered and administered by the Holy Spirit, but believers can only accomplish them as they cooperate (Matthew 25:35-40; 1 Corinthians 14:32).

This clothing of white linen reminds us of Christ's desire that His believers could come before Him "not having spot, or wrinkle, or any such thing" (Ephesians 5:27).

There is also a contrast here to the false woman, the great prostitute Babylon who corrupted, seduced, and destroyed the earth with her depraved moral and religious fornication or prostitution. The Church shows she is different because she prepares herself by good works that glorify God and bear witness to Christ (Acts 1:8; Ephesians 2:10).

**9. And he saith unto me, Write, Blessed [are] they which are called:** . . . The angel said to me, −NORL . . . Write this down, −SEB . . . are the guests, −NOLI . . . who are invited, −BRKL, −KLST . . . who have been bidden, −MNTG.

**unto the marriage supper of the Lamb:** . . . to the wedding banquet, −BRKL . . . to the Lamb's wedding dinner, −BECK . . . wedding-feast, −TCNT . . . To the marriage-feast, −WMCK

**And he saith unto me, These are the true sayings of God:** . . . And he added, −NORL . . . Again he said to me, −KLST . . . These words of mine, −LAMS . . . the true declarations, −FNTN . . . the true words, −WMCK

**19:9.** The same angelic voice now commands John to write. Some think this means that John was to give a special word to the seven churches of the Roman province of Asia. More likely, it is to all churches. The great and the mighty of this world may ignore believers, but the believers are the blessed ones, for they are called to the Marriage Supper of the Lamb and will partake of its joys that will last forever.

The word "called" here implies that these blessed ones have not only received the invitation, they have accepted it. The marriage supper will celebrate the fact that the Church shall "ever be with the Lord" (1 Thessalonians 4:17). God's love that sent Jesus to die on the cross for believers' sins made it possible for them to be saved from perishing in the lake of fire. It also made it possible for them to respond to that love and enter into and share the joy and triumph of the Lord. But entering into a living relationship with Jesus must be as individuals, not as a body or a group. These

promises of the Marriage Supper of the Lamb are the true sayings of God.

**10. And I fell at his feet to worship him:** . . . I prostrated before, −KLST . . . to pay him homage, −FNTN.

**And he said unto me, See [thou do it] not:** . . . Be careful! Don't do that! −BECK, −SEB . . . You must take care not to do that, −WLMS . . . Refrain from it! −FNTN . . . Never do that! −NORL.

**I am thy fellowservant:** . . . I am only a fellow-slave of yours, −WLMS . . . fellow servant with yourself, −NORL.

**and of thy brethren that have the testimony of Jesus:** . . . who possess the evidence, −FNTN . . . who hold, −MNTG . . . believing in, −NORL . . . who keep the witness of, −BB . . . who preserve the testimony borne by Jesus, −WADE . . . concerning Jesus, −KLST.

**worship God:** . . . God is the one to worship! −NORL . . . give worship to, −BB . . . it is to God that you must render worship, −WADE.

**for the testimony of Jesus is the spirit of prophecy:** . . . The testimony to God's Message borne by Jesus constitutes the inspiration of Christian Preaching which transmits that testimony, −WADE . . . for the witness of Jesus is the spirit of the prophet's word, −BB . . . for the evidence of Jesus is the life of preaching, −FNTN . . . The Gospel of Jesus is what has inspired prophecy, −NORL . . . is the vital breath of prophecy, −MNTG . . . is the inspiring spirit, −WLMS . . . is what inspires prophets, −SEB . . . is a sure mark of the prophetic spirit, −KLST.

**19:10.** The wonder, the glory, and the hope inspired by this vision so overwhelmed John that he fell at the feet of the angel in an attitude of worship. The angel rejected this immediately. He was only a fellow servant sent to serve John (Hebrews 1:14). Only God is worthy of worship. All the attention should be given to Jesus, just as the Spirit of prophecy in both the Old and New Testaments focuses its testimony or witness on Jesus.

"The testimony of Jesus is the spirit of prophecy" means that the purpose of prophecy is to bear witness to Jesus, to exalt Him, and to reveal His redemptive work. It does not exalt the prophet.

**11. And I saw heaven opened:** . . . lay open, −TCNT . . . wide open, −WADE.

**and behold a white horse:** . . . suddenly, −WADE . . . and lo! −MNTG . . . appeared, −FNTN.

**and he that sat upon him [was] called Faithful and True:** . . . its rider, −KLST . . . He that is mounted upon it is called . . . Reliable, −WADE . . . Certain, −BB.

**and in righteousness he doth judge and make war:** . . . in justice He passes judgment, −WLMS . . . He judges fairly, −SEB . . . He declares and wages war, −FNTN . . . and goes to battle, −BECK . . . He is the defender and champion of righteousness, −NOLI . . . judging and making war, −BB . . . execute judgment and wage war, −WADE . . . justly, −KLST.

**19:11.** The Bible does not describe the Marriage Supper of the Lamb here. Instead, it goes ahead in still another vision where John saw the heaven already opened and Jesus returning on a white horse, which means He comes as a mighty conqueror, the triumphant King of kings, and Lord of lords. He comes as the Mediator bringing the Father's victory and God's judgment which are necessary in order to clear the way before bringing in the Kingdom. (Compare Matthew 13:41-43; 2 Thessalonians 1:7; 2:8.)

As "Faithful and True" He comes establishing truth and justice. (Compare Psalm 96:13.) God's people have been waiting for this ever since God began to reveal His covenants and promises.

Jesus comes from heaven in righteousness; that is, He comes in relation to the fulfillment of God's promises and covenants. Righteousness in the Old Testament is often connected with faithfulness to God's covenants. In the New Testament it refers to His faithfulness. He is trustworthy. Full confidence can be placed in Him. That He is called "True" puts further emphasis on the same dependability. It also draws attention that He is true in contrast to the false prophets and false teachers of the world, but especially in contrast to the Antichrist and his false prophet. He is real in contrast to all the false gods and false things the world worships. His second coming is thus very real and will be a definite historical event. The New Testament makes it very clear so that it cannot be spiritualized away.

His purpose is first to judge and make war (compare John 5:30; 2 Thessalonians 1:7, 8). But all He does is in line with truth and carries out the truth already revealed in God's Word. Because the world under the Antichrist has turned its back totally on the true God and on the salvation He has provided through Christ's death and resurrection, their sin must be dealt with in judgment.

**12. His eyes [were] as a flame of fire:** ... His eyes blaze like fire, −NOLI ... a fiery flame, −FNTN.

**and on his head [were] many crowns:** ... many diadems, −BRKL, −WLMS ... many royal crowns, −TCNT.

**and he had a name written, that no man knew, but he himself:** ... a name in writing, of which no man has knowledge, −BB ... significant of His nature, −WADE ... having a name inscribed, which none except Himself could understand, −FNTN ... no one knows except, −NORL.

**19:12.** Eyes as a flame of fire indicate that nothing will escape Christ's righteous judgment. No one can hide from Him.

The many royal crowns (royal diadems) show He comes as King of kings to make David's throne eternal and to fulfill the many prophecies that He shall reign on the earth. They also show that Jesus is the fulfillment of the typology expressed in

Zechariah 6:9-15. As Zechariah prophesied, the One called the Branch (in fulfillment of Isaiah 11:1-10) will not only be King, but will reign as Priest upon His throne. He is already King at the Father's right hand, but He will be King on earth.

The name (or names, the word may be collective including a number of names no human being knew) speaks of the inner glory and divine nature He shares with the Father (Luke 10:22; John 17:5). The name or names were probably written on each of the diadems. The "names" of God and Christ are never mere empty designations. They are expressions of the divine nature and character. The fact that no one has known them and still does not know them except Christ himself means more than the names are secret. It means rather that no one knows them in their own personal experience. In other words, no human being shares these divine qualities which are inherent in the divine nature of Jesus. He is the unique Son of God, the Son of God in a special, one-of-a-kind way.

**13. And he [was] clothed with a vesture dipped in blood:** ... He is arrayed in, −NOLI ... in a garment, −KLST ... the garment with which He is clad is steeped in blood, −WADE ... clothed in a robe washed with blood, −BB ... The clothing He wore had been dipped, −NORL ... that has been sprinkled with, −TCNT.

**and his name is called The Word of God:** ... the Title by which He is called is The Expression of God's Purpose, −WADE ... and His appointed title is, −BRKL ... the name that He went by was, −NORL ... The Message of God, −SEB.

**19:13.** The vesture dipped in blood shows He is the same Jesus who shed His blood, rose from the dead, and ascended into heaven (Acts 1:9). "Dipped in blood" can also mean spattered by the blood of His enemies because He has come and judged them. (See also Isaiah 63:1-6.)

He is further identified for all to see as the Living Word of God (John 1:1, 14).

**14. And the armies [which were] in heaven followed him upon white horses:** ... The knights of heaven, −NOLI ... went after him, −BB ... and mounted on, −NORL.

**clothed in fine linen, white and clean:** ... dressed in pure, −BECK, −SEB ... delicate linen, −BB ... muslin, −FNTN.

**19:14.** The armies which were in heaven follow Jesus into this final Battle of Armageddon. They also ride white horses, for they already share in His triumph. Some think these armies are angels. However, 17:14 shows that believers, if not the whole army, are certainly included in it. Their clothing of fine linen, white and clean, identifies them with the "wife" of the Lamb (19:8). The emphasis on the fact that their clothing is clean also draws attention to their being made righteous and clean through the blood of the Lamb.

The Bible is full of assurance that when Jesus returns in glory to judge the nations, every faithful believer will be with Him. The plain statement in 1 Thessalonians 4:17 gives the assurance that those caught up to meet the Lord in the air will "ever be with the Lord."

**15. And out of his mouth goeth a sharp sword:** . . . issues, —NORL . . . from his lips, —MNTG . . . speech which cuts like, —WADE . . . had a sharp sword drawn out of its sheath, —FNTN.
**that with it he should smite the nations:** . . . with which to strike, —KLST . . . strike down, —BECK . . . smite the heathen, —FNTN, —NORL . . . overcomes the nations, —BB.
**and he shall rule them with a rod of iron:** . . . and he has rule over them with, —BB . . . He will shepherd them, —SEB . . . it is He Who will shepherd them with an iron mace, —WADE . . . govern them, —FNTN.
**and he treadeth the winepress:** . . . it is He Who treads, —WADE . . . he is crushing with his feet the grapes, —BB.
**of the fierceness and wrath of Almighty God:** . . . of the furious indignation of, —BRKL . . . of the passion of the anger of, —MNTG . . . of the strong wrath, —BB . . . the furious wrath, —NOLI . . . of the fierce anger, —NORL . . . of the fierce wrath of God, Sovereign Supreme, —WADE . . . of the All-ruling God, —FNTN.

**19:15.** This verse gives three pictures of the terribleness of the judgment that Jesus will bring when He returns in triumph. The sharp sword out of the mouth of the rider on the white horse will smite (strike down, slay) the nations. The sharp sword represents "the sword of the Spirit, which is the Word of God" (Ephesians 6:17).

The sharp sword smiting the nations is parallel to the shattering of the nations with a rod of iron (Psalm 2:9). To rule with a rod of iron is literally to act the part of a shepherd with a rod of iron and means to destroy the enemies of the sheep. (See 2:27; 12:5.) This must be done before Christ brings in the Kingdom. Many prophecies show that the Kingdom must be brought in through judgment. (See also 1 Peter 2:25; Hebrews 13:20.)

The third picture emphasizes the same thing in an even stronger way. Treading the winepress of the fierceness and wrath of Almighty God is a picture of a harvest of judgment that is deliberate and continuous until the judgment is complete. (Compare Matthew 24:29, 30; Isaiah 63:1, 2; Zechariah 14:3, 4.) The severity of the judgment to come will demonstrate how much God hates sin. He is indeed a God of love and is longsuffering and patient. Because of this His love is reaching out to sinners. He wants them to come to repentance (2 Peter 3:9). But His patience does not

mean He tolerates sin. The Day of Judgment must eventually come (2 Peter 3:10).

**16. And he hath on [his] vesture and on his thigh a** name **written:** . . . on his robe and on his leg is a name, —BB . . . on his garment . . . a name inscribed, —KLST . . . And He has upon His raiment, and upon His hip, a Title written, —WADE . . . On His cloak and on His thigh this title is given Him, —NORL.
**KING OF KINGS, AND LORD OF LORDS:**

**19:16.** The One who is the Living Word is also King of kings and Lord of lords. This name is in plain sight for all to see. The apostle Paul recognized earlier that this name belonged to Jesus (1 Timothy 6:15). John has previously stated that Jesus will overcome (17:14).

Beasley-Murray believes the name is written in two places: on His robe and on His thigh, a practice not uncommon in the ancient world (*New Century Bible, Revelation,* pp. 283f.). It is true that He will not wear an ordinary sword, for He will win the victory with the sword of His mouth, the powerful Word of God. "On his thigh" probably means on the robe spread over His thigh as He rides on the white horse.

Believers remember with joy that Jesus came as a baby. Believers remember with gratitude that Jesus died on the cross, and that God raised Him from the dead for their justification. But He is no longer the babe in the manger. He is no longer on the cross. He is risen, ascended, glorified, and exalted at the right hand of the Father as the believers' Advocate interceding for them (1 John 2:1). He is the King *now.* Every believer has accepted Him as Lord. But they look with anticipation for the day when He will return as King of kings and Lord of lords.

**17. And I saw an angel standing in the sun:** . . . a single Angel, —WADE . . . as he stood in, —NORL . . . taking his place in, —BB . . . stationed, —FNTN . . . on the sun, —KLST.
**and he cried with a loud voice:** . . . was crying, —BB . . . shouted very loudly, —SEB . . . in loud tones he cried thus, —WADE.
**saying to all the fowls that fly in the midst of heaven:** . . . calling, —FNTN . . . to all the birds flying around in the middle of the air, —SEB . . . all the vultures which fly, —NOLI . . . that fly in the zenith, —WADE . . . in flight in the heavens, —BB . . . in midheaven, —KLST.
**Come and gather yourselves together unto the supper of the great God:** . . . be collected, —FNTN . . . flock to the great banquet of God, —WADE . . . Come together to the great feast, —BB . . . assemble for the great supper God has prepared, —KLST . . . for God's great banquet, —BECK, —BRKL . . . the great supper of divine retribution! —NOLI.

**19:17.** The next vision John was given presents a striking contrast to the Marriage Supper of the Lamb. It reveals an angel already standing in the sun, which may mean he was actually in the sun, or it may mean the light of the sun was focused upon him. He is there as a messenger of God, for the Battle of Armageddon will soon be over. This angel calls loudly for all the birds that fly in the midheaven to come to another great supper. The "supper" of the great God refers to another result of the Battle of Armageddon. It is a supper for all the birds, but especially for the vultures and other birds of prey. The language used to describe this vision reflects a number of prophecies of the Old Testament, though not all of them may refer directly to this battle. (See Jeremiah 51:27-36; Ezekiel 39:17-20; Joel 3:9-15; Zephaniah 3:8; Zechariah 14:3-5; Revelation 14:14-20; 16:13-16; 17:14.)

18. **That ye may eat the flesh of kings:** ... in order to, *—KLST* ... So that you may take for your food, *—BB* ... devour, *—FNTN* ... the bodies of, *—EVRD.*
**and the flesh of captains:** ... of commanders, *—SEB* ... chief captains, *—NORL* ... generals, *—MNTG.*
**and the flesh of mighty men:** ... and famous men, *—EVRD* ... of strong men, *—SEB* ... warriors, *—WADE* ... of the mighty, *—KLGS.*
**and the flesh of horses, and of them that sit on them:** ... Come to eat the bodies of, *—EVRD* ... of steeds and of those who are mounted upon them, *—WADE* ... those who are seated on them, *—BB* ... and their riders, *—WMCK*
**and the flesh of all [men, both] free and bond:** ... of all the enemies of the Lamb, *—WADE* ... of all people, *—BECK* ... of all sorts of men, *—ADAM* ... all mankind, *—NORL* ... free men and slaves, *—TNT* ... Some are free and some are not free, *—NLTG* ... and unfree, *—BB* ... and enslaved, Fenton.
**both small and great:** ... low and high, *—WADE.*

**19:18.** The birds of prey will not distinguish between the victims of the Battle of Armageddon. They will feast on the flesh of kings, captains (captains of thousands, tribunes, generals), mighty warriors, horses, and horsemen, and all kinds of people who will follow the Antichrist into this battle, whether they are slave or free, small or great, unimportant or important. None of them will have an honorable burial. There will be no tombs with their names inscribed, no monuments erected to their memory.

Barnhouse points out the similarity of the description here to that in Ezekiel 39:17-20 and takes this to mean that the battle of Gog and Magog described by Ezekiel and the Battle of Armageddon are the same (p. 362). Others, however, think there are too many differences and that Ezekiel 38 and 39 refer to a battle at the beginning of the Tribulation or just preceding it.

19. **And I saw the beast:** ... the Wild Beast, *—WADE* ... animal, *—NLTG.*
**and the kings of the earth, and their armies:** ... muster, *—NORL.*
**gathered together to make war against him that sat on the horse:** ... come together, *—BB* ... assemble, *—KLST* ... mustered to wage war, *—BRKL, —WADE* ... They were ready to fight against, *—NLTG* ... against the horse's rider, *—TNT* ... the rider on the horse, *—EVRD.*
**and against his army:** ... with His army, *—ADAM* ... and his armies, *—KLGS.*

**19:19.** The birds of prey are called in anticipation for the battle. They will be ready and waiting when the wild beast (the Antichrist) comes into the great valley just south of Nazareth. The Antichrist will be accompanied by his false prophet and the kings (and other rulers) of the nations left in the world at the end of the Tribulation. These kings were already subject to the Antichrist (17:13). At the end of the Tribulation they will be summoned and brought together by demonic spirits sent from the mouth of the Antichrist and his false prophet. The armies of all the nations left in the world will thus join together under the Antichrist's banner to defy the Christ who comes on His white horse of triumph accompanied by His true followers.

Demonic agencies will actually do what God wants by gathering the nations to the region of Armageddon to prepare for war. (See Jeremiah 25:32, 33; Joel 3:2; Zephaniah 3:8; Zechariah 14:2, 3; Revelation 16:12, 16.) The war will end with the defeat of the Antichrist and his armies. God's judgment will also affect the rest of the world (Jeremiah 25:29-33).

Many of the false teachers of the world say good will gradually overcome evil. Many say that more and better education will bring peace and continued prosperity in a better world. Many well-meaning Bible believers take only the promises of hope and suppose that the gospel will convert the world before Jesus comes. There will indeed be good ground where the seed of God's Word will bear fruit. There will be times of refreshing right down to the time of Christ's return (Acts 3:19). But it is contrary to the plain teachings of the Bible to suppose that the world as a whole will be converted. Rather, the world as a whole will follow the Antichrist and take the mark of the beast. Thus, Jesus must come in judgment when He comes to reign.

20. **And the beast was taken:** ... The wild animal was taken, *—NLTG* ... was captured, *—BECK* ... was overpowered, *—FNTN* ... was seized, *—MNTG, —TNT.*
**and with him the false prophet that wrought miracles before him:** ... who in his sight produced

the wonders, —*FNTN*...who performed, —*MNTG*...who did the signs, —*BB*...before his eyes, —*WADE*...in his presence, —*NORL.*

**with which he deceived them that had received the mark of the beast:** ... by means of which he led astray, —*BRKL* ... by which he had misled those, —*NORL*...by which he deluded those who had received, —*WADE*... by which they were turned from the true way who had, —*BB*...who accepted, —*KLST*...the animal's brand, —*BECK.*

**and them that worshipped his image:** ... and who gave worship, —*BB* ... who adored his image, —*FNTN*...worshiped its statue, —*KLST.*

**These both were cast alive into a lake of fire burning with brimstone:**...The two were thrown alive ... blazing with brimstone, —*MNTG* ... these two were put living into the sea of everburning fire, —*BB* ... were hurled, —*KLST* ... were flung alive, —*BRKL* ... into the fiery lake of burning sulfur, —*BECK*...burning with Divine anger, —*FNTN.*

**19:20.** The battle will not last long. The wild beast (the Antichrist) and his false prophet will be captured (seized and taken into custody).

The false prophet is the last of a long line of false christs and false prophets who have shown deceptive signs and wonders, as Jesus himself foretold would happen (Matthew 24:24). His miracles will deceive many (Revelation 13:13-15; 2 Thessalonians 2:9, 10). Done in the presence of the Antichrist they will deceive those who receive the mark of the beast and who become worshipers of his image. But the miracles of the Antichrist's false prophet will not enable him to escape. He too will be taken. Then both the Antichrist and his false prophet will be thrown alive into the lake of fire burning with sulfur.

Though the lake of fire was prepared for the devil and his angels, these agents of Satan actually precede him into it. Satan will not be cast into it until after the thousand years are over (20:10). At that time the Antichrist and his false prophet will still be there, still in torment. The rest of the wicked dead will be cast into it after the Great White Throne Judgment (20:15). However, basing their view on 14:9-11, some believe it possible that those who took the mark of the beast will suffer the same fate as the beast and the false prophet.

The lake of fire is the final state of the wicked. In the King James Version of the New Testament two words, *hadēs* and *geenna*, are translated "hell." A third term, *tartaroō*, is translated "cast into hell" (*Tartarus*). Hades refers to the intermediate state where the wicked go now when they die (Matthew 11:23; 16:18; Luke 10:15; 16:23; Acts 2:27, 31; Revelation 1:18; 6:8; 20:13, 14). It sometimes translates the Old Testament Hebrew word *sheôl*. *Tartarus* is apparently the depths of Hades, for it is also an intermediate state (2 Peter 2:4). *Gehenna*,

however, is the final state, and the fires of Gehenna refer to the lake of fire (Matthew 5:22, 29, 30; 10:28; 18:9; 23:15, 33; Mark 9:43, 45, 47; Luke 12:5; James 3:6).

**21. And the remnant were slain with the sword of him that sat upon the horse:**...the remainder were slaughtered, —*FNTN*...And the rest were put to death with, —*BB* ... were killed by the broad-sword of him Who was mounted...that is, by the speech, cutting as any sword, —*WADE*...of the rider of the horse, —*KLST*...killed the rest, —*BECK.*

**which [sword] proceeded out of his mouth:**...that shot from, —*WLMS*...which He drew from its sheath, —*FNTN*...which issued from his lips, —*MNTG*...that comes from, —*KLST.*

**and all the fowls were filled with their flesh:**...all the birds were gorged with, —*WLMS*...gorged themselves on their bodies, —*BECK*, —*BRKL* ... All the birds ate up their flesh, —*SEB* ... were glutted, —*KLST*, —*WADE*...were made full, —*BB*...were gorged with the flesh of these fiends, —*NOLI.*

**19:21.** The rest of the followers of the Antichrist will not escape. The remnant of the kings of the earth and their armies will be slain. All Jesus will need to do is use the sword of His mouth; that is, He will speak the Word of God, and the sword of divine judgment will strike them all down.

These are all people who rejected the truth of the gospel that was preached during the Tribulation by an angel from heaven who proclaimed the everlasting gospel "to every nation, and kindred, and tongue, and people" (14:6). Thus, all of these who are slain at Armageddon will have heard the gospel. But because of their rejection of Christ they are given "strong delusion, that they should believe a lie; that they all might be damned who believed not the truth" (2 Thessalonians 2:11, 12). They are among those who have turned away from Christ because their deeds are evil (John 3:19, 20). By their unrighteous lifestyle and the lusts of the flesh that they practice, they have cut themselves off from any possibility of having any inheritance in the kingdom of God (1 Corinthians 6:9-11; Galatians 5:21).

## Chapter 20

**1. And I saw an angel come down from heaven:**...I saw, too, —*NORL*...descending, —*FNTN*...out of, —*WADE.*

**having the key of the bottomless pit:**...holding in his hand, —*NORL*...of the abyss, —*WADE*...of the great deep, —*BB.*

**and a great chain in his hand:** ... and carrying...upon his arm, —*WADE*...an enormous chain, —*BRKL.*

**20:1.** Chapter 20:1-10 deals with the judgment of Satan, which will take place in two stages: first a thousand-year imprisonment, then, after a short time of release, his eternal judgment in the lake of fire.

The first stage will be initiated by an angel from heaven who comes with the key to the abyss and a great chain in his hand.

**2. And he laid hold on the dragon:** ... seized, *—TCNT, —LAMS* ... took, *—BB* ... gripped, *—MNTG* ... He grabbed, *—SEB* ... overpowered, *—FNTN.*

**that old serpent, which is the Devil, and Satan:** ... the ancient serpent, *—WLMS* ... the Serpent of ancient days, *—WADE* ... who is none other than, *—NORL* ... the old snake, which is the Evil one, *—BB.*

**and bound him a thousand years:** ... and tied him up, *—SEB* ... and fettered him, *—WADE* ... and chained him, *—NOLI* ... put chains on him, *—BB* ... and secured him, *—FNTN.*

**20:2.** Daniel 2 shows that the present world system must be completely destroyed and swept away before the new order of Christ's kingdom can be established on earth. Revelation 19 shows that the Battle of Armageddon at the end of the Tribulation will bring the fall and end of the Antichrist and his false prophet. Chapter 20 shows the real troublemaker has been Satan all along. He is the adversary who is identified as the dragon, or snake, behind the Antichrist and his false prophet. He is further identified as the same old serpent who tempted Eve. He is also the devil (the slanderer). As the slanderer he spreads lies and false charges about God's people. As the adversary he opposes believers in all their battles for the Lord and for truth and right (Ephesians 6:12, 16). The earth cannot know the blessings of Christ's kingdom until Satan is out of the way.

After Christ's victory over the Antichrist and his armies Satan himself will be taken and bound for a thousand years. For the various views concerning the millennial period, see the *Overview.*

**3. And cast him into the bottomless pit:** ... He hurled him, *—BRKL* ... and flung him, *—MNTG* ... He then thrust him down into the pit, *—NORL* ... threw him into the great deep, *—WMCK* ... into the Abyss, *—WADE.*

**and shut him up, and set a seal upon him:** ... and locked, *—BECK* ... closed the mouth of the pit above him, making it secure with a seal, *—WADE* ... it was shut and locked, *—BB* ... closed and sealed it above him, *—FNTN* ... and sealed it over him, *—WLMS* ... and sealed the door of his dungeon, *—NOLI.*

**that he should deceive the nations no more:** ... to keep him from deceiving, *—BECK* ... so that he should seduce, *—MNTG* ... so that he might put the nations in error no longer, *—BB* ... any longer, *—NORL* ... mislead the nations, *—KLST* ... to prevent him from deluding ... any more, *—WADE.*

**till the thousand years should be fulfilled:** ... until the completion of, *—FNTN* ... had come

to an end, *—NORL* ... were ended, *—BB* ... should expire, *—WADE.*

**and after that he must be loosed a little season:** ... liberated, *—FNTN* ... set free, *—TCNT* ... it is necessary to loose him, *—MNTG* ... he must be free for awhile, *—NLTG* ... he is to be released for a short time, *—KLST* ... for a little while, *—BRKL* ... a little time, *—BB.*

**20:3.** After he is bound, Satan will be cast into the abyss, where he will be shut up, locked up, and sealed over. This will not allow him any activity on earth for the thousand years. During that time he will no longer be able to deceive the nations, nor will he have any influence on them or on anything else in the world for the entire period of the Millennium. Thus the Millennium will be completely free from all the lies and impulses to evil that come from the one who is the father or author of lies (John 8:44). "Millennium" is a term derived from the Latin mille meaning "thousand," and ennium, "years." It will be a time very different from the present age. God will restore Israel to her land and give her a spiritual restoration as well (Isaiah 54:11-14; 58:8; Ezekiel 36:33-38; 37:1-28; Zechariah 9:16). The desert will be restored to fertility and beauty (Isaiah 41:19, 20; 51:3). Even the animals will be changed (Isaiah 11:6-9), and undoubtedly even the atmosphere will be cleansed from all pollution.

"Nations" is a word often used in the Bible for the "Gentiles" who were outside of God's people and alienated from Him and His covenants and promises. The word "nations" here seems to mean those who followed Jesus and accepted His teachings as proclaimed by the apostles, prophets, evangelists, and pastor-teachers. John uses the same word in 21:24.

After the thousand years are over Satan will be released from the abyss for a short time. He will still be able to deceive those who desire to rebel against God's divine will and authority. Satan has always been a deceiver from the beginning (Genesis 3:13; compare Matthew 24:24; 2 Thessalonians 2:9, 10).

The "abyss," also called the "bottomless pit," is translated "the deep" in Luke 8:31 and Romans 10:7. It is "bottomless" only in the sense that it is unfathomable to the human eye and only God knows its limits. But it is capable of being sealed so Satan cannot leave it during the thousand years of the Millennium.

**4. And I saw thrones, and they sat upon them:** ... And I saw high seats, *—BB* ... I saw places where kings sit, *—NLTG* ... and men seated on them, *—KLST* ... and on them were seated, *—NORL* ... they took their seats upon them, *—WADE.*

**and judgment was given unto them:** ... a charge, *—FNTN* ... they were permitted to, *—MNTG* ... were given

**1367**

the power to say who is guilty, *–NLTG* . . . were given the authority to exercise judgment, *–KLST* . . . those who were to be judges, *–NORL* . . . they were empowered to deal judgment, *–WADE* . . . and the right of judging was given, *–BB*.

**and [I saw] the souls of them that were beheaded for the witness of Jesus:** . . . those who had been killed because they told about Jesus, *–NLTG* . . . for the witness of Jesus, *–BB* . . . because of the evidence, *–FNTN* . . . because of their love of Christ, *–NORL* . . . because of their testimony to, *–KLST* . . . for loyalty to the witness borne by Jesus, *–WADE*.

**and for the word of God:** . . . and preached the Word of God, *–NLTG* . . . and for loyalty to, *–WADE* . . . and because of the Message of God, *–FNTN*.

**and which had not worshipped the beast:** . . . who refused to worship, *–WLMS* . . . whoever had not paid homage, *–FNTN* . . . those who did not give worship, *–BB* . . . the wild animal, *–NLTG*.

**neither his image:** . . . or its statue, *–KLST* . . . false god, *–NLTG*.

**neither had received [his] mark upon their foreheads:** . . . because they did not bear his mark upon their brow, *–NORL* . . . his brand, *–MNTG*.

**or in their hands:** . . . upon, *–WADE* . . . that I saw, *–ADAM* . . . nor on his hand, *–KLGS*.

**and they lived and reigned with Christ a thousand years:** . . . They were restored to life, *–TCNT* . . . they returned to Life, *–WADE* . . . came to life once more and reigned as kings, *–NORL* . . . they were living and ruling, *–BB* . . . They lived again and were leaders along with the Christ, *–NLTG*.

**20:4.** Verses 4-6 speak of the reign of Christ with His saints during the thousand years of the Millennium. It will bring the fulfillment of many prophecies (Psalm 2:8; Isaiah 9:6, 7; 63:1-6; Jeremiah 23:5, 6; Daniel 2:44; Hosea 3:4, 5; Amos 9:11-15; Micah 4:1-8; Zechariah 8:1-9; Matthew 19:28; Acts 15:16-18; Revelation 2:25-28; 11:15).

Verse 4 deals with two groups of people. The first are those souls (that is, persons) who sit on thrones to judge (that is "rule," as the word so often means in the Old Testament). These are probably the believers from all churches of the Church Age who remain faithful and are overcomers, that is, conquerors, winners (2:26, 27; 3:21). They will include the resurrected saints and those who were still alive on earth at the time of that resurrection and the Rapture, all of whom will be with Christ when He comes to destroy the Antichrist's rule and establish the millennial kingdom (Revelation 19:14; cf. Matthew 24:31; 13:30, 41-43). Among them will be the 12 apostles of the Church judging (ruling) the 12 tribes of Israel (Luke 22:30). Israel will undoubtedly occupy all the land promised to Abraham (Genesis 15:18).

The second group includes those who were said to be faithful to Christ and who were martyred during the Tribulation (6:9; 12:17).

The two groups will be joined together to reign with Christ for a thousand years (Matthew 19:28; 2 Timothy 2:12; Revelation 2:26, 27; 3:21; 5:10; 20:4-6). This will be a time of peace and blessing with righteousness prevailing everywhere (Isaiah 2:2-4; Zechariah 9:10; Micah 4:3). The Holy Spirit will do a work of restoration. Even the natural world will reflect the order, perfection, and beauty God intended His creation to have (Isaiah 14:7, 8; 35:1, 2, 6, 7; 51:3; 55:12, 13; Psalms 96:11-13; 98:7-9; Romans 8:18-23). The animal world will also be changed (Isaiah 11:6-8; 65:25; Ezekiel 34:25). However, those born during the millennial reign of Christ on earth will still find it necessary to make their choice to follow Christ in faith and obedience. Even under these ideal conditions, some will rebel and disobey. Thus there will still be punishment and death (Isaiah 65:17-25). These will be sent to the lake of fire with the rest of the wicked dead after the Millennium is over (20:9, 10, 15).

Scholars differ as to whom John writes of here. Some believe there is only one group, the martyrs. Others add a main group of believers as well as the martyrs. The Bible shows that the Old Testament saints will be part of this main group (Isaiah 26:19-21; Ezekiel 37:12-14; Daniel 12:2, 13). To these a third view adds a group of living saints who have survived the Tribulation. According to dispensationalists one group is the 24 elders who are said to reign on the earth (5:10). They say Christ is the firstfruits of the first resurrection (1 Corinthians 15:23); the raptured and resurrected saints are the main harvest (1 Thessalonians 4:13-18); then the resurrection mentioned here is the gleanings or completion of the first resurrection.

**5.** **But the rest of the dead lived not again:** . . . The remainder of the dead will not live, *–FNTN* . . . As for the rest, *–NORL* . . . were not restored to life, *–TCNT* . . . did not come back to life, *–SEB* . . . did not return to Life, *–WADE*.

**until the thousand years were finished:** . . . were ended, *–TCNT* . . . had come to an end, *–NORL* . . . were completed, *–MNTG* . . . had expired, *–WADE*.

**This [is] the first resurrection:** . . . This is the first coming back from the dead, *–BB* . . . the first time many people are raised from the dead at the same time, *–NLTG* . . . the first rising again, *–KLGS*.

**20:5.** "The rest of the dead" includes all those not in the two groups mentioned in verse 4. That is, they are the wicked dead who died in their sins without ever accepting the saving grace of God. They will not live again, that is, be resurrected, until after the thousand years of Christ's kingdom on earth are over. Then they will be resurrected and brought before the Great White Throne for their final sentencing to the lake of fire.

"This is the first resurrection" means that those mentioned in verse 4 complete the first resurrection. Jesus spoke of two resurrections in John 5:29. He identified the first resurrection as the resurrection of life. It is for those who have done what God meant for them to do in accepting Christ and living for Him. The second resurrection is a resurrection of judgment for those who have done evil through unbelief. Just as the Old Testament prophets did not show the time difference between the first and second comings of Christ, so Jesus in this passage did not show the time difference between the two judgments. Not until Revelation 20 was it revealed that there will be at least a thousand years between them. In the Gospel of John Jesus was simply emphasizing the contrast between the two resurrections for the sake of encouraging people to live for God.

**6. Blessed and holy [is] he that hath part in the first resurrection:** . . . Those who are raised from the dead during this first time, *—NLTG* . . . is happy and holy, *—SEB* . . . and Hallowed, *—WADE* . . . he who share in, *—BRKL* . . . the holymen who share in this, *—NOLI* . . . is the participator in, *—FNTN* . . . in this first coming, *—BB* . . . the first rising again, *—KLGS.*
**on such the second death hath no power:** . . . over such, *—WADE* . . . has no authority, *—ADAM, —BB, —FNTN* . . . holds no sway, *—NORL* . . . over them, *—KLST.*
**but they shall be priests of God and of Christ:** . . . All these will be, *—NORL* . . . They will be religious leaders of God, *—NLTG* . . . ministers, *—FNTN* . . . God's priests and Christ's priests, *—ADAM.*
**and shall reign with him a thousand years:** . . . will rule with Him, *—BECK* . . . during the thousand years, *—WADE.*

**20:6.** The fullness of God's blessing will belong to those who have part in the first resurrection, which is the resurrection of the just (Luke 14:14). They are also holy, that is, dedicated to God and His will, for they worship and serve Him in spirit and in truth. Because their resurrection is like Christ's resurrection they rise to die no more. The second death will therefore have no power over them. They are king-priests, royal priests; priests of God and of Christ who will reign with Christ during the Millennium.

The word "blessed" here is in strong contrast to the word "miserable" used in 1 Corinthians 15:19. There Paul emphasized that the believer's resurrection and Christ's are closely tied together. If believers are not going to rise, then Christ did not rise. If He did not rise the faith of believers would be meaningless, and their sins would not be taken away. Christians would thus be miserable in the

sense that it is a miserable, pitiable thing to build one's faith on something that did not happen. But He did rise! His resurrection is a well-attested fact of history.

**7. And when the thousand years are expired:** . . . are over, *—BECK* . . . are finished, *—SEB* . . . come to an end, *—LAMS* . . . are completed, *—FNTN* . . . are ended, *—KLST.*
**Satan shall be loosed out of his prison:** . . . will be set free from, *—TCNT* . . . liberated, *—FNTN* . . . released from, *—KLST, —NORL.*

**20:7.** The Book of Revelation gives no further details of the Millennium, probably because previous prophecies are sufficient. For example, after revealing there will be a new heavens and a new earth Isaiah goes on to say the present Jerusalem will first have its fulfillment in a time of peace and joy (Isaiah 65:17-25, where the word "but" at the beginning of verse 18 is a strong adversative and indicates a strong contrast with the previous verse).

After the thousand years Satan will be loosed. Why he must be loosed can only be surmised. One reason may be that it is a final vindication of the justice of God. Also in every age man has been given the power to choose whom he will serve. This will be mankind's final test. Will he choose God or Satan? Some might say that surely since people know how wonderful Christ's reign will be they would all accept Him. But here it is clear that after a thousand years of Christ's glorious reign, some will follow Satan at their first opportunity. This shows they are rebels at heart. In justice, God can do nothing but separate them from His blessings forever in the outer darkness.

**8. And shall go out to deceive the nations:** . . . shall come out, *—FNTN* . . . to lead astray, *—BRKL* . . . to put in error, *—BB* . . . seduce, *—MNTG* . . . to mislead, *—KLST* . . . to delude, *—WADE* . . . the peoples, *—NORL.*
**which are in the four quarters of the earth, Gog and Magog:** . . . that live in, *—NORL* . . . in all four directions, *—SEB* . . . four corners of, *—KLST.*
**to gather them together to battle:** . . . He will assemble them, *—KLST* . . . to marshal them for war, *—MNTG* . . . to muster them to the war, *—FNTN.*
**the number of whom [is] as the sand of the sea:** . . . as many as the sands of the seashore, *—NORL.*

**20:8.** Satan will probably deceive himself into believing he can yet defeat God. As the great deceiver he will be allowed to go out and successfully deceive those who still want to exalt themselves against Christ and His righteous rule and reign.

This will be Satan's final attempt to deceive, and those who follow him will take part in his final defeat. Never again will there be any rebellion against God and His love.

Once again many will take the broad way of rebellion. Like so many during the ages of the past, they will reject God and His Word. They will refuse to learn from the examples of God's judgments on Adam and Eve, on the world of Noah's day, on Sodom and Gomorrah, on Egypt, on Israel, on Assyria, Babylon, Rome, and so many others.

The nations are identified here as Gog and Magog. The terms Gog and Magog are borrowed from Ezekiel chapters 38 and 39. The battle here is quite different, however. It may be that a comparison is being made meaning these people are acting like Gog and Magog.

**9. And they went up on the breadth of the earth:** ... And the future will show that they went up over, —WADE ... marched over the broad expanse of, —NORL ... spreading over the earth, —BECK ... over the broad plain, —KLST ... over the broad earth, —MNTG ... up over the face of the earth, —BB.

**and compassed the camp of the saints about:** ... and surrounded, —TCNT ... encircled the fortress of the holy, —FNTN ... made a circle about the tents of, —BB ... the encampment, —MNTG ... the camp of the saints, —NORL ... of the Lord's Hallowed People, —WADE.

**and the beloved city:** ... and the well loved town, —BB ... the city that is loved, —NLTG ... the city that he loves, —TNT ... the dearly loved city, —ADAM.

**and fire came down from God out of heaven:** ... flame descended, —WADE ... will fall from, —ADAM ... from the skies, —NORL.

**and devoured them:** ... for their destruction, —BB ... and consumed them, —BECK, —WLMS ... and swallowed them up, —WMCK ... and destroy them, —NLTG.

**20:9.** The armies of Satan will surround the camp (headquarters) of the saints and the beloved city (Jerusalem). There will be the godly remnant, just as there has been in every age. Jesus and the apostles foretold that many during the Church Age would depart from the Faith and leave the Church to go into all kinds of false doctrines and false cults (Matthew 24:10-12, 24; 2 Timothy 1:15; 4:1-4). The godly remnant will remain faithful and live in righteousness even in the midst of apostasy. So the saints of the Book of Revelation will be faithful whatever Satan may attempt to do.

God will send fire from heaven to devour the armies of Satan. So Satan will not be able to bring an end to Christ's reign of peace. All the Old Testament prophecies testify His reign will be eternal. His kingdom will continue on into the new heavens and the new earth.

**10. And the devil that deceived them:** ... the Evil One who put them in error, —BB ... who was leading them astray, —BRKL ... who misled them, —KLST.

**was cast into the lake of fire and brimstone:** ... was flung, —NORL ... hurled, —MNTG ... was thrown into ... fire and sulphur, —ADAM ... will be thrown into ... burning with sulphur, —NLTG ... was sent down into the sea of ever-burning fire, —BB.

**where the beast and the false prophet [are]:** ... where lie also, —MNTG ... The wild animal and the false preacher are already there, —NLTG.

**and shall be tormented:** ... there to be, —NORL ... they will suffer, —TNT ... tortured, —MNTG ... They will all be punished, —NLTG ... and their punishment will go on, —BB.

**day and night for ever and ever:** ... through the ages of the ages, —FNTN.

**20:10.** Not only will Satan's attempt fail, Satan's power and his deceptions will come to their final end when he is cast forever into the lake of fire and burning sulfur. Never will he be able to escape from its torments. Never again will he be able to accuse, deceive, tempt, oppose, or be an adversary to anyone. He will be finally and forever out of action.

In the lake of fire Satan will join the beast (the Antichrist) and the false prophet. They will have already been there for over a thousand years. They are still the same, still in torment. Clearly, the fires of the lake of fire have not cleansed, purified, or changed them. Only the blood of Jesus and the power of the Spirit can change anyone in a way that will affect his eternal destiny. It is also clear that after the thousand years they are still in existence. They have not been annihilated, but will continue in torment, along with Satan, for ever and ever throughout eternity.

**11. And I saw a great white throne:** ... Then I saw ... a great white seat, —NLTG ... white seat, —BB.

**and him that sat on it:** ... and One seated upon it, —BRKL ... Who sits on it, —ADAM.

**from whose face the earth and the heaven fled away:** ... from whose presence, —LAMS ... Both earth and sky fled from His sight so far, —NORL ... left Him in a hurry, —NLTG ... went in flight, —BB ... and vanished away, —TNT.

**and there was found no place for them:** ... that they could not be found, —NORL ... and not a trace of them remained, —BRCL ... and disappeared, —EVRD ... were found no more, —KNOX.

**20:11.** With Satan gone, the time comes for the final judgment of the wicked and the bringing in of the eternal state with the new heavens and the new earth. The Great White Throne is white because it is pure and holy and radiates the majesty and glory of God. It is God's final judgment throne. Yet the One who sits on it here must be the glorified King of kings and Lord of lords, the

Lord Jesus Christ. Jesus declared that "the Father judgeth no man, but hath committed all judgment unto the Son: that all men should honor the Son, even as they honor the Father" (John 5:22, 23). Jesus must be the one Mediator between God and man in this final judgment, just as He is now the one Mediator between God and man in redemption (1 Timothy 2:5), and just as He was the one Mediator in creation (John 1:3).

So great is the glory manifested at the Great White Throne, and so great is the fire of divine judgment that even the physical universe cannot stand before Him in His manifest presence.

There are different views of what is meant by the phrase "the earth and the heaven fled away." Some think they will go out of existence to make room for a completely new creation. Others aver they will go through a transformation and re-creation process.

There are strong arguments for both positions. If the universe is indeed to go out of existence it must be admitted it could not be more clearly stated than it is here. But on the other hand similar language is used in 6:14, yet a thousand years later the earth is continuing to exist (see 2 Peter 3:6, 7). Also many passages in both the Old and New Testaments speak of a renewal and restoration of this whole creation.

Perhaps Mounce is correct when he says: "Whether it simply passes away or is melted by fire is of minor import." What we do know is that this creation will be changed with a new heavens and a new earth. See the *Overview* for a further discussion.

**12. And I saw the dead, small and great, stand before God:** ... And I perceived, *–CNDT* ... Before this throne ... the dead must come, great and little alike, *–KNOX* ... all the dead people standing in front of, *–NLTG* ... important and unimportant, *–SEB* ... the high and the low, *–WADE* ... stationed in sight of, *–FNTN* ... taking their places before the high seat, *–BB* ... before the throne, *–EVRD, –LAMS.*

**and the books were opened:** ... record books, *–BRCL* ... as scrolls were opened, *–KLST* ... There were also other books opened, *–EVRD.*

**and another book was opened, which is [the book] of life:** ... Another scroll, *–KLST* ... the scroll of life, *–ADAM* ... the register of the living, *–BRCL.*

**and the dead were judged:** ... were told they were guilty, *–NLTG* ... were sentenced, *–NOLI.*

**out of those things which were written in the books:** ... on the basis of, *–BRCL* ... from the things that had been written, *–ADAM, –HNSN* ... from what was written, *–TNT* ... as the books recorded them, *–KNOX* ... as recorded on the scrolls, *–KLST.*

**according to their works:** ... even by their works, *–BB* ... in accord with their acts, *–CNDT* ... according to their conduct, *–BRKL* ... according to what they had done, *–BECK* ... to the way they had lived,

*–SEB* ... by what they had done, *–EVRD* ... their actions, *–TCNT* ... deeds, *–MRDK, –NORL.*

**20:12.** Standing before the throne are the dead, including "the rest of the dead" mentioned in 20:5, plus any who may have died during the Millennium, plus those who died when the fire from heaven destroyed the armies marshalled by Satan (20:8, 9). "The dead" are the small and great, which here must mean all the unbelievers, all the unsaved, all the lost of all the past ages of history, regardless of their station in life. The godly of the Old Testament and the believers of the Church Age, as well as the martyrs of the tribulation period cannot be included, for they will not be "dead" at this time. They will be alive forevermore, with new immortal bodies that cannot die or even decay (1 Corinthians 15:52-54). It seems the wicked dead will also receive some sort of body in this second resurrection, the resurrection to judgment and to shame and everlasting contempt (Daniel 12:2; John 5:29).

Though the wicked dead will stand before God, their judgment is still committed to Jesus. The books will be opened, and they will be judged according to the written record of their works. Their works will include their rejection of Christ and their following of Satan. But all their works will be included in the divinely kept records. The believer's sins are blotted out when they are confessed. Even the sins believers are unaware of are cleansed, forgiven, and gone (1 John 1:7, 10; 2:1). But that is not true of those whose sins have not been forgiven. Even the secret sins they thought no one knew about will be there on the books (Luke 8:17). There is no question but that their sentence will be eternal doom in the lake of fire.

There are those who speculate that any who are saved after the judgment seat of Christ during the Tribulation may also appear here for rewards, though the Bible does not say so here or elsewhere.

**13. And the sea gave up the dead which were in it:** ... The ocean yielded, *–SEB* ... delivered up, *–FNTN* ... gave back, *–BRCL* ... the dead people, *–NLTG* ... the corpses it contained, *–BRKL* ... that lay there, *–KNOX.*

**and death and hell delivered up the dead which were in them:** ... and the unseen, *–CNDT* ... hades gave up their dead, *–NORL* ... the unseen world gave up, *–ADAM* ... gave back, *–BRCL* ... the nether world ... the dead they imprisoned, *–KLST.*

**and they were judged every man according to their works:** ... Each one was told he was guilty, *–NLTG* ... they were condemned, each in accord with their acts, *–CNDT* ... all were judged, *–MNTG* ... to his doings, *–FNTN* ... judged by the record of, *–BRCL* ... everyone by what he had done, *–NORL* ... everyone was judged according to his actions, −*TNT*...to his conduct, −*NAB*...to his deeds, −*KLST.*

**20:13.** In order to further emphasize the fact that none of the wicked will escape this final Great White Throne Judgment, the Word says the sea will also give up the dead who were in it. Though their bodies were not preserved in a tomb, resurrection in the Bible is always bodily in nature. They will have a bodily resurrection so they can appear before God's throne to receive His sentence of judgment. Because death and hell will also give up the dead that were in them, it is clear that all the wicked dead of all past ages will be brought up before the Great White Throne also.

Again it is emphasized that they will all be judged individually by their works. All their works will be judged according to the principles of the gospel, with due consideration for their motives. There will be a difference in the sentencing and the degree of punishment, but not in the length of time of their punishment (Luke 12:47, 48). The fire of the lake of fire is by its very nature unquenchable, and their torment will last for ever and ever.

**14. And death and hell were cast into the lake of fire:**...and the Grave, −*FNTN*...and Hades were hurled into, −*BRCL*, −*MNTG*...and the unseen world, −*ADAM*...thrown into, −*NORL*...hurled, −*KLST*...were put into the sea of fire, −*BB*...the fiery lake, −*BECK*...the pool of fire, −*CNFT*, −*NAB.*
**This is the second death:**...[namely], −*MRDK*...This lake of fire, −*NORL*...pool, −*CNFT*...sea, −*BB.*

**20:14.** Since the final judgment removes all the wicked and rebels, and Satan himself is cast into the lake of fire, there will be no further sin or death. Thus death and hell (Greek, *Hadēs*) are cast into the lake of fire. That is, the lake of fire is the only place in the universe where death will exist. Hades, as the place of intermediate punishment with its fires, will be absorbed into the lake of fire.

**15. And whosoever was not found written in the book of life:**...Anyone whose name was not listed in, −*NOLI*...if any was not found, −*HNSN*...if anyone's name was not in, −*BB*...unless his name was found written, −*KNOX*...recorded in, −*BRKL*, −*KLST*...enrolled, −*MRDK*...inscribed, NAB...in the scroll of life, −*ADAM*, −*CNDT*...not found to be...in the book of the living, −*BRCL.*
**was cast into the lake of fire:**...everyone must be thrown into this lake of fire, −*KNOX*...were hurled into, −*TCNT*...he went down into the sea of fire, −*BB*...he was thrown into, −*TNT*...this lake, −*KLST*...the pool, −*CNFT*...the fiery lake, −*WLMS.*

**20:15.** Since death in the Bible means separation, the second death is the final separation from

God and from all He has prepared for those who love and serve Him. In the final analysis, there are only two destinies: eternal death or eternal life. Those who are not in the Book of Life will not inherit eternal life but will end in the lake of fire.

Jesus used the word *Gehenna* as a term for the final destiny of the wicked. Gehenna is a Greek form of the Hebrew word meaning "the Valley of Hinnom," a narrow ravine to the west and south of Jerusalem. During the decline of Judah's kingdom, apostate Israelites offered their children in a fiery sacrifice to the Ammonite god, Molech (2 Kings 23:10; Jeremiah 7:31). Because of the defiling effect of this idolatry, in New Testament times Jews used it as a city dump. A fire was always burning there, and it was full of putrefying matter.

The Bible is very careful to emphasize that the final destiny of the lost is terrible beyond imagination. It will involve tribulation, anguish, weeping, and gnashing of teeth (Romans 2:9; Matthew 22:13; 25:30). It is a furnace of fire (Matthew 13:42, 50), causing eternal loss or everlasting destruction (2 Thessalonians 1:9). Its fires, by their very nature, will be unquenchable (Mark 9:43), and the smoke of their torment will go up for ever and ever, so the inhabitants will have no rest (Revelation 14:11; 20:10).

The New Testament encourages believers to live with a conscious and continuing concern for those who are living in sin and doomed to eternal loss if they do not repent. This is still the greatest reason for carrying the good news of the gospel to the uttermost part of the world.

## Chapter 21

**1. And I saw a new heaven and a new earth:**...And I perceived, −*CNDT*...I saw in my vision, −*BRCL*...a new sky, −*FNTN*...a fresh new sky and a fresh new earth, −*ADAM.*
**for the first heaven and the first earth were passed away:**...The former heavens, −*TCNT*...for the first sky, −*ADAM*...old heaven, the old earth had vanished, −*KNOX*...were gone, −*BRCL*, −*SEB*, −*TNT*...had disappeared, −*EVRD*, −*PHLP*...were no more, −*NORL.*
**and there was no more sea:**...The ocean didn't exist anymore, either, −*SEB*...and the old sea had vanished, −*NOLI*...and the sea was gone too, −*ADAM*...no longer existed, −*TNT*...is no more, −*CNDT*, −*KLGS*...had passed away, −*NORL.*

**21:1.** In this vision John saw both a new heaven and a new earth, the first heaven and the first earth having passed away (come to an end, disappeared). The word "new" usually means brandnew, meaning marvelous and unheard of. However, many take this as a mere renovation of the surface of the present earth. Some even place it at the beginning of the Millennium as a regeneration (referring to Matthew 19:28). The word "regeneration" is indeed used both of spiritual rebirth (Titus 3:5) and also of the restitution or restoration (Acts 3:21) which brings in the millennial kingdom. But what is described here is clearly after the Millennium and after the Great White Throne Judgment.

Some point to passages such as Ecclesiastes 1:4 which speak of the earth abiding forever. But this probably means there will always be an earth even though the present earth may be replaced by a new one. The Psalmist declared that the present creation will perish (be destroyed, vanish). It will grow old like a garment, and God will change it the way we change clothes, that is, by putting on a new, different set of clothes (Psalm 102:25, 26). God also explained the same to Isaiah. God will make a new heaven and a new earth, and it is this new heaven and earth that will remain (Isaiah 51:6; 66:22). Jesus also said the present heaven and earth will pass away (Mark 13:31). So did Peter (2 Peter 3:10-12). Some believe the word "melt" (2 Peter 3:10) means "be untied, loosed, broken up" and say this is merely a renovation of the surface of the present earth. But 2 Peter 3:12 uses a different word for "melt" which in this context must mean to be melted away. The implication is that the total matter in the universe might be transformed into heat energy—something science shows to be perfectly possible.

The new earth will be completely different. That is seen by the fact that there will be no more sea. The ancients looked on the sea as being restless, unstable, full of danger (Isaiah 57:20; James 1:6). But the Bible does not always look on the sea as bad (Isaiah 11:9; 48:18; Habakkuk 2:14). Actually, the oceans are necessary for the replacing of oxygen in the atmosphere of the present earth (through multitudes of microscopic plant forms in the seas). The lack of the seas thus suggests that the whole economy of the new earth will be different.

**2. And I John saw the holy city, new Jerusalem:** ... I also saw, *–KLST* ... the holy town, *–BB* ... the fresh new, *–ADAM*.
**coming down from God out of heaven:** ... descending out of, *–BRKL* ... coming down out of the sky, *–ADAM*.
**prepared as a bride adorned for her husband:** ... dressed in all her finery for, *–BRCL* ... made ready like, *–MNTG* ... like a bride made beautiful for her husband, *–BB* ... dressed in beauty for, *–PHLP* ... all clothed in readiness, like a bride who has adorned herself to meet, *–KNOX* ... arrayed like, *–FNTN* ... dressed like, *–NORL* ... like a bride dressed for, *–EVRD* ... a bride decorated for, *–KLGS* ... ready to meet, *–BECK*.

**21:2.** The New Jerusalem is truly holy, set apart for God in a special sense. It already exists in heaven (Galatians 4:26). It is the city that Abraham and all God's people look for, and God himself is its architect and builder (Galatians 4:26; Philippians 3:20; Hebrews 11:10, 13, 16). It is a prepared place for a prepared people.

**3. And I heard a great voice out of heaven saying:** ... there came to my ears ... out of the high seat, *–BB* ... heard a mighty voice from, *–ADAM* ... loud voice, *–EVRD, –KLST* ... issuing from the throne, *–FNTN* ... from the throne crying, *–PHLP* ... speaking ... for all to hear, *–BRCL* ... from out of the Throne, exclaiming, *–WADE* ... announce, *–NORL* ... It said, *–NLTG*.
**Behold, the tabernacle of God [is] with men:** ... See, the Tent of God, *–BB* ... How wonderful! God's dwelling place is among, *–KLST* ... Look! God's sanctuary, *–SEB* ... Listen. God's sheltering Tabernacle is with mankind, *–WADE* ... God's tent, *–MNTG* ... God's home, *–NLTG*.
**and he will dwell with them:** ... and He will encamp among them, *–FNTN* ... and He will live with them, *–WLMS* ... and he will make his living-place with them, *–BB* ... he will tent with them, *–MNTG* ... shall make his home among them, *–KLST*.
**and they shall be bis people:** ... his peoples, *–MNTG*.
**and God himself shall be with them, [and be] their God:** ... will be among them, *–TCNT* ... shall abide in their midst, *–KLST*.

**21:3.** The tabernacle, the dwelling, of God from this point forward will be with men. In a sense, heaven and earth will merge. That is, the New Jerusalem at the new earth will become God's headquarters. No longer will believers be on earth with God's throne and special manifestation of His presence in heaven. He will be with His people forever (compare Leviticus 26:11, 12; Jeremiah 31:33; Ezekiel 37:27; Zechariah 14:9; Hebrews 8:2; 9:11).

**4. And God shall wipe away all tears from their eyes:** ... And God himself, *–NORL* ... And he will put an end to all their weeping, *–BB* ... will take away all their tears, *–NLTG*.
**and there shall be no more death:** ... None of these things will exist, *–SEB* ... shall exist no more, *–FNTN*.
**neither sorrow, nor crying:** ... nor anguish, *–FNTN* ... weeping, *–NORL* ... mourning, *–MNTG* ... nor will there be grief or outcry, *–WADE* ... or cry of anguish, *–KLST*.
**neither shall there be any more pain:** ... or distress, *–NORL* ... nor grief, shall exist any longer, *–FNTN* ... or trouble any more, *–WADE*.
**for the former things are passed away:** ... The old order, *–TCNT* ... The first order, *–WLMS* ... Old things, *–SEB* ... The former conditions, *–FNTN* ... the first things departed, *–RTHM* ... have come to an end, *–BB*.

**21:4.** John heard the great voice from heaven continue with wonderful comfort and assurance. God will wipe away all tears, every single tear from the believers' eyes. These include the tears shed on earth while they were enduring suffering for the sake of Christ and the gospel. The effects of sin will be forever removed. It will be the final and ultimate consummation of all that was purchased by Christ's death on the cross and guaranteed by His resurrection.

This means there will be no more death, for death is the wages of sin (Romans 6:23). This victory is a great triumph, for the last enemy to be destroyed is death (cf. 1 Corinthians 15:54). Since death involves separation, there will be no more separation from God or from the other members of the body of Christ. There will be no more sorrow (mourning) or crying, nor any pain (distress, affliction, hardship, fruitless toil, suffering), for never again will there be anything to cause sorrow, pain, grief, or guilt. In the New Jerusalem there will be no sin, and nothing will ever again mar the joy and fellowship believers will share with the Lord, for God will not allow it. (Compare Isaiah 35:10 which seems to show a partial fulfillment of this in the Millennium where "the ransomed of the Lord shall return, and come to Zion with songs and everlasting joy upon their heads; they shall obtain joy and gladness, and sorrow and sighing shall flee away"; also 65:19.) Possibly even the memory of those things will be gone, though undoubtedly the good things God has done will be remembered (Isaiah 65:17).

The fact that the "former things are passed away" means that all the evils which have beset mankind that have caused pain, heartache, sorrow, and death will have been eliminated. No wonder heaven will be a place of supreme joy.

**5. And he that sat upon the throne said:** ... Then the One sitting on His place as King, —*NLTG* ... the Occupant, —*FNTN* ... who was seated, —*KLST* ... on the high seat, —*BB*.

**Behold, I make all things new:** . . . See, —*KLST* ... Listen, I am renovating everything, —*NOLI*.

**And he said unto me, Write: for these words are true and faithful:** . . . Then he added, —*KLST* ... commanded me, —*FNTN* ... Record it, —*NORL* ... Put it in the book; for these words are certain, —*BB* ... are trustworthy, —*BRKL* ... are dependable and true, —*SEB* ... and genuine, —*RTHM* ... and reliable, —*WADE*.

**21:5.** Some believe the One sitting on the throne is the Lamb who is said to be in the midst of the throne (5:6). Others believe it is the Father, who is described as sitting on the throne in 4:2, 5:1, and quite clearly in 5:7. Both work together in perfect

harmony, of course. The Father is the Creator, but in the former creation He made all things through Christ as the Living Word (John 1:3). Both will work together in this new creation.

The speaker emphasizes how new the new heavens and the new earth are. He makes all things new. The word "make" is a word used often of God's creative acts (cf. Matthew 19:4). It speaks here of a new, recent creation. This, of course, does not include the outer darkness of the lake of fire prepared for the devil and his angels. That will continue on forever outside the whole new creation. But within the new creation all things will undoubtedly continue to be "new," for there will be no more death or decay (compare Romans 8:21, 22; Isaiah 25:8; see also 1 Corinthians 15:54 which states that death is swallowed up in victory).

The One on the throne commanded John again to write. These things are not the product of human reason or human imagination. They are divine revelation. God himself bears witness that they are "true and faithful," and therefore all He says will be brought to pass. The promises of the new creation are not to be spiritualized away. The new heavens and the new earth as well as the New Jerusalem will be real.

**6. And he said unto me, It is done:** ... He further said to me, —*WLMS* ... It has come! —*FNTN* ... has not come to pass, —*MNTG* ... They are fulfilled, —*TCNT* ... They are as good as realized, —*WADE* ... These things have happened! —*NLTG*.

**I am Alpha and Omega, the beginning and the end:** ... It is I Who am, —*WADE* ... the First and the Last! —*NORL* ... the start and the end, —*BB*.

**I will give unto him that is athirst of the fountain of the water of life freely:** ... I will freely give to the thirsty from, —*FNTN* ... It is I, Who to the thirsty will give a draught from the fountain of Life-imparting water without payment, —*WADE* ... I will freely give of the fountain of the water of life to him who is in need, —*BB* ... without cost ... from the springs of living water, —*WLMS* ... the fountain of life, —*NORL* ... free of charge, —*KLST* ... It is a free gift, —*NLTG*.

**21:6.** Jesus said on the cross, "It is finished." Now God says, "It is done." All that was revealed to John is as good as done because God has said it. God will be present to accomplish all these things because He is eternal. He declares himself to be the Alpha and Omega, the first and last letters of the Greek alphabet. They are combined here to indicate completeness.

The phrase "Alpha and Omega" also indicates that God (the entire Trinity—Father, Son, and Holy Spirit) is without beginning and without end. Christ was before all things, and by Him all things consist or hold together (Colossians 1:17).

Yet He is the beginning and the end. He was before all things and is the One who began all things. He is the source of all that is good. He is also the end in the sense of the goal and as the One who brings about the consummation of all things prophesied.

**7. He that overcometh shall inherit all things:** . . . The victor shall inherit all this, —BRKL . . . He who is victorious shall possess these blessings, —KLST . . . will have these things as his heritage, —NORL . . . The person who is victorious, —SEB . . . The conqueror, —FNTN . . . He who has power and wins will receive these things, —NLTG . . . will inherit these possessions, —WADE . . . will enter into possession of, —TCNT.
**and I will be his God, and he shall be my son:** . . . I will be to him his God, and he shall be to me a son, —WADE.

**21:7.** Those who overcome will inherit everything. In the letters to the seven churches Jesus promised the overcomers' inheritance will include eating of the tree of life in the paradise of God; not being hurt by the second death; eating of hidden manna; a white stone with a new name written on it; power over the nations; white raiment; one's name confessed before God the Father and His angels; being made a pillar in the temple of God with the name of God and the city and Christ's new name written on him; and the privilege of sitting with Jesus on His throne.

This is assured to believers because they are children of God, heirs of God, and joint-heirs with Christ (Romans 8:16, 17). Since Christ is the heir of all things (Hebrews 1:2; Psalm 2:8), believers as joint-heirs will also inherit all things. (See also 1 Corinthians 2:9, 10.)

The promise "I will be his God, and he shall be my son" will be the final climax and fulfillment of the promise that was first given to Israel, to the line of David, and then to the Church. (See Genesis 17:7; Exodus 19:5, 6; 2 Samuel 7:14; 2 Corinthians 6:16, 18; Galatians 3:29; 1 Peter 2:9, 10.)

**8. But the fearful:** . . . As for the cowardly, —BRKL . . . the timid, —RTHM . . . those who are full of fear, —BB . . . But those who are afraid, —NLTG.
**and unbelieving:** . . . the unfaithful, —WLMS . . . the faithless, —MNTG, —NOLI . . . and the untrustworthy, —WADE . . . and without faith, —BB.
**and the abominable:** . . . the polluted, —WLMS . . . perverts, —SEB . . . and depraved, —FNTN . . . the defiled, —NOLI . . . the unclean, —BB . . . and the sinful-minded people, —NLTG.
**and murderers:** . . . and takers of life, —BB . . . those who kill other people, —NLTG.
**and whoremongers:** . . . the sexually immoral, —WLMS . . . sexual sinners, —SEB . . . fornicators,

—NORL . . . immoral persons, —KLST . . . those who do the sins of the flesh, —BB . . . sex sins, —NLTG.
**and sorcerers:** . . . those who make use of evil powers, —BB . . . practice witchcraft, —BECK . . . the practicers of magic, —WLMS . . . those who follow occult practices, —SEB . . . poisoners, —FNTN.
**and idolaters:** . . . the worshipers of idols, —WLMS . . . who give worship to images, —BB . . . false gods, —NLTG.
**and all liars, shall have their part in the lake which burneth with fire and brimstone:** . . . all those who tell lies, —NLTG . . . everyone who is false . . . burns with fiery sulphur, —NORL . . . their lot is in the lake burning with Divine fire, —FNTN . . . their portion shall be in, —KLST . . . in the sea of everburning fire, —BB . . . that blazes with, —MNTG.
**which is the second death:** . . . This is, —KLST.

**21:8.** In contrast to the overcomers who will share the blessings of life in the eternal state, a list is given of those who will have their part in the lake of fire, that is, the second death. First on the list is the "fearful," the cowardly, those who are timid because of lack of faith. This will include those who have let the disapproval or threats of any person or of society cause them to turn away from Christ and the hope of glory. They have been more concerned about personal safety than loyalty to Christ. They have been quick to compromise with the truth. They are not overcomers. They are losers, not winners. (See Mark 8:35; 1 Thessalonians 2:4; 2 Timothy 2:12, 13.)

Second are the "unbelieving" who treat the gospel and the promises as something incredible. These will include the ones who have never believed, those who have rejected the truth of the gospel, and former believers who have fallen back into the practice of the lusts of the flesh, for those who make such things part of their lifestyle cannot inherit the kingdom of God (Galatians 5:19-21).

Third are the "abominable," those who are detestable to God and arouse His wrath. Both the Old and New Testaments show that to profess a faith in God and continue to practice evil or anything idolatrous is an abomination in the sight of the Lord. (In the Old Testament this word is often used of idolatry, but here it is more general.)

Fourth are "murderers" who have deliberately, willfully taken human life. Fifth are "whoremongers," including those who practice any kind of sexual impurity or sexual immorality. Sixth are "sorcerers" who use poisons, drugs, and magic potions. Seventh are "idolaters" who put something else in the place of God. Eighth are "all liars," especially including all false persons, such as false prophets, false apostles, and false teachers (2 Peter 2:1).

All of these eight classes of people will have their part outside the eternal kingdom of God.

Some religions, cults, churches, or denominations say a person can be immoral, adulterous, homosexual, or practice any of the lusts of the flesh and still be a true child of God. They suppose a loving God would not send anyone to hell. They are going against the Scriptures (1 Corinthians 6:9, 10; Galatians 5:19-21; Ephesians 5:5-7).

**9. And there came unto me one of the seven angels:** ... one from among, —WADE.
**which had the seven vials full of the seven last plagues:** ... had the seven bowls laden with, —NORL ... jars full of the seven last troubles, —NLTG ... vessels in which were the seven last punishments, —BB ... seven final plagues, —BRKL.
**and talked with me, saying:** ... came and said to me, —BB ... and he spoke to me, —MNTG.
**Come hither, I will show thee the bride, the Lamb's wife:** ... and see the bride, —BB ... let me show you, —NORL ... the spouse of, —KLST.

**21:9.** John's first vision of the New Jerusalem was very brief. Now one of the angels who heralded God's wrath showed him a new vision where he saw God's glory in the city. "In the spirit" (21:10) indicates a new, fresh vision.

The promise to show John the Bride was followed by a vision of the holy city, the New Jerusalem. Kiddle believes this great city, the holy New Jerusalem, is symbolic of the Church, and that no literal city is intended (*Moffatt New Testament Commentary, Revelation,* pp. 411f.). But in Old Testament language a city was often identified with its inhabitants. In the New Testament Jesus did the same as He wept over Jerusalem but had the people in mind. Even so the New Jerusalem will be just as real as the present Jerusalem, but the people who dwell in it will be what makes it a city. Thus the New Jerusalem will be the home city of the Church for all eternity.

**10. And he carried me away in the spirit to a great and high mountain:** ... Then, as in a trance, —NORL ... by him I was rapt away in a spiritual trance to a ... lofty, —WADE ... took me in ecstasy up to a large, —KLST ... conveyed me, —FNTN ... huge, —MNTG.
**and showed me that great city, the holy Jerusalem:** ... and let me see the holy town, —BB.
**descending out of heaven from God:** ... coming down, —FNTN ... out of the sky, —ADAM.

**21:10.** The angel then carried John away in spirit (or in the Spirit) to a great high mountain. From this position John saw a vision of the great city, the holy Jerusalem, coming down out of heaven from God. The heavens here must be the third heaven, the heaven beyond the starry heavens, where the throne of God is. It was coming down from heaven because its builder and maker is God. This is an important event, for the descent of this city will mark the beginning of the final, eternal state, the eternal kingdom of God.

**11. Having the glory of God:** ... with all God's glory upon it, —TNT ... invested with, —WADE ... She was surrounded with a divine aura, —NOLI ... It was filled with the shining greatness of God, —NLTG ... possessing the Divine glory, —FNTN.
**and her light [was] like unto a stone most precious:** ... Her luster resembled a most precious jewel, —BRKL ... shone like a most precious stone, —KLGS ... She sparkled with the radiance of, —NOLI ... The luster of it was like, —WLMS ... a brilliance like a very precious stone, —BECK ... its light was like that of a very valuable gem, —ADAM ... Its radiance was like that of, —TNT ... It shone like a stone worth much money, —NLTG ... with radiance like a very precious stone, —NORL ... It was shining like a very valuable jewel, —SEB ... like a stone of great price, —BB.
**even like a jasper stone, clear as crystal:** ... transparent as, —TCNT ... that of a crystalline jasper, —FNTN ... clear as glass, —BB ... something like a jasper that is clear, —ADAM ... like crystal-clear jasper, —TNT.

**21:11.** What a glorious city this will be! John saw it having the brilliant glory of God. His first impression was that its radiance was like a scintillating gem. Its light could only be compared to the most precious stone John knew. He called it (as the people of that day did) a crystal-clear jasper stone. This was different from the gem called jasper today. The name for it in English today would be a giant blue-white diamond, a most beautiful gem.

"Having the glory of God" is a statement that means it will have the glory of God by its nature. There is nothing temporary about the beautiful manifestation of the glory of God that fills this city and radiates out from it. When Moses and the people of Israel finished the work of building the tabernacle, a cloud covered it and the glory of the Lord filled it so that Moses was not able to enter it (Exodus 40:34, 35). When Solomon finished his prayer at the dedication of the temple "fire came down from heaven, and consumed the burnt offering and the sacrifices, and the glory of the Lord filled the house. And the priests could not enter into the house of the Lord, because the glory of the Lord had filled the Lord's house" (2 Chronicles 7:1, 2). That glory was still in the temple's Holy of Holies when Ezekiel saw it in vision in Jerusalem's temple. But he saw it leaving, and thus the temple became like any other building, so it was easily destroyed by Nebuchadnezzar (Ezekiel 10:18; 11:22, 23).

In another vision Ezekiel was taken to the land of Israel to see the millennial restoration of the land. There, at the eastern gate of Jerusalem, he also saw the glory returning to the millennial temple (Ezekiel 43:2-5), but the glory that filled that house was still only a partial manifestation compared to the glory that will fill the New Jerusalem.

**12. And had a wall great and high:** . . . It had a massive and high wall, —*KLST* . . . a great wall was raised high all round it, —*KNOX* . . . Around her she had a vast, —*PHLP* . . . and lofty wall, —*WADE* . . . huge and high, —*CNDT.*

**[and] had twelve gates, and at the gates twelve angels:** . . . in which were, —*ADAM* . . . with twelve huge gates, —*WLMS* . . . [large] gates, and . . . {there were stationed], —*AMPB* . . . with twelve doors, —*BB* . . . portals, —*CNDT*, —*HNSN* . . . gateways, —*PHLP*, —*WADE* . . . There were 12 angels at the gates, —*EVRD* . . . stood by the gates, —*NLTG* . . . messengers, —*KLGS.*

**and names written thereon:** . . . were carved on, —*NOLI* . . . inscribed over, —*PHLP* . . . written on the gates, —*NLTG* . . . On each gate was written the name of 1 of the 12, —*EVRD* . . . on the lintels, —*KNOX.*

**which are [the names] of the twelve tribes of the children of Israel:** . . . of the sons of, —*ADAM*, —*KLST* . . . the twelve family groups of the Jewish nation, —*NLTG.*

**21:12.** The great, high wall of the city indicates the security believers will have in the New Jerusalem. It also indicates that the city is real and has limits. The 12 gates indicate there is abundant entrance, free access in and out of the city. The city will be the home and headquarters for all the redeemed, but they will be free to go out into all the new earth. They certainly also will be able to explore and enjoy all the new heavens as well.

The angel at each gate does not seem to be a gatekeeper to keep anyone out, for nothing evil or sinful will exist in the new heavens and the new earth. It is true that only those qualified can enter, but the angels seem to be welcomers and encouragers. (Compare Isaiah 62:6 for similar language concerning watchmen on the walls of Jerusalem.)

**13. On the east three gates:** . . . three gates facing, —*NAB* . . . From the east are three portals, —*CNDT* . . . gateways, —*WADE* . . . There were three gates on each side, —*NLTG.*

**on the north three gates:** . . . upon the North, —*KLGS* . . . doors, —*BB.*

**on the south three gates:** . . . three south, —*NAB* . . . on the south side, —*NLTG.*

**and on the west three gates:** . . . three on the west, —*EVRD.*

**21:13.** The 3 gates on each side of the wall are a reminder of the way the camp of the 12 tribes of Israel was arranged and organized at Sinai for their journeys through the wilderness. Three tribes were on each side, arranged around the tabernacle in the center. The worship and the presence of God were to be central in the lives of the

people. The gates of the city John saw indicate that the New Jerusalem will be central for Israel and for all the redeemed during the eternal Kingdom. Ezekiel (48:31-35) saw the gates of the millennial Jerusalem named after the 12 tribes of Israel and he specified which tribes were on each side, but the city is much smaller. The present Jerusalem will have its fulfillment during the Millennium, but the New Jerusalem will not appear until after that.

**14. And the wall of the city had twelve foundations:** . . . The walls were on twelve stones, —*NLTG* . . . the city wall has, —*ADAM* . . . were built on, —*EVRD* . . . The wall of the city had twelve courses of stones as its foundation, —*NAB* . . . foundation courses, —*FNTN* . . . foundation stones, —*KLST*, —*KNOX* . . . had twelve bases, —*BB* . . . on them, —*HNSN.*

**and in them the names of the twelve apostles of the Lamb:** . . . one for each of the twelve, —*NORL* . . . the twelve names, —*MNTG* . . . of the twelve missionaries, —*NLTG.*

**21:14.** The 12 foundations with the names of the 12 apostles inscribed in them show that the New Jerusalem will be built on the foundation of the apostles and thus the New Jerusalem will be a proper home for the Church. The names of the apostles which are listed on the foundations will include Matthias since he was accepted as God's choice to replace Judas and must still have been among the Twelve when they are mentioned in Acts 6:2. The apostles will already have been judging or ruling over the 12 tribes of Israel during the Millennium in fulfillment of Christ's promise (Matthew 19:28; Luke 22:30). In the New Jerusalem they will be recognized as foundation apostles for the building of the Church and consequently their names will be put on the foundations of the city.

The Church even now is built on the foundation of the apostles and prophets and becomes a holy temple for the indwelling of God by His Spirit (Ephesians 2:20-22).

From this it is clear that all the true people of God of all ages (from both Old Testament and New Testament times) will be united in one body of people as the ultimate fulfillment of Galatians 3:28. Clearly, there is no longer a wall between Israel and the Church. There will be one city open to all God's people (compare Ephesians 2:11-22).

**15. And he that talked with me had a golden reed to measure the city:** . . . the speaker with me had a golden measuring rod, —*FNTN* . . . had a stick in his hand . . . used to find out how big, —*NLTG* . . . as a measure, a golden wand, —WADE . . . to take the measure of the town, —BB.

**and the gates thereof, and the wall thereof:** . . . its gates and its wall, —KLST . . . and of its doors, —BB.

**21:15.** The angel who was talking with John now came with a golden reed (made of gold but thin like a reed) as a measuring rod to measure the city, its walls, and its gates, and he did so as John watched. This is a further indication that John saw a literal city and not merely a spiritual symbol of the Church.

Everything about the city is amazing, and magnificent. It would be impossible for any human architect or builder to produce such a city, but the Bible is clear that its builder (designer, architect) and maker (craftsman, creator) is God. He prepared the city and its foundations. Its symmetry, size, perfection, and beauty will reflect not only His glory, but also His wonderful love for His people.

**16. And the city lieth foursquare:** . . . the town, —BB . . . He found out that the city was as wide as it was long, —NLTG . . . the city in plan is square, —WADE . . . was designed as a, —FNTN.

**and the length is as large as the breadth:** . . . it is as wide as it is long, —BB, —BECK . . . as high as it was wide, —NLTG . . . as great as, —KLST . . . the same as, —FNTN, —NORL.

**and he measured the city with the reed, twelve thousand furlongs:** . . . its extent amounted to one thousand four hundred miles, its proportions having the perfection of a cube, —WADE . . . It was as long as a man could walk in fifty days, —NLTG . . . it is fifteen hundred miles, —BECK . . . twelve hundred miles, —TCNT . . . one thousand five hundred miles, —NORL . . . stadia, —KLST.

**The length and the breadth and the height of it are equal:** . . . it is equally long and wide and high, —BB . . . It was the same each way, —NLTG . . . exactly the same in, —NORL . . . width, —FNTN . . . and elevation, —WADE . . . are the same, —BECK.

**21:16.** The size of the city is almost beyond comprehension. It will have plenty of room for all the believers of all time. It will be 12,000 furlongs. The English furlong is 220 yards, so the total equals 2,640,000 yards or 1,500 miles, the equivalent of 2,400 kilometers. This would stretch about halfway across the American or European continent. Some have speculated this would call for the new earth to be much larger than the present one. The Greek furlong (*stadion*) measured 607 feet, making the size 1380 miles instead of 1500.

The city is foursquare (laid out as a square, literally, four-cornered or four-angled, with the angles equal), with the length, width, and height equal. The word "foursquare" is used of squared stones prepared for building and for cubical objects.

Many believe this means the city will be a perfect cube, just as the Holy of Holies where God manifested His presence in the tabernacle and later in the temple was a perfect cube (1 Kings 6:20). This could point to the fact that God will fill the city with the manifestation of His glory and holiness, making it all a Holy of Holies.

Others think the city will be in the shape of a step pyramid with each level having slightly less area than the one below. This would make it possible to picture the river flowing down through the city from one level to another. However, because the pyramid shape in the Bible and in the nations of antiquity was always connected with heathen worship, some scholars believe it is not likely that the New Jerusalem would take that form.

Still others think the city will be a cube within a crystal sphere as a sort of moon revolving around the new earth. But this is speculation that has little to uphold it. The fact that it comes down from heaven seems to imply that the New Jerusalem comes to rest on the surface of the new earth (some think it will be suspended just above it). A further indication of this is the fact that the residents of the city go in and out of the gates freely.

Some suggest that since the form of the cube is the most likely, the size of the New Jerusalem would give a cubical space one-third of a mile on each side to each of 20 billion persons. But regardless of its shape and no matter how it is arranged, it is certain there will be room for all the saved.

**17. And he measured the wall thereof:** . . . The angel found out that the walls were, —NLTG.

**an hundred [and] forty [and] four cubits:** . . . two hundred and sixteen feet, —WLMS . . . its height reaching to seventy two yards, —WADE . . . the same as a man taking seventy-two long steps, —NLTG.

**[according to] the measure of a man, that is, of the angel:** . . . The angel used the same way to find out about the city as a man would have used, —NLTG . . . by human measurement, which the angel was using, —TNT . . . the measure of a man who is an angel, —FNTN . . . by such measure as is used by a man, [in this instance, by an angel], —WADE . . . man's measure, which is an angel's, —MNTG . . . by man's standard, which the angel used, —KLST.

**21:17.** The height of the wall is given in terms of the Hebrew cubit instead of the Greek stade. The cubit was about 18 inches. Thus 144 cubits of 18 inches would be about 216 feet or 65 meters. (Some think the wall of the city would have to be as high as the city, that is, about 1500 miles, and therefore suggest the thickness of the wall is what is measured here, rather than the height.)

The measure of a man means that though the wall was measured by the angel, the angel used human measuring standards that John could understand.

**18. And the building of the wall of it was [of] jasper:** ... The material in the wall, —NORL ... the fabric of its walls, —WADE ... the buttresses of its walls, —FNTN ... was constructed of, —LAMS.

**and the city [was] pure gold, like unto clear glass:** ... This gold was, —NLTG ... resembling pure glass, —FNTN ... and the town was clear gold, —BB ... clear as glass, —NORL ... in transparency, —WADE.

**21:18.** John testified the wall was built of jasper or, as it would be called today, of blue-white diamonds. John used the beauty and brilliance of these diamonds to describe the glory of the city as a whole (21:11), but verse 18 indicates the wall will be totally built of these diamonds. How beautifully they will reflect the glory of God!

John saw that the city within the walls "was pure gold like unto clear glass" (the Greek can also mean clear crystal). This seems to be a description of something in the new heavens and earth that is better than gold. The gold known in the present earth can be beaten until it is only a few molecules thick and then be put on a window as gold leaf, and it will not be transparent like the glass. John was using human language to describe something brand-new as best as it can be described. In its clarity and transparency it will also reflect the glory of God in a marvelous way.

**19. And the foundations of the wall of the city [were] garnished with all manner of precious stones:** ... The city was built on every kind of stone that was worth much money, —NLTG ... were decorated with, —FNTN ... were adorned with, —NOLI ... were ornamented with every kind of, —TCNT ... had ornaments of all sorts of beautiful stones, —BB ... are made beautiful, —BECK ... every sort of, —NORL ... every variety of, —WADE.

**The first foundation [was] jasper:** ... The first stone, —NLTG ... first course, —FNTN ... first base, —BB ... foundation stone, —KLST.

**the second, sapphire:**
**the third, a chalcedony:** ... agate, —BECK ... white agate, —BRKL.
**the fourth, an emerald:**

**21:19.** The 12 foundations of the wall inscribed with the names of the 12 apostles are also garnished (adorned, decorated) with all kinds of precious stones. This indicates that the foundations of the city will come to rest on the surface of the ground when the New Jerusalem comes down to the earth, so the foundations are glorious and beautiful, and are visible for all to see. With their jeweled adornment they will add wonderfully to the majesty of the city.

Jasper again is probably the blue-white diamond, though some believe the opal is meant in this verse.

Sapphire is not the modern sapphire but the ancient lapis lazuli, a deep blue stone sprinkled with brilliant bits of iron pyrite (fool's gold). It was prized in ancient Assyria and Egypt.

Chalcedony was a general term for a group of precious stones including carnelian, sardius, chrysoprase, agate, and onyx. Others identify it with a green copper silicate that was found near Chalcedon on the Bosporus not far from the modern city of Istanbul.

The emerald was a bright, light-green, transparent precious stone. It was actually a variety of beryl, but colored by chromium instead of iron. It was found in Egypt, Cyprus, and Ethiopia.

**20. The fifth, sardonyx:** ... was onyx, —EVRD.
**the sixth, sardius:** ... a carnelian, —TCNT.
**the seventh, chrysolyte; the eighth, beryl:**
**the ninth, a topaz:** ... peridot, —CNDT.
**the tenth, a chrysoprasus:** ... chrysoprase, —KLST ... chryso, —KLGS.
**the eleventh, a jacinth:** ... sapphire, —HNSN.
**the twelfth, an amethyst:** ... garnet, —CNDT.

**21:20.** The decorations of the 12 foundations continue with more precious stones.

Sardonyx is a variety of agate, or it may have been a layered stone of red sard and white onyx. The ancients prized it for making cameos.

Sardius is the carnelian or sard, a reddish to blood-red precious stone. It was often used for engraving.

Chrysolyte is the yellow topaz. Others think it was a golden jasper or a yellow topaz. It may have been a magnesium-iron silicate.

Beryl is a sea-green precious stone.

Topaz here is the golden topaz, sometimes greenish gold.

Chrysoprasus is a translucent, apple-green, fine-grained horn-stone (a variety of quartz). Others identify it as an apple-green, chromium colored variety of chalcedony.

Jacinth, also called hyacinth, was possibly a variety of zircon. Some were bluish, some bluish-purple like the modern sapphire, others orangish in color.

Amethyst was a clear purple or blue-violet, glassy quartz.

**21. And the twelve gates [were] twelve pearls:** ... twelve doors, —BB ... portals, —CNDT.
**every several gate was of one pearl:** ... Each one of the gates consisted of, —NOLI ... each one of the gate towers, —RTHM ... each separate gate, —FNTN ... each gate built of a single pearl, —WLMS ... Each one of the portals was respectively of one pearl,

−*CNDT*... was made out of, −*TNT*... made from one pearl, −*NLTG*... every door, −*BB*... each several gateway consisted of a single pearl, −*WADE*... made of, −*LAMS*.

**and the street of the city [was] pure gold:** ... the broad street of the city, −*MNTG*... The Broadway of the city, −*WLMS*... The avenues, −*KLST*... the square of the city is gold, −*CNDT*... was made of, −*EVRD*... the city street was pure gold, −*ADAM*... of the town was clear gold, −*BB*.

**as it were transparent glass:** ... but you could see through it like pure glass! −*SEB*... like translucent glass, −*WADE*... The gold was clear, −*EVRD*... as clear as, −*BB*, −*NLTG*... like shining glass, −*KLGS*.

**21:21.** The 12 gates with the names of the 12 tribes of Israel inscribed on them are each one a giant pearl. The pearl in ancient times was something owned only by the very wealthy. Jesus in a parable spoke of a pearl of great price, worth everything a person possessed (Matthew 13:45, 46). Such giant pearls will surely be a special creation, created by God himself.

The street John saw was wide and made of pure gold like transparent glass. The singular here may be used collectively for all the streets in the city.

**22. And I saw no temple therein:** ... I did not see a house of God, −*NLTG*... a temple I did not perceive in it, −*CNDT*... no Sanctuary in it, −*FNTN*... in the city, −*NORL*, −*TNT*.

**for the Lord God Almighty and the Lamb are the temple of it:** ... the Sovereign Supreme, −*WADE*... the Ruler of all, −*BB*... The All-powerful Lord... are the house of God in this city, −*NLTG*... and the Lambkin, −*CNDT*... are its Sanctuary, −*FNTN*... are the city's temple, −*EVRD*.

**21:22.** John saw no temple in the New Jerusalem. God, in Old Testament times, manifested His presence and glory in the Holy of Holies, the inner sanctuary of the tabernacle, then in the temple of Solomon. During the Church Age, the bodies of believers are temples (sanctuaries) of the Holy Spirit and whenever they come together in Christ's name they are the body of Christ. Together believers become the temple (sanctuary) where God manifests His presence through the Holy Spirit. But in the New Jerusalem, the whole city will become the temple, the sanctuary, the habitation of God and Christ. God's glory will be everywhere present in it. Those who dwell in it will be in constant direct contact with the Lord God Almighty and His Son, His Lamb, the Redeemer. Believers shall dwell in the temple, that is, in the midst of the manifestation of God's presence. This will also mean that all believers of all the ages shall continue to be a holy temple in the Lord, "builded together for a habitation of God through the Spirit" (Ephesians 2:20-22).

This fellowship in the immediate presence of God and Christ will surely be the greatest blessing and joy in the Holy City. The psalmist David recognized that in God's presence there is fullness of joy (Psalm 16:11). How much greater will be that fullness in the New Jerusalem!

**23. And the city had no need of the sun, neither of the moon, to shine in it:** ... does not need, −*TNT*... shine on her, −*NORL*... to give light to it, −*WADE*... to shine in the city, −*NLTG*... that they should be appearing in it, −*CNDT*.

**for the glory of God did lighten it:** ... The shining greatness of God makes it full of light, −*NLTG*... had illuminated it, −*TCNT*... illumined, −*WADE*... gives her light, −*NORL*... shines upon it, −*KLGS*... since God's glory enlightened it, −*ADAM*... has given it light, −*TNT*... lights it up, −*KLST*... did make it light, −*BB*... is its light, −*EVRD*.

**and the Lamb [is] the light thereof:** ... is its lamp, −*FNTN*... and the light of it is the Lamb, −*BB*... is the city's lamp, −*EVRD*... is the Lambkin, −*CNDT*.

**21:23.** The full revelation of God's glory will also mean the city will have no need of the sun or moon. In this present earth most of the energy needed for light and for all the life processes comes from the sun either directly or through the photosynthesis of plants. In the New Jerusalem, Christ will be the light (literally, the lamp). He will be the immediate source of all the power, energy, and light needed for the believers' lives and activities throughout eternity. The glorified bodies of believers will be like Christ's and will be able to stand the full impact of God's glory. (See Exodus 33:20-23; 1 John 3:2.) No intermediate source, such as the sun will be needed. So energized, there will be no longer a need for sleep or the succession of day and night. Jesus Christ who is the Light of the World spiritually now will be the light of the New Jerusalem and the new heaven and earth in a full and complete fulfillment. (Compare John 1:7-9; 3:19; 8:12; 12:35; 1 John 1:5-7.)

Isaiah saw a glimpse of this when he looked beyond even the millennial restoration of Zion to a time when "the sun shall be no more thy light by day; neither for brightness shall the moon give light unto thee: but the Lord shall be unto thee an everlasting light, and thy God thy glory.... Thy people also shall be all righteous: ... I the Lord will hasten it in his time" (Isaiah 60:19-22). "Thy God thy glory" is the central truth in this passage.

**24. And the nations of them which are saved shall walk in the light of it:** ... By its light the people of the world will walk, −*EVRD*... will go in its light, −*BB*... use its light to guide them, −*SEB*... will pursue their course of life by its light, —*WADE* . . . by means of its light, —*CNDT.*

**and the kings of the earth do bring their glory and honour into it:** . . . add, —*SEB* . . . will convey their splendor, —*BRKL* . . . will shine in her splendor, —*NOLI* . . . will offer their tribute of recognition to it, —*KLST* . . . are to bring their grandeur into the city, —*WADE* . . . are carrying their glory, —*CNDT* . . . will bring their greatness into it, —*NLTG.*

**21:24.** From this verse it is clear that the New Jerusalem will be the capital city, the headquarters of the believers. The glory of God that lights the city will be continuous and inexhaustible. Thus the nations (people) who are saved will continue to walk (and live) by means of this light forever. No longer will kings or people exalt themselves, but all their glory will be brought into the city that God's glory might be all in all.

"Nations" is a word often translated "Gentiles," but it is often used in a general sense (see Acts 17:26; Matthew 28:19; compare Acts 1:8) and would not exclude Israel. (Even the Old Testament word *gôyim,* "nations, Gentiles," sometimes includes the Jews.) It does not necessarily refer to nations in the sense of nationalistic states or to peoples with specific national identities. Thus, it is better to look at these "nations" as people with various backgrounds and from various parts of the present earth. The important thing here is that they are all saved and they all walk in the light of the glory of God.

Some writers think this verse means that only certain ones among the believers live in the city and that there are other nations and kings outside the city who walk in the light of it. That might be true of the present Jerusalem when it receives its fulfillment in the Millennium. However, the New Jerusalem is an entirely different city. The meaning here is rather that the nations or peoples who are saved are the same ones who are the redeemed residents in the city. This verse is simply saying all believers will be brought together in one, and whether they were ordinary people or kings in this life, whatever glory or honor they had, they will bring into the city and present it all to God, to whom it is due.

**25. And the gates of it shall not be shut at all by day:** . . . Her gates will never be shut by day, —*NOLI* . . . the doors of it, —*BB* . . . shall not be closed daily, —*FNTN* . . . will be wide open all the day long, —*KLST* . . . in the day time, —*WADE.*

**for there shall be no night there:** . . . for night is not there, —*FNTN* . . . which will never be brought to an end by night, —*KLST.*

**21:25.** Unlike the ancient cities of John's day whose gates were always shut at night, the gates

of the New Jerusalem will not be shut by day, and there will be no night. The gates will always be open, and the inhabitants of the city will be free to go in and out.

Notice that it is the city which does not need the light of the sun or moon, not necessarily the new earth. The city is independent of the earth and its sun. This city, which seems to be above the earth and casts its light upon it, is light itself because the glory of God provides its light.

Seiss says: "The glory of God's brightness envelops it like an unclouded halo, permeates it, and radiates through it and from it so that there is not a dark or obscure place about it. It shines like a new sun, inside and out, sending abroad its rays over all the earth, and into the depths of space, making our planet seem to distant worlds as if suddenly transformed into a brilliant luminary, whose brightness never wanes. But that shining is not from any material combustion, not from any consumption of fuel that needs to be replaced as one supply burns out, for it is the uncreated light of Him who is light, dispensed by and through the Lamb as the everlasting lamp."

**26. And they shall bring the glory and honour of the nations into it:** . . . present, —*FNTN* . . . The nations will lay at its feet all that is estimable and precious, —*KLST* . . . the greatness and honor of all the nations will be brought into it, —*NLTG* . . . the grandeur and costly possessions of the nations, —*WADE* . . . will come into it, —*BB.*

**21:26.** Again it is emphasized that the glory and honor of the nations, that is, of all who are saved, will be brought into the city.

**27. And there shall in no wise enter into it any thing that defileth:** . . . Never shall any unhallowed thing enter it, —*TCNT* . . . nothing unclean may come into it, —*BB* . . . into her anything profane, —*RTHM* . . . will be tolerated within her gates, —*NOLI* . . . will ever come into the city, —*NORL.*

**neither [whatsoever] worketh abomination, or [maketh] a lie:** . . . No person who is perverted will go in, —*SEB* . . . anyone whose works are cursed or false, —*BB* . . . or who practises depravity and falsehood, —*FNTN* . . . anyone who practices wicked and false living, —*NORL* . . . will ever gain entrance, —*KLST.*

**but they which are written in the Lamb's book of life:** . . . But only those, —*MNTG* . . . who are recorded, —*FNTN* . . . whose names are in, —*BB.*

**21:27.** Finally, the readers of the Book of Revelation are warned that when the New Jerusalem comes down from heaven, only those whose names are written in the Book of Life will share its glory. These are the redeemed of all ages. All others will be in outer darkness, completely outside the entire new heavens and new earth.

These who will never enter the city are specified here first as anything that defiles. This will include anything unclean, impure, or common (in the sense of being touched by any kind of impurity), that is, not cleansed by God (Acts 10:15, 28; 11:9, 18). Second, they will include whatever works abomination, whatever practices abomination, or whatever is detestable in God's sight. Third, they will include whatever or whoever makes a lie or practices falsehood or false religion or makes a false profession of loyalty to Christ.

God keeps records, and the names of all those who can enter the New Jerusalem will be in the Lamb's Book of Life.

## Chapter 22

1. **And he showed me a pure river of water of life:** ...And I saw a river of water of life, −BB...pointed out to me, −FNTN...of living water, −NORL...of Life-giving Water, −WADE.

**clear as crystal:** ...bright as, −BECK, −NORL...sparkling like, −FNTN...clear as glass, −BB, −NLTG.

**proceeding out of the throne of God and of the Lamb:** ...which continued to flow from, −WLMS ...coming from, −KLST ...issuing from, −TCNT...out of the high seat, −BB.

**22:1.** Inside the New Jerusalem the angel showed John a clear, beautiful, flowing river of the water of life coming from the throne of God and the Lamb. The throne seems to be in the midst of the city and the river flows out from it. The pure river of water of life is a literal river, but it also draws attention to the flow of the Holy Spirit and the life, blessing, and spiritual power He gives (compare Isaiah 44:3; Ezekiel 47:1-12; John 7:37-39; Revelation 7:17; 21:6; 22:17).

2. **In the midst of the street of it:** ...down the middle, −BECK...flowing in the centre of, −FNTN...of the Square within the city, −WADE ...of the city's Broadway, −WLMS...of the broad street, −MNTG.

**and on either side of the river, [was there] the tree of life:** ...on both sides, −FNTN...between the avenues and the river, −KLST ...is a grove of Life-sustaining Trees, −WADE.

**which bare twelve [manner of] fruits:** ...producing, −WADE...twelve kinds, −NORL...having twelve sorts of fruits, −BB.

**[and] yielded her fruit every month:** ...giving its fruit, −BB ...a different kind each month, −WLMS ...its own crop, −FNTN ...each yielding its special fruit every several month, −WADE...one crop each month, −KLST.

**and the leaves of the tree [were] for the healing of the nations:** ...serve for the cure of the ills of the nations, −WADE ...had a healing power for, −KLST...give life to, −BB.

**22:2.** The river of the water of life flows down through the middle of the great wide street of gold (which apparently winds down through the various levels of the city).

This river is a reminder that the inhabitants of the city are still as dependent on God and the Lamb for life as they ever were. The river John saw also gives the assurance that in the New Jerusalem the flow of the water of life will be always sufficient.

The tree of life has a similar meaning. Even though the believers' new bodies will be immortal and incorruptible, not capable of deterioration, they will never have life in themselves. "Tree" is probably collective, so that each side of the river will be lined with trees.

The leaves of the tree will be for the healing of the nations (people). Because 21:4 excludes the idea of sickness, pain, and death, there does not seem to be a healing process here. So some take the word to mean *health*. The leaves of the tree indicate that there will be nothing in the new creation to bring any physical or spiritual sickness, weakness, or harm.

3. **And there shall be no more curse:** ...Nothing that God has condemned will be found there, −SEB...No longer will any person or thing deserving of excration be found there, −KLST...nothing there with a curse on it, −NORL...Idolatry was abolished, −NOLI...And that which withers shall be no more, −LAMS...And no accursed thing shall any longer exist, −FNTN.

**but the throne of God and of the Lamb shall be in it:** ...and the high seat of God, −BB ...will be there, −NORL...shall be established in that city, −KLST.

**and his servants shall serve him:** ...His servants worshiped him, −NOLI...and His slaves will worship Him, −WLMS...will minister to him, −KLST...will render to Him worship, −WADE ...will be worshipping him, −BB.

**22:3.** Again it is clear that in the New Jerusalem there will be no more curse nor any of the effects of the curse, such as sickness and disease. This means the judgment on Adam and Eve will be completely removed. Work in the Garden of Eden was initially a joy. Adam was cursed to a life of toil that was often fruitless. Even today much work is disappointing, frustrating, and unrewarding. But in the New Jerusalem there will be joy not only in the presence of the throne of God and the Lamb, but joy in serving Him without hindrance or encumbrance.

Some have imagined the main occupation in eternity will be the playing of harps. But God will have far more for believers. God is infinite, and there will always be something new, fresh, and wonderful to do and enjoy in service for Him.

Serving the Lord does have a primary meaning of worshiping Him. Believers will be king-priests and ministers before Him, doing everything in a spirit of devotion to Him. Solomon caught a glimpse of what this will mean when he recognized that no earthly temple is sufficient for the full manifestation of God's glory, "seeing the heaven and heaven of heavens cannot contain him" (2 Chronicles 2:6). Isaiah saw the same thing, as did Stephen and Paul (Isaiah 6:1; 57:15; Acts 7:48-50; 17:24, 25). Believers too can have a foretaste through the Holy Spirit.

**4. And they shall see his face:** . . . look upon, —FNTN.

**and his name [shall be] in their foreheads:** . . . will be written, —NLTG . . . on their brows, —NORL.

**22:4.** "They shall see his face" refers first of all to Jesus, the Lamb in the midst of the throne, for God is Spirit (John 4:24). Moses was told that no one can see God and live (Exodus 33:20). In the present age worship is limited to what can be experienced and endured in these mortal bodies. But it must be remembered that in eternity believers will have spiritual bodies with capabilities beyond what we now have. We shall see both the Father and the Son. Worship there will be unlimited, unfettered, and full of the joy of seeing His face and experiencing the full impact of His glory. No darkness will ever hide His face, no cloud will ever obscure His glory, and believers shall be His forever.

There is no greater happiness or blessing than to be among the pure in heart who shall see God (Exodus 33:20, 23; Isaiah 33:17; Matthew 5:8; John 14:9; 1 John 3:2).

"His name shall be in their foreheads," identifying believers as belonging to Him forever. It also indicates that believers shall be like Him, with the fullness of the image of God restored in them, the image expressed in righteousness and true holiness as they see it expressed in Jesus (Ephesians 4:24; Hebrews 1:3). On the bases of 1 Corinthians 11:7 and Ezekiel 1:26-28 some interpret the image of God in mankind to be physical as well as spiritual. The Bible implies that human beings need a body for the full expression of their nature. Christ is God, but since His incarnation He has a body and will be the God-man for eternity (1 Corinthians 15:40-49). The full answer will have to wait until we are in the other world and know as we are known.

**5. And there shall be no night there:** . . . Night will cease to be, —TCNT . . . no night anymore,

—SEB . . . There will never be night again, —EVRD . . . shall exist no longer, —FNTN . . . will be no more, —MNTG.

**and they need no candle:** . . . and so they will have no need of the light of, —KLST . . . they will need no lamplight, —WLMS.

**neither light of the sun:** . . . or of the shining of the sun, —BB . . . nor sunlight, —WLMS . . . or sunshine, —HNSN.

**for the Lord God giveth them light:** . . . our God illuminated them, —NOLI . . . since the Lord will lighten them, —ADAM . . . will shine on them, —KLST, —SEB . . . will illumine, —WADE . . . shall lighten it, —KLGS . . . will be their light, —NLTG.

**and they shall reign for ever and ever:** . . . They will be leaders forever, —NLTG . . . they will rule like kings, —EVRD . . . will be ruling, —BB . . . through the eternities of the eternities, —FNTN . . . for the eons of the eons, —CNDT . . . they shall reign to the aeons, —HNSN.

**22:5.** Again the Bible emphasizes that there will be "no night there." There will be no need of a candle (literally, a lamp; tallow and wax candles were not invented until long after John wrote). There will be no need of artificial light just as there will be no need for the light of the sun. God will be the source of all light.

Not only will it be a delight to worship and serve God, He will not treat believers as servants. Instead, He will give them all the joys, benefits, and privileges of kings. Only the saints will be present, but they shall all reign as kings, for all shall share Christ's royal throne.

**6. And he said unto me, These sayings [are] faithful and true:** . . . Then the angel said, —TNT . . . You can trust these words, —BECK . . . These declarations are . . . reliable, —WADE . . . These words are dependable, —SEB . . . these statements, —FNTN . . . are certain, —BB . . . may be trusted, —MNTG . . . may be relied upon, —TCNT . . . are trustworthy, —NORL . . . worthy of confidence, —AMPB . . . and genuine, —ADAM.

**and the Lord God of the holy prophets sent his angel:** . . . The Lord is the God of, —EVRD . . . of the spirits of the prophets, —ADAM, —HNSN . . . from whom prophetic gifts come, —KLST . . . of the early preachers, —NLTG . . . Who inspires the Prophets, —WADE . . . of the spirits of the prophets, —BB . . . commissions His messenger, —CNDT . . . sent His messenger, —FNTN.

**to show unto his servants the things which must shortly be done:** . . . his slaves, —MNTG . . . to make clear . . . the things which are now to come about, —BB . . . to make known to His servants what must come quickly, —FNTN . . . to show the workmen He owns what must happen soon, —NLTG . . . which must happen in the near future, —NOLI . . . that which has to come about with speed, —KLGS . . . the things that must soon take place, —NORL . . . that must speedily come to pass, —WADE.

**22:6.** This verse begins the concluding segment of the Book of Revelation. The wonderful hope given to the saints, the believers, all true followers of Christ, is absolutely certain. The promises of joy and fellowship in the New Jerusalem were confirmed to John by an angelic messenger from the same God who sent the holy prophets of the Old Testament. They gave prophecies of their own day and of the first coming of Christ which were fulfilled literally and completely. They also gave prophecies of the Second Coming, the millennial Kingdom, and the new heavens and the new earth. The fact that the prophecies given for their own day and for Christ's first coming were fulfilled is a further guarantee that the prophecies yet to be fulfilled will come to pass just as literally and completely. Once God's time comes they will be fulfilled shortly, quickly, without further delay.

7. **Behold, I come quickly:** . . . And, see, —*ADAM* . . . Listen, —*TNT* . . . I come speedily, —*RTHM* . . . Mark well, I am coming, —*KLST* . . . look, I come with speed, —*KLGS* . . . soon, —*FNTN.*

**blessed [is] he that keepeth the sayings of the prophecy of this book:** . . . Happy, —*FNTN* . . . A blessing on him who keeps the words of this book of the prophet, —*BB* . . . who heeds, —*NOLI* . . . The one who obeys what is written, —*NLTG* . . . who observes the words of, —*BRKL* . . . who practices the truths of, —*WLMS* . . . who keeps in mind the prophetic declarations, —*WADE.*

**22:7.** Now comes a special announcement from Jesus himself. He says, "Behold, I come quickly." What does this mean? Some believe it means that when He comes, it will be very suddenly. However, whenever the Greek word translated "quickly" occurs elsewhere it means "soon" or "in a short time." It is necessary to remember that God does not look at time the way mankind does. To Him a thousand years is only like a day (2 Peter 3:8). Figuring time that way means that in a sense it has been less than 2 days since Jesus gave the Great Commission to His followers and returned to heaven. He is counting on us to take the gospel to the world. He has no other plan.

However, the call is for believers to live in readiness, always realizing that "now is our salvation nearer than when we believed" (Romans 13:11). The times and seasons are under the Father's authority and therefore are His alone to bring to pass (Acts 1:7).

The believers' responsibility is given in Acts 1:8 and Matthew 28:18-20, and the Holy Spirit gives the enabling. The Holy Spirit also is always ready to give believers gifts that will build up the Church both spiritually and in numbers. They must occupy (do the Lord's business) until He comes (Luke 19:13). Nevertheless, once the final events begin they will be fulfilled at a rapid rate. When He does

come believers will be changed, "in a moment, in the twinkling of an eye" (1 Corinthians 15:51, 52).

The Book of Revelation began with a blessing on those who read the book aloud and on those who hear. Now the blessing is on those who not only hear but keep on keeping, observing, and obeying the words, the teachings, of the prophecies in this book.

8. **And I John saw these things, and heard [them]:** . . . It was I, —*NORL* . . . am he who heard and saw these sound and sights, —*WADE* . . . and to whose ears they came, —*BB.*

**And when I had heard and seen:** . . . given ear, —*BB* . . . and saw them, —*WADE.*

**I fell down to worship before the feet of the angel:** . . . went down on my face to give worship, —*BB* . . . I got down at the feet of . . . I was going to worship him, —*NLTG* . . . bowed down to pay homage at the feet of the messenger, —*FNTN* . . . threw myself down to render worship, —*WADE.*

**which showed me these things:** . . . who made them known to me, —*FNTN* . . . who revealed them to me, —*NOLI* . . . made these things clear to me, —*BB.*

**22:8.** John did not need convincing. In fact, the angel who brought this revelation was so full of the glory and power of God that John fell down before him to worship.

9. **Then saith he unto me, See [thou do it] not:** . . . he exclaimed to me, Refrain from it, —*FNTN* . . . But he told me, Don't do it! —*ADAM* . . . No, he said to me, you must not do that, —*NORL.*

**for I am thy fellowservant, and of thy brethren the prophets:** . . . am a brother-servant with you, —*BB* . . . as I am also of your brethren the prophets, —*NORL* . . . I am only a fellow slave with you and your brothers, —*MNTG.*

**and of them which keep the sayings of this book: worship God:** . . . who observe the messages, —*BRKL* . . . keep the words, —*KLST* . . . who obey the words, —*SEB* . . . preserve the statements of, —*FNTN* . . . It is God whom you must worship! —*NORL.*

**22:9.** The angel immediately stopped John from worshiping him. As an angel, a messenger of God, he was but a fellow servant of the Lord's as well as a servant sent to serve John and to serve John's brothers, the prophets (probably New Testament prophets) in the churches (Hebrews 1:13, 14). He was also sent to serve all who keep the sayings in the Book of Revelation.

The angel further commanded John to worship God. God alone deserves worship. Jesus responded to Satan's temptation to worship him by reminding Satan that it is written, "Thou shalt worship the Lord thy God, and him only shalt thou serve" (Matthew 4:10; Luke 4:8; Deuteronomy 6:13).

**10. And he saith unto me, Seal not the sayings of the prophecy of this book:**... He further said, —FNTN...Do not seal up as secrets, —WADE...Let not the words of this prophet's book be kept secret, —BB.

**for the time is at hand:**...The right time is near, —SEB...the period, —FNTN...the time of their fulfillment is drawing near, —NOLI...for the crisis is near, —MNTG.

**22:10.** The message of the Book of Revelation is not to be sealed. Its prophecies are to be proclaimed. Compare Daniel 12:4. Why was it so important that John not fail to reveal the contents of this prophecy? Because the Lord's return is imminent. The angel repeated the warning of Christ in 22:7 that He was coming quickly but sharpened it somewhat by saying, "The time is at hand." It almost seems he was saying, "It could happen any moment."

**11. He that is unjust, let him be unjust still:**...Until then let the unrighteous keep on being, —NORL...He who is wicked, —MNTG...Let him who does harm, continue to do so, —KLST...Let the wrongdoer still do wrong, —BECK...the person who is doing evil do evil still, —WLMS...Let the evil man go on in his evil, —BB...continue to do wrong, —TCNT...deal unjustly still, —WADE.

**and he which is filthy, let him be filthy still:**...the filthy-minded man, —TCNT...who is vile, —FNTN.

**and he that is righteous, let him be righteous still:**...who is just, —KLST...keep practicing righteousness, —BRKL...practise justice still, —WADE.

**and he that is holy, let him be holy still:**...and let the saint grow ever more holy, —BRKL...let the consecrated person still be consecrated, —WLMS...let him practise righteousness still, —FNTN...continue to do so, —KLST...keep himself holy still, —WADE.

**22:11.** In view of the Lord's soon coming the angel gave a warning which indicates that the time will come when it will be too late to be saved. The call to repentance, faith, and obedience is still going out today. This is still the day of salvation. There is still opportunity for a person to accept Christ as Saviour and Lord and be changed. But the day will come when the line will be drawn and destinies determined.

In a sense, however, people determine their destinies now by their own choices. "He that is unjust" is literally "the wrongdoer," and includes all who do what is contrary to what is right in God's eyes. By disregarding the teachings and warnings of God's Word and by repeated wrong choices the sinner becomes hardened in a pattern of doing what God says is wrong. This even includes the moral person who persecutes, despises, or just ignores the believers in Christ.

The filthy person is one whose habits and speech patterns are foul and unclean. It also includes the

avaricious. Such a person has no concern over purity and decency and becomes hardened in rejection of the Bible's exhortation to holiness and righteousness. Those who reject the message of the Book of Revelation will continue in their sins. When Jesus comes it will be too late.

On the other hand, the book is a great incentive for believers to continue in righteousness and holiness, looking for Christ to return. The person who is holy in dedicated worship and service to God develops habits that are pleasing to God. The righteous person is just, honest, and good because he is cleansed by the blood of Jesus and because of his cooperation with the Spirit in obedience and faith. The person who is holy, living a life dedicated to God, seeking to be like Jesus, seeking to do what is right in God's eyes, will go right on in the same kind of life when Jesus comes.

Verse 11 must also be understood in terms of verse 12. When Jesus comes His reward will be with Him. It will be too late then for anyone to change. Jesus brought out the same truth in the Parable of the Ten Virgins where the five who were not ready found the door shut against them forever (Matthew 25:11, 12). There will be no second chance if this life is spent making choices contrary to God's Word and will.

**12. And, behold, I come quickly:**...Mark my word, —KLST...I am coming soon, —LAMS...Listen! —WADE.

**and my reward [is] with me:**...I will bring, —NORL...bring rewards with me, —EVRD...the recompense which I award, —WADE...and My wages are with me, —FNTN...my payment is, —KLGS...I am bringing the pay, —NLTG.

**to give every man according as his work shall be:**...I will give to everyone for what he has done, —NLTG...I will recompense, —CMPB...I will repay each one, —EVRD...to render to each one, —CNFT...to requite each one, —KLST...to repay each one for whatever his work is, —KLGS...according to what his work is found to be, —WADE...to pay to each as his own work is, —FNTN...give to each man what his actions merit, —MNTG...just what their actions deserve, —TCNT...the outcome of his works, —BB...according to his deeds, —NORL.

**22:12.** This is the fifth time in the Book of Revelation that Jesus indicates His coming will be soon. (See 2:5, 16; 3:11; 22:7.) As before, "I come quickly" may refer to the sense of imminence that God wants believers to have throughout the Church Age. It may refer also to the suddenness and rapidity of the events that will take place at the time of His coming. Again, it must be remembered that God does not look at time the way we do. He can do in a day what men might expect Him to take a thousand years to do. He can stretch out to a thousand years what men might expect Him to do in a day. He is not limited by time (2 Peter 3:8). This is "the last time" dispensation (1 John 2:18). It has been the "last days" ever since the inauguration of the age of the Holy Spirit (Acts 2:17). In other words, this is the last age, the last dispensation, before Christ returns to establish His kingdom. The next great event on God's prophetic program is Christ's return to catch away His bride (1 Thessalonians 4:16, 17).

When He comes His reward will be with Him. In both the judgment seat of Christ (often called the Bema judgment from the Greek word for a judicial bench found in Romans 14:10 and 2 Corinthians 5:10) and the Great White Throne Judgment, the judgment will be according to a person's work. (See 1 Corinthians 3:15; 2 Corinthians 5:10; Revelation 20:12.) The judgment will be based, not on the amount of the works, but on the spirit, motivation, and love people show (Matthew 18:23-35; 25:14-30; 1 Corinthians 3:13-15; 13:3).

**13. I am Alpha and Omega, the beginning and the end:** ... Aleph and Tau, *—LAMS* ... the A and the Z, *—KLGS* ... the Origin and the Consummation, *—CNDT.* **the first and the last:** ... the start, *—BB.*

**22:13.** What Jesus said is confirmed further by His declaration of the fact that He is the Alpha and the Omega (the first and last letters of the Greek alphabet). He is the eternal One, set apart from all God's creation, like the Father always existent. He is the beginning and the end, the first and the last. The beginning, for God created all things through Him and apart from Him nothing was made that was made (John 1:3). Thus, He was before all things (Colossians 1:17). He is the ending, for He will bring all things to their God-appointed consummation or end. Looking at this from the standpoint of eternity, that end is at hand, and was so even in John's day.

**14. Blessed [are] they that do his commandments:** ... A blessing on those whose robes are washed, *—BB* ... those who wash their robes, *—ADAM, —WLMS* ... who obey, *—NOLI* ... Those who wash their clothes clean are happy (who are washed by the blood of the Lamb), *—NLTG* ... who are rinsing their robes, *—CNDT.* **that they may have right to the tree of life:** ... for theirs will be authority over, *—KLGS* ... it will be their license to the log of life, *—CNDT* ... so as to have the right to, *—NORL* ... to eat of the fruit of, *—EVRD, —NLTG* ... that they may be allowed to approach, *—FNTN* ... to go to the grove of Life-sustaining Trees, *—WADE.* **and may enter in through the gates into the city:** ... They will have the right, *—NLTG* ... and may go in by the doors into the town, *—BB* ... and that they may enter the city by the gates, *—ADAM* ... and they

may be entering the portals into the city, *—CNDT* ... by the gateways, *—WADE.*

**22:14.** Once again in verses 14 and 15 Jesus sets the two destinies before us. As a background for the final invitation, Jesus turns believers' attention to the New Jerusalem. Those who do (obey) His commandments out of a love for God, for their neighbors (including the foreigners), and especially for Jesus who has saved them (John 14:15, 21; 15:9-14; 1 John 2:3, 4; 3:22, 24; 5:2, 3), have the right to enter the city. In the city there is a fullness of blessing awaiting them. They shall have a right to the tree of life. Again it is emphasized that they will freely enter through the gates into the New Jerusalem.

Some ancient Greek manuscripts have "they who have washed their robes" instead of "they that do his commandments." The meaning and the results are really the same. (See 7:14-17.)

**15. For without [are] dogs, and sorcerers, and whoremongers, and murderers, and idolaters:** ... There will be no room for, *—NOLI* ... Outside the city are ... people who follow witchcraft and those who do sex sins and those who kill other people and those who worship false gods, *—NLTG* ... Excluded from it are the foul, *—WADE* ... Outside will be male prostitutes and those involved in magic and the sexually immoral, *—ADAM* ... dope peddlers and pimps ... and idol servers, *—KLGS* ... Outside will be the filthy, *—TCNT* ... the dogs, and the magicians, *—FNTN* ... occult people, sexual sinners, *—SEB* ... those who make use of evil powers ... make themselves unclean ... takers of life ... give worship to images, *—BB.*

**and whosoever loveth and maketh a lie:** ... all who love and practice lying, *—WLMS* ... and everyone whose delight is in what is false, *—BB* ... all who love to tell lies, *—ADAM* ... those who like lies and tell them, *—NLTG* ... loves and practices falsehood, *—KLST* ... and lives a lie, *—NORL.*

**22:15.** "Without" means outside the whole new heavens and new earth, in outer darkness. Separated forever from all the blessing of God will be unclean people referred to as dogs. Dogs were considered unclean animals under the law of Moses, and the term was applied to unclean persons. These include sodomites (Deuteronomy 23:17, 18; 1 Timothy 1:10) and false teachers holding low moral standards (Philippians 3:2). Outside also will be sorcerers, including those who use poisons or drugs to get what they want; whoremongers, including sexually immoral persons of various kinds; murderers; idolaters; and those who love and make a lie, including all who promote and practice falsehood and false religions.

The warning to those who love and make a lie is the climax of a series of warnings in chapters

21 and 22. Those who practice lying are only deceiving themselves. It is clear from these passages that all liars will have their part in the lake of fire (21:8). No one who makes a lie can ever enter the New Jerusalem (21:27). Those who love and practice lying will be forever outside, not only outside the city, but outside the entire new heavens and new earth.

Lying is the last sin condemned in the Bible. It was a lie of Satan that brought the fall of the human race (Genesis 3:1-5; John 8:44). Then when people turned away from the truth of God, took God off the throne of their lives and put self on the throne, they soon turned to idolatry. All idolatry is a lie and a denial of the true God.

16. **I Jesus have sent mine angel to testify unto you these things in the churches:** . . . have sent my messenger for you to witness these things in, —KLGS . . . to you with these words, —NLTG . . . to declare these events in, —FNTN . . . to you with this message to the churches, —NORL . . . to convey this, —WADE . . . to give you this testimony for, —MNTG . . . to give witness to you, —BB . . . declare these things to you for the benefit of, —TNT . . . concerning the congregations, —KLST . . . because of the assemblies, Rother-ham.

**I am the root and the offspring of David, [and] the bright and morning star:** . . . I belong to the line and family of David, —WLMS . . . I am the beginning of David, —NLTG . . . the Scion, —WADE . . . AND BRANCH . . . THE FIRST SHINING STAR, —KLGS . . . I am the descendant from the family, —SEB . . . I am the radiant morning star, —NOLI.

**22:16.** Jesus confirms that He has sent His angel to testify (bear witness concerning) these things to the churches; that is through what John writes here in the Book of Revelation. Jesus wants the invitation to go forth until He comes. It is the same invitation He gave while on earth. (See Matthew 11:28.)

Jesus further identifies himself as the root and offspring of David, the fulfillment of God's promises of One who would make David's throne eternal. He is also the bright and morning star and the promised "Sun of righteousness" (Malachi 4:2; see Psalm 84:11; Matthew 17:2; Revelation 1:16; 2 Peter 1:19).

17. **And the Spirit and the bride say, Come:**
**And let him that heareth say, Come:** . . . let the hearer respond, —FNTN . . . him who gives ear, —BB . . . anyone who hears, —TNT . . . he who hears this Call should say, —WADE.

**And let him that is athirst come:** . . . let him who is in need come, —BB . . . anyone who is thirsty, —TNT . . . should come, —WADE.

**And whosoever will, let him take the water of life freely:** . . . He that chooses, —RTHM . . . let everyone desiring it, —BB . . . let him who wishes, receive . . . as a free gift, —KLST . . . whoever may desire, let him accept the water of life for nothing, —FNTN . . . let anyone who wants, —TNT . . . wishes to drink of the Life-giving Water can do so without cost, —WADE . . . it costs nothing, —BECK.

**22:17.** The last mention of the Holy Spirit in the Bible draws attention to the greatest work and ministry of the Spirit in the Church Age. In view of Christ's witness to the things prophesied in the Book of Revelation the Holy Spirit inspires the Bride, the whole Church, to join Him in the invitation. The work of evangelism that needs to be done before Christ returns can only be done as it should be done by believers empowered by the Holy Spirit (Acts 1:5-8; 2:4). That is, for the invitation to be effective the Spirit must do the real work, and the Church must cooperate with the Spirit, not merely as a Body but as individuals. Then, everyone who hears (hears and responds) has the responsibility to join in spreading the invitation.

18. **For I testify unto every man that heareth the words of the prophecy of this book:** . . . I warn everyone, —BECK, —WLMS . . . I say emphatically to all, —TCNT . . . I declare to, —TNT . . . everyone who hears the words that are written in, —NLTG . . . to every man to whose ears have come the words of this prophet's book, —BB . . . I certify to every one listening to the statements of the prophecy of this book, —FNTN . . . who hears the prophetic declarations contained, —WADE.

**If any man shall add unto these things:** . . . make an addition, —FNTN . . . add anything to what is said, —NORL.

**God shall add unto him the plagues that are written in this book:** . . . then to whatever ill he now suffers, —WADE . . . will lay upon him, —FNTN . . . will inflict upon him all the plagues described, —NOLI . . . will put on him the punishments, —BB . . . the kinds of trouble that this book tells about, —NLTG . . . that have been described, —TCNT . . . that are recorded in, —NORL.

**22:18.** Because of Jesus' own witness to this Book of Revelation, we must be careful how we treat it. The final warning of the Book of Revelation stands in contrast to the blessing given at the beginning of the book. There those who read the prophecy aloud and those who hear and keep the things written in the book will indeed be blessed. But those who hear it read (and those who read it, of course) must be careful not to treat it as some ordinary book, for it is the inspired Word of God. If they add to it from their own ideas, if they add their own reasonings, their own speculations, if they twist or distort its teachings, or if they claim to have new revelations of their own and add them as if they were part of the inspired Word of God, God will bring on them the plagues of divine wrath written in the book. That is, they will remain to be deceived by the Antichrist and will come under the plagues of God's wrath written in chapters 6, 9, and 16 of this book.

In view of Jesus' warnings to His disciples that false prophets would come at the end of the age, this is a much needed warning now (Matthew 24:11). False teachers and false prophets will pervert the meaning of Scripture deliberately. They were already doing that when Paul wrote to the Galatians about A.D. 49 (Galatians 1:6-9). Many are still perverting the gospel. Like the Bereans, believers need to keep searching the Scriptures, so that they will not be led astray.

It should be noted also that He is not talking about different translations. Each language has its own way of saying things. Thus, when the Greek, Hebrew, and Aramaic of the Bible are put into English, for example, the ancient manuscripts must be compared and good English must be used in the translation. The important thing is for people to search the Scriptures and keep open to the Holy Spirit. On the other hand, if a person uses a verse here and a half-verse there, out of context, he can pervert the meaning of Scripture even using the best translation or even when he knows the original languages. This is treating the Bible as though it is not inspired, as though it is like books written by men. Adding one's own ideas to the Scriptures will bring the judgment of God.

19. **And if any man shall take away from the words of the book of this prophecy:** . . . if anyone detracts from, *—BRKL* . . . takes away anything from the declarations . . . containing this Prophecy, *—WADE* . . . takes away any part of this book that tells what will happen in the future, *—NLTG* . . . this prophetic book, *—KLST.*
**God shall take away his part out of the book of life:** . . . he will be deprived by God of, *—KLST* . . . God shall be eliminating his part from the log of life, *—CNDT* . . . will cancel, *—CNFT* . . . your share in, *—BECK* . . . that person's share, *—SEB* . . . his portion from, *—CNFT, —FNTN* . . . take away his share in the Life-sustaining Trees, *—WADE* . . . in the tree of life, *—BB.*
**and out of the holy city:** . . . and from the city of holiness, *—FNTN* . . . the holy town, *—BB.*
**and [from] the things which are written in this book:** . . . about which this book is written, *—MNTG* . . . as described in this book, *—BRKL, —TCNT* . . . promised in this book, *—CNFT* . . . in this scroll, *—ADAM.*

**22:19.** Some readers and hearers will want to take away or spiritualize away the prophecies of the Book of Revelation. If they do, God will take away their part in the promised inheritance. They will have no part in the Book of Life, no part or place in the Holy City, the New Jerusalem, and no part in the wonderful promises and blessings written in the Book of Revelation. Many ancient manuscripts draw attention to the fact they will

have no part in the tree of life. This means they will suffer eternal death.

Though verses 18 and 19 deal specifically with the prophecies and warnings of the Book of Revelation, the principle applies to all the Bible. Moses told the people of Israel, "Ye shall not add unto the word which I command you, neither shall ye diminish aught from it, that ye may keep the commandments of the Lord your God which I command you" (Deuteronomy 4:2). Jesus implied the same when He said, "Till heaven and earth pass, one jot or one tittle shall in no wise pass from the law, till all be fulfilled" (Matthew 5:18).

20. **He which testifieth these things:** . . . Jesus is the One who says that these things are true, *—EVRD* . . . He who affirms this says, *—BRKL* . . . The witness says, *—SEB* . . . who witnesses to these, *—KLGS* . . . He Who tells, *—NLTG* . . . who gives witness to this, *—NORL* . . . gives this testimony, *—WADE* . . . to all this, *—CNFT.*
**saith, Surely I come quickly. Amen:** . . . Now he says, *—EVRD* . . . It is true, *—CNFT* . . . Truly, *—BB* . . . Yes, *—FNTN, —HNSN* . . . Indeed, *—KLST* . . . Assuredly I am coming soon, *—TCNT* . . . Yes, I come with speed, *—KLGS* . . . is saying, Yea, I am coming swiftly, *—CNDT.*
**Even so, come, Lord Jesus:** . . . Certainly! *—BECK* . . . So be it, *—FNTN* . . . Let it be so, *—NLTG* . . . Amen, *—WADE.*

**22:20.** Jesus himself bears witness to the truth of all that is written in the Book of Revelation. "Surely" could be translated "Yes, indeed!" His final promise repeats His assurance that He is coming quickly. The ordinary meaning of this is that He is coming soon. Thus, the call for people to come is urgent because Jesus is indeed coming soon. He wants believers to keep that sense of imminency, that sense of urgency. Keeping an attitude of waiting for His coming, keeping the hope of His coming before them, will help them to purify themselves, "even as he (Christ) is pure" (1 John 3:2, 3).

The response Jesus wants to hear is the one John himself gave while on the bleak, rocky Isle of Patmos, a prayer for Him to come. He longed for that day to come. His prayer was also a recognition that believers must wait for His coming to bring the completion of their redemption. Not until He comes will evil and sin be overthrown and the Kingdom be brought in. Those who love Jesus, those who love His appearing, will put the same "Amen" to the Book of Revelation and to the promise that Jesus is coming soon.

We can be sure of the truth of the prophecies of this book also because the One who testifies to them is the Living Word of God (John 1:1, 14; Revelation 19:13). He is indeed coming in triumphant victory to reign as King of kings and Lord of lords (19:16).

Unbelievers may wonder why true followers of Christ do not join with them in their lusts, revellings, drunkenness, and other excesses. It is because they know they must give account to the One who will judge the living and the dead (1 Peter 4:3-5). It is because they see also the wonder and glory of the reward. In a world where evil, corruption, violence, and all kinds of dangers are getting worse, their blessed hope sustains them.

**21. The grace of our Lord Jesus Christ [be] with you all. Amen:** ...The love of, *—BECK*...May the blessing of, *—TCNT*...The favour of, *—HNSN, —RTHM*...May all of you have the loving favor of... Let it be so, *—NLTG*...The spiritual blessing...be with His people, *—WLMS*...be with everyone, *—SEB, —TNT*...be with His saints! *—NORL*...be with God's Hallowed People, *—WADE*...continue with the holy, *—FNTN*...So be it, *—BB*...be with all people, *—KLGS*...with all the saints, *—CNDT*...with his people, *—CNFT.*

**22:21.** The Book of Revelation ends with a benediction. It assures believers that the grace of our Lord Jesus will be with them until He comes. His grace includes not only His unmerited favor that provides the forgiveness of sins, but it also provides the power to live a holy life that endures to the end. May we all add our "Amen" to this as well.

# BIBLIOGRAPHIES

## Acts

Alexander, J. A. *Commentary on the Acts of the Apostles.* 1857. Reprint. London: Banner of Truth Trust. 1979.

Bruce, F. F. *Acts. The New International Commentary on the New Testament.* Ed. by F. F. Bruce. Grand Rapids: William B. Eerdmans Publishing Co. 1974.

Carter, Charles, and Ralph Earle. *The Acts of the Apostles.* Grand Rapids: Zondervan Publishing House. 1959.

DeWitt, Norman W. *St. Paul and Epicurus.* Minneapolis: University of Minnesota Press. 1954.

Earle, Ralph. *The Acts of the Apostles.* Kansas City: Beacon Hill Press. 1965.

Eusebius. *Ecclesiastical History.* Trans. by Kirsopp Lake. Loeb Classical Library. Cambridge: Harvard University Press. 1965.

Gordon, Cyrus H. *The Ancient Near East.* 3d ed. New York: W. W. Norton and Company, Inc. 1965.

Guthrie, Donald. *The Apostles.* Grand Rapids: Zondervan Publishing House. 1975.

Gutzke, Manford G. *Plain Talk on Acts.* Grand Rapids: Zondervan Publishing House. 1966.

Hackett, H. B. *A Commentary on the Acts of the Apostles.* Philadelphia: American Baptist Publication Society. 1882.

Haenchen, Ernst. *The Acts of the Apostles: A Commentary.* Trans. by Bernard Noble and Gerald Shinn. Philadelphia: The Westminster Press. 1971.

Harnack, Adolf. *The Acts of the Apostles.* Trans. by J. R. Wilkinson. London: Williams and Norgate. 1909.

Harrison, E. F. *Acts: The Expanding Church.* Chicago: Moody Press. 1975.

Horton, Stanley M. *What the Bible Says about the Holy Spirit.* Springfield, MO: Gospel Publishing House. 1976.

Lenski, P. C. H. *The Interpretation of the Acts of the Apostles.* Columbus, Ohio: The Wartburg Press. 1940.

Longenecker, R. N. *The Acts of the Apostles.* In *John–Acts.* Vol. 9 of *The Expositor's Bible Commentary.* Ed. by Frank E. Gaebelein. Grand Rapids: Zondervan Publishing House. 1981.

Longenecker, R. N. *Paul, Apostle of Liberty.* Grand Rapids: Baker Book House. 1976.

Metzger, Bruce M. *A Textual Commentary on the Greek New Testament.* 3d ed. New York: United Bible Societies. 1971.

Newman, B. M., and Eugene Nida. *A Translators Handbook on the Acts of the Apostles.* New York: United Bible Societies. 1972.

Pache, Rene. *The Person and Work of the Holy Spirit.* Rev. ed. Chicago: Moody Press. 1966.

Packer, J. W. *Acts of the Apostles.* Cambridge: Cambridge University Press. 1975.

Pink, A. W. *The Holy Spirit.* Grand Rapids: Baker Book House. 1970.

*Apostles.* Cambridge: Cambridge University Press. 1975.

Ramsay, W. M. *The Cities of Saint Paul.* 1901. Reprint. Grand Rapids: Baker Book House. 1964.

Rutherford, John. "Partition, the Middle Wall of." In *The International Standard Bible Encyclopedia.* Ed. by James Orr. 4 vols. Grand Rapids: William B. Eerdmans Publishing Co. 1943.

Thomas, David. *Acts of the Apostles.* 1870. Reprint. Grand Rapids: Baker Book House. 1956.

Willis, Barnstone, ed. *The Other Bible.* New York: Harper and Row. 1984.

## Romans, I Corinthians, and II Corinthians

Achtemeier, Paul J. *Romans.* Atlanta: John Knox. 1985.

Barclay, William. *The Letter to the Romans. The Daily Study Bible.* Philadelphia: The Westminster Press. 1957.

Barclay, William. *The Letters to the Corinthians. The Daily Study Bible.* Philadelphia: The Westminster Press. 1956.

Barclay, William. *The Mind of St. Paul.* New York: Harper & Row. 1975.

Barrett, C. K. *A Commentary on the Epistle to the Romans. Harper's New Testament Commentaries.* Ed. by Henry Chadwick. New York: Harper & Row. 1957.

Barrett, C. K. *A Commentary on the First Epistle to the Corinthians. Harper's New Testament Commentaries.* Ed. by Henry Chadwick. New York: Harper & Row. 1968.

Barrett, C. K. *From First to Last Adam: A Study in Pauline Theology.* London: Adam & Charles Black. 1962.

Barth, Karl. *The Epistle to the Romans.* 6th. ed. Ed. by Edwyn C. Hoskyns. Grand Rapids: William B. Eerdmans Publishing Co. 1972.

Black, Matthew. *Romans.* Vol. 37 of *New Century Bible.* Ed. by Ronald E. Clements and Matthew Black. London: Oliphants. 1973.

Blass, F., and A. Debrunner. *A Greek Grammar of the New Testament and Other Early Christian Literature.* Trans, by Robert W. Funk. Chicago: The University of Chicago Press. 1961.

Brown, Francis, S. R. Driver, and Charles A. Briggs. *A Hebrew and English Lexicon of the Old Testament.* Oxford: The Clarendon Press. 1972.

Bruce, F. F. *1 and 2 Corinthians.* Vol. 38 of *New Century Bible.* Ed. by Ronald E. Clements and Matthew Black. London: Oliphants. 1976.

Bruce, F. F. *The Epistle of Paul to the Romans.* Vol. 6 of *Tyndale New Testament Commentaries.* Ed. by R. V. G. Tasker. Grand Rapids: William B. Eerdmans Publishing Co. 1963.

Calvin, John. *Commentary on the Epistles of Paul the Apostle to the Corinthians.* Trans, by John Pringle. *Calvin's Commentaries.* Grand Rapids: William B. Eerdmans Publishing Co. 1948.

Calvin, John. *Commentaries on the Epistle of Paul the Apostle to the Romans.* Trans, by John Owen. *Calvin's Commentaries.* Grand Rapids: William B. Eerdmans Publishing Co. 1947.

Calvin, John. *Institutes of the Christian Religion.* 2 vols. Trans, by Henry Beveridge. Grand Rapids: William B. Eerdmans Publishing Co. 1949.

Carver, Frank G. *2 Corinthians.* In *Romans, 1 and 2 Corinthians.* Vol. 8 of *Beacon Bible Commentary.* Ed. by Ralph Earle. Kansas City: Beacon Hill Press of Kansas City. 1968.

Clarke, Adam. *Romans to the Revelations.* Vol. 6 of *Clarke's Commentary.* Nashville: Abingdon Press. N.d.

Conybeare, W. J. and J. S. Howson. *The Life and Epistles of St. Paul.* Grand Rapids: William B. Eerdmans Publishing Co. 1978.

Cranfield, C. E. B. *A Critical and Exegetical Commentary on the Epistle to the Romans.* Rev. ed. 2 vols. *International Critical Commentary.* Ed. by J. A. Emerton and C. E. B. Cranfield. Edinburgh: T. & T. Clark. 1977.

Davies, W. D. *Paul and Rabbinic Judaism.* Philadelphia: Fortress Press. 1980.

Denney, James. St. *Paul's Epistle to the Romans.* In *Acts, Romans, First Corinthians.* Vol. 2 of *The Expositor's Greek Testament.* Ed. by W. Robertson Nicoll. Grand Rapids: William B. Eerdmans Publishing Co. 1951.

*The Didache.* Trans. by Maxwell Staniforth. In *Early Christian Writings: The Apostolic Fathers.* New York: Penguin Books. 1978.

Dieter, Melvin E., et al. *Five Views on Sanctification.* Grand Rapids: Zondervan Publishing House. 1987.

Dodd, C. H. *The Epistle of Paul to the Romans. The Moffatt New Testament Commentary.* London: Hodder & Stoughton Limited. 1960.

Dodd, C. H. *The Meaning of Paul for Today.* New York: World Publishing. 1957.

Drummond, Henry. *Essays and Addresses.* New York: James Pott and Company. 1904.

Edersheim, Alfred. *The Life and Times of Jesus the Messiah.* 2 vols. Grand Rapids: William B. Eerdmans Publishing Co. 1959.

Fee, Gordon D. *The First Epistle to the Corinthians. The New International Commentary on the New Testament.* Ed. by F. F. Bruce. Grand Rapids: William B. Eerdmans Publishing Co. 1987.

Godet, Frederic Louis. *Commentary on First Corinthians.* Edinburgh: T. & T. Clark. 1889. Reprint. Grand Rapids: Kregel Publications. 1977.

Goudge, H. L. *The Second Epistle to the Corinthians. Westminster Commentaries.* Ed. by Walter Lock and D. C. Simpson. London: Methuen & Co. Ltd. 1928.

Grosheide, F. W. *Commentary on the First Epistle to the Corinthians. The New International Commentary on the New Testament.* Ed. by F. F. Bruce. Grand Rapids: William B. Eerdmans Publishing Co. 1974.

Guthrie, Donald. *New Testament Introduction.* Downers Grove, Illinois: Inter-Varsity Press. 1970.

Guthrie, Donald. *The Apostles.* Grand Rapids: Zondervan Publishing House. 1980.

Harris, Murray J. *2 Corinthians.* In *Romans—Galatians.* Vol. 10 of *The Expositor's Bible Commentary.* Ed. by Frank E. Gaebelein. Grand Rapids: Zondervan Publishing House. 1976.

Hendriksen, William. *Exposition of the Epistle of Paul to the Romans. New Testament Commentary.* Grand Rapids: Baker Book House. 1975.

Henry, Matthew. *Matthew Henry's Commentary on the Whole Bible.* 6 vols. New York: Flemming H. Revell Company. N.d.

Hodge, Charles. *Commentary on the Epistle to the Romans.* Philadelphia: H. B. Garner. 1886. Reprint. Grand Rapids: William B. Eerdmans Publishing Co. 1972.

Horton, Stanley. *What the Bible Says about the Holy Spirit.* Springfield, MO: Gospel Publishing House. 1976.

Hughes, Philip Edgcumbe. *Paul's Second Epistle to the Corinthians. The New London Commentary.* London: Marshall, Morgan, and Scott. 1962.

Hughes, Robert R. *Second Corinthians. Everyman's Bible Commentary.* Chicago: Moody Press. 1985.

Ironside, H. A. *Addresses on the Second Epistle to the Corinthians.* New York: Loizeaux Brothers, Inc. N.d.

Jewett, Robert. *Paul's Anthropological Terms.* Leiden: E. J. Brill. 1971.

Kent, Homer A., Jr. *A Heart Opened Wide.* Grand Rapids: Baker Book House. 1982.

Lenski, R. C. H. *The Interpretation of St. Paul's First and Second Epistles to the Corinthians.* Minneapolis: Augsburg Publishing House. 1963.

Lightfoot, J. B. *The Apostolic Fathers.* London: MacMillan and Company. 1890.

Luther, Martin. *Lectures on Galatians, Chapters 1-4.* Vol. 26 of *Luther's Works.* Ed. and trans, by Jaroslav Pelikan. St. Louis: Concordia Publishing House. 1963.

Luther, Martin. *Lectures on Romans.* Trans, by Walter G. Tillmanns and Jacob A. O. Preus. Vol. 25 of *Luther's Works.* Ed. by Hilton C. Oswald. St. Louis: Concordia Publishing House. 1972.

Martin, Ralph P. *Reconciliation: A Study of Paul's Theology. New Foundations Theological Library.* Atlanta: John Knox. 1981.

Manson, T. W. *Romans. Peake's Commentary on the Bible.* Ed. by Matthew Black. London: T. Nelson. 1962.

Mayor, Joseph B. *The Epistle of St. James.* Reprint. Minneapolis: Klock and Klock Christian Publishers. 1977.

Meyer, Heinrich August Wilhelm. *Critical and Exegetical Handbook to the Epistles to the Corinthians.* Vol. 6 of *Meyer's Commentary on the New Testament.* Funk & Wagnalls. 1884. Reprint. Winona Lake, Indiana: Alpha Publications. 1979.

Meyer, Joh. P. *Ministers of Christ.* Milwaukee: Northwestern Publishing House. 1963.

Miller, Patrick D., Jr. "The Most Important Word: The Yoke of the Kingdom." *The Iliff Review* 41 (1984): 17-30.

Moody, Dale. *Romans.* In *Acts—1 Corinthians.* Vol. 8 of *The Broadman's Bible Commentary.* Ed. by Clifton J. Allen, et al. Nashville: Broadman Press. 1970.

Morris, Leon. *The First Epistle of Paul to the Corinthians.* Vol. 7 of *Tyndale New Testament Commentaries.* Ed. by R. V. G. Tasker. Grand Rapids: William B. Eerdmans Publishing Co. 1975.

Moule, C. G. Handley. *The Epistle of Paul to the Romans. The Expositor's Bible.* Ed. by W. Robertson Nicoll. London: Hodder & Stoughton Limited. 1894.

Murray, John. *The Epistle to the Romans. The New International Commentary on the New Testament.* Ed. by F. F. Bruce. Grand Rapids: William B. Eerdmans Publishing Co. 1982.

Nicoll, W. Robertson, ed. *The Expositor's Greek Testament.* Vol. 2, *Apostles, Romans, First Corinthians.* Grand Rapids: William B. Eerdmans Publishing Co. 1951.

Nygren, Anders. *Commentary on Romans.* Philadelphia: Fortress Press. 1949.

Packer, J. I. "Justification." *Evangelical Dictionary of Theology.* Ed. by Walter A. Elwell. Grand Rapids: Baker Book House. 1984.

Pearlman, Myer. *Knowing the Doctrines of the Bible.* Springfield, MO: Gospel Publishing House. 1937.

Proctor, W. C. G. *Second Corinthians. The New Bible Commentary.* Ed. by Francis Davidson. Grand Rapids: William B. Eerdmans Publishing Co. 1958.

Prohl, Russell. *Women in the Church.* Grand Rapids: William B. Eerdmans Publishing Co. 1957.

Ramsay, William. *Pictures of the Apostolic Church.* London: 1910. Reprint. Grand Rapids: Baker Book House. 1959.

Robertson, Archibald, and Alfred Plummer. *A Critical and Exegetical Commentary on the First Epistle of Paul to the Corinthians. The International Critical Commentary.* 2nd. ed. Ed. by S. R. Driver, A. Plummer, and C. A. Briggs. Edinburgh: T. & T. Clark. 1975.

Rosenius, C. O. *The Believer Free from the Law.* Trans. by Adolf Hult. Rock Island, Illinois: Augustana Book Concern. 1923.

Sadler, M. F. *The First and Second Epistles to the Corinthians.* London: George Bell and Sons. 1889.

Sanday, William and Arthur C. Headlam. *A Critical and Exegetical Commentary on the Epistle to the Romans. International Critical Commentary.* 5th. ed. Ed. by S. R. Driver, A. Plummer, and C. A. Briggs. Edinburgh: T. & T. Clark. 1902.

Sanders, E. P. *Paul and Palestinian Judaism.* London: SCM Press Ltd. 1977.

Tasker, R. V. G. *The Second Epistle of Paul to the Corinthians.* Vol. 8 of *Tyndale New Testament Commentaries.* Ed. by R. V. G. Tasker. Grand Rapids: William B. Eerdmans Publishing Co. 1983.

Thayer, Joseph Henry. *Greek-English Lexicon of the New Testament.* Grand Rapids: Zondervan Publishing House. 1972.

*The Syriac Apocalypse of Baruch.* In *The Apocrypha and Pseudepigrapha of the Old Testament in English.* 2 vols. Ed. by R. H. Charles. Oxford: Clarendon Press. 1973.

Tozer, A. W. *The Knowledge of the Holy.* New York: Harper & Row. 1961.

Turner, Nigel. *Grammatical Insights into the New Testament.* Edinburgh: T. & T. Clark. 1965.

Vincent, Marvin R. *Word Studies in the New Testament.* 4 vols. Reprint. Grand Rapids: William B. Eerdmans Publishing Co. 1973.

Zahniser, Clarence H. *2 Corinthians.* In *Romans—Philemon.* Vol. 5 of *The Wesleyan Bible Commentary.* Ed. by Ralph Earle. Grand Rapids: William B. Eerdmans Publishing Co. 1971.

## Galatians through Philemon

Abbott, T. K. *A Critical and Exegetical Commentary on the Epistles to the Ephesians and to the Colossians. The International Critical Commentary.* Ed. by S. R. Driver, A. Plummer, and C. A. Briggs. Edinburgh: T. & T. Clark. 1968.

*The Apocryphon of John.* In *The Nag Hammadi Library in English.* Trans. by Frederik Wisse. New York: Harper & Row, Publishers. 1977.

*The Babylonian Talmud.* Trans. by I. Epstein. London: The Soncino Press. 1952.

Barclay, William. *The Letters to the Galatians and*

*Ephesians. The Daily Study Bible.* Rev. ed. Philadelphia: The Westminster Press. 1976.

Barclay, William. *The Letters to Timothy, Titus, and Philemon. The Daily Study Bible.* Rev. ed. Philadelphia: The Westminster Press. 1975.

Barrett, C. K. *Freedom and Obligation: A Study of the Epistle to the Galatians.* Philadelphia: The Westminster Press. 1985.

Barth, Markus. *Ephesians.* Vol. 24 of *The Anchor Bible.* Ed. by William Foxwell Albright and David Noel Freedman. Garden City, NY: Doubleday & Company, Inc. 1974.

Baxter, J. Sidlow. *The Strategic Grasp of the Bible.* Grand Rapids: Zondervan Publishing House. 1970. Beare, Frank W. *St. Paul and His Letters.* Nashville: Abingdon Press. 1971.

Best, Ernest. *A Commentary on the 1st and 2nd Epistles to the Thessalonians.* Vol. 10 of *Black's New Testament Commentaries.* London: Adam and Charles Black. 1972.

Betz, H. D. *A Commentary on Paul's Letter to the Churches in Galatia. Hermeneia.* Ed. by Helmut Koester, et al. Philadelphia: Fortress Press. 1979.

Bruce, F. F. *The Epistle to the Galatians. New International Greek Testament Commentary.* Ed. by I. Howard Marshall and W. Ward Gasque. Grand Rapids: William B. Eerdmans Publishing Co. 1982.

Bruce, F. F. *The Epistles to the Colossians, to Philemon, and to the Ephesians. The New International Commentary on the New Testament.* Ed. by F. F. Bruce. Grand Rapids: William B. Eerdmans Publishing Co. 1984.

Bruce, F. F. *1 and 2 Thessalonians.* Vol. 45 of *Word Biblical Commentary.* Ed. by David A. Hubbard, et al. Waco, TX: Word Books. 1982.

Burton, E. D. *A Critical and Exegetical Commentary on the Epistle to the Galatians. The International Critical Commentary.* Ed. by S. R. Driver, A. Plummer, and C. A. Briggs. Edinburgh: T. & T. Clark. 1975.

Carson, Herbert M. *The Epistles of Paul to the Colossians and Philemon.* Vol. 12 of *Tyndale New Testament Commentaries.* Ed. by R. V. G. Tasker. Grand Rapids: William B. Eerdmans Publishing Co. 1960.

Chrysostom, John. *Homilies on Thessalonians.* In *Chrysostom.* Vol. 13 of *The Nicene and Post-Nicene Fathers.* Ed. by Philip Schaff. Edinburgh, 1867. Reprint. Grand Rapids: William B. Eerdmans Publishing Co. 1969.

Clarke, Adam. *Romans to the Revelation.* Vol. 6 of *Clarke's Commentary.* Nashville: Abingdon Press. N.d.

Clement of Rome. *Epistle to the Corinthians.* In *The Apostolic Fathers.* Vol. 1 of *The Ante-Nicene Fathers.* Ed. by Alexander Roberts and James Donaldson. Edinburgh. 1867. Reprint. Grand Rapids: William B. Eerdmans Publishing Co. 1973.

Coleridge, H. N., ed. *Specimens of the Table Talk of the Late Samuel Taylor Coleridge.* London, 1835.

Conybeare, W. J., and J. S. Howson. *The Life and Epistles of St. Paul.* Grand Rapids: William B. Eerdmans Publishing Co. 1978.

Craddock, Fred B. *Philippians. Interpretation.* Ed. by J. L. Mays, et al. Atlanta: John Knox Press. 1985.

Davies, W. D. *Paul and Rabbinic Judaism.* London: S.P.C.K. 1955.

Dibelius, Martin, and Hans Conzelmann. *A Commentary on the Pastoral Epistles.* Trans. by P. Buttolph and A. Yarbro. *Hermenia.* Ed. by Helmut Koester, et al. Philadelphia: Fortress Press. 1972.

Eadie, John. *Commentary on the Greek Text of the Epistles of Paul to the Thessalonians.* Vol. 5 of *The John Eadie Greek Text Commentaries.* Ed. by William Young. Macmillan and Company. 1877. Reprint. Grand Rapids: Baker Book House. 1979.

Eerdman, Charles R. *The Epistles of Paul to the Thessalonians.* Philadelphia: The Westminster Press. 1935.

Ellingsworth, Paul, and Eugene Nida. *A Translator's Handbook on Paul's Letters to the Thessalonians.* Vol. 17 of *Helps for Translators.* Stuttgart: United Bible Societies. 1975.

Fee, Gordon D. *1 and 2 Timothy, Titus. A Good News Commentary.* Ed. by W. Ward Gasque. San Francisco: Harper & Row. 1984.

Foulkes, Francis. *The Epistle of Paul to the Ephesians.* Vol. 10 of *Tyndale New Testament Commentaries.* Ed. by R. V. G. Tasker. Grand Rapids: William B. Eerdmans Publishing Co. 1961.

Frame, James Everett. *A Critical and Exegetical Commentary on the Epistles of St. Paul to the Thessalonians. The International Critical Commentary.* Ed. by S. R. Driver, A. Plummer, and C. A. Briggs. Edinburgh: T. & T. Clark. 1970.

Fung, Ronald Y. *The Epistle to the Galatians. The New International Commentary on the New Testament.* Ed. by F. F. Bruce. Grand Rapids: William B. Eerdmans Publishing Co. 1988.

Gaebelein, Frank E., ed. *The Expositor's Bible Commentary.* Vol. 11, *Ephesians—Philemon.* Grand Rapids: Zondervan Publishing House. 1978.

Goodspeed, E. J. *The Meaning of Ephesians.* Chicago: The University of Chicago Press. 1933.

Gunther, John J. *St. Paul's Opponents and Their Backgrounds: A Study of Apocalyptic and Jewish Sectarian Teachings.* Vol. 35 of *Supplements Novum Testamentum.* Leiden: E. J. Brill. 1973.

Guthrie, Donald. *Galatians. New Century Bible.* Ed. by Ronald E. Clements and Matthew Black. Greenwood, SC: The Attic Press. 1977. Guthrie, Donald. *The Pastoral Epistles.* Vol. 14 of *Tyndale New Testament Commentaries.* Ed. by R. V. G. Tasker. Grand Rapids: William B. Eerdmans Publishing Co. 1957.

Harrison, Norman B. *Living: A Book of Christian*

*Culture for All Ages*. Minneapolis: The Harrison Service. 1944.

Harrison, Percy Neale. *The Problem of the Pastoral Epistles*. Oxford: Oxford University Press. 1921.

Hawthorne, Gerald F. *Philippians*. Vol. 43 of *Word Biblical Commentary*. Ed. by David A. Hubbard, et al. Waco, TX: Word Books. 1983.

Hendriksen, William. *Exposition of Colossians and Philemon. New Testament Commentary*. Grand Rapids: Baker Book House. 1975.

Hiebert, D. Edmond. *An Introduction to the Pauline Epistles*. Chicago: Moody Press. 1972.

Hiebert, D. Edmond. *First Timothy*. Chicago: Moody Press. 1957.

Horton, Stanley M. *Adult Teacher, 1971*. Vol. 7 of *Adult Teacher Commentary*. Springfield, MO: Gospel Publishing House. 1970.

Ignatius. *Epistle to Polycarp*. In *The Apostolic Fathers*. Vol. 1 of *The Ante-Nicene Fathers*. Ed. by Alexander Roberts and James Donaldson. Edinburgh. 1867. Reprint. Grand Rapids: William B. Eerdmans Publishing Co. 1973.

Irenaeus. *Against Heresies*. In *The Apostolic Fathers*. Vol. 1 of *The Ante-Nicene Fathers*. Ed. by Alexander Roberts and James Donaldson. Edinburgh. 1867. Reprint. Grand Rapids: William B. Eerdmans Publishing Co. 1973.

Josephus, F. *The Complete Works of Flavius Josephus*. Trans, by William Whiston. Grand Rapids: Kregel Publications. 1960.

Kelly, J. N. D. *The Oxford Dictionary of Popes*. Oxford: Oxford University Press. 1986.

Lenski, R. C. H. *The Interpretation of St. Paul's Epistles to the Colossians, to the Thessalonians, to Timothy, to Titus, and to Philemon*. Minneapolis: Augsburg Publishing House. 1961.

Lightfoot, J. B. *St. Paul's Epistles to the Colossians and to Philemon*. Rev. ed. New York: Macmillan and Company. 1829. Reprint. Grand Rapids: Zondervan Publishing House. 1959.

Lock, Walter. *A Critical and Exegetical Commentary on the Pastoral Epistles. The International Critical Commentary*. Ed. by S. R. Driver, A. Plummer, and C. A. Briggs. Edinburgh: T. & T. Clark. 1966.

Lohse, Eduard. *A Commentary on the Epistles to the Colossians and Philemon*. Trans. by W. R. Poehlmann and R. J. Karris. *Hermeneia*. Ed. by Helmut Koester, et al. Philadelphia: Fortress Press. 1971.

Louw, Johannes P. and Eugene A. Nida, eds. *Greek-English Lexicon of the New Testament Based on Semantic Domains*. 2 vols. New York: United Bible Societies. 1988.

Marshall, I. Howard. *1 and 2 Thessalonians. New Century Bible*. Ed. by Donald E. Clements and Matthew Black. Grand Rapids: William B. Eerdmans Publishing Co. 1983.

Martin, Ralph P. *Carmen Christi*. Rev. ed. Grand Rapids: William B. Eerdmans Publishing Co. 1983.

Martin, Ralph P. *The Epistle of Paul to the Philippians*. Vol. 11 of *Tyndale New Testament Commentaries*. Rev. ed. by Leon Morris. Grand Rapids: William B. Eerdmans Publishing Co. 1988.

Meyer, H. A. W. *Critical and Exegetical Hand-Book to the Epistle to the Ephesians*. Trans. by M. J. Evans. Rev. ed. by W. P. Dickson. New York: Funk and Wagnalls, Publishers. 1884. Reprint. Alpha Publications. 1979.

Michael, J. Hugh. *The Epistle of Paul to the Philippians. The Moffat New Testament Commentary*. London: Hodder and Stoughton. 1964.

Mitton, C. Leslie. *Ephesians. New Century Bible*. Ed. by Donald E. Clements and Matthew Black. London: Oliphants. 1976.

Mitton, C. Leslie. *The Epistle to the Ephesians: Its Authorship, Origin and Purpose*. Oxford: Oxford University Press. 1951.

Moffatt, James. *1 Thessalonians—James*. Vol. 4 of *The Expositor's Greek Testament*. Ed. by W. Robertson Nicoll. Grand Rapids: William B. Eerdmans Publishing Co. 1951.

Morris, Leon. *The First and Second Epistles to the Thessalonians. The New International Commentary on the New Testament*. Ed. by F. F. Bruce. Grand Rapids: William B. Eerdmans Publishing Co. 1959.

Moule, C. F. D. *The Epistles of Paul the Apostle to the Colossians and to Philemon*. Cambridge: Cambridge University Press. 1968.

Peake, A. S. "The Quintessence of Paulinism." *Bulletin of the John Rylands Library* 4(1917-1918): 285-211.

Polycarp. *Epistle to the Philippians*. In *The Apostolic Fathers*. Vol. 1 of *The Ante-Nicene Fathers*. Ed. by Alexander Roberts and James Donaldson. Edinburgh. 1867. Reprint. Grand Rapids: William B. Eerdmans Publishing Co. 1973.

Ramsay, William M. *A Historical Commentary on St. Paul's Epistle to the Galatians*. G. P. Putnam's Sons. 1900. Reprint. Minneapolis: Klock & Klock Christian Publishers. 1978.

Ridderbos, H. N. *The Epistle of Paul to the Churches of Galatia. The New International Commentary on the New Testament*. Ed. F. F. Bruce. Grand Rapids: William B. Eerdmans Publishing Co. 1953.

Robertson, Archibald Thomas. *Paul and the Intellectuals: The Epistle to the Colossians*. New York: Doubleday, Doran and Company. 1928.

Ryrie, Charles Caldwell. *First and Second Thessalonians*. Chicago: Moody Press. 1959.

Schaff, Philip. *Apostolic Christianity*. Vol. 1 of *History of the Christian Church*. Charles Scribner's Sons. 1910. Reprint. Grand Rapids: William B. Eerdmans Publishing Co. 1971.

Scott, E. F. *The Epistles of Paul to the Colossians, to Philemon and to the Ephesians. The Moffat New Testament Commentary*. London: Hodder and

Stoughton. 1930.

Stevens, William Arnold. *Commentary on the Epistles to the Thessalonians*. In *Corinthians to Thessalonians*. Vol. 5 of *An American Commentary on the New Testament*. Ed. by Alvah Hovey. Valley Forge, PA: The Judson Press. N.d.

Stibbs, A. M. *The Pastoral Epistles*. In *The New Bible Commentary: Revised*. 3rd ed. Ed. by Donald Guthrie, et al. Grand Rapids: William B. Eerdmans Publishing Co. 1970.

Stott, John R. W. The *Message of Galatians*. Downers Grove, Ill.: Inter-Varsity Press. 1968. Summers, Ray. *Essentials of New Testament Greek*. Nashville: Broadman Press. 1950.

Tertullian. *Against Marcion*. In *Latin Christianity: Its Founder Tertullian*. Vol. 3 of *The Ante-Nicene Fathers*. Ed. by Alexander Roberts and James Donaldson. Edinburgh. 1867. Reprint. Grand Rapids: William B. Eerdmans Publishing Co. 1973.

Unger, Merrill F. *Unger's Bible Dictionary*. Chicago: Moody Press. 1972.

Walvoord, John F. *The Thessalonian Epistles*. Grand Rapids: Zondervan Publishing House. 1967.

Wright, N. T. *The Epistles of Paul to the Colossians and to Philemon*. Vol. 12 of *Tyndale New Testament Commentaries*. Rev. ed. Ed. by Leon Morris. Grand Rapids: William B. Eerdmans Publishing Co. 1986.

Wuest, Kenneth S. *Galatians in the Greek New Testament*. Grand Rapids: William B. Eerdmans Publishing Co. 1944.

# Hebrews through Jude

*The Ascension of Isaiah the Prophet*. In *The Old Testament Pseudepigrapha*. Ed. by James H. Charlesworth. Garden City: Doubleday and Company, Inc. 1983.

Barclay, William. *The Letter to the Hebrews. The Daily Study Bible*. Philadelphia: The Westminster Press. 1957.

Brown, Raymond E. *The Epistles of John*. Vol. 30 of *The Anchor Bible*. Ed. by W. F. Albright and D. N. Freedman. Garden City: Doubleday and Company, Inc. 1982.

Bruce, A. B. *The Epistle to the Hebrews*. 2d ed. Edinburgh: T. and T. Clark. 1899.

Bruce, F. F. *The Epistle to the Hebrews. The New International Commentary on the New Testament*. Ed. by F. F. Bruce. Grand Rapids: William B. Eerdmans Publishing Co. 1964.

Bruce, F. F. *The Epistles of John*. Old Tappan, NJ: Revell. 1970.

Buchanan, George Wesley. *Hebrews*. Vol. 36 of *The Anchor Bible*. Ed. by W. F. Albright and D. N. Freedman. Garden City: Doubleday and Company, Inc. 1978.

Bullinger, E. W. *Great Cloud of Witnesses*. London: Eyre and Spottiswoode. 1911. Reprint. Grand Rapids: Kregel Publications. 1979.

Calvin, John. *Commentaries of the Epistle of Paul to the Hebrews. Calvin's Commentaries*. Trans. by John Owen. Grand Rapids: William B. Eerdmans Publishing Co. 1948.

Carter, Charles W. *The Epistle to the Hebrews*. In *Hebrews-Revelation*. Vol. 6 of *The Wesleyan Bible Commentary*. Ed. by Ralph Earle. Grand Rapids: William B. Eerdmans Publishing Co. 1972.

Clarke, Adam. *The General Epistle of James*. In *Romans to the Revelation*. Vol. 6 of *Clarke's Commentary*. Nashville: Abingdon Press. N.d.

Cross, Frank Moore. *The Ancient Library of Qumran and Modern Biblical Studies*. Garden City: Doubleday and Company, Inc. Reprint. Grand Rapids: Baker Book House. 1980

Davids, Peter H. *The Epistle of James. The New International Greek Testament Commentary*. Ed. by I. Howard Marshall and W. Ward Gasque. Grand Rapids: William B. Eerdmans Publishing Co. 1982.

Dibelius, Martin. *James*. Trans. by Michael A. Williams. *Hermeneia*. Ed. by Helmut Koester. Philadelphia: Fortress Press. 1976.

Eusebius. *The History of the Church*. Trans. by G. A. Williamson. New York: Penguin Books. 1981.

Green, M. *The Second Epistle General of Peter and the General Epistle of Jude*. Vol. 18 of *Tyndale New Testament Commentaries*. Ed. by R. V. G. Tasker. Grand Rapids: William B. Eerdmans Publishing Co. 1968.

Hart, J. H. A. *The First Epistle General of Peter*. In *First Peter-Revelation*. Vol. 5 of *The Expositor's Greek Testament*. Ed. by W. Robertson Nicoll. Grand Rapids: William B. Eerdmans Publishing Co. 1951.

Henry, Matthew. *Acts to Revelation*. Vol. 6 of *Matthew Henry's Commentary on the Whole Bible*. New York: Flemming H. Revell Company. N.d.

Horton, Stanley *Ready Always: A Devotional Commentary on the Epistles of Peter*. Springfield, Mo: Gospel Publishing House. 1974.

Hughes, Graham. *Hebrews and Hermeneutics*. Vol. 36 of *Society for New Testament Studies Monograph Series*. Ed. by M. Wilson and M. E. Thrall. New York: Cambridge University Press. 1979

Kaiser, Walter C. *The Use of the Old Testament in the New*. Chicago: Moody Press. 1985.

Kaseman, Ernst. *The Wandering People of God*. Trans. by R. A. Harrisville and I. L. Sandberg. Minneapolis: Augsburg Publishing House. 1984.

Kelly, J. N. D. *A Commentary on the Epistles of Peter and Jude. Black's New Testament Commentaries*. London: A. and C. Black. 1969.

Louw, Johannes P., and Eugene A. Nida, eds. *Greek-English Lexicon of the New Testament Based on Semantic Domains*. 2 vols. New York: United Bible Societies. 1988.

Luther, Martin. *The Catholic Epistles*. Vol. 30 of *Luther's Works*. Ed. by Jaroslav Pelikan and Walter Hansen. St. Louis: Concordia Publishing House. 1967.

Manson, William. *The Epistle to the Hebrews*. London: Hodder and Stoughton Ltd. 1951.

Marshall, I. Howard. *The Epistles of John. The New International Commentary on the New Testament*. Ed. by F. F. Bruce. Grand Rapids: William B. Eerdmans Publishing Co. 1978.

Martin, Ralph P. *James*. Vol. 48 of *Word Biblical Commentary*. Ed. by Ralph P. Martin. Waco: Word Books. 1988.

Mayor, Joseph B. *The Epistle of St. Jude and Second Epistle of Peter*. MacMillan and Company. 1907. Reprint. Minneapolis: Klock and Klock Christian Publishers. 1978.

Michel, Otto. *Der Brief and die Hebraer. Kritisch-Exegetischer Kommentar uber Das Neue Testament*. Gottingen: Vandenhoeck and Ruprecht. 1975.

Milligan, George. *The Theology of the Epistle to the Hebrews*. London: T. and T. Clark. 1899. Reprint. Minneapolis: James Family Publishing Company. 1978.

Moffatt, James. *Critical and Exegetical Commentary on the Epistle to the Hebrews. The International Critical Commentary*. Ed. by Alfred Plummer. Edinburgh: T. and T. Clark. 1975.

Moffatt, James. *The General Epistles. The Moffat New Testament Commentary*. Garden City: Doubleday, Doran and Company, Inc. 1928.

Montefiore, Hugh. *The Epistle to the Hebrews. Black's New Testament Commentaries*. Ed. by Henry Chadwick. London: Adam and Charles Black. 1964.

Moulton, James Hope, and George Milligan. *The Vocabulary of the Greek New Testament*. Reprint. Grand Rapids: William B. Eerdmans Publishing Co. 1972.

Mussner, Franz. *Der Jakobusbrief. Herders Theologischer Kommentar zum Neuen Testament*. Freiburg: Herder. 1975.

Odeberg, Hugo. *Pharisaism and Christianity*. Trans. by J. M. Moe. St. Louis: Concordia Publishing House. 1964.

Pfeiffer, Charles F. *The Epistle to the Hebrews*. Chicago: Moody Press. 1962.

Plummer, Alfred. *The Epistles of St. John. Cambridge Greek Testament*. Cambridge: Cambridge University Press. 1886.

Plummer, Alfred. *The General Epistles of James and Jude*. In *James, Jude, Peter*. Vol. 24 of *The Expositor's Bible*. Ed. by W. Robertson Nicoll. New York: Funk and Wagnalls Company. 1900.

Plumptre, E. H. *The General Epistle of James. The Cambridge Bible*. Ed. by J. J. S. Perowne. Cambridge: The University Press. 1901.

Reicke, Bo. *The Epistles of James, Peter, and Jude.* Vol. 37 of *The Anchor Bible*. Ed. by W. F. Albright and D. N. Freedman. Garden City: Doubleday and Company, Inc. 1973.

Robertson, A. T. *The First Epistle General of Peter*. In *The General Epistles and the Revelation of John*. Vol. 6 of *Word Pictures in the New Testament*. Nashville: Broadman Press. 1933.

Ropes, James Hardy. *The First Epistle of St. James. The International Critical Commentary*. Ed. by Alfred Plummer and Francis Brown. Edinburgh: T. and T. Clark. 1968.

Ryrie, Charles Caldwell. *Biblical Theology of the New Testament*. Chicago: Moody Press. 1959.

Sidebottom, E. M. *James, Jude, and 2 Peter*. Vol. 49 of *New Century Bible*. Ed. by H. H. Rowley and Matthew Black. London: Thomas Nelson and Sons, Ltd. 1967.

Stott, John R. W. *The Epistles of John*. Vol. 19 of *Tyndale New Testament Commentaries*. Ed. by R. V. G. Tasker. Grand Rapids: William B. Eerdmans Publishing Co. 1964.

Strachan, R. H. *The Second Epistle General of Peter*. In *First Peter-Revelation*. Vol. 5 of *The Expositor's Greek Testament*. Ed. by W. Robertson Nicoll. Grand Rapids: William B. Eerdmans Publishing Co. 1951.

Taylor, Richard S. *The Epistle to the Hebrews-Revelation*. Vol. 10 of *Beacon Bible Commentary*. Ed. by Ralph Earle. Kansas City: Beacon Hill Press. 1967.

*Testaments of the Twelve Patriarchs*. In *The Old Testament Pseudepigrapha*. Ed. by James H. Charlesworth. Garden City: Doubleday and Company, Inc. 1983.

Vermes, G., trans. *The Dead Sea Scrolls in English*. Baltimore: Penguin Books. 1975.

Wesley, John, et.al. *One Volume New Testament Commentary*. Grand Rapids: Baker Book House. 1957.

Westcott, Brooke Foss. *The Epistle to the Hebrews*. Reprint. Grand Rapids: William B. Eerdmans Publishing Co. 1984.

Wheaton, David H. *2 Peter*. In *The New Bible Commentary*. Ed. by Donald Guthrie. Rev. ed. Grand Rapids: William B. Eerdmans Publishing Co. 1970.

Windisch, H. *Der Hebraerbrief. Handbook zum Neuen Testament*. Tubingen: 1931.

Wuest. Kenneth S. *In the Last Days*. In *Philippians-Hebrews-The Pastoral Epistles-First Peter: In the Last Days*. Vol. 2 of *Wuest's Word Studies from the Greek New Testament*. Grand Rapids: William B. Eerdmans Publishing Co. 1973

## Revelation

Alford, Henry. *Hebrews-Revelation*. Vol. 4 of *The Greek Testament*. Cambridge: Deighton, Bell, and Co. 1866.

Augustine. *The Harmony of the Gospels.* In *St. Augustine: Sermon on the Mount, Harmony of the Gospels, Homilies on the Gospels.* Vol. 6 of *The Nicene and Post-Nicene Fathers.* Ed. by Philip Schaff. Edinburgh, 1867. Reprint. Grand Rapids: William B. Eerdmans Publishing Co. 1956.

*The Babylonian Talmud.* Trans. by I. Epstein. London: The Soncino Press. 1952.

Barclay, William. *The Revelation of John.* 2 vols. *The Daily Study Bible.* 2d ed. Philadelphia: The Westminster Press. 1960.

Barnhouse, Donald Grey. *Revelation: An Expository Dictionary.* Grand Rapids: Zondervan Publishing House. 1971.

Beasley-Murray, G. R. *The Book of Revelation. New Century Bible.* Greenwood, SC: The Attic Press, Inc. 1974.

Beckwith, Ibson T. *The Apocalypse of John.* New York: MacMillan Company. 1919. Reprint. Grand Rapids: Baker Book House. 1979.

Blass, F., and A. DeBrunner. *A Greek Grammar of the New Testament and Other Early Christian Literature.* Trans. by Robert W. Funk. Chicago: The University of Chicago Press. 1974.

Botterweck, G. Johannes, and Helmer Ringgren, eds. *Theological Dictionary of the Old Testament.* 5 vols. Trans. by Geoffrey Bromiley, et al. Grand Rapids: William B. Eerdmans Publishing Co. 1974.

Bromiley, G. W., et al., eds. *The International Standard Bible Encyclopedia.* 4 vols. Rev. ed. Grand Rapids: William B. Eerdmans Publishing Co. 1988.

Bullinger, E. W. *The Apocalypse.* Greenwood, SC: The Attic Press, Inc. 1972.

Caird, G. B. *The Revelation of St. John the Divine. Harper's New Testament Commentaries.* Ed. by Henry Chadwick. New York: Harper and Row. 1966.

Charles, R. H. *A Critical and Exegetical Commentary on the Revelation of St. John.* 2 vols. *The International Critical Commentary.* Ed. by S. R. Driver, A. Plummer, and C. A. Briggs. Edinburgh: T. and T. Clark. 1970.

Clement of Rome. *The First Epistle of Clement to the Corinthians.* In *The Apostolic Fathers with Justin Martyr and Irenaeus.* Vol. 1 of *The Ante-Nicene Fathers.* Ed. by Alexander Roberts and James Donaldson. Edinburgh. 1867. Reprint. Grand Rapids: William B. Eerdmans Publishing Co. 1973.

Darby, J. N. *The Rapture of the Saints.* In *Prophetic, no. 4.* Vol. 11 of *The Collected Writings of J. N. Darby.* Ed. by William Kelly. Reprint. Sunbury, PA: Believers Bookshelf. 1972.

Deissman, G. Adolf. *Bible Studies:* Trans. by Alexander Grieve. Edinburgh: T. and T. Clark. 1923. Reprint. Winona Lake, IN: Alpha Publications. 1979.

Dhorme, Edouard. *A Commentary on the Book of Job.* Trans. by Harold Knight. Nashville: Thomas Nelson Publishers. 1984.

*The Didache.* In vol. 1 of *The Apostolic Fathers.* Trans. by Krisopp Lake. *The Loeb Classical Library.* Cambridge: Harvard University Press. 1970.

Eusebius. *The Ecclesiastical History.* 2 vols. Trans. by Krisopp Lake and J. E. L. Oulton. *The Loeb Classical Library.* Cambridge: Harvard University Press. 1970.

Ford, J. Massyngberde. *Revelation.* Vol. 38 of *The Anchor Bible.* Ed. by William Foxwell Albright and David Noel Freedman. Garden City, NY: Doubleday and Company, Inc. 1975.

Harrington, Wilfrid J. *Understanding the Apocalypse.* Washington: Corpus Books. 1969.

Hatch, Edwin. *Essays in Biblical Greek.* Oxford: Clarendon Press. 1889.

Hippolytus. *Treatise on Christ and the Antichrist.* In *Fathers of the Third Century.* Vol. 5 of *The Ante-Nicene Fathers.* Ed. by Alexander Roberts and James Donaldson. Edinburgh. 1867. Reprint. Grand Rapids: William B. Eerdmans Publishing Co. 1971.

Irenaeus. *Against Heresies.* In *The Apostolic Fathers with Justin Martyr and Irenaeus.* Vol. 1 of *The Ante-Nicene Fathers.* Ed. by Alexander Roberts and James Donaldson. Edinburgh. 1867. Reprint. Grand Rapids: William B. Eerdmans Publishing Co. 1973.

Johnson, Alan F. *Revelation* In *Hebrews-Revelation.* Vol. 12 of *The Expositor's Bible Commentary.* Ed. by Frank E. Gaebelein. Grand Rapids: Zondervan Publishing House. 1981.

Kiddle, Martin. *The Revelation of St. John.* Vol. 17 of *The Moffat New Testament Commentary.* Ed. by James Moffatt. London: Hodder and Stoughton. 1963.

Ladd, George Eldon. *A Commentary on the Revelation of John.* Grand Rapids: William B. Eerdmans Publishing Co. 1972.

Lang, G. H. *The Revelation of Jesus Christ.* London: Oliphants Ltd. 1945.

Lenski, R. C. H. *The Interpretation of St. John's Revelation.* Minneapolis: Augsburg Publishing House. 1963.

Lilje, Hans. *The Last Book of the Bible.* Trans. by Olive Wyon. Philadelphia: Muhlenberg Press. 1957.

Martyr, Justin. *Dialogue with Trypho.* In *The Apostolic Fathers with Justin Martyr and Irenaeus.* Vol. 1 of *The Ante-Nicene Fathers.* Ed. by Alexander Roberts and James Donaldson. Edinburgh. 1867. Reprint. Grand Rapids: William B. Eerdmans Publishing Co. 1973.

*The Martyrdom of Polycarp.* In *The Apostolic Fathers with Justin Martyr and Irenaeus.* Vol. 1 of *The Ante-Nicene Fathers.* Ed. by Alexander Roberts and James Donaldson. Edinburgh. 1867.

Reprint. Grand Rapids: William B. Eerdmans Publishing Co. 1973.

Morris, Henry M. *The Revelation Record.* Wheaton: Tyndale House Publishers. 1983.

Mounce, Robert H. *The Book of Revelation. The New International Commentary on the New Testament* Ed. by F. F. Bruce. Grand Rapids: William B. Eerdmans Publishing Co. 1977.

Oates, Joan. *Babylon.* Vol. 94 of *Ancient People and Places.* Ed. by Glyn Daniel. London: Thames and Hudson, Ltd. 1979.

Poellot, Luther. *Revelation: The Last Book in the Bible.* St. Louis: Concordia Publishing House. 1962.

Pope, Marvin H. *Job.* Vol. 15 of *The Anchor Bible.* Ed. by W. F. Albright and D. N. Freedman. Garden City, NY: Doubleday and Company, Inc. 1973.

Ramsey, James B. *The Book of Revelation.* Carlisle, PA: The Banner of Truth Trust. 1977.

Sauer, Erich. The *Triumph of the Crucified.* Trans. by G. H. Lange. Grand Rapids: William B. Eerdmans Publishing Co. 1952.

Scott, C. Anderson. *The Book of Revelation. The Expositor's Library.* London: Hodder and Stoughton. N.d.

Seiss, J. A. *The Apocalypse.* Grand Rapids: Zondervan Publishing House. 1966.

Sweet, J. P. M. *Revelation. Westminster Pelican Commentaries.* Ed. by D. E. Nineham. Philadelphia: The Westminster Press. 1979.

Swete, Henry Barclay. *Commentary on Revelation.* London: MacMillan. 1911. Reprint. Grand Rapids: Kregel Publications. 1977.

Walvoord, John F. *The Revelation of Jesus Christ.* Chicago: Moody Press. 1966.

# General Bibliography

## Modern Greek Texts

Aland, K. et al. in cooperation with the Institute for New Testament Textual Research. *The Greek New Testament.* 2nd ed. London: United Bible Societies. 1968.

Aland, K. et al. in cooperation with the Institute for New Testament Textual Research. *The Greek New Testament.* 3rd ed. New York: United Bible Societies. 1975.

Nestle, E. and K. Aland. *Novum Testamentum Graece.* 25th ed. Stuttgart: Deutsche Bibelstiftung. 1963.

Nestle, E. and K. Aland, et al. *Novum Testamentum Graece.* 26th ed. Stuttgart: Deutsche Bibelstiftung. 1979.

## Reference Sources with Abbreviations

### BAGD

Bauer, W., W.F. Arndt and F.W. Gingrich. *A Greek-English Lexicon of the New Testament and Other Early Christian Literature.* 2nd ed. Revised and augmented by F.W. Gingrich and F.W. Danker. Chicago: University of Chicago Press. 1958.

### NIDNTT

Brown, Colin, ed. The *New International Dictionary of New Testament Theology.* 4 vols. Grand Rapids: Zondervan. 1975.

### TDNT

Kittel, G. and G. Friedrich. *Theological Dictionary of the New Testament.* Trans, by G.W. Bromiley. 10 vols. Grand Rapids: Wm. B. Eerdmans. 1964-72.

### LSJ

Liddell, H.G. and R. Scott. *A Greek-English Lexicon.* 9th ed., Ed. by H. Stuart Jones and R. McKenzie. Oxford: Clarendon. 1940.

### M-M

Moulton, J.H. and G. Milligan. *The Vocabulary of the Greek Testament Illustrated from the Papyri and Other Non-Literary Sources.* London: Hodder and Stoughton. 1914-30. Reprint. Grand Rapids: Wm. B. Eerdmans. 1985.

# Early Church Fathers

*Ambrosius,* deacon of Alexandria, and intimate friend of Origen, died 250.

*Athanasius,* was bishop of Alexandria, 326; died in 373.

*Athenagoras,* a Christian philosopher of Athens, flourished in 178.

*Augustine,* 354-430.

*Basil* the Great, bishop of Caesarea, born in Cappadocia, 329; died 379.

*Bede,* the Venerable, born 673.

*Chrysostom,* bishop of Constantinople, born 344; died 407.

*Clemens Alexandrinus,* Clement of Alexandria, the preceptor of Origen, died 212.

*Clemens Romanus,* Clement of Rome, supposed to have been fellow laborer with Peter and Paul, and bishop of Rome, 91.

*Cyprian,* bishop of Carthage, in 248; was martyred, 258.

*Cyrillus Alexandrinus,* this Cyril was patriarch of Alexandria 412; died 444.

*Cyrillus Hierosolymitanus,* Cyril, bishop of Jerusalem, was born 315; died 386.

*Ephraim Syrus,* Ephraim the Syrian, was deacon of Edessa; and died 373.

*Eu—SEBius* of Caesarea, c. 260-340.

*Gregory* the Great, bishop of Rome, flourished in 590.

*Gregory Thaumaturgus,* was a disciple of Origen, and bishop of Neocaesarea in 240.

*Hippolytus,* a Christian bishop, flourished 230; died 235.

## Bibliographies

*Ignatius,* bishop of Antioch, was martyred about 110.

*Irenaeus,* disciple of Polycarp; born in Greece about 140; martyred 202.

*Jerome,* also called Hieronymus, one of the most eminent of the Latin fathers; author of the translation of the Scriptures called the Vulgate; born about 342, died in 420.

*Justin Martyr,* a Christian philosopher, martyred 165.

*Origen,* one of the most eminent of the Greek fathers, 185-254.

*Tertullian,* a most eminent Latin father, died about 220.

# VARIOUS VERSIONS ACKNOWLEDGMENTS

Scripture quotations found in Various Versions were taken from the following sources with special permission as indicated. The sources listed may be found in one or all of the volumes of *The Complete Biblical Library*.

**AB - AB** Fitzmyer, Joseph A., S. J., trans. The Gospel According to Luke I-IX; (Anchor Bible). New York: Doubleday & Company, Inc. 1985. Reprinted with permission. ©1981, 1985.

**ADAM - ADAMS** Adams, Jay E. The Christian Counselor's New Testament: a New Translation in Everyday English with Notations, Marginal References, and Supplemental Helps. Grand Rapids, MI: Baker Book House. 1977. Reprinted with permission. ©1977.

**ALBA - ALBA** Condon, Kevin. *The Alba House New Testament.* Staten Island, NY: Alba House, Society of St. Paul copublished with The Mercier Press Ltd. 1972. Reprinted with permission. *The Mercier New Testament.* 4 Bridge Street. Cork, Ireland: The Mercier Press Ltd. ©1970.

**ALFD - ALFORD** Alford, Henry. The *New Testament of Our Lord and Saviour Jesus Christ: After the Authorized Version.* Newly compared with the original Greek, and revised. London: Daldy, Isbister. 1875.

**AMPB - AMPB** The *Amplified Bible.* Grand Rapids, MI: Zondervan Publishing House. 1958. Reprinted with permission from the *Amplified New Testament.* © The Lockman Foundation. 1954, 1958.

**ASV - ASV** (*American Standard Version*) *The Holy Bible Containing the Old and New Testaments:* Translated out of the original tongues; being the version set forth a.d. 1611, compared with the most ancient authorities and rev. a.d. 1881-1885. New York: Thomas Nelson Inc., Publishers. 1901, 1929.

**BRCL - BARCLAY** Barclay, William. *The New Testament: A New Translation.* Vol. 1, *The Gospels and the Acts of the Apostles.* London: William Collins Sons & Co. Ltd. 1968. Reprinted with permission. ©1968.

**BB - BB** The *Basic Bible: Containing the Old and New Testaments in Basic English.* New York: Dutton. 1950. Reprinted with permission. *The Bible In Basic English.* © Cambridge University Press. 1982.

**BECK - BECK** Beck, William F. *The New Testament in the Language of Today.* St. Louis, MO: Concordia Publishing House. 1963. Reprinted with permission. © Mrs. William Beck, *An American Translation.* Leader Publishing Company: New Haven, MO.

**BRKL - BERKELEY** *The Holy Bible: the Berkeley Version in Modern English Containing the Old and New Testaments.* Grand Rapids: Zondervan Publishing House. 1959. Used by permission. ©1945, 1959, 1969.

**BEZA - BEZA** *Iesv Christi, D.N. Novum Testamentum.* Geneva: Henricus Stephanus. 1565.

**BKWD - BLACKWELDER** Blackwelder, Boyce W. *The Four Gospels: An Exegetical Translation.* Anderson, IN: Warner Press, Inc. 1980.

**BLKW - BLACKWELL** Blackwell, Boyce W. *Letters from Paul: An Exegetical Translation.* Anderson, IN: Warner Press, 1971.

**BRUC - BRUCE** Bruce, F.F. *The Letters of Paul: An Expanded Paraphrase Printed in Parallel with the RV.* Grand Rapids: William B. Eerdmans Publishing Co. 1965. Reprinted with permission. F.F. Bruce. *An Expanded Paraphrase of the Epistles of Paul.* The Paternoster Press: Exeter, England. © 1965, 1981.

**CMPB - CAMPBELL** Campbell, Alexander. *The Sacred Writings of the Apostles and Evangelists of Jesus Christ commonly styled the New Testament:* Translated from the original Greek by Drs. G. Campbell, J. Macknight & P. Doddridge with prefaces, various emendations and an appendix by A. Campbell. Grand Rapids: Baker Book House. 1951 reprint of the 1826 edition.

**CKJB - CKJB** *The Children's 'King James' Bible: New Testament.* Translated by Jay Green. Evansville, IN: Modern Bible Translations, Inc. 1960.

**CLMT - CLEMENTSON** Clementson, Edgar Lewis. *The New Testament: a Translation.* Pittsburg, PA: Evangelization Society of Pittsburgh Bible Institute. 1938.

**CNDT - CONCORDANT** *Concordant Version: The Sacred Scriptures:* Designed to put the Englished reader in possession of all the vital facts of divine revelation without a former knowledge of Greek by means of a restored Greek text. Los Angeles: Concordant Publishing Concern. 1931. Reprinted with permission. *Concordant Literal New Testament.* Concordant Publishing Concern. 15570 Knochaven Road, Canyon Country, CA 91351. ©1931.

**CNFT - CONFRATERNITY** *The New Testament of Our Lord and Savior Jesus Christ:* Translated from the Latin Vulgate, a revision of the Challoner-Rheims Version edited by Catholic scholars under the patronage of the Episcopal Committee of the Confraternity Christian Doctrine. Paterson, NJ: St. Anthony Guild Press. 1941. Reprinted with permission by the Confraternity of Christian Doctrine, Washington, DC.

©1941.

**CNBR - CONYBEARE** Conybeare, W.J. and Rev. J.S. Howson D.D. *The Life and Epistles of St. Paul.* Rev. ed. 2 vols. London: Longman, Green, Longman, and Roberts. 1862.

**CVDL - COVERDALE** *The New Testament: The Coverdale Version.* N.p. 1535(?), 1557.

**CRNM - CRANMER** Cranmer or Great Bible. *The Byble in Englyshe, . . .* translated after the very-te of the Hebrue and Greke text, by ye dilygent studye of dyverse excellent learned men, expert in the forsayde tonges. Prynted by Richard Grafton & Edward Whitchurch. Cum privilegio ad Imprimendum solum. 1539.

**DRBY - DARBY** Darby, J.N. *The Holy Scriptures A New Translation from the Original Languages.* Lansing, Sussex, England: Kingston Bible Trust. 1975 reprint of the 1890 edition.

**DOUY - DOUAY** *The Holy Bible containing the Old and New Testaments:* Translated from the Latin Vulgate . . . and with the other translations diligently compared, with annotations, references and an historical and chronological index. New York: Kennedy & Sons. N.d.

**ET - ET** Editor's Translation. Gerard J. Flokstra, Jr., D.Min.

**EVRD - EVERYDAY** *The Everyday Bible: New Century Version.* Fort Worth: Worthy Publishing. 1987. Reprinted with permission. World Wide Publications. *The Everyday Study Bible: Special New Testament Study Edition.* Minneapolis: World Wide Publications. 1988.

**FNTN - FENTON** Fenton, Farrar. *The Holy Bible in Modern English.* London: A. & C. Black. 1944 reprint of the 1910 edition.

**GNVA - GENEVA** *The Geneva Bible:* a facsimile of the 1560 edition. Madison, WI: University of Wisconsin Press. 1969.

**GN57 - GENEVA (1557)** *The Nevve Testament of Ovr Lord Iesus Christ.* Printed by Conrad Badius. 1557.

**GDSP - GOODSPEED** *The Bible: An American Translation.* Translated by Edgar J. Goodspeed. Chicago: The University of Chicago Press. 1935.

**HNSN - HANSEN** Hansen, J.W. *The New Covenant.* 2nd. ed. 2 vols. Boston: Universalist Publishing House. 1888.

**HBIE - HBIE** *The Holy Bible containing the Old and New Testaments:* an improved edition (based in part on the Bible Union Version). Philadelphia: American Baptist Publication Society 1913.

**HNT - HISTNT** *The Historical New Testament:* Being the literature of the New Testament arranged in the order of its literary growth and according to the dates of the documents: a new translation by James Moffitt. Edinburgh: T & T Clark. 1901.

**HRBR - HOERBER** Hoerber, Robert G. *Saint Paul's Shorter Letters.* Fulton, MO: Robert G. Hoerber. 1954.

**JB - JB** *The Jerusalem Bible.* Garden City, NY: Darton, Longman & Todd, Ltd. and Doubleday and Co, Inc. 1966. Reprinted by permission of the publisher. ©1966.

**KJII - KJII** *King James II New Testament.* Grand Rapids: Associated Publishers and Authors, Inc. ©Jay P. Green. 1970.

**KLST - KLEIST** *The New Testament Rendered from the Original Greek with Explanatory Notes.* Translated by James A. Kleist and Joseph L. Lilly. Milwaukee: The Bruce Publishing Company. 1954.

**KLGS - KLINGENSMITH** Klingensmith, Don J. *Today's English New Testament.* New York: Vantage Press. 1972. Reprinted by permission of author. ©Don J. Klingensmith, 1972.

**KNOX - KNOX** Knox, R. A. *The New Testament of our Lord and Saviour Jesus Christ: A New Translation.* New York: Sheen and Ward. 1946. Reprinted by permission of The Liturgy Commission.

**LAMS - LAMSA** Lamsa, George M. The *Holy Bible From Ancient Eastern Text.* Translated from original Aramaic sources. Philadelphia: Holman. 1957. From The *Holy Bible From Ancient Eastern Text* by George Lamsa. ©1933 by Nina Shabaz; renewed 1961 by Nina Shabaz. ©1939 by Nina Shabaz; renewed 1967 by Nina Shabaz. ©1940 by Nina Shabaz; renewed 1968 by Nina Shabaz. ©1957 by Nina Shabaz. Reprinted by permission of Harper & Row, Publishers, Inc.

**LTMR - LATTIMORE** Lattimore, Richmond. *Four Gospels and The Revelation:* Newly translated from the Greek. New York: Farrar, Straus, Giroux, Inc. 1979. Reprinted by permission of the publisher. © Richard Lattimore, 1962, 1979.

**LBCH - LAUBACH** Laubach, Frank C. *The Inspired Letters in Clearest English.* Nashville: Thomas Nelson Publishers. 1956.

**LIVB - LIVB** *The Living Bible: Paraphrased.* Wheaton, IL: Tyndale House Publishers. 1973. Used by permission of the publisher. © Tyndale House Publishers. 1971.

**LOCK - LOCKE** Locke, John. *A Paraphrase and Notes on the Epistles of St. Paul to the Galatians, First and Second Corinthians, Romans, and Ephesians:* To which is prefixed an essay for the understanding of St. Paul's Epistles. Campbridge, England: Brown, Shattuck; Boston: Hilliard, Gray, and Co. 1832.

**MKNT - MACKNIGHT** Macknight, James. New *Literal Translation: From the original Greek, of all the Apostolical Epistles, with a commentary, and notes, philological, critical, explanatory, and practical. Philadelphia: Wardkem. 1841. Macknight, James. Harmony of the Four Gospels:* 2 vols. in which the natural order of each is preserved, with a paraphrase and notes. London: Longman, Hurst, Rees, Orme and Brown. 1819.

**MJV - MJV** *English Messianic Jewish Version.* May Your Name Be Inscribed in the Book of Life. Introduction and footnotes by The Messianic Vision. Washington, D.C.: © 1981. Bible text by Thomas Nelson, Inc. Nashville: Thomas Nelson Publishing Company. © 1979.

**MOFT - MOFFATT** *The New Testament: A New Translation.* New York: Harper and Row Publishers, Inc.; Kent, England: Hodder and Stoughton Ltd. c.1912. Reprinted with permission.

**MNTG - MONTGOMERY** Montgomery, Helen Barrett. *The Centenary Translation of the New Testament:* Published to signalize the completion of the first hundred years of work of the American Baptist Publication Society. Philadelphia: American Baptist Publishing Society. 1924. Used by permission of Judson Press. *The New Testament in Modern English* by Helen Barrett Montgomery. Valley Forge: Judson Press. 1924, 1952.

**MRDK - MURDOCK** Murdock, James. *The New Testament: The Book of the Holy Gospel of our Lord and Our God, Jesus the Messiah: A* literal translation from the Syriac Peshito version. New York: Stanford and Swords. 1851.

**NAB - NAB** *The New American Bible.* Translated from the original languages with critical use for all the ancient sources by members of the Catholic Biblical Association of America. Encino, California: Benzinger. 1970.

**NASB - NASB** *The New American Standard Bible.* Anaheim, CA: Lockman Foundation. 1960. Reprinted with permission. © The Lockman Foundation 1960, 1962, 1963, 1968, 1971, 1972, 1973, 1975, 1977.

**NCV - NCV** *The Word: New Century Version New Testament.* Fort Worth, TX: Sweet Publishing. 1984.

**NEB - NEB** The *New English Bible:* New Testament. Cambridge, England: Cambridge University Press. 1970. Reprinted by permission. ©The Delegates of the Oxford University Press and The Syndics of the Cambridge University Press 1961, 1970.

**NIV - NIV** *The Holy Bible: New International Version.* Grand Rapids: Zondervan Publishing House. 1978. Used by permission of Zondervan Bible Publishers. © 1973, 1978, International Bible Society.

**NKJB - NKJB** *The New King James Bible, New Testament.* Nashville, TN: Royal Pub. 1979. Reprinted from *The New King James Bible-New Testament.* ©1979, 1982, Thomas Nelson, Inc., Publishers.

**NLTG - NLT** *The New Life Testament.* Translated by Gleason H. Ledyard. Canby, Oregon: Christian Literature Foundation. 1969.

**NOLI - NOLI** Noli, S. *The New Testament of Our Lord and Savior Jesus Christ: Translated into English from the Approved Greek Text of the Church of Constantinople and the Church of Greece.* Boston: Albanian Orthodox Church in America. 1961.

**NORL - NORLIE** Norlie, Olaf M. *Simplified New Testament: In plain English for today's reader: A new translation from the Greek.* Grand Rapids: Zondervan Publishing House. 1961. Used by permission. ©1961.

**NRTN - NORTON** Norton, Andrews. *A Translation of the Gospels with Notes.* Boston: Little, Brown. 1856.

**NOYS - NOYES** Noyes, George R. *The New Testament:* Translated from the Greek text of Tischendorf. Boston: American Unitarian Association. 1873.

**NTPE - NTPE** *The New Testament: A New Translation in Plain English.* Translated by Charles Kingsley —WLMS. Grand Rapids: Wm. B. Eerdmans Publishing Company. 1963.

**PNIN - PANIN** Panin, Ivan., ed. *The New Testament from the Greek Text as Established by Bible Numerics.* Toronto, Canada: Clarke, Irwin. 1935.

**PHLP -PHILLIPS** Phillips, J.B., trans. *The New Testament in Modern English.* Rev. ed. New York: Macmillan Publishing Company, Inc. 1958. Reprinted with permission. ©J.B. Phillips 1958, 1960, 1972.

**PNT - PNT** *A Plain Translation of the New Testament by a Student.* Melbourne, Australia: McCarron, Bird. 1921.

**RHEM - RHEIMS** The New *Testament of Iesus Christ.* Translated faithfully into English, out of the authentical Latin, . . . In the English College of Rhemes. Printed at Rhemes by Iohn Fogny. Cum privilegio. 1582.

**RIEU - RIEU** Rieu, E.V. *The Four Gospels.* London: Penguin Books Ltd. 1952. Reprinted with permission. ©E.V. Rieu, 1952.

**RTHM - ROTHERHAM** Rotherham, Joseph B. *The New Testament:* Newly translated (from the Greek text of Tregelles) and critically emphasized, with an introduction and occasional notes. London: Samual Bagster. 1890.

**RPNT - RPNT** Johnson, Ben Cambell. *The Heart of Paul: A Relational Paraphrase of the New Testament.* Vol. 1. Waco: Word Books. 1976.

**RSV - RSV** *Revised Standard Version;* The New Covenant commonly called the New Testament of our Lord and Saviour Jesus Christ: Translated from the Greek being the version set forth a.d. 1611, revised a.d. 1881, a.d. 1901. New York: Thomas Nelson Inc. Publishers. 1953. Used by permission. © 1946, 1952, 1971, 1973 by the Division of Christian Education of the National Council of the Churches of Christ in the U.S.A.

**RV - RV** *The New Testament of our Lord and Savior Jesus Christ:* Translated out of the Greek . . . being the new version revised 1881. St. Louis, MO: Scammell. 1881.

**SAWR - SAWYER** Sawyer, Leicester Ambrose. *The New Testament: Translated from the original Greek,* with chronological arrangement of the sacred books, and improved divisions of chapters and verses. Boston: Walker, Wise. 1861.

**SCLT - SCARLETT** Scarlett, Nathaniel. *A translation of the New Testament from the original Greek:* humbly attempted. London: T. Gillett. 1798.

**SEB - SEB** *The Simple English™ Bible, New Testament:* American edition. New York: International Bible Translators, Inc. 1981. Used by permission from International Bible Translators, Inc.

**SWAN - SWANN** Swann, George. *New Testament of our Lord and Saviour Jesus Christ.* 4th. ed. Robards, KY: George Swann Company. 1947.

**TCNT - TCNT** *The Twentieth Century New Testament: a Translation into Modern English Made from the Original Greek:* (Westcott & Hort's text). New York: Revell. 1900.

**TEV - TEV** *The Good News Bible, Today's English Version.* New York: American Bible Society. 1976. Used by permission. © American Bible Society, 1966, 1971, 1976.

**TNT - TNT** *The Translator's New Testament.* London: The British and Foreign Bible Society. 1973.

**TORY - TORREY** Torrey, Charles Cutler. *The Four Gospels: A New Translation.* New York: Harper and Row Publishers Inc. 1933. Reprinted by permission. ©1933.

**TNDL - TYNDALE** Tyndale, William. *The Newe Testament dylygently corrected and compared with the Greke.* and fynesshed in the yere of oure Lorde God anno M.D. and XXXIIII in the month of Nouember. London: Reeves and Turner. 1888.

**TL26 - TYNDALE (1526)** *The First New Testament in the English Language (1525 or 1526).* Reprint. Bristol. 1862. Or Clevland: Barton. N.d.

**WADE - WADE** Wade, G. W. *The Documents of the New Testament: Translated & Historically Arranged with Critical Introductions.* N.p., n.d.

**WAY - WAY** Way, Arthur S., trans. *Letters of St. Paul: To seven churches and three friends with the letter to the Hebrews.* 8th ed. Chicago: Moody. 1950 reprint of the 1901 edition.

**WSLY - WESLEY** Wesley, John. *Explanatory notes upon the New Testament.* London: Wesleyan-Methodist Book-room. N.d.

**WEYM - WEYMOUTH** Weymouth, Richard Francis. *The New Testament in Modern Speech:* An idiomatic translation into everyday English from the text of the "Resultant Greek Testament." Revised by J. A. Robertson. London: James Clarke and Co. Ltd. and Harper and Row Publishers Inc. 1908. Reprinted by permission.

**WLMS - WILLIAMS** Williams, Charles B. *The New Testament: A Translation in the Language of the People.* Chicago: Moody Bible Institute of Chicago. 1957. Used by permission of Moody Press. Moody Bible Institute of Chicago. © 1937, 1966 by Mrs. Edith S. Williams.

**WMCK - WILLIAMS C. K.** Williams, Charles Kingsley. *The New Testament: A New Translation in Plain English.* Grand Rapids: William B. Eerdmans Publishing Co. 1963.

**WLSN - WILSON** Wilson, Benjamin. *The Emphatic Diaglott containing the original Greek Text of what is commonly styled the New Testament* (according to the recension of Dr. F.F. Griesback) with interlineary word for word English translation. New York: Fowler & Wells. 1902 reprint edition of the 1864 edition.

**WORL - WORRELL** Worrell, A.S. *The New Testament: Revised and Translated:* With notes and instructions; designed to aid the earnest reader in obtaining a clear understanding of the doctrines, ordinances, and primitive assemblies as revealed. Louisville, KY: A.S. Worrell. 1904.

**WUST - WUEST** Wuest, Kenneth S. *The New Testament: An Expanded Translation.* Grand Rapids: Wm. B. Eerdmans Publishing Company. 1961. Used by permission of the publisher. ©1961.

**WCLF - WYCLIF** Wyclif(fe), John. *The Holy Bible containing the Old and New Testaments with the Apocryphal Books:* in the earliest English version made from the Latin Vulgate by John Wycliffe and his followers. London: Reeves and Turner. 1888.

**YNG - YOUNG** Young, Robert. *Young's Literal Translation of the Holy Bible.* Grand Rapids: Baker Book House. 1953 reprint of the 1898 3rd edition.

## Books of the New and Old Testament and the Apocrypha

### New Testament Books

Matthew

Mark

Luke

John

Acts

Romans

1 Corinthians

2 Corinthians

Galatians

Ephesians

Philippians

Colossians

1 Thessalonians

2 Thessalonians

1 Timothy

2 Timothy

Titus

Philemon

Hebrews

James

1 Peter

2 Peter

1 John

2 John

3 John

Jude

Revelation

## Old Testament Books

Genesis

Exodus

Leviticus

Numbers

Deuteronomy

Joshua

Judges

Ruth

1 Samuel

2 Samuel

1 Kings

2 Kings

1 Chronicles

2 Chronicles

Ezra

Nehemiah

Esther

Job

Psalms

Proverbs

Ecclesiastes

Song of Solomon

Isaiah

Jeremiah

Lamentations

Ezekiel

Daniel

Hosea

Joel

Amos

Obadiah

Jonah

Micah

Nahum

Habakkuk

Zephaniah

Haggai

Zechariah

Malachi

## Books of the Apocrypha

1 & 2 Esdras

Tobit

Judith

Additions to Esther

Wisdom of Solomon

Ecclesiasticus or the Wisdom of Jesus Son of Sirach

Baruch

Prayer of Azariah and the Song of the Three Holy Children

Susanna

Bel and the Dragon

The Prayer of Manasses

1-4 Maccabees

# NOTES